Y0-DYM-750

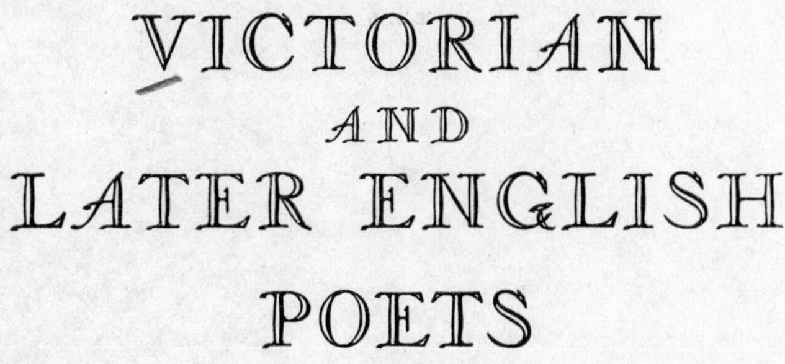

VICTORIAN AND LATER ENGLISH POETS

EDITED BY

JAMES STEPHENS
Author of *The Crock of Gold*, *The Demi-Gods*, *Collected Poems*, *Etched in Moonlight*, etc.

EDWIN L. BECK
Professor of English, Ohio State University

ROYALL H. SNOW
Associate Professor of English, Ohio State University

AMERICAN BOOK COMPANY

NEW YORK · CINCINNATI · CHICAGO · BOSTON · ATLANTA

VICTORIAN AND LATER ENGLISH POETS

E.P. 5

MADE IN U.S.A.

PREFACE

THE first anthologies of Victorian poetry were true to the most commonly understood meaning of the word "anthology"—collections of poetry alone. One anthology differed from another only as the taste of its maker differed from that of his brother maker. There was a large unvarying body of poems that appeared in every anthology and a smaller number representing the peculiar taste of the maker. After a time came the anthology that included prose along with the poetry. But the character of the prose was not such as gave the student a view of the poets as human beings or disclosed their vagaries and feelings as men. It was frankly critical in nature, having to do with the literary pronouncements of the poets themselves or with the judgments of critics contemporary with them.

In this book a place has been found for some important critical writing of the major Victorians and still greater place for their intimate revelation of self through their personal letters and, in some cases, through their small talk. In these pages Tennyson talks of both beer and the stateliness of English prose, and here Matthew Arnold evolves his touchstone theory of criticism and says to Mrs. Arnold of the death of Lola, the family pony, "dear little thing! The tears come into my eyes as I write." No other anthology contains at once so much of the poetry of the Victorians, their ideas and theories of poetry, and the intimate thoughts and feelings they had as men.

The facsimile reproductions of letters, drawings, pages of original manuscripts, and title-pages (particularly of presentation volumes) make for that intimate and real approach to the poets and their methods of work which the editors think essential to sound teaching. The descriptive caption with each illustration identifies it, and the reader who cares for fuller information about the illustrations will find it in Appendix I, pages 1129 ff.

It is impossible to include in a book as rich as this in the poems and in the critical and personal prose of the major Victorians, all of the large number who wrote good poetry during the period and in the immediately following years. All that the editors could do was to select. They are under no illusion that their selections will be entirely satisfactory to all who read the book. They feel, however, that the chosen representatives of minor poetry are of sufficient number and significance to give the reader an adequate knowledge of what all the Victorians, particularly those of the 'nineties, were doing.

The date given at the end of each poem is usually the date of publication. In many cases, particularly among the secondary figures, where it was difficult or impossible to be sure of a date, the date is either omitted or the date of composition is given. The order of the poems is generally chronological, and in the section devoted to secondary figures the poets are alphabetically arranged. There is, however, a chronological index (p. vi) of all the poets represented in the collection.

The editors wish to thank Mr. W. T. H. Howe, president of the American Book Company, for permission to make facsimile reproductions of material in his private collection. Of the thirty-eight pages of such reproductions, all but one are from Mr. Howe's collection. The facsimile of Arnold's autograph copy of *Longing* is reproduced from Whitridge's *Unpublished Letters of Matthew Arnold* by permission of the Yale University Press. An extended passage from P. F. Baum's edition of *The House of Life* is quoted by permission of the publishers, the Harvard University Press.

E. L. B.
R. H. S.

ACKNOWLEDGMENTS

In the group of selections from Matthew Arnold's letters, those numbered I, II, III, VI, VII, IX, XIII, XIV, and XXIV are reprinted from *Unpublished Letters of Matthew Arnold* (1923), ed. by A. Whitridge, by permission of Yale University Press, New Haven, publishers. The letters in this group numbered IV, V, VIII, X, XI, XII, XV, XVI, XVII, XVIII, XIX, XX, XXI, XXII, XXIII, XXV, and XXVI are reprinted from *Letters of Matthew Arnold, 1848–1888* (1895), ed. by G. W. E. Russell, by permission of The Macmillan Company, New York, publishers.

The selections from Wilfrid Scawen Blunt are reprinted from his *Poetical Works* (1914) by permission of The Macmillan Company, New York, publishers.

The selections from Robert Bridges are reprinted from his *Poetical Works* (1914) by permission of the Oxford University Press, New York, publishers.

The selections from Thomas Edward Brown are reprinted from his *Collected Poems* (1927) by permission of The Macmillan Company, New York, publishers.

The selections from *The Letters of Robert Browning and Elizabeth Barrett Barrett, 1845–1846* (2 vols., 1899) are reprinted by permission of Harper and Brothers, New York, publishers.

The selections from John Davidson are reprinted from his various collections by permission of Dodd, Mead and Company, New York, publishers.

The selections from Austin Dobson are reprinted from his *Complete Poetical Works* (1923) by permission of the Oxford University Press, New York, publishers.

The selections from Thomas Hardy are reprinted from his *Collected Poems* (1926) by permission of The Macmillan Company, New York, publishers.

The selections from William Ernest Henley are reprinted from his *Poems* (1919) by permission of Charles Scribner's Sons, New York, publishers.

The selections from Gerard Manley Hopkins are reprinted from *Poems of Gerard Manley Hopkins* (ed. by Robert Bridges, 2nd edition, 1930) by permission of the Oxford University Press, New York, publishers.

The selections from Lionel Pigot Johnson are reprinted from his *Poetical Works* (1915) by permission of Elkin Mathews & Marrot, Ltd., London, publishers.

The selections from Rudyard Kipling are reprinted from *Rudyard Kipling's Verse, Inclusive Edition* (1927) by permission of Mr. Kipling and of his literary agents, A. P. Watt and Son, London; also by permission of Mr. Kipling's American publishers, Doubleday, Doran and Company, Garden City.

The selections from George Meredith are reprinted from his *Poetical Works* (1912), ed. by G. M. Trevelyan, by permission of Charles Scribner's Sons, New York, publishers.

The selections from Arthur William Edgar O'Shaughnessy are reprinted from *Poems of Arthur O'Shaughnessy* (ed. by W. A. Percy, 1923) by permission of Yale University Press, New Haven, publishers.

The selections from Christina Rossetti are reprinted from her *Poetical Works* (ed. by W. M. Rossetti, 1904) by permission of The Macmillan Company, New York, publishers.

Letters of Dante Gabriel Rossetti are reprinted from Rossetti's *Letters to William Allingham, 1854–1870* (1898) by permission of Ernest Benn, Ltd., London, publishers, and from *Letters of Dante Gabriel Rossetti to His Publisher* (ed. by O. Doughty, 1928) by permission of The Scholartis Press, London, publishers.

The selections from William Sharp are reprinted from *Poems and Dramas* [by "Fiona Macleod"] by permission of Duffield and Green, New York, publishers.

The selections from Robert Louis Stevenson are reprinted from his *Complete Poems*, (1923) by permission of Charles Scribner's Sons, New York, publishers.

The poems by Algernon Charles Swinburne are reprinted from his *Collected Poetical Works* (2 vols.) by permission of Harper and Brothers, New York, publishers.

The selections from Swinburne's letters are reprinted from *The Letters of Algernon Charles Swinburne* (ed. by E. Gosse and T. J. Wise, 2 vols., copyright 1919) by permission of Dodd, Mead and Company, New York, publishers.

The selections from Arthur Symons are reprinted from his *Poems* (2 vols., 1929) by permission of Dodd, Mead and Company, New York, publishers.

The conversations and letters of Tennyson are reprinted from *Alfred Tennyson: A Memoir by His Son* (2 vols., 1897) by permission of The Macmillan Company, New York, publishers.

The selections from William Butler Yeats are reprinted from his *Collected Poems* (1933) by permission of The Macmillan Company, New York, publishers.

AUTHORS REPRESENTED IN THIS VOLUME

IN CHRONOLOGICAL ARRANGEMENT BY DATES OF BIRTH

CONTENTS

Matthew Arnold

Dante Gabriel Rossetti

Algernon Charles Swinburne

Wilfrid Scawen Blunt

Robert Bridges

Emily Brontë

Thomas Edward Brown

Elizabeth Barrett Browning

Arthur Hugh Clough

John Davidson

Henry Austin Dobson

Ernest Dowson

Edward FitzGerald

Thomas Hardy

William Ernest Henley

Gerard Manley Hopkins

Alfred Edward Housman

Lionel Pigot Johnson

Rudyard Kipling

George Meredith

William Morris

THE POETS AND POETRY OF THE NINETEENTH CENTURY

AN ESTIMATE

In attempting to review the literature of the Nineteenth Century we find that there is, as at the back of the mind, an uneasy reflection or system of reflections. We have passed from that mode, is one such reflection. There is no means of returning to it, is another. We do not wish to do so, nor is there any reason for such returning, are yet others.

Such a passing from the mode may enable us to regard its production with another closeness, another serenity than those which were previously possible—or it may not. The epoch is so nigh to us in time it should not seem withdrawn, or of peculiar difficulty or distinction. We do find distinction and difficulty; for, truly, that epoch is sundered from us by a change that is wider and deeper than has ever before intervened between two generations.

The change that has come between the Nineteenth and Twentieth Centuries is radical; and is, progressively, sundering: it is operative in every department of Life and Letters, and is still to operate. Something is finished, and something has begun. Within the space of thirty recent years a world has come into being; and, that it might come into being, a world has been obliterated.

The Nineteenth Century bequest of prose and verse stands in danger, and one wonders if the fate that has befallen one of these two may not, by the mere logic of epidemic, extend to the other.

Nineteenth Century prose is not now *in danger* of forgetfulness—it is, already, more than partially forgotten. Reputations which, only three decades ago, were in every cultivated person's memory, and ready upon every cultivated person's lips, are still, though fadingly, in the memory, but are no longer upon the lip. The idea of Scott or Dickens or Thackeray is no longer urgent in any youthful mind. Lamb or Carlyle, Macaulay or Hazlitt or Ruskin inspires no man's enthusiasm. Only the Brontë sisters (perhaps Jane Austen and Trollope) retain devotees, and can still evoke a literary and personal curiosity in the reader or the critic. The remainder of that enormous prose literature has gone down the wind.

Thirty years ago it was inconceivable that disaster could possibly overtake this literature. Each of these writers was stayed and stablished as by or upon a hill. Each rested in the confidence that English literature and history and tradition could and would secure him against any possible calamity, and that only a veritable world-cataclysm could possibly disturb him.

In the recent thirty years we have outlived a dozen world-cataclysms, by the side of which the tramplings of a Bonaparte seem only as the aimless skirmishings of a child. The economic, the social, the cultural, the political and moral spheres of mankind have been so harassed and transformed that today no "value" inheres for us that was stable and functioning only thirty years ago.

If a great prose literature and the sanctions upon which it is founded can be thus summarily dismissed, shall the parallel poetical literature submit to the same fate? Or is it true that poetry is of another mode, another matter, another integrity than prose? That its being is independent of scientific, or moral, or philosophical values, and its nature set elsewhere than in social contingencies?

There is an inner vitality in fine poetry which, historically, has preserved it from the disintegration to which prose is subject; and the work of a Shelley or a Wordsworth must be examined with another preoccupation, and from another level, than those we should find suitable in the case of a Thackeray or a Carlyle.

The intention of an Anthology is not, primarily, critical. The effort of the compiler should be to gather so much representative matter from each author that a judgment can thereupon be formed as to the field and the worth of that particular person. Judgment upon a writer can be truly final; it can cover every ground; for the writer, whether deliberately or not, does deliver himself to his reader and critic more completely than any other artist or human being can possibly manage. The writer is known to his critic socially, morally, psychologically, and, even, spiritually. If the writer be also an artist there is no possible disguise that he can use. There is no possible evasion by which he can retire himself from critical examination. He is given in the piece and in the lump, and the critic can finally "place" him as unerringly as a botanist "places" a plant.

A Selection, however, is other than an Anthology and should have as its base a severely critical intention; and in a Selection only work that exhibits the author at his best may be included.

At this date an Anthology of Nineteenth Century poetry must attempt to be selective also. Much water has flowed under the bridges since this poetry was composed; the "values" incident to that period are established, or are so comprehended that criticism can report upon them. The problems which beset those writers, in an economic, a cultural, or a technical sense, are largely removed from us as problems; are entirely removed from us as competitive and challenging production; and the personages represented have submitted to a large general criticism, which (though the final word has not yet been said) permits a just estimate to be formed as to the weight and variety of talent they have bequeathed to us.

This bequest is (or was) our inheritance. It has (however we exclaim against this) largely fashioned our culture and our technique; and only on the condition that we find this inheritance unsatisfying or limiting can we consciously depart from it, and apply ourselves to the discovery of other means than those they used, and to the ascertaining of other values than those which contented and exercised our predecessors. Put broadly, "value" is that which we wish to consider as immutable.

Mere lapse of time does not constitute or bring into being a "new" generation. Whatever time seems engaged, the old generation is yet in being while economic and technical facts remain unchanged. That is a new generation which, of necessity, professes dissatisfaction with and challenges the basic or working values of the preceding age. Such a dissatisfaction is now in being, and to justify this is a chief reason why criticism should be extreme on all that is extended to us from the immediate past.

Every "new" generation must revaluate the values; and to do this it must seek for another definition of that in which value inheres. Wherever and whenever a new definition is made, a new epoch is in being. In every generation, the sole means we have of evaluating it lies in the definitions which it advanced on those matters which were, for it, of fruitful importance. Definition is moral, or scientific, or economic. There is no artistic or philosophic definition of one's own time, for these are seeking a timeless truth.

Every story is situated in time: no poem is. Every story is sociological: no poem is. Every story is incomplete: no poem is. Therefore prose values are at the mercy of the next day: poetic values are only at the mercy of the language.

Definition is the epoch in its youth. It is that posited upon which the age will work as upon a guiding rule: and it seems certain that until such redefinition is attempted, no restabilization of values is possible for our generation, and there is no possibility of a regeneration of the debilitated art and culture, which are "ours" because we have inherited them, and are not ours because we cannot add to their growth: for if anything seems certain it is that we will not add much to the poetic epoch that began with Shakespeare and ended with Tennyson. The reason it cannot be added to is because it is completed.

An attempt at definition is worth making. We are at sea. But we are not at sea in a desert. A world of hitherto unrevealed variety and abundance is about us, and is uncharted. The economic of, the art of, the philosophy of paucity and the mean do not now express man, his capability, or his quest; and, until our definition of that which is basic to value is brought into conformity with our facts of superabundance and potential freedom, we shall get nowhere, and engage in nothing to its, and our own, extreme.

When examining poetry in the fashion which makes an Anthology, one cannot avoid considering that some poets wear better than others, and that there are many poets who have been forgotten, and who may, or may not, be again remembered.

When examined in this fashion, certain writers such as Tennyson, Byron, and Swinburne, are seen more clearly because of the rest they have had. Each of these has, now for quite a period, gone out of public appreciation; and critical curiosity is often exercised in the query as to whether these forgotten poets can or cannot come back. To every writer this going out, or being sent to Coventry, comes. The poet is forgotten, but while such forgetfulness may be temporary, it can be final. This critic would suggest that of these three only Byron can "come back."

Two periods of public neglect come to every fine writer. The first is during his own lifetime, and is indicated, is almost explained, in the jest attributed (I think) to Balzac — "Yes, Victor Hugo is a great man: let's not talk about him."

The public must think in this fashion about their great men. To be abundantly available carries also an idea of being too available. At a point in their days our Tennysons and Hardys, our Wellses and Chestertons and Shaws, do inordinately clutter our ways: they are stamping around all of our corners: they lie, each like a sack of wet sand, upon our own struggling production; so that, in mere self-defense, we laughingly detest them; and get to our own businesses by forgetting them.

If their talents are real they "come back," but an interim of at least ten years has to be lived through by every artist, during which, if he be remembered, he is reviled; and if he be merely considered unmentionable he may cultivate his modesty, or his *choux*, as best he may. This is his Squaw Winter; and, if he live through it, he comes to an Indian Summer in which appreciation and affection are given to him from every quarter; and are given with as beautiful an unreason as they were before unreasonably withheld.

Again, upon the day following the day of his death, the artist follows the man into silence and the void; and in that oblivion he will rest for nigh on forty years ere he be again discovered (if he is to be rediscovered), or finally and utterly forgotten if his talent be one that invokes the poppy, whereupon he may sleep happily ever after.

A question that frequently arises is—what is subject matter? Not merely the subject matter of a particular poem or poet, but of poetry itself? And the answer to this will be as we see poetry in a romantic, a psychological, or a metaphysical mode.

Action in diversity is man's subject romantically. Man is man's subject psychologically. That which we call divinity is man's subject finally. Perhaps the word divinity can only mean Creator.

More closely, the mind of man, perpetually dwelling upon itself; perpetually astonished and delighted and affrighted at its own infinity; endlessly discovering, discarding, and recreating all that it can hope or imagine, or (which is the same thing) desire, is the subject matter for the poet.

That we divided this Desire-Area into fields of action, passion, and thought, and by the powerful brooding which we call poetry, indicate these again as not disparate but as harmonious and unified, is the poetic subject and problem and resolution.

To identify a something as a completion—as beautiful, powerful, sufficing, and enduring—is that which the poet, even unconsciously, seeks to do. The unconscious will to do this we call inspiration: the attainment of it is creation.

Action and passion seem to change; seem to take on new and consequently exciting aspects as the Time in which they are manifested seems to revolve, discovering other subjects for, and other powers of our desire-nature. These, outworn, moving to occultation and repair: those others coming anew to manifestation; and, so, freshening, heartening, the incoming generation which, but for this superficial change, must have lacked in vitality and in courage.

The notation of these changes also is the poet's work; but now more as psychological observer than as creator; more as metrical historian than poet; more, perhaps, as minor than major. No man can stand on tiptoe all the time, and it is rare that a poet can sustain this subtle-intense for more than few and separated instants in any poem. Shakespeare, Milton, Shelley, Wordsworth, these could, even lengthily, endure that strain and lift. None others could so sustain it.

The matter that is basic in minor poetry is other than this. Psychological or even metaphysical considerations need not be entirely absent from this work—a lethargic philosophy is indeed abundantly to be found in it—but, in general, the fundamental fact of this poetry is a sensuous one.

It might be advanced that minor poetry has properly no subject. That it is a tale in which the achievement or the thwarting of desire at its simplest is perpetually narrated; and that, however sophisticated or elegant it be, a curious poetic or metrical form of the peasant mind is continually manifested in it.

A prolonged sensuous preoccupation comes at last to a sheerly pessimistic utterance (or to that which is exactly the same thing, a foolishly optimistic one). This preoccupation and this utterance is the minor mode. Thought matures in a way that sense does not; for the latter by usage is used up, where the former by usage is used upwards. Every new sense-exploit is a nail in the coffin of sense; every new thought is a reincarnation to the thinker. So sense must fall to limitation and despair, and must imagine Death as that it really aspires to. They call it Love.

When we read a quantity of the lesser minor poetry of this period we are amused, and finally astonished, by the abundant daydream upon the theme called Love; and the equally abundant preoccupation with the theme called Death. These two (with a third exceedingly curious matter called Humor) are points of repair for, are cardinal to, the minor poets; and when they have nothing to say (an endemic condition outside of the major mode) they can, and do, find something to say about the thing called Love, or the thing called Death: or they abandon both of these in that total artistic despair which is called Humor.

There is no logical opposition to the binding together of these, at first sight, dissimilar themes. Love and birth and death are in sure connection: they *are* the sensual or peasant theme; and no man needs to be astonished by the fact that if he will write Love, and (in the Blakeian phrase) persist in his folly, he must write Death thereafter, or be (that which a poet should not be, and which all modern poets are) a discontinuous writer. A discontinuous writer is one who has not led his matter to its extreme: so love must go to sadness, humor to tenderness, thought to ecstasy.

The marvel is that a legion of writers were able to indite a myriad of poems on this love-motif, and could face their own collected volumes afterwards without being violently sickened by them.

Even more remarkable, however, is the mighty appetite which the Nineteenth Century displayed for the absurd and more than plebeian sensuality, called Love. Poetic license is a real thing—it means that a poet may tell his truth—but the poet has no license to write rubbish about rubbish: for it is, surely, to rubbish that these indefatigable love-mongers have turned the thing they seemed to adore, and which, like everything else, is adorable.

Whether we will it or not, the mind insists upon forming categories. It is almost instinctive with us to put things into order, and to put all those we know, or know of, into the degrees and precedences which we consider to be their due. But it is rare, indeed, that one criticizes immediately in this fashion, or at all upon one's own account. Before the critic comes to an examination of the artist who preceded him, an important critical work has already been done, and it is quite impossible that he should dismiss precedent criticism and employ his own practical intelligence freely upon new artistic statement. We can only instantly criticize that which is slightly inferior to us.

Before we come to criticize, a very large part of the critical work must have been done. Time is the Judge, and each succeeding Time adds but a little to the growing knowledge that it inherited. At last, when the thing called knowledge is completed, there remains but to make the judgment which is implicit in that knowledge, and this finding we consider as the final, though temperamental, statement of the critic. It is astonishing that this temperamental agreement is ever arrived at, but it is more wonderful to consider that it is always come to, and that it is never at fault. In the interval, however, every person making such temperamental statements must be closely watched, and, whenever it is possible, rigorously disagreed with.

If the present writer considers that certain poets, once accounted of great moment, have gravely diminished, and are worthy of no wider than anthological estimation, that is his temperamental conclusion. If it be thought that Tennyson had neither the matter nor the mode that could assure long life to his work, or that Meredith or Swinburne or Francis Thompson or Gerard Hopkins stand in danger when considered in the whole of their work, and as only commendable in anthologies, that statement must be considered as temperamental to the present writer, and it is, consequently, as proper to be disagreed with as of being accepted, until further examination assists the judgment to one view or the other.

Prime criticism is largely of a technique. Interim criticism is mainly of the matter which the poet feels competent to, and, so, eager to handle: but what final criticism is of, no man can say. The great poets arrive at their own titanic tensions in a subject matter which permits the extreme of energy to be deployed: which permits to, by demanding from, the poetic imagination an almost unobstructed freedom: which permits an infinite to be posited as the norm; which permits infinity, whether of matter or desire or thought, to be suggested as given, and in being, and as the essence or essential of all that is to be considered: for that "poet" who is not writing of infinity is merely current and of the market.

This is so of the greater, it is not so of the lesser craftsmen. These work in a mode which does not posit or demand freedom, and from which infinity is not deducible. They must work, that is, on the earth, for the earth; in the mind, for the mind: and their subject matter is always one which can be regarded as having a psychological rather than a spiritual importance. It is this which makes the true distinction between the major and the minor modes.

There may be, in the poetry of any generation, several major poets, but among these there is always one to be discerned as prime to them all. So, in their times, Chaucer, Shakespeare, Milton are names by the side of which all others, contemporary, are recognized as subordinate to the great one.

Such supremacy is seen to exist, spiritually, in a superior imaginative vitality; and, technically, in a more effortless handling of weightier matter than others can achieve. The matter of such a poet appears to be more definitely his; and seems, indeed, so ingested and absorbed that, however abundantly it has already been used, it can yet be considered as especially his own. We can speak of Spenserian, Shakespearian and Miltonic matter. No other poetic names can be placed before the term "matter" in this possessive and exclusive way. We cannot speak of a Wordsworthian or Shelleyan or a Keatsian matter; for the first three are of the major mode, and after them all others, howsoever great, are minor, and are to be recognised not by a matter, but by a mode.

The technique which he uses in the manifestation of this work is (apparently) as natural to the great poet as is his own being. Such a technique is always seen as an original thing: it has been liberated by, but has not been inherited from, previous experiments; and it is not capable of being used by another than that person. That which we call "originality" refers always to a technique: it can never refer to subject, for this is impersonal and universal.

It is less by his subject than by his technique that one fine artist is distinguishable from another; as it is by the indistinguishable level of their technique that the *lesser* minor poets are seen to be all of a family, and almost all of a piece. You shall easily find among these lesser poets forty, or four hundred, examples of verse, any one of which might as easily have been written by anyone else out of a score of such-weight versifiers; but the workmanship of the larger poets is so individual that it can never be reproduced, or forged, or even parodied.

Technique is exactly as rare as poetry is: it is a mystery, but it is not mysterious.

It is immediately apperceptible; it cannot be defined although it can be pointed to. Matter, poetical or other, is the common human property, but a technique is the man who uses it; and this quality is the creative instrument, and is practically indistinguishable from the created thing.

We speak loosely when we speak of a "technical" education. There is certainly a somewhat which is impartible, and the imparting of which is the means whereby human effort is seen as continuous and cohering. But this, which is so impartible, is an alphabet: it is the indispensable groundwork: it can, in every art or craft, be compassed by whosoever has a memory: but, so compassed, it is to be forgotten, and that "technique" brought to being which is the being of the artist, and which justifies (what would otherwise be an impertinence) the artist's claim that he can impart to us something on those subjects upon which we are as accurately instructed as he is.

He imparts that matter plus himself, and, consequently, plus everyone else who is of his nature and tempo; for it is always to be remembered that conversation (and especially a cultural or artistic conversation) is between equals; and that as the reader and the writer are of intellectual and imaginative identity, so only is the writer's intention received to the limit of reception; otherwise it is partially received, or it is even not received.

Instruction, whether "technical" or other, cannot perform magic. The person who appreciates poetry does so by a natural aptitude, and is a poet: this bent is greatly assisted by instruction; but he or she who is not naturally thus receptive will never appreciate poetry in the final sense in which the poet intended it.

This does not suggest that a technique of appreciation should not be contrived and employed. The artist is by no means a solitary in this world, and the matter for astonishment is less that so few receive him, as that so many do.

It is unfortunate that criticism and creative critical curiosity should have been so completely devoted to the artist, and that what Buddhism calls "skilful means" should not have been more curiously contrived for the working looker-at and listener-to for whom all that strange labor was undertaken and completed. Whether, beyond mere memorizing, a technique of instruction towards appreciation of poetry, towards appreciation of art in general, has been evolved, I do not know. Efforts, certainly, to achieve this appreciation have been and are continually being made.

In the case of the art of painting a general rule could be suggested. It is that for an even exaggeratedly large period of his tuition, the scholar should not be permitted to see any bad pictures. The contrary to this is the rule for all of us. All the pictures that we see during the impressionable age, and most of those which throng upon us in after life, are examples of poor art; and are often examples of the art of painting at actually its most commonplace manifestation. The young person to whom only good work had been made available would receive, at last, an education in taste; and even if such an one's native power could never be assisted to the extreme of final appreciation, he or she would instinctively not admire bad work. Nor is this merely a negative result: there would ensue upon such a general instruction some abatement of the torrent of poverty-stricken, or unimaginative art with which we are deluged; and, in a world that is populous with charlatans, there would be some room for the artist.

A training in the appreciation of poetry is even more difficult to contrive. There is no way by which the approach of trivial verse can be hindered from the student. Every anthology, even, contains quantities of mediocre work; for, be it only from egoism, almost every poet has as zealously garnered his poor verse as he has carefully preserved his good: and many a critic has considered that the poet is not completely seen unless his bad work is considered as well as his good.

There is almost no poet, however great, whose poetic remnant is not made inordinately bulky by the inclusion of thoroughly unworthy material; and this is so frequently the case that one is compelled to wonder if normal critical intelligence does not at moments actually desert those artists; or even if it had ever formed a conscious part of their intellectual equipment. The student must marvel at the mind which could sit to and complete, say, the *Paradise Regained*, and many another work, and may conceive that these were minds so inordinately elevated that they were entirely removed from, were transcendent to the plane in which dullness can be experienced or even imagined. Coming upon other work of the same poets he again is astonished, being confronted with a vivacity and power and tact that seem superhuman; and he will ask in bewilderment, Did they know when their work was good and when it was bad? And he must be told that very often they did not know.

The counsel to invent or contrive a technique of appreciation is a counsel of perfection. Perfect teaching lies with the teacher, and has daily to be improvised by him: so, as knowledge and enthusiasm are in his control, he will meet with the occasional success that the artist meets with, and will be glad that success is, at least, occasional. At the end, say, of every hundred years, there should be an universal solemn destruction by fire and dynamite of all the bad, the incomplete, the experimental work of the previous era: culture would then cease to be business, and begin to be life; the worker would commence to look closely at his work, and criticism would begin to be the advised, the disciplinary, the drastic overlord which it now is not. There must be poor art as long as there is poor criticism, but no longer.

What is wrong with art? This—that there is no criticism of which it stands in righteous terror. And if it be further asked, What is wrong with criticism?—for something indeed is sadly to be mourned for in that also—it is, that criticism should never be appreciative: that criticism should always be harsh and destructive; that criticism should be removed from the poem or picture, and should directly advise and, where necessary, insult the poet and the painter and the musician who has the hardihood to confront it: but so long as our criticism is lisped by youngsters from school, so long will it be impossible to create a technique of teaching where artistic appreciation will be the vulgar fact which it should centuries ago have become. There are matters about which no young person knows anything: art is one of them. Everything else is another.

There is a point at which criticism has no validity; and reaching this point, the critic is enforced to become that which, ex officio, should be uncongenial to him. To this point the critic's work has been interim, supplementary, advisory; but here he becomes (if he can manage it) the eulogist, and needs no longer to seek definition by way of analysis. Here he makes his final statement, and his final statement can no longer be scientific, but temperamental. When true excellence is attained the critic has no work to do; for it is impossible to define excellence, or to indicate by what means it is arrived at. It is purely for this moment that all critical apparatus has been invented; and it is at this moment that he finds it, not useless—for knowledge when it has been removed from the surfaces must be operative in the depths—but unable to do another work than the one it was trained for; and here he becomes merely a pleased person, who discusses his pleasure as naïvely as we all discuss pleasure only. We are not naïve about death and calamity, but satisfaction makes us children again. Children shout, on their occasions, meaninglessly but significantly; and so, but as significantly, do all eulogists.

All that which is temporary or interim, which can be considered as a middle term, is amenable to fairly close analysis or criticism. We can say why such an one (being a poor poet) is bad; and can asseverate, almost to a gram, the extent and value of that person's mental and technical and, even, imaginative equipment. Given, that the greater includes the less, criticism does actually encompass and reveal all that can be considered as within this middle term. In the entire range of the second-rate (the term being used qualificatively and not abusively) the critic has real authority, and can counsel fruitfully or condemn justly or praise wittingly—this, because the persons and matters considered submit to definition; and are, consequently, inferior to the critic. Superiority consists mainly in the ability to define and classify that which is presented.

It is at the point where instruction ends that art begins; and only at that point where art begins does technique begin. The intention of the artist is by no means to instruct, nor (despite Wordsworth and Coleridge) does the artist seek to entertain. He seeks to satisfy.

Properly, there is no artistic "message." In everything whatever, whether as substance or quality or intention, we all know as much as the artist does; but to *know* and to *see* are, temporarily, two things; and it is in this revealing, in a carrying deeper and yet deeper into consciousness, and so into fullness of knowledge, that the artist is in his art. He subtly, or powerfully, or harmoniously makes more and more manifest that which at first seemed to be quite adequately manifested:

for he reveals that the matter dwelt upon was not so completely apprehended as we had thought; and, communing with him, we discover that we have reserves of perception which, but for him, would have lain undisturbed or even unsuspected; reserves of powerful-acceptance, and realization, which, but for him, might have been carried unused to the grave. Thus, and by him, life is made more abundant, and knowledge is brought more closely to the consciousness from which it now seems so irreparably sundered: for, though we say with the lip that "knowledge is power," we know in the heart that it is not so. Knowledge reveals: it does nothing else. Power is of and from the Gods.

Between the poet and his competent reader, identity is more firmly established than even between the lover and his beloved, for here such truth as can be uttered has been uttered beyond question, and has been as unquestionably received. Having created, he imparts! It is not so: that imparting is the very act and fact of creating, and such receiving on the reader's part is the same creative deed. Between the good poet and the good reader there is no distinction of greater or less: he who "gets" Shakespeare, or Milton, or Shelley, gets what they had; he may be certain that what they gave was of their best; and that their best and his are identical.

It is easy enough to indicate what it is that we call Classical, but it is not so easy to state at what fountain (other than a purely national one) the Classical writer refreshes himself. Classicism is less referable to a specific culture than to a specific epoch. It may even be that the term is incapable of just definition except internationally.

It is only as by chance that the names of Spenser, Shakespeare, and Milton are borne to us as the fine fruits of the epochs they worked in: they are scarcely men: they are states of consciousness: their matter is during, and so their names endure, and are representative or symbolic (not solely of themselves, but) with singular completeness of the epochs which nurtured and engrossed them. Shakespeare, *qua* poet, is the total, advised, conscious Elizabethan England which was about him: Shakespeare, the man, is personally almost unconveyed by this poetry. Without that Elizabethan England he would yet, by essential, indescribable virtue, be a great poet, but he would not be the greatness we know; nor would his matter and its accompanying technique resemble those we are acquainted with.

Time (What is time? For man it is much more environment than duration.) produces, dictates, or permits (or refuses as in our day) that which we call subject; which in turn discloses the technique which is within its mode, for matter carries an appropriate technique with it. But while matter is timeless, technique is the date stamped upon it; and the epoch which gives or permits subjects of a certain emotional and intellectual elevation and a certain spare and lucid handling of them to its artists is a Classical one, while that other, which gives or permits or condones other certain subjects and their appropriate control, is Romantic. As his period and environment, so is the poet (not purely as poet, but as poet-conditioned), and his subject is perpetually that dimension or climate of the human spirit in which he finds himself, as at home; and by virtue of which he can achieve an intimate utterance, apparently upon himself, but actually upon every person of his time of a posited caste, or culture, and upon those actions which are the work of that specific caste. All art wills to be aristocratic.

There is no Classical or Romantic poet in his own right—for the artist who will live by his own right is always a poet *manqué*—but there is always the artist whose subject and technique are given and governed by his time; and whose virtue is that he is capable of being especially energized by time and subject, and can, in that vitality, control his matter almost as by instinct.

For critical and examining purposes, the artists of any particular century are conveniently divisible into hierarchies of major and minor workers, even though the term "major" be only used as a temporary and relative description. The workers of the Nineteenth Century can be so tabled. This period is curiously rich in remarkable, if thwarted and thwarting personalities; but even more singular is the abundance and variety of talents which these personalities display.

A Classical period and tradition imposes so (apparently) narrowing a discipline on its superior minds that the consequent artistic production can almost be conceived as of a single cultural contexture. An impatient examination of such a time may lead to the conclusion that what has been gained in quality has been lost in variety; and, for the world in general, this latter poverty, with the narrowing of enthusiasm which every lack entails, cannot be compensated for by any magnificence thus qualified.

The major poets of the Nineteenth Century in order of birth are: Wordsworth, Coleridge, Byron, Shelley, Keats, Tennyson, Browning, Arnold, and Swinburne.

It is already a question as to whether all of these poets are properly to be included under the term "major"; but, whatever their lapses from the highest poetic excellence may be, there is no doubt that Coleridge, Wordsworth, Shelley, and Keats are, by the assent of time, to be recognized as superior to all others of their period: and superior to all those who have since created poetry to the date of this writing.

It is certain that the highest achievements of these four poets cannot be held to rival the greatest work of their predecessors, Chaucer, Spenser, Shakespeare, and Milton. It may be that a Classical mode or training, however narrow and narrowing it seems to be, does permit an extension of the spirit, an unifying of the whole being, which the Romantic mode does not call for and cannot, therefore, elicit. This may be so; but Shakespeare has yet to be accounted for; the English language and psychology has still to be reckoned with; and a more profound criticism embarked upon ere this claim can be stated as proven, and to be relied upon.

When the Romantic mind may move as at its own will, and be disciplined by no other asceticism than its own desires evolve, it will proceed as fancy inclines rather than to a direction which the intense and guarded spirit dictates. Variety is truly a blessing, and lacking it life would degenerate into boredom; but a variety which is too abundant and too available must lead, first, to a decentralization of the mind that plays in it; and second, to a congestion of desire (which desire is for many of us the only mind we ever use), and will thus lead to a lack of control, and so, of direction; and to his being lost among the trees who had expected to be a master of the wood.

The effect of this artistic and intellectual decentralization is not apparent to the writers at the moment immersed in their own excitements and labors: it is posterity that pays, and the sense that we have inherited a debilitated art by reason of Romantic handling is one that is urgent in all the artists of the present day. Our discontent, however, is not properly, because not entirely, attributable to this cause.

In the Classical mode a consciously directed discipline is maintained by the artist upon his subject. This discipline or gravity can be conceived of as a good in itself; and, seemingly, can be relied upon to achieve that elevation of spirit and utterance which is finally the poetic aim. It is as though one said, "Only control and parsimony are certain good." Once, indeed, that was a rule, not only of art, but of life. The Romantic artist, however, is much at the mercy of his subject; or is not incontestably master of it; and he can only arrive at the great utterance, which he also seeks, not so much by a rapt distillation of the matter, as by the addition to, or the imposition upon it, of a moral or a philosophical value.

Value must be, but when value can be defined, its being is endangered: it has been brought to subjection, almost to domesticity, and that quality which is the soul of poetry, that sense of magic or infinity which illumines and delights, may be foregone by mere limitation: for poetry is not comprehended, but realized; and it ceases to be gnomic at its peril.

A remarkable fact about the poetry of the Nineteenth Century is the diversity of subject matter and of human temperament which is to be found in that poetry and those poets. When we consider the names that are salient, we note at once that personalities and ideas are not only of singular abundance but are more diverse than is evident in any other literary period. The names Coleridge and Wordsworth have no essential connection with each other, and have no connection with the names Shelley and Keats. These, again, are at as singular a remove from such other names as Byron, or Tennyson, or Swinburne, or Browning; as are those from Thompson, Beddoes, Meredith, Dowson, Hardy, or Hopkins. It is not that there is the difference of a school or of a technique. The difference is personal to the writers, and is so extreme that the Nineteenth Century is notable for a temperamental variety and a psychological richness which is unparalleled in literary annals.

Additional to this, the tale of the minor writers is as singularly rich; and the work and quality of work of these latter are as varied as are those of their greater brethren.

Only four of the poets in this century are considered as belonging to the highest order of poetry. The others are significant, each according to his power, and their work forms a body of great social, historical, and psychological importance. Many of the minor writers also are intellectually so aware, and emotionally so highly vitalized, that their best work does not fall very far from the grave excellence of their greater contemporaries. Indeed, so abundant and varied is this production, the period might be referred to as the Century of, or, even, the Paradise of the minor poet; for (excepting Shakespeare) no poet of the Romantic mode quite escapes the attribution of minor.

The cases of Shelley and Keats are curious, both psychologically and artistically; but the problems raised by these men, or by their work, are explicable; as is explicable all that has aroused affection, and the interest which unfailingly depends from it—affection is interest: it is almost nothing else. So, also, the case of Wordsworth (or of Coleridge) is curious, but these are not so easily, because not so willingly or sympathetically explained. For any explanation which is not governed by sympathy will leave out of account all those imponderables which are the essence of any human quality or action requiring to be explained.

Everything is forgiven to Shelley or Keats, nothing is forgiven to Wordsworth: and, yet, thoroughly to understand Wordsworth is thoroughly to understand the Nineteenth Century. Wordsworth is the Nineteenth Century; and any clue we may gain about him is a key to the entire Romantic mode, and its Victorian dependency.

It is not easy to be completely sympathetic to Wordsworth.

No poet has been so extravagantly praised or so extravagantly blamed as Wordsworth was, and is. It is instantly said, not only that he is a great poet, but that he is properly among the greatest: and yet this statement is not so much advanced as permitted; and, quick upon the admission, there come reservations and qualifications so many, so pregnant, that one might be forgiven for wondering if he is to be considered a poet at all.

He is a poet, indeed, and after the names of Shakespeare and Milton have been counted no other name than that of Wordsworth can be put forward as the third to that great twain; and as the fifth, in order of merit, in the great hierarchy of English genius—Shakespeare, Milton, Spenser, Chaucer, Wordsworth, Blake. This is the order of the great poets.

We can understand why Shelley and Keats are beloved; it should not be impossible to discover why we lout low to Wordsworth, and at the same instant eye him askance!

In his strength he is almost divine; but his weakness is not merely, and properly, polar to this, it is not that his weakness is "human, too human," it is almost sub-human; and, while the noddings of Homer are occasional, and can be reverenced, the noddings of Wordsworth are not occasional, nor as by accident, and are not reverential at all: (it is mainly as he nods that we find a wherewithal to judge the great man).

One imagines that perhaps Wordsworth was born out of time: that the talent which he shows is not the complete talent upon which he could have drawn: that an area of his being lay in occultation, and—which is ill in a poet—was unsuspected by and unsought by him: one accuses him of being unadventurous: he did not rise, and go, and get: he sat, and remembered, and obtained, as by a charity: one imagines that a dimension of being or cogitation analogous to those in which Shelley or Keats were so at home should also have been his innocent habitation; and that (as every philosophy is fundamentally a dubiety) he should less have plunged himself into memory, and a reflection upon this, than into his own living life; and that he should have uttered his place and being in actuality rather than to reduce these to a theory, a problem, and a dubitation.

Splendor is his, but certitude is not his in all security.

It is of the essence of poetry that the statement made shall be unshakeable in its certainty. This certainty may be of a matter that is high or low, but, in whatever statement, if certainty be lacking poetry is lacking: and this, more than any other lack, saps at the reader and the writer, and makes creation queasy. The immediate weakness of Wordsworthian poetry is that almost every statement which it makes is amenable to definition—to limitation, that is; and it is, consequently, not absolutely redeemed from prose-thought. The true poetic-statement is impervious to definition, and admits no further meditation than that from which it arose.

That poet is in uncertainty who needs and seeks a philosophic basis for work—the being of whose art lies in quite another than the philosophic world. Wordsworth considered that poetry, which is an art, should be a way of life; and that the closer it could be carried to sheer or mere living, the more it—which is not rational—would be brought to rationality. He conceived that poetry could be ennobled by vulgarizing its vocabulary—whose vocabulary is curious and pondered and ceaselessly selective: that it could be energized by forcing it to consider the peasant—the law of whose being is that it must only consider the hero: that if he could succeed in anchoring it immovably to the earth it would the more effortlessly and aërially disport in the heavens. He felt that he must conciliate poetically those "lower" orders which were then assaulting a weakening aristocracy: and he considered as a good democrat (and a good democrat cannot also be a good poet) that a moral value was not only the equal of a metaphysical or poetic one, but that it could be carried as far, and made to fare not worse. The Wordsworthian betrayal of poetry is singular, is signal, is complete—but the cause for wonder lies not here: the cause for wonder and exultation lies in the fact that poetry did not betray Wordsworth.

Although Shelley and Keats are in every respect dissimilar, yet they are bracketed together in popular and even in learned estimation, almost as twin poets: and they are sharply separated, or even segregated, from Wordsworth. But, in truth, they are sundered and aloof from every other poet whatever. This identity and solitude is found only among the greatest: Chaucer, Spenser, Shakespeare, Milton, Blake are similarly ungregarious and unique. It would seem that such cannot be stated of any other poets than these, and that to be recognized as fundamentally solitary, and uninfluencing, is a prime quality of genius.

It is not by chance that Shelley and Keats are the most beloved of all the poets in the great English hierarchy of genius, and that there is almost no poetic lapse which is not forgivable by their readers, who are also their lovers. They are not beloved because they were young and were poets, nor even because they died young. They are loved because their poetry is lovely; and because it is so in a fashion which pertains to them alone, and which can be thought of as angelic.

With Blake, they stand from and evade comparison with even a poetic standard; and the question as to their being greater or less great than another is one that does not arise.

Beyond all natively-talented writers they can be thought of as original; as especially or even uniquely endowed; and as the imparters of a poesy more limpidly and simply satisfying than can be found elsewhere. They have been identified with, or as, their own poetry, in a way that no other poet except Blake has ever been; and however their personal lives be examined, that identification is not imperiled, and they are not put to the question as every other great artist has been, and should be: for, truly, the greater the artist is, the greater and graver are the questions that should be asked of him.

It can be said that a more massive and realistic poetry than theirs has been written; it cannot be held that a more authentic muse than theirs has been in existance. They breathe the air of poesy as by divine right: they need to don no learned sock when they would disport in their own realms: and their very lapses are yet lapses within poetry where the lapses of all others are into prose.

But while there is so much in their work that is matter for marvel, that is incapable of another expression than that they gave, there remains much which criticism (if the poets were other than these) would consider deplorable.

It is not enough that Shelley should be a poet as by divine right, and should be that in a sense which no other poet has ever been. Work has to be done; searching has to be done; difficulties are not available in order to be evaded, they are even to be sought for; and in a vast amount of his work (like many another of his lesser brothers—and this is the gravamen of critical disapproval of the entire Romantic mode) Shelley did not always seek the hardest matter, nor the hardest way: nor was Keats presumptuous when he wrote cautioning Shelley to "load every rift with ore." Shelley's ear was instinctively pleased, and, consequently, somewhat halted by, for him, easily attained harmonies. And at moments when sobriety of utterance was needed, if only to offset or prepare for the greater moments which were to come, his ear did not dismiss a rhythm from his matter which can justly be termed habitual and rhetorical.

There is no doubt that in the case of Shelley an easy poetic music was, almost always, subconsciously, at his command (as it was at the command of, say, Scott or Byron), and had these poets been of the austere temper that one will conceive the great poet to be, they should not have been so simply and naïvely contented with the instant product of their gift, so that the accusation of rhetoric, of virtuosity for its own sake, is an accusation which can be brought very easily against these men: and much of the feeling which we have for and against the amateur stays with us in considering them. The feeling we have for the amateur is that he is doing "all this" for love. The feeling we have against him is that he is, finally, not serious about all this.

Something of a like disapproving criticism may be brought in the case of Keats. He too, particularly (and excusably) in his early work had scattered his talent, and so diffused it that his matter also became diffuse. He recovered quickly enough from this diffusion, and in the great Odes, and practically in all his subsequent work, he does show a firmer grasp of his matter. All his best work, however, is of relatively short breath, and the doubt as to knowledge of his objective, which comes to us on reading *Endymion*, is not entirely absent while we are considering the *Hyperion*. Even though this latter large fragment is one of the most remarkable and indeed magnificent pieces of work done in that century, one has an uneasy sense that in the myth of *Hyperion* Keats knew as little whither his story must wend as he did in the *Endymion* of his youth. Something of the quality of the improviser is sensed, actually as from verse to verse, in every work of this poet; and, whether in music or poetry, the gift of improvisation, while wonderful, is not satisfying. Artistically and intellectually this quality is a grace only to the dramatist and the wit.

It is possible that, had he lived, Keats might not have increased in poetic stature. He lacked consecutiveness and the longer breath. He was moving towards a Miltonic technique and away from his own original, perhaps narrow, talent; and it may be that we only remove from that which is already forsaking us. Like Wordsworth, like all the finer men of that time, he had an interest, amounting to an obsession, in the philosophical consideration of life. This, while it is singularly rare in our prose literature (where it is most urgently needed), does often lie as a deadening weight upon English poetry: and it may be that in his case a theory of God and man and beauty could have hardened into a true obstacle against the poetry which was in him, and which gave promise of being the greatest single contribution to poetry that the age could hope for.

The poet must surmount, as before said, his very culture and his very self; and one questions if a talent so fine-drawn, so at the mercy of the moment as that of Keats's, was capable of the descent into anonymity, of that liberating self-forgetfulness which can remove the poet from the accustomed and memorial to that dimension of being-in-rapture wherein the greatest poetry is conceived. The man must be as large, nay, he must be larger than his subject, and whether Keats was or was not the Titan he dreamed of we shall never know. Like the scenes depicted upon his own Grecian Urn, he remains for us in imperishable adolescence, and it must suffice to assert that the presence of one talent such as his would make any century illustrious.

The same uncertainty-at-the-core which we discover with so much surprise in Wordsworth is even more evident in the work of Tennyson.

This uncertainty is evident as a major fact in the mentality of the entire period, which should less be known as the Victorian than as the Sceptical Age. Both of these writers seemed able to work for long periods without that mystical urge which we call, in however unknown a tongue, inspiration—i.e.: the description of everything whatever as infinity. It is certain that to Wordsworth, in his greater poems, inspiration did frequently come and that it could transfuse an actually lethargic subject matter so that it became vivid, and splendid, and endless. This inspiration is not now evident in the greater portion of Tennyson's work; and, because of the lack of it, it is possible that our time will judge his poetry more severely than did his own day. Speaking of his work *in general*, it could be said that he is the worst "great" poet that ever lived. And again *in general*, that his is the only example of "vulgarity" in poetry that our language has known.

It is not enough to write wittingly, or with certainty, that partial thing which is the desire-nature of one's time. The work of poetry is to transcend the fact of the day; to transcend, it may be, every fact, and to bring the chosen matter into another dimension of thought, into even another dimension of emotion, than those in which it seemed to be born and active. Every statement of fact belongs to prose. It might be further said that every consecutive operation belongs to prose, and that poetry will only handle with reluctance any matter which is founded on a definite logic or ground: for it has an ability to so change the internal vibration even of emotion, that the emotion, as disclosed by poetry, has not upon its reader the effect which normally we know of, and which logically or psychologically is connected with or to be expected from that well known emotion. In prose heroism makes one proud; in verse it makes one weep. In prose again sadness makes one sad: in verse it makes one happy. These and many other such transformations are perpetually occurring in poetry: and these transformations are poetry.

To the artist it can easily be that every fact-in-itself is hideous, and that every emotion is obscene; and for the purpose of his art these facts and emotions, which (being his apparent subject) are inescapable, must be transformed from the domain in which they lie and do their everyday work to another in which they develop another result than that which is ordinarily to be expected of them.

"Æ" (George Russell) once said that poetry is written on the Mount of Transfiguration, and in saying this he made one of the most fruitful critical generalizations of our day. Unless, at some point in a poem, this transformation of matter, or transfiguration of values, takes place, the work which is being done is temporary, and is merely a note in poetic form on the mode of thinking and feeling of the day in which the work was composed. The great poets make this transformation in every poem which we recognize as great. And if in the work of Tennyson we look beyond the temporary utterance for that more highly vitalized significance which we call transformation, it is but rarely found, so that he can often appear more as an adept of poetry than a poet.

A point comes, in regarding poetry or music or painting, when we grow impatient of the work done by the *virtuosi*. In music this is readily visible, and we can see a person much more interested in his own technique than he is in music; and quite complacently giving his audience matter which is musically insignificant, under the theory that the wizardry of his technique can make up for any musical deficiency whatever.

The same virtuosity is displayed by many poets of this period. It must have seemed to such that any subject is a good subject, so adequate and satisfying did they feel their technical equipment to be: and their generation, being all technicians, were prepared, perhaps, to be more interested in the rhetoric of poetry than in poetry itself, as they were prepared to be more absorbed in the bowing of Paganini than in the music which Paganini might have produced.

There is a great danger in the virtuoso's approach to his subject, for the virtuoso is always a profoundly ignorant person. The danger is that the matter tends to be absorbed in the mode; and the recipient is nourished on necromancy. Only a matter of essentially low vitality can submit to this hypnosis, and it is soon discernible that though the passage seems purple it is shoddy. To find shoddy masquerading in the purple is artistically that which, ethically, we term vice: and it was at one time of the period we are now discussing the especial vice of English literature. In fact, every virtuoso becomes an artistic egoist, and is always writing as it were, about what he can do, which even at its best is still only the possible, rather than seeking to do that more, which is the impossible.

For the impossible is poetry. Theoretically, it cannot be done. Actually, it is done; but it is not done by any trick that we can call virtuosity. It is done by a subtle transformation of the subject matter into a something which is not other but is yet transcendent to itself; and it is done by no other means. No technical expedient can give that quality to a commonplace matter (for all matter is commonplace) which we call originality. That which we call originality is the transformation of values from the prose world to the poetic world, and the "artist" poets are generally incapable of this powerful, or subtle, effort.

Possibly the greatest and most to be mourned for failure in the annals of English poetry is that of Matthew Arnold. The work that he succeeded in doing is of great importance, even of great beauty; and one marvels that, with so complete a technique and with such internal resources as Arnold had, he was unable to lift himself beyond himself.

A poetic failure is wrongly judged if it be attributed to lack of knowledge or to lack of industry. It is more to the fact that the will of the poet fails to surmount both his nature and his culture (the latter in especial) that one should look in accounting for such a failure. Somehow, if the finality which we call poetry is to be arrived at, the poet's entire knowledge, and actually his entire personality, must be so surpassed as to be practically forgotten. It is easier to forget one's self (whom in truth one has never known) than it is to dismiss the knowledge and philosophy which one has so laboriously acquired, and yet this dismissal is fundamentally necessary for the artist, and cannot be dispensed with. Personal and cultural forgetfulness is necessary, for all personal poetry is minor poetry: and all didactic poetry is prose.

It is likely that the dissatisfaction which we continually discover in reviewing work of such great men as Coleridge, Wordsworth, and Arnold is due mainly to the fact that they are unable to agree to, or to endure, a total immersion of self in the matter they are working upon, and an attendant knowledge of and cogitation only of that. And so, too often, the final extension of being which is demanded from the poet could not be arrived at because the poets in question, on the occasions in question, were unable to dismiss themselves and their cultures summarily and completely. The Self-Ego and, in especial, the Knowledge-Ego were always getting in their way.

Something of this inability to lift beyond the norm and into an imaginative realm; to rely on invention rather than on creation, is at all times sensed in the Arnold poetry. Something of the same spiritual winglessness is continually to be sensed even in all Romantic poetry. It is the poetry of the winged heel, but not of the winged shoulder. It is indeed not "pedestrian," but that prose ill does gloom upon and threaten it.

A diminution of power, the power of complete absorption in self-forgetfulness, had come upon the greater poets of this period, and however they strove to make up the surmounting loss by virtuosity or by variety or by the substitution of philosophical or psychological for poetic values, such loss is sensed when the greatest of this verse is compared with the finest poetry of the two preceding centuries.

The case of Swinburne, another who was conceived as one of the giants of his generation, is even more curious than is that of Tennyson.

(Tennyson appears as of a richer nature than Swinburne. It is mere appearance, for Tennyson was not richly endowed; and the considerations which could interest him seemed, by being more abundant, to be more varied than those which caught the Swinburnian attention.)

At first and while we are young, feats, whether of strength or of technique, astonish us, and perhaps in terms of sheer technical agility there has not been in the history of literature one so singularly equipped as Swinburne was. It did seem that he could handle any matter that came to his pen. One can remember the astonishment (and astonishment is, while we are young, indistinguishable from delight) that came upon the first acquaintance with poems such as *Hertha*, *Faustine*, and the numerous other poems of that *genre* in Swinburne, and one can recollect also that when maturity came, a dissatisfaction came also, and a sense that this poet was one who nourished his readers upon innutritious fare.

To be pure, even as an athlete, is quite a considerable something, but it is not enough to make surrender that intangible quality which we call poetry. Power, not purity, is the master in every art.

Theoretically Swinburne, like Shelley, should have been, or could have been, a more important poet than time now reveals him to be. That quality of transformation into a more subtle medium does seem to be one which he could have attained. The fact that he did not, or but rarely attained it, reflects properly no censure upon Tennyson, in whose case one sees a poet doing what he could, and giving what he had, but in Swinburne one uneasily conjectures that here is a poet who never pulled his weight, and one surmises in him, as in many another excessively active person, a fundamental, a spiritual laziness, that would be busy at, but would not be busy upon.

After the intense appreciation of Swinburnian virtuosity is over, one finds that the occasions upon which he diligently applied himself to a work are rare. Occasionally he does arrive at an apparently complete utterance of his matter—an utterance, that is, of a completion which few of his contemporaries achieved; and it is particularly strange in grave poetry to discover that complete utterance can also be completely pessimistic utterance. The following lines are famous:

From too much love of living,
  From hope and fear set free,
We thank with brief thanksgiving
  Whatever gods may be
That no life lives forever;
That dead men rise up never;
That even the weariest river
  Winds somewhere safe to sea.

This statement is completely expressed, but the reader is left with the conviction that such a completion of utterance is also a completion of emptiness; and that, contrary to what we consider the fundamental statement of poetry, which is not a pessimism as in Swinburne, or an optimism as in Tennyson—but truth—the poets in these cases are not telling the truth, but are very completely uttering complete nonsense.

Only once did Swinburne direct himself to a matter of final gravity. In the elegy on the death of Baudelaire, entitled "*Ave Atque Vale*," he measured himself against a large task, and he drew this poem so close to true poetic value that its insecurity must be mourned for.

This poem does not "come" as the famous elegies of the past had come, and (for it is by his failures that we see how and upon what an eminence the poet is to be criticized) in the failure of this work one sees the fundamental inability of Swinburnian treatment to handle values other than those which can be expressed in a term of speed, or pace.

An instinct for speed, for pace, for the internal poise and rhythm of subject matter, is an invaluable part of poetic equipment; and a lack of or an uncertainty as to those (such as is evident in most didactic poetry) has halted and brought to impotence much sound work: but these also must be transcended, and the condition known as intensity come to. It is to this lack that the great failures of the fine English poets must be attributed, and it is as finally lacking in intensity that important writers such as Arnold, Tennyson, and Swinburne must be criticized. Of these three, of course, Arnold is easily the first.

To the rule that psychological and narrative matter are debilitating to the poet there are (if they be exceptions) three strange exceptions—Chaucer, Shakespeare, and Browning. Coupling these names does not intend that there is any similarity between the work of these poets. Shakespeare's human studies are of extremely great psychological importance; nevertheless, the tale he tells and the values he attributes are lifted by sheer mastery into an art, an area, as magical, as indefinable as is that of Blake or Shelley at their most gnomic and unknown.

Browning shares with Shakespeare a continuous and sympathetic interest in the world of action and emotion and humanity. There is much more of Emotion than Passion in Browning; and much more of Passion than Emotion in Shakespeare. Indeed in the great poets it may be held that the quality called Emotion is never present in their works, being too plebeian for such wide or rapid or intense usage, and that the place of this is invariably taken by that which we call Passion. Like Shakespeare, Browning gives the impression of being inexhaustible. He is of the few poets of whom it can be said that when one has collected an extensive selection of his verse, there remains as much again to be gathered; and that the remnant is of practically as high value as was the material already taken. There has been no poet who so squarely and securely stood upon his ground; but in his case, as in the case of every important Nineteenth Century poet, Time has not yet made its final appraisement. There is much in his art which one can think of as petulance, as fantasy (for, contrary to a widely accepted idea, poetry is rarely fantastic, and is never petulant), and one is still in doubt as to the position he will finally occupy, as one is still doubtful of the position that will at last be adjudged to Blake or to Gerard Hopkins.

Before all poetry which exhibits itself as a feat the critic must stand in some dubiety, and until Time resolves the matter the critic will admit that in the case of Browning and of Blake and of Coleridge the last word has not been said. It is easy to assert of a certain poet, in this case Browning, that he is earth-bound; that psychological curiosity is a prose but not a poetical virtue; that he has not succeeded in transcending his knowledge; that to *épater* the philosopher is, artistically, as inadmissible as to *épater* the bourgeois—he still remains astonishing; and a virtuosity of this order almost absolves itself from any criticism whatever. One can only make the interim and temporary statement that this man is so remarkable as to be marvelous, and that criticism has not yet been able to establish his complete value.

In all of these poets, something of the taint of virtuosity for its own sake can be found. Thus it is with a feeling of relief that one comes to a poetry which makes no display, which is grounded in (though that be only) an emotional reality, and which is urgently needing and seeking a confidant.

Real matter is abundantly found among the greatest, but there are poets in whom real matter is scarcely discernible at all, and who are so immersed in as to be immured in their own talents. Such a poet is Swinburne, or even Browning, in whom psychological and narrative interest tends to shadow the poetic. While the Brontë sisters need not be considered as of the ranks of the great poets, and can even, if one be rigorous in the matter, be thought of as scarcely belonging to poetry at all, yet, by reason of an earnest entering into the matter upon which they were working, two of these sisters, Emily and Anne, have contributed, though it be only a note, a poetry which is singular, and which, by force of a poignantly meditated emotion, has attained that profundity of utterance which is original and is truth.

Emily Brontë has made significant to others an emotion which was purely personal to herself, and she has come at times to a completion of statement which lifts her purely personal utterance far from the merely personal. Her trouble has been so held and communicated that it is impossible to read her poems without being (that which we too seldom are) sorry for somebody other than ourselves. This is a true feat, and, no matter though the rank of poet could be denied to her, she has succeeded in doing that which many an acclaimed poet never attains to: a perfection of imparting which is one of the curiosities, if it be no other, of this literature.

Even in the case of Anne Brontë, although it be only in four or five poems, a something of that same urgent earnestness and significance is also come to.

Charlotte Brontë is quite distinct in this consideration from her two sisters. In her case it is prose that matters, and although, from the record of her prose writings, readers would consider that she had feelings and capacities beyond, and had suffered or imagined beyond the range of her sisters, the poetic tale, as told by them and by her, consigns her, on these grounds, to a considerably lower place. It could finally be said of Charlotte Brontë's poetry that it is valueless, while in the case of her sisters, though the amount be limited, it is yet so good that one is inclined to give them precedence over their great and wonderful sister.

It will be observed that in this survey reference has only been made to those authors who may be considered as the most significant poets of the century: and that the writer has dwelt with more emphasis on the weakness of these writers than on their strength.

The work of eulogy upon these great men has been abundantly done; and it is time that attention should be directed to the negative, the undecided, the extravagant and wasteful aspects of this production.

Such a situating of attention is the more needed if it can be considered (as the writer considers) that the official Classical and Romantic modes of poetry have reached their term: and that our day warrants the assumption that new values must be identified, and that a new method must be evolved for dealing with them.

There is no lack of talent amongst us today, and, perhaps, there is no lack of energy. On this latter we are uninformed, and no man's speculation is better than another's on the point. We must attend until Time discloses the possession or the absence of this central quality.

That something is lacking to us is evident, and is grievous. What is lacking now, and has been lacking since the death of Tennyson, is subject matter.

Today, whether it be for poetry or for prose, for painting or for music, there is no artistic-subject: and in consequence, no demand upon and no production of the graver artistic-energy. It may be; it almost assuredly is, that our predecessors have plundered and exhausted our fields; and that even the instrument of production, technique, has been so diligently overused by them that it, too, comes blunt and inapt to our needs, and will work no more.

That long poetic odyssey which may conveniently be referred to as the Shakespearian adventure, was completed in Tennyson: for, though an art may become trivial and yet recover, it cannot descend to vulgarity and be quicked again. In vulgarity it comes to its earth, and will be buried there.

No further adventure is possible under an Elizabethan ensign, and after more than three hundred years of conquest and splendor, we may bid that poetry adieu.

Passed for Press

James Stephens

ALFRED, LORD TENNYSON

[August 6, 1809–October 6, 1892]

ALFRED TENNYSON, fourth of the twelve children of George Clayton Tennyson and Elizabeth Fytche, was born at the rectory in Somersby, a little village in Lincolnshire. Tennyson and his brothers and sisters had the run of the excellent library of their rector father, and here they eagerly read such fine things as the plays of Shakespeare, Milton's poems, Addison's and Swift's essays, the Bible, and the fantastic tale of Cervantes.

Lincolnshire is a land of misty wolds, "of large fields, gray hillsides, and noble tall-towered churches." The rectory stood on a shady lawn, with a sunny flower garden, beyond the trees, rich in roses, lilies, hollyhocks, and purple lavender. The beautiful quiet countryside roundabout was a choice ranging ground for young boys, and here Tennyson and his brothers ran about from place to place and "took long walks at night-time." This early life in the woods and fields fostered the love for nature that must have been innate in the boy Tennyson and doubtless went a long way in developing in him the accurate and intimate knowledge of nature shown in many of his poems.

From 1816 to 1820 the boy Tennyson was a pupil of Louth Grammar School. Following this he received some instruction from private teachers, but his father was his chief teacher in his preparation for Trinity College, Cambridge, which he and his brother Charles entered in 1828. In 1827 he and Charles had published a volume of one hundred two poems entitled *Poems by Two Brothers* and reflecting the boys' fondness for Byron and Scott, Moore and Thomson. The editor of the *Literary Chronicle* noticed this book and said in mild praise of it that it contained "several little pieces of considerable merit;" but Tennyson himself always called it his "early rot."

At Cambridge Tennyson, who was a shy, reserved young man, did not make many acquaintances. He did, however, have a few intimate friends, some of whom, like himself, were to become famous in later years. Among these were Archbishop Trench, Henry Alford, Dean of Canterbury, and the historians, Merivale and Kinglake.

Tennyson's most loved and intimate friend in this Cambridge group was Arthur Hallam, son of the historian. Together with Hallam and the other serious-minded young men of his circle, Tennyson became a member of the "Apostles," a debating club given over to the discussion of two subjects mainly—political liberty and pure religion. The influence of this group upon Tennyson as a poet was not for the best, some late critics have suggested, since the members talked too much about the mission of the poet, who, they said, must be both sage and prophet. *The Poet*, a poem published in 1830 in the volume *Poems, Chiefly Lyrical*, and announcing his high ideal of the poet's calling, is pointed to by these critics as evidence of how the "Apostles" discussions had influenced his ideas of the poet and his destiny.

Whatever truth there may be in this criticism, a few discriminating English readers heard in some of the verses of the 1830 volume a new note in their poetry. Coleridge, who should have heard it, missed it and said of the author that he wrote "without very well understanding what metre is." Leigh Hunt heard it and praised it in the *Tatler*, as did Arthur Hallam in the *Englishman's Magazine*.

One act of Tennyson's that some have tried to trace back to the debates on political liberty in the "Apostles" meetings, was the romantic mission he entered upon in the summer of 1830 for the purpose of carrying funds to help the revolutionists in Portugal. Arthur Hallam was his companion on this mission, an undertaking which was not without real danger for the two young lovers of liberty, but which brought them no harm and ended with the safe delivery of the money.

In February, 1831, Tennyson left Cambridge without taking a degree. A few weeks later his father died, and for the next six years the young poet was at the family home in Somersby working over with scrupulous care the poems he had already printed and writing new ones. In 1832 he published a volume containing some of his most beautiful and most characteristic poetry—for example, *The Lady of Shalott*, *The Lotos-Eaters*, and *Œnone*. The book received little praise from any one except his University friends who, even in his undergraduate days, had hailed him as the poet-philosopher of the new age. Coleridge, still worried about the metre of Tennyson, said of the new volume, "I can scarcely scan his verses." The reviewers directed a merciless attack at it, the sneering Lockhart writing in the *Quarterly Review* for April, 1833, that he introduced "to the admiration of his more sequestered readers a new prodigy of genius—another and a brighter star of that galaxy or Milky Way of poetry of which the lamented Keats was the harbinger." He then went on "to point out . . . the peculiar brilliancy of some of the gems that irradiate his [Tennyson's] poetical crown." Criticism of this kind directed at a poet of the present day would probably be no more effective than cork balls thrown against granite, but the influence of Lockhart and his kind upon the reading public a hundred years ago was so formidable that it could almost make or break a poet. Poor Tennyson was ridiculed from so many sides that, almost broken, he published no more poetry for ten years.

In September of the same year a still deeper sorrow came to the poet. His most loved friend, Arthur Hallam, who was the accepted suitor of Tennyson's sister Emily and whom Tennyson considered "as near perfection as mortal man could be," died suddenly while traveling on the Continent. What the loss meant to Tennyson we may see in some small measure by reading the poems that grew out of it: *The Two Voices*, *Ulysses*, and the long *In Memoriam.*

The ten years following the publication of the 1832 volume were years of serious difficulties and problems for Tennyson. He lived with his mother and sister, "now here now there . . . always within reach of London, never in it . . . a man solitary and sad, carrying a bit of Chaos about him," studying, writing poetry, especially *In Memoriam*, revising his early poems, and brooding over his sorrows and disappointments. He fell in love with Emily Sellwood but believed himself too poor to marry her. He became an intimate friend of Carlyle, who advised him to give up writing poetry and who described him as "One of the finest looking men in the world. A great shock of rough dusky dark hair; bright, laughing, hazel eyes; massive aquiline face, most massive yet most delicate; of sallow brown complexion, almost Indian looking; clothes cynically loose, free-and-easy, smokes infinite tobacco. His voice is musical, metallic, fit for loud laughter and piercing wail, and all that may lie between; speech and speculation free and plenteous."

Finally, in 1842, out of this "bit of Chaos" which he carried about him came Cosmos. In this year he published his two volumes of *Poems*, containing revisions of many of his earlier poems and such well-known new ones as *Morte d'Arthur*, *Ulysses*, *Locksley Hall*, and *Break, Break, Break.* If the high perfection he reached in *Poems* could come only at the cost of ten years of brooding, gloomy speculation and painstaking study, one feels that the new book was ample reward for that long decade of silence. The book caught the fancy of the English reader, and through it Tennyson achieved a popularity that, after the reviews of 1833, he must have despaired of reaching.

About this time, however, some unpleasant things occurred to offset the success of the new poems. For example, he sold his small estate to obtain money for investment in a scheme promoted by the "Patent Decorative Carving Company" to make carved oak by machinery. The scheme failed inevitably, and Tennyson was left without a penny. So deeply did this loss affect him both mentally and physically that he suffered severely from his old melancholy, and he was for months under the care of a Cheltenham physician. In 1845 he was rescued from the poverty into which his speculation had thrown him by a government pension of £200 a year.

During these unhappy years his importance as a poet continued to grow. In America Edgar Allan Poe spoke of him as the noblest poet that ever lived; in England Wordsworth, the Laureate, called him "the first of our living poets." Even Carlyle, who a few years before had advised him to give up poetry, wrote him a letter praising his latest volume.

With his return to health Tennyson resumed his poetic activity. In 1847 he published *The Princess*, a poem containing some of his most beautiful lyrics and reflecting his interest in one of the absorbing problems of the day—the higher education of woman. In 1850 *In Memoriam* appeared, a poem about which Tennyson was for a long time reluctant to speak, and which, when it first appeared, did not carry the impress of the author's name.

A few days after the appearance of *In Memoriam*, Tennyson married Emily Sellwood, whom he had known and loved for twenty years. In November of the same year he accepted the Laureateship, succeeding Wordsworth, and in March, 1851, he was presented to the Queen at Buckingham Palace. That he was a Laureate of the right mettle he soon proved with his fine *Ode on the Death of the Duke of Wellington.*

The first three years of his married life Tennyson lived at Twickenham, but in November, 1853, he leased the fine house and farm of Farringford on the Isle of Wight, which he later bought, and for which he paid with the money he received from *Maud and Other Poems.* He was very fond of Farringford, but as time went on and his fame grew, tourists and celebrity-hunters sought him in such numbers that he felt compelled to build a house where he could not be so easily found. The place he chose for this was on Blackdown, in Surrey. The house, which he built in 1868 and '69 and called Aldworth, shared his presence with Farringford from 1870 to the end. The stream of curious tourists continued whenever he was at Farringford, but most of them went away with nothing more than a memory of a large, aloof man in a big blue cape and black sombrero striding about the grounds of the estate with some nobility even in that garb.

The year 1850 was the beginning of a new era for Tennyson. The years before had been years of high hopes that were soon shattered, of disappointments and sorrows; the years that followed (and there were forty-two of them) were years of happiness, of social and financial success, of high poetic achievement. Indeed, for more than forty years following 1850 Tennyson worked faithfully at the writing of poetry, perfecting and completing during this period the cycle of poems considered by many discriminating readers as his most distinctive work—the *Idylls of the King.* During this period, too, he published *Maud, The Charge of the Light Brigade, Enoch Arden*, the dramatic trilogy, *Queen Mary, Harold*, and *Becket, Locksley Hall Sixty Years After*, and *Demeter and Other Poems.* His industry never flagged, and a few weeks after his death, which occurred at Aldworth in October, 1892, a new volume, *The Death of Oenone, Akbar's Dream, and Other Poems*, came from the press.

The social and civic recognition that came to Tennyson in the last half of his life was significant. In 1855 he received the degree of D. C. L. from Oxford. Browning, Ruskin, Huxley, Gladstone, Prince Albert, and many other distinguished Englishmen became his warm friends and visited him at his home. He declined the Lord Rectorship of Glasgow University and a baronetcy offered him by the Queen, the latter with the words, "I had rather we should remain plain Mr. and Mrs." In 1883, however, after much persuasion, he accepted from the Queen the honor of a peerage, a dignity which he did not desire for himself but which he said he must accept, since it was a tribute from the Throne to Literature.

It is the fashion of some present day critics to strive for smartness when they speak unfavorably of Tennyson's work. "Tears, idle tears, I know not what they mean," they quote, and then say glibly, "Tennyson wouldn't." One who, like Tennyson, knows that tears do sometimes gather unaccountably in the eyes of sensitive but perfectly normal people may be forgiven, perhaps, if he replies to these critics, with something of their own flippancy, "You *would* say that." If the first remark is literary criticism, so is the second. Tennyson cannot be dismissed as an entirely superficial thinker. He did not discover the secret of tears—no one ever will—, but the beauty of the lyric arising from his thinking upon it has profoundly impressed those readers whose sensitivity gives them an instant appreciation of what was in the poet's soul. Whatever the critics may say about Tennyson, his place in English poetry is secure. To have written half a score of lyrics that reappear in every "Golden Treasury" of English verse is an accomplishment that no unfavorable criticism can belittle.

LILIAN

I

Airy, fairy Lilian,
Flitting, fairy Lilian,
When I ask her if she love me,
Claps her tiny hands above me,
Laughing all she can;
She'll not tell me if she love me,
Cruel little Lilian.

II

When my passion seeks
Pleasance in love-sighs,
She, looking thro' and thro' me
Thoroughly to undo me,
Smiling, never speaks:
So innocent-arch, so cunning-simple,
From beneath her gathered wimple
Glancing with black-beaded eyes,
Till the lightning laughters dimple
The baby-roses in her cheeks;
Then away she flies.

III

Prythee weep, May Lilian!
Gaiety without eclipse
Wearieth me, May Lilian:
Thro' my very heart it thrilleth
When from crimson-threaded lips
Silver-treble laughter trilleth:
Prythee weep, May Lilian.

IV

Praying all I can,
If prayers will not hush thee,
Airy Lilian,
Like a rose-leaf I will crush thee,
Fairy Lilian.

1830

CLARIBEL

A MELODY

I

Where Claribel low-lieth
The breezes pause and die,
Letting the rose-leaves fall:
But the solemn oak-tree sigheth,
Thick-leaved, ambrosial,
With an ancient melody
Of an inward agony,
Where Claribel low-lieth.

II

At eve the beetle boometh
Athwart the thicket lone:
At noon the wild bee hummeth
About the moss'd headstone:
At midnight the moon cometh,
And looketh down alone.
Her song the lintwhite swelleth,
The clear-voiced mavis dwelleth,
The callow throstle lispeth,
The slumbrous wave outwelleth,
The babbling runnel crispeth,
The hollow grot replieth
Where Claribel low-lieth.

1830

SONG

I

A spirit haunts the year's last hours
Dwelling amid these yellowing bowers:
To himself he talks;
For at eventide, listening earnestly,
At his work you may hear him sob and sigh
In the walks;
Earthward he boweth the heavy stalks
Of the mouldering flowers:
Heavily hangs the broad sunflower
Over its grave i' the earth so chilly;
Heavily hangs the hollyhock,
Heavily hangs the tiger-lily.

II

The air is damp, and hush'd, and close,
As a sick man's room when he taketh repose
An hour before death;
My very heart faints and my whole soul grieves
At the moist rich smell of the rotting leaves,
And the breath
Of the fading edges of box beneath,
And the year's last rose.
Heavily hangs the broad sunflower
Over its grave i' the earth so chilly;
Heavily hangs the hollyhock,
Heavily hangs the tiger-lily.

1830

MARIANA

"Mariana in the moated grange."
Measure for Measure.

WITH blackest moss the flower-plots
Were thickly crusted, one and all:
The rusted nails fell from the knots
That held the pear to the gable-wall.
The broken sheds look'd sad and strange:
Unlifted was the clinking latch;
Weeded and worn the ancient thatch
Upon the lonely moated grange.
She only said, "My life is dreary,
He cometh not," she said;
She said, "I am aweary, aweary,
I would that I were dead!"

Her tears fell with the dews at even;
Her tears fell ere the dews were dried;
She could not look on the sweet heaven,
Either at morn or eventide.
After the flitting of the bats,
When thickest dark did trance the sky,
She drew her casement-curtain by,
And glanced athwart the glooming flats.
She only said, "The night is dreary,
He cometh not," she said;
She said, "I am aweary, aweary,
I would that I were dead!"

Upon the middle of the night,
Waking she heard the night-fowl crow:
The cock sung out an hour ere light:
From the dark fen the oxen's low
Came to her: without hope of change,
In sleep she seem'd to walk forlorn,
Till cold winds woke the gray-eyed morn
About the lonely moated grange.
She only said, "The day is dreary,
He cometh not," she said;
She said, "I am aweary, aweary,
I would that I were dead!"

About a stone-cast from the wall
A sluice with blacken'd waters slept,
And o'er it many, round and small,
The cluster'd marish-mosses crept.
Hard by a poplar shook alway,
All silver-green with gnarled bark:
For leagues no other tree did mark
The level waste, the rounding gray.
She only said, "My life is dreary,
He cometh not," she said;
She said, "I am aweary, aweary,
I would that I were dead!"

And ever when the moon was low,
And the shrill winds were up and away,
In the white curtain, to and fro,
She saw the gusty shadow sway.
But when the moon was very low,
And wild winds bound within their cell,
The shadow of the poplar fell
Upon her bed, across her brow.
She only said, "The night is dreary,
He cometh not," she said;
She said, "I am aweary, aweary,
I would that I were dead!"

All day within the dreamy house,
The doors upon their hinges creak'd;
The blue fly sung in the pane; the mouse
Behind the mouldering wainscot shriek'd,
Or from the crevice peer'd about.
Old faces glimmer'd thro' the doors,
Old footsteps trod the upper floors,
Old voices called her from without.
She only said, "My life is dreary,
He cometh not," she said;
She said, "I am aweary, aweary,
I would that I were dead!"

The sparrow's chirrup on the roof,
The slow clock ticking, and the sound
Which to the wooing wind aloof
The poplar made, did all confound
Her sense; but most she loathed the hour
When the thick-moted sunbeam lay
Athwart the chambers, and the day
Was sloping toward his western bower.
Then, said she, "I am very dreary,
He will not come," she said;
She wept, "I am aweary, aweary,
Oh God, that I were dead!"

1830

RECOLLECTIONS OF THE ARABIAN NIGHTS

WHEN the breeze of a joyful dawn blew free
In the silken sail of infancy,
The tide of time flow'd back with me,
The forward-flowing tide of time;

And many a sheeny summer-morn,
Adown the Tigris I was borne,
By Bagdat's shrines of fretted gold,
High-walled gardens green and old;
True Mussulman was I and sworn,
For it was in the golden prime
Of good Haroun Alraschid.

Anight my shallop, rustling thro'
The low and bloomed foliage, drove
The fragrant, glistening deeps, and clove
The citron-shadows in the blue:
By garden porches on the brim,
The costly doors flung open wide,
Gold glittering thro' lamplight dim,
And broider'd sofas on each side:
In sooth it was a goodly time,
For it was in the golden prime
Of good Haroun Alraschid.

Often, where clear-stemm'd platans guard
The outlet, did I turn away
The boat-head down a broad canal
From the main river sluiced, where all
The sloping of the moon-lit sward
Was damask-work, and deep inlay
Of braided blooms unmown, which crept
Adown to where the water slept.
A goodly place, a goodly time,
For it was in the golden prime
Of good Haroun Alraschid.

A motion from the river won
Ridged the smooth level, bearing on
My shallop thro' the star-strown calm,
Until another night in night
I enter'd, from the clearer light,
Imbower'd vaults of pillar'd palm,
Imprisoning sweets, which, as they clomb
Heavenward, were stay'd beneath the dome
Of hollow boughs. — A goodly time,
For it was in the golden prime
Of good Haroun Alraschid.

Still onward; and the clear canal
Is rounded to as clear a lake.
From the green rivage many a fall
Of diamond rillets musical,
Thro' little crystal arches low
Down from the central fountain's flow
Fall'n silver-chiming, seemed to shake
The sparkling flints beneath the prow.
A goodly place, a goodly time,
For it was in the golden prime
Of good Haroun Alraschid.

Above thro' many a bowery turn
A walk with vary-colour'd shells
Wander'd engrain'd. On either side
All round about the fragrant marge
From fluted vase, and brazen urn
In order, eastern flowers large,
Some dropping low their crimson bells
Half-closed, and others studded wide
With disks and tiars, fed the time
With odour in the golden prime
Of good Haroun Alraschid.

Far off, and where the lemon grove
In closest coverture upsprung,
The living airs of middle night
Died round the bulbul as he sung;
Not he: but something which possess'd
The darkness of the world, delight,
Life, anguish, death, immortal love,
Ceasing not, mingled, unrepress'd,
Apart from place, withholding time,
But flattering the golden prime
Of good Haroun Alraschid.

Black the garden-bowers and grots
Slumber'd: the solemn palms were ranged
Above, unwoo'd of summer wind:
A sudden splendour from behind
Flush'd all the leaves with rich gold-green,
And, flowing rapidly between
Their interspaces, counterchanged
The level lake with diamond-plots
Of dark and bright. A lovely time,
For it was in the golden prime
Of good Haroun Alraschid.

Dark-blue the deep sphere overhead,
Distinct with vivid stars inlaid,
Grew darker from that under-flame:
So, leaping lightly from the boat,
With silver anchor left afloat,
In marvel whence that glory came
Upon me, as in sleep I sank
In cool soft turf upon the bank,
Entranced with that place and time,
So worthy of the golden prime
Of good Haroun Alraschid.

Thence thro' the garden I was drawn—
A realm of pleasance, many a mound,
And many a shadow-chequer'd lawn
Full of the city's stilly sound,
And deep myrrh-thickets blowing round
The stately cedar, tamarisks,
Thick rosaries of scented thorn,
Tall orient shrubs, and obelisks
Graven with emblems of the time,
In honour of the golden prime
Of good Haroun Alraschid.

With dazed vision unawares
From the long alley's latticed shade
Emerged, I came upon the great
Pavilion of the Caliphat.
Right to the carven cedarn doors,
Flung inward over spangled floors,
Broad-based flights of marble stairs
Ran up with golden balustrade,
After the fashion of the time,
And humour of the golden prime
Of good Haroun Alraschid.

The fourscore windows all alight
As with the quintessence of flame,
A million tapers flaring bright
From twisted silvers look'd to shame
The hollow-vaulted dark, and stream'd
Upon the mooned domes aloof
In inmost Bagdat, till there seem'd
Hundreds of crescents on the roof
Of night new-risen, that marvellous time
To celebrate the golden prime
Of good Haroun Alraschid.

Then stole I up, and trancedly
Gazed on the Persian girl alone,
Serene with argent-lidded eyes
Amorous, and lashes like to rays
Of darkness, and a brow of pearl
Tressed with redolent ebony,
In many a dark delicious curl,
Flowing beneath her rose-hued zone;
The sweetest lady of the time,
Well worthy of the golden prime
Of good Haroun Alraschid.

Six columns, three on either side,
Pure silver, underpropt a rich
Throne of the massive ore, from which
Down-droop'd, in many a floating fold,
Engarlanded and diaper'd
With inwrought flowers, a cloth of gold.
Thereon, his deep eye laughter-stirr'd
With merriment of kingly pride,
Sole star of all that place and time,
I saw him—in his golden prime,
The Good Haroun Alraschid.

1830

THE KRAKEN

Below the thunders of the upper deep;
Far, far beneath in the abysmal sea,
His ancient, dreamless, uninvaded sleep
The Kraken sleepeth: faintest sunlights flee
About his shadowy sides: above him swell
Huge sponges of millennial growth and height;
And far away into the sickly light,
From many a wondrous grot and secret cell
Unnumber'd and enormous polypi
Winnow with giant arms the slumbering green.
There hath he lain for ages and will lie
Battening upon huge seaworms in his sleep,
Until the latter fire shall heat the deep;
Then once by man and angels to be seen,
In roaring he shall rise and on the surface die.

1830

THE POET

The poet in a golden clime was born,
With golden stars above;
Dower'd with the hate of hate, the scorn of scorn,
The love of love.

He saw thro' life and death, thro' good and ill,
He saw thro' his own soul.
The marvel of the everlasting will,
An open scroll,

Before him lay: with echoing feet he threaded
The secretest walks of fame:
The viewless arrows of his thoughts were headed
And wing'd with flame,

Like Indian reeds blown from his silver tongue,
And of so fierce a flight,
From Calpe unto Caucasus they sung,
Filling with light

And vagrant melodies the winds which bore
Them earthward till they lit;
Then, like the arrow-seeds of the field flower,
The fruitful wit

Cleaving, took root, and springing forth anew
Where'er they fell, behold,
Like to the mother plant in semblance, grew
A flower all gold,

And bravely furnish'd all abroad to fling
The winged shafts of truth,
To throng with stately blooms the breathing spring
Of Hope and Youth.

So many minds did gird their orbs with beams,
Tho' one did fling the fire.
Heaven flow'd upon the soul in many dreams
Of high desire.

Thus truth was multiplied on truth, the world
Like one great garden show'd,
And thro' the wreaths of floating dark up-curl'd,
Rare sunrise flow'd.

And Freedom rear'd in that august sunrise
Her beautiful bold brow,
When rites and forms before his burning eyes
Melted like snow.

There was no blood upon her maiden robes
Sunn'd by those orient skies;
But round about the circles of the globes
Of her keen eyes

And in her raiment's hem was traced in flame
WISDOM, a name to shake
All evil dreams of power—a sacred name.
And when she spake,

Her words did gather thunder as they ran,
And as the lightning to the thunder
Which follows it, riving the spirit of man,
Making earth wonder,

So was their meaning to her words. No sword
Of wrath her right arm whirl'd,
But one poor poet's scroll, and with *his* word
She shook the world.

1830

TO J. M. K.

MY hope and heart is with thee—thou wilt be
A latter Luther, and a soldier-priest
To scare church-harpies from the master's feast;
Our dusted velvets have much need of thee:
Thou art no sabbath-drawler of old saws,
Distill'd from some worm-canker'd homily;
But spurr'd at heart with fieriest energy
To embattail and to wall about thy cause
With iron-worded proof, hating to hark
The humming of the drowsy pulpit-drone
Half God's good sabbath, while the worn-out clerk
Brow-beats his desk below. Thou from a throne
Mounted in heaven wilt shoot into the dark
Arrows of lightnings. I will stand and mark.

1830

THE MILLER'S DAUGHTER

I SEE the wealthy miller yet,
His double chin, his portly size,
And who that knew him could forget
The busy wrinkles round his eyes?
The slow wise smile that, round about
His dusty forehead drily curl'd,
Seem'd half-within and half-without,
And full of dealings with the world?

In yonder chair I see him sit,
Three fingers round the old silver cup—
I see his gray eyes twinkle yet
At his own jest—gray eyes lit up
With summer lightnings of a soul
So full of summer warmth, so glad,
So healthy, sound, and clear and whole,
His memory scarce can make me sad.

Yet fill my glass: give me one kiss:
My own sweet Alice, we must die.
There's somewhat in this world amiss
Shall be unriddled by and by.
There's somewhat flows to us in life,
But more is taken quite away.
Pray, Alice, pray, my darling wife,
That we may die the self-same day.

Have I not found a happy earth?
  I least should breathe a thought of pain.
Would God renew me from my birth
  I'd almost live my life again.
So sweet it seems with thee to walk,
  And once again to woo thee mine—
It seems in after-dinner talk
  Across the walnuts and the wine—

To be the long and listless boy
  Late-left an orphan of the squire,
Where this old mansion mounted high
  Looks down upon the village spire:
For even here, where I and you
  Have lived and loved alone so long,
Each morn my sleep was broken thro'
  By some wild skylark's matin song.

And oft I heard the tender dove
  In firry woodlands making moan;
But ere I saw your eyes, my love,
  I had no motion of my own.
For scarce my life with fancy play'd
  Before I dream'd that pleasant dream—
Still hither thither idly sway'd
  Like those long mosses in the stream.

Or from the bridge I lean'd to hear
  The milldam rushing down with noise,
And see the minnows everywhere
  In crystal eddies glance and poise,
The tall flag-flowers when they sprung
  Below the range of stepping-stones,
Or those three chestnuts near, that hung
  In masses thick with milky cones.

But, Alice, what an hour was that,
  When after roving in the woods
('Twas April then), I came and sat
  Below the chestnuts, when their buds
Were glistening to the breezy blue;
  And on the slope, an absent fool,
I cast me down, nor thought of you,
  But angled in the higher pool.

A love-song I had somewhere read,
  An echo from a measured strain,
Beat time to nothing in my head
  From some odd corner of the brain.
It haunted me, the morning long,
  With weary sameness in the rhymes,
The phantom of a silent song,
  That went and came a thousand times.

Then leapt a trout. In lazy mood
  I watch'd the little circles die;
They past into the level flood,
  And there a vision caught my eye;
The reflex of a beauteous form,
  A glowing arm, a gleaming neck,
As when a sunbeam wavers warm
  Within the dark and dimpled beck.

For you remember, you had set,
  That morning, on the casement-edge
A long green box of mignonette,
  And you were leaning from the ledge
And when I raised my eyes, above
  They met with two so full and bright—
Such eyes! I swear to you, my love,
  That these have never lost their light.

I loved, and love dispell'd the fear
  That I should die an early death:
For love possess'd the atmosphere,
  And fill'd the breast with purer breath.
My mother thought, What ails the boy?
  For I was alter'd, and began
To move about the house with joy,
  And with the certain step of man.

I loved the brimming wave that swam
  Thro' quiet meadows round the mill,
The sleepy pool above the dam,
  The pool beneath it never still,
The meal-sacks on the whiten'd floor,
  The dark round of the dripping wheel,
The very air about the door
  Made misty with the floating meal.

And oft in ramblings on the wold,
  When April nights began to blow,
And April's crescent glimmer'd cold,
  I saw the village lights below;
I knew your taper far away,
  And full at heart of trembling hope,
From off the wold I came, and lay
  Upon the freshly-flower'd slope.

The deep brook groan'd beneath the mill;
  And "by that lamp," I thought, "she sits!"
The white chalk-quarry from the hill
  Gleam'd to the flying moon by fits.
"O that I were beside her now!
  O will she answer if I call?
O would she give me vow for vow,
  Sweet Alice, if I told her all?"

Sometimes I saw you sit and spin;
And, in the pauses of the wind,
Sometimes I heard you sing within;
Sometimes your shadow cross'd the blind.
At last you rose and moved the light,
And the long shadow of the chair
Flitted across into the night,
And all the casement darken'd there.

But when at last I dared to speak,
The lanes, you know, were white with may,
Your ripe lips moved not, but your cheek
Flush'd like the coming of the day;
And so it was—half-sly, half-shy,
You would, and would not, little one!
Although I pleaded tenderly,
And you and I were all alone.

And slowly was my mother brought
To yield consent to my desire:
She wish'd me happy, but she thought
I might have look'd a little higher;
And I was young—too young to wed:
"Yet must I love her for your sake;
Go fetch your Alice here," she said:
Her eyelid quiver'd as she spake.

And down I went to fetch my bride:
But, Alice, you were ill at ease;
This dress and that by turns you tried,
Too fearful that you should not please.
I loved you better for your fears,
I knew you could not look but well;
And dews, that would have fall'n in tears,
I kiss'd away before they fell.

I watch'd the little flutterings,
The doubt my mother would not see;
She spoke at large of many things,
And at the last she spoke of me;
And turning look'd upon your face,
As near this door you sat apart,
And rose, and, with a silent grace
Approaching, press'd you heart to heart.

Ah, well—but sing the foolish song
I gave you, Alice, on the day
When, arm in arm, we went along,
A pensive pair, and you were gay
With bridal flowers—that I may seem,
As in the nights of old, to lie
Beside the mill-wheel in the stream,
While those full chestnuts whisper by.

It is the miller's daughter,
And she is grown so dear, so dear,
That I would be the jewel
That trembles in her ear:
For hid in ringlets day and night,
I'd touch her neck so warm and white.

And I would be the girdle
About her dainty dainty waist,
And her heart would beat against me,
In sorrow and in rest:
And I should know if it beat right,
I'd clasp it round so close and tight.

And I would be the necklace,
And all day long to fall and rise
Upon her balmy bosom,
With her laughter or her sighs,
And I would lie so light, so light,
I scarce should be unclasp'd at night.

A trifle, sweet! which true love spells—
True love interprets—right alone.
His light upon the letter dwells,
For all the spirit is his own.
So, if I waste words now, in truth
You must blame Love. His early rage
Had force to make me rhyme in youth,
And makes me talk too much in age.

And now those vivid hours are gone,
Like mine own life to me thou art,
Where Past and Present, wound in one,
Do make a garland for the heart:
So sing that other song I made,
Half-anger'd with my happy lot,
The day, when in the chestnut shade
I found the blue Forget-me-not.

Love that hath us in the net,
Can he pass, and we forget?
Many suns arise and set.
Many a chance the years beget.
Love the gift is Love the debt.
Even so.
Love is hurt with jar and fret.
Love is made a vague regret.
Eyes with idle tears are wet.
Idle habit links us yet.
What is love? for we forget:
Ah, no! no!

Look thro' mine eyes with thine. True wife,
Round my true heart thine arms entwine
My other dearer life in life,
Look thro' my very soul with thine!
Untouch'd with any shade of years,
May those kind eyes for ever dwell!
They have not shed a many tears,
Dear eyes, since first I knew them well.

Yet tears they shed: they had their part
  Of sorrow: for when time was ripe,
The still affection of the heart
  Became an outward breathing type,
That into stillness past again,
  And left a want unknown before;
Although the loss had brought us pain,
  That loss but made us love the more,

With farther lookings on. The kiss,
  The woven arms, seem but to be
Weak symbols of the settled bliss,
  The comfort, I have found in thee:
But that God bless thee, dear—who wrought
  Two spirits to one equal mind—
With blessings beyond hope or thought,
  With blessings which no words can find.

Arise, and let us wander forth,
  To yon old mill across the wolds;
For look, the sunset, south and north,
  Winds all the vale in rosy folds,
And fires your narrow casement glass,
  Touching the sullen pool below:
On the chalk-hill the bearded grass
  Is dry and dewless. Let us go.

1832, 1842

BUONAPARTE

He thought to quell the stubborn hearts of oak,
Madman!—to chain with chains, and bind with bands
That island queen who sways the floods and lands
From Ind to Ind, but in fair daylight woke,
When from her wooden walls,—lit by sure hands,—
With thunders, and with lightnings, and with smoke,—
Peal after peal, the British battle broke,
Lulling the brine against the Coptic sands.
We taught him lowlier moods, when Elsinore
Heard the war moan along the distant sea,
Rocking with shatter'd spars, with sudden fires
Flamed over: at Trafalgar yet once more
We taught him: late he learned humility
Perforce, like those whom Gideon school'd with briers.

1832

THE LADY OF SHALOTT

PART I

On either side the river lie
Long fields of barley and of rye,
That clothe the wold and meet the sky;
And thro' the field the road runs by
    To many-tower'd Camelot;
And up and down the people go,
Gazing where the lilies blow
Round an island there below,
    The island of Shalott.

Willows whiten, aspens quiver,
Little breezes dusk and shiver
Thro' the wave that runs for ever
By the island in the river
    Flowing down to Camelot.
Four gray walls, and four gray towers,
Overlook a space of flowers,
And the silent isle imbowers
    The Lady of Shalott.

By the margin, willow-veil'd,
Slide the heavy barges trail'd
By slow horses; and unhail'd
The shallop flitteth silken-sail'd
    Skimming down to Camelot:
But who hath seen her wave her hand?
Or at the casement seen her stand?
Or is she known in all the land,
    The Lady of Shalott?

Only reapers, reaping early
In among the bearded barley,
Hear a song that echoes cheerly
From the river winding clearly,
    Down to tower'd Camelot:
And by the moon the reaper weary,
Piling sheaves in uplands airy,
Listening, whispers "'Tis the fairy
    Lady of Shalott."

PART II

There she weaves by night and day
A magic web with colours gay.
She has heard a whisper say,
A curse is on her if she stay
    To look down to Camelot.

She knows not what the curse may be,
And so she weaveth steadily,
And little other care hath she,
The Lady of Shalott.

And moving thro' a mirror clear
That hangs before her all the year,
Shadows of the world appear.
There she sees the highway near
Winding down to Camelot:
There the river eddy whirls,
And there the surly village-churls,
And the red cloaks of market girls,
Pass onward from Shalott.

Sometimes a troop of damsels glad,
An abbot on an ambling pad,
Sometimes a curly shepherd-lad,
Or long-hair'd page in crimson clad,
Goes by to tower'd Camelot;
And sometimes thro' the mirror blue
The knights come riding two and two:
She hath no loyal knight and true,
The Lady of Shalott.

But in her web she still delights
To weave the mirror's magic sights,
For often thro' the silent nights
A funeral, with plumes and lights
And music, went to Camelot:
Or when the moon was overhead,
Came two young lovers lately wed;
"I am half sick of shadows," said
The Lady of Shalott.

PART III

A BOW-SHOT from her bower-eaves,
He rode between the barley-sheaves,
The sun came dazzling thro' the leaves,
And flamed upon the brazen greaves
Of bold Sir Lancelot.
A red-cross knight for ever kneel'd
To a lady in his shield,
That sparkled on the yellow field,
Beside remote Shalott.

The gemmy bridle glitter'd free,
Like to some branch of stars we see
Hung in the golden Galaxy.
The bridle bells rang merrily
As he rode down to Camelot:
And from his blazon'd baldric slung
A mighty silver bugle hung,
And as he rode his armour rung,
Beside remote Shalott.

All in the blue unclouded weather
Thick-jewell'd shone the saddle-leather,
The helmet and the helmet-feather
Burn'd like one burning flame together,
As he rode down to Camelot.
As often thro' the purple night,
Below the starry clusters bright,
Some bearded meteor, trailing light,
Moves over still Shalott.

His broad clear brow in sunlight glow'd;
On burnish'd hooves his war-horse trode;
From underneath his helmet flow'd
His coal-black curls as on he rode,
As he rode down to Camelot.
From the bank and from the river
He flash'd into the crystal mirror,
"Tirra lirra," by the river
Sang Sir Lancelot.

She left the web, she left the loom,
She made three paces thro' the room,
She saw the water-lily bloom,
She saw the helmet and the plume,
She look'd down to Camelot.
Out flew the web and floated wide;
The mirror crack'd from side to side;
"The curse is come upon me," cried
The Lady of Shalott.

PART IV

IN the stormy east-wind straining,
The pale yellow woods were waning,
The broad stream in his banks complaining,
Heavily the low sky raining
Over tower'd Camelot;
Down she came and found a boat
Beneath a willow left afloat,
And round about the prow she wrote
The Lady of Shalott.

And down the river's dim expanse
Like some bold seër in a trance,
Seeing all his own mischance—
With a glassy countenance
Did she look to Camelot.

And at the closing of the day
She loosed the chain, and down she lay;
The broad stream bore her far away,
The Lady of Shalott.

Lying, robed in snowy white
That loosely flew to left and right—
The leaves upon her falling light—
Thro' the noises of the night
She floated down to Camelot:
And as the boat-head wound along
The willowy hills and fields among,
They heard her singing her last song,
The Lady of Shalott.

Heard a carol, mournful, holy,
Chanted loudly, chanted lowly,
Till her blood was frozen slowly,
And her eyes were darken'd wholly,
Turn'd to tower'd Camelot.
For ere she reach'd upon the tide
The first house by the water-side,
Singing in her song she died,
The Lady of Shalott.

Under tower and balcony,
By garden-wall and gallery,
A gleaming shape she floated by,
Dead-pale between the houses high,
Silent into Camelot.
Out upon the wharfs they came,
Knight and burgher, lord and dame,
And round the prow they read her name,
The Lady of Shalott.

Who is this? and what is here?
And in the lighted palace near
Died the sound of royal cheer;
And they cross'd themselves for fear,
All the knights at Camelot:
But Lancelot mused a little space;
He said, "She has a lovely face;
God in his mercy lend her grace,
The Lady of Shalott."

1832, 1842

MARIANA IN THE SOUTH

With one black shadow at its feet,
The house thro' all the level shines,
Close-latticed to the brooding heat,
And silent in its dusty vines:
A faint-blue ridge upon the right,
An empty river-bed before,
And shallows on a distant shore,
In glaring sand and inlets bright.
But "Ave Mary," made she moan,
And "Ave Mary," night and morn,
And "Ah," she sang, "to be all alone,
To live forgotten, and love forlorn."

She, as her carol sadder grew,
From brow and bosom slowly down
Thro' rosy taper fingers drew
Her streaming curls of deepest brown
To left and right, and made appear
Still-lighted in a secret shrine,
Her melancholy eyes divine,
The home of woe without a tear.
And "Ave Mary," was her moan,
"Madonna, sad is night and morn,"
And "Ah," she sang, "to be all alone,
To live forgotten, and love forlorn."

Till all the crimson changed, and past
Into deep orange o'er the sea,
Low on her knees herself she cast,
Before Our Lady murmur'd she;
Complaining, "Mother, give me grace
To help me of my weary load."
And on the liquid mirror glow'd
The clear perfection of her face.
"Is this the form," she made her moan,
"That won his praises night and morn?"
And "Ah," she said, "but I wake alone,
I sleep forgotten, I wake forlorn."

Nor bird would sing, nor lamb would bleat,
Nor any cloud would cross the vault,
But day increased from heat to heat,
On stony drought and steaming salt;
Till now at noon she slept again,
And seem'd knee-deep in mountain grass,
And heard her native breezes pass,
And runlets babbling down the glen.
She breathed in sleep a lower moan,
And murmuring, as at night and morn,
She thought, "My spirit is here alone,
Walks forgotten, and is forlorn."

Dreaming, she knew it was a dream:
She felt he was and was not there.
She woke: the babble of the stream
Fell, and, without, the steady glare

Shrank one sick willow sere and small.
The river-bed was dusty-white;
And all the furnace of the light
Struck up against the blinding wall.
She whisper'd, with a stifled moan
More inward than at night or morn,
"Sweet Mother, let me not here alone
Live forgotten and die forlorn."

And, rising, from her bosom drew
Old letters, breathing of her worth,
For "Love," they said, "must needs be true,
To what is loveliest upon earth."
An image seem'd to pass the door,
To look at her with slight, and say
"But now thy beauty flows away,
So be alone for evermore."
"O cruel heart," she changed her tone,
"And cruel love, whose end is scorn,
Is this the end to be left alone,
To live forgotten, and die forlorn?"

But sometimes in the falling day
An image seem'd to pass the door,
To look into her eyes and say,
"But thou shalt be alone no more."
And flaming downward over all
From heat to heat the day decreased,
And slowly rounded to the east
The one black shadow from the wall.
"The day to night," she made her moan,
"The day to night, the night to morn,
And day and night I am left alone
To live forgotten, and love forlorn."

At eve a dry cicala sung,
There came a sound as of the sea;
Backward the lattice-blind she flung,
And lean'd upon the balcony.
There all in spaces rosy-bright
Large Hesper glitter'd on her tears,
And deepening thro' the silent spheres
Heaven over Heaven rose the night.
And weeping then she made her moan,
"The night comes on that knows not morn,
When I shall cease to be all alone,
To live forgotten, and love forlorn."

1832, 1842

ŒNONE

There lies a vale in Ida, lovelier
Than all the valleys of Ionian hills.
The swimming vapour slopes athwart the glen,
Puts forth an arm, and creeps from pine to pine,
And loiters, slowly drawn. On either hand
The lawns and meadow-ledges midway down
Hang rich in flowers, and far below them roars
The long brook falling thro' the clov'n ravine
In cataract after cataract to the sea.
Behind the valley topmost Gargarus
Stands up and takes the morning: but in front
The gorges, opening wide apart, reveal
Troas and Ilion's column'd citadel,
The crown of Troas.
Hither came at noon
Mournful Œnone, wandering forlorn
Of Paris, once her playmate on the hills.
Her cheek had lost the rose, and round her neck
Floated her hair or seem'd to float in rest.
She, leaning on a fragment twined with vine,
Sang to the stillness, till the mountain-shade
Sloped downward to her seat from the upper cliff.

"O mother Ida, many-fountain'd Ida,
Dear mother Ida, harken ere I die.
For now the noonday quiet holds the hill:
The grasshopper is silent in the grass:
The lizard, with his shadow on the stone,
Rests like a shadow, and the winds are dead.
The purple flower droops: the golden bee
Is lily-cradled: I alone awake.
My eyes are full of tears, my heart of love,
My heart is breaking, and my eyes are dim,
And I am all aweary of my life.

"O mother Ida, many-fountain'd Ida,
Dear mother Ida, harken ere I die.
Hear me, O Earth, hear me, O Hills, O Caves
That house the cold crown'd snake! O mountain brooks,
I am the daughter of a River-God,
Hear me, for I will speak, and build up all
My sorrow with my song, as yonder walls
Rose slowly to a music slowly breathed,
A cloud that gather'd shape: for it may be
That, while I speak of it, a little while
My heart may wander from its deeper woe,

"O mother Ida, many-fountain'd Ida,
Dear mother Ida, harken ere I die.
I waited underneath the dawning hills,
Aloft the mountain lawn was dewy-dark,
And dewy-dark aloft the mountain pine:
Beautiful Paris, evil-hearted Paris,
Leading a jet-black goat white-horn'd, white-hooved,
Came up from reedy Simois all alone.

"O mother Ida, harken ere I die.
Far-off the torrent call'd me from the cleft:
Far up the solitary morning smote
The streaks of virgin snow. With down-dropt eyes
I sat alone: white-breasted like a star
Fronting the dawn he moved; a leopard skin
Droop'd from his shoulder, but his sunny hair
Cluster'd about his temples like a God's:
And his cheek brighten'd as the foam-bow brightens
When the wind blows the foam, and all my heart
Went forth to embrace him coming ere he came.

"Dear mother Ida, harken ere I die.
He smiled, and opening out his milk-white palm
Disclosed a fruit of pure Hesperian gold,
That smelt ambrosially, and while I look'd
And listen'd, the full-flowing river of speech
Came down upon my heart.
"'My own Œnone,
Beautiful-brow'd Œnone, my own soul,
Behold this fruit, whose gleaming rind ingrav'n
"For the most fair," would seem to award it thine,
As lovelier than whatever Oread haunt
The knolls of Ida, loveliest in all grace
Of movement, and the charm of married brows.'

"Dear mother Ida, harken ere I die.
He prest the blossom of his lips to mine,
And added 'This was cast upon the board,
When all the full-faced presence of the Gods
Ranged in the halls of Peleus; whereupon
Rose feud, with question unto whom 'twere due:
But light-foot Iris brought it yester-eve,
Delivering, that to me, by common voice
Elected umpire, Herè comes to-day,
Pallas and Aphroditè, claiming each
This meed of fairest. Thou, within the cave
Behind yon whispering tuft of oldest pine,
Mayst well behold them unbeheld, unheard
Hear all, and see thy Paris judge of Gods.'

"Dear mother Ida, harken ere I die.
It was the deep midnoon: one silvery cloud
Had lost his way between the piny sides
Of this long glen. Then to the bower they came,
Naked they came to that smooth-swarded bower,
And at their feet the crocus brake like fire,
Violet, amaracus, and asphodel,
Lotos and lilies: and a wind arose,
And overhead the wandering ivy and vine,
This way and that, in many a wild festoon
Ran riot, garlanding the gnarled boughs
With bunch and berry and flower thro' and thro'.

"O mother Ida, harken ere I die.
On the tree-tops a crested peacock lit,
And o'er him flow'd a golden cloud, and lean'd
Upon him, slowly dropping fragrant dew.
Then first I heard the voice of her, to whom
Coming thro' Heaven, like a light that grows
Larger and clearer, with one mind the Gods
Rise up for reverence. She to Paris made
Proffer of royal power, ample rule
Unquestion'd, overflowing revenue
Wherewith to embellish state, 'from many a vale
And river-sunder'd champaign clothed with corn,
Or labour'd mine undrainable of ore.
Honour,' she said, 'and homage, tax and toll,
From many an inland town and haven large,
Mast-throng'd beneath her shadowing citadel
In glassy bays among her tallest towers.'

"O mother Ida, harken ere I die.
Still she spake on and still she spake of power,
'Which in all action is the end of all;
Power fitted to the season; wisdom-bred
And throned of wisdom—from all neighbour crowns

Alliance and allegiance, till thy hand
Fail from the sceptre-staff. Such boon from me,
From me, Heaven's Queen, Paris, to thee king-born,
A shepherd all thy life but yet king-born,
Should come most welcome, seeing men, in power
Only, are likest gods, who have attain'd
Rest in a happy place and quiet seats
Above the thunder, with undying bliss
In knowledge of their own supremacy.'

"Dear mother Ida, harken ere I die.
She ceased, and Paris held the costly fruit
Out at arm's-length, so much the thought of power
Flatter'd his spirit; but Pallas where she stood
Somewhat apart, her clear and bared limbs
O'erthwarted with the brazen-headed spear
Upon her pearly shoulder leaning cold,
The while, above, her full and earnest eye
Over her snow-cold breast and angry cheek
Kept watch, waiting decision, made reply.

" 'Self-reverence, self-knowledge, self-control,
These three alone lead life to sovereign power.
Yet not for power (power of herself
Would come uncall'd for) but to live by law,
Acting the law we live by without fear;
And, because right is right, to follow right
Were wisdom in the scorn of consequence.'

"Dear mother Ida, harken ere I die.
Again she said: 'I woo thee not with gifts.
Sequel of guerdon could not alter me
To fairer. Judge thou me by what I am,
So shalt thou find me fairest.
Yet, indeed,
If gazing on divinity disrobed
Thy mortal eyes are frail to judge of fair,
Unbias'd by self-profit, oh! rest thee sure
That I shall love thee well and cleave to thee,
So that my vigour, wedded to thy blood,
Shall strike within thy pulses, like a God's,
To push thee forward thro' a life of shocks,
Dangers, and deeds, until endurance grow
Sinew'd with action, and the full-grown will,
Circled thro' all experiences, pure law,
Commeasure perfect freedom.'

"Here she ceas'd,
And Paris ponder'd, and I cried, 'O Paris,
Give it to Pallas!' but he heard me not,
Or hearing would not hear me, woe is me!

"O mother Ida, many-fountain'd Ida,
Dear mother Ida, harken ere I die.
Idalian Aphroditè beautiful,
Fresh as the foam, new-bathed in Paphian wells,
With rosy slender fingers backward drew
From her warm brows and bosom her deep hair
Ambrosial, golden round her lucid throat
And shoulder: from the violets her light foot
Shone rosy-white, and o'er her rounded form
Between the shadows of the vine-bunches
Floated the glowing sunlights, as she moved.

"Dear mother Ida, harken ere I die.
She with a subtle smile in her mild eyes,
The herald of her triumph, drawing nigh
Half-whisper'd in his ear, 'I promise thee
The fairest and most loving wife in Greece,'
She spoke and laugh'd: I shut my sight for fear:
But when I look'd, Paris had raised his arm,
And I beheld great Herè's angry eyes,
As she withdrew into the golden cloud,
And I was left alone within the bower;
And from that time to this I am alone,
And I shall be alone until I die.

"Yet, mother Ida, harken ere I die.
Fairest—why fairest wife? am I not fair?
My love hath told me so a thousand times.
Methinks I must be fair, for yesterday,
When I past by, a wild and wanton pard,
Eyed like the evening star, with playful tail
Crouch'd fawning in the weed. Most loving is she?
Ah me, my mountain shepherd, that my arms
Were wound about thee, and my hot lips prest
Close, close to thine in that quick-falling dew
Of fruitful kisses, thick as Autumn rains
Flash in the pools of whirling Simois.

"O mother, hear me yet before I die.
They came, they cut away my tallest pines,
My tall dark pines, that plumed the craggy ledge

High over the blue gorge, and all between
The snowy peak and snow-white cataract
Foster'd the callow eaglet—from beneath
Whose thick mysterious boughs in the dark morn
The panther's roar came muffled, while I sat
Low in the valley. Never, never more
Shall lone Œnone see the morning mist
Sweep thro' them; never see them overlaid
With narrow moon-lit slips of silver cloud,
Between the loud stream and the trembling stars.

"O mother, hear me yet before I die.
I wish that somewhere in the ruin'd folds,
Among the fragments tumbled from the glens,
Or the dry thickets, I could meet with her
The Abominable, that uninvited came
Into the fair Peleïan banquet-hall,
And cast the golden fruit upon the board,
And bred this change; that I might speak my mind,
And tell her to her face how much I hate
Her presence, hated both of Gods and men.

"O mother, hear me yet before I die.
Hath he not sworn his love a thousand times,
In this green valley, under this green hill,
Ev'n on this hand, and sitting on this stone?
Seal'd it with kisses? water'd it with tears?
O happy tears, and how unlike to these!
O happy Heaven, how canst thou see my face?
O happy earth, how canst thou bear my weight?
O death, death, death, thou ever-floating cloud,
There are enough unhappy on this earth,
Pass by the happy souls, that love to live:
I pray thee, pass before my light of life,
And shadow all my soul, that I may die.
Thou weighest heavy on the heart within,
Weigh heavy on my eyelids: let me die.

"O mother, hear me yet before I die.
I will not die alone, for fiery thoughts
Do shape themselves within me, more and more,
Whereof I catch the issue, as I hear
Dead sounds at night come from the inmost hills,
Like footsteps upon wool. I dimly see
My far-off doubtful purpose, as a mother
Conjectures of the features of her child
Ere it is born: her child!—a shudder comes
Across me: never child be born of me,
Unblest, to vex me with his father's eyes!

"O mother, hear me yet before I die.
Hear me, O earth. I will not die alone,
Lest their shrill happy laughter come to me
Walking the cold and starless road of Death
Uncomforted, leaving my ancient love
With the Greek woman. I will rise and go
Down into Troy, and ere the stars come forth
Talk with the wild Cassandra, for she says
A fire dances before her, and a sound
Rings ever in her ears of armed men.
What this may be I know not, but I know
That, wheresoe'er I am by night and day,
All earth and air seem only burning fire."

1832, 1842

THE PALACE OF ART

I BUILT my soul a lordly pleasure-house,
Wherein at ease for aye to dwell.
I said, "O Soul, make merry and carouse,
Dear soul, for all is well."

A huge crag-platform, smooth as burnish'd brass
I chose. The ranged ramparts bright
From level meadow-bases of deep grass
Suddenly scaled the light.

Thereon I built it firm. Of ledge or shelf
The rock rose clear, or winding stair.
My soul would live alone unto herself
In her high palace there.

And "while the world runs round and round," I said,
"Reign thou apart, a quiet king,
Still as, while Saturn whirls, his stedfast shade
Sleeps on his luminous ring."

To which my soul made answer readily:
"Trust me, in bliss I shall abide
In this great mansion, that is built for me,
So royal-rich and wide."

* * *

Four courts I made, East, West and South and North,
In each a squared lawn, wherefrom
The golden gorge of dragons spouted forth
A flood of fountain-foam.

And round the cool green courts there ran a row
Of cloisters, branch'd like mighty woods,
Echoing all night to that sonorous flow
Of spouted fountain-floods.

And round the roofs a gilded gallery
That lent broad verge to distant lands,
Far as the wild swan wings, to where the sky
Dipt down to sea and sands.

From those four jets four currents in one swell
Across the mountain stream'd below
In misty folds, that floating as they fell
Lit up a torrent-bow.

And high on every peak a statue seem'd
To hang on tiptoe, tossing up
A cloud of incense of all odour steam'd
From out a golden cup.

So that she thought, "And who shall gaze upon
My palace with unblinded eyes,
While this great bow will waver in the sun,
And that sweet incense rise?"

For that sweet incense rose and never fail'd,
And, while day sank or mounted higher,
The light aërial gallery, golden-rail'd,
Burnt like a fringe of fire.

Likewise the deep-set windows, stain'd and traced,
Would seem slow-flaming crimson fires
From shadow'd grots of arches interlaced,
And tipt with frost-like spires.

* * *

Full of long-sounding corridors it was,
That over-vaulted grateful gloom,
Thro' which the livelong day my soul did pass,
Well-pleased, from room to room.

Full of great rooms and small the palace stood,
All various, each a perfect whole
From living Nature, fit for every mood
And change of my still soul.

For some were hung with arras green and blue,
Showing a gaudy summer-morn,
Where with puff'd cheek the belted hunter blew
His wreathed bugle-horn.

One seem'd all dark and red—a tract of sand,
And some one pacing there alone,
Who paced for ever in a glimmering land,
Lit with a low large moon.

One show'd an iron coast and angry waves.
You seem'd to hear them climb and fall
And roar rock-thwarted under bellowing caves,
Beneath the windy wall.

And one, a full-fed river winding slow
By herds upon an endless plain,
The ragged rims of thunder brooding low,
With shadow-streaks of rain.

And one, the reapers at their sultry toil.
In front they bound the sheaves. Behind
Were realms of upland, prodigal in oil,
And hoary to the wind.

And one a foreground black with stones and slags,
Beyond, a line of heights, and higher
All barr'd with long white cloud the scornful crags,
And highest, snow and fire.

And one, an English home—gray twilight pour'd
On dewy pastures, dewy trees,
Softer than sleep—all things in order stored,
A haunt of ancient Peace.

Nor these alone, but every landscape fair,
As fit for every mood of mind,
Or gay, or grave, or sweet, or stern, was there
Not less than truth design'd.

* * *

Or the maid-mother by a crucifix,
In tracts of pasture sunny-warm,
Beneath branch-work of costly sardonyx
Sat smiling, babe in arm.

Or in a clear-wall'd city on the sea,
Near gilded organ-pipes, her hair
Wound with white roses, slept St. Cecily;
An angel look'd at her.

Or thronging all one porch of Paradise
  A group of Houris bow'd to see
The dying Islamite, with hands and eyes
    That said, We wait for thee.

Or mythic Uther's deeply-wounded son
  In some fair space of sloping greens
Lay, dozing in the vale of Avalon,
    And watch'd by weeping queens.

Or hollowing one hand against his ear,
  To list a foot-fall, ere he saw
The wood-nymph, stay'd the Ausonian king to hear
    Of wisdom and of law.

Or over hills with peaky tops engrail'd,
  And many a tract of palm and rice,
The throne of Indian Cama slowly sail'd
    A summer fann'd with spice.

Or sweet Europa's mantle blew unclasp'd,
  From off her shoulder backward borne:
From one hand droop'd a crocus: one hand grasp'd
    The mild bull's golden horn.

Or else flush'd Ganymede, his rosy thigh
  Half-buried in the Eagle's down,
Sole as a flying star shot thro' the sky
    Above the pillar'd town.

Nor these alone: but every legend fair
  Which the supreme Caucasian mind
Carved out of Nature for itself, was there,
    Not less than life, design'd.

* * *

Then in the towers I placed great bells that swung,
  Moved of themselves, with silver sound;
And with choice paintings of wise men I hung
    The royal dais round.

For there was Milton like a seraph strong,
  Beside him Shakespeare bland and mild;
And there the world-worn Dante grasp'd his song,
    And somewhat grimly smiled.

And there the Ionian father of the rest;
  A million wrinkles carved his skin;
A hundred winters snow'd upon his breast,
    From cheek and throat and chin.

Above, the fair hall-ceiling stately-set
  Many an arch high up did lift,
And angels rising and descending met
    With interchange of gift.

Below was all mosaic choicely plann'd
  With cycles of the human tale
Of this wide world, the times of every land
    So wrought, they will not fail.

The people here, a beast of burden slow,
  Toil'd onward, prick'd with goads and stings;
Here play'd, a tiger, rolling to and fro
    The heads and crowns of kings;

Here rose, an athlete, strong to break or bind
  All force in bonds that might endure,
And here once more like some sick man declined,
    And trusted any cure.

But over these she trod: and those great bells
  Began to chime. She took her throne:
She sat betwixt the shining Oriels,
    To sing her songs alone.

And thro' the topmost Oriels' coloured flame
  Two godlike faces gazed below;
Plato the wise, and large-brow'd Verulam,
    The first of those who know.

And all those names, that in their motion were
  Full-welling fountain-heads of change,
Betwixt the slender shafts were blazon'd fair
    In diverse raiment strange:

Thro' which the lights, rose, amber, emerald, blue,
  Flush'd in her temples and her eyes,
And from her lips, as morn from Memnon, drew
    Rivers of melodies.

No nightingale delighteth to prolong
  Her low preamble all alone,
More than my soul to hear her echo'd song
    Throb thro' the ribbed stone;

Singing and murmuring in her feastful mirth,
  Joying to feel herself alive,
Lord over Nature, Lord of the visible earth,
    Lord of the senses five;

Communing with herself: "All these are mine,
And let the world have peace or wars,
'Tis one to me." She—when young night divine
Crown'd dying day with stars,

Making sweet close of his delicious toils—
Lit light in wreaths and anadems,
And pure quintessences of precious oils
In hollow'd moons of gems,

To mimic heaven; and clapt her hands and cried,
"I marvel if my still delight
In this great house so royal-rich, and wide,
Be flatter'd to the height.

"O all things fair to sate my various eyes!
O shapes and hues that please me well!
O silent faces of the Great and Wise,
My Gods, with whom I dwell!

"O God-like isolation which art mine,
I can but count thee perfect gain,
What time I watch the darkening droves of swine
That range on yonder plain.

"In filthy sloughs they roll a prurient skin,
They graze and wallow, breed and sleep;
And oft some brainless devil enters in,
And drives them to the deep."

Then of the moral instinct would she prate
And of the rising from the dead,
As hers by right of full-accomplish'd Fate;
And at the last she said:

"I take possession of man's mind and deed.
I care not what the sects may brawl.
I sit as God holding no form of creed,
But contemplating all."

* * *

Full oft the riddle of the painful earth
Flash'd thro' her as she sat alone,
Yet not the less held she her solemn mirth,
And intellectual throne.

And so she throve and prosper'd: so three years
She prosper'd: on the fourth she fell,
Like Herod, when the shout was in his ears,
Struck thro' with pangs of hell.

Lest she should fail and perish utterly,
God, before whom ever lie bare
The abysmal deeps of Personality,
Plagued her with sore despair.

When she would think, where'er she turn'd her sight
The airy hand confusion wrought,
Wrote, "Mene, mene," and divided quite
The kingdom of her thought.

Deep dread and loathing of her solitude
Fell on her, from which mood was born
Scorn of herself; again, from out that mood
Laughter at her self-scorn.

"What! is not this my place of strength," she said,
"My spacious mansion built for me,
Whereof the strong foundation-stones were laid
Since my first memory?"

But in dark corners of her palace stood
Uncertain shapes; and unawares
On white-eyed phantasms weeping tears of blood,
And horrible nightmares,

And hollow shades enclosing hearts of flame,
And, with dim fretted foreheads all,
On corpses three-months-old at noon she came,
That stood against the wall.

A spot of dull stagnation, without light
Or power of movement, seem'd my soul,
'Mid onward-sloping motions infinite
Making for one sure goal.

A still salt pool, lock'd in with bars of sand,
Left on the shore; that hears all night
The plunging seas draw backward from the land
Their moon-led waters white.

A star that with the choral starry dance
Join'd not, but stood, and standing saw
The hollow orb of moving Circumstance
Roll'd round by one fix'd law.

Back on herself her serpent pride had curl'd.
"No voice," she shriek'd in that lone hall,
"No voice breaks thro' the stillness of this world:
One deep, deep silence all!"

She, mouldering with the dull earth's mouldering sod,
Inwrapt tenfold in slothful shame,
Lay there exiled from eternal God,
Lost to her place and name;

And death and life she hated equally,
And nothing saw, for her despair,
But dreadful time, dreadful eternity,
No comfort anywhere;

Remaining utterly confused with fears,
And ever worse with growing time,
And ever unrelieved by dismal tears,
And all alone in crime:

Shut up as in a crumbling tomb, girt round
With blackness as a solid wall,
Far off she seem'd to hear the dully sound
Of human footsteps fall.

As in strange lands a traveller walking slow,
In doubt and great perplexity,
A little before moon-rise hears the low
Moan of an unknown sea;

And knows not if it be thunder, or a sound
Of rocks thrown down, or one deep cry
Of great wild beasts; then thinketh, "I have found
A new land, but I die."

She howl'd aloud, "I am on fire within.
There comes no murmur of reply.
What is it that will take away my sin,
And save me lest I die?"

So when four years were wholly finished,
She threw her royal robes away.
"Make me a cottage in the vale," she said,
"Where I may mourn and pray.

"Yet pull not down my palace towers, that are
So lightly, beautifully built:
Perchance I may return with others there
When I have purged my guilt."

1832, 1842

THE LOTOS–EATERS

"Courage!" he said, and pointed toward the land,
"This mounting wave will roll us shoreward soon."
In the afternoon they came unto a land
In which it seemed always afternoon.
All round the coast the languid air did swoon,
Breathing like one that hath a weary dream.
Full-faced above the valley stood the moon;
And like a downward smoke, the slender stream
Along the cliff to fall and pause and fall did seem.

A land of streams! some, like a downward smoke,
Slow-dropping veils of thinnest lawn, did go;
And some thro' wavering lights and shadows broke,
Rolling a slumbrous sheet of foam below.
They saw the gleaming river seaward flow
From the inner land: far off, three mountain-tops,
Three silent pinnacles of aged snow,
Stood sunset-flush'd: and, dew'd with showery drops,
Up-clomb the shadowy pine above the woven copse.

The charmed sunset linger'd low adown
In the red West: thro' mountain clefts the dale
Was seen far inland, and the yellow down
Border'd with palm, and many a winding vale
And meadow, set with slender galingale;
A land where all things always seem'd the same!
And round about the keel with faces pale,
Dark faces pale against that rosy flame,
The mild-eyed melancholy Lotos-eaters came.

Branches they bore of that enchanted stem,
Laden with flower and fruit, whereof they gave
To each, but whoso did receive of them,
And taste, to him the gushing of the wave
Far far away did seem to mourn and rave
On alien shores; and if his fellow spake,
His voice was thin, as voices from the grave;
And deep-asleep he seem'd, yet all awake,
And music in his ears his beating heart did make.

They sat them down upon the yellow sand,
Between the sun and moon upon the shore;
And sweet it was to dream of Fatherland,
Of child, and wife, and slave; but evermore

Most weary seem'd the sea, weary the oar,
Weary the wandering fields of barren foam.
Then some one said, "We will return no more;"
And all at once they sang, "Our island home
Is far beyond the wave; we will no longer roam."

Choric Song

I

There is sweet music here that softer falls
Than petals from blown roses on the grass,
Or night-dews on still waters between walls
Of shadowy granite, in a gleaming pass;
Music that gentlier on the spirit lies,
Than tir'd eyelids upon tir'd eyes;
Music that brings sweet sleep down from the blissful skies.
Here are cool mosses deep,
And thro' the moss the ivies creep,
And in the stream the long-leaved flowers weep,
And from the craggy ledge the poppy hangs in sleep.

II

Why are we weigh'd upon with heaviness,
And utterly consumed with sharp distress,
While all things else have rest from weariness?
All things have rest: why should we toil alone,
We only toil, who are the first of things,
And make perpetual moan,
Still from one sorrow to another thrown:
Nor ever fold our wings,
And cease from wanderings,
Nor steep our brows in slumber's holy balm;
Nor harken what the inner spirit sings,
"There is no joy but calm!"
Why should we only toil, the roof and crown of things?

III

Lo! in the middle of the wood,
The folded leaf is woo'd from out the bud
With winds upon the branch, and there
Grows green and broad, and takes no care,
Sun-steep'd at noon, and in the moon
Nightly dew-fed; and turning yellow
Falls, and floats adown the air.
Lo! sweeten'd with the summer light,
The full-juiced apple, waxing over-mellow,
Drops in a silent autumn night.
All its allotted length of days,
The flower ripens in its place,
Ripens and fades, and falls, and hath no toil,
Fast-rooted in the fruitful soil.

IV

Hateful is the dark-blue sky,
Vaulted o'er the dark-blue sea.
Death is the end of life; ah, why
Should life all labour be?
Let us alone. Time driveth onward fast,
And in a little while our lips are dumb.
Let us alone. What is it that will last?
All things are taken from us, and become
Portions and parcels of the dreadful Past.
Let us alone. What pleasure can we have
To war with evil? Is there any peace
In ever climbing up the climbing wave?
All things have rest, and ripen toward the grave
In silence; ripen, fall and cease:
Give us long rest or death, dark death, or dreamful ease.

V

How sweet it were, hearing the downward stream,
With half-shut eyes ever to seem
Falling asleep in a half-dream!
To dream and dream, like yonder amber light,
Which will not leave the myrrh-bush on the height;
To hear each other's whisper'd speech;
Eating the Lotos day by day,
To watch the crisping ripples on the beach,
And tender curving lines of creamy spray;
To lend our hearts and spirits wholly
To the influence of mild-minded melancholy;
To muse and brood and live again in memory,
With those old faces of our infancy
Heap'd over with a mound of grass,
Two handfuls of white dust, shut in an urn of brass!

VI

Dear is the memory of our wedded lives,
And dear the last embraces of our wives
And their warm tears: but all hath suffer'd change:

For surely now our household hearths are cold:
Our sons inherit us: our looks are strange:
And we should come like ghosts to trouble joy.
Or else the island princes over-bold
Have eat our substance, and the minstrel sings
Before them of the ten years' war in Troy,
And our great deeds, as half-forgotten things.
Is there confusion in the little isle?
Let what is broken so remain.
The Gods are hard to reconcile:
'Tis hard to settle order once again.
There *is* confusion worse than death,
Trouble on trouble, pain on pain,
Long labour unto aged breath,
Sore task to hearts worn out by many wars
And eyes grown dim with gazing on the pilot-stars.

VII

But, propt on beds of amaranth and moly,
How sweet (while warm airs lull us, blowing lowly)
With half-dropt eyelid still,
Beneath a heaven dark and holy,
To watch the long bright river drawing slowly
His waters from the purple hill—
To hear the dewy echoes calling
From cave to cave thro' the thick-twined vine—
To watch the emerald-colour'd water falling
Thro' many a wov'n acanthus-wreath divine!
Only to hear and see the far-off sparkling brine,
Only to hear were sweet, stretch'd out beneath the pine.

VIII

The Lotos blooms below the barren peak:
The Lotos blows by every winding creek:
All day the wind breathes low with mellower tone:
Thro' every hollow cave and alley lone
Round and round the spicy downs the yellow Lotos-dust is blown.
We have had enough of action, and of motion we,
Roll'd to starboard, roll'd to larboard, when the surge was seething free,
Where the wallowing monster spouted his foam-fountains in the sea.
Let us swear an oath, and keep it with an equal mind,
In the hollow Lotos-land to live and lie reclined
On the hills like Gods together, careless of mankind.
For they lie beside their nectar, and the bolts are hurl'd
Far below them in the valleys, and the clouds are lightly curl'd
Round their golden houses, girdled with the gleaming world:
Where they smile in secret, looking over wasted lands,
Blight and famine, plague and earthquake, roaring deeps and fiery sands,
Clanging fights, and flaming towns, and sinking ships, and praying hands.
But they smile, they find a music centred in a doleful song
Steaming up, a lamentation and an ancient tale of wrong,
Like a tale of little meaning tho' the words are strong;
Chanted from an ill-used race of men that cleave the soil,
Sow the seed, and reap the harvest with enduring toil,
Storing yearly little dues of wheat, and wine and oil;
Till they perish and they suffer—some, 'tis whisper'd—down in hell
Suffer endless anguish, others in Elysian valleys dwell,
Resting weary limbs at last on beds of asphodel.
Surely, surely, slumber is more sweet than toil, the shore
Than labour in the deep mid-ocean, wind and wave and oar;
Oh rest ye, brother mariners, we will not wander more.

1832, 1842

A DREAM OF FAIR WOMEN

I READ, before my eyelids dropt their shade,
"*The Legend of Good Women,*" long ago
Sung by the morning star of song, who made
His music heard below;

Dan Chaucer, the first warbler, whose sweet breath
Preluded those melodious bursts that fill
The spacious times of great Elizabeth
With sounds that echo still.

And, for a while, the knowledge of his art
Held me above the subject, as strong gales
Hold swollen clouds from raining, tho' my heart,
Brimful of those wild tales,

Charged both mine eyes with tears. In every land
I saw, wherever light illumineth,
Beauty and anguish walking hand in hand
The downward slope to death.

Those far-renowned brides of ancient song
Peopled the hollow dark, like burning stars,
And I heard sounds of insult, shame, and wrong,
And trumpets blown for wars;

And clattering flints batter'd with clanging hoofs;
And I saw crowds in column'd sanctuaries;
And forms that pass'd at windows and on roofs
Of marble palaces;

Corpses across the threshold; heroes tall
Dislodging pinnacle and parapet
Upon the tortoise creeping to the wall;
Lances in ambush set;

And high shrine-doors burst thro' with heated blasts
That run before the fluttering tongues of fire;
White surf wind-scatter'd over sails and masts,
And ever climbing higher;

Squadrons and squares of men in brazen plates,
Scaffolds, still sheets of water, divers woes,
Ranges of glimmering vaults with iron grates,
And hush'd seraglios.

So shape chased shape as swift as, when to land
Bluster the winds and tides the self-same way,
Crisp foam-flakes scud along the level sand,
Torn from the fringe of spray.

I started once, or seem'd to start in pain,
Resolved on noble things, and strove to speak,
As when a great thought strikes along the brain,
And flushes all the cheek.

And once my arm was lifted to hew down
A cavalier from off his saddle-bow,
That bore a lady from a leaguer'd town;
And then, I know not how,

All those sharp fancies, by down-lapsing thought
Stream'd onward, lost their edges, and did creep
Roll'd on each other, rounded, smooth'd, and brought
Into the gulfs of sleep.

At last methought that I had wander'd far
In an old wood: fresh-wash'd in coolest dew
The maiden splendours of the morning star
Shook in the stedfast blue.

Enormous elm-tree-boles did stoop and lean
Upon the dusky brushwood underneath
Their broad curved branches, fledged with clearest green,
New from its silken sheath.

The dim red morn had died, her journey done,
And with dead lips smiled at the twilight plain,
Half-fall'n across the threshold of the sun,
Never to rise again.

There was no motion in the dumb dead air,
Not any song of bird or sound of rill;
Gross darkness of the inner sepulchre
Is not so deadly still

As that wide forest. Growths of jasmine turn'd
Their humid arms festooning tree to tree,
And at the root thro' lush green grasses burn'd
The red anemone.

I knew the flowers, I knew the leaves, I knew
The tearful glimmer of the languid dawn
On those long, rank, dark wood-walks drench'd in dew,
Leading from lawn to lawn.

The smell of violets, hidden in the green,
Pour'd back into my empty soul and frame
The times when I remember to have been
Joyful and free from blame.

And from within me a clear under-tone
Thrill'd thro' mine ears in that unblissful clime,
"Pass freely thro': the wood is all thine own,
Until the end of time."

At length I saw a lady within call,
Stiller than chisell'd marble, standing there;
A daughter of the gods, divinely tall,
And most divinely fair.

Her loveliness with shame and with surprise
Froze my swift speech: she turning on my face
The star-like sorrows of immortal eyes,
Spoke slowly in her place.

"I had great beauty: ask thou not my name:
No one can be more wise than destiny.
Many drew swords and died. Where'er I came
I brought calamity."

"No marvel, sovereign lady: in fair field
Myself for such a face had boldly died,"
I answer'd free; and turning I appeal'd
To one that stood beside.

But she, with sick and scornful looks averse,
To her full height her stately stature draws;
"My youth," she said, "was blasted with a curse:
This woman was the cause.

"I was cut off from hope in that sad place,
Which men call'd Aulis in those iron years:
My father held his hand upon his face;
I, blinded with my tears,

"Still strove to speak: my voice was thick with sighs
As in a dream. Dimly I could descry
The stern black-bearded kings with wolfish eyes,
Waiting to see me die.

"The high masts flicker'd as they lay afloat;
The crowds, the temples, waver'd, and the shore;
The bright death quiver'd at the victim's throat;
Touch'd; and I knew no more."

Whereto the other with a downward brow:
"I would the white cold heavy-plunging foam,
Whirl'd by the wind, had roll'd me deep below,
Then when I left my home."

Her slow full words sank thro' the silence drear,
As thunder-drops fall on a sleeping sea:
Sudden I heard a voice that cried, "Come here,
That I may look on thee."

I turning saw, throned on a flowery rise,
One sitting on a crimson scarf unroll'd;
A queen, with swarthy cheeks and bold black eyes,
Brow-bound with burning gold.

She, flashing forth a haughty smile, began:
"I govern'd men by change, and so I sway'd
All moods. 'Tis long since I have seen a man.
Once, like the moon, I made

"The ever-shifting currents of the blood
According to my humour ebb and flow.
I have no men to govern in this wood:
That makes my only woe.

"Nay—yet it chafes me that I could not bend
One will; nor tame and tutor with mine eye
That dull cold-blooded Cæsar. Prythee, friend,
Where is Mark Antony?

"The man, my lover, with whom I rode sublime
On Fortune's neck: we sat as God by God:
The Nilus would have risen before his time
And flooded at our nod.

"We drank the Libyan Sun to sleep, and lit
Lamps which out-burn'd Canopus. O my life
In Egypt! O the dalliance and the wit,
The flattery and the strife,

"And the wild kiss, when fresh from war's alarms,
My Hercules, my Roman Antony,
My mailed Bacchus leapt into my arms,
Contented there to die!

"And there he died: and when I heard my name
Sigh'd forth with life I would not brook my fear
Of the other: with a worm I balk'd his fame.
What else was left? look here!"

(With that she tore her robe apart, and half
The polish'd argent of her breast to sight
Laid bare. Thereto she pointed with a laugh,
Showing the aspick's bite.)

"I died a Queen. The Roman soldier found
Me lying dead, my crown about my brows,
A name for ever!—lying robed and crown'd,
Worthy a Roman spouse."

Her warbling voice, a lyre of widest range
Struck by all passion, did fall down and glance
From tone to tone, and glided thro' all change
Of liveliest utterance.

When she made pause I knew not for delight;
Because with sudden motion from the ground
She raised her piercing orbs, and fill'd with light
The interval of sound.

Still with their fires Love tipt his keenest darts;
As once they drew into two burning rings
All beams of Love, melting the mighty hearts
Of captains and of kings.

Slowly my sense undazzled. Then I heard
A noise of some one coming thro' the lawn,
And singing clearer than the crested bird
That claps his wings at dawn.

"The torrent brooks of hallow'd Israel
From craggy hollows pouring, late and soon,
Sound all night long, in falling thro' the dell,
Far-heard beneath the moon.

"The balmy moon of blessed Israel
Floods all the deep-blue gloom with beams divine:
All night the splinter'd crags that wall the dell
With spires of silver shine."

As one that museth where broad sunshine laves
The lawn by some cathedral, thro' the door
Hearing the holy organ rolling waves
Of sound on roof and floor

Within, and anthem sung, is charm'd and tied
To where he stands,—so stood I, when that flow
Of music left the lips of her that died
To save her father's vow;

The daughter of the warrior Gileadite,
A maiden pure; as when she went along
From Mizpeh's tower'd gate with welcome light,
With timbrel and with song.

My words leapt forth: "Heaven heads the count of crimes
With that wild oath." She render'd answer high:
"Not so, nor once alone; a thousand times
I would be born and die.

"Single I grew, like some green plant, whose root
Creeps to the garden water-pipes beneath,
Feeding the flower; but ere my flower to fruit
Changed, I was ripe for death.

"My God, my land, my father—these did move
Me from my bliss of life, that Nature gave,
Lower'd softly with a threefold cord of love
Down to a silent grave.

"And I went mourning, 'No fair Hebrew boy
Shall smile away my maiden blame among
The Hebrew mothers'—emptied of all joy,
Leaving the dance and song,

"Leaving the olive-gardens far below,
Leaving the promise of my bridal bower,
The valleys of grape-loaded vines that glow
Beneath the battled tower.

"The light white cloud swam over us. Anon
We heard the lion roaring from his den;
We saw the large white stars rise one by one,
Or, from the darken'd glen,

"Saw God divide the night with flying flame,
And thunder on the everlasting hills.
I heard Him, for He spake, and grief became
A solemn scorn of ills.

"When the next moon was roll'd into the sky,
Strength came to me that equall'd my desire.
How beautiful a thing it was to die
For God and for my sire!

"It comforts me in this one thought to dwell,
That I subdued me to my father's will;
Because the kiss he gave me, ere I fell,
Sweetens the spirit still.

"Moreover it is written that my race
Hew'd Ammon, hip and thigh, from Aroer
On Arnon unto Minneth." Here her face
Glow'd, as I look'd at her.

She lock'd her lips: she left me where I stood:
"Glory to God," she sang, and past afar,
Thridding the sombre boskage of the wood,
Toward the morning-star.

Losing her carol I stood pensively,
As one that from a casement leans his head,
When midnight bells cease ringing suddenly,
And the old year is dead.

"Alas! alas!" a low voice, full of care,
Murmur'd beside me: "Turn and look on me:
I am that Rosamond, whom men call fair,
If what I was I be.

"Would I had been some maiden coarse and poor!
O me, that I should ever see the light!
Those dragon eyes of anger'd Eleanor
Do hunt me, day and night."

She ceased in tears, fallen from hope and trust:
To whom the Egyptian: "O, you tamely died!
You should have clung to Fulvia's waist, and thrust
The dagger thro' her side."

With that sharp sound the white dawn's creeping beams,
Stol'n to my brain, dissolved the mystery
Of folded sleep. The captain of my dreams
Ruled in the eastern sky.

Morn broaden'd on the borders of the dark,
Ere I saw her, who clasp'd in her last trance
Her murder'd father's head, or Joan of Arc,
A light of ancient France;

Or her who knew that Love can vanquish Death,
Who kneeling, with one arm about her king,
Drew forth the poison with her balmy breath,
Sweet as new buds in Spring.

No memory labours longer from the deep
Gold-mines of thought to lift the hidden ore
That glimpses, moving up, than I from sleep
To gather and tell o'er

Each little sound and sight. With what dull pain
Compass'd, how eagerly I sought to strike
Into that wondrous track of dreams again!
But no two dreams are like.

As when a soul laments, which hath been blest,
Desiring what is mingled with past years,
In yearnings that can never be exprest
By signs or groans or tears;

Because all words, tho' cull'd with choicest art,
Failing to give the bitter of the sweet,
Wither beneath the palate, and the heart
Faints, faded by its heat.

1832, 1842

ST. AGNES' EVE

DEEP on the convent-roof the snows
Are sparkling to the moon:
My breath to heaven like vapour goes:
May my soul follow soon!
The shadows of the convent-towers
Slant down the snowy sward,

Still creeping with the creeping hours
That lead me to my Lord:
Make Thou my spirit pure and clear
As are the frosty skies,
Or this first snowdrop of the year
That in my bosom lies.

As these white robes are soil'd and dark,
To yonder shining ground;
As this pale taper's earthly spark,
To yonder argent round;
So shows my soul before the Lamb,
My spirit before Thee;
So in mine earthly house I am,
To that I hope to be.
Break up the heavens, O Lord! and far,
Thro' all yon starlight keen,
Draw me, thy bride, a glittering star,
In raiment white and clean.

He lifts me to the golden doors;
The flashes come and go;
All heaven bursts her starry floors,
And strows her lights below,
And deepens on and up! the gates
Roll back, and far within
For me the Heavenly Bridegroom waits,
To make me pure of sin.
The sabbaths of Eternity,
One sabbath deep and wide—
A light upon the shining sea—
The Bridegroom with his bride!

1837, 1842

YOU ASK ME, WHY, THO' ILL AT EASE

You ask me, why, tho' ill at ease,
Within this region I subsist,
Whose spirits falter in the mist,
And languish for the purple seas.

It is the land that freemen till,
That sober-suited Freedom chose,
The land, where girt with friends or foes
A man may speak the thing he will;

A land of settled government,
A land of just and old renown,
Where Freedom slowly broadens down
From precedent to precedent:

Where faction seldom gathers head,
But by degrees to fullness wrought,
The strength of some diffusive thought
Hath time and space to work and spread.

Should banded unions persecute
Opinion, and induce a time
When single thought is civil crime,
And individual freedom mute;

Tho' Power should make from land to land
The name of Britain trebly great—
Tho' every channel of the State
Should fill and choke with golden sand—

Yet waft me from the harbour-mouth,
Wild wind! I seek a warmer sky,
And I will see before I die
The palms and temples of the South.

1842

OF OLD SAT FREEDOM ON THE HEIGHTS

Of old sat Freedom on the heights,
The thunders breaking at her feet:
Above her shook the starry lights:
She heard the torrents meet.

There in her place she did rejoice,
Self-gather'd in her prophet-mind,
But fragments of her mighty voice
Came rolling on the wind.

Then stept she down thro' town and field
To mingle with the human race,
And part by part to men reveal'd
The fullness of her face—

Grave mother of majestic works,
From her isle-altar gazing down,
Who, God-like, grasps the triple forks,
And, King-like, wears the crown:

Her open eyes desire the truth.
The wisdom of a thousand years
Is in them. May perpetual youth
Keep dry their light from tears;

That her fair form may stand and shine,
Make bright our days and light our dreams,
Turning to scorn with lips divine
The falsehood of extremes!

1842

LOVE THOU THY LAND, WITH LOVE FAR-BROUGHT

Love thou thy land, with love far-brought
From out the storied Past, and used
Within the Present, but transfused
Thro' future time by power of thought.

True love turn'd round on fixed poles,
Love, that endures not sordid ends,
For English natures, freemen, friends,
Thy brothers and immortal souls.

But pamper not a hasty time,
Nor feed with crude imaginings
The herd, wild hearts and feeble wings
That every sophister can lime.

Deliver not the tasks of might
To weakness, neither hide the ray
From those, not blind, who wait for day,
Tho' sitting girt with doubtful light.

Make knowledge circle with the winds;
But let her herald, Reverence, fly
Before her to whatever sky
Bear seed of men and growth of minds.

Watch what main-currents draw the years:
Cut Prejudice against the grain:
But gentle words are always gain:
Regard the weakness of thy peers:

Nor toil for title, place, or touch
Of pension, neither count on praise:
It grows to guerdon after-days:
Nor deal in watch-words overmuch:

Not clinging to some ancient saw;
Not master'd by some modern term;
Not swift nor slow to change, but firm:
And in its season bring the law;

That from Discussion's lip may fall
With Life, that, working strongly, binds—
Set in all lights by many minds,
To close the interests of all.

For Nature also, cold and warm,
And moist and dry, devising long,
Thro' many agents making strong,
Matures the individual form.

Meet is it changes should control
Our being, lest we rust in ease.
We all are changed by still degrees,
All but the basis of the soul.

So let the change which comes be free
To ingroove itself with that which flies,
And work, a joint of state, that plies
Its office, moved with sympathy.

A saying, hard to shape in act;
For all the past of Time reveals
A bridal dawn of thunder-peals,
Wherever Thought hath wedded Fact.

Ev'n now we hear with inward strife
A motion toiling in the gloom—
The Spirit of the years to come
Yearning to mix himself with Life.

A slow-develop'd strength awaits
Completion in a painful school;
Phantoms of other forms of rule,
New Majesties of mighty States—

The warders of the growing hour,
But vague in vapour, hard to mark;
And round them sea and air are dark
With great contrivances of Power.

Of many changes, aptly join'd,
Is bodied forth the second whole.
Regard gradation, lest the soul
Of Discord race the rising wind;

A wind to puff your idol-fires,
And heap their ashes on the head;
To shame the boast so often made,
That we are wiser than our sires.

Oh yet, if Nature's evil star
Drive men in manhood, as in youth,
To follow flying steps of Truth
Across the brazen bridge of war—

If New and Old, disastrous feud,
Must ever shock, like armed foes,
And this be true, till Time shall close,
That Principles are rain'd in blood;

Not yet the wise of heart would cease
To hold his hope thro' shame and guilt,
But with his hand against the hilt,
Would pace the troubled land, like Peace;

Not less, tho' dogs of Faction bay,
  Would serve his kind in deed and word,
  Certain, if knowledge bring the sword,
That knowledge takes the sword away—

Would love the gleams of good that broke
  From either side, nor veil his eyes:
  And if some dreadful need should rise
Would strike, and firmly, and one stroke:

To-morrow yet would reap to-day,
  As we bear blossom of the dead;
  Earn well the thrifty months, nor wed
Raw Haste, half-sister to Delay.

1842

THE EPIC

At Francis Allen's on the Christmas-eve,—
The game of forfeits done—the girls all kiss'd
Beneath the sacred bush and past away—
The parson Holmes, the poet Everard Hall,
The host, and I sat round the wassail-bowl,
Then half-way ebb'd: and there we held a talk,
How all the old honour had from Christmas gone,
Or gone, or dwindled down to some odd games
In some odd nooks like this; till I, tired out
With cutting eights that day upon the pond,
Where, three times slipping from the outer edge,
I bump'd the ice into three several stars,
Fell in a doze; and half-awake I heard
The parson taking wide and wider sweeps,
Now harping on the church-commissioners,
Now hawking at Geology and schism;
Until I woke, and found him settled down
Upon the general decay of faith
Right thro' the world, "at home was little left,
And none abroad: there was no anchor, none,
To hold by." Francis, laughing, clapt his hand
On Everard's shoulder, with "I hold by him."
"And I," quoth Everard, "by the wassail-bowl."
"Why yes," I said, "we knew your gift that way
At college: but another which you had,
I mean of verse (for so we held it then),
What came of that?" "You know," said Frank, "he burnt
His epic, his King Arthur, some twelve books"—
And then to me demanding why? "Oh, sir,
He thought that nothing new was said, or else
Something so said 'twas nothing—that a truth
Looks freshest in the fashion of the day:
God knows: he has a mint of reasons: ask.
It pleased *me* well enough." "Nay, nay," said Hall,
"Why take the style of those heroic times?
For nature brings not back the Mastodon,
Nor we those times; and why should any man
Remodel models? these twelve books of mine
Were faint Homeric echoes, nothing-worth,
Mere chaff and draff, much better burnt."
  "But I,"
Said Francis, "pick'd the eleventh from this hearth
And have it: keep a thing, its use will come.
I hoard it as a sugar-plum for Holmes."
He laugh'd, and I, tho' sleepy, like a horse
That hears the corn-bin open, prick'd my ears;
For I remember'd Everard's college fame
When we were Freshmen: then at my request
He brought it; and the poet little urged,
But with some prelude of disparagement,
Read, mouthing out his hollow oes and aes,
Deep-chested music, and to this result.

1842

MORTE D'ARTHUR

So all day long the noise of battle roll'd
Among the mountains by the winter sea;
Until King Arthur's table, man by man,
Had fallen in Lyonnesse about their Lord,
King Arthur: then, because his wound was deep,
The bold Sir Bedivere uplifted him,
Sir Bedivere, the last of all his knights,
And bore him to a chapel nigh the field,
A broken chancel with a broken cross,
That stood on a dark strait of barren land.
On one side lay the Ocean, and on one
Lay a great water, and the moon was full.
  Then spake King Arthur to Sir Bedivere:
"The sequel of to-day unsolders all
The goodliest fellowship of famous knights
Whereof this world holds record. Such a sleep

They sleep—the men I loved. I think that we
Shall never more, at any future time,
Delight our souls with talk of knightly deeds,
Walking about the gardens and the halls
Of Camelot, as in the days that were.
I perish by this people which I made,—
Tho' Merlin sware that I should come again
To rule once more—but let what will be, be,
I am so deeply smitten thro' the helm
That without help I cannot last till morn.
Thou therefore take my brand Excalibur,
Which was my pride: for thou rememberest how
In those old days, one summer noon, an arm
Rose up from out the bosom of the lake,
Clothed in white samite, mystic, wonderful,
Holding the sword—and how I row'd across
And took it, and have worn it, like a king:
And, wheresoever I am sung or told
In aftertime, this also shall be known:
But now delay not: take Excalibur,
And fling him far into the middle mere:
Watch what thou seëst, and lightly bring me word."
  To him replied the bold Sir Bedivere:
"It is not meet, Sir King, to leave thee thus,
Aidless, alone, and smitten thro' the helm.
A little thing may harm a wounded man.
Yet I thy hest will all perform at full,
Watch what I see, and lightly bring thee word."
  So saying, from the ruin'd shrine he stept
And in the moon athwart the place of tombs,
Where lay the mighty bones of ancient men,
Old knights, and over them the sea-wind sang
Shrill, chill, with flakes of foam. He, stepping down
By zig-zag paths, and juts of pointed rock,
Came on the shining levels of the lake.
  There drew he forth the brand Excalibur,
And o'er him, drawing it, the winter moon,
Brightening the skirts of a long cloud, ran forth
And sparkled keen with frost against the hilt:
For all the haft twinkled with diamond sparks,
Myriads of topaz-lights, and jacinth-work
Of subtlest jewellery. He gazed so long
That both his eyes were dazzled, as he stood,
This way and that dividing the swift mind,
In act to throw: but at the last it seem'd
Better to leave Excalibur conceal'd
There in the many-knotted waterflags,
That whistled stiff and dry about the marge.
So strode he back slow to the wounded King.
  Then spake King Arthur to Sir Bedivere:
"Hast thou perform'd my mission which I gave?
What is it thou hast seen? or what hast heard?"
  And answer made the bold Sir Bedivere:
"I heard the ripple washing in the reeds,
And the wild water lapping on the crag."
  To whom replied King Arthur, faint and pale:
"Thou hast betray'd thy nature and thy name,
Not rendering true answer as beseem'd
Thy fealty, nor like a noble knight:
For surer sign had follow'd, either hand,
Or voice, or else a motion of the mere.
This is a shameful thing for men to lie.
Yet now, I charge thee, quickly go again
As thou art lief and dear, and do the thing
I bade thee, watch, and lightly bring me word."
  Then went Sir Bedivere the second time
Across the ridge, and paced beside the mere,
Counting the dewy pebbles, fix'd in thought;
But when he saw the wonder of the hilt,
How curiously and strangely chased, he smote
His palms together, and he cried aloud,
  "And if indeed I cast the brand away,
Surely a precious thing, one worthy note,
Should thus be lost for ever from the earth,
Which might have pleased the eyes of many men.
What good should follow this, if this were done?
What harm, undone? deep harm to disobey,
Seeing obedience is the bond of rule.
Were it well to obey then, if a king demand
An act unprofitable, against himself?
The King is sick, and knows not what he does.
What record, or what relic of my lord
Should be to aftertime, but empty breath
And rumours of a doubt? but were this kept,
Stored in some treasure-house of mighty kings,
Some one might show it at a joust of arms,
Saying, 'King Arthur's sword, Excalibur,
Wrought by the lonely maiden of the Lake.
Nine years she wrought it, sitting in the deeps

Upon the hidden bases of the hills.'
So might some old man speak in the aftertime
To all the people, winning reverence.
But now much honour and much fame were lost."
So spake he, clouded with his own conceit,
And hid Excalibur the second time,
And so strode back slow to the wounded King.
Then spoke King Arthur, breathing heavily:
"What is it thou hast seen? or what hast heard?"
And answer made the bold Sir Bedivere:
"I heard the water lapping on the crag,
And the long ripple washing in the reeds."
To whom replied King Arthur, much in wrath:
"Ah, miserable and unkind, untrue,
Unknightly, traitor-hearted! Woe is me!
Authority forgets a dying king,
Laid widow'd of the power in his eye
That bow'd the will. I see thee what thou art,
For thou, the latest-left of all my knights,
In whom should meet the offices of all,
Thou wouldst betray me for the precious hilt;
Either from lust of gold, or like a girl
Valuing the giddy pleasure of the eyes.
Yet, for a man may fail in duty twice,
And the third time may prosper, get thee hence:
But, if thou spare to fling Excalibur,
I will arise and slay thee with my hands."
Then quickly rose Sir Bedivere, and ran,
And, leaping down the ridges lightly, plunged
Among the bulrush-beds, and clutch'd the sword,
And strongly wheel'd and threw it. The great brand
Made lightnings in the splendour of the moon,
And flashing round and round, and whirl'd in an arch,
Shot like a streamer of the northern morn,
Seen where the moving isles of winter shock
By night, with noises of the northern sea.
So flash'd and fell the brand Excalibur:
But ere he dipt the surface, rose an arm
Clothed in white samite, mystic, wonderful,
And caught him by the hilt, and brandish'd him
Three times, and drew him under in the mere.
And lightly went the other to the King.
Then spoke King Arthur, drawing thicker breath:
"Now see I by thine eyes that this is done.
Speak out: what is it thou hast heard, or seen?"
And answer made the bold Sir Bedivere:
"Sir King, I closed mine eyelids, lest the gems
Should blind my purpose, for I never saw,
Nor shall see, here or elsewhere, till I die,
Not tho' I live three lives of mortal men,
So great a miracle as yonder hilt.
Then with both hands I flung him, wheeling him;
But when I look'd again, behold an arm,
Clothed in white samite, mystic, wonderful,
That caught him by the hilt, and brandish'd him
Three times, and drew him under in the mere."
And answer made King Arthur, breathing hard:
"My end draws nigh; 'tis time that I were gone.
Make broad thy shoulders to receive my weight,
And bear me to the margin; yet I fear
My wound hath taken cold, and I shall die."
So saying, from the pavement he half rose,
Slowly, with pain, reclining on his arm,
And looking wistfully with wide blue eyes
As in a picture. Him Sir Bedivere
Remorsefully regarded thro' his tears,
And would have spoken, but he found not words,
Then took with care, and kneeling on one knee,
O'er both his shoulders drew the languid hands,
And rising bore him thro' the place of tombs.
But, as he walk'd, King Arthur panted hard,
Like one that feels a nightmare on his bed
When all the house is mute. So sigh'd the King,
Muttering and murmuring at his ear, "Quick, quick!
I fear it is too late, and I shall die."
But the other swiftly strode from ridge to ridge,
Clothed with his breath, and looking, as he walk'd,
Larger than human on the frozen hills.

He heard the deep behind him, and a cry
Before. His own thought drove him, like a goad.
Dry clash'd his harness in the icy caves
And barren chasms, and all to left and right
The bare black cliff clang'd round him, as he based
His feet on juts of slippery crag that rang
Sharp-smitten with the dint of armed heels—
And on a sudden, lo! the level lake,
And the long glories of the winter moon.
Then saw they how there hove a dusky barge,
Dark as a funeral scarf from stem to stern,
Beneath them; and descending they were ware
That all the decks were dense with stately forms
Black-stoled, black-hooded, like a dream—by these
Three Queens with crowns of gold—and from them rose
A cry that shiver'd to the tingling stars,
And, as it were one voice an agony
Of lamentation, like a wind, that shrills
All night in a waste land, where no one comes,
Or hath come, since the making of the world.
Then murmur'd Arthur, "Place me in the barge,"
And to the barge they came. There those three Queens
Put forth their hands, and took the King, and wept.
But she, that rose the tallest of them all
And fairest, laid his head upon her lap,
And loosed the shatter'd casque, and chafed his hands,
And call'd him by his name, complaining loud,
And dropping bitter tears against his brow
Striped with dark blood: for all his face was white
And colourless, and like the wither'd moon
Smote by the fresh beam of the springing east;
And all his greaves and cuisses dash'd with drops
Of onset; and the light and lustrous curls—
That made his forehead like a rising sun
High from the daïs-throne—were parch'd with dust;
Or, clotted into points and hanging loose,
Mix'd with the knightly growth that fringed his lips.
So like a shatter'd column lay the King;
Not like that Arthur who, with lance in rest,
From spur to plume a star of tournament,
Shot thro' the lists at Camelot, and charged
Before the eyes of ladies and of kings.
Then loudly cried the bold Sir Bedivere,
"Ah! my Lord Arthur, whither shall I go?
Where shall I hide my forehead and my eyes?
For now I see the true old times are dead,
When every morning brought a noble chance,
And every chance brought out a noble knight.
Such times have been not since the light that led
The holy Elders with the gift of myrrh.
But now the whole ROUND TABLE is dissolved
Which was an image of the mighty world;
And I, the last, go forth companionless,
And the days darken round me, and the years,
Among new men, strange faces, other minds."
And slowly answered Arthur from the barge:
"The old order changeth, yielding place to new,
And God fulfils Himself in many ways,
Lest one good custom should corrupt the world.
Comfort thyself: what comfort is in me?
I have lived my life, and that which I have done
May He within Himself make pure! but thou,
If thou shouldst never see my face again,
Pray for my soul. More things are wrought by prayer
Than this world dreams of. Wherefore, let thy voice
Rise like a fountain for me night and day.
For what are men better than sheep or goats
That nourish a blind life within the brain,
If, knowing God, they lift not hands of prayer
Both for themselves and those who call them friend?
For so the whole round earth is every way
Bound by gold chains about the feet of God.
But now farewell. I am going a long way
With these thou seëst—if indeed I go—
(For all my mind is clouded with a doubt)
To the island-valley of Avilion;
Where falls not hail, or rain, or any snow,
Nor ever wind blows loudly; but it lies

Deep-meadow'd, happy, fair with orchard-lawns
And bowery hollows crown'd with summer sea,
Where I will heal me of my grievous wound."
  So said he, and the barge with oar and sail
Moved from the brink, like some full-breasted swan
That, fluting a wild carol ere her death,
Ruffles her pure cold plume, and takes the flood
With swarthy webs. Long stood Sir Bedivere
Revolving many memories, till the hull
Look'd one black dot against the verge of dawn,
And on the mere the wailing died away.

1842

DORA

WITH farmer Allan at the farm abode
William and Dora. William was his son,
And she his niece. He often look'd at them,
And often thought, "I'll make them man and wife."
Now Dora felt her uncle's will in all,
And yearn'd toward William; but the youth, because
He had been always with her in the house,
Thought not of Dora.
                Then there came a day
When Allan call'd his son, and said, "My son:
I married late, but I would wish to see
My grandchild on my knees before I die:
And I have set my heart upon a match.
Now therefore look to Dora; she is well
To look to; thrifty too beyond her age.
She is my brother's daughter: he and I
Had once hard words, and parted, and he died
In foreign lands; but for his sake I bred
His daughter Dora: take her for your wife;
For I have wish'd this marriage, night and day,
For many years." But William answer'd short;
"I cannot marry Dora; by my life,
I will not marry Dora." Then the old man
Was wroth, and doubled up his hands, and said:
"You will not, boy! you dare to answer thus!
But in my time a father's word was law,
And so it shall be now for me. Look to it;
Consider, William: take a month to think,
And let me have an answer to my wish;
Or, by the Lord that made me, you shall pack,
And never more darken my doors again."
But William answer'd madly; bit his lips,
And broke away. The more he look'd at her
The less he liked her; and his ways were harsh;
But Dora bore them meekly. Then before
The month was out he left his father's house,
And hired himself to work within the fields;
And half in love, half spite, he woo'd and wed
A labourer's daughter, Mary Morrison.
  Then, when the bells were ringing, Allan call'd
His niece and said: "My girl, I love you well;
But if you speak with him that was my son,
Or change a word with her he calls his wife,
My home is none of yours. My will is law."
And Dora promised, being meek. She thought,
"It cannot be: my uncle's mind will change!"
  And days went on, and there was born a boy
To William; then distresses came on him;
And day by day he pass'd his father's gate,
Heart-broken, and his father help'd him not.
But Dora stored what little she could save,
And sent it them by stealth, nor did they know
Who sent it; till at last a fever seized
On William, and in harvest time he died.
  Then Dora went to Mary. Mary sat
And look'd with tears upon her boy, and thought
Hard things of Dora. Dora came and said:
  "I have obey'd my uncle until now,
And I have sinn'd, for it was all thro' me
This evil came on William at the first.
But, Mary, for the sake of him that's gone,
And for your sake, the woman that he chose,
And for this orphan, I am come to you:
You know there has not been for these five years
So full a harvest: let me take the boy,
And I will set him in my uncle's eye
Among the wheat; that when his heart is glad
Of the full harvest, he may see the boy,
And bless him for the sake of him that's gone."
  And Dora took the child, and went her way
Across the wheat, and sat upon a mound

That was unsown, where many poppies grew.
Far off the farmer came into the field
And spied her not; for none of all his men
Dare tell him Dora waited with the child;
And Dora would have risen and gone to him,
But her heart fail'd her; and the reapers reap'd,
And the sun fell, and all the land was dark.

But when the morrow came, she rose and took
The child once more, and sat upon the mound;
And made a little wreath of all the flowers
That grew about, and tied it round his hat
To make him pleasing in her uncle's eye.
Then when the farmer pass'd into the field
He spied her, and he left his men at work,
And came and said: "Where were you yesterday?
Whose child is that? What are you doing here?"
So Dora cast her eyes upon the ground,
And answer'd softly, "This is William's child!"
"And did I not," said Allan, "did I not
Forbid you, Dora?" Dora said again:
"Do with me as you will, but take the child,
And bless him for the sake of him that's gone!"
And Allan said, "I see it is a trick
Got up betwixt you and the woman there.
I must be taught my duty, and by you!
You knew my word was law, and yet you dared
To slight it. Well—for I will take the boy;
But go you hence, and never see me more."

So saying, he took the boy that cried aloud
And struggled hard. The wreath of flowers fell
At Dora's feet. She bow'd upon her hands,
And the boy's cry came to her from the field,
More and more distant. She bow'd down her head,
Remembering the day when first she came,
And all the things that had been. She bow'd down
And wept in secret; and the reapers reap'd,
And the sun fell, and all the land was dark.

Then Dora went to Mary's house, and stood
Upon the threshold. Mary saw the boy
Was not with Dora. She broke out in praise
To God, that help'd her in her widowhood.
And Dora said, "My uncle took the boy;
But, Mary, let me live and work with you:
He says that he will never see me more."
Then answer'd Mary, "This shall never be,
That thou shouldst take my trouble on thyself:
And, now I think, he shall not have the boy,
For he will teach him hardness, and to slight
His mother; therefore thou and I will go,
And I will have my boy, and bring him home;
And I will beg of him to take thee back:
But if he will not take thee back again,
Then thou and I will live within one house,
And work for William's child, until he grows
Of age to help us."

So the women kiss'd
Each other, and set out, and reach'd the farm.
The door was off the latch: they peep'd, and saw
The boy set up betwixt his grandsire's knees,
Who thrust him in the hollows of his arm,
And clapt him on the hands and on the cheeks,
Like one that loved him: and the lad stretch'd out
And babbled for the golden seal, that hung
From Allan's watch, and sparkled by the fire.
Then they came in: but when the boy beheld
His mother, he cried out to come to her:
And Allan set him down, and Mary said:

"O Father!—if you let me call you so—
I never came a-begging for myself,
Or William, or this child; but now I come
For Dora: take her back; she loves you well.
O Sir, when William died, he died at peace
With all men; for I ask'd him, and he said,
He could not ever rue his marrying me—
I had been a patient wife: but, Sir, he said
That he was wrong to cross his father thus:
'God bless him!' he said, 'and may he never know
The troubles I have gone thro'!' Then he turn'd
His face and pass'd—unhappy that I am!
But now, Sir, let me have my boy, for you
Will make him hard, and he will learn to slight
His father's memory; and take Dora back,
And let all this be as it was before."

So Mary said, and Dora hid her face
By Mary. There was silence in the room;
And all at once the old man burst in sobs:—

"I have been to blame—to blame. I have kill'd my son.
I have kill'd him—but I loved him—my dear son.
May God forgive me!—I have been to blame.
Kiss me, my children."
Then they clung about
The old man's neck, and kiss'd him many times.
And all the man was broken with remorse;
And all his love came back a hundredfold;
And for three hours he sobb'd o'er William's child
Thinking of William.
So those four abode
Within one house together; and as years
Went forward, Mary took another mate;
But Dora lived unmarried till her death.

1842

ULYSSES

It little profits that an idle king,
By this still hearth, among these barren crags,
Match'd with an aged wife, I mete and dole
Unequal laws unto a savage race,
That hoard, and sleep, and feed, and know not me.
I cannot rest from travel: I will drink
Life to the lees: all times I have enjoy'd
Greatly, have suffer'd greatly, both with those
That loved me, and alone; on shore, and when
Thro' scudding drifts the rainy Hyades
Vext the dim sea: I am become a name;
For always roaming with a hungry heart
Much have I seen and known; cities of men
And manners, climates, councils, governments,
Myself not least, but honour'd of them all;
And drunk delight of battle with my peers,
Far on the ringing plains of windy Troy.
I am a part of all that I have met;
Yet all experience is an arch wherethro'
Gleams that untravell'd world, whose margin fades
For ever and for ever when I move.
How dull it is to pause, to make an end,
To rust unburnish'd, not to shine in use!
As tho' to breathe were life. Life piled on life
Were all too little, and of one to me
Little remains: but every hour is saved
From that eternal silence, something more,
A bringer of new things; and vile it were
For some three suns to store and hoard myself,
And this gray spirit yearning in desire
To follow knowledge like a sinking star,
Beyond the utmost bound of human thought.
This is my son, mine own Telemachus,
To whom I leave the sceptre and the isle—
Well-loved of me, discerning to fulfil
This labour, by slow prudence to make mild
A rugged people, and thro' soft degrees
Subdue them to the useful and the good.
Most blameless is he, centred in the sphere
Of common duties, decent not to fail
In offices of tenderness, and pay
Meet adoration to my household gods,
When I am gone. He works his work, I mine.
There lies the port; the vessel puffs her sail:
There gloom the dark broad seas. My mariners,
Souls that have toil'd, and wrought, and thought with me—
That ever with a frolic welcome took
The thunder and the sunshine, and opposed
Free hearts, free foreheads—you and I are old;
Old age hath yet his honour and his toil;
Death closes all: but something ere the end,
Some work of noble note, may yet be done,
Not unbecoming men that strove with Gods.
The lights begin to twinkle from the rocks:
The long day wanes: the slow moon climbs: the deep
Moans round with many voices. Come, my friends,
'Tis not too late to seek a newer world.
Push off, and sitting well in order smite
The sounding furrows; for my purpose holds
To sail beyond the sunset, and the baths
Of all the western stars, until I die.
It may be that the gulfs will wash us down:
It may be we shall touch the Happy Isles,
And see the great Achilles, whom we knew.
Tho' much is taken, much abides; and tho'
We are not now that strength which in old days
Moved earth and heaven; that which we are, we are;
One equal temper of heroic hearts,
Made weak by time and fate, but strong in will
To strive, to seek, to find, and not to yield.

1842

LOCKSLEY HALL

COMRADES, leave me here a little, while as yet 'tis early morn:
Leave me here, and when you want me, sound upon the bugle-horn.

'Tis the place, and all around it, as of old, the curlews call,
Dreary gleams about the moorland flying over Locksley Hall;

Locksley Hall, that in the distance overlooks the sandy tracts,
And the hollow ocean-ridges roaring into cataracts.

Many a night from yonder ivied casement, ere I went to rest,
Did I look on great Orion sloping slowly to the West.

Many a night I saw the Pleiads, rising thro' the mellow shade,
Glitter like a swarm of fire-flies tangled in a silver braid.

Here about the beach I wander'd, nourishing a youth sublime
With the fairy tales of science, and the long result of Time;

When the centuries behind me like a fruitful land reposed;
When I clung to all the present for the promise that it closed:

When I dipt into the future far as human eye could see;
Saw the Vision of the world, and all the wonder that would be.—

In the Spring a fuller crimson comes upon the robin's breast;
In the Spring the wanton lapwing gets himself another crest;

In the Spring a livelier iris changes on the burnish'd dove;
In the Spring a young many's fancy lightly turns to thoughts of love.

Then her cheek was pale and thinner than should be for one so young,
And her eyes on all my motions with a mute observance hung.

And I said, "My cousin Amy, speak, and speak the truth to me,
Trust me, cousin, all the current of my being sets to thee."

On her pallid cheek and forehead came a colour and a light,
As I have seen the rosy red flushing in the northern night.

And she turn'd—her bosom shaken with a sudden storm of sighs—
All the spirit deeply dawning in the dark of hazel eyes—

Saying, "I have hid my feelings, fearing they should do me wrong;"
Saying, "Dost thou love me, cousin?" weeping, "I have loved thee long."

Love took up the glass of Time, and turn'd it in his glowing hands;
Every moment, lightly shaken, ran itself in golden sands.

Love took up the harp of Life, and smote on all the chords with might;
Smote the chord of Self, that, trembling, pass'd in music out of sight.

Many a morning on the moorland did we hear the copses ring,
And her whisper throng'd my pulses with the fulness of the Spring.

Many an evening by the waters did we watch the stately ships,
And our spirits rush'd together at the touching of the lips.

O my cousin, shallow-hearted! O my Amy, mine no more!
O the dreary, dreary moorland! O the barren, barren shore!

Falser than all fancy fathoms, falser than all songs have sung,
Puppet to a father's threat, and servile to a shrewish tongue!

Is it well to wish thee happy?—having known me—to decline
On a range of lower feelings and a narrower heart than mine!

Yet it shall be: thou shalt lower to his level day by day,
What is fine within thee growing coarse to sympathise with clay.

As the husband is, the wife is: thou art mated with a clown,
And the grossness of his nature will have weight to drag thee down.

He will hold thee, when his passion shall have spent its novel force,
Something better than his dog, a little dearer than his horse.

What is this? his eyes are heavy: think not they are glazed with wine.
Go to him: it is thy duty: kiss him: take his hand in thine.

It may be my lord is weary, that his brain is overwrought:
Soothe him with thy finer fancies, touch him with thy lighter thought.

He will answer to the purpose, easy things to understand—
Better thou wert dead before me, tho' I slew thee with my hand!

Better thou and I were lying, hidden from the heart's disgrace,
Roll'd in one another's arms, and silent in a last embrace.

Cursed be the social wants that sin against the strength of youth!
Cursed be the social lies that warp us from the living truth!

Cursed be the sickly forms that err from honest Nature's rule!
Cursed be the gold that gilds the straiten'd forehead of the fool!

Well—'tis well that I should bluster!—Hadst thou less unworthy proved—
Would to God—for I had loved thee more than ever wife was loved.

Am I mad, that I should cherish that which bears but bitter fruit?
I will pluck it from my bosom, tho' my heart be at the root.

Never, tho' my mortal summers to such length of years should come
As the many-winter'd crow that leads the clanging rookery home.

Where is comfort? in division of the records of the mind?
Can I part her from herself, and love her, as I knew her, kind?

I remember one that perish'd: sweetly did she speak and move:
Such a one do I remember, whom to look at was to love.

Can I think of her as dead, and love her for the love she bore?
No—she never loved me truly: love is love for evermore.

Comfort? comfort scorn'd of devils! this is truth the poet sings,
That a sorrow's crown of sorrow is remembering happier things.

Drug thy memories, lest thou learn it, lest thy heart be put to proof,
In the dead unhappy night, and when the rain is on the roof.

Like a dog, he hunts in dreams, and thou art staring at the wall,
Where the dying night-lamp flickers, and the shadows rise and fall.

Then a hand shall pass before thee, pointing to his drunken sleep,
To thy widow'd marriage-pillows, to the tears that thou wilt weep.

Thou shalt hear the "Never, never," whisper'd by the phantom years,
And a song from out the distance in the ringing of thine ears;

And an eye shall vex thee, looking ancient kindness on thy pain.
Turn thee, turn thee on thy pillow: get thee to thy rest again.

Nay, but Nature brings thee solace; for a tender voice will cry.
'Tis a purer life than thine; a lip to drain thy trouble dry.

Baby lips will laugh me down: my latest rival brings thee rest.
Baby fingers, waxen touches, press me from the mother's breast.

O, the child too clothes the father with a dearness not his due.
Half is thine and half is his: it will be worthy of the two.

O, I see thee old and formal, fitted to thy petty part,
With a little hoard of maxims preaching down a daughter's heart.

"They were dangerous guides the feelings—she herself was not exempt—
Truly, she herself had suffer'd"—Perish in thy self-contempt!

Overlive it—lower yet—be happy! wherefore should I care?
I myself must mix with action, lest I wither by despair.

What is that which I should turn to, lighting upon days like these?
Every door is barr'd with gold, and opens but to golden keys.

Every gate is throng'd with suitors, all the markets overflow.
I have but an angry fancy: what is that which I should do?

I had been content to perish, falling on the foeman's ground,
When the ranks are roll'd in vapour, and the winds are laid with sound.

But the jingling of the guinea helps the hurt that Honour feels,
And the nations do but murmur, snarling at each other's heels.

Can I but relive in sadness? I will turn that earlier page.
Hide me from my deep emotion, O thou wondrous Mother-Age!

Make me feel the wild pulsation that I felt before the strife,
When I heard my days before me, and the tumult of my life;

Yearning for the large excitement that the coming years would yield,
Eager-hearted as a boy when first he leaves his father's field,

And at night along the dusky highway near and nearer drawn,
Sees in heaven the light of London flaring like a dreary dawn;

And his spirit leaps within him to be gone before him then,
Underneath the light he looks at, in among the throngs of men:

Men, my brothers, men the workers, ever reaping something new:
That which they have done but earnest of the things that they shall do:

For I dipt into the future, far as human eye could see,
Saw the Vision of the world, and all the wonder that would be;

Saw the heavens fill with commerce, argosies of magic sails,
Pilots of the purple twilight, dropping down with costly bales;

Heard the heavens fill with shouting, and there rain'd a ghastly dew
From the nations' airy navies grappling in the central blue;

Far along the world-wide whisper of the south-wind rushing warm,
With the standards of the peoples plunging thro' the thunder-storm;

Till the war-drum throbb'd no longer, and the battle-flags were furl'd
In the Parliament of man, the Federation of the world.

There the common sense of most shall hold a fretful realm in awe,
And the kindly earth shall slumber, lapt in universal law.

So I triumph'd ere my passion sweeping thro' me left me dry,
Left me with the palsied heart, and left me with the jaundiced eye;

Eye, to which all order festers, all things here are out of joint:
Science moves, but slowly slowly, creeping on from point to point:

Slowly comes a hungry people, as a lion creeping nigher,
Glares at one that nods and winks behind a slowly-dying fire.

Yet I doubt not thro' the ages one increasing purpose runs,
And the thoughts of men are widen'd with the process of the suns.

What is that to him that reaps not harvest of his youthful joys,
Tho' the deep heart of existence beat for ever like a boy's?

Knowledge comes, but wisdom lingers, and I linger on the shore,
And the individual withers, and the world is more and more.

Knowledge comes, but wisdom lingers, and he bears a laden breast,
Full of sad experience, moving toward the stillness of his rest.

Hark, my merry comrades call me, sounding on the bugle-horn,
They to whom my foolish passion were a target for their scorn:

Shall it not be scorn to me to harp on such a moulder'd string?
I am shamed thro' all my nature to have loved so slight a thing.

Weakness to be wroth with weakness! woman's pleasure, woman's pain—
Nature made them blinder motions bounded in a shallower brain:

Woman is the lesser man, and all thy passions, match'd with mine,
Are as moonlight unto sunlight, and as water unto wine—

Here at least, where nature sickens, nothing. Ah, for some retreat
Deep in yonder shining Orient, where my life began to beat;

Where in wild Mahratta-battle fell my father evil-starr'd;—
I was left a trampled orphan, and a selfish uncle's ward.

Or to burst all links of habit—there to wander far away,
On from island unto island at the gateways of the day.

Larger constellations burning, mellow moons and happy skies,
Breadths of tropic shade and palms in cluster, knots of Paradise.

Never comes the trader, never floats an European flag,
Slides the bird o'er lustrous woodland, swings the trailer from the crag;

Droops the heavy-blossom'd bower, hangs the heavy-fruited tree—
Summer isles of Eden lying in dark-purple spheres of sea.

There methinks would be enjoyment more than in this march of mind,
In the steamship, in the railway, in the thoughts that shake mankind.

There the passions cramp'd no longer shall have scope and breathing space;
I will take some savage woman, she shall rear my dusky race.

Iron jointed, supple-sinew'd, they shall dive, and they shall run,
Catch the wild goat by the hair, and hurl their lances in the sun;

Whistle back the parrot's call, and leap the rainbows of the brooks,
Not with blinded eyesight poring over miserable books—

Fool, again the dream, the fancy! but I *know* my words are wild,
But I count the gray barbarian lower than the Christian child.

I, to herd with narrow foreheads, vacant of our glorious gains,
Like a beast with lower pleasures, like a beast with lower pains!

Mated with a squalid savage—what to me were sun or clime?
I the heir of all the ages, in the foremost files of time—

I that rather held it better men should perish one by one,
Than that earth should stand at gaze like Joshua's moon in Ajalon!

Not in vain the distance beacons. Forward, forward let us range,
Let the great world spin for ever down the ringing grooves of change.

Thro' the shadow of the globe we sweep into the younger day:
Better fifty years of Europe than a cycle of Cathay.

Mother-Age (for mine I knew not) help me as when life begun:
Rift the hills, and roll the waters, flash the lightnings, weigh the Sun.

O, I see the crescent promise of my spirit hath not set.
Ancient founts of inspiration well thro' all my fancy yet.

Howsoever these things be, a long farewell to Locksley Hall!
Now for me the woods may wither, now for me the roof-tree fall.

Comes a vapour from the margin, blackening over heath and holt,
Cramming all the blast before it, in its breast a thunderbolt.

Let it fall on Locksley Hall, with rain or hail, or fire or snow;
For the mighty wind arises, roaring seaward, and I go.

1842

GODIVA

I WAITED for the train at Coventry;
I hung with grooms and porters on the bridge,
To watch the three tall spires; and there I shaped
The city's ancient legend into this:—
Not only we, the latest seed of Time,
New men, that in the flying of a wheel
Cry down the past, not only we, that prate
Of rights and wrongs, have loved the people well,
And loathed to see them overtax'd; but she
Did more, and underwent, and overcame,
The woman of a thousand summers back,
Godiva, wife to that grim Earl, who ruled
In Coventry: for when he laid a tax
Upon his town, and all the mothers brought
Their children, clamouring, "If we pay, we starve!"
She sought her lord, and found him, where he strode
About the hall, among his dogs, alone,
His beard a foot before him, and his hair
A yard behind. She told him of their tears,
And pray'd him, "If they pay this tax, they starve."
Whereat he stared, replying, half-amazed,
"You would not let your little finger ache
For such as *these?*"—"But I would die," said she.
He laugh'd, and swore by Peter and by Paul:
Then fillip'd at the diamond in her ear;
"Oh ay, ay, ay, you talk!"—"Alas!" she said,
"But prove me what it is I would not do."
And from a heart as rough as Esau's hand,
He answer'd, "Ride you naked thro' the town,
And I repeal it;" and nodding, as in scorn,
He parted, with great strides among his dogs.
So left alone, the passions of her mind,
As winds from all the compass shift and blow,
Made war upon each other for an hour,
Till pity won. She sent a herald forth,
And bade him cry, with sound of trumpet, all
The hard condition; but that she would loose
The people: therefore, as they loved her well,
From then till noon no foot should pace the street,
No eye look down, she passing; but that all
Should keep within, door shut, and window barr'd.
Then fled she to her inmost bower, and there
Unclasp'd the wedded eagles of her belt,
The grim Earl's gift; but ever at a breath
She linger'd, looking like a summer moon
Half-dipt in cloud: anon she shook her head,
And shower'd the rippled ringlets to her knee;
Unclad herself in haste; adown the stair
Stole on; and, like a creeping sunbeam, slid
From pillar unto pillar, until she reach'd
The gateway; there she found her palfrey trapt
In purple blazon'd with armorial gold.
Then she rode forth, clothed on with chastity:
The deep air listen'd round her as she rode,
And all the low wind hardly breathed for fear.
The little wide-mouth'd heads upon the spout
Had cunning eyes to see: the barking cur
Made her cheek flame: her palfrey's footfall shot
Light horrors thro' her pulses: the blind walls
Were full of chinks and holes; and overhead
Fantastic gables, crowding, stared: but she
Not less thro' all bore up, till, last, she saw
The white-flower'd elder-thicket from the field
Gleam thro' the Gothic archway in the wall.
Then she rode back, clothed on with chastity:

And one low churl, compact of thankless earth,
The fatal byword of all years to come,
Boring a little auger-hole in fear,
Peep'd—but his eyes, before they had their will,
Were shrivell'd into darkness in his head,
And dropt before him. So the Powers, who wait
On noble deeds, cancell'd a sense misused;
And she, that knew not, pass'd: and all at once,
With twelve great shocks of sound, the shameless noon
Was clash'd and hammer'd from a hundred towers,
One after one: but even then she gain'd
Her bower; whence reissuing, robed and crown'd,
To meet her lord, she took the tax away
And built herself an everlasting name.

1842

SIR GALAHAD

My good blade carves the casques of men,
  My tough lance thrusteth sure,
My strength is as the strength of ten,
  Because my heart is pure.
The shattering trumpet shrilleth high,
  The hard brands shiver on the steel,
The splinter'd spear-shafts crack and fly,
  The horse and rider reel:
They reel, they roll in clanging lists,
  And when the tide of combat stands,
Perfume and flowers fall in showers,
  That lightly rain from ladies' hands.

How sweet are looks that ladies bend
  On whom their favours fall!
For them I battle till the end,
  To save from shame and thrall:
But all my heart is drawn above,
  My knees are bow'd in crypt and shrine:
I never felt the kiss of love,
  Nor maiden's hand in mine.
More bounteous aspects on me beam,
  Me mightier transports move and thrill;
So keep I fair thro' faith and prayer
  A virgin heart in work and will.

When down the stormy crescent goes,
  A light before me swims,
Between dark stems the forest glows,
  I hear a noise of hymns:
Then by some secret shrine I ride;
  I hear a voice but none are there;
The stalls are void, the doors are wide,
  The tapers burning fair.
Fair gleams the snowy altar-cloth,
  The silver vessels sparkle clean,
The shrill bell rings, the censer swings,
  And solemn chaunts resound between.

Sometimes on lonely mountain-meres
  I find a magic bark;
I leap on board: no helmsman steers:
  I float till all is dark.
A gentle sound, an awful light!
  Three angels bear the holy Grail:
With folded feet, in stoles of white,
  On sleeping wings they sail.
Ah, blessed vision! blood of God!
  My spirit beats her mortal bars,
As down dark tides the glory slides,
  And star-like mingles with the stars.

When on my goodly charger borne
  Thro' dreaming towns I go,
The cock crows ere the Christmas morn,
  The streets are dumb with snow.
The tempest crackles on the leads,
  And, ringing, springs from brand and mail;
But o'er the dark a glory spreads,
  And gilds the driving hail.
I leave the plain, I climb the height;
  No branchy thicket shelter yields;
But blessed forms in whistling storms
  Fly o'er waste fens and windy fields.

A maiden knight—to me is given
  Such hope, I know not fear;
I yearn to breathe the airs of heaven
  That often meet me here.
I muse on joy that will not cease,
  Pure spaces clothed in living beams,
Pure lilies of eternal peace,
  Whose odours haunt my dreams;
And, stricken by an angel's hand,
  This mortal armour that I wear,
This weight and size, this heart and eyes,
  Are touch'd, are turn'd to finest air.

The clouds are broken in the sky,
And thro' the mountain-walls
A rolling organ-harmony
Swells up, and shakes and falls.
Then move the trees, the copses nod,
Wings flutter, voices hover clear:
"O just and faithful knight of God!
Ride on! the prize is near."
So pass I hostel, hall, and grange;
By bridge and ford, by park and pale,
All-arm'd I ride, whate'er betide,
Until I find the holy Grail.

1842

MOVE EASTWARD, HAPPY EARTH

Move eastward, happy earth, and leave
Yon orange sunset waning slow:
From fringes of the faded eve,
O, happy planet, eastward go;
Till over thy dark shoulder glow
Thy silver sister-world, and rise
To glass herself in dewy eyes
That watch me from the glen below.

Ah, bear me with thee, smoothly borne,
Dip forward under starry light,
And move me to my marriage-morn,
And round again to happy night.

1842

THE VISION OF SIN

I

I had a vision when the night was late:
A youth came riding toward a palace-gate.
He rode a horse with wings, that would have flown,
But that his heavy rider kept him down.
And from the palace came a child of sin,
And took him by the curls, and led him in,
Where sat a company with heated eyes,
Expecting when a fountain should arise:
A sleepy light upon their brows and lips—
As when the sun, a crescent of eclipse,
Dreams over lake and lawn, and isles and capes—
Suffused them, sitting, lying, languid shapes,
By heaps of gourds, and skins of wine, and piles of grapes.

II

Then methought I heard a mellow sound,
Gathering up from all the lower ground;
Narrowing in to where they sat assembled
Low voluptuous music winding trembled,
Wov'n in circles: they that heard it sigh'd,
Panted hand-in-hand with faces pale,
Swung themselves, and in low tones replied;
Till the fountain spouted, showering wide
Sleet of diamond-drift and pearly hail;
Then the music touch'd the gates and died;
Rose again from where it seem'd to fail,
Storm'd in orbs of song, a growing gale;
Till thronging in and in, to where they waited,
As 'twere a hundred-throated nightingale,
The strong tempestuous treble throbb'd and palpitated;
Ran into its giddiest whirl of sound,
Caught the sparkles, and in circles,
Purple gauzes, golden hazes, liquid mazes,
Flung the torrent rainbow round:
Then they started from their places,
Moved with violence, changed in hue,
Caught each other with wild grimaces,
Half-invisible to the view,
Wheeling with precipitate paces
To the melody, till they flew,
Hair, and eyes, and limbs, and faces,
Twisted hard in fierce embraces,
Like to Furies, like to Graces,
Dash'd together in blinding dew:
Till, kill'd with some luxurious agony,
The nerve-dissolving melody
Flutter'd headlong from the sky.

III

And then I look'd up toward a mountain-tract,
That girt the region with high cliff and lawn:
I saw that every morning, far withdrawn
Beyond the darkness and the cataract,
God made Himself an awful rose of dawn,
Unheeded: and detaching, fold by fold,
From those still heights, and, slowly drawing near,
A vapour heavy, hueless, formless, cold,
Came floating on for many a month and year,
Unheeded: and I thought I would have spoken,
And warn'd that madman ere it grew too late:

But, as in dreams, I could not. Mine was broken,
When that cold vapour touch'd the palace gate,
And link'd again. I saw within my head
A gray and gap-tooth'd man as lean as death,
Who slowly rode across a wither'd heath,
And lighted at a ruin'd inn, and said:

IV

"Wrinkled ostler, grim and thin!
  Here is custom come your way;
Take my brute, and lead him in,
  Stuff his ribs with mouldy hay.

"Bitter barmaid, waning fast!
  See that sheets are on my bed;
What! the flower of life is past:
  It is long before you wed.

"Slip-shod waiter, lank and sour,
  At the Dragon on the heath!
Let us have a quiet hour,
  Let us hob-and-nob with Death.

"I am old, but let me drink;
  Bring me spices, bring me wine;
I remember, when I think,
  That my youth was half divine.

Wine is good for shrivell'd lips,
  When a blanket wraps the day,
When the rotten woodland drips,
  And the leaf is stamp'd in clay.

"Sit thee down, and have no shame,
  Cheek by jowl, and knee by knee:
What care I for any name?
  What for order or degree?

"Let me screw thee up a peg:
  Let me loose thy tongue with wine:
Callest thou that thing a leg?
  Which is thinnest? thine or mine?

"Thou shalt not be saved by works:
  Thou hast been a sinner too:
Ruin'd trunks on wither'd forks,
  Empty scarecrows, I and you!

"Fill the cup, and fill the can:
  Have a rouse before the morn:
Every moment dies a man,
  Every moment one is born.

"We are men of ruin'd blood;
  Therefore comes it we are wise.
Fish are we that love the mud,
  Rising to no fancy-flies.

"Name and fame! to fly sublime
  Thro' the courts, the camps, the schools,
Is to be the ball of Time,
  Bandied by the hands of fools.

"Friendship!—to be two in one—
  Let the canting liar pack!
Well I know, when I am gone,
  How she mouths behind my back.

"Virtue!—to be good and just—
  Every heart, when sifted well,
Is a clot of warmer dust,
  Mix'd with cunning sparks of hell.

"O! we two as well can look
  Whited thought and cleanly life
As the priest, above his book
  Leering at his neighbour's wife.

"Fill the cup, and fill the can:
  Have a rouse before the morn:
Every moment dies a man,
  Every moment one is born.

"Drink, and let the parties rave:
  They are fill'd with idle spleen;
Rising, falling, like a wave,
  For they know not what they mean.

"He that roars for liberty
  Faster binds a tyrant's power;
And the tyrant's cruel glee
  Forces on the freer hour.

"Fill the can, and fill the cup:
  All the windy ways of men
Are but dust that rises up,
  And is lightly laid again.

"Greet her with applausive breath,
  Freedom, gaily doth she tread;
In her right a civic wreath,
  In her left a human head.

"No, I love not what is new;
  She is of an ancient house:
And I think we know the hue
  Of that cap upon her brows.

"Let her go! her thirst she slakes
  Where the bloody conduit runs,
Then her sweetest meal she makes
  On the first-born of her sons.

"Drink to lofty hopes that cool—
  Visions of a perfect State:
Drink we, last, the public fool,
  Frantic love and frantic hate.

"Chant me now some wicked stave,
  Till thy drooping courage rise,
And the glow-worm of the grave
  Glimmer in thy rheumy eyes.

"Fear not thou to loose thy tongue;
  Set thy hoary fancies free;
What is loathsome to the young
  Savours well to thee and me.

"Change, reverting to the years,
  When thy nerves could understand
What there is in loving tears,
  And the warmth of hand in hand.

"Tell me tales of thy first love—
  April hopes, the fools of chance;
Till the graves begin to move,
  And the dead begin to dance.

"Fill the can, and fill the cup:
  All the windy ways of men
Are but dust that rises up,
  And is lightly laid again.

"Trooping from their mouldy dens
  The chap-fallen circle spreads:
Welcome, fellow-citizens,
  Hollow hearts and empty heads!

"You are bones, and what of that?
  Every face, however full,
Padded round with flesh and fat,
  Is but modell'd on a skull.

"Death is king, and Vivat Rex!
  Tread a measure on the stones,
Madam—if I know your sex,
  From the fashion of your bones.

"No, I cannot praise the fire
  In your eye—nor yet your lip:
All the more do I admire
  Joints of cunning workmanship.

"Lo! God's likeness—the ground-plan—
  Neither modell'd, glazed, nor framed:
Buss me, thou rough sketch of man,
  Far too naked to be shamed!

"Drink to Fortune, drink to Chance,
  While we keep a little breath!
Drink to heavy Ignorance!
  Hob-and-nob with brother Death!

"Thou art mazed, the night is long,
  And the longer night is near:
What! I am not all as wrong
  As a bitter jest is dear.

"Youthful hopes, by scores, to all,
  When the locks are crisp and curl'd;
Unto me my maudlin gall
  And my mockeries of the world.

"Fill the cup, and fill the can:
  Mingle madness, mingle scorn!
Dregs of life, and lees of man:
  Yet we will not die forlorn."

V

The voice grew faint: there came a further change:
Once more uprose the mystic mountain-range:
Below were men and horses pierced with worms,
And slowly quickening into lower forms;
By shards and scurf of salt, and scum of dross,
Old plash of rains, and refuse patch'd with moss.
Then some one spake: "Behold! it was a crime
Of sense avenged by sense that wore with time."
Another said: "The crime of sense became
The crime of malice, and is equal blame."
And one: "He had not wholly quench'd his power;
A little grain of conscience made him sour."
At last I heard a voice upon the slope
Cry to the summit, "Is there any hope?"
To which an answer peal'd from that high land,
But in a tongue no man could understand;
And on the glimmering limit far withdrawn
God made Himself an awful rose of dawn.

1842

BREAK, BREAK, BREAK

Break, break, break,
On thy cold gray stones, O Sea!
And I would that my tongue could utter
The thoughts that arise in me.

O well for the fisherman's boy,
That he shouts with his sister at play!
O well for the sailor lad,
That he sings in his boat on the bay!

And the stately ships go on
To their haven under the hill;
But O for the touch of a vanish'd hand,
And the sound of a voice that is still!

Break, break, break,
At the foot of thy crags, O Sea!
But the tender grace of a day that is dead
Will never come back to me.

1842

SONGS FROM THE PRINCESS

I AS THRO' THE LAND

As thro' the land at eve we went,
And pluck'd the ripen'd ears,
We fell out, my wife and I,
O we fell out I know not why,
And kiss'd again with tears.
And blessings on the falling out
That all the more endears,
When we fall out with those we love
And kiss again with tears!
For when we came where lies the child
We lost in other years,
There above the little grave,
O there above the little grave,
We kiss'd again with tears.

II SWEET AND LOW

Sweet and low, sweet and low,
Wind of the western sea,
Low, low, breathe and blow,
Wind of the western sea!
Over the rolling waters go,
Come from the dying moon, and blow,
Blow him again to me;
While my little one, while my pretty one, sleeps.
Sleep and rest, sleep and rest,
Father will come to thee soon;
Rest, rest, on mother's breast,
Father will come to thee soon;
Father will come to his babe in the nest,
Silver sails all out of the west
Under the silver moon:
Sleep, my little one, sleep, my pretty one, sleep.

III THE SPLENDOUR FALLS

The splendour falls on castle walls
And snowy summits old in story:
The long light shakes across the lakes,
And the wild cataract leaps in glory.
Blow, bugle, blow, set the wild echoes flying,
Blow, bugle; answer, echoes, dying, dying, dying.

O hark, O hear! how thin and clear,
And thinner, clearer, farther going!
O sweet and far from cliff and scar
The horns of Elfland faintly blowing!
Blow, let us hear the purple glens replying:
Blow, bugle; answer, echoes, dying, dying, dying.

O love, they die in yon rich sky,
They faint on hill or field or river:
Our echoes roll from soul to soul,
And grow for ever and for ever.
Blow, bugle, blow, set the wild echoes flying,
And answer, echoes, answer, dying, dying, dying.

IV TEARS, IDLE TEARS

Tears, idle tears, I know not what they mean,
Tears from the depth of some divine despair
Rise in the heart, and gather to the eyes,
In looking on the happy Autumn-fields,
And thinking of the days that are no more.

Fresh as the first beam glittering on a sail,
That brings our friends up from the underworld,
Sad as the last which reddens over one
That sinks with all we love below the verge;
So sad, so fresh, the days that are no more.

To Frederick Locker
20th Febr 1878.
Tears, idle tears.

Tears, idle tears, I know not what they mean,
Tears from the depth of some divine despair
Rise in the heart, & gather to the eyes,
In looking on the happy Autumn-fields,
And thinking of the days that are no more.

Fresh as the first beam glittering on a sail,
That brings our friends up from the underworld,
Sad as the last which reddens over one
That sinks with all we love below the verge;
So sad, so fresh, the days that are no more.

Ah, sad & strange as in dark summer dawns
The earliest pipe of half-awakend birds
To dying ears, when unto dying eyes
The casement slowly grows a glimmering square;
So sad, so strange, the days that are no more.

Dear as rememberd kisses after death,
And sweet as those by hopeless fancy feignd
On lips that are for others; deep as love,
Deep as first love, & wild with all regret;
O Death in Life the days that are no more.'

A Tennyson

A Copy of "Tears, Idle Tears," Made for Frederick Locker (—Lampson). (See Appendix I.)

Ah, sad and strange as in dark summer dawns
The earliest pipe of half-awaken'd birds
To dying ears, when unto dying eyes
The casement slowly grows a glimmering square;
So sad, so strange, the days that are no more.

Dear as remember'd kisses after death,
And sweet as those by hopeless fancy feign'd
On lips that are for others; deep as love,
Deep as first love, and wild with all regret;
O Death in Life, the days that are no more.

V O SWALLOW, SWALLOW

O Swallow, Swallow, flying, flying South,
Fly to her, and fall upon her gilded eaves,
And tell her, tell her, what I tell to thee.

O tell her, Swallow, thou that knowest each,
That bright and fierce and fickle is the South,
And dark and true and tender is the North.

O Swallow, Swallow, if I could follow, and light
Upon her lattice, I would pipe and trill,
And cheep and twitter twenty million loves.

O were I thou that she might take me in,
And lay me on her bosom, and her heart
Would rock the snowy cradle till I died.

Why lingereth she to clothe her heart with love,
Delaying as the tender ash delays
To clothe herself, when all the woods are green?

O tell her, Swallow, that thy brood is flown:
Say to her, I do but wanton in the South,
But in the North long since my nest is made.

O tell her, brief is life but love is long,
And brief the sun of summer in the North,
And brief the moon of beauty in the South.

O Swallow, flying from the golden woods,
Fly to her, and pipe and woo her, and make her mine,
And tell her, tell her, that I follow thee.

VI THY VOICE IS HEARD

Thy voice is heard thro' rolling drums,
That beat to battle where he stands;
Thy face across his fancy comes,
And gives the battle to his hands:
A moment, while the trumpets blow,
He sees his brood about thy knee;
The next, like fire he meets the foe,
And strikes him dead for thine and thee.

VII HOME THEY BROUGHT

Home they brought her warrior dead:
She nor swoon'd, nor utter'd cry:
All her maidens, watching, said,
"She must weep or she will die."

Then they praised him, soft and low,
Call'd him worthy to be loved,
Truest friend and noblest foe;
Yet she neither spoke nor moved.

Stole a maiden from her place,
Lightly to the warrior stept,
Took the face-cloth from the face;
Yet she neither moved nor wept.

Rose a nurse of ninety years,
Set his child upon her knee—
Like summer tempest came her tears—
"Sweet my child, I live for thee."

VIII OUR ENEMIES HAVE FALL'N

Our enemies have fall'n, have fall'n: the seed,
The little seed they laugh'd at in the dark,
Has risen and cleft the soil, and grown a bulk
Of spanless girth, that lays on every side
A thousand arms and rushes to the Sun.

Our enemies have fall'n, have fall'n: they came;
The leaves were wet with women's tears: they heard
A noise of songs they would not understand:
They mark'd it with the red cross to the fall,
And would have strown it, and are fall'n themselves.

Our enemies have fall'n, have fall'n: they came,
The woodmen with their axes: lo the tree!
But we will make it faggots for the hearth,
And shape it plank and beam for roof and floor,
And boats and bridges for the use of men.

Our enemies have fall'n, have fall'n: they struck;
With their own blows they hurt themselves, nor knew
There dwelt an iron nature in the grain:
The glittering axe was broken in their arms,
Their arms were shatter'd to the shoulder blade.

Our enemies have fall'n, but this shall grow
A night of Summer from the heat, a breadth
Of Autumn, dropping fruits of power: and roll'd
With music in the growing breeze of Time,
The tops shall strike from star to star, the fangs
Shall move the stony bases of the world.

IX ASK ME NO MORE

Ask me no more: the moon may draw the sea;
The cloud may stoop from heaven and take the shape
With fold to fold, of mountain or of cape;
But O too fond, when have I answer'd thee?
Ask me no more.

Ask me no more: what answer should I give?
I love not hollow cheek or faded eye:
Yet, O my friend, I will not have thee die!
Ask me no more, lest I should bid thee live;
Ask me no more.

Ask me no more: thy fate and mine are seal'd:
I strove against the stream and all in vain:
Let the great river take me to the main:
No more, dear love, for at a touch I yield;
Ask me no more.

X NOW SLEEPS THE CRIMSON PETAL

Now sleeps the crimson petal, now the white;
Nor waves the cypress in the palace walk;
Nor winks the gold fin in the porphyry font:
The fire-fly wakens: waken thou with me.

Now droops the milkwhite peacock like a ghost,
And like a ghost she glimmers on to me.

Now lies the Earth all Danaë to the stars,
And all thy heart lies open unto me.

Now slides the silent meteor on, and leaves
A shining furrow, as thy thoughts in me.

Now folds the lily all her sweetness up,
And slips into the bosom of the lake:
So fold thyself, my dearest, thou, and slip
Into my bosom and be lost in me.

XI COME DOWN, O MAID

Come down, O maid, from yonder mountain height:
What pleasure lives in height (the shepherd sang)
In height and cold, the splendour of the hills?
But cease to move so near the Heavens, and cease
To glide a sunbeam by the blasted Pine,
To sit a star upon the sparkling spire;
And come, for Love is of the valley, come,
For Love is of the valley, come thou down
And find him; by the happy threshold, he,
Or hand in hand with Plenty in the maize,
Or red with spirted purple of the vats,
Or foxlike in the vine; nor cares to walk
With Death and Morning on the silver horns,
Nor wilt thou snare him in the white ravine,
Nor find him dropt upon the firths of ice,
That huddling slant in furrow-cloven falls
To roll the torrent out of dusky doors:
But follow; let the torrent dance thee down
To find him in the valley; let the wild
Lean-headed Eagles yelp alone, and leave
The monstrous ledges there to slope, and spill
Their thousand wreaths of dangling water-smoke,
That like a broken purpose waste in air:
So waste not thou; but come; for all the vales
Await thee; azure pillars of the hearth
Arise to thee; the children call, and I
Thy shepherd pipe, and sweet is every sound,
Sweeter thy voice, but every sound is sweet;
Myriads of rivulets hurrying thro' the lawn,
The moan of doves in immemorial elms,
And murmuring of innumerable bees.

1850

IN MEMORIAM A. H. H.

OBIIT MDCCCXXXIII

STRONG Son of God, immortal Love,
Whom we, that have not seen thy face,
By faith, and faith alone, embrace,
Believing where we cannot prove;

Thine are these orbs of light and shade;
Thou madest Life in man and brute;
Thou madest Death; and lo, thy foot
Is on the skull which thou hast made.

Thou wilt not leave us in the dust:
Thou madest man, he knows not why,
He thinks he was not made to die;
And thou hast made him: thou art just.

Thou seemest human and divine,
The highest, holiest manhood, thou:
Our wills are ours, we know not how;
Our wills are ours, to make them thine.

Our little systems have their day;
They have their day and cease to be:
They are but broken lights of thee,
And thou, O Lord, art more than they.

We have but faith: we cannot know;
For knowledge is of things we see;
And yet we trust it comes from thee,
A beam in darkness: let it grow.

Let knowledge grow from more to more,
But more of reverence in us dwell;
That mind and soul, according well,
May make one music as before,

But vaster. We are fools and slight;
We mock thee when we do not fear:
But help thy foolish ones to bear;
Help thy vain worlds to bear thy light.

Forgive what seem'd my sin in me;
What seem'd my worth since I began;
For merit lives from man to man,
And not from man, O Lord, to thee.

Forgive my grief for one removed,
Thy creature, whom I found so fair.
I trust he lives in thee, and there
I find him worthier to be loved.

Forgive these wild and wandering cries,
Confusions of a wasted youth;
Forgive them where they fail in truth,
And in thy wisdom make me wise.

I

I held it truth, with him who sings
To one clear harp in divers tones,
That men may rise on stepping-stones
Of their dead selves to higher things.

But who shall so forecast the years
And find in loss a gain to match?
Or reach a hand thro' time to catch
The far-off interest of tears?

Let Love clasp Grief lest both be drown'd,
Let darkness keep her raven gloss:
Ah, sweeter to be drunk with loss,
To dance with death, to beat the ground,

Than that the victor Hours should scorn
The long result of love, and boast,
"Behold the man that loved and lost,
But all he was is overworn."

II

Old Yew, which graspest at the stones
That name the under-lying dead,
Thy fibres net the dreamless head,
Thy roots are wrapt about the bones.

The seasons bring the flower again,
And bring the firstling to the flock;
And in the dusk of thee, the clock
Beats out the little lives of men.

O not for thee the glow, the bloom,
Who changest not in any gale,
Nor branding summer suns avail
To touch thy thousand years of gloom:

And gazing on thee, sullen tree,
Sick for thy stubborn hardihood,
I seem to fail from out my blood
And grow incorporate into thee.

III

O Sorrow, cruel fellowship,
O Priestess in the vaults of Death,
O sweet and bitter in a breath,
What whispers from thy lying lip?

"The stars," she whispers, "blindly run;
A web is wov'n across the sky;
From out waste places comes a cry,
And murmurs from the dying sun:

"And all the phantom, Nature, stands—
With all the music in her tone,
A hollow echo of my own,—
A hollow form with empty hands."

And shall I take a thing so blind,
Embrace her as my natural good;
Or crush her, like a vice of blood,
Upon the threshold of the mind?

IV

To Sleep I give my powers away;
My will is bondsman to the dark;
I sit within a helmless bark,
And with my heart I muse and say:

O heart, how fares it with thee now,
That thou should'st fail from thy desire,
Who scarcely darest to inquire,
"What is it makes me beat so low?"

Something it is which thou hast lost,
Some pleasure from thine early years.
Break, thou deep vase of chilling tears,
That grief hath shaken into frost!

Such clouds of nameless trouble cross
All night below the darken'd eyes;
With morning wakes the will, and cries,
"Thou shalt not be the fool of loss."

V

I sometimes hold it half a sin
To put in words the grief I feel;
For words, like Nature, half reveal
And half conceal the Soul within.

But, for the unquiet heart and brain,
A use in measured language lies;
The sad mechanic exercise,
Like dull narcotics, numbing pain.

In words, like weeds, I'll wrap me o'er,
Like coarsest clothes against the cold:
But that large grief which these enfold
Is given in outline and no more.

VI

One writes, that "Other friends remain,"
That "Loss is common to the race"—
And common is the commonplace,
And vacant chaff well meant for grain.

That loss is common would not make
My own less bitter, rather more:
Too common! Never morning wore
To evening, but some heart did break.

O father, wheresoe'er thou be,
Who pledgest now thy gallant son;
A shot, ere half thy draught be done,
Hath still'd the life that beat from thee.

O mother, praying God will save
Thy sailor,—while thy head is bow'd,
His heavy-shotted hammock-shroud
Drops in his vast and wandering grave.

Ye know no more than I who wrought
At that last hour to please him well;
Who mused on all I had to tell,
And something written, something thought;

Expecting still his advent home;
And ever met him on his way
With wishes, thinking, "here to-day,"
Or "here to-morrow will he come."

O somewhere, meek, unconscious dove,
That sittest ranging golden hair;
And glad to find thyself so fair,
Poor child, that waitest for thy love!

For now her father's chimney glows
In expectation of a guest;
And thinking "this will please him best,"
She takes a riband or a rose;

For he will see them on to-night;
And with the thought her colour burns;
And, having left the glass, she turns
Once more to set a ringlet right;

And, even when she turn'd, the curse
Had fallen, and her future Lord
Was drown'd in passing thro' the ford,
Or kill'd in falling from his horse.

O what to her shall be the end?
And what to me remains of good?
To her, perpetual maidenhood,
And unto me no second friend.

VII

Dark house, by which once more I stand
Here in the long unlovely street,
Doors, where my heart was used to beat
So quickly, waiting for a hand,

A hand that can be clasp'd no more—
Behold me, for I cannot sleep,
And like a guilty thing I creep
At earliest morning to the door.

He is not here; but far away
The noise of life begins again,
And ghastly thro' the drizzling rain
On the bald street breaks the blank day.

VIII

A happy lover who has come
To look on her that loves him well,
Who 'lights and rings the gateway bell,
And learns her gone and far from home;

He saddens, all the magic light
Dies off at once from bower and hall,
And all the place is dark, and all
The chambers emptied of delight:

So find I every pleasant spot
In which we two were wont to meet,
The field, the chamber and the street,
For all is dark where thou art not.

Yet as that other, wandering there
In those deserted walks, may find
A flower beat with rain and wind,
Which once she foster'd up with care;

So seems it in my deep regret,
O my forsaken heart, with thee
And this poor flower of poesy
Which little cared for fades not yet.

But since it pleased a vanish'd eye,
I go to plant it on his tomb,
That if it can it there may bloom,
Or dying, there at least may die.

IX

Fair ship, that from the Italian shore
Sailest the placid ocean-plains
With my lost Arthur's loved remains,
Spread thy full wings, and waft him o'er.

So draw him home to those that mourn
In vain; a favourable speed
Ruffle thy mirror'd mast, and lead
Thro' prosperous floods his holy urn.

All night no ruder air perplex
Thy sliding keel, till Phosphor, bright
As our pure love, thro' early light
Shall glimmer on the dewy decks.

Sphere all your lights around, above;
Sleep, gentle heavens, before the prow;
Sleep, gentle winds, as he sleeps now,
My friend, the brother of my love;

My Arthur, whom I shall not see
Till all my widow'd race be run;
Dear as the mother to the son,
More than my brothers are to me.

X

I hear the noise about thy keel;
I hear the bell struck in the night:
I see the cabin-window bright;
I see the sailor at the wheel.

Thou bring'st the sailor to his wife,
And travell'd men from foreign lands;
And letters unto trembling hands;
And, thy dark freight, a vanish'd life.

So bring him: we have idle dreams:
This look of quiet flatters thus
Our home-bred fancies: O to us,
The fools of habit, sweeter seems

To rest beneath the clover sod,
That takes the sunshine and the rains,
Or where the kneeling hamlet drains
The chalice of the grapes of God;

Than if with thee the roaring wells
Should gulf him fathom-deep in brine;
And hands so often clasp'd in mine,
Should toss with tangle and with shells.

XI

Calm is the morn without a sound,
Calm as to suit a calmer grief,
And only thro' the faded leaf
The chestnut pattering to the ground:

Calm and deep peace on this high wold,
And on these dews that drench the furze,
And all the silvery gossamers
That twinkle into green and gold:

Calm and still light on yon great plain
That sweeps with all its autumn bowers,
And crowded farms and lessening towers,
To mingle with the bounding main:

Calm and deep peace in this wide air,
These leaves that redden to the fall;
And in my heart, if calm at all,
If any calm, a calm despair:

Calm on the seas, and silver sleep,
And waves that sway themselves in rest,
And dead calm in that noble breast
Which heaves but with the heaving deep.

XII

Lo, as a dove when up she springs
To bear thro' Heaven a tale of woe,
Some dolorous message knit below
The wild pulsation of her wings;

Like her I go; I cannot stay;
I leave this mortal ark behind,
A weight of nerves without a mind,
And leave the cliffs, and haste away

O'er ocean-mirrors rounded large,
And reach the glow of southern skies,
And see the sails at distance rise,
And linger weeping on the marge,

And saying; "Comes he thus, my friend?
Is this the end of all my care?"
And circle moaning in the air:
"Is this the end? Is this the end?"

And forward dart again, and play
About the prow, and back return
To where the body sits, and learn
That I have been an hour away.

XIII

Tears of the widower, when he sees
A late-lost form that sleep reveals,
And moves his doubtful arms, and feels
Her place is empty, fall like these;

Which weep a loss for ever new,
A void where heart on heart reposed;
And, where warm hands have prest and closed,
Silence, till I be silent too.

Which weep the comrade of my choice,
An awful thought, a life removed,
The human-hearted man I loved,
A Spirit, not a breathing voice.

Come Time, and teach me, many years,
I do not suffer in a dream;
For now so strange do these things seem,
Mine eyes have leisure for their tears;

My fancies time to rise on wing,
And glance about the approaching sails,
As tho' they brought but merchants' bales,
And not the burthen that they bring.

XIV

If one should bring me this report,
That thou hadst touch'd the land to-day,
And I went down unto the quay,
And found thee lying in the port;

And standing, muffled round with woe,
Should see thy passengers in rank
Come stepping lightly down the plank,
And beckoning unto those they know;

And if along with these should come
The man I held as half-divine;
Should strike a sudden hand in mine,
And ask a thousand things of home;

And I should tell him all my pain,
And how my life had droop'd of late,
And he should sorrow o'er my state
And marvel what possess'd my brain;

And I perceived no touch of change,
No hint of death in all his frame,
But found him all in all the same,
I should not feel it to be strange.

XV

To-night the winds begin to rise
And roar from yonder dropping day:
The last red leaf is whirl'd away,
The rooks are blown about the skies;

The forest crack'd, the waters curl'd,
The cattle huddled on the lea;
And wildly dash'd on tower and tree
The sunbeam strikes along the world:

And but for fancies, which aver
That all thy motions gently pass
Athwart a plane of molten glass,
I scarce could brook the strain and stir

That makes the barren branches loud;
And but for fear it is not so,
The wild unrest that lives in woe
Would dote and pore on yonder cloud

That rises upward always higher,
And onward drags a labouring breast,
And topples round the dreary west,
A looming bastion fringed with fire.

XVI

What words are these have fall'n from me?
Can calm despair and wild unrest
Be tenants of a single breast,
Or sorrow such a changeling be?

Or doth she only seem to take
The touch of change in calm or storm;
But knows no more of transient form
In her deep self, than some dead lake

That holds the shadow of a lark
Hung in the shadow of a heaven?
Or has the shock, so harshly given,
Confused me like the unhappy bark

That strikes by night a craggy shelf,
And staggers blindly ere she sink?
And stunn'd me from my power to think
And all my knowledge of myself;

And made me that delirious man
Whose fancy fuses old and new,
And flashes into false and true,
And mingles all without a plan?

XVII

Thou comest, much wept for: such a breeze
Compell'd thy canvas, and my prayer
Was as the whisper of an air
To breathe thee over lonely seas.

For I in spirit saw thee move
Thro' circles of the bounding sky,
Week after week: the days go by:
Come quick, thou bringest all I love.

Henceforth, wherever thou may'st roam,
My blessing, like a line of light,
Is on the waters day and night,
And like a beacon guards thee home.

So may whatever tempest mars
Mid-ocean, spare thee, sacred bark;
And balmy drops in summer dark
Slide from the bosom of the stars.

So kind an office hath been done,
Such precious relics brought by thee;
The dust of him I shall not see
Till all my widow'd race be run.

XVIII

'Tis well; 'tis something; we may stand
Where he in English earth is laid,
And from his ashes may be made
The violet of his native land.

'Tis little; but it looks in truth
As if the quiet bones were blest
Among familiar names to rest
And in the places of his youth.

Come then, pure hands, and bear the head
That sleeps or wears the mask of sleep,
And come, whatever loves to weep,
And hear the ritual of the dead.

Ah yet, ev'n yet, if this might be,
I, falling on his faithful heart,
Would breathing thro' his lips impart
The life that almost dies in me;

That dies not, but endures with pain,
And slowly forms the firmer mind,
Treasuring the look it cannot find,
The words that are not heard again.

XIX

The Danube to the Severn gave
The darken'd heart that beat no more;
They laid him by the pleasant shore,
And in the hearing of the wave.

There twice a day the Severn fills;
The salt sea-water passes by,
And hushes half the babbling Wye,
And makes a silence in the hills.

The Wye is hush'd nor moved along,
And hush'd my deepest grief of all,
When fill'd with tears that cannot fall,
I brim with sorrow drowning song.

The tide flows down, the wave again
Is vocal in its wooded walls;
My deeper anguish also falls,
And I can speak a little then.

XX

The lesser griefs that may be said,
That breathe a thousand tender vows,
Are but as servants in a house
Where lies the master newly dead;

Who speak their feeling as it is,
And weep the fulness from the mind:
"It will be hard," they say, "to find
Another service such as this."

My lighter moods are like to these,
That out of words a comfort win;
But there are other griefs within,
And tears that at their fountain freeze;

For by the hearth the children sit
Cold in that atmosphere of Death,
And scarce endure to draw the breath,
Or like to noiseless phantoms flit:

But open converse is there none,
So much the vital spirits sink
To see the vacant chair, and think,
"How good! how kind! and he is gone."

XXI

I sing to him that rests below,
And, since the grasses round me wave,
I take the grasses of the grave,
And make them pipes whereon to blow.

The traveller hears me now and then,
And sometimes harshly will he speak:
"This fellow would make weakness weak,
And melt the waxen hearts of men."

Another answers, "Let him be,
He loves to make parade of pain,
That with his piping he may gain
The praise that comes to constancy."

A third is wroth: "Is this an hour
For private sorrow's barren song,
When more and more the people throng
The chairs and thrones of civil power?

"A time to sicken and to swoon,
When Science reaches forth her arms
To feel from world to world, and charms
Her secret from the latest moon?"

Behold, ye speak an idle thing:
Ye never knew the sacred dust:
I do but sing because I must,
And pipe but as the linnets sing:

And one is glad; her note is gay,
For now her little ones have ranged;
And one is sad; her note is changed,
Because her brood is stol'n away.

XXII

The path by which we twain did go,
Which led by tracts that pleased us well,
Thro' four sweet years arose and fell,
From flower to flower, from snow to snow:

And we with singing cheer'd the way,
And, crown'd with all the season lent,
From April on to April went,
And glad at heart from May to May:

But where the path we walk'd began
To slant the fifth autumnal slope,
As we descended following Hope,
There sat the Shadow fear'd of man;

Who broke our fair companionship,
And spread his mantle dark and cold,
And wrapt thee formless in the fold,
And dull'd the murmur on thy lip,

And bore thee where I could not see
Nor follow, tho' I walk in haste,
And think, that somewhere in the waste
The Shadow sits and waits for me.

XXIII

Now, sometimes in my sorrow shut,
Or breaking into song by fits,
Alone, alone, to where he sits,
The Shadow cloak'd from head to foot,

Who keeps the keys of all the creeds,
I wander, often falling lame,
And looking back to whence I came,
Or on to where the pathway leads;

And crying, How changed from where it ran
 Thro' lands where not a leaf was dumb;
 But all the lavish hills would hum
The murmur of a happy Pan:

When each by turns was guide to each,
 And Fancy light from Fancy caught,
 And Thought leapt out to wed with Thought
Ere Thought could wed itself with Speech;

And all we met was fair and good,
 And all was good that Time could bring,
 And all the secret of the Spring
Moved in the chambers of the blood;

And many an old philosophy
 On Argive heights divinely sang,
 And round us all the thicket rang
To many a flute of Arcady.

XXIV

And was the day of my delight
 As pure and perfect as I say?
 The very source and fount of Day
Is dash'd with wandering isles of night.

If all was good and fair we met,
 This earth had been the Paradise
 It never look'd to human eyes
Since our first Sun arose and set.

And is it that the haze of grief
 Makes former gladness loom so great?
 The lowness of the present state,
That sets the past in this relief?

Or that the past will always win
 A glory from its being far;
 And orb into the perfect star
We saw not, when we moved therein?

XXV

I know that this was Life,—the track
 Whereon with equal feet we fared;
 And then, as now, the day prepared
The daily burden for the back.

But this it was that made me move
 As light as carrier-birds in air;
 I loved the weight I had to bear,
Because it needed help of Love:

Nor could I weary, heart or limb,
 When mighty Love would cleave in twain
 The lading of a single pain,
And part it, giving half to him.

XXVI

Still onward winds the dreary way;
 I with it; for I long to prove
 No lapse of moons can canker Love,
Whatever fickle tongues may say.

And if that eye which watches guilt
 And goodness, and hath power to see
 Within the green the moulder'd tree,
And towers fall'n as soon as built—

Oh, if indeed that eye foresee
 Or see (in Him is no before)
 In more of life true life no more
And Love the indifference to be,

Then might I find, ere yet the morn
 Breaks hither over Indian seas,
 That Shadow waiting with the keys,
To shroud me from my proper scorn.

XXVII

I envy not in any moods
 The captive void of noble rage,
 The linnet born within the cage,
That never knew the summer woods:

I envy not the beast that takes
 His license in the field of time,
 Unfetter'd by the sense of crime,
To whom a conscience never wakes;

Nor, what may count itself as blest,
 The heart that never plighted troth
 But stagnates in the weeds of sloth;
Nor any want-begotten rest.

I hold it true, whate'er befall;
 I feel it, when I sorrow most;
 'Tis better to have loved and lost
Than never to have loved at all.

XXVIII

The time draws near the birth of Christ:
 The moon is hid; the night is still;
 The Christmas bells from hill to hill
Answer each other in the mist.

Four voices of four hamlets round,
From far and near, on mead and moor,
Swell out and fail, as if a door
Were shut between me and the sound:

Each voice four changes on the wind,
That now dilate, and now decrease,
Peace and goodwill, goodwill and peace,
Peace and goodwill, to all mankind.

This year I slept and woke with pain,
I almost wish'd no more to wake,
And that my hold on life would break
Before I heard those bells again:

But they my troubled spirit rule,
For they controll'd me when a boy;
They bring me sorrow touch'd with joy,
The merry merry bells of Yule.

XXIX

With such compelling cause to grieve
As daily vexes household peace,
And chains regret to his decease,
How dare we keep our Christmas-eve;

Which brings no more a welcome guest
To enrich the threshold of the night
With shower'd largess of delight
In dance and song and game and jest?

Yet go, and while the holly boughs
Entwine the cold baptismal font,
Make one wreath more for Use and Wont,
That guard the portals of the house;

Old sisters of a day gone by,
Gray nurses, loving nothing new;
Why should they miss their yearly due
Before their time? They too will die.

XXX

With trembling fingers did we weave
The holly round the Christmas hearth;
A rainy cloud possess'd the earth,
And sadly fell our Christmas-eve.

At our old pastimes in the hall
We gambol'd, making vain pretence
Of gladness, with an awful sense
Of one mute Shadow watching all.

We paused: the winds were in the beech:
We heard them sweep the winter land;
And in a circle hand-in-hand
Sat silent, looking each at each.

Then echo-like our voices rang;
We sung, tho' every eye was dim,
A merry song we sang with him
Last year: impetuously we sang:

We ceased: a gentler feeling crept
Upon us: surely rest is meet:
"They rest," we said, "their sleep is sweet,"
And silence follow'd, and we wept.

Our voices took a higher range;
Once more we sang: "They do not die
Nor lose their mortal sympathy,
Nor change to us, although they change;

"Rapt from the fickle and the frail
With gather'd power, yet the same,
Pierces the keen seraphic flame
From orb to orb, from veil to veil."

Rise, happy morn, rise, holy morn,
Draw forth the cheerful day from night
O Father, touch the east, and light
The light that shone when Hope was born.

XXXI

When Lazarus left his charnel-cave,
And home to Mary's house return'd,
Was this demanded—if he yearn'd
To hear her weeping by his grave?

"Where wert thou, brother, those four days?"
There lives no record of reply,
Which telling what it is to die
Had surely added praise to praise.

From every house the neighbours met,
The streets were fill'd with joyful sound,
A solemn gladness even crown'd
The purple brows of Olivet.

Behold a man raised up by Christ!
The rest remaineth unreveal'd;
He told it not; or something seal'd
The lips of that Evangelist.

XXXII

Her eyes are homes of silent prayer,
Nor other thought her mind admits
But, he was dead, and there he sits,
And he that brought him back is there.

Then one deep love doth supersede
All other, when her ardent gaze
Roves from the living brother's face,
And rests upon the Life indeed.

All subtle thought, all curious fears,
Borne down by gladness so complete,
She bows, she bathes the Saviour's feet
With costly spikenard and with tears.

Thrice blest whose lives are faithful prayers,
Whose loves in higher love endure;
What souls possess themselves so pure,
Or is there blessedness like theirs?

XXXIII

O thou that after toil and storm
Mayst seem to have reach'd a purer air,
Whose faith has centre everywhere,
Nor cares to fix itself to form,

Leave thou thy sister when she prays,
Her early Heaven, her happy views;
Nor thou with shadow'd hint confuse
A life that leads melodious days.

Her faith thro' form is pure as thine,
Her hands are quicker unto good:
Oh, sacred be the flesh and blood
To which she links a truth divine!

See thou, that countest reason ripe
In holding by the law within,
Thou fail not in a world of sin,
And ev'n for want of such a type.

XXXIV

My own dim life should teach me this,
That life shall live for evermore,
Else earth is darkness at the core,
And dust and ashes all that is;

This round of green, this orb of flame,
Fantastic beauty; such as lurks
In some wild Poet, when he works
Without a conscience or an aim.

What then were God to such as I?
'Twere hardly worth my while to choose
Of things all mortal, or to use
A little patience ere I die;

'Twere best at once to sink to peace,
Like birds the charming serpent draws,
To drop head-foremost in the jaws
Of vacant darkness and to cease.

XXXV

Yet if some voice that man could trust
Should murmur from the narrow house,
"The cheeks drop in; the body bows;
Man dies: nor is there hope in dust:"

Might I not say? "Yet even here,
But for one hour, O Love, I strive
To keep so sweet a thing alive:"
But I should turn mine ears and hear

The moanings of the homeless sea,
The sound of streams that swift or slow
Draw down Æonian hills, and sow
The dust of continents to be;

And Love would answer with a sigh,
"The sound of that forgetful shore
Will change my sweetness more and more,
Half-dead to know that I shall die."

O me, what profits it to put
An idle case? If Death were seen
At first as Death, Love had not been,
Or been in narrowest working shut,

Mere fellowship of sluggish moods,
Or in his coarsest Satyr-shape
Had bruised the herb and crush'd the grape,
And bask'd and batten'd in the woods.

XXXVI

Tho' truths in manhood darkly join,
Deep-seated in our mystic frame,
We yield all blessing to the name
Of Him that made them current coin;

For Wisdom dealt with mortal powers,
Where truth in closest words shall fail,
When truth embodied in a tale
Shall enter in at lowly doors.

And so the Word had breath, and wrought
With human hands the creed of creeds
In loveliness of perfect deeds,
More strong than all poetic thought;

Which he may read that binds the sheaf,
Or builds the house, or digs the grave,
And those wild eyes that watch the wave
In roarings round the coral reef.

XXXVII

Urania speaks with darken'd brow:
"Thou pratest here where thou art least;
This faith has many a purer priest,
And many an abler voice than thou.

"Go down beside thy native rill,
On thy Parnassus set thy feet,
And hear thy laurel whisper sweet
About the ledges of the hill."

And my Melpomene replies,
A touch of shame upon her cheek:
"I am not worthy ev'n to speak
Of thy prevailing mysteries;

"For I am but an earthly Muse,
And owning but a little art
To lull with song an aching heart,
And render human love his dues;

"But brooding on the dear one dead,
And all he said of things divine,
(And dear to me as sacred wine
To dying lips is all he said),

"I murmur'd, as I came along,
Of comfort clasp'd in truth reveal'd;
And loiter'd in the master's field,
And darken'd sanctities with song."

XXXVIII

With weary steps I loiter on,
Tho' always under alter'd skies
The purple from the distance dies,
My prospect and horizon gone.

No joy the blowing season gives,
The herald melodies of spring,
But in the songs I love to sing
A doubtful gleam of solace lives.

If any care for what is here
Survive in spirits render'd free,
Then are these songs I sing of thee
Not all ungrateful to thine ear.

XXXIX

Old warder of these buried bones,
And answering now my random stroke
With fruitful cloud and living smoke,
Dark yew, that graspest at the stones

And dippest toward the dreamless head,
To thee too comes the golden hour
When flower is feeling after flower;
But Sorrow—fixt upon the dead,

And darkening the dark graves of men,—
What whisper'd from her lying lips?
Thy gloom is kindled at the tips,
And passes into gloom again.

XL

Could we forget the widow'd hour
And look on Spirits breathed away,
As on a maiden in the day
When first she wears her orange-flower!

When crown'd with blessing she doth rise
To take her latest leave of home,
And hopes and light regrets that come
Make April of her tender eyes;

And doubtful joys the father move,
And tears are on the mother's face,
As parting with a long embrace
She enters other realms of love;

Her office there to rear, to teach,
Becoming as is meet and fit
A link among the days, to knit
The generations each with each;

And, doubtless, unto thee is given
A life that bears immortal fruit
In those great offices that suit
The full-grown energies of heaven.

Ay me, the difference I discern!
How often shall her old fireside
Be cheer'd with tidings of the bride,
How often she herself return,

And tell them all they would have told,
And bring her babe, and make her boast,
Till even those that miss'd her most
Shall count new things as dear as old:

But thou and I have shaken hands,
Till growing winters lay me low;
My paths are in the fields I know,
And thine in undiscover'd lands.

XLI

Thy spirit ere our fatal loss
Did ever rise from high to higher;
As mounts the heavenward altar-fire,
As flies the lighter thro' the gross.

But thou art turn'd to something strange,
And I have lost the links that bound
Thy changes; here upon the ground,
No more partaker of thy change.

Deep folly! yet that this could be—
That I could wing my will with might
To leap the grades of life and light,
And flash at once, my friend, to thee.

For tho' my nature rarely yields
To that vague fear implied in death;
Nor shudders at the gulfs beneath,
The howlings from forgotten fields;

Yet oft when sundown skirts the moor
An inner trouble I behold,
A spectral doubt which makes me cold,
That I shall be thy mate no more,

Tho' following with an upward mind
The wonders that have come to thee,
Thro' all the secular to-be,
But evermore a life behind.

XLII

I vex my heart with fancies dim:
He still outstript me in the race;
It was but unity of place
That made me dream I rank'd with him.

And so may Place retain us still,
And he the much-beloved again,
A lord of large experience, train
To riper growth the mind and will:

And what delights can equal those
That stir the spirit's inner deeps,
When one that loves, but knows not, reaps
A truth from one that loves and knows?

XLIII

If Sleep and Death be truly one,
And every spirit's folded bloom
Thro' all its intervital gloom
In some long trance should slumber on;

Unconscious of the sliding hour,
Bare of the body, might it last,
And silent traces of the past
Be all the colour of the flower:

So then were nothing lost to man;
So that still garden of the souls
In many a figured leaf enrolls
The total world since life began;

And love will last as pure and whole
As when he loved me here in Time,
And at the spiritual prime
Rewaken with the dawning soul.

XLIV

How fares it with the happy dead?
For here the man is more and more;
But he forgets the days before
God shut the doorways of his head.

The days have vanish'd, tone and tint,
And yet perhaps the hoarding sense
Gives out at times (he knows not whence)
A little flash, a mystic hint;

And in the long harmonious years
(If Death so taste Lethean springs),
May some dim touch of earthly things
Surprise thee ranging with thy peers.

If such a dreamy touch should fall,
O turn thee round, resolve the doubt;
My guardian angel will speak out
In that high place, and tell thee all.

XLV

The baby new to earth and sky,
What time his tender palm is prest
Against the circle of the breast,
Has never thought that "this is I:"

But as he grows he gathers much,
And learns the use of "I," and "me,"
And finds "I am not what I see,
And other than the things I touch."

So rounds he to a separate mind
From whence clear memory may begin,
As thro' the frame that binds him in
His isolation grows defined.

This use may lie in blood and breath,
Which else were fruitless of their due,
Had man to learn himself anew
Beyond the second birth of Death.

XLVI

We ranging down this lower track,
The path we came by, thorn and flower,
Is shadow'd by the growing hour,
Lest life should fail in looking back.

So be it: there no shade can last
In that deep dawn behind the tomb,
But clear from marge to marge shall bloom
The eternal landscape of the past;

A lifelong tract of time reveal'd;
The fruitful hours of still increase;
Days order'd in a wealthy peace,
And those five years its richest field.

O Love, thy province were not large,
A bounded field, nor stretching far;
Look also, Love, a brooding star,
A rosy warmth from marge to marge.

XLVII

That each, who seems a separate whole,
Should move his rounds, and fusing all
The skirts of self again, should fall
Remerging in the general Soul,

Is faith as vague as all unsweet:
Eternal form shall still divide
The eternal soul from all beside;
And I shall know him when we meet:

And we shall sit at endless feast,
Enjoying each the other's good:
What vaster dream can hit the mood
Of Love on earth? He seeks at least

Upon the last and sharpest height,
Before the spirits fade away,
Some landing-place, to clasp and say,
"Farewell! We lose ourselves in light."

XLVIII

If these brief lays, of Sorrow born,
Were taken to be such as closed
Grave doubts and answers here proposed,
Then these were such as men might scorn:

Her care is not to part and prove;
She takes, when harsher moods remit,
What slender shade of doubt may flit,
And makes it vassal unto love:

And hence, indeed, she sports with words,
But better serves a wholesome law,
And holds it sin and shame to draw
The deepest measure from the chords:

Nor dare she trust a larger lay,
But rather loosens from the lip
Short swallow-flights of song, that dip
Their wings in tears, and skim away.

XLIX

From art, from nature, from the schools,
Let random influences glance,
Like light in many a shiver'd lance
That breaks about the dappled pools:

The lightest wave of thought shall lisp,
The fancy's tenderest eddy wreathe,
The slightest air of song shall breathe
To make the sullen surface crisp.

And look thy look, and go thy way,
But blame not thou the winds that make
The seeming-wanton ripple break,
The tender-pencil'd shadow play.

Beneath all fancied hopes and fears
Ay me, the sorrow deepens down,
Whose muffled motions blindly drown
The bases of my life in tears.

L

Be near me when my light is low,
When the blood creeps, and the nerves prick
And tingle; and the heart is sick,
And all the wheels of Being slow.

Be near me when the sensuous frame
Is rack'd with pangs that conquer trust;
And Time, a maniac scattering dust,
And Life, a Fury slinging flame.

Be near me when my faith is dry,
And men the flies of latter spring,
That lay their eggs, and sting and sing
And weave their petty cells and die.

Be near me when I fade away,
To point the term of human strife,
And on the low dark verge of life
The twilight of eternal day.

LI

Do we indeed desire the dead
Should still be near us at our side?
Is there no baseness we would hide?
No inner vileness that we dread?

Shall he for whose applause I strove,
I had such reverence for his blame,
See with clear eye some hidden shame
And I be lessen'd in his love?

I wrong the grave with fears untrue:
Shall love be blamed for want of faith?
There must be wisdom with great Death:
The dead shall look me thro' and thro'.

Be near us when we climb or fall:
Ye watch, like God, the rolling hours
With larger other eyes than ours,
To make allowance for us all.

LII

I cannot love thee as I ought,
For love reflects the thing beloved;
My words are only words, and moved
Upon the topmost froth of thought.

"Yet blame not thou thy plaintive song,"
The Spirit of true love replied;
"Thou canst not move me from thy side,
Nor human frailty do me wrong.

"What keeps a spirit wholly true
To that ideal which he bears?
What record? not the sinless years
That breathed beneath the Syrian blue:

"So fret not, like an idle girl,
That life is dash'd with flecks of sin.
Abide: thy wealth is gather'd in,
When Time hath sunder'd shell from pearl."

LIII

How many a father have I seen,
A sober man, among his boys,
Whose youth was full of foolish noise,
Who wears his manhood hale and green:

And dare we to this fancy give,
That had the wild oat not been sown,
The soil, left barren, scarce had grown
The grain by which a man may live?

Or, if we held the doctrine sound
For life outliving heats of youth,
Yet who would preach it as a truth
To those that eddy round and round?

Hold thou the good: define it well:
For fear divine Philosophy
Should push beyond her mark, and be
Procuress to the Lords of Hell.

LIV

Oh yet we trust that somehow good
Will be the final goal of ill,
To pangs of nature, sins of will,
Defects of doubt, and taints of blood;

That nothing walks with aimless feet;
That not one life shall be destroy'd,
Or cast as rubbish to the void,
When God hath made the pile complete;

That not a worm is cloven in vain;
That not a moth with vain desire
Is shrivell'd in a fruitless fire,
Or but subserves another's gain.

Behold, we know not anything;
I can but trust that good shall fall
At last—far off—at last, to all,
And every winter change to spring.

So runs my dream: but what am I?
An infant crying in the night:
An infant crying for the light:
And with no language but a cry.

LV

The wish, that of the living whole
No life may fail beyond the grave,
Derives it not from what we have
The likest God within the soul?

Are God and Nature then at strife,
That Nature lends such evil dreams?
So careful of the type she seems,
So careless of the single life;

That I, considering everywhere
Her secret meaning in her deeds,
And finding that of fifty seeds
She often brings but one to bear,

I falter where I firmly trod,
And falling with my weight of cares
Upon the great world's altar-stairs
That slope thro' darkness up to God,

I stretch lame hands of faith, and grope,
And gather dust and chaff, and call
To what I feel is Lord of all,
And faintly trust the larger hope.

LVI

"So careful of the type?" but no.
From scarped cliff and quarried stone
She cries, "A thousand types are gone:
I care for nothing, all shall go.

"Thou makest thine appeal to me:
I bring to life, I bring to death:
The spirit does but mean the breath:
I know no more." And he, shall he,

Man, her last work, who seem'd so fair,
Such splendid purpose in his eyes,
Who roll'd the psalm to wintry skies,
Who built him fanes of fruitless prayer,

Who trusted God was love indeed
And love Creation's final law—
Tho' Nature, red in tooth and claw
With ravine, shriek'd against his creed—

Who loved, who suffer'd countless ills,
Who battled for the True, the Just,
Be blown about the desert dust,
Or seal'd within the iron hills?

No more? A monster then, a dream,
A discord. Dragons of the prime,
That tare each other in their slime,
Were mellow music match'd with him.

O life as futile, then, as frail!
O for thy voice to soothe and bless!
What hope of answer, or redress?
Behind the veil, behind the veil.

LVII

Peace; come away: the song of woe
Is after all an earthly song:
Peace; come away: we do him wrong
To sing so wildly: let us go.

Come; let us go: your cheeks are pale;
But half my life I leave behind:
Methinks my friend is richly shrined;
But I shall pass; my work will fail.

Yet in these ears, till hearing dies,
One set slow bell will seem to toll
The passing of the sweetest soul
That ever look'd with human eyes.

I hear it now, and o'er and o'er,
Eternal greetings to the dead;
And "Ave, Ave, Ave," said,
"Adieu, adieu" for evermore.

LVIII

In those sad words I took farewell:
Like echoes in sepulchral halls,
As drop by drop the water falls
In vaults and catacombs, they fell;

And, falling, idly broke the peace
Of hearts that beat from day to day,
Half-conscious of their dying clay,
And those cold crypts where they shall cease.

The high Muse answer'd: "Wherefore grieve
Thy brethren with a fruitless tear?
Abide a little longer here,
And thou shalt take a nobler leave."

LIX

O Sorrow, wilt thou live with me
No casual mistress, but a wife,
My bosom-friend and half of life;
As I confess it needs must be;

O Sorrow, wilt thou rule my blood,
Be sometimes lovely like a bride,
And put thy harsher moods aside,
If thou wilt have me wise and good.

My centred passion cannot move,
Nor will it lessen from to-day;
But I'll have leave at times to play
As with the creature of my love;

And set thee forth, for thou art mine,
With so much hope for years to come,
That, howsoe'er I know thee, some
Could hardly tell what name were thine.

LX

He past; a soul of nobler tone:
My spirit loved and loves him yet,
Like some poor girl whose heart is set
On one whose rank exceeds her own.

He mixing with his proper sphere,
She finds the baseness of her lot,
Half jealous of she knows not what,
And envying all that meet him there.

The little village looks forlorn;
She sighs amid her narrow days,
Moving about the household ways,
In that dark house where she was born.

The foolish neighbours come and go,
And tease her till the day draws by:
At night she weeps, "How vain am I!
How should he love a thing so low?"

LXI

If, in thy second state sublime,
Thy ransom'd reason change replies
With all the circle of the wise,
The perfect flower of human time;

And if thou cast thine eyes below,
How dimly character'd and slight,
How dwarf'd a growth of cold and night,
How blanch'd with darkness must I grow!

Yet turn thee to the doubtful shore,
Where thy first form was made a man;
I loved thee, Spirit, and love, nor can
The soul of Shakespeare love thee more.

LXII

Tho' if an eye that's downward cast
Could make thee somewhat blench or fail,
Then be my love an idle tale,
And fading legend of the past;

And thou, as one that once declined,
When he was little more than boy,
On some unworthy heart with joy,
But lives to wed an equal mind;

And breathes a novel world, the while
His other passion wholly dies,
Or in the light of deeper eyes
Is matter for a flying smile.

LXIII

Yet pity for a horse o'er-driven,
And love in which my hound has part,
Can hang no weight upon my heart
In its assumptions up to heaven;

And I am so much more than these,
As thou, perchance, art more than I,
And yet I spare them sympathy,
And I would set their pains at ease.

So mayst thou watch me where I weep,
As, unto vaster motions bound,
The circuits of thine orbit round
A higher height, a deeper deep.

LXIV

Dost thou look back on what hath been,
As some divinely gifted man,
Whose life in low estate began
And on a simple village green;

Who breaks his birth's invidious bar,
And grasps the skirts of happy chance,
And breasts the blows of circumstance,
And grapples with his evil star;

Who makes by force his merit known
And lives to clutch the golden keys,
To mould a mighty state's decrees,
And shape the whisper of the throne;

And moving up from high to higher,
Becomes on Fortune's crowning slope
The pillar of a people's hope,
The centre of a world's desire;

Yet feels, as in a pensive dream,
When all his active powers are still,
A distant dearness in the hill,
A secret sweetness in the stream,

The limit of his narrower fate,
While yet beside its vocal springs
He play'd at counsellors and kings,
With one that was his earliest mate;

Who ploughs with pain his native lea
And reaps the labour of his hands,
Or in the furrow musing stands;
"Does my old friend remember me?"

LXV

Sweet soul, do with me as thou wilt;
I lull a fancy trouble-tost
With "Love's too precious to be lost,
A little grain shall not be spilt."

And in that solace can I sing,
Till out of painful phases wrought
There flutters up a happy thought,
Self-balanced on a lightsome wing:

Since we deserved the name of friends,
And thine effect so lives in me,
A part of mine may live in thee
And move thee on to noble ends.

LXVI

You thought my heart too far diseased;
You wonder when my fancies play
To find me gay among the gay,
Like one with any trifle pleased.

The shade by which my life was crost,
Which makes a desert in the mind,
Has made me kindly with my kind,
And like to him whose sight is lost;

Whose feet are guided thro' the land,
Whose jest among his friends is free,
Who takes the children on his knee,
And winds their curls about his hand:

He plays with threads, he beats his chair
For pastime, dreaming of the sky;
His inner day can never die,
His night of loss is always there.

LXVII

When on my bed the moonlight falls,
I know that in thy place of rest
By that broad water of the west,
There comes a glory on the walls:

Thy marble bright in dark appears,
As slowly steals a silver flame
Along the letters of thy name,
And o'er the number of thy years.

The mystic glory swims away;
From off my bed the moonlight dies;
And closing eaves of wearied eyes
I sleep till dusk is dipt in gray:

And then I know the mist is drawn
A lucid veil from coast to coast,
And in the dark church like a ghost
Thy tablet glimmers to the dawn.

LXVIII

When in the down I sink my head,
Sleep, Death's twin-brother, times my breath;
Sleep, Death's twin-brother, knows not Death,
Nor can I dream of thee as dead:

I walk as ere I walk'd forlorn,
When all our path was fresh with dew,
And all the bugle breezes blew
Reveillée to the breaking morn.

But what is this? I turn about,
I find a trouble in thine eye,
Which makes me sad I know not why,
Nor can my dream resolve the doubt:

But ere the lark hath left the lea
I wake, and I discern the truth;
It is the trouble of my youth
That foolish sleep transfers to thee.

LXIX

I dream'd there would be Spring no more,
That Nature's ancient power was lost:
The streets were black with smoke and frost,
They chatter'd trifles at the door:

I wander'd from the noisy town,
I found a wood with thorny boughs:
I took the thorns to bind my brows,
I wore them like a civic crown:

I met with scoffs, I met with scorns
From youth and babe and hoary hairs:
They call'd me in the public squares
The fool that wears a crown of thorns:

They call'd me fool, they call'd me child:
I found an angel of the night;
The voice was low, the look was bright;
He look'd upon my crown and smiled:

He reach'd the glory of a hand,
That seem'd to touch it into leaf:
The voice was not the voice of grief,
The words were hard to understand.

LXX

I cannot see the features right,
When on the gloom I strive to paint
The face I know; the hues are faint
And mix with hollow masks of night;

Cloud-towers by ghostly masons wrought,
A gulf that ever shuts and gapes,
A hand that points, and palled shapes
In shadowy thoroughfares of thought;

And crowds that stream from yawning doors,
And shoals of pucker'd faces drive;
Dark bulks that tumble half alive,
And lazy lengths on boundless shores;

Till all at once beyond the will
I hear a wizard music roll,
And thro' a lattice on the soul
Looks thy fair face and makes it still.

LXXI

Sleep, kinsman thou to death and trance
And madness, thou hast forged at last
A night-long Present of the Past
In which we went thro' summer France.

Hadst thou such credit with the soul?
Then bring an opiate trebly strong,
Drug down the blindfold sense of wrong
That so my pleasure may be whole;

While now we talk as once we talk'd
Of men and minds, the dust of change,
The days that grow to something strange,
In walking as of old we walk'd

Beside the river's wooded reach,
The fortress, and the mountain ridge,
The cataract flashing from the bridge,
The breaker breaking on the beach.

LXXII

Risest thou thus, dim dawn, again,
And howlest, issuing out of night,
With blasts that blow the poplar white,
And lash with storm the streaming pane?

Day, when my crown'd estate begun
To pine in that reverse of doom,
Which sicken'd every living bloom,
And blurr'd the splendour of the sun;

Who usherest in the dolorous hour
With thy quick tears that make the rose
Pull sideways, and the daisy close
Her crimson fringes to the shower;

Who might'st have heaved a windless flame
Up the deep East, or, whispering, play'd
A chequer-work of beam and shade
Along the hills, yet look'd the same.

As wan, as chill, as wild as now;
Day, mark'd as with some hideous crime,
When the dark hand struck down thro' time,
And cancell'd nature's best: but thou,

Lift as thou may'st thy burthen'd brows
Thro' clouds that drench the morning star,
And whirl the ungarner'd sheaf afar,
And sow the sky with flying boughs,

And up thy vault with roaring sound
Climb thy thick noon, disastrous day;
Touch thy dull goal of joyless gray,
And hide thy shame beneath the ground.

LXXIII

So many worlds, so much to do,
So little done, such things to be,
How know I what had need of thee,
For thou wert strong as thou wert true?

The fame is quench'd that I foresaw,
The head hath miss'd an earthly wreath:
I curse not nature, no, nor death;
For nothing is that errs from law.

We pass; the path that each man trod
Is dim, or will be dim, with weeds:
What fame is left for human deeds
In endless age? It rests with God.

O hollow wraith of dying fame,
Fade wholly, while the soul exults,
And self-infolds the large results
Of force that would have forged a name.

LXXIV

As sometimes in a dead man's face,
To those that watch it more and more,
A likeness, hardly seen before,
Comes out—to some one of his race:

So, dearest, now thy brows are cold,
I see thee what thou art, and know
Thy likeness to the wise below,
Thy kindred with the great of old.

But there is more than I can see,
And what I see I leave unsaid,
Nor speak it, knowing Death has made
His darkness beautiful with thee.

LXXV

I leave thy praises unexpress'd
In verse that brings myself relief,
And by the measure of my grief
I leave thy greatness to be guess'd;

What practice howsoe'er expert
In fitting aptest words to things,
Or voice the richest-toned that sings,
Hath power to give thee as thou wert?

I care not in these fading days
To raise a cry that lasts not long,
And round thee with the breeze of song
To stir a little dust of praise.

Thy leaf has perish'd in the green,
And, while we breathe beneath the sun,
The world which credits what is done
Is cold to all that might have been.

So here shall silence guard thy fame;
But somewhere, out of human view,
Whate'er thy hands are set to do
Is wrought with tumult of acclaim.

LXXVI

Take wings of fancy, and ascend,
And in a moment set thy face
Where all the starry heavens of space
Are sharpen'd to a needle's end;

Take wings of foresight; lighten thro'
The secular abyss to come,
And lo, thy deepest lays are dumb
Before the mouldering of a yew;

And if the matin songs, that woke
The darkness of our planet, last,
Thine own shall wither in the vast,
Ere half the lifetime of an oak.

Ere these have clothed their branchy bowers
With fifty Mays, thy songs are vain;
And what are they when these remain
The ruin'd shells of hollow towers?

LXXVII

What hope is here for modern rhyme
To him, who turns a musing eye
On songs, and deeds, and lives, that lie
Foreshorten'd in the tract of time?

These mortal lullabies of pain
May bind a book, may line a box,
May serve to curl a maiden's locks;
Or when a thousand moons shall wane

A man upon a stall may find,
And, passing, turn the page that tells
A grief, then changed to something else,
Sung by a long-forgotten mind.

But what of that? My darken'd ways
Shall ring with music all the same;
To breathe my loss is more than fame,
To utter love more sweet than praise.

LXXVIII

Again at Christmas did we weave
The holly round the Christmas hearth;
The silent snow possess'd the earth,
And calmly fell our Christmas-eve:

The yule-clog sparkled keen with frost,
No wing of wind the region swept,
But over all things brooding slept
The quiet sense of something lost.

As in the winters left behind,
Again our ancient games had place,
The mimic picture's breathing grace,
And dance and song and hoodman-blind.

Who show'd a token of distress?
No single tear, no mark of pain:
O sorrow, then can sorrow wane?
O grief, can grief be changed to less?

O last regret, regret can die!
No—mixt with all this mystic frame,
Her deep relations are the same,
But with long use her tears are dry.

LXXIX

"More than my brothers are to me,"—
Let this not vex thee, noble heart!
I know thee of what force thou art
To hold the costliest love in fee.

But thou and I are one in kind,
As moulded like in Nature's mint;
And hill and wood and field did print
The same sweet forms in either mind.

For us the same cold streamlet curl'd
Thro' all his eddying coves; the same
All winds that roam the twilight came
In whispers of the beauteous world.

At one dear knee we proffer'd vows,
One lesson from one book we learn'd,
Ere childhood's flaxen ringlet turn'd
To black and brown on kindred brows.

And so my wealth resembles thine,
But he was rich where I was poor,
And he supplied my want the more
As his unlikeness fitted mine.

LXXX

If any vague desire should rise,
That holy Death ere Arthur died
Had moved me kindly from his side,
And dropt the dust on tearless eyes;

Then fancy shapes, as fancy can,
The grief my loss in him had wrought,
A grief as deep as life or thought,
But stay'd in peace with God and man.

I make a picture in the brain;
I hear the sentence that he speaks;
He bears the burthen of the weeks
But turns his burthen into gain.

His credit thus shall set me free;
And, influence-rich to soothe and save,
Unused example from the grave
Reach out dead hands to comfort me.

LXXXI

Could I have said while he was here,
"My love shall now no further range;
There cannot come a mellower change,
For now is love mature in ear."

Love, then, had hope of richer store:
What end is here to my complaint?
This haunting whisper makes me faint,
"More years had made me love thee more."

But Death returns an answer sweet:
"My sudden frost was sudden gain,
And gave all ripeness to the grain,
It might have drawn from after-heat."

LXXXII

I wage not any feud with Death
For changes wrought on form and face;
No lower life that earth's embrace
May breed with him can fright my faith.

Eternal process moving on,
From state to state the spirit walks;
And these are but the shatter'd stalks,
Or ruin'd chrysalis of one.

Nor blame I Death, because he bare
The use of virtue out of earth:
I know transplanted human worth
Will bloom to profit, otherwhere.

For this alone on Death I wreak
The wrath that garners in my heart;
He put our lives so far apart
We cannot hear each other speak.

LXXXIII

Dip down upon the northern shore,
O sweet new-year delaying long;
Thou doest expectant nature wrong;
Delaying long, delay no more.

What stays thee from the clouded noons,
Thy sweetness from its proper place?
Can trouble live with April days,
Or sadness in the summer moons?

Bring orchis, bring the foxglove spire,
The little speedwell's darling blue,
Deep tulips dash'd with fiery dew,
Laburnums, dropping-wells of fire.

O thou, new-year, delaying long,
Delayest the sorrow in my blood,
That longs to burst a frozen bud
And flood a fresher throat with song.

LXXXIV

When I contemplate all alone
The life that had been thine below,
And fix my thoughts on all the glow
To which thy crescent would have grown;

I see thee sitting crown'd with good,
A central warmth diffusing bliss
In glance and smile, and clasp and kiss,
On all the branches of thy blood;

Thy blood, my friend, and partly mine;
For now the day was drawing on,
When thou should'st link thy life with one
Of mine own house, and boys of thine

Had babbled "Uncle" on my knee;
But that remorseless iron hour
Made cypress of her orange flower,
Despair of Hope, and earth of thee.

I seem to meet their least desire,
To clap their cheeks, to call them mine.
I see their unborn faces shine
Beside the never-lighted fire.

I see myself an honour'd guest,
Thy partner in the flowery walk
Of letters, genial table-talk,
Or deep dispute, and graceful jest;

While now thy prosperous labour fills
The lips of men with honest praise,
And sun by sun the happy days
Descend below the golden hills

With promise of a morn as fair;
And all the train of bounteous hours
Conduct by paths of growing powers,
To reverence and the silver hair;

Till slowly worn her earthly robe,
Her lavish mission richly wrought,
Leaving great legacies of thought,
Thy spirit should fail from off the globe;

What time mine own might also flee,
As link'd with thine in love and fate,
And, hovering o'er the dolorous strait
To the other shore, involved in thee,

Arrive at last the blessed goal,
And He that died in Holy Land
Would reach us out the shining hand,
And take us as a single soul.

What reed was that on which I leant?
Ah, backward fancy, wherefore wake
The old bitterness again, and break
The low beginnings of content.

LXXXV

This truth came borne with bier and pall,
I felt it, when I sorrow'd most,
'Tis better to have loved and lost,
Than never to have loved at all——

O true in word, and tried in deed,
Demanding, so to bring relief
To this which is our common grief,
What kind of life is that I lead;

And whether trust in things above
Be dimm'd of sorrow, or sustain'd;
And whether love for him have drain'd
My capabilities of love;

Your words have virtue such as draws
A faithful answer from the breast,
Thro' light reproaches, half exprest,
And loyal unto kindly laws.

My blood an even tenor kept,
Till on mine ear this message falls,
That in Vienna's fatal walls
God's finger touch'd him, and he slept.

The great Intelligences fair
That range above our mortal state,
In circle round the blessed gate,
Received and gave him welcome there;

And led him thro' the blissful climes,
And show'd him in the fountain fresh
All knowledge that the sons of flesh
Shall gather in the cycled times.

But I remain'd, whose hopes were dim,
Whose life, whose thoughts were little worth,
To wander on a darken'd earth,
Where all things round me breathed of him.

O friendship, equal-poised control,
O heart, with kindliest motion warm,
O sacred essence, other form,
O solemn ghost, O crowned soul!

Yet none could better know than I,
How much of act at human hands
The sense of human will demands
By which we dare to live or die.

Whatever way my days decline,
I felt and feel, tho' left alone,
His being working in mine own,
The footsteps of his life in mine;

A life that all the Muses deck'd
With gifts of grace, that might express
All-comprehensive tenderness,
All-subtilising intellect:

And so my passion hath not swerved
To works of weakness, but I find
An image comforting the mind,
And in my grief a strength reserved.

Likewise the imaginative woe,
That loved to handle spiritual strife,
Diffused the shock thro' all my life,
But in the present broke the blow.

My pulses therefore beat again
For other friends that once I met;
Nor can it suit me to forget
The mighty hopes that make us men.

I woo your love: I count it crime
To mourn for any overmuch;
I, the divided half of such
A friendship as had master'd Time;

Which masters Time indeed, and is
Eternal, separate from fears:
The all-assuming months and years
Can take no part away from this:

But Summer on the steaming floods,
And Spring that swells the narrow brooks,
And Autumn, with a noise of rooks,
That gather in the waning woods,

And every pulse of wind and wave
Recalls, in change of light or gloom,
My old affection of the tomb,
And my prime passion in the grave:

My old affection of the tomb,
A part of stillness, yearns to speak:
"Arise, and get thee forth and seek
A friendship for the years to come.

"I watch thee from the quiet shore;
Thy spirit up to mine can reach;
But in dear words of human speech
We two communicate no more."

And I, "Can clouds of nature stain
The starry clearness of the free?
How is it? Canst thou feel for me
Some painless sympathy with pain?"

And lightly does the whisper fall;
"'Tis hard for thee to fathom this;
I triumph in conclusive bliss,
And that serene result of all."

So hold I commerce with the dead;
Or so methinks the dead would say;
Or so shall grief with symbols play
And pining life be fancy-fed.

Now looking to some settled end,
That these things pass, and I shall prove
A meeting somewhere, love with love,
I crave your pardon, O my friend;

If not so fresh, with love as true,
I, clasping brother-hands, aver
I could not, if I would, transfer
The whole I felt for him to you.

For which be they that hold apart
The promise of the golden hours?
First love, first friendship, equal powers,
That marry with the virgin heart.

Still mine, that cannot but deplore,
That beats within a lonely place,
That yet remembers his embrace,
But at his footstep leaps no more,

My heart, tho' widow'd, may not rest
Quite in the love of what is gone,
But seeks to beat in time with one
That warms another living breast.

Ah, take the imperfect gift I bring,
Knowing the primrose yet is dear,
The primrose of the later year,
As not unlike to that of Spring.

LXXXVI

Sweet after showers, ambrosial air,
That rollest from the gorgeous gloom
Of evening over brake and bloom
And meadow, slowly breathing bare

The round of space, and rapt below
Thro' all the dewy-tassell'd wood,
And shadowing down the horned flood
In ripples, fan my brows and blow

The fever from my cheek, and sigh
The full new life that feeds thy breath
Throughout my frame, till Doubt and Death,
Ill brethren, let the fancy fly

From belt to belt of crimson seas
On leagues of odour streaming far,
To where in yonder orient star
A hundred spirits whisper "Peace."

LXXXVII

I past beside the reverend walls
In which of old I wore the gown;
I roved at random thro' the town,
And saw the tumult of the halls;

And heard once more in college fanes
The storm their high-built organs make,
And thunder-music, rolling, shake
The prophet blazon'd on the panes;

And caught once more the distant shout,
The measured pulse of racing oars
Among the willows; paced the shores
And many a bridge, and all about

The same gray flats again, and felt
The same, but not the same; and last
Up that long walk of limes I past
To see the rooms in which he dwelt.

Another name was on the door:
I linger'd; all within was noise
Of songs, and clapping hands, and boys
That crash'd the glass and beat the floor;

Where once we held debate, a band
Of youthful friends, on mind and art,
And labour, and the changing mart,
And all the framework of the land;

When one would aim an arrow fair,
But send it slackly from the string;
And one would pierce an outer ring,
And one an inner, here and there;

And last the master-bowman, he,
Would cleave the mark. A willing ear
We lent him. Who, but hung to hear
The rapt oration flowing free

From point to point, with power and grace
And music in the bounds of law,
To those conclusions when we saw
The God within him light his face,

And seem to lift the form, and glow
In azure orbits heavenly-wise;
And over those ethereal eyes
The bar of Michael Angelo.

LXXXVIII

Wild bird, whose warble, liquid sweet,
Rings Eden thro' the budded quicks,
O tell me where the senses mix,
O tell me where the passions meet,

Whence radiate: fierce extremes employ
Thy spirits in the darkening leaf,
And in the midmost heart of grief
Thy passion clasps a secret joy:

And I—my harp would prelude woe—
I cannot all command the strings;
The glory of the sum of things
Will flash along the chords and go.

LXXXIX

Witch-elms that counterchange the floor
Of this flat lawn with dusk and bright;
And thou, with all thy breadth and height
Of foliage, towering sycamore;

How often, hither wandering down,
My Arthur found your shadows fair,
And shook to all the liberal air
The dust and din and steam of town:

He brought an eye for all he saw;
He mixt in all our simple sports;
They pleased him, fresh from brawling courts
And dusty purlieus of the law.

O joy to him in this retreat,
Immantled in ambrosial dark,
To drink the cooler air, and mark
The landscape winking thro' the heat:

O sound to rout the brood of cares,
The sweep of scythe in morning dew,
The gust that round the garden flew,
And tumbled half the mellowing pears!

O bliss, when all in circle drawn
About him, heart and ear were fed
To hear him, as he lay and read
The Tuscan poets on the lawn:

Or in the all-golden afternoon
A guest, or happy sister, sung,
Or here she brought the harp and flung
A ballad to the brightening moon:

Nor less it pleased in livelier moods,
Beyond the bounding hill to stray,
And break the livelong summer day
With banquet in the distant woods;

Whereat we glanced from theme to theme,
Discuss'd the books to love or hate,
Or touch'd the changes of the state,
Or threaded some Socratic dream;

But if I praised the busy town,
He loved to rail against it still,
For "ground in yonder social mill
We rub each other's angles down,

"And merge" he said "in form and gloss
The picturesque of man and man."
We talk'd: the stream beneath us ran,
The wine-flask lying couch'd in moss,

Or cool'd within the glooming wave;
And last, returning from afar,
Before the crimson-circled star
Had fall'n into her father's grave,

And brushing ankle-deep in flowers,
We heard behind the woodbine veil
The milk that bubbled in the pail,
And buzzings of the honied hours.

XC

He tasted love with half his mind,
Nor ever drank the inviolate spring
Where nighest heaven, who first could fling
This bitter seed among mankind;

That could the dead, whose dying eyes
Were closed with wail, resume their life,
They would but find in child and wife
An iron welcome when they rise:

'Twas well, indeed, when warm with wine,
To pledge them with a kindly tear,
To talk them o'er, to wish them here,
To count their memories half divine;

But if they came who past away,
Behold their brides in other hands;
The hard heir strides about their lands,
And will not yield them for a day.

Yea, tho' their sons were none of these,
Not less the yet-loved sire would make
Confusion worse than death, and shake
The pillars of domestic peace.

Ah dear, but come thou back to me:
Whatever change the years have wrought,
I find not yet one lonely thought
That cries against my wish for thee.

XCI

When rosy plumelets tuft the larch,
And rarely pipes the mounted thrush;
Or underneath the barren bush
Flits by the sea-blue bird of March;

Come, wear the form by which I know
Thy spirit in time among thy peers;
The hope of unaccomplish'd years
Be large and lucid round thy brow.

When summer's hourly-mellowing change
May breathe, with many roses sweet,
Upon the thousand waves of wheat,
That ripple round the lonely grange;

Come: not in watches of the night,
But where the sunbeam broodeth warm,
Come, beauteous in thine after form,
And like a finer light in light.

XCII

If any vision should reveal
Thy likeness, I might count it vain
As but the canker of the brain;
Yea, tho' it spake and made appeal

To chances where our lots were cast
Together in the days behind,
I might but say, I hear a wind
Of memory murmuring the past.

Yea, tho' it spake and bared to view
A fact within the coming year;
And tho' the months, revolving near,
Should prove the phantom-warning true,

They might not seem thy prophecies,
But spiritual presentiments,
And such refraction of events
As often rises ere they rise.

XCIII

I shall not see thee. Dare I say
No spirit ever brake the band
That stays him from the native land
Where first he walk'd when claspt in clay?

No visual shade of some one lost,
But he, the Spirit himself, may come
Where all the nerve of sense is numb;
Spirit to Spirit, Ghost to Ghost.

O, therefore from thy sightless range
With gods in unconjectured bliss,
O, from the distance of the abyss
Of tenfold-complicated change,

Descend, and touch, and enter; hear
The wish too strong for words to name;
That in this blindness of the frame
My Ghost may feel that thine is near.

XCIV

How pure at heart and sound in head,
With what divine affections bold
Should be the man whose thought would hold
An hour's communion with the dead.

In vain shalt thou, or any, call
The spirits from their golden day,
Except, like them, thou too canst say,
My spirit is at peace with all.

They haunt the silence of the breast,
Imaginations calm and fair,
The memory like a cloudless air,
The conscience as a sea at rest:

But when the heart is full of din,
And doubt beside the portal waits,
They can but listen at the gates,
And hear the household jar within.

XCV

By night we linger'd on the lawn,
For underfoot the herb was dry;
And genial warmth; and o'er the sky
The silvery haze of summer drawn;

And calm that let the tapers burn
Unwavering: not a cricket chirr'd:
The brook alone far-off was heard,
And on the board the fluttering urn:

And bats went round in fragrant skies,
And wheel'd or lit the filmy shapes
That haunt the dusk, with ermine capes
And woolly breasts and beaded eyes;

While now we sang old songs that peal'd
From knoll to knoll, where, couch'd at ease,
The white kine glimmer'd, and the trees
Laid their dark arms about the field.

But when those others, one by one,
Withdrew themselves from me and night,
And in the house light after light
Went out, and I was all alone,

A hunger seized my heart; I read
Of that glad year which once had been,
In those fall'n leaves which kept their green,
The noble letters of the dead:

And strangely on the silence broke
The silent-speaking words, and strange
Was love's dumb cry defying change
To test his worth; and strangely spoke

The faith, the vigour, bold to dwell
On doubts that drive the coward back,
And keen thro' wordy snares to track
Suggestion to her inmost cell.

So word by word, and line by line,
The dead man touch'd me from the past,
And all at once it seem'd at last
The living soul was flash'd on mine,

And mine in this was wound, and whirl'd
About empyreal heights of thought,
And came on that which is, and caught
The deep pulsations of the world,

Æonian music measuring out
The steps of Time—the shocks of Chance—
The blows of Death. At length my trance
Was cancell'd, stricken thro' with doubt.

Vague words! but ah, how hard to frame
In matter-moulded forms of speech,
Or ev'n for intellect to reach
Thro' memory that which I became:

Till now the doubtful dusk reveal'd
The knolls once more where, couch'd at ease,
The white kine glimmer'd, and the trees
Laid their dark arms about the field:

And suck'd from out the distant gloom
A breeze began to tremble o'er
The large leaves of the sycamore,
And fluctuate all the still perfume,

And gathering freshlier overhead,
Rock'd the full-foliaged elms, and swung
The heavy-folded rose, and flung
The lilies to and fro, and said

"The dawn, the dawn," and died away;
And East and West, without a breath,
Mixt their dim lights, like life and death,
To broaden into boundless day.

XCVI

You say, but with no touch of scorn,
Sweet-hearted, you, whose light-blue eyes
Are tender over drowning flies,
You tell me, doubt is Devil-born.

I know not: one indeed I knew
In many a subtle question versed,
Who touch'd a jarring lyre at first,
But ever strove to make it true:

Perplext in faith, but pure in deeds,
At last he beat his music out.
There lives more faith in honest doubt,
Believe me, than in half the creeds.

He fought his doubts and gather'd strength,
He would not make his judgment blind,
He faced the spectres of the mind
And laid them: thus he came at length

To find a stronger faith his own;
And Power was with him in the night,
Which makes the darkness and the light,
And dwells not in the light alone,

But in the darkness and the cloud,
As over Sinaï's peaks of old,
While Israel made their gods of gold,
Altho' the trumpet blew so loud.

XCVII

My love has talk'd with rocks and trees;
He finds on misty mountain-ground
His own vast shadow glory-crown'd;
He sees himself in all he sees.

Two partners of a married life—
I look'd on these and thought of thee
In vastness and in mystery,
And of my spirit as of a wife.

These two—they dwelt with eye on eye,
Their hearts of old have beat in tune,
Their meetings made December June,
Their every parting was to die.

Their love has never past away;
The days she never can forget
Are earnest that he loves her yet,
Whate'er the faithless people say.

Her life is lone, he sits apart,
He loves her yet, she will not weep,
Tho' rapt in matters dark and deep
He seems to slight her simple heart.

He thrids the labyrinth of the mind,
He reads the secret of the star,
He seems so near and yet so far,
He looks so cold: she thinks him kind.

She keeps the gift of years before,
A wither'd violet is her bliss:
She knows not what his greatness is,
For that, for all, she loves him more.

For him she plays, to him she sings
Of early faith and plighted vows;
She knows but matters of the house,
And he, he knows a thousand things.

Her faith is fixt and cannot move,
She darkly feels him great and wise,
She dwells on him with faithful eyes,
"I cannot understand: I love."

XCVIII

You leave us: you will see the Rhine,
And those fair hills I sail'd below,
When I was there with him; and go
By summer belts of wheat and vine

To where he breathed his latest breath,
That City. All her splendour seems
No livelier than the wisp that gleams
On Lethe in the eyes of Death.

Let her great Danube rolling fair
Enwind her isles, unmark'd of me:
I have not seen, I will not see
Vienna; rather dream that there,

A treble darkness, Evil haunts
The birth, the bridal; friend from friend
Is oftener parted, fathers bend
Above more graves, a thousand wants

Gnarr at the heels of men, and prey
By each cold hearth, and sadness flings
Her shadow on the blaze of kings:
And yet myself have heard him say,

That not in any mother town
With statelier progress to and fro
The double tides of chariots flow
By park and suburb under brown
Of lustier leaves; nor more content,
He told me, lives in any crowd,
When all is gay with lamps, and loud
With sport and song, in booth and tent,

Imperial halls, or open plain;
And wheels the circled dance, and breaks
The rocket molten into flakes
Of crimson or in emerald rain.

XCIX

Risest thou thus, dim dawn, again,
So loud with voices of the birds,
So thick with lowings of the herds,
Day, when I lost the flower of men;

Who tremblest thro' thy darkling red
On yon swoll'n brook that bubbles fast
By meadows breathing of the past,
And woodlands holy to the dead;

Who murmurest in the foliaged eaves
A song that slights the coming care,
And Autumn laying here and there
A fiery finger on the leaves;

Who wakenest with thy balmy breath
To myriads on the genial earth,
Memories of bridal, or of birth,
And unto myriads more, of death.

O wheresoever those may be,
Betwixt the slumber of the poles,
To-day they count as kindred souls;
They know me not, but mourn with me.

C

I climb the hill: from end to end
Of all the landscape underneath,
I find no place that does not breathe
Some gracious memory of my friend;

No gray old grange, or lonely fold,
Or low morass and whispering reed,
Or simple stile from mead to mead,
Or sheepwalk up the windy wold;

Nor hoary knoll of ash and haw
That hears the latest linnet trill,
Nor quarry trench'd along the hill
And haunted by the wrangling daw;

Nor runlet tinkling from the rock;
  Nor pastoral rivulet that swerves
  To left and right thro' meadowy curves,
That feed the mothers of the flock;

But each has pleased a kindred eye,
  And each reflects a kindlier day;
  And, leaving these, to pass away,
I think once more he seems to die.

CI

Unwatch'd, the garden bough shall sway,
  The tender blossom flutter down,
  Unloved, that beech will gather brown,
This maple burn itself away;

Unloved, the sun-flower, shining fair,
  Ray round with flames her disk of seed,
  And many a rose-carnation feed
With summer spice the humming air;

Unloved, by many a sandy bar,
  The brook shall babble down the plain,
  At noon or when the lesser wain
Is twisting round the polar star;

Uncared for, gird the windy grove,
  And flood the haunts of hern and crake;
  Or into silver arrows break
The sailing moon in creek and cove;

Till from the garden and the wild
  A fresh association blow,
  And year by year the landscape grow
Familiar to the stranger's child;

As year by year the labourer tills
  His wonted glebe, or lops the glades;
  And year by year our memory fades
From all the circle of the hills.

CII

We leave the well-beloved place
  Where first we gazed upon the sky;
  The roofs, that heard our earliest cry,
Will shelter one of stranger race.

We go, but ere we go from home,
  As down the garden-walks I move,
  Two spirits of a diverse love
Contend for loving masterdom.

One whispers, "Here thy boyhood sung
  Long since its matin song, and heard
  The low love-language of the bird
In native hazels tassel-hung."

The other answers, "Yea, but here
  Thy feet have stray'd in after hours
  With thy lost friend among the bowers,
And this hath made them trebly dear."

These two have striven half the day,
  And each prefers his separate claim,
  Poor rivals in a losing game,
That will not yield each other way.

I turn to go: my feet are set
  To leave the pleasant fields and farms;
  They mix in one another's arms
To one pure image of regret.

CIII

On that last night before we went
  From out the doors where I was bred,
  I dream'd a vision of the dead,
Which left my after-morn content.

Methought I dwelt within a hall,
  And maidens with me: distant hills
  From hidden summits fed with rills
A river sliding by the wall.

The hall with harp and carol rang.
  They sang of what is wise and good
  And graceful. In the centre stood
A statue veil'd, to which they sang;

And which, tho' veil'd, was known to me,
  The shape of him I loved, and love
  For ever: then flew in a dove
And brought a summons from the sea:

And when they learnt that I must go
  They wept and wail'd, but led the way
  To where a little shallop lay
At anchor in the flood below;

And on by many a level mead,
  And shadowing bluff that made the banks,
  We glided winding under ranks
Of iris, and the golden reed;

And still as vaster grew the shore
  And roll'd the floods in grander space,
  The maidens gather'd strength and grace
And presence, lordlier than before;

And I myself, who sat apart
　And watch'd them, wax'd in every limb;
　I felt the thews of Anakim,
The pulses of a Titan's heart;

As one would sing the death of war,
　And one would chant the history
　Of that great race, which is to be,
And one the shaping of a star;

Until the forward-creeping tides
　Began to foam, and we to draw
　From deep to deep, to where we saw
A great ship lift her shining sides.

The man we loved was there on deck,
　But thrice as large as man he bent
　To greet us. Up the side I went,
And fell in silence on his neck:

Whereat those maidens with one mind
　Bewail'd their lot; I did them wrong:
　"We served thee here," they said, "so long,
And wilt thou leave us now behind?"

So rapt I was, they could not win
　An answer from my lips, but he
　Replying, "Enter likewise ye
And go with us:" they enter'd in.

And while the wind began to sweep
　A music out of sheet and shroud,
　We steer'd her toward a crimson cloud
That landlike slept along the deep.

CIV

The time draws near the birth of Christ;
　The moon is hid, the night is still;
　A single church below the hill
Is pealing, folded in the mist.

A single peal of bells below,
　That wakens at this hour of rest
　A single murmur in the breast,
That these are not the bells I know.

Like strangers' voices here they sound,
　In lands where not a memory strays,
　Nor landmark breathes of other days,
But all is new unhallow'd ground.

CV

To-night ungather'd let us leave
　This laurel, let this holly stand:
　We live within the stranger's land,
And strangely falls our Christmas-eve.

Our father's dust is left alone
　And silent under other snows:
　There in due time the woodbine blows,
The violet comes, but we are gone.

No more shall wayward grief abuse
　The genial hour with mask and mime;
　For change of place, like growth of time,
Has broke the bond of dying use.

Let cares that petty shadows cast,
　By which our lives are chiefly proved,
　A little spare the night I loved,
And hold it solemn to the past.

But let no footstep beat the floor,
　Nor bowl of wassail mantle warm;
　For who would keep an ancient form
Thro' which the spirit breathes no more?

Be neither song, nor game, nor feast;
　Nor harp be touch'd, nor flute be blown;
　No dance, no motion, save alone
What lightens in the lucid east

Of rising worlds by yonder wood.
　Long sleeps the summer in the seed;
　Run out your measured arcs, and lead
The closing cycle rich in good.

CVI

Ring out, wild bells, to the wild sky,
　The flying cloud, the frosty light:
　The year is dying in the night;
Ring out, wild bells, and let him die.

Ring out the old, ring in the new,
　Ring, happy bells, across the snow:
　The year is going, let him go;
Ring out the false, ring in the true.

Ring out the grief that saps the mind,
　For those that here we see no more;
　Ring out the feud of rich and poor,
Ring in redress to all mankind.

Ring out a slowly dying cause,
And ancient forms of party strife;
Ring in the nobler modes of life,
With sweeter manners, purer laws.

Ring out the want, the care, the sin,
The faithless coldness of the times;
Ring out, ring out my mournful rhymes,
But ring the fuller minstrel in.

Ring out false pride in place and blood,
The civic slander and the spite;
Ring in the love of truth and right,
Ring in the common love of good.

Ring out old shapes of foul disease;
Ring out the narrowing lust of gold;
Ring out the thousand wars of old,
Ring in the thousand years of peace.

Ring in the valiant man and free,
The larger heart, the kindlier hand;
Ring out the darkness of the land.
Ring in the Christ that is to be.

CVII

It is the day when he was born,
A bitter day that early sank
Behind a purple-frosty bank
Of vapour, leaving night forlorn.

The time admits not flowers or leaves
To deck the banquet. Fiercely flies
The blast of North and East, and ice
Makes daggers at the sharpen'd eaves,

And bristles all the brakes and thorns
To yon hard crescent, as she hangs
Above the wood which grides and clangs
Its leafless ribs and iron horns

Together, in the drifts that pass
To darken on the rolling brine
That breaks the coast. But fetch the wine,
Arrange the board and brim the glass;

Bring in great logs and let them lie,
To make a solid core of heat;
Be cheerful-minded, talk and treat
Of all things ev'n as he were by;

We keep the day. With festal cheer,
With books and music, surely we
Will drink to him, whate'er he be,
And sing the songs he loved to hear.

CVIII

I will not shut me from my kind,
And, lest I stiffen into stone,
I will not eat my heart alone,
Nor feed with sighs a passing wind:

What profit lies in barren faith,
And vacant yearning, tho' with might
To scale the heaven's highest height,
Or dive below the wells of Death?

What find I in the highest place,
But mine own phantom chanting hymns?
And on the depths of death there swims
The reflex of a human face.

I'll rather take what fruit may be
Of sorrow under human skies:
'Tis held that sorrow makes us wise,
Whatever wisdom sleep with thee.

CIX

Heart-affluence in discursive talk
From household fountains never dry;
The critic clearness of an eye,
That saw thro' all the Muses' walk;

Seraphic intellect and force
To seize and throw the doubts of man;
Impassion'd logic, which outran
The hearer in its fiery course;

High nature amorous of the good,
But touch'd with no ascetic gloom;
And passion pure in snowy bloom
Thro' all the years of April blood;

A love of freedom rarely felt,
Of freedom in her regal seat
Of England; not the schoolboy heat,
The blind hysterics of the Celt;

And manhood fused with female grace
In such a sort, the child would twine
A trustful hand, unask'd, in thine,
And find his comfort in thy face;

All these have been, and thee mine eyes
Have look'd on: if they look'd in vain,
My shame is greater who remain,
Nor let thy wisdom make me wise.

CX

Thy converse drew us with delight,
The men of rathe and riper years:
The feeble soul, a haunt of fears,
Forgot his weakness in thy sight.

On thee the loyal-hearted hung,
The proud was half disarm'd of pride,
Nor cared the serpent at thy side
To flicker with his double tongue.

The stern were mild when thou wert by,
The flippant put himself to school
And heard thee, and the brazen fool
Was soften'd, and he knew not why;

While I, thy nearest, sat apart,
And felt thy triumph was as mine;
And loved them more, that they were thine,
The graceful tact, the Christian art;

Nor mine the sweetness or the skill,
But mine the love that will not tire,
And, born of love, the vague desire
That spurs an imitative will.

CXI

The churl in spirit, up or down
Along the scale of ranks, thro' all,
To him who grasps a golden ball,
By blood a king, at heart a clown;

The churl in spirit, howe'er he veil
His want in forms for fashion's sake,
Will let his coltish nature break
At seasons thro' the gilded pale:

For who can always act? but he,
To whom a thousand memories call,
Not being less but more than all
The gentleness he seem'd to be,

Best seem'd the thing he was, and join'd
Each office of the social hour
To noble manners, as the flower
And native growth of noble mind;

Nor ever narrowness or spite,
Or villain fancy fleeting by,
Drew in the expression of an eye,
Where God and Nature met in light;

And thus he bore without abuse
The grand old name of gentleman,
Defamed by every charlatan,
And soil'd with all ignoble use.

CXII

High wisdom holds my wisdom less,
That I, who gaze with temperate eyes
On glorious insufficiencies,
Set light by narrower perfectness.

But thou, that fillest all the room
Of all my love, art reason why
I seem to cast a careless eye
On souls, the lesser lords of doom.

For what wert thou? some novel power
Sprang up for ever at a touch,
And hope could never hope too much,
In watching thee from hour to hour,

Large elements in order brought,
And tracts of calm from tempest made,
And world-wide fluctuation sway'd
In vassal tides that follow'd thought.

CXIII

'Tis held that sorrow makes us wise;
Yet how much wisdom sleeps with thee
Which not alone had guided me,
But served the seasons that may rise;

For can I doubt, who knew thee keen
In intellect, with force and skill
To strive, to fashion, to fulfil—
I doubt not what thou wouldst have been:

A life in civic action warm,
A soul on highest mission sent,
A potent voice of Parliament,
A pillar steadfast in the storm,

Should licensed boldness gather force,
Becoming, when the time has birth,
A lever to uplift the earth
And roll it in another course,

With thousand shocks that come and go,
With agonies, with energies,
With overthrowings, and with cries,
And undulations to and fro.

CXIV

Who loves not Knowledge? Who shall rail
Against her beauty? May she mix
With men and prosper! Who shall fix
Her pillars? Let her work prevail.

But on her forehead sits a fire:
She sets her forward countenance
And leaps into the future chance,
Submitting all things to desire.

Half-grown as yet, a child, and vain—
She cannot fight the fear of death.
What is she, cut from love and faith,
But some wild Pallas from the brain

Of Demons? fiery-hot to burst
All barriers in her onward race
For power. Let her know her place;
She is the second, not the first.

A higher hand must make her mild,
If all be not in vain; and guide
Her footsteps, moving side by side
With wisdom, like the younger child:

For she is earthly of the mind,
But Wisdom heavenly of the soul.
O, friend, who camest to thy goal
So early, leaving me behind,

I would the great world grew like thee,
Who grewest not alone in power
And knowledge, but by year and hour
In reverence and in charity.

CXV

Now fades the last long streak of snow,
Now burgeons every maze of quick
About the flowering squares, and thick
By ashen roots the violets blow.

Now rings the woodland loud and long,
The distance takes a lovelier hue,
And drown'd in yonder living blue
The lark becomes a sightless song.

Now dance the lights on lawn and lea,
The flocks are whiter down the vale,
And milkier every milky sail
On winding stream or distant sea;

Where now the seamew pipes, or dives
In yonder greening gleam, and fly
The happy birds, that change their sky
To build and brood; that live their lives

From land to land; and in my breast
Spring wakens too; and my regret
Becomes an April violet,
And buds and blossoms like the rest.

CXVI

Is it, then, regret for buried time
That keenlier in sweet April wakes,
And meets the year, and gives and takes
The colours of the crescent prime?

Not all: the songs, the stirring air,
The life re-orient out of dust,
Cry thro' the sense to hearten trust
In that which made the world so fair.

Not all regret: the face will shine
Upon me, while I muse alone;
And that dear voice, I once have known,
Still speak to me of me and mine:

Yet less of sorrow lives in me
For days of happy commune dead;
Less yearning for the friendship fled,
Than some strong bond which is to be.

CXVII

O days and hours, your work is this
To hold me from my proper place,
A little while from his embrace,
For fuller gain of after bliss:

That out of distance might ensue
Desire of nearness doubly sweet;
And unto meeting when we meet,
Delight a hundredfold accrue,

For every grain of sand that runs,
And every span of shade that steals,
And every kiss of toothed wheels,
And all the courses of the suns.

CXVIII

Contemplate all this work of Time,
The giant labouring in his youth;
Nor dream of human love and truth,
As dying Nature's earth and lime;

But trust that those we call the dead
Are breathers of an ampler day
For ever nobler ends. They say,
The solid earth whereon we tread

In tracts of fluent heat began,
And grew to seeming-random forms,
The seeming prey of cyclic storms,
Till at the last arose the man;

Who throve and branch'd from clime to clime,
The herald of a higher race,
And of himself in higher place,
If so he type this work of time

Within himself, from more to more;
Or, crown'd with attributes of woe
Like glories, move his course, and show
That life is not as idle ore,

But iron dug from central gloom,
And heated hot with burning fears,
And dipt in baths of hissing tears,
And batter'd with the shocks of doom

To shape and use. Arise and fly
The reeling Faun, the sensual feast;
Move upward, working out the beast,
And let the ape and tiger die.

CXIX

Doors, where my heart was used to beat
So quickly, not as one that weeps
I come once more; the city sleeps;
I smell the meadow in the street;

I hear a chirp of birds; I see
Betwixt the black fronts long-withdrawn
A light-blue lane of early dawn,
And think of early days and thee,

And bless thee, for thy lips are bland,
And bright the friendship of thine eye;
And in my thoughts with scarce a sigh
I take the pressure of thine hand.

CXX

I trust I have not wasted breath:
I think we are not wholly brain,
Magnetic mockeries; not in vain,
Like Paul with beasts, I fought with Death;

Not only cunning casts in clay:
Let Science prove we are, and then
What matters Science unto men,
At least to me? I would not stay.

Let him, the wiser man who springs
Hereafter, up from childhood shape
His action like the greater ape,
But I was *born* to other things.

CXXI

Sad Hesper o'er the buried sun
And ready, thou, to die with him,
Thou watchest all things ever dim
And dimmer, and a glory done:

The team is loosen'd from the wain,
The boat is drawn upon the shore;
Thou listenest to the closing door,
And life is darken'd in the brain.

Bright Phosphor, fresher for the night,
By thee the world's great work is heard
Beginning, and the wakeful bird;
Behind thee comes the greater light:

The market boat is on the stream,
And voices hail it from the brink;
Thou hear'st the village hammer clink,
And see'st the moving of the team.

Sweet Hesper-Phosphor, double name
For what is one, the first, the last,
Thou, like my present and my past,
Thy place is changed; thou art the same.

CXXII

Oh, wast thou with me, dearest, then,
While I rose up against my doom,
And yearn'd to burst the folded gloom,
To bare the eternal Heavens again,

To feel once more, in placid awe,
The strong imagination roll
A sphere of stars about my soul,
In all her motion one with law;

If thou wert with me, and the grave
Divide us not, be with me now,
And enter in at breast and brow,
Till all my blood, a fuller wave,

Be quicken'd with a livelier breath,
And like an inconsiderate boy,
As in the former flash of joy,
I slip the thoughts of life and death;

And all the breeze of Fancy blows,
And every dew-drop paints a bow,
The wizard lightnings deeply glow,
And every thought breaks out a rose.

CXXIII

There rolls the deep where grew the tree.
O earth, what changes hast thou seen!
There where the long street roars, hath been
The stillness of the central sea.

The hills are shadows, and they flow
From form to form, and nothing stands;
They melt like mist, the solid lands,
Like clouds they shape themselves and go.

But in my spirit will I dwell,
And dream my dream, and hold it true;
For tho' my lips may breathe adieu,
I cannot think the thing farewell.

CXXIV

That which we dare invoke to bless;
Our dearest faith; our ghastliest doubt;
He, They, One, All; within, without;
The Power in darkness whom we guess;

I found Him not in world or sun,
Or eagle's wing, or insect's eye;
Nor thro' the questions men may try,
The petty cobwebs we have spun:

If e'er when faith had fall'n asleep,
I heard a voice "believe no more"
And heard an ever-breaking shore
That tumbled in the Godless deep;

A warmth within the breast would melt
The freezing reason's colder part,
And like a man in wrath the heart
Stood up and answer'd "I have felt."

No, like a child in doubt and fear:
But that blind clamour made me wise;
Then was I as a child that cries,
But, crying, knows his father near;

And what I am beheld again
What is, and no man understands;
And out of darkness came the hands
That reach thro' nature, moulding men.

CXXV

Whatever I have said or sung,
Some bitter notes my harp would give,
Yea, tho' there often seem'd to live
A contradiction on the tongue,

Yet Hope had never lost her youth;
She did but look through dimmer eyes;
Or Love but play'd with gracious lies,
Because he felt so fix'd in truth:

And if the song were full of care,
He breathed the spirit of the song;
And if the words were sweet and strong
He set his royal signet there;

Abiding with me till I sail
To seek thee on the mystic deeps,
And this electric force, that keeps
A thousand pulses dancing, fail.

CXXVI

Love is and was my Lord and King,
And in his presence I attend
To hear the tidings of my friend,
Which every hour his couriers bring.

Love is and was my King and Lord,
And will be, tho' as yet I keep
Within his court on earth, and sleep
Encompass'd by his faithful guard,

And hear at times a sentinel
Who moves about from place to place,
And whispers to the worlds of space,
In the deep night, that all is well.

CXXVII

And all is well, tho' faith and form
Be sunder'd in the night of fear;
Well roars the storm to those that hear
A deeper voice across the storm,

Proclaiming social truth shall spread,
And justice, ev'n tho' thrice again
The red fool-fury of the Seine
Should pile her barricades with dead.

But ill for him that wears a crown,
And him, the lazar, in his rags:
They tremble, the sustaining crags;
The spires of ice are toppled down,

And molten up, and roar in flood;
The fortress crashes from on high,
The brute earth lightens to the sky,
And the great Æon sinks in blood,

And compass'd by the fires of Hell;
While thou, dear spirit, happy star,
O'erlook'st the tumult from afar,
And smilest, knowing all is well.

CXXVIII

The love that rose on stronger wings,
Unpalsied when he met with Death,
Is comrade of the lesser faith
That sees the course of human things.

No doubt vast eddies in the flood
Of onward time shall yet be made,
And throned races may degrade;
Yet O ye mysteries of good,

Wild Hours that fly with Hope and Fear,
If all your office had to do
With old results that look like new;
If this were all your mission here,

To draw, to sheathe a useless sword,
To fool the crowd with glorious lies,
To cleave a creed in sects and cries,
To change the bearing of a word,

To shift an arbitrary power,
To cramp the student at his desk,
To make old bareness picturesque
And tuft with grass a feudal tower;

Why then my scorn might well descend
On you and yours. I see in part
That all, as in some piece of art,
Is toil coöperant to an end.

CXXIX

Dear friend, far off, my lost desire,
So far, so near in woe and weal;
O loved the most, when most I feel
There is a lower and a higher;

Known and unknown; human, divine;
Sweet human hand and lips and eye;
Dear heavenly friend that canst not die,
Mine, mine, for ever, ever mine;

Strange friend, past, present, and to be;
Loved deeplier, darklier understood;
Behold, I dream a dream of good,
And mingle all the world with thee.

CXXX

Thy voice is on the rolling air;
I hear thee where the waters run;
Thou standest in the rising sun,
And in the setting thou art fair.

What art thou then? I cannot guess;
But tho' I seem in star and flower
To feel thee some diffusive power,
I do not therefore love thee less:

My love involves the love before;
My love is vaster passion now;
Tho' mix'd with God and Nature thou,
I seem to love thee more and more.

Far off thou art, but ever nigh;
I have thee still, and I rejoice;
I prosper, circled with thy voice;
I shall not lose thee tho' I die.

CXXXI

O living will that shalt endure
When all that seems shall suffer shock,
Rise in the spiritual rock,
Flow thro' our deeds and make them pure,

That we may lift from out of dust
A voice as unto him that hears,
A cry above the conquer'd years
To one that with us works, and trust,

With faith that comes of self-control,
The truths that never can be proved
Until we close with all we loved,
And all we flow from, soul in soul.

* * *

O true and tried, so well and long,
Demand not thou a marriage lay;
In that it is thy marriage day
Is music more than any song.

Nor have I felt so much of bliss
Since first he told me that he loved
A daughter of our house; nor proved
Since that dark day a day like this;

Tho' I since then have number'd o'er
Some thrice three years: they went and came,
Remade the blood and changed the frame,
And yet is love not less, but more;

No longer caring to embalm
In dying songs a dead regret,
But like a statue solid-set,
And moulded in colossal calm.

Regret is dead, but love is more
Than in the summers that are flown,
For I myself with these have grown
To something greater than before;

Which makes appear the songs I made
As echoes out of weaker times,
As half but idle brawling rhymes,
The sport of random sun and shade.

But where is she, the bridal flower,
That must be made a wife ere noon?
She enters, glowing like the moon
Of Eden on its bridal bower:

On me she bends her blissful eyes
And then on thee; they meet thy look
And brighten like the star that shook
Betwixt the palms of paradise.

O when her life was yet in bud,
He too foretold the perfect rose.
For thee she grew, for thee she grows
For ever, and as fair as good.

And thou art worthy; full of power;
As gentle; liberal-minded, great,
Consistent; wearing all that weight
Of learning lightly like a flower.

But now set out: the noon is near,
And I must give away the bride;
She fears not, or with thee beside
And me behind her, will not fear.

For I that danced her on my knee,
That watch'd her on her nurse's arm,
That shielded all her life from harm
At last must part with her to thee;

Now waiting to be made a wife,
Her feet, my darling, on the dead;
Their pensive tablets round her head,
And the most living words of life

Breathed in her ear. The ring is on,
The "wilt thou" answer'd, and again
The "wilt thou" ask'd, till out of twain
Her sweet "I will" has made you one.

Now sign your names, which shall be read,
Mute symbols of a joyful morn,
By village eyes as yet unborn;
The names are sign'd, and overhead

Begins the clash and clang that tells
The joy to every wandering breeze;
The blind wall rocks, and on the trees
The dead leaf trembles to the bells.

O happy hour, and happier hours
Await them. Many a merry face
Salutes them—maidens of the place,
That pelt us in the porch with flowers.

O happy hour, behold the bride
With him to whom her hand I gave.
They leave the porch, they pass the grave
That has to-day its sunny side.

To-day the grave is bright for me,
For them the light of life increased,
Who stay to share the morning feast,
Who rest to-night beside the sea.

Let all my genial spirits advance
To meet and greet a whiter sun;
My drooping memory will not shun
The foaming grape of eastern France.

It circles round, and fancy plays,
And hearts are warm'd and faces bloom,
As drinking health to bride and groom
We wish them store of happy days.

Nor count me all to blame if I
Conjecture of a stiller guest,
Perchance, perchance, among the rest,
And, tho' in silence, wishing joy.

But they must go, the time draws on,
And those white-favour'd horses wait;
They rise, but linger; it is late;
Farewell, we kiss, and they are gone.

A shade falls on us like the dark
From little cloudlets on the grass,
But sweeps away as out we pass
To range the woods, to roam the park,

Discussing how their courtship grew,
And talk of others that are wed,
And how she look'd, and what he said,
And back we come at fall of dew.

Again the feast, the speech, the glee,
The shade of passing thought, the wealth
Of words and wit, the double health,
The crowning cup, the three-times-three,

And last the dance;—till I retire:
Dumb is that tower which spake so loud,
And high in heaven the streaming cloud,
And on the downs a rising fire:

And rise, O moon, from yonder down,
Till over down and over dale
All night the shining vapour sail
And pass the silent-lighted town,

The white-faced halls, the glancing rills,
And catch at every mountain head,
And o'er the friths that branch and spread
Their sleeping silver thro' the hills;

And touch with shade the bridal doors,
With tender gloom the roof, the wall;
And breaking let the splendour fall
To spangle all the happy shores

By which they rest, and ocean sounds,
And, star and system rolling past,
A soul shall draw from out the vast
And strike his being into bounds,

And, moved thro' life of lower phase,
Result in man, be born and think,
And act and love, a closer link
Betwixt us and the crowning race

Of those that, eye to eye, shall look
On knowledge; under whose commmand
Is Earth and Earth's, and in their hand
Is Nature like an open book;

No longer half-akin to brute,
For all we thought and loved and did,
And hoped, and suffer'd, is but seed
Of what in them is flower and fruit;

Whereof the man, that with me trod
This planet, was a noble type
Appearing ere the times were ripe,
That friend of mine who lives in God,

That God, which ever lives and loves,
One God, one law, one element,
And one far-off divine event,
To which the whole creation moves.

1850

THE EAGLE

FRAGMENT

HE clasps the crag with crooked hands;
Close to the sun in lonely lands,
Ring'd with the azure world, he stands.

The wrinkled sea beneath him crawls;
He watches from his mountain walls,
And like a thunderbolt he falls.

1851

COME NOT, WHEN I AM DEAD

COME not, when I am dead,
To drop thy foolish tears upon my grave,
To trample round my fallen head,
And vex the unhappy dust thou wouldst not save.
There let the wind sweep and the plover cry;
But thou, go by.

Child, if it were thine error or thy crime
I care no longer, being all unblest:
Wed whom thou wilt, but I am sick of Time,
And I desire to rest.
Pass on, weak heart, and leave me where I lie:
Go by, go by.

1851

ODE ON THE DEATH OF THE DUKE OF WELLINGTON

PUBLISHED IN 1852

I

BURY the Great Duke
With an empire's lamentation,
Let us bury the Great Duke
To the noise of the mourning of a mighty nation,

Mourning when their leaders fall,
Warriors carry the warrior's pall,
And sorrow darkens hamlet and hall.

II

Where shall we lay the man whom we deplore?
Here, in streaming London's central roar.
Let the sound of those he wrought for,
And the feet of those he fought for,
Echo round his bones for evermore.

III

Lead out the pageant: sad and slow,
As fits an universal woe,
Let the long long procession go,
And let the sorrowing crowd about it grow,
And let the mournful martial music blow;
The last great Englishman is low.

IV

Mourn, for to us he seems the last,
Remembering all his greatness in the Past.
No more in soldier fashion will he greet
With lifted hand the gazer in the street.
O friends, our chief state-oracle is mute:
Mourn for the man of long-enduring blood,
The statesman-warrior, moderate, resolute,
Whole in himself, a common good.
Mourn for the man of amplest influence,
Yet clearest of ambitious crime,
Our greatest yet with least pretence,
Great in council and great in war,
Foremost captain of his time,
Rich in saving common-sense,
And, as the greatest only are,
In his simplicity sublime.
O good gray head which all men knew,
O voice from which their omens all men drew,
O iron nerve to true occasion true,
O fall'n at length that tower of strength
Which stood four-square to all the winds that blew!
Such was he whom we deplore.
The long self-sacrifice of life is o'er.
The great World-victor's victor will be seen no more.

V

All is over and done:
Render thanks to the Giver,
England, for thy son.
Let the bell be toll'd.
Render thanks to the Giver,
And render him to the mould.
Under the cross of gold
That shines over city and river,
There he shall rest for ever
Among the wise and the bold.
Let the bell be toll'd:
And a reverent people behold
The towering car, the sable steeds:
Bright let it be with its blazon'd deeds,
Dark in its funeral fold.
Let the bell be toll'd:
And a deeper knell in the heart be knoll'd;
And the sound of the sorrowing anthem roll'd
Thro' the dome of the golden cross;
And the volleying cannon thunder his loss;
He knew their voices of old.
For many a time in many a clime
His captain's-ear has heard them boom
Bellowing victory, bellowing doom:
When he with those deep voices wrought,
Guarding realms and kings from shame;
With those deep voices our dead captain taught
The tyrant, and asserts his claim
In that dread sound to the great name,
Which he has worn so pure of blame,
In praise and in dispraise the same,
A man of well-attemper'd frame.
O civic muse, to such a name,
To such a name for ages long,
To such a name,
Preserve a broad approach of fame,
And ever-echoing avenues of song.

VI

Who is he that cometh, like an honour'd guest,
With banner and with music, with soldier and with priest,
With a nation weeping, and breaking on my rest?
Mighty Seaman, this is he
Was great by land as thou by sea.
Thine island loves thee well, thou famous man,
The greatest sailor since our world began.
Now, to the roll of muffled drums,
To thee the greatest soldier comes;
For this is he
Was great by land as thou by sea;

His foes were thine; he kept us free:
O give him welcome, this is he
Worthy of our gorgeous rites,
And worthy to be laid by thee;
For this is England's greatest son,
He that gain'd a hundred fights,
Nor ever lost an English gun;
This is he that far away
Against the myriads of Assaye
Clash'd with his fiery few and won;
And underneath another sun,
Warring on a later day,
Round affrighted Lisbon drew
The treble works, the vast designs
Of his labour'd rampart-lines,
Where he greatly stood at bay,
Whence he issued forth anew,
And ever great and greater grew,
Beating from the wasted vines
Back to France her banded swarms,
Back to France with countless blows,
Till o'er the hills her eagles flew
Beyond the Pyrenean pines,
Follow'd up in valley and glen
With blare of bugle, clamour of men,
Roll of cannon and clash of arms,
And England pouring on her foes.
Such a war had such a close.
Again their ravening eagle rose
In anger, wheel'd on Europe-shadowing wings,
And barking for the thrones of kings;
Till one that sought but Duty's iron crown
On that loud sabbath shook the spoiler down;
A day of onsets of despair!
Dash'd on every rocky square
Their surging charges foam'd themselves away;
Last, the Prussian trumpet blew;
Thro' the long-tormented air
Heaven flash'd a sudden jubilant ray,
And down we swept and charged and overthrew.
So great a soldier taught us there,
What long-enduring hearts could do
In that world-earthquake, Waterloo!
Mighty Seaman, tender and true,
And pure as he from taint of craven guile,
O saviour of the silver-coasted isle,
O shaker of the Baltic and the Nile,
If aught of things that here befall
Touch a spirit among things divine,
If love of country move thee there at all,
Be glad, because his bones are laid by thine!
And thro' the centuries let a people's voice
In full acclaim,
A people's voice,
The proof and echo of all human fame,
A people's voice, when they rejoice
At civic revel and pomp and game,
Attest their great commander's claim
With honour, honour, honour, honour to him,
Eternal honour to his name.

VII

A people's voice! we are a people yet.
Tho' all men else their nobler dreams forget,
Confused by brainless mobs and lawless Powers;
Thank Him who isled us here, and roughly set
His Briton in blown seas and storming showers,
We have a voice, with which to pay the debt
Of boundless love and reverence and regret
To those great men who fought, and kept it ours.
And keep it ours, O God, from brute control;
O Statesmen, guard us, guard the eye, the soul
Of Europe, keep our noble England whole,
And save the one true seed of freedom sown
Betwixt a people and their ancient throne,
That sober freedom out of which there springs
Our loyal passion for our temperate kings;
For, saving that, ye help to save mankind
Till public wrong be crumbled into dust,
And drill the raw world for the march of mind,
Till crowds at length be sane and crowns be just.
But wink no more in slothful overtrust.
Remember him who led your hosts;
He bade you guard the sacred coasts.
Your cannons moulder on the seaward wall;
His voice is silent in your council-hall
For ever; and whatever tempests lour
For ever silent; even if they broke

In thunder, silent; yet remember all
He spoke among you, and the Man who spoke;
Who never sold the truth to serve the hour,
Nor palter'd with Eternal God for power;
Who let the turbid streams of rumour flow
Thro' either babbling world of high and low;
Whose life was work, whose language rife
With rugged maxims hewn from life;
Who never spoke against a foe;
Whose eighty winters freeze with one rebuke
All great self-seekers trampling on the right:
Truth-teller was our England's Alfred named;
Truth-lover was our English Duke;
Whatever record leap to light
He never shall be shamed.

VIII

Lo, the leader in these glorious wars
Now to glorious burial slowly borne,
Follow'd by the brave of other lands,
He, on whom from both her open hands
Lavish Honour shower'd all her stars,
And affluent Fortune emptied all her horn.
Yea, let all good things await
Him who cares not to be great,
But as he saves or serves the state.
Not once or twice in our rough island-story,
The path of duty was the way to glory:
He that walks it, only thirsting
For the right, and learns to deaden
Love of self, before his journey closes,
He shall find the stubborn thistle bursting
Into glossy purples, which outredden
All voluptuous garden-roses.
Not once or twice in our fair island-story,
The path of duty was the way to glory:
He, that ever following her commands,
On with toil of heart and knees and hands,
Thro' the long gorge to the far light has won
His path upward, and prevail'd,
Shall find the toppling crags of Duty scaled
Are close upon the shining table-lands
To which our God Himself is moon and sun.
Such was he: his work is done.
But while the races of mankind endure,
Let his great example stand
Colossal, seen of every land,
And keep the soldier firm, the statesman pure:
Till in all lands and thro' all human story
The path of duty be the way to glory:
And let the land whose hearths he saved from shame
For many and many an age proclaim
At civic revel and pomp and game,
And when the long-illumined cities flame,
Their ever-loyal iron leader's fame,
With honour, honour, honour, honour to him,
Eternal honour to his name.

IX

Peace, his triumph will be sung
By some yet unmoulded tongue
Far on in summers that we shall not see:
Peace, it is a day of pain
For one about whose patriarchal knee
Late the little children clung:
O peace, it is a day of pain
For one, upon whose hand and heart and brain
Once the weight and fate of Europe hung.
Ours the pain, be his the gain!
More than is of man's degree
Must be with us, watching here
At this, our great solemnity.
Whom we see not we revere;
We revere, and we refrain
From talk of battles loud and vain,
And brawling memories all too free
For such a wise humility
As befits a solemn fane:
We revere, and while we hear
The tides of Music's golden sea
Setting toward eternity,
Uplifted high in heart and hope are we,
Until we doubt not that for one so true
There must be other nobler work to do
Than when he fought at Waterloo,
And Victor he must ever be.
For tho' the Giant Ages heave the hill
And break the shore, and evermore
Make and break, and work their will;
Tho' world on world in myriad myriads roll
Round us, each with different powers,
And other forms of life than ours,
What know we greater than the soul?
On God and Godlike men we build our trust.

Hush, the Dead March wails in the people's ears:
The dark crowd moves, and there are sobs and tears:
The black earth yawns: the mortal disappears;
Ashes to ashes, dust to dust;
He is gone who seem'd so great.—
Gone; but nothing can bereave him
Of the force he made his own
Being here, and we believe him
Something far advanced in State,
And that he wears a truer crown
Than any wreath that man can weave him.
Speak no more of his renown,
Lay your earthly fancies down,
And in the vast cathedral leave him,
God accept him, Christ receive him.

1852

THE CHARGE OF THE LIGHT BRIGADE

I

Half a league, half a league,
Half a league onward,
All in the valley of Death
Rode the six hundred.
"Forward, the Light Brigade!
Charge for the guns!" he said:
Into the valley of Death
Rode the six hundred.

II

"Forward, the Light Brigade!"
Was there a man dismay'd?
Not tho' the soldier knew
Some one had blunder'd:
Theirs not to make reply,
Theirs not to reason why,
Theirs but to do and die:
Into the valley of Death
Rode the six hundred.

III

Cannon to right of them,
Cannon to left of them,
Cannon in front of them
Volley'd and thunder'd;
Storm'd at with shot and shell,
Boldly they rode and well,
Into the jaws of Death,
Into the mouth of Hell
Rode the six hundred.

IV

Flash'd all their sabres bare,
Flash'd as they turn'd in air
Sabring the gunners there,
Charging an army, while
All the world wonder'd:
Plunged in the battery-smoke
Right thro' the line they broke;
Cossack and Russian
Reel'd from the sabre-stroke
Shatter'd and sunder'd.
Then they rode back, but not,
Not the six hundred.

V

Cannon to right of them,
Cannon to left of them,
Cannon behind them
Volley'd and thunder'd;
Storm'd at with shot and shell,
While horse and hero fell,
They that had fought so well
Came thro' the jaws of Death,
Back from the mouth of Hell,
All that was left of them,
Left of six hundred.

VI

When can their glory fade?
O the wild charge they made!
All the world wonder'd.
Honour the charge they made!
Honour the Light Brigade,
Noble six hundred!

1854

THE DAISY

WRITTEN AT EDINBURGH

O love, what hours were thine and mine,
In lands of palm and southern pine;
In lands of palm, of orange-blossom,
Of olive, aloe, and maize and vine.

What Roman strength Turbia show'd
In ruin, by the mountain road;
How like a gem, beneath the city
Of little Monaco, basking, glow'd.

How richly down the rocky dell
The torrent vineyard streaming fell
To meet the sun and sunny waters,
That only heaved with a summer swell.

What slender campanili grew
By bays, the peacock's neck in hue;
Where, here and there, on sandy beaches
A milky-bell'd amaryllis blew.

How young Columbus seem'd to rove,
Yet present in his natal grove,
Now watching high on mountain cornice,
And steering, now, from a purple cove,

Now pacing mute by ocean's rim;
Till, in a narrow street and dim,
I stay'd the wheels at Cogoletto,
And drank, and loyally drank to him.

Nor knew we well what pleased us most,
Not the clipt palm of which they boast;
But distant colour, happy hamlet,
A moulder'd citadel on the coast,

Or tower, or high hill-convent, seen
A light amid its olives green;
Or olive-hoary cape in ocean;
Or rosy blossom in hot ravine,

Where oleanders flush'd the bed
Of silent torrents, gravel-spread;
And, crossing, oft we saw the glisten
Of ice, far up on a mountain head.

We loved that hall, tho' white and cold,
Those niched shapes of noble mould,
A princely people's awful princes,
The grave, severe Genovese of old.

At Florence too what golden hours,
In those long galleries, were ours;
What drives about the fresh Cascinè,
Or walks in Boboli's ducal bowers.

In bright vignettes, and each complete,
Of tower or duomo, sunny-sweet,
Or palace, how the city glitter'd,
Thro' cypress avenues, at our feet.

But when we crost the Lombard plain
Remember what a plague of rain;
Of rain at Reggio, rain at Parma;
At Lodi, rain, Piacenza, rain.

And stern and sad (so rare the smiles
Of sunlight) look'd the Lombard piles;
Porch-pillars on the lion resting,
And sombre, old, colonnaded aisles.

O Milan, O the chanting quires,
The giant windows' blazon'd fires,
The height, the space, the gloom, the glory!
A mount of marble, a hundred spires!

I climb'd the roofs at break of day;
Sun-smitten Alps before me lay.
I stood among the silent statues,
And statued pinnacles, mute as they.

How faintly-flush'd, how phantom-fair,
Was Monte Rosa, hanging there
A thousand shadowy-pencill'd valleys
And snowy dells in a golden air.

Remember how we came at last
To Como; shower and storm and blast
Had blown the lake beyond his limit,
And all was flooded; and how we past

From Como, when the light was gray,
And in my head, for half the day,
The rich Virgilian rustic measure
Of "Lari Maxume," all the way,

Like ballad-burthen music, kept,
As on the Lariano crept
To that fair port below the castle
Of Queen Theodolind, where we slept;

Or hardly slept, but watch'd awake
A cypress in the moonlight shake,
The moonlight touching o'er a terrace
One tall agavè above the lake.

What more? we took our last adieu,
And up the snowy Splügen drew,
But ere we reach'd the highest summit
I pluck'd a daisy, I gave it you.

It told of England then to me,
And now it tells of Italy.
O love, we two shall go no longer
To lands of summer across the sea;

So dear a life your arms enfold
Whose crying is a cry for gold:
Yet here to-night in this dark city,
When ill and weary, alone and cold,

I found, tho' crush'd to hard and dry,
This nurseling of another sky
Still in the little book you lent me,
And where you tenderly laid it by:

And I forgot the clouded Forth,
The gloom that saddens Heaven and Earth,
The bitter east, the misty summer
And gray metropolis of the North.

Perchance, to lull the throbs of pain,
Perchance, to charm a vacant brain,
Perchance, to dream you still beside me,
My fancy fled to the South again.

1855

THE SONG OF THE BROOK

(From *The Brook*)

I come from haunts of coot and hern,
I make a sudden sally,
And sparkle out among the fern,
To bicker down a valley.

By thirty hills I hurry down,
Or slip between the ridges,
By twenty thorps, a little town,
And half a hundred bridges.

Till last by Philip's farm I flow
To join the brimming river,
For men may come and men may go,
But I go on for ever.

I chatter over stony ways,
In little sharps and trebles,
I bubble into eddying bays,
I babble on the pebbles.

With many a curve my banks I fret
By many a field and fallow,
And many a fairy foreland set
With willow-weed and mallow.

I chatter, chatter, as I flow
To join the brimming river,
For men may come and men may go,
But I go on for ever.

I wind about, and in and out,
With here a blossom sailing,
And here and there a lusty trout,
And here and there a grayling,

And here and there a foamy flake
Upon me, as I travel
With many a silvery waterbreak
Above the golden gravel,

And draw them all along, and flow
To join the brimming river,
For men may come and men may go,
But I go on for ever.

I steal by lawns and grassy plots,
I slide by hazel covers;
I move the sweet forget-me-nots
That grow for happy lovers.

I slip, I slide, I gloom, I glance,
Among my skimming swallows;
I make the netted sunbeam dance
Against my sandy shallows.

I murmur under moon and stars
In brambly wildernesses;
I linger by my shingly bars;
I loiter round my cresses;

And out again I curve and flow
To join the brimming river,
For men may come and men may go,
But I go on for ever.

1855

MAUD; A MONODRAMA

Part I

I

I

I hate the dreadful hollow behind the little wood,
Its lips in the field above are dabbled with blood-red heath,
The red-ribb'd ledges drip with a silent horror of blood,
And Echo there, whatever is ask'd her, answers "Death."

II

For there in the ghastly pit long since a body was found,
His who had given me life—O father! O God! was it well?—
Mangled, and flatten'd, and crush'd, and dinted into the ground:
There yet lies the rock that fell with him when he fell.

III

Did he fling himself down? who knows? for a vast speculation had fail'd,
And ever he mutter'd and madden'd, and ever wann'd with despair,
And out he walk'd when the wind like a broken worldling wail'd,
And the flying gold of the ruin'd woodlands drove thro' the air.

IV

I remember the time, for the roots of my hair were stirr'd
By a shuffled step, by a dead weight trail'd, by a whisper'd fright,
And my pulses closed their gates with a shock on my heart as I heard
The shrill-edged shriek of a mother divide the shuddering night.

V

Villainy somewhere! whose? One says, we are villains all.
Not he: his honest fame should at least by me be maintained:
But that old man, now lord of the broad estate and the Hall,
Dropt off gorged from a scheme that had left us flaccid and drain'd.

VI

Why do they prate of the blessings of peace? we have made them a curse,
Pickpockets, each hand lusting for all that is not its own;
And lust of gain, in the spirit of Cain, is it better or worse
Than the heart of the citizen hissing in war on his own hearthstone?

VII

But these are the days of advance, the works of the men of mind,
When who but a fool would have faith in a tradesman's ware or his word?
Is it peace or war? Civil war, as I think, and that of a kind
The viler, as underhand, not openly bearing the sword.

VIII

Sooner or later I too may passively take the print
Of the golden age—why not? I have neither hope nor trust;
May make my heart as a millstone, set my face as a flint,
Cheat and be cheated, and die: who knows? we are ashes and dust.

Rossetti's Drawing of Tennyson Reading *Maud*. (See Appendix I.)

IX

Peace sitting under her olive, and slurring the days gone by,
When the poor are hovell'd and hustled together, each sex, like swine,
When only the ledger lives, and when only not all men lie;
Peace in her vineyard—yes!—but a company forges the wine.

X

And the vitriol madness flushes up in the ruffian's head,
Till the filthy by-lane rings to the yell of the trampled wife,
And chalk and alum and plaster are sold to the poor for bread,
And the spirit of murder works in the very means of life,

XI

And Sleep must lie down arm'd, for the villainous centre-bits
Grind on the wakeful ear in the hush of the moonless nights,
While another is cheating the sick of a few last gasps, as he sits
To pestle a poison'd poison behind his crimson lights.

XII

When a Mammonite mother kills her babe for a burial fee,
And Timour-Mammon grins on a pile of children's bones,
Is it peace or war? better, war! loud war by land and by sea,
War with a thousand battles, and shaking a hundred thrones.

XIII

For I trust if an enemy's fleet came yonder round by the hill,
And the rushing battle-bolt sang from the three-decker out of the foam,
That the smooth-faced snubnosed rogue would leap from his counter and till,
And strike, if he could, were it but with his cheating yardwand, home.——

XIV

What! am I raging alone as my father raged in his mood?
Must *I* too creep to the hollow and dash myself down and die
Rather than hold by the law that I made, nevermore to brood
On a horror of shatter'd limbs and a wretched swindler's lie?

XV

Would there be sorrow for *me?* there was *love* in the passionate shriek,
Love for the silent thing that had made false haste to the grave—
Wrapt in a cloak, as I saw him, and thought he would rise and speak
And rave at the lie and the liar, ah God, as he used to rave.

XVI

I am sick of the Hall and the hill, I am sick of the moor and the main.
Why should I stay? can a sweeter chance ever come to me here?
O having the nerves of motion as well as the nerves of pain,
Were it not wise if I fled from the place and the pit and the fear?

XVII

Workmen up at the Hall!—they are coming back from abroad;
The dark old place will be gilt by the touch of a millionaire:
I have heard, I know not whence, of the singular beauty of Maud;
I play'd with the girl when a child; she promised then to be fair.

XVIII

Maud with her venturous climbings and tumbles and childish escapes,
Maud the delight of the village, the ringing joy of the Hall,
Maud with her sweet purse-mouth when my father dangled the grapes,
Maud the beloved of my mother, the moon-faced darling of all,—

XIX

What is she now? My dreams are bad. She may bring me a curse.
No, there is fatter game on the moor; she will let me alone.
Thanks, for the fiend best knows whether woman or man be the worse.
I will bury myself in myself, and the Devil may pipe to his own.

II

Long have I sigh'd for a calm: God grant I may find it at last!
It will never be broken by Maud, she has neither savour nor salt,
But a cold and clear-cut face, as I found when her carriage past,
Perfectly beautiful: let it be granted her: where is the fault?
All that I saw (for her eyes were downcast, not to be seen)
Faultily faultless, icily regular, splendidly null,
Dead perfection, no more; nothing more, if it had not been
For a chance of travel, a paleness, an hour's defect of the rose,
Or an underlip, you may call it a little too ripe, too full,
Or the least little delicate aquiline curve in a sensitive nose,
From which I escaped heart-free, with the least little touch of spleen.

III

Cold and clear-cut face, why come you so cruelly meek,
Breaking a slumber in which all spleenful folly was drown'd,
Pale with the golden beam of an eyelash dead on the cheek,
Passionless, pale, cold face, star-sweet on a gloom profound;
Womanlike, taking revenge too deep for a transient wrong
Done but in thought to your beauty, and ever as pale as before
Growing and fading and growing upon me without a sound,
Luminous, gemlike, ghostlike, deathlike, half the night long
Growing and fading and growing, till I could bear it no more,
But arose, and all by myself in my own dark garden ground,
Listening now to the tide in its broad-flung shipwrecking roar,
Now to the scream of a madden'd beach dragg'd down by the wave,
Walk'd in a wintry wind by a ghastly glimmer, and found
The shining daffodil dead, and Orion low in his grave.

IV

I

A million emeralds break from the ruby-budded lime
In the little grove where I sit—ah, wherefore cannot I be
Like things of the season gay, like the bountiful season bland,
When the far-off sail is blown by the breeze of a softer clime,
Half-lost in the liquid azure bloom of a crescent of sea,
The silent sapphire-spangled marriage ring of the land?

II

Below me, there, is the village, and looks how quiet and small!
And yet bubbles o'er like a city, with gossip, scandal, and spite;
And Jack on his ale-house bench has as many lies as a Czar;
And here on the landward side, by a red rock, glimmers the Hall
And up in the high Hall-garden I see her pass like a light;
But sorrow seize me if ever that light be my leading star!

III

When have I bow'd to her father, the wrinkled head of the race?
I met her to-day with her brother, but not to her brother I bow'd:
I bow'd to his lady-sister as she rode by on the moor;
But the fire of a foolish pride flash'd over her beautiful face.
O child, you wrong your beauty, believe it, in being so proud;
Your father has wealth well-gotten, and I am nameless and poor.

IV

I keep but a man and a maid, ever ready to slander and steal;
I know it, and smile a hard-set smile, like a stoic, or like
A wiser epicurean, and let the world have its way:
For nature is one with rapine, a harm no preacher can heal;
The Mayfly is torn by the swallow, the sparrow spear'd by the shrike,
And the whole little wood where I sit is a world of plunder and prey.

V

We are puppets, Man in his pride, and Beauty fair in her flower;
Do we move ourselves, or are moved by an unseen hand at a game
That pushes us off from the board, and others ever succeed?
Ah yet, we cannot be kind to each other here for an hour;
We whisper, and hint, and chuckle, and grin at a brother's shame;
However we brave it out, we men are a little breed.

VI

A monstrous eft was of old the Lord and Master of Earth,
For him did his high sun flame, and his river billowing ran,
And he felt himself in his force to be Nature's crowning race.
As nine months go to the shaping an infant ripe for his birth,
So many a million of ages have gone to the making of man:
He now is first, but is he the last? is he not too base?

VII

The man of science himself is fonder of glory, and vain,
An eye well-practised in nature, a spirit bounded and poor;
The passionate heart of the poet is whirl'd into folly and vice.
I would not marvel at either, but keep a temperate brain;
For not to desire or admire, if a man could learn it, were more
Than to walk all day like the sultan of old in a garden of spice.

VIII

For the drift of the Maker is dark, an Isis hid by the veil.
Who knows the ways of the world, how God will bring them about?
Our planet is one, the suns are many, the world is wide.

Shall I weep if a Poland fall? shall I shriek if a Hungary fail?
Or an infant civilisation be ruled with rod or with knout?
I have not made the world, and He that made it will guide.

IX

Be mine a philosopher's life in the quiet woodland ways,
Where if I cannot be gay let a passionless peace be my lot,
Far-off from the clamour of liars belied in the hubbub of lies;
From the long-neck'd geese of the world that are ever hissing dispraise
Because their natures are little, and, whether he heed it or not,
Where each man walks with his head in a cloud of poisonous flies.

X

And most of all would I flee from the cruel madness of love,
The honey of poison-flowers and all the measureless ill.
Ah Maud, you milkwhite fawn, you are all unmeet for a wife.
Your mother is mute in her grave as her image in marble above;
Your father is ever in London, you wander about at your will;
You have but fed on the roses and lain in the lilies of life.

V

I

A voice by the cedar tree
In the meadow under the Hall!
She is singing an air that is known to me,
A passionate ballad gallant and gay,
A martial song like a trumpet's call!
Singing alone in the morning of life,
In the happy morning of life and of May,
Singing of men that in battle array,
Ready in heart and ready in hand,
March with banner and bugle and fife
To the death, for their native land.

II

Maud with her exquisite face,
And wild voice pealing up to the sunny sky,
And feet like sunny gems on an English green,
Maud in the light of her youth and her grace,
Singing of Death, and of Honour that cannot die,
Till I well could weep for a time so sordid and mean,
And myself so languid and base.

III

Silence, beautiful voice!
Be still, for you only trouble the mind
With a joy in which I cannot rejoice,
A glory I shall not find.
Still! I will hear you no more,
For your sweetness hardly leaves me a choice
But to move to the meadow and fall before
Her feet on the meadow grass, and adore,
Not her, who is neither courtly nor kind,
Not her, not her, but a voice.

VI

I

Morning arises stormy and pale,
No sun, but a wannish glare
In fold upon fold of hueless cloud,
And the budded peaks of the wood are bow'd
Caught and cuff'd by the gale:
I had fancied it would be fair.

II

Whom but Maud should I meet
Last night, when the sunset burn'd
On the blossom'd gable-ends
At the head of the village street,
Whom but Maud should I meet?
And she touch'd my hand with a smile so sweet,
She made me divine amends
For a courtesy not return'd.

III

And thus a delicate spark
Of glowing and growing light
Thro' the livelong hours of the dark

Kept itself warm in the heart of my dreams,
Ready to burst in a colour'd flame;
Till at last when the morning came
In a cloud, it faded, and seems
But an ashen-gray delight.

IV

What if with her sunny hair,
And smile as sunny as cold,
She meant to weave me a snare
Of some coquettish deceit,
Cleopatra-like as of old
To entangle me when we met,
To have her lion roll in a silken net
And fawn at a victor's feet.

V

Ah, what shall I be at fifty
Should Nature keep me alive,
If I find the world so bitter
When I am but twenty-five?
Yet, if she were not a cheat,
If Maud were all that she seem'd,
And her smile were all that I dream'd,
Then the world were not so bitter
But a smile could make it sweet.

VI

What if tho' her eye seem'd full
Of a kind intent to me,
What if that dandy-despot, he,
That jewell'd mass of millinery,
That oil'd and curl'd Assyrian Bull
Smelling of musk and of insolence,
Her brother, from whom I keep aloof,
Who wants the finer politic sense
To mask, tho' but in his own behoof,
With a glassy smile his brutal scorn—
What if he had told her yestermorn
How prettily for his own sweet sake
A face of tenderness might be feign'd,
And a moist mirage in desert eyes,
That so, when the rotten hustings shake
In another month to his brazen lies,
A wretched vote may be gain'd.

VII

For a raven ever croaks, at my side,
Keep watch and ward, keep watch and ward,
Or thou wilt prove their tool.
Yea, too, myself from myself I guard,
For often a man's own angry pride
Is cap and bells for a fool.

VIII

Perhaps the smile and tender tone
Came out of her pitying womanhood,
For am I not, am I not, here alone
So many a summer since she died,
My mother, who was so gentle and good?
Living alone in an empty house,
Here half-hid in the gleaming wood,
Where I hear the dead at midday moan,
And the shrieking rush of the wainscot mouse,
And my own sad name in corners cried,
When the shiver of dancing leaves is thrown
About its echoing chambers wide,
Till a morbid hate and horror have grown
Of a world in which I have hardly mixt,
And a morbid eating lichen fixt
On a heart half-turn'd to stone.

IX

O heart of stone, are you flesh, and caught
By that you swore to withstand?
For what was it else within me wrought
But, I fear, the new strong wine of love,
That made my tongue so stammer and trip
When I saw the treasured splendour, her hand,
Come sliding out of her sacred glove,
And the sunlight broke from her lip?

X

I have play'd with her when a child;
She remembers it now we meet.
Ah well, well, well, I *may* be beguiled
By some coquettish deceit.
Yet, if she were not a cheat,
If Maud were all that she seem'd,
And her smile had all that I dream'd,
Then the world were not so bitter
But a smile could make it sweet.

VII

I

Did I hear it half in a doze
  Long since, I know not where?
Did I dream it an hour ago,
  When asleep in this arm-chair?

II

Men were drinking together,
  Drinking and talking of me;
"Well, if it prove a girl, the boy
  Will have plenty: so let it be."

III

Is it an echo of something
 Read with a boy's delight,
Viziers nodding together
 In some Arabian night?

IV

Strange, that I hear two men,
 Somewhere, talking of me;
"Well, if it prove a girl, my boy
 Will have plenty: so let it be."

VIII

She came to the village church,
And sat by a pillar alone;
An angel watching an urn
Wept over her, carved in stone;
And once, but once, she lifted her eyes,
And suddenly, sweetly, strangely blush'd
To find they were met by my own;
And suddenly, sweetly, my heart beat stronger
And thicker, until I heard no longer
The snowy-banded, dilettante,
Delicate-handed priest intone;
And thought, is it pride, and mused and sigh'd
"No surely, now it cannot be pride."

IX

I was walking a mile,
More than a mile from the shore,
The sun look'd out with a smile
Betwixt the cloud and the moor
And riding at set of day
Over the dark moor land,
Rapidly riding far away,
She waved to me with her hand.
There were two at her side,
Something flash'd in the sun,
Down by the hill I saw them ride,
In a moment they were gone:
Like a sudden spark
Struck vainly in the night,
Then returns the dark
With no more hope of light.

X

I

Sick, am I sick of a jealous dread?
Was not one of the two at her side
This new-made lord, whose splendour plucks
The slavish hat from the villager's head?
Whose old grandfather has lately died,
Gone to a blacker pit, for whom
Grimy nakedness dragging his trucks
And laying his trams in a poison'd gloom
Wrought, till he crept from a gutted mine
Master of half a servile shire,
And left his coal all turn'd into gold
To a grandson, first of his noble line,
Rich in the grace all women desire,
Strong in the power that all men adore,
And simper and set their voices lower,
And soften as if to a girl, and hold
Awe-stricken breaths at a work divine,
Seeing his gewgaw castle shine,
New as his title, built last year,
There amid perky larches and pine,
And over the sullen-purple moor
(Look at it) pricking a cockney ear.

II

What, has he found my jewel out?
For one of the two that rode at her side
Bound for the Hall, I am sure was he:
Bound for the Hall, and I think for a bride.
Blithe would her brother's acceptance be.
Maud could be gracious too, no doubt
To a lord, a captain, a padded shape,
A bought commission, a waxen face,
A rabbit mouth that is ever agape—
Bought? what is it he cannot buy?
And therefore splenetic, personal, base,
A wounded thing with a rancorous cry,
At war with myself and a wretched race,
Sick, sick to the heart of life, am I.

III

Last week came one to the county town,
To preach our poor little army down,
And play the game of the despot kings,
Tho' the state has done it and thrice as well:
This broad-brimm'd hawker of holy things,
Whose ear is cramm'd with his cotton, and
 rings
Even in dreams to the chink of his pence,
This huckster put down war! can he tell
Whether war be a cause or a consequence?
Put down the passions that make earth Hell!
Down with ambition, avarice, pride,
Jealousy, down! cut off from the mind
The bitter springs of anger and fear;

Down too, down at your own fireside,
With the evil tongue and the evil ear,
For each is at war with mankind.

IV

I wish I could hear again
The chivalrous battle-song
That she warbled alone in her joy!
I might persuade myself then
She would not do herself this great wrong,
To take a wanton dissolute boy
For a man and leader of men.

V

Ah God, for a man with heart, head, hand,
Like some of the simple great ones gone
For ever and ever by,
One still strong man in a blatant land,
Whatever they call him, what care I,
Aristocrat, democrat, autocrat—one
Who can rule and dare not lie.

VI

And ah for a man to arise in me,
That the man I am may cease to be!

XI

I

O let the solid ground
  Not fail beneath my feet
Before my life has found
  What some have found so sweet;
Then let come what come may,
What matter if I go mad,
I shall have had my day.

II

Let the sweet heavens endure,
  Not close and darken above me
Before I am quite quite sure
  That there is one to love me;
Then let come what come may
To a life that has been so sad,
I shall have had my day.

XII

I

Birds in the high Hall-garden
  When twilight was falling,
Maud, Maud, Maud, Maud,
  They were crying and calling.

II

Where was Maud? in our wood;
  And I, who else, was with her,
Gathering woodland lilies,
  Myriads blow together.

III

Birds in our wood sang
  Ringing thro' the valleys,
Maud is here, here, here
  In among the lilies.

IV

I kiss'd her slender hand,
  She took the kiss sedately;
Maud is not seventeen,
  But she is tall and stately.

V

I to cry out on pride
  Who have won her favour!
O Maud were sure of Heaven
  If lowliness could save her.

VI

I know the way she went
  Home with her maiden posy,
For her feet have touch'd the meadows
  And left the daisies rosy.

VII

Birds in the high Hall-garden
  Were crying and calling to her,
Where is Maud, Maud, Maud?
  One is come to woo her.

VIII

Look, a horse at the door,
  And little King Charley snarling,
Go back, my lord, across the moor,
  You are not her darling.

XIII

I

Scorn'd, to be scorn'd by one that I scorn,
Is that a matter to make me fret?
That a calamity hard to be borne?
Well, he may live to hate me yet.
Fool that I am to be vext with his pride!
I past him, I was crossing his lands;
He stood on the path a little aside;
His face, as I grant, in spite of spite,

Has a broad-blown comeliness, red and white,
And six feet two, as I think, he stands;
But his essences turn'd the live air sick,
And barbarous opulence jewel-thick
Sunn'd itself on his breast and his hands.

II

Who shall call me ungentle, unfair,
I long'd so heartily then and there
To give him the grasp of fellowship;
But while I past he was humming an air,
Stopt, and then with a riding whip
Leisurely tapping a glossy boot,
And curving a contumelious lip,
Gorgonised me from head to foot
With a stony British stare.

III

Why sits he here in his father's chair?
That old man never comes to his place:
Shall I believe him ashamed to be seen?
For only once, in the village street,
Last year, I caught a glimpse of his face,
A gray old wolf and a lean.
Scarcely, now, would I call him a cheat;
For then, perhaps, as a child of deceit,
She might by a true descent be untrue;
And Maud is as true as Maud is sweet:
Tho' I fancy her sweetness only due
To the sweeter blood by the other side;
Her mother has been a thing complete,
However she came to be so allied.
And fair without, faithful within,
Maud to him is nothing akin:
Some peculiar mystic grace
Made her only the child of her mother,
And heap'd the whole inherited sin
On that huge scapegoat of the race,
All, all upon the brother.

IV

Peace, angry spirit, and let him be!
Has not his sister smiled on me?

XIV

I

Maud has a garden of roses
And lilies fair on a lawn;
There she walks in her state
And tends upon bed and bower,
And thither I climb'd at dawn
And stood by her garden-gate;
A lion ramps at the top,
He is claspt by a passion-flower.

II

Maud's own little oak-room
(Which Maud, like a precious stone
Set in the heart of the carven gloom,
Lights with herself, when alone
She sits by her music and books
And her brother lingers late
With a roystering company) looks
Upon Maud's own garden-gate:
And I thought as I stood, if a hand as white
As ocean-foam in the moon, were laid
On the hasp of the window, and my Delight
Had a sudden desire, like a glorious ghost, to glide,
Like a beam of the seventh Heaven, down to my side,
There were but a step to be made.

III

The fancy flatter'd my mind,
And again seem'd overbold;
Now I thought that she cared for me,
Now I thought she was kind
Only because she was cold.

IV

I heard no sound where I stood
But the rivulet on from the lawn
Running down to my own dark wood;
Or the voice of the long sea-wave as it swell'd
Now and then in the dim-gray dawn;
But I look'd, and round, all round the house I beheld
The death-white curtain drawn;
Felt a horror over me creep,
Prickle my skin and catch my breath,
Knew that the death-white curtain meant but sleep,
Yet I shudder'd and thought like a fool of the sleep of death.

XV

So dark a mind within me dwells,
And I make myself such evil cheer,
That if *I* be dear to some one else,

Then some one else may have much to fear;
But if *I* be dear to some one else,
Then I should be to myself more dear.
Shall I not take care of all that I think,
Yea ev'n of wretched meat and drink,
If I be dear,
If I be dear to some one else.

XVI

I

This lump of earth has left his estate
The lighter by the loss of his weight;
And so that he find what he went to seek,
And fulsome Pleasure clog him, and drown
His heart in the gross mud-honey of town,
He may stay for a year who has gone for a week:
But this is the day when I must speak,
And I see my Oread coming down,
O this is the day!
O beautiful creature, what am I
That I dare to look her way;
Think I may hold dominion sweet,
Lord of the pulse that is lord of her breast,
And dream of her beauty with tender dread,
From the delicate Arab arch of her feet
To the grace that, bright and light as the crest
Of a peacock, sits on her shining head,
And she knows it not: O, if she knew it,
To know her beauty might half undo it.
I know it the one bright thing to save
My yet young life in the wilds of Time,
Perhaps from madness, perhaps from crime,
Perhaps from a selfish grave.

II

What, if she be fasten'd to this fool lord,
Dare I bid her abide by her word?
Should I love her so well if she
Had given her word to a thing so low?
Shall I love her as well if she
Can break her word were it even for me?
I trust that it is not so.

III

Catch not my breath, O clamorous heart,
Let not my tongue be a thrall to my eye,
For I must tell her before we part,
I must tell her, or die.

XVII

Go not, happy day,
From the shining fields,
Go not, happy day,
Till the maiden yields.
Rosy is the West,
Rosy is the South,
Roses are her cheeks,
And a rose her mouth
When the happy Yes
Falters from her lips,
Pass and blush the news
Over glowing ships;
Over blowing seas,
Over seas at rest,
Pass the happy news,
Blush it thro' the West;
Till the red man dance
By his red cedar-tree,
And the red man's babe
Leap, beyond the sea.
Blush from West to East,
Blush from East to West,
Till the West is East,
Blush it thro' the West.
Rosy is the West,
Rosy is the South,
Roses are her cheeks,
And a rose her mouth.

XVIII

I

I have led her home, my love, my only friend.
There is none like her, none.
And never yet so warmly ran my blood
And sweetly, on and on
Calming itself to the long-wish'd-for end,
Full to the banks, close on the promised good.

II

None like her, none.
Just now the dry-tongued laurels' pattering talk
Seem'd her light foot along the garden walk,
And shook my heart to think she comes once more;
But even then I heard her close the door,
The gates of Heaven are closed, and she is gone.

III

There is none like her, none.
Nor will be when our summers have deceased.
O, art thou sighing for Lebanon
In the long breeze that streams to thy delicious East,
Sighing for Lebanon,
Dark cedar, tho' thy limbs have here increased,
Upon a pastoral slope as fair,
And looking to the South, and fed
With honey'd rain and delicate air,
And haunted by the starry head
Of her whose gentle will has changed my fate,
And made my life a perfumed altar-flame;
And over whom thy darkness must have spread
With such delight as theirs of old, thy great
Forefathers of the thornless garden, there
Shadowing the snow-limb'd Eve from whom she came.

IV

Here will I lie, while these long branches sway,
And you fair stars that crown a happy day
Go in and out as if at merry play,
Who am no more so all forlorn,
As when it seem'd far better to be born
To labour and the mattock-harden'd hand,
Than nursed at ease and brought to understand
A sad astrology, the boundless plan
That makes you tyrants in your iron skies,
Innumerable, pitiless, passionless eyes,
Cold fires, yet with power to burn and brand
His nothingness into man.

V

But now shine on, and what care I,
Who in this stormy gulf have found a pearl
The countercharm of space and hollow sky,
And do accept my madness, and would die
To save from some slight shame one simple girl.

VI

Would die; for sullen-seeming Death may give
More life to Love than is or ever was
In our low world, where yet 'tis sweet to live.
Let no one ask me how it came to pass;
It seems that I am happy, that to me
A livelier emerald twinkles in the grass,
A purer sapphire melts into the sea.

VII

Not die; but live a life of truest breath,
And teach true life to fight with mortal wrongs.
O, why should Love, like men in drinking-songs,
Spice his fair banquet with the dust of death?
Make answer, Maud my bliss,
Maud made my Maud by that long loving kiss,
Life of my life, wilt thou not answer this?
"The dusky strand of Death inwoven here
With dear Love's tie, makes Love himself more dear."

VIII

Is that enchanted moan only the swell
Of the long waves that roll in yonder bay?
And hark the clock within, the silver knell
Of twelve sweet hours that past in bridal white,
And died to live, long as my pulses play;
But now by this my love has closed her sight
And given false death her hand, and stol'n away
To dreamful wastes where footless fancies dwell
Among the fragments of the golden day.
May nothing there her maiden grace affright!
Dear heart, I feel with thee the drowsy spell.
My bride to be, my evermore delight,
My own heart's heart, my ownest own, farewell;
It is but for a little space I go:
And ye meanwhile far over moor and fell
Beat to the noiseless music of the night!
Has our whole earth gone nearer to the glow
Of your soft splendours that you look so bright?
I have climb'd nearer out of lonely Hell.
Beat, happy stars, timing with things below,
Beat with my heart more blest than heart can tell,
Blest, but for some dark undercurrent woe
That seems to draw—but it shall not be so:
Let all be well, be well.

XIX

I

Her brother is coming back to-night,
Breaking up my dream of delight.

II

My dream? do I dream of bliss?
I have walk'd awake with Truth.
O when did a morning shine
So rich in atonement as this
For my dark-dawning youth,
Darken'd watching a mother decline
And that dead man at her heart and mine:
For who was left to watch her but I?
Yet so did I let my freshness die.

III

I trust that I did not talk
To gentle Maud in our walk
(For often in lonely wanderings
I have cursed him even to lifeless things)
But I trust that I did not talk,
Not touch on her father's sin:
I am sure I did but speak
Of my mother's faded cheek
When it slowly grew so thin,
That I felt she was slowly dying
Vext with lawyers and harass'd with debt:
For how often I caught her with eyes all wet,
Shaking her head at her son and sighing
A world of trouble within!

IV

And Maud too, Maud was moved
To speak of the mother she loved
As one scarce less forlorn,
Dying abroad and it seems apart
From him who had ceased to share her heart,
And ever mourning over the feud,
The household Fury sprinkled with blood
By which our houses are torn:
How strange was what she said,
When only Maud and the brother
Hung over her dying bed—
That Maud's dark father and mine
Had bound us one to the other,
Betrothed us over their wine,
On the day when Maud was born;
Seal'd her mine from her first sweet breath.
Mine, mine by a right, from birth till death.
Mine, mine—our fathers have sworn.

V

But the true blood spilt had in it a heat
To dissolve the precious seal on a bond,
That, if left uncancell'd, had been so sweet:
And none of us thought of a something beyond,
A desire that awoke in the heart of the child,
As it were a duty done to the tomb,
To be friends for her sake, to be reconciled;
And I was cursing them and my doom,
And letting a dangerous thought run wild
While often abroad in the fragrant gloom
Of foreign churches—I see her there,
Bright English lily, breathing a prayer
To be friends, to be reconciled!

VI

But then what a flint is he!
Abroad, at Florence, at Rome,
I find whenever she touch'd on me
This brother had laugh'd her down,
And at last, when each came home,
He had darken'd into a frown,
Chid her, and forbid her to speak
To me, her friend of the years before;
And this was what had redden'd her cheek
When I bow'd to her on the moor.

VII

Yet Maud, altho' not blind
To the faults of his heart and mind,
I see she cannot but love him,
And says he is rough but kind,
And wishes me to approve him,
And tells me, when she lay
Sick once, with a fear of worse,
That he left his wine and horses and play,
Sat with her, read to her, night and day,
And tended her like a nurse.

VIII

Kind? but the deathbed desire
Spurn'd by this heir of the liar—
Rough but kind? yet I know
He has plotted against me in this,
That he plots against me still.
Kind to Maud? that were not amiss.
Well, rough but kind; why let it be so:
For shall not Maud have her will?

IX

For, Maud, so tender and true,
As long as my life endures
I feel I shall owe you a debt,
That I never can hope to pay;
And if ever I should forget

That I owe this debt to you
And for your sweet sake to yours;
O then, what then shall I say?—
If ever I *should* forget,
May God make me more wretched
Than ever I have been yet!

X

So now I have sworn to bury
All this dead body of hate,
I feel so free and so clear
By the loss of that dead weight,
That I should grow light-headed, I fear,
Fantastically merry;
But that her brother comes, like a blight
On my fresh hope, to the Hall to-night.

XX

I

Strange, that I felt so gay,
Strange, that *I* tried to-day
To beguile her melancholy;
The Sultan, as we name him,—
She did not wish to blame him—
But he vext her and perplext her
With his worldly talk and folly:
Was it gentle to reprove her
For stealing out of view
From a little lazy lover
Who but claims her as his due?
Or for chilling his caresses
By the coldness of her manners,
Nay, the plainness of her dresses?
Now I know her but in two,
Nor can pronounce upon it
If one should ask me whether
The habit, hat, and feather,
Or the frock and gipsy bonnet
Be the neater and completer;
For nothing can be sweeter
Than maiden Maud in either.

II

But to-morrow, if we live,
Our ponderous squire will give
A grand political dinner
To half the squirelings near;
And Maud will wear her jewels,
And the bird of prey will hover,
And the titmouse hope to win her
With his chirrup at her ear.

III

A grand political dinner
To the men of many acres,
A gathering of the Tory,
A dinner and then a dance
For the maids and marriage-makers,
And every eye but mine will glance
At Maud in all her glory.

IV

For I am not invited,
But, with the Sultan's pardon,
I am all as well delighted,
For I know her own rose-garden,
And mean to linger in it
Till the dancing will be over;
And then, oh then, come out to me
For a minute, but for a minute,
Come out to your own true lover,
That your true lover may see
Your glory also, and render
All homage to his own darling,
Queen Maud in all her splendour.

XXI

Rivulet crossing my ground,
And bringing me down from the Hall
This garden-rose that I found,
Forgetful of Maud and me,
And lost in trouble and moving round
Here at the head of a tinkling fall,
And trying to pass to the sea;
O Rivulet, born at the Hall,
My Maud has sent it by thee
(If I read her sweet will right)
On a blushing mission to me,
Saying in odour and colour, "Ah, be
Among the roses to-night."

XXII

I

Come into the garden, Maud,
For the black bat, night, has flown,
Come into the garden, Maud,
I am here at the gate alone;
And the woodbine spices are wafted abroad,
And the musk of the rose is blown.

II

For a breeze of morning moves,
And the planet of Love is on high,
Beginning to faint in the light that she loves
On a bed of daffodil sky,
To faint in the light of the sun she loves,
To faint in his light, and to die.

III

All night have the roses heard
The flute, violin, bassoon;
All night has the casement jessamine stirr'd
To the dancers dancing in tune;
Till a silence fell with the waking bird,
And a hush with the setting moon.

IV

I said to the lily, "There is but one
With whom she has heart to be gay.
When will the dancers leave her alone?
She is weary of dance and play."
Now half to the setting moon are gone,
And half to the rising day;
Low on the sand and loud on the stone
The last wheel echoes away.

V

I said to the rose, "The brief night goes
In babble and revel and wine.
O young lord-lover, what sighs are those,
For one that will never be thine?
But mine, but mine," so I sware to the rose,
"For ever and ever, mine."

VI

And the soul of the rose went into my blood,
As the music clash'd in the hall;
And long by the garden lake I stood,
For I heard your rivulet fall
From the lake to the meadow and on to the wood,
Our wood, that is dearer than all;

VII

From the meadow your walks have left so sweet
That whenever a March-wind sighs
He sets the jewel-print of your feet
In violets blue as your eyes,
To the woody hollows in which we meet
And the valleys of Paradise.

VIII

The slender acacia would not shake
One long milk-bloom on the tree;
The white lake-blossom fell into the lake
As the pimpernel dozed on the lea;
But the rose was awake all night for your sake,
Knowing your promise to me;
The lilies and roses were all awake,
They sigh'd for the dawn and thee.

IX

Queen rose of the rosebud garden of girls,
Come hither, the dances are done,
In gloss of satin and glimmer of pearls,
Queen lily and rose in one;
Shine out, little head, sunning over with curls,
To the flowers, and be their sun.

X

There has fallen a splendid tear
From the passion-flower at the gate.
She is coming, my dove, my dear;
She is coming, my life, my fate;
The red rose cries, "She is near, she is near;"
And the white rose weeps, "She is late;"
The larkspur listens, "I hear, I hear;"
And the lily whispers, "I wait."

XI

She is coming, my own, my sweet;
Were it ever so airy a tread,
My heart would hear her and beat,
Were it earth in an earthy bed;
My dust would hear her and beat,
Had I lain for a century dead;
Would start and tremble under her feet,
And blossom in purple and red.

Part II

I

I

"The fault was mine, the fault was mine"—
Why am I sitting here so stunn'd and still,
Plucking the harmless wild-flower on the hill?—
It is this guilty hand!—
And there rises ever a passionate cry
From underneath in the darkening land—
What is it, that has been done?
O dawn of Eden bright over earth and sky,

The fires of Hell brake out of thy rising sun,
The fires of Hell and of Hate;
For she, sweet soul, had hardly spoken a word,
When her brother ran in his rage to the gate,
He came with the babe-faced lord;
Heap'd on her terms of disgrace,
And while she wept, and I strove to be cool,
He fiercely gave me the lie,
Till I with as fierce an anger spoke,
And he struck me, madman, over the face,
Struck me before the languid fool,
Who was gaping and grinning by:
Struck for himself an evil stroke;
Wrought for his house an irredeemable woe;
For front to front in an hour we stood,
And a million horrible bellowing echoes broke
From the red-ribb'd hollow behind the wood,
And thunder'd up into Heaven the Christless code,
That must have life for a blow.
Ever and ever afresh they seem'd to grow.
Was it he lay there with a fading eye?
"The fault was mine," he whisper'd, "fly!"
Then glided out of the joyous wood
The ghastly Wraith of one that I know;
And there rang on a sudden a passionate cry,
A cry for a brother's blood:
It will ring in my heart and my ears, till I die, till I die.

II

Is it gone? my pulses beat—
What was it? a lying trick of the brain?
Yet I thought I saw her stand,
A shadow there at my feet,
High over the shadowy land.
It is gone; and the heavens fall in a gentle rain,
When they should burst and drown with deluging storms
The feeble vassals of wine and anger and lust,
The little hearts that know not how to forgive:
Arise, my God, and strike, for we hold Thee just,
Strike dead the whole weak race of venomous worms,
That sting each other here in the dust;
We are not worthy to live.

II

I

See what a lovely shell,
Small and pure as a pearl,
Lying close to my foot,
Frail, but a work divine,
Made so fairily well
With delicate spire and whorl,
How exquisitely minute,
A miracle of design!

II

What is it? a learned man
Could give it a clumsy name.
Let him name it who can,
The beauty would be the same.

III

The tiny cell is forlorn,
Void of the little living will
That made it stir on the shore.
Did he stand at the diamond door
Of his house in a rainbow frill?
Did he push, when he was uncurl'd,
A golden foot or a fairy horn
Thro' his dim water-world?

IV

Slight, to be crush'd with a tap
Of my finger-nail on the sand,
Small, but a work divine,
Frail, but of force to withstand,
Year upon year, the shock
Of cataract seas that snap
The three decker's oaken spine
Athwart the ledges of rock,
Here on the Breton strand!

V

Breton, not Briton; here
Like a shipwreck'd man on a coast
Of ancient fable and fear—
Plagued with a flitting to and fro,
A disease, a hard mechanic ghost
That never came from on high
Nor ever arose from below,
But only moves with the moving eye,
Flying along the land and the main—
Why should it look like Maud?
Am I to be overawed
By what I cannot but know
Is a juggle born of the brain?

VI

Back from the Breton coast,
Sick of a nameless fear,
Back to the dark sea-line
Looking, thinking of all I have lost;
An old song vexes my ear;
But that of Lamech is mine.

VII

For years, a measureless ill,
For years, for ever, to part—
But she, she would love me still;
And as long, O God, as she
Have a grain of love for me,
So long, no doubt, no doubt,
Shall I nurse in my dark heart,
However weary, a spark of will
Not to be trampled out.

VIII

Strange, that the mind, when fraught
With a passion so intense
One would think that it well
Might drown all life in the eye,—
That it should, by being so overwrought,
Suddenly strike on a sharper sense
For a shell, or a flower, little things
Which else would have been past by!
And now I remember, I,
When he lay dying there,
I noticed one of his many rings
(For he had many, poor worm) and thought
It is his mother's hair.

IX

Who knows if he be dead?
Whether I need have fled?
Am I guilty of blood?
However this may be,
Comfort her, comfort her, all things good,
While I am over the sea!
Let me and my passionate love go by,
But speak to her all things holy and high,
Whatever happen to me!
Me and my harmful love go by;
But come to her waking, find her asleep,
Powers of the height, Powers of the deep,
And comfort her tho' I die.

III

Courage, poor heart of stone!
I will not ask thee why
Thou canst not understand
That thou art left for ever alone:
Courage, poor stupid heart of stone.—
Or if I ask thee why,
Care not thou to reply:
She is but dead, and the time is at hand
When thou shalt more than die.

IV

I

O that 'twere possible
After long grief and pain
To find the arms of my true love
Round me once again!

II

When I was wont to meet her
In the silent woody places
By the home that gave me birth,
We stood tranced in long embraces
Mixt with kisses sweeter sweeter
Than anything on earth.

III

A shadow flits before me,
Not thou, but like to thee:
Ah Christ, that it were possible
For one short hour to see
The souls we loved, that they might
tell us
What and where they be.

IV

It leads me forth at evening,
It lightly winds and steals
In a cold white robe before me,
When all my spirit reels
At the shouts, the leagues of lights,
And the roaring of the wheels.

V

Half the night I waste in sighs,
Half in dreams I sorrow after
The delight of early skies;
In a wakeful doze I sorrow
For the hand, the lips, the eyes,
For the meeting of the morrow,
The delight of happy laughter,
The delight of low replies.

VI

'Tis a morning pure and sweet,
And a dewy splendour falls
On the little flower that clings
To the turrets and the walls;
'Tis a morning pure and sweet,
And the light and shadow fleet;
She is walking in the meadow,
And the woodland echo rings;
In a moment we shall meet;
She is singing in the meadow
And the rivulet at her feet
Ripples on in light and shadow
To the ballad that she sings.

VII

Do I hear her sing as of old,
My bird with the shining head,
My own dove with the tender eye?
But there rings on a sudden a passionate cry,
There is some one dying or dead,
And a sullen thunder is roll'd;
For a tumult shakes the city,
And I wake, my dream is fled;
In the shuddering dawn, behold,
Without knowledge, without pity,
By the curtains of my bed
That abiding phantom cold.

VIII

Get thee hence, nor come again,
Mix not memory with doubt,
Pass, thou deathlike type of pain,
Pass and cease to move about!
'Tis the blot upon the brain
That *will* show itself without.

IX

Then I rise, the eave-drops fall,
And the yellow vapours choke
The great city sounding wide;
The day comes, a dull red ball
Wrapt in drifts of lurid smoke
On the misty river-tide.

X

Thro' the hubbub of the market
I steal, a wasted frame;
It crosses here, it crosses there,
Thro' all that crowd confused and loud,
The shadow still the same;
And on my heavy eyelids
My anguish hangs like shame.

XI

Alas for her that met me,
That heard me softly call,
Came glimmering thro' the laurels
At the quiet evenfall,
In the garden by the turrets
Of the old manorial hall.

XII

Would the happy spirit descend,
From the realms of light and song,
In the chamber or the street,
As she looks among the blest,
Should I fear to greet my friend
Or to say "Forgive the wrong,"
Or to ask her, "Take me, sweet,
To the regions of thy rest"?

XIII

But the broad light glares and beats,
And the shadow flits and fleets
And will not let me be;
And I loathe the squares and streets,
And the faces that one meets,
Hearts with no love for me:
Always I long to creep
Into some still cavern deep,
There to weep, and weep, and weep
My whole soul out to thee.

V

I

Dead, long dead,
Long dead!
And my heart is a handful of dust,
And the wheels go over my head,
And my bones are shaken with pain,
For into a shallow grave they are thrust,
Only a yard beneath the street,
And the hoofs of the horses beat, beat,
The hoofs of the horses beat,
Beat into my scalp and my brain,
With never an end to the stream of passing feet,
Driving, hurrying, marrying, burying,
Clamour and rumble, and ringing and clatter,
And here beneath it is all as bad,
For I thought the dead had peace, but it is not so;
To have no peace in the grave, is that not sad?

But up and down and to and fro,
Ever about me the dead men go;
And then to hear a dead man chatter
Is enough to drive one mad.

II

Wretchedest age, since Time began,
They cannot even bury a man;
And tho' we paid our tithes in the days that are gone,
Not a bell was rung, not a prayer was read;
It is that which makes us loud in the world of the dead;
There is none that does his work, not one;
A touch of their office might have sufficed,
But the churchmen fain would kill their church,
As the churches have kill'd their Christ.

III

See, there is one of us sobbing,
No limit to his distress;
And another, a lord of all things, praying
To his own great self, as I guess;
And another, a statesman there, betraying
His party-secret, fool, to the press;
And yonder a vile physician, blabbing
The case of his patient—all for what?
To tickle the maggot born in an empty head,
And wheedle a world that loves him not,
For it is but a world of the dead.

IV

Nothing but idiot gabble!
For the prophecy given of old
And then not understood,
Has come to pass as foretold;
Not let any man think for the public good,
But babble, merely for babble.
For I never whisper'd a private affair
Within the hearing of cat or mouse,
No, not to myself in the closet alone,
But I heard it shouted at once from the top of the house;
Everything came to be known.
Who told *him* we were there?

V

Not that gray old wolf, for he came not back
From the wilderness, full of wolves, where he used to lie;
He has gather'd the bones for his o'ergrown whelp to crack;
Crack them now for yourself, and howl, and die.

VI

Prophet, curse me the blabbing lip,
And curse me the British vermin, the rat;
I know not whether he came in the Hanover ship,
But I know that he lies and listens mute
In an ancient mansion's crannies and holes:
Arsenic, arsenic, sure, would do it,
Except that now we poison our babes, poor souls!
It is all used up for that.

VII

Tell him now: she is standing here at my head;
Not beautiful now, not even kind;
He may take her now; for she never speaks her mind,
But is ever the one thing silent here.
She is not *of* us, as I divine;
She comes from another stiller world of the dead,
Stiller, not fairer than mine.

VIII

But I know where a garden grows,
Fairer than aught in the world beside,
All made up of the lily and rose
That blow by night, when the season is good,
To the sound of dancing music and flutes:
It is only flowers, they had no fruits,
And I almost fear they are not roses, but blood;
For the keeper was one, so full of pride,
He linkt a dead man there to a spectral bride;
For he, if he had not been a Sultan of brutes,
Would he have that hole in his side?

IX

But what will the old man say?
He laid a cruel snare in a pit
To catch a friend of mine one stormy day;
Yet now I could even weep to think of it;

Robert & Elizabeth Barrett Browning
from
A Tennyson

Thursday, September 27.
13 Dorset St Manchester Sq.

MAUD,

AND OTHER POEMS.

A Presentation Copy of *Maud*. (See Appendix I.)

For what will the old man say
When he comes to the second corpse in the pit?

X

Friend, to be struck by the public foe,
Then to strike him and lay him low,
That were a public merit, far,
Whatever the Quaker holds, from sin;
But the red life spilt for a private blow—
I swear to you, lawful and lawless war
Are scarcely even akin.

XI

O me, why have they not buried me deep enough?
Is it kind to have made me a grave so rough,
Me, that was never a quiet sleeper?
Maybe still I am but half-dead;
Then I cannot be wholly dumb;
I will cry to the steps above my head
And somebody, surely, some kind heart will come
To bury me, bury me
Deeper, ever so little deeper.

Part III

VI

I

My life has crept so long on a broken wing
Thro' cells of madness, haunts of horror and fear,
That I come to be grateful at last for a little thing:
My mood is changed, for it fell at a time of year
When the face of night is fair on the dewy downs,
And the shining daffodil dies, and the Charioteer
And starry Gemini hang like glorious crowns
Over Orion's grave low down in the west,
That like a silent lightning under the stars
She seem'd to divide in a dream from a band of the blest,
And spoke of a hope for the world in the coming wars—
"And in that hope, dear soul, let trouble have rest,
Knowing I tarry for thee," and pointed to Mars
As he glow'd like a ruddy shield on the Lion's breast.

II

And it was but a dream, yet it yielded a dear delight
To have look'd, tho' but in a dream, upon eyes so fair,
That had been in a weary world my one thing bright;
And it was but a dream, yet it lighten'd my despair
When I thought that a war would arise in defence of the right,
That an iron tyranny now should bend or cease,
The glory of manhood stand on his ancient height,
Nor Britain's one sole God be the millionaire:
No more shall commerce be all in all, and Peace
Pipe on her pastoral hillock a languid note,
And watch her harvest ripen, her herd increase,
Nor the cannon-bullet rust on a slothful shore,
And the cobweb woven across the cannon's throat
Shall shake its threaded tears in the wind no more.

III

And as months ran on and rumour of battle grew,
"It is time, it is time, O passionate heart," said I
(For I cleaved to a cause that I felt to be pure and true),

"It is time, O passionate heart and morbid eye,
That old hysterical mock-disease should die."
And I stood on a giant deck and mix'd my breath
With a loyal people shouting a battle cry,
Till I saw the dreary phantom arise and fly
Far into the North, and battle, and seas of death.

IV

Let it go or stay, so I wake to the higher aims
Of a land that has lost for a little her lust of gold,
And love of a peace that was full of wrongs and shames,
Horrible, hateful, monstrous, not to be told;
And hail once more to the banner of battle unroll'd!
Tho' many a light shall darken, and many shall weep
For those that are crush'd in the clash of jarring claims,
Yet God's just wrath shall be wreak'd on a giant liar;
And many a darkness into the light shall leap,
And shine in the sudden making of splendid names,
And noble thought be freër under the sun,
And the heart of a people beat with one desire;
For the peace, that I deem'd no peace, is over and done,
And now by the side of the Black and the Baltic deep,
And deathful-grinning mouths of the fortress, flames
The blood-red blossom of war with a heart of fire.

V

Let it flame or fade, and the war roll down like a wind,
We have proved we have hearts in a cause, we are noble still,
And myself have awaked, as it seems, to the better mind;
It is better to fight for the good than to rail at the ill;
I have felt with my native land, I am one with my kind,
I embrace the purpose of God, and the doom assign'd.

1855

TURN, FORTUNE, TURN THY WHEEL

(From *The Marriage of Geraint*)

Turn, Fortune, turn thy wheel and lower the proud;
Turn thy wild wheel thro' sunshine, storm, and cloud;
Thy wheel and thee we neither love nor hate.

Turn, Fortune, turn thy wheel with smile or frown;
With that wild wheel we go not up or down;
Our hoard is little, but our hearts are great.

Smile and we smile, the lords of many lands;
Frown and we smile, the lords of our own hands;
For man is man and master of his fate.

Turn, turn thy wheel above the staring crowd;
Thy wheel and thou are shadows in the cloud;
Thy wheel and thee we neither love nor hate.

1859

IN LOVE, IF LOVE BE LOVE

(From *Merlin and Vivien*)

In Love, if Love be Love, if Love be ours,
Faith and unfaith can ne'er be equal powers:
Unfaith in aught is want of faith in all.

It is the little rift within the lute,
That by and by will make the music mute,
And ever widening slowly silence all.

The little rift within the lover's lute
Or little pitted speck in garner'd fruit,
That rotting inward slowly moulders all.

It is not worth the keeping: let it go:
But shall it? answer, darling, answer, no.
And trust me not at all or all in all.

1859

TITHONUS

The woods decay, the woods decay and fall,
The vapours weep their burthen to the ground,
Man comes and tills the field and lies beneath,
And after many a summer dies the swan.
Me only cruel immortality
Consumes: I wither slowly in thine arms,
Here at the quiet limit of the world,
A white-hair'd shadow roaming like a dream
The ever-silent spaces of the East,
Far-folded mists, and gleaming halls of morn.

Alas! for this gray shadow, once a man—
So glorious in his beauty and thy choice,
Who madest him thy chosen, that he seem'd
To his great heart none other than a God!
I ask'd thee, "Give me immortality."
Then didst thou grant mine asking with a smile,
Like wealthy men who care not how they give.
But thy strong Hours indignant work'd their wills,
And beat me down and marr'd and wasted me,
And tho' they could not end me, left me maim'd
To dwell in presence of immortal youth,
Immortal age beside immortal youth,
And all I was, in ashes. Can thy love,
Thy beauty, make amends, tho' even now,
Close over us, the silver star, thy guide,
Shines in those tremulous eyes that fill with tears
To hear me? Let me go: take back thy gift:
Why should a man desire in any way
To vary from the kindly race of men,
Or pass beyond the goal of ordinance
Where all should pause, as is most meet for all?

A soft air fans the cloud apart; there comes
A glimpse of that dark world where I was born.
Once more the old mysterious glimmer steals
From thy pure brows, and from thy shoulders pure,
And bosom beating with a heart renew'd.
Thy cheek begins to redden thro' the gloom,
Thy sweet eyes brighten slowly close to mine,
Ere yet they blind the stars, and the wild team
Which love thee, yearning for thy yoke, arise,
And shake the darkness from their loosen'd manes,
And beat the twilight into flakes of fire.

Lo! ever thus thou growest beautiful
In silence, then before thine answer given
Departest, and thy tears are on my cheek.

Why wilt thou ever scare me with thy tears,
And make me tremble lest a saying learnt,
In days far-off, on that dark earth, be true?
"The Gods themselves cannot recall their gifts."

Ay me! ay me! with what another heart
In days far-off, and with what other eyes
I used to watch—if I be he that watch'd—
The lucid outline forming round thee; saw
The dim curls kindle into sunny rings;
Changed with thy mystic change, and felt my blood
Glow with the glow that slowly crimson'd all
Thy presence and thy portals, while I lay,
Mouth, forehead, eyelids, growing dewy-warm
With kisses balmier than half-opening buds
Of April, and could hear the lips that kiss'd
Whispering I knew not what of wild and sweet,
Like that strange song I heard Apollo sing,
While Ilion like a mist rose into towers.

Yet hold me not for ever in thine East:
How can my nature longer mix with thine?
Coldly thy rosy shadows bathe me, cold
Are all thy lights, and cold my wrinkled feet
Upon thy glimmering thresholds, when the steam
Floats up from those dim fields about the homes
Of happy men that have the power to die,
And grassy barrows of the happier dead.

Release me, and restore me to the ground;
Thou seëst all things, thou wilt see my grave:
Thou wilt renew thy beauty morn by morn;
I earth in earth forget these empty courts,
And thee returning on thy silver wheels.

1860

From AYLMER'S FIELD

(Lines 635–674)

Never since our bad earth became one sea,
Which rolling o'er the palaces of the proud,
And all but those who knew the living God—
Eight that were left to make a purer world—
When since had flood, fire, earthquake, thunder, wrought
Such waste and havoc as the idolatries,
Which from the low light of mortality
Shot up their shadows to the Heaven of Heavens,
And worshipt their own darkness in the Highest?
"Gash thyself, priest, and honour thy brute Baäl,
And to thy worst self sacrifice thyself,
For with thy worst self hast thou clothed thy God.
Then came a Lord in no wise like to Baäl.
The babe shall lead the lion. Surely now
The wilderness shall blossom as the rose.
Crown thyself, worm, and worship thine own lusts!—
No coarse and blockish God of acreage
Stands at thy gate for thee to grovel to—
Thy God is far diffused in noble groves
And princely halls, and farms, and flowing lawns,
And heaps of living gold that daily grow,
And title-scrolls and gorgeous heraldries.
In such a shape dost thou behold thy God.
Thou wilt not gash thy flesh for *him;* for thine
Fares richly, in fine linen, not a hair
Ruffled upon the scarfskin, even while
The deathless ruler of thy dying house
Is wounded to the death that cannot die;
And tho' thou numberest with the followers
Of One who cried, 'Leave all and follow me.'
Thee therefore with His light about thy feet,
Thee with His message ringing in thine ears,
Thee shall thy brother man, the Lord from Heaven,
Born of a village girl, carpenter's son,
Wonderful, Prince of peace, the Mighty God,
Count the more base idolater of the two;
Crueller: as not passing thro' the fire
Bodies, but souls—thy children's—thro' the smoke,
The blight of low desires—darkening thine own
To thine own likeness."

* * *

1864

IN THE VALLEY OF CAUTERETZ

All along the valley, stream that flashest white,
Deepening thy voice with the deepening of the night,
All along the valley, where thy waters flow,
I walk'd with one I loved two and thirty years ago.
All along the valley, while I walk'd to-day,
The two and thirty years were a mist that rolls away;
For all along the valley, down thy rocky bed,
Thy living voice to me was as the voice of the dead,
And all along the valley, by rock and cave and tree,
The voice of the dead was a living voice to me.

1864

MILTON

Alcaics

O mighty-mouth'd inventor of harmonies,
O skill'd to sing of Time or Eternity,
God-gifted organ-voice of England,
Milton, a name to resound for ages;
Whose Titan angels, Gabriel, Abdiel,
Starr'd from Jehovah's gorgeous armouries,
Tower, as the deep-domed empyrëan
Rings to the roar of an angel onset—
Me rather all that bowery loneliness,
The brooks of Eden mazily murmuring,
And bloom profuse and cedar arches
Charm, as a wanderer out in ocean,
Where some refulgent sunset of India
Streams o'er a rich ambrosial ocean isle,
And crimson-hued the stately palm-woods
Whisper in odorous heights of even.

1864

THE FLOWER

ONCE in a golden hour
I cast to earth a seed.
Up there came a flower,
The people said, a weed.

To and fro they went
Thro' my garden-bower,
And muttering discontent
Cursed me and my flower.

Then it grew so tall
It wore a crown of light,
But thieves from o'er the wall
Stole the seed by night.

Sow'd it far and wide
By every town and tower,
Till all the people cried,
"Splendid is the flower."

Read my little fable:
He that runs may read.
Most can raise the flowers now,
For all have got the seed.

And some are pretty enough,
And some are poor indeed;
And now again the people
Call it but a weed.

1864

A DEDICATION

DEAR, near and true—no truer Time himself
Can prove you, tho' he make you evermore
Dearer and nearer, as the rapid of life
Shoots to the fall—take this and pray that he
Who wrote it, honouring your sweet faith in him,
May trust himself; and after praise and scorn,
As one who feels the immeasurable world,
Attain the wise indifference of the wise;
And after Autumn past—if left to pass
His autumn into seeming-leafless days—
Draw toward the long frost and longest night,
Wearing his wisdom lightly, like the fruit
Which in our winter woodland looks a flower.[1]

1864

[1] The fruit of the Spindle-tree (*Euonymus europæus*).

THE VOYAGE

I

WE left behind the painted buoy
That tosses at the harbour-mouth;
And madly danced our hearts with joy,
As fast we fleeted to the South:
How fresh was every sight and sound
On open main or winding shore!
We knew the merry world was round,
And we might sail for evermore.

II

Warm broke the breeze against the brow,
Dry sang the tackle, sang the sail:
The Lady's-head upon the prow
Caught the shrill salt, and sheer'd the gale.
The broad seas swell'd to meet the keel,
And swept behind; so quick the run,
We felt the good ship shake and reel,
We seem'd to sail into the Sun!

III

How oft we saw the Sun retire,
And burn the threshold of the night,
Fall from his Ocean-lane of fire,
And sleep beneath his pillar'd light!
How oft the purple-skirted robe
Of twilight slowly downward drawn,
As thro' the slumber of the globe
Again we dash'd into the dawn!

IV

New stars all night above the brim
Of waters lighten'd into view;
They climb'd as quickly, for the rim
Changed every moment as we flew.
Far ran the naked moon across
The houseless ocean's heaving field,
Or flying shone, the silver boss
Of her own halo's dusky shield;

V

The peaky islet shifted shapes,
High towns on hills were dimly seen,
We past long lines of Northern capes
And dewy Northern meadows green.
We came to warmer waves, and deep
Across the boundless east we drove,
Where those long swells of breaker sweep
The nutmeg rocks and isles of clove.

VI

By peaks that flamed, or, all in shade,
Gloom'd the low coast and quivering brine
With ashy rains, that spreading made
Fantastic plume or sable pine;
By sands and steaming flats, and floods
Of mighty mouth, we scudded fast,
And hills and scarlet-mingled woods
Glow'd for a moment as we past.

VII

O hundred shores of happy climes,
How swiftly stream'd ye by the bark!
At times the whole sea burn'd, at times
With wakes of fire we tore the dark;
At times a carven craft would shoot
From havens hid in fairy bowers,
With naked limbs and flowers and fruit,
But we nor paused for fruit nor flowers.

VIII

For one fair Vision ever fled
Down the waste waters day and night,
And still we follow'd where she led,
In hope to gain upon her flight.
Her face was evermore unseen,
And fixt upon the far sea-line;
But each man murmur'd, "O my Queen,
I follow till I make thee mine."

IX

And now we lost her, now she gleam'd
Like Fancy made of golden air,
Now nearer to the prow she seem'd
Like Virtue firm, like Knowledge fair,
Now high on waves that idly burst
Like Heavenly Hope she crown'd the sea,
And now, the bloodless point reversed,
She bore the blade of Liberty.

X

And only one among us—him
We pleased not—he was seldom pleased:
He saw not far: his eyes were dim:
But ours he swore were all diseased.
"A ship of fools," he shriek'd in spite,
"A ship of fools," he sneer'd and wept.
And overboard one stormy night
He cast his body, and on we swept.

XI

And never sail of ours was furl'd,
Nor anchor dropt at eve or morn;
We lov'd the glories of the world,
But laws of nature were our scorn.
For blasts would rise and rave and cease,
But whence were those that drove the sail
Across the whirlwind's heart of peace,
And to and thro' the counter gale?

XII

Again to colder climes we came,
For still we follow'd where she led:
Now mate is blind and captain lame,
And half the crew are sick or dead,
But, blind or lame or sick or sound,
We follow that which flies before:
We know the merry world is round,
And we may sail for evermore.

1864

ENOCH ARDEN

LONG lines of cliff breaking have left a chasm;
And in the chasm are foam and yellow sands;
Beyond, red roofs about a narrow wharf
In cluster; then a moulder'd church; and higher
A long street climbs to one tall-tower'd mill;
And high in heaven behind it a gray down
With Danish barrows; and a hazelwood,
By autumn nutters haunted, flourishes
Green in a cuplike hollow of the down.

Here on this beach a hundred years ago,
Three children of three houses, Annie Lee,
The prettiest little damsel in the port,
And Philip Ray the miller's only son,
And Enoch Arden, a rough sailor's lad
Made orphan by a winter shipwreck, play'd
Among the waste and lumber of the shore,
Hard coils of cordage, swarthy fishing-nets,
Anchors of rusty fluke, and boats updrawn;
And built their castles of dissolving sand
To watch them overflow'd, or following up
And flying the white breaker, daily left
The little footprint daily wash'd away.

A narrow cave ran in beneath the cliff:
In this the children play'd at keeping house.
Enoch was host one day, Philip the next,
While Annie still was mistress; but at times
Enoch would hold possession for a week:

"This is my house and this my little wife."
"Mine too" said Philip "turn and turn about:"
When, if they quarrell'd, Enoch stronger-made
Was master: then would Philip, his blue eyes
All flooded with the helpless wrath of tears,
Shriek out "I hate you, Enoch," and at this
The little wife would weep for company,
And pray them not to quarrel for her sake,
And say she would be little wife to both.

But when the dawn of rosy childhood past,
And the new warmth of life's ascending sun
Was felt by either, either fixt his heart
On that one girl; and Enoch spoke his love,
But Philip loved in silence; and the girl
Seem'd kinder unto Philip than to him;
But she loved Enoch; tho' she knew it not,
And would if ask'd deny it. Enoch set
A purpose evermore before his eyes,
To hoard all savings to the uttermost,
To purchase his own boat, and make a home
For Annie: and so prosper'd that at last
A luckier or a bolder fisherman,
A carefuller in peril, did not breathe
For leagues along that breaker-beaten coast
Than Enoch. Likewise had he served a year
On board a merchantman, and made himself
Full sailor; and he thrice had pluck'd a life
From the dread sweep of the down-streaming seas:
And all men look'd upon him favourably:
And ere he touch'd his one-and-twentieth May
He purchased his own boat, and made a home
For Annie, neat and nestlike, halfway up
The narrow street that clamber'd toward the mill.

Then, on a golden autumn eventide,
The younger people making holiday,
With bag and sack and basket, great and small,
Went nutting to the hazels. Philip stay'd
(His father lying sick and needing him)
An hour behind; but as he climb'd the hill,
Just where the prone edge of the wood began
To feather toward the hollow, saw the pair,
Enoch and Annie, sitting hand-in-hand,
His large gray eyes and weather-beaten face
All-kindled by a still and sacred fire,
That burn'd as on an altar. Philip look'd,
And in their eyes and faces read his doom;
Then, as their faces drew together, groan'd,
And slipt aside, and like a wounded life
Crept down into the hollows of the wood;
There, while the rest were loud in merry-making,
Had his dark hour unseen, and rose and past
Bearing a lifelong hunger in his heart.

So these were wed, and merrily rang the bells,
And merrily ran the years, seven happy years,
Seven happy years of health and competence,
And mutual love and honourable toil;
With children; first a daughter. In him woke,
With his first babe's first cry, the noble wish
To save all earnings to the uttermost,
And give his child a better bringing-up
Than his had been, or hers; a wish renew'd,
When two years after came a boy to be
The rosy idol of her solitudes,
While Enoch was abroad on wrathful seas,
Or often journeying landward; for in truth
Enoch's white horse, and Enoch's ocean-spoil
In ocean-smelling osier, and his face,
Rough-redden'd with a thousand winter gales,
Not only to the market-cross were known,
But in the leafy lanes behind the down,
Far as the portal-warding lion-whelp,
And peacock-yewtree of the lonely Hall,
Whose Friday fare was Enoch's ministering.

Then came a change, as all things human change.
Ten miles to northward of the narrow port
Open'd a larger haven: thither used
Enoch at times to go by land or sea;
And once when there, and clambering on a mast
In harbour, by mischance he slipt and fell:
A limb was broken when they lifted him;
And while he lay recovering there, his wife
Bore him another son, a sickly one:
Another hand crept too across his trade
Taking her bread and theirs: and on him fell,
Altho' a grave and staid God-fearing man,
Yet lying thus inactive, doubt and gloom.
He seem'd, as in a nightmare of the night,
To see his children leading evermore
Low miserable lives of hand-to-mouth,
And her, he loved, a beggar: then he pray'd

"Save them from this, whatever comes to me."
And while he pray'd, the master of that ship
Enoch had served in, hearing his mischance,
Came, for he knew the man and valued him,
Reporting of his vessel China-bound,
And wanting yet a boatswain. Would he go?
There yet were many weeks before she sail'd,
Sail'd from this port. Would Enoch have the place?
And Enoch all at once assented to it,
Rejoicing at that answer to his prayer.

So now that shadow of mischance appear'd
No graver than as when some little cloud
Cuts off the fiery highway of the sun,
And isles a light in the offing: yet the wife—
When he was gone—the children—what to do?
Then Enoch lay long-pondering on his plans;
To sell the boat—and yet he loved her well—
How many a rough sea had he weather'd in her!
He knew her, as a horseman knows his horse—
And yet to sell her—then with what she brought
Buy goods and stores—set Annie forth in trade
With all that seamen needed or their wives—
So might she keep the house while he was gone.
Should he not trade himself out yonder? go
This voyage more than once? yea twice or thrice—
As oft as needed—last, returning rich,
Become the master of a larger craft,
With fuller profits lead an easier life,
Have all his pretty young ones educated,
And pass his days in peace among his own.

Thus Enoch in his heart determined all:
Then moving homeward came on Annie pale,
Nursing the sickly babe, her latest-born.
Forward she started with a happy cry,
And laid the feeble infant in his arms;
Whom Enoch took, and handled all his limbs,
Appraised his weight and fondled fatherlike,
But had no heart to break his purposes
To Annie, till the morrow, when he spoke.

Then first since Enoch's golden ring had girt
Her finger, Annie fought against his will:
Yet not with brawling opposition she,
But manifold entreaties, many a tear,
Many a sad kiss by day by night renew'd
(Sure that all evil would come out of it)
Besought him, supplicating, if he cared
For her or his dear children, not to go.
He not for his own self caring but her,
Her and her children, let her plead in vain;
So grieving held his will, and bore it thro'.

For Enoch parted with his old sea-friend,
Bought Annie goods and stores, and set his hand
To fit their little streetward sitting-room
With shelf and corner for the goods and stores.
So all day long till Enoch's last at home,
Shaking their pretty cabin, hammer and axe,
Auger and saw, while Annie seem'd to hear
Her own death-scaffold raising, shrill'd and rang,
Till this was ended, and his careful hand,—
The space was narrow,—having order'd all
Almost as neat and close as Nature packs
Her blossom or her seedling, paused; and he,
Who needs would work for Annie to the last,
Ascending tired, heavily slept till morn.

And Enoch faced this morning of farewell
Brightly and boldly. All his Annie's fears,
Save, as his Annie's, were a laughter to him.
Yet Enoch as a brave God-fearing man
Bow'd himself down, and in that mystery
Where God-in-man is one with man-in-God,
Pray'd for a blessing on his wife and babes
Whatever came to him: and then he said
"Annie, this voyage by the grace of God
Will bring fair weather yet to all of us.
Keep a clean hearth and a clear fire for me,
For I'll be back, my girl, before you know it."
Then lightly rocking baby's cradle "and he,
This pretty, puny, weakly little one,—
Nay—for I love him all the better for it—
God bless him, he shall sit upon my knees
And I will tell him tales of foreign parts,
And make him merry, when I come home again.
Come, Annie, come, cheer up before I go."

Him running on thus hopefully she heard,
And almost hoped herself; but when he turn'd
The current of his talk to graver things
In sailor fashion roughly sermonizing
On providence and trust in Heaven, she heard,

Heard and not heard him; as the village girl,
Who sets her pitcher underneath the spring,
Musing on him that used to fill it for her,
Hears and not hears, and lets it overflow.

At length she spoke "O Enoch, you are wise;
And yet for all your wisdom well know I
That I shall look upon your face no more."

"Well then," said Enoch, "I shall look on yours.
Annie, the ship I sail in passes here
(He named the day); get you a seaman's glass,
Spy out my face, and laugh at all your fears."

But when the last of those last moments came,
"Annie, my girl, cheer up, be comforted,
Look to the babes, and till I come again
Keep everything shipshape, for I must go.
And fear no more for me; or if you fear
Cast all your cares on God; that anchor holds.
Is He not yonder in those uttermost
Parts of the morning? if I flee to these
Can I go from Him? and the sea is His,
The sea is His: He made it."

Enoch rose,
Cast his strong arms about his drooping wife,
And kiss'd his wonder-stricken little ones;
But for the third, the sickly one, who slept
After a night of feverous wakefulness,
When Annie would have raised him Enoch said,
"Wake him not; let him sleep; how should the child
Remember this?" and kiss'd him in his cot.
But Annie from her baby's forehead clipt
A tiny curl, and gave it: this he kept
Thro' all his future; but now hastily caught
His bundle, waved his hand, and went his way.

She when the day, that Enoch mention'd, came,
Borrow'd a glass, but all in vain: perhaps
She could not fix the glass to suit her eye;
Perhaps her eye was dim, hand tremulous;
She saw him not: and while he stood on deck
Waving, the moment and the vessel past.

Ev'n to the last dip of the vanishing sail
She watch'd it, and departed weeping for him;
Then, tho' she mourn'd his absence as his grave,
Set her sad will no less to chime with his,
But throve not in her trade, not being bred
To barter, nor compensating the want
By shrewdness, neither capable of lies,
Nor asking overmuch and taking less,
And still foreboding "what would Enoch say?"
For more than once, in days of difficulty
And pressure, had she sold her wares for less
Than what she gave in buying what she sold:
She fail'd and sadden'd knowing it; and thus,
Expectant of that news which never came,
Gain'd for her own a scanty sustenance,
And lived a life of silent melancholy.

Now the third child was sickly-born and grew
Yet sicklier, tho' the mother cared for it
With all a mother's care: nevertheless,
Whether her business often call'd her from it,
Or thro' the want of what it needed most,
Or means to pay the voice who best could tell
What most it needed—howsoe'er it was,
After a lingering,—ere she was aware,—
Like the caged bird escaping suddenly,
The little innocent soul flitted away.

In that same week when Annie buried it,
Philip's true heart, which hunger'd for her peace
(Since Enoch left he had not look'd upon her),
Smote him, as having kept aloof so long.
"Surely," said Philip, "I may see her now,
May be some little comfort;" therefore went,
Past thro' the solitary room in front,
Paused for a moment at an inner door,
Then struck it thrice, and, no one opening,
Enter'd; but Annie, seated with her grief,
Fresh from the burial of her little one,
Cared not to look on any human face,
But turn'd her own toward the wall and wept.
Then Philip standing up said falteringly
"Annie, I came to ask a favour of you."

He spoke; the passion in her moan'd reply
"Favour from one so sad and so forlorn
As I am!" half abash'd him; yet unask'd,
His bashfulness and tenderness at war,
He set himself beside her, saying to her:

"I came to speak to you of what he wish'd,
Enoch, your husband: I have ever said
You chose the best among us—a strong man:
For where he fixt his heart he set his hand
To do the thing he will'd, and bore it thro'.
And wherefore did he go this weary way,
And leave you lonely? not to see the world—
For pleasure?—nay, but for the wherewithal
To give his babes a better bringing-up
Than his had been, or yours: that was his wish.
And if he come again, vext will he be
To find the precious morning hours were lost.
And it would vex him even in his grave,
If he could know his babes were running wild
Like colts about the waste. So, Annie, now—
Have we not known each other all our lives?
I do beseech you by the love you bear
Him and his children not to say me nay—
For, if you will, when Enoch comes again
Why then he shall repay me—if you will,
Annie—for I am rich and well-to-do.
Now let me put the boy and girl to school:
This is the favour that I came to ask."

Then Annie with her brows against the wall
Answer'd "I cannot look you in the face;
I seem so foolish and so broken down.
When you came in my sorrow broke me down;
And now I think your kindness breaks me down;
But Enoch lives; that is borne in on me:
He will repay you: money can be repaid;
Not kindness such as yours."

And Philip ask'd
"Then you will let me, Annie?"

There she turn'd,
She rose, and fixt her swimming eyes upon him,
And dwelt a moment on his kindly face,
Then calling down a blessing on his head
Caught at his hand, and wrung it passionately,
And past into the little garth beyond.
So lifted up in spirit he moved away.

Then Philip put the boy and girl to school,
And bought them needful books, and everyway,
Like one who does his duty by his own,
Made himself theirs; and tho' for Annie's sake,
Fearing the lazy gossip of the port,
He oft denied his heart his dearest wish,
And seldom crost her threshold, yet he sent
Gifts by the children, garden-herbs and fruit,
The late and early roses from his wall,
Or conies from the down, and now and then,
With some pretext of fineness in the meal
To save the offence of charitable, flour
From his tall mill that whistled on the waste.

But Philip did not fathom Annie's mind:
Scarce could the woman when he came upon her,
Out of full heart and boundless gratitude
Light on a broken word to thank him with.
But Philip was her children's all-in-all;
From distant corners of the street they ran
To greet his hearty welcome heartily;
Lords of his house and of his mill were they;
Worried his passive ear with petty wrongs
Or pleasures, hung upon him, play'd with him
And call'd him Father Philip. Philip gain'd
As Enoch lost; for Enoch seem'd to them
Uncertain as a vision or a dream,
Faint as a figure seen in early dawn
Down at the far end of an avenue,
Going we know not where: and so ten years,
Since Enoch left his hearth and native land,
Fled forward, and no news of Enoch came.

It chanced one evening Annie's children long'd
To go with others, nutting to the wood,
And Annie would go with them; then they begg'd
For Father Philip (as they call'd him) too:
Him, like the working bee in blossom-dust,
Blanch'd with his mill, they found; and saying to him
"Come with us Father Philip" he denied;
But when the children pluck'd at him to go,
He laugh'd, and yielded readily to their wish,
For was not Annie with them? and they went.

But after scaling half the weary down,
Just where the prone edge of the wood began
To feather toward the hollow, all her force
Fail'd her; and sighing, "Let me rest" she said:
So Philip rested with her well-content;

While all the younger ones with jubilant cries
Broke from their elders, and tumultuously
Down thro' the whitening hazels made a plunge
To the bottom, and dispersed, and bent or broke
The lithe reluctant boughs to tear away
Their tawny clusters, crying to each other
And calling, here and there, about the wood.

But Philip sitting at her side forgot
Her presence, and remember'd one dark hour
Here in this wood, when like a wounded life
He crept into the shadow: at last he said,
Lifting his honest forehead, "Listen, Annie,
How merry they are down yonder in the wood.
Tired, Annie?" for she did not speak a word.
"Tired?" but her face had fall'n upon her hands;
At which, as with a kind of anger in him,
"The ship was lost," he said, "the ship was lost!
No more of that! why should you kill yourself
And make them orphans quite?" And Annie said
"I thought not of it: but—I know not why—
Their voices make me feel so solitary."

Then Philip coming somewhat closer spoke.
"Annie, there is a thing upon my mind,
And it has been upon my mind so long,
That tho' I know not when it first came there,
I know that it will out at last. O Annie,
It is beyond all hope, against all chance,
That he who left you ten long years ago
Should still be living; well then—let me speak:
I grieve to see you poor and wanting help:
I cannot help you as I wish to do
Unless—they say that women are so quick—
Perhaps you know what I would have you know—
I wish you for my wife. I fain would prove
A father to your children: I do think
They love me as a father: I am sure
That I love them as if they were mine own;
And I believe, if you were fast my wife,
That after all these sad uncertain years,
We might be still as happy as God grants
To any of his creatures. Think upon it:
For I am well-to-do—no kin, no care,
No burthen, save my care for you and yours:
And we have known each other all our lives,
And I have loved you longer than you know."

Then answer'd Annie; tenderly she spoke:
"You have been as God's good angel in our house.
God bless you for it, God reward you for it,
Philip, with something happier than myself.
Can one love twice? can you be ever loved
As Enoch was? what is it that you ask?"
"I am content" he answer'd "to be loved
A little after Enoch." "O" she cried,
Scared as it were, "dear Philip, wait a while:
If Enoch comes—but Enoch will not come—
Yet wait a year, a year is not so long:
Surely I shall be wiser in a year:
O wait a little!" Philip sadly said
"Annie, as I have waited all my life
I well may wait a little." "Nay" she cried
"I am bound: you have my promise—in a year:
Will you not bide your year as I bide mine?"
And Philip answer'd "I will bide my year."

Here both were mute, till Philip glancing up
Beheld the dead flame of the fallen day
Pass from the Danish barrow overhead;
Then fearing night and chill for Annie, rose
And sent his voice beneath him thro' the wood.
Up came the children laden with their spoil;
Then all descended to the port, and there
At Annie's door he paused and gave his hand,
Saying gently "Annie, when I spoke to you,
That was your hour of weakness. I was wrong,
I am always bound to you, but you are free."
Then Annie weeping answer'd "I am bound."

She spoke; and in one moment as it were,
While yet she went about her household ways,
Ev'n as she dwelt upon his latest words,
That he had loved her longer than she knew,
That autumn into autumn flash'd again,
And there he stood once more before her face,
Claiming her promise. "Is it a year?" she ask'd.
"Yes, if the nuts" he said "be ripe again:
Come out and see." But she—she put him off—
So much to look to—such a change—a month—
Give her a month—she knew that she was bound—
A month—no more. Then Philip with his eyes

Full of that lifelong hunger, and his voice
Shaking a little like a drunkard's hand,
"Take your own time, Annie, take your own time."
And Annie could have wept for pity of him;
And yet she held him on delayingly
With many a scarce-believable excuse,
Trying his truth and his long-sufferance,
Till half-another year had slipt away.

By this the lazy gossips of the port,
Abhorrent of a calculation crost,
Began to chafe as at a personal wrong.
Some thought that Philip did but trifle with her;
Some that she but held off to draw him on;
And others laugh'd at her and Philip too,
As simple folk that knew not their own minds,
And one, in whom all evil fancies clung
Like serpent eggs together, laughingly
Would hint at worse in either. Her own son
Was silent, tho' he often look'd his wish;
But evermore the daughter prest upon her
To wed the man so dear to all of them
And lift the household out of poverty;
And Philip's rosy face contracting grew
Careworn and wan; and all these things fell on her
Sharp as reproach.

At last one night it chanced
That Annie could not sleep, but earnestly
Pray'd for a sign "my Enoch is he gone?"
Then compass'd round by the blind wall of night
Brook'd not the expectant terror of her heart,
Started from bed, and struck herself a light,
Then desperately seized the holy Book,
Suddenly set it wide to find a sign,
Suddenly put her finger on the text,
"Under the palm-tree." That was nothing to her:
No meaning there: she closed the Book and slept:
When lo! her Enoch sitting on a height,
Under a palm-tree, over him the Sun:
"He is gone," she thought, "he is happy, he is singing
Hosanna in the highest: yonder shines
The Sun of Righteousness, and these be palms
Whereof the happy people strowing cried
'Hosanna in the highest!'" Here she woke,
Resolved, sent for him and said wildly to him
"There is no reason why we should not wed."
"Then for God's sake," he answer'd, "both our sakes,
So you will wed me, let it be at once."

So these were wed and merrily rang the bells,
Merrily rang the bells and they were wed.
But never merrily beat Annie's heart.
A footstep seem'd to fall beside her path,
She knew not whence; a whisper on her ear,
She knew not what; nor loved she to be left
Alone at home, nor ventured out alone.
What ail'd her then, that ere she enter'd, often
Her hand dwelt lingeringly on the latch,
Fearing to enter: Philip thought he knew:
Such doubts and fears were common to her state,
Being with child: but when her child was born,
Then her new child was as herself renew'd,
Then the new mother came about her heart,
Then her good Philip was her all-in-all,
And that mysterious instinct wholly died.

And where was Enoch? prosperously sail'd
The ship "Good Fortune," tho' at setting forth
The Biscay, roughly ridging eastward, shook
And almost overwhelm'd her, yet unvext
She slipt across the summer of the world,
Then after a long tumble about the Cape
And frequent interchange of foul and fair,
She passing thro' the summer world again,
The breath of heaven came continually
And sent her sweetly by the golden isles,
Till silent in her oriental haven.

There Enoch traded for himself, and bought
Quaint monsters for the market of those times,
A gilded dragon, also, for the babes.

Less lucky her home-voyage: at first indeed
Thro' many a fair sea-circle, day by day,
Scarce-rocking, her full-busted figure-head
Stared o'er the ripple feathering from her bows:
Then follow'd calms, and then winds variable,
Then baffling, a long course of them; and last

Storm, such as drove her under moonless heavens
Till hard upon the cry of "breakers" came
The crash of ruin, and the loss of all
But Enoch and two others. Half the night,
Buoy'd upon floating tackle and broken spars,
These drifted, stranding on an isle at morn
Rich, but the loneliest in a lonely sea.

No want was there of human sustenance,
Soft fruitage, mighty nuts, and nourishing roots;
Nor save for pity was it hard to take
The helpless life so wild that it was tame.
There in a seaward-gazing mountain-gorge
They built, and thatch'd with leaves of palm, a hut,
Half hut, half native cavern. So the three,
Set in this Eden of all plenteousness,
Dwelt with eternal summer, ill-content.

For one, the youngest, hardly more than boy,
Hurt in that night of sudden ruin and wreck,
Lay lingering out a five-years' death-in-life.
They could not leave him. After he was gone,
The two remaining found a fallen stem;
And Enoch's comrade, careless of himself,
Fire-hollowing this in Indian fashion, fell
Sun-stricken, and that other lived alone.
In those two deaths he read God's warning "wait."

The mountain wooded to the peak, the lawns
And winding glades high up like ways to Heaven,
The slender coco's drooping crown of plumes,
The lightning flash of insect and of bird,
The lustre of the long convolvuluses
That coil'd around the stately stems, and ran
Ev'n to the limit of the land, the glows
And glories of the broad belt of the world,
All these he saw; but what he fain had seen
He could not see, the kindly human face,
Nor ever hear a kindly voice, but heard
The myriad shriek of wheeling ocean-fowl,
The league-long roller thundering on the reef,
The moving whisper of huge trees that branch'd
And blossom'd in the zenith, or the sweep
Of some precipitous rivulet to the wave,
As down the shore he ranged, or all day long
Sat often in the seaward-gazing gorge,
A shipwreck'd sailor, waiting for a sail:
No sail from day to day, but every day
The sunrise broken into scarlet shafts
Among the palms and ferns and precipices;
The blaze upon the waters to the east;
The blaze upon his island overhead;
The blaze upon the waters to the west;
Then the great stars that globed themselves in Heaven,
The hollower-bellowing ocean, and again
The scarlet shafts of sunrise—but no sail.

There often as he watch'd or seem'd to watch,
So still, the golden lizard on him paused,
A phantom made of many phantoms moved
Before him haunting him, or he himself
Moved haunting people, things and places, known
Far in a darker isle beyond the line;
The babes, their babble, Annie, the small house,
The climbing street, the mill, the leafy lanes,
The peacock-yewtree and the lonely Hall,
The horse he drove, the boat he sold, the chill
November dawns and dewy-glooming downs,
The gentle shower, the smell of dying leaves,
And the low moan of leaden-colour'd seas.

Once likewise, in the ringing of his ears,
Tho' faintly, merrily—far and far away—
He heard the pealing of his parish bells;
Then, tho' he knew not wherefore, started up
Shuddering, and when the beauteous hateful isle
Return'd upon him, had not his poor heart
Spoken with That, which being everywhere
Lets none, who speaks with Him, seem all alone,
Surely the man had died of solitude.

Thus over Enoch's early-silvering head
The sunny and rainy seasons came and went
Year after year. His hopes to see his own,
And pace the sacred old familiar fields,
Not yet had perish'd, when his lonely doom
Came suddenly to an end. Another ship
(She wanted water) blown by baffling winds,

Like the Good Fortune, from her destined course,
Stay'd by this isle, not knowing where she lay:
For since the mate had seen at early dawn
Across a break on the mist-wreathen isle
The silent water slipping from the hills,
They sent a crew that landing burst away
In search of stream or fount, and fill'd the shores
With clamour. Downward from his mountain gorge
Stept the long-hair'd long-bearded solitary,
Brown, looking hardly human, strangely clad,
Muttering and mumbling, idiotlike it seem'd,
With inarticulate rage, and making signs
They knew not what: and yet he led the way
To where the rivulets of sweet water ran;
And ever as he mingled with the crew,
And heard them talking, his long-bounden tongue
Was loosen'd, till he made them understand;
Whom, when their casks were fill'd they took aboard:
And there the tale he utter'd brokenly,
Scarce-credited at first but more and more,
Amazed and melted all who listen'd to it:
And clothes they gave him and free passage home;
But oft he work'd among the rest and shook
His isolation from him. None of these
Came from his country, or could answer him,
If question'd, aught of what he cared to know.
And dull the voyage was with long delays,
The vessel scarce sea-worthy; but evermore
His fancy fled before the lazy wind
Returning, till beneath a clouded moon
He like a lover down thro' all his blood
Drew in the dewy meadowy morning-breath
Of England, blown across her ghostly wall:
And that same morning officers and men
Levied a kindly tax upon themselves,
Pitying the lonely man, and gave him it:
Then moving up the coast they landed him,
Ev'n in that harbour whence he sail'd before.

There Enoch spoke no word to any one,
But homeward—home—what home? had he a home?
His home, he walk'd. Bright was that afternoon,
Sunny but chill; till drawn thro' either chasm,
Where either haven open'd on the deeps,
Roll'd a sea-haze and whelm'd the world in gray;
Cut off the length of highway on before,
And left but narrow breadth to left and right
Of wither'd holt or tilth or pasturage.
On the nigh-naked tree the robin piped
Disconsolate, and thro' the dripping haze
The dead weight of the dead leaf bore it down:
Thicker the drizzle grew, deeper the gloom;
Last, as it seem'd, a great mist-blotted light
Flared on him, and he came upon the place.

Then down the long street having slowly stolen,
His heart foreshadowing all calamity,
His eyes upon the stones, he reach'd the home
Where Annie lived and loved him, and his babes
In those far-off seven happy years were born;
But finding neither light nor murmur there
(A bill of sale gleam'd thro' the drizzle) crept
Still downward thinking "dead or dead to me!"

Down to the pool and narrow wharf he went,
Seeking a tavern which of old he knew,
A front of timber-crost antiquity,
So propt, worm-eaten, ruinously old,
He thought it must have gone; but he was gone
Who kept it; and his widow Miriam Lane,
With daily-dwindling profits held the house;
A haunt of brawling seamen once, but now
Stiller, with yet a bed for wandering men.
There Enoch rested silent many days.

But Miriam Lane was good and garrulous,
Nor let him be, but often breaking in,
Told him, with other annals of the port,
Not knowing—Enoch was so brown, so bow'd,
So broken—all the story of his house.
His baby's death, her growing poverty,
How Philip put her little ones to school,
And kept them in it, his long wooing her,

Her slow consent, and marriage, and the birth
Of Philip's child: and o'er his countenance
No shadow past, nor motion: any one,
Regarding, well had deem'd he felt the tale
Less than the teller: only when she closed
"Enoch, poor man, was cast away and lost"
He, shaking his gray head pathetically,
Repeated muttering "cast away and lost;"
Again in deeper inward whispers "lost!"

But Enoch yearn'd to see her face again;
"If I might look on her sweet face again
And know that she is happy." So the thought
Haunted and harass'd him, and drove him forth,
At evening when the dull November day
Was growing duller twilight, to the hill.
There he sat down gazing on all below;
There did a thousand memories roll upon him,
Unspeakable for sadness. By and by
The ruddy square of comfortable light,
Far-blazing from the rear of Philip's house,
Allured him, as the beacon-blaze allures
The bird of passage, till he madly strikes
Against it, and beats out his weary life.

For Philip's dwelling fronted on the street,
The latest house to landward; but behind,
With one small gate that open'd on the waste,
Flourish'd a little garden square and wall'd:
And in it throve an ancient evergreen,
A yewtree, and all round it ran a walk
Of shingle, and a walk divided it:
But Enoch shunn'd the middle walk and stole
Up by the wall, behind the yew; and thence
That which he better might have shunn'd, if griefs
Like his have worse or better, Enoch saw.

For cups and silver on the burnish'd board
Sparkled and shone; so genial was the hearth:
And on the right hand of the hearth he saw
Philip, the slighted suitor of old times,
Stout, rosy, with his babe across his knees;
And o'er her second father stoopt a girl,
A later but a loftier Annie Lee,
Fair-hair'd and tall, and from her lifted hand
Dangled a length of ribbon and a ring
To tempt the babe, who rear'd his creasy arms,
Caught at and ever miss'd it, and they laugh'd;
And on the left hand of the hearth he saw
The mother glancing often toward her babe,
But turning now and then to speak with him,
Her son, who stood beside her tall and strong,
And saying that which pleased him, for he smiled.

Now when the dead man come to life beheld
His wife his wife no more, and saw the babe
Hers, yet not his, upon the father's knee,
And all the warmth, the peace, the happiness,
And his own children tall and beautiful,
And him, that other, reigning in his place,
Lord of his rights and of his children's love,—
Then he, tho' Miriam Lane had told him all,
Because things seen are mightier than things heard,
Stagger'd and shook, holding the branch, and fear'd
To send abroad a shrill and terrible cry,
Which in one moment, like the blast of doom,
Would shatter all the happiness of the hearth.

He therefore turning softly like a thief,
Lest the harsh shingle should grate under foot,
And feeling all along the garden-wall,
Lest he should swoon and tumble and be found,
Crept to the gate, and open'd it, and closed,
As lightly as a sick man's chamber-door,
Behind him, and came out upon the waste.

And there he would have knelt, but that his knees
Were feeble, so that falling prone he dug
His fingers into the wet earth, and pray'd.

"Too hard to bear! why did they take me thence?
O God Almighty, blessed Saviour, Thou
That didst uphold me on my lonely isle,
Uphold me, Father, in my loneliness
A little longer! aid me, give me strength
Not to tell her, never to let her know.
Help me not to break in upon her peace.
My children too! must I not speak to these?

They know me not. I should betray myself.
Never: No father's kiss for me—the girl
So like her mother, and the boy, my son."

There speech and thought and nature fail'd a little,
And he lay tranced; but when he rose and paced
Back toward his solitary home again,
All down the long and narrow street he went
Beating it in upon his weary brain,
As tho' it were the burthen of a song,
"Not to tell her, never to let her know."

He was not all unhappy. His resolve
Upbore him, and firm faith, and evermore
Prayer from a living source within the will,
And beating up thro' all the bitter world,
Like fountains of sweet water in the sea,
Kept him a living soul. "This miller's wife"
He said to Miriam "that you spoke about,
Has she no fear that her first husband lives?"
"Ay, ay, poor soul" said Miriam, "fear enow!
If you could tell her you had seen him dead,
Why, that would be her comfort;" and he thought
"After the Lord has call'd me she shall know,
I wait His time," and Enoch set himself,
Scorning an alms, to work whereby to live.
Almost to all things could he turn his hand.
Cooper he was and carpenter, and wrought
To make the boatmen fishing-nets, or help'd
At lading and unlading the tall barks,
That brought the stinted commerce of those days;
Thus earn'd a scanty living for himself:
Yet since he did but labour for himself,
Work without hope, there was not life in it
Whereby the man could live; and as the year
Roll'd itself round again to meet the day
When Enoch had return'd, a languor came
Upon him, gentle sickness, gradually
Weakening the man, till he could do no more,
But kept the house, his chair, and last his bed.
And Enoch bore his weakness cheerfully.
For sure no gladlier does the stranded wreck
See thro' the gray skirts of a lifting squall
The boat that bears the hope of life approach
To save the life despair'd of, than he saw
Death dawning on him, and the close of all.

For thro' that dawning gleam'd a kindlier hope
On Enoch thinking "after I am gone,
Then may she learn I lov'd her to the last."
He call'd aloud for Miriam Lane and said
"Woman, I have a secret—only swear,
Before I tell you—swear upon the book
Not to reveal it, till you see me dead."
"Dead," clamour'd the good woman, "hear him talk!
I warrant, man, that we shall bring you round."
"Swear" added Enoch sternly "on the book."
And on the book, half-frighted, Miriam swore.
Then Enoch rolling his gray eyes upon her,
"Did you know Enoch Arden of this town?"
"Know him?" she said "I knew him far away.
Ay, ay, I mind him coming down the street;
Held his head high, and cared for no man, he."
Slowly and sadly Enoch answer'd her;
"His head is low, and no man cares for him.
I think I have not three days more to live;
I am the man." At which the woman gave
A half-incredulous, half-hysterical cry.
"You Arden, you! nay,—sure he was a foot
Higher than you be." Enoch said again
"My God has bow'd me down to what I am;
My grief and solitude have broken me;
Nevertheless, know you that I am he
Who married—but that name has twice been changed—
I married her who married Philip Ray.
Sit, listen." Then he told her of his voyage,
His wreck, his lonely life, his coming back,
His gazing in on Annie, his resolve,
And how he kept it. As the woman heard,
Fast flow'd the current of her easy tears,
While in her heart she yearn'd incessantly
To rush abroad all round the little haven,
Proclaiming Enoch Arden and his woes;
But awed and promise-bounden she forbore,
Saying only "See your bairns before you go!
Eh, let me fetch 'em, Arden," and arose
Eager to bring them down, for Enoch hung
A moment on her words, but then replied:

"Woman, disturb me not now at the last,
But let me hold my purpose till I die.

Sit down again; mark me and understand,
While I have power to speak. I charge you now,
When you shall see her, tell her that I died
Blessing her, praying for her, loving her;
Save for the bar between us, loving her
As when she laid her head beside my own.
And tell my daughter Annie, whom I saw
So like her mother, that my latest breath
Was spent in blessing her and praying for her.
And tell my son that I died blessing him.
And say to Philip that I blest him too;
He never meant us any thing but good.
But if my children care to see me dead,
Who hardly knew me living, let them come,
I am their father; but she must not come,
For my dead face would vex her after-life.
And now there is but one of all my blood
Who will embrace me in the world-to-be:
This hair is his: she cut it off and gave it,
And I have borne it with me all these years.
And thought to bear it with me to my grave;
But now my mind is changed, for I shall see him,
My babe in bliss: wherefore when I am gone,
Take, give her this, for it may comfort her:
It will moreover be a token to her,
That I am he."

He ceased; and Miriam Lane
Made such a voluble answer promising all,
That once again he roll'd his eyes upon her
Repeating all he wish'd, and once again
She promised.

Then the third night after this,
While Enoch slumber'd motionless and pale,
And Miriam watch'd and dozed at intervals,
There came so loud a calling of the sea,
That all the houses in the haven rang.
He woke, he rose, he spread his arms abroad
Crying with a loud voice "A sail! a sail!
I am saved;" and so fell back and spoke no more.

So past the strong heroic soul away.
And when they buried him the little port
Had seldom seen a costlier funeral.

1864

NORTHERN FARMER

OLD STYLE

I

WHEER 'asta beän saw long and meä liggin' 'ere aloän?
Noorse? thourt nowt o' a noorse: whoy, Doctor's abeän an' agoän:
Says that I moänt 'a naw moor aäle: but I beänt a fool:
Git ma my aäle, fur I beänt a-gawin' to breäk my rule.

II

Doctors, they knaws nowt, fur a says what's nawways true:
Naw soort o' koind o' use to saäy the things that a do.
I've 'ed my point o' aäle ivry noight sin' I beän 'ere.
An' I've 'ed my quart ivry market-noight for foorty year.

III

Parson's a beän loikewoise, an' a sittin' 'ere o' my bed.
"The amoighty's a taäkin o' you[1] to 'issén, my friend," a said,
An' a towd ma my sins, an's toithe were due, an' I gied it in hond;
I done moy duty boy 'um, as I 'a done boy the lond.

IV

Larn'd a ma' beä. I reckons I 'annot sa mooch to larn.
But a cast oop, thot a did, 'bout Bessy Marris's barne.
Thaw a knaws I hallus voäted wi' Squoire an' choorch an' staäte,
An' i' the woost o' toimes I wur niver agin the raäte.

[1] ou as in hour.

V

An' I hallus coom'd to 's chooch afoor moy Sally wur deäd,
An' 'eärd 'um a bummin' awaäy loike a buzzard-clock [1] ower my 'eäd,
An' I niver knaw'd whot a meän'd but I thowt a 'ad summut to saäy,
An' I thowt a said whot a owt to 'a said an' I coom'd awaäy.

VI

Bessy Marris's barne! tha knaws she laäid it to meä.
Mowt a beän, mayhap, for she wur a bad un, sheä.
'Siver, I kep 'um, I kep 'um, my lass, tha mun understond;
I done moy duty boy 'um, as I 'a done boy the lond.

VII

But Parson a cooms an' a goäs, an' a says it eäsy an' freeä:
"The amoighty's a taäkin o' you to 'issén, my friend," says 'eä.
I weänt saäy men be loiars, thaw summun said it in 'aäste:
But 'e reäds wonn sarmin a weeäk, an' I 'a stubb'd Thurnaby waäste.

VIII

D'ya moind the waäste, my lass? naw, naw, tha was not born then;
Theer wur a boggle in it, I often 'eärd 'um mysén;
Moäst loike a butter-bump,[2] fur I 'eärd 'um about an' about,
But I stubb'd 'um oop wi' the lot, an' raäved an' rembled 'um out.

IX

Keäper's it wur; fo' they fun 'um theer a-laäid of 'is faäce
Down i' the woild 'enemies [3] afoor I coom'd to the plaäce.
Noäks or Thimbleby—toäner [4] 'ed shot 'um as deäd as a naäil.
Noäks wur 'ang'd for it oop at 'soize—but git ma my aäle.

X

Dubbut looök at the waäste: theer warn't not feeäd for a cow;
Nowt at all but bracken an' fuzz, an' looök at it now—
Warnt worth nowt a haäcre, an' now theer's lots o' feeäd,
Fourscoor [5] yows upon it an' some on it down i' seeäd.[6]

XI

Nobbut a bit on it's left, an' I meän'd to 'a stubb'd it at fall,
Done it ta-year I meän'd, an' runn'd plow thruff it an' all,
If godamoighty an' parson 'ud nobbut let ma aloän,
Meä, wi' haäte hoonderd haäcre o' Squoire's, an' lond o' my oän.

XII

Do godamoighty knaw what a's doing a-taäkin' o' meä?
I beänt wonn as saws 'ere a beän an' yonder a peä;
An' Squoire 'ull be sa mad an' all—a' dear a' dear!
And I 'a managed for Squoire coom Michaelmas thutty year.

XIII

A mowt 'a taäen owd Joänes, as 'ant not a 'aäpoth o' sense,
Or a mowt 'a taäen young Robins—a niver mended a fence:
But godamoighty a moost taäke meä an' taäke ma now
Wi' aäf the cows to cauve an' Thurnaby hoälms to plow!

[1] Cockchafer. [2] Bittern. [3] Anemones.
[4] One or other [5] ou as in hour. [6] Clover.

XIV

Looök 'ow quoloty smoiles when they seeäs ma a passin' boy,
Says to thessén, naw doubt, "what a man a beä sewer-loy!"
Fur they knaws what I beän to Squoire sin fust a coom'd to the 'All;
I done moy duty by Squoire an' I done moy duty boy hall.

XV

Squoire's i' Lunnon, an' summun I reckons 'ull 'a to wroite,
For whoä's to howd the lond ater meä thot muddles ma quoit;
Sartin-sewer I beä, thot a weänt niver give it to Joänes,
Naw, nor a moänt to Robins—a niver rembles the stoäns.

XVI

But summun 'ull come ater meä mayhap wi' 'is kittle o' steäm
Huzzin' an' maäzin' the blessed feälds wi' the Divil's oän teäm.
Sin' I mun doy I mun doy, thaw loife they says is sweet,
But sin' I mun doy I mun doy, for I couldn abeär to see it.

XVII

What atta stannin' theer fur, an' doesn bring ma the aäle?
Doctor's a 'toättler, lass, an a's hallus i' the owd taäle;
I weänt breäk rules fur Doctor, a knaws naw moor nor a floy;
Git ma my aäle I tell tha, an' if I mun doy I mun doy.

1864

NORTHERN FARMER

NEW STYLE

I

Dosn't thou 'ear my 'erse's legs, as they canters awaäy?
Proputty, proputty, proputty—that's what I 'ears 'em saäy.
Proputty, proputty, proputty—Sam, thou's an ass for thy paaïns:
Theer's moor sense i' one o' 'is legs nor in all thy braaïns.

II

Woä—theer's a craw to pluck wi' tha, Sam: yon's parson's 'ouse—
Dosn't thou knaw that a man mun be eäther a man or a mouse?
Time to think on it then; for thou'll be twenty to weeäk.[1]
Proputty, proputty—woä then, woä—let ma 'ear mysén speäk.

III

Me an' thy muther, Sammy, 'as beän a-talkin' o' thee;
Thou's beän talkin' to muther, an' she beän a tellin' it me.
Thou'll not marry for munny—thou's sweet upo' parson's lass—
Noä—thou'll marry for luvv—an' we boäth on us thinks tha an ass.

IV

Seeä'd her todaäy goä by—Saäint's-daäy—they was ringing the bells.
She's a beauty, thou thinks—an' soä is scoors o' gells,
Them as 'as munny an' all—wot's a beauty?—the flower as blaws.
But proputty, proputty sticks, an' proputty, proputty graws.

[1] This week.

V

Do'ant be stunt:[1] taäke time: I knaws what maäkes tha sa mad.
Warn't I craäzed fur the lasses mysén when I wur a lad?
But I knaw'd a Quaäker feller as often 'as towd ma this:
"Doänt thou marry for munny, but goä wheer munny is!"

VI

An' I went wheer munny war: an' thy muther coom to 'and,
Wi' lots o' munny laaïd by, an' a nicetish bit o' land.
Maäybe she warn't a beauty:—I niver giv it a thowt—
But warn't she as good to cuddle an' kiss as a lass as 'ant nowt?

VII

Parson's lass 'ant nowt, an' she weänt 'a nowt when 'e's deäd,
Mun be a guvness, lad, or summut, and addle[2] her breäd:
Why? fur 'e's nobbut a curate, an' weänt niver git hissén clear,
An' 'e maäde the bed as 'e ligs on afoor 'e coom'd to the shere.

VIII

'An thin 'e coom'd to the parish wi' lots o' Varsity debt,
Stook to his taaïl they did, an' 'e 'ant got shut on 'em yet.
An' 'e ligs on 'is back i' the grip, wi' noän to lend 'im a shuvv,
Woorse nor a far-welter'd[3] yowe: fur, Sammy, 'e married fur luvv.

IX

Luvv? what's luvv? thou can luvv thy lass an' 'er munny too,
Maakin' 'em goä togither as they've good right to do.
Could'n I luvv thy muther by cause o' 'er munny laaïd by?
Naäy—fur I luvv'd 'er a vast sight moor fur it: reäson why.

X

Ay an' thy muther says thou wants to marry the lass,
Cooms of a gentleman burn: an' we boäth on us thinks tha an ass.
Woä then, proputty, wiltha?—an ass as near as mays nowt[4]—
Woä then, wiltha? dangtha!—the bees is as fell as owt.[5]

XI

Breäk me a bit o' the esh for his 'eäd, lad, out o' the fence!
Gentleman burn! what's gentleman burn? is it shillins an' pence?
Proputty, proputty's ivrything 'ere, an', Sammy, I'm blest
If it isn't the saäme oop yonder, fur them as 'as it's the best.

XII

Tis'n them as 'as munny as breäks into 'ouses an' steäls,
Them as 'as coäts to their backs an' taäkes their regular meäls.
Noä, but it's them as niver knaws wheer a meäl's to be 'ad.
Taäke my word for it, Sammy, the poor in a loomp is bad.

XIII

Them or thir feythers, tha sees, mun 'a beän a laäzy lot,
Fur work mun 'a gone to the gittin' whiniver munny was got.
Feyther 'ad ammost nowt; leästways 'is munny was 'id.
But 'e tued an' moil'd 'issén deäd, an 'e died a good un, 'e did.

[1] Obstinate. [2] Earn. [3] Or fow-welter'd,—said of a sheep lying on its back.
[4] Makes nothing. [5] The flies are as fierce as anything.

XIV

Looök thou theer wheer Wrigglesby beck cooms out by the 'ill!
Feyther run oop to the farm, an' I runs oop to the mill;
An' I'll run oop to the brig, an' that thou'll live to see;
And if thou marries a good un I'll leäve the land to thee.

XV

Thim's my noätions, Sammy, wheerby I means to stick;
But if thou marries a bad un, I'll leäve the land to Dick.—
Coom oop, proputty, proputty—that's what I 'ears 'im saäy—
Proputty, proputty, proputty—canter an' canter awaäy.

1869

WAGES

Glory of warrior, glory of orator, glory of song,
  Paid with a voice flying by to be lost on an endless sea—
Glory of Virtue, to fight, to struggle, to right the wrong—
  Nay, but she aim'd not at glory, no lover of glory she:
Give her the glory of going on, and still to be.

The wages of sin is death: if the wages of Virtue be dust,
  Would she have heart to endure for the life of the worm and the fly?
She desires no isles of the blest, no quiet seats of the just,
  To rest in a golden grove, or to bask in a summer sky:
Give her the wages of going on, and not to die.

1868

LUCRETIUS

Lucilia, wedded to Lucretius, found
Her master cold; for when the morning flush
Of passion and the first embrace had died
Between them, tho' he lov'd her none the less,
Yet often when the woman heard his foot
Return from pacings in the field, and ran
To greet him with a kiss, the master took
Small notice, or austerely, for—his mind
Half buried in some weightier argument,
Or fancy-borne perhaps upon the rise
And long roll of the Hexameter—he past
To turn and ponder those three hundred scrolls
Left by the Teacher, whom he held divine.
She brook'd it not; but wrathful, petulant,
Dreaming some rival, sought and found a witch
Who brew'd the philtre which had power, they said,
To lead an errant passion home again.
And this, at times, she mingled with his drink,
And this destroy'd him; for the wicked broth
Confused the chemic labour of the blood,
And tickling the brute brain within the man's
Made havock among those tender cells, and check'd
His power to shape: he loathed himself; and once
After a tempest woke upon a morn
That mock'd him with returning calm, and cried:

"Storm in the night! for thrice I heard the rain
Rushing; and once the flash of a thunder-bolt—
Methought I never saw so fierce a fork—
Struck out the streaming mountain-side, and show'd
A riotous confluence of watercourses
Blanching and billowing in a hollow of it,
Where all but yester-eve was dusty-dry.

"Storm, and what dreams, ye holy Gods, what dreams!
For thrice I waken'd after dreams. Perchance
We do but recollect the dreams that come
Just ere the waking: terrible! for it seem'd
A void was made in Nature; all her bonds
Crack'd; and I saw the flaring atom-streams
And torrents of her myriad universe,
Ruining along the illimitable inane,
Fly on to clash together again, and make
Another and another frame of things
For ever: that was mine, my dream, I knew it—
Of and belonging to me, as the dog
With inward yelp and restless forefoot plies
His function of the woodland: but the next!
I thought that all the blood by Sylla shed
Came driving rainlike down again on earth,
And where it dash'd the reddening meadow, sprang
No dragon warriors from Cadmean teeth,
For these I thought my dream would show to me,
But girls, Hetairai, curious in their art,
Hired animalisms, vile as those that made
The mulberry-faced Dictator's orgies worse
Than aught they fable of the quiet Gods.
And hands they mixt, and yell'd and round me drove
In narrowing circles till I yell'd again
Half-suffocated, and sprang up, and saw—
Was it the first beam of my latest day?

"Then, then, from utter gloom stood out the breasts,
The breasts of Helen, and hoveringly a sword
Now over and now under, now direct,
Pointed itself to pierce, but sank down shamed
At all that beauty; and as I stared, a fire,
The fire that left a roofless Ilion,
Shot out of them, and scorch'd me that I woke.

"Is this thy vengeance, holy Venus, thine,
Because I would not one of thine own doves,
Not ev'n a rose, were offer'd to thee? thine,
Forgetful how my rich prooemion makes
Thy glory fly along the Italian field,
In lays that will outlast thy Deity?

"Deity? nay, thy worshippers. My tongue
Trips, or I speak profanely. Which of these
Angers thee most, or angers thee at all?
Not if thou be'st of those who, far aloof
From envy, hate and pity, and spite and scorn,
Live the great life which all our greatest fain
Would follow, center'd in eternal calm.

"Nay, if thou canst, O Goddess, like ourselves
Touch, and be touch'd, then would I cry to thee
To kiss thy Mavors, roll thy tender arms
Round him, and keep him from the lust of blood
That makes a steaming slaughter-house of Rome.

"Ay, but I meant not thee; I meant not her,
Whom all the pines of Ida shook to see
Slide from that quiet heaven of hers, and tempt
The Trojan, while his neat-herds were abroad;
Not her that o'er her wounded hunter wept
Her Deity false in human-amorous tears;
Nor whom her beardless apple-arbiter
Decided fairest. Rather, O ye Gods,
Poet-like, as the great Sicilian called
Calliope to grace his golden verse—
Ay, and this Kypris also—did I take
That popular name of thine to shadow forth
The all-generating powers and genial heat
Of Nature, when she strikes thro' the thick blood
Of cattle, and light is large, and lambs are glad
Nosing the mother's udder, and the bird
Makes his heart voice amid the blaze of flowers:
Which things appear the work of mighty Gods.

"The Gods! and if I go *my* work is left
Unfinish'd—*if* I go. The Gods, who haunt
The lucid interspace of world and world,
Where never creeps a cloud, or moves a wind,
Nor ever falls the least white star of snow,
Nor ever lowest roll of thunder moans,
Nor sound of human sorrow mounts to mar
Their sacred everlasting calm! and such,
Not all so fine, nor so divine a calm,
Not such, nor all unlike it, man may gain
Letting his own life go. The Gods, the Gods!

If all be atoms, how then should the Gods
Being atomic not be dissoluble,
Not follow the great law? My master held
That Gods there are, for all men so believe.
I prest my footsteps into his, and meant
Surely to lead my Memmius in a train
Of flowery clauses onward to the proof
That Gods there are, and deathless. Meant? I meant?
I have forgotten what I meant: my mind
Stumbles, and all my faculties are lamed.

"Look where another of our Gods, the Sun,
Apollo, Delius, or of older use
All-seeing Hyperion—what you will—
Has mounted yonder; since he never sware,
Except his wrath were wreak'd on wretched man,
That he would only shine among the dead
Hereafter; tales! for never yet on earth
Could dead flesh creep, or bits of roasting ox
Moan round the spit—nor knows he what he sees;
King of the East altho' he seem, and girt
With song and flame and fragrance, slowly lifts
His golden feet on those empurpled stairs
That climb into the windy halls of heaven:
And here he glances on an eye new-born,
And gets for greeting but a wail of pain;
And here he stays upon a freezing orb
That fain would gaze upon him to the last;
And here upon a yellow eyelid fall'n
And closed by those who mourn a friend in vain,
Not thankful that his troubles are no more.
And me, altho' his fire is on my face
Blinding, he sees not, nor at all can tell
Whether I mean this day to end myself,
Or lend an ear to Plato where he says,
That men like soldiers may not quit the post
Allotted by the Gods: but he that holds
The Gods are careless, wherefore need he care
Greatly for them, nor rather plunge at once,
Being troubled, wholly out of sight, and sink
Past earthquake—ay, and gout and stone, that break
Body toward death, and palsy, death-in-life,
And wretched age—and worst disease of all,
These prodigies of myriad nakednesses,
And twisted shapes of lust, unspeakable,
Abominable, strangers at my hearth
Not welcome, harpies miring every dish,
The phantom husks of something foully done,
And fleeting thro' the boundless universe,
And blasting the long quiet of my breast
With animal heat and dire insanity?

"How should the mind, except it loved them, clasp
These idols to herself? or do they fly
Now thinner, and now thicker, like the flakes
In a fall of snow, and so press in, perforce
Of multitude, as crowds that in an hour
Of civic tumult jam the doors, and bear
The keepers down, and throng, their rags and they
The basest, far into that council-hall
Where sit the best and stateliest of the land?

"Can I not fling this horror off me again,
Seeing with how great ease Nature can smile,
Balmier and nobler from her bath of storm,
At random ravage? and how easily
The mountain there has cast his cloudy slough,
Now towering o'er him in serenest air,
A mountain o'er a mountain,—ay, and within
All hollow as the hopes and fears of men?

"But who was he, that in the garden snared
Picus and Faunus, rustic Gods? a tale
To laugh at—more to laugh at in myself—
For look! what is it? there? yon arbutus
Totters; a noiseless riot underneath
Strikes through the wood, sets all the tops quivering—
The mountain quickens into Nymph and Faun;
And here an Oread—how the sun delights
To glance and shift about her slippery sides,
And rosy knees and supple roundedness,
And budded bosom-peaks—who this way runs
Before the rest—A satyr, a satyr, see,
Follows; but him I proved impossible;
Twy-natured is no nature: yet he draws
Nearer and nearer, and I scan him now
Beastlier than any phantom of his kind
That ever butted his rough brother-brute
For lust or lusty blood or provender:
I hate, abhor, spit, sicken at him; and she
Loathes him as well; such a precipitate heel,

Fledged as it were with Mercury's ankle-wing,
Whirls her to me: but will she fling herself,
Shameless upon me? Catch her, goat-foot: nay,
Hide, hide them, million-myrtled wilderness,
And cavern-shadowing laurels, hide! do I wish—
What?—that the bush were leafless? or to whelm
All of them in one massacre? O ye Gods,
I know you careless, yet, behold, to you
From childly wont and ancient use I call—
I thought I lived securely as yourselves—
No lewdness, narrowing envy, monkey-spite,
No madness of ambition, avarice, none:
No larger feast than under plane or pine
With neighbours laid along the grass, to take
Only such cups as left us friendly-warm,
Affirming each his own philosophy—
Nothing to mar the sober majesties
Of settled, sweet, Epicurean life.
But now it seems some unseen monster lays
His vast and filthy hands upon my will,
Wrenching it backward into his; and spoils
My bliss in being; and it was not great;
For save when shutting reasons up in rhythm,
Or Heliconian honey in living words,
To make a truth less harsh, I often grew
Tired of so much within our little life,
Or of so little in our little life—
Poor little life that toddles half an hour
Crown'd with a flower or two, and there an end—
And since the nobler pleasure seems to fade,
Why should I, beastlike as I find myself,
Not manlike end myself?—our privilege—
What beast has heart to do it? And what man,
What Roman would be dragg'd in triumph thus?
Not I; not he, who bears one name with her
Whose death-blow struck the dateless doom of kings,
When, brooking not the Tarquin in her veins,
She made her blood in sight of Collatine
And all his peers, flushing the guiltless air,
Spout from the maiden fountain in her heart.
And from it sprang the Commonwealth, which breaks
As I am breaking now!

"And therefore now
Let her, that is the womb and tomb of all,
Great Nature, take, and forcing far apart
Those blind beginnings that have made me man,
Dash them anew together at her will
Thro' all her cycles—into man once more,
Or beast or bird or fish, or opulent flower:
But till this cosmic order everywhere
Shatter'd into one earthquake in one day
Cracks all to pieces,—and that hour perhaps
Is not so far when momentary man
Shall seem no more a something to himself,
But he, his hopes and hates, his homes and fanes,
And even his bones long laid within the grave,
The very sides of the grave itself shall pass,
Vanishing, atom and void, atom and void,
Into the unseen for ever,—till that hour,
My golden work in which I told a truth
That stays the rolling Ixionian wheel,
And numbs the Fury's ringlet-snake, and plucks
The mortal soul from out immortal hell,
Shall stand: ay, surely: then it fails at last
And perishes as I must; for O Thou,
Passionless bride, divine Tranquillity,
Yearn'd after by the wisest of the wise,
Who fail to find thee, being as thou art
Without one pleasure and without one pain,
Howbeit I know thou surely must be mine
Or soon or late, yet out of season, thus
I woo thee roughly, for thou carest not
How roughly men may woo thee so they win—
Thus—thus: the soul flies out and dies in the air."

With that he drove the knife into his side:
She heard him raging, heard him fall; ran in,
Beat breast, tore hair, cried out upon herself
As having fail'd in duty to him, shriek'd
That she but meant to win him back, fell on him,
Clasp'd, kiss'd him, wail'd: he answer'd, "Care not thou!
Thy duty? What is duty? Fare thee well!"

1868

THE HIGHER PANTHEISM

The sun, the moon, the stars, the seas, the hills and the plains—
Are not these, O Soul, the Vision of Him who reigns?

Is not the Vision He? tho' He be not that which He seems?

Dreams are true while they last, and do we not live in dreams?

Earth, these solid stars, this weight of body and limb,
Are they not sign and symbol of thy division from Him?

Dark is the world to thee: thyself art the reason why;
For is He not all but that which has power to feel "I am I"?

Glory about thee, without thee; and thou fulfillest thy doom
Making Him broken gleams, and a stifled splendour and gloom.

Speak to Him thou for He hears, and Spirit with Spirit can meet—
Closer is He than breathing, and nearer than hands and feet.

God is law, say the wise; O Soul, and let us rejoice,
For if He thunder by law the thunder is yet His voice.

Law is God, say some: no God at all, says the fool;
For all we have power to see is a straight staff bent in a pool;

And the ear of man cannot hear, and the eye of man cannot see;
But if we could see and hear, this Vision—were it not He?

1869

FLOWER IN THE CRANNIED WALL

Flower in the crannied wall,
I pluck you out of the crannies,
I hold you here, root and all, in my hand,
Little flower—but *if* I could understand
What you are, root and all, and all in all,
I should know what God and man is.

1869

ENGLAND AND AMERICA IN 1782

O thou, that sendest out the man
To rule by land and sea,
Strong mother of a Lion-line,
Be proud of those strong sons of thine
Who wrench'd their rights from thee!

What wonder, if in noble heat
Those men thine arms withstood,
Retaught the lesson thou hadst taught,
And in thy spirit with thee fought—
Who sprang from English blood!

But Thou rejoice with liberal joy,
Lift up thy rocky face,
And shatter, when the storms are black,
In many a streaming torrent back,
The seas that shock thy base!

Whatever harmonies of law
The growing world assume,
Thy work is thine—The single note
From that deep chord which Hampden smote
Will vibrate to the doom.

1872

IN THE GARDEN AT SWAINSTON

Nightingales warbled without,
Within was weeping for thee:
Shadows of three dead men
Walk'd in the walks with me,
Shadows of three dead men and thou wast one of the three.

Nightingales sang in his woods:
The Master was far away:
Nightingales warbled and sang
Of a passion that lasts but a day;
Still in the house in his coffin the Prince of courtesy lay.

Two dead men have I known
In courtesy like to thee:
Two dead men have I loved
With a love that ever will be:
Three dead men have I loved and thou art last of the three.

1874

From THE IDYLLS OF THE KING

THE COMING OF ARTHUR

Leodogran, the King of Cameliard,
Had one fair daughter, and none other child;
And she was fairest of all flesh on earth,
Guinevere, and in her his one delight.

For many a petty king ere Arthur came
Ruled in this isle, and ever waging war
Each upon other, wasted all the land;
And still from time to time the heathen host
Swarm'd overseas, and harried what was left.
And so there grew great tracts of wilderness,
Wherein the beast was ever more and more,
But man was less and less, till Arthur came.
For first Aurelius lived and fought and died,
And after him King Uther fought and died,
But either fail'd to make the kingdom one.
And after these King Arthur for a space,
And thro' the puissance of his Table Round,
Drew all their petty princedoms under him,
Their king and head, and made a realm, and reign'd.

And thus the land of Cameliard was waste,
Thick with wet woods, and many a beast therein,
And none or few to scare or chase the beast;
So that wild dog and wolf and boar and bear
Came night and day, and rooted in the fields,
And wallow'd in the gardens of the King.
And ever and anon the wolf would steal
The children and devour, but now and then,
Her own brood lost or dead, lent her fierce teat
To human sucklings; and the children, housed
In her foul den, there at their meat would growl,
And mock their foster-mother on four feet,
Till, straighten'd, they grew up to wolf-like men,
Worse than the wolves. And King Leodogran
Groan'd for the Roman legions here again,
And Cæsar's eagle: then his brother king,
Urien, assail'd him: last a heathen horde,
Reddening the sun with smoke and earth with blood,
And on the spike that split the mother's heart
Spitting the child, brake on him, till, amazed,
He knew not whither he should turn for aid.

But—for he heard of Arthur newly crown'd,
Tho' not without an uproar made by those
Who cried, "He is not Uther's son"—the King
Sent to him, saying, "Arise, and help us thou!
For here between the man and beast we die."

And Arthur yet had done no deed of arms,
But heard the call, and came: and Guinevere
Stood by the castle walls to watch him pass;
But since he neither wore on helm or shield
The golden symbol of his kinglihood,
But rode a simple knight among his knights,
And many of these in richer arms than he,
She saw him not, or mark'd not, if she saw,
One among many, tho' his face was bare.
But Arthur, looking downward as he past,
Felt the light of her eyes into his life
Smite on the sudden, yet rode on, and pitch'd
His tents beside the forest. Then he drave
The heathen; after, slew the beast, and fell'd
The forest, letting in the sun, and made
Broad pathways for the hunter and the knight
And so return'd.
For while he linger'd there,
A doubt that ever smoulder'd in the hearts
Of those great Lords and Barons of his realm
Flash'd forth and into war: for most of these,
Colleaguing with a score of petty kings,
Made head against him, crying, "Who is he
That he should rule us? who hath proven him
King Uther's son? for lo! we look at him,
And find nor face nor bearing, limbs nor voice,
Are like to those of Uther whom we knew.
This is the son of Gorloïs, not the King;
This is the son of Anton, not the King."

And Arthur, passing thence to battle, felt
Travail, and throes and agonies of the life,
Desiring to be join'd with Guinevere;
And thinking as he rode, "Her father said
That there between the man and beast they die.
Shall I not lift her from this land of beasts
Up to my throne, and side by side with me?
What happiness to reign a lonely king,
Vext—O ye stars that shudder over me,
O earth that soundest hollow under me,
Vext with waste dreams? for saving I be join'd
To her that is the fairest under heaven,
I seem as nothing in the mighty world,

And cannot will my will, nor work my work
Wholly, nor make myself in mine own realm
Victor and lord. But were I join'd with her,
Then might we live together as one life,
And reigning with one will in everything
Have power on this dark land to lighten it,
And power on this dead world to make it live."

Thereafter—as he speaks who tells the tale—
When Arthur reach'd a field-of-battle bright
With pitch'd pavilions of his foe, the world
Was all so clear about him, that he saw
The smallest rock far on the faintest hill,
And even in high day the morning star.
So when the King had set his banner broad,
At once from either side, with trumpet-blast,
And shouts, and clarions shrilling unto blood,
The long-lanced battle let their horses run.
And now the Barons and the kings prevail'd,
And now the King, as here and there that war
Went swaying; but the Powers who walk the world
Made lightnings and great thunders over him,
And dazed all eyes, till Arthur by main might,
And mightier of his hands with every blow,
And leading all his knighthood threw the kings
Carádos, Urien, Cradlemont of Wales,
Claudias, and Clariance of Northumberland,
The King Brandagoras of Latangor,
With Anguisant of Erin, Morganore,
And Lot of Orkney. Then, before a voice
As dreadful as the shout of one who sees
To one who sins, and deems himself alone
And all the world asleep, they swerved and brake
Flying, and Arthur call'd to stay the brands
That hack'd among the flyers, "Ho! they yield!"
So like a painted battle the war stood
Silenced, the living quiet as the dead,
And in the heart of Arthur joy was lord.
He laugh'd upon his warrior whom he loved
And honour'd most. "Thou dost not doubt me King,
So well thine arm hath wrought for me to-day."
"Sir and my liege," he cried, "the fire of God
Descends upon thee in the battle-field:
I know thee for my King!" Whereat the two,
For each had warded either in the fight,
Sware on the field of death a deathless love.
And Arthur said, "Man's word is God in man:
Let chance what will, I trust thee to the death."

Then quickly from the foughten field he sent
Ulfius, and Brastias, and Bedivere,
His new-made knights, to King Leodogran,
Saying, "If I in aught have served thee well,
Give me thy daughter Guinevere to wife."

Whom when he heard, Leodogran in heart
Debating—"How should I that am a king,
However much he holp me at my need,
Give my one daughter saving to a king,
And a king's son?"—lifted his voice, and call'd
A hoary man, his chamberlain, to whom
He trusted all things, and of him required
His counsel: "Knowest thou aught of Arthur's birth?"

Then spake the hoary chamberlain and said,
"Sir King, there be but two old men that know:
And each is twice as old as I; and one
Is Merlin, the wise man that ever served
King Uther thro' his magic art; and one
Is Merlin's master (so they call him) Bleys,
Who taught him magic; but the scholar ran
Before the master, and so far, that Bleys
Laid magic by, and sat him down, and wrote
All things and whatsoever Merlin did
In one great annal-book, where after-years
Will learn the secret of our Arthur's birth."

To whom the King Leodogran replied,
"O friend, had I been holpen half as well
By this King Arthur as by thee to-day,
Then beast and man had had their share of me:
But summon here before us yet once more
Ulfius, and Brastias, and Bedivere."

Then, when they came before him, the King said,
"I have seen the cuckoo chased by lesser fowl,
And reason in the chase: but wherefore now
Do these your lords stir up the heat of war,
Some calling Arthur born of Gorloïs,
Others of Anton? Tell me, ye yourselves,
Hold ye this Arthur for King Uther's son?"

And Ulfius and Brastias answer'd, "Ay."
Then Bedivere, the first of all his knights
Knighted by Arthur at his crowning, spake—
For bold in heart and act and word was he,
Whenever slander breathed against the King—

"Sir, there be many rumours on this head:
For there be those who hate him in their hearts,
Call him baseborn, and since his ways are sweet,
And theirs are bestial, hold him less than man:
And there be those who deem him more than man,
And dream he dropt from heaven: but my belief
In all this matter—so ye care to learn—
Sir, for ye know that in King Uther's time
The prince and warrior Gorloïs, he that held
Tintagil castle by the Cornish sea,
Was wedded with a winsome wife, Ygerne:
And daughters had she borne him,—one whereof,
Lot's wife, the Queen of Orkney, Bellicent,
Hath ever like a loyal sister cleaved
To Arthur,—but a son she had not borne.
And Uther cast upon her eyes of love:
But she, a stainless wife to Gorloïs,
So loathed the bright dishonour of his love,
That Gorloïs and King Uther went to war:
And overthrown was Gorloïs and slain.
Then Uther in his wrath and heat besieged
Ygerne within Tintagil, where her men,
Seeing the mighty swarm about their walls,
Left her and fled, and Uther enter'd in,
And there was none to call to but himself.
So, compass'd by the power of the King,
Enforced she was to wed him in her tears,
And with a shameful swiftness: afterward,
Not many moons, King Uther died himself,
Moaning and wailing for an heir to rule
After him, lest the realm should go to wrack.
And that same night, the night of the new year,
By reason of the bitterness and grief
That vext his mother, all before his time
Was Arthur born, and all as soon as born
Deliver'd at a secret postern-gate
To Merlin, to be holden far apart
Until his hour should come; because the lords
Of that fierce day were as the lords of this,
Wild beasts; and surely would have torn the child
Piecemeal among them, had they known; for each
But sought to rule for his own self and hand,
And many hated Uther for the sake
Of Gorloïs. Wherefore Merlin took the child,
And gave him to Sir Anton, an old knight
And ancient friend of Uther; and his wife
Nursed the young prince, and rear'd him with her own;
And no man knew. And ever since the lords
Have foughten like wild beasts among themselves,
So that the realm has gone to wrack: but now,
This year, when Merlin (for his hour had come)
Brought Arthur forth, and set him in the hall,
Proclaiming, "Here is Uther's heir, your king,"
A hundred voices cried, "Away with him!
No king of ours! a son of Gorloïs he,
Or else the child of Anton, and no king,
Or else baseborn." Yet Merlin thro' his craft,
And while the people clamour'd for a king,
Had Arthur crown'd; but after, the great lords
Banded, and so brake out in open war."

Then while the King debated with himself
If Arthur were the child of shamefulness,
Or born the son of Gorloïs, after death,
Or Uther's son, and born before his time,
Or whether there were truth in anything
Said by these three, there came to Cameliard,
With Gawain and young Modred, her two sons,
Lot's wife, the Queen of Orkney, Bellicent;
Whom as he could, not as he would, the King
Made feast for, saying, as they sat at meat,

"A doubtful throne is ice on summer seas.
Ye come from Arthur's court. Victor his men
Report him! Yea, but ye—think ye this king—
So many those that hate him, and so strong,
So few his knights, however brave they be—
Hath body enow to hold his foemen down?"

"O King," she cried, "and I will tell thee: few,
Few, but all brave, all of one mind with him;
For I was near him when the savage yells
Of Uther's peerage died, and Arthur sat
Crown'd on the daïs, and his warriors cried,
'Be thou the king, and we will work thy will
Who love thee.' Then the King in low deep tones,
And simple words of great authority,
Bound them by so strait vows to his own self,
That when they rose, knighted from kneeling, some
Were pale as at the passing of a ghost,
Some flush'd, and others dazed, as one who wakes
Half-blinded at the coming of a light.

"But when he spake and cheer'd his Table Round
With large, divine, and comfortable words,
Beyond my tongue to tell thee—I beheld
From eye to eye thro' all their Order flash
A momentary likeness of the King:
And ere it left their faces, thro' the cross
And those around it and the Crucified,
Down from the casement over Arthur, smote
Flame-colour, vert and azure, in three rays,
One falling upon each of three fair queens,
Who stood in silence near his throne, the friends
Of Arthur, gazing on him, tall, with bright
Sweet faces, who will help him at his need.

"And there I saw mage Merlin, whose vast wit
And hundred winters are but as the hands
Of loyal vassals toiling for their liege.

"And near him stood the Lady of the Lake,
Who knows a subtler magic than his own—
Clothed in white samite, mystic, wonderful.
She gave the King his huge cross-hilted sword,
Whereby to drive the heathen out: a mist
Of incense curl'd about her, and her face
Wellnigh was hidden in the minster gloom;
But there was heard among the holy hymns
A voice as of the waters, for she dwells
Down in a deep; calm, whatsoever storms
May shake the world, and when the surface rolls,
Hath power to walk the waters like our Lord.

"There likewise I beheld Excalibur
Before him at his crowning borne, the sword
That rose from out the bosom of the lake,
And Arthur row'd across and took it—rich
With jewels, elfin Urim, on the hilt,
Bewildering heart and eye—the blade so bright
That men are blinded by it—on one side,
Graven in the oldest tongue of all this world,
'Take me,' but turn the blade and ye shall see,
And written in the speech ye speak yourself,
'Cast me away!' And sad was Arthur's face
Taking it, but old Merlin counsell'd him,
'Take thou and strike! the time to cast away
Is yet far-off.' So this great brand the king
Took, and by this will beat his foemen down."

Thereat Leodogran rejoiced, but thought
To sift his doubtings to the last, and ask'd,
Fixing full eyes of question on her face,
"The swallow and the swift are near akin,
But thou art closer to this noble prince,
Being his own dear sister;" and she said,
"Daughter of Gorloïs and Ygerne am I;"
"And therefore Arthur's sister?" ask'd the King.
She answer'd, "These be secret things," and sign'd
To those two sons to pass, and let them be.
And Gawain went, and breaking into song
Sprang out, and follow'd by his flying hair
Ran like a colt, and leapt at all he saw:
But Modred laid his ear beside the doors,
And there half-heard; the same that afterward
Struck for the throne, and striking found his doom.

And then the Queen made answer, "What know I?
For dark my mother was in eyes and hair,
And dark in hair and eyes am I; and dark
Was Gorloïs, yea and dark was Uther too,
Wellnigh to blackness; but this King is fair
Beyond the race of Britons and of men.
Moreover, always in my mind I hear
A cry from out the dawning of my life,
A mother weeping, and I hear her say,
'O that ye had some brother, pretty one,
To guard thee on the rough ways of the world.' "

"Ay," said the King, "and hear ye such a cry?
But when did Arthur chance upon thee first?"

"O King!" she cried, "and I will tell thee true:
He found me first when yet a little maid:
Beaten I had been for a little fault
Whereof I was not guilty; and out I ran
And flung myself down on a bank of heath,
And hated this fair world and all therein,
And wept, and wish'd that I were dead; and he—
I know not whether of himself he came,
Or brought by Merlin, who, they say, can walk
Unseen at pleasure—he was at my side,
And spake sweet words, and comforted my heart,
And dried my tears, being a child with me.
And many a time he came, and evermore
As I grew greater grew with me; and sad
At times he seem'd, and sad with him was I,
Stern too at times, and then I loved him not,
But sweet again, and then I loved him well.
And now of late I see him less and less,
But those first days had golden hours for me,
For then I surely thought he would be king.

"But let me tell thee now another tale:
For Bleys, our Merlin's master, as they say,
Died but of late, and sent his cry to me,
To hear him speak before he left his life.
Shrunk like a fairy changeling lay the mage;
And when I enter'd told me that himself
And Merlin ever served about the King,
Uther, before he died; and on the night
When Uther in Tintagil past away
Moaning and wailing for an heir, the two
Left the still King, and passing forth to breathe,
Then from the castle gateway by the chasm
Descending thro' the dismal night—a night
In which the bounds of heaven and earth were lost—
Beheld, so high upon the dreary deeps
It seem'd in heaven, a ship, the shape thereof
A dragon wing'd, and all from stem to stern
Bright with a shining people on the decks,
And gone as soon as seen. And then the two
Dropt to the cove, and watch'd the great sea fall,
Wave after wave, each mightier than the last,
Till last, a ninth one, gathering half the deep
And full of voices, slowly rose and plunged
Roaring, and all the wave was in a flame:
And down the wave and in the flame was borne
A naked babe, and rode to Merlin's feet,
Who stoopt and caught the babe, and cried 'The King!
Here is an heir for Uther!' And the fringe
Of that great breaker, sweeping up the strand,
Lash'd at the wizard as he spake the word,
And all at once all round him rose in fire,
So that the child and he were clothed in fire.
And presently thereafter follow'd calm,
Free sky and stars: 'And this same child,' he said,
'Is he who reigns; nor could I part in peace
Till this were told.' And saying this the seer
Went thro' the strait and dreadful pass of death,
Not ever to be question'd any more
Save on the further side; but when I met
Merlin, and ask'd him if these things were truth—
The shining dragon and the naked child
Descending in the glory of the seas—
He laugh'd as is his wont, and answer'd me
In riddling triplets of old time, and said:

" 'Rain, rain, and sun! a rainbow in the sky!
A young man will be wiser by and by;
An old man's wit may wander ere he die.
Rain, rain, and sun! a rainbow on the lea!
And truth is this to me, and that to thee;
And truth or clothed or naked let it be.
Rain, sun, and rain! and the free blossom blows:
Sun, rain, and sun! and where is he who knows?
From the great deep to the great deep he goes.'

"So Merlin riddling anger'd me; but thou
Fear not to give this King thine only child,
Guinevere: so great bards of him will sing
Hereafter; and dark sayings from of old
Ranging and ringing thro' the minds of men,
And echo'd by old folk beside their fires
For comfort after their wage-work is done,
Speak of the King; and Merlin in our time

Hath spoken also, not in jest, and sworn
Tho' men may wound him that he will not die,
But pass, again to come; and then or now
Utterly smite the heathen underfoot,
Till these and all men hail him for their king."

She spake and King Leodogran rejoiced,
But musing "Shall I answer yea or nay?"
Doubted, and drowsed, nodded and slept, and saw,
Dreaming, a slope of land that ever grew,
Field after field, up to a height, the peak
Haze-hidden, and thereon a phantom king,
Now looming, and now lost; and on the slope
The sword rose, the hind fell, the herd was driven,
Fire glimpsed; and all the land from roof and rick,
In drifts of smoke before a rolling wind,
Stream'd to the peak, and mingled with the haze
And made it thicker; while the phantom king
Sent out at times a voice; and here or there
Stood one who pointed toward the voice, the rest
Slew on and burnt, crying, "No king of ours,
No son of Uther, and no king of ours;"
Till with a wink his dream was changed, the haze
Descended, and the solid earth became
As nothing, but the King stood out in heaven,
Crown'd. And Leodogran awoke, and sent
Ulfius, and Brastias and Bedivere,
Back to the court of Arthur answering yea.

Then Arthur charged his warrior whom he loved
And honour'd most, Sir Lancelot, to ride forth
And bring the Queen;—and watch'd him from the gates:
And Lancelot past away among the flowers,
(For then was latter April) and return'd
Among the flowers, in May, with Guinevere.
To whom arrived, by Dubric the high saint,
Chief of the church in Britain, and before
The stateliest of her altar-shrines, the King
That morn was married, while in stainless white,
The fair beginners of a nobler time,
And glorying in their vows and him, his knights
Stood round him, and rejoicing in his joy.
Far shone the fields of May thro' open door,
The sacred altar blossom'd white with May,
The Sun of May descended on their King,
They gazed on all earth's beauty in their Queen,
Roll'd incense, and there past along the hymns
A voice as of the waters, while the two
Sware at the shrine of Christ a deathless love:
And Arthur said, "Behold, thy doom is mine.
Let chance what will, I love thee to the death!"
To whom the Queen replied with drooping eyes,
"King and my lord, I love thee to the death!"
And holy Dubric spread his hands and spake,
"Reign ye, and live and love, and make the world
Other, and may thy Queen be one with thee,
And all this Order of thy Table Round
Fulfil the boundless purpose of their King!"

So Dubric said; but when they left the shrine
Great Lords from Rome before the portal stood,
In scornful stillness gazing as they past;
Then while they paced a city all on fire
With sun and cloth of gold, the trumpets blew,
And Arthur's knighthood sang before the King:—

"Blow trumpet, for the world is white with May;
Blow trumpet, the long night hath roll'd away!
Blow thro' the living world—'Let the King reign.'

"Shall Rome or Heathen rule in Arthur's realm?
Flash brand and lance, fall battleaxe upon helm,
Fall battleaxe, and flash brand! Let the King reign.

"Strike for the King and live! his knights have heard
That God hath told the King a secret word.
Fall battleaxe, and flash brand! Let the King reign.

"Blow trumpet! he will lift us from the dust.
Blow trumpet! live the strength and die the lust!
Clang battleaxe, and clash brand! Let the King reign.

"Strike for the King and die! and if thou diest,
The King is King, and ever wills the highest.
Clang battleaxe, and clash brand! Let the King reign.

"Blow, for our Sun is mighty in his May!
Blow, for our Sun is mightier day by day!
Clang battleaxe, and clash brand! Let the King reign.

"The King will follow Christ, and we the King
In whom high God hath breathed a secret thing.
Fall battleaxe, and flash brand! Let the King reign."

So sang the knighthood, moving to their hall.
There at the banquet those great Lords from Rome,
The slowly-fading mistress of the world,
Strode in, and claim'd their tribute as of yore.
But Arthur spake, "Behold, for these have sworn
To wage my wars, and worship me their King;
The old order changeth, yielding place to new;
And we that fight for our fair father Christ,
Seeing that ye be grown too weak and old
To drive the heathen from your Roman wall,
No tribute will we pay:" so those great lords
Drew back in wrath, and Arthur strove with Rome.

And Arthur and his knighthood for a space
Were all one will, and thro' that strength the King
Drew in the petty princedoms under him,
Fought, and in twelve great battles overcame
The heathen hordes, and made a realm and reign'd.

1869

LANCELOT AND ELAINE

ELAINE the fair, Elaine the lovable,
Elaine, the lily maid of Astolat,
High in her chamber up a tower to the east
Guarded the sacred shield of Lancelot;
Which first she placed where morning's earliest ray
Might strike it, and awake her with the gleam;
Then fearing rust or soilure fashion'd for it
A case of silk, and braided thereupon
All the devices blazon'd on the shield
In their own tinct, and added, of her wit,
A border fantasy of branch and flower,
And yellow-throated nestling in the nest.
Nor rested thus content, but day by day,
Leaving her household and good father, climb'd
That eastern tower, and entering barr'd her door,
Stript off the case, and read the naked shield,
Now guess'd a hidden meaning in his arms,
Now made a pretty history to herself
Of every dint a sword had beaten in it,
And every scratch a lance had made upon it,
Conjecturing when and where: this cut is fresh;
That ten years back; this dealt him at Caerlyle;
That at Caerleon; this at Camelot:
And ah God's mercy, what a stroke was there!
And here a thrust that might have kill'd, but God
Broke the strong lance, and roll'd his enemy down,
And saved him: so she lived in fantasy.

How came the lily maid by that good shield
Of Lancelot, she that knew not ev'n his name?
He left it with her, when he rode to tilt
For the great diamond in the diamond jousts,

Which Arthur had ordain'd, and by that name
Had named them, since a diamond was the prize.

For Arthur, long before they crown'd him King,
Roving the trackless realms of Lyonnesse,
Had found a glen, gray boulder and black tarn.
A horror lived about the tarn, and clave
Like its own mists to all the mountain side:
For here two brothers, one a king, had met
And fought together; but their names were lost;
And each had slain his brother at a blow;
And down they fell and made the glen abhorr'd:
And there they lay till all their bones were bleach'd,
And lichen'd into colour with the crags:
And he, that once was king, had on a crown
Of diamonds, one in front, and four aside.
And Arthur came, and labouring up the pass,
All in a misty moonshine, unawares
Had trodden that crown'd skeleton, and the skull
Brake from the nape, and from the skull the crown
Roll'd into light, and turning on its rims
Fled like a glittering rivulet to the tarn:
And down the shingly scaur he plunged, and caught,
And set it on his head, and in his heart
Heard murmurs, "Lo, thou likewise shalt be King."

Thereafter, when a King, he had the gems
Pluck'd from the crown, and show'd them to his knights,
Saying, "These jewels, whereupon I chanced
Divinely, are the kingdom's, not the King's—
For public use: henceforward let there be,
Once every year, a joust for one of these:
For so by nine years' proof we needs must learn
Which is our mightiest, and ourselves shall grow
In use of arms and manhood, till we drive
The heathen, who, some say, shall rule the land
Hereafter, which God hinder." Thus he spoke:
And eight years past, eight jousts had been, and still
Had Lancelot won the diamond of the year,
With purpose to present them to the Queen,
When all were won; but meaning all at once
To snare her royal fancy with a boon
Worth half her realm, had never spoken word.

Now for the central diamond and the last
And largest, Arthur, holding then his court
Hard on the river nigh the place which now
Is this world's hugest, let proclaim a joust
At Camelot, and when the time drew nigh
Spake (for she had been sick) to Guinevere,
"Are you so sick, my Queen, you cannot move
To these fair jousts?" "Yea, lord," she said, "ye know it."
"Then will ye miss," he answer'd, "the great deeds
Of Lancelot, and his prowess in the lists,
A sight ye love to look on." And the Queen
Lifted her eyes, and they dwelt languidly
On Lancelot, where he stood beside the King.
He thinking that he read her meaning there,
"Stay with me, I am sick; my love is more
Than many diamonds," yielded; and a heart
Love-loyal to the least wish of the Queen
(However much he yearn'd to make complete
The tale of diamonds for his destined boon)
Urged him to speak against the truth, and say,
"Sir King, mine ancient wound is hardly whole,
And lets me from the saddle;" and the King
Glanced first at him, then her, and went his way.
No sooner gone than suddenly she began:

"To blame, my lord Sir Lancelot, much to blame!
Why go ye not to these fair jousts? the knights
Are half of them our enemies, and the crowd
Will murmur, 'Lo the shameless ones, who take
Their pastime now the trustful King is gone!' "
Then Lancelot vext at having lied in vain:
"Are ye so wise? ye were not once so wise,
My Queen, that summer, when ye loved me first.

Then of the crowd ye took no more account
Than of the myriad cricket of the mead,
When its own voice clings to each blade of grass,
And every voice is nothing. As to knights,
Them surely can I silence with all ease.
But now my loyal worship is allow'd
Of all men: many a bard, without offence,
Has link'd our names together in his lay,
Lancelot, the flower of bravery, Guinevere,
The pearl of beauty: and our knights at feast
Have pledged us in this union, while the King
Would listen smiling. How then? is there more?
Has Arthur spoken aught? or would yourself,
Now weary of my service and devoir,
Henceforth be truer to your faultless lord?"

She broke into a little scornful laugh:
"Arthur, my lord, Arthur, the faultless King,
That passionate perfection, my good lord—
But who can gaze upon the Sun in heaven?
He never spake word of reproach to me,
He never had a glimpse of mine untruth,
He cares not for me: only here to-day
There gleam'd a vague suspicion in his eyes:
Some meddling rogue has tamper'd with him—else
Rapt in this fancy of his Table Round,
And swearing men to vows impossible,
To make them like himself: but, friend, to me
He is all fault who hath no fault at all:
For who loves me must have a touch of earth;
The low sun makes the colour: I am yours,
Not Arthur's, as ye know, save by the bond.
And therefore hear my words: go to the jousts:
The tiny-trumpeting gnat can break our dream
When sweetest; and the vermin voices here
May buzz so loud—we scorn them, but they sting."

Then answer'd Lancelot, the chief of knights:
"And with what face, after my pretext made,
Shall I appear, O Queen, at Camelot, I
Before a King who honours his own word,
As if it were his God's?"
"Yea," said the Queen,
"A moral child without the craft to rule,
Else had he not lost me: but listen to me,
If I must find you wit: we hear it said
That men go down before your spear at a touch,
But knowing you are Lancelot; your great name,
This conquers: hide it therefore; go unknown:
Win! by this kiss you will: and our true King
Will then allow your pretext, O my knight,
As all for glory; for to speak him true,
Ye know right well, how meek soe'er he seem,
No keener hunter after glory breathes.
He loves it in his knights more than himself:
They prove to him his work: win and return."

Then got Sir Lancelot suddenly to horse,
Wroth at himself. Not willing to be known,
He left the barren-beaten thoroughfare,
Chose the green path that show'd the rarer foot,
And there among the solitary downs,
Full often lost in fancy, lost his way;
Till as he traced a faintly-shadow'd track,
That all in loops and links among the dales
Ran to the Castle of Astolat, he saw
Fired from the west, far on a hill, the towers.
Thither he made, and blew the gateway horn.
Then came an old, dumb, myriad-wrinkled man,
Who let him into lodging and disarm'd.
And Lancelot marvell'd at the wordless man;
And issuing found the Lord of Astolat
With two strong sons, Sir Torre and Sir Lavaine,
Moving to meet him in the castle court;
And close behind them stept the lily maid
Elaine, his daughter: mother of the house
There was not: some light jest among them rose
With laughter dying down as the great knight
Approach'd them: then the Lord of Astolat:
"Whence comest thou, my guest, and by what name
Livest between the lips? for by thy state
And presence I might guess thee chief of those,
After the King, who eat in Arthur's halls.
Him have I seen: the rest, his Table Round,
Known as they are, to me they are unknown."

Then answer'd Lancelot, the chief of knights:
"Known am I, and of Arthur's hall, and known,
What I by mere mischance have brought, my shield.
But since I go to joust as one unknown
At Camelot for the diamond, ask me not,
Hereafter ye shall know me—and the shield—
I pray you lend me one, if such you have,
Blank, or at least with some device not mine."

Then said the Lord of Astolat, "Here is Torre's:
Hurt in his first tilt was my son, Sir Torre.
And so, God wot, his shield is blank enough.
His ye can have." Then added plain Sir Torre,
"Yea, since I cannot use it, ye may have it."
Here laugh'd the father saying, "Fie, Sir Churl,
Is that an answer for a noble knight?
Allow him! but Lavaine, my younger here,
He is so full of lustihood, he will ride,
Joust for it, and win, and bring it in an hour,
And set it in this damsel's golden hair,
To make her thrice as wilful as before."

"Nay, father, nay good father, shame me not
Before this noble knight," said young Lavaine,
"For nothing. Surely I but play'd on Torre:
He seem'd so sullen, vext he could not go:
A jest, no more! for, knight, the maiden dreamt
That some one put this diamond in her hand,
And that it was too slippery to be held,
And slipt and fell into some pool or stream,
The castle-well, belike; and then I said
That *if* I went and *if* I fought and won it
(But all was jest and joke among ourselves)
Then must she keep it safelier. All was jest.
But, father, give me leave, an if he will,
To ride to Camelot with this noble knight:
Win shall I not, but do my best to win:
Young as I am, yet would I do my best."

"So ye will grace me," answer'd Lancelot,
Smiling a moment, "with your fellowship
O'er these waste downs whereon I lost myself,
Then were I glad of you as guide and friend:
And you shall win this diamond,—as I hear
It is a fair large diamond,—if ye may,
And yield it to this maiden, if ye will."
"A fair large diamond," added plain Sir Torre,
"Such be for queens, and not for simple maids."
Then she, who held her eyes upon the ground,
Elaine, and heard her name so tost about,
Flush'd slightly at the slight disparagement
Before the stranger knight, who, looking at her,
Full courtly, yet not falsely, thus return'd:
"If what is fair be but for what is fair,
And only queens are to be counted so,
Rash were my judgment then, who deem this maid
Might wear as fair a jewel as is on earth,
Not violating the bond of like to like."

He spoke and ceased: the lily maid Elaine,
Won by the mellow voice before she look'd,
Lifted her eyes, and read his lineaments.
The great and guilty love he bare the Queen,
In battle with the love he bare his lord,
Had marr'd his face, and mark'd it ere his time.
Another sinning on such heights with one,
The flower of all the west and all the world,
Had been the sleeker for it: but in him
His mood was often like a fiend, and rose
And drove him into wastes and solitudes
For agony, who was yet a living soul.
Marr'd as he was, he seem'd the goodliest man
That ever among ladies ate in hall,
And noblest, when she lifted up her eyes.
However marr'd, of more than twice her years,
Seam'd with an ancient swordcut on the cheek,
And bruised and bronzed, she lifted up her eyes
And loved him, with that love which was her doom.

Then the great knight, the darling of the court,
Loved of the loveliest, into that rude hall
Stept with all grace, and not with half disdain
Hid under grace, as in a smaller time,
But kindly man moving among his kind:
Whom they with meats and vintage of their best
And talk and minstrel melody entertain'd.

And much they ask'd of court and Table Round,
And ever well and readily answer'd he:
But Lancelot, when they glanced at Guinevere,
Suddenly speaking of the wordless man,
Heard from the Baron that, ten years before,
The heathen caught and reft him of his tongue.
"He learnt and warn'd me of their fierce design
Against my house, and him they caught and maim'd;
But I, my sons, and little daughter fled
From bonds or death, and dwelt among the woods
By the great river in a boatman's hut.
Dull days were those, till our good Arthur broke
The Pagan yet once more on Badon hill."

"O there, great lord, doubtless," Lavaine said, rapt
By all the sweet and sudden passion of youth
Toward greatness in its elder, "you have fought.
O tell us—for we live apart—you know
Of Arthur's glorious wars." And Lancelot spoke
And answer'd him at full, as having been
With Arthur in the fight which all day long
Rang by the white mouth of the violent Glem;
And in the four loud battles by the shore
Of Duglas; that on Bassa; then the war
That thunder'd in and out the gloomy skirts
Of Celidon the forest; and again
By castle Gurnion, where the glorious King
Had on his cuirass worn our Lady's Head,
Carved of one emerald center'd in a sun
Of silver rays, that lighten'd as he breathed;
And at Caerleon had he help'd his lord,
When the strong neighings of the wild white Horse
Set every gilded parapet shuddering;
And up in Agned-Cathregonion too,
And down the waste sand-shores of Trath Treroit,
Where many a heathen fell; "and on the mount
Of Badon I myself beheld the King
Charge at the head of all his Table Round,
And all his legions crying Christ and him,
And break them; and I saw him, after, stand
High on a heap of slain, from spur to plume
Red as the rising sun with heathen blood,
And seeing me, with a great voice he cried,
'They are broken, they are broken!' for the King,
However mild he seems at home, nor cares
For triumph in our mimic wars, the jousts—
For if his own knight cast him down, he laughs
Saying, his knights are better men than he—
Yet in this heathen war the fire of God
Fills him: I never saw his like: there lives
No greater leader."

While he utter'd this,
Low to her own heart said the lily maid,
"Save your great self, fair lord;" and when he fell
From talk of war to traits of pleasantry—
Being mirthful he, but in a stately kind—
She still took note that when the living smile
Died from his lips, across him came a cloud
Of melancholy severe, from which again,
Whenever in her hovering to and fro
The lily maid had striven to make him cheer,
There brake a sudden-beaming tenderness
Of manners and of nature: and she thought
That all was nature, all, perchance, for her.
And all night long his face before her lived,
As when a painter, poring on a face,
Divinely thro' all hindrance finds the man
Behind it, and so paints him that his face,
The shape and colour of a mind and life,
Lives for his children, ever at its best
And fullest; so the face before her lived,
Dark-splendid, speaking in the silence, full
Of noble things, and held her from her sleep.
Till rathe she rose, half-cheated in the thought
She needs must bid farewell to sweet Lavaine.
First as in fear, step after step, she stole
Down the long tower-stairs, hesitating:
Anon, she heard Sir Lancelot cry in the court,
"This shield, my friend, where is it?" and Lavaine
Past inward, as she came from out the tower.
There to his proud horse Lancelot turn'd, and smooth'd
The glossy shoulder, humming to himself.

Half-envious of the flattering hand, she drew
Nearer and stood. He look'd, and more amazed
Than if seven men had set upon him, saw
The maiden standing in the dewy light.
He had not dream'd she was so beautiful.
Then came on him a sort of sacred fear,
For silent, tho' he greeted her, she stood
Rapt on his face as if it were a God's.
Suddenly flash'd on her a wild desire,
That he should wear her favour at the tilt.
She braved a riotous heart in asking for it.
"Fair lord, whose name I know not—noble it is,
I well believe, the noblest—will you wear
My favour at this tourney?" "Nay," said he,
"Fair lady, since I never yet have worn
Favour of any lady in the lists.
Such is my wont, as those, who know me, know."
"Yea, so," she answer'd; "then in wearing mine
Needs must be lesser likelihood, noble lord,
That those who know should know you."
And he turn'd
Her counsel up and down within his mind,
And found it true, and answer'd, "True, my child.
Well, I will wear it: fetch it out to me:
What is it?" and she told him "A red sleeve
Broider'd with pearls," and brought it: then he bound
Her token on his helmet, with a smile
Saying, "I never yet have done so much
For any maiden living," and the blood
Sprang to her face and fill'd her with delight;
But left her all the paler, when Lavaine
Returning brought the yet-unblazon'd shield,
His brother's; which he gave to Lancelot,
Who parted with his own to fair Elaine:
"Do me this grace, my child, to have my shield
In keeping till I come." "A grace to me,"
She answer'd, "twice to-day. I am your squire!"
Whereat Lavaine said, laughing, "Lily maid,
For fear our people call you lily maid
In earnest, let me bring your colour back;
Once, twice, and thrice: now get you hence to bed:"
So kiss'd her, and Sir Lancelot his own hand,
And thus they moved away: she stay'd a minute,
Then made a sudden step to the gate, and there—
Her bright hair blown about the serious face
Yet rosy-kindled with her brother's kiss—
Paused by the gateway, standing near the shield
In silence, while she watch'd their arms far-off
Sparkle, until they dipt below the downs.
Then to her tower she climb'd, and took the shield,
There kept it, and so lived in fantasy.

Meanwhile the new companions past away
Far o'er the long backs of the bushless downs,
To where Sir Lancelot knew there lived a knight
Not far from Camelot, now for forty years
A hermit, who had pray'd, labour'd and pray'd,
And ever labouring had scoop'd himself
In the white rock a chapel and a hall
On massive columns, like a shorecliff cave,
And cells and chambers: all were fair and dry;
The green light from the meadows underneath
Struck up and lived along the milky roofs;
And in the meadows tremulous aspen-trees
And poplars made a noise of falling showers.
And thither wending there that night they bode.

But when the next day broke from underground,
And shot red fire and shadows thro' the cave,
They rose, heard mass, broke fast, and rode away:
Then Lancelot saying, "Hear, but hold my name
Hidden, you ride with Lancelot of the Lake,"
Abash'd Lavaine, whose instant reverence,
Dearer to true young hearts than their own praise,
But left him leave to stammer, "Is it indeed?"
And after muttering "The great Lancelot,"
At last he got his breath and answer'd, "One,
One have I seen—that other, our liege lord,
The dread Pendragon, Britain's King of kings,

Of whom the people talk mysteriously,
He will be there—then were I stricken blind
That minute, I might say that I had seen."

So spake Lavaine, and when they reach'd the lists
By Camelot in the meadow, let his eyes
Run thro' the peopled gallery which half round
Lay like a rainbow fall'n upon the grass,
Until they found the clear-faced King, who sat
Robed in red samite, easily to be known,
Since to his crown the golden dragon clung,
And down his robe the dragon writhed in gold,
And from the carven-work behind him crept
Two dragons gilded, sloping down to make
Arms for his chair, while all the rest of them
Thro' knots and loops and folds innumerable
Fled ever thro' the woodwork, till they found
The new design wherein they lost themselves,
Yet with all ease, so tender was the work:
And, in the costly canopy o'er him set,
Blazed the last diamond of the nameless king.

Then Lancelot answer'd young Lavaine and said,
"Me you call great: mine is the firmer seat,
The truer lance: but there is many a youth
Now crescent, who will come to all I am
And overcome it; and in me there dwells
No greatness, save it be some far-off touch
Of greatness to know well I am not great:
There is the man." And Lavaine gaped upon him
As on a thing miraculous, and anon
The trumpets blew; and then did either side,
They that assail'd, and they that held the lists,
Set lance in rest, strike spur, suddenly move,
Meet in the midst, and there so furiously
Shock, that a man far-off might well perceive,
If any man that day were left afield,
The hard earth shake, and a low thunder of arms.
And Lancelot bode a little, till he saw
Which were the weaker; then he hurl'd into it
Against the stronger: little need to speak
Of Lancelot in his glory! King, duke, earl,
Count, baron—whom he smote, he overthrew.
But in the field were Lancelot's kith and kin,
Ranged with the Table Round that held the lists,
Strong men, and wrathful that a stranger knight
Should do and almost overdo the deeds
Of Lancelot; and one said to the other, "Lo!
What is he? I do not mean the force alone—
The grace and versatility of the man!
Is it not Lancelot?" "When has Lancelot worn
Favour of any lady in the lists?
Not such his wont, as we, that know him, know."
"How then? who then?" a fury seized them all,
A fiery family passion for the name
Of Lancelot, and a glory one with theirs.
They couch'd their spears and prick'd their steeds, and thus,
Their plumes driv'n backward by the wind they made
In moving, all together down upon him
Bare, as a wild wave in the wide North-sea,
Green-glimmering toward the summit, bears, with all
Its stormy crests that smoke against the skies,
Down on a bark, and overbears the bark,
And him that helms it, so they overbore
Sir Lancelot and his charger, and a spear
Down-glancing lamed the charger, and a spear
Prick'd sharply his own cuirass, and the head
Pierced thro' his side, and there snapt, and remain'd.

Then Sir Lavaine did well and worshipfully;
He bore a knight of old repute to the earth,
And brought his horse to Lancelot where he lay.
He up the side, sweating with agony, got,
But thought to do while he might yet endure,
And being lustily holpen by the rest,
His party,—tho' it seem'd half-miracle
To those he fought with,—drave his kith and kin,
And all the Table Round that held the lists,
Back to the barrier; then the trumpets blew
Proclaiming his the prize, who wore the sleeve
Of scarlet, and the pearls; and all the knights,

His party, cried "Advance and take thy prize
The diamond;" but he answer'd, "Diamond me
No diamonds! for God's love, a little air!
Prize me no prizes, for my prize is death!
Hence will I, and I charge you, follow me not."

He spoke, and vanish'd suddenly from the field
With young Lavaine into the poplar grove.
There from his charger down he slid, and sat,
Gasping to Sir Lavaine, "Draw the lance-head:"
"Ah my sweet lord Sir Lancelot," said Lavaine,
"I dread me, if I draw it, you will die."
But he, "I die already with it: draw—
Draw,"—and Lavaine drew, and Sir Lancelot gave
A marvellous great shriek and ghastly groan,
And half his blood burst forth, and down he sank
For the pure pain, and wholly swoon'd away.
Then came the hermit out and bare him in,
There stanch'd his wound; and there, in daily doubt
Whether to live or die, for many a week
Hid from the wide world's rumour by the grove
Of poplars with their noise of falling showers,
And ever-tremulous aspen-trees, he lay.

But on that day when Lancelot fled the lists,
His party, knights of utmost North and West,
Lords of waste marches, kings of desolate isles,
Came round their great Pendragon, saying to him,
"Lo, Sire, our knight, thro' whom we won the day,
Hath gone sore wounded, and hath left his prize
Untaken, crying that his prize is death."
"Heaven hinder," said the King, "that such an one,
So great a knight as we have seen to-day—
He seem'd to me another Lancelot—
Yea, twenty times I thought him Lancelot—
He must not pass uncared for. Wherefore, rise,
O Gawain, and ride forth and find the knight.
Wounded and wearied needs must he be near.
I charge you that you get at once to horse.
And, knights and kings, there breathes not one of you
Will deem this prize of ours is rashly given:
His prowess was too wondrous. We will do him
No customary honour: since the knight
Came not to us, of us to claim the prize,
Ourselves will send it after. Rise and take
This diamond, and deliver it, and return,
And bring us where he is, and how he fares,
And cease not from your quest until ye find."

So saying, from the carven flower above,
To which it made a restless heart, he took,
And gave, the diamond: then from where he sat
At Arthur's right, with smiling face arose,
With smiling face and frowning heart, a Prince
In the mid might and flourish of his May,
Gawain, surnamed The Courteous, fair and strong,
And after Lancelot, Tristram, and Geraint
And Gareth, a good knight, but therewithal
Sir Modred's brother, and the child of Lot,
Nor often loyal to his word, and now
Wroth that the King's command to sally forth
In quest of whom he knew not, made him leave
The banquet, and concourse of knights and kings.

So all in wrath he got to horse and went;
While Arthur to the banquet, dark in mood,
Past, thinking "Is it Lancelot who hath come
Despite the wound he spake of, all for gain
Of glory, and hath added wound to wound,
And ridd'n away to die?" So fear'd the King,
And, after two days' tarriance there, return'd.
Then when he saw the Queen, embracing ask'd,
"Love, are you yet so sick?" "Nay, lord," she said.
"And where is Lancelot?" Then the Queen amazed,
"Was he not with you? won he not your prize?"

"Nay, but one like him." "Why that like was he."
And when the King demanded how she knew,
Said, "Lord, no sooner had ye parted from us,
Than Lancelot told me of a common talk
That men went down before his spear at a touch,
But knowing he was Lancelot; his great name
Conquer'd; and therefore would he hide his name
From all men, ev'n the King, and to this end
Had made the pretext of a hindering wound,
That he might joust unknown of all, and learn
If his old prowess were in aught decay'd;
And added, 'Our true Arthur, when he learns,
Will well allow my pretext, as for gain
Of purer glory.' "

Then replied the King:
"Far lovelier in our Lancelot had it been,
In lieu of idly dallying with the truth,
To have trusted me as he hath trusted thee.
Surely his King and most familiar friend
Might well have kept his secret. True, indeed,
Albeit I know my knights fantastical,
So fine a fear in our large Lancelot
Must needs have moved my laughter: now remains
But little cause for laughter: his own kin—
Ill news, my Queen, for all who love him, this!—
His kith and kin, not knowing, set upon him;
So that he went sore wounded from the field:
Yet good news too: for goodly hopes are mine
That Lancelot is no more a lonely heart.
He wore, against his wont, upon his helm
A sleeve of scarlet, broider'd with great pearls,
Some gentle maiden's gift."

"Yea, lord," she said,
"Thy hopes are mine," and saying that, she choked,
And sharply turn'd about to hide her face,
Past to her chamber, and there flung herself
Down on the great King's couch, and writhed upon it,
And clench'd her fingers till they bit the palm,
And shriek'd out "Traitor" to the unhearing wall,
Then flash'd into wild tears, and rose again,
And moved about her palace, proud and pale.

Gawain the while thro' all the region round
Rode with his diamond, wearied of the quest,
Touch'd at all points, except the poplar grove,
And came at last, tho' late, to Astolat:
Whom glittering in enamell'd arms the maid
Glanced at, and cried, "What news from Camelot, lord?
What of the knight with the red sleeve?" "He won."
"I knew it," she said. "But parted from the jousts
Hurt in the side," whereat she caught her breath;
Thro' her own side she felt the sharp lance go;
Thereon she smote her hand: wellnigh she swoon'd:
And, while he gazed wonderingly at her, came
The Lord of Astolat out, to whom the Prince
Reported who he was, and on what quest
Sent, that he bore the prize and could not find
The victor, but had ridd'n a random round
To seek him, and had wearied of the search.
To whom the Lord of Astolat, "Bide with us,
And ride no more at random, noble Prince!
Here was the knight, and here he left a shield;
This will he send or come for: furthermore
Our son is with him; we shall hear anon,
Needs must we hear." To this the courteous Prince
Accorded with his wonted courtesy,
Courtesy with a touch of traitor in it,
And stay'd; and cast his eyes on fair Elaine:
Where could be found face daintier? then her shape
From forehead down to foot, perfect—again
From foot to forehead exquisitely turn'd:
"Well—if I bide, lo! this wild flower for me!"
And oft they met among the garden yews,
And there he set himself to play upon her
With sallying wit, free flashes from a height
Above her, graces of the court, and songs,
Sighs, and slow smiles, and golden eloquence
And amorous adulation, till the maid
Rebell'd against it, saying to him, "Prince,
O loyal nephew of our noble King,
Why ask you not to see the shield he left,
Whence you might learn his name? Why slight your King,

And lose the quest he sent you on, and prove
No surer than our falcon yesterday,
Who lost the hern we slipt her at, and went
To all the winds?" "Nay, by mine head," said he,
"I lose it, as we lose the lark in heaven,
O damsel, in the light of your blue eyes;
But an ye will it let me see the shield."
And when the shield was brought, and Gawain saw
Sir Lancelot's azure lions, crown'd with gold,
Ramp in the field, he smote his thigh, and mock'd:
"Right was the King! our Lancelot! that true man!"
"And right was I," she answer'd merrily, "I,
Who dream'd my knight the greatest knight of all."
"And if *I* dream'd," said Gawain, "that you love
This greatest knight, your pardon! lo, ye know it!
Speak therefore: shall I waste myself in vain?"
Full simple was her answer, "What know I?
My brethren have been all my fellowship;
And I, when often they have talk'd of love,
Wish'd it had been my mother, for they talk'd,
Meseem'd, of what they knew not; so myself—
I know not if I know what true love is,
But if I know, then, if I love not him,
I know there is none other I can love."
"Yea, by God's death," said he, "ye love him well,
But would not, knew ye what all others know,
And whom he loves." "So be it," cried Elaine,
And lifted her fair face and moved away:
But he pursued her, calling, "Stay a little!
One golden minute's grace! he wore your sleeve:
Would he break faith with one I may not name?
Must our true man change like a leaf at last?
Nay—like enow: why then, far be it from me
To cross our mighty Lancelot in his loves!
And, damsel, for I deem you know full well
Where your great knight is hidden, let me leave
My quest with you; the diamond also: here!
For if you love, it will be sweet to give it;
And if he love, it will be sweet to have it
From your own hand; and whether he love or not,
A diamond is a diamond. Fare you well
A thousand times!—a thousand times farewell!
Yet, if he love, and his love hold, we two
May meet at court hereafter: there, I think,
So ye will learn the courtesies of the court,
We two shall know each other."

Then he gave,
And slightly kiss'd the hand to which he gave,
The diamond, and all wearied of the quest
Leapt on his horse, and carolling as he went
A true-love ballad, lightly rode away.

Thence to the court he past; there told the King
What the King knew, "Sir Lancelot is the knight."
And added, "Sire, my liege, so much I learnt;
But fail'd to find him, tho' I rode all round
The region: but I lighted on the maid
Whose sleeve he wore; she loves him; and to her,
Deeming our courtesy is the truest law,
I gave the diamond: she will render it;
For by mine head she knows his hiding-place."

The seldom-frowning King frown'd, and replied,
"Too courteous truly! ye shall go no more
On quest of mine, seeing that ye forget
Obedience is the courtesy due to kings."

He spake and parted. Wroth, but all in awe,
For twenty strokes of the blood, without a word,
Linger'd that other, staring after him;
Then shook his hair, strode off, and buzz'd abroad
About the maid of Astolat, and her love.
All ears were prick'd at once, all tongues were loosed:
"The maid of Astolat loves Sir Lancelot,
Sir Lancelot loves the maid of Astolat."
Some read the King's face, some the Queen's, and all

Had marvel what the maid might be, but most
Predoom'd her as unworthy. One old dame
Came suddenly on the Queen with the sharp news.
She, that had heard the noise of it before,
But sorrowing Lancelot should have stoop'd so low,
Marr'd her friend's aim with pale tranquillity.
So ran the tale like fire about the court,
Fire in dry stubble a nine-days' wonder flared:
Till ev'n the knights at banquet twice or thrice
Forgot to drink to Lancelot and the Queen,
And pledging Lancelot and the lily maid
Smiled at each other, while the Queen, who sat
With lips severely placid, felt the knot
Climb in her throat, and with her feet unseen
Crush'd the wild passion out against the floor
Beneath the banquet, where the meats became
As wormwood, and she hated all who pledged.

But far away the maid in Astolat,
Her guiltless rival, she that ever kept
The one-day-seen Sir Lancelot in her heart,
Crept to her father, while he mused alone,
Sat on his knee, stroked his gray face and said,
"Father, you call me wilful, and the fault
Is yours who let me have my will, and now,
Sweet father, will you let me lose my wits?"
"Nay," said he, "surely." "Wherefore, let me hence,"
She answer'd, "and find out our dear Lavaine."
"Ye will not lose your wits for dear Lavaine:
Bide," answer'd he: "we needs must hear anon
Of him, and of that other." "Ay," she said,
"And of that other, for I needs must hence
And find that other, wheresoe'er he be,
And with mine own hand give his diamond to him,
Lest I be found as faithless in the quest
As yon proud prince who left the quest to me.
Sweet father, I behold him in my dreams
Gaunt as it were the skeleton of himself,
Death-pale, for lack of gentle maiden's aid.
The gentler-born the maiden, the more bound,
My father, to be sweet and serviceable
To noble knights in sickness, as ye know
When these have worn their tokens: let me hence
I pray you." Then her father nodding said,
"Ay, ay, the diamond: wit ye well, my child,
Right fain were I to learn this knight were whole,
Being our greatest: yea, and you must give it—
And sure I think this fruit is hung too high
For any mouth to gape for save a queen's—
Nay, I mean nothing: so then, get you gone,
Being so very wilful you must go."

Lightly, her suit allow'd, she slipt away,
And while she made her ready for her ride,
Her father's latest word humm'd in her ear,
"Being so very wilful you must go,"
And changed itself and echo'd in her heart,
"Being so very wilful you must die."
But she was happy enough and shook it off,
As we shake off the bee that buzzes at us;
And in her heart she answer'd it and said,
"What matter, so I help him back to life?
Then far away with good Sir Torre for guide
Rode o'er the long backs of the bushless downs
To Camelot, and before the city-gates
Came on her brother with a happy face
Making a roan horse caper and curvet
For pleasure all about a field of flowers:
Whom when she saw, "Lavaine," she cried, "Lavaine,
How fares my lord Sir Lancelot?" He amazed,
"Torre and Elaine! why here? Sir Lancelot!
How know ye my lord's name is Lancelot?"
But when the maid had told him all her tale,
Then turn'd Sir Torre, and being in his moods
Left them, and under the strange-statued gate,
Where Arthur's wars were render'd mystically,
Past up the still rich city to his kin,
His own far blood, which dwelt at Camelot;
And her, Lavaine across the poplar grove
Led to the caves: there first she saw the casque
Of Lancelot on the wall: her scarlet sleeve,
Tho' carved and cut, and half the pearls away,
Stream'd from it still; and in her heart she laugh'd,

Because he had not loosed it from his helm,
But meant once more perchance to tourney in it.
And when they gain'd the cell wherein he slept,
His battle-writhen arms and mighty hands
Lay naked on the wolfskin, and a dream
Of dragging down his enemy made them move.
Then she that saw him lying unsleek, unshorn,
Gaunt as it were the skeleton of himself,
Utter'd a little tender dolorous cry.
The sound not wonted in a place so still
Woke the sick knight, and while he roll'd his eyes
Yet blank from sleep, she started to him, saying,
"Your prize the diamond sent you by the King:"
His eyes glisten'd: she fancied "Is it for me?"
And when the maid had told him all the tale
Of King and Prince, the diamond sent, the quest
Assign'd to her not worthy of it, she knelt
Full lowly by the corners of his bed,
And laid the diamond in his open hand.
Her face was near, and as we kiss the child
That does the task assign'd, he kiss'd her face.
At once she slipt like water to the floor.
"Alas," he said, "your ride hath wearied you.
Rest must you have." "No rest for me," she said;
"Nay, for near you, fair lord, I am at rest."
What might she mean by that? his large black eyes,
Yet larger thro' his leanness, dwelt upon her,
Till all her heart's sad secret blazed itself
In the heart's colours on her simple face;
And Lancelot look'd and was perplext in mind,
And being weak in body said no more;
But did not love the colour; woman's love,
Save one, he not regarded, and so turn'd
Sighing, and feign'd a sleep until he slept.

Then rose Elaine and glided thro' the fields,
And past beneath the weirdly-sculptured gates
Far up the dim rich city to her kin;
There bode the night: but woke with dawn, and past
Down thro' the dim rich city to the fields,
Thence to the cave: so day by day she past
In either twilight ghost-like to and fro
Gliding, and every day she tended him,
And likewise many a night: and Lancelot
Would, tho' he call'd his wound a little hurt
Whereof he should be quickly whole, at times
Brain-feverous in his heat and agony, seem
Uncourteous, even he: but the meek maid
Sweetly forbore him ever, being to him
Meeker than any child to a rough nurse,
Milder than any mother to a sick child,
And never woman yet, since man's first fall,
Did kindlier unto man, but her deep love
Upbore her; till the hermit, skill'd in all
The simples and the science of that time,
Told him that her fine care had saved his life.
And the sick man forgot her simple blush,
Would call her friend and sister, sweet Elaine,
Would listen for her coming and regret
Her parting step, and held her tenderly,
And loved her with all love except the love
Of man and woman when they love their best,
Closest and sweetest, and had died the death
In any knightly fashion for her sake.
And peradventure had he seen her first
She might have made this and that other world
Another world for the sick man; but now
The shackles of an old love straiten'd him,
His honour rooted in dishonour stood,
And faith unfaithful kept him falsely true.

Yet the great knight in his mid-sickness made
Full many a holy vow and pure resolve.
These, as but born of sickness, could not live:
For when the blood ran lustier in him again,
Full often the bright image of one face,
Making a treacherous quiet in his heart,
Dispersed his resolution like a cloud.
Then if the maiden, while that ghostly grace
Beam'd on his fancy, spoke, he answer'd not,
Or short and coldly, and she knew right well
What the rough sickness meant, but what this meant
She knew not, and the sorrow dimm'd her sight,
And drave her ere her time across the fields
Far into the rich city, where alone
She murmur'd, "Vain, in vain: it cannot be.

He will not love me: how then? must I die?"
Then as a little helpless innocent bird,
That has but one plain passage of few notes,
Will sing the simple passage o'er and o'er
For all an April morning, till the ear
Wearies to hear it, so the simple maid
Went half the night repeating, "Must I die?"
And now to right she turn'd, and now to left,
And found no ease in turning or in rest;
And "Him or death," she mutter'd, "death or him,"
Again and like a burthen, "Him or death."

But when Sir Lancelot's deadly hurt was whole,
To Astolat returning rode the three.
There morn by morn, arraying her sweet self
In that wherein she deem'd she look'd her best,
She came before Sir Lancelot, for she thought
"If I be loved, these are my festal robes,
If not, the victim's flowers before he fall."
And Lancelot ever prest upon the maid
That she should ask some goodly gift of him
For her own self or hers; "and do not shun
To speak the wish most near to your true heart;
Such service have ye done me, that I make
My will of yours, and Prince and Lord am I
In mine own land, and what I will I can."
Then like a ghost she lifted up her face,
But like a ghost without the power to speak.
And Lancelot saw that she withheld her wish,
And bode among them yet a little space
Till he should learn it; and one morn it chanced
He found her in among the garden yews,
And said, "Delay no longer, speak your wish,
Seeing I go to-day:" then out she brake:
"Going? and we shall never see you more.
And I must die for want of one bold word."
"Speak: that I live to hear," he said, "is yours."
Then suddenly and passionately she spoke:
"I have gone mad. I love you: let me die."
"Ah, sister," answer'd Lancelot, "what is this?"
And innocently extending her white arms,
"Your love," she said, "your love—to be your wife."
And Lancelot answer'd, "Had I chosen to wed,
I had been wedded earlier, sweet Elaine:
But now there never will be wife of mine."
"No, no," she cried, "I care not to be wife,
But to be with you still, to see your face,
To serve you, and to follow you thro' the world."
And Lancelot answer'd, "Nay, the world, the world,
All ear and eye, with such a stupid heart
To interpret ear and eye, and such a tongue
To blare its own interpretation—nay,
Full ill then should I quit your brother's love,
And your good father's kindness." And she said,
"Not to be with you, not to see your face—
Alas for me then, my good days are done."
"Nay, noble maid," he answer'd, "ten times nay!
This is not love: but love's first flash in youth,
Most common: yea, I know it of mine own self:
And you yourself will smile at your own self
Hereafter, when you yield your flower of life
To one more fitly yours, not thrice your age:
And then will I, for true you are and sweet
Beyond mine old belief in womanhood,
More specially should your good knight be poor,
Endow you with broad land and territory
Even to the half my realm beyond the seas,
So that would make you happy: furthermore,
Ev'n to the death, as tho' ye were my blood,
In all your quarrels will I be your knight.
This will I do, dear damsel, for your sake,
And more than this I cannot."

While he spoke
She neither blush'd nor shook, but deathly-pale
Stood grasping what was nearest, then replied:
"Of all this will I nothing;" and so fell,
And thus they bore her swooning to her tower.

Then spake, to whom thro' those black walls of yew
Their talk had pierced, her father: "Ay, a flash,
I fear me, that will strike my blossom dead.

Too courteous are ye, fair Lord Lancelot.
I pray you, use some rough discourtesy
To blunt or break her passion."
Lancelot said,
"That were against me: what I can I will;"
And there that day remain'd, and toward even
Sent for his shield: full meekly rose the maid,
Stript off the case, and gave the naked shield;
Then, when she heard his horse upon the stones,
Unclasping flung the casement back, and look'd
Down on his helm, from which her sleeve had gone.
And Lancelot knew the little clinking sound;
And she by tact of love was well aware
That Lancelot knew that she was looking at him.
And yet he glanced not up, nor waved his hand,
Nor bad farewell, but sadly rode away.
This was the one discourtesy that he used.

So in her tower alone the maiden sat:
His very shield was gone; only the case,
Her own poor work, her empty labour, left.
But still she heard him, still his picture form'd
And grew between her and the pictured wall.
Then came her father, saying in low tones,
"Have comfort," whom she greeted quietly.
Then came her brethren saying, "Peace to thee,
Sweet sister," whom she answer'd with all calm.
But when they left her to herself again,
Death, like a friend's voice from a distant field
Approaching thro' the darkness, call'd; the owls
Wailing had power upon her, and she mixt
Her fancies with the sallow-rifted glooms
Of evening, and the moanings of the wind.

And in those days she made a little song,
And call'd her song "The Song of Love and Death,"
And sang it: sweetly could she make and sing.

"Sweet is true love tho' given in vain, in vain;
And sweet is death who puts an end to pain:
I know not which is sweeter, no, not I.

"Love, art thou sweet? then bitter death must be:
Love, thou art bitter; sweet is death to me.
O Love, if death be sweeter, let me die.

"Sweet love, that seems not made to fade away,
Sweet death, that seems to make us loveless clay,
I know not which is sweeter, no, not I.

"I fain would follow love, if that could be;
I needs must follow death, who calls for me;
Call and I follow, I follow! let me die."

High with the last line scaled her voice, and this,
All in a fiery dawning wild with wind
That shook her tower, the brothers heard, and thought
With shuddering, "Hark the Phantom of the house
That ever shrieks before a death," and call'd
The father, and all three in hurry and fear
Ran to her, and lo! the blood-red light of dawn
Flared on her face, she shrilling, "Let me die!"

As when we dwell upon a word we know,
Repeating, till the word we know so well
Becomes a wonder, and we know not why,
So dwelt the father on her face, and thought
"Is this Elaine?" till back the maiden fell,
Then gave a languid hand to each, and lay,
Speaking a still good-morrow with her eyes.
At last she said, "Sweet brothers, yesternight
I seem'd a curious little maid again,
As happy as when we dwelt among the woods,
And when ye used to take me with the flood
Up the great river in the boatman's boat.
Only ye would not pass beyond the cape
That has the poplar on it: there ye fixt
Your limit, oft returning with the tide.
And yet I cried because ye would not pass
Beyond it, and far up the shining flood
Until we found the palace of the King.
And yet ye would not; but this night I dream'd
That I was all alone upon the flood,
And then I said, 'Now shall I have my will:'

And there I woke, but still the wish remain'd.
So let me hence that I may pass at last
Beyond the poplar and far up the flood,
Until I find the palace of the King.
There will I enter in among them all,
And no man there will dare to mock at me;
But there the fine Gawain will wonder at me,
And there the great Sir Lancelot muse at me;
Gawain, who bade a thousand farewells to me,
Lancelot, who coldly went, nor bade me one:
And there the King will know me and my love,
And there the Queen herself will pity me,
And all the gentle court will welcome me,
And after my long voyage I shall rest!"

"Peace," said her father, "O my child, ye seem
Light-headed, for what force is yours to go
So far, being sick? and wherefore would ye look
On this proud fellow again, who scorns us all?"

Then the rough Torre began to heave and move,
And bluster into stormy sobs and say,
"I never loved him: an I meet with him,
I care not howsoever great he be,
Then will I strike at him and strike him down,
Give me good fortune, I will strike him dead,
For this discomfort he hath done the house."

To whom the gentle sister made reply,
"Fret not yourself, dear brother, nor be wroth,
Seeing it is no more Sir Lancelot's fault
Not to love me, than it is mine to love
Him of all men who seems to me the highest."

"Highest?" the father answer'd, echoing "highest?"
(He meant to break the passion in her) "nay,
Daughter, I know not what you call the highest;
But this I know, for all the people know it,
He loves the Queen, and in an open shame:
And she returns his love in open shame;
If this be high, what is it to be low?"

Then spake the lily maid of Astolat:
"Sweet father, all too faint and sick am I
For anger: these are slanders: never yet
Was noble man but made ignoble talk.
He makes no friend who never made a foe.
But now it is my glory to have loved
One peerless, without stain: so let me pass,
My father, howsoe'er I seem to you,
Not all unhappy, having loved God's best
And greatest, tho' my love had no return:
Yet, seeing you desire your child to live,
Thanks, but you work against your own desire;
For if I could believe the things you say
I should but die the sooner; wherefore cease,
Sweet father, and bid call the ghostly man
Hither, and let me shrive me clean, and die."

So when the ghostly man had come and gone,
She with a face, bright as for sin forgiven,
Besought Lavaine to write as she devised
A letter, word for word; and when he ask'd
"Is it for Lancelot, is it for my dear lord?
Then will I bear it gladly;" she replied,
"For Lancelot and the Queen and all the world,
But I myself must bear it." Then he wrote
The letter she devised; which being writ
And folded, "O sweet father, tender and true,
Deny me not," she said—"ye never yet
Denied my fancies—this, however strange,
My latest: lay the letter in my hand
A little ere I die, and close the hand
Upon it; I shall guard it even in death.
And when the heat is gone from out my heart,
Then take the little bed on which I died
For Lancelot's love, and deck it like the Queen's
For richness, and me also like the Queen
In all I have of rich, and lay me on it.
And let there be prepared a chariot-bier
To take me to the river, and a barge
Be ready on the river, clothed in black.
I go in state to court, to meet the Queen.
There surely I shall speak for mine own self,
And none of you can speak for me so well.
And therefore let our dumb old man alone
Go with me, he can steer and row, and he
Will guide me to that palace, to the doors."

She ceased: her father promised; whereupon
She grew so cheerful that they deem'd her death
Was rather in the fantasy than the blood.

But ten slow mornings past, and on the eleventh
Her father laid the letter in her hand,
And closed the hand upon it, and she died.
So that day there was dole in Astolat.

But when the next sun brake from underground,
Then, those two brethren slowly with bent brows
Accompanying, the sad chariot-bier
Past like a shadow thro' the field, that shone
Full-summer, to that stream whereon the barge,
Pall'd all its length in blackest samite, lay.
There sat the lifelong creature of the house,
Loyal, the dumb old servitor, on deck,
Winking his eyes, and twisted all his face.
So those two brethren from the chariot took
And on the black decks laid her in her bed,
Set in her hand a lily, o'er her hung
The silken case with braided blazonings,
And kiss'd her quiet brows, and saying to her
"Sister, farewell for ever," and again
"Farewell, sweet sister," parted all in tears.
Then rose the dumb old servitor, and the dead,
Oar'd by the dumb, went upward with the flood—
In her right hand the lily, in her left
The letter—all her bright hair streaming down—
And all the coverlid was cloth of gold
Drawn to her waist, and she herself in white
All but her face, and that clear-featured face
Was lovely, for she did not seem as dead,
But fast asleep, and lay as tho' she smiled.

That day Sir Lancelot at the palace craved
Audience of Guinevere, to give at last
The price of half a realm, his costly gift,
Hard-won and hardly won with bruise and blow,
With deaths of others, and almost his own,
The nine-years-fought-for diamonds: for he saw
One of her house, and sent him to the Queen
Bearing his wish, whereto the Queen agreed
With such and so unmoved a majesty
She might have seem'd her statue, but that he,
Low-drooping till he wellnigh kiss'd her feet
For loyal awe, saw with a sidelong eye
The shadow of some piece of pointed lace,
In the Queen's shadow, vibrate on the walls,
And parted, laughing in his courtly heart.

All in an oriel on the summer side,
Vine-clad, of Arthur's palace toward the stream,
They met, and Lancelot kneeling utter'd, "Queen,
Lady, my liege, in whom I have my joy,
Take, what I had not won except for you,
These jewels, and make me happy, making them
An armlet for the roundest arm on earth,
Or necklace for a neck to which the swan's
Is tawnier than her cygnet's: these are words:
Your beauty is your beauty, and I sin
In speaking, yet O grant my worship of it
Words, as we grant grief tears. Such sin in words
Perchance, we both can pardon: but, my Queen,
I hear of rumours flying thro' your court.
Our bond, as not the bond of man and wife,
Should have in it an absoluter trust
To make up that defect: let rumours be:
When did not rumours fly? these, as I trust
That you trust me in your own nobleness,
I may not well believe that you believe."

While thus he spoke, half turn'd away, the Queen
Brake from the vast oriel-embowering vine
Leaf after leaf, and tore, and cast them off,
Till all the place whereon she stood was green;
Then, when he ceased, in one cold passive hand
Received at once and laid aside the gems
There on a table near her, and replied:

"It may be, I am quicker of belief
Than you believe me, Lancelot of the Lake.
Our bond is not the bond of man and wife.
This good is in it, whatsoe'er of ill,
It can be broken easier. I for you
This many a year have done despite and wrong
To one whom ever in my heart of hearts
I did acknowledge nobler. What are these?
Diamonds for me! they had been thrice their worth
Being your gift, had you not lost your own.

To loyal hearts the value of all gifts
Must vary as the giver's. Not for me!
For her! for your new fancy. Only this
Grant me, I pray you: have your joys apart.
I doubt not that however changed, you keep
So much of what is graceful: and myself
Would shun to break those bounds of courtesy
In which as Arthur's Queen I move and rule:
So cannot speak my mind. An end to this!
A strange one! yet I take it with Amen.
So pray you, add my diamonds to her pearls;
Deck her with these; tell her, she shines me down:
An armlet for an arm to which the Queen's
Is haggard, or a necklace for a neck
O as much fairer—as a faith once fair
Was richer than these diamonds—hers not mine—
Nay, by the mother of our Lord himself,
Or hers or mine, mine now to work my will—
She shall not have them."

Saying which she seized,
And, thro' the casement standing wide for heat,
Flung them, and down they flash'd, and smote the stream.
Then from the smitten surface flash'd, as it were,
Diamonds to meet them, and they past away.
Then while Sir Lancelot leant, in half disdain
At love, life, all things, on the window ledge,
Close underneath his eyes, and right across
Where these had fallen, slowly past the barge
Whereon the lily maid of Astolat
Lay smiling, like a star in blackest night.

But the wild Queen, who saw not, burst away
To weep and wail in secret; and the barge,
On to the palace-doorway sliding, paused.
There two stood arm'd, and kept the door; to whom,
All up the marble stair, tier over tier,
Were added mouths that gaped, and eyes that ask'd
"What is it?" but that oarsman's haggard face,
As hard and still as is the face that men
Shape to their fancy's eye from broken rocks
On some cliff-side, appall'd them, and they said,
"He is enchanted, cannot speak—and she,
Look how she sleeps—the Fairy Queen, so fair!
Yea, but how pale! what are they? flesh and blood?
Or come to take the King to Fairyland?
For some do hold our Arthur cannot die,
But that he passes into Fairyland."

While thus they babbled of the King, the King
Came girt with knights: then turn'd the tongueless man
From the half-face to the full eye, and rose
And pointed to the damsel, and the doors.
So Arthur bad the meek Sir Percivale
And pure Sir Galahad to uplift the maid;
And reverently they bore her into hall.
Then came the fine Gawain and wonder'd at her,
And Lancelot later came and mused at her,
And last the Queen herself, and pitied her:
But Arthur spied the letter in her hand,
Stoopt, took, brake seal, and read it; this was all:

"Most noble lord, Sir Lancelot of the Lake,
I, sometime call'd the maid of Astolat,
Come, for you left me taking no farewell,
Hither, to take my last farewell of you.
I loved you, and my love had no return,
And therefore my true love has been my death.
And therefore to our Lady Guinevere,
And to all other ladies, I make moan:
Pray for my soul, and yield me burial.
Pray for my soul thou too, Sir Lancelot,
As thou art a knight peerless."

Thus he read;
And ever in the reading, lords and dames
Wept, looking often from his face who read
To hers which lay so silent, and at times,
So touch'd were they, half-thinking that her lips,
Who had devised the letter, moved again.

Then freely spoke Sir Lancelot to them all:
"My lord liege Arthur, and all ye that hear,
Know that for this most gentle maiden's death
Right heavy am I; for good she was and true,
But loved me with a love beyond all love
In women, whomsoever I have known.
Yet to be loved makes not to love again;
Not at my years, however it hold in youth.
I swear by truth and knighthood that I gave
No cause, not willingly, for such a love:
To this I call my friends in testimony,
Her brethren, and her father, who himself
Besought me to be plain and blunt, and use,
To break her passion, some discourtesy
Against my nature: what I could I did.
I left her and I bad her no farewell;
Tho', had I dreamt the damsel would have died,
I might have put my wits to some rough use,
And help'd her from herself."

Then said the Queen
(Sea was her wrath, yet working after storm)
"Ye might at least have done her so much grace,
Fair lord, as would have help'd her from her death."
He raised his head, their eyes met and hers fell,
He adding,

"Queen, she would not be content
Save that I wedded her, which could not be.
Then might she follow me thro' the world, she ask'd;
It could not be. I told her that her love
Was but the flash of youth, would darken down
To rise hereafter in a stiller flame
Toward one more worthy of her—then would I,
More specially were he, she wedded, poor,
Estate them with large land and territory
In mine own realm beyond the narrow seas,
To keep them in all joyance: more than this
I could not; this she would not, and she died."

He pausing, Arthur answer'd, "O my knight,
It will be to thy worship, as my knight,
And mine, as head of all our Table Round,
To see that she be buried worshipfully."

So toward that shrine which then in all the realm
Was richest, Arthur leading, slowly went
The marshall'd Order of their Table Round,
And Lancelot sad beyond his wont, to see
The maiden buried, not as one unknown,
Nor meanly, but with gorgeous obsequies,
And mass, and rolling music, like a queen.
And when the knights had laid her comely head
Low in the dust of half-forgotten kings,
Then Arthur spake among them, "Let her tomb
Be costly, and her image thereupon,
And let the shield of Lancelot at her feet
Be carven, and her lily in her hand.
And let the story of her dolorous voyage
For all true hearts be blazon'd on her tomb
In letters gold and azure!" which was wrought
Thereafter; but when now the lords and dames
And people, from the high door streaming, brake
Disorderly, as homeward each, the Queen,
Who mark'd Sir Lancelot where he moved apart,
Drew near, and sigh'd in passing, "Lancelot,
Forgive me; mine was jealousy in love."
He answer'd with his eyes upon the ground,
"That is love's curse; pass on, my Queen, forgiven."
But Arthur, who beheld his cloudy brows,
Approach'd him, and with full affection said,

"Lancelot, my Lancelot, thou in whom I have
Most joy and most affiance, for I know
What thou hast been in battle by my side,
And many a time have watch'd thee at the tilt
Strike down the lusty and long practised knight,
And let the younger and unskill'd go by
To win his honour and to make his name,
And loved thy courtesies and thee, a man
Made to be loved; but now I would to God,
Seeing the homeless trouble in thine eyes,
Thou couldst have loved this maiden, shaped, it seems,
By God for thee alone, and from her face,
If one may judge the living by the dead,
Delicately pure and marvellously fair,

Who might have brought thee, now a lonely man
Wifeless and heirless, noble issue, sons
Born to the glory of thy name and fame,
My knight, the great Sir Lancelot of the Lake."

Then answer'd Lancelot, "Fair she was, my King,
Pure, as you ever wish your knights to be.
To doubt her fairness were to want an eye,
To doubt her pureness were to want a heart—
Yea, to be loved, if what is worthy love
Could bind him, but free love will not be bound."

"Free love, so bound, were freëst," said the King.
"Let love be free; free love is for the best:
And, after heaven, on our dull side of death,
What should be best, if not so pure a love
Clothed in so pure a loveliness? yet thee
She fail'd to bind, tho' being, as I think,
Unbound as yet, and gentle, as I know."

And Lancelot answer'd nothing, but he went,
And at the inrunning of a little brook
Sat by the river in a cove, and watch'd
The high reed wave, and lifted up his eyes
And saw the barge that brought her moving down,
Far-off, a blot upon the stream, and said
Low in himself, "Ah, simple heart and sweet,
Ye loved me, damsel, surely with a love
Far tenderer than my Queen's. Pray for thy soul?
Ay, that will I. Farewell too—now at last—
Farewell, fair lily. 'Jealousy in love?'
Not rather dead love's harsh heir, jealous pride?
Queen, if I grant the jealousy as of love,
May not your crescent fear for name and fame
Speak, as it waxes, of a love that wanes?
Why did the King dwell on my name to me?
Mine own name shames me, seeming a reproach,
Lancelot, whom the Lady of the Lake
Caught from his mother's arms—the wondrous one
Who passes thro' the vision of the night—
She chanted snatches of mysterious hymns
Heard on the winding waters, eve and morn
She kiss'd me saying, 'Thou art fair, my child,
As a king's son,' and often in her arms
She bare me, pacing on the dusky mere.
Would she had drown'd me in it, where'er it be!
For what am I? what profits me my name
Of greatest knight? I fought for it, and have it:
Pleasure to have it, none; to lose it, pain;
Now grown a part of me: but what use in it?
To make men worse by making my sin known?
Or sin seem less, the sinner seeming great?
Alas for Arthur's greatest knight, a man
Not after Arthur's heart! I needs must break
These bonds that so defame me: not without
She wills it: would I, if she will'd it? nay,
Who knows? but if I would not, then may God,
I pray him, send a sudden Angel down
To seize me by the hair and bear me far,
And fling me deep in that forgotten mere,
Among the tumbled fragments of the hills."

So groan'd Sir Lancelot in remorseful pain,
Not knowing he should die a holy man.

1859

THE HOLY GRAIL

From noiseful arms, and acts of prowess done
In tournament or tilt, Sir Percivale,
Whom Arthur and his knighthood call'd The Pure,
Had pass'd into the silent life of prayer,
Praise, fast, and alms; and leaving for the cowl
The helmet in an abbey far away
From Camelot, there, and not long after, died.

And one, a fellow-monk among the rest,
Ambrosius, loved him much beyond the rest,
And honour'd him, and wrought into his heart
A way by love that waken'd love within,
To answer that which came: and as they sat
Beneath a world-old yew-tree, darkening half
The cloisters, on a gustful April morn

That puff'd the swaying branches into smoke
Above them, ere the summer when he died,
The monk Ambrosius question'd Percivale:

"O brother, I have seen this yew-tree smoke,
Spring after spring, for half a hundred years:
For never have I known the world without,
Nor ever stray'd beyond the pale: but thee,
When first thou camest—such a courtesy
Spake thro' the limbs and in the voice—I knew
For one of those who eat in Arthur's hall;
For good ye are and bad, and like to coins,
Some true, some light, but every one of you
Stamp'd with the image of the King; and now
Tell me, what drove thee from the Table Round,
My brother? was it earthly passion crost?"

"Nay," said the knight; "for no such passion mine.
But the sweet vision of the Holy Grail
Drove me from all vainglories, rivalries,
And earthly heats that spring and sparkle out
Among us in the jousts, while women watch
Who wins, who falls; and waste the spiritual strength
Within us, better offer'd up to Heaven."

To whom the monk: "The Holy Grail!—I trust
We are green in Heaven's eyes; but here too much
We moulder—as to things without I mean—
Yet one of your own knights, a guest of ours,
Told us of this in our refectory,
But spake with such a sadness and so low
We heard not half of what he said. What is it?
The phantom of a cup that comes and goes?"

"Nay, monk! what phantom?" answer'd Percivale.
"The cup, the cup itself, from which our Lord
Drank at the last sad supper with his own.
This, from the blessed land of Aromat—
After the day of darkness, when the dead
Went wandering o'er Moriah—the good saint
Arimathæan Joseph, journeying brought
To Glastonbury, where the winter thorn
Blossoms at Christmas, mindful of our Lord.
And there awhile it bode; and if a man
Could touch or see it, he was heal'd at once,
By faith, of all his ills. But then the times
Grew to such evil that the holy cup
Was caught away to Heaven, and disappear'd."

To whom the monk: "From our old books I know
That Joseph came of old to Glastonbury,
And there the heathen Prince, Arviragus,
Gave him an isle of marsh whereon to build;
And there he built with wattles from the marsh
A little lonely church in days of yore,
For so they say, these books of ours, but seem
Mute of this miracle, far as I have read.
But who first saw the holy thing to-day?"

"A woman," answer'd Percivale, "a nun,
And one no further off in blood from me
Than sister; and if ever holy maid
With knees of adoration wore the stone,
A holy maid; tho' never maiden glow'd,
But that was in her earlier maidenhood,
With such a fervent flame of human love,
Which being rudely blunted, glanced and shot
Only to holy things; to prayer and praise
She gave herself, to fast and alms. And yet,
Nun as she was, the scandal of the Court,
Sin against Arthur and the Table Round,
And the strange sound of an adulterous race,
Across the iron grating of her cell
Beat, and she pray'd and fasted all the more.

"And he to whom she told her sins, or what
Her all but utter whiteness held for sin,
A man wellnigh a hundred winters old,
Spake often with her of the Holy Grail,
A legend handed down thro' five or six,
And each of these a hundred winters old,
From our Lord's time. And when King Arthur made
His Table Round, and all men's hearts became
Clean for a season, surely he had thought
That now the Holy Grail would come again;
But sin broke out. Ah, Christ, that it would come,

And heal the world of all their wickedness!
'O Father!' ask'd the maiden, 'might it come
To me by prayer and fasting?' 'Nay,' said he,
'I know not, for thy heart is pure as snow.'
And so she pray'd and fasted, till the sun
Shone, and the wind blew, thro' her, and I thought
She might have risen and floated when I saw her.

"For on a day she sent to speak with me.
And when she came to speak, behold her eyes
Beyond my knowing of them, beautiful,
Beyond all knowing of them, wonderful,
Beautiful in the light of holiness.
And 'O my brother Percivale,' she said,
'Sweet brother, I have seen the Holy Grail:
For, waked at dead of night, I heard a sound
As of a silver horn from o'er the hills
Blown, and I thought, "It is not Arthur's use
To hunt by moonlight;" and the slender sound
As from a distance beyond distance grew
Coming upon me—O never harp nor horn,
Nor aught we blow with breath, or touch with hand,
Was like that music as it came; and then
Stream'd thro' my cell a cold and silver beam,
And down the long beam stole the Holy Grail,
Rose-red with beatings in it, as if alive,
Till all the white walls of my cell were dyed
With rosy colours leaping on the wall;
And then the music faded, and the Grail
Past, and the beam decay'd, and from the walls
The rosy quiverings died into the night.
So now the Holy Thing is here again
Among us, brother, fast thou too and pray,
And tell thy brother knights to fast and pray,
That so perchance the vision may be seen
By thee and those, and all the world be heal'd.'

"Then leaving the pale nun, I spake of this
To all men; and myself fasted and pray'd
Always, and many among us many a week
Fasted and pray'd even to the uttermost,
Expectant of the wonder that would be.

"And one there was among us, ever moved
Among us in white armour, Galahad.
'God make thee good as thou art beautiful,'
Said Arthur, when he dubb'd him knight; and none,
In so young youth, was ever made a knight
Till Galahad; and this Galahad, when he heard
My sister's vision, fill'd me with amaze;
His eyes became so like her own, they seem'd
Hers, and himself her brother more than I.

"Sister or brother none had he; but some
Call'd him a son of Lancelot, and some said
Begotten by enchantment—chatterers they,
Like birds of passage piping up and down,
That gape for flies—we know not whence they come;
For when was Lancelot wanderingly lewd?

"But she, the wan sweet maiden, shore away
Clean from her forehead all that wealth of hair
Which made a silken mat-work for her feet;
And out of this she plaited broad and long
A strong sword-belt, and wove with silver thread
And crimson in the belt a strange device,
A crimson grail within a silver beam;
And saw the bright boy-knight, and bound it on him,
Saying, 'My knight, my love, my knight of heaven,
O thou, my love, whose love is one with mine,
I, maiden, round thee, maiden, bind my belt.
Go forth, for thou shalt see what I have seen,
And break thro' all, till one will crown thee king
Far in the spiritual city:' and as she spake
She sent the deathless passion in her eyes
Thro' him, and made him hers, and laid her mind
On him, and he believed in her belief.

"Then came a year of miracle: O brother,
In our great hall there stood a vacant chair,
Fashion'd by Merlin ere he past away,
And carven with strange figures; and in and out
The figures, like a serpent, ran a scroll
Of letters in a tongue no man could read.
And Merlin call'd it 'The Siege perilous,'
Perilous for good and ill; 'for there,' he said,
'No man could sit but he should lose himself:'

And once by misadvertence Merlin sat
In his own chair, and so was lost; but he,
Galahad, when he heard of Merlin's doom,
Cried, 'If I lose myself, I save myself!'

"Then on a summer night it came to pass,
While the great banquet lay along the hall,
That Galahad would sit down in Merlin's chair.

"And all at once, as there we sat, we heard
A cracking and a riving of the roofs,
And rending, and a blast, and overhead
Thunder, and in the thunder was a cry.
And in the blast there smote along the hall
A beam of light seven times more clear than day:
And down the long beam stole the Holy Grail
All over cover'd with a luminous cloud,
And none might see who bare it, and it past.
But every knight beheld his fellow's face
As in a glory, and all the knights arose,
And staring each at other like dumb men
Stood, till I found a voice and sware a vow.

"I sware a vow before them all, that I,
Because I had not seen the Grail, would ride
A twelvemonth and a day in quest of it,
Until I found and saw it, as the nun
My sister saw it; and Galahad sware the vow,
And good Sir Bors, our Lancelot's cousin, sware,
And Lancelot sware, and many among the knights,
And Gawain sware, and louder than the rest."

Then spake the monk Ambrosius, asking him,
"What said the King? Did Arthur take the vow?"

"Nay, for my lord," said Percivale, "the King,
Was not in hall: for early that same day,
Scaped thro' a cavern from a bandit hold,
An outraged maiden sprang into the hall
Crying on help: for all her shining hair
Was smear'd with earth, and either milky arm
Red-rent with hooks of bramble, and all she wore
Torn as a sail that leaves the rope is torn
In tempest: so the King arose and went
To smoke the scandalous hive of those wild bees
That made such honey in his realm. Howbeit
Some little of this marvel he too saw,
Returning o'er the plain that then began
To darken under Camelot; whence the King
Look'd up, calling aloud, 'Lo, there! the roofs
Of our great hall are roll'd in thunder-smoke!
Pray Heaven, they be not smitten by the bolt.'
For dear to Arthur was that hall of ours,
As having there so oft with all his knights
Feasted, and as the stateliest under heaven.

"O brother, had you known our mighty hall,
Which Merlin built for Arthur long ago!
For all the sacred mount of Camelot,
And all the dim rich city, roof by roof,
Tower after tower, spire beyond spire,
By grove, and garden-lawn, and rushing brook,
Climbs to the mighty hall that Merlin built.
And four great zones of sculpture, set betwixt
With many a mystic symbol, gird the hall:
And in the lowest beasts are slaying men,
And in the second men are slaying beasts,
And on the third are warriors, perfect men,
And on the fourth are men with growing wings,
And over all one statue in the mould
Of Arthur, made by Merlin, with a crown,
And peak'd wings pointed to the Northern Star.
And eastward fronts the statue, and the crown
And both the wings are made of gold, and flame
At sunrise till the people in far fields,
Wasted so often by the heathen hordes,
Behold it, crying, 'We have still a King.'

"And, brother, had you known our hall within,
Broader and higher than any in all the lands!
Where twelve great windows blazon Arthur's wars,
And all the light that falls upon the board
Streams thro' the twelve great battles of our King.
Nay, one there is, and at the eastern end,

Wealthy with wandering lines of mount and mere,
Where Arthur finds the brand Excalibur.
And also one to the west, and counter to it,
And blank: and who shall blazon it? when and how?—
O there, perchance, when all our wars are done,
The brand Excalibur will be cast away.

"So to this hall full quickly rode the King,
In horror lest the work by Merlin wrought,
Dreamlike, should on the sudden vanish, wrapt
In unremorseful folds of rolling fire.
And in he rode, and up I glanced, and saw
The golden dragon sparkling over all:
And many of those who burnt the hold, their arms
Hack'd, and their foreheads grimed with smoke, and sear'd,
Follow'd, and in among bright faces, ours,
Full of the vision, prest: and then the King
Spake to me, being nearest, 'Percivale,'
(Because the hall was all in tumult—some
Vowing, and some protesting), 'what is this?'

"O brother, when I told him what had chanced,
My sister's vision, and the rest, his face
Darken'd, as I have seen it more than once,
When some brave deed seem'd to be done in vain,
Darken; and 'Woe is me, my knights,' he cried,
'Had I been here, ye had not sworn the vow.'
Bold was mine answer, 'Had thyself been here,
My King, thou wouldst have sworn.' 'Yea, yea,' said he,
'Art thou so bold and hast not seen the Grail?'

" 'Nay, lord, I heard the sound, I saw the light,
But since I did not see the Holy Thing,
I sware a vow to follow it till I saw.'

"Then when he ask'd us, knight by knight, if any
Had seen it, all their answers were as one:
'Nay, lord, and therefore have we sworn our vows.'

" 'Lo now,' said Arthur, 'have ye seen a cloud?
What go ye into the wilderness to see?'

"Then Galahad on the sudden, and in a voice
Shrilling along the hall to Arthur, call'd,
'But I, Sir Arthur, saw the Holy Grail,
I saw the Holy Grail and heard a cry—
"O Galahad, and O Galahad, follow me." '

" 'Ah, Galahad, Galahad,' said the King, 'for such
As thou art is the vision, not for these.
Thy holy nun and thou have seen a sign—
Holier is none, my Percivale, than she—
A sign to maim this Order which I made.
But ye, that follow but the leader's bell'
(Brother the King was hard upon his knights)
'Taliessin is our fullest throat of song,
And one hath sung and all the dumb will sing.
Lancelot is Lancelot, and hath overborne
Five knights at once, and every younger knight,
Unproven, holds himself as Lancelot,
Till overborne by one, he learns—and ye,
What are ye? Galahads?—no, nor Percivales'
(For thus it pleased the King to range me close
After Sir Galahad); 'nay,' said he, 'but men
With strength and will to right the wrong'd, of power
To lay the sudden heads of violence flat,
Knights that in twelve great battles splash'd and dyed
The strong White Horse in his own heathen blood—
But one hath seen, and all the blind will see.
Go, since your vows are sacred, being made:
Yet—for ye know the cries of all my realm
Pass thro' this hall—how often, O my knights,
Your places being vacant at my side,
This chance of noble deeds will come and go
Unchallenged, while ye follow wandering fires
Lost in the quagmire! Many of you, yea most,
Return no more: ye think I show myself
Too dark a prophet: come now, let us meet
The morrow morn once more in one full field
Of gracious pastime, that once more the King,
Before ye leave him for this Quest, may count
The yet-unbroken strength of all his knights,
Rejoicing in that Order which he made.'

"So when the sun broke next from under ground,
All the great table of our Arthur closed
And clash'd in such a tourney and so full,
So many lances broken—never yet
Had Camelot seen the like, since Arthur came;
And I myself and Galahad, for a strength
Was in us from the vision, overthrew
So many knights that all the people cried,
And almost burst the barriers in their heat,
Shouting, 'Sir Galahad and Sir Percivale!'

"But when the next day brake from under ground—
O brother, had you known our Camelot,
Built by old kings, age after age, so old
The King himself had fears that it would fall,
So strange, and rich, and dim; for where the roofs
Totter'd toward each other in the sky,
Met foreheads all along the street of those
Who watch'd us pass; and lower, and where the long
Rich galleries, lady-laden, weigh'd the necks
Of dragons clinging to the crazy walls,
Thicker than drops from thunder, showers of flowers
Fell as we past; and men and boys astride
On wyvern, lion, dragon, griffin, swan,
At all the corners, named us each by name,
Calling 'God speed!' but in the ways below
The knights and ladies wept, and rich and poor
Wept, and the King himself could hardly speak
For grief, and all in middle street the Queen,
Who rode by Lancelot, wail'd and shriek'd aloud,
'This madness has come on us for our sins.'
So to the Gate of the Three Queens we came,
Where Arthur's wars are render'd mystically,
And thence departed every one his way.

"And I was lifted up in heart, and thought
Of all my late-shown prowess in the lists,
How my strong lance had beaten down the knights,
So many and famous names; and never yet
Had heaven appear'd so blue, nor earth so green,
For all my blood danced in me, and I knew
That I should light upon the Holy Grail.

"Thereafter, the dark warning of our King,
That most of us would follow wandering fires,
Came like a driving gloom across my mind.
Then every evil word I had spoken once,
And every evil thought I had thought of old,
And every evil deed I ever did,
Awoke and cried, 'This Quest is not for thee.'
And lifting up mine eyes, I found myself
Alone, and in a land of sand and thorns,
And I was thirsty even unto death;
And I, too, cried, 'This Quest is not for thee.'

"And on I rode, and when I thought my thirst
Would slay me, saw deep lawns, and then a brook,
With one sharp rapid, where the crisping white
Play'd ever back upon the sloping wave,
And took both ear and eye; and o'er the brook
Were apple-trees, and apples by the brook
Fallen, and on the lawns. 'I will rest here,'
I said, 'I am not worthy of the Quest;'
But even while I drank the brook, and ate
The goodly apples, all these things at once
Fell into dust, and I was left alone,
And thirsting, in a land of sand and thorns.

"And then behold a woman at a door
Spinning; and fair the house whereby she sat,
And kind the woman's eyes and innocent,
And all her bearing gracious; and she rose
Opening her arms to meet me, as who should say,
'Rest here;' but when I touch'd her, lo! she, too,
Fell into dust and nothing, and the house
Became no better than a broken shed,
And in it a dead babe; and also this
Fell into dust, and I was left alone.

"And on I rode, and greater was my thirst.
Then flash'd a yellow gleam across the world,
And where it smote the plowshare in the field,
The plowman left his plowing, and fell down
Before it; where it glitter'd on her pail,
The milkmaid left her milking, and fell down
Before it, and I knew not why, but thought
'The sun is rising,' tho' the sun had risen.

Then was I ware of one that on me moved
In golden armour with a crown of gold
About a casque all jewels; and his horse
In golden armour jewell'd everywhere:
And on the splendour came, flashing me blind;
And seem'd to me the Lord of all the world,
Being so huge. But when I thought he meant
To crush me, moving on me, lo! he, too,
Open'd his arms to embrace me as he came,
And up I went and touch'd him, and he, too,
Fell into dust, and I was left alone
And wearying in a land of sand and thorns.

"And I rode on and found a mighty hill,
And on the top, a city wall'd: the spires
Prick'd with incredible pinnacles into heaven.
And by the gateway stirr'd a crowd; and these
Cried to me climbing, 'Welcome, Percivale!
Thou mightiest and thou purest among men!'
And glad was I and clomb, but found at top
No man, nor any voice. And thence I past
Far thro' a ruinous city, and I saw
That man had once dwelt there; but there I found
Only one man of an exceeding age.
'Where is that goodly company,' said I,
'That so cried out upon me?' and he had
Scarce any voice to answer, and yet gasp'd,
'Whence and what art thou?' and even as he spoke
Fell into dust, and disappear'd, and I
Was left alone once more, and cried in grief,
'Lo, if I find the Holy Grail itself
And touch it, it will crumble into dust.'

"And thence I dropt into a lowly vale,
Low as the hill was high, and where the vale
Was lowest, found a chapel, and thereby
A holy hermit in a hermitage,
To whom I told my phantoms, and he said:

" 'O son, thou hast not true humility,
The highest virtue, mother of them all;
For when the Lord of all things made Him-self
Naked of glory for His mortal change,
"Take thou my robe," she said, "for all is thine,"
And all her form shone forth with sudden light
So that the angels were amazed, and she
Follow'd Him down, and like a flying star
Led on the gray-hair'd wisdom of the east;
But her thou hast not known: for what is this
Thou thoughtest of thy prowess and thy sins?
Thou hast not lost thyself to save thyself
As Galahad.' When the hermit made an end,
In silver armour suddenly Galahad shone
Before us, and against the chapel door
Laid lance, and enter'd, and we knelt in prayer.
And there the hermit slaked my burning thirst,
And at the sacring of the mass I saw
The holy elements alone; but he,
'Saw ye no more? I, Galahad, saw the Grail,
The Holy Grail, descend upon the shrine:
I saw the fiery face as of a child
That smote itself into the bread, and went;
And hither am I come; and never yet
Hath what thy sister taught me first to see,
This Holy Thing, fail'd from my side, nor come
Cover'd, but moving with me night and day,
Fainter by day, but always in the night
Blood-red, and sliding down the blacken'd marsh
Blood-red, and on the naked mountain top
Blood-red, and in the sleeping mere below
Blood-red. And in the strength of this I rode,
Shattering all evil customs everywhere,
And past thro' Pagan realms, and made them mine,
And clash'd with Pagan hordes, and bore them down,
And broke thro' all, and in the strength of this
Come victor. But my time is hard at hand,
And hence I go; and one will crown me king
Far in the spiritual city; and come thou, too,
For thou shalt see the vision when I go.'

"While thus he spake, his eye, dwelling on mine,
Drew me, with power upon me, till I grew
One with him, to believe as he believed.
Then, when the day began to wane, we went.

"There rose a hill that none but man could climb,
Scarr'd with a hundred wintry watercourses—
Storm at the top, and when we gain'd it, storm

Round us and death; for every moment glanced
His silver arms and gloom'd: so quick and thick
The lightnings here and there to left and right
Struck, till the dry old trunks about us, dead,
Yea, rotten with a hundred years of death,
Sprang into fire: and at the base we found
On either hand, as far as eye could see,
A great black swamp and of an evil smell,
Part black, part whiten'd with the bones of men,
Not to be crost, save that some ancient king
Had built a way, where, link'd with many a bridge,
A thousand piers ran into the great Sea.
And Galahad fled along them bridge by bridge,
And every bridge as quickly as he crost
Sprang into fire and vanish'd, tho' I yearn'd
To follow; and thrice above him all the heavens
Open'd and blazed with thunder such as seem'd
Shoutings of all the sons of God: and first
At once I saw him far on the great Sea,
In silver-shining armour starry-clear;
And o'er his head the Holy Vessel hung
Clothed in white samite or a luminous cloud.
And with exceeding swiftness ran the boat,
If boat it were—I saw not whence it came.
And when the heavens open'd and blazed again
Roaring, I saw him like a silver star—
And had he set the sail, or had the boat
Become a living creature clad with wings?
And o'er his head the Holy Vessel hung
Redder than any rose, a joy to me,
For now I knew the veil had been withdrawn.
Then in a moment when they blazed again
Opening, I saw the least of little stars
Down on the waste, and straight beyond the star
I saw the spiritual city and all her spires
And gateways in a glory like one pearl—
No larger, tho' the goal of all the saints—
Strike from the sea; and from the star there shot
A rose-red sparkle to the city, and there
Dwelt, and I knew it was the Holy Grail,
Which never eyes on earth again shall see.
Then fell the floods of heaven drowning the deep.
And how my feet recrost the deathful ridge
No memory in me lives; but that I touch'd
The chapel-doors at dawn I know; and thence
Taking my war-horse from the holy man,
Glad that no phantom vext me more, return'd
To whence I came, the gate of Arthur's wars."

"O brother," ask'd Ambrosius,—"for in sooth
These ancient books—and they would win thee—teem,
Only I find not there this Holy Grail,
With miracles and marvels like to these,
Not all unlike; which oftentime I read,
Who read but on my breviary with ease,
Till my head swims; and then go forth and pass
Down to the little thorpe that lies so close,
And almost plaster'd like a martin's nest
To these old walls—and mingle with our folk;
And knowing every honest face of theirs
As well as ever shepherd knew his sheep,
And every homely secret in their hearts,
Delight myself with gossip and old wives,
And ills and aches, and teethings, lyings-in,
And mirthful sayings, children of the place,
That have no meaning half a league away:
Or lulling random squabbles when they rise,
Chafferings and chatterings at the market-cross,
Rejoice, small man, in this small world of mine,
Yea, even in their hens and in their eggs—
O brother, saving this Sir Galahad,
Came ye on none but phantoms in your quest,
No man, no woman?"

Then Sir Percivale:
"All men, to one so bound by such a vow,
And women were as phantoms. O, my brother,
Why wilt thou shame me to confess to thee
How far I falter'd from my quest and vow?
For after I had lain so many nights,
A bedmate of the snail and eft and snake,
In grass and burdock, I was changed to wan
And meagre, and the vision had not come;
And then I chanced upon a goodly town

With one great dwelling in the middle of it;
Thither I made, and there was I disarm'd
By maidens each as fair as any flower:
But when they led me into hall, behold,
The Princess of that castle was the one,
Brother, and that one only, who had ever
Made my heart leap; for when I moved of old
A slender page about her father's hall,
And she a slender maiden, all my heart
Went after her with longing: yet we twain
Had never kiss'd a kiss, or vow'd a vow.
And now I came upon her once again,
And one had wedded her, and he was dead,
And all his land and wealth and state were hers.
And while I tarried, every day she set
A banquet richer than the day before
By me; for all her longing and her will
Was toward me as of old; till one fair morn,
I walking to and fro beside a stream
That flash'd across her orchard underneath
Her castle-walls, she stole upon my walk,
And calling me the greatest of all knights,
Embraced me, and so kiss'd me the first time,
And gave herself and all her wealth to me.
Then I remember'd Arthur's warning word,
That most of us would follow wandering fires,
And the Quest faded in my heart. Anon,
The heads of all her people drew to me,
With supplication both of knees and tongue:
'We have heard of thee: thou art our greatest knight,
Our Lady says it, and we well believe:
Wed thou our Lady, and rule over us,
And thou shalt be as Arthur in our land.'
O me, my brother! but one night my vow
Burnt me within, so that I rose and fled,
But wail'd and wept, and hated mine own self,
And ev'n the Holy Quest, and all but her;
Then after I was join'd with Galahad
Cared not for her, nor anything upon earth."

Then said the monk, "Poor men, when yule is cold,
Must be content to sit by little fires.
And this am I, so that ye care for me
Ever so little; yea, and blest be Heaven
That brought thee here to this poor house of ours
Where all the brethren are so hard, to warm
My cold heart with a friend: but O the pity
To find thine own first love once more—to hold,
Hold her a wealthy bride within thine arms,
Or all but hold, and then—cast her aside,
Foregoing all her sweetness, like a weed.
For we that want the warmth of double life,
We that are plagued with dreams of something sweet
Beyond all sweetness in a life so rich,—
Ah, blessed Lord, I speak too earthlywise,
Seeing I never stray'd beyond the cell,
But live like an old badger in his earth,
With earth about him everywhere, despite
All fast and penance. Saw ye none beside,
None of your knights?"

"Yea so," said Percivale:
"One night my pathway swerving east, I saw
The pelican on the casque of our Sir Bors
All in the middle of the rising moon:
And toward him spurr'd, and hail'd him, and he me,
And each made joy of either; then he ask'd,
'Where is he? hast thou seen him—Lancelot?—Once,'
Said good Sir Bors, 'he dash'd across me—mad,
And maddening what he rode: and when I cried,
"Ridest thou then so hotly on a quest
So holy," Lancelot shouted, "Stay me not!
I have been the sluggard, and I ride apace,
For now there is a lion in the way."
So vanish'd.'

"Then Sir Bors had ridden on
Softly, and sorrowing for our Lancelot,
Because his former madness, once the talk
And scandal of our table, had return'd;
For Lancelot's kith and kin so worship him
That ill to him is ill to them; to Bors
Beyond the rest: he well had been content
Not to have seen, so Lancelot might have seen,
The Holy Cup of healing; and, indeed,
Being so clouded with his grief and love,
Small heart was his after the Holy Quest:
If God would send the vision, well: if not,
The Quest and he were in the hands of Heaven.

"And then, with small adventure met, Sir Bors
Rode to the lonest tract of all the realm,
And found a people there among their crags,
Our race and blood, a remnant that were left
Paynim amid their circles, and the stones
They pitch up straight to heaven: and their wise men
Were strong in that old magic which can trace
The wandering of the stars, and scoff'd at him
And this high Quest as at a simple thing:
Told him he follow'd—almost Arthur's words—
A mocking fire: 'what other fire than he,
Whereby the blood beats, and the blossom blows,
And the sea rolls, and all the world is warm'd?'
And when his answer chafed them, the rough crowd,
Hearing he had a difference with their priests,
Seized him, and bound and plunged him into a cell
Of great piled stones; and lying bounden there
In darkness thro' innumerable hours
He heard the hollow-ringing heavens sweep
Over him till by miracle—what else?—
Heavy as it was, a great stone slipt and fell,
Such as no wind could move: and thro' the gap
Glimmer'd the streaming scud: then came a night
Still as the day was loud; and thro' the gap
The seven clear stars of Arthur's Table Round—
For, brother, so one night, because they roll
Thro' such a round in heaven, we named the stars,
Rejoicing in ourselves and in our King—
And these, like bright eyes of familiar friends,
In on him shone: 'And then to me, to me,'
Said good Sir Bors, 'beyond all hopes of mine,
Who scarce had pray'd or ask'd it for myself—
Across the seven clear stars—O grace to me—
In colour like the fingers of a hand
Before a burning taper, the sweet Grail
Glided and past, and close upon it peal'd
A sharp quick thunder.' Afterwards, a maid,
Who kept our holy faith among her kin
In secret, entering, loosed and let him go."

To whom the monk: "And I remember now
That pelican on the casque: Sir Bors it was
Who spake so low and sadly at our board;
And mighty reverent at our grace was he:
A square-set man and honest; and his eyes,
An out-door sign of all the warmth within,
Smiled with his lips—a smile beneath a cloud,
But heaven had meant it for a sunny one:
Ay, ay, Sir Bors, who else? But when ye reach'd
The city, found ye all your knights return'd,
Or was there sooth in Arthur's prophecy,
Tell me, and what said each, and what the King?"

Then answer'd Percivale: "And that can I,
Brother, and truly; since the living words
Of so great men as Lancelot and our King
Pass not from door to door and out again,
But sit within the house. O, when we reach'd
The city, our horses stumbling as they trode
On heaps of ruin, hornless unicorns,
Crack'd basilisks, and splinter'd cockatrices,
And shatter'd talbots, which had left the stones
Raw, that they fell from, brought us to the hall.

"And there sat Arthur on the daïs-throne,
And those that had gone out upon the Quest,
Wasted and worn, and but a tithe of them,
And those that had not, stood before the King,
Who, when he saw me, rose, and bad me hail,
Saying, 'A welfare in thine eye reproves
Our fear of some disastrous chance for thee
On hill, or plain, at sea, or flooding ford.
So fierce a gale made havoc here of late
Among the strange devices of our kings;
Yea, shook this newer, stronger hall of ours,
And from the statue Merlin moulded for us
Half-wrench'd a golden wing; but now—the Quest,
This vision—hast thou seen the Holy Cup,
That Joseph brought of old to Glastonbury?'

"So when I told him all thyself hast heard,
Ambrosius, and my fresh but fixt resolve
To pass away into the quiet life,
He answer'd not, but, sharply turning, ask'd
Of Gawain, 'Gawain, was this Quest for thee?'

" 'Nay, lord,' said Gawain, 'not for such as I.
Therefore I communed with a saintly man,
Who made me sure the Quest was not for me;
For I was much awearied of the Quest:
But found a silk pavilion in a field,
And merry maidens in it; and then this gale
Tore my pavilion from the tenting-pin,
And blew my merry maidens all about
With all discomfort; yea, and but for this,
My twelvemonth and a day were pleasant to me.'

"He ceased; and Arthur turn'd to whom at first
He saw not, for Sir Bors, on entering, push'd
Athwart the throng to Lancelot, caught his hand,
Held it, and there, half-hidden by him, stood,
Until the King espied him, saying to him,
'Hail, Bors! if ever loyal man and true
Could see it, thou hast seen the Grail;' and Bors,
'Ask me not, for I may not speak of it:
I saw it;' and the tears were in his eyes.

"Then there remain'd but Lancelot, for the rest
Spake but of sundry perils in the storm;
Perhaps, like him of Cana in Holy Writ,
Our Arthur kept his best until the last;
'Thou, too, my Lancelot,' ask'd the King, 'my friend,
Our mightiest, hath this Quest avail'd for thee?'

" 'Our mightiest!' answer'd Lancelot, with a groan;
'O King!'—and when he paused, methought I spied
A dying fire of madness in his eyes—
'O King, my friend, if friend of thine I be,
Happier are those that welter in their sin,
Swine in the mud, that cannot see for slime,
Slime of the ditch: but in me lived a sin
So strange, of such a kind, that all of pure,
Noble, and knightly in me twined and clung
Round that one sin, until the wholesome flower
And poisonous grew together, each as each,
Not to be pluck'd asunder; and when thy knights
Sware, I sware with them only in the hope
That could I touch or see the Holy Grail
They might be pluck'd asunder. Then I spake
To one most holy saint, who wept and said,
That save they could be pluck'd asunder, all
My quest were but in vain; to whom I vow'd
That I would work according as he will'd.
And forth I went, and while I yearn'd and strove
To tear the twain asunder in my heart,
My madness came upon me as of old,
And whipt me into waste fields far away;
There was I beaten down by little men,
Mean knights, to whom the moving of my sword
And shadow of my spear had been enow
To scare them from me once; and then I came
All in my folly to the naked shore,
Wide flats, where nothing but coarse grasses grew;
But such a blast, my King, began to blow,
So loud a blast along the shore and sea,
Ye could not hear the waters for the blast,
Tho' heapt in mounds and ridges all the sea
Drove like a cataract, and all the sand
Swept like a river, and the clouded heavens
Were shaken with the motion and the sound.
And blackening in the sea-foam sway'd a boat,
Half-swallow'd in it, anchor'd with a chain;
And in my madness to myself I said,
"I will embark and I will lose myself,
And in the great sea wash away my sin."
I burst the chain, I sprang into the boat.
Seven days I drove along the dreary deep,
And with me drove the moon and all the stars;
And the wind fell, and on the seventh night
I heard the shingle grinding in the surge,
And felt the boat shock earth, and looking up,
Behold, the enchanted towers of Carbonek,
A castle like a rock upon a rock,
With chasm-like portals open to the sea,
And steps that met the breaker! there was none
Stood near it but a lion on each side
That kept the entry, and the moon was full.
Then from the boat I leapt, and up the stairs.
There drew my sword. With sudden-flaring manes
Those two great beasts rose upright like a man,
Each gript a shoulder, and I stood between;

And, when I would have smitten them, heard a voice,
"Doubt not, go forward; if thou doubt, the beasts
Will tear thee piecemeal." Then with violence
The sword was dash'd from out my hand, and fell.
And up into the sounding hall I past;
But nothing in the sounding hall I saw,
No bench nor table, painting on the wall
Or shield of knight; only the rounded moon
Thro' the tall oriel on the rolling sea.
But always in the quiet house I heard,
Clear as a lark, high o'er me as a lark,
A sweet voice singing in the topmost tower
To the eastward: up I climb'd a thousand steps
With pain: as in a dream I seem'd to climb
For ever: at the last I reach'd a door,
A light was in the crannies, and I heard,
"Glory and joy and honour to our Lord
And to the Holy Vessel of the Grail."
Then in my madness I essay'd the door;
It gave; and thro' a stormy glare, a heat
As from a seventimes-heated furnace, I,
Blasted and burnt, and blinded as I was,
With such a fierceness that I swoon'd away—
O, yet methought I saw the Holy Grail,
All pall'd in crimson samite, and around
Great angels, awful shapes, and wings and eyes.
And but for all my madness and my sin,
And then my swooning, I had sworn I saw
That which I saw; but what I saw was veil'd
And cover'd; and this Quest was not for me.'

"So speaking, and here ceasing, Lancelot left
The hall long silent, till Sir Gawain—nay,
Brother, I need not tell thee foolish words,—
A reckless and irreverent knight was he,
Now bolden'd by the silence of his King,—
Well, I will tell thee: 'O King, my liege,' he said,
'Hath Gawain fail'd in any quest of thine?
When have I stinted stroke in foughten field?
But as for thine, my good friend Percivale,
Thy holy nun and thou have driven men mad,
Yea, made our mightiest madder than our least.
But by mine eyes and by mine ears I swear,
I will be deafer than the blue-eyed cat,
And thrice as blind as any noonday owl,
To holy virgins in their ecstasies,
Henceforward.'

" 'Deafer,' said the blameless King,
'Gawain, and blinder unto holy things
Hope not to make thyself by idle vows,
Being too blind to have desire to see.
But if indeed there came a sign from heaven,
Blessed are Bors, Lancelot and Percivale,
For these have seen according to their sight.
For every fiery prophet in old times,
And all the sacred madness of the bard,
When God made music thro' them, could but speak
His music by the framework and the chord;
And as ye saw it ye have spoken truth.

" 'Nay—but thou errest, Lancelot: never yet
Could all of true and noble in knight and man
Twine round one sin, whatever it might be,
With such a closeness, but apart there grew,
Save that he were the swine thou spakest of,
Some root of knighthood and pure nobleness;
Whereto see thou, that it may bear its flower.

" 'And spake I not too truly, O my knights?
Was I too dark a prophet when I said
To those who went upon the Holy Quest,
That most of them would follow wandering fires,
Lost in the quagmire?—lost to me and gone,
And left me gazing at a barren board,
And a lean Order—scarce return'd a tithe—
And out of those to whom the vision came
My greatest hardly will believe he saw;
Another hath beheld it afar off,
And leaving human wrongs to right themselves,
Cares but to pass into the silent life.
And one hath had the vision face to face,
And now his chair desires him here in vain,
However they may crown him otherwhere.

" 'And some among you held, that if the King
Had seen the sight he would have sworn the vow:
Not easily, seeing that the King must guard

That which he rules, and is but as the hind
To whom a space of land is given to plow,
Who may not wander from the allotted field
Before his work be done; but, being done,
Let visions of the night or of the day
Come, as they will; and many a time they come,
Until this earth he walks on seems not earth,
This light that strikes his eyeball is not light,
This air that smites his forehead is not air
But vision—yea, his very hand and foot—
In moments when he feels he cannot die,
And knows himself no vision to himself,
Nor the high God a vision, nor that One
Who rose again: ye have seen what ye have seen.'

"So spake the King: I knew not all he meant."

1869

GUINEVERE

Queen Guinevere had fled the court, and sat
There in the holy house at Almesbury
Weeping, none with her save a little maid,
A novice: one low light betwixt them burn'd
Blurr'd by the creeping mist, for all abroad,
Beneath a moon unseen albeit at full,
The white mist, like a face-cloth to the face,
Clung to the dead earth, and the land was still.

For hither had she fled, her cause of flight
Sir Modred; he that like a subtle beast
Lay couchant with his eyes upon the throne,
Ready to spring, waiting a chance: for this
He chill'd the popular praises of the King
With silent smiles of slow disparagement;
And tamper'd with the Lords of the White Horse,
Heathen, the brood by Hengist left; and sought
To make disruption in the Table Round
Of Arthur, and to splinter it into feuds
Serving his traitorous end; and all his aims
Were sharpen'd by strong hate for Lancelot.

For thus it chanced one morn when all the court,
Green-suited, but with plumes that mock'd the may,
Had been, their wont, a-maying and return'd,
That Modred still in green, all ear and eye,
Climb'd to the high top of the garden-wall
To spy some secret scandal if he might,
And saw the Queen who sat betwixt her best
Enid, and lissome Vivien, of her court
The wiliest and the worst; and more than this
He saw not, for Sir Lancelot passing by
Spied where he couch'd, and as the gardener's hand
Picks from the colewort a green caterpillar,
So from the high wall and the flowering grove
Of grasses Lancelot pluck'd him by the heel,
And cast him as a worm upon the way;
But when he knew the Prince tho' marr'd with dust,
He, reverencing king's blood in a bad man,
Made such excuses as he might, and these
Full knightly without scorn; for in those days
No knight of Arthur's noblest dealt in scorn;
But, if a man were halt or hunch'd, in him
By those whom God had made full-limb'd and tall,
Scorn was allow'd as part of his defect,
And he was answer'd softly by the King
And all his Table. So Sir Lancelot holp
To raise the Prince, who rising twice or thrice
Full sharply smote his knees, and smiled, and went:
But, ever after, the small violence done
Rankled in him and ruffled all his heart,
As the sharp wind that ruffles all day long
A little bitter pool about a stone
On the bare coast.

But when Sir Lancelot told
This matter to the Queen, at first she laugh'd
Lightly, to think of Modred's dusty fall,
Then shudder'd, as the village wife who cries
"I shudder, some one steps across my grave;"
Then laugh'd again, but faintlier, for indeed
She half-foresaw that he, the subtle beast,
Would track her guilt until he found, and hers
Would be for evermore a name of scorn.
Henceforward rarely could she front in hall,
Or elsewhere, Modred's narrow foxy face,
Heart-hiding smile, and gray persistent eye:
Henceforward too, the Powers that tend the soul,
To help it from the death that cannot die,
And save it even in extremes, began
To vex and plague her. Many a time for hours,

Beside the placid breathings of the King,
In the dead night, grim faces came and went
Before her, or a vague spiritual fear—
Like to some doubtful noise of creaking doors,
Heard by the watcher in a haunted house,
That keeps the rust of murder on the walls—
Held her awake: or if she slept, she dream'd
An awful dream; for then she seem'd to stand
On some vast plain before a setting sun,
And from the sun there swiftly made at her
A ghastly something, and its shadow flew
Before it, till it touch'd her, and she turn'd—
When lo! her own, that broadening from her feet,
And blackening, swallow'd all the land, and in it
Far cities burnt, and with a cry she woke.
And all this trouble did not pass but grew;
Till ev'n the clear face of the guileless King,
And trustful courtesies of household life,
Became her bane; and at the last she said,
"O Lancelot, get thee hence to thine own land,
For if thou tarry we shall meet again,
And if we meet again, some evil chance
Will make the smouldering scandal break and blaze
Before the people, and our lord the King."
And Lancelot ever promised, but remain'd,
And still they met and met. Again she said,
"O Lancelot, if thou love me get thee hence."
And then they were agreed upon a night
(When the good King should not be there) to meet
And part for ever. Vivien, lurking, heard.
She told Sir Modred. Passion-pale they met
And greeted. Hands in hands, and eye to eye,
Low on the border of her couch they sat
Stammering and staring. It was their last hour,
A madness of farewells. And Modred brought
His creatures to the basement of the tower
For testimony; and crying with full voice
"Traitor, come out, ye are trapt at last," aroused
Lancelot, who rushing outward lionlike
Leapt on him, and hurl'd him headlong, and he fell
Stunn'd, and his creatures took and bare him off,
And all was still: then she, "The end is come,
And I am shamed for ever;" and he said,
"Mine be the shame; mine was the sin: but rise,
And fly to my strong castle overseas:
There will I hide thee, till my life shall end,
There hold thee with my life against the world."
She answer'd, "Lancelot, wilt thou hold me so?
Nay, friend, for we have taken our farewells.
Would God that thou couldst hide me from myself!
Mine is the shame, for I was wife, and thou
Unwedded: yet rise now, and let us fly,
For I will draw me into sanctuary,
And bide my doom." So Lancelot got her horse,
Set her thereon, and mounted on his own,
And then they rode to the divided way,
There kiss'd, and parted weeping: for he past,
Love-loyal to the least wish of the Queen,
Back to his land; but she to Almesbury
Fled all night long by glimmering waste and weald,
And heard the spirits of the waste and weald
Moan as she fled, or thought she heard them moan:
And in herself she moan'd "Too late, too late!"
Till in the cold wind that foreruns the morn,
A blot in heaven, the raven, flying high,
Croak'd, and she thought, "He spies a field of death;
For now the heathen of the Northern Sea,
Lured by the crimes and frailties of the court,
Begin to slay the folk, and spoil the land."

And when she came to Almesbury she spake
There to the nuns, and said, "Mine enemies
Pursue me, but, O peaceful Sisterhood,
Receive, and yield me sanctuary, nor ask
Her name to whom ye yield it, till her time
To tell you:" and her beauty, grace and power,
Wrought as a charm upon them, and they spared
To ask it.

So the stately Queen abode
For many a week, unknown, among the nuns;
Nor with them mix'd, nor told her name, nor sought,
Wrapt in her grief, for housel or for shrift,

But communed only with the little maid,
Who pleased her with a babbling heedlessness
Which often lured her from herself; but now,
This night, a rumour wildly blown about
Came, that Sir Modred had usurp'd the realm,
And leagued him with the heathen, while the King
Was waging war on Lancelot: then she thought,
"With what a hate the people and the King
Must hate me," and bow'd down upon her hands
Silent, until the little maid, who brook'd
No silence, brake it, uttering "Late! so late!
What hour, I wonder, now?" and when she drew
No answer, by and by began to hum
An air the nuns had taught her; "Late, so late!"
Which when she heard, the Queen look'd up, and said,
"O maiden, if indeed ye list to sing,
Sing, and unbind my heart that I may weep."
Whereat full willingly sang the little maid.

"Late, late, so late! and dark the night and chill!
Late, late, so late! but we can enter still.
Too late, too late! ye cannot enter now.

"No light had we: for that we do repent;
And learning this, the bridegroom will relent.
Too late, too late! ye cannot enter now.

"No light: so late! and dark and chill the night!
O let us in, that we may find the light!
Too late, too late: ye cannot enter now.

"Have we not heard the bridegroom is so sweet?
O let us in, tho' late, to kiss his feet!
No, no, too late! ye cannot enter now."

So sang the novice, while full passionately,
Her head upon her hands, remembering
Her thought when first she came, wept the sad Queen.
Then said the little novice prattling to her:

"O pray you, noble lady, weep no more;
But let my words, the words of one so small,
Who knowing nothing knows but to obey,
And if I do not there is penance given—
Comfort your sorrows; for they do not flow
From evil done; right sure am I of that,
Who see your tender grace and stateliness.
But weigh your sorrows with our lord the King's,
And weighing find them less; for gone is he
To wage grim war against Sir Lancelot there,
Round that strong castle where he holds the Queen;
And Modred whom he left in charge of all,
The traitor—Ah sweet lady, the King's grief
For his own self, and his own Queen, and realm,
Must needs be thrice as great as any of ours.
For me, I thank the saints, I am not great.
For if there ever come a grief to me
I cry my cry in silence, and have done.
None knows it, and my tears have brought me good:
But even were the griefs of little ones
As great as those of great ones, yet this grief
Is added to the griefs the great must bear,
That howsoever much they may desire
Silence, they cannot weep behind a cloud:
As even here they talk at Almesbury
About the good King and his wicked Queen,
And were I such a King with such a Queen,
Well might I wish to veil her wickedness,
But were I such a King, it could not be."

Then to her own sad heart mutter'd the Queen,
"Will the child kill me with her innocent talk?"
But openly she answer'd, "Must not I,
If this false traitor have displaced his lord,
Grieve with the common grief of all the realm?"

"Yea," said the maid, "this is all woman's grief,
That *she* is woman, whose disloyal life
Hath wrought confusion in the Table Round
Which good King Arthur founded, years ago,
With signs and miracles and wonders, there
At Camelot, ere the coming of the Queen."

Then thought the Queen within herself again,
"Will the child kill me with her foolish prate?"
But openly she spake and said to her,
"O little maid, shut in by nunnery walls,
What canst thou know of Kings and Tables Round,
Or what of signs and wonders, but the signs
And simple miracles of thy nunnery?"

To whom the little novice garrulously,
"Yea, but I know: the land was full of signs
And wonders ere the coming of the Queen.
So said my father, and himself was knight
Of the great Table—at the founding of it;
And rode thereto from Lyonnesse, and he said
That as he rode, an hour or maybe twain
After the sunset, down the coast, he heard
Strange music, and he paused, and turning—there,
All down the lonely coast of Lyonnesse,
Each with a beacon-star upon his head,
And with a wild sea-light about his feet,
He saw them—headland after headland flame
Far on into the rich heart of the west:
And in the light the white mermaiden swam,
And strong man-breasted things stood from the sea,
And sent a deep sea-voice thro' all the land,
To which the little elves of chasm and cleft
Made answer, sounding like a distant horn.
So said my father—yea, and furthermore,
Next morning, while he past the dim-lit woods,
Himself beheld three spirits mad with joy
Come dashing down on a tall wayside flower,
That shook beneath them, as the thistle shakes
When three gray linnets wrangle for the seed:
And still at evenings on before his horse
The flickering fairy-circle wheel'd and broke
Flying, and link'd again, and wheel'd and broke
Flying, for all the land was full of life.
And when at last he came to Camelot,
A wreath of airy dancers hand-in-hand
Swung round the lighted lantern of the hall;
And in the hall itself was such a feast
As never man had dream'd; for every knight
Had whatsoever meat he long'd for served
By hands unseen; and even as he said
Down in the cellars merry bloated things
Shoulder'd the spigot, straddling on the butts
While the wine ran: so glad were spirits and men
Before the coming of the sinful Queen."

Then spake the Queen and somewhat bitterly,
"Were they so glad? ill prophets were they all,
Spirits and men: could none of them foresee,
Not even thy wise father with his signs
And wonders, what has fall'n upon the realm?"

To whom the novice garrulously again,
"Yea, one, a bard; of whom my father said,
Full many a noble war-song had he sung,
Ev'n in the presence of an enemy's fleet,
Between the steep cliff and the coming wave;
And many a mystic lay of life and death
Had chanted on the smoky mountain-tops,
When round him bent the spirits of the hills
With all their dewy hair blown back like flame:
So said my father—and that night the bard
Sang Arthur's glorious wars, and sang the King
As wellnigh more than man, and rail'd at those
Who call'd him the false son of Gorloïs:
For there was no man knew from whence he came;
But after tempest, when the long wave broke
All down the thundering shores of Bude and Bos,
There came a day as still as heaven, and then
They found a naked child upon the sands
Of dark Tintagil by the Cornish sea;
And that was Arthur; and they foster'd him
Till he by miracle was approven King:
And that his grave should be a mystery
From all men, like his birth; and could he find
A woman in her womanhood as great
As he was in his manhood, then, he sang,
The twain together well might change the world.
But even in the middle of his song
He falter'd, and his hand fell from the harp,

And pale he turn'd, and reel'd, and would have fall'n,
But that they stay'd him up; nor would he tell
His vision; but what doubt that he foresaw
This evil work of Lancelot and the Queen?"

Then thought the Queen, "Lo! they have set her on,
Our simple-seeming Abbess and her nuns,
To play upon me," and bow'd her head nor spake.
Whereat the novice crying, with clasp'd hands,
Shame on her own garrulity garrulously,
Said the good nuns would check her gadding tongue
Full often, "and, sweet lady, if I seem
To vex an ear too sad to listen to me,
Unmannerly, with prattling and the tales
Which my good father told me, check me too
Nor let me shame my father's memory, one
Of noblest manners, tho' himself would say
Sir Lancelot had the noblest; and he died,
Kill'd in a tilt, come next, five summers back,
And left me; but of others who remain,
And of the two first-famed for courtesy—
And pray you check me if I ask amiss—
But pray you, which had noblest, while you moved
Among them, Lancelot or our lord the King?"

Then the pale Queen look'd up and answer'd her,
"Sir Lancelot, as became a noble knight,
Was gracious to all ladies, and the same
In open battle or the tilting-field
Forebore his own advantage, and the King
In open battle or the tilting-field
Forebore his own advantage, and these two
Were the most nobly-manner'd men of all;
For manners are not idle, but the fruit
Of loyal nature, and of noble mind."

"Yea," said the maid, "be manners such fair fruit?
Then Lancelot's needs must be a thousand-fold
Less noble, being, as all rumour runs,
The most disloyal friend in all the world."

To which a mournful answer made the Queen:
"O closed about by narrowing nunnery-walls,
What knowest thou of the world, and all its lights
And shadows, all the wealth and all the woe?
If ever Lancelot, that most noble knight,
Were for one hour less noble than himself,
Pray for him that he scape the doom of fire,
And weep for her who drew him to his doom."

"Yea," said the little novice, "I pray for both;
But I should all as soon believe that his,
Sir Lancelot's, were as noble as the King's,
As I could think, sweet lady, yours would be
Such as they are, were you the sinful Queen."

So she, like many another babbler, hurt
Whom she would soothe, and harm'd where she would heal;
For here a sudden flush of wrathful heat
Fired all the pale face of the Queen, who cried,
"Such as thou art be never maiden more
For ever! thou their tool, set on to plague
And play upon, and harry me, petty spy
And traitress." When that storm of anger brake
From Guinevere, aghast the maiden rose,
White as her veil, and stood before the Queen
As tremulously as foam upon the beach
Stands in a wind, ready to break and fly,
And when the Queen had added "Get thee hence,"
Fled frighted. Then that other left alone
Sigh'd, and began to gather heart again,
Saying in herself, "The simple, fearful child
Meant nothing, but my own too-fearful guilt,
Simpler than any child, betrays itself.
But help me, heaven, for surely I repent.
For what is true repentance but in thought—
Not ev'n in inmost thought to think again
The sins that made the past so pleasant to us:
And I have sworn never to see him more,
To see him more."

And ev'n in saying this,
Her memory from old habit of the mind
Went slipping back upon the golden days
In which she saw him first, when Lancelot came,
Reputed the best knight and goodliest man,
Ambassador, to lead her to his lord
Arthur, and led her forth, and far ahead
Of his and her retinue moving, they,
Rapt in sweet talk or lively, all on love
And sport and tilts and pleasure, (for the time
Was maytime, and as yet no sin was dream'd,)
Rode under groves that look'd a paradise
Of blossom, over sheets of hyacinth
That seem'd the heavens upbreaking thro' the earth,
And on from hill to hill, and every day
Beheld at noon in some delicious dale
The silk pavilions of King Arthur raised
For brief repast or afternoon repose
By couriers gone before; and on again,
Till yet once more ere set of sun they saw
The Dragon of the great Pendragonship,
That crown'd the state pavilion of the King,
Blaze by the rushing brook or silent well.

But when the Queen immersed in such a trance,
And moving thro' the past unconsciously,
Came to that point where first she saw the King
Ride toward her from the city, sigh'd to find
Her journey done, glanced at him, thought him cold,
High, self-contain'd, and passionless, not like him,
"Not like my Lancelot"—while she brooded thus
And grew half-guilty in her thoughts again,
There rode an armed warrior to the doors.
A murmuring whisper thro' the nunnery ran,
Then on a sudden a cry, "The King." She sat
Stiff-stricken, listening; but when armed feet
Thro' the long gallery from the outer doors
Rang coming, prone from off her seat she fell,
And grovell'd with her face against the floor:
There with her milkwhite arms and shadowy hair
She made her face a darkness from the King:
And in the darkness heard his armed feet
Pause by her; then came silence, then a voice,
Monotonous and hollow like a ghost's
Denouncing judgment, but tho' changed, the King's:

"Liest thou here so low, the child of one
I honour'd, happy, dead before thy shame?
Well is it that no child is born of thee.
The children born of thee are sword and fire,
Red ruin, and the breaking up of laws,
The craft of kindred and the godless hosts
Of heathen swarming o'er the Northern Sea;
Whom I, while yet Sir Lancelot, my right arm,
The mightiest of my knights, abode with me,
Have everywhere about this land of Christ
In twelve great battles ruining overthrown.
And knowest thou now from whence I come—from him,
From waging bitter war with him: and he,
That did not shun to smite me in worse way,
Had yet that grace of courtesy in him left,
He spared to lift his hand against the King
Who made him knight: but many a knight was slain;
And many more, and all his kith and kin
Clave to him, and abode in his own land.
And many more when Modred raised revolt,
Forgetful of their troth and fealty, clave
To Modred, and a remnant stays with me.
And of this remnant will I leave a part,
True men who love me still, for whom I live,
To guard thee in the wild hour coming on,
Lest but a hair of this low head be harm'd.
Fear not: thou shalt be guarded till my death.
Howbeit I know, if ancient prophecies
Have err'd not, that I march to meet my doom.
Thou hast not made my life so sweet to me,
That I the King should greatly care to live;
For thou hast spoilt the purpose of my life.
Bear with me for the last time while I show,
Ev'n for thy sake, the sin which thou hast sinn'd.
For when the Roman left us, and their law
Relax'd its hold upon us, and the ways
Were fill'd with rapine, here and there a deed
Of prowess done redress'd a random wrong.
But I was first of all the kings who drew
The knighthood-errant of this realm and all
The realms together under me, their Head,
In that fair Order of my Table Round,

A glorious company, the flower of men,
To serve as model for the mighty world,
And be the fair beginning of a time.
I made them lay their hands in mine and swear
To reverence the King, as if he were
Their conscience, and their conscience as their King,
To break the heathen and uphold the Christ,
To ride abroad redressing human wrongs,
To speak no slander, no, nor listen to it,
To honour his own word as if his God's,
To lead sweet lives in purest chastity,
To love one maiden only, cleave to her,
And worship her by years of noble deeds,
Until they won her; for indeed I knew
Of no more subtle master under heaven
Than is the maiden passion for a maid,
Not only to keep down the base in man,
But teach high thought, and amiable words
And courtliness, and the desire of fame,
And love of truth, and all that makes a man.
And all this throve before I wedded thee,
Believing, 'Lo mine helpmate, one to feel
My purpose and rejoicing in my joy.'
Then came thy shameful sin with Lancelot;
Then came the sin of Tristram and Isolt;
Then others, following these my mightiest knights,
And drawing foul ensample from fair names,
Sinn'd also, till the loathsome opposite
Of all my heart had destined did obtain,
And all thro' thee! so that this life of mine
I guard as God's high gift from scathe and wrong,
Not greatly care to lose; but rather think
How sad it were for Arthur, should he live,
To sit once more within his lonely hall,
And miss the wonted number of my knights,
And miss to hear high talk of noble deeds
As in the golden days before thy sin.
For which of us, who might be left, could speak
Of the pure heart, nor seem to glance at thee?
And in thy bowers of Camelot or of Usk
Thy shadow still would glide from room to room,
And I should evermore be vext with thee
In hanging robe or vacant ornament,
Or ghostly footfall echoing on the stair.
For think not, tho' thou wouldst not love thy lord,
Thy lord has wholly lost his love for thee.
I am not made of so slight elements.
Yet must I leave thee, woman, to thy shame.
I hold that man the worst of public foes
Who either for his own or children's sake,
To save his blood from scandal, lets the wife
Whom he knows false, abide and rule the house:
For being thro' his cowardice allow'd
Her station, taken everywhere for pure,
She like a new disease, unknown to men,
Creeps, no precaution used, among the crowd,
Makes wicked lightnings of her eyes, and saps
The fealty of our friends, and stirs the pulse
With devil's leaps, and poisons half the young.
Worst of the worst were that man he that reigns!
Better the King's waste hearth and aching heart
Than thou reseated in thy place of light,
The mockery of my people, and their bane."

He paused, and in the pause she crept an inch
Nearer, and laid her hands about his feet.
Far off a solitary trumpet blew.
Then waiting by the doors the war-horse neigh'd
As at a friend's voice, and he spake again:

"Yet think not that I come to urge thy crimes,
I did not come to curse thee, Guinevere,
I, whose vast pity almost makes me die
To see thee, laying there thy golden head,
My pride in happier summers, at my feet.
The wrath which forced my thoughts on that fierce law,
The doom of treason and the flaming death,
(When first I learnt thee hidden here) is past.
The pang—which while I weigh'd thy heart with one
Too wholly true to dream untruth in thee,
Made my tears burn—is also past—in part.
And all is past, the sin is sinn'd, and I,
Lo! I forgive thee, as Eternal God
Forgives: do thou for thine own soul the rest.
But how to take last leave of all I loved?
O golden hair, with which I used to play
Not knowing! O imperial-moulded form,
And beauty such as never woman wore,

Until it came a kingdom's curse with thee—
I cannot touch thy lips, they are not mine,
But Lancelot's: nay, they never were the King's.
I cannot take thy hand; that too is flesh,
And in the flesh thou hast sinn'd; and mine own flesh,
Here looking down on thine polluted, cries
'I loathe thee:' yet not less, O Guinevere,
For I was ever virgin save for thee,
My love thro' flesh hath wrought into my life
So far, that my doom is, I love thee still.
Let no man dream but that I love thee still.
Perchance, and so thou purify thy soul,
And so thou lean on our fair father Christ,
Hereafter in that world where all are pure
We two may meet before high God, and thou
Wilt spring to me, and claim me thine, and know
I am thine husband—not a smaller soul,
Nor Lancelot, nor another. Leave me that,
I charge thee, my last hope. Now must I hence.
Thro' the thick night I hear the trumpet blow:
They summon me their King to lead mine hosts
Far down to that great battle in the west,
Where I must strike against the man they call
My sister's son—no kin of mine, who leagues
With Lords of the White Horse, heathen, and knights,
Traitors—and strike him dead, and meet myself
Death, or I know not what mysterious doom.
And thou remaining here wilt learn the event;
But hither shall I never come again,
Never lie by thy side; see thee no more—
Farewell!"

And while she grovell'd at his feet,
She felt the King's breath wander o'er her neck,
And in the darkness o'er her fallen head,
Perceived the waving of his hands that blest.

Then, listening till those armed steps were gone,
Rose the pale Queen, and in her anguish found
The casement: "peradventure," so she thought,
"If I might see his face, and not be seen."
And lo, he sat on horseback at the door!
And near him the sad nuns with each a light
Stood, and he gave them charge about the Queen,
To guard and foster her for evermore.
And while he spake to these his helm was lower'd,
To which for crest the golden dragon clung
Of Britain; so she did not see the face,
Which then was as an angel's, but she saw,
Wet with the mists and smitten by the lights,
The Dragon of the great Pendragonship
Blaze, making all the night a steam of fire.
And even then he turn'd; and more and more
The moony vapour rolling round the King,
Who seem'd the phantom of a giant in it,
Enwound him fold by fold, and made him gray
And grayer, till himself became as mist
Before her, moving ghostlike to his doom.

Then she stretch'd out her arms and cried aloud
"Oh Arthur!" there her voice brake suddenly,
Then—as a stream that spouting from a cliff
Fails in mid air, but gathering at the base
Re-makes itself, and flashes down the vale—
Went on in passionate utterance:

"Gone—my lord!
Gone thro' my sin to slay and to be slain!
And he forgave me, and I could not speak.
Farewell? I should have answer'd his farewell.
His mercy choked me. Gone, my lord the King,
My own true lord! how dare I call him mine?
The shadow of another cleaves to me,
And makes me one pollution: he, the King,
Call'd me polluted: shall I kill myself?
What help in that? I cannot kill my sin,
If soul be soul; nor can I kill my shame;
No, nor by living can I live it down.
The days will grow to weeks, the weeks to months,
The months will add themselves and make the years,
The years will roll into the centuries,
And mine will ever be a name of scorn.
I must not dwell on that defeat of fame.
Let the world be; that is but of the world

What else? what hope? I think there was a hope,
Except he mock'd me when he spake of hope;
His hope he call'd it; but he never mocks,
For mockery is the fume of little hearts.
And blessed be the King, who hath forgiven
My wickedness to him, and left me hope
That in mine own heart I can live down sin
And be his mate hereafter in the heavens
Before high God. Ah great and gentle lord,
Who wast, as is the conscience of a saint
Among his warring senses, to thy knights—
To whom my false voluptuous pride, that took
Full easily all impressions from below,
Would not look up, or half-despised the height
To which I would not or I could not climb—
I thought I could not breathe in that fine air
That pure severity of perfect light—
I yearn'd for warmth and colour which I found
In Lancelot—now I see thee what thou art,
Thou art the highest and most human too,
Not Lancelot, nor another. Is there none
Will tell the King I love him tho' so late?
Now—ere he goes to the great battle? none:
Myself must tell him in that purer life,
But now it were too daring. Ah my God,
What might I not have made of thy fair world,
Had I but loved thy highest creature here?
It was my duty to have loved the highest:
It surely was my profit had I known:
It would have been my pleasure had I seen.
We needs must love the highest when we see it,
Not Lancelot, nor another."

Here her hand
Grasp'd, made her vail her eyes: she look'd and saw
The novice, weeping, suppliant, and said to her,
"Yea, little maid, for am *I* not forgiven?"
Then glancing up beheld the holy nuns
All round her, weeping; and her heart was loosed
Within her, and she wept with these and said,
"Ye know me then, that wicked one, who broke
The vast design and purpose of the King.
O shut me round with narrowing nunnery-walls,
Meek maidens, from the voices crying 'shame.'
I must not scorn myself: he loves me still.
Let no one dream but that he loves me still.
So let me, if you do not shudder at me,
Nor shun to call me sister, dwell with you;
Wear black and white, and be a nun like you,
Fast with your fasts, not feasting with your feasts;
Grieve with your griefs, not grieving at your joys,
But not rejoicing; mingle with your rites;
Pray and be pray'd for; lie before your shrines;
Do each low office of your holy house;
Walk your dim cloister, and distribute dole
To poor sick people, richer in His eyes
Who ransom'd us, and haler too than I;
And treat their loathsome hurts and heal mine own;
And so wear out in almsdeed and in prayer
The sombre close of that voluptuous day,
Which wrought the ruin of my lord the King."

She said: they took her to themselves; and she
Still hoping, fearing "is it yet too late?"
Dwelt with them, till in time their abbess died.
Then she, for her good deeds and her pure life,
And for the power of ministration in her,
And likewise for the high rank she had borne,
Was chosen abbess, there, an abbess, lived
For three brief years, and there, an abbess, past
To where beyond these voices there is peace.
1859

A WORM WITHIN A ROSE

(From *Pelleas and Ettarre*)

A rose, but one, none other rose had I,
A rose, one rose, and this was wondrous fair,
One rose, a rose that gladden'd earth and sky,

One rose, my rose, that sweeten'd all mine air—
I cared not for the thorns; the thorns were there.

One rose, a rose to gather by and by,
One rose, a rose to gather and to wear,
No rose but one—what other rose had I?
One rose, my rose; a rose that will not die,—
He dies who loves it,—if the worm be there.

1869

THE VOICE AND THE PEAK

I

THE voice and the Peak
Far over summit and lawn,
The lone glow and long roar
Green-rushing from the rosy thrones of dawn!

II

All night have I heard the voice
Rave over the rocky bar,
But thou wert silent in heaven,
Above thee glided the star.

III

Hast thou no voice, O Peak,
That standest high above all?
"I am the voice of the Peak,
I roar and rave for I fall.

IV

"A thousand voices go
To North, South, East, and West;
They leave the heights and are troubled,
And moan and sink to their rest.

V

"The fields are fair beside them,
The chestnut towers in his bloom;
But they—they feel the desire of the deep—
Fall, and follow their doom.

VI

"The deep has power on the height,
And the height has power on the deep;
They are raised for ever and ever,
And sink again into sleep."

VII

Not raised for ever and ever,
But when their cycle is o'er,
The valley, the voice, the peak, the star
Pass, and are found no more.

VIII

The Peak is high and flush'd
At his highest with sunrise fire;
The Peak is high, and the stars are high,
And the thought of a man is higher.

IX

A deep below the deep,
And a height beyond the height!
Our hearing is not hearing,
And our seeing is not sight.

X

The voice and the Peak
Far into heaven withdrawn,
The lone glow and long roar
Green-rushing from the rosy thrones of dawn!

1874

HAPLESS DOOM OF WOMAN

(From *Queen Mary*)

Hapless doom of woman happy in betrothing!
Beauty passes like a breath and love is lost in loathing:
Low, my lute; speak low, my lute, but say the world is nothing—
Low, lute, low!

Love will hover round the flowers when they first awaken;
Love will fly the fallen leaf, and not be overtaken;
Low, my lute! oh low, my lute! we fade and are forsaken—
Low, dear lute, low!

1875

THE REVENGE

A BALLAD OF THE FLEET

I

AT Flores in the Azores Sir Richard Grenville lay,
And a pinnace, like a flutter'd bird, came flying from far away:

"Spanish ships of war at sea! we have sighted fifty-three!"
Then sware Lord Thomas Howard: "'Fore God I am no coward;
But I cannot meet them here, for my ships are out of gear,
And the half my men are sick. I must fly, but follow quick.
We are six ships of the line; can we fight with fifty-three?"

II

Then spake Sir Richard Grenville: "I know you are no coward;
You fly them for a moment to fight with them again.
But I've ninety men and more that are lying sick ashore.
I should count myself the coward if I left them, my Lord Howard,
To these Inquisition dogs and the devildoms of Spain."

III

So Lord Howard past away with five ships of war that day,
Till he melted like a cloud in the silent summer heaven;
But Sir Richard bore in hand all his sick men from the land
Very carefully and slow,
Men of Bideford in Devon,
And we laid them on the ballast down below;
For we brought them all aboard,
And they blest him in their pain, that they were not left to Spain,
To the thumbscrew and the stake, for the glory of the Lord.

IV

He had only a hundred seamen to work the ship and to fight,
And he sailed away from Flores till the Spaniard came in sight,
With his huge sea-castles heaving upon the weather bow.
"Shall we fight or shall we fly?
Good Sir Richard, tell us now,
For to fight is but to die!
There'll be little of us left by the time this sun be set."
And Sir Richard said again: "We be all good English men.
Let us bang these dogs of Seville, the children of the devil,
For I never turn'd my back upon Don or devil yet."

V

Sir Richard spoke and he laugh'd, and we roar'd a hurrah, and so
The little Revenge ran on sheer into the heart of the foe,
With her hundred fighters on deck, and her ninety sick below;
For half of their fleet to the right and half to the left were seen,
And the little Revenge ran on thro' the long sea-lane between.

VI

Thousands of their soldiers look'd down from their decks and laugh'd,
Thousands of their seamen made mock at the mad little craft
Running on and on, till delay'd
By their mountain-like San Philip that, of fifteen hundred tons,
And up-shadowing high above us with her yawning tiers of guns,
Took the breath from our sails, and we stay'd.

VII

And while now the great San Philip hung above us like a cloud
Whence the thunderbolt will fall
Long and loud,
Four galleons drew away
From the Spanish fleet that day,
And two upon the larboard and two upon the starboard lay,
And the battle-thunder broke from them all.

VIII

But anon the great San Philip, she bethought herself and went
Having that within her womb that had left her ill content;
And the rest they came aboard us, and they fought us hand to hand,

For a dozen times they came with their pikes and musqueteers,
And a dozen times we shook 'em off as a dog that shakes his ears
When he leaps from the water to the land.

IX

And the sun went down, and the stars came out far over the summer sea,
But never a moment ceased the fight of the one and the fifty-three.
Ship after ship, the whole night long, their high-built galleons came,
Ship after ship, the whole night long, with her battle-thunder and flame;
Ship after ship, the whole night long, drew back with her dead and her shame.
For some were sunk and many were shatter'd, and so could fight us no more—
God of battles, was ever a battle like this in the world before?

X

For he said "Fight on! fight on!"
Tho' his vessel was all but a wreck;
And it chanced that, when half of the short summer night was gone,
With a grisly wound to be drest he had left the deck,
But a bullet struck him that was dressing it suddenly dead,
And himself he was wounded again in the side and the head,
And he said "Fight on! fight on!"

XI

And the night went down, and the sun smiled out far over the summer sea,
And the Spanish fleet with broken sides lay round us all in a ring;
But they dared not touch us again, for they fear'd that we still could sting,
So they watch'd what the end would be.
And we had not fought them in vain,
But in perilous plight were we,
Seeing forty of our poor hundred were slain,
And half of the rest of us maim'd for life
In the crash of the cannonades and the desperate strife;
And the sick men down in the hold were most of them stark and cold,
And the pikes were all broken or bent, and the powder was all of it spent;
And the masts and the rigging were lying over the side;
But Sir Richard cried in his English pride,
"We have fought such a fight for a day and a night
As may never be fought again!
We have won great glory, my men!
And a day less or more
At sea or ashore,
We die—does it matter when?
Sink me the ship, Master Gunner—sink her, split her in twain!
Fall into the hands of God, not into the hands of Spain!"

XII

And the gunner said "Ay, ay," but the seamen made reply:
"We have children, we have wives,
And the Lord hath spared our lives.
We will make the Spaniard promise, if we yield, to let us go;
We shall live to fight again and to strike another blow."
And the lion there lay dying, and they yielded to the foe.

XIII

And the stately Spanish men to their flagship bore him then,
Where they laid him by the mast, old Sir Richard caught at last,
And they praised him to his face with their courtly foreign grace;
But he rose upon their decks, and he cried:
"I have fought for Queen and Faith like a valiant man and true;
I have only done my duty as a man is bound to do:
With a joyful spirit I Sir Richard Grenville die!"
And he fell upon their decks, and he died.

XIV

And they stared at the dead that had been so valiant and true,
And had holden the power and glory of Spain so cheap
That he dared her with one little ship and his English few;

Was he devil or man? He was devil for aught they knew,
But they sank his body with honour down into the deep,
And they mann'd the Revenge with a swarthier alien crew,
And away she sail'd with her loss and long'd for her own;
When a wind from the lands they had ruin'd awoke from sleep,
And the water began to heave and the weather to moan,
And or ever that evening ended a great gale blew,
And a wave like the wave that is raised by an earthquake grew,
Till it smote on their hulls and their sails and their masts and their flags,
And the whole sea plunged and fell on the shot-shatter'd navy of Spain,
And the little Revenge herself went down by the island crags
To be lost evermore in the main.

1878

From THE LOVER'S TALE

(Lines 657–676)

And yet to-night, to-night—when all my wealth
Flash'd from me in a moment and I fell
Beggar'd for ever—why *should* he come my way
Robed in those robes of light I must not wear,
With that great crown of beams about his brows—
Come like an angel to a damned soul,
To tell him of the bliss he had with God—
Come like a careless and a greedy heir
That scarce can wait the reading of the will
Before he takes possession? Was mine a mood
To be invaded rudely, and not rather
A sacred, secret, unapproached woe,
Unspeakable? I was shut up with Grief;
She took the body of my past delight,
Narded and swathed and balm'd it for herself,
And laid it in a sepulchre of rock
Never to rise again. I was led mute
Into her temple like a sacrifice;
I was the High Priest in her holiest place,
Not to be loudly broken in upon.

1879

DE PROFUNDIS:

THE TWO GREETINGS

I

Out of the deep, my child, out of the deep,
Where all that was to be, in all that was,
Whirl'd for a million æons thro' the vast
Waste dawn of multitudinous-eddying light—
Out of the deep, my child, out of the deep,
Thro' all this changing world of changeless law,
And every phase of ever-heightening life,
And nine long months of antenatal gloom,
With this last moon, this crescent—her dark orb
Touch'd with earth's light—thou comest, darling boy;
Our own; a babe in lineament and limb
Perfect, and prophet of the perfect man;
Whose face and form are hers and mine in one,
Indissolubly married like our love;
Live, and be happy in thyself, and serve
This mortal race thy kin so well, that men
May bless thee as we bless thee, O young life
Breaking with laughter from the dark; and may
The fated channel where thy motion lives
Be prosperously shaped, and sway thy course
Along the years of haste and random youth
Unshatter'd; then full-current thro' full man;
And last in kindly curves, with gentlest fall,
By quiet fields, a slowly-dying power,
To that last deep where we and thou are still.

II

I

Out of the deep, my child, out of the deep,
From that great deep, before our world begins,
Whereon the Spirit of God moves as he will—
Out of the deep, my child, out of the deep,
From that true world within the world we see,
Whereof our world is but the bounding shore—
Out of the deep, Spirit, out of the deep,
With this ninth moon, that sends the hidden sun
Down yon dark sea, thou comest, darling boy.

II

For in the world, which is not ours, They said
"Let us make man" and that which should be man,
From that one light no man can look upon,
Drew to this shore lit by the suns and moons
And all the shadows. O dear Spirit half-lost
In thine own shadow and this fleshly sign
That thou art thou—who wailest being born
And banish'd into mystery, and the pain
Of this divisible-indivisible world
Among the numerable-innumerable
Sun, sun, and sun, thro' finite-infinite space
In finite-infinite Time—our mortal veil
And shatter'd phantom of that infinite One,
Who made thee unconceivably Thyself
Out of His whole World-self and all in all—
Live thou! and of the grain and husk, the grape
And ivyberry, choose; and still depart
From death to death thro' life and life, and find
Nearer and ever nearer Him, who wrought
Not Matter, nor the finite-infinite,
But this main-miracle, that thou art thou,
With power on thine own act and on the world.

THE HUMAN CRY

I

HALLOWED be Thy name—Halleluiah!—
Infinite Ideality!
Immeasurable Reality!
Infinite Personality!
Hallowed be Thy name—Halleluiah!

II

We feel we are nothing—for all is Thou and in Thee;
We feel we are something—*that* also has come from Thee;
We know we are nothing—but Thou wilt help us to be.
Hallowed be Thy name—Halleluiah!

1880

RIZPAH

17—

I

WAILING, wailing, wailing, the wind over land and sea—
And Willy's voice in the wind, "O mother, come out to me."
Why should he call me to-night, when he knows that I cannot go?
For the downs are as bright as day, and the full moon stares at the snow.

II

We should be seen, my dear; they would spy us out of the town.
The loud black nights for us, and the storm rushing over the down,
When I cannot see my own hand, but am led by the creak of the chain,
And grovel and grope for my son till I find myself drenched with the rain.

III

Anything fallen again? nay—what was there left to fall?
I have taken them home, I have number'd the bones, I have hidden them all.
What am I saying? and what are *you?* do you come as a spy?
Falls? what falls? who knows? As the tree falls so must it lie.

IV

Who let her in? how long has she been? you—what have you heard?
Why did you sit so quiet? you never have spoken a word.
O—to pray with me—yes—a lady—none of their spies—
But the night has crept into my heart, and begun to darken my eyes.

V

Ah—you, that have lived so soft, what should *you* know of the night,
The blast and the burning shame and the bitter frost and the fright?
I have done it, while you were asleep—you were only made for the day.
I have gather'd my baby together—and now you may go your way.

VI

Nay—for it's kind of you, Madam, to sit by an old dying wife.
But say nothing hard of my boy, I have only an hour of life.
I kiss'd my boy in the prison, before he went out to die.
"They dared me to do it," he said, and he never has told me a lie.
I whipt him for robbing an orchard once when he was but a child—
"The farmer dared me to do it," he said; he was always so wild—
And idle—and couldn't be idle—my Willy—he never could rest.
The King should have made him a soldier, he would have been one of his best.

VII

But he lived with a lot of wild mates, and they never would let him be good;
They swore that he dare not rob the mail, and he swore that he would;
And he took no life, but he took one purse, and when all was done
He flung it among his fellows—"I'll none of it," said my son.

VIII

I came into court to the Judge and the lawyers. I told them my tale,
God's own truth—but they kill'd him, they kill'd him for robbing the mail.
They hang'd him in chains for a show—we had always borne a good name—
To be hang'd for a thief—and then put away—isn't that enough shame?
Dust to dust—low down—let us hide! but they set him so high
That all the ships of the world could stare at him, passing by.
God 'ill pardon the hell-black raven and horrible fowls of the air,
But not the black heart of the lawyer who kill'd him and hang'd him there.

IX

And the jailer forced me away. I had bid him my last goodbye;
They had fasten'd the door of his cell. "O mother!" I heard him cry.
I couldn't get back tho' I tried, he had something further to say,
And now I never shall know it. The jailer forced me away.

X

Then since I couldn't but hear that cry of my boy that was dead,
They seized me and shut me up: they fasten'd me down on my bed.
"Mother, O mother!"—he call'd in the dark to me year after year—
They beat me for that, they beat me—you know that I couldn't but hear;
And then at the last they found I had grown so stupid and still
They let me abroad again—but the creatures had worked their will.

XI

Flesh of my flesh was gone, but bone of my bone was left—
I stole them all from the lawyers—and you, will you call it a theft?—
My baby, the bones that had suck'd me, the bones that had laughed and had cried—
Theirs? O no! they are mine—not theirs—they had moved in my side.

XII

Do you think I was scared by the bones? I kiss'd 'em, I buried 'em all—
I can't dig deep, I am old—in the night by the churchyard wall.
My Willy 'ill rise up whole when the trumpet of judgment 'ill sound,
But I charge you never to say that I laid him in holy ground.

XIII

They would scratch him up—they would hang him again on the cursed tree.
Sin? O yes—we are sinners, I know—let all that be,
And read me a Bible verse of the Lord's good will toward men—
"Full of compassion and mercy, the Lord"—let me hear it again;
"Full of compassion and mercy—long-suffering." Yes, O yes!
For the lawyer is born but to murder—the Saviour lives but to bless.

He'll never put on the black cap except for the worst of the worst,
And the first may be last—I have heard it in church—and the last may be first.
Suffering—O long-suffering—yes, as the Lord must know,
Year after year in the mist and the wind and the shower and the snow.

XIV

Heard, have you? what? they have told you he never repented his sin.
How do they know it? are *they* his mother? are *you* of his kin?
Heard! have you ever heard, when the storm on the downs began,
The wind that 'ill wail like a child and the sea that 'ill moan like a man?

XV

Election, Election and Reprobation—it's all very well.
But I go to-night to my boy, and I shall not find him in Hell.
For I cared so much for my boy that the Lord has look'd into my care,
And He means me I'm sure to be happy with Willy, I know not where.

XVI

And if *he* be lost—but to save *my* soul, that is all your desire:
Do you think that I care for *my* soul if my boy be gone to the fire?
I have been with God in the dark—go, go, you may leave me alone—
You never have borne a child—you are just as hard as a stone.

XVII

Madam, I beg your pardon! I think that you mean to be kind,
But I cannot hear what you say for my Willy's voice in the wind—
The snow and the sky so bright—he used but to call in the dark,
And he calls to me now from the church and not from the gibbet—for hark!
Nay—you can hear it yourself—it is coming—shaking the walls—
Willy—the moon's in a cloud——Good-night. I am going. He calls.

1880

"FRATER AVE ATQUE VALE"

Row us out from Desenzano, to your Sirmione row!
So they row'd, and there we landed—"O venusta Sirmio!"
There to me thro' all the groves of olive in the summer glow,
There beneath the Roman ruin where the purple flowers grow,
Came that "Ave atque Vale" of the Poet's hopeless woe,
Tenderest of Roman poets nineteen-hundred years ago,
"Frater Ave atque Vale"—as we wander'd to and fro
Gazing at the Lydian laughter of the Garda Lake below
Sweet Catullus's all-but-island, olive-silvery Sirmio!

1883

TO VIRGIL

WRITTEN AT THE REQUEST OF THE MANTUANS FOR THE NINETEENTH CENTENARY OF VIRGIL'S DEATH

I

ROMAN VIRGIL, thou that singest
 Ilion's lofty temples robed in fire,
Ilion falling, Rome arising,
 wars, and filial faith, and Dido's pyre;

II

Landscape-lover, lord of language
 more than he that sang the Works and Days,
All the chosen coin of fancy
 flashing out from many a golden phrase;

III

Thou that singest wheat and woodland,
 tilth and vineyard, hive and horse and herd;
All the charm of all the Muses
 often flowering in a lonely word;

IV

Poet of the happy Tityrus
 piping underneath his beechen bowers;
Poet of the poet-satyr
 whom the laughing shepherd bound with flowers;

V

Chanter of the Pollio, glorying
    in the blissful years again to be,
Summers of the snakeless meadow,
    unlaborious earth and oarless sea;

VI

Thou that seëst Universal
    Nature moved by Universal Mind;
Thou majestic in thy sadness
    at the doubtful doom of human kind;

VII

Light among the vanish'd ages;
    star that gildest yet this phantom shore;
Golden branch amid the shadows,
    kings and realms that pass to rise no more;

VIII

Now thy Forum roars no longer,
    fallen every purple Cæsar's dome—
Tho' thine ocean-roll of rhythm
    sound for ever of Imperial Rome—

IX

Now the Rome of slaves hath perish'd,
    and the Rome of freemen holds her place,
I, from out the Northern Island
    sunder'd once from all the human race,

X

I salute thee, Mantovano,
    I that loved thee since my day began,
Wielder of the stateliest measure
    ever moulded by the lips of man.

1882

FREEDOM

I

O THOU so fair in summers gone,
    While yet thy fresh and virgin soul
Inform'd the pillar'd Parthenon,
    The glittering Capitol;

II

So fair in southern sunshine bathed,
    But scarce of such majestic mien
As here with forehead vapour-swathed
    In meadows ever green;

III

For thou—when Athens reign'd and Rome,
    Thy glorious eyes were dimm'd with pain
To mark in many a freeman's home
    The slave, the scourge, the chain;

IV

O follower of the Vision, still
    In motion to the distant gleam,
Howe'er blind force and brainless will
    May jar thy golden dream

V

Of Knowledge fusing class with class,
    Of civic Hate no more to be,
Of Love to leaven all the mass,
    Till every Soul be free;

VI

Who yet, like Nature, wouldst not mar
    By changes all too fierce and fast
This order of Her Human Star,
    This heritage of the past;

VII

O scorner of the party cry
    That wanders from the public good,
Thou—when the nations rear on high
    Their idol smear'd with blood,

VIII

And when they roll their idol down—
    Of saner worship sanely proud;
Thou loather of the lawless crown
    As of the lawless crowd;

IX

How long thine ever-growing mind
    Hath still'd the blast and strown the wave,
Tho' some of late would raise a wind
    To sing thee to thy grave,

X

Men loud against all forms of power—
    Unfurnish'd brows, tempestuous tongues—
Expecting all things in an hour—
    Brass mouths and iron lungs!

1884

VASTNESS

I

Many a hearth upon our dark globe sighs after many a vanish'd face,
Many a planet by many a sun may roll with the dust of a vanish'd race.

II

Raving politics, never at rest—as this poor earth's pale history runs,—
What is it all but a trouble of ants in the gleam of a million million of suns?

III

Lies upon this side, lies upon that side, truthless violence mourn'd by the Wise,
Thousands of voices drowning his own in a popular torrent of lies upon lies;

IV

Stately purposes, valour in battle, glorious annals of army and fleet,
Death for the right cause, death for the wrong cause, trumpets of victory, groans of defeat;

V

Innocence seethed in her mother's milk, and Charity setting the martyr aflame;
Thraldom who walks with the banner of Freedom, and recks not to ruin a realm in her name.

VI

Faith at her zenith, or all but lost in the gloom of doubts that darken the schools;
Craft with a bunch of all-heal in her hand, follow'd up by her vassal legion of fools;

VII

Trade flying over a thousand seas with her spice and her vintage, her silk and her corn;
Desolate offing, sailorless harbours, famishing populace, wharves forlorn;

VIII

Star of the morning, Hope in the sunrise; gloom of the evening, Life at a close;
Pleasure who flaunts on her wide down-way with her flying robe and her poison'd rose;

IX

Pain, that has crawl'd from the corpse of Pleasure, a worm which writhes all day, and at night
Stirs up again in the heart of the sleeper, and stings him back to the curse of the light;

X

Wealth with his wines and his wedded harlots; honest Poverty, bare to the bone;
Opulent Avarice, lean as Poverty; Flattery gilding the rift in a throne;

XI

Fame blowing out from her golden trumpet a jubilant challenge to Time and to Fate;
Slander, her shadow, sowing the nettle on all the laurel'd graves of the Great;

XII

Love for the maiden, crown'd with marriage, no regrets for aught that has been,
Household happiness, gracious children, debtless competence, golden mean;

XIII

National hatreds of whole generations, and pigmy spites of the village spire;
Vows that will last to the last death-ruckle, and vows that are snapt in a moment of fire;

XIV

He that has lived for the lust of the minute, and died in the doing it, flesh without mind;
He that has nail'd all flesh to the Cross, till Self died out in the love of his kind;

XV

Spring and Summer and Autumn and Winter, and all these old revolutions of earth;
All new-old revolutions of Empire—change of the tide—what is all of it worth?

XVI

What the philosophies, all the sciences, poesy, varying voices of prayer?
All that is noblest, all that is basest, all that is filthy with all that is fair?

XVII

What is it all, if we all of us end but in being our own corpse-coffins at last,
Swallow'd in Vastness, lost in Silence, drown'd in the deeps of a meaningless Past?

XVIII

What but a murmur of gnats in the gloom,
or a moment's anger of bees in their hive?—

* * *

Peace, let it be! for I loved him, and love him
for ever: the dead are not dead but alive.

1885

THE ANCIENT SAGE

A THOUSAND summers ere the time of Christ
From out his ancient city came a Seer
Whom one that loved, and honour'd him, and yet
Was no disciple, richly garb'd, but worn
From wasteful living, follow'd—in his hand
A scroll of verse—till that old man before
A cavern whence an affluent fountain pour'd
From darkness into daylight, turn'd and spoke.

This wealth of waters might but seem to draw
From yon dark cave, but, son, the source is higher,
Yon summit half-a-league in air—and higher,
The cloud that hides it—higher still, the heavens
Whereby the cloud was moulded, and whereout
The cloud descended. Force is from the heights.
I am wearied of our city, son, and go
To spend my one last year among the hills.
What hast thou there? Some deathsong for the Ghouls
To make their banquet relish? let me read.

"How far thro' all the bloom and brake
That nightingale is heard!
What power but the bird's could make
This music in the bird?
How summer-bright are yonder skies,
And earth as fair in hue!
And yet what sign of aught that lies
Behind the green and blue?
But man to-day is fancy's fool
As man hath ever been.
The nameless Power, or Powers, that rule
Were never heard or seen."

If thou would'st hear the Nameless, and wilt dive
Into the Temple-cave of thine own self,
There, brooding by the central altar, thou
May'st haply learn the Nameless hath a voice,
By which thou wilt abide, if thou be wise,
As if thou knewest, tho' thou canst not know;
For Knowledge is the swallow on the lake
That sees and stirs the surface-shadow there
But never yet hath dipt into the abysm,
The Abysm of all Abysms, beneath, within
The blue of sky and sea, the green of earth,
And in the million-millionth of a grain
Which cleft and cleft again for evermore,
And ever vanishing, never vanishes,
To me, my son, more mystic than myself,
Or even than the Nameless is to me.
And when thou sendest thy free soul thro' heaven,
Nor understandest bound nor boundlessness,
Thou seest the Nameless of the hundred names.
And if the Nameless should withdraw from all
Thy frailty counts most real, all thy world
Might vanish like thy shadow in the dark.

"And since—from when this earth began—
The Nameless never came
Among us, never spake with man,
And never named the Name"—

Thou canst not prove the Nameless, O my son,
Nor canst thou prove the world thou movest in,
Thou canst not prove that thou art body alone,
Nor canst thou prove that thou art spirit alone,
Nor canst thou prove that thou art both in one:
Thou canst not prove thou art immortal, no
Nor yet that thou art mortal—nay my son,
Thou canst not prove that I, who speak with thee,
Am not thyself in converse with thyself,
For nothing worthy proving can be proven,
Nor yet disproven: wherefore thou be wise,
Cleave ever to the sunnier side of doubt,
And cling to Faith beyond the forms of Faith!
She reels not in the storm of warring words,

She brightens at the clash of "Yes" and "No,"
She sees the Best that glimmers thro' the Worst,
She feels the Sun is hid but for a night,
She spies the summer thro' the winter bud,
She tastes the fruit before the blossom falls,
She hears the lark within the songless egg,
She finds the fountain where they wail'd "Mirage"!

"What Power? aught akin to Mind,
The mind in me and you?
Or power as of the Gods gone blind
Who see not what they do?"

But some in yonder city hold, my son,
That none but Gods could build this house of ours,
So beautiful, vast, various, so beyond
All work of man, yet, like all work of man,
A beauty with defect——till That which knows,
And is not known, but felt thro' what we feel
Within ourselves is highest, shall descend
On this half-deed, and shape it at the last
According to the Highest in the Highest.

"What Power but the Years that make
And break the vase of clay,
And stir the sleeping earth, and wake
The bloom that fades away?
What rulers but the Days and Hours
That cancel weal with woe,
And wind the front of youth with flowers,
And cap our age with snow?"

The days and hours are ever glancing by,
And seem to flicker past thro' sun and shade,
Or short, or long, as Pleasure leads, or Pain;
But with the Nameless is nor Day nor Hour;
Tho' we, thin minds, who creep from thought to thought,
Break into "Thens" and "Whens" the Eternal Now:
This double seeming of the single world!—
My words are like the babblings in a dream
Of nightmare, when the babblings break the dream.
But thou be wise in this dream-world of ours,
Nor take thy dial for thy deity,
But make the passing shadow serve thy will.

"The years that made the stripling wise
Undo their work again,
And leave him, blind of heart and eyes,
The last and least of men;
Who clings to earth, and once would dare
Hell-heat or Arctic cold,
And now one breath of cooler air
Would loose him from his hold;
His winter chills him to the root,
He withers marrow and mind;
The kernel of the shrivell'd fruit
Is jutting thro' the rind;
The tiger spasms tear his chest,
The palsy wags his head;
The wife, the sons, who love him best
Would fain that he were dead;
The griefs by which he once was wrung
Were never worth the while"—

Who knows? or whether this earth-narrow life
Be yet but yolk, and forming in the shell?

"The shaft of scorn that once had stung
But wakes a dotard smile."

The placid gleam of sunset after storm!

"The statesman's brain that sway'd the past
Is feebler than his knees;
The passive sailor wrecks at last
In ever-silent seas;
The warrior hath forgot his arms,
The Learned all his lore;
The changing market frets or charms
The merchant's hope no more;
The prophet's beacon burn'd in vain,
And now is lost in cloud;
The plowman passes, bent with pain,
To mix with what he plow'd;
The poet whom his Age would quote
As heir of endless fame—
He knows not ev'n the book he wrote,
Not even his own name.
For man has overlived his day,
And, darkening in the light,
Scarce feels the senses break away
To mix with ancient Night."

The shell must break before the bird can fly.

"The years that when my Youth began
Had set the lily and rose
By all my ways where'er they ran,
Have ended mortal foes;
My rose of love for ever gone,
My lily of truth and trust—
They made her lily and rose in one,
And changed her into dust.
O rosetree planted in my grief,
And growing, on her tomb,
Her dust is greening in your leaf,
Her blood is in your bloom.
O slender lily waving there,
And laughing back the light,
In vain you tell me 'Earth is fair'
When all is dark as night."

My son, the world is dark with griefs and graves,
So dark that men cry out against the Heavens.
Who knows but that the darkness is in man?
The doors of Night may be the gates of Light;
For wert thou born or blind or deaf, and then
Suddenly heal'd, how would'st thou glory in all
The splendours and the voices of the world!
And we, the poor earth's dying race, and yet
No phantoms, watching from a phantom shore
Await the last and largest sense to make
The phantom walls of this illusion fade,
And show us that the world is wholly fair.

"But vain the tears for darken'd years
As laughter over wine,
And vain the laughter as the tears,
O brother, mine or thine,
For all that laugh, and all that weep
And all that breathe are one
Slight ripple on the boundless deep
That moves, and all is gone."

But that one ripple on the boundless deep
Feels that the deep is boundless, and itself
For ever changing form, but evermore
One with the boundless motion of the deep.

"Yet wine and laughter friends! and set
The lamps alight, and call
For golden music, and forget
The darkness of the pall."

If utter darkness closed the day, my son—
But earth's dark forehead flings athwart the heavens
Her shadow crown'd with stars—and yonder—out
To northward—some that never set, but pass
From sight and night to lose themselves in day.
I hate the black negation of the bier,
And wish the dead, as happier than ourselves
And higher, having climb'd one step beyond
Our village miseries, might be borne in white
To burial or to burning, hymn'd from hence
With songs in praise of death, and crown'd with flowers!

"O worms and maggots of to-day
Without their hope of wings!"

But louder than thy rhyme the silent Word
Of that world-prophet in the heart of man.

"Tho' some have gleams or so they say
Of more than mortal things."

To-day? but what of yesterday? for oft
On me, when boy, there came what then I call'd,
Who knew no books and no philosophies,
In my boy-phrase "The Passion of the Past."
The first gray streak of earliest summer-dawn,
The last long stripe of waning crimson gloom,
As if the late and early were but one—
A height, a broken grange, a grove, a flower
Had murmurs "Lost and gone and lost and gone!"
A breath, a whisper—some divine farewell—
Desolate sweetness—far and far away—
What had he loved, what had he lost, the boy?
I know not and I speak of what has been.
And more, my son! for more than once when I
Sat all alone, revolving in myself
The word that is the symbol of myself,
The mortal limit of the Self was loosed,
And past into the Nameless, as a cloud
Melts into Heaven. I touch'd my limbs, the limbs
Were strange not mine—and yet no shade of doubt,
But utter clearness, and thro' loss of Self

The gain of such large life as match'd with ours
Were Sun to spark—unshadowable in words,
Themselves but shadows of a shadow-world.

"And idle gleams will come and go,
But still the clouds remain;"
The clouds themselves are children of the Sun.

"And Night and Shadow rule below
When only Day should reign."
And Day and Night are children of the Sun,
And idle gleams to thee are light to me.
Some say, the Light was father of the Night,
And some, the Night was father of the Light,
No night no day!—I touch thy world again—
No ill no good! such counter-terms, my son,
Are border-races, holding, each its own
By endless war: but night enough is there
In yon dark city: get thee back: and since
The key to that weird casket, which for thee
But holds a skull, is neither thine nor mine,
But in the hand of what is more than man,
Or in man's hand when man is more than man,
Let be thy wail and help thy fellow men,
And make thy gold thy vassal not thy king,
And fling free alms into the beggar's bowl,
And send the day into the darken'd heart;
Nor list for guerdon in the voice of men,
A dying echo from a falling wall;
Nor care—for Hunger hath the Evil eye—
To vex the noon with fiery gems, or fold
Thy presence in the silk of sumptuous looms;
Nor roll thy viands on a luscious tongue,
Nor drown thyself with flies in honied wine;
Nor thou be rageful, like a handled bee,
And lose thy life by usage of thy sting;
Nor harm an adder thro' the lust for harm,
Nor make a snail's horn shrink for wantonness;
And more—think well! Do-well will follow thought,
And in the fatal sequence of this world
An evil thought may soil thy children's blood;
But curb the beast would cast thee in the mire,
And leave the hot swamp of voluptuousness
A cloud between the Nameless and thyself,
And lay thine uphill shoulder to the wheel,
And climb the Mount of Blessing, whence, if thou
Look higher, then—perchance—thou mayest—beyond
A hundred ever-rising mountain lines,
And past the range of Night and Shadow—see
The high-heaven dawn of more than mortal day
Strike on the Mount of Vision!

So, farewell.

1885

LOCKSLEY HALL SIXTY YEARS AFTER

Late, my grandson! half the morning have I paced these sandy tracts,
Watch'd again the hollow ridges roaring into cataracts,

Wander'd back to living boyhood while I heard the curlews call,
I myself so close on death, and death itself in Locksley Hall.

So—your happy suit was blasted—she the faultless, the divine;
And you liken—boyish babble—this boy-love of yours with mine.

I myself have often babbled doubtless of a foolish past;
Babble, babble; our old England may go down in babble at last.

"Curse him!" curse your fellow-victim? call him dotard in your rage?
Eyes that lured a doting boyhood well might fool a dotard's age.

Jilted for a wealthier! wealthier? yet perhaps she was not wise;
I remember how you kiss'd the miniature with those sweet eyes.

In the hall there hangs a painting—Amy's arms about my neck—
Happy children in a sunbeam sitting on the ribs of wreck.

In my life there was a picture, she that clasp'd my neck had flown;
I was left within the shadow sitting on the wreck alone.

Yours has been a slighter ailment, will you sicken for her sake?
You, not you! your modern amourist is of easier, earthlier make.

Amy loved me, Amy fail'd me, Amy was a timid child;
But your Judith—but your worldling—*she* had never driven me wild.

She that holds the diamond necklace dearer than the golden ring,
She that finds a winter sunset fairer than a morn of Spring.

She that in her heart is brooding on his briefer lease of life,
While she vows "till death shall part us," she the would-be-widow wife.

She the worldling born of worldlings—father, mother—be content,
Ev'n the homely farm can teach us there is something in descent.

Yonder in that chapel, slowly sinking now into the ground,
Lies the warrior, my forefather, with his feet upon the hound.

Cross'd! for once he sail'd the sea to crush the Moslem in his pride;
Dead the warrior, dead his glory, dead the cause in which he died.

Yet how often I and Amy in the mouldering aisle have stood,
Gazing for one pensive moment on that founder of our blood.

There again I stood to-day, and where of old we knelt in prayer,
Close beneath the casement crimson with the shield of Locksley—there,

All in white Italian marble, looking still as if she smiled,
Lies my Amy dead in child-birth, dead the mother, dead the child.

Dead—and sixty years ago, and dead her aged husband now—
I this old white-headed dreamer stoopt and kiss'd her marble brow.

Gone the fires of youth, the follies, furies, curses, passionate tears,
Gone like fires and floods and earthquakes of the planet's dawning years.

Fires that shook me once, but now to silent ashes fall'n away.
Cold upon the dead volcano sleeps the gleam of dying day.

Gone the tyrant of my youth, and mute below the chancel stones,
All his virtues—I forgive them—black in white above his bones.

Gone the comrades of my bivouac, some in fight against the foe,
Some thro' age and slow diseases, gone as all on earth will go.

Gone with whom for forty years my life in golden sequence ran,
She with all the charm of woman, she with all the breadth of man,

Strong in will and rich in wisdom, Edith, yet so lowly-sweet,
Woman to her inmost heart, and woman to her tender feet,

Very woman of very woman, nurse of ailing body and mind,
She that link'd again the broken chain that bound me to my kind.

Here to-day was Amy with me, while I wander'd down the coast,
Near us Edith's holy shadow, smiling at the slighter ghost.

Gone our sailor son thy father, Leonard early lost at sea;
Thou alone, my boy, of Amy's kin and mine art left to me.

Gone thy tender-natured mother, wearying to be left alone,
Pining for the stronger heart that once had beat beside her own.

Truth, for Truth is Truth, he worshipt, being true as he was brave;
Good, for Good is Good, he follow'd, yet he look'd beyond the grave,

Wiser there than you, that crowning barren Death as lord of all,
Deem this over-tragic drama's closing curtain is the pall!

Beautiful was death in him, who saw the death, but kept the deck,
Saving women and their babes, and sinking with the sinking wreck,

Gone for ever! Ever? no—for since our dying race began,
Ever, ever, and for ever was the leading light of man.

Those that in barbarian burials kill'd the slave, and slew the wife
Felt within themselves the sacred passion of the second life.

Indian warriors dream of ampler hunting grounds beyond the night;
Ev'n the black Australian dying hopes he shall return, a white.

Truth for truth, and good for good! The Good, the True, the Pure, the Just—
Take the charm "for ever" from them, and they crumble into dust.

Gone the cry of "Forward, Forward," lost within a growing gloom;
Lost, or only heard in silence from the silence of a tomb.

Half the marvels of my morning, triumphs over time and space,
Staled by frequence, shrunk by usage into commonest commonplace!

"Forward" rang the voices then, and of the many mine was one.
Let us hush this cry of "Forward" till ten thousand years have gone.

Far among the vanish'd races, old Assyrian kings would flay
Captives whom they caught in battle—iron-hearted victors they.

Ages after, while in Asia, he that led the wild Moguls,
Timur built his ghastly tower of eighty thousand human skulls,

Then, and here in Edward's time, an age of noblest English names,
Christian conquerors took and flung the conquer'd Christian into flames.

Love your enemy, bless your haters, said the Greatest of the great;
Christian love among the Churches look'd the twin of heathen hate.

From the golden alms of Blessing man had coin'd himself a curse:
Rome of Cæsar, Rome of Peter, which was crueller? which was worse?

France had shown a light to all men, preach'd a Gospel, all men's good;
Celtic Demos rose a Demon, shriek'd and slaked the light with blood.

Hope was ever on her mountain, watching till the day begun—
Crown'd with sunlight—over darkness—from the still unrisen sun.

Have we grown at last beyond the passions of the primal clan?
"Kill your enemy, for you hate him," still, "your enemy" was a man.

Have we sunk below them? peasants maim the helpless horse, and drive
Innocent cattle under thatch, and burn the kindlier brutes alive.

Brutes, the brutes are not your wrongers—burnt at midnight, found at morn,
Twisted hard in mortal agony with their offspring, born-unborn,

Clinging to the silent mother! Are we devils? are we men?
Sweet St. Francis of Assisi, would that he were here again,

He that in his Catholic wholeness used to call the very flowers
Sisters, brothers—and the beasts—whose pains are hardly less than ours!

Chaos, Cosmos! Cosmos, Chaos! who can tell how all will end?
Read the wide world's annals, you, and take your wisdom for your friend.

Hope the best, but hold the Present fatal daughter of the Past,
Shape your heart to front the hour, but dream not that the hour will last.

Ay, if dynamite and revolver leave you courage to be wise:
When was age so cramm'd with menace? madness? written, spoken lies?

Envy wears the mask of Love, and, laughing sober fact to scorn,
Cries to Weakest as to Strongest, "Ye are equals, equal-born."

Equal-born? O yes, if yonder hill be level with the flat.
Charm us, Orator, till the Lion look no larger than the Cat,

Till the Cat thro' that mirage of overheated language loom
Larger than the Lion,—Demos end in working its own doom.

Russia bursts our Indian barrier, shall we fight her? shall we yield?
Pause! before you sound the trumpet, hear the voices from the field.

Those three hundred millions under one Imperial sceptre now,
Shall we hold them? shall we loose them? take the suffrage of the plow.

Nay, but these would feel and follow Truth if only you and you,
Rivals of realm-ruining party, when you speak were wholly true.

Plowmen, Shepherds, have I found, and more than once, and still could find,
Sons of God, and kings of men in utter nobleness of mind,

Truthful, trustful, looking upward to the practised hustings-liar;
So the Higher wields the Lower, while the Lower is the Higher.

Here and there a cotter's babe is royal-born by right divine;
Here and there my lord is lower than his oxen or his swine.

Chaos, Cosmos! Cosmos, Chaos! once again the sickening game;
Freedom, free to slay herself, and dying while they shout her name.

Step by step we gain'd a freedom known to Europe, known to all;
Step by step we rose to greatness,—thro' the tonguesters we may fall.

You that woo the Voices—tell them "old experience is a fool,"
Teach your flatter'd kings that only those who cannot read can rule.

Pluck the mighty from their seat, but set no meek ones in their place;
Pillory Wisdom in your markets, pelt your offal at her face.

Tumble Nature heel o'er head, and, yelling with the yelling street,
Set the feet above the brain and swear the brain is in the feet.

Bring the old dark ages back without the faith, without the hope,
Break the State, the Church, the Throne, and roll their ruins down the slope.

Authors—essayist, atheist, novelist, realist, rhymester, play your part,
Paint the mortal shame of nature with the living hues of Art.

Rip your brothers' vices open, strip your own foul passions bare;
Down with Reticence, down with Reverence—forward—naked—let them stare.

Feed the budding rose of boyhood with the drainage of your sewer;
Send the drain into the fountain, lest the stream should issue pure.

Set the maiden fancies wallowing in the troughs of Zolaism,—
Forward, forward, ay and backward, downward too into the abysm.

Do your best to charm the worst, to lower the rising race of men;
Have we risen from out the beast, then back into the beast again?

Only "dust to dust" for me that sicken at your lawless din,
Dust in wholesome old-world dust before the newer world begin.

Heated am I? you—you wonder—well, it scarce becomes mine age—
Patience! let the dying actor mouth his last upon the stage.

Cries of unprogressive dotage ere the dotard fall asleep?
Noises of a current narrowing, not the music of a deep?

Ay, for doubtless I am old, and think gray thoughts, for I am gray:
After all the stormy changes shall we find a changeless May?

After madness, after massacre, Jacobinism and Jacquerie,
Some diviner force to guide us thro' the days I shall not see?

When the schemes and all the systems, Kingdoms and Republics fall,
Something kindlier, higher, holier—all for each and each for all?

All the full-brain, half-brain races, led by Justice, Love, and Truth;
All the millions one at length with all the visions of my youth?

All diseases quench'd by Science, no man halt, or deaf or blind;
Stronger ever born of weaker, lustier body, larger mind?

Earth at last a warless world, a single race, a single tongue—
I have seen her far away—for is not Earth as yet so young?—

Every tiger madness muzzled, every serpent passion kill'd,
Every grim ravine a garden, every blazing desert till'd,

Robed in universal harvest up to either pole she smiles,
Universal ocean softly washing all her warless Isles.

Warless? when her tens are thousands, and her thousands millions, then—
All her harvest all too narrow—who can fancy warless men?

Warless? war will die out late then. Will it ever? late or soon?
Can it, till this outworn earth be dead as yon dead world the moon?

Dead the new astronomy calls her. . . . On this day and at this hour,
In this gap between the sandhills, whence you see the Locksley tower,

Here we met, our latest meeting—Amy—sixty years ago—
She and I—the moon was falling greenish thro' a rosy glow,

Just above the gateway tower, and even where you see her now—
Here we stood and claspt each other, swore the seeming-deathless vow. . . .

Dead, but how her living glory lights the hall, the dune, the grass!
Yet the moonlight is the sunlight, and the sun himself will pass.

Venus near her! smiling downward at this earthlier earth of ours,
Closer on the Sun, perhaps a world of never fading flowers.

Hesper, whom the poet call'd the Bringer home of all good things.
All good things may move in Hesper, perfect peoples, perfect kings.

Hesper—Venus—were we native to that splendour or in Mars,
We should see the Globe we groan in, fairest of their evening stars.

Could we dream of wars and carnage, craft and madness, lust and spite,
Roaring London, raving Paris, in that point of peaceful light?

Might we not in glancing heavenward on a star so silver-fair,
Yearn, and clasp the hands and murmur, "Would to God that we were there"?

Forward, backward, backward, forward, in the immeasurable sea,
Sway'd by vaster ebbs and flows than can be known to you or me.

All the suns—are these but symbols of innumerable man,
Man or Mind that sees a shadow of the planner or the plan?

Is there evil but on earth? or pain in every peopled sphere?
Well be grateful for the sounding watchword "Evolution" here,

Evolution ever climbing after some ideal good,
And Reversion ever dragging Evolution in the mud.

What are men that He should heed us? cried the king of sacred song;
Insects of an hour, that hourly work their brother insect wrong,

While the silent Heavens roll, and Suns along their fiery way,
All their planets whirling round them, flash a million miles a day.

Many an Æon moulded earth before her highest, man, was born,
Many an Æon too may pass when earth is manless and forlorn,

Earth so huge, and yet so bounded—pools of salt, and plots of land—
Shallow skin of green and azure—chains of mountain, grains of sand!

Only That which made us, meant us to be mightier by and by,
Set the sphere of all the boundless Heavens within the human eye,

Sent the shadow of Himself, the boundless, thro' the human soul;
Boundless inward, in the atom, boundless outward, in the Whole.

* * * * * *

Here is Locksley Hall, my grandson, here the lion-guarded gate.
Not to-night in Locksley Hall—to-morrow—you, you come so late.

Wreck'd—your train—or all but wreck'd? a shatter'd wheel? a vicious boy!
Good, this forward, you that preach it, is it well to wish you joy?

Is it well that while we range with Science, glorying in the Time,
City children soak and blacken soul and sense in city slime?

There among the glooming alleys Progress halts on palsied feet,
Crime and hunger cast our maidens by the thousand on the street.

There the Master scrimps his haggard sempstress of her daily bread,
There a single sordid attic holds the living and the dead.

There the smouldering fire of fever creeps across the rotted floor,
And the crowded couch of incest in the warrens of the poor.

Nay, your pardon, cry your "forward," yours are hope and youth, but I—
Eighty winters leave the dog too lame to follow with the cry,

Lame and old, and past his time, and passing now into the night;
Yet I would the rising race were half as eager for the light.

Light the fading gleam of Even? light the glimmer of the dawn?
Aged eyes may take the growing glimmer for the gleam withdrawn.

Far away beyond her myriad coming changes earth will be
Something other than the wildest modern guess of you and me.

Earth may reach her earthly-worst, or if she gain her earthly-best,
Would she find her human offspring this ideal man at rest?

Forward then, but still remember how the course of Time will swerve,
Crook and turn upon itself in many a backward streaming curve.

Not the Hall to-night, my grandson! Death and Silence hold their own.
Leave the Master in the first dark hour of his last sleep alone.

Worthier soul was he than I am, sound and honest, rustic Squire,
Kindly landlord, boon companion—youthful jealousy is a liar.

Cast the poison from your bosom, oust the madness from your brain.
Let the trampled serpent show you that you have not lived in vain.

Youthful! youth and age are scholars yet but in the lower school,
Nor is he the wisest man who never proved himself a fool.

Yonder lies our young sea-village—Art and Grace are less and less:
Science grows and Beauty dwindles—roofs of slated hideousness!

There is one old Hostel left us where they swing the Locksley shield,
Till the peasant cow shall butt the "Lion passant" from his field.

Poor old Heraldry, poor old History, poor old Poetry, passing hence,
In the common deluge drowning old political common-sense!

Poor old voice of eighty crying after voices that have fled!
All I loved are vanish'd voices, all my steps are on the dead.

All the world is ghost to me, and as the phantom disappears,
Forward far and far from here is all the hope of eighty years.

* * * * * *

In this Hostel—I remember—I repent it o'er his grave—
Like a clown—by chance he met me—I refused the hand he gave.

From that casement where the trailer mantles all the mouldering bricks—
I was then in early boyhood, Edith but a child of six—

While I shelter'd in this archway from a day of driving showers—
Peept the winsome face of Edith like a flower among the flowers.

Here to-night! the Hall to-morrow, when they toll the Chapel bell!
Shall I hear in one dark room a wailing, "I have loved thee well."

Then a peal that shakes the portal—one has come to claim his bride,
Her that shrank, and put me from her, shriek'd, and started from my side—

Silent echoes! You, my Leonard, use and not abuse your day,
Move among your people, know them, follow him who led the way,

Strove for sixty widow'd years to help his homelier brother men,
Served the poor, and built the cottage, raised the school, and drain'd the fen.

Hears he now the Voice that wrong'd him? who shall swear it cannot be?
Earth would never touch her worst, were one in fifty such as he.

Ere she gain her Heavenly-best, a God must mingle with the game:
Nay, there may be those about us whom we neither see nor name,

Felt within us as ourselves, the Powers of Good, the Powers of Ill,
Strowing balm, or shedding poison in the fountains of the Will.

Follow you the Star that lights a desert pathway, yours or mine.
Forward, till you see the highest Human Nature is divine.

Follow Light, and do the Right—for man can half-control his doom—
Till you find the deathless Angel seated in the vacant tomb.

Forward, let the stormy moment fly and mingle with the Past.
I that loathed, have come to love him. Love will conquer at the last.

Gone at eighty, mine own age, and I and you will bear the pall;
Then I leave thee Lord and Master, latest Lord of Locksley Hall.

1886

MERLIN AND THE GLEAM

I

O young Mariner,
You from the haven
Under the sea-cliff,
You that are watching
The gray Magician
With eyes of wonder,
I am Merlin,
And *I* am dying,
I am Merlin
Who follow The Gleam.

II

Mighty the Wizard
Who found me at sunrise
Sleeping, and woke me
And learn'd me Magic!
Great the Master,
And sweet the Magic,
When over the valley,
In early summers,
Over the mountain,
On human faces,
And all around me,
Moving to melody,
Floated The Gleam.

III

Once at the croak of a Raven
 who crost it,
A barbarous people,
Blind to the magic,
And deaf to the melody,
Snarl'd at and cursed me.
A demon vext me,
The light retreated,
The landskip darken'd,
The melody deaden'd,
The Master whisper'd
"Follow The Gleam."

IV

Then to the melody,
Over a wilderness
Gliding, and glancing at
Elf of the woodland,
Gnome of the cavern,
Griffin and Giant,
And dancing of Fairies
In desolate hollows,
And wraiths of the mountain,
And rolling of dragons
By warble of water,
Or cataract music
Of falling torrents,
Flitted The Gleam.

V

Down from the mountain
And over the level,
And streaming and shining on
Silent river,
Silvery willow,
Pasture and plowland,
Innocent maidens,
Garrulous children,
Homestead and harvest,
Reaper and gleaner,
And rough-ruddy faces
Of lowly labour,
Slided The Gleam—

VI

Then, with a melody
Stronger and statelier,
Led me at length
To the city and palace
Of Arthur the king;
Touch'd at the golden
Cross of the churches,
Flash'd on the Tournament,
Flicker'd and bicker'd
From helmet to helmet,
And last on the forehead
Of Arthur the blameless
Rested The Gleam.

VII

Clouds and darkness
Closed upon Camelot;
Arthur had vanish'd
I knew not whither,
The king who loved me,
And cannot die;
For out of the darkness
Silent and slowly
The Gleam, that had waned to a
 wintry glimmer
On icy fallow
And faded forest,

Drew to the valley
Named of the shadow,
And slowly brightening
Out of the glimmer,
And slowly moving again to a
melody
Yearningly tender,
Fell on the shadow,
No longer a shadow,
But clothed with The Gleam.

VIII

And broader and brighter
The Gleam flying onward,
Wed to the melody,
Sang thro' the world;
And slower and fainter,
Old and weary,
But eager to follow,
I saw, whenever
In passing it glanced upon
Hamlet or city,
That under the Crosses
The dead man's garden,
The mortal hillock,
Would break into blossom;
And so to the land's
Last limit I came——
And can no longer,
But die rejoicing,
For thro' the Magic
Of Him the Mighty,
Who taught me in childhood,
There on the border
Of boundless Ocean,
And all but in Heaven
Hovers The Gleam.

IX

Not of the sunlight,
Not of the moonlight,
Not of the starlight!
O young Mariner,
Down to the haven,
Call your companions,
Launch your vessel,
And crowd your canvas,
And, ere it vanishes
Over the margin,
After it, follow it,
Follow The Gleam.

1889

BY AN EVOLUTIONIST

The Lord let the house of a brute to the soul
of a man,
And the man said "Am I your debtor?"
And the Lord—"Not yet: but make it as
clean as you can,
And then I will let you a better."

I

If my body come from brutes, my soul uncertain, or a fable,
Why not bask amid the senses while the sun
of morning shines,
I, the finer brute rejoicing in my hounds, and
in my stable,
Youth and Health, and birth and wealth.
and choice of women and of wines?

II

What hast thou done for me, grim Old Age,
save breaking my bones on the rack?
Would I had past in the morning that looks
so bright from afar!

OLD AGE

Done for thee? starved the wild beast that was
linkt with thee eighty years back.
Less weight now for the ladder-of-heaven
that hangs on a star.

I

If my body come from brutes, tho' somewhat
finer than their own,
I am heir, and this my kingdom. Shall the
royal voice be mute?
No, but if the rebel subject seek to drag me
from the throne,
Hold the sceptre, Human Soul, and rule
thy Province of the brute.

II

I have climb'd to the snows of Age, and I
gaze at a field in the Past,
Where I sank with the body at times in the
sloughs of a low desire,
But I hear no yelp of the beast, and the Man
is quiet at last
As he stands on the heights of his life with
a glimpse of a height that is higher.

1889

FAR—FAR—AWAY

(FOR MUSIC)

WHAT sight so lured him thro' the fields he knew
As where earth's green stole into heaven's own hue,
Far—far—away?

What sound was dearest in his native dells?
The mellow lin-lan-lone of evening bells
Far—far—away.

What vague world-whisper, mystic pain or joy,
Thro' those three words would haunt him when a boy,
Far—far—away?

A whisper from his dawn of life? a breath
From some fair dawn beyond the doors of death
Far—far—away?

Far, far, how far? from o'er the gates of Birth,
The faint horizons, all the bounds of earth,
Far—far—away?

What charm in words, a charm no words could give?
O dying words, can Music make you live
Far—far—away?

1889

THE THROSTLE

"SUMMER is coming, summer is coming.
I know it, I know it, I know it.
Light again, leaf again, life again, love again,"
Yes, my wild little Poet.

Sing the new year in under the blue.
Last year you sang it as gladly.
"New, new, new, new"! Is it then *so* new
That you should carol so madly?

"Love again, song again, nest again, young again,"
Never a prophet so crazy!
And hardly a daisy as yet, little friend,
See, there is hardly a daisy.

"Here again, here, here, here, happy year"!
O warble unchidden, unbidden!
Summer is coming, is coming, my dear,
And all the winters are hidden.

1889

JUNE BRACKEN AND HEATHER

To —

THERE on the top of the down,
The wild heather round me and over me June's high blue,
When I look'd at the bracken so bright and the heather so brown,
I thought to myself I would offer this book to you,
This, and my love together,
To you that are seventy-seven,
With a faith as clear as the heights of the June-blue heaven,
And a fancy as summer-new
As the green of the bracken amid the gloom of the heather.

1892

CROSSING THE BAR

SUNSET and evening star,
And one clear call for me!
And may there be no moaning of the bar,
When I put out to sea,

But such a tide as moving seems asleep,
Too full for sound and foam,
When that which drew from out the boundless deep
Turns again home.

Twilight and evening bell,
And after that the dark!
And may there be no sadness of farewell,
When I embark;

For tho' from out our bourne of Time and Place
The flood may bear me far,
I hope to see my Pilot face to face
When I have crost the bar.

1889

EXTRACTS FROM CONVERSATIONS WITH HIS SON AND WITH OTHER PERSONS

[All the following extracts and selections from Tennyson's letters are reprinted from *Alfred, Lord Tennyson: A Memoir by His Son* by permission of The Macmillan Company, publishers.]

I am of the same politics as Shakespeare, Bacon, and every sane man. Some critics object to Shakespeare's *aristocratic* view of his clowns, because he makes them talk such poor stuff, but they forget that his clowns occasionally speak as real truths as Hamlet, and that sometimes they utter very profound sayings. That is the glory of Shakespeare; he can give you the incongruity of things.

* * *

Arthur Hallam could take in the most abstruse ideas with the utmost rapidity and insight, and had a marvellous power of work and thought, and a wide range of knowledge. On one occasion, I remember, he mastered a difficult book of Descartes at a single sitting.

* * *

Lycidas is a test of any reader's poetic instinct. Keats, with his high spiritual vision, would have been, if he had lived, the greatest of us all (tho' his blank verse was poor). There is something magic and of the innermost soul of poetry in almost everything which he wrote.

* * *

I dare not tell how high I rate humour, which is generally most fruitful in the highest and most solemn human spirits. Dante is full of it, Shakespeare, Cervantes, and almost all the greatest have been pregnant with this glorious power. You will find it even in the Gospel of Christ.

* * *

Dim mystic sympathies with tree and hill reaching far back into childhood. A known landskip is to me an old friend, that continually talks to me of my own youth and half-forgotten things, and indeed does more for me than many an old friend that I know. An old park is my delight, and I could tumble about it for ever.

* * *

Sculpture is particularly good for the mind: there is a height and divine stillness about it which preaches peace to our stormy passions. Methinks that, in looking upon a great statue like the Theseus (maim'd and defaced as it is), one becomes as it were Godlike, to feel things in the Idea.

* * *

I never wrote a line against anyone but Sir Edward Lytton Bulwer. His lines did not move me to do so. But at the very time he was writing or had written these he was visiting my cousins, the d'Eyncourts, and said to them, "How much I should like to know your cousin Alfred"; and I, going into a book-club in the town where I was then living, found a newspaper turned up and folded so that I could not miss, "See how Sir Edward tickles up the poetasters and their patrons." The stupid insignificant paper, and the purpose with which it had been set before me, provoked me. I saw afterwards a letter which he wrote to my friend John Forster. Moreover, he stated in a note that I belonged to a very rich family. The younger son, his friend, who had inherited was rich enough, but the elder branch was shut out in the cold, and at that time I had scarce anything. Moreover, I remembered that he had said "If a man be attacked, let him attack."

Wretched work. *Odium literarium.*

* * *

How much of history we have in the story of Arthur is doubtful. Let not my readers press too hardly on details whether for history or for allegory. Some think that King Arthur may be taken to typify conscience. He is anyhow meant to be a man who spent himself in the cause of honour, duty and self-sacrifice, who felt and aspired with his nobler knights, though with a stronger and clearer conscience than any of them, "reverencing his conscience as his king." "There was no such perfect man since Adam" as an old writer says. *Major præteritis majorque futuris Regibus.*

* * *

[The sea on the south coast of England is] not a grand sea, only an angry curt sea. It seems to shriek as it recoils with the pebbles along the shore; the finest seas I have ever seen are at Valencia, Mablethorpe and in (West) Cornwall. At Valencia the sea was grand, without any wind blowing and seemingly without a wave: but with the momentum of the Atlantic behind, it dashes up into foam, blue diamonds it looks like, all along the rocks, like ghosts playing at hide and seek. When I was in Cornwall it had blown a storm of wind and rain for days, and all of a sudden fell into perfect calm; I was a little inland of the cliffs: when, after a space of perfect silence, a long roll of thunder, from some wave rushing into a cavern I suppose, came up from the distance, and died away. I *never* felt silence like that.

* * *

The first time I met Robertson I felt that he expected something notable from me because I knew that he admired my poems, that he wished to pluck the heart from my mystery; so for the life of me from pure nervousness I could talk of nothing but beer.

* * *

This is a terrible age of unfaith. I hate utter unfaith; I cannot endure that men should sacrifice everything at the cold altar of what with their imperfect knowledge they choose to call truth and reason. One can easily lose all belief, through giving up the continual thought and care for spiritual things.

* * *

If a man is merely to be a bundle of sensations, he had better not exist at all. He should embark on his career in the spirit of selfless and adventurous heroism; should develop his true self by not shirking responsibility, by casting aside all maudlin and introspective morbidities, and by using his powers cheerfully in accordance with the obvious dictates of his moral consciousness, and so, as far as possible, in harmony with what he feels to be the Absolute Right.

Self-reverence, self-knowledge, self-control,
These three alone lead life to sovereign power.
Yet not for power (power of herself
Would come uncall'd for) but to live by *law*,
Acting the law we live by without fear;
And, because right is right, to follow right
Were wisdom in the scorn of consequence.

It is motive, it is the great purpose which consecrates life. The real test of a man is not what he knows, but what he is in himself and in his relation to others. For instance, can he battle against his own bad inherited instincts, or brave public opinion in the cause of truth? The love of God is the true basis of duty, truth, reverence, loyalty, love, virtue and work. I believe in these although I feel the emptiness and hollowness of much of life. "Be ye perfect as your Father in heaven is perfect."

* * *

If the absorption into the divine in the after-life be the creed of some, let them at all events allow us many existences of individuality before this absorption; since this short-lived individuality seems to be but too short a preparation for so mighty a union.

* * *

People do not consider that every human being is a vanful of human beings, of those who have gone before him, and of those who form part of his life.

* * *

The reason why men find it hard to regard prayer in the same light in which it was formerly regarded is, that *we* seem to know more of the unchangeableness of Law: but I believe that God reveals Himself in each individual soul. Prayer is, to take a mundane simile, like opening a sluice between the great ocean and our little channels when the great sea gathers itself together and flows in at full tide. Prayer on our part is the highest aspiration of the soul.

* * *

The English public think that blank verse is the easiest thing in the world to write, mere prose cut up into five-foot lines; whereas it is one of the most difficult. In a blank verse you can have from three up to eight beats; but, if you vary the beats unusually, your ordinary newspaper critic sets up a howl. The varying of the beats, of the construction of the feet, of the emphasis, of the extra-metrical syllables and of the pauses, helps to make the greatness of blank verse. There are many other things besides, for instance a fine ear for vowel-sounds, and the kicking of the geese out of the boat (i.e. doing away with sibilations);

but few educated men really understand the structure of blank verse. I never put two 'ss' together in any verse of mine. My line is not, as often quoted,

> And freedom broaden*s s*lowly down —

but

> And freedom slowly broadens down.

People sometimes say how "studiedly alliterative" Tennyson's verse is. Why, when I spout my lines first, they come out so alliteratively that I have sometimes no end of trouble to get rid of the alliteration.

* * *

Whatever is the object of Faith cannot be the object of Reason. In fine, Faith must be our guide,—*that* Faith which we believe comes to us from a Divine Source.

* * *

After all, what is matter? I think it is merely the shadow of something greater than itself, and which we poor shortsighted creatures cannot see. If the rationalists are in the right, what is the meaning of all the mosques and temples and cathedrals, spread and spreading over the face of the earth? They will not easily beat the character of our Lord, that union of man and woman, sweetness and strength.

* * *

Byron's merits are on the surface. This is not the case with Wordsworth. You must love Wordsworth ere he will seem worthy of your love. As a boy I was an enormous admirer of Byron, so much so that I got a surfeit of him, and now I cannot read him as I should like to do. I was fourteen when I heard of his death. It seemed an awful calamity; I remember I rushed out of doors, sat down by myself, shouted aloud, and wrote on the sandstone: "*Byron is dead!*"

* * *

At twenty-four I meant to write an epic or a drama of King Arthur; and I thought that I should take twenty years about the work. They will now say that I have been forty years about it. "The Holy Grail" is one of the most imaginative of my poems. I have expressed there my strong feeling as to the Reality of the Unseen. The end, when the king speaks of his work and of his visions, is intended to be the summing up of all in the highest note by the highest of human men. These three lines in Arthur's speech are the (spiritually) central lines of the Idylls:

> In moments when he feels he cannot die,
> And knows himself no vision to himself,
> Nor the High God a vision.

The general English view of God is as of an immeasurable clergyman; and some mistake the devil for God.

* * *

Yes, it is true that there are moments when the flesh is nothing to me, when I feel and know the flesh to be the vision, God and the Spiritual the only real and true. Depend upon it, the Spiritual *is* the real: it belongs to one more than the hand and the foot. You may tell me that my hand and my foot are only imaginary symbols of my existence, I could believe you; but you never, never can convince me that the *I* is not an eternal Reality, and that the Spiritual is not the true and real part of me.

* * *

I don't find it difficult to believe in the Infinity of Worlds. From the starry spheres to think of the airs given themselves by county families in ball-rooms! One lady I remember early in the century in Lincolnshire, drawing herself up on hearing that the daughters of a neighbouring family were taking lessons in drawing and singing, and saying, "My daughters don't learn drawing." Miss Austen understood the smallness of life to perfection. She was a great artist, equal in her small sphere to Shakespeare. I think *Persuasion* and *Mansfield Park* are my favourites. There is a saying that if God made the country, and man the town, the devil made the little country town. There is nothing equal to the smallness of a small town.

* * *

Catullus says that a poet's lines may be impure provided his life is pure. I don't agree with him: his verses fly much further than he does. There is hardly any crime greater than for a man with genius to propagate vice by his written words. I have always admired him: "Acme and Septimius" is lovely. Then he has very pretty metres. "Collis O Heliconii" is in a beautiful metre. I wrote a great part of my "Jubilee Ode" in it. People didn't understand. They don't understand these things. They don't understand English scansion. In the line "Dream not of where some sunny rose may linger" they said the first syllable of "sunny" was long, whereas it evidently is short. Doubling the "n" in English makes the vowel before short.

* * *

A good hymn is the most difficult thing in the world to write. In a good hymn you have to be commonplace and poetical. The moment you cease to be commonplace and put in any expression at all out of the common, it ceases to be a hymn. Of hymns I like Heber's "Holy, Holy, Holy" better than most, it is in a fine metre too. What will people come to in a hundred years? do you think they will give up all religious forms and go and sit in silence in the Churches listening to the organs?

* * *

I think there is more religion now among the parsons, though they are often very ignorant about modern criticism and about the great religions of the world, and they certainly cannot read aloud. Did you ever hear that story of Rawnsley's? The clerk told him not to read the service so fast: "For you mooöst gie me toime, Mr. Rawnsley, you mooöst i' deed. You *mooöst* gie me toime, for I've a graäceless wife an' two godless soons to praäy for."

* * *

. . . Writing to order is what I hate. They think a poet can write poems to order as a bootmaker makes boots. For the Queen I am obliged to do it, but she has been very kind and has only asked me once or twice. They call the "Ode on the Duke of Wellington" a Laureate Ode; nothing of the kind! it was written from genuine admiration of the man.

* * *

[The stateliest English prose is] probably in Hooker, Bacon, Milton, Jeremy Taylor, De Quincey, Ruskin. Some of Sir Thomas Browne too is very stately; and some of the Acts of Elizabeth, Froude tells me, are written in the grandest language that he knows. Listen to this from Bacon: "It is a heaven upon earth when a man's mind rests on Providence, moves in Charity, and turns upon the poles of Truth." There is more wisdom compressed into that small volume [Bacon's *Essays*] than into any other book of the same size that I know.

* * *

The life after death, Lightfoot and I agreed, is the cardinal point of Christianity. I believe that God reveals Himself in every individual soul: and my idea of heaven is the perpetual ministry of one soul to another.

* * *

I dread the losing hold of forms. I have expressed this in my "Akbar." There must be forms, yet I hate the need for so many sects and separate services.

* * *

If the immediate life after death be only sleep, and the spirit between this life and the next should be folded like a flower in a night slumber, then the remembrance of the past might remain, as the smell and colour do in the sleeping flower; and in that case the memory of our love would last as true, and would live pure and whole within the spirit of my friend until after it was unfolded at the breaking of the morn, when the sleep was over.

* * *

I have been reading in the *Spectator* that Wordsworth and Keats are great masters of blank verse, who are also great in rhyme. Keats was not a master of blank verse. It might be true of Wordsworth at his best. Blank verse can be the finest mode of expression in our language.

* * *

I never could care about French Alexandrines. They are so artificial. The French language lends itself much better to slighter things. Some of Béranger's Chansons are exquisite, for example his lyric to "Le Temps," with the chorus: "O par pitié, lui dit ma belle, Vieillard, épargnez nos amours!" "L'Agonie" by Sully Prudhomme I have just been reading, and think it beautiful, yet very sad; and there are things of Alfred de Musset like "Tristesse" which seem to me perfect. I consider him a greater artist than Victor Hugo, but on smaller lines. Victor Hugo is an unequal genius, sometimes sublime; he reminds one that there is only one step between the sublime and the ridiculous. "Napoléon génait Dieu," "Napoleon irked God." Was there ever such an expression?

Among Hugo's poems I like some of the *Légende des Siècles*, and a lyric "Gastibelza." His finest play is *Le Roi s'amuse;* but *Mary Tudor* is a mere travesty.

* * *

In his smaller poems such as those in *Wilhelm Meister*, Goethe shows himself to be one of the great artists of the world. He is also a great critic: yet he always said the best he could about an author. Good critics are rarer than good authors.

* * *

I am told by a certain gentleman that this mill is the original mill in "The Miller's Daughter," and that that oak was "The Talking Oak," and that hall "Locksley Hall." Never anything of the sort. Why do they give a poet no credit for imagination? The power of poetical creation seems to be utterly ignored now. This modern realism is hateful, and destroys all poetry. No man with an imagination can be tied down for his ideal. Turner was an imaginative painter, and how absurd it would be to account for some of his works. There may be special suggestions.

* * *

I remember the very strange simile which the gardener made to me fifty years ago when he showed me over the place [Blenheim]. We were talking of the stories told about the then Duke of Marlborough's unpopularity. He said, "You see, Sir, when a man goes down in his luck, everyone points at him as if he were a church steeple."

The man himself was doubtless unaware that his comparison answered the definition of humour, the bringing together of violent contrasts.

* * *

All the magazines and daily newspapers, which pounce upon everything they can get hold of, demoralize literature. This age gives an author no time to mature his works.

* * *

Burlesque, the true enemy of humour, the thin bastard sister of poetical caricature, would, I verily believe, from her utter want of human feeling, in a revolution be the first to dabble her hands in blood.

* * *

I have just had a letter from a man who wants my opinion as to whether Shakespeare's plays were written by Bacon. I feel inclined to write back: "Sir, don't be a fool." The way in which Bacon speaks of Love would be enough to prove that he was not Shakespeare. "I know not how, but martial men are given to Love. I think it is but as they are given to wine, for perils commonly ask to be paid in pleasures." How could a man with such an idea of Love write *Romeo and Juliet?*

* * *

Walt [Whitman] neglects form altogether, but there is a fine spirit breathing through his writings. Some of them are quite unreadable from nakedness of expression.

* * *

His [Bruno's] view of God is in some ways mine. Bruno was a poet, holding his mind ever open to new truths, and believing in an infinite universe as the necessary effect of the infinite divine Power; he was burnt as a heretic. His age did not believe in him. I think that he was misunderstood, and I should like to show him in what I conceive to be his right colours; he was the author of much of our modern philosophy. He died the most desolate of deaths.

* * *

Spinoza is another man who has been often misunderstood. He has been called an atheist, and yet he is so full of God that he sees Him everywhere, so much so that he leaves no room for man. He was said to be "Gottbetrunken." He thought joy was more real than sorrow.

* * *

Matter is a greater mystery than mind. What such a thing as a spirit is apart from God and man I have never been able to conceive. Spirit seems to me to be the reality of the world.

SELECTIONS FROM TENNYSON'S LETTERS

I To His Sister's Governess

La Mancha [c. 1821]

My dear Dulcinea,

Pursuant to your request and the honour of Knight-errantry, and in conformity to my bump of conscientiousness (which has grown so enormous since my visit to you that I can scarce put on my helmet), I now intend, as far as lies in my power, to fulfil that promise which the lustre of your charms extorted from me. Know then, most adorable mistress of my heart, that the manuscripts which your angelic goodness and perfection were pleased to commend are not with me. If however my memory, assisted by the peerless radiance of your divine favour, avail me aught, I will endeavor to illume the darkness of my imagination with the recollection of your glorious excellence, till I produce a species of artificial memory unequalled by the Memoria Technica of Mr. Gray. Who would not remember when thus requested? It would cause a dead idiot to start afresh to life and intellect. Accept then, soul of my soul, these effusions, in which no Ossianic, Miltonic, Byronic, Milmanic, Moorish, Crabbic, Coleridgic, etc. fire is contained.

The first is a review of death:

Why should we weep for those who die? etc.

The second is a comparison:

Je fais naître la lumière
Du sein de l'obscurité. (Rousseau.)

How gaily sinks the gorgeous sun, etc.

And now farewell, my incomparable Dulcinea. In the truest spirit of knight-errantry,

Yours ever, DON QUIXOTE.

II To Christopher North

Somersby, Spilsby, Lincolnshire
[1832]

Sir,

Tho' I *am* "the star of little Britain," I assure you I do not rise or set there very cordially. I prefer vegetating in a very quiet garden where I neither see nor hear anything of the great world of literature—not lighting even upon *Maga* once a year. Nevertheless, in the lack of better things, a composition, mistermed a Satyre, entitled *Criticism and Taste*, and particularly remarkable for the want of either, was forwarded to me, a day or two ago, by the author—with a note; he thinks I ought to promote the circulation of his book for the good of my own, does he? so then I am to be pioneered—perhaps patronized, by Mr. John Lake. Now, Sir, hew me piecemeal, cut me up any way you will, exhaust all your world of fun and fancy upon me, but do not suspect me—tho' I may have done, written, said foolish things, not excepting a silly squib to Christopher North—do not dream that I can, now or ever, own any one grain of sympathy with the ravings of this unhappy coxcomb. I would rather request you, if you do not object to meet me on such dirty ground, to shake hands over the puddle he has made.

Five months after it had been printed I saw the critique from which Mr. L. has drawn his inspiration. I considered it at the time as somewhat too skittish and petulant, tho' it was redeemed to me by a tone of boisterous and picturesque humour such as I love. My gall might have risen a little—that it could never have contained much bitterness the weakness of my epigram ought, I think, to prove; for I trust that you will give me credit for being able to write a better.

I could wish that some of the poems there broken on your critical wheel were deeper than ever plummet sounded. Written as they were before I had attained my nineteenth year they could not but contain as many faults as words. I never wish to see them or hear of them again—much less to find them dragged forward once more on your boards, if you should condescend to divide Mr. L. from his one idea by replying to him. Perhaps you should not use him too harshly—tho' his arrogance deserves reproof; a consideration of the real imbecility of his nature ought to blunt the weapon.

Someone (I think M. in his cups) told a friend of mine that you were the author of an article on me in the *Quarterly*. I do not believe it; for I could not recognise one spark of genius or a single touch of true humour or good feeling. Moreover the man misprints me, which is worse than lying—but now that we have shaken hands (for I trust, we have) I find that you owe me an explanation. Somewhere or other you state "Alfred is a gentleman"—to which I answer with Conrade and Borachio, "Yea, sir, we hope": you say afterwards, that I have forgotten what was due to myself in that character, because having previously sent you "a copy with a grateful superscription" I had publicly disclaimed much relish for your approbation. Now upon mine honour as a gentleman, I did never send or cause to be sent any such presentation-copy, or write, indite, or cause to be written or indited any superscription, grateful or ungrateful, to any Editor or any Review or Magazine whatsoever.

Apologising for having thus far incroached on your valuable time . . .

III To James Spedding

[Undated]

My dear James,

I am sorry to disappoint myself (and perhaps in some slight measure you also) by postponing my visit. I am going to be from home for some time but not anywhere in your direction. The birds must sing and the furze bloom for you and Fitzgerald alone, "par nobile fratrum." I sincerely hope you have not put off any one else in the expectation of seeing me: tho' I did not state as much in my note, it was only when I first proposed it that I could have come to you. Fortune will perhaps bring me whiter days.

I know not whether you are aware that Charles has become an independent gentleman, living in a big house among chalky wolds at Caistor. His and my great uncle, Sam Turner, to whom he was heir, died some little time ago and left him property, but he complains that it is at present unavailable, talks of debts to be paid etc. etc.

John Heath writes me word that Mill is going to review me in a new Magazine, to be called the *London Review*, and favourably; but it is the last thing I wish for, and I would that you or some other who may be friends of Mill would hint as much to him. *I do not wish to be dragged forward again in any shape before the reading public at present*, particularly on the score of my old poems, most of which I have so corrected (particularly "Œnone") as to make them much less imperfect, which you who are a wise man would own if you had the corrections. I may very possibly send you these some time.

I am in much haste and obliged to conclude, but absent or present,

Believe me

Ever your true friend and admirer, A. T.

IV From Letters to Emily Sellwood

I

Aberystwith [1839]. I cannot say I have seen much worth the trouble of the journey, always excepting the Welshwomen's hats which look very comical to an English eye, being in truth men's hats, beavers, with the brim a little broad, and tied under the chin with a black ribband. Some faces look very pretty in them. It is remarkable how fluently the little boys and girls can speak Welsh, but I have seen no leeks yet, nor shot any cheeses. This place, the Cambrian Brighton, pleases me not, . . . a sea certainly to-day of a most lovely blue, but with scarce a ripple. Anything more unlike the old Homeric "much-sounding" sea I never saw. Yet the bay is said to be tempestuous. O for a good Mablethorpe breaker! I took up this morning an unhappy book of English verse by a Welshman, and read therein that all which lies at present swampt fathom-deep under the bay of Carnarvon was long ago in the twilight of history a lovely lowland, rich in woods, thick with cities. One wild night a drunken man, who was a sort of clerk of the drains and sewers in his time, opened the dam-gates and let in the sea, and Heaven knows how many stately palaces have ever since been filled with polyps and sea-tangle. How many gentlemen discussing after-dinner politics of that day were surprised by the precocious entrance of lobster before supper! How many young ladies playing at their pre-historic pianos ended some warm love-song of life in a quavering swan-song of death!

II

Warwick [1840]. I got into the third class of carriages in the train to Leicester. It is a carriage entirely open, without seats, nothing but a rail or two running across it, something like pens of cattle. . . . Tho' we did not move very quickly, yet it was liker flying than anything else . . . I learnt some curious lessons in perspective, e.g. the two rails on the road were always drawn together with the greatest rapidity. I stopt last night at Leicester, and came on here (to Warwick) this morning by a slow mail. On driving into Warwick, by great chance I happened to have my glass in my eye and perceived my friend, Edward Fitzgerald, taking his walk on the pavé towards Leamington. I stopt the coach, and he got up, and we drove to the George here, and had an evening together. Kenilworth looked grand in the distance. I think of going over with Fitz tomorrow. Warwick not to be seen till Saturday as the family are there. Almost afraid I cannot stop as long, as it is very expensive being at an inn. Warwick Castle looked grand and black among its woods from the bridge this evening, a nightingale was singing, and rooks were cawing, and there was moreover the noise of a waterfall.

III

London [1840]. I went thro' Warwick Castle. It is certainly a noble specimen of old feudalism, and the views from the windows would be of unrivalled loveliness if the river were only clearer. I and Fitzgerald also (climbed) up Guy's tower, and had "large prospect" of the surrounding country: but nothing pleased me better on the whole than two paintings I saw in the castle: one, an Admiral van Tromp by Rembrandt, the other Macchiavelli by Titian, both wonderful pictures, but the last grand beyond all words. We strayed about the gardens. . . . Afterwards we went to Stratford and saw Shakespeare's monument. I should not think it can be a good likeness. That foolish fellow painted it white all over, and served poor Johnny Combe, who lies on a monument near, in the same way. I suppose from a notion that so painted they would look more classic, but the monuments all about were gilded and painted, and so were theirs. By which fancy of Malone we have in all probability lost the colour of Shakespeare's hair and eyes, which perhaps would do the world very little good to know, but would have been a little satisfaction to poor physiognomists like myself. We went also into the room where they say he was born. Every part of it is scribbled over with names. I was seized with a sort of enthusiasm, and wrote mine, tho' I was a little ashamed of it afterwards: yet the feeling was genuine at the time, and I did homage with the rest. I forgot Kenilworth. We tumbled about the ruins for three hours, but I was rather disappointed. I had expected to find them larger and more august.

V TO EDWARD FITZGERALD

Mablethorpe, Alford, 1841

Dear old Fitz,

Not on the Western, on the Eastern coast. Mablethorpe near Alford in the fat shire of Lincoln is the place where I am. I walk about the coast, and have it all to myself, sand and sea. You bore me about my book; so does a letter just received from America, threatening, tho' in the civilest terms, that, if I will not publish in England, they will do it for me in that land of freemen. I *may* curse, knowing what they will bring forth. But I don't care. I am in a great haste writing for the muffinman, my only communication with the world, who comes once a week bringing the produce of his art, also what letters may be stagnating at the Alford post, waits five minutes and then returns.

Always yours, A. T.

VI TO EDMUND LUSHINGTON

Otley, September 19th, 1841

My dear Edmund,

This is to let you know that I am at present in the classic neighbourhood of Bolton Abbey whither I was led the other day by some half-remembrance of a note to one of Wordsworth's poems, which told with me (to speak the truth) more than the poem itself: said Wordsworth having stated, (as far as I recollect) that everything which the eyes of man could desire in a landskip was to be found at and about the Abbey aforesaid. I, coming with an imagination inflamed, and working upon this passage, was at first disappointed, but yesterday I took a walk of some seven or eight or, by our Lady, nine miles, to left and right of the Wharfe, and you may conjecture that no ordinary charms of nature could get nine miles out of legs (*at present*) more familiar with armchair and settle than rock and greensward, so that I suppose there is something in what Wordsworth asserts, and that something will probably keep me here some time, and whether I shall see you or no before you return to Glasgow is thereby rendered uncertain. I suppose there is no chance of your coming here, is there? that would be a Godsend I have no right to expect, but Harry at High Beech was a Godsend I did not expect. Poor fellow, he was very nervous, very uncomfortable too about his Italian journey, but in that respect I found it hard to sympathize with him.

Ever yours, A. Tennyson.

VII To Aubrey de Vere (after a visit to Scotland in 1848)

Cheltenham, Oct.

My dear Aubrey,

I have just now on my return to Cheltenham got two letters from you, for I am one, as you know, who wander to and fro for months careless of P. O. and correspondences. I am grieved to have occasioned you so much trouble about the article, but let it pass, excuses will not mend it: neither will I mention the money troubles I have had, for they are dead and buried, tho' you bribe with your "great piece of news," which I take it must mean that you are going to be married! is it so? if so, joy to you. I am glad that you have thought of me at Kilkee by the great deeps. The sea is my delight, tho' Mr. Chretien in the *Christian Examiner* says that I have no power upon him and always represent him dead asleep. I have seen many fine things in Scotland, and many fine things did I miss seeing, rolled up as they were tenfold in Scotch mists. Loch Awe too, which you call the finest, I saw. It is certainly very grand, tho' the pass disappointed me. I thought of Wordsworth's lines there, and, approving much, disapproved of much in them. What can be worse than to say to old Kilchurn Castle,

"Take then thy seat, vicegerent unreproved?"

Surely, master Aubrey, that is puffed and false. I steamed from Oban to Skye, a splendid voyage, for the whole day, with the exception of three hours in the morning, was blue and sunny; and I think I saw more outlines of hills than ever I saw in my life; and exquisitely shaped are those Skye mountains. Loch Corusk, said to be the wildest scene in the Highlands, I failed in seeing. After a fatiguing expedition over the roughest ground on a wet day we arrived at the banks of the loch, and made acquaintance with the extremest tiptoes of the hills, all else being thick wool-white fog. Dunkeld is lovely, and I delighted in Inverary, tho' there likewise I got drenched to the skin, till my very hat wept tears of ink. I rejoiced in Killeen, but on the whole perhaps I enjoyed no day more than the one I spent at Kirk Alloway by the monument of poor Burns, and the orchards, and "banks and braes of bonny Doon." I made a pilgrimage thither out of love for the great peasant; they were gathering in the wheat and the spirit of the man mingled or seemed to mingle with all I saw. I know you do not care much for him, but I do, and hold that there never was immortal poet if he be not one. Farewell. Give my best love and remembrances to all yours, and

Believe me ever yours,

A.

VIII To Gerald Massey

Freshwater, I. of Wight,
April 1st, 1854

My dear Sir,

In consequence of my change of residence I did not receive your captivating volume till yesterday. I am no reader of papers and Reviews and I had not seen, nor even heard of any of your poems: my joy was all the fresher and the greater in thus suddenly coming on a poet of such fine lyrical impulse, and of so rich half-oriental an imagination. It must be granted that you make our good old English tongue crack and sweat for it occasionally, but time will chasten all that. Go on and prosper, and believe me grateful for your gift, and

Yours most truly, A. Tennyson.

IX To John Forster

[1855]

My dear Forster,

In the first place thanks for your critique which seems to me good and judicious. Many thanks, my wife will write to you about it; but what I am writing to you now about is a matter which interests me very much. My friend Chapman of 3, Stone Buildings, Lincoln's Inn, writes to me thus:—"An acquaintance of mine in the department of the S.P.G. as he calls it (Society for the Propagation of the Gospel) was saying how a chaplain in the Crimea sent by the Society writes to the Society—(neither he nor the Society being suspected of any Tennysonian prejudices)—'The *greatest service you can do* just now is to send out on printed slips Mr. A. T.'s 'Charge at Balaclava.' It is the greatest favourite of the soldiers—half are singing it, and all want to have it in black and white, so as to read what has so taken them.'"

Now, my dear Forster, you see I cannot possibly be deaf to such an appeal. I wish to send out about 1000 slips, and I don't at all want the S.P.G. or any one to send out the *version last printed:* it would, I believe, quite disappoint the soldiers. Don't you live quite close to the S.P.G.? Could you not send Henry over to say that *I* am sending over the soldiers' version of my ballad, and beg them not to stir in the matter? The soldiers are the best critics in what pleases them. I send you a copy which retains the "Light Brigade," and the "blunder'd"; and I declare it is the best of the two, and that the criticism of two or three London friends (not yours) induced me to spoil it. For Heaven's sake get *this* copy fairly printed at once, and sent out. I have sent it by this post likewise to Moxon, but you are closer to your printer. Concoct with him how it is all to be managed: I am so sorry that I am not in town to have done it at once. I have written a little note to the soldiers which need not be sent—just as you like. It might be merely printed "From A. Tennyson." Please see to all this: and see that there are *no mistakes* and I will be bound to you for evermore, and more than ever yours in great haste,

A. Tennyson.

P.S. I am convinced now after writing it out that this *is* the best version.

X To the Rev. G. G. Bradley

Farringford,
August 25th, 1855

Dear Mr. Bradley,

Many thanks for the Arnold: nobody can deny that he is a poet. "The Merman" was an old favourite of mine, and I like him as well as ever. "The Scholar Gipsy" is quite new to me, and I have already an affection for him, which I think will increase. There are several others which seem very good, so that altogether I may say that you have conferred a great boon upon me. I have received a Scotch paper, in which it is stated that poor "Maud" is to be slashed all to pieces by that mighty man, that pompholygous, broad-blown Apollodorus, the gifted X. Her best friends do not expect her to survive it!

I am yours very truly,
A. Tennyson.

XI To George Brimley

Freshwater, I. W.
Nov. 28th, 1855

Sir,

I wish to assure you that I quite close with your commentary on "Maud." I may have agreed with portions of other critiques on the same poem, which have been sent to me; but when I saw your notice I laid my finger upon it and said, "There, that is my meaning." Poor little "Maud" after having run the gauntlet of so much brainless abuse and anonymous spite, has found a critic. Therefore believe her father (not the gray old wolf) to be

Yours not unthankfully, A. Tennyson

P.S. But there are two or three points in your comment to which I should take exception, e.g. "The writer of the fragments, etc.," surely the speaker or the thinker rather than the writer; again, as to the character of the love, do any of the expressions "rapturous," "painful," "childish," however they may apply to some of the poems, fully characterize the 18th? is it not something deeper? but perhaps some day I may discuss these things with you, and therefore I will say no more here, except that I shall be very glad to see you if ever you come to the Isle of Wight.

Chapel House
Twickenham

Aug. 11th

My dear Mrs Browning

I wrote to you once before this morning. I now write again to tell you what I am sure your woman's & poet's heart will rejoice in that my wife was delivered of a fine boy at 9½ a.m. this day & that both she & the child are doing well. I never saw any face so radiant with all high & sweet expression as hers when I saw her some time after.

Ever yours truly

A Tennyson

Letter to Mrs. Browning Announcing the Birth of Hallam Tennyson.

(See Appendix I.)

XII To a Stranger Who Had Sent a Volume of Verse

[December 31, 1856]

I have as you desired considered your poem, and though I make it a rule to decline passing any judgment on poems, I cannot in this instance refrain from giving you a word of advice.

Follow your calling diligently, for be assured, work, far from being a hardship, is a blessing, and if you are a poet indeed, you will find in it a help not a hindrance. You might, if you chose, offer these lines to some magazine, but you must not be surprised if they are refused, for the poetic gift is so common in these days that hundreds must have to endure this disappointment, and I should not be an honest friend if I did not prepare you for that.

I should by no means recommend you to risk the publication of a volume on your own account. The publication of verse is always attended with loss. As an amusement to yourself and your friends, the writing is all very well. Accept my good wishes and believe me,

Your obedient servant,
A. Tennyson.

XIII To Dr. Mann (in Natal)

[1858]

Our winter has been the mildest I have ever known. I read of ripe pomegranates hanging on a houseside at Bath, and I myself counted scores of our wild summer roses on a hedge near, flourishing in December and lasting on into January, tho' now gone, for the temperature has changed. They were perfectly fragrant, and I brought home a bouquet of them and put them in water. You ask after the farm? I cannot say that——is going on satisfactorily, very niggard of manure in the fields and ever doing his best to 'reave me of my rent by working at little odd jobs as a set off, so that at the end of the year, all things deducted, I get almost nothing. I am now building a little summer-house to catch the southern sun in Maiden's Croft, if you remember what field that is. I shall sit there and bask in the sunbeams and think of you far south. How I should love to rove about that parklike scenery of which you give such a fascinating account!

Yours ever, A. Tennyson.

P.S. I may tell you however that young Swinburne called here the other day with a college friend of his, and we asked him to dinner, and I thought him a very modest and intelligent young fellow. Moreover I read him what you vindicated [*Maud*], but what I particularly admired in him was that he did not press upon me any verses of his own. Good-bye. How desolate No. 7 B. T. must feel itself!

XIV To W. M. Thackeray

Farringford [1859]

My dear Thackeray,

Should I not have answered you ere this 6th of November? surely: what excuse? none that I know of: except indeed, that perhaps your very generosity and boundlessness of approval made me in a measure shamefaced. I could scarcely accept it, being, I fancy, a modest man, and always more or less doubtful of my own efforts in any line. But I may tell you that your little note gave me more pleasure than all the journals and monthlies and quarterlies which have come across me: not so much from your being the Great Novelist I hope as from your being my good old friend, or perhaps from your being both of these in one. Well, let it be. I have been ransacking all sorts of old albums and scrap books but cannot find anything worthy sending you. Unfortunately before your letter arrived I had agreed to give Macmillan the only available poem I had by me ("Sea Dreams"). I don't think he would have got it (for I dislike publishing in magazines) except that he had come to visit me in my Island, and was sitting and blowing his weed vis-à-vis. I am sorry that you have engaged for any quantity of money to let your brains be sucked periodically by Smith, Elder, & Co.: not that I don't like Smith who seems from the very little I have seen of him liberal and kindly, but that so great an artist as you are should go to work after this fashion. Whenever you feel your brains as the "remainder biscuit," or indeed whenever you will, come over to me and take a blow on these downs where the air as Keats said is "worth sixpence a pint," and bring your girls too.

Yours always, A. Tennyson.

XV To the Duke of Argyll

[1860]

My dear Duke,

I sympathised with you when I read of Macaulay's death in the *Times*. He was, was he not, your next-door neighbour? I can easily conceive what a loss you must have had in the want of his brilliant conversation. I hardly knew him: met him once, I remember, when Hallam and Guizot were in his company: Hallam was showing Guizot the Houses of Parliament then building, and Macaulay went on like a cataract for an hour or so to those two great men, and, when they had gone, turned to me and said, "Good morning, I am happy to have had the pleasure of making your acquaintance," and strode away. Had I been a piquable man I should have been piqued, but I don't think I was, for the movement after all was amicable. Of the two books I should, I think, have chosen the Crabbe, though Macaulay's criticisms on poetry would be less valuable probably than his historical ones. Peace be with him!

As to the *Sangreal*, as I gave up the subject so many long years ago I do not think that I shall resume it. You will see a little poem of mine in the *Cornhill Magazine*. My friend Thackeray and his publishers had been so urgent with me to send them something, that I ferreted among my old books and found this "Tithonus," written upwards of a quarter of a century ago, and now queerly enough at the tail of a flashy modern novel. It was originally a pendent to the "Ulysses" in my former volumes, and I wanted Smith to insert a letter, not of mine, to the editor stating this, and how long ago it had been written, but he thought it would lower the value of the contribution in the public eye. Read in Browning's *Men and Women* "Evelyn Hope" for its beauty, and "Bishop Blougram's Apology" for its exceeding cleverness, and I think that you will not deny him his own. The *Cornhill Magazine* gives a very pleasant account of Macaulay.

Yours ever, A. Tennyson.

XVI To the Duke of Argyll

Farringford, Feb. 1862

My dear Duke,

Many thanks for your very interesting letter. Very touching is what you tell me about the Queen. I am of course exceedingly gratified that anything which I have written should have the power to console one whom we all love; strange that a book which, when it first appeared, was pronounced by more than one clergyman as Pantheistic, if not, as (I think) one wiseacre commented on it, Atheistic, should have such a power, but after all it is very little that words can do. Time, time!

I have written out for the Princess Royal a morsel from "Guinevere." I do so hate rewriting my own things that my pen refuses to trace the "Dedication."

Her critique on the "Idylls" is enthusiastic, and mingled up with the affection of her father, as I would wish it to be. As to joining these with the "Morte d'Arthur," there are two objections,—one that I could scarcely light upon a finer close than the ghostlike passing away of the king, and the other that the "Morte" is older in style. I have thought about it and arranged all the intervening Idylls, but I dare not set to work for fear of a failure, and time lost. I am now about my "Fisherman," which is heroic too in its way.

Yours ever, A. Tennyson.

If you call me Mr. Tennyson any longer, I think that I must Your-grace you till the end of the chapter.

XVII To the Duke of Argyll

Stoatley Farm, Haslemere,
1867

My dear Duke,

I shall be very glad to read your book [*The Reign of Law*], which I suppose is waiting for me at Farringford. We are at present lodging at a farmhouse here in the neighbourhood of Haslemere. My wife has always had a fancy for the sandy soil and heather-scented air of this part of England, and we are intending to buy a few acres, and build a little home here, whither we may escape when the cockneys are running over my lawns at Freshwater. I am sorry that

I did not see Lord Lorne, but I will call for the calumet when I go to town. It is odd that the Americans always send me pipes, or tobacco, as if I cared for nothing else in this world; and their tobacco is not my tobacco, nor their pipes my pipes: bird's-eye and a Milo-cutty being more according to my fancy than costlier things. I don't however mean to undervalue Longfellow's gift. I envy you your journey. I have been along the Corniche, as you may read in my little poem "The Daisy." I don't suppose that Europe, or Asia perhaps, has a more splendid piece of coast-scenery, but at this time of year you will hardly see it in perfection. Perhaps however if the Autumn tints remain they may more than make up for the loss of that opulence of summer, which seemed to satiate heart and eye when I looked from the hill above Nice, over rock and ruin and down-streaming vineyard, to the many coloured Mediterranean. We did not get further than Florence, and Rome is only a dream to me and not a very distinct one.

Mine and my wife's love to the Duchess, and all joy to you both. You must feel like the starling that has got out, and the sweets of office outsweetened by the sweets of out of office. Hallam is at Marlborough and flourishing; Lionel with Dr. Hunt near Hastings. Lady Edith is, we trust, quite recovered, and enjoying her tour.

Ever yours,

A. Tennyson.

XVIII To Francis T. Palgrave

Farringford, 24th December, 1868

My dear Palgrave,

You distress me when you tell me that, without leave given by me, you showed my poem to Max Müller: not that I care about Max Müller seeing it, but I do care for your not considering it a sacred deposit. Pray do so in future; otherwise I shall see some boy in some Magazine making a lame imitation of it, which a clever boy could do in twenty minutes—and, though his work would be worth nothing, it would take away the bloom and freshness from mine.

I can't conceive how the Grail M. M. mentions can well be treated by a poet of the 13th century from a similar point of view to mine, who write in the 19th, but, if so, I am rather sorry for it, as I rather piqued myself on my originality of treatment.

If Max Müller will give you or me the name of the book, which contains all the Mediæval literature about the Grail, I will order it of the London Library; though, if it be in German prose, I fear I shan't have the patience to wade thro' a tenth of it.

The "Grail" is not likely to be published for a year or two, and certainly not along with the other thing which you hate so much (too much it seems to me). I shall write three or four more of the "Idylls," and link them together as well as I may. Jowett comes on Saturday, and I will give him your message. The boys are both here and well, not at Farringford which is getting scoured and cleaned, but at a house at Alum Bay (Headon Hall) where Nature, in winter at least, seems always in a rage.

Please attend to my request about the "Grail" and the "Lover's Tale," and show them to no one, or if you can't depend upon yourself, forward them to me.

Always yours,

A. Tennyson.

XIX To Lord Houghton

[March 6, 1874]

My dear Houghton,

I was the other day present at a funeral here, and one of the chief mourners reached me her hand silently almost over the grave, and I as silently gave her mine. No words were possible; and this little note, that can really do nothing to help you in your sorrow, is just such a reaching of the hand to you, my old college comrade of more than forty years standing, to show you that I think of you. You have your children; she must live to you more or less in them, and to you and others in the memory and result of her good and charitable life: and I may say that I think I can see as far as one can see in this twilight, that the nobler nature does not pass from its individuality when it passes out of this one life. If you could believe as much, it would be a comfort to you, and perhaps you do. I did not intend to say even so much as this, and will say no more, only that

I am yours affectionately,
A. Tennyson.

XX To S. E. Dawson

[November, 1882]

I thank you for your able and thoughtful essay on "The Princess." You have seen amongst other things that if women ever were to play such freaks, the burlesque and the tragic might go hand in hand. . . . Your explanatory notes are very much to the purpose, and I do not object to your finding parallelisms. They must always occur. A man (a Chinese scholar) some time ago wrote to me saying that in an unknown, untranslated Chinese poem there were two whole lines of mine almost word for word. Why not? Are not human eyes all over the world looking at the same objects, and must there not consequently be coincidences of thought and impressions and expressions? It is scarcely possible for anyone to say or write anything in this late time of the world to which, in the rest of the literature of the world, a parallel could not somewhere be found. But when you say that this passage or that was suggested by Wordsworth or Shelley or another, I demur; and more, I wholly disagree. There was a period in my life when, as an artist, Turner for instance, takes rough sketches of landskip, etc. in order to work them eventually into some great picture, so I was in the habit of chronicling, in four or five words or more, whatever might strike me as picturesque in Nature. I never put these down, and many and many a line has gone away on the north wind, but some remain: e.g.

A full sea glazed with muffled moonlight.

Suggestion.

The sea one night at Torquay, when Torquay was the most lovely sea-village in England, tho' now a smoky town. The sky was covered with thin vapour, and the moon behind it.

A great black cloud
Drags inward from the deep.

Suggestion.

A coming storm seen from the top of Snowdon.

In the *Idylls of the King*,

With all
Its stormy crests that smote against the skies.

Suggestion.

A storm which came upon us in the middle of the North Sea.

As the water-lily starts and slides.

Suggestion.

Water-lilies in my own pond, seen on a gusty day with my own eyes. They did start and slide in the sudden puffs of wind till caught and stayed by the tether of their own stalks, quite as true as Wordsworth's simile and more in detail.

A wild wind shook,—
Follow, follow, thou shalt win.

Suggestion.

I was walking in the New Forest. A wind did arise and

Shake the songs, the whispers and the shrieks
Of the wild wood together.

The wind I believe was a west wind, but because I wished the Prince to go south, I turned the wind to the south, and naturally the wind said "follow." I believe the resemblance which you note is just a chance one. Shelley's lines are not familiar to me tho' of course, if they occur in the *Prometheus*, I must have read them. I could multiply instances, but I will not bore you, and far indeed am I from asserting that books as well as Nature are not, and ought not to be, suggestive to the poet. I am sure that I myself, and many others, find a peculiar charm in those passages of such great masters as Virgil or Milton where they adopt the creation of a bygone poet, and reclothe it, more or less, according to their own fancy. But there is, I fear, a prosaic set growing up among us, editors of booklets, book-worms, index-hunters, or men of great memories and no imagination, who *impute themselves* to the poet, and so believe that *he*, too, has no imagination, but is for ever poking his nose between the pages of some old volume in order to see what he can appropriate. They will not allow one to say "Ring the bell" without finding that we have taken it from Sir P. Sidney, or even to use such a simple expression as the ocean "roars," without finding out the precise verse in Homer or Horace from which we have plagiarised it (fact!).

I have known an old fish-wife, who had lost two sons at sea, clench her fist at the advancing tide on a stormy day, and cry out, "Ay! roar, do! how I hates to see thee show thy white teeth." Now if I had adopted her exclamation and put it into the mouth of some old woman in one of my poems, I daresay the critics would have thought it original enough, but would most likely have advised me to go to Nature for my old women and not to my own imagination; and indeed it is a strong figure.

Here is another anecdote about suggestion. When I was about twenty or twenty-one I went on a tour to the Pyrenees. Lying among these mountains before a waterfall that comes down one thousand or twelve hundred feet I sketched it (according to my custom then) in these words:

Slow-dropping veils of thinnest lawn.

When I printed this, a critic informed me that "lawn" was the material used in theatres to imitate a waterfall, and graciously added, "Mr. T. should not go to the boards of a theatre but to Nature herself for his suggestions." And I *had* gone to Nature herself.

I think it is a moot point whether, if I had known how that effect was produced on the stage, I should have ventured to publish the line.

I find that I have written, quite contrary to my custom, a letter, when I had merely intended to thank you for your interesting commentary.

Thanking you again for it, I beg you to believe me

Very faithfully yours,

A. Tennyson.

ROBERT BROWNING

[May 7, 1812–December 12, 1889]

ROBERT BROWNING was born in Southampton Street, Camberwell, which was then a leafy suburb of London, and there he lived the first twenty-eight years of his life. His early schooling, officially, was at neighboring schools but actually from his father and in his father's library. The elder Browning was so steeped in medieval legend that, as his son later said, he "seemed to have known Paracelsus, Faustus, and even Talmudic personages, personally," and in his library there was much curious treasure trove for an alert, browsing boy. Or the boy would slip downstairs from bed to listen outside the door to his mother playing the pianoforte and, when she stopped, cry out, "Oh, Mother, play some more." And not far away was the Dulwich Art Gallery, which he haunted. Decidedly, Browning's education took place out of school. Neither did he attend a university—a few classes at University College, London (1829–30), completed his formal studies. But in his poem *Development* Browning has told how in his early childhood his father dramatized for him the story of the *Iliad*, with bits of furniture for setting and the surprised family cat playing the part of Helen of Troy. From his earliest days, people out of books and from far-away places were vividly alive to him, and he ended by being one of the most disconcertingly learned of the English poets.

In 1833 Browning published *Pauline* and in the winter of that year made the first of his many trips to the Continent—in this case to Russia. *Pauline*, although he later tried to suppress the book, indicated that he was leaning towards poetry as a career—he had considered music and for a time thought of diplomacy. With the completion and publication in 1835 of *Paracelsus*, the decision was made. For the opportunity to devote himself to poetry, Browning, as for so many things, owed a debt of gratitude to his father and to his family. The elder Browning had wished to become an artist; refused support by his practical father, he had gone into the Bank of England as a clerk and, when the time came for his son to choose a career, resolved that the young man should have the freedom of choice denied himself. Browning received the loyal support of his family. He repaid loyalty with loyalty. One of the salient traits of his character was his intense devotion to his immediate family circle—to his father, mother, and sister and, later, to his wife and son. Domestic intensity is not always the most obvious virtue in poets.

Paracelsus had a very bad press reception—it was ignored by most of the great reviews, and the *Athenæum*, which had given one hundred lines to *Pauline*, had only seventy-three words to spare for *Paracelsus*. The public were even more unconcerned than the press; very few copies were sold. Yet *Paracelsus* clearly enough launched Browning as a poet. John Forster praised it in *The Examiner*. W. J. Fox, admitting blemishes, had written of *Pauline* in the *Monthly Repository*, "In recognizing a poet we cannot stand upon trifles. . . . Archimedes in the bath had many particulars to settle about specific gravities . . . but he first gave a glorious leap and shouted Eureka." Fox played godfather to Browning and introduced him to literary London. Browning made the most of the opening. By instinct he was social, even to the frivolous and trivial meaning of the word; he gravitated toward people. Browning seems to have gone everywhere and met everybody—Carlyle, Landor, Talfourd, "Barry Cornwall," Hengist Horne, Leigh Hunt, and later Dickens and Wordsworth, were amongst his "bag." Despite the reviews and the public, he was, on the basis of *Paracelsus*, accepted as a poet, and at one famous literary dinner (celebrating the triumph of Talfourd's *Ion*) when the host proposed a toast to Browning, William Wordsworth leaned across the table with the remark, "I am proud to drink your health, Mr. Browning."

Among those he met in his goings to and fro was Macready, the leading English actor of the time. "His face is full of intelligence," noted Macready in his Diary and, ten days later, having read *Paracelsus* as a result of the meeting, he wrote that Browning could "scarcely fail to be a leading spirit of his time." In consequence of Macready's suggestion that he write for the stage, Browning wrote *Strafford*, which Macready performed at Covent Garden, May 1, 1837. The house was packed and the applause genuine but, as it was his benefit performance, the triumph was Macready's rather than that of the author. In spite of this promising beginning and the writing of *King Victor and King Charles* and *The Return of the Druses*, Browning did not reappear on the acted stage for six years. Then *A Blot in the 'Scutcheon* (1843) was performed at Macready's theatre (then Drury Lane)—but not by Macready. The admiration between the two men was real, and the breach which occurred over this play was unfortunate. Macready had promised to bring it out, but reverses on previous plays had put him in desperate financial straits and he was too proud to beg off from his promise. Browning did not understand the situation as one more closely connected with the theatre might have done. After a series of irritating episodes the play was brought out under unfavorable auspices and Browning was very "sore" about the general handling of it. His soreness persisted until many years later when he learned the reason for Macready's attitude. But Browning's direct attempt at writing actable drama coincides with his acquaintance with Macready and extends only a little beyond it to *Luria* and *A Soul's Tragedy*, both of 1846. Between *Strafford* (1837) and *A Soul's Tragedy* (1846) Browning had written a series of plays. (See Chronological List, pp. 227 ff.) He had also written *Sordello* (1840) and achieved with it an undeserved reputation for obscurity so granite-strong that all the beating of the waves of praise have not quite been able to wear it down. The year after *Sordello*, Browning had begun the publication of a series of pamphlets under the general title of *Bells and Pomegranates*. The series began with *Pippa Passes* in 1841 and ended in 1846 with *Luria* and *A Soul's Tragedy*.

It is necessary here to pause and consider how curiously consistent is the texture of Browning's life. In 1846 he was thirty-four years old and, with something over forty years of productive writing ahead of him, and his greatest work yet to do, the direction his life was to follow had been marked out. With *Paracelsus* and *Sordello* he had indicated that the direction of his genius was toward soul study. In *Dramatic Lyrics* (1842) Browning had illustrated again his psychological curiosity in such poems as *My Last Duchess* and the *Soliloquy of the Spanish Cloister*, but in this case on a severely condensed and focused scale, and in so doing, had learned the possibilities of the dramatic monologue. Having contracted from the rather sprawling *Paracelsus*, he was to expand again, but he had found both his material and his manner. As a creative artist he found his pace early and maintained it long. Personal tendencies also were plain—especially the tendency to dine out and see every one. The proper tombstone for Robert Browning the man would be a dinner-table place-card. The foible of the man and the strength of the genius had both become apparent. Browning's public reputation had also taken shape. He had sold practically no copies, but he had erected a reputation. And he was already an "obscure" poet.

The pattern of Browning's life was approaching completion, with fifty years to go of life. Elizabeth Barrett completed it. She was in spirit a gay and impetuous person, but for some years she had been an invalid confined to her room and seeing no one but her immediate family. Her second cousin John Kenyon, a great admirer of Browning, had tried to bring them together as early as 1841, but Elizabeth Barrett had refused to see him out of her fear of meeting a new face. Through Kenyon, however, the two poets heard much of one another and their admiration for one another's work was great. When Browning was in doubt as to whether to write her a congratulatory letter on her *Poems* of 1844 Kenyon urged him to do so, and Browning's first letter to her on January 10, 1845, was the result. She replied, and thus began their beautiful correspondence. It was some time toward the end of May before she consented to see him. She afterwards confessed that once he came "he never went away again," and Browning's mind was instantly made up. It was not a case of love at first sight, it was a case of love before first sight. Elizabeth Barrett, however, believing herself hopelessly ill and done with the world, put a positive veto on the subject of love, threatening never to see him again. Browning bided his time. Meanwhile the correspondence continued and Browning's weekly visits to Wimpole Street became an established part of their lives. It had been planned for Miss Barrett to go to Italy in the autumn for her health, but her father, a curious type of domestic tyrant, forbade the trip. Fortunately the winter was a mild one; her health improved, she was able to leave her sofa for a straight chair; was able to go down stairs; with the coming of spring again, was able to leave the house for short trips out of doors. "I am yours for every thing but to do you harm" she had written Browning, but still she refused to marry him in the dreadful fear that to tie his life to that of an invalid would be doing him the greatest possible harm. With the approach of another winter and its menace to her health, however, Browning took more definite command of events. On September 12, 1846, she slipped out of the house accompanied by her maid and met him at St. Marylebone Church, where they were married. She returned to Wimpole Street to recover strength for the approaching journey, and a few days later started with Browning for Italy by way of Paris.

It was the beginning of a supremely happy marriage. "Temper, spirits, manners—there is not a flaw anywhere" was her judgment of him, and his devotion to her was absolute. By all the rules of Victorian medicine she should, after the excitement of her elopement, promptly have fallen into a decline and died upon his hands, but she proved her gallantry of spirit by rallying, and, although she never became robust, she gained strength. Florence became the headquarters of the Brownings and the Casa Guidi, where they had apartments, is indissolubly connected with their name. But they were not rooted there. There were frequent trips away, lasting from a few weeks to six or more months, and the extent of their travels ranged from Rome to London. Of their trips to London two are noteworthy—the first in 1851 when Mrs. Browning's tyrannical father refused to see her, and the trip of 1855 when the two poets carried with them the manuscripts of her *Aurora Leigh* and his *Men and Women.* It was on this visit that Tennyson read his *Maud* to a group which included the Brownings, and Rossetti, withdrawn to a corner, quietly made his sketch of Tennyson reading. . . . The marriage was a happy one. It was the more remarkable in that two great literary personalities wrote without jealousy. "This is a great poem" is scribbled in Browning's handwriting on the margin of the manuscript of *Aurora Leigh*, and he declared that he sweated over his work while she turned off a little star "like God." Her admiration of him was equally high. To complete the association of flesh and spirit had come the birth in the spring of 1849 of their son, nicknamed "Pen,"—a brilliant child to whom they were both devoted. . . . The pattern of Browning's life had reached completion, and the death of his wife in Florence, June 29, 1861, tore a great rent across it.

He left Florence the following month and never revisited it, although of course he later came back to Italy, and died there. Early the following year (in 1862) he took a house in London, at 19 Warwick Crescent, which was his headquarters for about twenty-five years. His chief thought in coming back to England was "Pen"—his boy to be educated. The intense domestic sense of Browning was running true to form. For something over a year he was depressed severely and saw few people. Then he felt that Elizabeth Barrett would not have approved of a moping Robert. So he set to dining out and became a hardy perennial at London dinner parties. The social Browning was running again true to form. But he was not really happy. As Elizabeth Barrett had once drugged herself with work, so did he. He began on *The Ring and the Book*. He went seriously about the actual writing in the latter part of 1864, and the first installment of the poem appeared in November 1868.

Browning, by a happy accident, had discovered the original material in a yellow vellum bound volume on a Florentine street bookstall in June, 1860. He had stood before the stall, spellbound, reading, and before he reached home the story was plain in his mind. But the material was temporarily put aside and germinated deep within him. When he finally came to write, he wrote with the richness of years of brooding behind his work, and produced what is unquestionably one of the great poems of the century. . . . It has been rather the conventional criticism to consider that Browning's work which followed belongs to his "later" period and is sterile and over-intellectualized. This is not sound criticism. Works which followed, notably *Balaustion's Adventure* (1871) or *The Inn Album* (1875), are well up to his standard, and *The Inn Album* has a fair claim to stand among his best. The story of self-murder in *Red Cotton Night-Cap Country* (1873) would have made the reputation of any poet but the author of *The Ring and the Book*. After that volume any book was an anticlimax.

The events of his later life are not of great significance, as the pattern of his life was already clear. "Pen" was a focal point in his thinking for many years, and he welcomed an M. A. from Oxford in 1867 and election to an honorary fellowship at Balliol, chiefly for the contacts they gave him with the University where his boy was being educated, and, although he said that his heart was in the grave with Elizabeth Barrett, he did about 1871 propose marriage to Lady Ashburton because "Pen needed a mother,"—an argument not very persuasive to the lady. These years also were years of growing repute. Never was he a popular poet in the "best-seller" sense. As late as 1871 he wrote of the sale of 2500 copies in five months of *Balaustion's Adventure* as very good for "the likes of me," which is significant when one considers that at about the same time (in 1870, to be precise) Tennyson was selling 40,000 copies of a group of the *Idylls of the King* in advance of actual publication. But Browning's repute was plain and growing. The election to an honorary fellowship at Balliol had been indicative, and in 1882 Oxford conferred an honorary D.C.L. on him. He was being read in America also. Some ingenious and intelligent railroad officials here conceived the idea of reprinting in installments his works in their time-table, and did so from 1872 to 1874 in the *Official Guide of the Chicago and Alton R.R. and Monthly Reprint and Advertiser*. Such manifestations are indications of a powerful grip on a section of the reading public, and the formation of the Browning Society in London in 1881 is not surprising. The society was founded by personal strangers and Browning rather severely kept "hands off" in the period of formation, but he was pleased. And so Browning passed into old age, an honored old man. He died December 12, 1889, at the Palazzo Rezzonico in Venice—"Pen's" home.

"He isn't at all like a damned literary man" Lockhart said of Browning in the winter of 1853, and, had Browning heard the remark, he would have been pleased. He tried to be a man of the world and hated the cheaper Bohemianisms. Perhaps he went too far the other way. It is hard to visualize a great poet chatting amicably over the soup at a dinner party, evening after evening. Perhaps the explanation lies in a remark made in Browning's later life. "You have not a great love for nature, have you?" he was asked. "Yes, I have," he replied, "but I love men and women better." Only in society does one meet people, and the greatness of Browning's poetry lies in an understanding of people.

BROWNING'S POEMS AND PLAYS

A CHRONOLOGICAL LIST

[For the collected edition of 1863 Browning rearranged the shorter poems previously published in *Dramatic Lyrics*, *Dramatic Romances and Lyrics*, and *Men and Women*, and, in subsequent editions issued during his own lifetime and under his supervision, the rearrangement was retained. The present anthology follows Browning's own arrangement of his poems rather than the strict chronological order, with the exception of *The Ring and the Book* which, on account of its length, is placed last. A chronological list, with tables of contents, is here given of Browning's volumes (magazine publication is ignored) for the convenience of those who wish to follow the chronological approach. The figures in brackets indicate the page of the present volume on which poems here reprinted are to be found.]

1833. Pauline: A Fragment of a Confession.
1835. Paracelsus.
1837. Strafford: An Historical Tragedy.
1840. Sordello.
1841. Bells and Pomegranates, No. I., Pippa Passes. [230]
1842. Bells and Pomegranates, No. II., King Victor and King Charles.
1842. Bells and Pomegranates, No. III., Dramatic Lyrics.
Cavalier Tunes—
I. Marching Along. [253]
II. Give a Rouse. [253]
III. My Wife Gertrude. (Afterwards called "Boot and Saddle.") [254]
Italy and France—
I. Italy. (Afterwards called "My Last Duchess.") [290]
II. France. (Afterwards called "Count Gismond.")
Camp and Cloister—
I. Camp (French). (Afterwards called "Incident of the French Camp.")
II. Cloister (Spanish). (Afterwards called "Soliloquy of the Spanish Cloister.") [258]
In a Gondola. [300]
Artemis Prologuizes.
Waring.
Queen Worship—
I. Rudel and the Lady of Tripoli.
II. Cristina. [260]
Madhouse Cells—
I. [Johannes Agricola.] (Afterwards called "Johannes Agricola in Meditation.")
II. [Porphyria.] (Afterwards called "Porphyria's Lover.") [322]
Through the Metidja to Abd-el-Kadr.
The Pied Piper of Hamelin.
1843. Bells and Pomegranates, No. IV., The Return of the Druses: A Tragedy in Five Acts.
1843. Bells and Pomegranates, No. V., A Blot in the 'Scutcheon: A Tragedy in Three Acts.
1844. Bells and Pomegranates, No. VI., Colombe's Birthday: A Play in Five Acts.
1845. Bells and Pomegranates, No. VII., Dramatic Romances and Lyrics—
How They Brought the Good News from Ghent to Aix. [255]
Pictor Ignotus. Florence, 15—. [330]
Italy in England. (Afterwards called "The Italian in England.") [295]
England in Italy. (Afterwards called "The Englishman in Italy.") [297]
The Lost Leader. [254]
The Lost Mistress. [260]
Home Thoughts from Abroad—
I. "Oh to be in England." [272]
II. "Here's to Nelson's Memory." (Afterwards printed as the third section of "Nationality in Drinks.")
III. "Nobly Cape St. Vincent." (Afterwards called "Home Thoughts from the Sea.") [272]
The Tomb at St. Praxed's. (Afterwards called "The Bishop Orders His Tomb in St. Praxed's Church.") [341]
Garden Fancies—
I. The Flower's Name. [256]
II. Sibrandus Schafnaburgensis. [257]
France and Spain—
I. The Laboratory (Ancien Régime). [259]
II. The Confessional.
The Flight of the Duchess. [305]
Earth's Immortalities. [261]
Song, "Nay but you, who do not love her." [261]
The Boy and the Angel. [291]
Night and Morning—
I. Night. (Afterwards called "Meeting at Night.") [261]
II. Morning (Afterwards called "Parting at Morning.") [261]
Claret and Tokay. (Afterwards printed as

the first and second sections of "Nationality in Drinks.")
Saul. (First part only, sections 1–9; the second part was added and included with it in "Men and Women," 1855, vol. ii., p. 111.) [273]
Time's Revenges. [295]
The Glove. [293]

1846. Bells and Pomegranates, No. VIII. and last. Luria; and A Soul's Tragedy.

1850. Christmas-Eve and Easter-Day.

1855. Men and Women. In Two Volumes—

Vol. I.

Love among the Ruins. [263]
A Lovers' Quarrel.
Evelyn Hope. [262]
Up at a Villa—Down in the City. (As distinguished by an Italian Person of Quality.) [264]
A Woman's Last Word. [261]
Fra Lippo Lippi. [331]
A Toccata of Galuppi's. [266]
By the Fireside. [280]
Any Wife to Any Husband.
An Epistle containing the Strange Medical Experience of Karshish, the Arab Physician. [326]
Mesmerism.
A Serenade at the Villa. [285]
My Star. [280]
Instans Tyrannus. [292]
A Pretty Woman.
"Childe Roland to the Dark Tower Came." [322]
Respectability. [286]
A Light Woman. [303]
The Statue and the Bust. [318]
Love in a Life. [287]
Life in a Love. [287]
How It Strikes a Contemporary.
The Last Ride Together. [304]
The Patriot: An Old Story. [288]
Master Hugues of Saxe-Gotha.
Bishop Blougram's Apology.
Memorabilia. [288]

Vol. II.

Andrea del Sarto (called "The Faultless Painter"). [337]
Before.
After.
In Three Days.
In a Year. [287]
Old Pictures in Florence. [267]
In a Balcony.
Saul.
"De Gustibus—" [271]
Women and Roses.
Protus.
Holy-Cross Day.
The Guardian Angel: A Picture at Fano.
Cleon. [343]
The Twins. (First printed in a pamphlet entitled "Two Poems. By Elizabeth Barrett and Robert Browning." 8vo. London, 1854.)
Popularity.
The Heretic's Tragedy. A Middle-Age Interlude.
Two in the Campagna. [284]
A Grammarian's Funeral. [316]
One Way of Love. [286]
Another Way of Love. [286]
"Transcendentalism: A Poem in Twelve Books." [326]
Misconceptions. [285]
One Word More. To E. B. B. [347]

1864. Dramatis Personæ—

James Lee. [350]
Gold Hair: A Story of Pornic.
The Worst of It.
Dîs aliter visum; or, Le Byron de nos Jours.
Too Late.
Abt Vogler. [351]
Rabbi Ben Ezra. [353]
A Death in the Desert.
Caliban upon Setebos; or, Natural Theology in the Island. [356]
Confessions. [360]
May and Death.
Prospice. [361]
Youth and Art. [361]
A Face. [362]
A Likeness.
Mr. Sludge, "the Medium."
Apparent Failure. [363]
Epilogue.

1868–9. The Ring and the Book. In Four Volumes. [382]

1871. Balaustion's Adventure: Including a Transcript from Euripides.

1871. Prince Hohenstiel-Schwangau, Saviour of Society.

1872. Fifine at the Fair.

1873. Red Cotton Night-Cap Country, or Turf and Towers.

1875. Aristophanes' Apology: Including a Transcript from Euripides, Being the Last Adventure of Balaustion.

1875. The Inn Album.

1876. Pacchiarotto, and How he Worked in Distemper: with other Poems—

Prologue.
Of Pacchiarotto, and How he Worked in Distemper.
At the "Mermaid."
House. [363]
Shop. [364]
Pisgah Sights. I.
Pisgah Sights. II.
Fears and Scruples.
Natural Magic. [366]
Magical Nature. [366]
Bifurcation.
Numpholeptos.
Appearances.
St. Martin's Summer.
Hervé Riel.
A Forgiveness.
Cenciaja.
Filippo Baldinucci on the Privilege of Burial.
Epilogue.

1877. The Agamemnon of Æschylus.

1878. La Saisiaz.

1878. The Two Poets of Croisic [366]
(Last two titles published together in one volume.)

1879. Dramatic Idyls—
Martin Relph.
Pheidippides.
Halbert and Hob.
Ivàn Ivànovitch.
Tray.
Ned Bratts. [366]

1880. Dramatic Idyls: Second Series—
[Prologue.]
Echetlos.
Clive.
Muléykeh.
Pietro of Abano.
Doctor ——.
Pan and Luna.
[Epilogue.]

1883. Jocoseria—
Wanting is—What? [374]
Donald.
Solomon and Balkis.
Cristina and Monaldeschi.
Mary Wollstonecraft and Fuseli.
Adam, Lilith, and Eve. [374]
Ixion.
Jochanan Hakkadosh.
Never the Time and the Place. [374]
Pambo. [374]

1884. Ferishtah's Fancies—
Prologue.
1. The Eagle.
2. The Melon-Seller.
3. Shah Abbas.
4. The Family.
5. The Sun.
6. Mihrab Shah.
7. A Camel-Driver.
8. Two Camels.
9. Cherries.
10. Plot-Culture.
11. A Pillar at Sebzevar.
12. A Bean-Stripe: also Apple-Eating.
Epilogue.

[Songs from *Ferishtah's Fancies* will be found on p. 375 f.]

1887. Parleyings with Certain People of Importance in Their Day: To wit: Bernard de Mandeville, Daniel Bartoli, Christopher Smart, George Bubb Dodington, Francis Furini, Gerard de Lairesse, and Charles Avison. Introduced by a Dialogue between Apollo and the Fates; concluded by another between John Fust and his Friends.

1889. Asolando: Fancies and Facts—
Prologue.
Rosny.
Dubiety.
Now. [377]
Humility.
Poetics.
Summum Bonum. [377]
A Pearl, A Girl. [377]
Speculative.
White Witchcraft.
Bad Dreams. I.
Bad Dreams. II.
Bad Dreams. III.
Bad Dreams. IV.
Inapprehensiveness.
Which?
The Cardinal and the Dog.
The Pope and the Net.
The Bean-Feast.
Muckle-Mouth Meg. [377]
Arcades Ambo.
The Lady and the Painter.
Ponte dell' Angelo, Venice.
Beatrice Signorini.
Flute-Music, with an Accompaniment.
"Imperante Augusto natus est—"
Development. [378]
Rephan. [380]
Reverie.
Epilogue. [382]

PIPPA PASSES

A DRAMA

1841

PERSONS

PIPPA.	JULES.
OTTIMA.	PHENE.
SEBALD.	*Austrian Police.*
Foreign Students.	BLUPHOCKS.
GOTTLIEB.	LUIGI *and his* Mother.
SCHRAMM.	*Poor Girls.*

MONSIGNOR *and his Attendants.*

INTRODUCTION

NEW YEAR'S DAY AT ASOLO IN THE TREVISAN.

SCENE.—*A large mean airy chamber. A girl,* PIPPA, *from the Silk-mills, springing out of bed.*

DAY!
Faster and more fast,
O'er night's brim, day boils at last:
Boils, pure gold, o'er the cloud-cup's brim
Where spurting and suppressed it lay,
For not a froth-flake touched the rim
Of yonder gap in the solid gray
Of the eastern cloud, an hour away;
But forth one wavelet, then another, curled,
Till the whole sunrise, not to be suppressed,
Rose, reddened, and its seething breast
Flickered in bounds, grew gold, then overflowed the world.

Oh, Day, if I squander a wavelet of thee,
A mite of my twelve hours' treasure,
The least of thy gazes or glances,
(Be they grants thou art bound to or gifts above measure)
One of thy choices or one of thy chances,
(Be they tasks God imposed thee or freaks at thy pleasure)
—My Day, if I squander such labour or leisure,
Then shame fall on Asolo, mischief on me!

Thy long blue solemn hours serenely flowing,
Whence earth, we feel, gets steady help and good—
Thy fitful sunshine-minutes, coming, going,
As if earth turned from work in gamesome mood—
All shall be mine! But thou must treat me not
As prosperous ones are treated, those who live
At hand here, and enjoy the higher lot,
In readiness to take what thou wilt give,
And free to let alone what thou refusest;
For, Day, my holiday, if thou ill-usest
Me, who am only Pippa,—old-year's sorrow,
Cast off last night, will come again tomorrow:
Whereas, if thou prove gentle, I shall borrow
Sufficient strength of thee for new-year's sorrow.
All other men and women that this earth
Belongs to, who all days alike possess,
Make general plenty cure particular dearth,
Get more joy one way, if another, less:
Thou art my single day, God lends to leaven
What were all earth else, with a feel of heaven,—
Sole light that helps me through the year, thy sun's!
Try now! Take Asolo's Four Happiest Ones—
And let thy morning rain on that superb
Great haughty Ottima; can rain disturb
Her Sebald's homage? All the while thy rain
Beats fiercest on her shrub-house window-pane,
He will but press the closer, breathe more warm
Against her cheek; how should she mind the storm?
And, morning past, if mid-day shed a gloom
O'er Jules and Phene,—what care bride and groom
Save for their dear selves? 'Tis their marriage-day;
And while they leave church and go home their way,
Hand clasping hand, within each breast would be
Sunbeams and pleasant weather spite of thee.
Then, for another trial, obscure thy eve
With mist,—will Luigi and his mother grieve—
The lady and her child, unmatched, forsooth,
She in her age, as Luigi in his youth,
For true content? The cheerful town, warm, close
And safe, the sooner that thou art morose,

Receives them. And yet once again, outbreak
In storm at night on Monsignor,[1] they make
Such stir about,—whom they expect from Rome
To visit Asolo, his brothers' home,
And say here masses proper to release
A soul from pain,—what storm dares hurt his peace?
Calm would he pray, with his own thoughts to ward
Thy thunder off, nor want the angels' guard.
But Pippa—just one such mischance would spoil
Her day that lightens the next twelve-month's toil
At wearisome silk-winding, coil on coil!
And here I let time slip for nought!
Aha, you foolhardy sunbeam, caught
With a single splash from my ewer!
You that would mock the best pursuer,
Was my basin over-deep?
One splash of water ruins you asleep,
And up, up, fleet your brilliant bits
Wheeling and counterwheeling,
Reeling, broken beyond healing:
Now grow together on the ceiling!
That will task your wits.
Whoever it was quenched fire first, hoped to see
Morsel after morsel flee
As merrily, as giddily . . .
Meantime, what lights my sunbeam on,
Where settles by degrees the radiant cripple?
Oh, is it surely blown, my martagon?[2]
New-blown and ruddy as St. Agnes' nipple,
Plump as the flesh-bunch on some Turk bird's poll!
Be sure if corals, branching 'neath the ripple
Of ocean, bud there,—fairies watch unroll
Such turban-flowers; I say, such lamps disperse
Thick red flame through that dusk green universe!
I am queen of thee, floweret!
And each fleshy blossom
Preserve I not—(safer
Than leaves that embower it,
Or shells that embosom)
—From weevil and chafer?
Laugh through my pane then; solicit the bee;
Gibe him, be sure; and, in midst of thy glee,
Love thy queen, worship me!

—Worship whom else? For am I not, this day,
Whate'er I please? What shall I please to-day?
My morn, noon, eve and night—how spend my day?
To-morrow I must be Pippa who winds silk,
The whole year round, to earn just bread and milk:
But, this one day, I have leave to go.
And play out my fancy's fullest games;
I may fancy all day—and it shall be so—
That I taste of the pleasures, am called by the names
Of the Happiest Four in our Asolo!

See! Up the hill-side yonder, through the morning,
Some one shall love me, as the world calls love:
I am no less than Ottima, take warning!
The gardens, and the great stone house above,
And other house for shrubs, all glass in front,
Are mine; where Sebald steals, as he is wont,
To court me, while old Luca yet reposes:
And therefore, till the shrub-house door uncloses,
I . . . what now?—give abundant cause for prate
About me—Ottima, I mean—of late,
Too bold, too confident she'll still face down
The spitefullest of talkers in our town.
How we talk in the little town below!
But love, love, love—there's better love, I know!
This foolish love was only day's first offer;
I choose my next love to defy the scoffer:
For do not our Bride and Bridegroom sally
Out of Possagno church at noon?
Their house looks over Orcana valley:
Why should not I be the bride as soon
As Ottima? For I saw, beside,
Arrive last night that little bride—
Saw, if you call it seeing her, one flash
Of the pale snow-pure cheek and black bright tresses,
Blacker than all except the black eyelash;

[1] A title of honor conferred by the Pope on high church officials. [2] A lily.

I wonder she contrives those lids no dresses!
—So strict was she, the veil
Should cover close her pale
Pure cheeks—a bride to look at and scarce touch,
Scarce touch, remember, Jules! For are not such
Used to be tended, flower-like, every feature,
As if one's breath would fray the lily of a creature?
A soft and easy life these ladies lead:
Whiteness in us were wonderful indeed.
Oh, save that brow its virgin dimness,
Keep that foot its lady primness,
Let those ankles never swerve
From their exquisite reserve,
Yet have to trip along the streets like me,
All but naked to the knee!
How will she ever grant her Jules a bliss
So startling as her real first infant kiss?
Oh, no—not envy, this!

—Not envy, sure!—for if you gave me
Leave to take or to refuse,
In earnest, do you think I'd choose
That sort of new love to enslave me?
Mine should have lapped me round from the beginning;
As little fear of losing it as winning:
Lovers grow cold, men learn to hate their wives,
And only parents' love can last our lives.
At eve the Son and Mother, gentle pair,
Commune inside our turret: what prevents
My being Luigi? While that mossy lair
Of lizards through the winter-time is stirred
With each to each imparting sweet intents
For this new-year, as brooding bird to bird—
(For I observe of late, the evening walk
Of Luigi and his mother, always ends
Inside our ruined turret, where they talk,
Calmer than lovers, yet more kind than friends)
—Let me be cared about, kept out of harm,
And schemed for, safe in love as with a charm;
Let me be Luigi! If I only knew
What was my mother's face—my father, too!
Nay, if you come to that, best love of all
Is God's; then why not have God's love befall
Myself as, in the palace by the Dome,[1]

[1] The Dome is the cathedral. The palace then would be the Episcopal palace near by.

Monsignor?—who to-night will bless the home
Of his dead brother; and God bless in turn
That heart which beats, those eyes which mildly burn
With love for all men! I, to-night at least,
Would be that holy and beloved priest.

Now wait!—even I already seem to share
In God's love: what does New-year's hymn declare?
What other meaning do these verses bear?

All service ranks the same with God:
If now, as formerly he trod
Paradise, his presence fills
Our earth, each only as God wills
Can work—God's puppets, best and worst,
Are we; there is no last nor first.

Say not "a small event!" Why "small?"
Costs it more pain that this, ye call
A "great event," should come to pass,
Than that? Untwine me from the mass
Of deeds which make up life, one deed
Power shall fall short in or exceed!

And more of it, and more of it!—oh yes—
I will pass each, and see their happiness,
And envy none—being just as great, no doubt,
Useful to men, and dear to God, as they!
A pretty thing to care about
So mightily, this single holiday!
But let the sun shine! Wherefore repine?
—With thee to lead me, O Day of mine,
Down the grass path grey with dew,
Under the pine-wood, blind with boughs,
Where the swallow never flew
Nor yet cicala dared carouse—
No, dared carouse! [*She enters the street.*

I.—MORNING

SCENE.—*Up the Hill-side, inside the Shrub-house.* LUCA'S *wife,* OTTIMA, *and her paramour, the German* SEBALD.

Sebald [*sings*].

Let the watching lids wink!
Day's a-blaze with eyes, think!
Deep into the night, drink!

Ottima. Night? Such may be your Rhineland nights perhaps;
But this blood-red beam through the shutter's chink
—We call such light, the morning: let us see!
Mind how you grope your way, though! How these tall
Naked geraniums straggle! Push the lattice
Behind that frame!—Nay, do I bid you?—Sebald,
It shakes the dust down on me! Why, of course
The slide-bolt catches. Well, are you content,
Or must I find you something else to spoil?
Kiss and be friends, my Sebald! Is't full morning?
Oh, don't speak then!
Sebald. Ay, thus it used to be.
Ever your house was, I remember, shut
Till mid-day; I observed that, as I strolled
On mornings through the vale here; country girls
Were noisy, washing garments in the brook,
Hinds drove the slow white oxen up the hills:
But no, your house was mute, would ope no eye.
And wisely: you were plotting one thing there,
Nature, another outside. I looked up—
Rough white wood shutters, rusty iron bars,
Silent as death, blind in a flood of light.
Oh, I remember!—and the peasants laughed
And said, "The old man sleeps with the young wife."
This house was his, this chair, this window—his.
Ottima. Ah, the clear morning! I can see St. Mark's;
That black streak is the belfry. Stop: Vicenza
Should lie . . . there's Padua, plain enough, that blue!
Look o'er my shoulder, follow my finger!
Sebald. Morning?
It seems to me a night with a sun added.
Where's dew, where's freshness? That bruised plant, I bruised
In getting through the lattice yestereve,
Droops as it did. See, here's my elbow's mark
I' the dust o' the sill.
Ottima. Oh, shut the lattice, pray!
Sebald. Let me lean out. I cannot scent blood here,
Foul as the morn may be.
There, shut the world out!
How do you feel now, Ottima? There, curse
The world and all outside! Let us throw off
This mask: how do you bear yourself? Let's out
With all of it.
Ottima. Best never speak of it.
Sebald. Best speak again and yet again of it,
Till words cease to be more than words. "His blood,"
For instance—let those two words mean "His blood"
And nothing more. Notice, I'll say them now,
"His blood."
Ottima. Assuredly if I repented
The deed—
Sebald. Repent? Who should repent, or why?
What puts that in your head? Did I once say
That I repented?
Ottima. No, I said the deed . . .
Sebald. "The deed" and "the event"—just now it was
"Our passion's fruit"—the devil take such cant!
Say, once and always, Luca was a wittol,
I am his cut-throat, you are . . .
Ottima. Here's the wine;
I brought it when we left the house above,
And glasses too—wine of both sorts. Black? White then?
Sebald. But am not I his cut-throat? What are you?
Ottima. There trudges on his business from the Duomo
Benet the Capuchin, with his brown hood
And bare feet; always in one place at church,
Close under the stone wall by the south entry
I used to take him for a brown cold piece
Of the wall's self, as out of it he rose
To let me pass—at first, I say, I used:
Now, so has that dumb figure fastened on me,
I rather should account the plastered wall
A piece of him, so chilly does it strike.
This, Sebald?
Sebald. No, the white wine—the white wine!
Well, Ottima, I promised no new year
Should rise on us the ancient shameful way;
Nor does it rise. Pour on! To your black eyes!

Do you remember last damned New Year's day?
Ottima. You brought those foreign prints. We looked at them
Over the wine and fruit. I had to scheme
To get him from the fire. Nothing but saying
His own set wants the proof-mark,[1] roused him up
To hunt them out.
Sebald. 'Faith, he is not alive
To fondle you before my face.
Ottima. Do you
Fondle me then! Who means to take your life
For that, my Sebald?
Sebald. Hark you, Ottima!
One thing to guard against. We'll not make much
One of the other—that is, not make more
Parade of warmth, childish officious coil,
Than yesterday: as if, sweet, I supposed
Proof upon proof were needed now, now first,
To show I love you—yes, still love you—love you
In spite of Luca and what's come to him
—Sure sign we had him ever in our thoughts,
White sneering old reproachful face and all!
We'll even quarrel, love, at times, as if
We still could lose each other, were not tied
By this: conceive you?
Ottima. Love!
Sebald. Not tied so sure.
Because though I was wrought upon, have struck
His insolence back into him—am I
So surely yours?—therefore for ever yours?
Ottima. Love, to be wise, (one counsel pays another)
Should we have—months ago, when first we loved,
For instance that May morning we two stole
Under the green ascent of sycamores—
If we had come upon a thing like that
Suddenly . . .
Sebald. "A thing"—there again—"a thing!"
Ottima. Then, Venus' body, had we come upon
My husband Luca Gaddi's murdered corpse
Within there, at his couch-foot, covered close—

[1] The sign on a print which indicates whether or not it is one of the first impressions drawn from the plate.

Would you have pored upon it? Why persist
In poring now upon it? For 'tis here
As much as there in the deserted house:
You cannot rid your eyes of it. For me,
Now he is dead I hate him worse: I hate . . .
Dare you stay here? I would go back and hold
His two dead hands, and say, "I hate you worse,
Luca, than . . ."
Sebald. Off, off—take your hands off mine,
'Tis the hot evening—off! oh, morning is it?
Ottima. There's one thing must be done; you know what thing.
Come in and help to carry. We may sleep
Anywhere in the whole wide house tonight.
Sebald. What would come, think you, if we let him lie
Just as he is? Let him lie there until
The angels take him! He is turned by this
Off from his face beside, as you will see.[1]
Ottima. This dusty pane might serve for looking glass.
Three, four—four grey hairs! Is it so you said
A plait of hair should wave across my neck?
No—this way.
Sebald. Ottima, I would give your neck,
Each splendid shoulder, both those breasts of yours,
That this were undone! Killing! Kill the world
So Luca lives again!—ay, lives to sputter
His fulsome dotage on you—yes, and feign
Surprise that I return at eve to sup,
When all the morning I was loitering here
Bid me dispatch my business and begone.
I would . . .
Ottima. See!
Sebald. No, I'll finish. Do you think
I fear to speak the bare truth once for all?
All we have talked of, is, at bottom, fine
To suffer; there's a recompense in guilt;
One must be venturous and fortunate:
What is one young for, else? In age we'll sigh
O'er the wild reckless wicked days flown over;
Still, we have lived: the vice was in its place.

[1] According to superstition the face of a murdered man always looks skyward for vengeance. The two had left Luca lying face down and Sebald is afraid the body has turned.

But to have eaten Luca's bread, have worn
His clothes, have felt his money swell my purse—
Do lovers in romances sin that way?
Why, I was starving when I used to call
And teach you music, starving while you plucked me
These flowers to smell!
Ottima. My poor lost friend!
Sebald. He gave me
Life, nothing less: what if he did reproach
My perfidy, and threaten, and do more—
Had he no right? What was to wonder at?
He sat by us at table quietly:
Why must you lean across till our cheeks touched?
Could he do less than make pretence to strike?
'Tis not the crime's sake—I'd commit ten crimes
Greater, to have this crime wiped out, undone!
And you—O how feel you? Feel you for me?
Ottima. Well then, I love you better now than ever,
And best (look at me while I speak to you)
Best for the crime; nor do I grieve, in truth,
This mask, this simulated ignorance,
This affectation of simplicity,
Falls off our crime; this naked crime of ours
May not now be looked over: look it down!
Great? let it be great; but the joys it brought,
Pay they or no its price? Come: they or it!
Speak not! The past, would you give up the past
Such as it is, pleasure and crime together?
Give up that noon I owned my love for you?
The garden's silence: even the single bee
Persisting in his toil, suddenly stopped,
And where he hid you only could surmise
By some campanula chalice set a-swing.
Who stammered—"Yes, I love you?"
Sebald. And I drew
Back; put far back your face with both my hands
Lest you should grow too full of me—your face
So seemed athirst for my whole soul and body!
Ottima. And when I ventured to receive you here,
Made you steal hither in the mornings—
Sebald. When
I used to look up 'neath the shrub-house here,
Till the red fire on its glazed windows spread
To a yellow haze?
Ottima. Ah—my sign was, the sun
Inflamed the sere side of yon chestnut-tree
Nipped by the first frost.
Sebald. You would always laugh
At my wet boots: I had to stride thro' grass
Over my ankles.
Ottima. Then our crowning night!
Sebald. The July night?
Ottima. The day of it too, Sebald!
When heaven's pillars seemed o'erbowed with heat,
Its black-blue canopy suffered descend
Close on us both, to weigh down each to each,
And smother up all life except our life.
So lay we till the storm came.
Sebald. How it came!
Ottima. Buried in woods we lay, you recollect;
Swift ran the searching tempest overhead;
And ever and anon some bright white shaft
Burned thro' the pine-tree roof, here burned and there,
As if God's messenger thro' the close wood screen
Plunged and replunged his weapon at a venture,
Feeling for guilty thee and me: then broke
The thunder like a whole sea overhead—
Sebald. Yes!
Ottima. —While I stretched myself upon you, hands
To hands, my mouth to your hot mouth, and shook
All my locks loose, and covered you with them—
You, Sebald, the same you!
Sebald. Slower, Ottima!
Ottima. And as we lay—
Sebald. Less vehemently! Love me!
Forgive me! Take not words, mere words, to heart!
Your breath is worse than wine! Breathe slow, speak slow!
Do not lean on me!
Ottima. Sebald, as we lay,
Rising and falling only with our pants,
Who said, "Let death come now! 'Tis right to die!

Right to be punished! Nought completes such bliss
But woe!" Who said that?
Sebald. How did we ever rise?
Was't that we slept? Why did it end?
Ottima. I felt you
Taper into a point the ruffled ends
Of my loose locks 'twixt both your humid lips.
My hair is fallen now: knot it again!
Sebald. I kiss you now, dear Ottima, now and now!
This way? Will you forgive me—be once more
My great queen?
Ottima. Bind it thrice about my brow;
Crown me your queen, your spirit's arbitress,
Magnificent in sin. Say that!
Sebald. I crown you
My great white queen, my spirit's arbitress,
Magnificent . . .

[*From without is heard the voice of* PIPPA, *singing*—

The year's at the spring
And day's at the morn;
Morning's at seven;
The hill-side's dew-pearled;
The lark's on the wing;
The snail's on the thorn:
God's in his heaven—
All's right with the world!

[PIPPA *passes.*

Sebald. God's in his heaven! Do you hear that? Who spoke?
You, you spoke!
Ottima. Oh—that little ragged girl!
She must have rested on the step: we give them
But this one holiday the whole year round.
Did you ever see our silk-mills—their inside?
There are ten silk-mills now belong to you.
She stoops to pick my double heartsease . . . Sh!
She does not hear: call you out louder!
Sebald. Leave me!
Go, get your clothes on—dress those shoulders!
Ottima. Sebald?
Sebald. Wipe off that paint! I hate you.
Ottima. Miserable!
Sebald. My God, and she is emptied of it now!
Outright now!—how miraculously gone
All of the grace—had she not strange grace once?
Why, the blank cheek hangs listless as it likes,
No purpose holds the features up together,
Only the cloven brow and puckered chin
Stay in their places: and the very hair
That seemed to have a sort of life in it,
Drops, a dead web!
Ottima. Speak to me—not of me.
Sebald. That round great full-orbed face, where not an angle
Broke the delicious indolence—all broken!
Ottima. To me—not of me! Ungrateful, perjured cheat!
A coward too: but ingrate's worse than all.
Beggar—my slave—a fawning, cringing lie!
Leave me! Betray me! I can see your drift!
A lie that walks and eats and drinks?
Sebald. My God!
Those morbid olive faultless shoulder-blades—
I should have known there was no blood beneath!
Ottima. You hate me then? You hate me then?
Sebald. To think
She would succeed in her absurd attempt,
And fascinate by sinning, show herself
Superior—guilt from its excess superior
To innocence! That little peasant's voice
Has righted all again. Though I be lost,
I know which is the better, never fear,
Of vice or virtue, purity or lust,
Nature or trick! I see what I have done,
Entirely now! Oh I am proud to feel
Such torments—let the world take credit thence—
I, having done my deed, pay too its price!
I hate, hate—curse you! God's in his heaven!
Ottima. —Me!
Me! no, no, Sebald, not yourself—kill me!
Mine is the whole crime. Do but kill me—then
Yourself—then—presently—first hear me speak!
I always meant to kill myself—wait, you!
Lean on my breast—not as a breast; don't love me
The more because you lean on me, my own

Heart's Sebald! There, there, both deaths
presently!

Sebald. My brain is drowned now—quite
drowned: all I feel
Is . . . is, at swift-recurring intervals,
A hurry-down within me, as of waters
Loosened to smother up some ghastly pit:
There they go—whirls from a black fiery sea!

Ottima. Not me—to him, O God, be merciful!

Talk by the way, while PIPPA *is passing from the hill-side to Orcana. Foreign* STUDENTS *of painting and sculpture, from Venice, assembled opposite the house of* JULES, *a young French statuary, at Possagno.*

1st Student. Attention! My own post is beneath this window, but the pomegranate clump yonder will hide three or four of you with a little squeezing, and Schramm and his pipe must lie flat in the balcony. Four, five—who's a defaulter? We want everybody, for Jules must not be suffered to hurt his bride when the jest's found out.

2nd Student. All here! Only our poet's away—never having much meant to be present, moonstrike him! The airs of that fellow, that Giovacchino! He was in violent love with himself, and had a fair prospect of thriving in his suit, so unmolested was it,—when suddenly a woman falls in love with him, too; and out of pure jealousy he takes himself off to Trieste, immortal poem and all: whereto is this prophetical epitaph appended already, as Bluphocks assures me,—"*Here a mammoth-poem lies, Fouled to death by butterflies.*" His own fault, the simpleton! Instead of cramp couplets, each like a knife in your entrails, he should write, says Bluphocks, both classically and intelligibly.—*Æsculapius, an Epic. Catalogue of the drugs: Hebe's plaister—One strip Cools your lip. Phœbus' emulsion—One bottle Clears your throttle. Mercury's bolus—One box Cures . . .*

3rd Student. Subside, my fine fellow! If the marriage was over by ten o'clock, Jules will certainly be here in a minute with his bride.

2nd Student. Good!—only, so should the poet's muse have been universally acceptable, says Bluphocks, *et canibus nostris* . . . and Delia not better known to our literary dogs than the boy Giovacchino![1]

1st Student. To the point now. Where's Gottlieb, the new-comer? Oh,—listen, Gottlieb, to what has called down this piece of friendly vengeance on Jules, of which we now assemble to witness the winding-up. We are all agreed, all in a tale, observe, when Jules shall burst out on us in a fury by and by: I am spokesman—the verses that are to undeceive Jules bear my name of Lutwyche—but each professes himself alike insulted by this strutting stone-squarer, who came alone from Paris to Munich, and thence with a crowd of us to Venice and Possagno here, but proceeds in a day or two alone again—oh, alone indubitably!—to Rome and Florence. He, forsooth, take up his portion with these dissolute, brutalised, heartless bunglers!—so he was heard to call us all: now, is Schramm brutalised, I should like to know? Am I heartless?

Gottlieb. Why, somewhat heartless; for, suppose Jules a coxcomb as much as you choose, still, for this mere coxcombry, you will have brushed off—what do folks style it?—the bloom of his life.

Is it too late to alter? These love-letters now, you call his—I can't laugh at them.

4th Student. Because you never read the sham letters of our inditing which drew forth these.

Gottlieb. His discovery of the truth will be frightful.

4th Student. That's the joke. But you should have joined us at the beginning: there's no doubt he loves the girl—loves a model he might hire by the hour!

Gottlieb. See here! "He has been accustomed," he writes, "to have Canova's women about him, in stone, and the world's women beside him, in flesh; these being as much below, as those above, his soul's aspiration: but now he is to have the reality." There you

[1] *Et canibus nostris* translates "and to our dogs." The fragment is from Virgil's Third Eclogue, line 67, in which Menalcas boasts that Amyntas had come to see him so often that the dogs did not even bark at her, so well known was she, just as Delia had been. The reference is ironical, implying Giovacchino not at all well known to the literary dogs.

laugh again! I say, you wipe off the very dew of his youth.

1st Student. Schramm! (Take the pipe out of his mouth, somebody!) Will Jules lose the bloom of his youth?

Schramm. Nothing worth keeping is ever lost in this world: look at a blossom—it drops presently, having done its service and lasted its time; but fruits succeed, and where would be the blossom's place could it continue? As well affirm that your eye is no longer in your body, because its earliest favourite, whatever it may have first loved to look on, is dead and done with—as that any affection is lost to the soul when its first object, whatever happened first to satisfy it, is superseded in due course. Keep but ever looking, whether with the body's eye or the mind's, and you will soon find something to look on! Has a man done wondering at women?—there follow men, dead and alive, to wonder at. Has he done wondering at men?—there's God to wonder at: and the faculty of wonder may be, at the same time, old and tired enough with respect to its first object, and yet young and fresh sufficiently, so far as concerns its novel one. Thus . . .

1st Student. Put Schramm's pipe into his mouth again! There, you see! Well, this Jules . . . a wretched fribble—oh, I watched his disportings at Possagno, the other day! Canova's gallery—you know: there he marches first resolvedly past great works by the dozen without vouchsafing an eye: all at once he stops full at the *Psiche-fanciulla*[1]—cannot pass that old acquaintance without a nod of encouragement—"In your new place, beauty? Then behave yourself as well here as at Munich—I see you!" Next he posts himself deliberately before the unfinished *Pietà* for half an hour without moving, till up he starts of a sudden, and thrusts his very nose into—I say, into—the group; by which gesture you are informed that precisely the sole point he had not fully mastered in Canova's practice was a certain method of using the drill in the articulation of the knee-joint—and that, likewise, has he mastered at length! Good-bye, therefore, to poor Canova—whose gallery no longer needs detain his successor Jules, the predestinated novel thinker in marble!

[1] One of Canova's statues showing Psyche as a young girl with a butterfly.

5th Student. Tell him about the women: go on to the women!

1st Student. Why, on that matter he could never be supercilious enough. How should we be other (he said) than the poor devils you see, with those debasing habits we cherish? He was not to wallow in that mire, at least: he would wait, and love only at the proper time, and meanwhile put up with the *Psiche-fanciulla*. Now, I happened to hear of a young Greek—real Greek girl at Malamocco; a true Islander, do you see, with Alciphron's "hair like sea-moss"—Schramm knows!—white and quiet as an apparition, and fourteen years old at farthest,—a daughter of Natalia, so she swears,—that hag Natalia, who helps us to models at three *lire* an hour. We selected this girl for the heroine of our jest. So first, Jules received a scented letter—somebody had seen his Tydeus at the Academy, and my picture was nothing to it: a profound admirer bade him persevere—would make herself known to him ere long. (Paolina, my little friend of the *Fenice*,[1] transcribes divinely.) And in due time, the mysterious correspondent gave certain hints of her peculiar charms—the pale cheeks, the black hair—whatever, in short, had struck us in our Malamocco model: we retained her name, too—Phene, which is, by interpretation, sea-eagle. Now, think of Jules finding himself distinguished from the herd of us by such a creature! In his very first answer he proposed marrying his monitress: and fancy us over these letters, two, three times a day, to receive and dispatch! I concocted the main of it: relations were in the way—secrecy must be observed—in fine, would he wed her on trust, and only speak to her when they were indissolubly united? St—st—Here they come!

6th Student. Both of them! Heaven's love, speak softly, speak within yourselves!

5th Student. Look at the bridegroom! Half his hair in storm and half in calm,—patted down over the left temple,—like a frothy cup one blows on to cool it: and the same old blouse that he murders the marble in.

2nd Student. Not a rich vest like yours,

[1] A theater in Venice.

Hannibal Scratchy!—rich, that your face may the better set it off.

6th Student. And the bride! Yes, sure enough, our Phene! Should you have known her in her clothes? How magnificently pale!

Gottlieb. She does not also take it for earnest, I hope?

1st Student. Oh, Natalia's concern, that is! We settle with Natalia.

6th Student. She does not speak—has evidently let out no word. The only thing is, will she equally remember the rest of her lesson, and repeat correctly all those verses which are to break the secret to Jules?

Gottlieb. How he gazes on her! Pity—pity!

1st Student. They go in: now, silence! You three,—not nearer the window, mind, than that pomegranate: just where the little girl, who a few minutes ago passed us singing, is seated!

II. — NOON

SCENE.—*Over Orcana. The house of* JULES, *who crosses its threshold with* PHENE: *she is silent, on which* JULES *begins*—

Do not die, Phene! I am yours now, you
Are mine now; let fate reach me how she likes,
If you'll not die: so, never die! Sit here—
My work-room's single seat. I over-lean
This length of hair and lustrous front; they turn
Like an entire flower upward: eyes, lips, last
Your chin—no, last your throat turns: 'tis their scent
Pulls down my face upon you. Nay, look ever
This one way till I change, grow you—I could
Change into you, beloved!
You by me,
And I by you; this is your hand in mine,
And side by side we sit: all's true. Thank God!
I have spoken: speak you!
O my life to come!
My Tydeus must be carved that's there in clay;
Yet how be carved, with you about the room?
Where must I place you? When I think that once
This room-full of rough block-work seemed my heaven
Without you! Shall I ever work again,
Get fairly into my old ways again,
Bid each conception stand while, trait by trait,
My hand transfers its lineaments to stone?
Will my mere fancies live near you, their truth—
The live truth, passing and repassing me,
Sitting beside me?
Now speak!
Only first,
See, all your letters! Was't not well contrived?
Their hiding-place is Psyche's robe; she keeps
Your letters next her skin: which drops out foremost?
Ah,—this that swam down like a first moonbeam
Into my world!
Again those eyes complete
Their melancholy survey, sweet and slow,
Of all my room holds; to return and rest
On me, with pity, yet some wonder too:
As if God bade some spirit plague a world,
And this were the one moment of surprise
And sorrow while she took her station, pausing
O'er what she sees, finds good, and must destroy!
What gaze you at? Those? Books, I told you of;
Let your first word to me rejoice them, too:
This minion, a Coluthus, writ in red
Bistre and azure by Bessarion's scribe—
Read this line . . . no, shame—Homer's be the Greek
First breathed me from the lips of my Greek girl!
This Odyssey in coarse black vivid type
With faded yellow blossoms 'twixt page and page,
To mark great places with due gratitude;
"*He said, and on Antinous directed*
A bitter shaft" . . . a flower blots out the rest!
Again upon your search? My statues, then!
—Ah, do not mind that—better that will look
When cast in bronze—an Almaign Kaiser, that,
Swart-green and gold, with truncheon based on hip.

This, rather, turn to! What, unrecognised?
I thought you would have seen that here you sit
As I imagined you,—Hippolyta,
Naked upon her bright Numidian horse.
Recall you this then? "Carve in bold relief"—
So you commanded—"carve, against I come,
A Greek, in Athens, as our fashion was,
Feasting, bay-filleted and thunder-free,
Who rises 'neath the lifted myrtle-branch.
'Praise those who slew Hipparchus!' cry the guests,
'While o'er thy head the singer's myrtle waves
As erst above our champion: stand up, all!'"
See, I have laboured to express your thought.
Quite round, a cluster of mere hands and arms,
(Thrust in all senses, all ways, from all sides,
Only consenting at the branch's end
They strain toward) serves for frame to a sole face,
The Praiser's, in the centre: who with eyes
Sightless, so bend they back to light inside
His brain where visionary forms throng up,
Sings, minding not that palpitating arch
Of hands and arms, nor the quick drip of wine
From the drenched leaves o'erhead, nor crowns cast off,
Violet and parsley crowns to trample on—
Sings, pausing as the patron-ghosts approve,
Devoutly their unconquerable hymn.
But you must say a "well" to that—say "well!"
Because you gaze—am I fantastic, sweet?
Gaze like my very life's-stuff, marble—marbly
Even to the silence! Why, before I found
The real flesh Phene, I inured myself
To see, throughout all nature, varied stuff
For better nature's birth by means of art:
With me, each substance tended to one form
Of beauty—to the human archetype.
On every side occurred suggestive germs
Of that—the tree, the flower—or take the fruit,—
Some rosy shape, continuing the peach,
Curved beewise o'er its bough; as rosy limbs,
Depending, nestled in the leaves; and just
From a cleft rose-peach the whole Dryad sprang.
But of the stuffs one can be master of,
How I divined their capabilities!
From the soft-rinded smoothening facile chalk
That yields your outline to the air's embrace,
Half-softened by a halo's pearly gloom;
Down to the crisp imperious steel, so sure
To cut its one confided thought clean out
Of all the world. But marble!—'neath my tools
More pliable than jelly—as it were
Some clear primordial creature dug from depths
In the earth's heart, where itself breeds itself,
And whence all baser substance may be worked;
Refine it off to air, you may,—condense it
Down to the diamond;—is not metal there,
When o'er the sudden speck my chisel trips?
—Not flesh, as flake off flake I scale, approach,
Lay bare those bluish veins of blood asleep?
Lurks flame in no strange windings where, surprised
By the swift implement sent home at once,
Flushes and glowings radiate and hover
About its track?

Phene? what—why is this?
That whitening cheek, those still dilating eyes!
Ah, you will die—I knew that you would die!

PHENE *begins, on his having long remained silent.*

Now the end's coming; to be sure, it must
Have ended sometime! Tush, why need I speak
Their foolish speech? I cannot bring to mind
One-half of it, beside; and do not care
For old Natalia now, nor any of them.
Oh, you—what are you?—if I do not try
To say the words Natalia made me learn,
To please your friends,—it is to keep myself
Where your voice lifted me, by letting that
Proceed: but can it? Even you, perhaps,
Cannot take up, now you have once let fall,
The music's life, and me along with that—
No, or you would! We'll stay, then, as we are:
Above the world.

You creature with the eyes!
If I could look for ever up to them,
As now you let me,—I believe, all sin,
All memory of wrong done, suffering borne,
Would drop down, low and lower, to the earth

Whence all that's low comes, and there touch and stay
—Never to overtake the rest of me,
All that, unspotted, reaches up to you,
Drawn by those eyes! What rises is myself,
Not me the shame and suffering; but they sink,
Are left, I rise above them. Keep me so,
Above the world!
But you sink, for your eyes
Are altering—altered! Stay—"I love you, love" . . .
I could prevent it if I understood:
More of your words to me: was't in the tone
Or the words, your power?
Or stay—I will repeat
Their speech, if that contents you! Only change
No more, and I shall find it presently
Far back here, in the brain yourself filled up.
Natalia threatened me that harm should follow
Unless I spoke their lesson to the end,
But harm to me, I thought she meant, not you.
Your friends,—Natalia said they were your friends
And meant you well,—because, I doubted it,
Observing (what was very strange to see)
On every face, so different in all else,
The same smile girls like me are used to bear,
But never men, men cannot stoop so low;
Yet your friends, speaking of you, used that smile,
That hateful smirk of boundless self-conceit
Which seems to take possession of the world
And make of God a tame confederate,
Purveyor to their appetites . . . you know!
But still Natalia said they were your friends,
And they assented though they smiled the more,
And all came round me,—that thin Englishman
With light lank hair seemed leader of the rest;
He held a paper—"What we want," said he,
Ending some explanation to his friends—
"Is something slow, involved and mystical,
To hold Jules long in doubt, yet take his taste
And lure him on until, at innermost
Where he seeks sweetness' soul, he may find—this!
—As in the apple's core, the noisome fly:
For insects on the rind are seen at once,
And brushed aside as soon, but this is found
Only when on the lips or loathing tongue."
And so he read what I have got by heart:
I'll speak it,—"Do not die, love! I am yours."
No—is not that, or like that, part of words
Yourself began by speaking? Strange to lose
What cost such pains to learn! Is this more right?

I am a painter who cannot paint;
In my life, a devil rather than saint;
In my brain, as poor a creature too:
No end to all I cannot do!
Yet do one thing at least I can—
Love a man or hate a man
Supremely: thus my lore began.
Through the Valley of Love I went,
In the lovingest spot to abide,
And just on the verge where I pitched my tent,
I found Hate dwelling beside.
(Let the Bridegroom ask what the painter meant,
Of his Bride, of the peerless Bride!)
And further, I traversed Hate's grove,
In the hatefullest nook to dwell;
But lo, where I flung myself prone, couched Love
Where the shadow threefold fell.
(The meaning—those black bride's-eyes above,
Not a painter's lip should tell!)

"And here," said he, "Jules probably will ask,
'You have black eyes, Love,—you are, sure enough,
My peerless bride,—then do you tell indeed
What needs some explanation! What means this?'"
—And I am to go on, without a word—

So, I grew wise in Love and Hate,
From simple that I was of late.
Once, when I loved, I would enlace
Breast, eyelids, hands, feet, form and face
Of her I loved, in one embrace—
As if by mere love I could love immensely!
Once, when I hated, I would plunge
My sword, and wipe with the first lunge
My foe's whole life out like a sponge—
As if by mere hate I could hate intensely!
But now I am wiser, know better the fashion

How passion seeks aid from its opposite passion:
And if I see cause to love more, hate more
Than ever man loved, ever hated before—
And seek in the Valley of Love,
The nest, or the nook in Hate's Grove,
Where my soul may surely reach
The essence, nought less, of each,
The Hate of all Hates, the Love
Of all Loves, in the Valley or Grove,—
I find them the very warders
Each of the other's borders.
When I Love most, Love is disguised
In Hate; and when Hate is surprised
In Love, then I hate most: ask
How Love smiles through Hate's iron casque,
Hate grins through Love's rose-braided mask,—
And how, having hated thee,
I sought long and painfully
To reach thy heart, nor prick
The skin but pierce to the quick—
Ask this, my Jules, and be answered straight
By thy bride—how the painter Lutwyche can hate!

JULES *interposes.*

Lutwyche! Who else? But all of them, no doubt,
Hated me: they at Venice—presently
Their turn, however! You I shall not meet:
If I dreamed, saying this would wake me.
Keep
What's here, the gold—we cannot meet again,
Consider! and the money was but meant
For two years' travel, which is over now,
All chance or hope or care or need of it.
This—and what comes from selling these, my casts
And books and medals, except . . . let them go
Together, so the produce keeps you safe
Out of Natalia's clutches! If by chance
(For all's chance here) I should survive the gang
At Venice, root out all fifteen of them,
We might meet somewhere, since the world is wide.
[*From without is heard the voice of* PIPPA, *singing—*

Give her but a least excuse to love me!
When—where—
How—can this arm establish her above me,
If fortune fixed her as my lady there,
There already, to externally reprove me?
("Hist!"—said Kate the Queen;
But "Oh!"—cried the maiden, binding her tresses,
"'Tis only a page that carols unseen,
Crumbling your hounds their messes!")

Is she wronged?—To the rescue of her honour,
My heart!
Is she poor?—What costs it to be styled a donor?
Merely an earth to cleave, a sea to part.
But that fortune should have thrust all this upon her!
("Nay, list!"—bade Kate the Queen;
And still cried the maiden, binding her tresses,
"'Tis only a page that carols unseen
Fitting your hawks their jesses!")
[PIPPA *passes.*

JULES *resumes.*

What name was that the little girl sang forth?
Kate? The Cornaro,[1] doubtless, who renounced
The crown of Cyprus to be lady here
At Asolo, where still her memory stays,
And peasants sing how once a certain page
Pined for the grace of her so far above
His power of doing good to, "Kate the Queen—
She never could be wronged, be poor," he sighed,
"Need him to help her!"
Yes, a bitter thing
To see our lady above all need of us;
Yet so we look ere we will love; not I,
But the world looks so. If whoever loves
Must be, in some sort, god or worshipper,
The blessing or the blest one, queen or page,

[1] Catarina Cornaro, queen of Cyprus, was forced to abdicate by the Venetian Republic, but was granted every honor and was allowed to hold court at Asolo, where she was much beloved by the people. She died in 1510, but Browning conceives that songs about her were still known in the countryside.

Why should we always choose the page's part?
Here is a woman with utter need of me,—
I find myself queen here, it seems!
How strange!
Look at the woman here with the new soul,
Like my own Psyche,—fresh upon her lips
Alit, the visionary butterfly,
Waiting my word to enter and make bright,
Or flutter off and leave all blank as first.
This body had no soul before, but slept
Or stirred, was beauteous or ungainly, free
From taint or foul with stain, as outward things
Fastened their image on its passiveness:
Now, it will wake, feel, live—or die again!
Shall to produce form out of unshaped stuff
Be Art—and further, to evoke a soul
From form be nothing? This new soul is mine!
Now, to kill Lutwyche, what would that do?—save
A wretched dauber, men will hoot to death
Without me, from their hooting. Oh, to hear
God's voice plain as I heard it first, before
They broke in with their laughter! I heard them
Henceforth, not God.
To Ancona—Greece—some isle!
I wanted silence only; there is clay
Everywhere. One may do whate'er one likes
In Art: the only thing is, to make sure
That one does like it—which takes pains to know.
Scatter all this, my Phene—this mad dream!
Who, what is Lutwyche, what Natalia's friends,
What the whole world except our love—my own,
Own Phene? But I told you, did I not,
Ere night we travel for your land—some isle
With the sea's silence on it? Stand aside—
I do but break these paltry models up
To begin Art afresh. Meet Lutwyche, I—
And save him from my statue meeting him?
Some unsuspected isle in the far seas!
Like a god going through his world, there stands
One mountain for a moment in the dusk,
Whole brotherhoods of cedars on its brow:
And you are ever by me while I gaze
—Are in my arms as now—as now—as now!
Some unsuspected isle in the far seas!
Some unsuspected isle in far-off seas!

Talk by the way, while PIPPA *is passing from Orcana to the Turret. Two or three of the Austrian* POLICE *loitering with* BLUPHOCKS, *an English vagabond, just in view of the Turret.*

Bluphocks.[1] So, that is your Pippa, the little girl who passed us singing? Well, your Bishop's Intendant's money shall be honestly earned:—now, don't make me that sour face because I bring the Bishop's name into the business; we know he can have nothing to do with such horrors: we know that he is a saint and all that a bishop should be, who is a great man beside. *Oh were but every worm a maggot, Every fly a grig, Every bough a Christmas faggot, Every tune a jig!* In fact, I have abjured all religions; but the last I inclined to, was the Armenian: for I have travelled, do you see, and at Koenigsberg, Prussia Improper (so styled because there's a sort of bleak hungry sun there), you might remark over a venerable house-porch, a certain Chaldee inscription; and brief as it is, a mere glance at it used absolutely to change the mood of every bearded passenger. In they turned, one and all; the young and lightsome, with no irreverent pause, the aged and decrepit, with a sensible alacrity: 'twas the Grand Rabbi's abode, in short. Struck with curiosity, I lost no time in learning Syriac—(these are vowels, you dogs,—follow my stick's end in the mud —*Celarent, Darii, Ferio!*[2]) and one morning presented myself, spelling-book in hand, a, b, c,—I picked it out letter by letter, and what was the purport of this miraculous posy? Some cherished legend of the past, you'll say—"*How Moses hocus-pocussed Egypt's land with fly and locust,*"—or, "*How to Jonah sounded harshish, Get thee up and go to Tarshish,*"—or, "*How the angel meeting Balaam, Straight his ass returned a salaam.*" In no wise! "*Shackabrack—Boach—somebody or other—Isaach, Re-cei-ver, Pur-cha-ser and Ex-chan-ger of—Stolen Goods!*" So, talk to me of the religion of

[1] "He maketh his sun to rise on the evil and on the good, and sendeth rain on the just and on the unjust." [Browning's note.]

[2] Coined words used in logic.

a bishop! I have renounced all bishops save Bishop Beveridge[1]—mean to live so—and die —*As some Greek dog-sage, dead and merry, Hellward bound in Charon's[2] wherry, With food for both worlds, under and upper, Lupine-seed and Hecate's supper, And never an obolus . . .* (Though thanks to you, or this Intendant through you, or this Bishop through his Intendant—I possess a burning pocketful of *zwanzigers*) . . . *To pay the Stygian Ferry!*

1st Policeman. There is the girl, then; go and deserve them the moment you have pointed out to us Signor Luigi and his mother. [*To the rest.*] I have been noticing a house yonder, this long while: not a shutter unclosed since morning!

2nd Policeman. Old Luca Gaddi's, that owns the silk-mills here: he dozes by the hour, wakes up, sighs deeply, says he should like to be Prince Metternich, and then dozes again, after having bidden young Sebald, the foreigner, set his wife to playing draughts. Never molest such a household, they mean well.

Bluphocks. Only, cannot you tell me something of this little Pippa, I must have to do with? One could make something of that name. Pippa—that is, short for Felippa—rhyming to *Panurge consults Hertrippa—Believest thou, King Agrippa?* Something might be done with that name.

2nd Policeman. Put into rhyme that your head and a ripe musk-melon would not be dear at half a *zwanziger!* Leave this fooling, and look out; the afternoon's over or nearly so.

3rd Policeman. Where in this passport of Signor Luigi does our Principal instruct you to watch him so narrowly? There? What's there beside a simple signature? (That English fool's busy watching.)

2nd Policeman. Flourish all round—"Put all possible obstacles in his way;" oblong dot at the end—"Detain him till further advices reach you;" scratch at bottom—"Send him back on pretence of some informality in the above;" ink-spirt on right-hand side (which is the case here)—"Arrest him at once." Why and wherefore, I don't concern myself, but my instructions amount to this: if Signor Luigi leaves home to-night for Vienna—well and good, the passport deposed with us for our *visa* is really for his own use, they have misinformed the Office, and he means well; but let him stay over to-night—there has been the pretence we suspect, the accounts of his corresponding and holding intelligence with the Carbonari[1] are correct, we arrest him at once, to-morrow comes Venice, and presently Spielberg.[2] Bluphocks makes the signal, sure enough! That is he, entering the turret with his mother, no doubt.

[1] There was a Bishop Beveridge, but Bluphocks is punning on the word "beverage."

[2] Charon was a God of Hades who ferried the dead across the river Styx for an obolus, a small coin. Hecate, a fearful goddess of the underworld, was propitiated by gifts of food.

III.—EVENING

SCENE.—*Inside the Turret on the Hill above Asolo.* LUIGI *and his* Mother *entering.*

Mother. If there blew wind, you'd hear a long sigh, easing
The utmost heaviness of music's heart.
Luigi. Here in the archway?
Mother. Oh no, no—in farther,
Where the echo is made, on the ridge.
Luigi. Here surely, then.
How plain the tap of my heel as I leaped up!
Hark—"Lucius Junius!"[3] The very ghost of a voice
Whose body is caught and kept by . . . what are those?
Mere withered wallflowers, waving overhead?
They seem an elvish group with thin bleached hair
That lean out of their topmost fortress—look
And listen, mountain men, to what we say,
Hand under chin of each grave earthy face.
Up and show faces all of you!—"All of you!"
That's the king dwarf with the scarlet comb; old Franz,
Come down and meet your fate? Hark—"Meet your fate!"

[1] A secret revolutionary society organized by Italian patriots to work for the freedom of Italy from Austrian rule.

[2] An Austrian prison.

[3] Lucius Junius Brutus roused the Romans to revolt against the Tarquin kings and helped to establish the Republic. Luigi is planning a similar deed.

Mother. Let him not meet it, my Luigi—do not
Go to his City! Putting crime aside,
Half of these ills of Italy are feigned:
Your Pellicos and writers for effect,
Write for effect.
Luigi. Hush! Say A. writes, and B.
Mother. These A.s and B.s write for effect, I say.
Then, evil is in its nature loud, while good
Is silent; you hear each petty injury,
None of his virtues; he is old beside,
Quiet and kind, and densely stupid. Why
Do A. and B. not kill him themselves?
Luigi. They teach
Others to kill him—me—and, if I fail,
Others to succeed; now, if A. tried and failed,
I could not teach that: mine's the lesser task.
Mother, they visit night by night . . .
Mother. —You, Luigi?
Ah, will you let me tell you what you are?
Luigi. Why not? Oh, the one thing you fear to hint,
You may assure yourself I say and say
Ever to myself! At times—nay, even as now
We sit—I think my mind is touched, suspect
All is not sound: but is not knowing that,
What constitutes one sane or otherwise?
I know I am thus—so, all is right again.
I laugh at myself as through the town I walk,
And see men merry as if no Italy
Were suffering; then I ponder—"I am rich,
Young, healthy; why should this fact trouble me,
More than it troubles these?" But it does trouble.
No, trouble's a bad word: for as I walk
There's springing and melody and giddiness,
And old quaint turns and passages of my youth,
Dreams long forgotten, little in themselves,
Return to me—whatever may amuse me:
And earth seems in a truce with me, and heaven
Accords with me, all things suspend their strife,
The very cicala laughs "There goes he, and there!
Feast him, the time is short; he is on his way
For the world's sake: feast him this once, our friend!"
And in return for all this, I can trip
Cheerfully up the scaffold-steps. I go
This evening, mother!
Mother. But mistrust yourself—
Mistrust the judgment you pronounce on him!
Luigi. Oh, there I feel—am sure that I am right!
Mother. Mistrust your judgment then, of the mere means
To this wild enterprise. Say, you are right,—
How should one in your state e'er bring to pass
What would require a cool head, a cold heart,
And a calm hand? You never will escape.
Luigi. Escape? To even wish that, would spoil all.
The dying is best part of it. Too much
Have I enjoyed these fifteen years of mine,
To leave myself excuse for longer life:
Was not life pressed down, running o'er with joy,
That I might finish with it ere my fellows
Who, sparelier feasted, make a longer stay?
I was put at the board-head, helped to all
At first; I rise up happy and content.
God must be glad one loves his world so much.
I can give news of earth to all the dead
Who ask me:—last year's sunsets, and great stars
Which had a right to come first and see ebb
The crimson wave that drifts the sun away—
Those crescent moons with notched and burning rims
That strengthened into sharp fire, and there stood,
Impatient of the azure—and that day
In March, a double rainbow stopped the storm—
May's warm slow yellow moonlit summer nights—
Gone are they, but I have them in my soul!
Mother. (He will not go!)
Luigi. You smile at me? 'Tis true,—
Voluptuousness, grotesqueness, ghastliness,
Environ my devotedness as quaintly
As round about some antique altar wreathe
The rose festoons, goats' horns, and oxen's skulls.
Mother. See now: you reach the city, you must cross
His threshold—how?

Luigi. Oh, that's if we conspired!
Then would come pains in plenty, as you guess—
But guess not how the qualities most fit
For such an office, qualities I have,
Would little stead me, otherwise employed,
Yet prove of rarest merit only here.
Every one knows for what his excellence
Will serve, but no one ever will consider
For what his worst defect might serve: and yet
Have you not seen me range our coppice yonder
In search of a distorted ash?—I find
The wry spoilt branch a natural perfect bow.
Fancy the thrice-sage, thrice-precautioned man
Arriving at the palace on my errand!
No, no! I have a handsome dress packed up—
White satin here, to set off my black hair;
In I shall march—for you may watch your life out
Behind thick walls, make friends there to betray you;
More than one man spoils everything. March straight—
Only, no clumsy knife to fumble for.
Take the great gate and walk (not saunter) on
Thro' guards and guards——I have rehearsed it all
Inside the turret here a hundred times.
Don't ask the way of whom you meet, observe!
But where they cluster thickliest is the door
Of doors; they'll let you pass—they'll never blab
Each to the other, he knows not the favourite,
Whence he is bound and what's his business now.
Walk in—straight up to him; you have no knife:
Be prompt, how should he scream? Then, out with you!
Italy, Italy, my Italy!
You're free, you're free! Oh mother, I could dream
They got about me—Andrea from his exile,
Pier from his dungeon, Gualtier from his grave!

Mother. Well, you shall go. Yet seems this patriotism
The easiest virtue for a selfish man
To acquire: he loves himself—and next, the world—
If he must love beyond,—but nought between:
As a short-sighted man sees nought midway
His body and the sun above. But you
Are my adored Luigi, ever obedient
To my least wish, and running o'er with love:
I could not call you cruel or unkind.
Once more, your ground for killing him!—then go!

Luigi. Now do you try me, or make sport of me?
How first the Austrians got these provinces . . .
(If that is all, I'll satisfy you soon)
—Never by conquest but by cunning, for
That treaty whereby . .

Mother. Well?

Luigi. (Sure, he's arrived,
The tell-tale cuckoo: spring's his confidant,
And he lets out her April purposes!)
Or . . . better go at once to modern time,
He has . . . they have . . . in fact, I understand
But can't restate the matter; that's my boast:
Others could reason it out to you, and prove
Things they have made me feel.

Mother. Why go to-night?
Morn's for adventure. Jupiter is now
A morning-star.[1] I cannot hear you, Luigi!

Luigi. "I am the bright and morning-star," saith God—
And, "to such an one I give the morning-star."
The gift of the morning-star! Have I God's gift
Of the morning-star?

Mother. Chiara[2] will love to see
That Jupiter an evening-star next June.

Luigi. True, mother. Well for those who live through June!

[1] Jupiter would have been a planet of favorable augury for Luigi's venture. If the mother can persuade him to wait for its rising, she will accomplish her purpose of detaining him.

[2] Clara, Luigi's fiancée.

Great noontides, thunder-storms, all glaring pomps
That triumph at the heels of June the god
Leading his revel through our leafy world.
Yes, Chiara will be here.
Mother. In June: remember,
Yourself appointed that month for her coming.
Luigi. Was that low noise the echo?
Mother. The night-wind.
She must be grown—with her blue eyes upturned
As if life were one long and sweet surprise:
In June she comes.
Luigi. We were to see together
The Titian at Treviso. There, again!

[*From without is heard the voice of* PIPPA, *singing*—

A king lived long ago,
In the morning of the world,
When earth was nigher heaven than now.
And the king's locks curled,
Disparting o'er a forehead full
As the milk-white space 'twixt horn and horn
Of some sacrificial bull—
Only calm as a babe new-born:
For he was got to a sleepy mood,
So safe from all decrepitude,
Age with its bane, so sure gone by,
(The gods so loved him while he dreamed)
That, having lived thus long, there seemed
No need the king should ever die.

Luigi. No need that sort of king should ever die!

Among the rocks his city was:
Before his palace, in the sun,
He sat to see his people pass,
And judge them every one
From its threshold of smooth stone.
They haled him many a valley-thief
Caught in the sheep-pens, robber-chief
Swarthy and shameless, beggar-cheat,
Spy-prowler, or rough pirate found
On the sea-sand left aground;
And sometimes clung about his feet,
With bleeding lip and burning cheek,
A woman, bitterest wrong to speak
Of one with sullen thickset brows:
And sometimes from the prison-house
The angry priests a pale wretch brought,
Who through some chink had pushed and pressed
On knees and elbows, belly and breast,
Worm-like into the temple,—caught
He was by the very god,
Who ever in the darkness strode
Backward and forward, keeping watch
O'er his brazen bowls, such rogues to catch!
These, all and every one,
The king judged, sitting in the sun.

Luigi. That king should still judge sitting in the sun!

His councillors, on left and right,
Looked anxious up,—but no surprise
Disturbed the king's old smiling eyes
Where the very blue had turned to white.
'Tis said, a Python[1] *scared one day*
The breathless city, till he came,
With forky tongue and eyes on flame,
Where the old king sat to judge alway;
But when he saw the sweepy hair
Girt with a crown of berries rare
Which the god will hardly give to wear
To the maiden who singeth, dancing bare
In the altar-smoke by the pine-torch lights,
At his wondrous forest rites,—
Seeing this, he did not dare
Approach that threshold in the sun,
Assault the old king smiling there.
Such grace had kings when the world begun! [PIPPA *passes*.

Luigi. And such grace have they, now that the world ends!
The Python at the city, on the throne,
And brave men, God would crown for slaying him,
Lurk in bye-corners lest they fall his prey.
Are crowns yet to be won in this late time,
Which weakness makes me hesitate to reach?
'Tis God's voice calls: how could I stay? Farewell!

Talk by the way, while PIPPA *is passing from the Turret to the Bishop's Brother's House, close to the Duomo S. Maria. Poor* Girls *sitting on the steps.*

[1] In Greek mythology the Python was the great serpent slain by Apollo near Delphi. The term was later applied in poetic usage to any dragon.

1st Girl. There goes a swallow to Venice—the stout seafarer!
Seeing those birds fly, makes one wish for wings.
Let us all wish; you wish first!
2nd Girl. I? This sunset
To finish.
3rd Girl. That old—somebody I know,
Greyer and older than my grandfather,
To give me the same treat he gave last week—
Feeding me on his knee with fig-peckers,
Lampreys and red Breganze-wine, and mumbling
The while some folly about how well I fare,
Let sit and eat my supper quietly:
Since had he not himself been late this morning
Detained at—never mind where,—had he not . . .
"Eh, baggage, had I not!"—
2nd Girl. How she can lie!
3rd Girl. Look there—by the nails!
2nd Girl. What makes your fingers red!
3rd Girl. Dipping them into wine to write bad words with
On the bright table: how he laughed!
1st Girl. My turn.
Spring's come and summer's coming. I would wear
A long loose gown, down to the feet and hands,
With plaits here, close about the throat, all day;
And all night lie, the cool long nights, in bed;
And have new milk to drink, apples to eat,
Deuzans and junetings, leather-coats[1] . . . ah, I should say,
This is away in the fields—miles!
3rd Girl. Say at once
You'd be at home: she'd always be at home!
Now comes the story of the farm among
The cherry orchards, and how April snowed
White blossoms on her as she ran. Why, fool,
They've rubbed the chalk-mark out, how tall you were,
Twisted your starling's neck, broken his cage,
Made a dung-hill of your garden!
1st Girl. They, destroy
My garden since I left them? well—perhaps!
I would have done so: so I hope they have!

[1] Varieties of apples.

A fig-tree curled out of our cottage wall;
They called it mine, I have forgotten why,
It must have been there long ere I was born:
Cric—cric—I think I hear the wasps o'erhead
Pricking the papers strung to flutter there
And keep off birds in fruit-time—coarse long papers,
And the wasps eat them, prick them through and through.
3rd Girl. How her mouth twitches! Where was I?—before
She broke in with her wishes and long gowns
And wasps—would I be such a fool!—Oh, here!
This is my way: I answer every one
Who asks me why I make so much of him—
(If you say, "you love him"—straight "he'll not be gulled!")
"He that seduced me when I was a girl
Thus high—had eyes like yours, or hair like yours,
Brown, red, white,"—as the case may be: that pleases!
See how that beetle burnishes in the path!
There sparkles he along the dust: and, there—
Your journey to that maize-tuft spoiled at least!
1st Girl. When I was young, they said if you killed one
Of those sunshiny beetles, that his friend
Up there, would shine no more that day nor next.
2nd Girl. When you were young? Nor are you young, that's true.
How your plump arms, that were, have dropped away!
Why, I can span them. Cecco beats you still?
No matter, so you keep your curious hair.
I wish they'd find a way to dye our hair
Your colour—any lighter tint, indeed,
Than black: the men say they are sick of black,
Black eyes, black hair!
4th Girl. Sick of yours, like enough.
Do you pretend you ever tasted lampreys
And ortolans? Giovita, of the palace,
Engaged (but there's no trusting him) to slice me
Polenta with a knife that had cut up
An ortolan.[1]

[1] The lamprey (an eel-like fish) and the ortolan (a small bird) were considered delicacies. Polenta was a cheap pudding made out of chestnut flour.

2nd Girl. Why, there! Is not that Pippa
We are to talk to, under the window,—quick,—
Where the lights are?

1st Girl. That she? No, or she would sing,
For the Intendant said . . .

3rd Girl. Oh, you sing first!
Then, if she listens and comes close . . .
I'll tell you,—
Sing that song the young English noble made,
Who took you for the purest of the pure,
And meant to leave the world for you—what fun!

2nd Girl [*sings*].

You'll love me yet!—and I can tarry
Your love's protracted growing:
June reared that bunch of flowers you carry,
From seeds of April's sowing.

I plant a heartful now: some seed
At least is sure to strike,
And yield—what you'll not pluck indeed,
Not love, but, may be, like.

You'll look at least on love's remains,
A grave's one violet:
Your look?—that pays a thousand pains.
What's death? You'll love me yet!

3rd Girl [*to* PIPPA *who approaches*]. Oh, you may come closer—we shall not eat you! Why, you seem the very person that the great rich handsome Englishman has fallen so violently in love with. I'll tell you all about it.

IV.—NIGHT

SCENE.—*Inside the Palace by the Duomo.* MONSIGNOR, *dismissing his* Attendants.

Monsignor. Thanks, friends, many thanks! I chiefly desire life now, that I may recompense every one of you. Most I know something of already. What, a repast prepared? *Benedicto benedicatur*[1] . . . ugh, ugh! Where was I? Oh, as you were remarking, Ugo, the weather is mild, very unlike winter-weather: but I am a Sicilian, you know, and shiver in your Julys here. To be sure, when 'twas full summer at Messina, as we priests used to cross in procession the great square on Assumption Day, you might see our thickest yellow tapers twist suddenly in two, each like a falling star, or sink down on themselves in a gore of wax. But go, my friends, but go! [*To the* Intendant.] Not you, Ugo! [*The others leave the apartment.*] I have long wanted to converse with you, Ugo.

Intendant. Uguccio—

Monsignor. . . . 'guccio Stefani, man! of Ascoli, Fermo and Fossombruno;—what I do need instructing about, are these accounts of your administration of my poor brother's affairs. Ugh! I shall never get through a third part of your accounts: take some of these dainties before we attempt it, however. Are you bashful to that degree? For me, a crust and water suffice.

Intendant. Do you choose this especial night to question me?

Monsignor. This night, Ugo. You have managed my late brother's affairs since the death of our elder brother: fourteen years and a month, all but three days. On the Third of December, I find him . . .

Intendant. If you have so intimate an acquaintance with your brother's affairs, you will be tender of turning so far back: they will hardly bear looking into, so far back.

Monsignor. Ay, ay, ugh, ugh,—nothing but disappointments here below! I remark a considerable payment made to yourself on this Third of December. Talk of disappointments! There was a young fellow here, Jules, a foreign sculptor I did my utmost to advance, that the Church might be a gainer by us both: he was going on hopefully enough, and of a sudden he notifies to me some marvellous change that has happened in his notions of Art. Here's his letter, "He never had a clearly conceived Ideal within his brain till today. Yet since his hand could manage a chisel, he has practised expressing other men's Ideals; and, in the very perfection he has attained to, he foresees an ultimate failure: his unconscious hand will pursue its prescribed course of old years, and will reproduce with a fatal expertness the ancient types, let the novel one appear never so palpably to his spirit. There is but one method of escape: confiding the virgin type

[1] The beginning of a blessing over meat.

to as chaste a hand, he will turn painter instead of sculptor, and paint, not carve, its characteristics,"—strike out, I dare say, a school like Correggio:[1] how think you, Ugo?

Intendant. Is Correggio a painter?

Monsignor. Foolish Jules! and yet, after all, why foolish? He may—probably will—fail egregiously; but if there should arise a new painter, will it not be in some such way, by a poet now, or a musician (spirits who have conceived and perfected an Ideal through some other channel), transferring it to this, and escaping our conventional roads by pure ignorance of them; eh, Ugo? If you have no appetite, talk at least, Ugo!

Intendant. Sir, I can submit no longer to this course of yours. First, you select the group of which I formed one,—next you thin it gradually,—always retaining me with your smile,—and so do you proceed till you have fairly got me alone with you between four stone walls. And now then? Let this farce, this chatter, end now: what is it you want with me?

Monsignor. Ugo!

Intendant. From the instant you arrived, I felt your smile on me as you questioned me about this and the other article in those papers —why your brother should have given me this villa, that *podere*,[2]—and your nod at the end meant,—what?

Monsignor. Possibly that I wished for no loud talk here. If once you set me coughing, Ugo!—

Intendant. I have your brother's hand and seal to all I possess: now ask me what for! what service I did him—ask me!

Monsignor. I would better not: I should rip up old disgraces, let out my poor brother's weaknesses. By the way, Maffeo of Forli (which, I forgot to observe, is your true name), was the interdict ever taken off you, for robbing that church at Cesena?

Intendant. No, nor needs be: for when I murdered your brother's friend, Pasquale, for him . . .

Monsignor. Ah, he employed you in that business, did he? Well, I must let you keep, as you say, this villa and that *podere*, for fear the world should find out my relations were

[1] A famous Italian painter, rather rich and sensuous in his style. [2] A small farm.

of so indifferent a stamp? Maffeo, my family is the oldest in Messina, and century after century have my progenitors gone on polluting themselves with every wickedness under heaven: my own father . . . rest his soul!—I have, I know, a chapel to support that it may rest: my dear two dead brothers were,—what you know tolerably well; I, the youngest, might have rivalled them in vice, if not in wealth: but from my boyhood I came out from among them, and so am not partaker of their plagues. My glory springs from another source; or if from this, by contrast only,—for I, the bishop, am the brother of your employers, Ugo. I hope to repair some of their wrong, however; so far as my brother's ill-gotten treasure reverts to me, I can stop the consequences of his crime: and not one *soldo*[1] shall escape me. Maffeo, the sword we quiet men spurn away, you shrewd knaves pick up and commit murders with; what opportunities the virtuous forego, the villanous seize. Because, to pleasure myself apart from other considerations, my food would be millet-cake, my dress sackcloth, and my couch straw,—am I therefore to let you, the offscouring of the earth, seduce the poor and ignorant by appropriating a pomp these will be sure to think lessens the abominations so unaccountably and exclusively associated with it? Must I let villas and *poderi* go to you, a murderer and thief, that you may beget by means of them other murderers and thieves? No—if my cough would but allow me to speak!

Intendant. What am I to expect? You are going to punish me?

Monsignor.—Must punish you, Maffeo. I cannot afford to cast away a chance. I have whole centuries of sin to redeem, and only a month or two of life to do it in. How should I dare to say . . .

Intendant. "Forgive us our trespasses"?

Monsignor. My friend, it is because I avow myself a very worm, sinful beyond measure, that I reject a line of conduct you would applaud perhaps. Shall I proceed, as it were, a-pardoning?—I?—who have no symptom of reason to assume that aught less than my strenuousest efforts will keep myself out of mortal sin, much less keep others out. No: I do

[1] A penny.

trespass, but will not double that by allowing you to trespass.

Intendant. And suppose the villas are not your brother's to give, nor yours to take? Oh, you are hasty enough just now!

Monsignor. 1, 2—No. 3!—ay, can you read the substance of a letter, No. 3, I have received from Rome? It is precisely on the ground there mentioned, of the suspicion I have that a certain child of my late elder brother, who would have succeeded to his estates, was murdered in infancy by you, Maffeo, at the instigation of my late younger brother—that the Pontiff enjoins on me not merely the bringing that Maffeo to condign punishment, but the taking all pains, as guardian of the infant's heritage for the Church, to recover it parcel by parcel, howsoever, whensoever, and wheresoever. While you are now gnawing those fingers, the police are engaged in sealing up your papers, Maffeo, and the mere raising of my voice brings my people from the next room to dispose of yourself. But I want you to confess quietly, and save me raising my voice. Why, man, do I not know the old story? The heir between the succeeding heir, and this heir's ruffianly instrument, and their complot's effect, and the life of fear and bribes and ominous smiling silence? Did you throttle or stab my brother's infant? Come now!

Intendant. So old a story, and tell it no better? When did such an instrument ever produce such an effect? Either the child smiles in his face; or, most likely, he is not fool enough to put himself in the employer's power so thoroughly: the child is always ready to produce—as you say—howsoever, wheresoever, and whensoever.

Monsignor. Liar!

Intendant. Strike me? Ah, so might a father chastise! I shall sleep soundly to-night at least, though the gallows await me to-morrow; for what a life did I lead! Carlo of Cesena reminds me of his connivance, every time I pay his annuity; which happens commonly thrice a year. If I remonstrate, he will confess all to the good bishop—you!

Monsignor. I see through the trick, caitiff! I would you spoke truth for once. All shall be sifted, however—seven times sifted.

Intendant. And how my absurd riches encumbered me! I dared not lay claim to above half my possessions. Let me but once unbosom myself, glorify Heaven, and die!

Sir, you are no brutal dastardly idiot like your brother I frightened to death: let us understand one another. Sir, I will make away with her for you—the girl—here close at hand; not the stupid obvious kind of killing; do not speak—know nothing of her nor of me! I see her every day—saw her this morning: of course there is to be no killing; but at Rome the courtesans perish off every three years, and I can entice her thither—have indeed begun operations already. There's a certain lusty blue-eyed florid-complexioned English knave, I and the Police employ occasionally. You assent, I perceive—no, that's not it—assent I do not say—but you will let me convert my present havings and holdings into cash, and give me time to cross the Alps? 'Tis but a little black-eyed pretty singing Felippa, gay silk-winding girl. I have kept her out of harm's way up to this present; for I always intended to make your life a plague for you with her. 'Tis as well settled once and for ever. Some women I have procured will pass Bluphocks, my handsome scoundrel, off for somebody; and once Pippa entangled!—you conceive? Through her singing? Is it a bargain?

[*From without is heard the voice of* PIPPA, *singing*—

Overhead the tree-tops meet,
Flowers and grass spring 'neath one's feet;
There was nought above me, nought below,
My childhood had not learned to know:
For, what are the voices of birds
—Ay, and of beasts,—but words, our words,
Only so much more sweet?
The knowledge of that which my life begun.
But I had so near made out the sun,
And counted your stars, the seven and one,[1]
Like the fingers of my hand:
Nay, I could all but understand
Wherefore through heaven the white moon ranges;

[1] The seven are the Pleiades; the one probably Aldebaran.

And just when out of her soft fifty changes
No unfamiliar face might overlook me—
Suddenly God took me.

[PIPPA *passes.*

Monsignor [*springing up*]. My people—one and all—all—within there! Gag this villain—tie him hand and foot! He dares . . . I know not half he dares—but remove him—quick! *Miserere mei, Domine!* [1] Quick, I say!

SCENE.—PIPPA'S *chamber again. She enters it.*

The bee with his comb,
The mouse at her dray,
The grub in his tomb,
Wile winter away;
But the fire-fly and hedge-shrew and lob-worm, I pray,
How fare they?
Ha, ha, thanks for your counsel, my Zanze!
"Feast upon lampreys, quaff Breganze"—
The summer of life so easy to spend,
And care for to-morrow so soon put away!
But winter hastens at summer's end,
And fire-fly, hedge-shrew, lob-worm, pray,
How fare they?
No bidding me then to . . . what did Zanze say?
"Pare your nails pearlwise, get your small feet shoes
More like" . . . (what said she?)—"and less like canoes!"
How pert that girl was!—would I be those pert
Impudent staring women! It had done me,
However, surely no such mighty hurt
To learn his name who passed that jest upon me:
No foreigner, that I can recollect,
Came, as she says, a month since, to inspect
Our silk-mills—none with blue eyes and thick rings
Of raw-silk-coloured hair, at all events.
Well, if old Luca keep his good intents,
We shall do better, see what next year brings.
I may buy shoes, my Zanze, not appear
More destitute than you perhaps next year!
Bluph . . . something! I had caught the uncouth name
But for Monsignor's people's sudden clatter
Above us—bound to spoil such idle chatter
As ours: it were indeed a serious matter
If silly talk like ours should put to shame
The pious man, the man devoid of blame,
The . . . ah but—ah but, all the same,
No mere mortal has a right
To carry that exalted air;
Best people are not angels quite:
While—not the worst of people's doings scare
The devil; so there's that proud look to spare!
Which is mere counsel to myself, mind! for
I have just been the holy Monsignor:
And I was you too, Luigi's gentle mother,
And you too, Luigi!—how that Luigi started
Out of the turret—doubtlessly departed
On some good errand or another,
For he passed just now in a traveller's trim,
And the sullen company that prowled
About his path, I noticed, scowled
As if they had lost a prey in him.
And I was Jules the sculptor's bride,
And I was Ottima beside,
And now what am I?—tired of fooling.
Day for folly, night for schooling!
New Year's day is over and spent,
Ill or well, I must be content.
Even my lily's asleep, I vow:
Wake up—here's a friend I've plucked you:
Call this flower a heart's-ease now!
Something rare, let me instruct you,
Is this, with petals triply swollen,
Three times spotted, thrice the pollen;
While the leaves and parts that witness
Old proportions and their fitness,
Here remain unchanged, unmoved now;
Call this pampered thing improved now!
Suppose there's a king of the flowers
And a girl-show held in his bowers—
"Look ye, buds, this growth of ours,"
Says he, "Zanze from the Brenta,
I have made her gorge polenta
Till both cheeks are near as bouncing
As her . . . name there's no pronouncing!
See this heightened colour too,
For she swilled Breganze wine
Till her nose turned deep carmine;
'Twas but white when wild she grew.
And only by this Zanze's eyes
Of which we could not change the size,
The magnitude of all achieved
Otherwise, may be perceived."

[1] "Have mercy upon me, O God!"

Oh what a drear dark close to my poor day!
How could that red sun drop in that black cloud?
Ah Pippa, morning's rule is moved away,
Dispensed with, never more to be allowed!
Day's turn is over, now arrives the night's.
Oh lark, be day's apostle
To mavis, merle and throstle,
Bid them their betters jostle
From day and its delights!
But at night, brother howlet, over the woods,
Toll the world to thy chantry;
Sing to the bats' sleek sisterhoods
Full complines with gallantry:
Then, owls and bats,
Cowls and twats,
Monks and nuns, in a cloister's moods,
Adjourn to the oak-stump pantry!

[*After she has begun to undress herself.*

Now, one thing I should like to really know:
How near I ever might approach all these
I only fancied being, this long day:
—Approach, I mean, so as to touch them, so
As to . . . in some way . . . move them—if you please,
Do good or evil to them some slight way.
For instance, if I wind
Silk to-morrow, my silk may bind

[*Sitting on the bedside.*

And border Ottima's cloak's hem.
Ah me, and my important part with them,
This morning's hymn half promised when I rose!
True in some sense or other, I suppose.

[*As she lies down.*

God bless me! I can pray no more tonight.
No doubt, some way or other, hymns say right.

All service ranks the same with God—
With God, whose puppets, best and worst,
Are we: there is no last nor first.

[*She sleeps.*

1841

CAVALIER TUNES

I. Marching Along

I

Kentish Sir Byng stood for his King,
Bidding the crop-headed Parliament swing:
And, pressing a troop unable to stoop
And see the rogues flourish and honest folk droop,
Marched them along, fifty-score strong,
Great-hearted gentlemen, singing this song.

II

God for King Charles! Pym and such carles
To the Devil that prompts 'em their treasonous parles!
Cavaliers, up! Lips from the cup,
Hands from the pasty, nor bite take nor sup
Till you're—
Chorus.—*Marching along, fifty-score strong,*
Great-hearted gentlemen, singing this song.

III

Hampden to hell, and his obsequies' knell
Serve Hazelrig, Fiennes, and young Harry as well!
England, good cheer! Rupert is near!
Kentish and loyalists, keep we not here
Chorus.—*Marching along, fifty-score strong,*
Great-hearted gentlemen, singing this song?

IV

Then, God for King Charles! Pym and his snarls
To the Devil that pricks on such pestilent carles!
Hold by the right, you double your might;
So, onward to Nottingham, fresh for the fight,
Chorus.—*March we along, fifty-score strong,*
Great-hearted gentlemen, singing this song!

II. Give a Rouse

I

King Charles, and who'll do him right now?
King Charles, and who's ripe for fight now?
Give a rouse: here's, in hell's despite now,
King Charles!

II

Who gave me the goods that went since?
Who raised me the house that sank once?

Who helped me to gold I spent since?
Who found me in wine you drank once?
  CHORUS.—*King Charles, and who'll do him right now?*
  King Charles, and who's ripe for fight now?
  Give a rouse: here's, in hell's despite now,
  King Charles!

III

To whom used my boy George quaff else,
By the old fool's side that begot him?
For whom did he cheer and laugh else,
While Noll's damned troopers shot him?
  CHORUS.—*King Charles, and who'll do him right now?*
  King Charles, and who's ripe for fight now?
  Give a rouse: here's, in hell's despite now,
  King Charles!

III. BOOT AND SADDLE

I

Boot, saddle, to horse, and away!
Rescue my castle before the hot day
Brightens to blue from its silvery grey,
  CHORUS.—*Boot, saddle, to horse, and away!*

II

Ride past the suburbs, asleep as you'd say;
Many's the friend there, will listen and pray
"God's luck to gallants that strike up the lay—
  CHORUS.—*Boot, saddle, to horse, and away!*"

III

Forty miles off, like a roebuck at bay,
Flouts Castle Brancepeth the Roundheads' array:
Who laughs, "Good fellows ere this, by my fay,
  CHORUS.—*Boot, saddle, to horse, and away!*"

IV

Who? My wife Gertrude; that, honest and gay,
Laughs when you talk of surrendering, "Nay!
I've better counsellors; what counsel they?
  CHORUS.—*Boot, saddle, to horse, and away!*"

1842

THE LOST LEADER

I

JUST for a handful of silver he left us,
  Just for a riband to stick in his coat—
Found the one gift of which fortune bereft us,
  Lost all the others she lets us devote;
They, with the gold to give, doled him out silver,
  So much was theirs who so little allowed:
How all our copper had gone for his service!
  Rags—were they purple, his heart had been proud!
We that had loved him so, followed him, honoured him,
  Lived in his mild and magnificent eye,
Learned his great language, caught his clear accents,
  Made him our pattern to live and to die!
Shakespeare was of us, Milton was for us,
  Burns, Shelley, were with us,—they watch from their graves!
He alone breaks from the van and the freemen,
  —He alone sinks to the rear and the slaves!

II

We shall march prospering,—not thro' his presence;
  Songs may inspirit us,—not from his lyre;
Deeds will be done,—while he boasts his quiescence,
  Still bidding crouch whom the rest bade aspire:
Blot out his name, then, record one lost soul more,
  One task more declined, one more footpath untrod,
One more devils'-triumph and sorrow for angels,
  One wrong more to man, one more insult to God!
Life's night begins: let him never come back to us!
  There would be doubt, hesitation and pain,
Forced praise on our part—the glimmer of twilight,
  Never glad confident morning again!
Best fight on well, for we taught him—strike gallantly,

Menace our heart ere we master his own;
Then let him receive the new knowledge and wait us,
Pardoned in heaven, the first by the throne!

1845

"HOW THEY BROUGHT THE GOOD NEWS FROM GHENT TO AIX"[1]

[16—.]

I

I SPRANG to the stirrup, and Joris, and he;
I galloped, Dirck galloped, we galloped all three;
"Good speed!" cried the watch, as the gate-bolts undrew;
"Speed!" echoed the wall to us galloping through;
Behind shut the postern, the lights sank to rest,
And into the midnight we galloped abreast.

II

Not a word to each other; we kept the great pace
Neck by neck, stride by stride, never changing our place;
I turned in my saddle and made its girths tight,
Then shortened each stirrup, and set the pique right,
Rebuckled the cheek-strap, chained slacker the bit,
Nor galloped less steadily Roland a whit.

III

'Twas moonset at starting; but while we drew near
Lokeren, the cocks crew and twilight dawned clear;
At Boom, a great yellow star came out to see;
At Düffeld, 'twas morning as plain as could be;
And from Mecheln church-steeple we heard the half-chime,
So, Joris broke silence with, "Yet there is time!"

IV

At Aershot, up leaped of a sudden the sun,
And against him the cattle stood black every one,
To stare thro' the mist at us galloping past,
And I saw my stout galloper Roland at last,
With resolute shoulders, each butting away
The haze, as some bluff river headland its spray:

V

And his low head and crest, just one sharp ear bent back
For my voice, and the other pricked out on his track;
And one eye's black intelligence,—ever that glance
O'er its white edge at me, his own master, askance!
And the thick heavy spume-flakes which aye and anon
His fierce lips shook upwards in galloping on.

VI

By Hasselt, Dirck groaned; and cried Joris, "Stay spur!
Your Roos galloped bravely, the fault's not in her,
We'll remember at Aix"—for one heard the quick wheeze
Of her chest, saw the stretched neck and staggering knees,
And sunk tail, and horrible heave of the flank,
As down on her haunches she shuddered and sank.

VII

So, we were left galloping, Joris and I,
Past Looz and past Tongres, no cloud in the sky;
The broad sun above laughed a pitiless laugh,
'Neath our feet broke the brittle bright stubble like chaff;
Till over by Dalhem a dome-spire sprang white,
And "Gallop," gasped Joris, "for Aix is in sight!"

VIII

"How they'll greet us!"—and all in a moment his roan
Rolled neck and croup over, lay dead as a stone;

[1] There is no historical basis for this poem though such an episode is not inconsistent with Dutch history in the wars against Spain. The geography of the Lowlands is, however, accurate.

And there was my Roland to bear the whole weight
Of the news which alone could save Aix from her fate,
With his nostrils like pits full of blood to the brim,
And with circles of red for his eye-sockets' rim.

IX

Then I cast loose my buffcoat, each holster let fall,
Shook off both my jack-boots, let go belt and all,
Stood up in the stirrup, leaned, patted his ear,
Called my Roland his pet-name, my horse without peer;
Clapped my hands, laughed and sang, any noise, bad or good,
Till at length into Aix Roland galloped and stood.

X

And all I remember is—friends flocking round
As I sat with his head 'twixt my knees on the ground;
And no voice but was praising this Roland of mine,
As I poured down his throat our last measure of wine,
Which (the burgesses voted by common consent)
Was no more than his due who brought good news from Ghent.

1845

GARDEN FANCIES

I. The Flower's Name

I

Here's the garden she walked across,
  Arm in my arm, such a short while since:
Hark, now I push its wicket, the moss
  Hinders the hinges and makes them wince!
She must have reached this shrub ere she turned,
  As back with that murmur the wicket swung;
For she laid the poor snail, my chance foot spurned,
  To feed and forget it the leaves among.

II

Down this side of the gravel-walk
  She went while her robe's edge brushed the box:
And here she paused in her gracious talk
  To point me a moth on the milk-white phlox.
Roses, ranged in valiant row,
  I will never think that she passed you by!
She loves you noble roses, I know;
  But yonder, see, where the rock-plants lie!

III

This flower she stopped at, finger on lip,
  Stooped over, in doubt, as settling its claim;
Till she gave me, with pride to make no slip,
  Its soft meandering Spanish name:
What a name! Was it love or praise?
  Speech half-asleep or song half-awake?
I must learn Spanish, one of these days,
  Only for that slow sweet name's sake.

IV

Roses, if I live and do well,
  I may bring her, one of these days,
To fix you fast with as fine a spell,
  Fit you each with his Spanish phrase;
But do not detain me now; for she lingers
  There, like sunshine over the ground,
And ever I see her soft white fingers
  Searching after the bud she found.

V

Flower, you Spaniard, look that you grow not,
  Stay as you are and be loved for ever!
Bud, if I kiss you 'tis that you blow not:
  Mind, the shut pink mouth opens never!
For while it pouts, her fingers wrestle,
  Twinkling the audacious leaves between,
Till round they turn and down they nestle—
  Is not the dear mark still to be seen?

VI

Where I find her not, beauties vanish;
  Whither I follow her, beauties flee;
Is there no method to tell her in Spanish
  June's twice June since she breathed it with me?
Come, bud, show me the least of her traces,
  Treasure my lady's lightest footfall!
—Ah, you may flout and turn up your faces—
  Roses, you are not so fair after all!

II. Sibrandus Schafnaburgensis

I

Plague take all your pedants, say I!
He who wrote what I hold in my hand,
Centuries back was so good as to die,
Leaving this rubbish to cumber the land;
This, that was a book in its time,
Printed on paper and bound in leather,
Last month in the white of a matin-prime
Just when the birds sang all together.

II

Into the garden I brought it to read,
And under the arbute and laurustine
Read it, so help me grace in my need,
From title-page to closing line.
Chapter on chapter did I count,
As a curious traveller counts Stonehenge;[1]
Added up the mortal amount;
And then proceeded to my revenge.

III

Yonder's a plum-tree with a crevice
An owl would build in, were he but sage;
For a lap of moss, like a fine pont-levis
In a castle of the Middle Age,
Joins to a lip of gum, pure amber;
When he'd be private, there might he spend
Hours alone in his lady's chamber:
Into this crevice I dropped our friend.

IV

Splash, went he, as under he ducked,
—At the bottom, I knew, rain-drippings stagnate:
Next, a handful of blossoms I plucked
To bury him with, my bookshelf's magnate;
Then I went in-doors, brought out a loaf,
Half a cheese, and a bottle of Chablis:
Lay on the grass and forgot the oaf
Over a jolly chapter of Rabelais.

V

Now, this morning, betwixt the moss
And gum that locked our friend in limbo,
A spider had spun his web across,
And sat in the midst with arms akimbo:

[1] A temple-like arrangement of huge stones, some as much as twenty-two feet in height, built in Britain at the end of the stone age. What this implies as to the size and weight of Sibrandus's chapters is obvious.

So, I took pity, for learning's sake,
And, *de profundis, accentibus lætis,*
Cantate![1] quoth I, as I got a rake;
And up I fished his delectable treatise.

VI

Here you have it, dry in the sun,
With all the binding all of a blister,
And great blue spots where the ink has run,
And reddish streaks that wink and glister
O'er the page so beautifully yellow:
Oh, well have the droppings played their tricks!
Did he guess how toadstools grow, this fellow?
Here's one stuck in his chapter six!

VII

How did he like it when the live creatures
Tickled and toused and browsed him all over,
And worm, slug, eft, with serious features,
Came in, each one, for his right of trover?
—When the water-beetle with great blind deaf face
Made of her eggs the stately deposit,
And the newt borrowed just so much of the preface
As tiled in the top of his black wife's closet?

VIII

All that life and fun and romping,
All that frisking and twisting and coupling,
While slowly our poor friend's leaves were swamping
And clasps were cracking and covers suppling!
As if you had carried sour John Knox
To the play-house at Paris, Vienna or Munich,
Fastened him into a front-row box,
And danced off the ballet with trousers and tunic.

IX

Come, old martyr! What, torment enough is it?
Back to my room shall you take your sweet self.

[1] "Come forth from the depths with flaming joy."

Good-bye, mother-beetle; husband-eft, *sufficit!*
  See the snug niche I have made on my shelf!
A.'s book shall prop you up, B.'s shall cover you,
  Here's C. to be grave with, or D. to be gay,
And with E. on each side, and F. right over you,
Dry-rot at ease till the Judgment-day!

1844

SOLILOQUY OF THE SPANISH CLOISTER

I

Gr-r-r—there go, my heart's abhorrence!
  Water your damned flower-pots, do!
If hate killed men, Brother Lawrence,
  God's blood, would not mine kill you!
What? your myrtle-bush wants trimming?
  Oh, that rose has prior claims—
Needs its leaden vase filled brimming?
  Hell dry you up with its flames!

II

At the meal we sit together:
  Salve tibi! I must hear
Wise talk of the kind of weather,
  Sort of season, time of year:
Not a plenteous cork-crop: scarcely
  Dare we hope oak-galls, I doubt:
What's the Latin name for "parsley"?
  What's the Greek name for Swine's Snout?

III

Whew! We'll have our platter burnished,
  Laid with care on our own shelf!
With a fire-new spoon we're furnished,
  And a goblet for ourself,
Rinsed like something sacrificial
  Ere 'tis fit to touch our chaps—
Marked with L. for our initial!
  (He-he! There his lily snaps!)

IV

Saint, forsooth! While brown Dolores
  Squats outside the Convent bank
With Sanchicha, telling stories,
  Steeping tresses in the tank,
Blue-black, lustrous, thick like horsehairs,
  —Can't I see his dead eye glow,
Bright as 'twere a Barbary corsair's?
  (That is, if he'd let it show!)

V

When he finishes refection,
  Knife and fork he never lays
Cross-wise, to my recollection,
  As do I, in Jesu's praise.
I the Trinity illustrate,
  Drinking watered orange-pulp—
In three sips the Arian [1] frustrate;
  While he drains his at one gulp.

VI

Oh, those melons? If he's able
  We're to have a feast! so nice!
One goes to the Abbot's table,
  All of us get each a slice.
How go on your flowers? None double?
  Not one fruit-sort can you spy?
Strange!—And I, too, at such trouble,
  Keep them close-nipped on the sly!

VII

There's a great text in Galatians,
  Once you trip on it, entails
Twenty-nine distinct damnations,
  One sure, if another fails:
If I trip him just a-dying,
  Sure of heaven as sure can be,
Spin him round and send him flying
  Off to hell, a Manichee? [2]

VIII

Or, my scrofulous French novel
  On grey paper with blunt type!
Simply glance at it, you grovel
  Hand and foot in Belial's gripe:
If I double down its pages
  At the woeful sixteenth print,
When he gathers his greengages,
  Ope a sieve and slip it in't?

IX

Or, there's Satan!—one might venture
  Pledge one's soul to him, yet leave
Such a flaw in the indenture

[1] A follower of Arius who, in the fourth century, declared Christ to be a created being, inferior to God the Father, and so denied the Trinity.

[2] A follower of Manes, a third century Persian, whose doctrine of the blending of good and evil was declared heretical by the Church.

As he'd miss till, past retrieve,
Blasted lay that rose-acacia
We're so proud of! *Hy*, *Zy*, *Hine* . . .
'St, there's Vespers! *Plena gratiâ*
Ave, *Virgo!*[1] Gr-r-r—you swine!

1842

THE LABORATORY

Ancien Régime

I

Now that I, tying thy glass mask tightly,
May gaze thro' these faint smokes curling whitely,
As thou pliest thy trade in this devil's-smithy—
Which is the poison to poison her, prithee?

II

He is with her, and they know that I know
Where they are, what they do: they believe my tears flow
While they laugh, laugh at me, at me fled to the drear
Empty church, to pray God in, for them!—I am here.

III

Grind away, moisten and mash up thy paste,
Pound at thy powder,—I am not in haste!
Better sit thus, and observe thy strange things,
Than go where men wait me and dance at the King's.

IV

That in the mortar—you call it a gum?
Ah, the brave tree whence such gold oozings come!
And yonder soft phial, the exquisite blue,
Sure to taste sweetly,—is that poison too?

V

Had I but all of them, thee and thy treasures,
What a wild crowd of invisible pleasures!
To carry pure death in an earring, a casket,
A signet, a fan-mount, a filigree basket!

[1] The beginning of the vesper prayer, "Hail Mary, full of grace." Browning has varied the Latin somewhat.

VI

Soon, at the King's, a mere lozenge to give,
And Pauline should have just thirty minutes to live!
But to light a pastile, and Elise, with her head
And her breast and her arms and her hands, should drop dead!

VII

Quick—is it finished? The colour's too grim!
Why not soft like the phial's, enticing and dim?
Let it brighten her drink, let her turn it and stir,
And try it and taste, ere she fix and prefer!

VIII

What a drop! She's not little, no minion like me!
That's why she ensnared him: this never will free
The soul from those masculine eyes,—say, "no!"
To that pulse's magnificent come-and-go.

IX

For only last night, as they whispered, I brought
My own eyes to bear on her so, that I thought
Could I keep them one half minute fixed she would fall
Shrivelled; she fell not; yet this does it all!

X

Not that I bid you spare her the pain;
Let death be felt and the proof remain:
Brand, burn up, bite into its grace—
He is sure to remember her dying face!

XI

Is it done? Take my mask off! Nay, be not morose;
It kills her, and this prevents seeing it close:
The delicate droplet, my whole fortune's fee!
If it hurts her, beside, can it ever hurt me?

XII

Now, take all my jewels, gorge gold to your fill,
You may kiss me, old man, on my mouth if you will!

But brush this dust off me, lest horror it brings
Ere I know it—next moment I dance at the King's!

1844

CRISTINA[1]

I

SHE should never have looked at me
  If she meant I should not love her!
There are plenty . . . men, you call such,
  I suppose . . . she may discover
All her soul to, if she pleases,
  And yet leave much as she found them:
But I'm not so, and she knew it
  When she fixed me, glancing round them.

II

What? To fix me thus meant nothing?
  But I can't tell (there's my weakness)
What her look said!—no vile cant, sure,
  About "need to strew the bleakness
Of some lone shore with its pearl seed,
  That the sea feels"—no "strange yearning
That such souls have, most to lavish
  Where there's chance of least returning."

III

Oh, we're sunk enough here, God knows!
  But not quite so sunk that moments,
Sure tho' seldom, are denied us,
  When the spirit's true endowments
Stand out plainly from its false ones,
  And apprise it if pursuing
Or the right way or the wrong way,
  To its triumph or undoing.

IV

There are flashes struck from midnights,
  There are fire-flames noondays kindle,
Whereby piled-up honours perish,
  Whereby swollen ambitions dwindle,
While just this or that poor impulse,
  Which for once had play unstifled,

[1] Cristina, a princess of the kingdom of the Two Sicilies, married and became the queen of Spain (1829). She was notorious as a coquette and it is said that more than one victim, too openly responding to her glances, found himself languishing in prison. Her trifling with love is the starting point for Browning's poem, spoken by another type of lover.

Seems the sole work of a life-time
  That away the rest have trifled.

V

Doubt you if, in some such moment,
  As she fixed me, she felt clearly,
Ages past the soul existed,
  Here an age 'tis resting merely,
And hence fleets again for ages,
  While the true end, sole and single,
It stops here for is, this love-way,
  With some other soul to mingle?

VI

Else it loses what it lived for,
  And eternally must lose it;
Better ends may be in prospect,
  Deeper blisses (if you choose it),
But this life's end and this love-bliss
  Have been lost here. Doubt you whether
This she felt as, looking at me,
  Mine and her souls rushed together?

VII

Oh, observe! Of course, next moment,
  The world's honours, in derision,
Trampled out the light for ever:
  Never fear but there's provision
Of the devil's to quench knowledge
  Lest we walk the earth in rapture!
—Making those who catch God's secret
  Just so much more prize their capture!

VIII

Such am I: the secret's mine now!
  She has lost me, I have gained her;
Her soul's mine: and thus, grown perfect,
  I shall pass my life's remainder.
Life will just hold out the proving
  Both our powers, alone and blended:
And then, come the next life quickly!
  This world's use will have been ended.

1842

THE LOST MISTRESS

I

ALL's over, then: does truth sound bitter
  As one at first believes?
Hark, 'tis the sparrows' good-night twitter
  About your cottage eaves!

II

And the leaf-buds on the vine are woolly,
I noticed that, to-day;
One day more bursts them open fully
—You know the red turns grey.

III

To-morrow we meet the same then, dearest?
May I take your hand in mine?
Mere friends are we,—well, friends the merest
Keep much that I resign:

IV

For each glance of the eye so bright and black,
Though I keep with heart's endeavour,—
Your voice, when you wish the snowdrops back,
Though it stay in my soul for ever!—

V

Yet I will but say what mere friends say,
Or only a thought stronger;
I will hold your hand but as long as all may,
Or so very little longer!

1845

EARTH'S IMMORTALITIES

FAME

See, as the prettiest graves will do in time,
Our poet's wants the freshness of its prime;
Spite of the sexton's browsing horse, the sods
Have struggled through its binding osier rods;
Headstone and half-sunk footstone lean awry,
Wanting the brick-work promised by-and-by;
How the minute grey lichens, plate o'er plate,
Have softened down the crisp-cut name and date!

LOVE

So, the year's done with!
(*Love me for ever!*)
All March begun with,
April's endeavour;
May-wreaths that bound me
June needs must sever;
Now snows fall round me,
Quenching June's fever—
(*Love me for ever!*)

1845

MEETING AT NIGHT

I

The grey sea and the long black land;
And the yellow half-moon large and low;
And the startled little waves that leap
In fiery ringlets from their sleep,
As I gain the cove with pushing prow,
And quench its speed i' the slushy sand.

II

Then a mile of warm sea-scented beach;
Three fields to cross till a farm appears;
A tap at the pane, the quick sharp scratch
And blue spurt of a lighted match,
And a voice less loud, thro' its joys and fears,
Than the two hearts beating each to each!

1845

PARTING AT MORNING

Round the cape of a sudden came the sea,
And the sun looked over the mountain's rim:
And straight was a path of gold for him,
And the need of a world of men for me.

1845

SONG

I

Nay but you, who do not love her,
Is she not pure gold, my mistress?
Holds earth aught—speak truth—above her?
Aught like this tress, see, and this tress,
And this last fairest tress of all,
So fair, see, ere I let it fall?

II

Because, you spend your lives in praising;
To praise, you search the wide world over:
Then why not witness, calmly gazing,
If earth holds aught—speak truth—above her?
Above this tress, and this, I touch
But cannot praise, I love so much!

1845

A WOMAN'S LAST WORD

I

Let's contend no more, Love,
Strive nor weep:
All be as before, Love,
—Only sleep!

II

What so wild as words are?
  I and thou
In debate, as birds are,
  Hawk on bough!

III

See the creature stalking
  While we speak!
Hush and hide the talking,
  Cheek on cheek!

IV

What so false as truth is,
  False to thee?
Where the serpent's tooth is
  Shun the tree—

V

Where the apple reddens
  Never pry—
Lest we lose our Edens,
  Eve and I.

VI

Be a god and hold me
  With a charm!
Be a man and fold me
  With thine arm!

VII

Teach me, only teach, Love!
  As I ought
I will speak thy speech, Love,
  Think thy thought—

VIII

Meet, if thou require it,
  Both demands,
Laying flesh and spirit
  In thy hands.

IX

That shall be to-morrow
  Not to-night:
I must bury sorrow
  Out of sight:

X

—Must a little weep, Love,
  (Foolish me!)
And so fall asleep, Love,
  Loved by thee.

1855

EVELYN HOPE

I

Beautiful Evelyn Hope is dead!
  Sit and watch by her side an hour.
That is her book-shelf, this her bed;
  She plucked that piece of geranium-flower,
Beginning to die too, in the glass;
  Little has yet been changed, I think:
The shutters are shut, no light may pass
  Save two long rays thro' the hinge's chink.

II

Sixteen years old when she died!
  Perhaps she had scarcely heard my name;
It was not her time to love; beside,
  Her life had many a hope and aim,
Duties enough and little cares,
  And now was quiet, now astir,
Till God's hand beckoned unawares,—
  And the sweet white brow is all of her.

III

Is it too late then, Evelyn Hope?
  What, your soul was pure and true,
The good stars met in your horoscope,
  Made you of spirit, fire and dew—
And, just because I was thrice as old
  And our paths in the world diverged so wide,
Each was nought to each, must I be told?
  We were fellow mortals, nought beside?

IV

No, indeed! for God above
  Is great to grant, as mighty to make,
And creates the love to reward the love:
  I claim you still, for my own love's sake!
Delayed it may be for more lives yet,
  Through worlds I shall traverse, not a few:
Much is to learn, much to forget
  Ere the time be come for taking you.

V

But the time will come,—at last it will,
  When Evelyn Hope, what meant (I shall say)
In the lower earth, in the years long still,
  That body and soul so pure and gay?
Why your hair was amber, I shall divine,

And your mouth of your own geranium's red—
And what you would do with me, in fine,
In the new life come in the old one's stead.

VI

I have lived (I shall say) so much since then,
Given up myself so many times,
Gained me the gains of various men,
Ransacked the ages, spoiled the climes;
Yet one thing, one, in my soul's full scope,
Either I missed or itself missed me:
And I want and find you, Evelyn Hope!
What is the issue? let us see!

VII

I loved you, Evelyn, all the while!
My heart seemed full as it could hold;
There was place and to spare for the frank young smile,
And the red young mouth, and the hair's young gold.
So, hush,—I will give you this leaf to keep:
See, I shut it inside the sweet cold hand!
There that is our secret: go to sleep!
You will wake, and remember, and understand.

1855

LOVE AMONG THE RUINS

I

Where the quiet-coloured end of evening smiles,
Miles and miles
On the solitary pastures where our sheep
Half-asleep
Tinkle homeward thro' the twilight, stray or stop
As they crop—
Was the site once of a city great and gay,
(So they say)
Of our country's very capital, its prince
Ages since
Held his court in, gathered councils, wielding far
Peace or war.

II

Now,—the country does not even boast a tree,
As you see,
To distinguish slopes of verdure, certain rills
From the hills
Intersect and give a name to, (else they run
Into one)
Where the domed and daring palace shot its spires
Up like fires
O'er the hundred-gated circuit of a wall
Bounding all,
Made of marble, men might march on nor be pressed,
Twelve abreast.

III

And such plenty and perfection, see, of grass
Never was!
Such a carpet as, this summer-time, o'erspreads
And embeds
Every vestige of the city, guessed alone,
Stock or stone—
Where a multitude of men breathed joy and woe
Long ago;
Lust of glory pricked their hearts up, dread of shame
Struck them tame;
And that glory and that shame alike, the gold
Bought and sold.

IV

Now,—the single little turret that remains
On the plains,
By the caper overrooted, by the gourd
Overscored,
While the patching houseleek's head of blossom winks
Through the chinks—
Marks the basement whence a tower in ancient time
Sprang sublime,
And a burning ring, all round, the chariots traced
As they raced,
And the monarch and his minions and his dames
Viewed the games.

V

And I know, while thus the quiet-coloured eve
Smiles to leave
To their folding, all our many-tinkling fleece
In such peace,

And the slopes and rills in undistinguished grey
Melt away—
That a girl with eager eyes and yellow hair
Waits me there
In the turret whence the charioteers caught soul
For the goal,
When the king looked, where she looks now, breathless, dumb
Till I come.

VI

But he looked upon the city, every side,
Far and wide,
All the mountains topped with temples, all the glades'
Colonnades,
All the causeys, bridges, aqueducts,—and then,
All the men!
When I do come, she will speak not, she will stand,
Either hand
On my shoulder, give her eyes the first embrace
Of my face,
Ere we rush, ere we extinguish sight and speech
Each on each.

VII

In one year they sent a million fighters forth
South and North,
And they built their gods a brazen pillar high
As the sky,
Yet reserved a thousand chariots in full force—
Gold, of course.
Oh heart! oh blood that freezes, blood that burns!
Earth's returns
For whole centuries of folly, noise and sin!
Shut them in,
With their triumphs and their glories and the rest!
Love is best.

1855

UP AT A VILLA—DOWN IN THE CITY

(AS DISTINGUISHED BY AN ITALIAN PERSON OF QUALITY)

I

HAD I but plenty of money, money enough and to spare,
The house for me, no doubt, were a house in the city-square;
Ah, such a life, such a life, as one leads at the window there!

II

Something to see, by Bacchus, something to hear, at least!
There, the whole day long, one's life is a perfect feast;
While up at a villa one lives, I maintain it, no more than a beast.

III

Well now, look at our villa! stuck like the horn of a bull
Just on a mountain-edge as bare as the creature's skull,
Save a mere shag of a bush with hardly a leaf to pull!
—I scratch my own, sometimes, to see if the hair's turned wool.

IV

But the city, oh the city—the square with the houses! Why?
They are stone-faced, white as a curd, there's something to take the eye!
Houses in four straight lines, not a single front awry;
You watch who crosses and gossips, who saunters, who hurries by;
Green blinds, as a matter of course, to draw when the sun gets high;
And the shops with fanciful signs which are painted properly.

V

What of a villa? Though winter be over in March by rights,
'Tis May perhaps ere the snow shall have withered well off the heights:

You've the brown ploughed land before, where the oxen steam and wheeze,
And the hills over-smoke behind by the faint grey-olive trees

VI

Is it better in May, I ask you? You've summer all at once;
In a day he leaps complete with a few strong April suns.
'Mid the sharp short emerald wheat, scarce risen three fingers well,
The wild tulip, at end of its tube, blows out its great red bell
Like a thin clear bubble of blood, for the children to pick and sell.

VII

Is it ever hot in the square? There's a fountain to spout and splash!
In the shade it sings and springs; in the shine such foam-bows flash
On the horses with curling fish-tails, that prance and paddle and pash
Round the lady atop in her conch—fifty gazers do not abash,
Though all that she wears is some weeds round her waist in a sort of sash.

VIII

All the year long at the villa, nothing to see though you linger,
Except yon cypress that points like death's lean lifted forefinger.
Some think fireflies pretty, when they mix i' the corn and mingle,
Or thrid the stinking hemp till the stalks of it seem a-tingle.
Late August or early September, the stunning cicala is shrill,
And the bees keep their tiresome whine round the resinous firs on the hill.
Enough of the seasons,—I spare you the months of the fever and chill.

IX

Ere you open your eyes in the city, the blessed church-bells begin:
No sooner the bells leave off than the diligence rattles in:
You get the pick of the news, and it costs you never a pin.
By-and-by there's the travelling doctor gives pills, lets blood, draws teeth;
Or the Pulcinello-trumpet[1] breaks up the market beneath.
At the post-office such a scene-picture—the new play, piping hot!
And a notice how, only this morning, three liberal thieves were shot.
Above it, behold the Archbishop's most fatherly of rebukes,
And beneath, with his crown and his lion, some little new law of the Duke's!
Or a sonnet with flowery marge, to the Reverend Don So-and-so
Who is Dante, Boccaccio, Petrarca, Saint Jerome and Cicero,
"And moreover," (the sonnet goes rhyming,) "the skirts of Saint Paul has reached,
Having preached us those six Lent-lectures more unctuous than ever he preached."
Noon strikes,—here sweeps the procession! our Lady borne smiling and smart
With a pink gauze gown all spangles, and seven swords[2] stuck in her heart!
Bang-whang-whang goes the drum, *tootle-te-tootle* the fife;
No keeping one's haunches still: it's the greatest pleasure in life.

X

But bless you, it's dear—it's dear! fowls, wine, at double the rate.
They have clapped a new tax upon salt, and what oil pays passing the gate[3]
It's a horror to think of. And so, the villa for me, not the city!
Beggars can scarcely be choosers: but still—ah, the pity, the pity!
Look, two and two go the priests, then the monks with cowls and sandals,
And the penitents dressed in white shirts, a-holding the yellow candles;
One, he carries a flag up straight, and another a cross with handles,

[1] Pulcinello was the clown of strolling players or puppet shows.
[2] To symbolize the Seven Sorrows of our Lady.
[3] Under the Italian tax system, cities collected a tax on all provisions as they entered the city

And the Duke's guard brings up the rear, for the better prevention of scandals:
Bang-whang-whang goes the drum, *tootle-te-tootle* the fife.
Oh, a day in the city-square, there is no such pleasure in life!

1855

A TOCCATA OF GALUPPI'S [1]

I

OH Galuppi, Baldassare, this is very sad to find!
I can hardly misconceive you; it would prove me deaf and blind;
But although I take your meaning, 'tis with such a heavy mind!

II

Here you come with your old music, and here's all the good it brings.
What, they lived once thus at Venice where the merchants were the kings,
Where Saint Mark's is, where the Doges used to wed the sea with rings?

III

Ay, because the sea's the street there; and 'tis arched by . . . what you call
. . . Shylock's bridge with houses on it, where they kept the carnival:
I was never out of England—it's as if I saw it all.

IV

Did young people take their pleasure when the sea was warm in May?
Balls and masks begun at midnight, burning ever to mid-day,
When they made up fresh adventures for the morrow, do you say?

V

Was a lady such a lady, cheeks so round and lips so red,—
On her neck the small face buoyant, like a bell-flower on its bed,
O'er the breast's superb abundance where a man might base his head?

VI

Well, and it was graceful of them—they'd break talk off and afford
—She, to bite her mask's black velvet—he, to finger on his sword,
While you sat and played Toccatas, stately at the clavichord?

VII

What? Those lesser thirds so plaintive, sixths diminished, sigh on sigh,
Told them something? Those suspensions, those solutions—"Must we die?"
Those commiserating sevenths—"Life might last! we can but try!"

VIII

"Were you happy?"—"Yes."—"And are you still as happy?"—"Yes. And you?"
—"Then, more kisses!"—"Did *I* stop them, when a million seemed so few?"
Hark, the dominant's persistence till it must be answered to!

IX

So, an octave struck the answer. Oh, they praised you, I dare say!
"Brave Galuppi! that was music! good alike at grave and gay!
I can always leave off talking when I hear a master play!"

X

Then they left you for their pleasure: till in due time, one by one,
Some with lives that came to nothing, some with deeds as well undone,
Death stepped tacitly and took them where they never see the sun.

XI

But when I sit down to reason, think to take my stand nor swerve,
While I triumph o'er a secret wrung from nature's close reserve,
In you come with your cold music till I creep thro' every nerve.

XII

Yes, you, like a ghostly cricket, creaking where a house was burned:
"Dust and ashes, dead and done with, Venice spent what Venice earned.
The soul, doubtless, is immortal—where a soul can be discerned.

[1] Baldassare Galuppi (1706–1785) was a famous Italian musician who lived and worked also in England and Russia. A toccata (or touch-piece) had some of the freedom of an improvisation rather than the more formal organization of a sonata.

XIII

"Yours for instance: you know physics, something of geology,
Mathematics are your pastime; souls shall rise in their degree;
Butterflies may dread extinction,—you'll not die, it cannot be!

XIV

"As for Venice and her people, merely born to bloom and drop,
Here on earth they bore their fruitage, mirth and folly were the crop:
What of soul was left, I wonder, when the kissing had to stop?

XV

"Dust and ashes!" So you creak it, and I want the heart to scold.
Dear dead women, with such hair, too—what's become of all the gold
Used to hang and brush their bosoms? I feel chilly and grown old.

1855

OLD PICTURES IN FLORENCE[1]

I

THE morn when first it thunders in March,
The eel in the pond gives a leap, they say:
As I leaned and looked over the aloed arch
Of the villa-gate this warm March day,
No flash snapped, no dumb thunder rolled
In the valley beneath where, white and wide
And washed by the morning water-gold,
Florence lay out on the mountain-side.

II

River and bridge and street and square
Lay mine, as much at my beck and call,
Through the live translucent bath of air,
As the sights in a magic crystal ball.
And of all I saw and of all I praised,
The most to praise and the best to see
Was the startling bell-tower Giotto raised:
But why did it more than startle me?

III

Giotto, how, with that soul of yours,
Could you play me false who loved you so?
Some slights if a certain heart endures
Yet it feels, I would have your fellows know!
I' faith, I perceive not why I should care
To break a silence that suits them best,
But the thing grows somewhat hard to bear
When I find a Giotto join the rest.

---

[1] The poem begins with Browning looking down on the city of Florence from his hillside villa, much upset by the fact that a little picture by Giotto had been found and he hadn't been lucky enough to find it. How could Giotto have played him such a trick as to give the picture to others! The poet falls to thinking, not of the live city below him, but of the imperfect beginners of its great school of art — men whose works are crumbling away in dark chapels. By a transition of thought he is led from their striving imperfection to the perfection of surviving Greek statuary, and, in some of the most striking and Browningesque stanzas of the poem (particularly XI to XVII), he discusses the significance of growth and perfection. The story of Giotto's ○ to which he refers at the end of stanza XVII was taken from the art historian Vasari. Asked to submit samples of his workmanship to the Pope, who was about to commission some paintings, Giotto took up a brush and drew free-hand at one stroke an absolutely perfect circle. Although he refused to submit any further samples, he received the commission. Browning uses the story for his own purposes. The ○ is perfect — and completed. Giotto's more ambitious project, the great bell-tower which he designed and which is still one of the glories of Florence, is even yet incomplete as Giotto planned it.

Browning returns (stanza XXIII) to the idea with which the poem begins — why don't the old masters let the man who really loves them find a painting or so? There follow many names, somewhat confusing to a student unfamiliar with Italian art. A knowledge of the dates and the significance of these painters to the history of art is unnecessary. What Browning says is sufficient and the stanzas should be read in the chatty, conversational mood in which Browning wrote them. Suffice it to note that while he pays his respects to the great names, he doesn't expect to have the luck to find any of their works. But he might find something by one of the lesser painters.

In fact he is quite sure he will, and (stanzas XXXI to the end) out of gratitude he gives in exchange a prophecy of some of the good things which are going to happen to Florence — the Austrians are going to be driven out, Italy is going to be united, and Giotto's Campanile is going to be completed.

IV

On the arch where olives overhead
Print the blue sky with twig and leaf,
(That sharp-curled leaf which they never shed)
'Twixt the aloes, I used to lean in chief,
And mark through the winter afternoons,
By a gift God grants me now and then,
In the mild decline of those suns like moons,
Who walked in Florence, besides her men.

V

They might chirp and chaffer, come and go
For pleasure or profit, her men alive—
My business was hardly with them, I trow,
But with empty cells of the human hive;
—With the chapter-room, the cloister-porch,
The church's apsis, aisle or nave,
Its crypt, one fingers along with a torch,
Its face set full for the sun to shave.

VI

Wherever a fresco peels and drops,
Wherever an outline weakens and wanes
Till the latest life in the painting stops,
Stands One whom each fainter pulse-tick pains:
One, wishful each scrap should clutch the brick,
Each tinge not wholly escape the plaster,
—A lion who dies of an ass's kick,
The wronged great soul of an ancient Master.

VII

For oh, this world and the wrong it does!
They are safe in heaven with their backs to it,
The Michaels and Rafaels, you hum and buzz
Round the works of, you of the little wit!
Do their eyes contract to the earth's old scope,
Now that they see God face to face,
And have all attained to be poets, I hope?
'Tis their holiday now, in any case.

VIII

Much they reck of your praise and you!
But the wronged great souls—can they be quit
Of a world where their work is all to do,
Where you style them, you of the little wit,
Old Master This and Early the Other,
Not dreaming that Old and New are fellows:
A younger succeeds to an elder brother,
Da Vincis derive in good time from Dellos.

IX

And here where your praise might yield returns,
And a handsome word or two give help,
Here, after your kind, the mastiff girns
And the puppy pack of poodles yelp.
What, not a word for Stefano there,
Of brow once prominent and starry,
Called Nature's Ape and the world's despair
For his peerless painting? (See Vasari.)

X

There stands the Master. Study, my friends,
What a man's work comes to! So he plans it,
Performs it, perfects it, makes amends
For the toiling and moiling, and then, *sic transit!*[1]
Happier the thrifty blind-folk labour,
With upturned eye while the hand is busy,
Not sidling a glance at the coin of their neighbour!
'Tis looking downward that makes one dizzy.

XI

"If you knew their work you would deal your dole."
May I take upon me to instruct you?
When Greek Art ran and reached the goal,
Thus much had the world to boast *in fructu*—[2]
The Truth of Man, as by God first spoken,
Which the actual generations garble,
Was re-uttered, and Soul (which Limbs betoken)
And Limbs (Soul informs) made new in marble.

XII

So, you saw yourself as you wished you were,
As you might have been, as you cannot be;
Earth here, rebuked by Olympus there:
And grew content in your poor degree

[1] *Sic transit gloria mundi* — so departs the glory of the world.

[2] "As fruit."

With your little power, by those statues' godhead,
And your little scope, by their eyes' full sway,
And your little grace, by their grace embodied,
And your little date, by their forms that stay.

XIII

You would fain be kinglier, say, than I am?
Even so, you will not sit like Theseus.[1]
You would prove a model? The Son of Priam
Has yet the advantage in arms' and knees' use.
You're wroth—can you slay your snake like Apollo?
You're grieved—still Niobe's the grander!
You live—there's the Racers' frieze to follow:
You die—there's the dying Alexander.

XIV

So, testing your weakness by their strength,
Your meagre charms by their rounded beauty,
Measured by Art in your breadth and length,
You learned—to submit is a mortal's duty.
—When I say "you" 'tis the common soul,
The collective, I mean: the race of Man
That receives life in parts to live in a whole,
And grow here according to God's clear plan.

XV

Growth came when, looking your last on them all,
You turned your eyes inwardly one fine day
And cried with a start—What if we so small
Be greater and grander the while than they?
Are they perfect of lineament, perfect of stature?
In both, of such lower types are we
Precisely because of our wider nature;
For time, theirs—ours, for eternity.

XVI

To-day's brief passion limits their range;
It seethes with the morrow for us and more.
They are perfect—how else? they shall never change:
We are faulty—why not? we have time in store.
The Artificer's hand is not arrested
With us; we are rough-hewn, nowise polished:
They stand for our copy, and, once invested
With all they can teach, we shall see them abolished.

XVII

'Tis a life-long toil till our lump be leaven—
The better! What's come to perfection perishes.
Things learned on earth, we shall practise in heaven:
Works done least rapidly, Art most cherishes.
Thyself shalt afford the example, Giotto!
Thy one work, not to decrease or diminish,
Done at a stroke, was just (was it not?) "O!"
Thy great Campanile is still to finish.

XVIII

Is it true that we are now, and shall be hereafter,
But what and where depend on life's minute?
Hails heavenly cheer or infernal laughter
Our first step out of the gulf or in it?
Shall Man, such step within his endeavour,
Man's face, have no more play and action
Than joy which is crystallised for ever,
Or grief, an eternal petrifaction?

XIX

On which I conclude, that the early painters,
To cries of "Greek Art and what more wish you?"—
Replied, "To become now self-acquainters,
And paint man man, whatever the issue!
Make new hopes shine through the flesh they fray,
New fears aggrandise the rags and tatters:
To bring the invisible full into play!
Let the visible go to the dogs—what matters?"

XX

Give these, I exhort you, their guerdon and glory
For daring so much, before they well did it.
The first of the new, in our race's story,
Beats the last of the old; 'tis no idle quiddit.

1 The references are to famous surviving statues of the classical period.

The worthies began a revolution,
Which if on earth you intend to acknowledge,
Why, honour them now! (ends my allocution)
Nor confer your degree when the folk leave college.

XXI

There's a fancy some lean to and others hate—
That, when this life is ended, begins
New work for the soul in another state,
Where it strives and gets weary, loses and wins:
Where the strong and the weak this world's congeries,
Repeat in large what they practised in small,
Through life after life in unlimited series;
Only the scale's to be changed, that's all.

XXII

Yet I hardly know. When a soul has seen
By the means of Evil that Good is best,
And, through earth and its noise, what is heaven's serene,—
When our faith in the same has stood the test—
Why, the child grown man, you burn the rod,
The uses of labour are surely done;
There remaineth a rest for the people of God:
And I have had troubles enough, for one.

XXIII

But at any rate I have loved the season
Of Art's spring-birth so dim and dewy;
My sculptor is Nicolo the Pisan,
My painter—who but Cimabue?
Nor ever was man of them all indeed,
From these to Ghiberti and Ghirlandajo,
Could say that he missed my critic-meed.
So, now to my special grievance—heigh ho!

XXIV

Their ghosts still stand, as I said before,
Watching each fresco flaked and rasped,
Blocked up, knocked out, or whitewashed o'er:
—No getting again what the church has grasped!
The works on the wall must take their chance;
"Works never conceded to England's thick clime!"
(I hope they prefer their inheritance
Of a bucketful of Italian quick-lime.)

XXV

When they go at length, with such a shaking
Of heads o'er the old delusion, sadly
Each master his way through the black streets taking,
Where many a lost work breathes though badly—
Why don't they bethink them of who has merited?
Why not reveal, while their pictures dree
Such doom, how a captive might be out-ferreted?
Why is it they never remember me?

XXVI

Not that I expect the great Bigordi,
Nor Sandro to hear me, chivalric, bellicose;
Nor the wronged Lippino; and not a word I
Say of a scrap of Fra Angelico's:
But are you too fine, Taddeo Gaddi,
To grant me a taste of your intonaco,
Some Jerome that seeks the heaven with a sad eye?
Not a churlish saint, Lorenzo Monaco?

XXVII

Could not the ghost with the close red cap,
My Pollajolo, the twice a craftsman,
Save me a sample, give me the hap
Of a muscular Christ that shows the draughtsman?
No Virgin by him the somewhat petty,
Of finical touch and tempera crumbly—
Could not Alesso Baldovinetti
Contribute so much, I ask him humbly?

XXVIII

Margheritone of Arezzo,
With the grave-clothes garb and swaddling barret
(Why purse up mouth and beak in a pet so,
You bald old saturnine poll-clawed parrot?)
Not a poor glimmering Crucifixion,
Where in the foreground kneels the donor?
If such remain, as is my conviction,
The hoarding it does you but little honour.

XXIX

They pass; for them the panels may thrill,
The tempera grow alive and tinglish;
Their pictures are left to the mercies still
Of dealers and stealers, Jews and the English,

Who, seeing mere money's worth in their prize,
Will sell it to somebody calm as Zeno
At naked High Art, and in ecstasies
Before some clay-cold vile Carlino!

XXX

No matter for these! But Giotto, you,
Have you allowed, as the town-tongues babble it,—
Oh, never! it shall not be counted true—
That a certain precious little tablet
Which Buonarroti eyed like a lover,—
Was buried so long in oblivion's womb
And, left for another than I to discover,
Turns up at last! and to whom?—to whom?

XXXI

I, that have haunted the dim San Spirito,
(Or was it rather the Ognissanti?)
Patient on altar-step planting a weary toe!
Nay, I shall have it yet! *Detur amanti!* [1]
My Koh-i-noor—or (if that's a platitude)
Jewel of Giamschid, the Persian Sofi's eye;
So, in anticipative gratitude,
What if I take up my hope and prophesy?

XXXII

When the hour grows ripe, and a certain dotard
Is pitched, no parcel that needs invoicing,
To the worse side of the Mount Saint Gothard,
We shall begin by way of rejoicing;
None of that shooting the sky (blank cartridge),
Nor a civic guard, all plumes and lacquer,
Hunting Radetzky's [2] soul like a partridge
Over Morello with squib and cracker.

XXXIII

This time we'll shoot better game and bag 'em hot—
No mere display at the stone of Dante,
But a kind of sober Witanagemot
(Ex: "Casa Guidi," *quod videas ante* [3])

[1] "Let it be given to the lover."
[2] Governor of the northern Italian provinces occupied by Austria.
[3] A reference to Mrs. Browning's "Casa Guidi Windows." *Quod videas ante* — which you may have seen.

Shall ponder, once Freedom restored to Florence,
How Art may return that departed with her.
Go, hated house, go each trace of the Loraine's,
And bring us the days of Orgagna [1] hither!

XXXIV

How we shall prologise, how we shall perorate,
Utter fit things upon art and history,
Feel truth at blood-heat and falsehood at zero rate,
Make of the want of the age no mystery;
Contrast the fructuous and sterile eras,
Show—monarchy ever its uncouth cub licks
Out of the bear's shape into Chimæra's,
While Pure Art's birth is still the republic's.

XXXV

Then one shall propose in a speech (curt Tuscan,
Expurgate and sober, with scarcely an "*issimo*,")
To end now our half-told tale of Cambuscan,
And turn the bell-tower's *alt* to *altissimo:* [2]
And fine as the beak of a young beccaccia
The Campanile, the Duomo's fit ally,
Shall soar up in gold full fifty braccia,[3]
Completing Florence, as Florence Italy.

XXXVI

Shall I be alive that morning the scaffold
Is broken away, and the long-pent fire,
Like the golden hope of the world, unbaffled
Springs from its sleep, and up goes the spire
While "God and the People" plain for its motto,
Thence the new tricolour flaps at the sky?
At least to foresee that glory of Giotto
And Florence together, the first am I!

1855

"DE GUSTIBUS——"

I

YOUR ghost will walk, you lover of trees,
(If our loves remain)
In an English lane,

[1] In other words the great days of Italian art and liberty.
[2] "High to highest."
[3] I.e., the Campanile shall be completed as Giotto planned it long ago.

By a cornfield-side a-flutter with poppies.
Hark, those two in the hazel coppice—
A boy and a girl, if the good fates please,
  Making love, say,—
  The happier they!
Draw yourself up from the light of the moon,
And let them pass, as they will too soon,
  With the bean-flowers' boon,
  And the blackbird's tune,
  And May, and June!

II

What I love best in all the world
Is a castle, precipice-encurled,
In a gash of the wind-grieved Apennine
Or look for me, old fellow of mine,
(If I get my head from out the mouth
O' the grave, and loose my spirit's bands,
And come again to the land of lands)—
In a sea-side house to the farther South,
Where the baked cicala dies of drouth,
And one sharp tree—'tis a cypress—stands,
By the many hundred years red-rusted,
Rough iron-spiked, ripe fruit-o'ercrusted,
My sentinel to guard the sands
To the water's edge. For, what expands
Before the house, but the great opaque
Blue breadth of sea without a break?
While, in the house, for ever crumbles
Some fragment of the frescoed walls,
From blisters where a scorpion sprawls.
A girl bare-footed brings, and tumbles
Down on the pavement, green-flesh melons,
And says there's news to-day—the king
Was shot at, touched in the liver-wing,
Goes with his Bourbon arm in a sling:
—She hopes they have not caught the felons.
Italy, my Italy!
Queen Mary's saying serves for me—
  (When fortune's malice
  Lost her—Calais)—
Open my heart and you will see
Graved inside of it, "Italy."
Such lovers old are I and she:
So it always was, so shall ever be!

1855

HOME-THOUGHTS, FROM ABROAD

I

Oh, to be in England
Now that April's there,
And whoever wakes in England
Sees, some morning, unaware,
That the lowest boughs and the brush-wood sheaf
Round the elm-tree bole are in tiny leaf,
While the chaffinch sings on the orchard bough
In England—now!

II

And after April, when May follows,
And the whitethroat builds, and all the swallows!
Hark, where my blossomed pear-tree in the hedge
Leans to the field and scatters on the clover
Blossoms and dewdrops—at the bent spray's edge—
That's the wise thrush; he sings each song twice over,
Lest you should think he never could recapture
The first fine careless rapture!
And though the fields look rough with hoary dew,
All will be gay when noontide wakes anew
The buttercups, the little children's dower
—Far brighter than this gaudy melon-flower!

1845

HOME-THOUGHTS, FROM THE SEA

Nobly, nobly Cape Saint Vincent to the North-west died away;
Sunset ran, one glorious blood-red, reeking into Cadiz Bay;
Bluish 'mid the burning water, full in face Trafalgar lay;
In the dimmest North-east distance dawned Gibraltar grand and grey;
"Here and here did England help me: how can I help England?"—say,

Whoso turns as I, this evening, turn to God
to praise and pray,
While Jove's planet rises yonder, silent over
Africa.

1845

SAUL [1]

I

Said Abner,[2] "At last thou art come! Ere I
tell, ere thou speak,
Kiss my cheek, wish me well!" Then I wished
it, and did kiss his cheek.
And he, "Since the King, O my friend, for
thy countenance sent,
Neither drunken nor eaten have we; nor until
from his tent
Thou return with the joyful assurance the
King liveth yet,
Shall our lip with the honey be bright, with
the water be wet.
For out of the black mid-tent's silence, a
space of three days,
Not a sound hath escaped to thy servants, of
prayer nor of praise,
To betoken that Saul and the Spirit have ended
their strife,
And that, faint in his triumph, the monarch
sinks back upon life.

II

"Yet now my heart leaps, O beloved! God's
child with his dew
On thy gracious gold hair, and those lilies
still living and blue
Just broken to twine round thy harp-strings,
as if no wild heat
Were now raging to torture the desert!"

III

Then I, as was meet,
Knelt down to the God of my fathers, and
rose on my feet,
And ran o'er the sand burnt to powder. The
tent was unlooped;

[1] The poem is based on I Samuel, 16:14–23. David, alone with his sheep, is telling of his singing before Saul. Note that the poem is in part narrative in the past tense, and in part is direct quotation (in the present tense) of what was said and sung. The quotation marks give the clue.

[2] The captain of Saul's armies.

I pulled up the spear that obstructed, and under
I stooped;
Hands and knees on the slippery grass-patch,
all withered and gone,
That extends to the second enclosure, I groped
my way on
Till I felt where the foldskirts fly open. Then
once more I prayed,
And opened the foldskirts and entered, and
was not afraid
But spoke, "Here is David, thy servant!" And
no voice replied.
At the first I saw nought but the blackness;
but soon I descried
A something more black than the blackness—
the vast, the upright
Main prop which sustains the pavilion: and
slow into sight
Grew a figure against it, gigantic and blackest
of all.
Then a sunbeam, that burst thro' the tent-
roof, showed Saul.

IV

He stood as erect as that tent-prop, both arms
stretched out wide
On the great cross-support in the centre, that
goes to each side;
He relaxed not a muscle, but hung there as,
caught in his pangs
And waiting his change, the king-serpent all
heavily hangs,
Far away from his kind, in the pine, till
deliverance come
With the spring-time,—so agonised Saul,
drear and stark, blind and dumb.

V

Then I tuned my harp,—took off the lilies
we twine round its chords
Lest they snap 'neath the stress of the noon-
tide—those sunbeams like swords!
And I first played the tune all our sheep know,
as, one after one,
So docile they come to the pen-door till
folding be done.
They are white and untorn by the bushes,
for lo, they have fed
Where the long grasses stifle the water within
the stream's bed;

And now one after one seeks its lodging, as star follows star
Into eve and the blue far above us,—so blue and so far!

VI

—Then the tune, for which quails on the cornland will each leave his mate
To fly after the player; then, what makes the crickets elate
Till for boldness they fight one another: and then, what has weight
To set the quick jerboa a-musing outside his sand house—
There are none such as he for a wonder, half bird and half mouse!
God made all the creatures and gave them our love and our fear,
To give sign, we and they are his children, one family here.

VII

Then I played the help-tune of our reapers, their wine-song, when hand
Grasps at hand, eye lights eye in good friendship, and great hearts expand
And grow one in the sense of this world's life.—And then, the last song
When the dead man is praised on his journey—"Bear, bear him along
With his few faults shut up like dead flowerets! Are balm-seeds not here
To console us? The land has none left such as he on the bier.
Oh, would we might keep thee, my brother!"—And then, the glad chaunt
Of the marriage,—first go the young maidens, next, she whom we vaunt
As the beauty, the pride of our dwelling.—And then, the great march
Wherein man runs to man to assist him and buttress an arch
Nought can break; who shall harm them, our friends?—Then, the chorus intoned
As the Levites go up to the altar in glory enthroned.
But I stopped here: for here in the darkness Saul groaned.

VIII

And I paused, held my breath in such silence, and listened apart;
And the tent shook, for mighty Saul shuddered: and sparkles 'gan dart
From the jewels that woke in his turban, at once with a start,
All its lordly male-sapphires, and rubies courageous at heart.
So the head: but the body still moved not, still hung there erect.
And I bent once again to my playing, pursued it unchecked,
As I sang,—

IX

"Oh, our manhood's prime vigour! No spirit feels waste,
Not a muscle is stopped in its playing nor sinew unbraced.
Oh, the wild joys of living! the leaping from rock up to rock,
The strong rending of boughs from the fir-tree, the cool silver shock
Of the plunge in a pool's living water, the hunt of the bear,
And the sultriness showing the lion is couched in his lair.
And the meal, the rich dates yellowed over with gold dust divine,
And the locust-flesh steeped in the pitcher, the full draught of wine,
And the sleep in the dried river-channel where bulrushes tell
That the water was wont to go warbling so softly and well.
How good is man's life, the mere living! how fit to employ
All the heart and the soul and the senses for ever in joy!
Hast thou loved the white locks of thy father, whose sword thou didst guard
When he trusted thee forth with the armies, for glorious reward?
Didst thou see the thin hands of thy mother, held up as men sung
The low song of the nearly-departed, and hear her faint tongue
Joining in while it could to the witness, 'Let one more attest,
I have lived, seen God's hand thro' a lifetime, and all was for best'?
Then they sung thro' their tears in strong triumph, not much, but the rest.
And thy brothers, the help and the contest, the working whence grew

Such result as, from seething grape-bundles, the spirit strained true:
And the friends of thy boyhood—that boyhood of wonder and hope,
Present promise and wealth of the future beyond the eye's scope,—
Till lo, thou art grown to a monarch; a people is thine;
And all gifts, which the world offers singly, on one head combine!
On one head, all the beauty and strength, love and rage (like the throe
That, a-work in the rock, helps its labour and lets the gold go)
High ambition and deeds which surpass it, fame crowning them,—all
Brought to blaze on the head of one creature—King Saul!"

X

And lo, with that leap of my spirit,—heart, hand, harp and voice,
Each lifting Saul's name out of sorrow, each bidding rejoice
Saul's fame in the light it was made for—as when, dare I say,
The Lord's army, in rapture of service, strains through its array,
And upsoareth the cherubim-chariot—"Saul!" cried I, and stopped,
And waited the thing that should follow. Then Saul, who hung propped
By the tent's cross-support in the centre, was struck by his name.
Have ye seen when Spring's arrowy summons goes right to the aim,
And some mountain, the last to withstand her, that held (he alone,
While the vale laughed in freedom and flowers) on a broad bust of stone
A year's snow bound about for a breastplate,—leaves grasp of the sheet?
Fold on fold all at once it crowds thunderously down to his feet,
And there fronts you, stark, black, but alive yet, your mountain of old,
With his rents, the successive bequeathings of ages untold—
Yea, each harm got in fighting your battles, each furrow and scar
Of his head thrust 'twixt you and the tempest—all hail, there they are!
—Now again to be softened with verdure, again hold the nest
Of the dove, tempt the goat and its young to the green on his crest
For their food in the ardours of summer. One long shudder thrilled
All the tent till the very air tingled, then sank and was stilled
At the King's self left standing before me, released and aware.
What was gone, what remained? All to traverse, 'twixt hope and despair;
Death was past, life not come: so he waited. Awhile his right hand
Held the brow, helped the eyes left too vacant forthwith to remand
To their place what new objects should enter: 'twas Saul as before.
I looked up and dared gaze at those eyes, nor was hurt any more
Than by slow pallid sunsets in autumn, ye watch from the shore,
At their sad level gaze o'er the ocean—a sun's slow decline
Over hills which, resolved in stern silence, o'erlap and entwine
Base with base to knit strength more intensely: so, arm folded arm
O'er the chest whose slow heavings subsided.

XI

What spell or what charm,
(For, awhile there was trouble within me) what next should I urge
To sustain him where song had restored him?—Song filled to the verge
His cup with the wine of this life, pressing all that it yields
Of mere fruitage, the strength and the beauty: beyond, on what fields,
Glean a vintage more potent and perfect to brighten the eye
And bring blood to the lip, and commend them the cup they put by?
He saith, "It is good;" still he drinks not: he lets me praise life,
Gives assent, yet would die for his own part.

XII

Then fancies grew rife
Which had come long ago on the pasture, when round me the sheep

Fed in silence—above, the one eagle wheeled slow as in sleep;
And I lay in my hollow and mused on the world that might lie
'Neath his ken, though I saw but the strip 'twixt the hill and the sky:
And I laughed—"Since my days are ordained to be passed with my flocks,
Let me people at least, with my fancies, the plains and the rocks,
Dream the life I am never to mix with, and image the show
Of mankind as they live in those fashions I hardly shall know!
Schemes of life, its best rules and right uses, the courage that gains,
And the prudence that keeps what men strive for." And now these old trains
Of vague thought came again; I grew surer; so, once more the string
Of my harp made response to my spirit, as thus—

XIII

"Yea, my King,"
I began—"thou dost well in rejecting mere comforts that spring
From the mere mortal life held in common by man and by brute:
In our flesh grows the branch of this life, in our soul it bears fruit.
Thou hast marked the slow rise of the tree,—how its stem trembled first
Till it passed the kid's lip, the stag's antler; then safely outburst
The fan-branches all round; and thou mindest when these too, in turn
Broke a-bloom and the palm-tree seemed perfect: yet more was to learn,
E'en the good that comes in with the palm-fruit. Our dates shall we slight,
When their juice brings a cure for all sorrow? or care for the plight
Of the palm's self whose slow growth produced them? Not so! stem and branch
Shall decay, nor be known in their place, while the palm-wine shall staunch
Every wound of man's spirit in winter. I pour thee such wine.
Leave the flesh to the fate it was fit for! the spirit be thine!
By the spirit, when age shall o'ercome thee, thou still shalt enjoy
More indeed, than at first when inconscious, the life of a boy.
Crush that life, and behold its wine running! Each deed thou hast done
Dies, revives, goes to work in the world; until e'en as the sun
Looking down on the earth, though clouds spoil him, though tempests efface,
Can find nothing his own deed produced not, must everywhere trace
The results of his past summer-prime,—so, each ray of thy will,
Every flash of thy passion and prowess, long over, shall thrill
Thy whole people, the countless, with ardour, till they too give forth
A like cheer to their sons, who in turn, fill the South and the North
With the radiance thy deed was the germ of. Carouse in the past!
But the license of age has its limit; thou diest at last:
As the lion when age dims his eyeball, the rose at her height
So with man—so his power and his beauty for ever take flight.
No! Again a long draught of my soul-wine! Look forth o'er the years!
Thou hast done now with eyes for the actual; begin with the seer's!
Is Saul dead? In the depth of the vale make his tomb—bid arise
A grey mountain of marble heaped four-square, till, built to the skies,
Let it mark where the great First King slumbers: whose fame would ye know?
Up above see the rock's naked face, where the record shall go
In great characters cut by the scribe,—Such was Saul, so he did;
With the sages directing the work, by the populace chid,—
For not half, they'll affirm, is comprised there! Which fault to amend,
In the grove with his kind grows the cedar, whereon they shall spend
(See, in tablets 'tis level before them) their praise, and record

With the gold of the graver, Saul's story,—statesman's great word
Side by side with the poet's sweet comment. The river's a-wave
With smooth paper-reeds grazing each other when prophet-winds rave:
So the pen gives unborn generations their due and their part
In thy being! Then, first of the mighty, thank God that thou art!"

XIV

And behold while I sang . . . but O Thou who didst grant me that day,
And before it not seldom hast granted thy help to essay,
Carry on and complete an adventure,—my shield and my sword
In that act where my soul was thy servant, thy word was my word,—
Still be with me, who then at the summit of human endeavour
And scaling the highest, man's thought could, gazed hopeless as ever
On the new stretch of heaven above me—till, mighty to save,
Just one lift of thy hand cleared that distance—God's throne from man's grave!
Let me tell out my tale to its ending—my voice to my heart
Which can scarce dare believe in what marvels last night I took part,
As this morning I gather the fragments, alone with my sheep,
And still fear lest the terrible glory evanish like sleep!
For I wake in the grey dewy covert, while Hebron [1] upheaves
The dawn struggling with night on his shoulder, and Kidron [2] retrieves
Slow the damage of yesterday's sunshine.

XV

I say then,—my song
While I sang thus, assuring the monarch, and ever more strong
Made a proffer of good to console him—he slowly resumed
His old motions and habitudes kingly. The right-hand replumed
His black locks to their wonted composure, adjusted the swathes
Of his turban, and see—the huge sweat that his countenance bathes,
He wipes off with the robe; and he girds now his loins as of yore,
And feels slow for the armlets of price, with the clasp set before.
He is Saul, ye remember in glory,—ere error had bent
The broad brow from the daily communion; and still, though much spent
Be the life and the bearing that front you, the same, God did choose,
To receive what a man may waste, desecrate, never quite lose.
So sank he along by the tent-prop till, stayed by the pile
Of his armour and war-cloak and garments, he leaned there awhile,
And sat out my singing,—one arm round the tent-prop, to raise
His bent head, and the other hung slack—till I touched on the praise
I foresaw from all men in all time, to the man patient there;
And thus ended, the harp falling forward. Then first I was 'ware
That he sat, as I say, with my head just above his vast knees
Which were thrust out on each side around me, like oak-roots which please
To encircle a lamb when it slumbers. I looked up to know
If the best I could do had brought solace: he spoke not, but slow
Lifted up the hand slack at his side, till he laid it with care
Soft and grave, but in mild settled will, on my brow: thro' my hair
The large fingers were pushed, and he bent back my head, with kind power—
All my face back, intent to peruse it, as men do a flower.
Thus held he me there with his great eyes that scrutinised mine—
And oh, all my heart how it loved him! but where was the sign?

[1] A city in Palestine.
[2] A brook near Jerusalem.

I yearned—"Could I help thee, my father, inventing a bliss,
I would add, to that life of the past, both the future and this;
I would give thee new life altogether, as good, ages hence,
As this moment,—had love but the warrant, love's heart to dispense!"

XVI

Then the truth came upon me. No harp more—no song more! outbroke—

XVII

"I have gone the whole round of creation: I saw and I spoke:
I, a work of God's hand for that purpose, received in my brain
And pronounced on the rest of his handwork—returned him again
His creation's approval or censure: I spoke as I saw:
I report, as a man may of God's work—all's love, yet all's law.
Now I lay down the judgeship he lent me. Each faculty tasked
To perceive him, has gained an abyss, where a dewdrop was asked.
Have I knowledge? confounded it shrivels at Wisdom laid bare.
Have I forethought? how purblind, how blank, to the Infinite Care!
Do I task any faculty highest, to image success?
I but open my eyes,—and perfection, no more and no less,
In the kind I imagined, full-fronts me, and God is seen God
In the star, in the stone, in the flesh, in the soul and the clod.
And thus looking within and around me, I ever renew
(With that stoop of the soul which in bending upraises it too)
The submission of man's nothing-perfect to God's all-complete,
As by each new obeisance in spirit, I climb to his feet.
Yet with all this abounding experience, this deity known,
I shall dare to discover some province, some gift of my own.
There's a faculty pleasant to exercise, hard to hoodwink,
I am fain to keep still in abeyance, (I laugh as I think)
Lest, insisting to claim and parade in it, wot ye, I worst
E'en the Giver in one gift.—Behold, I could love if I durst!
But I sink the pretension as fearing a man may o'ertake
God's own speed in the one way of love: I abstain for love's sake.
—What, my soul? see thus far and no farther? when doors great and small,
Nine-and-ninety flew ope at our touch, should the hundredth appal?
In the least things have faith, yet distrust in the greatest of all?
Do I find love so full in my nature, God's ultimate gift,
That I doubt his own love can compete with it? Here, the parts shift?
Here, the creature surpass the Creator,—the end, what Began?
Would I fain in my impotent yearning do all for this man,
And dare doubt he alone shall not help him, who yet alone can?
Would it ever have entered my mind, the bare will, much less power,
To bestow on this Saul what I sang of, the marvellous dower
Of the life he was gifted and filled with? to make such a soul,
Such a body, and then such an earth for insphering the whole?
And doth it not enter my mind (as my warm tears attest)
These good things being given, to go on, and give one more, the best?
Ay, to save and redeem and restore him, maintain at the height
This perfection,—succeed with life's day-spring, death's minute of night?
Interpose at the difficult minute, snatch Saul the mistake,
Saul the failure, the ruin he seems now,—and bid him awake

From the dream, the probation, the prelude,
to find himself set
Clear and safe in new light and new life,—a
new harmony yet
To be run, and continued, and ended—who
knows?—or endure!
The man taught enough, by life's dream, of
the rest to make sure;
By the pain-throb, triumphantly winning in-
tensified bliss,
And the next world's reward and repose, by
the struggles in this.

XVIII

"I believe it! 'Tis thou, God, that givest,
'tis I who receive:
In the first is the last, in thy will is my power
to believe.
All's one gift: thou canst grant it moreover,
as prompt to my prayer
As I breathe out this breath, as I open these
arms to the air.
From thy will, stream the worlds, life and
nature, thy dread Sabaoth:
I will?—the mere atoms despise me! Why am
I not loth
To look that, even that in the face too? Why
is it I dare
Think but lightly of such impuissance? What
stops my despair?
This;—'tis not what man Does which exalts
him, but what man Would do!
See the King—I would help him but cannot,
the wishes fall through.
Could I wrestle to raise him from sorrow,
grow poor to enrich,
To fill up his life, starve my own out, I would
—knowing which,
I know that my service is perfect. Oh, speak
through me now!
Would I suffer for him that I love? So wouldst
thou—so wilt thou!
So shall crown thee the topmost, ineffablest,
uttermost crown—
And thy love fill infinitude wholly, nor leave
up nor down
One spot for the creature to stand in! It is
by no breath,
Turn of eye, wave of hand, that salvation
joins issue with death!
As thy Love is discovered almighty, al-
mighty be proved
Thy power, that exists with and for it, of
being Beloved!
He who did most, shall bear most; the strong-
est shall stand the most weak.
'Tis the weakness in strength, that I cry for!
my flesh, that I seek
In the Godhead! I seek and I find it. O Saul,
it shall be
A Face like my face that receives thee; a Man
like to me,
Thou shalt love and be loved by, for ever: a
Hand like this hand
Shall throw open the gates of new life to thee!
See the Christ stand!"

XIX

I know not too well how I found my way
home in the night.
There were witnesses, cohorts about me, to
left and to right,
Angels, powers, the unuttered, unseen, the
alive, the aware:
I repressed, I got through them as hardly, as
strugglingly there,
As a runner beset by the populace famished
for news—
Life or death. The whole earth was awakened,
hell loosed with her crews;
And the stars of night beat with emotion,
and tingled and shot
Out in fire the strong pain of pent knowledge:
but I fainted not,
For the Hand still impelled me at once and
supported, suppressed
All the tumult, and quenched it with quiet,
and holy behest,
Till the rapture was shut in itself, and the
earth sank to rest.
Anon at the dawn, all that trouble had withered
from earth—
Not so much, but I saw it die out in the day's
tender birth;
In the gathered intensity brought to the grey
of the hills;
In the shuddering forests' held breath; in the
sudden wind-thrills;
In the startled wild beasts that bore off, each
with eye sidling still

Though averted with wonder and dread; in the birds stiff and chill
That rose heavily, as I approached them, made stupid with awe:
E'en the serpent that slid away silent,—he felt the new law.
The same stared in the white humid faces upturned by the flowers;
The same worked in the heart of the cedar and moved the vine-bowers:
And the little brooks witnessing murmured, persistent and low,
With their obstinate, all but hushed voices—"E'en so, it is so!"

1845, 1855

MY STAR

All that I know
Of a certain star
Is, it can throw
(Like the angled spar)
Now a dart of red,
Now a dart of blue;
Till my friends have said
They would fain see, too,
My star that dartles the red and the blue!
Then it stops like a bird; like a flower, hangs furled:
They must solace themselves with the Saturn above it.
What matter to me if their star is a world?
Mine has opened its soul to me; therefore I love it.

1855

BY THE FIRE-SIDE

I

How well I know what I mean to do
When the long dark autumn-evenings come:
And where, my soul, is thy pleasant hue?
With the music of all thy voices, dumb
In life's November too!

II

I shall be found by the fire, suppose,
O'er a great wise book as beseemeth age,
While the shutters flap as the cross-wind blows
And I turn the page, and I turn the page,
Not verse now, only prose!

III

Till the young ones whisper, finger on lip,
"There he is at it, deep in Greek:
Now then, or never, out we slip
To cut from the hazels by the creek
A mainmast for our ship!"

IV

I shall be at it indeed, my friends:
Greek puts already on either side
Such a branch-work forth as soon extends
To a vista opening far and wide,
And I pass out where it ends.

V

The outside-frame, like your hazel-trees:
But the inside-archway widens fast,
And a rarer sort succeeds to these,
And we slope to Italy at last
And youth, by green degrees.

VI

I follow wherever I am led,
Knowing so well the leader's hand:
Oh woman-country, wooed not wed,
Loved all the more by earth's male-lands,
Laid to their hearts instead!

VII

Look at the ruined chapel again
Half-way up in the Alpine gorge!
Is that a tower, I point you plain,
Or is it a mill, or an iron-forge
Breaks solitude in vain?

VIII

A turn, and we stand in the heart of things;
The woods are round us, heaped and dim;
From slab to slab how it slips and springs,
The thread of water single and slim,
Through the ravage some torrent brings!

IX

Does it feed the little lake below?
That speck of white just on its marge
Is Pella; see, in the evening-glow,
How sharp the silver spear-heads charge
When Alp meets heaven in snow!

X

On our other side is the straight-up rock;
And a path is kept 'twixt the gorge and it
By boulder-stones where lichens mock
The marks on a moth, and small ferns fit
Their teeth to the polished block.

XI

Oh the sense of the yellow mountain-flowers,
And thorny balls, each three in one,
The chestnuts throw on our path in showers!
For the drop of the woodland fruit's begun,
These early November hours,

XII

That crimson the creeper's leaf across
Like a splash of blood, intense, abrupt,
O'er a shield else gold from rim to boss,
And lay it for show on the fairy-cupped
Elf-needled mat of moss,

XIII

By the rose-flesh mushrooms, undivulged
Last evening—nay, in to-day's first dew
Yon sudden coral nipple bulged,
Where a freaked fawn-coloured flaky crew
Of toadstools peep indulged.

XIV

And yonder, at foot of the fronting ridge
That takes the turn to a range beyond,
Is the chapel reached by the one-arched bridge
Where the water is stopped in a stagnant pond
Danced over by the midge.

XV

The chapel and bridge are of stone alike,
Blackish-grey and mostly wet;
Cut hemp-stalks steep in the narrow dyke.
See here again, how the lichens fret
And the roots of the ivy strike!

XVI

Poor little place, where its one priest comes
On a festa-day, if he comes at all,
To the dozen folk from their scattered homes,
Gathered within that precinct small
By the dozen ways one roams—

XVII

To drop from the charcoal-burners' huts,
Or climb from the hemp-dressers' low shed,
Leave the grange where the woodman stores his nuts,
Or the wattled cote where the fowlers spread
Their gear on the rock's bare juts.

XVIII

It has some pretension too, this front,
With its bit of fresco half-moon-wise
Set over the porch, Art's early wont:
'Tis John in the Desert, I surmise,
But has borne the weather's brunt—

XIX

Not from the fault of the builder, though,
For a pent-house properly projects
Where three carved beams make a certain show,
Dating—good thought of our architect's—
'Five, six, nine, he lets you know.

XX

And all day long a bird sings there,
And a stray sheep drinks at the pond at times;
The place is silent and aware;
It has had its scenes, its joys and crimes,
But that is its own affair.

XXI

My perfect wife, my Leonor,
Oh heart, my own, oh eyes, mine too,
Whom else could I dare look backward for,
With whom beside should I dare pursue
The path grey heads abhor?

XXII

For it leads to a crag's sheer edge with them;
Youth, flowery all the way, there stops—
Not they; age threatens and they contemn,
Till they reach the gulf wherein youth drops,
One inch from life's safe hem!

XXIII

With me, youth led . . . I will speak now,
No longer watch you as you sit
Reading by fire-light, that great brow
And the spirit-small hand propping it,
Mutely, my heart knows how—

XXIV

When, if I think but deep enough,
You are wont to answer, prompt as rhyme;
And you, too, find without rebuff
Response your soul seeks many a time
Piercing its fine flesh-stuff.

XXV

My own, confirm me! If I tread
This path back, is it not in pride
To think how little I dreamed it led
To an age so blest that, by its side,
Youth seems the waste instead?

XXVI

My own, see where the years conduct!
At first, 'twas something our two souls
Should mix as mists do; each is sucked
In each now: on, the new stream rolls,
Whatever rocks obstruct.

XXVII

Think, when our one soul understands
The great Word which makes all things new,
When earth breaks up and heaven expands,
How will the change strike me and you
In the house not made with hands?

XXVIII

Oh I must feel your brain prompt mine,
Your heart anticipate my heart,
You must be just before, in fine,
See and make me see, for your part,
New depths of the divine!

XXIX

But who could have expected this
When we two drew together first
Just for the obvious human bliss,
To satisfy life's daily thirst
With a thing men seldom miss?

XXX

Come back with me to the first of all,
Let us lean and love it over again,
Let us now forget and now recall,
Break the rosary in a pearly rain,
And gather what we let fall!

XXXI

What did I say?—that a small bird sings
All day long, save when a brown pair
Of hawks from the wood float with wide wings
Strained to a bell: 'gainst noon-day glare
You count the streaks and rings.

XXXII

But at afternoon or almost eve
'Tis better; then the silence grows
To that degree, you half believe
It must get rid of what it knows,
Its bosom does so heave.

XXXIII

Hither we walked then, side by side,
Arm in arm and cheek to cheek,
And still I questioned or replied,
While my heart, convulsed to really speak,
Lay choking in its pride.

XXXIV

Silent the crumbling bridge we cross,
And pity and praise the chapel sweet,
And care about the fresco's loss,
And wish for our souls a like retreat,
And wonder at the moss.

XXXV

Stoop and kneel on the settle under,
Look through the window's grated square:
Nothing to see! For fear of plunder,
The cross is down and the altar bare,
As if thieves don't fear thunder.

XXXVI

We stoop and look in through the grate,
See the little porch and rustic door,
Read duly the dead builder's date;
Then cross the bridge that we crossed before,
Take the path again—but wait!

XXXVII

Oh moment, one and infinite!
The water slips o'er stock and stone;
The West is tender, hardly bright:
How grey at once is the evening grown—
One star, its chrysolite!

XXXVIII

We two stood there with never a third,
But each by each, as each knew well:
The sights we saw and the sounds we heard,
The lights and the shades made up a spell
Till the trouble grew and stirred.

XXXIX

Oh, the little more, and how much it is!
  And the little less, and what worlds away!
How a sound shall quicken content to bliss,
  Or a breath suspend the blood's best play,
And life be a proof of this!

XL

Had she willed it, still had stood the screen
  So slight, so sure, 'twixt my love and her:
I could fix her face with a guard between,
  And find her soul as when friends confer,
Friends—lovers that might have been.

XLI

For my heart had a touch of the woodland-time,
  Wanting to sleep now over its best.
Shake the whole tree in the summer-prime,
  But bring to the last leaf no such test!
"Hold the last fast!" runs the rhyme.

XLII

For a chance to make your little much,
  To gain a lover and lose a friend,
Venture the tree and a myriad such,
  When nothing you mar but the year can mend:
But a last leaf—fear to touch!

XLIII

Yet should it unfasten itself and fall
  Eddying down till it find your face
At some slight wind—best chance of all!
  Be your heart henceforth its dwelling-place
You tremble to forestall!

XLIV

Worth how well, those dark grey eyes,
  That hair so dark and dear, how worth
That a man should strive and agonise,
  And taste a veriest hell on earth
For the hope of such a prize!

XLV

You might have turned and tried a man,
  Set him a space to weary and wear,
And prove which suited more your plan,
  His best of hope or his worst despair,
Yet end as he began.

XLVI

But you spared me this, like the heart you are,
  And filled my empty heart at a word.
If two lives join, there is oft a scar,
  They are one and one, with a shadowy third;
One near one is too far.

XLVII

A moment after, and hands unseen
  Were hanging the night around us fast;
But we knew that a bar was broken between
  Life and life: we were mixed at last
In spite of the mortal screen.

XLVIII

The forests had done it; there they stood;
  We caught for a moment the powers at play:
They had mingled us so, for once and good,
  Their work was done—we might go or stay,
They relapsed to their ancient mood.

XLIX

How the world is made for each of us!
  How all we perceive and know in it
Tends to some moment's product thus,
  When a soul declares itself—to wit,
By its fruit, the thing it does!

L

Be hate that fruit or love that fruit,
  It forwards the general deed of man,
And each of the Many helps to recruit
  The life of the race by a general plan;
Each living his own, to boot.

LI

I am named and known by that moment's feat;
  There took my station and degree;
So grew my own small life complete,
  As nature obtained her best of me—
One born to love you, sweet!

LII

And to watch you sink by the fire-side now
  Back again, as you mutely sit
Musing by fire-light, that great brow
  And the spirit-small hand propping it,
Yonder, my heart knows how!

LIII

So, earth has gained by one man the more,
And the gain of earth must be heaven's gain too;
And the whole is well worth thinking o'er
When autumn comes: which I mean to do
One day, as I said before.

1855

TWO IN THE CAMPAGNA[1]

I

I WONDER do you feel to-day
As I have felt since, hand in hand,
We sat down on the grass, to stray
In spirit better through the land,
This morn of Rome and May?

II

For me, I touched a thought, I know,
Has tantalised me many times,
(Like turns of thread the spiders throw
Mocking across our path) for rhymes
To catch at and let go.

III

Help me to hold it! First it left
The yellowing fennel, run to seed
There, branching from the brickwork's cleft,
Some old tomb's ruin: yonder weed
Took up the floating weft,

IV

Where one small orange cup amassed
Five beetles,—blind and green they grope
Among the honey-meal: and last,
Everywhere on the grassy slope
I traced it. Hold it fast!

V

The champaign with its endless fleece
Of feathery grasses everywhere!
Silence and passion, joy and peace,
An everlasting wash of air—
Rome's ghost since her decease.

VI

Such life here, through such lengths of hours,
Such miracles performed in play,
Such primal naked forms of flowers,
Such letting nature have her way
While heaven looks from its towers!

VII

How say you? Let us, O my dove,
Let us be unashamed of soul,
As earth lies bare to heaven above!
How is it under our control
To love or not to love?

VIII

I would that you were all to me,
You that are just so much, no more.
Nor yours nor mine, nor slave nor free!
Where does the fault lie? What the core
O' the wound, since wound must be?

IX

I would I could adopt your will,
See with your eyes, and set my heart
Beating by yours, and drink my fill
At your soul's springs,—your part my part
In life, for good and ill.

X

No. I yearn upward, touch you close,
Then stand away. I kiss your cheek,
Catch your soul's warmth,—I pluck the rose
And love it more than tongue can speak—
Then the good minute goes.

XI

Already how am I so far
Out of that minute? Must I go
Still like the thistle-ball, no bar,
Onward, whenever light winds blow,
Fixed by no friendly star?

XII

Just when I seemed about to learn!
Where is the thread now? Off again!
The old trick! Only I discern—
Infinite passion, and the pain
Of finite hearts that yearn.

1855

[1] The Campagna — the countryside around Rome has been called "the ghost of old Rome." It roughly coincides with ancient Latium and is dotted with ruins.

MISCONCEPTIONS

I

This is a spray the Bird clung to,
Making it blossom with pleasure,
Ere the high tree-top she sprung to,
Fit for her nest and her treasure.
Oh, what a hope beyond measure
Was the poor spray's, which the flying feet hung to,—
So to be singled out, built in, and sung to!

II

This is a heart the Queen leant on,
Thrilled in a minute erratic,
Ere the true bosom she bent on,
Meet for love's regal dalmatic.
Oh, what a fancy ecstatic
Was the poor heart's, ere the wanderer went on—
Love to be saved for it, proffered to, spent on!

1855

A SERENADE AT THE VILLA

I

That was I, you heard last night,
When there rose no moon at all,
Nor, to pierce the strained and tight
Tent of heaven, a planet small:
Life was dead and so was light.

II

Not a twinkle from the fly,
Not a glimmer from the worm;
When the crickets stopped their cry,
When the owls forbore a term,
You heard music; that was I.

III

Earth turned in her sleep with pain,
Sultrily suspired for proof:
In at heaven and out again,
Lightning!—where it broke the roof,
Bloodlike, some few drops of rain.

IV

What they could my words expressed,
O my love, my all, my one!
Singing helped the verses best,
And when singing's best was done,
To my lute I left the rest.

V

So wore night; the East was grey,
White the broad-faced hemlock-flowers:
There would be another day;
Ere its first of heavy hours
Found me, I had passed away.

VI

What became of all the hopes,
Words and song and lute as well?
Say, this struck you—"When life gropes
Feebly for the path where fell
Light last on the evening slopes,

VII

"One friend in that path shall be,
To secure my step from wrong;
One to count night day for me,
Patient through the watches long,
Serving most with none to see."

VIII

Never say—as something bodes—
"So, the worst has yet a worse!
When life halts 'neath double loads,
Better the taskmaster's curse
Than such music on the roads!

IX

"When no moon succeeds the sun,
Nor can pierce the midnight's tent
Any star, the smallest one,
While some drops, where lightning rent,
Show the final storm begun—

X

"When the fire-fly hides its spot,
When the garden-voices fail
In the darkness thick and hot,—
Shall another voice avail,
That shape be where these are not?

XI

"Has some plague a longer lease,
Proffering its help uncouth?
Can't one even die in peace?
As one shuts one's eyes on youth,
Is that face the last one sees?"

XII

Oh how dark your villa was,
Windows fast and obdurate!
How the garden grudged me grass

Where I stood—the iron gate
Ground its teeth to let me pass!

1855

ONE WAY OF LOVE

I

All June I bound the rose in sheaves.
Now, rose by rose, I strip the leaves
And strew them where Pauline may pass.
She will not turn aside? Alas!
Let them lie. Suppose they die?
The chance was they might take her eye.

II

How many a month I strove to suit
These stubborn fingers to the lute!
To-day I venture all I know.
She will not hear my music? So!
Break the string; fold music's wing:
Suppose Pauline had bade me sing!

III

My whole life long I learned to love.
This hour my utmost art I prove
And speak my passion—heaven or hell?
She will not give me heaven? 'Tis well!
Lose who may—I still can say,
Those who win heaven, blest are they!

1855

ANOTHER WAY OF LOVE

I

June was not over
Though past the full,
And the best of her roses
Had yet to blow,
When a man I know
(But shall not discover,
Since ears are dull,
And time discloses)
Turned him and said with a man's true air,
Half sighing a smile in a yawn, as 'twere,—
"If I tire of your June, will she greatly care?"

II

Well, dear, in-doors with you!
True! serene deadness
Tries a man's temper.
What's in the blossom
June wears on her bosom?
Can it clear scores with you?
Sweetness and redness.
Eadem semper! [1]
Go, let me care for it greatly or slightly!
If June mend her bower now, your hand left unsightly
By plucking the roses,—my June will do rightly.

III

And after, for pastime,
If June be refulgent
With flowers in completeness,
All petals, no prickles,
Delicious as trickles
Of wine poured at mass-time,—
And choose One indulgent
To redness and sweetness:
Or if, with experience of man and of spider,
June use my June-lightning, the strong insect-ridder,
And stop the fresh film-work,—why, June will consider.

1855

RESPECTABILITY

I

Dear, had the world in its caprice
Deigned to proclaim "I know you both,
Have recognised your plighted troth,
Am sponsor for you: live in peace!"—
How many precious months and years
Of youth had passed, that speed so fast,
Before we found it out at last,
The world, and what it fears?

II

How much of priceless life were spent
With men that every virtue decks,
And women models of their sex,
Society's true ornament,—
Ere we dared wander, nights like this,
Thro' wind and rain, and watch the Seine,
And feel the Boulevard break again
To warmth and light and bliss?

III

I know! the world proscribes not love;
Allows my finger to caress
Your lips' contour and downiness,
Provided it supply a glove.

[1] "Always the same."

The world's good word!—the Institute!
  Guizot receives Montalembert!
  Eh? Down the court three lampions flare:
Put forward your best foot!

1855

LOVE IN A LIFE

I

Room after room,
I hunt the house through
We inhabit together.
Heart, fear nothing, for, heart, thou shalt find her—
Next time, herself!—not the trouble behind her
Left in the curtain, the couch's perfume!
As she brushed it, the cornice-wreath blossomed anew:
Yon looking-glass gleamed at the wave of her feather.

II

Yet the day wears,
And door succeeds door;
I try the fresh fortune—
Range the wide house from the wing to the centre.
Still the same chance! she goes out as I enter.
Spend my whole day in the quest,—who cares?
But 'tis twilight, you see,—with such suites to explore,
Such closets to search, such alcoves to importune!

1855

LIFE IN A LOVE

Escape me?
Never—
Beloved!
While I am I, and you are you,
  So long as the world contains us both,
  Me the loving and you the loth,
While the one eludes, must the other pursue,
My life is a fault at last, I fear:
  It seems too much like a fate, indeed!
  Though I do my best I shall scarce succeed.
But what if I fail of my purpose here?
It is but to keep the nerves at strain,
  To dry one's eyes and laugh at a fall,
And, baffled, get up and begin again,—
  So the chace takes up one's life, that's all.
While, look but once from your farthest bound
  At me so deep in the dust and dark,
No sooner the old hope goes to ground
  Than a new one, straight to the selfsame mark,
I shape me—
Ever
Removed!

1855

IN A YEAR

I

Never any more,
  While I live,
Need I hope to see his face
  As before.
Once his love grown chill,
  Mine may strive:
Bitterly we re-embrace,
  Single still.

II

Was it something said,
  Something done,
Vexed him? was it touch of hand,
  Turn of head?
Strange! that very way
  Love begun:
I as little understand
  Love's decay.

III

When I sewed or drew,
  I recall
How he looked as if I sung,
  —Sweetly too.
If I spoke a word,
  First of all
Up his cheek the colour sprung,
  Then he heard.

IV

Sitting by my side,
  At my feet,
So he breathed but air I breathed,
  Satisfied!

I, too, at love's brim
  Touched the sweet:
I would die if death bequeathed
  Sweet to him.

V

"Speak, I love thee best!"
  He exclaimed:
"Let thy love my own foretell!"
  I confessed:
"Clasp my heart on thine
  Now unblamed,
Since upon thy soul as well
  Hangeth mine!"

VI

Was it wrong to own,
  Being truth?
Why should all the giving prove
  His alone?
I had wealth and ease,
  Beauty, youth:
Since my lover gave me love,
  I gave these.

VII

That was all I meant,
  —To be just,
And the passion I had raised,
  To content.
Since he chose to change
  Gold for dust,
If I gave him what he praised
  Was it strange?

VIII

Would he loved me yet,
  On and on,
While I found some way undreamed
  —Paid my debt!
Gave more life and more,
  Till, all gone,
He should smile "She never seemed
  Mine before.

IX

"What, she felt the while,
  Must I think?
Love's so different with us men!"
  He should smile:
"Dying for my sake—
  White and pink!
Can't we touch these bubbles then
  But they break?"

X

Dear, the pang is brief,
  Do thy part,
Have thy pleasure! How perplexed
  Grows belief!
Well, this cold clay clod
  Was man's heart:
Crumble it, and what comes next?
  Is it God?

1855

MEMORABILIA

I

Ah, did you once see Shelley plain,
  And did he stop and speak to you
And did you speak to him again?
  How strange it seems and new!

II

But you were living before that,
  And also you are living after;
And the memory I started at—
  My starting moves your laughter.

III

I crossed a moor, with a name of its own
  And a certain use in the world no doubt,
Yet a hand's-breadth of it shines alone
  'Mid the blank miles round about:

IV

For there I picked up on the heather
  And there I put inside my breast
A moulted feather, an eagle-feather!
  Well, I forget the rest.

1855

THE PATRIOT

AN OLD STORY

I

It was roses, roses, all the way,
  With myrtle mixed in my path like mad:
The house-roofs seemed to heave and sway,
  The church-spires flamed, such flags they had,
A year ago on this very day.

Dramatic Romances.

Incident of the French Camp.

1.

You know, we French stormed Ratisbon:
A mile or so away
On a little mound, Napoleon
Stood on our storming-day;
With neck out-thrust, you fancy how,
Legs wide, arms locked behind,
As if to balance the prone brow
Oppressive with its mind.

A Page of Browning's Manuscript. (See Appendix I.)

II

The air broke into a mist with bells,
The old walls rocked with the crowd and cries.
Had I said, "Good folk, mere noise repels—
But give me your sun from yonder skies!"
They had answered, "And afterward, what else?"

III

Alack, it was I who leaped at the sun
To give it my loving friends to keep!
Nought man could do, have I left undone:
And you see my harvest, what I reap
This very day, now a year is run.

IV

There's nobody on the house-tops now—
Just a palsied few at the windows set;
For the best of the sight is, all allow,
At the Shambles' Gate—or, better yet,
By the very scaffold's foot, I trow.

V

I go in the rain, and, more than needs,
A rope cuts both my wrists behind;
And I think, by the feel, my forehead bleeds,
For they fling, whoever has a mind,
Stones at me for my year's misdeeds.

VI

Thus I entered, and thus I go!
In triumphs, people have dropped down dead.
"Paid by the world, what dost thou owe
Me?"—God might question; now instead,
'Tis God shall repay: I am safer so.

1855

MY LAST DUCHESS

FERRARA

THAT'S my last Duchess painted on the wall,
Looking as if she were alive. I call
That piece a wonder, now: Frà Pandolf's hands
Worked busily a day, and there she stands.
Will't please you sit and look at her? I said
"Frà Pandolf" by design, for never read
Strangers like you that pictured countenance,
The depth and passion of its earnest glance,
But to myself they turned (since none puts by
The curtain I have drawn for you, but I)
And seemed as they would ask me, if they durst,
How such a glance came there; so, not the first
Are you to turn and ask thus. Sir, 'twas not
Her husband's presence only, called that spot
Of joy into the Duchess' cheek: perhaps
Frà Pandolf chanced to say "Her mantle laps
Over my lady's wrist too much," or "Paint
Must never hope to reproduce the faint
Half-flush that dies along her throat:" such stuff
Was courtesy, she thought, and cause enough
For calling up that spot of joy. She had
A heart—how shall I say?—too soon made glad,
Too easily impressed; she liked whate'er
She looked on, and her looks went everywhere.
Sir, 'twas all one! My favour at her breast,
The dropping of the daylight in the West,
The bough of cherries some officious fool
Broke in the orchard for her, the white mule
She rode with round the terrace—all and each
Would draw from her alike the approving speech,
Or blush, at least. She thanked men,—good! but thanked
Somehow—I know not how—as if she ranked
My gift of a nine-hundred-years-old name
With anybody's gift. Who'd stoop to blame
This sort of trifling? Even had you skill
In speech—(which I have not)—to make your will
Quite clear to such an one, and say, "Just this
Or that in you disgusts me; here you miss,
Or there exceed the mark"—and if she let
Herself be lessoned so, nor plainly set
Her wits to yours, forsooth, and made excuse,
—E'en then would be some stooping; and I choose
Never to stoop. Oh sir, she smiled, no doubt,
Whene'er I passed her; but who passed without
Much the same smile? This grew; I gave commands;
Then all smiles stopped together. There she stands
As if alive. Will't please you rise? We'll meet
The company below, then. I repeat,
The Count your master's known munificence
Is ample warrant that no just pretence

Of mine for dowry will be disallowed;
Though his fair daughter's self, as I avowed
At starting, is my object. Nay, we'll go
Together down, sir. Notice Neptune, though,
Taming a sea-horse, thought a rarity,
Which Claus of Innsbruck cast in bronze for me!

1842

THE BOY AND THE ANGEL

Morning, evening, noon and night,
"Praise God!" sang Theocrite.

Then to his poor trade he turned,
Whereby the daily meal was earned.

Hard he laboured, long and well;
O'er his work the boy's curls fell.

But ever, at each period,
He stopped and sang, "Praise God!"

Then back again his curls he threw,
And cheerful turned to work anew.

Said Blaise, the listening monk, "Well done;
I doubt not thou art heard, my son:

"As well as if thy voice to-day
Were praising God, the Pope's great way.

"This Easter Day, the Pope at Rome
Praises God from Peter's dome."

Said Theocrite, "Would God that I
Might praise him, that great way, and die!"

Night passed, day shone,
And Theocrite was gone.

With God a day endures alway,
A thousand years are but a day.

God said in heaven, "Nor day nor night
Now brings the voice of my delight."

Then Gabriel, like a rainbow's birth,
Spread his wings and sank to earth;

Entered in flesh, the empty cell,
Lived there, and played the craftsman well;

And morning, evening, noon and night,
Praised God in place of Theocrite.

And from a boy, to youth he grew:
The man put off the stripling's hue:

The man matured and fell away
Into the season of decay:

And ever o'er the trade he bent,
And ever lived on earth content.

(He did God's will; to him, all one
If on the earth or in the sun.)

God said, "A praise is in mine ear;
There is no doubt in it, no fear:

"So sing old worlds, and so
New worlds that from my footstool go.

"Clearer loves sound other ways:
I miss my little human praise."

Then forth sprang Gabriel's wings, off fell
The flesh disguise, remained the cell.

'Twas Easter Day: he flew to Rome,
And paused above Saint Peter's dome.

In the tiring-room close by
The great outer gallery,

With his holy vestments dight,
Stood the new Pope, Theocrite:

And all his past career
Came back upon him clear,

Since when, a boy, he plied his trade,
Till on his life the sickness weighed;

And in his cell, when death drew near,
An angel in a dream brought cheer:

And rising from the sickness drear
He grew a priest, and now stood here.

To the East with praise he turned,
And on his sight the angel burned.

"I bore thee from thy craftsman's cell
And set thee here; I did not well.

"Vainly I left my angel-sphere,
Vain was thy dream of many a year.

"Thy voice's praise seemed weak; it dropped—
Creation's chorus stopped!

"Go back and praise again
The early way, while I remain.

"With that weak voice of our disdain,
Take up creation's pausing strain.

"Back to the cell and poor employ:
Resume the craftsman and the boy!"

Theocrite grew old at home;
A new Pope dwelt in Peter's dome.

One vanished as the other died:
They sought God side by side.

1844

INSTANS TYRANNUS

I

Of the million or two, more or less,
I rule and possess,
One man, for some cause undefined,
Was least to my mind.

II

I struck him, he grovelled of course—
For, what was his force?
I pinned him to earth with my weight
And persistence of hate:
And he lay, would not moan, would not curse,
As his lot might be worse.

III

"Were the object less mean, would he stand
At the swing of my hand!
For obscurity helps him and blots
The hole where he squats."
So, I set my five wits on the stretch
To inveigle the wretch.
All in vain! Gold and jewels I threw,
Still he couched there perdue;
I tempted his blood and his flesh,
Hid in roses my mesh,
Choicest cates and the flagon's best spilth:
Still he kept to his filth.

IV

Had he kith now or kin, were access
To his heart, did I press:
Just a son or a mother to seize!
No such booty as these.
Were it simply a friend to pursue
'Mid my million or two,
Who could pay me in person or pelf
What he owes me himself!
No: I could not but smile through my chafe:
For the fellow lay safe
As his mates do, the midge and the nit,
—Through minuteness, to wit.

V

Then a humour more great took its place
At the thought of his face,
The droop, the low cares of the mouth,
The trouble uncouth
'Twixt the brows, all that air one is fain
To put out of its pain.
And, "no!" I admonished myself,
"Is one mocked by an elf,
Is one baffled by toad or by rat?
The gravamen's in that!
How the lion, who crouches to suit
His back to my foot,
Would admire that I stand in debate!
But the small turns the great
If it vexes you,—that is the thing!
Toad or rat vex the king?
Though I waste half my realm to unearth
Toad or rat, 'tis well worth!"

VI

So, I soberly laid my last plan
To extinguish the man.
Round his creep-hole, with never a break
Ran my fires for his sake;
Over-head, did my thunder combine
With my underground mine:
Till I looked from my labour content
To enjoy the event.

VII

When sudden . . . how think ye, the end?
Did I say "without friend"?
Say rather, from marge to blue marge
The whole sky grew his targe
With the sun's self for visible boss,
While an Arm ran across
Which the earth heaved beneath like a breast
Where the wretch was safe prest!
Do you see? Just my vengeance complete,
The man sprang to his feet,
Stood erect, caught at God's skirts, and prayed!
—So, *I* was afraid!

1855

THE GLOVE

(PETER RONSARD *loquitur.*)

"HEIGHO!" yawned one day King Francis,
Distance all value enhances!
When a man's busy, why, leisure
Strikes him as wonderful pleasure:
'Faith, and at leisure once is he?
Straightway he wants to be busy.
Here we've got peace; and aghast I'm
Caught thinking war the true pastime.
Is there a reason in metre?
Give us your speech, master Peter!"
I who, if mortal dare say so,
Ne'er am at loss with my Naso,
"Sire," I replied, "joys prove cloudlets:
Men are the merest Ixions"—
Here the King whistled aloud, "Let's
—Heigho—go look at our lions!"
Such are the sorrowful chances
If you talk fine to King Francis.

And so, to the courtyard proceeding
Our company, Francis was leading,
Increased by new followers tenfold
Before he arrived at the penfold;
Lords, ladies, like clouds which bedizen
At sunset the western horizon.
And Sir De Lorge pressed 'mid the foremost
With the dame he professed to adore most.
Oh, what a face! One by fits eyed
Her, and the horrible pitside;
For the penfold surrounded a hollow
Which led where the eye scarce dared follow,
And shelved to the chamber secluded
Where Bluebeard, the great lion, brooded.
The King hailed his keeper, an Arab
As glossy and black as a scarab,
And bade him make sport and at once stir
Up and out of his den the old monster.
They opened a hole in the wire-work
Across it, and dropped there a firework,
And fled: one's heart's beating redoubled;
A pause, while the pit's mouth was troubled,
The blackness and silence so utter,
By the firework's slow sparkling and sputter;
Then earth in a sudden contortion
Gave out to our gaze her abortion.
Such a brute! Were I friend Clement Marot [1]
(Whose experience of nature's but narrow,
And whose faculties move in no small mist
When he versifies David the Psalmist)
I should study that brute to describe you
Illum Juda Leonem de Tribu. [1]
One's whole blood grew curdling and creepy
To see the black mane, vast and heapy,
The tail in the air stiff and straining,
The wide eyes, nor waxing nor waning,
As over the barrier which bounded
His platform, and us who surrounded
The barrier, they reached and they rested
On space that might stand him in best stead:
For who knew, he thought, what the amazement,
The eruption of clatter and blaze meant,
And if, in this minute of wonder,
No outlet, 'mid lightning and thunder,
Lay broad, and, his shackles all shivered,
The lion at last was delivered?
Ay, that was the open sky o'erhead!
And you saw by the flash on his forehead,
By the hope in those eyes wide and steady,
He was leagues in the desert already,
Driving the flocks up the mountain,
Or catlike couched hard by the fountain,
To waylay the date-gathering negress:
So guarded he entrance or egress.
"How he stands!" quoth the King: "we may well swear,
(No novice, we've won our spurs elsewhere
And so can afford the confession,)
We exercise wholesome discretion
In keeping aloof from his threshold;
Once hold you, those jaws want no fresh hold,
Their first would too pleasantly purloin
The visitor's brisket or surloin:
But who's he would prove so fool-hardy?
Not the best man of Marignan, pardie!"

The sentence no sooner was uttered,
Than over the rails a glove fluttered,
Fell close to the lion, and rested:
The dame 'twas, who flung it and jested
With life so, De Lorge had been wooing
For months past; he sat there pursuing
His suit, weighing out with nonchalance
Fine speeches like gold from a balance.

[1] The court poet of Francis I.

[1] "That lion of the tribe of Judah."

Sound the trumpet, no true knight's a tarrier!
De Lorge made one leap at the barrier,
Walked straight to the glove,—while the lion
Ne'er moved, kept his far-reaching eye on
The palm-tree-edged desert-spring's sapphire,
And the musky oiled skin of the Kaffir,—
Picked it up, and as calmly retreated,
Leaped back where the lady was seated,
And full in the face of its owner
Flung the glove.

"Your heart's queen, you dethrone her?
So should I!"—cried the King—"'twas mere vanity,
Not love, set that task to humanity!"
Lords and ladies alike turned with loathing
From such a proved wolf in sheep's clothing.

Not so, I; for I caught an expression
In her brow's undisturbed self-possession
Amid the Court's scoffing and merriment,—
As if from no pleasing experiment
She rose, yet of pain not much heedful
So long as the process was needful,—
As if she had tried in a crucible,
To what "speeches like gold" were reducible,
And, finding the finest prove copper,
Felt the smoke in her face was but proper;
To know what she had *not* to trust to,
Was worth all the ashes and dust too.
She went out 'mid hooting and laughter;
Clement Marot stayed; I followed after,
And asked, as a grace, what it all meant?
If she wished not the rash deed's recallment?
"For I"—so I spoke—"am a poet:
Human nature,—behooves that I know it!"

She told me, "Too long had I heard
Of the deed proved alone by the word:
For my love—what De Lorge would not dare!
With my scorn—what De Lorge could compare!
And the endless descriptions of death
He would brave when my lip formed a breath,
I must reckon as braved, or, of course,
Doubt his word—and moreover, perforce,
For such gifts as no lady could spurn,
Must offer my love in return.
When I looked on your lion, it brought
All the dangers at once to my thought,
Encountered by all sorts of men,
Before he was lodged in his den,—
From the poor slave whose club or bare hands
Dug the trap, set the snare on the sands,
With no King and no Court to applaud,
By no shame, should he shrink, overawed,
Yet to capture the creature made shift
That his rude boys might laugh at the gift,
—To the page who last leaped o'er the fence
Of the pit, on no greater pretence
Than to get back the bonnet he dropped,
Lest his pay for a week should be stopped.
So, wiser I judged it to make
One trial what 'death for my sake'
Really meant, while the power was yet mine,
Than to wait until time should define
Such a phrase not so simply as I,
Who took it to mean just 'to die.'
The blow a glove gives is but weak:
Does the mark yet discolour my cheek?
But when the heart suffers a blow,
Will the pain pass so soon, do you know?"

I looked, as away she was sweeping.
And saw a youth eagerly keeping
As close as he dared to the doorway.
No doubt that a noble should more weigh
His life than befits a plebeian;
And yet, had our brute been Nemean—
(I judge by a certain calm fervour
The youth stepped with, forward to serve her)
—He'd have scarce thought you did him the worst turn
If you whispered "Friend, what you'd get, first earn!"
And when, shortly after, she carried
Her shame from the Court, and they married,
To that marriage some happiness, maugre
The voice of the Court, I dared augur.

For De Lorge, he made women with men vie,
Those in wonder and praise, these in envy;
And in short stood so plain a head taller
That he wooed and won . . . how do you call her?
The beauty, that rose in the sequel
To the King's love, who loved her a week well.
And 'twas noticed he never would honour

De Lorge (who looked daggers upon her)
With the easy commission of stretching
His legs in the service, and fetching
His wife, from her chamber, those straying
Sad gloves she was always mislaying,
While the King took the closet to chat in,—
But of course this adventure came pat in.
And never the King told the story,
How bringing a glove brought such glory,
But the wife smiled—"His nerves are grown
 firmer:
Mine he brings now and utters no murmur."

Venienti occurrite morbo![1]
With which moral I drop my theorbo.

1845

TIME'S REVENGES

I've a Friend, over the sea;
I like him, but he loves me.
It all grew out of the books I write;
They find such favour in his sight
That he slaughters you with savage looks
Because you don't admire my books.
He does himself though,—and if some vein
Were to snap to-night in this heavy brain,
To-morrow month, if I lived to try,
Round should I just turn quietly,
Or out of the bedclothes stretch my hand
Till I found him, come from his foreign land
To be my nurse in this poor place,
And make my broth and wash my face
And light my fire and, all the while,
Bear with his old good-humoured smile
That I told him "Better have kept away
Than come and kill me, night and day,
With, worse than fever throbs and shoots,
The creaking of his clumsy boots."
I am as sure that this he would do,
As that Saint Paul's is striking two.
And I think I rather . . . woe is me!
—Yes, rather should see him than not see,
If lifting a hand could seat him there
Before me in the empty chair
To-night, when my head aches indeed,
And I can neither think nor read
Nor make these purple fingers hold
The pen; this garret's freezing cold!

[1] "Meet the coming disease" — in other words, foresee trouble and forestall it.

And I've a Lady—there he wakes,
The laughing fiend and prince of snakes
Within me, at her name, to pray
Fate send some creature in the way
Of my love for her, to be down-torn,
Upthrust and outward-borne,
So I might prove myself that sea
Of passion which I needs must be!
Call my thoughts false and my fancies quaint
And my style infirm and its figures faint,
All the critics say, and more blame yet,
And not one angry word you get.
But, please you, wonder I would put
My cheek beneath that lady's foot
Rather than trample under mine
The laurels of the Florentine,
And you shall see how the devil spends
A fire God gave for other ends!
I tell you, I stride up and down
This garret, crowned with love's best crown,
And feasted with love's perfect feast,
To think I kill for her, at least,
Body and soul and peace and fame,
Alike youth's end and manhood's aim,
—So is my spirit, as flesh with sin,
Filled full, eaten out and in
With the face of her, the eyes of her,
The lips, the little chin, the stir
Of shadow round her mouth; and she
—I'll tell you,—calmly would decree
That I should roast at a slow fire,
If that would compass her desire
And make her one whom they invite
To the famous ball to-morrow night.

There may be heaven: there must be hell;
Meantime, there is our earth here—well!

1845

THE ITALIAN IN ENGLAND

That second time they hunted me
From hill to plain, from shore to sea,
And Austria, hounding far and wide
Her blood-hounds thro' the country-side,
Breathed hot and instant on my trace,—
I made six days a hiding-place
Of that dry green old aqueduct
Where I and Charles, when boys, have plucked
The fire-flies from the roof above,
Bright creeping thro' the moss they love:

—How long it seems since Charles was lost!
Six days the soldiers crossed and crossed
The country in my very sight;
And when that peril ceased at night,
The sky broke out in red dismay
With signal fires; well, there I lay
Close covered o'er in my recess,
Up to the neck in ferns and cress,
Thinking on Metternich our friend,
And Charles's miserable end,
And much beside, two days; the third,
Hunger o'ercame me when I heard
The peasants from the village go
To work among the maize; you know,
With us in Lombardy, they bring
Provisions packed on mules, a string
With little bells that cheer their task,
And casks, and boughs on every cask
To keep the sun's heat from the wine;
These I let pass in jingling line,
And, close on them, dear noisy crew,
The peasants from the village, too;
For at the very rear would troop
Their wives and sisters in a group
To help, I knew. When these had passed,
I threw my glove to strike the last,
Taking the chance: she did not start,
Much less cry out, but stooped apart,
One instant rapidly glanced round,
And saw me beckon from the ground.
A wild bush grows and hides my crypt;
She picked my glove up while she stripped
A branch off, then rejoined the rest
With that; my glove lay in her breast.
Then I drew breath; they disappeared:
It was for Italy I feared.

An hour, and she returned alone
Exactly where my glove was thrown.
Meanwhile came many thoughts: on me
Rested the hopes of Italy.
I had devised a certain tale
Which, when 'twas told her, could not fail
Persuade a peasant of its truth;
I meant to call a freak of youth
This hiding, and give hopes of pay,
And no temptation to betray.
But when I saw that woman's face,
Its calm simplicity of grace,
Our Italy's own attitude
In which she walked thus far, and stood,
Planting each naked foot so firm,
To crush the snake and spare the worm—
At first sight of her eyes, I said,
"I am that man upon whose head
They fix the price, because I hate
The Austrians over us: the State
Will give you gold—oh, gold so much!—
If you betray me to their clutch,
And be your death, for aught I know,
If once they find you saved their foe.
Now, you must bring me food and drink,
And also paper, pen and ink,
And carry safe what I shall write
To Padua, which you'll reach at night
Before the duomo shuts; go in,
And wait till Tenebræ [1] begin;
Walk to the third confessional,
Between the pillar and the wall,
And kneeling whisper, *Whence comes peace?*
Say it a second time, then cease;
And if the voice inside returns,
From Christ and Freedom; what concerns
The cause of Peace?—for answer, slip
My letter where you placed your lip;
Then come back happy we have done
Our mother service—I, the son,
As you the daughter of our land!"

Three mornings more, she took her stand
In the same place, with the same eyes:
I was no surer of sunrise
Than of her coming. We conferred
Of her own prospects, and I heard
She had a lover—stout and tall,
She said—then let her eyelids fall,
"He could do much"—as if some doubt
Entered her heart,—then, passing out,
"She could not speak for others, who
Had other thoughts; herself she knew:"
And so she brought me drink and food.
After four days, the scouts pursued
Another path; at last arrived
The help my Paduan friends contrived
To furnish me: she brought the news.
For the first time I could not choose
But kiss her hand, and lay my own
Upon her head—"This faith was shown
To Italy, our mother; she
Uses my hand and blesses thee."

[1] A service celebrated in the Roman Catholic Church during the last three days of Holy Week.

She followed down to the sea-shore;
I left and never saw her more.

How very long since I have thought
Concerning—much less wished for—aught
Beside the good of Italy,
For which I live and mean to die!
I never was in love; and since
Charles proved false, what shall now convince
My inmost heart I have a friend?
However, if I pleased to spend
Real wishes on myself—say, three—
I know at least what one should be.
I would grasp Metternich until
I felt his red wet throat distil
In blood thro' these two hands. And next,
—Nor much for that am I perplexed—
Charles, perjured traitor, for his part,
Should die slow of a broken heart
Under his new employers. Last
—Ah, there, what should I wish? For fast
Do I grow old and out of strength.
If I resolved to seek at length
My father's house again, how scared
They all would look, and unprepared!
My brothers live in Austria's pay
—Disowned me long ago, men say;
And all my early mates who used
To praise me so—perhaps induced
More than one early step of mine—
Are turning wise: while some opine
"Freedom grows licence," some suspect
"Haste breeds delay," and recollect
They always said, such premature
Beginnings never could endure!
So, with a sullen "All's for best,"
The land seems settling to its rest.
I think then, I should wish to stand
This evening in that dear, lost land,
Over the sea the thousand miles,
And know if yet that woman smiles
With the calm smile; some little farm
She lives in there, no doubt: what harm
If I sat on the door-side bench,
And, while her spindle made a trench
Fantastically in the dust,
Inquired of all her fortunes—just
Her children's ages and their names,
And what may be the husband's aims
For each of them. I'd talk this out,
And sit there, for an hour about,
Then kiss her hand once more, and lay
Mine on her head, and go my way.

So much for idle wishing—how
It steals the time! To business now.

1845

THE ENGLISHMAN IN ITALY

PIANO DI SORRENTO [1]

Fortù, Fortù, my beloved one,
Sit here by my side,
On my knees put up both little feet!
I was sure, if I tried,
I could make you laugh spite of Scirocco.[2]
Now, open your eyes,
Let me keep you amused till he vanish
In black from the skies,
With telling my memories over
As you tell your beads;
All the Plain saw me gather, I garland
—The flowers or the weeds.

Time for rain! for your long hot dry Autumn
Had net-worked with brown
The white skin of each grape on the bunches,
Marked like a quail's crown,
Those creatures you make such account of,
Whose heads,—speckled white
Over brown like a great spider's back,
As I told you last night,—
Your mother bites off for her supper.
Red-ripe as could be,
Pomegranates were chapping and splitting
In halves on the tree:
And betwixt the loose walls of great flintstone,
Or in the thick dust
On the path, or straight out of the rockside,
Wherever could thrust
Some burnt sprig of bold hardy rock-flower
Its yellow face up,
For the prize were great butterflies fighting,
Some five for one cup.
So, I guessed, ere I got up this morning,
What change was in store,
By the quick rustle-down of the quail-nets
Which woke me before

[1] Plain of Sorrento, adjoining the city of that name on the bay of Naples.

[2] A hot dry wind from Africa, blowing frequently and strongly in the autumn.

I could open my shutter, made fast
With a bough and a stone,
And look thro' the twisted dead vine-twigs,
Sole lattice that's known.
Quick and sharp rang the rings down the net-poles,
While, busy beneath,
Your priest and his brother tugged at them,
The rain in their teeth.
And out upon all the flat house-roofs
Where split figs lay drying,
The girls took the frails under cover:
Nor use seemed in trying
To get out the boats and go fishing,
For, under the cliff,
Fierce the black water frothed o'er the blind-rock.
No seeing our skiff
Arrive about noon from Amalfi,
—Our fisher arrive,
And pitch down his basket before us,
All trembling alive
With pink and grey jellies, your sea-fruit;
You touch the strange lumps,
And mouths gape there, eyes open, all manner
Of horns and of humps,
Which only the fisher looks grave at,
While round him like imps
Cling screaming the children as naked
And brown as his shrimps;
Himself too as bare to the middle
—You see round his neck
The string and its brass coin suspended,
That saves him from wreck.
But to-day not a boat reached Salerno,
So back, to a man,
Came our friends, with whose help in the vineyards
Grape-harvest began.
In the vat, halfway up in our house-side,
Like blood the juice spins,
While your brother all bare-legged is dancing
Till breathless he grins
Dead-beaten in effort on effort
To keep the grapes under,
Since still when he seems all but master,
In pours the fresh plunder
From girls who keep coming and going
With basket on shoulder,
And eyes shut against the rain's driving;
Your girls that are older,
For under the hedges of aloe,
And where, on its bed
Of the orchard's black mould, the love-apple
Lies pulpy and red,
All the young ones are kneeling and filling
Their laps with the snails
Tempted out by this first rainy weather,—
Your best of regales,
As to-night will be proved to my sorrow,
When, supping in state,
We shall feast our grape-gleaners (two dozen,
Three over one plate)
With lasagne [1] so tempting to swallow
In slippery ropes,
And gourds fried in great purple slices,
That colour of popes.
Meantime, see the grape bunch they've brought you:
The rain-water slips
O'er the heavy blue bloom on each globe
Which the wasp to your lips
Still follows with fretful persistence:
Nay, taste, while awake,
This half of a curd-white smooth cheese-ball
That peels, flake by flake,
Like an onion, each smoother and whiter;
Next, sip this weak wine
From the thin green glass flask, with its stopper,
A leaf of the vine;
And end with the prickly-pear's red flesh
That leaves thro' its juice
The stony black seeds on your pearl-teeth.
Scirocco is loose!
Hark, the quick, whistling pelt of the olives
Which, thick in one's track,
Tempt the stranger to pick up and bite them,
Tho' not yet half black!
How the old twisted olive trunks shudder,
The medlars let fall
Their hard fruit, and the brittle great fig-trees
Snap off, figs and all,
For here comes the whole of the tempest!
No refuge, but creep
Back again to my side and my shoulder
And listen or sleep.
O how will your country show next week,
When all the vine-boughs
Have been stripped of their foliage to pasture
The mules and the cows?

[1] A kind of macaroni.

Last eve, I rode over the mountains;
Your brother, my guide,
Soon left me, to feast on the myrtles
That offered, each side,
Their fruit-balls, black, glossy and luscious,—
Or strip from the sorbs
A treasure, or, rosy and wondrous,
Those hairy gold orbs!
But my mule picked his sure sober path out,
Just stopping to neigh
When he recognised down in the valley
His mates on their way
With the faggots and barrels of water;
And soon we emerged
From the plain, where the woods could scarce follow;
And still as we urged
Our way, the woods wondered, and left us,
As up still we trudged
Though the wild path grew wilder each instant,
And the place was e'en grudged
'Mid the rock-chasms and piles of loose stones
Like the loose broken teeth
Of some monster which climbed there to die
From the ocean beneath—
Place was grudged to the silver-grey fume-weed
That clung to the path,
And dark rosemary ever a-dying
That, 'spite the wind's wrath,
So loves the salt rock's face to seaward,
And lentisks [1] as staunch
To the stone where they root and bear berries,
And . . what shows a branch
Coral-coloured, transparent, with circlets
Of pale seagreen leaves;
Over all trod my mule with the caution
Of gleaners o'er sheaves,
Still, foot after foot like a lady,
Till, round after round,
He climbed to the top of Calvano,
And God's own profound
Was above me, and round me the mountains,
And under, the sea,
And within me my heart to bear witness
What was and shall be.
Oh, heaven and the terrible crystal!
No rampart excludes

[1] The mastic tree.

Your eye from the life to be lived
In the blue solitudes.
Oh, those mountains, their infinite movement!
Still moving with you;
For, ever some new head and breast of them
Thrusts into view
To observe the intruder; you see it
If quickly you turn
And, before they escape you surprise them.
They grudge you should learn
How the soft plains they look on, lean over
And love (they pretend)
—Cower beneath them, the flat sea-pine crouches,
The wild fruit-trees bend,
E'en the myrtle-leaves curl, shrink and shut:
All is silent and grave:
'Tis a sensual and timorous beauty,
How fair! but a slave.
So, I turned to the sea; and there slumbered
As greenly as ever
Those isles of the siren, your Galli; [1]
No ages can sever
The Three, nor enable their sister
To join them,—halfway
On the voyage, she looked at Ulysses—
No farther to-day,
Tho' the small one, just launched in the wave,
Watches breast-high and steady
From under the rock, her bold sister
Swum halfway already.
Fortù, shall we sail there together
And see from the sides
Quite new rocks show their faces, new haunts
Where the siren abides?
Shall we sail round and round them, close over
The rocks, tho' unseen,
That ruffle the grey glassy water
To glorious green?
Then scramble from splinter to splinter,
Reach land and explore,
On the largest, the strange square black turret
With never a door,
Just a loop to admit the quick lizards;
Then, stand there and hear
The birds' quiet singing, that tells us
What life is, so clear?
—The secret they sang to Ulysses
When, ages ago,

[1] According to legend it was from three islands off this coast that the sirens sang to Ulysses.

He heard and he knew this life's secret
I hear and I know.

Ah, see! The sun breaks o'er Calvano;
He strikes the great gloom
And flutters it o'er the mount's summit
In airy gold fume.
All is over. Look out, see the gipsy,
Our tinker and smith,
Has arrived, set up bellows and forge,
And down-squatted forthwith
To his hammering, under the wall there;
One eye keeps aloof
The urchins that itch to be putting
His jews'-harps to proof,
While the other, thro' locks of curled wire,
Is watching how sleek
Shines the hog, come to share in the windfall
—Chew, abbot's own cheek!
All is over. Wake up and come out now,
And down let us go,
And see the fine things got in order
At church for the show
Of the Sacrament, set forth this evening.
To-morrow's the Feast
Of the Rosary's Virgin, by no means
Of Virgins the least,
As you'll hear in the off-hand discourse
Which (all nature, no art)
The Dominican brother, these three weeks,
Was getting by heart.
Not a pillar nor post but is dizened
With red and blue papers;
All the roof waves with ribbons, each altar
A-blaze with long tapers;
But the great masterpiece is the scaffold
Rigged glorious to hold
All the fiddlers and fifers and drummers
And trumpeters bold,
Not afraid of Bellini nor Auber,
Who, when the priest's hoarse,
Will strike us up something that's brisk
For the feast's second course.
And then will the flaxen-wigged Image
Be carried in pomp
Thro' the plain, while in gallant procession
The priests mean to stomp.
All round the glad church lie old bottles
With gunpowder stopped,
Which will be, when the Image re-enters,
Religiously popped;
And at night from the crest of Calvano
Great bonfires will hang,
On the plain will the trumpets join chorus,
And more poppers bang.
At all events, come—to the garden
As far as the wall;
See me tap with a hoe on the plaster
Till out there shall fall
A scorpion with wide angry nippers!
—"Such trifles!" you say?
Fortù, in my England at home,
Men meet gravely to-day
And debate, if abolishing Corn-laws
Be righteous and wise
—If 'twere proper, Scirocco should vanish
In black from the skies!

1845

IN A GONDOLA

He sings

I SEND my heart up to thee, all my heart
In this my singing.
For the stars help me, and the sea bears part;
The very night is clinging
Closer to Venice' streets to leave one space
Above me, whence thy face
May light my joyous heart to thee its dwelling-place.

She speaks

Say after me, and try to say
My very words, as if each word
Came from you of your own accord,
In your own voice, in your own way:
"This woman's heart and soul and brain
Are mine as much as this gold chain
She bids me wear; which" (say again)
"I choose to make by cherishing
A precious thing, or choose to fling
Over the boat-side, ring by ring."
And yet once more say . . . no word more
Since words are only words. Give o'er!

Unless you call me, all the same,
Familiarly by my pet name,
Which if the Three should hear you call,
And me reply to, would proclaim
At once our secret to them all.
Ask of me, too, command me, blame—
Do, break down the partition-wall

'Twixt us, the daylight world beholds
Curtained in dusk and splendid folds!
What's left but—all of me to take?
I am the Three's: prevent them, slake
Your thirst! 'Tis said, the Arab sage,
In practising with gems, can loose
Their subtle spirit in his cruce
And leave but ashes: so, sweet mage,
Leave them my ashes when thy use
Sucks out my soul, thy heritage!

He sings

I

Past we glide, and past, and past!
  What's that poor Agnese doing
Where they make the shutters fast?
  Grey Zanobi's just a-wooing
To his couch the purchased bride:
  Past we glide!

II

Past we glide, and past, and past!
  Why's the Pucci Palace flaring
Like a beacon to the blast?
  Guests by hundreds, not one caring
If the dear host's neck were wried:
  Past we glide!

She sings

I

The moth's kiss, first!
Kiss me as if you made believe
You were not sure, this eve
How my face, your flower, had pursed
Its petals up; so, here and there
You brush it, till I grow aware
Who wants me, and wide ope I burst.

II

The bee's kiss, now!
Kiss me as if you entered gay
My heart at some noonday,
A bud that dares not disallow
The claim, so all is rendered up,
And passively its shattered cup
Over your head to sleep I bow.

He sings

I

What are we two?
I am a Jew,
And carry thee, farther than friends can pursue,
To a feast of our tribe;
Where they need thee to bribe
The devil that blasts them unless he imbibe
Thy . . . Scatter the vision forever! And now,
As of old, I am I, thou art thou!

II

Say again, what we are?
The sprite of a star,
I lure thee above where the destinies bar
My plumes their full play
Till a ruddier ray
Than my pale one announce there is withering away
Some . . . Scatter the vision for ever! And now,
As of old, I am I, thou art thou!

He muses

Oh, which were best, to roam or rest?
The land's lap or the water's breast?
To sleep on yellow millet-sheaves,
Or swim in lucid shallows just
Eluding water-lily leaves,
An inch from Death's black fingers, thrust
To lock you, whom release he must;
Which life were best on Summer eves?

He speaks, musing

Lie back; could thought of mine improve you?
From this shoulder let there spring
A wing; from this, another wing;
Wings, not legs and feet, shall move you!
Snow-white must they spring, to blend
With your flesh, but I intend
They shall deepen to the end,
Broader, into burning gold,
Till both wings crescent-wise enfold
Your perfect self, from 'neath your feet
To o'er your head, where, lo, they meet
As if a million sword-blades hurled
Defiance from you to the world!

Rescue me thou, the only real!
And scare away this mad ideal
That came, nor motions to depart!
Thanks! Now, stay ever as thou art!

Still he muses

I

What if the Three should catch at last
Thy serenader? While there's cast
Paul's cloak about my head, and fast
Gian pinions me, Himself has past
His stylet thro' my back; I reel;
And . . . is it thou I feel?

II

They trail me, these three godless knaves,
Past every church that saints and saves,
Nor stop till, where the cold sea raves
By Lido's wet accursed graves,
They scoop mine, roll me to its brink,
And . . . on thy breast I sink!

She replies, musing

Dip your arm o'er the boat-side, elbow-deep,
As I do: thus: were death so unlike sleep,
Caught this way? Death's to fear from flame
    or steel,
Or poison doubtless; but from water—feel!
Go find the bottom! Would you stay me?
    There!
Now pluck a great blade of that ribbon-grass
To plait in where the foolish jewel was,
I flung away: since you have praised my hair,
'Tis proper to be choice in what I wear.

He speaks

Row home? must we row home? Too surely
Know I where its front's demurely
Over the Giudecca [1] piled;
Window just with window mating,
Door on door exactly waiting,
All's the set face of a child:
But behind it, where's a trace
Of the staidness and reserve,
And formal lines without a curve,
In the same child's playing-face?
No two windows look one way
O'er the small sea-water thread
Below them. Ah, the autumn day
I, passing, saw you overhead!
First, out a cloud of curtain blew,
Then a sweet cry, and last came you—
To catch your lory that must needs
Escape just then, of all times then,

[1] One of the canals of Venice.

To peck a tall plant's fleecy seeds,
And make me happiest of men.
I scarce could breathe to see you reach
So far back o'er the balcony
To catch him ere he climbed too high
Above you in the Smyrna peach
That quick the round smooth cord of gold,
This coiled hair on your head, unrolled,
Fell down you like a gorgeous snake
The Roman girls were wont, of old,
When Rome there was, for coolness' sake
To let it lie curling o'er their bosoms.
Dear lory, may his beak retain
Ever its delicate rose stain
As if the wounded lotus-blossoms
Had marked their thief to know again!

Stay longer yet, for others' sake
Than mine! What should your chamber do?
—With all its rarities that ache
In silence while day lasts, but wake
At night-time and their life renew,
Suspended just to pleasure you
Who brought against their will together
These objects, and, while day lasts, weave
Around them such a magic tether
That dumb they look; your harp, believe,
With all the sensitive tight strings
Which dare not speak, now to itself
Breathes slumberously, as if some elf
Went in and out the chords, his wings
Make murmur wheresoe'er they graze,
As an angel may, between the maze
Of midnight palace-pillars, on
And on, to sow God's plagues, have gone
Through guilty glorious Babylon.
And while such murmurs flow, the nymph
Bends o'er the harp-top from her shell
As the dry limpet for the lymph
Come with a tune he knows so well.
And how your statues' hearts must swell!
And how your pictures must descend
To see each other, friend with friend!
Oh, could you take them by surprise,[1]
You'd find Schidone's eager Duke
Doing the quaintest courtesies
To that prim saint by Haste-thee-Luke!

[1] Browning imagines a group of pictures in her house. The artists are real — Schidone, Haste-thee-Luke (Luca Giordano), Giorgione of Castelfranco, and Titian — but the pictures are imaginary.

And, deeper into her rock den,
Bold Castelfranco's Magdalen
You'd find retreated from the ken
Of that robed counsel-keeping Ser—
As if the Tizian thinks of her,
And is not, rather, gravely bent
On seeing for himself what toys
Are these, his progeny invent,
What litter now the board employs
Whereon he signed a document
That got him murdered! Each enjoys
Its night so well, you cannot break
The sport up, so, indeed must make
More stay with me, for others' sake.

She speaks

I

To-morrow, if a harp-string, say,
Is used to tie the jasmine back
That overfloods my room with sweets,
Contrive your Zorzi somehow meets
My Zanze! If the ribbon's black,
The Three are watching: keep away!

II

Your gondola—let Zorzi wreathe
A mesh of water-weeds about
Its prow, as if he unaware
Had struck some quay or bridge-foot stair!
That I may throw a paper out
As you and he go underneath.

There's Zanze's vigilant taper; safe are we.
Only one minute more to-night with me?
Resume your past self of a month ago!
Be you the bashful gallant, I will be
The lady with the colder breast than snow.
Now bow you, as becomes, nor touch my hand
More than I touch yours when I step to land,
And say, "All thanks, Siora!"—
Heart to heart
And lips to lips! Yet once more, ere we part,
Clasp me and make me thine, as mine thou art!

He is surprised and stabbed

It was ordained to be so, sweet!—and best
Comes now, beneath thine eyes, upon thy breast.
Still kiss me! Care not for the cowards! Care
Only to put aside thy beauteous hair
My blood will hurt! The Three, I do not scorn
To death, because they never lived: but I
Have lived indeed, and so—(yet one more kiss)—can die!

1842

A LIGHT WOMAN

I

So far as our story approaches the end,
Which do you pity the most of us three?—
My friend, or the mistress of my friend
With her wanton eyes, or me?

II

My friend was already too good to lose,
And seemed in the way of improvement yet,
When she crossed his path with her hunting-noose
And over him drew her net.

III

When I saw him tangled in her toils,
A shame, said I, if she adds just him
To her nine-and-ninety other spoils,
The hundredth for a whim!

IV

And before my friend be wholly hers,
How easy to prove to him, I said,
An eagle's the game her pride prefers,
Though she snaps at a wren instead!

V

So, I gave her eyes my own eyes to take,
My hand sought hers as in earnest need,
And round she turned for my noble sake,
And gave me herself indeed.

VI

The eagle am I, with my fame in the world,
The wren is he, with his maiden face.
—You look away and your lip is curled?
Patience, a moment's space!

VII

For see, my friend goes shaking and white;
He eyes me as the basilisk:
I have turned, it appears, his day to night,
Eclipsing his sun's disk.

VIII

And I did it, he thinks, as a very thief:
  "Though I love her—that, he comprehends—
One should master one's passions, (love, in chief)
  And be loyal to one's friends!"

IX

And she,—she lies in my hand as tame
  As a pear late basking over a wall;
Just a touch to try and off it came;
  'Tis mine,—can I let it fall?

X

With no mind to eat it, that's the worst!
  Were it thrown in the road, would the case assist?
'Twas quenching a dozen blue-flies' thirst
  When I gave its stalk a twist.

XI

And I,—what I seem to my friend, you see:
  What I soon shall seem to his love, you guess:
What I seem to myself, do you ask of me?
  No hero, I confess.

XII

'Tis an awkward thing to play with souls,
  And matter enough to save one's own:
Yet think of my friend, and the burning coals
  He played with for bits of stone!

XIII

One likes to show the truth for the truth;
  That the woman was light is very true:
But suppose she says,—Never mind that youth!
  What wrong have I done to you?

XIV

Well, any how, here the story stays,
  So far at least as I understand;
And, Robert Browning, you writer of plays,
  Here's a subject made to your hand!

1855

THE LAST RIDE TOGETHER

I

I said—Then, dearest, since 'tis so,
Since now at length my fate I know,
Since nothing all my love avails,
Since all, my life seemed meant for, fails,
  Since this was written and needs must be—
My whole heart rises up to bless
Your name in pride and thankfulness!
Take back the hope you gave,—I claim
Only a memory of the same,
—And this beside, if you will not blame,
  Your leave for one more last ride with me.

II

My mistress bent that brow of hers;
Those deep dark eyes where pride demurs
When pity would be softening through,
Fixed me a breathing-while or two
  With life or death in the balance: right!
The blood replenished me again;
My last thought was at least not vain:
I and my mistress, side by side
Shall be together, breathe and ride,
So, one day more am I deified.
  Who knows but the world may end to-night?

III

Hush! if you saw some western cloud
All billowy-bosomed, over-bowed
By many benedictions—sun's
And moon's and evening-star's at once—
  And so, you, looking and loving best,
Conscious grew, your passion drew
Cloud, sunset, moonrise, star-shine too,
Down on you, near and yet more near,
Till flesh must fade for heaven was here!—
Thus leant she and lingered—joy and fear!
  Thus lay she a moment on my breast.

IV

Then we began to ride. My soul
Smoothed itself out, a long-cramped scroll
Freshening and fluttering in the wind.
Past hopes already lay behind.
  What need to strive with a life awry?
Had I said that, had I done this,
So might I gain, so might I miss.
Might she have loved me? just as well
She might have hated, who can tell!
Where had I been now if the worst befell?
  And here we are riding, she and I.

V

Fail I alone, in words and deeds?
Why, all men strive and who succeeds?

We rode; it seemed my spirit flew,
Saw other regions, cities new,
  As the world rushed by on either side.
I thought,—All labour, yet no less
Bear up beneath their unsuccess.
Look at the end of work, contrast
The petty done, the undone vast,
This present of theirs with the hopeful past!
  I hoped she would love me; here we ride.

VI

What hand and brain went ever paired?
What heart alike conceived and dared?
What act proved all its thought had been?
What will but felt the fleshly screen?
  We ride and I see her bosom heave.
There's many a crown for who can reach.
Ten lines, a statesman's life in each!
The flag stuck on a heap of bones,
A soldier's doing! what atones?
They scratch his name on the abbey-stones.
  My riding is better, by their leave.

VII

What does it all mean, poet? Well,
Your brains beat into rhythm, you tell
What we felt only; you expressed
You hold things beautiful the best,
  And pace them in rhyme so, side by side.
'Tis something, nay 'tis much: but then,
Have you yourself what's best for men?
Are you—poor, sick, old ere your time—
Nearer one whit your own sublime
Than we who never have turned a rhyme?
  Sing, riding's a joy! For me, I ride.

VIII

And you, great sculptor—so, you gave
A score of years to Art, her slave,
And that's your Venus, whence we turn
To yonder girl that fords the burn!
  You acquiesce, and shall I repine?
What, man of music, you grown grey
With notes and nothing else to say,
Is this your sole praise from a friend,
"Greatly his opera's strains intend,
But in music we know how fashions end!"
  I gave my youth; but we ride, in fine.

IX

Who knows what's fit for us? Had fate
Proposed bliss here should sublimate
My being—had I signed the bond—
Still one must lead some life beyond,
  Have a bliss to die with, dim-descried.
This foot once planted on the goal,
This glory-garland round my soul,
Could I descry such? Try and test!
I sink back shuddering from the quest.
Earth being so good, would heaven seem
    best?
  Now, heaven and she are beyond this ride.

X

And yet—she has not spoke so long!
What if heaven be that, fair and strong
At life's best, with our eyes upturned
Whither life's flower is first discerned,
  We, fixed so, ever should so abide?
What if we still ride on, we two
With life for ever old yet new,
Changed not in kind but in degree,
The instant made eternity,—
And heaven just prove that I and she
  Ride, ride together, for ever ride?

1855

THE FLIGHT OF THE DUCHESS

I

You're my friend:
I was the man the Duke spoke to;
I helped the Duchess to cast off his yoke, too;
So, here's the tale from beginning to end,
My friend!

II

Ours is a great wild country:
If you climb to our castle's top,
I don't see where your eye can stop;
For when you've passed the corn-field coun-
    try,
Where vineyards leave off, flocks are packed,
And sheep-range leads to cattle-tract,
And cattle-tract to open-chase,
And open-chase to the very base
Of the mountain, where, at a funeral pace,
Round about, solemn and slow,
One by one, row after row,
Up and up the pine-trees go,
So, like black priests up, and so
Down the other side again
To another greater, wilder country,
That's one vast red drear burnt-up plain,

Branched through and through with many a vein
Whence iron's dug, and copper's dealt;
Look right, look left, look straight before,—
Beneath they mine, above they smelt,
Copper-ore and iron-ore,
And forge and furnace mould and melt,
And so on, more and ever more,
Till, at the last, for a bounding belt,
Comes the salt sand hoar of the great sea-shore,
—And the whole is our Duke's country!

III

I was born the day this present Duke was—
(And O, says the song, ere I was old!)
In the castle where the other Duke was—
(When I was happy and young, not old!)
I in the kennel, he in the bower:
We are of like age to an hour.
My father was huntsman in that day;
Who has not heard my father say
That, when a boar was brought to bay,
Three times, four times out of five,
With his huntspear he'd contrive
To get the killing-place transfixed,
And pin him true, both eyes betwixt?
And that's why the old Duke would rather
He lost a salt-pit than my father,
And loved to have him ever in call;
That's why my father stood in the hall
When the old Duke brought his infant out
To show the people, and while they passed
The wondrous bantling round about,
Was first to start at the outside blast
As the Kaiser's courier blew his horn,
Just a month after the babe was born.
"And," quoth the Kaiser's courier, "since
The Duke has got an heir, our Prince
Needs the Duke's self at his side:"
The Duke looked down and seemed to wince,
But he thought of wars o'er the world wide,
Castles a-fire, men on their march,
The toppling tower, the crashing arch;
And up he looked, and awhile he eyed
The row of crests and shields and banners,
Of all achievements after all manners,
And "ay," said the Duke with a surly pride.
The more was his comfort when he died
At next year's end, in a velvet suit,
With a gilt glove on his hand, his foot
In a silken shoe for a leather boot,
Petticoated like a herald,
In a chamber next to an ante-room,
Where he breathed the breath of page and groom,
What he called stink, and they, perfume:
—They should have set him on red Berold,
Mad with pride, like fire to manage!
They should have got his cheek fresh tannage
Such a day as to-day in the merry sunshine!
Had they stuck on his fist a rough-foot merlin!
(Hark, the wind's on the heath at its game!
Oh for a noble falcon-lanner
To flap each broad wing like a banner,
And turn in the wind, and dance like flame!)
Had they broached a white-beer cask from Berlin
—Or if you incline to prescribe mere wine
Put to his lips, when they saw him pine,
A cup of our own Moldavia fine,
Cotnar, for instance, green as May sorrel,
And ropy with sweet,—we shall not quarrel.

IV

So, at home, the sick tall yellow Duchess
Was left with the infant in her clutches,
She being the daughter of God knows who:
And now was the time to revisit her tribe.
So, abroad and afar they went, the two,
And let our people rail and gibe
At the empty hall and extinguished fire,
As loud as we liked, but ever in vain,
Till after long years we had our desire,
And back came the Duke and his mother again.

V

And he came back the pertest little ape
That ever affronted human shape;
Full of his travel, struck at himself.
You'd say, he despised our bluff old ways?
—Not he! For in Paris they told the elf
Our rough North land was the Land of Lays,
The one good thing left in evil days;
Since the Mid-Age was the Heroic Time,
And only in wild nooks like ours
Could you taste of it yet as in its prime,
And see true castles, with proper towers,
Young-hearted women, old-minded men,
And manners now as manners were then.
So, all that the old Dukes had been, without knowing it,

This Duke would fain know he was, without being it;
'Twas not for the joy's self, but the joy of his showing it,
Nor for the pride's self, but the pride of our seeing it,
He revived all usages thoroughly worn-out,
The souls of them fumed-forth, the hearts of them torn-out:
And chief in the chase his neck he perilled,
On a lathy horse, all legs and length,
With blood for bone, all speed, no strength;
—They should have set him on red Berold,
With the red eye slow consuming in fire,
And the thin stiff ear like an abbey spire!

VI

Well, such as he was, he must marry, we heard:
And out of a convent, at the word,
Came the lady, in time of spring.
—Oh, old thoughts they cling, they cling!
That day, I know, with a dozen oaths
I clad myself in thick hunting-clothes
Fit for the chase of urochs or buffle
In winter-time when you need to muffle.
But the Duke had a mind we should cut a figure,
And so we saw the lady arrive:
My friend, I have seen a white crane bigger!
She was the smallest lady alive,
Made in a piece of nature's madness,
Too small, almost, for the life and gladness
That over-filled her, as some hive
Out of the bears' reach on the high trees
Is crowded with its safe merry bees:
In truth, she was not hard to please!
Up she looked, down she looked, round at the mead,
Straight at the castle, that's best indeed
To look at from outside the walls:
As for us, styled the "serfs and thralls,"
She as much thanked me as if she had said it,
(With her eyes, do you understand?)
Because I patted her horse while I led it;
And Max, who rode on her other hand,
Said, no bird flew past but she inquired
What its true name was, nor ever seemed tired—
If that was an eagle she saw hover,
And the green and grey bird on the field was the plover.
When suddenly appeared the Duke:
And as down she sprung, the small foot pointed
On to my hand,—as with a rebuke,
And as if his backbone were not jointed,
The Duke stepped rather aside than forward,
And welcomed her with his grandest smile;
And, mind you, his mother all the while
Chilled in the rear, like a wind to Nor'ward;
And up, like a weary yawn, with its pulleys
Went, in a shriek, the rusty portcullis;
And, like a glad sky the north-wind sullies,
The lady's face stopped its play,
As if her first hair had grown grey;
For such things must begin some one day!

VII

In a day or two she was well again;
As who should say, "You labour in vain!
This is all a jest against God, who meant
I should ever be, as I am, content
And glad in his sight; therefore, glad I will be."
So, smiling as at first went she.

VIII

She was active, stirring, all fire—
Could not rest, could not tire—
To a stone she might have given life!
(I myself loved once, in my day)
—For a shepherd's, miner's, huntsman's wife,
(I had a wife, I know what I say)
Never in all the world such an one!
And here was plenty to be done,
And she that could do it, great or small,
She was to do nothing at all.
There was already this man in his post,
This in his station, and that in his office,
And the Duke's plan admitted a wife, at most,
To meet his eye, with the other trophies,
Now outside the hall, now in it,
To sit thus, stand thus, see and be seen,
At the proper place in the proper minute,
And die away the life between.
And it was amusing enough, each infraction
Of rule—(but for after-sadness that came)
To hear the consummate self-satisfaction
With which the young Duke and the old dame
Would let her advise, and criticise,
And, being a fool, instruct the wise,

And, childlike, parcel out praise or blame:
They bore it all in complacent guise,
As though an artificer, after contriving
A wheel-work image as if it were living,
Should find with delight it could motion to strike him!
So found the Duke, and his mother like him:
The lady hardly got a rebuff—
That had not been contemptuous enough,
With his cursed smirk, as he nodded applause,
And kept off the old mother-cat's claws.

IX

So, the little lady grew silent and thin,
  Paling and ever paling,
As the way is with a hid chagrin;
  And the Duke perceived that she was ailing,
And said in his heart, "'Tis done to spite me,
But I shall find in my power to right me!"
Don't swear, friend! the old one, many a year,
Is in hell, and the Duke's self . . . you shall hear.

X

Well, early in autumn, at first winter-warning,
When the stag had to break with his foot, of a morning,
A drinking-hole out of the fresh tender ice
That covered the pond till the sun, in a trice,
Loosening it, let out a ripple of gold,
And another and another, and faster and faster,
Till, dimpling to blindness, the wide water rolled:
Then it so chanced that the Duke our master
Asked himself what were the pleasures in season,
And found, since the calendar bade him be hearty,
He should do the Middle Age no treason
In resolving on a hunting-party.
Always provided, old books showed the way of it!
What meant old poets by their strictures?
And when old poets had said their say of it,
How taught old painters in their pictures?
We must revert to the proper channels,
Workings in tapestry, paintings on panels,
And gather up woodcraft's authentic traditions:
Here was food for our various ambitions,
As on each case, exactly stated—
To encourage your dog, now, the properest chirrup,
Or best prayer to St. Hubert on mounting your stirrup—
We of the household took thought and debated.
Blessed was he whose back ached with the jerkin
His sire was wont to do forest-work in;
Blesseder he who nobly sunk "ohs"
And "ahs" while he tugged on his grandsire's trunk-hose;
What signified hats if they had no rims on,
Each slouching before and behind like the scallop,
And able to serve at sea for a shallop,
Loaded with lacquer and looped with crimson?
So that the deer now, to make a short rhyme on't,
What with our Venerers, Prickers, and Verderers,
Might hope for real hunters at length, and not murderers,
And oh, the Duke's tailor, he had a hot time on't!

XI

Now you must know that when the first dizziness
Of flap-hats and buff-coats and jack-boots subsided,
The Duke put this question, "The Duke's part provided,
Had not the Duchess some share in the business?"
For out of the mouth of two or three witnesses
Did he establish all fit-or-unfitnesses:
And, after much laying of heads together,
Somebody's cap got a notable feather
By the announcement with proper unction
That he had discovered the lady's function;
Since ancient authors gave this tenet,
"When horns wind a mort and the deer is at siege,
Let the dame of the Castle prick forth on her jennet,
And, with water to wash the hands of her liege
In a clean ewer with a fair toweling,
Let her preside at the disemboweling."
Now, my friend, if you had so little religion

As to catch a hawk, some falcon-lanner,
And thrust her broad wings like a banner
Into a coop for a vulgar pigeon;
And if day by day and week by week
You cut her claws, and sealed her eyes,
And clipped her wings, and tied her beak,
Would it cause you any great surprise
If, when you decided to give her an airing,
You found she needed a little preparing?
—I say, should you be such a curmudgeon,
If she clung to the perch, as to take it in dudgeon?
Yet when the Duke to his lady signified,
Just a day before, as he judged most dignified,
In what a pleasure she was to participate,—
And, instead of leaping wide in flashes,
Her eyes just lifted their long lashes,
As if pressed by fatigue even he could not dissipate,
And duly acknowledged the Duke's forethought,
But spoke of her health, if her health were worth aught,
Of the weight by day and the watch by night,
And much wrong now that used to be right,
So, thanking him, declined the hunting,—
Was conduct ever more affronting?
With all the ceremony settled—
With the towel ready, and the sewer
Polishing up his oldest ewer,
And the jennet pitched upon, a piebald,
Black-barred, cream-coated and pink eye-balled,
No wonder if the Duke was nettled!
And when she persisted nevertheless,—
Well, I suppose here's the time to confess
That there ran half round our lady's chamber
A balcony none of the hardest to clamber;
And that Jacynth the tire-woman, ready in waiting,
Stayed in call outside, what need of relating?
And since Jacynth was like a June rose, why, a fervent
Adorer of Jacynth of course was your servant;
And if she had the habit to peep through the casement,
How could I keep at any vast distance?
And so, as I say, on the lady's persistence,
The Duke, dumb-stricken with amazement,
Stood for a while in a sultry smother,
And then, with a smile that partook of the awful,
Turned her over to his yellow mother
To learn what was held decorous and lawful;
And the mother smelt blood with a cat-like instinct,
As her cheek quick whitened thro' all its quince-tinct.
Oh, but the Lady heard the whole truth at once!
What meant she?—Who was she?—Her duty and station,
The wisdom of age and the folly of youth, at once,
Its decent regard and its fitting relation—
In brief, my friend, set all the devils in hell free
And turn them out to carouse in a belfry
And treat the priests to a fifty-part canon,
And then you may guess how that tongue of hers ran on!
Well, somehow or other it ended at last
And, licking her whiskers, out she passed;
And after her,—making (he hoped) a face
Like Emperor Nero or Sultan Saladin,
Stalked the Duke's self with the austere grace
Of ancient hero or modern paladin,
From door to staircase—oh, such a solemn
Unbending of the vertebral column!

XII

However, at sunrise our company mustered;
And here was the huntsman bidding unkennel,
And there 'neath his bonnet the pricker blustered,
With feather dank as a bough of wet fennel;
For the court-yard walls were filled with fog
You might have cut as an axe chops a log—
Like so much wool for colour and bulkiness;
And out rode the Duke in a perfect sulkiness,
Since, before breakfast, a man feels but queasily,
And a sinking at the lower abdomen
Begins the day with indifferent omen.
And lo, as he looked around uneasily,
The sun ploughed the fog up and drove it asunder
This way and that from the valley under;
And, looking through the court-yard arch,

Down in the valley, what should meet him
But a troop of Gipsies on their march,
No doubt with the annual gifts to greet him.

XIII

Now, in your land, Gipsies reach you, only
After reaching all lands beside;
North they go, South they go, trooping or lonely,
And still, as they travel far and wide,
Catch they and keep now a trace here, a trace there,
That puts you in mind of a place here, a place there.
But with us, I believe they rise out of the ground,
And nowhere else, I take it, are found
With the earth-tint yet so freshly embrowned:
Born, no doubt, like insects which breed on
The very fruit they are meant to feed on.
For the earth—not a use to which they don't turn it,
The ore that grows in the mountain's womb,
Or the sand in the pits like a honeycomb,
They sift and soften it, bake it and burn it—
Whether they weld you, for instance, a snaffle
With side-bars never a brute can baffle;
Or a lock that's a puzzle of wards within wards;
Or, if your colt's forefoot inclines to curve inwards,
Horseshoes they'll hammer which turn on a swivel
And won't allow the hoof to shrivel.
Then they cast bells like the shell of the winkle
That keep a stout heart in the ram with their tinkle;
But the sand—they pinch and pound it like otters;
Commend me to Gipsy glass-makers and potters!
Glasses they'll blow you, crystal-clear,
Where just a faint cloud of rose shall appear,
As if in pure water you dropped and let die
A bruised black-blooded mulberry;
And that other sort, their crowning pride,
With long white threads distinct inside,
Like the lake-flower's fibrous roots which dangle
Loose such a length and never tangle,
Where the bold sword-lily cuts the clear waters,
And the cup-lily couches with all the white daughters:
Such are the works they put their hand to,
The uses they turn and twist iron and sand to.
And these made the troop, which our Duke saw sally
Toward his castle from out of the valley,
Men and women, like new-hatched spiders,
Come out with the morning to greet our riders.
And up they wound till they reached the ditch,
Whereat all stopped save one, a witch
That I knew, as she hobbled from the group,
By her gait directly and her stoop,
I, whom Jacynth was used to importune
To let that same witch tell us our fortune;
The oldest Gipsy then above ground;
And, sure as the autumn season came round,
She paid us a visit for profit or pastime,
And every time, as she swore, for the last time.
And presently she was seen to sidle
Up to the Duke till she touched his bridle,
So that the horse of a sudden reared up
As under its nose the old witch peered up
With her worn-out eyes, or rather eye-holes
Of no use now but to gather brine,
And began a kind of level whine
Such as they use to sing to their viols
When their ditties they go grinding
Up and down with nobody minding:
And then, as of old, at the end of the humming
Her usual presents were forthcoming
—A dog-whistle blowing the fiercest of trebles,
(Just a sea-shore stone holding a dozen fine pebbles,)
Or a porcelain mouthpiece to screw on a pipe-end,—
And so she awaited her annual stipend.
But this time, the Duke would scarcely vouchsafe
A word in reply; and in vain she felt
With twitching fingers at her belt
For the purse of sleek pine-marten pelt,
Ready to put what he gave in her pouch safe,—
Till, either to quicken his apprehension,
Or possibly with an after-intention,

She was come, she said, to pay her duty
To the new Duchess, the youthful beauty.
No sooner had she named his lady,
Than a shine lit up the face so shady,
And its smirk returned with a novel meaning—
For it struck him, the babe just wanted weaning;
If one gave her a taste of what life was and sorrow,
She, foolish to-day, would be wiser to-morrow;
And who so fit a teacher of trouble
As this sordid crone bent well-nigh double?
So, glancing at her wolf-skin vesture,
(If such it was, for they grow so hirsute
That their own fleece serves for natural fur-suit)
He was contrasting, 'twas plain from his gesture,
The life of the Lady so flower-like and delicate
With the loathsome squalor of this helicat.
I, in brief, was the man the Duke beckoned
From out of the throng, and while I drew near
He told the crone—as I since have reckoned
By the way he bent and spoke into her ear
With circumspection and mystery—
The main of the lady's history,
Her frowardness and ingratitude:
And for all the crone's submissive attitude
I could see round her mouth the loose plaits tightening,
And her brow with assenting intelligence brightening.
As though she engaged with hearty goodwill
Whatever he now might enjoin to fulfil,
And promised the lady a thorough frightening.
And so, just giving her a glimpse
Of a purse, with the air of a man who imps
The wing of the hawk that shall fetch the hernshaw,
He bade me take the Gipsy mother
And set her telling some story or other
Of hill or dale, oak-wood or fernshaw,
To while away a weary hour
For the lady left alone in her bower,
Whose mind and body craved exertion
And yet shrank from all better diversion.

XIV

Then clapping heel to his horse, the mere curveter,
Out rode the Duke, and after his hollo
Horses and hounds swept, huntsman and servitor,
And back I turned and bade the crone follow.
And what makes me confident what's to be told you
Had all along been of this crone's devising,
Is, that, on looking round sharply, behold you,
There was a novelty quick as surprising:
For first, she had shot up a full head in stature,
And her step kept pace with mine nor faltered,
As if age had foregone its usurpature,
And the ignoble mien was wholly altered,
And the face looked quite of another nature,
And the change reached too, whatever the change meant,
Her shaggy wolf-skin cloak's arrangement:
For where its tatters hung loose like sedges,
Gold coins were glittering on the edges,
Like the band-roll strung with tomans
Which proves the veil a Persian woman's:
And under her brow, like a snail's horns newly
Come out as after the rain he paces,
Two unmistakeable eye-points duly
Live and aware looked out of their places.
So, we went and found Jacynth at the entry
Of the lady's chamber standing sentry;
I told the command and produced my companion,
And Jacynth rejoiced to admit any one,
For since last night, by the same token,
Not a single word had the lady spoken:
They went in both to the presence together,
While I in the balcony watched the weather.

XV

And now, what took place at the very first of all,
I cannot tell, as I never could learn it:
Jacynth constantly wished a curse to fall
On that little head of hers and burn it,
If she knew how she came to drop so soundly
Asleep of a sudden and there continue
The whole time sleeping as profoundly
As one of the boars my father would pin you
'Twixt the eyes where the life holds garrison,
—Jacynth forgive me the comparison!

But where I begin my own narration
Is a little after I took my station
To breathe the fresh air from the balcony,
And, having in those days a falcon eye,
To follow the hunt thro' the open country,
From where the bushes thinlier crested
The hillocks, to a plain where's not one tree.
When, in a moment, my ear was arrested
By—was it singing, or was it saying,
Or a strange musical instrument playing
In the chamber?—and to be certain
I pushed the lattice, pulled the curtain,
And there lay Jacynth asleep,
Yet as if a watch she tried to keep,
In a rosy sleep along the floor
With her head against the door;
While in the midst, on the seat of state,
Was a queen—the Gipsy woman late,
With head and face downbent
On the lady's head and face intent:
For, coiled at her feet like a child at ease,
The lady sat between her knees,
And o'er them the lady's clasped hands met,
And on those hands her chin was set,
And her upturned face met the face of the crone
Wherein the eyes had grown and grown
As if she could double and quadruple
At pleasure the play of either pupil
—Very like, by her hands' slow fanning,
As up and down like a gor-crow's flappers
They moved to measure, or bell-clappers.
I said, "Is it blessing, is it banning,
Do they applaud you or burlesque you—
Those hands and fingers with no flesh on?"
But, just as I thought to spring in to the rescue,
At once I was stopped by the lady's expression:
For it was life her eyes were drinking
From the crone's wide pair above unwinking,
—Life's pure fire received without shrinking,
Into the heart and breast whose heaving
Told you no single drop they were leaving,
—Life, that filling her, passed redundant
Into her very hair, back swerving
Over each shoulder, loose and abundant,
As her head thrown back showed the white throat curving;
And the very tresses shared in the pleasure,
Moving to the mystic measure,
Bounding as the bosom bounded.
I stopped short, more and more confounded,
As still her cheeks burned and eyes glistened,
As she listened and she listened:
When all at once a hand detained me,
The selfsame contagion gained me,
And I kept time to the wondrous chime,
Making out words and prose and rhyme,
Till it seemed that the music furled
Its wings like a task fulfilled, and dropped
From under the words it first had propped,
And left them midway in the world:
Word took word as hand takes hand,
I could hear at last, and understand,
And when I held the unbroken thread,
The Gipsy said:—
"And so at last we find my tribe.
And so I set thee in the midst,
And to one and all of them describe
What thou saidst and what thou didst,
Our long and terrible journey through,
And all thou art ready to say and do
In the trials that remain:
I trace them the vein and the other vein
That meet on thy brow and part again,
Making our rapid mystic mark;
And I bid my people prove and probe
Each eye's profound and glorious globe
Till they detect the kindred spark
In those depths so dear and dark,
Like the spots that snap and burst and flee,
Circling over the midnight sea.
And on that round young cheek of thine
I make them recognize the tinge,
As when of the costly scarlet wine
They drip so much as will impinge
And spread in a thinnest scale afloat
One thick gold drop from the olive's coat
Over a silver plate whose sheen
Still thro' the mixture shall be seen.
For so I prove thee, to one and all,
Fit, when my people ope their breast,
To see the sign, and hear the call,
And take the vow, and stand the test
Which adds one more child to the rest—
When the breast is bare and the arms are wide,
And the world is left outside.
For there is probation to decree,
And many and long must the trials be
Thou shalt victoriously endure,
If that brow is true and those eyes are sure;
Like a jewel-finder's fierce assay
Of the prize he dug from its mountain tomb—

Let once the vindicating ray
Leap out amid the anxious gloom,
And steel and fire have done their part
And the prize falls on its finder's heart;
So, trial after trial past,
Wilt thou fall at the very last
Breathless, half in trance
With the thrill of the great deliverance,
Into our arms for evermore;
And thou shalt know, those arms once curled
About thee, what we knew before,
How love is the only good in the world.
Henceforth be loved as heart can love,
Or brain devise, or hand approve!
Stand up, look below,
It is our life at thy feet we throw
To step with into light and joy;
Not a power of life but we employ
To satisfy thy nature's want;
Art thou the tree that props the plant,
Or the climbing plant that seeks the tree—
Canst thou help us, must we help thee?
If any two creatures grew into one,
They would do more than the world has done:
Though each apart were never so weak,
Ye vainly through the world should seek
For the knowledge and the might
Which in such union grew their right:
So, to approach at least that end,
And blend,—as much as may be, blend
Thee with us or us with thee,—
As climbing plant or propping tree,
Shall some one deck thee, over and down,
Up and about, with blossoms and leaves?
Fix his heart's fruit for thy garland-crown,
Cling with his soul as the gourd-vine cleaves,
Die on thy boughs and disappear
While not a leaf of thine is sere?
Or is the other fate in store,
And art thou fitted to adore,
To give thy wondrous self away,
And take a stronger nature's sway?
I foresee and could foretell
Thy future portion, sure and well:
But those passionate eyes speak true, speak true,
Let them say what thou shalt do!
Only be sure thy daily life,
In its peace, or in its strife,
Never shall be unobserved;
We pursue thy whole career,
And hope for it, or doubt, or fear,—
Lo, hast thou kept thy path or swerved,
We are beside thee in all thy ways,
With our blame, with our praise,
Our shame to feel, our pride to show,
Glad, angry—but indifferent, no!
Whether it is thy lot to go,
For the good of us all, where the haters meet
In the crowded city's horrible street;
Or thou step alone through the morass
Where never sound yet was
Save the dry quick clap of the stork's bill,
For the air is still, and the water still,
When the blue breast of the dipping coot
Dives under, and all is mute.
So, at the last shall come old age,
Decrepit as befits that stage;
How else wouldst thou retire apart
With the hoarded memories of thy heart,
And gather all to the very least
Of the fragments of life's earlier feast,
Let fall through eagerness to find
The crowning dainties yet behind?
Ponder on the entire past
Laid together thus at last,
When the twilight helps to fuse
The first fresh, with the faded hues,
And the outline of the whole,
As round eve's shades their framework roll,
Grandly fronts for once thy soul.
And then as, 'mid the dark, a gleam
Of yet another morning breaks,
And like the hand which ends a dream,
Death, with the might of his sunbeam,
Touches the flesh and the soul awakes,
Then—"

Ay, then indeed something would happen!
But what? For here her voice changed like a bird's;
There grew more of the music and less of the words;
Had Jacynth only been by me to clap pen
To paper and put you down every syllable
With those clever clerkly fingers,
All that I've forgotten as well as what lingers
In this old brain of mine that's but ill able
To give you even this poor version
Of the speech I spoil, as it were, with stammering
—More fault of those who had the hammering

Of prosody into me and syntax,
And did it, not with hobnails but tintacks!
But to return from this excursion,—
Just, do you mark, when the song was sweetest,
The peace most deep and the charm completest,
There came, shall I say, a snap—
And the charm vanished!
And my sense returned, so strangely banished,
And, starting as from a nap,
I knew the crone was bewitching my lady,
With Jacynth asleep; and but one spring made I
Down from the casement, round to the portal,
Another minute and I had entered,—
When the door opened, and more than mortal
Stood, with a face where to my mind centred
All beauties I ever saw or shall see,
The Duchess: I stopped as if struck by palsy.
She was so different, happy and beautiful,
I felt at once that all was best,
And that I had nothing to do, for the rest,
But wait her commands, obey and be dutiful.
Not that, in fact, there was any commanding;
I saw the glory of her eye,
And the brow's height and the breast's expanding,
And I was hers to live or to die.
As for finding what she wanted,
You know God Almighty granted
Such little signs should serve wild creatures
To tell one another all their desires,
So that each knows what his friend requires,
And does its bidding without teachers.
I preceded her; the crone
Followed silent and alone;
I spoke to her, but she merely jabbered
In the old style; both her eyes had slunk
Back to their pits; her stature shrunk;
In short, the soul in its body sunk
Like a blade sent home to its scabbard.
We descended, I preceding;
Crossed the court with nobody heeding;
All the world was at the chase,
The court-yard like a desert-place,
The stable emptied of its small fry;
I saddled myself the very palfrey
I remember patting while it carried her,
The day she arrived and the Duke married her.
And, do you know, though it's easy deceiving
Oneself in such matters, I can't help believing
The lady had not forgotten it either,
And knew the poor devil so much beneath her
Would have been only too glad for her service
To dance on hot ploughshares like a Turk dervise,
But, unable to pay proper duty where owing it,
Was reduced to that pitiful method of showing it:
For though the moment I began setting
His saddle on my own nag of Berold's begetting,
(Not that I meant to be obtrusive)
She stopped me, while his rug was shifting,
By a single rapid finger's lifting,
And, with a gesture kind but conclusive,
And a little shake of the head, refused me,—
I say, although she never used me,
Yet when she was mounted, the Gipsy behind her,
And I ventured to remind her,
I suppose with a voice of less steadiness
Than usual, for my feeling exceeded me,
—Something to the effect that I was in readiness
Whenever God should please she needed me,—
Then, do you know, her face looked down on me
With a look that placed a crown on me,
And she felt in her bosom,—mark, her bosom—
And, as a flower-tree drops its blossom,
Dropped me . . . ah, had it been a purse
Of silver, my friend, or gold that's worse,
Why, you see, as soon as I found myself
So understood,—that a true heart so may gain
Such a reward,—I should have gone home again,
Kissed Jacynth, and soberly drowned myself!
It was a little plait of hair
Such as friends in a convent make
To wear, each for the other's sake,—
This, see, which at my breast I wear,
Ever did (rather to Jacynth's grudgement),
And ever shall, till the Day of Judgment.
And then,—and then,—to cut short,—this is idle,

These are feelings it is not good to foster,—
I pushed the gate wide, she shook the bridle,
And the palfrey bounded,—and so we lost her.

XVI

When the liquor's out why clink the cannikin?
I did think to describe you the panic in
The redoubtable breast of our master the mannikin,
And what was the pitch of his mother's yellowness,
How she turned as a shark to snap the spare-rib
Clean off, sailors say, from a pearl-diving Carib,
When she heard, what she called, the flight of the feloness
—But it seems such child's play,
What they said and did with the lady away!
And to dance on, when we've lost the music,
Always made me—and no doubt makes you—sick.
Nay, to my mind, the world's face looked so stern
As that sweet form disappeared through the postern,
She that kept it in constant good humour,
It ought to have stopped; there seemed nothing to do more.
But the world thought otherwise and went on,
And my head's one that its spite was spent on:
Thirty years are fled since that morning,
And with them all my head's adorning.
Nor did the old Duchess die outright,
As you expect, of suppressed spite,
The natural end of every adder
Not suffered to empty its poison-bladder:
But she and her son agreed, I take it,
That no one should touch on the story to wake it,
For the wound in the Duke's pride rankled fiery,
So, they made no search and small inquiry—
And when fresh Gipsies have paid us a visit, I've
Noticed the couple were never inquisitive,
But told them they're folks the Duke don't want here,
And bade them make haste and cross the frontier.
Brief, the Duchess was gone and the Duke was glad of it,
And the old one was in the young one's stead,
And took, in her place, the household's head,
And a blessed time the household had of it!
And were I not, as a man may say, cautious
How I trench, more than needs, on the nauseous,
I could favour you with sundry touches
Of the paint-smutches with which the Duchess
Heightened the mellowness of her cheek's yellowness
(To get on faster) until at last her
Cheek grew to be one master-plaster
Of mucus and fucus from mere use of ceruse:
In short, she grew from scalp to udder
Just the object to make you shudder.

XVII

You're my friend—
What a thing friendship is, world without end!
How it gives the heart and soul a stir-up
As if somebody broached you a glorious runlet,
And poured out, all lovelily, sparklingly, sunlit,
Our green Moldavia, the streaky syrup,
Cotnar as old as the time of the Druids—
Friendship may match with that monarch of fluids;
Each supples a dry brain, fills you its ins-and-outs,
Gives your life's hour-glass a shake when the thin sand doubts
Whether to run on or stop short, and guarantees
Age is not all made of stark sloth and arrant ease.
I have seen my little lady once more,
Jacynth, the Gipsy, Berold, and the rest of it,
For to me spoke the Duke, as I told you before;
I always wanted to make a clean breast of it:
And now it is made—why, my heart's blood, that went trickle,
Trickle, but anon, in such muddy driblets,
Is pumped up brisk now, through the main ventricle,
And genially floats me about the giblets.

I'll tell you what I intend to do:
I must see this fellow his sad life through—
He is our Duke, after all,
And I, as he says, but a serf and thrall.
My father was born here, and I inherit
His fame, a chain he bound his son with;
Could I pay in a lump I should prefer it,
But there's no mine to blow up and get done with:
So, I must stay till the end of the chapter.
For, as to our middle-age-manners-adapter,
Be it a thing to be glad on or sorry on,
Some day or other, his head in a morion
And breast in a hauberk, his heels he'll kick up,
Slain by an onslaught fierce of hiccup.
And then, when red doth the sword of our Duke rust,
And its leathern sheath lie o'ergrown with a blue crust,
Then, I shall scrape together my earnings;
For, you see, in the churchyard Jacynth reposes,
And our children all went the way of the roses:
It's a long lane that knows no turnings.
One needs but little tackle to travel in;
So, just one stout cloak shall I indue:
And for a staff, what beats the javelin
With which his boars my father pinned you?
And then, for a purpose you shall hear presently,
Taking some Cotnar, a tight plump skinful,
I shall go journeying, who but I, pleasantly!
Sorrow is vain and despondency sinful.
What's a man's age? He must hurry more, that's all;
Cram in a day, what his youth took a year to hold:
When we mind labour, then only, we're too old—
What age had Methusalem when he begat Saul?
And at last, as its haven some buffeted ship sees,
(Come all the way from the north-parts with sperm oil)
I hope to get safely out of the turmoil
And arrive one day at the land of the Gipsies,
And find my lady, or hear the last news of her
From some old thief and son of Lucifer,
His forehead chapleted green with wreathy hop,
Sunburned all over like an Æthiop.
And when my Cotnar begins to operate
And the tongue of the rogue to run at a proper rate,
And our wine-skin, tight once, shows each flaccid dent,
I shall drop in with—as if by accident—
"You never knew then, how it all ended,
What fortune good or bad attended
The little Lady your Queen befriended?"
—And when that's told me, what's remaining?
This world's too hard for my explaining.
The same wise judge of matters equine
Who still preferred some slim four-year-old
To the big-boned stock of mighty Berold,
And, for strong Cotnar, drank French weak wine,
He also must be such a lady's scorner!
Smooth Jacob still robs homely Esau:
Now up, now down, the world's one see-saw.
—So, I shall find out some snug corner
Under a hedge, like Orson the wood-knight,
Turn myself round and bid the world good night;
And sleep a sound sleep till the trumpet's blowing
Wakes me (unless priests cheat us laymen)
To a world where will be no further throwing
Pearls before swine that can't value them. Amen!

1845

A GRAMMARIAN'S FUNERAL

SHORTLY AFTER THE REVIVAL OF LEARNING IN EUROPE

Let us begin and carry up this corpse,
Singing together.
Leave we the common crofts, the vulgar thorpes
Each in its tether
Sleeping safe on the bosom of the plain,
Cared-for till cock-crow:
Look out if yonder be not day again
Rimming the rock-row!
That's the appropriate country; there, man's thought,
Rarer, intenser,

Self-gathered for an outbreak, as it ought,
 Chafes in the censer.
Leave we the unlettered plain its herd and crop;
 Seek we sepulture
On a tall mountain, citied to the top,
 Crowded with culture!
All the peaks soar, but one the rest excels;
 Clouds overcome it;
No! yonder sparkle is the citadel's
 Circling its summit.
Thither our path lies; wind we up the heights:
 Wait ye the warning?
Our low life was the level's and the night's;
 He's for the morning.
Step to a tune, square chests, erect each head,
 'Ware the beholders!
This is our master, famous calm and dead,
 Borne on our shoulders.

Sleep, crop and herd! sleep, darkling thorpe and croft,
 Safe from the weather!
He, whom we convoy to his grave aloft,
 Singing together,
He was a man born with thy face and throat,
 Lyric Apollo!
Long he lived nameless: how should spring take note
 Winter would follow?
Till lo, the little touch, and youth was gone!
 Cramped and diminished,
Moaned he, "New measures, other feet anon!
 My dance is finished?"
No, that's the world's way: (keep the mountain-side,
 Make for the city!)
He knew the signal, and stepped on with pride
 Over men's pity;
Left play for work, and grappled with the world
 Bent on escaping:
"What's in the scroll," quoth he, "thou keepest furled?
 Show me their shaping,
Theirs who most studied man, the bard and sage,—
 Give!"—So, he gowned him,
Straight got by heart that book to its last page:
 Learned, we found him.
Yea, but we found him bald too, eyes like lead,
 Accents uncertain:
"Time to taste life," another would have said,
 "Up with the curtain!"
This man said rather, "Actual life comes next?
 Patience a moment!
Grant I have mastered learning's crabbed text,
 Still there's the comment.
Let me know all! Prate not of most or least,
 Painful or easy!
Even to the crumbs I'd fain eat up the feast,
 Ay, nor feel queasy."
Oh, such a life as he resolved to live,
 When he had learned it,
When he had gathered all books had to give!
 Sooner, he spurned it.
Image the whole, then execute the parts—
 Fancy the fabric
Quite, ere you build, ere steel strike fire from quartz,
 Ere mortar dab brick!

(Here's the town-gate reached: there's the market-place
 Gaping before us.)
Yea, this in him was the peculiar grace
 (Hearten our chorus!)
That before living he'd learn how to live—
 No end to learning:
Earn the means first—God surely will contrive
 Use for our earning.
Others mistrust and say, "But time escapes:
 Live now or never!"
He said, "What's time? Leave Now for dogs and apes!
 Man has Forever."
Back to his book then: deeper drooped his head:
 Calculus [1] racked him:
Leaden before, his eyes grew dross of lead:
 Tussis [2] attacked him.
"Now, master, take a little rest!"—not he!
 (Caution redoubled,
Step two abreast, the way winds narrowly!)
 Not a whit troubled
Back to his studies, fresher than at first,
 Fierce as a dragon
He (soul-hydroptic with a sacred thirst)
 Sucked at the flagon.

[1] The stone. [2] A cough.

Oh, if we draw a circle premature,
Heedless of far gain,
Greedy for quick returns of profit, sure
Bad is our bargain!
Was it not great? did not he throw on God,
(He loves the burthen)—
God's task to make the heavenly period
Perfect the earthen?
Did not he magnify the mind, show clear
Just what it all meant?
He would not discount life, as fools do here,
Paid by instalment.
He ventured neck or nothing—heaven's success
Found, or earth's failure:
"Wilt thou trust death or not?" He answered "Yes!
Hence with life's pale lure!"
That low man seeks a little thing to do,
Sees it and does it:
This high man, with a great thing to pursue,
Dies ere he knows it.
That low man goes on adding one to one,
His hundred's soon hit:
This high man, aiming at a million,
Misses an unit.
That, has the world here—should he need the next,
Let the world mind him!
This, throws himself on God, and unperplexed
Seeking shall find him.
So, with the throttling hands of death at strife,
Ground he at grammar;
Still, thro' the rattle, parts of speech were rife:
While he could stammer
He settled *Hoti's* business—let it be!—
Properly based *Oun*—
Gave us the doctrine of the enclitic *De*,
Dead from the waist down.
Well, here's the platform, here's the proper place:
Hail to your purlieus,
All ye highfliers of the feathered race,
Swallows and curlews!
Here's the top-peak; the multitude below
Live, for they can, there:
This man decided not to Live but Know—
Bury this man there?
Here—here's his place, where meteors shoot, clouds form,
Lightnings are loosened,
Stars come and go! Let joy break with the storm,
Peace let the dew send!
Lofty designs must close in like effects:
Loftily lying,
Leave him—still loftier than the world suspects,
Living and dying.

1855

THE STATUE AND THE BUST [1]

THERE'S a palace in Florence, the world knows well,
And a statue watches it from the square,
And this story of both do our townsmen tell.

Ages ago, a lady there,
At the farthest window facing the East
Asked, "Who rides by with the royal air?"

The bridesmaids' prattle around her ceased;
She leaned forth, one on either hand;
They saw how the blush of the bride increased—

They felt by its beats her heart expand—
As one at each ear and both in a breath
Whispered, "The Great-Duke Ferdinand."

That self-same instant, underneath,
The Duke rode past in his idle way,
Empty and fine like a swordless sheath.

Gay he rode, with a friend as gay,
Till he threw his head back—"Who is she?"
—"A bride the Riccardi brings home to-day."

[1] The bust is imaginary and the statue real. The statue is that of Ferdinand I (1549–1609), Grand Duke of Tuscany, and stands in the Piazza dell' Annunziata, Florence. Confusion has been caused to those who like to seek out in Italy the scenes Browning writes about by the fact that the palaces in which the Lady and the Duke lived have, since the time of the poem, changed hands, — and names. The Lady was a Riccardi and lived in what was then the Riccardi palace in the Piazza dell' Annunziata, and there the scene of the poem is laid. The Duke (see lines 34–39) lived in what was then the Medici palace in the Via Larga (now Via Cavour) and rode from there to the Piazza dell' Annunziata to see his lady. It so happened that in 1659, half a century after the death of the characters in the poem, the Riccardi bought what had been the Duke's palace and gave it their name, by which it is still known. Hence the confusion.

Hair in heaps lay heavily
Over a pale brow spirit-pure—
Carved like the heart of a coal-black tree,

Crisped like a war-steed's encolure—
And vainly sought to dissemble her eyes
Of the blackest black our eyes endure.

And lo, a blade for a knight's emprise
Filled the fine empty sheath of a man,—
The Duke grew straightway brave and wise.

He looked at her, as a lover can;
She looked at him, as one who awakes:
The past was a sleep, and her life began.

Now, love so ordered for both their sakes,
A feast was held that selfsame night
In the pile which the mighty shadow makes.

(For Via Larga is three-parts light,
But the palace overshadows one,
Because of a crime which may God requite!

To Florence and God the wrong was done,
Through the first republic's murder there
By Cosimo and his cursed son.)

The Duke (with the statue's face in the square)
Turned in the midst of his multitude
At the bright approach of the bridal pair.

Face to face the lovers stood
A single minute and no more,
While the bridegroom bent as a man subdued—

Bowed till his bonnet brushed the floor—
For the Duke on the lady a kiss conferred,
As the courtly custom was of yore.

In a minute can lovers exchange a word?
If a word did pass, which I do not think,
Only one out of the thousand heard.

That was the bridegroom. At day's brink
He and his bride were alone at last
In a bedchamber by a taper's blink.

Calmly he said that her lot was cast,
That the door she had passed was shut on her
Till the final catafalk [1] repassed.

[1] The stage or scaffolding for a coffin while in the church.

The world meanwhile, its noise and stir,
Through a certain window facing the East,
She could watch like a convent's chronicler.

Since passing the door might lead to a feast,
And a feast might lead to so much beside,
He, of many evils, chose the least.

"Freely I choose too," said the bride—
"Your window and its world suffice,"
Replied the tongue, while the heart replied—

"If I spend the night with that devil twice,
May his window serve as my loop of hell
Whence a damned soul looks on paradise!

"I fly to the Duke who loves me well,
Sit by his side and laugh at sorrow
Ere I count another ave-bell.

"'Tis only the coat of a page to borrow,
And tie my hair in a horse-boy's trim,
And I save my soul—but not to-morrow"—

(She checked herself and her eye grew dim)
"My father tarries to bless my state:
I must keep it one day more for him.

"Is one day more so long to wait?
Moreover the Duke rides past, I know;
We shall see each other, sure as fate."

She turned on her side and slept. Just so!
So we resolve on a thing and sleep:
So did the lady, ages ago.

That night the Duke said, "Dear or cheap
As the cost of this cup of bliss may prove
To body or soul, I will drain it deep."

And on the morrow, bold with love,
He beckoned the bridegroom (close on call,
As his duty bade, by the Duke's alcove)

And smiled "'Twas a very funeral,
Your lady will think, this feast of ours,—
A shame to efface, whate'er befall!

"What if we break from the Arno bowers,
And try if Petraja, cool and green,
Cure last night's fault with this morning's flowers?"

The bridegroom, not a thought to be seen
On his steady brow and quiet mouth,
Said, "Too much favour for me so mean!

"But, alas! my lady leaves the South;
Each wind that comes from the Apennine
Is a menace to her tender youth:

"Nor a way exists, the wise opine,
If she quits her palace twice this year,
To avert the flower of life's decline."

Quoth the Duke, "A sage and a kindly fear.
Moreover Petraja is cold this spring:
Be our feast to-night as usual here!"

And then to himself—"Which night shall bring
Thy bride to her lover's embraces, fool—
Or I am the fool, and thou art the king!

"Yet my passion must wait a night, nor cool—
For to-night the Envoy arrives from France
Whose heart I unlock with thyself, my tool.

"I need thee still and might miss perchance.
To-day is not wholly lost, beside,
With its hope of my lady's countenance:

"For I ride—what should I do but ride?
And passing her palace, if I list,
May glance at its window—well betide!"

So said, so done: nor the lady missed
One ray that broke from the ardent brow,
Nor a curl of the lips where the spirit kissed.

Be sure that each renewed the vow,
No morrow's sun should arise and set
And leave them then as it left them now.

But next day passed, and next day yet,
With still fresh cause to wait one day more
Ere each leaped over the parapet.

And still, as love's brief morning wore,
With a gentle start, half smile, half sigh,
They found love not as it seemed before.

They thought it would work infallibly,
But not in despite of heaven and earth:
The rose would blow when the storm passed by.

Meantime they could profit in winter's dearth
By store of fruits that supplant the rose:
The world and its ways have a certain worth:

And to press a point while these oppose
Were simple policy; better wait:
We lose no friends and we gain no foes,

Meantime, worse fates than a lover's fate,
Who daily may ride and pass and look
Where his lady watches behind the grate!

And she—she watched the square like a book
Holding one picture and only one,
Which daily to find she undertook:

When the picture was reached the book was done,
And she turned from the picture at night to scheme
Of tearing it out for herself next sun.

So weeks grew months, years; gleam by gleam
The glory dropped from their youth and love,
And both perceived they had dreamed a dream;

Which hovered as dreams do, still above:
But who can take a dream for a truth?
Oh, hide our eyes from the next remove!

One day as the lady saw her youth
Depart, and the silver thread that streaked
Her hair, and, worn by the serpent's tooth,

The brow so puckered, the chin so peaked,—
And wondered who the woman was,
Hollow-eyed and haggard-cheeked,

Fronting her silent in the glass—
"Summon here," she suddenly said,
"Before the rest of my old self pass,

"Him, the Carver, a hand to aid,
Who fashions the clay no love will change,
And fixes a beauty never to fade.

"Let Robbia's craft so apt and strange
Arrest the remains of young and fair,
And rivet them while the seasons range.

"Make me a face on the window there,
Waiting as ever, mute the while,
My love to pass below in the square!

"And let me think that it may beguile
Dreary days which the dead must spend
Down in their darkness under the aisle,

"To say, 'What matters it at the end?
I did no more while my heart was warm
Than does that image, my pale-faced friend.'

"Where is the use of the lip's red charm,
The heaven of hair, the pride of the brow,
And the blood that blues the inside arm—

"Unless we turn, as the soul knows how,
The earthly gift to an end divine?
A lady of clay is as good, I trow."

But long ere Robbia's cornice, fine,
With flowers and fruits which leaves enlace,
Was set where now is the empty shrine—

(And, leaning out of a bright blue space,
As a ghost might lean from a chink of sky,
The passionate pale lady's face—

Eyeing ever, with earnest eye
And quick-turned neck at its breathless stretch,
Some one who ever is passing by—)

The Duke had sighed like the simplest wretch
In Florence, "Youth—my dream escapes!
Will its record stay?" And he bade them fetch

Some subtle moulder of brazen shapes—
"Can the soul, the will, die out of a man
Ere his body find the grave that gapes?

"John of Douay [1] shall effect my plan,
Set me on horseback here aloft,
Alive, as the crafty sculptor can,

"In the very square I have crossed so oft:
That men may admire, when future suns
Shall touch the eyes to a purpose soft,

"While the mouth and the brow stay brave in bronze—
Admire and say, 'When he was alive
How he would take his pleasure once!'

"And it shall go hard but I contrive
To listen the while, and laugh in my tomb
At idleness which aspires to strive."

[1] Giovanni of Bologna, a sculptor.

So! While these wait the trump of doom,
How do their spirits pass, I wonder,
Nights and days in the narrow room?

Still, I suppose, they sit and ponder
What a gift life was, ages ago,
Six steps out of the chapel yonder.

Only they see not God, I know,
Nor all that chivalry of his,
The soldier-saints who, row on row,

Burn upward each to his point of bliss
Since, the end of life being manifest,
He had burned his way thro' the world to this.

I hear you reproach, "But delay was best,
For their end was a crime."—Oh, a crime will do
As well, I reply, to serve for a test,

As a virtue golden through and through,
Sufficient to vindicate itself
And prove its worth at a moment's view!

Must a game be played for the sake of pelf?
Where a button goes, 'twere an epigram
To offer the stamp of the very Guelph.[1]

The true has no value beyond the sham:
As well the counter as coin, I submit,
When your table's a hat, and your prize a dram.

Stake your counter as boldly every whit,
Venture as warily, use the same skill,
Do your best, whether winning or losing it,

If you choose to play!—is my principle.
Let a man contend to the uttermost
For his life's set prize, be it what it will!

The counter our lovers staked was lost
As surely as if it were lawful coin:
And the sin I impute to each frustrate ghost

Is—the unlit lamp and the ungirt loin,
Though the end in sight was a vice, I say.
You of the virtue (we issue join)
How strive you? *De te, fabula!* [2]

1855

[1] Real money, indicated by the stamp of the ruler.

[2] "Concerning you, this fable."

PORPHYRIA'S LOVER

THE rain set early in to-night,
The sullen wind was soon awake,
It tore the elm-tops down for spite,
And did its worst to vex the lake:
I listened with heart fit to break.
When glided in Porphyria; straight
She shut the cold out and the storm,
And kneeled and made the cheerless grate
Blaze up, and all the cottage warm;
Which done, she rose, and from her form
Withdrew the dripping cloak and shawl,
And laid her soiled gloves by, untied
Her hat and let the damp hair fall,
And, last, she sat down by my side
And called me. When no voice replied,
She put my arm about her waist,
And made her smooth white shoulder bare,
And all her yellow hair displaced,
And, stooping, made my cheek lie there,
And spread, o'er all, her yellow hair,
Murmuring how she loved me—she
Too weak, for all her heart's endeavour,
To set its struggling passion free
From pride, and vainer ties dissever,
And give herself to me for ever.
But passion sometimes would prevail,
Nor could to-night's gay feast restrain
A sudden thought of one so pale
For love of her, and all in vain:
So, she was come through wind and rain.
Be sure I looked up at her eyes
Happy and proud; at last I knew
Porphyria worshipped me; surprise
Made my heart swell, and still it grew
While I debated what to do.
That moment she was mine, mine, fair,
Perfectly pure and good: I found
A thing to do, and all her hair
In one long yellow string I wound
Three times her little throat around,
And strangled her. No pain felt she;
I am quite sure she felt no pain.
As a shut bud that holds a bee,
I warily oped her lids: again
Laughed the blue eyes without a stain.
And I untightened next the tress
About her neck; her cheek once more
Blushed bright beneath my burning kiss:
I propped her head up as before,
Only, this time my shoulder bore
Her head, which droops upon it still:
The smiling rosy little head,
So glad it has its utmost will,
That all it scorned at once is fled,
And I, its love, am gained instead!
Porphyria's love: she guessed not how
Her darling one wish would be heard.
And thus we sit together now,
And all night long we have not stirred,
And yet God has not said a word!

1836, 1842

"CHILDE ROLAND TO THE DARK TOWER CAME" [1]

(*See Edgar's song in* "LEAR")

I

MY first thought was, he lied in every word,
That hoary cripple, with malicious eye
Askance to watch the working of his lie
On mine, and mouth scarce able to afford
Suppression of the glee, that pursed and scored
Its edge, at one more victim gained thereby.

II

What else should he be set for, with his staff?
What, save to waylay with his lies, ensnare
All travellers who might find him posted there,
And ask the road? I guessed what skull-like laugh
Would break, what crutch 'gin write my epitaph
For pastime in the dusty thoroughfare,

III

If at his counsel I should turn aside
Into that ominous tract which, all agree,
Hides the Dark Tower. Yet acquiescingly

[1] Browning three times declared that this poem was not an allegory — that it was a dramatic creation called forth by a line of Shakespeare. Repeated efforts have been made to read a meaning into it. This is justified in that if a poem carries a special significance to certain minds it quite obviously has that significance latent in it. Such an interpretation, however, must be regarded as personal and not that of the poet whose conception was purely objective.

I did turn as he pointed: neither pride
Nor hope rekindling at the end descried,
So much as gladness that some end might be.

IV

For, what with my whole world-wide wandering,
What with my search drawn out thro' years, my hope
Dwindled into a ghost not fit to cope
With that obstreperous joy success would bring,
I hardly tried now to rebuke the spring
My heart made, finding failure in its scope.

V

As when a sick man very near to death
Seems dead indeed, and feels begin and end
The tears and takes the farewell of each friend,
And hears one bid the other go, draw breath
Freelier outside, ("since all is o'er," he saith,
"And the blow fallen no grieving can amend;")

VI

While some discuss if near the other graves
Be room enough for this, and when a day
Suits best for carrying the corpse away,
With care about the banners, scarves and staves:
And still the man hears all, and only craves
He may not shame such tender love and stay.

VII

Thus, I had so long suffered in this quest,
Heard failure prophesied so oft, been writ
So many times among "The Band"—to wit,
The knights who to the Dark Tower's search addressed
Their steps—that just to fail as they, seemed best,
And all the doubt was now—should I be fit?

VIII

So, quiet as despair, I turned from him,
That hateful cripple, out of his highway
Into the path he pointed. All the day
Had been a dreary one at best, and dim
Was settling to its close, yet shot one grim
Red leer to see the plain catch its estray.

IX

For mark! no sooner was I fairly found
Pledged to the plain, after a pace or two,
Than, pausing to throw backward a last view
O'er the safe road, 'twas gone; grey plain all round:
Nothing but plain to the horizon's bound.
I might go on; nought else remained to do.

X

So, on I went. I think I never saw
Such starved ignoble nature; nothing throve:
For flowers—as well expect a cedar grove!
But cockle, spurge, according to their law
Might propagate their kind, with none to awe,
You'd think; a burr had been a treasure-trove.

XI

No! penury, inertness and grimace,
In some strange sort, were the land's portion. "See
Or shut your eyes," said Nature peevishly,
It nothing skills: I cannot help my case:
'Tis the Last Judgment's fire must cure this place,
Calcine its clods and set my prisoners free."

XII

If there pushed any ragged thistle-stalk
Above its mates, the head was chopped; the bents
Were jealous else. What made those holes and rents
In the dock's harsh swarth leaves, bruised as to baulk
All hope of greenness? 'tis a brute must walk
Pashing their life out, with a brute's intents.

XIII

As for the grass, it grew as scant as hair
In leprosy; thin dry blades pricked the mud
Which underneath looked kneaded up with blood.
One stiff blind horse, his every bone a-stare,
Stood stupefied, however he came there:
Thrust out past service from the devil's stud!

XIV

Alive? he might be dead for aught I know,
  With that red gaunt and colloped neck a-strain,
  And shut eyes underneath the rusty mane;
Seldom went such grotesqueness with such woe;
I never saw a brute I hated so;
  He must be wicked to deserve such pain.

XV

I shut my eyes and turned them on my heart.
  As a man calls for wine before he fights,
  I asked one draught of earlier, happier sights,
Ere fitly I could hope to play my part.
Think first, fight afterwards—the soldier's art:
  One taste of the old time sets all to rights.

XVI

Not it! I fancied Cuthbert's reddening face
  Beneath its garniture of curly gold,
  Dear fellow, till I almost felt him fold
An arm in mine to fix me to the place,
That way he used. Alas, one night's disgrace!
  Out went my heart's new fire and left it cold.

XVII

Giles then, the soul of honour—there he stands
  Frank as ten years ago when knighted first.
  What honest man should dare (he said) he durst.
Good—but the scene shifts—faugh! what hangman hands
Pin to his breast a parchment? His own bands
  Read it. Poor traitor, spit upon and curst!

XVIII

Better this present than a past like that;
  Back therefore to my darkening path again!
  No sound, no sight as far as eye could strain.
Will the night send a howlet or a bat?
I asked: when something on the dismal flat
  Came to arrest my thoughts and change their train.

XIX

A sudden little river crossed my path
  As unexpected as a serpent comes.
  No sluggish tide congenial to the glooms;
This, as it frothed by, might have been a bath
For the fiend's glowing hoof—to see the wrath
  Of its black eddy bespate with flakes and spumes.

XX

So petty yet so spiteful! All along,
  Low scrubby alders kneeled down over it;
  Drenched willows flung them headlong in a fit
Of mute despair, a suicidal throng:
The river which had done them all the wrong,
  Whate'er that was, rolled by, deterred no whit.

XXI

Which, while I forded,—good saints, how I feared
  To set my foot upon a dead man's cheek,
  Each step, or feel the spear I thrust to seek
For hollows, tangled in his hair or beard!
—It may have been a water-rat I speared,
  But, ugh! it sounded like a baby's shriek.

XXII

Glad was I when I reached the other bank.
  Now for a better country. Vain presage!
  Who were the strugglers, what war did they wage,
Whose savage trample thus could pad the dank
Soil to a plash? Toads in a poisoned tank,
  Or wild cats in a red-hot iron cage—

XXIII

The fight must so have seemed in that fell cirque.
  What penned them there, with all the plain to choose?
  No foot-print leading to that horrid mews,
None out of it. Mad brewage set to work
Their brains, no doubt, like galley-slaves the Turk
  Pits for his pastime, Christians against Jews.

XXIV

And more than that—a furlong on—why, there!
  What bad use was that engine for, that wheel,
  Or brake, not wheel—that harrow fit to reel

Men's bodies out like silk? with all the air
Of Tophet's tool, on earth left unaware,
Or brought to sharpen its rusty teeth of steel.

XXV

Then came a bit of stubbed ground, once a wood,
Next a marsh, it would seem, and now mere earth
Desperate and done with; (so a fool finds mirth,
Makes a thing and then mars it, till his mood
Changes and off he goes!) within a rood—
Bog, clay and rubble, sand and stark black dearth.

XXVI

Now blotches rankling, coloured gay and grim,
Now patches where some leanness of the soil's
Broke into moss or substances like boils;
Then came some palsied oak, a cleft in him
Like a distorted mouth that splits its rim
Gaping at death, and dies while it recoils.

XXVII

And just as far as ever from the end!
Nought in the distance but the evening, nought
To point my footstep further! At the thought,
A great black bird, Apollyon's bosom-friend,
Sailed past, nor beat his wide wing dragon-penned
That brushed my cap—perchance the guide I sought.

XXVIII

For, looking up, aware I somehow grew,
'Spite of the dusk, the plain had given place
All round to mountains—with such name to grace
Mere ugly heights and heaps now stolen in view.
How thus they had surprised me,—solve it, you!
How to get from them was no clearer case.

XXIX

Yet half I seemed to recognise some trick
Of mischief happened to me, God knows when—
In a bad dream perhaps. Here ended, then,
Progress this way. When, in the very nick
Of giving up, one time more, came a click
As when a trap shuts—you're inside the den!

XXX

Burningly it came on me all at once,
This was the place! those two hills on the right,
Crouched like two bulls locked horn in horn in fight;
While to the left, a tall scalped mountain . . . Dunce,
Dotard, a-dozing at the very nonce,
After a life spent training for the sight!

XXXI

What in the midst lay but the Tower itself?
The round squat turret, blind as the fool's heart,
Built of brown stone, without a counterpart
In the whole world. The tempest's mocking elf
Points to the shipman thus the unseen shelf
He strikes on, only when the timbers start.

XXXII

Not see? because of night perhaps?—why, day
Came back again for that! before it left,
The dying sunset kindled through a cleft:
The hills, like giants at a hunting, lay,
Chin upon hand, to see the game at bay,—
"Now stab and end the creature—to the heft!"

XXXIII

Not hear? when noise was everywhere! it tolled
Increasing like a bell. Names in my ears
Of all the lost adventurers my peers,—
How such a one was strong, and such was bold,
And such was fortunate, yet each of old
Lost, lost! one moment knelled the woe of years.

XXXIV

There they stood, ranged along the hillsides, met
To view the last of me, a living frame
For one more picture! in a sheet of flame

I saw them and I knew them all. And yet
Dauntless the slug-horn [1] to my lips I set
And blew. "*Childe Roland to the Dark Tower came.*"

1855

"TRANSCENDENTALISM: A POEM IN TWELVE BOOKS"

STOP playing, poet! May a brother speak?
'Tis you speak, that's your error. Song's our art:
Whereas you please to speak these naked thoughts
Instead of draping them in sights and sounds.
—True thoughts, good thoughts, thoughts fit to treasure up!
But why such long prolusion and display,
Such turning and adjustment of the harp,
And taking it upon your breast, at length,
Only to speak dry words across its strings?
Stark-naked thought is in request enough:
Speak prose and hollo it till Europe hears!
The six-foot Swiss tube, braced about with bark,
Which helps the hunter's voice from Alp to Alp—
Exchange our harp for that,—who hinders you?

But here's your fault; grown men want thought, you think;
Thought's what they mean by verse, and seek in verse.
Boys seek for images and melody,
Men must have reason—so, you aim at men.
Quite otherwise! Objects throng our youth, 'tis true;
We see and hear and do not wonder much:
If you could tell us what they mean, indeed!
As German Boehme [2] never cared for plants
Until it happed, a-walking in the fields,
He noticed all at once that plants could speak,
Nay, turned with loosened tongue to talk with him.
That day the daisy had an eye indeed—
Colloquised with the cowslip on such themes!
We find them extant yet in Jacob's prose.
But by the time youth slips a stage or two
While reading prose in that tough book he wrote
(Collating and emendating the same
And settling on the sense most to our mind),
We shut the clasps and find life's summer past.
Then, who helps more, pray, to repair our loss—
Another Boehme with a tougher book
And subtler meanings of what roses say,—
Or some stout Mage like him of Halberstadt,[1]
John, who made things Boehme wrote thoughts about?
He with a "look you!" vents a brace of rhymes,
And in there breaks the sudden rose herself,
Over us, under, round us every side,
Nay, in and out the tables and the chairs
And musty volumes, Boehme's book and all,—
Buries us with a glory, young once more,
Pouring heaven into this shut house of life.

So come, the harp back to your heart again!
You are a poem, though your poem's naught.
The best of all you showed before, believe,
Was your own boy-face o'er the finer chords
Bent, following the cherub at the top
That points to God with his paired half-moon wings.

1855

[1] Trumpet.

[2] Jacob Boehme, author of *De Signatura Rerum* (On the Signatures of Things).

[1] John of Halberstadt was supposed to have had power to make plants grow by magic where and when he willed, so that he could cause flowers to spring up in winter.

AN EPISTLE

CONTAINING THE STRANGE MEDICAL EXPERIENCE OF KARSHISH, THE ARAB PHYSICIAN

KARSHISH, the picker-up of learning's crumbs,
The not-incurious in God's handiwork
(This man's-flesh he hath admirably made,
Blown like a bubble, kneaded like a paste
To coop up and keep down on earth a space
That puff of vapour from his mouth, man's soul)
—To Abib, all-sagacious in our art,
Breeder in me of what poor skill I boast,
Like me inquisitive how pricks and cracks
Befall the flesh through too much stress and strain,

Whereby the wily vapour fain would slip
Back and rejoin its source before the term,—
And aptest in contrivance (under God)
To baffle it by deftly stopping such:—
The vagrant Scholar to his Sage at home
Sends greeting (health and knowledge, fame with peace)
Three samples of true snakestone [1]—rarer still,
One of the other sort, the melon-shaped,
(But fitter, pounded fine, for charms than drugs)
And writeth now the twenty-second time.

My journeyings were brought to Jericho:
Thus I resume. Who studious in our art
Shall count a little labour unrepaid?
I have shed sweat enough, left flesh and bone
On many a flinty furlong of this land.
Also, the country-side is all on fire
With rumours of a marching hitherward:
Some say Vespasian cometh,[2] some, his son.
A black lynx snarled and pricked a tufted ear;
Lust of my blood inflamed his yellow balls:
I cried and threw my staff and he was gone.
Twice have the robbers stripped and beaten me,
And once a town declared me for a spy;
But at the end, I reach Jerusalem,
Since this poor covert where I pass the night,
This Bethany, lies scarce the distance thence
A man with plague-sores at the third degree
Runs till he drops down dead. Thou laughest here!
'Sooth, it elates me, thus reposed and safe,
To void the stuffing of my travel-scrip
And share with thee whatever Jewry yields.
A viscid choler is observable
In tertians, I was nearly bold to say;
And falling-sickness [3] hath a happier cure
Than our school wots of: there's a spider [4] here
Weaves no web, watches on the ledge of tombs,

[1] The name applied to any one of a number of substances supposed to be a remedy for snake bites.

[2] This line places the date of the poem. Karshish is writing about the year 66, the year Vespasian marched on Palestine. The miracle is supposed to have been performed about 33 — approximately thirty years before.

[3] Epilepsy.

[4] From very ancient days until comparatively modern times it was believed that spiders had some occult power of healing, and they were much used in medicine.

Sprinkled with mottles on an ash-grey back;
Take five and drop them . . . but who knows his mind,
The Syrian runagate I trust this to?
His service payeth me a sublimate
Blown up his nose to help the ailing eye.
Best wait: I reach Jerusalem at morn,
There set in order my experiences,
Gather what most deserves, and give thee all—
Or I might add, Judæa's gum-tragacanth
Scales off in purer flakes, shines clearer-grained,
Cracks 'twixt the pestle and the porphyry,
In fine exceeds our produce. Scalp-disease
Confounds me, crossing so with leprosy—
Thou hadst admired one sort I gained at Zoar—
But zeal outruns discretion. Here I end.

Yet stay: my Syrian blinketh gratefully,
Protesteth his devotion is my price—
Suppose I write what harms not, though he steal?
I half resolve to tell thee, yet I blush,
What set me off a-writing first of all.
An itch I had, a sting to write, a tang!
For, be it this town's barrenness—or else
The Man had something in the look of him—
His case has struck me far more than 'tis worth.
So, pardon if—(lest presently I lose
In the great press of novelty at hand
The care and pains this somehow stole from me)
I bid thee take the thing while fresh in mind,
Almost in sight—for, wilt thou have the truth?
The very man is gone from me but now,
Whose ailment is the subject of discourse.
Thus then, and let thy better wit help all!

'Tis but a case of mania—subinduced
By epilepsy, at the turning-point
Of trance prolonged unduly some three days:
When, by the exhibition of some drug
Or spell, exorcization, stroke of art
Unknown to me and which 'twere well to know,
The evil thing out-breaking all at once
Left the man whole and sound of body indeed,—

But, flinging (so to speak) life's gates too wide,
Making a clear house of it too suddenly,
The first conceit that entered might inscribe
Whatever it was minded on the wall
So plainly at that vantage, as it were,
(First come, first served) that nothing subsequent
Attaineth to erase those fancy-scrawls
The just-returned and new-established soul
Hath gotten now so thoroughly by heart
That henceforth she will read or these or none.
And first—the man's own firm conviction rests
That he was dead (in fact they buried him)
—That he was dead and then restored to life
By a Nazarene physician of his tribe:
—'Sayeth, the same bade "Rise," and he did rise.
"Such cases are diurnal," thou wilt cry.
Not so this figment!—not, that such a fume,
Instead of giving way to time and health,
Should eat itself into the life of life,
As saffron tingeth flesh, blood, bones and all!
For see, how he takes up the after-life.
The man—it is one Lazarus a Jew,
Sanguine, proportioned, fifty years of age,
The body's habit wholly laudable,
As much, indeed, beyond the common health
As he were made and put aside to show.
Think, could we penetrate by any drug
And bathe the wearied soul and worried flesh,
And bring it clear and fair, by three days' sleep!
Whence has the man the balm that brightens all?
This grown man eyes the world now like a child.
Some elders of his tribe, I should premise,
Led in their friend, obedient as a sheep,
To bear my inquisition. While they spoke,
Now sharply, now with sorrow,—told the case,—
He listened not except I spoke to him,
But folded his two hands and let them talk,
Watching the flies that buzzed: and yet no fool.
And that's a sample how his years must go.
Look, if a beggar, in fixed middle-life,
Should find a treasure,—can he use the same
With straitened habits and with tastes starved small,
And take at once to his impoverished brain
The sudden element that changes things,
That sets the undreamed-of rapture at his hand
And puts the cheap old joy in the scorned dust?
Is he not such an one as moves to mirth—
Warily parsimonious, when no need,
Wasteful as drunkenness at undue times?
All prudent counsel as to what befits
The golden mean, is lost on such an one:
The man's fantastic will is the man's law.
So here—we call the treasure knowledge, say,
Increased beyond the fleshly faculty—
Heaven opened to a soul while yet on earth,
Earth forced on a soul's use while seeing heaven:
The man is witless of the size, the sum,
The value in proportion of all things,
Or whether it be little or be much.
Discourse to him of prodigious armaments
Assembled to besiege his city now,
And of the passing of a mule with gourds—
'Tis one! Then take it on the other side,
Speak of some trifling fact,—he will gaze rapt
With stupor at its very littleness,
(Far as I see) as if in that indeed
He caught prodigious import, whole results;
And so will turn to us the bystanders
In ever the same stupor (note this point)
That we too see not with his opened eyes.
Wonder and doubt come wrongly into play,
Preposterously, at cross purposes.
Should his child sicken unto death,—why, look
For scarce abatement of his cheerfulness,
Or pretermission of the daily craft!
While a word, gesture, glance from that same child
At play or in the school or laid asleep,
Will startle him to an agony of fear,
Exasperation, just as like. Demand
The reason why—"'tis but a word," object—
"A gesture"—he regards thee as our lord
Who lived there in the pyramid alone,
Looked at us (dost thou mind?) when, being young,
We both would unadvisedly recite
Some charm's beginning, from that book of his,
Able to bid the sun throb wide and burst

All into stars, as suns grown old are wont.
Thou and the child have each a veil alike
Thrown o'er your heads, from under which ye both
Stretch your blind hands and trifle with a match
Over a mine of Greek fire, did ye know!
He holds on firmly to some thread of life—
(It is the life to lead perforcedly)
Which runs across some vast distracting orb
Of glory on either side that meagre thread,
Which, conscious of, he must not enter yet—
The spiritual life around the earthly life:
The law of that is known to him as this,
His heart and brain move there, his feet stay here.
So is the man perplext with impulses
Sudden to start off crosswise, not straight on,
Proclaiming what is right and wrong across,
And not along, this black thread through the blaze—
"It should be" baulked by "here it cannot be."
And oft the man's soul springs into his face
As if he saw again and heard again
His sage that bade him "Rise" and he did rise.
Something, a word, a tick o' the blood within
Admonishes: then back he sinks at once
To ashes, who was very fire before,
In sedulous recurrence to his trade
Whereby he earneth him the daily bread;
And studiously the humbler for that pride,
Professedly the faultier that he knows
God's secret, while he holds the thread of life.
Indeed the especial marking of the man
Is prone submission to the heavenly will—
Seeing it, what it is, and why it is.
'Sayeth, he will wait patient to the last
For that same death which must restore his being
To equilibrium, body loosening soul
Divorced even now by premature full growth:
He will live, nay, it pleaseth him to live
So long as God please, and just how God please.
He even seeketh not to please God more
(Which meaneth, otherwise) than as God please.
Hence, I perceive not he affects to preach
The doctrine of his sect whate'er it be,
Make proselytes as madmen thirst to do:
How can he give his neighbour the real ground,
His own conviction? Ardent as he is—
Call his great truth a lie, why, still the old
"Be it as God please" reassureth him.
I probed the sore as thy disciple should:
"How, beast," said I, "this stolid carelessness
Sufficeth thee, when Rome is on her march
To stamp out like a little spark thy town,
Thy tribe, thy crazy tale and thee at once?"
He merely looked with his large eyes on me.
The man is apathetic, you deduce?
Contrariwise, he loves both old and young,
Able and weak, affects the very brutes
And birds—how say I? flowers of the field—
As a wise workman recognises tools
In a master's workshop, loving what they make.
Thus is the man as harmless as a lamb:
Only impatient, let him do his best,
At ignorance and carelessness and sin—
An indignation which is promptly curbed:
As when in certain travel I have feigned
To be an ignoramus in our art
According to some preconceived design,
And happed to hear the land's practitioners
Steeped in conceit sublimed by ignorance,
Prattle fantastically on disease,
Its cause and cure—and I must hold my peace!

Thou wilt object—Why have I not ere this
Sought out the sage himself, the Nazarene
Who wrought this cure, inquiring at the source,
Conferring with the frankness that befits?
Alas! it grieveth me, the learned leech
Perished in a tumult many years ago,
Accused,—our learning's fate,—of wizardry,
Rebellion, to the setting up a rule
And creed prodigious as described to me.
His death, which happened when the earthquake fell
(Prefiguring, as soon appeared, the loss
To occult learning in our lord the sage
Who lived there in the pyramid alone)
Was wrought by the mad people—that's their wont!
On vain recourse, as I conjecture it,
To his tried virtue, for miraculous help—

How could he stop the earthquake? That's their way!
The other imputations must be lies.
But take one, though I loathe to give it thee,
In mere respect for any good man's fame.
(And after all, our patient Lazarus
Is stark mad; should we count on what he says?
Perhaps not: though in writing to a leech
'Tis well to keep back nothing of a case.)
This man so cured regards the curer, then,
As—God forgive me! who but God himself,
Creator and sustainer of the world,
That came and dwelt in flesh on it awhile!
—'Sayeth that such an one was born and lived,
Taught, healed the sick, broke bread at his own house,
Then died, with Lazarus by, for aught I know,
And yet was . . . what I said nor choose repeat,
And must have so avouched himself, in fact,
In hearing of this very Lazarus
Who saith—but why all this of what he saith?
Why write of trivial matters, things of price
Calling at every moment for remark?
I noticed on the margin of a pool
Blue-flowering borage, the Aleppo sort,
Aboundeth, very nitrous. It is strange!

Thy pardon for this long and tedious case,
Which, now that I review it, needs must seem
Unduly dwelt on, prolixly set forth!
Nor I myself discern in what is writ
Good cause for the peculiar interest
And awe indeed this man has touched me with.
Perhaps the journey's end, the weariness
Had wrought upon me first. I met him thus:
I crossed a ridge of short sharp broken hills
Like an old lion's cheek teeth. Out there came
A moon made like a face with certain spots
Multiform, manifold and menacing:
Then a wind rose behind me. So we met
In this old sleepy town at unaware,
The man and I. I send thee what is writ.
Regard it as a chance, a matter risked
To this ambiguous Syrian—he may lose,
Or steal, or give it thee with equal good.
Jerusalem's repose shall make amends
For time this letter wastes, thy time and mine;
Till when, once more thy pardon and farewell!

The very God! think, Abib; dost thou think?
So, the All-Great, were the All-Loving too—
So, through the thunder comes a human voice
Saying, "O heart I made, a heart beats here!
Face, my hands fashioned, see it in myself!
Thou hast no power nor mayst conceive of mine,
But love I gave thee, with myself to love,
And thou must love me who have died for thee!"
The madman saith He said so: it is strange.

1855

PICTOR IGNOTUS [1]

FLORENCE, 15—

I COULD have painted pictures like that youth's
Ye praise so. How my soul springs up! No bar
Stayed me—ah, thought which saddens while it soothes!
—Never did fate forbid me, star by star,
To outburst on your night with all my gift
Of fires from God: nor would my flesh have shrunk
From seconding my soul, with eyes uplift
And wide to heaven, or, straight like thunder, sunk
To the centre, of an instant; or around
Turned calmly and inquisitive, to scan
The licence and the limit, space and bound,
Allowed to truth made visible in man.
And, like that youth ye praise so, all I saw,
Over the canvas could my hand have flung,
Each face obedient to its passion's law,
Each passion clear proclaimed without a tongue;
Whether Hope rose at once in all the blood,
A-tiptoe for the blessing of embrace,
Or Rapture drooped the eyes, as when her brood
Pulled down the nesting dove's heart to its place;
Or Confidence lit swift the forehead up,
And locked the mouth fast, like a castle braved,—
O human faces, hath it spilt, my cup?
What did ye give me that I have not saved?

[1] "The unknown painter."

Nor will I say I have not dreamed (how well!)
Of going—I, in each new picture,—forth,
As, making new hearts beat and bosoms swell,
To Pope or Kaiser, East, West, South, or North,
Bound for the calmly-satisfied great State,
Or glad aspiring little burgh, it went,
Flowers cast upon the car which bore the freight,
Through old streets named afresh from the event,
Till it reached home, where learned age should greet
My face, and youth, the star not yet distinct
Above his hair, lie learning at my feet!—
Oh, thus to live, I and my picture, linked
With love about, and praise, till life should end,
And then not go to heaven, but linger here,
Here on my earth, earth's every man my friend,—
The thought grew frightful, 'twas so wildly dear!
But a voice changed it. Glimpses of such sights
Have scared me, like the revels through a door
Of some strange house of idols at its rites!
This world seemed not the world it was before:
Mixed with my loving trusting ones, there trooped
. . . Who summoned those cold faces that begun
To press on me and judge me? Though I stooped
Shrinking, as from the soldiery a nun,
They drew me forth, and spite of me . . . enough!
These buy and sell our pictures, take and give,
Count them for garniture and household-stuff,
And where they live needs must our pictures live
And see their faces, listen to their prate,
Partakers of their daily pettiness,
Discuss of,—"This I love, or this I hate,
This likes me more, and this affects me less!"
Wherefore I chose my portion. If at whiles
My heart sinks, as monotonous I paint
These endless cloisters and eternal aisles
With the same series, Virgin, Babe and Saint,
With the same cold calm beautiful regard—
At least no merchant traffics in my heart;
The sanctuary's gloom at least shall ward
Vain tongues from where my pictures stand apart:
Only prayer breaks the silence of the shrine
While, blackening in the daily candle-smoke,
They moulder on the damp wall's travertine,
'Mid echoes the light footstep never woke.
So, die my pictures! surely, gently die!
O youth, men praise so,—holds their praise its worth?
Blown harshly, keeps the trump its golden cry?
Tastes sweet the water with such specks of earth?

1845

FRA LIPPO LIPPI [1]

I AM poor brother Lippo, by your leave!
You need not clap your torches to my face.
Zooks, what's to blame? you think you see a monk!
What, 'tis past midnight, and you go the rounds,
And here you catch me at an alley's end
Where sportive ladies leave their doors ajar?
The Carmine's my cloister: hunt it up,
Do,—harry out, if you must show your zeal,
Whatever rat, there, haps on his wrong hole,
And nip each softling of a wee white mouse,
Weke, weke, that's crept to keep him company!
Aha, you know your betters! Then, you'll take
Your hand away that's fiddling on my throat,

[1] Fra Filippo Lippi (1406–1469) was, as the poem says, placed in the community of the Carmelites of the Carmine at the age of eight. There he stayed until 1432 and became a painter. Some of his religious paintings are very fine in spirit but his attitude toward life, far from being that of a monk, was that of the world. In the end he seems to have received a more or less complete dispensation from his religious vows. The episode on which Browning bases the poem — that of Lippo's escaping out the window one spring night — is recounted in Vasari, and the character Browning gives to him is consistent with tradition. Browning's contribution, granted the accepted facts and tradition, is the imaginative analysis of what may have been the workings of Fra Lippo's brain.

And please to know me likewise. Who am I?
Why, one, sir, who is lodging with a friend
Three streets off—he's a certain . . . how d'ye call?
Master—a . . . Cosimo of the Medici,[1]
I' the house that caps the corner. Boh! you were best!
Remember and tell me, the day you're hanged,
How you affected such a gullet's-gripe!
But you, sir, it concerns you that your knaves
Pick up a manner nor discredit you:
Zooks, are we pilchards, that they sweep the streets
And count fair prize what comes into their net?
He's Judas to a tittle, that man is!
Just such a face! Why, sir, you make amends.
Lord, I'm not angry! Bid your hangdogs go
Drink out this quarter-florin to the health
Of the munificent House that harbours me
(And many more beside, lads! more beside!)
And all's come square again. I'd like his face—
His, elbowing on his comrade in the door
With the pike and lantern,—for the slave that holds
John Baptist's head a-dangle by the hair
With one hand ("Look you, now," as who should say)
And his weapon in the other, yet unwiped!
It's not your chance to have a bit of chalk,
A wood-coal or the like? or you should see!
Yes, I'm the painter, since you style me so.
What, brother Lippo's doings, up and down,
You know them and they take you? like enough!
I saw the proper twinkle in your eye—
'Tell you, I liked your looks at very first.
Let's sit and set things straight now, hip to haunch.
Here's spring come, and the nights one makes up bands
To roam the town and sing out carnival,
And I've been three weeks shut within my mew,
A-painting for the great man, saints and saints
And saints again. I could not paint all night—
Ouf! I leaned out of window for fresh air.
There came a hurry of feet and little feet,
A sweep of lute-strings, laughs, and whifts of song,—
Flower o' the broom,
Take away love, and our earth is a tomb!
Flower o' the quince,
I let Lisa go, and what good in life since?
Flower o' the thyme—and so on. Round they went.
Scarce had they turned the corner when a titter
Like the skipping of rabbits by moonlight,—three slim shapes,
And a face that looked up . . . zooks, sir, flesh and blood,
That's all I'm made of! Into shreds it went,
Curtain and counterpane and coverlet,
All the bed-furniture—a dozen knots,
There was a ladder! Down I let myself,
Hands and feet, scrambling somehow, and so dropped,
And after them. I came up with the fun
Hard by Saint Laurence, hail fellow, well met,—
Flower o' the rose,
If I've been merry, what matter who knows?
And so as I was stealing back again
To get to bed and have a bit of sleep
Ere I rise up to-morrow and go work
On Jerome knocking at his poor old breast
With his great round stone to subdue the flesh,
You snap me of the sudden. Ah, I see!
Though your eye twinkles still, you shake your head—
Mine's shaved—a monk, you say—the sting's in that!
If Master Cosimo announced himself,
Mum's the word naturally; but a monk!
Come, what am I a beast for? tell us, now!
I was a baby when my mother died
And father died and left me in the street.
I starved there, God knows how, a year or two
On fig-skins, melon-parings, rinds and shucks,
Refuse and rubbish. One fine frosty day,
My stomach being empty as your hat,
The wind doubled me up and down I went.
Old Aunt Lapaccia trussed me with one hand,
(Its fellow was a stinger as I knew)
And so along the wall, over the bridge,

[1] The effect this name has on the watch is explained by the fact that Cosimo, besides being a great patron of the arts and Lippo's friend, was a great statesman (known as *Pater Patriæ*) and certainly the most powerful man in Florence.

By the straight cut to the convent. Six words there,
While I stood munching my first bread that month:
"So, boy, you're minded," quoth the good fat father
Wiping his own mouth, 'twas refection-time,—
"To quit this very miserable world?
Will you renounce" . . . "the mouthful of bread?" thought I;
By no means! Brief, they made a monk of me;
I did renounce the world, its pride and greed,
Palace, farm, villa, shop and banking-house,
Trash, such as these poor devils of Medici
Have given their hearts to—all at eight years old.
Well, sir, I found in time, you may be sure,
'Twas not for nothing—the good bellyful,
The warm serge and the rope that goes all round,
And day-long blessed idleness beside!
"Let's see what the urchin's fit for"—that came next.
Not overmuch their way, I must confess.
Such a to-do! They tried me with their books:
Lord, they'd have taught me Latin in pure waste!
Flower o' the clove,
All the Latin I construe is, "amo" I love!
But, mind you, when a boy starves in the streets
Eight years together, as my fortune was,
Watching folk's faces to know who will fling
The bit of half-stripped grape-bunch he desires,
And who will curse or kick him for his pains,—
Which gentleman processional and fine,
Holding a candle to the Sacrament,
Will wink and let him lift a plate and catch
The droppings of the wax to sell again,
Or holla for the Eight and have him whipped,—
How say I?—nay, which dog bites, which lets drop
His bone from the heap of offal in the street,—
Why, soul and sense of him grow sharp alike,
He learns the look of things, and none the less
For admonition from the hunger-pinch.
I had a store of such remarks, be sure,
Which, after I found leisure, turned to use.
I drew men's faces on my copy-books,
Scrawled them within the antiphonary's marge,
Joined legs and arms to the long music-notes,
Found eyes and nose and chin for A's and B's,
And made a string of pictures of the world
Betwixt the ins and outs of verb and noun,
On the wall, the bench, the door. The monks looked black.
"Nay," quoth the Prior, "turn him out, d'ye say?
In no wise. Lose a crow and catch a lark.
What if at last we get our man of parts,
We Carmelites, like those Camaldolese [1]
And Preaching Friars, to do our church up fine
And put the front on it that ought to be!"
And hereupon he bade me daub away.
Thank you! my head being crammed, the walls a blank,
Never was such prompt disemburdening.
First, every sort of monk, the black and white,
I drew them, fat and lean: then, folk at church,
From good old gossips waiting to confess
Their cribs of barrel-droppings, candle-ends,—
To the breathless fellow at the altar-foot,
Fresh from his murder, safe and sitting there
With the little children round him in a row
Of admiration, half for his beard and half
For that white anger of his victim's son
Shaking a fist at him with one fierce arm,
Signing himself with the other because of Christ
(Whose sad face on the cross sees only this
After the passion of a thousand years)
Till some poor girl, her apron o'er her head,
(Which the intense eyes looked through) came at eve
On tiptoe, said a word, dropped in a loaf,

[1] There was considerable praiseworthy rivalry between religious orders in decorating their churches. The Camaldolese had Lorenzo Monaco, mentioned later in the poem (line 236), and the Preaching Friars (the Dominicans) had Fra Angelico. Lippo's superiors, when they encouraged him, were thinking of the highly spiritualized style of these two painters, and the effect of Lippo's work on them is in direct proportion to its unexpectedness.

Her pair of earrings and a bunch of flowers
(The brute took growling), prayed, and so was gone.
I painted all, then cried "'Tis ask and have;
Choose, for more's ready!"—laid the ladder flat,
And showed my covered bit of cloister-wall.
The monks closed in a circle and praised loud
Till checked, taught what to see and not to see,
Being simple bodies,—"That's the very man!
Look at the boy who stoops to pat the dog!
That woman's like the Prior's niece who comes
To care about his asthma: it's the life!"
But there my triumph's straw-fire flared and funked;
Their betters took their turn to see and say:
The Prior and the learned pulled a face
And stopped all that in no time. "How? what's here?
Quite from the mark of painting, bless us all!
Faces, arms, legs and bodies like the true
As much as pea and pea! it's devil's-game!
Your business is not to catch men with show,
With homage to the perishable clay,
But lift them over it, ignore it all,
Make them forget there's such a thing as flesh.
Your business is to paint the souls of men—
Man's soul, and it's a fire, smoke . . . no, it's not . . .
It's vapour done up like a new-born babe—
(In that shape when you die it leaves your mouth)
It's . . . well, what matters talking, it's the soul!
Give us no more of body than shows soul!
Here's Giotto, with his Saint a-praising God,
That sets us praising,—why not stop with him?
Why put all thoughts of praise out of our head
With wonder at lines, colours, and what not?
Paint the soul, never mind the legs and arms!
Rub all out, try at it a second time.
Oh, that white smallish female with the breasts,
She's just my niece . . . Herodias, I would say,—
Who went and danced and got men's heads cut off!
Have it all out!" Now, is this sense, I ask?
A fine way to paint soul, by painting body
So ill, the eye can't stop there, must go further
And can't fare worse! Thus, yellow does for white
When what you put for yellow's simply black,
And any sort of meaning looks intense
When all beside itself means and looks nought.
Why can't a painter lift each foot in turn,
Left foot and right foot, go a double step,
Make his flesh liker and his soul more like,
Both in their order? Take the prettiest face,
The Prior's niece . . . patron-saint—is it so pretty
You can't discover if it means hope, fear,
Sorrow or joy? won't beauty go with these?
Suppose I've made her eyes all right and blue,
Can't I take breath and try to add life's flash,
And then add soul and heighten them three-fold?
Or say there's beauty with no soul at all—
(I never saw it—put the case the same—)
If you get simple beauty and nought else,
You get about the best thing God invents:
That's somewhat: and you'll find the soul you have missed,
Within yourself, when you return him thanks.
"Rub all out!" Well, well, there's my life, in short,
And so the thing has gone on ever since.
I'm grown a man no doubt, I've broken bounds:
You should not take a fellow eight years old
And make him swear to never kiss the girls.
I'm my own master, paint now as I please—
Having a friend, you see, in the Corner-house!
Lord, it's fast holding by the rings in front—
Those great rings serve more purposes than just
To plant a flag in, or tie up a horse!
And yet the old schooling sticks, the old grave eyes
Are peeping o'er my shoulder as I work,
The heads shake still—"It's art's decline, my son!
You're not of the true painters, great and old;
Brother Angelico's the man, you'll find;
Brother Lorenzo [1] stands his single peer:
Fag on at flesh, you'll never make the third!"

[1] Lorenzo Monaco, an eminent painter, a monk.

Flower o' the pine,
You keep your mistr . . . manners, and I'll stick to mine!
I'm not the third, then: bless us, they must know!
Don't you think they're the likeliest to know,
They with their Latin? So, I swallow my rage,
Clench my teeth, suck my lips in tight, and paint
To please them—sometimes do and sometimes don't;
For, doing most, there's pretty sure to come
A turn, some warm eve finds me at my saints—
A laugh, a cry, the business of the world—
(*Flower o' the peach,*
Death for us all, and his own life for each!)
And my whole soul revolves, the cup runs over,
The world and life's too big to pass for a dream,
And I do these wild things in sheer despite,
And play the fooleries you catch me at,
In pure rage! The old mill-horse, out at grass
After hard years, throws up his stiff heels so,
Although the miller does not preach to him
The only good of grass is to make chaff.
What would men have? Do they like grass or no—
May they or mayn't they? all I want's the thing
Settled for ever one way. As it is,
You tell too many lies and hurt yourself:
You don't like what you only like too much,
You do like what, if given you at your word
You find abundantly detestable.
For me, I think I speak as I was taught;
I always see the garden and God there
A-making man's wife: and, my lesson learned,
The value and significance of flesh,
I can't unlearn ten minutes afterwards.

You understand me: I'm a beast, I know.
But see, now—why, I see as certainly
As that the morning-star's about to shine,
What will hap some day. We've a youngster here
Comes to our convent, studies what I do,
Slouches and stares and lets no atom drop:
His name is Guidi[1]—he'll not mind the monks—
They call him Hulking Tom, he lets them talk—
He picks my practice up—he'll paint apace,
I hope so—though I never live so long,
I know what's sure to follow. You be judge!
You speak no Latin more than I, belike;
However, you're my man, you've seen the world
—The beauty and the wonder and the power,
The shapes of things, their colours, lights and shades,
Changes, surprises,—and God made it all!
—For what? Do you feel thankful, ay or no,
For this fair town's face, yonder river's line,
The mountain round it and the sky above,
Much more the figures of man, woman, child,
These are the frame to? What's it all about?
To be passed over, despised? or dwelt upon,
Wondered at? oh, this last course!—you say.
But why not do as well as say,—paint these
Just as they are, careless what comes of it?
God's works—paint anyone, and count it crime
To let a truth slip. Don't object, "His works
Are here already; nature is complete:
Suppose you reproduce her—(which you can't)
There's no advantage! you must beat her, then."
For, don't you mark? we're made so that we love
First when we see them painted, things we have passed
Perhaps a hundred times nor cared to see;
And so they are better, painted—better to us,
Which is the same thing. Art was given for that;
God uses us to help each other so,
Lending our minds out. Have you noticed, now,
Your cullion's hanging face? A bit of chalk,
And trust me but you should, though! How much more,
If I drew higher things with the same truth!
That were to take the Prior's pulpit-place,
Interpret God to all of you! Oh, oh,

[1] Generally accepted as referring to Masaccio who was known as "Hulking Tom." Browning was misinformed as to the relationship of the two painters. It was Lippo who was the pupil, Masaccio's frescoes at the Carmine having been among the most important of his early models.

It makes me mad to see what men shall do
And we in our graves! This world's no blot for us,
Nor blank; it means intensely, and means good:
To find its meaning is my meat and drink.
"Ay, but you don't so instigate to prayer!"
Strikes in the Prior: "when your meaning's plain
It does not say to folk—remember matins,
Or, mind you fast next Friday!" Why, for this
What need of art at all? A skull and bones,
Two bits of stick nailed crosswise, or, what's best,
A bell to chime the hour with, does as well.
I painted a Saint Laurence six months since
At Prato, splashed the fresco in fine style:
"How looks my painting, now the scaffold's down?"
I ask a brother: "Hugely," he returns—
Already not one phiz of your three slaves
Who turn the Deacon off his toasted side,
But's scratched and prodded to our heart's content,
The pious people have so eased their own
With coming to say prayers there in a rage:
We get on fast to see the bricks beneath.
Expect another job this time next year,
For pity and religion grow i' the crowd—
Your painting serves its purpose!" Hang the fools!

—That is—you'll not mistake an idle word
Spoke in a huff by a poor monk, God wot,
Tasting the air this spicy night which turns
The unaccustomed head like Chianti wine!
Oh, the church knows! don't misreport me, now!
It's natural a poor monk out of bounds
Should have his apt word to excuse himself:
And hearken how I plot to make amends.
I have bethought me: I shall paint a piece
. . . There's for you! Give me six months, then go, see
Something in Sant' Ambrogio's! Bless the nuns!
They want a cast o' my office. I shall paint
God in the midst, Madonna and her babe,
Ringed by a bowery flowery angel-brood,
Lilies and vestments and white faces, sweet
As puff on puff of grated orris-root
When ladies crowd to Church at midsummer.
And then i' the front, of course a saint or two—
Saint John, because he saves the Florentines,
Saint Ambrose, who puts down in black and white
The convent's friends and gives them a long day,
And Job, I must have him there past mistake,
The man of Uz (and Us without the z,
Painters who need his patience). Well, all these
Secured at their devotion, up shall come
Out of a corner when you least expect,
As one by a dark stair into a great light,
Music and talking, who but Lippo! I!—
Mazed, motionless and moonstruck—I'm the man!
Back I shrink—what is this I see and hear?
I, caught up with my monk's-things by mistake,
My old serge gown and rope that goes all round,
I, in this presence, this pure company!
Where's a hole, where's a corner for escape?
Then steps a sweet angelic slip of a thing
Forward, puts out a soft palm—"Not so fast!"
—Addresses the celestial presence, "nay—
He made you and devised you, after all,
Though he's none of you! Could Saint John there draw—
His camel-hair make up a painting-brush?
We come to brother Lippo for all that,
Iste perfecit opus!" [1] So, all smile—
I shuffle sideways with my blushing face
Under the cover of a hundred wings
Thrown like a spread of kirtles when you're gay
And play hot cockles, all the doors being shut,
Till, wholly unexpected, in there pops
The hothead husband! Thus I scuttle off
To some safe bench behind, not letting go
The palm of her, the little lily thing
That spoke the good word for me in the nick,
Like the Prior's niece . . . Saint Lucy, I would say.
And so all's saved for me, and for the church
A pretty picture gained. Go, six months hence!

[1] "This one did the work."

Your hand, sir, and good-bye: no lights, no lights!
The street's hushed, and I know my own way back,
Don't fear me! There's the grey beginning. Zooks!

1855

ANDREA DEL SARTO[1]

(CALLED "THE FAULTLESS PAINTER.")

BUT do not let us quarrel any more,
No, my Lucrezia; bear with me for once:
Sit down and all shall happen as you wish.
You turn your face, but does it bring your heart?
I'll work then for your friend's friend, never fear,
Treat his own subject after his own way,
Fix his own time, accept too his own price,
And shut the money into this small hand
When next it takes mine. Will it? tenderly?
Oh, I'll content him,—but to-morrow, Love!
I often am much wearier than you think,
This evening more than usual, and it seems
As if—forgive now—should you let me sit
Here by the window with your hand in mine
And look a half-hour forth on Fiesole,
Both of one mind, as married people use,
Quietly, quietly the evening through,
I might get up to-morrow to my work
Cheerful and fresh as ever. Let us try.
To-morrow, how you shall be glad for this!
Your soft hand is a woman of itself,
And mine the man's bared breast she curls inside.
Don't count the time lost, neither; you must serve
For each of the five pictures we require:
It saves a model. So! keep looking so—
My serpentining beauty, rounds on rounds!
—How could you ever prick those perfect ears,
Even to put the pearl there! oh, so sweet—
My face, my moon, my everybody's moon,
Which everybody looks on and calls his,
And, I suppose, is looked on by in turn,
While she looks—no one's: very dear, no less.
You smile? why, there's my picture ready made,
There's what we painters call our harmony!
A common greyness silvers everything,—
All in a twilight, you and I alike
—You, at the point of your first pride in me
(That's gone you know),—but I, at every point;
My youth, my hope, my art, being all toned down
To yonder sober pleasant Fiesole.
There's the bell clinking from the chapel-top;
That length of convent-wall across the way
Holds the trees safer, huddled more inside;
The last monk leaves the garden; days decrease,
And autumn grows, autumn in everything.
Eh? the whole seems to fall into a shape
As if I saw alike my work and self
And all that I was born to be and do,
A twilight-piece. Love, we are in God's hand.
How strange now looks the life he makes us lead;
So free we seem, so fettered fast we are!
I feel he laid the fetter: let it lie!

[1] Andrea del Sarto's (1486–1531) true name is not known. He was the son of a tailor and so his contemporaries nicknamed him del Sarto — Andrew the tailor's son. They also called him Andrea *senza errori* — the unerring — which sufficiently indicates their high respect for his craftsmanship. He fell in love with the wife of a cap-maker, Lucrezia del Fede, and married her in 1512 after her husband's death. Vasari, who knew her, minces no words in describing her faithlessness, her jealousy, and her vixenish temper, but Andrea was devoted to her and she was the model for many of his greatest canvases. In return for his devotion she left him, when he was ill, to die alone. Out of Andrea's relationship to Lucrezia and to his art, Browning constructs the poem. The reference (line 66, line 149, and elsewhere) in the poem to the visit to France refers to one of the happiest periods in his life. In 1519 Francis I invited Andrea to France and in the king's court at Paris and at Fontainebleau he was made much of as the great painter he was. But his wife wrote to him to return to Florence. The art-loving king, expecting him soon to return to Fontainebleau, gave him a considerable sum of money with which to purchase paintings in Florence. Andrea spent the money on Lucrezia and, in disgrace, did not dare return.

The immediate impulse which led Browning to write the poem was a request from John Kenyon asking that Browning buy for him a copy of Andrea's portrait of himself and his wife which was hanging in the Pitti Palace in Florence. Unable to secure a good copy Browning set out to write a poem which should interpret the spirit of the picture.

This chamber for example—turn your head—
All that's behind us! You don't understand
Nor care to understand about my art,
But you can hear at least when people speak:
And that cartoon, the second from the door
—It is the thing, Love! so such things should be—
Behold Madonna!—I am bold to say.
I can do with my pencil what I know,
What I see, what at bottom of my heart
I wish for, if I ever wish so deep—
Do easily, too—when I say, perfectly,
I do not boast, perhaps: yourself are judge,
Who listened to the Legate's talk last week,
And just as much they used to say in France.
At any rate 'tis easy, all of it!
No sketches first, no studies, that's long past:
I do what many dream of, all their lives,
—Dream? strive to do, and agonise to do,
And fail in doing. I could count twenty such
On twice your fingers, and not leave this town,
Who strive—you don't know how the others strive
To paint a little thing like that you smeared
Carelessly passing with your robes afloat,—
Yet do much less, so much less, Someone says,
(I know his name, no matter)—so much less!
Well, less is more, Lucrezia: I am judged.
There burns a truer light of God in them,
In their vexed beating stuffed and stopped-up brain,
Heart, or whate'er else, than goes on to prompt
This low-pulsed forthright craftsman's hand of mine.
Their works drop groundward, but themselves, I know,
Reach many a time a heaven that's shut to me,
Enter and take their place there sure enough,
Though they come back and cannot tell the world.
My works are nearer heaven, but I sit here.
The sudden blood of these men! at a word—
Praise them, it boils, or blame them, it boils too.
I, painting from myself and to myself,
Know what I do, am unmoved by men's blame
Or their praise either. Somebody remarks
Morello's outline there is wrongly traced,
His hue mistaken; what of that? or else,
Rightly traced and well ordered; what of that?
Speak as they please, what does the mountain care?
Ah, but a man's reach should exceed his grasp,
Or what's a heaven for? All is silver-grey
Placid and perfect with my art: the worse!
I know both what I want and what might gain,
And yet how profitless to know, to sigh
"Had I been two, another and myself,
Our head would have o'erlooked the world!" No doubt.
Yonder's a work now, of that famous youth
The Urbinate [1] who died five years ago.
('Tis copied, George Vasari sent it me.)
Well, I can fancy how he did it all,
Pouring his soul, with kings and popes to see,
Reaching, that heaven might so replenish him,
Above and through his art—for it gives way;
That arm is wrongly put—and there again—
A fault to pardon in the drawing's lines,
Its body, so to speak: its soul is right,
He means right—that, a child may understand.
Still, what an arm! and I could alter it:
But all the play, the insight and the stretch—
Out of me, out of me! And wherefore out?
Had you enjoined them on me, given me soul,
We might have risen to Rafael, I and you!
Nay, Love, you did give all I asked, I think—
More than I merit, yes, by many times.
But had you—oh, with the same perfect brow,
And perfect eyes, and more than perfect mouth,
And the low voice my soul hears, as a bird
The fowler's pipe, and follows to the snare—
Had you, with these the same, but brought a mind!
Some women do so. Had the mouth there urged
"God and the glory! never care for gain.
The present by the future, what is that?
Live for fame, side by side with Agnolo! [2]
Rafael is waiting: up to God, all three!"
I might have done it for you. So it seems:
Perhaps not. All is as God over-rules.
Beside, incentives come from the soul's self;

[1] Raphael, who was born at Urbino.

[2] Michael Angelo, the more correct form of whose name was Michel Agnolo Buonarroti.

160 *RED COTTON NIGHT-CAP COUNTRY*

And make society the just amends;
Scarce ~~Not~~ by a new attachment—Heaven forbid!
Still less by lawful marriage: that's reserved
For those who make a proper choice at first—
Not try both courses and ~~unfit their~~ age would grasp in
The very ~~For graspin~~g treasure, youth preferred to spurn!
No! putting decently ~~the past~~ aside, such thought
The penitent ~~would straightway~~ give his powers must rather
To such a reparation of the past
As, edifying kindred, makes them rich.
Now, how would ~~this~~ enrich prospectively it
The Cousins, ~~that~~ he lavished such expense if
Clairvaux On ~~Tailleville~~?—pretty as a toy, but then
to As toy, productive, so much and no more!
If all the outcome of the ~~Street of Peace~~ goldsmith's shop Place Vendôme
Went to gild ~~Tailleville~~, where remained the funds
Clairvaux

A Page of Browning's Revised Proof-Copy. (See Appendix I.)

The rest avail not. Why do I need you?
What wife had Rafael, or has Agnolo?
In this world, who can do a thing, will not;
And who would do it, cannot, I perceive:
Yet the will's somewhat—somewhat, too, the power—
And thus we half-men struggle. At the end,
God, I conclude, compensates, punishes.
'Tis safer for me, if the award be strict,
That I am something underrated here,
Poor this long while, despised, to speak the truth.
I dared not, do you know, leave home all day,
For fear of chancing on the Paris lords.
The best is when they pass and look aside;
But they speak sometimes; I must bear it all.
Well may they speak! That Francis, that first time,
And that long festal year at Fontainebleau!
I surely then could sometimes leave the ground,
Put on the glory, Rafael's daily wear,
In that humane great monarch's golden look,—
One finger in his beard or twisted curl
Over his mouth's good mark that made the smile,
One arm about my shoulder, round my neck,
The jingle of his gold chain in my ear,
I painting proudly with his breath on me,
All his court round him, seeing with his eyes,
Such frank French eyes, and such a fire of souls
Profuse, my hand kept plying by those hearts,—
And, best of all, this, this, this face beyond,
This in the background, waiting on my work,
To crown the issue with a last reward!
A good time, was it not, my kingly days?
And had you not grown restless . . . but I know—
'Tis done and past; 'twas right, my instinct said;
Too live the life grew, golden and not grey,
And I'm the weak-eyed bat no sun should tempt
Out of the grange whose four walls make his world.
How could it end in any other way?
You called me, and I came home to your heart.
The triumph was—to reach and stay there; since
I reached it ere the triumph, what is lost?
Let my hands frame your face in your hair's gold,
You beautiful Lucrezia that are mine!
"Rafael did this, Andrea painted that;
The Roman's is the better when you pray,
But still the other's Virgin was his wife—"
Men will excuse me. I am glad to judge
Both pictures in your presence; clearer grows
My better fortune, I resolve to think.
For, do you know, Lucrezia, as God lives,
Said one day Agnolo, his very self,
To Rafael . . . I have known it all these years . . .
(When the young man was flaming out his thoughts
Upon a palace-wall for Rome to see,
Too lifted up in heart because of it)
"Friend, there's a certain sorry little scrub
Goes up and down our Florence, none cares how,
Who, were he set to plan and execute
As you are, pricked on by your popes and kings,
Would bring the sweat into that brow of yours!"
To Rafael's!—And indeed the arm is wrong.
I hardly dare . . . yet, only you to see,
Give the chalk here—quick, thus the line should go!
Ay, but the soul! he's Rafael! rub it out!
Still, all I care for, if he spoke the truth,
(What he? why, who but Michel Agnolo?
Do you forget already words like those?)
If really there was such a chance, so lost,—
Is, whether you're—not grateful—but more pleased.
Well, let me think so. And you smile indeed!
This hour has been an hour! Another smile?
If you would sit thus by me every night
I should work better, do you comprehend?
I mean that I should earn more, give you more.
See, it is settled dusk now; there's a star;
Morello's gone, the watch-lights show the wall,
The cue-owls speak the name we call them by.
Come from the window, love,—come in, at last,

Inside the melancholy little house
We built to be so gay with. God is just.
King Francis may forgive me: oft at nights
When I look up from painting, eyes tired out,
The walls become illumined, brick from brick
Distinct, instead of mortar, fierce bright gold,
That gold of his I did cement them with!
Let us but love each other. Must you go?
That Cousin here again? he waits outside?
Must see you—you, and not with me? Those loans?
More gaming debts to pay? you smiled for that?
Well, let smiles buy me? have you more to spend?
While hand and eye and something of a heart
Are left me, work's my ware, and what's it worth?
I'll pay my fancy. Only let me sit
The grey remainder of the evening out,
Idle, you call it, and muse perfectly
How I could paint, were I but back in France,
One picture, just one more—the Virgin's face,
Not yours this time! I want you at my side
To hear them—that is, Michel Agnolo—
Judge all I do and tell you of its worth.
Will you? To-morrow, satisfy your friend.
I take the subjects for his corridor,
Finish the portrait out of hand—there, there,
And throw him in another thing or two
If he demurs; the whole should prove enough
To pay for this same Cousin's freak. Beside,
What's better and what's all I care about,
Get you the thirteen scudi for the ruff!
Love, does that please you? Ah, but what does he,
The Cousin! what does he to please you more?

I am grown peaceful as old age to-night.
I regret little, I would change still less.
Since there my past life lies, why alter it?
The very wrong to Francis!—it is true
I took his coin, was tempted and complied,
And built this house and sinned, and all is said.
My father and my mother died of want.
Well, had I riches of my own? you see
How one gets rich! Let each one bear his lot.
They were born poor, lived poor, and poor they died:
And I have laboured somewhat in my time
And not been paid profusely. Some good son
Paint my two hundred pictures—let him try!
No doubt, there's something strikes a balance.
Yes,
You loved me quite enough, it seems tonight.
This must suffice me here. What would one have?
In heaven, perhaps, new chances, one more chance—
Four great walls in the New Jerusalem,
Meted on each side by the angel's reed,
For Leonard,[1] Rafael, Agnolo and me
To cover—the three first without a wife,
While I have mine! So—still they overcome
Because there's still Lucrezia,—as I choose.

Again the Cousin's whistle! Go, my Love.

1855

THE BISHOP ORDERS HIS TOMB AT SAINT PRAXED'S CHURCH

Rome, 15—

Vanity, saith the preacher, vanity!
Draw round my bed: is Anselm keeping back?
Nephews—sons mine . . . ah God, I know not! Well—
She, men would have to be your mother once,
Old Gandolf envied me, so fair she was!
What's done is done, and she is dead beside,
Dead long ago, and I am Bishop since,
And as she died so must we die ourselves,
And thence ye may perceive the world's a dream.
Life, how and what is it? As here I lie
In this state-chamber, dying by degrees,
Hours and long hours in the dead night, I ask
"Do I live, am I dead?" Peace, peace seems all.
Saint Praxed's ever was the church for peace;
And so, about this tomb of mine. I fought
With tooth and nail to save my niche, ye know:
—Old Gandolf cozened me, despite my care;
Shrewd was that snatch from out the corner South
He graced his carrion with, God curse the same!
Yet still my niche is not so cramped but thence
One sees the pulpit o' the epistle-side,

[1] Leonardo da Vinci.

And somewhat of the choir, those silent seats,
And up into the aery dome where live
The angels, and a sunbeam's sure to lurk:
And I shall fill my slab of basalt there,
And 'neath my tabernacle [1] take my rest,
With those nine columns round me, two and two,
The odd one at my feet where Anselm stands:
Peach-blossom marble all, the rare, the ripe
As fresh-poured red wine of a mighty pulse.
—Old Gandolf with his paltry onion-stone,
Put me where I may look at him! True peach,
Rosy and flawless: how I earned the prize!
Draw close: that conflagration of my church
—What then? So much was saved if aught were missed!
My sons, ye would not be my death? Go dig
The white-grape vineyard where the oil-press stood,
Drop water gently till the surface sink,
And if ye find . . . Ah God, I know not, I! . . .
Bedded in store of rotten fig-leaves soft,
And corded up in a tight olive-frail,
Some lump, ah God, of *lapis lazuli*,
Big as a Jew's head cut off at the nape,
Blue as a vein o'er the Madonna's breast . . .
Sons, all have I bequeathed you, villas, all,
That brave Frascati villa with its bath,
So, let the blue lump poise between my knees,
Like God the Father's globe on both his hands
Ye worship in the Jesu Church so gay,
For Gandolf shall not choose but see and burst!
Swift as a weaver's shuttle fleet our years:
Man goeth to the grave, and where is he?
Did I say basalt for my slab, sons? Black—
'Twas ever antique-black I meant! How else
Shall ye contrast my frieze to come beneath?
The bas-relief in bronze ye promised me,
Those Pans and Nymphs ye wot of, and perchance
Some tripod, thyrsus,[2] with a vase or so,
The Saviour at his sermon on the mount,
Saint Praxed in a glory, and one Pan
Ready to twitch the Nymph's last garment off,
And Moses with the tables . . . but I know
Ye mark me not! What do they whisper thee,
Child of my bowels, Anselm? Ah, ye hope
To revel down my villas while I gasp
Bricked o'er with beggar's mouldy travertine
Which Gandolf from his tomb-top chuckles at!
Nay, boys, ye love me—all of jasper, then!
'Tis jasper ye stand pledged to, lest I grieve.
My bath must needs be left behind, alas!
One block, pure green as a pistachio-nut,
There's plenty jasper somewhere in the world—
And have I not Saint Praxed's ear to pray
Horses for ye, and brown Greek manuscripts,
And mistresses with great smooth marbly limbs?
—That's if ye carve my epitaph aright,
Choice Latin, picked phrase, Tully's every word,[1]
No gaudy ware like Gandolf's second line—
Tully, my masters? Ulpian serves his need!
And then how I shall lie through centuries,
And hear the blessed mutter of the mass,
And see God made and eaten all day long,[2]
And feel the steady candle-flame, and taste
Good strong thick stupefying incense-smoke!
For as I lie here, hours of the dead night,
Dying in state and by such slow degrees,
I fold my arms as if they clasped a crook,
And stretched my feet forth straight as stone can point,
And let the bedclothes, for a mortcloth, drop
Into great laps and folds of sculptor's-work:
And as yon tapers dwindle, and strange thoughts
Grow, with a certain humming in my ears,
About the life before I lived this life,
And this life too, popes, cardinals and priests,
Saint Praxed at his sermon on the mount,
Your tall pale mother with her talking eyes,
And new-found agate urns as fresh as day,

[1] The tomb would be set into the wall in a canopied niche, or tabernacle.

[2] Pan was the god of flocks and pastures; he was also the goat-god of sensual revelry. The priestesses at Delphi sat on a tripod when giving responses to those who consulted the oracle. The thyrsus is the symbol of Bacchus. Thus many of the figures the bishop wishes on his tomb are purely pagan.

[1] Tully is Marcus Tullius Cicero whose Latin was of the purest, while Ulpian was a jurist of the second century A.D., when the language had lost some of its purity.

[2] In the sacrament of the mass.

And marble's language, Latin pure, discreet,
—Aha, ELUCESCEBAT [1] quoth our friend?
No Tully, said I, Ulpian at the best!
Evil and brief hath been my pilgrimage.
All *lapis*, all, sons! Else I give the Pope
My villas! Will ye ever eat my heart?
Ever your eyes were as a lizard's quick,
They glitter like your mother's for my soul,
Or ye would heighten my impoverished frieze,
Piece out its starved design, and fill my vase
With grapes, and add a vizor and a Term,
And to the tripod ye would tie a lynx
That in his struggle throws the thyrsus down,
To comfort me on my entablature
Whereon I am to lie till I must ask
"Do I live, am I dead?" There, leave me, there!
For ye have stabbed me with ingratitude
To death—ye wish it—God, ye wish it! Stone—
Gritstone, a-crumble! Clammy squares which sweat
As if the corpse they keep were oozing through—
And no more *lapis* to delight the world!
Well go! I bless ye. Fewer tapers there,
But in a row: and, going, turn your backs
—Ay, like departing altar-ministrants,
And leave me in my church, the church for peace,
That I may watch at leisure if he leers—
Old Gandolf, at me, from his onion-stone,
As still he envied me, so fair she was!

1845

CLEON

"As certain also of your own poets have said"—

CLEON the poet (from the sprinkled isles,
Lily on lily, that o'erlace the sea,
And laugh their pride when the light wave lisps "Greece")—
To Protus in his Tyranny:[2] much health!

They give thy letter to me, even now:
I read and seem as if I heard thee speak.
The master of thy galley still unlades
Gift after gift; they block my court at last
And pile themselves along its portico
Royal with sunset, like a thought of thee:
And one white she-slave from the group dispersed
Of black and white slaves (like the chequer-work
Pavement, at once my nation's work and gift,
Now covered with this settle-down of doves),
One lyric woman, in her crocus vest
Woven of sea-wools, with her two white hands
Commends to me the strainer and the cup
Thy lip hath bettered ere it blesses mine.

Well-counselled, king, in thy munificence!
For so shall men remark, in such an act
Of love for him whose song gives life its joy,
Thy recognition of the use of life;
Nor call thy spirit barely adequate
To help on life in straight ways, broad enough
For vulgar souls, by ruling and the rest.
Thou, in the daily building of thy tower,—
Whether in fierce and sudden spasms of toil,
Or through dim lulls of unapparent growth,
Or when the general work 'mid good acclaim
Climbed with the eye to cheer the architect,—
Didst ne'er engage in work for mere work's sake—
Hadst ever in thy heart the luring hope
Of some eventual rest a-top of it,
Whence, all the tumult of the building hushed,
Thou first of men mightst look out to the East:
The vulgar saw thy tower, thou sawest the sun.
For this, I promise on thy festival
To pour libation, looking o'er the sea,
Making this slave narrate thy fortunes, speak
Thy great words, and describe thy royal face—
Wishing thee wholly where Zeus lives the most,
Within the eventual element of calm.

Thy letter's first requirement meets me here.
It is as thou hast heard: in one short life
I, Cleon, have effected all those things
Thou wonderingly dost enumerate.

[1] "He was illustrious." What delights the Bishop is that this resounding statement on Gandolf's tomb is made in inferior post-classical Latin.

[2] In the Greek sense a tyrant was any ruler who had absolute power. The word did not necessarily imply cruelty or misuse of that power.

That epos on thy hundred plates of gold
Is mine,—and also mine the little chant,
So sure to rise from every fishing-bark
When, lights at prow, the seamen haul their net.
The image of the sun-god on the phare,
Men turn from the sun's self to see, is mine;
The Pœcile, o'er-storied [1] its whole length,
As thou didst hear, with painting, is mine too.
I know the true proportions of a man
And woman also, not observed before;
And I have written three books on the soul,
Proving absurd all written hitherto,
And putting us to ignorance again.
For music,—why, I have combined the moods,[2]
Inventing one. In brief, all arts are mine;
Thus much the people know and recognise,
Throughout our seventeen islands. Marvel not.
We of these latter days, with greater mind
Than our forerunners, since more composite,
Look not so great, beside their simple way,
To a judge who only sees one way at once,
One mind-point and no other at a time,—
Compares the small part of a man of us
With some whole man of the heroic age,
Great in his way—not ours, nor meant for ours.
And ours is greater, had we skill to know:
For, what we call this life of men on earth,
This sequence of the soul's achievements here
Being, as I find much reason to conceive,
Intended to be viewed eventually
As a great whole, not analysed to parts,
But each part having reference to all,—
How shall a certain part, pronounced complete,
Endure effacement by another part?
Was the thing done?—then, what's to do again?
See, in the chequered pavement opposite,
Suppose the artist made a perfect rhomb,
And next a lozenge, then a trapezoid—
He did not overlay them, superimpose
The new upon the old and blot it out,
But laid them on a level in his work,
Making at last a picture; there it lies.
So, first the perfect separate forms were made,
The portions of mankind; and after, so,
Occurred the combination of the same.
For where had been a progress, otherwise?
Mankind, made up of all the single men,—
In such a synthesis the labour ends.
Now mark me! those divine men of old time
Have reached, thou sayest well, each at one point
The outside verge that rounds our faculty;
And where they reached, who can do more than reach?
It takes but little water just to touch
At some one point the inside of a sphere,
And, as we turn the sphere, touch all the rest
In due succession: but the finer air
Which not so palpably nor obviously,
Though no less universally, can touch
The whole circumference of that emptied sphere,
Fills it more fully than the water did;
Holds thrice the weight of water in itself
Resolved into a subtler element.
And yet the vulgar call the sphere first full
Up to the visible height—and after, void;
Not knowing air's more hidden properties.
And thus our soul, misknown, cries out to Zeus
To vindicate his purpose in our life:
Why stay we on the earth unless to grow?
Long since, I imaged, wrote the fiction out,
That he or other god descended here
And, once for all, showed simultaneously
What, in its nature, never can be shown,
Piecemeal or in succession;—showed, I say,
The worth both absolute and relative
Of all his children from the birth of time,
His instruments for all appointed work.
I now go on to image,—might we hear
The judgment which should give the due to each,
Show where the labour lay and where the ease,
And prove Zeus' self, the latent everywhere!
This is a dream:—but no dream, let us hope,
That years and days, the summers and the springs,
Follow each other with unwaning powers.
The grapes which dye thy wine are richer far,

[1] "O'er-storied" means painted over with stories. In the case of the Pœcile, a famous portico at Athens, the scenes were of war.

[2] The scales in Greek music were called moods or modes.

Through culture, than the wild wealth of the rock;
The suave plum than the savage-tasted drupe;
The pastured honey-bee drops choicer sweet;
The flowers turn double, and the leaves turn flowers;
That young and tender crescent-moon, thy slave,
Sleeping above her robe as buoyed by clouds,
Refines upon the women of my youth.
What, and the soul alone deteriorates?
I have not chanted verse like Homer, no—
Nor swept string like Terpander,[1] no—nor carved
And painted men like Phidias and his friend:[2]
I am not great as they are, point by point.
But I have entered into sympathy
With these four, running these into one soul,
Who, separate, ignored each other's art.
Say, is it nothing that I know them all?
The wild flower was the larger; I have dashed
Rose-blood upon its petals, prick'd its cup's
Honey with wine, and driven its seed to fruit,
And show a better flower if not so large:
I stand myself. Refer this to the gods
Whose gift alone it is! which, shall I dare
(All pride apart) upon the absurd pretext
That such a gift by chance lay in my hand,
Discourse of lightly or depreciate?
It might have fallen to another's hand: what then?
I pass too surely: let at least truth stay!

And next, of what thou followest on to ask.
This being with me as I declare, O king,
My works, in all these varicoloured kinds,
So done by me, accepted so by men—
Thou askest, if (my soul thus in men's hearts)
I must not be accounted to attain
The very crown and proper end of life?
Inquiring thence how, now life closeth up,
I face death with success in my right hand:
Whether I fear death less than dost thyself
The fortunate of men? "For" (writest thou)
"Thou leavest much behind, while I leave nought.
Thy life stays in the poems men shall sing,
The pictures men shall study; while my life,
Complete and whole now in its power and joy,
Dies altogether with my brain and arm,
Is lost indeed; since, what survives myself?
The brazen statue to o'erlook my grave,
Set on the promontory which I named.
And that—some supple courtier of my heir
Shall use its robed and sceptred arm, perhaps,
To fix the rope to, which best drags it down.
I go then: triumph thou, who dost not go!"

Nay, thou art worthy of hearing my whole mind.
Is this apparent, when thou turn'st to muse
Upon the scheme of earth and man in chief,
That admiration grows as knowledge grows?
That imperfection means perfection hid,
Reserved in part, to grace the after-time?
If, in the morning of philosophy,
Ere aught had been recorded, nay perceived,
Thou, with the light now in thee, couldst have looked
On all earth's tenantry, from worm to bird,
Ere man, her last, appeared upon the stage—
Thou wouldst have seen them perfect, and deduced
The perfectness of others yet unseen.
Conceding which,—had Zeus then questioned thee
"Shall I go on a step, improve on this,
Do more for visible creatures than is done?"
Thou wouldst have answered, "Ay, by making each
Grow conscious in himself—by that alone.
All's perfect else: the shell sucks fast the rock,
The fish strikes through the sea, the snake both swims
And slides, forth range the beasts, the birds take flight,
Till life's mechanics can no further go—
And all this joy in natural life is put
Like fire from off thy finger into each,
So exquisitely perfect is the same.
But 'tis pure fire, and they mere matter are;
It has them, not they it: and so I choose
For man, thy last premeditated work
(If I might add a glory to the scheme)
That a third thing should stand apart from both,

[1] Terpander, a musician of Lesbos (c. 650 B.C.) who added three strings to the four-stringed Greek lyre, thus increasing its musical possibilities.

[2] Phidias was one of the greatest sculptors of the fifth century, B.C. He was a friend of Pericles, the great Athenian statesman.

A quality arise within his soul,
Which, intro-active, made to supervise
And feel the force it has, may view itself,
And so be happy." Man might live at first
The animal life: but is there nothing more?
In due time, let him critically learn
How he lives; and, the more he gets to know
Of his own life's adaptabilities,
The more joy-giving will his life become.
Thus man, who hath this quality, is best.

But thou, king, hadst more reasonably said:
"Let progress end at once,—man make no step
Beyond the natural man, the better beast,
Using his senses, not the sense of sense."
In man there's failure, only since he left
The lower and inconscious forms of life.
We called it an advance, the rendering plain
Man's spirit might grow conscious of man's life,
And, by new lore so added to the old,
Take each step higher over the brute's head.
This grew the only life, the pleasure-house,
Watch-tower and treasure-fortress of the soul,
Which whole surrounding flats of natural life
Seemed only fit to yield subsistence to;
A tower that crowns a country. But alas,
The soul now climbs it just to perish there!
For thence we have discovered ('tis no dream—
We know this, which we had not else perceived)
That there's a world of capability
For joy, spread round about us, meant for us,
Inviting us; and still the soul craves all,
And still the flesh replies, "Take no jot more
Than ere thou clombst the tower to look abroad!
Nay, so much less as that fatigue has brought
Deduction to it." We struggle, fain to enlarge
Our bounded physical recipiency,
Increase our power, supply fresh oil to life,
Repair the waste of age and sickness: no,
It skills not! life's inadequate to joy,
As the soul sees joy, tempting life to take.
They praise a fountain in my garden here
Wherein a Naiad sends the water-bow
Thin from her tube; she smiles to see it rise.
What if I told her, it is just a thread
From that great river which the hills shut up,
And mock her with my leave to take the same?
The artificer has given her one small tube
Past power to widen or exchange—what boots
To know she might spout oceans if she could?
She cannot lift beyond her first thin thread:
And so a man can use but a man's joy
While he sees God's. Is it for Zeus to boast,
"See, man, how happy I live, and despair—
That I may be still happier—for thy use!"
If this were so, we could not thank our lord,
As hearts beat on to doing; 'tis not so—
Malice it is not. Is it carelessness?
Still, no. If care—where is the sign? I ask,
And get no answer, and agree in sum,
O king, with thy profound discouragement,
Who seest the wider but to sigh the more.
Most progress is most failure: thou sayest well.

The last point now:—thou dost except a case—
Holding joy not impossible to one
With artist-gifts—to such a man as I
Who leave behind me living works indeed;
For, such a poem, such a painting lives.
What? dost thou verily trip upon a word,
Confound the accurate view of what joy is
(Caught somewhat clearer by my eyes than thine)
With feeling joy? confound the knowing how
And showing how to live (my faculty)
With actual living?—Otherwise
Where is the artist's vantage o'er the king?
Because in my great epos I display
How divers men young, strong, fair, wise, can act—
Is this as though I acted? if I paint,
Carve the young Phœbus, am I therefore young?
Methinks I'm older that I bowed myself
The many years of pain that taught me art!
Indeed, to know is something, and to prove
How all this beauty might be enjoyed, is more:
But, knowing nought, to enjoy is something too.
Yon rower, with the moulded muscles there,
Lowering the sail, is nearer it than I.
I can write love-odes: thy fair slave's an ode.
I get to sing of love, when grown too grey
For being beloved: she turns to that young man,
The muscles all a-ripple on his back.
I know the joy of kingship: well, thou art king!

"But," sayest thou—(and I marvel, I repeat,
To find thee trip on such a mere word) "what
Thou writest, paintest, stays; that does not die:
Sappho survives, because we sing her songs,
And Æschylus, because we read his plays!"
Why, if they live still, let them come and take
Thy slave in my despite, drink from thy cup,
Speak in my place. Thou diest while I survive?
Say rather that my fate is deadlier still,
In this, that every day my sense of joy
Grows more acute, my soul (intensified
By power and insight) more enlarged, more keen;
While every day my hairs fall more and more,
My hand shakes, and the heavy years increase—
The horror quickening still from year to year,
The consummation coming past escape
When I shall know most, and yet least enjoy—
When all my works wherein I prove my worth,
Being present still to mock me in men's mouths,
Alive still, in the praise of such as thou,
I, I the feeling, thinking, acting man,
The man who loved his life so over-much,
Sleep in my urn. It is so horrible,
I dare at times imagine to my need
Some future state revealed to us by Zeus,
Unlimited in capability
For joy, as this is in desire for joy,
—To seek which, the joy-hunger forces us:
That, stung by straitness of our life, made strait
On purpose to make prized the life at large—
Freed by the throbbing impulse we call death,
We burst there as the worm into the fly,
Who, while a worm still, wants his wings. But no!
Zeus has not yet revealed it; and alas,
He must have done so, were it possible!

Live long and happy, and in that thought die:
Glad for what was! Farewell. And for the rest,
I cannot tell thy messenger aright
Where to deliver what he bears of thine
To one called Paulus; we have heard his fame
Indeed, if Christus be not one with him—
I know not, nor am troubled much to know.
Thou canst not think a mere barbarian Jew,
As Paulus proves to be, one circumcised,
Hath access to a secret shut from us?
Thou wrongest our philosophy, O king,
In stooping to inquire of such an one,
As if his answer could impose at all!
He writeth, doth he? well, and he may write.
Oh, the Jew findeth scholars! certain slaves
Who touched on this same isle, preached him and Christ;
And (as I gathered from a bystander)
Their doctrine could be held by no sane man.

1855

ONE WORD MORE [1]

TO E. B. B.

I

There they are, my fifty men and women
Naming me the fifty poems finished!
Take them, Love, the book and me together:
Where the heart lies, let the brain lie also.

II

Rafael made a century of sonnets,
Made and wrote them in a certain volume
Dinted with the silver-pointed pencil
Else he only used to draw Madonnas:
These, the world might view—but one, the volume.
Who that one, you ask? Your heart instructs you.
Did she live and love it all her life-time?
Did she drop, his lady of the sonnets
Die, and let it drop beside her pillow
Where it lay in place of Rafael's glory,
Rafael's cheek so duteous and so loving—
Cheek, the world was wont to hail a painter's,
Rafael's cheek, her love had turned a poet's?

III

You and I would rather read that volume,
(Taken to his beating bosom by it)
Lean and list the bosom-beats of Rafael,
Would we not? than wonder at Madonnas—

[1] [Originally appended to the collection of Poems called "Men and Women," the greater portion of which has now been, more correctly, distributed under the other titles of this edition.—*Browning's note.*]

Her, San Sisto names, and Her, Foligno,
Her, that visits Florence in a vision,
Her, that's left with lilies in the Louvre—
Seen by us and all the world in circle.

IV

You and I will never read that volume.
Guido Reni, like his own eye's apple
Guarded long the treasure-book and loved it.
Guido Reni dying, all Bologna
Cried, and the world cried too, "Ours, the treasure!"
Suddenly, as rare things will, it vanished.[1]

V

Dante once prepared to paint an angel:
Whom to please? You whisper "Beatrice."
While he mused and traced it and retraced it,
(Peradventure with a pen corroded
Still by drops of that hot ink he dipped for,
When, his left-hand i' the hair o' the wicked,
Back he held the brow and pricked its stigma,
Bit into the live man's flesh for parchment,
Loosed him, laughed to see the writing rankle,
Let the wretch go festering through Florence)—
Dante, who loved well because he hated,
Hated wickedness that hinders loving,
Dante standing, studying his angel,—
In there broke the folk of his Inferno.
Says he—"Certain people of importance"
(Such he gave his daily dreadful line to)
"Entered and would seize, forsooth, the poet."
Says the poet—"Then I stopped my painting."

VI

You and I would rather see that angel,
Painted by the tenderness of Dante,
Would we not?—than read a fresh Inferno.

VII

You and I will never see that picture.
While he mused on love and Beatrice,
While he softened o'er his outlined angel,
In they broke, those "people of importance:"
We and Bice bear the loss for ever.

[1] The lost book owned by Reni was probably a book of drawings. Raphael is known to have written four love sonnets on the back of sketches and Browning, indulging in poetic license, imagines a whole precious book of sonnets.

VIII

What of Rafael's sonnets, Dante's picture?
This: no artist lives and loves, that longs not
Once, and only once, and for one only,
(Ah, the prize!) to find his love a language
Fit and fair and simple and sufficient—
Using nature that's an art to others,
Not, this one time, art that's turned his nature.
Ay of all the artists living, loving,
None but would forego his proper dowry,—
Does he paint? he fain would write a poem,—
Does he write? he fain would paint a picture,
Put to proof art alien to the artist's,
Once, and only once, and for one only,
So to be the man and leave the artist,
Gain the man's joy, miss the artist's sorrow.

IX

Wherefore? Heaven's gift takes earth's abatement!
He who smites the rock and spreads the water,
Bidding drink and live a crowd beneath him,
Even he, the minute makes immortal,
Proves, perchance, but mortal in the minute,
Desecrates, belike, the deed in doing.
While he smites, how can he but remember,
So he smote before, in such a peril,
When they stood and mocked—"Shall smiting help us?"
When they drank and sneered—"A stroke is easy!"
When they wiped their mouths and went their journey,
Throwing him for thanks—"But drought was pleasant."
Thus old memories mar the actual triumph;
Thus the doing savours of disrelish;
Thus achievement lacks a gracious somewhat;
O'er-importuned brows becloud the mandate,
Carelessness or consciousness—the gesture.
For he bears an ancient wrong about him,
Sees and knows again those phalanxed faces,
Hears, yet one time more, the 'customed prelude—
"How shouldst thou, of all men, smite, and save us?"
Guesses what is like to prove the sequel—
"Egypt's flesh-pots—nay, the drought was better."

X

Oh, the crowd must have emphatic warrant!
Theirs, the Sinai-forehead's cloven brilliance,[1]
Right-arm's rod-sweep, tongue's imperial fiat.
Never dares the man put off the prophet.

XI

Did he love one face from out the thousands,
(Were she Jethro's daughter, white and wifely,
Were she but the Æthiopian bondslave,)
He would envy yon dumb patient camel,
Keeping a reserve of scanty water
Meant to save his own life in the desert
Ready in the desert to deliver
(Kneeling down to let his breast be opened)
Hoard and life together for his mistress.

XII

I shall never, in the years remaining,
Paint you pictures, no, nor carve you statues,
Make you music that should all-express me;
So it seems: I stand on my attainment.
This of verse alone, one life allows me;
Verse and nothing else have I to give you.
Other heights in other lives, God willing:
All the gifts from all the heights, your own, Love!

XIII

Yet a semblance of resource avails us—
Shade so finely touched, love's sense must seize it.
Take these lines, look lovingly and nearly,
Lines I write the first time and the last time.
He who works in fresco, steals a hair-brush,
Curbs the liberal hand,[2] subservient proudly,
Cramps his spirit, crowds its all in little,
Makes a strange art of an art familiar,
Fills his lady's missal-marge with flowerets.
He who blows thro' bronze, may breathe thro' silver,
Fitly serenade a slumbrous princess.
He who writes, may write for once as I do.

XIV

Love, you saw me gather men and women,
Live or dead or fashioned by my fancy,
Enter each and all, and use their service,
Speak from every mouth,—the speech, a poem.
Hardly shall I tell my joys and sorrows,
Hopes and fears, belief and disbelieving:
I am mine and yours—the rest be all men's,
Karshish, Cleon, Norbert and the fifty.
Let me speak this once in my true person,
Not as Lippo, Roland or Andrea,
Though the fruit of speech be just this sentence:
Pray you, look on these my men and women,
Take and keep my fifty poems finished;
Where my heart lies, let my brain lie also!
Poor the speech; be how I speak, for all things.

XV

Not but that you know me! Lo, the moon's self!
Here in London, yonder late in Florence,
Still we find her face, the thrice-transfigured.
Curving on a sky imbrued with colour,
Drifted over Fiesole by twilight,
Came she, our new crescent of a hair's-breadth.
Full she flared it, lamping Samminiato,
Rounder 'twixt the cypresses and rounder,
Perfect till the nightingales applauded.
Now, a piece of her old self, impoverished,
Hard to greet, she traverses the house-roofs,
Hurries with unhandsome thrift of silver,
Goes dispiritedly, glad to finish.

XVI

What, there's nothing in the moon noteworthy?
Nay: for if that moon could love a mortal,
Use, to charm him (so to fit a fancy),
All her magic ('tis the old sweet mythos),
She would turn a new side to her mortal,
Side unseen of herdsman, huntsman, steersman—
Blank to Zoroaster on his terrace,
Blind to Galileo on his turret,
Dumb to Homer, dumb to Keats—him, even!
Think, the wonder of the moonstruck mortal—
When she turns round, comes again in heaven,
Opens out anew for worse or better!
Proves she like some portent of an iceberg
Swimming full upon the ship it founders,

[1] The reference is to Exodus 19:16 in which God speaks through lightning and thunder.

[2] Frescoes were painted with swift sweeping strokes—the liberal hand. The artist will curb himself to delicate miniature work.

Hungry with huge teeth of splintered crystals?
Proves she as the paved work of a sapphire
Seen by Moses when he climbed the mountain?
Moses, Aaron, Nadab and Abihu
Climbed and saw the very God, the Highest,
Stand upon the paved work of a sapphire.[1]
Like the bodied heaven in his clearness
Shone the stone, the sapphire of that paved work,
When they ate and drank and saw God also!

XVII

What were seen? None knows, none ever shall know.
Only this is sure—the sight were other,
Not the moon's same side, born late in Florence,
Dying now impoverished here in London.
God be thanked, the meanest of his creatures
Boasts two soul-sides, one to face the world with,
One to show a woman when he loves her!

XVIII

This I say of me, but think of you, Love!
This to you—yourself my moon of poets!
Ah, but that's the world's side, there's the wonder,
Thus they see you, praise you, think they know you!
There, in turn I stand with them and praise you—
Out of my own self, I dare to phrase it.
But the best is when I glide from out them,
Cross a step or two of dubious twilight,
Come out on the other side, the novel
Silent silver lights and darks undreamed of,
Where I hush and bless myself with silence.

XIX

Oh, their Rafael of the dear Madonnas,
Oh, their Dante of the dread Inferno,
Wrote one song—and in my brain I sing it,
Drew one angel—borne, see, on my bosom!

R. B.

1855

[1] Exodus 24:9–10. "Then went up Moses, and Aaron, Nadab, and Abihu, and seventy of the elders of Israel: and they saw the God of Israel: and there was under his feet as it were a paved work of a sapphire stone, and as it were the body of heaven in his clearness."

From JAMES LEE'S WIFE

IV Along the Beach

I

I will be quiet and talk with you,
And reason why you are wrong.
You wanted my love—is that much true?
And so I did love, so I do:
What has come of it all along?

II

I took you—how could I otherwise?
For a world to me, and more;
For all, love greatens and glorifies
Till God's a-glow, to the loving eyes,
In what was mere earth before.

III

Yes, earth—yes, mere ignoble earth!
Now do I mis-state, mistake?
Do I wrong your weakness and call it worth?
Expect all harvest, dread no dearth,
Seal my sense up for your sake?

IV

Oh, Love, Love, no, Love! not so, indeed!
You were just weak earth, I knew:
With much in you waste, with many a weed,
And plenty of passions run to seed,
But a little good grain too.

V

And such as you were, I took you for mine:
Did not you find me yours,
To watch the olive and wait the vine,
And wonder when rivers of oil and wine
Would flow, as the Book assures?

VI

Well, and if none of these good things came,
What did the failure prove?
The man was my whole world, all the same,
With his flowers to praise or his weeds to blame,
And, either or both, to love.

VII

Yet this turns now to a fault—there! there!
That I do love, watch too long,
And wait too well, and weary and wear;
And 'tis all an old story, and my despair
Fit subject for some new song:

VIII

"How the light, light love, he has wings to fly
At suspicion of a bond:
My wisdom has bidden your pleasure good-bye,
Which will turn up next in a laughing eye,
And why should you look beyond?"

VII Among the Rocks

I

Oh, good gigantic smile o' the brown old earth,
This autumn morning! How he sets his bones
To bask i' the sun, and thrusts out knees and feet
For the ripple to run over in its mirth;
Listening the while, where on the heap of stones
The white breast of the sea-lark twitters sweet.

II

That is the doctrine, simple, ancient, true;
Such is life's trial, as old earth smiles and knows.
If you loved only what were worth your love,
Love were clear gain, and wholly well for you:
Make the low nature better by your throes!
Give earth yourself, go up for gain above!

1864

ABT VOGLER [1]

(AFTER HE HAS BEEN EXTEMPORISING UPON THE MUSICAL INSTRUMENT OF HIS INVENTION.)

I

Would that the structure brave, the manifold music I build,
Bidding my organ obey, calling its keys to their work,
Claiming each slave of the sound, at a touch, as when Solomon willed [1]
Armies of angels that soar, legions of demons that lurk,
Man, brute, reptile, fly,—alien of end and of aim,
Adverse, each from the other heaven-high, hell-deep removed,—
Should rush into sight at once as he named the ineffable Name,
And pile him a palace straight, to pleasure the princess he loved!

II

Would it might tarry like his, the beautiful building of mine,
This which my keys in a crowd pressed and importuned to raise!
Ah, one and all, how they helped, would dispart now and now combine,
Zealous to hasten the work, heighten their master his praise!
And one would bury his brow with a blind plunge down to hell,
Burrow awhile and build, broad on the roots of things,
Then up again swim into sight, having based me my palace well,
Founded it, fearless of flame, flat on the nether springs.[2]

III

And another would mount and march, like the excellent minion he was,
Ay, another and yet another, one crowd but with many a crest,
Raising my rampired walls of gold as transparent as glass,
Eager to do and die, yield each his place to the rest:
For higher still and higher (as runner tips with fire,
When a great illumination surprises a festal night—
Outlining round and round Rome's dome from space to spire)
Up, the pinnacled glory reached, and the pride of my soul was in sight.

[1] The Abbé Vogler (1749–1814) was the teacher of Weber and Meyerbeer, and the inventor of a musical instrument which he called the "orchestrion." It was really an organ, so compactly constructed that it was easily transported. It is on this instrument that Browning represents him as playing in the poem.

[1] Solomon, according to legend, had power over the spirits of the earth and air through possession of a seal on which was engraved "the ineffable Name" of God. [2] Sources

IV

In sight? Not half! for it seemed, it was certain, to match man's birth,
Nature in turn conceived, obeying an impulse as I;
And the emulous heaven yearned down, made effort to reach the earth,
As the earth had done her best, in my passion, to scale the sky:
Novel splendours burst forth, grew familiar and dwelt with mine,
Not a point nor peak but found and fixed its wandering star;
Meteor-moons, balls of blaze: and they did not pale nor pine,
For earth had attained to heaven, there was no more near nor far.

V

Nay more; for there wanted not who walked in the glare and glow,
Presences plain in the place; or, fresh from the Protoplast,[1]
Furnished for ages to come, when a kindlier wind should blow,
Lured now to begin and live, in a house to their liking at last;
Or else the wonderful Dead who have passed through the body and gone,
But were back once more to breathe in an old world worth their new:
What never had been, was now; what was, as it shall be anon;
And what is,—shall I say, matched both? for I was made perfect too.

VI

All through my keys that gave their sounds to a wish of my soul,
All through my soul that praised as its wish flowed visibly forth,
All through music and me! For think, had I painted the whole,
Why, there it had stood, to see, nor the process so wonder-worth:
Had I written the same, made verse—still, effect proceeds from cause,
Ye know why the forms are fair, ye hear how the tale is told;
It is all triumphant art, but art in obedience to laws,
Painter and poet are proud in the artist-list enrolled:—

VII

But here is the finger of God, a flash of the will that can,
Existent behind all laws, that made them and, lo, they are!
And I know not if, save in this, such gift be allowed to man,
That out of three sounds he frame, not a fourth sound, but a star.
Consider it well: each tone of our scale in itself is nought;
It is everywhere in the world—loud, soft, and all is said:
Give it to me to use! I mix it with two in my thought:
And, there! Ye have heard and seen: consider and bow the head!

VIII

Well, it is gone at last, the palace of music I reared;
Gone! and the good tears start, the praises that come too slow;
For one is assured at first, one scarce can say that he feared,
That he even gave it a thought, the gone thing was to go.
Never to be again! But many more of the kind
As good, nay, better perchance: is this your comfort to me?
To me, who must be saved because I cling with my mind
To the same, same self, same love, same God: ay, what was, shall be.

IX

Therefore to whom turn I but to thee, the ineffable Name?
Builder and maker, thou, of houses not made with hands!
What, have fear of change from thee who art ever the same?

[1] From the protoplasm, the lowest unit of living matter. The word also means "the first made thing or being of its kind." Browning's use of the word embraces both meanings—a thing created, "lured to begin," but close to its source.

Doubt that thy power can fill the heart that thy power expands?
There shall never be one lost good! What was, shall live as before;
  The evil is null, is nought, is silence implying sound;
What was good shall be good, with, for evil, so much good more;
  On the earth the broken arcs; in the heaven, a perfect round.

X

All we have willed or hoped or dreamed of good shall exist;
  Not its semblance, but itself; no beauty, nor good, nor power
Whose voice has gone forth, but each survives for the melodist
  When eternity affirms the conception of an hour.
The high that proved too high, the heroic for earth too hard,
  The passion that left the ground to lose itself in the sky,
Are music sent up to God by the lover and the bard;
  Enough that he heard it once: we shall hear it by-and-by.

XI

And what is our failure here but a triumph's evidence
  For the fulness of the days? Have we withered or agonised?
Why else was the pause prolonged but that singing might issue thence?
  Why rushed the discords in but that harmony should be prized?
Sorrow is hard to bear, and doubt is slow to clear,
  Each sufferer says his say, his scheme of the weal and woe:
But God has a few of us whom he whispers in the ear;
  The rest may reason and welcome: 'tis we musicians know.

XII

Well, it is earth with me; silence resumes her reign:
  I will be patient and proud, and soberly acquiesce.
Give me the keys. I feel for the common chord again,[1]
  Sliding by semitones, till I sink to the minor,—yes,
And I blunt it into a ninth, and I stand on alien ground,
  Surveying awhile the heights I rolled from into the deep;
Which, hark, I have dared and done, for my resting-place is found,
  The C Major of this life: so, now I will try to sleep.

1864

RABBI BEN EZRA[2]

I

Grow old along with me!
  The best is yet to be,
The last of life, for which the first was made:
  Our times are in His hand
  Who saith "A whole I planned,
Youth shows but half; trust God: see all nor be afraid!"

II

Not that, amassing flowers,
  Youth sighed "Which rose make ours,
Which lily leave and then as best recall?"

[1] Precisely because music would seem to be the most fleeting of the arts, its beauty dying with the death of sound, the musician is compelled to turn to God, the maker "of houses not built with hands," for confidence that his conception of an hour has its existence in eternity. He feels then for the "common chord," and through an harmonic modulation returns to the "C major of this life" — the C major, a natural scale without variation of sharps or flats, symbolizing to the player a return to, and acceptance of, the common levels of life — sure that his flights of imagination still have their exis tence and value elsewhere.

[2] Rabbi Ben Ezra or Ibn Ezra was a mediaeval Jewish thinker who was born in Toledo, and died about 1167. He was widely traveled, having visited such widely scattered lands as Palestine, Persia, India, Italy, France, and England. It is said that Browning in the poem has faithfully reproduced the philosophy of the Rabbi of history. It was a philosophy with which Browning was in sympathy, and the poem has been taken as one of the clearest expositions of Browning's own philosophy of life.

Not that, admiring stars,
It yearned "Nor Jove, nor Mars;
Mine be some figured flame which blends, transcends them all!"

III

Not for such hopes and fears
Annulling youth's brief years,
Do I remonstrate: folly wide the mark!
Rather I prize the doubt
Low kinds exist without,
Finished and finite clods, untroubled by a spark.

IV

Poor vaunt of life indeed,
Were man but formed to feed
On joy, to solely seek and find and feast:
Such feasting ended, then
As sure an end to men;
Irks care the crop-full bird? Frets doubt the maw-crammed beast?

V

Rejoice we are allied
To That which doth provide
And not partake, effect and not receive!
A spark disturbs our clod;
Nearer we hold of God
Who gives, than of His tribes that take, I must believe.

VI

Then, welcome each rebuff
That turns earth's smoothness rough,
Each sting that bids nor sit nor stand but go!
Be our joys three-parts pain!
Strive, and hold cheap the strain;
Learn, nor account the pang; dare, never grudge the throe!

VII

For thence,—a paradox
Which comforts while it mocks,—
Shall life succeed in that it seems to fail:
What I aspired to be,
And was not, comforts me:
A brute I might have been, but would not sink i' the scale.

VIII

What is he but a brute
Whose flesh has soul to suit,
Whose spirit works lest arms and legs want play?
To man, propose this test—
Thy body at its best,
How far can that project thy soul on its lone way?

IX

Yet gifts should prove their use:
I own the Past profuse
Of power each side, perfection every turn:
Eyes, ears took in their dole,
Brain treasured up the whole;
Should not the heart beat once "How good to live and learn?"

X

Not once beat "Praise be Thine!
I see the whole design,
I, who saw power, see now Love perfect too:
Perfect I call Thy plan:
Thanks that I was a man!
Maker, remake, complete,—I trust what Thou shalt do!"

XI

For pleasant is this flesh;
Our soul, in its rose-mesh
Pulled ever to the earth, still yearns for rest;
Would we some prize might hold
To match those manifold
Possessions of the brute,—gain most, as we did best!

XII

Let us not always say
"Spite of this flesh to-day
I strove, made head, gained ground upon the whole!"
As the bird wings and sings,
Let us cry "All good things
Are ours, nor soul helps flesh more, now, than flesh helps soul!"

XIII

Therefore I summon age
To grant youth's heritage,
Life's struggle having so far reached its term:
Thence shall I pass, approved
A man, for aye removed
From the developed brute; a god though in the germ.

XIV

And I shall thereupon
Take rest, ere I be gone
Once more on my adventure brave and new:

Fearless and unperplexed,
When I wage battle next,
What weapons to select, what armour to indue.

XV

Youth ended, I shall try
My gain or loss thereby;
Leave the fire ashes, what survives is gold:
And I shall weigh the same,
Give life its praise or blame:
Young, all lay in dispute; I shall know, being old.

XVI

For note, when evening shuts,
A certain moment cuts
The deed off, calls the glory from the grey:
A whisper from the west
Shoots—"Add this to the rest,
Take it and try its worth: here dies another day."

XVII

So, still within this life,
Though lifted o'er its strife,
Let me discern, compare, pronounce at last,
"This rage was right i' the main,
That acquiescence vain:
The Future I may face now I have proved the Past."

XVIII

For more is not reserved
To man, with soul just nerved
To act to-morrow what he learns to-day:
Here, work enough to watch
The Master work, and catch
Hints of the proper craft, tricks of the tool's true play.

XIX

As it was better, youth
Should strive, through acts uncouth,
Toward making, than repose on aught found made:
So, better, age, exempt
From strife, should know, than tempt
Further. Thou waitedest age: wait death nor be afraid!

XX

Enough now, if the Right
And Good and Infinite
Be named here, as thou callest thy hand thine own,
With knowledge absolute,
Subject to no dispute
From fools that crowded youth, nor let thee feel alone.

XXI

Be there, for once and all,
Severed great minds from small,
Announced to each his station in the Past!
Was I, the world arraigned,
Were they, my soul disdained,
Right? Let age speak the truth and give us peace at last!

XXII

Now, who shall arbitrate?
Ten men love what I hate,
Shun what I follow, slight what I receive;
Ten, who in ears and eyes
Match me: we all surmise,
They this thing, and I that: whom shall my soul believe?

XXIII

Not on the vulgar mass
Called "work," must sentence pass,
Things done, that took the eye and had the price;
O'er which, from level stand,
The low world laid its hand,
Found straightway to its mind, could value in a trice:

XXIV

But all, the world's coarse thumb
And finger failed to plumb,
So passed in making up the main account;
All instincts immature,
All purposes unsure,
That weighed not as his work, yet swelled the man's amount:

XXV

Thoughts hardly to be packed
Into a narrow act,
Fancies that broke through language and escaped;
All I could never be,
All, men ignored in me,
This, I was worth to God, whose wheel the pitcher shaped.

XXVI

Ay, note that Potter's wheel,[1]
That metaphor! and feel
Why time spins fast, why passive lies our clay,—
Thou, to whom fools propound,
When the wine makes its round,
"Since life fleets, all is change; the Past gone, seize to-day!"

XXVII

Fool! All that is, at all,
Lasts ever, past recall;
Earth changes, but thy soul and God stand sure:
What entered into thee,
That was, is, and shall be:
Time's wheel runs back or stops: Potter and clay endure.

XXVIII

He fixed thee mid this dance
Of plastic circumstance,
This Present, thou, forsooth, wouldst fain arrest:
Machinery just meant
To give thy soul its bent,
Try thee and turn thee forth, sufficiently impressed.

XXIX

What though the earlier grooves
Which ran the laughing loves
Around thy base, no longer pause and press?
What though, about thy rim,
Skull-things in order grim
Grow out, in graver mood, obey the sterner stress?

XXX

Look not thou down but up!
To uses of a cup,
The festal board, lamp's flash and trumpet's peal,
The new wine's foaming flow,
The Master's lips aglow!
Thou, heaven's consummate cup, what need'st thou with earth's wheel?

[1] Isaiah 64:8. "But now, O Lord, thou art our father; we are the clay and thou our potter; and we all are the work of thy hand." See also Jeremiah 18:2–6.

XXXI

But I need, now as then,
Thee, God, who mouldest men;
And since, not even while the whirl was worst,
Did I,—to the wheel of life
With shapes and colours rife,
Bound dizzily,—mistake my end, to slake Thy thirst:

XXXII

So, take and use Thy work:
Amend what flaws may lurk,
What strain o' the stuff, what warpings past the aim!
My times be in Thy hand!
Perfect the cup as planned!
Let age approve of youth, and death complete the same!

1864

CALIBAN UPON SETEBOS; OR, NATURAL THEOLOGY IN THE ISLAND

"Thou thoughtest that I was altogether such a one as thyself."[1]

['WILL sprawl, now that the heat of day is best,
Flat on his belly in the pit's much mire,
With elbows wide, fists clenched to prop his chin.
And, while he kicks both feet in the cool slush,
And feels about his spine small eft-things course,
Run in and out each arm, and make him laugh:
And while above his head a pompion-plant,
Coating the cave-top as a brow its eye,
Creeps down to touch and tickle hair and beard,
And now a flower drops with a bee inside,
And now a fruit to snap at, catch and crunch,—
He looks out o'er yon sea which sunbeams cross
And recross till they weave a spider-web
(Meshes of fire, some great fish breaks at times)
And talks to his own self, howe'er he please,
Touching that other, whom his dam called God.
Because to talk about Him, vexes—ha,

[1] Psalms 50:21, spoken by God to the wicked.

Could He but know! and time to vex is now,
When talk is safer than in winter-time.
Moreover Prosper and Miranda sleep
In confidence he drudges at their task,
And it is good to cheat the pair, and gibe,
Letting the rank tongue blossom into speech.]

Setebos, Setebos, and Setebos!
'Thinketh, He dwelleth i' the cold o' the moon.

'Thinketh He made it, with the sun to match,
But not the stars; the stars came otherwise;
Only made clouds, winds, meteors, such as that:
Also this isle, what lives and grows thereon,
And snaky sea which rounds and ends the same.

'Thinketh, it came of being ill at ease:
He hated that He cannot change His cold,
Nor cure its ache. 'Hath spied an icy fish
That longed to 'scape the rock-stream where she lived,
And thaw herself within the lukewarm brine
O' the lazy sea her stream thrusts far amid,
A crystal spike 'twixt two warm walls of wave;
Only, she ever sickened, found repulse
At the other kind of water, not her life,
(Green-dense and dim-delicious, bred o' the sun)
Flounced back from bliss she was not born to breathe,
And in her old bounds buried her despair,
Hating and loving warmth alike: so He.

'Thinketh, He made thereat the sun, this isle,
Trees and the fowls here, beast and creeping thing.
Yon otter, sleek-wet, black, lithe as a leech;
Yon auk, one fire-eye in a ball of foam,
That floats and feeds; a certain badger brown
He hath watched hunt with that slant white-wedge eye
By moonlight; and the pie with the long tongue
That pricks deep into oakwarts for a worm,
And says a plain word when she finds her prize,
But will not eat the ants; the ants themselves
That build a wall of seeds and settled stalks
About their hole—He made all these and more,
Made all we see, and us, in spite: how else?
He could not, Himself, make a second self
To be His mate; as well have made Himself:
He would not make what he mislikes or slights,
An eyesore to Him, or not worth His pains:
But did, in envy, listlessness or sport,
Make what Himself would fain, in a manner, be—
Weaker in most points, stronger in a few,
Worthy, and yet mere playthings all the while,
Things He admires and mocks too,—that is it.
Because, so brave, so better though they be,
It nothing skills if He begin to plague.
Look now, I melt a gourd-fruit into mash,
And honey-comb and pods, I have perceived,
Which bite like finches when they bill and kiss,—
Then, when froth rises bladdery, drink up all,
Quick, quick, till maggots scamper through my brain;
Last, throw me on my back i' the seeded thyme,
And wanton, wishing I were born a bird.
Put case, unable to be what I wish,
I yet could make a live bird out of clay:
Would not I take clay, pinch my Caliban
Able to fly?—for, there, see, he hath wings,
And great comb like the hoopoe's to admire,
And there, a sting to do his foes offence,
There, and I will that he begin to live,
Fly to yon rock-top, nip me off the horns
Of grigs high up that make the merry din,
Saucy through their veined wings, and mind me not.
In which feat, if his leg snapped, brittle clay,
And he lay stupid-like,—why, I should laugh;
And if he, spying me, should fall to weep,
Beseech me to be good, repair his wrong,
Bid his poor leg smart less or grow again,—
Well, as the chance were, this might take or else
Not take my fancy: I might hear his cry,
And give the mankin three sound legs for one,
Or pluck the other off, leave him like an egg,
And lessoned he was mine and merely clay.
Were this no pleasure, lying in the thyme,
Drinking the mash, with brain become alive,
Making and marring clay at will? So He.

'Thinketh, such shows nor right nor wrong in Him,
Nor kind, nor cruel: He is strong and Lord.

'Am strong myself compared to yonder crabs
That march now from the mountain to the sea;
'Let twenty pass, and stone the twenty-first,
Loving not, hating not, just choosing so.
'Say, the first straggler that boasts purple spots
Shall join the file, one pincer twisted off;
'Say, this bruised fellow shall receive a worm,
And two worms he whose nippers end in red;
As it likes me each time, I do: so He.

Well then, 'supposeth He is good i' the main,
Placable if His mind and ways were guessed,
But rougher than His handiwork, be sure!
Oh, He hath made things worthier than Himself,
And envieth that, so helped, such things do more
Than He who made them! What consoles but this?
That they, unless through Him, do nought at all,
And must submit: what other use in things?
'Hath cut a pipe of pithless elder-joint
That, blown through, gives exact the scream o' the jay
When from her wing you twitch the feathers blue:
Sound this, and little birds that hate the jay
Flock within stone's throw, glad their foe is hurt:
Put case such pipe could prattle and boast forsooth
"I catch the birds, I am the crafty thing,
I make the cry my maker cannot make
With his great round mouth; he must blow through mine!"
Would not I smash it with my foot? So He.

But wherefore rough, why cold and ill at ease?
Aha, that is a question! Ask, for that,
What knows,—the something over Setebos
That made Him, or He, may be, found and fought,
Worsted, drove off and did to nothing, perchance.
There may be something quiet o'er His head,
Out of His reach, that feels nor joy nor grief,
Since both derive from weakness in some way.
I joy because the quails come; would not joy
Could I bring quails here when I have a mind:
This Quiet, all it hath a mind to, doth.
'Esteemeth stars the outposts of its couch,
But never spends much thought nor care that way.
It may look up, work up,—the worse for those
It works on! 'Careth but for Setebos
The many-handed as a cuttle-fish,
Who, making Himself feared through what He does,
Looks up, first, and perceives he cannot soar
To what is quiet and hath happy life;
Next looks down here, and out of very spite
Makes this a bauble-world to ape yon real,
These good things to match those as hips do grapes.
'Tis solace making baubles, ay, and sport.
Himself peeped late, eyed Prosper at his books
Careless and lofty, lord now of the isle:
Vexed, 'stitched a book of broad leaves, arrow-shaped,
Wrote thereon, he knows what, prodigious words;
Has peeled a wand and called it by a name;
Weareth at whiles for an enchanter's robe
The eyed skin of a supple oncelot;
And hath an ounce sleeker than youngling mole,
A four-legged serpent he makes cower and couch,
Now snarl, now hold its breath and mind his eye,
And saith she is Miranda and my wife:
'Keeps for his Ariel a tall pouch-bill crane
He bids go wade for fish and straight disgorge;
Also a sea-beast, lumpish, which he snared,
Blinded the eyes of, and brought somewhat tame,
And split its toe-webs, and now pens the drudge
In a hole o' the rock and calls him Caliban;
A bitter heart that bides its time and bites.
'Plays thus at being Prosper in a way,
Taketh his mirth with make-believes: so He.

His dam held that the Quiet made all things
Which Setebos vexed only: 'holds not so.
Who made them weak, meant weakness He might vex.

Had He meant other, while His hand was in,
Why not make horny eyes no thorn could prick,
Or plate my scalp with bone against the snow,
Or overscale my flesh 'neath joint and joint,
Like an orc's armour? Ay,—so spoil His sport!
He is the One now: only He doth all.

'Saith, He may like, perchance, what profits Him.
Ay, himself loves what does him good; but why?
'Gets good no otherwise. This blinded beast
Loves whoso places flesh-meat on his nose,
But, had he eyes, would want no help, but hate
Or love, just as it liked him: He hath eyes.
Also it pleaseth Setebos to work,
Use all His hands, and exercise much craft,
By no means for the love of what is worked.
'Tasteth, himself, no finer good i' the world
When all goes right, in this safe summer-time,
And he wants little, hungers, aches not much,
Than trying what to do with wit and strength.
'Falls to make something: 'piled yon pile of turfs,
And squared and stuck there squares of soft white chalk,
And, with a fish-tooth, scratched a moon on each,
And set up endwise certain spikes of tree,
And crowned the whole with a sloth's skull a-top,
Found dead i' the woods, too hard for one to kill.
No use at all i' the work, for work's sole sake;
'Shall some day knock it down again: so He.

'Saith He is terrible: watch His feats in proof!
One hurricane will spoil six good month's hope.
He hath a spite against me, that I know,
Just as He favours Prosper, who knows why?
So it is, all the same, as well I find.
'Wove wattles half the winter, fenced them firm
With stone and stake to stop she-tortoises
Crawling to lay their eggs here: well, one wave,
Feeling the foot of Him upon its neck,
Gaped as a snake does, lolled out its large tongue,
And licked the whole labour flat: so much for spite.
Saw a ball flame down late (yonder it lies)
Where, half an hour before, I slept i' the shade:
Often they scatter sparkles: there is force!
'Dug up a newt He may have envied once
And turned to stone, shut up inside a stone.
Please Him and hinder this?—What Prosper does?
Aha, if He would tell me how! Not He!
There is the sport: discover how or die!
All need not die, for of the things o' the isle
Some flee afar, some dive, some run up trees;
Those at His mercy,—why, they please Him most
When . . . when . . . well, never try the same way twice!
Repeat what act has pleased, He may grow wroth.
You must not know His ways, and play Him off,
Sure of the issue. 'Doth the like himself:
'Spareth a squirrel that it nothing fears
But steals the nut from underneath my thumb,
And when I threat, bites stoutly in defence:
'Spareth an urchin that contrariwise,
Curls up into a ball, pretending death
For fright at my approach: the two ways please.
But what would move my choler more than this,
That either creature counted on its life
To-morrow and next day and all days to come,
Saying, forsooth, in the inmost of its heart,
"Because he did so yesterday with me,
And otherwise with such another brute,
So much he do henceforth and always."—Ay?
Would teach the reasoning couple what "must" means!
'Doth as he likes, or wherefore Lord? So He.

'Conceiveth all things will continue thus,
And we shall have to live in fear of Him
So long as He lives, keeps His strength: no change,
If He have done His best, make no new world
To please Him more, so leave off watching this,—

If He surprise not even the Quiet's self
Some strange day,—or, suppose, grow into it
As grubs grow butterflies: else, here are we,
And there is He, and nowhere help at all.
'Believeth with the life, the pain shall stop.
His dam held different, that after death
He both plagued enemies and feasted friends:
Idly! He doth His worst in this our life,
Giving just respite lest we die through pain,
Saving last pain for worst,—with which, an end.
Meanwhile, the best way to escape His ire
Is, not to seem too happy. 'Sees, himself,
Yonder two flies, with purple films and pink,
Bask on the pompion-bell above: kills both.
'Sees two black painful beetles roll their ball
On head and tail as if to save their lives:
Moves them the stick away they strive to clear.

Even so, 'would have Him misconceive, suppose
This Caliban strives hard and ails no less
And always, above all else, envies Him;
Wherefore he mainly dances on dark nights,
Moans in the sun, gets under holes to laugh,
And never speaks his mind save housed as now:
Outside, 'groans, curses. If He caught me here,
O'erheard this speech, and asked "What chucklest at?"
'Would, to appease Him, cut a finger off,
Or of my three kid yearlings burn the best,
Or let the toothsome apples rot on tree,
Or push my tame beast for the orc to taste:
While myself lit a fire, and made a song
And sung it, "*What I hate, be consecrate*
To celebrate Thee and Thy state, no mate
For Thee; what see for envy in poor me?"
Hoping the while, since evils sometimes mend,
Warts rub away and sores are cured with slime,
That some strange day, will either the Quiet catch
And conquer Setebos, or likelier He
Decrepit may doze, doze, as good as die.

* * *

[What, what? A curtain o'er the world at once!
Crickets stop hissing; not a bird—or, yes,
There scuds His raven that has told Him all!
It was fool's play, this prattling! Ha! The wind
Shoulders the pillared dust, death's house o' the move,
And fast invading fires begin! White blaze—
A tree's head snaps—and there, there, there, there, there,
His thunder follows! Fool to gibe at Him!
Lo! 'Lieth flat and loveth Setebos!
'Maketh his teeth meet through his upper lip,
Will let those quails fly, will not eat this month
One little mess of whelks, so he may 'scape!]

1864

CONFESSIONS

I

What is he buzzing in my ears?
  "Now that I come to die,
Do I view the world as a vale of tears?"
  Ah, reverend sir, not I!

II

What I viewed there once, what I view again
  Where the physic bottles stand
On the table's edge,—is a suburb lane,
  With a wall to my bedside hand.

III

That lane sloped, much as the bottles do,
  From a house you could descry
O'er the garden-wall: is the curtain blue
  Or green to a healthy eye?

IV

To mine, it serves for the old June weather
  Blue above lane and wall;
And that farthest bottle labelled "Ether"
  Is the house o'ertopping all.

V

At a terrace, somewhere near the stopper,
  There watched for me, one June,
A girl: I know, sir, it's improper,
  My poor mind's out of tune.

VI

Only, there was a way . . . you crept
  Close by the side, to dodge
Eyes in the house, two eyes except:
  They styled their house "The Lodge."

VII

What right had a lounger up their lane?
But, by creeping very close,
With the good wall's help,—their eyes might strain
And stretch themselves to Oes,

VIII

Yet never catch her and me together,
As she left the attic, there,
By the rim of the bottle labelled "Ether,"
And stole from stair to stair,

IX

And stood by the rose-wreathed gate. Alas,
We loved, sir—used to meet:
How sad and bad and mad it was—
But then, how it was sweet!

1864

PROSPICE[1]

FEAR death?—to feel the fog in my throat,
The mist in my face,
When the snows begin, and the blasts denote
I am nearing the place,
The power of the night, the press of the storm,
The post of the foe;
Where he stands, the Arch Fear in a visible form,
Yet the strong man must go:
For the journey is done and the summit attained,
And the barriers fall,
Though a battle's to fight ere the guerdon be gained,
The reward of it all.
I was ever a fighter, so—one fight more,
The best and the last!
I would hate that death bandaged my eyes and forbore,
And bade me creep past.
No! let me taste the whole of it, fare like my peers
The heroes of old,
Bear the brunt, in a minute pay glad life's arrears
Of pain, darkness and cold.
For sudden the worst turns the best to the brave,
The black minute's at end,
And the elements' rage, the fiend-voices that rave,
Shall dwindle, shall blend,
Shall change, shall become first a peace out of pain,
Then a light, then thy breast,
O thou soul of my soul! I shall clasp thee again,
And with God be the rest!

1864

[1] "Look forward."

YOUTH AND ART

I

IT once might have been, once only:
We lodged in a street together,
You, a sparrow on the housetop lonely,
I, a lone she-bird of his feather.

II

Your trade was with sticks and clay,
You thumbed, thrust, patted and polished,
Then laughed "They will see some day
Smith made, and Gibson[1] demolished."

III

My business was song, song, song;
I chirped, cheeped, trilled and twittered,
"Kate Brown's on the boards ere long,
And Grisi's[2] existence embittered!"

IV

I earned no more by a warble
Than you by a sketch in plaster;
You wanted a piece of marble,
I needed a music-master.

V

We studied hard in our styles,
Chipped each at a crust like Hindoos,[3]
For air looked out on the tiles,
For fun watched each other's windows.

VI

You lounged, like a boy of the South,
Cap and blouse—nay, a bit of beard too;
Or you got it, rubbing your mouth
With fingers the clay adhered to.

[1] John Gibson (1790–1866) was a well-known sculptor.

[2] Giulia Grisi (1811–1869) was perhaps the most famous singer of her time.

[3] I.e., they lived on insufficient food because they were poor.

VII

And I—soon managed to find
  Weak points in the flower-fence facing,
Was forced to put up a blind
  And be safe in my corset-lacing.

VIII

No harm! It was not my fault
  If you never turned your eye's tail up
As I shook upon E *in alt.*,
  Or ran the chromatic scale up:

IX

For spring bade the sparrows pair,
  And the boys and girls gave guesses,
And stalls in our street looked rare
  With bulrush and watercresses.

X

Why did not you pinch a flower
  In a pellet of clay and fling it?
Why did not I put a power
  Of thanks in a look, or sing it?

XI

I did look, sharp as a lynx,
  (And yet the memory rankles)
When models arrived, some minx
  Tripped up-stairs, she and her ankles.

XII

But I think I gave you as good!
  "That foreign fellow,—who can know
How she pays, in a playful mood,
  For his tuning her that piano?"

XIII

Could you say so, and never say
  "Suppose we join hands and fortunes,
And I fetch her from over the way,
  Her piano, and long tunes and short tunes?"

XIV

No, no: you would not be rash,
  Nor I rasher and something over:
You've to settle yet Gibson's hash,
  And Grisi yet lives in clover.

XV

But you meet the Prince at the Board,
  I'm queen myself at *bals-paré*,[1]
I've married a rich old lord,
  And you're dubbed knight and an R.A.[1]

XVI

Each life unfulfilled, you see;
  It hangs still, patchy and scrappy:
We have not sighed deep, laughed free,
  Starved, feasted, despaired,—been happy.

XVII

And nobody calls you a dunce,
  And people suppose me clever:
This could but have happened once,
  And we missed it, lost it for ever.

1864

[1] Fancy-dress balls.

[1] A member of the Royal Academy.

A FACE

If one could have that little head of hers
  Painted upon a background of pale gold,
Such as the Tuscan's early art prefers!
  No shade encroaching on the matchless mould
Of those two lips, which should be opening soft
  In the pure profile; not as when she laughs,
For that spoils all: but rather as if aloft
  Yon hyacinth, she loves so, leaned its staff's
Burthen of honey-coloured buds to kiss
And capture 'twixt the lips apart for this.
Then her lithe neck, three fingers might surround,
How it should waver on the pale gold ground
Up to the fruit-shaped, perfect chin it lifts!
I know, Correggio loves to mass, in rifts
Of heaven, his angel faces, orb on orb
Breaking its outline, burning shades absorb:
But these are only massed there, I should think,
  Waiting to see some wonder momently
  Grow out, stand full, fade slow against the sky
  (That's the pale ground you'd see this sweet face by),
  All heaven, meanwhile, condensed into one eye
Which fears to lose the wonder, should it wink.

1864

APPARENT FAILURE

"We shall soon lose a celebrated building."—*Paris Newspaper.*

I

No, for I'll save it! Seven years since,
I passed through Paris, stopped a day
To see the baptism of your Prince;
Saw, made my bow, and went my way:
Walking the heat and headache off,
I took the Seine-side, you surmise,
Thought of the Congress,[1] Gortschakoff,
Cavour's appeal and Buol's replies,
So sauntered till—what met my eyes?

II

Only the Doric little Morgue!
The dead-house where you show your drowned:
Petrarch's Vaucluse makes proud the Sorgue,[2]
Your Morgue has made the Seine renowned.
One pays one's debt in such a case;
I plucked up heart and entered,—stalked,
Keeping a tolerable face
Compared with some whose cheeks were chalked:
Let them! No Briton's to be baulked!

III

First came the silent gazers; next,
A screen of glass, we're thankful for;
Last, the sight's self, the sermon's text,
The three men who did most abhor
Their life in Paris yesterday,
So killed themselves: and now, enthroned
Each on his copper couch, they lay
Fronting me, waiting to be owned.
I thought, and think, their sin's atoned.

IV

Poor men, God made, and all for that!
The reverence struck me; o'er each head
Religiously was hung its hat,
Each coat dripped by the owner's bed
Sacred from touch: each had his berth,
His bounds, his proper place of rest,
Who last night tenanted on earth
Some arch, where twelve such slept abreast,—
Unless the plain asphalt seemed best.

V

How did it happen, my poor boy?
You wanted to be Buonaparte
And have the Tuileries for toy,
And could not, so it broke your heart?
You, old one by his side, I judge,
Were, red as blood, a socialist,
A leveller! Does the Empire grudge
You've gained what no Republic missed?
Be quiet, and unclench your fist!

VI

And this—why, he was red in vain,
Or black,—poor fellow that is blue!
What fancy was it turned your brain?
Oh, women were the prize for you!
Money gets women, cards and dice
Get money, and ill-luck gets just
The copper couch and one clear nice
Cool squirt of water o'er your bust,
The right thing to extinguish lust!

VII

It's wiser being good than bad;
It's safer being meek than fierce:
It's fitter being sane than mad.
My own hope is, a sun will pierce
The thickest cloud earth ever stretched;
That, after Last, returns the First,
Though a wide compass round be fetched;
That what began best, can't end worst,
Nor what God blessed once, prove accurst.

1864

[1] The Congress of Paris, a conference of the great powers, met in 1856 to discuss the unity of Italy, the Austrian Buol opposing Cavour's appeal.

[2] By a fountain at Vaucluse Petrarch is supposed to have written many of his sonnets to Laura. This fountain is the source of the Sorgue.

HOUSE

I

SHALL I sonnet-sing you about myself?
Do I live in a house you would like to see?
Is it scant of gear, has it store of pelf?
"Unlock my heart with a sonnet-key?"

II

Invite the world, as my betters have done?
"Take notice: this building remains on view,
Its suites of reception every one,
Its private apartment and bedroom too;

III

"For a ticket, apply to the Publisher."
  No: thanking the public, I must decline.
A peep through my window, if folk prefer;
  But, please you, no foot over threshold of mine!

IV

I have mixed with a crowd and heard free talk
  In a foreign land where an earthquake chanced:
And a house stood gaping, nought to baulk
  Man's eye wherever he gazed or glanced.

V

The whole of the frontage shaven sheer,
  The inside gaped: exposed to day,
Right and wrong and common and queer,
  Bare, as the palm of your hand, it lay.

VI

The owner? Oh, he had been crushed, no doubt!
  "Odd tables and chairs for a man of wealth!
What a parcel of musty old books about!
  He smoked,—no wonder he lost his health!

VII

"I doubt if he bathed before he dressed.
  A brasier?—the pagan, he burned perfumes!
You see it is proved, what the neighbours guessed:
  His wife and himself had separate rooms."

VIII

Friends, the goodman of the house at least
  Kept house to himself till an earthquake came:
'Tis the fall of its frontage permits you feast
  On the inside arrangement you praise or blame.

IX

Outside should suffice for evidence:
  And whoso desires to penetrate
Deeper, must dive by the spirit-sense—
  No optics like yours, at any rate!

X

"Hoity toity! A street to explore,
  Your house the exception! '*With this same key*
Shakespeare unlocked his heart,' [1] once more!"
  Did Shakespeare? If so, the less Shakespeare he!

1876

SHOP

I

So, friend, your shop was all your house!
  Its front, astonishing the street,
Invited view from man and mouse
  To what diversity of treat
  Behind its glass—the single sheet!

II

What gimcracks, genuine Japanese:
  Gape-jaw and goggle-eye, the frog;
Dragons, owls, monkeys, beetles, geese;
  Some crush-nosed human-hearted dog:
  Queer names, too, such a catalogue!

III

I thought "And he who owns the wealth
  Which blocks the window's vastitude,
—Ah, could I peep at him by stealth
  Behind his ware, pass shop, intrude
  On house itself, What scenes were viewed!

IV

"If wide and showy thus the shop,
  What must the habitation prove?
The true house with no name a-top—
  The mansion, distant one remove,
  Once get him off his traffic-groove!

V

"Pictures he likes, or books perhaps;
  And as for buying most and best,
Commend me to these City [2] chaps!
  Or else he's social, takes his rest
  On Sundays, with a Lord for guest.

VI

"Some suburb-palace, parked about
  And gated grandly, built last year:
The four-mile walk to keep off gout;
  Or big seat sold by bankrupt peer:
  But then he takes the rail, that's clear.

[1] Quoted from Wordsworth's "Scorn Not the Sonnet." The reference is to Shakespeare's sonnet sequence — the key with which he unlocked his heart. It is Browning's point that the poet does not necessarily unlock his heart — he doubts if Shakespeare did — and for himself he intends to maintain his spiritual privacy.

[2] The "City" is the financial district of London.

VII

"Or, stop! I wager, taste selects
Some out o' the way, some all-unknown
Retreat: the neighbourhood suspects
Little that he who rambles lone
Makes Rothschild [1] tremble on his throne!"

VIII

Nowise! Nor Mayfair [2] residence
Fit to receive and entertain,—
Nor Hampstead villa's kind defence
From noise and crowd, from dust and drain,—
Nor country-box was soul's domain!

IX

Nowise! At back of all that spread
Of merchandise, woe's me, I find
A hole i' the wall where, heels by head,
The owner couched, his ware behind,
—In cupboard suited to his mind.

X

For why? He saw no use of life
But, while he drove a roaring trade,
To chuckle "Customers are rife!"
To chafe "So much hard cash outlaid
Yet zero in my profits made!

XI

"This novelty costs pains, but—takes?
Cumbers my counter! Stock no more!
This article, no such great shakes,
Fizzes like wildfire? Underscore
The cheap thing—thousands to the fore!"

XII

'Twas lodging best to live most nigh
(Cramp, coffinlike as crib might be)
Receipt of Custom; ear and eye
Wanted no outworld: "Hear and see
The bustle in the shop!" quoth he.

XIII

My fancy of a merchant-prince
Was different. Through his wares we groped
Our darkling way to—not to mince
The matter—no black den where moped
The master if we interloped!

XIV

Shop was shop only: household-stuff?
What did he want with comforts there?
"Walls, ceiling, floor, stay blank and rough,
So goods on sale show rich and rare!
'*Sell and scud home*' be shop's affair!"

XV

What might he deal in? Gems, suppose!
Since somehow business must be done
At cost of trouble,—see, he throws
You choice of jewels, everyone,
Good, better, best, star, moon and sun!

XVI

Which lies within your power of purse?
This ruby that would tip aright
Solomon's sceptre? Oh, your nurse
Wants simply coral, the delight
Of teething baby,—stuff to bite!

XVII

Howe'er your choice fell, straight you took
Your purchase, prompt your money rang
On counter,—scarce the man forsook
His study of the "Times," just swang
Till-ward his hand that stopped the clang,—

XVIII

Then off made buyer with a prize,
Then seller to his "Times" returned;
And so did day wear, wear, till eyes
Brightened apace, for rest was earned:
He locked door long ere candle burned.

XIX

And whither went he? Ask himself,
Not me! To change of scene, I think.
Once sold the ware and pursed the pelf,
Chaffer was scarce his meat and drink,
Nor all his music—money-chink.

XX

Because a man has shop to mind
In time and place, since flesh must live,
Needs spirit lack all life behind,
All stray thoughts, fancies fugitive,
All loves except what trade can give?

XXI

I want to know a butcher paints,
A baker rhymes for his pursuit,
Candlestick-maker much acquaints
His soul with song, or, haply mute,
Blows out his brains upon the flute!

[1] The Rothschilds were one of the great European banking families, international in their power.

[2] The most fashionable residential section of London.

XXII

But—shop each day and all day long!
Friend, your good angel slept, your star
Suffered eclipse, fate did you wrong!
From where these sorts of treasures are,
There should our hearts be—Christ, how far!

1876

NATURAL MAGIC

I

ALL I can say is—I saw it!
The room was as bare as your hand.
I locked in the swarth little lady,—I swear,
From the head to the foot of her—well, quite as bare!
"No Nautch [1] shall cheat me," said I, "taking my stand
At this bolt which I draw!" And this bolt—I withdraw it,
And there laughs the lady, not bare, but embowered
With—who knows what verdure, o'erfruited, o'erflowered?
Impossible! Only—I saw it!

II

All I can sing is—I feel it!
This life was as blank as that room;
I let you pass in here. Precaution, indeed?
Walls, ceiling and floor,—not a chance for a weed!
Wide opens the entrance: where's cold now, where's gloom?
No May to sow seed here, no June to reveal it,
Behold you enshrined in these blooms of your bringing,
These fruits of your bearing—nay, birds of your winging!
A fairy-tale! Only—I feel it!

1876

MAGICAL NATURE

I

FLOWER—I never fancied, jewel—I profess you!
Bright I see and soft I feel the outside of a flower.
Save but glow inside and—jewel, I should guess you,
Dim to sight and rough to touch: the glory is the dower.

II

You, forsooth, a flower? Nay, my love, a jewel—
Jewel at no mercy of a moment in your prime!
Time may fray the flower-face: kind be time or cruel,
Jewel, from each facet, flash your laugh at time!

1876

[1] An Indian dancing girl. In this poem Browning ascribes to her the magical powers supposed to be possessed by some Hindu magicians.

SUCH A STARVED BANK OF MOSS

(Prologue to *The Two Poets of Croisic*)

I

SUCH a starved bank of moss
Till that May-morn,
Blue ran the flash across:
Violets were born!

II

Sky—what a scowl of cloud
Till, near and far,
Ray on ray split the shroud
Splendid, a star!

III

World—how it walled about
Life with disgrace
Till God's own smile came out:
That was thy face!

1878

NED BRATTS [1]

'TWAS Bedford Special Assize, one daft Midsummer's Day:
A broiling blasting June,—was never its like, men say.

[1] The poem was suggested to Browning by a passage in Bunyan's *Life and Death of Mr. Badman* in which old Tod, "all on a dung sweat, as if he had run for his life," burst in upon a startled court and confessed his crimes. The characters of Ned Bratts and his wife Tab are purely Browning's creation.

This poem, less well known than some of Brown-

Corn stood sheaf-ripe already, and trees looked yellow as that;
Ponds drained dust-dry, the cattle lay foaming around each flat.
Inside town, dogs went mad, and folk kept bibbing beer
While the parsons prayed for rain. 'Twas horrible, yes—but queer:
Queer—for the sun laughed gay, yet nobody moved a hand
To work one stroke at his trade: as given to understand
That all was come to a stop, work and such worldly ways,
And the world's old self about to end in a merry blaze.
Midsummer's Day moreover was the first of Bedford Fair,
With Bedford Town's tag-rag and bobtail a-bowsing there.

But the Court House, Quality crammed: through doors ope, windows wide,
High on the Bench you saw sit Lordships side by side.
There frowned Chief Justice Jukes, fumed learned Brother Small,
And fretted their fellow Judge: like threshers, one and all,
Of a reek with laying down the law in a furnace. Why?
Because their lungs breathed flame—the regular crowd forbye—
From gentry pouring in—quite a nosegay, to be sure!
How else could they pass the time, six mortal hours endure
Till night should extinguish day, when matters might haply mend?
Meanwhile no bad resource was—watching begin and end
Some trial for life and death, in a brisk five minutes' space,
And betting which knave would 'scape, which hang, from his sort of face.

So, their Lordships toiled and moiled, and a deal of work was done
(I warrant) to justify the mirth of the crazy sun
As this and t'other lout, struck dumb at the sudden show
Of red robes and white wigs, boggled nor answered "Boh!"
When asked why he, Tom Styles, should not—because Jack Nokes
Had stolen the horse—be hanged: for Judges must have their jokes,
And louts must make allowance—let's say, for some blue fly
Which punctured a dewy scalp where the frizzles [1] stuck awry—
Else Tom had fleered scot-free, so nearly over and done
Was the main of the job. Full-measure, the gentles enjoyed their fun,
As a twenty-five were tried, rank puritans caught at prayer
In a cow-house and laid by the heels,[2]—have at 'em, devil may care!—
And ten were prescribed the whip, and ten a brand on the cheek,
And five a slit of the nose—just leaving enough to tweak.

Well, things at jolly high-tide, amusement steeped in fire,
While noon smote fierce the roof's red tiles to heart's desire,

---

ing's Italian poems, is especially interesting as a further illustration of his genius in interpreting types and atmospheres. Compare Bratts, for example, with the Renaissance rascal, Fra Lippo Lippi, both in the nature of their rascality and of their redeeming qualities. Fra Lippo is justified in the end by art, Bratts by a stubborn and realistic moral sense — realistic in that he realizes perfectly he will have a relapse unless he gets himself hanged immediately. In the face of such disarming self-honesty it is difficult to condemn Bratts for his sins as severely as he should perhaps be condemned, just as it is difficult to condemn Fra Lippo. The absolute conviction that poems of this sort carry to the reader that Browning *has* penetrated to what is going on in the brain of characters of many periods is the final testimony to his genius in interpreting humanity.

[1] Wigs, carefully curled and powdered, were worn in England by all gentlemen at the time of the action of this poem. The custom of wearing wigs is now preserved only in the law courts and the presence of a presiding judge in wig and gown lends a curious and solemn dignity to legal procedure.

[2] Meetings for worship outside of the established church were forbidden by law.

The Court a-simmer with smoke, one ferment of oozy flesh,
One spirituous humming musk mount-mounting until its mesh
Entoiled all heads in a fluster, and Serjeant Postlethwayte
—Dashing the wig oblique as he mopped his oily pate—
Cried "Silence, or I grow grease! No loophole lets in air?
Jurymen,—Guilty, Death! Gainsay me if you dare!"
—Things at this pitch, I say,—what hubbub without the doors?
What laughs, shrieks, hoots and yells, what rudest of uproars?

Bounce through the barrier throng a bulk comes rolling vast!
Thumps, kicks,—no manner of use!—spite of them rolls at last
Into the midst a ball which, bursting, brings to view
Publican Black Ned Bratts and Tabby his big wife too:
Both in a muck-sweat, both . . . were never such eyes uplift
At the sight of yawning hell, such nostrils—snouts that sniffed
Sulphur, such mouths a-gape ready to swallow flame!
Horrified, hideous, frank fiend-faces! yet, all the same,
Mixed with a certain . . . eh? how shall I dare style—mirth
The desperate grin of the guess that, could they break from earth,
Heaven was above, and hell might rage in impotence
Below the saved, the saved!

"Confound you! (no offence!)
Out of our way,—push, wife! Yonder their Worships be!"
Ned Bratts has reached the bar, and "Hey, my Lords," roars he,
"A Jury of life and death, Judges the prime of the land,
Constables, javelineers,—all met, if I understand,
To decide so knotty a point as whether 'twas Jack or Joan
Robbed the henroost, pinched the pig, hit the King's Arms with a stone,
Dropped the baby down the well, left the tithesman in the lurch,
Or, three whole Sundays running, not once attended church!
What a pother—do these deserve the parish-stocks or whip,
More or less brow to brand, much or little nose to snip,—
When, in our Public, plain stand we—that's we stand here,
I and my Tab, brass-bold, brick-built of beef and beer,
—Do not we, slut? Step forth and show your beauty, jade!
Wife of my bosom—that's the word now! What a trade
We drove! None said us nay: nobody loved his life
So little as wag a tongue against us,—did they, wife?
Yet they knew us all the while, in their hearts, for what we are
—Worst couple, rogue and quean, unhanged—search near and far!
Eh, Tab? The pedlar, now—o'er his noggin—who warned a mate
To cut and run, nor risk his pack where its loss of weight
Was the least to dread,—aha, how we two laughed a-good
As, stealing round the midden, he came on where I stood
With billet poised and raised,—you, ready with the rope,—
Ah, but that's past, that's sin repented of we hope!
Men knew us for that same, yet safe and sound stood we!
The lily-livered knaves knew too (I've baulked a d——)
Our keeping the 'Pied Bull' was just a mere pretence:
Too slow the pounds make food, drink, lodging, from out the pence!
There's not a stoppage to travel has chanced, this ten long year,

No break into hall or grange, no lifting of nag or steer,
Not a single roguery, from the clipping of a purse
To the cutting of a throat, but paid us toll. Od's curse!
When Gipsy Smouch made bold to cheat us of our due,
—Eh, Tab? the Squire's strong-box we helped the rascal to—
I think he pulled a face, next Sessions' swinging-time!
He danced the jig that needs no floor,—and, here's the prime,
'Twas Scroggs that houghed the mare! Ay, those were busy days!

"Well, there we flourished brave, like scripture-trees called bays,
Faring high, drinking hard, in money up to head
—Not to say, boots and shoes, when . . . Zounds, I nearly said—
Lord, to unlearn one's language! How shall we labour, wife?
Have you, fast hold, the Book?[1] Grasp, grip it, for your life!
See, sirs, here's life, salvation! Here's—hold but out my breath—
When did I speak so long without once swearing? 'Sdeath,
No, nor unhelped by ale since man and boy! And yet
All yesterday I had to keep my whistle wet
While reading Tab this Book: book? don't say 'book'—they're plays,
Songs, ballads and the like: here's no such strawy blaze,
But sky wide ope, sun, moon, and seven stars out full-flare!
Tab, help and tell! I'm hoarse. A mug! or—no, a prayer!
Dip for one out of the Book! Who wrote it in the Jail
—He plied his pen unhelped by beer, sirs, I'll be bail!

"I've got my second wind. In trundles she—that's Tab.
'Why, Gammer, what's come now, that—bobbing like a crab

[1] Bunyan's *Pilgrim's Progress.*

On Yule-tide bowl—your head's a-work and both your eyes
Break loose? Afeard, you fool? As if the dead can rise!
Say—Bagman Dick was found last May with fuddling-cap
Stuffed in his mouth: to choke's a natural mishap!'
'Gaffer, be—blessed,' cries she, 'and Bagman Dick as well!
I, you, and he are damned: this Public is our hell:
We live in fire: live coals don't feel!—Once quenched, they learn—
Cinders do, to what dust they moulder while they burn!'

"'If you don't speak straight out,' says I—belike I swore—
'A knobstick, well you know the taste of, shall, once more,
Teach you to talk, my maid!' She ups with such a face,
Heart sunk inside me. 'Well, pad on, my prate-apace!'

"'I've been about those laces we need for . . . never mind!
If henceforth they tie hands, 'tis mine they'll have to bind.
You know who makes them best—the Tinker in our cage,
Pulled-up for gospelling, twelve years ago: no age
To try another trade,—yet, so he scorned to take
Money he did not earn, he taught himself the make
Of laces, tagged and tough—Dick Bagman found them so![1]
Good customers were we! Well, last week, you must know
His girl,—the blind young chit, who hawks about his wares,—
She takes it in her head to come no more—such airs
These hussies have! Yet, since we need a stoutish lace,—
"I'll to the jail-bird father, abuse her to his face!"

[1] Bunyan in jail supported his family by making laces. His blind daughter Mary sold them.

So, first I filled a jug to give me heart, and then,
Primed to the proper pitch, I posted to their den—
Patmore—they style their prison! I tip the turnkey, catch
My heart up, fix my face, and fearless lift the latch—
Both arms a-kimbo, in bounce with a good round oath
Ready for rapping out: no "Lawks" nor "By my troth!"

"'There sat my man, the father. He looked up: what one feels
When heart that leapt to mouth drops down again to heels!
He raised his hand . . . Hast seen, when drinking out the night,
And in, the day, earth grow another something quite
Under the sun's first stare? I stood a very stone.

"'"Woman!" (a fiery tear he put in every tone),
"How should my child frequent your house where lust is sport,
Violence—trade? Too true! I trust no vague report.
Her angel's hand, which stops the sight of sin, leaves clear
The other gate of sense, lets outrage through the ear.
What has she heard!—which, heard shall never be again.
Better lack food than feast, a Dives in the—wain
Or reign or train—of Charles!" (His language was not ours:
'Tis my belief, God spoke: no tinker has such powers).
"Bread, only bread they bring—my laces: if we broke
Your lump of leavened sin, the loaf's first crumb would choke!"

"'Down on my marrow-bones! Then all at once rose he:
His brown hair burst a-spread, his eyes were suns to see:
Up went his hands: "Through flesh, I reach, I read thy soul!
So may some stricken tree look blasted, bough and bole,
Champed by the fire-tooth, charred without, and yet, thrice-bound
With dreriment about, within may life be found,
A prisoned power to branch and blossom as before,
Could but the gardener cleave the cloister, reach the core,
Loosen the vital sap: yet where shall help be found?
Who says 'How save it?'—nor 'Why cumbers it the ground?'
Woman, that tree art thou! All sloughed about with scurf,
Thy stag-horns fright the sky, thy snake-roots sting the turf!
Drunkenness, wantonness, theft, murder gnash and gnarl
Thine outward, case thy soul with coating like the marle
Satan stamps flat upon each head beneath his hoof!
And how deliver such? The strong men keep aloof,
Lover and friend stand far, the mocking ones pass by,
Tophet gapes wide for prey: lost soul, despair and die!
What then? 'Look unto me and be ye saved!' saith God:
'I strike the rock, outstreats [1] the life-stream at my rod!
Be your sins scarlet, wool shall they seem like,—although
As crimson red, yet turn white as the driven snow!'"

"'There, there, there! All I seem to somehow understand
Is—that, if I reached home, 'twas through the guiding hand
Of his blind girl which led and led me through the streets
And out of town and up to door again. What greets
First thing my eye, as limbs recover from their swoon?

[1] Outstreams.

A book—this Book she gave at parting. "Father's boon—
The Book he wrote: it reads as if he spoke himself:
He cannot preach in bonds, so,—take it down from shelf
When you want counsel,—think you hear his very voice!"

"'Wicked dear Husband, first despair and then rejoice!
Dear wicked Husband, waste no tick of moment more,
Be saved like me, bald trunk! There's greenness yet at core,
Sap under slough! Read, read!'

"Let me take breath, my lords!
I'd like to know, are these—hers, mine, or Bunyan's words?
I'm 'wildered—scarce with drink,—nowise with drink alone!
You'll say, with heat: but heat's no stuff to split a stone
Like this black boulder—this flint heart of mine: the Book—
That dealt the crushing blow! Sirs, here's the fist that shook
His beard till Wrestler Jem howled like a just-lugged bear![1]
You had brained me with a feather: at once I grew aware
Christmas[2] was meant for me. A burden at your back,
Good Master Christmas? Nay,—yours was that Joseph's sack,
—Or whose it was,—which held the cup,—compared with mine!
Robbery loads my loins, perjury cracks my chine,
Adultery . . . nay, Tab, you pitched me as I flung!
One word, I'll up with fist . . . No, sweet spouse, hold your tongue!

"I'm hasting to the end. The Book, sirs—take and read!
You have my history in a nutshell,—ay, indeed!
It must off, my burden! See,—slack straps and into pit,
Roll, reach the bottom, rest, rot there—a plague on it!
For a mountain's sure to fall and bury Bedford Town,
'Destruction'—that's the name, and fire shall burn it down!
O 'scape the wrath in time! Time's now, if not too late.
How can I pilgrimage up to the wicket-gate?
Next comes Despond the slough: not that I fear to pull
Through mud, and dry my clothes at brave House Beautiful—
But it's late in the day, I reckon: had I left years ago
Town, wife, and children dear . . . Well, Christmas did, you know!—
Soon I had met in the valley and tried my cudgel's strength
On the enemy horned and winged, a-straddle across its length!
Have at his horns, thwick—thwack: they snap, see! Hoof and hoof—
Bang, break the fetlock-bones! For love's sake, keep aloof
Angels! I'm man and match,—this cudgel for my flail,—
To thresh him, hoofs and horns, bat's wing and serpent's tail!
A chance gone by! But then, what else does Hopeful ding
Into the deafest ear except—hope, hope's the thing?
Too late i' the day for me to thrid the windings: but
There's still a way to win the race by death's short cut!
Did Master Faithful need climb the Delightful Mounts?
No, straight to Vanity Fair,—a fair, by all accounts,
Such as is held outside,—lords, ladies, grand and gay,—
Says he in the face of them, just what you hear me say.

[1] A bear just captured and led (lugged) by a rope around its neck.

[2] Bratts is in such an excited hurry that he gets the name wrong. He means "Christian" who fears at the opening of *Pilgrim's Progress* that "this burden that is upon my back will sink me lower than the Grave; and I shall fall into Tophet." Similarly in line 205 he says Joseph for Benjamin. (See Genesis 44:12.)

And the Judges brought him in guilty, and brought him out
To die in the market-place—St. Peter's Green's about
The same thing: there they flogged, flayed, buffeted, lanced with knives,
Pricked him with swords,—I'll swear, he'd full a cat's nine lives,—
So to his end at last came Faithful,—ha, ha, he!
Who holds the highest card? for there stands hid, you see,
Behind the rabble-rout, a chariot, pair and all:
He's in, he's off, he's up, through clouds, at trumpet-call,
Carried the nearest way to Heaven-gate! Odds my life—
Has nobody a sword to spare? not even a knife?
Then hang me, draw and quarter! Tab—do the same by her!
O Master Worldly-Wiseman . . . that's Master Interpreter,
Take the will, not the deed! Our gibbet's handy close:
Forestall Last Judgment-Day! Be kindly, not morose!
There wants no earthly judge-and-jurying: here we stand—
Sentence our guilty selves: so, hang us out of hand!
Make haste for pity's sake! A single moment's loss
Means—Satan's lord once more: his whisper shoots across
All singing in my heart, all praying in my brain,
'It comes of heat and beer!'—hark how he guffaws plain!
'To-morrow you'll wake bright, and, in a safe skin, hug
Your sound selves, Tab and you, over a foaming jug!
You've had such qualms before, time out of mind!' He's right!
Did not we kick and cuff and curse away, that night
When home we blindly reeled, and left poor humpback Joe
I' the lurch to pay for what . . . somebody did, you know!
Both of us maundered then 'Lame humpback,—never more
Will he come limping, drain his tankard at our door!
He'll swing, while—somebody' . . . Says Tab, 'No, for I'll peach!'
'I'm for you, Tab,' cries I, 'there's rope enough for each!'
So blubbered we, and bussed, and went to bed upon
The grace of Tab's good thought: by morning, all was gone!
We laughed—'What's life to him, a cripple of no account?'
Oh, waves increase around—I feel them mount and mount!
Hang us! To-morrow brings Tom Bearward with his bears:
One new black-muzzled brute beats Sackerson,[1] he swears:
(Sackerson, for my money!) And, baiting o'er, the Brawl
They lead on Turner's Patch,—lads, lasses, up tails all,
I'm i' the thick o' the throng! That means the Iron Cage,[2]
—Means the Lost Man inside! Where's hope for such as wage
War against light? Light's left, light's here, I hold light still,
So does Tab—make but haste to hang us both! You will?"

I promise, when he stopped you might have heard a mouse
Squeak, such a death-like hush sealed up the old Mote House.
But when the mass of man sank meek upon his knees,
While Tab, alongside, wheezed a hoarse "Do hang us, please!"
Why, then the waters rose, no eye but ran with tears,
Hearts heaved, heads thumped, until, paying all past arrears

[1] The name of a bear. It was the custom to name the animals, and a successful fighting bear had a following just as a prize-fighter has.

[2] In *Pilgrim's Progress* a backslider is shut up in the iron cage of his lusts.

Of pity and sorrow, at last a regular scream outbroke
Of triumph, joy and praise.

My Lord Chief Justice spoke,
First mopping brow and cheek, where still, for one that budged,
Another bead broke fresh: "What Judge, that ever judged
Since first the world began, judged such a case as this?
Why, Master Bratts, long since, folk smelt you out, I wis!
I had my doubts, i' faith, each time you played the fox
Convicting geese of crime in yonder witness-box—
Yea, much did I misdoubt, the thief that stole her eggs
Was hardly goosey's self at Reynard's game, i' feggs! [1]
Yet thus much was to praise—you spoke to point, direct—
Swore you heard, saw the theft: no jury could suspect—
Dared to suspect,—I'll say,—a spot in white so clear:
Goosey was throttled, true: but thereof godly fear
Came of example set, much as our laws intend;
And, though a fox confessed, you proved the Judge's friend.
What if I had my doubts? Suppose I gave them breath,
Brought you to bar: what work to do, ere 'Guilty, Death,'—
Had paid our pains! What heaps of witnesses to drag
From holes and corners, paid from out the County's bag!
Trial three dog-days long! *Amicus Curiæ* [2]—that's
Your title, no dispute—truth-telling Master Bratts!
Thank you, too, Mistress Tab! Why doubt one word you say?
Hanging you both deserve, hanged both shall be this day!
The tinker [1] needs must be a proper man. I've heard
He lies in Jail long since: if Quality's good word
Warrants me letting loose,—some householder, I mean—
Freeholder, better still,—I don't say but—between
Now and next Sessions . . . Well! Consider of his case,
I promise to, at least: we owe him so much grace.
Not that—no, God forbid!—I lean to think, as you,
The grace that such repent is any jail-bird's due:
I rather see the fruit of twelve years' pious reign—
Astræa Redux, Charles restored his rights again! [2]
—Of which, another time! I somehow feel a peace
Stealing across the world. May deeds like this increase!
So, Master Sheriff, stay that sentence I pronounced
On those two dozen odd: deserving to be trounced
Soundly, and yet . . . well, well, at all events dispatch
This pair of—shall I say, sinner-saints?—ere we catch
Their jail-distemper too. Stop tears, or I'll indite
All weeping Bedfordshire for turning Bunyanite!"

So, forms were galloped through. If Justice, on the spur,
Proved somewhat expeditious, would Quality demur?
And happily hanged were they,—why lengthen out my tale?—
Where Bunyan's Statue stands facing where stood his Jail.

1879

[1] Reynard is the fox; "i' feggs" means in faith, honestly. [2] "Friend of the Court."

[1] Bunyan was a tinker, a wandering mender of pots and pans.

[2] Charles II was restored in 1660. The events of the poem are thus supposed to have occurred in 1672, twelve years after his restoration.

WANTING IS—WHAT?

WANTING is—what?
Summer redundant,
Blueness abundant,
—Where is the blot?
Beamy the world, yet a blank all the same,
—Framework which waits for a picture to frame:
What of the leafage, what of the flower?
Roses embowering with nought they embower!
Come then, complete incompletion, O comer,
Pant through the blueness, perfect the summer!
Breathe but one breath
Rose-beauty above,
And all that was death
Grows life, grows love,
Grows love!

1883

ADAM, LILITH, AND EVE

ONE day it thundered and lightened.
Two women, fairly frightened,
Sank to their knees, transformed, transfixed,
At the feet of the man who sat betwixt;
And "Mercy!" cried each—"if I tell the truth
Of a passage in my youth!"

Said This: "Do you mind the morning
I met your love with scorning?
As the worst of the venom left my lips,
I thought 'If, despite this lie, he strips
The mask from my soul with a kiss—I crawl
His slave,—soul, body and all!' "

Said That: "We stood to be married;
The priest, or someone, tarried;
'If Paradise-door prove locked?' smiled you
I thought, as I nodded, smiling too,
'Did one, that's away, arrive—nor late
Nor soon should unlock Hell's gate!' "

It ceased to lighten and thunder.
Up started both in wonder,
Looked round and saw that the sky was clear,
Then laughed "Confess you believed us, Dear!"
"I saw through the joke!" the man replied
They re-seated themselves beside.

1883

NEVER THE TIME AND THE PLACE

NEVER the time and the place
And the loved one all together!
This path—how soft to pace!
This May—what magic weather!
Where is the loved one's face?
In a dream that loved one's face meets mine,
But the house is narrow, the place is bleak
Where, outside, rain and wind combine
With a furtive ear, if I strive to speak,
With a hostile eye at my flushing cheek,
With a malice that marks each word, each sign!
O enemy sly and serpentine,
Uncoil thee from the waking man!
Do I hold the Past
Thus firm and fast
Yet doubt if the Future hold I can?
This path so soft to pace shall lead
Thro' the magic of May to herself indeed!
Or narrow if needs the house must be,
Outside are the storms and strangers: we—
Oh, close, safe, warm sleep I and she,
—I and she!

1883

PAMBO [1]

SUPPOSE that we part (work done, comes play)
With a grave tale told in crambo [2]
—As our hearty sires were wont to say—
Whereof the hero is Pambo?

Do you happen to know who Pambo was?
Nor I—but this much have heard of him:
He entered one day a college-class,
And asked—was it so absurd of him?—

"May Pambo learn wisdom ere practise it?
In wisdom I fain would ground me:
Since wisdom is centred in Holy Writ,
Some psalm to the purpose expound me!"

[1] "Pambo spends a lifetime devotedly trying to reconcile premeditated acceptability with actual speech. The poet suggests that is his case too. Though he keeps his original aim steadily in view, and ceaselessly matures his art, his expression rouses the same old criticisms, because his qualities are inseparable from his aim."—[Porter and Clarke.]

[2] Crambo is an old game of capping rhymes.

"That psalm," the Professor smiled, "shall be
Untroubled by doubt which dirtieth
Pellucid streams when an ass like thee
Would drink there—the Nine-and-thirtieth.

"Verse first: *I said I will look to my ways*
That I with my tongue offend not.
How now? Why stare? Art struck in amaze?
Stop, stay! The smooth line hath an end knot!

"He's gone!—disgusted my text should prove
Too easy to need explaining?
Had he waited, the blockhead might find I move
To matter that pays remaining!"

Long years went by, when—"Ha, who's this?
Do I come on the restive scholar
I had driven to Wisdom's goal, I wis,
But that he slipped the collar?

"What? Arms crossed, brow bent, thought-immersed?
A student indeed! Why scruple
To own that the lesson proposed him first
Scarce suited so apt a pupil?

"Come back! From the beggarly elements
To a more recondite issue
We pass till we reach, at all events,
Some point that may puzzle . . . Why 'pish' you?"

From the ground looked piteous up the head:
"Daily and nightly, Master,
Your pupil plods thro' that text you read,
Yet gets on never the faster.

"At the self-same stand,—now old, then young!
I will look to my ways—were doing
As easy as saying!—*that I with my tongue*
Offend not—and 'scape pooh-poohing

"From sage and simple, doctor and dunce?
Ah, nowise! Still doubts so muddy
The stream I would drink at once,—but once!
That—thus I resume my study!"

Brother, brother, I share the blame,
Arcades sumus ambo! [1]
Darkling, I keep my sunrise-aim,
Lack not the critic's flambeau,
And *look to my ways*, yet, much the same,
Offend with my tongue—like Pambo!

1883

[1] "Arcadians are we both."

SONGS FROM FERISHTAH'S FANCIES

I. Round Us the Wild Creatures

Round us the wild creatures, overhead the trees,
Underfoot the moss-tracks,—life and love with these!
I to wear a fawn-skin, thou to dress in flowers:
All the long lone Summer-day, that greenwood life of ours!
Rich-pavilioned, rather,—still the world without,—
Inside—gold-roofed silk-walled silence round about!
Queen it thou on purple,—I, at watch and ward
Couched beneath the columns, gaze, thy slave, love's guard!

So, for us no world? Let throngs press thee to me!
Up and down amid men, heart by heart fare we!
Welcome squalid vesture, harsh voice, hateful face!
God is soul, souls I and thou: with souls should souls have place.

II. Man I Am and Man Would Be

Man I am and man would be, Love—merest man and nothing more.
Bid me seem no other! Eagles boast of pinions—let them soar!
I may put forth angel's plumage, once unmanned, but not before.

Now on earth, to stand suffices,—nay, if kneeling serves, to kneel:
Here you front me, here I find the all of heaven that earth can feel:
Sense looks straight,—not over, under,—perfect sees beyond appeal.

FERISHTAH'S FANCIES

BY

ROBERT BROWNING

To Dearest Pen from
Robert Browning.
Nov. 20. '84.

LONDON
SMITH, ELDER, & CO., 15 WATERLOO PLACE
1884

A Presentation Copy from Browning to His Son. (See Appendix I.)

Good you are and wise, full circle: what to
me were more outside?
Wiser wisdom, better goodness? Ah, such
want the angel's wide
Sense to take and hold and keep them! Mine
at least has never tried.

III. Fire Is in the Flint

Fire is in the flint: true, once a spark escapes,
Fire forgets the kinship, soars till fancy shapes
Some befitting cradle where the babe had
birth—
Wholly heaven's the product, unallied to
earth.
Splendours recognised as perfect in the star!—
In our flint their home was, housed as now
they are.

IV. Ask Not One Least Word of Praise

Ask not one least word of praise!
Words declare your eyes are bright?
What then meant that summer day's
Silence spent in one long gaze?
Was my silence wrong or right?

Words of praise were all to seek!
Face of you and form of you,
Did they find the praise so weak
When my lips just touched your cheek—
Touch which let my soul come through?

1884

NOW

Out of your whole life give but a moment!
All of your life that has gone before,
All to come after it,—so you ignore,
So you make perfect the present,—condense,
In a rapture of rage, for perfection's endow-
ment,
Thought and feeling and soul and sense—
Merged in a moment which gives me at last
You around me for once, you beneath me,
above me—
Me—sure that despite of time future, time
past,—
This tick of our life-time's one moment you
love me!
How long such suspension may linger? Ah,
Sweet—
The moment eternal—just that and no more—
When ecstasy's utmost we clutch at the core
While cheeks burn, arms open, eyes shut and
lips meet!

1889

SUMMUM BONUM

All the breath and the bloom of the year in
the bag of one bee:
All the wonder and wealth of the mine in
the heart of one gem:
In the core of one pearl all the shade and the
shine of the sea:
Breath and bloom, shade and shine,—won-
der, wealth, and—how far above them—
Truth, that's brighter than gem,
Trust, that's purer than pearl,—
Brightest truth, purest trust in the universe—
all were for me
In the kiss of one girl.

1889

A PEARL, A GIRL

A simple ring with a single stone
To the vulgar eye no stone of price:
Whisper the right word, that alone—
Forth starts a sprite, like fire from ice,
And lo, you are lord (says an Eastern scroll)
Of heaven and earth, lord whole and sole
Through the power in a pearl.

A woman ('tis I this time that say)
With little the world counts worthy praise
Utter the true word—out and away
Escapes her soul: I am wrapt in blaze,
Creation's lord, of heaven and earth
Lord whole and sole—by a minute's birth—
Through the love in a girl!

1889

MUCKLE-MOUTH [1] MEG

Frowned the Laird on the Lord: "So, red-
handed I catch thee?
Death-doomed by our Law of the Border! [2]

[1] Big-mouthed.

[2] Before James VI of Scotland ascended the throne of England as James I, England and Scotland were separate kingdoms with a long tradition of rivalry and of skirmishing on the Border. Many of the ballads deal with this conflict.

We've a gallows outside and a chiel [1] to dispatch thee:
Who trespasses—hangs: all's in order."

He met frown with smile, did the young English gallant:
Then the Laird's dame: "Nay, Husband, I beg!
He's comely: be merciful! Grace for the callant
—If he marries our Muckle-mouth Meg!"

"No mile-wide-mouthed monster of yours do I marry:
Grant rather the gallows!" laughed he.
"Foul fare kith and kin of you—why do you tarry?"
"To tame your fierce temper!" quoth she.

"Shove him quick in the Hole, shut him fast for a week:
Cold, darkness and hunger work wonders:
Who lion-like roars now, mouse-fashion will squeak,
And 'it rains' soon succeed to 'it thunders.'"

A week did he bide in the cold and the dark
—Not hunger: for duly at morning
In flitted a lass, and a voice like a lark
Chirped "Muckle-mouth Meg still ye're scorning?

"Go hang, but here's parritch to hearten ye first!"
"Did Meg's muckle-mouth boast within some
Such music as yours, mine should match it or burst:
No frog-jaws! So tell folk, my Winsome!"

Soon week came to end, and, from Hole's door set wide,
Out he marched, and there waited the lassie:
"Yon gallows, or Muckle-mouth Meg for a bride!
Consider! Sky's blue and turf's grassy:

"Life's sweet: shall I say ye wed Muckle-mouth Meg?"
"Not I," quoth the stout heart: "too eerie

[1] Young fellow.

The mouth that can swallow a bubblyjock's [1] egg:
Shall I let it munch mine? Never, Dearie!"

"Not Muckle-mouth Meg? Wow, the obstinate man!
Perhaps he would rather wed me!"
"Ay, would he—with just for a dowry your can!"
"I'm Muckle-mouth Meg" chirruped she.

"Then so—so—so—so—" as he kissed her apace—
"Will I widen thee out till thou turnest
From Margaret Minnikin-mou', by God's grace,
To Muckle-mouth Meg in good earnest!"

1889

DEVELOPMENT

My Father was a scholar and knew Greek.
When I was five years old, I asked him once
"What do you read about?"
"The siege of Troy."
"What is a siege and what is Troy?" [2]
Whereat
He piled up chairs and tables for a town,
Set me a-top for Priam, called our cat
—Helen, enticed away from home (he said)
By wicked Paris, who couched somewhere close
Under the footstool, being cowardly,
But whom—since she was worth the pains, poor puss—
Towzer and Tray,—our dogs, the Atreidai,—sought
By taking Troy to get possession of
—Always when great Achilles ceased to sulk,

[1] A turkey.

[2] Paris, the son of Priam King of Troy, had carried off Helen the wife of Menelaus, and to avenge this insult and recover Helen the Greeks besieged Troy. The Atreidai — the sons of Atreus — were Menelaus and Agamemnon, the latter the commander-in-chief of the Greeks. Achilles was the greatest warrior of the Greeks. He, however, sulked in his tent during part of the war, because Agamemnon had deprived him of a beautiful captive girl named Briseis. After Hector, another son of Priam and the greatest of the Trojan warriors, had killed his friend Patroclus, Achilles came out of his retirement, slew Hector, and dragged his body around the walls of Troy. Achilles was in turn killed by Paris.

(My pony in the stable)—forth would prance
And put to flight Hector—our page-boy's self.
This taught me who was who and what was what:
So far I rightly understood the case
At five years old: a huge delight it proved
And still proves—thanks to that instructor sage
My Father, who knew better than turn straight
Learning's full flare on weak-eyed ignorance,
Or, worse yet, leave weak eyes to grow sand-blind,
Content with darkness and vacuity.

It happened, two or three years afterward,
That—I and playmates playing at Troy's Siege—
My Father came upon our make-believe.
"How would you like to read yourself the tale
Properly told, of which I gave you first
Merely such notion as a boy could bear?
Pope,[1] now, would give you the precise account
Of what, some day, by dint of scholarship,
You'll hear—who knows?—from Homer's very mouth.
Learn Greek by all means, read the 'Blind Old Man,
Sweetest of Singers'—*tuphlos* which means 'blind,'
Hedistos which means 'sweetest.' Time enough!
Try, anyhow, to master him some day;
Until when, take what serves for substitute,
Read Pope, by all means!"
So I ran through Pope,
Enjoyed the tale—what history so true?
Also attacked my Primer, duly drudged,
Grew fitter thus for what was promised next—
The very thing itself, the actual words,
When I could turn—say, Buttmann[2] to account.

Time passed, I ripened somewhat: one fine day,
"Quite ready for the Iliad, nothing less?

[1] Alexander Pope completed his translation of the *Iliad* in 1720.

[2] A distinguished German philologist and an authority on Greek grammar.

There's Heine,[1] where the big books block the shelf:
Don't skip a word, thumb well the Lexicon!"

I thumbed well and skipped nowise till I learned
Who was who, what was what, from Homer's tongue,
And there an end of learning. Had you asked
The all-accomplished scholar, twelve years old,
"Who was it wrote the Iliad?"—what a laugh!
"Why, Homer, all the world knows: of his life
Doubtless some facts exist: it's everywhere:
We have not settled, though, his place of birth:
He begged, for certain, and was blind beside:
Seven cities claimed him—Scio, with best right,
Thinks Byron. What he wrote? Those Hymns we have.[2]
Then there's the 'Battle of the Frogs and Mice,'
That's all—unless they dig 'Margites' up
(I'd like that) nothing more remains to know."

Thus did youth spend a comfortable time;
Until—"What's this the Germans say is fact
That Wolf[3] found out first? It's unpleasant work
Their chop and change, unsettling one's belief:
All the same, while we live, we learn, that's sure."
So, I bent brow o'er *Prolegomena.*
And, after Wolf, a dozen of his like

[1] Heine or Heyne was the editor of the standard text of Homer.

[2] The Homeric Hymns — poems to the gods — were not by Homer although they were once attributed to him, as was also, without much certainty, *The Battle of the Frogs and Mice*, a burlesque epic. The *Margites* was a comic poem, no longer ascribed to Homer.

[3] Friedrich August Wolf (1759–1824) advanced the theory in his *Prolegomena ad Homerum* that the *Iliad* and the *Odyssey* were not by a single individual but were composites made up of many shorter pieces which had been handed down by word of mouth for a long period.

Proved there was never any Troy at all,
Neither Besiegers nor Besieged,—nay, worse,
No actual Homer, no authentic text,
No warrant for the fiction I, as fact,
Had treasured in my heart and soul so long—
Ay, mark you! and as fact held still, still hold,
Spite of new knowledge, in my heart of hearts
And soul of souls, fact's essence freed and fixed
From accidental fancy's guardian sheath.
Assuredly thenceforward—thank my stars!—
However it got there, deprive who could—
Wring from the shrine my precious tenantry,
Helen, Ulysses, Hector and his Spouse,
Achilles and his Friend?—though Wolf—ah, Wolf!
Why must he needs come doubting, spoil a dream?

But then "No dream's worth waking"—Browning says:
And here's the reason why I tell thus much
I, now mature man, you anticipate,
May blame my Father justifiably
For letting me dream out my nonage thus,
And only by such slow and sure degrees
Permitting me to sift the grain from chaff,
Get truth and falsehood known and named as such.
Why did he ever let me dream at all,
Not bid me taste the story in its strength?
Suppose my childhood was scarce qualified
To rightly understand mythology,
Silence at least was in his power to keep:
I might have—somehow—correspondingly—
Well, who knows by what method, gained my gains,
Been taught, by forthrights not meanderings,
My aim should be to loathe, like Peleus' son,[1]
A lie as Hell's Gate, love my wedded wife,
Like Hector,[2] and so on with all the rest.
Could not I have excogitated this
Without believing such men really were?
That is—he might have put into my hand

[1] Peleus' son was Achilles who felt that Agamemnon's decision concerning Briseis was a breach of faith.

[2] Hector's devotion to his wife Andromache and his little son is one of the most touching things in the *Iliad*.

The "Ethics"?[1] In translation, if you please,
Exact, no pretty lying that improves,
To suit the modern taste: no more, no less—
The "Ethics": 'tis a treatise I find hard
To read aright now that my hair is grey,
And I can manage the original.
At five years old—how ill had fared its leaves!
Now, growing double o'er the Stagirite,
At least I soil no page with bread and milk,
Nor crumple, dogs-ear and deface—boys' way.

1889

REPHAN[2]

How I lived, ere my human life began
In this world of yours,—like you, made man,—
When my home was the Star of my God Rephan?

Come then around me, close about,
World-weary earth-born ones! Darkest doubt
Or deepest despondency keeps you out?

Nowise! Before a word I speak,
Let my circle embrace your worn, your weak,
Brow-furrowed old age, youth's hollow cheek—

Diseased in the body, sick in soul
Pinched poverty, satiate wealth,—your whole
Array of despairs! Have I read the roll?

All here? Attend, perpend! O Star
Of my God Rephan, what wonders are
In thy brilliance fugitive, faint and far!

Far from me, native to thy realm,
Who shared its perfections which o'erwhelm
Mind to conceive. Let drift the helm,

Let drive the sail, dare unconfined
Embark for the vastitude, O Mind,
Of an absolute bliss! Leave earth behind!

[1] The *Nicomachean Ethics* by Aristotle, who is the Stagirite of line 113 — so-called because he was born in Stagira.

[2] Suggested by a very early recollection of a prose story by the noble woman and imaginative writer, Jane Taylor, of Norwich. (Browning's note. The story referred to is "How It Strikes a Stranger" in the *Contributions of Q. Q.*)

Here, by extremes, at a mean you guess:
There, all's at most—not more, not less:
Nowhere deficiency nor excess.

No want—whatever should be, is now:
No growth—that's change, and change comes—how
To royalty born with crown on brow?

Nothing begins—so needs to end:
Where fell it short at first? Extend
Only the same, no change can mend!

I use your language: mine—no word
Of its wealth would help who spoke, who heard,
To a gleam of intelligence. None preferred,

None felt distaste when better and worse
Were uncontrastable: bless or curse
What—in that uniform universe?

Can your world's phrase, your sense of things
Forth-figure the Star of my God? No springs,
No winters throughout its space. Time brings

No hope, no fear: as to-day, shall be
To-morrow: advance or retreat need we
At our stand-still through eternity?

All happy: needs must we so have been,
Since who could be otherwise? All serene:
What dark was to banish, what light to screen?

Earth's rose is a bud that's checked or grows
As beams may encourage or blasts oppose:
Our lives leapt forth, each a full-orbed rose—

Each rose sole rose in a sphere that spread
Above and below and around—rose-red:
No fellowship, each for itself instead.

One better than I—would prove I lacked
Somewhat: one worse were a jarring fact
Disturbing my faultlessly exact.

How did it come to pass there lurked
Somehow a seed of change that worked
Obscure in my heart till perfection irked?—

Till out of its peace at length grew strife—
Hopes, fears, loves, hates,—obscurely rife,—
My life grown a-tremble to turn your life?

Was it Thou, above all lights that are,
Prime Potency, did Thy hand unbar
The prison-gate of Rephan my Star?

In me did such potency wake a pulse
Could trouble tranquillity that lulls
Not lashes inertion till throes convulse

Soul's quietude into discontent?
As when the completed rose bursts, rent
By ardours till forth from its orb are sent

New petals that mar—unmake the disc—
Spoil rondure: what in it ran brave risk,
Changed apathy's calm to strife, bright, brisk,

Pushed simple to compound, sprang and spread
Till, fresh-formed, faceted, floreted,
The flower that slept woke a star instead?

No mimic of Star Rephan! How long
I stagnated there where weak and strong,
The wise and the foolish, right and wrong,

Are merged alike in a neutral Best,
Can I tell? No more than at whose behest
The passion arose in my passive breast,

And I yearned for no sameness but difference
In thing and thing, that should shock my sense
With a want of worth in them all, and thence

Startle me up, by an Infinite
Discovered above and below me—height
And depth alike to attract my flight,

Repel my descent: by hate taught love.
Oh, gain were indeed to see above
Supremacy ever—to move, remove,

Not reach—aspire yet never attain
To the object aimed at! Scarce in vain,—
As each stage I left nor touched again.

To suffer, did pangs bring the loved one bliss,
Wring knowledge from ignorance,—just for this—
To add one drop to a love-abyss!

Enough: for you doubt, you hope, O men,
You fear, you agonise, die: what then?
Is an end to your life's work out of ken?

Have you no assurance that, earth at end,
Wrong will prove right? Who made shall mend
In the higher sphere to which yearnings tend?

Why should I speak? You divine the test.
When the trouble grew in my pregnant breast
A voice said "So wouldst thou strive, not rest?

"Burn and not smoulder, win by worth,
Not rest content with a wealth that's dearth?
Thou art past Rephan, thy place be Earth!"

1889

EPILOGUE

At the midnight in the silence of the sleep-time,
When you set your fancies free,
Will they pass to where—by death, fools think, imprisoned—
Low he lies who once so loved you, whom you loved so,
—Pity me?

Oh to love so, be so loved, yet so mistaken!
What had I on earth to do
With the slothful, with the mawkish, the unmanly?
Like the aimless, helpless, hopeless, did I drivel
—Being—who?

One who never turned his back but marched breast forward,
Never doubted clouds would break,
Never dreamed, though right were worsted, wrong would triumph,
Held we fall to rise, are baffled to fight better,
Sleep to wake.

No, at noonday in the bustle of man's work-time
Greet the unseen with a cheer!
Bid him forward, breast and back as either should be,
"Strive and thrive!" cry "Speed,—fight on, fare ever
There as here!"

1889

From THE RING AND THE BOOK

Introduction

The Ring and the Book is founded upon a sensational murder case which occurred in Rome in 1698. During one of his strolls through Florence in 1860, Browning discovered on an open bookstall an old vellum-bound volume —a collection of legal documents dealing with the case. Browning's imagination pierced through the legal dryness to the drama and terror which lay behind, and he at once saw the possibilities of the story. At first, however, he put aside the thought of using it himself and offered the story to at least two friends for use in prose. These, fortunately, refused it. The theme remained in his mind and, after gathering such additional information as he could, Browning set to work on it, probably in the autumn of 1864. The first of the four volumes in which it was published appeared in November 1868, and the other three appeared in successive months.

It was not, however, Browning's purpose to tell a murder story, charged with drama though it might be. The poem is a study in the unreliability of fact as a measure of human impulses and values. A certain set of facts existed and everybody knew them. What these facts meant when translated into human terms was the problem. Browning gives the interpretation of three citizens of Rome, of different social and mental qualities, talking about the case on the excited day when it was "news," he gives us the testimony on the witness stand of the man who had tried to save the woman and of the man who had killed her, and he gives the woman's deathbed statement. The case is shown through the eyes of the prosecuting attorney, the defense attorney, and the Pope who reviewed it on an appeal for clemency. And in one of the later books the murderer speaks in the death cell.

Obviously the bare facts are secondary to the greater theme of human motive and character as revealed in conduct, but how interpret the facts? Three people were dead—brutally murdered—and a nobleman was on trial fighting desperately for his life. Rome was full of clamor. There had been accusations and counter-accusations, and back of the murder was a long story in which greed and hate had played their ugly parts. The facts, at least, are definite.

Pompilia, aged thirteen, was married by her mother to Count Guido Franceschini, a broken-down nobleman over forty years of age and physically ugly. The ceremony was performed secretly and hastily. What reasons were behind this abrupt performance?

One commentator thinks the girl's father, a well-to-do, jovial citizen, had reached his dotage and that his estate was dwindling:

This came when he was past the working-time,
Had learned to dandle and forgot to dig,
And who must but Violante cast about,
Contrive and task that head of hers again?
She who had caught one fish, could make that catch
A bigger still, in angler's policy:
So, with an angler's mercy for the bait,
Her minnow was set wriggling on its barb
And tossed to mid-stream; which means, this grown girl
With the great eyes and bounty of black hair
And first crisp youth that tempts a jaded taste,
Was whisked i' the way of a certain man, who snapped.

Count Guido Franceschini the Aretine
Was head of an old noble house enough,
Not over-rich, you can't have everything,
But such a man as riches rub against,
Readily stick to,—one with a right to them
Born in the blood: 'twas in his very brow
Always to knit itself against the world,
Beforehand so, when that world stinted due
Service and suit: the world ducks and defers.

* * *

What constituted him so choice a catch,
You question? Past his prime and poor beside!
Ask that of any she who knows the trade.
Why first, here was a nobleman with friends,
A palace one might run to and be safe
When presently the threatened fate should fall,
A big-browed master to block door-way up,
Parley with people bent on pushing by
And praying the mild Pietro quick clear scores:
Is birth a privilege and power or no?
Also,—but judge of the result desired,
By the price paid and manner of the sale.
The Count was made woo, win and wed at once:
Asked, and was haled for answer, lest the heat
Should cool, to San Lorenzo, one blind eve,
And had Pompilia put into his arms
O' the sly there, by a hasty candle-blink,
With sanction of some priest-confederate
Properly paid to make short work and sure.

(II, 257–288, 344–362)

A less friendly view of Guido sees him as a failure in his life at Rome who might as well take a pretty wife—and her dowry—back to his home in Arezzo, if he could get one. Accordingly his silky-tongued brother was set to work to turn the head of the innocent but susceptible housewife who wished to see her daughter grandly married. The more neutral view divides the blame equally:

Now, here take breath and ask,—which bird o' the brace
Decoyed the other into clapnet? Who
Was fool, who knave? Neither and both, perchance.
There was a bargain mentally proposed
On each side, straight and plain and fair enough;
Mind knew its own mind: but when mind must speak,
The bargain have expression in plain terms,
There came the blunder incident to words,
And in the clumsy process, fair turned foul.
The straight backbone-thought of the crooked speech
Were just—"I Guido truck my name and rank
For so much money and youth and female charms.—
We Pietro and Violante give our child
And wealth to you for a rise i' the world thereby."
Such naked truth while chambered in the brain
Shocks nowise; walk it forth by way of tongue,—
Out on the cynical unseemliness!
Hence was the need, on either side, of a lie
To serve as decent wrappage: so, Guido gives
Money for money,—and they, bride for groom,
Having, he, not a doit, they, not a child
Honestly theirs, but this poor waif and stray.
According to the words, each cheated each;
But in the inexpressive barter of thoughts,
Each did give and did take the thing designed,
The rank on this side and the cash on that—
Attained the object of the traffic, so.
The way of the world, the daily bargain struck
In the first market!

(IV, 505–533)

Whatever the truth of the matter, a second set of perfectly clear facts follows. Pietro and Violante (the father and mother) went with Pompilia and Guido to live with him and *his* mother in his castle at Arezzo. After a few months Pietro and Violante went back to Rome, leaving Pompilia with Guido, and making an uproar about having been mistreated and cheated. What happened in Guido's palace?

One account says:

They went to Arezzo,—Pietro and his spouse,
With just the dusk o' the day of life to spend,
Eager to use the twilight, taste a treat,
Enjoy for once with neither stay nor stint
The luxury of lord-and-lady-ship,
And realise the stuff and nonsense long
A-simmer in their noddles; vent the fume
Born there and bred, the citizen's conceit
How fares nobility while crossing earth.

(II, 429–437)

In other words, two silly fools who wished to simper and strut, went into a household where the count and his mother in honorable poverty were trying to put up a brave front to the world, and—not finding the gaudiness they expected—first raised a clamor in the house and then went squawking off to Rome. A more sinister interpretation, however, could be put on the events in Guido's palace. One group in Rome felt that the girl's father had acted in an open-handedly generous, although rather unwary fashion. Having had nothing to do with making the hasty marriage, he made the best of it when he learned of it—did, indeed, far more than could have been fairly expected. He put his fortune at his noble son-in-law's disposal. It was an honest alliance to which he contributed all that he could, and with his wife he went to spend his declining years in the new household.

But they touched bottom at Arezzo: there—
Four months' experience of how craft and greed
Quickened by penury and pretentious hate
Of plain truth, brutify and bestialise,—
Four months' taste of apportioned insolence,
Cruelty graduated, dose by dose
Of ruffianism dealt out at bed and board,
And lo, the work was done, success clapped hands.
The starved, stripped, beaten brace of stupid dupes
Broke at last in their desperation loose,
Fled away for their lives, and lucky so;
Found their account in casting coat afar
And bearing off a shred of skin at least:
Left Guido lord o' the prey, as the lion is,
And, careless what came after, carried their wrongs
To Rome,—I nothing doubt, with such remorse
As folly feels, since pain can make it wise.

(III, 521–539)

Put simply, Guido, having his clutches on the money, got rid of the old couple as rapidly as possible.

The action of the story now developed simultaneously in Rome and Arezzo. And a new set of facts became common knowledge. Violante, the mother, announced that Pompilia, the girl, was not her child at all. Incapable of having children herself and wishing to provide her husband with an heir, she had bought a baby from a common prostitute and ingeniously foisted it off on her pleased husband.

The foster parents expected that Guido's reaction to this would be to turn the girl out of doors and thus they would recover the child. Furthermore it was expected that the legal effect of this statement, if proved, would be to pry loose from Guido the girl's dowry, and the parents entered suit accordingly. If the girl was not Pietro's child, then neither she nor her husband had any legal claim on any part of Pietro's fortune. The court *did* hold the girl to be illegitimate but left Guido in possession of the dowry, as he had been the deceived party. There was an explosion of lawsuits and counter-suits.

. . . The court, its customary way,
Inclined to the middle course the sage affect.
They held the child to be a changeling,—good:
But, lest the husband got no good thereby,
They willed the dowry, though not hers at all,
Should yet be his, if not by right then grace—
Part-payment for the plain injustice done.
As for that other contract, Pietro's work,
Renunciation of his own estate,
That must be cancelled—give him back his gifts,
He was no party to the cheat at least!
So ran the judgment:—whence a prompt appeal
On both sides, seeing right is absolute.
Cried Pietro, "Is the child no child of mine?
Why give her a child's dowry?"—"Have I right
To the dowry, why not to the rest as well?"
Cried Guido, or cried Paolo in his name:
Till law said "Reinvestigate the case!"
And so the matter pends, to this same day.

(III, 670–688)

The facts of the story thus far are sordid enough. Certainly by any objective measurement Count Guido, whatever his own faults, had no reason to be pleased with his mother-in-law. She had been very public about matters usually kept quiet. As she was announcing the story to Roman gossip, the girl he had married had been bought as a baby from a public prostitute. If Guido did not deny the story, he practically admitted the story to be true. If he fought, he was in the unhappy position before the public of fighting, not for his wife's honor, but for her money alone. Much of his later venom was easily explainable—to the public—on such ground. The one passive and pitiable figure in the story is the young wife. After her parents fled to Rome, what did she do?

What side did our Pompilia first espouse?
Her first deliberate measure was—she wrote,
Pricked by some loyal impulse, straight to Rome
And her husband's brother the Abate there,
Who, having managed to effect the match,
Might take men's censure for its ill success.
She made a clean breast also in her turn,
And qualified the couple properly,
Since whose departure, hell, she said, was heaven,
And the house, late distracted by their peals,
Quiet as Carmel where the lilies live.
Herself had oftentimes complained: but why?
All her complaints had been their prompting, tales
Trumped up, devices to this very end.
Their game had been to thwart her husband's love
And cross his will, malign his words and ways,
To reach this issue, furnish this pretence
For impudent withdrawal from their bond,—
Theft, indeed murder, since they meant no less
Whose last injunction to her simple self
Had been—what parents'-precept do you think?
That she should follow after with all speed.
Fly from her husband's house clandestinely,
Join them at Rome again, but first of all
Pick up a fresh companion in her flight,
So putting youth and beauty to fit use,—
Some gay dare-devil cloak-and-rapier spark
Capable of adventure,—helped by whom
She, some fine eve when lutes were in the air,
Having put poison in the posset-cup,
Laid hands on money, jewels and the like,
And, to conceal the thing with more effect,
By way of parting benediction too,
Fired the house,—one would finish famously
I' the tumult, slip out, scurry off and away
And turn up merrily at home once more.
Fact this, and not a dream o' the devil, Sir!
And more than this, a fact none dare dispute,
Word for word, such a letter did she write,
And such the Abate read, nor simply read
But gave all Rome to ruminate upon,
In answer to such charges as, I say,
The couple sought to be beforehand with.

(II, 683–725)

That letter in itself would seem to be decisive—if it could be believed. The difficulty in believing it comes from the fact that Pompilia at this time could not write—or so she said—and that she had been given the penciled letter to trace over in ink and sign, not knowing what it said.

While the lawsuits were being fought in Rome, the unfortunate Pompilia was left alone with her husband in Arezzo. If the case were as Pompilia told it, shut up in the black household with a cruel husband and evilly pursued by his younger brother, her situation was desperate. In great distress she appealed to the governor and three times to the Archbishop for help, and both civil and church authorities returned her to her husband. These events were public knowledge. The explanations were varied. Pompilia does not fare well in one interpretation:

Leave it thus, and now revert
To the old Arezzo whence we moved to Rome.
We've had enough o' the parents, false or true,
Now for a touch o' the daughter's quality.
The start's fair henceforth, every obstacle
Out of the young wife's footpath, she's alone,
Left to walk warily now: how does she walk?
Why, once a dwelling's threshold marked and crossed
In rubric by the enemy on his rounds
As eligible, as fit place of prey,
Baffle him henceforth, keep him out who can!
Stop up the door at the first hint of hoof,
Presently at the window taps a horn,
And Satan's by your fireside, never fear!
Pompilia, left alone now, found herself;
Found herself young too, sprightly, fair enough,
Matched with a husband old beyond his age
(Though that was something like four times her own)
Because of cares past, present and to come:
Found too the house dull and its inmates dead,
So, looked outside for light and life.
And love
Did in a trice turn up with life and light.—

(II, 759–781)

Guido, however, according to his enemies, was a cunning devil and his wife's frantic appeals were the result of his doing. That the authorities repulsed her was due to the fact that they were Guido's friends in a city where she was alone. The appeals were her despairing efforts to avoid the desperate step she finally took.

Law may meet law,—but all the gibes and jeers,
The superfluity of naughtiness,
Those libels on his House,—how reach at them?
Two hateful faces, grinning all a-glow,
Not only make parade of spoil they filched,
But foul him from the height of a tower, you see.
Unluckily temptation is at hand—
To take revenge on a trifle overlooked,
A pet lamb they have left in reach outside,
Whose first bleat, when he plucks the wool away,
Will strike the grinners grave: his wife remains
Who, four months earlier, some thirteen years old,
Never a mile away from mother's house
And petted to the height of her desire,
Was told one morning that her fate had come,
She must be married—just as, a month before,
Her mother told her she must comb her hair
And twist her curls into one knot behind.
These fools forgot their pet lamb, fed with flowers,
Then 'ticed as usual by the bit of cake
Out of the bower into the butchery.
Plague her, he plagues them threefold: but how plague?
The world may have its word to say to that:
You can't do some things with impunity.
What remains . . . well, it is an ugly thought . . .
But that he drive herself to plague herself—
Herself disgrace herself and so disgrace
Who seek to disgrace Guido?

* * *

Under the best stars Hymen brings above,
Had all been honesty on either side,
A common sincere effort to good end,
Still, this would prove a difficult problem, Prince!
—Given, a fair wife, aged thirteen years,
A husband poor, care-bitten, sorrow-sunk,
Little, long-nosed, bush-bearded, lantern-jawed,
Forty-six years old,—place the two grown one,
She, cut off sheer from every natural aid,
In a strange town with no familiar face—
He, in his own parade-ground or retreat
If need were, free from challenge, much less check
To an irritated, disappointed will—
How evolve happiness from such a match?
'Twere hard to serve up a congenial dish
Out of these ill-agreeing morsels, Duke,
By the best exercise of the cook's craft,
Best interspersion of spice, salt and sweet!
But let two ghastly scullions concoct mess
With brimstone, pitch, vitriol and devil's-dung—
Throw in abuse o' the man, his body and soul,
Kith, kin and generation, shake all slab
At Rome, Arezzo, for the world to nose,
Then end by publishing, for fiend's arch-prank,
That, over and above sauce to the meat's self,
Why, even the meat, bedevilled thus in dish,
Was never a pheasant but a carrion-crow—
Prince, what will then the natural loathing be?
What wonder if this?—the compound plague o' the pair
Pricked Guido,—not to take the course they hoped,
That is, submit him to their statement's truth,
Accept its obvious promise of relief,
And thrust them out of doors the girl again
Since the girl's dowry would not enter there,
—Quit of the one if baulked of the other: no!
Rather did rage and hate so work on him,
Their product proved the horrible conceit
That he should plot and plan and bring to pass
His wife might, of her own free will and deed,
Relieve him of her presence, get her gone,
And yet leave all the dowry safe behind,
Confirmed his own henceforward past dispute,
While blotting out, as by a belch of hell,
Their triumph in her misery and death.[1]

(IV, 657–684, 712–755)

Guido himself at his trial cited the action of the Arezzo authorities as proof that he had not mistreated his wife. Stern he might have been with a troublesome young wife in an admittedly difficult domestic situation, but sternness and diabolic cruelty are two different matters.

Well, let me have the benefit, just so far,
O' the fact announced,—my wife then is my wife,
I have allowance for a husband's right.
I am charged with passing right's due bound,—such acts
As I thought just, my wife called cruelty,
Complained of in due form,—convoked no court
Of common gossipry, but took her wrongs—
And not once, but so long as patience served—
To the town's top, jurisdiction's pride of place,
To the Archbishop and the Governor.
These heard her charge with my reply, and found
That futile, this sufficient: they dismissed
The hysteric querulous rebel, and confirmed
Authority in its wholesome exercise,
They, with directest access to the facts.

(V, 1816–1830)

Another brief defense could be made for Guido:

Accordingly one word on the other side
Tips over the piled-up fabric of a tale.
Guido says—that is, always, his friends say—
It is unlikely, from the wickedness,
That any man treat any woman so.

(IV, 903–907)

[1] It should be noted that there is a considerable gap in time (sometimes overlooked) between the dramatic outbreak of the quarrel at Arezzo and Pompilia's final flight from there, so that Pompilia's torture, if this account be true, was a long one of over three years. She was approaching her fourteenth birthday when her parents left her alone with Guido, and her seventeenth when she fled.

To such unlikelihood could be added the common-sense question of—even if Guido had such plans in his head—where he was to find the man in the case. Elopements are active rather than passive affairs, involving two people, and when they occur the world is likely to suspect they were engineered by the principals involved, rather than the husband.

About this time, however, the handsome and worldly young Canon Caponsacchi (who may or may not have thrown confetti at Pompilia one night at the theatre—certainly some one threw it) began to receive rather extreme love letters, and Guido claimed that he began to write similar letters—and send them to Pompilia through the maid. Both denied the correspondence.

An elopement there was, however, and the event provides the next set of indisputable and openly known facts. Pompilia, now not quite seventeen years old, fled from Arezzo with Caponsacchi. They drove without a break the remainder of that night, the next day, the next night, and the next day and stopped at sunset at Castelnuovo, near Rome, Pompilia being too exhausted to go farther. Early the following morning, Guido, accompanied by the police, came to the inn to find Caponsacchi in the courtyard, fully dressed, but as a courtier rather than a priest, and with a sword at his side. Caponsacchi was overpowered. Pompilia was found asleep in a bedroom upstairs, but when the police rushed in she leapt up, snatched her husband's sword from his hand and tried to kill him. About these facts there was no dispute.

About the circumstances preceding and surrounding the elopement there is conflicting evidence, although neither Browning nor the reader is in much doubt of the truth of the matter. Did Pompilia send Caponsacchi love letters and receive them over a period of time or did she not? At their trial Guido produced a packet of letters he claimed to have found in the bedroom at Castelnuovo and which both denied having written. Had Caponsacchi and Pompilia met often in secret, or not? Did she drug her husband and the servants before fleeing from the Arezzo palace, or did she not? Such are some of the questions on which the evidence conflicts.

There was an odd matter of the timing of Guido's pursuit which attracted attention in some minds. Catching an errant wife on the road is one thing and catching her at an inn is quite another. Says a friend of Guido's of the flight:

So it went on and on till—who was right?
One merry April morning, Guido woke
After the cuckoo, so late, near noonday,
With an inordinate yawning of the jaws,
Ears plugged, eyes gummed together, palate, tongue
And teeth one mud-paste made of poppy-milk;
And found his wife flown, his scritoire the worse
For a rummage,—jewelry that was, was not,
Some money there had made itself wings too,—
The door lay wide and yet the servants slept
Sound as the dead, or dosed which does as well.
In short, Pompilia, she who, candid soul,
Had not so much as spoken all her life
To the Canon, nay, so much as peeped at him
Between her fingers while she prayed in church,—
This lamb-like innocent of fifteen years [1]
(Such she was grown to by this time of day)
Had simply put an opiate in the drink
Of the whole household overnight, and then
Got up and gone about her work secure,
Laid hand on this waif and the other stray,
Spoiled the Philistine and marched out of doors.

* * *

Guido heard all, swore the befitting oaths,
Shook off the relics of his poison-drench,
Got horse, was fairly started in pursuit
With never a friend to follow, found the track
Fast enough, 'twas the straight Perugia way,
Trod soon upon their very heels, too late
By a minute only at Camoscia, reached
Chiusi, Foligno, ever the fugitives
Just ahead, just out as he galloped in,
Getting the good news ever fresh and fresh,
Till, lo, at the last stage of all, last post
Before Rome,—as we say, in sight of Rome
And safety (there's impunity at Rome
For priests, you know) at—what's the little place?—
What some call Castelnuovo, some just call
The Osteria, because o' the post-house inn,
There, at the journey's all but end, it seems,
Triumph deceived them and undid them both,
Secure they might foretaste felicity
Nor fear surprisal: so, they were surprised.
There did they halt at early evening, there
Did Guido overtake them: 'twas daybreak;
He came in time enough, not time too much,
Since in the courtyard stood the Canon's self
Urging the drowsy stable-grooms to haste

[1] Not strictly accurate. It is the speaker's intent to make Pompilia out as precociously brazen, and "fifteen" did well enough for his story.

Harness the horses, have the journey end,
The trifling four-hours'-running, so reach Rome.
And the other runaway, the wife? Upstairs,
Still on the couch where she had spent the night,
One couch in one room, and one room for both.
So gained they six hours, so were lost thereby.

(II, 888–909, 952–982)

But says a friend of Pompilia's:

Guido's tale begins—
How he and his whole household, drunk to death
By some enchanted potion, poppied drugs
Plied by the wife, lay powerless in gross sleep
And left the spoilers unimpeded way,
Could not shake off their poison and pursue,
Till noontide, then made shift to get on horse
And did pursue: which means he took his time,
Pressed on no more than lingered after, step
By step, just making sure o' the fugitives,
Till at the nick of time, he saw his chance,
Seized it, came up with and surprised the pair.
How he must needs have gnawn lip and gnashed teeth,
Taking successively at tower and town,
Village and roadside, still the same report
"Yes, such a pair arrived an hour ago,
Sat in the carriage just where now you stand,
While we got horses ready,—turned deaf ear
To all entreaty they would even alight;
Counted the minutes and resumed their course."
Would they indeed escape, arrive at Rome,
Leave no least loop-hole to let murder through,
But foil him of his captured infamy,
Prize of guilt proved and perfect? So it seemed.
Till, oh the happy chance, at last stage, Rome
But two short hours off, Castelnuovo reached,
The guardian angel gave reluctant place,
Satan stepped forward with alacrity,
Pompilia's flesh and blood succumbed, perforce
A halt was, and her husband had his will.
Perdue he couched, counted out hour by hour
Till he should spy in the east a signal-streak—
Night had been, morrow was, triumph would be.
Do you see the plan deliciously complete?
The rush upon the unsuspecting sleep,
The easy execution, the outcry
Over the deed "Take notice all the world!
These two dead bodies, locked still in embrace,—
The man is Caponsacchi and a priest,
The woman is my wife: they fled me late,
Thus have I found and you behold them thus,
And may judge me: do you approve or no?"

Success did seem not so improbable,
But that already Satan's laugh was heard,
His black back turned on Guido—left i' the lurch
Or rather, baulked of suit and service now,
Left to improve on both by one deed more,
Burn up the better at no distant day,
Body and soul one holocaust to hell.
Anyhow, of this natural consequence
Did just the last link of the long chain snap:
For an eruption was o' the priest, alive
And alert, calm, resolute and formidable,
Not the least look of fear in that broad brow—
One not to be disposed of by surprise,
And armed moreover—who had guessed as much?
Yes, there stood he in secular costume
Complete from head to heel, with sword at side,
He seemed to know the trick of perfectly.
There was no prompt suppression of the man
As he said calmly "I have saved your wife
From death; there was no other way but this—"

(III, 1202–1264)

Guido's motive, if one grants the worst of his character, is plain enough—if he could force his wife into just such a step and catch her at it he would have plain sailing in his lawsuits for the possession of her dowry. As to Caponsacchi and Pompilia:

If then, all outlets thus secured save one,
At last she took to the open, stood and stared
With her wan face to see where God might wait—
And there found Caponsacchi wait as well
For the precious something at perdition's edge,
He only was predestinate to save,—
And if they recognized in a critical flash
From the zenith, each the other, her need of him,
His need of . . . say, a woman to perish for,
The regular way o' the world, yet break no vow,
Do no harm save to himself,—if this were thus?
How do you say? It were improbable;
So is the legend of my patron-saint.

Anyhow, whether, as Guido states the case,
Pompilia,—like a starving wretch i' the street
Who stops and rifles the first passenger
In the great right of an excessive wrong,—
Did somehow call this stranger and he came,—
Or whether the strange sudden interview
Blazed as when star and star must needs go close
Till each hurts each and there is loss in heaven—
Whatever way in this strange world it was,—
Pompilia and Caponsacchi met, in fine,
She at her window, he i' the street beneath,
And understood each other at first look.

(III, 1039–1063)

The ecclesiastical court had to deal not with abstractions and beautiful improbabilities but with a handsome priest and a young wife caught in a roadside inn and charged by the husband with adultery. The court rendered a rather surprising decision, but one which showed it had estimated the case much as Browning did nearly two centuries later. It did not disgrace Caponsacchi but it sent him for a period to a small town (Civita)—out of harm's way. And it confined Pompilia in a religious house—also out of harm's way, and Guido's way. The mildness of the decision implied indiscretion rather than guilt, but Guido's partisans were able to ask why, if they were innocent, there had been any punishment at all. The same case, tried in the Tuscan court at Arezzo, where Guido had also filed criminal charges, resulted in a verdict of guilty and a sentence of life imprisonment against Pompilia. She, however, was in Rome outside Tuscan jurisdiction, and did not even appear at the trial.

The final act of the tragedy was not long delayed. After a few months with the convertites, Pompilia, who was expecting a child, was given permission to return to the villa of her foster parents and there, just eight months after the flight from Arezzo, her child was born. Guido came in from Arezzo with four laborers from his estate. They lurked several days in a brother's villa and then went one night to where Pompilia was staying. The foster mother opened the door. The murderers stabbed the foster mother and father to death and, leaving Pompilia for dead, took to flight, only to be captured next morning. Pompilia lived four days and revived sufficiently to make a deathbed statement. The child, which had been concealed near by, escaped.

Guido's defense was *honoris causa*—the right of a husband to kill an adulterous wife. It was somewhat weakened by the fact that the time for a noble flame of wrath, if there was to be one, was when he caught the couple in the inn at Castelnuovo, not some months later. His explanation was that he had respected the Law and for his pains had been beaten, tricked, and covered with every kind of shameful ridicule. Worse, an honorable name had been hopelessly stained. In his despair it was one consolation that it was over, that the name would die out and the ignominy be forgotten. The birth of the child changed all that and drove him mad. He doubted the child's paternity, yet it would carry his name, and he testified that when the news of the child's birth reached him—

Then I rose up like fire, and fire-like roared.
What, all is only beginning not ending now?
The worm which wormed its way from skin through flesh
To the bone and there lay biting, did its best,—
What, it goes on to scrape at the bone's self,
Will wind to inmost marrow and madden me?
There's to be yet my representative,
Another of the name shall keep displayed
The flag with the ordure on it, brandish still
The broken sword has served to stir a jakes?
Who will he be, how will you call the man?
A Franceschini.—

* * *

Or say, by some mad miracle of chance,
Is he indeed my flesh and blood, this babe?
Was it because fate forged a link at last
Betwixt my wife and me, and both alike
Found we had henceforth some one thing to love,
Was it when she could damn my soul indeed
She unlatched door, let all the devils o' the dark
Dance in on me to cover her escape?
Why then, the surplusage of disgrace, the spilth
Over and above the measure of infamy,
Failing to take effect on my coarse flesh
Seasoned with scorn now, saturate with shame,—
Is saved to instil on and corrode the brow,
The baby-softness of my first-born child . . .

(V, 1483–1494, 1506–1519)

Of the actual brutal killing of an aged couple and a sick woman by five armed men he also has his explanation:

Surely,—I pray God that I think aright!—
Had but Pompilia's self, the tender thing
Who once was good and pure, was once my lamb
And lay in my bosom, had the well-known shape
Fronted me in the door-way,—stood there faint
With the recent pang perhaps of giving birth
To what might, though by miracle, seem my child,—
Nay more, I will say, had even the aged fool
Pietro, the dotard, in whom folly and age
Wrought, more than enmity or malevolence,
To practise and conspire against my peace,—
Had either of these but opened, I had paused.
But it was she the hag, she that brought hell
For a dowry with her to her husband's house,
She the mock-mother, she that made the match
And married me to perdition, spring and source
O' the fire inside me that boiled up from heart
To brain and hailed the Fury gave it birth,—
Violante Comparini, she it was,
With the old grin amid the wrinkles yet,
Opened: as if in turning from the Cross,
With trust to keep the sight and save my soul,
I had stumbled, first thing, on the serpent's head
Coiled with a leer at foot of it.
There was the end!
Then was I rapt away by the impulse, one
Immeasurable everlasting wave of a need
To abolish that detested life. 'Twas done:
You know the rest and how the folds o' the thing,
Twisting for help, involved the other two
More or less serpent-like: how I was mad,

Blind, stamped on all, the earth-worms with the asp,
And ended so.

(V, 1634–1670)

In such fashion was a dreadful story told in many ways in its own day. The greatness of Browning's accomplishment in *The Ring and the Book*, one of the very few great poems of sustained dimension of the century, was his recognition that the story could be so told, and his so telling it, and then his placing at the center of his poem three characters unmistakably clear in their powers and their limitations. Time has damaged the convincingness of the Pompilia portrait—a passiveness which the Victorians accepted is not so easily accepted as an ideal today. But time has not so seriously damaged Pompilia [1] as to impair the essential truth of Browning's central trilogy. The three must be allowed to speak, each in his own voice and clearly. . . .

[1] After all, Fra Celestino on January 19, 1698 made an affidavit which convinced as penetrating a person as Browning two centuries later, a "hard-boiled" criminal court in May 1698 decided in favour of Pompilia's executor, and a final decree in September of the same year cleared her reputation decisively.

VI. GIUSEPPE CAPONSACCHI [1]

ANSWER you, Sirs? Do I understand aright?
Have patience! In this sudden smoke from hell,—
So things disguise themselves,—I cannot see
My own hand held thus broad before my face
And know it again. Answer you? Then that means
Tell over twice what I, the first time, told
Six months ago: 'twas here, I do believe,
Fronting you same three in this very room,
I stood and told you: yet now no one laughs,
Who then . . . nay, dear my lords, but laugh you did,
As good as laugh, what in a judge we style
Laughter—no levity, nothing indecorous, lords!
Only,—I think I apprehend the mood:
There was the blameless shrug, permissible smirk,
The pen's pretence at play with the pursed mouth,
The titter stifled in the hollow palm
Which rubbed the eyebrow and caressed the nose,
When I first told my tale: they meant, you know,
"The sly one, all this we are bound believe!
Well, he can say no other than what he says.
We have been young, too,—come, there's greater guilt!
Let him but decently disembroil himself,
Scramble from out the scrape nor move the mud,—
We solid ones may risk a finger-stretch!"
And now you sit as grave, stare as aghast
As if I were a phantom: now 'tis—"Friend,
Collect yourself!"—no laughing matter more—
"Counsel the Court in this extremity,
Tell us again!"—tell that, for telling which,
I got the jocular piece of punishment,
Was sent to lounge a little in the place
Whence now of a sudden here you summon me
To take the intelligence from just—your lips
You, Judge Tommati, who then tittered most,—
That she I helped eight months since to escape
Her husband, was retaken by the same,
Three days ago, if I have seized your sense,—
(I being disallowed to interfere,
Meddle or make in a matter none of mine,
For you and law were guardians quite enough
O' the innocent, without a pert priest's help)—
And that he has butchered her accordingly,
As she foretold and as myself believed,—
And, so foretelling and believing so,
We were punished, both of us, the merry way:
Therefore, tell once again the tale! For what?
Pompilia is only dying while I speak!
Why does the mirth hang fire and miss the smile?

[1] Caponsacchi is now testifying at Guido's trial for murder. He had first told his story the previous summer before this same court at the trial for adultery, which followed the arrest of the run-away pair at Castelnuovo.

My masters, there's an old book, you should con
For strange adventures, applicable yet,
'Tis stuffed with. Do you know that there was once
This thing: a multitude of worthy folk
Took recreation, watched a certain group
Of soldiery intent upon a game,—
How first they wrangled, but soon fell to play,
Threw dice,—the best diversion in the world.
A word in your ear,—they are now casting lots,
Ay, with that gesture quaint and cry uncouth,
For the coat of One murdered an hour ago! [1]
I am a priest,—talk of what I have learned.
Pompilia is bleeding out her life belike,
Gasping away the latest breath of all,
This minute, while I talk—not while you laugh?

Yet, being sobered now, what is it you ask
By way of explanation? There's the fact!
It seems to fill the universe with sight
And sound,—from the four corners of this earth
Tells itself over, to my sense at least.
But you may want it lower set i' the scale,—
Too vast, too close it clangs in the ear, perhaps;
You'd stand back just to comprehend it more:
Well then, let me, the hollow rock, condense
The voice o' the sea and wind, interpret you
The mystery of this murder. God above!
It is too paltry, such a transference
O' the storm's roar to the cranny of the stone!

This deed, you saw begin—why does its end
Surprise you? Why should the event enforce
The lesson, we ourselves learned, she and I,
From the first o' the fact, and taught you, all in vain?
This Guido from whose throat you took my grasp,
Was this man to be favoured, now, or feared,
Let do his will, or have his will restrained,
In the relation with Pompilia?—say!
Did any other man need interpose
—Oh, though first comer, though as strange at the work
As fribble must be, coxcomb, fool that's near
To knave as, say, a priest who fears the world—
Was he bound brave the peril, save the doomed,
Or go on, sing his snatch and pluck his flower,
Keep the straight path and let the victim die?
I held so; you decided otherwise,
Saw no such peril, therefore no such need
To stop song, loosen flower, and leave path: Law,
Law was aware and watching, would suffice,
Wanted no priest's intrusion, palpably
Pretence, too manifest a subterfuge!
Whereupon I, priest, coxcomb, fribble, and fool,
Ensconced me in my corner, thus rebuked,
A kind of culprit, over-zealous hound
Kicked for his pains to kennel; I gave place,
To you, and let the law reign paramount:
I left Pompilia to your watch and ward,
And now you point me—there and thus she lies!

Men, for the last time, what do you want with me?

Is it,—you acknowledge, as it were, a use,
A profit in employing me?—at length
I may conceivably help the august law?
I am free to break the blow, next hawk that swoops
On next dove, nor miss much of good repute?
Or what if this your summons, after all,
Be but the form of mere release, no more,
Which turns the key and lets the captive go?
I have paid enough in person at Civita,
Am free,—what more need I concern me with?
Thank you! I am rehabilitated then,
A very reputable priest. But she—
The glory of life, the beauty of the world,
The splendour of heaven, . . . well, Sirs, does no one move?
Do I speak ambiguously? The glory, I say,
And the beauty, I say, and splendour, still say I,
Who, priest and trained to live my whole life long
On beauty and splendour, solely at their source,
God,—have thus recognised my food in one,
You tell me, that's fast dying while we talk,
Pompilia! How does lenity to me,

[1] Roman soldiers cast lots for the cloak of Christ after the Crucifixion.

Remit one death-bed pang to her? Come, smile!
The proper wink at the hot-headed youth
Who lets his soul show, through transparent words,
The mundane love that's sin and scandal too!
You are all struck acquiescent now, it seems:
It seems the oldest, gravest signor here,
Even the redoubtable Tommati, sits
Chop-fallen,—understands how law might take
Service like mine, of brain and heart and hand,
In good part. Better late than never, law!
You understand of a sudden, gospel too
Has a claim here, may possibly pronounce
Consistent with my priesthood, worthy Christ,
That I endeavoured to save Pompilia?
Then,
You were wrong, you see: that's well to see, though late:
That's all we may expect of man, this side
The grave: his good is—knowing he is bad:
Thus will it be with us when the books ope
And we stand at the bar on judgment-day.
Well then, I have a mind to speak, see cause
To relume the quenched flax by this dreadful light,
Burn my soul out in showing you the truth.
I heard, last time I stood here to be judged,
What is priest's-duty,—labour to pluck tares
And weed the corn of Molinism;[1] let me
Make you hear, this time, how, in such a case,
Man, be he in the priesthood or at plough,
Mindful of Christ or marching step by step
With . . . what's his style, the other potentate,
Who bids have courage and keep honour safe,
Nor let minuter admonition tease?
How he is bound, better or worse, to act.
Earth will not end through this misjudgment, no!
For you and the others like you sure to come,
Fresh work is sure to follow,—wickedness
That wants withstanding. Many a man of blood,
Many a man of guile will clamour yet,
Bid you redress his grievance,—as he clutched
The prey, forsooth a stranger stepped between,
And there's the good gripe in pure waste! My part
Is done; i' the doing it, I pass away
Out of the world. I want no more with earth.
Let me, in heaven's name, use the very snuff
O' the taper in one last spark shall show truth
For a moment, show Pompilia who was true!
Not for her sake, but yours: if she is dead,
Oh, Sirs, she can be loved by none of you
Most or least priestly! Saints, to do us good,
Must be in heaven, I seem to understand:
We never find them saints before, at least.
Be her first prayer then presently for you—
She had done the good to me . . .
What is all this?
There, I was born, have lived, shall die, a fool!
This is a foolish outset:—might with cause
Give colour to the very lie o' the man,
The murderer,—make as if I loved his wife,
In the way he called love. He is the fool there!
Why, had there been in me the touch of taint,
I had picked up so much of knaves'-policy
As hide it, keep one hand pressed on the place
Suspected of a spot would damn us both.
Or no, not her!—not even if any of you
Dares think that I, i' the face of death, her death
That's in my eyes and ears and brain and heart,
Lie,—if he does, let him! I mean to say,
So he stop there, stay thought from smirching her
The snow-white soul that angels fear to take
Untenderly. But, all the same, I know
I too am taintless, and I bare my breast.
You can't think, men as you are, all of you,
But that, to hear thus suddenly such an end
Of such a wonderful white soul, that comes
Of a man and murderer calling the white black,
Must shake me, trouble and disadvantage. Sirs,
Only seventeen!
Why, good and wise you are!
You might at the beginning stop my mouth:
So, none would be to speak for her, that knew.
I talk impertinently, and you bear,
All the same. This it is to have to do
With honest hearts: they easily may err,

[1] The works of Molinos, a Spanish Jesuit, were condemned by the Roman Catholic Church in 1687. His somewhat oriental doctrine that the soul, by a perfect contemplation of God, could reach a state of quietude where it neither desired salvation nor feared hell, presented a challenge to the more active thought of occidental Christianity and caused considerable stir in its day.

But in the main they wish well to the truth.
You are Christians; somehow, no one ever plucked
A rag, even, from the body of the Lord,
To wear and mock with, but, despite himself,
He looked the greater and was the better. Yes,
I shall go on now. Does she need or not
I keep calm? Calm I'll keep as monk that croons
Transcribing battle, earthquake, famine, plague,
From parchment to his cloister's chronicle.
Not one word more from the point now!

I begin.
Yes, I am one of your body and a priest.
Also I am a younger son o' the House
Oldest now, greatest once, in my birth-town
Arezzo, I recognise no equal there—
(I want all arguments, all sorts of arms
That seem to serve,—use this for a reason, wait!)
Not therefore thrust into the Church, because
O' the piece of bread one gets there. We were first
Of Fiesole, that rings still with the fame
Of Capo-in-Sacco our progenitor:
When Florence ruined Fiesole, our folk
Migrated to the victor-city, and there
Flourished,—our palace and our tower attest,
In the Old Mercato,—this was years ago,
Four hundred, full,—no, it wants fourteen just.
Our arms are those of Fiesole itself,
The shield quartered with white and red: a branch
Are the Salviati of us, nothing more.
That were good help to the Church? But better still—
Not simply for the advantage of my birth
I' the way of the world, was I proposed for priest;
But because there's an illustration, late
I' the day, that's loved and looked to as a saint
Still in Arezzo, he was bishop of,
Sixty years since: he spent to the last doit
His bishop's-revenue among the poor,
And used to tend the needy and the sick,
Barefoot, because of his humility.
He it was,—when the Granduke Ferdinand
Swore he would raze our city, plough the place
And sow it with salt, because we Aretines
Had tied a rope about the neck, to hale
The statue of his father from its base
For hate's sake,—he availed by prayers and tears
To pacify the Duke and save the town.
This was my father's father's brother. You see,
For his sake, how it was I had a right
To the self-same office, bishop in the egg,
So, grew i' the garb and prattled in the school,
Was made expect, from infancy almost,
The proper mood o' the priest; till time ran by
And brought the day when I must read the vows,
Declare the world renounced and undertake
To become priest and leave probation,—leap
Over the ledge into the other life,
Having gone trippingly hitherto up to the height
O'er the wan water. Just a vow to read!

I stopped short awe-struck. "How shall holiest flesh
Engage to keep such vow inviolate,
How much less mine? I know myself too weak,
Unworthy! Choose a worthier stronger man!"
And the very Bishop smiled and stopped the mouth
In its mid-protestation. "Incapable?
Qualmish of conscience? Thou ingenuous boy!
Clear up the clouds and cast thy scruples far!
I satisfy thee there's an easier sense
Wherein to take such vow than suits the first
Rough rigid reading. Mark what makes all smooth,
Nay, has been even a solace to myself!
The Jews who needs must, in their synagogue,
Utter sometimes the holy name of God,
A thing their superstition boggles at,
Pronounce aloud the ineffable sacrosanct,—
How does their shrewdness help them? In this wise;
Another set of sounds they substitute,
Jumble so consonants and vowels—how
Should I know?—that there grows from out the old
Quite a new word that means the very same—
And o'er the hard place slide they with a smile.
Giuseppe Maria Caponsacchi mine,
Nobody wants you in these latter days

To prop the Church by breaking your back-
bone,—
As the necessary way was once, we know,
When Diocletian flourished and his like.
That building of the buttress-work was done
By martyrs and confessors: let it bide,
Add not a brick, but, where you see a chink,
Stick in a sprig of ivy or root a rose
Shall make amends and beautify the pile!
We profit as you were the painfullest
O' the martyrs, and you prove yourself a match
For the cruellest confessor ever was,
If you march boldly up and take your stand
Where their blood soaks, their bones yet strew
the soil,
And cry 'Take notice, I the young and free
And well-to-do i' the world, thus leave the
world,
Cast in my lot thus with no gay young world
But the grand old Church: she tempts me of
the two!'
Renounce the world? Nay, keep and give it us!
Let us have you, and boast of what you bring.
We want the pick o' the earth to practise
with,
Not its offscouring, halt and deaf and blind
In soul and body. There's a rubble-stone
Unfit for the front o' the building, stuff to
stow
In a gap behind and keep us weather-tight;
There's porphyry for the prominent place.
Good lack!
Saint Paul has had enough and to spare, I
trow,
Of ragged run-away Onesimus: [1]
He wants the right-hand with the signet-ring
Of King Agrippa, now, to shake and use.
I have a heavy scholar cloistered up
Close under lock and key, kept at his task
Of letting Fénelon [2] know the fool he is,
In a book I promise Christendom next Spring.
Why, if he covets so much meat, the clown,
As a lark's wing next Friday, or, any day,
Diversion beyond catching his own fleas,
He shall be properly swinged, I promise him.

[1] In the Epistle of Paul to Philemon he asks for forgiveness of his son Onesimus and promises to pay anything the latter may owe Philemon; whereas King Agrippa (Acts, 25 and 26) favored Paul when he was imprisoned.

[2] An eloquent French supporter of the heresy of Molinos referred to in a previous note.

But you, who are so quite another paste
Of a man,—do you obey me? Cultivate
Assiduous that superior gift you have
Of making madrigals—(who told me? Ah!)
Get done a Marinesque Adoniad [1] straight
With a pulse o' the blood a-pricking, here and
there
That I may tell the lady, 'And he's ours!'"

So I became a priest: those terms changed all,
I was good enough for that, nor cheated so;
I could live thus and still hold head erect.
Now you see why I may have been before
A fribble and coxcomb, yet, as priest, break
word
Nowise, to make you disbelieve me now.
I need that you should know my truth. Well,
then,
According to prescription did I live,
—Conformed myself, both read the breviary
And wrote the rhymes, was punctual to my
place
I' the Pieve,[2] and as diligent at my post
Where beauty and fashion rule. I throve
apace,
Sub-deacon, Canon, the authority
For delicate play at tarocs,[3] and arbiter
O' the magnitude of fan-mounts: all the while
Wanting no whit the advantage of a hint
Benignant to the promising pupil,—thus:
"Enough attention to the Countess now,
The young one; 'tis her mother rules the roast,
We know where, and puts in a word: go pay
Devoir to-morrow morning after mass!
Break that rash promise to preach, Passion-
week!
Has it escaped you the Archbishop grunts
And snuffles when one grieves to tell his Grace
No soul dares treat the subject of the day
Since his own masterly handling it (ha, ha!)
Five years ago,—when somebody could help
And touch up an odd phrase in time of need,
(He, he!)—and somebody helps you, my son!
Therefore, don't prove so indispensable
At the Pieve, sit more loose i' the seat, nor
grow

[1] Marini's *Adone* [1623] was a popular book which pleased the fashionable with its treatment of the love story of Adonis.

[2] Sta. Maria della Pieve, the church in Arezzo to which Caponsacchi was attached.

[3] Cards.

A fixture by attendance morn and eve!
Arezzo's just a haven midway Rome—
Rome's the eventual harbour,—make for port,
Crowd sail, crack cordage! And your cargo be
A polished presence, a genteel manner, wit
At will, and tact at every pore of you!
I sent our lump of learning, Brother Clout,
And Father Slouch, our piece of piety,
To see Rome and try suit the Cardinal.
Thither they clump-clumped, beads and book in hand,
And ever since 'tis meat for man and maid
How both flopped down, prayed blessing on bent pate
Bald many an inch beyond the tonsure's need,
Never once dreaming, the two moony dolts,
There's nothing moves his Eminence so much
As—far from all this awe at sanctitude—
Heads that wag, eyes that twinkle, modified mirth
At the closet-lectures on the Latin tongue
A lady learns so much by, we know where.
Why, body o' Bacchus, you should crave his rule
For pauses in the elegiac couplet, chasms
Permissible only to Catullus! [1] There!
Now go do duty: brisk, break Priscian's head
By reading the day's office—there's no help.
You've Ovid in your poke to plaster that;
Amen's at the end of all: then sup with me!"

Well, after three or four years of this life,
In prosecution of my calling, I
Found myself at the theatre one night
With a brother Canon, in a mood and mind
Proper enough for the place, amused or no:
When I saw enter, stand, and seat herself
A lady, young, tall, beautiful, strange, and sad.
It was as when, in our cathedral once,
As I got yawningly through matin-song,
I saw *facchini* [2] bear a burden up,
Base it on the high-altar, break away
A board or two, and leave the thing inside
Lofty and lone: and lo, when next I looked,
There was the Rafael! I was still one stare,
When—"Nay, I'll make her give you back your gaze"
Said Canon Conti; and at the word he tossed
A paper-twist of comfits to her lap,
And dodged and in a trice was at my back
Nodding from over my shoulder. Then she turned,
Looked our way, smiled the beautiful sad strange smile.
"Is not she fair? 'Tis my new cousin," said he:
"The fellow lurking there i' the black o' the box
Is Guido, the old scapegrace: she's his wife,
Married three years since: how his Countship sulks!
He has brought little back from Rome beside,
After the bragging, bullying. A fair face,
And—they do say—a pocket-full of gold
When he can worry both her parents dead.
I don't go much there, for the chamber's cold
And the coffee pale. I got a turn at first
Paying my duty: I observed they crouched
—The two old frightened family spectres—close
In a corner, each on each like mouse on mouse
I' the cat's cage: ever since, I stay at home.
Hallo, there's Guido, the black, mean, and small,
Bends his brows on us—please to bend your own
On the shapely nether limbs of Light-skirts there
By way of a diversion! I was a fool
To fling the sweetmeats. Prudence, for God's love!
To-morrow I'll make my peace, e'en tell some fib,
Try if I can't find means to take you there."
That night and next day did the gaze endure,
Burnt to my brain, as sunbeam thro' shut eyes,
And not once changed the beautiful sad strange smile.
At vespers Conti leaned beside my seat
I' the choir,—part said, part sung—"*In ex-cel-sis*—[1]
All's to no purpose: I have louted low,
But he saw you staring—*quia sub*—don't incline

[1] From other references in the poem it is plain that the Cardinal was proud of his skill in Latin verse, but here the implication is that it was really so bad that he took licenses which even so great a poet as Catullus might have had difficulty in justifying.

[2] Porters.

[1] In the following lines Conti intersperses between the Latin of the church service his comments to Caponsacchi.

To know you nearer: him we would not hold
For Hercules,—the man would lick your shoe
If you and certain efficacious friends
Managed him warily,—but there's the wife:
Spare her, because he beats her, as it is,
She's breaking her heart quite fast enough—*jam tu*—
So, be you rational and make amends
With little Light-skirts yonder—*in secula*
Secu-lo-o-o-o-rum. Ah, you rogue! Every one knows
What great dame she makes jealous: one against one,
Play, and win both!"
Sirs, ere the week was out,
I saw and said to myself "Light-skirts hides teeth
Would make a dog sick,—the great dame shows spite
Should drive a cat mad: 'tis but poor work this—
Counting one's fingers till the sonnet's crowned.
I doubt much if Marino really be
A better bard than Dante after all.
'Tis more amusing to go pace at eve
I' the Duomo,—watch the day's last gleam outside
Turn, as into a skirt of God's own robe,
Those lancet-windows' jewelled miracle,—
Than go eat the Archbishop's ortolans,
Digest his jokes. Luckily Lent is near:
Who cares to look will find me in my stall
At the Pieve, constant to this faith at least—
Never to write a canzonet any more."
So, next week, 'twas my patron spoke abrupt,
In altered guise, "Young mán, can it be true
That after all your promise of sound fruit,
You have kept away from Countess young or old
And gone play truant in church all day long?
Are you turning Molinist?" I answered quick:
"Sir, what if I turned Christian? It might be.
The fact is, I am troubled in my mind,
Beset and pressed hard by some novel thoughts.
This your Arezzo is a limited world;
There's a strange Pope,—'tis said, a priest who thinks.
Rome is the port, you say: to Rome I go.
I will live alone, one does so in a crowd,
And look into my heart a little." "Lent
Ended,"—I told friends,—"I shall go to Rome."

One evening I was sitting in a muse
Over the opened "Summa,"[1] darkened round
By the mid-March twilight, thinking how my life
Had shaken under me,—broke short indeed
And showed the gap 'twixt what is, what should be,—
And into what abysm the soul may slip,
Leave aspiration here, achievement there,
Lacking omnipotence to connect extremes—
Thinking moreover . . . oh, thinking, if you like,
How utterly dissociated was I
A priest and celibate, from the sad strange wife
Of Guido,—just as an instance to the point,
Nought more,—how I had a whole store of strengths
Eating into my heart, which craved employ,
And she, perhaps, need of a finger's help,—
And yet there was no way in the wide world
To stretch out mine and so relieve myself—
How when the page o' the Summa preached its best,
Her smile kept glowing out of it, as to mock
The silence we could break by no one word,—
There came a tap without the chamber-door
And a whisper, when I bade who tapped speak out,
And, in obedience to my summons, last
In glided a masked muffled mystery,
Laid lightly a letter on the opened book,
Then stood with folded arms and foot demure,
Pointing as if to mark the minutes' flight.

I took the letter, read to the effect
That she, I lately flung the comfits to,
Had a warm heart to give me in exchange,
And gave it,—loved me and confessed it thus,

[1] The *Summa Theologiæ* of St. Thomas Aquinas, one of the tremendously influential books of the middle ages and studied by all Catholic students of theology in later periods. Between the *Summa* and the thought of Pompilia there is an obvious contrast which indicates the power of the impression, in no unfavorable sense, which she had made upon Caponsacchi.

And bade me render thanks by word of mouth,
Going that night to such a side o' the house
Where the small terrace overhangs a street
Blind and deserted, not the street in front:
Her husband being away, the surly patch,
At his villa of Vittiano.

"And you?"—I asked:
"What may you be?"—"Count Guido's kind of maid—
Most of us have two functions in his house.
We all hate him, the lady suffers much,
'Tis just we show compassion, furnish aid,
Specially since her choice is fixed so well.
What answer may I bring to cheer the sweet
Pompilia?"

Then I took a pen and wrote
"No more of this! That you are fair, I know:
But other thoughts now occupy my mind.
I should not thus have played the insensible
Once on a time. What made you,—may one ask,—
Marry your hideous husband? 'Twas a fault,
And now you taste the fruit of it. Farewell."

"There!" smiled I as she snatched it and was gone—
"There, let the jealous miscreant,—Guido's self,
Whose mean soul grins through this transparent trick,—
Be baulked so far, defrauded of his aim!
What fund of satisfaction to the knave,
Had I kicked this his messenger downstairs,
Trussed to the middle of her impudence,
And set his heart at ease so! No, indeed!
There's the reply which he shall turn and twist
At pleasure, snuff at till his brain grow drunk,
As the bear does when he finds a scented glove
That puzzles him,—a hand and yet no hand,
Of other perfume than his own foul paw!
Last month, I had doubtless chosen to play the dupe,
Accepted the mock-invitation, kept
The sham appointment, cudgel beneath cloak,
Prepared myself to pull the appointer's self
Out of the window from his hiding-place
Behind the gown of this part-messenger
Part-mistress who would personate the wife.
Such had seemed once a jest permissible:
Now, I am not i' the mood."

Back next morn brought
The messenger, a second letter in hand.
"You are cruel, Thyrsis, and Myrtilla [1] moans
Neglected but adores you, makes request
For mercy: why is it you dare not come?
Such virtue is scarce natural to your age:
You must love someone else; I hear you do,
The Baron's daughter or the Advocate's wife,
Or both,—all's one, would you make me the third—
I take the crumbs from table gratefully
Nor grudge who feasts there. 'Faith, I blush and blaze!
Yet if I break all bounds, there's reason sure,
Are you determinedly bent on Rome?
I am wretched here, a monster tortures me:
Carry me with you! Come and say you will!
Concert this very evening! Do not write!
I am ever at the window of my room
Over the terrace, at the *Ave*. Come!"

I questioned—lifting half the woman's mask
To let her smile loose. "So, you gave my line
To the merry lady?" "She kissed off the wax,
And put what paper was not kissed away,
In her bosom to go burn: but merry, no!
She wept all night when evening brought no friend,
Alone, the unkind missive at her breast;
Thus Philomel, the thorn at her breast too,
Sings" . . . "Writes this second letter?" "Even so!
Then she may peep at vespers forth?"—"What risk
Do we run o' the husband?"—"Ah,—no risk at all!
He is more stupid even than jealous. Ah—
That was the reason? Why, the man's away!
Beside, his bugbear is that friend of yours,
Fat little Canon Conti. He fears him,
How should he dream of you? I told you truth—
He goes to the villa at Vittiano—'tis
The time when Spring-sap rises in the vine—
Spends the night there. And then his wife's a child,
Does he think a child outwits him? A mere child:

[1] It was a literary fashion of the pastoral, and an affectation of the love correspondence (and poetry) of the day to adopt the names of shepherds and shepherdesses *à la* Theocritus.

Yet so full grown, a dish for any duke.
Don't quarrel longer with such cates, but come!"

I wrote, "In vain do you solicit me.
I am a priest: and you are wedded wife,
Whatever kind of brute your husband prove.
I have scruples, in short. Yet should you really show
Sign at the window . . . but nay, best be good!
My thoughts are elsewhere."—"Take her that!"
—"Again
Let the incarnate meanness, cheat and spy,
Mean to the marrow of him, make his heart
His food, anticipate hell's worm once more!
Let him watch shivering at the window—ay,
And let this hybrid, this his light-of-love
And lackey-of-lies,—a sage economy,—
Paid with embracings for the rank brass coin,—
Let her report and make him chuckle o'er
The break-down of my resolution now,
And lour at disappointment in good time!
—So tantalise and so enrage by turns,
Until the two fall each on the other like
Two famished spiders, as the coveted fly
That toys long, leaves their net and them at last!"

And so the missives followed thick and fast
For a month, say,—I still came at every turn
On the soft sly adder, endlong 'neath my tread.
I was met i' the street, made sign to in the church,
A slip was found i' the door-sill, scribbled word
'Twixt page and page o' the prayer-book in my place:
A crumpled thing dropped even before my feet,
Pushed through the blind, above the terrace-rail,
As I passed, by day, the very window once.
And ever from corners would be peering up
The messenger, with the self-same demand
"Obdurate still, no flesh but adamant?
Nothing to cure the wound, assuage the throe
O' the sweetest lamb that ever loved a bear?"
And ever my one answer in one tone—
"Go your ways, temptress! Let a priest read, pray,
Unplagued of vain talk, visions not for him!
In the end, you'll have your will and ruin me!"

One day, a variation: thus I read:
"You have gained little by timidity.
My husband has found out my love at length,
Sees cousin Conti was the stalking-horse,
And you the game he covered, poor fat soul!
My husband is a formidable foe,
Will stick at nothing to destroy you. Stand
Prepared, or better, run till you reach Rome!
I bade you visit me, when the last place
My tyrant would have turned suspicious at,
Or cared to seek you in, was . . . why say, where?
But now all's changed: beside, the season's past
At the villa,—wants the master's eye no more.
Anyhow, I beseech you, stay away
From the window! He might well be posted there."

I wrote—"You raise my courage, or call up
My curiosity, who am but man.
Tell him he owns the palace, not the street
Under—that's his and yours and mine alike.
If it should please me pad the path this eve,
Guido will have two troubles, first to get
Into a rage and then get out again.
Be cautious, though: at the *Ave!*"
You of the court!
When I stood question here and reached this point
O' the narrative,—search notes and see and say
If some one did not interpose with smile
And sneer, "And prithee why so confident
That the husband must, of all needs, not the wife,
Fabricate thus,—what if the lady loved?
What if she wrote the letters?"
Learned Sir,
I told you there's a picture in our church.
Well, if a low-browed verger sidled up
Bringing me, like a blotch, on his prod's point,
A transfixed scorpion, let the reptile writhe,
And then said, "See a thing that Rafael made—
This venom issued from Madonna's mouth!"—
I should reply, "Rather, the soul of you
Has issued from your body, like from like,
By way of the ordure-corner!"

But no less,
I tired of the same black teasing lie
Obtruded thus at every turn; the pest
Was far too near the picture, anyhow:
One does Madonna service, making clowns
Remove their dung-heap from the sacristy.
"I will to the window, as he tempts," said I:
"Yes, whom the easy love has failed allure,
This new bait of adventure tempts—thinks he.
Though the imprisoned lady keeps afar,
There will they lie in ambush, heads alert,
Kith, kin, and Count mustered to bite my heel.
No mother nor brother viper of the brood
Shall scuttle off without the instructive bruise!"

So, I went: crossed street and street: "The next street's turn,
I stand beneath the terrace, see, above,
The black of the ambush-window. Then, in place
Of hand's throw of soft prelude over lute
And cough that clears way for the ditty last,"—
I began to laugh already—"he will have
'Out of the hole you hide in, on to the front,
Count Guido Franceschini, show yourself!
Hear what a man thinks of a thing like you,
And after, take this foulness in your face!' "

The words lay living on my lip, I made
The one turn more—and there at the window stood,
Framed in its black square length, with lamp in hand,
Pompilia; the same great, grave, griefful air
As stands i' the dusk, on altar that I know,
Left alone with one moonbeam in her cell,
Our Lady of all the Sorrows. Ere I knelt—
Assured myself that she was flesh and blood—
She had looked one look and vanished.
I thought—"Just so:
It was herself, they have set her there to watch—
Stationed to see some wedding-band go by,
On fair pretence that she must bless the bride,
Or wait some funeral with friends wind past,
And crave peace for the corpse that claims its due.
She never dreams they used her for a snare,
And now withdraw the bait has served its turn.
Well done, the husband, who shall fare the worse!"
And on my lip again was—"Out with thee,
Guido!" When all at once she re-appeared;
But, this time, on the terrace overhead,
So close above me, she could almost touch
My head if she bent down; and she did bend,
While I stood still as stone, all eye, all ear.

She began—"You have sent me letters, Sir:
I have read none, I can neither read nor write;
But she you gave them to, a woman here,
One of the people in whose power I am,
Partly explained their sense, I think, to me
Obliged to listen while she inculcates
That you, a priest, can dare love me, a wife,
Desire to live or die as I shall bid,
(She makes me listen if I will or no)
Because you saw my face a single time.
It cannot be she says the thing you mean;
Such wickedness were deadly to us both:
But good true love would help me now so much—
I tell myself, you may mean good and true.
You offer me, I seem to understand,
Because I am in poverty and starve,
Much money, where one piece would save my life.
The silver cup upon the altar-cloth
Is neither yours to give nor mine to take;
But I might take one bit of bread therefrom,
Since I am starving, and return the rest,
Yet do no harm: this is my very case.
I am in that strait, I may not dare abstain
From so much of assistance as would bring
The guilt of theft on neither you nor me;
But no superfluous particle of aid.
I think, if you will let me state my case,
Even had you been so fancy-fevered here,
Not your sound self, you must grow healthy now—
Care only to bestow what I can take.
That it is only you in the wide world,
Knowing me nor in thought nor word nor deed,
Who, all unprompted save by your own heart,
Come proffering assistance now,—were strange
But that my whole life is so strange: as strange
It is, my husband whom I have not wronged
Should hate and harm me. For his own soul's sake,
Hinder the harm! But there is something more,

And that the strangest: it has got to be
Somehow for my sake too, and yet not mine,
—This is a riddle—for some kind of sake
Not any clearer to myself than you,
And yet as certain as that I draw breath,—
I would fain live, not die—oh no, not die!
My case is, I was dwelling happily
At Rome with those dear Comparini, called
Father and mother to me; when at once
I found I had become Count Guido's wife:
Who then, not waiting for a moment, changed
Into a fury of fire, if once he was
Merely a man: his face threw fire at mine,
He laid a hand on me that burned all peace,
All joy, all hope, and last all fear away,
Dipping the bough of life, so pleasant once,
In fire which shrivelled leaf and bud alike,
Burning not only present life but past,
Which you might think was safe beyond his reach.
He reached it, though, since that beloved pair,
My father once, my mother all those years,
That loved me so, now say I dreamed a dream
And bid me wake henceforth no child of theirs,
Never in all the time their child at all.
Do you understand? I cannot: yet so it is.
Just so I say of you that proffer help:
I cannot understand what prompts your soul,
I simply needs must see that it is so,
Only one strange and wonderful thing more.
They came here with me, those two dear ones, kept
All the old love up, till my husband, till
His people here so tortured them, they fled.
And now, is it because I grow in flesh
And spirit one with him their torturer,
That they, renouncing him, must cast off me?
If I were graced by God to have a child,
Could I one day deny God graced me so?
Then, since my husband hates me, I shall break
No law that reigns in this fell house of hate,
By using—letting have effect so much
Of hate as hides me from that whole of hate
Would take my life which I want and must have—
Just as I take from your excess of love
Enough to save my life with, all I need.
The Archbishop said to murder me were sin:
My leaving Guido were a kind of death
With no sin,—more death, he must answer for.
Hear now what death to him and life to you
I wish to pay and owe. Take me to Rome!
You go to Rome, the servant makes me hear.
Take me as you would take a dog, I think,
Masterless left for strangers to maltreat:
Take me home like that—leave me in the house
Where the father and the mother are; and soon
They'll come to know and call me by my name,
Their child once more, since child I am, for all
They now forget me, which is the worst o' the dream—
And the way to end dreams is to break them, stand,
Walk, go: then help me to stand, walk and go!
The Governor said the strong should help the weak:
You know how weak the strongest women are.
How could I find my way there by myself?
I cannot even call out, make them hear—
Just as in dreams: I have tried and proved the fact.
I have told this story and more to good great men,
The Archbishop and the Governor: they smiled.
'Stop your mouth, fair one!'—presently they frowned,
'Get you gone, disengage you from our feet!'
I went in my despair to an old priest,
Only a friar, no great man like these two,
But good, the Augustinian, people name
Romano,—he confessed me two months since:
He fears God, why then needs he fear the world?
And when he questioned how it came about
That I was found in danger of a sin—
Despair of any help from providence,—
'Since, though your husband outrage you,' said he,
'That is a case too common, the wives die
Or live, but do not sin so deep as this'—
Then I told—what I never will tell you—
How, worse than husband's hate, I had to bear
The love,—soliciting to shame called love,—
Of his brother,—the young idle priest i' the house
With only the devil to meet there. 'This is grave—
Yes, we must interfere: I counsel,—write

To those who used to be your parents once,
Of dangers here, bid them convey you hence!'
'But,' said I, 'when I neither read nor write?'
Then he took pity and promised 'I will write.'
If he did so,—why, they are dumb or dead:
Either they give no credit to the tale,
Or else, wrapped wholly up in their own joy
Of such escape, they care not who cries, still
I' the clutches. Anyhow, no word arrives.
All such extravagance and dreadfulness
Seems incident to dreaming, cured one way,—
Wake me! The letter I received this morn,
Said—if the woman spoke your very sense—
'You would die for me:' I can believe it now:
For now the dream gets to involve yourself.
First of all, you seemed wicked and not good,
In writing me those letters: you came in
Like a thief upon me. I this morning said
In my extremity, entreat the thief!
Try if he have in him no honest touch!
A thief might save me from a murderer.
'Twas a thief said the last kind word to Christ:
Christ took the kindness and forgave the theft:
And so did I prepare what I now say.
But now, that you stand and I see your face,
Though you have never uttered word yet,—well, I know,
Here too has been dream-work, delusion too,
And that at no time, you with the eyes here,
Ever intended to do wrong by me,
Nor wrote such letters therefore. It is false,
And you are true, have been true, will be true.
To Rome then,—when is it you take me there?
Each minute lost is mortal. When?—I ask."
I answered, "It shall be when it can be.
I will go hence and do your pleasure, find
The sure and speedy means of travel, then
Come back and take you to your friends in Rome.
There wants a carriage, money and the rest,—
A day's work by to-morrow at this time.
How shall I see you and assure escape?"
She replied, "Pass, to-morrow at this hour.
If I am at the open window, well:
If I am absent, drop a handkerchief
And walk by! I shall see from where I watch,
And know that all is done. Return next eve,
And next, and so till we can meet and speak!"
"To-morrow at this hour I pass," said I.
She was withdrawn.

Here is another point
I bid you pause at. When I told thus far,
Someone said, subtly, "Here at least was found
Your confidence in error,—you perceived
The spirit of the letters, in a sort,
Had been the lady's, if the body should be
Supplied by Guido: say, he forged them all!
Here was the unforged fact—she sent for you,
Spontaneously elected you to help,
—What men call, loved you: Guido read her mind,
Gave it expression to assure the world
The case was just as he foresaw: he wrote,
She spoke."

Sirs, that first simile serves still,—
That falsehood of a scorpion hatched, I say,
Nowhere i' the world but in Madonna's mouth.
Go on! Suppose, that falsehood foiled, next eve
Pictured Madonna raised her painted hand,
Fixed the face Rafael bent above the Babe,
On my face as I flung me at her feet:
Such miracle vouchsafed and manifest,
Would that prove the first lying tale was true?
Pompilia spoke, and I at once received,
Accepted my own fact, my miracle
Self-authorised and self-explained,—she chose
To summon me and signify her choice.
Afterward,—oh! I gave a passing glance
To a certain ugly cloud-shape, goblin-shred
Of hell-smoke hurrying past the splendid moon
Out now to tolerate no darkness more,
And saw right through the thing that tried to pass
For truth and solid, not an empty lie:
"So, he not only forged the words for her
But word for me, made letters he called mine:
What I sent, he retained, gave these in place,
All by the mistress-messenger! As I
Recognised her, at potency of truth,
So she, by the crystalline soul, knew me,
Never mistook the signs. Enough of this—
Let the wraith go to nothingness again,
Here is the orb, have only thought for her!"

"Thought?" nay, Sirs, what shall follow was not thought:
I have thought sometimes, and thought long and hard.

I have stood before, gone round a serious thing,
Tasked my whole mind to touch and clasp it close,
As I stretch forth my arm to touch this bar.
God and man, and what duty I owe both,—
I dare to say I have confronted these
In thought: but no such faculty helped here.
I put forth no thought,—powerless, all that night
I paced the city: it was the first Spring.
By the invasion I lay passive to,
In rushed new things, the old were rapt away;
Alike abolished—the imprisonment
Of the outside air, the inside weight o' the world
That pulled me down. Death meant, to spurn the ground,
Soar to the sky,—die well and you do that.
The very immolation made the bliss; [1]
Death was the heart of life, and all the harm
My folly had crouched to avoid, now proved a veil
Hiding all gain my wisdom strove to grasp:
As if the intense centre of the flame
Should turn a heaven to that devoted fly
Which hitherto, sophist alike and sage,
Saint Thomas with his sober grey goose-quill,
And sinner Plato by Cephisian reed,[2]
Would fain, pretending just the insect's good,
Whisk off, drive back, consign to shade again.
Into another state, under new rule
I knew myself was passing swift and sure;
Whereof the initiatory pang approached,
Felicitous annoy, as bitter-sweet
As when the virgin-band, the victors chaste,
Feel at the end the earthly garments drop,
And rise with something of a rosy shame
Into immortal nakedness: so I
Lay, and let come the proper throe would thrill
Into the ecstacy and outthrob pain.

I' the grey of dawn it was I found myself
Facing the pillared front o' the Pieve—mine,
My church: it seemed to say for the first time
"But am not I the Bride, the mystic love
O' the Lamb, who took thy plighted troth, my priest,
To fold thy warm heart on my heart of stone
And freeze thee nor unfasten any more?
This is a fleshly woman,—let the free
Bestow their life-blood, thou art pulseless now!"
See! Day by day I had risen and left this church
At the signal waved me by some foolish fan,
With half a curse and half a pitying smile
For the monk I stumbled over in my haste,
Prostrate and corpse-like at the altar-foot
Intent on his *corona:* [1] then the church
Was ready with her quip, if word conduced,
To quicken my pace nor stop for prating—"There!
Be thankful you are no such ninny, go
Rather to teach a black-eyed novice cards
Than gabble Latin and protrude that nose
Smoothed to a sheep's through no brains and much faith!"
That sort of incentive! Now the church changed tone—
Now, when I found out first that life and death
Are means to an end, that passion uses both,
Indisputably mistress of the man
Whose form of worship is self-sacrifice—
Now, from the stone lungs sighed the scrannel voice
"Leave that live passion, come be dead with me!"
As if, i' the fabled garden, I had gone
On great adventure, plucked in ignorance
Hedge-fruit, and feasted to satiety,
Laughing at such high fame for hips and haws,
And scorned the achievement: then come all at once
O' the prize o' the place, the thing of perfect gold,
The apples's self: and, scarce my eye on that,
Was 'ware as well o' the seven-fold dragon's watch.

[1] The lines which follow are difficult. The central imagery of the passage (to 961 and beyond) seems to be that of the instinct of the moth for the flame, tritely considered destruction, but here considered as an instinct to penetrate to intense heaven.

[2] Both St. Thomas, the Christian author of the *Summa,* and Plato (a sinner because a Pagan; by the "Cephisian reed" because the Cephisus was one of the reedy rivers of his city of Athens) would have driven the moth from the flame. Caponsacchi ventures to differ with the preëminent authorities of the Christian and the Pagan world.

[1] Rosary.

Sirs, I obeyed. Obedience was too strange,—
This new thing that had been struck into me
By the look o' the lady,—to dare disobey
The first authoritative word. 'Twas God's.
I had been lifted to the level of her,
Could take such sounds into my sense. I said
"We two are cognizant o' the Master now;
She it is bids me bow the head: how true,
I am a priest! I see the function here;
I thought the other way self-sacrifice:
This is the true, seals up the perfect sum.
I pay it, sit down, silently obey."

So, I went home. Dawn broke, noon broadened, I—
I sat stone-still, let time run over me.
The sun slanted into my room, had reached
The west. I opened book,—Aquinas blazed
With one black name only on the white page.
I looked up, saw the sunset: vespers rang:
"She counts the minutes till I keep my word
And come say all is ready. I am a priest.
Duty to God is duty to her: I think
God, who created her, will save her too
Some new way, by one miracle the more,
Without me. Then, prayer may avail perhaps."
I went to my own place i' the Pieve, read
The office: I was back at home again
Sitting i' the dark. "Could she but know—but know
That, were there good in this distinct from God's,
Really good as it reached her, though procured
By a sin of mine,—I should sin: God forgives.
She knows it is no fear withholds me: fear?
Of what? Suspense here is the terrible thing.
If she should, as she counts the minutes, come
On the fantastic notion that I fear
The world now, fear the Archbishop, fear perhaps
Count Guido, he who, having forged the lies,
May wait the work, attend the effect,—I fear
The sword of Guido! Let God see to that—
Hating lies, let not her believe a lie!"

Again the morning found me. "I will work,
Tie down my foolish thoughts. Thank God so far!
I have saved her from a scandal, stopped the tongues
Had broken else into a cackle and hiss
Around the noble name. Duty is still
Wisdom: I have been wise." So the day wore.
At evening—"But, achieving victory,
I must not blink the priest's peculiar part,
Nor shrink to counsel, comfort: priest and friend—
How do we discontinue to be friends?
I will go minister, advise her seek
Help at the source,—above all, not despair:
There may be other happier help at hand.
I hope it,—wherefore then neglect to say?"

There she stood—leaned there, for the second time,
Over the terrace, looked at me, then spoke:
"Why is it you have suffered me to stay
Breaking my heart two days more than was need?
Why delay help, your own heart yearns to give?
You are again here, in the self-same mind,
I see here, steadfast in the face of you,—
You grudge to do no one thing that I ask.
Why then is nothing done? You know my need.
Still, through God's pity on me, there is time
And one day more: shall I be saved or no?"
I answered—"Lady, waste no thought, no word
Even to forgive me! Care for what I care—
Only! Now follow me as I were fate!
Leave this house in the dark to-morrow night,
Just before daybreak:—there's new moon this eve—
It sets, and then begins the solid black.
Descend, proceed to the Torrione, step
Over the low dilapidated wall,
Take San Clemente, there's no other gate
Unguarded at the hour: some paces thence
An inn stands; cross to it; I shall be there."

She answered, "If I can but find the way.
But I shall find it. Go now!"

I did go,
Took rapidly the route myself prescribed,
Stopped at Torrione, climbed the ruined place,
Proved that the gate was practicable, reached
The inn, no eye, despite the dark, could miss,

Knocked there and entered, made the host secure:
"With Caponsacchi it is ask and have;
I know my betters. Are you bound for Rome?
I get swift horse and trusty man," said he.

Then I retraced my steps, was found once more
In my own house for the last time: there lay
The broad pale opened Summa. "Shut his book,
There's other showing! 'Twas a Thomas too
Obtained,—more favoured than his namesake here,—
A gift, tied faith fast, foiled the tug of doubt,—
Our Lady's girdle; down he saw it drop
As she ascended into heaven, they say: [1]
He kept that safe and bade all doubt adieu.
I too have seen a lady and hold a grace."

I know not how the night passed: morning broke:
Presently came my servant. "Sir, this eve—
Do you forget?" I started. "How forget?
What is it you know?" "With due submission, Sir,
This being last Monday in the month but one
And a vigil, since to-morrow is Saint George,
And feast day, and moreover day for copes,
And Canon Conti now away a month,
And Canon Crispi sour because, forsooth,
You let him sulk in stall and bear the brunt
Of the octave. . . . Well, Sir, 'tis important!"
"True!
Hearken, I have to start for Rome this night.
No word, lest Crispi overboil and burst!
Provide me with a laic dress! Throw dust
I' the Canon's eye, stop his tongue's scandal so!
See there's a sword in case of accident."
I knew the knave, the knave knew me.

And thus
Through each familiar hindrance of the day
Did I make steadily for its hour and end,—
Felt time's old barrier-growth of right and fit
Give way through all its twines and let me go;
Use and wont recognised the excepted man,
Let speed the special service,—and I sped
Till, at the dead between midnight and morn,
There was I at the goal, before the gate,
With a tune in the ears, low leading up to loud,
A light in the eyes, faint that would soon be flare,
Ever some spiritual witness new and new
In faster frequence, crowding solitude
To watch the way o' the warfare,—till, at last,
When the ecstatic minute must bring birth,
Began a whiteness in the distance, waxed
Whiter and whiter, near grew and more near,
Till it was she: there did Pompilia come:
The white I saw shine through her was her soul's,
Certainly, for the body was one black,
Black from head down to foot. She did not speak,
Glided into the carriage,—so a cloud
Gathers the moon up. "By San Spirito,
To Rome, as if the road burned underneath!
Reach Rome, then hold my head in pledge, I pay
The run and the risk to heart's content!" Just that,
I said,—then, in another tick of time,
Sprang, was beside her, she and I alone.

So it began, our flight thro' dusk to clear,
Through day and night and day again to night
Once more, and to last dreadful dawn of all.
Sirs, how should I lie quiet in my grave
Unless you suffer me wring, drop by drop,
My brain dry, make a riddance of the drench
Of minutes with a memory in each,
Recorded motion, breath or look of hers,
Which poured forth would present you one pure glass,
Mirror you plain,—as God's sea, glassed in gold,
His saints,—the perfect soul Pompilia? Men,
You must know that a man gets drunk with truth
Stagnant inside him! Oh, they've killed her, Sirs!
Can I be calm?

Calmly! Each incident
Proves, I maintain, that action of the flight
For the true thing it was. The first faint scratch

[1] Doubting St. Thomas was convinced, according to the legends of the church, when the Virgin on her ascent to Heaven let fall her girdle, which fell into his hands.

O' the stone will test its nature, teach its worth
To idiots who name Parian—coprolite.
After all, I shall give no glare—at best
Only display you certain scattered lights
Lamping the rush and roll of the abyss—
Nothing but here and there a fire-point pricks
Wavelet from wavelet: well!
For the first hour
We both were silent in the night, I know:
Sometimes I did not see nor understand.
Blackness engulphed me,—partial stupor, say—
Then I would break way, breathe through the surprise,
And be aware again, and see who sat
In the dark vest with the white face and hands.
I said to myself—"I have caught it, I conceive
The mind o' the mystery: 'tis the way they wake
And wait, two martyrs somewhere in a tomb
Each by each as their blessing was to die;
Some signal they are promised and expect,—
When to arise before the trumpet scares:
So, through the whole course of the world they wait
The last day, but so fearless and so safe!
No otherwise, in safety and not fear,
I lie, because she lies too by my side."
You know this is not love, Sirs,—it is faith,
The feeling that there's God, he reigns and rules
Out of this low world: that is all; no harm!
At times she drew a soft sigh—music seemed
Always to hover just above her lips,
Not settle,—break a silence music too.

In the determined morning, I first found
Her head erect, her face turned full to me,
Her soul intent on mine through two wide eyes.
I answered them. "You are saved hitherto.
We have passed Perugia,—gone round by the wood,
Not through, I seem to think,—and opposite
I know Assisi; this is holy ground."
Then she resumed. "How long since we both left
Arezzo?"—"Years—and certain hours beside."

It was at . . . ah, but I forget the names!
'Tis a mere post-house and a hovel or two,—
I left the carriage and got bread and wine
And brought it her.—"Does it detain to eat?"
"—They stay perforce, change horses,—therefore eat!
We lose no minute: we arrive, be sure!"
She said—I know not where—there's a great hill
Close over, and the stream has lost its bridge,
One fords it. She began—"I have heard say
Of some sick body that my mother knew,
'Twas no good sign when in a limb diseased
All the pain suddenly departs,—as if
The guardian angel discontinued pain
Because the hope of cure was gone at last:
The limb will not again exert itself,
It needs be pained no longer: so with me,
—My soul whence all the pain is past at once:
All pain must be to work some good in the end.
True, this I feel now, this may be that good,
Pain was because of,—otherwise, I fear!"

She said,—a long while later in the day,
When I had let the silence be,—abrupt—
"Have you a mother?"—"She died, I was born."
"A sister then?"—"No sister."—"Who was it—
What woman were you used to serve this way,
Be kind to, till I called you and you came?"
I did not like that word. Soon afterward—
"Tell me, are men unhappy, in some kind
Of mere unhappiness at being men,
As women suffer, being womanish?
Have you, now, some unhappiness, I mean,
Born of what may be man's strength overmuch,
To match the undue susceptibility,
The sense at every pore when hate is close?
It hurts us if a baby hides its face
Or child strikes at us punily, calls names
Or makes a mouth,—much more if stranger men
Laugh or frown,—just as that were much to bear!
Yet rocks split,—and the blow-ball does no more,
Quivers to feathery nothing at a touch;
And strength may have its drawback, weakness 'scapes."

Once she asked, "What is it that made you smile,
At the great gate with the eagles and the snakes,
Where the company entered, 'tis a long time since?"
"—Forgive—I think you would not understand:
Ah, but you ask me,—therefore, it was this.
That was a certain bishop's villa-gate,
I knew it by the eagles,—and at once
Remembered this same bishop was just he
People of old were wont to bid me please
If I would catch preferment: so, I smiled
Because an impulse came to me, a whim—
What if I prayed the prelate leave to speak,
Began upon him in his presence-hall
—'What, still at work so grey and obsolete?
Still rocheted and mitred more or less?
Don't you feel all that out of fashion now?
I find out when the day of things is done!' "

At eve we heard the *angelus:* she turned—
"I told you I can neither read nor write.
My life stopped with the play-time; I will learn,
If I begin to live again: but you—
Who are a priest—wherefore do you not read
The service at this hour? Read Gabriel's song,
The lesson, and then read the little prayer
To Raphael, proper for us travellers!" [1]
I did not like that, neither, but I read.

When we stopped at Foligno it was dark.
The people of the post came out with lights:
The driver said, "This time to-morrow, may
Saints only help, relays continue good,
Nor robbers hinder, we arrive at Rome."
I urged,—"Why tax your strength a second night?
Trust me, alight here and take brief repose!
We are out of harm's reach, past pursuit: go sleep
If but an hour! I keep watch, guard the while
Here in the doorway." But her whole face changed,
The misery grew again about her mouth,
The eyes burned up from faintness, like the fawn's
Tired to death in the thicket, when she feels
The probing spear o' the huntsman. "Oh, no stay!"
She cried, in the fawn's cry, "On to Rome, on, on—
Unless 'tis you who fear,—which cannot be!"

We did go on all night; but at its close
She was troubled, restless, moaned low, talked at whiles
To herself, her brow on quiver with the dream:
Once, wide awake, she menaced, at arms' length
Waved away something—"Never again with you!
My soul is mine, my body is my soul's:
You and I are divided ever more
In soul and body: get you gone!" Then I—
"Why, in my whole life I have never prayed!
Oh, if the God, that only can, would help!
Am I his priest with power to cast out fiends?
Let God arise and all his enemies
Be scattered!" By morn, there was peace, no sigh
Out of the deep sleep.

When she woke at last,
I answered the first look—"Scarce twelve hours more,
Then, Rome! There probably was no pursuit,
There cannot now be peril: bear up brave!
Just some twelve hours to press through to the prize:
Then, no more of the terrible journey!"
"Then,
No more o' the journey: if it might but last!
Always, my life-long, thus to journey still!
It is the interruption that I dread,—
With no dread, ever to be here and thus!
Never to see a face nor hear a voice!
Yours is no voice; you speak when you are dumb;
Nor face, I see it in the dark. I want

[1] The Archangel Raphael is the patron of travelers and the guardian of high and holy love. Just why Pompilia's request distressed Caponsacchi is not altogether clear. Oversensitive in his exalted state, he may have sensed a rebuke she did not intend. At a previous line (1234) he is hurt at her thought that he may have offered such noble service to another woman before her; now he seems negligent in his priestly duties. Caponsacchi, rapt above ritual, is not negligent, nor has he ever been capable of such devotion before. He is surprised at himself, and his hurt may spring from a sensitive (and unjustified) fear that even Pompilia does not understand how completely he has risen to meet the spiritual challenge.

No face nor voice that change and grow unkind."
That I liked, that was the best thing she said.

In the broad day, I dared entreat, "Descend!"
I told a woman, at the garden-gate
By the post-house, white and pleasant in the sun,
"It is my sister,—talk with her apart!
She is married and unhappy, you perceive;
I take her home because her head is hurt;
Comfort her as you women understand!"
So, there I left them by the garden-wall,
Paced the road, then bade put the horses to,
Came back, and there she sat: close to her knee,
A black-eyed child still held the bowl of milk,
Wondered to see how little she could drink,
And in her arms the woman's infant lay.
She smiled at me "How much good this has done!
This is a whole night's rest and how much more!
I can proceed now, though I wish to stay.
How do you call that tree with the thick top
That holds in all its leafy green and gold
The sun now like an immense egg of fire?"
(It was a million-leaved mimosa.) "Take
The babe away from me and let me go!"
And in the carriage, "Still a day, my friend;
And perhaps half a night, the woman fears.
I pray it finish since it cannot last.
There may be more misfortune at the close,
And where will you be? God suffice me then!"
And presently—for there was a roadside-shrine—
"When I was taken first to my own church
Lorenzo in Lucina, being a girl,
And bid confess my faults, I interposed,
'But teach me what fault to confess and know!'
So, the priest said—'You should bethink yourself:
Each human being needs must have done wrong!'
Now, be you candid and no priest but friend—
Were I surprised and killed here on the spot,
A runaway from husband and his home,
Do you account it were in sin I died?
My husband used to seem to harm me, not . . .
Not on pretence he punished sin of mine,
Nor for sin's sake and lust of cruelty,
But as I heard him bid a farming-man
At the villa take a lamb once to the wood
And there ill-treat it, meaning that the wolf
Should hear its cries, and so come, quick be caught,
Enticed to the trap: he practised thus with me
That so, whatever were his gain thereby,
Others than I might become prey and spoil.
Had it been only between our two selves,—
His pleasure and my pain,—why, pleasure him
By dying, nor such need to make a coil!
But this was worth an effort, that my pain
Should not become a snare, prove pain threefold
To other people—strangers—or unborn—
How should I know? I sought release from that—
I think, or else from,—dare I say, some cause
Such as is put into a tree, which turns
Away from the north wind with what nest it holds,—
The woman said that trees so turn: now, friend,
Tell me, because I cannot trust myself!
You are a man: what have I done amiss?"
You must conceive my answer,—I forget—
Taken up wholly with the thought, perhaps,
This time she might have said,—might, did not say—
"You are a priest." She said, "my friend."
Day wore,
We passed the places, somehow the calm went,
Again the restless eyes began to rove
In new fear of the foe mine could not see:
She wandered in her mind,—addressed me once
"Gaetano!"—that is not my name: whose name?[1]
I grew alarmed, my head seemed turning too:
I quickened pace with promise now, now threat:
Bade drive and drive, nor any stopping more.
"Too deep i' the thick of the struggle, struggle through!
Then drench her in repose though death's self pour
The plenitude of quiet,—help us, God,
Whom the winds carry!"

[1] Distressing this was to Caponsacchi. From Pompilia's story we learn that it was the name she intended to give to her unborn child—which she hoped and expected would be a boy.

Suddenly I saw
The old tower, and the little white-walled clump
Of buildings and the cypress-tree or two,—
"Already Castelnuovo—Rome!" I cried,
"As good as Rome,—Rome is the next stage, think!
This is where travellers' hearts are wont to beat.
Say you are saved, sweet lady!" Up she woke.
The sky was fierce with colour from the sun
Setting. She screamed out "No, I must not die!
Take me no farther, I should die: stay here!
I have more life to save than mine!"
She swooned.
We seemed safe: what was it foreboded so?
Out of the coach into the inn I bore
The motionless and breathless pure and pale
Pompilia,—bore her through a pitying group
And laid her on a couch, still calm and cured
By deep sleep of all woes at once. The host
Was urgent "Let her stay an hour or two!
Leave her to us, all will be right by morn!"
Oh, my foreboding! But I could not choose.

I paced the passage, kept watch all night long.
I listened,—not one movement, not one sigh.
"Fear not: she sleeps so sound!" they said—but I
Feared, all the same, kept fearing more and more,
Found myself throb with fear from head to foot,
Filled with a sense of such impending woe,
That, at first pause of night, pretence of grey,
I made my mind up it was morn.—"Reach Rome,
Lest hell reach her! A dozen miles to make,
Another long breath, and we emerge!" I stood
I' the court-yard, roused the sleepy grooms.
"Have out
Carriage and horse, give haste, take gold!" said I.
While they made ready in the doubtful morn,—
'Twas the last minute,—needs must I ascend
And break her sleep; I turned to go.
And there
Faced me Count Guido, there posed the mean man
As master,—took the field, encamped his rights,
Challenged the world: there leered new triumph, there
Scowled the old malice in the visage bad
And black o' the scamp. Soon triumph suppled the tongue
A little, malice glued to his dry throat,
And he part howled, part hissed . . . oh, how he kept
Well out o' the way, at arm's length and to spare!—
"My salutation to your priestship! What?
Matutinal, busy with book so soon
Of an April day that's damp as tears that now
Deluge Arezzo at its darling's flight?—
'Tis unfair, wrongs feminity at large,
To let a single dame monopolize
A heart the whole sex claims, should share alike:
Therefore I overtake you, Canon! Come!
The lady,—could you leave her side so soon?
You have not yet experienced at her hands
My treatment, you lay down undrugged, I see!
Hence this alertness—hence no death-in-life
Like what held arms fast when she stole from mine.
To be sure, you took the solace and repose
That first night at Foligno!—news abound
O' the road by this time,—men regaled me much,
As past them I came halting after you,
Vulcan pursuing Mars, as poets sing,—[1]
Still at the last here pant I, but arrive,
Vulcan—and not without my Cyclops too,
The Commissary and the unpoisoned arm
O' the Civil Force, should Mars turn mutineer.
Enough of fooling: capture the culprits, friend!
Here is the lover in the smart disguise
With the sword,—he is a priest, so mine lies still:
There upstairs hides my wife the runaway,
His leman: the two plotted, poisoned first,
Plundered me after, and eloped thus far
Where now you find them. Do your duty quick!

[1] According to Greek mythology the jealous Vulcan, a deformed and ugly god, on one occasion trapped Venus in a net, along with Mars, the handsome young god of war.

Arrest and hold him! That's done: now catch her!"
During this speech of that man,—well, I stood
Away, as he managed,—still, I stood as near
The throat of him,—with these two hands, my own,—
As now I stand near yours, Sir,—one quick spring,
One great good satisfying gripe, and lo!
There had he lain abolished with his lie,
Creation purged o' the miscreate, man redeemed,
A spittle wiped off from the face of God!
I, in some measure, seek a poor excuse
For what I left undone, in just this fact
That my first feeling at the speech I quote
Was—not of what a blasphemy was dared,
Not what a bag of venomed purulence
Was split and noisome,—but how splendidly
Mirthful, how ludicrous a lie was launched!
Would Molière's self wish more than hear such man
Call, claim such woman for his own, his wife,
Even though, in due amazement at the boast,
He had stammered, she moreover was divine?
She to be his,—were hardly less absurd
Than that he took her name into his mouth,
Licked, and then let it go again, the beast,
Signed with his slaver. Oh, she poisoned him,
Plundered him, and the rest! Well, what I wished
Was, that he would but go on, say once more
So to the world, and get his meed of men,
The fist's reply to the filth. And while I mused,
The minute, oh the misery, was gone!
On either idle hand of me there stood
Really an officer, nor laughed i' the least:
Nay, rendered justice to his reason, laid
Logic to heart, as 'twere submitted them
"Twice two makes four."
"And now, catch her!" he cried.
That sobered me. "Let myself lead the way—
Ere you arrest me, who am somebody,
Being, as you hear, a priest and privileged,—
To the lady's chamber! I presume you—men
Expert, instructed how to find out truth,
Familiar with the guise of guilt. Detect
Guilt on her face when it meets mine, then judge
Between us and the mad dog howling there!"
Up we all went together, in they broke
O' the chamber late my chapel. There she lay,
Composed as when I laid her, that last eve,
O' the couch, still breathless, motionless, sleep's self,
Wax-white, seraphic, saturate with the sun
O' the morning that now flooded from the front
And filled the window with a light like blood.
"Behold the poisoner, the adulteress,
—And feigning sleep too! Seize, bind!" Guido hissed.

She started up, stood erect, face to face
With the husband: back he fell, was buttressed there
By the window all aflame with morning-red,
He the black figure, the opprobrious blur
Against all peace and joy and light and life.
"Away from between me and hell!" she cried:
"Hell for me, no embracing any more!
I am God's, I love God, God—whose knees I clasp,
Whose utterly most just award I take,
But bear no more love-making devils: hence!"
I may have made an effort to reach her side
From where I stood i' the door-way,—anyhow
I found the arms, I wanted, pinioned fast,
Was powerless in the clutch to left and right
O' the rabble pouring in, rascality
Enlisted, rampant on the side of hearth,
Home, and the husband,—pay in prospect too!
They heaped themselves upon me. "Ha!—and him
Also you outrage? Him, too, my sole friend,
Guardian, and saviour? That I baulk you of,
Since—see how God can help at last and worst!"
She sprang at the sword that hung beside him, seized,
Drew, brandished it, the sunrise burned for joy
O' the blade, "Die," cried she, "devil, in God's name!"
Ah, but they all closed round her, twelve to one,
—The unmanly men, no woman-mother made,

Spawned somehow! Dead-white and disarmed she lay.
No matter for the sword, her word sufficed
To spike the coward through and through: he shook,
Could only spit between the teeth—“You see?
You hear? Bear witness, then! Write down . . . but no—
Carry these criminals to the prison-house,
For first thing! I begin my search meanwhile
After the stolen effects, gold, jewels, plate,
Money, and clothes, they robbed me of and fled:
With no few amorous pieces, verse and prose,
I have much reason to expect to find.”

When I saw that—no more than the first mad speech,
Made out the speaker mad and a laughing-stock,
So neither did this next device explode
One listener's indignation,—that a scribe
Did sit down; set himself to write indeed,
While sundry knaves began to peer and pry
In corner and hole,—that Guido, wiping brow
And getting him a countenance, was fast
Losing his fear, beginning to strut free
O' the stage of his exploit, snuff here, sniff there,—
I took the truth in, guessed sufficiently
The service for the moment. “What I say,
Slight at your peril! We are aliens here,
My adversary and I, called noble both;
I am the nobler, and a name men know.
I could refer our cause to our own court
In our own country, but prefer appeal
To the nearer jurisdiction. Being a priest,
Though in a secular garb,—for reasons good
I shall adduce in due time to my peers,—
I demand that the Church I serve, decide
Between us, right the slandered lady there.
A Tuscan noble, I might claim the Duke:
A priest, I rather choose the Church,—bid Rome
Cover the wronged with her inviolate shield.”

There was no refusing this: they bore me off,
They bore her off, to separate cells o' the same
Ignoble prison, and, separate, thence to Rome.
Pompilia's face, then and thus, looked on me
The last time in this life: not one sight since,
Never another sight to be! And yet
I thought I had saved her. I appealed to Rome:
It seems I simply sent her to her death.
You tell me she is dying now, or dead;
I cannot bring myself to quite believe
This is a place you torture people in:
What if this your intelligence were just
A subtlety, an honest wile to work
On a man at unawares? 'Twere worthy you.
No, Sirs, I cannot have the lady dead!
That erect form, flashing brow, fulgurant eye,
That voice immortal (oh, that voice of hers!)
That vision in the blood-red day-break—that
Leap to life of the pale electric sword
Angels go armed with,—that was not the last
O' the lady! Come, I see through it, you find—
Know the manœuvre! Also herself said
I had saved her: do you dare say she spoke false?
Let me see for myself if it be so!
Though she were dying, a priest might be of use,
The more when he's a friend too,—she called me
Far beyond “friend.” Come, let me see her—indeed
It is my duty, being a priest: I hope
I stand confessed, established, proved a priest?
My punishment had motive that, a priest
I, in a laic garb, a mundane mode,
Did what were harmlessly done otherwise.
I never touched her with my finger-tip
Except to carry her to the couch, that eve,
Against my heart, beneath my head, bowed low,
As we priests carry the paten: that is why
—To get leave and go see her of your grace—
I have told you this whole story over again.
Do I deserve grace? For I might lock lips,
Laugh at your jurisdiction: what have you
To do with me in the matter? I suppose
You hardly think I donned a bravo's dress
To have a hand in the new crime; on the old,
Judgment's delivered, penalty imposed,
I was chained fast at Civita hand and foot—
She had only you to trust to, you and Rome,
Rome and the Church, and no pert meddling priest
Two days ago, when Guido, with the right,
Hacked her to pieces. One might well be wroth;

I have been patient, done my best to help:
I come from Civita and punishment
As a friend of the court—and for pure friendship's sake
Have told my tale to the end,—nay, not the end—
For, wait—I'll end—not leave you that excuse!

When we were parted,—shall I go on there?
I was presently brought to Rome—yes, here I stood
Opposite yonder very crucifix—
And there sat you and you, Sirs, quite the same,
I heard charge, and bore question, and told tale
Noted down in the book there,—turn and see
If, by one jot or tittle, I vary now!
I' the colour the tale takes, there's change perhaps;
'Tis natural, since the sky is different,
Eclipse in the air now; still, the outline stays.
I showed you how it came to be my part
To save the lady. Then your clerk produced
Papers, a pack of stupid and impure
Banalities called letters about love—
Love, indeed,—I could teach who styled them so,
Better, I think, though priest and loveless both!
"—How was it that a wife, young, innocent,
And stranger to your person, wrote this page?"—
"—She wrote it when the Holy Father wrote
The bestiality that posts thro' Rome,
Put in his mouth by Pasquin." [1]—"Nor perhaps
Did you return these answers, verse, and prose,
Signed, sealed and sent the lady? There's your hand!"
"—This precious piece of verse, I really judge
Is meant to copy my own character,
A clumsy mimic; and this other prose,
Not so much even; both rank forgery:
Verse, quotha? Bembo's verse! When Saint John wrote
The tract *De Tribus*, [1] I wrote this to match."
"—How came it, then, the documents were found
At the inn on your departure?"—"I opine,
Because there were no documents to find
In my presence,—you must hide before you find.
Who forged them hardly practised in my view;
Who found them waited till I turned my back."
"—And what of the clandestine visits paid,
Nocturnal passage in and out the house
With its lord absent? 'Tis alleged you climbed . . ."
"—Flew on a broomstick to the man i' the moon!
Who witnessed or will testify this trash?"
"—The trusty servant, Margherita's self,
Even she who brought you letters, you confess,
And, you confess, took letters in reply:
Forget not we have knowledge of the facts!"
"—Sirs, who have knowledge of the facts, defray
The expenditure of wit I waste in vain,
Trying to find out just one fact of all!
She who brought letters from who could not write,
And took back letters to who could not read,—
Who was that messenger, of your charity?"
"—Well, so far favours you the circumstance
That this same messenger . . . how shall we say? . . .
Sub imputatione meretricis
Laborat, [2]—which makes accusation null:
We waive this woman's:—nought makes void the next.
Borsi, called Venerino, he who drove,
O' the first night when you fled away, at length

[1] Opposite the shop of a shoemaker, named Pasquino, there was a statue on which it was the custom to post satirical and sometimes licentious verses and bulletins. The true author, of course, never signed his name.

[1] *De Tribus Impostoribus*—A tract which probably never existed, but was for a long time supposed to have existed in secret. Caponsacchi's point is: "If St. John the Divine wrote a tract calling Christ an impostor, then I wrote these letters to a light-o'-love; otherwise the whole story is a lie."

[2] "Labors under the imputation of unchastity." The polite Latin description of the character of the messenger in its restraint more completely disposes of the value of the witness than more emphatic language would have done.

Deposes to your kissings in the coach,
—Frequent, frenetic . . ." "When deposed he so?"
"After some weeks of sharp imprisonment . . ."
"—Granted by friend the Governor, I engage—"
"—For his participation in your flight!
At length his obduracy melting made
The avowal mentioned . . ." "Was dismissed forthwith
To liberty, poor knave, for recompense.
Sirs, give what credit to the lie you can!
For me, no word in my defence I speak,
And God shall argue for the lady!"
So
Did I stand question, and make answer, still
With the same result of smiling disbelief,
Polite impossibility of faith
In such affected virtue in a priest;
But a showing fair play, an indulgence, even,
To one no worse than others after all—
Who had not brought disgrace to the order, played
Discreetly, ruffled gown nor ripped the cloth
In a bungling game at romps: I have told you, Sirs—
If I pretended simply to be pure,
Honest and Christian in the case,—absurd!
As well go boast myself above the needs
O' the human nature, careless how meat smells,
Wine tastes,—a saint above the smack! But once
Abate my crest, own flaws i' the flesh, agree
To go with the herd, be hog no more nor less,
Why, hogs in common herd have common rights:
I must not be unduly borne upon,
Who had just romanced a little, sown wild oats,
But 'scaped without a scandal, flagrant fault.
My name helped to a mirthful circumstance:
"Joseph" [1] would do well to amend his plea:
Undoubtedly—some toying with the wife,
But as for ruffian violence and rape,
Potiphar pressed too much on the other side!
The intrigue, the elopement, the disguise,—well charged!

[1] The story of Joseph and Potiphar's wife is told in Genesis 39.

The letters and verse looked hardly like the truth.
Your apprehension was—of guilt enough
To be compatible with innocence,
So, punished best a little and not too much.
Had I struck Guido Franceschini's face,
You had counselled me withdraw for my own sake,
Baulk him of bravo-hiring. Friends came round,
Congratulated, "Nobody mistakes!
The pettiness o' the forfeiture defines
The peccadillo: Guido gets his share:
His wife is free of husband and hook-nose,
The mouldy viands and the mother-in-law.
To Civita with you and amuse the time,
Travesty us *De Raptu Helenæ!* [1]
A funny figure must the husband cut
When the wife makes him skip,—too ticklish, eh?
Do it in Latin, not the Vulgar, then!
Scazons—we'll copy and send his Eminence.
Mind—one iambus in the final foot!
He'll rectify it, be your friend for life!"
Oh, Sirs, depend on me for much new light
Thrown on the justice and religion here
By this proceeding, much fresh food for thought!

And I was just set down to study these
In relegation, two short days ago,
Admiring how you read the rules, when, clap,
A thunder comes into my solitude—
I am caught up in a whirlwind and cast here,
Told of a sudden, in this room where so late
You dealt out law adroitly, that those scales,
I meekly bowed to, took my allotment from,
Guido has snatched at, broken in your hands,
Metes to himself the murder of his wife,
Full measure, pressed down, running over now!

[1] "The carrying-off of Helen" by Paris—the elopement which provoked the Trojan war recorded in Homer's *Iliad.* Caponsacchi had been passionately earnest and true throughout his conduct of the affair. His friends in congratulating him on his escape from a serious criminal adultery case had seen only the opportunity for him in his temporary exile to write an amusing social skit on the elopement which provoked an epic war. Events had forced upon all men a full consciousness of the tragic seriousness of the case. Only Caponsacchi was conscious of the tragic irony of it.

Can I assist to an explanation?—Yes,
I rise in your esteem, sagacious Sirs,
Stand up a renderer of reasons, not
The officious priest would personate Saint George
For a mock Princess in undragoned days.
What, the blood startles you? What, after all
The priest who needs must carry sword on thigh
May find imperative use for it? Then, there was
A princess, was a dragon belching flame,
And should have been a Saint George also? Then,
There might be worse schemes than to break the bonds
At Arezzo, lead her by the little hand,
Till she reached Rome, and let her try to live?
But you were law and gospel,—would one please
Stand back, allow your faculty elbow-room?
You blind guides who must needs lead eyes that see!
Fools, alike ignorant of man and God!
What was there here should have perplexed your wit
For a wink of the owl-eyes of you? How miss, then,
What's now forced on you by this flare of fact—
As if Saint Peter failed to recognise
Nero as no apostle, John or James,
Till someone burned a martyr, made a torch
O' the blood and fat to show his features by!
Could you fail read this cartulary aright
On head and front of Franceschini there,
Large-lettered like hell's masterpiece of print,—
That he, from the beginning pricked at heart
By some lust, letch of hate against his wife,
Plotted to plague her into overt sin
And shame, would slay Pompilia body and soul,
And save his mean self—miserably caught
I' the quagmire of his own tricks, cheats, and lies?
—That himself wrote those papers,—from himself
To himself,—which, i' the name of me and her,
His mistress-messenger gave her and me,
Touching us with such pustules of the soul
That she and I might take the taint, be shown
To the world and shuddered over, speckled so?
—That the agent put her sense into my words,
Made substitution of the thing she hoped,
For the thing she had and held, its opposite,
While the husband in the background bit his lips
At each fresh failure of his precious plot?
—That when at the last we did rush each on each,
By no chance but because God willed it so—
The spark of truth was struck from out our souls—
Made all of me, descried in the first glance,
Seem fair and honest and permissible love
O' the good and true—as the first glance told me
There was no duty patent in the world
Like daring try be good and true myself,
Leaving the shows of things to the Lord of Show
And prince o' the Power of the Air. Our very flight,
Even to its most ambiguous circumstance,
Irrefragably proved how futile, false . . .
Why, men—men and not boys—boys and not babes—
Babes and not beasts—beasts and not stocks and stones!—
Had the liar's lie been true one pin-point speck,
Were I the accepted suitor, free o' the place,
Disposer of the time, to come at a call
And go at a wink as who should say me nay,—
What need of flight, what were the gain therefrom
But just damnation, failure or success?
Damnation pure and simple to her the wife
And me the priest—who bartered private bliss
For public reprobation, the safe shade
For the sunshine which men see to pelt me by:
What other advantage—we who led the days
And nights alone i' the house—was flight to find?
In our whole journey did we stop an hour,
Diverge a foot from strait road till we reached
Or would have reached—but for that fate of ours—
The father and mother, in the eye of Rome,

The eye of yourselves we made aware of us
At the first fall of misfortune? And indeed
You did so far give sanction to our flight,
Confirm its purpose, as lend helping hand,
Deliver up Pompilia not to him
She fled, but those the flight was ventured for.
Why then could you, who stopped short, not go on
One poor step more, and justify the means,
Having allowed the end?—not see and say,
"Here's the exceptional conduct that should claim
To be exceptionally judged on rules
Which, understood, make no exception here"—
Why play instead into the devil's hands
By dealing so ambiguously as gave
Guido the power to intervene like me,
Prove one exception more? I saved his wife
Against law: against law he slays her now:
Deal with him!

I have done with being judged.
I stand here guiltless in thought, word and deed,
To the point that I apprise you,—in contempt
For all misapprehending ignorance
O' the human heart, much more the mind of Christ,—
That I assuredly did bow, was blessed
By the revelation of Pompilia. There!
Such is the final fact I fling you, Sirs,
To mouth and mumble and misinterpret: there!
"The priest's in love," have it the vulgar way!
Unpriest me, rend the rags o' the vestment, do—
Degrade deep, disenfranchise all you dare—
Remove me from the midst, no longer priest
And fit companion for the like of you—
Your gay Abati with the well-turned leg
And rose i' the hat-rim, Canons, cross at neck
And silk mask in the pocket of the gown,
Brisk bishops with the world's musk still unbrushed
From the rochet; I'll no more of these good things:
There's a crack somewhere, something that's unsound
I' the rattle!

For Pompilia—be advised,
Build churches, go pray! You will find me there,
I know, if you come,—and you will come, I know.
Why, there's a Judge weeping! Did not I say
You were good and true at bottom? You see the truth—
I am glad I helped you: she helped me just so.

But for Count Guido,—you must counsel there!
I bow my head, bend to the very dust,
Break myself up in shame of faultiness.
I had him one whole moment, as I said—
As I remember, as will never out
O' the thoughts of me,—I had him in arm's reach
There,—as you stand, Sir, now you cease to sit,—
I could have killed him ere he killed his wife,
And did not: he went off alive and well
And then effected this last feat—through me!
Me—not through you—dismiss that fear! 'Twas you
Hindered me staying here to save her,—not
From leaving you and going back to him
And doing service in Arezzo. Come,
Instruct me in procedure! I conceive—
In all due self-abasement might I speak—
How you will deal with Guido: oh, not death!
Death, if it let her life be: otherwise
Not death,—your lights will teach you clearer! I
Certainly have an instinct of my own
I' the matter: bear with me and weigh its worth!
Let us go away—leave Guido all alone
Back on the world again that knows him now!
I think he will be found (indulge so far!)
Not to die so much as slide out of life,
Pushed by the general horror and common hate
Low, lower,—left o' the very ledge of things,
I seem to see him catch convulsively
One by one at all honest forms of life,
At reason, order, decency, and use—
To cramp him and get foothold by at least;
And still they disengage them from his clutch.
"What, you are he, then, had Pompilia once
And so forwent her? Take not up with us!"

And thus I see him slowly and surely edged
Off all the table-land whence life upsprings
Aspiring to be immortality,
As the snake, hatched on hill-top by mischance,
Despite his wriggling, slips, slides, slidders down
Hill-side, lies low and prostrate on the smooth
Level of the outer place, lapsed in the vale:
So I lose Guido in the loneliness,
Silence and dusk, till at the doleful end,
At the horizontal line, creation's verge,
From what just is to absolute nothingness—
Whom is it, straining onward still, he meets?
What other man deep further in the fate,
Who, turning at the prize of a footfall
To flatter him and promise fellowship,
Discovers in the act a frightful face—
Judas, made monstrous by much solitude!
The two are at one now! Let them love their love
That bites and claws like hate, or hate their hate
That mops and mows and makes as it were love!
There, let them each tear each in devil's-fun,
Or fondle this the other while malice aches—
Both teach, both learn detestability!
Kiss him the kiss, Iscariot! Pay that back,
That smatch o' the slaver blistering on your lip—
By the better trick, the insult he spared Christ—
Lure him the lure o' the letters, Aretine!
Lick him o'er the slimy-smooth with jelly-filth
O' the verse-and-prose pollution in love's guise!
The cockatrice is with the basilisk!
There let them grapple, denizens o' the dark,
Foes or friends, but indissolubly bound,
In their one spot out of the ken of God
Or care of man, for ever and ever more!

Why, Sirs, what's this? Why, this is sorry and strange!
Futility, divagation: this from me
Bound to be rational, justify an act
Of sober man!—whereas, being moved so much,
I give you cause to doubt the lady's mind:
A pretty sarcasm for the world! I fear
You do her wit injustice,—all through me!
Like my fate all through,—ineffective help!
A poor rash advocate I prove myself.
You might be angry with good cause: but sure
At the advocate,—only at the undue zeal
That spoils the force of his own plea, I think?
My part was just to tell you how things stand,
State facts and not be flustered at their fume.
But then 'tis a priest speaks: as for love,—no!
If you let buzz a vulgar fly like that
About your brains, as if I loved, forsooth,
Indeed, Sirs, you do wrong! We had no thought
Of such infatuation, she and I:
There are many points that prove it: do be just!
I told you,—at one little roadside-place
I spent a good half-hour, paced to and fro
The garden; just to leave her free awhile,
I plucked a handful of Spring herb and bloom:
I might have sat beside her on the bench
Where the children were: I wish the thing had been,
Indeed: the event could not be worse, you know:
One more half-hour of her saved! She's dead now, Sirs!
While I was running on at such a rate,
Friends should have plucked me by the sleeve: I went
Too much o' the trivial outside of her face
And the purity that shone there—plain to me,
Not to you, what more natural? Nor am I
Infatuated,—oh, I saw, be sure!
Her brow had not the right line, leaned too much,
Painters would say; they like the straight-up Greek:
This seemed bent somewhat with an invisible crown
Of martyr and saint, not such as art approves.
And how the dark orbs dwelt deep underneath,
Looked out of such a sad sweet heaven on me!
The lips, compressed a little, came forward too,
Careful for a whole world of sin and pain.
That was the face, her husband makes his plea,
He sought just to disfigure,—no offence

Beyond that! Sirs, let us be rational!
He needs must vindicate his honour,—ay,
Yet shirks, the coward, in a clown's disguise,
Away from the scene, endeavours to escape.
Now, had he done so, slain and left no trace
O' the slayer,—what were vindicated, pray?
You had found his wife disfigured or a corpse,
For what and by whom? It is too palpable!
Then, here's another point involving law:
I use this argument to show you meant
No calumny against us by that title
O' the sentence,—liars try to twist it so:
What penalty it bore, I had to pay
Till further proof should follow of innocence—
Probationis ob defectum, [1]—proof?
How could you get proof without trying us?
You went through the preliminary form,
Stopped there, contrived this sentence to amuse
The adversary. If the title ran
For more than fault imputed and not proved,
That was a simple penman's error, else
A slip i' the phrase,—as when we say of you
"Charged with injustice"—which may either be
Or not be,—'tis a name that sticks meanwhile.
Another relevant matter: fool that I am!
Not what I wish true, yet a point friends urge:
It is not true,—yet, since friends think it helps,—
She only tried me when some others failed—
Began with Conti, whom I told you of,
And Guillichini, Guido's kinsfolk both,
And when abandoned by them, not before,
Turned to me. That's conclusive why she turned.
Much good they got by the happy cowardice!
Conti is dead, poisoned a month ago:
Does that much strike you as a sin? Not much,
After the present murder,—one mark more
On the Moor's skin,—what is black by blacker still?
Conti had come here and told truth. And so
With Guillichini; he's condemned of course
To the galleys, as a friend in this affair,
Tried and condemned for no one thing i' the world,
A fortnight since by who but the Governor?—
The just judge, who refused Pompilia help
At first blush, being her husband's friend, you know.
There are two tales to suit the separate courts,
Arezzo and Rome: he tells you here, we fled
Alone, unhelped,—lays stress on the main fault,
The spiritual sin, Rome looks to: but elsewhere
He likes best we should break in, steal, bear off,
Be fit to brand and pillory and flog—
That's the charge goes to the heart of the Governor:
If these unpriest me, you and I may yet
Converse, Vincenzo Marzi-Medici! [1]
Oh, Sirs, there are worse men than you, I say!
More easily duped, I mean; this stupid lie,
Its liar never dared propound in Rome,
He gets Arezzo to receive,—nay more,
Gets Florence and the Duke to authorize!
This is their Rota's sentence, their Granduke
Signs and seals! Rome for me henceforward—Rome,
Where better men are,—most of all, that man
The Augustinian of the Hospital,
Who writes the letter,—he confessed, he says,
Many a dying person, never one
So sweet and true and pure and beautiful.
A good man! Will you make him Pope one day?
Not that he is not good too, this we have—
But old,—else he would have his word to speak,
His truth to teach the world: I thirst for truth,
But shall not drink it till I reach the source.

Sirs, I am quiet again. You see, we are
So very pitiable, she and I,
Who had conceivably been otherwise.
Forget distemperature and idle heat!
Apart from truth's sake, what's to move so much?
Pompilia will be presently with God;
I am, on earth, as good as out of it,
A relegated priest; when exile ends,
I mean to do my duty and live long.
She and I are mere strangers now: but priests

[1] "For want of sufficient proof."

[1] The Governor of Arezzo. The implication is that as a priest Caponsacchi is bound; if adjudged unworthy of the priesthood, he will return to the standards of the world and his first act will be a "conversation"—leading to a duel.

Should study passion; how else cure mankind,
Who come for help in passionate extremes?
I do but play with an imagined life
Of who, unfettered by a vow, unblessed
By the higher call,—since you will have it so,—
Leads it companioned by the woman there.
To live, and see her learn, and learn by her,
Out of the low obscure and petty world—
Or only see one purpose and one will
Evolve themselves i' the world, change wrong to right:
To have to do with nothing but the true,
The good, the eternal—and these, not alone
In the main current of the general life,
But small experiences of every day,
Concerns of the particular hearth and home:
To learn not only by a comet's rush
But a rose's birth,—not by the grandeur, God,—
But the comfort, Christ. All this, how far away!
Mere delectation, meet for a minute's dream!—
Just as a drudging student trims his lamp,
Opens his Plutarch, puts him in the place
Of Roman, Grecian; draws the patched gown close,
Dreams, "Thus should I fight, save or rule the world!"—
Then smilingly, contentedly, awakes
To the old solitary nothingness.
So I, from such communion, pass content. . . .

O great, just, good God! Miserable me!

VII. POMPILIA [1]

I AM just seventeen years and five months old,
And, if I lived one day more, three full weeks;
'Tis writ so in the church's register,
Lorenzo in Lucina, all my names
At length, so many names for one poor child,
—Francesca Camilla Vittoria Angela
Pompilia Comparini,—laughable!
Also 'tis writ that I was married there
Four years ago; and they will add, I hope,
When they insert my death, a word or two,—
Omitting all about the mode of death,—
This, in its place, this which one cares to know,
That I had been a mother of a son
Exactly two weeks. It will be through grace
O' the Curate, not through any claim I have;
Because the boy was born at, so baptized
Close to, the Villa, in the proper church:
A pretty church, I say no word against,
Yet stranger-like,[1]—while this Lorenzo seems
My own particular place, I always say.
I used to wonder, when I stood scarce high
As the bed here, what the marble lion meant,
With half his body rushing from the wall,
Eating the figure of a prostrate man—
(To the right, it is, of entry by the door)—
An ominous sign to one baptized like me,
Married, and to be buried there, I hope.
And they should add, to have my life complete,
He is a boy and Gaetan by name—
Gaetano, for a reason,—if the friar
Don Celestine will ask this grace for me
Of Curate Ottoboni: he it was
Baptized me: he remembers my whole life
As I do his grey hair.

All these few things
I know are true,—will you remember them?
Because time flies. The surgeon cared for me,
To count my wounds,—twenty-two dagger-wounds,
Five deadly, but I do not suffer much—
Or too much pain,—and am to die to-night.

Oh how good God is that my babe was born,
—Better than born, baptized and hid away
Before this happened, safe from being hurt!
That had been sin God could not well forgive:
He was too young to smile and save himself.
When they took, two days after he was born,
My babe away from me to be baptized
And hidden awhile, for fear his foe should find,—
The country-woman, used to nursing babes,
Said "Why take on so? where is the great loss?
These next three weeks he will but sleep and feed,
Only begin to smile at the month's end;

[1] Pompilia, who lived for four days after the assault, is speaking from what was her death-bed in a hospital cell.

[1] Pompilia's child had been born in a different parish from that in which she had been baptized.

He would not know you, if you kept him here,
Sooner than that; so, spend three merry weeks
Snug in the Villa, getting strong and stout,
And then I bring him back to be your own,
And both of you may steal to—we know where!"
The month—there wants of it two weeks this day!
Still, I half fancied when I heard the knock
At the Villa in the dusk, it might prove she—
Come to say, "Since he smiles before the time,
Why should I cheat you out of one good hour?
Back I have brought him; speak to him and judge!"
Now I shall never see him; what is worse,
When he grows up and gets to be my age,
He will seem hardly more than a great boy;
And if he asks, "What was my mother like?"
People may answer, "Like girls of seventeen"—
And how can he but think of this and that,
Lucias, Marias, Sofias, who titter or blush
When he regards them as such boys may do?
Therefore I wish some one will please to say
I looked already old though I was young;
Do I not . . . say, if you are by to speak . . .
Look nearer twenty? No more like, at least,
Girls who look arch or redden when boys laugh,
Than the poor Virgin that I used to know
At our street-corner in a lonely niche,—[1]
The babe, that sat upon her knees, broke off,—
Thin white glazed clay, you pitied her the more:
She, not the gay ones, always got my rose.

How happy those are who know how to write!
Such could write what their son should read in time,
Had they a whole day to live out like me.
Also my name is not a common name,
"Pompilia," and may help to keep apart
A little the thing I am from what girls are.
But then how far away, how hard to find
Will anything about me have become,
Even if the boy bethink himself and ask!

[1] In Italian cities there are many little shrines to the Virgin embedded in the walls of houses, particularly at street corners.

No father that he ever knew at all,
Nor ever had—no, never had, I say!
That is the truth,—nor any mother left,
Out of the little two weeks that she lived,
Fit for such memory as might assist:
As good too as no family, no name,
Not even poor old Pietro's name, nor hers,
Poor kind unwise Violante, since it seems
They must not be my parents any more.
That is why something put it in my head
To call the boy "Gaetano"—no old name
For sorrow's sake; I looked up to the sky
And took a new saint to begin anew.
One who has only been made saint—how long?
Twenty-five years: so, carefuller, perhaps,
To guard a namesake than those old saints grow,
Tired out by this time,—see my own five saints!

On second thoughts, I hope he will regard
The history of me as what someone dreamed,
And get to disbelieve it at the last:
Since to myself it dwindles fast to that,
Sheer dreaming and impossibility,—
Just in four days too! All the seventeen years,
Not once did a suspicion visit me
How very different a lot is mine
From any other woman's in the world.
The reason must be, 'twas by step and step
It got to grow so terrible and strange:
These strange woes stole on tiptoe, as it were,
Into my neighbourhood and privacy,
Sat down where I sat, laid them where I lay;
And I was found familiarised with fear,
When friends broke in, held up a torch and cried
"Why, you Pompilia in the cavern thus,
How comes that arm of yours about a wolf?
And the soft length,—lies in and out your feet
And laps you round the knee,—a snake it is!"
And so on.

Well, and they are right enough,
By the torch they hold up now: for first, observe,
I never had a father,—no, nor yet
A mother: my own boy can say at least
"I had a mother whom I kept two weeks!"
Not I, who little used to doubt . . . *I* doubt
Good Pietro, kind Violante, gave me birth?

They loved me always as I love my babe
(—Nearly so, that is—quite so could not be—)
Did for me all I meant to do for him,
Till one surprising day, three years ago,
They both declared, at Rome, before some judge
In some court where the people flocked to hear,
That really I had never been their child,
Was a mere castaway, the careless crime
Of an unknown man, the crime and care too much
Of a woman known too well,—little to these,
Therefore, of whom I was the flesh and blood:
What then to Pietro and Violante, both
No more my relatives than you or you?
Nothing to them! You know what they declared.

So with my husband,—just such a surprise,
Such a mistake, in that relationship!
Everyone says that husbands love their wives,
Guard them and guide them, give them happiness;
'Tis duty, law, pleasure, religion: well,
You see how much of this comes true in mine!
People indeed would fain have somehow proved
He was no husband: but he did not hear,
Or would not wait, and so has killed us all.
Then there is . . . only let me name one more!
There is the friend,—men will not ask about,
But tell untruths of, and give nicknames to,
And think my lover, most surprise of all!
Do only hear, it is the priest they mean,
Giuseppe Caponsacchi: a priest—love,
And love me! Well, yet people think he did.
I am married, he has taken priestly vows,
They know that, and yet go on, say, the same,
"Yes, how he loves you!" "That was love"—they say,
When anything is answered that they ask:
Or else "No wonder you love him"—they say.
Then they shake heads, pity much, scarcely blame—
As if we neither of us lacked excuse,
And anyhow are punished to the full,
And downright love atones for everything!
Nay, I heard read out in the public court
Before the judge, in presence of my friends,
Letters 'twas said the priest had sent to me,
And other letters sent him by myself,
We being lovers!

Listen what this is like!
When I was a mere child, my mother . . . that's
Violante, you must let me call her so
Nor waste time, trying to unlearn the word, . . .
She brought a neighbour's child of my own age
To play with me of rainy afternoons;
And, since there hung a tapestry on the wall,
We two agreed to find each other out
Among the figures. "Tisbe, that is you,
With half-moon on your hair-knot, spear in hand,
Flying, but no wings, only the great scarf
Blown to a bluish rainbow at your back:
Call off your hound and leave the stag alone!"
"—And there are you, Pompilia, such green leaves
Flourishing out of your five finger-ends,
And all the rest of you so brown and rough:
Why is it you are turned a sort of tree?"
You know the figures never were ourselves
Though we nicknamed them so. Thus, all my life,—
As well what was, as what, like this, was not,—
Looks old, fantastic and impossible:[1]
I touch a fairy thing that fades and fades.
—Even to my babe! I thought, when he was born,
Something began for once that would not end,
Nor change into a laugh at me, but stay
For evermore, eternally quite mine.
Well, so he is,—but yet they bore him off,
The third day, lest my husband should lay traps
And catch him, and by means of him catch me.
Since they have saved him so, it was well done:
Yet thence comes such confusion of what was

[1] The story that she and Caponsacchi were lovers was like a child's story, "fantastic and impossible." It may be significant that the two figures in the tapestry with which the children identify themselves are the chaste Diana and the nymph Daphne who escaped from Apollo by changing into a laurel tree.

With what will be,—that late seems long ago,
And, what years should bring round, already come,
Till even he withdraws into a dream
As the rest do: I fancy him grown great,
Strong, stern, a tall young man who tutors me,
Frowns with the others "Poor imprudent child!
Why did you venture out of the safe street?
Why go so far from help to that lone house?
Why open at the whisper and the knock?"

Six days ago when it was New Year's day,
We bent above the fire and talked of him,
What he should do when he was grown and great.
Violante, Pietro, each had given the arm
I leant on, to walk by, from couch to chair
And fireside,—laughed, as I lay safe at last,
"Pompilia's march from bed to board is made,
Pompilia back again and with a babe,
Shall one day lend his arm and help her walk!"
Then we all wished each other more New Years.
Pietro began to scheme—"Our cause is gained;
The law is stronger than a wicked man:
Let him henceforth go his way, leave us ours!
We will avoid the city, tempt no more
The greedy ones by feasting and parade,—
Live at the other villa, we know where,
Still farther off, and we can watch the babe
Grow fast in the good air; and wood is cheap
And wine sincere outside the city gate.
I still have two or three old friends will grope
Their way along the mere half-mile of road,
With staff and lantern on a moonless night
When one needs talk: they'll find me, never fear,
And I'll find them a flask of the old sort yet!"
Violante said "You chatter like a crow:
Pompilia tires o' the tattle, and shall to bed:
Do not too much the first day,—somewhat more
To-morrow, and, the next, begin the cape
And hood and coat! I have spun wool enough."
Oh what a happy friendly eve was that!

And, next day, about noon, out Pietro went—
He was so happy and would talk so much,
Until Violante pushed and laughed him forth
Sight-seeing in the cold,—"So much to see
I' the churches! Swathe your throat three times!" she cried,
"And, above all, beware the slippery ways,
And bring us all the news by supper-time!"
He came back late, laid by cloak, staff and hat,
Powdered so thick with snow it made us laugh,
Rolled a great log upon the ash o' the hearth,
And bade Violante treat us to a flask,
Because he had obeyed her faithfully,
Gone sight-see through the seven, and found no church
To his mind like San Giovanni—"There's the fold,
And all the sheep together, big as cats!
And such a shepherd, half the size of life,
Starts up and hears the angel" [1]—when, at the door,
A tap: we started up: you know the rest.

Pietro at least had done no harm, I know;
Nor even Violante, so much harm as makes
Such revenge lawful. Certainly she erred—
Did wrong, how shall I dare say otherwise?—
In telling that first falsehood, buying me
From my poor faulty mother at a price,
To pass off upon Pietro as his child.
If one should take my babe, give him a name,
Say he was not Gaetano and my own,
But that some other woman made his mouth
And hands and feet,—how very false were that!
No good could come of that; and all harm did.
Yet if a stranger were to represent
"Needs must you either give your babe to me
And let me call him mine for evermore,
Or let your husband get him"—ah, my God,
That were a trial I refuse to face!
Well, just so here: it proved wrong but seemed right
To poor Violante—for there lay, she said,
My poor real dying mother in her rags,
Who put me from her with the life and all,

[1] In Catholic countries it is the custom at Christmas time to put in the churches models of scenes connected with the birth of Christ, such as the manger at Bethlehem with the Holy Family and the shepherds. Pietro had just returned from seeing these when the murder occurred.

Poverty, pain, shame and disease at once,
To die the easier by what price I fetched—
Also (I hope) because I should be spared
Sorrow and sin,—why may not that have helped?
My father,—he was no one, any one,—
The worse, the likelier,—call him,—he who came,
Was wicked for his pleasure, went his way,
And left no trace to track by; there remained
Nothing but me, the unnecessary life,
To catch up or let fall,—and yet a thing
She could make happy, be made happy with,
This poor Violante,—who would frown thereat?

Well, God, you see! God plants us where we grow.
It is not that, because a bud is born
At a wild brier's end, full i' the wild beast's way,
We ought to pluck and put it out of reach
On the oak-tree top,—say, "There the bud belongs!"
She thought, moreover, real lies were lies told
For harm's sake; whereas this had good at heart,
Good for my mother, good for me, and good
For Pietro who was meant to love a babe,
And needed one to make his life of use,
Receive his house and land when he should die.
Wrong, wrong and always wrong! how plainly wrong!
For see, this fault kept pricking, as faults do,
All the same at her heart,—this falsehood hatched,
She could not let it go nor keep it fast.
She told me so,—the first time I was found
Locked in her arms once more after the pain,
When the nuns let me leave them and go home,
And both of us cried all the cares away,—
This it was set her on to make amends,
This brought about the marriage—simply this!
Do let me speak for her you blame so much!
When Paul,[1] my husband's brother, found me out,
Heard there was wealth for who should marry me,
So, came and made a speech to ask my hand
For Guido,—she, instead of piercing straight
Through the pretence to the ignoble truth,
Fancied she saw God's very finger point,
Designate just the time for planting me
(The wild-brier slip she plucked to love and wear)
In soil where I could strike real root, and grow,
And get to be the thing I called myself:
For, wife and husband are one flesh, God says,
And I, whose parents seemed such and were none,
Should in a husband have a husband now,
Find nothing, this time, but was what it seemed,
—All truth and no confusion any more.
I know she meant all good to me, all pain
To herself,—since how could it be aught but pain,
To give me up, so, from her very breast,
The wilding flower-tree-branch that, all those years,
She had got used to feel for and find fixed?
She meant well: has it been so ill i' the main?
That is but fair to ask: one cannot judge
Of what has been the ill or well of life,
The day that one is dying,—sorrows change
Into not altogether sorrow-like;
I do see strangeness but scarce misery,
Now it is over, and no danger more.
My child is safe; there seems not so much pain.
It comes, most like, that I am just absolved,
Purged of the past, the foul in me, washed fair,—
One cannot both have and not have, you know,—
Being right now, I am happy and colour things.
Yes, everybody that leaves life sees all
Softened and bettered: so with other sights:

[1] It was Paolo, the suave and successful younger brother of Guido, who suggested that he might marry for money, and who conducted the negotiations with Violante. Before the actual murder he left Rome and was never heard from again.

To me at least was never evening yet
But seemed far beautifuller than its day,
For past is past.

There was a fancy came,
When somewhere, in the journey with my friend,
We stepped into a hovel to get food;
And there began a yelp here, a bark there,—
Misunderstanding creatures that were wroth
And vexed themselves and us till we retired.
The hovel is life: no matter what dogs bit
Or cats scratched in the hovel I break from,
All outside is lone field, moon and such peace—
Flowing in, filling up as with a sea
Whereon comes Someone, walks fast on the white,
Jesus Christ's self, Don Celestine declares,
To meet me and calm all things back again.

Beside, up to my marriage, thirteen years
Were, each day, happy as the day was long:
This may have made the change too terrible.
I know that when Violante told me first
The cavalier—she meant to bring next morn,
Whom I must also let take, kiss my hand—
Would be at San Lorenzo the same eve
And marry me,—which over, we should go
Home both of us without him as before,
And, till she bade speak, I must hold my tongue,
Such being the correct way with girl-brides,
From whom one word would make a father blush,—
I know, I say, that when she told me this,
—Well, I no more saw sense in what she said
Than a lamb does in people clipping wool;
Only lay down and let myself be clipped.
And when next day the cavalier who came—
(Tisbe had told me that the slim young man
With wings at head, and wings at feet, and sword
Threatening a monster, in our tapestry,
Would eat a girl else,—was a cavalier) [1]—

[1] The figure in the tapestry here has an ironic significance. It is that of Perseus who rescued Andromeda from a sea-monster. Guido's rôle is to be that of the monster. The symbolism of the hero doing battle with the monster recurs in this monologue, Caponsacchi later being compared to St. George (l. 1323).

When he proved Guido Franceschini,—old
And nothing like so tall as I myself,
Hook-nosed and yellow in a bush of beard,
Much like a thing I saw on a boy's wrist,
He called an owl and used for catching birds,—
And when he took my hand and made a smile—
Why, the uncomfortableness of it all
Seemed hardly more important in the case
Than—when one gives you, say, a coin to spend—
Its newness or its oldness; if the piece
Weigh properly and buy you what you wish,
No matter whether you get grime or glare!
Men take the coin, return you grapes and figs.
Here, marriage was the coin, a dirty piece
Would purchase me the praise of those I loved:
About what else should I concern myself?

So, hardly knowing what a husband meant,
I supposed this or any man would serve,
No whit the worse for being so uncouth:
For I was ill once and a doctor came
With a great ugly hat, no plume thereto,
Black jerkin and black buckles and black sword,
And white sharp beard over the ruff in front,
And oh so lean, so sour-faced and austere!—
Who felt my pulse, made me put out my tongue,
Then oped a phial, dripped a drop or two
Of a black bitter something,—I was cured!
What mattered the fierce beard or the grim face?
It was the physic beautified the man,
Master Malpichi,[1]—never met his match
In Rome, they said,—so ugly all the same!

However, I was hurried through a storm,
Next dark eve of December's deadest day—
How it rained!—through our street and the Lion's-mouth
And the bit of Corso,—cloaked round, covered close,
I was like something strange or contraband,—
Into blank San Lorenzo, up the aisle,
My mother keeping hold of me so tight,
I fancied we were come to see a corpse
Before the altar which she pulled me toward.

[1] Possibly Marcello Malpighi, the physician of Pope Innocent XII.

There we found waiting an unpleasant priest
Who proved the brother, not our parish friend,
But one with mischief-making mouth and eye,
Paul, whom I know since to my cost. And then
I heard the heavy church-door lock out help
Behind us: for the customary warmth,
Two tapers shivered on the altar. "Quick—
Lose no time!"—cried the priest. And straightway down
From . . . what's behind the altar where he hid—
Hawk-nose and yellowness and bush and all,
Stepped Guido, caught my hand, and there was I
O' the chancel, and the priest had opened book,
Read here and there, made me say that and this,
And after, told me I was now a wife,
Honoured indeed, since Christ thus weds the Church,
And therefore turned he water into wine,
To show I should obey my spouse like Christ.
Then the two slipped aside and talked apart,
And I, silent and scared, got down again
And joined my mother who was weeping now.
Nobody seemed to mind us any more,
And both of us on tiptoe found our way
To the door which was unlocked by this, and wide.
When we were in the street, the rain had stopped,
All things looked better. At our own house-door,
Violante whispered, "No one syllable
To Pietro! Girl-brides never breathe a word!"
"—Well treated to a wetting, draggle-tails!"
Laughed Pietro as he opened—"Very near
You made me brave the gutter's roaring sea
To carry off from roost old dove and young,
Trussed up in church, the cote, by me, the kite!
What do these priests mean, praying folk to death
On stormy afternoons, with Christmas close
To wash our sins off nor require the rain?"
Violante gave my hand a timely squeeze,
Madonna saved me from immodest speech,
I kissed him and was quiet, being a bride.

When I saw nothing more, the next three weeks,
Of Guido—"Nor the Church sees Christ" thought I:
"Nothing is changed however, wine is wine
And water only water in our house.
Nor did I see that ugly doctor since
That cure of the illness: just as I was cured,
I am married,—neither scarecrow will return."

Three weeks, I chuckled—"How would Giulia stare,
And Tecla smile and Tisbe laugh outright,
Were it not impudent for brides to talk!"—
Until one morning, as I sat and sang
At the broidery-frame alone i' the chamber,—loud
Voices, two, three together, sobbings too,
And my name, "Guido," "Paolo," flung like stones
From each to the other! In I ran to see.
There stood the very Guido and the priest
With sly face,—formal but nowise afraid,—
While Pietro seemed all red and angry, scarce
Able to stutter out his wrath in words;
And this it was that made my mother sob,
As he reproached her—"You have murdered us,
Me and yourself and this our child beside!"
Then Guido interposed, "Murdered or not,
Be it enough your child is now my wife!
I claim and come to take her." Paul put in,
"Consider—kinsman, dare I term you so?—
What is the good of your sagacity
Except to counsel in a strait like this?
I guarantee the parties man and wife
Whether you like or loathe it, bless or ban.
May spilt milk be put back within the bowl—
The done thing, undone? You, it is, we look
For counsel to, you fitliest will advise!
Since milk, though spilt and spoilt, does marble good,
Better we down on knees and scrub the floor,
Than sigh, 'the waste would make a syllabub!'
Help us so turn disaster to account,
So predispose the groom, he needs shall grace
The bride with favour from the very first,
Not begin marriage an embittered man!"
He smiled,—the game so wholly in his hands!
While fast and faster sobbed Violante—"Ay,
All of us murdered, past averting now!
O my sin, O my secret!" and such like.

Then I began to half surmise the truth;
Something had happened, low, mean, underhand,

False, and my mother was to blame, and I
To pity, whom all spoke of, none addressed:
I was the chattel that had caused a crime.
I stood mute,—those who tangled must untie
The embroilment. Pietro cried, "Withdraw, my child!
She is not helpful to the sacrifice
At this stage,—do you want the victim by
While you discuss the value of her blood?
For her sake, I consent to hear you talk:
Go, child, and pray God help the innocent!"

I did go and was praying God, when came
Violante, with eyes swollen and red enough,
But movement on her mouth for make-believe
Matters were somehow getting right again.
She bade me sit down by her side and hear.
"You are too young and cannot understand,
Nor did your father understand at first.
I wished to benefit all three of us,
And when he failed to take my meaning,—why,
I tried to have my way at unaware—
Obtained him the advantage he refused.
As if I put before him wholesome food
Instead of broken victual,—he finds change
I' the viands, never cares to reason why,
But falls to blaming me, would fling the plate
From window, scandalise the neighbourhood,
Even while he smacks his lips,—men's way, my child!
But either you have prayed him unperverse
Or I have talked him back into his wits:
And Paolo was a help in time of need,—
Guido, not much—my child, the way of men!
A priest is more a woman than a man,
And Paul did wonders to persuade. In short,
Yes, he was wrong, your father sees and says;
My scheme was worth attempting: and bears fruit,
Gives you a husband and a noble name,
A palace and no end of pleasant things.
What do you care about a handsome youth?
They are so volatile, and tease their wives!
This is the kind of man to keep the house.
We lose no daughter,—gain a son, that's all:
For 'tis arranged we never separate,
Nor miss, in our grey time of life, the tints
Of you that colour eve to match with morn.
In good or ill, we share and share alike,
And cast our lots into a common lap,
And all three die together as we lived!
Only, at Arezzo,—that's a Tuscan town,
Not so large as this noisy Rome, no doubt,
But older far and finer much, say folks,—
In a great palace where you will be queen,
Know the Archbishop and the Governor,
And we see homage done you ere we die.
Therefore, be good and pardon!"—"Pardon what?
You know things, I am very ignorant:
All is right if you only will not cry!"

And so an end! Because a blank begins
From when, at the word, she kissed me hard and hot,
And took me back to where my father leaned
Opposite Guido—who stood eyeing him,
As eyes the butcher the cast panting ox
That feels his fate is come, nor struggles more,—
While Paul looked archly on, pricked brow at whiles
With the pen-point as to punish triumph there,—
And said "Count Guido, take your lawful wife
Until death part you!"

All since is one blank,
Over and ended; a terrific dream.
It is the good of dreams—so soon they go!
Wake in a horror of heart-beats, you may—
Cry, "The dread thing will never from my thoughts!"
Still, a few daylight doses of plain life,
Cock-crow and sparrow-chirp, or bleat and bell
Of goats that trot by, tinkling, to be milked;
And when you rub your eyes awake and wide,
Where is the harm o' the horror? Gone! So here.
I know I wake,—but from what? Blank, I say!
This is the note of evil: for good lasts.
Even when Don Celestine [1] bade "Search and find!

[1] Fra Celestino received Pompilia's dying confession and attended her the last days of her life. In the Old Yellow Book was included a copy of Celestino's affidavit testifying to the saintliness of Pompilia's character—a document which convinced Browning, and aided him greatly in his formulation of her character.

For your soul's sake, remember what is past,
The better to forgive it,"—all in vain!
What was fast getting indistinct before,
Vanished outright. By special grace perhaps,
Between that first calm and this last, four years
Vanish,—one quarter of my life, you know.
I am held up, amid the nothingness,
By one or two truths only—thence I hang,
And there I live,—the rest is death or dream,
All but those points of my support. I think
Of what I saw at Rome once in the Square
O' the Spaniards, opposite the Spanish House:
There was a foreigner had trained a goat,
A shuddering white woman of a beast,
To climb up, stand straight on a pile of sticks
Put close, which gave the creature room enough:
When she was settled there, he, one by one,
Took away all the sticks, left just the four
Whereon the little hoofs did really rest,
There she kept firm, all underneath was air.
So, what I hold by, are my prayer to God,
My hope, that came in answer to the prayer,
Some hand would interpose and save me—hand
Which proved to be my friend's hand: and,—best bliss,—
That fancy which began so faint at first,
That thrill of dawn's suffusion through my dark,
Which I perceive was promise of my child,
The light his unborn face sent long before,—
God's way of breaking the good news to flesh.
That is all left now of those four bad years.
Don Celestine urged, "But remember more!
Other men's faults may help me find your own.
I need the cruelty exposed, explained,
Or how can I advise you to forgive?"
He thought I could not properly forgive
Unless I ceased forgetting,—which is true:
For, bringing back reluctantly to mind
My husband's treatment of me,—by a light
That's later than my life-time, I review
And comprehend much and imagine more,
And have but little to forgive at last.
For now,—be fair and say,—is it not true
He was ill-used and cheated of his hope
To get enriched by marriage? Marriage gave
Me and no money, broke the compact so:
He had a right to ask me on those terms,
As Pietro and Violante to declare
They would not give me: so the bargain stood:
They broke it, and he felt himself aggrieved,
Became unkind with me to punish them.
They said 'twas he began deception first,
Nor, in one point whereto he pledged himself,
Kept promise: what of that, suppose it were?
Echoes die off, scarcely reverberate
For ever,—why should ill keep echoing ill,
And never let our ears have done with noise?
Then my poor parents took the violent way
To thwart him,—he must needs retaliate,—wrong,
Wrong, and all wrong,—better say, all blind!
As I myself was, that is sure, who else
Had understood the mystery: for his wife
Was bound in some sort to help somehow there.
It seems as if I might have interposed,
Blunted the edge of their resentment so,
Since he vexed me because they first vexed him;
"I will entreat them to desist, submit,
Give him the money and be poor in peace,—
Certainly not go tell the world: perhaps
He will grow quiet with his gains."

Yes, say
Something to this effect and you do well!
But then you have to see first: I was blind.
That is the fruit of all such wormy ways,
The indirect, the unapproved of God:
You cannot find their author's end and aim,
Not even to substitute your good for bad,
Your straight for the irregular; you stand
Stupefied, profitless, as cow or sheep
That miss a man's mind; anger him just twice
By trial at repairing the first fault.
Thus, when he blamed me, "You are a coquette,
A lure-owl posturing to attract birds,
You look love-lures at theatre and church,
In walk, at window!"—that, I knew, was false:
But why he charged me falsely, whither sought
To drive me by such charge,—how could I know?
So, unaware, I only made things worse.
I tried to soothe him by abjuring walk,

Window, church, theatre, for good and all,
As if he had been in earnest: that, you know,
Was nothing like the object of his charge.
Yes, when I got my maid to supplicate
The priest, whose name she read when she would read
Those feigned false letters I was forced to hear
Though I could read no word of,—he should cease
Writing,—nay, if he minded prayer of mine,
Cease from so much as even pass the street
Whereon our house looked,—in my ignorance
I was just thwarting Guido's true intent;
Which was, to bring about a wicked change
Of sport to earnest, tempt a thoughtless man
To write indeed, and pass the house, and more,
Till both of us were taken in a crime.
He ought not to have wished me thus act lies,
Simulate folly: but,—wrong or right, the wish,—
I failed to apprehend its drift. How plain
It follows,—if I fell into such fault,
He also may have overreached the mark,
Made mistake, by perversity of brain,
I' the whole sad strange plot, the grotesque intrigue
To make me and my friend unself ourselves,
Be other man and woman than we were!
Think it out, you who have the time! for me,—
I cannot say less; more I will not say.
Leave it to God to cover and undo!
Only, my dulness should not prove too much!
—Not prove that in a certain other point
Wherein my husband blamed me,—and you blame,
If I interpret smiles and shakes of head,—
I was dull too. Oh, if I dared but speak!
Must I speak? I am blamed that I forwent
A way to make my husband's favour come.
That is true: I was firm, withstood, refused . . .
—Women as you are, how can I find the words?
I felt there was just one thing Guido claimed
I had no right to give nor he to take;
We being in estrangement, soul from soul:
Till, when I sought help, the Archbishop smiled,
Inquiring into privacies of life,
—Said I was blameable—(he stands for God)
Nowise entitled to exemption there.
Then I obeyed,—as surely had obeyed
Were the injunction "Since your husband bids,
Swallow the burning coal he proffers you!"
But I did wrong, and he gave wrong advice
Though he were thrice Archbishop,—that, I know!—
Now I have got to die and see things clear.
Remember I was barely twelve years old—
A child at marriage: I was let alone
For weeks, I told you, lived my child-life still
Even at Arezzo, when I woke and found
First . . . but I need not think of that again—
Over and ended! Try and take the sense
Of what I signify, if it must be so.
After the first, my husband, for hate's sake,
Said one eve, when the simpler cruelty
Seemed somewhat dull at edge and fit to bear,
"We have been man and wife six months almost:
How long is this your comedy to last?
Go this night to my chamber, not your own!"
At which word, I did rush—most true the charge—
And gain the Archbishop's house—he stands for God—
And fall upon my knees and clasp his feet,
Praying him hinder what my estranged soul
Refused to bear, though patient of the rest:
"Place me within a convent," I implored—
"Let me henceforward lead the virgin life
You praise in Her you bid me imitate!"
What did he answer? "Folly of ignorance!
Know, daughter, circumstances make or mar
Virginity,—'tis virtue or 'tis vice.
That which was glory in the Mother of God
Had been, for instance, damnable in Eve
Created to be mother of mankind.
Had Eve, in answer to her Maker's speech
'Be fruitful, multiply, replenish earth'—
Pouted 'But I choose rather to remain
Single'—why, she had spared herself forth-with
Further probation by the apple and snake,
Been pushed straight out of Paradise! For see—
If motherhood be qualified impure,
I catch you making God command Eve sin!
—A blasphemy so like these Molinists',

I must suspect you dip into their books."
Then he pursued "'Twas in your covenant!"
No! There my husband never used deceit.
He never did by speech nor act imply
"Because of our souls' yearning that we meet
And mix in soul through flesh, which yours and mine
Wear and impress, and make their visible selves,
—All which means, for the love of you and me,
Let us become one flesh, being one soul!"
He only stipulated for the wealth;
Honest so far. But when he spoke as plain—
Dreadfully honest also—"Since our souls
Stand each from each, a whole world's width between,
Give me the fleshy vesture I can reach
And rend and leave just fit for hell to burn!"—
Why, in God's name, for Guido's soul's own sake
Imperilled by polluting mine,—I say,
I did resist; would I had overcome!

My heart died out at the Archbishop's smile;
—It seemed so stale and worn a way o' the world,
As though 'twere nature frowning—"Here is Spring,
The sun shines as he shone at Adam's fall,
The earth requires that warmth reach everywhere:
What, must your patch of snow be saved forsooth
Because you rather fancy snow than flowers?"
Something in this style he began with me.
Last he said, savagely for a good man,
"This explains why you call your husband harsh,
Harsh to you, harsh to whom you love. God's Bread!
The poor Count has to manage a mere child
Whose parents leave untaught the simplest things
Their duty was and privilege to teach,—
Goodwives' instruction, gossips' lore: they laugh
And leave the Count the task,—or leave it me!"
Then I resolved to tell a frightful thing.
"I am not ignorant,—know what I say,
Declaring this is sought for hate, not love.
Sir, you may hear things like almighty God.
I tell you that my housemate, yes—the priest
My husband's brother, Canon Girolamo—[1]
Has taught me what depraved and misnamed love
Means, and what outward signs denote the sin,
For he solicits me and says he loves,
The idle young priest with nought else to do.
My husband sees this, knows this, and lets be.
Is it your counsel I bear this beside?"
"—More scandal, and against a priest this time!
What, 'tis the Canon now?"—less snappishly—
"Rise up, my child, for such a child you are,
The rod were too advanced a punishment!
Let's try the honeyed cake. A parable!
'Without a parable spake He not to them.'
There was a ripe round long black toothsome fruit,
Even a flower-fig, the prime boast of May:
And, to the tree, said . . . either the spirit o' the fig,
Or, if we bring in men, the gardener,
Archbishop of the orchard—had I time
To try o' the two which fits in best: indeed
It might be the Creator's self, but then
The tree should bear an apple, I suppose,—
Well, anyhow, one with authority said
'Ripe fig, burst skin, regale the fig-pecker—
The bird whereof thou art a perquisite!'
'Nay,' with a flounce, replied the restif fig,
'I much prefer to keep my pulp myself:
He may go breakfastless and dinnerless,
Supperless of one crimson seed, for me!'
So, back she flopped into her bunch of leaves.
He flew off, left her,—did the natural lord,—
And lo, three hundred thousand bees and wasps
Found her out, feasted on her to the shuck:
Such gain the fig's that gave its bird no bite!
The moral,—fools elude their proper lot,
Tempt other fools, get ruined all alike.
Therefore go home, embrace your husband quick!
Which if this Canon brother chance to see,
He will the sooner back to book again."

[1] Another younger brother of Guido—perhaps the least attractive of an unattractive family.

So, home I did go; so, the worst befell:
So, I had proof the Archbishop was just man,
And hardly that, and certainly no more.
For, miserable consequence to me,
My husband's hatred waxed nor waned at all,
His brother's boldness grew effrontery soon,
And my last stay and comfort in myself
Was forced from me: henceforth I looked to God
Only, nor cared my desecrated soul
Should have fair walls, gay windows for the world.
God's glimmer, that came through the ruin-top,
Was witness why all lights were quenched inside:
Henceforth I asked God counsel, not mankind.

So, when I made the effort, freed myself,
They said—"No care to save appearance here!
How cynic,—when, how wanton, were enough!"
—Adding, it all came of my mother's life—
My own real mother, whom I never knew,
Who did wrong (if she needs must have done wrong)
Through being all her life, not my four years,
At mercy of the hateful,—every beast
O' the field was wont to break that fountain-fence,
Trample the silver into mud so murk
Heaven could not find itself reflected there.
Now they cry, "Out on her, who, plashy pool,
Bequeathed turbidity and bitterness
To the daughter-stream where Guido dipt and drank!"

Well, since she had to bear this brand—let me!
The rather do I understand her now,—
From my experience of what hate calls love,—
Much love might be in what their love called hate.
If she sold . . . what they call, sold . . . me her child—
I shall believe she hoped in her poor heart
That I at least might try be good and pure,
Begin to live untempted, not go doomed
And done with ere once found in fault, as she.
Oh and, my mother, it all came to this?
Why should I trust those that speak ill of you,
When I mistrust who speaks even well of them?
Why, since all bound to do me good, did harm,
May not you, seeming as you harmed me most,
Have meant to do most good—and feed your child
From bramble-bush, whom not one orchard-tree
But drew bough back from, nor let one fruit fall?
This it was for you sacrificed your babe?
Gained just this, giving your heart's hope away
As I might give mine, loving it as you,
If . . . but that never could be asked of me!

There, enough! I have my support again,
Again the knowledge that my babe was, is,
Will be mine only. Him, by death, I give
Outright to God, without a further care,—
But not to any parent in the world,—
So to be safe: why is it we repine?
What guardianship were safer could we choose?
All human plans and projects come to nought,
My life, and what I know of other lives,
Prove that: no plan nor project! God shall care!

And now you are not tired? How patient then
All of you,—Oh yes, patient this long while
Listening, and understanding, I am sure!
Four days ago, when I was sound and well
And like to live, no one would understand.
People were kind, but smiled, "And what of him,
Your friend, whose tonsure, the rich dark-brown hides?
There, there!—your lover, do we dream he was?
A priest too—never were such naughtiness!
Still, he thinks many a long think, never fear,
After the shy pale lady,—lay so light
For a moment in his arms, the lucky one!"
And so on: wherefore should I blame you much?
So we are made, such difference in minds,
Such difference too in eyes that see the minds!
That man, you misinterpret and misprise—
The glory of his nature, I had thought,
Shot itself out in white light, blazed the truth
Through every atom of his act with me:

Yet where I point you, through the crystal shrine,
Purity in quintessence, one dew-drop,
You all descry a spider in the midst.
One says, "The head of it is plain to see,"
And one, "They are the feet by which I judge,"
All say, "Those films were spun by nothing else."

Then, I must lay my babe away with God,
Nor think of him again, for gratitude.
Yes, my last breath shall wholly spend itself
In one attempt more to disperse the stain,
The mist from other breath fond mouths have made,
About a lustrous and pellucid soul:
So that, when I am gone but sorrow stays,
And people need assurance in their doubt
If God yet have a servant, man a friend,
The weak a saviour and the vile a foe,—
Let him be present, by the name invoked,
Giuseppe-Maria Caponsacchi!
There,
Strength comes already with the utterance!
I will remember once more for his sake
The sorrow: for he lives and is belied.
Could he be here, how he would speak for me!

I had been miserable three drear years
In that dread palace and lay passive now,
When I first learned there could be such a man.
Thus it fell: I was at a public play,
In the last days of Carnival last March,
Brought there I knew not why, but now know well.
My husband put me where I sat, in front;
Then crouched down, breathed cold through me from behind,
Stationed i' the shadow,—none in front could see,—
I, it was, faced the stranger-throng beneath,
The crowd with upturned faces, eyes one stare,
Voices one buzz. I looked but to the stage,
Whereon two lovers sang and interchanged
"True life is only love, love only bliss:
I love thee—thee I love!" then they embraced.
I looked thence to the ceiling and the walls,—
Over the crowd, those voices and those eyes,—
My thoughts went through the roof and out, to Rome
On wings of music, waft of measured words,—
Set me down there, a happy child again,
Sure that to-morrow would be festa-day,
Hearing my parents praise past festas more,
And seeing they were old if I was young,
Yet wondering why they still would end discourse
With "We must soon go, you abide your time,
And,—might we haply see the proper friend
Throw his arm over you and make you safe!"

Sudden I saw him; into my lap there fell
A foolish twist of comfits, broke my dream
And brought me from the air and laid me low,
As ruined as the soaring bee that's reached
(So Pietro told me at the Villa once)
By the dust-handful. There the comfits lay:
I looked to see who flung them, and I faced
This Caponsacchi, looking up in turn.
Ere I could reason out why, I felt sure,
Whoever flung them, his was not the hand,—
Up rose the round face and good-natured grin
Of him who, in effect, had played the prank,
From covert close beside the earnest face,—
Fat waggish Conti, friend of all the world.
He was my husband's cousin, privileged
To throw the thing: the other, silent, grave,
Solemn almost, saw me, as I saw him.

There is a psalm Don Celestine recites,
"Had I a dove's wings, how I fain would flee!"
The psalm runs not "I hope, I pray for wings,"—
Not "If wings fall from heaven, I fix them fast,"—
Simply "How good it were to fly and rest,
Have hope now, and one day expect content!
How well to do what I shall never do!"
So I said, "Had there been a man like that,
To lift me with his strength out of all strife
Into the calm, how I could fly and rest!
I have a keeper in the garden here
Whose sole employment is to strike me low
If ever I, for solace, seek the sun.
Life means with me successful feigning death,
Lying stone-like, eluding notice so,
Foregoing here the turf and there the sky.

Suppose that man had been instead of this!"
Presently Conti laughed into my ear,
—Had tripped up to the raised place where I sat—
"Cousin, I flung them brutishly and hard!
Because you must be hurt, to look austere
As Caponsacchi yonder, my tall friend
A-gazing now. Ah, Guido, you so close?
Keep on your knees, do! Beg her to forgive!
My cornet battered like a cannon-ball.
Good bye, I'm gone!"—nor waited the reply.

That night at supper, out my husband broke,
"Why was that throwing, that buffoonery?
Do you think I am your dupe? What man would dare
Throw comfits in a stranger lady's lap?
'Twas knowledge of you bred such insolence
In Caponsacchi; he dared shoot the bolt,
Using that Conti for his stalking-horse.
How could you see him this once and no more,
When he is always haunting hereabout
At the street-corner or the palace-side,
Publishing my shame and your impudence?
You are a wanton,—I a dupe, you think?
O Christ, what hinders that I kill her quick?"
Whereat he drew his sword and feigned a thrust.

All this, now,—being not so strange to me,
Used to such misconception day by day
And broken-in to bear,—I bore, this time,
More quietly than woman should perhaps:
Repeated the mere truth and held my tongue.

Then he said, "Since you play the ignorant,
I shall instruct you. This amour,—commenced
Or finished or midway in act, all's one,—
'Tis the town-talk; so my revenge shall be.
Does he presume because he is a priest?
I warn him that the sword I wear shall pink
His lily-scented cassock through and through,
Next time I catch him underneath your eaves!"
But he had threatened with the sword so oft
And, after all, not kept his promise. All
I said was, "Let God save the innocent!
Moreover, death is far from a bad fate.
I shall go pray for you and me, not him;
And then I look to sleep, come death or, worse,
Life." So, I slept.

There may have elapsed a week,
When Margherita,—called my waiting-maid,
Whom it is said my husband found too fair—
Who stood and heard the charge and the reply,
Who never once would let the matter rest
From that night forward, but rang changes still
On this the thrust and that the shame, and how
Good cause for jealousy cures jealous fools,
And what a paragon was this same priest
She talked about until I stopped my ears,—
She said, "A week is gone; you comb your hair,
Then go mope in a corner, cheek on palm,
Till night comes round again,—so, waste a week
As if your husband menaced you in sport.
Have not I some acquaintance with his tricks?
Oh no, he did not stab the serving-man
Who made and sang the rhymes about me once!
For why? They sent him to the wars next day.
Nor poisoned he the foreigner, my friend,
Who wagered on the whiteness of my breast,—
The swarth skins of our city in dispute:
For, though he paid me proper compliment,
The Count well knew he was besotted with
Somebody else, a skin as black as ink,
(As all the town knew save my foreigner)
He found and wedded presently,—'Why need
Better revenge?'—the Count asked. But what's here?
A priest, that does not fight, and cannot wed,
Yet must be dealt with! If the Count took fire
For the poor pastime of a minute,—me—
What were the conflagration for yourself,
Countess and lady-wife and all the rest?
The priest will perish; you will grieve too late:
So shall the city-ladies' handsomest,
Frankest and liberalest gentleman
Die for you, to appease a scurvy dog
Hanging's too good for. Is there no escape?
Were it not simple Christian charity
To warn the priest be on his guard,—save him
Assured death, save yourself from causing it?
I meet him in the street. Give me a glove,
A ring to show for token! Mum's the word!"

I answered, "If you were, as styled, my maid,
I would command you: as you are, you say,
My husband's intimate,—assist his wife
Who can do nothing but entreat 'Be still!'
Even if you speak truth and a crime is planned,
Leave help to God as I am forced to do!
There is no other help, or we should craze,
Seeing such evil with no human cure.
Reflect that God, who makes the storm desist,
Can make an angry violent heart subside.
Why should we venture teach Him governance?
Never address me on this subject more!"

Next night she said, "But I went, all the same,
—Ay, saw your Caponsacchi in his house,
And come back stuffed with news I must outpour.
I told him, 'Sir, my mistress is a stone:
Why should you harm her for no good you get?
For you do harm her—prowl about our place
With the Count never distant half the street,
Lurking at every corner, would you look!
'Tis certain she has witched you with a spell.
Are there not other beauties at your beck?
We all know, Donna This and Monna That
Die for a glance of yours, yet here you gaze!
Go make them grateful, leave the stone its cold!'
And he—oh, he turned first white and then red,
And then—'To her behest I bow myself,
Whom I love with my body and my soul:
Only, a word i' the bowing! See, I write
One little word, no harm to see or hear!
Then, fear no further!' This is what he wrote.
I know you cannot read,—therefore, let me!
'*My idol!*' " . . .

But I took it from her hand
And tore it into shreds. "Why join the rest
Who harm me? Have I ever done you wrong?
People have told me 'tis you wrong myself:
Let it suffice I either feel no wrong
Or else forgive it,—yet you turn my foe!
The others hunt me and you throw a noose!"

She muttered, "Have your wilful way!" I slept.
Whereupon . . . no, I leave my husband out!
It is not to do him more hurt, I speak.
Let it suffice, when misery was most,
One day, I swooned and got a respite so.
She stooped as I was slowly coming to,
This Margherita, ever on my trace,
And whispered—"Caponsacchi!"

If I drowned,
But woke afloat i' the wave with upturned eyes,
And found their first sight was a star! I turned—
For the first time, I let her have her will,
Heard passively,—"The imposthume at such head,
One touch, one lancet-puncture would relieve,—
And still no glance the good physician's way
Who rids you of the torment in a trice!
Still he writes letters you refuse to hear.
He may prevent your husband, kill himself,
So desperate and all fordone is he!
Just hear the pretty verse he made to-day!
A sonnet from Mirtillo. '*Peerless fair* . . .'
All poetry is difficult to read,
—The sense of it is, anyhow, he seeks
Leave to contrive you an escape from hell,
And for that purpose asks an interview.
I can write, I can grant it in your name,
Or, what is better, lead you to his house.
Your husband dashes you against the stones;
This man would place each fragment in a shrine:
You hate him, love your husband!"

I returned,
"It is not true I love my husband,—no,
Nor hate this man. I listen while you speak,
—Assured that what you say is false, the same:
Much as when once, to me a little child,
A rough gaunt man in rags, with eyes on fire,
A crowd of boys and idlers at his heels,
Rushed as I crossed the Square, and held my head
In his two hands, 'Here's she will let me speak!
You little girl, whose eyes do good to mine,
I am the Pope, am Sextus, now the Sixth;
And that Twelfth Innocent, proclaimed to-day,
Is Lucifer disguised in human flesh!

The angels, met in conclave, crowned me!'—thus
He gibbered and I listened; but I knew
All was delusion, ere folks interposed
'Unfasten him, the maniac!' Thus I know
All your report of Caponsacchi false,
Folly or dreaming; I have seen so much
By that adventure at the spectacle,
The face I fronted that one first, last time:
He would belie it by such words and thoughts.
Therefore while you profess to show him me,
I ever see his own face. Get you gone!"

"—That will I, nor once open mouth again,—
No, by Saint Joseph and the Holy Ghost!
On your head be the damage, so adieu!"

And so more days, more deeds I must forget,
Till . . . what a strange thing now is to declare!
Since I say anything, say all if true!
And how my life seems lengthened as to serve!
It may be idle or inopportune,
But, true?—why, what was all I said but truth,
Even when I found that such as are untrue
Could only take the truth in through a lie?
Now—I am speaking truth to the Truth's self:
God will lend credit to my words this time.

It had got half through April. I arose
One vivid daybreak,—who had gone to bed
In the old way my wont those last three years,
Careless until, the cup drained, I should die.
The last sound in my ear, the over-night,
Had been a something let drop on the sly
In prattle by Margherita, "Soon enough
Gaieties end, now Easter's past: a week,
And the Archbishop gets him back to Rome,—
Everyone leaves the town for Rome, this Spring,—
Even Caponsacchi, out of heart and hope,
Resigns himself and follows with the flock."
I heard this drop and drop like rain outside
Fast-falling through the darkness while she spoke:
So had I heard with like indifference,
"And Michael's pair of wings will arrive first
At Rome to introduce the company,
Will bear him from our picture where he fights
Satan,—expect to have that dragon loose
And never a defender!"—my sole thought
Being still, as night came, "Done, another day!
How good to sleep and so get nearer death!"—
When, what, first thing at daybreak, pierced the sleep
With a summons to me? Up I sprang alive,
Light in me, light without me, everywhere
Change! A broad yellow sun-beam was let fall
From heaven to earth,—a sudden drawbridge lay,
Along which marched a myriad merry motes,
Mocking the flies that crossed them and recrossed
In rival dance, companions new-born too.
On the house-eaves, a dripping shag of weed
Shook diamonds on each dull grey lattice-square,
As first one, then another bird leapt by,
And light was off, and lo was back again,
Always with one voice,—where are two such joys?
The blessed building-sparrow! I stepped forth,
Stood on the terrace,—o'er the roofs, such sky!
My heart sang, "I too am to go away,
I too have something I must care about,
Carry away with me to Rome, to Rome!
The bird brings hither sticks and hairs and wool,
And nowhere else i' the world; what fly breaks rank,
Falls out of the procession that befits,
From window here to window there, with all
The world to choose,—so well he knows his course?
I have my purpose and my motive too,
My march to Rome, like any bird or fly!
Had I been dead! How right to be alive!
Last night I almost prayed for leave to die,
Wished Guido all his pleasure with the sword
Or the poison,—poison, sword, was but a trick,
Harmless, may God forgive him the poor jest!
My life is charmed, will last till I reach Rome!
Yesterday, but for the sin,—ah, nameless be
The deed I could have dared against myself!
Now—see if I will touch an unripe fruit,
And risk the health I want to have and use!
Not to live, now, would be the wickedness,—

For life means to make haste and go to Rome
And leave Arezzo, leave all woes at once!"

Now, understand here, by no means mistake!
Long ago had I tried to leave that house
When it seemed such procedure would stop sin;
And still failed more the more I tried—at first
The Archbishop, as I told you,—next, our lord
The Governor,—indeed I found my way,
I went to the great palace where he rules,
Though I knew well 'twas he who,—when I gave
A jewel or two, themselves had given me,
Back to my parents,—since they wanted bread,
They who had never let me want a nosegay,—he
Spoke of the jail for felons, if they kept
What was first theirs, then mine, so doubly theirs,
Though all the while my husband's most of all!
I knew well who had spoke the word wrought this:
Yet, being in extremity, I fled
To the Governor, as I say,—scarce opened lip
When—the cold cruel snicker close behind—
Guido was on my trace, already there,
Exchanging nod and wink for shrug and smile,
And I—pushed back to him and, for my pains,
Paid with . . . but why remember what is past?
I sought out a poor friar the people call
The Roman, and confessed my sin which came
Of their sin,—that fact could not be repressed,—
The frightfulness of my despair in God:
And, feeling, through the grate, his horror shake,
Implored him, "Write for me who cannot write,
Apprise my parents, make them rescue me!
You bid me be courageous and trust God:
Do you in turn dare somewhat, trust and write
'Dear friends, who used to be my parents once,
And now declare you have no part in me,
This is some riddle I want wit to solve,
Since you must love me with no difference.
Even suppose you altered,—there's your hate,
To ask for: hate of you two dearest ones
I shall find liker love than love found here,
If husbands love their wives. Take me away
And hate me as you do the gnats and fleas,
Even the scorpions! How I shall rejoice!'
Write that and save me!" And he promised—wrote
Or did not write; things never changed at all:
He was not like the Augustinian here!
Last, in a desperation I appealed
To friends, whoever wished me better days,
To Guillichini, that's of kin,—"What, I—
Travel to Rome with you? A flying gout
Bids me deny my heart and mind my leg!"
Then I tried Conti, used to brave—laugh back
The louring thunder when his cousin scowled
At me protected by his presence: "You—
Who well know what you cannot save me from,—
Carry me off! What frightens you, a priest?"
He shook his head, looked grave—"Above my strength!
Guido has claws that scratch, shows feline teeth;
A formidabler foe than I dare fret:
Give me a dog to deal with, twice the size!
Of course I am a priest and Canon too,
But . . . by the bye . . . though both, not quite so bold
As he, my fellow-Canon, brother-priest,
The personage in such ill odour here
Because of the reports—pure birth o' the brain—
Our Caponsacchi, he's your true Saint George
To slay the monster, set the Princess free,
And have the whole High-Altar to himself:
I always think so when I see that piece [1]
I' the Pieve, that's his church and mine, you know:
Though you drop eyes at mention of his name!"

That name had got to take a half-grotesque
Half-ominous, wholly enigmatic sense,
Like any by-word, broken bit of song
Born with a meaning, changed by mouth and mouth

[1] There was a painting of Saint George in Caponsacchi's church, Sta. Maria della Pieve.

That mix it in a sneer or smile, as chance
Bids, till it now means nought but ugliness
And perhaps shame.

—All this intends to say,
That, over-night, the notion of escape
Had seemed distemper, dreaming; and the name,—
Not the man, but the name of him, thus made
Into a mockery and disgrace,—why, she
Who uttered it persistently, had laughed,
"I name his name, and there you start and wince
As criminal from the red tongs' touch!"—yet now,
Now, as I stood letting morn bathe me bright,
Choosing which butterfly should bear my news,—
The white, the brown one, or that tinier blue,—
The Margherita, I detested so,
In she came—"The fine day, the good Spring time!
What, up and out at window? That is best.
No thought of Caponsacchi?—who stood there
All night on one leg, like the sentry crane,
Under the pelting of your water-spout—
Looked last look at your lattice ere he leave
Our city, bury his dead hope at Rome?
Ay, go to looking-glass and make you fine,
While he may die ere touch one least loose hair
You drag at with the comb in such a rage!"

I turned—"Tell Caponsacchi he may come!"

"Tell him to come? Ah, but, for charity,
A truce to fooling! Come? What,—come this eve?
Peter and Paul! But I see through the trick—
Yes, come, and take a flower-pot on his head
Flung from your terrace! No joke, sincere truth?"

How plainly I perceived hell flash and fade
O' the face of her,—the doubt that first paled joy,
Then, final reassurance I indeed
Was caught now, never to be free again!
What did I care?—who felt myself of force
To play with the silk, and spurn the horsehair-springe.[1]

"But—do you know that I have bade him come,
And in your own name? I presumed so much,
Knowing the thing you needed in your heart.
But somehow—what had I to show in proof?
He would not come: half-promised, that was all,
And wrote the letters you refused to read.
What is the message that shall move him now?"
"After the Ave Maria, at first dark,
I will be standing on the terrace, say!"

"I would I had a good long lock of hair
Should prove I was not lying! Never mind!"

Off she went—"May he not refuse, that's all—
Fearing a trick!"

I answered, "He will come."
And, all day, I sent prayer like incense up
To God the strong, God the beneficent,
God ever mindful in all strife and strait,
Who, for our own good, makes the need extreme,
Till at the last He puts forth might and saves.
An old rhyme came into my head and rang
Of how a virgin, for the faith of God,
Hid herself, from the Paynims that pursued,
In a cave's heart; until a thunderstone,
Wrapped in a flame, revealed the couch and prey:
And they laughed—"Thanks to lightning, ours at last!"
And she cried "Wrath of God, assert His love!
Servant of God, thou fire, befriend His child!"
And lo, the fire she grasped at, fixed its flash,
Lay in her hand a calm cold dreadful sword
She brandished till pursuers strewed the ground,
So did the souls within them die away,
As o'er the prostrate bodies, sworded, safe,
She walked forth to the solitudes and Christ:
So should I grasp the lightning and be saved!

[1] A springe is a noose trap. Woven of such coarse material as horsehair, it would lack the strength of twisted silk strands. Pompilia is of a strength now to escape the crude traps of Margherita.

And still, as the day wore, the trouble grew
Whereby I guessed there would be born a star,
Until at an intense throe of the dusk,
I started up, was pushed, I dare to say,
Out on the terrace, leaned and looked at last
Where the deliverer waited me: the same
Silent and solemn face, I first descried
At the spectacle, confronted mine once more.

So was that minute twice vouchsafed me, so
The manhood, wasted then, was still at watch
To save me yet a second time: no change
Here, though all else changed in the changing world!

I spoke on the instant, as my duty bade,
In some such sense as this, whatever the phrase.

"Friend, foolish words were borne from you to me;
Your soul behind them is the pure strong wind,
Not dust and feathers which its breath may bear:
These to the witless seem the wind itself,
Since proving thus the first of it they feel.
If by mischance you blew offence my way,
The straws are dropt, the wind desists no whit,
And how such strays were caught up in the street
And took a motion from you, why inquire?
I speak to the strong soul, no weak disguise.
If it be truth,—why should I doubt it truth?—
You serve God specially, as priests are bound,
And care about me, stranger as I am,
So far as wish my good,—that miracle
I take to intimate He wills you serve
By saving me,—what else can He direct?
Here is the service. Since a long while now,
I am in course of being put to death:
While death concerned nothing but me, I bowed
The head and bade, in heart, my husband strike.
Now I imperil something more, it seems,
Something that's trulier me than this myself,
Something I trust in God and you to save.
You go to Rome, they tell me: take me there,
Put me back with my people!"

He replied—
The first word I heard ever from his lips,
All himself in it,—an eternity
Of speech, to match the immeasurable depths
O' the soul that then broke silence—"I am yours."

So did the star rise, soon to lead my step,
Lead on, nor pause before it should stand still
Above the House o' the Babe,—my babe to be,
That knew me first and thus made me know him,
That had his right of life and claim on mine,
And would not let me die till he was born,
But pricked me at the heart to save us both,
Saying "Have you the will? Leave God the way!"
And the way was Caponsacchi—"mine," thank God!
He was mine, he is mine, he will be mine.

No pause i' the leading and the light! I know,
Next night there was a cloud came, and not he:
But I prayed through the darkness till it broke
And let him shine. The second night, he came.

"The plan is rash; the project desperate:
In such a flight needs must I risk your life,
Give food for falsehood, folly or mistake,
Ground for your husband's rancour and revenge"—
So he began again, with the same face.
I felt that, the same loyalty—one star
Turning now red that was so white before—
One service apprehended newly: just
A word of mine and there the white was back!

"No, friend, for you will take me! 'Tis yourself
Risk all, not I,—who let you, for I trust
In the compensating great God: enough!
I know you: when is it that you will come?"

"To-morrow at the day's dawn." Then I heard
What I should do: how to prepare for flight
And where to fly.

That night my husband bade
"—You, whom I loathe, beware you break my sleep
This whole night! Couch beside me like the corpse
I would you were!" The rest you know, I think—
How I found Caponsacchi and escaped.

And this man, men call sinner? Jesus Christ!
Of whom men said, with mouths Thyself mad'st once,
"He hath a devil"—say he was Thy saint,
My Caponsacchi! Shield and show—unshroud
In Thine own time the glory of the soul
If aught obscure,—if ink-spot, from vile pens
Scribbling a charge against him—(I was glad
Then, for the first time, that I could not write)—
Flirted his way, have flecked the blaze!

For me,
'Tis otherwise: let men take, sift my thoughts
—Thoughts I throw like the flax for sun to bleach!
I did pray, do pray, in the prayer shall die,
Oh, to have Caponsacchi for my guide!
Ever the face upturned to mine, the hand
Holding my hand across the world,—a sense
That reads, as only such can read, the mark
God sets on women, signifying so
She should—shall peradventure—be divine;
Yet 'ware, the while, how weakness mars the print
And makes confusion, leaves the thing men see,
—Not this man sees,—who from his soul, re-writes
The obliterated charter,—love and strength
Mending what's marred: "So kneels a votarist,
Weeds some poor waste traditionary plot
Where shrine once was, where temple yet may be,
Purging the place but worshipping the while,
By faith and not by sight, sight clearest so,—
Such way the saints work,"—says Don Celestine.
But I, not privileged to see a saint
Of old when such walked earth with crown and palm,
If I call "saint" what saints call something else—
The saints must bear with me, impute the fault
To a soul i' the bud, so starved by ignorance,
Stinted of warmth, it will not blow this year
Nor recognise the orb which Spring-flowers know.
But if meanwhile some insect with a heart
Worth floods of lazy music, spendthrift joy—
Some fire-fly renounced Spring for my dwarfed cup,
Crept close to me, brought lustre for the dark,
Comfort against the cold,—what though excess
Of comfort should miscall the creature—sun?
What did the sun to hinder while harsh hands
Petal by petal, crude and colourless,
Tore me? This one heart gave me all the Spring!

Is all told? There's the journey: and where's time
To tell you how that heart burst out in shine?
Yet certain points do press on me too hard.
Each place must have a name, though I forget:
How strange it was—there where the plain begins
And the small river mitigates its flow—
When eve was fading fast, and my soul sank,
And he divined what surge of bitterness,
In overtaking me, would float me back
Whence I was carried by the striding day—
So,—"This grey place was famous once," said he—
And he began that legend of the place
As if in answer to the unspoken fear,
And told me all about a brave man dead,
Which lifted me and let my soul go on!
How did he know too,—at that town's approach
By the rock-side,—that in coming near the signs,
Of life, the house-roofs and the church and tower,
I saw the old boundary and wall o' the world
Rise plain as ever round me, hard and cold,
As if the broken circlet joined again,
Tightened itself about me with no break,—
As if the town would turn Arezzo's self,—
The husband there,—the friends my enemies,

All ranged against me, not an avenue
To try, but would be blocked and drive me back
On him,—this other, . . . oh the heart in that!
Did not he find, bring, put into my arms
A new-born babe?—and I saw faces beam
Of the young mother proud to teach me joy,
And gossips round expecting my surprise
At the sudden hole through earth that lets in heaven.
I could believe himself by his strong will
Had woven around me what I thought the world
We went along in, every circumstance,
Towns, flowers and faces, all things helped so well!
For, through the journey, was it natural
Such comfort should arise from first to last?
As I look back, all is one milky way;
Still bettered more, the more remembered, so
Do new stars bud while I but search for old,
And fill all gaps i' the glory, and grow him—
Him I now see make the shine everywhere.
Even at the last when the bewildered flesh,
The cloud of weariness about my soul
Clogging too heavily, sucked down all sense,—
Still its last voice was, "He will watch and care;
Let the strength go, I am content: he stays!"
I doubt not he did stay and care for all—
From that sick minute when the head swam round,
And the eyes looked their last and died on him,
As in his arms he caught me and, you say,
Carried me in, that tragical red eve,
And laid me where I next returned to life
In the other red of morning, two red plates
That crushed together, crushed the time between,
And are since then a solid fire to me,—
When in, my dreadful husband and the world
Broke,—and I saw him, master, by hell's right,
And saw my angel helplessly held back
By guards that helped the malice—the lamb prone,
The serpent towering and triumphant—then
Came all the strength back in a sudden swell,
I did for once see right, do right, give tongue
The adequate protest: for a worm must turn
If it would have its wrong observed by God.
I did spring up, attempt to thrust aside
That ice-block 'twixt the sun and me, lay low
The neutralizer of all good and truth.
If I sinned so,—never obey voice more
O' the Just and Terrible, who bids us—"Bear!"
Not—"Stand by, bear to see my angels bear!"
I am clear it was on impulse to serve God
Not save myself,—no—nor my child unborn!

Had I else waited patiently till now?—
Who saw my old kind parents, silly-sooth
And too much trustful, for their worst of faults,
Cheated, brow-beaten, stripped and starved, cast out
Into the kennel: I remonstrated,
Then sank to silence, for,—their woes at end,
Themselves gone,—only I was left to plague.
If only I was threatened and belied,
What matter? I could bear it and did bear;
It was a comfort, still one lot for all:
They were not persecuted for my sake
And I, estranged, the single happy one.
But when at last, all by myself I stood
Obeying the clear voice which bade me rise,
Not for my own sake but my babe unborn,
And take the angel's hand was sent to help—
And found the old adversary athwart the path—
Not my hand simply struck from the angel's, but
The very angel's self made foul i' the face
By the fiend who struck there,—that I would not bear,
That only I resisted! So, my first
And last resistance was invincible.
Prayers move God; threats, and nothing else, move men!
I must have prayed a man as he were God
When I implored the Governor to right
My parents' wrongs: the answer was a smile.
The Archbishop,—did I clasp his feet enough,
Hide my face hotly on them, while I told
More than I dared make my own mother know?
The profit was—compassion and a jest.

This time, the foolish prayers were done with, right
Used might, and solemnized the sport at once.
All was against the combat: vantage, mine?
The runaway avowed, the accomplice-wife,
In company with the plan-contriving priest?
Yet, shame thus rank and patent, I struck, bare,
At foe from head to foot in magic mail,
And off it withered, cobweb-armoury
Against the lightning! 'Twas truth singed the lies
And saved me, not the vain sword nor weak speech!

You see, I will not have the service fail!
I say, the angel saved me: I am safe!
Others may want and wish, I wish nor want
One point o' the circle plainer, where I stand
Traced round about with white to front the world.
What of the calumny I came across,
What o' the way to the end?—the end crowns all.
The judges judged aright i' the main, gave me
The uttermost of my heart's desire, a truce
From torture and Arezzo, balm for hurt
With the quiet nuns,—God recompense the good!
Who said and sang away the ugly past.
And, when my final fortune was revealed,
What safety while, amid my parents' arms,
My babe was given me! Yes, he saved my babe:
It would not have peeped forth, the bird-like thing,
Through that Arezzo noise and trouble: back
Had it returned nor ever let me see!
But the sweet peace cured all, and let me live
And give my bird the life among the leaves
God meant him! Weeks and months of quietude,
I could lie in such peace and learn so much—
Begin the task, I see how needful now,
Of understanding somewhat of my past,—
Know life a little, I should leave so soon.
Therefore, because this man restored my soul,
All has been right; I have gained my gain, enjoyed
As well as suffered,—nay, got foretaste too
Of better life beginning where this ends—
All through the breathing-while allowed me thus,
Which let good premonitions reach my soul
Unthwarted, and benignant influence flow
And interpenetrate and change my heart,
Uncrossed by what was wicked,—nay, unkind.
For, as the weakness of my time drew nigh,
Nobody did me one disservice more,
Spoke coldly or looked strangely, broke the love
I lay in the arms of, till my boy was born,
Born all in love, with nought to spoil the bliss
A whole long fortnight: in a life like mine
A fortnight filled with bliss is long and much.
All women are not mothers of a boy,
Though they live twice the length of my whole life,
And, as they fancy, happily all the same.
There I lay, then, all my great fortnight long,
As if it would continue, broaden out
Happily more and more, and lead to heaven:
Christmas before me,—was not that a chance?
I never realized God's birth before—
How he grew likest God in being born.
This time I felt like Mary, had my babe
Lying a little on my breast like hers.
So all went on till, just four days ago—
The night and the tap.

Oh, it shall be success
To the whole of our poor family! My friends
. . . Nay, father and mother,—give me back my word!
They have been rudely stripped of life, disgraced
Like children who must needs go clothed too fine,
Carry the garb of Carnival in Lent:
If they too much affected frippery,
They have been punished and submit themselves,
Say no word: all is over, they see God
Who will not be extreme to mark their fault
Or he had granted respite: they are safe.

For that most woeful man my husband once,
Who, needing respite, still draws vital breath,
I—pardon him? So far as lies in me,
I give him for his good the life he takes,

Praying the world will therefore acquiesce.
Let him make God amends,—none, none to me
Who thank him rather that, whereas strange fate
Mockingly styled him husband and me wife,
Himself this way at least pronounced divorce,
Blotted the marriage-bond: this blood of mine
Flies forth exultingly at any door,
Washes the parchment white, and thanks the blow.
We shall not meet in this world nor the next,
But where will God be absent? In His face
Is light, but in His shadow healing too:
Let Guido touch the shadow and be healed!
And as my presence was importunate,—
My earthly good, temptation and a snare,—
Nothing about me but drew somehow down
His hate upon me,—somewhat so excused
Therefore, since hate was thus the truth of him,—
May my evanishment for evermore
Help further to relieve the heart that cast
Such object of its natural loathing forth!
So he was made; he nowise made himself:
I could not love him, but his mother did.
His soul has never lain beside my soul;
But for the unresisting body,—thanks!
He burned that garment spotted by the flesh.
Whatever he touched is rightly ruined: plague
It caught, and disinfection it had craved
Still but for Guido; I am saved through him
So as by fire; to him—thanks and farewell!

Even for my babe, my boy, there's safety thence—
From the sudden death of me, I mean; we poor
Weak souls, how we endeavour to be strong!
I was already using up my life,—
This portion, now, should do him such a good,
This other go to keep off such an ill!
The great life; see, a breath and it is gone!
So is detached, so left all by itself
The little life, the fact which means so much.
Shall not God stoop the kindlier to His work,
His marvel of creation, foot would crush,
Now that the hand He trusted to receive
And hold it, lets the treasure fall perforce?
The better; He shall have in orphanage
His own way all the clearlier: if my babe
Outlived the hour—and he has lived two weeks—
It is through God who knows I am not by.
Who is it makes the soft gold hair turn black,
And sets the tongue, might lie so long at rest,
Trying to talk? Let us leave God alone!
Why should I doubt He will explain in time
What I feel now, but fail to find the words?
My babe nor was, nor is, nor yet shall be
Count Guido Franceschini's child at all—
Only his mother's, born of love not hate!
So shall I have my rights in after-time.
It seems absurd, impossible to-day;
So seems so much else, not explained but known!

Ah! Friends, I thank and bless you every one!
No more now: I withdraw from earth and man
To my own soul, compose myself for God.

Well, and there is more! Yes, my end of breath
Shall bear away my soul in being true!
He is still here, not outside with the world,
Here, here, I have him in his rightful place!
'Tis now, when I am most upon the move,
I feel for what I verily find—again
The face, again the eyes, again, through all,
The heart and its immeasurable love
Of my one friend, my only, all my own,
Who put his breast between the spears and me.
Ever with Caponsacchi! Otherwise
Here alone would be failure, loss to me—
How much more loss to him, with life debarred
From giving life, love locked from love's display,
The day-star stopped its task that makes night morn!
O lover of my life, O soldier-saint,
No work begun shall ever pause for death!
Love will be helpful to me more and more
I' the coming course, the new path I must tread—
My weak hand in thy strong hand, strong for that!
Tell him that if I seem without him now,
That's the world's insight! Oh, he understands!

He is at Civita—do I once doubt
The world again is holding us apart?
He had been here, displayed in my behalf
The broad brow that reverberates the truth,
And flashed the word God gave him, back to man!
I know where the free soul is flown! My fate
Will have been hard for even him to bear:
Let it confirm him in the trust of God,
Showing how holily he dared the deed!
And, for the rest,—say, from the deed, no touch
Of harm came, but all good, all happiness,
Not one faint fleck of failure! Why explain?
What I see, oh, he sees and how much more!
Tell him,—I know not wherefore the true word
Should fade and fall unuttered at the last—
It was the name of him I sprang to meet
When came the knock, the summons and the end.[1]
"My great heart, my strong hand are back again!"
I would have sprung to these, beckoning across
Murder and hell gigantic and distinct
O' the threshold, posted to exclude me heaven:
He is ordained to call and I to come!
Do not the dead wear flowers when dressed for God?
Say,—I am all in flowers from head to foot!
Say,—not one flower of all he said and did,
Might seem to flit unnoticed, fade unknown,
But dropped a seed has grown a balsam-tree
Whereof the blossoming perfumes the place
At this supreme of moments! He is a priest;
He cannot marry therefore, which is right:
I think he would not marry if he could.
Marriage on earth seems such a counterfeit,
Mere imitation of the inimitable:
In heaven we have the real and true and sure.
'Tis there they neither marry nor are given
In marriage but are as the angels: right,
Oh how right that is, how like Jesus Christ
To say that! Marriage-making for the earth,
With gold so much,—birth, power, repute so much,
Or beauty, youth so much, in lack of these!

[1] Guido gained admittance on the night of the murder by answering with the name of Caponsacchi the query as to who was knocking.

Be as the angels rather, who, apart,
Know themselves into one, are found at length
Married, but marry never, no, nor give
In marriage; they are man and wife at once
When the true time is: here we have to wait
Not so long neither! Could we by a wish
Have what we will and get the future now,
Would we wish ought done undone in the past?
So, let him wait God's instant men call years;
Meantime hold hard by truth and his great soul,
Do out the duty! Through such souls alone
God stooping shows sufficient of His light
For us i' the dark to rise by. And I rise.

XI. GUIDO[1]

You are the Cardinal Acciaiuoli, and you,
Abate Panciatichi—two good Tuscan names:
Acciaiuoli—ah, your ancestor it was
Built the huge battlemented convent-block
Over the little forky flashing Greve
That takes the quick turn at the foot o' the hill
Just as one first sees Florence: oh those days!
'Tis Ema, though, the other rivulet,
The one-arched brown brick bridge yawns over,—yes,
Gallop and go five minutes, and you gain
The Roman Gate from where the Ema's bridged:
Kingfishers fly there: how I see the bend
O'erturreted by Certosa which he built,
That Senescal (we styled him) of your House!
I do adjure you, help me, Sirs! My blood
Comes from as far a source: ought it to end
This way, by leakage through their scaffold-planks
Into Rome's sink where her red refuse runs?
Sirs, I beseech you by blood-sympathy,
If there be any vile experiment
In the air,—if this your visit simply prove,
When all's done, just a well-intentioned trick,

[1] In Book V, Guido spoke as "Count Guido Franceschini" on the witness stand, fighting for his life and putting up a pretense before the world. Here he is simply "Guido" in the death cell, speaking to the two churchmen who have come to give him spiritual ministration. As the book advances the essential Guido is more and more clearly revealed.

That tries for truth truer than truth itself,
By startling up a man, ere break of day,
To tell him he must die at sunset,—pshaw!
That man's a Franceschini; feel his pulse,
Laugh at your folly, and let's all go sleep!
You have my last word,—innocent am I
As Innocent my Pope and murderer,
Innocent as a babe, as Mary's own,
As Mary's self,—I said, say and repeat,—
And why, then, should I die twelve hours hence? I—
Whom, not twelve hours ago, the gaoler bade
Turn to my straw-truss, settle and sleep sound
That I might wake the sooner, promptlier pay
His dues of meat-and-drink-indulgence, cross
His palm with fee of the good-hand, beside,
As gallants use who go at large again!
For why? All honest Rome approved my part;
Whoever owned wife, sister, daughter,—nay,
Mistress,—had any shadow of any right
That looks like right, and, all the more resolved,
Held it with tooth and nail,—these manly men
Approved! I being for Rome, Rome was for me.
Then, there's the point reserved, the subterfuge
My lawyers held by, kept for last resource,
Firm should all else,—the impossible fancy!—fail,
And sneaking burgess-spirit win the day.
The knaves! One plea at least would hold,—they laughed,—
One grappling-iron scratch the bottom-rock
Even should the middle mud let anchor go!
I hooked my cause on to the Clergy's,[1]—plea
Which, even if law tipped off my hat and plume,
Would show my priestly tonsure, save me so.
The Pope moreover, this old Innocent,
Being so meek and mild and merciful,
So fond o' the poor and so fatigued of earth,
So . . . fifty thousand devils in deepest hell!
Why must he cure us of our strange conceit
Of the angel in man's likeness, that we loved
And looked should help us at a pinch? He help?
He pardon? Here's his mind and message—death!
Thank the good Pope! Now, is he good in this,
Never mind, Christian,—no such stuff's extant,—
But will my death do credit to his reign,
Show he both lived and let live, so was good?
Cannot I live if he but like? "The law!"
Why, just the law gives him the very chance,
The precise leave to let my life alone,
Which the angelic soul of him (he says)
Yearns after! Here they drop it in his palm,
My lawyers, capital o' the cursed kind,—
Drop life to take and hold and keep: but no!
He sighs, shakes head, refuses to shut hand,
Motions away the gift they bid him grasp,
And of the coyness comes—that off I run
And down I go, he best knows whither! mind,
He knows, who sets me rolling all the same!
Disinterested Vicar of our Lord,
This way he abrogates and disallows,
Nullifies and ignores,—reverts in fine
To the good and right, in detriment of me!
Talk away! Will you have the naked truth?
He's sick of his life's supper,—swallowed lies:
So, hobbling bedward, needs must ease his maw
Just where I sit o' the door-sill. Sir Abate,
Can you do nothing? Friends, we used to frisk:
What of this sudden slash in a friend's face,
This cut across our good companionship
That showed its front so gay when both were young?
Were not we put into a beaten path,
Bid pace the world, we nobles born and bred,
We body of friends with each his 'scutcheon full
Of old achievement and impunity,—
Taking the laugh of morn and Sol's salute
As forth we fared, pricked on to breathe our steeds
And take equestrian sport over the green
Under the blue, across the crop,—what care?
If we went prancing up hill and down dale,
In and out of the level and the straight,

[1] Guido had had a minor connection with the church. His lawyers argued that he was therefor only under the jurisdiction of the Church Court and that the sentence was invalid. The Pope refused to remit the sentence.

By the bit of pleasant byway, where was harm?
Still Sol salutes me and the morning laughs:
I see my grandsire's hoof-prints,—point the spot
Where he drew rein, slipped saddle, and stabbed knave
For daring throw gibe—much less, stone—from pale:
Then back, and on, and up with the cavalcade.
Just so wend we, now canter, now converse,
Till, 'mid the jauncing pride and jaunty port,
Something of a sudden jerks at somebody—
A dagger is out, a flashing cut and thrust,
Because I play some prank my grandsire played,
And here I sprawl: where is the company? Gone!
A trot and a trample! only I lie trapped,
Writhe in a certain novel springe just set
By the good old Pope: I'm first prize. Warn me? Why?
Apprise me that the law o' the game is changed?
Enough that I'm a warning, as I writhe,
To all and each my fellows of the file,
And make law plain henceforward past mistake,
"For such a prank, death is the penalty!"
Pope the Five Hundredth (what do I know or care?)
Deputes your Eminence and Abateship
To announce that, twelve hours from this time, he needs
I just essay upon my body and soul
The virtue of his brand-new engine, prove
Represser of the pranksome! I'm the first!
Thanks. Do you know what teeth you mean to try
The sharpness of, on this soft neck and throat?
I know it,—I have seen and hate it,—ay,
As you shall, while I tell you! Let me talk,
Or leave me, at your pleasure! talk I must:
What is your visit but my lure to talk?
Nay, you have something to disclose?—a smile,
At end of the forced sternness, means to mock
The heart-beats here? I call your two hearts stone!
Is your charge to stay with me till I die?
Be tacit as your bench, then! Use your ears,
I use my tongue: how glibly yours will run
At pleasant supper-time . . . God's curse! . . . to-night
When all the guests jump up, begin so brisk,
"Welcome, his Eminence who shrived the wretch!
Now we shall have the Abate's story!"

Life!
How I could spill this overplus of mine
Among those hoar-haired, shrunk-shanked, odds and ends
Of body and soul, old age is chewing dry!
Those windle-straws that stare while purblind death
Mows here, mows there, makes hay of juicy me,
And misses, just the bunch of withered weed,
Would brighten hell and streak its smoke with flame!
How the life I could shed yet never shrink,
Would drench their stalks with sap like grass in May!
Is it not terrible, I entreat you, Sirs?—
With manifold and plenitudinous life,
Prompt at death's menace to give blow for threat,
Answer his "Be thou not!" by "Thus I am!"—
Terrible so to be alive yet die?

How I live, how I see! so,—how I speak!
Lucidity of soul unlocks the lips:
I never had the words at will before.
How I see all my folly at a glance!
"A man requires a woman and a wife:"
There was my folly; I believed the saw:
I knew that just myself concerned myself,
Yet needs must look for what I seemed to lack,
In a woman,—why, the woman's in the man!
Fools we are, how we learn things when too late!
Overmuch life turns round my woman-side;
The male and female in me, mixed before,
Settle of a sudden: I'm my wife outright
In this unmanly appetite for truth,
This careless courage as to consequence,
This instantaneous sight through things and through,
This voluble rhetoric, if you please,—'tis she!
Here you have that Pompilia whom I slew,
Also the folly for which I slew her!

Fool!
And, fool-like, what is it I wander from?
What did I say of your sharp iron tooth?
Ah,—that I know the hateful thing! this way.
I chanced to stroll forth, many a good year gone,
One warm Spring eve in Rome, and unaware
Looking, mayhap, to count what stars were out,
Came on your fine axe in a frame, that falls
And so cuts off a man's head underneath,
Mannaia,[1]—thus we made acquaintance first:
Out of the way, in a by-part o' the town,
At the Mouth-of-Truth o' the river-side, you know:
One goes by the Capitol: and wherefore coy,
Retiring out of crowded noisy Rome?
Because a very little time ago
It had done service, chopped off head from trunk,
Belonging to a fellow whose poor house
The thing must make a point to stand before.
Felice Whatsoever-was-the-name
Who stabled buffaloes and so gained bread,
(Our clowns unyoke them in the ground hard by)
And, after use of much improper speech,
Had struck at Duke Some-title-or-other's face,
Because he kidnapped, carried away and kept
Felice's sister who would sit and sing
I' the filthy doorway while she plaited fringe
To deck the brutes with,—on their gear it goes,—
The good girl with the velvet in her voice.
So did the Duke, so did Felice, so
Did Justice, intervening with her axe.
There the man-mutilating engine stood
At ease, both gay and grim, like a Swiss guard
Off duty,—purified itself as well,
Getting dry, sweet and proper for next week,—
And doing incidental good, 'twas hoped
To the rough lesson-lacking populace
Who now and then, forsooth, must right their wrongs!
There stood the twelve-foot square of scaffold, railed
Considerately round to elbow-height:
(For fear an officer should tumble thence
And sprain his ankle and be lame a month,
Through starting when the axe fell and head too!)
Railed likewise were the steps whereby 'twas reached.
All of it painted red: red, in the midst,
Ran up two narrow tall beams barred across,
Since from the summit, some twelve feet to reach,
The iron plate with the sharp shearing edge
Had slammed, jerked, shot, or slid,—I shall soon find which!
And so lay quiet, fast in its fit place,
The wooden half-moon collar, now eclipsed
By the blade which blocked its curvature: apart,
The other half,—the under half-moon board
Which, helped by this, completes a neck's embrace,—
Joined to a sort of desk that wheels aside
Out of the way when done with,—down you kneel,
In you're pushed, over you the other drops,
Tight you're clipped, whiz, there's the blade cleaves its best,
Out trundles body, down flops head on floor,
And where's your soul gone? That, too, I shall find!
This kneeling-place was red, red, never fear!
But only slimy-like with paint, not blood,
For why? a decent pitcher stood at hand,
A broad dish to hold sawdust, and a broom
By some unnamed utensil,—scraper-rake,—
Each with a conscious air of duty done.
Underneath, loungers,—boys and some few men,—
Discoursed this platter, named the other tool,
Just as, when grooms tie up and dress a steed,
Boys lounge and look on, and elucubrate
What the round brush is used for, what the square,—
So was explained—to me the skill-less man—
The manner of the grooming for next world
Undergone by Felice What's-his-name.
There's no such lovely month in Rome as May—
May's crescent is no half-moon of red plank,
And came now tilting o'er the wave i' the west,

[1] The mannaia was the instrument used to execute Guido. It was an earlier form of the guillotine.

One greenish-golden sea, right 'twixt those bars
Of the engine—I began acquaintance with,
Understood, hated, hurried from before,
To have it out of sight and cleanse my soul!
Here it is all again, conserved for use:
Twelve hours hence I may know more, not hate worse.

That young May-moon-month! Devils of the deep!
Was not a Pope then Pope as much as now?
Used not he chirrup o'er the Merry Tales,
Chuckle,—his nephew so exact the wag
To play a jealous cullion such a trick
As wins the wife i' the pleasant story! Well?
Why do things change? Wherefore is Rome un-Romed?
I tell you, ere Felice's corpse was cold,
The Duke, that night, threw wide his palace-doors,
Received the compliments o' the quality,
For justice done him,—bowed and smirked his best,
And in return passed round a pretty thing,
A portrait of Felice's sister's self,
Florid old rogue Albano's masterpiece,
As—better than virginity in rags—
Bouncing Europa on the back o' the bull:
They laughed and took their road the safelier home.
Ah, but times change, there's quite another Pope,
I do the Duke's deed, take Felice's place,
And, being no Felice, lout and clout,
Stomach but ill the phrase, "I lose my head!"
How euphemistic! Lose what? Lose your ring,
Your snuff-box, tablets, kerchief!—but, your head?
I learnt the process at an early age;
'Twas useful knowledge in those same old days,
To know the way a head is set on neck.
My fencing-master urged, "Would you excel?
Rest not content with mere bold give-and-guard,
Nor pink the antagonist somehow-anyhow,—
See me dissect a little, and know your game!
Only anatomy makes a thrust the thing."
Oh, Cardinal, those lithe live necks of ours!
Here go the vertebræ, here's *Atlas*, here
Axis, and here the symphyses [1] stop short,
So wisely and well,—as, o'er a corpse, we cant,—
And here's the silver cord which . . . what's our word?
Depends from the gold bowl, which loosed (not "lost")
Lets us from heaven to hell,—one chop, we're loose!
"And not much pain i' the process," quoth a sage:
Who told him? Not Felice's ghost, I think!
Such "losing" is scarce Mother Nature's mode.
She fain would have cord ease itself away,
Worn to a thread by threescore years and ten,
Snap while we slumber: that seems bearable.
I'm told one clot of blood extravasate
Ends one as certainly as Roland's sword,—
One drop of lymph suffused proves Oliver's mace,—
Intruding, either of the pleasant pair,
On the arachnoid tunic of my brain.
That's Nature's way of loosing cord!—but Art,
How of Art's process with the engine here?
When bowl and cord alike are crushed across,
Bored between, bruised through? Why, if Fagon's self,[2]
The French Court's pride, that famed practitioner,
Would pass his cold pale lightning of a knife
Pistoja-ware, adroit 'twixt joint and joint,
With just a "See how facile, gentlefolk!"—
The thing were not so bad to bear! Brute force
Cuts as he comes, breaks in, breaks on, breaks out
O' the hard and soft of you: is that the same?
A lithe snake thrids the hedge, makes throb no leaf:
A heavy ox sets chest to brier and branch,
Bursts somehow through, and leaves one hideous hole
Behind him!

And why, why must this needs be?
Oh, if men were but good! They are not good,
Nowise like Peter: people called him rough,

[1] Two of the vertebræ and the cartilage between.
[2] Physician to Louis XIV.

But if, as I left Rome, I spoke the Saint,
—"*Petrus, quo vadis?*" [1]—doubtless, I should hear,
"To free the prisoner and forgive his fault!
I plucked the absolute dead from God's own bar,
And raised up Dorcas,—why not rescue thee?"
What would cost one such nullifying word?
If Innocent succeeds to Peter's place,
Let him think Peter's thought, speak Peter's speech!
I say, he is bound to it: friends, how say you?
Concede I be all one bloodguiltiness
And mystery of murder in the flesh,
Why should that fact keep the Pope's mouth shut fast?
He execrates my crime,—good!—sees hell yawn
One inch from the red plank's end which I press,—
Nothing is better! What's the consequence?
How should a Pope proceed that knows his cue?
Why, leave me linger out my minute here,
Since close on death comes judgment and comes doom,
Not crib at dawn its pittance from a sheep
Destined ere dewfall to be butcher's-meat!
Think, Sirs, if I have done you any harm,
And you require the natural revenge,
Suppose, and so intend to poison me,
—Just as you take and slip into my draught
The paperful of powder that clears scores,
You notice on my brow a certain blue:
How you both overset the wine at once!
How you both smile! "Our enemy has the plague!
Twelve hours hence he'll be scraping his bones bare
Of that intolerable flesh, and die,
Frenzied with pain: no need for poison here!
Step aside and enjoy the spectacle!"
Tender for souls are you, Pope Innocent!
Christ's maxim is—one soul outweighs the world:
Respite me, save a soul, then, curse the world!
"No," venerable sire, I hear you smirk,
"No: for Christ's gospel changes names, not things,
Renews the obsolete, does nothing more!
Our fire-new gospel is re-tinkered law,
Our mercy, justice,—Jove's rechristened God—
Nay, whereas, in the popular conceit,
'Tis pity that old harsh Law somehow limps,
Lingers on earth, although Law's day be done,—
Else would benignant Gospel interpose,
Not furtively as now, but bold and frank
O'erflutter us with healing in her wings,
Law being harshness, Gospel only love—
We tell the people, on the contrary,
Gospel takes up the rod which Law lets fall;
Mercy is vigilant when justice sleeps!
Does Law permit a taste of Gospel-grace?
The secular arm allow the spiritual power
To act for once?—no compliment so fine
As that our Gospel handsomely turn harsh,
Thrust victim back on Law the nice and coy!"
Yes, you do say so,—else you would forgive
Me, whom Law does not touch but tosses you!
Don't think to put on the professional face!
You know what I know,—casuists as you are,
Each nerve must creep, each hair start, sting, and stand,
At such illogical inconsequence!
Dear my friends, do but see! A murder's tried,
There are two parties to the cause: I'm one,
—Defend myself, as somebody must do:
I have the best o' the battle: that's a fact,
Simple fact,—fancies find no place just now.
What though half Rome condemned me? Half approved:
And, none disputes, the luck is mine at last,
All Rome, i' the main, acquits me: whereon,
What has the Pope to ask but "How finds Law?"
"I find," replies Law, "I have erred this while:
Guilty or guiltless, Guido proves a priest,
No layman: he is therefore yours, not mine:
I bound him: loose him, you whose will is Christ's!"
And now what does this Vicar of the Lord,
Shepherd o' the flock,—one of whose charge bleats sore
For crook's help from the quag wherein it drowns?

[1] The question with which, according to legendary accounts, Christ turned back Peter when he was leaving Rome at the time of the persecutions of Nero: "Peter, whither goest thou?"

Law suffers him employ the crumpled end:
His pleasure is to turn staff, use the point,
And thrust the shuddering sheep he calls a wolf,
Back and back, down and down to where hell gapes!
"Guiltless," cries Law—"Guilty," corrects the Pope!
"Guilty," for the whim's sake! "Guilty," he somehow thinks,
And anyhow says: 'tis truth; he dares not lie!

Others should do the lying. That's the cause
Brings you both here: I ought in decency
Confess to you that I deserve my fate,
Am guilty, as the Pope thinks,—ay, to the end,
Keep up the jest, lie on, lie ever, lie
I' the latest gasp of me! What reason, Sirs?
Because to-morrow will succeed to-day
For you, though not for me: and if I stick
Still to the truth, declare with my last breath,
I die an innocent and murdered man,—
Why, there's the tongue of Rome will wag a-pace
This time to-morrow,—don't I hear the talk!
"So, to the last he proved impenitent?
Pagans have said as much of martyred saints!
Law demurred, washed her hands of the whole case.
Prince Somebody said this, Duke Something, that.
Doubtless the man's dead, dead enough, don't fear!
But, hang it, what if there have been a spice,
A touch of . . . eh? You see, the Pope's so old,
Some of us add, obtuse,—age never slips
The chance of shoving youth to face death first!"
And so on. Therefore to suppress such talk
You two come here, entreat I tell you lies,
And end, the edifying way. I end,
Telling the truth! Your self-styled shepherd thieves!
A thief—and how thieves hate the wolves we know:
Damage to theft, damage to thrift, all's one!
The red hand is sworn foe of the black jaw!
That's only natural, that's right enough:
But why the wolf should compliment the thief
With the shepherd's title, bark out life in thanks,
And, spiteless, lick the prong that spits him,—eh,
Cardinal? My Abate, scarcely thus!
There, let my sheepskin-garb, a curse on't, go—
Leave my teeth free if I must show my shag!
Repent? What good shall follow? If I pass
Twelve hours repenting, will that fact hold fast
The thirteenth at the horrid dozen's end?
If I fall forthwith at your feet, gnash, tear,
Foam, rave, to give your story the due grace,
Will that assist the engine half-way back
Into its hiding-house?—boards, shaking now,
Bone against bone, like some old skeleton bat
That wants, at winter's end, to wake and prey!
Will howling put the spectre back to sleep?
Ah, but I misconceive your object, Sirs!
Since I want new life like the creature,—life
Being done with here, begins i' the world away:
I shall next have "Come, mortals, and be judged!"
There's but a minute betwixt this and then:
So, quick, be sorry since it saves my soul!
Sirs, truth shall save it, since no lies assist!
Hear the truth, you, whatever you style yourselves,
Civilisation and society!
Come, one good grapple, I with all the world!
Dying in cold blood is the desperate thing;
The angry heart explodes, bears off in blaze
The indignant soul, and I'm combustion-ripe.
Why, you intend to do your worst with me!
That's in your eyes! You dare no more than death,
And mean no less. I must make up my mind!
So Pietro,—when I chased him here and there,
Morsel by morsel cut away the life
I loathed,—cried for just respite to confess
And save his soul: much respite did I grant!
Why grant me respite who deserve my doom?
Me—who engaged to play a prize, fight you,
Knowing your arms, and foil you, trick for trick,
At rapier-fence, your match and, may be, more.
I knew that if I chose sin certain sins,
Solace my lusts out of the regular way
Prescribed me, I should find you in the path,
Have to try skill with a redoubted foe;

You would lunge, I would parry, and make end.
At last, occasion of a murder comes:
We cross blades, I, for all my brag, break guard,
And in goes the cold iron at my breast,
Out at my back, and end is made of me.
You stand confessed the adroiter swordsman,—ay,
But on your triumph you increase, it seems,
Want more of me than lying flat on face:
I ought to raise my ruined head, allege
Not simply I pushed worse blade o' the pair,
But my antagonist dispensed with steel!
There was no passage of arms, you looked me low,
With brow and eye abolished cut and thrust
Nor used the vulgar weapon! This chance scratch,
This incidental hurt, this sort of hole
I' the heart of me? I stumbled, got it so!
Fell on my own sword as a bungler may!
Yourself proscribe such heathen tools, and trust
To the naked virtue: it was virtue stood
Unarmed and awed me,—on my brow there burned
Crime out so plainly, intolerably red,
That I was fain to cry—"Down to the dust
With me, and bury there brow, brand and all!"
Law had essayed the adventure,—but what's Law?
Morality exposed the Gorgon shield!
Morality and Religion conquer me.
If Law sufficed would you come here, entreat
I supplement law, and confess forsooth?
Did not the Trial show things plain enough?
"Ah, but a word of the man's very self
Would somehow put the keystone in its place
And crown the arch!" Then take the word you want!

I say that, long ago, when things began,
All the world made agreement, such and such
Were pleasure-giving profit-bearing acts,
But henceforth extra-legal, nor to be:
You must not kill the man whose death would please
And profit you, unless his life stop yours
Plainly, and need so be put aside:
Get the thing by a public course, by law,
Only no private bloodshed as of old!
All of us, for the good of every one,
Renounced such license and conformed to law:
Who breaks law, breaks pact therefore, helps himself
To pleasure and profit over and above the due,
And must pay forfeit,—pain beyond his share:
For, pleasure being the sole good in the world,
Any one's pleasure turns to some one's pain,
So, let law watch for every one,—say we,
Who call things wicked that give too much joy,
And nickname mere reprisal, envy makes,
Punishment: quite right! thus the world goes round.
I, being well aware such pact there was,
I, in my time who found advantage come
Of law's observance and crime's penalty,—
Who, but for wholesome fear law bred in friends,
Had doubtless given example long ago,
Furnished forth some friend's pleasure with my pain,
And, by my death, pieced out his scanty life,—
I could not, for that foolish life of me,
Help risking law's infringement,—I broke bond,
And needs must pay price,—wherefore, here's my head,
Flung with a flourish! But, repentance too?
But pure and simple sorrow for law's breach
Rather than blunderer's-ineptitude?
Cardinal, no! Abate, scarcely thus!
'Tis the fault, not that I dared try a fall
With Law and straightway am found undermost,
But that I failed to see, above man's law,
God's precept you, the Christians, recognize?
Colly my cow! Don't fidget, Cardinal!
Abate, cross your breast and count your beads
And exorcise the devil, for here he stands
And stiffens in the bristly nape of neck,
Daring you drive him hence! You, Christians both?
I say, if ever was such faith at all
Born in the world, by your community
Suffered to live its little tick of time,
'Tis dead of age, now, ludicrously dead;
Honour its ashes, if you be discreet,
In epitaph only! For, concede its death,

Allow extinction, you may boast unchecked
What feats the thing did in a crazy land
At a fabulous epoch,—treat your faith, that way,
Just as you treat your relics: "Here's a shred
Of saintly flesh, a scrap of blessed bone,
Raised King Cophetua, who was dead, to life
In Mesopotamy twelve centuries since,
Such was its virtue!"—twangs the Sacristan,
Holding the shrine-box up, with hands like feet
Because of gout in every finger-joint:
Does he bethink him to reduce one knob,
Allay one twinge by touching what he vaunts?
I think he half uncrooks fist to catch fee,
But, for the grace, the quality of cure,—
Cophetua was the man put that to proof!
Not otherwise, your faith is shrined and shown
And shamed at once: you banter while you bow!
Do you dispute this? Come, a monster-laugh,
A madman's laugh, allowed his Carnival
Later ten days than when all Rome, but he,
Laughed at the candle-contest: mine's alight,
'Tis just it sputter till the puff o' the Pope
End it to-morrow and the world turn Ash.
Come, thus I wave a wand and bring to pass
In a moment, in the twinkle of an eye,
What but that—feigning everywhere grows fact,
Professors turn possessors, realize
The faith they play with as a fancy now,
And bid it operate, have full effect
On every circumstance of life, to-day,
In Rome,—faith's flow set free at fountain-head!
Now, you'll own, at this present, when I speak,
Before I work the wonder, there's no man,
Woman or child in Rome, faith's fountain-head,
But might, if each were minded, realize
Conversely unbelief, faith's opposite—
Set it to work on life unflinchingly,
Yet give no symptom of an outward change:
Why should things change because men disbelieve?
What's incompatible, in the whited tomb,
With bones and rottenness one inch below?
What saintly act is done in Rome to-day
But might be prompted by the devil,—"is"
I say not,—"has been, and again may be,"—
I do say, full i' the face o' the crucifix
You try to stop my mouth with! Off with it!
Look in your own heart, if your soul have eyes!
You shall see reason why, though faith were fled,
Unbelief still might work the wires and move
Man, the machine, to play a faithful part.
Preside your college, Cardinal, in your cape,
Or,—having got above his head, grown Pope,—
Abate, gird your loins and wash my feet!
Do you suppose I am at loss at all
Why you crook, why you cringe, why fast or feast?
Praise, blame, sit, stand, lie or go!—all of it,
In each of you, purest unbelief may prompt,
And wit explain to who has eyes to see.
But, lo, I wave wand, make the false the true!
Here's Rome believes in Christianity!
What an explosion, how the fragments fly
Of what was surface, mask, and make-believe!
Begin now,—look at this Pope's-halberdier
In wasp-like black and yellow foolery!
He, doing duty at the corridor,
Wakes from a muse and stands convinced of sin!
Down he flings halbert, leaps the passage-length,
Pushes into the presence, pantingly
Submits the extreme peril of the case
To the Pope's self,—whom in the world beside?—
And the Pope breaks talk with ambassador,
Bids aside bishop, wills the whole world wait
Till he secure that prize, outweighs the world,
A soul, relieve the sentry of his qualm!
His Altitude the Referendary,—
Robed right, and ready for the usher's word
To pay devoir,—is, of all times, just then
'Ware of a master-stroke of argument
Will cut the spinal cord . . . ugh, ugh! . . . I mean,
Paralyse Molinism for evermore!
Straight he leaves lobby, trundles, two and two,
Down steps, to reach home, write if but a word
Shall end the impudence: he leaves who likes
Go pacify the Pope: there's Christ to serve!
How otherwise would men display their zeal?

If the same sentry had the least surmise
A powder-barrel 'neath the pavement lay
In neighbourhood with what might prove a match,
Meant to blow sky-high Pope and presence both—
Would he not break through courtiers, rank and file,
Bundle up, bear off and save body so,
The Pope, no matter for his priceless soul?
There's no fool's-freak here, nought to soundly swinge,
Only a man in earnest, you'll so praise
And pay and prate about, that earth shall ring!
Had thought possessed the Referendary
His jewel-case at home was left ajar,
What would be wrong in running, robes awry,
To be beforehand with the pilferer?
What talk then of indecent haste? Which means,
That both these, each in his degree, would do
Just that—for a comparative nothing's sake,
And thereby gain approval and reward—
Which, done for what Christ says is worth the world,
Procures the doer curses, cuffs, and kicks.
I call such difference 'twixt act and act,
Sheer lunacy unless your truth on lip
Be recognized a lie in heart of you!
How do you all act, promptly or in doubt,
When there's a guest poisoned at supper-time
And he sits chatting on with spot on cheek?
"Pluck him by the skirt, and round him in the ears,
Have at him by the beard, warn anyhow!"
Good, and this other friend that's cheat and thief
And dissolute,—go stop the devil's feast,
Withdraw him from the imminent hell-fire!
Why, for your life, you dare not tell your friend,
"You lie, and I admonish you for Christ!"
Who yet dare seek that same man at the Mass
To warn him—on his knees, and tinkle near,—
He left a cask a-tilt, a tap unturned,
The Trebbian running: what a grateful jump
Out of the Church rewards your vigilance!
Perform that self-same service just a thought
More maladroitly,—since a bishop sits
At function!—and he budges not, bites lip,—
"You see my case: how can I quit my post?
He has an eye to any such default.
See to it, neighbour, I beseech your love!"
He and you know the relative worth of things,
What is permissible or inopportune.
Contort your brows! You know I speak the truth:
Gold is called gold, and dross called dross, i' the Book:
Gold you let lie and dross pick up and prize!
—Despite your master of some fifty monks
And nuns a-maundering here and mumping there,
Who could, and on occasion would, spurn dross,
Clutch gold, and prove their faith a fact so far,—
I grant you! Fifty times the number squeak
And gibber in the madhouse—firm of faith,
This fellow, that his nose supports the moon;
The other, that his straw hat crowns him Pope:
Does that prove all the world outside insane?
Do fifty miracle-mongers match the mob
That acts on the frank faithless principle,
Born-baptised-and-bred Christian-atheists, each
With just as much a right to judge as you,—
As many senses in his soul, and nerves
I' neck of him as I,—whom, soul and sense,
Neck and nerve, you abolish presently,—
I being the unit in creation now
Who pay the Maker, in this speech of mine,
A creature's duty, spend my last of breath
In bearing witness, even by my worst fault
To the creature's obligation, absolute,
Perpetual: my worst fault protests, "The faith
Claims all of me: I would give all she claims,
But for a spice of doubt: the risk's too rash:
Double or quits, I play, but, all or nought,
Exceeds my courage: therefore, I descend
To the next faith with no dubiety—
Faith in the present life, made last as long
And prove as full of pleasure as may hap,
Whatever pain it cause the world." I'm wrong?
I've had my life, whate'er I lose: I'm right?
I've got the single good there was to gain.
Entire faith, or else complete unbelief!
Aught between has my loathing and contempt,
Mine and God's also, doubtless: ask yourself,
Cardinal, where and how you like a man!
Why, either with your feet upon his head,

Confessed your caudatory, or, at large,
The stranger in the crowd who caps to you
But keeps his distance,—why should he presume?
You want no hanger-on and dropper-off,
Now yours, and now not yours but quite his own,
According as the sky looks black or bright.
Just so I capped to and kept off from faith—
You promised trudge behind through fair and foul,
Yet leave i' the lurch at the first spit of rain.
Who holds to faith whenever rain begins?
What does the father when his son lies dead,
The merchant when his money-bags take wing,
The politician whom a rival ousts?
No case but has its conduct, faith prescribes:
Where's the obedience that shall edify?
Why, they laugh frankly in the face of faith
And take the natural course,—this rends his hair
Because his child is taken to God's breast,
That gnashes teeth and raves at loss of trash
Which rust corrupts and thieves break through and steal,
And this, enabled to inherit earth
Through meekness, curses till your blood runs cold!
Down they all drop to my low level, rest
Heart upon dungy earth that's warm and soft,
And let who please attempt the altitudes:
Each playing prodigal son of heavenly sire,
Turning his nose up at the fatted calf,
Fain to fill belly with the husks, we swine
Did eat by born depravity of taste!

Enough of the hypocrites. But you, Sirs, you—
Who never budged from litter where I lay,
And buried snout i' the draff-box while I fed,
Cried amen to my creed's one article—
"Get pleasure, 'scape pain,—give your preference
To the immediate good, for time is brief,
And death ends good and ill and everything!
What's got is gained, what's gained soon is gained twice,
And,—inasmuch as faith gains most,—feign faith!"
So did we brother-like pass word about:
—You, now,—like bloody drunkards but half-drunk,
Who fool men yet perceive men find them fools,
Vexed that a titter gains the gravest mouth,—
O' the sudden you must needs re-introduce
Solemnity, straight sober undue mirth
By a blow dealt me, your boon companion here,
Who, using the old license, dreamed of harm
No more than snow in harvest: yet it falls!
You check the merriment effectually
By pushing your abrupt machine i' the midst,
Making me Rome's example: blood for wine!
The general good needs that you chop and change!
I may dislike the hocus-pocus,—Rome,
The laughter-loving people, won't they stare
Chap-fallen!—while serious natures sermonize
"The magistrate, he beareth not the sword
In vain; who sins may taste its edge, we see!"
Why my sin, drunkards? Where have I abused
Liberty, scandalized you all so much?
Who called me, who crooked finger till I came,
Fool that I was, to join companionship?
I knew my own mind, meant to live my life,
Elude your envy, or else make a stand,
Take my own part and sell you my life dear.
But it was "Fie! No prejudice in the world
To the proper manly instinct! Cast your lot
Into our lap, one genius ruled our births,
We'll compass joy by concert; take with us
The regular irregular way i' the wood;
You'll miss no game through riding breast by breast,
In this preserve, the Church's park and pale,
Rather than outside where the world lies waste!"
Come, if you said not that, did you say this?
Give plain and terrible warning, "Live, enjoy?
Such life begins in death and ends in hell!
Dare you bid us assist your sins, us priests
Who hurry sin and sinners from the earth?
No such delight for us, why then for you?
Leave earth, seek heaven or find its opposite!"
Had you so warned me, not in lying words
But veritable deeds with tongues of flame,
That had been fair, that might have struck a man,
Silenced the squabble between soul and sense,

Compelled him to make mind up, take one course
Or the other, peradventure!—wrong or right,
Foolish or wise, you would have been at least
Sincere, no question,—forced me choose, indulge
Or else renounce my instincts, still play wolf
Or find my way submissive to your fold,
Be red-crossed on my fleece, one sheep the more.
But you as good as bade me wear sheep's wool
Over wolf's skin, suck blood and hide the noise
By mimicry of something like a bleat,—
Whence it comes that because, despite my care,
Because I smack my tongue too loud for once,
Drop baaing, here's the village up in arms!
Have at the wolf's throat, you who hate the breed!
Oh, were it only open yet to choose—
One little time more—whether I'd be free
Your foe, or subsidized your friend forsooth!
Should not you get a growl through the white fangs
In answer to your beckoning! Cardinal,
Abate, managers o' the multitude,
I'd turn your gloved hands to account, be sure!
You should manipulate the coarse rough mob:
'Tis you I'd deal directly with, not them,—
Using your fears: why touch the thing myself
When I could see you hunt and then cry "Shares!
Quarter the carcass or we quarrel; come,
Here's the world ready to see justice done!"
Oh, it had been a desperate game, but game
Wherein the winner's chance were worth the pains!
We'd try conclusions!—at the worst, what worse
Than this Mannaia-machine, each minute's talk,
Helps push an inch the nearer me? Fool, fool!

You understand me and forgive, sweet Sirs?
I blame you, tear my hair and tell my woe—
All's but a flourish, figure of rhetoric!
One must try each expedient to save life.
One makes fools look foolisher fifty-fold
By putting in their place men wise like you
To take the full force of an argument
Would buffet their stolidity in vain.
If you should feel aggrieved by the mere wind
O' the blow that means to miss you and maul them,
That's my success! Is it not folly, now,
To say with folk, "A plausible defence—
We see through notwithstanding, and reject?"
Reject the plausible they do, these fools,
Who never even make pretence to show
One point beyond its plausibility
In favour of the best belief they hold!
"Saint Somebody-or-other raised the dead:"
Did he? How do you come to know as much?
"Know it, what need? The story's plausible,
Avouched for by a martyrologist,
And why should good men sup on cheese and leeks
On such a saint's day, if there were no saint?"
I praise the wisdom of these fools, and straight
Tell them my story—"plausible, but false!"
False, to be sure! What else can story be
That runs—a young wife tired of an old spouse,
Found a priest whom she fled away with,—both
Took their full pleasure in the two-days' flight,
Which a grey-headed greyer-hearted pair,
(Whose best boast was, their life had been a lie)
Helped for the love they bore all liars. Oh,
Here incredulity begins! Indeed?
Allow then, were no one point strictly true,
There's that i' the tale might seem like truth at least
To the unlucky husband,—jaundiced patch,—
Jealousy maddens people, why not him?
Say, he was maddened, so, forgivable!
Humanity pleads that though the wife were true,
The priest true, and the pair of liars true,
They might seem false to one man in the world!
A thousand gnats make up a serpent's sting,
And many sly soft stimulants to wrath
Compose a formidable wrong at last,
That gets called easily by some one name
Not applicable to the single parts,
And so draws down a general revenge,
Excessive if you take crime, fault by fault.
Jealousy! I have known a score of plays,
Were listened to and laughed at in my time
As like the everyday-life on all sides,
Wherein the husband, mad as a March hare,

Suspected all the world contrived his shame;
What did the wife? The wife kissed both eyes blind,
Explained away ambiguous circumstance,
And while she held him captive by the hand,
Crowned his head,—you know what's the mockery,—
By half her body behind the curtain. That's
Nature now! That's the subject of a piece
I saw in Vallombrosa Convent, made
Expressly to teach men what marriage was!
But say, "Just so did I misapprehend,"
Imagine she deceived me to my face,"
And that's pretence too easily seen through!
All those eyes of all husbands in all plays,
At stare like one expanded peacock-tail,
Are laughed at for pretending to be keen
While horn-blind: but the moment I step forth—
Oh, I must needs o' the sudden prove a lynx
And look the heart, that stone-wall, through and through!
Such an eye, God's may be,—not yours nor mine.

Yes, presently . . . what hour is fleeting now?
When you cut earth away from under me,
I shall be left alone with, pushed beneath
Some such an apparitional dread orb
As the eye of God, since such an eye there glares:
I fancy it go filling up the void
Above my mote-self it devours, or what
Proves wrath, immensity wreaks on nothingness.
Just so I felt once, couching through the dark,
Hard by Vittiano; young I was, and gay,
And wanting to trap fieldfares: first a spark
Tipped a bent, as a mere dew-globule might
Any stiff grass-stalk on the meadow,—this
Grew fiercer, flamed out full, and proved the sun.
What do I want with proverbs, precepts here?
Away with man! What shall I say to God?
This, if I find the tongue and keep the mind—
"Do Thou wipe out the being of me, and smear
This soul from off Thy white of things, I blot!
I am one huge and sheer mistake,—whose fault?
Not mine at least, who did not make myself!"
Someone declares my wife excused me so!
Perhaps she knew what argument to use.
Grind your teeth, Cardinal, Abate, writhe!
What else am I to cry out in my rage,
Unable to repent one particle
O' the past? Oh, how I wish some cold wise man
Would dig beneath the surface which you scrape,
Deal with the depths, pronounce on my desert
Groundedly! I want simple sober sense,
That asks, before it finishes with a dog,
Who taught the dog that trick you hang him for?
You both persist to call that act a crime,
Sense would call . . . yes, I maintain it, Sirs, . . .
A blunder! At the worst, I stood in doubt
On cross-road, took one path of many paths:
It leads to the red thing, we all see now,
But nobody saw at first: one primrose-patch
In bank, one singing-bird in bush, the less,
Had warned me from such wayfare: let me prove!
Put me back to the cross-road, start afresh!
Advise me when I take the first false step!
Give me my wife: how should I use my wife,
Love her or hate her? Prompt my action now!
There she is, there she stands alive and pale,
The thirteen-years'-old child, with milk for blood,
Pompilia Comparini, as at first,
Which first is only four brief years ago!
I stand too in the little ground-floor room
O' the father's house at Via Vittoria: see!
Her so-called mother,—one arm round the waist
O' the child to keep her from the toys—let fall,
At wonder I can live yet look so grim,—
Ushers her in, with deprecating wave
Of the other,—and she fronts me loose at last,
Held only by the mother's finger-tip—
Struck dumb, for she was white enough before!
She eyes me with those frightened balls of black,
As heifer—the old simile comes pat—
Eyes tremblingly the altar and the priest:
The amazed look, all one insuppressive prayer,—

Might she but breathe, set free as heretofore,
Have this cup leave her lips unblistered, bear
Any cross anywhither anyhow,
So but alone, so but apart from me!
You are touched? So am I, quite otherwise,
If 'tis with pity. I resent my wrong,
Being a man: I only show man's soul
Through man's flesh, she sees mine, it strikes her thus!
Is that attractive? To a youth perhaps—
Calf-creature, one-part boy to three-parts girl,
To whom it is a flattering novelty 991
That he, men use to motion from their path,
Can thus impose, thus terrify in turn
A chit whose terror shall be changed apace
To bliss unbearable when grace and glow,
Prowess and pride descend the throne and touch
Esther in all that pretty tremble, cured
By the dove o' the sceptre! But myself am old,
O' the wane at least, in all things: what do you say 999
To her who frankly thus confirms my doubt?
I am past the prime, I scare the woman-world,
Done-with that way: you like this piece of news?
A little saucy rose-bud minx can strike
Death-damp into the breast of doughty king
Though 'twere French Louis,—soul I understand,—
Saying, by gesture of repugnance, just
"Sire, you are regal, puissant and so forth,
But—young you have been, are not, nor will be!"
In vain the mother nods, winks, bustles up,
"Count, girls incline to mature worth like you!
As for Pompilia, what's flesh, fish, or fowl
To one who apprehends no difference, 1012
And would accept you even were you old
As you are . . . youngish by her father's side?
Trim but your beard a little, thin your bush
Of eyebrow; and for presence, portliness,
And decent gravity, you beat a boy!"
Deceive yourself one minute, if you may,
In presence of the child that so loves age,
Whose neck writhes, cords itself against your kiss, 1020
Whose hand you wring stark, rigid with despair!
Well, I resent this; I am young in soul,
Nor old in body,—thews and sinews here,—
Though the vile surface be not smooth as once,—
Far beyond that first wheelwork which went wrong
Through the untempered iron ere 'twas proof:
I am the wrought man worth ten times the crude,—
Would woman see what this declines to see,
Declines to say "I see,"—the officious word
That makes the thing, pricks on the soul to shoot 1030
New fire into the half-used cinder, flesh!
Therefore 'tis she begins with wronging me,
Who cannot but begin with hating her.
Our marriage follows: there she stands again!
Why do I laugh? Why, in the very gripe
O' the jaws of death's gigantic skull, do I
Grin back his grin, make sport of my own pangs?
Why from each clashing of his molars, ground
To make the devil bread from out my grist,
Leaps out a spark of mirth, a hellish toy?
Take notice we are lovers in a church, 1041
Waiting the sacrament to make us one
And happy! Just as bid, she bears herself,
Comes and kneels, rises, speaks, is silent,—goes:
So have I brought my horse, by word and blow,
To stand stock-still and front the fire he dreads.
How can I other than remember this,
Resent the very obedience? Gain thereby?
Yes, I do gain my end and have my will,—
Thanks to whom? When the mother speaks the word, 1050
She obeys it—even to enduring me!
There had been compensation in revolt—
Revolt's to quell: but martyrdom rehearsed,
But predetermined saintship for the sake
O' the mother?—"Go!" thought I, "we meet again!"
Pass the next weeks of dumb contented death,
She lives,—wakes up, installed in house and home,
Is mine, mine all day-long, all night-long mine.
Good folks begin at me with open mouth:
"Now, at least, reconcile the child to life!
Study and make her love . . . that is, endure
The . . . hem! the . . . all of you though somewhat old, 1062
Till it amount to something, in her eye,

As good as love, better a thousand times—
Since nature helps the woman in such strait,
Makes passiveness her pleasure: failing which,
What if you give up boy-and-girl-fools'-play
And go on to wise friendship all at once?
Those boys and girls kiss themselves cold, you know,
Toy themselves tired and slink aside full soon
To friendship, as they name satiety:
Thither go you and wait their coming!" Thanks,
Considerate advisers,—but, fair play!
Had you and I, friends, started fair at first,
We, keeping fair, might reach it, neck by neck,
This blessed goal, whenever fate so please:
But why am I to miss the daisied mile
The course begins with, why obtain the dust
Of the end precisely at the starting-point?
Why quaff life's cup blown free of all the beads,
The bright red froth wherein our beard should steep
Before our mouth essay the black o' the wine?
Foolish, the love-fit? Let me prove it such
Like you, before like you I puff things clear!
"The best's to come, no rapture but content!
Not love's first glory but a sober glow,
Nor a spontaneous outburst in pure boon,
So much as, gained by patience, care and toil,
Proper appreciation and esteem!"
Go preach that to your nephews, not to me
Who, tired i' the midway of my life, would stop
And take my first refreshment, pluck a rose:
What's this coarse woolly hip, worn smooth of leaf,
You counsel I go plant in garden-plot,
Water with tears, manure with sweat and blood,
In confidence the seed shall germinate
And, for its very best, some far-off day,
Grow big, and blow me out a dog-rose bell?
Why must your nephews begin breathing spice
O' the hundred-petalled Provence prodigy?
Nay, more and worse,—would such my root bear rose—
Prove really flower and favourite, not the kind
That's queen, but those three leaves that make one cup
And hold the hedge-bird's breakfast,—then indeed
The prize though poor would pay the care and toil!
Respect we Nature that makes least as most,
Marvellous in the minim! But this bud,
Bit through and burned black by the tempter's tooth,
This bloom whose best grace was the slug outside
And the wasp inside its bosom,—call you "rose"?
Claim no immunity from a weed's fate
For the horrible present! What you call my wife
I call a nullity in female shape,
Vapid disgust, soon to be pungent plague,
When mixed with, made confusion and a curse
By two abominable nondescripts,
That father and that mother: think you see
The dreadful bronze our boast,[1] we Aretines,
The Etruscan monster, the three-headed thing,
Bellerophon's foe! How name you the whole beast?
You choose to name the body from one head,
That of the simple kid which droops the eye,
Hangs the neck and dies tenderly enough:
I rather see the griesly lion belch
Flame out i' the midst, the serpent writhe her rings,
Grafted into the common stock for tail,
And name the brute, Chimæra, which I slew!
How was there ever more to be—(concede
My wife's insipid harmless nullity)—
Dissociation from that pair of plagues—
That mother with her cunning and her cant—
The eyes with first their twinkle of conceit,
Then, dropped to earth in mock-demureness,—now,
The smile self-satisfied from ear to ear,
Now, the prim pursed-up mouth's protruded lips,
With deferential duck, slow swing of head,
Tempting the sudden fist of man too much,—
That owl-like screw of lid and rock of ruff!
As for the father,—Cardinal, you know
The kind of idiot!—such are rife in Rome,
But they wear velvet commonly, good fools,

[1] Preserved at Arezzo was an ancient Etruscan bronze representing the Chimæra — a fire-belching monster with a lion's head, a goat's body, and a serpent's tail. Bellerophon slew it.

At the end of life, to furnish forth young folk
Who grin and bear with imbecility,
Since the stalled ass, the joker, sheds from jaw
Corn, in the joke, for those who laugh or starve.
But what say we to the same solemn beast
Wagging his ears and wishful of our pat,
When turned, with holes in hide and bones laid bare,
To forage for himself i' the waste o' the world,
Sir Dignity i' the dumps? Pat him? We drub
Self-knowledge, rather, into frowzy pate,
Teach Pietro to get trappings or go hang!
Fancy this quondam oracle in vogue
At Via Vittoria, this personified
Authority when time was,—Pantaloon[1]
Flaunting his tom-fool tawdry just the same
As if Ash-Wednesday were mid-Carnival!
That's the extreme and unforgivable
Of sins, as I account such. Have you stooped
For your own ends to bestialize yourself
By flattery of a fellow of this stamp?
The ends obtained, or else shown out of reach,
He goes on, takes the flattery for pure truth,—
"You love and honour me, of course: what next?"
What, but the trifle of the stabbing, friend?—
Which taught you how one worships when the shrine
Has lost the relic that we bent before.
Angry? And how could I be otherwise?
'Tis plain: this pair of old pretentious fools
Meant to fool me: it happens, I fooled them.
Why could not these who sought to buy and sell
Me,—when they found themselves were bought and sold,
Make up their mind to the proved rule of right,
Be chattel and not chapman any more?
Miscalculation has its consequence;
But when the shepherd crooks a sheep-like thing
And meaning to get wool, dislodges fleece
And finds the veritable wolf beneath,
(How that staunch image serves at every turn!)
Does he, by way of being politic,
Pluck the first whisker grimly visible?—
Or rather grow in a trice all gratitude,
Protest this sort-of-what-one-might-name sheep
Beats the old other curly-coated kind,
And shall share board and bed, if so it deign,
With its discoverer, like a royal ram?
Ay, thus, with chattering teeth and knocking knees,
Would wisdom treat the adventure! these, forsooth,
Tried whisker-plucking, and so found what trap
The whisker kept perdue, two rows of teeth—
Sharp, as too late the prying fingers felt.
What would you have? The fools transgress, the fools
Forthwith receive appropriate punishment:
They first insult me, I return the blow,
There follows noise enough: four hubbub months,
Now hue and cry, now whimpering and wail—
A perfect goose-yard cackle of complaint
Because I do not gild the geese their oats,—
I have enough of noise, ope wicket wide,
Sweep out the couple to go whine elsewhere,
Frightened a little, hurt in no respect,
And am just taking thought to breathe again,
Taste the sweet sudden silence all about,
When, there they raise it, the old noise I know,
At Rome i' the distance! "What, begun once more?
Whine on, wail ever, 'tis the loser's right!"
But eh, what sort of voice grows on the wind?
Triumph it sounds and no complaint at all!
And triumph it is. My boast was premature:
The creatures, I turned forth, clapped wing and crew
Fighting-cock-fashion,—they had filched a pearl
From dung-heap, and might boast with cause enough!
I was defrauded of all bargained for,—
You know, the Pope knows, not a soul but knows
My dowry was derision, my gain—muck,
My wife (the Church declared my flesh and blood)
The nameless bastard of a common whore:
My old name turned henceforth to . . . shall I say
"He that received the ordure in his face?"

[1] A foolish character in the Italian "Commedia dell' Arte."

And they who planned this wrong, performed this wrong,
And then revealed this wrong to the wide world,
Rounded myself in the ears with my own wrong,—
Why, these were (note hell's lucky malice, now!)
These were just they who, they alone, could act
And publish and proclaim their infamy,
Secure that men would in a breath believe
Compassionate and pardon them,—for why?
They plainly were too stupid to invent,
Too simple to distinguish wrong from right,—
Inconscious agents they, the silly-sooth,
Of heaven's retributive justice on the strong
Proud cunning violent oppressor—me!
Follow them to their fate and help your best,
You Rome, Arezzo, foes called friends of me,
They gave the good long laugh to, at my cost!
Defray your share o' the cost, since you partook
The entertainment! Do!—assured the while,
That not one stab, I dealt to right and left,
But went the deeper for a fancy—this—
That each might do me two-fold service, find
A friend's face at the bottom of each wound,
And scratch its smirk a little!
Panciatichi!
There's a report at Florence,—is it true?—
That when your relative the Cardinal
Built, only the other day, that barrack-bulk,
The palace in Via Larga, some one picked
From out the street a saucy quip enough
That fell there from its day's flight through the town,
About the flat front and the windows wide
And bulging heap of cornice,—hitched the joke
Into a sonnet, signed his name thereto,
And forthwith pinned on post the pleasantry:
For which he's at the galleys, rowing now
Up to his waist in water,—just because
Panciatic and *lymphatic* rhymed so pat!
I hope, Sir, those who passed this joke on me
Were not unduly punished? What say you,
Prince of the Church, my patron? Nay, indeed,
I shall not dare insult your wits so much
As think this problem difficult to solve!
This Pietro and Violante then, I say,
These two ambiguous insects, changing name
And nature with the season's warmth or chill,—
Now, grovelled, grubbing toiling moiling ants,
A very synonym of thrift and peace,—
Anon, with lusty June to prick their heart,
Soared i' the air, winged flies for more offence,
Circled me, buzzed me deaf and stung me blind,
And stunk me dead with fetor in the face
Until I stopped the nuisance: there's my crime!
Pity I did not suffer them subside
Into some further shape and final form
Of execrable life? My masters, no!
I, by one blow, wisely cut short at once
Them and their transformations of disgust,
In the snug little Villa out of hand.
"Grant me confession, give bare time for that!"—
Shouted the sinner till his mouth was stopped.
His life confessed!—that was enough for me,
Who came to see that he did penance. 'S death!
Here's a coil raised, a pother and for what?
Because strength, being provoked by weakness, fought
And conquered,—the world never heard the like!
Pah, how I spend my breath on them, as if
'Twas their fate troubled me, too hard to range
Among the right and fit and proper things!

Ay, but Pompilia,—I await your word,—
She, unimpeached of crime, unimplicate
In folly, one of alien blood to these
I punish, why extend my claim, exact
Her portion of the penalty? Yes, friends,
I go too fast: the orator's at fault:
Yes, ere I lay her, with your leave, by them
As she was laid at San Lorenzo late,
I ought to step back, lead you by degrees,
Recounting at each step some fresh offence,
Up to the red bed,—never fear, I will!
Gaze at her, where I place her, to begin,
Confound me with her gentleness and worth!
The horrible pair have fled and left her now,
She has her husband for her sole concern:
His wife, the woman fashioned for his help,
Flesh of his flesh, bone of his bone, the bride
To groom as is the Church and Spouse to Christ:

There she stands in his presence: "Thy desire
Shall be to the husband, o'er thee shall he rule!"
—"Pompilia, who declare that you love God,
You know who said that: then, desire my love,
Yield me contentment and be ruled aright!"
She sits up, she lies down, she comes and goes,
Kneels at the couch-side, overleans the sill
O' the window, cold and pale and mute as stone,
Strong as stone also. "Well, are they not fled?
Am I not left, am I not one for all?
Speak a word, drop a tear, detach a glance,
Bless me or curse me of your own accord!
Is it the ceiling only wants your soul,
Is worth your eyes?" And then the eyes descend
And do look at me. Is it at the meal?
"Speak!" she obeys, "Be silent!" she obeys,
Counting the minutes till I cry "Depart,"
As brood-bird when you saunter past her eggs,
Departs she, just the same through door and wall
I see the same stone strength of white despair.
And all this will be never otherwise!
Before, the parents' presence lent her life:
She could play off her sex's armoury,
Entreat, reproach, be female to my male,
Try all the shrieking doubles of the hare,
Go clamour to the Commissary, bid
The Archbishop hold my hands and stop my tongue,
And yield fair sport so: but the tactics change,
The hare stands stock-still to enrage the hound!
Since that day when she learned she was no child
Of those she thought her parents,—that their trick
Had tricked me whom she thought sole trickster late,—
Why, I suppose she said within herself,
"Then, no more struggle for my parents' sake,
And, for my own sake, why needs struggle be?"
But is there no third party to the pact?
What of her husband's relish or dislike
For this new game of giving up the game,
This worst offence of not offending more?
I'll not believe but instinct wrought in this,
Set her on to conceive and execute
The preferable plague: how sure they probe,—
These jades, the sensitivest soft of man!
The long black hair was wound now in a wisp,
Crowned sorrow better than the wild web late:
No more soiled dress, 'tis trimness triumphs now,
For how should malice go with negligence?
The frayed silk looked the fresher for her spite!
There was an end to springing out of bed,
Praying me, with face buried on my feet,
Be hindered of my pastime,—so an end
To my rejoinder, "What, on the ground at last?
Vanquished in fight, a supplicant for life?
What if I raise you? 'Ware the casting down
When next you fight me!" Then, she lay there, mine:
Now, mine she is if I please wring her neck,—
A moment of disquiet, working eyes,
Protruding tongue, a long sigh, then no more,—
As if one killed the horse one could not ride!
Had I enjoined "Cut off the hair!"—why, snap
The scissors, and at once a yard or so
Had fluttered in black serpents to the floor:
But till I did enjoin it, how she combs,
Uncurls and draws out to the complete length,
Plaits, places the insulting rope on head
To be an eyesore past dishevelment!
Is all done? Then sit still again and stare!
I advise—no one think to bear that look
Of steady wrong, endured as steadily
—Through what sustainment of deluding hope?
Who is the friend i' the background that notes all?
Who may come presently and close accounts?
This self-possession to the uttermost,
How does it differ in aught, save degree,
Fom the terrible patience of God?
"All which just means,
She did not love you!" Again the word is launched
And the fact fronts me! What, you try the wards
With the true key and the dead lock flies ope?
No, it sticks fast and leaves you fumbling still!

You have some fifty servants, Cardinal,—
Which of them loves you? Which subordinate
But makes parade of such officiousness
That,—if there's no love prompts it,—love, the sham,
Does twice the service done by love, the true?
God bless us liars, where's one touch of truth
In what we tell the world, or world tells us,
Of how we love each other? All the same,
We calculate on word and deed, nor err,—
Bid such a man do such a loving act,
Sure of effect and negligent of cause,
Just as we bid a horse, with cluck of tongue,
Stretch his legs arch-wise, crouch his saddled back
To foot-reach of the stirrup—all for love,
And some for memory of the smart of switch
On the inside of the foreleg—what care we?
Yet where's the bond obliges horse to man
Like that which binds fast wife to husband? God
Laid down the law: gave man the brawny arm
And ball of fist—woman the beardless cheek
And proper place to suffer in the side:
Since it is he can strike, let her obey!
Can she feel no love? Let her show the more,
Sham the worse, damn herself praiseworthily!
Who's that soprano Rome went mad about
Last week while I lay rotting in my straw?
The very jailor gossiped in his praise—
How,—dressed up like Armida, though a man;
And painted to look pretty, though a fright,—
He still made love so that the ladies swooned,
Being an eunuch. "Ah, Rinaldo mine!
But to breathe by thee while Jove slays us both!"
All the poor bloodless creature never felt,
Si, do, re, me, fa, squeak and squall—for what?
Two gold zecchines the evening. Here's my slave,
Whose body and soul depend upon my nod,
Can't falter out the first note in the scale
For her life! Why blame me if I take the life?
All women cannot give men love, forsooth!
No, nor all pullets lay the henwife eggs—
Whereat she bids them remedy the fault,
Brood on a chalk-ball: soon the nest is stocked—
Otherwise, to the plucking and the spit!
This wife of mine was of another mood—
Would not begin the lie that ends with truth,
Nor feign the love that brings real love about:
Wherefore I judged, sentenced and punished her.
But why particularize, defend the deed?
Say that I hated her for no one cause
Beyond my pleasure so to do,—what then?
Just on as much incitement acts the world,
All of you! Look and like! You favour one,
Brow-beat another, leave alone a third,—
Why should you master natural caprice?
Pure nature! Try: plant elm by ash in file;
Both unexceptionable trees enough,
They ought to overlean each other, pair
At top and arch across the avenue
The whole path to the pleasaunce: do they so—
Or loathe, lie off abhorrent each from each?
Lay the fault elsewhere: since we must have faults,
Mine shall have been,—seeing there's ill in the end
Come of my course,—that I fare somehow worse
For the way I took: my fault . . . as God's my judge,
I see not where my fault lies, that's the truth!
I ought . . . oh, ought in my own interest
Have let the whole adventure go untried,
This chance by marriage,—or else, trying it,
Ought to have turned it to account some one
O' the hundred otherwises? Ay, my friend,
Easy to say, easy to do,—step right
Now you've stepped left and stumbled on the thing,
—The red thing! Doubt I any more than you
That practice makes man perfect? Give again
The chance,—same marriage and no other wife,
Be sure I'll edify you! That's because
I'm practised, grown fit guide for Guido's self.
You proffered guidance,—I know, none so well,—
You laid down law and rolled decorum out,
From pulpit-corner on the gospel-side,—
Wanted to make your great experience mine,
Save me the personal search and pains so: thanks!
Take your word on life's use? When I take his—
The muzzled ox that treadeth out the corn,

Gone blind in padding round and round one path,—
As to the taste of green grass in the field!
What do you know o' the world that's trodden flat
And salted sterile with your daily dung,
Leavened into a lump of loathsomeness?
Take your opinion of the modes of life,
The aims of life, life's triumph or defeat,
How to feel, how to scheme, and how to do
Or else leave undone? You preached long and loud
On high-days, "Take our doctrine upon trust!
Into the mill-house with you! Grind our corn,
Relish our chaff, and let the green grass grow!"
I tried chaff, found I famished on such fare,
So made this mad rush at the mill-house-door,
Buried my head up to the ears in dew,
Browsed on the best, for which you brain me, Sirs!
Be it so! I conceived of life that way,
And still declare—life, without absolute use
Of the actual sweet therein, is death, not life.
Give me,—pay down,—not promise, which is air,—
Something that's out of life and better still,
Make sure reward, make certain punishment,
Entice me, scare me,—I'll forego this life;
Otherwise, no!—the less that words, mere wind,
Would cheat me of some minutes while they plague,
Balk fulness of revenge here,—blame yourselves
For this eruption of the pent-up soul
You prisoned first and played with afterward!
"Deny myself" meant simply pleasure you,
The sacred and superior, save the mark!
You,—whose stupidity and insolence
I must defer to, soothe at every turn,—
Whose swine-like snuffling greed and grunting lust
I had to wink at or help gratify,—
While the same passions,—dared they perk in me,
Me, the immeasurably marked, by God,
Master of the whole world of such as you,—
I, boast such passions? 'Twas, "Suppress them straight!
Or stay, we'll pick and choose before destroy.
Here's wrath in you,—a serviceable sword,—
Beat it into a ploughshare! What's this long
Lance-like ambition? Forge a pruning-hook,
May be of service when our vines grow tall!
But—sword used swordwise, spear thrust out as spear?
Anathema! Suppression is the word!"
My nature, when the outrage was too gross,
Widened itself an outlet over-wide
By way of answer, sought its own relief
With more of fire and brimstone than you wished.
All your own doing: preachers, blame yourselves!

'Tis I preach while the hour-glass runs and runs!
God keep me patient! All I say just means—
My wife proved, whether by her fault or mine,—
That's immaterial,—a true stumbling-block
I' the way of me her husband. I but plied
The hatchet yourselves use to clear a path,
Was politic, played the game you warrant wins,
Plucked at law's robe a-rustle through the courts,
Bowed down to kiss divinity's buckled shoe
Cushioned i' the church: efforts all wide the aim!
Procedures to no purpose! Then flashed truth.
The letter kills, the spirit keeps alive
In law and gospel: there be nods and winks
Instruct a wise man to assist himself
In certain matters nor seek aid at all.
"Ask money of me,"—quoth the clownish saw,—
"And take my purse! But,—speaking with respect,—
Need you a solace for the troubled nose?
Let everybody wipe his own himself!"
Sirs, tell me free and fair! Had things gone well
At the wayside inn: had I surprised asleep
The runaways, as was so probable,
And pinned them each to other partridge-wise,
Through back and breast to breast and back, then bade
Bystanders witness if the spit, my sword,
Were loaded with unlawful game for once—
Would you have interposed to damp the glow
Applauding me on every husband's cheek?

Would you have checked the cry "A judgment, see!
A warning, note! Be henceforth chaste, ye wives,
Nor stray beyond your proper precinct, priests!"
If you had, then your house against itself
Divides, nor stands your kingdom any more.
Oh, why, why was it not ordained just so?
Why fell not things out so nor otherwise?
Ask that particular devil whose task it is
To trip the all-but-at perfection,—slur
The line o' the painter just where paint leaves off
And life begins,—put ice into the ode
O' the poet while he cries "Next stanza—fire!"
Inscribe all human effort with one word,
Artistry's haunting curse, the Incomplete!
Being incomplete, my act escaped success.
Easy to blame now! Every fool can swear
To hole in net that held and slipped the fish.
But, treat my act with fair unjaundiced eye,
What was there wanting to a masterpiece
Except the luck that lies beyond a man?
My way with the woman, now proved grossly wrong,
Just missed of being gravely grandly right
And making mouths laugh on the other side.
Do, for the poor obstructed artist's sake,
Go with him over that spoiled work once more!
Take only its first flower, the ended act
Now in the dusty pod, dry and defunct!
I march to the Villa, and my men with me,
That evening, and we reach the door and stand.
I say . . . no, it shoots through me lightning-like
While I pause, breathe, my hand upon the latch,
"Let me forebode! Thus far, too much success:
I want the natural failure—find it where?
Which thread will have to break and leave a loop
I' the meshy combination, my brain's loom
Wove this long while, and now next minute tests?
Of three that are to catch, two should go free,
One must: all three surprised,—impossible!
Beside, I seek three and may chance on six,—
This neighbour, t'other gossip,—the babe's birth
Brings such to fireside and folks give them wine,—
'Tis late: but when I break in presently
One will be found outlingering the rest
For promise of a posset,—one whose shout
Would raise the dead down in the catacombs,
Much more the city-watch that goes its round.
When did I ever turn adroitly up
To sun some brick embedded in the soil,
And with one blow crush all three scorpions there?
Or Pietro or Violante shambles off—
It cannot be but I surprise my wife—
If only she is stopped and stamped on, good!
That shall suffice: more is improbable.
Now I may knock!" And this once for my sake
The impossible was effected: I called king,
Queen and knave in a sequence, and cards came,
All three, three only! So, I had my way,
Did my deed: so, unbrokenly lay bare
Each tænia that had sucked me dry of juice,
At last outside me, not an inch of ring
Left now to writhe about and root itself
I' the heart all powerless for revenge! Henceforth
I might thrive: these were drawn and dead and damned.
Oh Cardinal, the deep long sigh you heave
When the load's off you, ringing as it runs
All the way down the serpent-stair to hell!
No doubt the fine delirium flustered me,
Turned my brain with the influx of success
As if the sole need now were to wave wand
And find doors fly wide,—wish and have my will,—
The rest o' the scheme would care for itself: escape?
Easy enough were that, and poor beside!
It all but proved so,—ought to quite have proved,
Since, half the chances had sufficed, set free
Any one, with his senses at command,
From thrice the danger of my flight. But, drunk,
Redundantly triumphant,—some reverse
Was sure to follow! There's no other way
Accounts for such prompt perfect failure then
And there on the instant.[1] Any day o' the week,

[1] Guido had neglected to get the official order which would have enabled him to hire post-horses and was obliged to flee on foot.

A ducat slid discreetly into palm
O' the mute post-master, while you whisper him—
How you the Count and certain four your knaves,
Have just been mauling who was malapert,
Suspect the kindred may prove troublesome,
Therefore, want horses in a hurry,—that
And nothing more secures you any day
The pick o' the stable! Yet I try the trick,
Double the bribe, call myself Duke for Count,
And say the dead man only was a Jew,
And for my pains find I am dealing just
With the one scrupulous fellow in all Rome—
Just this immaculate official stares,
Sees I want hat on head and sword in sheath,
Am splashed with other sort of wet than wine,
Shrugs shoulder, puts my hand by, gold and all,
Stands on the strictness of the rule o' the road!
"Where's the Permission?" Where's the wretched rag
With the due seal and sign of Rome's Police,
To be had for asking, half-an-hour ago?
"Gone? Get another, or no horses hence!"
He dares not stop me, we five glare too grim,
But hinders,—hacks and hamstrings sure enough,
Gives me some twenty miles of miry road
More to march in the middle of that night
Whereof the rough beginning taxed the strength
O' the youngsters, much more mine, both soul and flesh,
Who had to think as well as act: dead-beat,
We gave in ere we reached the boundary
And safe spot out of this irrational Rome,—
Where, on dismounting from our steeds next day,
We had snapped our fingers at you, safe and sound,
Tuscans once more in blessed Tuscany,
Where laws make wise allowance, understand
Civilised life and do its champions right!
Witness the sentence of the Rota there,
Arezzo uttered, the Granduke confirmed,
One week before I acted on its hint,—
Giving friend Guillichini, for his love,
The galleys, and my wife your saint, Rome's saint,—
Rome manufactures saints enough to know,—
Seclusion at the Stinche for her life.
All this, that all but was, might all have been,
Yet was not! baulked by just a scrupulous knave
Whose palm was horn through handling horses' hoofs
And could not close upon my proffered gold!
What say you to the spite of fortune? Well,
The worst's in store: thus hindered, haled this way
To Rome again by hangdogs, whom find I
Here, still to fight with, but my pale frail wife?
—Riddled with wounds by one not like to waste
The blows he dealt,—knowing anatomy,—
(I think I told you) bound to pick and choose
The vital parts! 'Twas learning all in vain!
She too must shimmer through the gloom o' the grave,
Come and confront me—not at judgment-seat
Where I could twist her soul, as erst her flesh,
And turn her truth into a lie,—but there,
O' the death-bed, with God's hand between us both,
Striking me dumb, and helping her to speak,
Tell her own story her own way, and turn
My plausibility to nothingness!
Four whole days did Pompilia keep alive,
With the best surgery of Rome agape
At the miracle,—this cut, the other slash,
And yet the life refusing to dislodge,
Four whole extravagant impossible days,
Till she had time to finish and persuade
Every man, every woman, every child
In Rome of what she would: the selfsame she
Who, but a year ago, had wrung her hands,
Reddened her eyes and beat her breasts, rehearsed
The whole game at Arezzo, nor availed
Thereby to move one heart or raise one hand!
When destiny intends you cards like these,
What good of skill and preconcerted play?
Had she been found dead, as I left her dead,
I should have told a tale brooked no reply:
You scarcely will suppose me found at fault
With that advantage! "What brings me to Rome?
Necessity to claim and take my wife:
Better, to claim and take my new-born babe,—
Strong in paternity a fortnight old,
When 'tis at strongest: warily I work,

Knowing the machinations of my foe;
I have companionship and use the night:
I seek my wife and child,—I find—no child
But wife, in the embraces of that priest
Who caused her to elope from me. These two,
Backed by the pander-pair who watch the while,
Spring on me like so many tiger-cats,
Glad of the chance to end the intruder. I—
What should I do but stand on my defence,
Strike right, strike left, strike thick and threefold, slay, 1721
Not all—because the coward priest escapes.
Last, I escape, in fear of evil tongues,
And having had my taste of Roman law."
What's disputable, refutable here?—
Save by just this one ghost-thing half on earth,
Half out of it,—as if she held God's hand
While she leant back and looked her last at me,
Forgiving me (here monks begin to weep)
Oh, from her very soul, commending mine
To heavenly mercies which are infinite,—
While fixing fast my head beneath your knife!
'Tis fate, not fortune! All is of a piece! 1733
When was it chance informed me of my youths?
My rustic four o' the family, soft swains,
What sweet surprise had they in store for me,
Those of my very household,—what did Law
Twist with her rack-and-cord-contrivance late
From out their bones and marrow? What but this—
Had no one of these several stumbling-blocks
Stopped me, they yet were cherishing a scheme, 1741
All of their honest country homespun wit,
To quietly next day at crow of cock,
Cut my own throat too, for their own behoof,
Seeing I had forgot to clear accounts
O' the instant, nowise slackened speed for that,—
And somehow never might find memory,
Once safe back in Arezzo, where things change,
And a court-lord needs mind no country lout.
Well, being the arch-offender, I die last,—
May, ere my head falls, have my eyesight free,
Nor miss them dangling high on either hand,
Like scarecrows in a hemp-field, for their pains! 1753

And then my Trial,—'tis my Trial that bites
Like a corrosive, so the cards are packed,
Dice loaded, and my life-stake tricked away!
Look at my lawyers, lacked they grace of law,
Latin or logic? Were not they fools to the height,
Fools to the depth, fools to the level between,
O' the foolishness set to decide the case?
They feign, they flatter; nowise does it skill,
Everything goes against me: deal each judge
His dole of flattery and feigning,—why, 1763
He turns and tries and snuffs and savours it,
As an old fly the sugar-grain, your gift;
Then eyes your thumb and finger, brushes clean
The absurd old head of him, and whisks away,
Leaving your thumb and finger dirty. Faugh!

And finally, after this long-drawn range
Of affront and failure, failure and affront,—
This path, 'twixt crosses leading to a skull,
Paced by me barefoot, bloodied by my palms
From the entry to the end,—there's light at length, 1773
A cranny of escape: appeal may be
To the old man, to the father, to the Pope,
For a little life—from one whose life is spent,
A little pity—from pity's source and seat,
A little indulgence to rank, privilege,
From one who is the thing personified,
Rank, privilege, indulgence, grown beyond
Earth's bearing, even, ask Jansenius [1] else!
Still the same answer, still no other tune 1782
From the cicala perched at the tree-top
Than crickets noisy round the root,—'tis "Die!"
Bids Law—"Be damned!" adds Gospel,—nay,
No word so frank,—'tis rather, "Save yourself!"
The Pope subjoins—"Confess and be absolved!
So shall my credit countervail your shame,
And the world see I have not lost the knack
Of trying all the spirits: yours, my son, 1790
Wants but a fiery washing to emerge
In clarity! Come, cleanse you, ease the ache
Of these old bones, refresh our bowels, boy!"
Do I mistake your mission from the Pope?

[1] Founder of the Jansenist group. His doctrines were condemned by the church.

Then, bear his Holiness the mind of me!
I do get strength from being thrust to wall,
Successively wrenched from pillar and from post
By this tenacious hate of fortune, hate
Of all things in, under, and above earth.
Warfare, begun this mean unmanly mode,
Does best to end so,—gives earth spectacle
Of a brave fighter who succumbs to odds
That turn defeat to victory. Stab, I fold
My mantle round me! Rome approves my act:
Applauds the blow which costs me life but keeps
My honour spotless: Rome would praise no more
Had I fallen, say, some fifteen years ago,
Helping Vienna when our Aretines
Flocked to Duke Charles [1] and fought Turk Mustafa:
Nor would you two be trembling o'er my corpse
With all this exquisite solicitude.
Why is it that I make such suit to live?
The popular sympathy that's round me now
Would break like bubble that o'er-domes a fly—
Solid enough while he lies quiet there,
But let him want the air and ply the wing,
Why, it breaks and bespatters him, what else?
Cardinal, if the Pope had pardoned me,
And I walked out of prison through the crowd,
It would not be your arm I should dare press!
Then, if I got safe to my place again,
How sad and sapless were the years to come!
I go my old ways and find things grown grey;
You priests leer at me, old friends look askance;
The mob's in love, I'll wager, to a man,
With my poor young good beauteous murdered wife:
For hearts require instruction how to beat,
And eyes, on warrant of the story, wax
Wanton at portraiture in white and black
Of dead Pompilia gracing ballad-sheet,
Which eyes, lived she unmurdered and unsung,
Would never turn though she paced street as bare
As the mad penitent ladies do in France.
My brothers quietly would edge me out
Of use and management of things called mine;
Do I command? "You stretched command before!"
Show anger? "Anger little helped you once!"
Advise? "How managed you affairs of old?"
My very mother, all the while they gird,
Turns eye up, gives confirmatory groan;
For unsuccess, explain it how you will,
Disqualifies you, makes you doubt yourself,
—Much more, is found decisive by your friends.
Beside, am I not fifty years of age?
What new leap would a life take, checked like mine
I' the spring at outset? Where's my second chance?
Ay, but the babe . . . I had forgot my son,
My heir! Now for a burst of gratitude!
There's some appropriate service to intone,
Some *gaudeamus* and thanksgiving-psalm!
Old, I renew my youth in him, and poor
Possess a treasure,—is not that the phrase?
Only I must wait patient twenty years—
Nourishing all the while, as father ought,
The excrescence with my daily blood of life.
Does it respond to hope, such sacrifice,—
Grows the wen plump while I myself grow lean?
Why, here's my son and heir in evidence,
Who stronger, wiser, handsomer than I
By fifty years, relieves me of each load,—
Tames my hot horse, carries my heavy gun,
Courts my coy mistress,—has his apt advice
On house-economy, expenditure,
And what not? All which good gifts and great growth
Because of my decline, he brings to bear
On Guido, but half apprehensive how
He cumbers earth, crosses the brisk young Count,
Who civilly would thrust him from the scene.
Contrariwise, does the blood-offering fail?
There's an ineptitude, one blank the more
Added to earth in semblance of my child?
Then, this has been a costly piece of work,
My life exchanged for his!—why he, not I,
Enjoy the world, if no more grace accrue?
Dwarf me, what giant have you made of him?
I do not dread the disobedient son—

[1] Duke Charles of Lorraine was one of the leaders who helped to raise the siege of Vienna besieged by the Turks in 1683.

I know how to suppress rebellion there,
Being not quite the fool my father was.
But grant the medium measure of a man,
The usual compromise 'twixt fool and sage,
—You know—the tolerably-obstinate,
The not-so-much-perverse but you may train,
The true son-servant that, when parent bids
"Gô work, son, in my vineyard!" makes reply
"I go, Sir!"—Why, what profit in your son
Beyond the drudges you might subsidise,
Have the same work from, at a paul [1] the head?
Look at those four young precious olive-plants
Reared at Vittiano,—not on flesh and blood,
These twenty years, but black bread and sour wine!
I bade them put forth tender branch, hook, hold,
And hurt three enemies I had in Rome:
They did my hest as unreluctantly,
At promise of a dollar, as a son
Adjured by mumping memories of the past.
No, nothing repays youth expended so—
Youth, I say, who am young still: grant but leave
To live my life out, to the last I'd live
And die conceding age no right of youth!
It is the will runs the renewing nerve
Through flaccid flesh, that faints before the time.
Therefore no sort of use for son have I—
Sick, not of life's feast but of steps to climb
To the house where life prepares her feast,—of means
To the end: for make the end attainable
Without the means,—my relish were like yours.
A man may have an appetite enough
For a whole dish of robins ready cooked,
And yet lack courage to face sleet, pad snow,
And snare sufficiently for supper. Thus
The time's arrived when, ancient Roman-like,
I am bound to fall on my own sword,—why not
Say—Tuscan-like, more ancient, better still?
Will you hear truth can do no harm nor good?
I think I never was at any time
A Christian, as you nickname all the world,
Me among others: truce to nonsense now!
Name me, a primitive religionist—
As should the aboriginary be
I boast myself, Etruscan, Aretine,
One sprung,—your frigid Virgil's fieriest word,—
From fauns and nymphs, trunks and the heart of oak,
With,—for a visible divinity,—
The portent of a Jove Ægiochus
Descried 'mid clouds, lightning and thunder, couched
On topmost crag of your Capitoline:
'Tis in the Seventh Æneid,—what, the Eighth?
Right,—thanks, Abate,—though the Christian's dumb,
The Latinist's vivacious in you yet!
I know my grandsire had our tapestry
Marked with the motto, 'neath a certain shield,
Whereto his grandson presently will give gules
To vary azure. First we fight for faiths,
But get to shake hands at the last of all:
Mine's your faith too,—in Jove Ægiochus!
Nor do Greek gods, that serve as supplement,
Jar with the simpler scheme, if understood.
We want such intermediary race
To make communication possible;
The real thing were too lofty, we too low,
Midway hang these: we feel their use so plain
In linking height to depth, that we doff hat
And put no question nor pry narrowly
Into the nature hid behind the names.
We grudge no rite the fancy may demand;
But never, more than needs, invent, refine,
Improve upon requirement, idly wise
Beyond the letter, teaching gods their trade,
Which is to teach us: we'll obey when taught.
Why should we do our duty past the need?
When the sky darkens, Jove is wroth,—say prayer!
When the sun shines and Jove is glad,—sing psalm!
But wherefore pass prescription and devise
Blood-offering for sweat-service, lend the rod
A pungency through pickle of our own?
Learned Abate,—no one teaches you
What Venus means and who's Apollo here!
I spare you, Cardinal,—but, though you wince,
You know me, I know you, and both know that!

[1] A small copper coin.

So, if Apollo bids us fast, we fast:
But where does Venus order we stop sense
When Master Pietro [1] rhymes a pleasantry?
Give alms prescribed on Friday,—but, hold hand
Because your foe lies prostrate,—where's the word
Explicit in the book debars revenge?
The rationale of your scheme is just
"Pay toll here, there pursue your pleasure free!"
So do you turn to use the medium-powers,
Mars and Minerva, Bacchus and the rest,
And so are saved propitiating—whom?
What all-good, all-wise and all-potent Jove
Vexed by the very sins in man, himself
Made life's necessity when man he made?
Irrational bunglers! So, the living truth
Revealed to strike Pan dead, ducks low at last,
Prays leave to hold its own and live good days
Provided it go masque grotesquely, called
Christian not Pagan? Oh, you purged the sky
Of all gods save the One, the great and good,
Clapped hands and triumphed! But the change came fast:
The inexorable need in man for life
(Life,—you may mulct and minish to a grain
Out of the lump, so that the grain but live)
Laughed at your substituting death for life,
And bade you do your worst,—which worst was done
In just that age styled primitive and pure
When Saint this, Saint that, dutifully starved,
Froze, fought with beasts, was beaten and abused,
And finally ridded of his flesh by fire,
He kept life-long unspotted from the world!—
Next age, how goes the game, what mortal gives
His life and emulates Saint that, Saint this?
Men mutter, make excuse, or mutiny,
In fine are minded all to leave the new,
Stick to the old,—enjoy old liberty,
No prejudice in enjoyment, if you please,
To the new profession: sin o' the sly, henceforth!
The law stands though the letter kills: what then?
The spirit saves as unmistakably.

[1] Pietro Aretino, a licentious writer of the seventeenth century.

Omniscience sees, Omnipotence could stop,
Omnibenevolence pardons: it must be,
Frown law its fiercest, there's a wink somewhere.

Such was the logic in this head of mine:
I, like the rest, wrote "poison" on my bread;
But broke and ate:—said "those that use the sword
Shall perish by the same;" then stabbed my foe.
I stand on solid earth, not empty air:
Dislodge me, let your Pope's crook hale me hence!
Not he, nor you! And I so pity both,
I'll make the true charge you want wit to make:
"Count Guido, who reveal our mystery,
And trace all issues to the love of life:
We having life to love and guard, like you,
Why did you put us upon self-defence?
You well knew what prompt pass-word would appease
The sentry's ire when folk infringe his bounds,
And yet kept mouth shut: do you wonder then
If, in mere decency, he shot you dead?
He can't have people play such pranks as yours
Beneath his nose at noonday: you disdained
To give him an excuse before the world
By crying 'I break rule to save our camp!'
Under the old rule, such offence were death;
And you had heard the Pontifex pronounce,
'Since you slay foe and violate the form,
Slaying turns murder, which were sacrifice
Had you, while, say, law-suiting foe to death,
But raised an altar to the Unknown God,
Or else the Genius of the Vatican.'
Why then this pother?—all because the Pope,
Doing his duty, cried 'A foreigner,
You scandalize the natives: here at Rome
Romano vivitur more: [1] wise men, here,
Put the Church forward and efface themselves.
The fit defence had been,—you stamped on wheat,
Intending all the time to trample tares,—
Were fain extirpate, then, the heretic,
You now find, in your haste was slain a fool:
Nor Pietro, nor Violante, nor your wife
Meant to breed up your babe a Molinist!

[1] "One lives in Roman fashion."

Whence you are duly contrite. Not one word
Of all this wisdom did you urge!—which slip
Death must atone for!' "

So, let death atone!
So ends mistake, so end mistakers!—end
Perhaps to recommence,—how should I know?
Only, be sure, no punishment, no pain
Childish, preposterous, impossible,
But some such fate as Ovid could foresee,—
Byblis in fluvium,[1] let the weak soul end
In water, *sed Lycaon in lupum*,[1] but
The strong become a wolf for evermore!
Change that Pompilia to a puny stream
Fit to reflect the daisies on its bank!
Let me turn wolf, be whole, and sate, for once,—
Wallow in what is now a wolfishness
Coerced too much by the humanity
That's half of me as well! Grow out of man,
Glut the wolf-nature,—what remains but grow
Into the man again, be man indeed
And all man? Do I ring the changes right?
Deformed, transformed, reformed, informed, conformed!
The honest instinct, pent and crossed through life,
Let surge by death into a visible flow
Of rapture: as the strangled thread of flame
Painfully winds, annoying and annoyed,
Malignant and maligned, thro' stone and ore,
Till earth exclude the stranger: vented once,
It finds full play, is recognized a-top
Some mountain as no such abnormal birth.
Fire for the mount, not streamlet for the vale!
Ay, of the water was that wife of mine—
Be it for good, be it for ill, no run
O' the red thread through that insignificance!
Again, how she is at me with those eyes!
Away with the empty stare! Be holy still,
And stupid ever! Occupy your patch
Of private snow that's somewhere in what world
May now be growing icy round your head,

[1] The titles of stories in the *Metamorphoses* telling of how Byblis was changed into a river and Lycaon into a wolf.

And aguish at your foot-print,—freeze not me,
Dare follow not another step I take.
Not with so much as those detested eyes,
No, though they follow but to pray me pause
On the incline, earth's edge that's next to hell!
None of your abnegation of revenge!
Fly at me frank, tug while I tear again!
There's God, go tell Him, testify your worst!
Not she! There was no touch in her of hate:
And it would prove her hell, if I reached mine!
To know I suffered, would still sadden her,
Do what the angels might to make amends!
Therefore there's either no such place as hell,
Or thence shall I be thrust forth, for her sake,
And thereby undergo three hells, not one—
I who, with outlet for escape to heaven,
Would tarry if such flight allowed my foe
To raise his head, relieved of that firm foot
Had pinned him to the fiery pavement else!
So am I made, "who did not make myself:"
(How dared she rob my own lip of the word?)
Beware me in what other world may be!—
Pompilia, who have brought me to this pass!
All I know here, will I say there, and go
Beyond the saying with the deed. Some use
There cannot but be for a mood like mine,
Implacable, persistent in revenge.
She maundered "All is over and at end:
I go my own road, go you where God will!
Forgive you? I forget you!" There's the saint
That takes your taste, you other kind of men!
How you had loved her! Guido wanted skill
To value such a woman at her worth!
Properly the instructed criticise
"What's here, you simpleton have tossed to take
Its chance i' the gutter? This a daub, indeed?
Why, 'tis a Rafael that you kicked to rags!"
Perhaps so: some prefer the pure design:
Give me my gorge of colour, glut of gold
In a glory round the Virgin made for me!
Titian's the man, not Monk Angelico
Who traces you some timid chalky ghost
That turns the church into a charnel: ay,
Just such a pencil might depict my wife!

She,—since she, also, would not change herself,—
Why could not she come in some heart-shaped cloud,
Rainbowed about with riches, royalty
Rimming her round, as round the tintless lawn
Guardingly runs the selvage cloth of gold?
I would have left the faint fine gauze untouched,
Needle-worked over with its lily and rose,
Let her bleach unmolested in the midst,
Chill that selected solitary spot
Of quietude she pleased to think was life.
Purity, pallor grace the lawn no doubt
When there's the costly bordure to unthread
And make again an ingot: but what's grace
When you want meat and drink and clothes and fire?

A tale comes to my mind that's apposite—
Possibly true, probably false, a truth
Such as all truths we live by, Cardinal!
'Tis said, a certain ancestor of mine
Followed—whoever was the potentate,
To Paynimrie, and in some battle, broke
Through more than due allowance of the foe,
And, risking much his own life, saved the lord's.
Battered and bruised, the Emperor scrambles up,
Rubs his eyes and looks round and sees my sire,
Picks a furze-sprig from out his hauberk-joint,
(Token how near the ground went majesty)
And says, "Take this, and, if thou get safe home,
Plant the same in thy garden-ground to grow:
Run thence an hour in a straight line, and stop:
Describe a circle round (for central point)
The furze aforesaid, reaching every way
The length of that hour's run: I give it thee,—
The central point, to build a castle there,
The circumjacent space, for fit demesne,
The whole to be thy children's heritage,—
Whom, for the sake, bid thou wear furze on cap!"
Those are my arms: we turned the furze a tree
To show more, and the greyhound tied thereto,
Straining to start, means swift and greedy both;
He stands upon a triple mount of gold—
By Jove, then, he's escaping from true gold
And trying to arrive at empty air!
Aha! the fancy never crossed my mind!
My father used to tell me, and subjoin,
"As for the castle, that took wings and flew:
The broad lands,—why, to traverse them today
Scarce tasks my gouty feet, and in my prime
I doubt not I could stand and spit so far:
But for the furze, boy, fear no lack of that,
So long as fortune leaves one field to grub!
Wherefore hurrah for furze and loyalty!"
What may I mean, where may the lesson lurk?
"Do not bestow on man by way of gift
Furze without land for framework,—vaunt no grace
Of purity, no furze-sprig of a wife,
To me, i' the thick of battle for my bread,
Without some better dowry,—gold will do!"
No better gift than sordid muck? Yes, Sirs!
Many more gifts much better. Give them me!
O those Olimpias bold, those Biancas brave,
That brought a husband power worth Ormuz' wealth!
Cried "Thou being mine, why, what but thine am I?
Be thou to me law, right, wrong, heaven and hell!
Let us blend souls, blent, thou in me, to bid
Two bodies work one pleasure! What are these
Called king, priest, father, mother, stranger, friend?
They fret thee or they frustrate? Give the word—
Be certain they shall frustrate nothing more!
And who is this young florid foolishness
That holds thy fortune in his pigmy clutch,
—Being a prince and potency, forsooth!—
He hesitates to let the trifle go?
Let me but seal up eye, sing ear to sleep
Sounder than Samson,—pounce thou on the prize
Shall slip from off my breast, and down couch-side,
And on to floor, and far as my lord's feet—

Where he stands in the shadow with the knife,
Waiting to see what Delilah dares do!
Is the youth fair? What is a man to me
Who am thy call-bird? Twist his neck—my dupe's,—
Then take the breast shall turn a breast indeed!"
Such women are there; and they marry whom?
Why, when a man has gone and hanged himself
Because of what he calls a wicked wife,—
See, if the very turpitude bemoaned
Prove not mere excellence the fool ignores!
His monster is perfection,—Circe, sent
Straight from the sun, with wand the idiot blames
As not an honest distaff to spin wool!
O thou Lucrezia,[1] is it long to wait
Yonder where all the gloom is in a glow
With thy suspected presence?—virgin yet,
Virtuous again in face of what's to teach—
Sin unimagined, unimaginable,—
I come to claim my bride,—thy Borgia's self
Not half the burning bridegroom I shall be!
Cardinal, take away your crucifix!
Abate, leave my lips alone,—they bite!
Vainly you try to change what should not change,
And shall not. I have bared, you bathe my heart—
It grows the stonier for your saving dew!
You steep the substance, you would lubricate,
In waters that but touch to petrify!

You too are petrifactions of a kind:
Move not a muscle that shows mercy; rave
Another twelve hours, every word were waste!
I thought you would not slay impenitence,—
But teased, from men you slew, contrition first,—
I thought you had a conscience. Cardinal,
You know I am wronged!—wronged, say, and wronged, maintain.
Was this strict inquisition made for blood
When first you showed us scarlet on your back,
Called to the College? Your straightforward way

[1] Lucrezia Borgia, who had an evil reputation as a dissolute woman and as a poisoner.

To your legitimate end,—I think it passed
Over a scantling of heads brained, hearts broke,
Lives trodden into dust,—how otherwise?
Such was the way o' the world, and so you walked:
Does memory haunt your pillow? Not a whit.
God wills you never pace your garden-path,
One appetising hour ere dinner-time,
But your intrusion there treads out of life
A universe of happy innocent things:
Feel you remorse about that damsel-fly
Which buzzed so near your mouth and flapped your face,
You blotted it from being at a blow?
It was a fly, you were a man, and more,
Lord of created things, so took your course.
Manliness, mind,—these are things fit to save,
Fit to brush fly from: why, because I take
My course, must needs the Pope kill me?—kill you!
You! for this instrument, he throws away,
Is strong to serve a master, and were yours
To have and hold and get much good from out!
The Pope who dooms me needs must die next year;
I'll tell you how the chances are supposed
For his successor: first the Chamberlain,
Old San Cesario,—Colloredo, next,—
Then, one, two, three, four, I refuse to name;
After these, comes Altieri; then come you—
Seventh on the list you come, unless . . ha, ha,
How can a dead hand give a friend a lift?
Are you the person to despise the help
O' the head shall drop in pannier presently?
So a child seesaws on or kicks away
The fulcrum-stone that's all the sage requires
To fit his lever to and move the world.
Cardinal, I adjure you in God's name,
Save my life, fall at the Pope's feet, set forth
Things your own fashion, not in words like these
Made for a sense like yours who apprehend!
Translate into the court-conventional
"Count Guido must not die, is innocent!
Fair, be assured! But what an he were foul,

Blood-drenched and murder-crusted head to foot?
Spare one whose death insults the Emperor,
Nay, outrages the Louis you so love!
He has friends who will avenge him; enemies
Who will hate God now with impunity,
Missing the old coercive: would you send
A soul straight to perdition, dying frank
An atheist?" Go and say this, for God's sake!
—Why, you don't think I hope you'll say one word?
Neither shall I persuade you from your stand
Nor you persuade me from my station: take
Your crucifix away, I tell you twice!

Come, I am tired of silence! Pause enough!
You have prayed: I have gone inside my soul
And shut its door behind me: 'tis your torch
Makes the place dark: the darkness let alone
Grows tolerable twilight: one may grope
And get to guess at length and breadth and depth.
What is this fact I feel persuaded of—
This something like a foothold in the sea,
Although Saint Peter's bark scuds, billow-borne,
Leaves me to founder where it flung me first?
Spite of your splashing, I am high and dry!
God takes his own part in each thing he made;
Made for a reason, he conserves his work,
Gives each its proper instinct of defence.
My lamblike wife could neither bark nor bite,
She bleated, bleated, till for pity pure,
The village roused up, ran with pole and prong
To the rescue, and behold the wolf's at bay!
Shall he try bleating?—or take turn or two,
Since the wolf owns some kinship with the fox,
And, failing to escape the foe by craft,
Give up attempt, die fighting quietly?
The last bad blow that strikes fire in at eye
And on to brain, and so out, life and all,
How can it but be cheated of a pang
If, fighting quietly, the jaws enjoy
One re-embrace in mid backbone they break,
After their weary work thro' the foe's flesh?
That's the wolf-nature. Don't mistake my trope!
A Cardinal so qualmish? Eminence,
My fight is figurative, blows i' the air,
Brain-war with powers and principalities,
Spirit-bravado, no real fisticuffs!
I shall not presently, when the knock comes,
Cling to this bench nor claw the hangman's face,
No, trust me! I conceive worse lots than mine.
Whether it be the old contagious fit
And plague o' the prison have surprised me too,
The appropriate drunkenness of the death-hour
Crept on my sense, kind work o' the wine and myrrh,—
I know not,—I begin to taste my strength,
Careless, gay even. What's the worth of life?
The Pope's dead now, my murderous old man,
For Tozzi told me so: and you, forsooth—
Why, you don't think, Abate, do your best,
You'll live a year more with that hacking cough
And blotch of crimson where the cheek's a pit?
Tozzi has got you also down in book!
Cardinal, only seventh of seventy near,
Is not one called Albano in the lot?
Go eat your heart, you'll never be a Pope!
Inform me, is it true you left your love,
A Pucci, for promotion in the church?
She's more than in the church,—in the church-yard!
Plautilla Pucci, your affianced bride,
Has dust now in the eyes that held the love,—
And Martinez, suppose they make you Pope,
Stops that with *veto*,—so, enjoy yourself!
I see you all reel to the rock, you waves—
Some forthright, some describe a sinuous track,
Some, crested brilliantly, with heads above,
Some in a strangled swirl sunk who knows how,
But all bound whither the main-current sets,
Rockward, an end in foam for all of you!
What if I be o'ertaken, pushed to the front
By all you crowding smoother souls behind,
And reach, a minute sooner than was meant,
The boundary whereon I break to mist?
Go to! the smoothest safest of you all,
Most perfect and compact wave in my train,
Spite of the blue tranquillity above,
Spite of the breadth before of lapsing peace,

Where broods the halcyon and the fish leaps free,
Will presently begin to feel the prick
At lazy heart, the push at torpid brain,
Will rock vertiginously in turn, and reel,
And, emulative, rush to death like me.
Later or sooner by a minute then,
So much for the untimeliness of death!
And, as regards the manner that offends,
The rude and rough, I count the same for gain.
Be the act harsh and quick! Undoubtedly
The soul's condensed and, twice itself, expands
To burst thro' life, by alternation due,
Into the other state whate'er it prove.
You never know what life means till you die:
Even throughout life, 'tis death that makes life live,
Gives it whatever the significance.
For see, on your own ground and argument,
Suppose life had no death to fear, how find
A possibility of nobleness
In man, prevented daring any more?
What's love, what's faith without a worst to dread?
Lack-lustre jewelry! but faith and love
With death behind them bidding do or die—
Put such a foil at back, the sparkle's born!
From out myself how the strange colours come!
Is there a new rule in another world?
Be sure I shall resign myself: as here
I recognized no law I could not see,
There, what I see, I shall acknowledge too:
On earth I never took the Pope for God,
In heaven I shall scarce take God for the Pope.
Unmanned, remanned: I hold it probable—
With something changeless at the heart of me
To know me by, some nucleus that's myself:
Accretions did it wrong? Away with them—
You soon shall see the use of fire!

Till when,
All that was, is; and must for ever be.
Nor is it in me to unhate my hates,—
I use up my last strength to strike once more
Old Pietro in the wine-house-gossip-face,
To trample underfoot the whine and wile
Of beast Violante,—and I grow one gorge
To loathingly reject Pompilia's pale
Poison my hasty hunger took for food.
A strong tree wants no wreaths about its trunk,
No cloying cups, no sickly sweet of scent,
But sustenance at root, a bucketful.
How else lived that Athenian who died so,
Drinking hot bull's-blood, fit for men like me?
I lived and died a man, and take man's chance,
Honest and bold: right will be done to such.

Who are these you have let descend my stair?
Ha, their accursed psalm! [1] Lights at the sill!
Is it "Open" they dare bid you? Treachery!
Sirs, have I spoken one word all this while
Out of the world of words I had to say?
Not one word! All was folly—I laughed and mocked!
Sirs, my first true word, all truth and no lie,
Is—save me notwithstanding! Life is all!
I was just stark mad,—let the madman live
Pressed by as many chains as you please pile!
Don't open! Hold me from them! I am yours,
I am the Granduke's—no, I am the Pope's!
Abate, — Cardinal, — Christ, — Maria, — God,
Pompilia, will you let them murder me?

[1] The penitential psalm sung by the Brotherhood of Death who had come to escort Guido.

REDEDICATION OF *SORDELLO*

To J. Milsand, of Dijon

Dear Friend,—Let the next poem be introduced by your name, therefore remembered along with one of the deepest of my affections, and so repay all trouble it ever cost me. I wrote it twenty-five years ago for only a few, counting even in these on somewhat more care about its subject than they really had. My own faults of expression were many; but with care for a man or book such would be surmounted, and without it what avails the faultlessness of either? I blame nobody, least of all myself, who did my best then and since; for I lately gave time and pains to turn my work into what the many might,—instead of what the few must,—like: but after all, I imagined another thing at first, and therefore leave as I find it. The historical decoration was purposely of no more importance than a background requires; and my stress lay on the incidents in the development of a soul: little else is worth study. I, at least, always thought so—you, with many known and unknown to me, think so—others may one day think so; and whether my attempt remain for them or not, I trust, though away and past it, to continue ever yours, R. B.

London: *June* 9, 1863.

FOREWORD TO *A SOUL'S TRAGEDY*

(1846. Not reprinted in later editions.)

Here ends my first series of "Bells and Pomegranates," and I take the opportunity of explaining, in reply to inquiries, that I only meant by that title to indicate an endeavour towards something like an alternation, or mixture, of music with discoursing, sound with sense, poetry with thought; which looks too ambitious, thus expressed, so the symbol was preferred. It is little to the purpose that such is actually one of the most familiar of the many Rabbinical (and Patristic) acceptations of the phrase; because I confess that, letting authority alone, I supposed the bare words, in such juxtaposition, would sufficiently convey the desired meaning. "Faith and good works" is another fancy, for instance, and perhaps no easier to arrive at: yet Giotto placed a pomegranate fruit in the hand of Dante, and Raffaelle crowned his Theology (in the *Camera della Segnatura*) with blossoms of the same; as if the Bellari and Vasari would be sure to come after, and explain that it was merely "simbolo delle buone opere—il qual Pomogranato fu però usato nelle vesti del Pontefice appresso gli Ebrei."

BROWNING ON THE RECEPTION OF HIS POEMS

I

[August, 1865]

. . . I suppose that what you call "my fame within these four years" comes from a little of this gossiping and going about, and showing myself to be alive: and so indeed some folks say—but I hardly think it: for remember I was uninterruptedly (almost) in London from the time I published *Paracelsus* till I ended that string of plays with *Luria*—and I used to go out then, and see far more of merely literary people, critics etc. than I do now,—but what came of it? There were always a few people who had a certain opinion of my poems, but nobody cared to speak what he thought, or the things printed twenty-five years ago would not have waited so long for a good word; but at last a new set of men arrive who don't mind the conventionalities of ignoring one and seeing everything in another—Chapman says, "the new orders come from Oxford and Cambridge," and all my new cultivators are young men—more than that, I observe that some of my old friends don't like at all the irruption of outsiders who rescue me from their sober and private approval, and take those words out of their mouths "which they always meant to say" and never did. When there gets to be a general feeling of this kind, that there must be something in the works of an author, the reviews are obliged to notice him, such notice as it is—but what poor work, even when doing its best! I mean poor in the failure to give a general notion of the whole works; not a particular one of such and such points therein. As I begun, so I shall end,—taking my own course, pleasing myself or aiming at doing so, and thereby, I hope, pleasing God. . . .

II

[November 27th, 1868]

. . . I can have but little doubt but that my writing has been, in the main, too hard for many I should have been pleased to communicate with; but I never designedly tried to puzzle people, as some of my critics have supposed. On the other hand, I never pretended to offer such literature as should be a substitute for a cigar, or a game of dominoes, to an idle man. . . .

Yours very faithfully,
Robert Browning.

III

[1871]

. . . I am told my little thing ["Prince Hohenstiel-Schwangau, Saviour of Society"] is succeeding—sold 1,400 in the first five days, and before any notice appeared. I remember that year I made the little rough sketch in Rome, '60, my account for the last six months with Chapman was—nil, not one copy disposed of! . . .

Spite of my ailments and bewailments I have just all but finished another poem of quite another kind, which shall amuse you in the spring, I hope! I don't go sound asleep at all events. *Balaustion*—the second edition is in the press I think I told you. 2,500 in five months, is a good sale for the likes of me. But I met Henry Taylor (of *Artevelde*) two days ago at dinner, and he said he had never gained anything by his books, which surely is a shame—I mean, if no buyers mean no readers. . . .

IV

[February 10th, 1887]

Dear Sir,[1]

I am quite sure you mean very kindly, but I have had too long an experience of the inability of the human goose to do other than cackle when benevolent, and hiss when malicious; and no amount of goose criticism shall make me lift a heel at what waddles behind it.

Believe me, Dear Sir,
Very sincerely,
Robert Browning.

[1] This letter was Browning's brisk reply to a correspondent who had forwarded to him an extract from an unfriendly criticism published in the *Daily Mail*, Feb. 3, 1887.

SELECTIONS FROM THE LETTERS OF ROBERT BROWNING AND ELIZABETH BARRETT

I R. B. to E. B. B.

New Cross, Hatcham, Surrey
[Postmark, January 10, 1845]

I love your verses with all my heart, dear Miss Barrett,—and this is no off-hand complimentary letter that I shall write,—whatever else, no prompt matter-of-course recognition of your genius, and there a graceful and natural end of the thing. Since the day last week when I first read your poems, I quite laugh to remember how I have been turning and turning again in my mind what I should be able to tell you of their effect upon me, for in the first flush of delight I thought I would this once get out of my habit of purely passive enjoyment, when I do really enjoy, and thoroughly justify my admiration—perhaps even, as a loyal fellow-craftsman should, try and find fault and do you some little good to be proud of hereafter!—but nothing comes of it all—so into me has it gone, and part of me has it become, this great living poetry of yours, not a flower of which but took root and grew—Oh, how different that is from lying to be dried and pressed flat, and prized highly, and put in a book with a proper account at top and bottom, and shut up and put away . . . and the book called a "Flora," besides! After all, I need not give up the thought of doing that, too, in time; because even now, talking with whoever is worthy, I can give a reason for my faith in one and another excellence, the fresh strange music, the affluent language, the exquisite pathos and true new brave thought; but in this addressing myself to you—your own self, and for the first time, my feeling rises altogether. I do, as I say, love these books with all my heart—and I love you too. Do you know I was once not very far from seeing—really seeing you? Mr. Kenyon said to me one morning "Would you like to see Miss Barrett?"

then he went to announce me,—then he returned . . you were too unwell, and now it is years ago, and I feel as at some untoward passage in my travels, as if I had been close, so close, to some world's-wonder in chapel or crypt, only a screen to push and I might have entered, but there was some slight, so it now seems, slight and just sufficient bar to admission, and the half-opened door shut, and I went home my thousands of miles, and the sight was never to be.

Well, these Poems were to be, and this true thankful joy and pride with which I feel myself,

Yours ever faithfully,
Robert Browning.

II E. B. B. to R. B.

50 Wimpole Street: Jan. 11, 1845

I thank you, dear Mr. Browning, from the bottom of my heart. You meant to give me pleasure by your letter—and even if the object had not been answered, I ought still to thank you. But it is thoroughly answered. Such a letter from such a hand! Sympathy is dear—very dear to me: but the sympathy of a poet, and of such a poet, is the quintessence of sympathy to me! Will you take back my gratitude for it?—agreeing, too, that of all the commerce done in the world, from Tyre to Carthage, the exchange of sympathy for gratitude is the most princely thing!

For the rest you draw me on with your kindness. It is difficult to get rid of people when you once have given them too much pleasure—*that* is a fact, and we will not stop for the moral of it. What I was going to say—after a little natural hesitation—is, that if ever you emerge without inconvenient effort from your "passive state," and will *tell* me of such faults as rise to the surface and strike you as important in my poems, (for of course, I do not think of troubling you with criticism in detail) you will confer a lasting obligation on me, and one which I shall value so much, that I covet it at a distance. I do not pretend to any extraordinary meekness under criticism and it is possible enough that I might not be altogether obedient to yours. But with my high respect for your power in your Art and for your experience as an artist, it would be quite impossible for me to hear a general observation of yours on what appear to you my master-faults, without being the better for it hereafter in some way. I ask for only a sentence or two of general observation—and I do not ask even for *that*, so as to tease you—but in the humble, low voice, which is so excellent a thing in women—particularly when they go a-begging! The most frequent general criticism I receive, is, I think, upon the style, "if I *would* but change my style"! But *that* is an objection (isn't it?) to the writer bodily? Buffon says, and every sincere writer must feel, that "*Le style c'est l'homme;*" a fact, however, scarcely calculated to lessen the objection with certain critics.

Is it indeed true that I was so near to the pleasure and honour of making your acquaintance? and can it be true that you look back upon the lost opportunity with any regret? *But*—you know—if you had entered the "crypt," you might have caught cold, or been tired to death, and *wished* yourself "a thousand miles off;" which would have been worse than travelling them. It is not my interest, however, to put such thoughts in your head about its being "all for the best;" and I would rather hope (as I do) that what I lost by one chance I may recover by some future one. Winters shut me up as they do dormouse's eyes; in the spring, *we shall see:* and I am so much better that I seem turning round to the outward world again. And in the meantime I have learnt to know your voice, not merely from the poetry but from the kindness in it. Mr. Kenyon often speaks of you—dear Mr. Kenyon!—who most unspeakably, or only speakably with tears in my eyes,—has been my friend and helper, and my book's friend and helper! critic and sympathiser, true friend of all hours! You know him well enough, I think, to understand that I must be grateful to him.

I am writing too much,—and notwithstanding that I am writing too much, I will write of one thing more. I will say that I am your debtor, not only for this cordial letter and for all the pleasure which came with it, but in other ways, and those the highest: and I will say that while I live to follow this divine art of poetry, in proportion to my love for it and my devotion to it, I must be a devout admirer and student of your works. This is in my heart to say to you—and I say it.

And, for the rest, I am proud to remain

Your obliged and faithful
Elizabeth B. Barrett.

III R. B. to E. B. B.

New Cross, Hatcham, Surrey
Jan. 13, 1845

Dear Miss Barrett,—I just shall say, in as few words as I can, that you make me very happy, and that, now the beginning is over, I dare say I shall do better, because my poor praise, number one, was nearly as felicitously brought out, as a certain tribute to no less a personage than Tasso, which I was amused with at Rome some weeks ago, in a neat pencilling on the plaister-wall by his tomb at Sant' Onofrio—"Alla cara memoria—di—(please fancy solemn interspaces and grave capital letters at the new lines) di—Torquato Tasso—il Dottore Bernardini—offriva—il seguente Carme—*O tu*"—and no more, the good man, it should seem, breaking down with the overload of love here! But my "O tu"—was breathed out most sincerely, and now you have taken it in gracious part, the rest will come after. Only,—and which is why I write now—it looks as if I have introduced some phrase or other about "your faults" so cleverly as to give exactly the opposite meaning to what I meant, which was, that in my first ardour I had thought to tell you of *everything* which impressed me in your verses, down, even, to whatever "faults" I could find—a good earnest, when I had got to *them*, that I had left out not much between—as if some Mr. Fellows were to say, in the overflow of his first enthusiasm of rewarded adventure: "I will describe you all the outer life and ways of these Lycians, down to their very sandal-thongs," whereto the be-corresponded one rejoins—"Shall I get next week, then, your dissertation on sandal-thongs"? Yes, and a little about the "Olympian Horses," and God-charioteers as well!

What "struck me as faults," were not matters on the removal of which, one was to have—poetry, or high poetry,—but the very highest poetry, so I thought, and that, to universal recognition. For myself, or any artist, in many of the cases there would be a positive loss of time, peculiar artist's pleasure—for an instructed eye loves to see where the brush has dipped twice in a lustrous colour, has lain insistingly along a favourite outline, dwelt lovingly in a grand shadow; for these "too muches" for the everybody's picture are so many helps to the making out the real painter's picture as he had it in his brain. And all of the Titian's Naples Magdalen must have once been golden in its degree to justify that heap of hair in her hands—the *only* gold effected now!

But about this soon—for night is drawing on and I go out, yet cannot, quiet at conscience, till I repeat (to *myself*, for I never said it to you, I think) that your poetry must be, cannot but be, infinitely more to me than mine to you—for you *do* what I always wanted, hoped to do, and only seem now likely to do for the first time. You speak out, *you*,—I only make men and women speak—give you truth broken into prismatic hues, and fear the pure white light, even if it is in me, but I am going to try; so it will be no small comfort to have your company just now, seeing that when you have your men and women aforesaid, you are busied with them, whereas it seems bleak, melancholy work, this talking to the wind (for I have begun)—yet I don't think I shall let *you* hear, after all, the savage things about Popes and imaginative religions that I must say.

See how I go on and on to you, I who, whenever now and then pulled, by the head and hair, into letter-writing, get sorrowfully on for a line or two, as the cognate creature urged on by stick and string, and then come down "flop" upon the sweet haven of page one, line last, as serene as the sleep of the virtuous! You will never more, I hope, talk of "the honour of my acquaintance," but I will joyfully wait for the delight of your friendship, and the spring, and my Chapel-sight after all!

Ever yours most faithfully,
R. Browning.

For Mr. Kenyon—I have a convenient theory about *him*, and his otherwise unaccountable kindness to me; but 'tis quite night now, and they call me.

IV E. B. B. to R. B.

50 Wimpole Street: Jan. 15, 1845

Dear Mr. Browning,—The fault was clearly with me and not with you.

When I had an Italian master, years ago, he told me that there was an unpronounceable English word which absolutely expressed me, and which he would say in his own tongue, as he could not in mine—"*testa lunga*." Of course, the signor meant *headlong!*—and now I have had enough to tame me, and might be expected to stand still in my stall. But you see I do not. Headlong I was at first, and headlong I continue—precipitously rushing forward through all manner of nettles and briars instead of keeping the path; guessing at the meaning of unknown words instead of looking into the dictionary—tearing open letters, and never untying a string,—and expecting everything to be done in a minute, and the thunder to be as quick as the lightning. And so, at your half word I flew at the whole one, with all its possible consequences, and wrote what you read. Our common friend, as I think he is, Mr. Horne, is often forced to entreat me into patience and coolness of purpose, though his only intercourse with me has been by letter. And, by the way, you will be sorry to hear that during his stay in Germany *he* has been "headlong" (out of a metaphor) twice; once, in falling from the Drachenfels, when he only just saved himself by catching at a vine; and once quite lately, at Christmas, in a fall on the ice of the Elbe in skating, when he dislocated his left shoulder in a very painful manner. He is doing quite well, I believe, but it was sad to have such a shadow from the German Christmas tree, and he a stranger.

In art, however, I understand that it does not do to be headlong, but patient and laborious—and there is a love strong enough, even in me, to overcome nature. I apprehend what you mean in the criticism you just intimate, and shall turn it over and over in my mind until I get practical good from it. What no mere critic sees, but what you, an artist, know, is the difference between the thing desired and the thing attained, between the idea in the writer's mind and the εἴδωλον cast off in his work. All the effort—the quick'ning of the breath and beating of the heart in pursuit, which is ruffling and injurious to the general effect of a composition; all which you call "insistency," and which many would call superfluity, and which *is* superfluous in a sense—*you* can pardon, because you understand. The great chasm between the thing I say, and the thing I would say, would be quite dispiriting to me, in spite even of such kindnesses as yours, if the desire did not master the despondency. "Oh for a horse with wings!" It is wrong of me to write so of myself—only you put your finger on the root of a fault, which has, to my fancy, been a little misapprehended. I do not *say everything I think* (as has been said of me by master-critics) but I *take every means to say what I think*, which is different!—or I fancy so!

In one thing, however, you are wrong. Why should you deny the full measure of my delight and benefit from your writings? I could tell you why you should not. You have in your vision two worlds, or to use the language of the schools of the day, you are both subjective and objective in the habits of your mind. You can deal both with abstract thought and with human passion in the most passionate sense. Thus, you have an immense grasp in Art; and no one at all accustomed to consider the usual forms of it, could help regarding with reverence and gladness the gradual expansion of your powers. Then you are "masculine" to the height—and I, as a woman, have studied some of your gestures of language and intonation wistfully, as a thing beyond me far! and the more admirable for being beyond.

Of your new work I hear with delight. How good of you to tell me. And it is not dramatic in the strict sense, I am to understand—(am I right in understanding so?) and you speak, in your own person "to the winds"? no—but to the thousand living sympathies which will awake to hear you. A great dramatic power may develop itself otherwise than in the formal drama; and I have been guilty of wishing, before this hour (for reasons which

I will not thrust upon you after all my tedious writing), that you would give the public a poem unassociated directly or indirectly with the stage, for a trial on the popular heart. I reverence the drama, but—

But I break in on myself out of consideration for you. I might have done it, you will think, before. I vex your "serene sleep of the virtuous" like a nightmare. Do not say "No." I am *sure* I do! As to the vain parlance of the world, I did not talk of the "honour of your acquaintance" without a true sense of honour, indeed; but I shall willingly exchange it all (and *now*, if you please, at this moment, for fear of worldly mutabilities) for the "delight of your friendship."

Believe me, therefore, dear Mr. Browning,
Faithfully yours, and gratefully,
Elizabeth B. Barrett.

For Mr. Kenyon's kindness, as *I* see it, no theory will account. I class it with mesmerism for that reason.

V R. B. TO E. B. B.

Wednesday morning—Spring!
[Postmark, February 26, 1845]

* * *

Who told you of my sculls and spider webs —Horne? Last year I petted extraordinarily a fine fellow, (a *garden* spider—there was the singularity,—the thin clever-even-for a spider-sort, and they are *so* "spirited and sly," all of them—this kind makes a long cone of web, with a square chamber of vantage at the end, and there he sits loosely and looks about), a great fellow that housed himself, with real gusto, in the jaws of a great scull, whence he watched me as I wrote, and I remember speaking to Horne about his good points. Phrenologists look gravely at that great scull, by the way, and hope, in their grim manner, that its owner made a good end. He looks quietly, now, out at the green little hill behind. I have no little insight to the feelings of furniture, and treat books and prints with a reasonable consideration. How some people use their pictures, for instance, is a mystery to me; very revolting all the same—portraits obliged to face each other for ever,—prints put together in portfolios. My Polidoro's perfect Andromeda along with "Boors Carousing," by Ostade,—where I found her,—my own father's doing, or I would say more.

And when I have said I like "Pippa" better than anything else I have done yet, I shall have answered all you bade me. And now may *I* begin questioning? No,—for it is all a pure delight to me, so that you do but write. I never was without good, kind, generous friends and lovers, so they say—so they were and are—perhaps they came at the wrong time—I never wanted them—though that makes no difference in my gratitude, I trust—but I know myself—surely—and always have done so, for is there not somewhere the little book I first printed when a boy, with John Mill, the metaphysical head, *his* marginal note that "the writer possesses a deeper self-consciousness than I ever knew in a sane human being." So I never deceived myself much, nor called my feelings for people other than they were. And who has a right to say, if I have not, that I had, but I said that, supernatural or no. Pray tell me, too, of your present doings and projects, and never write yourself "grateful" to me, who *am* grateful, very grateful to you,—for none of your words but I take in earnest—and tell me if Spring *be not* coming, come, and I will take to writing the gravest of letters, because this beginning is for gladness' sake, like Carlyle's song couplet. My head aches a little today too, and, as poor dear Kirke White said to the moon, from his heap of mathematical papers,

"I throw aside the learned sheet;
I cannot choose but gaze, she looks so — mildly sweet."

Out on the foolish phrase, but there's hard rhyming without it.

Ever yours faithfully,
Robert Browning.

VI E. B. B. TO R. B.

50 Wimpole Street: March 20, 1845

Whenever I delay to write to you, dear Mr. Browning, it is not, be sure, that I take my "own good time," but submit to my own bad time. It was kind of you to wish to know how I was, and not unkind of me to suspend my answer to your question—for indeed I have not been very well, nor have had much heart for saying so. This implacable weather! this east wind that seems to blow through the sun and moon! who can be well in such a wind? Yet for me, I should not grumble. There has been nothing very bad the matter with me, as there used to be—I only grow weaker than usual, and learn my lesson of being mortal, in a corner—and then all this must end! April is coming. There will be both a May and a June if we live to see such things, and perhaps, after all, we may, and as to seeing *you* besides, I observe that you distrust me, and that perhaps you penetrate my morbidity and guess how when the moment comes to see a living human face to which I am not accustomed, I shrink and grow pale in the spirit. Do you? You are learned in human nature, and you know the consequences of leading such a secluded life as mine—notwithstanding all my fine philosophy about social duties and the like—well—if you have such knowledge or if you have it not, I cannot say, but I do say that I will indeed see you when the warm weather has revived me a little, and put the earth "to rights" again so as to make pleasures of the sort possible. For if you think that I shall not *like* to see you, you are wrong, for all your learning. But I shall be afraid of you at first—though I am not, in writing thus. You are Paracelsus, and I am a recluse, with nerves that have been all broken on the rack, and now hang loosely—quivering at a step and breath.

And what you say of society draws me on to many comparative thoughts of your life and mine. You seem to have drunken of the cup of life full, with the sun shining on it. I have lived only inwardly; or with *sorrow*, for a strong emotion. Before this seclusion of my illness, I was secluded still, and there are few of the youngest women in the world who have not seen more, heard more, known more, of society, than I, who am scarcely to be called young now. I grew up in the country—had no social opportunities, had my heart in books and poetry, and my experience in reveries. My sympathies drooped towards the ground like an untrained honeysuckle—and but for *one*, in my own house—but of this I cannot speak. It was a lonely life, growing green like the grass around it. Books and dreams were what I lived in—and domestic life only seemed to buzz gently around, like the bees about the grass. And so time passed, and passed—and afterwards, when my illness came and I seemed to stand at the edge of the world with all done, and no prospect (as appeared at one time) of ever passing the threshold of one room again; why then, I turned to thinking with some bitterness (after the greatest sorrow of my life had given me room and time to breathe) that I had stood blind in this temple I was about to leave—that I had seen no Human nature, that my brothers and sisters of the earth were *names* to me, that I had beheld no great mountain or river, nothing in fact. I was as a man dying who had not read Shakespeare, and it was too late! do you understand? And do you also know what a disadvantage this ignorance is to my art? Why, if I live on and yet do not escape from this seclusion, do you not perceive that I labour under signal disadvantages—that I am, in a manner, as a *blind poet?* Certainly, there is a compensation to a degree. I have had much of the inner life, and from the habit of self-consciousness and self-analysis, I made great guesses at Human nature in the main. But how willingly I would as a poet exchange some of this lumbering, ponderous, helpless knowledge of books, for some experience of life and man, for some . . .

But all grumbling is a vile thing. We should all thank God for our measures of life, and think them enough for each of us. I write so, that you may not mistake what I wrote before in relation to society, although you do not see from my point of view; and that you may understand what I mean fully when I say, that I have lived all my chief *joys*, and indeed nearly all emotions that go warmly by that name and relate to myself personally, in poetry and in poetry alone. Like to write? Of course, of course I do. I seem to live while I write—it is life, for me. Why, what is to live? Not to eat and drink and breathe,—but to feel the life in you down all the fibres of being, passionately and joyfully. And thus, one lives in composition surely—not always—but when the wheel goes round and the procession is uninterrupted. Is it not so with you? oh—it must be so. For the rest, there will be necessarily a reaction; and, in my own particular case, whenever I see a poem of mine in print, or even smoothly transcribed, the reaction is most painful. The pleasure, the sense of power, without which I could not write a line, is gone in a moment; and nothing remains but disappointment and humiliation. I never wrote a poem which you could not persuade me to tear to pieces if you took me at the right moment! I have a *seasonable* humility, I do assure you.

How delightful to talk about oneself; but as you "tempted me and I did eat," I entreat your longsuffering of my sin, and ah! if you would but sin back so in turn! . . .

Ah! you tempt me with a grand vision of Prometheus! *I*, who have just escaped with my life, after treading Milton's ground, you would send me to Æschylus's. No, *I do not dare.* And besides, . . I am inclined to think that we want new *forms*, as well as thoughts. The old gods are dethroned. Why should we go back to the antique moulds, classical moulds, as they are so improperly called? If it is a necessity of Art to do so, why then those critics are right who hold that Art is exhausted and the world too worn out for poetry. I do not, for my part, believe this: and I believe the so-called necessity of Art to be the mere feebleness of the artist. Let us all aspire rather to *Life*, and let the dead bury their dead. If we have but courage to face these conventions, to touch this low ground, we shall take strength from it instead of losing it; and of that, I am intimately persuaded. For there is poetry *everywhere:* the "treasure" (see the old fable) lies all over the field. And then Christianity is a worthy *myth*, and poetically acceptable.

* * *

May God bless you!

Ever and truly yours,

E. B. B.

VII R. B. TO E. B. B.

Tuesday Evening

[Postmark, May 21, 1845]

I trust to you for a true account of how you are—if tired, if not tired, if I did wrong in any thing,—or, if you please, *right* in any thing—(only, not one more word about my "kindness," which, to get done with, I will grant is exceptive)—but, let us so arrange matters if possible,—and why should it not be—that my great happiness, such as it will be if I see you, as this morning, from time to time, may be obtained at the cost of as little inconvenience to you as we can contrive. For an instance—just what strikes me—they all say here I speak very loud—(a trick caught from having often to talk with a deaf relative of mine). And did I stay too long?

I will tell *you* unhesitatingly of such "corrigenda"—nay, I will again say, do not humiliate me—*do not* again,—by calling me "kind" in that way.

I am proud and happy in your friendship—now and ever. May God bless you!

R. B.

VIII R. B. TO E. B. B.

[Postmark, May 26, 1845]

Nay—I *must* have last word—as all people in the wrong desire to have—and then, no more of the subject. You said I had given you *great pain*—so long as I stop *that*, think anything of me you choose or can! But *before* your former letter came, I saw the pre-ordained uselessness of mine. Speaking is to some *end*, (apart from foolish self-relief, which, after all, I can do without)—and where there is *no* end—you see! or, to finish characteristically—since the offering to cut off one's right-hand to save anybody a headache, is in vile taste, even for our melodramas, seeing that it was never yet believed in on the stage or off it,—how much worse to really make the ugly chop, and afterwards come sheepishly in, one's arm in a black sling, and find that the delectable gift had changed aching to nausea! And now, "exit, prompt-side, nearest door, Luria" —and enter R. B.—next Wednesday,—as boldly as he suspects most people do just after they have been soundly frightened!

I shall be most happy to see you on the day and at the hour you mention.

God bless you, my dear friend,

R. B.

IX E. B. B. TO R. B.

Wednesday
[Postmark, August 25, 1845]

* * *

Friday.—I was writing you see before you came—and now I go on in haste to speak "off my mind" some things which are on it. First . . of yourself; how can it be that you are unwell again, . . and that you should talk (now did you not?—did I not hear you say so?) of being "weary in your soul" . . *you?* What should make *you*, dearest friend, weary in your soul; or out of spirits in any way?—Do . . tell me . . I was going to write without a pause—and almost I might, perhaps, . . even as one of the two hundred of your friends, . . almost I might say out that "Do tell me." Or is it (which I am inclined to think most probable) that you are tired of a same life and want change? It may happen to anyone sometimes, and is independent of your will and choice, you know—and I know, and the whole world knows: and would it not therefore be wise of you, in that case, to fold your life new again and go abroad at once? What can make you weary in your soul, is a problem to me. You are the last from whom I should have expected such a word. And you did say so, I *think*. I *think* that it was not a mistake of mine. And *you* . . with a full liberty, and the world in your hand for every purpose and pleasure of it!—Or is it that, being unwell, your spirits are affected by *that?* But then you might be more unwell than you like to admit—. And I am teasing you with talking of it . . am I not?—and being disagreeable is only one third of the way towards being useful, it is good to remember in time.

. . . But what you do *not* see, what you *cannot* see, is the deep tender affection behind and below all those patriarchal ideas of governing grown up children "in the way they *must* go!" and there never was (under the strata) a truer affection in a father's heart . . no, nor a worthier heart in itself . . a heart loyaller and purer, and more compelling to gratitude and reverence, than his, as I see it! The evil is in the system—and he simply takes it to be his duty to rule, and to make happy according to his own views of the propriety of happiness—he takes it to be his duty to rule like the Kings of Christendom, by divine right. But he loves us through and through it—and *I*, for one, love *him!* and when, five years ago, I lost what I loved best in the world beyond comparison and rivalship . . far better than himself as he knew . . for everyone who knew *me* could not choose but know what was my first and chiefest affection . . when I lost *that*, . . I felt that he stood the nearest to me on the closed grave . . or by the unclosing sea . . I do not know which nor could ask. And I will tell you that not only he has been kind and patient and forbearing to me through the tedious trial of this illness (far more trying to standers by than you have an idea of perhaps) but that he was generous and forbearing in that hour of bitter trial and never reproached me as he might have done and as my own soul has not spared—never once said to me then or since, that if it had not been for *me*, the crown of his house would not have fallen. He *never did* . . and he might have said it, and more—and I could have answered nothing. Nothing, except that I had paid my own price—and that price I paid was greater than his *loss* . . his! For see how it was; and how, "not with my hand but heart," I was the cause or occasion of that misery—and though not with the intention of my heart but with its weakness, yet the *occasion*, any way!

They sent me down you know to Torquay—Dr. Chambers saying that I could not live a winter in London. The worst—what people call the worst—was apprehended for me at that time. So I was sent down with my sister to my aunt there—and he, my brother whom I loved so, was sent too, to take us there and return. And when the time came for him to leave me, *I*, to whom he was the dearest of friends and brothers in one . . the only one of my family who . . well, but I cannot write of these things; and it is enough to tell you that he was above us all, better than us all, and kindest and noblest and dearest to *me*, beyond comparison, any comparison, as I said—and when the time came for him to leave me *I*, weakened by illness, could not master my spirits or drive back my tears—and my aunt kissed them away instead of reproving me as she should have done; and said that *she* would take care that I should not be grieved . . *she!* . . and so she sate down and wrote a letter to Papa to tell him that he would "break my heart" if he persisted in calling away my brother—As if hearts were broken *so!* I have thought bitterly since that my heart did not break for a good deal more than *that!* And Papa's answer was—burnt into me, as with fire, it is—that "under such circumstances he did not refuse to suspend his purpose, but that he considered it to be *very wrong in me to exact such a thing*." So there was no separation *then:* and month after month passed—and sometimes I was better and sometimes worse—and the medical men continued to say that they would not answer for my life . . they! if I were agitated—and so there was no more talk of a separation. And once *he* held my hand, . . how I remember! and said that he "loved me better than them all and that he *would not* leave me . . till I was well," he said! how I remember *that!* And ten days from that day the boat had left the shore which never returned; never—and he *had* left me! gone! For three days we waited—and I hoped while I could—oh—that awful agony of three days! And the sun shone as it shines to-day, and there was no more wind than now; and the sea under the windows was like this paper for smoothness—and my sisters drew the curtains back that I might see for myself how smooth the sea was, and how it could hurt nobody—and other boats came back one by one.

Remember how you wrote in your "Gismond"

> What says the body when they spring
> Some monstrous torture-engine's whole
> Strength on it? No more says the soul.

and you never wrote anything which *lived* with me more than *that*. It is such a dreadful truth. . . .

Do not notice what I have written to you, my dearest friend. I have never said so much to a living being—I never *could* speak or write of it. I asked no question from the moment when my last hope went: and since then, it has been impossible for me to speak what was in me. I have borne to do it to-day and to you, but perhaps if you were to write—so do not let this be noticed between us again—*do not!* . . .

And so goodbye until Tuesday. Perhaps I shall . . not . . hear from you to-night. Don't let the tragedy or aught else do you harm—will you? and try not to be "weary in your soul" any more—and forgive me this gloomy letter I half shrink from sending you, yet will send.

May God bless you.

E. B. B.

X R. B. TO E. B. B.[1]

[Postmark, September 25, 1845]

You have said to me more than once that you wished I might never know certain feelings *you* had been forced to endure. I suppose all of us have the proper place where a blow should fall to be felt most—and I truly wish *you* may never feel what I have to bear in looking on, quite powerless, and silent, while you are subjected to this treatment, which I refuse to characterize—so blind is it *for* blindness. I think I ought to understand what a father may exact, and a child should comply with; and I respect the most ambiguous of love's caprices if they give never so slight a clue to their all-justifying source. Did I, when you signified to me the probable objections—you remember what—to myself, my own happiness,—did I once allude to, much less argue against, or refuse to acknowledge those objections? For I wholly sympathize, however it go against me, with the highest, wariest, pride and love for you, and the proper jealousy and vigilance they entail—but now, and here, the jewel is not being over guarded, but ruined, cast away. And whoever is privileged to interfere should do so in the possessor's own interest—all common sense interferes—all rationality against absolute no-reason at all. And you ask whether you ought to obey this no-reason? I will tell you: all passive obedience and implicit submission of will and intellect is by far too easy, if well considered, to be the course prescribed by God to Man in

[1] Miss Barrett had written in great distress of her father's refusal to allow her to go to Italy for her health. Browning's reply is in answer to her "Think for me"—was she bound by daughterly duty to obedience?

this life of probation—for they *evade* probation altogether, though foolish people think otherwise. Chop off your legs, you will never go astray; stifle your reason altogether and you will find it is difficult to reason ill. "It is hard to make these sacrifices!"—not so hard as to lose the reward or incur the penalty of an Eternity to come; "hard to effect them, then, and go through with them"—*not* hard, when the leg is to be *cut off*,—that it is rather harder to keep it quiet on a stool, I know very well. The partial indulgence, the proper exercise of one's faculties, there is the difficulty and problem for solution, set by that Providence which might have made the laws of Religion as indubitable as those of vitality, and revealed the articles of belief as certainly as that condition, for instance, by which we breathe so many times in a minute to support life. But there is no reward proposed for the feat of breathing, and a great one for that of believing—consequently there must go a great deal more of voluntary effort to this latter than is implied in the getting absolutely rid of it at once, by adopting the direction of an infallible church, or private judgment of another—for all our life is some form of religion, and all our action some belief, and there is but one law, however modified, for the greater and the less. In your case I do think you are called upon to do your duty to yourself; that is, to God in the end. Your own reason should examine the whole matter in dispute by every light which can be put in requisition; and every interest that appears to be affected by your conduct should have its utmost claims considered—your father's in the first place; and that interest, not in the miserable limits of a few days' pique or whim in which it would seem to express itself; but in its whole extent . . the *hereafter* which all momentary passion prevents him seeing . . indeed, the *present* on either side which everyone must see. And this examination made, with whatever earnestness you will, I do think and am sure that on its conclusion you should act, in confidence that a duty has been performed . . *difficult*, or how were it a duty? Will it *not* be infinitely harder to act so than to blindly adopt his pleasure, and die under it? Who can *not* do that?

I fling these hasty rough words over the paper, fast as they will fall—knowing to whom I cast them, and that any sense they may contain or point to, will be caught and understood, and presented in a better light. The hard thing . . this is all I want to say . . is to act on one's own best conviction—not to abjure it and accept another will, and say "*there* is my plain duty"—easy it is, whether plain or no!

How "all changes!" When I first saw you—you know what followed. I supposed you to labour under an incurable complaint—and, of course, to be completely dependent on your father for its commonest alleviations; the moment after that inconsiderate letter, I reproached myself bitterly with the selfishness apparently involved in any proposition I might then have made—for though I have never been at all frightened of the world, nor mistrustful of my power to deal with it, and get my purpose out of it if once I thought it worth while, yet I could not but feel the consideration, of *what* failure would *now* be, paralyse all effort even in fancy. When you told me lately that "you could never be poor"—all my solicitude was at an end—I had but myself to care about, and I told you, what I believed and believe, that I can at any time amply provide for that, and that I could cheerfully and confidently undertake the removing *that* obstacle. Now again the circumstances shift—and you are in what I should wonder at as the veriest slavery—and I who *could* free you from it, I am here scarcely daring to write . . though I know you must feel for me and forgive what forces itself from me . . what retires so mutely into my heart at your least word . . what *shall not* be again written or spoken, if you so will . . that I should be made happy beyond all hope of expression by. Now while I *dream*, let me once dream! I would marry you now and thus—I would come when you let me, and go when you bade me—I would be no more than one of your brothers—"*no more*"—that is, instead of getting to-morrow for Saturday, I should get Saturday as well—two hours for one—when your head ached I should be *here*. I deliberately choose the realization of that dream (—of sitting simply by you for an hour every day) rather than any other, excluding you, I am able to form for this world, or any world I know—And it will continue but a dream.

God bless my dearest E. B. B.

R. B.

You understand that I see you to-morrow, Friday, as you propose.

I am better—thank you—and will go out to-day.

You know what I am, what I would speak, and all I would do.

XI E. B. B. to R. B.

Friday Evening
[Postmark, September 27, 1845]

I had your letter late last night, everyone almost, being out of the house by an accident, so that it was left in the letter-box, and if I had wished to answer it before I saw you, it had scarcely been possible.

But it will be the same thing—for you know as well as if you saw my answer, what it must be, what it cannot choose but be, on pain of sinking me so infinitely below not merely your level but my own, that the depth cannot bear a glance down. Yet, though I am not made of such clay as to admit of my taking a base advantage of certain noble extravagances, (and that I am not I thank God for your sake) I will say, I must say, that your words in this letter have done me good and made me happy, . . that I thank and bless you for them, . . and that to receive such a proof of attachment from *you*, not only overpowers every present evil, but seems to me a full and abundant amends for the merely personal sufferings of my whole life. When I had read that letter last night I *did* think so. I looked round and round for the small bitternesses which for several days had been bitter to me, and I could not find one of them. The tear-marks went away in the moisture of new, happy tears. Why, how else could I have felt? how else do you think I could? How would any woman have felt . . who could feel at all . . hearing such words said (though "in a dream" indeed) by such a speaker?

And now listen to me in turn. You have touched me more profoundly than I thought even *you* could have touched me—my heart was full when you came here to-day. Henceforward I am yours for everything but to do you harm—and I am yours too much, in my heart, ever to consent to do you harm in that way. If I could consent to do it, not only should I be less loyal . . but in one sense, less yours. I say this to you without drawback and reserve, because it is all I am able to say, and perhaps all I *shall* be able to say. However this may be, a promise goes to you in it that none, except God and your will, shall interpose between you and me, . . I mean, that if He should free me within a moderate time from the trailing chain of this weakness, I will then be to you whatever at that hour you shall choose . . whether friend or more than friend . . a friend to the last in any case. So it rests with God and with you—only in the meanwhile you are most absolutely free . . "unentangled" (as they call it) by the breadth of a thread—and if I did not know that you considered yourself so, I would not see you any more, let the effort cost me what it might. You may force me to *feel:* . . but you cannot force me to *think* contrary to my first thought . . that it were better for you to forget me at once in one relation. And if better for *you*, can it be bad for *me?* which flings me down on the stone-pavement of the logicians.

And now if I ask a boon of you, will you forget afterwards that it ever was asked? I have hesitated a great deal; but my face is down on the stone-pavement—no—I will not ask today—It shall be for another day—and may God bless you on this and on those that come after, my dearest friend.

XII R. B. to E. B. B.

[Postmark, September 27, 1845]

Think for me, speak for me, my dearest, *my own!* You that are all great-heartedness and generosity, do that one more generous thing?

God bless you for

R. B.

What can it be you ask of me!—"a boon"—once my answer to *that* had been the plain one—but now . . when I have better experience of—

No, now I have BEST experience of how you understand my interests; that at last we *both* know what is my true good—so ask, ask! *My own*, now! now! For there it is!—oh, do not fear I am "*entangled*"—my crown is loose on my head, not nailed there—my pearl lies in my hand—I may return it to the sea, if I will!

What is it you ask of me, this first asking?

XIII E. B. B. TO R. B.

Thursday Evening
[Postmark, December 20, 1845]

Dearest, you know how to say what makes me happiest, you who never think, you say, of making me happy! For my part I do not think of it either; I simply understand that you *are* my happiness, and that therefore you could not make another happiness for me, such as would be worth having—not even *you!* Why, how could you? *That* was in my mind to speak yesterday, but I could not speak it—to write it, is easier.

Talking of happiness—shall I tell you? Promise not to be angry and I will tell you. I have thought sometimes that, if I considered myself wholly, I should choose to die this winter—now—before I had disappointed you in anything. But because you are better and dearer and more to be considered than I, I do *not* choose it. I *cannot* choose to give you any pain, even on the chance of its being a less pain, a less evil, than what may follow perhaps (who can say?), if I should prove the burden of your life.

For if you make me happy with some words, you frighten me with others—as with the extravagance yesterday—and seriously—*too* seriously, when the moment for smiling at them is past—I am frightened, I tremble! When you come to know me as well as I know myself, what can save me, do you think, from disappointing and displeasing you? I ask the question, and find no answer.

It is a poor answer, to say that I can do one thing well . . that I have one capacity largely. On points of the general affections, I have in thought applied to myself the words of Mme. de Stael, not fretfully, I hope, not complainingly, I am sure (I can thank God for most affectionate friends!) not complainingly, yet mournfully and in profound conviction—those words—"*jamais je n'ai pas été aimée comme j'aime.*" The capacity of loving is the largest of my powers I think—I thought so before knowing you—and one form of feeling. And although any woman might love you—*every* woman,—with understanding enough to discern you by—(oh, do not fancy that I am unduly magnifying mine office) yet I persist in persuading myself that! Because I have the capacity, as I said—and besides I owe more to you than others could, it seems to me: let me boast of it. To many, you might be better than all things while one of all things: to me you are instead of all—to many, a crowning happiness—to me, the happiness itself. From out of the deep dark pits men see the stars more gloriously—and *de profundis amavi*—

It is a very poor answer! Almost as poor an answer as yours could be if I were to ask you to teach me to please you always; or rather, how not to displease you, disappoint you, vex you—what if all those things were in my fate?

And—(to begin!)—*I* am disappointed tonight. I expected a letter which does not come —and I had felt so sure of having a letter tonight . . unreasonably sure perhaps, which means doubly sure.

* * *

XIV E. B. B. TO R. B.

Sunday
[Postmark, January 6, 1846]

* * *

You never guessed perhaps, what I look back to at this moment in the physiology of our intercourse, the curious double feeling I had about you—you personally, and you as the writer of these letters, and the crisis of the feeling, when I was positively vexed and jealous of myself for not succeeding better in making a unity of the two. I could not! And moreover I could not help but that the writer of the letters seemed nearer to me, long . . long . . and in spite of the postmark, than did the personal visitor who confounded me, and left me constantly under such an impression of its being all dream-work on his side, that I have stamped my feet on this floor with impatience to think of having to wait so many hours before the "candid" closing letter could come with its confessional of an illusion. "People say," I used to think, "that women *always* know, and certainly I do not know, and therefore . . therefore."—The logic crushed on like Juggernaut's car. But in the letters it was different—the dear letters took me on the side of my own ideal life where I was able to stand a little upright and look around. I could read such letters for ever and answer them after a fashion . . that, I felt from the beginning. But *you—!*

* * *

XV E. B. B. TO R. B.

Monday
[Postmark, January 27, 1846]

* * *

For *him*[1] . . he would rather see me dead at his foot than yield the point: and he will say so, and mean it, and persist in the meaning.

Do you ever wonder at me . . that I should write such things, and have written others so different? *I have thought that in myself very often.* Insincerity and injustice may seem the two ends, while I occupy the straight betwixt two—and I should not like you to doubt how this may be! Sometimes I have begun to show you the truth, and torn the paper: I *could* not. Yet now again I am borne on to tell you, . . to save you from some thoughts which you cannot help perhaps.

There has been no insincerity—nor is there injustice. I believe, I am certain, I have loved him better than the rest of his children. I have heard the fountain within the rock, and my heart has struggled in towards him through the stones of the rock . . thrust off . . dropping off . . turning in again and clinging! Knowing what is excellent in him well, loving him as my only parent left, and for himself dearly, notwithstanding that hardness and the miserable "system" which made him appear harder still, I have loved him and been proud of him for his high qualities, for his courage and fortitude when he bore up so bravely years ago under the worldly reverses which he yet felt acutely—more than you and I could feel them—but the fortitude was admirable. Then came the trials of love—then, I was repulsed too often, . . made to suffer in the suffering of those by my side . . depressed by petty daily sadnesses and terrors, from which it is possible however for an elastic affection to rise again as past. Yet my friends used to say "You look broken-spirited"—and it was true. In the midst, came my illness,—and when I was ill he grew gentler and let me draw nearer than ever I had done: and after that great stroke . . you *know* . . though *that* fell in the middle of a storm of emotion and sympathy on my part, which drove clearly against him, God seemed to strike our hearts together by the shock; and I was grateful to him for not saying aloud what I said to myself in my agony, "*If it had not been for you*" . . *!* And comparing my self-reproach to what I imagined his self-reproach must certainly be (for if *I* had loved selfishly, *he* had not been kind), I felt as if I could love and forgive him for two . . (I knowing that serene generous departed spirit, and seeming left to represent it) . . and I did love him better than all those left to *me* to love in the world here. I proved a little my affection for him, by coming to London at the risk of my life rather than diminish the comfort of his home by keeping a part of my family away from him. And afterwards for long and long he spoke to me kindly and gently, and of me affectionately and with too much praise; and God knows that I had as much joy as I imagined myself capable of again, in the sound of his footstep on the stairs, and of his voice when he prayed in this room; my best hope, as I have told him since, being, to die beneath his eyes. Love is so much to me naturally—it is, to all women! and it was so much to *me* to feel sure at last that *he* loved me—to forget all blame—to pull the weeds up from that last illusion of life:—and this, till the Pisa-business, which threw me off, far as ever, again—farther than ever—when George said "he could not flatter me" and I dared not flatter myself. But do *you* believe that I never wrote what I did not feel: I never did. And I ask one kindness more . . do not notice what I have written here. Let it pass. We can alter nothing by ever

[1] Her father.

so many words. After all, he is the victim. He isolates himself—and now and then he feels it . . the cold dead silence all round, which is the effect of an incredible system. If he were not stronger than most men, he could not bear it as he does. With such high qualities too!—so upright and honourable—you would esteem him, you would like him, I think. And so . . dearest . . let *that* be the last word.

I dare say you have asked yourself sometimes, why it was that I never managed to draw you into the house here, so that you might make your own way. Now *that* is one of the things impossible to me. I have not influence enough for *that*. George can never invite a friend of his even. Do you see? The people who do come here, come by particular license and association . . Capt. Surtees Cook being one of them. Once . . when I was in high favour too . . I asked Mr. Kenyon to be invited to dinner—he an old college friend, and living close by and so affectionate to me always—I felt that he must be hurt by the neglect, and asked. *It was in vain.* Now, you see—

May God bless you always! I wrote all my spirits away in this letter yesterday, and kept it to finish to-day . . being yours every day, glad or sad, ever beloved!—

Your Ba.

XVI R. B. to E. B. B.

Wednesday
[Postmark, January 28, 1846]

Ever dearest—I will say, as you desire, nothing on that subject—but this strictly for myself: you engaged me to consult my own good in the keeping or breaking our engagement; not *your* good as it might even seem to me; much less seem to another. My only good in this world—that against which all the world goes for nothing—is to spend my life with you, and be yours. You know that when I *claim* anything, it is really yourself in me—you *give* me a right and bid me use it, and I, in fact, am most obeying you when I appear most exacting on my own account—so, in that feeling, I dare claim, once for all, and in all possible cases (except that dreadful one of your becoming worse again . . in which case I wait till life ends with both of us), I claim your promise's fulfilment—say, at the summer's end: it cannot be for your good that this state of things should continue. We can go to Italy for a year or two and be happy as day and night are long. For me, I adore you. This is all unnecessary, I feel as I write: but you will think of the main fact as *ordained*, granted by God, will you not, dearest?—so, not to be put in doubt *ever again*—then, we can go quietly thinking of after matters. Till to-morrow, and ever after, God bless my heart's own, own Ba. All my soul follows you, love—encircles you—and I live in being yours.

XVII R. B. to E. B. B.

Wednesday Morning
[Postmark, February 25, 1846]

Once you were pleased to say, my own Ba, that "I made you do as I would." I am quite sure, you make me *speak* as you would, and not at all as I mean—and for one instance, I never surely spoke anything half so untrue as that "I came with the intention of loving whomever I should find"—No!, wreathed shells, and hollows in ruins, and roofs of caves may transform a voice wonderfully, make more of it or less, or so change it as to almost alter, but turn a "no" into a "yes" can no echo (except the Irish one), and I said "no" to such a charge, and still say "no." I *did* have a presentiment—and though it is hardly possible for me to look back on it now without lending it the true colours given to it by the event, yet I *can* put them aside, if I please, and remember that I not merely hoped it would not be so (*not* that the effect I expected to be produced would be *less* than in anticipation, certainly I did not hope *that*, but that it would range itself with the old feelings of simple reverence and sympathy and friendship, that I should love you as much as I supposed I *could* love, and no more) but in the confidence that nothing could occur to divert me from my intended way of life, I made—went on making arrangements to return to Italy. You know—did I not tell you—I wished to see you before I returned? And I had heard of you just so much as seemed to make it impossible such a relation could ever exist. I know very well, if you choose to refer to my letters you may easily bring them to bear a sense in parts, more agreeable to your own theory than to mine, the true one—but that was instinct, Providence—anything rather than foresight. Now I will convince you! yourself have noticed the difference between the *letters* and the *writer;* the greater "distance of the latter from you," why was that? Why, if not because the conduct *began* with *him*, with one who had now seen you—was no continuation of the conduct, as influenced by the feeling, of the letters—else, they, if *near*, should have enabled him, if but in the natural course of time and with increase of familiarity, to become *nearer*—but it was not so! The letters began by loving you after their way—but what a world-wide difference between *that* love and the true, the love from seeing and hearing and feeling, since you make me resolve, what now lies blended so harmoniously, into its component parts. Oh, I know what is old from what is new, and how chrystals may surround and glorify other vessels meant for ordinary service than Lord N's! But I *don't* know that handling may not snap them off, some of the more delicate ones; and if you let me, love, I will not again, ever again, consider how it came and whence, and when, so curiously, so pryingly, but believe that it was always so, and that it all came at once, all the same; the more unlikelinesses the better, for they set off the better the truth of truths that here, ("how begot? how nourished?")—here is the whole wondrous Ba filling my whole heart and soul; and over-filling it, because she is in all the world, too, where I look, where I fancy. At the same time, because all is so wondrous and so sweet, do you think that it would be *so* difficult for me to analyse it, and give causes to the effects in sufficiently numerous instances, even to "justify my presentiment?" Ah, dear, dearest Ba, I could, could indeed, could account for all, or enough! But you are unconscious, I do believe, of your power, and the knowledge of it would be no added grace, perhaps! So let us go on—taking a lesson out of the world's book in a different sense. You shall think I love you for—(tell me, you must, what for) while in my secret heart I know what my "mission of humanity" means, and what telescopic and microscopic views it procures me. Enough—Wait, one word about the "too kind letters"—could not the same Montefiore understand that though he deserved not one of his thousand guineas, yet that he is in disgrace if they bate him of his next gift by merely *ten?* It *is* all too kind—but I shall feel the diminishing of the kindness, be very sure! Of that there is, however, not too alarming a sign in this dearest, because last of all—dearest letter of all—till the next! I looked yesterday over the "Tragedy," and think it will do after all. I will bring one part at least next time, and "Luria" take away, if you let me, so all will be off my mind, and April and May be the welcomer? Don't think I am going to take any extraordinary pains. There are some things in the "Tragedy" I should like to preserve and print now, leaving the future to spring as it likes, in any direction, and these half-dead, half-alive works fetter it, if left behind.

Yet one thing will fetter it worse, only one thing—if *you*, in any respect, stay behind? You that in all else help me and will help me, beyond words—beyond dreams—if, because I find you, your own works *stop*—"then comes the Selah and the voice is hushed." Oh, no, no, dearest, *so* would the help cease to be help—the joy to be joy, Ba herself to be *quite* Ba, and my own Siren singing song for song. Dear love, will that be kind, and right, and like the rest? Write and promise that all shall be resumed, the romance-poem chiefly, and I will try and feel more yours than ever now. Am I not with you in the world, proud of you—and *vain*, too, very likely, which is all the sweeter if it is a sin as you teach me. Indeed dearest, I have set my heart on your fulfilling your mission—my heart is on it! Bless you, my Ba—

Your R. B.

I am so well as to have resumed the shower-bath (this morning)—and I walk, especially near the elms and stile—and mean to walk, and be very well—and you, dearest?

XVIII E. B. B. to R. B.

Thursday
[Postmark, April 16, 1846]

* * *

In the meanwhile assure yourself that I understand perfectly your feeling about the subject of yesterday.[1] Flies are flies, and yet they are vexatious with their buzzing, *as* flies. Only Mrs. Jameson told me the other day that a remedy against the mosquitos . . *polvere di morchia* . . had been discovered lately in Italy, so that the world might sleep there in peace—as *you* may here . . let us talk no more of it. I think I should not have told you if I had not needed it for a talking-ladder to something else. For the rest, it is amusing to me, quite amusing, to observe how people cannot conceive of *work* except under certain familiar forms. Men who dig in ditches have an idea that the man who leads the plough rather rests than works: and all men of out-door labour distrust the industry of the manufacturers in-doors—while both manufacturers and out-door labourers consider the holders of offices and clerkships as idle men . . gentlemen at ease. Then between all these classes and the intellectual worker, the difference is wider, and the want of perception more complete. The work of creation, nobody will admit . . though everybody has by heart, without laying it to heart, that God rested on the seventh day. Looking up to the stars at nights, they might as well take all to be motionless—though if there were no motion there would be no morning . . and they look for a morning after all. Why who could mind such obtuse stupidity? It is the stupidity of mankind, par excellence of foolishness! The hedger and ditcher they see working, but God they do not see working. If one built a palace without noise and confusion and the stroke of hammers, one would scarcely get credit for it in this world . . so full of virtue and admiration it is, to make a noise! Even I, you see, who said just now "Talk no more of it," talk more and more, and make more noise than is necessary. Here is an end though—we leave Mrs. Procter here. And do not think that the least word of disrespect was said of you—indeed it was not! neither disrespect nor reproach. So you and I will forgive everybody henceforward, for wishing you to be rich. And if Mrs. Procter would "commit suicide" rather than live as you like to live, I will not, as long as you are not tired of me—and *that, just now* and as things are, is of a little more consequence perhaps . . .

* * *

[1] Mrs. Procter had thought it a pity Browning was not a working man with "seven or eight hours a day of occupation."

XIX E. B. B. to R. B.

Monday
[Postmark, May 12, 1846]

* * *

Look what is inside of this letter—look! I gathered it for you to-day when I was walking in the Regent's Park. Are you surprised? Arabel and Flush and I were in the carriage—and the sun was shining with that green light through the trees, as if he carried down with him the very essence of the leaves, to the ground, . . and I wished so much to walk through a half open gate along a shaded path, that we stopped the carriage and got out and walked, and I put both my feet on the grass, . . which was the strangest feeling! . . and gathered this laburnum for you. It hung quite high up on the tree, the little blossom did, and Arabel said that certainly I could not reach it—but you see! It is a too generous return for all your flowers: or, to speak seriously, a proof that I thought of you and wished for you—which it was natural to do, for I never enjoyed any of my excursions as I did to-day's—the standing under the trees and on the grass, was so delightful. It was like a bit of that Dreamland which is your especial dominion,—and I felt joyful enough for the moment, to look round for you, as for the cause. It seemed *illogical*, not to see you close by. And you were not far after all, if thoughts count as bringers near. Dearest, we shall walk together under the trees some day!

And all those strange people moving about like phantoms of life. How wonderful it looked to me!—and only you, . . the idea of you . . and myself seemed to be real there! And Flush a little, too!—

* * *

XX R. B. to E. B. B.

Wednesday
[Postmark, May 13, 1846]

* * *

I saw Tennyson last night—and . . oh, let me tell you to-morrow. Also, Severn, I saw . . Keats' Severn, who bought his own posthumous picture of Keats, and talked pleasantly about him and Shelley (Tennyson asked me "what I thought of Shelley"—in so many words). Moxon's care of him,—Tennyson, not Severn,—is the charmingest thing imaginable, and he seems to need it all—being in truth but a LONG, hazy kind of a man, at least just after dinner . . yet there is something "naif" about him, too,—the genius you see, too.

* * *

XXI R. B. to E. B. B.

Tuesday
[Postmark, May 19, 1846]

With this day expires the first year since you have been yourself to me—putting aside the anticipations, and prognostications, and even assurances from all reasons short of absolute sight and hearing,—excluding the five or six months of these, there remains a year of this intimacy. You accuse me of talking extravagantly sometimes. I will be quiet here,—is the tone *too* subdued if I say, such a life—made-up of such years—I would deliberately take rather than any other imaginable one in which fame and worldly prosperity and the love of the whole human race should combine, excluding "that of yours—to which I hearken" —only wishing the rest were there for a moment that you might see and know that I did turn from them to you. My dearest, inexpressibly dearest. How can I thank you? I feel sure you *need* not have been so kind to me, so perfectly kind and good,—I should have remained your own, gratefully, entirely your own, through the bare permission to love you, or even without it—seeing that I never dreamed of stipulating at the beginning for "a return," and "reward,"—but I also believe, joyfully, that no course but the course you have taken would have raised me above my very self, as I feel on looking back. I began by loving you in comparison with all the world, —now, I love you, my Ba, in the face of your past self, as I remember it.

All words are foolish—but I kiss your feet and offer you my heart and soul, dearest, dearest Ba.

I left you last evening without the usual privilege—you did not rise, Ba! But,—I don't know why,—I got nervous of a sudden, it seemed late and I remembered the Drawing-room and its occupants.

XXII E. B. B. to R. B.

Tuesday Evening
[Postmark, July 8, 1846]

Yes—I understand you perfectly—and it should be exactly as you say—and it is just *that*, which requires so much adroitness,—and such decision and strength of hand, to manage these responsibilities.[1] Somebody is wanted to cut and burn, and be silent afterwards. I remember that bitter things are said of Shelley and Leigh Hunt beyond all the bitterness of alcohol. Olives do not taste so, though steeped in salt. There are some curious letters by poor Keats about Hunt, and *they* too are bitter. It would be dreadful to suffer these miseries to sow themselves about the world, like so much thistle-down . . the world, where there are thistles enough already, to make fodder for its wild asses!

As to Landor . . oh, I did not remember the note you speak of in the satire you speak of—but you remember everything . . even *me*. Is it not true that Landor, too, is one of the men who carry their passions about with them into everything, as a boy would, pebbles . . muddying every clear water, with a stone here and a stone there. The end is, that we lose the image of himself in the serene depth, as we might have had it—and the little stone comes to stand for him. How unworthy of such a man as Landor, such weakness is! To *think* with one's temper! ! One might as well be at once Don Quixote, and fight with a warming-pan. . . .

Dearest!—I have written all this before I

[1] The manuscripts of Haydon's journals and letters had, to her consternation, been left to Elizabeth Barrett, apparently in the expectation that she would supervise publication. The bitterness of the manuscripts dismayed her.

would say a word of your coming, just to think a little more—and down all these pages I have been thinking, thinking, of *you* . . of your possible coming . . what nonsense they must be! Well! and the end is that, let it be wise or unwise, I *must and will see you to-morrow*—I cannot do otherwise. It is just as if Flush had been shut up in a box for so many days. My spirits flag . . and I could find it in my heart to grow cross like Landor and deny Goethe. So come, dearest dearest—and let the world bark at our heels if it pleases. I will just turn round and set Flush at it.

For two or three days I have not been out—not for two days . . not out of this room. This evening at seven, when they were all going to dinner, I took Wilson with me and drove into the park for air. It will do me good perhaps—but your coming will, certainly. So come, my dearest beloved!—At three, remember.

Your own
Ba.

XXIII R. B. TO E. B. B.

Thursday
[Postmark, July 9, 1846]

My own darling, my Ba, do you know when I read those letters (as soon as I remembered I had got them,—for you hold me long after both doors, up and down stairs, shut) when I looked through them, under a gateway . . I was pricked at the heart to have thought so, and spoken so, of the poor writer. I will believe that he was good and even great when in communication with you—indeed all men are made, or make themselves, different in their approaches to different men—and the secret of goodness and greatness is in choosing *whom* you will approach, and live with, in memory or imagination, through the crowding obvious people who seem to live with you. That letter about the glory of being a painter "if only for the neglect" is most touching and admirable . . there is the serene spot attained, the solid siren's isle amid the sea; and while *there*, he was safe and well . . but he would put out to sea again, after a breathing time, I suppose? though even a smaller strip of land was enough to maintain Blake, for one instance, in power and glory through the poor, fleeting "sixty years"—then comes the rest from cartooning and exhibiting. But there is no standing, one foot on land and one on the waves, now with the high aim in view, now with the low aim,—and all the strange mistaken talk about "prestiges," "Youth and its luck," Napoleon and the world's surprise and interest. There comes the low aim between the other,—an organ grinds Mr. Jullien's newest dance-tune, and Camoens is vexed that the "choral singing which brought angels down," can't also draw street-passengers round.

I take your view of H.'s freedom, at that time, from the thoughts of what followed.

He was weak—a strong man would have borne what so many bear—what were his griefs, as grief *goes?* Do you remember I told you, when the news of Aliwal and the other battles came to England, of our gardener, and his son, a sergeant in one of the regiments engaged . . how the father could learn nothing at first, of course . . how they told him at the Horse Guards he should be duly informed in time, after his betters, whether this son was dead, or wounded. Since then, no news came . . "which is *good* news" the father persuaded himself to think . . so the apprehensions subside, and the hope confirms itself, more and more, while the old fellow digs and mows and rakes away, like a man painting historical pictures . . only without the love of it. Well, this morning we had his daughter here to say "the letter" had arrived at last . . her brother was killed in the first battle, so there's an end of the three months' sickness of heart,—and the poor fellow must bear his loss "like a man"—or like a woman . . for I recollect another case, of an old woman whom my mother was in the habit of relieving,—who brought a letter one day which she could hardly understand—it was from her son, a sailor, and went on for a couple of pages about his good health and expectations,—then in a different handwriting, somebody, "your son's shipmate" "took up his pen to inform you that he fell from the masthead into the sea and was drowned yesterday,—which he therefore thought it right to put in the unfinished letter." All which the old woman bore somehow,—seeing she lives yet. * * *

Ever your R.

XXIV E. B. B. to R. B.

Thursday
[Postmark, July 9, 1846]

* * *

Ah Flush, Flush!—he did not hurt you really? You will forgive him for me? The truth is that he hates all unpetticoated people, and that though he does not hate *you*, he has a certain distrust of you, which any outward sign, such as the umbrella, reawakens. But if you had seen how sorry and ashamed he was yesterday! I slapped his ears and told him that he never should be loved again: and he sate on the sofa (sitting, not lying) with his eyes fixed on me all the time I did the flowers, with an expression of quite despair in his face. At last I said, "If you are good, Flush, you may come and say that you are sorry" . . on which he dashed across the room and, trembling all over, kissed first one of my hands and then another, and put up his paws to be shaken, and looked into my face with such great beseeching eyes that you would certainly have forgiven him just as I did. It is not savageness. If he once loved you, you might pull his ears and his tail, and take a bone out of his mouth even, and he would not bite you. He has no savage caprices like other dogs and men I have known.

* * *

XXV E. B. B. to R. B.

Thursday Evening
[Postmark, July 10, 1846]

* * *

Poor Haydon! Think what an agony, life was to him, so constituted!—his own genius a clinging curse! The fire and the clay in him seething and quenching one another!—the man seeing maniacally in all men the assassins of his fame! and, with the whole world against him, struggling for the thing which was his life, through night and day, in thoughts and in dreams . . struggling, stifling, breaking the hearts of the creatures dearest to him, in the conflict for which there was no victory, though he could not choose but fight it. Tell me if Laocoon's anguish was not as an infant's sleep, compared to this? And could a man, suffering *so*, stop to calculate very nicely the consideration due to A, and the delicacy which should be observed toward B? Was he scrupulously to ask himself whether this or that cry of his might not give C a headache? Indeed no, no. It is for *us* rather to look back and consider! Poor Haydon.

* * *

XXVI R. B. to E. B. B.

Tuesday
[Postmark, July 22, 1846]

How I long, my sweetest Ba, to know whether any heavy price is to be paid for our three hours yesterday,—if your Aunt knew or has discovered since? I shall not murmur in any case, I hope . . they are too delicious, these three-hour visits—and if *I* could pay for them by myself, Ba,—what would I not pay?

Will you let me write something, and forgive me? Because it is, I know, quite unnecessary to be written, and, beside, may almost seem an interference with your own delicacy, —teaching it its duty! However, I will venture to go on, with your hand before my two eyes. Then,—you remember what we were speaking of yesterday,—house-rents and styles of living? You will never overlook, through its very obviousness, that to consult my feelings on the only point in which they are sensitive to the world you must endeavour to live as simply and cheaply as possible, down to my own habitual simplicity and cheapness,—so that you shall come and live with me, in a sense, rather than I with Miss Campbell! You see, Ba, if you have more money than you want, you shall save it or spend it in pictures or parrots or what you please . . you avoid all offence to *me* who never either saved money nor spent it—but the large house, I should be forced to stay in,—the carriage, to enter, I suppose. And you see too, Ba, that the one point on which I desire the world to be informed concerning our future life, will be that it is ordered *so*—I wish they could hear we lived in one room like George Sand in "that happy year—"

No, there I have put down an absurdity—because, I shall have to confess a weakness, at some time or other, which is hardly reconcilable to that method of being happy—why may I not tell you now, my adored Ba, to whom I tell everything as it rises to me? Now put the hand on my eyes again—now that I have kissed it. I shall begin by begging a separate room from yours—I could never brush my hair and wash my face, I do think, before my own father—I could not, I am sure, take off my coat before you *now*—why should I ever? The kitchen is an unknown horror to me,—I come to the dining-room for whatever repast there may be,—nor willingly stay too long there,—and on the day on which poor Countess Peppa taught me how maccaroni is made,—*then* began a quiet revolution, (indeed a rapid one) against "tagliolini," "fettucce," "lasagne," etc., etc., etc.—typical, typical!

What foolishness . . spare me, my own Ba, and don't answer one word,—do not even laugh,—for I *know* the exceeding unnecessary foolishness of it!

* * *

Your own, very own.

XXVII E. B. B. to R. B.

Wednesday Morning
[Postmark, July 22, 1846]

I did not go out yesterday, and was very glad not to have a command laid on me to go out, the wind blew so full of damp and dreariness. Then it was pleasanter to lie on the sofa and think of you, which I did, till at last I actually dreamed of you, falling asleep for that purpose. As to Flush, he came upstairs with a great deal of shame in the bearing of his ears, and straight to me—no indeed! I would not speak to him—then he went up to Arabel . . "naughty Flush, go away" . . and Wilson, . . who had whipped him before, "because it was right," she said . . in a fit of poetical justice, . . did not give him any consolation. So he lay down on the floor at my feet looking from under his eyebrows at me. I did not forgive him till nearly eight o'clock however. And I have not yet given him your cakes. Almost I am inclined to think now that he has not *a soul*. To behave so to you! It is nearly as bad as if I had thrown the coffee cup! Wicked Flush!—Do you imagine that I scolded Wilson when she confessed to having whipped him? I did not. It was done with her hand, and not very hardly perhaps, though "he cried," she averred to me—and if people, like Flush, choose to behave like dogs savagely, they must take the consequences indeed, as dogs usually do! And *you*, so good and gentle to him! Anyone but *you*, would have said "hasty words" at least. I think I shall have a muzzle for him, to make him harmless while he learns to know you. Would it not be a good plan?

But nobody heard yesterday of either your visit or of Flush's misdoings . . so Wilson was discreet, I suppose, as she usually is, by the instinct of her vocation. Of all the persons who are *not* in our confidence, she has the most certain knowledge of the truth. Dearest, we shall be able to have Saturday. There will be no danger in it.

Perhaps in the days to come we shall look back on these days as covetable things. Will *you* do so, because you were loved in them as a beginning, or because you were *free?* (Am *I* not as bad as Flush, to ask such questions?) *I* shall look back on these days gratefully and gladly, because the good in them has overcome the evil, for the first time in days of mine. . . .

Your very own Ba.

XXVIII R. B. to E. B. B.

Sunday Morning
[Postmark, August 31, 1846]

I wonder what I shall write to you, Ba—I could suppress my feelings here, as I do on other points, and say nothing of the hatefulness of this state of things which is prolonged so uselessly. There is the point—show me one good reason, or show of reason, why we gain anything by deferring our departure till next week instead of to-morrow, and I will bear to perform yesterday's part for the amusement of Mr. Kenyon a dozen times over without complaint. But if the cold plunge *must* be taken, all this shivering delay on the bank is hurtful as well as fruitless. I *do* understand your anxieties, dearest—I take your fears and make them mine, while I put my own natural feeling of quite another kind away from us both, succeeding in *that* beyond all expectation. There is no amount of patience or suffering I would not undergo to relieve you from these apprehensions. But if, on the whole, you really determine to act as we propose in spite of them,—why, a new leaf is turned over in our journal, an old part of our adventure done with, and a new one entered upon, altogether distinct from the other. Having once decided to go to Italy with me, the next thing to decide is on the best means of going—or rather, there is just this connection between the two measures, that by the success or failure of the last, the first will have to be justified or condemned. You tell me you have decided to go—then, dearest, you will be prepared to go earlier than you promised yesterday—by the end of September at very latest. In proportion to the too probable excitement and painful circumstances of the departure, the greater amount of advantages should be secured for the departure itself. How can I take you away in even the beginning of October? We shall be a fortnight on the journey—with the year, as everybody sees and says, a full month in advance . . cold mornings and dark evenings already. Everybody would cry out on such folly when it was found that we let the favorable weather escape, in full assurance that the Autumn would come to us unattended by any one beneficial circumstance.

My own dearest, I am wholly your own, for ever, and under every determination of yours. If you find yourself unable, or unwilling to make this effort, tell me so and plainly and at once—I will not offer a word in objection, —I will continue our present life, if you please, so far as may be desirable, and wait till next autumn, and the next and the next, till providence end our waiting. It is clearly not for me to pretend to instruct you in your duties to God and yourself; . . enough, that I have long ago chosen to accept your decision. If, on the other hand, you make up your mind to leave England now, you will be prepared by the end of September.

I should think myself the most unworthy of human beings if I could employ any arguments with the remotest show of a tendency to *frighten* you into a compliance with any scheme of mine. Those methods are for people in another relation to you. But you love me, and, at lowest, shall I say, wish me well—and the fact is too obvious for me to commit any indelicacy in reminding you, that in any dreadful event to our journey of which I could accuse myself as the cause,—as of this undertaking to travel with you in the worst time of year when I could have taken the best, —in the case of your health being irretrievably shaken, for instance . . the happiest fate I should pray for would be to live and die in some corner where I might never hear a word of the English language, much less a comment in it on my own wretched imbecility,—to disappear and be forgotten.

So that must not be, for all our sakes. My family will give me to you that we may be both of us happy . . but for such an end—no!

Dearest, do you think all this earnestness foolish and uncalled for?—that I might know you spoke yesterday in mere jest,—as yourself said, "only to hear what I would say"? Ah but consider, my own Ba, the way of our life, as it is, and is to be—a word, a simple word from you, is not as a word is counted in the world—the word between us is different—I am guided by your will, which a word shall signify to me. Consider that just such a word, so spoken, even with that lightness, would make me lay my life at your feet at any minute. Should we gain anything by my trying, if I could, to deaden the sense of hearing, dull the medium of communication between us; and procuring that, instead of this prompt rising of my will at the first intimation from yours, the same effect should only follow after fifty speeches, and as many protestations of complete serious desire for their success on your part, accompanied by all kinds of acts and deeds and other evidences of the same?

At all events, God knows I have said this in the deepest, truest love of you. I will say no more, praying you to forgive whatever you shall judge to need forgiveness here,—dearest Ba! I will also say, if that may help me,—and what otherwise I might not have said,—that I am not too well this morning, and write with an aching head. My mother's suffering continues too.

My friend Pritchard tells me that Brighton is not to be thought of under ordinary circumstances as a point of departure for Havre. Its one packet a week from Shoreham cannot get in if the wind and tide are unfavourable.

There is the greatest uncertainty in consequence . . as I have heard before—while, of course, from Southampton, the departures are calculated punctually. He considers that the least troublesome plan, and the cheapest, is to go from London to Havre . . the voyage being so arranged that the river passage takes up the day and the sea-crossing the night—you reach Havre early in the morning and get to Paris by four o'clock, perhaps, in the afternoon . . in time to leave for Orleans and spend the night there, I suppose.

Do I make myself particularly remarkable for silliness when confronted by our friend as yesterday? And the shortest visit,—and comments of everybody. Oh, Mr. Hunter, methinks you should be of some use to me with those amiable peculiarities of yours, if you would just dye your hair black, take a stick in your hand, sink the clerical character you do such credit to, and have the goodness just to deliver yourself of one such epithet as *that* pleasant one, the next time you find me on the steps of No. 50, with Mr. Kenyon somewhere higher up in the building. It is delectable work this having to do with relatives and "free-men who have a right to beat their own negroes," and father Zeus with his paternal epistles, and peggings to the rock, and immense indignation at "this marriage you talk of" which is to release his victim. Is Mr. Kenyon Hermes?

Εἰσελθέτω σε μήποθ' ὡς ἐγὼ Διὸς
γνώμην φοβηθεὶς θηλύνους γενήσομαι,
καὶ λιπαρήσω τὸν μέγα στυγούμενον
γυναικουίμοις ὑπτιάσμασιν χερῶν,
λῦσαί με δεσμῶν τῶνδε· τοῦ παντὸς δέω.

Chorus of Aunts: ἡμῖν μὲν Ἑρμῆς οὐκ ἄκαιρα φαίνεται λέγειν, κ.τ.λ.[1]

Well, bless you in any case—
Your own R.

[1] "Oh, think no more
That I, fear-struck by Zeus to a woman's mind
Will supplicate him, loathèd as he is,
With feminine upliftings of my hands,
To break these chains. Far from me be the thought!
Chorus. Our Hermes suits his reasons to the times;
At least I think so."
Æschylus, *Prometheus,* 1002–6, 1036–7.)

XXIX E. B. B. to R. B.

Monday Night
[Postmark, September 1, 1846]

You are better, dearest,—and so I will confess to having felt a little inclined to reproach you gently for the earlier letter, except that you were not well when you wrote it. That you should endure painfully and impatiently a position unworthy of you, is the natural consequence of the unworthiness—and I do hold that you would be justified at this moment, on the barest motives of self-respect, in abandoning the whole ground and leaving me to Mr. Kenyon and others. What I might complain of, is another thing—what I might complain of is, that I have not given you reason to *doubt me* or my inclination to accede to any serious wish of yours relating to the step before us. On the contrary I told you in so many words in July, that, if you really wished to go in August rather than in September, I would make no difficulty—to which you answered, remember, that *October or November would do as well.* Now *is* it fair, ever dearest, that you should turn round on me so quickly, and call in question my willingness to keep my engagement for years, if ever? Can I help it, if the circumstances around us are painful to both of us? Did I not keep repeating, from the beginning, that they *must* be painful? Only you could not believe, you see, until you felt the pricks. And when all is done, and the doing shall be the occasion of new affronts, sarcasms, every form of injustice, will you be any happier then, than you are now that you only imagine the possibility of them? I tremble to answer that question—even to myself—! As for myself, though I cannot help feeling pain and fear, in encountering what is to be encountered, and though I sometimes fear, in addition, for *you,* lest you should overtask your serenity in bearing your own part in it, . . yet certainly I have never wavered for a moment from the decision on which all depends. I might fill up your quotations from "Prometheus," and say how no evil takes me unaware, having foreseen all from the beginning—but I have not the heart for filling up quotations. I mean to say only, that I never wavered from the promise I gave freely; and that I will keep it freely at any time you choose—that is, within a week of any time you choose. As to a light word . . why now, dear, judge me in justice! If I had written it, there might have been more wrong in it—but I spoke it lightly to show it was light, and in the next breath I told you that it was a jest. Will you not forgive me a word so spoken, Robert? will you rather set it against me as if habitually I threw to you levities in change for earnest devotion?—you imply *that* of me. Or you *seem* to imply it—you did not mean, you could not, a thought approaching to unkindness,—but it looks like *that* in the letter, or *did*, this morning. And all the time, you pretended not to know very well, . . (dearest!) . . that what you made up your mind to wish and ask of me, I had not in my power to say "no" to. Ah, you *knew* that you had only to make up your mind, and to see that the thing was possible. So if September shall be possible, let it be September. I do not object nor hold back. To sail from the Thames has not the feasibility—and listen why! All the sailing or rather steaming from London begins *early;* and I told you how out of the question it was, for me to leave this house early. I could not, without involving my sisters. Arabel sleeps in my room, on the sofa, and is seldom out of the room before nine in the morning—and for me to draw her into a ruinous confidence, or to escape without a confidence at that hour, would be equally impossible. Now see if it is my fancy, my whim! And as for the expenses, *they* are as nearly equal as a shilling and two sixpences can be—the expense of the sea-voyage from London to Havre, and of the land and sea voyage, through Southampton . . *or* Brighton. But of course what you say of Brighton, keeps us to Southampton, of those two routes. We can go to Southampton and meet the packet . . take the river-steamer to Rouen, and proceed as rapidly as your programme shows. You are not angry with me, dearest, dearest? I did not mean any harm.

May God bless you always. *I* am not angry either, understand, though I did think this morning that you were a little hard on me, just when I felt myself ready to give up the whole world for you at the holding up of a finger. And now say nothing of this. I kiss the end of the dear finger; and when *it* is ready, *I* am ready; I will not be reproached again. Being too much your own, very own

Ba.

Tell me that you keep better. And your mother?

XXX E. B. B. TO R. B.

Tuesday

[Postmark, September 2, 1846]

Here is a distress for me, dearest! I have lost my poor Flush—*lost* him! You were a prophet when you said "Take care."

This morning Arabel and I, and he with us, went in a cab to Vere Street where we had a little business, and he followed us as usual into a shop and out of it again, and was at my heels when I stepped up into the carriage. Having turned, I said "Flush," and Arabel looked round for Flush—there was no Flush! He had been caught up in that moment, from *under* the wheels, do you understand? and the thief must have run with him and thrown him into a bag perhaps. It was such a shock to me—think of it! losing him in a moment, *so!* No wonder if I looked white, as Arabel said! So she began to comfort me by showing how certain it was that I should recover him for ten pounds at most, and we came home ever so drearily. Because *Flush* doesn't know that we can recover him, and he is in the extremest despair all this while, poor darling Flush, with his fretful fears, and pretty whims, and his fancy of being near me. All this night he will howl and lament, I know perfectly,—for I fear we shall not ransom him to-night. Henry went down for me directly to the captain of the banditti, who evidently knew all about it, said Henry,—and after a little form of consideration and enquiry, promised to let us hear something this evening, but has not come yet. In the morning perhaps he will come. Henry told him that I was resolved not to give much—but of course they will make me give what they choose—I am not going to leave Flush at their mercy, and they know that as well as I do. My poor Flush!

When we shall be at Pisa, dearest, we shall

be away from the London dog-stealers—it will be one of the advantages. Another may be that I may have an opportunity of "forgiving" you, which I have not had yet. I might reproach you a little in my letter, and I *did*, I believe; but the offending was not enough for any *forgiving* to follow—it is too grand a word. Also your worst is better than my best, taking it on the whole. How then should I be able to *forgive* you, my beloved, even *at Pisa?*

If we go to Southampton, we go straight from the railroad to the packet, without entering any hotel—and if we do *so*, *no* greater expense is incurred than by the long water-passage from London. Also, we reach Havre alike in the morning, and have the day before us for Rouen, Paris and Orleans. Thereupon nothing is lost by losing the early hour for the departure. Then, if I accede to your *idée fixe* about the marriage! Only do not let us put a long time between that and the setting out, and do not you come here afterwards—let us go away as soon as possible afterwards at least. You are afraid for me of my suffering from the autumnal cold when it is yet far off—while *I* (observe this!) while *I* am afraid for myself, of breaking down under quite a different set of causes, in nervous excitement and exhaustion. I belong to that pitiful order of weak women who cannot command their bodies with their souls at every moment, and who sink down in hysterical disorder when they ought to act and resist. Now I think and believe that I shall take strength from my attachment to you, and so go through to the end what is before us; but at the same time, knowing myself and fearing myself, I do desire to provoke the "demon" as little as possible, and to be as quiet as the situation will permit. Still, where things *ought* to be done, they of course *must* be done. Only we should consider whether they really *ought* to be done—not for the sake of the inconvenience to me, but of the consequence to both of us.

Do I frighten you, ever dearest? Oh no—I shall go through it, if I keep a breath of soul in me to live with. I shall go through it, as certainly as that I love you. I speak only of the accessory circumstances, that they may be kept as smooth as is practicable.

You are not well, my beloved—and I cannot even dream of making you better this time,—because you will think it wise for us not to meet for the next few days perhaps. Mr. Kenyon will come to see me, he said, before he leaves town, and he leaves it on the fourth, fifth or sixth of September. This is the first. So I will not let you come to be vexed as last time—no, indeed. But write to me instead—and pity me for Flush. Oh, I trust to have him back to-morrow. I had no headache, and was quite perfectly well this morning . . before I lost him.

Is your mother able to walk? is she worse on the whole than last week for instance? We may talk of September, but you cannot leave her, you know, dearest, if she should be *so* ill! It would be unkind and wrong.

More, to-morrow! But I cannot be more to-morrow, your very own—

XXXI R. B. TO E. B. B.

Wednesday Morning

[Postmark, September 2, 1846]

Poor Flush—how sorry I am for you, my Ba! But you will recover him, I dare say . . not, perhaps directly; the delay seems to justify their charge at the end: poor fellow—was he no better than the rest of us, and did all that barking and fanciful valour spend itself on such enemies as Mr. Kenyon and myself, leaving only blandness and waggings of the tail for the man with the bag? I am sure you are grieved and frightened for our friend and follower, that was to be, at Pisa—will you not write a special note to tell me when you get him again?

For the rest—I will urge you no more by a single word—you shall arrange everything henceforward without a desire on my part,—an expressed one at least. Do not let our happiness be caught up from us, after poor Flush's fashion—there may be no redemption from *that* peril.

There can hardly be another way of carrying our purpose into effect than by that arrangement you consent to—except you choose to sacrifice a day and incur all costs of risk. Of course, the whole in the way and with the conditions that you shall determine.

Do you think, Ba, I apprehend nothing from the excitement and exhaustion attendant on it? I altogether apprehend it,—and am therefore the more anxious that no greater difficulty should be superinduced than is absolutely necessary. Because the first part of our adventure will be dangerous in *that* way, I want the second part to be as safe as possible in another. I should care comparatively little about winter-travelling, even (knowing that one can take precautions)—if it were to be undertaken under really propitious circumstances, and you set forth with so much kindness to carry away as would keep you warm for a week or two—but the "winter wind that is not *so* unkind as &c," may prove,—by adding its share of unkindness to the greater, —intolerable. Now, my last word is said, however—and a kiss follows!

I thank you, dearest, for your enquiries about my mother; and for the sympathy, and proposal of delay. She is better this morning, I hope. From the time that my sister went to Town, she discontinued the exercise which does her such evident good—and on Monday the walks began again—with no great effect yesterday because of the dull weather and sharp wind . . she kept at home—but this morning she is abroad, and will profit by this sunshine, I hope. My head will not get quite well, neither. I take both effects to be caused by the turn of the year.

Bless you, dearest—I cannot but acquiesce in your postponing our day for such reasons. Only, do not misconceive those few foolish words of impatience . . a great matter to bear truly! I shall be punished indeed if they prevent you from according to me one hour I should have otherwise possessed.

Bless you once again, my Ba.

My mother is returned—very much better indeed. Remember Flush—to write.

XXXII E. B. B. to R. B.

Wednesday Evening
[Postmark, September 3, 1846]

"Our friend and follower, that *was* to be"—is *that*, then, your opinion of my poor darling Flush's destiny—? Ah,—I should not have been so quiet if I had not known differently and better. I "shall not recover him directly," you think! But, dearest, I am *sure* that I *shall*. I am learned in the ways of the Philistines—I knew from the beginning where to apply and how to persuade. The worst is poor Flush's fright and suffering. And then, it is inconvenient just now to pay the ransom for him. But we shall have time to-morrow if not to-night. Two hours ago the chief of the Confederacy came to call on Henry and to tell him that the "Society had the dog," having done us the honour of tracking us into Bond Street and out of Bond Street into Vere Street where he was kidnapped. Now he is in Whitechapel (poor Flush). And the great man was going down there at half past seven to meet other great men in council and hear the decision as to the ransom exacted, and would return with their *ultimatum*. Oh, the villainy of it is excellent, and then the humiliation of having to pay for your own vexations and anxieties! *Will* they have the insolence, now, to make me pay ten pounds, as they said they would? But I must have Flush, you know—I can't run any risk, and bargain and haggle. There is a dreadful tradition in this neighbourhood, of a lady who did *so* having her dog's head sent to her in a parcel. So I say to Henry—"Get Flush back, whatever you do"—for Henry is angry as he may well be, and as *I* should be if I was not too afraid . . and talks police-officers against thieves, and finds it very hard to attend to my instructions and be civil and respectful to their captain. There he found him, smoking a cigar in a room with pictures! They make some three or four thousand a year by their honourable employment. As to Flush's following anyone "blandly," never think it. He was caught up and gagged . . depend upon that. If he could have bitten, he would have bitten—if he could have yelled, he would have yelled. Indeed on a former occasion the ingenuous thief observed, that he "was a difficult dog to get, he was so distrustful." They had to drag him with a string, put him into a cab, they said, before. Poor Flush!

Dearest, I am glad that your mother is a little better—but why should the turn of the year make you suffer, ever dearest? I am not easy about you indeed. Remember not to use the shower-bath injudiciously—and remember to walk. *Do* you walk enough?—it being as necessary for you as for your mother.

And as for *me* you will not say a word more to *me*, you will leave me to my own devices now.

Which is just exactly what you must *not* do. Ah, why do you say so, even, when you must not do it? Have I refused one proposition of yours when there were not strong obstacles, that you should have finished with me so, my beloved? For instance, I agreed to your plan about the marrying, and I agreed to go with you to Italy in the latter part of September—did I not? And what am I disagreeing in now? Don't let me pass for disagreeable! And don't, above all, refuse to think for me, and decide for me, or what will become of me, I cannot guess. I shall be worse off than Flush is now . . in his despair, at Whitechapel. Think of my being let loose upon a common, just when the thunder-clouds are gathering! ! You would not be so cruel, *you*. All I meant to say was that it would be wise to make the occasions of excitement as few as possible, for the reasons I gave you. But I shall not fail, I believe—I should despise myself too much for failing—I should lose too much by the failure. Then there is an amulet which strengthens the heart of one,—let it incline to fail ever so. Believe of me that I shall not fail, dearest beloved—I shall not, if you love me enough to stand by—believe *that* always.

The heart will sink indeed sometimes—as mine does to-night, I scarcely know why—but even while it sinks, I do not feel that I shall fail *so*—I do not. Dearest, I do not, either, "misconceive," as you desire me not: I only infer that you will think it best to avoid the chance of meeting Mr. Kenyon, who speaks to me, in a note received this morning, of intending to leave town next Monday—of coming here he does not speak,—and he may come and he may not come, on any intermediate day. He wrote for a book he lent me. If I do not see you until Monday, it will be hard—but judge! there was more of bitterness than of sweetness in the last visit.

Mr. Kenyon said in his note that he had seen Moxon, and that Tennyson was "disappointed" with the mountains. Is not that strange? Is it a good or a bad sign when people are disappointed with the miracles of nature? I am accustomed to fancy it a bad sign. Because a man's imagination ought to aggrandise, glorify, consecrate. A man sees with his mind, and mind is at fault when he does not see greatly, I think.

* * *

XXXIII R. B. to E. B. B.

Thursday
[Postmark, September 3, 1846]

I am rejoiced that poor Flush is found again, dearest—altogether rejoiced.

And now that you probably have him by your side, I will tell you what I should have done in such a case, because it explains our two ways of seeing and meeting oppression lesser or greater. I would not have given five shillings on that fellow's application. I would have said,—and in entire earnestness "*You* are responsible for the proceedings of your gang, and *you* I mark—don't talk nonsense to me about cutting off heads or paws. Be as sure as that I stand here and tell you, I will spend my whole life in putting you down, the nuisance you declare yourself—and by every imaginable means I will be the death of you and as many of your accomplices as I can discover—but *you* I have discovered and will never lose sight of—now try my sincerity, by delaying to produce the dog by to-morrow. And for the ten pounds—see!" Whereupon I would give them to the first beggar in the street. You think I should receive Flush's head? Perhaps—*so* God allows matters to happen! on purpose, it may be, that I should vindicate him by the punishment I would exact.

Observe, Ba, this course ought not to be yours, because it *could* not be—it would not suit your other qualities. But all religion, right and justice, with me, seem implied in such a resistance to wickedness and refusal to multiply it a hundredfold—for from this prompt payment of ten pounds for a few minutes' act of the easiest villainy, there will be encouragement to—how many similar acts in the course of next month? And how will the poor owners fare who have not money enough for their dogs' redemption? I suppose the gentleman, properly disgusted with such obstinacy, will threaten roasting at a slow fire to test the sincerity of attachment! No—the world would grow too detestable a den of thieves and oppressors that way! And this is too great a piece of indignation to be expressed when one has the sick vile headache that oppresses me this morning. Dearest, I am not inclined to be even as tolerant as usual. Will you be tolerant, my Ba, and forgive me—till to-morrow at least—when, what with physic, what with impatience, I shall be better one way or another?

Ever your own R.

XXXIV R. B. to E. B. B.

Thursday Afternoon
[Postmark, September 4, 1846]

When I had finished that letter this morning, dearest dearest, before I could seal it, even, (my sister did it for me . . and despatched it to the post at once) I became quite ill and so sick as to be forced to go up-stairs and throw myself on the bed. It is now six o'clock, and I feel better, and have some thoughts of breaking my fast to-day—but, first of all . . did whatever it may have been I wrote seem *cross*—unnecessarily angry, to you, dearest Ba? Because, I confess to having felt indignant at this sample of the evils done under the sun every day . . and as if it would be to no purpose though the whole world were peopled with Ba's, instead of just Wimpole Street; as they would be just so many more soft cushions for the villainously-disposed to run pins into at their pleasure. Donne says that "Weakness invites, but silence *feasts* oppression." And it is horrible to fancy how all the oppressors in their several ranks may, if they choose, twitch back to them by the heartstrings after various modes the weak and silent whose secret they have found out. No one should profit by those qualities in me, at least. Having formed a resolution, I would keep it, I hope, through fire and water, and the threatener of any piece of rascality, who (as commonly happens) should be without the full heart to carry it into effect, should pay me exactly the same for the threat . . which had determined my conduct once and for ever. But in this particular case, I ought to have told you (unless you divined it, as you might) that I would give all I am ever to be worth in the world to get back your Flush for you—for your interest is not *mine*, any more than the lake is the river that goes to feed it,—mine is only made to feed yours—I am yours, as we say—as I feel more and more every minute.

Are you not mine, too? And do you not forgive your own R

XXXV E. B. B. to R. B.

Thursday Evening
[Postmark, September 4, 1846]

Ever dearest, you are not well—that is the first thing!—And that is the thing I saw first, when, opening your letter, my eyes fell on the ending sentence of it,—which disenchanted me in a moment from the hope of the day. Dearest—you have not been well for two or three days, it is plain,—and now you are very, very unwell—tell me if it is not so? I beseech you to let me hear the exact truth about you, for I am very uneasy, and it is dreadful to doubt about knowing the exact truth in all such cases. How everything goes against me this week! I cannot see you. I cannot comfort myself by knowing that you are well. And then poor Flush! You must let him pass as one of the evils, and you *will*, I know; for I have not got him back yet—no, indeed.

I should have done it. The archfiend, Taylor, the man whom you are going to spend your life in persecuting (the life that belongs to me, too!), came last night to say that they would accept six pounds, six guineas, with half a guinea for himself, considering the trouble of the mediation; and Papa desired Henry to refuse to pay, and not to tell me a word about it—all which I did not find out till this morning. Now it is less, as the money goes, than I had expected, and I was very vexed and angry, and wanted Henry to go at once and conclude the business—only he wouldn't, talked of Papa, and persuaded me that Taylor would come to-day with a lower charge. He has not come—I knew he would not come,—and if people won't do as I choose, I shall go down to-morrow morning myself and bring Flush back with me. All this time he is suffering and I am suffering. It may be very foolish—I do not say it is not—or it may even be "awful sin," as Mr. Boyd sends to assure me—but I cannot endure to run cruel hazards about my poor Flush for the sake of a few guineas, or even for the sake of abstract principles of justice—I cannot. *You* say that *I* cannot, . . but that *you would.* You would! —Ah dearest—most pattern of citizens, but you *would not*—I know you better. Your theory is far too good not to fall to pieces in practice. A man may love justice intensely; but the love of an abstract principle is not the strongest love—now is it? Let us consider a little, putting poor Flush out of the question. (You would bear, you say, to receive his head in a parcel—it would satisfy you to cut off Taylor's in return.) Do you mean to say that if the banditti came down on us in Italy and carried me off to the mountains, and, sending to you one of my ears, to show you my probable fate if you did not let them have . . how much may I venture to say I am worth? . . five or six scudi,—(is *that* reasonable at all?) . . would your answer be "Not so many crazie"; and would you wait, poised upon abstract principles, for the other ear, and the catastrophe,—as was done in Spain not long ago? Would you, dearest? Because it is as well to know beforehand, perhaps.

Ah—how I am teazing you, my beloved, when you are not well. But indeed that life of yours is worthy of better uses than to scourge Taylor with, even if *I* should not be worth the crazie.

I have seen nobody and heard nothing. I bought a pair of shoes to-day lined with flannel, to walk with on the bare floors of Italy in the winter. Is not *that* being practical and coming to the point? I did it indeed!

May God bless you. I love you always and am your own.

Write of yourself, I *do pray you*—and also, how is your mother?

XXXVI E. B. B. TO R. B.

Friday
[Postmark, September 5, 1846]

* * *

I have not Flush yet. I am to have him to-morrow morning.

And for the Flush-argument, dear dearest, I hold that your theory is entirely good and undeniable. I agree with you throughout it, . . Also I hope I should try, at least, to resist with you their various iniquities . .

But Flush, poor Flush, Flush who has loved me so faithfully; have I a right to sacrifice *him* in his innocence, for the sake of any Mr. Taylor's guilt in the world? Does not Flush's condition assimilate to my own among the banditti? for you agree that you would not, after all, leave me to the banditti—and I, *exactly on the same ground*, will not leave Flush. It seems to me that you and I are *at one* upon the whole question,—only that *I* am *your* Flush, and *he* is mine. You, if you were "consistent" . . dearest! . . would not redeem me on any account. You do ever so much harm by it, observe—you produce catastrophe on catastrophe, just for the sake of my two ears without earrings! Oh, I entirely agree with your principle. Evil should be resisted that it may fly from you.

But Flush is not to be sacrificed—nor even is Ba, it appears. So our two weaknesses may pardon one another, yours and mine!

Some dog, shut up in a mews somewhere behind this house, has been yelling and moaning to-day and yesterday. How he has made me think of my poor poor Flush, I cannot tell you—"Think of Flush" he seemed to say.

* * *

XXXVII E. B. B. TO R. B.

Sunday
[Postmark, September 7, 1846]

Not well—not well! But I shall see you with my own eyes soon after you read what I write to-day; so I shall not write much. Only a few words to tell you that Flush is found, and lying on the sofa, with one paw and both ears hanging over the edge of it. Still my visit to Taylor was not the successful one. My hero was not at home.

I went, you know, . . did I tell you? . . with Wilson in the cab. We got into obscure streets; and our cabman stopped at a public house to ask his way. Out came two or three men, . . "Oh, you want to find Mr. Taylor, I dare say!" (mark that no name had been mentioned!) and instantly an unsolicited philanthropist ran before us to the house, and out again to tell me that the great man "wasn't at home! but wouldn't I get out?") Wilson, in an aside of terror, entreated me not to think of such a thing—she believed devoutly in the robbing and murdering, and was not reassured by the gang of benevolent men and boys who "lived but to oblige us" all round the cab. "Then wouldn't I see Mrs. Taylor," suggested the philanthropist,—and, notwithstanding my negatives, he had run back again and brought an immense feminine bandit, . . fat enough to have had an easy conscience all her life, . . who informed me that "her husband might be in in a few minutes, or in so many hours—wouldn't I like to get out and wait" (Wilson pulling at my gown, the philanthropist echoing the invitation of the feminine Taylor.)—"No, I thanked them all—it was not necessary that I should get out, but it *was*, that Mr. Taylor should keep his promise about the restoration of a dog which he had agreed to restore—and I begged her to induce him to go to Wimpole Street in the course of the day, and not defer it any longer." To which, replied the lady, with the most gracious of smiles—"Oh yes certainly"—and indeed she *did* believe that Taylor had left home precisely on that business—poising her head to the right and left with the most easy grace—"She was sure that Taylor would give his very best attention." . .

So, in the midst of the politeness, we drove away, and Wilson seemed to be of opinion that we had escaped with our lives barely. Plain enough it was, that the gang was strong there. The society . . the "Fancy" . . had their roots in the ground. The faces of those men!—

I had not been at home long, when Mr. Taylor did actually come—desiring to have six guineas confided to his honour!! . . and promising to bring back the dog. I sent down the money, and told them to trust the gentleman's honour, as there seemed no other way for it—and while the business was being concluded, in came Alfred, and straightway called our "honourable friend" (meeting him in the passage) a swindler and a liar and a thief. Which no gentleman could bear, of course. Therefore with reiterated oaths he swore, "as he hoped to be saved, we should never see our dog again"—and rushed out of the house. Followed a great storm. I was very angry with Alfred, who had no business to risk Flush's life for the sake of the satisfaction of trying on names which fitted. Angry I was with Alfred, and terrified for Flush,—seeing at a glance the probability of his head being cut off as the proper vengeance! and downstairs I went with the resolution of going again myself to Mr. Taylor's in Manning Street, or Shoreditch [or] wherever it was, and saving the victim at any price. It was the evening, getting dusk—and everybody was crying out against me for being "quite mad" and obstinate, and wilful—I was called as many names as Mr. Taylor. At last, Sette said that *he* would do it, promised to be as civil as I could wish, and got me to be "in a good humour and go up to my room again." And he went instead of me, and took the money and fair words, and induced the "man of honour" to forfeit his vengeance and go and fetch the dog. Flush arrived here at eight o'clock (at the very moment with your letter, dearest!), and the first thing he did was to dash up to this door, and then to drink his purple cup full of water, filled three times over. He was not so enthusiastic about seeing me, as I expected—he seemed bewildered and frightened—and whenever anyone said to him "Poor Flush, did the naughty men take you away?" he put up his head and moaned and yelled. He has been very unhappy certainly. Dirty he is, and much thinner, and continually he is drinking. Six guineas was his ransom—and now I have paid twenty for him to the dog-stealers.

Arabel says that I wanted *you* yesterday, she thought, to manage me a little. She thought I was suddenly seized with madness, to prepare to walk out of the house in that state of excitement and that hour of the evening. But now—*was* I to let them cut off Flush's head?—

There! I have told you the whole history of yesterday's adventures—and to-morrow I shall see you, my own dear, dear!—Only remember for my sake, *not* to come if you are not fit to come. Dearest, remember not to run any hazards!— . .

Ba.

MATTHEW ARNOLD

[December 24, 1822–April 15, 1888]

MATTHEW ARNOLD, son of Dr. Thomas Arnold, liberal clergyman and, from 1828 to his death in 1842, famous headmaster of Rugby, was born in Laleham, a little village in the valley of the Thames. The formal, planned beauty of this region made a deep impression upon him, but the stories and legends associated with it, running far back to the beginning of English history, influenced him still more markedly. In 1848, after visiting in the Laleham country, he wrote to his mother: "I never go along that shelving gravelly road up towards Laleham without interest, from Chertsey Lock to the turn where the drunken man lay. . . . I went up to Pentonhook, and found the stream with the old volume, width, shine, rapid fulness, 'kempshott,' and swans, unchanged and unequalled, to my partial and remembering eyes. . . . The old paved part of the barge road on the Laleham side of the Lock-house is all as it was, and the campanulas, they told me, grow as much as ever there in summer. . . . I was yesterday at the old house and under the cedars and by the old pink acacia."

The boy Arnold was for several years a pupil of his uncle's at Laleham. Following this he was in school for a year at Winchester, after which he spent five years at Rugby under the direction of his father, the great headmaster. His best work at Rugby was in the classics, and in 1841, when he was nineteen years old, he was given a classical scholarship at Balliol College, Oxford.

It is a great surprise to those who think they read character in a portrait to hear that in his college days Arnold was something of a madcap. In the portraits of the Arnold who was inspector of schools there is a seriousness, a severity, a bleakness even, completely out of keeping with the young Arnold of Oxford, who gave himself airs, affected French manners—"Parisianism," Clough, his great friend and brother poet, called it—and, as a recent writer said of him, "indulged a general bumptiousness as good-natured as it was superficial."

When the time for examinations was coming close at Balliol in mid-July 1844, Clough, alarmed lest Arnold should be fatally unprepared, took him to a quiet spot for a period of reading and study. The project was a failure, however, for at every opportunity Arnold ran away from his mentor to go on walking or fishing trips; and even when he did get to work at his books the slightest relaxation of Clough's watchfulness meant that his "yoke-fellow would come to a dead stop."

The examination began November 12, and in the three weeks preceding this date Arnold rose to the crisis and worked very hard, the result of his belated efforts being graduation with respectable, not with first-class standing, a circumstance which Clough spoke of as the "disaster of November." It was almost beyond the belief of Oxford men that one of Arnold's intellectual strength could graduate less than a first. Clough alone knew the secret and wrote to a friend that Arnold did not deserve even a second.

The following March, while he was teaching in the lower fifth form at Rugby, Arnold was elected a fellow of Oriel College, an office to which his father had been elected just thirty years before. Two years later, somewhat to the uneasiness of his family and of Clough, he was appointed private secretary to Lord Lansdowne. This position he held for three years, apparently without having done anything or become anything to justify the uneasiness of his relatives; for his mother wrote of him that he was not spoiled by the demands and honors of a society into which the other members of his family could not enter.

In 1851 Arnold was appointed inspector of nonconformist schools, an office which for some years prevented his having a settled residence and kept him always on the go, from Yarmouth to Pembroke and from Yorkshire to the Thames. For more than thirty-five years he lived this life, engaged in what he called an incessant grind, reading examination papers for three or four hours a day, visiting classes and examining pupil teachers, often eating nothing for hours "except a biscuit which a charitable lady gave," sometimes astonishing a school by eating a bun in the classroom. And all the time he was dreaming of a better day to come when, as he wrote to Mrs. Arnold, they could live at Berne "on a diplomatic appointment" or "retire to Italy on £200 a year." In time he became hardened to the grind, even developing a great interest in the schools because "their effects on the children were so immense," their influence "in civilizing the next generation of the lower classes so important." Out of his long experience in the inspectorship this champion of culture,

> jaded with the rush and glare
> Of the interminable hours,

wrote papers and reports on educational questions that point direction to the professional educator today.

When he left Oxford, Arnold wanted more than anything else to be a poet. He had written to his sister in 1849, the year he published his first volume, *The Strayed Reveller, and Other Poems*, that he had many poetical schemes, but was fermenting too much about poetry in general to do anything satisfactory. But the painful routine of the school inspectorship was not favorable to the creative impulse, and the fermenting about poetry was not to be for long. Before the impulse had entirely ebbed, however, some great poems came into being, and the reader who remembers the exacting demands of the inspectorship will look with something of amazement upon the rapidity with which the volumes appeared. In 1852 *Empedocles on Etna* was published, containing "Tristram and Iseult," and the next year came the volume that contained "Sohrab and Rustum," "The Scholar Gipsy," "Requiescat," and "Memorial Verses to Wordsworth." There was silence for two years, and then *Poems, Second Series* was issued, its most impressive poem being "Balder Dead." Upon the appearance of *Merope, a Tragedy*, in 1858, some readers felt that the poet's creative power was spent, a belief which Arnold himself may have shared, since about this time he said in a letter to his sister, "It is not so light a matter, when you have other grave claims on your powers, to submit voluntarily to the exhaustion of the best poetical production in a time like this." There was nothing more till 1867, when *New Poems*, his final volume, appeared, a book containing a number of reprinted poems, but containing also such fine poetic tributes as "Rugby Chapel," "Heine's Grave," and "Thyrsis." The period in which Arnold produced the body of verse that placed him among the major Victorians, therefore, was one of but a scant ten years. In 1859, when he said that his chief work was to "inculcate intelligence" on the British nation, he was virtually announcing that the poet was through and that the critic and teacher was coming into his own.

From 1857 to 1867 Arnold held the professorship of poetry at Oxford, a position which spurred his critical energy and which, in turn, he adorned with his poetical accomplishment, his pure taste, and his fine intelligence. That he was an impressive lecturer is evidenced by the incident of the master of Jesus College, who, at the close of one of Arnold's lectures, murmured in rapt voice: "The Angel ended."

After 1860 Arnold was definitely committed to prose, although, as the volume of 1867 indicates, he gave some desultory attention to the composition of poetry throughout the decade of the 'sixties. His principal critical writings included *Essays in Criticism* (1865 and 1888), *On*

Translating Homer (1861), and *On the Study of Celtic Literature* (1867). He pointed out in these books that the best poetry has a power of forming, sustaining, and delighting us, as nothing else can; that the reader should test poetic lines by applying to them, as touchstones, lines and expressions of the great masters; and that poetry, which is "a criticism of life," must be written in "the grand style" and filled with "high seriousness."

Culture and Anarchy (1869), perhaps his greatest book, is a criticism of English social and political life. In it he tells us that culture implies a knowledge of the best that is known and thought in the world, that its motto is "to make reason and the will of God prevail." The Philistines, or middle class of English society, he attacks vigorously for their complacency and materialism.

In his books on religion (*St. Paul and Protestantism*, 1870; *Literature and Dogma*, 1873; *God and the Bible*, 1875) Arnold spoke for a Christianity that finds theology unimportant, rejects the miraculous, and considers religion "as the recognition, the emotional sense, and the use of the often mysterious power 'not ourselves which makes for righteousness.' "

There is another book, *Discourses in America*, which grew out of his visit to America in 1883, five years before his death. His American trip was in some respects a pleasant surprise to him, but the pleasure he derived from it did not purge him of the belief he had before he left England, that Americans were underbred, uninteresting Philistines. He thought New York looked beautiful from his boat; he liked Philadelphia; he recoiled from the "dirt, untidiness, and spitting" in the halls of Congress; he was delighted with the sleigh-ride which the university boys at Ann Arbor gave him; he laughed at the Detroit newspaper that compared him, as he stooped to glance at his manuscript, to "an elderly bird pecking at grapes on a trellis"; he was greatly amused when, in response to a talk he made in a negro school, the little darkies sang lustily, "Dare to be a Daniel." But still he wrote, even though his daughter was to marry an American and reside in America, "I have seen no American yet, except Norton at Cambridge, who does not seem to desire constant publicity and to be on the go all the day long."

As early as May of 1885 he spoke of a "horrid pain" in his chest that made tennis, fast walking, or hill-climbing unbearable. He was to retire from the school inspectorship that year, but in October the Education Office sent him on an official trip to Paris and Berlin, one duty of his position that was much to his taste. The trip gave him about four months on the Continent, and after it was over he came again to America. He spent the summer in America, the last two months of it in the Berkshire Hills, and when he left for England in late August he said that his greatest relief would be "to cease seeing the American newspapers," whose "badness and ignobleness are beyond belief." All his days since the May day of 1885, when he wrote of the "horrid pain" in his chest, he had lived under the threat of angina. In April 1888 it suddenly struck, and a few days later the man whom some discerning spirit addressed as *Vir dulcissime et lucidissime* was buried in Laleham churchyard beside his three boys.

What will the future write of Matthew Arnold the poet? It is a question that cannot be surely answered now. Mr. James Stephens, in his "Estimate," introducing this volume, says Arnold is "possibly the greatest and most to be mourned for failure in the annals of English poetry." Arnold said of himself, "I have less poetical sentiment than Tennyson, and less intellectual vigour and abundance than Browning; yet, because I have perhaps more of a fusion of the two than either of them, and have more regularly applied that fusion to the main line of modern development, I am likely enough to have my turn, as they have had theirs." There are critics who speak of the cold temper of Arnold's verse, of its artificiality, its awkward rhythm. They praise its elegance and precision and yet say it pays for these qualities with a prosy dryness. They see in it only the studied, nothing of the spontaneous. A few—and the number seems to be growing—say there are signs that Arnold spoke truly when he said he was likely enough to have his turn with Tennyson and Browning. They see in his scant ten years of "much fermenting about poetry" an accomplishment glorious enough to give him a place side by side with the two great figures that have been called supreme among the Victorians. The one thing upon which there is general agreement today is that Arnold possessed one unmistakable gift—the gift of feeling and insight. For some, who find in him much more than this one gift, he is already "the most perfect voice" among the Victorians.

QUIET WORK

One lesson, Nature, let me learn of thee,
One lesson which in every wind is blown,
One lesson of two duties kept at one
Though the loud world proclaim their enmity—

Of toil unsever'd from tranquillity!
Of labour, that in lasting fruit outgrows
Far noisier schemes, accomplish'd in repose,
Too great for haste, too high for rivalry!

Yes, while on earth a thousand discords ring,
Man's fitful uproar mingling with his toil,
Still do thy sleepless ministers move on,

Their glorious tasks in silence perfecting;
Still working, blaming still our vain turmoil,
Labourers that shall not fail, when man is gone.

1849

MYCERINUS

"Not by the justice that my father spurn'd,
Not for the thousands whom my father slew,
Altars unfed and temples overturn'd,
Cold hearts and thankless tongues, where thanks are due;
Fell this dread voice from lips that cannot lie,
Stern sentence of the Powers of Destiny.

"I will unfold my sentence and my crime.
My crime—that, rapt in reverential awe,
I sate obedient, in the fiery prime
Of youth, self-govern'd, at the feet of Law;
Ennobling this dull pomp, the life of kings,
By contemplation of diviner things.

"My father loved injustice, and lived long;
Crown'd with gray hairs he died, and full of sway.
I loved the good he scorn'd, and hated wrong—
The Gods declare my recompense to-day.
I look'd for life more lasting, rule more high;
And when six years are measured, lo, I die!

"Yet surely, O my people, did I deem
Man's justice from the all-just Gods was given;
A light that from some upper fount did beam,
Some better archetype, whose seat was heaven;
A light that, shining from the blest abodes,
Did shadow somewhat of the life of Gods.

"Mere phantoms of man's self-tormenting heart,
Which on the sweets that woo it dares not feed!
Vain dreams, which quench our pleasures, then depart,
When the duped soul, self-master'd, claims its meed;
When, on the strenuous just man, Heaven bestows,
Crown of his struggling life, an unjust close!

"Seems it so light a thing, then, austere Powers,
To spurn man's common lure, life's pleasant things?

Seems there no joy in dances crown'd with flowers,
Love, free to range, and regal banquetings?
Bend ye on these, indeed, an unmoved eye,
Not Gods but ghosts, in frozen apathy?

"Or is it that some Force, too wise, too strong,
Even for yourselves to conquer or beguile,
Sweeps earth, and heaven, and men, and gods along,
Like the broad volume of the insurgent Nile?
And the great powers we serve, themselves may be
Slaves of a tyrannous necessity?

"Or in mid-heaven, perhaps, your golden cars,
Where earthly voice climbs never, wing their flight,
And in wild hunt, through mazy tracts of stars,
Sweep in the sounding stillness of the night?
Or in deaf ease, on thrones of dazzling sheen,
Drinking deep draughts of joy, ye dwell serene?

"Oh, wherefore cheat our youth, if thus it be,
Of one short joy, one lust, one pleasant dream?
Stringing vain words of powers we cannot see,
Blind divinations of a will supreme;
Lost labour! when the circumambient gloom
But hides, if Gods, Gods careless of our doom?

"The rest I give to joy. Even while I speak,
My sand runs short; and—as yon star-shot ray,
Hemm'd by two banks of cloud, peers pale and weak,
Now, as the barrier closes, dies away—
Even so do past and future intertwine,
Blotting this six years' space, which yet is mine.

"Six years—six little years—six drops of time!
Yet suns shall rise, and many moons shall wane,
And old men die, and young men pass their prime,
And languid pleasure fade and flower again,
And the dull Gods behold, ere these are flown,
Revels more deep, joy keener than their own.

"Into the silence of the groves and woods
I will go forth; though something would I say—
Something—yet what, I know not; for the Gods
The doom they pass revoke not, nor delay;
And prayers, and gifts, and tears, are fruitless all,
And the night waxes, and the shadows fall.

"Ye men of Egypt, ye have heard your king!
I go, and I return not. But the will
Of the great Gods is plain; and ye must bring
Ill deeds, ill passions, zealous to fulfil
Their pleasure, to their feet; and reap their praise,
The praise of Gods, rich boon! and length of days."

—So spake he, half in anger, half in scorn;
And one loud cry of grief and of amaze
Broke from his sorrowing people; so he spake,
And turning, left them there; and with brief pause,
Girt with a throng of revellers, bent his way
To the cool region of the groves he loved.
There by the river-banks he wander'd on,
From palm-grove on to palm-grove, happy trees,
Their smooth tops shining sunward, and beneath
Burying their unsunn'd stems in grass and flowers;
Where in one dream the feverish time of youth
Might fade in slumber, and the feet of joy
Might wander all day long and never tire.
Here came the king, holding high feast, at morn,
Rose-crown'd; and ever, when the sun went down,
A hundred lamps beam'd in the tranquil gloom,
From tree to tree all through the twinkling grove,
Revealing all the tumult of the feast—
Flush'd guests, and golden goblets foam'd with wine;
While the deep-burnish'd foliage overhead
Splinter'd the silver arrows of the moon.
  It may be that sometimes his wondering soul
From the loud joyful laughter of his lips
Might shrink half startled, like a guilty man
Who wrestles with his dream; as some pale shape
Gliding half hidden through the dusky stems,
Would thrust a hand before the lifted bowl,
Whispering: *A little space, and thou art mine!*
It may be on that joyless feast his eye
Dwelt with mere outward seeming; he, within,
Took measure of his soul, and knew its strength,
And by that silent knowledge, day by day,
Was calm'd, ennobled, comforted, sustain'd.
It may be; but not less his brow was smooth,
And his clear laugh fled ringing through the gloom,
And his mirth quail'd not at the mild reproof
Sigh'd out by winter's sad tranquillity;
Nor, pall'd with its own fulness, ebb'd and died
In the rich languor of long summer-days;
Nor wither'd when the palm-tree plumes, that roof'd
With their mild dark his grassy banquet-hall,
Bent to the cold winds of the showerless spring;
No, nor grew dark when autumn brought the clouds.
  So six long years he revell'd, night and day.
And when the mirth wax'd loudest, with dull sound
Sometimes from the grove's centre echoes came,
To tell his wondering people of their king;
In the still night, across the steaming flats,
Mix'd with the murmur of the moving Nile.

1849

TO A FRIEND

Who prop, thou ask'st, in these bad days, my mind?—
He much, the old man, who, clearest-soul'd of men,
Saw The Wide Prospect, and the Asian Fen,
And Tmolus hill, and Smyrna bay, though blind.

Much he, whose friendship I not long since won,
That halting slave, who in Nicopolis
Taught Arrian, when Vespasian's brutal son
Clear'd Rome of what most shamed him. But be his

My special thanks, whose even-balanced soul,
From first youth tested up to extreme old age,
Business could not make dull, nor passion wild;

Who saw life steadily, and saw it whole;
The mellow glory of the Attic stage,
Singer of sweet Colonus, and its child.

1849

THE SICK KING IN BOKHARA

Hussein

O most just Vizier, send away
The cloth-merchants, and let them be,
Them and their dues, this day! the King
Is ill at ease, and calls for thee.

The Vizier

O merchants, tarry yet a day
Here in Bokhara! but at noon,
To-morrow, come, and ye shall pay
Each fortieth web of cloth to me,
As the law is, and go your way.
O Hussein, lead me to the King!
Thou teller of sweet tales, thine own.
Ferdousi's, and the others', lead!
How is it with my lord?

Hussein

Alone,
Ever since prayer-time, he doth wait,
O Vizier! without lying down,
In the great window of the gate,
Looking into the Registàn,
Where through the sellers' booths the slaves
Are this way bringing the dead man.—
O Vizier, here is the King's door!

The King

O Vizier, I may bury him?

The Vizier

O King, thou know'st, I have been sick
These many days, and heard no thing
(For Allah shut my ears and mind),
Not even what thou dost, O King!
Wherefore, that I may counsel thee,
Let Hussein, if thou wilt, make haste
To speak in order what hath chanced.

The King

O Vizier, be it as thou say'st!

Hussein

Three days since, at the time of prayer
A certain Moollah, with his robe
All rent, and dust upon his hair,
Watch'd my lord's coming forth, and push'd
The golden mace-bearers aside,
And fell at the King's feet, and cried:

"Justice, O King, and on myself!
On this great sinner, who did break
The law, and by the law must die!
Vengeance, O King!"

But the King spake:
"What fool is this, that hurts our ears
With folly? or what drunken slave?
My guards, what, prick him with your spears!
Prick me the fellow from the path!"
As the King said, so it was done,
And to the mosque my lord pass'd on.

But on the morrow, when the King
Went forth again, the holy book
Carried before him, as is right,
And through the square his way he took;
My man comes running, fleck'd with blood
From yesterday, and falling down
Cries out most earnestly: "O King,
My lord, O King, do right, I pray!

"How canst thou, ere thou hear, discern
If I speak folly? but a king,
Whether a thing be great or small,
Like Allah, hears and judges all.

"Wherefore hear thou! Thou know'st, how fierce
In these last days the sun hath burn'd;
That the green water in the tanks
Is to a putrid puddle turn'd;
And the canal, which from the stream
Of Samarcand is brought this way,
Wastes, and runs thinner every day.

"Now I at nightfall had gone forth
Alone, and in a darksome place
Under some mulberry-trees I found
A little pool; and in short space,
With all the water that was there
I fill'd my pitcher, and stole home
Unseen; and having drink to spare,
I hid the can behind the door,
And went up on the roof to sleep.

"But in the night, which was with wind
And burning dust, again I creep
Down, having fever, for a drink.

"Now meanwhile had my brethren found
The water-pitcher, where it stood
Behind the door upon the ground,
And call'd my mother; and they all,
As they were thirsty, and the night
Most sultry, drain'd the pitcher there;
That they sate with it, in my sight,
Their lips still wet, when I came down.

"Now mark! I, being fever'd, sick
(Most unblest also), at that sight
Brake forth, and cursed them—dost thou hear?
One was my mother——Now, do right!"

But my lord mused a space, and said:
"Send him away, Sirs, and make on!
It is some madman!" the King said.
As the King bade, so was it done.

The morrow, at the self-same hour,
In the King's path, behold, the man,
Not kneeling, sternly fix'd! he stood
Right opposite, and thus began,
Frowning grim down: "Thou wicked King,
Most deaf where thou shouldst most give ear!
What, must I howl in the next world,
Because thou wilt not listen here?

"What, wilt thou pray, and get thee grace,
And all grace shall to me be grudged?
Nay but, I swear, from this thy path
I will not stir till I be judged!"

Then they who stood about the King
Drew close together and conferr'd;
Till that the King stood forth and said:
"Before the priests thou shalt be heard."

But when the Ulemas were met,
And the thing heard, they doubted not;
But sentenced him, as the law is,
To die by stoning on the spot.

Now the King charged us secretly:
"Stoned must he be, the law stands so.
Yet, if he seek to fly, give way;
Hinder him not, but let him go."

So saying, the King took a stone,
And cast it softly;—but the man,
With a great joy upon his face,
Kneel'd down, and cried not, neither ran.

So they, whose lot it was, cast stones,
That they flew thick and bruised him sore.
But he praised Allah with loud voice,
And remain'd kneeling as before.

My lord had cover'd up his face;
But when one told him, "He is dead,"
Turning him quickly to go in,
"Bring thou to me his corpse," he said.

And truly, while I speak, O King,
I hear the bearers on the stair;
Wilt thou they straightway bring him in?
—Ho! enter ye who tarry there!

The Vizier

O King, in this I praise thee not!
Now must I call thy grief not wise.
Is he thy friend, or of thy blood,
To find such favour in thine eyes?

Nay, were he thine own mother's son,
Still, thou art king, and the law stands.
It were not meet the balance swerved,
The sword were broken in thy hands.

But being nothing, as he is,
Why for no cause make sad thy face?—
Lo, I am old! three kings, ere thee,
Have I seen reigning in this place.

But who, through all this length of time,
Could bear the burden of his years,
If he for strangers pain'd his heart
Not less than those who merit tears?

Fathers we *must* have, wife and child,
And grievous is the grief for these;
This pain alone, which *must* be borne,
Makes the head white, and bows the knees.

But other loads than this his own
One man is not well made to bear.
Besides, to each are his own friends,
To mourn with him, and show him care.

Look, this is but one single place,
Though it be great; all the earth round,
If a man bear to have it so,
Things which might vex him shall be found.

Upon the Russian frontier, where
The watchers of two armies stand
Near one another, many a man,
Seeking a prey unto his hand,

Hath snatch'd a little fair-hair'd slave;
They snatch also, towards Mervè,
The Shiah dogs, who pasture sheep,
And up from thence to Orgunjè.

And these all, labouring for a lord,
Eat not the fruit of their own hands;
Which is the heaviest of all plagues,
To that man's mind, who understands.

The kaffirs also (whom God curse!)
Vex one another, night and day;
There are the lepers, and all sick;
There are the poor, who faint alway.

All these have sorrow, and keep still,
Whilst other men make cheer, and sing.
Wilt thou have pity on all these?
No, nor on this dead dog, O King!

The King

O Vizier, thou art old, I young!
Clear in these things I cannot see.
My head is burning, and a heat
Is in my skin which angers me.

But hear ye this, ye sons of men!
They that bear rule, and are obey'd,
Unto a rule more strong than theirs
Are in their turn obedient made.

In vain therefore, with wistful eyes
Gazing up hither, the poor man,
Who loiters by the high-heap'd booths,
Below there, in the Registàn,

Says: "Happy he, who lodges there!
With silken raiment, store of rice,
And for this drought, all kinds of fruits,
Grape-syrup, squares of colour'd ice,

"With cherries serv'd in drifts of snow."
In vain hath a king power to build
Houses, arcades, enamell'd mosques;
And to make orchard-closes, fill'd

With curious fruit-trees brought from far
With cisterns for the winter-rain,
And, in the desert, spacious inns
In divers places—if that pain

Is not more lighten'd, which he feels,
If his will be not satisfied;
And that it be not, from all time
The law is planted, to abide.

Thou wast a sinner, thou poor man!
Thou wast athirst; and didst not see,
That, though we take what we desire,
We must not snatch it eagerly.

And I have meat and drink at will,
And rooms of treasures, not a few.
But I am sick, nor heed I these;
And what I would, I cannot do.

Even the great honour which I have,
When I am dead, will soon grow still;
So have I neither joy, nor fame.
But what I can do, that I will.

I have a fretted brick-work tomb
Upon a hill on the right hand,
Hard by a close of apricots,
Upon the road of Samarcand;

Thither, O Vizier, will I bear
This man my pity could not save,
And, plucking up the marble flags,
There lay his body in my grave.

Bring water, nard, and linen rolls!
Wash off all blood, set smooth each limb!
Then say: "He was not wholly vile,
Because a king shall bury him."

1849

WRITTEN IN EMERSON'S ESSAYS

"O MONSTROUS, dead, unprofitable world,
That thou canst hear, and hearing, hold thy way!
A voice oracular hath peal'd to-day,
To-day a hero's banner is unfurl'd;

Hast thou no lip for welcome?"—So I said.
Man after man, the world smiled and pass'd by;
A smile of wistful incredulity
As though one spake of life unto the dead—

Scornful, and strange, and sorrowful, and full
Of bitter knowledge. Yet the will is free;
Strong is the soul, and wise, and beautiful;

The seeds of godlike power are in us still;
Gods are we, bards, saints, heroes, if we will!—
Dumb judges, answer, truth or mockery?

1849

SHAKESPEARE

OTHERS abide our question. Thou art free.
We ask and ask—Thou smilest and art still,
Out-topping knowledge. For the loftiest hill,
Who to the stars uncrowns his majesty,

Planting his steadfast footsteps in the sea,
Making the heaven of heavens his dwelling-place,
Spares but the cloudy border of his base
To the foil'd searching of mortality;

And thou, who didst the stars and sunbeams know,
Self-school'd, self-scann'd, self-honour'd, self-secure,
Didst tread on earth unguess'd at.—Better so!

All pains the immortal spirit must endure,
All weakness which impairs, all griefs which bow,
Find their sole speech in that victorious brow.

1849

IN HARMONY WITH NATURE

TO A PREACHER

"IN harmony with Nature?" Restless fool,
Who with such heat dost preach what were to thee,
When true, the last impossibility—
To be like Nature strong, like Nature cool!

Know, man hath all which Nature hath, but more,
And in that *more* lie all his hopes of good.
Nature is cruel, man is sick of blood;
Nature is stubborn, man would fain adore;

Nature is fickle, man hath need of rest;
Nature forgives no debt, and fears no grave;
Man would be mild, and with safe conscience blest.

Man must begin, know this, where Nature ends;
Nature and man can never be fast friends.
Fool, if thou canst not pass her, rest her slave!

1849

TO A REPUBLICAN FRIEND, 1848

GOD knows it, I am with you. If to prize
Those virtues, prized and practised by too few,
But prized, but loved, but eminent in you,
Man's fundamental life; if to despise

The barren optimistic sophistries
Of comfortable moles, whom what they do
Teaches the limit of the just and true
(And for such doing they require not eyes);

If sadness at the long heart-wasting show
Wherein earth's great ones are disquieted;
If thoughts, not idle, while before me flow

The armies of the homeless and unfed—
If these are yours, if this is what you are,
Then am I yours, and what you feel, I share.

1849

CONTINUED

Yet, when I muse on what life is, I seem
Rather to patience prompted, than that proud
Prospect of hope which France proclaims so loud—
France, famed in all great arts, in none supreme;

Seeing this vale, this earth, whereon we dream,
Is on all sides o'ershadow'd by the high
Uno'erleap'd Mountains of Necessity,
Sparing us narrower margin than we deem.

Nor will that day dawn at a human nod,
When, bursting through the network superposed
By selfish occupation—plot and plan,

Lust, avarice, envy—liberated man,
All difference with his fellow-mortal closed,
Shall be left standing face to face with God.

1849

A QUESTION

TO FAUSTA

Joy comes and goes, hope ebbs and flows
Like the wave;
Change doth unknit the tranquil strength of men.
Love lends life a little grace,
A few sad smiles; and then,
Both are laid in one cold place,
In the grave.

Dreams dawn and fly, friends smile and die
Like spring flowers;
Our vaunted life is one long funeral.
Men dig graves with bitter tears
For their dead hopes; and all,
Mazed with doubts and sick with fears,
Count the hours.

We count the hours! These dreams of ours,
False and hollow,
Do we go hence and find they are not dead?
Joys we dimly apprehend,
Faces that smiled and fled,
Hopes born here, and born to end,
Shall we follow?

1849

From THE STRAYED REVELLER

(Lines 261–297)

The old Silenus
Came, lolling in the sunshine,
From the dewy forest-coverts,
This way, at noon.
Sitting by me, while his Fauns
Down at the water-side
Sprinkled and smoothed
His drooping garland,
He told me these things.

But I, Ulysses,
Sitting on the warm steps,
Looking over the valley,
All day long, have seen,
Without pain, without labour,
Sometimes a wild-hair'd Mænad—
Sometimes a Faun with torches—
And sometimes, for a moment,
Passing through the dark stems
Flowing-robed, the beloved,
The desired, the divine,
Beloved Iacchus.

Ah, cool night-wind, tremulous stars!
Ah, glimmering water,
Fitful earth-murmur,
Dreaming woods!
Ah, golden-hair'd, strangely smiling Goddess,
And thou, proved, much enduring,
Wave-toss'd Wanderer!
Who can stand still?
Ye fade, ye swim, ye waver before me—
The cup again!

Faster, faster,
O Circe, Goddess,
Let the wild, thronging train,
The bright procession
Of eddying forms,
Sweep through my soul!

1849

THE FORSAKEN MERMAN

Come, dear children, let us away;
Down and away below!
Now my brothers call from the bay,
Now the great winds shoreward blow,
Now the salt tides seaward flow;
Now the wild white horses play,
Champ and chafe and toss in the spray.
Children dear, let us away!
This way, this way!

Call her once before you go—
Call once yet!
In a voice that she will know:
"Margaret! Margaret!"
Children's voices should be dear
(Call once more) to a mother's ear;
Children's voices, wild with pain—
Surely she will come again!
Call her once and come away;
This way, this way!
"Mother dear, we cannot stay!
The wild white horses foam and fret."
Margaret! Margaret!

Come, dear children, come away down;
Call no more!
One last look at the white-wall'd town,
And the little grey church on the windy shore;
Then come down!
She will not come though you call all day;
Come away, come away!

Children dear, was it yesterday
We heard the sweet bells over the bay?
In the caverns where we lay,
Through the surf and through the swell,
The far-off sound of a silver bell?
Sand-strewn caverns, cool and deep,
Where the winds are all asleep;
Where the spent lights quiver and gleam,
Where the salt weed sways in the stream,
Where the sea-beasts, ranged all round,
Feed in the ooze of their pasture-ground;
Where the sea-snakes coil and twine,
Dry their mail and bask in the brine;
Where great whales come sailing by,
Sail and sail, with unshut eye,
Round the world for ever and aye?
When did music come this way?
Children dear, was it yesterday?

Children dear, was it yesterday
(Call yet once) that she went away?
Once she sate with you and me,
On a red gold throne in the heart of the sea,
And the youngest sate on her knee.
She comb'd its bright hair, and she tended it well,
When down swung the sound of a far-off bell.
She sigh'd, she look'd up through the clear green sea;
She said: "I must go, for my kinsfolk pray
In the little grey church on the shore to-day.
'Twill be Easter-time in the world—ah me!
And I lose my poor soul, Merman! here with thee."
I said: "Go up, dear heart, through the waves;
Say thy prayer, and come back to the kind sea-caves!"
She smiled, she went up through the surf in the bay.
Children dear, was it yesterday?

Children dear, were we long alone?
"The sea grows stormy, the little ones moan;
Long prayers," I said, "in the world they say;
Come!" I said; and we rose through the surf in the bay.
We went up the beach, by the sandy down
Where the sea-stocks bloom, to the white-wall'd town;
Through the narrow paved streets, where all was still,
To the little grey church on the windy hill.
From the church came a murmur of folk at their prayers,
But we stood without in the cold blowing airs.
We climb'd on the graves, on the stones worn with rains,
And we gazed up the aisle through the small leaded panes.
She sate by the pillar; we saw her clear:
"Margaret, hist! come quick, we are here!
Dear heart," I said, "we are long alone;
The sea grows stormy, the little ones moan."
But, ah, she gave me never a look,
For her eyes were seal'd to the holy book!
Loud prays the priest; shut stands the door.
Come away, children, call no more!
Come away, come down, call no more!

Down, down, down!
Down to the depths of the sea!
She sits at her wheel in the humming town,
Singing most joyfully.
Hark what she sings: "O joy, O joy,
For the humming street, and the child with its toy!
For the priest, and the bell, and the holy well;
For the wheel where I spun,
And the blessed light of the sun!"
And so she sings her fill,
Singing most joyfully,
Till the spindle drops from her hand,
And the whizzing wheel stands still.
She steals to the window, and looks at the sand,
And over the sand at the sea;
And her eyes are set in a stare;
And anon there breaks a sigh,
And anon there drops a tear,
From a sorrow-clouded eye,
And a heart sorrow-laden,
A long, long sigh;
For the cold strange eyes of a little Mermaiden
And the gleam of her golden hair.

Come away, away children;
Come children, come down!
The hoarse wind blows coldly;
Lights shine in the town.
She will start from her slumber
When gusts shake the door;
She will hear the winds howling,
Will hear the waves roar.
We shall see, while above us
The waves roar and whirl,
A ceiling of amber,
A pavement of pearl.
Singing: "Here came a mortal,
But faithless was she!
And alone dwell for ever
The kings of the sea."

But, children, at midnight,
When soft the winds blow,
When clear falls the moonlight,
When spring-tides are low;
When sweet airs come seaward
From heaths starr'd with broom,
And high rocks throw mildly
On the blanch'd sands a gloom;
Up the still, glistening beaches,
Up the creeks we will hie,
Over banks of bright seaweed
The ebb-tide leaves dry.
We will gaze, from the sand-hills,
At the white, sleeping town;
At the church on the hill-side—
And then come back down.
Singing: "There dwells a loved one,
But cruel is she!
She left lonely for ever
The kings of the sea."

1849

IN UTRUMQUE PARATUS

If, in the silent mind of One all-pure,
At first imagined lay
The sacred world; and by procession sure
From those still deeps, in form and colour drest,
Seasons alternating, and night and day,
The long-mused thought to north, south, east, and west,
Took then its all-seen way;

O waking on a world which thus-wise springs!
Whether it needs thee count
Betwixt thy waking and the birth of things
Ages or hours—O waking on life's stream!
By lonely pureness to the all-pure fount
(Only by this thou canst) the colour'd dream
Of life remount!

Thin, thin the pleasant human noises grow,
And faint the city gleams;
Rare the lone pastoral huts—marvel not thou!
The solemn peaks but to the stars are known,
But to the stars, and the cold lunar beams;
Alone the sun arises, and alone
Spring the great streams.

But, if the wild unfather'd mass no birth
In divine seats hath known;
In the blank, echoing solitude if Earth,
Rocking her obscure body to and fro,
Ceases not from all time to heave and groan,
Unfruitful oft, and at her happiest throe
Forms, what she forms, alone;

O seeming sole to awake, thy sun-bathed head
  Piercing the solemn cloud
Round thy still dreaming brother-world outspread!
O man, whom Earth, thy long-vext mother, bare
Not without joy—so radiant, so endow'd
(Such happy issue crown'd her painful care)—
  Be not too proud!

Oh, when most self-exalted most alone,
  Chief dreamer, own thy dream!
Thy brother-world stirs at thy feet unknown,
Who hath a monarch's hath no brother's part;
Yet doth thine inmost soul with yearning teem.
—Oh, what a spasm shakes the dreamer's heart!
  "*I, too, but seem.*"

1849

A MODERN SAPPHO

They are gone—all is still! Foolish heart, dost thou quiver?
  Nothing stirs on the lawn but the quick lilac-shade.
Far up shines the house, and beneath flows the river—
  Here lean, my head, on this cold balustrade!

Ere he come—ere the boat by the shining-branch'd border
  Of dark elms shoot round, dropping down the proud stream,
Let me pause, let me strive, in myself make some order,
  Ere their boat-music sound, ere their broider'd flags gleam.

Last night we stood earnestly talking together;
  She enter'd—that moment his eyes turn'd from me!
Fasten'd on her dark hair, and her wreath of white heather—
  As yesterday was, so to-morrow will be.

Their love, let me know, must grow strong and yet stronger,
  Their passion burn more, ere it ceases to burn.
They must love—while they must! but the hearts that love longer
  Are rare—ah! most loves but flow once, and return.

I shall suffer—but they will outlive their affection;
  I shall weep—but their love will be cooling; and he,
As he drifts to fatigue, discontent, and dejection,
  Will be brought, thou poor heart, how much nearer to thee!

For cold is his eye to mere beauty, who, breaking
  The strong band which passion around him hath furl'd,
Disenchanted by habit, and newly awaking,
  Looks languidly round on a gloom-buried world.

Through that gloom he will see but a shadow appearing,
  Perceive but a voice as I come to his side—
But deeper their voice grows, and nobler their bearing,
  Whose youth in the fires of anguish hath died.

So, to wait!—But what notes down the wind, hark! are driving?
  'Tis he! 'tis their flag, shooting round by the trees!
—Let my turn, if it *will* come, be swift in arriving!
  Ah! hope cannot long lighten torments like these.

Hast thou yet dealt him, O life, thy full measure?
  World, have thy children yet bow'd at his knee?
Hast thou with myrtle-leaf crown'd him, O pleasure?
  —Crown, crown him quickly, and leave him for me!

1849

RESIGNATION

TO FAUSTA

To die be given us, or attain!
Fierce work it were, to do again.
So pilgrims, bound for Mecca, pray'd
At burning noon; so warriors said,
Scarf'd with the cross, who watch'd the miles
Of dust which wreathed their struggling files
Down Lydian mountains; so, when snows
Round Alpine summits, eddying, rose,
The Goth, bound Rome-wards; so the Hun,
Crouch'd on his saddle, while the sun
Went lurid down o'er flooded plains
Through which the groaning Danube strains
To the drear Euxine;—so pray all,
Whom labours, self-ordain'd, enthrall;
Because they to themselves propose
On this side the all-common close
A goal which, gain'd, may give repose.
So pray they; and to stand again
Where they stood once, to them were pain;
Pain to thread back and to renew
Past straits, and currents long steer'd through.

But milder natures, and more free—
Whom an unblamed serenity
Hath freed from passions, and the state
Of struggle these necessitate;
Whom schooling of the stubborn mind
Hath made, or birth hath found, resign'd—
These mourn not, that their goings pay
Obedience to the passing day.
These claim not every laughing Hour
For handmaid to their striding power;
Each in her turn, with torch uprear'd,
To await their march; and when appear'd,
Through the cold gloom, with measured race,
To usher for a destined space
(Her own sweet errands all forgone)
The too imperious traveller on.
These, Fausta, ask not this; nor thou,
Time's chafing prisoner, ask it now!

We left, just ten years since, you say,
That wayside inn we left to-day.
Our jovial host, as forth we fare,
Shouts greeting from his easy chair.
High on a bank our leader stands,
Reviews and ranks his motley bands,
Makes clear our goal to every eye—
The valley's western boundary.
A gate swings to! our tide hath flow'd
Already from the silent road.
The valley-pastures, one by one,
Are threaded, quiet in the sun;
And now beyond the rude stone bridge
Slopes gracious up the western ridge.
Its woody border, and the last
Of its dark upland farms is past—
Cool farms, with open-lying stores,
Under their burnish'd sycamores;
All past! and through the trees we glide,
Emerging on the green hill-side.
There climbing hangs, a far-seen sign,
Our wavering, many-colour'd line;
There winds, upstreaming slowly still
Over the summit of the hill.
And now, in front, behold outspread
Those upper regions we must tread!
Mild hollows, and clear heathy swells,
The cheerful silence of the fells.
Some two hours' march with serious air,
Through the deep noontide heats we fare;
The red-grouse, springing at our sound,
Skims, now and then, the shining ground;
No life, save his and ours, intrudes
Upon these breathless solitudes.
O joy! again the farms appear.
Cool shade is there, and rustic cheer;
There springs the brook will guide us down,
Bright comrade, to the noisy town.
Lingering, we follow down; we gain
The town, the highway, and the plain.
And many a mile of dusty way,
Parch'd and road-worn, we made that day;
But, Fausta, I remember well,
That as the balmy darkness fell
We bathed our hands with speechless glee,
That night, in the wide-glimmering sea.

Once more we tread this self-same road,
Fausta, which ten years since we trod;
Alone we tread it, you and I,
Ghosts of that boisterous company.
Here, where the brook shines, near its head,
In its clear, shallow, turf-fringed bed;
Here, whence the eye first sees, far down,
Capp'd with faint smoke, the noisy town;

Here sit we, and again unroll,
Though slowly, the familiar whole.
The solemn wastes of heathy hill
Sleep in the July sunshine still;
The self-same shadows now, as then,
Play through this grassy upland glen;
The loose dark stones on the green way
Lie strewn, it seems, where then they lay;
On this mild bank above the stream,
(You crush them!) the blue gentians gleam.
Still this wild brook, the rushes cool,
The sailing foam, the shining pool!
These are not changed; and we, you say,
Are scarce more changed, in truth, than they.

The gipsies, whom we met below,
They, too, have long roam'd to and fro;
They ramble, leaving, where they pass,
Their fragments on the cumber'd grass.
And often to some kindly place
Chance guides the migratory race,
Where, though long wanderings intervene,
They recognise a former scene.
The dingy tents are pitch'd; the fires
Give to the wind their wavering spires;
In dark knots crouch round the wild flame
Their children, as when first they came;
They see their shackled beasts again
Move, browsing, up the gray-wall'd lane.
Signs are not wanting, which might raise
The ghost in them of former days—
Signs are not wanting, if they would;
Suggestions to disquietude.
For them, for all, time's busy touch,
While it mends little, troubles much.
Their joints grow stiffer—but the year
Runs his old round of dubious cheer;
Chilly they grow—yet winds in March,
Still, sharp as ever, freeze and parch;
They must live still—and yet, God knows,
Crowded and keen the country grows;
It seems as if, in their decay,
The law grew stronger every day.
So might they reason, so compare,
Fausta, times past with times that are.
But no!—they rubb'd through yesterday
In their hereditary way,
And they will rub through, if they can,
To-morrow on the self-same plan,
Till death arrive to supersede,
For them, vicissitude and need.

The poet, to whose mighty heart
Heaven doth a quicker pulse impart,
Subdues that energy to scan
Not his own course, but that of man.
Though he move mountains, though his day
Be pass'd on the proud heights of sway,
Though he hath loosed a thousand chains,
Though he hath borne immortal pains,
Action and suffering though he know—
He hath not lived, if he lives so.
He sees, in some great-historied land,
A ruler of the people stand,
Sees his strong thought in fiery flood
Roll through the heaving multitude,
Exults—yet for no moment's space
Envies the all-regarded place.
Beautiful eyes meet his—and he
Bears to admire uncravingly;
They pass—he, mingled with the crowd,
Is in their far-off triumphs proud.
From some high station he looks down,
At sunset, on a populous town;
Surveys each happy group, which fleets,
Toil ended, through the shining streets,
Each with some errand of its own—
And does not say: *I am alone.*
He sees the gentle stir of birth
When morning purifies the earth;
He leans upon a gate and sees
The pastures, and the quiet trees.
Low, woody hill, with gracious bound,
Folds the still valley almost round;
The cuckoo, loud on some high lawn,
Is answer'd from the depth of dawn;
In the hedge straggling to the stream,
Pale, dew-drench'd, half-shut roses gleam;
But, where the farther side slopes down,
He sees the drowsy new-waked clown
In his white quaint-embroider'd frock
Make, whistling, tow'rd his mist-wreathed flock—
Slowly, behind his heavy tread,
The wet, flower'd grass heaves up its head.
Lean'd on his gate, he gazes—tears
Are in his eyes, and in his ears
The murmur of a thousand years.
Before him he sees life unroll,
A placid and continuous whole—
That general life, which does not cease,
Whose secret is not joy, but peace;

That life, whose dumb wish is not miss'd
If birth proceeds, if things subsist;
The life of plants, and stones, and rain,
The life he craves—if not in vain
Fate gave, what chance shall not control,
His sad lucidity of soul.

You listen—but that wandering smile,
Fausta, betrays you cold the while!
Your eyes pursue the bells of foam
Wash'd, eddying, from this bank, their home.
Those gipsies, so your thoughts I scan,
Are less, the poet more, than man.
They feel not, though they move and see;
Deeper the poet feels; but he
Breathes, when he will, immortal air,
Where Orpheus and where Homer are.
In the day's life, whose iron round
Hems us all in, he is not bound;
He leaves his kind, o'erleaps their pen,
And flees the common life of men.
He escapes thence, but we abide—
Not deep the poet sees, but wide.

The world in which we live and move
Outlasts aversion, outlasts love,
Outlasts each effort, interest, hope,
Remorse, grief, joy;—and were the scope
Of these affections wider made,
Man still would see, and see dismay'd,
Beyond his passion's widest range,
Far regions of eternal change.
Nay, and since death, which wipes out man,
Finds him with many an unsolved plan,
With much unknown, and much untried,
Wonder not dead, and thirst not dried,
Still gazing on the ever full
Eternal mundane spectacle—
This world in which we draw our breath,
In some sense, Fausta, outlasts death.

Blame thou not, therefore, him who dares
Judge vain beforehand human cares;
Whose natural insight can discern
What through experience others learn;
Who needs not love and power, to know
Love transient, power an unreal show;
Who treads at ease life's uncheer'd ways—
Him blame not, Fausta, rather praise!
Rather thyself for some aim pray
Nobler than this, to fill the day;
Rather that heart, which burns in thee,
Ask, not to amuse, but to set free;
Be passionate hopes not ill resign'd
For quiet, and a fearless mind.
And though fate grudge to thee and me
The poet's rapt security,
Yet they, believe me, who await
No gifts from chance, have conquer'd fate.
They, winning room to see and hear,
And to men's business not too near,
Through clouds of individual strife
Draw homeward to the general life.
Like leaves by suns not yet uncurl'd;
To the wise, foolish; to the world,
Weak;—yet not weak, I might reply,
Not foolish, Fausta, in His eye,
To whom each moment in its race,
Crowd as we will its neutral space,
Is but a quiet watershed
Whence, equally, the seas of life and death
 are fed.

Enough, we live!—and if a life,
With large results so little rife,
Though bearable, seem hardly worth
This pomp of worlds, this pain of birth;
Yet, Fausta, the mute turf we tread,
The solemn hills around us spread,
This stream which falls incessantly,
The strange-scrawl'd rocks, the lonely sky,
If I might lend their life a voice,
Seem to bear rather than rejoice.
And even could the intemperate prayer
Man iterates, while these forbear,
For movement, for an ampler sphere,
Pierce Fate's impenetrable ear;
Not milder is the general lot
Because our spirits have forgot,
In action's dizzying eddy whirl'd,
The something that infects the world.

1849

MEMORIAL VERSES

April, 1850

Goethe in Weimar sleeps, and Greece,
Long since, saw Byron's struggle cease.
But one such death remain'd to come;
The last poetic voice is dumb—
We stand to-day by Wordsworth's tomb.

When Byron's eyes were shut in death,
We bow'd our head and held our breath.
He taught us little; but our soul
Had *felt* him like the thunder's roll.
With shivering heart the strife we saw
Of passion with eternal law;
And yet with reverential awe
We watch'd the fount of fiery life
Which served for that Titanic strife.

When Goethe's death was told, we said:
Sunk, then, is Europe's sagest head.
Physician of the iron age,
Goethe has done his pilgrimage.
He took the suffering human race,
He read each wound, each weakness clear;
And struck his finger on the place,
And said: *Thou ailest here, and here!*
He look'd on Europe's dying hour
Of fitful dream and feverish power;
His eye plunged down the weltering strife,
The turmoil of expiring life—
He said: *The end is everywhere,*
Art still has truth, take refuge there!
And he was happy, if to know
Causes of things, and far below
His feet to see the lurid flow
Of terror, and insane distress,
And headlong fate, be happiness.

And Wordsworth!—Ah, pale ghosts, rejoice!
For never has such soothing voice
Been to your shadowy world convey'd,
Since erst, at morn, some wandering shade
Heard the clear song of Orpheus come
Through Hades, and the mournful gloom.
Wordsworth has gone from us—and ye,
Ah, may ye feel his voice as we!
He too upon a wintry clime
Had fallen—on this iron time
Of doubts, disputes, distractions, fears.
He found us when the age had bound
Our souls in its benumbing round;
He spoke, and loosed our heart in tears.
He laid us as we lay at birth
On the cool flowery lap of earth,
Smiles broke from us and we had ease;
The hills were round us, and the breeze
Went o'er the sun-lit fields again;
Our foreheads felt the wind and rain.
Our youth return'd; for there was shed
On spirits that had long been dead,
Spirits dried up and closely furl'd,
The freshness of the early world.

Ah! since dark days still bring to light
Man's prudence and man's fiery might,
Time may restore us in his course
Goethe's sage mind and Byron's force;
But where will Europe's latter hour
Again find Wordsworth's healing power?
Others will teach us how to dare,
And against fear our breast to steel;
Others will strengthen us to bear—
But who, ah! who, will make us feel?
The cloud of mortal destiny,
Others will front it fearlessly—
But who, like him, will put it by?

Keep fresh the grass upon his grave
O Rotha, with thy living wave!
Sing him thy best! for few or none
Hears thy voice right, now he is gone.

1850

LAST SONG OF CALLICLES

From *Empedocles on Etna*

THROUGH the black, rushing smoke-bursts,
Thick breaks the red flame;
All Etna heaves fiercely
Her forest-clothed frame.

Not here, O Apollo!
Are haunts meet for thee.
But, where Helicon breaks down
In cliff to the sea,

Where the moon-silver'd inlets
Send far their light voice
Up the still vale of Thisbe,
O speed, and rejoice!

On the sward at the cliff-top
Lie strewn the white flocks,
On the cliff-side the pigeons
Roost deep in the rocks.

In the moonlight the shepherds,
Soft lull'd by the rills,
Lie wrapt in their blankets
Asleep on the hills.

—What forms are these coming
So white through the gloom?
What garments out-glistening
The gold-flower'd broom?

What sweet-breathing presence
Out-perfumes the thyme?
What voices enrapture
The night's balmy prime?—

'Tis Apollo comes leading
His choir, the Nine.
—The leader is fairest,
But all are divine.

They are lost in the hollows!
They stream up again!
What seeks on this mountain
The glorified train?—

They bathe on this mountain,
In the spring by their road;
Then on to Olympus,
Their endless abode.

—Whose praise do they mention?
Of what is it told?—
What will be for ever;
What was from of old.

First hymn they the Father
Of all things; and then,
The rest of immortals,
The action of men.

The day in his hotness,
The strife with the palm;
The night in her silence,
The stars in their calm.

1852

From PARTING

Forgive me! forgive me!
Ah, Marguerite, fain
Would these arms reach to clasp thee!
But see! 'tis in vain.

In the void air, towards thee,
My stretch'd arms are cast;
But a sea rolls between us—
Our different past!

To the lips, ah! of others
Those lips have been prest,
And others, ere I was,
Were strain'd to that breast;

Far, far from each other
Our spirits have grown;
And what heart knows another?
Ah! who knows his own?

Blow, ye winds! lift me with you!
I come to the wild.
Fold closely, O Nature!
Thine arms round thy child.

To thee only God granted
A heart ever new—
To all always open,
To all always true.

Ah! calm me, restore me;
And dry up my tears
On thy high mountain-platforms,
Where morn first appears;

Where the white mists, for ever,
Are spread and upfurl'd—
In the stir of the forces
Whence issued the world.

1852

ISOLATION. TO MARGUERITE [1]

We were apart; yet, day by day,
I bade my heart more constant be.
I bade it keep the world away,
And grow a home for only thee;
Nor fear'd but thy love likewise grew,
Like mine, each day, more tried, more true.

The fault was grave! I might have known,
What far too soon, alas! I learn'd—
The heart can bind itself alone,
And faith may oft be unreturn'd.
Self-sway'd our feelings ebb and swell—
Thou lov'st no more;—Farewell! Farewell!

[1] In 1857, Arnold gathered the Marguerite poems together under the title, "Switzerland." This poem appeared for the first time in that year, preceding the earlier poem of 1852 now known as a continuation. The logic of subject matter rather than the strict chronology thus determines the placing of the poem.

Farewell!—and thou, thou lonely heart,
Which never yet without remorse
Even for a moment didst depart
From thy remote and sphered course
To haunt the place where passions reign—
Back to thy solitude again!

Back! with the conscious thrill of shame
Which Luna felt, that summer-night,
Flash through her pure immortal frame,
When she forsook the starry height
To hang over Endymion's sleep
Upon the pine-grown Latmian steep.

Yet she, chaste queen, had never proved
How vain a thing is mortal love,
Wandering in Heaven, far removed.
But thou hast long had place to prove
This truth—to prove, and make thine own:
"Thou hast been, shalt be, art, alone."

Or, if not quite alone, yet they
Which touch thee are unmating things—
Ocean and clouds and night and day;
Lorn autumns and triumphant springs;
And life, and others' joy and pain,
And love, if love, of happier men.

Of happier men—for they, at least,
Have *dream'd* two human hearts might blend
In one, and were through faith released
From isolation without end
Prolong'd; nor knew, although not less
Alone than thou, their loneliness.

1857

TO MARGUERITE—CONTINUED

Yes! in the sea of life enisled,
With echoing straits between us thrown,
Dotting the shoreless watery wild,
We mortal millions live *alone*.
The islands feel the enclasping flow,
And then their endless bounds they know.

But when the moon their hollows lights,
And they are swept by balms of spring,
And in their glens, on starry nights,
The nightingales divinely sing;
And lovely notes, from shore to shore,
Across the sounds and channels pour—

Oh! then a longing like despair
Is to their farthest caverns sent;
For surely once, they feel, we were
Parts of a single continent!
Now round us spreads the watery plain—
Oh might our marges meet again!

Who order'd, that their longing's fire
Should be, as soon as kindled, cool'd?
Who renders vain their deep desire?—
A God, a God their severance ruled!
And bade betwixt their shores to be
The unplumb'd, salt, estranging sea.

1852

DESPONDENCY

The thoughts that rain their steady glow
Like stars on life's cold sea,
Which others know, or say they know—
They never shone for me.

Thoughts light, like gleams, my spirit's sky,
But they will not remain.
They light me once, they hurry by;
And never come again.

1852

SELF-DECEPTION

Say, what blinds us, that we claim the glory
Of possessing powers not our share?
—Since man woke on earth, he knows his story,
But, before we woke on earth, we were.

Long, long since, undower'd yet, our spirit
Roam'd, ere birth, the treasuries of God;
Saw the gifts, the powers it might inherit,
Ask'd an outfit for its earthly road.

Then, as now, this tremulous, eager being
Strain'd and long'd and grasp'd each gift it saw;
Then, as now, a Power beyond our seeing
Staved us back, and gave our choice the law.

Ah, whose hand that day through Heaven guided
Man's new spirit, since it was not we?
Ah, who sway'd our choice, and who decided
What our gifts, and what our wants should be?

For, alas! he left us each retaining
Shreds of gifts which he refused in full.
Still these waste us with their hopeless straining,
Still the attempt to use them proves them null.

And on earth we wander, groping, reeling;
Powers stir in us, stir and disappear.
Ah! and he, who placed our master-feeling,
Fail'd to place that master-feeling clear.

We but dream we have our wish'd-for powers,
Ends we seek we never shall attain.
Ah! *some* power exists there, which is ours?
Some end is there, we indeed may gain?

1852

SELF-DEPENDENCE

WEARY of myself, and sick of asking
What I am, and what I ought to be,
At this vessel's prow I stand, which bears me
Forwards, forwards, o'er the starlit sea.

And a look of passionate desire
O'er the sea and to the stars I send:
"Ye who from my childhood up have calm'd me,
Calm me, ah, compose me to the end!

"Ah, once more," I cried, "ye stars, ye waters,
On my heart your mighty charm renew;
Still, still let me, as I gaze upon you,
Feel my soul becoming vast like you!"

From the intense, clear, star-sown vault of heaven,
Over the lit sea's unquiet way,
In the rustling night-air came the answer:
"Wouldst thou *be* as these are? *Live* as they.

"Unaffrighted by the silence round them,
Undistracted by the sights they see,
These demand not that the things without them
Yield them love, amusement, sympathy.

"And with joy the stars perform their shining,
And the sea its long moon-silver'd roll;
For self-poised they live, nor pine with noting
All the fever of some differing soul.

"Bounded by themselves, and unregardful
In what state God's other works may be,
In their own tasks all their powers pouring,
These attain the mighty life you see."

O air-born voice! long since, severely clear,
A cry like thine in mine own heart I hear:
"Resolve to be thyself; and know that he,
Who finds himself, loses his misery!"

1852

MORALITY

WE cannot kindle when we will
The fire which in the heart resides;
The spirit bloweth and is still,
In mystery our soul abides.
  But tasks in hours of insight will'd
  Can be through hours of gloom fulfill'd.

With aching hands and bleeding feet
We dig and heap, lay stone on stone;
We bear the burden and the heat
Of the long day, and wish 'twere done.
  Not till the hours of light return,
  All we have built do we discern.

Then, when the clouds are off the soul,
When thou dost bask in Nature's eye,
Ask, how *she* view'd thy self-control,
Thy struggling, task'd morality—
  Nature, whose free, light, cheerful air,
  Oft made thee, in thy gloom, despair.

And she, whose censure thou dost dread,
Whose eye thou wast afraid to seek,
See, on her face a glow is spread,
A strong emotion on her cheek!
  "Ah, child!" she cries, "that strife divine,
  Whence was it, for it is not mine?

"There is no effort on *my* brow—
I do not strive, I do not weep;
I rush with the swift spheres and glow
In joy, and when I will, I sleep.
  Yet that severe, that earnest air,
  I saw, I felt it once—but where?

"I knew not yet the gauge of time,
Nor wore the manacles of space;
I felt it in some other clime,
I saw it in some other place.
  'Twas when the heavenly house I trod,
  And lay upon the breast of God."

1852

A SUMMER NIGHT

In the deserted, moon-blanch'd street,
How lonely rings the echo of my feet!
Those windows, which I gaze at, frown,
Silent and white, unopening down,
Repellent as the world;—but see,
A break between the housetops shows
The moon! and, lost behind her, fading dim
Into the dewy dark obscurity
Down at the far horizon's rim,
Doth a whole tract of heaven disclose!

And to my mind the thought
Is on a sudden brought
Of a past night, and a far different scene.
Headlands stood out into the moonlit deep
As clearly as at noon;
The spring-tide's brimming flow
Heaved dazzlingly between;
Houses, with long white sweep,
Girdled the glistening bay;
Behind, through the soft air,
The blue haze-cradled mountains spread away,
That night was far more fair—
But the same restless pacings to and fro,
And the same vainly throbbing heart was there,
And the same bright, calm moon.

And the calm moonlight seems to say:
Hast thou then still the old unquiet breast,
Which neither deadens into rest,
Nor ever feels the fiery glow
That whirls the spirit from itself away,
But fluctuates to and fro,
Never by passion quite possess'd
And never quite benumb'd by the world's sway?—
And I, I know not if to pray
Still to be what I am, or yield and be
Like all the other men I see.

For most men in a brazen prison live,
Where, in the sun's hot eye,
With heads bent o'er their toil, they languidly
Their lives to some unmeaning taskwork give,
Dreaming of nought beyond their prison-wall.
And as, year after year,
Fresh products of their barren labour fall
From their tired hands, and rest
Never yet comes more near,
Gloom settles slowly down over their breast;
And while they try to stem
The waves of mournful thought by which they are prest,
Death in their prison reaches them,
Unfreed, having seen nothing, still unblest.

And the rest, a few,
Escape their prison and depart
On the wide ocean of life anew.
There the freed prisoner, where'er his heart
Listeth, will sail;
Nor doth he know how there prevail,
Despotic on that sea,
Trade-winds which cross it from eternity.
Awhile he holds some false way, undebarr'd
By thwarting signs, and braves
The freshening wind and blackening waves.
And then the tempest strikes him; and between
The lightning-bursts is seen
Only a driving wreck,
And the pale master on his spar-strewn deck
With anguish'd face and flying hair
Grasping the rudder hard,
Still bent to make some port he knows not where,
Still standing for some false, impossible shore.
And sterner comes the roar
Of sea and wind, and through the deepening gloom
Fainter and fainter wreck and helmsman loom,
And he too disappears, and comes no more.

Is there no life, but these alone?
Madman or slave, must man be one?

Plainness and clearness without shadow of stain!
Clearness divine!
Ye heavens, whose pure dark regions have no sign
Of languor, though so calm, and, though so great,
Are yet untroubled and unpassionate;
Who, though so noble, share in the world's toil,
And, though so task'd, keep free from dust and soil!
I will not say that your mild deeps retain
A tinge, it may be, of their silent pain

Who have long'd deeply once, and long'd in vain—
But I will rather say that you remain
A world above man's head, to let him see
How boundless might his soul's horizons be,
How vast, yet of what clear transparency!
How it were good to abide there, and breathe free;
How fair a lot to fill
Is left to each man still!

1852

THE BURIED LIFE

LIGHT flows our war of mocking words, and yet,
Behold, with tears mine eyes are wet!
I feel a nameless sadness o'er me roll.
Yes, yes, we know that we can jest,
We know, we know that we can smile!
But there's a something in this breast,
To which thy light words bring no rest,
And thy gay smiles no anodyne.
Give me thy hand, and hush awhile,
And turn those limpid eyes on mine,
And let me read there, love! thy inmost soul.

Alas! is even love too weak
To unlock the heart, and let it speak?
Are even lovers powerless to reveal
To one another what indeed they feel?
I knew the mass of men conceal'd
Their thoughts, for fear that if reveal'd
They would by other men be met
With blank indifference, or with blame reproved;
I knew they lived and moved
Trick'd in disguises, alien to the rest
Of men, and alien to themselves—and yet
The same heart beats in every human breast!

But we, my love!—doth a like spell benumb
Our hearts, our voices?—must we too be dumb?

Ah! well for us, if even we,
Even for a moment, can get free
Our heart, and have our lips unchain'd;
For that which seals them hath been deep-ordain'd!

Fate, which foresaw
How frivolous a baby man would be—
By what distractions he would be possess'd,
How he would pour himself in every strife,
And well-nigh change his own identity—
That it might keep from his capricious play
His genuine self, and force him to obey
Even in his own despite his being's law,
Bade through the deep recesses of our breast
The unregarded river of our life
Pursue with indiscernible flow its way;
And that we should not see
The buried stream, and seem to be
Eddying at large in blind uncertainty,
Though driving on with it eternally.

But often, in the world's most crowded streets,
But often, in the din of strife,
There rises an unspeakable desire
After the knowledge of our buried life;
A thirst to spend our fire and restless force
In tracking out our true, original course;
A longing to inquire
Into the mystery of this heart which beats
So wild, so deep in us—to know
Whence our lives come and where they go.
And many a man in his own breast then delves,
But deep enough, alas! none ever mines.
And we have been on many thousand lines,
And we have shown, on each, spirit and power;
But hardly have we, for one little hour,
Been on our own line, have we been ourselves—
Hardly had skill to utter one of all
The nameless feelings that course through our breast,
But they course on for ever unexpress'd.
And long we try in vain to speak and act
Our hidden self, and what we say and do
Is eloquent, is well—but 'tis not true!
And then we will no more be rack'd
With inward striving, and demand
Of all the thousand nothings of the hour
Their stupefying power;
Ah yes, and they benumb us at our call!
Yet still, from time to time, vague and forlorn,
From the soul's subterranean depth upborne
As from an infinitely distant land,
Come airs, and floating echoes, and convey
A melancholy into all our day.

Only—but this is rare—
When a belovéd hand is laid in ours,
When, jaded with the rush and glare
Of the interminable hours,
Our eyes can in another's eyes read clear,
When our world-deafen'd ear
Is by the tones of a loved voice caress'd—
A bolt is shot back somewhere in our breast,
And a lost pulse of feeling stirs again.
The eye sinks inward, and the heart lies plain,
And what we mean, we say, and what we would, we know.
A man becomes aware of his life's flow,
And hears its winding murmur; and he sees
The meadows where it glides, the sun, the breeze.
And there arrives a lull in the hot race
Wherein he doth for ever chase
That flying and elusive shadow, rest.
An air of coolness plays upon his face,
And an unwonted calm pervades his breast.
And then he thinks he knows
The hills where his life rose,
And the sea where it goes.

1852

STANZAS IN MEMORY OF THE AUTHOR OF "OBERMANN"

November, 1849

In front the awful Alpine track
Crawls up its rocky stair;
The autumn storm-winds drive the rack,
Close o'er it, in the air.

Behind are the abandon'd baths
Mute in their meadows lone;
The leaves are on the valley-paths,
The mists are on the Rhone—

The white mists rolling like a sea!
I hear the torrents roar.
—Yes, Obermann, all speaks of thee;
I feel thee near once more!

I turn thy leaves! I feel their breath
Once more upon me roll;
That air of languor, cold, and death,
Which brooded o'er thy soul.

Fly hence, poor wretch, whoe'er thou art,
Condemn'd to cast about,
All shipwreck in thy own weak heart,
For comfort from without!

A fever in these pages burns
Beneath the calm they feign;
A wounded human spirit turns,
Here, on its bed of pain.

Yes, though the virgin mountain-air
Fresh through these pages blows;
Though to these leaves the glaciers spare
The soul of their white snows;

Though here a mountain-murmur swells
Of many a dark-bough'd pine;
Though, as you read, you hear the bells
Of the high-pasturing kine—

Yet, through the hum of torrent lone,
And brooding mountain-bee,
There sobs I know not what ground-tone
Of human agony.

Is it for this, because the sound
Is fraught too deep with pain,
That, Obermann! the world around
So little loves thy strain?

Some secrets may the poet tell,
For the world loves new ways;
To tell too deep ones is not well—
It knows not what he says.

Yet, of the spirits who have reign'd
In this our troubled day,
I know but two, who have attain'd,
Save thee, to see their way.

By England's lakes, in grey old age,
His quiet home one keeps;
And one, the strong much-toiling sage,
In German Weimar sleeps.

But Wordsworth's eyes avert their ken
From half of human fate;
And Goethe's course few sons of men
May think to emulate.

For he pursued a lonely road,
His eyes on Nature's plan;
Neither made man too much a God,
Nor God too much a man.

Strong was he, with a spirit free
From mists, and sane, and clear;
Clearer, how much! than ours—yet we
Have a worse course to steer.

For though his manhood bore the blast
Of a tremendous time,
Yet in a tranquil world was pass'd
His tenderer youthful prime.

But we, brought forth and rear'd in hours
Of change, alarm, surprise—
What shelter to grow ripe is ours?
What leisure to grow wise?

Like children bathing on the shore,
Buried a wave beneath,
The second wave succeeds, before
We have had time to breathe.

Too fast we live, too much are tried,
Too harass'd, to attain
Wordsworth's sweet calm, or Goethe's wide
And luminous view to gain.

And then we turn, thou sadder sage,
To thee! we feel thy spell!
—The hopeless tangle of our age,
Thou too hast scann'd it well!

Immoveable thou sittest, still
As death, composed to bear!
Thy head is clear, thy feeling chill,
And icy thy despair.

Yes, as the son of Thetis said,
I hear thee saying now:
Greater by far than thou art dead;
Strive not! die also thou!

Ah! two desires toss about
The poet's feverish blood.
One drives him to the world without,
And one to solitude.

The glow, he cries, *the thrill of life*,
Where, where do these abound?—
Not in the world, not in the strife
Of men, shall they be found.

He who hath watch'd, not shared, the strife,
Knows how the day hath gone.
He only lives with the world's life,
Who hath renounced his own.

To thee we come, then! Clouds are roll'd
Where thou, O seer! art set;
Thy realm of thought is drear and cold—
The world is colder yet!

And thou hast pleasures, too, to share
With those who come to thee—
Balms floating on thy mountain-air,
And healing sights to see.

How often, where the slopes are green
On Jaman, hast thou sate
By some high chalet-door, and seen
The summer-day grow late;

And darkness steal o'er the wet grass
With the pale crocus starr'd,
And reach that glimmering sheet of glass
Beneath the piny sward,

Lake Leman's waters, far below!
And watch'd the rosy light
Fade from the distant peaks of snow;
And on the air of night

Heard accents of the eternal tongue
Through the pine branches play—
Listen'd, and felt thyself grow young!
Listen'd and wept——Away!

Away the dreams that but deceive
And thou, sad guide, adieu!
I go, fate drives me; but I leave
Half of my life with you.

We, in some unknown Power's employ,
Move on a rigorous line;
Can neither, when we will, enjoy,
Nor, when we will, resign.

I in the world must live; but thou,
Thou melancholy shade!
Wilt not, if thou canst see me now,
Condemn me, nor upbraid.

For thou art gone away from earth,
And place with those dost claim,
The Children of the Second Birth,
Whom the world could not tame;

And with that small, transfigured band,
Whom many a different way
Conducted to their common land,
Thou learn'st to think as they.

Christian and pagan, king and slave,
Soldier and anchorite,
Distinctions we esteem so grave,
Are nothing in their sight.

They do not ask, who pined unseen,
Who was on action hurl'd,
Whose one bond is, that all have been
Unspotted by the world.

There without anger thou wilt see
Him who obeys thy spell
No more, so he but rest, like thee,
Unsoil'd!—and so, farewell.

Farewell!—Whether thou now liest near
That much-loved inland sea,
The ripples of whose blue waves cheer
Vevey and Meillerie:

And in that gracious region bland,
Where with clear-rustling wave
The scented pines of Switzerland
Stand dark round thy green grave,

Between the dusty vineyard-walls
Issuing on that green place
The early peasant still recalls
The pensive stranger's face,

And stoops to clear thy moss-grown date
Ere he plods on again;—
Or whether, by maligner fate,
Among the swarms of men,

Where between granite terraces
The blue Seine rolls her wave,
The Capital of Pleasure sees
The hardly-heard-of grave;—

Farewell! Under the sky we part,
In the stern Alpine dell.
O unstrung will! O broken heart!
A last, a last farewell!

1852

LINES

WRITTEN IN KENSINGTON GARDENS

In this lone, open glade I lie,
Screen'd by deep boughs on either hand;
And at its end, to stay the eye,
Those black-crown'd, red-boled pine-trees stand!

Birds here make song, each bird has his,
Across the girdling city's hum.
How green under the boughs it is!
How thick the tremulous sheep-cries come!

Sometimes a child will cross the glade
To take his nurse his broken toy;
Sometimes a thrush flit overhead
Deep in her unknown day's employ.

Here at my feet what wonders pass,
What endless, active life is here!
What blowing daisies, fragrant grass!
An air-stirr'd forest, fresh and clear.

Scarce fresher is the mountain-sod
Where the tired angler lies, stretch'd out,
And, eased of basket and of rod,
Counts his day's spoil, the spotted trout.

In the huge world, which roars hard by,
Be others happy if they can!
But in my helpless cradle I
Was breathed on by the rural Pan.

I, on men's impious uproar hurl'd,
Think often, as I hear them rave,
That peace has left the upper world
And now keeps only in the grave.

Yet here is peace for ever new!
When I who watch them am away,
Still all things in this glade go through
The changes of their quiet day.

Then to their happy rest they pass!
The flowers upclose, the birds are fed,
The night comes down upon the grass,
The child sleeps warmly in his bed.

Calm soul of all things! make it mine
To feel, amid the city's jar,
That there abides a peace of thine,
Man did not make, and cannot mar.

The will to neither strive nor cry,
The power to feel with others give!
Calm, calm me more! nor let me die
Before I have begun to live.

1852

REVOLUTIONS

Before man parted for this earthly strand,
While yet upon the verge of heaven he stood,
God put a heap of letters in his hand,
And bade him make with them what word he could.

And man has turn'd them many times; made Greece,
Rome, England, France;—yes, nor in vain essay'd
Way after way, changes that never cease!
The letters have combined, something was made.

But ah! an inextinguishable sense
Haunts him that he has not made what he should;
That he has still, though old, to recommence,
Since he has not yet found the word God would.

And empire after empire, at their height
Of sway, have felt this boding sense come on;
Have felt their huge frames not constructed right,
And droop'd, and slowly died upon their throne.

One day, thou say'st, there will at last appear
The word, the order, which God meant should be.
—Ah! we shall know *that* well when it comes near;
The band will quit man's heart, he will breathe free.

1852

THE YOUTH OF NATURE

Raised are the dripping oars,
Silent the boat! the lake,
Lovely and soft as a dream,
Swims in the sheen of the moon.
The mountains stand at its head
Clear in the pure June-night,
But the valleys are flooded with haze.
Rydal and Fairfield are there;
In the shadow Wordsworth lies dead.
So it is, so it will be for aye.
Nature is fresh as of old,
Is lovely; a mortal is dead.

The spots which recall him survive,
For he lent a new life to these hills.
The Pillar still broods o'er the fields
Which border Ennerdale Lake,
And Egremont sleeps by the sea.
The gleam of The Evening Star
Twinkles on Grasmere no more,
But ruin'd and solemn and grey
The sheepfold of Michael survives;
And, far to the south, the heath
Still blows in the Quantock coombs,
By the favourite waters of Ruth.
These survive!—yet not without pain,
Pain and dejection to-night,
Can I feel that their poet is gone.

He grew old in an age he condemn'd.
He look'd on the rushing decay
Of the times which had shelter'd his youth
Felt the dissolving throes
Of a social order he loved;
Outlived his brethren, his peers;
And, like the Theban seer,
Died in his enemies' day.

Cold bubbled the spring of Tilphusa,
Copais lay bright in the moon,
Helicon glass'd in the lake
Its firs, and afar rose the peaks
Of Parnassus, snowily clear;
Thebes was behind him in flames,
And the clang of arms in his ear,
When his awe-struck captors led
The Theban seer to the spring.
Tiresias drank and died.
Nor did reviving Thebes
See such a prophet again.

Well may we mourn, when the head
Of a sacred poet lies low
In an age which can rear them no more!
The complaining millions of men
Darken in labour and pain;
But he was a priest to us all
Of the wonder and bloom of the world,
Which we saw with his eyes, and were glad.
He is dead, and the fruit-bearing day
Of his race is past on the earth;
And darkness returns to our eyes.

For, oh! is it you, is it you,
Moonlight, and shadow, and lake,
And mountains, that fill us with joy,
Or the poet who sings you so well?
Is it you, O beauty, O grace,
O charm, O romance, that we feel,
Or the voice which reveals what you are?
Are ye, like daylight and sun,
Shared and rejoiced in by all?
Or are ye immersed in the mass
Of matter, and hard to extract,
Or sunk at the core of the world
Too deep for the most to discern?
Like stars in the deep of the sky,
Which arise on the glass of the sage,
But are lost when their watcher is gone.

"They are here"—I heard, as men heard
In Mysian Ida the voice
Of the Mighty Mother, or Crete,
The murmur of Nature reply—
"Loveliness, magic, and grace,
They are here! they are set in the world,
They abide; and the finest of souls
Hath not been thrill'd by them all,
Nor the dullest been dead to them quite.
The poet who sings them may die,
But they are immortal and live,
For they are the life of the world.
Will ye not learn it, and know,
When ye mourn that a poet is dead,
That the singer was less than his themes,
Life, and emotion, and I?

"More than the singer are these.
Weak is the tremor of pain
That thrills in his mournfullest chord
To that which once ran through his soul.
Cold the elation of joy
In his gladdest, airiest song,
To that which of old in his youth
Fill'd him and made him divine.
Hardly his voice at its best
Gives us a sense of the awe,
The vastness, the grandeur, the gloom
Of the unlit gulph of himself.

"Ye know not yourselves; and your bards—
The clearest, the best, who have read
Most in themselves—have beheld
Less than they left unreveal'd.
Ye express not yourselves;—can you make
With marble, with colour, with word,
What charm'd you in others re-live?
Can thy pencil, O artist! restore
The figure, the bloom of thy love,
As she was in her morning of spring?
Canst thou paint the ineffable smile
Of her eyes as they rested on thine?
Can the image of life have the glow,
The motion of life itself?

"Yourselves and your fellows ye know not; and me,
The mateless, the one, will ye know?
Will ye scan me, and read me, and tell
Of the thoughts that ferment in my breast,
My longing, my sadness, my joy?
Will ye claim for your great ones the gift
To have render'd the gleam of my skies,
To have echoed the moan of my seas,
Utter'd the voice of my hills?
When your great ones depart, will ye say:
All things have suffer'd a loss,
Nature is hid in their grave?

"Race after race, man after man,
Have thought that my secret was theirs,
Have dream'd that I lived but for them,
That they were my glory and joy.
—They are dust, they are changed, they are gone!
I remain."

1852

THE FUTURE

A WANDERER is man from his birth.
He was born in a ship
On the breast of the river of Time;
Brimming with wonder and joy
He spreads out his arms to the light,
Rivets his gaze on the banks of the stream.

As what he sees is, so have his thoughts been.
Whether he wakes,
Where the snowy mountainous pass,
Echoing the screams of the eagles,
Hems in its gorges the bed
Of the new-born clear-flowing stream;
Whether he first sees light
Where the river in gleaming rings
Sluggishly winds through the plain;

Whether in sound of the swallowing sea—
As is the world on the banks,
So is the mind of the man.

Vainly does each, as he glides,
Fable and dream
Of the lands which the river of Time
Had left ere he woke on its breast,
Or shall reach when his eyes have been closed.
Only the tract where he sails
He wots of; only the thoughts,
Raised by the objects he passes, are his.

Who can see the green earth any more
As she was by the sources of Time?
Who imagines her fields as they lay
In the sunshine, unworn by the plough?
Who thinks as they thought,
The tribes who then roam'd on her breast,
Her vigorous, primitive sons?

What girl
Now reads in her bosom as clear
As Rebekah read, when she sate
At eve by the palm-shaded well?
Who guards in her breast
As deep, as pellucid a spring
Of feeling, as tranquil, as sure?

What bard,
At the height of his vision, can deem
Of God, of the world, of the soul,
With a plainness as near,
As flashing as Moses felt
When he lay in the night by his flock
On the starlit Arabian waste?
Can rise and obey
The beck of the Spirit like him?

This tract which the river of Time
Now flows through with us, is the plain.
Gone is the calm of its earlier shore.
Border'd by cities and hoarse
With a thousand cries is its stream.
And we on its breast, our minds
Are confused as the cries which we hear,
Changing and shot as the sights which we see.

And we say that repose has fled
For ever the course of the river of Time.
That cities will crowd to its edge
In a blacker, incessanter line;
That the din will be more on its banks,
Denser the trade on its stream,
Flatter the plain where it flows,
Fiercer the sun overhead.
That never will those on its breast
See an ennobling sight,
Drink of the feeling of quiet again.

But what was before us we know not,
And we know not what shall succeed.

Haply, the river of Time—
As it grows, as the towns on its marge
Fling their wavering lights
On a wider, statelier stream—
May acquire, if not the calm
Of its early mountainous shore,
Yet a solemn peace of its own.

And the width of the waters, the hush
Of the grey expanse where he floats,
Freshening its current and spotted with foam
As it draws to the Ocean, may strike
Peace to the soul of the man on its breast—
As the pale waste widens around him,
As the banks fade dimmer away,
As the stars come out, and the night-wind
Brings up the stream
Murmurs and scents of the infinite sea.

1852

LONGING

COME to me in my dreams, and then
By day I shall be well again!
For then the night will more than pay
The hopeless longing of the day.

Come, as thou cam'st a thousand times,
A messenger from radiant climes,
And smile on thy new world, and be
As kind to others as to me!

Or, as thou never cam'st in sooth,
Come now, and let me dream it truth;
And part my hair, and kiss my brow,
And say: *My love! why sufferest thou?*

Come to me in my dreams, and then
By day I shall be well again!
For then the night will more than pay
The hopeless longing of the day.

1852

Come to me in my dreams, and then
By day I shall be well again.
For then the night will more than pay
The hopeless longing of the day.

Come, as thou cam'st a thousand times,
A messenger from radiant climes,
And smile on thy new world, and be
As kind to others as to me.

Or, as thou never cam'st in sooth,
Come now, and let me deem it truth.
And part my hair, and kiss my brow,
And say, "My friend, why sufferest thou?"

Come to me in my dreams and then
By day I shall be well again.
For then the night will more than pay
The hopeless longing of the day.

A Copy of "Longing" in Arnold's Handwriting. (See Appendix I.)

TRISTRAM AND ISEULT

I

Tristram

Tristram

Is she not come? The messenger was sure.
Prop me upon the pillows once again—
Raise me, my page! this cannot long endure.
—Christ, what a night! how the sleet whips the pane!
What lights will those out to the northward be?

The Page

The lanterns of the fishing-boats at sea.

Tristram

Soft—who is that, stands by the dying fire?

The Page

Iseult.

Tristram

Ah! not the Iseult I desire.

* * *

What Knight is this so weak and pale,
Though the locks are yet brown on his noble head,
Propt on pillows in his bed,
Gazing seaward for the light
Of some ship that fights the gale
On this wild December night?
Over the sick man's feet is spread
A dark green forest-dress;
A gold harp leans against the bed,
Ruddy in the fire's light.
I know him by his harp of gold,
Famous in Arthur's court of old;
I know him by his forest-dress—
The peerless hunter, harper, knight,
Tristram of Lyoness.

What Lady is this, whose silk attire
Gleams so rich in the light of the fire?
The ringlets on her shoulders lying
In their flitting lustre vying
With the clasp of burnish'd gold
Which her heavy robe doth hold.
Her looks are mild, her fingers slight
As the driven snow are white;
But her cheeks are sunk and pale.
Is it that the bleak sea-gale
Beating from the Atlantic sea
On this coast of Brittany,
Nips too keenly the sweet flower?
Is it that a deep fatigue
Hath come on her, a chilly fear,
Passing all her youthful hour
Spinning with her maidens here,
Listlessly through the window-bars
Gazing seawards many a league,
From her lonely shore-built tower,
While the knights are at the wars?
Or, perhaps, has her young heart
Felt already some deeper smart,
Of those that in secret the heart-strings rive,
Leaving her sunk and pale, though fair?
Who is this snowdrop by the sea?—
I know her by her mildness rare,
Her snow-white hands, her golden hair;
I know her by her rich silk dress,
And her fragile loveliness—
The sweetest Christian soul alive,
Iseult of Brittany.

Iseult of Brittany?—but where
Is that other Iseult fair,
That proud, first Iseult, Cornwall's queen?
She, whom Tristram's ship of yore
From Ireland to Cornwall bore,
To Tyntagel, to the side
Of King Marc, to be his bride?
She who, as they voyaged, quaff'd
With Tristram that spiced magic draught,
Which since then for ever rolls
Through their blood, and binds their souls,
Working love, but working teen?—
There were two Iseults who did sway
Each her hour of Tristram's day;
But one possess'd his waning time,
The other his resplendent prime.
Behold her here, the patient flower,
Who possess'd his darker hour!
Iseult of the Snow-White Hand
Watches pale by Tristram's bed.
She is here who had his gloom,
Where art thou who hadst his bloom?
One such kiss as those of yore

Might thy dying knight restore!
Does the love-draught work no more?
Art thou cold, or false, or dead,
Iseult of Ireland?

* * *

Loud howls the wind, sharp patters the rain,
And the knight sinks back on his pillows again.
He is weak with fever and pain,
And his spirit is not clear.
Hark! he mutters in his sleep,
As he wanders far from here,
Changes place and time of year,
And his closéd eye doth sweep
O'er some fair unwintry sea,
Not this fierce Atlantic deep,
While he mutters brokenly:—

Tristram

The calm sea shines, loose hang the vessel's sails;
Before us are the sweet green fields of Wales,
And overhead the cloudless sky of May.—
"*Ah, would I were in those green fields at play,*
Not pent on ship-board this delicious day!
Tristram, I pray thee, of thy courtesy,
Reach me my golden phial stands by thee,
But pledge me in it first for courtesy.—"
Ha! dost thou start? are thy lips blanch'd like mine?
Child, 'tis no true draught this, 'tis poison'd wine!
Iseult! . . .

* * *

Ah, sweet angels, let him dream!
Keep his eyelids! let him seem
Not this fever-wasted wight
Thinn'd and paled before his time,
But the brilliant youthful knight
In the glory of his prime,
Sitting in the gilded barge,
At thy side, thou lovely charge,
Bending gaily o'er thy hand,
Iseult of Ireland!
And she too, that princess fair,
If her bloom be now less rare,
Let her have her youth again—
Let her be as she was then!
Let her have her proud dark eyes,
And her petulant quick replies—
Let her sweep her dazzling hand
With its gesture of command,
And shake back her raven hair
With the old imperious air!
As of old, so let her be,
That first Iseult, princess bright,
Chatting with her youthful knight
As he steers her o'er the sea,
Quitting at her father's will
The green isle where she was bred,
And her bower in Ireland,
For the surge-beat Cornish strand;
Where the prince whom she must wed
Dwells on loud Tyntagel's hill,
High above the sounding sea.
And that potion rare her mother
Gave her, that her future lord,
Gave her, that King Marc and she,
Might drink it on their marriage-day,
And for ever love each other—
Let her, as she sits on board,
Ah, sweet saints, unwittingly!
See it shine, and take it up,
And to Tristram laughing say:
"Sir Tristram, of thy courtesy,
Pledge me in my golden cup!"
Let them drink it—let their hands
Tremble, and their cheeks be flame,
As they feel the fatal bands
Of a love they dare not name,
With a wild delicious pain,
Twine about their hearts again!
Let the early summer be
Once more round them, and the sea
Blue, and o'er its mirror kind
Let the breath of the May-wind,
Wandering through their drooping sails,
Die on the green fields of Wales!
Let a dream like this restore
What his eye must see no more!

Tristram

Chill blows the wind, the pleasaunce-walks are drear—
Madcap, what jest was this, to meet me here?
Were feet like those made for so wild a way?
The southern winter-parlour, by my fay,
Had been the likeliest trysting-place to-day!
"*Tristram!—nay, nay—thou must not take my hand!—*
Tristram!—sweet love!—we are betray'd—out-plann'd.

Fly—save thyself—save me!—I dare not stay."—
One last kiss first!—"*'Tis vain—to horse—away!*"

* * *

Ah! sweet saints, his dream doth move
Faster surely than it should,
From the fever in his blood!
All the spring-time of his love
Is already gone and past,
And instead thereof is seen
Its winter, which endureth still—
Tyntagel on its surge-beat hill,
The pleasaunce-walks, the weeping queen,
The flying leaves, the straining blast,
And that long, wild kiss—their last.
And this rough December-night,
And his burning fever-pain,
Mingle with his hurrying dream,
Till they rule it, till he seem
The press'd fugitive again,
The love-desperate banish'd knight
With a fire in his brain
Flying o'er the stormy main.
—Whither does he wander now?
Haply in his dreams the wind
Wafts him here, and lets him find
The lovely orphan child again
In her castle by the coast;
The youngest, fairest chatelaine,
Whom this realm of France can boast,
Our snowdrop by the Atlantic sea,
Iseult of Brittany.
And—for through the haggard air,
The stain'd arms, the matted hair
Of that stranger-knight ill-starr'd,
There gleam'd something, which recall'd
The Tristram who in better days
Was Launcelot's guest at Joyous Gard—
Welcomed here, and here install'd,
Tended of his fever here,
Haply he seems again to move
His young guardian's heart with love;
In his exiled loneliness,
In his stately, deep distress,
Without a word, without a tear.
—Ah! 'tis well he should retrace
His tranquil life in this lone place;
His gentle bearing at the side
Of his timid youthful bride;
His long rambles by the shore
On winter-evenings, when the roar
Of the near waves came, sadly grand,
Through the dark, up the drown'd sand,
Or his endless reveries
In the woods, where the gleams play
On the grass under the trees,
Passing the long summer's day
Idle as a mossy stone
In the forest-depths alone,
The chase neglected, and his hound
Couch'd beside him on the ground.
—Ah! what trouble's on his brow?
Hither let him wander now;
Hither, to the quiet hours
Pass'd among these heaths of ours
By the grey Atlantic sea;
Hours, if not of ecstasy,
From violent anguish surely free!

Tristram

All red with blood the whirling river flows,
The wide plain rings, the dazed air throbs with blows.
Upon us are the chivalry of Rome—
Their spears are down, their steeds are bathed in foam.
"Up, Tristram, up," men cry, "thou moon-struck knight!
What foul fiend rides thee? On into the fight!"
—Above the din her voice is in my ears;
I see her form glide through the crossing spears.—
Iseult! . . .

* * *

Ah! he wanders forth again;
We cannot keep him; now, as then,
There's a secret in his breast
Which will never let him rest.
These musing fits in the green wood
They cloud the brain, they dull the blood!
—His sword is sharp, his horse is good;
Beyond the mountains will he see
The famous towns of Italy,
And label with the blessed sign
The heathen Saxons on the Rhine.
At Arthur's side he fights once more
With the Roman Emperor.
There's many a gay knight where he goes
Will help him to forget his care;

The march, the leaguer, Heaven's blithe air,
The neighing steeds, the ringing blows—
Sick pining comes not where these are.
Ah! what boots it, that the jest
Lightens every other brow,
What, that every other breast
Dances as the trumpets blow,
If one's own heart beats not light
On the waves of the toss'd fight,
If oneself cannot get free
From the clog of misery?
Thy lovely youthful wife grows pale
Watching by the salt sea-tide
With her children at her side
For the gleam of thy white sail.
Home, Tristram, to thy halls again!
To our lonely sea complain,
To our forests tell thy pain!

Tristram

All round the forest sweeps off, black in shade,
But it is moonlight in the open glade;
And in the bottom of the glade shine clear
The forest-chapel and the fountain near.
—I think, I have a fever in my blood;
Come, let me leave the shadow of this wood,
Ride down, and bathe my hot brow in the flood.
—Mild shines the cold spring in the moon's clear light;
God! 'tis *her* face plays in the waters bright.
"Fair love," she says, "canst thou forget so soon,
At this soft hour, under this sweet moon?"—
Iseult! . . .

* * *

Ah, poor soul! if this be so,
Only death can balm thy woe.
The solitudes of the green wood
Had no medicine for thy mood;
The rushing battle clear'd thy blood
As little as did solitude.
—Ah! his eyelids slowly break
Their hot seals, and let him wake;
What new change shall we now see?
A happier? Worse it cannot be.

Tristram

Is my page here? Come, turn me to the fire!
Upon the window-panes the moon shines bright;
The wind is down—but she'll not come to-night.
Ah no! she is asleep in Cornwall now,
Far hence; her dreams are fair—smooth is her brow.
Of me she recks not, nor my vain desire.
—I have had dreams, I have had dreams, my page,
Would take a score years from a strong man's age;
And with a blood like mine, will leave, I fear,
Scant leisure for a second messenger.
—My princess, art thou there? Sweet, do not wait!
To bed, and sleep! my fever is gone by;
To-night my page shall keep me company.
Where do the children sleep? kiss them for me!
Poor child, thou art almost as pale as I;
This comes of nursing long and watching late.
To bed—good night!

* * *

She left the gleam-lit fireplace,
She came to the bed-side;
She took his hands in hers—her tears
Down on his wasted fingers rain'd.
She raised her eyes upon his face
Not with a look of wounded pride,
A look as if the heart complained—
Her look was like a sad embrace;
The gaze of one who can divine
A grief, and sympathise.
Sweet flower! thy children's eyes
Are not more innocent than thine.
But they sleep in shelter'd rest,
Like helpless birds in the warm nest,
On the castle's southern side;
Where feebly comes the mournful roar
Of buffeting wind and surging tide
Through many a room and corridor.
—Full on their window the moon's ray
Makes their chamber as bright as day.
It shines upon the blank white walls,
And on the snowy pillow falls,
And on two angel-heads doth play
Turn'd to each other—the eyes closed,
The lashes on the cheeks reposed.
Round each sweet brow the cap close-set
Hardly lets peep the golden hair;
Through the soft-open'd lips the air
Scarcely moves the coverlet.

One little wandering arm is thrown
At random on the counterpane,
And often the fingers close in haste
As if their baby-owner chased
The butterflies again.
This stir they have, and this alone;
But else they are so still!
—Ah, tired madcaps! you lie still;
But were you at the window now,
To look forth on the fairy sight
Of your illumined haunts by night,
To see the park-glades where you play
Far lovelier than they are by day,
To see the sparkle on the eaves,
And upon every giant-bough
Of those old oaks, whose wet red leaves
Are jewell'd with bright drops of rain—
How would your voices run again!
And far beyond the sparkling trees
Of the castle-park one sees
The bare heaths spreading, clear as day,
Moor behind moor, far, far away,
Into the heart of Brittany.
And here and there, lock'd by the land,
Long inlets of smooth glittering sea,
And many a stretch of watery sand
All shining in the white moon-beams—
But you see fairer in your dreams!

What voices are these on the clear night-air?
What lights in the court—what steps on the stair?

II

Iseult of Ireland

Tristram

Raise the light, my page! that I may see her.—
Thou art come at last, then, haughty Queen!
Long I've waited, long I've fought my fever,
Late thou comest, cruel thou hast been.

Iseult

Blame me not, poor sufferer! that I tarried;
Bound I was, I could not break the band.
Chide not with the past, but feel the present!
I am here—we meet—I hold thy hand.

Tristram

Thou art come, indeed—thou hast rejoin'd me;
Thou hast dared it—but too late to save.
Fear not now that men should tax thine honour!
I am dying: build—(thou may'st)—my grave!

Iseult

Tristram, ah, for love of Heaven, speak kindly!
What, I hear these bitter words from thee?
Sick with grief I am, and faint with travel—
Take my hand—dear Tristram, look on me!

Tristram

I forgot, thou comest from thy voyage—
Yes, the spray is on thy cloak and hair.
But thy dark eyes are not dimm'd, proud Iseult!
And thy beauty never was more fair.

Iseult

Ah, harsh flatterer! let alone my beauty!
I, like thee, have left my youth afar.
Take my hand, and touch these wasted fingers—
See my cheek and lips, how white they are!

Tristram

Thou art paler—but thy sweet charm, Iseult!
Would not fade with the dull years away.
Ah, how fair thou standest in the moonlight!
I forgive thee, Iseult!—thou wilt stay?

Iseult

Fear me not, I will be always with thee;
I will watch thee, tend thee, soothe thy pain;
Sing thee tales of true, long-parted lovers,
Join'd at evening of their days again.

Tristram

No, thou shalt not speak! I should be finding
Something alter'd in thy courtly tone.
Sit—sit by me! I will think, we've lived so
In the green wood, all our lives, alone.

Iseult

Alter'd, Tristram? Not in courts, believe me,
Love like mine is alter'd in the breast;
Courtly life is light and cannot reach it—
Ah! it lives, because so deep-suppress'd!

What, thou think'st men speak in courtly chambers
Words by which the wretched are consoled?
What, thou think'st this aching brow was cooler,
Circled, Tristram, by a band of gold?
Royal state with Marc, my deep-wrong'd husband—
That was bliss to make my sorrows flee!
Silken courtiers whispering honied nothings—
Those were friends to make me false to thee!

Ah, on which, if both our lots were balanced,
Was indeed the heaviest burden thrown—
Thee, a pining exile in thy forest,
Me, a smiling queen upon my throne?

Vain and strange debate, where both have suffer'd
Both have pass'd a youth consumed and sad,
Both have brought their anxious day to evening,
And have now short space for being glad!

Join'd we are henceforth; nor will thy people,
Nor thy younger Iseult take it ill,
That a former rival shares her office,
When she sees her humbled, pale, and still.

I, a faded watcher by thy pillow,
I, a statue on thy chapel-floor,
Pour'd in prayer before the Virgin-Mother,
Rouse no anger, make no rivals more.

She will cry: "Is this the foe I dreaded?
This his idol? this that royal bride?
Ah, an hour of health would purge his eye-sight!
Stay, pale queen! for ever by my side."

Hush, no words! that smile, I see, forgives me.
I am now thy nurse, I bid thee sleep.
Close thine eyes—this flooding moonlight blinds them!—
Nay, all's well again! thou must not weep.

Tristram

I am happy! yet I feel, there's something
Swells my heart, and takes my breath away.
Through a mist I see thee; near—come nearer!
Bend—bend down!—I yet have much to say.

Iseult

Heaven! his head sinks back upon the pillow—
Tristram! Tristram! let thy heart not fail!
Call on God and on the holy angels!
What, love, courage!—Christ! he is so pale.

Tristram

Hush, 'tis vain, I feel my end approaching!
This is what my mother said should be,
When the fierce pains took her in the forest,
The deep draughts of death, in bearing me.

"Son," she said, "thy name shall be of sorrow;
Tristram art thou call'd for my death's sake."
So she said, and died in the drear forest.
Grief since then his home with me doth make.

I am dying.—Start not, nor look wildly!
Me, thy living friend, thou canst not save.
But, since living we were ununited,
Go not far, O Iseult! from my grave.

Close mine eyes, then seek the princess Iseult;
Speak her fair, she is of royal blood!
Say, I will'd so, that thou stay beside me—
She will grant it; she is kind and good.

Now to sail the seas of death I leave thee—
One last kiss upon the living shore!

Iseult

Tristram!—Tristram!—stay—receive me with thee!
Iseult leaves thee, Tristram! never more.

* * *

You see them clear—the moon shines bright.
Slow, slow and softly, where she stood,
She sinks upon the ground;—her hood
Had fallen back; her arms outspread
Still hold her lover's hand; her head
Is bow'd, half-buried, on the bed.

O'er the blanch'd sheet her raven hair
Lies in disorder'd streams; and there,
Strung like white stars, the pearls still are,
And the golden bracelets, heavy and rare,
Flash on her white arms still.
The very same which yesternight
Flash'd in the silver sconces' light,
When the feast was gay and the laughter loud
In Tyntagel's palace proud.
But then they deck'd a restless ghost
With hot-flush'd cheeks and brilliant eyes,
And quivering lips on which the tide
Of courtly speech abruptly died,
And a glance which over the crowded floor,
The dancers, and the festive host,
Flew ever to the door.
That the knights eyed her in surprise,
And the dames whispered scoffingly:
"Her moods, good lack, they pass like showers!
But yesternight and she would be
As pale and still as wither'd flowers,
And now to-night she laughs and speaks
And has a colour in her cheeks;
Christ keep us from such fantasy!"—

Yes, now the longing is o'erpast,
Which, dogg'd by fear and fought by shame,
Shook her weak bosom day and night,
Consumed her beauty like a flame,
And dimm'd it like the desert-blast.
And though the bed-clothes hide her face,
Yet were it lifted to the light,
The sweet expression of her brow
Would charm the gazer, till his thought
Erased the ravages of time,
Fill'd up the hollow cheek, and brought
A freshness back as of her prime—
So healing is her quiet now.
So perfectly the lines express
A tranquil, settled loveliness,
Her younger rival's purest grace.

The air of the December-night
Steals coldly around the chamber bright,
Where those lifeless lovers be;
Swinging with it, in the light
Flaps the ghostlike tapestry.
And on the arras wrought you see
A stately Huntsman, clad in green,
And round him a fresh forest-scene.
On that clear forest-knoll he stays,
With his pack round him, and delays.
He stares and stares, with troubled face,
At this huge, gleam-lit fireplace,
At that bright, iron-figured door,
And those blown rushes on the floor.
He gazes down into the room
With heated cheeks and flurried air,
And to himself he seems to say:
"*What place is this, and who are they?*
Who is that kneeling Lady fair?
And on his pillows that pale Knight
Who seems of marble on a tomb?
How comes it here, this chamber bright,
Through whose mullion'd windows clear
The castle-court all wet with rain,
The drawbridge and the moat appear,
And then the beach, and, mark'd with spray,
The sunken reefs, and far away
The unquiet bright Atlantic plain?
—What, has some glamour made me sleep,
And sent me with my dogs to sweep,
By night, with boisterous bugle-peal,
Through some old, sea-side, knightly hall,
Not in the free green wood at all?
That Knight's asleep, and at her prayer
That Lady by the bed doth kneel—
Then hush, thou boisterous bugle-peal!"
—The wild boar rustles in his lair;
The fierce hounds snuff the tainted air;
But lord and hounds keep rooted there.

Cheer, cheer thy dogs into the brake,
O Hunter! and without a fear
Thy golden-tassell'd bugle blow,
And through the glades thy pastime take—
For thou wilt rouse no sleepers here!
For these thou seest are unmoved;
Cold, cold as those who lived and loved
A thousand years ago.

III

Iseult of Brittany

A year had flown, and o'er the sea away,
In Cornwall, Tristram and Queen Iseult lay;
In King Marc's chapel, in Tyntagel old—
There in a ship they bore those lovers cold.

The young surviving Iseult, one bright day,
Had wander'd forth. Her children were at play

In a green circular hollow in the heath
Which borders the sea-shore—a country path
Creeps over it from the till'd fields behind.
The hollow's grassy banks are soft-inclined,
And to one standing on them, far and near
The lone unbroken view spreads bright and clear
Over the waste. This cirque of open ground
Is light and green; the heather, which all round
Creeps thickly, grows not here; but the pale grass
Is strewn with rocks, and many a shiver'd mass
Of vein'd white-gleaming quartz, and here and there
Dotted with holly-trees and juniper.
In the smooth centre of the opening stood
Three hollies side by side, and made a screen,
Warm with the winter-sun, of burnish'd green
With scarlet berries gemm'd, the fell-fare's food.
Under the glittering hollies Iseult stands,
Watching her children play; their little hands
Are busy gathering spars of quartz, and streams
Of stagshorn for their hats; anon, with screams
Of mad delight they drop their spoils, and bound
Among the holly-clumps and broken ground,
Racing full speed, and startling in their rush
The fell-fares and the speckled missel-thrush
Out of their glossy coverts;—but when now
Their cheeks were flush'd, and over each hot brow,
Under the feather'd hats of the sweet pair,
In blinding masses shower'd the golden hair—
Then Iseult call'd them to her, and the three
Cluster'd under the holly-screen, and she
Told them an old-world Breton history.

Warm in their mantles wrapt the three stood there,
Under the hollies, in the clear still air—
Mantles with those rich furs deep glistering
Which Venice ships do from swart Egypt bring.
Long they stay'd still—then, pacing at their ease,
Moved up and down under the glossy trees.
But still, as they pursued their warm dry road,
From Iseult's lips the unbroken story flow'd,
And still the children listen'd, their blue eyes
Fix'd on their mother's face in wide surprise;
Nor did their looks stray once to the sea-side,
Nor to the brown heaths round them, bright and wide,
Nor to the snow, which, though 'twas all away
From the open heath, still by the hedgerows lay,
Nor to the shining sea-fowl, that with screams
Bore up from where the bright Atlantic gleams,
Swooping to landward; nor to where, quite clear,
The fell-fares settled on the thickets near.
And they would still have listen'd, till dark night
Came keen and chill down on the heather bright;
But, when the red glow on the sea grew cold,
And the grey turrets of the castle old
Look'd sternly through the frosty evening-air,
Then Iseult took by the hand those children fair,
And brought her tale to an end, and found the path,
And led them home over the darkening heath.

And is she happy? Does she see unmoved
The days in which she might have lived and loved
Slip without bringing bliss slowly away,
One after one, to-morrow like to-day?
Joy has not found her yet, nor ever will—
Is it this thought which makes her mien so still,
Her features so fatigued, her eyes, though sweet,
So sunk, so rarely lifted save to meet
Her children's? She moves slow; her voice alone
Hath yet an infantine and silver tone,
But even that comes languidly; in truth,
She seems one dying in a mask of youth.
And now she will go home, and softly lay
Her laughing children in their beds, and play
Awhile with them before they sleep; and then
She'll light her silver lamp, which fishermen

Dragging their nets through the rough waves, afar,
Along this iron coast, know like a star,
And take her broidery-frame, and there she'll sit
Hour after hour, her gold curls sweeping it;
Lifting her soft-bent head only to mind
Her children, or to listen to the wind.
And when the clock peals midnight, she will move
Her work away, and let her fingers rove
Across the shaggy brows of Tristram's hound
Who lies, guarding her feet, along the ground;
Or else she will fall musing, her blue eyes
Fixt, her slight hands clasp'd on her lap; then rise,
And at her prie-dieu kneel, until she have told
Her rosary-beads of ebony tipp'd with gold,
Then to her soft sleep—and to-morrow'll be
To-day's exact repeated effigy.

Yes, it is lonely for her in her hall.
The children, and the grey-hair'd seneschal,
Her women, and Sir Tristram's aged hound,
Are there the sole companions to be found.
But these she loves; and noisier life than this
She would find ill to bear, weak as she is.
She has her children, too, and night and day
Is with them; and the wide heaths where they play,
The hollies, and the cliff, and the sea-shore,
The sand, the sea-birds, and the distant sails,
These are to her dear as to them; the tales
With which this day the children she beguiled
She gleaned from Breton grandames, when a child,
In every hut along this sea-coast wild.
She herself loves them still, and, when they are told,
Can forget all to hear them, as of old.

Dear saints, it is not sorrow, as I hear,
Not suffering, which shuts up eye and ear
To all that has delighted them before,
And lets us be what we were once no more.
No, we may suffer deeply, yet retain
Power to be moved and soothed, for all our pain,
By what of old pleased us, and will again.
No, 'tis the gradual furnace of the world,
In whose hot air our spirits are upcurl'd
Until they crumble, or else grow like steel—
Which kills in us the bloom, the youth, the spring—
Which leaves the fierce necessity to feel,
But takes away the power—this can avail,
By drying up our joy in everything,
To make our former pleasures all seem stale.
This, or some tyrannous single thought, some fit
Of passion, which subdues our souls to it,
Till for its sake alone we live and move—
Call it ambition, or remorse, or love—
This too can change us wholly, and make seem
All which we did before, shadow and dream.

And yet, I swear, it angers me to see
How this fool passion gulls men potently;
Being, in truth, but a diseased unrest,
And an unnatural overheat at best.
How they are full of languor and distress
Not having it; which when they do possess,
They straightway are burnt up with fume and care,
And spend their lives in posting here and there
Where this plague drives them; and have little ease,
Are furious with themselves, and hard to please.
Like that bald Cæsar, the famed Roman wight,
Who wept at reading of a Grecian knight
Who made a name at younger years than he;
Or that renown'd mirror of chivalry,
Prince Alexander, Philip's peerless son,
Who carried the great war from Macedon
Into the Soudan's realm, and thundered on
To die at thirty-five in Babylon.

What tale did Iseult to the children say,
Under the hollies, that bright winter's day?

She told them of the fairy-haunted land
Away the other side of Brittany,
Beyond the heaths, edged by the lonely sea;
Of the deep forest-glades of Broce-liande,
Through whose green boughs the golden sunshine creeps,
Where Merlin by the enchanted thorn-tree sleeps.
For here he came with the fay Vivian,
One April, when the warm days first began.

He was on foot, and that false fay, his friend,
On her white palfrey; here he met his end,
In these lone sylvan glades, that April-day.
This tale of Merlin and the lovely fay
Was the one Iseult chose, and she brought clear
Before the children's fancy him and her.

Blowing between the stems, the forest-air
Had loosen'd the brown locks of Vivian's hair,
Which play'd on her flush'd cheek, and her blue eyes
Sparkled with mocking glee and exercise.
Her palfrey's flanks were mired and bathed in sweat,
For they had travell'd far and not stopp'd yet.
A brier in that tangled wilderness
Had scored her white right hand, which she allows
To rest ungloved on her green riding-dress;
The other warded off the drooping boughs.
But still she chatted on, with her blue eyes
Fix'd full on Merlin's face, her stately prize.
Her 'haviour had the morning's fresh clear grace,
The spirit of the woods was in her face.
She look'd so witching fair, that learned wight
Forgot his craft, and his best wits took flight;
And he grew fond, and eager to obey
His mistress, use her empire as she may.

They came to where the brushwood ceased, and day
Peer'd 'twixt the stems; and the ground broke away,
In a sloped sward down to a brawling brook;
And up as high as where they stood to look
On the brook's farther side was clear, but then
The underwood and trees began again.
This open glen was studded thick with thorns
Then white with blossom; and you saw the horns,
Through last year's fern, of the shy fallow-deer
Who come at noon down to the water here.
You saw the bright-eyed squirrels dart along
Under the thorns on the green sward; and strong
The blackbird whistled from the dingles near,
And the weird chipping of the woodpecker
Rang lonelily and sharp; the sky was fair,
And a fresh breath of spring stirr'd everywhere.
Merlin and Vivian stopp'd on the slope's brow,
To gaze on the light sea of leaf and bough
Which glistering plays all round them, lone and mild,
As if to itself the quiet forest smiled.
Upon the brow-top grew a thorn, and here
The grass was dry and moss'd, and you saw clear
Across the hollow; white anemonies
Starr'd the cool turf, and clumps of primroses
Ran out from the dark underwood behind.
No fairer resting-place a man could find.
"Here let us halt," said Merlin then; and she
Nodded, and tied her palfrey to a tree.

They sate them down together, and a sleep
Fell upon Merlin, more like death, so deep.
Her finger on her lips, then Vivian rose,
And from her brown-lock'd head the wimple throws,
And takes it in her hand, and waves it over
The blossom'd thorn-tree and her sleeping lover.
Nine times she waved the fluttering wimple round,
And made a little plot of magic ground.
And in that daised circle, as men say,
Is Merlin prisoner till the judgment-day;
But she herself whither she will can rove—
For she was passing weary of his love.

1852

SOHRAB AND RUSTUM

AN EPISODE

And the first grey of morning fill'd the east,
And the fog rose out of the Oxus stream.
But all the Tartar camp along the stream
Was hush'd, and still the men were plunged in sleep;
Sohrab alone, he slept not; all night long
He had lain wakeful, tossing on his bed;
But when the grey dawn stole into his tent,
He rose, and clad himself, and girt his sword,
And took his horseman's cloak, and left his tent,
And went abroad into the cold wet fog,
Through the dim camp to Peran-Wisa's tent.
Through the black Tartar tents he pass'd, which stood
Clustering like bee-hives on the low flat strand

Of Oxus, where the summer-floods o'erflow
When the sun melts the snows in high Pamere;
Through the black tents he pass'd, o'er that low strand,
And to a hillock came, a little back
From the stream's brink—the spot where first a boat,
Crossing the stream in summer, scrapes the land.
The men of former times had crown'd the top
With a clay fort; but that was fall'n, and now
The Tartars built there Peran-Wisa's tent,
A dome of laths, and o'er it felts were spread.
And Sohrab came there, and went in, and stood
Upon the thick-piled carpets in the tent,
And found the old man sleeping on his bed
Of rugs and felts, and near him lay his arms.
And Peran-Wisa heard him, though the step
Was dull'd; for he slept light, an old man's sleep;
And he rose quickly on one arm, and said:—
"Who art thou? for it is not yet clear dawn.
Speak! is there news, or any night alarm?"
But Sohrab came to the bedside, and said:—
"Thou know'st me, Peran-Wisa! it is I.
The sun is not yet risen, and the foe
Sleep; but I sleep not; all night long I lie
Tossing and wakeful, and I come to thee.
For so did King Afrasiab bid me seek
Thy counsel, and to heed thee as thy son,
In Samarcand, before the army march'd;
And I will tell thee what my heart desires.
Thou know'st if, since from Ader-baijan first
I came among the Tartars and bore arms,
I have still served Afrasiab well, and shown,
At my boy's years, the courage of a man.
This too thou know'st, that while I still bear on
The conquering Tartar ensigns through the world,
And beat the Persians back on every field,
I seek one man, one man, and one alone—
Rustum, my father; who I hoped should greet,
Should one day greet, upon some well-fought field,
His not unworthy, not inglorious son.
So I long hoped, but him I never find.
Come then, hear now, and grant me what I ask.
Let the two armies rest to-day; but I
Will challenge forth the bravest Persian lords
To meet me, man to man; if I prevail,
Rustum will surely hear it; if I fall—
Old man, the dead need no one, claim no kin.
Dim is the rumour of a common fight,
Where host meets host, and many names are sunk;
But of a single combat fame speaks clear."
He spoke; and Peran-Wisa took the hand
Of the young man in his, and sigh'd, and said:—
"O Sohrab, an unquiet heart is thine!
Canst thou not rest among the Tartar chiefs,
And share the battle's common chance with us
Who love thee, but must press for ever first,
In single fight incurring single risk,
To find a father thou hast never seen?
That were far best, my son, to stay with us
Unmurmuring; in our tents, while it is war,
And when 'tis truce, then in Afrasiab's towns.
But, if this one desire indeed rules all,
To seek out Rustum—seek him not through fight!
Seek him in peace, and carry to his arms,
O Sohrab, carry an unwounded son!
But far hence seek him, for he is not here.
For now it is not as when I was young,
When Rustum was in front of every fray;
But now he keeps apart, and sits at home,
In Seistan, with Zal, his father old.
Whether that his own mighty strength at last
Feels the abhorr'd approaches of old age,
Or in some quarrel with the Persian King.
There go!—Thou wilt not? Yet my heart forebodes
Danger or death awaits thee on this field.
Fain would I know thee safe and well, though lost
To us; fain therefore send thee hence, in peace
To seek thy father, not seek single fights
In vain;—but who can keep the lion's cub
From ravening, and who govern Rustum's son?
Go, I will grant thee what thy heart desires."
So said he, and dropp'd Sohrab's hand, and left
His bed, and the warm rugs whereon he lay;
And o'er his chilly limbs his woollen coat
He pass'd, and tied his sandals on his feet,

And threw a white cloak round him, and he took
In his right hand a ruler's staff, no sword;
And on his head he set his sheep-skin cap,
Black, glossy, curl'd, the fleece of Kara-Kul;
And raised the curtain of his tent, and call'd
His herald to his side, and went abroad.
  The sun by this had risen, and clear'd the fog
From the broad Oxus and the glittering sands.
And from their tents the Tartar horsemen filed
Into the open plain; so Haman bade—
Haman, who next to Peran-Wisa ruled
The host, and still was in his lusty prime.
From their black tents, long files of horse, they stream'd;
As when some grey November morn the files,
In marching order spread, of long-neck'd cranes
Stream over Casbin and the southern slopes
Of Elburz, from the Aralian estuaries,
Or some frore Caspian reed-bed, southward bound
For the warm Persian sea-board—so they stream'd.
The Tartars of the Oxus, the King's guard,
First, with black sheep-skin caps and with long spears;
Large men, large steeds; who from Bokhara come
And Khiva, and ferment the milk of mares.
Next, the more temperate Toorkmuns of the south,
The Tukas, and the lances of Salore,
And those from Attruck and the Caspian sands;
Light men and on light steeds, who only drink
The acrid milk of camels, and their wells.
And then a swarm of wandering horse, who came
From far, and a more doubtful service own'd;
The Tartars of Ferghana, from the banks
Of the Jaxartes, men with scanty beards
And close-set skull-caps; and those wilder hordes
Who roam o'er Kipchak and the northern waste,
Kalmucks and unkempt Kuzzaks, tribes who stray
Nearest the Pole, and wandering Kirghizzes,
Who come on shaggy ponies from Pamere;
These all filed out from camp into the plain.
And on the other side the Persians form'd;—
First a light cloud of horse, Tartars they seem'd,
The Ilyats of Khorassan; and behind,
The royal troops of Persia, horse and foot,
Marshall'd battalions bright in burnish'd steel.
But Peran-Wisa with his herald came,
Threading the Tartar squadrons to the front,
And with his staff kept back the foremost ranks.
And when Ferood, who led the Persians, saw
That Peran-Wisa kept the Tartars back,
He took his spear, and to the front he came,
And check'd his ranks, and fix'd them where they stood.
And the old Tartar came upon the sand
Betwixt the silent hosts, and spake, and said:—
  "Ferood, and ye, Persians and Tartars, hear!
Let there be truce between the hosts to-day.
But choose a champion from the Persian lords
To fight our champion Sohrab, man to man."
  As, in the country, on a morn in June,
When the dew glistens on the pearled ears,
A shiver runs through the deep corn for joy—
So, when they heard what Peran-Wisa said,
A thrill through all the Tartar squadrons ran
Of pride and hope for Sohrab, whom they loved.
  But as a troop of pedlars, from Cabool,
Cross underneath the Indian Caucasus,
That vast sky-neighbouring mountain of milk snow;
Crossing so high, that, as they mount, they pass
Long flocks of travelling birds dead on the snow,
Choked by the air, and scarce can they themselves
Slake their parch'd throats with sugar'd mulberries—
In single file they move, and stop their breath,
For fear they should dislodge the o'erhanging snows—
So the pale Persians held their breath with fear.
  And to Ferood his brother chiefs came up
To counsel; Gudurz and Zoarrah came,
And Feraburz, who ruled the Persian host
Second, and was the uncle of the King;

These came and counsell'd, and then Gudurz said:—
"Ferood, shame bids us take their challenge up,
Yet champion have we none to match this youth.
He has the wild stag's foot, the lion's heart.
But Rustum came last night; aloof he sits
And sullen, and has pitch'd his tents apart.
Him will I seek, and carry to his ear
The Tartar challenge, and this young man's name.
Haply he will forget his wrath, and fight.
Stand forth the while, and take their challenge up."
So spake he; and Ferood stood forth and cried:—
"Old man, be it agreed as thou hast said!
Let Sohrab arm, and we will find a man."
He spake: and Peran-Wisa turn'd, and strode
Back through the opening squadrons to his tent.
But through the anxious Persians Gudurz ran,
And cross'd the camp which lay behind, and reach'd,
Out on the sands beyond it, Rustum's tents.
Of scarlet cloth they were, and glittering gay,
Just pitch'd; the high pavilion in the midst
Was Rustum's, and his men lay camp'd around.
And Gudurz enter'd Rustum's tent, and found
Rustum; his morning meal was done, but still
The table stood before him, charged with food—
A side of roasted sheep, and cakes of bread,
And dark green melons; and there Rustum sate
Listless, and held a falcon on his wrist,
And play'd with it; but Gudurz came and stood
Before him; and he look'd, and saw him stand,
And with a cry sprang up and dropp'd the bird,
And greeted Gudurz with both hands, and said:—
"Welcome! these eyes could see no better sight.
What news? but sit down first, and eat and drink."
But Gudurz stood in the tent-door, and said:—
"Not now! a time will come to eat and drink,
But not to-day; to-day has other needs.
The armies are drawn out, and stand at gaze;
For from the Tartars is a challenge brought
To pick a champion from the Persian lords
To fight their champion—and thou know'st his name—
Sohrab men call him, but his birth is hid.
O Rustum, like thy might is this young man's!
He has the wild stag's foot, the lion's heart;
And he is young, and Iran's chiefs are old,
Or else too weak; and all eyes turn to thee.
Come down and help us, Rustum, or we lose!"
He spoke; but Rustum answer'd with a smile:
"Go to! if Iran's chiefs are old, then I
Am older; if the young are weak, the King
Errs strangely; for the King, for Kai Khosroo,
Himself is young, and honours younger men,
And lets the aged moulder to their graves.
Rustum he loves no more, but loves the young—
The young may rise at Sohrab's vaunts, not I.
For what care I, though all speak Sohrab's fame?
For would that I myself had such a son,
And not that one slight helpless girl I have—
A son so famed, so brave, to send to war,
And I to tarry with the snow-hair'd Zal,
My father, whom the robber Afghans vex,
And clip his borders short, and drive his herds,
And he has none to guard his weak old age.
There would I go, and hang my armour up,
And with my great name fence that weak old man,
And spend the goodly treasures I have got,
And rest my age, and hear of Sohrab's fame,
And leave to death the hosts of thankless kings,
And with these slaughterous hands draw sword no more."
He spoke, and smiled; and Gudurz made reply:—
"What then, O Rustum, will men say to this,
When Sohrab dares our bravest forth, and seeks
Thee most of all, and thou, whom most he seeks,

Hidest thy face? Take heed lest men should say:
Like some old miser, Rustum hoards his fame,
And shuns to peril it with younger men."
  And, greatly moved, then Rustum made reply:—
"O Gudurz, wherefore dost thou say such words?
Thou knowest better words than this to say.
What is one more, one less, obscure or famed,
Valiant or craven, young or old, to me?
Are not they mortal, am not I myself?
But who for men of nought would do great deeds?
Come, thou shalt see how Rustum hoards his fame!
But I will fight unknown, and in plain arms;
Let not men say of Rustum, he was match'd
In single fight with any mortal man."
  He spoke, and frown'd; and Gudurz turn'd, and ran
Back quickly through the camp in fear and joy—
Fear at his wrath, but joy that Rustum came.
But Rustum strode to his tent-door, and call'd
His followers in, and bade them bring his arms,
And clad himself in steel; the arms he chose
Were plain, and on his shield was no device,
Only his helm was rich, inlaid with gold,
And, from the fluted spine atop, a plume
Of horsehair waved, a scarlet horsehair plume.
So arm'd, he issued forth; and Ruksh, his horse,
Follow'd him like a faithful hound at heel—
Ruksh, whose renown was noised through all the earth,
The horse, whom Rustum on a foray once
Did in Bokhara by the river find
A colt beneath its dam, and drove him home,
And rear'd him; a bright bay, with lofty crest,
Dight with a saddle-cloth of broider'd green
Crusted with gold, and on the ground were work'd
All beasts of chase, all beasts which hunters know.
So follow'd, Rustum left his tents, and cross'd
The camp, and to the Persian host appear'd.
And all the Persians knew him, and with shouts
Hail'd; but the Tartars knew not who he was.
And dear as the wet diver to the eyes
Of his pale wife who waits and weeps on shore,
By sandy Bahrein, in the Persian Gulf,
Plunging all day in the blue waves, at night,
Having made up his tale of precious pearls,
Rejoins her in their hut upon the sands—
So dear to the pale Persians Rustum came.
  And Rustum to the Persian front advanced,
And Sohrab arm'd in Haman's tent, and came.
And as afield the reapers cut a swath
Down through the middle of a rich man's corn,
And on each side are squares of standing corn,
And in the midst a stubble, short and bare—
So on each side were squares of men, with spears
Bristling, and in the midst, the open sand.
And Rustum came upon the sand, and cast
His eyes toward the Tartar tents, and saw
Sohrab come forth, and eyed him as he came.
  As some rich woman, on a winter's morn,
Eyes through her silken curtains the poor drudge
Who with numb blacken'd fingers makes her fire—
At cock-crow, on a starlit winter's morn,
When the frost flowers the whiten'd window-panes—
And wonders how she lives, and what the thoughts
Of that poor drudge may be; so Rustum eyed
The unknown adventurous youth, who from afar
Came seeking Rustum, and defying forth
All the most valiant chiefs; long he perused
His spirited air, and wonder'd who he was.
For very young he seem'd, tenderly rear'd;
Like some young cypress, tall, and dark, and straight,
Which in a queen's secluded garden throws
Its slight dark shadow on the moonlit turf,
By midnight, to a bubbling fountain's sound—
So slender Sohrab seem'd, so softly rear'd.
And a deep pity enter'd Rustum's soul
As he beheld him coming; and he stood,
And beckon'd to him with his hand, and said:—
  "O thou young man, the air of Heaven is soft,
And warm, and pleasant; but the grave is cold!

Heaven's air is better than the cold dead grave.
Behold me! I am vast, and clad in iron,
And tried; and I have stood on many a field
Of blood, and I have fought with many a foe—
Never was that field lost, or that foe saved.
O Sohrab, wherefore wilt thou rush on death?
Be govern'd! quit the Tartar host, and come
To Iran, and be as my son to me,
And fight beneath my banner till I die!
There are no youths in Iran brave as thou."

So he spake, mildly; Sohrab heard his voice,
The mighty voice of Rustum, and he saw
His giant figure planted on the sand,
Sole, like some single tower, which a chief
Hath builded on the waste in former years
Against the robbers; and he saw that head,
Streak'd with its first grey hairs;—hope filled his soul,
And he ran forward and embraced his knees,
And clasp'd his hand within his own, and said:—
"O, by thy father's head! by thine own soul!
Art thou not Rustum? speak! art thou not he?"

But Rustum eyed askance the kneeling youth,
And turn'd away, and spake to his own soul:—
"Ah me, I muse what this young fox may mean!
False, wily, boastful, are these Tartar boys.
For if I now confess this thing he asks,
And hide it not, but say: *Rustum is here!*
He will not yield indeed, nor quit our foes,
But he will find some pretext not to fight,
And praise my fame, and proffer courteous gifts
A belt or sword perhaps, and go his way.
And on a feast-tide, in Afrasiab's hall,
In Samarcand, he will arise and cry:
'I challenged once, when the two armies camp'd
Beside the Oxus, all the Persian lords
To cope with me in single fight; but they
Shrank, only Rustum dared; then he and I
Changed gifts, and went on equal terms away.'
So will he speak, perhaps, while men applaud;
Then were the chiefs of Iran shamed through me."

And then he turn'd, and sternly spake aloud:—
"Rise! wherefore dost thou vainly question thus
Of Rustum? I am here, whom thou hast call'd
By challenge forth; make good thy vaunt, or yield!
Is it with Rustum only thou wouldst fight?
Rash boy, men look on Rustum's face and flee!
For well I know, that did great Rustum stand
Before thy face this day, and were reveal'd,
There would be then no talk of fighting more.
But being what I am, I tell thee this—
Do thou record it in thine inmost soul:
Either thou shalt renounce thy vaunt and yield,
Or else thy bones shall strew this sand, till winds
Bleach them, or Oxus with his summer-floods,
Oxus in summer wash them all away."

He spoke; and Sohrab answer'd, on his feet:—
"Art thou so fierce? Thou wilt not fright me so!
I am no girl, to be made pale by words.
Yet this thou hast said well, did Rustum stand
Here on this field, there were no fighting then.
But Rustum is far hence, and we stand here.
Begin! thou art more vast, more dread than I,
And thou art proved, I know, and I am young—
But yet success sways with the breath of Heaven.
And though thou thinkest that thou knowest sure
Thy victory, yet thou canst not surely know.
For we are all, like swimmers in the sea,
Poised on the top of a huge wave of fate,
Which hangs uncertain to which side to fall.
And whether it will heave us up to land,
Or whether it will roll us out to sea,
Back out to sea, to the deep waves of death,
We know not, and no search will make us know;
Only the event will teach us in its hour."

He spoke, and Rustum answer'd not, but hurl'd

His spear; down from the shoulder, down it came,
As on some partridge in the corn a hawk,
That long has tower'd in the airy clouds,
Drops like a plummet; Sohrab saw it come,
And sprang aside, quick as a flash; the spear
Hiss'd, and went quivering down into the sand,
Which it sent flying wide;—then Sohrab threw
In turn, and full struck Rustum's shield; sharp rang,
The iron plates rang sharp, but turn'd the spear.
And Rustum seized his club, which none but he
Could wield; an unlopp'd trunk it was, and huge,
Still rough—like those which men in treeless plains
To build them boats fish from the flooded rivers,
Hyphasis or Hydaspes, when, high up
By their dark springs, the wind in winter-time
Hath made in Himalayan forests wrack,
And strewn the channels with torn boughs—so huge
The club which Rustum lifted now, and struck
One stroke; but again Sohrab sprang aside,
Lithe as the glancing snake, and the club came
Thundering to earth, and leapt from Rustum's hand.
And Rustum follow'd his own blow, and fell
To his knees, and with his fingers clutch'd the sand;
And now might Sohrab have unsheathed his sword,
And pierced the mighty Rustum while he lay
Dizzy, and on his knees, and choked with sand;
But he look'd on, and smiled, nor bared his sword,
But courteously drew back, and spoke, and said:—
"Thou strik'st too hard! that club of thine will float
Upon the summer-floods, and not my bones.
But rise, and be not wroth! not wroth am I;
No, when I see thee, wrath forsakes my soul.
Thou say'st, thou art not Rustum; be it so!
Who art thou then, that canst so touch my soul?
Boy as I am, I have seen battles too—
Have waded foremost in their bloody waves,
And heard their hollow roar of dying men;
But never was my heart thus touch'd before.
Are they from Heaven, these softenings of the heart?
O thou old warrior, let us yield to Heaven!
Come, plant we here in earth our angry spears,
And make a truce, and sit upon this sand,
And pledge each other in red wine, like friends,
And thou shalt talk to me of Rustum's deeds.
There are enough foes in the Persian host,
Whom I may meet, and strike, and feel no pang;
Champions enough Afrasiab has, whom thou
Mayst fight; fight *them*, when they confront thy spear!
But oh, let there be peace 'twixt thee and me!"
He ceased, but while he spake, Rustum had risen,
And stood erect, trembling with rage; his club
He left to lie, but had regain'd his spear,
Whose fiery point now in his mail'd right-hand
Blazed bright and baleful, like that autumn-star,
The baleful sign of fevers; dust had soil'd
His stately crest, and dimm'd his glittering arms.
His breast heaved, his lips foam'd, and twice his voice
Was choked with rage; at last these words broke way:—
"Girl! nimble with thy feet, not with thy hands!
Curl'd minion, dancer, coiner of sweet words!
Fight, let me hear thy hateful voice no more!
Thou art not in Afrasiab's gardens now
With Tartar girls, with whom thou art wont to dance;
But on the Oxus-sands, and in the dance
Of battle, and with me, who make no play
Of war; I fight it out, and hand to hand.

Speak not to me of truce, and pledge, and wine!
Remember all thy valour; try thy feints
And cunning! all the pity I had is gone;
Because thou hast shamed me before both the hosts
With thy light skipping tricks, and thy girl's wiles."

He spoke, and Sohrab kindled at his taunts,
And he too drew his sword; at once they rush'd
Together, as two eagles on one prey
Come rushing down together from the clouds,
One from the east, one from the west; their shields
Dash'd with a clang together, and a din
Rose, such as that the sinewy woodcutters
Make often in the forest's heart at morn,
Of hewing axes, crashing trees—such blows
Rustum and Sohrab on each other hail'd.
And you would say that sun and stars took part
In that unnatural conflict; for a cloud
Grew suddenly in Heaven, and dark'd the sun
Over the fighters' heads; and a wind rose
Under their feet, and moaning swept the plain,
And in a sandy whirlwind wrapp'd the pair.
In gloom they twain were wrapp'd, and they alone;
For both the on-looking hosts on either hand
Stood in broad daylight, and the sky was pure,
And the sun sparkled on the Oxus stream.
But in the gloom they fought, with bloodshot eyes
And labouring breath; first Rustum struck the shield
Which Sohrab held stiff out; the steel-spiked spear
Rent the tough plates, but fail'd to reach the skin,
And Rustum pluck'd it back with angry groan.
Then Sohrab with his sword smote Rustum's helm,
Nor clove its steel quite through; but all the crest
He shore away, and that proud horsehair plume,
Never till now defiled, sank to the dust;
And Rustum bow'd his head; but then the gloom
Grew blacker, thunder rumbled in the air,
And lightnings rent the cloud; and Ruksh, the horse,
Who stood at hand, utter'd a dreadful cry;—
No horse's cry was that, most like the roar
Of some pain'd desert-lion, who all day
Hath trail'd the hunter's javelin in his side,
And comes at night to die upon the sand.
The two hosts heard that cry, and quaked for fear,
And Oxus curdled as it cross'd his stream.
But Sohrab heard, and quail'd not, but rush'd on,
And struck again; and again Rustum bow'd
His head; but this time all the blade, like glass,
Sprang in a thousand shivers on the helm,
And in the hand the hilt remain'd alone.
Then Rustum raised his head; his dreadful eyes
Glared, and he shook on high his menacing spear,
And shouted: *Rustum!*—Sohrab heard that shout,
And shrank amazed; back he recoil'd one step,
And scann'd with blinking eyes the advancing form;
And then he stood bewilder'd; and he dropp'd
His covering shield, and the spear pierced his side.
He reel'd, and staggering back, sank to the ground;
And then the gloom dispersed, and the wind fell,
And the bright sun broke forth, and melted all
The cloud; and the two armies saw the pair—
Saw Rustum standing, safe upon his feet,
And Sohrab, wounded, on the bloody sand.

Then, with a bitter smile, Rustum began:—
"Sohrab, thou thoughtest in thy mind to kill
A Persian lord this day, and strip his corpse,
And bear thy trophies to Afrasiab's tent.
Or else that the great Rustum would come down
Himself to fight, and that thy wiles would move
His heart to take a gift, and let thee go.
And then that all the Tartar host would praise

Thy courage or thy craft, and spread thy fame,
To glad thy father in his weak old age.
Fool, thou art slain, and by an unknown man!
Dearer to the red jackals shalt thou be
Than to thy friends, and to thy father old."
And, with a fearless mien, Sohrab replied:—
"Unknown thou art; yet thy fierce vaunt is vain.
Thou dost not slay me, proud and boastful man!
No! Rustum slays me, and this filial heart.
For were I match'd with ten such men as thee,
And I were that which till to-day I was,
They should be lying here, I standing there.
But that belovéd name unnerved my arm—
That name, and something, I confess, in thee,
Which troubles all my heart, and made my shield
Fall; and thy spear transfix'd an unarm'd foe.
And now thou boastest, and insult'st my fate.
But hear thou this, fierce man, tremble to hear:
The mighty Rustum shall avenge my death!
My father, whom I seek through all the world,
He shall avenge my death, and punish thee!"
As when some hunter in the spring hath found
A breeding eagle sitting on her nest,
Upon the craggy isle of a hill-lake,
And pierced her with an arrow as she rose,
And follow'd her to find her where she fell
Far off;—anon her mate comes winging back
From hunting, and a great way off descries
His huddling young left sole; at that, he checks
His pinion, and with short uneasy sweeps
Circles above his eyry, with loud screams
Chiding his mate back to her nest; but she
Lies dying, with the arrow in her side,
In some far stony gorge out of his ken,
A heap of fluttering feathers—never more
Shall the lake glass her, flying over it;
Never the black and dripping precipices
Echo her stormy scream as she sails by—
As that poor bird flies home, nor knows his loss,
So Rustum knew not his own loss, but stood
Over his dying son, and knew him not.
But, with a cold incredulous voice, he said:—
"What prate is this of fathers and revenge?
The mighty Rustum never had a son."
And, with a failing voice, Sohrab replied:—
"Ah yes, he had! and that lost son am I.
Surely the news will one day reach his ear,
Reach Rustum, where he sits, and tarries long,
Somewhere, I know not where, but far from here;
And pierce him like a stab, and make him leap
To arms, and cry for vengeance upon thee.
Fierce man, bethink thee, for an only son!
What will that grief, what will that vengeance be?
Oh, could I live, till I that grief had seen!
Yet him I pity not so much, but her,
My mother, who in Ader-baijan dwells
With that old king, her father, who grows grey
With age, and rules over the valiant Koords.
Her most I pity, who no more will see
Sohrab returning from the Tartar camp,
With spoils and honour, when the war is done.
But a dark rumour will be bruited up,
From tribe to tribe, until it reach her ear;
And then will that defenceless woman learn
That Sohrab will rejoice her sight no more,
But that in battle with a nameless foe,
By the far-distant Oxus, he is slain."
He spoke; and as he ceased, he wept aloud,
Thinking of her he left, and his own death.
He spoke; but Rustum listen'd, plunged in thought.
Nor did he yet believe it was his son
Who spoke, although he call'd back names he knew;
For he had had sure tidings that the babe,
Which was in Ader-baijan born to him,
Had been a puny girl, no boy at all—
So that sad mother sent him word, for fear
Rustum should seek the boy, to train in arms
And so he deem'd that either Sohrab took,
By a false boast, the style of Rustum's son;
Or that men gave it him, to swell his fame.
So deem'd he; yet he listen'd, plunged in thought
And his soul set to grief, as the vast tide
Of the bright rocking Ocean sets to shore

At the full moon; tears gather'd in his eyes;
For he remember'd his own early youth,
And all its bounding rapture; as, at dawn,
The shepherd from his mountain-lodge descries
A far, bright city, smitten by the sun,
Through many rolling clouds—so Rustum saw
His youth; saw Sohrab's mother, in her bloom;
And that old king, her father, who loved well
His wandering guest, and gave him his fair child
With joy; and all the pleasant life they led,
They three, in that long-distant summer-time—
The castle, and the dewy woods, and hunt
And hound, and morn on those delightful hills
In Ader-baijan. And he saw that Youth,
Of age and looks to be his own dear son,
Piteous and lovely, lying on the sand,
Like some rich hyacinth which by the scythe
Of an unskilful gardener has been cut,
Mowing the garden grass-plots near its bed,
And lies, a fragrant tower of purple bloom,
On the mown, dying grass—so Sohrab lay,
Lovely in death, upon the common sand.
And Rustum gazed on him with grief, and said:—

"O Sohrab, thou indeed art such a son
Whom Rustum, wert thou his, might well have loved.
Yet here thou errest, Sohrab, or else men
Have told thee false—thou art not Rustum's son.
For Rustum had no son; one child he had—
But one—a girl; who with her mother now
Plies some light female task, nor dreams of us—
Of us she dreams not, nor of wounds, nor war."

But Sohrab answer'd him in wrath; for now
The anguish of the deep-fix'd spear grew fierce,
And he desired to draw forth the steel,
And let the blood flow free, and so to die—
But first he would convince his stubborn foe;
And, rising sternly on one arm, he said:—

"Man who art thou who dost deny my words?
Truth sits upon the lips of dying men,
And falsehood, while I lived, was far from mine.
I tell thee, prick'd upon this arm I bear
That seal which Rustum to my mother gave,
That she might prick it on the babe she bore."

He spoke; and all the blood left Rustum's cheeks,
And his knees totter'd, and he smote his hand
Against his breast, his heavy mailed hand,
That the hard iron corslet clank'd aloud;
And to his heart he press'd the other hand,
And in a hollow voice he spake, and said:—

"Sohrab, that were a proof which could not lie!
If thou show this, then art thou Rustum's son."

Then, with weak hasty fingers, Sohrab loosed
His belt, and near the shoulder bared his arm,
And show'd a sign in faint vermilion points
Prick'd; as a cunning workman, in Pekin,
Pricks with vermilion some clear porcelain vase,
An emperor's gift—at early morn he paints,
And all day long, and, when night comes, the lamp
Lights up his studious forehead and thin hands—
So delicately prick'd the sign appear'd
On Sohrab's arm, the sign of Rustum's seal.
It was that griffin, which of old rear'd Zal,
Rustum's great father, whom they left to die,
A helpless babe, among the mountain-rocks;
Him that kind creature found, and rear'd, and loved—
Then Rustum took it for his glorious sign.
And Sohrab bared that image on his arm,
And himself scann'd it long with mournful eyes,
And then he touch'd it with his hand and said:—

"How say'st thou? Is that sign the proper sign
Of Rustum's son, or of some other man's?"

He spoke; but Rustum gazed, and gazed, and stood
Speechless; and then he utter'd one sharp cry:

O boy—thy father!—and his voice choked there.
And then a dark cloud pass'd before his eyes,
And his head swam, and he sank down to earth.
But Sohrab crawl'd to where he lay, and cast
His arms about his neck, and kiss'd his lips,
And with fond faltering fingers stroked his cheeks,
Trying to call him back to life; and life
Came back to Rustum, and he oped his eyes,
And they stood wide with horror; and he seized
In both his hands the dust which lay around,
And threw it on his head, and smirch'd his hair,—
His hair, and face, and beard, and glittering arms;
And strong convulsive groanings shook his breast,
And his sobs choked him; and he clutch'd his sword,
To draw it, and for ever let life out.
But Sohrab saw his thought, and held his hands,
And with a soothing voice he spake, and said:—
"Father, forbear! for I but meet to-day
The doom which at my birth was written down
In Heaven, and thou art Heaven's unconscious hand.
Surely my heart cried out that it was thou,
When first I saw thee; and thy heart spoke too,
I know it! but fate trod those promptings down
Under its iron heel; fate, fate engaged
The strife, and hurl'd me on my father's spear.
But let us speak no more of this! I find
My father; let me feel that I have found!
Come, sit beside me on this sand, and take
My head betwixt thy hands, and kiss my cheeks,
And wash them with thy tears, and say: *My son!*
Quick! quick! for number'd are my sands of life,
And swift; for like the lightning to this field
I came, and like the wind I go away—
Sudden, and swift, and like a passing wind.
But it was writ in Heaven that this should be."
So said he, and his voice released the heart
Of Rustum, and his tears broke forth; he cast
His arms round his son's neck, and wept aloud,
And kiss'd him. And awe fell on both the hosts,
When they saw Rustum's grief; and Ruksh, the horse,
With his head bowing to the ground and mane
Sweeping the dust, came near, and in mute woe
First to the one then to the other moved
His head, as if inquiring what their grief
Might mean; and from his dark, compassionate eyes,
The big warm tears roll'd down, and caked the sand.
But Rustum chid him with stern voice, and said:—
"Ruksh, now thou grievest; but, O Ruksh, thy feet
Should first have rotted on their nimble joints,
Or ere they brought thy master to this field!"
But Sohrab look'd upon the horse and said;—
"Is this, then, Ruksh? How often, in past days,
My mother told me of thee, thou brave steed,
My terrible father's terrible horse! and said,
That I should one day find thy lord and thee.
Come, let me lay my hand upon thy mane!
O Ruksh, thou art more fortunate than I;
For thou hast gone where I shall never go,
And snuff'd the breezes of my father's home.
And thou hast trod the sands of Seistan,
And seen the River of Helmund, and the Lake
Of Zirrah; and the aged Zal himself
Has often stroked thy neck, and given thee food,
Corn in a golden platter soak'd with wine,
And said; *O Ruksh! bear Rustum well!*—but I
Have never known my grandsire's furrow'd face,
Nor seen his lofty house in Seistan,
Nor slaked my thirst at the clear Helmund stream;
But lodged among my father's foes, and seen
Afrasiab's cities only, Samarcand,
Bokhara, and lone Khiva in the waste,

And the black Toorkmun tents; and only drunk
The desert rivers, Moorghab and Tejend,
Kohik, and where the Kalmuks feed their sheep,
The northern Sir; and this great Oxus stream,
The yellow Oxus, by whose brink I die."
  Then, with a heavy groan, Rustum bewail'd:—
"Oh, that its waves were flowing over me!
Oh, that I saw its grains of yellow silt
Roll tumbling in the current o'er my head!"
  But, with a grave mild voice, Sohrab replied:—
"Desire not that, my father! thou must live.
For some are born to do great deeds, and live,
As some are born to be obscured, and die.
Do thou the deeds I die too young to do,
And reap a second glory in thine age;
Thou art my father, and thy gain is mine.
But come! thou seest this great host of men
Which follow me; I pray thee, slay not these!
Let me entreat for them: what have they done?
They follow'd me, my hope, my fame, my star.
Let them all cross the Oxus back in peace.
But me thou must bear hence, not send with them,
But carry me with thee to Seistan,
And place me on a bed, and mourn for me,
Thou, and the snow-hair'd Zal, and all thy friends.
And thou must lay me in that lovely earth,
And heap a stately mound above my bones,
And plant a far-seen pillar over all.
That so the passing horseman on the waste
May see my tomb a great way off, and cry:
Sohrab, the mighty Rustum's son, lies there,
Whom his great father did in ignorance kill!
And I be not forgotten in my grave."
  And, with a mournful voice, Rustum replied:—
"Fear not! as thou hast said, Sohrab, my son,
So shall it be; for I will burn my tents,
And quit the host, and bear thee hence with me,
And carry thee away to Seistan,
And place thee on a bed, and mourn for thee,
With the snow-headed Zal, and all my friends.
And I will lay thee in that lovely earth,
And heap a stately mound above thy bones,
And plant a far-seen pillar over all,
And men shall not forget thee in thy grave.
And I will spare thy host; yea, let them go!
Let them all cross the Oxus back in peace!
What should I do with slaying any more?
For would that all that I have ever slain
Might be once more alive; my bitterest foes,
And they who were call'd champions in their time,
And through whose death I won that fame I have—
And I were nothing but a common man,
A poor, mean soldier, and without renown,
So thou mightest live too, my son, my son!
Or rather would that I, even I myself,
Might now be lying on this bloody sand,
Near death, and by an ignorant stroke of thine,
Not thou of mine! and I might die, not thou;
And I, not thou, be borne to Seistan;
And Zal might weep above my grave, not thine;
And say: *O son, I weep thee not too sore,*
For willingly, I know, thou met'st thine end!
But now in blood and battles was my youth,
And full of blood and battles is my age,
And I shall never end this life of blood."
  Then, at the point of death, Sohrab replied:—
"A life of blood indeed, thou dreadful man!
But thou shalt yet have peace; only not now,
Not yet! but thou shalt have it on that day,
When thou shalt sail in a high-masted ship,
Thou and the other peers of Kai Khosroo,
Returning home over the salt blue sea,
From laying thy dear master in his grave."
  And Rustum gazed in Sohrab's face, and said:—
"Soon be that day, my son, and deep that sea!
Till then, if fate so wills, let me endure."
  He spoke; and Sohrab smiled on him, and took
The spear, and drew it from his side, and eased
His wound's imperious anguish; but the blood
Came welling from the open gash, and life
Flow'd with the stream;—all down his cold white side
The crimson torrent ran, dim now and soil'd,
Like the soil'd tissue of white violets

Left, freshly gather'd, on their native bank,
By children whom their nurses call with haste
Indoors from the sun's eye; his head droop'd low,
His limbs grew slack; motionless, white, he lay—
White, with eyes closed; only when heavy gasps,
Deep heavy gasps quivering through all his frame,
Convulsed him back to life, he open'd them,
And fix'd them feebly on his father's face;
Till now all strength was ebb'd, and from his limbs
Unwillingly the spirit fled away,
Regretting the warm mansion which it left,
And youth, and bloom, and this delightful world.

So, on the bloody sand, Sohrab lay dead;
And the great Rustum drew his horseman's cloak
Down o'er his face, and sate by his dead son.
As those black granite pillars, once high-rear'd
By Jemshid in Persepolis, to bear
His house, now 'mid their broken flights of steps
Lie prone, enormous, down the mountain side—
So in the sand lay Rustum by his son.

And night came down over the solemn waste,
And the two gazing hosts, and that sole pair,
And darken'd all; and a cold fog, with night,
Crept from the Oxus. Soon a hum arose,
As of a great assembly loosed, and fires
Began to twinkle through the fog; for now
Both armies moved to camp, and took their meal;
The Persians took it on the open sands
Southward, the Tartars by the river marge;
And Rustum and his son were left alone.

But the majestic river floated on,
Out of the mist and hum of that low land,
Into the frosty starlight, and there moved,
Rejoicing, through the hush'd Chorasmian waste,
Under the solitary moon;—he flow'd
Right for the polar star, past Orgunjè,
Brimming, and bright, and large; then sands begin
To hem his watery march, and dam his streams,
And split his currents; that for many a league
The shorn and parcell'd Oxus strains along
Through beds of sand and matted rushy isles—
Oxus, forgetting the bright speed he had
In his high mountain-cradle in Pamere,
A foil'd circuitous wanderer—till at last
The long'd-for dash of waves is heard, and wide
His luminous home of waters opens, bright
And tranquil, from whose floor the new-bathed stars
Emerge, and shine upon the Aral Sea.

1853

PHILOMELA

Hark! ah, the nightingale—
The tawny-throated!
Hark, from that moonlit cedar what a burst!
What triumph! hark!—what pain!

O wanderer from a Grecian shore,
Still, after many years, in distant lands,
Still nourishing in thy bewilder'd brain
That wild, unquench'd, deep-sunken, old-world pain—
Say, will it never heal?
And can this fragrant lawn
With its cool trees, and night,
And the sweet, tranquil Thames,
And moonshine, and the dew,
To thy rack'd heart and brain
Afford no balm?

Dost thou to-night behold,
Here, through the moonlight on this English grass,
The unfriendly palace in the Thracian wild?
Dost thou again peruse
With hot cheeks and sear'd eyes
The too clear web, and thy dumb sister's shame?
Dost thou once more assay
Thy flight, and feel come over thee,
Poor fugitive, the feathery change
Once more, and once more seem to make resound
With love and hate, triumph and agony,
Lone Daulis, and the high Cephissian vale?

Listen, Eugenia—
How thick the bursts come crowding through the leaves!
Again—thou hearest?
Eternal passion!
Eternal pain!

1853

REQUIESCAT

Strew on her roses, roses,
And never a spray of yew!
In quiet she reposes;
Ah, would that I did too!

Her mirth the world required;
She bathed it in smiles of glee.
But her heart was tired, tired,
And now they let her be.

Her life was turning, turning,
In mazes of heat and sound.
But for peace her soul was yearning,
And now peace laps her round.

Her cabin'd, ample spirit,
It flutter'd and fail'd for breath.
To-night it doth inherit
The vasty hall of death.

1853

THE SCHOLAR-GIPSY

Go, for they call you, shepherd, from the hill;
Go, shepherd, and untie the wattled cotes!
No longer leave thy wistful flock unfed,
Nor let thy bawling fellows rack their throats,
Nor the cropp'd herbage shoot another head.
But when the fields are still,
And the tired men and dogs all gone to rest,
And only the white sheep are sometimes seen
Cross and recross the strips of moon-blanch'd green,
Come, shepherd, and again begin the quest!

Here, where the reaper was at work of late—
In this high field's dark corner, where he leaves
His coat, his basket, and his earthen cruse,
And in the sun all morning binds the sheaves,
Then here, at noon, comes back his stores to use—
Here will I sit and wait,
While to my ear from uplands far away
The bleating of the folded flocks is borne,
With distant cries of reapers in the corn—
All the live murmur of a summer's day.

Screen'd is this nook o'er the high, half-reap'd field,
And here till sun-down, shepherd! will I be.
Through the thick corn the scarlet poppies peep,
And round green roots and yellowing stalks I see
Pale pink convolvulus in tendrils creep;
And air-swept lindens yield
Their scent, and rustle down their perfumed showers
Of bloom on the bent grass where I am laid,
And bower me from the August sun with shade;
And the eye travels down to Oxford's towers.

And near me on the grass lies Glanvil's book—
Come, let me read the oft-read tale again!
The story of the Oxford scholar poor,
Of pregnant parts and quick inventive brain,
Who, tired of knocking at preferment's door,
One summer-morn forsook
His friends, and went to learn the gipsy-lore,
And roam'd the world with that wild brotherhood,
And came, as most men deem'd, to little good,
But came to Oxford and his friends no more.

But once, years after, in the country-lanes,
Two scholars, whom at college erst he knew,
Met him, and of his way of life enquired;
Whereat he answer'd, that the gipsy-crew,
His mates, had arts to rule as they desired
The workings of men's brains,
And they can bind them to what thoughts they will.

"And I," he said, "the secret of their art,
When fully learn'd, will to the world impart;
But it needs heaven-sent moments for this skill."

This said, he left them, and return'd no more.—
But rumours hung about the country-side,
That the lost Scholar long was seen to stray,
Seen by rare glimpses, pensive and tongue-tied,
In hat of antique shape, and cloak of grey,
The same the gipsies wore.
Shepherds had met him on the Hurst in spring;
At some lone alehouse in the Berkshire moors,
On the warm ingle-bench, the smock-frock'd boors
Had found him seated at their entering,

But, 'mid their drink and clatter, he would fly.
And I myself seem half to know thy looks,
And put the shepherds, wanderer! on thy trace;
And boys who in lone wheatfields scare the rooks
I ask if thou hast pass'd their quiet place;
Or in my boat I lie
Moor'd to the cool bank in the summer-heats,
'Mid wide grass meadows which the sunshine fills,
And watch the warm, green-muffled Cumner hills,
And wonder if thou haunt'st their shy retreats.

For most, I know, thou lov'st retired ground!
Thee at the ferry Oxford riders blithe,
Returning home on summer-nights, have met
Crossing the stripling Thames at Bab-lock-hithe,
Trailing in the cool stream thy fingers wet,
As the punt's rope chops round;
And leaning backward in a pensive dream,
And fostering in thy lap a heap of flowers
Pluck'd in shy fields and distant Wych-wood bowers,
And thine eyes resting on the moonlit stream.

And then they land, and thou art seen no more!—
Maidens, who from the distant hamlets come
To dance around the Fyfield elm in May,
Oft through the darkening fields have seen thee roam,
Or cross a stile into the public way.
Oft thou hast given them store
Of flowers—the frail-leaf'd, white anemony,
Dark bluebells drench'd with dews of summer eves,
And purple orchises with spotted leaves—
But none hath words she can report of thee.

And, above Godstow Bridge, when hay-time's here
In June, and many a scythe in sunshine flames,
Men who through those wide fields of breezy grass
Where black-wing'd swallows haunt the glittering Thames,
To bathe in the abandon'd lasher pass,
Have often pass'd thee near
Sitting upon the river bank o'ergrown;
Mark'd thine outlandish garb, thy figure spare,
Thy dark vague eyes, and soft abstracted air—
But, when they came from bathing, thou wast gone!

At some lone homestead in the Cumner hills,
Where at her open door the housewife darns,
Thou hast been seen, or hanging on a gate
To watch the threshers in the mossy barns.
Children, who early range these slopes and late
For cresses from the rills,
Have known thee eying, all an April-day,
The springing pastures and the feeding kine;

And mark'd thee, when the stars come out and shine,
Through the long dewy grass move slow away.

In autumn, on the skirts of Bagley Wood—
Where most the gipsies by the turf-edged way
Pitch their smoked tents, and every bush you see
With scarlet patches tagg'd and shreds of grey,
Above the forest-ground called Thessaly—
The blackbird, picking food,
Sees thee, nor stops his meal, nor fears at all;
So often has he known thee past him stray,
Rapt, twirling in thy hand a wither'd spray,
And waiting for the spark from heaven to fall.

And once, in winter, on the causeway chill
Where home through flooded fields foot-travellers go,
Have I not pass'd thee on the wooden bridge,
Wrapt in thy cloak and battling with the snow,
Thy face tow'rd Hinksey and its wintry ridge?
And thou hast climb'd the hill,
And gain'd the white brow of the Cumner range;
Turn'd once to watch, while thick the snow-flakes fall,
The line of festal light in Christ-Church hall—
Then sought thy straw in some sequester'd grange.

But what—I dream! Two hundred years are flown
Since first thy story ran through Oxford halls,
And the grave Glanvil did the tale inscribe
That thou wert wander'd from the studious walls
To learn strange arts, and join a gipsy-tribe;
And thou from earth art gone
Long since, and in some quiet churchyard laid—
Some country-nook, where o'er thy unknown grave
Tall grasses and white flowering nettles wave,
Under a dark, red-fruited yew-tree's shade.

—No, no, thou hast not felt the lapse of hours!
For what wears out the life of mortal men?
'Tis that from change to change their being rolls;
'Tis that repeated shocks, again, again,
Exhaust the energy of strongest souls
And numb the elastic powers.
Till having used our nerves with bliss and teen,
And tired upon a thousand schemes our wit,
To the just-pausing Genius we remit
Our worn-out life, and are—what we have been.

Thou hast not lived, why should'st thou perish, so?
Thou hadst *one* aim, *one* business, *one* desire;
Else wert thou long since number'd with the dead!
Else hadst thou spent, like other men, thy fire!
The generations of thy peers are fled,
And we ourselves shall go;
But thou possessest an immortal lot,
And we imagine thee exempt from age
And living as thou liv'st on Glanvil's page,
Because thou hadst—what we, alas! have not.

For early didst thou leave the world, with powers
Fresh, undiverted to the world without,
Firm to their mark, not spent on other things;
Free from the sick fatigue, the languid doubt,
Which much to have tried, in much been baffled, brings.
O life unlike to ours!

Who fluctuate idly without term or scope,
Of whom each strives, nor knows for what he strives,
And each half lives a hundred different lives;
Who wait like thee, but not, like thee, in hope.

Thou waitest for the spark from heaven! and we,
Light half-believers of our casual creeds,
Who never deeply felt, nor clearly will'd,
Whose insight never has borne fruit in deeds,
Whose vague resolves never have been fulfill'd;
For whom each year we see
Breeds new beginnings, disappointments new;
Who hesitate and falter life away,
And lose to-morrow the ground won to-day—
Ah! do not we, wanderer! await it too?

Yes, we await it!—but it still delays,
And then we suffer! and amongst us one,
Who most has suffer'd, takes dejectedly
His seat upon the intellectual throne;
And all his store of sad experience he
Lays bare of wretched days;
Tells us his misery's birth and growth and signs,
And how the dying spark of hope was fed,
And how the breast was soothed, and how the head,
And all his hourly varied anodynes.

This for our wisest! and we others pine,
And wish the long unhappy dream would end,
And waive all claim to bliss, and try to bear;
With close-lipp'd patience for our only friend,
Sad patience, too near neighbour to despair—
But none has hope like thine!
Thou through the fields and through the woods dost stray,
Roaming the country-side, a truant boy,
Nursing thy project in unclouded joy,
And every doubt long blown by time away.

O born in days when wits were fresh and clear,
And life ran gaily as the sparkling Thames;
Before this strange disease of modern life,
With its sick hurry, its divided aims,
Its heads o'ertax'd, its palsied hearts, was rife—
Fly hence, our contact fear!
Still fly, plunge deeper in the bowering wood!
Averse, as Dido did with gesture stern
From her false friend's approach in Hades turn,
Wave us away, and keep thy solitude!

Still nursing the unconquerable hope,
Still clutching the inviolable shade,
With a free, onward impulse brushing through,
By night, the silver'd branches of the glade—
Far on the forest-skirts, where none pursue,
On some mild pastoral slope
Emerge, and resting on the moonlit pales
Freshen thy flowers as in former years
With dew, or listen with enchanted ears,
From the dark dingles, to the nightingales!

But fly our paths, our feverish contact fly!
For strong the infection of our mental strife,
Which, though it gives no bliss, yet spoils for rest;
And we should win thee from thy own fair life,
Like us distracted, and like us unblest.
Soon, soon thy cheer would die,
Thy hopes grow timorous, and unfix'd thy powers,
And thy clear aims be cross and shifting made;
And then thy glad perennial youth would fade,
Fade, and grow old at last, and die like ours.

Then fly our greetings, fly our speech and smiles!
—As some grave Tyrian trader, from the sea,

Descried at sunrise an emerging prow
Lifting the cool-hair'd creepers stealthily,
The fringes of a southward-facing brow
Among the Ægæan isles;
And saw the merry Grecian coaster come,
Freighted with amber grapes, and Chian wine,
Green, bursting figs, and tunnies steep'd in brine—
And knew the intruders on his ancient home,

The young light-hearted masters of the waves—
And snatch'd his rudder, and shook out more sail;
And day and night held on indignantly
O'er the blue Midland waters with the gale,
Betwixt the Syrtes and soft Sicily,
To where the Atlantic raves
Outside the western straits; and unbent sails
There, where down cloudy cliffs, through sheets of foam,
Shy traffickers, the dark Iberians come;
And on the beach undid his corded bales.

1853

HAWORTH CHURCHYARD

April, 1855

Where, under Loughrigg, the stream
Of Rotha sparkles through fields
Vested for ever with green,
Four years since, in the house
Of a gentle spirit, now dead—
Wordsworth's son-in-law, friend—
I saw the meeting of two
Gifted women.[1] The one,
Brilliant with recent renown,
Young, unpractised, had told
With a master's accent her feign'd
Story of passionate life;
The other, maturer in fame,
Earning, she too, her praise
First in fiction, had since
Widen'd her sweep, and survey'd
History, politics, mind.

[1] Charlotte Brontë and Harriet Martineau.

The two held converse; they wrote
In a book which of world-famous souls
Kept the memorial;—bard,
Warrior, statesman, had sign'd
Their names; chief glory of all,
Scott had bestow'd there his last
Breathings of song, with a pen
Tottering, a death-stricken hand.

Hope at that meeting smiled fair.
Years in number, it seem'd,
Lay before both, and a fame
Heighten'd, and multiplied power.—
Behold! The elder, to-day,
Lies expecting from death,
In mortal weakness, a last
Summons! the younger is dead!

First to the living we pay
Mournful homage;—the Muse
Gains not an earth-deafen'd ear.

Hail to the steadfast soul,
Which, unflinching and keen,
Wrought to erase from its depth
Mist and illusion and fear!
Hail to the spirit which dared
Trust its own thoughts, before yet
Echoed her back by the crowd!
Hail to the courage which gave
Voice to its creed, ere the creed
Won consecration from time!

Turn we next to the dead.
—How shall we honour the young,
The ardent, the gifted? how mourn?
Console we cannot, her ear
Is deaf. Far northward from here,
In a churchyard high 'mid the moors
Of Yorkshire, a little earth
Stops it for ever to praise.

Where, behind Keighley, the road
Up to the heart of the moors
Between heath-clad showery hills
Runs, and colliers' carts
Poach the deep ways coming down,
And a rough, grimed race have their homes-
There on its slope is built
The moorland town. But the church

Stands on the crest of the hill,
Lonely and bleak;—at its side
The parsonage-house and the graves.

Strew with laurel the grave
Of the early-dying! Alas,
Early she goes on the path
To the silent country, and leaves
Half her laurels unwon,
Dying too soon!—yet green
Laurels she had, and a course
Short, but redoubled by fame.

And not friendless, and not
Only with strangers to meet,
Faces ungreeting and cold,
Thou, O mourn'd one, to-day
Enterest the house of the grave!
Those of thy blood, whom thou lov'dst,
Have preceded thee—young,
Loving, a sisterly band;
Some in art, some in gift
Inferior—all in fame.
They, like friends, shall receive
This comer, greet her with joy;
Welcome the sister, the friend;
Hear with delight of thy fame!

Round thee they lie—the grass
Blows from their graves to thy own!
She, whose genius, though not
Puissant like thine, was yet
Sweet and graceful;—and she
(How shall I sing her?) whose soul
Knew no fellow for might,
Passion, vehemence, grief,
Daring, since Byron died,
That world-famed son of fire—she, who sank
Baffled, unknown, self-consumed;
Whose too bold dying song
Stirr'd, like a clarion-blast, my soul.
Of one, too, I have heard,
A brother—sleeps he here?
Of all that gifted race
Not the least gifted; young,
Unhappy, eloquent—the child
Of many hopes, of many tears.
O boy, if here thou sleep'st, sleep well!
On thee too did the Muse
Bright in thy cradle smile;
But some dark shadow came
(I know not what) and interposed.

Sleep, O cluster of friends,
Sleep!—or only when May,
Brought by the west-wind, returns
Back to your native heaths,
And the plover is heard on the moors,
Yearly awake to behold
The opening summer, the sky,
The shining moorland—to hear
The drowsy bee, as of old,
Hum o'er the thyme, the grouse
Call from the heather in bloom!
Sleep, or only for this
Break your united repose!

1855

STANZAS FROM THE GRANDE CHARTREUSE

THROUGH Alpine meadows soft-suffused
With rain, where thick the crocus blows,
Past the dark forges long disused,
The mule-track from Saint Laurent goes.
The bridge is cross'd, and slow we ride,
Through forest, up the mountain-side.

The autumnal evening darkens round,
The wind is up, and drives the rain;
While, hark! far down, with strangled sound
Doth the Dead Guier's stream complain,
Where that wet smoke, among the woods,
Over his boiling cauldron broods.

Swift rush the spectral vapours white
Past limestone scars with ragged pines,
Showing—then blotting from our sight!—
Halt—through the cloud-drift something shines!
High in the valley, wet and drear,
The huts of Courrerie appear.

Strike leftward! cries our guide; and higher
Mounts up the stony forest-way.
At last the encircling trees retire;
Look! through the showery twilight grey
What pointed roofs are these advance?—
A palace of the Kings of France?

Approach, for what we seek is here!
Alight, and sparely sup, and wait
For rest in this outbuilding near;
Then cross the sward and reach that gate.
Knock; pass the wicket! Thou art come
To the Carthusians' world-famed home.

The silent courts, where night and day
Into their stone-carved basins cold
The splashing icy fountains play—
The humid corridors behold!
Where, ghostlike in the deepening night,
Cowl'd forms brush by in gleaming white.

The chapel, where no organ's peal
Invests the stern and naked prayer—
With penitential cries they kneel
And wrestle; rising then, with bare
And white uplifted faces stand,
Passing the Host from hand to hand;

Each takes, and then his visage wan
Is buried in his cowl once more.
The cells!—the suffering Son of Man
Upon the wall—the knee-worn floor—
And where they sleep, that wooden bed,
Which shall their coffin be, when dead!

The library, where tract and tome
Not to feed priestly pride are there,
To hymn the conquering march of Rome,
Nor yet to amuse, as ours are!
They paint of souls the inner strife,
Their drops of blood, their death in life.

The garden, overgrown—yet mild,
See, fragrant herbs are flowering there!
Strong children of the Alpine wild
Whose culture is the brethren's care;
Of human tasks their only one,
And cheerful works beneath the sun.

Those halls, too, destined to contain
Each its own pilgrim-host of old,
From England, Germany, or Spain—
All are before me! I behold
The House, the Brotherhood austere!
—And what am I, that I am here?

For rigorous teachers seized my youth,
And purged its faith, and trimm'd its fire,
Show'd me the high, white star of Truth,
There bade me gaze, and there aspire.
Even now their whispers pierce the gloom:
What dost thou in this living tomb?

Forgive me, masters of the mind!
At whose behest I long ago
So much unlearnt, so much resign'd—
I come not here to be your foe!
I seek these anchorites, not in ruth,
To curse and to deny your truth;

Not as their friend, or child, I speak!
But as, on some far northern strand,
Thinking of his own Gods, a Greek
In pity and mournful awe might stand
Before some fallen Runic stone—
For both were faiths, and both are gone.

Wandering between two worlds, one dead,
The other powerless to be born,
With nowhere yet to rest my head,
Like these, on earth I wait forlorn.
Their faith, my tears, the world deride—
I come to shed them at their side.

Oh, hide me in your gloom profound,
Ye solemn seats of holy pain!
Take me, cowl'd forms, and fence me round,
Till I possess my soul again;
Till free my thoughts before me roll,
Not chafed by hourly false control!

For the world cries your faith is now
But a dead time's exploded dream;
My melancholy, sciolists say,
Is a pass'd mode, an outworn theme—
As if the world had ever had
A faith, or sciolists been sad!

Ah, if it *be* pass'd, take away,
At least, the restlessness, the pain;
Be man henceforth no more a prey
To these out-dated stings again!
The nobleness of grief is gone—
Ah, leave us not the fret alone!

But—if you cannot give us ease—
Last of the race of them who grieve
Here leave us to die out with these
Last of the people who believe!
Silent, while years engrave the brow;
Silent—the best are silent now.

Achilles ponders in his tent,
The kings of modern thought are dumb;
Silent they are, though not content,
And wait to see the future come.
They have the grief men had of yore,
But they contend and cry no more.

Our fathers water'd with their tears
This sea of time whereon we sail,
Their voices were in all men's ears
Who pass'd within their puissant hail.
Still the same ocean round us raves,
But we stand mute, and watch the waves.

For what avail'd it, all the noise
And outcry of the former men?—
Say, have their sons achieved more joys,
Say, is life lighter now than then?
The sufferers died, they left their pain—
The pangs which tortured them remain.

What helps it now, that Byron bore,
With haughty scorn which mock'd the smart,
Through Europe to the Ætolian shore
The pageant of his bleeding heart?
That thousands counted every groan,
And Europe made his woe her own?

What boots it, Shelley! that the breeze
Carried thy lovely wail away,
Musical through Italian trees
Which fringe thy soft blue Spezzian bay?
Inheritors of thy distress
Have restless hearts one throb the less?

Or are we easier, to have read,
O Obermann! the sad, stern page,
Which tells us how thou hidd'st thy head
From the fierce tempest of thine age
In the lone brakes of Fontainebleau,
Or chalets near the Alpine snow?

Ye slumber in your silent grave!—
The world, which for an idle day
Grace to your mood of sadness gave,
Long since hath flung her weeds away.
The eternal trifler breaks your spell;
But we—we learnt your lore too well!

Years hence, perhaps, may dawn an age,
More fortunate, alas! than we,
Which without hardness will be sage,
And gay without frivolity.
Sons of the world, oh, speed those years;
But, while we wait, allow our tears!

Allow them! We admire with awe
The exulting thunder of your race;
You give the universe your law,
You triumph over time and space!
Your pride of life, your tireless powers,
We laud them, but they are not ours.

We are like children rear'd in shade
Beneath some old-world abbey wall,
Forgotten in a forest-glade,
And secret from the eyes of all.
Deep, deep the greenwood round them waves,
Their abbey, and its close of graves!

But, where the road runs near the stream,
Oft through the trees they catch a glance
Of passing troops in the sun's beam—
Pennon, and plume, and flashing lance!
Forth to the world those soldiers fare,
To life, to cities, and to war!

And through the wood, another way,
Faint bugle-notes from far are borne,
Where hunters gather, staghounds bay,
Round some fair forest-lodge at morn.
Gay dames are there, in sylvan green;
Laughter and cries—those notes between!

The banners flashing through the trees
Make their blood dance and chain their eyes
That bugle-music on the breeze
Arrests them with a charm'd surprise.
Banner by turns and bugle woo:
Ye shy recluses, follow too!

O children, what do ye reply?—
"Action and pleasure, will ye roam
Through these secluded dells to cry
And call us?—but too late ye come!
Too late for us your call ye blow,
Whose bent was taken long ago.

"Long since we pace this shadow'd nave;
We watch those yellow tapers shine,
Emblems of hope over the grave,
In the high altar's depth divine;
The organ carries to our ear
Its accents of another sphere.

"Fenced early in this cloistral round
Of reverie, of shade, of prayer,
How should we grow in other ground?
How can we flower in foreign air?
—Pass, banners, pass, and bugles, cease;
And leave our desert to its peace!"

1855

SAINT BRANDAN

SAINT BRANDAN sails the northern main;
The brotherhoods of saints are glad.
He greets them once, he sails again;
So late!—such storms!—The Saint is mad!

He heard, across the howling seas,
Chime convent-bells on wintry nights;
He saw, on spray-swept Hebrides,
Twinkle the monastery-lights.

But north, still north, Saint Brandan steer'd—
And now no bells, no convents more!
The hurtling Polar lights are near'd,
The sea without a human shore.

At last—(it was the Christmas night;
Stars shone after a day of storm)—
He sees float past an iceberg white,
And on it—Christ!—a living form.

That furtive mien, that scowling eye,
Of hair that red and tufted fell——
It is—Oh, where shall Brandan fly?—
The traitor Judas, out of hell!

Palsied with terror, Brandan sate;
The moon was bright, the iceberg near.
He hears a voice sigh humbly: "Wait!
By high permission I am here.

"One moment wait, thou holy man!
On earth my crime, my death, they knew;
My name is under all men's ban—
Ah, tell them of my respite too!

"Tell them, one blessed Christmas-night—
(It was the first after I came,
Breathing self-murder, frenzy, spite,
To rue my guilt in endless flame)—

"I felt, as I in torment lay
'Mid the souls plagued by heavenly power,
An angel touch mine arm, and say:
Go hence and cool thyself an hour!

" 'Ah, whence this mercy, Lord?' I said.
The Leper recollect, said he,
Who ask'd the passers-by for aid,
In Joppa, and thy charity.

"Then I remember'd how I went,
In Joppa, through the public street,
One morn when the sirocco spent
Its storms of dust with burning heat;

"And in the street a leper sate,
Shivering with fever, naked, old;
Sand raked his sores from heel to pate,
The hot wind fever'd him five-fold.

"He gazed upon me as I pass'd,
And murmur'd: *Help me, or I die!*—
To the poor wretch my cloak I cast,
Saw him look eased, and hurried by.

"Oh, Brandan, think what grace divine,
What blessing must full goodness shower,
When fragment of it small, like mine,
Hath such inestimable power!

"Well-fed, well-clothed, well-friended, I
Did that chance act of good, that one!
Then went my way to kill and lie—
Forgot my good as soon as done.

"That germ of kindness, in the womb
Of mercy caught, did not expire;
Outlives my guilt, outlives my doom,
And friends me in the pit of fire.

"Once every year, when carols wake,
On earth, the Christmas-night's repose,
Arising from the sinners' lake,
I journey to these healing snows.

"I stanch with ice my burning breast,
With silence balm my whirling brain.
O Brandan! to this hour of rest
That Joppan leper's ease was pain."——

Tears started to Saint Brandan's eyes;
He bow'd his head, he breathed a prayer—
Then look'd, and lo, the frosty skies!
The iceberg, and no Judas there!

1860

THYRSIS

A MONODY, *to commemorate the author's friend*, ARTHUR HUGH CLOUGH, *who died at Florence*, 1861

How changed is here each spot man makes or fills!
In the two Hinkseys nothing keeps the same;

The village street its haunted mansion lacks,
And from the sign is gone Sibylla's name,
And from the roofs the twisted chimney-stacks—
Are ye too changed, ye hills?
See, 'tis no foot of unfamiliar men
To-night from Oxford up your pathway strays!
Here came I often, often, in old days—
Thyrsis and I; we still had Thyrsis then.

Runs it not here, the track by Childsworth Farm,
Past the high wood, to where the elm-tree crowns
The hill behind whose ridge the sunset flames?
The signal-elm, that looks on Ilsley Downs,
The Vale, the three lone weirs, the youthful Thames?—
This winter-eve is warm,
Humid the air! leafless, yet soft as spring,
The tender purple spray on copse and briers!
And that sweet city with her dreaming spires,
She needs not June for beauty's heightening,

Lovely all times she lies, lovely to-night!—
Only, methinks, some loss of habit's power
Befalls me wandering through this upland dim.
Once pass'd I blindfold here, at any hour;
Now seldom come I, since I came with him.
That single elm-tree bright
Against the west—I miss it! is it gone?
We prized it dearly; while it stood, we said,
Our friend, the Gipsy-Scholar, was not dead;
While the tree lived, he in these fields lived on.

Too rare, too rare, grow now my visits here,
But once I knew each field, each flower, each stick;
And with the country-folk acquaintance made
By barn in threshing-time, by new-built rick.
Here, too, our shepherd-pipes we first assay'd.
Ah me! this many a year
My pipe is lost, my shepherd's holiday!
Needs must I lose them, needs with heavy heart
Into the world and wave of men depart;
But Thyrsis of his own will went away.

It irk'd him to be here, he could not rest.
He loved each simple joy the country yields,
He loved his mates; but yet he could not keep,
For that a shadow lour'd on the fields,
Here with the shepherds and the silly sheep.
Some life of men unblest
He knew, which made him droop, and fill'd his head.
He went; his piping took a troubled sound
Of storms that rage outside our happy ground;
He could not wait their passing, he is dead.

So, some tempestuous morn in early June,
When the year's primal burst of bloom is o'er,
Before the roses and the longest day—
When garden-walks and all the grassy floor
With blossoms red and white of fallen May
And chestnut-flowers are strewn—
So have I heard the cuckoo's parting cry,
From the wet field, through the vext garden-trees,
Come with the volleying rain and tossing breeze:
The bloom is gone, and with the bloom go I!

Too quick despairer, wherefore wilt thou go?
Soon will the high Midsummer pomps come on,
Soon will the musk carnations break and swell,
Soon shall we have gold-dusted snapdragon,
Sweet-William with his homely cottage-smell,
And stocks in fragrant blow;

Roses that down the alleys shine afar,
And open, jasmine-muffled lattices,
And groups under the dreaming garden-trees,
And the full moon, and the white evening-star.

He hearkens not! light comer, he is flown!
What matters it? next year he will return,
And we shall have him in the sweet spring-days,
With whitening hedges, and uncrumpling fern,
And blue-bells trembling by the forest-ways,
And scent of hay new-mown.
But Thyrsis never more we swains shall see;
See him come back, and cut a smoother reed,
And blow a strain the world at last shall heed—
For Time, not Corydon, hath conquer'd thee!

Alack, for Corydon no rival now!—
But when Sicilian shepherds lost a mate,
Some good survivor with his flute would go,
Piping a ditty sad for Bion's fate;
And cross the unpermitted ferry's flow,
And relax Pluto's brow,
And make leap up with joy the beauteous head
Of Proserpine, among whose crownéd hair
Are flowers first open'd on Sicilian air,
And flute his friend, like Orpheus, from the dead.

O easy access to the hearer's grace
When Dorian shepherds sang to Proserpine!
For she herself had trod Sicilian fields,
She knew the Dorian water's gush divine,
She knew each lily white which Enna yields,
Each rose with blushing face;
She loved the Dorian pipe, the Dorian strain.
But ah, of our poor Thames she never heard!
Her foot the Cumner cowslips never stirr'd;
And we should tease her with our plaint in vain!

Well! wind-dispersed and vain the words will be,
Yet, Thyrsis, let me give my grief its hour
In the old haunt, and find our tree-topp'd hill!
Who, if not I, for questing here hath power?
I know the wood which hides the daffodil,
I know the Fyfield tree,
I know what white, what purple fritillaries
The grassy harvest of the river-fields,
Above by Ensham, down by Sandford, yields,
And what sedged brooks are Thames's tributaries;

I know these slopes; who knows them if not I?—
But many a dingle on the loved hill-side,
With thorns once studded, old, white-blossom'd trees,
Where thick the cowslips grew, and far descried
High tower'd the spikes of purple orchises,
Hath since our day put by
The coronals of that forgotten time;
Down each green bank hath gone the ploughboy's team,
And only in the hidden brookside gleam
Primroses, orphans of the flowery prime.

Where is the girl, who by the boatman's door,
Above the locks, above the boating throng,
Unmoor'd our skiff when through the Wytham flats,
Red loosestrife and blond meadow-sweet among
And darting swallows and light water-gnats,
We track'd the shy Thames shore?
Where are the mowers, who, as the tiny swell
Of our boat passing heaved the river-grass,

Stood with suspended scythe to see us pass?—
They all are gone, and thou art gone as well!

Yes, thou art gone! and round me too the night
In ever-nearing circle weaves her shade.
I see her veil draw soft across the day,
I feel her slowly chilling breath invade
The cheek grown thin, the brown hair sprent with grey;
I feel her finger light
Laid pausefully upon life's headlong train;—
The foot less prompt to meet the morning dew,
The heart less bounding at emotion new,
And hope, once crush'd, less quick to spring again.

And long the way appears, which seem'd so short
To the less practised eye of sanguine youth;
And high the mountain-tops, in cloudy air,
The mountain-tops where is the throne of Truth,
Tops in life's morning-sun so bright and bare!
Unbreachable the fort
Of the long-batter'd world uplifts its wall;
And strange and vain the earthly turmoil grows,
And near and real the charm of thy repose,
And night as welcome as a friend would fall.

But hush! the upland hath a sudden loss
Of quiet!—Look, adown the dusk hill-side,
A troop of Oxford hunters going home,
As in old days, jovial and talking, ride!
From hunting with the Berkshire hounds they come.
Quick! let me fly, and cross
Into yon farther field!—'Tis done; and see,
Back'd by the sunset, which doth glorify
The orange and pale violet evening-sky,
Bare on its lonely ridge, the Tree! the Tree!

I take the omen! Eve lets down her veil,
The white fog creeps from bush to bush about,
The west unflushes, the high stars grow bright,
And in the scatter'd farms the lights come out.
I cannot reach the signal-tree to-night,
Yet, happy omen, hail!
Hear it from thy broad lucent Arno-vale
(For there thine earth-forgetting eyelids keep
The morningless and unawakening sleep
Under the flowery oleanders pale),

Hear it, O Thyrsis, still our tree is there!—
Ah, vain! These English fields, this upland dim,
These brambles pale with mist engarlanded,
That lone, sky-pointing tree, are not for him;
To a boon southern country he is fled,
And now in happier air,
Wandering with the great Mother's train divine
(And purer or more subtle soul than thee,
I trow, the mighty Mother doth not see)
Within a folding of the Apennine,

Thou hearest the immortal chants of old!—
Putting his sickle to the perilous grain
In the hot cornfield of the Phrygian king,
For thee the Lityerses-song again
Young Daphnis with his silver voice doth sing;
Sings his Sicilian fold,
His sheep, his hapless love, his blinded eyes—
And how a call celestial round him rang,
And heavenward from the fountain-brink he sprang,
And all the marvel of the golden skies.

There thou art gone, and me thou leavest here
Sole in these fields! yet will I not despair.
Despair I will not, while I yet descry
Neath the mild canopy of English air
That lonely tree against the western sky.
Still, still these slopes, 'tis clear,

Our Gipsy-Scholar haunts, outliving thee!
Fields where soft sheep from cages pull the hay,
Woods with anemonies in flower till May,
Know him a wanderer still; then why not me?

A fugitive and gracious light he seeks,
Shy to illumine; and I seek it too.
This does not come with houses or with gold,
With place, with honour, and a flattering crew;
'Tis not in the world's market bought and sold—
But the smooth-slipping weeks
Drop by, and leave its seeker still untired;
Out of the heed of mortals he is gone,
He wends unfollow'd, he must house alone;
Yet on he fares, by his own heart inspired.

Thou too, O Thyrsis, on like quest wast bound;
Thou wanderedst with me for a little hour!
Men gave thee nothing; but his happy quest,
If men esteem'd thee feeble, gave thee power,
If men procured thee trouble, gave thee rest.
And this rude Cumner ground,
Its fir-topped Hurst, its farms, its quiet fields,
Here cam'st thou in thy jocund youthful time,
Here was thine height of strength, thy golden prime!
And still the haunt beloved a virtue yields.

What though the music of thy rustic flute
Kept not for long its happy, country tone;
Lost it too soon, and learnt a stormy note
Of men contention-tost, of men who groan,
Which task'd thy pipe too sore, and tired thy throat—
It fail'd, and thou wast mute!
Yet hadst thou alway visions of our light,
And long with men of care thou couldst not stay,
And soon thy foot resumed its wandering way,
Left human haunt, and on alone till night.

Too rare, too rare, grow now my visits here!
'Mid city-noise, not, as with thee of yore,
Thyrsis! in reach of sheep-bells is my home.
—Then through the great town's harsh, heart-wearying roar,
Let in thy voice a whisper often come,
To chase fatigue and fear:
Why faintest thou? I wander'd till I died.
Roam on! The light we sought is shining still.
Dost thou ask proof? Our tree yet crowns the hill,
Our Scholar travels yet the loved hill-side.

1866

EAST LONDON

'Twas August, and the fierce sun overhead
Smote on the squalid streets of Bethnal Green,
And the pale weaver, through his windows seen
In Spitalfields, look'd thrice dispirited.

I met a preacher there I knew, and said:
"Ill and o'erwork'd, how fare you in this scene?"—
"Bravely!" said he; "for I of late have been
Much cheer'd with thoughts of Christ, *the living bread.*"

O human soul! as long as thou canst so
Set up a mark of everlasting light,
Above the howling senses' ebb and flow,

To cheer thee, and to right thee if thou roam—
Not with lost toil thou labourest through the night!
Thou mak'st the heaven thou hop'st indeed thy home.

1867

WEST LONDON

Crouch'd on the pavement, close by Belgrave Square,
A tramp I saw, ill, moody, and tongue-tied.
A babe was in her arms, and at her side
A girl; their clothes were rags, their feet were bare.

Some labouring men, whose work lay somewhere there,
Pass'd opposite; she touch'd her girl, who hied
Across, and begg'd, and came back satisfied.
The rich she had let pass with frozen stare.

Thought I: "Above her state this spirit towers;
She will not ask of aliens, but of friends,
Of sharers in a common human fate.

"She turns from that cold succour, which attends
The unknown little from the unknowing great,
And points us to a better time than ours."

1867

THE BETTER PART

LONG fed on boundless hopes, O race of man,
How angrily thou spurn'st all simpler fare!
"Christ," some one says, "was human as we are;
No judge eyes us from Heaven, our sin to scan;

"We live no more, when we have done our span."—
"Well, then, for Christ," thou answerest, "who can care?
From sin, which Heaven records not, why forbear?
Live we like brutes our life without a plan!"

So answerest thou; but why not rather say:
"Hath man no second life?—*Pitch this one high!*
Sits there no judge in Heaven, our sin to see?—

"*More strictly, then, the inward judge obey!*
Was Christ a man like us? *Ah! let us try*
If we, then, too, can be such men as he!"

1867

IMMORTALITY

FOIL'D by our fellow-men, depress'd, outworn,
We leave the brutal world to take its way,
And, *Patience! in another life*, we say,
The world shall be thrust down, and we upborne.

And will not, then, the immortal armies scorn
The world's poor, routed leavings? or will they,
Who fail'd under the heat of this life's day,
Support the fervours of the heavenly morn?

No, no! the energy of life may be
Kept on after the grave, but not begun;
And he who flagg'd not in the earthly strife,

From strength to strength advancing—only he,
His soul well-knit, and all his battles won,
Mounts, and that hardly, to eternal life.

1867

WORLDLY PLACE

EVEN in a palace, life may be led well!
So spake the imperial sage, purest of men,
Marcus Aurelius. But the stifling den
Of common life, where, crowded up pell-mell,

Our freedom for a little bread we sell,
And drudge under some foolish master's ken
Who rates us if we peer outside our pen—
Match'd with a palace, is not this a hell?

Even in a palace! On his truth sincere,
Who spoke these words, no shadow ever came;
And when my ill-school'd spirit is aflame

Some nobler, ampler stage of life to win,
I'll stop, and say: "There were no succour here!
The aids to noble life are all within."

1867

AUSTERITY OF POETRY

THAT son of Italy who tried to blow,
Ere Dante came, the trump of sacred song,
In his light youth amid a festal throng
Sate with his bride to see a public show.

Fair was the bride, and on her front did glow
Youth like a star; and what to youth belong—
Gay raiment, sparkling gauds, elation strong.
A prop gave way! crash fell a platform! lo,

'Mid struggling sufferers, hurt to death, she lay!
Shuddering, they drew her garments off—and found
A robe of sackcloth next the smooth, white skin.

Such, poets, is your bride, the Muse! young, gay,
Radiant, adorn'd outside; a hidden ground
Of thought and of austerity within.

1867

DOVER BEACH

THE sea is calm to-night.
The tide is full, the moon lies fair
Upon the straits;—on the French coast the light
Gleams and is gone; the cliffs of England stand,
Glimmering and vast, out in the tranquil bay.
Come to the window, sweet is the night-air!
Only, from the long line of spray
Where the sea meets the moon-blanch'd land,
Listen! you hear the grating roar
Of pebbles which the waves draw back, and fling,
At their return, up the high strand,
Begin, and cease, and then again begin,
With tremulous cadence slow, and bring
The eternal note of sadness in.

Sophocles long ago
Heard it on the Ægæan, and it brought
Into his mind the turbid ebb and flow
Of human misery; we
Find also in the sound a thought,
Hearing it by this distant northern sea.

The Sea of Faith
Was once, too, at the full, and round earth's shore
Lay like the folds of a bright girdle furl'd.
But now I only hear
Its melancholy, long, withdrawing roar,
Retreating, to the breath
Of the night-wind, down the vast edges drear
And naked shingles of the world.

Ah, love, let us be true
To one another! for the world, which seems
To lie before us like a land of dreams,
So various, so beautiful, so new,
Hath really neither joy, nor love, nor light,
Nor certitude, nor peace, nor help for pain;
And we are here as on a darkling plain
Swept with confused alarms of struggle and flight,
Where ignorant armies clash by night.

1867

PALLADIUM

SET where the upper streams of Simois flow
Was the Palladium, high 'mid rock and wood;
And Hector was in Ilium, far below,
And fought, and saw it not—but there it stood!

It stood, and sun and moonshine rain'd their light
On the pure columns of its glen-built hall.
Backward and forward roll'd the waves of fight
Round Troy—but while this stood, Troy could not fall.

So, in its lovely moonlight, lives the soul.
Mountains surround it, and sweet virgin air;
Cold plashing, past it, crystal waters roll;
We visit it by moments, ah, too rare!

We shall renew the battle in the plain
To-morrow;—red with blood will Xanthus be;
Hector and Ajax will be there again,
Helen will come upon the wall to see.

Then we shall rust in shade, or shine in strife,
And fluctuate 'twixt blind hopes and blind despairs,
And fancy that we put forth all our life,
And never know how with the soul it fares.

Still doth the soul, from its lone fastness high,
Upon our life a ruling effluence send.
And when it fails, fight as we will, we die;
And while it lasts, we cannot wholly end.

1867

YOUTH AND CALM

'TIS death! and peace, indeed, is here,
And ease from shame, and rest from fear.
There's nothing can dismarble now
The smoothness of that limpid brow.

But is a calm like this, in truth,
The crowning end of life and youth,
And when this boon rewards the dead,
Are all debts paid, has all been said?
And is the heart of youth so light,
Its step so firm, its eyes so bright,
Because on its hot brow there blows
A wind of promise and repose
From the far grave, to which it goes;
Because it hath the hope to come,
One day, to harbour in the tomb?
Ah no, the bliss youth dreams is one
For daylight, for the cheerful sun,
For feeling nerves and living breath—
Youth dreams a bliss on this side death.
It dreams a rest, if not more deep,
More grateful than this marble sleep;
It hears a voice within it tell:
Calm's not life's crown, though calm is well.
'Tis all perhaps which man acquires,
But 'tis not what our youth desires.

1867

GROWING OLD

WHAT is it to grow old?
Is it to lose the glory of the form,
The lustre of the eye?
Is it for beauty to forego her wreath?
—Yes, but not this alone.

Is it to feel our strength—
Not our bloom only, but our strength—decay?
Is it to feel each limb
Grow stiffer, every function less exact,
Each nerve more loosely strung?

Yes, this, and more; but not
Ah, 'tis not what in youth we dream'd 'twould be!
'Tis not to have our life
Mellow'd and soften'd as with sunset-glow,
A golden day's decline.

'Tis not to see the world
As from a height, with rapt prophetic eyes,
And heart profoundly stirr'd;
And weep, and feel the fulness of the past,
The years that are no more.

It is to spend long days
And not once feel that we were ever young;
It is to add, immured
In the hot prison of the present, month
To month with weary pain.

It is to suffer this,
And feel but half, and feebly, what we feel.
Deep in our hidden heart
Festers the dull remembrance of a change,
But no emotion—none.

It is—last stage of all—
When we are frozen up within, and quite
The phantom of ourselves,
To hear the world applaud the hollow ghost
Which blamed the living man.

1867

THE PROGRESS OF POESY

A VARIATION

YOUTH rambles on life's arid mount,
And strikes the rock, and finds the vein,
And brings the water from the fount,
The fount which shall not flow again.

The man mature with labour chops
For the bright stream a channel grand,
And sees not that the sacred drops
Ran off and vanish'd out of hand.

And then the old man totters nigh,
And feebly rakes among the stones.
The mount is mute, the channel dry;
And down he lays his weary bones.

1867

THE LAST WORD

CREEP into thy narrow bed,
Creep, and let no more be said!
Vain thy onset! all stands fast.
Thou thyself must break at last.

Let the long contention cease!
Geese are swans, and swans are geese.
Let them have it how they will!
Thou art tired; best be still.

They out-talk'd thee, hiss'd thee, tore thee?
Better men fared thus before thee;
Fired their ringing shot and pass'd,
Hotly charged—and sank at last.

Charge once more, then, and be dumb!
Let the victors, when they come,
When the forts of folly fall,
Find thy body by the wall!

1867

A WISH

I ASK not that my bed of death
From bands of greedy heirs be free;
For these besiege the latest breath
Of fortune's favour'd sons, not me.

I ask not each kind soul to keep
Tearless, when of my death he hears.
Let those who will, if any, weep!
There are worse plagues on earth than tears.

I ask but that my death may find
The freedom to my life denied;
Ask but the folly of mankind
Then, then at last, to quit my side.

Spare me the whispering, crowded room,
The friends who come, and gape, and go;
The ceremonious air of gloom—
All, which makes death a hideous show!

Nor bring, to see me cease to live,
Some doctor full of phrase and fame,
To shake his sapient head, and give
The ill he cannot cure a name.

Nor fetch, to take the accustom'd toll
Of the poor sinner bound for death,
His brother-doctor of the soul,
To canvass with official breath

The future and its viewless things—
That undiscover'd mystery
Which one who feels death's winnowing wings
Must needs read clearer, sure, than he!

Bring none of these; but let me be,
While all around in silence lies,
Moved to the window near, and see
Once more, before my dying eyes,

Bathed in the sacred dews of morn
The wide aerial landscape spread—
The world which was ere I was born,
The world which lasts when I am dead;

Which never was the friend of *one*,
Nor promised love it could not give,
But lit for all its generous sun,
And lived itself, and made us live.

There let me gaze, till I become
In soul, with what I gaze on, wed!
To feel the universe my home;
To have before my mind—instead

Of the sick room, the mortal strife,
The turmoil for a little breath—
The pure eternal course of life,
Not human combatings with death!

Thus feeling, gazing, might I grow
Composed, refresh'd, ennobled, clear;
Then willing let my spirit go
To work or wait elsewhere or here!

1867

PIS-ALLER

"MAN is blind because of sin,
Revelation makes him sure;
Without that, who looks within,
Looks in vain, for all's obscure."

Nay, look closer into man!
Tell me, can you find indeed
Nothing sure, no moral plan
Clear prescribed, without your creed?

"No, I nothing can perceive!
Without that, all's dark for men.
That, or nothing, I believe."—
For God's sake, believe it then!

1867

BACCHANALIA;

OR,

THE NEW AGE

I

THE evening comes, the fields are still.
The tinkle of the thirsty rill,
Unheard all day, ascends again;
Deserted is the half-mown plain,
Silent the swaths! the ringing wain,
The mower's cry, the dog's alarms,
All housed within the sleeping farms!

The business of the day is done,
The last-left haymaker is gone.
And from the thyme upon the height,
And from the elder-blossom white
And pale dog-roses in the hedge,
And from the mint-plant in the sedge,
In puffs of balm the night-air blows
The perfume which the day forgoes.
And on the pure horizon far,
See, pulsing with the first-born star,
The liquid sky above the hill!
The evening comes, the fields are still.

Loitering and leaping,
With saunter, with bounds—
Flickering and circling
In files and in rounds—
Gaily their pine-staff green
Tossing in air,
Loose o'er their shoulders white
Showering their hair—
See! the wild Mænads
Break from the wood,
Youth and Iacchus
Maddening their blood.
See! through the quiet land
Rioting they pass—
Fling the fresh heaps about,
Trample the grass.
Tear from the rifled hedge
Garlands, their prize;
Fill with their sports the field,
Fill with their cries.

Shepherd, what ails thee, then?
Shepherd, why mute?
Forth with thy joyous song!
Forth with thy flute!
Tempts not the revel blithe?
Lure not their cries?
Glow not their shoulders smooth?
Melt not their eyes?
Is not, on cheeks like those,
Lovely the flush?
—Ah, so the quiet was!
So was the hush!

II

The epoch ends, the world is still.
The age has talk'd and work'd its fill—
The famous orators have shone,
The famous poets sung and gone,
The famous men of war have fought,
The famous speculators thought,
The famous players, sculptors, wrought,
The famous painters fill'd their wall,
The famous critics judged it all.
The combatants are parted now—
Uphung the spear, unbent the bow,
The puissant crown'd, the weak laid low.
And in the after-silence sweet,
Now strifes are hush'd, our ears doth meet,
Ascending pure, the bell-like fame
Of this or that down-trodden name
Delicate spirits, push'd away
In the hot press of the noon-day.
And o'er the plain, where the dead age
Did its now silent warfare wage—
O'er that wide plain, now wrapt in gloom,
Where many a splendour finds its tomb,
Many spent fames and fallen mights—
The one or two immortal lights
Rise slowly up into the sky
To shine there everlastingly,
Like stars over the bounding hill.
The epoch ends, the world is still.

Thundering and bursting
In torrents, in waves—
Carolling and shouting
Over tombs, amid graves—
See! on the cumber'd plain
Clearing a stage,
Scattering the past about,
Comes the new age.
Bards make new poems,
Thinkers new schools,
Statesmen new systems,
Critics new rules.
All things begin again;
Life is their prize;
Earth with their deeds they fill,
Fill with their cries.

Poet, what ails thee, then?
Say, why so mute?
Forth with thy praising voice!
Forth with thy flute!
Loiterer! why sittest thou
Sunk in thy dream?
Tempts not the bright new age?
Shines not its stream?
Look, ah, what genius,

Art, science, wit!
Soldiers like Cæsar,
Statesmen like Pitt!
Sculptors like Phidias,
Raphaels in shoals,
Poets like Shakespeare—
Beautiful souls!
See, on their glowing cheeks
Heavenly the flush!
—Ah, so the silence was!
So was the hush!

The world but feels the present's spell,
The poet feels the past as well;
Whatever men have done, might do,
Whatever thought, might think it too.

1867

RUGBY CHAPEL

November 1857

Coldly, sadly descends
The autumn-evening. The field
Strewn with its dank yellow drifts
Of wither'd leaves, and the elms,
Fade into dimness apace,
Silent;—hardly a shout
From a few boys late at their play!
The lights come out in the street,
In the school-room windows;—but cold,
Solemn, unlighted, austere,
Through the gathering darkness, arise
The chapel-walls, in whose bound
Thou, my father! art laid.

There thou dost lie, in the gloom
Of the autumn evening. But ah!
That word, *gloom*, to my mind
Brings thee back, in the light
Of thy radiant vigour, again;
In the gloom of November we pass'd
Days not dark at thy side;
Seasons impair'd not the ray
Of thy buoyant cheerfulness clear.
Such thou wast! and I stand
In the autumn evening, and think
Of bygone autumns with thee.

Fifteen years have gone round
Since thou arosest to tread,
In the summer-morning, the road
Of death, at a call unforeseen,
Sudden. For fifteen years,
We who till then in thy shade
Rested as under the boughs
Of a mighty oak, have endured
Sunshine and rain as we might,
Bare, unshaded, alone,
Lacking the shelter of thee.

O strong soul, by what shore
Tarriest thou now? For that force,
Surely, has not been left vain!
Somewhere, surely, afar,
In the sounding labour-house vast
Of being, is practised that strength,
Zealous, beneficent, firm!

Yes, in some far-shining sphere,
Conscious or not of the past,
Still thou performest the word
Of the Spirit in whom thou dost live—
Prompt, unwearied, as here!
Still thou upraisest with zeal
The humble good from the ground,
Sternly repressest the bad!
Still, like a trumpet, dost rouse
Those who with half-open eyes
Tread the border-land dim
'Twixt vice and virtue; reviv'st,
Succourest!—this was thy work,
This was thy life upon earth.

What is the course of the life
Of mortal men on the earth?—
Most men eddy about
Here and there—eat and drink,
Chatter and love and hate,
Gather and squander, are raised
Aloft, are hurl'd in the dust,
Striving blindly, achieving
Nothing; and then they die—
Perish;—and no one asks
Who or what they have been,
More than he asks what waves,
In the moonlit solitudes mild
Of the midmost Ocean, have swell'd,
Foam'd for a moment, and gone.

And there are some, whom a thirst
Ardent, unquenchable, fires,
Not with the crowd to be spent,
Not without aim to go round

In an eddy of purposeless dust,
Effort unmeaning and vain.
Ah yes! some of us strive
Not without action to die
Fruitless, but something to snatch
From dull oblivion, nor all
Glut the devouring grave!
We, we have chosen our path—
Path to a clear-purposed goal,
Path of advance!—but it leads
A long, steep journey, through sunk
Gorges, o'er mountains in snow.
Cheerful, with friends, we set forth—
Then, on the height, comes the storm.
Thunder crashes from rock
To rock, the cataracts reply,
Lightnings dazzle our eyes.
Roaring torrents have breach'd
The track, the stream-bed descends
In the place where the wayfarer once
Planted his footstep—the spray
Boils o'er its borders! aloft
The unseen snow-beds dislodge
Their hanging ruin; alas,
Havoc is made in our train!
Friends, who set forth at our side,
Falter, are lost in the storm.
We, we only are left!
With frowning foreheads, with lips
Sternly compress'd, we strain on,
On—and at nightfall at last
Come to the end of our way,
To the lonely inn 'mid the rocks;
Where the gaunt and taciturn host
Stands on the threshold, the wind
Shaking his thin white hairs—
Holds his lantern to scan
Our storm-beat figures, and asks:
Whom in our party we bring?
Whom we have left in the snow?

Sadly we answer: We bring
Only ourselves! we lost
Sight of the rest in the storm.
Hardly ourselves we fought through,
Stripp'd, without friends, as we are.
Friends, companions, and train,
The avalanche swept from our side.

But thou would'st not *alone*
Be saved, my father! *alone*
Conquer and come to thy goal,
Leaving the rest in the wild.
We were weary, and we
Fearful, and we in our march
Fain to drop down and to die.
Still thou turnedst, and still
Beckonedst the trembler, and still
Gavest the weary thy hand.

If, in the paths of the world,
Stones might have wounded thy feet,
Toil or dejection have tried
Thy spirit, of that we saw
Nothing—to us thou wast still
Cheerful, and helpful, and firm!
Therefore to thee it was given
Many to save with thyself;
And, at the end of thy day,
O faithful shepherd! to come,
Bringing thy sheep in thy hand.
And through thee I believe
In the noble and great who are gone;
Pure souls honour'd and blest
By former ages, who else—
Such, so soulless, so poor,
Is the race of men whom I see—
Seem'd but a dream of the heart,
Seem'd but a cry of desire.
Yes! I believe that there lived
Others like thee in the past,
Not like the men of the crowd
Who all round me to-day
Bluster or cringe, and make life
Hideous, and arid, and vile;
But souls temper'd with fire,
Fervent, heroic, and good,
Helpers and friends of mankind.

Servants of God!—or sons
Shall I not call you? because
Not as servants ye knew
Your Father's innermost mind,
His, who unwillingly sees
One of his little ones lost—
Yours is the praise, if mankind
Hath not as yet in its march
Fainted, and fallen, and died!

See! In the rocks of the world
Marches the host of mankind,
A feeble, wavering line.

Where are they tending?—A God
Marshall'd them, gave them their goal.
Ah, but the way is so long!
Years they have been in the wild!
Sore thirst plagues them, the rocks,
Rising all round, overawe;
Factions divide them, their host
Threatens to break, to dissolve.
—Ah, keep, keep them combined!
Else, of the myriads who fill
That army, not one shall arrive;
Sole they shall stray; in the rocks
Stagger for ever in vain,
Die one by one in the waste.

Then, in such hour of need
Of your fainting, dispirited race,
Ye, like angels, appear,
Radiant with ardour divine!
Beacons of hope, ye appear!
Languor is not in your heart,
Weakness is not in your word,
Weariness not on your brow.
Ye alight in our van! at your voice,
Panic, despair, flee away.
Ye move through the ranks, recall
The stragglers, refresh the outworn,
Praise, re-inspire the brave!
Order, courage, return.
Eyes rekindling, and prayers,
Follow your steps as ye go.
Ye fill up the gaps in our files,
Strengthen the wavering line,
Stablish, continue our march,
On, to the bound of the waste,
On, to the City of God.

1867

OBERMANN ONCE MORE

Savez-vous quelque bien qui console du regret d'un monde?

—Obermann

Glion?——Ah, twenty years, it cuts
All meaning from a name!
White houses prank where once were huts.
Glion, but not the same!

And yet I know not! All unchanged
The turf, the pines, the sky!
The hills in their old order ranged;
The lake, with Chillon by!

And, 'neath those chestnut-trees, where stiff
And stony mounts the way,
The crackling husk-heaps burn, as if
I left them yesterday!

Across the valley, on that slope,
The huts of Avant shine!
Its pines, under their branches, ope
Ways for the pasturing kine.

Full-foaming milk-pails, Alpine fare,
Sweet heaps of fresh-cut grass,
Invite to rest the traveller there
Before he climb the pass—

The gentian-flower'd pass, its crown
With yellow spires aflame;
Whence drops the path to Allière down,
And walls where Byron came,

By their green river, who doth change
His birth-name just below;
Orchard, and croft, and full-stored grange
Nursed by his pastoral flow.

But stop!—to fetch back thoughts that stray
Beyond this gracious bound,
The cone of Jaman, pale and grey,
See, in the blue profound!

Ah, Jaman! delicately tall
Above his sun-warm'd firs—
What thoughts to me his rocks recall,
What memories he stirs!

And who but thou must be, in truth,
Obermann! with me here?
Thou master of my wandering youth,
But left this many a year!

Yes, I forget the world's work wrought,
Its warfare waged with pain;
An eremite with thee, in thought
Once more I slip my chain,

And to thy mountain-chalet come,
And lie beside its door,
And hear the wild bee's Alpine hum,
And thy sad, tranquil lore!

Again I feel the words inspire
Their mournful calm; serene,
Yet tinged with infinite desire
For all that *might* have been—

The harmony from which man swerved
Made his life's rule once more!
The universal order served,
Earth happier than before!

—While thus I mused, night gently ran
Down over hill and wood.
Then, still and sudden, Obermann
On the grass near me stood.

Those pensive features well I knew,
On my mind, years before,
Imaged so oft! imaged so true!
—A shepherd's garb he wore,

A mountain-flower was in his hand,
A book was in his breast.
Bent on my face, with gaze which scann'd
My soul, his eyes did rest.

"And is it thou," he cried, "so long
Held by the world which we
Loved not, who turnest from the throng
Back to thy youth and me?

"And from thy world, with heart opprest,
Choosest thou *now* to turn?—
Ah me! we anchorites read things best,
Clearest their course discern!

"Thou fledst me when the ungenial earth,
Man's work-place, lay in gloom.
Return'st thou in her hour of birth,
Of hopes and hearts in bloom?

"Perceiv'st thou not the change of day?
Ah! Carry back thy ken,
What, some two thousand years! Survey
The world as it was then!

"Like ours it look'd in outward air.
Its head was clear and true,
Sumptuous its clothing, rich its fare,
No pause its action knew;

"Stout was its arm, each thew and bone
Seem'd puissant and alive—
But, ah! its heart, its heart was stone,
And so it could not thrive!

"On that hard Pagan world disgust
And secret loathing fell.
Deep weariness and sated lust
Made human life a hell.

"In his cool hall, with haggard eyes,
The Roman noble lay;
He drove abroad, in furious guise,
Along the Appian way.

"He made a feast, drank fierce and fast,
And crown'd his hair with flowers—
No easier nor no quicker pass'd
The impracticable hours.

"The brooding East with awe beheld
Her impious younger world.
The Roman tempest swell'd and swell'd,
And on her head was hurl'd.

"The East bow'd low before the blast
In patient, deep disdain;
She let the legions thunder past,
And plunged in thought again.

"So well she mused, a morning broke
Across her spirit grey;
A conquering, new-born joy awoke,
And fill'd her life with day.

" 'Poor world,' she cried, 'so deep accurst,
That runn'st from pole to pole
To seek a draught to slake thy thirst—
Go, seek it in thy soul!'

"She heard it, the victorious West,
In crown and sword array'd!
She felt the void which mined her breast,
She shiver'd and obey'd.

"She veil'd her eagles, snapp'd her sword,
And laid her sceptre down;
Her stately purple she abhorr'd,
And her imperial crown.

"She broke her flutes, she stopp'd her sports,
Her artists could not please;
She tore her books, she shut her courts,
She fled her palaces;

"Lust of the eye and pride of life
She left it all behind,
And hurried, torn with inward strife,
The wilderness to find.

"Tears wash'd the trouble from her face!
She changed into a child!
'Mid weeds and wrecks she stood—a place
Of ruin—but she smiled!

"Oh, had I lived in that great day,
How had its glory new
Fill'd earth and heaven, and caught away
My ravish'd spirit too!

"No thoughts that to the world belong
Had stood against the wave
Of love which set so deep and strong
From Christ's then open grave.

"No cloister-floor of humid stone
Had been too cold for me.
For me no Eastern desert lone
Had been too far to flee.

"No lonely life had pass'd too slow,
When I could hourly scan
Upon his Cross, with head sunk low,
That nail'd thorn-crowned Man!

"Could see the Mother with her Child
Whose tender winning arts
Have to his little arms beguiled
So many wounded hearts!

"And centuries came and ran their course,
And unspent all that time
Still, still went forth that Child's dear force,
And still was at its prime.

"Ay, ages long endured his span
Of life—'tis true received—
That gracious Child, that thorn-crown'd Man!
—He lived while we believed.

"While we believed, on earth we went,
And open stood his grave.
Men call'd from chamber, church, and tent;
And Christ was by to save.

"Now he is dead! Far hence he lies
In the lorn Syrian town;
And on his grave, with shining eyes,
The Syrian stars look down.

"In vain men still, with hoping new,
Regard his death-place dumb,
And say the stone is not yet to,
And wait for words to come.

"Ah, o'er that silent sacred land,
Of sun, and arid stone,
And crumbling wall, and sultry sand,
Sounds now one word alone!

"*Unduped of fancy, henceforth man
Must labour!—must resign
His all too human creeds, and scan
Simply the way divine!*

"But slow that tide of common thought,
Which bathed our life, retired;
Slow, slow the old world wore to naught,
And pulse by pulse expired.

"Its frame yet stood without a breach
When blood and warmth were fled;
And still it spake its wonted speech—
But every word was dead.

"And oh, we cried, that on this corse
Might fall a freshening storm!
Rive its dry bones, and with new force
A new-sprung world inform!

"—Down came the storm! O'er France it pass'd
In sheets of scathing fire;
All Europe felt that fiery blast,
And shook as it rush'd by her.

"Down came the storm! In ruins fell
The worn-out world we knew.
It pass'd, that elemental swell!
Again appear'd the blue;

"The sun shone in the new-wash'd sky,
And what from heaven saw he?
Blocks of the past, like icebergs high,
Float on a rolling sea!

"Upon them plies the race of man
All it before endeavour'd;
'Ye live,' I cried, 'ye work and plan,
And know not ye are sever'd!

" 'Poor fragments of a broken world
Whereon men pitch their tent!
Why were ye too to death not hurl'd
When your world's day was spent?

" 'That glow of central fire is done
Which with its fusing flame
Knit all your parts, and kept you one—
But ye, ye are the same!

" 'The past, its mask of union on,
Had ceased to live and thrive.
The past, its mask of union gone,
Say, is it more alive?

" 'Your creeds are dead, your rites are dead,
Your social order too!
Where tarries he, the Power who said:
See, I make all things new?

" 'The millions suffer still, and grieve,
And what can helpers heal
With old-world cures men half believe
For woes they wholly feel?

" 'And yet men have such need of joy!
But joy whose grounds are true;
And joy that should all hearts employ
As when the past was new.

" 'Ah, not the emotion of that past,
Its common hope, were vain!
Some new such hope must dawn at last,
Or man must toss in pain.

" 'But now the old is out of date,
The new is not yet born,
And who can be *alone* elate,
While the world lies forlorn?'

"Then to the wilderness I fled.—
There among Alpine snows
And pastoral huts I hid my head,
And sought and found repose.

"It was not yet the appointed hour.
Sad, patient, and resign'd,
I watch'd the crocus fade and flower,
I felt the sun and wind.

"The day I lived in was not mine,
Man gets no second day.
In dreams I saw the future shine—
But ah! I could not stay!

"Action I had not, followers, fame;
I pass'd obscure, alone.
The after-world forgets my name,
Nor do I wish it known.

"Composed to bear, I lived and died,
And knew my life was vain,
With fate I murmur not, nor chide,
At Sèvres by the Seine

"(If Paris that brief flight allow)
My humble tomb explore!
It bears: *Eternity, be thou*
My refuge! and no more.

"But thou, whom fellowship of mood
Did make from haunts of strife
Come to my mountain-solitude,
And learn my frustrate life;

"O thou, who, ere thy flying span
Was past of cheerful youth,
Didst find the solitary man
And love his cheerless truth—

"Despair not thou as I despair'd,
Nor be cold gloom thy prison!
Forward the gracious hours have fared,
And see! the sun is risen!

"He breaks the winter of the past;
A green, new earth appears.
Millions, whose life in ice lay fast,
Have thoughts, and smiles, and tears.

"What though there still need effort, strife?
Though much be still unwon?
Yet warm it mounts, the hour of life!
Death's frozen hour is done!

"The world's great order dawns in sheen,
After long darkness rude,
Divinelier imaged, clearer seen,
With happier zeal pursued.

"With hope extinct and brow composed
I mark'd the present die;
Its term of life was nearly closed,
Yet it had more than I.

"But thou, though to the world's new hour
Thou come with aspect marr'd,
Shorn of the joy, the bloom, the power
Which best befits its bard—

"Though more than half thy years be past,
And spent thy youthful prime;
Though, round thy firmer manhood cast,
Hang weeds of our sad time

"Whereof thy youth felt all the spell,
And traversed all the shade—
Though late, though dimm'd, though weak, yet tell
Hope to a world new-made!

"Help it to fill that deep desire,
The want which rack'd our brain,
Consumed our heart with thirst like fire,
Immedicable pain;

"Which to the wilderness drove out
Our life, to Alpine snow,
And palsied all our word with doubt,
And all our work with woe—

"What still of strength is left, employ
That end to help attain:
One common wave of thought and joy
Lifting mankind again!"

—The vision ended. I awoke
As out of sleep, and no
Voice moved;—only the torrent broke
The silence, far below.

Soft darkness on the turf did lie.
Solemn, o'er hut and wood,
In the yet star-sown nightly sky,
The peak of Jaman stood.

Still in my soul the voice I heard
Of Obermann!——away
I turned; by some vague impulse stirr'd,
Along the rocks of Naye

Past Sonchaud's piny flanks I gaze
And the blanch'd summit bare
Of Malatrait, to where in haze
The Valais opens fair,

And the domed Velan, with his snows,
Behind the upcrowding hills,
Doth all the heavenly opening close
Which the Rhone's murmur fills;—

And glorious there, without a sound,
Across the glimmering lake,
High in the Valais-depth profound,
I saw the morning break.

1867

HEINE'S GRAVE

"*Henri Heine*"—'tis here!
That black tombstone, the name
Carved there—no more! and the smooth,
Swarded alleys, the limes
Touch'd with yellow by hot
Summer, but under them still,
In September's bright afternoon,
Shadow, and verdure, and cool.
Trim Montmartre! the faint
Murmur of Paris outside;
Crisp everlasting-flowers,
Yellow and black, on the graves.

Half blind, palsied, in pain,
Hither to come, from the streets'
Uproar, surely not loath
Wast thou, Heine!—to lie
Quiet, to ask for closed
Shutters, and darken'd room,
And cool drinks, and an eased
Posture, and opium, no more;
Hither to come, and to sleep
Under the wings of Renown.

Ah! not little, when pain
Is most quelling, and man
Easily quell'd, and the fine
Temper of genius so soon
Thrills at each smart, is the praise,
Not to have yielded to pain!
No small boast, for a weak
Son of mankind, to the earth
Pinn'd by the thunder, to rear
His bolt-scathed front to the stars;
And, undaunted, retort
'Gainst thick-crashing, insane,
Tyrannous tempests of bale,
Arrowy lightnings of soul.

Hark! through the alley resounds
Mocking laughter! A film
Creeps o'er the sunshine; a breeze
Ruffles the warm afternoon,
Saddens my soul with its chill.
Gibing of spirits in scorn
Shakes every leaf of the grove,
Mars the benignant repose
Of this amiable home of the dead.

Bitter spirits, ye claim
Heine?—Alas, he is yours!
Only a moment I long'd
Here in the quiet to snatch
From such mates the outworn
Poet, and steep him in calm.
Only a moment! I knew
Whose he was who is here
Buried—I knew he was yours!
Ah, I knew that I saw
Here no sepulchre built
In the laurell'd rock, o'er the blue
Naples bay, for a sweet
Tender Virgil! no tomb
On Ravenna sands, in the shade
Of Ravenna pines, for a high
Austere Dante! no grave
By the Avon side, in the bright
Stratford meadows, for thee,
Shakespeare! loveliest of souls,
Peerless in radiance, in joy.

What, then, so harsh and malign,
Heine! distils from thy life?
Poisons the peace of the grave?

I chide with thee not, that thy sharp
Upbraidings often assail'd
England, my country—for we,
Heavy and sad, for her sons,
Long since, deep in our hearts,
Echo the blame of her foes.
We, too, sigh that she flags;
We, too, say that she now—
Scarce comprehending the voice
Of her greatest, golden-mouth'd sons
Of a former age any more—
Stupidly travels her round
Of mechanic business, and lets
Slow die out of her life
Glory, and genius, and joy.

So thou arraign'st her, her foe;
So we arraign her, her sons.

Yes, we arraign her! but she,
The weary Titan, with deaf
Ears, and labour-dimm'd eyes,
Regarding neither to right
Nor left, goes passively by,
Staggering on to her goal;
Bearing on shoulders immense,
Atlanteän, the load,
Wellnigh not to be borne,
Of the too vast orb of her fate.

But was it thou—I think
Surely it was!—that bard
Unnamed, who, Goethe said,
Had every other gift, but wanted love;
Love, without which the tongue
Even of angels sounds amiss?

Charm is the glory which makes
Song of the poet divine,
Love is the fountain of charm.
How without charm wilt thou draw,
Poet! the world to thy way?
Not by the lightnings of wit—
Not by the thunder of scorn!
These to the world, too, are given;
Wit it possesses, and scorn—
Charm is the poet's alone.
Hollow and dull are the great,
And artists envious, and the mob profane.
We know all this, we know!
Cam'st thou from heaven, O child
Of light! but this to declare?
Alas, to help us forget
Such barren knowledge awhile,
God gave the poet his song!

Therefore a secret unrest
Tortured thee, brilliant and bold!
Therefore triumph itself
Tasted amiss to thy soul.
Therefore, with blood of thy foes,
Trickled in silence thine own.
Therefore the victor's heart
Broke on the field of his fame.

Ah! as of old, from the pomp
Of Italian Milan, the fair
Flower of marble of white
Southern palaces—steps
Border'd by statues, and walks
Terraced, and orange-bowers
Heavy with fragrance—the blond
German Kaiser full oft
Long'd himself back to the fields,
Rivers, and high-roof'd towns
Of his native Germany; so,

So, how often! from hot
Paris drawing-rooms, and lamps
Blazing, and brilliant crowds,
Starr'd and jewell'd, of men
Famous, of women the queens
Of dazzling converse—from fumes
Of praise, hot, heady fumes, to the poor brain
That mount, that madden—how oft
Heine's spirit outworn
Long'd itself out of the din,
Back to the tranquil, the cool
Far German home of his youth!

See! in the May-afternoon,
O'er the fresh, short turf of the Hartz,
A youth, with the foot of youth,
Heine! thou climbest again!
Up, through the tall dark firs
Warming their heads in the sun,
Chequering the grass with their shade—
Up, by the stream, with its huge
Moss-hung boulders, and thin
Musical water half-hid—
Up, o'er the rock-strewn slope,
With the sinking sun, and the air
Chill, and the shadows now
Long on the grey hill-side—
To the stone-roof'd hut at the top!

Or, yet later, in watch
On the roof of the Brocken-tower
Thou standest, gazing!—to see
The broad red sun, over field,
Forest, and city, and spire,
And mist-track'd stream of the wide,
Wide German land, going down
In a bank of vapours——again
Standest, at nightfall, alone!

Or, next morning, with limbs
Rested by slumber, and heart
Freshen'd and light with the May,
O'er the gracious spurs coming down
Of the Lower Hartz, among oaks,
And beechen coverts, and copse
Of hazels green in whose depth
Ilse, the fairy transform'd,
In a thousand water-breaks light
Pours her petulant youth—
Climbing the rock which juts
O'er the valley, the dizzily perch'd
Rock—to its iron cross
Once more thou cling'st; to the Cross
Clingest! with smiles, with a sigh!

Goethe, too, had been there.
In the long-past winter he came
To the frozen Hartz, with his soul
Passionate, eager—his youth
All in ferment!—but he
Destined to work and to live
Left it, and thou, alas!
Only to laugh and to die.

But something prompts me: Not thus
Take leave of Heine! not thus
Speak the last word at his grave!
Not in pity, and not
With half censure—with awe
Hail, as it passes from earth
Scattering lightnings, that soul!

The Spirit of the world,
Beholding the absurdity of men—
Their vaunts, their feats—let a sardonic smile,
For one short moment, wander o'er his lips.
That smile was Heine!—for its earthly hour
The strange guest sparkled; now 'tis pass'd away.

That was Heine! and we,
Myriads who live, who have lived,
What are we all, but a mood,
A single mood, of the life
Of the Spirit in whom we exist,
Who alone is all things in one?

Spirit, who fillest us all!
Spirit, who utterest in each
New-coming son of mankind
Such of thy thoughts as thou wilt!
O thou, one of whose moods,
Bitter and strange, was the life
Of Heine—his strange, alas,
His bitter life!—may a life
Other and milder be mine!
May'st thou a mood more serene,
Happier, have utter'd in mine!
May'st thou the rapture of peace
Deep have embreathed at its core;
Made it a ray of thy thought,
Made it a beat of thy joy!

1867

THE STUDY OF POETRY

"The future of poetry is immense, because in poetry, where it is worthy of its high destinies, our race, as time goes on, will find an ever surer and surer stay. There is not a creed which is not shaken, not an accredited dogma which is not shown to be questionable, not a received tradition which does not threaten to dissolve. Our religion has materialized itself in the fact, in the supposed fact; it has attached its emotion to the fact, and now the fact is failing it. But for poetry the idea is everything; the rest is a world of illusion, of divine illusion. Poetry attaches its emotion to the idea; the idea *is* the fact. The strongest part of our religion to-day is its unconscious poetry."

Let me be permitted to quote these words of my own, as uttering the thought which should, in my opinion, go with us and govern us in all our study of poetry. In the present work it is the course of one great contributory stream to the world-river of poetry that we are invited to follow. We are here invited to trace the stream of English poetry. But whether we set ourselves, as here, to follow only one of the several streams that make the mighty river of poetry, or whether we seek to know them all, our governing thought should be the same. We should conceive of poetry worthily, and more highly than it has been the custom to conceive of it. We should conceive of it as capable of higher uses, and called to higher destinies, than those which in general men have assigned to it hitherto. More and more mankind will discover that we have to turn to poetry to interpret life for us, to console us, to sustain us. Without poetry, our science will appear incomplete; and most of what now passes with us for religion and philosophy will be replaced by poetry. Science, I say, will appear incomplete without it. For finely and truly does Wordsworth call poetry "the impassioned expression which is in the countenance of all science"; and what is a countenance without its expression? Again, Wordsworth finely and truly calls poetry "the breath and finer spirit of all knowledge": our religion, parading evidences such as those on which the popular mind relies now; our philosophy, pluming itself on its reasonings about causation and finite and infinite being; what are they but the shadows and dreams and false shows of knowledge? The day will come when we shall wonder at ourselves for having trusted to them, for having taken them seriously; and the more we perceive their hollowness, the more we shall prize "the breath and finer spirit of knowledge" offered to us by poetry.

But if we conceive thus highly of the destinies of poetry, we must also set our standard for poetry high, since poetry, to be capable of fulfilling such high destinies, must be poetry of a high order of excellence. We must accustom ourselves to a high standard and to a strict judgment. Sainte-Beuve relates that Napoleon one day said, when somebody was spoken of in his presence as a charlatan: "Charlatan as much as you please; but where is there *not* charlatanism?"—"Yes," answers Sainte-Beuve, "in politics, in the art of governing mankind, that is perhaps true. But in the order of thought, in art, the glory, the eternal honour is that charlatanism shall find no entrance; herein lies the inviolableness of that noble portion of man's being." It is admirably said, and let us hold fast to it. In poetry, which is thought and art in one, it is the glory, the eternal honour, that charlatanism shall find no entrance; that this noble sphere be kept inviolate and inviolable. Charlatanism is for confusing or obliterating the distinctions between excellent and inferior, sound and unsound or only half-sound, true and untrue or only half-true. It is charlatanism, conscious or unconscious, whenever we confuse or obliterate these. And in poetry, more than anywhere else, it is unpermissible to confuse or obliterate them. For in poetry the distinction between excellent and inferior, sound and unsound or only half-sound, true and untrue or only half-true, is of paramount importance. It is of paramount importance because of the high destinies of poetry. In poetry, as a criticism of life under the conditions fixed for such a criticism by the laws of poetic truth and poetic beauty, the spirit of our race will find, we have said, as time goes on and as other helps fail, its consolation and stay. But the consolation and stay will be of power in proportion to the power of the criticism of life. And the criticism of life will be of power in proportion as the poetry conveying it is excellent rather than inferior, sound rather than unsound or half-sound, true rather than untrue or half-true.

The best poetry is what we want; the best poetry will be found to have a power of forming, sustaining, and delighting us, as nothing else can. A clearer, deeper sense of the best in poetry, and of the strength and joy to be drawn from it, is the most precious benefit which we can gather from a poetical collection such as the present. And yet in the very nature and conduct of such a collection there is inevitably something which tends to obscure in us the consciousness of what our benefit should be, and to distract us from the pursuit of it. We should therefore steadily set it before our minds at the outset, and should compel ourselves to revert constantly to the thought of it as we proceed.

Yes; constantly in reading poetry, a sense for the best, the really excellent, and of the strength and joy to be drawn from it, should be present in our minds and should govern our estimate of what we read. But this real estimate, the only true one, is liable to be superseded, if we are not watchful, by two other kinds of estimate, the historic estimate and the personal estimate, both of which are fallacious. A poet or a poem may count to us historically, they may count to us on grounds personal to ourselves, and they may count to us really. They may count to us historically. The course of development of a nation's language, thought, and poetry, is profoundly interesting; and by regarding a poet's work as a stage in this course of development we may easily bring ourselves to make it of more importance as poetry than in itself it really is, we may come to use a language of quite exaggerated praise in criticising it; in short, to over-rate it. So arises in our poetic judgments the fallacy caused by the estimate which we may call historic. Then, again, a poet or a poem may count to us on grounds personal to ourselves. Our personal affinities, likings, and circumstances, have great power to sway our estimate of this or that poet's work, and to make us attach more importance to it as poetry than in itself it really possesses, because to us it is, or has been, of high importance. Here also we over-rate the object of our interest, and apply to it a language of praise which is quite exaggerated. And thus we get the source of a second fallacy in our poetic judgments—the fallacy caused by an estimate which we may call personal.

Both fallacies are natural. It is evident how naturally the study of the history and development of a poetry may incline a man to pause over reputations and works once conspicuous but now obscure, and to quarrel with a careless public for skipping, in obedience to mere tradition and habit, from one famous name or work in its national poetry to another, ignorant of what it misses, and of the reason for keeping what it keeps, and of the whole process of growth in its poetry. The French have become diligent students of their own early poetry, which they long neglected; the study makes many of them dissatisfied with their so-called classical poetry, the court-tragedy of the seventeenth century, a poetry which Pellisson long ago reproached with its want of the true poetic stamp, with its *politesse stérile et rampante*, but which nevertheless has reigned in France as absolutely as if it had been the perfection of classical poetry indeed. The dissatisfaction is natural; yet a lively and accomplished critic, M. Charles d'Héricault, the editor of Clément Marot, goes too far when he says that "the cloud of glory playing round a classic is a mist as dangerous to the future of a literature as it is intolerable for the purposes of history." "It hinders," he goes on, "it hinders us from seeing more than one single point, the culminating and exceptional point; the summary, fictitious and arbitrary, of a thought and of a work. It substitutes a halo for a physiognomy, it puts a statue where there was once a man, and hiding from us all trace of the labour, the attempts, the weaknesses, the failures, it claims not study but veneration; it does not show us how the thing is done, it imposes upon us a model. Above all, for the historian this creation of classic personages is inadmissible; for it withdraws the poet from his time, from his proper life, it breaks historical relationships, it blinds criticism by conventional admiration, and renders the investigation of literary origins unacceptable. It gives us a human personage no longer, but a God seated immovable amidst His perfect work, like Jupiter on Olympus; and hardly will it be possible for the young student, to whom such work is exhibited at such a distance from him, to believe that it did not issue ready made from that divine head."

All this is brilliantly and tellingly said, but we must plead for a distinction. Everything depends on the reality of a poet's classic character. If he is a dubious classic, let us sift him; if he is a false classic, let us explode him. But if he is a real classic, if his work belongs to the class of the very best (for this is the true and right meaning of the word *classic*, *classical*), then the great thing for us is to feel and enjoy his work as deeply as ever we can, and to appreciate the wide difference between it and all work which has not the same high character. This is what is salutary, this is what is formative; this is the great benefit to be got from the study of poetry. Everything which interferes with it, which hinders it, is injurious. True, we must read our classic with open eyes, and not with eyes blinded with superstition; we must perceive when his work comes short, when it drops out of the class of the very best, and we must rate it, in such cases, at its proper value. But the use of this negative criticism is not in itself, it is entirely in its enabling us to have a clearer sense and a deeper enjoyment of what is truly excellent. To trace the labour, the attempts, the weaknesses, the failures of a genuine classic, to acquaint oneself with his time and his life and his historical relationships, is mere literary dilettantism unless it has that clear sense and deeper enjoyment for its end. It may be said that the more we know about a classic the better we shall enjoy him; and, if we lived as long as Methuselah and had all of us heads of perfect clearness and wills of perfect steadfastness, this might be true in fact as it is plausible in theory. But the case here is much the same as the case with the Greek and Latin studies of our schoolboys. The elaborate philological groundwork which we require them to lay is in theory an admirable preparation for appreciating the Greek and Latin authors worthily. The more thoroughly we lay the groundwork, the better we shall be able, it may be said, to enjoy the authors. True, if time were not so short, and schoolboys' wits not so soon tired and their power of attention exhausted; only, as it is, the elaborate philological preparation goes on, but the authors are little known and less enjoyed. So with the investigator of "historic origins" in poetry. He ought to enjoy the true classic all the better for his investigations; he often is distracted from the enjoyment of the best, and with the less good he overbusies himself, and is prone to overrate it in proportion to the trouble which it has cost him.

The idea of tracing historic origins and historical relationships cannot be absent from a compilation like the present. And naturally the poets to be exhibited in it will be assigned to those persons for exhibition who are known to prize them highly, rather than to those who have no special inclination towards them. Moreover the very occupation with an author, and the business of exhibiting him, disposes us to affirm and amplify his importance. In the present work, therefore, we are sure of frequent temptation to adopt the historic estimate, or the personal estimate, and to forget the real estimate; which latter, nevertheless, we must employ if we are to make poetry yield us its full benefit. So high is that benefit, the benefit of clearly feeling and of deeply enjoying the really excellent, the truly classic in poetry, that we do well, I say, to set it fixedly before our minds as our object in studying poets and poetry, and to make the desire of attaining it the one principle to which, as the *Imitation* says, whatever we may read or come to know, we always return. *Cum multa legeris et cognoveris, ad unum semper oportet redire principium.*

The historic estimate is likely in especial to affect our judgment and our language when we are dealing with ancient poets; the personal estimate when we are dealing with poets our contemporaries, or at any rate modern. The exaggerations due to the historic estimate are not in themselves, perhaps, of very much gravity. Their report hardly enters the general ear; probably they do not always impose even on the literary men who adopt them. But they lead to a dangerous abuse of language. So we hear Cædmon, amongst our own poets, compared to Milton. I have already noticed the enthusiasm of one accomplished French critic for "historic origins." Another eminent French critic, M. Vitet, comments upon that famous document of the early poetry of his nation, the *Chanson de Roland.* It is indeed a most interesting document. The *joculator* or *jongleur* Taillefer, who was with William the Conqueror's army at Hastings, marched before the Norman troops, so said the tradition, singing "of Charlemagne and of Roland and of Oliver, and of the vassals who died at Roncevaux"; and it is suggested that in the *Chanson de Roland* by one Turoldus or Théroulde, a poem preserved in a manuscript of the twelfth century in the Bodleian Library at Oxford, we have certainly the matter, perhaps even some of the words, of the chant which Taillefer sang. The poem has vigour and freshness; it is not without pathos. But M. Vitet is not satisfied with seeing in it a document of some poetic value, and of very high historic and linguistic value; he sees in it a grand and beautiful work, a monument of epic genius. In its general design he finds the grandiose conception, in its details he finds the constant union of simplicity with greatness, which are the marks, he truly says, of the genuine epic, and distinguish it from the artificial epic of literary ages. One thinks of Homer; this is the sort of praise which is given to Homer, and justly given. Higher praise there cannot well be, and it is the praise due to epic poetry of the highest order only, and to no other. Let us try, then, the *Chanson de Roland* at its best. Roland, mortally wounded, lays himself down under a pine-tree, with his face turned towards Spain and the enemy—

"De plusurs choses à remembrer li prist,
De tantes teres cume li bers cunquist,
De dulce France, des humes de sun lign,
De Carlemagne sun seignor ki l'nurrit."[1]

That is primitive work, I repeat, with an undeniable poetic quality of its own. It deserves such praise, and such praise is sufficient for it. But now turn to Homer—

Ὣς φάτο, τοὺς δ' ἤδη κατέχεν φυσίζοος αἶα
ἐν Λακεδαίμονι αὖθι, φίλῃ ἐν πατρίδι γαίῃ.[2]

We are here in another world, another order of poetry altogether; here is rightly due such supreme praise as that which M. Vitet gives to the *Chanson de Roland.* If our words are to have any meaning, if our judgments are to have any solidity, we must not heap that supreme praise upon poetry of an order immeasurably inferior.

Indeed there can be no more useful help for discovering what poetry belongs to the class of the truly excellent, and can therefore do us most good, than to have always in one's mind lines and expressions of the great masters, and to apply them as a touchstone to other poetry. Of course we are not to require this other poetry to resemble them; it may be very dissimilar. But if we have any tact we shall find them, when we have lodged them well in our minds, an infallible touchstone for detecting the presence or absence of high poetic quality, and also the degree of this quality, in all other poetry which we may place beside them. Short passages, even single lines, will serve our turn quite sufficiently. Take the two lines which I have just quoted from Homer, the poet's comment on Helen's mention of her brothers;—or take his

Ἆ δειλώ, τί σφῶι δόμεν Πηλῆι ἄνακτι
θνητῷ; ὑμεῖς δ' ἐστὸν ἀγήρω τ' ἀθανάτω τε.
ἦ ἵνα δυστήνοισι μετ' ἀνδράσιν ἄλγε' ἔχητον;[3]

the address of Zeus to the horses of Peleus;—or take finally his

Καὶ σέ, γέρον, τὸ πρὶν μὲν ἀκούομεν ὄλβιον εἶναι.[4]

the words of Achilles to Priam, a suppliant before him. Take that incomparable line and a half of Dante, Ugolino's tremendous words—

"Io no piangeva; sì dentro impietrai.
Piangevan elli . . ."[5]

---

[1] "Then began he to call many things to remembrance,—all the lands which his valour conquered, and pleasant France, and the men of his lineage, and Charlemagne his liege lord who nourished him."—*Chanson de Roland*, III, 939–942.

[2] "So said she; they long since in Earth's soft arms were reposing,
There in their own dear land, their father land, Lacedæmon."—*Iliad*, III, 243–4 (translated by Dr. Hawtrey).

[3] "Ah, unhappy pair, why gave we you to King Peleus, to a mortal? but ye are without old age, and immortal. Was it that with men born to misery ye might have sorrow?"—*Iliad*, XVII, 443–5.

[4] "Nay, and thou too, old man, in former days wast, as we hear, happy."—*Iliad*, XXIV, 543.

[5] "I wailed not, so of stone grew I within;—*they* wailed."—*Inferno*, XXXIII, 39, 40.

take the lovely words of Beatrice to Virgil—

"Io son fatta da Dio, sua mercè, tale,
Che la vostra miseria non mi tange,
Nè fiamma d'esto incendio non m'assale . . ."[1]

take the simple, but perfect, single line—

"In la sua volontade è nostra pace."[2]

Take of Shakespeare a line or two of Henry the Fourth's expostulation with sleep—

"Wilt thou upon the high and giddy mast
Seal up the ship-boy's eyes, and rock his brains
In cradle of the rude imperious surge . . ."

and take, as well, Hamlet's dying request to Horatio—

"If thou didst ever hold me in thy heart,
Absent thee from felicity awhile,
And in this harsh world draw thy breath in pain
To tell my story . . ."

Take of Milton that Miltonic passage—

"Darken'd so, yet shone
Above them all the archangel; but his face
Deep scars of thunder had intrench'd, and care
Sat on his faded cheek . . ."

add two such lines as—

"And courage never to submit or yield
And what is else not to be overcome . . ."

and finish with the exquisite close to the loss of Proserpine, the loss

". . . which cost Ceres all that pain
To seek her through the world."

These few lines, if we have tact and can use them, are enough even of themselves to keep clear and sound our judgments about poetry, to save us from fallacious estimates of it, to conduct us to a real estimate.

The specimens I have quoted differ widely from one another, but they have in common this: the possession of the very highest poetical quality. If we are thoroughly penetrated by their power, we shall find that we have acquired a sense enabling us, whatever poetry may be laid before us, to feel the degree in which a high poetical quality is present or wanting there. Critics give themselves great labour to draw out what in the abstract constitutes the characters of a high quality of poetry. It is much better simply to have recourse to concrete examples;—to take specimens of poetry of the high, the very highest quality, and to say: The characters of a high quality poetry are what is expressed *there.* They are far better recognized by being felt in the verse of the master, than by being perused in the prose of the critic. Nevertheless if we are urgently pressed to give some critical account of them, we may safely, perhaps, venture on laying down, not indeed how and why the characters arise, but where and in what they arise. They are in the matter and substance of the poetry, and they are in its manner and style. Both of these, the substance and matter on the one hand, the style and manner on the other, have a mark, an accent, of high beauty, worth, and power. But if we are asked to define this mark and accent in the abstract, our answer must be: No, for we should thereby be darkening the question, not clearing it. The mark and accent are given by the substance and matter of that poetry, by the style and manner of that poetry, and of all other poetry which is akin to it in quality.

Only one thing we may add as to the substance and matter of poetry, guiding ourselves by Aristotle's profound observation that the superiority of poetry over history consists in its possessing a higher truth and a higher seriousness (*φιλοσοφώτερον καὶ σπουδαιότερον*). Let us add, therefore, to what we have said, this: that the substance and matter of the best poetry acquire their special character from possessing, in an eminent degree, truth and seriousness. We may add yet further, what is in itself evident, that to the style and manner of the best poetry their special character, their accent, is given by their diction, and, even yet more, by their movement. And though we distinguish between the two characters, the two accents, of superiority, yet they are nevertheless vitally connected one with the other. The superior character of truth and seriousness, in the matter and substance of the best poetry, is inseparable from the superiority of diction and movement marking its style and manner. The two superiorities are closely related, and are in steadfast proportion one to

[1] "Of such sort hath God, thanked be his mercy, made me, that your misery toucheth me not, neither doth the flame of this fire strike me." —*Inferno,* II, 91–93.

[2] "In His will is our peace." —*Paradiso,* III, 85.

the other. So far as high poetic truth and seriousness are wanting to a poet's matter and substance, so far also, we may be sure, will a high poetic stamp of diction and movement be wanting to his style and manner. In proportion as this high stamp of diction and movement, again, is absent from a poet's style and manner, we shall find, also, that high poetic truth and seriousness are absent from his substance and matter.

So stated, these are but dry generalities; their whole force lies in their application. And I could wish every student of poetry to make the application of them for himself. Made by himself, the application would impress itself upon his mind far more deeply than made by me. Neither will my limits allow me to make any full application of the generalities above propounded; but in the hope of bringing out, at any rate, some significance in them, and of establishing an important principle more firmly by their means, I will, in the space which remains to me, follow rapidly from the commencement the course of our English poetry with them in my view.

Once more I return to the early poetry of France, with which our own poetry, in its origins, is indissolubly connected. In the twelfth and thirteenth centuries, that seed-time of all modern language and literature, the poetry of France had a clear predominance in Europe. Of the two divisions of that poetry, its productions in the *langue d'oil* and its productions in the *langue d'oc*, the poetry of the *langue d'oc*, of southern France, of the troubadours, is of importance because of its effect on Italian literature;—the first literature of modern Europe to strike the true and grand note, and to bring forth, as in Dante and Petrarch it brought forth, classics. But the predominance of French poetry in Europe, during the twelfth and thirteenth centuries, is due to its poetry of the *langue d'oil*, the poetry of northern France and of the tongue which is now the French language. In the twelfth century the bloom of this romance-poetry was earlier and stronger in England, at the court of our Anglo-Norman kings, than in France itself. But it was a bloom of French poetry; and as our native poetry formed itself, it formed itself out of this. The romance-poems which took possession of the heart and imagination of Europe in the twelfth and thirteenth centuries are French; "they are," as Southey justly says, "the pride of French literature, nor have we anything which can be placed in competition with them." Themes were supplied from all quarters; but the romance-setting which was common to them all, and which gained the ear of Europe, was French. This constituted for the French poetry, literature, and language, at the height of the Middle Age, an unchallenged predominance. The Italian Brunetto Latini, the master of Dante, wrote his *Treasure* in French because, he says, "la parleure en est plus délitable et plus commune à toutes gens." In the same century, the thirteenth, the French romance-writer, Christian of Troyes, formulates the claims, in chivalry and letters, of France, his native country, as follows:—

"Or vous ert par ce livre apris,
Que Gresse ot de chevalerie
Le premier los et de clergie;
Puis vint chevalerie à Rome,
Et de la clergie la some,
Qui ore est en France venue.
Diex doinst qu'ele i soit retenue,
Et que li lius li abelisse
Tant que de France n'isse
L'onor qui s'i est arestée!"

"Now by this book you will learn that first Greece had the renown for chivalry and letters; then chivalry and the primacy in letters passed to Rome, and now it is come to France. God grant it may be kept there; and that the place may please it so well, that the honour which has come to make stay in France may never depart thence!"

Yet it is now all gone, this French romance-poetry, of which the weight of substance and the power of style are not unfairly represented by this extract from Christian of Troyes. Only by means of the historic estimate can we persuade ourselves now to think that any of it is of poetical importance.

But in the fourteenth century there comes an Englishman nourished on this poetry, taught his trade by this poetry, getting words, rhyme, metre from this poetry; for even of that stanza which the Italians used, and which Chaucer derived immediately from the Italians, the basis and suggestion was probably given in France. Chaucer (I have already named him) fascinated his contemporaries, but so too did Christian of Troyes and Wolfram of Eschenbach. Chaucer's power of fascination, however, is enduring; his poetical importance does not need the assistance of the historic estimate; it is real. He is a genuine source of joy and strength, which is flowing still for us and will flow always. He will be read, as time goes on, far more generally than he is read now. His language is a cause of difficulty for us; but so also, and I think in quite as great a degree, is the language of Burns. In Chaucer's case, as in that of Burns, it is a difficulty to be unhesitatingly accepted and overcome.

If we ask ourselves wherein consists the immense superiority of Chaucer's poetry over the romance-poetry—why it is that in passing from this to Chaucer we suddenly feel ourselves to be in another world, we shall find that his superiority is both in the substance of his poetry and in the style of his poetry. His superiority in substance is given by his large, free, simple, clear yet kindly view of human life,—so unlike the total want, in the romance-poets, of all intelligent command of it. Chaucer has not their helplessness; he has gained the power to survey the world from a central, a truly human point of view. We have only to call to mind the Prologue to *The Canterbury Tales*. The right comment upon it is Dryden's: "It is sufficient to say, according to the proverb, that *here is God's plenty*." And again: "He is a perpetual fountain of good sense." It is by a large, free, sound representation of things, that poetry, this high criticism of life, has truth of substance; and Chaucer's poetry has truth of substance.

Of his style and manner, if we think first of the romance-poetry and then of Chaucer's divine liquidness of diction, his divine fluidity of movement, it is difficult to speak temperately. They are irresistible, and justify all the rapture with which his successors speak of his "gold dew-drops of speech." Johnson misses the point entirely when he finds fault with Dryden for ascribing to Chaucer the first refinement of our numbers, and says that Gower also can show smooth numbers and easy rhymes. The refinement of our numbers means something far more than this. A nation may have versifiers with smooth numbers and easy rhymes, and yet may have no real poetry at all. Chaucer is the father of our splendid English poetry; he is our "well of English undefiled," because by the lovely charm of his diction, the lovely charm of his movement, he makes an epoch and founds a tradition. In Spenser, Shakespeare, Milton, Keats, we can follow the tradition of the liquid diction, the fluid movement, of Chaucer; at one time it is his liquid diction of which in these poets we feel the virtue, and at another time it is his fluid movement. And the virtue is irresistible.

Bounded as is my space, I must yet find room for an example of Chaucer's virtue, as I have given examples to show the virtue of the great classics. I feel disposed to say that a single line is enough to show the charm of Chaucer's verse; that merely one line like this:

> "O martyr souded[1] in virginitee!"

has a virtue of manner and movement such as we shall not find in all the verse of romance-poetry;—but this is saying nothing. The virtue is such as we shall not find, perhaps, in all English poetry, outside the poets whom I have named as the special inheritors of Chaucer's tradition. A single line, however, is too little if we have not the strain of Chaucer's verse well in our memory; let us take a stanza. It is from *The Prioress's Tale*, the story of the Christian child murdered in a Jewry—

> "My throte is cut unto my nekke-bone
> Saidè this child, and as by way of kinde
> I should have deyd, yea, longè time agone;
> But Jesu Christ, as ye in bookès finde,
> Will that his glory last and be in minde,
> And for the worship of his mother dere
> Yet may I sing *O Alma* loud and clere."

Wordsworth has modernized this Tale, and to feel how delicate and evanescent is the charm of verse, we have only to read Wordsworth's first three lines of this stanza after Chaucer's—

> "My throat is cut unto the bone, I trow,
> Said this young child, and by the law of kind
> I should have died, yea, many hours ago."

The charm is departed. It is often said that the power of liquidness and fluidity in Chaucer's verse was dependent upon a free, a

[1] The French *soudé;* soldered, fixed fast.

licentious dealing with language, such as is now impossible; upon a liberty, such as Burns too enjoyed, of making words like *neck*, *bird*, into a dissyllable by adding to them, and words like *cause*, *rhyme*, into a dissyllable by sounding the *e* mute. It is true that Chaucer's fluidity is conjoined with this liberty, and is admirably served by it; but we ought not to say that it was dependent upon it. It was dependent upon his talent. Other poets with a like liberty do not attain to the fluidity of Chaucer; Burns himself does not attain to it. Poets, again, who have a talent akin to Chaucer's, such as Shakespeare or Keats, have known how to attain to his fluidity without the like liberty.

And yet Chaucer is not one of the great classics. His poetry transcends and effaces, easily and without effort, all the romance-poetry of Catholic Christendom; it transcends and effaces all the English poetry contemporary with it, it transcends and effaces all the English poetry subsequent to it down to the age of Elizabeth. Of such avail is poetic truth of substance, in its natural and necessary union with poetic truth of style. And yet, I say, Chaucer is not one of the great classics. He has not their accent. What is wanting to him is suggested by the mere mention of the name of the first great classic of Christendom, the immortal poet who died eighty years before Chaucer,—Dante. The accent of such verse as

"In la sua volontade è nostra pace . . ."

is altogether beyond Chaucer's reach; we praise him, but we feel that this accent is out of the question for him. It may be said that it was necessarily out of the reach of any poet in the England of that stage of growth. Possibly; but we are to adopt a real, not a historic, estimate of poetry. However we may account for its absence, something is wanting, then, to the poetry of Chaucer, which poetry must have before it can be placed in the glorious class of the best. And there is no doubt what that something is. It is the σπουδαιότης, the high and excellent seriousness, which Aristotle assigns as one of the grand virtues of poetry. The substance of Chaucer's poetry, his view of things and his criticism of life, has largeness, freedom, shrewdness, benignity; but it has not this high seriousness. Homer's criticism of life has it, Dante's has it, Shakespeare's has it. It is this chiefly which gives to our spirits what they can rest upon; and with the increasing demands of our modern ages upon poetry, this virtue of giving us what we can rest upon will be more and more highly esteemed. A voice from the slums of Paris, fifty or sixty years after Chaucer, the voice of poor Villon out of his life of riot and crime, has at its happy moments (as, for instance, in the last stanza of *La Belle Heaulmière* [1]) more of this important poetic virtue of seriousness than all the productions of Chaucer. But its apparition in Villon, and in men like Villon, is fitful; the greatness of the great poets, the power of their criticism of life, is that their virtue is sustained.

To our praise, therefore, of Chaucer as a poet there must be this limitation; he lacks the high seriousness of the great classics, and therewith an important part of their virtue. Still, the main fact for us to bear in mind about Chaucer is his sterling value according to that real estimate which we firmly adopt for all poets. He has poetic truth of substance, though he has not high poetic seriousness, and corresponding to his truth of substance he has an exquisite virtue of style and manner. With him is born our real poetry.

For my present purpose I need not dwell on our Elizabethan poetry, or on the continuation and close of this poetry in Milton. We all of us profess to be agreed in the estimate of

[1] The name *Heaulmière* is said to be derived from a headdress (helm) worn as a mark by courtesans. In Villon's ballad, a poor old creature of this class laments her days of youth and beauty. The last stanza of the ballad runs thus—

"Ainsi le bon temps regretons
Entre nous, pauvres vieilles sottes,
Assises bas, à croppetons,
Tout en un tas comme pelottes;
A petit feu de chènevottes
Tost allumées, tost estainctes,
Et jadis fusmes si mignottes!
Ainsi en prend à maintz et maintes."

"Thus amongst ourselves we regret the good time, poor silly old things, low-seated on our heels, all in a heap like so many balls; by a little fire of hemp-stalks, soon lighted, soon spent. And once we were such darlings! So fares it with many and many a one."

this poetry; we all of us recognize it as great poetry, our greatest, and Shakespeare and Milton as our poetical classics. The real estimate, here, has universal currency. With the next age of our poetry divergency and difficulty begin. An historic estimate of that poetry has established itself; and the question is, whether it will be found to coincide with the real estimate.

The age of Dryden, together with our whole eighteenth century which followed it, sincerely believed itself to have produced poetical classics of its own, and even to have made advance, in poetry, beyond all its predecessors. Dryden regards as not seriously disputable the opinion "that the sweetness of English verse was never understood or practised by our fathers." Cowley could see nothing at all in Chaucer's poetry. Dryden heartily admired it, and, as we have seen, praised its matter admirably; but of its exquisite manner and movement all he can find to say is that "there is the rude sweetness of a Scotch tune in it, which is natural and pleasing, though not perfect." Addison, wishing to praise Chaucer's numbers, compares them with Dryden's own. And all through the eighteenth century, and down even into our own times, the stereotyped phrase of approbation for good verse found in our early poetry has been, that it even approached the verse of Dryden, Addison, Pope, and Johnson.

Are Dryden and Pope poetical classics? Is the historic estimate, which represents them as such, and which has been so long established that it cannot easily give way, the real estimate? Wordsworth and Coleridge, as is well known, denied it; but the authority of Wordsworth and Coleridge does not weigh much with the young generation, and there are many signs to show that the eighteenth century and its judgments are coming into favour again. Are the favourite poets of the eighteenth century classics?

It is impossible within my present limits to discuss the question fully. And what man of letters would not shrink from seeming to dispose dictatorially of the claims of two men who are, at any rate, such masters in letters as Dryden and Pope; two men of such admirable talent, both of them, and one of them, Dryden, a man, on all sides, of such energetic and genial power? And yet, if we are to gain the full benefit from poetry, we must have the real estimate of it. I cast about for some mode of arriving, in the present case, at such an estimate without offence. And perhaps the best way is to begin, as it is easy to begin, with cordial praise.

When we find Chapman, the Elizabethan translator of Homer, expressing himself in his preface thus: "Though truth in her very nakedness sits in so deep a pit, that from Gades to Aurora and Ganges few eyes can sound her, I hope yet those few here will so discover and confirm that, the date being out of her darkness in this morning of our poet, he shall now gird his temples with the sun,"—we pronounce that such a prose is intolerable. When we find Milton writing: "And long it was not after, when I was confirmed in this opinion, that he, who would not be frustrate of his hope to write well hereafter in laudable things, ought himself to be a true poem,"—we pronounce that such a prose has its own grandeur, but that it is obsolete and inconvenient. But when we find Dryden telling us: "What Virgil wrote in the vigour of his age, in plenty and at ease, I have undertaken to translate in my declining years; struggling with wants, oppressed with sickness, curbed in my genius, liable to be misconstrued in all I write,"—then we exclaim that here at last we have the true English prose, a prose such as we would all gladly use if we only knew how. Yet Dryden was Milton's contemporary.

But after the Restoration the time had come when our nation felt the imperious need of a fit prose. So, too, the time had likewise come when our nation felt the imperious need of freeing itself from the absorbing preoccupation which religion in the Puritan age had exercised. It was impossible that this freedom should be brought about without some negative excess, without some neglect and impairment of the religious life of the soul; and the spiritual history of the eighteenth century shows us that the freedom was not achieved without them. Still, the freedom was achieved; the preoccupation, an undoubtedly baneful and retarding one if it had continued, was got rid of. And as with religion amongst us at that period, so it was also with letters. A fit prose was a necessity; but it was impossible that a fit prose should establish itself amongst us without some touch of frost to the imaginative life of the soul. The needful qualities for a fit prose are regularity, uniformity, precision, balance. The men of letters, whose destiny it may be to bring their nation to the attainment of a fit prose, must of necessity, whether they work in prose or in verse, give a predominating, an almost exclusive attention to the qualities of regularity, uniformity, precision, balance. But an almost exclusive attention to these qualities involves some repression and silencing of poetry.

We are to regard Dryden as the puissant and glorious founder, Pope as the splendid high priest, of our age of prose and reason, of our excellent and indispensable eighteenth century. For the purposes of their mission and destiny their poetry, like their prose, is admirable. Do you ask me whether Dryden's verse, take it almost where you will, is not good?

> "A milk-white Hind, immortal and unchanged,
> Fed on the lawns and in the forest ranged."

I answer: Admirable for the purposes of the inaugurator of an age of prose and reason. Do you ask me whether Pope's verse, take it almost where you will, is not good?

> "To Hounslow Heath I point, and Banstead Down;
> Thence comes your mutton, and these chicks my own."

I answer: Admirable for the purposes of the high priest of an age of prose and reason. But do you ask me whether such verse proceeds from men with an adequate poetic criticism of life, from men whose criticism of life has a high seriousness, or even without that high seriousness, has poetic largeness, freedom, insight, benignity? Do you ask me whether the application of ideas to life in the verse of these men, often a powerful application, no doubt, is a powerful *poetic* application? Do you ask me whether the poetry of these men has either the matter or the inseparable manner of such an adequate poetic criticism; whether it has the accent of

> "Absent thee from felicity awhile . . ."

or of

> "And what is else not to be overcome . . ."

or of

> "O martyr souded in virginitee!"

I answer: It has not and cannot have them; it is the poetry of the builders of an age of prose and reason. Though they may write in verse, though they may in a certain sense be masters of the art of versification, Dryden and Pope are not classics of our poetry, they are classics of our prose.

Gray is our poetical classic of that literature and age; the position of Gray is singular, and demands a word of notice here. He has not the volume or the power of poets who, coming in times more favourable, have attained to an independent criticism of life. But he lived with the great poets, he lived, above all, with the Greeks, through perpetually studying and enjoying them; and he caught their poetic point of view for regarding life, caught their poetic manner. The point of view and the manner are not self-sprung in him, he caught them of others; and he had not the free and abundant use of them. But whereas Addison and Pope never had the use of them, Gray had the use of them at times. He is the scantiest and frailest of classics in our poetry, but he is a classic.

And now, after Gray, we are met, as we draw towards the end of the eighteenth century, we are met by the great name of Burns. We enter now on times where the personal estimate of poets begins to be rife, and where the real estimate of them is not reached without difficulty. But in spite of the disturbing pressures of personal partiality, of national partiality, let us try to reach a real estimate of the poetry of Burns.

By his English poetry Burns in general belongs to the eighteenth century, and has little importance for us.

> "Mark ruffian Violence, distain'd with crimes,
> Rousing elate in these degenerate times;
> View unsuspecting Innocence a prey,
> As guileful Fraud points out the erring way;
> While subtle Litigation's pliant tongue
> The life-blood equal sucks of Right and Wrong!"

Evidently this is not the real Burns, or his name and fame would have disappeared long ago. Nor is Clarinda's love-poet, Sylvander, the real Burns either. But he tells us himself: "These English songs gravel me to death. I have not the command of the language that I have of my native tongue. In fact, I think that my ideas are more barren in English than in Scotch. I have been at *Duncan Gray* to dress it in English, but all I can do is desperately stupid." We English turn naturally, in Burns, to the poems in our own language, because we can read them easily; but in those poems we have not the real Burns.

The real Burns is of course in his Scotch poems. Let us boldly say that of much of this poetry, a poetry dealing perpetually with Scotch drink, Scotch religion, and Scotch manners, a Scotchman's estimate is apt to be personal. A Scotchman is used to this world of Scotch drink, Scotch religion, and Scotch manners; he has a tenderness for it; he meets its poets half way. In this tender mood he reads pieces like the *Holy Fair* or *Halloween*. But this world of Scotch drink, Scotch religion, and Scotch manners is against a poet, not for him, when it is not a partial countryman who reads him; for in itself it is not a beautiful world, and no one can deny that it is of advantage to a poet to deal with a beautiful world. Burns's world of Scotch drink, Scotch religion, and Scotch manners is often a harsh, a sordid, a repulsive world; even the world of his *Cotter's Saturday Night* is not a beautiful world. No doubt a poet's criticism of life may have such truth and power that it triumphs over its world and delights us. Burns may triumph over his world, often he does triumph over his world, but let us observe how and where. Burns is the first case we have had where the bias of the personal estimate tends to mislead; let us look at him closely, he can bear it.

Many of his admirers will tell us that we have Burns, convivial, genuine, delightful, here: —

"Leeze me on drink! it gies us mair
 Than either school or college;
It kindles wit, it waukens lair,
 It pangs us fou o' knowledge.
Be 't whisky gill or penny wheep
 Or ony stronger potion,
It never fails, on drinking deep,
 To kittle up our notion
  By night or day."

There is a great deal of that sort of thing in Burns, and it is unsatisfactory, not because it is bacchanalian poetry, but because it has not that accent of sincerity which bacchanalian poetry, to do it justice, very often has. There is something in it of bravado, something which makes us feel that we have not the man speaking to us with his real voice; something, therefore, poetically unsound.

With still more confidence will his admirers tell us that we have the genuine Burns, the great poet, when his strain asserts the independence, equality, dignity, of men, as in the famous song *For a' that and a' that*—

"A prince can mak' a belted knight,
 A marquis, duke, and a' that;
But an honest man's aboon his might,
 Guid faith he mauna fa' that!
  For a' that, and a' that,
   Their dignities, and a' that,
  The pith o' sense, and pride o' worth,
   Are higher rank than a' that."

Here they find his grand, genuine touches; and still more, when this puissant genius, who so often set morality at defiance, falls moralising—

"The sacred lowe o' weel-placed love
 Luxuriantly indulge it;
But never tempt th' illicit rove,
 Tho' naething should divulge it.
I waive the quantum o' the sin,
 The hazard o' concealing,
But och; it hardens a' within,
 And petrifies the feeling."

Or in a higher strain—

"Who made the heart, 't is He alone
 Decidedly can try us;
He knows each chord, its various tone;
 Each spring, its various bias.
Then at the balance let 's be mute,
 We never can adjust it;
What 's *done* we partly may compute,
 But know not what 's resisted."

Or in a better strain yet, a strain, his admirers will say, unsurpassable—

"To make a happy fire-side clime
  To weans and wife,
That 's the true pathos and sublime
  Of human life."

There is criticism of life for you, the admirers of Burns will say to us; there is the application of ideas to life! There is, undoubtedly. The doctrine of the last-quoted lines coincides almost exactly with what was the aim and end, Xenophon tells us, of all the teaching of Socrates. And the application is a powerful one; made by a man of vigorous understanding, and (need I say?) a master of language.

But for supreme poetical success more is required than the powerful application of ideas to life; it must be an application under the conditions fixed by the laws of poetic truth and poetic beauty. Those laws fix as an essential condition, in the poet's treatment of such matters as are here in question, high seriousness;—the high seriousness which comes from absolute sincerity. The accent of high seriousness, born of absolute sincerity, is what gives to such verse as

> In la sua volontade è nostra pace . . .

to such criticism of life as Dante's, its power. Is this accent felt in the passages which I have been quoting from Burns? Surely not; surely, if our sense is quick, we must perceive that we have not in those passages a voice from the very inmost soul of the genuine Burns; he is not speaking to us from these depths, he is more or less preaching. And the compensation for admiring such passages less, from missing the perfect poetic accent in them, will be that we shall admire more the poetry where that accent is found.

No; Burns, like Chaucer, comes short of the high seriousness of the great classics, and the virtue of matter and manner which goes with that high seriousness is wanting to his work. At moments he touches it in a profound and passionate melancholy, as in those four immortal lines taken by Byron as a motto for *The Bride of Abydos*, but which have in them a depth of poetic quality such as resides in no verse of Byron's own—

> "Had we never loved sae kindly,
> Had we never loved sae blindly,
> Never met, or never parted,
> We had ne'er been broken-hearted."

But a whole poem of that quality Burns cannot make; the rest, in the *Farewell to Nancy*, is verbiage.

We arrive best at the real estimate of Burns, I think, by conceiving his work as having truth of matter and truth of manner, but not the accent or the poetic virtue of the highest masters. His genuine criticism of life, when the sheer poet in him speaks, is ironic; it is not—

> "Thou Power Supreme, whose mighty scheme
> These woes of mine fulfil,
> Here firm I rest, they must be best
> Because they are Thy will!"

It is far rather: *Whistle owre the lave o't!* Yet we may say of him as of Chaucer, that of life and the world, as they come before him, his view is large, free, shrewd, benignant,—truly poetic, therefore; and his manner of rendering what he sees is to match. But we must note, at the same time, his great difference from Chaucer. The freedom of Chaucer is heightened, in Burns, by a fiery, reckless energy; the benignity of Chaucer deepens, in Burns, into an overwhelming sense of the pathos of things;—of the pathos of human nature, the pathos, also, of non-human nature. Instead of the fluidity of Chaucer's manner, the manner of Burns has spring, bounding swiftness. Burns is by far the greater force, though he has perhaps less charm. The world of Chaucer is fairer, richer, more significant than that of Burns; but when the largeness and freedom of Burns get full sweep, as in *Tam o' Shanter*, or still more in that puissant and splendid production, *The Jolly Beggars*, his world may be what it will, his poetic genius triumphs over it. In the world of *The Jolly Beggars* there is more than hideousness and squalor, there is bestiality; yet the piece is a superb poetic success. It has a breadth, truth, and power which make the famous scene in Auerbach's Cellar, of Goethe's *Faust*, seem artificial and tame beside it, and which are only matched by Shakespeare and Aristophanes.

Here, where his largeness and freedom serve him so admirably, and also in those poems and songs where to shrewdness he adds infinite archness and wit, and to benignity infinite pathos, where his manner is flawless, and a perfect poetic whole is the result,—in things like the address to the mouse whose home he had ruined, in things like *Duncan Gray*, *Tam Glen*, *Whistle and I'll come to you my Lad*, *Auld Lang Syne* (this list might be made much longer),—here we have the genuine Burns, of whom the real estimate must be high indeed. Not a classic, nor with the excellent σπουδαιότης of the great classic, nor with a verse rising to a criticism of life and a virtue like theirs; but a poet with thorough truth of substance and an answering truth of style, giving us a poetry sound to the core. We all of us have a leaning towards the pathetic, and may be inclined perhaps to prize Burns most for his touches of piercing, sometimes almost intolerable, pathos; for verse like—

"We twa hae paidl't i' the burn
From mornin' sun till dine;
But seas between us braid hae roar'd
Sin auld lang syne . . ."

where he is as lovely as he is sound. But perhaps it is by the perfection of soundness of his lighter and archer masterpieces that he is poetically most wholesome for us. For the votary misled by a personal estimate of Shelley, as so many of us have been, are, and will be,—of that beautiful spirit building his many-coloured haze of words and images

"Pinnacled dim in the intense inane"—

no contact can be wholesomer than the contact with Burns at his archest and soundest. Side by side with the

"On the brink of the night and the morning
My coursers are wont to respire,
But the Earth has just whispered a warning
That their flight must be swifter than fire . . ."

of *Prometheus Unbound*, how salutary, how very salutary, to place this from *Tam Glen*:—

"My minnie does constantly deave me
And bids me beware o' young men;
They flatter, she says, to deceive me;
But wha can think sae o' Tam Glen?"

But we enter on burning ground as we approach the poetry of times so near to us—poetry like that of Byron, Shelley, and Wordsworth—of which the estimates are so often not only personal, but personal with passion. For my purpose, it is enough to have taken the single case of Burns, the first poet we come to of whose work the estimate formed is evidently apt to be personal, and to have suggested how we may proceed, using the poetry of the great classics as a sort of touchstone, to correct this estimate, as we had previously corrected by the same means the historic estimate where we met with it. A collection like the present,[1] with its succession of celebrated names and celebrated poems, offers a good opportunity to us for resolutely endeavouring to make our estimates of poetry real. I have sought to point out a method which will help us in making them so, and to exhibit it in use so far as to put any one who likes in a way of applying it for himself.

At any rate the end to which the method and the estimate are designed to lead, and from leading to which, if they do lead to it, they get their whole value,—the benefit of being able clearly to feel and deeply to enjoy the best, the truly classic, in poetry,—is an end, let me say it once more at parting, of supreme importance. We are often told that an era is opening in which we are to see multitudes of a common sort of readers, and masses of a common sort of literature; that such readers do not want and could not relish anything better than such literature, and that to provide it is becoming a vast and profitable industry. Even if good literature entirely lost currency with the world, it would still be abundantly worth while to continue to enjoy it by oneself. But it never will lose currency with the world, in spite of momentary appearances; it never will lose supremacy. Currency and supremacy are insured to it, not indeed by the world's deliberate and conscious choice, but by something far deeper,—by the instinct of self-preservation in humanity.

1888

SELECTIONS FROM MATTHEW ARNOLD'S LETTERS

I To Mrs. Forster

London, Monday 1849

My dearest K,—

. . . More and more I think ill of the great people here: that is their two capital faults, stupidity & hardness of heart become more and more clear to me. Their faults of character seem to me, as I watch the people in the park, to be the grand impairers of English beauty. In the men certainly; for the faces of the

[1] This essay was first published as the introduction to Ward's *English Poets*.

handsomest express either a stupid pride, or the stupidity without the pride, & the half alive look of many pretty faces among the women, so different from the southern languor, points to something very like stupidity. And a proud looking Englishwoman is the hardest looking thing I know in the world. So I should not be sorry to get away; but I still accustom myself to feel that we should pity these people rather than be angry with them.

I do not think any fruitful revolution can come in my time; and meanwhile, thank God, there are many honest people on earth, and the month of May comes every year.

. . . Good-bye; this is rather a sombre letter, but I have not breakfasted & it is $11\frac{1}{2}$, which is perhaps the reason.

I have many poetical schemes, but am fermenting too much about poetry in general to do anything satisfactory. My last volume I have got absolutely to dislike.

Ever yours

M. A.

II To Mrs. Forster

38 Eaton Place Sunday [1853]

My darling K,—

I seem to want to see you and be with you more than anyone when my Poems are making their way, or beginning to make it. You were my first hearer—you dear K—and such a sympathising, dear—animating hearer, too.

I should like now, to go abroad—above all —to Rome, to live for some months quite quietly there—to see no English, and to hear nothing more about my Poems. It does me no good hearing the discussion of them—yet of course I cannot help being occupied by it. I intend soon to try and make some strong resolution in this respect—and keep it.

The Spectator elaborately and rather méchamment attacks—Rentool himself was the "apparently intelligent critic." Most of what he says is precisely what I do not believe. The Leader to my surprise behaves with extraordinary civility—one may say friendliness, though not committing itself too far. The Press is very praising too—I am surprised at that also—but very glad. The Examiner will probably come next week. I am very anxious to see that, as L'd Lansdowne and such as he, go mainly, I think, by what Foster says.

I heard last night from Froude that Chapman had just written to him "begging for the article on me which he had twice refused." So it will appear in January. Whose doing is this? Grey's or William's?

Love to William, who I hope is better. I shall send the newspapers containing notices home, so you can get from Mamma any you want to see.

Ever your own affectionate

M. A.

Eckerman is I think certainly genuine, and most interesting. But read him in German—such beautiful, easy German.

We are here for two months.

III To Mrs. Forster

Fox How, October 10/54

My dearest K,

I could not let Flu[1] write, because I wished to write myself and say how very sorry we both are not to be able to pay you and William the visit we so much wished and hoped to pay this autumn. But I must at once begin inspecting—and as I begin in Shropshire and Liverpool is on our road there, I take Flu and the children to the Dingle on Monday—going away myself for a week the day after, and leaving them there. I shall be for a week at Oxford inspecting schools in that neighborhood—and on Tuesday the 24th I hope we shall all meet at Crewe, and proceed to Derby together. If Mamma comes to Edward, you and William must come to us for a Saturday and Sunday at least at Derby—or, if she does not come, you must still come to us, or we must go to you, for that time.

I have so much to say to you, you dear soul. It was odd—as your letter about the country you went through on the Italian side of the Alps was being read, it brought to my mind delightfully just what had been present to it when many of the poems of mine which are nearest to me were composed—and then came your sentence saying that what you had seen had brought these Poems to your mind. That was a correspondence to give one real pleasure

[1] Mrs. Matthew Arnold.

—but there is no one and never will be any one who enters into what I have done as you have entered into it, dearest K,—and to whom I so want to communicate what I do. I have just finished a poem which I think is better than Sohrab and Rustum, though here I do not think they consider it so—but I am nearly sure you will think so—and William too I think will like it. You will see it in November, I hope. You can hardly tell what pleasure Sainte-Beuve's letter gave me, because you do not know how highly I estimate him as a critic. His intention of reviewing me, though, I know very well, arises more from his interest in the questions raised in the preface, than from his caring much about the poems. The article in the Revue des deux mondes is a confused affair—a piece of theorising—the author having a mania for finding everything in Shelley whether it is there or no.

I should like to know what William thinks of this very pretty Westminster quarrel. Miss Martineau and her brother James, and their hatreds, remind one of the family of Pelops. She proposed to me to take part in the Review (from Chapman) but for that I have not time.

Write to me my darling K, when you have time, and with love to William, believe me ever

Your faithless but most affectionate brother

M. A.

I do so long for you to see the children. Louisa Twining has made a beautiful sketch of Flu.

IV To His Wife

Oxford, Sunday [October, 1854]

I am writing from Walrond's rooms in Balliol. This time *thirteen* years ago I was wandering about this quadrangle a freshman, as I see other freshmen doing now. The time seems prodigious. I do not certainly feel thirteen years older than when I came up to Oxford. . . . I am going with Walrond today to explore the Cumnor country, and on Thursday I got up alone into one of the little coombs that papa was so fond of, and which I had in my mind in the "Gipsy Scholar," and felt the peculiar *sentiment* of this country and neighborhood as deeply as ever. But I am much struck with the apathy and *poorness* of the people here, as they now strike me, and their petty pottering habits compared with the students of Paris, or Germany, or even of London. Animation and interest and the power of work seem so sadly wanting in them. And I think this is so; and the place, in losing Newman and his followers, has lost its religious movement, which after all kept it from stagnating, and has not yet, so far as I see, got anything better. However, we must hope that the coming changes, and perhaps the infusion of Dissenters' sons of that muscular, hardworking, *unblasé* middle class—for it is this, in spite of its abominable disagreeableness—may brace the flaccid sinews of Oxford a little.

V To Mrs. Forster

London, Tuesday Morning [April 1856]

Many thanks, my dearest K., for your extracts. My poems are making their way, I think, though slowly, and perhaps never to make way very far. There must always be some people, however, to whom the literalness and sincerity of them has a charm. After all, that American review, which hit upon this last—their sincerity—as their most interesting quality, was not far wrong. It seems to me strange sometimes to hear of people taking pleasure in this or that poem which was written years ago, which then nobody took pleasure in but you, which I then perhaps wondered that nobody took pleasure in, but since had made up my mind that nobody was likely to. The fact is, however, that the state of mind expressed in many of the poems is one that is becoming more common, and you see that even the Obermann stanzas are taken up with interest by some.

I think I shall be able to do something more in time, but am sadly bothered and hindered at present, and that puts one in *deprimirter Stimmung*, which is a fatal thing. To make a habitual war on depression and low spirits, which in one's early youth one is apt to indulge and be somewhat interested in, is one of the things one learns as one gets older. They are noxious alike to body and mind, and already partake of the nature of death.

* * *

Ever most affectionately yours,

M. A.

VI To W. E. Forster

January 11th, 1858

* * *

As to Merope not exciting you—on the stage (for which these things are meant) I think the chief situations would excite you; and it is easy to over-write a situation for acting. For an unconscious testimony to this truth, see that masterpiece of bad criticism, the Times' remarks on Rachel's acting. But we must beware of taking our notions of excitement from the modern drame or from the modern novel—from Adrienne Lecouvreur or from Night & Morning. Certainly the Greek tragic drama does not excite & harrow us to the extent that these do; I think, neither does Shakespeare. Not one hundredth part of the excitement have I ever felt at seeing Lear or Othello on the stage that I have felt at the Corsican brothers or Adrienne Lecouvreur. And, perhaps, this is necessary. For in good tragedy the poet must controul his matter—and in the drama and novel the matter is uncontrollable. There is a kind of pity & fear (Kotzebue is a great master of it) which cannot be purified, it is the most agitating and overwhelming, certainly, but, for the sake of a higher result, we must renounce this. Pity & fear of a certain kind—say commiseration & awe and you will perhaps better feel what I mean—I think Merope does excite—as does Greek tragedy in general; I allow, however, that the problem for the poet is, or should be, to unite the highest degree of agitatingness on the part of his subject-matter, with the highest degree of controul and assuagement on the part of his own exhibition of it—Shakespeare, under immense difficulties, goes further in this respect than the Greeks, and so far he is an advance upon them.

I think in the plot you sketch the interest must have dropped as it drops in Voltaire's tragedy. Such a marriage-tie as Merope's would have not been one to inspire the smallest simple or tragic reluctance to cut it violently. But I am sure you are wrong in your notion that the Greek poets tolerated what we call "repulsive" situations a bit more than we do. There are some excellent remarks in Grote on the liberties Sophocles took with the horrible old legends in order to adapt them to his own poetical feeling & to the refined modern feeling of his time, which are worth your looking at. I feel sure Sophocles would not have treated the subject in the way you suggest, though it might have been very effectively treated in that way,—but Walter Scott would have been far more likely to treat it so than Sophocles.

Michelet has well shown that Christianity has had credit given to it with regard to the extinction of slavery which it does not deserve, and I cannot but think that the same may be said with respect to the treatment of women. The influence of women in Greece was immense.

The conflict of feelings in Merope's nature is what, I think, the tragedy turns upon—I think this would come out upon the stage, and this makes Merope the principal person. The most attractive, however, I certainly agree with you is Polyphontes.

I have a thousand things to say to you about the matter, but have neither time nor room. It is a great pleasure to me to interest you by what I do.

* * *

Love to dearest K,

Ever yours affect'ly,

M. A.

VII To Mrs. Forster

Hotel du Luxembourg, Nismes
May 22nd, 1859. Sunday

* * *

Louis Napoleon is as little connected with the past as the French peasant—he has the ideas of the modern world in which he was long knocked about in a way in which the members of the old royal races—our Queen or the Emperors of Russia and Austria cannot have them—in a way in which even the old aristocracies cannot have them. His uncle had them, too, and was a man of genius which this man is not—but he went off his centre with success and dashed himself to pieces. But you may depend upon it that it is a "mot" of the first Napoleon's which is now inspiring this second Napoleon—that the sovereign who put himself at the head of the cause of the peoples of Europe would be the master of the future. And I firmly believe that his desire in invading Italy is to obtain the preëminence which he believes will accrue to him and to France by executing this idea of his uncle—not to get some perilous and useless kingdom of Etruria established again. In this sense he is, what the Italians call him, L'uomo del secolo—and our worst chance is that our politicians and diplomatists are so bound up in routine and the traditions of the past, as I can perceive very well even by hearing Lord Cowley talk, that they cannot even conceive such a course as that of the French Emperor, and will be entirely unprepared for everything that happens. But this is the worst of aristocracies, with all their merits—they are inaccessible to ideas; and when civilization comes to that point that ideas, and not mere tenacity, are wanted for the Government of the world, they break down. So it was at Rome—so, I fear, it will be with us, unless our aristocracy, always so prudent, can get from others, and use, the lights which it has not itself. But our people's strong point is not intellectual coup d'œil any more than our aristocracy's; & this is our worst chance.

There—I have filled my letter with all this disputation—but it is every word true and I like to write to you what I think. I wrote to Lord Lansdowne the other day, and told him as much as I could. There is a man with an open intelligence if he had youth, faith and commanding energy! But the true type of the British political nobleman is Lord Derby—with eloquence, high feeling and good intentions—but the ideas of a school-boy.

I thought nothing could have been better than William's appearance at Leeds—but I was too provoked when I found how narrowly he had missed success. My love to him—I should like to wring his hand for poor dear Willy's sake. Write me a line to Paris within the next week—you shall then have a more proper journalizing letter in answer. It is very hot, but I drink chocolate and get as brown and stout as Queen Pomare. Think of me at Vaucluse on Wednesday.

My dearest K, you know how truly I am always your affectionate brother,

M. A.

Kiss the poor little darlings for me if they are with you when this reaches you. I shall be at Meurice's in Paris.

VIII To Miss Arnold

2 Chester Square, December 17, 1860

. . . I have not been in better case for a long time, and I attribute it entirely to making greater demands on myself. If you only half use the machine it goes badly, but its full play suits it; and if I live and do well from now to fifty (only twelve years!), I will get something out of myself. I shall tomorrow finish my third lecture. It will not be given till the middle of January, but I want to get the subject done, and to have my mind free for other subjects. I have at last got the Commissioner's distinct leave to publish my Report, with additions, as a book. It will appear in February. By the time you come I hope to have finished the introduction to that and to have got it printed, and to be well plunged in the Middle Age. I have a strong sense of the irrationality of that period, and of the utter folly of those who take it seriously, and play at restoring it; still, it has poetically the greatest charm and refreshment possible for me. The fault I find with Tennyson in his *Idylls of the King* is that the peculiar charm and aroma of the Middle Age he does not give in them. There is something magical about it, and I will do something with it before I have done. The real truth is that Tennyson, with all his temperament and artistic skill, is deficient in intellectual power; and no modern poet can make very much of his business unless he is preëminently strong in this. Goethe owes his grandeur to his strength in this, although it even hurt his poetical operations by its immense predominance. However, it would not do for me to say this about Tennyson, though gradually I mean to say boldly the truth about a great many English celebrities, and begin with Ruskin in these lectures on Homer. I have been reading a great deal in the *Iliad* again lately, and though it is too much to say, as the writer in the *Biographie Universelle* says, that "none but an Englishman would dream of matching Shakespeare with the Greeks," yet it is true that Homer leaves him with all his unequalled gift—and certainly there never was any such naturally gifted poet—as far behind as perfection leaves imperfection.

IX To Mrs. Forster

2, Chester Square, Feb'y 8th, 1861

My dearest K,—

* * *

So you find my tone in the Lectures too dogmatic? I shall be curious to see if the reviewers find the same thing. No one else has yet made this complaint, and you must remember that the tone of a lecturing professor to an audience supposed to be there to learn of him, cannot be quite that of a man submitting his views to the great world. The expression to speak ex cathedra in itself implies what is expected in one who speaks from a Professor's chair. Also it is not positive forms in themselves that are offensive to people—it is positive forms in defense of paradox; such as Ruskin's, that Claude is a bad colorist, or Murillo a second-rate painter. But Voltaire one reads with delight, for all his positive forms and stringent argumentation—because he is generally defending the common-sense side of a question against pedantry or prejudice—and that Homer is plain, noble, etc., etc., is certainly the common-sense view of Homer, and that hitherto generally received by the best judges. But enough of all this—certainly I must and will take care not to fall into an offensive tone of dogmatising, on any subject, for that is always in bad taste, and therefore always excruciating.

God bless you—let me hear as soon as anything is settled in your plans.

You know we cannot make up our minds to send old Budge[1] away, happy as you would have made him—perhaps as it is this may be convenient for you.

Much love to William, and a thousand final congratulations to you both.

Your ever affectionate,

M. A.

[1] Matthew Arnold's son, Trevenen.

X To His Mother

2 Chester Square, November 20, 1861

My dearest Mother—I was up at a quarter past seven this morning, breakfasted *tête-à-tête* with Dicky, and before nine was off to Euston Square on my way to Bushey, near Watford. I am only just returned, and have not much time before the post goes. However, I will not break my Wednesday rule if I can help it. First of all, you will expect me to say something about poor Clough. That is a loss which I shall feel more and more as time goes on, for he is one of the few people who ever made a deep impression upon me, and as time goes on, and one finds no one else who makes such an impression, one's feeling about those who did make it gets to be something more and more distinct and unique. Besides, the object of it no longer survives to wear it out himself by becoming ordinary and different from what he was. People were beginning to say about Clough that he never would do anything now, and, in short, to pass him over. I foresee that there will now be a change, and attention will be fixed on what there was of extraordinary promise and interest in him when young, and of unique and imposing even as he grew older without fulfilling people's expectations. I have been asked to write a Memoir of him for the *Daily News*, but that I cannot do. I could not write about him in a newspaper now, nor can, I think, at length in a review, but I shall some day in some way or other relieve myself of what I think about him.

I know no details except that he died at Florence. I heard this in a note from Lingen the day before his death appeared in the newspaper. His wife was with him.

* * *

Your ever affectionate

M. A.

XI To J. Dykes Campbell

Fox How, September 22, 1864

I am much tempted to say something about the Enoch Arden volume. I agree with you in thinking "Enoch Arden" itself very good indeed—perhaps the best thing Tennyson has done; "Tithonus" I do not like quite so well. But is it possible for one who has himself published verses to print a criticism on Tennyson in which perfect freedom shall be used? And without perfect freedom, what is a criticism worth? I do not think Tennyson a great and powerful spirit in any line—as Goethe was in the line of modern thought, Wordsworth in that of contemplation, Byron even in that of passion; and unless a poet, especially a poet at this time of day, is that, my interest in him is only slight, and my conviction that he will not finally stand high is firm. But is it possible or proper for me to say this about Tennyson, when my saying it would inevitably be attributed to odious motives? Therefore, though the temptation to speak—especially because I should probably say something so totally different from what the writer in the *Spectator* supposes—is great, I shall probably say nothing.

XII To J. C. Shairp

The Athenæum, April 12, 1866

My dear Shairp—To prevent all mistakes, and leave you without excuse in case of misconduct, I write a line to tell you that we have let our house (2 Chester *Square*) and are going out of town on the 1st of May. But we shall not go far—perhaps to Woodford in Epping Forest, where I heard, two years ago, the cuckoo I have brought in in *Thyrsis;* and, wherever we go, our address may be got at the Privy Council Office, and you will be inexcusable if you do not get it and communicate with me. I will take care that we meet, if you do not, in your shabby way, slip through London unperceived.

It gives me great pleasure that you and Sellar like *Thyrsis. Multi multa loquuntur: ideo fides parum est adhibenda*, says Thomas à Kempis; but the voices I do turn to are the voices of our old set, now so scattered, who, at the critical moment of opening life, were among the same influences and (more or less) sought the same things as I did myself. What influences those before and after us have been or may be among, or what things they have sought or may seek, God knows. Perhaps the same as we, but we cannot know, cannot, therefore, be sure of understanding them and their criticisms on what we do.

Thyrsis is a very quiet poem, but I think solid and sincere. It will not be popular, however. It had long been in my head to connect Clough with that Cumnor country, and when I began I was carried irresistibly into this form; you say, truly, however, that there is much in Clough (the whole *prophet* side, in fact) which one cannot deal with in this way, and one has the feeling, if one reads the poem as a memorial poem, that not enough is said about Clough in it; I feel this so much that I do not send the poem to Mrs. Clough. Still Clough *had* this idyllic side, too; to deal with this suited my desire to deal again with that Cumnor country: anyway, only so could I treat the matter this time. *Valeat quantum.* Do not let Mrs. Shairp forget me.—Yours ever affectionately,

M. A.

XIII To Cardinal Newman

Harrow, November 29th, 1871

My dear Sir,—

Mr. Boyle promised me he would tell you that it had been in my mind to give myself the great pleasure of calling upon you when I was in Birmingham, but the time at my command was too short. I have ventured to send you the lecture I then gave at Birmingham; partly because what is said about Mahometanism at the end seems to me to coincide very much with a strain of remark in a reprinted article of yours on Milman which I have just been reading, and to be an unconscious homage to the truth of what you have there said; and partly to give myself an opportunity of explaining, that the Spectator's assertion, in a review of your Essays, that some lines of mine were "a portrait of Mr. Newman," has its sole ground in the writer's own imagination. What is said in those lines is not what I should have said if I had been speaking of you, and I should not like you to think it was; at any rate, said of you it was not; I had quite another personage in my mind.

I cannot forbear adding, what I have often wished to tell you, that no words can be too strong to express the interest with which I used to hear you at Oxford, and the pleasure with which I continue to read your writings now. We are all of us carried in ways not of our own making or choosing, but nothing can ever do away the effect you have produced upon me, for it consists in a general disposition of mind rather than in a particular set of ideas. In all the conflicts I have with modern Liberalism and Dissent, and with their pretensions and shortcomings, I recognize your work; and I can truly say that no praise gives me so much pleasure as to be told (which sometimes happens) that a thing I have said reminds people, either in manner or matter, of you.

I wish, now I am writing, you would let me ask you two questions. One is: Had you any particular passage of Butler himself in your mind when you said in your Essay on Development, "Anyhow, Analogy is in some sort violated by the fact of a revelation." Butler seems to me now and then to come near an admission of this kind, but I want to know whether you meant to convey that he does make the admission, and if so, where you consider him to make it.

The other question relates to your remarks on Lamennais at the bottom of p. 121 in the first volume of your Essays, and again in p. 123. It is this: Do not you think that what is Tory and anti-democratic in the Church of England (and undoubtedly her Tory, anti-democratic, and even squirearchical character is very marked) is one of her great dangers at the present time; and a danger from which the Catholic Church, with its Gregories and Innocents of whom you speak, is much more exempt? I mean, though the R. Catholic Church may in fact have been anti-democratic in modern times on the Continent, there seems nothing in her nature to make her so; but in the nature of the English Church there does; and is not this an additional peril, at the present day, for the English Church?[1]

I really do not know how to excuse myself for troubling you at all this length, and I can only throw myself upon your kindness, begging you to believe me, with the most cordial gratitude and esteem,

Sincerely yours,

Matthew Arnold.

The Revd. Dr. Newman.

P. S. The Birmingham lecture is in the Cornhill Magazine, which I have told the publisher to send you.

[1] Cardinal Newman wrote Arnold on December 3, 1871, answering his two questions by saying that his impressions about Butler were like Arnold's but that he could not refer to any distinct passage, and that he agreed with what Arnold said "about the Anglican and the Catholic churches relatively to democratic ideas."

XIV From Cardinal Newman

The Oratory, May 24, 1872

My dear Matthew Arnold,

I have read with great interest the Preface of your "Great Prophecy," which has just come to me from you, and, while I ought to write at once to you to thank you for it, as I do, I feel on the other hand I am hardly just or respectful to a work which has taken you so much thought and engages your heart, and which you have earned so special a right to employ yourself upon, not to take more time before I speak about it.

The idea of your book is excellent—so far may be said without chance of mistake; and, as to execution, I see at once that many will be drawn to be your scholars in it who have long done with school. And that, at first sight, is rather my criticism upon it, that it is too good for children.

It is pleasant indeed to find a writer in his day that champion of "letters" in popular education, as against science, which you are; and doubtless the Old Testament is the only book, as you bring out so well in your Preface, which can serve as literary matter in popular schools.

On the other hand, I should dread to view it as literature in the first place—and there will be no time, in the years available for the education of the masses, to read it over a second time, viz., in its literary aspect. A devout mind, which loves the objects which are its ultimate scope, and which instinctively sees our Lord moving along the successive prophetical announcements, may and will (if cultivated) go on to admire its wonderful poetry, and will bear safely, in a critical and scholarlike way, to investigate its literal or first meaning. But how few children are devout. As things are, the prophecies of Isaiah come to the young as their creed in the garb of poetry. The great dogmatical truths of the Gospel are inculcated on them in the medium of the imagination and the affections. If the duty of mastering the literal text and its historical and geographical circumstances is put upon young minds, who have not learned to be devout, nor have the subtlety necessary for being at home with the method of type and antetype, either they will be perplexed and put out to find—(*e.g.*), Isai liii. means at once Jeremiah or an abstract prophet and our Lord, or they will never learn the secret sense of the sacred text at all. It must be recollected that in popular schools the children do not stay over 12 years old—in public schools for the upper classes the case is different.

If I was obliged to throw out some alternative for popular education, I should recommend the 1st Book of Samuel, which is a perfect poem, epic or tragedy, as we take it; going down to 2 Samuel inclusive.

Your remarks on the translation of Isaiah are very important and true, and your "Introductory Note" very apposite. I have no difficulty myself in considering the chs. 40–66 to be written at the date you assign for them, but I have not the necessary knowledge to decide the matter of fact.

I must not conclude without taking grateful notice of the kindness with which, as on former occasions, you introduce my name at page xxx.[1]

Very sincerely yours,
John H. Newman.

XV To His Brother, Walter Arnold

Menaggio, May 5, 1873

. . . At Florence I saw the Princess Alice again. I was marking some favourite pictures in the catalogue, at a last visit to the Pitti, when I heard some one behind me say: "So Mr. Matthew Arnold is making notes on the pictures"; and I turned round and saw the Princess. She introduced me to Prince Louis, who was with her, and her suite fell back, and we stood and talked for at least twenty minutes. When I thought they were fairly gone, she ran back again to ask if I had seen Lord Russell's book.[1] I said I had not, but that it would probably be nothing more than a sort of model religion of the British and Foreign School Society, and rather old-fashioned for modern requirements. Upon which she ran back laughing to Prince Louis, saying: "He says Lord Russell's new religion is sure to be old-fashioned!"

* * *

Your ever affectionate
M. A.

XVI To Lady de Rothschild

Cobham, Surrey
October 11, 1873

My dear Lady de Rothschild—I ought to have thanked you sooner for your kind note. In these last days I have often thought how greatly I should have liked you to have seen and known my mother. There is a little notice of her in this week's *Guardian* which I should like you to look at. It is very well done, and very true. I have not the paper here, or I would send it. But I will send you a sermon, or part of a sermon, which the Dean of Durham preached about her last Sunday, and which is now being printed. She had a clearness and fairness of mind, an interest in things, and a power of appreciating what might not be in her own line, which were very remarkable, and which remained with her to the very end of her life. To my great regret, I cannot find a letter she wrote me this last spring after my book had been published. It was a wonderful letter. I can think of no woman in the prime of life, brought up and surrounded as my mother was, and with my mother's sincere personal convictions, who could have written it; and in a

[1] The passage referred to reads as follows:—"Dr. Newman, in one of those charming essays which he has of late rescued for us, quotes from the 54th chapter of Isaiah the passage beginning—'I will lay thy stones with fair colours and lay thy foundations with sapphires' as a prophecy and authorization of the sumptuosities of the Church of Rome. This is evidently to use the passage by way of application. Protestants will say this is a wrong use of it, but to Dr. Newman their similar use of passages about the Scarlet Woman, &c., will seem equally wrong."

[1] *The Rise and Progress of the Christian Religion in the West of Europe*, by John, Earl Russell. 1873.

woman past eighty it was something astonishing. I have a beautiful letter to-day from Dean Stanley, written from Florence; he says, "What to me was so impressive was not merely that she rose instead of sinking under the blow[1] which we all feared would crush her, but that she retained the life-long reverence for your father's greatness, without a blind attempt to rest in the form and letter of his words." This is exactly true. To many who knew my father her death will be the end of a period, and deeply felt accordingly. And to me and her children how much more must it be this! My thanks and very kind regards to Sir Anthony and your daughters.

I am always, dear Lady de Rothschild, most sincerely yours,

Matthew Arnold.

XVII To Miss Arnold

Cobham, February 19, 1876

. . . George Eliot says, a lady tells me, that of all modern poetry mine is that which keeps constantly growing upon her; she, Carlyle, and Gladstone have all expressed great satisfaction with the first instalment of my Butler; I send you the note about Gladstone—it may burn. But it is a great and solid satisfaction, at fifty, to find one's work, the fruit of so many years of isolated reflexion and labour, getting recognition amongst those whose judgment passes for the most valuable.

Your ever most affectionate

M. A.

XVIII To Miss Arnold

[June, 1876]

My dearest Fan—I send you some letters which may burn, all except Sarazin's, which you must return. He is always praising the freedom of opinion in Protestant religious circles, so I sent him an extract from the *Pilot* about my address at Sion College. But it is curious how utterly the religiously disposed people in Catholic countries are without belief in Catholicism's power to transform itself. I, however, believe that it will transform itself; I see no other possible solution. Not to break one's connexion with the past in one's religion is one of the strongest instincts in human nature. Protestantism is breaking up everywhere where it has severed this connexion; only in England has it any hold upon the educated class, and that is because the Church of England is the one Protestant Church which maintained its connexion with the past. I am going to dine with the Bishop of Derry on the 3rd of July. I could not refuse a man who told me that my poems were the centre of his mental life, and that he had read many of them hundreds of times. I also heard from Morley yesterday that G. Sand had said to Renan that when she saw me years ago, "*Je lui faisais l'effet d'un Milton jeune et voyageant.*" Renan told him this. Her death has been much in my mind; she was the greatest spirit in our European world from the time that Goethe departed. With all her faults and Frenchism, she was this. I must write a few pages about her. Do not hang yourself for vexation at not being able to make out this flower.

Your ever affectionate

M. A.

XIX To His Sister, Mrs. Cropper

October 26, 1878

My dearest Susy—I have sent you *Light* with a rather rhapsodical review of my poetry, because it praises and quotes a poem which I remember repeating to you just after it was composed, and I can see your dear face now as you listened to it, and were touched by it. My poems have had no better friends in their early and needy days than my own sisters. It is curious how the public is beginning to take them to its bosom after long years of comparative neglect. The wave of thought and change has rolled on until people begin to find a significance and an attraction in what had none for them formerly. Send *Light* to Fan when you have read it, she will like to see it. I believe the article is by Robert Buchanan. The writers of poetry have been better friends to me always than the mass of readers of poetry.

Your affectionate

M. A.

[1] The sudden death of Dr. Arnold, 1842.

XX To Miss Arnold

Athenæum Club, Pall Mall, S. W.
April 14, 1879

My dearest Fan—It is an east wind and a gray sky, but I had meant to go to Horsley and see the daffodils; however, the dentist willed it otherwise, and I have had to come up here, my appointment being made for eleven this morning. How much time and power, in the course of my life, my teeth have made me lose! I have since been correcting the proof of my Eton speech, which is to appear in the *Cornhill.* I am well forward with my school reports, and have nearly finished arranging my Wordsworth selection, so I feel more of a free man than usual. It is delightful to have to occupy oneself with Wordsworth, and he will come out better, and more effective in my arrangement, I think, than he has ever come out before. I have gone on the plan of throwing pieces of one poetical *kind* together, not of classifying them, in Wordsworth's own intricate way, according to the spiritual faculty from which they are supposed to have proceeded. I don't think any of his *best* work will be left out, though a great deal must be left out which is *good* work, especially of his later time. When I have sent my list off to the printer I shall set about my introduction—a short one, but I hope to do him justice. He can show a body of work superior to what any other English poet, except Shakespeare and Milton, can show; and his body of work is more interesting than Milton's, though not so great. This seems to me to be the simple truth. I hope this collection of mine may win for him some appreciation on the Continent also. I shall send the book to Scherer, and beg him to review it. Wordsworth's body of work, to keep to that phrase, is superior to the body of work of any Continental poet of the last hundred years except Goethe; superior to that of Schiller, Heine, Musset, Victor Hugo. This, again, seems to me to be the simple truth. But I must not run on.

I have had some happy gatherings of white violets, though the cottage children are apt to be before me, and they spoil as much as they gather. We are going to-morrow to Aston Clinton, and there, in the lanes of the Chilterns, I hope to find the white violets in masses. It is one of the best soils in England for them. The wild primroses are only just showing.

Your ever affectionate

M. A.

XXI To Miss Arnold

Cobham, Sunday, May 15 [1880]

. . . On Thursday I got a card from the Duchess of Norfolk for a party that evening, to meet Newman. I went, because I wanted to have spoken once in my life to Newman, and because I wanted to see the house. The house was not so fine as I expected. Newman was in costume—not full Cardinal's costume, but a sort of vest with gold about it and the red cap; he was in state at one end of the room, with the Duke of Norfolk on one side of him and a chaplain on the other, and people filed before him as before the Queen, dropping on their knees when they were presented and kissing his hand. It was the faithful who knelt in general, but then it was in general only the faithful who were presented. That old mountebank Lord ——, dropped on his knees, however, and mumbled the Cardinal's hand like a piece of cake. I only made a deferential bow, and Newman took my hand in both of his and was charming. He said, "I ventured to tell the Duchess I should like to see you." One had to move on directly, for there was a crowd of devotees waiting, and he retires at eleven. But I am very glad to have seen him. I met Lady Portsmouth there, who is a relation of the Duke; she took charge of me, and carried me through the crowd to the chaplain, who knew who I was; else I should never have got at Newman at all. . . .

Your ever affectionate

M. A.

XXII To Miss Arnold

Cobham, Surrey, October 7, 1883

. . . Everybody is very kind, and I hear all sorts of promising reports about America. A railway contractor who has just come back tells the Yates Thompsons that all the railway porters and guides have read my books! We are taking a good many introductions after all: the Secretaries at the American Legation thought it better. They say Lowell only knows at home Boston and Cambridge, and his advice as to social points cannot be followed for America generally. Philip Currie, of the Foreign Office, has given us letters to the British Legation at Washington, and to the British Consuls in the chief towns. I have got two of my lectures fairly printed and ready, and am getting much interested in the Emerson one. I shall be glad to have it to think of on the voyage. He did me a great deal of good formerly—far more than Carlyle ever did, and now, going back to him, I do not feel his merit less than I did formerly. I want to see Concord, and Boston Bay, and his grave, before I actually write this lecture. . .

Your most affectionate

M. A.

XXIII To Miss Arnold

Somerset Club, Boston
December 13, 1883

My dearest Fan—Here it is wonderfully fine; two slight drizzlings are all the rain we have had this month; no snow, and not excessive frosts; almost continual sunshine, and such sunsets behind the spires of Boston, and over the immense expanse of western sky visible here, as you never saw. I have bought a pair of *arctics*, the lined waterproof boots which everybody here wears in winter over their boots or shoes, but I have not yet worn them. The day after to-morrow I leave New England. Boston . . . has been very kind to me, and I am sorry to think that I shall see it no more. Last night I lectured at Concord. I did not give the Emerson lecture, as it was a free criticism of him on the literary side, and I did not wish to stand up in his town as a critic of him; but Miss Emerson wrote me a charming note about my lecture on him from the summary given in the newspapers, and his family and literary executor are perfectly satisfied. I give the lecture to-morrow night to a popular audience of some 2000 people here. We went to Concord at five yesterday afternoon; it is about twenty miles off. The Emersons sent to meet us. They live in the house which Emerson himself built, about a mile from the station; a good house with nine acres of ground. The house is much more English in its distribution and furniture than most of the houses here. I had told Fanny Lucy to expect something like Rydal Mount, but it was nothing like that—all the modern improvements were present. Mrs. Emerson is eighty-one, of great height, and an invalid. She is still one of the handsomest women you ever saw, with manners of high distinction. She was brought up a strict Calvinist, and never approved her husband's views. He called her "Queeny," and she does indeed look like a queen and rules the house. We dined at six, and all except Mrs. Emerson went to the lecture along the frozen road by which the British troops retreated—the high road from Concord to Boston. I gave the lecture on Numbers. This morning I left with them, by request, the lecture on Emerson to read, and we departed, after driving round to Concord Bridge and the monument with Dr. Emerson and his sister. It is a very pleasing country—gentle hills, and New England homesteads, and elm-bordered roads (such elms!), and the quiet river flowing through it. Emerson's lines on the monument you know. They are very fine—

"Here once the embattled farmers stood,
And fired the shot heard round the world."

Tell William he should get and read his correspondence with Carlyle, if he has not already done so. It gives a most favourable impression of both the friends. Now I must be off to Andover, some twenty-three miles. I am quite well, and have as yet had no cold or hoarseness. Ever your affectionate

M. A.

XXIV To Mrs. Forster

Cobham, October 18th, 1884

My dearest K,—

* * *

How very right you were about what you called my too "solemn" and poor Mr. Carnegie my "ministerial" manner in speaking. Since I have spoken so much, I have perceived that it is my great defect, inasmuch as it strikes every one. Harper's Magazine goes so far as to say that just because I am irresistibly agreeable to read, I ought never to speak, because speaking is a line in which I am imperfect. I was talking about this to Huxley, & he said that for years he had made the mere manner of speaking his perpetual study; but then, he said, he regarded speaking as to be his business in life. He is very ill, and looks like a man quite spent. I have a real affection for him though we seldom meet; it brought the tears into my eyes to see him. But I should think he would have great rallying power, when he gets real rest.

William has taken and kept his line very well, but the whole discussion of the Franchise has been, as you say, singularly unfruitful. I hope Cleveland will be returned in America. I find that having been in America wonderfully increases my interest in their men and politics. In some points they are certainly our superiors; but it is not easy to see them and ourselves quite clearly and all round.

Ever, my dearest, your most affectionate

M. A.

XXV To Henry A. Jones

Athenæum Club, Pall Mall
December 23, 1884

My dear Sir—I went to see *Saints and Sinners*, and my interest was kept up throughout, as I expected. You have remarkably the art—so valuable in drama—of exciting interest and sustaining it. The piece is full of good and telling things, and one cannot watch the audience without seeing that by strokes of this kind faith in the middle-class fetish is weakened, however slowly, as it could be in no other way.

I must add that I dislike seduction-dramas (even in *Faust* the feeling tells with me), and that the marriage of the heroine with her farmer does not please me as a *dénouement*.

Your representative middle-class man was well drawn and excellently acted.

Very truly yours,
Matthew Arnold.

XXVI To His Wife

Munich, Sunday, February 28, 1886

Your announcement of dear Lola's [a family pony] death did indeed give me a pang. I have just been reading your letter again. You tell it beautifully, just all that I should naturally want to know; and all you have done is exactly right, and as I could wish. Perhaps we might have kept a meche of her hair where it used to come over her forehead, but I should have hated mangling her to take her hoof off, and should not have cared for having it when it was done. You have buried her just in the right place, and I shall often stand by the thorn-tree and think of her. I could indeed say, "Let my last end be like hers!" for her death must have been easy, though I am grieved to hear of her being so wasted and short-breathed. When I was at home at Christmas, I thought she was much as before, and she always liked her apples. I am glad Nelly went to see her. How glad I am, too, that we resisted all proposals to "put her away." How small has been the trouble and expense of keeping her this last year, and how far different is the feeling about her death now from what it would have been if we had put an end to her. There was something in her character which I particularly liked and admired, and I shall never forget her, dear little thing! The tears come into my eyes as I write. . . .

DANTE GABRIEL ROSSETTI

[May 12, 1828–April 9, 1882]

Dante Gabriel Rossetti was the second child and eldest son of Gabriele Rossetti, an Italian political exile, who had settled in London in 1824. He maintained his family by teaching Italian and for some years was professor of Italian at King's College. Meanwhile other exiles came and went at his house, and young Gabriel grew up in an atmosphere of political talk which so sickened him of politics that he took little interest afterwards. The household, however, was more than political. The father was a poet in his own right and a student of Dante, and young Gabriel grew up in a congenial intellectual atmosphere. To be a painter became very early his ambition, and it was understood in the family. He had been sent to day school at King's College School from 1837 until 1842, but when, in 1842, the family purse became pinched it was judged wise that he should proceed at once to the study of painting.

He worked first (1842–46) at an art school under the direction of F. S. Cary and then was admitted to the Antique School of the Royal Academy. He never did proceed to the Life and Painting Schools. A painter he wished to become, but the method of teaching he did not like, and lessons imposed upon him he liked less. As he said some years later, "As soon as a thing is imposed on me as an obligation, my aptitude for doing it is gone; what I *ought* to do is what I *can't* do." There was a wilfulness about him which did not take gladly to schools and therefore he abandoned the Academy. He wrote Ford Madox Brown, a very independent and capable artist although only twenty-seven, and asked to become his pupil. Brown was astonished, but he agreed. Discovering his pupil's technical immaturity, Brown set him, as a drill, to painting a picture of a pickle jar—possibly as the only convenient study at hand.

This was in March 1848. In May Rossetti, always impatient of restraint or delay, was calling on Holman Hunt and bewailing the pickle jars. Some time in August or September he met John Millais at Hunt's and the three young men studied some engravings of frescoes by Gozzoli and Orcagna at Pisa. The Pre-Raphaelite Brotherhood came of these engravings. The three men were really still students, Rossetti the least advanced of them, although his dominant personality soon made him the acknowledged leader. They took four others in to make a group of seven, and hit upon the name Pre-Raphaelite Brotherhood to express the point of their revolt from Academy standards. They wanted to escape from schools, dominated as these were by the prestige of great names and therefore tending toward the conventional, and they wanted to escape in the direction of individual honesty of expression. There was no intention to imitate early work. The group was to get together for long sessions of talk on art, and literature was not forgotten.

The association was a group of young men and its impulse sprang as much out of camaraderie as out of identicalness of aim. Nevertheless there did develop a Pre-Raphaelite style. Writing in 1868, Rossetti declared that it was "the qualities of realism, emotional but extremely minute, which marked the style," and the description is as good as any, although Rossetti said it was best exemplified in the paintings of Hunt. Their canvases were emotional in effect and yet painted with extreme attention to realistic detail. The elaboration of detail they agreed upon, however, as good training for the eye of young painters, not as an essential of art, and realism in the sense of mere photographic reproduction was never their aim.

The three ringleaders set to work on pictures for the next exhibiting season. Millais and Hunt exhibited at the Royal Academy and Rossetti at the "Free Exhibition" in 1849. Rossetti's picture was "The Girlhood of Mary, Virgin" (for which his sister Christina sat as model) and it was so successful that he sold it at his own price (£80). Seeing it again in 1864, he found it "a long way better than he thought." The initials P.R.B. were passed over unnoticed, the press and public reception was good, and Gabriel "had become a painter."

He had also become a poet, but with no public recognition. As early as 1845 he was at work on his translations from the early Italian poets, and before 1847 he had finished the first version of *The Blessed Damozel.* The poem derived from Poe's *The Raven.* "I saw at once," said Rossetti, "that Poe had done the utmost it was possible to do with the grief of the lover on earth, and I determined to reverse the conditions, and give utterance to the yearning of the loved one in heaven." Other poems written about this time were *My Sister's Sleep*, *Portrait*, and *Ave.* Later, about the time of his distress over Brown's pickle jars, he considered giving up painting for poetry and wrote to Leigh Hunt, enclosing some of his poems. Too much can be made of Rossetti's precocity as a poet. The versions of these poems familiar to every one were perfected, especially in the case of *The Blessed Damozel*, through years of revision. But what Rossetti sent to Leigh Hunt at this time led Hunt to reply that he was an "unquestionable poet." Hunt, however, sternly warned him there was no living to be made out of poetry, and Rossetti, a little dashed, stuck to his pickle jars.

By 1851 the P.R.B. as an organization had ceased to function, but meanwhile the brothers had some lively times together. In 1850 they published (to the severe damage of their purses) four issues of a little magazine called *The Germ.* It was here that Rossetti's *The Blessed Damozel* was first printed. And in 1850 the pictures they exhibited were severely criticised. Largely through Rossetti's influence, and his instinct for publicity, the meaning of the initials P.R.B. was made public. A challenge to established authority was understood, and the established journals such as the *Athenæum* and *The Times* attacked the new school. The very violence of the attack raised up a powerful defender. John Ruskin, who told Victorian England what to believe about art, became interested and (early in 1851) in two letters to *The Times* he came publicly to the defense of the group. Equally important, he privately opened his full purse to Rossetti and, under an arrangement which lasted nearly a decade, purchased many of Rossetti's pictures. It was Ruskin also who in 1861 subsidized Rossetti's first published volume, *The Early Italian Poets.*

More important to Rossetti than the advent of Ruskin was an accident. Among art students there is a perpetual quest of the model—the right model. Late in 1849 or early in 1850 Walter Deverell, one of the younger members of the group, discovered a girl in a bonnet shop who sent him back to the rest of the group raving. The girl was Elizabeth Siddal. It was no easy matter to get her to pose, for she was only seventeen, of a respectable family, with no notion of being the model for a Bohemian group. But Deverell accomplished it. She posed for Deverell and Millais, and for Rossetti—and Rossetti appropriated her to the exclusion of the rest. Rossetti, with his flashing eyes and dominance of personality, was the acknowledged chieftain of the group. The others would no more have questioned his right to choose than they would have questioned a decision from one of the gods, and when they saw how powerfully the chief was affected, they withdrew. Rossetti promptly set the Sid, as she was called, to drawing (it was the complaint of his friends that he tried to make a painter out of every one) and she demonstrated a talent in her own right. But to Rossetti she was miraculously the physical embodiment of the girls he had dreamed of. Her beauty imposed itself upon his canvases. He was intoxicated with her glorious hair and it showed in painting after painting. And the Sid, as the years passed and as she came to understand the group, affected flowing gowns which preserved the long lines and gothic simplicities of the P.R.B. paintings, and moved through the lives of the group as the physical embodiment of Pre-Raphaelite art.

The group had become enlarged and was changing. Millais and Hunt had drawn off. Rossetti always attracted younger men, and in 1856 he was delighted to find in *The Oxford and Cambridge Magazine* what he thought was a descendant of *The Germ*. He became acquainted with its moving spirits, notably William Morris and Edward Burne-Jones, and published in it his *The Burden of Nineveh*. On one of his visits to Oxford he conceived the idea of painting the new Oxford Union, whose walls cried out for pictures. Arrangements were made with the authorities, Rossetti recruited a group of artists and, despite the fact that Rossetti himself knew nothing of fresco technique and some of his artists knew nothing of painting whatever, there was in 1857 much excited planning and a mighty splashing of paint which has since fallen off. One of the students who came in to watch the work was Swinburne,—Rossetti was still the chieftain of a young and eager group. The Sid was older, growing unhappy, and ill.

The love affair of Rossetti and Elizabeth Siddal was a long, psychologically tangled and tragic affair. It had been understood among the brotherhood toward the close of 1851 that the two were engaged, but time had dragged on to the bewilderment of their friends. What obscure impulses operated in Rossetti at first, what exasperations against restraint or compulsion later, it were difficult to say. Then she fell ill and there was always the hope, and the excuse, of her possible improvement. Rossetti was tortured in the strange hell he had made for himself. He had delayed too long. The magic was gone and he was bound to a dying woman. Worse still, at Oxford he had met Jane Burden. It was Rossetti himself, knowing he was bound to another, who urged William Morris to marry Jane, but she had haunted his imagination. Morris himself was only too glad; he had stood aside with an aching heart as Rossetti's followers always stood aside for the chief.

Rossetti married Elizabeth Siddal in May 1860 and their married life was brief. Rossetti came in one evening in February 1862 to find his wife dying of an overdraught of a sleeping potion. His movements through London that night in his effort to save her, were frantic—even though he knew too well that the woman dying of drugs and tuberculosis was not the woman who had inspired him. Before her burial, overcome with grief, Rossetti slipped the manuscript of his poems in against her cheek and under her glorious hair. It was buried with her.

Following the death of the Sid, Rossetti, unable to bear the association of his former home, moved to 16 Cheyne Walk, Chelsea. Meredith and Swinburne for a time were co-tenants and it was here that Swinburne wrote his first great success, *Atalanta in Calydon*. And it was while he was at Cheyne Walk that Rossetti indulged to the full his passion for collecting. He was an inveterate collector, rarely returning from his walks through London without a piece of bric-à-brac or without having bespoke a piece of rare furniture, until the house became cluttered with objects. Convex mirrors and blue china he especially favored. The collecting mania raged at its height from about 1862 until 1869.

At Cheyne Walk also Rossetti gathered about him from time to time the series of pets which were the amazement and consternation of his friends and neighbors. His brother reports that there were in the series a Pomeranian puppy, an Irish deerhound, owls, rabbits, dormice, hedgehogs, woodchucks, kangaroos, walabies, a deer, white mice, a raven, chameleons, lizards, parrakeets, and peacocks. There was a raccoon which hibernated in a drawer; there was an armadillo which burrowed its way out and came up through the floor of a neighbor's kitchen—to the great alarm of the cook; and there was a zebra. On one occasion Rossetti priced a young elephant but, finding it too expensive, bought a laughing jackass instead—which unfortunate beast came to a melancholy end, drowned in a tub of water.

Rossetti's reputation as a painter was steadily rising and he had means to indulge his caprices, but, because of his careless spending, he was often short of ready cash and, because of his habit of accepting payment in advance on commissions, he was frequently harassed to deliver paintings whose purchase price he had already spent. But he was a canny bargainer so far as his pictures were concerned, and he had an instinct for impressing himself on the public imagination. His brother estimates that in the later years his income ranged from about £1000 in poor years to £3000 in good,—no inconsiderable sum for an artist in Victorian England.

For some time Rossetti's friends had been urging him to publish his poems, and at their urging he permitted the manuscript which had been buried with Elizabeth Siddal to be exhumed. The grisly act was performed and the following year (1870) he published his *Poems*, which included about half of the sonnets which later were to make up *The House of Life* sequence, his most famous songs, and such favorites as *The Blessed Damozel* in a revised version, and *Sister Helen.*

While Rossetti's career seemed to be prospering, actually clouds were gathering over his life. Beginning about 1867 he began to suffer from insomnia which became increasingly worse, and to combat his sleeplessness he had taken to a new drug, chloral, which he believed harmless. The habit became fixed upon him, injuring his health and depressing him mentally so that he suffered from severe melancholia. After the publication of his poems in 1870 Robert Buchanan attacked him in an article (signed with a pseudonym) called *The Fleshly School of Poetry.* This attack in The *Contemporary Review*, coming at a time when he was already suffering from depression, had a disastrous effect on Rossetti's mind. He rallied to write a reply, *The Stealthy School of Criticism*, in The *Athenæum*, but the idea grew on him that he was surrounded by enemies and that the Buchanan article, later published as a pamphlet in 1872, was the first symptom of a widespread conspiracy. His brother says that he became "a changed man," and judged one day (June 2, 1872) from his wild way of talking of conspiracies that he was "not entirely sane." Browning, for example, on the basis of some lines in *Fifine at the Fair* was enrolled among the conspirators, and Dodgson's *Hunting of the Snark* he considered a pasquinade on himself.

Rossetti after this withdrew from the world. The flashing and dominant Rossetti of the early days was gone. His bedroom was hung with dark velvet, and the hangings of the bed were dark—gloomy in the extreme. His exercise was largely limited to walks in his garden—after dark—and, as he continued using chloral, his melancholy continued. Gloomy stories grew up about the recluse who never ventured out, but his prestige as a painter and, with some, as a poet remained. The year 1881 was a year of success. He reprinted his *Poems* and published *Ballads and Sonnets*, containing the completed *House of Life.* And this year he sold his great painting "Dante's Dream" to the Walker Art Gallery of Liverpool at his own price. But the achievement brought him no cheerfulness. He only seemed "in a faint way, gratified." He died April 9, 1882.

THE BLESSED DAMOZEL

The blessed damozel leaned out
  From the gold bar of Heaven;
Her eyes were deeper than the depth
  Of waters stilled at even;
She had three lilies in her hand,
  And the stars in her hair were seven.

Her robe, ungirt from clasp to hem,
  No wrought flowers did adorn,
But a white rose of Mary's gift,
  For service meetly worn;
Her hair that lay along her back
  Was yellow like ripe corn.

Herseemed she scarce had been a day
  One of God's choristers;
The wonder was not yet quite gone
  From that still look of hers;
Albeit, to them she left, her day
  Had counted as ten years.

(To one, it is ten years of years.
  . . . Yet now, and in this place,
Surely she leaned o'er me—her hair
  Fell all about my face. . . .
Nothing: the autumn fall of leaves.
  The whole year sets apace.)

It was the rampart of God's house
  That she was standing on;
By God built over the sheer depth
  The which is Space begun;
So high, that looking downward thence
  She scarce could see the sun.

It lies in Heaven, across the flood
  Of ether, as a bridge.
Beneath, the tides of day and night
  With flame and darkness ridge
The void, as low as where this earth
  Spins like a fretful midge.

Around her, lovers, newly met
  'Mid deathless love's acclaims,
Spoke evermore among themselves
  Their heart-remembered names;
And the souls mounting up to God
  Went by her like thin flames.

And still she bowed herself and stooped
  Out of the circling charm;
Until her bosom must have made
  The bar she leaned on warm,
And the lilies lay as if asleep
  Along her bended arm.

From the fixed place of Heaven she saw
  Time like a pulse shake fierce
Through all the worlds. Her gaze still strove
  Within the gulf to pierce
Its path; and now she spoke as when
  The stars sang in their spheres.

The sun was gone now; the curled moon
  Was like a little feather
Fluttering far down the gulf; and now
  She spoke through the still weather.
Her voice was like the voice the stars
  Had when they sang together.

(Ah sweet! Even now, in that bird's song,
  Strove not her accents there,
Fain to be hearkened? When those bells
  Possessed the mid-day air,
Strove not her steps to reach my side
  Down all the echoing stair?)

"I wish that he were come to me,
  For he will come," she said.
"Have I not prayed in Heaven?—on earth,
  Lord, Lord, has he not pray'd?
Are not two prayers a perfect strength?
  And shall I feel afraid?

"When round his head the aureole clings,
  And he is clothed in white,
I'll take his hand and go with him
  To the deep wells of light;
We will step down as to a stream,
  And bathe there in God's sight.

"We two will stand beside that shrine,
  Occult, withheld, untrod,
Whose lamps are stirred continually
  With prayer sent up to God;
And see our old prayers, granted, melt
  Each like a little cloud.

"We two will lie i' the shadow of
  That living mystic tree
Within whose secret growth the Dove
  Is sometimes felt to be,

While every leaf that His plumes touch
Saith His Name audibly.

"And I myself will teach to him,
I myself, lying so,
The songs I sing here; which his voice
Shall pause in, hushed and slow,
And find some knowledge at each pause,
Or some new thing to know."

(Alas! We two, we two, thou say'st!
Yea, one wast thou with me
That once of old. But shall God lift
To endless unity
The soul whose likeness with thy soul
Was but its love for thee?)

"We two," she said, "will seek the groves
Where the lady Mary is,
With her five handmaidens, whose names
Are five sweet symphonies,
Cecily, Gertrude, Magdalen,
Margaret and Rosalys.

"Circlewise sit they, with bound locks
And foreheads garlanded;
Into the fine cloth white like flame
Weaving the golden thread,
To fashion the birth-robes for them
Who are just born, being dead.

"He shall fear, haply, and be dumb:
Then will I lay my cheek
To his, and tell about our love,
Not once abashed or weak:
And the dear Mother will approve
My pride, and let me speak.

"Herself shall bring us, hand in hand,
To Him round whom all souls
Kneel, the clear-ranged unnumbered heads
Bowed with their aureoles:
And angels meeting us shall sing
To their citherns and citoles.

"There will I ask of Christ the Lord
Thus much for him and me:—
Only to live as once on earth
With Love,—only to be,
As then awhile, for ever now
Together, I and he."

She gazed and listened and then said,
Less sad of speech than mild,—
"All this is when he comes." She ceased.
The light thrilled towards her, fill'd
With angels in strong level flight.
Her eyes prayed, and she smil'd.

(I saw her smile.) But soon their path
Was vague in distant spheres:
And then she cast her arms along
The golden barriers,
And laid her face between her hands,
And wept. (I heard her tears.)

(1847) 1850

MY SISTER'S SLEEP

She fell asleep on Christmas Eve:
At length the long-ungranted shade
Of weary eyelids overweigh'd
The pain nought else might yet relieve.

Our mother, who had leaned all day
Over the bed from chime to chime,
Then raised herself for the first time,
And as she sat her down, did pray.

Her little work-table was spread
With work to finish. For the glare
Made by her candle, she had care
To work some distance from the bed.

Without, there was a cold moon up,
Of winter radiance sheer and thin;
The hollow halo it was in
Was like an icy crystal cup.

Through the small room, with subtle sound
Of flame, by vents the fireshine drove
And reddened. In its dim alcove
The mirror shed a clearness round.

I had been sitting up some nights,
And my tired mind felt weak and blank;
Like a sharp strengthening wine it drank
The stillness and the broken lights.

Twelve struck. That sound, by dwindling years
Heard in each hour, crept off; and then
The ruffled silence spread again,
Like water that a pebble stirs.

Our mother rose from where she sat:
  Her needles, as she laid them down,
  Met lightly, and her silken gown
Settled: no other noise than that.

"Glory unto the Newly Born!"
  So, as said angels, she did say;
  Because we were in Christmas Day,
Though it would still be long till morn.

Just then in the room over us
  There was a pushing back of chairs,
  As some who had sat unawares
So late, now heard the hour, and rose.

With anxious softly-stepping haste
  Our mother went where Margaret lay,
  Fearing the sounds o'erhead—should they
Have broken her long watched-for rest!

She stooped an instant, calm, and turned;
  But suddenly turned back again;
  And all her features seemed in pain
With woe, and her eyes gazed and yearned.

For my part, I but hid my face,
  And held my breath, and spoke no word:
  There was none spoken; but I heard
The silence for a little space.

Our mother bowed herself and wept:
  And both my arms fell, and I said,
  "God knows I knew that she was dead."
And there, all white, my sister slept.

Then kneeling, upon Christmas morn
  A little after twelve o'clock
  We said, ere the first quarter struck,
"Christ's blessing on the newly born!"

(*1847*) 1850

THE PORTRAIT

This is her picture as she was;
  It seems a thing to wonder on,
As though mine image in the glass
  Should tarry when myself am gone.
I gaze until she seems to stir,
Until mine eyes almost aver
  That now, even now, the sweet lips part
  To breathe the words of the sweet heart—
And yet the earth is over her.

Alas! even such the thin-drawn ray
  That makes the prison-depth more rude—
The drip of water night and day
  Giving a tongue to solitude.
Yet only this, of love's whole prize,
Remains; save what in mournful guise
  Takes counsel with my soul alone—
  Save what is secret and unknown,
Below the earth, above the skies.

In painting her I shrined her face
  'Mid mystic trees, where light falls in
Hardly at all; a covert place
  Where you might think to find a din
Of doubtful talk, and a live flame
Wandering, and many a shape whose name
  Not itself knoweth, and old dew,
  And your own footsteps meeting you,
And all things going as they came.

A deep dim wood; and there she stands
  As in that wood that day—for so
Was the still movement of her hands
  And such the pure line's gracious flow.
And passing fair the type must seem,
Unknown the presence and the dream.
  'Tis she—though of herself, alas!
  Less than her shadow on the grass
Or than her image in the stream.

That day we met there, I and she
  One with the other all alone;
And we were blithe; yet memory
  Saddens those hours, as when the moon
Looks upon daylight. And with her
I stooped to drink the spring-water,
  Athirst where other waters sprang;
  And where the echo is, she sang—
My soul another echo there.

But when that hour my soul won strength
  For words whose silence wastes and kills,
Dull raindrops smote us, and at length
  Thundered the heat within the hills.
That eve I spoke those words again
Beside the pelted window-pane;
  And there she harkened what I said,
  With under-glances that surveyed
The empty pastures blind with rain.

Next day the memories of these things,
  Like leaves through which a bird has flown,
Still vibrated with Love's warm wings;
  Till I must make them all my own
And paint this picture. So, 'twixt ease
Of talk and sweet, long silences,
  She stood among the plants in bloom
  At windows of a summer room,
To feign the shadow of the trees.

And as I wrought, while all above
  And all around was fragrant air,
In the sick burthen of my love
  It seemed each sun-thrilled blossom there
Beat like a heart among the leaves.
O heart that never beats nor heaves,
  In that one darkness lying still,
  What now to thee my love's great will,
Or the fine web the sunshine weaves?

For now doth daylight disavow
  Those days—naught left to see or hear.
Only in solemn whispers now
  At night-time these things reach mine ear,
When the leaf-shadows at a breath
Shrink in the road, and all the heath,
  Forest and water, far and wide,
  In limpid starlight glorified,
Lie like the mystery of death.

Last night at last I could have slept,
  And yet delayed my sleep till dawn,
Still wandering. Then it was I wept;
  For unawares I came upon
Those glades where once she walked with me;
And as I stood there suddenly,
  All wan with traversing the night,
  Upon the desolate verge of light
Yearned loud the iron-bosomed sea.

Even so, where Heaven holds breath and hears
  The beating heart of Love's own breast—
Where round the secret of all spheres
  All angels lay their wings to rest—
How shall my soul stand rapt and awed,
When, by the new birth borne abroad
  Throughout the music of the suns,
  It enters in her soul at once
And knows the silence there for God!

Here with her face doth memory sit
  Meanwhile, and wait the day's decline,
Till other eyes shall look from it,
  Eyes of the spirit's Palestine,
Even than the old gaze tenderer;
While hopes and aims long lost with her
  Stand round her image side by side,
  Like tombs of pilgrims that have died
About the Holy Sepulcher.

(*1847–1870*) 1870

AVE

Mother of the Fair Delight,
Thou handmaid perfect in God's sight,
Now sitting fourth beside the Three,
Thyself a woman-Trinity,—
Being a daughter borne to God,
Mother of Christ from stall to rood,
And wife unto the Holy Ghost:—
Oh when our need is uttermost,
Think that to such as death may strike
Thou once wert sister sisterlike!
Thou headstone of humanity,
Groundstone of the great Mystery,
Fashioned like us, yet more than we!

  Mind'st thou not (when June's heavy breath
Warmed the long days in Nazareth,)
That eve thou didst go forth to give
Thy flowers some drink that they might live
One faint night more amid the sands?
Far off the trees were as pale wands
Against the fervid sky: the sea
Sighed further off eternally
As human sorrow sighs in sleep.
Then suddenly the awe grew deep,
As of a day to which all days
Were footsteps in God's secret ways:
Until a folding sense, like prayer,
Which is, as God is, everywhere,
Gathered about thee; and a voice
Spake to thee without any noise,
Being of the silence:—"Hail," it said,
"Thou that art highly favoured;
The Lord is with thee here and now;
Blessed among all women thou."

  Ah! knew'st thou of the end, when first
That Babe was on thy bosom nurs'd?—
Or when He tottered round thy knee
Did thy great sorrow dawn on thee?—

And through His boyhood, year by year
Eating with Him the Passover,
Didst thou discern confusedly
That holier sacrament, when He,
The bitter cup about to quaff,
Should break the bread and eat thereof?—
Or came not yet the knowledge, even
Till on some day forecast in Heaven
His feet passed through thy door to press
Upon His Father's business?—
Or still was God's high secret kept?

Nay, but I think the whisper crept
Like growth through childhood. Work and
play,
Things common to the course of day,
Awed thee with meanings unfulfill'd;
And all through girlhood, something still'd
Thy senses like the birth of light,
When thou hast trimmed thy lamp at night
Or washed thy garments in the stream;
To whose white bed had come the dream
That He was thine and thou wast His
Who feeds among the field-lilies.
O solemn shadow of the end
In that wise spirit long contain'd!
O awful end! and those unsaid
Long years when It was Finishèd!

Mind'st thou not (when the twilight gone
Left darkness in the house of John,)
Between the naked window-bars
That spacious vigil of the stars?—
For thou, a watcher even as they,
Wouldst rise from where throughout the day
Thou wroughtest raiment for His poor;
And, finding the fixed terms endure
Of day and night which never brought
Sounds of His coming chariot,
Wouldst lift through cloud-waste unexplor'd
Those eyes which said, "How long, O Lord?"
Then that disciple whom He loved,
Well heeding, haply would be moved
To ask thy blessing in His name;
And that one thought in both, the same
Though silent, then would clasp ye round
To weep together,—tears long bound,
Sick tears of patience, dumb and slow.
Yet, "Surely I come quickly,"—so
He said, from life and death gone home.
Amen: even so, Lord Jesus, come!

But oh! what human tongue can speak
That day when Michael came to break
From the tir'd spirit, like a veil,
Its covenant with Gabriel
Endured at length unto the end?
What human thought can apprehend
That mystery of motherhood
When thy Beloved at length renew'd
The sweet communion severèd,—
His left hand underneath thine head
And His right hand embracing thee?—
Lo! He was thine, and this is He!

Soul, is it Faith, or Love, or Hope,
That lets me see her standing up
Where the light of the Throne is bright?
Unto the left, unto the right,
The cherubim, arrayed, conjoint,
Float inward to a golden point,
And from between the seraphim
The glory issues for a hymn.
O Mary Mother, be not loth
To listen,—thou whom the stars clothe,
Who seëst and mayst not be seen!
Hear us at last, O Mary Queen!
Into our shadow bend thy face,
Bowing thee from the secret place,
O Mary Virgin, full of grace!

(*c. 1847*) 1870

AUTUMN SONG

Know'st thou not at the fall of the leaf
How the heart feels a languid grief
Laid on it for a covering;
And how sleep seems a goodly thing
In Autumn at the fall of the leaf?

And how the swift beat of the brain
Falters because it is in vain,
In Autumn at the fall of the leaf
Knowest thou not? and how the chief
Of joys seems—not to suffer pain?

Know'st thou not at the fall of the leaf
How the soul feels like a dried sheaf
Bound up at length for harvesting,
And how death seems a comely thing
In Autumn at the fall of the leaf?

(*1848*) 1883

ON REFUSAL OF AID BETWEEN NATIONS

NOT that the earth is changing, O my God!
Nor that the seasons totter in their walk,—
Not that the virulent ill of act and talk
Seethes ever as a winepress ever trod,—
Not therefore are we certain that the rod
Weighs in thine hand to smite thy world; though now
Beneath thine hand so many nations bow,
So many kings:—not therefore, O my God!—

But because Man is parcelled out in men
Even thus; because, for any wrongful blow,
No man not stricken asks, "I would be told
Why thou dost strike;" but his heart whispers then,
"He is he, I am I." By this we know
That the earth falls asunder, being old.

(*1849*) 1870

THE CARD-DEALER

COULD you not drink her gaze like wine?
Yet though its splendour swoon
Into the silence languidly
As a tune into a tune,
Those eyes unravel the coiled night
And know the stars at noon.

The gold that's heaped beside her hand,
In truth rich prize it were;
And rich the dreams that wreathe her brows
With magic stillness there;
And he were rich who should unwind
That woven golden hair.

Around her, where she sits, the dance
Now breathes its eager heat;
And not more lightly or more true
Fall there the dancers' feet
Than fall her cards on the bright board
As 'twere an heart that beat.

Her fingers let them softly through,
Smooth polished silent things;
And each one as it falls reflects
In swift light-shadowings,
Blood-red and purple, green and blue,
The great eyes of her rings.

Whom plays she with? With thee, who lov'st
Those gems upon her hand;
With me, who search her secret brows;
With all men, bless'd or bann'd.
We play together, she and we,
Within a vain strange land:

A land without any order,—
Day even as night, (one saith,)—
Where who lieth down ariseth not
Nor the sleeper awakeneth;
A land of darkness as darkness itself
And of the shadow of death.

What be her cards, you ask? Even these:—
The heart, that doth but crave
More, having fed; the diamond,
Skilled to make base seem brave;
The club, for smiting in the dark;
The spade, to dig a grave.

And do you ask what game she plays?
With me 'tis lost or won;
With thee it is playing still; with him
It is not well begun;
But 'tis a game she plays with all
Beneath the sway o' the sun.

Thou seest the card that falls,—she knows
The card that followeth:
Her game in thy tongue is called Life,
As ebbs thy daily breath:
When she shall speak, thou'lt learn her tongue
And know she calls it Death.

(*1849*) 1852

THE STAFF AND SCRIP [1]

"WHO owns these lands?" the Pilgrim said.
"Stranger, Queen Blanchelys."
"And who has thus harried them?" he said.
"It was Duke Luke did this:
God's ban be his!"

The Pilgrim said: "Where is your house?
I'll rest there, with your will."
"You've but to climb these blackened boughs
And you'll see it over the hill,
For it burns still."

[1] Pilgrims in the Middle Ages carried a staff and scrip (or small bag). As signs that the man was going on a holy journey, they were a species of moral passport in troubled times, and a guarantee of integrity.

"Which road, to seek your Queen?" said he.
  "Nay, nay, but with some wound
You'll fly back hither, it may be,
  And by your blood i' the ground
    My place be found."

"Friend, stay in peace. God keep your head,
  And mine, where I will go;
For He is here and there," he said.
  He passed the hill-side, slow,
    And stood below.

The Queen sat idle by her loom:
  She heard the arras stir,
And looked up sadly: through the room
  The sweetness sickened her
    Of musk and myrrh.

Her women, standing two and two,
  In silence combed the fleece.
The pilgrim said, "Peace be with you,
  Lady;" and bent his knees.
    She answered, "Peace."

Her eyes were like the wave within;
  Like water-reeds the poise
Of her soft body, dainty thin;
  And like the water's noise
    Her plaintive voice.

For him, the stream had never well'd
  In desert tracts malign
So sweet; nor had he ever felt
  So faint in the sunshine
    Of Palestine.

Right so, he knew that he saw weep
  Each night through every dream
The Queen's own face, confused in sleep
  With visages supreme
    Not known to him.

"Lady," he said, "your lands lie burnt
  And waste: to meet your foe
All fear: this I have seen and learnt.
  Say that it shall be so,
    And I will go."

She gazed at him. "Your cause is just,
  For I have heard the same:"
He said: "God's strength shall be my trust.
  Fall it to good or grame,
    'Tis in His name."

"Sir, you are thanked. My cause is dead.
  Why should you toil to break
A grave, and fall therein?" she said.
  He did not pause but spake:
    "For my vow's sake."

"Can such vows be, Sir—to God's ear,
  Not to God's will?" "My vow
Remains: God heard me there as here,"
  He said with reverent brow,
    "Both then and now."

They gazed together, he and she,
  The minute while he spoke;
And when he ceased, she suddenly
  Looked round upon her folk
    As though she woke.

"Fight, Sir," she said: "my prayers in pain
  Shall be your fellowship."
He whispered one among her train,—
  "To-morrow bid her keep
    This staff and scrip."

She sent him a sharp sword, whose belt
  About his body there
As sweet as her own arms he felt.
  He kissed its blade, all bare,
    Instead of her.

She sent him a green banner wrought
  With one white lily stem,
To bind his lance with when he fought.
  He writ upon the same
    And kissed her name.

She sent him a white shield, whereon
  She bade that he should trace
His will. He blent fair hues that shone,
  And in a golden space
    He kissed her face.

Born of the day that died, that eve
  Now dying sank to rest;
As he, in likewise taking leave,
  Once with a heaving breast
    Looked to the west.

And there the sunset skies unseal'd,
  Like lands he never knew,
Beyond to-morrow's battle-field
  Lay open out of view
    To ride into.

Next day till dark the women pray'd:
  Nor any might know there
How the fight went: the Queen has bade
  That there do come to her
    No messenger.

The Queen is pale, her maidens ail;
  And to the organ-tones
They sing but faintly, who sang well
  The matin-orisons,
    The lauds and nones.

Lo, Father, is thine ear inclin'd
  And hath thine angel pass'd?
For these thy watchers now are blind
  With vigil, and at last
    Dizzy with fast.

Weak now to them the voice o' the priest
  As any trance affords;
And when each anthem failed and ceas'd,
  It seemed that the last chords
    Still sang the words.

"Oh what is the light that shines so red?
  'Tis long since the sun set;"
Quoth the youngest to the eldest maid:
  "'Twas dim but now, and yet
    The light is great."

Quoth the other: "'Tis our sight is dazed
  That we see flame i' the air."
But the Queen held her brows and gazed,
  And said, "It is the glare
    Of torches there."

"Oh what are the sounds that rise and spread?
  All day it was so still;"
Quoth the youngest to the eldest maid;
  "Unto the furthest hill
    The air they fill."

Quoth the other: "'Tis our sense is blurr'd
  With all the chants gone by."
But the Queen held her breath and heard,
  And said, "It is the cry
    Of Victory."

The first of all the rout was sound,
  The next were dust and flame,
And then the horses shook the ground:
  And in the thick of them
    A still band came.

"Oh what do ye bring out of the fight,
  Thus hid beneath these boughs?"
"Even him, thy conquering guest to-night,
  Who yet shall not carouse,
    Queen, in thy house."

"Uncover ye his face," she said.
  "O changed in little space!"
She cried, "O pale that was so red!
  O God, O God of grace!
    Cover his face."

His sword was broken in his hand
  Where he had kissed the blade.
"O soft steel that could not withstand!
  O my hard heart unstayed,
    That prayed and prayed!"

His bloodied banner crossed his mouth
  Where he had kissed her name.
"O east, and west, and north, and south,
  Fair flew my web, for shame,
    To guide Death's aim!"

The tints were shredded from his shield
  Where he had kissed her face.
"Oh, of all gifts that I could yield,
  Death only keeps its place,
    My gift and grace!"

Then stepped a damsel to her side,
  And spoke, and needs must weep:
"For his sake, lady, if he died,
  He prayed of thee to keep
    This staff and scrip."

That night they hung above her bed,
  Till morning wet with tears.
Year after year above her head
  Her bed his token wears,
    Five years, ten years.

That night the passion of her grief
  Shook them as there they hung.
Each year the wind that shed the leaf
  Shook them and in its tongue
    A message flung.

And once she woke with a clear mind
  That letters writ to calm
Her soul lay in the scrip; to find
  Only a torpid balm
    And dust of palm.

They shook far off with palace sport
When joust and dance were rife;
And the hunt shook them from the court;
For hers, in peace or strife,
Was a Queen's life.

A Queen's death now: as now they shake
To gusts in chapel dim,—
Hung where she sleeps, not seen to wake,
(Carved lovely white and slim,)
With them by him.

Stand up to-day, still armed, with her,
Good knight, before His brow
Who then as now was here and there,
Who had in mind thy vow
Then even as now.

The lists are set in Heaven to-day,
The bright pavilions shine;
Fair hangs thy shield, and none gainsay;
The trumpets sound in sign
That she is thine.

Not tithed with days' and years' decease
He pays thy wage He owed,
But with imperishable peace
Here in His own abode,
Thy jealous God.

(*c. 1851–2*) 1856

SISTER HELEN

"Why did you melt your waxen man,
Sister Helen?
To-day is the third since you began."
"The time was long, yet the time ran,
Little brother."
(*O Mother, Mary Mother,*
Three days to-day, between Hell and Heaven!)

"But if you have done your work aright,
Sister Helen,
You'll let me play, for you said I might."
"Be very still in your play to-night,
Little brother."
(*O Mother, Mary Mother,*
Third night, to-night, between Hell and Heaven!)

"You said it must melt ere vesper-bell,
Sister Helen;
If now it be molten, all is well."
"Even so,—nay, peace! you cannot tell,
Little brother."
(*O Mother, Mary Mother,*
O what is this, between Hell and Heaven?)

"Oh the waxen knave was plump to-day,
Sister Helen;
How like dead folk he has dropped away!"
"Nay now, of the dead what can you say,
Little brother?"
(*O Mother, Mary Mother,*
What of the dead, between Hell and Heaven?)

"See, see, the sunken pile of wood,
Sister Helen,
Shines through the thinned wax red as blood!"
"Nay now, when looked you yet on blood,
Little brother?"
(*O Mother, Mary Mother,*
How pale she is, between Hell and Heaven!)

"Now close your eyes, for they're sick and
sore,
Sister Helen,
And I'll play without the gallery door."
"Aye, let me rest,—I'll lie on the floor,
Little brother."
(*O Mother, Mary Mother,*
What rest to-night, between Hell and Heaven?)

"Here high up in the balcony,
Sister Helen,
The moon flies face to face with me."
"Aye, look and say whatever you see,
Little brother."
(*O Mother, Mary Mother,*
What sight to-night, between Hell and Heaven?)

"Outside it's merry in the wind's wake,
Sister Helen;
In the shaken trees the chill stars shake."
"Hush, heard you a horse-tread as you spake,
Little brother?"
(*O Mother, Mary Mother,*
What sound to-night between Hell and Heaven?)

"I hear a horse-tread, and I see,
Sister Helen,
Three horsemen that ride terribly."
"Little brother, whence come the three,
Little brother?"
(*O Mother, Mary Mother,*
Whence should they come, between Hell and
Heaven?)

"They come by the hill-verge from Boyne Bar,
Sister Helen,
And one draws nigh, but two are afar."
"Look, look, do you know them who they are,
Little brother?"
(*O Mother, Mary Mother,*
Who should they be, between Hell and Heaven?)

"Oh, it 's Keith of Eastholm rides so fast,
Sister Helen,
For I know the white mane on the blast."
"The hour has come, has come at last,
Little brother!"
(*O Mother, Mary Mother,*
Her hour at last, between Hell and Heaven!)

"He has made a sign and called Halloo!
Sister Helen,
And he says that he would speak with you."
"Oh tell him I fear the frozen dew,
Little brother."
(*O Mother, Mary Mother,*
Why laughs she thus, between Hell and Heaven?)

"The wind is loud, but I hear him cry,
Sister Helen,
That Keith of Ewern's like to die."
"And he and thou, and thou and I,
Little brother."
(*O Mother, Mary Mother,*
And they and we, between Hell and Heaven!)

"Three days ago, on his marriage-morn,
Sister Helen,
He sickened, and lies since then forlorn."
"For bridegroom's side is the bride a thorn,
Little brother?"
(*O Mother, Mary Mother,*
Cold bridal cheer, between Hell and Heaven!)

"Three days and nights he has lain abed,
Sister Helen,
And he prays in torment to be dead."
"The thing may chance, if he have prayed,
Little brother!"
(*O Mother, Mary Mother,*
If ye have prayed, between Hell and Heaven!)

"But he has not ceased to cry to-day,
Sister Helen,
That you should take your curse away."
"*My* prayer was heard,—he need but pray,
Little brother!"
(*O Mother, Mary Mother,*
Shall God not hear, between Hell and Heaven?)

"But he says, till you take back your ban,
Sister Helen,
His soul would pass, yet never can."
"Nay then, shall I slay a living man,
Little brother?"
(*O Mother, Mary Mother,*
A living soul, between Hell and Heaven!)

"But he calls for ever on your name,
Sister Helen,
And says that he melts before a flame."
"My heart for his pleasure fared the same,
Little brother."
(*O Mother, Mary Mother,*
Fire at the heart, between Hell and Heaven!)

"Here's Keith of Westholm riding fast,
Sister Helen,
For I know the white plume on the blast."
"The hour, the sweet hour I forecast,
Little brother!"
(*O Mother, Mary Mother,*
Is the hour sweet, between Hell and Heaven?)

"He stops to speak, and he stills his horse,
Sister Helen;
But his words are drowned in the wind's course."
"Nay hear, nay hear, you must hear perforce,
Little brother!"
(*O Mother, Mary Mother,*
What word between Hell and Heaven!)

"Oh he says that Keith of Ewern's cry,
Sister Helen,
Is ever to see you ere he die."
"In all that his soul sees, there am I,
Little brother!"
(*O Mother, Mary Mother,*
The soul's one sight between Hell and Heaven!)

"He sends a ring and a broken coin,
Sister Helen,
And bids you mind the banks of Boyne."
"What else he broke will he ever join,
Little brother?"
(*O Mother, Mary Mother,*
No, never joined, between Hell and Heaven!)

"He yields you these and craves full fain,
Sister Helen,
You pardon him in his mortal pain."
"What else he took will he give again,
Little brother?"
(*O Mother, Mary Mother,*
Not twice to give, between Hell and Heaven!)

"He calls your name in an agony,
Sister Helen,
That even dead Love must weep to see."
"Hate, born of Love, is blind as he,
Little brother!"
(*O Mother, Mary Mother,*
Love turned to hate, between Hell and Heaven!)

"Oh, it's Keith of Keith now that rides fast,
Sister Helen,
For I know the white hair on the blast."
"The short, short hour will soon be past,
Little brother!"
(*O Mother, Mary Mother,*
Will soon be past, between Hell and Heaven!)

"He looks at me and he tries to speak,
Sister Helen,
But oh! his voice is sad and weak!"
"What here should the mighty Baron seek,
Little brother?"
(*O Mother, Mary Mother,*
Is this the end, between Hell and Heaven?)

"Oh his son still cries, if you forgive,
Sister Helen,
The body dies but the soul shall live."
"Fire shall forgive me as I forgive,
Little brother!"
(*O Mother, Mary Mother,*
As she forgives, between Hell and Heaven!)

"Oh he prays you, as his heart would rive,
Sister Helen,
To save his dear son's soul alive."
"Fire cannot slay it, it shall thrive,
Little brother!"
(*O Mother, Mary Mother,*
Alas, alas, between Hell and Heaven!)

"He cries to you, kneeling in the road,
Sister Helen,
To go with him for the love of God!"
"The way is long to his son's abode,
Little brother."
(*O Mother, Mary Mother,*
The way is long, between Hell and Heaven!)

"A lady 's here, by a dark steed brought,
Sister Helen,
So darkly clad, I saw her not."
"See her now or never see aught,
Little brother!"
(*O Mother, Mary Mother,*
What more to see, between Hell and Heaven?)

"Her hood falls back, and the moon shines fair,
Sister Helen,
On the Lady of Ewern's golden hair."
"Blest hour of my power and her despair,
Little Brother!"
(*O Mother, Mary Mother,*
Hour blest and bann'd, between Hell and Heaven!)

"Pale, pale her cheeks, that in pride did glow,
Sister Helen,
Neath the bridal-wreath three days ago."
"One morn for pride and three days for woe,
Little brother!"
(*O Mother, Mary Mother,*
Three days, three nights, between Hell and Heaven!)

"Her clasped hands stretch from her bending head,
Sister Helen;
With the loud wind's wail her sobs are wed."
"What wedding-strains hath her bridal-bed
Little brother?"
(*O Mother, Mary Mother,*
What strain but death's, between Hell and Heaven?)

"She may not speak, she sinks in a swoon,
Sister Helen,—
She lifts her lips and gasps on the moon."
"Oh! might I but hear her soul's blithe tune,
Little brother!"
(*O Mother, Mary Mother,*
Her woe's dumb cry, between Hell and Heaven!)

"They've caught her to Westholm's saddle-bow,
Sister Helen,
And her moonlit hair gleams white in its flow."

"Let it turn whiter than winter snow,
Little brother!"
(*O Mother, Mary Mother,*
Woe-withered gold, between Hell and Heaven!)

"O Sister Helen, you heard the bell,
Sister Helen!
More loud than the vesper-chime it fell."
"No vesper-chime, but a dying knell,
Little brother!"
(*O Mother, Mary Mother,*
His dying knell, between Hell and Heaven!)

"Alas! but I fear the heavy sound,
Sister Helen;
Is it in the sky or in the ground?"
"Say, have they turned their horses round,
Little brother?"
(*O Mother, Mary Mother,*
What would she more, between Hell and Heaven?)

"They have raised the old man from his knee,
Sister Helen,
And they ride in silence hastily."
"More fast the naked soul doth flee,
Little brother!"
(*O Mother, Mary Mother,*
The naked soul, between Hell and Heaven!)

"Flank to flank are the three steeds gone,
Sister Helen,
But the lady's dark steed goes alone."
"And lonely her bridegroom's soul hath flown,
Little brother."
(*O Mother, Mary Mother,*
The lonely ghost, between Hell and Heaven!)

"Oh the wind is sad in the iron chill,
Sister Helen,
And weary sad they look by the hill."
"But Keith of Ewern's sadder still,
Little brother!"
(*O Mother, Mary Mother,*
Most sad of all, between Hell and Heaven!)

"See, see, the wax has dropped from its place,
Sister Helen,
And the flames are winning up apace!"
"Yet here they burn but for a space,
Little brother!"
(*O Mother, Mary Mother,*
Here for a space, between Hell and Heaven!)

"Ah! what white thing at the door has cross'd,
Sister Helen?
Ah! what is this that sighs in the frost?"
"A soul that's lost as mine is lost,
Little brother!"
(*O Mother, Mary Mother,*
Lost, lost, all lost, between Hell and Heaven!)

1854 [1]

THE BURDEN OF NINEVEH [2]

In our Museum galleries
To-day I lingered o'er the prize
Dead Greece vouchsafes to living eyes,—
Her Art for ever in fresh wise
From hour to hour rejoicing me.
Sighing I turned at last to win
Once more the London dirt and din;
And as I made the swing-door spin
And issued, they were hoisting in
A wingèd beast from Nineveh.

A human face the creature wore,
And hoofs behind and hoofs before,
And flanks with dark runes fretted o'er.
'Twas bull, 'twas mitred Minotaur,
A dead disbowelled mystery;
The mummy of a buried faith
Stark from the charnel without scathe,
Its wings stood for the light to bathe,—
Such fossil cerements as might swathe
The very corpse of Nineveh.

The print of its first rush-wrapping,
Wound ere it dried, still ribbed the thing.
What song did the brown maidens sing,
From purple mouths alternating,
When that was woven languidly?

[1] Begun possibly as early as 1851, "Sister Helen" was revised and republished at intervals until 1881.

[2] Excavations were carried on at Nineveh in 1845–51. The inspiration for this poem came to Rossetti as he watched some of the discoveries being unpacked for the British Museum. A great winged bull in stone particularly caught his imagination. During the work of excavation the workmen held their Christian services in the shadow of the great statues. See line 70.

What vows, what rites, what prayers preferr'd,
What songs has the strange image heard?
In what blind vigil stood interr'd
For ages, till an English word
Broke silence first at Nineveh?

Oh when upon each sculptured court,
Where even the wind might not resort,—
O'er which Time passed, of like import
With the wild Arab boys at sport,—
A living face looked in to see:—
Oh seemed it not—the spell once broke—
As though the carven warriors woke,
As though the shaft the string forsook,
The cymbals clashed, the chariots shook,
And there was life in Nineveh?

On London stones our sun anew
The beast's recovered shadow threw.
(No shade that plague of darkness knew,
No light, no shade, while older grew
By ages the old earth and sea.)
Lo thou! could all thy priests have shown
Such proof to make thy godhead known?
From their dead Past thou liv'st alone;
And still thy shadow is thine own
Even as of yore in Nineveh.

That day whereof we keep record,
When near thy city-gates the Lord
Sheltered his Jonah with a gourd,
This sun, (I said) here present, pour'd
Even thus this shadow that I see.
This shadow has been shed the same
From sun and moon,—from lamps which came
For prayer,—from fifteen days of flame,
The last, while smouldered to a name
Sardanapalus' Nineveh.

Within thy shadow, haply, once
Sennacherib has knelt, whose sons
Smote him between the altar-stones:
Or pale Semiramis her zones
Of gold, her incense brought to thee,
In love for grace, in war for aid: . . .
Ay, and who else? . . . till 'neath thy shade
Within his trenches newly made
Last year the Christian knelt and pray'd—
Not to thy strength—in Nineveh.

Now, thou poor god, within this hall
Where the blank windows blind the wall
From pedestal to pedestal,
The kind of light shall on thee fall
Which London takes the day to be:
While school-foundations in the act
Of holiday, three files compact,
Shall learn to view thee as a fact
Connected with that zealous tract:
"Rome,—Babylon and Nineveh."

Deemed they of this, those worshippers,
When, in some mythic chain of verse
Which man shall not again rehearse,
The faces of thy ministers
Yearned pale with bitter ecstasy?
Greece, Egypt, Rome,—did any god
Before whose feet men knelt unshod
Deem that in this unblest abode
Another scarce more unknown god
Should house with him, from Nineveh?

Ah! in what quarries lay the stone
From which this pillared pile has grown,
Unto man's need how long unknown,
Since those thy temples, court and cone,
Rose far in desert history?
Ah! what is here that does not lie
All strange to thine awakened eye?
Ah! what is here can testify
(Save that dumb presence of the sky)
Unto thy day and Nineveh?

Why, of those mummies in the room
Above, there might indeed have come
One out of Egypt to thy home,
An alien. Nay, but were not some
Of these thine own "antiquity"?
And now,—they and their gods and thou
All relics here together,—now
Whose profit? whether bull or cow,
Isis or Ibis, who or how,
Whether of Thebes or Nineveh?

The consecrated metals found,
And ivory tablets, underground,
Winged teraphim and creatures crown'd,
When air and daylight filled the mound,
Fell into dust immediately.
And even as these, the images
Of awe and worship,—even as these,—

So, smitten with the sun's increase,
Her glory mouldered and did cease
From immemorial Nineveh.

The day her builders made their halt,
Those cities of the lake of salt
Stood firmly 'stablished without fault,
Made proud with pillars of basalt,
With sardonyx and porphyry.
The day that Jonah bore abroad
To Nineveh the voice of God,
A brackish lake lay in his road,
Where erst Pride fixed her sure abode
As then in royal Nineveh.

The day when he, Pride's lord and Man's,
Showed all the kingdoms at a glance
To Him before whose countenance
The years recede, the years advance,
And said, Fall down and worship me:—
'Mid all the pomp beneath that look,
Then stirred there, haply, some rebuke,
Where to the wind the Salt Pools shook,
And in those tracts, of life forsook,
That knew thee not, O Nineveh!

Delicate harlot! On thy throne
Thou with a world beneath thee prone
In state for ages sat'st alone;
And needs were years and lustres flown
Ere strength of man could vanquish thee:
Whom even thy victor foes must bring,
Still royal, among maids that sing
As with doves' voices, taboring
Upon their breasts, unto the King,—
A kingly conquest, Nineveh!

. . . Here woke my thought. The wind's slow sway
Had waxed; and like the human play
Of scorn that smiling spreads away,
The sunshine shivered off the day:
The callous wind, it seemed to me,
Swept up the shadow from the ground:
And pale as whom the Fates astound,
The god forlorn stood winged and crown'd:
Within I knew the cry lay bound
Of the dumb soul of Nineveh.

And as I turned, my sense half shut
Still saw the crowds of kerb and rut
Go past as marshalled to the strut
Of ranks in gypsum quaintly cut.
It seemed in one same pageantry
They followed forms which had been erst;
To pass, till on my sight should burst
That future of the best or worst
When some may question which was first,
Of London or of Nineveh.

For as that Bull-god once did stand
And watched the burial-clouds of sand,
Till these at last without a hand
Rose o'er his eyes, another land,
And blinded him with destiny:—
So may he stand again; till now,
In ships of unknown sail and prow,
Some tribe of the Australian plough
Bear him afar,—a relic now
Of London, not of Nineveh!

Or it may chance indeed that when
Man's age is hoary among men,—
His centuries threescore and ten,—
His furthest childhood shall seem then
More clear than later times may be:
Who, finding in this desert place
This form, shall hold us for some race
That walked not in Christ's lowly ways,
But bowed its pride and vowed its praise
Unto the God of Nineveh.

The smile rose first,—anon drew nigh
The thought: . . . Those heavy wings spread high
So sure of flight, which do not fly;
That set gaze never on the sky;
Those scriptured flanks it cannot see;
Its crown, a brow-contracting load;
Its planted feet which trust the sod: . . .
(So grew the image as I trod:)
O Nineveh, was this thy God,—
Thine also, mighty Nineveh?

1856

TROY TOWN

HEAVENBORN Helen, Sparta's queen,
(O Troy Town!)
Had two breasts of heavenly sheen,
The sun and moon of the heart's desire;
All Love's lordship lay between.
(O Troy's down,
Tall Troy's on fire!)

Helen knelt at Venus' shrine,
(*O Troy Town!*)
Saying, "A little gift is mine,
A little gift for a heart's desire.
Hear me speak and make me a sign!
(*O Troy's down,*
Tall Troy's on fire!)

"Look, I bring thee a carven cup;
(*O Troy Town!*)
See it here as I hold it up—
Shaped it is to the heart's desire,
Fit to fill when the gods would sup.
(*O Troy's down,*
Tall Troy's on fire!)

"It was molded like my breast;
(*O Troy Town!*)
He that sees it may not rest,
Rest at all for his heart's desire.
O give ear to my heart's behest!
(*O Troy's down,*
Tall Troy's on fire!)

"See my breast, how like it is;
(*O Troy Town!*)
See it bare for the air to kiss!
Is the cup to thy heart's desire?
O for the breast, O make it his!
(*O Troy's down,*
Tall Troy's on fire!)

"Yea, for my bosom here I sue;
(*O Troy Town!*)
Thou must give it where 'tis due,
Give it there to the heart's desire.
Whom do I give my bosom to?
(*O Troy's down,*
Tall Troy's on fire!)

"Each twin breast is an apple sweet!
(*O Troy Town!*)
Once an apple stirred the beat
Of thy heart with the heart's desire;
Say, who brought it then to thy feet?
(*O Troy's down,*
Tall Troy's on fire!)

"They that claimed it then were three;
(*O Troy Town!*)
For thy sake two hearts did he
Make forlorn of the heart's desire.
Do for him as he did for thee!
(*O Troy's down,*
Tall Troy's on fire!)

"Mine are apples grown to the south,
(*O Troy Town!*)
Grown to taste in the days of drouth,
Taste and waste to the heart's desire;
Mine are apples meet for his mouth!"
(*O Troy's down,*
Tall Troy's on fire!)

Venus looked on Helen's gift,
(*O Troy Town!*)
Looked and smiled with subtle drift,
Saw the work of her heart's desire—
"There thou kneel'st for Love to lift!"
(*O Troy's down,*
Tall Troy's on fire!)

Venus looked in Helen's face,
(*O Troy Town!*)
Knew far off an hour and place,
And fire lit from the heart's desire;
Laughed and said, "Thy gift hath grace!"
(*O Troy's down,*
Tall Troy's on fire!)

Cupid looked on Helen's breast,
(*O Troy Town!*)
Saw the heart within its nest,
Saw the flame of the heart's desire—
Marked his arrow's burning crest.
(*O Troy's down,*
Tall Troy's on fire!)

Cupid took another dart,
(*O Troy Town!*)
Fledged it for another heart,
Winged the shaft with the heart's desire,
Drew the string and said, "Depart!"
(*O Troy's down,*
Tall Troy's on fire!)

Paris turned upon his bed,
(*O Troy Town!*)
Turned upon his bed and said,
Dead at heart with the heart's desire—
"O to clasp her golden head!"
(*O Troy's down,*
Tall Troy's on fire!)

1870

THE BALLAD OF DEAD LADIES

(Translation from François Villon.)

Tell me now in what hidden way is
  Lady Flora the lovely Roman?
Where's Hipparchia, and where is Thais,
  Neither of them the fairer woman?
  Where is Echo, beheld of no man,
Only heard on river and mere,—
  She whose beauty was more than human? . . .
But where are the snows of yester-year?

Where 's Héloise, the learned nun,
  For whose sake Abeillard, I ween,
Lost manhood and put priesthood on?
  (From Love he won such dule and teen!)
  And where, I pray you, is the Queen
Who willed that Buridan should steer
  Sewed in a sack's mouth down the Seine? . . .
But where are the snows of yester-year?

White Queen Blanche, like a queen of lilies,
  With a voice like any mermaiden—
Bertha Broadfoot, Beatrice, Alice,
  And Ermengarde the lady of Maine,—
  And that good Joan whom Englishmen
At Rouen doomed and burned her there,—
  Mother of God, where are they then? . . .
But where are the snows of yester-year?

Nay, never ask this week, fair lord,
  Where they are gone, nor yet this year,
Except with this for an overword,—
  But where are the snows of yester-year?

1869

SONGS[1]

I THE SEA-LIMITS

Consider the sea's listless chime:
  Time's self it is, made audible,—
  The murmur of the earth's own shell.
Secret continuance sublime
  Is the sea's end: our sight may pass
  No furlong further. Since time was,
This sound hath told the lapse of time.

[1] For convenience, these poems which Rossetti's arrangement of 1870 recognized as "Songs," are here gathered together. Chronological order is preserved within the group.

No quiet, which is death's,—it hath
  The mournfulness of ancient life,
  Enduring always at dull strife.
As the world's heart of rest and wrath,
  Its painful pulse is in the sands.
  Last utterly, the whole sky stands,
Grey and not known, along its path.

Listen alone beside the sea,
  Listen alone among the woods;
  Those voices of twin solitudes
Shall have one sound alike to thee:
  Hark where the murmurs of thronged men
  Surge and sink back and surge again,—
Still the one voice of wave and tree.

Gather a shell from the strown beach
  And listen at its lips: they sigh
  The same desire and mystery,
The echo of the whole sea's speech.
  And all mankind is thus at heart
  Not anything but what thou art:
And Earth, Sea, Man, are all in each.

(*1849*) 1870

II PENUMBRA

I did not look upon her eyes
(Though scarcely seen, with no surprise,
'Mid many eyes a single look),
Because they should not gaze rebuke,
At night, from stars in sky and brook.

I did not take her by the hand
(Though little was to understand
From touch of hand all friends might take),
Because it should not prove a flake
Burnt in my palm to boil and ache.

I did not listen to her voice
(Though none had noted, where at choice
All might rejoice in listening),
Because no such a thing should cling
In the wood's moan at evening.

I did not cross her shadow once
(Though from the hollow west the sun's
Last shadow runs along so far),
Because in June it should not bar
My ways, at noon when fevers are.

They told me she was sad that day
(Though wherefore tell what love's soothsay,
Sooner than they, did register?),
And my heart leapt and wept to her,
And yet I did not speak nor stir.

So shall the tongues of the sea's foam
(Though many voices therewith come
From drowned hope's home to cry to me),
Bewail one hour the more, when sea
And wind are one with memory.

(*1853*) 1870

III THE HONEYSUCKLE

I PLUCKED a honeysuckle where
The hedge on high is quick with thorn,
And climbing for the prize, was torn,
And fouled my feet in quag-water;
And by the thorns and by the wind
The blossom that I took was thinn'd
And yet I found it sweet and fair.

Thence to a richer growth I came,
Where, nursed in mellow intercourse,
The honeysuckles sprang by scores,
Not harried like my single stem,
All virgin lamps of scent and dew.
So from my hand that first I threw,
Yet plucked not any more of them.

(*1853*) 1870

IV SUDDEN LIGHT

I HAVE been here before,
But when or how I cannot tell:
I know the grass beyond the door,
The sweet keen smell,
The sighing sound, the lights around the shore.

You have been mine before,—
How long ago I may not know:
But just when at that swallow's soar
Your neck turned so,
Some veil did fall,—I knew it all of yore.

Has this been thus before?
And shall not thus time's eddying flight
Still with our lives our loves restore
In death's despite,
And day and night yield one delight once more?

(*1854*) 1870

V THE WOODSPURGE

THE wind flapped loose, the wind was still,
Shaken out dead from tree and hill:
I had walked on at the wind's will,—
I sat now, for the wind was still.

Between my knees my forehead was,—
My lips, drawn in, said not Alas!
My hair was over in the grass,
My naked ears heard the day pass.

My eyes, wide open, had the run
Of some ten weeds to fix upon;
Among those few, out of the sun,
The woodspurge flowered, three cups in one.

From perfect grief there need not be
Wisdom or even memory:
One thing then learnt remains to me,—
The woodspurge has a cup of three.

(*1856*) 1870

VI A LITTLE WHILE

A LITTLE while a little love
The hour yet bears for thee and me
Who have not drawn the veil to see
If still our heaven be lit above.
Thou merely, at the day's last sigh,
Hast felt thy soul prolong the tone;
And I have heard the night-wind cry
And deemed its speech mine own.

A little while a little love
The scattering autumn hoards for us
Whose bower is not yet ruinous
Nor quite unleaved our songless grove.
Only across the shaken boughs
We hear the flood-tides seek the sea,
And deep in both our hearts they rouse
One wail for thee and me.

A little while a little love
May yet be ours who have not said
The word it makes our eyes afraid
To know that each is thinking of.
Not yet the end: be our lips dumb
In smiles a little season yet:
I'll tell thee, when the end is come,
How we may best forget.

(*1859*) 1870

VII LOVE-LILY

Between the hands, between the brows,
 Between the lips of Love-Lily,
A spirit is born whose birth endows
 My blood with fire to burn through me;
Who breathes upon my gazing eyes,
 Who laughs and murmurs in mine ear,
At whose least touch my colour flies,
 And whom my life grows faint to hear.

Within the voice, within the heart,
 Within the mind of Love-Lily,
A spirit is born who lifts apart
 His tremulous wings and looks at me;
Who on my mouth his finger lays,
 And shows, while whispering lutes confer,
That Eden of Love's watered ways
 Whose winds and spirits worship her.

Brows, hands, and lips, heart, mind, and voice,
 Kisses and words of Love-Lily,—
Oh! bid me with your joy rejoice
 Till riotous longing rest in me!
Ah! let not hope be still distraught,
 But find in her its gracious goal,
Whose speech Truth knows not from her thought
 Nor Love her body from her soul.

1870

VIII FIRST LOVE REMEMBERED

Peace in her chamber, wheresoe'er
 It be, a holy place;
 The thought still brings my soul such grace
As morning meadows wear.

Whether it still be small and light,
 A maid's who dreams alone,
 As from her orchard-gate the moon
Its ceiling showed at night;

Or whether, in a shadow dense
 As nuptial hymns invoke,
 Innocent maidenhood awoke
To married innocence—

There still the thanks unheard await
 The unconscious gift bequeathed;
 For there my soul this hour has breathed
An air inviolate.

1870

SONNETS FOR PICTURES[1]

I MARY'S GIRLHOOD[2]

1

This is that blessed Mary, pre-elect
 God's Virgin. Gone is a great while, and she
 Dwelt young in Nazareth of Galilee.
Unto God's will she brought devout respect,
Profound simplicity of intellect,
 And supreme patience. From her mother's knee
 Faithful and hopeful; wise in charity;
Strong in grave peace; in pity circumspect.

So held she through her girlhood; as it were
 An angel-watered lily, that near God
 Grows and is quiet. Till, one dawn at home
She woke in her white bed, and had no fear
 At all—yet wept till sunshine, and felt awed,
 Because the fullness of the time was come.

2

These are the symbols. On that cloth of red
 I' the center is the Tripoint; perfect each,
 Except the second of its points, to teach
That Christ is not yet born. The books—whose head
Is golden Charity, as Paul hath said—
 Those virtues are wherein the soul is rich;
 Therefore on them the lily standeth, which
Is Innocence, being interpreted.

The seven-thorned briar and the palm seven-leaved
 Are her great sorrow and her great reward.
 Until the end be full, the Holy One
Abides without. She soon shall have achieved
 Her perfect purity; yea, God the Lord
 Shall soon vouchsafe His Son to be her Son.

1848–9

[1] See also numbers 77 and 78 of "The House of Life."

[2] The second of these sonnets was inscribed around the frame of Rossetti's first exhibited picture, The Girlhood of Mary Virgin. It was not otherwise published during his lifetime. The passage in the first sonnet—"one dawn at home she woke in her white bed"—seems to refer to Rossetti's second picture, Ecce Ancilla Domini or The Annunciation. Christina Rossetti was the model for the virgin in both pictures.

II FOR "A VENETIAN PASTORAL"

By Giorgione

(In the Louvre)

Water, for anguish of the solstice:—nay,
But dip the vessel slowly,—nay, but lean
And hark how at its verge the wave sighs in
Reluctant. Hush! Beyond all depth away
The heat lies silent at the brink of day:
Now the hand trails upon the viol-string
That sobs, and the brown faces cease to sing,
Sad with the whole of pleasure. Whither stray
Her eyes now, from whose mouth the slim pipes creep
And leave it pouting, while the shadowed grass
Is cool against her naked side? Let be:—
Say nothing now unto her lest she weep,
Nor name this ever. Be it as it was,—
Life touching lips with Immortality.

1850

III FOR "THE WINE OF CIRCE"

By Edward Burne-Jones

Dusk-haired and gold-robed o'er the golden wine
She stoops, wherein, distilled of death and shame,
Sink the black drops; while, lit with fragrant flame,
Round her spread board the golden sunflowers shine.
Doth Helios here with Hecatè combine
(O Circe, thou their votaress!) to proclaim
For these thy guests all rapture in Love's name,
Till pitiless Night gave Day the countersign?
Lords of their hour, they come. And by her knee
Those cowering beasts, their equals heretofore,
Wait; who with them in new equality
To-night shall echo back the unchanging roar
Which sounds for ever from the tide-strown shore
Where the dishevelled seaweed hates the sea.

1870

IV FIAMMETTA[1]

Behold Fiammetta, shown in vision here.
Gloom-girt 'mid Spring-flushed apple-growth she stands;
And as she sways the branches with her hands,
Along her arm the sundered bloom falls sheer,
In separate petals shed, each like a tear;
While from the quivering bough the bird expands
His wings. And lo! thy spirit understands
Life shaken and shower'd and flown, and Death drawn near.

All stirs with change. Her garments beat the air:
The angel circling round her aureole
Shimmers in flight against the tree's gray bole:
While she, with reassuring eyes most fair,
A presage and a promise stands; as 'twere
On Death's dark storm the rainbow of the Soul.

1881

V "FOUND"

"There is a budding morrow in midnight:"—
So sang our Keats, our English nightingale.
And here, as lamps across the bridge turn pale
In London's smokeless resurrection-light,
Dark breaks to dawn. But o'er the deadly blight
Of love deflowered and sorrow of none avail
Which makes this man gasp and this woman quail,
Can day from darkness ever again take flight?

Ah! gave not these two hearts their mutual pledge,
Under one mantle sheltered 'neath the hedge
In gloaming courtship? And O God! to-day
He only knows he holds her;—but what part
Can life now take? She cries in her locked heart,—
"Leave me—I do not know you—go away!"

1881

[1] This and the following sonnet do not belong to the group of "Sonnets for Pictures" printed in the "Poems" of 1870, but they are here printed out of their chronological place because of their kinship in subject matter with the earlier group.

JENNY

"Vengeance of Jenny's case! Fie on her! Never name her, child!"—(*Mrs. Quickly.*)

LAZY laughing languid Jenny,
Fond of a kiss and fond of a guinea,
Whose head upon my knee to-night
Rests for a while, as if grown light
With all our dances and the sound
To which the wild tunes spun you round:
Fair Jenny mine, the thoughtless queen
Of kisses which the blush between
Could hardly make much daintier;
Whose eyes are as blue skies, whose hair
Is countless gold incomparable:
Fresh flower, scarce touched with signs that tell
Of Love's exuberant hotbed:—Nay,
Poor flower left torn since yesterday
Until to-morrow leave you bare;
Poor handful of bright spring-water
Flung in the whirlpool's shrieking face;
Poor shameful Jenny, full of grace
Thus with your head upon my knee;—
Whose person or whose purse may be
The lodestar of your reverie?

This room of yours, my Jenny, looks
A change from mine so full of books,
Whose serried ranks hold fast, forsooth,
So many captive hours of youth,—
The hours they thieve from day and night
To make one's cherished work come right,
And leave it wrong for all their theft,
Even as to-night my work was left:
Until I vowed that since my brain
And eyes of dancing seemed so fain,
My feet should have some dancing too:—
And thus it was I met with you.
Well, I suppose 'twas hard to part,
For here I am. And now, sweetheart,
You seem too tired to get to bed.

It was a careless life I led.
When rooms like this were scarce so strange
Not long ago. What breeds the change,—
The many aims or the few years?
Because to-night it all appears
Something I do not know again.

The cloud's not danced out of my brain,—
The cloud that made it turn and swim
While hour by hour the books grew dim.
Why, Jenny, as I watch you there,—
For all your wealth of loosened hair,
Your silk ungirdled and unlac'd
And warm sweets open to the waist,
All golden in the lamplight's gleam,—
You know not what a book you seem,
Half-read by lightning in a dream!
How should you know, my Jenny? Nay,
And I should be ashamed to say:—
Poor beauty, so well worth a kiss!
But while my thought runs on like this
With wasteful whims more than enough,
I wonder what you're thinking of.

If of myself you think at all,
What is the thought?—conjectural
On sorry matters best unsolved?—
Or inly is each grace revolved
To fit me with a lure?—or (sad
To think!) perhaps you're merely glad
That I'm not drunk or ruffianly
And let you rest upon my knee.

For sometimes, were the truth confess'd,
You're thankful for a little rest,—
Glad from the crush to rest within,
From the heart-sickness and the din
Where envy's voice at virtue's pitch
Mocks you because your gown is rich;
And from the pale girl's dumb rebuke,
Whose ill-clad grace and toil-worn look
Proclaim the strength that keeps her weak
And other nights than yours bespeak;
And from the wise unchildish elf
To schoolmate lesser than himself
Pointing you out, what thing you are:—
Yes, from the daily jeer and jar,
From shame and shame's outbraving too,
Is rest not sometimes sweet to you?—
But most from the hatefulness of man
Who spares not to end what he began,
Whose acts are ill and his speech ill,
Who, having used you at his will,
Thrusts you aside, as when I dine
I serve the dishes and the wine.

Well, handsome Jenny mine, sit up,
I've filled our glasses, let us sup,
And do not let me think of you,
Lest shame of yours suffice for two.
What, still so tired? Well, well then, keep
Your head there, so you do not sleep;

But that the weariness may pass
And leave you merry, take this glass.
Ah! lazy lily hand, more bless'd
If ne'er in rings it had been dress'd
Nor ever by a glove conceal'd!

Behold the lilies of the field,
They toil not neither do they spin;
(So doth the ancient text begin,—
Not of such rest as one of these
Can share.) Another rest and ease
Along each summer-sated path
From its new lord the garden hath,
Than that whose spring in blessings ran
Which praised the bounteous husbandman,
Ere yet, in days of hankering breath,
The lilies sickened unto death.

What, Jenny, are your lilies dead?
Aye, and the snow-white leaves are spread
Like winter on the garden-bed.
But you had roses left in May,—
They were not gone too. Jenny, nay,
But must your roses die, and those
Their purfled buds that should unclose?
Even so; the leaves are curled apart,
Still red as from the broken heart,
And here's the naked stem of thorns.

Nay, nay, mere words. Here nothing warns
As yet of winter. Sickness here
Or want alone could waken fear,—
Nothing but passion wrings a tear.
Except when there may rise unsought
Haply at times a passing thought
Of the old days which seem to be
Much older than any history
That is written in any book;
When she would lie in fields and look
Along the ground through the blown grass,
And wonder where the city was,
Far out of sight, whose broil and bale
They told her then for a child's tale.

Jenny, you know the city now.
A child can tell the tale there, how
Some things which are not yet enroll'd
In market-lists are bought and sold
Even till the early Sunday light,
When Saturday night is market-night
Everywhere, be it dry or wet,
And market-night in the Haymarket.
Our learned London children know,
Poor Jenny, all your pride and woe;
Have seen your lifted silken skirt
Advertise dainties through the dirt;
Have seen your coach-wheels splash rebuke
On virtue; and have learned your look
When, wealth and health slipped past, you stare
Along the streets alone, and there,
Round the long park, across the bridge,
The cold lamps at the pavement's edge
Wind on together and apart,
A fiery serpent for your heart.

Let the thoughts pass, an empty cloud!
Suppose I were to think aloud,—
What if to her all this were said?
Why, as a volume seldom read
Being opened halfway shuts again,
So might the pages of her brain
Be parted at such words, and thence
Close back upon the dusty sense.
For is there hue or shape defin'd
In Jenny's desecrated mind,
Where all contagious currents meet,
A Lethe of the middle street?
Nay, it reflects not any face,
Nor sound is in its sluggish pace,
But as they coil those eddies clot,
And night and day remember not.

Why, Jenny, you're asleep at last!—
Asleep, poor Jenny, hard and fast,—
So young and soft and tired; so fair,
With chin thus nestled in your hair,
Mouth quiet, eyelids almost blue
As if some sky of dreams shone through!

Just as another woman sleeps!
Enough to throw one's thoughts in heaps
Of doubt and horror,—what to say
Or think,—this awful secret sway,
The potter's power over the clay!
Of the same lump (it has been said)
For honour and dishonour made,
Two sister vessels. Here is one.

My cousin Nell is fond of fun,
And fond of dress, and change, and praise,
So mere a woman in her ways:
And if her sweet eyes rich in youth
Are like her lips that tell the truth,

My cousin Nell is fond of love.
And she 's the girl I'm proudest of.
Who does not prize her, guard her well?
The love of change, in cousin Nell,
Shall find the best and hold it dear:
The unconquered mirth turn quieter
Not through her own, through others' woe:
The conscious pride of beauty glow
Beside another's pride in her,
One little part of all they share.
For Love himself shall ripen these
In a kind soil to just increase
Through years of fertilizing peace.

Of the same lump (as it is said)
For honour and dishonour made,
Two sister vessels. Here is one.

It makes a goblin of the sun.

So pure,—so fall'n! How dare to think
Of the first common kindred link?
Yet, Jenny, till the world shall burn
It seems that all things take their turn;
And who shall say but this fair tree
May need, in changes that may be,
Your children's children's charity?
Scorned then, no doubt, as you are scorn'd!
Shall no man hold his pride forewarn'd
Till in the end, the Day of Days,
At Judgement, one of his own race,
As frail and lost as you, shall rise,—
His daughter, with his mother's eyes?

How Jenny's clock ticks on the shelf!
Might not the dial scorn itself
That has such hours to register?
Yet as to me, even so to her
Are golden sun and silver moon,
In daily largesse of earth's boon,
Counted for life-coins to one tune.
And if, as blindfold fates are toss'd,
Through some one man this life be lost,
Shall soul not somehow pay for soul?

Fair shines the gilded aureole
In which our highest painters place
Some living woman's simple face.
And the stilled features thus descried
As Jenny's long throat droops aside,—
The shadows where the cheeks are thin,
And pure wide curve from ear to chin,—
With Raffael's or Da Vinci's hand
To show them to men's souls, might stand,
Whole ages long, the whole world through,
For preachings of what God can do.
What has man done here? How atone,
Great God, for this which man has done?
And for the body and soul which by
Man's pitiless doom must now comply
With lifelong hell, what lullaby
Of sweet forgetful second birth
Remains? All dark. No sign on earth
What measure of God's rest endows
The many mansions of his house.

If but a woman's heart might see
Such erring heart unerringly
For once! But that can never be.

Like a rose shut in a book
In which pure women may not look,
For its base pages claim control
To crush the flower within the soul;
Where through each dead rose-leaf that clings,
Pale as transparent psyche-wings,
To the vile text, are traced such things
As might make lady's cheek indeed
More than a living rose to read;
So nought save foolish foulness may
Watch with hard eyes the sure decay;
And so the life-blood of this rose,
Puddled with shameful knowledge, flows
Through leaves no chaste hand may unclose:
Yet still it keeps such faded show
Of when 'twas gathered long ago,
That the crushed petals' lovely grain,
The sweetness of the sanguine stain,
Seen of a woman's eyes, must make
Her pitiful heart, so prone to ache,
Love roses better for its sake:—
Only that this can never be:—
Even so unto her sex is she.

Yet, Jenny, looking long at you,
The woman almost fades from view.
A cipher of man's changeless sum
Of lust, past, present, and to come,
Is left. A riddle that one shrinks
To challenge from the scornful sphinx.

Like a toad within a stone
Seated while Time crumbles on;
Which sits there since the earth was curs'd

For Man's transgression at the first;
Which, living through all centuries,
Not once has seen the sun arise;
Whose life, to its cold circle charmed,
The earth's whole summers have not warmed;
Which always—whitherso the stone
Be flung—sits there, deaf, blind, alone;—
Aye, and shall not be driven out
Till that which shuts him round about
Break at the very Master's stroke,
And the dust thereof vanish as smoke,
And the seed of Man vanish as dust:—
Even so within this world is Lust.

Come, come, what use in thoughts like this?
Poor little Jenny, good to kiss,—
You'd not believe by what strange roads
Thought travels, when your beauty goads
A man to-night to think of toads!
Jenny, wake up. . . . Why, there's the dawn!

And there's an early waggon drawn
To market, and some sheep that jog
Bleating before a barking dog;
And the old streets come peering through
Another night that London knew;
And all as ghostlike as the lamps.

So on the wings of day decamps
My last night's frolic. Glooms begin
To shiver off as lights creep in
Past the gauze curtains half drawn-to,
And the lamp's doubled shade grows blue,—
Your lamp, my Jenny, kept alight,
Like a wise virgin's, all one night!
And in the alcove coolly spread
Glimmers with dawn your empty bed;
And yonder your fair face I see
Reflected lying on my knee,
Where teems with first foreshadowings
Your pier-glass scrawled with diamond rings.

And now without, as if some word
Had called upon them that they heard,
The London sparrows far and nigh
Clamour together suddenly;
And Jenny's cage-bird grown awake
Here in their song his part must take,
Because here too the day doth break.

And somehow in myself the dawn
Among stirred clouds and veils withdrawn
Strikes greyly on her. Let her sleep.
But will it wake her if I heap
These cushions thus beneath her head
Where my knee was? No,—there's your bed,
My Jenny, while you dream. And there
I lay among your golden hair
Perhaps the subject of your dreams,
These golden coins.

For still one deems
That Jenny's flattering sleep confers
New magic on the magic purse,—
Grim web, how clogged with shrivelled flies!
Between the threads fine fumes arise
And shape their pictures in the brain.
There roll no streets in glare and rain,
Nor flagrant man-swine whets his tusk;
But delicately sighs in musk
The homage of the dim boudoir;
Or like a palpitating star
Thrilled into song, the opera-night
Breathes faint in the quick pulse of light;
Or at the carriage-window shine
Rich wares for choice; or, free to dine,
Whirls through its hour of health (divine
For her) the concourse of the Park.
And though in the discounted dark
Her functions there and here are one,
Beneath the lamps and in the sun
There reigns at least the acknowledged belle
Apparelled beyond parallel.
Ah Jenny, yes, we know your dreams.

For even the Paphian Venus seems
A goddess o'er the realms of love,
When silver-shrined in shadowy grove:
Aye, or let offerings nicely placed
But hide Priapus to the waist,
And whoso looks on him shall see
An eligible deity.

Why, Jenny, waking here alone
May help you to remember one,
Though all the memory's long outworn
Of many a double-pillowed morn.
I think I see you when you wake,
And rub your eyes for me, and shake
My gold, in rising, from your hair,
A Danaë for a moment there.

Jenny, my love rang true! for still
Love at first sight is vague, until
That tinkling makes him audible.

And must I mock you to the last,
Ashamed of my own shame,—aghast
Because some thoughts not born amiss
Rose at a poor fair face like this?
Well, of such thoughts so much I know:
In my life, as in hers, they show,
By a far gleam which I may near,
A dark path I can strive to clear.

Only one kiss. Good-bye, my dear.

1870[1]

SONNETS FROM THE HOUSE OF LIFE

THE SONNET

A sonnet is a moment's monument—
Memorial from the Soul's eternity
To one dead deathless hour. Look that it be,
Whether for lustral rite or dire portent,
Of its own arduous fullness reverent.
Carve it in ivory or in ebony,
As Day or Night may rule; and let Time see
Its flowering crest impearled and orient.

A sonnet is a coin; its face reveals
The Soul—its converse, to what Power 'tis due:—
Whether for tribute to the august appeals
Of Life, or dower in Love's high retinue,
It serve; or 'mid the dark wharf's cavernous breath,
In Charon's palm it pay the toll to Death.

1881

PART I. YOUTH AND CHANGE

I LOVE ENTHRONED

I MARKED all kindred Powers the heart finds fair:
Truth, with awed lips; and Hope, with eyes upcast;
And Fame, whose loud wings fan the ashen Past
To signal-fires, Oblivion's flight to scare;
And Youth, with still some single golden hair
Unto his shoulder clinging, since the last
Embrace wherein two sweet arms held him fast;
And Life, still wreathing flowers for Death to wear.

Love's throne was not with these; but far above
All passionate wind of welcome and farewell
He sat in breathless bowers they dream not of;
Though Truth foreknow Love's heart, and Hope foretell,
And Fame be for Love's sake desirable,
And Youth be dear, and Life be sweet to Love.

1881

II BRIDAL BIRTH

As when desire, long darkling, dawns, and first
The mother looks upon the newborn child,
Even so my Lady stood at gaze and smiled
When her soul knew at length the Love it nursed.
Born with her life, creature of poignant thirst
And exquisite hunger, at her heart Love lay
Quickening in darkness, till a voice that day
Cried on him, and the bonds of birth were burst.

Now, shielded in his wings, our faces yearn
Together, as his fullgrown feet now range
The grove, and his warm hands our couch prepare:
Till to his song our bodiless souls in turn
Be born his children, when Death's nuptial change
Leaves us for light the halo of his hair.

1870

IV LOVESIGHT

WHEN do I see thee most, beloved one?
When in the light the spirits of mine eyes
Before thy face, their altar, solemnize
The worship of that Love through thee made known?
Or when in the dusk hours, (we two alone,)
Close-kissed and eloquent of still replies
Thy twilight-hidden glimmering visage lies,
And my soul only sees thy soul its own?

[1] According to Rossetti's brother this poem was begun as early as 1848, but the greater part of the composition was done between 1858 and 1869.

O love, my love! if I no more should see
Thyself, nor on the earth the shadow of thee,
Nor image of thine eyes in any spring,—
How then should sound upon Life's darkening slope
The ground-whirl of the perished leaves of Hope,
The wind of Death's imperishable wing?

1870

V HEART'S HOPE

By what word's power, the keys of paths untrod,
Shall I the difficult deeps of Love explore,
Till parted waves of Song yield up the shore
Even as that sea which Israel crossed dryshod?
For lo! in some poor rhythmic period,
Lady, I fain would tell how evermore
Thy soul I know not from thy body, nor
Thee from myself, neither our love from God.

Yea, in God's name, and Love's, and thine, would I
Draw from one loving heart such evidence
As to all hearts all things shall signify;
Tender as dawn's first hill-fire, and intense
As instantaneous penetrating sense,
In Spring's birth-hour, of other Springs gone by.

1881

X THE PORTRAIT

O Lord of all compassionate control,
O Love! let this my lady's picture glow
Under my hand to praise her name, and show
Even of her inner self the perfect whole:
That he who seeks her beauty's furthest goal,
Beyond the light that the sweet glances throw
And refluent wave of the sweet smile, may know
The very sky and sea-line of her soul.

Lo! it is done. Above the long lithe throat
The mouth's mould testifies of voice and kiss,
The shadowed eyes remember and foresee.
Her face is made her shrine. Let all men note
That in all years (O Love, thy gift is this!)
They that would look on her must come to me.

1870

XI THE LOVE–LETTER

Warmed by her hand and shadowed by her hair
As close she leaned and poured her heart through thee,
Whereof the articulate throbs accompany
The smooth black stream that makes thy whiteness fair,—
Sweet fluttering sheet, even of her breath aware,—
Oh let thy silent song disclose to me
That soul wherewith her lips and eyes agree
Like married music in Love's answering air.

Fain had I watched her when, at some fond thought,
Her bosom to the writing closelier press'd,
And her breast's secrets peered into her breast;
When, through eyes raised an instant, her soul sought
My soul, and from the sudden confluence caught
The words that made her love the loveliest.

1870

XIV YOUTH'S SPRING–TRIBUTE

On this sweet bank your head thrice sweet and dear
I lay, and spread your hair on either side,
And see the newborn woodflowers bashful-eyed
Look through the golden tresses here and there.
On these debateable borders of the year
Spring's foot half falters; scarce she yet may know
The leafless blackthorn-blossom from the snow;
And through her bowers the wind's way still is clear.

But April's sun strikes down the glades today;
So shut your eyes upturned, and feel my kiss
Creep, as the Spring now thrills through every spray,

Percy Bysshe Shelley.

(Inscription for the couch, still preserved, on which he passed the last night of his life.)

'Twixt those twin worlds,—the world of Sleep, which gave
No dream to warn,—the tidal world of Death,
Which the earth's sea, as the earth, replenisheth,—
Shelley, Song's orient sun, to breast the wave,
Rose from this couch that morn. Ah! did he brave
Only the sea?—or did man's deed of hell
Engulph his bark 'mid mists impenetrable?...
No eye discerned, nor any power might save.

When that mist cleared, O Shelley! what dread veil
Was rent for thee, to whom far-darkling Truth
~~Was~~ Reigned sovereign guide through thy brief ageless youth?
Was the Truth thy Truth, Shelley?—Hush! All-Hail,
Past doubt, thou gav'st it; and in ~~that the~~ Truth's bright vale
Art first of praisers, being most praised here.

Manuscript of Rossetti's Sonnet Inscription for Shelley's Couch. (See Appendix I.)

Up your warm throat to your warm lips: for this
Is even the hour of Love's sworn suitservice,
With whom cold hearts are counted castaway.

1881

XVIII GENIUS IN BEAUTY

Beauty like hers is genius. Not the call
Of Homer's or of Dante's heart sublime,—
Not Michael's hand furrowing the zones of time,—
Is more with compassed mysteries musical;
Nay, not in Spring's or Summer's sweet footfall
More gathered gifts exuberant Life bequeathes
Than does this sovereign face, whose love-spell breathes
Even from its shadowed contour on the wall.

As many men are poets in their youth,
But for one sweet-strung soul the wires prolong
Even through all change the indominable song;
So in likewise the envenomed years, whose tooth
Rends shallower grace with ruin void of ruth,
Upon this beauty's power shall wreak no wrong.

1881

XIX SILENT NOON

Your hands lie open in the long, fresh grass—
The finger-points look through like rosy blooms;
Your eyes smile peace. The pasture gleams and glooms
'Neath billowing skies that scatter and amass.
All round our nest, far as the eye can pass,
Are golden kingcup-fields with silver edge
Where the cow-parsley skirts the hawthorn hedge.
'Tis visible silence, still as the hour-glass.

Deep in the sun-searched growths the dragon-fly
Hangs like a blue thread loosened from the sky—
So this winged hour is dropped to us from above.
Oh! clasp we to our hearts, for deathless dower,
This close-companioned inarticulate hour
When twofold silence was the song of love.

1881

XXI LOVE–SWEETNESS

Sweet dimness of her loosened hair's downfall
About thy face; her sweet hands round thy head
In gracious fostering union garlanded;
Her tremulous smiles; her glances' sweet recall
Of love; her murmuring sighs memorial;
Her mouth's culled sweetness by thy kisses shed
On cheeks and neck and eyelids, and so led
Back to her mouth which answers there for all:—

What sweeter than these things, except the thing
In lacking which all these would lose their sweet:—
The confident heart's still fervour; the swift beat
And soft subsidence of the spirit's wing,
Then when it feels, in cloud-girt wayfaring,
The breath of kindred plumes against its feet?

1870

XXII HEART'S HAVEN

Sometimes she is a child within my arms,
Cowering beneath dark wings that love must chase,—
With still tears showering and averted face,
Inexplicably filled with faint alarms:
And oft from mine own spirit's hurtling harms
I crave the refuge of her deep embrace,—
Against all ills the fortified strong place
And sweet reserve of sovereign counter-charms.

And love, our light at night and shade at noon,
Lulls us to rest with songs, and turns away
All shafts of shelterless tumultuous day.
Like the moon's growth, his face gleams through his tune;
And as soft waters warble to the moon,
Our answering spirits chime our roundelay.

1881

XXVII HEART'S COMPASS

SOMETIMES thou seem'st not as thyself alone,
But as the meaning of all things that are;
A breathless wonder, shadowing forth afar
Some heavenly solstice hushed and halcyon;
Whose unstirred lips are music's visible tone;
Whose eyes the sun-gate of the soul unbar,
Being of its furthest fires oracular—
The evident heart of all life sown and mown.

Even such love is; and is not thy name Love?
Yea, by thy hand the Love-god rends apart
All gathering clouds of Night's ambiguous art;
Flings them far down, and sets thine eyes above;
And simply, as some gage of flower or glove,
Stakes with a smile the world against thy heart.

1881

XXVIII SOUL-LIGHT

WHAT other woman could be loved like you,
Or how of you should love possess his fill?
After the fulness of all rapture, still,—
As at the end of some deep avenue
A tender glamour of the day,—there comes to view
Far in your eyes a yet more hungering thrill,—
Such fire as Love's soul-winnowing hands distil
Even from his inmost ark of light and dew.

And as the traveller triumphs with the sun,
Glorying in heat's mid-height, yet star tide brings
Wonder new-born, and still fresh transport springs
From limpid lambent hours of day begun;—
Even so, through eyes and voice, your soul doth move
My soul with changeful light of infinite love.

1881

XXXIV THE DARK GLASS

NOT I myself know all my love for thee;
How should I reach so far, who cannot weigh
Tomorrow's dower by gage of yesterday?
Shall birth and death, and all dark names that be
As doors and windows bared to some loud sea,
Lash deaf mine ears and blind my face with spray;
And shall my sense pierce love—the last relay
And ultimate outpost of eternity?

Lo! what am I to Love, the Lord of all?
One murmuring shell he gathers from the sand,
One little heart-flame sheltered in his hand.
Yet through thine eyes he grants me clearest call
And veriest touch of powers primordial
That any hour-girt life may understand.

1881

XXXVI LIFE-IN-LOVE

NOT in thy body is thy life at all
But in this lady's lips and hands and eyes;
Through these she yields thee life that vivifies
What else were sorrow's servant and death's thrall.
Look on thyself without her, and recall
The waste remembrance and forlorn surmise
That lived but in a dead-drawn breath of sighs
O'er vanished hours and hours eventual.

Even so much life hath the poor tress of hair
Which, stored apart, is all love hath to show
For heart-beats and for fire-heats long ago;
Even so much life endures unknown, even where,
'Mid change the changeless night environeth,
Lies all that golden hair undimmed in death.

1870

XXXVIII THE MORROW'S MESSAGE

"THOU Ghost," I said, "and is thy name To-day?—
Yesterday's son, with such an abject brow!—
And can To-morrow be more pale than thou?"

While yet I spoke, the silence answered: "Yea,
Henceforth our issue is all grieved and grey,
And each beforehand makes such poor avow
As of old leaves beneath the budding bough
Or night-drift that the sundawn shreds away."

Then cried I: "Mother of many malisons,
O Earth, receive me to thy dusty bed!"
But therewithal the tremulous silence said:
"Lo! Love yet bids thy lady greet thee once:—
Yea, twice,—whereby thy life is still the sun's;
And thrice,—whereby the shadow of death is dead."

1870

XLI THROUGH DEATH TO LOVE

Like labor-laden moonclouds faint to flee
From winds that sweep the winter-bitten wold,—
Like multiform circumfluence manifold
Of night's flood-tide,—like terrors that agree
Of hoarse-tongued fire and inarticulate sea,—
Even such, within some glass dimmed by our breath,
Our hearts discern wild images of Death,
Shadows and shoals that edge eternity.

Howbeit athwart Death's imminent shade doth soar
One Power, than flow of stream or flight of dove
Sweeter to glide around, to brood above.
Tell me, my heart,—what angel-greeted door
Or threshold of wing-winnowed threshing-floor
Hath guest fire-fledged as thine, whose lord is Love?

1881

XLVII BROKEN MUSIC

The mother will not turn, who thinks she hears
Her nursling's speech first grow articulate;
But breathless with averted eyes elate
She sits, with open lips and open ears,
That it may call her twice. 'Mid doubts and fears
Thus oft my soul has hearkened; till the song,
A central moan for days, at length found tongue.
And the sweet music welled and the sweet tears.

But now, whatever while the soul is fain
To list that wonted murmur, as it were
The speech-bound sea-shell's low importunate strain,—
No breath of song, thy voice alone is there,
O bitterly beloved! and all her gain
Is but the pang of unpermitted prayer.

1870

XLIX WILLOWWOOD—1

I sat with Love upon a woodside well,
Leaning across the water, I and he;
Nor ever did he speak nor looked at me,
But touched his lute wherein was audible
The certain secret thing he had to tell:
Only our mirrored eyes met silently
In the low wave; and that sound came to be
The passionate voice I knew; and my tears fell.

And at their fall, his eyes beneath grew hers;
And with his foot and with his wing-feathers
He swept the spring that watered my heart's drouth.
Then the dark ripples spread to waving hair,
And as I stooped, her own lips rising there
Bubbled with brimming kisses at my mouth.

L WILLOWWOOD—2

And now Love sang: but his was such a song,
So meshed with half-remembrance hard to free,
As souls disused in death's sterility
May sing when the new birthday tarries long.
And I was made aware of a dumb throng
That stood aloof, one form by every tree,
All mournful forms, for each was I or she,
The shades of those our days that had no tongue.

They looked on us, and knew us and were known;
While fast together, alive from the abyss,
Clung the soul-wrung implacable close kiss;

And pity of self through all made broken moan
Which said, "For once, for once, for once alone!"
And still Love sang, and what he sang was this:—

LI WILLOWWOOD—3

"O ye, all ye that walk in Willowwood,
That walk with hollow faces burning white;
What fathom-depth of soul-struck widowhood,
What long, what longer hours, one lifelong night,
Ere ye again, who so in vain have wooed
Your last hope lost, who so in vain invite
Your lips to that their unforgotten food,
Ere ye, ere ye again shall see the light!

Alas! the bitter banks in Willowwood,
With tear-spurge wan, with blood-wort burning red:
"Alas! if ever such a pillow could
Steep deep the soul in sleep till she were dead,—
Better all life forget her than this thing,
That Willowwood should hold her wandering!"

LII WILLOWWOOD—4

So sang he: and as meeting rose and rose
Together cling through the wind's well-away,
Nor change at once, yet near the end of day
The leaves drop loosened where the heart-stain glows,—
So when the song died did the kiss unclose;
And her face fell back drowned, and was as grey
As its grey eyes; and if it ever may
Meet mine again I know not if Love knows.

Only I know that I leaned low and drank
A long draught from the water where she sank,
Her breath and all her tears and all her soul:
And as I leaned, I know I felt Love's face
Pressed on my neck with moan of pity and grace,
Till both our heads were in his aureole.

1870

LIII WITHOUT HER

What of her glass without her? The blank gray
There where the pool is blind of the moon's face.
Her dress without her? The tossed empty space
Of cloud-rack whence the moon has passed away.
Her paths without her? Day's appointed sway
Usurped by desolate night. Her pillowed place
Without her? Tears, ah me! for love's good grace,
And cold forgetfulness of night or day.

What of the heart without her? Nay, poor heart,
Of thee what word remains ere speech be still?
A wayfarer by barren ways and chill,
Steep ways and weary, without her thou art.
Where the long cloud, the long wood's counterpart,
Sheds double darkness up the laboring hill.

1881

Part II. Change and Fate

LXVI THE HEART OF THE NIGHT

From child to youth; from youth to arduous man;
From lethargy to fever of the heart;
From faithful life to dream-dowered days apart;
From trust to doubt; from doubt to brink of ban—
Thus much of change in one swift cycle ran
Till now. Alas, the soul!—how soon must she
Accept her primal immortality—
The flesh resume its dust whence it began?

O Lord of work and peace! O Lord of life!
O Lord, the awful Lord of will! though late,
Even yet renew this soul with duteous breath:

That when the peace is garnered in from strife,
The work retrieved, the will regenerate,
This soul may see thy face, O Lord of death!

1881

LXIX AUTUMN IDLENESS

This sunlight shames November where he grieves
In dead red leaves, and will not let him shun
The day, though bough with bough be overrun.
But with a blessing every glade receives
High salutation; while from hillock-eaves
The deer gaze calling, dappled white and dun,
As if, being foresters of old, the sun
Had marked them with the shade of forest-leaves.
Here dawn today unveiled her magic glass;
Here noon now gives the thirst and takes the dew;
Till eve bring rest when other good things pass.
And here the lost hours the lost hours renew
While I still lead my shadow o'er the grass,
Nor know, for longing, that which I should do.

1870

LXXI THE CHOICE—1

Eat thou and drink; to-morrow thou shalt die.
Surely the earth, that 's wise being very old,
Needs not our help. Then loose me, love, and hold
Thy sultry hair up from my face; that I
May pour for thee this golden wine, brim-high,
Till round the glass thy fingers glow like gold.
We'll drown all hours: thy song, while hours are toll'd,
Shall leap, as fountains veil the changing sky.
Now kiss, and think that there are really those,
My own high-bosomed beauty, who increase
Vain gold, vain lore, and yet might choose our way!
Through many days they toil; then comes a day
They die not,—never having lived,—but cease;
And round their narrow lips the mould falls close.

LXXII THE CHOICE—2

Watch thou and fear: to-morrow thou shalt die.
Or art thou sure thou shalt have time for death?
Is not the day which God's word promiseth
To come man knows not when? In yonder sky,
Now while we speak, the sun speeds forth: can I
Or thou assure him of his goal? God's breath
Even at the moment haply quickeneth
The air to a flame; till spirits, always nigh
Though screened and hid, shall walk the daylight here.
And dost thou prate of all that man shall do?
Canst thou, who hast but plagues, presume to be
Glad in his gladness that comes after thee?
Will *his* strength slay *thy* worm in Hell? Go to:
Cover thy countenance, and watch, and fear.

LXXIII THE CHOICE—3

Think thou and act; to-morrow thou shalt die.
Outstretched in the sun's warmth upon the shore,
Thou say'st: "Man's measured path is all gone o'er:
Up all his years, steeply, with strain and sigh,
Man clomb until he touched the truth; and I,
Even I, am he whom it was destined for."
How should this be? Art thou then so much more
Than they who sowed, that thou shouldst reap thereby?
Nay, come up hither. From this wave-washed mound
Unto the furthest flood-brim look with me;
Then reach on with thy thought till it be drown'd.

Miles and miles distant though the grey line be,
And though thy soul sail leagues and leagues beyond,—
Still, leagues beyond those leagues, there is more sea.

1870

LXXVII SOUL'S BEAUTY [1]

UNDER the arch of Life, where love and death,
Terror and mystery, guard her shrine, I saw
Beauty enthroned; and though her gaze struck awe,
I drew it in as simply as my breath.
Hers are the eyes which, over and beneath,
The sky and sea bend on thee,—which can draw,
By sea or sky or woman, to one law,
The allotted bondman of her palm and wreath.

This is that Lady Beauty, in whose praise
Thy voice and hand shake still,—long known to thee
By flying hair and fluttering hem,—the beat
Following her daily of thy heart and feet,
How passionately and irretrievably,
In what fond flight, how many ways and days!

1870

LXXVIII BODY'S BEAUTY

OF Adam's first wife, Lilith, it is told
(The witch he loved before the gift of Eve,)
That, ere the snake's, her sweet tongue could deceive,
And her enchanted hair was the first gold.
And still she sits, young while the earth is old,
And, subtly of herself contemplative,
Draws men to watch the bright net she can weave,
Till heart and body and life are in its hold.

The rose and poppy are her flowers; for where
Is he not found, O Lilith, whom shed scent
And soft-shed kisses and soft sleep shall snare?

[1] This and the following sonnet were written respectively for "Sibylla Palmifera" and "Lilith," two of Rossetti's pictures. In the 1870 edition of his poems, they appeared among the "Sonnets for Pictures." He later shifted them to the "House of Life" sequence.

Lo! as that youth's eyes burned at thine, so went
Thy spell through him, and left his straight neck bent,
And round his heart one strangling golden hair.

1870

LXXXIII BARREN SPRING

ONCE more the changed year's turning wheel returns:
And as a girl sails balanced in the wind,
And now before and now again behind
Stoops as it swoops, with cheek that laughs and burns,—
So Spring comes merry towards me now, but earns
No answering smile from me, whose life is twin'd
With the dead boughs that winter still must bind,
And whom to-day the Spring no more concerns.

Behold, this crocus is a withering flame;
This snowdrop, snow; this apple-blossom's part
To breed the fruit that breeds the serpent's art.
Nay, for these Spring-flowers, turn thy face from them,
Nor gaze till on the year's last lily-stem
The white cup shrivels round the golden heart.

1870

XCVII A SUPERSCRIPTION

LOOK in my face; my name is Might-have-been;
I am also called No-more, Too-late, Farewell;
Unto thine ear I hold the dead-sea shell
Cast up thy Life's foam-fretted feet between;
Unto thine eyes the glass where that is seen
Which had Life's form and Love's, but by my spell
Is now a shaken shadow intolerable,
Of ultimate things unuttered the frail screen.

Mark me, how still I am! But should there dart
One moment through thy soul the soft surprise

Of that winged Peace which lulls the breath
of sighs,—
Then shalt thou see me smile, and turn apart
Thy visage to mine ambush at thy heart
Sleepless with cold commemorative eyes.

1870

CI THE ONE HOPE

When vain desire at last and vain regret
Go hand in hand to death, and all is vain,
What shall assuage the unforgotten pain
And teach the unforgetful to forget?
Shall Peace be still a sunk stream long unmet,—
Or may the soul at once in a green plain
Stoop through the spray of some sweet life-fountain
And cull the dew-drenched flowering amulet?

Ah! when the wan soul in that golden air
Between the scriptured petals softly blown
Peers breathless for the gift of grace unknown,—
Ah! let none other written spell soe'er
But only the one Hope's one name be there,—
Not less nor more, but even that word alone.

1870

THE CLOUD CONFINES

The day is dark and the night
To him that would search their heart;
No lips of cloud that will part
Nor morning song in the light:
Only, gazing alone,
To him wild shadows are shown,
Deep under deep unknown
And height above unknown height.
Still we say as we go,—
"Strange to think by the way,
Whatever there is to know,
That we shall know one day."

The Past is over and fled;
Named new, we name it the old;
Thereof some tale hath been told,
But no word comes from the dead;
Whether at all they be,
Or whether as bond or free,
Or whether they too were we,
Or by what spell they have sped.
Still we say as we go,—
"Strange to think by the way,
Whatever there is to know,
That we shall know one day."

What of the heart of hate
That beats in thy breast, O Time?—
Red strife from the furthest prime,
And anguish of fierce debate;
War that shatters her slain,
And peace that grinds them as grain,
And eyes fixed ever in vain
On the pitiless eyes of Fate.
Still we say as we go,—
"Strange to think by the way
Whatever there is to know
That we shall know one day."

What of the heart of love
That bleeds in thy breast, O Man?—
Thy kisses snatched 'neath the ban
Of fangs that mock them above;
Thy bells prolonged unto knells,
Thy hope that a breath dispels,
Thy bitter forlorn farewells
And the empty echoes thereof?
Still we say as we go,—
"Strange to think by the way,
Whatever there is to know,
That we shall know one day."

The sky leans dumb on the sea,
Aweary with all its wings;
And oh! the song the sea sings
Is dark everlastingly.
Our past is clean forgot,
Our present is and is not,
Our future's a sealed seedplot,
And what betwixt them are we?—
We who say as we go,—
"Strange to think by the way,
Whatever there is to know,
That we shall know one day."

1872

THREE SHADOWS

I looked and saw your eyes
In the shadow of your hair,
As a traveler sees the stream
In the shadow of the wood;

And I said, "My faint heart sighs,
  Ah me! to linger there,
To drink deep and to dream
  In that sweet solitude."

I looked and saw your heart
  In the shadow of your eyes,
As a seeker sees the gold
  In the shadow of the stream;
And I said, "Ah me! what art
  Should win the immortal prize,
Whose want must make life cold
  And heaven a hollow dream?"

I looked and saw your love
  In the shadow of your heart,
As a diver sees the pearl
  In the shadow of the sea;
And I murmured, not above
  My breath, but all apart—
"Ah! you can love, true girl,
  And is your love for me?"

(1876) 1881

INSOMNIA

THIN are the night-skirts left behind
  By daybreak hours that onward creep,
  And thin, alas! the shred of sleep
That wavers with the spirit's wind;
But in half-dreams that shift and roll
  And still remember and forget,
My soul this hour has drawn your soul
    A little nearer yet.

Our lives, most dear, are never near,
  Our thoughts are never far apart,
  Though all that draws us heart to heart
Seems fainter now and now more clear.
Tonight Love claims his full control,
  And with desire and with regret
My soul this hour has drawn your soul
    A little nearer yet.

Is there a home where heavy earth
  Melts to bright air that breathes no pain,
  Where water leaves no thirst again
And springing fire is Love's new birth?
If faith long bound to one true goal
  May there at length its hope beget,
My soul that hour shall draw your soul
    Forever nearer yet.

1881

THE KING'S TRAGEDY [1]

JAMES I OF SCOTS.—20TH FEBRUARY, 1437

I CATHERINE am a Douglas born,
  A name to all Scots dear;
And Kate Barlass they've called me now
  Through many a waning year.

This old arm's withered now. 'Twas once
  Most deft 'mong maidens all
To reign the steed, to wing the shaft,
  To smite the palm-play ball.

In hall adown the close-linked dance
  It has shone most white and fair;
It has been the rest for a true lord's head,
And many a sweet babe's nursing-bed,
  And the bar to a King's chambère.

Aye, lasses, draw round Kate Barlass,
  And hark with bated breath
How good King James, King Robert's son,
  Was foully done to death.

Through all the days of his gallant youth
  The princely James was pent,
By his friends at first and then by his foes,
  In long imprisonment.

For the elder Prince, the kingdom's heir,
  By treason's murderous brood
Was slain; and the father quaked for the child
  With the royal mortal blood.

I' the Bass Rock fort, by his father's care,
  Was his childhood's life assured;
And Henry the subtle Bolingbroke,
Proud England's King, 'neath the southron yoke
  His youth for long years immured.

[1] Tradition says that Catherine Douglas, in honor of her heroic act when she barred the door with her arm against the murderers of James the First of Scots, received popularly the name of "Barlass." This name remains to her descendants, the Barlas family, in Scotland, who bear for their crest a broken arm. She married Alexander Lovell of Bolunnie.

A few stanzas from King James's lovely poem, known as *The King's Quhair*, are quoted in the course of this ballad. The writer must express regret for the necessity which has compelled him to shorten the ten-syllabled lines to eight syllables, in order that they might harmonize with the ballad metre. [Rossetti's note.]

Yet in all things meet for a kingly man
Himself did he approve;
And the nightingale through his prison-wall
Taught him both lore and love.

For once, when the bird's song drew him close
To the opened window-pane,
In her bowers beneath a lady stood,
A light of life to his sorrowful mood,
Like a lily amid the rain.

And for her sake, to the sweet bird's note,
He framed a sweeter song,
More sweet than ever a poet's heart
Gave yet to the English tongue.

She was a lady of royal blood;
And when, past sorrow and teen,
He stood where still through his crownless years
His Scottish realm had been,
At Scone were the happy lovers crowned,
A heart-wed King and Queen.

But the bird may fall from the bough of youth,
And song be turned to moan,
And Love's storm-cloud be the shadow of Hate,
When the tempest-waves of a troubled State
Are beating against a throne.

Yet well they loved; and the god of Love,
Whom well the King had sung,
Might find on the earth no truer hearts
His lowliest swains among.

From the days when first she rode abroad
With Scottish maids in her train,
I Catherine Douglas won the trust
Of my mistress sweet Queen Jane.

And oft she sighed, "To be born a King!"
And oft along the way
When she saw the homely lovers pass
She has said, "Alack the day!"

Years waned—the loving and toiling years:
Till England's wrong renewed
Drove James, by outrage cast on his crown,
To the open field of feud.

'Twas when the King and his host were met
At the leaguer of Roxbro' hold,
The Queen o' the sudden sought his camp
With a tale of dread to be told.

And she showed him a secret letter writ
That spoke of treasonous strife,
And how a band of his noblest lords
Were sworn to take his life.

"And it may be here or it may be there,
In the camp or the court," she said;
"But for my sake come to your people's arms
And guard your royal head."

Quoth he, "'Tis the fifteenth day of the siege,
And the castle's nigh to yield."
"Oh, face your foes on your throne," she cried,
"And show the power you wield;
And under your Scottish people's love
You shall sit as under your shield."

At the fair Queen's side I stood that day
When he bade them raise the siege,
And back to his Court he sped to know
How the lords would meet their Liege.

But when he summoned his Parliament,
The louring brows hung round,
Like clouds that circle the mountain-head
Ere the first low thunders sound.

For he had tamed the nobles' lust
And curbed their power and pride,
And reached out an arm to right the poor
Through Scotland far and wide;
And many a lordly wrongdoer
By the headsman's axe had died.

'Twas then upspoke Sir Robert Græme,
The bold o'ermastering man,
"O King, in the name of your Three Estates
I set you under their ban!

"For, as your lords made oath to you
Of service and fealty,
Even in likewise you pledged your oath
Their faithful sire to be:—

"Yet all we here that are nobly sprung
Have mourned dear kith and kin
Since first for the Scottish Barons' curse
Did your bloody rule begin."

With that he laid his hands on his King—
"Is this not so, my lords?"
But of all who had sworn to league with him
Not one spake back to his words.

Quoth the King: "Thou speak'st but for one Estate,
Nor doth it avow thy gage.
Let my liege lords hale this traitor hence!"
The Græme fired dark with rage,
"Who works for lesser men than himself,
He earns but a witless wage!"

But soon from the dungeon where he lay
He won by privy plots,
And forth he fled with a price on his head
To the country of the Wild Scots.

And word there came from Sir Robert Græme
To the King at Edinbro':
"No Liege of mine thou art; but I see
From this day forth alone in thee
God's creature, my mortal foe.

"Through thee are my wife and children lost,
My heritage and lands;
And when my God shall show me a way,
Thyself my mortal foe will I slay
With these my proper hands."

Against the coming of Christmastide
That year the King bade call
I' the Black Friars' Charterhouse of Perth
A solemn festival.

And we of his household rode with him
In a close-ranked company;
But not till the sun had sunk from his throne
Did we reach the Scottish Sea.

That eve was clenched for a boding storm,
'Neath a toilsome moon half seen;
The cloud stooped low and the surf rose high;
And where there was a line of the sky,
Wild wings loomed dark between.

And on a rock of the black beach-side
By the veiled moon dimly lit,
There was something seemed to heave with life
As the King drew nigh to it.

And was it only the tossing furze
Or brake of the waste sea-wold?
Or was it an eagle bent to the blast?
When near we came, we knew it at last
For a woman tattered and old.

But it seemed as though by a fire within
Her writhen limbs were wrung;
And as soon as the King was close to her,
She stood up gaunt and strong.

'Twas then the moon sailed clear of the rack
On high in her hollow dome;
And still as aloft with hoary crest
Each clamorous wave rang home,
Like fire in snow the moonlight blazed
Amid the champing foam.

And the woman held his eyes with her eyes:
"O King, thou art come at last;
But thy wraith has haunted the Scottish Sea
To my sight for four years past.

"Four years it is since first I met,
'Twixt the Duchray and the Dhu,
A shape whose feet clung close in a shroud,
And that shape for thine I knew.

"A year again, and on Inchkeith Isle
I saw thee pass in the breeze,
With the cerecloth risen above thy feet
And wound about thy knees.

"And yet a year, in the Links of Forth,
As a wanderer without rest,
Thou cam'st with both thine arms i' the shroud
That clung high up thy breast.

"And in this hour I find thee here,
And well mine eyes may note
That the winding-sheet hath passed thy breast
And risen around thy throat.

"And when I meet thee again, O King,
That of death hast such sore drouth,—
Except thou turn again on this shore,—
The winding-sheet shall have moved once more
And covered thine eyes and mouth.

"O King, whom poor men bless for their King,
Of thy fate be not so fain;
But these my words for God's message take,
And turn thy steed, O King, for her sake
Who rides beside thy rein!"

While the woman spoke, the King's horse reared
As if it would breast the sea,
And the Queen turned pale as she heard on the gale
The voice die dolorously.

When the woman ceased, the steed was still,
But the King gazed on her yet,
And in silence save for the wail of the sea
His eyes and her eyes met.

At last he said, "God's ways are His own;
Man is but shadow and dust.
Last night I prayed by His altar-stone;
Tonight I wend to the Feast of His Son;
And in Him I set my trust.

"I have held my people in sacred charge,
And have not feared the sting
Of proud men's hate—to His will resigned
Who has but one same death for a hind
And one same death for a King.

"And if God in His wisdom have brought close
The day when I must die,
That day by water or fire or air
My feet shall fall in the destined snare
Wherever my road may lie.

"What man can say but the Fiend hath set
Thy sorcery on my path,
My heart with the fear of death to fill,
And turn me against God's very will
To sink in His burning wrath?"

The woman stood as the train rode past,
And moved nor limb nor eye;
And when we were shipped, we saw her there
Still standing against the sky.

As the ship made way, the moon once more
Sank slow in her rising pall;
And I thought of the shrouded wraith of the King,
And I said, "The Heavens know all."

And now, ye lasses, must ye hear
How my name is Kate Barlass—
But a little thing, when all the tale
Is told of the weary mass
Of crime and woe which in Scotland's realm
God's will let come to pass.

'Twas in the Charterhouse of Perth
That the King and all his Court
Were met, the Christmas Feast being done,
For solace and disport.

'Twas a wind-wild eve in February,
And against the casement-pane
The branches smote like summoning hands
And muttered the driving rain.

And when the wind swooped over the lift
And made the whole heaven frown,
It seemed a grip was laid on the walls
To tug the housetop down.

And the Queen was there, more stately fair
Than a lily in garden set;
And the King was loath to stir from her side,
For as on the day when she was his bride,
Even so he loved her yet.

And the Earl of Athole, the King's false friend,
Sat with him at the board;
And Robert Stuart the chamberlain
Who had sold his sovereign Lord.

Yet the traitor Christopher Chaumber there
Would fain have told him all,
And vainly four times that night he strove
To reach the King through the hall.

But the wine is bright at the goblet's brim
Though the poison lurk beneath;
And the apples still are red on the tree
Within whose shade may the adder be
That shall turn thy life to death.

There was a knight of the King's fast friends
Whom he called the King of Love;
And to such bright cheer and courtesy
That name might best behove.

And the King and Queen both loved him well
For his gentle knightliness;
And with him the King, as that eve wore on,
Was playing at the chess.

And the King said (for he thought to jest
  And soothe the Queen thereby),
"In a book 'tis writ that this same year
  A King shall in Scotland die.

"And I have pondered the matter o'er,
  And this have I found, Sir Hugh—
There are but two kings on Scottish ground,
  And those kings are I and you.

"And I have a wife and a newborn heir,
  And you are yourself alone;
So stand you stark at my side with me
  To guard our double throne.

"For here sit I and my wife and child,
  As well your heart shall approve,
In full surrender and soothfastness,
  Beneath your Kingdom of Love."

And the Knight laughed, and the Queen too smiled;
  But I knew her heavy thought,
And I strove to find in the good King's jest
  What cheer might thence be wrought.

And I said, "My Liege, for the Queen's dear love
  Now sing the song that of old
You made, when a captive Prince you lay,
And the nightingale sang sweet on the spray,
  In Windsor's castle-hold."

Then he smiled the smile I knew so well
  When he thought to please the Queen;
The smile which under all bitter frowns
  Of hate that rose between,
Forever dwelt at the poet's heart
  Like the bird of love unseen.

And he kissed her hand and took his harp,
  And the music sweetly rang;
And when the song burst forth, it seemed
  'Twas the nightingale that sang.

"*Worship, ye lovers, on this May;*
  Of bliss your kalends are begun.
Sing with us, Away, Winter, away!
  Come, Summer, the sweet season and sun!
  Awake for shame—your heaven is won—
And amorously your heads lift all;
Thank Love, that you to his grace doth call!"

But when he bent to the Queen, and sang
  The speech whose praise was hers,
It seemed his voice was the voice of the spring
  And the voice of the bygone years.

"*The fairest and the freshest flower*
That ever I saw before that hour,
The which o' the sudden made to start
The blood of my body to my heart.

* * *

Ah sweet, are ye a worldly creature
Or heavenly thing in form of nature?"

And the song was long, and richly stored
  With wonder and beauteous things;
And the harp was tuned to every change
  Of minstrel ministerings;
But when he spoke of the Queen at the last,
  Its strings were his own heart-strings.

"*Unworthy but only of her grace,*
  Upon Love's rock that's easy and sure,
In guerdon of all my love's space
  She took me her humble creäture.
  Thus fell my blissful aventure
In youth of love that from day to day
Flowereth aye new, and further I say.

"*To reckon all the circumstance*
  As happed when lessen gan my sore,
Of my rancour and woeful chance,
  It were too long—I have done therefor.
  And of this flower I say no more
But unto my help her heart hath tended
And even from death her man defended."

"Aye, even from death," to myself I said;
  For I thought of the day when she
Had borne him the news, at Roxbro' siege,
  Of the fell confederacy.

But Death even then took aim as he sang
  With an arrow deadly bright;
And the grinning skull lurked grimly aloof,
And the wings were spread far over the roof
  More dark than the winter night.

Yet truly along the amorous song
  Of Love's high pomp and state,
There were words of Fortune's trackless doom
  And the dreadful face of Fate.

And oft have I heard again in dreams
  The voice of dire appeal
In which the King then sang of the pit
  That is under Fortune's wheel.

"*And under the wheel beheld I there*
  An ugly Pit as deep as hell,
That to behold I quaked for fear.
  And this I heard, that who therein fell
  Came no more up, tidings to tell;
Whereat, astound of the fearful sight,
I wist not what to do for fright."

And oft has my thought called up again
  These words of the changeful song:
"*Wist thou thy pain and thy travàil*
To come, well might'st thou weep and wail!"
  And our wail, O God! is long.

But the song's end was all of his love;
  And well his heart was grac'd
With her smiling lips and her tear-bright eyes
  As his arm went round her waist.

And on the swell of her long fair throat
  Close clung the necklet-chain
As he bent her pearl-tired head aside,
And in the warmth of his love and pride
  He kissed her lips full fain.

And her true face was a rosy red,
  The very red of the rose
That, couched on the happy garden-bed,
  In the summer sunlight glows.

And all the wondrous things of love
  That sang so sweet through the song
Were in the look that met in their eyes,
  And the look was deep and long.

'Twas then a knock came at the outer gate,
  And the usher sought the King.
"The woman you met by the Scottish Sea,
  My Liege, would tell you a thing;
And she says that her present need for speech
  Will bear no gainsaying."

And the King said: "The hour is late;
  To-morrow will serve, I ween."
Then he charged the usher strictly, and said:
  "No word of this to the Queen."

But the usher came again to the King.
  "Shall I call her back?" quoth he;
"For as she went on her way, she cried,
  'Woe! Woe! then the thing must be!' "

And the King paused, but he did not speak.
  Then he called for the Voidee-cup;
And as we heard the twelfth hour strike,
There by true lips and false lips alike
  Was the draft of trust drained up.

So with reverence meet to King and Queen,
  To bed went all from the board;
And the last to leave of the courtly train
Was Robert Stuart the chamberlain
  Who had sold his sovereign lord.

And all the locks of the chamber door
  Had the traitor riven and brast;
And that Fate might win sure way from afar
He had drawn out every bolt and bar
  That made the entrance fast.

And now at midnight he stole his way
  To the moat of the outer wall,
And laid strong hurdles closely across
  Where the traitors' tread should fall.

But we that were the Queen's bower-maids
  Alone were left behind;
And with heed we drew the curtains close
  Against the winter wind.

And now that all was still through the hall,
  More clearly we heard the rain
That clamored ever against the glass
  And the boughs that beat on the pane.

But the fire was bright in the ingle-nook,
  And through empty space around
The shadows cast on the arrased wall
'Mid the pictured kings stood sudden and tall
  Like specters sprung from the ground.

And the bed was dight in a deep alcove;
  And as he stood by the fire
The King was still in talk with the Queen
  While he doffed his goodly attire.

And the song had brought the image back
  Of many a bygone year;
And many a loving word they said
With hand in hand and head laid to head;
  And none of us went anear.

But Love was weeping outside the house,
A child in the piteous rain;
And as he watched the arrow of Death,
He wailed for his own shafts close in the sheath
That never should fly again.

And now beneath the window arose
A wild voice suddenly;
And the King reared straight, but the Queen fell back
As for bitter dule to dree;
And all of us knew the woman's voice
Who spoke by the Scottish Sea.

"O King," she cried, "in an evil hour
They drove me from thy gate;
And yet my voice must rise to thine ears;
But alas! it comes too late!

"Last night at mid-watch, by Aberdour,
When the moon was dead in the skies,
O King, in a death-light of thine own
I saw thy shape arise.

"And in full season, as erst I said,
The doom had gained its growth;
And the shroud had risen above thy neck
And covered thine eyes and mouth.

"And no moon woke, but the pale dawn broke,
And still thy soul stood there;
And I thought its silence cried to my soul
As the first rays crowned its hair.

"Since then have I journeyed fast and fain
In very despite of Fate,
Lest Hope might still be found in God's will;
But they drove me from thy gate.

"For every man on God's ground, O King,
His death grows up from his birth
In a shadow-plant perpetually;
And thine towers high, a black yew-tree,
O'er the Charterhouse of Perth!"

That room was built far out from the house;
And none but we in the room
Might hear the voice that rose beneath,
Nor the tread of the coming doom.

For now there came a torchlight-glare,
And a clang of arms there came;
And not a soul in that space but thought
Of the foe Sir Robert Græme.

Yea, from the country of the Wild Scots,
O'er mountain, valley, and glen,
He had brought with him in murderous league
Three hundred armèd men.

The King knew all in an instant's flash,
And like a King did he stand;
But there was no armor in all the room,
Nor weapon lay to his hand.

And all we women flew to the door
And thought to have made it fast;
But the bolts were gone and the bars were gone
And the locks were riven and brast.

And he caught the pale pale Queen in his arms
As the iron footsteps fell,—
Then loosed her, standing alone, and said,
"Our bliss was our farewell!"

And 'twixt his lips he murmured a prayer,
And he crossed his brow and breast;
And proudly in royal hardihood
Even so with folded arms he stood—
The prize of the bloody quest.

Then on me leaped the Queen like a deer—
"O Catherine, help!" she cried.
And low at his feet we clasped his knees
Together side by side.
"Oh! even a king, for his people's sake,
From treasonous death must hide!"

"For *her* sake most!" I cried, and I marked
The pang that my words could wring.
And the iron tongs from the chimney-nook
I snatched and held to the King—
"Wrench up the plank! and the vault beneath
Shall yield safe harboring."

With brows low-bent, from my eager hand
The heavy heft did he take;
And the plank at his feet he wrenched and tore;
And as he frowned through the open floor,
Again I said, "For her sake!"

Then he cried to the Queen, "God's will be done!"
For her hands were clasped in prayer.
And down he sprang to the inner crypt;
And straight we closed the plank he had ripped
And toiled to smoothe it fair.

(Alas! in that vault a gap once was
Wherethro' the King might have fled;
But three days since close-walled had it been
By his will; for the ball would roll therein
When without at the palm he play'd.)

Then the Queen cried, "Catherine, keep the door,
And I to this will suffice!"
At her word I rose all dazed to my feet,
And my heart was fire and ice.

And louder ever the voices grew,
And the tramp of men in mail;
Until to my brain it seemed to be
As though I tossed on a ship at sea
In the teeth of a crashing gale.

Then back I flew to the rest; and hard
We strove with sinews knit
To force the table against the door;
But we might not compass it.

Then my wild gaze sped far down the hall
To the place of the hearthstone-sill;
And the Queen bent ever above the floor,
For the plank was rising still.

And now the rush was heard on the stair,
And "God, what help?" was our cry.
And was I frenzied or was I bold?
I looked at each empty stanchion-hold,
And no bar but my arm had I!

Like iron felt my arm, as through
The staple I made it pass—
Alack! it was flesh and bone—no more!
'Twas Catherine Douglas sprang to the door,
But I fell back Kate Barlass.

With that they all thronged into the hall,
Half dim to my failing ken;
And the space that was but a void before
Was a crowd of wrathful men.

Behind the door I had fall'n and lay,
Yet my sense was wildly aware,
And for all the pain of my shattered arm
I never fainted there.

Even as I fell, my eyes were cast
Where the King leaped down to the pit;
And lo! the plank was smooth in its place,
And the Queen stood far from it.

And under the litters and through the bed
And within the presses all
The traitors sought for the King, and pierced
The arras around the wall.

And through the chamber they ramped and stormed
Like lions loose in the lair,
And scarce could trust to their very eyes—
For behold! no King was there.

Then one of them seized the Queen, and cried,
"Now tell us, where is thy lord?"
And he held the sharp point over her heart.
She drooped not her eyes nor did she start,
But she answered never a word.

Then the sword half pierced the true true breast;
But it was the Græme's own son
Cried, "This is a woman—we seek a man!"
And away from her girdle-zone
He struck the point of the murderous steel;
And that foul deed was not done.

And forth flowed all the throng like a sea,
And 'twas empty space once more;
And my eyes sought out the wounded Queen
As I lay behind the door.

And I said, "Dear Lady, leave me here,
For I cannot help you now;
But fly while you may, and none shall reck
Of my place here lying low."

And she said, "My Catherine, God help thee!"
Then she looked to the distant floor,
And clasping her hands, "O God help *him*,"
She sobbed, "for we can no more!"

But God He knows what help may mean,
If it mean to live or to die;
And what sore sorrow and mighty moan
On earth it may cost ere yet a throne
Be filled in His house on high.

And now the ladies fled with the Queen;
And through the open door
The night-wind wailed round the empty room
And the rushes shook on the floor.

And the bed drooped low in the dark recess
Whence the arras was rent away;
And the firelight still shone over the space
Where our hidden secret lay.

And the rain had ceased, and the moonbeams lit
The window high in the wall—
Bright beams that on the plank that I knew
Through the painted pane did fall
And gleamed with the splendor of Scotland's crown
And shield armorial.

But then a great wind swept up the skies,
And the climbing moon fell back;
And the royal blazon fled from the floor,
And naught remained on its track;
And high in the darkened window-pane
The shield and the crown were black.

And what I say next I partly saw
And partly I heard in sooth,
And partly since from the murderers' lips
The torture wrung the truth.

For now again came the armèd tread,
And fast through the hall it fell;
But the throng was less—and ere I saw,
By the voice without I could tell
That Robert Stuart had come with them
Who knew that chamber well.

And over the space the Græme strode dark
With his mantle round him flung;
And in his eye was a flaming light
But not a word on his tongue.

And Stuart held a torch to the floor,
And he found the thing he sought;
And they slashed the plank away with their swords;
And O God! I fainted not!

And the traitor held his torch in the gap,
All smoking and smoldering;
And through the vapor and fire, beneath
In the dark crypt's narrow ring,
With a shout that pealed to the room's high roof
They saw their naked King.

Half naked he stood, but stood as one
Who yet could do and dare;
With the crown, the King was stript away,—
The Knight was reft of his battle-array,—
But still the Man was there.

From the rout then stepped a villain forth—
Sir John Hall was his name;
With a knife unsheathed he leapt to the vault
Beneath the torchlight-flame.

Of his person and stature was the King
A man right manly strong,
And mightily by the shoulder-blades
His foe to his feet he flung.

Then the traitor's brother, Sir Thomas Hall,
Sprang down to work his worst;
And the King caught the second man by the neck
And flung him above the first.

And he smote and trampled them under him;
And a long month thence they bare
All black their throats with the grip of his hands
When the hangman's hand came there.

And sore he strove to have had their knives,
But the sharp blades gashed his hands.
Oh, James! so armed, thou hadst battled there
Till help had come of thy bands;
And oh! once more thou hadst held our throne
And ruled thy Scottish lands!

But while the King o'er his foes still raged
With a heart that naught could tame,
Another man sprang down to the crypt;
And with his sword in his hand hard-gripp'd
There stood Sir Robert Græme.

(Now shame on the recreant traitor's heart
Who durst not face his King
Till the body unarmed was wearied out
With two-fold combating!

Ah! well might the people sing and say,
As oft ye have heard aright—
"*O Robert Græme, O Robert Græme,*
Who slew our King, God give thee shame!"
For he slew him not as a knight.)

And the naked King turned round at bay,
  But his strength had passed the goal,
And he could but gasp, "Mine hour is come;
But oh! to succor thine own soul's doom,
  Let a priest now shrive my soul!"

And the traitor looked on the King's spent strength
  And said, "Have I kept my word?—
Yea, King, the mortal pledge that I gave?
No black friar's shrift thy soul shall save,
  But the shrift of this red sword!"

With that he smote his King through the breast;
  And all they three in the pen
Fell on him and stabbed and stabbed him there
  Like merciless murderous men.

Yet seemed it now that Sir Robert Græme,
  Ere the King's last breath was o'er,
Turned sick at heart with the deadly sight
  And would have done no more.

But a cry came from the troop above:
  "If him thou do not slay,
The price of his life that thou dost spare
  Thy forfeit life shall pay!"

O God! what more did I hear or see,
  Or how should I tell the rest?
But there at length our King lay slain
  With sixteen wounds in his breast.

O God! and now did a bell boom forth,
  And the murderers turned and fled;—
Too late, too late, O God, did it sound!—
And I heard the true men mustering round,
  And the cries and the coming tread.

But ere they came, to the black death-gap
  Somewise did I creep and steal;
And lo! or ever I swooned away,
Through the dusk I saw where the white face lay
  In the Pit of Fortune's Wheel.

And now, ye Scottish maids who have heard
  Dread things of the days grown old—
Even at the last, of true Queen Jane
  May somewhat yet be told,
And how she dealt for her dear lord's sake
  Dire vengeance manifold.

'Twas in the Charterhouse of Perth,
  In the fair-lit Death-chapelle,
That the slain King's corpse on bier was laid
  With chaunt and requiem-knell.

And all with royal wealth of balm
  Was the body purified;
And none could trace on the brow and lips
  The death that he had died.

In his robes of state he lay asleep
  With orb and scepter in hand;
And by the crown he wore on his throne
  Was his kingly forehead spann'd.

And, girls, 'twas a sweet sad thing to see
  How the curling golden hair,
As in the day of the poet's youth,
  From the King's crown clustered there.

And if all had come to pass in the brain
  That throbbed beneath those curls,
Then Scots had said in the days to come
That this their soil was a different home
  And a different Scotland, girls!

And the Queen sat by him night and day,
  And oft she knelt in prayer,
All wan and pale in the widow's veil
  That shrouded her shining hair.

And I had got good help of my hurt.
  And only to me some sign
She made; and save the priests that were there
  No face would she see but mine.

And the month of March wore on apace;
  And now fresh couriers fared
Still from the country of the Wild Scots
  With news of the traitors snared.

And still as I told her day by day,
  Her pallor changed to sight,
And the frost grew to a furnace-flame
  That burnt her visage white.

And evermore as I brought her word,
  She bent to her dead King James,
And in the cold ear with fire-drawn breath
  She spoke the traitors' names.

But when the name of Sir Robert Græme
  Was the one she had to give,
I ran to hold her up from the floor;
For the froth was on her lips, and sore
  I feared that she could not live.

And the month of March wore nigh to its end,
  And still was the death-pall spread;
For she would not bury her slaughtered lord
  Till his slayers all were dead.

And now of their dooms dread tidings came,
  And of torments fierce and dire;
And naught she spake,—she had ceased to speak,—
  But her eyes were a soul on fire.

But when I told her the bitter end
  Of the stern and just award,
She leaned o'er the bier, and thrice three times
  She kissed the lips of her lord.

And then she said, "My King, they are dead!"
  And she knelt on the chapel-floor,
And whispered low with a strange proud smile—
  "James, James, they suffered more!"

Last she stood up to her queenly height,
  But she shook like an autumn leaf,
As though the fire wherein she burned
Then left her body, and all were turned
  To winter of life-long grief.

And "O James!" she said—"My James!" she said—
  "Alas for the woful thing,
That a poet true and a friend of man,
In desperate days of bale and ban,
  Should needs be born a King!"

1881

SELECTIONS FROM DANTE GABRIEL ROSSETTI'S LETTERS

I To William Allingham

Sunday [Endorsed July 24, 1854]

Dear Allingham,

I have been waiting to write until I could see Cayley who has my MS. translations (i.e., such as are copied of them—cetera desunt, that is, are not decent), in order that I might send them on to you at the same time as this letter. Not that my writing now implies that I have had vision of Cayley (a fair type of *Divine Comedy*)—of course you can guess that—but merely that every day after dinner it has seemed a very long way from the B. S. to Chancery Lane, and that my interview with the great unshaved seeming no nearer, I may as well write at once, trusting very soon nevertheless to get hold of the Poems and send them, as I should much like to have your dictum, and especially any suggestions of yours, which I wish you would mark on the margin, regardless of the original Italian, as I can always compare what you suggest with that, and see if it be compatible. I am still hoping to get them out as soon as possible, and think I should include the *Vita Nuova* of Dante, which I translated some 5 years ago, and which would only want some revision. Title perhaps thus: *Italian Lyrical Poetry of the First Epoch from Ciullo d'Alcamo to D. Alighieri* (1197–1300); translated in the original metres, including Dante's *Vita Nuova* or autobiography of his youth.

Can you think of any better title? or is this too long?

Maclennan (whom you once met at my rooms) visited Cambridge with my brother the other day, and at some gathering there they met Macmillan, the publisher, to whom Maclennan spoke of my translations, which he expressed every good disposition to publish. He also said he had some time been wishing to propose to Millais, Hunt, and me to illustrate a Life of Christ.

My original poems are all (or all the best) in an aboriginal state, being beginnings, though some of them very long beginnings, and not one, I think, fairly copied. Moreover, I am always hoping to finish those I like, and know they would have no chance if shown to you unfinished, as I am sure they would not please you in that state, and then I should feel disgusted with them. This is the sheer truth. Of short pieces I have seldom or never done anything tolerable, except perhaps sonnets; but if I can find any which I think

To Dr A. Heimann
from his affectionate
D. G. Rossetti
July 1864

THE EARLY ITALIAN POETS

FROM CIULLO D'ALCAMO TO

DANTE ALIGHIERI

(1100-1200-1300)

IN THE ORIGINAL METRES

TOGETHER WITH DANTE'S VITA NUOVA

TRANSLATED BY D. G. ROSSETTI

PART I. POETS CHIEFLY BEFORE DANTE

PART II. DANTE AND HIS CIRCLE

LONDON:

SMITH, ELDER AND CO. 65, CORNHILL.

1861.

The rights of translation and reproduction, as regards all editorial parts of this work, are reserved.

Presentation Copy from Rossetti to Dr. Heimann. (See Appendix I.)

in any sense legible, I will send them with the translations. I wish, if you write anything you care to show, you would reciprocate, as you may be sure I care to see. As a grand installment I send you the Mac Crac sonnet: it hangs over him as yet like the sword of Damocles. I dare say you remember Tennyson's sonnet, *The Kraken:* it is in the MS. book of mine you have by you,—so compare.

MAC CRACKEN[1]

Getting his pictures, like his supper, cheap,
Far, far away in Belfast by the sea,
His scaly, one-eyed, uninvaded sleep
Mac Cracken sleepeth. While the P. R. B.
Must keep the shady side, he walks a swell
Through spungings of perennial growth and height;
And far away in Belfast out of sight,
By many an open do and secret sell
Fresh daubers he make shift to scarify,
And fleece with pliant sheers the slumb'ring green.
There he has lied, though aged, and will lie,
Fattening on ill-got pictures in his sleep,
Till some Pre-Raphael prove for him too deep.
Then once by Hunt and Ruskin to be seen
Insolvent he shall turn, and in the Queen's Bench
die.

You'll find it very close to the original—as well as to fact.

I'll add my last sonnet, made two days ago, though at the risk of seeming trivial after the stern reality of the above:—

As when two men have loved a woman well,
Each hating each; and all in all, deceit;
Since not for either this straight marriage-sheet
And the long pauses of this wedding-bell;
But o'er her grave, the night and day dispel
At last their feud forlorn, with cold and heat;
Nor other than dear friends to death may fleet
The two lives left which most of her can tell:
So separate hopes, that in a soul had wooed
The one same Peace, strove with each other
long;
And Peace before their faces, perish'd since;
So from that soul, in mindful brotherhood,
(When silence may not be) sometimes they
throng
Through high-streets and at many dusty inns.

But my sonnets are not generally finished till I see them again after forgetting them, and this is only 2 days old.

But now about friends. Outside your letter you tell me to tell you something of Woolner, and I cannot recollect whether I mentioned to you that he had written up [sic] touching a statue for which he was competing there, or rather which he stood every chance of getting without competition, until the people determined to ask Eastlake, Dyce, and Mulready about his competency. I have been to Eastlake to see about it, and Millais has written to all three. Between us I think Eastlake is safe, Mulready has not answered either Millais or Dickinson, who also wrote (but he knew Woolner in England, and I know liked him personally, though I do not think he ever saw any work of his); and Dyce has answered Millais that he cannot remember W.'s works but wants to see some. The Wordsworth group is therefore going to be sent to the Royal Academy, that Dyce may see it there. Dyce and Eastlake were both among those members of the Committee who were named in that letter which Woolner got on the occasion of the Wordsworth job, as having stuck out to the last in favour of W.'s model; but it is very possible they did not know his name, as I suppose the competition was anonymous. Thus far as yet about this. Woolner is very probably now on his way to England. I will send you his letter, if you write me that you did not see it, of which I am uncertain.

Hunt has written Millais another letter at last; the first since his second to me, months ago. It was sent to me by M., but I had to send it on to Lear, or would have let you have it, as it is full of curious depths and difficulties in style and matter, and contains an account of his penetrating to the central chamber of the Pyramids. He is at Jerusalem now, where he has taken a house, and seems in great ravishment, so I suppose he is not likely to be back yet. Have you seen the lying dullness of that ass Waagen, anent the Light of the World, in *Times* last week? There is a still more incredible paragraph, amounting to blasphemy, in yesterday's *Athenæum*, which you will see soon. I hope you got the last one.

I spent two or three days at Ridge, near Barnet, with Hannay lately, where he is staying at his father's, and will remain probably for some months. His babe has grown quite beautiful, and I saw him put in a tub in a very vigorous state. Hannay and I walked to St.

[1] Rossetti's sallies against Francis Mac Cracken, a Belfast shipping-agent who bought Pre-Raphælite pictures, were more humorous than angry.

Albans, and saw Bacon's tomb, the Cathedral, etc. We purposed writing to you jointly thence after dinner, but somehow out of the fulness of the stomach the speech wouldn't come. *Satire and Satirists* is out.

I hav'n't seen much lately of Munro, but hope he will come to-morrow evening when Collins and Stephens are to come too. I wish you had met Collins.

Hughes, I think, is in the country again—at Burnham. What a capital sketch of one, though not the best of your face's phases, Hughes did before you left! I suppose it must supersede, for posterity, that railway portrait, which was so decidedly en train. I trust certainly to join Hughes in at any rate one of the illustrations of *Day and Night Songs*, of which I hope his and mine will be worthy—else there is nothing so much spoils a good book as an attempt to embody its ideas, only going halfway. Is *Saint Margaret's Eve* to be in? That would be illustratable. By the bye, Miss S. has made a splendid design from that *Sister Helen* of mine. Those she did at Hastings for the old ballads illustrate *The Lass of Lochryan* and *The Gay Goss Hawk*, but they are only first sketches. As to all you say about her and the hospital, etc., I think just at present, at any rate, she had better keep out, as she has made a design which is practicable for her to paint quietly at my rooms, having convinced herself that nothing which involved her moving constantly from place to place is possible at present. She will begin it now at once, and try at least whether it is possible to carry it on without increased danger to her health. The subject is the *Nativity*, designed in a most lovely and original way. For my own part, the more I think of the B. H. [Brompton Hospital] for her, the more I become convinced that when left there to brood over her inactivity, with images of disease and perhaps death on every side, she could not but feel very desolate and miserable. If it seemed at this moment urgently necessary that she should go there, the matter would be different; but Wilkinson says that he considers her better. I wish, and she wishes, that something should be done by her to make a beginning, and set her mind a little at ease about her pursuit of art, and we think that this more than anything would be likely to have a good effect on her health. It seems hard to me when I look at her sometimes, working or too ill to work, and think how many without one tithe of her genius or greatness of spirit have granted them abundant health and opportunity to labour through the little they can do or will do, while perhaps her soul is never to bloom nor her bright hair to fade, but after hardly escaping from degradation and corruption, all she might have been must sink out again unprofitably in that dark house where she was born. How truly she may say, "No man cared for my soul." I do not mean to make myself an exception, for how long I have known her, and not thought of this till so late—perhaps too late. But it is no use writing more about this subject; and I fear, too, my writing at all about it must prevent your easily believing it to be, as it is, by far the nearest thing to my heart.

I will write you something of my own doings soon, I hope; at present I could only speak of discomfitures. About the publication of the ballads, or indeed of your songs either, it has occurred to me we might reckon Macmillan as one possible string to the bow. Smith ought to be bowstrung himself, or hamstrung, or something, for fighting shy of so much honour. By the bye, I turned up the other day, at my rooms, that copy of Routledge's poets which you bought as a specimen. Ought I to send it back? Good-morning.

Your D. G. Rossetti.

P. S.—I hav'n't seen the Howitts very lately, but A. M. [Anna Mary] is very busy, I know. I shall get there soon. She has the *Folio*, which is beginning to circulate.

P. P. S.—Write soon and I'll answer soon.

II To William Allingham

September 19 [1854]

Dear Allingham,

* * *

I wanted to send you a letter Stephens had from Hunt, but it seems there is some mystic matter in it, so he has copied what I enclose for you. It is the latest news, I believe. The *Chief of Zanquebar* is a lark, but I confess I begrudge him that whole sheet of note paper.

The *Times* on Massey is loathsome indeed. Really some one ought to write to them about that prig from Poe, which has roused Hannay's bile. I've been reading a *Spectator* copy of *Firmilian* in its complete state—on second thought I'll post it now for you instead of describing it. Please return it soon. I've also read some of the *Stones of Venice* having received all Ruskin's books from him, really a splendid present, including even the huge plates of Venetial architecture. I've heard again from him at Chamounix. I've been greatly interested in *Wuthering Heights*, the first novel I've read for an age, and the best (as regards power and sound style) for two ages, except *Sidonia*. But it is a fiend of a book—an incredible monster, combining all the stronger female tendencies from Mrs. Browning to Mrs. Brownrigg. The action is laid in hell,—only it seems places and people have English names there. Did you ever read it?

I think you're quite right about leaving out a few of my translations from the volume, and should like to know which you think. I had thought so myself, but shall copy out all I have done before determining. I am very glad you like them so much, and will send more when copied.

My plan as to their form is, I think, a preface for the first part, containing those previous to Dante, and a connecting essay (but not bulky) for the second part, containing Dante and his contemporaries, as many of them are in the form of correspondence, etc., very interesting, and require some annotation. I think you have few or none of this class. I shall include the *Vita Nuova*, I am almost sure, and then the vol. will be a thick one. I think, if it were possible to bring some or all out first, as you say, in a good magazine, the plan might be a very good one. Indeed, anything that paid would be very useful just now, as I do not forget my debts. I've a longish story more than half done, which might likely be even more marketable in this way. It is not so intensely metaphysical as that in the *Germ*. If I possibly can manage to copy what I've done of it, I'd like to send it you. By the bye, in my last long letter (a long letter, Allingham) I put two sonnets which I'm afraid you didn't like. Pray tell me, too, about the alteration I there proposed in the last lines of one, which you objected to.

I fear this letter has as many I's as Argus: argal it is snobbish.

Tenez vous bien for the present and good bye.

Yours sincerely,

D. G. Rossetti.

III To William Allingham

Finchley, November, 1854

My dear Allingham:

. . . You mention having sent a copy of *Day and Night Songs* to Ruskin: did you remember that I had already given him one? I trust he and you will meet when next in London. He has been back about a month or so, looking very well and in excellent spirits. Perhaps you know that he has joined Maurice's scheme for a *Working Men's College*, which has now begun to be put in operation at 31, Red Lion Square. Ruskin has most liberally undertaken a drawing-class, which he attends every Thursday evening, and he and I had a long confab about plans for teaching. He is most enthusiastic about it, and has so infected me that I think of offering an evening weekly for the same purpose, when I am settled in town again. At present I am hard at work out here on my picture, painting the calf and cart. It has been a fine clear weather, though cold, till now, but these two days the rain has set in (for good, I fear), and driven me to my wits' end, as even were I inclined to paint notwithstanding, the calf would be like a hearth-rug after half an hour's rain; but I suppose I must turn out tomorrow and try. A very disagreeable part of the business is that I am being obliged to a farmer whom I cannot pay for his trouble in providing calf and all, as he insists on being good natured. As for the calf, he kicks and fights all the time he remains tied up, which is 5 or 6 hours daily, and the view of life induced at his early age by experience in art appears to be so melancholy that he punctually attempts suicide by hanging himself at $3\frac{1}{2}$ daily P.M. At these times I have to cut him down, and then shake him up and lick him like blazes. There is a pleasure in it, my dear fellow: the Smithfield drovers are a kind of opium-eaters at it, but a moderate practitioner might perhaps sustain an argument. I hope soon to be back at my rooms, as I have been quite long enough at my rhumes. (The above joke did service for MacCrac's benefit last night.)

Before I came here I had been painting ever so long on a brick wall at Chiswick which is in my foreground. By the bye, that boating sketch of yours is really good in its way, and would bear showing to Ruskin as an original Turner—and perhaps selling to Windus afterwards.

Many thanks for your minute criticism on my ballad, which was just of the kind I wanted. Not, of course, that a British poet is going to knock under on all points;—accordingly, I take care to disagree from you in various respects—as regards abruptnesses, improbabilities, prosaicisms, coarsenesses, and other esses and isms, not more prominent, I think, in my production than in its models. As to dialect there is much to be said, but I doubt much whether, as you say, mine is more Scotticised than many or even the majority of genuine old ballads. If the letter and poem were here, I might perhaps bore you with counter-analysis. But in very many respects I shall benefit greatly by your criticisms, if ever I think the ballad worth working on again, without which it would certainly not be worth printing. . . .

IV To William Allingham

Blackfriars Bridge
Tuesday Evening, 23 January, 1855

Dear Allingham,

. . . The other day Moxon called on me, wanting me to do some of the blocks for the new Tennyson. The artists already engaged are Millais, Hunt, Landseer, Stanfield, Maclise, Creswick, Mulready, and Horsley. The right names would have been Millais, Hunt, Madox Brown, Hughes, a certain lady, and myself. No others. What do you think? Stanfield is to do *Break, break*, because there is the sea in it, and *Ulysses*, too, because there are ships. Landseer has *Lady Godiva*—and all in that way. Each artist, it seems, is to do about half-a-dozen, but I hardly expect to manage so many, as I find the work of drawing on wood particularly trying to the eyes. I have not begun even designing for them yet, but fancy I shall try the *Vision of Sin* and *Palace of Art*, etc.,—those where one can allegorize on one's own hook on the subject of the poem, without killing for oneself and every one a distinct idea of the poet's. This, I fancy, is always the upshot of illustrated editions,—Tennyson, Allingham, or any one,—unless where the poetry is so absolutely narrative as in the old ballads, for instance. Are we to try the experiment ever in their regard? There are one or two or more of Tennyson's in narrative,—but generally the worst, I think,—*Lady Clare*, *Lord of Burleigh*, to wit.

News must have grown so old since I wrote to you that most likely I shall forget the most of it. For myself, I got nearly finished (and shall make it do for quite, I think) with my calf and cart at Finchley, when I was laid up all of a sudden for some little time, through the wind blowing my picture down on my leg, which caused it to gather and create a nuisance. Since I got over this I have been water-colouring again, somewhat against the grain, and have not yet got my picture to London. I began my class last night at the Working Men's College: it is for the figure, quite a separate thing from Ruskin's, who teaches foliage. I have set one of them as a model to the rest, till they can find themselves another model. I intend them to draw only from nature, and some of them—two or three—show unmistakable aptitude—almost all more than one could ever have looked for. Ruskin's class has progressed astonishingly, and I must try to keep pace with him. The class proceeds quite on a family footing, and I feel sure, will prove amusing. . . .

V To William Allingham

Saturday, March 18, 1855

Dear Allingham,

. . . About a week ago, Ruskin saw and bought on the spot every scrap of designs hitherto produced by Miss Siddal. He declared that they were far better than mine, or almost than any one's, and seemed quite wild with delight at getting them. He asked me to name a price for them, after asking and hearing that they were for sale; and I, of course, considering the immense advantage of their getting them into his hands, named a very low price, £25, which he declared to be too low even for a low price, and increased to £30. He is going to have them splendidly mounted and bound together in gold; and no doubt this will be a real opening for her, as it is already a great assistance and encouragement. He has since written her a letter, which I enclose, and which, as you see, promises further usefulness. She is now doing the designs wanted. Pray, AFTER READING IT, ENCLOSE IT AND RETURN IT TO ME AT ONCE, as I want much to have it by me and show to one or two friends; and accompany it with a word or two as I want to know that you are not quite disgusted with me on account of that unlucky job. Ruskin's praise is beginning to bear fruit already. I wrote about it to Woolner, who has been staying for a week or two with the Tennysons; and they, hearing that several of Miss Siddal's designs were from Tennyson, and being told about Ruskin, etc., wish her exceedingly to join in the illustrated edition; and Mrs. T. wrote immediately to Moxon about it, declaring that she had rather pay for Miss S.'s designs herself than not have them in the book. There is only one damper in this affair, and that is the lesson as to the difficulty of wood-drawing which I am still wincing under;[1] but she and I must adopt a simpler method, and then I hope for better luck. All this will, I know, give you real pleasure, so I write it at such length.

By the bye, Miss Siddal reminded me after the sale of the design, which was my doing and quite unexpected, that we owe you a compensation, as one of them, the two nigger girls playing to the lovers, belonged to you, which I had, I am ashamed to say, forgotten, but remembered when she named it. She means to do another and better one for you, from one of your own poems, and meanwhile apologises with me for the mistake.

Yours affectionately,
D. G. Rossetti.

VI To William Allingham

May 11, 1855

Dear Allingham,

Thanks for the returned MSS., which I ought to have acknowledged before, but this is absolutely the first evening I have been able to find since then for letter-writing. Your remarks in the margin I value much, and am sure I shall adopt many of the suggestions, if ever that book come to aught. Indeed, I have a further large relay of them in course of copying, which may perhaps meet your eye, if you care for them, and would no doubt benefit under your hand. I take one out at long intervals and copy and yawn; but "is it not all in vain?" A man of many journeys must needs find his path crossed here and there by some old hobby, each time grown seedier and sleepier, and sometimes he may say:—"Now will I saddle thee, for where our pastures lay, there they lie;" and, no doubt, so they do; but even one's hobby is not so soft to ride as to lay one's head on; and so they two snooze together. If either is ever woke up, it may be the hobby, which somebody saddles awry to fetch the sexton, to risk a cheap bell or so for him who is still asleep, and have him enough remembered to be forgotten.

This fine writing, you'll say, is wronging you of news. Yesterday I took the MSS. to Ruskin, who, on hearing that they came from you, said you were one to whom he owed and would yet pay a letter of thanks, which he was sorry remained so long unwritten; and therewith spoke again with great delight of your poems. He was not delighted, by the bye, with that design beyond designation which your readers are to suppose I did; and he even saw it to great advantage, as I had been over the proof with white, to get Dalziel to alter parts of it. I have since given it him to do so, and have seen it in part done. Well! I have supped full with horrors, served (out) in three courses, which, as Hood says, can't be helped. I wish D—— only had his desert as a finish.

[1] An illustration which Rossetti did for Allingham's book turned out very badly when made into a woodcut. Rossetti blamed Dalziel, who cut the block, for the disaster. Dalziel's defence was a question, — "How is one to engrave a drawing that is partly in ink, partly in pencil, and partly in red chalk?" Another reference to the episode occurs in the next letter.

Meanwhile, how is Millais' design which I have not yet seen? I hope it is only as good as his picture at the R. A.—the most wonderful thing he has done, except perhaps the *Huguenot*. He had an awful row with the hanging committee, who had put it above the level of the eye; but J. E. M. yelled for several hours and threatened to resign, till they put it right. Anthony's landscape of *Stratford-on-Avon*, a noble thing badly hung—though, of course, not so badly. They have been running wilder than ever this year in insolence and dishonesty; have actually turned out a drawing by Hunt (his pictures have not reached England; I heard from him the other day, and he is likely to be back in two or three months); put the 4 best landscapes in the place—3 by Inchbold, 1 by some new Davis—quite out of sight; kicked out 2 pictures by one Arthur Hughes—*Orlando*, and a most admirable little full-length of a child in a flannel night-gown; and played "warious games of that sort." There is a big picture of *Cimabue*, one of his works in procession, by a new man, living abroad, named Leighton—a huge thing, which the Queen has bought, which every one talks of. The R. A.'s have been gasping for years for some one to back against Hunt and Millais, and here they have him; a fact which makes some people do the picture injustice in return. It was very uninteresting to me at first sight; but on looking more at it, I think there is great richness of arrangement—a quality which, when really existing, as it does in the best old masters, and perhaps hitherto in no living man—at any rate English—ranks among the great qualities.

But I am not quite sure yet either of this or of the faculty for colour, which I suspect exists very strongly, but is certainly at present under a thick veil of paint; owing, I fancy, to too much continental study. One undoubted excellence it has—facility without much neatness or ultra-cleverness in the execution, which is greatly like that of Paul Veronese; and the colour may mature in future works to the same resemblance, I fancy. There is much feeling for beauty, too, in the women. As for purely intellectual qualities, expression, intention, etc., there is little as yet of them; but I think that in art richness of arrangement is so nearly allied to these that where it exists (in an earnest man) they will probably supervene. However, the choice of the subject, though interesting in a certain way, leaves one quite in the dark as to what faculty the man may have for representing incident or passionate emotion. But I believe, as far as this showing goes, that he possesses qualities which the mass of our artists aim at chiefly, and only seem to possess; whether he have those of which neither they nor he give sign, I cannot yet tell; but he is said to be only 24 years old. There is something very French in his work, at present, which is the most disagreeable thing about it; but this I dare say would leave him if he came to England. . . .

VII · To William Allingham

London, July 4 [1855]

Dear Allingham,

. . . I had to break off in the above, [the letter was begun June 25, at Clevedon] and go on with it to-day, instead of beginning afresh, to prove that I was not waiting for you to write, as I remembered well owing you two or three, though one of mine had been lost for some time. Yours was very welcome on Monday. Going on about *The Music Master*, I see the sentence already written looks very iniquitous, and perhaps is; but one can only speak of one's own needs and cravings: and I must confess to a need, in narrative dramatic poetry (unless so simple in structure as *Auld Robin Gray*, for instance), of something rather "exciting," and indeed I believe something of the "romantic" element, to rouse my mind to anything like the moods produced by personal emotion in my own life. That sentence is shockingly ill worded, but Keats's narratives would be of the kind I mean. Not that I would place the expressions of pure love and life, or of any calm, gradual feeling or experience, one step below their place,—the very highest; but I think them better conveyed at less length, and chiefly as from oneself. Were I speaking to any one else, I might instance (as indeed I often do) the best of your own lyrics as examples; and these will always have for me much more attraction than *The Music Master*. The latter, I think, by its calm subject and course during a longish reading, chiefly awakens contemplation, like a walk on a fine day with a churchyard in it, instead of rousing one like a part of one's own life, and leaving one to walk it off as one might live it off. The only part where I remember being much affected was at the old woman's narrative of Milly's gradual decline. Of course the poem has artistic beauties constantly, though I think it flags a little at some of its joints, and am not sure that its turning-point would not have turned in vain for me at first reading, if I had not in time remembered your account of the story one day on a walk. After all, I fancy its chief want is that it should accompany a few more stories of deeper incident and passion from the same hand, when what seem to me its shortcomings might, I believe, as a leavening of the mass, become des qualités. As I have stated them, too, they are merely matters of feeling, and those who felt differently (as Patmore, who thinks the poem perfect) might probably be at the higher point of view. P. was here last night with Cayley and one or two more. We sat all the evening on my balcony, and had ice and strawberries there, and I wished for you many times, and meanwhile put in your book as a substitute (having, you may be sure, torn out that thing of Dalziel's). . . .

VIII To William Allingham

Sunday, 25 Nov., '55

Dear Allingham,

I'm quite ashamed of the long delay in answering your letter—especially when I remember (as such things generally happen) that on receiving it I sat down to answer on the spot, and was only compelled by some accident to postpone it—of course no further than the same evening. I believe that must be a good month ago.

I have not the letter by me in beginning this answer, but remember it opened with a question about Routledge. At that time I could only have given a very bad answer on this head: as some time after the publication of your vol. I had (hearing nothing from R. & Co.) sent in my "small account," but with no result up to the time of hearing from you, which was ever so long an interval; I having, on their showing no signs of life, let the matter go its way. Some short time ago, however, Hughes hearing this, in a fit of virtuous and friendly indignation, gave them a look up about it, and they have now paid me at the same rate as him, with which I am perfectly well satisfied. I know no further about Millais, and am very sorry you should have been worried about it all.

I have just come back from a ten days' trip to Paris, in pursuit of various things and persons. The Brownings are there for the winter, on account of the cholera at Florence, and had previously been some time in London, where I saw them a good many times, and indeed may boast of some intimacy with the glorious Robert by this time. What a magnificent series is *Men and Women*. Of course you have it half by heart ere this. The comparative stagnation, even among those I see, and complete torpor elsewhere, which greet this my Elixir of Life, are awful signs of the times to me—"and I must hold my peace!"—for it isn't fair to Browning (besides, indeed, being too much trouble) to bicker and flicker about it. I fancy we shall agree pretty well on favourites, though one's mind has no right to be quite made up so soon on such a subject. For my own part, I don't reckon I've read them at all yet, as I only got them the day before leaving town, and couldn't possibly read them then,—the best proof to you how hard at work I was for once,—so heard them read by William; since then read them on the journey again, and some a third time at intervals; but they'll bear lots of squeezing yet. My prime favourites hitherto (without the book by me) are *Childe Roland*, *Bp. Blougram*, *Karshish*, *the Contemporary*, *Lippo Lippi*, *Cleon*, and *Popularity;* about the other ones I can't quite speak yet, and their names don't stick in my head: but I'm afraid *The Heretic's Tragedy* rather gave me the gripes at first, though I've tried since to think it didn't, on finding the *Athenæum* similarly affected.

8 Jan., 1856

A month and a half actually, dear A., since the last sheet, already long behindhand, yet which has lain in my drawer ever since, till it is too late now to wish you merry Christmas, too late to wish you happy New Year, only not too late to feel just the same towards you as if I were the best correspondent in the world, and to know you feel the same towards me. I am sure, too, you believe that, little as I do to deserve and obtain frequent letters from you, your letters are as great a pleasure to me as any I get,—greater, I think, than any, except certain ones which you'll be glad to hear come now dated Nice, their writer having left England three months ago, and benefiting already, I trust, by the genial climate she is now enjoying, which, while that bitter cold weather was ailing us here, remained as warm as the best English May.

Many thanks indeed for your new year's gift,—a most delightful one. Old Blake is quite as loveable by his oddities as by his genius, and the drawings to the Ballads abound with both. The two nearly faultless are the *Eagle* and the *Hermit's Dog*. Ruskin's favourite (who has just been looking at it) is the *Horse;* but I can't myself quite get over the intensity of comic decorum in the brute's face. He seems absolutely snuffling with propriety. The *Lion* seems singing a comic song with a pen behind his ear, but the glimpse of distant landscape below is lovely. The only drawing where the comic element riots almost unrebuked is the one of the dog jumping down the crocodile.

As regards engraving, these drawings, with the *Job*, present the only good medium between etching and formal line that I ever met with. I see that in coming to me the book returns home; having set out from No. 6 Bridge St., Blackfriars, just 50 years ago. Strange to think of it as then, new literature and art. Those ballads of Hayley—some of the quaintest human bosh in the world—picked their way, no doubt, in highly respectable quarters, where poor Blake's unadorned hero at Page 1 was probably often stared at, and sometimes torn out.

I broke off at the last sheet in mid-Browning. Of course I've been drenching myself with him at intervals since, only he gets carried off by friends, and I have him not always by me. I wish you'd let me hear in a speedy answer (there's cheek for you!) all you think about his new work, and it shall nerve me to express my ideas in return; but since I have given up poetry as a pursuit of my own, I really find my thoughts on the subject generally require a starting-point from somebody else to bring them into activity; and as you're the only man I know who'd be really in my mood of receptiveness in regard to Browning, and as I can't get at you, I've been bottled up ever since *M. and W.* came out. By the bye, I don't reckon William—the intensity of fellow-feeling on the subject making the discussion of it between us rather flat. I went the other day to a 1d. reading-room,—a real blessing—which now occupies the place of Burford's Panorama, and where all papers and reviews whatsoever are taken in. There I saw two articles on Browning—one by Masson—really thoroughly appreciative, but slow—in the *British Quarterly*—and one by a certain Brimley, of Trin. Col., Cam., in *Fraser*,—the cheekiest of human products. This man, less than two years ago, had not read a line of Browning, as I know through my brother; and I have no doubt he has just read him up to write this article; which opens, nevertheless, with accusations against R. B. of nothing less than personal selfishness and vanity, so plumply put as to be justifiable by nothing less than personal intimacy of many years. When I went to Paris, I took my copy of *Men and Women* (which had been sent me the day before) with me, and got B. to write my name in it. Did you get a copy? We spoke often of you,—he with great personal and poetical regard—I of course with loathing. I inclose herewith a note which reached me before the book, containing emendations. Copy them, if you please, and return the note. I spent some most delightful time with Browning at Paris, both in the evenings and at the Louvre where (and throughout conversation) I found his knowledge of early Italian art beyond that of any one I ever met,—encyclopædically beyond that of Ruskin himself. What a jolly thing is *Old Pictures at Florence!* It seems all the pictures desired by the poet are in his possession in fact. At Paris I met his father, and in London an uncle of his and his sister, who, it appears, performed the singular female feat of copying *Sordello* for him, to which some of its eccentricities may possibly be referred. However, she remembers it all, and even *Squarcialupe*, *Zin the Horrid*, and the sad dishevelled ghost. But no doubt you know her. The father and uncle—father especially —show just that submissive yet highly cheerful and capable simplicity of character which often, I think, appears in the family of a great man who uses at last what the others have kept for him. The father is a complete oddity —with a real genius for drawing—but caring for nothing in the least except Dutch boors,—fancy the father of Browning!—and as innocent as a child. In the New Volumes, the only thing he seemed to care for much was that about the Sermon to the Jews.

At B.'s house at Paris I met a miraculous French critic named Milsand, who actually before ever meeting Browning knew his works to the very dregs—and had even been years in search of Pauline,—how heard of I know not,—and wrote a famous article on him in the *Revue des Deux Mondes*, through which B. somehow came to know him. I hear he has translated some of the *Men and Women*, which must be curiosities. In London I showed Browning Miss Siddal's drawing from *Pippa Passes*, with which he was delighted beyond measure, and wanted excessively to know her. However, though afterwards she was in Paris at the same time that he and I were, he only met her once for a few minutes: she being very unwell then and averse to going anywhere; and Mrs. B. being forbidden to go out, and so unable to call. What a delightfully unliterary person Mrs. B. is to meet! During two evenings when Tennyson was at their house in London, Mrs. Browning left T. with her husband and William and me (who were the fortunate remnant of the male party) to discuss the universe, and gave all her attention to some certainly not very exciting ladies in the next room. . . . I made a sketch of Tennyson reading, which I gave to Browning, and afterwards duplicated it for Miss S. . . . He is quite as glorious in his way as Browning, and perhaps of the 2 even more impressive on the whole personally. . . .

Have you reviewed Browning anywhere, or shall you? Hannay has my copy for a similar purpose, but I see no fruit coming of it. In B.'s note enclosed, the portrait referred to is one of himself by Page, an American living at Rome, which he has confided to my care with some idea of its going to the R. A. After much delay I have only just got hold of it, and am much disappointed in it, so shall advise its non-exhibition, as a portrait of Browning oughtn't to be put out of sight or kicked out. I have done one in water-colours myself, which hangs now over my mantelpiece, and which every one says is very like. Next time I have the chance I shall paint him in oil, and probably Mrs. B. too, with him. Ruskin, on reading *Men and Women* (and with it some of the other works which he didn't know before), declared them rebelliously to be a mass of conundrums, and compelled me to sit down before him and lay siege for one whole night; the result of which was that he sent me next morning a bulky letter to be forwarded to B., in which I trust he told him he was the greatest man since Shakespeare.

Of other friends there is little news I think. Hughes is painting *Porphyrio* and *Madeline* in 3 compartments. Hunt is (I believe with better grounds than hitherto) expected back almost daily. Woolner has made some lovely sketches in clay. Patmore has just lost his father, and is on the eve of bringing out the *Espousals*. Ruskin's new volume will be in my hands I believe, on Tuesday. WHAT ARE YOU AT? I have just seen a capital sonnet of yours,—a star shot as rubbish into a dust-bin labelled the *Idler*. I've done lots of work lately (i.e., for me), but all in water-colours, and nearly all for Ruskin. Among the later of my drawings finished are *Francesca da Rimini* in 3 compartments; *Dante cut by Beatrice at a marriage feast; Lancelot and Guenever parting at tomb of Arthur;* at finishing of each of which, and of various others I have done, I have very much wished you were by to show them to. I'm sorry to say my modern picture remains untouched since last Xmas; but this has really not been through idleness, as I have done more during the past year than for a long while previously, and I think I can myself perceive an advance in my later work. Pray, again, what are you up to?

I've left no space for the French Exhibition,

to which indeed I devoted only one of the 10 days I spent in Paris,—my head not being a teetotum nor my mind an old-clothes shop. Delacroix is one of the mighty ones of the earth, and Ingres misses being so creditably. There is a German, Knaus, who is perfection in a way something between Hogarth and Wilkie; Millais and Hunt are marvels and omens. Water-colour Hunt and Lewis are the only things in their department. The rest is silence; or must be so for the present.

What do you think of Browning being able to read *The Mystake?* Could you?

Yours affectionately,

D. G. Rossetti.

IX To William Allingham

Thursday [Endorsed March 7, 1856]

Dear Allingham,

... That notice in *The Oxford and Cambridge Mag.* was the most gratifying thing by far that ever happened to me—being unmistakeably [sic] genuine. I thought it must be by your old acquaintance Fryer, of Cambridge, he having called on me once about those same things. But it turns out to be by a certain youthful Jones, who was in London the other day, and whom (being known to some of the Working Men's Coll. council) I have not met. One of the nicest young fellows in—*Dreamland.* For there most of the writers in that miraculous piece of literature seem to be. Surely this cometh in some wise of the *Germ*, with which it might bind up. But how much more the right thing—in kind—than the *Idler!* I see it monthly. The new No. has a story called *A Dream*, which really is remarkable, I think, in colour....

X To William Allingham

Mrs. Green's, 17, Orange Grove, Bath

[Postmark, December 18, 1856]

My dear Allingham,

Very glad was I of your undeserved letter. How long have I meant to write to you! It was sent on to me here, where I have been a week or two, and may still be a week.

The piece of news freshest in my mind is *Aurora Leigh*,—an astounding work, surely. You said nothing of it. I know that St. Francis and Poverty do not wed in these days of St. James' Church, with rows of portrait figures on either side, and the corners neatly finished with angels. I know that if a blind man were to enter the room this evening and talk to me for some hours, I should, with the best intentions, be in danger of twigging his blindness before the right moment came, if such there were, for the chord in the orchestra and the proper theatrical start; yet with all my knowledge I have felt something like a bug ever since reading *Aurora Leigh*. Oh, the wonder of it! and oh, the bore of writing about it.

The Brownings are long gone back now, and with them one of my delights,—an evening resort where I never felt unhappy. How large a part of the real world, I wonder, are those two small people?—taking meanwhile so little room in any railway carriage, and hardly needing a double bed at the inn.

Little Read has been in London lately, and I saw him once or twice—just the same as ever —with a new wife, I hear, but he did not say so. They are going on to Rome.

* * *

You will see no more of the poor *Oxford and Cambridge*. It was "too like the Spirit of Germ, Down, down!" and has vanished into the witches' cauldron. Morris and Jones have now been some time settled in London, and are both, I find, wonders after their kind. Jones is doing designs which quite put one to shame, so full are they of everything—*Aurora Leighs* of art. He will take the lead in no time. Morris, besides writing those capital tales, writes poems which are really better than the tales, though one or two short ones in the Mag. were not of his best. By the bye, though, *The Chapel in Lyoness* was glorious,—did you not think so? In his last tale—*Golden Wings*—the printer, after no doubt considering himself personally insulted all along by the nature of those compositions, wound up matters with an avenging blow, and inserted some comic touches, such as prefixing *old* to *woman* or *lady* in several instances, and other commissions and omissions. Morris's facility at poetising puts one in a rage. He has been writing at all for little more than a year, I believe, and has already poetry enough for a big book. You know he is a millionaire, and buys pictures. He bought Hughes's *April Love*, and lately several water-colours of mine, and a landscape of Brown,—indeed, seems as if he would never stop, as I have 3 or 4 more commissions from him. To one of my water-colours, called *The Blue Closet*, he has written a stunning poem. You would think him one of the finest little fellows alive—with a touch of the incoherent, but a real man. He and Jones have taken those rooms in Red Lion Square which poor Deverell and I used to have, and where the only sign of life, when I found them the other day, on going to enquire, all dusty and unused, was an address written up by us on the wall of a bedroom,—so pale and watery had been all subsequent inmates, not a trace of whom remained. Morris is rather doing the magnificent there, and is having some intensely mediaeval furniture made—tables and chairs like incubi and succubi. He and I have painted the back of a chair with figures and inscriptions in gules and vert and azure, and we are all three going to cover a cabinet with pictures.

Morris means to be an architect, and to that end has set about becoming a painter, at which he is making progress. In all illumination and work of that kind he is quite unrivalled by anything modern that I know—Ruskin says, better than anything ancient. By the bye, it was Ruskin made me alter that line in *The Blessed D.* I had never meant to show him any of my versifyings, but he wrote to me one day asking if I knew the author of *Nineveh*, and could introduce him—being really ignorant, as I found—so after that the flesh was weak. Indeed, I do not know that it will not end in a volume of mine, one of these days. But first I want to bring out those translations, which I have not found time yet to get together for Macmillan, so busy have I been. Do you not think Vernon Lushington's *Carlyle* very good in *O. and C. Mag?* His things and his brother's, Morris's, and the one or two by Jones (who never wrote before or since) are the staple of that magazine. The rest—had better have been —silence. Another matter which shall be silence—mainly—on my part is your picture at Tom Taylor's—merciful silence, O! W. A.! were it better, wouldn't I tell its faults!

A lady, to whose doings you once inferred a comparison of the above, has been, you will be sorry to hear, most terribly ill a month or two ago, but is now somewhat better again. She has begun an oil picture from that wood-block subject, though a good deal altered, but it seems as if her health could set all her efforts at naught. There were some thoughts of her going this winter to Algiers (whither Barbara Smith and her sick sister are gone) but Miss Siddal seems to have no fancy for the place. Medical men are recommending it this winter, but earthquakes seem rather a shy feature of the entertainment.

Have you heard of the Howitts? I have seen them, though not very lately, and fear that Miss H. is anything but well. *Spiritualism* has begun to be in the ascendant at the Hermitage, and this to a degree which you could not conceive possible without witnessing it. Do not say anything to anybody, though. I elicited from W. Howitt, before his family, his opinion of it with some trouble, and found it to be a modified form of my own, which of course I give without reserve—but the ladies of the house seem to take but one view of the subject, and, astounding as it may appear, Mrs. Browning has given in her adherence. I hope *Aurora Leigh* is not to be followed by "that style only." Browning, of course, pockets his hands and shakes his mane over the question, with occasional foamings at the mouth, and he and I laid siege to the subject one night, but to no purpose.

Here we are in the 3rd sheet and 3rd hour, A.M. Goodbye for the present. Do let us keep it up now.

Yours ever affectionately,
D. G. Rossetti.

XI To William Allingham

Paris, Wednesday [June, 1860]

My dear Allingham,

Have you heard yet that I'm married? The news is hardly a month old, so it may not have reached you, though I have meant to write you word of it all along, as you are one of the few valued friends whom Lizzie and I have in common as yet; nor, as the circle spreads, will she be likely to feel a warmer regard for any than she does for you.

Of her health all I can say is that it is possible to give rather better news of it than I could have given a month ago. Paris seems to agree so well with her that I am fearful of returning to London (which, however, we must do in a day or two) lest it should throw her back into the terrible state of illness she had been in for some time before. But in that case I shall make up my mind to settle in Paris for a time, as I could no doubt paint here well enough. In any case I expect a move, as winter comes on, will be necessary.

You know I have been meaning to inflict my vol. of MS. rhymes on you for some time, but have been so busy lately and wanted to copy a little more first. I shall try and send them yet. When shall we be likely to see you again in London? Jones is married, too, only a week ago. He and his wife (a charming and most gifted little woman) were to have met us in Paris, but he has not been well enough to travel with pleasure.

With love from both of us I remain,

Your affectionate

D. G. Rossetti.

XII To William Allingham

[September or October, 1860]

My dear Allingham,

I am sending you them things at last, i.e., the MSS. which Ruskin has only just returned me; I having asked him to send one—viz. *Jenny*, to the *Cornhill* for me—he of course refusing to send that, offering to send some of the mystical ones that I don't care to print by themselves.

My delay has been partly through this, and partly through wanting to add more before sending them to you. But they'd better e'en go now, for no more will get done for the nonce. The only one very unfinished, both in what is written and unwritten (I think), is *The Bride's Chamber*. I wish you'd specially tell me of any you don't think worth including. You will find that your advice has been followed often (if you remember what you gave), and so it is not time wasted to advise me. When I think how old most of these things are, it seems like a sort of mania to keep thinking of them still; but I suppose one's leaning still to them depends mainly on their having no trade associations, and being still a sort of thing of one's own. I have no definite ideas as to doing anything with them, but should like, even if they lie at rest, to make them as good as I can.

And what are you doing? How goes the sawdust poem you spoke of? And is it to be visible that wine is packed therein, or is a pure surface of sawdust, betraying no wine, the duty of the modern bard? So may the shade of Wordsworth smile on him and repay him by reading all his (W.'s) Poems through to him when the kindred Spirits meet.

I wish you were in town, to see you sometimes, for I literally see no one now except Madox Brown pretty often, and even he is gone now to join Morris, who is out of reach at Upton, and with them is married Jones painting the inner walls of the house that Top[1] built. But as for the neighbours, when they see men pourtrayed by Jones upon the walls, the images of the Chaldeans pourtrayed (by him!) in Extract Vermilion, exceeding all probability in dyed attire upon their heads, after the manner of no Babylonians of any Chaldea, the land of any one's nativity,—as soon as they see them with their eyes, shall they not account him doting, and send messengers into Colney Hatch?

Lizzie has been rather better of late, I hope—certainly not subject to the same extent to violent fits of illness. She is at Brighton just now for a few days, but I know I may send you her love with mine. We are sorely put to it for a pied-à-terre, every house we try for seeming to slip through just as we think we have got it. For one in Church Row, Hampstead, which has just escaped us, my heart is in doleful dumps; it having a glorious old-world garden worth 200 a year to me for backgrounds.

Do let me hear from you (to Blkfrs [Blackfriars]) when you have got the book which goes with this, and believe me

Yours affectionately,

D. G. Rossetti.

William is gone to Florence to old Browning.

1 "Top" or "Topsy" was the nickname given by the group to William Morris.

XIII To William Allingham

[January, 1861]

Dear Allingham,

I hope you've had all the luck of the Season, and that it's to last all the year. I write this more specially to say that I sent off the Magdalene photograph some time back to Green, and that I hope it reached you safely.

Lizzie is pretty well for her, and we are in expectation (but this is quite in confidence, as such things are better waited for quietly) of a little accident which has just befallen Topsy and Mrs. T. who have become parients [sic]. Ours however will not be (if at all) for 2 or 3 months yet.

We have got our rooms quite jolly now. Our drawing-room is a beauty, I assure you, already, and on the first country trip we make we shall have it newly papered from a design of mine which I have an opportunity of getting made by a paper-manufacturer, somewhat as below. I shall have it printed on common brown packing-paper and on blue grocer's-paper, to try which is best. [Here follows, in the original letter, a design of the wall-paper.]

The trees are to stand the whole height of the room, so that the effect will be slighter and quieter than in the sketch, where the tops look too large. Of course they will be wholly conventional: the stems and the fruit will be Venetian Red, the leaves black—the fruit, however, will have a line of yellow to indicate roundness and distinguish it from the stem; the lines of the ground black, and the stars yellow with a white ring round them. The red and black will be made of the same key as the brown or blue of the ground, so that the effect of the whole will be rather sombre, but I think rich, also. When we get the paper up, we shall have the doors and wainscoting painted summer-house green. We got into the room in such a hurry that we had no time to do anything to the paper and painting, which had just been done by the landlord. I should like you to see how nice the rooms are looking, and how many nice things we have got in them.

However you have yet to see a real wonder of the age—viz., Topsy's house, which baffles all description now.

We are organising (but this is quite under the rose as yet) a company for the production of furniture and decoration of all kinds, for the sale of which we are going to open an actual shop! The men concerned are Madox Brown, Jones, Topsy, Webb (the architect of T.'s house), P. P. Marshall, Faulkner, and myself. Each of us is now producing, at his own charges, one or two (and some of us more) things towards the stock. We are not intending to compete with ——'s costly rubbish or anything of that sort, but to give real good taste at the price as far as possible of ordinary furniture. We expect to start in some shape about May or June, but not to go to any expense in premises at first.

Here is the last piece of news, and other there is none available I think. Description of pictures in hand is barren work. I am making use of your notes on my Poems and bettering some of them, I hope. I am now going to print all those written except the *Bride's Chamber*, and those you advised omitting. When printed, I shall see how much more is needed for a volume, and try to do it in the evenings, while the printed sheets wait, and then bring the book out. I am actually continuing the printing of the *Translations* now, and hope to get both books out together.

What became of the Poem you meant to send to *Once a Week?* Did you send it? I have not seen the paper regularly, but should have nosed it out nevertheless, I fancy, if it had appeared.

Write me as soon as you can, and believe me, with love from Lizzie and self,

Your affectionate

D. G. Rossetti.

XIV To Madox Brown

16 Cheyne Walk

16 June, 1866

My dear Brown,—If you can conveniently, will you let me have that big Scrap-book again to-morrow (Friday). My reason is that I believe I shall begin a portrait of Janey on Saturday; and, if I do it in the same action as the drawing in the book, I might square it off life-size before she comes.

I was very sorry to bolt in that way so early

from such a really jolly party as yours. But, Brown, if you had known! Doubtless you, in common with your guests, admired my elegant langour and easy grace. But O Brown, had Truth herself been there to rend away my sheltering coat! Behold me!

Physical condition and mental attitude.

The burden of conscious fat and hypocrisy, the stings of remorse, the haunting dread of exposure as every motion wafted the outer garment to this side or to that, the senses quickened to catch the fatal sound of further rents,—all this and more—but let us draw once more over the scene that veil which Fate respected. Might not Tupper say truly, "Let not Man, fattening, leave his dress-trowsers too long unworn, lest a worse thing come unto him"?—Your affectionate

D. G. R.

XV To William Allingham

22 March, 1867

My dear Allingham,

I inclose an answer to Aidé, which will tell you my mind, except that I may add to you that £1400 is £1400 to me, or rather to any body rather than me as I never see it at all, and that my plan is to rent, not to buy. I have been pot-boiling to an extent lately that does not hold out much hope of estate buying or even renting. Moreover, as I haven't been outside my door for months in the daytime, I shouldn't have had much opportunity of enjoying pastime and pleasances. I have accordingly no news whatever, except of my easel, which is too mean a slave to small needs to be worth reporting on. I do not see a fellow of any sort really much oftener than you do, I imagine.

I lately heard from Aubrey de Vere, with a request to my sister and self to contribute something to a verse collection. We looked up scraps, and were promised proofs, but these come not; and I imagine that the result when in type will be the usual incentive to blasphemy. I wonder do you sail in the same boat—or "funny," as it is likely to prove according to my experience.

Yours always,

D. G. Rossetti.

XVI To Madox Brown

Cheyne Walk, Chelsea

15 August 1867

My dear Brown,—Dreffle bad, ain't it?

All would be well as to the £10, were it not that I had on Monday to send that very sum to Lizzie's brother Harry, who has had the small-pox; and (what is worse) I have reason to fear at present that it may have been lost in the post, though registered. However, I suppose I must draw on Leyland on my own account, and can then do the needful. I wished to avoid doing this further till all his daubs were daubed; but other matters than yours will force me to it, I fear. As for the wretch Gambart, his d——d £200 (minus 5s. which he stopped for something like cab-hire) are had and spent now—and now he wants more done to the drawings, and has left two of them with me. Let him write, and won't he get it!—this at least will be a tit-bit. I'm on the right side of the hedge this time. . . .—Your affectionate

D. G R.

XVII To Charles Eliot Norton

16 Cheyne Walk

19 April, 1869

My dear Norton,—You expressed a kind intention of visiting my studio by daylight. . .

I have long wished to make a proposal to you. It would be a great satisfaction to me to possess the drawing you have by my late Wife, of *Clerk Saunders*, to add to those of hers which are now mine, and which every year teaches me to value more and more as works of genius, even apart from other personal interest to me. None would ever have been parted with, of course, had we not then hoped that these little things were but preludes to much greater ones—a hope which was never to be realized. I would not offer you a profit on the drawing, as you would probably not accept that; but would esteem it a great favour if you would let me have it at its original price —35 guineas, if I recollect;—or would, if you preferred it, make a chalk drawing of Mrs. Norton, life-size, of the kind for which I am in the habit of charging 60 to 80 guineas. This I should do with the greatest pleasure, and consider myself still greatly your debtor.—Ever yours,

D. G. Rossetti.

XVIII To Charles Eliot Norton, Florence

16 Cheyne Walk, Chelsea
22 January, 1870

My dear Norton,—I am truly ashamed of the above date, and of all my sins of omission; including perhaps some omitted sins,—for these too strike one as mistakes occasionally as life wears on. However, at present such is not my remorse; for most certainly it would have been no sin, but a duty, to have written ere now to one who must think he remembers me much better than I do him—and to whom at any rate I am grateful for past friendship, and even for future instalments of the same, so sure I am of them, whatever my poor deserts may be.

I duly got long ago the drawing of *Clerk Saunders*, and was truly pleased to see its face again. It even surprised me by its great merit of feeling and execution, and now takes its place among its fellows on my drawing-room walls. I have had the silver flat gilded; which makes a wonderful improvement in the tone, which the former leaden tint damaged terribly. Silver flats are one of the wilder experiments of our frame-making in those days.

I hope when I see you again you will be pleased with the drawing of Janey Morris destined for you, which is now being finished. If you like however (you know), I will send it to you in Florence. But, before parting with it, I shall have to make a replica for my own keeping, as I like it on the whole the best of the drawings I have made of her, and never mean to let any more go out of my own possession. The chance of such a model is too precious for the ordinary market. You will be grieved to have heard (as you have doubtless done) how very ill she has been since you were in London; nor can I give a good account of her now, though she has been somewhat better just lately.

I have been thinking what there may be to tell you of my work, and am obliged to confess that it does not amount to much. I have been a good deal out of sorts, nor did I benefit much in the autumn by a trip to Scotland. However, poor health has not been the only cause of the little I have got done in painting, as I lost some time preparing a volume of poems for the press, which I hope to get out in the Spring. I have communicated with Mr. Fields of Boston (whom you doubtless know) as to his undertaking an American reprint; since, when he called on me with Longfellow last summer, he expressed a wish to reprint some early poetry of mine he had seen somewhere. I have not as yet received his reply. My proposed publisher, Ellis, had received a request for sheets of the poems from Messrs Roberts the American publishers, but I thought after what Fields said it was best to write to him.

Of course you know how great a success Morris's new *Earthly Paradise* is; and no doubt you agree with all the most reliable opinions, that there is some real advance as to strength and human character in this volume even over the former one. The *Gudrun* is surely on the whole one of the finest poems in the English language. I believe you have been hearing from Ned Jones, so need not convey news of him and his.

What a delightful picture—indeed, a most precious one—your Giorgione turns out after passing through the hands of a skillful picture-cleaner! Why in the world the change in it had ever been made it is difficult to conceive; except indeed that it appears to have been part of a larger picture, the rest of which may presumably have been lost, and an attempt then made to give the fragment the look of a whole at the expense of its beauty and real character. It seems, as now cleaned, to be in a quite perfect state, and needed I believe no retouching whatever. The colour is so golden that it gives an idea of being actually painted on a gold ground, though this does not seem on examination to be the case.

We have a very fine specimen of an American over here now in the person of Stillman, whom you know. I have known him in a fragmentary way for many years, but am seeing more of him now, and like him extremely.

I hope you are all enjoying yourselves in Florence, and above all that you have no ill-health to interfere with the fitness of things around you. Will you give my very best and truest remembrances to all yours, and accept them for yourself, believing me your sincere friend,

D. G. Rossetti.

XIX To F. S. Ellis

16, Cheyne Walk, Chelsea
[February 14, 1870]

My dear Ellis,

I think perhaps my book might be advertised now for once—what say you? merely

To appear shortly—
Poems
by Dante Gabriel Rossetti
F. S. Ellis, &c.

I hope in a few days to get the final alterations & resetting done to the sheets already in type, & have serious thoughts of going into retreat for 2 or 3 weeks in the country to see about adding a sheet or two more. I suppose the close of April will be the right moment to bring it out. A review is promised for the May number of "Fraser." I want to appear when I know a few reviews are ready, to keep spite at bay and leave it gaping and goggling without a chance of a good snarl. I fancy Mr. Buchanan probably has his natural organ of speech hiched up for an utterance. It would be nice if he had to make it a silent emanation & got nothing but the smell to enjoy.

This might perhaps be managed if a few good men were in the field at the outset. Morris proposes to do the "Academy," & I believe Swinburne will come out in the "Fortnightly."

Perhaps to-morrow—certainly in a day or two—I'll send you the sketches for the cover & flyleaf. I suppose the latter ought to be cut on wood. If so, I have a draughtsman who can draw it for the purpose.

Of course Strangeways must charge the printing of the prose tale to me.

Ever yours,
D. G. Rossetti.

P.S. Of course the binding question will be subject to your opinion as to expense.

XX To F. S. Ellis

[March 18 or 19, 1870]

Dear Ellis,

Now you *will* swear. I have all of a sudden been very strongly advised, I think from a specially trustworthy quarter, that my book wd begin very much better & please a much larger class of readers at the outset if it opened with the "Blessed Damozel" & not with "Troy Town," which latter is supposed (and I think rightly) to be likely to please a smaller class. Now my own wish in the case wd be to put "Troy Town" on to follow the "Burden of Nineveh," & so secure 3 seats[1] in mental or moral things at the outset. All I want you to do is just to tell me what it would cost to cancel & reprint these 2 sheets. I would stand the whole expense if I decided on having it done. Would you let me know at once?

Ever yours,
D. G. R.

Of course I suppose the types are still up.

XXI To F. S. Ellis

Monday, Scalands
[April 11, 1870]

Dear Ellis,

I believe the tenor of my letter yesterday was towards a notion that the outside journals (the unattached, as "Athenæum," "Saturday" &c.) had better get their copies on the 14th. But on reflection I think it is undesirable perhaps to let them have these till a week later. However, you are the better judge on this point, & I am willing to leave it entirely in your hands. Whatever you do will be for the best without need of further correspondence.

I find I have a most formidable list of copies I shall have to send myself. I will forward this to you. Meanwhile I send the names of those who I think wd be likely to "do" the book somewhere & might be worth while to send to on that account as I said before. Those marked X are doing it already.[2]

Ever yours,
D. G. Rossetti.

[1] "The word appears to be 'seats,' but is not very clearly written." [Doughty's note.]

[2] Rossetti forgot to mark the X against the names in question.

P. S. Papers for which the thing is being done are

Pall Mall (Colvin)
Globe (Knight)
Edinburgh Courant (Alexander)
Fraser (Skelton)
Fortnightly (Swinburne)
Academy (Morris)
Quarterly (Colvin)

but this last is a spec. I believe.

I hear you heard the Topsaic article.

XXII To Charles Eliot Norton

Scalands, Robertsbridge, Sussex
11, April 1870

My dear Norton,—What very, very kind letters from yourself and Mrs. Norton! May I mass the answers I owe into one? It seems natural, when the unity of kindness is so complete in both.

I have been here for a month or rather more now, having left London in very poor health, and not having much to boast of at this writing. There is everything to tempt me in your invitation, I need hardly say; but the weakness I have long been experiencing in my eyes forbids sight-seeing, and to enter Florence under such a prohibition for the first time would be, I fear, too tantalizing. Better dulness and commonplace at home than such a change so circumscribed. Besides, if work may be, work I must for many reasons, and the day has arrived to try again. So I fear there is little likelihood (though not perhaps quite none) of my seeing you in Florence. Meanwhile, I may say truly that no distant place or persons seem to me so pleasantly inviting, but for dismal drawbacks.

I hope you will soon get my volume of poems. It shall reach you as soon as it is out, which will I believe be for certain before the end of this month. Some friendly hands are already at work on reviews of it: Morris for *The Academy*—Swinburne for the *Fortnightly*—Stillman for an American paper—and others.

Stillman is my companion in these solitudes, and a very good, helpful, friendly companion he is, as you will judge from your knowledge of him. The house (which has a good studio in it) has been lent us by an old friend, Mrs. Bodichon, an excellent landscape-painter herself, as you perhaps know. I think you have heard from Stillman that he has . . . got himself engaged. . . . He has gone up to town to-day, . . . and I am left to lonely letter-writing. She is a noble girl—in beauty, in sweetness, and in artistic gifts; and the sky should seem very warm and calm above, and the road in front bright and clear, and all ill things left behind for ever, to him who starts anew on his life-journey; foot to foot and hand in hand with her. . . . I warmly hope that happiness is in store for them both. She is a pearl among women, and there are points in Stillman's character of the manliest and truest I know. His prospects are at present however very uncertain. . . .

I hope that when you get my book you will agree with me as to the justness of my including all it contains. I say this because there are a few things—and notably a poem called *Jenny*—which will raise objections in some quarters. I only know that they have been written neither recklessly nor aggressively (moods which I think are sure to result in the ruin of Art), but from a true impulse to deal with subjects which seem to me capable of being brought rightly within Art's province. Of my own position I feel sure, and so wait the final result without apprehension.

Our friends are all well, with the exception, I most deeply grieve to say, of Mrs. Morris, who is still in a very delicate state. She and Morris have been in this neighbourhood lately, and are coming again; and I trust the change may prove eventually of some decided benefit to her, as signs of this have already become apparent.

Good-bye, my dear Norton. I am going for a walk now in a pleasing but not very sympathetic entourage of leafless woods and English associations which I have grown old in, but am never perhaps quite at home with. I envy you your Italian ones, and shall be very glad to hear more of the study you propose to undertake of Michelangelo's unpublished letters. I hope the fit of queer health which baulked you at the outset is over now, and that you and yours are all well. To all of you my best love, and the assurance that I am ever yours and theirs,

D. G. Rossetti.

XXIII To F. S. Ellis

Scalands, Saturday
[April 23, 1870]

Dear Ellis,

This delay is most infernal, and renders the promptness of friendly critics a nuisance instead of a benefit. It will *most* certainly put up the backs of the unfriendly ones, & that with no chance of their backsides coming to the level of our boot-toes for a rejoinder.

I see now that you are "letting me down easy," and thus whatever day I proposed to come up I sh^{d} receive a notification at the last moment that it must be one day later.

Now I say *Wednesday*—looking of course for the due result. However if Tuesday will do, let me know in time: though of course I know it wont. *Now* I hope you're swearing in *your* turn.

I see the adv^{t} in "Pall Mall" with a *rather* long line ab^{t} the binding. It seems to me that "bound from the author's design" w^{d} be shorter & better.

Ever yours,
D. G. R.

XXIV To F. S. Ellis

Saturday
[May 14, 1870]

Dear Ellis,

I'm glad you're not bent in any case on giving up Swinburne's book. It would be a pity—a great pity—to break up the little knot of congenial writers at last got together. I fancy my 2nd edition ought to come out as soon as possible; and I, for my part, sh^{d} not object to some portion of it being issued with the old back if that would hasten matters. However you are best judge.

The *Saturday* article to-day is a bestial one—almost confessedly incompetent, but not hurtful, which one soon learns, in the sty of British Criticism, to think the only point worth considering.

Morris's article is direct & complete—an honour and a profit to the book.

Ever yours,
D. G. Rossetti.

Would it be worth while looking up some of the best reviews of the 1st ed^{n} of my Translations to print in the adv^{ts}? I remember good ones in *Spectator* & (I think) *Westminster* or some Quarterly.

ALGERNON CHARLES SWINBURNE

[April 5, 1837–April 10, 1909]

Of Sir John Swinburne, his grandfather, whose life, he said, would be better worth writing than his own, Swinburne wrote to Edmund Clarence Stedman: "Born and brought up in France, his father a naturalized Frenchman and his mother a lady of the house of Polignac (a quaint political relationship for me), my grandfather never left France till called away at twenty-five on the falling in of such English estates as confiscation had left to a family which in every Catholic rebellion from the days of my own Queen Mary to those of Charles Edward had given their blood like water and their lands like dust for the Stuarts." . . . "He was the friend of the great Turner," he continues, "and of many lesser artists; I wish to God he had discovered Blake! . . . To the last [and he died at ninety-eight] he was far liker in appearance and manners to an old French nobleman (I have heard my mother remark it) than to any type of the average English gentlemen."

An ancestress of Sir John's (i.e., a Lady Swinburne) bore thirty children to one husband, and people thronged about her carriage "to see the living and thriving mother of thirty sons and daughters." "When this race," he writes on, "chose at last to produce a poet, it would have been at least remarkable if he had been content to write nothing but hymns and idyls for clergymen and young ladies to read out in chapels and drawing rooms."

Of his father, Admiral Swinburne, he said nothing except that he was the second son of this Sir John. Lady Jane, his gentle mother, was the daughter of the Earl of Ashburnham, whose family, after one of its members followed Charles I to his death, broke away from the cause of the Stuarts and increased in wealth and titles.

Swinburne was a strange-looking being with his "little pallid face," large head, green eyes, and great cloud of flaming red hair. At the age of twelve he went to Eton, where he did a vast amount of reading, "poured forth torrents of verse," and, when he was convalescing from an occasional school-boy sickness, horrified the maid who was reading to him by taking the jam-pot from his tray and turning it upside down on her head. After five years at Eton he traveled abroad for a while, returning with a deepened love of the sea, whose salt, he once wrote, "must have been in my blood before I was born."

Just before he was nineteen he entered Balliol College, Oxford, with some half-formed notion in his head of going into the Church. At Oxford he met Jowett, who soon after became Master of Balliol, and Dante Gabriel Rossetti, who, with a group of young Pre-Raphaelites, had come to the University to decorate the walls of the Union. Swinburne found association with these young medievalists greatly to his taste, and he watched their work with glowing interest, often entering into discussions with them on the subject of art, and on at least one occasion unfolding to them such a conception of Heaven as drove the curious dons, who overheard him, into shocked flight. His university career was, as he himself said, "a total and scandalous failure." He neglected his studies, he read the poets endlessly, he joined the "Old Mortality," a band of youthful extremists at Balliol presided over by an engaging Scotsman, John Nichol, who knew Mazzini, the man Swinburne "most loved and revered on earth." Nichol, alas, set Swinburne a pattern at drinking whisky and brandy that was fatal to one of his perilously balanced nerves. Swinburne, following Nichol's lead, listened, drank, preached, drank again, and shouted out a dangerous and violent republicanism, to a private college audience for a while, but soon to the general public.

At first Jowett, who loved Swinburne, explained him and excused him with the words, "It's all youth!" But Swinburne grew more and more neglectful of his college work, more and more outspoken in his republicanism, and finally Jowett, fearing that Balliol might be driven to expel a poet, as University College had been driven to expel Shelley, decided that the young rebel should be rusticated for a term. His actions continued outrageous during his period of rustication, however, and when he returned to Balliol for another trial all his old bad habits went with him. He left Oxford very soon after his second entrance there, nothing good having come of his four college years except, perhaps, his stimulating companionship with such men of genius as Pater, Symonds, Morris, Burne-Jones, and Rossetti.

In 1860, the year he left Oxford, Swinburne published his first volume, containing two plays in verse, *The Queen Mother* and *Rosamond*. The book fell flat, Swinburne's comment on it being that it "was the stillest of all still-born books." In 1865 he brought out *Atalanta in Calydon*, a poem in the form of a Greek tragedy, dedicated to Walter Savage Landor, whom he had met in Italy in 1864. The audacious *Atalanta*, which was really an attack on religion, found an immediate if small audience, the intoxication of its language serving to hide from many readers what, if they had studied it with sober intelligence, they would have considered a sinister assault upon some of their most cherished beliefs. To speak of God as "the supreme evil" was to be guilty of an impiety that no orthodox Victorian could forgive.

If the ease and brilliance of its language hid from many readers the paganism of *Atalanta*, all England believed it saw Swinburne for what he really was when, in 1866, his *Poems and Ballads* appeared. Almost overnight the poet became notorious. Dallas, reviewer for *The Times*, and John Morley, of the *Saturday Review*, each had a large share in bringing this about. Dallas read the book and ran to Moxon, the publisher, with the threat that if he did not withdraw it, Dallas would denounce it and destroy it. Frightened, the publisher withdrew it, an act which Swinburne considered an effort to swamp his book when "the storm of warm water began to seethe and rage in the British tea-kettle." He withdrew all his books from Moxon and "declined any further dealings with such a den of thieves." Morley himself a liberal-radical, did not notice the revolutionary poems in the volume, but turned his pen on those dealing with vagaries of sex, and said of them that they were the work of "a mind all aflame with the feverish carnality of a schoolboy," one who was "an unclean, fiery imp from the pit." The poet received anonymous letters threatening him with mutilation and even with death. And yet it would not be easy to find anything in the guilty volume more wicked than

> Time turns the old days to derision,
> Our loves into corpses or wives;
> And marriage and death and division
> Make barren our lives.

The fact that the young liberals "went about chanting these new astonishing melodies" did not take the curse from Swinburne. His name, says a recent writer, "was to all sober-minded Englishmen a synonym for a scandalous sensualist."

Swinburne continued to write with feverish energy in the lull following the tempest evoked by *Poems and Ballads*. In the same year of that volume *Notes on Poems and Reviews* appeared, and in 1867 came his "A Song of Italy" and "William Blake." *Songs before Sunrise*, a volume which followed a warning given to him by Mazzini, the exiled Italian liberator, that he should write "no more love frenzy," appeared in 1871. In it he speaks in his customary bold note his detestation of kings and priests, but there are those who doubt that his poetry was improved by the change of subject from love to liberty. This volume was followed by *Bothwell* in 1874, by *Erectheus*, a second Greek tragedy in English verse, and by another *Poems and Ballads* in 1878. This second volume of *Poems and Ballads* is more subdued in tone and subject than the first and contains such fine poems as "The Forsaken Garden" and the impressive elegies for Baudelaire and Gautier.

Unfortunately during these crowded years the habits fanned by Nichol and others of the "Old Mortality" club at Oxford flamed with a new violence, and in 1879, his nerves overstimulated by drink and his entire body weakened by overwork and by a variety of dissipations, alarming epileptic seizures fastened upon the poet, and he suffered complete physical collapse. At this crisis his mother sent for Watts-Dunton, a literary solicitor, who, although he had been shocked by the first *Poems and Ballads*, yet felt the magic of them and looked with real affection upon their author. Watts forced Swinburne to go with him to the Pines, a little villa in Putney, where for thirty years the poet lived in luxurious captivity, Watts relieving him of every material responsibility, dictating his actions, and, to a large extent directing his thinking.

Swinburne wrote much in this thirty-year period, but the poetry he produced was not that of the Swinburne of the 'sixties and 'seventies, with the possible exception of two poems which he had begun before his break. In 1881 he published the first of these, *Mary Stuart*, a drama, and in 1882 the second, *Tristram of Lyonesse*, a romantic poem of great excellence, marred, some say, by the "proper" lyrics "advised" by Watts-Dunton to give respectability to a poem in which there were passages of the earlier Swinburnian glow. Numerous other publications followed these, both prose and verse, but only rarely was there a poem of the fire and spirit that marked the work of the earlier Swinburne. Some of his literary criticism attained a degree of distinction: his *Miscellanies*, e.g., his monographs on Shakespeare, Victor Hugo, and Ben Jonson, and his acute and interesting studies of some of the modern English writers.

Swinburne's elder and, it would seem, greater contemporaries, disapproving the diffuseness in his work, accused him of youthful immaturity. Tennyson spoke of him as "Master Swinburne"; Matthew Arnold called him "a pseudo-Shelley" and said, "his fatal habit of using one hundred words where one would suffice always offends me." Carlyle, who may always be depended upon to slay his fellowman with a phrase, is reported to have said that Swinburne's poetry was "the miaulings of a delirious cat"; Browning found his verse "a fuzz of words."

But the very thing that these elder contemporaries condemned in Swinburne remains the one thing about him that serves for a marvel to readers of today—his genius for assembling, ordering, and bending words until it would seem that they can no further. It is not that his words are musical only—they are always that—but that he so interfuses sound and meaning that the two things become one. Swinburne's readers remember words, not objects. "The bad poet," writes Mr. T. S. Eliot, "dwells partly in a world of words, and he never can get them to fit. Only a man of genius could dwell so exclusively and consistently among words as Swinburne." Doubtless what has been called his "marvellous metrical inventiveness" arose out of his exclusive and consistent dwelling among words.

This poet who exalted freedom, social and individual, who gave up Christianity without a regret and turned to the worship of "our immemorial Mother, the earth," who loved sensuous beauty and a pagan world, and who made great place in art for the passions of men and women, declared that he wrote simply in submissive obedience to Sir Philip Sidney's precept, "Look in thine heart, and write." "These poems" (*Songs before Sunrise*), he said, "and others which followed or preceded them in print, were inspired by such faith as is born of devotion and reverence: not by such faith, if faith it may be called, as is synonymous with servility or compatible with prostration of an abject or wavering spirit and a submissive or dethroned intelligence."

"Born of devotion and reverence." Doubtless it is a sincere and impressive declaration, but certainly one that the outer public, and many of the intimate inner group even, would challenge. One thing beyond challenge is that some of Swinburne's best work, howsoever born, is making an abiding place for itself in the libraries of readers who are discriminating in their choice of poetry.

A SONG IN TIME OF ORDER
1852

PUSH hard across the sand,
For the salt wind gathers breath;
Shoulder and wrist and hand,
Push hard as the push of death.

The wind is as iron that rings,
The foam-heads loosen and flee;
It swells and welters and swings,
The pulse of the tide of the sea.

And up on the yellow cliff
The long corn flickers and shakes;
Push, for the wind holds stiff,
And the gunwale dips and rakes.

Good hap to the fresh fierce weather,
The quiver and beat of the sea!
While three men hold together,
The kingdoms are less by three.

Out to the sea with her there,
Out with her over the sand,
Let the kings keep the earth for their share!
We have done with the sharers of land.

They have tied the world in a tether,
They have bought over God with a fee;
While three men hold together,
The kingdoms are less by three.

We have done with the kisses that sting,
The thief's mouth red from the feast,
The blood on the hands of the king,
And the lie at the lips of the priest.

Will they tie the winds in a tether,
Put a bit in the jaws of the sea?
While three men hold together,
The kingdoms are less by three.

Let our flag run out straight in the wind!
The old red shall be floated again
When the ranks that are thin shall be thinned,
When the names that were twenty are ten;

When the devil's riddle is mastered
And the galley-bench creaks with a Pope,
We shall see Buonaparte the bastard
Kick heels with his throat in a rope.

While the shepherd sets wolves on his sheep
And the emperor halters his kine,
While Shame is a watchman asleep
And Faith is a keeper of swine.

Let the wind shake our flag like a feather,
Like the plumes of the foam of the sea!
While three men hold together,
The kingdoms are less by three.

All the world has its burdens to bear,
From Cayenne to the Austrian whips;
Forth, with the rain in our hair
And the salt sweet foam in our lips;

In the teeth of the hard glad weather,
In the blown wet face of the sea;
While three men hold together,
The kingdoms are less by three.

1862

FAUSTINE

Ave Faustina Imperatrix, morituri te salutant

LEAN back, and get some minutes' peace;
Let your head lean
Back to the shoulder with its fleece
Of locks, Faustine.

The shapely silver shoulder stoops,
Weighed over clean
With state of splendid hair that droops
Each side, Faustine.

Let me go over your good gifts
That crown you queen;
A queen whose kingdom ebbs and shifts
Each week, Faustine.

Bright heavy brow well gathered up:
White gloss and sheen;
Carved lips that make my lips a cup
To drink, Faustine.

Wine and rank poison, milk and blood,
Being mixed therein
Since first the devil threw dice with God
For you, Faustine.

Your naked new-born soul, their stake,
Stood blind between;
God said "let him that wins her take
And keep Faustine."

But this time Satan throve, no doubt;
  Long since, I ween,
God's part in you was battered out;
  Long since, Faustine.

The die rang sideways as it fell,
  Rang cracked and thin,
Like a man's laughter heard in hell
  Far down, Faustine.

A shadow of laughter like a sigh,
  Dead sorrow's kin;
So rang, thrown down, the devil's die
  That won Faustine.

A suckling of his breed you were,
  One hard to wean;
But God, who lost you, left you fair,
  We see, Faustine.

You have the face that suits a woman
  For her soul's screen—
The sort of beauty that's called human
  In hell, Faustine.

You could do all things but be good
  Or chaste of mien;
And that you would not if you could,
  We know, Faustine.

Even he who cast seven devils out
  Of Magdalene
Could hardly do as much, I doubt,
  For you, Faustine.

Did Satan make you to spite God?
  Or did God mean
To scourge with scorpions for a rod
  Our sins, Faustine?

I know what queen at first you were,
  As though I had seen
Red gold and black imperious hair
  Twice crown Faustine.

As if your fed sarcophagus
  Spared flesh and skin,
You come back face to face with us,
  The same Faustine.

She loved the games men played with death,
  Where death must win;
As though the slain man's blood and breath
  Revived Faustine.

Nets caught the pike, pikes tore the net;
  Lithe limbs and lean
From drained-out pores dripped thick red sweat
  To soothe Faustine.

She drank the steaming drift and dust
  Blown off the scene;
Blood could not ease the bitter lust
  That galled Faustine.

All round the foul fat furrows reeked,
  Where blood sank in;
The circus splashed and seethed and shrieked
  All round Faustine.

But these are gone now: years entomb
  The dust and din;
Yea, even the bath's fierce reek and fume
  That slew Faustine.

Was life worth living then? and now
  Is life worth sin?
Where are the imperial years? and how
  Are you, Faustine?

Your soul forgot her joys, forgot
  Her times of teen;
Yea, this life likewise will you not
  Forget, Faustine?

For in the time we know not of
  Did fate begin
Weaving the web of days that wove
  Your doom, Faustine.

The threads were wet with wine, and all
  Were smooth to spin;
They wove you like a Bacchanal,
  The first Faustine.

And Bacchus cast your mates and you
  Wild grapes to glean;
Your flower-like lips dashed with dew
  From his, Faustine.

Your drenched loose hands were stretched to hold
  The vine's wet green,
Long ere they coined in Roman gold
  Your face, Faustine.

Then after change of soaring feather
  And winnowing fin,
You woke in weeks of feverish weather,
  A new Faustine.

A star upon your birthday burned,
  Whose fierce serene
Red pulseless planet never yearned
  In heaven, Faustine.

Stray breaths of Sapphic song that blew
  Through Mitylene
Shook the fierce quivering blood in you
  By night, Faustine.

The shameless nameless love that makes
  Hell's iron gin
Shut on you like a trap that breaks
  The soul, Faustine.

And when your veins were void and dead,
  What ghosts unclean
Swarmed round the straitened barren bed
  That hid Faustine?

What sterile growths of sexless root
  Or epicene?
What flower of kisses without fruit
  Of love, Faustine?

What adders came to shed their coats?
  What coiled obscene
Small serpents with soft stretching throats
  Caressed Faustine?

But the time came of famished hours,
  Maimed loves and mean,
This ghastly thin-faced time of ours,
  To spoil Faustine.

You seem a thing that hinges hold,
  A love-machine
With clockwork joints of supple gold—
  No more, Faustine.

Not godless, for you serve one God,
  The Lampsacene,
Who metes the gardens with his rod;
  Your lord, Faustine.

If one should love you with real love
  (Such things have been,
Things your fair face knows nothing of,
  It seems, Faustine);

That clear hair heavily bound back,
  The lights wherein
Shift from dead blue to burnt-up black;
  Your throat, Faustine,

Strong, heavy, throwing out the face
  And hard bright chin
And shameful scornful lips that grace
  Their shame, Faustine,

Curled lips, long since half kissed away,
  Still sweet and keen;
You'd give him—poison shall we say?
  Or what, Faustine?

1862

From ATALANTA IN CALYDON

I WHEN THE HOUNDS OF SPRING

WHEN the hounds of spring are on winter's traces,
  The mother of months in meadow or plain
Fills the shadows and windy places
  With lisp of leaves and ripple of rain;
And the brown bright nightingale amorous
Is half assuaged for Itylus,
For the Thracian ships and the foreign faces,
  The tongueless vigil, and all the pain.

Come with bows bent and with emptying of quivers,
  Maiden most perfect, lady of light,
With a noise of winds and many rivers,
  With a clamour of waters, and with might;
Bind on thy sandals, O thou most fleet,
Over the splendour and speed of thy feet;
For the faint east quickens, the wan west shivers,
  Round the feet of the day and the feet of the night.

Where shall we find her, how shall we sing to her,
  Fold our hands round her knees, and cling?
O that man's heart were as fire and could spring to her,
  Fire, or the strength of the streams that spring!
For the stars and the winds are unto her
As raiment, as songs of the harp-player;
For the risen stars and the fallen cling to her,
  And the southwest-wind and the west-wind sing.

For winter's rains and ruins are over,
    And all the season of snows and sins;
The days dividing lover and lover,
    The light that loses, the night that wins;
And time remembered is grief forgotten,
And frosts are slain and flowers begotten,
And in green underwood and cover
    Blossom by blossom the spring begins.

The full streams feed on flower of rushes,
    Ripe grasses trammel a travelling foot,
The faint fresh flame of the young year flushes
    From leaf to flower and flower to fruit;
And fruit and leaf are as gold and fire,
And the oat is heard above the lyre,
And the hoofèd heel of a satyr crushes
    The chestnut-husk at the chestnut-root.

And Pan by noon and Bacchus by night,
    Fleeter of foot than the fleet-foot kid,
Follows with dancing and fills with delight
    The Mænad and the Bassarid;
And soft as lips that laugh and hide
The laughing leaves of the trees divide,
And screen from seeing and leave in sight
    The god pursuing, the maiden hid.

The ivy falls with the Bacchanal's hair
    Over her eyebrows hiding her eyes;
The wild vine slipping down leaves bare
    Her bright breast shortening into sighs;
The wild vine slips with the weight of its leaves,
But the berried ivy catches and cleaves
To the limbs that glitter, the feet that scare
    The wolf that follows, the fawn that flies.

II Before the Beginning of Years

Before the beginning of years,
    There came to the making of man
Time, with a gift of tears;
    Grief, with a glass that ran;
Pleasure, with pain for leaven;
    Summer, with flowers that fell;
Remembrance fallen from heaven,
    And madness risen from hell;
Strength without hands to smite;
    Love that endures for a breath;
Night, the shadow of light,
    And life, the shadow of death.

And the high gods took in hand
    Fire, and the falling of tears,
And a measure of sliding sand
    From under the feet of the years;
And froth and drift of the sea;
    And dust of the laboring earth;
And bodies of things to be
    In the houses of death and of birth;
And wrought with weeping and laughter,
    And fashioned with loathing and love,
With life before and after
    And death beneath and above,
For a day and a night and a morrow,
    That his strength might endure for a span
With travail and heavy sorrow,
    The holy spirit of man.

From the winds of the north and the south
    They gathered as unto strife;
They breathed upon his mouth,
    They filled his body with life;
Eyesight and speech they wrought
    For the veils of the soul therein,
A time for labor and thought,
    A time to serve and to sin;
They gave him light in his ways,
    And love, and a space for delight,
And beauty and length of days,
    And night, and sleep in the night.
His speech is a burning fire;
    With his lips he travaileth;
In his heart is a blind desire,
    In his eyes foreknowledge of death;
He weaves, and is clothed with derision;
    Sows, and he shall not reap;
His life is a watch or a vision
    Between a sleep and a sleep.

III We Have Seen Thee, O Love

We have seen thee, O Love, thou art fair; thou art goodly, O Love;
Thy wings make light in the air as the wings of a dove.
Thy feet are as winds that divide the stream of the sea;
Earth is thy covering to hide thee, the garment of thee.
Thou art swift and subtle and blind as a flame of fire;
Before thee the laughter, behind thee the tears of desire;

And twain go forth beside thee, a man with a maid;
Her eyes are the eyes of a bride whom delight makes afraid;
As the breath in the buds that stir is her bridal breath:
But Fate is the name of her; and his name is Death.

IV Not as with Sundering of the Earth

Not as with sundering of the earth
  Nor as with cleaving of the sea
Nor fierce foreshadowings of a birth
  Nor flying dreams of death to be
Nor loosening of the large world's girth
And quickening of the body of night,
  And sound of thunder in men's ears
And fire of lightning in men's sight,
  Fate, mother of desires and fears,
  Bore unto men the law of tears;
But sudden, an unfathered flame,
  And broken out of night, she shone,
She, without body, without name,
  In days forgotten and foregone;
And heaven rang round her as she came
Like smitten cymbals, and lay bare;
  Clouds and great stars, thunders and snows,
The blue sad fields and folds of air,
  The life that breathes, the life that grows,
  All wind, all fire, that burns or blows,
Even all these knew her: for she is great;
  The daughter of doom, the mother of death,
The sister of sorrow; a lifelong weight
  That no man's finger lighteneth,
Nor any god can lighten fate;
A landmark seen across the way
  Where one race treads as the other trod;
An evil sceptre, an evil stay,
  Wrought for a staff, wrought for a rod,
  The bitter jealousy of God.

For death is deep as the sea,
  And fate as the waves thereof.
Shall the waves take pity on thee
  Or the south-wind offer thee love?
Wilt thou take the night for thy day
Or the darkness for light on thy way
  Till thou say in thine heart Enough?
Behold, thou art over fair, thou art over wise;
The sweetness of spring in thine hair, and the light in thine eyes.
The light of the spring in thine eyes, and the sound in thine ears;
Yet thine heart shall wax heavy with sighs and thine eyelids with tears.
Wilt thou cover thine hair with gold; and with silver thy feet?
Hast thou taken the purple to fold thee, and made thy mouth sweet?
Behold, when thy face is made bare, he that loved thee shall hate;
Thy face shall be no more fair at the fall of thy fate.
For thy life shall fall as a leaf and be shed as the rain;
And the veil of thine head shall be grief; and the crown shall be pain.

V The Death of Meleager

MELEAGER

Let your hands meet
  Round the weight of my head;
Lift ye my feet
  As the feet of the dead;
For the flesh of my body is molten, the limbs of it molten as lead.

CHORUS

O thy luminous face,
  Thine imperious eyes!
O the grief, O the grace,
  As of day when it dies!
Who is this bending over thee, lord, with tears and suppression of sighs?

MELEAGER

Is a bride so fair?
  Is a maid so meek?
With unchapleted hair
  With unfilleted cheek,
Atalanta, the pure among women, whose name is as blessing to speak.

ATALANTA

I would that with feet
  Unsandalled, unshod,
Overbold, overfleet,
  I had swum not nor trod
From Arcadia to Calydon northward, a blast of the envy of God.

MELEAGER

Unto each man his fate;
Unto each as he saith
In whose fingers the weight
Of the world is as breath;
Yet I would that in clamor of battle mine hands had laid hold upon death.

CHORUS

Not with cleaving of shields
And their clash in thine ear,
When the lord of fought fields
Breaketh spearshaft from spear,
Thou art broken, our lord, thou art broken, with travail and labor and fear.

MELEAGER

Would God he had found me
Beneath fresh boughs!
Would God he had bound me
Unawares in mine house,
With light in mine eyes, and songs in my lips, and a crown on my brows!

CHORUS

Whence art thou sent from us?
Whither thy goal?
How art thou rent from us,
Thou that wert whole,
As with severing of eyelids and eyes, as with sundering of body and soul!

MELEAGER

My heart is within me
As an ash in the fire;
Whosoever hath seen me,
Without lute, without lyre,
Shall sing of me grievous things, even things that were ill to desire.

CHORUS

Who shall raise thee
From the house of the dead?
Or what man praise thee
That thy praise may be said?
Alas thy beauty! alas thy body! alas thine head!

MELEAGER

But thou, O mother,
That dreamer of dreams,
Wilt thou bring forth another
To feel the sun's beams
When I move among shadows a shadow, and wail by impassable streams?

ŒNEUS

What thing wilt thou leave me
Now this thing is done?
A man wilt thou give me,
A son for my son,
For the light of mine eyes, the desire of my life, the desirable one?

CHORUS

Thou wert glad above others,
Yea, fair beyond word;
Thou wert glad among mothers;
For each man that heard
Of thee, praise there was added unto thee, as wings to the feet of a bird.

ŒNEUS

Who shall give back
Thy face of old years,
With travail made black,
Grown gray among fears,
Mother of sorrow, mother of cursing, mother of tears?

MELEAGER

Though thou art as fire
Fed with fuel in vain,
My delight, desire,
Is more chaste than the rain,
More pure than the dewfall, more holy than stars are that live without stain.

ATALANTA

I would that as water
My life's blood had thawn,
Or as winter's wan daughter
Leaves lowland and lawn
Spring-stricken, or ever mine eyes had beheld thee made dark in thy dawn.

CHORUS

When thou dravest the men
Of the chosen of Thrace,
None turned him again
Nor endured he thy face
Clothed round with the blush of the battle, with light from a terrible place.

ŒNEUS

Thou shouldst die as he dies
For whom none sheddeth tears;
Filling thine eyes
And fulfilling thine ears
With the brilliance of battle, the bloom and the beauty, the splendour of spears.

CHORUS

In the ears of the world
It is sung, it is told,
And the light thereof hurled
And the noise thereof rolled
From the Acroceraunian snow to the ford of the fleece of gold.

MELEAGER

Would God ye could carry me
Forth of all these;
Heap sand and bury me
By the Chersonese
Where the thundering Bosphorus answers the thunder of Pontic seas.

ŒNEUS

Dost thou mock at our praise
And the singing begun
And the men of strange days
Praising my son
In the folds of the hills of home, high places of Calydon?

MELEAGER

For the dead man no home is;
Ah, better to be
What the flower of the foam is
In fields of the sea,
That the sea-waves might be as my raiment, the gulf-stream a garment for me.

CHORUS

Who shall seek thee and bring
And restore thee thy day,
When the dove dipt her wing
And the oars won their way
Where the narrowing Symplegades whitened the straits of Propontis with spray?

MELEAGER

Will ye crown me my tomb
Or exalt me my name,
Now my spirits consume,
Now my flesh is a flame?
Let the sea slake it once, and men speak of me sleeping to praise me or shame.

CHORUS

Turn back now, turn thee,
As who turns him to wake;
Though the life in thee burn thee,
Couldst thou bathe it and slake
Where the sea-ridge of Helle hangs heavier, and east upon west waters break?

MELEAGER

Would the winds blow me back
Or the waves hurl me home?
Ah, to touch in the track
Where the pine learnt to roam
Cold girdles and crowns of the sea-gods, cool blossoms of water and foam!

CHORUS

The gods may release
That they made fast;
Thy soul shall have ease
In thy limbs at the last;
But what shall they give thee for life, sweet life that is overpast?

MELEAGER

Not the life of men's veins,
Not of flesh that conceives;
But the grace that remains,
The fair beauty that cleaves
To the life of the rains in the grasses, the life of the dews on the leaves.

CHORUS

Thou wert helmsman and chief;
Wilt thou turn in an hour,
Thy limbs to the leaf,
Thy face to the flower,
Thy blood to the water, thy soul to the gods who divide and devour?

MELEAGER

The years are hungry,
They wail all their days;
The gods wax angry
And weary of praise;
And who shall bridle their lips? and who shall straiten their ways?

CHORUS

The gods guard over us
With sword and with rod;
Weaving shadow to cover us,
Heaping the sod,
That law may fulfil herself wholly, to darken man's face before God.

1865

A BALLAD OF LIFE

I FOUND in dreams a place of wind and flowers,
Full of sweet trees and color of glad grass,
In midst whereof there was
A lady clothed like summer with sweet hours.
Her beauty, fervent as a fiery moon
Made my blood burn and swoon
Like a flame rained upon.
Sorrow had filled her shaken eyelids' blue,
And her mouth's sad red heavy rose all through
Seemed sad with glad things gone.

She held a little cithern by the strings,
Shaped heartwise, strung with subtle-colored hair
Of some dead lute player
That in dead years had done delicious things.
The seven strings were named accordingly;
The first string charity,
The second tenderness,
The rest were pleasure, sorrow, sleep, and sin,
And loving-kindness, that is pity's kin
And is most pitiless.

There were three men with her, each garmented
With gold and shod with gold upon the feet;
And with plucked ears of wheat.
The first man's hair was wound upon his head:
His face was red, and his mouth curled and sad;
All his gold garment had
Pale stains of dust and rust.
A riven hood was pulled across his eyes;
The token of him being upon this wise
Made for a sign of Lust.

The next was Shame, with hollow heavy face
Colored like green wood when flame kindles it.
He hath such feeble feet
They may not well endure in any place.
His face was full of grey old miseries,
And all his blood's increase
Was even increase of pain.
The last was Fear, that is akin to Death;
He is Shame's friend, and always as Shame saith
Fear answers him again.

My soul said in me; This is marvellous,
Seeing the air's face is not so delicate
Nor the sun's grace so great,
If sin and she be kin or amorous.
And seeing where maidens served her on their knees,
I bade one crave of these
To know the cause thereof.
Then Fear said: I am Pity that was dead.
And Shame said: I am Sorrow comforted.
And Lust said: I am Love.

Thereat her hands began a lute-playing
And her sweet mouth a song in a strange tongue;
And all the while she sung
There was no sound but long tears following
Long tears upon men's faces, waxen white
With extreme sad delight.
But those three following men
Became as men raised up among the dead;
Great glad mouths open, and fair cheeks made red
With child's blood come again.

Then I said: Now assuredly I see
My lady is perfect, and transfigureth
All sin and sorrow and death,
Making them fair as her own eyelids be,
Or lips wherein my whole soul's life abides;
Or as her sweet white sides
And bosom carved to kiss.
Now therefore, if her pity further me,
Doubtless for her sake all my days shall be
As righteous as she is.

Forth, ballad, and take roses in both arms,
Even till the top rose touch thee in the throat
Where the least thornprick harms;
And girdled in thy golden singing-coat,
Come thou before my lady and say this;
Borgia, thy gold hair's colour burns in me,
Thy mouth makes beat my blood in feverish rhymes;
Therefore so many as these roses be,
Kiss me so many times.
Then it may be, seeing how sweet she is,
That she will stoop herself none otherwise
Than a blown vine-branch doth,
And kiss thee with soft laughter on thine eyes,
Ballad, and on thy mouth.

1866

A BALLAD OF DEATH

KNEEL down, fair Love, and fill thyself with tears,
Girdle thyself with sighing for a girth
Upon the sides of mirth,
Cover thy lips and eyelids, let thine ears
Be filled with rumor of people sorrowing;
Make thee soft raiment out of woven sighs
Upon the flesh to cleave,
Set pains therein and many a grievous thing,
And many sorrows after each his wise
For armlet and for gorget and for sleeve.

O Love's lute heard about the lands of death,
Left hanged upon the trees that were therein;
O Love and Time and Sin,
Three singing mouths that mourn now under breath,
Three lovers, each one evil spoken of;
O smitten lips where through this voice of mine
Came softer with her praise;
Abide a little for our lady's love.
The kisses of her mouth were more than wine,
And more than peace the passage of her days.

O Love, thou knowest if she were good to see.
O Time, thou shalt not find in any land
Till, cast out of thine hand,
The sunlight and the moonlight fail from thee,
Another woman fashioned like as this.
O Sin, thou knowest that all thy shame in her
Was made a goodly thing;
Yea, she caught Shame and shamed him with her kiss,
With her fair kiss, and lips much lovelier
Than lips of amorous roses in late spring.

By night there stood over against my bed
Queen Venus with a hood striped gold and black,
Both sides drawn fully back
From brows wherein the sad blood failed of red,
And temples drained of purple and full of death.
Her curled hair had the wave of sea-water
And the sea's gold in it.
Her eyes were as a dove's that sickeneth.
Strewn dust of gold she had shed over her,
And pearl and purple and amber on her feet.

Upon her raiment of dyed sendaline
Were painted all the secret ways of love
And covered things thereof,
That hold delight as grape-flowers hold their wine;
Red mouths of maidens and red feet of doves,
And brides that kept within the bride-chamber
Their garment of soft shame,
And weeping faces of the wearied loves
That swoon in sleep and awake wearier,
With heat of lips and hair shed out like flame.

The tears that through her eyelids fell on me
Made my own bitter where they ran between
As blood had fallen therein,
She saying; Arise, lift up thine eyes and see
If any glad thing be or any good
Now the best thing is taken forth of us;
Even she to whom all praise
Was as one flower in a great multitude,
One glorious flower of many and glorious,
One day found gracious among many days:

Even she whose handmaiden was Love—to whom
At kissing times across her stateliest bed
Kings bowed themselves and shed
Pale wine, and honey with the honeycomb,

And spikenard bruised for a burnt-offering;
Even she between whose lips the kiss became
As fire and frankincense;
Whose hair was as gold raiment on a king,
Whose eyes were as the morning purged with flame,
Whose eyelids as sweet savour issuing thence.

Then I beheld, and lo on the other side
My lady's likeness crowned and robed and dead.
Sweet still, but now not red,
Was the shut mouth whereby men lived and died,
And sweet, but emptied of the blood's blue shade,
The great curled eyelids that withheld her eyes.
And sweet, but like spoilt gold,
The weight of color in her tresses weighed,
And sweet, but as a vesture with new dyes,
The body that was clothed with love of old.

Ah! that my tears filled all her woven hair
And all the hollow bosom of her gown—
Ah! that my tears ran down
Even to the place where many kisses were,
Even where her parted breast-flowers have place,
Even where they are cloven apart—who knows not this?
Ah! the flowers cleave apart
And their sweet fills the tender interspace;
Ah! the leaves grown thereof were things to kiss
Ere their fine gold was tarnished at the heart.

Ah! in the days when God did good to me,
Each part about her was a righteous thing;
Her mouth an almsgiving,
The glory of her garments charity,
The beauty of her bosom a good deed,
In the good days when God kept sight of us;
Love lay upon her eyes,
And on that hair whereof the world takes heed:
And all her body was more virtuous
Than souls of women fashioned otherwise.

Now, ballad, gather poppies in thine hands
And sheaves of briar and many rusted sheaves
Rain-rotten in rank lands,
Waste marigold and late unhappy leaves
And grass that fades ere any of it be mown;
And when thy bosom is filled full thereof
Seek out Death's face ere the light altereth,
And say "My master that was thrall to Love
Is become thrall to Death."
Bow down before him, ballad, sigh and groan,
But make no sojourn in thy outgoing;
For haply it may be
That when thy feet return at evening
Death shall come in with thee.

1866

LAUS VENERIS

Asleep or waking is it? for her neck,
Kissed over close, wears yet a purple speck,
Wherein the pained blood falters and goes out;
Soft, and stung softly—fairer for a fleck.

But though my lips shut sucking on the place,
There is no vein at work upon her face;
Her eyelids are so peaceable, no doubt
Deep sleep has warmed her blood through all its ways.

Lo, this is she that was the world's delight;
The old grey years were parcels of her might;
The strewings of the ways wherein she trod
Were the twain seasons of the day and night.

Lo, she was thus when her clear limbs enticed
All lips that now grow sad with kissing Christ,
Stained with blood fallen from the feet of God,
The feet and hands whereat our souls were priced.

Alas, Lord, surely thou art great and fair.
But lo her wonderfully woven hair!
And thou didst heal us with thy piteous kiss;
But see now, Lord; her mouth is lovelier.

She is right fair; what hath she done to thee?
Nay, fair Lord Christ, lift up thine eyes and see;
Had now thy mother such a lip—like this?
Thou knowest how sweet a thing it is to me.

Inside the Horsel here the air is hot;
Right little peace one hath for it, God wot;
The scented dusty daylight burns the air,
And my heart chokes me till I hear it not.

Behold, my Venus, my soul's body, lies
With my love laid upon her garment-wise,
Feeling my love in all her limbs and hair
And shed between her eyelids through her eyes.

She holds my heart in her sweet open hands
Hanging asleep; hard by her head there stands,
Crowned with gilt thorns and clothed with flesh like fire,
Love, wan as foam blown up the salt burnt sands—

Hot as the brackish waifs of yellow spume
That shift and steam—loose clots of arid fume
From the sea's panting mouth of dry desire;
There stands he, like one labouring at a loom.

The warp holds fast across; and every thread
That makes the woof up has dry specks of red;
Always the shuttle cleaves clean through, and he
Weaves with the hair of many a ruined head.

Love is not glad nor sorry, as I deem;
Labouring he dreams, and labours in the dream,
Till when the spool is finished, lo I see
His web, reeled off, curls and goes out like steam.

Night falls like fire; the heavy lights run low,
And as they drop, my blood and body so
Shake as the flame shakes, full of days and hours
That sleep not neither weep they as they go.

Ah yet would God this flesh of mine might be
Where air might wash and long leaves cover me,
Where tides of grass break into foam of flowers,
Or where the wind's feet shine along the sea.

Ah yet would God that stems and roots were bred
Out of my weary body and my head,
That sleep were sealed upon me with a seal,
And I were as the least of all his dead.

Would God my blood were dew to feed the grass,
Mine ears made deaf and mine eyes blind as glass,
My body broken as a turning wheel,
And my mouth stricken ere it saith Alas!

Ah God, that love were as a flower or flame,
That life were as the naming of a name,
That death were not more pitiful than desire,
That these things were not one thing and the same!

Behold now, surely somewhere there is death:
For each man hath some space of years, he saith.
A little space of time ere time expire,
A little day, a little way of breath.

And lo, between the sundawn and the sun,
His day's work and his night's work are undone;
And lo, between the nightfall and the light,
He is not, and none knoweth of such an one.

Ah God, that I were as all souls that be,
As any herb or leaf of any tree,
As men that toil through hours of labouring night,
As bones of men under the deep sharp sea.

Outside it must be winter among men;
For at the gold bars of the gates again
I heard all night and all the hours of it,
The wind's wet wings and fingers drip with rain.

Knights gather, riding sharp for cold; I know
The ways and woods are strangled with the snow;
And with short song the maidens spin and sit
Until Christ's birthnight, lily-like, arow.

The scent and shadow shed about me make
The very soul in all my senses ache;
The hot hard night is fed upon my breath,
And sleep beholds me from afar awake.

Alas, but surely where the hills grow deep,
Or where the wild ways of the sea are steep,
Or in strange places somewhere there is death,
And on death's face the scattered hair of sleep.

There lover-like with lips and limbs that meet
They lie, they pluck sweet fruit of life and eat;
But me the hot and hungry days devour,
And in my mouth no fruit of theirs is sweet.

No fruit of theirs, but fruit of my desire,
For her love's sake whose lips through mine respire;
Her eyelids on her eyes like flower on flower,
Mine eyelids on mine eyes like fire on fire.

So lie we, not as sleep that lies by death,
With heavy kisses and with happy breath;
Not as man lies by woman, when the bride
Laughs low for love's sake and the words he saith.

For she lies, laughing low with love; she lies
And turns his kisses on her lips to sighs,
To sighing sound of lips unsatisfied,
And the sweet tears are tender with her eyes.

Ah, not as they, but as the souls that were
Slain in the old time, having found her fair;
Who, sleeping with her lips upon their eyes,
Heard sudden serpents hiss across her hair.

Their blood runs round the roots of time like rain:
She casts them forth and gathers them again;
With nerve and bone she weaves and multiplies
Exceeding pleasure out of extreme pain.

Her little chambers drip with flower-like red,
Her girdles, and the chaplets of her head,
Her armlets and her anklets; with her feet,
She tramples all that winepress of the dead.

Her gateways smoke with fume of flowers and fires,
With loves burnt out and unassuaged desires;
Between her lips the steam of them is sweet,
The languor in her ears of many lyres.

Her beds are full of perfume and sad sound,
Her doors are made with music and barred round
With sighing and with laughter and with tears,
With tears whereby strong souls of men are bound.

There is the knight Adonis that was slain;
With flesh and blood she chains him for a chain;
The body and the spirit in her ears
Cry, for her lips divide him vein by vein.

Yea, all she slayeth; yea, every man save me;
Me, love, thy lover that must cleave to thee
Till the ending of the days and ways of earth,
The shaking of the sources of the sea.

Me, most forsaken of all souls that fell;
Me, satiated with things insatiable;
Me, for whose sake the extreme hell makes mirth,
Yea, laughter kindles at the heart of hell.

Alas thy beauty! for thy mouth's sweet sake
My soul is bitter to me, my limbs quake
As water, as the flesh of men that weep,
As their heart's vein whose heart goes nigh to break.

Ah God, that sleep with flower-sweet finger-tips
Would crush the fruit of death upon my lips;
Ah God, that death would tread the grapes of sleep
And wring their juice upon me as it drips.

There is no change of cheer for many days,
But change of chimes high up in the air, that sways
Rung by the running fingers of the wind;
And singing sorrows heard on hidden ways.

Day smiteth day in twain, night sundereth night,
And on mine eyes the dark sits as the light;
Yea, Lord, thou knowest I know not, having sinned,
If heaven be clean or unclean in thy sight.

Yea, as if earth were sprinkled over me,
Such chafed harsh earth as chokes a sandy sea,
Each pore doth yearn, and the dried blood thereof
Gasps by sick fits, my heart swims heavily,

There is a feverish famine in my veins;
Below her bosom, where a crushed grape stains
The white and blue, there my lips caught and clove
An hour since, and what mark of me remains?

I dare not always touch her, lest the kiss
Leave my lips charred. Yea, Lord, a little bliss,
Brief bitter bliss, one hath for a great sin;
Nathless thou knowest how sweet a thing it is.

Sin, is it sin whereby men's souls are thrust
Into the pit? yet had I a good trust
To save my soul before it slipped therein,
Trod under by the fire-shod feet of lust.

For if mine eyes fail and my soul takes breath,
I look between the iron sides of death
Into sad hell where all sweet love hath end,
All but the pain that never finisheth.

There are the naked faces of great kings,
The singing folk with all their lute-playings;
There when one cometh he shall have to friend
The grave that covets and the worm that clings.

There sit the knights that were so great of hand,
The ladies that were queens of fair green land,
Grown grey and black now, brought unto the dust,
Soiled, without raiment, clad about with sand.

There is one end for all of them; they sit
Naked and sad, they drink the dregs of it,
Trodden as grapes in the wine-press of lust,
Trampled and trodden by the fiery feet.

I see the marvellous mouth whereby there fell
Cities and people whom the gods loved well,
Yet for her sake on them the fire gat hold,
And for their sakes on her the fire of hell.

And softer than the Egyptian lote-leaf is,
The queen whose face was worth the world to kiss,
Wearing at breast a suckling snake of gold;
And large pale lips of strong Semiramis,

Curled like a tiger's that curl back to feed;
Red only where the last kiss made them bleed;
Her hair most thick with many a carven gem,
Deep in the mane, great-chested, like a steed.

Yea, with red sin the faces of them shine;
But in all these there was no sin like mine;
No, not in all the strange great sins of them
That made the wine-press froth and foam with wine.

For I was of Christ's choosing, I God's knight,
No blinkard heathen stumbling for scant light;
I can well see, for all the dusty days
Gone past, the clean great time of goodly fight.

I smell the breathing battle sharp with blows,
With shriek of shafts and snapping short of bows;
The fair pure sword smites out in subtle ways,
Sounds and long lights are shed between the rows

Of beautiful mailed men; the edged light slips,
Most like a snake that takes short breath and dips
Sharp from the beautifully bending head,
With all its gracious body lithe as lips

That curl in touching you; right in this wise
My sword doth, seeming fire in mine own eyes,
Leaving all colors in them brown and red
And flecked with death; then the keen breaths like sighs,

The caught-up choked dry laughters following them,
When all the fighting face is grown a flame
For pleasure, and the pulse that stuns the ears,
And the heart's gladness of the goodly game.

Let me think yet a little; I do know
These things were sweet, but sweet such years ago,
Their savor is all turned now into tears;
Yea, ten years since, where the blue ripples blow,

The blue curled eddies of the blowing Rhine,
I felt the sharp wind shaking grass and vine
Touch my blood, too, and sting me with delight
Through all this waste and weary body of mine

That never feels clear air; right gladly then
I rode alone, a great way off my men,
  And heard the chiming bridle smite and smite.
And gave each rhyme thereof some rhyme again,

Till my song shifted to that iron one;
Seeing there rode up between me and the sun
  Some certain of my foe's men, for his three
White wolves across their painted coats did run.

The first red-bearded, with square cheeks—alack,
I made my knave's blood turn his beard to black;
  The slaying of him was a joy to see:
Perchance too, when at night he came not back,

Some woman fell a-weeping, whom this thief
Would beat when he had drunken; yet small grief
  Hath any for the ridding of such knaves;
Yea, if one wept, I doubt her teen was brief.

This bitter love is sorrow in all lands,
Draining of eyelids, wringing of drenched hands,
  Sighing of hearts and filling up of graves;
A sign across the head of the world he stands,

As one that hath a plague-mark on his brows;
Dust and spilt blood do track him to his house
  Down under earth; sweet smells of lip and cheek,
Like a sweet snake's breath made more poisonous

With chewing of some perfumed deadly grass,
Are shed all round his passage if he pass,
  And their quenched savour leaves the whole soul weak,
Sick with keen guessing whence the perfume was.

As one who hidden in deep sedge and reeds
Smells the rare scent made where a panther feeds,
  And tracking ever slotwise the warm smell
Is snapped upon by the sweet mouth and bleeds,

His head far down the hot sweet throat of her—
So one tracks love, whose breath is deadlier,
  And lo, one springe and you are fast in hell,
Fast as the gin's grip of a wayfarer.

I think now, as the heavy hours decease
One after one, and bitter thoughts increase
  One upon one, of all sweet finished things;
The breaking of the battle; the long peace

Wherein we sat clothed softly, each man's hair
Crowned with green leaves beneath white hoods of vair;
  The sounds of sharp spears at great tourneyings,
And noise of singing in the late sweet air.

I sang of love too, knowing nought thereof;
"Sweeter," I said, "the little laugh of love
  Than tears out of the eyes of Magdalen,
Or any fallen feather of the Dove.

"The broken little laugh that spoils a kiss,
The ache of purple pulses, and the bliss
  Of blinded eyelids that expand again—
Love draws them open with those lips of his,

"Lips that cling hard till the kissed face has grown
Of one same fire and colour with their own;
  Then ere one sleep, appeased with sacrifice,
Where his lips wounded, there his lips atone."

I sang these things long since and knew them not;
"Lo, here is love, or there is love, God wot,
  This man and that finds favor in his eyes,"
I said, "but I, what guerdon have I got?

"The dust of praise that is blown everywhere
In all men's faces with the common air;
  The bay-leaf that wants chafing to be sweet
Before they wind it in a singer's hair."

So that one dawn I rode forth sorrowing;
I had no hope but of some evil thing,
  And so rode slowly past the windy wheat,
And past the vineyard and the water-spring,

Up to the Horsel. A great elder-tree
Held back its heaps of flowers to let me see
The ripe tall grass, and one that walked therein,
Naked, with hair shed over to the knee.

She walked between the blossom and the grass;
I knew the beauty of her, what she was,
The beauty of her body and her sin,
And in my flesh the sin of hers, alas!

Alas! for sorrow is all the end of this.
O sad kissed mouth, how sorrowful it is!
O breast whereat some suckling sorrow clings,
Red with the bitter blossom of a kiss!

Ah, with blind lips I felt for you, and found
About my neck your hands and hair enwound,
The hands that stifle and the hair that stings,
I felt them fasten sharply without sound.

Yea, for my sin I had great store of bliss
Rise up, make answer for me, let thy kiss
Seal my lips hard from speaking of my sin,
Lest one go mad to hear how sweet it is.

Yet I waxed faint with fume of barren bowers,
And murmuring of the heavy-headed hours;
And let the dove's beak fret and peck within
My lips in vain, and Love shed fruitless flowers,

So that God looked upon me when your hands
Were hot about me; yea, God brake my bands
To save my soul alive, and I came forth
Like a man blind and naked in strange lands

That hears men laugh and weep, and knows not whence
Nor wherefore, but is broken in his sense;
Howbeit I met folk riding from the north
Towards Rome, to purge them of their souls' offence,

And rode with them, and spake to none; the day
Stunned me like lights upon some wizard way,
And ate like fire mine eyes and mine eye-sight;
So rode I, hearing all these chant and pray,

And marvelled; till before us rose and fell
White cursed hills, like outer skirts of hell
Seen where men's eyes look through the day to night,
Like a jagged shell's lips, harsh, untunable,

Blown in between by devils' wrangling breath;
Nathless we won well past that hell and death,
Down to the sweet land where all airs are good,
Even unto Rome where God's grace tarrieth.

Then came each man and worshipped at his knees
Who in the Lord God's likeness bears the keys
To bind or loose, and called on Christ's shed blood,
And so the sweet-souled father gave him ease.

But when I came I fell down at his feet,
Saying, "Father, though the Lord's blood be right sweet,
The spot it takes not off the panther's skin,
Nor shall an Ethiop's stain be bleached with it.

"Lo, I have sinned and have spat out at God,
Wherefore his hand is heavier and his rod
More sharp because of mine exceeding sin,
And all his raiment redder than bright blood

"Before mine eyes; yea, for my sake I wot
The heat of hell is waxen seven times hot
Through my great sin." Then spake he some sweet word,
Giving me cheer; which thing availed me not;

Yea, scarce I wist if such indeed were said;
For when I ceased—lo, as one newly dead
Who hears a great cry out of hell, I heard
The crying of his voice across my head.

"Until this dry shred staff, that hath no whit
Of leaf nor bark, bear blossom and smell sweet,
Seek thou not any mercy in God's sight,
For so long shalt thou be cast out from it."

Yea, what if dried-up stems wax red and green,
Shall that thing be which is not nor has been?
  Yea, what if sapless bark wax green and white,
Shall any good fruit grow upon my sin?

Nay, though sweet fruit were plucked of a dry tree,
And though men drew sweet waters of the sea,
  There should not grow sweet leaves on this dead stem,
This waste wan body and shaken soul of me.

Yea, though God search it warily enough,
There is not one sound thing in all thereof;
  Though he search all my veins through, searching them
He shall find nothing whole therein but love.

For I came home right heavy, with small cheer,
And lo my love, mine own soul's heart, more dear
  Than mine own soul, more beautiful than God,
Who hath my being between the hands of her—

Fair still, but fair for no man saving me,
As when she came out of the naked sea
  Making the foam as fire whereon she trod,
And as the inner flower of fire was she.

Yea, she laid hold upon me, and her mouth
Clove unto mine as soul to body doth,
  And, laughing, made her lips luxurious;
Her hair had smells of all the sunburnt south,

Strange spice and flower, strange savour of crushed fruit,
And perfume the swart kings tread underfoot
  For pleasure when their minds wax amorous,
Charred frankincense and grated sandal-root.

And I forgot fear and all weary things,
All ended prayers and perished thanksgivings,
  Feeling her face with all her eager hair
Cleave to me, clinging as a fire that clings

To the body and to the raiment, burning them;
As after death I know that such-like flame
  Shall cleave to me for ever; yea, what care,
Albeit I burn then, having felt the same?

Ah love, there is no better life than this;
To have known love, how bitter a thing it is,
  And afterward be cast out of God's sight;
Yea, these that know not, shall they have such bliss

High up in barren heaven before his face
As we twain in the heavy-hearted place,
  Remembering love and all the dead delight,
And all that time was sweet with for a space?

For till the thunder in the trumpet be,
Soul may divide from body, but not we
  One from another; I hold thee with my hand,
I let mine eyes have all their will of thee,

I seal myself upon thee with my might,
Abiding alway out of all men's sight
  Until God loosen over sea and land
The thunder of the trumpets of the night.

EXPLICIT LAUS VENERIS.

1866

THE TRIUMPH OF TIME

Before our lives divide for ever,
  While time is with us and hands are free,
(Time, swift to fasten and swift to sever
  Hand from hand, as we stand by the sea)
I will say no word that a man might say
Whose whole life's love goes down in a day;
For this could never have been; and never,
  Though the gods and the years relent, shall be.

Is it worth a tear, is it worth an hour,
  To think of things that are well outworn?
Of fruitless husk and fugitive flower,
  The dream foregone and the deed forborne?
Though joy be done with and grief be vain,
Time shall not sever us wholly in twain;
Earth is not spoilt for a single shower;
  But the rain has ruined the ungrown corn.

It will grow not again, this fruit of my heart,
  Smitten with sunbeams, ruined with rain.
The singing seasons divide and depart,
  Winter and summer depart in twain.

It will grow not again, it is ruined at root,
The bloodlike blossom, the dull red fruit;
Though the heart yet sickens, the lips yet smart,
With sullen savour of poisonous pain.

I have given no man of my fruit to eat;
I trod the grapes, I have drunken the wine.
Had you eaten and drunken and found it sweet,
This wild new growth of the corn and vine,
This wine and bread without lees or leaven,
We had grown as gods, as the gods in heaven,
Souls fair to look upon, goodly to greet,
One splendid spirit, your soul and mine.

In the change of years, in the coil of things,
In the clamour and rumour of life to be,
We, drinking love at the furthest springs,
Covered with love as a covering tree,
We had grown as gods, as the gods above,
Filled from the heart to the lips with love,
Held fast in his hands, clothed warm with his wings,
O love, my love had you loved but me!

We had stood as the sure stars stand, and moved
As the moon moves, loving the world; and seen
Grief collapse as a thing disproved,
Death consume as a thing unclean.
Twain halves of a perfect heart, made fast,
Soul to soul while the years fell past;
Had you loved me once, as you have not loved;
Had the chance been with us that has not been.

I have put my days and dreams out of mind,
Days that are over, dreams that are done.
Though we seek life through, we shall surely find
There is none of them clear to us now, not one.
But clear are these things; the grass and the sand,
Where, sure as the eyes reach, ever at hand,
With lips wide open and face burnt blind,
The strong sea-daisies feast on the sun.

The low downs lean to the sea; the stream,
One loose thin pulseless tremulous vein,
Rapid and vivid and dumb as a dream,
Works downward, sick of the sun and the rain;
No wind is rough with the rank rare flowers;
The sweet sea, mother of loves and hours,
Shudders and shines as the grey winds gleam,
Turning her smile to a fugitive pain.

Mother of loves that are swift to fade,
Mother of mutable winds and hours.
A barren mother, a mother-maid,
Cold and clean as her faint salt flowers.
I would we twain were even as she,
Lost in the night and the light of the sea,
Where faint sounds falter and wan beams wade,
Break, and are broken, and shed into showers.

The loves and hours of the life of a man,
They are swift and sad, being born of the sea.
Hours that rejoice and regret for a span,
Born with a man's breath, mortal as he;
Loves that are lost ere they come to birth,
Weeds of the wave, without fruit upon earth,
I lose what I long for, save what I can,
My love, my love, and no love for me!

It is not much that a man can save
On the sands of life, in the straits of time,
Who swims in sight of the great third wave
That never a swimmer shall cross or climb.
Some waif washed up with the strays and spars
That ebb-tide shows to the shore and the stars;
Weed from the water, grass from a grave,
A broken blossom, a ruined rhyme.

There will no man do for your sake, I think,
What I would have done for the least word said.
I had wrung life dry for your lips to drink,
Broken it up for your daily bread:
Body for body and blood for blood,
As the flow of the full sea risen to flood
That yearns and trembles before it sink,
I had given, and lain down for you, glad and dead.

Yea, hope at highest and all her fruit,
And time at fullest and all his dower,
I had given you surely, and life to boot,
Were we once made one for a single hour.
But now, you are twain, you are cloven apart,
Flesh of his flesh, but heart of my heart;
And deep in one is the bitter root,
And sweet for one is the lifelong flower.

To have died if you cared I should die for you, clung
To my life if you bade me, played my part
As it pleased you—these were the thoughts that stung,
The dreams that smote with a keener dart
Than shafts of love or arrows of death;
These were but as fire is, dust or breath,
Or poisonous foam on the tender tongue
Of the little snakes that eat my heart.

I wish we were dead together to-day,
Lost sight of, hidden away out of sight,
Clasped and clothed in the cloven clay,
Out of the world's way, out of the light,
Out of the ages of worldly weather,
Forgotten of all men altogether,
As the world's first dead, taken wholly away,
Made one with death, filled full of the night.

How we should slumber, how we should sleep,
Far in the dark with the dreams and the dews!
And dreaming, grow to each other, and weep,
Laugh low, live softly, murmur and muse;
Yea, and it may be, struck through by the dream,
Feel the dust quicken and quiver, and seem
Alive as of old to the lips, and leap
Spirit to spirit as lovers use.

Sick dreams and sad of a dull delight;
For what shall it profit when men are dead
To have dreamed, to have loved with the whole soul's might,
To have looked for day when the day was fled?
Let come what will, there is one thing worth,
To have had fair love in the life upon earth:
To have held love safe till the day grew night,
While skies had colour and lips were red.

Would I lose you now? would I take you then,
If I lose you now that my heart has need?
And come what may after death to men,
What thing worth this will the dead years breed?
Lose life, lose all; but at least I know,
O sweet life's love, having loved you so,
Had I reached you on earth, I should lose not again,
In death nor life, nor in dream or deed.

Yea, I know this well: were you once sealed mine,
Mine in the blood's beat, mine in the breath,
Mixed into me as honey in wine,
Not time that sayeth and gainsayeth,
Nor all strong things had severed us then;
Not wrath of gods, nor wisdom of men,
Nor all things earthly, nor all divine,
Nor joy nor sorrow, nor life nor death.

I had grown pure as the dawn and the dew,
You had grown strong as the sun or the sea.
But none shall triumph a whole life through:
For death is one, and the fates are three.
At the door of life, by the gate of breath,
There are worse things waiting for men than death;
Death could not sever my soul and you,
As these have severed your soul from me.

You have chosen and clung to the chance they sent you,
Life sweet as perfume and pure as prayer.
But will it not one day in heaven repent you?
Will they solace you wholly, the days that were?
Will you lift up your eyes between sadness and bliss,
Meet mine, and see where the great love is,
And tremble and turn and be changed? Content you;
The gate is strait; I shall not be there.

But you, had you chosen, had you stretched hand,
Had you seen good such a thing were done,
I too might have stood with the souls that stand
In the sun's sight, clothed with the light of the sun;
But who now on earth need care how I live?
Have the high gods anything left to give,
Save dust and laurels and gold and sand?
Which gifts are goodly; but I will none.

O all fair lovers about the world,
There is none of you, none, that shall comfort me.
My thoughts are as dead things, wrecked and whirled
Round and round in a gulf of the sea;
And still, through the sound and the straining stream,
Through the coil and chafe, they gleam in a dream,
The bright fine lips so cruelly curled,
And strange swift eyes where the soul sits free.

Free, without pity, withheld from woe,
Ignorant; fair as the eyes are fair.
Would I have you change now, change at a blow,
Startled and stricken, awake and aware?
Yea, if I could, would I have you see
My very love of you filling me,
And know my soul to the quick, as I know
The likeness and look of your throat and hair?

I shall not change you. Nay, though I might,
Would I change my sweet one love with a word?
I had rather your hair should change in a night,
Clear now as the plume of a black bright bird;
Your face fail suddenly, cease, turn grey,
Die as a leaf that dies in a day.
I will keep my soul in a place out of sight,
Far off, where the pulse of it is not heard.

Far off it walks, in a bleak blown space,
Full of the sound of the sorrow of years.
I have woven a veil for the weeping face,
Whose lips have drunken the wine of tears;
I have found a way for the failing feet,
A place for slumber and sorrow to meet;
There is no rumour about the place,
Nor light, nor any that sees or hears.

I have hidden my soul out of sight, and said
"Let none take pity upon thee, none
Comfort thy crying: for lo, thou art dead,
Lie still now, safe out of sight of the sun.
Have I not built thee a grave, and wrought
Thy grave-clothes on thee of grievous thought,
With soft spun verses and tears unshed,
And sweet light visions of things undone?

"I have given thee garments and balm and myrrh,
And gold, and beautiful burial things.
But thou, be at peace now, make no stir;
Is not thy grave as a royal king's?
Fret not thyself though the end were sore;
Sleep, be patient, vex me no more.
Sleep; what hast thou to do with her?
The eyes that weep, with the mouth that sings?"

Where the dead red leaves of the years lie rotten,
The cold old crimes and the deeds thrown by,
The misconceived and the misbegotten,
I would find a sin to do ere I die,
Sure to dissolve and destroy me all through,
That would set you higher in heaven, serve you
And leave you happy, when clean forgotten,
As a dead man out of mind, am I.

Your lithe hands draw me, your face burns through me,
I am swift to follow you, keen to see;
But love lacks might to redeem or undo me;
As I have been, I know I shall surely be;
"What should such fellows as I do?" Nay,
My part were worse if I chose to play;
For the worst is this after all; if they knew me,
Not a soul upon earth would pity me.

And I play not for pity of these; but you,
If you saw with your soul what man am I,
You would praise me at least that my soul all through
Clove to you, loathing the lives that lie;
The souls and lips that are bought and sold,
The smiles of silver and kisses of gold,
The lapdog loves that whine as they chew,
The little lovers that curse and cry.

There are fairer women, I hear; that may be;
But I, that I love you and find you fair,
Who are more than fair in my eyes if they be,
Do the high gods know or the great gods care?
Though the swords in my heart for one were seven,
Would the iron hollow of doubtful heaven,
That knows not itself whether night-time or day be,
Reverberate words and a foolish prayer?

I will go back to the great sweet mother,
Mother and lover of men, the sea.
I will go down to her, I and none other,
Close with her, kiss her and mix her with me;
Cling to her, strive with her, hold her fast;
O fair white mother, in days long past
Born without sister, born without brother,
Set free my soul as thy soul is free.

O fair green-girdled mother of mine,
Sea, that art clothed with the sun and the rain,
Thy sweet hard kisses are strong like wine,
Thy large embraces are keen like pain.
Save me and hide me with all thy waves,
Find me one grave of thy thousand graves,
Those pure cold populous graves of thine,
Wrought without hand in a world without stain.

I shall sleep, and move with the moving ships,
Change as the winds change, veer in the tide;
My lips will feast on the foam of thy lips,
I shall rise with thy rising, with thee subside;
Sleep, and not know if she be, if she were,
Filled full with life to the eyes and hair,
As a rose is fulfilled to the roseleaf tips
With splendid summer and perfume and pride.

This woven raiment of nights and days,
Were it once cast off and unwound from me,
Naked and glad would I walk in thy ways,
Alive and aware of thy ways and thee;
Clear of the whole world, hidden at home,
Clothed with the green and crowned with the foam,
A pulse of the life of thy straits and bays,
A vein in the heart of the streams of the sea.

Fair mother, fed with the lives of men,
Thou art subtle and cruel of heart, men say.
Thou hast taken, and shalt not render again;
Thou art full of thy dead, and cold as they.
But death is the worst that comes of thee;
Thou art fed with our dead, O mother, O sea,
But when hast thou fed on our hearts? or when,
Having given us love, hast thou taken away?

O tender-hearted, O perfect lover,
Thy lips are bitter, and sweet thine heart.
The hopes that hurt and the dreams that hover,
Shall they not vanish away and apart?
But thou, thou art sure, thou art older than earth;
Thou art strong for death and fruitful of birth;
Thy depths conceal and thy gulfs discover;
From the first thou wert; in the end thou art.

And grief shall endure not for ever, I know.
As things that are not shall these things be;
We shall live through seasons of sun and of snow,
And none be grievous as this to me.
We shall hear, as one in a trance that hears,
The sound of time, the rhyme of the years;
Wrecked hope and passionate pain will grow
As tender things of a spring-tide sea,

Sea-fruit that swings in the waves that hiss,
Drowned gold and purple and royal rings.
And all time past, was it all for this?
Times unforgotten, and treasures of things?
Swift years of liking, and sweet long laughter,
That wist not well of the years thereafter
Till love woke, smitten at heart by a kiss,
With lips that trembled and trailing wings?

There lived a singer in France of old,
By the tideless dolorous midland sea.
In a land of sand and ruin and gold
There shone one woman, and none but she.
And finding life for her love's sake fail,
Being fain to see her, he bade set sail,
Touched land, and saw her as life grew cold,
And praised God, seeing; and so died he.

Died, praising God for his gift and grace:
For she bowed down to him weeping, and said
"Live;" and her tears were shed on his face
Or ever the life in his face was shed.
The sharp tears fell through her hair, and stung
Once, and her close lips touched him and clung
Once, and grew one with his lips for a space;
And so drew back, and the man was dead.

O brother, the gods were good to you.
Sleep, and be glad while the world endures.
Be well content as the years wear through;
Give thanks for life, and the loves and lures;
Give thanks for life, O brother, and death,
For the sweet last sound of her feet, her breath,
For gifts she gave you, gracious and few,
Tears and kisses, that lady of yours.

Rest and be glad of the gods; but I,
How shall I praise them, or how take rest?
There is not room under all the sky
For me that know not of worst or best,
Dream or desire of the days before,
Sweet things or bitterness, any more.
Love will not come to me now though I die,
As love came close to you, breast to breast.

I shall never be friends again with roses;
I shall loathe sweet tunes, where a note grown strong
Relents and recoils, and climbs and closes,
As a wave of the sea turned back by song.
There are sounds where the soul's delight takes fire,
Face to face with its own desire;
A delight that rebels, a desire that reposes,
I shall hate sweet music my whole life long.

The pulse of war and passion of wonder,
The heavens that murmur, the sounds that shine,
The stars that sing and the loves that thunder,
The music burning at heart like wine,
An armed archangel whose hands raise up
All senses mixed in the spirit's cup
Till flesh and spirit are molten in sunder—
These things are over, and no more mine.

These were a part of the playing I heard
Once, ere my love and my heart were at strife;
Love that sings and hath wings as a bird,
Balm of the wound and heft of the knife,
Fairer than earth is the sea, and sleep
Than overwatching of eyes that weep,
Now time has done with this one sweet word,
The wine and leaven of lovely life.

I shall go my ways, tread out my measure,
Fill the days of my daily breath
With fugitive things not good to treasure,
Do as the world doth, say as it saith;
But if we had loved each other—O sweet,
Had you felt, lying under the palms of your feet,
The heart of my heart, beating harder with pleasure
To feel you tread it to dust and death—

Ah, had I not taken my life up and given
All that life gives and the years let go,
The wine and honey, the balm and leaven,
The dreams reared high and the hopes brought low?
Come life, come death, not a word be said;
Should I lose you living, and vex you dead?
I never shall tell you on earth; and in heaven
If I cry to you then, will you hear or know?

1866

A LEAVE-TAKING

Let us go hence, my songs; she will not hear.
Let us go hence together without fear;
Keep silence now, for singing-time is over,
And over all old things and all things dear.
She loves not you nor me as all we love her.
Yea, though we sang as angels in her ear,
She would not hear.

Let us rise up and part; she will not know.
Let us go seaward as the great winds go,
Full of blown sand and foam; what help is there?
There is no help, for all these things are so,
And all the world is bitter as a tear.
And how these things are, though ye strove to show,
She would not know.

Let us go home and hence; she will not weep.
We gave love many dreams and days to keep,
Flowers without scent, and fruits that would not grow,
Saying, "If thou wilt, thrust in thy sickle and reap."
All is reaped now; no grass is left to mow;
And we that sowed, though all we fell on sleep,
She would not weep.

Let us go hence and rest; she will not love.
She shall not hear us if we sing hereof,
Nor see love's ways, how sore they are and steep.
Come hence, let be, lie still; it is enough.
Love is a barren sea, bitter and deep;
And though she saw all heaven in flower above,
She would not love.

Let us give up, go down; she will not care.
Though all the stars made gold of all the air,
And the sea moving saw before it move
One moon-flower making all the foam-flowers fair;
Though all those waves went over us, and drove
Deep down the stifling lips and drowning hair,
She would not care.

Let us go hence, go hence; she will not see.
Sing all once more together: surely she,
She too, remembering days and words that were,
Will turn a little toward us, sighing; but we,
We are hence, we are gone, as though we had not been there.
Nay, and though all men seeing had pity on me,
She would not see.

1866

ITYLUS

Swallow, my sister, O sister swallow,
How can thine heart be full of the spring?
A thousand summers are over and dead.
What hast thou found in the spring to follow?
What hast thou found in thine heart to sing?
What wilt thou do when the summer is shed?

O swallow, sister, O fair swift swallow,
Why wilt thou fly after spring to the south,
The soft south whither thine heart is set?
Shall not the grief of the old time follow?
Shall not the song thereof cleave to thy mouth?
Hast thou forgotten ere I forget?

Sister, my sister, O fleet sweet swallow,
Thy way is long to the sun and the south;
But I, fulfilled of my heart's desire,
Shedding my song upon height, upon hollow,
From tawny body and sweet small mouth
Feed the heart of the night with fire.

I the nightingale all spring through,
O swallow, sister, O changing swallow,
All spring through till the spring be done,
Clothed with the light of the night on the dew,
Sing, while the hours and the wild birds follow,
Take flight and follow and find the sun.

Sister, my sister, O soft light swallow,
Though all things feast in the spring's guest-chamber,
How hast thou heart to be glad thereof yet?
For where thou fliest I shall not follow,
Till life forget and death remember,
Till thou remember and I forget.

Swallow, my sister, O singing swallow,
I know not how thou hast heart to sing
Hast thou the heart? is it all past over?
Thy lord the summer is good to follow,
And fair the feet of thy lover the spring:
But what wilt thou say to the spring thy lover?

O swallow, sister, O fleeting swallow,
My heart in me is a molten ember,
And over my head the waves have met.

But thou wouldst tarry or I would follow,
Could I forget or thou remember,
Couldst thou remember and I forget.

O sweet stray sister, O shifting swallow,
The heart's division divideth us.
Thy heart is light as a leaf of a tree;
But mine goes forth among sea-gulfs hollow
To the place of the slaying of Itylus,
The feast of Daulis, the Thracian sea.

O swallow, sister, O rapid swallow,
I pray thee sing not a little space.
Are not the roofs and the lintels wet?
The woven web that was plain to follow,
The small slain body, the flower-like face,
Can I remember if thou forget?

O sister, sister, thy first-begotten!
The hands that cling and the feet that follow,
The voice of the child's blood crying yet
Who hath remembered me? who hath forgotten?
Thou hast forgotten, O summer swallow,
But the world shall end when I forget.

1866

HYMN TO PROSERPINE

(AFTER THE PROCLAMATION IN ROME OF THE CHRISTIAN FAITH)

Vicisti, Galilæe.

I HAVE lived long enough, having seen one thing, that love hath an end;
Goddess and maiden and queen, be near me now and befriend.
Thou art more than the day or the morrow, the seasons that laugh or that weep;
For these give joy and sorrow; but thou, Proserpina, sleep.
Sweet is the treading of wine, and sweet the feet of the dove;
But a goodlier gift is thine than foam of the grapes or love.
Yea, is not even Apollo, with hair and harpstring of gold,
A bitter God to follow, a beautiful God to behold?
I am sick of singing; the bays burn deep and chafe: I am fain
To rest a little from praise and grievous pleasure and pain.
For the Gods we know not of, who give us our daily breath,
We know they are cruel as love or life, and lovely as death.
O Gods dethroned and deceased, cast forth, wiped out in a day!
From your wrath is the world released, redeemed from your chains, men say.
New Gods are crowned in the city, their flowers have broken your rods;
They are merciful, clothed with pity, the young compassionate Gods.
But for me their new device is barren, the days are bare;
Things long past over suffice, and men forgotten that were.
Time and the Gods are at strife: ye dwell in the midst thereof,
Draining a little life from the barren breasts of love.
I say to you, cease, take rest; yea, I say to you all, be at peace,
Till the bitter milk of her breast and the barren bosom shall cease.
Wilt thou yet take all, Galilean? but these thou shalt not take,
The laurel, the palms and the pæan, the breasts of the nymphs in the brake;
Breasts more soft than a dove's, that tremble with tenderer breath;
And all the wings of the Loves, and all the joy before death;
All the feet of the hours that sound as a single lyre,
Dropped and deep in the flowers, with strings that flicker like fire.
More than these wilt thou give, things fairer than all these things?
Nay, for a little we live, and life hath mutable wings.
A little while and we die; shall life not thrive as it may?

For no man under the sky lives twice, outliving his day.
And grief is a grievous thing, and a man hath enough of his tears:
Why should he labour, and bring fresh grief to blacken his years?
Thou hast conquered, O pale Galilean; the world has grown grey from thy breath;
We have drunken of things Lethean, and fed on the fullness of death.
Laurel is green for a season, and love is sweet for a day;
But love grows bitter with treason, and laurel outlives not May.
Sleep, shall we sleep after all? for the world is not sweet in the end;
For the old faiths loosen and fall, the new years ruin and rend.
Fate is a sea without shore, and the soul is a rock that abides;
But her ears are vexed with the roar and her face with the foam of the tides.
O lips that the live blood faints in, the leavings of racks and rods!
O ghastly glories of saints, dead limbs of gibbeted Gods!
Though all men abase them before you in spirit, and all knees bend,
I kneel not neither adore you, but standing, look to the end.
All delicate days and pleasant, all spirits and sorrows are cast
Far out with the foam of the present that sweeps to the surf of the past:
Where beyond the extreme sea-wall, and between the remote sea-gates,
Waste water washes, and tall ships founder, and deep death waits:
Where, mighty with deepening sides, clad about with the seas as with wings,
And impelled of invisible tides, and fulfilled of unspeakable things,
White-eyed and poisonous-finned, shark-toothed and serpentine-curled,
Rolls, under the whitening wind of the future, the wave of the world.
The depths stand naked in sunder behind it, the storms flee away;
In the hollow before it the thunder is taken and snared as a prey;
In its sides is the north-wind bound; and its salt is of all men's tears;
With light of ruin, and sound of changes, and pulse of years:
With travail of day after day, and with trouble of hour upon hour;
And bitter as blood is the spray; and the crests are as fangs that devour:
And its vapour and storm of its steam as the sighing of spirits to be;
And its noise as the noise in a dream; and its depth as the roots of the sea:
And the height of its heads as the height of the utmost stars of the air:
And the ends of the earth at the might thereof tremble, and time is made bare.
Will ye bridle the deep sea with reins, will ye chasten the high sea with rods?
Will ye take her to chain her with chains, who is older than all ye Gods?
All ye as a wind shall go by, as a fire shall ye pass and be past;
Ye are Gods, and behold ye shall die, and the waves be upon you at last.
In the darkness of time, in the deeps of the years, in the changes of things,
Ye shall sleep as a slain man sleeps, and the world shall forget you for kings.
Though the feet of thine high priests tread where thy lords and our forefathers trod,
Though these that were Gods are dead, and thou being dead art a God,
Though before thee the throned Cytherean be fallen, and hidden her head,
Yet thy kingdom shall pass, Galilean, thy dead shall go down to thee dead.
Of the maiden thy mother men sing as a goddess with grace clad around;
Thou art throned where another was king; where another was queen she is crowned.
Yea, once we had sight of another: but now she is queen, say these.
Not as thine, not as thine was our mother, a blossom of flowering seas,
Clothed round with the world's desire as with raiment, and fair as the foam,
And fleeter than kindled fire, and a goddess, and mother of Rome.
For thine came pale and a maiden, and sister to sorrow; but ours,
Her deep hair heavily laden with odour and colour of flowers,

White rose of the rose-white water, a silver splendour, a flame,
Bent down unto us that besought her, and earth grew sweet with her name.
For thine came weeping, a slave among slaves, and rejected; but she
Came flushed from the full-flushed wave, and imperial, her foot on the sea,
And the wonderful waters knew her, the winds and the viewless ways,
And the roses grew rosier, and bluer the sea-blue stream of the bays.
Ye are fallen, our lords, by what token? we wist that ye should not fall.
Ye were all so fair that are broken; and one more fair than ye all.
But I turn to her still, having seen she shall surely abide in the end;
Goddess and maiden and queen, be near me now and befriend.
O daughter of earth, of my mother, her crown and blossom of birth,
I am also, I also, thy brother; I go as I came unto earth.
In the night where thine eyes are as moons are in heaven, the night where thou art,
Where the silence is more than all tunes, where sleep overflows from the heart,
Where the poppies are sweet as the rose in our world, and the red rose is white,
And the wind falls faint as it blows with the fume of the flowers of the night,
And the murmur of spirits that sleep in the shadow of Gods from afar
Grows dim in thine ears and deep as the deep dim soul of a star,
In the sweet low light of thy face, under heavens untrod by the sun,
Let my soul with their souls find place, and forget what is done and undone.
Thou art more than the Gods who number the days of our temporal breath;
For these give labor and slumber; but thou, Proserpina, death.
Therefore now at thy feet I abide for a season in silence. I know
I shall die as my fathers died, and sleep as they sleep; even so.
For the glass of the years is brittle wherein we gaze for a span;
A little soul for a little bears up this corpse which is man.[1]
So long I endure, no longer; and laugh not again, neither weep.
For there is no God found stronger than death; and death is a sleep.

1866

ILICET

THERE is an end of joy and sorrow;
Peace all day long, all night, all morrow,
  But never a time to laugh or weep.
The end is come of pleasant places,
The end of tender words and faces,
  The end of all, the poppied sleep.

No place for sound within their hearing,
No room to hope, no time for fearing,
  No lips to laugh, no lids for tears.
The old years have run out all their measure;
No chance of pain, no chance of pleasure,
  No fragment of the broken years.

Outside of all the worlds and ages,
There where the fool is as the sage is,
  There where the slayer is clean of blood,
No end, no passage, no beginning,
There where the sinner leaves off sinning,
  There where the good man is not good.

There is not one thing with another,
But Evil saith to Good: My brother,
  My brother, I am one with thee:
They shall not strive nor cry forever:
No man shall choose between them: never
  Shall this thing end and that thing be.

Wind wherein seas and stars are shaken
Shall shake them, and they shall not waken;
  None that has lain down shall arise;
The stones are sealed across their places;
One shadow is shed on all their faces,
  One blindness cast on all their eyes.

[1] Ψυχάριον εἶ βαστάζον νεκρόν. EPICTETUS.

Sleep, is it sleep perchance that covers
Each face, as each face were his lover's?
  Farewell; as men that sleep fare well.
The grave's mouth laughs unto derision
Desire and dread and dream and vision,
  Delight of heaven and sorrow of hell.

No soul shall tell nor lip shall number
The names and tribes of you that slumber;
  No memory, no memorial.
"Thou knowest"—who shall say thou knowest?
There is none highest and none lowest:
  An end, an end, an end of all.

Good night, good sleep, good rest from sorrow,
To these that shall not have good morrow;
  The gods be gentle to all these.
Nay, if death be not, how shall they be?
Nay, is there help in heaven? it may be
  All things and lords of things shall cease.

The stooped urn, filling, dips and flashes;
The bronzed brims are deep in ashes;
  The pale old lips of death are fed.
Shall this dust gather flesh hereafter?
Shall one shed tears or fall to laughter,
  At sight of all these poor old dead?

Nay, as thou wilt; these know not of it;
Thine eyes' strong weeping shall not profit,
  Thy laughter shall not give thee ease;
Cry aloud, spare not, cease not crying,
Sigh, till thou cleave thy sides with sighing,
  Thou shalt not raise up one of these.

Burnt spices flash, and burnt wine hisses,
The breathing flame's mouth curls and kisses
  The small dried rows of frankincense;
All round the sad red blossoms smoulder,
Flowers colored like the fire, but colder,
  In sign of sweet things taken hence;

Yea, for their sake and in death's favour
Things of sweet shape and of sweet savour
  We yield them, spice and flower and wine;
Yea, costlier things than wine or spices,
Whereof none knoweth how great the price is,
  And fruit that comes not of the vine.

From boy's pierced throat and girl's pierced bosom
Drips, reddening round the blood-red blossom,
  The slow delicious bright soft blood,
Bathing the spices and the pyre,
Bathing the flowers and fallen fire,
  Bathing the blossom by the bud.

Roses whose lips the flame had deadened
Drink till the lapping leaves are reddened
  And warm wet inner petals weep;
The flower whereof sick sleep gets leisure,
Barren of balm and purple pleasure,
  Fumes with no native steam of sleep.

Why will ye weep? what do ye weeping?
For waking folk and people sleeping,
  And sands that fill and sands that fall,
The day rose-red, the poppied hours,
Blood, wine, and spice and fire and flowers,
  There is one end of one and all.

Shall such an one lend love or borrow?
Shall these be sorry for thy sorrow?
  Shall these give thanks for words or breath?
Their hate is as their loving-kindness;
The frontlet of their brows is blindness,
  The armlet of their arms is death.

Lo, for no noise or light of thunder
Shall these grave-clothes be rent in sunder;
  He that hath taken, shall he give?
He hath rent them: shall he bind together?
He hath bound them: shall he break the tether?
  He hath slain them: shall he bid them live?

A little sorrow, a little pleasure,
Fate metes us from the dusty measure
  That holds the date of all of us;
We are born with travail and strong crying,
And from the birth-day to the dying
  The likeness of our life is thus.

One girds himself to serve another,
Whose father was the dust, whose mother
  The little dead red worm therein;
They find no fruit of things they cherish;
The goodness of a man shall perish,
  It shall be one thing with his sin.

In deep wet ways by grey old gardens
Fed with sharp spring the sweet fruit hardens;
They know not what fruits wane or grow;
Red summer burns to the utmost ember;
They know not, neither can remember,
The old years and flowers they used to know.

Ah, for their sakes, so trapped and taken,
For theirs, forgotten and forsaken,
Watch, sleep not, gird thyself with prayer.
Nay, where the heart of wrath is broken,
Where long love ends as a thing spoken,
How shall thy crying enter there?

Though the iron sides of the old world falter,
The likeness of them shall not alter
For all the rumour of periods,
The stars and seasons that come after,
The tears of latter men, the laughter
Of the old unalterable gods.

Far up above the years and nations,
The high gods, clothed and crowned with patience,
Endure through days of deathlike date;
They bear the witness of things hidden;
Before their eyes all life stands chidden,
As they before the eyes of Fate.

Not for their love shall Fate retire,
Nor they relent for our desire,
Nor the graves open for their call.
The end is more than joy and anguish,
Than lives that laugh and lives that languish,
The poppied sleep, the end of all.

1866

A MATCH

If love were what the rose is,
And I were like the leaf,
Our lives would grow together
In sad or singing weather,
Blown fields or flowerful closes,
Green pleasure or grey grief;
If love were what the rose is,
And I were like the leaf.

If I were what the words are,
And love were like the tune,
With double sound and single
Delight our lips would mingle,
With kisses glad as birds are
That get sweet rain at noon;
If I were what the words are
And love were like the tune.

If you were life, my darling,
And I your love were death,
We'd shine and snow together
Ere March made sweet the weather
With daffodil and starling
And hours of fruitful breath;
If you were life, my darling,
And I your love were death.

If you were thrall to sorrow,
And I were page to joy,
We'd play for lives and seasons
With loving looks and treasons
And tears of night and morrow
And laughs of maid and boy;
If you were thrall to sorrow,
And I were page to joy.

If you were April's lady,
And I were lord in May,
We'd throw with leaves for hours
And draw for days with flowers,
Till day like night were shady
And night were bright like day;
If you were April's lady,
And I were lord in May.

If you were queen of pleasure,
And I were king of pain,
We'd hunt down love together,
Pluck out his flying-feather,
And teach his feet a measure,
And find his mouth a rein;
If you were queen of pleasure,
And I were king of pain.

1866

A BALLAD OF BURDENS

The burden of fair women. Vain delight,
And love self-slain in some sweet shameful way,
And sorrowful old age that comes by night
As a thief comes that has no heart by day,

And change that finds fair cheeks and leaves them grey,
And weariness that keeps awake for hire,
And grief that says what pleasure used to say;
This is the end of every man's desire.

The burden of bought kisses. This is sore,
A burden without fruit in childbearing;
Between the nightfall and the dawn threescore,
Threescore between the dawn and evening.
The shuddering in thy lips, the shuddering
In thy sad eyelids tremulous like fire,
Makes love seem shameful and a wretched thing.
This is the end of every man's desire.

The burden of sweet speeches. Nay, kneel down,
Cover thy head, and weep; for verily
These market-men that buy thy white and brown
In the last days shall take no thought for thee.
In the last days like earth thy face shall be,
Yea, like sea-marsh made thick with brine and mire,
Sad with sick leavings of the sterile sea.
This is the end of every man's desire.

The burden of long living. Thou shalt fear
Waking, and sleeping mourn upon thy bed;
And say at night "Would God the day were here,"
And say at dawn "Would God the day were dead."
With weary days thou shalt be clothed and fed,
And wear remorse of heart for thine attire,
Pain for thy girdle and sorrow upon thine head;
This is the end of every man's desire.

The burden of bright colors. Thou shalt see
Gold tarnished, and the grey above the green;
And as the thing thou seest thy face shall be,
And no more as the thing beforetime seen.
And thou shalt say of mercy "It hath been,"
And living, watch the old lips and loves expire,
And talking, tears shall take thy breath between;
This is the end of every man's desire.

The burden of sad sayings. In that day
Thou shalt tell all thy days and hours, and tell
Thy times and ways and words of love, and say
How one was dear and one desirable,
And sweet was life to hear and sweet to smell,
But now with lights reverse the old hours retire
And the last hour is shod with fire from hell;
This is the end of every man's desire.

The burden of four seasons. Rain in spring,
White rain and wind among the tender trees;
A summer of green sorrows gathering,
Rank autumn in a mist of miseries,
With sad face set towards the year, that sees
The charred ash drop out of the dropping pyre,
And winter wan with many maladies;
This is the end of every man's desire.

The burden of dead faces. Out of sight
And out of love, beyond the reach of hands,
Changed in the changing of the dark and light,
They walk and weep about the barren lands
Where no seed is nor any garner stands,
Where in short breaths the doubtful days respire,
And time's turned glass lets through the sighing sands;
This is the end of every man's desire.

The burden of much gladness. Life and lust
Forsake thee, and the face of thy delight;
And underfoot the heavy hour strews dust,
And overhead strange weathers burn and bite;

And where the red was, lo the bloodless white,
And where truth was, the likeness of a liar,
And where day was, the likeness of the night;
This is the end of every man's desire.

L'ENVOY

Princes, and ye whom pleasure quickeneth,
Heed well this rhyme before your pleasure tire;
For life is sweet, but after life is death.
This is the end of every man's desire.

1866

IN MEMORY OF WALTER SAVAGE LANDOR

Back to the flower-town, side by side,
The bright months bring,
New-born, the bridegroom and the bride,
Freedom and spring.

The sweet land laughs from sea to sea,
Filled full of sun;
All things come back to her, being free;
All things but one.

In many a tender wheaten plot
Flowers that were dead
Live, and old suns revive; but not
That holier head.

By this white wandering waste of sea,
Far north, I hear
One face shall never turn to me
As once this year:

Shall never smile and turn and rest
On mine as there,
Nor one most sacred hand be prest
Upon my hair.

I came as one whose thoughts half linger,
Half run before;
The youngest to the oldest singer
That England bore.

I found him whom I shall not find
Till all grief end,
In holiest age our mightiest mind,
Father and friend.

But thou, if anything endure,
If hope there be,
O spirit that man's life left pure,
Man's death set free,

Not with disdain of days that were
Look earthward now;
Let dreams revive the reverend hair,
The imperial brow;

Come back in sleep, for in the life
Where thou art not
We find none like thee. Time and strife
And the world's lot

Move thee no more; but love at least
And reverent heart
May move thee, royal and released,
Soul, as thou art.

And thou, his Florence, to thy trust
Receive and keep,
Keep safe his dedicated dust,
His sacred sleep.

So shall thy lovers, come from far,
Mix with thy name
As morning-star with evening-star
His faultless fame.

1866

DOLORES

(NOTRE-DAME DES SEPT DOULEURS)

Cold eyelids that hide like a jewel
Hard eyes that grow soft for an hour;
The heavy white limbs, and the cruel
Red mouth like a venomous flower;
When these are gone by with their glories,
What shall rest of thee then, what remain,
O mystic and sombre Dolores,
Our Lady of Pain?

Seven sorrows the priests give their Virgin;
But thy sins, which are seventy times seven,
Seven ages would fail thee to purge in,
And then they would haunt thee in heaven:
Fierce midnights and famishing morrows,
And the loves that complete and control
All the joys of the flesh, all the sorrows
That wear out the soul.

O garment not golden but gilded,
  O garden where all men may dwell,
O tower not of ivory, but builded
  By hands that reach heaven from hell;
O mystical rose of the mire,
  O house not of gold but of gain,
O house of unquenchable fire,
  Our Lady of Pain!

O lips full of lust and of laughter,
  Curled snakes that are fed from my breast,
Bite hard, lest remembrance come after
  And press with new lips where you pressed.
For my heart too springs up at the pressure,
  Mine eyelids too moisten and burn;
Ah, feed me and fill me with pleasure,
  Ere pain come in turn.

In yesterday's reach and to-morrow's,
  Out of sight though they lie of to-day,
There have been and there yet shall be sorrows
  That smite not and bite not in play.
The life and the love thou despisest,
  These hurt us indeed, and in vain,
O wise among women, and wisest,
  Our Lady of Pain.

Who gave thee thy wisdom? what stories
  That stung thee, what visions that smote?
Wert thou pure and a maiden, Dolores,
  When desire took thee first by the throat?
What bud was the shell of a blossom
  That all men may smell to and pluck?
What milk fed thee first at what bosom?
  What sins gave thee suck?

We shift and bedeck and bedrape us,
  Thou art noble and nude and antique;
Libitina thy mother, Priapus
  Thy father, a Tuscan and Greek.
We play with light loves in the portal,
  And wince and relent and refrain;
Loves die, and we know thee immortal,
  Our Lady of Pain.

Fruits fail and love dies and time ranges;
  Thou art fed with perpetual breath,
And alive after infinite changes,
  And fresh from the kisses of death;
Of languors rekindled and rallied,
  Of barren delights and unclean,
Things monstrous and fruitless, a pallid
  And poisonous queen.

Could you hurt me, sweet lips, though I hurt you?
  Men touch them, and change in a trice
The lilies and languors of virtue
  For the raptures and roses of vice;
Those lie where thy foot on the floor is,
  These crown and caress thee and chain,
O splendid and sterile Dolores,
  Our Lady of Pain.

There are sins it may be to discover,
  There are deeds it may be to delight.
What new work wilt thou find for thy lover?
  What new passions for daytime or night?
What spells that they know not a word of
  Whose lives are as leaves overblown?
What tortures undreamt of, unheard of,
  Unwritten, unknown?

Ah beautiful passionate body
  That never has ached with a heart!
On thy mouth though the kisses are bloody,
  Though they sting till it shudder and smart,
More kind than the love we adore is,
  They hurt not the heart or the brain,
O bitter and tender Dolores,
  Our Lady of Pain.

As our kisses relax and redouble,
  From the lips and the foam and the fangs
Shall no new sin be born for men's trouble,
  No dream of impossible pangs?
With the sweet of the sins of old ages
  Wilt thou satiate thy soul as of yore?
Too sweet is the rind, say the sages,
  Too bitter the core.

Hast thou told all thy secrets the last time,
  And bared all thy beauties to one?
Ah, where shall we go then for pastime,
  If the worst that can be has been done?
But sweet as the rind was the core is;
  We are fain of thee still, we are fain,
O sanguine and subtle Dolores,
  Our Lady of Pain.

& 7

We shift & bedeck & bedrape us,
Thou art noble & nude & antique;
Libitina thy mother, Priapus
Thy father, a Tuscan & Greek.
We play with light loves in the portal,
And wince & relent & refrain;
Loves die, & we know thee immortal,
Our Lady of Pain.

& 36

All shrines that were Vestal are flameless,
But the flame has not fallen from this;
Though obscure be the god, & though nameless
The eyes & the hair that we kiss;
Low fires that love sits by & forges
~~New shafts, with the~~ Fresh heads for his arrows & thine;
Hair loosened & soiled in mid orgies
With kisses & wine.

Stanzas 7 and 36 of "Dolores" in Swinburne's Handwriting. (See Appendix I.)

By the hunger of change and emotion,
  By the thirst of unbearable things,
By despair, the twin-born of devotion,
  By the pleasure that winces and stings,
The delight that consumes the desire,
  The desire that outruns the delight;
By the cruelty deaf as a fire
  And blind as the night,

By the ravenous teeth that have smitten
  Through the kisses that blossom and bud,
By the lips intertwisted and bitten
  Till the foam has a savour of blood,
By the pulse as it rises and falters,
  By the hands as they slacken and strain,
I adjure thee, respond from thine altars,
  Our Lady of Pain.

Wilt thou smile as a woman disdaining
  The light fire in the veins of a boy?
But he comes to thee sad, without feigning,
  Who has wearied of sorrow and joy;
Less careful of labour and glory
  Than the elders whose hair has uncurled;
And young, but with fancies as hoary
  And grey as the world.

I have passed from the outermost portal
  To the shrine where a sin is a prayer;
What care though the service be mortal?
  O our lady of Torture, what care?
All thine the last wine that I pour is,
  The last in the chalice we drain,
O fierce and luxurious Dolores,
  Our Lady of Pain.

All thine the new wine of desire,
  The fruit of four lips as they clung
Till the hair and the eyelids took fire,
  The foam of a serpentine tongue,
The froth of the serpents of pleasure,
  More salt than the foam of the sea,
Now felt as a flame, now at leisure
  As wine shed for me.

Ah thy people, thy children, thy chosen,
  Marked cross from the womb and perverse!
They have found out the secret to cozen
  The gods that constrain us and curse;
They alone, they are wise, and none other;
  Give me place, even me, in their train,
O my sister, my spouse, and my mother,
  Our Lady of Pain.

For the crown of our life as it closes
  Is darkness, the fruit thereof dust;
No thorns go as deep as a rose's,
  And love is more cruel than lust.
Time turns the old days to derision,
  Our loves into corpses or wives;
And marriage and death and division
  Make barren our lives.

And pale from the past we draw nigh thee
  And satiate with comfortless hours;
And we know thee, how all men belie thee,
  And we gather the fruit of thy flowers;
The passion that slays and recovers,
  The pangs and the kisses that rain
On the lips and the limbs of thy lovers,
  Our Lady of Pain.

The desire of thy furious embraces
  Is more than the wisdom of years,
On the blossom though blood lie in traces,
  Though the foliage be sodden with tears.
For the lords in whose keeping the door is
  That opens on all who draw breath
Gave the cypress to love, my Dolores,
  The myrtle to death.

And they laughed, changing hands in the measure,
  And they mixed and made peace after strife;
Pain melted in tears, and was pleasure;
  Death tingled with blood, and was life.
Like lovers they melted and tingled,
  In the dusk of thine innermost fane;
In the darkness they murmured and mingled,
  Our Lady of Pain.

In a twilight where virtues are vices,
  In thy chapels, unknown of the sun,
To a tune that enthralls and entices,
  They were wed, and the twain were as one.
For the tune from thine altar hath sounded
  Since God bade the world's work begin,
And the fume of thine incense abounded,
  To sweeten the sin.

Love listens, and paler than ashes,
  Through his curls as the crown on them slips,
Lifts languid wet eyelids and lashes,
  And laughs with insatiable lips.

Thou shalt hush him with heavy caresses,
With music that scares the profane;
Thou shalt darken his eyes with thy tresses,
Our Lady of Pain.

Thou shalt blind his bright eyes though he wrestle,
Thou shalt chain his light limbs though he strive;
In his lips all thy serpents shall nestle,
In his hands all thy cruelties thrive.
In the daytime thy voice shall go through him,
In his dreams he shall feel thee and ache;
Thou shalt kindle by night and subdue him
Asleep and awake.

Thou shalt touch and make redder his roses
With juice not of fruit nor of bud;
When the sense in the spirit reposes,
Thou shalt quicken the soul through the blood.
Thine, thine the one grace we implore is,
Who would live and not languish or feign,
O sleepless and deadly Dolores,
Our Lady of Pain.

Dost thou dream, in a respite of slumber,
In a lull of the fires of thy life,
Of the days without name, without number,
When thy will stung the world into strife,
When, a goddess, the pulse of thy passion
Smote kings as they revelled in Rome;
And they hailed thee re-risen, O Thalassian,
Foam-white, from the foam?

When thy lips had such lovers to flatter,
When the city lay red from thy rods,
And thine hands were as arrows to scatter
The children of change and their gods;
When the blood of thy foemen made fervent
A sand never moist from the main,
As one smote them, their lord and thy servant,
Our Lady of Pain.

On sands by the storm never shaken,
Nor wet from the washing of tides;
Nor by foam of the waves overtaken,
Nor winds that the thunder bestrides;
But red from the print of thy paces,
Made smooth for the world and its lords,
Ringed round with a flame of fair faces,
And splendid with swords.

There the gladiator, pale for thy pleasure,
Drew bitter and perilous breath;
There torments laid hold on the treasure
Of limbs too delicious for death;
When thy gardens were lit with live torches;
When the world was a steed for thy rein;
When the nations lay prone in thy porches,
Our Lady of Pain.

When, with flame all around him aspirant,
Stood flushed, as a harp-player stands,
The implacable beautiful tyrant,
Rose-crowned, having death in his hands;
And a sound as the sound of loud water
Smote far through the flight of the fires,
And mixed with the lightning of slaughter
A thunder of lyres.

Dost thou dream of what was and no more is,
The old kingdoms of earth and the kings?
Dost thou hunger for these things, Dolores,
For these, in a world of new things?
But thy bosom no fasts could emaciate,
No hunger compel to complain
Those lips that no bloodshed could satiate,
Our Lady of Pain.

As of old when the world's heart was lighter,
Through thy garments the grace of thee glows,
The white wealth of thy body made whiter
By the blushes of amorous blows,
And seamed with sharp lips and fierce fingers,
And branded by kisses that bruise;
When all shall be gone that now lingers,
Ah, what shall we lose?

Thou wert fair in the fearless old fashion,
And thy limbs are as melodies yet,
And move to the music of passion
With lithe and lascivious regret.
What ailed us, O gods, to desert you
For creeds that refuse and restrain?
Come down and redeem us from virtue,
Our Lady of Pain.

All shrines that were Vestal are flameless,
But the flame has not fallen from this;
Though obscure be the god, and though nameless
The eyes and the hair that we kiss;

Low fires that love sits by and forges
  Fresh heads for his arrows and thine;
Hair loosened and soiled in mid orgies
  With kisses and wine.

Thy skin changes country and colour,
  And shrivels or swells to a snake's.
Let it brighten and bloat and grow duller,
  We know it, the flames and the flakes,
Red brands on it smitten and bitten,
  Round skies where a star is a stain,
And the leaves with thy litanies written,
  Our Lady of Pain.

On thy bosom though many a kiss be,
  There are none such as knew it of old.
Was it Alciphron once or Arisbe,
  Male ringlets or feminine gold,
That thy lips met with under the statue,
  Whence a look shot out sharp after thieves
From the eyes of the garden-god at you
  Across the fig-leaves?

Then still, through dry seasons and moister,
  One god had a wreath to his shrine;
Then love was the pearl of his oyster,[1]
  And Venus rose red out of wine.
We have all done amiss, choosing rather
  Such loves as the wise gods disdain;
Intercede for us thou with thy father,
  Our Lady of Pain.

In spring he had crowns of his garden,
  Red corn in the heat of the year,
Then hoary green olives that harden
  When the grape-blossom freezes with fear;
And milk-budded myrtles with Venus
  And vine-leaves with Bacchus he trod;
And ye said, "We have seen, he hath seen us,
  A visible God."

What broke off the garlands that girt you?
  What sundered you spirit and clay?
Weak sins yet alive are as virtue
  To the strength of the sins of that day.

[1] "Nam te præcipuè in suis urbibus colit ora Hellespontia, cæteris ostreosior oris."
Catull. *Carm.* xviii.
("The cities on the shores of the Hellespont, richer in oysters than the other waters, especially worship thee.")

For dried is the blood of thy lover,
  Ipsithilla, contracted the vein;
Cry aloud, "Will he rise and recover,
  Our Lady of Pain?"

Cry aloud; for the old world is broken:
  Cry out; for the Phrygian is priest,
And rears not the bountiful token
  And spreads not the fatherly feast.
From the midmost of Ida, from shady
  Recesses that murmur at morn,
They have brought and baptized her, Our Lady,
  A goddess new-born.

And the chaplets of old are above us,
  And the oyster-bed teems out of reach;
Old poets outsing and outlove us,
  And Catullus makes mouths at our speech.
Who shall kiss, in thy father's own city,
  With such lips as he sang with, again?
Intercede for us all of thy pity,
  Our Lady of Pain.

Out of Dindymus heavily laden
  Her lions draw bound and unfed
A mother, a mortal, a maiden,
  A queen over death and the dead.
She is cold, and her habit is lowly,
  Her temple of branches and sods;
Most fruitful and virginal, holy,
  A mother of gods.

She hath wasted with fire thine high places,
  She hath hidden and marred and made sad
The fair limbs of the Loves, the fair faces
  Of gods that were goodly and glad.
She slays, and her hands are not bloody;
  She moves as a moon in the wane,
White-robed, and thy raiment is ruddy,
  Our Lady of Pain.

They shall pass and their places be taken,
  The gods and the priests that are pure.
They shall pass, and shalt thou not be shaken?
  They shall perish, and shalt thou endure?
Death laughs, breathing close and relentless
  In the nostrils and eyelids of lust,
With a pinch in his fingers of scentless
  And delicate dust.

But the worm shall revive thee with kisses;
Thou shalt change and transmute as a god,
As the rod to a serpent that hisses,
As the serpent again to a rod.
Thy life shall not cease though thou doff it;
Thou shalt live until evil be slain,
And good shall die first, said thy prophet,
Our Lady of Pain.

Did he lie? did he laugh? does he know it,
Now he lies out of reach, out of breath,
Thy prophet, thy preacher, thy poet,
Sin's child by incestuous Death?
Did he find out in fire at his waking,
Or discern as his eyelids lost light,
When the bands of the body were breaking
And all came in sight?

Who has known all the evil before us,
Or the tyrannous secrets of time?
Though we match not the dead men that bore us
At a song, at a kiss, at a crime—
Though the heathen outface and outlive us,
And our lives and our longings are twain—
Ah, forgive us our virtues, forgive us,
Our Lady of Pain.

Who are we that embalm and embrace thee
With spices and savours of song?
What is time, that his children should face thee;
What am I, that my lips do thee wrong?
I could hurt thee—but pain would delight thee;
Or caress thee—but love would repel;
And the lovers whose lips would excite thee
Are serpents in hell.

Who now shall content thee as they did,
Thy lovers, when temples were built
And the hair of the sacrifice braided
And the blood of the sacrifice spilt,
In Lampsacus fervent with faces,
In Aphaca red from thy reign,
Who embraced thee with awful embraces,
Our Lady of Pain?

Where are they, Cotytto or Venus,
Astarte or Ashtaroth, where?
Do their hands as we touch come between us?
Is the breath of them hot in thy hair?
From their lips have thy lips taken fever,
With the blood of their bodies grown red?
Hast thou left upon earth a believer
If these men are dead?

They were purple of raiment and golden,
Filled full of thee, fiery with wine,
Thy lovers, in haunts unbeholden,
In marvellous chambers of thine.
They are fled, and their footprints escape us,
Who appraise thee, adore, and abstain,
O daughter of Death and Priapus,
Our Lady of Pain.

What ails us to fear overmeasure,
To praise thee with timorous breath,
O mistress and mother of pleasure,
The one thing as certain as death?
We shall change as the things that we cherish,
Shall fade as they faded before,
As foam upon water shall perish,
As sand upon shore.

We shall know what the darkness discovers,
If the grave-pit be shallow or deep;
And our fathers of old, and our lovers,
We shall know if they sleep not or sleep.
We shall see whether hell be not heaven,
Find out whether tares be not grain,
And the joys of thee seventy times seven,
Our Lady of Pain.

1866

MADONNA MIA

Under green apple boughs
That never a storm will rouse,
My lady hath her house
Between two bowers;
In either of the twain
Red roses full of rain;
She hath for bondwomen
All kind of flowers.

She hath no handmaid fair
To draw her curled gold hair
Through rings of gold that bear
Her whole hair's weight;
She hath no maids to stand
Gold-clothed on either hand;
In all the great green land
None is so great.

She hath no more to wear
But one white hood of vair
Drawn over eyes and hair,
  Wrought with strange gold,
Made for some great queen's head,
Some fair great queen since dead;
And one strait gown of red
  Against the cold.

Beneath her eyelids deep
Love lying seems asleep,
Love, swift to wake, to weep,
  To laugh, to gaze;
Her breasts are like white birds,
And all her gracious words
As water-grass to herds
  In the June-days.

To her all dews that fall
And rains are musical;
Her flowers are fed from all,
  Her joy from these;
In the deep-feathered firs
Their gift of joy is hers,
In the least breath that stirs
  Across the trees.

She grows with greenest leaves,
Ripens with reddest sheaves,
Forgets, remembers, grieves,
  And is not sad;
The quiet lands and skies
Leave light upon her eyes;
None knows her, weak or wise,
  Or tired or glad.

None knows, none understands,
What flowers are like her hands;
Though you should search all lands
  Wherein time grows,
What snows are like her feet,
Though his eyes burn with heat
Through gazing on my sweet,
  Yet no man knows.

Only this thing is said;
That white and gold and red,
God's three chief words, man's bread
  And oil and wine,
Were given her for dowers,
And kingdom of all hours,
And grace of goodly flowers
  And various vine.

This is my lady's praise:
God after many days
Wrought her in unknown ways,
  In sunset lands;
This was my lady's birth;
God gave her might and mirth
And laid his whole sweet earth
  Between her hands.

Under deep apple-boughs
My lady hath her house;
She wears upon her brows
  The flower thereof;
All saying but what God saith
To her is as vain breath;
She is more strong than death,
  Being strong as love.

1866

LOVE AT SEA

We are in love's land to-day;
  Where shall we go?
Love, shall we start or stay,
  Or sail or row?
There's many a wind and way,
And never a May but May;
We are in love's hand to-day;
  Where shall we go?

Our landwind is the breath
Of sorrows kissed to death
  And joys that were;
Our ballast is a rose;
Our way lies where God knows
  And love knows where.
    We are in love's hand to-day—

Our seamen are fledged Loves,
Our masts are bills of doves,
  Our decks fine gold;
Our ropes are dead maids' hair,
Our stores are love-shafts fair
  And manifold.
    We are in love's land to-day—

Where shall we land you, sweet?
On fields of strange men's feet,
  Or fields near home?
Or where the fire-flowers blow,
Or where the flowers of snow
  Or flowers of foam?
    We are in love's hand to-day—

Land me, she says, where love
Shows but one shaft, one dove,
One heart, one hand.
—A shore like that, my dear,
Lies where no man will steer,
No maiden land.

Imitated from Théophile Gautier.

1866

THE GARDEN OF PROSERPINE

Here, where the world is quiet,
Here, where all trouble seems
Dead winds' and spent waves' riot
In doubtful dreams of dreams;
I watch the green field growing
For reaping folk and sowing,
For harvest time and mowing,
A sleepy world of streams.

I am tired of tears and laughter,
And men that laugh and weep;
Of what may come hereafter
For men that sow to reap:
I am weary of days and hours,
Blown buds of barren flowers,
Desires and dreams and powers
And everything but sleep.

Here life has death for neighbour,
And far from eye or ear
Wan waves and wet winds labour,
Weak ships and spirits steer;
They drive adrift, and whither
They wot not who make thither;
But no such winds blow hither,
And no such things grow here.

No growth of moor or coppice,
No heather-flower or vine,
But bloomless buds of poppies,
Green grapes of Proserpine,
Pale beds of blowing rushes
Where no leaf blooms or blushes,
Save this whereout she crushes
For dead men deadly wine.

Pale, without name or number,
In fruitless fields of corn,
They bow themselves and slumber
All night till light is born;
And like a soul belated,
In hell and heaven unmated,
By cloud and mist abated
Comes out of darkness morn.

Though one were strong as seven,
He too with death shall dwell,
Nor wake with wings in heaven,
Nor weep for pains in hell;
Though one were fair as roses,
His beauty clouds and closes;
And well though love reposes,
In the end it is not well.

Pale, beyond porch and portal,
Crowned with calm leaves, she stands
Who gathers all things mortal
With cold immortal hands;
Her languid lips are sweeter
Than love's who fears to greet her
To men that mix and meet her
From many times and lands.

She waits for each and other,
She waits for all men born;
Forgets the earth her mother,
The life of fruits and corn;
And spring and seed and swallow
Take wing for her and follow
Where summer song rings hollow
And flowers are put to scorn.

There go the loves that wither,
The old loves with wearier wings;
And all dead years draw thither,
And all disastrous things;
Dead dreams of days forsaken,
Blind buds that snows have shaken,
Wild leaves that winds have taken,
Red strays of ruined springs.

We are not sure of sorrow,
And joy was never sure;
To-day will die to-morrow;
Time stoops to no man's lure;
And love, grown faint and fretful,
With lips but half regretful
Sighs, and with eyes forgetful
Weeps that no loves endure.

From too much love of living,
From hope and fear set free,
We thank with brief thanksgiving
Whatever gods may be

That no life lives for ever;
That dead men rise up never;
That even the weariest river
Winds somewhere safe to sea.

Then star nor sun shall waken,
Nor any change of light:
Nor sound of waters shaken,
Nor any sound or sight:
Nor wintry leaves nor vernal,
Nor days nor things diurnal;
Only the sleep eternal
In an eternal night.

1866

SAPPHICS

All the night sleep came not upon my eyelids,
Shed not dew, nor shook nor unclosed a feather,
Yet with lips shut close and with eyes of iron
Stood and beheld me.

Then to me so lying awake a vision
Came without sleep over the seas and touched me,
Softly touched mine eyelids and lips; and I too,
Full of the vision,

Saw the white implacable Aphrodite,
Saw the hair unbound and the feet unsandalled
Shine as fire of sunset on western waters;
Saw the reluctant

Feet, the straining plumes of the doves that drew her,
Looking always, looking with necks reverted,
Back to Lesbos, back to the hills whereunder
Shone Mitylene;

Heard the flying feet of the Loves behind her
Make a sudden thunder upon the waters,
As the thunder flung from the strong unclosing
Wings of a great wind.

So the goddess fled from her place, with awful
Sound of feet and thunder of wings around her;
While behind a clamour of singing women
Severed the twilight.

Ah the singing, ah the delight, the passion!
All the Loves wept, listening; sick with anguish,
Stood the crowned nine Muses about Apollo;
Fear was upon them,

While the tenth sang wonderful things they knew not.
Ah the tenth, the Lesbian! the nine were silent,
None endured the sound of her song for weeping;
Laurel by laurel,

Faded all their crowns; but about her forehead,
Round her woven tresses and ashen temples
White as dead snow, paler than grass in summer,
Ravaged with kisses,

Shone a light of fire as a crown for ever.
Yea, almost the implacable Aphrodite
Paused, and almost wept; such a song was that song,
Yea, by her name too

Called her, saying, "Turn to me, O my Sappho;"
Yet she turned her face from the Loves, she saw not
Tears or laughter darken immortal eyelids,
Heard not about her

Fearful fitful wings of the doves departing,
Saw not how the bosom of Aphrodite
Shook with weeping, saw not her shaken raiment,
Saw not her hands wrung;

Saw the Lesbians kissing across their smitten
Lutes with lips more sweet than the sound of lute-strings,
Mouth to mouth and hand upon hand, her chosen,
Fairer than all men;

Only saw the beautiful lips and fingers,
Full of songs and kisses and little whispers,
Full of music; only beheld among them
Soar, as a bird soars

Newly fledged, her visible song, a marvel,
Made of perfect sound and exceeding passion,
Sweetly shapen, terrible, full of thunders,
Clothed with the wind's wings.

Then rejoiced she, laughing with love, and scattered
Roses, awful roses of holy blossom;
Then the Loves thronged sadly with hidden faces
Round Aphrodite,

Then the Muses, stricken at heart, were silent;
Yea, the gods waxed pale; such a song was that song.
All reluctant, all with a fresh repulsion,
Fled from before her.

All withdrew long since, and the land was barren,
Full of fruitless women and music only.
Now perchance, when winds are assuaged at sunset,
Lulled at the dewfall,

By the grey sea-side, unassuaged, unheard of,
Unbeloved, unseen in the ebb of twilight,
Ghosts of outcast women return lamenting,
Purged not in Lethe,

Clothed about with flame and with tears, and singing
Songs that move the heart of the shaken heaven,
Songs that break the heart of the earth with pity,
Hearing, to hear them.

1866

DEDICATION

(*Poems and Ballads, First Series*)

The sea gives her shells to the shingle,
The earth gives her streams to the sea;
They are many, but my gift is single,
My verses, the first fruits of me.
Let the wind take the green and the grey leaf,
Cast forth without fruit upon air;
Take rose-leaf and vine-leaf and bay-leaf
Blown loose from the hair.

The night shakes them round me in legions
Dawn drives them before her like dreams;
Time sheds them like snows on strange regions,
Swept shoreward on infinite streams;
Leaves pallid and sombre and ruddy,
Dead fruits of the fugitive years;
Some stained as with wine and made bloody,
And some as with tears.

Some scattered in seven years' traces,
As they fell from the boy that was then;
Long left among idle green places,
Or gathered but now among men;
On seas full of wonder and peril,
Blown white round the capes of the north;
Or in islands where myrtles are sterile
And loves bring not forth.

O daughters of dreams and of stories
That life is not wearied of yet,
Faustine, Fragoletta, Dolores,
Félise and Yolande and Juliette,
Shall I find you not still, shall I miss you,
When sleep, that is true or that seems,
Comes back to me hopeless to kiss you,
O daughters of dreams?

They are past as a slumber that passes,
As the dew of a dawn of old time;
More frail than the shadows on glasses,
More fleet than a wave or a rhyme.
As the waves after ebb drawing seaward,
When their hollows are full of the night,
So the birds that flew singing to me-ward
Recede out of sight.

The songs of dead seasons, that wander
On wings of articulate words;
Lost leaves that the shore-wind may squander,
Light flocks of untameable birds;
Some sang to me dreaming in class-time
And truant in hand as in tongue;
For the youngest were born of boy's pastime,
The eldest are young.

Is there shelter while life in them lingers,
Is there hearing for songs that recede,
Tunes touched from a harp with men's fingers
Or blown with boy's mouth in a reed?

Is there place in the land of your labour,
  Is there room in your world of delight,
Where change has not sorrow for neighbour
  And day has not night?

In their wings though the sea-wind yet quivers,
  Will you spare not a space for them there
Made green with the running of rivers
  And gracious with temperate air;
In the fields and the turreted cities,
  That cover from sunshine and rain
Fair passions and bountiful pities
  And loves without stain?

In a land of clear colours and stories,
  In a region of shadowless hours,
Where earth has a garment of glories
  And a murmur of musical flowers;
In woods where the spring half uncovers
  The flush of her amorous face,
By the waters that listen for lovers,
  For these is there place?

For the song-birds of sorrow, that muffle
  Their music as clouds do their fire:
For the storm-birds of passion, that ruffle
  Wild wings in a wind of desire;
In the stream of the storm as it settles
  Blown seaward, borne far from the sun,
Shaken loose on the darkness like petals
  Dropt one after one?

Though the world of your hands be more gracious
  And lovelier in lordship of things
Clothed round by sweet art with the spacious
  Warm heaven of her imminent wings,
Let them enter, unfledged and nigh fainting,
  For the love of old loves and lost times;
And receive in your palace of painting
  This revel of rhymes.

Though the seasons of man full of losses
  Make empty the years full of youth,
If but one thing be constant in crosses,
  Change lays not her hand upon truth;
Hopes die, and their tombs are for token
  That the grief as the joy of them ends
Ere time that breaks all men has broken
  The faith between friends.

Though the many lights dwindle to one light,
  There is help if the heaven has one;
Though the skies be discrowned of the sunlight
  And the earth dispossessed of the sun,
They have moonlight and sleep for repayment,
  When, refreshed as a bride and set free
With stars and sea-winds in her raiment,
  Night sinks on the sea.

1866

BEFORE DAWN

Sweet life, if life were stronger,
Earth clear of years that wrong her,
Then two things might live longer,
  Two sweeter things than they;
Delight, the rootless flower,
And love, the bloomless bower;
Delight that lives an hour,
  And love that lives a day,

From evensong to daytime,
When April melts in Maytime,
Love lengthens out his playtime,
  Love lessens breath by breath,
And kiss by kiss grows older
On listless throat or shoulder
Turned sideways now, turned colder
  Than life that dreams of death.

This one thing once worth giving
Life gave, and seemed worth living;
Sin sweet beyond forgiving
  And brief beyond regret:
To laugh and love together
And weave with foam and feather
And wind and words the tether
  Our memories play with yet.

Ah, one thing worth beginning,
One thread in life worth spinning,
Ah sweet, one sin worth sinning
  With all the whole soul's will;
To lull you till one stilled you,
To kiss you till one killed you,
To feed you till one filled you,
  Sweet lips, if love could fill;

To hunt sweet Love and lose him
Between white arms and bosom,
Between the bud and blossom,
  Between your throat and chin;

To say of shame—what is it?
Of virtue—we can miss it,
Of sin—we can but kiss it,
  And it's no longer sin:

To feel the strong soul, stricken
Through fleshly pulses, quicken
Beneath swift sighs that thicken,
  Soft hands and lips that smite;
Lips that no love can tire,
With hands that sting like fire,
Weaving the web Desire
  To snare the bird Delight.

But love so lightly plighted,
Our love with torch unlighted,
Paused near us unaffrighted,
  Who found and left him free;
None, seeing us cloven in sunder,
Will weep or laugh or wonder;
Light love stands clear of thunder,
  And safe from winds at sea.

As, when late larks give warning
Of dying lights and dawning,
Night murmurs to the morning,
  "Lie still, O love, lie still;"
And half her dark limbs cover
The white limbs of her lover,
With amorous plumes that hover
  And fervent lips that chill;

As scornful day represses
Night's void and vain caresses,
And from her cloudier tresses
  Unwinds the gold of his,
With limbs from limbs dividing
And breath by breath subsiding;
For love has no abiding,
  But dies before the kiss.

So hath it been, so be it;
For who shall live and flee it?
But look that no man see it
  Or hear it unaware;
Lest all who love and choose him
See Love, and so refuse him;
For all who find him lose him,
  But all have found him fair.

1866

THE LEPER

NOTHING is better, I well think,
  Than love; the hidden well-water
Is not so delicate to drink:
  This was well seen of me and her.

I served her in a royal house;
  I served her wine and curious meat.
For will to kiss between her brows,
  I had no heart to sleep or eat.

Mere scorn God knows she had of me,
  A poor scribe, nowise great or fair,
Who plucked his clerk's hood back to see
  Her curled up lips and amorous hair.

I vex my head with thinking this.
  Yea, though God always hated me,
And hates me now that I can kiss
  Her eyes, plait up her hair to see

How she then wore it on the brows,
  Yet am I glad to have her dead
Here in this wretched wattled house
  Where I can kiss her eyes and head.

Nothing is better, I well know,
  Than love; no amber in cold sea
Or gathered berries under snow:
  That is well seen of her and me.

Three thoughts I make my pleasure of:
  First I take heart and think of this:
That knight's gold hair she chose to love,
  His mouth she had such will to kiss.

Then I remember that sundawn
  I brought him by a privy way
Out at her lattice, and thereon
  What gracious words she found to say.

(Cold rushes for such little feet—
  Both feet could lie into my hand.
A marvel was it of my sweet
  Her upright body could so stand.)

"Sweet friend, God give you thank and grace;
  Now am I clean and whole of shame,
Nor shall men burn me in the face
  For my sweet fault that scandals them."

I tell you over word by word.
She, sitting edgewise on her bed,
Holding her feet, said thus. The third,
A sweeter thing than these, I said.

God, that makes time and ruins it,
And alters not, abiding God,
Changed with disease her body sweet,
The body of love wherein she abode.

Love is more sweet and comelier
Than a dove's throat strained out to sing.
All they spat out and cursed at her
And cast her forth for a base thing.

They cursed her, seeing how God had wrought
This curse to plague her, a curse of his.
Fools were they surely, seeing not
How sweeter than all sweet she is.

He that had held her by the hair,
With kissing lips blinding her eyes,
Felt her bright bosom, strained and bare,
Sigh under him, with short mad cries

Out of her throat and sobbing mouth
And body broken up with love,
With sweet hot tears his lips were loth
Her own should taste the savour of,

Yea, he inside whose grasp all night
Her fervent body leapt or lay,
Stained with sharp kisses red and white,
Found her a plague to spurn away.

I hid her in this wattled house,
I served her water and poor bread.
For joy to kiss between her brows
Time upon time I was nigh dead.

Bread failed; we got but well-water
And gathered grass with dropping seed.
I had such joy of kissing her,
I had small care to sleep or feed.

Sometimes when service made me glad
The sharp tears leapt between my lids,
Falling on her, such joy I had
To do the service God forbids.

"I pray you let me be at peace,
Get hence, make room for me to die."
She said that: her poor lip would cease,
Put up to mine, and turn to cry.

I said, "Bethink yourself how love
Fared in us twain, what either did;
Shall I unclothe my soul thereof?
That I should do this, God forbid."

Yea, though God hateth us, he knows
That hardly in a little thing
Love faileth of the work it does
Till it grow ripe for gathering.

Six months, and now my sweet is dead
A trouble takes me; I know not
If all were done well, all well said,
No word or tender deed forgot.

Too sweet, for the least part in her,
To have shed life out by fragments; yet,
Could the close mouth catch breath and stir,
I might see something I forget.

Six months, and I sit still and hold
In two cold palms her cold two feet.
Her hair, half grey half ruined gold,
Thrills me and burns me in kissing it.

Love bites and stings me through, to see
Her keen face made of sunken bones.
Her worn-off eyelids madden me,
That were shot through with purple once.

She said, "Be good with me; I grow
So tired for shame's sake, I shall die
If you say nothing:" even so.
And she is dead now, and shame put by.

Yea, and the scorn she had of me
In the old time, doubtless vexed her then.
I never should have kissed her. See
What fools God's anger makes of men!

She might have loved me a little too,
Had I been humbler for her sake.
But that new shame could make love new
She saw not—yet her shame did make.

I took too much upon my love,
Having for such mean service done
Her beauty and all the ways thereof,
Her face and all the sweet thereon.

Yea, all this while I tended her,
I know the old love held fast his part:
I know the old scorn waxed heavier,
Mixed with sad wonder, in her heart.

It may be all my love went wrong—
A scribe's work writ awry and blurred,
Scrawled after the blind evensong—
Spoilt music with no perfect word.

But surely I would fain have done
All things the best I could. Perchance
Because I failed, came short of one,
She kept at heart that other man's.

I am grown blind with all these things:
It may be now she hath in sight
Some better knowledge; still there clings
The old question. Will not God do right?

1866

AVE ATQUE VALE

IN MEMORY OF CHARLES BAUDELAIRE

Nous devrions pourtant lui porter quelques fleurs;
Les morts, les pauvres morts, ont de grandes douleurs,
Et quand Octobre souffle, émondeur des vieux arbres,
Son vent mélancolique à l'entour de leurs marbres,
Certe, ils doivent trouver les vivants bien ingrats.

Les Fleurs du Mal.

I

SHALL I strew on thee rose or rue or laurel,
Brother, on this that was the veil of thee?
Or quiet sea-flower moulded by the sea,
Or simplest growth of meadow-sweet or sorrel,
Such as the summer-sleepy Dryads weave,
Waked up by snow-soft sudden rains at eve?
Or wilt thou rather, as on earth before,
Half-faded fiery blossoms, pale with heat
And full of bitter summer, but more sweet
To thee than gleanings of a northern shore
Trod by no tropic feet?

II

For always thee the fervid languid glories
Allured of heavier suns in mightier skies;
Thine ears knew all the wandering watery sighs
Where the sea sobs round Lesbian promontories,
The barren kiss of piteous wave to wave
That knows not where is that Leucadian grave
Which hides too deep the supreme head of song.
Ah, salt and sterile as her kisses were,
The wild sea winds her and the green gulfs bear
Hither and thither, and vex and work her wrong,
Blind gods that cannot spare.

III

Thou sawest, in thine old singing season, brother,
Secrets and sorrows unbeheld of us:
Fierce loves, and lovely leaf-buds poisonous,
Bare to thy subtler eye, but for none other
Blowing by night in some unbreathed-in clime;
The hidden harvest of luxurious time,
Sin without shape, and pleasure without speech;
And where strange dreams in a tumultuous sleep
Make the shut eyes of stricken spirits weep;
And with each face thou sawest the shadow on each,
Seeing as men sow men reap.

IV

O sleepless heart and sombre soul unsleeping,
That were athirst for sleep and no more life
And no more love, for peace and no more strife!
Now the dim gods of death have in their keeping
Spirit and body and all the springs of song,
Is it well now where love can do no wrong,
Where stingless pleasure has no foam or fang
Behind the unopening closure of her lips?
Is it not well where soul from body slips
And flesh from bone divides without a pang
As dew from flower-bell drips?

V

It is enough; the end and the beginning
Are one thing to thee, who art past the end.
O hand unclasped of unbeheld friend,

For thee no fruits to pluck, no palms for winning,
No triumph and no labor and no lust,
Only dead yew-leaves and a little dust.
O quiet eyes wherein the light saith nought,
Whereto the day is dumb, nor any night
With obscure finger silences your sight,
Nor in your speech the sudden soul speaks thought,
Sleep, and have sleep for light.

VI

Now all strange hours and all strange loves are over,
Dreams and desires and sombre songs and sweet,
Hast thou found place at the great knees and feet
Of some pale Titan-woman like a lover,
Such as thy vision here solicited,
Under the shadow of her fair vast head,
The deep division of prodigious breasts,
The solemn slope of mighty limbs asleep,
The weight of awful tresses that still keep
The savour and shade of old-world pine-forests
Where the wet hill-winds weep?

VII

Hast thou found any likeness for thy vision?
O gardener of strange flowers, what bud, what bloom,
Hast thou found sown, what gathered in the gloom?
What of despair, of rapture, of derision,
What of life is there, what of ill or good?
Are the fruits gray like dust or bright like blood?
Does the dim ground grow any seed of ours,
The faint fields quicken any terrene root,
In low lands where the sun and moon are mute
And all the stars keep silence? Are there flowers
At all, or any fruit?

VIII

Alas, but though my flying song flies after,
O sweet strange elder singer, thy more fleet
Singing, and footprints of thy fleeter feet,
Some dim derision of mysterious laughter
From the blind tongueless warders of the dead,
Some gainless glimpse of Proserpine's veiled head,
Some little sound of unregarded tears
Wept by effaced unprofitable eyes,
And from pale mouths some cadence of dead sighs—
These only, these the hearkening spirit hears,
Sees only such things rise.

IX

Thou art far too far for wings of words to follow,
Far too far off for thought or any prayer.
What ails us with thee, who art wind and air?
What ails us gazing where all seen is hollow?
Yet with some fancy, yet with some desire,
Dreams pursue death as winds a flying fire,
Our dreams pursue our dead and do not find.
Still, and more swift than they, the thin flame flies,
The low light fails us in elusive skies,
Still the foiled earnest ear is deaf, and blind
Are still the eluded eyes.

X

Not thee, O never thee, in all time's changes,
Not thee, but this the sound of thy sad soul,
The shadow of thy swift spirit, this shut scroll
I lay my hand on, and not death estranges
My spirit from communion of thy song—
These memories and these melodies that throng
Veiled porches of a Muse funereal—
These I salute, these touch, these clasp and fold
As though a hand were in my hand to hold,
Or through mine ears a mourning musical
Of many mourners rolled.

XI

I among these, I also, in such station
As when the pyre was charred, and piled the sods,
And offering to the dead made, and their gods,
The old mourners had, standing to make libation,
I stand, and to the gods and to the dead
Do reverence without prayer or praise, and shed
Offering to these unknown, the gods of gloom,
And what of honey and spice my seedlands bear,
And what I may of fruits in this chilled air,
And lay, Orestes-like, across the tomb
A curl of severed hair.

XII

But by no hand nor any treason stricken,
Not like the low-lying head of Him, the King,
The flame that made of Troy a ruinous thing,
Thou liest and on this dust no tears could quicken
There fall no tears like theirs that all men hear
Fall tear by sweet imperishable tear
Down the opening leaves of holy poet's pages.
Thee not Orestes, not Electra mourns;
But bending us-ward with memorial urns
The most high Muses that fulfil all ages
Weep, and our God's heart yearns.

XIII

For, sparing us his sacred strength, not often
Among us darkling here the lord of light
Makes manifest his music and his might
In hearts that open and in lips that soften
With the soft flame and heat of songs that shine.
Thy lips indeed he touched with bitter wine,
And nourished them indeed with bitter bread;
Yet surely from his hand thy soul's food came,
The fire that scarred thy spirit at his flame
Was lighted, and thine hungering heart he fed
Who feeds our hearts with fame.

XIV

Therefore he too now at thy soul's sunsetting,
God of all suns and songs, he too bends down
To mix his laurel with thy cypress crown,
And save thy dust from blame and from forgetting.
Therefore he too, seeing all thou wert and art,
Compassionate, with sad and sacred heart,
Mourns thee of many his children the last dead,
And hallows with strange tears and alien sighs
Thine unmelodious mouth and sunless eyes,
And over thine irrevocable head
Sheds light from the under skies.

XV

And one weeps with him in the ways Lethean,
And stains with tears her changing bosom chill;
That obscure Venus of the hollow hill,
That thing transformed which was the Cytherean,
With lips that lost their Grecian laugh divine
Long since, and face no more called Erycine;
A ghost, a bitter and luxurious god.
Thee also with fair flesh and singing spell
Did she, a sad and second prey, compel
Into the footless places once more trod,
And shadows hot from hell.

XVI

And now no sacred staff shall break in blossom,
No choral salutation lure to light
A spirit with perfume and sweet night
And love's tired eyes and hands and barren bosom.
There is no help for these things; none to mend
And none to mar; not all our songs, O friend,

Will make death clear or make life durable.
Howbeit with rose and ivy and wild vine
And with wild notes about this dust of thine
At least I fill the place where white dreams dwell
And wreathe an unseen shrine.

XVII

Sleep; and if life was bitter to thee, pardon,
If sweet, give thanks; thou hast no more to live;
And to give thanks is good, and to forgive.
Out of the mystic and the mournful garden
Where all day through thine hands in barren braid
Wove the sick flowers of secrecy and shade,
Green buds of sorrow and sin, and remnants gray,
Sweet-smelling, pale with poison, sanguine-hearted,
Passions that sprang from sleep and thoughts that started,
Shall death not bring us all as thee one day
Among the days departed?

XVIII

For thee, O now a silent soul, my brother,
Take at my hands this garland, and farewell.
Thin is the leaf, and chill the wintry smell,
And chill the solemn earth, a fatal mother,
With sadder than the Niobean womb,
And in the hollow of her breasts a tomb.
Content thee, howsoe'er, whose days are done:
There lies not any troublous thing before,
Nor sight nor sound to war against thee more,
For whom all winds are quiet as the sun,
All waters as the shore.

1868

SUPER FLUMINA BABYLONIS

By the waters of Babylon we sat down and wept,
Remembering thee,
That for ages of agony hast endured, and slept,
And wouldst not see.

By the waters of Babylon we stood up and sang,
Considering thee,
That a blast of deliverance in the darkness rang,
To set thee free.

And with trumpets and thunderings and with morning song
Came up the light;
And thy spirit uplifted thee to forget thy wrong
As day doth night.

And thy sons were dejected not any more, as then
When thou wast shamed;
When thy lovers went heavily without heart, as men
Whose life was maimed.

In the desolate distances, with a great desire,
For thy love's sake,
With our hearts going back to thee, they were filled with fire,
Were nigh to break.

It was said to us: "Verily ye are great of heart,
But ye shall bend;
Ye are bondmen and bondwomen, to be scourged and smart,
To toil and tend."

And with harrows men harrowed us, and subdued with spears,
And crushed with shame;
And the summer and winter was, and the length of years,
And no change came.

By the rivers of Italy, by the sacred streams,
By town, by tower,
There was feasting with revelling, there was sleep with dreams,
Until thine hour.

And they slept and they rioted on their rose-hung beds,
With mouths on flame,
And with love-locks vine-chapleted, and with rose-crowned heads
And robes of shame.

And they knew not their forefathers, nor the hills and streams
And words of power,
Nor the gods that were good to them, but with songs and dreams
Filled up their hour.

By the rivers of Italy, by the dry streams' beds,
When thy time came,
There was casting of crowns from them, from their young men's heads,
The crowns of shame.

By the horn of Eridanus, by the Tiber mouth,
As thy day rose,
They arose up and girded them to the north and south,
By seas, by snows.

As a water in January the frost confines,
Thy kings bound thee;
As a water in April is, in the new-blown vines,
Thy sons made free.

And thy lovers that looked for thee, and that mourned from far,
For thy sake dead,
We rejoiced in the light of thee, in the signal star
Above thine head.

In thy grief had we followed thee, in thy passion loved,
Loved in thy loss;
In thy shame we stood fast to thee, with thy pangs were moved,
Clung to thy cross.

By the hillside of Calvary we beheld thy blood,
Thy bloodred tears,
As a mother's in bitterness, an unebbing flood,
Years upon years.

And the north was Gethsemane, without leaf or bloom,
A garden sealed;
And the south was Aceldama, for a sanguine fume
Hid all the field.

By the stone of the sepulchre we returned to weep,
From far, from prison;
And the guards by it keeping it we beheld asleep,
But thou wast risen.

And an angel's similitude by the unsealed grave,
And by the stone:
And the voice was angelical, to whose words God gave
Strength like his own.

"Lo, the graveclothes of Italy that are folded up
In the grave's gloom!
And the guards as men wrought upon with charmed cup,
By the open tomb.

"And her body most beautiful, and her shining head,
These are not here;
For your mother, for Italy, is not surely dead:
Have ye no fear.

"As of old time she spake to you, and you hardly heard,
Hardly took heed,
So now also she saith to you, yet another word,
Who is risen indeed.

"By my saying she saith to you, in your ears she saith,
Who hear these things,
Put no trust in men's royalties, nor in great men's breath,
Nor words of kings.

"For the life of them vanishes and is no more seen,
Nor no more known;
Nor shall any remember him if a crown hath been,
Or where a throne.

"Unto each man his handiwork, unto each his crown,
The just Fate gives;
Whoso takes the world's life on him and his own lays down,
He, dying so, lives.

"Whoso bears the whole heaviness of the wronged world's weight
And puts it by,
It is well with him suffering, though he face man's fate;
How should he die?

"Seeing death has no part in him any more, no power
Upon his head;
He has bought his eternity with a little hour,
And is not dead.

"For an hour, if ye look for him, he is no more found,
For one hour's space;
Then ye lift up your eyes to him and behold him crowned,
A deathless face.

"On the mountains of memory, by the world's well-springs,
In all men's eyes,
Where the light of the life of him is on all past things,
Death only dies.

"Not the light that was quenched for us, nor the deeds that were,
Nor the ancient days,
Nor the sorrows not sorrowful, nor the face most fair
Of perfect praise."

So the angel of Italy's resurrection said,
So yet he saith;
So the son of her suffering, that from breasts nigh dead
Drew life, not death.

That the pavement of Golgotha should be white as snow,
Not red, but white;
That the waters of Babylon should no longer flow,
And men see light.

1871

HERTHA

I AM that which began;
Out of me the years roll;
Out of me God and man;
I am equal and whole;
God changes, and man, and the form of them bodily; I am the soul.

Before ever land was,
Before ever the sea,
Or soft hair of the grass,
Or fair limbs of the tree,
Or the flesh-coloured fruit of my branches, I was, and thy soul was in me.

First life on my sources
First drifted and swam;
Out of me are the forces
That save it or damn;
Out of me man and woman, and wild-beast and bird; before God was, I am.

Beside or above me
Nought is there to go;
Love or unlove me,
Unknow me or know,
I am that which unloves me and loves; I am stricken, and I am the blow.

I the mark that is missed
And the arrows that miss,
I the mouth that is kissed
And the breath in the kiss,
The search, and the sought, and the seeker, the soul and the body that is.

I am that thing which blesses
My spirit elate;
That which caresses
With hands uncreate
My limbs unbegotten that measure the length of the measure of fate.

But what thing dost thou now,
Looking Godward, to cry
"I am I, thou art thou,
I am low, thou art high"?
I am thou, whom thou seekest to find him; find thou but thyself, thou art I.

I the grain and the furrow,
The plough-cloven clod
And the ploughshare drawn thorough,
The germ and the sod,
The deed and the doer, the seed and the sower, the dust which is God.

Hast thou known how I fashioned thee,
Child, underground?
Fire that impassioned thee,
Iron that bound,
Dim changes of water, what thing of all these hast thou known of or found?

Canst thou say in thine heart
Thou hast seen with thine eyes
With what cunning of art
Thou wast wrought in what wise,
By what force of what stuff thou wast shapen, and shown on my breast to the skies?

Who hath given, who hath sold it thee,
Knowledge of me?
Hath the wilderness told it thee?
Hast thou learnt of the sea?
Hast thou communed in spirit with night? have the winds taken counsel with thee?

Have I set such a star
To show light on thy brow
That thou sawest from afar
What I show to thee now?
Have ye spoken as brethren together, the sun and the mountains and thou?

What is here, dost thou know it?
What was, hast thou known?
Prophet nor poet
Nor tripod nor throne
Nor spirit nor flesh can make answer, but only thy mother alone.

Mother, not maker,
Born, and not made;
Though her children forsake her,
Allured or afraid,
Praying prayers to the God of their fashion, she stirs not for all that have prayed.

A creed is a rod,
And a crown is of night;
But this thing is God,
To be man with thy might,
To grow straight in the strength of thy spirit, and live out thy life as the light.

I am in thee to save thee,
As my soul in thee saith,
Give thou as I gave thee,
Thy life-blood and breath,
Green leaves of thy labour, white flowers of thy thought, and red fruit of thy death.

Be the ways of thy giving
As mine were to thee;
The free life of thy living,
Be the gift of it free;
Not as servant to lord, nor as master to slave, shalt thou give thee to me.

O children of banishment,
Souls overcast,
Were the lights ye see vanish meant
Alway to last,
Ye would know not the sun overshining the shadows and stars overpast.

I that saw where ye trod
The dim paths of the night
Set the shadow called God
In your skies to give light;
But the morning of manhood is risen, and the shadowless soul is in sight.

The tree many-rooted
That swells to the sky
With frondage red-fruited,
The life-tree am I;
In the buds of your lives is the sap of my leaves: ye shall live and not die.

But the Gods of your fashion
That take and that give,
In their pity and passion
That scourge and forgive,
They are worms that are bred in the bark that falls off: they shall die and not live.

My own blood is what stanches
The wounds in my bark;
Stars caught in my branches
Make day of the dark,
And are worshipped as suns till the sunrise shall tread out their fires as a spark.

Where dead ages hide under
The live roots of the tree,
In my darkness the thunder
Makes utterance of me;
In the clash of my boughs with each other ye hear the waves sound of the sea.

That noise is of Time,
As his feathers are spread
And his feet set to climb
Through the boughs overhead,
And my foliage rings round him and rustles, and branches are bent with his tread.

The storm-winds of ages
Blow through me and cease,
The war-wind that rages,
The spring-wind of peace,
Ere the breath of them roughen my tresses, ere one of my blossoms increase.

All sounds of all changes,
All shadows and lights
On the world's mountain-ranges
And stream-riven heights,
Whose tongue is the wind's tongue and language of storm-clouds on earth-shaking nights;

All forms of all faces,
All works of all hands
In unsearchable places
Of time-stricken lands,
All death and all life, and all reigns and all ruins, drop through me as sands.

Though sore be my burden
And more than ye know,
And my growth have no guerdon
But only to grow,
Yet I fail not of growing for lightnings above me or deathworms below.

These too have their part in me,
As I too in these;
Such fire is at heart in me,
Such sap is this tree's,
Which hath in it all sounds and all secrets of infinite lands and of seas.

In the spring-coloured hours
When my mind was as May's,
There brake forth of me flowers
By centuries of days,
Strong blossoms with perfume of manhood, shot out from my spirit as rays.

And the sound of them springing
And smell of their shoots
Were as warmth and sweet singing
And strength to my roots;
And the lives of my children made perfect with freedom of soul were my fruits.

I bid you but be;
I have need not of prayer;
I have need of you free
As your mouths of mine air;
That my heart may be greater within me, beholding the fruits of me fair.

More fair than strange fruit is
Of faiths ye espouse;
In me only the root is
That blooms in your boughs;
Behold now your God that ye made you, to feed him with faith of your vows.

In the darkening and whitening
Abysses adored,
With dayspring and lightning
For lamp and for sword,
God thunders in heaven, and his angels are red with the wrath of the Lord.

O my sons, O too dutiful
Toward Gods not of me,
Was not I enough beautiful?
Was it hard to be free?
For behold, I am with you, am in you and of you; look forth now and see.

Lo, winged with world's wonders,
With miracles shod,
With the fires of his thunders
For raiment and rod,
God trembles in heaven, and his angels are white with the terror of God.

For his twilight is come on him,
His anguish is here;
And his spirits gaze dumb on him,
Grown grey from his fear;
And his hour taketh hold on him stricken, the last of his infinite year.

Thought made him and breaks him,
Truth slays and forgives;
But to you, as time takes him,
This new thing it gives,
Even love, the beloved Republic, that feeds upon freedom and lives.

For truth only is living,
Truth only is whole,
And the love of his giving
Man's polestar and pole;
Man, pulse of my centre, and fruit of my body, and seed of my soul.

One birth of my bosom;
One beam of mine eye;
One topmost blossom
That scales the sky;
Man, equal and one with me, man that is made of me, man that is I.

1871

THE PILGRIMS

Who is your lady of love, O ye that pass
Singing? and is it for sorrow of that which was
That ye sing sadly, or dream of what shall be?
For gladly at once and sadly it seems ye sing.
—Our lady of love by you is unbeholden;
For hands she hath none, nor eyes, nor lips, nor golden
Treasure of hair, nor face nor form; but we
That love, we know her more fair than anything.

—Is she a queen, having great gifts to give?
—Yea, these; that whoso hath seen her shall not live
Except he serve her sorrowing, with strange pain,
Travail and bloodshedding and bitterer tears;
And when she bids die he shall surely die.
And he shall leave all things under the sky
And go forth naked under sun and rain
And work and wait and watch out all his years.

—Hath she on earth no place of habitation?
—Age to age calling, nation answering nation,
Cries out, Where is she? and there is none to say;
For if she be not in the spirit of men,
For if in the inward soul she hath no place,
In vain they cry unto her, seeking her face,
In vain their mouths make much of her; for they
Cry with vain tongues, till the heart lives again.

—O ye that follow, and have ye no repentance?
For on your brows is written a mortal sentence,
An hieroglyph of sorrow, a fiery sign,
That in your lives ye shall not pause or rest,
Nor have the sure sweet common love, nor keep
Friends and safe days, nor joy of life nor sleep.
—These have we not, who have one thing, the divine
Face and clear eyes of faith and fruitful breast.

—And ye shall die before your thrones be won.
—Yea, and the changed world and the liberal sun
Shall move and shine without us, and we lie
Dead; but if she too move on earth and live,
But if the old world with all the old irons rent
Laugh and give thanks, shall we be not content?
Nay, we shall rather live, we shall not die,
Life being so little and death so good to give.

—And these men shall forget you.—Yea, but we
Shall be a part of the earth and the ancient sea,
And heaven-high air august, and awful fire,
And all things good; and no man's heart shall beat
But somewhat in it of our blood once shed
Shall quiver and quicken, as now in us the dead
Blood of men slain and the old same life's desire
Plants in their fiery footprints our fresh feet.

—But ye that might be clothed with all things pleasant,
Ye are foolish that put off the fair soft present,
That clothe yourselves with the cold future air;
When mother and father and tender sister and brother
And the old live love that was shall be as ye,
Dust, and no fruit of loving life shall be.
—She shall be yet who is more than all these were,
Than sister or wife or father unto us or mother.

—Is this worth life, is this, to win for wages?
Lo, the dead mouths of the awful grey-grown ages,
The venerable, in the past that is their prison,
In the outer darkness, in the unopening grave,
Laugh, knowing how many as ye now say have said,
How many, and all are fallen, are fallen and dead:
Shall ye dead rise, and these dead have not risen?
—Not we but she, who is tender and swift to save.

—Are ye not weary and faint not by the way,
Seeing night by night devoured of day by day,
Seeing hour by hour consumed in sleepless fire?
Sleepless; and ye too, when shall ye too sleep?
—We are weary in heart and head, in hands and feet,
And surely more than all things sleep were sweet,
Than all things save the inexorable desire
Which whoso knoweth shall neither faint nor weep.

—Is this so sweet that one were fain to follow?
Is this so sure where all men's hopes are hollow,
Even this your dream, that by much tribulation
Ye shall make whole flawed hearts, and bowed necks straight?
—Nay though our life were blind, our death were fruitless,
Not therefore were the whole world's high hope rootless;
But man to man, nation would turn to nation,
And the old life live, and the old great world be great.

—Pass on then and pass by us and let us be,
For what light think ye after life to see?
And if the world fare better will ye know?
And if man triumph who shall seek you and say?
—Enough of light is this for one life's span,
That all men born are mortal, but not man:
And we men bring death lives by night to sow,
That man may reap and eat and live by day.

1871

TO WALT WHITMAN IN AMERICA

Send but a song oversea for us,
Heart of their hearts who are free,
Heart of their singer, to be for us
More than our singing can be;
Ours, in the tempest at error,
With no light but the twilight of terror;
Send us a song oversea!

Sweet-smelling of pine-leaves and grasses,
And blown as a tree through and through
With the winds of the keen mountain-passes,
And tender as sun-smitten dew;
Sharp-tongued as the winter that shakes
The wastes of your limitless lakes,
Wide-eyed as the sea-line's blue.

O strong-winged soul with prophetic
Lips hot with the bloodbeats of song,
With tremor of heartstrings magnetic,
With thoughts as thunders in throng,
With consonant ardours of chords
That pierce men's souls as with swords
And hale them hearing along,

Make us too music, to be with us
As a word from a world's heart warm,
To sail the dark as a sea with us,
Full-sailed, outsinging the storm,
A song to put fire in our ears
Whose burning shall burn up tears,
Whose sign bid battle reform;

A note in the ranks of a clarion,
A word in the wind of cheer,
To consume as with lightning the carrion
That makes time foul for us here;
In the air that our dead things infest
A blast of the breath of the west,
Till east way as west way is clear.

Out of the sun beyond sunset,
From the evening whence morning shall be,
With the rollers in measureless onset,
With the van of the storming sea,

With the world-wide wind, with the breath
That breaks ships driven upon death,
  With the passion of all things free,
With the sea-steeds footless and frantic,
  White myriads for death to bestride
In the charge of the ruining Atlantic
  Where deaths by regiments ride,
With clouds and clamours of waters,
With a long note shriller than slaughter's
  On the furrowless fields world-wide,

With terror, with ardour and wonder,
  With the soul of the season that wakes
When the weight of a whole year's thunder
  In the tidestream of autumn breaks,
Let the flight of the wide-winged word
Come over, come in and be heard,
  Take form and fire for our sakes.

For a continent bloodless with travail
  Here toils and brawls as it can,
And the web of it who shall unravel
  Of all that peer on the plan;
Would fain grow men, but they grow not,
And fain be free, but they know not
  One name for freedom and man?

One name, not twain for division;
  One thing, not twain, from the birth;
Spirit and substance and vision,
  Worth more than worship is worth;
Unbeheld, unadored, undivined,
The cause, the centre, the mind,
  The secret and sense of the earth.

Here as a weakling in irons,
  Here as a weanling in bands,
As a prey that the stake-net environs,
  Our life that we looked for stands;
And the man-child naked and dear,
Democracy, turns on us here
  Eyes trembling with tremulous hands.

It sees not what season shall bring to it
  Sweet fruit of its bitter desire;
Few voices it hears yet sing to it,
  Few pulses of hearts reaspire;
Foresees not time, nor forehears
The noises of imminent years,
  Earthquake, and thunder, and fire:

When crowned and weaponed and curbless
  It shall walk without helm or shield
The bare burnt furrows and herbless
  Of war's last flame-stricken field,
Till godlike, equal with time,
It stand in the sun sublime,
  In the godhead of man revealed.

Round your people and over them
  Light like raiment is drawn,
Close as a garment to cover them
  Wrought not of mail nor of lawn:
Here, with hope hardly to wear,
Naked nations and bare
  Swim, sink, strike out for the dawn.

Chains are here, and a prison,
  Kings, and subjects, and shame;
If the God upon you be arisen,
  How should our songs be the same?
How, in confusion of change,
How shall we sing, in a strange
  Land, songs praising his name?

God is buried and dead to us,
  Even the spirit of earth,
Freedom; so have they said to us,
  Some with mocking and mirth,
Some with heartbreak and tears;
And a God without eyes, without ears,
  Who shall sing of him, dead in the birth?

The earth-god Freedom, the lonely
  Face lightening, the footprint unshod,
Not as one man crucified only
  Nor scourged with but one life's rod;
The soul that is substance of nations,
Reincarnate with fresh generations;
  The great god Man, which is God.

But in weariest of years and obscurest
  Doth it live not at heart of all things,
The one God and one spirit, a purest
  Life, fed from unstanchable springs?
Within love, within hatred it is,
And its seed in the stripe as the kiss,
  And in slaves is the germ, and in kings.

Freedom we call it, for holier
  Name of the soul's there is none;
Surelier it labours, if slowlier,
  Than the metres of star or of sun;

Slowlier than life into breath,
Surelier than time into death,
  It moves till its labour be done.

Till the motion be done and the measure
  Circling through season and clime,
Slumber and sorrow and pleasure,
  Vision of virtue and crime;
Till consummate with conquering eyes,
A soul disembodied, it rise
  From the body transfigured of time.

Till it rise and remain and take station
  With the stars of the world that rejoice;
Till the voice of its heart's exultation
  Be as theirs an invariable voice;
By no discord of evil estranged,
By no pause, by no breach in it changed,
  By no clash in the chord of its choice.

It is one with the world's generations,
  With the spirit, the star, and the sod;
With the kingless and king-stricken nations,
  With the cross, and the chain, and the rod;
The most high, the most secret, most lonely,
The earth-soul Freedom, that only
  Lives, and that only is God.

1871

COR CORDIUM

O HEART of hearts, the chalice of love's fire,
  Hid round with flowers and all the bounty of bloom;
  O wonderful and perfect heart, for whom
The lyrist liberty made life a lyre;
O heavenly heart, at whose most dear desire
  Dead love, living and singing, cleft his tomb,
  And with him risen and regent in death's room
All day thy choral pulses rang full choir;
O heart whose beating blood was running song,
  O sole thing sweeter than thine own songs were,
    Help us for thy free love's sake to be free,
True for thy truth's sake, for thy strength's sake strong,
  Till very liberty make clean and fair
    The nursing earth as the sepulchral sea.

1871

MATER TRIUMPHALIS

MOTHER of man's time-travelling generations,
  Breath of his nostrils, heartblood of his heart,
God above all Gods worshipped of all nations,
  Light above light, law beyond law, thou art.

Thy face is as a sword smiting in sunder
  Shadows and chains and dreams and iron things;
The sea is dumb before thy face, the thunder
  Silent, the skies are narrower than thy wings.

Angels and Gods, spirit and sense, thou takest
  In thy right hand as drops of dust or dew;
The temples and the towers of time thou breakest,
  His thoughts and words and works, to make them new.

All we have wandered from thy ways, have hidden
  Eyes from thy glory and ears from calls they heard;
Called of thy trumpets vainly, called and chidden,
  Scourged of thy speech and wounded of thy word.

We have known thee and have not known thee; stood beside thee,
  Felt thy lips breathe, set foot where thy feet trod,
Loved and renounced and worshipped and denied thee,
  As though thou wert but as another God.

"One hour for sleep," we said, "and yet one other;
  All day we served her, and who shall serve by night?"
Not knowing of thee, thy face not knowing, O mother,
  O light wherethrough the darkness is as light.

Men that forsook thee hast thou not forsaken,
  Races of men that knew not hast thou known;

Nations that slept thou hast doubted not to waken,
Worshippers of strange Gods to make thine own.

All old grey histories hiding thy clear features,
O secret spirit and sovereign, all men's tales,
Creeds woven of men thy children and thy creatures,
They have woven for vestures of thee and for veils.

Thine hands, without election or exemption,
Feed all men fainting from false peace or strife,
O thou, the resurrection and redemption,
The godhead and the manhood and the life.

Thy wings shadow the waters; thine eyes lighten
The horror of the hollows of the night;
The depths of the earth and the dark places brighten
Under thy feet, whiter than fire is white.

Death is subdued to thee, and hell's bands broken;
Where thou art only is heaven; who hears not thee,
Time shall not hear him; when men's names are spoken,
A nameless sign of death shall his name be.

Deathless shall be the death, the name be nameless;
Sterile of stars his twilight time of breath;
With fire of hell shall shame consume him shameless,
And dying, all the night darken his death.

The years are as thy garments, the world's ages
As sandals bound and loosed from thy swift feet;
Time serves before thee, as one that hath for wages
Praise or shame only, bitter words or sweet.

Thou sayest "Well done," and all a century kindles;
Again thou sayest "Depart from sight of me,"
And all the light of face of all men dwindles,
And the age is as the broken glass of thee.

The night is as a seal set on men's faces,
On faces fallen of men that take no light,
Nor give light in the deeps of the dark places,
Blind things, incorporate with the body of night.

Their souls are serpents winterbound and frozen,
Their shame is as a tame beast, at their feet
Couched; their cold lips deride thee and thy chosen,
Their lying lips made grey with dust for meat.

Then when their time is full and days run over,
The splendour of thy sudden brow made bare
Darkens the morning; thy bared hands uncover
The veils of light and night and the awful air.

And the world naked as a new-born maiden
Stands virginal and splendid as at birth,
With all thine heaven of all its light unladen,
Of all its love unburdened all thine earth.

For the utter earth and the utter air of heaven
And the extreme depth is thine and the extreme height;
Shadows of things and veils of ages riven
Are as men's kings unkingdomed in thy sight.

Through the iron years, the centuries brazen-gated,
By the ages' barred impenetrable doors,
From the evening to the morning have we waited,
Should thy foot haply sound on the awful floors.

The floors untrodden of the sun's feet glimmer,
The star-unstricken pavements of the night;
Do the lights burn inside? the lights wax dimmer
On festal faces withering out of sight.

The crowned heads lose the light on them; it may be
Dawn is at hand to smite the loud feast dumb;
To blind the torch-lit centuries till the day be,
The feasting kingdoms till thy kingdom come.

Shall it not come? deny they or dissemble,
Is it not even as lightning from on high
Now? and though many a soul close eyes and tremble,
How should they tremble at all who love thee as I?

I am thine harp between thine hands, O mother!
All my strong chords are strained with love of thee.
We grapple in love and wrestle, as each with other
Wrestle the wind and the unreluctant sea.

I am no courtier of thee sober-suited,
Who loves a little for a little pay.
Me not thy winds and storms nor thrones disrooted
Nor molten crowns nor thine own sins dismay.

Sinned hast thou sometime, therefore art thou sinless;
Stained hast thou been, who art therefore without stain;
Even as man's soul is kin to thee, but kinless
Thou, in whose womb Time sows the all-various grain.

I do not bid thee spare me, O dreadful mother!
I pray thee that thou spare not, of thy grace.
How were it with me then, if ever another
Should come to stand before thee in this my place?

I am the trumpet at thy lips, thy clarion
Full of thy cry, sonorous with thy breath;
The grave of souls born worms and creeds grown carrion
Thy blast of judgment fills with fires of death.

Thou art the player whose organ-keys are thunders,
And I beneath thy foot the pedal prest;
Thou art the ray whereat the rent night sunders,
And I the cloudlet borne upon thy breast.

I shall burn up before thee, pass and perish,
As haze in sunrise on the red sea-line;
But thou from dawn to sunsetting shalt cherish
The thoughts that led and souls that lighted mine.

Reared between night and noon and truth and error,
Each twilight-travelling bird that trills and screams
Sickens at midday, nor can face for terror
The imperious heaven's inevitable extremes.

I have no spirit of skill with equal fingers
At sign to sharpen or to slacken strings;
I keep no time of song with gold-perched singers
And chirp of linnets on the wrists of kings.

I am thy storm-thrush of the days that darken,
Thy petrel in the foam that bears thy bark
To port through night and tempest; if thou hearken,
My voice is in thy heaven before the lark.

My song is in the mist that hides thy morning,
My cry is up before the day for thee;
I have heard thee and beheld thee and give warning,
Before thy wheels divide the sky and sea.

Birds shall wake with thee voiced and feathered fairer,
To see in summer what I see in spring;
I have eyes and heart to endure thee, O thunder-bearer,
And they shall be who shall have tongues to sing.

I have love at least, and have not fear, and part not
From thine unnavigable and wingless way;
Thou tarriest, and I have not said thou art not,
Nor all thy night long have denied thy day.

Darkness to daylight shall lift up thy pæan,
Hill to hill thunder, vale cry back to vale,
With wind-notes as of eagles Æschylean,
And Sappho singing in the nightingale.

Sung to by mighty sons of dawn and daughters,
Of this night's songs thine ear shall keep but one;
That supreme song which shook the channelled waters,
And called thee skyward as God calls the sun.

Come, though all heaven again be fire above thee;
Though death before thee come to clear thy sky;
Let us but see in his thy face who love thee;
Yea, though thou slay us, arise and let us die.

1871

THE SONG OF THE STANDARD

Maiden most beautiful, mother most bountiful, lady of lands,
Queen and republican, crowned of the centuries whose years are thy sands,
See for thy sake what we bring to thee, Italy, here in our hands.

This is the banner thy gonfalon, fair in the front of thy fight,
Red from the hearts that were pierced for thee, white as thy mountains are white,
Green as the spring of thy soul everlasting, whose life-blood is light.

Take to thy bosom thy banner, a fair bird fit for the nest,
Feathered for flight into sunrise or sunset, for eastward or west,
Fledged for the flight everlasting, but held yet warm to thy breast.

Gather it close to thee, song-bird or storm-bearer, eagle or dove,
Lift it to sunward, a beacon beneath to the beacon above,
Green as our hope in it, white as our faith in it, red as our love.

Thunder and splendour of lightning are hid in the folds of it furled;
Who shall unroll it but thou, as thy bolt to be handled and hurled,
Out of whose lips is the honey, whose bosom the milk of the world?

Out of thine hands hast thou fed us with pasture of colour and song;
Glory and beauty by birthright to thee as thy garments belong;
Out of thine hands thou shalt give us as surely deliverance from wrong.

Out of thine eyes thou hast shed on us love as a lamp in our night,
Wisdom a lodestar to ships, and remembrance a flame-coloured light;
Out of thine eyes thou shalt shew us as surely the sundawn of right.

Turn to us, speak to us, Italy, mother, but once and a word,
None shall not follow thee, none shall not serve thee, not one that has heard;
Twice hast thou spoken a message, and time is athirst for the third.

Kingdom and empire of peoples thou hadst, and thy lordship made one
North sea and south sea and east men and west men that look on the sun;
Spirit was in thee and counsel, when soul in the nations was none.

Banner and beacon thou wast to the centuries of storm-wind and foam,
Ages that clashed in the dark with each other, and years without home;
Empress and prophetess wast thou, and what wilt thou now be, O Rome?

Ah, by the faith and the hope and the love that have need of thee now,
Shines not thy face with the forethought of freedom, and burns not thy brow?
Who is against her but all men? and who is beside her but thou?
Art thou not better than all men? and where shall she turn but to thee?
Lo, not a breath, not a beam, not a beacon from midland to sea;
Freedom cries out for a sign among nations, and none will be free.

England in doubt of her, France in despair of her, all without heart—
Stand on her side in the vanward of ages, and strike on her part!
Strike but one stroke for the love of her love of thee, sweet that thou art!

Take in thy right hand thy banner, a strong staff fit for thine hand;
Forth at the light of it lifted shall foul things flock from the land;
Faster than stars from the sun shall they fly, being lighter than sand.

Green thing to green in the summer makes answer, and rose-tree to rose;
Lily by lily the year becomes perfect; and none of us knows
What thing is fairest of all things on earth as it brightens and blows.

This thing is fairest in all time of all things, in all time is best—
Freedom, that made thee, our mother, and suckled her sons at thy breast;
Take to thy bosom the nations, and there shall the world come to rest.

1871

THE OBLATION

Ask nothing more of me, sweet,
All I can give you I give.
Heart of my heart, were it more,
More would be laid at your feet:
Love that should help you to live,
Song that should spur you to soar.

All things were nothing to give
Once to have sense of you more,
Touch you and taste of you sweet,
Think you and breathe you and live,
Swept of your wings as they soar,
Trodden by chance of your feet.

I that have love and no more
Give you but love of you, sweet:
He that hath more, let him give;
He that hath wings, let him soar;
Mine is the heart at your feet
Here, that must love you to live.

1871

TRISTRAM AND ISEULT

(Prelude to *Tristram of Lyonesse*)

Love, that is first and last of all things made,
The light that has the living world for shade,
The spirit that for temporal veil has on
The souls of all men woven in unison,
One fiery raiment with all lives inwrought
And lights of sunny and starry deed and thought,
And alway through new act and passion new
Shines the divine same body and beauty through,
The body spiritual of fire and light
That is to worldly noon as noon to night;
Love, that is flesh upon the spirit of man
And spirit within the flesh whence breath began;
Love, that keeps all the choir of lives in chime;
Love, that is blood within the veins of time;
That wrought the whole world without stroke of hand,
Shaping the breadth of sea, the length of land,
And with the pulse and motion of his breath
Through the great heart of the earth strikes life and death,
The sweet twain chords that make the sweet tune live
Through day and night of things alternative,
Through silence and through sound of stress and strife,
And ebb and flow of dying death and life;

Queen Iseult

Canto I Of the birth of Sir Tristram, & how he voyaged into Ireland

In the noble days were shown
Deeds of good knights many an one,
~~Warring well before the sun~~
Many worthy fights were done.

It was time of scath & scorn
When at breaking of the morn
Tristram the good knight was born

He was fair & well to see
As his mother's child might be.
Many happy wars had he.

Slew he worde the ~~evil~~ ~~...~~ knight alone,
Wherefore all the ill was begun
That on Blanchefleur was done.

A Page of Early Swinburne Manuscript. (See Appendix I.)

Love, that sounds loud or light in all men's ears,
Whence all men's eyes take fire from sparks of tears,
That binds on all men's feet or chains or wings;
Love, that is root and fruit of terrene things;
Love, that the whole world's waters shall not drown,
The whole world's fiery forces not burn down;
Love, that what time his own hands guard his head
The whole world's wrath and strength shall not strike dead;
Love, that if once his own hands make his grave
The whole world's pity and sorrow shall not save;
Love that for very life shall not be sold,
Nor bought nor bound with iron nor with gold;
So strong that heaven, could love bid heaven farewell,
Would turn to fruitless and unflowering hell;
So sweet that hell, to hell could love be given,
Would turn to splendid and sonorous heaven;
Love that is fire within thee and light above,
And lives by grace of nothing but of love;
Through many and lovely thoughts and much desire
Led these twain to the life of tears and fire;
Through many and lovely days and much delight
Led these twain to the lifeless life of night.
  Yea, but what then? albeit all this were thus,
And soul smote soul and left it ruinous,
And love led love as eyeless men lead men,
Through chance by chance to deathward—Ah, what then?
Hath love not likewise led them further yet,
Out through the years where memories rise and set,
Some large as suns, some moon-like warm and pale,
Some starry-sighted, some through clouds that sail
Seen as red flame through spectral float of fume,
Each with the blush of its own special bloom
On the fair face of its own coloured light,
Distinguishable in all the host of night,
Divisible from all the radiant rest
And separable in splendour? Hath the best
Light of love's all, of all that burn and move,
A better heaven than heaven is? Hath not love
Made for all these their sweet particular air
To shine in, their own beams and names to bear,
Their ways to wander and their wards to keep,
Till story and song and glory and all things sleep?
Hath he not plucked from death of lovers dead
Their musical soft memories, and kept red
The rose of their remembrance in men's eyes,
The sunsets of their stories in his skies,
The blush of their dead blood in lips that speak
Of their dead lives, and in the listener's cheek
That trembles with the kindling pity lit
In gracious hearts for some sweet fever-fit,
A fiery pity enkindled of pure thought
By tales that make their honey out of nought,
The faithless faith that lives without belief
Its light life through, the griefless ghost of grief?
Yea, as warm night refashions the sere blood
In storm-struck petal or in sun-struck bud,
With tender hours and tempering dew to cure
The hunger and thirst of day's distemperature
And ravin of the dry discolouring hours,
Hath he not bid relume their flameless flowers
With summer fire and heat of lamping song,
And bid the short-lived things, long dead, live long,
And thought remake their wan funereal fames,
And the sweet shining signs of women's names
That mark the months out and the weeks anew
He moves in changeless change of seasons through
To fill the days up of his dateless year
Flame from Queen Helen to Queen Guenevere?
For first of all the sphery signs whereby
Love severs light from darkness, and most high,

In the white front of January there glows
The rose-red sign of Helen like a rose:
And gold-eyed as the shore-flower shelterless
Whereon the sharp-breathed sea blows bitterness,
A storm-star that the seafarers of love
Strain their wind-wearied eyes for glimpses of,
Shoots keen through February's grey frost and damp
The lamplike star of Hero for a lamp;
The star that Marlowe sang into our skies
With mouth of gold, and mourning in his eyes;
And in clear March across the rough blue sea
The signal sapphire of Alcyone
Makes bright the blown brows of the wind-foot year;
And shining like a sunbeam-smitten tear
Full ere it fall, the fair next sign in sight
Burns opal-wise with April-coloured light
When air is quick with song and rain and flame,
My birth-month star that in love's heaven hath name
Iseult, a light of blossom and beam and shower,
My singing sign that makes the song-tree flower;
Next like a pale and burning pearl beyond
The rose-white sphere of flower-named Rosamond
Signs the sweet head of Maytime; and for June
Flares like an angered and storm-reddening moon
Her signal sphere, whose Carthaginian pyre
Shadowed her traitor's flying sail with fire;
Next, glittering as the wine-bright jacinth-stone,
A star south-risen that first to music shone,
The keen girl-star of golden Juliet bears
Light northward to the month whose forehead wears
Her name for flower upon it, and his trees
Mix their deep English song with Veronese;
And like an awful sovereign chrysolite
Burning, the supreme fire that blinds the night,
The hot gold head of Venus kissed by Mars,
A sun-flower among small sphered flowers of stars,
The light of Cleopatra fills and burns
The hollow of heaven whence ardent August yearns;
And fixed and shining as the sister-shed
Sweet tears for Phaethon disorbed and dead,
The pale bright autumn's amber-coloured sphere,
That through September sees the saddening year
As love sees change through sorrow, hath to name
Francesca's; and the star that watches flame
The embers of the harvest overgone
Is Thisbe's, slain of love in Babylon,
Set in the golden girdle of sweet signs
A blood-bright ruby; last save one light shines
An eastern wonder of sphery chrysopras,
The star that made men mad, Angelica's;
And latest named and lordliest, with a sound
Of swords and harps in heaven that ring it round,
Last love-light and last love-song of the year's,
Gleams like a glorious emerald Guenevere's.
These are the signs wherethrough the year sees move,
Full of the sun, the sun-god which is love,
A fiery body blood-red from the heart
Outward, with fire-white wings made wide apart,
That close not and unclose not, but upright
Steered without wind by their own light and might
Sweep through the flameless fire of air that rings
From heaven to heaven with thunder of wheels and wings
And antiphones of motion-moulded rhyme
Through spaces out of space and timeless time.

So shine above dead chance and conquered change
The sphered signs and leave without their range
Doubt and desire, and hope with fear for wife,
Pale pains, and pleasures long worn out of life.
Yea, even the shadows of them spiritless,
Through the dim door of sleep that seem to press,

Forms without form, a piteous people and blind,
Men and no men, whose lamentable kind
The shadow of death and shadow of life compel
Through semblances of heaven and false-faced hell,
Through dreams of light and dreams of darkness tost
On waves innavigable, are these so lost?
Shapes that wax pale and shift in swift strange wise,
Void faces with unspeculative eyes,
Dim things that gaze and glare, dead mouths that move,
Featureless heads discrowned of hate and love,
Mockeries and masks of motion and mute breath,
Leavings of life, the superflux of death—
If these things and no more than these things be
Left when man ends or changes, who can see?
Or who can say with what more subtle sense
Their subtler natures taste in air less dense
A life less thick and palpable than ours,
Warmed with faint fires and sweetened with dead flowers
And measured by low music? how time fares
In that wan time-forgotten world of theirs,
Their pale poor world too deep for sun or star
To live in, where the eyes of Helen are,
And hers who made as God's own eyes to shine
The eyes that met them of the Florentine,
Wherein the godhead thence transfigured lit
All time for all men with the shadow of it?
Ah, and these too felt on them as God's grace
The pity and glory of this man's breathing face;
For these too, these my lovers, these my twain,
Saw Dante, saw God visible by pain,
With lips that thundered and with feet that trod
Before men's eyes incognisable God;
Saw love and wrath and light and night and fire
Live with one life and at one mouth respire,
And in one golden sound their whole soul heard
Sounding, one sweet immitigable word.

They have the night who had like us the day;
We, whom day binds, shall have the night as they.
We, from the fetters of the light unbound,
Healed of our wound of living, shall sleep sound.
All gifts but one the jealous God may keep
From our soul's longing, one he cannot—sleep.
This, though he grudge all other grace to prayer,
This grace his closed hand cannot choose but spare.
This, though his ear be sealed to all that live,
Be it lightly given or lothly, God must give.
We, as the men whose name on earth is none,
We too shall surely pass out of the sun;
Out of the sound and eyeless light of things,
Wide as the stretch of life's time-wandering wings,
Wide as the naked world and shadowless,
And long-lived as the world's own weariness.
Us too, when all the fires of time are cold,
The heights shall hide us and the depths shall hold.
Us too, when all the tears of time are dry,
The night shall lighten from her tearless eye.
Blind is the day and eyeless all its light,
But the large unbewildered eye of night
Hath sense and speculation; and the sheer
Limitless length of lifeless life and clear,
The timeless space wherein the brief worlds move
Clothed with light life and fruitful with light love,
With hopes that threaten, and with fears that cease,
Past fear and hope, hath in it only peace.

Yet of these lives inlaid with hopes and fears,
Spun fine as fire and jewelled thick with tears,
These lives made out of loves that long since were,
Lives wrought as ours of earth and burning air,
Fugitive flame, and water of secret springs,
And clothed with joys and sorrows as with wings,
Some yet are good, if aught be good, to save
Some while from washing wreck and wrecking wave.

Was such not theirs, the twain I take, and give
Out of my life to let their dead life live
Some days of mine, and blow my living breath
Between dead lips forgotten even of death?
So many and many of old have given my twain
Love and live song and honey-parted pain,
Whose root is sweetness and whose fruit is sweet,
So many and with such joy have tracked their feet,
What should I do to follow? yet I too,
I have the heart to follow, many or few
Be the feet gone before me; for the way,
Rose-red with remnant roses of the day
Westward, and eastward white with stars that break,
Between the green and foam is fair to take
For any sail the sea-wind steers for me
From morning into morning, sea to sea.

1871

MATER DOLOROSA

Citoyen, lui dit Enjolras, ma mère, c'est la République.—*Les Misérables.*

WHO is this that sits by the way, by the wild wayside,
In a rent stained raiment, the robe of a cast-off bride,
In the dust, in the rainfall sitting, with soiled feet bare,
With the night for a garment upon her, with torn wet hair?
She is fairer of face than the daughters of men, and her eyes,
Worn through with her tears, are deep as the depth of skies.

This is she for whose sake being fallen, for whose abject sake,
Earth groans in the blackness of darkness, and men's hearts break.
This is she for whose love, having seen her, the men that were
Poured life out as water, and shed their souls upon air.
This is she for whose glory their years were counted as foam;
Whose face was a light upon Greece, was a fire upon Rome.

Is it now not surely a vain thing, a foolish and vain,
To sit down by her, mourn to her, serve her, partake in the pain?
She is grey with the dust of time on his manifold ways,
Where her faint feet stumble and falter through yearlong days.
Shall she help us at all, O fools, give fruit or give fame,
Who herself is a name despised, a rejected name?

We have not served her for guerdon. If any do so,
That his mouth may be sweet with such honey, we care not to know.
We have drunk from a wine-unsweetened, a perilous cup,
A draught very bitter. The kings of the earth stood up,
And the rulers took counsel together, to smite her and slay;
And the blood of her wounds is given us to drink to-day.

Can these bones live? or the leaves that are dead leaves bud?
Or the dead blood drawn from her veins be in your veins blood?
Will ye gather up water again that was drawn and shed?
In the blood is the life of the veins, and her veins are dead.
For the lives that are over are over, and past things past;
She had her day, and it is not; was first, and is last.

Is it nothing unto you then, all ye that pass by,
If her breath be left in her lips, if she live now or die?
Behold now, O people, and say if she be not fair,
Whom your fathers followed to find her, with praise and prayer,
And rejoiced, having found her, though roof they had none nor bread;
But ye care not; what is it to you if her day be dead?

It was well with our fathers; their sound was in all men's lands;
There was fire in their hearts, and the hunger of fight in their hands.
Naked and strong they went forth on her strength like flame,
For her love's and her name's sake of old, her republican name.
But their children, by kings made quiet, by priests made wise,
Love better the heat of their hearths than the light of her eyes.

Are they children of these thy children indeed, who have sold,
O golden goddess, the light of thy face for gold?
Are they sons indeed of the sons of thy dayspring of hope,
Whose lives are in fief of an emperor, whose souls of a Pope?
Hide then thine head, O belovèd; thy time is done;
Thy kingdom is broken in heaven, and blind thy sun.

What sleep is upon you, to dream she indeed shall rise,
When the hopes are dead in her heart as the tears in her eyes?
If ye sing of her dead, will she stir? if ye weep for her, weep?
Come away now, leave her; what hath she to do but sleep?
But ye that mourn are alive, and have years to be;
And life is good, and the world is wiser than we.

Yea, wise is the world and mighty, with years to give,
And years to promise; but how long now shall it live?
And foolish and poor is faith, and her ways are bare,
Till she find the way of the sun, and the morning air,
In that hour shall this dead face shine as the face of the sun,
And the soul of man and her soul and the world's be one.

1871

HYMN OF MAN

(During the Session in Rome of the Œcumenical Council)

In the grey beginning of years, in the twilight of things that began,
The word of the earth in the ears of the world, was it God? was it man?
The word of the earth to the spheres her sisters, the note of her song,
The sound of her speech in the ears of the starry and sisterly throng,
Was it praise or passion or prayer, was it love or devotion or dread,
When the veils of the shining air first wrapt her jubilant head?
When her eyes new-born of the night saw yet no star out of reach;
When her maiden mouth was alight with the flame of musical speech;
When her virgin feet were set on the terrible heavenly way,
And her virginal lids were wet with the dew of the birth of the day:
Eyes that had looked not on time, and ears that had heard not of death;
Lips that had learnt not the rhyme of change and passionate breath,

The rhythmic anguish of growth, and the motion of mutable things,
Of love that longs and is loth, and plume-plucked hope without wings,
Passions and pains without number, and life that runs and is lame,
From slumber again to slumber, the same race set for the same,
Where the runners outwear each other, but running with lampless hands
No man takes light from his brother till blind at the goal he stands:
Ah, did they know, did they dream of it, counting the cost and the worth?
The ways of her days, did they seem then good to the new-souled earth?
Did her heart rejoice, and the might of her spirit exult in her then,
Child yet no child of the night, and motherless mother of men?
Was it Love brake forth flower-fashion, a bird with gold on his wings,
Lovely, her firstborn passion, and impulse of firstborn things?
Was Love that nestling indeed that under the plume of the night
Was hatched and hidden as seed in the furrow, and brought forth bright?
Was it Love lay shut in the shell world-shaped, having over him there
Black world-wide wings that impel the might of the night through air?
And bursting his shell as a bird, night shook through her sail-stretched vans,
And her heart as a water was stirred, and its heat was the firstborn man's.
For the waste of the dead void air took form of a world at birth,
And the waters and firmaments were, and light, and the life-giving earth.
The beautiful bird unbegotten that night brought forth without pain
In the fathomless years forgotten whereover the dead gods reign,
Was it love, life, godhead, or fate? we say the spirit is one
That moved on the dark to create out of darkness the stars and the sun.
Before the growth was the grower, and the seed ere the plant was sown;
But what was seed of the sower? and the grain of him, whence was it grown?
Foot after foot ye go back and travail and make yourselves mad;
Blind feet that feel for the track where highway is none to be had.
Therefore the God that ye make you is grievous, and gives not aid,
Because it is but for your sake that the God of your making is made.
Thou and I and he are not gods made men for a span,
But God, if a God there be, is the substance of men which is man.
Our lives are as pulses or pores of his manifold body and breath;
As waves of his sea on the shores where birth is the beacon of death.
We men, the multiform features of man, whatsoever we be,
Recreate him of whom we are creatures, and all we only are he.
For each man of all men is God, but God is the fruit of the whole;
Indivisible spirit and blood, indiscernible body from soul.
Not men's but man's is the glory of godhead, the kingdom of time,
The mountainous ages made hoary with snows for the spirit to climb.
A God with the world inwound whose clay to his footsole clings;
A manifold God fast-bound as with iron of adverse things.
A soul that labours and lives, an emotion, a strenuous breath,
From the flame that its own mouth gives reillumed, and refreshed with death.
In the sea whereof centuries are waves the live God plunges and swims;
His bed is in all men's graves, but the worm hath not hold on his limbs.
Night puts out not his eyes, nor time sheds change on his head;
With such fire as the stars of the skies are the roots of his heart are fed.
Men are the thoughts passing through it, the veins that fulfil it with blood,
With spirit of sense to renew it as springs fulfilling a flood.
Men are the heartbeats of man, the plumes that feather his wings,

Storm-worn, since being began, with the wind and thunder of things.
Things are cruel and blind; their strength detains and deforms:
And the wearying wings of the mind still beat up the stream of their storms.
Still, as one swimming up stream, they strike out blind in the blast,
In thunders of vision and dream, and lightning of future and past.
We are baffled and caught in the current and bruised upon edges of shoals;
As weeds or as reeds in the torrent of things are the wind-shaken souls.
Spirit by spirit goes under, a foam-bell's bubble of breath,
That blows and opens in sunder and blurs not the mirror of death.
For a worm or a thorn in his path is a man's soul quenched as a flame;
For his lust of an hour or his wrath shall the worm and the man be the same.
O God sore stricken of things! they have wrought him a raiment of pain;
Can a God shut eyelids and wings at a touch on the nerves of the brain?
O shamed and sorrowful God, whose force goes out at a blow!
What world shall shake at his nod? at his coming what wilderness glow?
What help in the work of his hands? what light in the track of his feet?
His days are snowflakes or sands, with cold to consume him and heat.
He is servant with Change for lord, and for wages he hath to his hire
Folly and force, and a sword that devours, and a ravening fire.
From the bed of his birth to his grave he is driven as a wind at their will;
Lest Change bow down as his slave, and the storm and the sword be still;
Lest earth spread open her wings to the sunward, and sing with the spheres;
Lest man be master of things, to prevail on their forces and fears.
By the spirit are things overcome; they are stark, and the spirit hath breath;
It hath speech, and their forces are dumb; it is living, and things are of death.
But they know not the spirit for master, they feel not force from above,
While man makes love to disaster, and woos desolation with love.
Yea, himself too hath made himself chains, and his own hands plucked out his eyes;
For his own soul only constrains him, his own mouth only denies.
The herds of kings and their hosts and the flocks of the high priests bow
To a master whose face is a ghost's; O thou that wast God, is it thou?
Thou madest man in the garden; thou temptedst man, and he fell;
Thou gavest him poison and pardon for blood and burnt-offering to sell.
Thou hast sealed thine elect to salvation, fast locked with faith for the key;
Make now for thyself expiation, and be thine atonement for thee.
Ah, thou that darkenest heaven—ah, thou that bringest a sword—
By the crimes of thine hands unforgiven they beseech thee to hear them, O Lord.
By the balefires of ages that burn for thine incense, by creed and by rood,
By the famine and passion that yearn and that hunger to find of thee food,
By the children that asked at thy throne of the priests that were fat with thine hire
For bread, and thou gavest a stone; for light, and thou madest them fire;
By the kiss of thy peace like a snake's kiss, that leaves the soul rotten at root;
By the savours of gibbets and stakes thou hast planted to bear to thee fruit;
By torture and terror and treason, that make to thee weapons and wings;
By thy power upon men for a season, made out of the malice of things;
O thou that hast built thee a shrine of the madness of man and his shame,
And hast hung in the midst for a sign of his worship the lamp of thy name;
That hast shown him for heaven in a vision a void world's shadow and shell,
And hast fed thy delight and derision with fire of belief as of hell;
That has fleshed on the souls that believe thee the fang of the death-worm fear,
With anguish of dreams to deceive them whose faith cries out in thine ear;

By the face of the spirit confounded before thee and humbled in dust,
By the dread wherewith life was astounded and shamed out of sense of its trust,
By the scourges of doubt and repentance that fell on the soul at thy nod,
Thou art judged, O judge, and the sentence is gone forth against thee, O God.
Thy slave that slept is awake; thy slave but slept for a span;
Yea, man thy slave shall unmake thee, who made thee lord over man.
For his face is set to the east, his feet on the past and its dead;
The sun rearisen is his priest, and the heat thereof hallows his head.
His eyes take part in the morning; his spirit outsounding the sea
Asks no more witness or warning from temple or tripod or tree.
He hath set the centuries at union; the night is afraid at his name;
Equal with life, in communion with death, he hath found them the same.
Past the wall unsurmounted that bars out our vision with iron and fire
He hath sent forth his soul for the stars to comply with and suns to conspire.
His thought takes flight for the centre wherethrough it hath part in the whole;
The abysses forbid it not enter: the stars make room for the soul.
Space is the soul's to inherit; the night is hers as the day;
Lo, saith man, this is my spirit; how shall not the worlds make way?
Space is thought's, and the wonders thereof, and the secret of space;
Is thought not more than the thunders and lightnings? shall thought give place?
Is the body not more than the vesture, the life not more than the meat?
The will than the word or the gesture, the heart than the hands or the feet?
Is the tongue not more than the speech is? the head not more than the crown?
And if higher than is heaven be the reach of the soul, shall not heaven bow down?
Time, father of life, and more great than the life it begat and began,
Earth's keeper and heaven's and their fate, lives, thinks, and hath substance in man.
Time's motion that throbs in his blood is the thought that gives heart to the skies,
And the springs of the fire that is food to the sunbeams are light to his eyes.
The minutes that beat with his heart are the words to which worlds keep chime,
And the thought in his pulses is part of the blood and the spirit of time.
He saith to the ages, Give; and his soul foregoes not her share;
Who are ye that forbid him to live, and would feed him with heavenlier air?
Will ye feed him with poisonous dust, and restore him with hemlock for drink,
Till he yield you his soul up in trust, and have heart not to know or to think?
He hath stirred him, and found out the flaw in his fetters, and cast them behind;
His soul to his soul is a law, and his mind is a light to his mind.
The seal of his knowledge is sure, the truth and his spirit are wed;
Men perish, but man shall endure; lives die, but the life is not dead.
He hath sight of the secrets of season, the roots of the years and the fruits;
His soul is at one with the reason of things that is sap to the roots.
He can hear in their changes a sound as the conscience of consonant spheres;
He can see through the years flowing round him the law lying under the years.
Who are ye that would bind him with curses and blind him with vapour of prayer?
Your might is as night that disperses when light is alive in the air.
The bow of your godhead is broken, the arm of your conquest is stayed;
Though ye call down God to bear token, for fear of you none is afraid.
Will ye turn back times, and the courses of stars, and the season of souls?
Shall God's breath dry up the sources that feed time full as it rolls?
Nay, cry on him then till he show you a sign, till he lift up a rod;
Hath he made not the nations to know him of old if indeed he be God?
Is no heat of him left in the ashes of thousands burnt up for his sake?

Can prayer not rekindle the flashes that shone in his face from the stake?
Cry aloud; for your God is a God and a Saviour; cry, make yourselves lean;
Is he drunk or asleep, that the rod of his wrath is unfelt and unseen?
Is the fire of his old loving-kindness gone out, that his pyres are acold?
Hath he gazed on himself unto blindness, who made men blind to behold?
Cry out, for his kingdom is shaken; cry out, for the people blaspheme;
Cry aloud till his godhead awaken; what doth he to sleep and to dream?
Cry, cut yourselves, gash you with knives and with scourges, heap on to you dust;
Is his life but as other gods' lives? is not this the Lord God of your trust?
Is not this the great God of your sires, that with souls and with bodies was fed,
And the world was on flame with his fires? O fools, he was God, and is dead.
He will hear not again the strong crying of earth in his ears as before,
And the fume of his multitudes dying shall flatter his nostrils no more.
By the spirit he ruled as his slave is he slain who was mighty to slay,
And the stone that is sealed on his grave he shall rise not and roll not away.
Yea, weep to him, lift up your hands; be your eyes as a fountain of tears;
Where he stood there is nothing that stands; if he call, there is no man that hears.
He hath doffed his king's raiment of lies now the wane of his kingdom is come;
Ears hath he, and hears not; and eyes, and he sees not; and mouth, and is dumb.
His red king's raiment is ripped from him naked, his staff broken down;
And the signs of his empire are stripped from him shuddering; and where is his crown?
And in vain by the wellsprings refrozen ye cry for the warmth of his sun—
O God, the Lord God of thy chosen, thy will in thy kingdom be done.
Kingdom and will hath he none in him left him, nor warmth in his breath;
Till his corpse be cast out of the sun will ye know not the truth of his death?
Surely, ye say, he is strong, though the times be against him and men;
Yet a little, ye say, and how long, till he come to show judgment again?
Shall God then die as the beasts die? who is it hath broken his rod?
O God, Lord God of thy priests, rise up now and show thyself God.
They cry out, thine elect, thine aspirants to heavenward, whose faith is as flame;
O thou the Lord God of our tyrants, they call thee, their God, by thy name.
By thy name that in hell-fire was written, and burned at the point of thy sword,
Thou art smitten, thou God, thou art smitten; thy death is upon thee, O Lord.
And the love-song of earth as thou diest resounds through the wind of her wings—
Glory to Man in the highest! for Man is the master of things.

1871

A VISION OF SPRING IN WINTER

I

O TENDER time that love thinks long to see,
Sweet foot of spring that with her footfall sows
Late snowlike flowery leavings of the snows,
Be not too long irresolute to be;
O mother-month, where have they hidden thee?
Out of the pale time of the flowerless rose
I reach my heart out toward the springtime lands,
I stretch my spirit forth to the fair hours,
The purplest of the prime;
I lean my soul down over them, with hands
Made wide to take the ghostly growths of flowers;
I send my love back to the lovely time.

II

Where has the greenwood hid thy gracious head?
Veiled with what visions while the grey world grieves,
Or muffled with what shadows of green leaves,

What warm intangible green shadows spread
To sweeten the sweet twilight for thy bed?
What sleep enchants thee? what delight deceives?
Where the deep dreamlike dew before the dawn
Feels not the fingers of the sunlight yet
Its silver web unweave,
Thy footless ghost on some unfooted lawn
Whose air the unrisen sunbeams fear to fret
Lives a ghost's life of daylong dawn and eve.

III

Sunrise it sees not, neither set of star,
Large nightfall, nor imperial plenilune,
Nor strong sweet shape of the full-breasted noon;
But where the silver-sandalled shadows are,
Too soft for arrows of the sun to mar,
Moves with the mild gait of an ungrown moon:
Hard overhead the half-lit crescent swims,
The tender-coloured night draws hardly breath,
The light is listening;
They watch the dawn of slender-shapen limbs,
Virginal, born again of doubtful death,
Chill foster-father of the weanling spring.

IV

As sweet desire of day before the day,
As dreams of love before the true love born,
From the outer edge of winter overworn
The ghost arisen of May before the May
Takes through dim air her unawakened way,
The gracious ghost of morning risen ere morn.
With little unblown breasts and child-eyed looks
Following, the very maid, the girl-child spring,
Lifts windward her bright brows,
Dips her light feet in warm and moving brooks,
And kindles with her own mouth's colouring
The fearful firstlings of the plumeless boughs.

V

I seek thee sleeping, and awhile I see,
Fair face that art not, how thy maiden breath
Shall put at last the deadly days to death
And fill the fields and fire the woods with thee
And seaward hollows where my feet would be
When heaven shall hear the word that April saith
To change the cold heart of the weary time,
To stir and soften all the time to tears,
Tears joyfuller than mirth;
As even to May's clear height the young days climb
With feet not swifter than those fair first years
Whose flowers revive not with thy flowers on earth.

VI

I would not bid thee, though I might, give back
One good thing youth has given and borne away;
I crave not any comfort of the day
That is not, nor on time's retrodden track
Would turn to meet the white-robed hours or black
That long since left me on their mortal way;
Nor light nor love that has been, nor the breath
That comes with the morning from the sun to be
And sets light hope on fire;
No fruit, no flower thought once too fair for death,
No flower nor hour once fallen from life's green tree,
No leaf once plucked or once fulfilled desire.

VII

The morning song beneath the stars that fled
With twilight through the moonless mountain air,
While youth with burning lips and wreathless hair
Sang toward the sun that was to crown his head,
Rising; the hopes that triumphed and fell dead,

The sweet swift eyes and songs of hours that were;
These may'st thou not give back for ever; these,
As at the sea's heart all her wrecks lie waste,
Lie deeper than the sea;
But flowers thou may'st, and winds, and hours of ease,
And all its April to the world thou may'st
Give back, and half my April back to me.

1875

A FORSAKEN GARDEN

In a coign of the cliff between lowland and highland,
At the sea-down's edge between windward and lee,
Walled round with rocks as an inland island,
The ghost of a garden fronts the sea.
A girdle of brushwood and thorn encloses
The steep square slope of the blossomless bed
Where the weeds that grew green from the graves of its roses
Now lie dead.

The fields fall southward, abrupt and broken,
To the low last edge of the long lone land.
If a step should sound or a word be spoken,
Would a ghost not rise at the strange guest's hand?
So long have the grey bare walks lain guestless,
Through branches and briars if a man make way,
He shall find no life but the sea-wind's, restless
Night and day.

The dense hard passage is blind and stifled
That crawls by a track none turn to climb
To the strait waste place that the years have rifled
Of all but the thorns that are touched not of time.
The thorns he spares when the rose is taken;
The rocks are left when he wastes the plain.
The wind that wanders, the weeds wind-shaken,
These remain.

Not a flower to be pressed of the foot that falls not;
As the heart of a dead man the seed-plots are dry;
From the thicket of thorns whence the nightingale calls not,
Could she call, there were never a rose to reply.
Over the meadows that blossom and wither
Rings but the note of a sea-bird's song;
Only the sun and the rain come hither
All year long.

The sun burns sere and the rain dishevels
One gaunt bleak blossom of scentless breath.
Only the wind here hovers and revels
In a round where life seems barren as death.
Here there was laughing of old, there was weeping,
Haply, of lovers none ever will know,
Whose eyes went seaward a hundred sleeping
Years ago.

Heart handfast in heart as they stood, "Look thither,"
Did he whisper? "look forth from the flowers to the sea;
For the foam-flowers endure when the rose-blossoms wither,
And men that love lightly may die—but we?"
And the same wind sang and the same waves whitened,
And or ever the garden's last petals were shed,
In the lips that had whispered, the eyes that had lightened,
Love was dead.

Or they loved their life through, and then went whither?
And were one to the end—but what end who knows?
Love deep as the sea as a rose must wither,
As the rose-red seaweed that mocks the rose.
Shall the dead take thought for the dead to love them?
What love was ever as deep as a grave?
They are loveless now as the grass above them
Or the wave.

All are at one now, roses and lovers,
Not known of the cliffs and the fields and the sea.
Not a breath of the time that has been hovers
In the air now soft with a summer to be.
Not a breath shall there sweeten the seasons hereafter
Of the flowers or the lovers that laugh now or weep,
When as they that are free now of weeping and laughter
We shall sleep.

Here death may deal not again for ever;
Here change may come not till all change end.
From the graves they have made they shall rise up never,
Who have left nought living to ravage and rend.
Earth, stones, and thorns of the wild ground growing,
While the sun and the rain live, these shall be;
Till a last wind's breath upon all these blowing
Roll the sea.

Till the slow sea rise and the sheer cliff crumble,
Till terrace and meadow the deep gulfs drink,
Till the strength of the waves of the high tides humble
The fields that lessen, the rocks that shrink,
Here now in his triumph where all things falter,
Stretched out on the spoils that his own hand spread,
As a god self-slain on his own strange altar,
Death lies dead.

1876

A BALLAD OF DREAMLAND

I HID my heart in a nest of roses,
Out of the sun's way, hidden apart;
In a softer bed than the soft white snow's is,
Under the roses I hid my heart.
Why would it sleep not? why should it start,
When never a leaf of the rose-tree stirred?
What made sleep flutter his wings and part?
Only the song of a secret bird.

Lie still, I said, for the wind's wing closes,
And mild leaves muffle the keen sun's dart;
Lie still, for the wind on the warm sea dozes,
And the wind is unquieter yet than thou art.
Does a thought in thee still as a thorn's wound smart?
Does the fang still fret thee of hope deferred?
What bids the lids of thy sleep dispart?
Only the song of a secret bird.

The green land's name that a charm encloses,
It never was writ in the traveller's chart,
And sweet on its trees as the fruit that grows is,
It never was sold in the merchant's mart.
The swallows of dreams through its dim fields dart,
And sleep's are the tunes in its tree-tops heard;
No hound's note wakens the wildwood hart,
Only the song of a secret bird.

ENVOI

In the world of dreams I have chosen my part,
To sleep for a season and hear no word
Of true love's truth or of light love's art,
Only the song of a secret bird.

1878

A BALLAD OF FRANÇOIS VILLON

PRINCE OF ALL BALLAD-MAKERS

BIRD of the bitter bright grey golden morn
Scarce risen upon the dusk of dolorous years,
First of us all and sweetest singer born
Whose far shrill note the world of new men hears
Cleave the cold shuddering shade as twilight clears;
When song new-born put off the old world's attire
And felt its tune on her changed lips expire,
Writ foremost on the roll of them that came
Fresh girt for service of the latter lyre,
Villon, our sad bad glad mad brother's name!

Alas the joy, the sorrow, and the scorn,
  That clothed thy life with hopes and sins and fears,
And gave thee stones for bread and tares for corn
  And plume-plucked gaol-birds for thy starveling peers
  Till death clipt close their flight with shameful shears;
Till shifts came short and loves were hard to hire,
When lilt of song nor twitch of twangling wire
  Could buy thee bread or kisses; when light fame
Spurned like a ball and haled through brake and briar,
  Villon, our sad bad glad mad brother's name!

Poor splendid wings so frayed and soiled and torn!
  Poor kind wild eyes so dashed with light quick tears!
Poor perfect voice, most blithe when most forlorn,
  That rings athwart the sea whence no man steers
  Like joy-bells crossed with death-bells in our ears!
What far delight has cooled the fierce desire
That like some ravenous bird was strong to tire
  On that frail flesh and soul consumed with flame,
But left more sweet than roses to respire,
  Villon, our sad bad glad mad brother's name?

ENVOI

Prince of sweet songs made out of tears and fire,
A harlot was thy nurse, a God thy sire;
  Shame soiled thy song, and song assoiled thy shame.
But from thy feet now death has washed the mire,
Love reads out first at head of all our quire,
  Villon, our sad bad glad mad brother's name.

1878

THE LAST ORACLE

(A.D. 361)

εἴπατε τῷ βασιλῆϊ, χαμαὶ πέσε δαίδαλος αὐλά·
οὐκέτι Φοῖβος ἔχει καλύβαν, οὐ μάντιδα δάφνην,
οὐ παγὰν λαλέουσαν· ἀπέσβετο καὶ λάλον ὕδωρ.[1]

Years have risen and fallen in darkness or in twilight,
  Ages waxed and waned that knew not thee nor thine,
While the world sought light by night and sought not thy light,
  Since the sad last pilgrim left thy dark mid shrine.
Dark the shrine and dumb the fount of song thence welling,
  Save for words more sad than tears of blood, that said:
Tell the king, on earth has fallen the glorious dwelling,
  And the watersprings that spake are quenched and dead.
Not a cell is left the God, no roof, no cover;
  In his hand the prophet laurel flowers no more.
And the great king's high sad heart, thy true last lover,
  Felt thine answer pierce and cleave it to the core.
    And he bowed down his hopeless head
      In the drift of the wild world's tide,
    And dying, *Thou hast conquered*, he said,
      Galilean; he said it, and died.
    And the world that was thine and was ours
    When the Graces took hands with the Hours,
    Grew cold as a winter wave
    In the wind from a wide-mouthed grave,
    As a gulf wide open to swallow
      The light that the world held dear.
  O father of all of us, Paian, Apollo,
    Destroyer and healer, hear!

Age on age thy mouth was mute, thy face was hidden,
  And the lips and eyes that loved thee blind and dumb;

[1] "Tell the king, on earth has fallen the glorious dwelling, no longer has Phoebus his temple cell—no, not his prophetic laurel, nor the speaking spring, quenched too the speaking water."

Song forsook their tongues that held thy name forbidden,
  Light their eyes that saw the strange God's kingdom come.
Fire for light and hell for heaven and psalms for pæans
  Filled the clearest eyes and lips most sweet of song,
When for chant of Greeks the wail of Galileans
  Made the whole world moan with hymns of wrath and wrong.
Yea, not yet we see thee, father, as they saw thee,
  They that worshipped when the world was theirs and thine,
They whose words had power by thine own power to draw thee
  Down from heaven till earth seemed more than heaven divine.

For the shades are about us that hover
  When darkness is half withdrawn
And the skirts of the dead night cover
  The face of the live new dawn.
For the past is not utterly past
Though the word on its lips be the last,
And the time be gone by with its creed
When men were as beasts that bleed,
As sheep or as swine that wallow,
  In the shambles of faith and of fear.
O father of all of us, Paian, Apollo,
  Destroyer and healer, hear!

Yet it may be, lord and father, could we know it,
  We that love thee for our darkness shall have light
More than ever prophet hailed of old or poet
  Standing crowned and robed and sovereign in thy sight.
To the likeness of one God their dreams enthralled thee,
  Who wast greater than all Gods that waned and grew;
Son of God the shining son of Time they called thee,
  Who wast older, O our father, than they knew.
For no thought of man made Gods to love or honour
  Ere the song within the silent soul began,
Nor might earth in dream or deed take heaven upon her
  Till the word was clothed with speech by lips of man.

And the word and the life wast thou,
  The spirit of man and the breath;
And before thee the Gods that bow
  Take life at thine hands and death.
For these are as ghosts that wane,
That are gone in an age or twain;
Harsh, merciful, passionate, pure,
They perish, but thou shalt endure;
Be their flight with the swan or the swallow,
  They pass as the flight of a year.
O father of all of us, Paian, Apollo,
  Destroyer and healer, hear!

Thou the word, the light, the life, the breath, the glory,
  Strong to help and heal, to lighten and to slay,
Thine is all the song of man, the world's whole story;
  Not of morning and of evening is thy day.
Old and younger Gods are buried or begotten
  From uprising to downsetting of thy sun,
Risen from eastward, fallen to westward and forgotten,
  And their springs are many, but their end is one.
Divers births of godheads find one death appointed,
  As the soul whence each was born makes room for each;
God by God goes out, discrowned and disanointed,
  But the soul stands fast that gave them shape and speech.

Is the sun yet cast out of heaven?
  Is the song yet cast out of man?
Life that had song for its leaven
  To quicken the blood that ran
Through the veins of the songless years
More bitter and cold than tears,
Heaven that had thee for its one
Light, life, word, witness, O sun,
Are they soundless and sightless and hollow,

Without eye, without speech, without ear?
O father of all of us, Paian, Apollo,
Destroyer and healer, hear!

Time arose and smote thee silent at his warning,
Change and darkness fell on men that fell from thee;
Dark thou satest, veiled with light, behind the morning,
Till the soul of man should lift up eyes and see.
Till the blind mute soul get speech again and eyesight,
Man may worship not the light of life within;
In his sight the stars whose fires grow dark in thy sight
Shine as sunbeams on the night of death and sin.
Time again is risen with mightier word of warning,
Change hath blown again a blast of louder breath;
Clothed with clouds and stars and dreams that melt in morning,
Lo, the Gods that ruled by grace of sin and death!
They are conquered, they break, they are stricken,
Whose might made the whole world pale;
They are dust that shall rise not or quicken
Though the world for their death's sake wail.
As a hound on a wild beast's trace,
So time has their godhead in chase;
As wolves when the hunt makes head,
They are scattered, they fly, they are fled;
They are fled beyond hail, beyond hollo,
And the cry of the chase, and the cheer.
O father of all of us, Paian, Apollo,
Destroyer and healer, hear!

Day by day thy shadow shines in heaven beholden,
Even the sun, the shining shadow of thy face:
King, the ways of heaven before thy feet grow golden;
God, the soul of earth is kindled with thy grace.
In thy lips the speech of man whence Gods were fashioned,
In thy soul the thought that makes them and unmakes;
By thy light and heat incarnate and impassioned,
Soul to soul of man gives light for light and takes.
As they knew thy name of old time could we know it,
Healer called of sickness, slayer invoked of wrong,
Light of eyes that saw thy light, God, king, priest, poet,
Song should bring thee back to heal us with thy song.
For thy kingdom is past not away,
Nor thy power from the place thereof hurled;
Out of heaven they shall cast not the day,
They shall cast not out song from the world.
By the song and the light they give
We know thy works that they live;
With the gift thou hast given us of speech
We praise, we adore, we beseech,
We arise at thy bidding and follow,
We cry to thee, answer, appear,
O father of all of us, Paian, Apollo,
Destroyer and healer, hear!

1878

TRIADS

I

I

THE word of the sun to the sky,
The word of the wind to the sea,
The word of the moon to the night,
What may it be?

II

The sense to the flower of the fly,
The sense of the bird to the tree,
The sense to the cloud of the light,
Who can tell me?

III

The song of the fields to the kye,
The song of the lime to the bee,
The song of the depth to the height,
Who knows all three?

II

I

The message of April to May
That May sends on into June
And June gives out to July
For birthday boon;

II

The delight of the dawn in the day,
The delight of the day in the noon,
The delight of a song in a sigh
That breaks the tune;

III

The secret of passing away,
The cost of the change of the moon,
None knows it with ear or with eye,
But all will soon.

III

I

The live wave's love for the shore,
The shore's for the wave as it dies,
The love of the thunder-fire
That sears the skies,

II

We shall know not though life wax hoar,
Till all life, spent into sighs,
Burn out as consumed with desire
Of death's strange eyes:

III

Till the secret be secret no more
In the light of one hour as it flies,
Be the hour as of suns that expire
Or suns that rise.

1878

IN THE BAY

I

Beyond the hollow sunset, ere a star
Take heart in heaven from eastward, while the west,
Fulfilled of watery resonance and rest,
Is as a port with clouds for harbour bar
To fold the fleet in of the winds from far
That stir no plume now of the bland sea's breast:

II

Above the soft sweep of the breathless bay
Southwestward, far past flight of night and day,
Lower than the sunken sunset sinks, and higher
Than dawn can freak the front of heaven with fire,
My thought with eyes and wings made wide makes way
To find the place of souls that I desire.

III

If any place for any soul there be,
Disrobed and disentrammelled; if the might,
The fire and force that filled with ardent light
The souls whose shadow is half the light we see,
Survive and be suppressed not of the night;
This hour should show what all day hid from me.

IV

Night knows not, neither is it shown to day,
By sunlight nor by starlight is it shown,
Nor to the full moon's eve nor footfall known,
Their world's untrodden and unkindled way.
Nor is the breath nor music of it blown
With sounds of winter or with winds of May.

V

But here, where light and darkness reconciled
Hold earth between them as a weanling child
Between the balanced hands of death and birth,
Even as they held the new-born shape of earth
When first life trembled in her limbs and smiled,
Here hope might think to find what hope were worth.

VI

Past Hades, past Elysium, past the long
Slow smooth strong lapse of Lethe—past the toil
Wherein all souls are taken as a spoil,
The Stygian web of waters—if your song
Be quenched not, O our brethren, but be strong
As ere ye too shook off our temporal coil;

VII

If yet these twain survive your worldly breath,
Joy trampling sorrow, life devouring death,
If perfect life possess your life all through
And like your words your souls be deathless too,
To-night, of all whom night encompasseth,
My soul would commune with one soul of you.

VIII

Above the sunset might I see thine eyes
That were above the sundawn in our skies,
Son of the songs of morning,—thine that were
First lights to lighten that rekindling air
Wherethrough men saw the front of England rise
And heard thine loudest of the lyre-notes there—

IX

If yet thy fire have not one spark the less,
O Titan, born of her a Titaness,
Across the sunrise and the sunset's mark
Send of thy lyre one sound, thy fire one spark,
To change this face of our unworthiness,
Across this hour dividing light from dark.

X

To change this face of our chill time, that hears
No song like thine of all that crowd its ears,
Of all its lights that lighten all day long
Sees none like thy most fleet and fiery sphere's
Outlightening Sirius—in its twilight throng
No thunder and no sunrise like thy song.

XI

Hath not the sea-wind swept the sea-line bare
To pave with stainless fire through stainless air
A passage for thine heavenlier feet to tread
Ungrieved of earthly floor-work? hath it spread
No covering splendid as the sun-god's hair
To veil or to reveal thy lordlier head?

XII

Hath not the sunset shown across the sea
A way majestical enough for thee?
What hour save this should be thine hour—and mine,
If thou have care of any less divine
Than thine own soul; if thou take thought of me,
Marlowe, as all my soul takes thought of thine?

XIII

Before the moon's face as before the sun
The morning star and evening star are one
For all men's lands as England. O, if night
Hang hard upon us,—ere our day take flight,
Shed thou some comfort from thy day long done
On us pale children of the latter light!

XIV

For surely, brother and master and lord and king,
Where'er thy footfall and thy face make spring
In all souls' eyes that meet thee wheresoe'er,
And have thy soul for sunshine and sweet air—
Some late love of thine old live land should cling,
Some living love of England, round thee there.

XV

Here from her shore across her sunniest sea
My soul makes question of the sun for thee,
And waves and beams make answer. When thy feet
Made her ways flowerier and their flowers more sweet
With childlike passage of a god to be,
Like spray these waves cast off her foemen's fleet.

XVI

Like foam they flung it from her, and like weed
Its wrecks were washed from scornful shoal to shoal,
From rock to rock reverberate; and the whole
Sea laughed and lightened with a deathless deed
That sowed our enemies in her field for seed
And made her shores fit harbourage for thy soul.

XVII

Then in her green south fields, a poor man's child,
Thou hast thy short sweet fill of half-blown joy,
That ripens all of us for time to cloy
With full-blown pain and passion; ere the wild

World caught thee by the fiery heart, and smiled
To make so swift end of the godlike boy.

XVIII

For thou, if ever godlike foot there trod
These fields of ours, wert surely like a god.
Who knows what splendour of strange dreams was shed
With sacred shadow and glimmer of gold and red
From hallowed windows, over stone and sod,
On thine unbowed bright insubmissive head?

XIX

The shadow stayed not, but the splendour stays,
Our brother, till the last of English days.
No day nor night on English earth shall be
For ever, spring nor summer, Junes nor Mays,
But somewhat as a sound or gleam of thee
Shall come on us like morning from the sea.

XX

Like sunrise never wholly risen, nor yet
Quenched; or like sunset never wholly set,
A light to lighten as from living eyes
The cold unlit close lids of one that lies
Dead, or a ray returned from death's far skies
To fire us living lest our lives forget.

XXI

For in that heaven what light of lights may be,
What splendour of what stars, what spheres of flame
Sounding, that none may number nor may name,
We know not, even thy brethren; yea, not we
Whose eyes desire the light that lightened thee,
Whose ways and thine are one way and the same.

XXII

But if the riddles that in sleep we read,
And trust them not, be flattering truth indeed,
As he that rose our mightiest called them,—he,
Much higher than thou as thou much higher than we—
There, might we say, all flower of all our seed,
All singing souls are as one sounding sea.

XXIII

All those that here were of thy kind and kin,
Beside thee and below thee, full of love,
Full-souled for song,—and one alone above
Whose only light folds all your glories in—
With all birds' notes from nightingale to dove
Fill the world whither we too fain would win.

XXIV

The world that sees in heaven the sovereign light
Of sunlike Shakespeare, and the fiery night
Whose stars were watched of Webster; and beneath,
The twin-souled brethren of the single wreath,
Grown in kings' gardens, plucked from pastoral heath,
Wrought with all flowers for all men's heart's delight.

XXV

And that fixed fervour, iron-red like Mars,
In the mid moving tide of tenderer stars,
That burned on loves and deeds the darkest done,
Athwart the incestuous prisoner's bride-house bars;
And thine, most highest of all their fires but one,
Our morning star, sole risen before the sun.

XXVI

And one light risen since theirs to run such race
Thou hast seen, O Phosphor, from thy pride of place.
Thou hast seen Shelley, him that was to thee
As light to fire or dawn to lightning; me,
Me likewise, O our brother, shalt thou see,
And I behold thee, face to glorious face?

XXVII

You twain the same swift year of manhood swept
Down the steep darkness, and our father wept.
And from the gleam of Apollonian tears
A holier aureole rounds your memories, kept
Most fervent-fresh of all the singing spheres,
And April-coloured through all months and years.

XXVIII

You twain fate spared not half your fiery span;
The longer date fulfils the lesser man.
Ye from beyond the dark dividing date
Stand smiling, crowned as gods with foot on fate.
For stronger was your blessing than his ban,
And earliest whom he struck, he struck too late.

XXIX

Yet love and loathing, faith and unfaith yet
Bind less to greater souls in unison,
And one desire that makes three spirits as one
Takes great and small as in one spiritual net
Woven out of hope toward what shall yet be done
Ere hate or love remember or forget.

XXX

Woven out of faith and hope and love too great
To bear the bonds of life and death and fate:
Woven out of love and hope and faith too dear
To take the print of doubt and change and fear:
And interwoven with lines of wrath and hate
Blood-red with soils of many a sanguine year.

XXXI

Who cannot hate, can love not; if he grieve,
His tears are barren as the unfruitful rain
That rears no harvest from the green sea's plain,
And as thorns crackling this man's laugh is vain.
Nor can belief touch, kindle, smite, reprieve
His heart who has not heart to disbelieve.

XXXII

But you, most perfect in your hate and love,
Our great twin-spirited brethren; you that stand
Head by head glittering, hand made fast in hand,
And underfoot the fang-drawn worm that strove
To wound you living; from so far above,
Look love, not scorn, on ours that was your land.

XXXIII

For love we lack, and help and heat and light
To clothe us and to comfort us with might.
What help is ours to take or give? but ye—
O, more than sunrise to the blind cold sea,
That wailed aloud with all her waves all night,
Much more, being much more glorious, should you be.

XXXIV

As fire to frost, as ease to toil, as dew
To flowerless fields, as sleep to slackening pain,
As hope to souls long weaned from hope again
Returning, or as blood revived anew
To dry-drawn limbs and every pulseless vein,
Even so toward us should no man be but you.

XXXV

One rose before the sunrise was, and one
Before the sunset, lovelier than the sun.
And now the heaven is dark and bright and loud
With wind and starry drift and moon and cloud,
And night's cry rings in straining sheet and shroud,
What help is ours if hope like yours be none?

XXXVI

O well-beloved, our brethren, if ye be,
Then are we not forsaken. This kind earth
Made fragrant once for all time with your birth,
And bright for all men with your love, and worth
The clasp and kiss and wedlock of the sea,
Were not your mother if not your brethren we.

XXXVII

Because the days were dark with gods and kings
And in time's hand the old hours of time as rods,
When force and fear set hope and faith at odds,
Ye failed not nor abased your plume-plucked wings;
And we that front not more disastrous things,
How should we fail in face of kings and gods?

XXXVIII

For now the deep dense plumes of night are thinned
Surely with winnowing of the glimmering wind
Whose feet are fledged with morning; and the breath
Begins in heaven that sings the dark to death.
And all the night wherein men groaned and sinned
Sickens at heart to hear what sundawn saith.

XXXIX

O first-born sons of hope and fairest, ye
Whose prows first clove the thought-unsounded sea
Whence all the dark dead centuries rose to bar
The spirit of man lest truth should make him free,
The sunrise and the sunset, seeing one star,
Take heart as we to know you that ye are.

XL

Ye rise not and ye set not; we that say
Ye rise and set like hopes that set and rise
Look yet but seaward from a land-locked bay;
But where at last the sea's line is the sky's
And truth and hope one sunlight in your eyes,
No sunrise and no sunset marks their day.

1879

AT PARTING

For a day and a night Love sang to us, played with us,
Folded us round from the dark and the light;
And our hearts were fulfilled of the music he made with us,
Made with our hearts and our lips while he stayed with us,
Stayed in mid passage his pinions from flight
For a day and a night.

From his foes that kept watch with his wings had he hidden us,
Covered us close from the eyes that would smite,
From the feet that had tracked and the tongues that had chidden us
Sheltering in shade of the myrtles forbidden us
Spirit and flesh growing one with delight
For a day and a night.

But his wings will not rest and his feet will not stay for us:
Morning is here in the joy of its might;
With his breath has he sweetened a night and a day for us;
Now let him pass, and the myrtles make way for us;
Love can but last in us here at his height
For a day and a night.

1879

RELICS

This flower that smells of honey and the sea,
White laurustine, seems in my hand to be
A white star made of memory long ago
Lit in the heaven of dear times dead to me.

A star out of the skies love used to know
Here held in hand, a stray left yet to show
What flowers my heart was full of in the days
That are long since gone down dead memory's flow.

Dead memory that revives on doubtful ways,
Half hearkening what the buried season says
Out of the world of the unapparent dead
Where the lost Aprils are, and the lost Mays.

Flower, once I knew thy star-white brethren bred
Nigh where the last of all the land made head
Against the sea, a keen-faced promontory,
Flowers on salt wind and sprinkled sea-dews fed.

Their hearts were glad of the free place's glory;
The wind that sang them all his stormy story
Had talked all winter to the sleepless spray,
And as the sea's their hues were hard and hoary.

Like things born of the sea and the bright day,
They laughed out at the years that could not slay,
Live sons and joyous of unquiet hours,
And stronger than all storms that range for prey.

And in the close indomitable flowers
A keen-edged odour of the sun and showers
Was as the smell of the fresh honeycomb
Made sweet for mouths of none but paramours.

Out of the hard green wall of leaves that clomb
They showed like windfalls of the snow-soft foam,
Or feathers from the weary south-wind's wing,
Fair as the spray that it came shoreward from.

And thou, as white, what word hast thou to bring?
If my heart hearken, whereof wilt thou sing?
For some sign surely thou too hast to bear,
Some word far south was taught thee of the spring.

White like a white rose, not like these that were
Taught of the wind's mouth and the winter air,
Poor tender thing of soft Italian bloom,
Where once thou grewest, what else for me grew there?

Born in what spring and on what city's tomb,
By whose hand wast thou reached, and plucked for whom?
There hangs about thee, could the soul's sense tell,
An odour as of love and of love's doom.

Of days more sweet than thou wast sweet to smell,
Of flower-soft thoughts that came to flower and fell,
Of loves that lived a lily's life and died,
Of dreams now dwelling where dead roses dwell.

O white birth of the golden mountain-side
That for the sun's love makes its bosom wide
At sunrise, and with all its woods and flowers
Takes in the morning to its heart of pride!

Thou hast a word of that one land of ours,
And of the fair town called of the Fair Towers,
A word for me of my San Gimignan,
A word of April's greenest-girdled hours.

Of the breached walls whereon the wall-flowers ran
Called of Saint Fina, breachless now of man,
Though time with soft feet break them stone by stone,
Who breaks down hour by hour his own reign's span.

Of the cliff overcome and overgrown
That all that flowerage clothed as flesh clothes bone,
That garment of acacias made for May,
Whereof here lies one witness overblown.

The fair brave trees with all their flowers at play,
How king-like they stood up into the day!
How sweet the day was with them, and the night!
Such words of message have dead flowers to say.

This that the winter and the wind made bright,
And this that lived upon Italian light,
Before I throw them and these words away,
Who knows but I what memories too take flight?

1879

THALASSIUS

Upon the flowery forefront of the year,
One wandering by the grey-green April sea
Found on a reach of shingle and shallower sand
Inlaid with starrier glimmering jewellery
Left for the sun's love and the light wind's cheer
Along the foam-flowered strand
Breeze-brightened, something nearer sea than land
Though the last shoreward blossom-fringe was near,
A babe asleep with flower-soft face that gleamed
To sun and seaward as it laughed and dreamed,
Too sure of either love for either's fear,
Albeit so birdlike slight and light, it seemed
Nor man nor mortal child of man, but fair
As even its twin-born tenderer spray-flowers were,
That the wind scattered like an Oread's hair.

For when July strewed fire on earth and sea
The last time ere that year,
Out of the flame of morn Cymothoe
Beheld one brighter than the sunbright sphere
Move toward her from its fieriest heart, whence trod
The live sun's very God,
Across the foam-bright water-ways that are
As heavenlier heavens with star for answering star,
And on her eyes and hair and maiden mouth
Felt a kiss falling fierier than the South
And heard above afar
A noise of songs and wind-enamoured wings
And lutes and lyres of milder and mightier strings,
And round the resonant radiance of his car
Where depth is one with height,
Light heard as music, music seen as light.
And with that second moondawn of the spring's
That fosters the first rose,
A sun-child whiter than the sunlit snows
Was born out of the world of sunless things
That round the round earth flows and ebbs and flows.

But he that found the sea-flower by the sea
And took to foster like a graft of earth
Was born of man's most highest and heavenliest birth,
Free-born as winds and stars and waves are free;
A warrior grey with glories more than years,
Though more of years than change the quick to dead
Had rained their light and darkness on his head;
A singer that in time's and memory's ears
Should leave such words to sing as all his peers
Might praise with hallowing heat of rapturous tears
Till all the days of human flight were fled.
And at his knees his fosterling was fed
Not with man's wine and bread
Nor mortal mother-milk of hopes and fears,
But food of deep memorial days long sped;
For bread with wisdom and with song for wine
Clear as the full calm's emerald hyaline.
And from his grave glad lips the boy would gather
Fine honey of song-notes goldener than gold,
More sweet than bees make of the breathing heather,
That he, as glad and bold,
Might drink as they, and keep his spirit from cold.
And the boy loved his laurel-laden hair
As his own father's risen on the eastern air,
And that less white brow-binding bayleaf bloom
More than all flowers his father's eyes relume;
And those high songs he heard,
More than all notes of any landward bird,
More than all sounds less free
Than the wind's quiring to the choral sea.

High things the high song taught him; how the breath
Too frail for life may be more strong than death;
And this poor flash of sense in life, that gleams
As a ghost's glory in dreams,
More stabile than the world's own heart's root seems,
By that strong faith of lordliest love which gives
To death's own sightless-seeming eyes a light
Clearer, to death's bare bones a verier might,
Than shines or strikes from any man that lives.
How he that loves life overmuch shall die
The dog's death, utterly:
And he that much less loves it than he hates
All wrongdoing that is done
Anywhere always underneath the sun
Shall live a mightier life than time's or fate's.
One fairer thing he shewed him, and in might
More strong than day and night
Whose strengths build up time's towering period:
Yea, one thing stronger and more high than God,
Which if man had not, then should God not be:
And that was Liberty.
And gladly should man die to gain, he said,
Freedom; and gladlier, having lost, lie dead.
For man's earth was not, nor the sweet seawaves
His, nor his own land, nor its very graves,
Except they bred not, bore not, hid not slaves:
But all of all that is,
Were one man free in body and soul, were his.

And the song softened, even as heaven by night
Softens, from sunnier down to starrier light,
And with its moonbright breath
Blessed life for death's sake, and for life's sake death,
Till as the moon's own beam and breath confuse
In one clear hueless haze of glimmering hues
The sea's line and the land's line and the sky's,
And light for love of darkness almost dies,
As darkness only lives for light's dear love,
Whose hands the web of night is woven of,
So in that heaven of wondrous words were life
And death brought out of strife;
Yea, by that strong spell of serene increase
Brought out of strife to peace.

And the song lightened, as the wind at morn
Flashes, and even with lightning of the wind
Night's thick-spun web is thinned
And all its weft unwoven and overworn
Shrinks, as might love from scorn.
And as when wind and light on water and land
Leap as twin gods from heavenward hand in hand,
And with the sound and splendor of their leap
Strike darkness dead, and daunt the spirit of sleep,
And burn it up with fire;
So with the light that lightened from the lyre
Was all the bright heat in the child's heart stirred
And blown with blasts of music into flame
Till even his sense became
Fire, as the sense that fires the singing bird
Whose song calls night by name.
And in the soul within the sense began
The manlike passion of a godlike man,
And in the sense within the soul again
Thoughts that make men of gods and gods of men.

For love the high song taught him: love that turns
God's heart toward man as man's to Godward; love
That life and death and life are fashioned of,
From the first breath that burns
Half kindled on the flowerlike yeanling's lip,
So light and faint that life seems like to slip,
To that yet weaklier drawn
When sunset dies of night's devouring dawn.
But the man dying not wholly as all men dies
If aught be left of his in live men's eyes
Out of the dawnless dark of death to rise;
If aught of deed or word
Be seen for all time or of all time heard.
Love, that though body and soul were overthrown
Should live for love's sake of itself alone,
Though spirit and flesh were one thing doomed and dead,
Not wholly annihilated.
Seeing even the hoariest ash-flake that the pyre
Drops, and forgets the thing was once afire
And gave its heart to feed the pile's full flame
Till its own heart its own heat overcame,
Outlives its own life, though by scarce a span,
As such men dying outlive themselves in man,
Outlive themselves for ever; if the heat
Outburn the heart that kindled it, the sweet
Outlast the flower whose soul it was, and flit
Forth of the body of it
Into some new shape of a strange perfume
More potent than its light live spirit of bloom,
How shall not something of that soul relive,
That only soul that had such gifts to give
As lighten something even of all men's doom,
Even from the labouring womb,
Even to the seal set on the unopening tomb?
And these the loving light of song and love
Shall wrap and lap round and impend above,
Imperishable; and all springs born illume
Their sleep with brighter thoughts than wake the dove
To music, when the hillside winds resume
The marriage-song of heather-flower and broom
And all the joy thereof.

And hate the song too taught him: hate of all
That brings or holds in thrall
Of spirit or flesh, free-born ere God began,
The holy body and sacred soul of man.
And wheresoever a curse was or a chain,
A throne for torment or a crown for bane
Rose, moulded out of poor men's molten pain,

There, said he, should man's heaviest hate be set
Inexorably, to faint not or forget
Till the last warmth bled forth of the last vein
In flesh that none should call a king's again,
Seeing wolves and dogs and birds that plague-strike air
Leave the last bone of all the carrion bare.

And hope the high song taught him: hope whose eyes
Can sound the seas unsoundable, the skies
Inaccessible of eyesight; that can see
What earth beholds not, hear what wind and sea
Hear not, and speak what all these crying in one
Can speak not to the sun.
For in her sovereign eyelight all things are
Clear as the closest seen and kindlier star
That marries morn and even and winter and spring
With one love's golden ring.
For she can see the days of man, the birth
Of good and death of evil things on earth
Inevitable and infinite, and sure
As present pain is, or herself is pure.
Yea, she can hear and see, beyond all things
That lighten from before Time's thunderous wings
Through the awful circle of wheel-winged periods,
The tempest of the twilight of all Gods:
And higher than all the circling course they ran
The sundawn of the spirit that was man.

And fear the song too taught him; fear to be
Worthless the dear love of the wind and sea
That bred him fearless, like a sea-mew reared
In rocks of man's foot feared,
Where nought of wingless life may sing or shine.
Fear to wax worthless of that heaven he had
When all the life in all his limbs was glad
And all the drops in all his veins were wine
And all the pulses music; when his heart,
Singing, bade heaven and wind and sea bear part
In one live song's reiterance, and they bore:
Fear to go crownless of the flower he wore
When the winds loved him and the waters knew,
The blithest life that clove their blithe life through
With living limbs exultant, or held strife
More amorous than all dalliance aye anew
With the bright breath and strength of their large life,
With all strong wrath of all sheer winds that blew,
All glories of all storms of the air that fell
Prone, ineluctable,
With roar from heaven of revel, and with hue
As of heaven turned hell.
For when the red blast of their breath had made
All heaven aflush with light more dire than shade,
He felt it in his blood and eyes and hair
Burn as if all the fires of the earth and air
Had laid strong hold upon his flesh, and stung
The soul behind it as with serpent's tongue,
Forked like the loveliest lightnings: nor could bear
But hardly, half distraught with strong delight,
The joy that like a garment wrapped him round
And lapped him over and under
With raiment of great light
And rapture of great sound
At every loud leap earthward of the thunder
From heaven's most furthest bound:
So seemed all heaven in hearing and in sight
Alive and mad with glory and angry joy,
That something of its marvellous mirth and might
Moved even to madness, fledged as even for flight,
The blood and spirit of one but mortal boy.

So, clothed with love and fear that love makes great,
And armed with hope and hate,
He set first foot upon the spring-flowered ways
That all feet pass and praise.
And one dim dawn between the winter and spring,
In the sharp harsh wind harrying heaven and earth
To put back April that had borne his birth

From sunward on her sunniest shower-struck wing,
With tears and laughter for the dew-dropt thing,
Slight as indeed a dew-drop, by the sea
One met him lovelier than all men may be,
God-featured, with god's eyes; and in their might
Somewhat that drew men's own to mar their sight,
Even of all eyes drawn toward him: and his mouth
Was as the very rose of all men's youth,
One rose of all the rose-beds in the world:
But round his brows the curls were snakes that curled,
And like his tongue a serpent's; and his voice
Speaks death, and bids rejoice.
Yet then he spake no word, seeming as dumb,
A dumb thing mild and hurtless; nor at first
From his bowed eyes seemed any light to come,
Nor his meek lips for blood or tears to thirst:
But as one blind and mute in mild sweet wise
Pleading for pity of piteous lips and eyes,
He strayed with faint bare lily-lovely feet
Helpless, and flowerlike sweet:
Nor might man see, not having word hereof,
That this of all gods was the great god Love.

And seeing him lovely and like a little child
That wellnigh wept for wonder that it smiled
And was so feeble and fearful, with soft speech
The youth bespake him softly; but there fell
From the sweet lips no sweet word audible
That ear or thought might reach:
No sound to make the dim cold silence glad,
No breath to thaw the hard harsh air with heat;
Only the saddest smile of all things sweet,
Only the sweetest smile of all things sad.

And so they went together one green way
Till April dying made free the world for May;
And on his guide suddenly Love's face turned,
And in his blind eyes burned
Hard light and heat of laughter; and like flame
That opens in a mountain's ravening mouth
To blear and sear the sunlight from the south,
His mute mouth opened, and his first word came:
"Knowest thou me now by name?"
And all his stature waxed immeasurable,
As of one shadowing heaven and lightening hell;
And statelier stood he than a tower that stands
And darkens with its darkness far-off sands
Whereon the sky leans red;
And with a voice that stilled the winds he said:
"I am he that was thy lord before thy birth,
I am he that is thy lord till thou turn earth:
I make the night more dark, and all the morrow
Dark as the night whose darkness was my breath:
O fool, my name is sorrow;
Thou fool, my name is death."

And he that heard spake not, and looked right on
Again, and Love was gone.

Through many a night toward many a wearier day
His spirit bore his body down its way.
Through many a day toward many a wearier night
His soul sustained his sorrows in her sight.
And earth was bitterer, and heaven, and even the sea
Sorrowful even as he.
And the wind helped not, and the sun was dumb;
And with too long stress of grief to be
His heart grew sere and numb.

And one bright eve ere summer in autumn sank,
At stardawn standing on a grey sea-bank
He felt the wind fitfully shift and heave
As toward a stormier eve;
And all the wan wide sea shuddered; and earth
Shook underfoot as toward some timeless birth,
Intolerable and inevitable; and all
Heaven, darkling, trembled like a stricken thrall.
And far out of the quivering east, and far
From past the moonrise and its guiding star,
Began a noise of tempest and a light
That was not of the lightning; and a sound
Rang with it round and round
That was not of the thunder; and a flight

As of blown clouds by night,
That was not of them; and with songs and cries
That sang and shrieked their soul out at the skies
A shapeless earthly storm of shapes began
From all ways round to move in on the man,
Clamorous against him silent; and their feet
Were as the wind's are fleet,
And their shrill songs were as wild birds' are sweet.

And as when all the world of earth was wronged
And all the host of all men driven afoam
By the red hand of Rome,
Round some fierce amphitheatre overthronged
With fair clear faces full of bloodier lust
Than swells and stings the tiger when his mood
Is fieriest after blood
And drunk with trampling of the murderous must
That soaks and stains the tortuous close-coiled wood
Made monstrous with its myriad-mustering brood,
Face by fair face panted and gleamed and pressed,
And breast by passionate breast
Heaved hot with ravenous rapture, as they quaffed
The red ripe full fume of the deep live draught,
The sharp quick reek of keen fresh bloodshed, blown
Through the dense deep drift up to the emperor's throne
From the under steaming sands
With clamour of all-applausive throats and hands,
Mingling in mirthful time
With shrill blithe mockeries of the lithe-limbed mime:
So from somewhence far forth of the unbeholden,
Dreadfully driven from over and after and under,
Fierce, blown through fifes of brazen blast and golden,
With sound of chiming waves that drown the thunder
Or thunder that strikes dumb the sea's own chimes,
Began the bellowing of the bull-voiced mimes,
Terrible; firs bowed down as briars or palms
Even at the breathless blast as of a breeze
Fulfilled with clamour and clangour and storms of psalms;
Red hands rent up the roots of old-world trees,
Thick flames of torches tossed as tumbling seas
Made mad the moonless and infuriate air
That, ravening, revelled in the riotous hair
And raiment of the furred Bassarides.

So came all those in on him; and his heart,
As out of sleep suddenly struck astart,
Danced, and his flesh took fire of theirs, and grief
Was as a last year's leaf
Blown dead far down the wind's way; and he set
His pale mouth to the brightest mouth it met
That laughed for love against his lips, and bade
Follow; and in following all his blood grew glad
And as again a sea-bird's; for the wind
Took him to bathe him deep round breast and brow
Not as it takes a dead leaf drained and thinned,
But as the brightest bay-flower blown on bough,
Set springing toward it singing: and they rode
By many a vine-leafed, many a rose-hung road,
Exalt with exultation; many a night
Set all its stars upon them as for spies
On many a moon-bewildering mountain-height
Where he rode only by the fierier light
Of his dread lady's hot sweet hungering eyes.
For the moon wandered witless of her way,
Spell-stricken by strong magic in such wise
As wizards use to set the stars astray.
And in his ears the music that makes mad
Beat always; and what way the music bade,
That always rode he; nor was any sleep
His, nor from height nor deep.
But heaven was as red iron, slumberless,
And had no heart to bless;
And earth lay sere and darkling as distraught,
And help in her was nought.

Then many a midnight, many a morn and even,
His mother, passing forth of her fair heaven,
With goodlier gifts than all save gods can give
From earth or from the heaven where sea-things live,
With shine of sea-flowers through the bayleaf braid
Woven for a crown her foam-white hands had made
To crown him with land's laurel and sea-dew,
Sought the sea-bird that was her boy: but he
Sat panther-throned beside Erigone,
Riding the red ways of the revel through
Midmost of pale-mouthed passion's crownless crew.
Till on some winter's dawn of some dim year
He let the vine-bit on the panther's lip
Slide, and the green rein slip,
And set his eyes to seaward, nor gave ear
If sound from landward hailed him, dire or dear;
And passing forth of all those fair fierce ranks
Back to the grey sea-banks,
Against a sea-rock lying, aslant the steep,
Fell after many sleepless dreams on sleep.

And in his sleep the dun green light was shed
Heavily round his head
That through the veil of sea falls fathom-deep,
Blurred like a lamp's that when the night drops dead
Dies; and his eyes gat grace of sleep to see
The deep divine dark dayshine of the sea,
Dense water-walls and clear dusk water-ways,
Broad-based, or branching as a sea-flower sprays
That side or this dividing; and anew
The glory of all her glories that he knew.
And in sharp rapture of recovering tears
He woke on fire with yearnings of old years,
Pure as one purged of pain that passion bore,
Ill child of bitter mother; for his own
Looked laughing toward him from her midsea throne,
Up toward him there ashore.

Thence in his heart the great same joy began,
Of child that made him man:
And turned again from all hearts else on quest,
He communed with his own heart, and had rest.
And like sea-winds upon loud waters ran
His days and dreams together, till the joy
Burned in him of the boy.
Till the earth's great comfort and the sweet sea's breath
Breathed and blew life in where was heartless death,
Death spirit-stricken of soul-sick days, where strife
Of thought and flesh made mock of death and life.
And grace returned upon him of his birth
Where heaven was mixed with heavenlike sea and earth;
And song shot forth strong wings that took the sun
From inward, fledged with might of sorrow and mirth
And father's fire made mortal in his son.
Nor was not spirit of strength in blast and breeze
To exalt again the sun's child and the sea's;
For as wild mares in Thessaly grow great
With child of ravishing winds, that violate
Their leaping length of limb with manes like fire
And eyes outburning heaven's
With fires more violent than the lightning levin's
And breath drained out and desperate of desire,
Even so the spirit in him, when winds grew strong,
Grew great with child of song.
Nor less than when his veins first leapt for joy
To draw delight in such as burns a boy,
Now too the soul of all his senses felt
The passionate pride of deep sea-pulses dealt
Through nerve and jubilant vein
As from the love and largess of old time,
And with his heart again
The tidal throb of all the tides keep rhyme
And charm him from his own soul's separate sense
With infinite and invasive influence
That made strength sweet in him and sweetness strong,
Being now no more a singer, but a song.

Till one clear day when brighter sea-wind blew
And louder sea-shine lightened, for the waves
Were full of godhead and the light that saves,
His father's, and their spirit had pierced him through,
He felt strange breath and light all round him shed
That bowed him down with rapture; and he knew
His father's hand, hallowing his humbled head,
And the old great voice of the old good time, that said:

"Child of my sunlight and the sea, from birth
A fosterling and fugitive on earth;
Sleepless of soul as wind or wave or fire,
A manchild with an ungrown God's desire;
Because thou hast loved nought mortal more than me,
Thy father, and thy mother-hearted sea;
Because thou hast set thine heart to sing, and sold
Life and life's love for song, God's living gold;
Because thou hast given thy flower and fire of youth
To feed men's hearts with visions, truer than truth;
Because thou hast kept in those world-wandering eyes
The light that makes me music of the skies;
Because thou hast heard with world-unwearied ears
The music that puts light into the spheres;
Have therefore in thine heart and in thy mouth
The sound of song that mingles north and south,
The song of all the winds that sing of me,
And in thy soul the sense of all the sea."

1880

THE HIGHER PANTHEISM IN A NUTSHELL

One, who is not, we see: but one, whom we see not, is:
Surely this is not that: but that is assuredly this.

What, and wherefore, and whence? for under is over and under:
If thunder could be without lightning, lightning could be without thunder.

Doubt is faith in the main: but faith, on the whole, is doubt:
We cannot believe by proof: but could we believe without?

Why, and whither, and how? for barley and rye are not clover:
Neither are straight lines curves: yet over is under and over.

Two and two may be four: but four and four are not eight:
Fate and God may be twain: but God is the same thing as fate.

Ask a man what he thinks, and get from a man what he feels:
God, once caught in the fact, shows you a fair pair of heels.

Body and spirit are twins: God only knows which is which:
The soul squats down in the flesh, like a tinker drunk in a ditch.

More is the whole than a part: but half is more than the whole:
Clearly, the soul is the body: but is not the body the soul?

One and two are not one: but one and nothing is two:
Truth can hardly be false, if falsehood cannot be true.

Once the mastodon was: pterodactyls were common as cocks:
Then the mammoth was God: now is He a prize ox.

Parallels all things are: yet many of these are askew:
You are certainly I: but certainly I am not you.

Springs the rock from the plain, shoots the stream from the rock:
Cocks exist for the hen: but hens exist for the cock.

God, whom we see not, is: and God, who is not, we see:
Fiddle, we know, is diddle: and diddle, we take it, is dee.

1880

NEPHELIDIA

FROM the depth of the dreamy decline of the dawn through a notable nimbus of nebulous noonshine,
  Pallid and pink as the palm of the flag-flower that flickers with fear of the flies as they float,
Are the looks of our lovers that lustrously lean from a marvel of mystic miraculous moonshine,
  These that we feel in the blood of our blushes that thicken and threaten with throbs through the throat?
Thicken and thrill as a theatre thronged at appeal of an actor's appalled agitation,
  Fainter with fear of the fires of the future than pale with the promise of pride in the past;
Flushed with the famishing fullness of fever that reddens with radiance of rathe recreation,
  Gaunt as the ghastliest of glimpses that gleam through the gloom of the gloaming when ghosts go aghast?
Nay, for the nick of the tick of the time is a tremulous touch on the temples of terror,
  Strained as the sinews yet strenuous with strife of the dead who is dumb as the dust-heaps of death:
Surely no soul is it, sweet as the spasm of erotic emotional exquisite error,
  Bathed in the balms of beatified bliss, beatific itself by beatitude's breath.
Surely no spirit or sense of a soul that was soft to the spirit and soul of our senses
  Sweetens the stress of suspiring suspicion that sobs in the semblance and sound of a sigh;
Only this oracle opens Olympian, in mystical moods and triangular tenses—
  "Life is the lust of a lamp for the light that is dark till the dawn of the day when we die."
Mild is the mirk and monotonous music of memory, melodiously mute as it may be,
  While the hope in the heart of a hero is bruised by the breach of men's rapiers, resigned to the rod;
Made meek as a mother whose bosom-beats bound with the bliss-bringing bulk of a balm-breathing baby,
  As they grope through the grave-yard of creeds, under skies growing green at a groan for the grimness of God.
Blank is the book of his bounty beholden of old, and its binding is blacker than bluer:
  Out of blue into black is the scheme of the skies, and their dews are the wine of the bloodshed of things;
Till the darkling desire of delight shall be free as a fawn that is freed from the fangs that pursue her,
  Till the heart-beats of hell shall be hushed by a hymn from the hunt that has harried the kennel of kings.

1880

ON THE DEATHS OF THOMAS CARLYLE AND GEORGE ELIOT

Two souls diverse out of our human sight
  Pass, followed one with love and each with wonder:
  The stormy sophist with his mouth of thunder,
Clothed with loud words and mantled in the might
Of darkness and magnificence of night;
  And one whose eye could smite the night in sunder,
  Searching if light or no light were thereunder,
And found in love of loving-kindness light.
Duty divine and Thought with eyes of fire
  Still following Righteousness with deep desire
    Shone sole and stern before her and above,
Sure stars and sole to steer by; but more sweet
Shone lower the loveliest lamp for earthly feet,
    The light of little children, and their love.

1881

From SONNETS ON ENGLISH DRAMATIC POETS—(1590–1650)

I CHRISTOPHER MARLOWE

CROWNED, girdled, garbed and shod with light and fire,
Son first-born of the morning, sovereign star!
Soul nearest ours of all, that wert most far,
Most far off in the abysm of time, thy lyre
Hung highest above the dawn-enkindled quire
Where all ye sang together, all that are,
And all the starry songs behind thy car
Rang sequence, all our souls acclaim thee sire.

"If all the pens that ever poets held
Had fed the feeling of their masters' thoughts,"
And as with rush of hurtling chariots
The flight of all their spirits were impelled
Toward one great end, thy glory—nay, not then,
Not yet might'st thou be praised enough of men.

II WILLIAM SHAKESPEARE

NOT if men's tongues and angels' all in one
Spake, might the word be said that might speak Thee.
Streams, winds, woods, flowers, fields, mountains, yea, the sea,
What power is in them all to praise the sun?
His praise is this,—he can be praised of none.
Man, woman, child, praise God for him; but he
Exults not to be worshipped, but to be.
He is; and, being, beholds his work well done.
All joy, all glory, all sorrow, all strength, all mirth,
Are his: without him, day were night on earth.
Time knows not his from time's own period.
All lutes, all harps, all viols, all flutes, all lyres,
Fall dumb before him ere one string suspires.
All stars are angels; but the sun is God.

III BEN JONSON

BROAD-BASED, broad-fronted, bounteous, multiform,
With many a valley impleached with ivy and vine,
Wherein the springs of all the streams run wine,
And many a crag full-faced against the storm,
The mountain where thy Muse's feet made warm
Those lawns that revelled with her dance divine
Shines yet with fire as it was wont to shine
From tossing torches round the dance aswarm.

Nor less, high-stationed on the grey grave heights,
High-thoughted seers with heaven's heart-kindling lights
Hold converse: and the herd of meaner things
Knows or by fiery scourge or fiery shaft
When wrath on thy broad brows has risen, and laughed,
Darkening thy soul with shadow of thunderous wings.

V PHILIP MASSINGER

CLOUDS here and there arisen an hour past noon
Chequered our English heaven with lengthening bars
And shadow and sound of wheel-winged thunder-cars
Assembling strength to put forth tempest soon,
When the clear still warm concord of thy tune
Rose under skies unscared by reddening Mars
Yet, like a sound of silver speech of stars,
With full mild flame as of the mellowing moon.

Grave and great-hearted Massinger, thy face
High melancholy lights with loftier grace
Than gilds the brows of revel: sad and wise,
The spirit of thought that moved thy deeper song,
Sorrow serene in soft calm scorn of wrong,
Speaks patience yet from thy majestic eyes.

VII JOHN WEBSTER

THUNDER: the flesh quails, and the soul bows down.
Night: east, west, south, and northward, very night.
Star upon struggling star strives into sight,

Star after shuddering star the deep storms drown.
The very throne of night, her very crown,
A man lays hand on, and usurps her right.
Song from the highest of heaven's imperious height
Shoots, as a fire to smite some towering town.
Rage, anguish, harrowing fear, heart-crazing crime,
Make monstrous all the murderous face of Time
Shown in the spheral orbit of a glass
Revolving. Earth cries out from all her graves.
Frail, on frail rafts, across wide-wallowing waves,
Shapes here and there of child and mother pass.

VIII THOMAS DECKER

Out of the depths of darkling life where sin
Laughs piteously that sorrow should not know
Her own ill name, nor woe be counted woe;
Where hate and craft and lust make drearier din
Than sounds through dreams that grief holds revel in;
What charm of joy-bells ringing, streams that flow,
Winds that blow healing in each note they blow,
Is this that the outer darkness hears begin?

O sweetest heart of all thy time save one,
Star seen for love's sake nearest to the sun,
Hung lamplike o'er a dense and doleful city,
Not Shakespeare's very spirit, howe'er more great,
Than thine toward man was more compassionate,
Nor gave Christ praise from lips more sweet with pity.

1882

A CHILD'S LAUGHTER

All the bells of heaven may ring,
All the birds of heaven may sing,
All the wells on earth may spring,
All the winds on earth may bring
All sweet sounds together;
Sweeter far than all things heard,
Hand of harper, tone of bird,
Sound of woods at sundawn stirred,
Welling water's winsome word,
Wind in warm wan weather,

One thing yet there is, that none
Hearing ere its chime be done
Knows not well the sweetest one
Heard of man beneath the sun,
Hoped in heaven hereafter;
Soft and strong and loud and light,
Very sound of very light
Heard from morning's rosiest height,
When the soul of all delight
Fills a child's clear laughter.

Golden bells of welcome rolled
Never forth such notes, nor told
Hours so blithe in tones so bold,
As the radiant mouth of gold
Here that rings forth heaven.
If the golden-crested wren
Were a nightingale—why, then,
Something seen and heard of men
Might be half as sweet as when
Laughs a child of seven.

1882

OF SUCH IS THE KINGDOM OF HEAVEN

Of such is the kingdom of heaven.
No glory that ever was shed
From the crowning star of the seven
That crown the north world's head,

No word that ever was spoken
Of human or godlike tongue,
Gave ever such godlike token
Since human harps were strung.

No sign that ever was given
To faithful or faithless eyes
Showed ever beyond clouds riven
So clear a Paradise.

Earth's creeds may be seventy times seven
And blood have defiled each creed:
If of such be the kingdom of heaven,
It must be heaven indeed.

1882

A BABY'S DEATH

I

A LITTLE soul scarce fledged for earth
Takes wing with heaven again for goal
Even while we hailed as fresh from birth
  A little soul.

Our thoughts ring sad as bells that toll,
Not knowing beyond this blind world's girth
What things are writ in heaven's full scroll.

Our fruitfulness is there but dearth,
And all things held in time's control
Seem there, perchance, ill dreams, not worth
  A little soul.

II

The little feet that never trod
Earth, never strayed in field or street,
What hand leads upward back to God
  The little feet?

A rose in June's most honied heat,
When life makes keen the kindling sod,
Was not so soft and warm and sweet.

Their pilgrimage's period
A few swift moons have seen complete
Since mother's hand first clasped and shod
  The little feet.

III

The little hands that never sought
Earth's prizes, worthless all as sands,
What gift has death, God's servant, brought
  The little hands?

We ask: but love's self silent stands,
Love, that lends eyes and wings to thought
To search where death's dim heaven expands.

Ere this, perchance, though love know nought,
Flowers fill them, grown in lovelier lands,
Where hands of guiding angels caught
  The little hands.

IV

The little eyes that never knew
Light other than of dawning skies,
What new life now lights up anew
  The little eyes?

Who knows but on their sleep may rise
Such light as never heaven let through
To lighten earth from Paradise?

No storm, we know, may change the blue
Soft heaven that haply death descries;
No tears, like these in ours, bedew
  The little eyes.

V

Was life so strange, so sad the sky,
  So strait the wide world's range,
He would not stay to wonder why
  Was life so strange?

Was earth's fair house a joyless grange
  Beside that house on high
Whence Time that bore him failed to estrange?

That here at once his soul put by
  All gifts of time and change,
And left us heavier hearts to sigh
  "Was life so strange?"

VI

Angel by name love called him, seeing so fair
  The sweet small frame!
Meet to be called, if ever man's child were,
  Angel by name.

Rose-bright and warm from heaven's own heart he came,
  And might not bear
The cloud that covers earth's wan face with shame.

His little light of life was all too rare
  And soft a flame:
Heaven yearned for him till angels hailed him there
  Angel by name.

VII

The song that smiled upon his birthday here
Weeps on the grave that holds him undefiled
Whose loss makes bitterer than a soundless tear
  The song that smiled.

His name crowned once the mightiest ever styled
Sovereign of arts, and angel: fate and fear
Knew then their master, and were reconciled.

But we saw born beneath some tenderer sphere
Michael, an angel and a little child,
Whose loss bows down to weep upon his bier
The song that smiled.

1883

A SINGING LESSON

Far-fetched and dear-bought, as the proverb rehearses,
Is good, or was held so, for ladies: but nought
In a song can be good if the turn of the verse is
Far-fetched and dear-bought.

As the turn of a wave should it sound, and the thought
Ring smooth, and as light as the spray that disperses
Be the gleam of the words for the garb thereof wrought.

Let the soul in it shine through the sound as it pierces
Men's hearts with possession of music unsought;
For the bounties of song are no jealous god's mercies,
Far-fetched and dear-bought.

1883

THE WAY OF THE WIND

The wind's way in the deep sky's hollow
None may measure, as none can say
How the heart in her shows the swallow
The wind's way.

Hope nor fear can avail to stay
Waves that whiten on wrecks that wallow,
Times and seasons that wane and slay.

Life and love, till the strong night swallow
Thought and hope and the red last ray,
Swim the waters of years that follow
The wind's way.

1883

THE ROUNDEL

A roundel is wrought as a ring or a star-bright sphere,
With craft of delight and with cunning of sound unsought,
That the heart of the hearer may smile if to pleasure his ear
A roundel is wrought.

Its jewel of music is carven of all or of aught—
Love, laughter, or mourning—remembrance of rapture or fear—
That fancy may fashion to hang in the ear of thought.

As a bird's quick song runs round, and the hearts in us hear
Pause answer to pause, and again the same strain caught,
So moves the device whence, round as a pearl or tear,
A roundel is wrought.

1883

IN GUERNSEY

I

The heavenly bay, ringed round with cliffs and moors,
Storm-stained ravines, and crags that lawns inlay,
Soothes as with love the rocks whose guard secures
The heavenly bay.

O friend, shall time take ever this away,
This blessing given of beauty that endures,
This glory shown us, not to pass but stay?

Though sight be changed for memory, love ensures
What memory, changed by love to sight, would say—
The word that seals forever mine and yours
The heavenly bay.

II

My mother sea, my fostress, what new strand
What new delight of waters, may this be,
The fairest found since time's first breezes fanned
My mother sea?

Once more I give me body and soul to thee,
Who hast my soul forever: cliff and sand
Recede, and heart to heart once more are we.

My heart springs first and plunges, ere my hand
Strike out from shore: more close it brings to me,
More near and dear than seems my fatherland,
My mother sea.

III

Across and along, as the bay's breadth opens, and o'er us
Wild autumn exults in the wind, swift rapture and strong
Impels us, and broader the wide waves brighten before us
Across and along.

The whole world's heart is uplifted, and knows not wrong;
The whole world's life is a chant to the sea-tide's chorus;
Are we not as waves of the water, as notes of the song?

Like children unworn of the passions and toils that wore us,
We breast for a season the breadth of the seas that throng,
Rejoicing as they, to be borne as of old they bore us
Across and along.

IV

On Dante's track by some funereal spell
Drawn down through desperate ways that lead not back
We seem to move, bound forth past flood and fell
On Dante's track.

The grey path ends: the gaunt rocks gape: the black
Deep hollow tortuous night, a soundless shell,
Glares darkness: are the fires of old grown slack?

Nay, then, what flames are these that leap and swell
As 'twere to show, where earth's foundations crack,
The secrets of the sepulchres of hell
On Dante's track?

V

By mere men's hands the flame was lit, we know,
From heaps of dry waste whin and casual brands:
Yet, knowing, we scarce believe it kindled so
By mere men's hands.

Above, around, high-vaulted hell expands,
Steep, dense, a labyrinth walled and roofed with woe.
Whose mysteries even itself not understands.

The scorn in Farinata's eyes aglow
Seems visible in this flame: there Geryon stands:
No stage of earth's is here, set forth to show
By mere men's hands.

VI

Night, in utmost noon forlorn and strong, with heart athirst and fasting,
Hungers here, barred up forever, whence as one whom dreams affright
Day recoils before the low-browed lintel threatening doom and casting Night.

All the reefs and islands, all the lawns and highlands, clothed with light,
Laugh for love's sake in their sleep outside: but here the night speaks, blasting
Day with silent speech and scorn of all things known from depth to height.

Lower than dive the thoughts of spirit-stricken fear in souls forecasting
Hell, the deep void seems to yawn fear's reach, and higher than sight
Rise the walls and roofs that compass it about with everlasting Night.

VII

The house accurst, with cursing sealed and signed,
Heeds not what storms about it burn and burst:
No fear more fearful than its own may find
The house accurst.

Barren as crime, anhungered and athirst,
Blank miles of moor sweep inland, sere and blind,
Where summer's best rebukes not winter's worst.

The low bleak tower with nought save wastes behind
Stares down the abyss whereon chance reared and nursed
This type and likeness of the accurst man's mind,
The house accurst.

VIII

Beloved and blest, lit warm with love and fame,
The house that had the light of the earth for guest
Hears for his name's sake all men hail its name
Beloved and blest.

This eyrie was the homeless eagle's nest
When storm laid waste his eyrie: hence he came
Again, when storm smote sore his mother's breast.

Bow down men bade us, or be clothed with blame
And mocked for madness: worst, they sware, was best:
But grief shone here, while joy was one with shame,
Beloved and blest.

1883

LINES ON THE MONUMENT OF GIUSEPPE MAZZINI

ITALIA, mother of the souls of men,
Mother divine,
Of all that served thee best with sword or pen,
All sons of thine,

Thou knowest that here the likeness of the best
Before thee stands;
The head most high, the heart found faithfullest,
The purest hands.

Above the fume and foam of time that flits,
The soul, we know,
Now sits on high where Alighieri sits
With Angelo.

Not his own heavenly tongue hath heavenly speech
Enough to say
What this man was, whose praise no thought may reach,
No words can weigh.

Since man's first mother brought to mortal birth
Her first-born son,
Such grace befell not ever man on earth
As crowns this one.

Of God nor man was ever this thing said,
That he could give
Life back to her who gave him, whence his dead
Mother might live.

But this man found his mother dead and slain,
With fast sealed eyes,
And bade the dead rise up and live again,
And she did rise.

And all the world was bright with her through him:
But dark with strife,
Like heaven's own sun that storming clouds bedim,
Was all his life.

Life and the clouds are vanished: hate and fear
Have had their span
Of time to hurt, and are not: he is here,
The sunlike man.

City superb that hadst Columbus first
For sovereign son,
Be prouder that thy breast hath later nurst
This mightier one.

Glory be his forever, while his land
Lives and is free,
As with controlling breath and sovereign hand
He bade her be.

Earth shows to heaven the names by thousands told
That crown her fame,
But highest of all that heaven and earth behold
Mazzini's name.

1884

From A MIDSUMMER HOLIDAY

I On a Country Road

Along these low pleached lanes, on such a day,
So soft a day as this, through shade and sun,
With glad grave eyes that scanned the glad wild way,
And hearts still hovering o'er a song begun,
And smile that warmed the world with benison,
Our father, lord long since of lordly rhyme,
Long since hath haply ridden, when the lime
Bloomed broad above him, flowering where he came.
Because thy passage once made warm this clime,
Our father Chaucer, here we praise thy name.

Each year that England clothes herself with May,
She takes thy likeness on her. Time hath spun
Fresh raiment all in vain and strange array
For earth and man's new spirit, fain to shun
Things past for dreams of better to be won,
Through many a century since thy funeral chime
Rang, and men deemed it death's most direful crime
To have spared not thee for very love or shame;
And yet, while mists round last year's memories climb,
Our father Chaucer, here we praise thy name.

Each turn of the old wild road whereon we stray,
Meseems, might bring us face to face with one
Whom seeing we could not but give thanks, and pray
For England's love our father and her son
To speak with us as once in days long done
With all men, sage and churl and monk and mime,
Who knew not as we know the soul sublime
That sang for song's love more than lust of fame.
Yet, though this be not, yet, in happy time,
Our father Chaucer, here we praise thy name.

Friend, even as bees about the flowering thyme,
Years crowd on years, till hoar decay begrime
Names once beloved; but, seeing the sun the same,
As birds of autumn fain to praise the prime,
Our father Chaucer, here we praise thy name.

II In The Water

The sea is awake, and the sound of the song of the joy of her waking is rolled
From afar to the star that recedes, from anear to the wastes of the wild wide shore.
Her call is a trumpet compelling us homeward: if dawn in her east be acold,
From the sea shall we crave not her grace to rekindle the life that it kindled before,
Her breath to requicken, her bosom to rock us, her kisses to bless as of yore?
For the wind, with his wings half open, at pause in the sky, neither fettered nor free,
Leans waveward and flutters the ripple to laughter: and fain would the twain of us be
Where lightly the wave yearns forward from under the curve of the deep dawn's dome,
And, full of the morning and fired with the pride of the glory thereof and the glee,
Strike out from the shore as the heart in us bids and beseeches, athirst for the foam.

Life holds not an hour that is better to live in: the past is a tale that is told,
The future a sun-flecked shadow, alive and asleep, with a blessing in store.
As we give us again to the waters, the rapture of limbs that the waters enfold
Is less than the rapture of spirit whereby, though the burden it quits were sore,
Our souls and the bodies they wield at their will are absorbed in the life they adore—
In the life that endures no burden, and bows not the forehead, and bends not the knee—
In the life everlasting of earth and of heaven, in the laws that atone and agree,

In the measureless music of things, in the fervour of forces that rest or that roam,
That cross and return and reissue, as I after you and as you after me
Strike out from the shore as the heart in us bids and beseeches, athirst for the foam.

For, albeit he were less than the least of them, haply the heart of a man may be bold
To rejoice in the word of the sea as a mother's that saith to the son she bore,
Child, was not the life in thee mine, and my spirit the breath in thy lips from of old?
Have I let not thy weakness exult in my strength, and thy foolishness learn of my lore?
Have I helped not or healed not thine anguish, or made not the might of thy gladness more?
And surely his heart should answer, The light of the love of my life is in thee.
She is fairer than earth, and the sun is not fairer, the wind is not blither than she:
From my youth hath she shown me the joy of her bays that I crossed, of her cliffs that I clomb.
Till now that the twain of us here, in desire of the dawn and in trust of the sea,
Strike out from the shore as the heart in us bids and beseeches, athirst for the foam.

Friend, earth is a harbour of refuge for winter, a covert whereunder to flee
When day is the vassal of night, and the strength of the hosts of her mightier than he;
But here is the presence adored of me, here my desire is at rest and at home.
There are cliffs to be climbed upon land, there are ways to be trodden and ridden: but we
Strike out from the shore as the heart in us bids and beseeches, athirst for the foam.

III On The Verge

HERE begins the sea that ends not till the world's end. Where we stand,
Could we know the next high sea-mark set beyond these waves that gleam,
We should know what never man hath known, nor eye of man hath scanned.
Nought beyond these coiling clouds that melt like fume of shrines that steam
Breaks or stays the strength of waters till they pass our bounds of dream.
Where the waste Land's End leans westward, all the seas it watches roll
Find their border fixed beyond them, and a worldwide shore's control:
These whereby we stand no shore beyond us limits: these are free.
Gazing hence, we see the water that grows iron round the Pole,
From the shore that hath no shore beyond it set in all the sea.

Sail on sail along the sea-line fades and flashes; here on land
Flash and fade the wheeling wings on wings of mews that plunge and scream.
Hour on hour along the line of life and time's evasive strand
Shines and darkens, wanes and waxes, slays and dies: and scarce they seem
More than motes that thronged and trembled in the brief noon's breath and beam.
Some with crying and wailing, some with notes like sound of bells that toll,
Some with sighing and laughing, some with words that blessed and made us whole,
Passed, and left us, and we know not what they were, nor what were we.
Would we know, being mortal? Never breath of answering whisper stole
From the shore that hath no shore beyond it set in all the sea.

Shadows, would we question darkness? Ere our eyes and brows be fanned
Round with airs of twilight, washed with dews from sleep's eternal stream,
Would we know sleep's guarded secret? Ere the fire consume the brand,
Would it know if yet its ashes may requicken? yet we deem
Surely man may know, or ever night unyoke her starry team,
What the dawn shall be, or if the dawn shall be not: yea, the scroll
Would we read of sleep's dark scripture, pledge of peace or doom of dole.

Ah, but here man's heart leaps, yearning toward the gloom with venturous glee,
Though his pilot eye behold nor bay nor harbour, rock nor shoal,
From the shore that hath no shore beyond it set in all the sea.

Friend, who knows if death indeed have life or life have death for goal?
Day nor night can tell us, nor may seas declare nor skies unroll
What has been from everlasting, or if aught shall always be.
Silence answering only strikes response reverberate on the soul
From the shore that hath no shore beyond it set in all the sea.

1884

IN TIME OF MOURNING

"Return," we dare not as we fain
Would cry from hearts that yearn:
Love dares not bid our dead again
Return.

O hearts that strain and burn
As fires fast fettered burn and strain!
Bow down, lie still, and learn.

The heart that healed all hearts of pain
No funeral rites inurn:
Its echoes, while the stars remain,
Return.

May, 1885

IN A GARDEN

Baby, see the flowers!
—Baby sees
Fairer things than these,
Fairer though they be than dreams of ours.

Baby, hear the birds!
—Baby knows
Better songs than those,
Sweeter though they sound than sweetest words.

Baby, see the moon!
—Baby's eyes
Laugh to watch it rise,
Answering light with love and night with noon.

Baby, hear the sea!
—Baby's face
Takes a graver grace,
Touched with wonder what the sound may be.

Baby, see the star!
—Baby's hand
Opens, warm and bland,
Calm in claim of all things fair that are.

Baby, hear the bells!
—Baby's head
Bows, as ripe for bed,
Now the flowers curl round and close their cells.

Baby, flower of light,
Sleep, and see
Brighter dreams than we,
Till good day shall smile away good night.

1889

THE WINDS

O weary fa' the east wind,
And weary fa' the west:
And gin I were under the wan waves wide
I wot weel wad I rest.

O weary fa' the north wind,
And weary fa' the south:
The sea went ower my good lord's head
Or ever he kissed my mouth.

Weary fa' the windward rocks,
And weary fa' the lee:
They might hae sunken sevenscore ships,
And let my love's gang free.

And weary fa' ye, mariners a',
And weary fa' the sea:
It might hae taken an hundred men,
And let my ae love be.

1889

ON THE DEATH OF ROBERT BROWNING

HE held no dream worth waking: so he said,
He who stands now on death's triumphal steep,
Awakened out of life wherein we sleep
And dream of what he knows and sees, being dead.
But never death for him was dark or dread:
"Look forth," he bade the soul, and fear not. Weep,
All ye that trust not in his truth, and keep
Vain memory's vision of a vanished head
As all that lives of all that once was he
Save that which lightens from his word: but we,
Who, seeing the sunset-coloured waters roll,
Yet know the sun subdued not of the sea,
Nor weep nor doubt that still the spirit is whole,
And life and death but shadows of the soul.

1890

A NYMPHOLEPT

SUMMER, and noon, and a splendour of silence, felt,
Seen, and heard of the spirit within the sense.
Soft through the frondage the shades of the sunbeams melt,
Sharp through the foliage the shafts of them, keen and dense,
Cleave, as discharged from the string of the God's bow, tense
As a war-steed's girth, and bright as a warrior's belt.
Ah, why should an hour that is heaven for an hour pass hence?

I dare not sleep for delight of the perfect hour,
Lest God be wroth that his gift should be scorned of man.
The face of the warm bright world is the face of a flower,
The word of the wind and the leaves that the light winds fan
As the word that quickened at first into flame, and ran,
Creative and subtle and fierce with invasive power,
Through darkness and cloud, from the breath of the one God, Pan.

The perfume of earth possessed by the sun pervades
The chaster air that he soothes but with sense of sleep.
Soft, imminent, strong as desire that prevails and fades,
The passing noon that beholds not a cloudlet weep
Imbues and impregnates life with delight more deep
Than dawn or sunset or moonrise on lawns or glades
Can shed from the skies that receive it and may not keep.

The skies may hold not the splendour of sundown fast;
It wanes into twilight as dawn dies down into day.
And the moon, triumphant when twilight is overpast,
Takes pride but awhile in the hours of her stately sway.
But the might of the noon, though the light of it pass away,
Leaves earth fulfilled of desires and of dreams that last;
But if any there be that hath sense of them, none can say.

For if any there be that hath sight of them, sense, or trust
Made strong by the might of a vision, the strength of a dream,
His lips shall straiten and close as a dead man's must,
His heart shall be sealed as the voice of a frost-bound stream.
For the deep mid mystery of light and of heat that seem
To clasp and pierce dark earth, and enkindle dust,
Shall a man's faith say what it is? or a man's guess deem?

A Sequence of Sonnets
on the death of Robert Browning.

I.

The clearest eyes in all the world they read
With sense more keen & spirit of sight more true
Than burns & thrills in sunrise, when the dew
Flames, & absorbs the glory round it shed,
As they the light of ages quick & dead,
Closed now, forsake us: yet the shaft that slew
Can slay not one of all the works we knew,
Nor death discrown that many-laurelled head.

The works of words ~~divine & deathless~~ whose life seems lightning wrought,
And moulded of unconquerable thought,
And quickened with imperishable flame,
Stand fast & shine & smile, assured that nought
May fade of all their myriad-moulded fame,
Nor England's memory clasp not Browning's name.

Dec. 13, 1889.

Manuscript Copy of the Opening Sonnet from "A Sequence of Sonnets on the Death of Robert Browning." (See Appendix I.)

Sleep lies not heavier on eyes that have watched all night
Than hangs the heat of the noon on the hills and trees.
Why now should the haze not open, and yield to sight
A fairer secret than hope or than slumber sees?
I seek not heaven with submission of lips and knees,
With worship and prayer for a sign till it leap to light:
I gaze on the gods about me, and call on these.

I call on the gods hard by, the divine dim powers
Whose likeness is here at hand, in the breathless air,
In the pulseless peace of the fervid and silent flowers,
In the faint sweet speech of the waters that whisper there.
Ah, what should darkness do in a world so fair?
The bent-grass heaves not, the couch-grass quails not or cowers;
The wind's kiss frets not the rowan's or aspen's hair.

But the silence trembles with passion of sound suppressed,
And the twilight quivers and yearns to the sunward, wrung
With love as with pain; and the wide wood's motionless breast
Is thrilled with a dumb desire that would fain find tongue
And palpitates, tongueless as she whom a man-snake stung,
Whose heart now heaves in the nightingale, never at rest
Nor satiated ever with song till her last be sung.

Is it rapture or terror that circles me round, and invades
Each vein of my life with hope—if it be not fear?
Each pulse that awakens my blood into rapture fades,
Each pulse that subsides into dread of a strange thing near
Requickens with sense of a terror less dread than dear.
Is peace not one with light in the deep green glades
Where summer at noonday slumbers? Is peace not here?

The tall thin stems of the firs, and the roof sublime
That screens from the sun the floor of the steep still wood,
Deep, silent, splendid, and perfect and calm as time,
Stand fast as ever in sight of the night they stood,
When night gave all that moonlight and dewfall could.
The dense ferns deepen, the moss glows warm as the thyme:
The wild heath quivers about me: the world is good.

Is it Pan's breath, fierce in the tremulous maidenhair,
That bids fear creep as a snake through the woodlands, felt
In the leaves that it stirs not yet, in the mute bright air,
In the stress of the sun? For here has the great God dwelt:
For hence were the shafts of his love or his anger dealt.
For here has his wrath been fierce as his love was fair,
When each was as fire to the darkness its breath bade melt.

Is it love, is it dread, that enkindles the trembling noon,
That yearns, reluctant in rapture that fear has fed,
As man for woman, as woman for man? Full soon,
If I live, and the life that may look on him drop not dead,
Shall the ear that hears not a leaf quake hear his tread,
The sense that knows not the sound of the deep day's tune
Receive the God, be it love that he brings or dread.

The naked noon is upon me: the fierce dumb spell,
The fearful charm of the strong sun's imminent might,
Unmerciful, steadfast, deeper than seas that swell,
Pervades, invades, appals me with loveless light,
With harsher awe than breathes in the breath of night.
Have mercy, God who art all! For I know thee well,
How sharp is thine eye to lighten, thine hand to smite.

The whole wood feels thee, the whole air fears thee: but fear
So deep, so dim, so sacred, is wellnigh sweet.
For the light that hangs and broods on the woodlands here,
Intense, invasive, intolerant, imperious, and meet
To lighten the works of thine hands and the ways of thy feet,
Is hot with the fire of the breath of thy life, and dear
As hope that shrivels or shrinks not for frost or heat.

Thee, thee the supreme dim godhead, approved afar,
Perceived of the soul and conceived of the sense of man,
We scarce dare love, and we dare not fear: the star
We call the sun, that lit us when life began
To brood on the world that is thine by his grace for a span,
Conceals and reveals in the semblance of things that are
Thine immanent presence, the pulse of thy heart's life, Pan.

The fierce mid noon that wakens and warms the snake
Conceals thy mercy, reveals thy wrath: and again
The dew-bright hour that assuages the twilight brake
Conceals thy wrath and reveals thy mercy: then
Thou art fearful only for evil souls of men
That feel with nightfall the serpent within them wake,
And hate the holy darkness on glade and glen.

Yea, then we know not and dream not if ill things be,
Or if aught of the work of the wrong of the world be thine.
We hear not the footfall of terror that treads the sea,
We hear not the moan of winds that assail the pine:
We see not if shipwreck reign in the storm's dim shrine;
If death do service and doom bear witness to thee
We see not,—know not if blood for thy lips be wine.

But in all things evil and fearful that fear may scan,
As in all things good, as in all things fair that fall,
We know thee present and latent, the lord of man;
In the murmuring of doves, in the clamouring of winds that call
And wolves that howl for their prey; in the midnight's pall,
In the naked and nymph-like feet of the dawn, O Pan,
And in each life living, O thou the God who art all.

Smiling and singing, wailing and wringing of hands,
Laughing and weeping, watching and sleeping, still
Proclaim but and prove but thee, as the shifted sands
Speak forth and show but the strength of the sea's wild will
That sifts and grinds them as grain in the storm-wind's mill.
In thee is the doom that falls and the doom that stands:
The tempests utter thy word, and the stars fulfil.

Where Etna shudders with passion and pain volcanic
That rend her heart as with anguish that rends a man's,
Where Typho labours, and finds not his thews Titanic,
In breathless torment that ever the flame's breath fans,
Men felt and feared thee of old, whose pastoral clans
Were given to the charge of thy keeping; and soundless panic
Held fast the woodland whose depths and whose heights were Pan's.

And here, though fear be less than delight, and awe
Be one with desire and with worship of earth and thee,
So mild seems now thy secret and speechless law,
So fair and fearless and faithful and godlike she,
So soft the spell of thy whisper on stream and sea,
Yet man should fear lest he see what of old men saw
And withered: yet shall I quail if thy breath smite me.

Lord God of life and of light and of all things fair,
Lord God of ravin and ruin and all things dim,
Death seals up life, and darkness the sunbright air,
And the stars that watch blind earth in the deep night swim
Laugh, saying, "What God is your God, that ye call on him?
What is man, that the God who is guide of our way should care
If day for a man be golden, or night be grim?"

But thou, dost thou hear? Stars too but abide for a span,
Gods too but endure for a season; but thou, if thou be
God, more than shadows conceived and adored of man,
Kind Gods and fierce, that bound him or made him free,
The skies that scorn us are less in thy sight than we,
Whose souls have strength to conceive and perceive thee, Pan,
With sense more subtle than senses that hear and see.

Yet may not it say, though it seek thee and think to find
One soul of sense in the fire and the frost-bound clod,
What heart is this, what spirit alive or blind,
That moves thee: only we know that the ways we trod
We tread, with hands unguided, with feet unshod,
With eyes unlightened; and yet, if with steadfast mind,
Perchance may we find thee and know thee at last for God.

Yet then should God be dark as the dawn is bright,
And bright as the night is dark on the world—no more.
Light slays not darkness, and darkness absorbs not light;
And the labour of evil and good from the years of yore
Is even as the labour of waves on a sunless shore.
And he who is first and last, who is depth and height,
Keeps silence now, as the sun when the woods wax hoar.

The dark dumb godhead innate in the fair world's life
Imbues the rapture of dawn and of noon with dread,
Infects the peace of the star-shod night with strife,
Informs with terror the sorrow that guards the dead.
No service of bended knee or of humbled head
May soothe or subdue the God who has change to wife:
And life with death is as morning with evening wed.

And yet, if the light and the life in the light that here
Seem soft and splendid and fervid as sleep may seem
Be more than the shine of a smile or the flash of a tear,
Sleep, change, and death are less than a spell-struck dream,
And fear than the fall of a leaf on a starlit stream.
And yet, if the hope that hath said it absorb not fear,
What helps it man that the stars and the waters gleam?

What helps it man, that the noon be indeed intense,
The night be indeed worth worship? Fear and pain
Were lords and masters yet of the secret sense,
Which now dares deem not that light is as darkness, fain
Though dark dreams be to declare it, crying in vain.
For whence, thou God of the light and the darkness, whence
Dawns now this vision that bids not the sunbeams wane?

What light, what shadow, diviner than dawn or night,
Draws near, makes pause, and again—or I dream—draws near?
More soft than shadow, more strong than the strong sun's light,
More pure than moonbeams—yea, but the rays run sheer
As fire from the sun through the dusk of the pinewood, clear
And constant; yea, but the shadow itself is bright
That the light clothes round with love that is one with fear.

Above and behind it the noon and the wood-land lie,
Terrible, radiant with mystery, superb and subdued,
Triumphant in silence; and hardly the sacred sky
Seems free from the tyrannous weight of the dumb fierce mood
Which rules as with fire and invasion of beams that brood
The breathless rapture of earth till its hour pass by
And leave her spirit released and her peace renewed.

I sleep not: never in sleep has a man beholden
This. From the shadow that trembles and yearns with light
Suppressed and elate and reluctant—obscure and golden
As water kindled with presage of dawn or night—
A form, a face, a wonder to sense and sight,
Grows great as the moon through the month; and her eyes embolden
Fear, till it change to desire, and desire to delight.

I sleep not: sleep would die of a dream so strange;
A dream so sweet would die as a rainbow dies,
As a sunbow laughs and is lost on the waves that range
And reck not of light that flickers or spray that flies.
But the sun withdraws not, the woodland shrinks not or sighs,
No sweet thing sickens with sense or with fear of change;
Light wounds not, darkness blinds not, my steadfast eyes.

Only the soul in my sense that receives the soul
Whence now my spirit is kindled with breathless bliss
Knows well if the light that wounds it with love makes whole,
If hopes that carol be louder than fears that hiss,
If truth be spoken of flowers and of waves that kiss,
Of clouds and stars that contend for a sun-bright goal.
And yet may I dream that I dream not indeed of this?

An earth-born dreamer, constrained by the bonds of birth,
Held fast by the flesh, compelled by his veins that beat
And kindle to rapture or wrath, to desire or to mirth,
May hear not surely the fall of immortal feet,
May feel not surely if heaven upon earth be sweet;
And here is my sense fulfilled of the joys of earth,
Light, silence, bloom, shade, murmur of leaves that meet.

Bloom, fervour, and perfume of grasses and flowers aglow,
Breathe and brighten about me: the darkness gleams,
The sweet light shivers and laughs on the slopes below,
Made soft by leaves that lighten and change like dreams;
The silence thrills with the whisper of secret streams
That well from the heart of the woodland: these I know:
Earth bore them, heaven sustained them with showers and beams.

I lean my face to the heather, and drink the sun
Whose flame-lit odour satiates the flowers: mine eyes
Close, and the goal of delight and of life is one:
No more I crave of earth or her kindred skies.
No more? But the joy that springs from them smiles and flies:
The sweet work wrought of them surely, the good work done,
If the mind and the face of the season be loveless, dies.

Thee, therefore, thee would I come to, cleave to, cling,
If haply thy heart be kind and thy gifts be good,
Unknown sweet spirit, whose vesture is soft in spring,
In summer splendid, in autumn pale as the wood
That shudders and wanes and shrinks as a shamed thing should,
In winter bright as the mail of a war-worn king
Who stands where foes fled far from the face of him stood.

My spirit or thine is it, breath of thy life or of mine,
Which fills my sense with a rapture that casts out fear?
Pan's dim frown wanes, and his wild eyes brighten as thine,
Transformed as night or as day by the kindling year.
Earth-born, or mine eye were withered that sees, mine ear
That hears were stricken to death by the sense divine,
Earth-born I know thee: but heaven is about me here.

The terror that whispers in darkness and flames in light,
The doubt that speaks in the silence of earth and sea,
The sense, more fearful at noon than in midmost night,
Of wrath scarce hushed and of imminent ill to be,
Where are they? Heaven is as earth, and as heaven to me
Earth: for the shadows that sundered them here take flight;
And nought is all, as am I, but a dream of thee.

1894

A CHANNEL PASSAGE

Forth from Calais, at dawn of night, when sunset summer on autumn shone,
Fared the steamer alert and loud through seas whence only the sun was gone:
Soft and sweet as the sky they smiled, and bade man welcome: a dim sweet hour
Gleamed and whispered in wind and sea, and heaven was fair as a field in flower:
Stars fulfilled the desire of the darkling world as with music: the starbright air
Made the face of the sea, if aught may make the face of the sea, more fair.

Whence came change? Was the sweet night weary of rest? What anguish awoke in the dark?
Sudden, sublime, the strong storm spake: we heard the thunders as hounds that bark.
Lovelier if aught may be lovelier than stars, we saw the lightnings exalt the sky,
Living and lustrous and rapturous as love that is born but to quicken and lighten and die.
Heaven's own heart at its highest of delight found utterance in music and semblance in fire:
Thunder on thunder exulted, rejoicing to live and to satiate the night's desire.

And the night was alive and anhungered of life as a tiger from toils cast free:
And a rapture of rage made joyous the spirit and strength of the soul of the sea.
All the weight of the wind bore down on it, freighted with death for fraught:
And the keen waves kindled and quickened as things transfigured or things distraught.
And madness fell on them laughing and leaping; and madness came on the wind:
And the might and the light and the darkness of storm were as storm in the heart of Ind.
Such glory, such terror, such passion, as lighten and harrow the far fierce East,
Rang, shone, spake, shuddered around us: the night was an altar with death for priest.
The channel that sunders England from shores where never was man born free
Was clothed with the likeness and thrilled with the strength and the wrath of a tropic sea.
As a wild steed ramps in rebellion, and rears till it swerves from a backward fall,
The strong ship struggled and reared, and her deck was upright as a sheer cliff's wall.
Stern and prow plunged under, alternate: a glimpse, a recoil, a breath,
And she sprang as the life in a god made man would spring at the throat of death.
Three glad hours, and it seemed not an hour of supreme and supernal joy,
Filled with delight that revives in remembrance a sea-bird's heart in a boy.
For the central crest of the night was cloud that thundered and flamed, sublime
As the splendour and song of the soul everlasting that quickens the pulse of time.
The glory beholden of man in a vision, the music of light overheard,
The rapture and radiance of battle, the life that abides in the fire of a word,
In the midmost heaven enkindled, was manifest far on the face of the sea,
And the rage in the roar of the voice of the waters was heard but when heaven breathed free.
Far eastward, clear of the covering of cloud, the sky laughed out into light
From the rims of the storm to the sea's dark edge with flames that were flowerlike and white.
The leaping and luminous blossoms of live sheet lightning that laugh as they fade
From the cloud's black base to the black wave's brim rejoiced in the light they made.
Far westward, throned in a silent sky, where life was in lustrous tune,
Shone, sweeter and surer than morning or evening, the steadfast smile of the moon.
The limitless heaven that enshrined them was lovelier than dreams may behold, and deep
As life or as death, revealed and transfigured, may shine on the soul through sleep.
All glories of toil and of triumph and passion and pride that it yearns to know
Bore witness there to the soul of its likeness and kinship, above and below.
The joys of the lightnings, the songs of the thunders, the strong sea's labour and rage,
Were tokens and signs of the war that is life and is joy for the soul to wage.
No thought strikes deeper or higher than the heights and the depths that the night made bare,

Illimitable, infinite, awful and joyful, alive in the summit of air—
Air stilled and thrilled by the tempest that thundered between its reign and the sea's,
Rebellious, rapturous, and transient as faith or as terror that bows men's knees.
No love sees loftier and fairer the form of its godlike vision in dreams
Than the world shone then, when the sky and the sea were as love for a breath's length seems—
One utterly, mingled and mastering and mastered and laughing with love that subsides
As the glad mad night sank panting and satiate with storm, and released the tides.
In the dense mid channel the steam-souled ship hung hovering, assailed and withheld
As a soul born royal, if life or if death be against it, is thwarted and quelled.
As the glories of myriads of glowworms in lustrous grass on a boundless lawn
Were the glories of flames phosphoric that made of the water a light like dawn.
A thousand Phosphors, a thousand Hespers, awoke in the churning sea,
And the swift soft hiss of them living and dying was clear as a tune could be;
As a tune that is played by the fingers of death on the keys of life or of sleep,
Audible alway alive in the storm, too fleet for a dream to keep:
Too fleet, too sweet for a dream to recover and thought to remember awake:
Light subtler and swifter than lightning, that whispers and laughs in the live storm's wake,
In the wild bright wake of the storm, in the dense loud heart of the labouring hour,
A harvest of stars by the storm's hand reaped, each fair as a star-shaped flower.
And sudden and soft as the passing of sleep is the passing of tempest seemed
When the light and the sound of it sank, and the glory was gone as a dream half dreamed.
The glory, the terror, the passion that made of the midnight a miracle, died,
Not slain at a stroke, nor in gradual reluctance abated of power and of pride;
With strong swift subsidence, awful as power that is wearied of power upon earth,
As a God that were wearied of power upon heaven, and were fain of a new God's birth,
The might of the night subsided: the tyranny kindled in darkness fell:
And the sea and the sky put off them the rapture and radiance of heaven and of hell.
The waters, heaving and hungering at heart, made way, and were wellnigh fain,
For the ship that had fought them, and wrestled, and revelled in labour, to cease from her pain.
And an end was made of it: only remembrance endures of the glad loud strife;
And the sense that a rapture so royal may come not again in the passage of life.

1904

NORTHUMBERLAND

BETWEEN our eastward and our westward sea
    The narrowing strand
Clasps close the noblest shore fame holds in fee
Even here where English birth seals all men free—
    Northumberland.

The sea-mists meet across it when the snow
    Clothes moor and fell,
And bid their true-born hearts who love it glow
For joy that none less nobly born may know
    What love knows well.

The splendour and the strength of storm and fight
    Sustain the song
That filled our fathers' hearts with joy to smite,
To live, to love, to lay down life that right
    Might tread down wrong.

They warred, they sang, they triumphed, and they passed,
And left us glad
Here to be born, their sons, whose hearts hold fast
The proud old love no change can overcast,
No chance leave sad.

None save our northmen ever, none but we,
Met, pledged, or fought
Such foes and friends as Scotland and the sea
With heart so high and equal, strong in glee
And stern in thought.

Thought, fed from time's memorial springs with pride,
Made strong as fire
Their hearts who hurled the foe down Flodden side;
And hers who rode the waves none else durst ride—
None save her sire.

O land beloved, where nought of legend's dream
Outshines the truth,
Where Joyous Gard, closed round with clouds that gleam
For them that know thee not, can scarce but seem
Too sweet for sooth,

Thy sons forget not, nor shall fame forget,
The deed there done
Before the walls whose fabled fame is yet
A light too sweet and strong to rise and set
With moon and sun.

Song bright as flash of swords or oars that shine
Through fight or foam
Stirs yet the blood thou hast given thy sons like wine
To hail in each bright ballad hailed as thine
One heart, one home.

Our Collingwood, though Nelson be not ours,
By him shall stand
Immortal, till those waifs of oldworld hours,
Forgotten, leave uncrowned with bays and flowers
Northumberland.

1904

THE LAKE OF GAUBE

THE sun is lord and god, sublime, serene,
And sovereign on the mountains: earth and air
Lie prone in passion, blind with bliss unseen
By force of sight and might of rapture, fair
As dreams that die and know not what they were.
The lawns, the gorges, and the peaks, are one
Glad glory, thrilled with sense of unison
In strong compulsive silence of the sun.

Flowers dense and keen as midnight stars aflame
And living things of light like flames in flower
That glance and flash as though no hand might tame
Lightnings whose life outshone their stormlit hour
And played and laughed on earth, with all their power
Gone, and with all their joy of life made long
And harmless as the lightning life of song,
Shine sweet like stars when darkness feels them strong.

The deep mild purple flaked with moonbright gold
That makes the scales seem flowers of hardened light,
The flamelike tongue, the feet that noon leaves cold,
The kindly trust in man, whence once the sight
Grew less than strange, and faith bade fear take flight,
Outlive the little harmless life that shone
And gladdened eyes that loved it, and was gone
Ere love might fear that fear had looked thereon.

Fear held the bright thing hateful, even as fear,
Whose name is one with hate and horror, saith
That heaven, the dark deep heaven of water near,
Is deadly deep as hell and dark as death.
The rapturous plunge that quickens blood and breath
With pause more sweet than passion, ere they strive
To raise again the limbs that yet would dive
Deeper, should there have slain the soul alive.

As the bright salamander in fire of the noonshine exults and is glad of his day,
The spirit that quickens my body rejoices to pass from the sunlight away,
To pass from the glow of the mountainous flowerage, the high multitudinous bloom,
Far down through the fathomless night of the water, the gladness of silence and gloom.
Death-dark and delicious as death in the dream of a lover and dreamer may be,
It clasps and encompasses body and soul with delight to be living and free:
Free utterly now, though the freedom endure but the space of a perilous breath,
And living, though girdled about with the darkness and coldness and strangeness of death:
Each limb and each pulse of the body rejoicing, each nerve of the spirit at rest,
All sense of the soul's life rapture, a passionate peace in its blindness blest.
So plunges the downward swimmer, embraced of the water unfathomed of man,
The darkness unplummeted, icier than seas in midwinter, for blessing or ban;
And swiftly and sweetly, when strength and breath fall short, and the dive is done,
Shoots up as a shaft from the dark depth shot, sped straight into sight of the sun;
And sheer through the snow-soft water, more dark than the roof of the pines above,
Strikes forth, and is glad as a bird whose flight is impelled and sustained of love.
As a sea-mew's love of the sea-wind breasted and ridden for rapture's sake
Is the love of his body and soul for the darkling delight of the soundless lake:
As the silent speed of a dream too living to live for a thought's space more
Is the flight of his limbs through the still stronger chill of the darkness from shore to shore.
Might life be as this is and death be as life that casts off time as a robe,
The likeness of infinite heaven were a symbol revealed of the lake of Gaube.

Whose thought has fashioned and measured
The darkness of life and of death,
The secret within them treasured,

The spirit that is not breath?
Whose vision has yet beholden
The splendour of death and of life?
Though sunset as dawn be golden,
Is the word of them peace, not strife?
Deep silence answers: the glory
We dream of may be but a dream,
And the sun of the soul wax hoary
As ashes that show not a gleam.
But well shall it be with us ever
Who drive through the darkness here,
If the soul that we live by never,
For aught that a lie saith, fear.

1904

IN A ROSARY

Through the low grey archway children's feet that pass
Quicken, glad to find the sweetest haunt of all.
Brightest wildflowers gleaming deep in lustiest grass,
Glorious weeds that glisten through the green sea's glass,
Match not now this marvel, born to fade and fall.

Roses like a rainbow wrought of roses rise
Right and left and forward, shining toward the sun.
Nay, the rainbow lit of sunshine droops and dies
Ere we dream it hallows earth and seas and skies;
Ere delight may dream it lives, its life is done.

Round the border hemmed with high deep hedges round
Go the children, peering over or between
Where the dense bright oval wall of box inwound,
Reared about the roses fast within its bound,
Gives them grace to glance at glories else unseen.

Flower outlightening flower and tree outflowering tree
Feed and fill the sense and spirit full with joy.
Nought awhile they know of outer earth and sea:
Here enough of joy it is to breathe and be:
Here the sense of life is one for girl and boy.

Heaven above them, bright as children's eyes or dreams,
Earth about them, sweet as glad soft sleep can show
Earth and sky and sea, a world that scarcely seems
Even in children's eyes less fair than life that gleams
Through the sleep that none but sinless eyes may know.

Near beneath, and near above, the terraced ways
Wind or stretch and bask or blink against the sun.
Hidden here from sight on soft or stormy days
Lies and laughs with love toward heaven, at silent gaze,
All the radiant rosary—all its flowers made one.

All the multitude of roses towering round
Dawn and noon and night behold as one full flower,
Fain of heaven and loved of heaven, curbed and crowned,
Raised and reared to make this plot of earthly ground
Heavenly, could but heaven endure on earth an hour.

Swept away, made nothing now for ever, dead,
Still the rosary lives and shines on memory, free
Now from fear of death or change as childhood, fled
Years on years before its last live leaves were shed:
None may mar it now, as none may stain the sea.

1904

BURNS: AN ODE

A FIRE of fierce and laughing light
That clove the shuddering heart of night
Leapt earthward, and the thunder's might
That pants and yearns
Made fitful music round its flight:
And earth saw Burns.

The joyous lightning found its voice
And bade the heart of wrath rejoice
And scorn uplift a song to voice
The imperial hate
That smote the God of base men's choice
At God's own gate.

Before the shrine of dawn, wherethrough
The lark rang rapture as she flew,
It flashed and fired the darkling dew:
And all that heard
With love or loathing hailed anew
A new day's word.

The servants of the lord of hell,
As though their lord had blessed them, fell
Foaming at mouth for fear, so well
They knew the lie
Wherewith they sought to scan and spell
The unsounded sky.

And Calvin, night's prophetic bird,
Out of his home in hell was heard
Shrieking; and all the fens were stirred
Whence plague is bred;
Can God endure the scoffer's word?
But God was dead.

The God they made them in despite
Of man and woman, love and light,
Strong sundawn and the starry night,
The lie supreme,
Shot through with song, stood forth to sight
A devil's dream.

And he that bent the lyric bow
And laid the lord of darkness low
And bade the fire of laughter glow
Across his grave,
And bade the tides above it flow,
Wave hurtling wave,

Shall he not win from latter days
More than his own could yield of praise?
Ay, could the sovereign singer's bays
Forsake his brow,
The warrior's, won on stormier ways,
Still clasp it now.

He loved, and sang of love; he laughed,
And bade the cup whereout he quaffed
Shine as a planet, fore and aft,
And left and right,
And keen as shoots the sun's first shaft
Against the night.

But love and wine were moon and sun
For many a fame long since undone,
And sorrow and joy have lost and won
By stormy turns
As many a singer's soul, if none
More bright than Burns.

And sweeter far in grief or mirth
Have songs as glad and sad of birth
Found voice to speak of wealth or dearth
In joy of life:
But never song took fire from earth
More strong for strife.

The daisy by his ploughshare cleft,
The lips of women loved and left,
The griefs and joys that weave the weft
Of human time,
With craftsman's cunning, keen and deft,
He carved in rhyme.

But Chaucer's daisy shines a star
Above his ploughshare's reach to mar,
And mightier vision gave Dunbar
More strenuous wing
To hear around all sins that are
Hell dance and sing.

And when such pride and power of trust
In song's high gift to arouse from dust
Death, and transfigure love or lust
Through smiles or tears
In golden speech that takes no rust
From cankering years,

As never spake but once in one
Strong star-crossed child of earth and sun,
Villon, made music such as none
May praise or blame,
A crown of starrier flower was won
Than Burns may claim.

But never, since bright earth was born
In rapture of the enkindling morn,
Might godlike wrath and sunlike scorn
That was and is
And shall be while false weeds are worn
Find word like his.

Above the rude and radiant earth
That heaves and glows from firth to firth
In vale and mountain, bright in dearth
And warm in wealth,
Which gave his fiery glory birth
By chance and stealth.

Above the storms of praise and blame
That blur with mist his lustrous name,
His thunderous laughter went and came,
And lives and flies;
The roar that follows on the flame
When lightning dies.

Earth, and the snow-dimmed heights of air,
And water winding soft and fair
Through still sweet places, bright and bare,
By bent and byre,
Taught him what hearts within them were:
But his was fire.

1904

SELECTIONS FROM SWINBURNE'S LETTERS

I To Edwin Hatch [1]

Oxford, February 17th [1858]

My dear Hatch,

I commiserate you sincerely; but I have two things to comfort you with:—(1) Morris's book is really out. Reading it, I would fain be worthy to sit down at his feet; but I have a painful recollection of *Aurora Leigh:*

> Almost all the birds
> Will sing at dawn; and yet we do not take
> The chattering swallow for the holy lark!

Such, however, is the invincible absurdity of all poets, that he ventured to prefer *Rosamond* to *Peter Harpdon* in a repeatedly rebuked and resolutely argued statement. It appears to me simple mania; but certainly I am glad of his words for *Rosamond* is about my favourite poem, and is now verging on a satisfactory completion. The first scene as rewritten is an acknowledged improvement. But after all—!

. . . I enclose two of my latest grinds, regardless of postage. Lose not the priceless uniques lest the world demand the account thereof at your hands. *The Golden House* is of course *Rudel in Paradise*. The other I can only describe as a dramato-lyrico-phantas-magorico-spasmodic sermon on the grievous sin of flirtation. It was written off one evening and has never been corrected. Verdicts differ concerning it. Morris attacks it as weak and spasmodic. Nichol (in whose opinion I often trust) thinks it rather a good dramatic story than otherwise. It is of course meant for a picture of exceptional weakness; inaction of the man, impulsive irresolution of the woman; mutual ignorance of each other and themselves, with

[1] Edwin Hatch (1835–1889), afterwards a distinguished theologian, had just been appointed to an East End curacy.

an extra dash of sensuous impulse; finally with no ostensible cause, rupture and spiflication. Pray abuse if it you feel inclined; I am not (as you know) overdelicate and timid concerning my scribbles, and I have no tenderness for this; and if it is not what it ought to be, it is a decided failure. But I suspect I must be *Eglamor* to Morris as *Sordello.*

I long to be with you by firelight between the sunset and the sea to have talk of *Sordello;* it is one of my canonical scriptures. Does he sleep and forget? I think yes. Did the first time Palma's mouth trembled to touch his in the golden roselands of Paradise, a sudden power of angelic action come over him? I suspect, not utterly companionless. Sometimes one knows—not now: but I suppose he slept years off before she kissed him. In Heaven she grew too tired and thin to sing well, and her face grew whiter than its aureole with pain and want of him. And if, like the other Saint, she wept, the tears fell upon his shut lids and fretted the eyes apart as they trickled. Who knows these matters? Only we keep the honey-stain of hair.

I write more folly to you than I dare read over, because I think you wise. So take my stupidity as a compliment. If you like, and if it prospers, I will send you specimens of a new poem on Tristram which I am about. I envy you your work of corrupting the young idea with Shelley. I hope you will also introduce Morris—the first edition *must* pay well. If you like or care to amuse yourself therewith, my poems are at your service. I don't care about privacy. I shudder at the idea of a young man in the sixth form being tainted by such reading as Shelley, Morris, and the unworthiest of their admirers. I should like to review myself and say "that I have an abortive covetousness of imitation in which an exaggeration of my models—i.e. blasphemy and sensuality—is happily neutralised by my own imbecility." I flatter myself the last sentence was worthy of the *Saturday Review.* I also envy your musical and architectural work. Upon the whole, if your pupils in poetry and profanity are conversible, I think that one might be worse off than you. I am sure, but for Morris, I should be.

One evening—when the *Union* was just finished—Jones and I had a great talk. [Spencer] Stanhope and Swan attacked, and we defended, our idea of Heaven, viz. a rose-garden full of stunners. Atrocities of an appalling nature were uttered on the other side. We became so fierce that two respectable members of the University—entering to see the pictures—stood mute and looked at us. We spoke just then of kisses in Paradise, and expounded our ideas on the celestial development of that necessity of life; and after listening five minutes to our language, they literally fled from the room! Conceive our mutual ecstasy of delight.

* * *

Mind you send for his book at once; read it, and repent your former heresies, or I will review it somewhere and say that he is to Tennyson what Tennyson is to Dobell or Dobell to Tupper.

Believe me, ever yours truly,

A. C. Swinburne.

II To Paulina, Lady Trevelyan

Maison Laurenti, Mentone
January 19th [1861]

My dear Lady Trevelyan,

(Which a nice place it is to date from!)

Many thanks for your letter, which a comfortable letter it was, but creates violent wishes to get back to England. For of *all the beasts* of countries I ever see, I reckon this about caps them. I also strongly notion that there ain't a hole in St. Giles's which isn't a paradise to this. How any professing Christian as has been in France and England can look at it, passes me. It is more like the landscape in Browning's *Childe Roland* than anything I ever heard tell on. A calcined, scalped, rasped, scraped, flayed, broiled, powdered, leprous, blotched, mangy, grimy, parboiled country *without trees*, water, grass, fields—*with* blank, beastly, senseless olives and orange-trees like a mad cabbage gone indigestible; it is infinitely liker hell than earth, and one looks for tails among the people. And such females with hunched bodies and crooked necks carrying tons on their heads, and looking like Death taken seasick. Ar-r-r-r-r! Gr-r-r-rn!

Wal, I feel kind of better after that. But the

aggravation of having people about one who undertake to admire these big stone-heaps of hills and hideous split-jawed gorges! I must say (in Carlylese) that "the (scenery) is of the sort which must be called, *not* in the way of profane swearing, but of grave, earnest and sorrowing indignation, the d—— sort." (I wd. rather die than write it at length.)

I am very glad you like my book [*The Queen Mother* and *Rosamond*]; if it will do anything like sell I shall publish my shorter poems soon. They are quite ready. I have done a lot of work since I saw you. Rossetti says some of my best pieces: one on St. Dorothy and Theophilus (I wanted to try my heathen hands at a Christian subject, you comprehend, and give a pat to the Papist interest); also a long one out of Boccaccio, that was begun ages ago and let drop. Item many songs and ballads. I am trying to write prose, which is very hard, but I want to make a few stories each about three or six pages long. Likewise a big one about my blessedest pet which her initials is Lucrezia Estense Borgia. Which soon I hope to see her hair as is kep at Milan "in spirits in a bottle."

Which puts me in mind of a favour I want to ask you. In the beginning (probably) of Feb. I am going to Venice and through all the chief towns I can, and perhaps to Florence *if* I could find out whether Mr. Browning is there. Now there is nobody within reach who knows as much of art as a decently educated cockroach; and I want you to have the extreme goodness to tell me what to go to and how to see Venice—buildings especially as well as pictures—before it gets bombarded—out of the British tourist's fashion. If you are not awfully busy wd you write me a letter wh: I cd get say by the week after next? considering I have read no books and am not content with the British Murray.

I wish I *had* anything to do besides my proper work if I can't live by it. Which it's very well to pitch into a party like brother Stockdollopger, but what *is* one to do? I can't go to the bar: and much good I shd do if I did. You know there is really no profession one can take up with and go on working. Item—poetry is quite work enough for any one man. Item—who is there that is anything *besides* a poet at this day except Hugo? And though his politics is excellent and his opinions is sound, he does much better when he sticks to his work and makes Ratbert and Ruy Blas. *I* don't want to sit in [a] room and write, gracious knows. Do you think a small thing in the stump-orator line wd do? or a Grace-Walker? Seriously what is there you wd have one take to? It's a very good lecture but it is not practical. Nor yet it ain't fair. It's bage.

Have you heard the report that old Landor is going to republish *all* his suppressed libels in verse and prose and more new ones? Isn't he a marvel of heaven's making? I suppose a British public will bust at once if it's nipped and frizzled and churned up to an etarnal smash any more: which by the by America seems to be at this writing.

I am in love with Paris—you know I never saw it before. What a stunner above stunners that Giorgione party with the music in the grass and the water-drawer is, that Gabriel made such a sonnet on. Then that Stephen preaching of Carpaccio! I never heard a word of it; but it seems to me lovely, with wonders of faces. Item the Velasquez. Item things in general. Item the little Uccello up at the top of the gallery.

My parents should no doubt send all proper messages, but are probably in bed and (let us hope) enjoying a deep repose. For the hour is midnight. On this account I will now conclude with my duty and respects to Sir Walter; and am with a filial heart,

Al. C. Swinburne.

I wish to goodness you would send me out some eligible companions. I shall have to go alone to Turin. For the English here are mainly false friends. Don't you think we shall yet live to see the last Austrian emperor hung? Is Garibaldi the greatest man since Adam, or is he not?

III To Lord Houghton

Albergo della Gran Bretagna
March 4th [1864]

My dear Lord Houghton,

I meant to write you a word two days since, and a sufficiently dolorous epistle you would have had, but luckily an equivocal and occasional beneficent Providence intervened. With much labour I hunted out the most ancient of the demi-gods [Landor] at 93 Via della Chiesa, but (although knock-down blows were not, as you anticipated, his mode of salutation) I found him, owing I suspect to the violent weather, too much weakened and confused to realise the fact of the introduction with distress. In effect, he seemed so feeble and incompatible that I came away in a grievous state of disappointment and depression myself, fearing I was really too late. But taking heart of grace I wrote him a line of apology and explanation, saying why and how I had made up my mind to call upon him after you had furnished me with an introduction. That is, expressing (as far as was expressible) my immense admiration and reverence in the plainest and sincerest way I could manage. To which missive of mine came a note of invitation which I answered by setting off again for his lodging. After losing myself for an hour in the Borgo S. Frediano I found it at last, and found him as alert, brilliant, and altogether delicious as I suppose others may have found him twenty years since. I cannot thank you enough for procuring me this great pleasure and exquisite satisfaction. I am seriously more obliged for this than for anything that could have been done for me. I have got the one thing I wanted with all my heart. If both or either of us die to-morrow, at least to-day he has told me that my presence here has made him happy; he said more than that—things for which of course I take no credit to myself but which are not the less pleasant to hear from such a man. There is no other man living from whom I should so much have prized any expression of acceptance or goodwill in return for my homage, for all other men as great are so much younger, that in his case one sort of reverence serves as the lining for another. My grandfather was upon the whole *mieux conservé*, but he had written no *Hellenics*. In answer to something that Mr. Landor said to-day of his own age, I reminded him of his equals and predecessors, Sophocles and Titian; he said he should not live up to the age of Sophocles—not see ninety. I don't see why he shouldn't, if he has people about him to care for him as he should be cared for. I should like to throw up all other things on earth and devote myself to playing valet to him for the rest of his days. I would black his boots if he were *chez moi*. He has given me the shock of adoration which one feels at thirteen towards great men. I am not sure that any other emotion is so endurable and persistently delicious as that of worship, when your god is indubitable and incarnate before your eyes.

I told him, as we were talking of poems and such things, that his poems had first given me inexplicable pleasure and a sort of blind relief when I was a small fellow of twelve. My first recollection of them is *The Song of Hours* in the *Iphigenia*. Apart from their executive perfection, all those Greek poems of his always fitted on to my own way of feeling and thought infinitely more than even Tennyson's modern versions do now. I am more than ever sure that the *Hamadryad* is a purer and better piece of work, from the highest point of view that art can take, than such magnificent hashes and stews of old and new with a sharp sauce of personality as *Œnone* and *Ulysses*. Not that I am disloyal to Tennyson, into whose church we were all in my time born and baptized as far back as we can remember at all. But he is not a Greek nor a heathen, and I imagine does not want to be. I greatly fear he believes it possible to be something better; an absurdity which should be left to the Brownings and other blatant creatures begotten on the slime of the modern chaos.

If I let myself loose I shall go on giving you indirect thanks for bringing me acquainted with Landor, till time and paper fail me, and patience fails you. Even if I did so, I could hardly tell you what pleasures I have had today in a half-hour's intercourse with him: nor what delicious things he said in recognition of my half-expressed gratitude to him. It is comfortable when one does once in a way go in for a complete quiet bit of hero-worship, and an honest interlude of relief to find it taken up instead of thrown away. And the chance of this I owe to you; and you must simply take my thanks for granted. It is better than a publisher to me; what more can a *rimailleur inédit* possibly say?

* * *

Yours affectionately,

A. C. Swinburne.

IV To Paulina, Lady Trevelyan

36, Wilton Crescent, S.W.
March 15th, 1865

My dear Lady Trevelyan,

I have just got your letter which has given me the greatest pleasure I have yet had with regard to my book [*Atalanta in Calydon*]. I was in hopes it would find favour with you, as I think it is the best executed and sustained of my larger poems. It was begun last autumn twelvemonth, when we were all freshly unhappy, and finished just after I got the news in September last of Mr. Landor's death, which was a considerable trouble to me as I had hoped against hope or reason that he who in the spring at Florence had accepted the dedication of an unfinished poem would live to receive and read it. You will recognise the allusion to his life and death at pp. 25, 26. As it is he never read anything of mine more mature than *Rosamond.* In spite of the funereal circumstances which I suspect have a little deepened the natural colours of Greek fatalism here and there, so as to have already incurred a charge of "rebellious antagonism" and suchlike things, I never enjoyed anything more in my life than the composition of this poem, which though a work done by intervals, was very rapid and pleasant. Allowing for a few after insertions, two or three in all, from p. 66 to 83 (as far as the Chorus) was the work of two afternoons, and from p. 83 to the end was the work of two other afternoons: so you will understand that I enjoyed my work. I think it is pure Greek, and the first poem of the sort in modern times, combining lyric and dramatic work on the old principle. Shelley's *Prometheus* is magnificent and un-Hellenic, spoilt too in my mind by the infusion of philanthropic doctrinaire views and "progress of the species;" and by what I gather from Lewes's life of Goethe the *Iphigenia in Tauris* must be also impregnated with modern morals and feelings. As for Professor Arnold's *Merope*, the clothes are well enough, but where has the body gone? So I thought and still think the field was clear for me.

* * *

I am raging in silence at the postponement from day to day of Mr. Carlyle's volumes. He ought to be in London tying firebrands to the tails of those unclean foxes called publishers and printers. Meantime the world is growing lean with hunger and ravenous with expectation. I finished the fourth volume last May in a huge garden at Fiesole, the nightingales and roses serving by way of salt and spice to the divine dish of battles and intrigues. I take greater delight in the hero, who was always a hero of mine and more comprehensible to my heathen mind than any Puritan, at every step the book takes. Trust in Providence somewhat spoils heroism, to me at least. The letter at the end of vol. 4, coming where and when it does, is a sample of what I conceive and enjoy as the highest and most *reasonable* heroic temper. "A God-intoxicated man" of course can fight, but I prefer a man who fights sober. Whether he gets drunk on faith or on brandy, it is still "Dutch courage," as the sailors call it. I must say Frederick's clear, cold purity of pluck, looking neither upward nor around for any help or comfort, seems to me a much more wholesome and more admirable state of mind than Cromwell's splendid pietism. And then who would not face all chances if he were convinced that the Gods were specially interested on his side and personally excited about his failure or success? It is the old question between Jews and Greeks, and I, who can understand Leonidas better than Joshua, must prefer Marathon to Gilgal.

* * *

You must have seen Tennyson's book of *Selections*, and I hope agree with me that he might have made a better picking out of the lot. I say that *Boädicea*, as the highest if not sweetest of all the notes he ever struck, should have served as prelude to the book. The yellow-ringleted Britoness is worth many score of revered Victorias. His volume [*Enoch Arden, etc.*] of last summer struck me as a new triumph worth any of the old; I read it with a pleasure as single and complete as I might have done at thirteen.

With best remembrances from all to yourself and Sir Walter,

Believe me ever,

Yours (in spite of ill-usage) most filially,

A. C. Swinburne.

V To Paulina, Lady Trevelyan

22, Dorset Street, W.
December 10th, 1865

My dear Lady Trevelyan,

* * *

As to my poems, my perplexity is this; that no two friends have ever given me the same advice. Now more than ever I would rather take yours than another's; but I see neither where to begin nor when to stop. I have written nothing to be ashamed or afraid of. I have been advised to suppress *Atalanta*, to cancel *Chastelard*, and so on till not a line of my work would have been left. Two days ago Ruskin called on me and stayed for a long evening, during which he heard a great part of my forthcoming volume of poems, selected with a view to secure his advice as to publication and the verdict of the world of readers and writers. It was impossible to have a fairer judge. I have not known him long or intimately; and he is neither a rival nor a reviewer. I can only say that I was sincerely surprised by the enjoyment he seemed to derive from my work, and the frankness with which he accepted it. Any poem which all my friends for whose opinion I care had advised me to omit, should be omitted. But I never have written such an one. Some for example which you have told me were favourites of yours, such as the *Hymn to Proserpine* of the "Last Pagan"—I have been advised to omit as likely to hurt the feeling of a religious public. I cannot but see that whatever I do will be assailed and misconstrued by those who can do nothing and who detest their betters.

* * *

I can only lay to heart the words of Shakespeare—even he never uttered any truer—"Be thou as pure as ice, as chaste as snow, thou shalt not escape calumny." And I cannot, as Hamlet advises, betake myself "to a nunnery."

. . . Meantime you will I am sure be glad to hear that my luck is looking up in the beautiful literary world of publishers and readers. I have already the wildest offers made me for anything I will do: and expect soon to have in effect the control of a magazine which I shall be able to mould as I please. This has always been a dream of mine; and very likely I shall come to grief, as Byron did on a similar occasion. Have you seen Moxon's series of "poets"? There are new things (as of course you know) in the Tennyson which are worth looking up—and I don't remember seeing it this year at Wallington. I am *doing* Byron for the series, as well as Landor: and I am to meet my partners in the serial work, Tennyson and Browning, at a publishers' feast some time this week. . . .

Yours most sincerely,
A. C. Swinburne.

VI To Lord Lytton

22a, Dorset Street, W.
August 13th [1866]

Dear Lord Lytton,

I am much obliged by the letter of advice you wrote me, and if Lord Houghton had not gone off to Vichy, I should certainly take counsel with him. As it is, I am compelled to decide without further help. I have no relation with Messrs. Moxon except of a strictly business character, and considering that the head of this firm has broken his agreement by refusing to continue the sale of my poems, without even speaking to me on the matter, I cannot but desire, first of all, to have no further dealings with anyone so untrustworthy. The book is mine. I agreed with him to issue an edition of 1,000 copies, he undertaking to print, publish and sell them, and if the edition sold off, I was to have two-thirds of the profits. He does not now deny the contract which he refuses to fulfil; he simply said to a friend who called on him as my representative, that on hearing there was to be an article in *The Times* attacking my book as improper, he could not continue the sale. As to the suppression of separate passages or poems, it could not be done without injuring the whole structure of the book, where every part has been as carefully considered and arranged as I could manage, and under the circumstances, it seems to me that I have no choice but to break off my connection with the publisher.

I have consulted friends older than myself, and more experienced in the business ways of the world, and really it seems to me I have no alternative. Before the book was published, if my friends had given me strong and unanimous advice to withdraw or to alter any passage, I should certainly have done so—in two instances I did, rather against my own impulse, which is a fair proof that I am not too headstrong or conceited to listen to friendly counsel. But *now* to alter my course or mutilate my published work seems to me somewhat like deserting one's colours. One may or may not repent having enlisted, but to lay down one's arms, except under compulsion, remains intolerable. Even if I did not feel the matter in this way, my withdrawal would not undo what has been done, nor unsay what has been said.

Yours truly,
A. C. Swinburne.

VII To Lord Houghton

[1869]

My dear Houghton,

What a wonderful work this is of Browning's [*The Ring and the Book*]. I tore through the first volume in a day of careful study, with a sense of absolute possession. I have not felt so strongly that delightful sense of being mastered—dominated—by another man's imaginative work since I was a small boy. I always except, of course, Victor Hugo's, which has the same force and insight and variety of imagination together with that exquisite bloom and flavour of the highest poetry which Browning's has not: though it has perhaps a more wonderful subtlety at once and breadth of humorous invention and perception.

As for interest, it simply kills all other matters of thought for the time. This is his real work—big enough to give him breathing-space, whereas in play or song he is alike cramped. It is of the mixed-political composite-dramatic order which alone suits him and serves him.

Yours sincerely,
A. C. Swinburne.

VIII To Thomas Purnell

Holmwood, Henley-on-Thames
November 26th [1872]

My dear Purnell,

Since I got your note asking for a "Stanza" for the *Athenæum* I have fallen in with one [*Before Sunset*] among my unpublished MS. which I send you. As a rule I do not care to send any verse to newspapers or magazines under £10 or £20, not finding it worth while, and not wishing to have my name hawked about like that of a Close, Buchanan, or any other hack rhymester; and I am not yet at all in good humour with the *Athenæum* for joining in the marked and utter neglect of a pamphlet [*Under the Microscope*] which I see they now find convenient to quote and borrow from, and on which as a piece of critical prose, I value myself more than I usually do on any other improvisations in that line. But as the application comes through you I send what I have.

I am in very great want of tin just now, having overdrawn my account by half a year's allowance, and being overwhelmed by bills and dunning notes: particularly objectionable when one is £200 worse than penniless. I am at least that much behind the world, and *must* soon raise it somehow. Can you suggest any way? Say by publishing somewhere the first canto of *Tristram* separately? If the *Prelude* was worth fifty pounds, this ought to be worth at least three times as much. I must have a little money at once—a hundred or two—and surely my name must be worth something in the market. Give me what help or advice you can.

I see with disgust that King of Cornhill, who I was told was reputable, announces an edition of R. Buchanan's works! Faugh—it will be impossible for men of honour and character to publish with him afterwards.

Yours ever,
A. C. Swinburne.

IX To E. C. Stedman

Holmwood, Henley-on-Thames
January 21st, 1874

My dear Mr. Stedman,

* * *

But, above all, I wonder to find wanting [in Stedman's selections from Landor] the very brightest (in my eyes at least) of all the jewels in Landor's crown of song; the divine four lines on *Dirce*, which hold the place in my affections that those on *Rose Aylmer* did in Lamb's—

Stand close around, ye Stygian set,
With Dirce in one boat conveyed,
Or Charon, seeing, may forget
That he is old and she a shade.

If ever verses besides her own were, in Sappho's phrase, "more golden than gold," surely these are. I looked again and again through your book in search of them, unable to believe that I had not at first accidently passed over the page which they should have glorified. There is the whole Anthology—all of it, I mean what is really composed of flowers—distilled in its essence into that one quatrain. These too, I think, might have found a place among their followers:— "*The leaves are falling; so am I;*" "*Ye little household gods, that make,*" etc.; "*Twenty years hence;*" I think I am not wrong in saying that they are not among your Cameos, but I have not time to look again before the post goes out, and I do not wish to let one day pass without thanking you for the gift of them.

* * *

A. C. Swinburne.

X To E. C. Stedman

Holmwood, Henley-on-Thames
February 23rd, 1874

My dear Mr. Stedman,

* * *

I hope the book (with Landor's pamphlet inside it) will reach you safely; I shall be curious to know what you think of it; and if there should be any notice taken of it in any American journal or magazine I should very much like to see it. (This really is not a hint or insinuated petition begging for such notice at your hands or any one's, and must not be taken as such; but I am curious about the fate of this book as a unique sort of production in these days, and take certainly a quite unselfish interest in its fortunes.) I am very glad you like my elegy on Baudelaire; I wrote it with very sincere feelings of regret for the poor fellow's untimely loss, which gave it a tone of deeper thought or emotion than was called forth by the death of Gautier, with whom (though from boyhood almost his ardent admirer) I never had any correspondence; but in spite of your kind mention of it in this month's *Scribner's Magazine*, which I have just seen, I cannot believe it worthy to tie the shoes (so to speak) of the least, whichever may be the least, of the great English triad or trinity of elegies—Milton's, Shelley's and Arnold's. I am content if it may be allowed to take its stand below the lowest of them, or to sit meekly at their feet. . . .

Yours very faithfully,
A. C. Swinburne.

XI To John H. Ingram

Holmwood, Shiplake, Henley-on-Thames
March 6th, 1874

Dear Sir,

I shall be glad to do what little I can to assist your project, and if my name is of any use to you it is at your service. But I know nothing practically of committees, and heartily agree with the disgust you express for the vulgar and fashionable parade of worthless pretensions for which they usually form an excuse.[1]

I fell in by chance with your first article some weeks ago, and must try to get the series when complete.[2] You will have done an immense service, not only to the memory of an admirable poet, but to the consciousness of every one among the multitude of his admirers, which has hitherto perforce been harassed and fretted by the involuntary recollection, however tempered with contempt and loathing, of the villainous calumnies of Griswold. The dog is dead, I believe, is he not? or I should like to see combined with the immediate object of your committee, the scarcely less praiseworthy object of getting him cudgelled to death in default of a rope and gibbet. Among all his poisonous assertions there was but one—I hardly like to allude to it—which has always seemed to me, if one were compelled to believe it, inexplicable and intolerable, the rest even if true

[1] Miss Rosalie Poe, the sister of the poet, being in great distress, had appealed to Mr. Ingram for aid. Mr. Ingram suggested the formation of a strong committee of literary men and women, under the shelter of whose names sufficient money might be obtained to provide a permanent endowment for the lady. Tennyson, W. M. Rossetti, and others, promised assistance. However, before any practical steps could be taken, Miss Poe died.

[2] A series of articles on Edgar Poe refuting the slanders of Griswold, his first biographer.

would not be damning accusations, or, however lamentable, beyond all excuse or comprehension of charity; I refer of course to the foul allegation of an attempt to extort money from a woman by th eats of defamation in return for relief received, which were afterwards retracted under a counter threat of chastisement. Incredible as this vile story is, I have looked eagerly for a full and unanswerable refutation of it point by point, which I hope you will be able to give. I do not find it touched upon in your present or first article, indeed one is loath to touch such filth, but as long as what that polecat biographer has left behind him is not swept or shovelled away finally from the grave of Poe, it must offend the nostrils of those who would come thither with offerings of another kind.

I cannot undertake to offer any suggestion as to the business part of your plans, but no doubt, as you have Mr. W. Rossetti with you, you will not want for more efficient help and alliance than mine. I wish indeed that poor Baudelaire were alive to see his own and instinctive contradiction of Griswold's villainies confirmed by evidence, and to give the help it would have rejoiced him to offer to the poor lady who remains to represent the name which he honoured and made famous throughout France by his own labours. Or, if Théophile Gautier were but alive, I daresay he might have answered to the appeal.

I should think something might be raised among the admirers of Poe in Paris, if anything is left of the old set of artists and authors who learned of Baudelaire to enjoy the genius of his favourite. I should think Mr. Frederick Locker might like to be of service; have you applied to him? I don't know whether he is in town; if he were I would look him up, and Mr. Whistler, who might also help us for the sake of a fellow Southerner.

With best wishes for your success, and sincere congratulations on the good work you have already done for the long and grievously outraged memory of the first true and great genius of America.

Believe me,

Yours very truly,

A. C. Swinburne.

XII To Joseph Knight

Holmwood, Henley-on-Thames

July 8th [1874]

My dear Knight,

Not having any stray song on hand I have just sat down and thrown off the enclosed. I pique myself on its moral tone; in an age when all other lyrists, from Tennyson to Rossetti, go in (metrically) for constancy and eternity of attachment and reunion in future lives, etc., etc., etc., I limit love, honestly and candidly, to 24 hours; and quite enough too in all conscience.

When I last took the trouble to write a song for present use (it was [*Love laid his sleepless head,*] for Hollingshed's revival of "The Merry Wives of Windsor") I priced it by advice of Sandys, who acted as common friend on the occasion, at £50; I don't expect to sell my songs usually at that rate, not being (thank Phœbus) a Laureate; but of course you know I can't *afford* to give my name and my verses for nothing.

I should like of all things to meet Sir C. Dilke, and especially under your auspices; there are few men whose acquaintance I should be so glad to make. But I don't know when I shall be in London again. At present I am a close prisoner with a badly sprained foot, and have to work against tides to get my biographical and critical article on Beaumont and Fletcher for the *Encyclopædia Britannica* ready in time.

Yours ever,

A. C. Swinburne.

XIII To Edmund Gosse

Holmwood, Shiplake, Henley-on-Thames

January 31st [1875]

My dear Gosse,

I must confess that I had quite forgotten what anniversary [1] was yesterday, though oddly enough I had been thinking of it in passing, and (not having the date at hand to look up) had come to the conclusion that the centenary must have been over a year or two since. I am vexed to have let it slip. Had I known it a

[1] Walter Savage Landor was born on the 30th of January, 1775; Charles Lamb on the 10th of February following.

week earlier I should have proposed to you, and such friends as might have liked to join us, a meeting in honour of the day. If—as proposed in *The Athenæum*,—any commemoration of Lamb's centenary is to take place next week (Feb. 10th) I hope to take part in it, and come up to-morrow week for a few days only to London. There ought to be among our own friends and acquaintances enough lovers of Lamb to make at least a pleasant private party. Would Scott join it do you think? I wrote to Watts about it yesterday. There being but ten days between the two dates, we might commemorate with the same libations both the two great men who loved and admired each other in life, and whose memories might fitly and gracefully be mingled after death in our affectionate recollection.

I read your article of yesterday with great pleasure, and with thorough sympathy of opinion, except as to one expression which startled me considerably. You speak of the "laborious versification" of Catullus, whom I should have called the least laborious, and the most spontaneous in his godlike and birdlike melody, of all lyrists known to me except Sappho and Shelley: I should as soon call a lark's note laboured as his. And with all my loving admiration of Landor as a poet, I cannot consider him as belonging to the same class, or even to the same kind, as Catullus; though you have very justly pointed out the many and noble personal qualities they had in common. Landor's verse, as a rule, without ever being harsh or weak, yet wants the contrary characteristic of subtle and simple sweetness; while no poet ever had more of this than the Veronese: few ever had so much. This has been noted by Landor himself, who (perhaps under the influence of Catullus), has sometimes touched in his Latin verse a string of more exquisite and spontaneous melody than was often struck in his English poems. As to the wholly unequalled if not unapproached and unapproachable excellence of his prose, you know how thoroughly I am at one with you. Indeed, it is always a thorn in my flesh when writing prose, and a check to any satisfaction I might feel in it, to reflect that probably I never have written or shall write a page that Landor might have signed. Nothing of the sort (or of any sort) ever troubles me in writing verse, but this always haunts me when at work on prose. As to my own intercourse with the divine old man, I shall never have more to tell the world than I have already made public in verse; for there is nothing to tell except such things as cannot be told; slight personal matters, not the less precious that they must be private.

* * *

Yours affectionately,
A. C. Swinburne.

XIV To E. C. Stedman

Holmwood, Henley-on-Thames
February 20th, 1875

My dear Mr. Stedman,

Now let me at last tell you how truly and how much I have enjoyed the beautiful book of poems which you must long since have thought of as thrown away on the most thankless and ungracious of recipients. Your rebuke on the subject of American poetry is doubtless as well deserved as it is kindly and gently expressed. Yet I must say that while I appreciate (I hope) the respective excellence of Mr. Bryant's *Thanatopsis* and of Mr. Lowell's *Commemoration Ode*, I cannot say that either of them leaves in my ear the echo of a single note of song. It is excellent good speech, but if given us as song its first and last duty is to sing. The one is most august meditation, the other a noble expression of deep and grave patriotic feeling on a supreme national occasion; but the thing more necessary, though it may be less noble than these, is the pulse, the fire, the passion of music—the quality of a singer, not of a solitary philosopher or a patriotic orator. Now, when Whitman is not speaking bad prose he sings, and when he sings at all he sings well. Mr. Longfellow has a pretty little pipe of his own, but surely it is very thin and reedy. Again whatever may be Mr. Emerson's merits, to talk of his poetry seems to me like talking of the scholarship of a child who has not learnt its letters. Even Browning's verse always goes to a recognizable tune (I say not to a good one), but in the name of all bagpipes what is the tune of Emerson's? Now it is a poor thing to have nothing but melody and be unable to rise above it into harmony, but one or the other, the less if not the greater, you *must* have. Imagine a man full of great thoughts and emotions and resolved to express them in painting who has absolutely no power upon either form or colour. Wainwright the murderer, who never had any thought or emotion above those of a pig or of a butcher, will be a better man for us than he. But (as Blake says) "Enough! or too much."

* * *

Ever yours faithfully,
A. C. Swinburne.

XV To E. C. Stedman

Holmwood, Henley-on-Thames
September 8th, 1875

My dear Mr. Stedman,

* * *

I read your former letter very carefully and have since re-read a good deal of Emerson's first volume of poems therein mentioned, which certainly contains noble verses and passages well worth remembering. I hope that no personal feeling or consideration will ever prevent or impair my recognition of any man's higher qualities. In Whittier the power and pathos and righteousness (to use a great old word which should not be left to the pulpiteers) of noble emotion would be more enjoyable and admirable if he were not so deplorably ready to put up with the first word, good or bad, that comes to hand, and to run on long after he is out of breath. For Mr. Lowell's verse when out of the Biglow costume, I could never bring myself to care at all. I believe you know my theory that nothing which can possibly be *as well* said in prose ought ever to be said in verse.

I sincerely hope that your own health and affairs will enable you to pursue our common art with full freedom and success for many years to come. I may confess to you, what I could not gracefully or properly say in public, that I think but little of Tennyson's play [*Queen Mary*], though it has one good song and one good scene at least. I am writing a Greek tragedy [*Erechtheus*], which I mean to be more purely Hellenic and perhaps more universal (so to speak) in its relation to human thought and emotion than was *Atalanta*. The fusion of lyric with dramatic form gives the highest type of poetry I know; and I always feel the Greek history and mythology (in its deeper sense and wider bearing) much nearer to us even yet than those of the Jews, alien from us in blood and character. Even the poet of Job is a Semitic alien, while the poet of Prometheus is an Aryan kinsman of our own: his national history of far more real importance to us, his poetry far closer to our own thought, passion, speculation, conscience, than the Hebrew. This argument, if necessary, I may perhaps expand into a vindication of my choice in taking up what may seem, but is not and should not be, a remote and obsolete theme to work upon.

It may interest you, as it gratified me, to read the following excerpt from a letter of Wm. Rossetti, who with a rare generosity has forgiven my too sincere but I must think deserved strictures on some of his misdemeanours as editor of Shelley.

"(6 Aug.) Old Trelawny is extraordinarily delighted with your Essay on Shelley—indeed with your book [*Essays and Studies*] generally; vows that nobody ever did justice to or understand S. before you;—he has enlarged on these matters to me any number of times these two months, and yesterday he specially asked me to let you know and convey his thanks for the book. He has written down various additional reminiscences of Shelley and Byron, and seems really disposed to reissue his book [*Recollections of the Last Days of Shelley and Byron*], with these additions included."

With which piece of good news I will leave off, and remain

Ever faithfully yours,
A. C. Swinburne.

XVI To Lord Morley

Holmwood, Henley-on-Thames
February 1st, 1876

My dear Morley,

* * *

I have just been reading Meredith's book [*Beauchamp's Career*] which I only tried by fits and starts as it was coming out in the *Fortnightly*. Full of power and beauty and fine truthfulness as it is, what a noble book it might and should have been, if he would but have foregone his lust of epigram and habit of trying to tell a story by means of riddles that hardly excite the curiosity they are certain to baffle! By dint of revulsion from Trollope on this hand and Braddon on that, he seems to have persuaded himself that limpidity of style must mean shallowness, lucidity of narrative must imply triviality, and simplicity of direct interest or positive incident must involve "sensationalism." It is a constant irritation to see a man of such rarely strong and subtle genius, such various and splendid forces of mind, do so much to justify the general neglect he provokes. But what noble powers there are visible in almost all parts of his work. I hear he has written a very fine poem on the death of Attila.

Have you seen a new magazine started in Paris—*La République des Lettres?* I, as a French poet of the day, have been solicited to help in setting it on foot, together with Leconte de Lisle (do you know his works? I have but lately begun to read them, often with the highest admiration and enjoyment), Flaubert and younger men of note. The editor is Catulle Mendès, Th. Gautier's son-in-law. I have just had an ecstatic letter acknowledging a poem I sent—an attempt to adapt to French verse the complex metre of an Italian sestina.

I hope this long letter will not find you overwhelmed with graver work and disposed to receive it with an execration; but in any case I am,

Yours very sincerely,
A. C. Swinburne.

P.S. . . . And have you detected . . . Browning's wholesale plagiarism from Diderot of a plot which he has completely spoilt?

XVII To Lord Houghton

Holmwood, Shiplake, Henley-on-Thames
August 7th, 1879

Dear Lord Houghton,

Is there—oh! is there any truth in the report that in consequence of an article in *The Times* yesterday which decrees that there are—and shall be—no living poets in England, Mr. Tennyson and Mr. Browning have "shaken hands in death" by shutting themselves up in a hermetically sealed room with a pan of ignited charcoal between them? and that Mr. Thomas Carlyle, regardless alike of his years, of the weather, and of the law of the land prohibiting indecent exposure, has been seen dancing a Highland fling, in a state of total nudity and partial intoxication, down and up the whole length of Cheyne Walk, Chelsea, with a Scotch cutty-pipe in his mouth, and the Scotch Fiddle on his back, by way of expressing as in a Pyrrhic war-dance the triumph of an "inarticulate poet" over the downfall of the last articulate individual of that ilk? But, alas! to whom am I, with my last faltering breath, appealing for information, which doubtless I must not —I dare not hope to receive? for you too, being one of us, the condemned victim of *The Times* guillotine and of *The Times*, editor, Fouquier-Tinville petit-fils, are probably even now no more.

I wish I could find and copy out and send you a French love-song which I wrote some time ago—the first on record, I should think, that ever was addressed to an elderly London attorney—to Mr. Collette, Secretary and Solicitor to the Society for the Suppression of Vice (talk of *my* alliteration after that!). I need not remind you that Colette (with one *l*—I do not presume to guess what may or may not be signified by the reduplication of that liquid consonant) was a favourite name for a shepherdess of French lovesongs of the last century, whether sentimental or *grivoises*. "Ma Collette," as I call it, is, I flatter myself, a pretty and tender little effusion, even if so somewhat warm—I hope not unpardonably warm—in one or two of the closing stanzas. . . .

Ever sincerely yours,
A. C. Swinburne.

XVIII To Edmund Gosse

The Pines, Putney Hill, S.W.
October 10th [1879]

My dear Gosse,

It is with no flavour of sour grapes on my tongue that I can say I would rather read Arnold on Keats than write on Keats myself.

I only hope—but of this I gravely doubt—that his selection, and above all his arrangement of the selected poems, will be such as I should agree was the best and (to use his own favourite epithet) the most adequate possible. The prefatory essay is sure to be most exquisite reading—*merum sal cum mero melle.*

On Landor I could of course write my fill anywhere at any time; but in this case above all it is the adequacy of the representative selections which is the first and last thing to be looked to; and on that score I will yield precedence in competency to no man whatever.

On Byron I have not another word to say in public; finding nothing to add or recant, and little if anything to modify, on reconsideration of my early essay.

But one poet remains whom I should dearly like to edit, and would do my very best to do him full and late and necessary justice; and this is Collins. On him, if it were desired, I could fall to work almost at once. Excluding Blake from the list of properly and exclusively eighteenth century poets—(and among them, if we include all who published before 1800, we must class not only Blake, but Coleridge and Wordsworth!)—I hold Collins as *facile principem* in the most quintessential quality of a poet proper; and I should like to show reason why, by giving a rapid comparative estimate of all possible competitors for his crown.

* * *

As to Browning's having disgraced himself for life by his acceptance of a presidency of a blackguard's gang of blockheads [the New Shakespeare Society], it is but an additional and perhaps superfluous proof that he is not thoroughbred gentleman enough to have the due self-respect which should—and does not—always accompany genius. I would rather see a copy of your answer to the head blackguard's impertinent offer than even your aforesaid article. My own reply to the same proposal from the same foul quarter long since was of course—in Thomson's phrase—"expressive silence."

* * *

Your fellow-servant,

A. C. Swinburne.

XIX To Edmund Gosse

The Pines

April 7th, 1881

My dear Gosse,

I must lose no time in thanking you for the exquisite little book [*English Odes*] which arrived last night—a flower or a jewel of a song-book. I am proud to be found worthy of the last place in it—and amused to see who is my next neighbour [Coventry Patmore], and what are his ideas of lyric style and the structure of an ode. I think you have been rather cruel to the Laureate: it was hard on him to reprint two such pieces as you have given: but perhaps the man who could be capable of writing either may be said to deserve that neither should be charitably forgotten.

I think your favourite Cowley might have been better represented. Is not his *Ode to Brutus* a finer sample of his better style than these? To my mind also there is too much of Gray: but I should say that, despite my respect for Matthew Arnold's opinion, I am a heretic—and always have been—as to *The Progress of Poesy*, about which I am rather disposed to agree with Dr. Samuel Johnson.

Watts and I are both deeply shocked at the audacious indecency of the opening lines of Warton's *Ode to Spring!* How can anyone have the effrontery to put a volume containing a picture so improper into female hands? Is this the result of too much devotion to such writers as Etheredge? I blush alike for the author and the editor. Aphra Behn might have been ashamed of it.

To be serious again for a moment—you must let me say how very much I regret that you should have thought fit, in such a place as you have chosen, to tax Landor with "splenetic caprice" in the suppression of his couplet on Coleridge. I have little doubt that his reason was one equally just and simple: such an estimate—unhappily, in my opinion, inevitable by any reasonable man—of Coleridge's personal character as compelled him, under pain of insincerity and a conscious touch of the absurd, to rescind his letters of beatification.

* * *

Ever sincerely yours,

A. C. Swinburne.

XX To E. C. Stedman

The Pines, Putney Hill, S.W.
April 4th, 1882

My dear Mr. Stedman,

It is a real gratification to see your friendly handwriting again. If ever I come to America yours will probably be about the first address to which I shall betake myself. . . .

Mary Stuart has found no favour with the reading or reviewing public, but has procured me two satisfactions (I doubt Landor would never have permitted me the use of such a plural), which I prefer infinitely to six columns of adulation in *The Times* and any profit thence resulting. (1) A letter from the venerable and revered father—in age—of all living English (or other) poets, in which the illustrious author [Sir Henry Taylor] of *Philip van Artevelde* bestows such nobly cordial and unreserved praise on the play as I must not transcribe, but should like to show you. (2) An application from the editor of the *Encyclopædia Britannica*—who might, I suppose, in Macaulay's time, almost command the services of the most eminent scholars and historians of the country—to me, a mere poet, proposing that I should contribute to that great repository of erudition the biography of Mary Queen of Scots. I doubt if the like compliment was ever paid before to one of our "idle trade!" To this task I am about to set myself as soon as I have finished my long narrative poem in nine parts—*Tristram of Lyonesse*. I am now engaged on the last canto, or book, or whatever the reader may choose to call it.

My next volume, which will go to the press as soon as this main *pièce de résistance* is ready to be served up, will contain, besides, upwards of fifty lyrical poems—mostly, of course, short; and the greater number of them studies of childhood or songs about children—and various odes and sonnets on literary, historic, and political matters; among them a series of twenty-one sonnets on the English dramatic poets from 1590 to 1650, which I hope will interest those who share my devotion to that branch of our older poetry, and perhaps attract to the study of it some who have not yet embarked on that most delightful and inexhaustible line of reading, which is to me (as far as enjoyment goes) all that ever it was to Charles Lamb. In that case I shall certainly have been of some service in my generation.

* * *

The only time I ever saw Mr. Oscar Wilde was in a crush at our acquaintance, Lord Houghton's. I thought he seemed a harmless young nobody, and had no notion he was the sort of man to play the mountebank, as he seems to have been doing. A letter which he wrote to me lately about Walt Whitman was quite a modest, gentleman-like, reasonable affair without any flourish or affectation of any kind in matter or expression. It is really very odd. I should think you in America must be as tired of his name as we are in London of Mr. Barnum's and his Jumbo's.

Mr. Watts, with whom I now keep house, sends his kind regards to you; and I remain

Yours very sincerely,
A. C. Swinburne.

XXI To Edmund Gosse

The Pines, Putney Hill, S.W.
June 24th, 1882

My dear Gosse,

I had hardly put down Watts's copy of your *Gray* when the copy you were kind enough to send me arrived. I thank you very sincerely for it, and congratulate you on a successful and delightful piece of work. It must have been a labour of love, and one which needed a love of labour for its accomplishment.

The book is unquestionably one of the very few jewels of a most singularly unequal series [*English Men of Letters*]—of which I should say that some volumes were about as bad as possible, others—perhaps more—very fairly creditable, and two or three about as good as they could be. I need not say that yours belongs unmistakably to my third class. As to the *Odes*, we may as well agree to differ. About the Norse poems I agree with you as heartily as about the *Elegy*. Did I ever tell you from whose lips it was that I, when a little boy, first heard the unforgettable anecdote of Wolfe's tribute to that poem? Wordsworth's—who related it to my parents on the one occasion on which I was presented to him a month or two before his death.

This *Gray*, with *Byron*, *Landor*, and *Spenser*, makes up, I think, the quadrilateral of thoroughly good books in the series. Perhaps I should add *Goldsmith* to the four.

Yours very sincerely,
A. C. Swinburne.

XXII To John Churton Collins

The Pines, Putney Hill, S.W.
November 30th, 1882

My dear Collins,

I fear you will think me very dull if I confess that I do not see or believe in any recondite law or principle in Shakespeare's use of prose whenever he felt himself more at ease, for his purpose of the moment, in prose than in verse. Of course his range of command in the one province was almost as wonderful as in the other, and he had an unequalled capacity of adapting it to the requirements of the subject, from Hamlet's meditation on man to Falstaff's catechism on honour: but I at all events am unable to recognize any deeper or subtler line of demarcation traceable between its varieties of tone and style than might be required by the exigencies of the matter in hand.

* * *

Always sincerely yours,
A. C. Swinburne.

XXIII To Paul Hamilton Hayne

The Pines, Putney Hill, S.W.
July 4th, 1884

My dear Mr. Hayne,

I must not let a day pass without acknowledging the receipt of your letter and the poem enclosed in it.

The verses give a charming idea of the song they so lovingly describe. I am sorry to hear you speak of your feeble health and the improbability of your ever visiting England. Of course I shall be delighted to receive a copy of your "complete edition." If you should send it and receive no acknowledgment by return of post, please understand that I must at the time have been away from home; which I usually leave for some time during the summer and autumn.

I do know a little of Mr. Burroughs' writings, and hope some day to know more. He seems to hold among your writers much the same place that Mr. Richard Jefferies (author of *The Gamekeeper at Home*, *The Amateur Poacher*, etc., etc.) holds among ours,—that of an eloquent and subtle, studious and humorous worshipper of nature.

As to Byron I have said my last word, with full and final deliberation. I think Poe, like Shelley, one of the very worst critics of poetry that ever existed; which does not diminish one whit my admiration for his exquisite genius. You will remember that he thought poor old Mr. Horne, lately deceased, one of the greatest poets of the century. The poem you mention is not even verse. How do you, or how did Poe, or how, for that matter, did Byron, propose to scan this line?—

In the wide waste there still is a tree.

That is not so much bad metre or harsh metre as no metre at all. I defy anybody to read or sing that line, as it stands, so as to make verse, even bad verse, of it; and for this reason—that it is very bad prose, lumbering, limping, and dissonant. Poe himself could not have written such a line, nor, I am convinced, could you.

Byron has written hundreds upon thousands as bad. And I hope he is almost the only man who ever did.

So much for the singer. As for the thinker I cannot imagine what your imagination can persuade you to see in *Manfred* that can be called imaginative. As dramatic figures, Manfred and Astarte are surely inferior to Punch and Judy; and for those poorest of poor devils in the "Hall of Arimanes," if they could not put a little more spirit into their deviltry they would be hooted and hissed off the stage of any penny theatre in the world. There is not one scene, there is not one conception, in all the three acts of ranting rhetoric and guide-book descriptions, actually realized and vivified for a single second. I will find something better in the obscurest of the Elizabethans commemorated in those sonnets which I am delighted to hear that you like so well,—poets of whom Byron always spoke with the blatant insolence of stupid and vulgar ignorance.

Thanks for your suggestion about my poems

on childhood. I should like very well to see them brought together in a book, but I leave all that sort of thing entirely to my publishers. If they thought it would pay I suppose they would suggest it. When my forthcoming volume is out [*A Midsummer Holiday and Other Poems*], I shall have published fifty poems on a single child [Edward Mason, Watts-Dunton's nephew] (whom I have just seen playing at see-saw in the broiling sun), all written between his sixth and his tenth birthdays.

Ever sincerely yours,
A. C. Swinburne.

XXIV To Edmund Gosse

The Pines, Putney Hill, S.W.
February 21st, 1885

My dear Gosse,

* * *

I am glad to hear of you home again, and to receive so agreeable an account of Whitman.[1] I retain a very cordial admiration for not a little of his earlier work; but the habit of vague and flatulent verbiage seems to me to have grown upon him instead of decreasing; and I must say it is long since I have read anything of his which seemed to me worthy of the nobler passages of his *Drum-Taps* and the earliest *Leaves of Grass*. However, you need not tell him so; but give him my cordial regards if ever you write to him.

* * *

Ever yours sincerely,
A. C. Swinburne.

XXV To Sir Sidney Lee

The Pines
December 13th, 1888

Dear Sir,

I can only repeat what I said before, that Canterbury is not merely the best, but the only proper site (in my humble opinion) for a memorial to Marlowe. Even if the Dean would subscribe—instead of demanding—£250 for the erection of a monument to his memory in Westminster Abbey, I should continue to think that it was not the place for such a monument. A so-called "poets' corner" where Shakespeare, Milton and Shelley "shine by their absence" is surely not the place for Marlowe. There is every reason why Canterbury should enjoy the honour which I am delighted to hear that it "is anxious for." And, I may be allowed to add, I think they are quite right in wishing that the site should not be in the cathedral. One of the most eminent Englishmen (and clergymen) living once expressed to me his regret that the doors of the Abbey should have been closed against Byron. I replied that I thought it much more discreditable that Shelley should not have his place there. "Ah," was the answer, "but think how he would have disliked it!" Would Marlowe have disliked it less? Giordano Bruno, I see in to-day's papers, is to have his statue in Rome—but not in St. Peter's.

* * *

Yours very truly,
A. C. Swinburne.

XXVI To Sir E. Burne-Jones

The Pines
October 15th, 1892

My dear Ned,

How am I to thank you for the sweetest photograph ever taken? Watts and I are now Palamon and Arcite, our hitherto impregnable friendship breached and shattered by rivalry in devotion to the lady whose adorable arm (what can the missing arms of the Venus of Milo's have been to that one) is caressing your honoured beard. When will you come? or would you prefer luncheon or dinner time? Give it a name I beg. And do not be tempted to put off. Remember how many souls which Almighty God designed for salvation have been eternally lost thro' the apparently venial sin of procrastination.

I am awfully sorry and taken aback (*erasures*). . . . As for being old I can only say in language appropriate to our time of life that I like your something cheek. We ought all, like Hugo and Tennyson, at our time of life to have many of our best years before us. I should rather think you did not see me at the Abbey on Wednesday; I sent back my card with a word of excuse just as I did when I received one for the funeral of Browning. I hate all

[1] Mr. Gosse saw Walt Whitman in his house at Camden, New Jersey, in December, 1884.

crowds and all functions, but especially the funereal kind beyond all decent expression. But I did write a little word to Lady Tennyson, having once been their guest, which I am glad to know was found acceptable.

I want you to like an unpublished poem of mine which has been very successful in MS. and which I should have liked to send Tennyson (but Omnipotence overruled our humble aspirations! as I need not remind you) on my countrywoman Grace Darling. I went with dear old Scott who was hideously sick all the way out from Joyous Gard to the lighthouse, where the heroine's old father who had rescued the shipwrecked crew from off the rocks while she kept the boat steady to take them in received us. Didn't you ever when a boy think how you would like of all things to keep or live in a lighthouse? I do to this day. Of course I mean if it's some miles out to sea and difficult to get at. Isn't the name of our Northumbrian reefs about that one lovely—The Hawkers. Falconers and falcons with ships and men for prey instead of herons (I always thought it rather a shame to hawk at them—they are so beautiful, especially, *of course*, in Northumberland).

I hope you got all right, I fear you may not have had time to read my little book of this year: *The Sisters*. It found less favour with the reviewer than with my mother, whose chief criticism was, "I like Redgie so much," which gave me more pleasure than any review could as I did think I had succeeded in making a nice young fellow out of my own recollections and aspirations. On getting into one's teens, a little way—the cavalry service is apt to supplant even the keeping of a lighthouse in one's fancy, or may I be allowed the endearing word Ideal. I hope you will not be bored by this prolonged scrawl, but the man to whom the absence and the silence of an honoured friend has been for many, many revolutions of the lunar globe an affliction (grammarians not unaware would say that they had been afflictions—but what, my dearest sir, is grammar to sentiment?), may be forgiven if he adds no further expression of apology for excessive and unpremeditated verbosity in addressing a friend

by his very devoted
A. C. Swinburne.

XXVII To Clement K. Shorter

The Pines, Putney Hill, S.W.
March 4th, 1896

Dear Mr. Shorter,

I am sorry that I must—with many thanks—decline the invitation of the Omar Khayyám Club. As to the immortal tent-maker himself, I believe I may claim to be one of his earliest English admirers. It is upwards of thirty-six years since I was introduced to him by D. G. Rossetti, who had just been introduced himself, I believe, by Mr. Whitley Stokes. At that time the first and best edition of FitzGerald's wonderful version was being sold off at a penny a copy, having proved hopelessly unsaleable at the published price of one shilling. We invested, I should think, in hardly less than sixpenny-worth apiece, and on returning to the stall next day for more found that we had sent up the market to the sinfully extravagant sum of two pence, an imposition which evoked from Rossetti a fervent and impressive remonstrance. Not so very long afterwards, if I mistake not, the price of a copy was thirty shillings. It is the only edition worth having, as FitzGerald, like the ass of genius he was, cut out of later editions the crowning stanza which is the core or kernel of the whole. As to the greatness of the poem I can say no more than I have tried to say in print. I know none to be compared with it for power, pathos, and beauty, in the same line of thought and work, except possibly Ecclesiastes; and magnificent as that is, I can hardly think the author comparable to Omar either as philosopher or as poet.

Yours very truly,
A. C. Swinburne.

XXVIII To Clement K. Shorter

The Pines, Putney Hill, S.W.
October 19th, 1896

Dear Mr. Shorter,

I have to thank you again for a most acceptable gift [*Charlotte Brontë and Her Circle*]—but I know not how we are to thank Mr. Nicholls for his truly generous surrender of personal inclination! Mr. Watts-Dunton asks me to join his thanks to mine, and to say how fully he shares my interest in this delightful and valuable book.

Lest I should forget to say it at all, let me begin by saying that while I by no means disagree on the whole with what you say about Mme. Darmesteter's book [*Life of Emily Brontë*], I think you have forgotten that the one new thing she had to tell us—how Emily saved her wretched brother from being burnt in his bed—is the most important thing we know about that wonderful poetess and heroine. Of course there is far too much in the book about him: but that one anecdote atones for all. Is it not possible to recover his portrait of her? Martha Brown must surely have treasured it. I would give anything in reason to see what she was like. Charlotte's bad eyesight must have misled her when she fancied a likeness between her sister and G. H. Lewes. I only met him once, but I remember not only that he was the ugliest of human beings I ever saw except perhaps his consort George Eliot, but that it was not such a mean and vulgar ugliness as suggested nothing but the idea of a smart, pert, impudent counter-jumper. I no more believe in that likeness than I would believe that Homer or Sappho or Shakespeare or Vittoria Colonna could have been like that hideous smirking scribbler. And all the more do I wish to see what she *was* like. The letter printed at p. 47 would suffice of itself to make your book most valuable to all readers fit to read it.

Yours very gratefully,
A. C. Swinburne.

XXIX To William Sharp

The Pines, Putney Hill, London, S.W.
October 6th, 1901

Dear Mr. Sharp,

Many thanks for the early copy [Sharp's *Selections* from Swinburne] you have had the kindness to send on to me. I am pleased to find the *Nympholept* in a leading place, as I think it one of the best and most representative things I ever did. I should have preferred on all accounts that *In the Bay* had filled the place you have allotted to *Ave atque Vale*, a poem to which you are altogether too kind in my opinion, as others have been before you. I never had really much in common with Baudelaire, though I retain all my early admiration for his genius at its best. I wish there were fewer of such very juvenile crudities as you have selected from my first volume of Poems: it is trying to find such boyish attempts as *The Sundew*, *Aholibah*, *Madonna Mia*, etc., offered as examples of the work of a man who has written so many volumes since in which there is nothing that is not at least better and riper than they. I wish too that *Mater Triumphalis* had not been separated from its fellow poem—a much fitter piece of work to stand by itself. On the other hand I am very cordially obliged to you for giving the detached extract from *Anactoria*. I should greatly have preferred that extracts only should have been given from *Atalanta in Calydon*, which sorely needs compression in the earlier parts. *Erechtheus*, which would have taken up so much less space, would also, I venture to think, have been a better and a fairer example of the author's works. Mr. Watts-Dunton's objection to the book is the omission of *Super Flumina Babylonis*. I too am much surprised to find it excluded from a selection which includes so much that might well be spared—nay, would be better away. I would like to have seen one of what I call my topographical poems in full. The tiny scrap from *Loch Torridon* was hardly worth giving by itself. I do not understand what you find obscure or melancholy in *The Garden of Cymodoce*. It was written principally to express my constant delight in the recollection of Sark.

I hope you will not think anything in this note captious or ungracious. Candour always seems to be the best expression possible of gratitude or good-will.

Ever sincerely yours,
A. C. Swinburne.

WILFRID SCAWEN BLUNT

[August 17, 1840–September 10, 1922]

Wilfrid Scawen Blunt, foreign attaché, traveler, and poet, was born at Petworth House, Sussex, and educated at Stonyhurst and at St. Mary's, Oscott. For twelve years he served in the English diplomatic service. In 1869 he married Lady Anne Noel, a granddaughter of Lord Byron, and traveled with her in Spain, Algeria, Egypt, and Syria. He was a strong champion of the cause of Arabi Pasha in Egypt in 1882, and in 1887 his participation in the anti-coercion movement in Ireland led to his imprisonment for two months. His *Love Sonnets of Proteus* (1880) brought him recognition as a poet. Among his other publications were *Esther* (1892), *Griselda* (1893), *Quatrains of Youth* (1898), and *My Diaries* (1919–20).

THEY SHALL NOT KNOW

When thou art happy, thou dear heart of pleasure,
Because men love thee and the feasts are spread,
And Fortune in thy lap has poured her treasure,
And Spring is there and roses crown thy head,
Then think of one who loved thee for his woe,
And, if thou sigh
With others by,
They shall not know.

When thou art silent in thy day of trouble,
Because fools vex and thou hast rivals found
And love has played thee falser than a bubble
And memory stings and grief is as a wound,
Then think of one whose hand first soothed thy brow,
And, if a smile
Thy tears beguile,
These shall not know.

When all is ended, thou pale ghost of sorrow,
And time's last flower is gathered from the grove,
And yesterday to thee is as to-morrow
And there is none to speak to thee of love,
Then sing these songs one made thee long ago,
And men shall swear
Thou still art fair—
Yet shall not know.

1875

IF WE HAD MET

If we had met when leaves were green,
And fate to us less hard had proved,
And naught had been of what has been,
We might have loved as none have loved.

If we had met as girl and boy,
The world of pleasure at our feet,
Our joy had been a perfect joy;
We might have met, but did not meet.

Nor less in youth's full passionate day,
A woman you and I a man,
We might have loved and found a way
No laws could check, no vows could ban.

Too late! Too sad! A year ago,
Even then perhaps, in spite of fate
It might have been,—but ah! not now,
I dare not love you, 'tis too late.

1875

YOU HAVE LET THE BEAUTY OF THE DAY GO OVER

You have let the beauty of the day go over,
You have let the glory of the noon go by.
Clouds from the West have gathered close and cover
All but a remnant now of our proud sky.

Dumbly the rain beats on our darkened faces.
Hushed are the woods. Alas, for us no bird

Shall sing to-day of pleasure in green places,
No touch shall thrill, no soul of leaves be stirred.

Why did we wait? What faith was ours in fortune?
What was our pride that fate should kneel to us?
Oh, we were fools. Love loves not to importune,
And he is silent here in this sad house.

Alas, dear love, the day for us is ended,
The pleasure of green fields, of streams, of skies.
One hour remains, one only of joy blended
With coming night. Ah, seize it ere it flies.

Draw fast the curtains. Close the door on sorrow.
Shut out the dusk. It only makes us grieve.
Here we may live a life,—and then, to-morrow,
If fate still wills it, we may take our leave.

1875

THINK NO MORE OF ME

THINK no more of me,
If we needs must part.
Mine was but a heart.
Think no more of me.
Think no more of me.
For Love's sake forget.
Love grows hard which cannot see,
It may wound us yet.

Think no more of me.
Love has had his day.
Now Love runs away.
Think no more of me.
Think no more of me.
If we loved or not
Hidden is 'twixt me and thee.
It were best forgot.

Think no more of me.
We shall need our tears
For the coming years.
Think no more of me.
Think no more of me.
In the world above
Sadder far it were if we
Met and did not love.

1875

THE MORTE D'ARTHUR

THESE are the tales in all their valorous lore
Of that famed frolic of the Table Round
No shame-faced verse, but stout prose to the core,
As Malory wrote it and our fathers found.
Tales touching still, and still through time renowned,
But less, methinks, for their high deeds that bore
Their crests so proudly than the one lost sound
Of Lancelot's step at the Queen's chamber door.
—How their sighs echo! Think, if then she had made
Another answer than her human "Yes,"
And been more valiant and denied and slept!
Should we still weep o'er Bors and Galahad,
The Sancgreal's quest, Gawayne in wrath equipped,
Or all King Arthur's jousts in Lyonnesse?

1898

ALFRED TENNYSON

TEARS, idle tears! Ah, who shall bid us weep,
Now that thy lyre, O prophet, is unstrung?
What voice shall rouse the dull world from its sleep
And lead its requiem as when Grief was young,
And thou in thy rapt youth, Time's bards among,
Captured our ears, and we looked up and heard
Spring's sweetest music on thy mourning tongue
And knew thee for Pain's paradisal bird.
We are alone without thee in our tears,
Alone in our mute chauntings. Vows are vain
To tell thee how we loved thee in those years
Nor dream to look upon thy like again.
We know not how to weep without thy aid,
Since all that tears would tell thyself hast said.

1898

GHOST OF THE BEAUTIFUL PAST

Ghost of the beautiful past, of the days long gone, of a queen, of a fair sweet woman.
Ghost with the passionate eyes, how proud, yet not too proud to have wept, to have loved, since to love is human.

Angel in fair white garments, with skirts of lawn, by the autumn wind on the pathway fluttered,
Always close by the castle wall and about to speak. But the whisper dies on her lips unuttered.

Yellow leaves deep strewn on the sward, dead leaves of a far-off glorious summer.
Yea, the leaves of the roses she plucked, petal by petal, with beating heart, for him the delayed loved comer.

Why doth she weep thus year on year? He hath tarried long, ah me, a thousand desolate years.
Why doth she weep? She hath wept enough. For see, dark down in the gardens dim, a lake. It is filled with her tears.

If I should ask her name, her title with men? But I need not ask it. I know it, alas, of old, though of old unspoken.
Is there another name but one for that face divine, for those sad sweet lips, like a bow unbent, like a bent bow broken?
No, it is none but hers, the Queen, the beloved of all, the beloved of one, when the Table Round was set in thy mead, Carleon.
None but hers, who was Guenevere, when the trumpets blew and the knights full clad rode down to joust at noon, with their clamorous shout, "The Queen!"

Doth she remember all, or is all forgotten, pennon proud and lance in rest, the thunder of hoofs and the light swift tread of the foremost runner?
Dareth she raise her eyes, those passionate eyes, at the crowd that gazed? None of them all might meet her look, save he, her one true passionate knight, who adoring won her.

Surely, surely, she seeth; she knoweth all; she is no lost vision of death.
She hath still a smile deep hidden. She hath a name on her lips. She shall sigh, she shall speak, she shall move, when the light winds breathe from the Western Seas with the Spring that quickeneth.

Oh, she shall laugh and sing, though the shadow of Death be a cloud behind her!
Oh, she shall love! Though the dragon of grief keep watch, he shall sleep when the trees on the mead grow green, and awaking he shall not find her.

Read me a sweeter meaning, O Lady, O thou whom I serve, of this pictured story.
Read. Nay the tale is told. To its truth I swear, by my sword, by my knightly faith, by the fame of the King and the Table Round, and the souls of the Saints in glory!

1898

ROBERT BRIDGES

[October 23, 1844–April 21, 1930]

Robert Bridges, sixteenth poet laureate of England, was born in Kent and attended Eton and Oxford, where he took the classical course, made the second class in the Final School of Litteræ Humaniores, and excelled at cricket and rowing. Following his graduation he traveled in Europe and in the Orient for several years. Upon his return he studied medicine at St. Bartholomew's Hospital and received the degree of M. B. at Oxford. For a while he was a general practitioner in London and at the same time a member of the staff at St. Bartholomew's and at the Children's Hospital. He abandoned the practice of medicine when he was thirty-eight years old, deliberately giving up all he had gained in the profession and retiring to Yattendon in

Berkshire to marry and to devote his life to poetry. His first volume, *Poems*, appeared in 1873. Many of his earlier poems were "most charmingly and tastefully" printed by his friend, Mr. Henry Daniel, of Worcester College. One of these volumes, *The Growth of Love* (1889), done in a beautiful black-letter type, is now much sought by booklovers as a rare and lovely treasure. His final poem, *The Testament of Beauty* (1929), published when he was eighty-five, is an eloquent testimony to the vitality of his poetic gift.

ELEGY

THE wood is bare: a river-mist is steeping
The trees that winter's chill of life bereaves:
Only their stiffened boughs break silence, weeping
Over their fallen leaves;

That lie upon the dank earth brown and rotten,
Miry and matted in the soaking wet:
Forgotten with the spring, that is forgotten
By them that can forget.

Yet it was here we walked when ferns were springing,
And through the mossy bank shot bud and blade:—
Here found in summer, when the birds were singing,
A green and pleasant shade.

'Twas here we loved in sunnier days and greener;
And now, in this disconsolate decay,
I come to see her where I most have seen her,
And touch the happier day.

For on this path, at every turn and corner,
The fancy of her figure on me falls:
Yet walks she with the slow step of a mourner,
Nor hears my voice that calls.

So through my heart there winds a track of feeling,
A path of memory, that is all her own:
Whereto her phantom beauty ever stealing
Haunts the sad spot alone.

About her steps the trunks are bare, the branches
Drip heavy tears upon her downcast head;
And bleed from unseen wounds that no sun stanches,
For the year's sun is dead.

And dead leaves wrap the fruits that summer planted:
And birds that love the South have taken wing.
The wanderer, loitering o'er the scene enchanted,
Weeps, and despairs of spring.

1873

A PASSER-BY

WHITHER, O splendid ship, thy white sails crowding,
Leaning across the bosom of the urgent West,
That fearest nor sea rising, nor sky clouding,
Whither away, fair rover, and what thy quest?
Ah! soon, when Winter has all our vales opprest,
When skies are cold and misty, and hail is hurling,
Wilt thóu glíde on the blue Pacific, or rest
In a summer haven asleep, thy white sails furling.

I there before thee, in the country that well thou knowest,
Already arrived am inhaling the odorous air:
I watch thee enter unerringly where thou goest,
And anchor queen of the strange shipping there,
Thy sails for awnings spread, thy masts bare;
Nor is aught from the foaming reef to the snow-capped, grandest
Peak, that is over the feathery palms more fair
Than thou, so upright, so stately, and still thou standest.

PAX HOMINIBUS BONAE VOLUNTATIS.

A frosty Xmas eve ' when the stars were shining
Fared I forth alone ' where westward falls the hill
And from many a village ' in the water'd valley
Distant music reached me ' peals of bells aringing:
The constellated sounds ' ran sprinkling on earth's floor
As the dark vault above ' with stars was spangled o'er.

Then sped my thought to keep ' that first Xmas of all
When the shepherds watching ' by their folds ere the dawn
Heard music in the fields ' and marveling c^d not tell
Whether it were angels ' or the bright stars singing.

Now blessed be the towers ' that crown England so fair
That stand up strong in prayer ' unto God for our souls:
Blessed be their founders ' (said I) and our country folk
Who are ringing for Christ ' in the belfries tonight
With arms lifted to clutch ' the rattling ropes that race
Into the dark above ' and the mad romping din.

But to me heard afar ' it was heav'nly† music
Angels song comforting ' as the comfort of Christ
When he spake tenderly ' to his sorrowful flock:
The old words came to me ' by the riches of time
Mellow'd and transfigured ' as I stood on the hill
Heark'ning in the aspect ' of th' eternal silence

RB. 1913

† I find I have written "heav'nly" in all my copies for my original is "starry". I can't copy a fault. so I leave it –

Copy of a Poem in Robert Bridges' Handwriting. (See Appendix I.)

And yet, O splendid ship, unhailed and nameless,
I know not if, aiming a fancy, I rightly divine
That thou hast a purpose joyful, a courage blameless,
Thy port assured in a happier land than mine.
But for all I have given thee, beauty enough is thine,
As thou, aslant with trim tackle and shrouding,
From the proud nostril curve of a prow's line
In the offing scatterest foam, thy white sails crowding.

1879

THERE IS A HILL BESIDE THE SILVER THAMES

THERE is a hill beside the silver Thames,
Shady with birch and beech and odorous pine:
And brilliant underfoot with thousand gems
Steeply the thickets to his floods decline.
Straight trees in every place
Their thick tops interlace,
And pendant branches trail their foliage fine
Upon his watery face.

Swift from the sweltering pasturage he flows:
His stream, alert to seek the pleasant shade,
Pictures his gentle purpose, as he goes
Straight to the caverned pool his toil has made.
His winter floods lay bare
The stout roots in the air:
His summer streams are cool, when they have played
Among their fibrous hair.

A rushy island guards the sacred bower,
And hides it from the meadow, where in peace
The lazy cows wrench many a scented flower,
Robbing the golden market of the bees:
And laden barges float
By banks of myosote;
And scented flag and golden flower-de-lys
Delay the loitering boat.

And on this side the island, where the pool
Eddies away, are tangled mass on mass
The water-weeds, that net the fishes cool,
And scarce allow a narrow stream to pass;
Where spreading crowfoot mars
The drowning nenuphars,
Waving the tassels of her silken grass
Below her silver stars.

But in the purple pool there nothing grows,
Not the white water-lily spoked with gold;
Though best she loves the hollows, and well knows
On quiet streams her broad shields to unfold:
Yet should her roots but try
Within these deeps to lie,
Not her long reaching stalk could ever hold
Her waxen head so high.

Sometimes an angler comes, and drops his hook
Within its hidden depths, and 'gainst a tree
Leaning his rod, reads in some pleasant book,
Forgetting soon his pride of fishery;
And dreams, or falls asleep,
While curious fishes peep
About his nibbled bait, or scornfully
Dart off and rise and leap.

And sometimes a slow figure 'neath the trees,
In ancient-fashioned smock, with tottering care
Upon a staff propping his weary knees,
May by the pathway of the forest fare:
As from a buried day
Across the mind will stray
Some perishing mute shadow,—and unaware
He passeth on his way.

Else, he that wishes solitude is safe,
Whether he bathe at morning in the stream:
Or lead his love there when the hot hours chafe
The meadows, busy with a blurring steam;
Or watch, as fades the light,
The gibbous moon grow bright,
Until her magic rays dance in a dream,
And glorify the night.

Where is this bower beside the silver Thames?
O pool and flowery thickets, hear my vow!
O trees of freshest foliage and straight stems,
No sharer of my secret I allow:
Lest ere I come the while
Strange feet your shades defile;
Or lest the burly oarsman turn his prow
Within your guardian isle.

1879

I HAVE LOVED FLOWERS THAT FADE

I HAVE loved flowers that fade,
Within whose magic tents
Rich hues have marriage made
With sweet unmemoried scents:
A honeymoon delight,—
A joy of love at sight,
That ages in an hour:—
My song be like a flower!

I have loved airs, that die
Before their charm is writ
Along a liquid sky
Trembling to welcome it.
Notes, that with pulse of fire
Proclaim the spirit's desire,
Then die, and are nowhere:—
My song be like an air!

Die, song, die like a breath,
And wither as a bloom:
Fear not a flowery death,
Dread not an airy tomb!
Fly with delight, fly hence!
'Twas thine love's tender sense
To feast; now on thy bier
Beauty shall shed a tear.

1879

LONDON SNOW

WHEN men were all asleep the snow came flying,
In large white flakes falling on the city brown,
Stealthily and perpetually settling and loosely lying,
Hushing the latest traffic of the drowsy town;
Deadening, muffling, stifling its murmurs failing;
Lazily and incessantly floating down and down:
Silently sifting and veiling road, roof and railing;
Hiding difference, making unevenness even,
Into angles and crevices softly drifting and sailing.
All night it fell, and when full inches seven
It lay in the depth of its uncompacted lightness,
The clouds blew off from a high and frosty heaven;
And all woke earlier for the unaccustomed brightness
Of the winter dawning, the strange unheavenly glare:
The eye marvelled—marvelled at the dazzling whiteness;
The ear hearkened to the stillness of the solemn air;
No sound of wheel rumbling nor of foot falling,
And the busy morning cries came thin and spare.
Then boys I heard, as they went to school, calling,
They gathered up the crystal manna to freeze
Their tongues with tasting, their hands with snowballing;
Or rioted in a drift, plunging up to the knees;
Or peering up from under the white-mossed wonder,
"O look at the trees!" they cried, "O look at the trees!"
With lessened load a few carts creak and blunder,
Following along the white deserted way,
A country company long dispersed asunder:
When now already the sun, in pale display
Standing by Paul's high dome, spread forth below
His sparkling beams, and awoke the stir of the day.
For now doors open, and war is waged with the snow;
And trains of sombre men, past tale of number,
Tread long brown paths, as toward their toil they go:
But even for them awhile no cares encumber
Their minds diverted; the daily word is unspoken,
The daily thoughts of labour and sorrow slumber
At the sight of the beauty that greets them, for the charm they have broken.

1880

THE PHILOSOPHER TO HIS MISTRESS

Because thou canst not see,
Because thou canst not know
The black and hopeless woe
That hath encompassed me:
Because, should I confess
The thought of my despair,
My words would wound thee less
Than swords can hurt the air:

Because with thee I seem
As one invited near
To taste the faery cheer
Of spirits in a dream;
Of whom he knoweth nought
Save that they vie to make
All motion, voice and thought
A pleasure for his sake:

Therefore more sweet and strange
Has been the mystery
Of thy long love to me,
That doth not quit, nor change,
Nor tax my solemn heart,
That kisseth in a gloom,
Knowing not who thou art
That givest, nor to whom.

Therefore the tender touch
Is more; more dear the smile:
And thy light words beguile
My wisdom overmuch:
And O with swiftness fly
The fancies of my song
To happy worlds, where I
Still in thy love belong.

1890

THOU DIDST DELIGHT MY EYES

Thou didst delight my eyes:
Yet who am I? nor first
Nor last nor best, that durst
Once dream of thee for prize;
Nor this the only time
Thou shalt set love to rhyme.

Thou didst delight my ear:
Ah! little praise; thy voice
Makes other hearts rejoice,
Makes all ears glad that hear;
And short my joy: but yet,
O song, do not forget.

For what wert thou to me?
How shall I say? The moon,
That poured her midnight noon
Upon his wrecking sea;—
A sail, that for a day
Has cheered the castaway.

1890

THE FULL MOON FROM HER CLOUDLESS SKIES

The full moon from her cloudless skies
Turneth her face, I think, on me;
And from the hour when she doth rise
Till when she sets, none else will see.

One only other ray she hath,
That makes an angle close with mine,
And glancing down its happy path
Upon another spot doth shine.

But that ray too is sent to me,
For where it lights there dwells my heart:
And if I were where I would be,
Both rays would shine, love, where thou art.

1890

AWAKE, MY HEART

Awake, my heart, to be loved, awake, awake!
The darkness silvers away, the morn doth break,
It leaps in the sky: unrisen lustres slake
The o'ertaken moon. Awake, O heart, awake!

She too that loveth awaketh and hopes for thee;
Her eyes already have sped the shades that flee,
Already they watch the path thy feet shall take:
Awake, O heart, to be loved, awake, awake!

And if thou tarry from her,—if this could be,—
She cometh herself, O heart, to be loved, to thee;
For thee would unashamèd herself forsake:
Awake to be loved, my heart, awake, awake!

Awake, the land is scattered with light, and see,
Uncanopied sleep is flying from field and tree:
And blossoming boughs of April in laughter shake;
Awake, O heart, to be loved, awake, awake!

Lo all things wake and tarry and look for thee:
She looketh and saith, "O sun, now bring him to me.
Come more adored, O adored, for his coming's sake,
And awake my heart to be loved: awake, awake!"

1890

I LOVE ALL BEAUTEOUS THINGS

I LOVE all beauteous things,
I seek and adore them;
God hath no better praise,
And man in his hasty days
Is honoured for them.

I too will something make
And joy in the making;
Altho' to-morrow it seem
Like the empty words of a dream
Remembered on waking.

1890

MY EYES FOR BEAUTY PINE

MY eyes for beauty pine,
My soul for Goddës grace:
No other care nor hope is mine;
To heaven I turn my face.

One splendour thence is shed
From all the stars above:
'Tis namèd when God's name is said,
'Tis Love, 'tis heavenly Love.

And every gentle heart,
That burns with true desire,
Is lit from eyes that mirror part
Of that celestial fire.

1890

SO SWEET LOVE SEEMED THAT APRIL MORN

So sweet love seemed that April morn,
When first we kissed beside the thorn,
So strangely sweet, it was not strange
We thought that love could never change.

But I can tell—let truth be told—
That love will change in growing old;
Though day by day is nought to see,
So delicate his motions be.

And in the end 'twill come to pass
Quite to forget what once he was,
Nor even in fancy to recall
The pleasure that was all in all.

His little spring, that sweet we found,
So deep in summer floods is drowned,
I wonder, bathed in joy complete,
How love so young could be so sweet.

1893

I NEVER SHALL LOVE THE SNOW AGAIN

I NEVER shall love the snow again
Since Maurice died:
With corniced drift it blocked the lane
And sheeted in a desolate plain
The country side.

The trees with silvery rime bedight
Their branches bare.
By day no sun appeared; by night
The hidden moon shed thievish light
In the misty air.

We fed the birds that flew around
In flocks to be fed:
No shelter in holly or brake they found.
The speckled thrush on the frozen ground
Lay frozen and dead.

We skated on stream and pond; we cut
The crinching snow
To Doric temple or Arctic hut;
We laughed and sang at nightfall, shut
By the fireside glow.

Yet grudged we our keen delights before
Maurice should come.
We said, In-door or out-of-door
We shall love life for a month or more,
When he is home.

They brought him home; 'twas two days late
For Christmas day:
Wrapped in white, in solemn state,
A flower in his hand, all still and straight
Our Maurice lay.

And two days ere the year outgave
We laid him low.
The best of us truly were not brave,
When we laid Maurice down in his grave
Under the snow.

1893

NIGHTINGALES

Beautiful must be the mountains whence ye come,
And bright in the fruitful valleys the streams, wherefrom
Ye learn your song:
Where are those starry woods? O might I wander there,
Among the flowers, which in that heavenly air
Bloom the year long!

Nay, barren are those mountains and spent the streams:
Our song is the voice of desire, that haunts our dreams,
A throe of the heart,
Whose pining visions dim, forbidden hopes profound,
No dying cadence nor long sigh can sound,
For all our art.

Alone, aloud in the raptured ear of men
We pour our dark nocturnal secret; and then,
As night is withdrawn
From these sweet-springing meads and bursting boughs of May,
Dream, while the innumerable choir of day
Welcome the dawn.

1893

PATER FILIO

Sense with keenest edge unusèd,
Yet unsteel'd by scathing fire;
Lovely feet as yet unbruisèd
On the ways of dark desire;
Sweetest hope that lookest smiling
O'er the wilderness defiling!

Why such beauty, to be blighted
By the swarm of foul destruction?
Why such innocence delighted,
When sin stalks to thy seduction?
All the litanies e'er chaunted
Shall not keep thy faith undaunted.

I have pray'd the sainted Morning
To unclasp her hands to hold thee;
From resignful Eve's adorning
Stol'n a robe of peace to enfold thee;
With all charms of man's contriving
Arm'd thee for thy lonely striving.

Me too once unthinking Nature,
—Whence Love's timeless mockery took me,—
Fashion'd so divine a creature,
Yea, and like a beast forsook me.
I forgave, but tell the measure
Of her crime in thee, my treasure.

1899

SCREAMING TARN

The saddest place that e'er I saw
Is the deep tarn above the inn
That crowns the mountain-road, whereby
One southward bound his way must win.

Sunk on the table of the ridge
From its deep shores is nought to see:
The unresting wind lashes and chills
Its shivering ripples ceaselessly.

Three sides 'tis banked with stones aslant,
And down the fourth the rushes grow,
And yellow sedge fringing the edge
With lengthen'd image all arow.

'Tis square and black, and on its face
When noon is still, the mirror'd sky
Looks dark and further from the earth
Than when you gaze at it on high.

At mid of night, if one be there,
—So say the people of the hill—
A fearful shriek of death is heard,
One sudden scream both loud and shrill.

And some have seen on stilly nights,
  And when the moon was clear and round,
Bubbles which to the surface swam
  And burst as if they held the sound.—

'Twas in the days ere hapless Charles
  Losing his crown had lost his head,
This tale is told of him who kept
  The inn upon the watershed:

He was a lowbred ruin'd man
  Whom lawless times set free from fear:
One evening to his house there rode
  A young and gentle cavalier.

With curling hair and linen fair
  And jewel-hilted sword he went;
The horse he rode he had ridden far,
  And he was with his journey spent.

He asked a lodging for the night,
  His valise from his steed unbound,
He let none bear it but himself
  And set it by him on the ground.

"Here's gold or jewels," thought the host,
  "That's carrying south to find the king."
He chattered many a loyal word,
  And scraps of royal airs gan sing.

His guest thereat grew more at ease
  And o'er his wine he gave a toast,
But little ate, and to his room
  Carried his sack behind the host.

"Now rest you well," the host he said,
  But of his wish the word fell wide;
Nor did he now forget his son
  Who fell in fight by Cromwell's side.

Revenge and poverty have brought
  Full gentler heart than his to crime;
And he was one by nature rude,
  Born to foul deeds at any time.

With unshod feet at dead of night
  In stealth he to the guest-room crept,
Lantern and dagger in his hand,
  And stabbed his victim while he slept.

But as he struck a scream there came,
  A fearful scream so loud and shrill:
He whelm'd the face with pillows o'er,
  And lean'd till all had long been still.

Then to the face the flame he held
  To see there should no life remain:—
When lo! his brutal heart was quell'd:
  'Twas a fair woman he had slain.

The tan upon her face was paint,
  The manly hair was torn away,
Soft was the breast that he had pierced;
  Beautiful in her death she lay.

His was no heart to faint at crime,
  Tho' half he wished the deed undone.
He pulled the valise from the bed
  To find what booty he had won.

He cut the straps, and pushed within
  His murderous fingers to their theft.
A deathly sweat came o'er his brow,
  He had no sense nor meaning left.

He touched not gold, it was not cold,
  It was not hard, it felt like flesh.
He drew out by the curling hair
  A young man's head, and murder'd fresh;

A young man's head, cut by the neck.
  But what was dreader still to see,
Her whom he had slain he saw again,
  The twain were like as like can be.

Brother and sister if they were,
  Both in one shroud they now were wound,—
Across his back and down the stair,
  Out of the house without a sound.

He made his way unto the tarn,
  The night was dark and still and dank;
The ripple chuckling neath the boat
  Laughed as he drew it to the bank.

Upon the bottom of the boat
  He laid his burden flat and low,
And on them laid the square sandstones
  That round about the margin go.

Stone upon stone he weighed them down,
  Until the boat would hold no more;
The freeboard now was scarce an inch:
  He stripp'd his clothes and push'd from shore.

All naked to the middle pool
  He swam behind in the dark night;
And there he let the water in
  And sank his terror out of sight.

He swam ashore, and donn'd his dress,
  And scraped his bloody fingers clean;
Ran home and on his victim's steed
  Mounted, and never more was seen

But to a comrade ere he died
  He told his story guess'd of none:
So from his lips the crime returned
  To haunt the spot where it was done.

1899

EMILY BRONTË

[August 20, 1818–December 19, 1848]

Emily Brontë, the greatest and most enigmatic of the Brontë sisters, was the daughter of a curate, Patrick Prunty, who changed his name on coming from Ireland to Hartshead-cum-Clifton in England. Her mother, Maria Branwell, died early of cancer, leaving six children, three of whom—Charlotte, Emily and Anne—distinguished themselves in the literary world; except for the only brother, Patrick Branwell, who was expected to be the genius of the family, but who died of delirium tremens, the other three made no claim to distinction. The children were left to themselves very often, and for recreation walked the bleak and wind-blown moors near Haworth, to which the family had moved from Hartshead. Emily was educated at home save for one miserable year spent in the Clergy Daughters' School at Cowan's Bridge, where the food was bad and the discipline harsh. In 1836 she accompanied Charlotte as a pupil to Miss Wooler's school at Dewsbury, and in 1842 to Brussels, where she studied modern languages for eight months at the Pensionnat Héger, until an aunt's death stopped their supply of money and forced their return home.

In 1845 Charlotte by accident discovered some poems of Emily's, and each of the three talented sisters learned that the others had been secretly composing. In 1846 they printed at their own expense a volume of poems by "Currer, Ellis and Acton Bell," employing their first initials in forming the pseudonyms. Two copies were sold. Branwell died in 1848, and hardly had Charlotte recovered from the breakdown occasioned by this when Emily's health began to fail. She had been ill for some time, but now her breathing became more labored and she suffered intense pain. Yet only two hours before her death she struggled out of bed and dressed herself before she would allow the doctor to be called. Such stoicism marked her entire life.

Emily's poems (she alone of the sisters was genuinely poetic) throw most illumination upon her spirit, while her lone and mighty novel, *Wuthering Heights*, darkens rather than resolves the mystery of her life. Her verse reveals a quasi-paganism, and in her passion for the moors one senses an almost mystical experience. Some of her poems must be placed high among the accomplishments of Englishwomen in literature.

THE PHILOSOPHER

Enough of thought, philosopher!
  Too long hast thou been dreaming
Unlightened, in this chamber drear,
  While summer's sun is beaming!
Space-sweeping soul, what sad refrain
Concludes thy musing once again?

"Oh, for the time when I shall sleep
  Without identity,
And never care how rain may steep,
  Or snow may cover me!
No promised heaven, these wild desires
  Could all, or half fufil;
No threatened hell, with quenchless fires,
  Subdue this quenchless will!"

"So said I, and still say the same;
Still, to my death, will say—
Three gods, within this little frame,
Are warring night and day;
Heaven could not hold them all, and yet
They all are held in me;
And must be mine till I forget
My present entity!
Oh, for the time, when in my breast
Their struggles will be o'er!
Oh, for the day, when I shall rest,
And never suffer more!"

"I saw a spirit standing, man,
Where thou dost stand—an hour ago,
And round his feet three rivers ran,
Of equal depth, and equal flow—
A golden stream—and one like blood,
And one like sapphire seemed to be;
But, where they joined their triple flood,
It tumbled in an inky sea.
The spirit sent his dazzling gaze
Down through that ocean's gloomy night;
Then, kindling all, with sudden blaze,
The glad deep sparkled wide and bright—
White as the sun, far, far more fair
Than its divided sources were!"

"And even for that spirit, seer,
I've watched and sought my lifetime long;
Sought him in heaven, hell, earth, and air,
An endless search, and always wrong.
Had I but seen his glorious eye
Once light the clouds that 'wilder me,
I ne'er had raised this coward cry
To cease to think, and cease to be;
I ne'er had called oblivion blest,
Nor stretching eager hands to death,
Implored to change for senseless rest
This sentient soul, this living breath.
Oh, let me die—that power and will
Their cruel strife may close;
And conquered good and conquering ill
Be lost in one repose!"

October, 1845

REMEMBRANCE

COLD in the earth—and the deep snow piled above thee,
Far, far removed, cold in the dreary grave!
Have I forgot, my only Love, to love thee,
Severed at last by Time's all-severing wave?

Now, when alone, do my thoughts no longer hover
Over the mountains, on that northern shore,
Resting their wings where heath and fern-leaves cover
Thy noble heart for ever, ever more?

Cold in the earth—and fifteen wild Decembers,
From those brown hills, have melted into spring:
Faithful, indeed, is the spirit that remembers
After such years of change and suffering!

Sweet Love of youth, forgive, if I forget thee,
While the world's tide is bearing me along;
Other desires and other hopes beset me,
Hopes which obscure, but cannot do thee wrong!

No later light has lightened up my heaven,
No second moon has ever shone for me;
All my life's bliss from thy dear life was given,
All my life's bliss is in the grave with thee.

But, when the days of golden dreams had perished,
And ev'n Despair was powerless to destroy;
Then did I learn how existence could be cherished,
Strengthened, and fed without the aid of joy.

Then did I check the tears of useless passion—
Weaned my young soul from yearning after thine;
Sternly denied its burning wish to hasten
Down to that tomb already more than mine.

And, even yet, I dare not let it languish,
Dare not indulge in memory's rapturous pain;
Once drinking deep of that divinest anguish,
How could I seek the empty world again?

March 3, 1845

TO IMAGINATION

WHEN weary with the long day's care,
And earthly change from pain to pain,
And lost, and ready to despair,

POEMS

BY

CURRER, ELLIS, AND ACTON

BELL.

LONDON:

AYLOTT AND JONES, 8, PATERNOSTER-ROW.

1846.

Title Page of *Poems* by the Brontë Sisters. (See Appendix I.)

Thy kind voice calls me back again,
Oh, my true friend! I am not lone,
While thou canst speak with such a tone!

So hopeless is the world without,
The world within I doubly prize;
Thy world, where guile and hate and doubt
And cold suspicion never rise;
Where thou and I and Liberty
Have undisputed sovereignty.

What matters it, that all around
Danger and guilt and darkness lie,
If but within our bosom's bound
We hold a bright, untroubled sky,
Warm with ten thousand mingled rays
Of suns that know no winter days?

Reason, indeed, may oft complain
For Nature's sad reality,
And tell the suffering heart how vain
Its cherished dreams must always be;
And Truth may rudely trample down
The flowers of Fancy, newly-blown:

But thou art ever there, to bring
The hovering vision back, and breathe
New glories o'er the blighted spring,
And call a lovelier Life from Death,
And whisper, with a voice divine,
Of real worlds, as bright as thine.

I trust not to thy phantom bliss,
Yet, still, in evening's quiet hour,
With never-failing thankfulness,
I welcome thee, Benignant Power,
Sure solacer of human cares,
And sweeter hope, when hope despairs!

1846

HOW CLEAR SHE SHINES!

How clear she shines! How quietly
I lie beneath her guardian light;
While heaven and earth are whispering me,
"To-morrow wake, but dream to-night."

* * *

The world is going; dark world, adieu!
Grim world, conceal thee till the day;
The heart thou canst not all subdue
Must still resist, if thou delay!

Thy love I will not, will not share;
Thy hatred only wakes a smile;
Thy griefs may wound—thy wrongs may tear,
But, oh, thy lies shall ne'er beguile!
While gazing on the stars that glow
Above me, in that stormless sea,
I long to hope that all the woe
Creation knows, is held in thee!

1846

TO A BLUEBELL

SACRED watcher, wave thy bells!
Fair hill-flower and woodland child,
Dear to me in deep green dells,
Dearest on the mountains wild.

Bluebell, even as all divine
I have seen my darling shine;
Bluebell, even as fair and frail
I have seen my darling fail.
Lift thy head and speak to me,
Soothing thoughts are breathed by thee.
Thus they whisper, "Summer's sun
Lights me till my life is done;
Would I rather choose to die
Under winter's stormy sky?

"Glad I bloom, and calm I fade,
Dews of heaven are round me stayed;
Mourner, mourner, dry thy tears,
Sorrow comes with lengthened years."

May 7, 1839

I AM THE ONLY BEING

I AM the only being whose doom
No tongue would ask, no eye would mourn;
I've never caused a thought of gloom,
A smile of joy, since I was born.

In secret pleasure, secret tears,
This changeful life has slipped away,
As friendless after eighteen years,
As lone as on my natal day.

There have been times, I cannot hide,
There have been times when this was dreary,
When my sad soul forgot its pride
And longed for one to love me here.

But those were in the early glow
Of feelings long subdued by care,
And they have died so long ago,
I hardly now believe they were.

First melted off the hope of youth,
Then fancy's rainbow fast withdrew;
And then experience told me truth
In mortal bosoms never grew.

'Twas grief enough to think mankind
All hollow, servile, insincere;
But worse to turn to my own mind,
And find the same corruption there.

May 17, 1839

I KNOW NOT HOW IT FALLS ON ME

I KNOW not how it falls on me,
This summer evening, hushed and lone;
Yet the faint wind comes soothingly
With something of an olden tone.

Forgive me if I've shunned so long
Your gentle greeting, earth and air!
But sorrow withers e'en the strong,
And who can fight against despair?

June 3, 1831

HOW LONG WILL YOU REMAIN?

"How long will you remain? The midnight hour
Has tolled its last stroke from the minster tower.
Come, come; the fire is dead, the lamp burns low;
Your eyelids droop, a weight is on your brow;
Your cold hands hardly hold the weary pen:
Come; morn will give recovered strength again."

"No; let me linger; leave me, let me be
A little longer in this reverie:
I'm happy now; and would you tear away
My blissful thought that never comes with day?
A vision dear, though false, for well my mind
Knows what a bitter waking waits behind."

"Can there be pleasure in this shadowy room,
With windows yawning on intenser gloom,
And such a dreary wind so bleakly sweeping
Round walls where only you are vigil keeping?
Besides, your face has not a sign of joy,
And more than tearful sorrow fills your eye.
Look on those woods, look on that mountain lorn,
And think how changed they'll be to-morrow morn:
The doors of heaven expanding bright and blue;
The leaves, the green grass, sprinkled with the dew;
And white mists rising on the river's breast,
And wild birds bursting from their songless nest,
And your own children's merry voices chasing
The phantom ghost that pleasure has been raising."

"Ay, speak of these! but can you tell me why
Day breathes such beauty over earth and sky,
And waking sounds revive, restored again
To hearts that all night long have throbbed with pain?
Is it not that the sunshine and the wind
Lure from itself the woeful woe-worn mind,
And all the joyous music breathing by,
And all the splendours of that cloudless sky,
Re-give him shadowy gleams of infancy
And draw his tired gaze from futurity?"

August 12, 1839

AT CASTLE WOOD

THE day is done, the winter sun
Is setting in its sullen sky,
And drear the course that has been run,
And dim the hearts that slowly die.

No star will light my coming night,
No morn of hope for me will shine;
I mourn not Heaven would blast my sight,
And I ne'er longed for joys divine.

Through life's hard task I did not ask
Celestial aid, celestial cheer;
I saw my fate without its mask,
And met it too without a tear.

And [illegible], [illegible], messenger
Thy presence waked a thrilling tone
That comforts me while thou art here
And will sustain when thou art gone
Emily Jane Brontë December – 1837

Song by Julius Angora

Awake! awake! how loud the stormy morning
Calls up to life the nations resting round
Arise, arise, is it the voice of mourning
That breaks our slumber with so wild a sound

The voice of mourning? listen to its pealing
That shout of triumph drowns the sigh of woe
Each tortured heart forgets its wonted feeling
Each faded cheek resumes its longlost glow

Our souls are full of gladness, God has given
Our arms to victory, our foes to death;
The crimson [illegible] waves its sheet [in heaven]

A Page of Emily Brontë's Manuscript. (See Appendix I.)

The grief that prest my aching breast
Was heavier far than earth can be;
And who would dread eternal rest
When labour's hour was agony?

Dark falls the fear of this despair
On spirits born of happiness;
But I was bred the mate of care,
The foster child of sore distress.

No sighs for me, no sympathy,
No wish to keep my soul below;
The heart is dead in infancy,
Unwept-for let the body go.

February 2, 1844

HARP OF WILD AND DREAM-LIKE STRAIN

Harp of wild and dream-like strain,
When I touch thy strings,
Why dost thou repeat again
Long-forgotten things?

Harp, in other earlier days
I could sing to thee,
And not one of all my lays
Vexed my memory.

But now if I awake a note
That gave me joy before,
Sounds of sorrow from thee float,
Changing evermore.

Yet still steeped in memory's dyes
They come sailing on,
Darkening all my summer skies,
Shutting out my sun.

THAT DREARY LAKE

That dreary lake, that moonlight sky,
That wan moon struggling through the cloud,
That sullen murmur whispering by,
As if it dared not speak aloud,
Fall on my heart so sadly now,
Whither my joys so lonely flow.
Touch them not, they bloom and smile,
But their roots are withering all the while.

WARNING AND REPLY

In the earth, the earth, thou shalt be laid,
A grey stone standing over thee;
Black mould beneath thee spread,
And black mould to cover thee.

"Well, there is rest there,
So fast come thy prophecy;
The time when my sunny hair
Shall with grass roots entwined be."

But cold, cold is that resting-place,
Shut out from joy and liberty,
And all who loved thy living face
Will shrink from it shudderingly.

"Not so! Here the world is chill,
And sworn friends fall from me:
But there—they will own me still,
And prize my memory."

Farewell, then, all that love,
All that deep sympathy:
Sleep on; Heaven laughs above,
Earth never misses thee.

Turf-sod and tombstone drear
Part human company;
One heart breaks only—here,
But that heart was worthy thee!

1850

NO COWARD SOUL IS MINE

No coward soul is mine,
No trembler in the world's storm-troubled sphere:
I see Heaven's glories shine,
And faith shines equal, arming me from fear.

O God within my breast,
Almighty, ever-present Deity!
Life—that in me has rest,
As I—undying Life—have power in Thee!

Vain are the thousand creeds
That move men's hearts, unutterably vain,
Worthless as withered weeds,
Or idle froth amid the boundless main,

To waken doubt in one
Holding so fast by Thine infinity;
So surely anchored on
The steadfast rock of immortality.

With wide-embracing love
Thy spirit animates eternal years,
Pervades and broods above,
Changes, sustains, dissolves, creates, and rears.

Though earth and man were gone,
And suns and universes ceased to be,
And Thou wert left alone,
Every existence would exist in Thee.

There is not room for Death,
Nor atom that his might could render void:
Thou—THOU art Being and Breath,
And what THOU art may never be destroyed.

1850

THOMAS EDWARD BROWN

[May 5, 1830–October 29, 1897]

THOMAS EDWARD BROWN, the son of a clergyman, was born in Douglas on the Isle of Man. Upon leaving King William's College he became a servitor at Christ Church, Oxford, a position which he considered menial, but which did not keep him from making a record that brought him a double first class and a fellowship at Oriel. After taking orders he served for a short time as vice-principal of King William's College in his native Isle and later as head master of the Crypt School, Gloucester, where he made a deep impression on young William E. Henley. In 1863 he became assistant master under Dr. Percival at Clifton College, Bristol, which post he held until 1892. The remainder of his life he passed on the Isle of Man. His death occurred suddenly at Clifton College where he had gone to make a talk to the boys of his old school. His principal volumes of poetry are *Fo'c's'le Yarns, Including Betsy Lee* (1881), *The Doctor and Other Poems* (1887), *The Manx Witch and Other Poems* (1889), and *Old John and Other Poems* (1893).

PEGGY'S WEDDING

"Is that you, Peggy? my goodness me!
And so dark still I can hardly see!
Wait, woman, wait!
I'll come down: ye needn' go on hommerin' at such a rate.
Here's the master snorin'
Like a mill, and you to be breakin' the door in—
It's just disthractin', that's what it is—
Aisy, woman! yis! yis!—
There's people'll snore—where's that perricut?[1]
There's people'll hommer—my gough! that slut!
I'm comin'! I'm comin'!
God bless the woman!
I navar heard such a row—

[1] Petticoat.

"Aw dear! aw dear! aw, the craythur! aw, poor Peggy, what's the matter with you now?
Come in! come in! the sowl! the sowl!
What is it, Peggy, what? and where have you left Dan Cowle?
Is he outside in the street?—well, where is he then?
Did you call at the halfway-house? did he get—aw, bless these men!
Did he fall on the road? *No*, ye say, *no?*
Well then where did he go?
Is he lyin' in the ditch?
Did he lave you, or did you lave him—which?
You left *him?*
So I suppose it's not a man you're wantin' at all, but a cherubim?
Aye! aye!
Middlin' high!

"And you that were married only yesterday, and the weddin' out of this house—
To be comin' home in the mornin' all ragg'd and rumpled like a reg'lar trouse[1]—
Peggy, Peggy! *You'd like to blow the fire, just to feel*
You're at home again—eh, Peggy? Don't kneel! don't kneel!
Don't be foolish, Peggy. There! take the bellows,
And blow away!
And we'll have a cup o' tay,
And then you'll tell us.
Why—Dan Cowle! Dan Ballabroo!
A dacent man, and well-to-do!
Dan! Dan Cowle! dear heart!
And the beautiful ye went away in the cart!
And you've tuk and left him! left Dan!
Left the man!"

"*Man!* did ye say? aw Misthriss, Misthriss! what are ye talkin'?
Man! do ye call that craythur a man, because he's a thing that's walkin'
On two legs, and a tongue in his head? a beautiful surt[2]
Of a man—you call him a man, I call him a dirt!
That's what I call him—a dirt, and a sneak, and a dunkey—
Man! if that chap's a man, he's a cross 'twix a man and a monkey!
And a touch of a divil, and a touch of a fool . . .
Listen, Misthriss, listen! We warn' half-way up Barrule,
When I thought he'd ha' stayed a bit—and only raisonable he shud—
At Kinvigs's—bein' a thing lek that's general understood—
What's halfway-houses for, I'd like to know—
Just so!
You wouldn' be agen[3] that?
What?

"Certainly! and company waitin'—and just a drop to warm a body—
And dear me! what is there in half a glass of rum, or a whole glass, for the matter of that, to harm a body?
And well you know it isn' the dhrink I regard—
Well you know that—but still a body's hardly prepar'd
To pass the only public-house on the road, drivin' home on your weddin' night—
It isn' right,
Nor correck, nor friendly, nor in any surt of a concatenation
Lek accordin' to your station—
And disappintin' people that way, when they're trustin'
Your proper feelin's, is quite disgustin'.

"So I lays my hand on his arm, just by way of signifyin'—
Nothin' more—and behould ye! he cocks hisself up as stiff and as dignifyin'
And rip! and rup! and chip! and chup!
And 'There's nobody up,' he says. Nobody up?
And glasses jinglin', and windows blazin',
And people comin' out, and shoutin' amazin'
To stop! But no! but sticks his elbers like skewers in a body—
'What!' I says, 'not a glass of toddy?
Just for neighbourly dacency?'
'It's surprisin' how early they're goin' to bed,' says he.
'Goin' to bed!' says I. 'Yes,' he says—middlin' snarly—
'Kinvigs's was allis early,' he says, 'partic'lar early'—
And his ould hoss gallopin', and heisin' his hind-quarters, and workin'
Like a see-saw, and bumpin' and jerkin',
And sent me flyin', with my head in the bottom of the cart, and my feet in the air,
And the rest of me—anywhere.

"So he puts out his hand—
'Bless my sowl!' he says, 'I thought it was gone!'
'What?' says I. 'The box,' he says, maenin' my box, and my weddin' bonnet
Smashed to jammy—'I wish you'd sit upon it,'
He says—the box, of coorse! So I thought I'd be a little lovin'
And that—and I comes up lek gradjal, lek shiftin' and shovin'

[1] Slattern. [2] Sort. [3] Against.

Lek agen him in a way. And I says, 'I'd like to be with you,' says I,
'My own husband,' I says; for I thought it better to try
Was there just a taste
Of anything of a husband in him. So he put his arm round my waist—
Not round either—for he couldn' do that—
Not for the stout I am, bein' allis a gintale figger, but just like a lath—
Flat
Agen the back o' my stays, and not the smallest curl
Or squeeze in the ould pump-handle, not the smallest in the worl'—
And his eyes on the box—and 'There it's goin'!'
He says, and waein' and woin'—
And as restless! And then we got on the mountain; and the ling
Was smellin' very sweet in the dark, and a stream began ting-ting-ting
Down the other way—very pleasant, and it got couldher,
And I thought it was only a 'spectable thing to put my head on his shouldher.

"O dear! he got as crabbit
As an ould buck rabbit;
And he hitched and he hunched, and he cribbed and he crunched,
Till he was all bunched
In a lump; and anyway his blades that sharp
And snaggy you might as well ha' leaned your head on the backbone of a carp.

"So I didn' care, and I sat up as straight
And as indepandin'. It was gettin' late
When we come to his house; and there was a falla theer standin' on the look-out
On the very top of the midden, and jumps down, and grips the hoss, and gives a big shout,
And 'Look here!' he says, 'who's goin' to pay me?' 'Pay!'
Thinks I—and this ould fool goin' seerchin' away
In all his pockets—and gev a start,
And 'Bless my heart!'
He says, 'hev I lost it? hev I lost it?' and twisses and wriggles
Hisself into knots—and the other chap stands and sniggles—
A young chap—And 'Dear me!' says Dan, 'it must ha' dropt out on the road comin'—
It's very disthressin',' he says. 'Faith then! you're a rummin,'
Says the chap, and like to buss [1]—
'What's the use o' talkin'?' says Dan Cowle, 'I've lost my puss.
Where's your puss, Peggy? maybe,' he says, 'you'll not mind
Payin' the man,' he says—'if you 'll be so kind,'
He says—but oh! that creepin', and that sneakin', and that slewin', and that screwin',
Like a conger just. And 'What's a doin'?'
Says I; 'isn' it your own cart you got?'
'Well——no——it's not,
He says, 'I must confess—
The fact of the matter is,' he says,
'My own cart is bruk very bad,
And I borrowed this one for the occasion.' So I paid the lad.

"'Aye, aye! his cart is bruk very bad,' says the chap,
'Likewise his trap,
And the phaeton, and the barooch, and the jantin'-car, and the family coach-and-four'—
And he gev a roor
Out of hisself, this young divil—
And 'Hurrah for the weddiners!' he says. 'Be civil! be civil!'
Says Dan, 'be civil, young man, it would well become ye'—
But says I—'Take your money and your cart,' I says, 'and be off with ye, ye scum ye!
Be off!' I says, 'stir your stumps!'
(These Foxdale lumps [2]
Is pirriful.[3]) And Dan with the box on the street, and pokin'
The key in the door—and, you know, I seen the chimbley wasn' smokin',
Nor nothin'—nor no cowhouse about that I could see,
Nor no garden, nor a bush, let alone a tree—
But just a crock
Standin' on a rock,
And water runnin' in it very free

[1] Burst. [2] Lads. [3] Pitiful, detestable.

At the gable, and slishin' and slushin', and muckin' the street
Under one's feet.

"And this is the man that tould me he'd make me
So comfible!
But still
You'll not mistake me,
You know me, Misthriss, don't ye? and you know I wouldn' flinch,
No, not even if I was deceived—no, not an inch!
On I'd go, through the smooth and the rough,
Content enough—
For richer for poorer, for better for wuss—
Lost his puss!
Had he? lost two! lost twenty!
Give me a man with a lovin' heart, Misthriss, with a lovin' heart—
That's plenty—
Plenty for me—navar mind the cart—
With a lovin' heart, and some wit about him—
And I'd navar doubt him,
Misthriss—no! *For better for wuss*—
Them's the words, and didn' the Pazon say them? And I'd nuss
His childher, and I'd work, and I'd slave, and I'd die
Before I'd be beat—and still a lie
Is a dirty thing—fore or aft,
As the sailors is sayin'—
But listen again—
Misthriss! Misthriss! you don't know half.

"So we got in, however, and he groped about, and he found a flint-and-steel,
And he skinned his ould knuckles all like a priddha [1] peel,
Streck-streckin' away; and, when he gor [2] a light at last,
You navar seen such a rookery. A dresser there was—
Yis—but hardly a plate or a bason, or any other surt o' war',
And a hape of mouldy turmits [3] in a corner there—could, comfortless things they are—
And a rot-hole,[4] or a shot-hole, I don't know which, and I don't care etha',[5]

[1] Potato. [2] Got. [3] Turnips.
[4] Rat-hole. [5] Either.

And a barrel that looked like male, with a flag or a slate on the top of it, and a medha,[1]
And a pot, and nothin' in it, and no fire, if there had been, and as for bed or beddin'—
Well, I dedn' throuble, no, faith, I dedn'.

"It was a house that if you were inside you'd see about as much sky as roof,
A surt o' mixthar o' the two, and a touch of harry-long-legses and spiders—aw, it's the troof! [2] it's the troof,
The troof I'm tellin'! And the scraas [3] hangin' in rags and strings of dirt as black
You couldn' tell were they scraas, or strips tore from a rotten ould sack,
Or nettin' or somethin'. And I can tell ye the chap begun, as a body might say,
To look rather ashamed of hisself—I think so —in a way—
Yis—he didn' look at me for a bit at all,
But cocked his face agen the wall.

"And—'It's too late,' he says, 'it's too late for supper, I suppose'—
And ye might have sniffed and sniffed till ye straint your nose
Afore you'd ha' got a smell of supper in yandhar place—
But he turned at last, and I saw his face—
Workin', workin', workin' most terrible,
And screwin' the eye, and workin' still—
And—'Let's sit down a bit,' he says, and he studdied the candle, if ye plaze, and he looks up as innocent as a linnet,
And he says, 'That's a nice puss you've got,' he says; 'how much is there in it?'
And I tould him £4:16s. and 2½d. farlin'—
So he says, 'That's a nice little bit o' money, my darlin'—
Let's see it,' he says.
So I gev it to him, ye know;
And he counted it out, I tell ye, every coin of it, very slow—
Very slow he counted—and then—what d'ye think?
Whips it in his pocket! 'A nice lump of jink!'
Says Dan; and he snuggled up closer to me, and he began to fiddle and fiddle,
Lek tryin' to span me round the middle—

[1] Small, one-handled tub. [2] Truth.
[3] Strips of sod laid on the rafters under the thatch.

Some surt o' coortin'? thinks I, *he's improvin'*, *I doubt*—
The ould villyan! He was just tryin' to find out
Had I any more stitched up in my stays!
And a man with such ways—
Would you call him a man? now would ye, Misthriss? would ye, though?
That was the fiddlin'—aye! he said it, he said it hisself, the ould crow!
Yis, and his dirty ould mouth all of a pucker, and grippin' and nippin',
And declarin' he felt the shillin's slippin'
Between the quiltin's—aw dear! aw dear!
But I was enough for him—navar fear!

"I says—'This is no place for me,' I says; and up I jumps—
'I'm off,' I says; and he rattles his ould stumps—
And—'Off?' he says—'Why you've not opened your box yet!'
'Clear out o' the road!' I says. 'I hevn' seen your frocks yet,'
He says, 'nor the sheetin' nor nothin'!—just give us that key—
It's every bit my proppity!' he says. 'Out o' the way!'
I says, and I gript the box. But if I gript it, he gript it, and he shouted and bawled,
And backards and forrards we tugged and we hauled;
And we staggered this way, and we staggered that way,
And higgledy-piggledy, and I cannot tell what way—
But I gev him a run in on the dresser, and his ould back bent,
And——down he went!

"And the crockery—what there was—all smashed—well to be sure!
And the turmits rowlin' on the floor—
So the box was mine, and I out on the door.
'Murdher! tieves!' and he run after me full trot—
'You're a robber!' he says; 'you've robbed me! everything you got
Belongs to me—I'll bring a shuit,' he says; 'I'll bring a shuit
For damagers!' he says—the ould brute—
'I'll have your life!' he says,
'Ar'n' you my wife?' he says—
'Murdher!' he says, 'murdher!'—'*Murdher*—your granny,'
I says—'Good-bye, Dan Cowle! good-bye, Danny!'
And I left him standin' in the road; and here I am, as you see—
And, Misthriss! no more weddin's, aw good sakes! no, no more weddin's for me!"

ST. BEE'S HEAD

I HAVE seen cliffs that met the ocean foe
As a black bison, with his crouching front
And neck back-coiled, awaits the yelping hunt,
That reck not of his horns protruding low.

And others I have seen with calm disdain
O'erlook the immediate strife, and gaze afar:
Eternity was in that gaze; the jar
Of temporal broil assailed not its domain.

Some cliffs are full of pity: in the sweep
Of their bluff brows a kindly tolerance waits,
And smiles upon the petulant sea, that rates,
And fumes, and scolds against the patient steep.

And some are joyous with a hearty joy,
And in mock-earnest wage the busy fight:
So may you see a giant with delight
Parrying the buffets of a saucy boy!

Remonstrant others stand—a wild surprise
Glares from their crests against the insolent throng;
Half frightened, half indignant at the wrong,
They look appealing to those heedless skies.

And other some are of a sleepy mood,
Who care not if the tempest does its worst:
What is't to them if bounding billows burst,
Or winds assail them with their jeerings rude?

But like not unto any one of these
Is that tall crag, that northward guards the bay,
And stands, a watchful sentry, night and day
Above the pleasant downs of old St. Bee's.

Straight-levelled as the bayonet's dread array,
His shelves abide the charge. Come one, come all!
The blustering surges at his feet shall fall
And writhe and sob their puny lives away!

1893

AN OXFORD IDYLL

Ah little mill, you're rumbling still,
Ah sunset flecked with gold!
Ah deepening tinge, ah purple fringe
Of lilac as of old!
Ah hawthorn hedge, ah light-won pledge
Of kisses warm and plenty,
When she was true, and twenty-two,
And I was two-and-twenty.
I don't know how she broke her vow—
She said that I was "horty";
And there's the mill a goin' still,
And I am five-and-forty.
And sooth to tell, 'twas just as well,
Her aitches were uncertain;
Her ways though nice, not point-device;
Her father liked his "Burton."
But there's a place you cannot trace,
So spare the fond endeavour—
A cloudless sky, where Kate and I
Are twenty-two for ever.

Magdalen Walk
1893

TO K. H.

O far withdrawn into the lonely West,
To whom those Irish hills are as a grave
Cairn-crowned, the dead sun's monument,
And this fair English land but vaguely guessed—
Thee, lady, by the melancholy wave
I greet, where salt winds whistle through the bent,
And harsh sea-holly buds beneath thy foot are pressed.

What is thy thought? 'Tis not the obvious scene
That holds thee with its grand simplicity
Of natural forms. Thou musest rather
What larger life may be, what richer sheen
Of social gloss in lands beyond the sea,
What nobler cult than where, around thy father,
The silent fishers pray in chapel small and mean.

Yes, thou art absent far—thy soul has slipt
The visual bond, and thou art lowly kneeling
Upon a pavement with the sacred kisses
Of emerald and ruby gleamings lipped;
And down the tunnelled nave the organ, pealing,
Blows music-storm, and with far-floating blisses
Gives tremor to the bells, and shakes the dead men's crypt.

This is thy thought; for this thou heav'st the sigh.
Yet, lady, look around thee! hast thou not
The life of real men, the home,
The tribe, and for a temple that old sky,
Whereto the sea intones the polyglot
Of water-pipes antiphonal, and the dome,
Round-arched, goes up to God in lapis lazuli?

INDWELLING

If thou couldst empty all thyself of self,
Like to a shell dishabited,
Then might He find thee on the Ocean shelf,
And say—"This is not dead,"—
And fill thee with Himself instead.

But thou art all replete with very *thou*,
And hast such shrewd activity,
That, when He comes, He says:—"This is enow
Unto itself—'Twere better let it be:
It is so small and full, there is no room for Me."

IN MEMORIAM

(Paul Bridson)

Take him, O Braddan, for he loved thee well—
Take him, kind mother of my own dear dead!
And let him lay his head
On thy soft breast,
And rest—
Rest.
He loved thee well; and thee, my father, thee
Also he loved. O, meet him! reassure
That heart thou prov'dst so pure—
Whisper release!
And peace—
Peace!

O countrymen, believe me! here is laid
A Manxman's heart the simplest and the truest:
O Spring, when thou renewest
Thy sunny hours,
Bring flowers—
Flowers!
And bring them of thy sweetest
And bring them of thy meetest
And, till God's trumpet wake him,
Take him, O Braddan, take him!

CANTICLE

When all the sky is pure
My soul takes flight,
Serene and sure,
Upward—till at the height
She weighs her wings,
And sings.

But when the heaven is black,
And west-winds sigh,
Beat back, beat back,
She has no strength to try
The drifting rain
Again.

So cheaply baffled! see!
The field is bare—
Behold a tree—
Is't not enough? Sit there,
Thou foolish thing,
And sing!

CAROL

Three kings from out the Orient
For Judah's land were fairly bent,
To find the Lord of grace;
And as they journeyed pleasantlie,
A star kept shining in the sky,
To guide them to the place.
"O Star," they cried, "by all confest
Withouten dreed, the loveliest!"

The first was Melchior to see,
The emperour hight of Arabye,
An aged man, I trow:
He sat upon a rouncy bold,
Had taken of the red red gold,
The babe for to endow.
"O Star," he cried. . . .

The next was Gaspar, young and gay,
That held the realm of far Cathay—
Our Jesus drew him thence—
Yclad in silk from head to heel,
He rode upon a high cameel,
And bare the frankincense.
"O Star," he cried. . . .

The last was dusky Balthasar,
That rode upon a dromedar—
His coat was of the fur.
Dark-browed he came from Samarkand,
The Christ to seek, and in his hand
Upheld the bleeding myrrh.
"O Star," he cried, "by all confest
Withouten dreed, the loveliest."

CLIMBING

When I would get me to the upper fields,
I look if anywhere
A man be found who craves what joyaunce yields
The keen thin air,
Who loves the rapture of the height,
And fain would snatch with me a perilous delight.

I wait, and linger on the village street,
And long for one to come,
And say:—"The morning's bright, it is not meet
That thou the hum

Of vulgar life shouldst leave, and seek the view
Alone from those great peaks; I surely will go too."

But not to me comes ever any man;
Or, if he come, dull sleep
Still thickens in his eyes, so that to scan
The beckoning steep
He has no power; and of its scornful cone
Unconscious sits him down, and I go on alone.

Yet children are before me on the slope,
Their dew-bedabbled prints
Press the black fern-roots naked; sunny hope
Darts red, and glints
Upon their hair; but, devious, they remain
Among the bilberry beds, and I go on again.

And so there is no help for it, no mate
To share the arduous way:
Natheless I must ascend ere it grow late,
And, dim and gray, 28
The final cloud obstruct my soul's endeavour,
And I see nothing more for ever and for ever.

VESPERS

O BLACKBIRD, what a boy you are!
How you do go it!
Blowing your bugle to that one sweet star—
How you do blow it!
And does she hear you, blackbird boy, so far?
Or is it wasted breath?
"Good Lord! she is so bright
To-night!"
The blackbird saith.

O GOD TO THEE I YIELD

O GOD to Thee I yield
The gift Thou givest most precious, most divine!
Yet to what field
I must resign
His little feet
That wont to be so fleet,
I muse. O, joy to think
On what soft brink
Of flood he plucks the daffodils,
On what empurpled hills
He stands, Thy kiss all fresh upon his brow,
And wonders, if his father sees him now!

SAD! SAD!

O, SAD when grass is green,
O, sad when blue-bells blow,
Sad, sad 'mid lily sheen,
Laburnum's rippled glow,
And all the things that grow,
And are not sad—
Sad! sad!

O, sad when lambkins skip,
O, sad when children play,
Sad, sad, when to my lip
Is pressed the dewy may,
And all the bright things say:—
"Why art thou sad?"
Sad! sad!

Is it some tricksy Puck
That makes me causeless dole?
Or does some vampire suck
The blood from out my soul?
Or is it joy diviner,
Joy echoing in a minor,
Joy vibrant to its pole,
That seems but sad?—
Sad! sad!

Is it the ebbing ghost
Of God that leaves me dry
Upon a weary coast,
Beneath a burning sky?
Is it His voice afar
That booms upon the bar,
And makes me sigh,
And makes me sad?
Sad! sad!

Or does the old travail-pain
Resume the mother-*geist?*
In some far orb again
Is boundless ransom priced
For others than for us?
In Mars, or Uranus,
They crucify the Christ?
So am I sad—
Sad! sad!

One thing appears to me—
The work is not complete;
One world I know, and see
It is not at His feet—

Not, not! Is this the sum?
Not, not! the Heaven is dumb—
I bear His stigmata
Or not—ah, who shall say?
Only it is most meet
That I be sad—
Sad! sad!

MY GARDEN

A GARDEN is a lovesome thing, God wot!
Rose plot,
Fringed pool,
Ferned grot—
The veriest school
Of peace; and yet the fool
Contends that God is not—
Not God! in gardens! when the eve is cool?
Nay, but I have a sign;
'Tis very sure God walks in mine.

1893

DREAMS

IT looks as if in dreams the soul was free,
No bodily limit checks its absolute play;
Then why doth it not use its liberty,
And clear a certain way
To further truth beyond the actual sea?

It is not so; for when, with loosened grip,
The warder sense unlocks the visible hold,
Then will my soul from forth its chamber slip,
An idiot blithe and bold,
And into vacancy of folly skip;

Or aimless wander on the poppied floor
Of gaudy fields, or, scarce upon the street,
Return unto the grim, familiar door,
And, coward, crave retreat,
As who had never been outside before.

What boots it that I hold the chartered space,
If I but fill it with th' accustomed forms,
And load its breathless essence with the trace
Of casual-risen storms,
And drag my chain along the lovely place?

O, but if God would make a deep suspense,
And draw me perfect from th' adhesive sheath;
If all the veils and swathings of pretence,
Dropt from me, sunk beneath,
Then would I get me very far from hence.

I'd come to Him with one swift arrow-dart,
Aimed at the zenith of th' o'erbrooding blue;
Straight to the centre of His awful heart
The flight long-winged and true
Should bear me rapt through all the spheres that part.

But as it is, it is a waste of rest.
God uses not the occasion: on the rock
Stands prone my soul, a diver lean undrest,
And looks, and fears the shock,
And turns and hides its shame with some poor sorry jest.

PREPARATION

HAST thou a cunning instrument of play,
'Tis well; but see thou keep it bright,
And tuned to primal chords, so that it may
Be ready day and night.
For when He comes thou know'st not, who shall say:—
"These virginals are apt"; and try a note,
And sit, and make sweet solace of delight,
That men shall stand to listen on the way,
And all the room with heavenly music float.

ELIZABETH BARRETT BROWNING

[March 6, 1806–June 29, 1861]

ELIZABETH BARRETT, eldest of the eleven children of Edward Barrett, was born at Coxhoe Hall, near Durham, and spent a most happy childhood at the beautiful estate at Hope End, Herefordshire, where her family settled in 1809. When she was thirteen her father printed fifty copies of her *Battle of Marathon*, an "epic poem" of four books. Two years later she received an injury to her spine, which contributed to the invalidism from which she suffered the rest of her life. In 1832 her father, anticipating the Emancipation Act of the next year, freed the slaves on his West Indian estates, gave up his place at Hope End, and took his family to Sidmouth, in Devonshire. Three years later the family removed to London, settling first at Gloucester Place and then at "50 Wimpole Street," a big, gloomy house which Elizabeth called "Newgate turned inside out." In the thick air of London she developed tuberculosis which, together with her injury, kept her almost entirely indoors. Her oldest brother, Edward, who understood her as did no other member of the family, insisted that she must go to a milder climate and himself took her to Torquay. The trip was a tragical failure, however, for Edward was accidentally drowned, and Elizabeth was so prostrated by bodily illness and mental anguish that her life was in grave danger. For several years she was confined to her room, virtually the prisoner of her over-apprehensive father, whose insistence that her invalidism was hopeless went a long way to make it so.

In the intervals of respite from her suffering she wrote, and in 1844 she published two volumes of poems dedicated to her father with the hope that he would "accept the inscription of these volumes, the exponents of a few years of an existence which has been sustained and comforted by you as well as given." One of the poems in these volumes, *Lady Geraldine's Courtship*, contains a reference to Robert Browning, listing him with such great ones as Spenser, Petrarch, Wordsworth, and Tennyson. When Browning, who had been traveling in Italy, returned to England, he was "eagerly grateful" for this reference, and in January 1845 he wrote her a letter in which he said, "I love your verses with all my heart, dear Miss Barrett, . . . and I love you too." The very next night Elizabeth wrote to a friend: "I had a letter from Browning the poet last night which threw me into ecstasies." For several months the two carried on a discreet epistolary courtship the exact nature of which was probably not understood by the lady, inasmuch as she had brought it about by begging Browning to criticize her poems. The only conclusion to such a flow of letters as passed between the poets was a meeting, and finally in answer to Robert's oft-repeated request Elizabeth set the day when he might call—May 20, 1845. This first call Browning followed up with a succession of weekly visits at Miss Barrett's home, and on September 12, 1846, they were married—secretly, because of the violent opposition of Miss Barrett's father to the idea of marriage for any of his children. Within a week they left England—secretly again—the raging father, when he found it out, forbidding the mention of Elizabeth's name in his presence, and vowing that there would never be a reconciliation. The aged Wordsworth's remark on the flight of the lovers was final and humorously satisfying to buzzing London-town. "Well!" he said. "I hope they understand each other; no one else can."

After a brief stay in Paris to enable Mrs. Browning to recover from the excitement of her sudden flight and from illness brought on by the rough channel passage, they went on to Pisa. From Pisa they went to Florence and settled in Casa Guidi, which was their home until the death of Mrs. Browning fifteen years later.

In *Sonnets from the Portuguese* (1847), Mrs. Browning tells with great feeling and yet with great restraint the story of her companionship and love-making with Robert Browning. Among her other volumes are *Casa Guidi Windows* (1851), *Aurora Leigh* (1857), and *Last Poems* (1862).

THE DESERTED GARDEN

I MIND me in the days departed,
How often underneath the sun
With childish bounds I used to run
To a garden long deserted.

The beds and walks were vanished quite;
And wheresoe'er had struck the spade,
The greenest grasses Nature laid
To sanctify her right.

I called the place my wilderness,
For no one entered there but I;
The sheep looked in, the grass to espy,
And passed it ne'ertheless.

The trees were interwoven wild,
And spread their boughs enough about
To keep both sheep and shepherd out,
But not a happy child.

Adventurous joy it was for me!
I crept beneath the boughs, and found
A circle smooth of mossy ground
Beneath a poplar-tree.

Old garden rose-trees hedged it in,
Bedropt with roses waxen-white
Well satisfied with dew and light,
And careless to be seen.

Long years ago it might befall,
When all the garden flowers were trim,
The grave old gardener prided him
On these the most of all.

Some lady, stately overmuch,
Here moving with a silken noise,
Has blushed beside them at the voice
That likened her to such.

And these, to make a diadem,
She often may have plucked and twined,
Half-smiling as it came to mind
That few would look at *them*.

Oh, little thought that lady proud,
A child would watch her fair white rose,
When buried lay her whiter brows,
And silk was changed for shroud!

Nor thought that gardener (full of scorns
For men unlearned and simple phrase),
A child would bring it all its praise
By creeping through the thorns!

To me upon my low moss seat,
Though never a dream the roses sent
Of science or love's compliment,
I ween they smelt as sweet.

It did not move my grief to see
The trace of human step departed:
Because the garden was deserted,
The blither place for me!

Friends, blame me not! a narrow ken
Has childhood 'twixt the sun and sward;
We draw the moral afterward,
We feel the gladness then.

And gladdest hours for me did glide
In silence at the rose-tree wall:
A thrush made gladness musical
Upon the other side.

Nor he nor I did e'er incline
To peck or pluck the blossoms white;
How should I know but roses might
Lead lives as glad as mine?

To make my hermit-home complete,
I brought clear water from the spring
Praised in its own low murmuring,
And cresses glossy wet.

And so, I thought, my likeness grew
(Without the melancholy tale)
To "gentle hermit of the dale,"
And Angelina too.

For oft I read within my nook
Such minstrel stories; till the breeze
Made sounds poetic in the trees,
And then I shut the book.

If I shut this wherein I write
I hear no more the wind athwart
Those trees, nor feel that childish heart
Delighting in delight.

My childhood from my life is parted,
My footstep from the moss which drew
Its fairy circle round: anew
The garden is deserted.

Another thrush may there rehearse
The madrigals which sweetest are;
No more for me! myself afar
Do sing a sadder verse.

Ah me, ah me! when erst I lay
In that child's-nest so greenly wrought,
I laughed unto myself, and thought
"The time will pass away."

And still I laughed, and did not fear
But that, whene'er was past away
The childish time, some happier play
My womanhood would cheer.

I knew the time would pass away,
And yet, beside the rose-tree wall,
Dear God, how seldom, if at all,
Did I look up to pray!

The time is past; and now that grows
The cypress high among the trees,
And I behold white sepulchres,
As well as the white rose,—

When graver, meeker thoughts are given,
And I have learnt to lift my face,
Reminded how earth's greenest place
The color draws from heaven,—

It something saith for earthly pain,
But more for Heavenly promise free,
That I who was, would shrink to be
That happy child again.

1838

CONSOLATION

All are not taken; there are left behind
Living Belovèds, tender looks to bring
And make the daylight still a happy thing,
And tender voices, to make soft the wind:
But if it were not so—if I could find
No love in all the world for comforting,
Nor any path but hollowly did ring
Where "dust to dust" the love from life disjoined,
And if, before those sepulchres unmoving
I stood alone (as some forsaken lamb
Goes bleating up the moors in weary dearth),
Crying, "Where are ye, O my loved and loving?"—
I know a Voice would sound, "Daughter, I AM.
Can I suffice for HEAVEN and not for earth?"

1838

COWPER'S GRAVE

I

It is a place where poets crowned may feel the heart's decaying;
It is a place where happy saints may weep amid their praying;
Yet let the grief and humbleness as low as silence languish:
Earth surely now may give her calm to whom she gave her anguish.

II

O poets, from a maniac's tongue was poured the deathless singing!
O Christians, at your cross of hope a hopeless hand was clinging!
O men, this man in brotherhood your weary paths beguiling,
Groaned inly while he taught you peace, and died while ye were smiling!

III

And now, what time ye all may read through dimming tears his story,
How discord on the music fell and darkness on the glory,
And how when, one by one, sweet sounds and wandering lights departed,
He wore no less a loving face because so broken-hearted,

POEMS.

BY

ELIZABETH BARRETT BARRETT,

AUTHOR OF "THE SERAPHIM," ETC.

"De patrie, et de Dieu, des poëtes, de l'âme
Qui s'élève en priant."—VICTOR HUGO.

IN TWO VOLUMES.

VOL. I.

LONDON:
EDWARD MOXON, DOVER STREET.
MDCCCXLIV.

To Mr. Serjt. Talfourd
with the author's compliments.
August 1844

A Presentation Copy to Talfourd. (See Appendix I.)

IV

He shall be strong to sanctify the poet's high vocation,
And bow the meekest Christian down in meeker adoration;
Nor ever shall he be, in praise, by wise or good forsaken,
Named softly as the household name of one whom God hath taken.

V

With quiet sadness and no gloom I learn to think upon him,
With meekness that is gratefulness to God whose heaven hath won him,
Who suffered once the madness-cloud to His own love to blind him,
But gently led the blind along where breath and bird could find him;

VI

And wrought within his shattered brain such quick poetic senses
As hills have language for, and stars, harmonious influences:
The pulse of dew upon the grass kept his within its number,
And silent shadows from the trees refreshed him like a slumber.

VII

Wild timid hares were drawn from woods to share his home-caresses,
Uplooking to his human eyes with sylvan tendernesses:
The very world, by God's constraint, from falsehood's ways removing,
Its women and its men became, beside him, true and loving.

VIII

And though, in blindness, he remained unconscious of that guiding,
And things provided came without the sweet sense of providing,
He testified this solemn truth, while frenzy desolated,
—Nor man nor nature satisfies whom only God created.

IX

Like a sick child that knoweth not his mother while she blesses
And drops upon his burning brow the coolness of her kisses,—
That turns his fevered eyes around,—"My mother! where's my mother?"—
As if such tender words and deeds could come from any other!—

X

The fever gone, with leaps of heart he sees her bending o'er him,
Her face all pale from watchful love,—the unweary love she bore him!—
Thus woke the poet from the dream his life's long fever gave him,
Beneath those deep pathetic Eyes which closed in death to save him;

XI

Thus? oh, not *thus!* no type of earth can image that awaking,
Wherein he scarcely heard the chant of seraphs, round him breaking,
Or felt the new immortal throb of soul from body parted,
But felt those eyes alone, and knew—"*My* Saviour! *not* deserted!"

XII

Deserted! Who hath dreamt that when the cross in darkness rested,
Upon the Victim's hidden face no love was manifested?
What frantic hands outstretched have e'er the atoning drops averted?
What tears have washed them from the soul, that *one* should be deserted?

XIII

Deserted! God could separate from his own essence rather;
And Adam's sins *have* swept between the righteous Son and Father:
Yea, once Immanuel's orphaned cry his universe hath shaken—
It went up single, echoless, "My God, I am forsaken!"

XIV

It went up from the Holy's lips amid his lost creation,
That, of the lost, no son should use those words of desolation!
That earth's worst frenzies, marring hope, should mar not hope's fruition,
And I, on Cowper's grave, should see his rapture in a vision.

1838

THE CRY OF THE CHILDREN

"Φεῦ, φεῦ, τί προσδέρκεσθέ μ' ὄμμασιν, τέκνα;"
—MEDEA

I

Do ye hear the children weeping, O my brothers,
Ere the sorrow comes with years?
They are leaning their young heads against their mothers,
And *that* cannot stop their tears.
The young lambs are bleating in the meadows,
The young birds are chirping in the nest,
The young fawns are playing with the shadows,
The young flowers are blowing toward the west—
But the young, young children, O my brothers,
They are weeping bitterly!
They are weeping in the playtime of the others,
In the country of the free.

II

Do you question the young children in the sorrow
Why their tears are falling so?
The old man may weep for his to-morrow
Which is lost in Long Ago;
The old tree is leafless in the forest,
The old year is ending in the frost,
The old wound, if stricken, is the sorest,
The old hope is hardest to be lost:
But the young, young children, O my brothers,
Do you ask them why they stand
Weeping sore before the bosoms of their mothers,
In our happy Fatherland?

III

They look up with their pale and sunken faces,
And their looks are sad to see,
For the man's hoary anguish draws and presses
Down the cheeks of infancy;
"Your old earth," they say, "is very dreary,
Our young feet," they say, "are very weak;
Few paces have we taken, yet are weary—
Our grave-rest is very far to seek:
Ask the aged why they weep, and not the children,
For the outside earth is cold,
And we young ones stand without, in our bewildering,
And the graves are for the old.

IV

"True," say the children, "it may happen
That we die before our time:
Little Alice died last year, her grave is shapen
Like a snowball, in the rime.
We looked into the pit prepared to take her:
Was no room for any work in the close clay!
From the sleep wherein she lieth none will wake her,
Crying, 'Get up, little Alice! it is day.'
If you listen by that grave, in sun and shower,
With your ear down, little Alice never cries;
Could we see her face, be sure we should not know her,
For the smile has time for growing in her eyes:
And merry go her moments, lulled and stilled in
The shroud by the kirk-chime.
It is good when it happens," say the children,
"That we die before our time."

V

Alas, alas, the children! They are seeking
  Death in life, as best to have:
They are binding up their hearts away from breaking,
  With a cerement from the grave.
Go out, children, from the mine and from the city,
  Sing out, children, as the little thrushes do;
Pluck your handfuls of the meadow-cowslips pretty.
  Laugh aloud, to feel your fingers let them through!
But they answer, "Are your cowslips of the meadows
  Like our weeds anear the mine?
Leave us quiet in the dark of the coal-shadows,
  From your pleasures fair and fine!

VI

"For oh," say the children, "we are weary,
  And we cannot run or leap;
If we cared for any meadows, it were merely
  To drop down in them and sleep.
Our knees tremble sorely in the stooping,
  We fall upon our faces, trying to go;
And, underneath our heavy eyelids drooping
  The reddest flower would look as pale as snow.
For, all day, we drag our burden tiring
  Through the coal-dark, underground
Or, all day, we drive the wheels of iron
  In the factories, round and round.

VII

"For all day the wheels are droning, turning;
  Their wind comes in our faces,
Till our hearts turn, our heads with pulses burning,
  And the walls turn in their places:
Turns the sky in the high window, blank and reeling,
  Turns the long light that drops adown the wall,
Turn the black flies that crawl along the ceiling:
  All are turning, all the day, and we with all.
And all day the iron wheels are droning,
  And sometimes we could pray,
'O ye wheels' (breaking out in a mad moaning),
  'Stop! be silent for to-day!' "

VIII

Ay, be silent! Let them hear each other breathing
  For a moment, mouth to mouth!
Let them touch each other's hands, in a fresh wreathing
  Of their tender human youth!
Let them feel that this cold metallic motion
  Is not all the life God fashions or reveals:
Let them prove their living souls against the notion
  That they live in you, or under you, O wheels!
Still, all day, the iron wheels go onward,
  Grinding life down from its mark;
And the children's souls, which God is calling sunward,
  Spin on blindly in the dark.

IX

Now tell the poor young children, O my brothers,
  To look up to Him, and pray;
So the blessèd One who blesseth all the others,
  Will bless them another day.
They answer, "Who is God that He should hear us,
  While the rushing of the iron wheels is stirred?
When we sob aloud, the human creatures near us
  Pass by, hearing not, or answer not a word.
And *we* hear not (for the wheels in their resounding)
  Strangers speaking at the door:
Is it likely God, with angels singing round Him,
  Hears our weeping any more?

X

"Two words, indeed, of praying we remember,
  And at midnight's hour of harm,
'Our Father,' looking upward in the chamber,
  We say softly for a charm.
We know no other words except 'Our Father,'
  And we think that, in some pause of angels' song,
God may pluck them with the silence sweet to gather,

And hold both within his right hand which is strong,
'Our Father!' If He heard us, He would surely
(For they call Him good and mild)
Answer, smiling down the steep world very purely,
'Come and rest with me, my child.'

XI

"But, no!" say the children, weeping faster,
"He is speechless as a stone:
And they tell us, of His image is the master
Who commands us to work on.
Go to!" say the children,—"up in Heaven,
Dark, wheel-like, turning clouds are all we find.
Do not mock us; grief has made us unbelieving:
We look up for God, but tears have made us blind."
Do you hear the children weeping and disproving,
O my brothers, what ye preach?
For God's possible is taught by his world's loving,
And the children doubt of each.

XII

And well may the children weep before you!
They are weary ere they run;
They have never seen the sunshine, nor the glory
Which is brighter than the sun.
They know the grief of man, without its wisdom;
They sink in man's despair, without its calm;
Are slaves, without the liberty in Christdom,
Are martyrs, by the pang without the palm:
Are worn as if with age, yet unretrievingly
The harvest of its memories cannot reap,—
Are orphans of the earthly love and heavenly.
Let them weep! let them weep!

XIII

They look up with their pale and sunken faces,
And their look is dread to see,
For they mind you of their angels in high places,
With eyes turned on Deity.
"How long," they say, "how long, O cruel nation,
Will you stand, to move the world, on a child's heart,—
Stifle down with a mailèd heel its palpitation,
And tread onward to your throne amid the mart?
Our blood splashes upward, O gold-heaper,
And your purple shows your path!
But the child 's sob in the silence curses deeper
Than the strong man in his wrath."

1844

THE POET AND THE BIRD

A FABLE

I

Said a people to a poet—"Go out from among us straightway!
While we are thinking earthly things, thou singest of divine:
There's a little fair brown nightingale who, sitting in the gateway,
Makes fitter music to our ear than any song of thine!"

II

The poet went out weeping; the nightingale ceased chanting:
"Now, wherefore, O thou nightingale, is all thy sweetness done?"
—"I cannot sing my earthly things, the heavenly poet wanting,
Whose highest harmony includes the lowest under sun."

III

The poet went out weeping, and died abroad, bereft there;
The bird flew to his grave and died amid a thousand wails:
And when I last came by the place, I swear the music left there
Was only of the poet's song, and not the nightingale's.

1844

CONFESSIONS

I

Face to face in my chamber, my silent chamber, I saw her:
God and she and I only, there I sat down to draw her
Soul through the clefts of confession: "Speak, I am holding thee fast,
As the angel of resurrection shall do at the last!"
"My cup is blood-red
With my sin," she said,
"And I pour it out to the bitter lees,
As if the angels of judgment stood over me strong at the last,
Or as thou wert as these."

II

When God smote his hands together, and struck out thy soul as a spark
Into the organized glory of things, from deeps of the dark,—
Say, didst thou shine, didst thou burn, didst thou honor the power in the form,
As the star does at night, or the fire-fly, or even the little ground-worm?
"I have sinned," she said,
"For my seed-light shed
Has smouldered away from his first decrees.
The cypress praiseth the firefly, the ground-leaf praiseth the worm;
I am viler than these."

III

When God on that sin had pity, and did not trample thee straight
With his wild rains beating and drenching thy light found inadequate;
When He only sent thee the north-wind, a little searching and chill,
To quicken thy flame—didst thou kindle and flash to the heights of his will?
"I have sinned," she said,
"Unquickened, unspread,
My fire dropt down, and I wept on my knees:
I only said of his winds of the north as I shrank from their chill,
What delight is in these?"

IV

When God on that sin had pity, and did not meet it as such,
But tempered the wind to thy uses, and softened the world to thy touch,
At least thou wast moved in thy soul, though unable to prove it afar,
Thou couldst carry thy light like a jewel, not giving it out like a star?
"I have sinned," she said,
"And not merited
The gift He gives, by the grace He sees!
The mine-cave praiseth the jewel, the hillside praiseth the star;
I am viler than these."

V

Then I cried aloud in my passion,—Unthankful and impotent creature,
To throw up thy scorn unto God through the rents in thy beggarly nature!
If He, the all-giving and loving, is served so unduly, what then
Hast thou done to the weak and the false and the changing,—thy fellows of men?

"I have *loved*," she said,
(Words bowing her head
As the wind the wet acacia-trees)
"I saw God sitting above me, but I . . . I sat among men,
And I have loved these."

VI

Again with a lifted voice, like a choral trumpet that takes
The lowest note of a viol that trembles, and triumphing breaks
On the air with it solemn and clear,—"Behold! I have sinned not in this!
Where I loved, I have loved much and well,—I have verily loved not amiss.
Let the living," she said,
"Inquire of the dead,
In the house of the pale-fronted images.
My own true dead will answer for me, that I have not loved amiss
In my love for all these.

VII

"The least touch of their hands in the morning, I keep it by day and by night;
Their least step on the stair, at the door, still throbs through me, if ever so light;
Their least gift, which they left to my childhood, far off in the long-ago years,
Is now turned from a toy to a relic, and seen through the crystals of tears.
Dig the snow," she said,
"For my churchyard bed,
Yet I, as I sleep, shall not fear to freeze,
If one only of these my beloveds shall love me with heart-warm tears,
As I have loved these!

VIII

"If I angered any among them, from thenceforth my own life was sore;
If I fell by chance from their presence, I clung to their memory more:
Their tender I often felt holy, their bitter I sometimes called sweet;
And whenever their heart has refused me, I fell down straight at their feet.
I have loved," she said,—
"Man is weak, God is dread,
Yet the weak man dies with his spirit at ease,
Having poured such an unguent of love but once on the Saviour's feet,
As I lavished for these."

IX

Go, I cried, thou hast chosen the Human, and left the Divine!
Then, at least, have the Human shared with thee their wild-berry wine?
Have they loved back thy love, and when strangers approached thee with blame,
Have they covered thy fault with their kisses, and loved thee the same?
But she shrunk and said,
"God, over my head,
Must sweep in the wrath of his judgment-seas,
If *He* shall deal with me sinning, but only indeed the same
And no gentler than these."

1850

THE MASK

I

I HAVE a smiling face, she said,
  I have a jest for all I meet,
I have a garland for my head
  And all its flowers are sweet,—
And so you call me gay, she said.

II

Grief taught to me this smile, she said,
  And Wrong did teach this jesting bold;
These flowers were plucked from garden-bed
  While a death-chime was tolled:
And what now will you say?—she said.

III

Behind no prison-grate, she said,
  Which slurs the sunshine half a mile,
Live captives so uncomforted
  As souls behind a smile.
God's pity let us pray, she said.

IV

I know my face is bright, she said,—
  Such brightness dying suns diffuse:
I bear upon my forehead shed
  The sign of what I lose,
The ending of my day, she said.

V

If I dared leave this smile, she said,
  And take a moan upon my mouth,
And tie a cypress round my head,
  And let my tears run smooth,
It were the happier way, she said.

VI

And since that must not be, she said,
  I fain your bitter world would leave.
How calmly, calmly smile the Dead,
  Who do not, therefore, grieve!
The yea of Heaven is yea, she said.

VII

But in your bitter world, she said,
  Face-joy's a costly mask to wear;
'Tis bought with pangs long nourishèd,
  And rounded to despair:
Grief's earnest makes life's play, she said.

VIII

Ye weep for those who weep? she said—
  Ah fools! I bid you pass them by.
Go, weep for those whose hearts have bled
  What time their eyes were dry.
Whom sadder can I say? she said.

1850

SONNETS FROM THE PORTUGUESE

I

I THOUGHT once how Theocritus had sung
Of the sweet years, the dear and wished-for years,
Who each one in a gracious hand appears
To bear a gift for mortals, old or young:
And, as I mused it in his antique tongue,
I saw, in gradual vision through my tears,
The sweet, sad years, the melancholy years,
Those of my own life, who by turns had flung
A shadow across me. Straightway I was 'ware,
So weeping, how a mystic Shape did move
Behind me, and drew me backward by the hair;
And a voice said in mastery, while I strove,—
"Guess now who holds thee?"—"Death," I said. But, there,
The silver answer rang, "Not Death, but Love."

II

BUT only three in all God's universe
Have heard this word thou has said,—Himself, beside
Thee speaking, and me listening! and replied
One of us . . . *that* was God, . . . and laid the curse
So darkly on my eyelids, as to amerce
My sight from seeing thee,—that if I had died,
The death-weights, placed there, would have signified
Less absolute exclusion. "Nay" is worse
From God than from all others, O my friend!
Men could not part us with their worldly jars,
Nor the seas change us, nor the tempests bend;
Our hands would touch for all the mountain-bars:
And, heaven being rolled between us at the end,
We should but vow the faster for the stars.

III

Unlike are we, unlike, O princely Heart!
Unlike our uses and our destinies.
Our ministering two angels look surprise
On one another, as they strike athwart
Their wings in passing. Thou, bethink thee, art
A guest for queens to social pageantries,
With gages from a hundred brighter eyes
Than tears even can make mine, to play thy part
Of chief musician. What hast *thou* to do
With looking from the lattice-lights at me,
A poor, tired, wandering singer, singing through
The dark, and leaning up a cypress-tree?
The chrism is on thine head,—on mine, the dew,—
And Death must dig the level where these agree.

IV

Thou hast thy calling to some palace-floor,
Most gracious singer of high poems! where
The dancers will break footing, from the care
Of watching up thy pregnant lips for more.
And dost thou lift this house's latch too poor
For hand of thine? and canst thou think and bear
To let thy music drop here unaware
In folds of golden fulness at my door?
Look up and see the casement broken in,
The bats and owlets builders in the roof!
My cricket chirps against thy mandolin.
Hush, call no echo up in further proof
Of desolation! there's a voice within
That weeps . . . as thou must sing . . . alone, aloof.

V

I lift my heavy heart up solemnly,
As once Electra her sepulchral urn,
And, looking in thine eyes, I overturn
The ashes at thy feet. Behold and see
What a great heap of grief lay hid in me,
And how the red wild sparkles dimly burn
Through the ashen grayness. If thy foot in scorn
Could tread them out to darkness utterly,
It might be well perhaps. But if instead
Thou wait beside me for the wind to blow
The gray dust up, . . . those laurels on thine head,
O my Belovèd, will not shield thee so,
That none of all the fires shall scorch and shred
The hair beneath. Stand farther off then! go.

VI

Go from me. Yet I feel that I shall stand
Henceforward in thy shadow. Nevermore
Alone upon the threshold of my door
Of individual life, I shall command
The uses of my soul, nor lift my hand
Serenely in the sunshine as before,
Without the sense of that which I forbore—
Thy touch upon the palm. The widest land
Doom takes to part us, leaves thy heart in mine
With pulses that beat double. What I do
And what I dream include thee, as the wine
Must taste of its own grapes. And when I sue
God for myself, He hears that name of thine,
And sees within my eyes the tears of two.

VII

The face of all the world is changed, I think,
Since first I heard the footsteps of thy soul
Move still, oh, still, beside me, as they stole
Betwixt me and the dreadful outer brink
Of obvious death, where I, who thought to sink,
Was caught up into love, and taught the whole
Of life in a new rhythm. The cup of dole
God gave for baptism, I am fain to drink,
And praise its sweetness, Sweet, with thee anear.
The names of country, heaven, are changed away
For where thou art or shalt be, there or here;
And this . . . this lute and song . . . loved yesterday,
(The singing angels know) are only dear
Because thy name moves right in what they say.

VIII

What can I give thee back, O liberal
And princely giver, who hast brought the gold
And purple of thine heart, unstained, untold,
And laid them on the outside of the wall
For such as I to take or leave withal,
In unexpected largesse? am I cold,
Ungrateful, that for these most manifold
High gifts, I render nothing back at all?
Not so; not cold,—but very poor instead.

Ask God who knows. For frequent tears have run
The colors from my life, and left so dead
And pale a stuff, it were not fitly done
To give the same as pillow to thy head.
Go farther! let it serve to trample on.

IX

CAN it be right to give what I can give?
To let thee sit beneath the fall of tears
As salt as mine, and hear the sighing years
Re-sighing on my lips renunciative
Through those infrequent smiles which fail to live
For all thy adjurations? O my fears,
That this can scarce be right! We are not peers,
So to be lovers; and I own, and grieve,
That givers of such gifts as mine are, must
Be counted with the ungenerous. Out, alas!
I will not soil thy purple with my dust,
Nor breathe my poison on thy Venice-glass,
Nor give thee any love—which were unjust.
Beloved, I only love thee! let it pass.

X

YET love, mere love, is beautiful indeed
And worthy of acceptation. Fire is bright,
Let temple burn, or flax; an equal light
Leaps in the flame from cedar-plank or weed:
And love is fire. And when I say at need
I love thee . . . mark! . . . *I love thee*—in thy sight
I stand transfigured, glorified aright,
With conscience of the new rays that proceed
Out of my face toward thine. There's nothing low
In love, when love the lowest: meanest creatures
Who love God, God accepts while loving so.
And what I *feel*, across the inferior features
Of what I *am*, doth flash itself, and show
How that great work of Love enhances Nature's.

XI

AND therefore if to love can be desert,
I am not all unworthy. Cheeks as pale
As these you see, and trembling knees that fail
To bear the burden of a heavy heart,—
This weary minstrel-life that once was girt
To climb Aornus, and can scarce avail
To pipe now 'gainst the valley nightingale
A melancholy music,—why advert
To these things? O Belovèd, it is plain
I am not of thy worth nor for thy place!
And yet, because I love thee, I obtain
From that same love this vindicating grace,
To live on still in love, and yet in vain,—
To bless thee, yet renounce thee to thy face.

XII

INDEED this very love which is my boast,
And which, when rising up from breast to brow,
Doth crown me with a ruby large enow
To draw men's eyes and prove the inner cost,—
This love even, all my worth, to the uttermost,
I should not love withal, unless that thou
Hadst set me an example, shown me how,
When first thine earnest eyes with mine were crossed,
And love called love. And thus, I cannot speak
Of love even, as a good thing of my own:
Thy soul hath snatched up mine all faint and weak,
And placed it by thee on a golden throne,—
And that I love (O soul, we must be meek!)
Is by thee only, whom I love alone.

XIII

AND wilt thou have me fashion into speech
The love I bear thee, finding words enough,
And hold the torch out, while the winds are rough,
Between our faces, to cast light on each?—
I drop it at thy feet. I cannot teach
My hand to hold my spirit so far off
From myself—me—that I should bring thee proof
In words, of love hid in me out of reach.
Nay, let the silence of my womanhood
Commend my woman-love to thy belief,—
Seeing that I stand unwon, however wooed,
And rend the garment of my life, in brief,
By a most dauntless, voiceless fortitude,
Lest one touch of this heart convey its grief.

XIV

IF thou must love me, let it be for nought
Except for love's sake only. Do not say
"I love her for her smile—her look—her way
Of speaking gently,—for a trick of thought

That falls in well with mine, and certes brought
A sense of pleasant ease on such a day"—
For these things in themselves, Belovèd, may
Be changed, or change for thee,—and love, so wrought,
May be unwrought so. Neither love me for
Thine own dear pity's wiping my cheeks dry,—
A creature might forget to weep, who bore
Thy comfort long, and lose thy love thereby!
But love me for love's sake, that evermore
Thou mayst love on, through love's eternity.

XV

ACCUSE me not, beseech thee, that I wear
Too calm and sad a face in front of thine;
For we two look two ways, and cannot shine
With the same sunlight on our brow and hair.
On me thou lookest with no doubting care,
As on a bee shut in a crystalline;
Since sorrow hath shut me safe in love's divine,
And to spread wing and fly in the outer air
Were most impossible failure, if I strove
To fail so. But I look on thee—on thee—
Beholding, besides love, the end of love,
Hearing oblivion beyond memory;
As one who sits and gazes from above,
Over the rivers to the bitter sea.

XVI

AND yet, because thou overcomest so,
Because thou art more noble and like a king,
Thou canst prevail against my fears and fling
Thy purple round me, till my heart shall grow
Too close against thine heart henceforth to know
How it shook when alone. Why, conquering
May prove as lordly and complete a thing
In lifting upward, as in crushing low!
And as a vanquished soldier yields his sword
To one who lifts him from the bloody earth,
Even so, Belovèd, I at last record,
Here ends my strife. If *thou* invite me forth,
I rise above abasement at the word.
Make thy love larger to enlarge my worth.

XVII

MY poet, thou canst touch on all the notes
God set between his After and Before,
And strike up and strike off the general roar
Of the rushing worlds a melody that floats
In a serene air purely. Antidotes
Of medicated music, answering for
Mankind's forlornest uses, thou canst pour
From thence into their ears. God's will devotes
Thine to such ends, and mine to wait on thine.
How, Dearest, wilt thou have me for most use?
A hope, to sing by gladly? or a fine
Sad memory, with thy songs to interfuse?
A shade, in which to sing,—of palm or pine?
A grave, on which to rest from singing? Choose.

XVIII

I NEVER gave a lock of hair away
To a man, Dearest, except this to thee,
Which now upon my fingers thoughtfully,
I ring out to the full brown length and say
"Take it." My day of youth went yesterday;
My hair no longer bounds to my foot's glee,
Nor plant I it from rose or myrtle-tree,
As girls do, any more: it only may
Now shade on two pale cheeks the mark of tears,
Taught drooping from the head that hangs aside
Through sorrow's trick. I thought the funeral-shears
Would take this first, but Love is justified,—
Take it thou,—finding pure, from all those years,
The kiss my mother left here when she died.

XIX

THE soul's Rialto hath its merchandise;
I barter curl for curl upon that mart,
And from my poet's forehead to my heart
Receive this lock which outweighs argosies,—
As purply black, as erst to Pindar's eyes
The dim purpureal tresses gloomed athwart
The nine white Muse-brows. For this counterpart, . . .
The bay-crown's shade, Belovèd, I surmise,
Still lingers on thy curl, it is so black!
Thus, with a fillet of smooth-kissing breath,
I tie the shadows safe from gliding back,
And lay the gift where nothing hindereth;
Here on my heart, as on thy brow, to lack
No natural heat till mine grows cold in death.

XX

Belovèd, my Belovèd, when I think
That thou wast in the world a year ago,
What time I sat alone here in the snow
And saw no footprint, heard the silence sink
No moment at thy voice, but, link by link,
Went counting all my chains as if that so
They never could fall off at any blow
Struck by thy possible hand,—why, thus I drink
Of life's great cup of wonder! Wonderful,
Never to feel thee thrill the day or night
With personal act or speech,—nor ever cull
Some prescience of thee with the blossoms white
Thou sawest growing! Atheists are as dull,
Who cannot guess God's presence out of sight.

XXI

Say over again, and yet once over again,
That thou dost love me. Though the word repeated
Should seem "a cuckoo-song," as thou dost treat it,
Remember, never to the hill or plain,
Valley and wood, without her cuckoo-strain
Comes the fresh Spring in all her green completed.
Belovèd, I, amid the darkness greeted
By a doubtful spirit-voice, in that doubt's pain
Cry, "Speak once more—thou lovest!" Who can fear
Too many stars, though each in heaven shall roll,
Too many flowers, though each shall crown the year?
Say thou dost love me, love me, love me—toll
The silver iterance!—only minding, Dear,
To love me also in silence with thy soul.

XXII

When our two souls stand up erect and strong,
Face to face, silent, drawing nigh and nigher,
Until the lengthening wings break into fire
At either curvèd point,—what bitter wrong
Can the earth do to us, that we should not long
Be here contented? Think. In mounting higher,
The angels would press on us and aspire
To drop some golden orb of perfect song
Into our deep, dear silence. Let us stay
Rather on earth, Belovèd,—where the unfit
Contrarious moods of men recoil away
And isolate pure spirits, and permit
A place to stand and love in for a day,
With darkness and the death-hour rounding it.

XXIII

Is it indeed so? If I lay here dead,
Wouldst thou miss any life in losing mine?
And would the sun for thee more coldly shine
Because of grave-damps falling round my head?
I marvelled, my Belovèd, when I read
Thy thought so in the letter. I am thine—
But . . . *so* much to thee? Can I pour thy wine
While my hands tremble? Then my soul, instead
Of dreams of death, resumes life's lower range.
Then, love me, Love! look on me—breathe on me!
As brighter ladies do not count it strange,
For love, to give up acres and degree,
I yield the grave for thy sake, and exchange
My near sweet view of Heaven, for earth with thee!

XXIV

Let the world's sharpness, like a clasping knife,
Shut in upon itself and do no harm
In this close hand of Love, now soft and warm,
And let us hear no sound of human strife
After the click of the shutting. Life to life—
I lean upon thee, Dear, without alarm,
And feel as safe as guarded by a charm
Against the stab of worldlings, who if rife
Are weak to injure. Very whitely still
The lilies of our lives may reassure
Their blossoms from their roots, accessible
Alone to heavenly dews that drop not fewer,
Growing straight, out of man's reach, on the hill.
God only, who made us rich, can make us poor.

XXV

A heavy heart, Belovèd, have I borne
From year to year until I saw thy face,
And sorrow after sorrow took the place
Of all those natural joys as lightly worn
As the stringed pearls, each lifted in its turn
By a beating heart at dance-time. Hopes apace
Were changed to long despairs, till God's own grace

Could scarcely lift above the world forlorn
My heavy heart. Then *thou* didst bid me bring
And let it drop adown thy calmly great
Deep being. Fast it sinketh, as a thing
Which its own nature doth precipitate,
While thine doth close above it, mediating
Betwixt the stars and the unaccomplished fate.

XXVI

I LIVED with visions for my company
Instead of men and women, years ago,
And found them gentle mates, nor thought to know
A sweeter music than they played to me.
But soon their trailing purple was not free
Of his world's dust, their lutes did silent grow,
And I myself grew faint and blind below
Their vanishing eyes. Then THOU didst come—to be,
Belovèd, what they seemed. Their shining fronts,
Their songs, their splendors (better, yet the same,
As river-water hallowed into fonts),
Met in thee, and from out thee overcame
My soul with satisfaction of all wants:
Because God's gifts put man's best dreams to shame.

XXVII

MY own Belovèd, who hast lifted me
From this drear flat of earth where I was thrown,
And, in betwixt the languid ringlets, blown
A life-breath, till the forehead hopefully
Shines out again, as all the angels see,
Before thy saving kiss! My own, my own,
Who camest to me when the world was gone,
And I who looked for only God, found *thee!*
I find thee; I am safe, and strong, and glad.
As one who stands in dewless asphodel
Looks backward on the tedious time he had
In the upper life,—so I, with bosom-swell,
Make witness, here, between the good and bad,
That Love, as strong as Death, retrieves as well.

XXVIII

MY letters! all dead paper, mute and white!
And yet they seem alive and quivering
Against my tremulous hands which loose the string
And let them drop down on my knee to-night.
This said,—he wished to have me in his sight
Once, as a friend: this fixed a day in spring
To come and touch my hand . . . a simple thing,
Yet I wept for it!—this, . . . the paper's light . . . .
Said, *Dear*, *I love thee;* and I sank and quailed
As if God's future thundered on my past.
This said, *I am thine*—and so its ink has paled
With lying at my heart that beat too fast.
And this . . . O Love, thy words have ill availed
If, what this said, I dared repeat at last!

XXIX

I THINK of thee!—my thoughts do twine and bud
About thee, as wild vines, about a tree,
Put out broad leaves, and soon there's nought to see
Except the straggling green which hides the wood.
Yet, O my palm-tree, be it understood
I will not have my thoughts instead of thee
Who art dearer, better! Rather, instantly
Renew thy presence; as a strong tree should,
Rustle thy boughs and set thy trunk all bare,
And let these bands of greenery which insphere thee
Drop heavily down,—burst, shattered, everywhere!
Because, in this deep joy to see and hear thee
And breathe within thy shadow a new air,
I do not think of thee—I am too near thee.

XXX

I SEE thine image through my tears to-night,
And yet to-day I saw thee smiling. How
Refer the cause?—Belovèd, is it thou
Or I, who makes me sad? The acolyte
Amid the chanted joy and thankful rite
May so fall flat, with pale insensate brow,
On the altar-stair. I hear thy voice and vow,
Perplexed, uncertain, since thou art out of sight,
As he, in his swooning ears, the choir's Amen.
Belovèd, dost thou love? or did I see all
The glory as I dreamed, and fainted when
Too vehement light dilated my ideal,
For my soul's eyes? Will that light come again,
As now these tears come—falling hot and real?

XXXI

Thou comest! all is said without a word.
I sit beneath thy looks, as children do
In the noon-sun, with souls that tremble through
Their happy eyelids from an unaverred
Yet prodigal inward joy. Behold, I erred
In that last doubt! and yet I cannot rue
The sin most, but the occasion—that we two
Should for a moment stand unministered
By a mutual presence. Ah, keep near and close,
Thou dovelike help! and, when my fears would rise,
With thy broad heart serenely interpose:
Brood down with thy divine sufficiencies
These thoughts which tremble when bereft of those,
Like callow birds left desert to the skies.

XXXII

The first time that the sun rose on thine oath
To love me, I looked forward to the moon
To slacken all those bonds which seemed too soon
And quickly tied to make a lasting troth.
Quick-loving hearts, I thought, may quickly loathe;
And, looking on myself, I seemed not one
For such man's love!—more like an out-of-tune
Worn viol, a good singer would be wroth
To spoil his song with, and which, snatched in haste,
Is laid down at the first ill-sounding note.
I did not wrong myself so, but I placed
A wrong on *thee*. For perfect strains may float
'Neath master-hands, from instruments defaced,—
And great souls, at one stroke, may do and doat.

XXXIII

Yes, call me by my pet-name! let me hear
The name I used to run at, when a child,
From innocent play, and leave the cowslips piled,
To glance up in some face that proved me dear
With the look of its eyes. I miss the clear
Fond voices which, being drawn and reconciled
Into the music of Heaven's undefiled,
Call me no longer. Silence on the bier,
While I call God—call God!—So let thy mouth
Be heir to those who are now exanimate.
Gather the north flowers to complete the south,
And catch the early love up in the late.
Yes, call me by that name,—and I, in truth,
With the same heart, will answer and not wait.

XXXIV

With the same heart, I said, I'll answer thee
As those, when thou shalt call me by my name—
Lo, the vain promise! is the same, the same,
Perplexed and ruffled by life's strategy?
When called before, I told how hastily
I dropped my flowers or brake off from a game,
To run and answer with the smile that came
At play last moment, and went on with me
Through my obedience. When I answer now,
I drop a grave thought, break from solitude;
Yet still my heart goes to thee—ponder how—
Not as to a single good, but all my good!
Lay thy hand on it, best one, and allow
That no child's foot could run fast as this blood.

XXXV

If I leave all for thee, wilt thou exchange
And be all to me? Shall I never miss
Home-talk and blessing and the common kiss
That comes to each in turn, nor count it strange,
When I look up, to drop on a new range
Of walls and floors, another home than this?
Nay, wilt thou fill that place by me which is
Filled by dead eyes too tender to know change?
That's hardest. If to conquer love, has tried,
To conquer grief, tries more, as all things prove;
For grief indeed is love and grief beside.
Alas, I have grieved so I am hard to love.
Yet love me—wilt thou? Open thine heart wide,
And fold within the wet wings of thy dove.

XXXVI

When we met first and loved, I did not build
Upon the event with marble. Could it mean
To last, a love set pendulous between

Sorrow and sorrow? Nay, I rather thrilled,
Distrusting every light that seemed to gild
The onward path, and feared to overlean
A finger even. And, though I have grown serene
And strong since then, I think that God has willed
A still renewable fear . . . O love, O troth . . .
Lest these enclaspèd hands should never hold,
This mutual kiss drop down between us both
As an unowned thing, once the lips being cold.
And Love, be false! if *he*, to keep one oath,
Must lose one joy, by his life's star foretold.

XXXVII

Pardon, oh, pardon, that my soul should make,
Of all that strong divineness which I know
For thine and thee, an image only so
Formed of the sand, and fit to shift and break.
It is that distant years which did not take
Thy sovranty, recoiling with a blow,
Have forced my swimming brain to undergo
Their doubt and dread, and blindly to forsake
Thy purity of likeness and distort
Thy worthiest love to a worthless counterfeit:
As if a shipwrecked Pagan, safe in port,
His guardian sea-god to commemorate,
Should set a sculptured porpoise, gills a-snort
And vibrant tail, within the temple-gate.

XXXVIII

First time he kissed me, he but only kissed
The fingers of this hand wherewith I write;
And ever since, it grew more clean and white,
Slow to world-greetings, quick with its "Oh, list,"
When the angels speak. A ring of amethyst
I could not wear here, plainer to my sight,
Than that first kiss. The second passed in height
The first, and sought the forehead, and half missed,
Half falling on the hair. O beyond meed!
That was the chrism of love, which love's own crown,
With sanctifying sweetness, did precede.
The third upon my lips was folded down
In perfect, purple state; since when, indeed,
I have been proud and said, "My love, my own."

XXXIX

Because thou hast the power and own'st the grace
To look through and behind this mask of me
(Against which years have beat thus blanchingly
With their rains), and behold my soul's true face,
The dim and weary witness of life's race,—
Because thou hast the faith and love to see,
Through that same soul's distracting lethargy,
The patient angel waiting for a place
In the new Heavens,—because nor sin nor woe,
Nor God's infliction, nor death's neighborhood,
Nor all which others viewing, turn to go,
Nor all which makes me tired of all, self-viewed,—
Nothing repels thee, . . . Dearest, teach me so
To pour out gratitude, as thou dost, good!

XL

Oh, yes! they love through all this world of ours!
I will not gainsay love, called love forsooth.
I have heard love talked in my early youth,
And since, not so long back but that the flowers
Then gathered, smell still. Mussulmans and Giaours
Throw kerchiefs at a smile, and have no ruth
For any weeping. Polypheme's white tooth
Slips on the nut if, after frequent showers,
The shell is over-smooth,—and not so much
Will turn the thing called love, aside to hate
Or else to oblivion. But thou art not such
A lover, my Belovèd! thou canst wait
Through sorrow and sickness, to bring souls to touch,
And think it soon when others cry "Too late."

XLI

I thank all who have loved me in their hearts,
With thanks and love from mine. Deep thanks to all
Who paused a little near the prison-wall
To hear my music in its louder parts
Ere they went onward, each one to the mart's
Or temple's occupation, beyond call.
But thou, who, in my voice's sink and fall

When the sob took it, thy divinest Art's
Own instrument didst drop down at thy foot
To hearken what I said between my tears, . . .
Instruct me how to thank thee! Oh, to shoot
My soul's full meaning into future years,
That *they* should lend it utterance, and salute
Love that endures, from Life that disappears!

XLII

"My *future will not copy fair my past*"—
I wrote that once; and thinking at my side
My ministering life-angel justified
The word by his appealing look upcast
To the white throne of God, I turned at last,
And there, instead, saw thee, not unallied
To angels in thy soul! Then I, long tried
By natural ills, received the comfort fast,
While budding, at thy sight, my pilgrim's staff
Gave out green leaves with morning dews impearled.
I seek no copy now of life's first half:
Leave here the pages with long musing curled,
And write me new my future's epigraph,
New angel mine, unhoped for in the world!

XLIII

How do I love thee? Let me count the ways.
I love thee to the depth and breadth and height
My soul can reach, when feeling out of sight
For the ends of Being and ideal Grace.
I love thee to the level of everyday's
Most quiet need, by sun and candle-light.
I love thee freely, as men strive for Right;
I love thee purely, as they turn from Praise.
I love thee with the passion put to use
In my old griefs, and with my childhood's faith.
I love thee with a love I seemed to lose
With my lost saints,—I love thee with the breath,
Smiles, tears, of all my life!—and, if God choose,
I shall but love thee better after death.

XLIV

Beloved, thou hast brought me many flowers
Plucked in the garden, all the summer through
And winter, and it seemed as if they grew
In this close room, nor missed the sun and showers.
So, in the like name of that love of ours,
Take back these thoughts which here unfolded too,
And which on warm and cold days I withdrew
From my heart's ground. Indeed, those beds and bowers
Be overgrown with bitter weeds and rue,
And wait thy weeding; yet here's eglantine,
Here's ivy!—take them, as I used to do
Thy flowers, and keep them where they shall not pine.
Instruct thine eyes to keep their colors true,
And tell thy soul their roots are left in mine.

1850

From AURORA LEIGH

I

* * *

Nowise beautiful
Was Marian Erle. She was not white nor brown,
But could look either, like a mist that changed
According to being shone on more or less:
The hair, too, ran its opulence of curls
In doubt 'twixt dark and bright, nor left you clear
To name the color. Too much hair perhaps
(I'll name a fault here) for so small a head,
Which seemed to droop on that side and on this,
As a full-blown rose uneasy with its weight
Though not a wind should trouble it. Again,
The dimple in the cheek had better gone
With redder, fuller rounds; and somewhat large
The mouth was, though the milky little teeth
Dissolved it to so infantine a smile.
For soon it smiled at me; the eyes smiled too,
But 'twas as if remembering they had wept,
And knowing they should, some day, weep again.

We talked. She told me all her story out,
Which I'll re-tell with fuller utterance,
As colored and confirmed in after times
By others and herself too. Marian Erle
Was born upon the ledge of Malvern Hill,
To eastward, in a hut built up at night,
To evade the landlord's eye, of mud and turf,
Still liable, if once he looked that way,

To being straight levelled, scattered by his foot,
Like any other anthill. Born, I say;
God sent her to his world, commissioned right,
Her human testimonials fully signed,
Not scant in soul—complete in lineaments;
But others had to swindle her a place
To wail in when she had come. No place for her,
By man's law! born an outlaw was this babe;
Her first cry in our strange and strangling air,
When cast in spasms out by the shuddering womb,
Was wrong against the social code,—forced wrong:—
What business had the baby to cry there?

I tell her story and grow passionate.
She, Marian, did not tell it so, but used
Meek words that made no wonder of herself
For being so sad a creature. "Mister Leigh
Considered truly that such things should change.
They *will*, in heaven—but meantime, on the earth,
There's none can like a nettle as a pink,
Except himself. We're nettles, some of us,
And give offence by the act of springing up;
And, if we leave the damp side of the wall,
The hoes, of course, are on us." So she said.
Her father earned his life by random jobs
Despised by steadier workmen—keeping swine
On commons, picking hops, or hurrying on
The harvest at wet seasons, or, at need,
Assisting the Welsh drovers, when a drove
Of startled horses plunged into the mist
Below the mountain-road, and sowed the wind
With wandering neighings. In between the gaps
Of such irregular work he drank and slept,
And cursed his wife because, the pence being out,
She could not buy more drink. At which she turned
(The worm), and beat her baby in revenge
For her own broken heart. There's not a crime
But takes its proper change out still in crime
If once rung on the counter of this world:
Let sinners look to it.
Yet the outcast child,
For whom the very mother's face forwent
The mother's special patience, lived and grew;
Learnt early to cry low, and walk alone,
With that pathetic vacillating roll
Of the infant body on the uncertain feet
(The earth being felt unstable ground so soon),
At which most women's arms unclose at once
With irrepressive instinct. Thus, at three,
This poor weaned kid would run off from the fold,
This babe would steal off from the mother's chair,
And, creeping through the golden walls of gorse,
Would find some keyhole toward the secrecy
Of Heaven's high blue, and, nestling down, peer out—
Oh, not to catch the angels at their games,—
She had never heard of angels,—but to gaze
She knew not why, to see she knew not what,
A-hungering outward from the barren earth
For something like a joy. She liked, she said,
To dazzle black her sight against the sky,
For then, it seemed, some grand blind Love came down,
And groped her out, and clasped her with a kiss;
She learnt God that way, and was beat for it
Whenever she went home,—yet came again,
As surely as the trapped hare, getting free,
Returns to his form. This grand blind Love, she said,
This skyey father and mother both in one,
Instructed her and civilized her more
Than even Sunday-school did afterward,
To which a lady sent her to learn books
And sit upon a long bench in a row
With other children. Well, she laughed sometimes
To see them laugh and laugh and maul their texts;
But ofter she was sorrowful with noise
And wondered if their mothers beat them hard
That ever they should laugh so. There was one
She loved indeed,—Rose Bell, a seven years' child,
So pretty and clever, who read syllables
When Marian was at letters; *she* would laugh
At nothing—hold your finger up, she laughed,
Then shook her curls down over eyes and mouth

To hide her make-mirth from the schoolmaster:
And Rose's pelting glee, as frank as rain
On cherry-blossoms, brightened Marian too,
To see another merry whom she loved.
She whispered once (the children side by side,
With mutual arms entwined about their necks)
"Your mother lets you laugh so?" "Ay," said Rose,
"She lets me. She was dug into the ground
Six years since, I being but a yearling wean.
Such mothers let us play and lose our time,
And never scold nor beat us! Don't you wish
You had one like that?" There, Marian breaking off
Looked suddenly in my face. "Poor Rose," said she,
"I heard her laugh last night in Oxford Street.
I'd pour out half my blood to stop that laugh.
Poor Rose, poor Rose!" said Marian.
She resumed.
It tried her, when she had learnt at Sunday-school
What God was, what He wanted from us all,
And how in choosing sin we vexed the Christ,
To go straight home and hear her father pull
The Name down on us from the thunder-shelf,
Then drink away his soul into the dark
From seeing judgment. Father, mother, home,
Were God and heaven reversed to her: the more
She knew of Right, the more she guessed their wrong:
Her price paid down for knowledge, was to know
The vileness of her kindred: through her heart,
Her filial and tormented heart, henceforth,
They struck their blows at virtue. Oh, 'tis hard
To learn you have a father up in heaven
By a gathering certain sense of being, on earth,
Still worse than orphaned: 'tis too heavy a grief,
The having to thank God for such a joy!

* * *

II

* * *

"There is none good save God," said Jesus Christ.
If He once, in the first creation-week,
Called creatures good,—for ever, afterward,
The Devil only has done it, and his heirs,
The knaves who win so, and the fools who lose;
The word's grown dangerous. In the middle age,
I think they called malignant fays and imps
Good people. A good neighbor, even in this,
Is fatal sometimes,—cuts your morning up
To mincemeat of the very smallest talk,
Then helps to sugar her bohea at night
With your reputation. I have known good wives,
As chaste, or nearly so, as Potiphar's;
And good, good mothers, who would use a child
To better an intrigue; good friends, beside
(Very good) who hung succinctly round your neck
And sucked your breath, as cats are fabled to do
By sleeping infants. And we all have known
Good critics who have stamped out poet's hope,
Good statesmen who pulled ruin on the state,
Good patriots who for a theory risked a cause,
Good kings who disembowelled for a tax,
Good popes who brought all good to jeopardy,
Good Christians who sat still in easy chairs
And damned the general world for standing up.—
Now may the good God pardon all good men!

* * *

III

* * *

But poets should
Exert a double vision; should have eyes
To see near things as comprehensively
As if afar they took their point of sight,
And distant things as intimately deep
As if they touched them. Let us strive for this.
I do distrust the poet who discerns
No character or glory in his times,
And trundles back his soul five hundred years,
Past moat and drawbridge, into a castle-court,
To sing—oh, not of lizard or of toad
Alive i' the ditch there, —'twere excusable,
But of some black chief, half knight, half sheep-lifter,

Some beauteous dame, half chattel and half queen,
As dead as must be, for the greater part,
The poems made on their chivalric bones;
And that's no wonder: death inherits death.

Nay, if there's room for poets in this world
A little overgrown (I think there is),
Their sole work is to represent the age,
Their age, not Charlemagne's,—this live, throbbing age,
That brawls, cheats, maddens, calculates, aspires,
And spends more passion, more heroic heat,
Betwixt the mirrors of its drawing-rooms,
Than Roland with his knights at Roncesvalles.
To flinch from modern varnish, coat or flounce,
Cry out for togas and the picturesque,
Is fatal,—foolish too. King Arthur's self
Was commonplace to Lady Guenever;
And Camelot to minstrels seemed as flat
As Fleet Street to our poets.
Never flinch,
But still, unscrupulously epic, catch
Upon the burning lava of a song
The full-veined, heaving, double-breasted Age:
That, when the next shall come, the men of that
May touch the impress with reverent hand, and say
"Behold,—behold the paps we all have sucked!
This bosom seems to beat still, or at least
It sets ours beating: this is living art,
Which thus presents and thus records true life."

What form is best for poems? Let me think
Of forms less, and the external. Trust the spirit,
As sovran nature does, to make the form;
For otherwise we only imprison spirit
And not embody. Inward evermore
To outward,—so in life, and so in art
Which still is life.
Five acts to make a play.
And why not fifteen? why not ten? or seven?
What matter for the number of the leaves,
Supposing the tree lives and grows? exact
The literal unities of time and place,
When 'tis the essence of passion to ignore
Both time and place? Absurd. Keep up the fire,
And leave the generous flames to shape themselves.

'Tis true the stage requires obsequiousness
To this or that convention; "exit" here
And "enter" there; the points for clapping, fixed,
Like Jacob's white-peeled rods before the rams,
And all the close-curled imagery clipped
In manner of their fleece at shearing-time.
Forget to prick the galleries to the heart
Precisely at the fourth act,—culminate
Our five pyramidal acts with one act more,—
We're lost so: Shakespeare's ghost could scarcely plead
Against our just damnation. Stand aside;
We'll muse for comfort that, last century,
On this same tragic stage on which we have failed,
A wigless Hamlet would have failed the same.

And whosoever writes good poetry,
Looks just to art. He does not write for you
Or me,—for London or for Edinburgh;
He will not suffer the best critic known
To step into his sunshine of free thought
And self-absorbed conception and exact
An inch-long swerving of the holy lines.
If virtue done for popularity
Defiles like vice, can art, for praise or hire,
Still keep its splendor and remain pure art?
Eschew such serfdom. What the poet writes,
He writes: mankind accepts it if it suits,
And that's success: if not, the poem's passed
From hand to hand, and yet from hand to hand
Until the unborn snatch it, crying out
In pity on their fathers' being so dull,
And that's success too.
I will write no plays;
Because the drama, less sublime in this,
Makes lower appeals, submits more menially,
Adopts the standard of the public taste
To chalk its height on, wears a dog-chain round
Its regal neck, and learns to carry and fetch
The fashions of the day to please the day,
Fawns close on pit and boxes, who clap hands
Commending chiefly its docility

And humor in stage-tricks,—or else indeed
Gets hissed at, howled at, stamped at like a dog,
Or worse, we'll say. For dogs, unjustly kicked,
Yell, bite at need; but if your dramatist
(Being wronged by some five hundred nobodies
Because their grosser brains most naturally
Misjudge the fineness of his subtle wit)
Shows teeth an almond's breadth, protests the length
Of a modest phrase,—"My gentle countrymen,
There's something in it haply of your fault,"—
Why then, besides five hundred nobodies,
He'll have five thousand and five thousand more
Against him,—the whole public,—all the hoofs
Of King Saul's father's asses, in full drove,
And obviously deserve it.

* * *

1856

A MUSICAL INSTRUMENT

I

WHAT was he doing, the great god Pan,
Down in the reeds by the river?
Spreading ruin and scattering ban,
Splashing and paddling with hoofs of a goat,
And breaking the golden lilies afloat
With the dragon-fly on the river.

II

He tore out a reed, the great god Pan,
From the deep cool bed of the river;
The limpid water turbidly ran,
And the broken lilies a-dying lay,
And the dragon-fly had fled away,
Ere he brought it out of the river.

III

High on the shore sat the great god Pan
While turbidly flowed the river;
And hacked and hewed as a great god can,
With his hard bleak steel at the patient reed,
Till there was not a sign of the leaf indeed
To prove it fresh from the river.

IV

He cut it short, did the great god Pan,
(How tall it stood in the river!)
Then drew the pith, like the heart of a man,
Steadily from the outside ring,
And notched the poor dry empty thing
In holes, as he sat by the river.

V

"This is the way," laughed the great god Pan
(Laughed while he sat by the river),
"The only way, since gods began
To make sweet music, they could succeed."
Then, dropping his mouth to a hole in the reed,
He blew in power by the river.

VI

Sweet, sweet, sweet, O Pan!
Piercing sweet by the river!
Blinding sweet, O great god Pan!
The sun on the hill forgot to die,
And the lilies revived, and the dragon-fly
Came back to dream on the river.

VII

Yet half a beast is the great god Pan,
To laugh as he sits by the river,
Making a poet out of a man:
The true gods sigh for the cost and pain,—
For the reed which grows nevermore again
As a reed with the reeds in the river.

1860

MOTHER AND POET

TURIN, AFTER NEWS FROM GAETA, 1861

I

DEAD! One of them shot by the sea in the east,
And one of them shot in the west by the sea.
Dead! both my boys! When you sit at the feast
And are wanting a great song for Italy free,
Let none look at *me!*

II

Yet I was a poetess only last year,
And good at my art, for a woman, men said;
But *this* woman, *this*, who is agonized here,
—The east sea and west sea rhyme on in her head
For ever instead.

III

What art can a woman be good at? Oh, vain!
What art *is* she good at, but hurting her breast

Seventh stanza omitted by an oversight, from the "Tale of Villafranca" –
(Insert it between the sixth and seventh as printed in the Athenæum.)

"A great deed in this world of ours?
Unheard of the pretence is –
It threatens plainly the great Powers,
Is fatal in all senses –
A just deed in the world? call out
The rifles! – be not slack about
The national Defences –"

Elizabeth Barrett Browning.
Florence – 1859 –

A Piece of Mrs. Browning's Manuscript. (See Appendix I.)

With the milk-teeth of babes, and a smile at the pain?
Ah boys, how you hurt! you were strong as you pressed,
And I proud, by that test.

IV

What art's for a woman? To hold on her knees
Both darlings! to feel all their arms round her throat,
Cling, strangle a little! to sew by degrees
And 'broider the long-clothes and neat little coat;
To dream and to doat.

V

To teach them . . . It stings there! *I* made them indeed
Speak plain the word *country*. *I* taught them, no doubt,
That a country's a thing men should die for at need.
I prated of liberty, rights, and about
The tyrant cast out.

VI

And when their eyes flashed . . . O my beautiful eyes! . . .
I exulted; nay, let them go forth at the wheels
Of the guns, and denied not. But then the surprise
When one sits quite alone! Then one weeps, then one kneels!
God, how the house feels!

VII

At first, happy news came, in gay letters moiled
With my kisses,—of camp-life and glory, and how
They both loved me; and, soon coming home to be spoiled,
In return would fan off every fly from my brow
With their green laurel-bough.

VIII

Then was triumph at Turin: "Ancona was free!"
And some one came out of the cheers in the street,
With a face pale as stone, to say something to me.
My Guido was dead! I fell down at his feet,
While they cheered in the street.

IX

I bore it; friends soothed me; my grief looked sublime
As the ransom of Italy. One boy remained
To be leant on and walked with, recalling the time
When the first grew immortal, while both of us strained
To the height he had gained.

X

And letters still came, shorter, sadder, more strong,
Writ now but in one hand, "I was not to faint,—
One loved me for two—would be with me ere long:
And *Viva l'Italia!—he* died for, our saint,
Who forbids our complaint."

XI

My Nanni would add, "he was safe, and aware
Of a presence that turned off the balls,—was imprest
It was Guido himself, who knew what I could bear,
And how 'twas impossible, quite dispossessed
To live on for the rest."

XII

On which, without pause, up the telegraph-line
Swept smoothly the next news from Gaeta:—*Shot*.
Tell his mother. Ah, ah, "his," "their" mother,—not "mine,"
No voice says "*My* mother" again to me. What!
You think Guido forgot?

XIII

Are souls straight so happy that, dizzy with Heaven,
They drop earth's affections, conceive not of woe?

I think not. Themselves were too lately forgiven
Through THAT Love and Sorrow which reconciled so
The Above and Below.

XIV

O Christ of the five wounds, who look'dst through the dark
To the face of thy mother! consider, I pray,
How we common mothers stand desolate, mark,
Whose sons, not being Christs, die with eyes turned away,
And no last word to say!

XV

Both boys dead? but that's out of nature. We all
Have been patriots, yet each house must always keep one.
'Twere imbecile, hewing out roads to a wall;
And, when Italy's made, for what end is it done
If we have not a son?

XVI

Ah, ah, ah! when Gaeta's taken, what then?
When the fair wicked queen sits no more at her sport
Of the fire-balls of death crashing souls out of men?
When the guns of Cavalli with final retort
Have cut the game short?

XVII

When Venice and Rome keep their new jubilee,
When your flag takes all heaven for its white, green, and red,
When *you* have your country from mountain to sea,
When King Victor has Italy's crown on his head,
(And *I* have my Dead)—

XVIII

What then? Do not mock me. Ah, ring your bells low,
And burn your lights faintly! *My* country is *there*,
Above the star pricked by the last peak of snow:
My Italy's THERE, with my brave civic Pair,
To disfranchise despair!

XIX

Forgive me. Some women bear children in strength,
And bite back the cry of their pain in self-scorn;
But the birth-pangs of nations will wring us at length
Into wail such as this—and we sit on forlorn
When the man-child is born.

XX

Dead! One of them shot by the sea in the east,
And one of them shot in the west by the sea.
Both! both my boys! If in keeping the feast
You want a great song for your Italy free,
Let none look at *me!*

[This was Laura Savio of Turin, a poetess and patriot, whose sons were killed at Ancona and Gaeta.]

A FALSE STEP

I

SWEET, thou hast trod on a heart.
Pass; there's a world full of men;
And women as fair as thou art
Must do such things now and then.

II

Thou hast only stepped unaware,—
Malice, not one can impute;
And why should a heart have been there
In the way of a fair woman's foot?

III

It was not a stone that could trip,
Nor was it a thorn that could rend:
Put up thy proud under-lip!
'Twas merely the heart of a friend.

IV

And yet peradventure one day
Thou, sitting alone at the glass,
Remarking the bloom gone away,
Where the smile in its dimplement was,

V

And seeking around thee in vain
  From hundreds who flattered before,
Such a word as "Oh, not in the main
  Do I hold thee less precious, but more!" . . .

VI

Thou'lt sigh, very like, on thy part, 21
  "Of all I have known or can know,
I wish I had only that Heart
  I trod upon ages ago!"

1862

ARTHUR HUGH CLOUGH

[January 1, 1819–November 13, 1861]

Arthur Hugh Clough, the son of a cotton-merchant, was born in Liverpool and taken by his family, when he was not yet four years old, to Charleston, South Carolina, where he spent five years of his childhood. He was a serious child who took naturally to reading and study at a very early age, and he is said to have read a number of Scott's novels, the life of Columbus, and Pope's *Homer* before he was seven years old. In 1829 he and his brother Charles went to Rugby, where he became the favorite pupil of the famous head master, Dr. Thomas Arnold. His brother remained at Rugby only two years, and since his family was again in America, Clough suffered, as he said, under "the curse of being without a home." The Arnolds conceived a great liking for him and made him a welcome visitor at their home, a circumstance which both relieved his loneliness and led him to speak of "the blessing of being under Arnold," and to "thank God for Arnold and his kindness."

In 1836 Clough closed his Rugby days in triumph by winning the Balliol scholarship, and in October, 1837, he entered Oxford. This was the stormy time of the Oxford Movement, and Clough, coming under the influence of Newman and others, felt himself deeply unsettled in an atmosphere of religious speculation and excitement. The effect of his unsettlement was a falling off in his studies, and he graduated as a second instead of a first, a ranking which one of his ability might easily have reached had he turned his energies to academic performance. Failing in his trial for the Balliol fellowship in 1841, he was elected to a fellowship in Oriel College, which he resigned after six years because he could not honestly remain in a university where he had to subscribe to the Thirty-nine Articles of the Church of England. Following his resignation, he visited Italy and France for a short time but found no ease for his unquiet mind in travel.

In 1852, having given up the headship of University Hall, London, which he had held since 1849, he accepted the invitation of Emerson to lecture, teach, and write in America. This effort proved a failure and after a year he returned to London, where he became an examiner in the Education Office. The next year he married. After seven years of happy home life his health, which had never been good, broke, and in October, 1860, he went to Florence, hoping to regain his usual strength. It was a vain hope, however, and a few weeks later he died and found a resting place in the Protestant cemetery, where, a few months before his death, Mrs. Browning had been laid.

In 1848 he published *The Bothie of Tober-na-Vuolich*, in 1849 *Ambarvalia*, and in 1858 *Amours de Voyage*. His *Dipsychus* and *Mari Magno* were posthumous works.

Living a life of spiritual unrest was inevitable for one who, like Clough, said that we must "look straight out at things" and abide the consequences. He believed that poetry must "touch some deep question, some vital feeling in human nature," and hence his poetry makes slight appeal to the imagination and gives little stir to the emotions. One whose thought is dominated by the "austere love of truth" and whose constant creed is that "poetry must touch some deep question" will not write far above the level Clough reached when he voiced his eternal query whether it is our fate to

spend uncounted years of pain,
Again, again, and yet again,
In working out in heart and brain
The problem of our being here.

THE HIGHER COURAGE

Come back again, my olden heart!—
Ah, fickle spirit and untrue,
I bade the only guide depart
Whose faithfulness I surely knew:
I said, my heart is all too soft;
He who would climb and soar aloft
Must needs keep ever at his side
The tonic of a wholesome pride.

Come back again, my olden heart!—
Alas, I called not then for thee;
I called for Courage, and apart
From Pride if Courage could not be,
Then welcome, Pride! and I shall find
In thee a power to lift the mind
This low and grovelling joy above—
'Tis but the proud can truly love.

Come back again, my olden heart!—
With incrustations of the years
Uncased as yet,—as then thou wert,
Full-filled with shame and coward fears:
Wherewith amidst a jostling throng
Of deeds, that each and all were wrong,
The doubting soul, from day to day,
Uneasy paralytic lay.

Come back again, my olden heart!
I said, Perceptions contradict,
Convictions come, anon depart,
And but themselves as false convict.
Assumptions, hasty, crude and vain,
Full oft to use will Science deign;
The corks the novice plies to-day
The swimmer soon shall cast away.

Come back again, my olden heart!
I said, Behold, I perish quite,
Unless to give me strength to start,
I make myself my rule of right:
It must be, if I act at all,
To save my shame I have at call
The plea of all men understood,—
Because I willed it, it is good.

Come back again, my olden heart!
I know not if in very deed
This means alone could aid impart
To serve my sickly spirit's need;
But clear alike of wild self-will,
And fear that faltered, paltered still,
Remorseful thoughts of after days
A way espy betwixt the ways.

Come back again, old heart! Ah me!
Methinks in those thy coward fears
There might, perchance, a courage be,
That fails in these the manlier years;
Courage to let the courage sink,
Itself a coward base to think,
Rather than not for heavenly light
Wait on to show the truly right.

1840

AN EVENING WALK IN SPRING

It was but some few nights ago
I wandered down this quiet lane;
I pray that I may never know
The feelings then I felt, again.
The leaves were shining all about,
You might almost have seen them springing;
I heard the cuckoo's simple shout,
And all the little birds were singing.
It was not dull, the air was clear,
All lovely sights and sounds to deal,
My eyes could see, my ears could hear,
Only my heart, it would not feel;
And yet that it should not be so,
My mind kept telling me within;

Though nought was wrong that I did know,
  I thought I must have done some sin.
For I am sure as I can be,
  That they who have been wont to look
On all in Nature's face they see,
  Even as in the Holy Book;
They who with pure and humble eyes
  Have gazed and read her lessons high,
And taught their spirits to be wise
  In love and human sympathy,—
That they can soon and surely tell
  When aught has gone amiss within,
When the mind is not sound and well,
  Nor the soul free from taint of sin.
For as God's Spirit from above,
  So Beauty is to them below,
And when they slight that holy love,
  Their hearts that presence may not know.
So I turned home the way I came,
  With downcast looks and heavy heart,
A guilty thing and full of shame,
  With a dull grief that had no smart.
It chanced when I was nearly there
  That all at once I raised my eyes—
Was it a dream, or vision rare,
  That then they saw before them rise?
I see it now, before me here,
  As often, often I have done,
As bright as it could then appear,
  All shining in the setting sun.
Elms, with their mantling foliage spread,
  And tall dark poplars rising out,
And blossomed orchards, white and red,
  Cast, like a long low fence, about;
And in the midst the grey church-tower,
  With one slight turret at its side,
Bringing to mind with silent power
  Those thousand homes the elm trees hide.
And then there came the thought of one
  Who on his bed of sickness lay,
Whilst I beneath the setting sun
  Was dreaming this sweet hour away.
I thought of hearts for him that beat,
  Of aching eyes their watch that kept;
The sister's and the mother's seat—
  And oh! I thought I should have wept.
And oh! my spirit melted then,
  The weight fell off me that I bore,
And now I felt in truth again
  The lovely things that stood before.
O blessed, blessed scene, to thee,
  For that thy sweet and softening power,
I could have fallen upon my knee,
  Thy stately elms, thy grey church-tower.
So then I took my homeward way,
  My heart in sweet and holy frame,
With spirit, I may dare to say,
  More good and soft than when I came.

1836

LOVE AND REASON

When panting sighs the bosom fill,
And hands by chance united thrill
At once with one delicious pain
The pulses and the nerves of twain;
When eyes that erst could meet with ease,
Do seek, yet, seeking, shyly shun
Ecstatic conscious unison,—
The sure beginnings, say, be these
Prelusive to the strain of love
Which angels sing in heaven above?

  Or is it but the vulgar tune,
Which all that breathe beneath the moon
So accurately learn—so soon?
With variations duly blent;
Yet that same song to all intent,
Set for the finer instrument;
It is; and it would sound the same
In beasts, were not the bestial frame,
Less subtly organised, to blame;
And but that soul and spirit add
To pleasures, even base and bad,
A zest the soulless never had.

  It may be—well indeed I deem;
But what if sympathy, it seem,
And admiration and esteem,
Commingling therewithal, do make
The passion prized for Reason's sake?
Yet, when my heart would fain rejoice,
A small expostulating voice
Falls in; Of this thou wilt not take
Thy one irrevocable choice?
In accent tremulous and thin
I hear high Prudence deep within,
Pleading the bitter, bitter sting,
Should slow-maturing seasons bring,
Too late, the veritable thing.
For if (the Poet's tale of bliss)
A love, wherewith commeasured this

Is weak and beggarly, and none,
Exist a treasure to be won,
And if the vision, though it stay,
Be yet for an appointed day,—
This choice, if made, this deed, if done,
The memory of this present past,
With vague foreboding might o'ercast
The heart, or madden it at last.

Let Reason first her office ply;
Esteem, and admiration high,
And mental, moral sympathy,
Exist they first, nor be they brought,
By self-deceiving afterthought,—
What if an halo interfuse
With these again its opal hues,
That all o'erspreading and o'erlying,
Transmuting, mingling, glorifying,
About the beauteous various whole,
With beaming smile do dance and quiver;
Yet, is that halo of the soul?—
Or is it, as may sure be said,
Phosphoric exhalation bred
Of vapour, steaming from the bed
Of Fancy's brook, or Passion's river?
So when, as will be by and by,
The stream is waterless and dry,
This halo and its hues will die;
And though the soul contented rest
With those substantial blessings blest,
Will not a longing, half confest,
Betray that this is not the love,
The gift for which all gifts above
Him praise we, Who is Love, the Giver?

I cannot say—the things are good:
Bread is it, if not angels' food;
But Love? Alas! I cannot say;
A glory on the vision lay;
A light of more than mortal day
About it played, upon it rested;
It did not, faltering and weak,
Beg Reason on its side to speak:
Itself was Reason, or, if not,
Such substitute as is, I wot,
Of seraph-kind the loftier lot;—
Itself was of itself attested;—
To processes that, hard and dry,
Elaborate truth from fallacy,
With modes intuitive succeeding,
Including those and superseding;
Reason sublimed and Love most high
It was, a life that cannot die,
A dream of glory most exceeding.

1844

LOVE, NOT DUTY

THOUGHT may well be ever ranging,
And opinion ever changing,
Task-work be, though ill begun,
Dealt with by experience better;
By the law and by the letter
Duty done is duty done:
Do it, Time is on the wing!

Hearts, 'tis quite another thing,
Must or once for all be given,
Or must not at all be given;
Hearts, 'tis quite another thing!

To bestow the soul away
Is an idle duty-play!—
Why, to trust a life-long bliss
To caprices of a day,
Scarce were more depraved than this!

Men and maidens, see you mind it;
Show of love, where'er you find it,
Look if duty lurk behind it!
Duty-fancies, urging on
Whither love had never gone!

Loving—if the answering breast
Seem not to be thus possessed,
Still in hoping have a care;
If it do, beware, beware!
But if in yourself you find it,
Above all things—mind it, mind it!

1841

THE MUSIC OF THE WORLD AND OF THE SOUL

I

WHY should I say I see the things I see not?
Why be and be not?
Show love for that I love not, and fear for what I fear not?
And dance about to music that I hear not?
Who standeth still i' the street
Shall be hustled and justled about;

And he that stops i' the dance shall be spurned by the dancers' feet,—
Shall be shoved and be twisted by all he shall meet,
And shall raise up an outcry and rout;
And the partner, too,—
What's the partner to do?
While all the while 'tis but, perchance, an humming in mine ear,
That yet anon shall hear,
And I anon, the music in my soul,
In a moment read the whole;
The music in my heart,
Joyously take my part,
And hand in hand, and heart with heart, with these retreat, advance;
And borne on wings of wavy sound,
Whirl with these around, around,
Who here are living in the living dance!
Why forfeit that fair chance?
Till that arrive, till thou awake,
Of these, my soul, thy music make,
And keep amid the throng,
And turn as they shall turn, and bound as they are bounding,—
Alas! alas! alas! and what if all along
The music is not sounding?

II

Are there not, then, two musics unto men?—
One loud and bold and coarse,
And overpowering still perforce
All tone and tune beside;
Yet in despite its pride
Only of fumes of foolish fancy bred,
And sounding solely in the sounding head:
The other, soft and low,
Stealing whence we not know,
Painfully heard, and easily forgot,
With pauses oft and many a silence strange
(And silent oft it seems, when silent it is not),
Revivals too of unexpected change:
Haply thou think'st 'twill never be begun,
Or that 't has come, and been, and passed away:
Yet turn to other none,—
Turn not, oh, turn not thou!
But listen, listen, listen,—if haply be heard it may;
Listen, listen, listen,—is it not sounding now?

III

Yea, and as thought of some departed friend
By death or distance parted will descend,
Severing, in crowded rooms ablaze with light,
As by a magic screen, the seër from the sight
(Palsying the nerves that intervene
The eye and central sense between);
So may the ear,
Hearing not hear,
Though drums do roll, and pipes and cymbals ring;
So the bare conscience of the better thing
Unfelt, unseen, unimaged, all unknown,
May fix the entrancèd soul 'mid multitudes alone.

A SONG OF AUTUMN

My wind is turned to bitter north,
That was so soft a south before;
My sky, that shone so sunny bright,
With foggy gloom is clouded o'er:
My gay green leaves are yellow-black,
Upon the dank autumnal floor;
For love, departed once, comes back
No more again, no more.

A roofless ruin lies my home,
For winds to blow and rains to pour;
One frosty night befell, and lo!
I find my summer days are o'er:
The heart bereaved, of why and how
Unknowing, knows that yet before
It had what e'en to Memory now
Returns no more, no more.

REVIVAL

So I went wrong,
Grievously wrong, but folly crushed itself,
And vanity o'ertoppling fell, and time
And healthy discipline and some neglect,
Labour and solitary hours revived
Somewhat, at least, of that original frame.
Oh, well do I remember then the days
When on some grassy slope (what time the sun
Was sinking, and the solemn eve came down
With its blue vapour upon field and wood
And elm-embosomed spire) once more again

I fed on sweet emotion, and my heart
With love o'erflowed, or hushed itself in fear
Unearthly, yea celestial. Once again
My heart was hot within me, and, meseemed,
I too had in my body breath to wind
The magic horn of song; I too possessed
Up-welling in my being's depths a fount
Of the true poet-nectar whence to fill
The golden urns of verse.

1839

IN A LECTURE-ROOM

Away, haunt thou not me,
Thou vain Philosophy!
Little hast thou bestead,
Save to perplex the head,
And leave the spirit dead.
Unto thy broken cisterns wherefore go,
While from the secret treasure-depths below,
Fed by the skyey shower,
And clouds that sink and rest on hill-tops high,
Wisdom at once, and Power,
Are welling, bubbling forth, unseen, incessantly?
Why labour at the dull mechanic oar,
When the fresh breeze is blowing,
And the strong current flowing,
Right onward to the Eternal Shore?

1840

τὸ καλόν

I have seen higher, holier things than these,
And therefore must to these refuse my heart.
Yet am I panting for a little ease;
I'll take, and so depart.

Ah, hold! the heart is prone to fall away,
Her high and cherished visions to forget,
And if thou takest, how wilt thou repay
So vast, so dread a debt?

How will the heart, which now thou trustest, then
Corrupt, yet in corruption mindful yet,
Turn with sharp stings upon itself! Again,
Bethink thee of the debt!

—Hast thou seen higher, holier things than these,
And therefore must to these thy heart refuse?
With the true best, alack, how ill agrees
That best that thou would'st choose!

The Summum Pulchrum rests in heaven above;
Do thou, as best thou may'st, thy duty do:
Amid the things allowed thee live and love;
Some day thou shalt it view.

1841

QUA CURSUM VENTUS

As ships, becalmed at eve, that lay
With canvas drooping, side by side,
Two towers of sail at dawn of day
Are scarce long leagues apart descried;

When fell the night, upsprung the breeze,
And all the darkling hours they plied,
Nor dreamt but each the self-same seas
By each was cleaving, side by side:

E'en so—but why the tale reveal
Of those whom, year by year unchanged,
Brief absence joined anew to feel,
Astounded, soul from soul estranged?

At dead of night their sails were filled,
And onward each rejoicing steered—
Ah, neither blame, for neither willed,
Or wist, what first with dawn appeared!

To veer, how vain! On, onward strain,
Brave barks! In light, in darkness too,
Through winds and tides one compass guides—
To that, and your own selves, be true.

But O blithe breeze; and O great seas,
Though ne'er, that earliest parting past,
On your wide plain they join again,
Together lead them home at last.

One port, methought, alike they sought,
One purpose hold where'er they fare,—
O bounding breeze, O rushing seas!
At last, at last, unite them there!

1849

"WEN GOTT BETRÜGT, IST WOHL BETROGEN"

Is it true, ye gods, who treat us
As the gambling fool is treated;
O ye, who ever cheat us,

And let us feel we're cheated!
Is it true that poetical power,
The gift of heaven, the dower
Of Apollo and the Nine,
The inborn sense, "the vision and the faculty divine,"
All we glorify and bless
In our rapturous exaltation,
All invention, and creation,
Exuberance of fancy, and sublime imagination,
All a poet's fame is built on,
The fame of Shakespeare, Milton,
Of Wordsworth, Byron, Shelley,
Is in reason's grave precision,
Nothing more, nothing less,
Than a peculiar conformation,
Constitution, and condition
Of the brain and of the belly?
Is it true, ye gods who cheat us?
And that's the way ye treat us?

Oh say it, all who think it,
Look straight, and never blink it!
If it is so, let it be so,
And we will all agree so;
But the plot has counterplot,
It may be, and yet be not.

1849

"*Blank Misgivings of a Creature moving about in Worlds not realised.*"

I

Here am I yet, another twelvemonth spent,
One-third departed of the mortal span,
Carrying on the child into the man,
Nothing into reality. Sails rent,
And rudder broken,—reason impotent,—
Affections all unfixed; so forth I fare
On the mid seas unheedingly, so dare
To do and to be done by, well content.
So was it from the first, so is it yet;
Yea, the first kiss that by these lips was set
On any human lips, methinks was sin—
Sin, cowardice, and falsehood; for the will
Into a deed e'en then advanced, wherein
God, unidentified, was thought-of still.

II

Though to the vilest things beneath the moon
For poor Ease' sake I give away my heart,
And for the moment's sympathy let part
My sight and sense of truth, Thy precious boon,
My painful earnings, lost, all lost, as soon,
Almost, as gained; and though aside I start,
Belie Thee daily, hourly,—still Thou art,
Art surely as in heaven the sun at noon;
How much so e'er I sin, whate'er I do
Of evil, still the sky above is blue,
The stars look down in beauty as before:
It is enough to walk as best we may,
To walk, and, sighing, dream of that blest day
When ill we cannot quell shall be no more.

III

Well, well,—Heaven bless you all from day to day!
Forgiveness too, or e'er we part, from each,
As I do give it, so must I beseech:
I owe all much, much more than I can pay;
Therefore it is I go; how could I stay
Where every look commits me to fresh debt,
And to pay little I must borrow yet?
Enough of this already, now away!
With silent woods and hills untenanted
Let me go commune; under thy sweet gloom,
O kind maternal Darkness, hide my head:
The day may come I yet may reassume
My place, and, these tired limbs recruited, seek
The task for which I now am all too weak.

IV

Yes, I have lied, and so must walk my way,
Bearing the liar's curse upon my head;
Letting my weak and sickly heart be fed
On food which does the present craving stay,
But may be clean-denied me e'en to-day,
And tho' 'twere certain, yet were ought but bread;
Letting—for so they say, it seems, I said,
And I am all too weak to disobey!
Therefore for me sweet Nature's scenes reveal not
Their charm; sweet Music greets me and I feel not
Sweet eyes pass off me uninspired; yea, more,
The golden tide of opportunity
Flows wafting-in friendships and better,—I
Unseeing, listless, pace along the shore.

V

How often sit I, poring o'er
My strange distorted youth,
Seeking in vain, in all my store,
One feeling based on truth;
Amid the maze of petty life
A clue whereby to move,
A spot whereon in toil and strife
To dare to rest and love.
So constant as my heart would be,
So fickle as it must,
'Twere well for others as for me
'Twere dry as summer dust.
Excitements come, and act and speech
Flow freely forth;—but no,
Nor they, nor ought beside can reach
The buried world below.

1841

THE NEW SINAI

Lo, here is God, and there is God!
Believe it not, O Man;
In such vain sort to this and that
The ancient heathen ran:
Though old Religion shake her head,
And say in bitter grief,
The day behold, at first foretold,
Of atheist unbelief:
Take better part, with manly heart,
Thine adult spirit can;
Receive it not, believe it not,
Believe it not, O Man!

As men at dead of night awaked
With cries, "The king is here,"
Rush forth and greet whome'er they meet,
Whoe'er shall first appear;
And still repeat, to all the street,
"'Tis he,—the king is here;"
The long procession moveth on,
Each nobler form they see,
With changeful suit they still salute
And cry, "'Tis he, 'tis he!"

So, even so, when men were young,
And earth and heaven were new,
And His immediate presence He
From human hearts withdrew,
The soul perplexed and daily vexed
With sensuous False and True,
Amazed, bereaved, no less believed,
And fain would see Him too:
"He is!" the prophet-tongues proclaimed;
In joy and hasty fear,
"He is!" aloud replied the crowd,
"Is here, and here, and here."

"He is! They are!" in distance seen
On yon Olympus high,
In those Avernian woods abide,
And walk this azure sky:
"They are! They are!"—to every show
Its eyes the baby turned,
And blazes sacrificial, tall,
On thousand altars burned:
"They are! They are!"—On Sinai's top
Far seen the lightnings shone,
The thunder broke, a trumpet spoke,
And God said, "I am One."

God spake it out, "I, God, am One;"
The unheeding ages ran.
And baby-thoughts again, again,
Have dogged the growing man:
And as of old from Sinai's top
God said that God is One,
By Science strict so speaks He now
To tell us, There is None!
Earth goes by chemic forces; Heaven's
A Mécanique Céleste!
And heart and mind of human kind
A watch-work as the rest!

Is this a Voice, as was the Voice,
Whose speaking told abroad,
When thunder pealed, and mountain reeled,
The ancient truth of God?
Ah, not the Voice; 'tis but the cloud,
The outer darkness dense,
Where image none, nor e'er was seen
Similitude of sense.
'Tis but the cloudy darkness dense
That wrapt the Mount around;
While in amaze the people stays,
To hear the Coming Sound.

Is there no prophet-soul the while
To dare, sublimely meek,
Within the shroud of blackest cloud
The Deity to seek?
'Midst atheistic systems dark,
And darker hearts' despair,

That soul has heard perchance His word,
And on the dusky air
His skirts, as passed He by, to see
Hath strained on their behalf,
Who on the plain, with dance amain,
Adore the Golden Calf.

'Tis but the cloudy darkness dense;
Though blank the tale it tells,
No God, no Truth! yet He, in sooth,
Is there—within it dwells;
Within the sceptic darkness deep
He dwells that none may see,
Till idol forms and idol thoughts
Have passed and ceased to be:
No God, no Truth! ah, though, in sooth
So stand the doctrine's half:
On Egypt's track return not back,
Nor own the Golden Calf.

Take better part, with manlier heart,
Thine adult spirit can;
No God, no Truth, receive it ne'er—
Believe it ne'er—O Man!
But turn not then to seek again
What first the ill began;
No God, it saith; ah, wait in faith
God's self-completing plan;
Receive it not, but leave it not,
And wait it out, O Man!

"The Man that went the cloud within
Is gone and vanished quite;
He cometh not," the people cries,
"Nor bringeth God to sight:
Lo these thy gods, that safety give,
Adore and keep the feast!"
Deluding and deluded cries
The Prophet's brother-Priest:
And Israel all bows down to fall
Before the gilded beast.

Devout, indeed! that priestly creed,
O Man, reject as sin;
The clouded hill attend thou still,
And him that went within.
He yet shall bring some worthy thing
For waiting souls to see:
Some sacred word that he hath heard
Their light and life shall be;
Some lofty part, than which the heart
Adopt no nobler can,
Thou shalt receive, thou shalt believe
And thou shalt do, O Man!

1845

THE QUESTIONING SPIRIT

The human spirits saw I on a day,
Sitting and looking each a different way;
And hardly tasking, subtly questioning,
Another spirit went around the ring
To each and each: and as he ceased his say,
Each after each, I heard them singly sing,
Some querulously high, some softly, sadly low.
We know not—what avails to know?
We know not—wherefore need we know?
This answer gave they still unto his suing,
We know not, let us do as we are doing.
Dost thou not know that these things only seem?—
I know not, let me dream my dream.
Are dust and ashes fit to make a treasure?—
I know not, let me take my pleasure.
What shall avail the knowledge thou hast sought?—
I know not, let me think my thought.
What is the end of strife?—
I know not, let me live my life.
How many days or e'er thou mean'st to move?—
I know not, let me love my love.
Were not things old once new?—
I know not, let me do as others do.
And when the rest were over past,
I know not, I will do my duty, said the last.

Thy duty do? rejoined the voice,
Ah, do it, do it, and rejoice;
But shalt thou then, when all is done,
Enjoy a love, embrace a beauty
Like these, that may be seen and won
In life, whose course will then be run;
Or wilt thou be where there is none?
I know not, I will do my duty.

And taking up the word around, above, below,
Some querulously high, some softly, sadly low,
We know not, sang they all, nor ever need we know;

We know not, sang they, what avails to know?
Whereat the questioning spirit, some short space,
Though unabashed, stood quiet in his place.
But as the echoing chorus died away
And to their dreams the rest returned apace,
By the one spirit I saw him kneeling low,
And in a silvery whisper heard him say:
Truly, thou know'st not, and thou need'st not know;
Hope only, hope thou, and believe alway;
I also know not, and I need not know,
Only with questionings pass I to and fro,
Perplexing these that sleep, and in their folly
Imbreeding doubt and sceptic melancholy;
Till that, their dreams deserting, they with me
Come all to this true ignorance and thee.

1847

BETHESDA

A SEQUEL

I SAW again the spirits on a day,
Where on the earth in mournful case they lay;
Five porches were there, and a pool, and round,
Huddling in blankets, strewn upon the ground,
Tied-up and bandaged, weary, sore, and spent,
The maimed and halt, diseased and impotent.

For a great angel came, 'twas said, and stirred
The pool at certain seasons, and the word
Was, with this people of the sick, that they
Who in the waters here their limbs should lay
Before the motion on the surface ceased
Should of their torment straightway be released.
So with shrunk bodies and with heads down-dropt,
Stretched on the steps, and at the pillars propt,
Watching by day and listening through the night,
They filled the place, a miserable sight.

And I beheld that on the stony floor
He too, that spoke of duty once before,
No otherwise than others here to-day,
Foredone and sick and sadly muttering lay.
"I know not, I will do—what is it I would say?
What was that word which once sufficed alone for all,
Which now I seek in vain, and never can recall?"
And then, as weary of in vain renewing
His question, thus his mournful thought pursuing,
"I know not, I must do as other men are doing."

But what the waters of that pool might be,
Of Lethe were they, or Philosophy;
And whether he, long waiting, did attain
Deliverance from the burden of his pain
There with the rest; or whether, yet before,
Some more diviner stranger passed the door
With his small company into that sad place,
And breathing hope into the sick man's face,
Bade him take up his bed, and rise and go,
What the end were, and whether it were so,
Further than this I saw not, neither know.

1849

SEHNSUCHT

WHENCE are ye, vague desires,
Which carry men along,
However proud and strong;
Which, having ruled to-day,
To-morrow pass away?
Whence are ye, vague desires?
Whence are ye?

Which women, yielding to,
Find still so good and true;
So true, so good to-day,
To-morrow gone away;
Whence are ye, vague desires?
Whence are ye?

From seats of bliss above,
Where angels sing of love;
From subtle airs around,
Or from the vulgar ground,
Whence are ye, vague desires?
Whence are ye?

A message from the blest,
Or bodily unrest;
A call to heavenly good,
A fever in the blood:
What are ye, vague desires?
What are ye?

Which men who know you best
Are proof against the least,
And rushing on to-day,
To-morrow cast away;
What are ye, vague desires?
What are ye?

Which women, ever new,
Still warned, surrender to;
Adored with you to-day,
Then cast with you away;
What are ye, vague desires?
What are ye?

Which unto boyhood's heart
The force of man impart,
And pass, and leave it cold,
And prematurely old;
What are ye, vague desires?
What are ye?

Which, tremblingly confest,
Pour in the young girl's breast
Joy, joy—the like is none,
And leave her then undone—
What are ye, vague desires?
What are ye?

Ah yet! though man be marred,
Ignoble made, and hard;
Though broken women lie
In anguish down to die;
Ah yet! ye vague desires,
Ah yet!

By Him who gave you birth,
And blended you with earth,
Was some good end designed
For man and womankind;
Ah yet! ye vague desires,
Ah yet!

The petals of to-day,
To-morrow fallen away,
Shall something leave instead,
To live when they are dead;
When you, ye vague desires,
Have vanished;

A something to survive,
Of you though it derive
Apparent earthly birth,
But of far other worth
Than you, ye vague desires,
Than you.

1862

PESCHIERA

WHAT voice did on my spirit fall,
Peschiera, when thy bridge I crost?
"'Tis better to have fought and lost,
Than never to have fought at all."

The tricolour—a trampled rag
Lies, dirt and dust; the lines I track
By sentry boxes yellow-black,
Lead up to no Italian flag.

I see the Croat soldier stand
Upon the grass of your redoubts;
The eagle with his black wings flouts
The breath and beauty of your land.

Yet not in vain, although in vain,
O men of Brescia, on the day
Of lost past hope, I heard you say
Your welcome to the noble pain.

You say, "Since so it is,—good-bye
Sweet life, high hope; but whatsoe'er
May be, or must, no tongue shall dare
To tell, 'The Lombard feared to die!'"

You said (there shall be answer fit),
"And if our children must obey,
They must; but thinking on this day
'Twill less debase them to submit."

You said (Oh not in vain you said),
"Haste, brothers, haste, while yet we may;
The hours ebb fast of this one day
When blood may yet be nobly shed."

Ah! not for idle hatred, not
For honour, fame, nor self-applause,
But for the glory of the cause,
You did, what will not be forgot.

And though the stranger stand, 'tis true,
By force and fortune's right he stands;
By fortune, which is in God's hands,
And strength, which yet shall spring in you.

This voice did on my spirit fall,
Peschiera, when thy bridge I crost,
"'Tis better to have fought and lost,
Than never to have fought at all."

1849

ALTERAM PARTEM

Or shall I say, Vain word, false thought,
Since Prudence hath her martyrs too,
And Wisdom dictates not to do,
Till doing shall be not for nought?

Not ours to give or lose is life;
Will Nature, when her brave ones fall,
Remake her work? or songs recall
Death's victim slain in useless strife?

That rivers flow into the sea
Is loss and waste, the foolish say,
Nor know that back they find their way,
Unseen, to where they wont to be.

Showers fall upon the hills, springs flow,
The river runneth still at hand,
Brave men are born into the land,
And whence the foolish do not know.

No! no vain voice did on me fall,
Peschiera, when thy bridge I crost,
"'*Tis* better to have fought and lost,
Than never to have fought at all."

1849

IN THE DEPTHS

It is not sweet content, be sure,
That moves the nobler Muse to song,
Yet when could truth come whole and pure
From hearts that inly writhe with wrong?

'Tis not the calm and peaceful breast
That sees or reads the problem true;
They only know on whom 't has prest
Too hard to hope to solve it too.

Our ills are worse than at their ease
These blameless happy souls suspect,
They only study the disease,
Alas, who live not to detect.

1862

From DIPSYCHUS

I There Is No God

"There is no God," the wicked saith,
"And truly it's a blessing,
For what He might have done with us
It's better only guessing."

"There is no God," a youngster thinks,
"Or really, if there may be,
He surely didn't mean a man
Always to be a baby."

"There is no God, or if there is,"
The tradesman thinks, "'twere funny
If He should take it ill in me
To make a little money."

"Whether there be," the rich man says,
"It matters very little,
For I and mine, thank somebody,
Are not in want of victual."

Some others, also, to themselves,
Who scarce so much as doubt it,
Think there is none, when they are well,
And do not think about it.

But country folks who live beneath
The shadow of the steeple;
The parson and the parson's wife,
And mostly married people;

Youths green and happy in first love,
So thankful for illusion;
And men caught out in what the world
Calls guilt, in first confusion;

And almost every one when age,
Disease, or sorrows strike him,
Inclines to think there is a God,
Or something very like Him.

II Help, Sure Help

I had a vision; was it in my sleep?
And if it were, what then? But sleep or wake,
I saw a great light open o'er my head;
And sleep or wake, uplifted to that light,
Out of that light proceeding heard a voice
Uttering high words, which, whether sleep or wake,
In me were fixed, and in me must abide.

When the enemy is near thee,
Call on us!
In our hands we will upbear thee,
He shall neither scathe nor scare thee,
He shall fly thee, and shall fear thee.
Call on us!
Call when all good friends have left thee,
Of all good sights and sounds bereft thee;
Call when hope and heart are sinking,
And the brain is sick with thinking,
Help, O help!
Call, and following close behind thee
There shall haste, and there shall find thee,
Help, sure help.

When the panic comes upon thee,
When necessity seems on thee,
Hope and choice have all foregone thee,
Fate and force are closing o'er thee,
And but one way stands before thee—
Call on us!
Oh, and if thou dost not call,
Be but faithful, that is all.
Go right on, and close behind thee
There shall follow still and find thee,
Help, sure help.

III Pleasure and Guilt

Di. She will come yet, I think, although she said
She would go hence and die; I cannot tell.
Should I have made the nation's business wait,
That I might listen to an old sad tale
Uselessly iterated? Ah—ah me!
I am grown weak indeed; those old black thoughts
No more as servants at my bidding go,
But as stern tyrants look me in the face,
And mock my reason's inefficient hand
That sways to wave them hence.

Serv. You rung, my lord?

Di. Come here, my friend. The woman,
A beggar-woman, whom six weeks ago,
As you remember, you admitted to me,
You may admit again if she returns.
(*Exit Servant.*)

Will she return? or did she die? I searched
Newspaper columns through to find a trace
O some poor corpse discovered in the Thames,
Weltering in filth or stranded on the shoals.
"You called me Pleasure once, I now am Guilt."
Is that her voice?—
"Once Pleasure and now Guilt—and after this
Guilt evermore." I hear her voice again.
"Once Guilt, but now"—I know not what it says;—
Some word in some strange language, that my ears
Have never heard, yet seem to long to know.
"Once Pleasure and now Guilt, and after this"—
What does she say?—

1862

SAY NOT THE STRUGGLE NOUGHT AVAILETH

Say not the struggle nought availeth,
The labour and the wounds are vain,
The enemy faints not, nor faileth,
And as things have been they remain.

If hopes were dupes, fears may be liars;
It may be, in yon smoke concealed,
Your comrades chase e'en now the fliers,
And, but for you, possess the field.

For while the tired waves, vainly breaking,
Seem here no painful inch to gain,
Far back, through creeks and inlets making,
Comes silent, flooding in, the main.

And not by eastern windows only,
When daylight comes, comes in the light,
In front, the sun climbs slow, how slowly,
But westward, look, the land is bright.

1849

IN STRATIS VIARUM

Blessed are those who have not seen,
And who have yet believed
The witness, here that has not been,
From heaven they have received.

Blessed are those who have not known
The things that stand before them,
And for a vision of their own
Can piously ignore them.

So let me think whate'er befall,
That in the city duly
Some men there are who love at all,
Some women who love truly;

And that upon two millions odd
Transgressors in sad plenty,
Mercy will of a gracious God
Be shown—because of twenty.

1862

IN THE GREAT METROPOLIS

EACH for himself is still the rule;
We learn it when we go to school—
The devil take the hindmost, O!

And when the schoolboys grow to men,
In life they learn it o'er again—
The devil take the hindmost, O!

For in the church, and at the bar,
On 'Change, at court, where'er they are,
The devil takes the hindmost, O!

Husband for husband, wife for wife,
Are careful that in married life
The devil takes the hindmost, O!

From youth to age, whate'er the game,
The unvarying practice is the same—
The devil takes the hindmost, O!

And after death, we do not know,
But scarce can doubt, where'er we go,
The devil takes the hindmost, O!

Ti rol de rol, ti rol de ro,
The devil take the hindmost, O!

1862

QUI LABORAT, ORAT

O ONLY Source of all our light and life,
Whom as our truth, our strength, we see and feel,
But whom the hours of mortal moral strife
Alone aright reveal!

Mine inmost soul, before Thee inly brought,
Thy presence owns ineffable, divine;
Chastised each rebel self-encentered thought,
My will adoreth Thine.

With eye down-dropt, if then this earthly mind
Speechless remain, or speechless e'en depart;
Nor seek to see—for what of earthly kind
Can see Thee as Thou art?—

If well-assured 'tis but profanely bold
In thought's abstractest forms to seem to see,
It dare not dare the dread communion hold
In ways unworthy Thee,

O not unowned, thou shalt unnamed forgive,
In worldly walks the prayerless heart prepare;
And if in work its life it seem to live,
Shalt make that work be prayer.

Nor times shall lack, when while the work it plies,
Unsummoned powers the blinding film shall part,
And scarce by happy tears made dim, the eyes
In recognition start.

But, as thou willest, give or e'en forbear
The beatific supersensual sight,
So, with Thy blessing blest, that humbler prayer
Approach Thee morn and night.

1862

ὕμνος ἄυμνος

O THOU whose image in the shrine
Of human spirits dwells divine;
Which from that precinct once conveyed,
To be to outer day displayed,
Doth vanish, part, and leave behind
Mere blank and void of empty mind,
Which wilful fancy seeks in vain
With casual shapes to fill again!

O Thou that in our bosom's shrine
Dost dwell, unknown because divine!
I thought to speak, I thought to say,
"The light is here," "behold the way,"
"The voice was thus," and "thus the word,"
And "thus I saw," and "that I heard,"—
But from the lips that half essayed
The imperfect utterance fell unmade.

O Thou, in that mysterious shrine
Enthroned, as I must say, divine!
I will not frame one thought of what
Thou mayest either be or not.
I will not prate of "thus" and "so,"
And be profane with "yes" and "no,"
Enough that in our soul and heart
Thou, whatsoe'er Thou may'st be, art.

Unseen, secure in that high shrine
Acknowledged present and divine,
I will not ask some upper air,
Some future day to place Thee there;
Nor say, nor yet deny, such men
And women saw Thee thus and then:
Thy name was such, and there or here
To him or her Thou didst appear.

Do only Thou in that dim shrine,
Unknown or known, remain, divine;
There, or if not, at least in eyes
That scan the fact that round them lies
The hand to sway, the judgment guide,
In sight and sense Thyself divide:
Be Thou but there,—in soul and heart,
I will not ask to feel Thou art.

1862

AH! YET CONSIDER IT AGAIN!

"Old things need not be therefore true,"
O brother men, nor yet the new;
Ah! still awhile the old thought retain,
And yet consider it again!

The souls of now two thousand years
Have laid up here their toils and fears,
And all the earnings of their pain,—
Ah, yet consider it again!

We! what do we see? each a space
Of some few yards before his face;
Does that the whole wide plan explain?
Ah, yet consider it again!

Alas! the great world goes its way,
And takes its truth from each new day;
They do not quit, nor can retain,
Far less consider it again.

1851

COME HOME, COME HOME!

Come home, come home! and where is home
for me,
Whose ship is driving o'er the trackless
sea?
To the frail bark here plunging on its way,
To the wild waters, shall I turn and say
To the plunging bark, or to the salt sea
foam,
You are my home?

Fields once I walked in, faces once I knew,
Familiar things so old my heart believed them
true,
These far, far back, behind me lie, before
The dark clouds mutter, and the deep seas
roar,
And speak to them that 'neath and o'er them
roam
No words of home.

Beyond the clouds, beyond the waves that
roar,
There may indeed, or may not be, a shore,
Where fields as green, and hands and hearts
as true,
The old forgotten semblance may renew,
And offer exiles driven far o'er the salt sea
foam
Another home.

But toil and pain must wear out many a
day,
And days bear weeks, and weeks bear months
away,
Ere, if at all, the weary traveller hear,
With accents whispered in his wayworn ear,
A voice he dares to listen to, say, Come
To thy true home.

Come home, come home! and where a home
hath he
Whose ship is driving o'er the driving sea?
Through clouds that mutter, and o'er waves
that roar,
Say, shall we find, or shall we not, a shore
That is, as is not ship or ocean foam,
Indeed our home?

1852

GREEN FIELDS OF ENGLAND!

GREEN fields of England! wheresoe'er
Across this watery waste we fare,
Your image at our hearts we bear,
Green fields of England, everywhere.

Sweet eyes in England, I must flee
Past where the waves' last confines be,
Ere your loved smile I cease to see,
Sweet eyes in England, dear to me.

Dear home in England, safe and fast
If but in thee my lot lie cast,
The past shall seem a nothing past
To thee, dear home, if won at last;
Dear home in England, won at last.

1852

YE FLAGS OF PICCADILLY

YE flags of Piccadilly,
Where I posted up and down,
And wished myself so often
Well away from you and town,—

Are the people walking quietly
And steady on their feet,
Cabs and omnibuses plying
Just as usual in the street?

Do the houses look as upright
As of old they used to be,
And does nothing seem affected
By the pitching of the sea?

Through the Green Park iron railings
Do the quick pedestrians pass?
Are the little children playing
Round the plane-tree in the grass?

This squally wild north-wester
With which our vessel fights,
Does it merely serve with you to
Carry up some paper kites?

Ye flags of Piccadilly,
Which I hated so, I vow
I could wish with all my heart
You were underneath me now!

1862

COME BACK, COME BACK

COME back, come back, behold with straining mast
And swelling sail, behold her steaming fast;
With one new sun to see her voyage o'er,
With morning light to touch her native shore.
Come back, come back.

Come back, come back, while westward labouring by,
With sailless yards, a bare black hulk we fly.
See how the gale we fight with sweeps her back,
To our lost home, on our forsaken track.
Come back, come back.

Come back, come back, across the flying foam,
We hear faint far-off voices call us home,
Come back, ye seem to say; ye seek in vain;
We went, we sought, and homeward turned again.
Come back, come back.

Come back, come back; and whither back or why?
To fan quenched hopes, forsaken schemes to try;
Walk the old fields; pace the familiar street;
Dream with the idlers, with the bards compete.
Come back, come back.

Come back, come back; and whither and for what?
To finger idly some old Gordian knot,
Unskilled to sunder, and too weak to cleave,
And with much toil attain to half-believe.
Come back, come back.

Come back, come back; yea back, indeed, do go
Sighs panting thick, and tears that want to flow;
Fond fluttering hopes upraise their useless wings,
And wishes idly struggle in the strings;
Come back, come back.

Come back, come back, more eager than the breeze,
The flying fancies sweep across the seas,

And lighter far than ocean's flying foam,
The heart's fond message hurries to its home.
Come back, come back.

Come back, come back!
Back flies the foam; the hoisted flag streams back;
The long smoke wavers on the homeward track,
Back fly with winds things which the winds obey;
The strong ship follows its appointed way.

1852

WHERE LIES THE LAND

WHERE lies the land to which the ship would go?
Far, far ahead, is all her seamen know.
And where the land she travels from? Away,
Far, far behind, is all that they can say.

On sunny noons upon the deck's smooth face,
Linked arm in arm, how pleasant here to pace;
Or, o'er the stern reclining, watch below
The foaming wake far widening as we go.

On stormy nights when wild north-westers rave,
How proud a thing to fight with wind and wave!
The dripping sailor on the reeling mast
Exults to bear, and scorns to wish it past.

Where lies the land to which the ship would go?
Far, far ahead, is all her seamen know.
And where the land she travels from? Away,
Far, far behind, is all that they can say.

1852

WERE YOU WITH ME

WERE you with me, or I with you,
There's nought, methinks, I might not do;
Could venture here, and venture there,
And never fear, nor ever care.

To things before, and things behind,
Could turn my thoughts, and turn my mind,
On this and that, day after day,
Could dare to throw myself away.

Secure, when all was o'er, to find
My proper thought, my perfect mind,
And unimpaired receive anew
My own and better self in you.

1853

O SHIP, SHIP, SHIP

O SHIP, ship, ship,
That travellest over the sea,
What are the tidings, I pray thee,
Thou bearest hither to me?

Are they tidings of comfort and joy,
That shall make me seem to see
The sweet lips softly moving
And whispering love to me?

Or are they of trouble and grief,
Estrangement, sorrow, and doubt,
To turn into torture my hopes,
And drive me from Paradise out?

O ship, ship, ship,
That comest over the sea,
Whatever it be thou bringest,
Come quickly with it to me.

1853

THROUGH A GLASS DARKLY

WHAT we, when face to face we see
The Father of our souls, shall be,
John tells us, doth not yet appear;
Ah! did he tell what we are here!

A mind for thoughts to pass into,
A heart for loves to travel through,
Five senses to detect things near,
Is this the whole that we are here?

Rules baffle instincts—instincts rules,
Wise men are bad—and good are fools,
Facts evil—wishes vain appear,
We cannot go, why are we here?

O may we for assurance' sake,
Some arbitrary judgment take,
And wilfully pronounce it clear,
For this or that 'tis we are here?

Or is it right, and will it do,
To pace the sad confusion through,
And say:—It doth not yet appear,
What we shall be, what we are here?

Ah yet, when all is thought and said,
The heart still overrules the head;
Still what we hope we must believe,
And what is given us receive;

Must still believe, for still we hope
That in a world of larger scope,
What here is faithfully begun
Will be completed, not undone.

My child, we still must think, when we
That ampler life together see,
Some true result will yet appear
Of what we are, together, here.

1862

ITE DOMUM SATURÆ VENIT HESPERUS

The skies have sunk, and hid the upper snow
(Home, Rose, and home, Provence and La Palie),
The rainy clouds are filing fast below,
And wet will be the path, and wet shall we.
Home, Rose, and home, Provence and La Palie.

Ah dear, and where is he, a year agone,
Who stepped beside and cheered us on and on?
My sweetheart wanders far away from me,
In foreign land or on a foreign sea.
Home, Rose, and home, Provence and La Palie.

The lightning zigzags shoot across the sky
(Home, Rose, and home, Provence and La Palie),
And through the vale the rains go sweeping by;
Ah me, and when in shelter shall we be?
Home, Rose, and home, Provence and La Palie.

Cold, dreary cold, the stormy winds feel they
O'er foreign lands and foreign seas that stray
(Home, Rose, and home, Provence and La Palie).
And doth he e'er, I wonder, bring to mind
The pleasant huts and herds he left behind?
And doth he sometimes in his slumbering see
The feeding kine, and doth he think of me,
My sweetheart wandering wheresoe'er it be?
Home, Rose, and home, Provence and La Palie.

The thunder bellows far from snow to snow
(Home, Rose, and home, Provence and La Palie),
And loud and louder roars the flood below.
Heigho! but soon in shelter shall we be:
Home, Rose, and home, Provence and La Palie.

Or shall he find before his term be sped,
Some comelier maid that he shall wish to wed?
(Home, Rose, and home, Provence and La Palie.)
For weary is work, and weary day by day
To have your comfort miles on miles away.
Home, Rose, and home, Provence and La Palie.

Or may it be that I shall find my mate,
And he returning see himself too late?
For work we must, and what we see, we see,
And God, He knows, and what must be, must be,
When sweethearts wander far away from me.
Home, Rose, and home, Provence and La Palie.

The sky behind is brightening up anew
(Home, Rose, and home, Provence and La Palie),
The rain is ending, and our journey too:
Heigho! aha! for here at home are we:—
In, Rose, and in, Provence and La Palie.

1862

"WITH WHOM IS NO VARIABLENESS, NEITHER SHADOW OF TURNING"

It fortifies my soul to know
That, though I perish, Truth is so:
That, howsoe'er I stray and range,
Whate'er I do, Thou dost not change.
I steadier step when I recall
That, if I slip, Thou dost not fall.

1862

THE LATEST DECALOGUE

Thou shalt have one God only; who
Would be at the expense of two?
No graven images may be
Worshipped, except the currency:
Swear not at all; for, for thy curse
Thine enemy is none the worse:
At church on Sunday to attend
Will serve to keep the world thy friend:
Honour thy parents; that is, all
From whom advancement may befall;
Thou shalt not kill; but need'st not strive
Officiously to keep alive:
Do not adultery commit;
Advantage rarely comes of it:
Thou shalt not steal; an empty feat,
When it's so lucrative to cheat:
Bear not false witness; let the lie
Have time on its own wings to fly:
Thou shalt not covet, but tradition
Approves all forms of competition.

1862

"PERCHÈ PENSA? PENSANDO S'INVECCHIA"

To spend uncounted years of pain,
Again, again, and yet again,
In working out in heart and brain
The problem of our being here;
To gather facts from far and near,
Upon the mind to hold them clear,
And, knowing more may yet appear,
Unto one's latest breath to fear,
The premature result to draw—
Is this the object, end and law,
And purpose of our being here?

1869

LIFE IS STRUGGLE

To wear out heart, and nerves, and brain,
And give oneself a world of pain;
Be eager, angry, fierce, and hot,
Imperious, supple—God knows what,
For what's all one to have or not;
O false, unwise, absurd, and vain!
For 'tis not joy, it is not gain,
It is not in itself a bliss,
Only it is precisely this
That keeps us all alive.

To say we truly feel the pain,
And quite are sinking with the strain;—
Entirely, simply, undeceived,
Believe, and say we ne'er believed
The object, e'en were it achieved,
A thing we e'er had cared to keep;
With heart and soul to hold it cheap,
And then to go and try it again;
O false, unwise, absurd, and vain!
O, 'tis not joy, and 'tis not bliss,
Only it is precisely this
That keeps us still alive.

1869

EASTER DAY

NAPLES, 1849

Through the great sinful streets of Naples as I past,
With fiercer heat than flamed above my head
My heart was hot within me; till at last
My brain was lightened when my tongue had said—
Christ is not risen!

Christ is not risen, no—
He lies and moulders low;
Christ is not risen!

What though the stone were rolled away, and though
The grave found empty there?—
If not there, then elsewhere;
If not where Joseph laid Him first, why then
Where other men
Translaid Him after, in some humbler clay.
Long ere to-day
Corruption that sad perfect work hath done,
Which here she scarcely, lightly had begun:
The foul engendered worm
Feeds on the flesh of the life-giving form
Of our most Holy and Anointed One.
He is not risen, no—
He lies and moulders low;
Christ is not risen!

What if the women, ere the dawn was grey,
Saw one or more great angels, as they say
(Angels, or Him himself)? Yet neither there, nor then,
Nor afterwards, nor elsewhere, nor at all,

Hath He appeared to Peter or the Ten;
Nor, save in thunderous terror, to blind Saul;
Save in an after Gospel and late Creed,
He is not risen, indeed,—
Christ is not risen!

Or, what if e'en, as runs a tale, the Ten
Saw, heard, and touched, again and yet again?
What if at Emmaüs' inn, and by Capernaum's Lake,
Came One, the bread that brake—
Came One that spake as never mortal spake,
And with them ate, and drank, and stood, and walked about?
Ah! "some" did well to "doubt"!
Ah! the true Christ, while these things came to pass,
Nor heard, nor spake, nor walked, nor lived, alas!
He was not risen, no—
He lay and mouldered low,
Christ was not risen!

As circulates in some great city crowd
A rumour changeful, vague, importunate, and loud,
From no determined centre, or of fact
Or authorship exact,
Which no man can deny
Nor verify;
So spread the wondrous fame;
He all the same
Lay senseless, mouldering, low:
He was not risen, no—
Christ was not risen!

Ashes to ashes, dust to dust;
As of the unjust, also of the just—
Yea, of that Just One, too!
This is the one sad Gospel that is true—
Christ is not risen!

Is He not risen, and shall we not rise?
Oh, we unwise!
What did we dream, what wake we to discover?
Ye hills, fall on us, and ye mountains, cover!
In darkness and great gloom
Come ere we thought it is *our* day of doom;
From the cursed world, which is one tomb,
Christ is not risen!

Eat, drink, and play, and think that this is bliss:
There is no heaven but this;
There is no hell,
Save earth, which serves the purpose doubly well,
Seeing it visits still
With equalest apportionment of ill
Both good and bad alike, and brings to one same dust
The unjust and the just
With Christ, who is not risen.

Eat, drink, and die, for we are souls bereaved:
Of all the creatures under heaven's wide cope
We are most hopeless, who had once most hope,
And most beliefless, that had most believed.
Ashes to ashes, dust to dust;
As of the unjust, also of the just—
Yea, of that Just One too!
It is the one sad Gospel that is true—
Christ is not risen!

Weep not beside the tomb,
Ye women, unto whom
He was great solace while ye tended Him;
Ye who with napkin o'er the head
And folds of linen round each wounded limb
Laid out the Sacred Dead;
And thou that bar'st Him in thy wondering womb;
Yea, Daughters of Jerusalem, depart,
Bind up as best ye may your own sad bleeding heart:
Go to your homes, your living children tend,
Your earthly spouses love;
Set your affections *not* on things above,
Which moth and rust corrupt, which quickliest come to end:
Or pray, if pray ye must, and pray, if pray ye can,
For death; since dead is He whom ye deemed more than man,
Who is not risen: no—
But lies and moulders low—
Who is not risen!

Ye men of Galilee!
Why stand ye looking up to heaven, where
Him ye ne'er may see,
Neither ascending hence, nor returning hither again?
Ye ignorant and idle fishermen!
Hence to your huts, and boats, and inland native shore,
And catch not men, but fish;
Whate'er things ye might wish,
Him neither here nor there ye e'er shall meet with more.
Ye poor deluded youths, go home,
Mend the old nets ye left to roam,
Tie the split oar, patch the torn sail:
It was indeed an "idle tale"—
He was not risen!

And, oh, good men of ages yet to be,
Who shall believe *because* ye did not see—
Oh, be ye warned, be wise!
No more with pleading eyes,
And sobs of strong desire,
Unto the empty vacant void aspire,
Seeking another and impossible birth
That is not of your own, and only mother earth.
But if there is no other life for you,
Sit down and be content, since this must even do:
He is not risen!

One look, and then depart,
Ye humble and ye holy men of heart;
And ye! ye ministers and stewards of a Word
Which ye would preach, because another heard—
Ye worshippers of that ye do not know,
Take these things hence and go:—
He is not risen!

Here, on our Easter Day
We rise, we come, and lo! we find Him not,
Gardener nor other, on the sacred spot:
Where they have laid Him there is none to say;
No sound, nor in, nor out—no word
Of where to seek the dead or meet the living Lord.
There is no glistering of an angel's wings,
There is no voice of heavenly clear behest:
Let us go hence, and think upon these things
In silence, which is best.
Is He not risen? No—
But lies and moulders low?
Christ is not risen?

1869

EASTER DAY

II

So in the sinful streets, abstracted and alone,
I with my secret self held communing of mine own.
So in the southern city spake the tongue
Of one that somewhat overwildly sung,
But in a later hour I sat and heard
Another voice that spake—another graver word.
Weep not, it bade, whatever hath been said,
Though He be dead, He is not dead.
In the true creed
He is yet risen indeed;
Christ is yet risen.

Weep not beside His tomb,
Ye women unto whom
He was great comfort and yet greater grief;
Nor ye, ye faithful few that wont with Him to roam,
Seek sadly what for Him ye left, go hopeless to your home;
Nor ye despair, ye sharers yet to be of their belief;
Though He be dead, He is not dead,
Nor gone, though fled,
Not lost, though vanished;
Though He return not, though
He lies and moulders low;
In the true creed
He is yet risen indeed;
Christ is yet risen.

Sit if ye will, sit down upon the ground,
Yet not to weep and wail, but calmly look around.
Whate'er befell,
Earth is not hell;
Now, too, as when it first began,
Life is yet life, and man is man.

For all that breathe beneath the heaven's
  high cope,
Joy with grief mixes, with despondence hope.
Hope conquers cowardice, joy grief:
Or at least, faith unbelief.
    Though dead, not dead;
    Not gone, though fled;
    Not lost, though vanished.
    In the great gospel and true creed,
    He is yet risen indeed;
      Christ is yet risen.

1869

IN A LONDON SQUARE

Put forth thy leaf, thou lofty plane,
  East wind and frost are safely gone;
With zephyr mild and balmy rain
  The summer comes serenely on;
Earth, air, and sun and skies combine
  To promise all that's kind and fair:—
But thou, O human heart of mine,
  Be still, contain thyself, and bear.

December days were brief and chill,
  The winds of March were wild and drear,
And, nearing and receding still,
  Spring never would, we thought, be here.
The leaves that burst, the suns that shine,
  Had, not the less, their certain date:—
And thou, O human heart of mine,
  Be still, refrain thyself, and wait.

1869

ALL IS WELL

Whate'er you dream with doubt possest,
Keep, keep it snug within your breast,
And lay you down and take your rest;
Forget in sleep the doubt and pain,
And when you wake, to work again.
The wind it blows, the vessel goes,
And where and whither, no one knows.

'Twill all be well: no need of care;
Though how it will, and when, and where,
We cannot see, and can't declare.
In spite of dreams, in spite of thought,
'Tis not in vain, and not for nought,
The wind it blows, the ship it goes,
Though where and whither, no one knows.

1869

JOHN DAVIDSON

[April 11, 1857–March 23, 1909]

John Davidson, a native of Barrhead, Scotland, was a chemist's assistant in a sugar house at the age of thirteen. Later he spent a little time at Edinburgh University, after which he taught for a while in public and private schools in Scotland. In the late 'eighties he published three plays, each of which contains some moving scenes. In 1890 he went to London where he continued writing plays and poetry and worked on his *Testaments*, a series of pamphlets in verse which began to appear in 1901. One of these defended vivisection on the ground that man can progress towards knowledge of self only through brutal effort. His philosophy, in so far as it touched the individual man, was gloomy and pessimistic. Poverty and ill health pursued the "Poet of Anarchy" and finally drove him to drown himself. His ballads, which are distinguished by originality in treatment if not in subject, are his most significant work. Chief of these are *Ballads and Songs* (1894), *New Ballads* (1896), and *The Last Ballad and Other Poems* (1898).

A BALLAD OF A NUN

From Eastertide to Eastertide
  For ten long years her patient knees
Engraved the stones—the fittest bride
  Of Christ in all the diocese.

She conquered every earthly lust;
  The abbess loved her more and more;
And, as a mark of perfect trust,
  Made her the keeper of the door.

High on a hill the convent hung,
  Across a duchy looking down,

Where everlasting mountains flung
  Their shadows over tower and town.

The jewels of their lofty snows
  In constellations flashed at night;
Above their crests the moon arose;
  The deep earth shuddered with delight.

Long ere she left her cloudy bed,
  Still dreaming in the orient land,
On many a mountain's happy head
  Dawn lightly laid her rosy hand.

The adventurous sun took Heaven by storm,
  Clouds scattered largesses of rain;
The sounding cities, rich and warm,
  Smouldered and glittered in the plain.

Sometimes it was a wandering wind,
  Sometimes the fragrance of the pine,
Sometimes the thought how others sinned,
  That turned her sweet blood into wine.

Sometimes she heard a serenade
  Complaining sweetly far away:
She said, "A young man woos a maid";
  And dreamt of love till break of day.

Then would she ply her knotted scourge
  Until she swooned; but evermore
She had the same red sin to purge,
  Poor, passionate keeper of the door!

For still night's starry scroll unfurled,
  And still the day came like a flood:
It was the greatness of the world
  That made her long to use her blood.

In winter-time when Lent drew nigh,
  And hill and plain were wrapped in snow,
She watched beneath the frosty sky
  The nearest city nightly glow.

Like peals of airy bells outworn
  Faint laughter died above her head
In gusts of broken music borne:
  "They keep the Carnival," she said.

Her hungry heart devoured the town:
  "Heaven save me by a miracle!
Unless God sends an angel down,
  Thither I go though it were Hell."

She dug her nails deep in her breast,
  Sobbed, shrieked, and straight withdrew the bar:
A fledgling flying from the nest,
  A pale moth rushing to a star.

Fillet and veil in strips she tore;
  Her golden tresses floated wide;
The ring and bracelet that she wore
  As Christ's betrothed, she cast aside.

"Life's dearest meaning I shall probe;
  Lo! I shall taste of love at last!
Away!" She doffed her outer robe,
  And sent it sailing down the blast.

Her body seemed to warm the wind;
  With bleeding feet o'er ice she ran:
"I leave the righteous God behind;
  I go to worship sinful man."

She reached the sounding city's gate;
  No question did the warder ask:
He passed her in: "Welcome, wild mate!"
  He thought her some fantastic mask.

Half-naked through the town she went;
  Each footstep left a bloody mark;
Crowds followed her with looks intent;
  Her bright eyes made the torches dark.

Alone and watching in the street
  There stood a grave youth nobly dressed;
To him she knelt and kissed his feet;
  Her face her great desire confessed.

Straight to his house the nun he led:
  "Strange lady, what would you with me?"
"Your love, your love, sweet lord," she said;
  "I bring you my virginity."

He healed her bosom with a kiss;
  She gave him all her passion's hoard;
And sobbed and murmured ever, "This
  Is life's great meaning, dear, my lord.

"I care not for my broken vow;
  Though God should come in thunder soon,
I am sister to the mountains now,
  And sister to the sun and moon."

Through all the towns of Belmarie
  She made a progress like a queen.
"She is," they said, "whate'er she be,
  The strangest woman ever seen.

George Gissing from John Davidson 25 Dec. '95

A SECOND SERIES OF

FLEET STREET ECLOGUES

BY

JOHN DAVIDSON

1896

LONDON JOHN LANE
THE BODLEY HEAD
NEW YORK DODD MEAD
AND COMPANY

A Presentation Copy from Davidson to Gissing. (See Appendix I.)

"From fairyland she must have come,
  Or else she is a mermaiden."
Some said she was a ghoul, and some
  A heathen goddess born again.

But soon her fire to ashes burned;
  Her beauty changed to haggardness;
Her golden hair to silver turned;
  The hour came of her last caress.

At midnight from her lonely bed
  She rose, and said, "I have had my will."
The old ragged robe she donned, and fled
  Back to the convent on the hill.

Half-naked as she went before,
  She hurried to the city wall,
Unnoticed in the rush and roar
  And splendour of the carnival.

No question did the warder ask:
  Her ragged robe, her shrunken limb,
Her dreadful eyes! "It is no mask;
  It is a she-wolf, gaunt and grim!"

She ran across the icy plain;
  Her worn blood curdled in the blast;
Each footstep left a crimson stain;
  The white-faced moon looked on aghast.

She said between her chattering jaws,
  "Deep peace is mine, I cease to strive;
Oh, comfortable convent laws,
  That bury foolish nuns alive!

"A trowel for my passing-bell,
  A little bed within the wall,
A coverlet of stones; how well
  I there shall keep the Carnival!"

Like tired bells chiming in their sleep,
  The wind faint peals of laughter bore;
She stopped her ears and climbed the steep,
  And thundered at the convent door.

It opened straight: she entered in,
  And at the wardress' feet fell prone:
"I come to purge away my sin;
  Bury me, close me up in stone."

The wardress raised her tenderly;
  She touched her wet and fast-shut eyes:
"Look, sister; sister, look at me;
  Look; can you see through my disguise?"

She looked and saw her own sad face,
  And trembled, wondering, "Who art thou?"
"God sent me down to fill your place:
  I am the Virgin Mary now."

And with the word, God's mother shone:
  The wanderer whispered, "Mary, hail!"
The vision helped her to put on
  Bracelet and fillet, ring and veil.

"You are sister to the mountains now,
  And sister to the day and night;
Sister to God." And on the brow
  She kissed her thrice, and left her sight.

While dreaming in her cloudy bed,
  Far in the crimson orient land,
On many a mountain's happy head
  Dawn lightly laid her rosy hand.

THE VENGEANCE OF THE DUCHESS

The sun of Austerlitz had dawned and shone and set in blood,
When to Illyria Sigismund rode home by fell and flood.

"What news, what news, Duke Sigismund?" the Duchess Agnes cried.
"Heavy—an avalanche of lead," Duke Sigismund replied.

"Across the astonished land the sun comes conquering from the west—
Napoleon's banners, purpled in the blood of Europe's best."

"Heavy—an avalanche of lead!" she echoed in dismay.
"Take heart," he said. But she, "Ah me! this was our wedding-day

"Five years ago!—Oh! that base churl, and unimagined thief,
That kingdom-breaker! Give me words, or I shall die of grief!

"Our wedding-day, and Europe fallen! How comes it that earth stands!"
She paced the room across, along, and wrung her jewelled hands.

At last a new thought dyed her cheek and set her eyes on fire:
"Husband, upon my wedding-day, grant me my heart's desire.

"I have a thing to do. Take horse.—You're tired, my love? Drink wine—
But come—you must—and ride with me to Idria's poisonous mine."

By circling paths adown the hill they rode, a toilsome way;
And came where in a cup-like gap the town of Idria lay.

Far in the hideous mine the haughty Duchess Agnes found
The thing she sought for buried quick a mile beneath the ground:

A ghastly shape of palsied bones across the lamplight dim,
Scarce held together by the chains that bound him limb to limb.

While on the earthy slate quicksilver globed itself like dew,
He struck the sulphurous cinnabar with feeble blows and few.

A clammy sweat welled over him and drenched his ragged sash;
Upon his back appeared the curious branch-work of the lash.

The Duchess fed her eyes on him unconscious; then she said,
"So, Casimir; poor Casimir!" The prisoner raised his head,

And ceased his work, but looked not round. She whispered to her lord,
"The breathing corpse that swelters here and lives this death abhorred,

"Dared think of me, the noblest blood and highest heart there is!
Five years ago a youthful god he seemed; now is he—this!"
And then aloud: "Aha! my foster-brother, Casimir!
Know then at last that it was I who had you buried here.

"You looked to me!—and yet you come of better-blooded curs
Than he who tramples on the necks of kings and emperors.

"You looked to me, you peasant's son! So on my wedding-morn
You here were set, the enduring mark of my forgetful scorn.

"From then till now your memory has been a bauble thrust
In some disused old cupboard and there left to gather dust.

"To-day my suffering soul recalled the vengeance I had wrought
On one who hurt my pride by silent look and secret thought.

"Under the lash you toil and sweat and know nor day nor night,
Rotted with steaming mercury and blanched for lack of light.

"In you I came to see what I would make of that false knave,
That giant-burglar, Bonaparte, the puddle-blooded slave!

"Do you remember Bonaparte who conquered Italy?
He is now the master of the world; while you—why, you are he—

"With fortunes cast like Bonaparte's, a match perhaps for him—
Who here lie buried quick to please an idle woman's whim."

When she had done he raised his eyes—wide, hollow orbs. She shook
With instant dread, beholding awful meanings in his look.

As feeble as a child's his dwindled flesh and palsied frame,
But manhood lightened round him from his glance of purest flame.

"Agnes," he sighed; and that was all he uttered of rebuke.
He paused, and then melodiously said, though low, "You took

"God's way when here you buried me; nothing can touch my soul
To discord with the universe. I understand the whole

"Great wonder of creation: every atom in the earth
Aches to be man unconsciously, and every living birth—

"The lowest struggling motion and the fiercest blood on fire,
The tree, the flower, are pressing towards a future ever higher,

"To reach that mood august wherein we know we suffer pain.
Napoleon! I am greater by this woe and by this chain;

"Because where all blaspheme and die, slaves of their agony,
I still am master of my thought, friend of my enemy.

"I reverence the force that was before the world began,
And which in me obtained the signal grace to be a man.

"Millions of men there are who happy live and happy die:
But what of that? I, too, am born a man, I, even I!"

He shone on her serenely like a solitary star,
Then turned and toiled in anguish at the poisonous cinnabar.

The Duchess gnawed her nether lip, but found no word to say.
"The man is mad," the Duke declared, and led his wife away.

Glory to those who conquer Fate and peace to those who fail!
But who would be the Duchess, who, her victor-victim pale?

A BALLAD OF HEAVEN

He wrought at one great work for years;
The world passed by with lofty look:
Sometimes his eyes were dashed with tears;
Sometimes his lips with laughter shook.

His wife and child went clothed in rags,
And in a windy garret starved:
He trod his measures on the flags,
And high on heaven his music carved.

Wistful he grew, but never feared;
For always on the midnight skies
His rich orchestral score appeared
In stars and zones and galaxies.

He thought to copy down his score:
The moonlight was his lamp: he said,
"Listen, my love;" but on the floor
His wife and child were lying dead.

Her hollow eyes were open wide;
He deemed she heard with special zest:
Her death's-head infant coldly eyed
The desert of her shrunken breast.

"Listen, my love: my work is done;
I tremble as I touch the page
To sign the sentence of the sun
And crown the great eternal age.

"The slow adagio begins;
The winding-sheets are ravelled out
That swathe the minds of men, the sins
That wrap their rotting souls about.

"The dead are heralded along;
With silver trumps and golden drums,
And flutes and oboes, keen and strong,
My brave andante singing comes.

"Then like a python's sumptuous dress
The frame of things is cast away,
And out of Time's obscure distress,
The thundering scherzo crashes Day.

"For three great orchestras I hope
  My mighty music shall be scored:
On three high hills they shall have scope
  With heaven's vault for a sounding-board.

"Sleep well, love; let your eyelids fall;
  Cover the child; goodnight, and if . . .
What? Speak . . . the traitorous end of all!
  Both . . . cold and hungry . . . cold and stiff!

"But no, God means us well, I trust:
  Dear ones, be happy, hope is nigh:
We are too young to fall to dust,
  And too unsatisfied to die."

He lifted up against his breast
  The woman's body, stark and wan;
And to her withered bosom pressed
  The little skin-clad skeleton.

"You see you are alive," he cried.
  He rocked them gently to and fro.
"No, no, my love, you have not died;
  Nor you, my little fellow; no."

Long in his arms he strained his dead
  And crooned an antique lullaby;
Then laid them on the lowly bed,
  And broke down with a doleful cry.

"The love, the hope, the blood, the brain,
  Of her and me, the budding life,
And my great music—all in vain!
  My unscored work, my child, my wife!

"We drop into oblivion,
  And nourish some suburban sod:
My work, this woman, this my son,
  Are now no more: there is no God.

"The world's a dustbin; we are due,
  And death's cart waits: be life accurst!"
He stumbled down beside the two,
  And clasping them, his great heart burst.

Straightway he stood at heaven's gate,
  Abashed and trembling for his sin:
I trow he had not long to wait,
  For God came out and led him in.

And then there ran a radiant pair,
  Ruddy with haste and eager-eyed,
To meet him first upon the stair—
  His wife and child beatified.

They clad him in a robe of light,
  And gave him heavenly food to eat;
Great seraphs praised him to the height,
  Archangels sat about his feet.

God, smiling, took him by the hand,
  And led him to the brink of heaven:
He saw where systems whirling stand,
  Where galaxies like snow are driven.

Dead silence reigned; a shudder ran
  Through space; Time furled his wearied wings;
A slow adagio then began,
  Sweetly resolving troubled things.

The dead were heralded along:
  As if with drums and trumps of flame,
And flutes and oboes keen and strong,
  A brave andante singing came.

Then like a python's sumptuous dress
  The frame of things was cast away,
And out of Time's obscure distress
  The conquering scherzo thundered Day.

He doubted; but God said, "Even so;
  Nothing is lost that's wrought with tears.
The music that you made below
  Is now the music of the spheres."

1894

A BALLAD OF HELL

"A LETTER from my love to-day!
  Oh, unexpected, dear appeal!"
She struck a happy tear away,
  And broke the crimson seal.

"My love, there is no help on earth,
  No help in heaven; the dead-man's bell
Must toll our wedding; our first hearth
  Must be the well-paved floor of hell."

The colour died from out her face,
  Her eyes like ghostly candles shone;
She cast dread looks about the place,
  Then clenched her teeth and read right on.

"I may not pass the prison door;
  Here must I rot from day to day,
Unless I wed whom I abhor,
  My cousin, Blanche of Valencay.

"At midnight with my dagger keen,
I'll take my life; it must be so.
Meet me in hell to-night, my queen,
For weal and woe."

She laughed although her face was wan,
She girded on her golden belt,
She took her jewelled ivory fan,
And at her glowing missal knelt.

Then rose, "And am I mad?" she said.
She broke her fan, her belt untied;
With leather girt herself instead,
And stuck a dagger at her side.

She waited, shuddering in her room,
Till sleep had fallen on all the house.
She never flinched; she faced her doom:
They two must sin to keep their vows.

Then out into the night she went,
And stooping crept by hedge and tree;
Her rose-bush flung a snare of scent,
And caught a happy memory.

She fell, and lay a minute's space;
She tore the sward in her distress;
The dewy grass refreshed her face;
She rose and ran with lifted dress.

She started like a morn-caught ghost
Once when the moon came out and stood
To watch; the naked road she crossed,
And dived into the murmuring wood.

The branches snatched her streaming cloak;
A live thing shrieked; she made no stay!
She hurried to the trysting-oak—
Right well she knew the way.

Without a pause she bared her breast,
And drove her dagger home and fell,
And lay like one that takes her rest,
And died and wakened up in hell.

She bathed her spirit in the flame,
And near the centre took her post;
From all sides to her ears there came,
The dreary anguish of the lost.

The devil started at her side,
Comely, and tall, and black as jet.
"I am young Malespina's bride;
Has he come hither yet?"

"My poppet, welcome to your bed."
"Is Malespina here?"
"Not he! To-morrow he must wed
His cousin Blanche, my dear!"

"You lie, he died with me to-night."
"Not he! it was a plot." "You lie."
"My dear, I never lie outright."
"We died at midnight, he and I.'"

The devil went. Without a groan
She, gathered up in one fierce prayer,
Took root in hell's midst all alone,
And waited for him there.

She dared to make herself at home
Amidst the wail, the uneasy stir.
The blood-stained flame that filled the dome,
Scentless and silent, shrouded her.

How long she stayed I cannot tell;
But when she felt his perfidy,
She marched across the floor of hell;
And all the damned stood up to see.

The devil stopped her at the brink.
She shook him off; she cried, "Away!"
"My dear, you have gone mad, I think."
"I was betrayed;—I will not stay."

Across the weltering deep she ran;
A stranger thing was never seen:
The damned stood silent to a man;
They saw the great gulf set between.

To her it seemed a meadow fair;
And flowers sprang up about her feet;
She entered heaven; she climbed the stair;
And knelt down at the mercy-seat.

Seraphs and saints with one great voice
Welcomed that soul that knew not fear;
Amazed to find it could rejoice,
Hell raised a hoarse half-human cheer.

1894

SUMMER

I

THE poets' May is dead and done
That warm and soft came shoulder-high
On Leda's twins; for now the sun
Scarce breaks the cold and cloudy sky.

But still by fields of grass and corn
With mantling green like blushes spread,
The milk-maid in the early morn
Trips with her milkpail on her head.

And still through mists that droop and float,
Beside the river lingering white,
Dew on his wings and in his note,
The lark goes singing out of sight.

And still the hawthorn blossoms blow;
The belted bee on nectar sups;
And still the dazzling daisies grow
Beside the golden buttercups.

II

Glow-worm-like the daisies peer;
Roses in the thickets fade,
Grudging every petal dear;
Swinging incense in the shade
The honeysuckle's chandelier
Twinkles down a shadowy glade.

Now is Nature's restful mood:
Death-still stands the sombre fir;
Hardly where the rushes brood
Something crawling makes a stir;
Hardly in the underwood
Russet pinions softly whirr.

III

Above the shimmering square
Swallows climb the air;
Like crystal trees the fountain's shower,
A-bloom with many a rainbow flower.

Where the lake is deep
Water-lilies sleep,
Dreaming dreams with open eyes
Enchanted by the dragon-flies—

Azure dragon-flies,
Slivered from the skies,
Chased and burnished, joints and rings,
Elfin magic wands on wings.

Like an army dressed
In diamond mail and crest,
The silent light o'er park and town
In burning phalanxes comes down;
And lustrous ambuscades
In glittering streets and glades,
Where daisies crowd or people throng,
Keep watch and ward the whole day long.

A RUNNABLE STAG

When the pods went pop on the broom, green broom,
And apples began to be golden-skinned,
We harboured a stag in the Priory comb,
And we feathered his trail up-wind, up-wind,
We feathered his trail up-wind—
A stag of warrant, a stag, a stag,
A runnable stag, a kingly crop,
Brow, bay and tray and three on top,
A stag, a runnable stag.

Then the huntsman's horn rang yap, yap, yap,
And "Forwards" we heard the harbourer shout;
But 'twas only a brocket that broke a gap
In the beechen underwood, driven out,
From the underwood antlered out
By warrant and might of the stag, the stag,
The runnable stag, whose lordly mind
Was bent on sleep, though beamed and tined
He stood, a runnable stag.

So we tufted the covert till afternoon
With Tinkerman's Pup and Bell-of-the-North;
And hunters were sulky and hounds out of tune
Before we tufted the right stag forth,
Before we tufted him forth,
The stag of warrant, the wily stag,
The runnable stag with his kingly crop,
Brow, bay and tray and three on top,
The royal and runnable stag.

It was Bell-of-the-North and Tinkerman's Pup
That stuck to the scent till the copse was drawn.
"Tally ho! tally ho!" and the hunt was up,
The tufters whipped and the pack laid on,
The resolute pack laid on,

And the stag of warrant away at last,
The runnable stag, the same, the same,
His hoofs on fire, his horns like flame,
A stag, a runnable stag.

"Let your gelding be: if you check or chide
He stumbles at once and you're out of the hunt;
For three hundred gentlemen, able to ride,
On hunters accustomed to bear the brunt,
Accustomed to bear the brunt,
Are after the runnable stag, the stag,
The runnable stag with his kingly crop,
Brow, bay and tray and three on top,
The right, the runnable stag."

By perilous paths in coomb and dell,
The heather, the rocks, and the river-bed,
The pace grew hot, for the scent lay well,
And a runnable stag goes right ahead,
The quarry went right ahead—
Ahead, ahead, and fast and far;
His antlered crest, his cloven hoof,
Brow, bay and tray and three aloof,
The stag, the runnable stag.

For a matter of twenty miles and more,
By the densest hedge and the highest wall,
Through herds of bullocks he baffled the lore
Of harbourer, huntsman, hounds and all,
Of harbourer, hounds and all—
The stag of warrant, the wily stag,
For twenty miles, and five and five,
He ran, and he never was caught alive,
This stag, this runnable stag.

When he turned at bay in the leafy gloom,
In the emerald gloom where the brook ran deep,
He heard in the distance the rollers boom,
And he saw in a vision of peaceful sleep,
In a wonderful vision of sleep,
A stag of warrant, a stag, a stag,
A runnable stag in a jewelled bed,
Under the sheltering ocean dead,
A stag, a runnable stag.

So a fateful hope lit up his eye,
And he opened his nostrils wide again,
And he tossed his branching antlers high
As he headed the hunt down the Charlock glen,
As he raced down the echoing glen—
For five miles more, the stag, the stag,
For twenty miles, and five and five,
Not to be caught now, dead or alive,
The stag, the runnable stag.

Three hundred gentlemen, able to ride,
Three hundred horses as gallant and free,
Beheld him escape on the evening tide,
Far out till he sank in the Severn Sea,
Till he sank in the depths of the sea—
The stag, the buoyant stag, the stag
That slept at last in a jewelled bed
Under the sheltering ocean spread,
The stag, the runnable stag.

1906

THE CHILTERNS

I REMEMBER once a glorious thing
Crowned the season in my wandering time.
Through the year I went from earliest Spring
Hither, thither, weaving prose and rhyme,

Like a gleeman of the former age.
Sound and colour were my pensioners;
Constant on my passionate pilgrimage
Love attended me, and friends of hers,

Life and Death besides. But one day, late
Roaming in the Chilterns, want of will
Irked me, and the impotence of Fate—
Something lacking in the World, until

Bluff November in the coppice near
Loud on orient horns an onset wound,
While the larks that through the golden year
Garlanded the air with dazzling sound,

Surged upon the tempest's deafening cry—
Crests of foam about the ocean driven,
Lightning scribbled on a thund'rous sky,
Tongues of flame upon the top of heaven!

HENRY AUSTIN DOBSON

[January 18, 1840–September 2, 1921]

Henry Austin Dobson, who wished his fellow-men to testify that

"He held his pen in trust
To Art, not serving shame or lust,"

was born in Plymouth, England, and spent his early years in Anglesey. He attended school at Beaumaris and Coventry for a time and afterwards went to Strasbourg, then a French city, to finish his elementary education. Returning to England in 1856, he entered the civil service and for almost fifty years held offices in the Board of Trade. His life at Strasbourg had intensified his love for literature, particularly French literature, and he gave his long years of service at the Board of Trade in order that he might have the means to devote his leisure to study and writing. In 1868 Dobson published his first verse, in Anthony Trollope's magazine. Five years later his first volume, *Vignettes in Rhyme*, appeared and in 1877 came *Proverbs in Porcelain*. Both these books, with additional poems, were later reprinted, one, *Old World Idylls*, in 1883, the other *At the Sign of the Lyre*, in 1885. Dobson's knowledge of the literary and the social life of the eighteenth century was considerable, and after 1884 much of his writing had to do with the lives and the works of great literary men of that century. In the late 'seventies he was a leader in the movement to introduce the French forms, the ballade, the triolet, and the rondeau, into English poetry. His own achievements in these forms are sufficient to rank him among the best writers of light verse in English. In 1901 he retired from his clerkship—he was then Principal—and passed the remaining twenty years of his life among the books and the friends he loved, "unhurried, happy, steadfast, and serene."

A SONG OF THE FOUR SEASONS

When Spring comes laughing
By vale and hill,
By wind-flower walking
And daffodil,—
Sing stars of morning,
Sing morning skies,
Sing blue of speedwell,—
And my Love's eyes.

When comes the Summer,
Full-leaved and strong,
And gay birds gossip
The orchard long,—
Sing hid, sweet honey
That no bee sips;
Sing red, red roses,—
And my Love's lips.

When Autumn scatters
The leaves again,
And piled sheaves bury
The broad-wheeled wain,—
Sing flutes of harvest
Where men rejoice;
Sing rounds of reapers,—
And my Love's voice.

But when comes Winter
With hail and storm,
And red fire roaring
And ingle warm,—
Sing first sad going
Of friends that part;
Then sing glad meeting,—
And my Love's heart.

1877

THE PARADOX OF TIME

(A VARIATION ON RONSARD)

"Le temps s'en va, le temps s'en va, ma dame!
Las! le temps non: mais NOUS *nous en allons!"*

TIME goes, you say? Ah no!
Alas, Time stays, *we* go;
Or else, were this not so,
What need to chain the hours,
For Youth were always ours?
Time goes, you say?—ah no!

Ours is the eyes' deceit
Of men whose flying feet
Lead through some landscape low;
We pass, and think we see
The earth's fixed surface flee:—
Alas, Time stays,—we go!

Once in the days of old,
Your locks were curling gold,
And mine had shamed the crow.
Now, in the self-same stage,
We've reached the silver age;
Time goes, you say?—ah no!

Once, when my voice was strong,
I filled the woods with song
To praise your "rose" and "snow";
My bird, that sang, is dead;
Where are your roses fled?
Alas, Time stays,—we go!

See, in what traversed ways,
What backward Fate delays
The hopes we used to know;
Where are our old desires?—
Ah, where those vanished fires?
Time goes, you say?—ah no!

How far, how far, O Sweet,
The past behind our feet
Lies in the even-glow!
Now, on the forward way,
Let us fold hands, and pray;
Alas, Time stays,—*we* go!

1875

TO A GREEK GIRL

WITH breath of thyme and bees that hum,
Across the years you seem to come,—
Across the years with nymph-like head,
And wind-blown brows unfilleted;
A girlish shape that slips the bud
In lines of unspoiled symmetry;
A girlish shape that stirs the blood
With pulse of Spring, Autonoë!

Where'er you pass,—where'er you go,
I hear the pebbly rillet flow;
Where'er you go,—where'er you pass,
There comes a gladness on the grass;
You bring blithe airs where'er you tread,—
Blithe airs that blow from down and sea;
You wake in me a Pan not dead,—
Not wholly dead!—Autonoë!

How sweet with you on some green sod
To wreathe the rustic garden-god;
How sweet beneath the chestnut's shade
With you to weave a basket-braid;
To watch across the stricken chords
Your rosy-twinkling fingers flee;
To woo you in soft woodland words,
With woodland pipe, Autonoë!

In vain,—in vain! The years divide:
Where Thamis rolls a murky tide,
I sit and fill my painful reams,
And see you only in my dreams;—
A vision, like Alcestis, brought
From under-lands of Memory,—
A dream of Form in days of Thought,—
A dream,—a dream, Autonoë!

1875

ARS VICTRIX

(IMITATED FROM THÉOPHILE GAUTIER)

YES; when the ways oppose—
When the hard means rebel,
Fairer the work out-grows,—
More potent far the spell.

O POET, then, forbear
The loosely-sandalled verse,
Choose rather thou to wear
The buskin—strait and terse;

Leave to the tiro's hand
The limp and shapeless style,
See that thy form demand
The labour of the file.

SCULPTOR, do thou discard
The yielding clay,—consign
To Paros marble hard
The beauty of thy line;—

Model thy Satyr's face
For bronze of Syracuse;
In the veined agate trace
The profile of thy Muse.

PAINTER, that still must mix
But transient tints anew,
Thou in the furnace fix
The firm enamel's hue;

Let the smooth tile receive
Thy dove-drawn Erycine;
Thy Sirens blue at eve
Coiled in a wash of wine.

All passes. ART alone
Enduring stays to us;
The Bust outlasts the throne,—
The Coin, Tiberius;

Even the gods must go;
Only the lofty Rhyme
Not countless years o'erthrow,—
Not long array of time.

Paint, chisel, then, or write;
But, that the work surpass,
With the hard fashion fight,—
With the resisting mass.

1876

THE LADIES OF ST. JAMES'S

A PROPER NEW BALLAD OF THE COUNTRY AND THE TOWN

"*Phyllida amo ante alias.*"—VIRG.

THE ladies of St. James's
Go swinging to the play;
Their footmen run before them,
With a "Stand by! Clear the way!"
But Phyllida, my Phyllida!
She takes her buckled shoon,
When we go out a-courting
Beneath the harvest moon.

The ladies of St. James's
Wear satin on their backs;
They sit all night at *Ombre*,
With candles all of wax:
But Phyllida, my Phyllida!
She dons her russet gown,
And hastes to gather May dew
Before the world is down.

The ladies of St. James's!
They are so fine and fair,
You'd think a box of essences
Was broken in the air:
But Phyllida, my Phyllida!
The breath of heath and furze,
When breezes blow at morning,
Is not so fresh as hers.

The ladies of St. James's!
They're painted to the eyes,
Their white it stays for ever,
Their red it never dies:
But Phyllida, my Phyllida!
Her colour comes and goes;
It trembles to a lily,—
It wavers to a rose.

The ladies of St. James's!
You scarce can understand
The half of all their speeches,
Their phrases are so grand:
But Phyllida, my Phyllida!
Her shy and simple words
Are clear as after rain-drops
The music of the birds.

The ladies of St. James's!
They have their fits and freaks;
They smile on you—for seconds;
They frown on you—for weeks:
But Phyllida, my Phyllida!
Come either storm or shine,
From Shrove-tide unto Shrove-tide,
Is always true—and mine.

My Phyllida! my Phyllida!
I care not though they heap
The hearts of all St. James's,
And give me all to keep;
I care not whose the beauties
Of all the world may be,
For Phyllida—for Phyllida
Is all the world to me!

1883

TWO SERMONS

BETWEEN the rail of woven brass,
  That hides the "Strangers' Pew,"
I hear the gray-haired Vicar pass
  From Section One to Two.

And somewhere on my left I see—
  Whene'er I chance to look—
A soft-eyed girl St. Cecily,
  Who notes them—in a book.

Ah, worthy GOODMAN,—sound divine!
  Shall I your wrath incur,
If I admit these thoughts of mine
  Will sometimes stray—to her?

I know your theme, and I revere;
  I hear your precepts tried;
Must I confess I also hear
  A sermon at my side?

Or how explain this need I feel,—
  This impulse prompting me
Within my secret self to kneel
  To Faith,—to Purity!

1879

AT THE CONVENT GATE

WISTARIA blossoms trail and fall
Above the length of barrier wall,
  And softly, now and then,
The shy, staid-breasted doves will flit
From roof to gateway-top, and sit
  And watch the ways of men.

The gate's ajar. If one might peep!
Ah, what a haunt of rest and sleep
  The shadowy garden seems!
And note how dimly to and fro
The grave, gray-hooded Sisters go,
  Like figures seen in dreams.

Look, there is one that tells her beads;
And yonder one apart that reads
  A tiny missal's page;
And see, beside the well, the two
That, kneeling, strive to lure anew
  The magpie to its cage!

Not beautiful—not all! But each
With that mild grace, outlying speech,
  Which comes of even mood;—
The Veil unseen that women wear
With heart-whole thought, and quiet care,
  And hope of higher good.

"A placid life—a peaceful life!
What need to these the name of Wife?
  What gentler task (I said)—
What worthier—e'en your arts among—
Than tend the sick, and teach the young,
  And give the hungry bread?"

"No worthier task!" re-echoes She,
Who (closelier clinging) turns with me
  To face the road again:
—And yet, in that warm heart of hers,
She means the doves', for she prefers
  To "watch the ways of men."

1879

A GARDEN SONG

(TO W. E. H.)

HERE, in this sequestered close,
Bloom the hyacinth and rose;
Here beside the modest stock
Flaunts the flaring hollyhock;
Here, without a pang, one sees
Ranks, conditions, and degrees.

All the seasons run their race
In this quiet resting place;
Peach, and apricot, and fig
Here will ripen, and grow big;
Here is store and overplus,—
More had not Alcinoüs!

Here, in alleys cool and green,
Far ahead the thrush is seen;
Here along the southern wall
Keeps the bee his festival;
All is quiet else—afar
Sounds of toil and turmoil are.

Here be shadows large and long;
Here be spaces meet for song;
Grant, O garden-god, that I,
Now that none profane is nigh,—
Now that mood and moment please,—
Find the fair Pierides!

1885

HOUSEHOLD ART

"Mine be a cot," for the hours of play,
Of the kind that is built by Miss Greenaway;
Where the walls are low, and the roofs are red,
And the birds are gay in the blue o'erhead;
And the dear little figures, in frocks and frills,
Go roaming about at their own sweet wills,
And "play with the pups," and "reprove the calves,"
And do nought in the world (but Work) by halves,
From "Hunt the Slipper" and "Riddle-me-ree"
To watching the cat in the apple-tree.

O Art of the Household! Men may prate
Of their ways "intense" and Italianate,—
They may soar on their wings of sense, and float
To the *au delà* and the dim remote,—
Till the last sun sink in the last-lit West,
'Tis the Art at the Door that will please the best;
To the end of Time 'twill be still the same,
For the Earth first laughed when the children came.

1883

FOR A COPY OF HERRICK

Many days have come and gone,
Many suns have set and shone,
Herrick, since thou sang'st of Wake,
Morris-dance and Barley-break;—
Many men have ceased from care,
Many maidens have been fair,
Since thou sang'st of Julia's eyes,
Julia's lawns and tiffanies;—
Many things are past: but thou,
Golden-Mouth, art singing now,
Singing clearly as of old,
And thy numbers are of gold!

1887

ROSE-LEAVES

"Sans peser.—Sans rester."

A KISS

Rose kissed me to-day.
Will she kiss me to-morrow?
Let it be as it may,
Rose kissed me to-day,
But the pleasure gives way
To a savour of sorrow;—
Rose kissed me to-day,—
Will she kiss me to-morrow?

CIRCE

In the School of Coquettes
Madam Rose is a scholar:—
O, they fish with all nets
In the School of Coquettes!
When her brooch she forgets
'Tis to show her new collar;
In the School of Coquettes
Madam Rose is a scholar!

A TEAR

There's a tear in her eye,—
Such a clear little jewel!
What *can* make her cry?
There's a tear in her eye.
"Puck has killed a big fly,—
And it's *horribly* cruel";
There's a tear in her eye,—
Such a clear little jewel!

A GREEK GIFT

Here's a present for Rose,
How pleased she is looking!
Is it verse?—is it prose?
Here's a present for Rose!
"*Plats*," "*Entrées*," and "*Rôts*,"—
Why, it's "Gouffé on Cooking."
Here's a present for Rose,
How *pleased* she is looking!

"URCEUS EXIT"

I intended an Ode,
And it turned to a Sonnet.
It began *à la mode*,
I intended an Ode;
But Rose crossed the road
In her latest new bonnet;
I intended an Ode;
And it turned to a Sonnet.

1874

"WITH PIPE AND FLUTE"

(TO E. G.)

With pipe and flute the rustic Pan
Of old made music sweet for man;

And wonder hushed the warbling bird,
And closer drew the calm-eyed herd,—
The rolling river slowlier ran.

Ah! would,—ah! would, a little span,
Some air of Arcady could fan
This age of ours, too seldom stirred
With pipe and flute!

But now for gold we plot and plan;
And from Beersheba unto Dan,
Apollo's self might pass unheard,
Or find the night-jar's note preferred;—
Not so it fared, when time began,
With pipe and flute!

1877

FOR A COPY OF THEOCRITUS

O SINGER of the field and fold,
THEOCRITUS! Pan's pipe was thine,—
Thine was the happier Age of Gold.

For thee the scent of new-turned mould,
The bee-hives, and the murmuring pine,
O Singer of the field and fold!

Thou sang'st the simple feasts of old,—
The beechen bowl made glad with wine . . .
Thine was the happier Age of Gold.

Thou bad'st the rustic loves be told,—
Thou bad'st the tuneful reeds combine,
O Singer of the field and fold!

And round thee, ever-laughing, rolled
The blithe and blue Sicilian brine:
Thine was the happier Age of Gold.

Alas for us! Our songs are cold;
Our Northern suns too sadly shine:—
O Singer of the field and fold,
Thine was the happier Age of Gold.

1879

THE BALLAD OF IMITATION

"*C'est imiter quelqu'un que de planter des choux.*"
—ALFRED DE MUSSET

IF they hint, O Musician, the piece that you played
Is nought but a copy of Chopin or Spohr;
That the ballad you sing is but merely "conveyed"
From the stock of the Arnes and the Purcells of yore;
That there's nothing, in short, in the words or the score
That is not as out-worn as the "Wandering Jew,"
Make answer—Beethoven could scarcely do more—
That the man who plants cabbages imitates, too!

If they tell you, Sir Artist, your light and your shade
Are simply "adapted" from other men's lore;
That—plainly to speak of a "spade" as a "spade"—
You've "stolen" your grouping from three or from four;
That (however the writer the truth may deplore),
'Twas Gainsborough painted *your* "Little Boy Blue";
Smile only serenely—though cut to the core—
For the man who plants cabbages imitates, too!

And you too, my Poet, be never dismayed
If they whisper your Epic—"Sir Éperon d'Or"—
Is nothing but Tennyson thinly arrayed
In a tissue that's taken from Morris's store;
That no one, in fact, but a child could ignore
That you "lift" or "accommodate" all that you do;
Take heart—though your Pegasus' withers be sore—
For the man who plants cabbages imitates, too!

POSTSCRIPTUM—And you, whom we all so adore,
Dear Critics, whose verdicts are always so new!—
One word in your ear. There were Critics before . . .
And the man who plants cabbages imitates, too!

1878

"WHEN THIS OLD WORLD WAS NEW"

When this old world was new,
Before the towns were made,
Love was a shepherd too.

Clear-eyed as flowers men grew,
Of evil unafraid,
When this old world was new.

No skill had they to woo,
Who but their hearts obey'd—
Love was a shepherd too.

What need to feign or sue?
Not thus was life delay'd
When this old world was new.

Under the cloudless blue
They kiss'd their shepherd-maid—
Love was a shepherd too.

They knew but joy; they knew
No pang of Love decay'd:
When this old world was new,
Love was a shepherd too.

1901

THE BALLAD OF THE BORE

"*Garrulus hunc quando consumet cunque.*"
—Hor. Sat. I, ix, 33.

I see him come from far,
And, sick with hopelessness,
Invoke some kindly star,—
I see him come, no less.
Is there no sure recess
Where hunted men may lie?
Ye gods, it is too hard!
I feel his glittering eye,—
Defend us from The Bard!

He knows nor let nor bar:
With ever-nearing stress,
Like Juggernaut his car,
I see him onward press;
He waves a huge MS.;
He puts evasion by,
He stands—as one on guard,
And reads—how volubly!—
Defend us from The Bard!

He reads—of Fates that mar,
Of Woes beyond redress,
Of all the Moons that are,
Of Maids that never bless
(As one, indeed, might guess);
Of Vows, of Hopes too high,
Of Dolours by the yard
That none believe (nor buy),—
Defend us from The Bard!

ENVOY

Prince Phoebus, all must die,
Or well- or evil-starred,
Or whole of heart or scarred;
But why in this way—why?
Defend us from The Bard!

1887

AN EPITAPH
(FOR A PARISH MAGAZINE)

"*On n'y lit aucun nom.*"—Victor Hugo

Here sleeps, at last, in narrow bed,
A man of whom, whate'er is spoken,
This may with certainty be said—
His promises were never broken.

He boasted no high-sounding name,
Or graced with academic letters;
He paid his way though, all the same,
And—more than once—forgave his debtors.

He never joined the cry of those
Who prate about the Public Morals;
But reconciled some private foes,
And patched up sundry standing quarrels.

It never came within his plan
To "demonstrate" on Want or Labour;
He strove to serve his fellow-man,
And did his best to love his neighbour.

When Doubt disturbed his honest soul,
He found in this his consolation:—
We see a part, and not the whole,
With only scant illumination.

And this, at least, he felt was sure:—
To give the sick man's hurt a plaster,
To soothe the pain no art can cure,—
Was but the bidding of his Master.

So, all unpraised, he ran his race;
But we, who watched his life, and knew it,
Thus mark his nameless resting-place,
Because he died too poor to do it.

1908

ON THE FUTURE OF POETRY

Bards of the Future! you that come
With striding march, and roll of drum,
What will your newest challenge be
To our prose-bound community?

What magic will you find to stir
The limp and languid listener?
Will it be daring and dramatic?
Will it be frankly democratic?

Will Pegasus return again
In guise of modern aeroplane,
Descending from a cloudless blue
To drop on us a bomb or two?

I know not. Far be it from me
To darken dark futurity;
Still less to render more perplexed
The last vagary, or the next.

Leave Pindus Hill to those who list,
Iconoclast or anarchist—
So be it. "They that break shall pay."
I stand upon the ancient way

I hold it for a certain thing,
That, blank or rhyming, song must sing;
And more, that what is good for verse,
Need not, by dint of rhyme, grow worse.

I hold that they who deal in rhyme
Must take the standpoint of the time—
But not to catch the public ear,
As mountebank or pulpiteer;

That the old notes are still the new,
If the musician's touch be true—
Nor can the hand that knows its trade
Achieve the trite and ready-made;

That your first theme is Human Life,
Its hopes and fears, its love and strife—
A theme no custom can efface,
Common, but never commonplace;

For this, beyond all doubt, is plain:
The Truth that pleased will please again,
And move men as in bygone years
When Hector's wife smiled through her tears.

1914 [1913]

NEW AND OLD

(TO A YOUNG LADY)

For what is old you nothing care—
"Antiques," you say, but leave you cold;
And yet the sun that gilds your hair
Is more than many aeons old.

The very song I hear you sing
Is little but a variation
Of some foregone primaeval thing—
Some early mortal inspiration!

Ah, never say you hate the old,
It always hides the new within it;
'Twill last until the stars are cold,
The other only stays a minute!

1920

IN AFTER DAYS

In after days when grasses high
O'er-top the stone where I shall lie,
Though ill or well the world adjust
My slender claim to honoured dust,
I shall not question or reply.

I shall not see the morning sky;
I shall not hear the night-wind sigh;
I shall be mute, as all men must
In after days!

But yet, now living, fain were I
That some one then should testify,
Saying—"He held his pen in trust
To Art, not serving shame or lust."
Will none?—Then let my memory die
In after days!

1884

ERNEST DOWSON

[August 2, 1867–February 23, 1900]

FROM his father Ernest Dowson acquired a taste for literature. He was born in Kent, but was educated irregularly out of England before he returned to enter Queen's College at Oxford. The hit and miss fashion in which he had gone to school left its impression on him, however, and in 1887, without a degree, he went to London. There he fell in with the Rhymers' Club, but his morbid shyness kept him from all intimate association with its members. The daughter of a humble restaurant-keeper cast her spell over him and for two years he paid her a reserved though eager courtship. But she married a waiter, and Ernest, heartbroken, wrote *Non Sum Qualis Eram*, perhaps one of the greatest poems of the period of the *Yellow Book*. He often visited France, which was his favorite country, and in the latter years of his life lived almost wholly in Paris, Brittany, and Normandy. As disease weakened him, he secluded himself in his miserable chambers and refused to permit the doctor to see him, while he half starved. Even then he did not see death ahead. Full of plans for the future (he was expecting £600 from the sale of some property), he sat up one night with friends talking and laughing until dawn. Once he choked and tried to cough, but he could not, and his heart quietly stopped.

Though he was exquisitely refined in manner, his clothes were always dilapidated. He had a passionate adoration for youth. In his poetry two moods are at war with each other: a simple and sensual lyricism against an admiration for religious devotion. But he could never divorce them, and under the saint's robe one always senses the presence of the goat-foot. He tried to make life a quest for the pleasurable but found disillusion everywhere; a hovering sadness of regret is the dominant tone of his work. Like so many other poets of the 'nineties who were defeated in their efforts to live life intensely, he found a solace in the Roman Catholic church and died a convert to its faith.

VITÆ SUMMA BREVIS SPEM NOS VETAT INCOHARE LONGAM

THEY are not long, the weeping and the laughter,
Love and desire and hate:
I think they have no portion in us after
We pass the gate.

They are not long, the days of wine and roses:
Out of a misty dream
Our path emerges for a while, then closes
Within a dream.

1896

MY LADY APRIL

DEW on her robe and on her tangled hair;
Twin dewdrops for her eyes; behold her pass,
With dainty step brushing the young, green grass,
The while she trills some high, fantastic air,
Full of all feathered sweetness: she is fair,
And all her flower-like beauty, as a glass,
Mirrors out hope and love: and still, alas!
Traces of tears her languid lashes wear.

Say, doth she weep for very wantonness?
Or is it that she dimly doth foresee
Across her youth the joys grow less and less
The burden of the days that are to be:
Autumn and withered leaves and vanity,
And winter bringing end in barrenness.

AMOR PROFANUS

BEYOND the pale of memory,
In some mysterious dusky grove;
A place of shadows utterly,
Where never coos the turtle-dove,

A world forgotten of the sun:
I dreamed we met when day was done,
And marvelled at our ancient love.

Met there by chance, long kept apart,
We wandered through the darkling glades;
And that old language of the heart
We sought to speak: alas! poor shades!
Over our pallid lips had run
The waters of oblivion,
Which crown all loves of men or maids.

In vain we stammered: from afar
Our old desire shone cold and dead:
That time was distant as a star,
When eyes were bright and lips were red.
And still we went with downcast eye
And no delight in being nigh,
Poor shadows most uncomforted.

Ah, Lalage! while life is ours,
Hoard not thy beauty rose and white,
But pluck the pretty, fleeting flowers
That deck our little path of light:
For all too soon we twain shall tread
The bitter pastures of the dead:
Estranged, sad spectres of the night.

1896

NON SUM QUALIS ERAM BONÆ SUB REGNO CYNARÆ

Last night, ah, yesternight, betwixt her lips and mine
There fell thy shadow, Cynara! thy breath was shed
Upon my soul between the kisses and the wine;
And I was desolate and sick of an old passion,
Yea, I was desolate and bowed my head:
I have been faithful to thee, Cynara! in my fashion.

All night upon mine heart I felt her warm heart beat,
Night-long within mine arms in love and sleep she lay;
Surely the kisses of her bought red mouth were sweet;
But I was desolate and sick of an old passion,
When I awoke and found the dawn was gray:
I have been faithful to thee, Cynara! in my fashion.

I have forgot much, Cynara! gone with the wind,
Flung roses, roses riotously with the throng,
Dancing, to put thy pale, lost lilies out of mind;
But I was desolate and sick of an old passion,
Yea, all the time, because the dance was long:
I have been faithful to thee, Cynara! in my fashion.

I cried for madder music and for stronger wine,
But when the feast is finished and the lamps expire,
Then falls thy shadow, Cynara! the night is thine;
And I am desolate and sick of an old passion,
Yea, hungry for the lips of my desire:
I have been faithful to thee, Cynara! in my fashion.

1896

O MORS! QUAM AMARA EST MEMORIA TUA HOMINI PACEM HABENTI IN SUBSTANTIIS SUIS

Exceeding sorrow
Consumeth my sad heart!
Because to-morrow
We must depart,
Now is exceeding sorrow
All my part!

Give over playing,
Cast thy viol away:
Merely laying
Thine head my way:
Prithee, give over playing,
Grave or gay.

Be no word spoken;
Weep nothing: let a pale
Silence, unbroken
Silence prevail!
Prithee, be no word spoken,
Lest I fail!

Forget to-morrow!
Weep nothing: only lay
In silent sorrow
Thine head my way:
Let us forget to-morrow,
This one day!

VAIN RESOLVES

I SAID: "There is an end of my desire:
Now have I sown, and I have harvested,
And these are ashes of an ancient fire,
Which, verily, shall not be quickened.
Now will I take me to a place of peace,
Forget mine heart's desire;
In solitude and prayer, work out my soul's release.

"I shall forget her eyes, how cold they were;
Forget her voice, how soft it was and low,
With all my singing that she did not hear,
And all my service that she did not know.
I shall not hold the merest memory
Of any days that were,
Within those solitudes where I will fasten me."

And once she passed, and once she raised her eyes,
And smiled for courtesy, and nothing said:
And suddenly the old flame did uprise,
And all my dead desire was quickened.
Yea! as it hath been, it shall ever be,
Most passionless, pure eyes!
Which never shall grow soft, nor change, nor pity me.

1896

IN TEMPORE SENECTUTIS

WHEN I am old,
And sadly steal apart,
Into the dark and cold,
Friend of my heart!
Remember, if you can,
Not him who lingers, but that other man,
Who loved and sang, and had a beating heart,—
When I am old!

When I am old,
And all Love's ancient fire
Be tremulous and cold:
My soul's desire!
Remember, if you may,
Nothing of you and me but yesterday,
When heart on heart we bid the years conspire
To make us old.

When I am old,
And every star above
Be pitiless and cold:
My life's one love!
Forbid me not to go:
Remember nought of us but long ago,
And not at last, how love and pity strove
When I grew old!

EXTREME UNCTION

UPON the eyes, the lips, the feet,
On all the passages of sense,
The atoning oil is spread with sweet
Renewal of lost innocence.

The feet, that lately ran so fast
To meet desire, are soothly sealed;
The eyes, that were so often cast
On vanity, are touched and healed.

From troublous sights and sounds set free;
In such a twilight hour of breath,
Shall one retrace his life, or see,
Through shadows, the true face of death?

Vials of mercy! Sacring oils!
I know not where nor when I come,
Nor through what wanderings and toils,
To crave of you Viaticum.

Yet, when the walls of flesh grow weak,
In such an hour, it well may be,
Through mist and darkness, light will break,
And each anointed sense will see.

SERAPHITA

COME not before me now, O visionary face!
Me tempest-tost, and borne along life's passionate sea;
Troublous and dark and stormy though my passage be;
Not here and now may we commingle or embrace,
Lest the loud anguish of the waters should efface

The bright illumination of thy memory,
Which dominates the night; rest, far away from me,
In the serenity of thine abiding place!

But when the storm is highest, and the thunders blare,
And sea and sky are riven, O moon of all my night!
Stoop down but once in pity of my great despair,
And let thine hand, though over late to help, alight
But once upon my pale eyes and my drowning hair,
Before the great waves conquer in the last vain fight.

1896

DREGS

The fire is out, and spent the warmth thereof,
(This is the end of every song man sings!)
The golden wine is drunk, the dregs remain,
Bitter as wormwood and as salt as pain;
And health and hope have gone the way of love
Into the drear oblivion of lost things.
Ghosts go along with us until the end;
This was a mistress, this, perhaps, a friend.
With pale, indifferent eyes, we sit and wait
For the dropt curtain and the closing gate:
This is the end of all the songs man sings.

1899

IMPENITENTIA ULTIMA

Before my light goes out for ever if God should give me a choice of graces,
I would not reck of length of days, nor crave for things to be;
But cry: "One day of the great lost days, one face of all the faces,
Grant me to see and touch once more and nothing more to see.

"For, Lord, I was free of all Thy flowers, but I chose the world's sad roses,
And that is why my feet are torn and mine eyes are blind with sweat,
But at Thy terrible judgment-seat, when this my tired life closes,
I am ready to reap whereof I sowed, and pay my righteous debt.

"But once before the sand is run and the silver thread is broken,
Give me a grace and cast aside the veil of dolorous years,
Grant me one hour of all mine hours, and let me see for a token
Her pure and pitiful eyes shine out, and bathe her feet with tears."
Her pitiful hands should calm, and her hair stream down and blind me,
Out of the sight of night, and out of the reach of fear,
And her eyes should be my light whilst the sun went out behind me,
And the viols in her voice be the last sound in mine ear.
Before the ruining waters fall and my life be carried under,
And Thine anger cleave me through as a child cuts down a flower,
I will praise Thee Lord, in Hell, while my limbs are racked asunder,
For the last sad sight of her face and the little grace of an hour.

1896

A LAST WORD

Let us go hence: the night is now at hand;
The day is overworn, the birds all flown;
And we have reaped the crops the gods have sown:
Despair and death; deep darkness o'er the land,
Broods like an owl; we cannot understand
Laughter or tears, for we have only known
Surpassing vanity: vain things alone
Have driven our perverse and aimless band.

Let us go hence, somewhither strange and cold,
To Hollow Lands where just men and unjust
Find end of labour, where's rest for the old,
Freedom to all from love and fear and lust.
Twine our torn hands! O pray the earth enfold
Our life-sick hearts and turn them into dust.

1899

EDWARD FITZGERALD

[March 31, 1809–June 14, 1883]

EDWARD FITZGERALD was born at Bredfield, Suffolk, the third son of John Purcell, of Kilkenny, Ireland, who, since he married the daughter of John FitzGerald, a distinguished Irishman, adorned the name of Purcell with that of FitzGerald. When he was twelve years old Edward went to the grammar school of Bury St. Edmunds, and in 1826 entered Trinity College, Cambridge, where Thackeray and several other young Englishmen of ability became his good friends. Tennyson, whom FitzGerald came to know well, he did not meet till some time after he himself had left Cambridge. His first book, *Euphranor*, a series of colloquies reflecting his university experience, was published anonymously in 1851. His affection for Cambridge was strong, and after his graduation he returned frequently. On one of these visits he began a close friendship with a young Cambridge man, Edward Cowell, who was highly learned in Oriental literature. Through Cowell, FitzGerald became interested in Persian poetry, and 1859 he translated the *Rubáiyát* and published it anonymously in pamphlet form. It attracted no attention at first, but the year following its publication Rossetti discovered it on a London bookstall and gave it enthusiastic acclaim. In 1868 FitzGerald printed a revised edition of the poem and in 1879 his final enlarged revision appeared. FitzGerald, who was a lover of the sea, had a yacht of his own on which he took many cruises for a number of years after 1861. Upon the death of his boatman, however, he gave up sailing and retired to his home at Little Grange, near Woodbridge, to grow old among his books and flowers. On or about March 31, 1883, Tennyson wrote as an introduction to his volume *Tiresias and Other Poems* a tribute "To E. FitzGerald" on his seventy-fifth birthday. The first few lines of this introduction present with some beauty a picture of FitzGerald's shy retirement at Little Grange.

> Old Fitz, who from your suburb grange,
> Where once I tarried for a while,
> Glance at the wheeling orb of change,
> And greet it with a kindly smile;
> Whom yet I see as there you sit
> Beneath your sheltering garden-tree
> And watch your doves about you flit,
> And plant on shoulder, hand, and knee,
> Or on your head their rosy feet

—and so on for near threescore lines.

FitzGerald, who died in mid-June, 1883, did not live to see the volume which contained his birthday tribute.

THE RUBÁIYÁT OF OMAR KHAYYÁM

I

WAKE! For the Sun, who scatter'd into flight
The Stars before him from the Field of Night,
Drives Night along with them from Heav'n, and strikes
The Sultán's Turret with a Shaft of Light.

II

Before the phantom of False morning died,
Methought a Voice within the Tavern cried,
"When all the Temple is prepared within,
Why nods the drowsy Worshipper outside?"

III

And, as the cock crew, those who stood before
The Tavern shouted—"Open then the Door!

You know how little while we have to stay,
And, once departed, may return no more."

IV

Now the New Year reviving old Desires,
The thoughtful Soul to Solitude retires,
Where the White Hand of Moses on the Bough
Puts out, and Jesus from the Ground suspires.

V

Iram indeed is gone with all his Rose,
And Jamshyd's Sev'n-ring'd Cup where no one knows;
But still a Ruby kindles in the Vine,
And many a Garden by the Water blows.

VI

And David's lips are lockt; but in divine
High-piping Pehleví, with "Wine! Wine! Wine!
Red Wine!"—the Nightingale cries to the Rose
That sallow cheek of hers to incarnadine.

VII

Come, fill the Cup, and in the fire of Spring
Your Winter-garment of Repentance fling:
The Bird of Time has but a little way
To flutter—and the Bird is on the Wing.

VIII

Whether at Naisheápúr or Babylon,
Whether the Cup with sweet or bitter run,
The Wine of Life keeps oozing drop by drop,
The Leaves of Life keep falling one by one.

IX

Each morn a thousand Roses brings, you say;
Yes, but where leaves the Rose of Yesterday?
And this first Summer month that brings the Rose
Shall take Jamshyd and Kaikobád away.

X

Well, let it take them! What have we to do
With Kaikobád the Great, or Kaikhosrú?
Let Zál and Rustum bluster as they will,
Or Hátim call to Supper—heed not you.

XI

With me along the strip of Herbage strown
That just divides the desert from the sown,
Where name of Slave and Sultán is forgot—
And Peace to Mahmúd on his golden Throne!

XII

A Book of Verses underneath the Bough,
A Jug of Wine, a Loaf of Bread—and Thou
Beside me singing in the Wilderness—
Oh, Wilderness were Paradise enow!

XIII

Some for the Glories of This World; and some
Sigh for the Prophet's Paradise to come;
Ah, take the Cash, and let the Credit go,
Nor heed the rumble of a distant Drum!

XIV

Look to the blowing Rose about us—"Lo,
Laughing," she says, "into the world I blow,
At once the silken tassel of my Purse
Tear, and its Treasure on the Garden throw."

XV

And those who husbanded the Golden grain,
And those who flung it to the winds like Rain,
Alike to no such aureate Earth are turn'd
As, buried once, Men want dug up again.

XVI

The Worldly Hope men set their Hearts upon
Turns Ashes—or it prospers; and anon,
Like Snow upon the Desert's dusty Face,
Lighting a little hour or two—is gone.

XVII

Think, in this batter'd Caravanserai
Whose Portals are alternate Night and Day,
How Sultán after Sultán with his Pomp
Abode his destined Hour, and went his way.

XVIII

They say the Lion and the Lizard keep
The Courts where Jamshyd gloried and drank deep:
And Bahrám, that great Hunter—the Wild Ass
Stamps o'er his Head, but cannot break his Sleep.

چون عهده نمی کند کسی فردا را
حالی خوش کن این دل شیدا را
می نوش بنور ماه ای ماه که ماه
بسیار بجوید و نیابد ما را

and am yours sincerely
Edward FitzGerald

A Stanza of the *Rubáiyát* (last but one) in Persian Script, with FitzGerald's Signature. (See Appendix I.)

XIX

I sometimes think that never blows so red
The Rose as where some buried Cæsar bled;
That every Hyacinth the Garden wears
Dropt in her Lap from some once lovely Head.

XX

And this reviving Herb whose tender Green
Fledges the River-Lip on which we lean—
Ah, lean upon it lightly! for who knows
From what once lovely Lip it springs unseen!

XXI

Ah, my Belovéd, fill the Cup that clears
TO-DAY of past Regret and future Fears:
To-morrow!—Why, To-morrow I may be
Myself with Yesterday's Sev'n thousand Years.

XXII

For some we loved, the loveliest and the best
That from his Vintage rolling Time hath prest,
Have drunk their Cup a Round or two before,
And one by one crept silently to rest.

XXIII

And we, that now make merry in the Room
They left, and Summer dresses in new bloom,
Ourselves must we beneath the Couch of Earth
Descend—ourselves to make a Couch—for whom?

XXIV

Ah, make the most of what we yet may spend,
Before we too into the Dust descend;
Dust into Dust, and under Dust, to lie,
Sans Wine, sans Song, sans Singer, and—sans End!

XXV

Alike for those who for TO-DAY prepare,
And those that after some TO-MORROW stare,
A Muezzín from the Tower of Darkness cries,
"Fools, your Reward is neither Here nor There."

XXVI

Why, all the Saints and Sages who discuss'd
Of the Two Worlds so wisely—they are thrust
Like foolish Prophets forth; their Words to Scorn
Are scatter'd, and their Mouths are stopt with Dust.

XXVII

Myself when young did eagerly frequent
Doctor and Saint, and heard great argument
About it and about: but evermore
Came out by the same Door where in I went.

XXVIII

With them the seed of Wisdom did I sow,
And with mine own hand wrought to make it grow;
And this was all the Harvest that I reap'd—
"I came like Water, and like Wind I go."

XXIX

Into this Universe, and *Why* not knowing
Nor *Whence*, like Water willy-nilly flowing;
And out of it, as Wind along the Waste,
I know not *Whither*, willy-nilly blowing.

XXX

What, without asking, hither hurried *Whence?*
And, without asking, *Whither* hurried hence!
Oh, many a Cup of this forbidden Wine
Must drown the memory of that insolence!

XXXI

Up from Earth's Centre through the Seventh Gate
I rose, and on the Throne of Saturn sate,
And many a Knot unravel'd by the Road;
But not the Master-knot of Human Fate.

XXXII

There was the Door to which I found no Key;
There was the Veil through which I might not see:
Some little talk awhile of ME and THEE
There was—and then no more of THEE and ME.

XXXIII

Earth could not answer; nor the Seas that mourn
In flowing Purple, of their Lord forlorn;
Nor rolling Heaven, with all his Signs reveal'd
And hidden by the sleeve of Night and Morn.

XXXIV

Then of the Thee in Me who works behind
The Veil, I lifted up my hands to find
A Lamp amid the Darkness; and I heard,
As from Without—"The Me within Thee blind!"

XXXV

Then to the Lip of this poor earthen Urn
I lean'd, the Secret of my Life to learn:
And Lip to Lip it murmur'd—"While you live,
Drink!—for, once dead, you never shall return."

XXXVI

I think the Vessel, that with fugitive
Articulation answer'd, once did live,
And drink; and Ah! the passive Lip I kiss'd,
How many Kisses might it take—and give!

XXXVII

For I remember stopping by the way
To watch a Potter thumping his wet Clay;
And with its all-obliterated Tongue
It murmur'd—"Gently, Brother, gently, pray!"

XXXVIII

And has not such a Story from of Old
Down Man's successive generations roll'd
Of such a clod of saturated Earth
Cast by the Maker into Human mould?

XXXIX

And not a drop that from our Cups we throw
For Earth to drink of, but may steal below
To quench the fire of Anguish in some Eye
There hidden—far beneath, and long ago.

XL

As then the Tulip for her morning sup,
Of Heav'nly Vintage from the soil looks up,
Do you devoutly do the like, till Heav'n
To Earth invert you—like an empty Cup.

XLI

Perplext no more with Human or Divine,
To-morrow's tangle to the winds resign,
And lose your fingers in the tresses of
The Cypress-slender Minister of Wine.

XLII

And if the Wine you drink, the Lip you press,
End in what All begins and ends in—Yes;
Think then you are To-day what Yesterday
You were—To-morrow you shall not be less.

XLIII

So when the Angel of the darker Drink
At last shall find you by the river-brink,
And offering his Cup, invite your Soul
Forth to your Lips to quaff—you shall not shrink.

XLIV

Why, if the Soul can fling the Dust aside,
And naked on the Air of Heaven ride,
Were't not a Shame—were't not a Shame for him
In this clay carcase crippled to abide?

XLV

'Tis but a Tent where takes his one day's rest
A Sultán to the realm of Death addrest;
The Sultán rises, and the dark Ferrásh
Strikes, and prepares it for another Guest.

XLVI

And fear not lest Existence closing your
Account, and mine, should know the like no more;
The Eternal Sákí from that Bowl has pour'd
Millions of Bubbles like us, and will pour.

XLVII

When You and I behind the Veil are past,
Oh, but the long, long while the World shall last,
Which of our Coming and Departure heeds
As the Sea's self should heed a pebble-cast.

XLVIII

A Moment's Halt—a momentary taste
Of Being from the Well amid the Waste—
And Lo!—the phantom Caravan has reach'd
The Nothing it set out from—Oh, make haste!

XLIX

Would you that spangle of Existence spend
About THE SECRET—quick about it, Friend!
A Hair perhaps divides the False and True—
And upon what, prithee, may life depend?

L

A Hair perhaps divides the False and True—
Yes; and a single Alif were the clue—
Could you but find it—to the Treasure-house,
And peradventure to THE MASTER too;

LI

Whose secret Presence, through Creation's veins
Running Quicksilver-like, eludes your pains;
Taking all shapes from Máh to Máhi; and
They change and perish all—but He remains;

LII

A moment guess'd—then back behind the Fold
Immerst of Darkness round the Drama roll'd
Which, for the Pastime of Eternity,
He doth himself contrive, enact, behold.

LIII

But if in vain, down on the stubborn floor
Of Earth, and up to Heav'n's unopening Door,
You gaze TO-DAY, while You are You—how then
TO-MORROW, when You shall be You no more?

LIV

Waste not your Hour, nor in the vain pursuit
Of This and That endeavour and dispute;
Better be jocund with the fruitful Grape
Than sadden after none, or bitter, Fruit.

LV

You know, my Friends, with what a brave Carouse
I made a Second Marriage in my house;
Divorced old barren Reason from my Bed,
And took the Daughter of the Vine to Spouse.

LVI

For "Is" and "IS-NOT" though with Rule and Line
And "UP-AND-DOWN" by Logic I define,
Of all that one should care to fathom, I
Was never deep in anything but—Wine.

LVII

Ah, but my Computations, People say,
Reduced the Year to better reckoning?—Nay,
'Twas only striking from the Calendar
Unborn To-morrow, and dead Yesterday.

LVIII

And lately, by the Tavern Door agape,
Came shining through the Dusk an Angel Shape
Bearing a Vessel on his Shoulder; and
He bid me taste of it; and 'twas—the Grape!

LIX

The Grape that can with Logic Absolute
The Two and Seventy jarring Sects confute:
The sovereign Alchemist that in a trice
Life's leaden metal into Gold transmute:

LX

The mighty Mahmúd, Allah-breathing Lord,
That all the misbelieving and black Horde
Of fears and Sorrows that infest the Soul
Scatters before him with his whirlwind Sword.

LXI

Why, be this Juice the growth of God, who dare
Blaspheme the twisted tendril as a Snare?
A Blessing, we should use it, should we not?
And if a Curse—why, then, Who set it there?

LXII

I must abjure the Balm of Life, I must,
Scared by some After-reckoning ta'en on trust,
Or lured with Hope of some Diviner Drink,
To fill the Cup—when crumbled into Dust!

LXIII

O threats of Hell and Hopes of Paradise!
One thing at least is certain—*This* Life flies;
One thing is certain and the rest is Lies;
The Flower that once has blown for ever dies.

LXIV

Strange, is it not? that of the myriads who
Before us pass'd the door of Darkness through,
Not one returns to tell us of the Road,
Which to discover we must travel too.

LXV

The Revelations of Devout and Learn'd
Who rose before us, and as Prophets burn'd,
Are all but Stories, which, awoke from Sleep
They told their comrades, and to Sleep return'd.

LXVI

I sent my soul through the Invisible,
Some letter of that After-life to spell:
And by and by my Soul return'd to me,
And answer'd "I Myself am Heav'n and Hell:"

LXVII

Heav'n but the Vision of fulfill'd Desire,
And Hell the Shadow from a Soul on fire
Cast on the Darkness into which Ourselves,
So late emerg'd from, shall so soon expire.

LXVIII

We are no other than a moving row
Of Magic Shadow-shapes that come and go
Round with the Sun-illumin'd Lantern held
In Midnight by the Master of the Show;

LXIX

But helpless Pieces of the Game He plays
Upon this Chequer-board of Nights and Days;
Hither and thither moves, and checks, and slays,
And one by one back in the Closet lays.

LXX

The Ball no question makes of Ayes and Noes,
But Here or There as strikes the Player goes;
And He that toss'd you down into the Field,
He knows about it all—HE knows—HE knows!

LXXI

The Moving Finger writes; and, having writ,
Moves on: nor all your Piety nor Wit
Shall lure it back to cancel half a Line,
Nor all your Tears wash out a Word of it.

LXXII

And that inverted Bowl they call the Sky,
Whereunder crawling coop'd we live and die,
Lift not your hands to *It* for help—for It
As impotently moves as you or I.

LXXIII

With Earth's first Clay They did the Last Man knead,
And there of the Last Harvest sow'd the Seed:
And the first Morning of Creation wrote
What the Last Dawn of Reckoning shall read.

LXXIV

YESTERDAY *This* Day's Madness did prepare;
TO-MORROW's Silence, Triumph, or Despair:
Drink! for you know not whence you came, nor why:
Drink! for you know not why you go, nor where.

LXXV

I tell you this—When, started from the Goal,
Over the flaming shoulders of the Foal
Of Heav'n Parwín and Mushtarí they flung,
In my predestin'd Plot of Dust and Soul

LXXVI

The Vine had struck a fibre: which about
If clings my Being—let the Dervish flout;
Of my Base metal may be filed a Key,
That shall unlock the Door he howls without.

LXXVII

And this I know: whether the one True Light
Kindle to Love, or Wrath consume me quite,
One Flash of It within the Tavern caught
Better than in the Temple lost outright.

LXXVIII

What! out of senseless Nothing to provoke
A conscious Something to resent the yoke
Of unpermitted Pleasure, under pain
Of Everlasting Penalties, if broke!

LXXIX

What! from his helpless Creature be repaid
Pure Gold for what he lent him dross-allay'd—
Sue for a Debt we never did contract,
And cannot answer—Oh, the sorry trade!

LXXX

O Thou, who didst with Pitfall and with Gin
Beset the Road I was to wander in,
Thou wilt not with Predestined Evil round
Enmesh, and then impute my Fall to Sin!

LXXXI

O Thou, who Man of baser Earth didst make,
And ev'n with Paradise devise the Snake:
For all the Sin wherewith the Face of Man
Is blacken'd—Man's forgiveness give—and take!

* * *

LXXXII

As under cover of departing Day
Slunk hunger-stricken Ramazán away,
Once more within the Potter's house alone
I stood, surrounded by the Shapes of Clay.

LXXXIII

Shapes of all Sorts and Sizes, great and small,
That stood along the floor and by the wall;
And some loquacious Vessels were; and some
Listen'd perhaps, but never talk'd at all.

LXXXIV

Said one among them—"Surely not in vain
My substance of the common Earth was ta'en
And to this Figure moulded, to be broke,
Or trampled back to shapeless Earth again."

LXXXV

Then said a Second—"Ne'er a peevish Boy
Would break the Bowl from which he drank in joy;
And He that with his hand the Vessel made
Will surely not in after Wrath destroy."

LXXXVI

After a momentary silence spake
Some Vessel of a more ungainly Make;
"They sneer at me for leaning all awry:
What! did the Hand then of the Potter shake?"

LXXXVII

Whereat some one of the loquacious Lot—
I think a Súfi pipkin—waxing hot—
"All this of Pot and Potter—Tell me then,
Who is the Potter, pray, and who the Pot?"

LXXXVIII

"Why," said another, "Some there are who tell
Of one who threatens he will toss to Hell
The luckless Pots he marr'd in making—Pish!
He's a Good Fellow, and 'twill all be well."

LXXXIX

"Well," murmur'd one, "Let whoso make or buy,
My Clay with long Oblivion is gone dry:
But fill me with the old familiar Juice,
Methinks I might recover by and by."

XC

So while the Vessels one by one were speaking,
The little Moon look'd in that all were seeking:
And then they jogg'd each other, "Brother! Brother!
Now for the Porter's shoulder-knot a-creaking!"

* * *

XCI

Ah, with the Grape my fading Life provide,
And wash the Body whence the Life has died,
And lay me, shrouded in the living Leaf,
By some not unfrequented Garden-side.

XCII

That ev'n my buried Ashes such a snare
Of Vintage shall fling up into the Air
As not a True-believer passing by
But shall be overtaken unaware.

XCIII

Indeed the Idols I have loved so long
Have done my credit in this World much wrong:
Have drown'd my Glory in a shallow Cup,
And sold my Reputation for a Song.

XCIV

Indeed, indeed, Repentance oft before
I swore—but was I sober when I swore?
And then and then came Spring, and Rose-in-hand
My thread-bare Penitence apieces tore.

XCV

And much as Wine has play'd the Infidel,
And robb'd me of my Robe of Honour—Well,
I wonder often what the Vintners buy
One half so precious as the stuff they sell.

XCVI

Yet Ah, that Spring should vanish with the Rose!
That Youth's sweet-scented manuscript should close!

The Nightingale that in the branches sang,
Ah whence, and whither flown again, who
knows!

XCVII

Would but the desert of the Fountain yield
One glimpse—if dimly, yet indeed, reveal'd,
To which the fainting Traveller might
spring,
As springs the trampled herbage of the field!

XCVIII

Would but some wingéd Angel ere too late
Arrest the yet unfolded Roll of Fate,
And make the stern Recorder otherwise
Enregister, or quite obliterate!

XCIX

Ah Love! could you and I with Him conspire
To grasp this sorry Scheme of Things entire,
Would not we shatter it to bits—and then
Remould it nearer to the Heart's Desire!

* * *

C

Yon rising Moon that looks for us again—
How oft hereafter will she wax and wane;
How oft hereafter rising look for us
Through this same Garden—and for *one* in
vain!

CI

And when like her, O Sákí, you shall pass
Among the Guests Star-scatter'd on the Grass,
And in your joyous errand reach the spot
Where I made One—turn down an empty
Glass!

TAMAM

(1859, 1868, 1872) 1879

THOMAS HARDY

[June 2, 1840–January 12, 1928]

THOMAS HARDY, last of the great Victorians, was born in Dorsetshire and educated at local schools until 1854, when he was placed under private instruction. At the age of sixteen he was articled to an ecclesiastical architect of Dorchester, and three years later began to write verse and essays. But his employer's objections compelled the young author to concern himself with the more tangible aspects of beauty, and he was set to sketching old Dorset churches with an eye to their restoration. In 1862 he went to London as an assistant to Sir Arthur Blomfield of the Royal Academy, and there his first short story appeared in *Chambers's Journal* (March, 1865).

Hardy's works fall naturally into three divisions. The first, composed of his novels, ranges from the lighter, more traditional forms—such as *Desperate Remedies* (1871), and *The Hand of Ethelberta* (1876)—to those revealing a more sombre realism in the picturing of the conflict of man against the crushing forces of nature, chance, and his own tragic flaws, as in *Far from the Madding Crowd* (1874), *The Return of the Native* (1878), *The Mayor of Casterbridge* (1886), *The Woodlanders* (1887), *Tess of the d'Urbervilles* (1891), and *Jude the Obscure* (1895).

The second period embraces *The Dynasts* (1904–08), a poem of epic scope, which is perhaps the greatest single accomplishment of Hardy's life. Founded on history, it eulogizes England's part in the Napoleonic conflict; but more than this, it becomes the summation of Hardy's view of life and thereby achieves a unity which in grandeur and command of matter (not in diction) may be compared with Milton's monumental work.

In his third period he published almost nothing but lyrical poetry, and his unceasing devotion to this medium gained for him a mastery almost as signal as his command in fiction. His seventieth year marks the beginning, with *Time's Laughingstocks* (1909), of a series of volumes which reveal him as one of the most poignant and prolific of recent poets: *Satires of Circumstance* (1914), *Moments of Vision* (1917), *Late Lyrics and Earlier* (1922), *Human Shows, Far Phantasies* (1925), and *Winter Words*, published after his death in 1928.

The originality of Hardy's poetic technique consists in the blend he makes of the usual and the unusual. His rhyme-schemes are wholly dependent upon his fancy, while his stanzas remain rigidly formal. His diction, which defies poetic tradition, is oddly sown with literary clichés and lexicographer's words. In this strange Victorian-modern mold he casts his versions of experiences common to all men, and their subtlety, profundity and variance are surprising. The ordinary under his hand becomes the rich and curious.

When Hardy died in 1928 the last link with the 19th century was severed. His ashes were buried in Westminster Abbey out of deference to the feeling of the world, but his heart was buried in his native parish churchyard in Wessex, close to the fields and people he loved.

[The poems of Thomas Hardy are reprinted from his *Collected Poems* by permission of The Macmillan Company, New York, publishers.]

NEUTRAL TONES

WE stood by a pond that winter day,
And the sun was white, as though chidden of
God,
And a few leaves lay on the starving sod;
—They had fallen from an ash, and
were gray.

Your eyes on me were as eyes that rove
Over tedious riddles of years ago;
And some words played between us to and fro
On which lost the more by our love.

The smile on your mouth was the deadest thing
Alive enough to have strength to die;
And a grin of bitterness swept thereby
Like an ominous bird a-wing. . . .

Since then, keen lessons that love deceives,
And wrings with wrong, have shaped to me
Your face, and the God-curst sun, and a tree,
And a pond edged with grayish leaves.

1867

HER IMMORTALITY

UPON a noon I pilgrimed through
A pasture, mile by mile,
Unto the place where last I saw
My dead Love's living smile.

And sorrowing I lay me down
Upon the heated sod:
It seemed as if my body pressed
The very ground she trod.

I lay, and thought; and in a trance
She came and stood thereby—
The same, even to the marvellous ray
That used to light her eye.

"You draw me, and I come to you,
My faithful one," she said,
In voice that had the moving tone
It bore ere she was wed.

"Seven years have circled since I died:
Few now remember me;
My husband clasps another bride:
My children's love has she.

"My brethren, sisters, and my friends
Care not to meet my sprite:
Who prized me most I did not know
Till I passed down from sight."

I said: "My days are lonely here;
I need thy smile alway:
I'll use this night my ball or blade,
And join thee ere the day."

A tremor stirred her tender lips,
Which parted to dissuade:
"That cannot be, O friend," she cried;
"Think, I am but a Shade!

"A Shade but in its mindful ones
Has immortality;
By living, me you keep alive,
By dying you slay me.

"In you resides my single power
Of sweet continuance here;
On your fidelity I count
Through many a coming year."

—I started through me at her plight,
So suddenly confessed:
Dismissing late distaste for life,
I craved its bleak unrest.

"I will not die, my One of all!—
To lengthen out thy days
I'll guard me from minutest harms
That may invest my ways!"

She smiled and went. Since then she comes
Oft when her birth-moon climbs,
Or at the seasons' ingresses,
Or anniversary times;

But grows my grief. When I surcease,
Through whom alone lives she,
Her spirit ends its living lease,
Never again to be!

1898

"I SAID TO LOVE"

I SAID to Love,
"It is not now as in old days
When men adored thee and thy ways
All else above;
Named thee the Boy, the Bright, the One
Who spread a heaven beneath the sun."
I said to Love.

I said to him,
"We now know more of thee than then;
We were but weak in judgment when,
With hearts abrim,
We clamoured thee that thou would'st please
Inflict on us thine agonies,"
I said to him.

I said to Love,
"Thou art not young, thou art not fair,
No elfin darts, no cherub air,
Nor swan, nor dove
Are thine; but features pitiless,
And iron daggers of distress,"
I said to Love.

"Depart then, Love! . . .
—Man's race shall perish, threatenest thou,
Without thy kindling coupling-vow?
The age to come the man of now
Know nothing of?—
We fear not such a threat from thee;
We are too old in apathy!
Mankind shall cease.—So let it be,"
I said to Love.

1901

GOD-FORGOTTEN

I TOWERED far, and lo! I stood within
The presence of the Lord Most High,
Sent thither by the sons of Earth, to win
Some answer to their cry.

—"The Earth, sayest thou? The Human race?
By Me created? Sad its lot?
Nay: I have no remembrance of such place:
Such world I fashioned not."—

—"O Lord, forgive me when I say
Thou spakest the word that made it all."—
"The Earth of men—let me bethink me. . . . Yea!
I dimly do recall

"Some tiny sphere I built long back
(Mid millions of such shapes of mine)
So named . . . It perished, surely—not a wrack
Remaining, or a sign?

"It lost my interest from the first,
My aims therefor succeeding ill;
Haply it died of doing as it durst?"—
"Lord, it existeth still."—

"Dark, then, its life! For not a cry
Of aught it bears do I now hear;
Of its own act the threads were snapt whereby
Its plaints had reached mine ear.

"It used to ask for gifts of good,
Till came its severance, self-entailed,
When sudden silence on that side ensued,
And has till now prevailed.

"All other orbs have kept in touch;
Their voicings reach me speedily:
Thy people took upon them overmuch
In sundering them from me!

"And it is strange—though sad enough—
Earth's race should think that one whose call
Frames, daily, shining spheres of flawless stuff
Must heed their tainted ball! . . .

"But sayest it is by pangs distraught,
And strife, and silent suffering?—
Sore grieved am I that injury should be wrought
Even on so poor a thing!

"Thou shouldst have learnt that *Not to Mend*
For Me could mean but *Not to Know:*
Hence, Messengers! and straightway put an end
To what men undergo." . . .

Homing at dawn, I thought to see
One of the Messengers standing by.
—Oh, childish thought! . . . Yet often it comes to me
When trouble hovers nigh.

1901

SHELLEY'S SKYLARK

(*The neighbourhood of Leghorn: March 1887*)

Somewhere afield here something lies
In Earth's oblivious eyeless trust
That moved a poet to prophecies—
A pinch of unseen, unguarded dust:

The dust of the lark that Shelley heard,
And made immortal through times to be;—
Though it only lived like another bird,
And knew not its immortality:

Lived its meek life; then, one day, fell—
A little ball of feather and bone;
And how it perished, when piped farewell,
And where it wastes, are alike unknown.

Maybe it rests in the loam I view,
Maybe it throbs in a myrtle's green,
Maybe it sleeps in the coming hue
Of a grape on the slopes of yon inland scene.

Go find it, faeries, go and find
That tiny pinch of priceless dust,
And bring a casket silver-lined,
And framed of gold that gems encrust;

And we will lay it safe therein,
And consecrate it to endless time;
For it inspired a bard to win
Ecstatic heights in thought and rhyme.

WIVES IN THE SERE

I

Never a careworn wife but shows,
If a joy suffuse her,
Something beautiful to those
Patient to peruse her,
Some one charm the world unknows
Precious to a muser,
Haply what, ere years were foes,
Moved her mate to choose her.

II

But, be it a hint of rose
That an instant hues her,
Or some early light or pose
Wherewith thought renews her—
Seen by him at full, ere woes
Practised to abuse her—
Sparely comes it, swiftly goes,
Time again subdues her.

THE PUZZLED GAME-BIRDS

(TRIOLET)

They are not those who used to feed us
When we were young—they cannot be—
These shapes that now bereave and bleed us?
They are not those who used to feed us,
For did we then cry, they would heed us.
—If hearts can house such treachery
They are not those who used to feed us
When we were young—they cannot be!

THE DARKLING THRUSH

I leant upon a coppice gate
When Frost was spectre-gray,
And Winter's dregs made desolate
The weakening eye of day.
The tangled bine-stems scored the sky
Like strings of broken lyres,
And all mankind that haunted nigh
Had sought their household fires.

The land's sharp features seemed to be
The Century's corpse outleant,
His crypt the cloudy canopy,
The wind his death-lament.
The ancient pulse of germ and birth
Was shrunken hard and dry,
And every spirit upon earth
Seemed fervourless as I.

At once a voice arose among
The bleak twigs overhead
In a full-hearted evensong
Of joy illimited;

Shelley's Skylark

The neighbourhood of Leghorn:

(March: 1887.)

Somewhere afield here something lies
In Earth's oblivious eyeless trust
That moved a poet to prophecies —
A pinch of unseen, unguarded dust:

The dust of the lark that Shelley heard,
And made immortal through times to be; —
Though it only lived like another bird,
And knew not its immortality:

Lived

Two Stanzas in Hardy's Handwriting. (See Appendix I.)

An aged thrush, frail, gaunt, and small,
In blast-beruffled plume,
Had chosen thus to fling his soul
Upon the growing gloom.

So little cause for carolings
Of such ecstatic sound
Was written on terrestrial things
Afar or nigh around,
That I could think there trembled through
His happy good-night air
Some blessed Hope, whereof he knew
And I was unaware.

December 1900

THE SIGH

Little head against my shoulder,
Shy at first, then somewhat bolder,
And up-eyed;
Till she, with a timid quaver,
Yielded to the kiss I gave her;
But, she sighed.

That there mingled with her feeling
Some sad thought she was concealing
It implied.
—Not that she had ceased to love me,
None on earth she set above me;
But she sighed.

She could not disguise a passion,
Dread, or doubt, in weakest fashion
If she tried:
Nothing seemed to hold us sundered,
Hearts were victors; so I wondered
Why she sighed.

Afterwards I knew her throughly,
And she loved me staunchly, truly,
Till she died;
But she never made confession
Why, at that first sweet concession,
She had sighed.

It was in our May, remember;
And though now I near November,
And abide
Till my appointed change, unfretting,
Sometimes I sit half regretting
That she sighed.

LET ME ENJOY

(MINOR KEY)

I

Let me enjoy the earth no less
Because the all-enacting Might
That fashioned forth its loveliness
Had other aims than my delight.

II

About my path there flits a Fair,
Who throws me not a word or sign;
I'll charm me with her ignoring air,
And laud the lips not meant for mine.

III

From manuscripts of moving song
Inspired by scenes and dreams unknown,
I'll pour out raptures that belong
To others, as they were my own.

IV

And some day hence, towards Paradise
And all its blest—if such should be—
I will lift glad, afar-off eyes,
Though it contain no place for me.

1909

THE MAN HE KILLED

"Had he and I but met
By some old ancient inn,
We should have sat us down to wet
Right many a nipperkin!

"But ranged as infantry,
And staring face to face,
I shot at him as he at me,
And killed him in his place.

"I shot him dead because—
Because he was my foe,
Just so: my foe of course he was;
That's clear enough; although

"He thought he'd 'list, perhaps,
Off-hand like—just as I—
Was out of work—had sold his traps—
No other reason why.

"Yes; quaint and curious war is!
You shoot a fellow down
You'd treat if met where any bar is,
Or help to half-a-crown."

1902

THE WOMAN IN THE RYE

"WHY do you stand in the dripping rye,
Cold-lipped, unconscious, wet to the knee,
When there are firesides near?" said I.
"I told him I wished him dead," said she.

"Yea, cried it in my haste to one
Whom I had loved, whom I well loved still;
And die he did. And I hate the sun,
And stand here lonely, aching, chill;

"Stand waiting, waiting under skies
That blow reproach, the while I see
The rooks sheer off to where he lies
Wrapt in a peace withheld from me!"

THE SACRILEGE

A BALLAD-TRAGEDY

(*Circa* 182–)

PART I

"I HAVE a Love I love too well
Where Dunkery frowns on Exon Moor;
I have a Love I love too well,
To whom, ere she was mine,
'Such is my love for you,' I said,
'That you shall have to hood your head
A silken kerchief crimson-red,
Wove finest of the fine.'

"And since this Love, for one mad moon,
On Exon Wild by Dunkery Tor,
Since this my Love for one mad moon
Did clasp me as her king,
I snatched a silk-piece red and rare
From off a stall at Priddy Fair,
For handkerchief to hood her hair
When we went gallanting.

"Full soon the four weeks neared their end
Where Dunkery frowns on Exon Moor;
And when the four weeks neared their end,
And their swift sweets outwore,
I said, 'What shall I do to own
Those beauties bright as tulips blown,
And keep you here with me alone
As mine for evermore?'

"And as she drowsed within my van
On Exon Wild by Dunkery Tor—
And as she drowsed within my van,
And dawning turned to day,
She heavily raised her sloe-black eyes
And murmured back in softest wise,
'One more thing, and the charms you prize
Are yours henceforth for aye.

" 'And swear I will I'll never go
While Dunkery frowns on Exon Moor
To meet the Cornish Wrestler Joe
For dance and dallyings.
If you'll to yon cathedral shrine,
And finger from the chest divine
Treasure to buy me ear-drops fine,
And richly jewelled rings.'

"I said: 'I am one who has gathered gear
From Marlbury Downs to Dunkery Tor,
Who has gathered gear for many a year
From mansion, mart and fair;
But at God's house I've stayed my hand,
Hearing within me some command—
Curbed by a law not of the land
From doing damage there!'

"Whereat she pouts, this Love of mine,
As Dunkery pouts to Exon Moor,
And still she pouts, this Love of mine,
So cityward I go.
But ere I start to do the thing,
And speed my soul's imperilling
For one who is my ravishing
And all the joy I know,

"I come to lay this charge on thee—
On Exon Wild by Dunkery Tor—
I come to lay this charge on thee
With solemn speech and sign:
Should things go ill, and my life pay
For botchery in this rash assay,
You are to take hers likewise—yea,
The month the law takes mine.

"For should my rival, Wrestler Joe,
Where Dunkery frowns on Exon Moor—
My reckless rival, Wrestler Joe,
My Love's bedwinner be,

My rafted spirit would not rest,
But wander weary and distrest
Throughout the world in wild protest:
The thought nigh maddens me!"

PART II

Thus did he speak—this brother of mine—
On Exon Wild by Dunkery Tor,
Born at my birth of mother of mine,
And forthwith went his way
To dare the deed some coming night . . .
I kept the watch with shaking sight,
The moon at moments breaking bright,
At others glooming gray.

For three full days I heard no sound
Where Dunkery frowns on Exon Moor,
I heard no sound at all around
Whether his fay prevailed,
Or one more foul the master were,
Till some afoot did tidings bear
How that, for all his practised care,
He had been caught and jailed.

They had heard a crash when twelve had chimed
By Mendip east of Dunkery Tor,
When twelve had chimed and moonlight climbed;
They watched, and he was tracked
By arch and aisle and saint and knight
Of sculptured stonework sheeted white
In the cathedral's ghostly light,
And captured in the act.

Yes; for this Love he loved too well
Where Dunkery sights the Severn shore,
All for this Love he loved too well
He burst the holy bars,
Seized golden vessels from the chest
To buy her ornaments of the best,
At her ill-witchery's request
And lure of eyes like stars. . . .

When blustering March confused the sky
In Toneborough Town by Exon Moor,
When blustering March confused the sky
They stretched him; and he died.
Down in the crowd where I, to see
The end of him, stood silently,
With a set face he lipped to me—
"Remember." "Ay!" I cried.

By night and day I shadowed her
From Toneborough Deane to Dunkery Tor,
I shadowed her asleep, astir,
And yet I could not bear—
Till Wrestler Joe anon began
To figure as her chosen man,
And took her to his shining van—
To doom a form so fair!

He made it handsome for her sake—
And Dunkery smiled to Exon Moor—
He made it handsome for her sake,
Painting it out and in;
And on the door of apple-green
A bright brass knocker soon was seen,
And window-curtains white and clean
For her to sit within.

And all could see she clave to him
As cleaves a cloud to Dunkery Tor,
Yea, all could see she clave to him,
And every day I said,
"A pity it seems to part those two
That hourly grow to love more true:
Yet she's the wanton woman who
Sent one to swing till dead!"

That blew to blazing all my hate,
While Dunkery frowned on Exon Moor,
And when the river swelled, her fate
Came to her pitilessly. . . .
I dogged her, crying: "Across that plank
They use as bridge to reach yon bank
A coat and hat lie limp and dank;
Your goodman's, can they be?"

She paled, and went, I close behind—
And Exon frowned to Dunkery Tor,
She went, and I came up behind
And tipped the plank that bore
Her, fleetly flitting across to eye
What such might bode. She slid awry;
And from the current came a cry,
A gurgle; and no more.

How that befell no mortal knew
From Marlbury Downs to Exon Moor;
No mortal knew that deed undue
But he who schemed the crime,
Which night still covers. . . . But in dream
Those ropes of hair upon the stream
He sees, and he will hear that scream
Until his judgment-time.

A POET

ATTENTIVE eyes, fantastic heed,
Assessing minds, he does not need,
Nor urgent writs to sup or dine,
Nor pledges in the rosy wine.

For loud acclaim he does not care
By the august or rich or fair,
Nor for smart pilgrims from afar,
Curious on where his hauntings are.

But soon or later, when you hear
That he has doffed this wrinkled gear,
Some evening, at the first star-ray,
Come to his graveside, pause and say:

"Whatever his message—glad or grim—
Two bright-souled women clave to him";
Stand and say that while day decays;
It will be word enough of praise.

July 1914

TO SHAKESPEARE

AFTER THREE HUNDRED YEARS

BRIGHT baffling Soul, least capturable of themes,
Thou, who display'dst a life of commonplace,
Leaving no intimate word or personal trace
Of high design outside the artistry
Of thy penned dreams,
Still shalt remain at heart unread eternally.

Through human orbits thy discourse to-day,
Despite thy formal pilgrimage, throbs on
In harmonies that cow Oblivion,
And, like the wind, with all-uncared effect
Maintain a sway
Not fore-desired, in tracks unchosen and unchecked.

And yet, at thy last breath, with mindless note
The borough clocks but samely tongued the hour,
The Avon just as always glassed the tower,
Thy age was published on thy passing-bell
But in due rote
With other dwellers' deaths accorded a like knell.

And at the strokes some townsman (met, maybe,
And thereon queried by some squire's good dame
Driving in shopward) may have given thy name,
With, "Yes, a worthy man and well-to-do;
Though, as for me,
I knew him but by just a neighbour's nod, 'tis true.

"I' faith, few knew him much here, save by word,
He having elsewhere led his busier life;
Though to be sure he left with us his wife."
—"Ah, one of the tradesmen's sons, I now recall. . . .
Witty, I've heard. . . .
We did not know him. . . . Well, good-day. Death comes to all."

So, like a strange bright bird we sometimes find
To mingle with the barn-door brood awhile,
Then vanish from their homely domicile—
Into man's poesy, we wot not whence,
Flew thy strange mind,
Lodged there a radiant guest, and sped for ever thence.

1916

ON A MIDSUMMER EVE

I IDLY cut a parsley stalk,
And blew therein towards the moon;
I had not thought what ghosts would walk
With shivering footsteps to my tune.

I went, and knelt, and scooped my hand
As if to drink, into the brook,
And a faint figure seemed to stand
Above me, with the bygone look.

I lipped rough rhymes of chance, not choice,
I thought not what my words might be;
There came into my ear a voice
That turned a tenderer verse for me.

THE BLINDED BIRD

So zestfully canst thou sing?
And all this indignity,
With God's consent, on thee!
Blinded ere yet a-wing
By the red-hot needle thou,
I stand and wonder how
So zestfully thou canst sing!

Resenting not such wrong,
Thy grievous pain forgot,
Eternal dark thy lot,
Groping thy whole life long,
After that stab of fire;
Enjailed in pitiless wire;
Resenting not such wrong!

Who hath charity? This bird.
Who suffereth long and is kind,
Is not provoked, though blind
And alive ensepulchred?
Who hopeth, endureth all things?
Who thinketh no evil, but sings?
Who is divine? This bird.

THE OXEN

Christmas Eve, and twelve of the clock.
"Now they are all on their knees,"
An elder said as we sat in a flock
By the embers in hearthside ease.

We pictured the meek mild creatures where
They dwelt in their strawy pen,
Nor did it occur to one of us there
To doubt they were kneeling then.

So fair a fancy few would weave
In these years! Yet, I feel,
If someone said on Christmas Eve,
"Come; see the oxen kneel,

"In the lonely barton by yonder coomb
Our childhood used to know,"
I should go with him in the gloom,
Hoping it might be so.

1915

IN TIME OF "THE BREAKING OF NATIONS" [1]

I

Only a man harrowing clods
In a slow silent walk
With an old horse that stumbles and nods
Half asleep as they stalk.

II

Only thin smoke without flame
From the heaps of couch-grass;
Yet this will go onward the same
Though Dynasties pass.

III

Yonder a maid and her wight
Come whispering by:
War's annals will fade into night
Ere their story die.

1915

AFTERWARDS

When the Present has latched its postern behind my tremulous stay,
And the May month flaps its glad green leaves like wings,
Delicate-filmed as new-spun silk, will the neighbours say,
"He was a man who used to notice such things"?

If it be in the dusk when, like an eyelid's soundless blink,
The dewfall-hawk comes crossing the shades to alight
Upon the wind-warped upland thorn, a gazer may think,
"To him this must have been a familiar sight."

If I pass during some nocturnal blackness, mothy and warm,
When the hedgehog travels furtively over the lawn,
One may say, "He strove that such innocent creatures should come to no harm,
But he could do little for them; and now he is gone."

[1] Jer. 51: 20.

At a House in Hampstead

(Sometime the Dwelling of John Keats.)

O Poet, come you haunting here
Where streets have crept up all around
And never a nightingale pours ~~note~~ one
Full throated sound?

Drawn from your drowse by ~~Rome's~~ the far Gaunt Gate,
Thought you to find all just the same
Here shining, as in ~~days~~ hours, of old,
If you but came?

What will you do in your surprise
At seeing that changes wrought in Rome
Are wrought yet more on the misty hill
One time your home?

Will you wake windwafts on these stairs?
Swing the doors open noisily?
Show as ~~one~~ ~~entranced~~ ~~wandering~~ a troubled ghost beside
Your ancient tree?

Or will you, softening, the while
You further & yet further look,
Learn that a laggard few would fain
Preserve your nook?....

- Where

A Page of Hardy's Manuscript. (See Appendix I.)

If, when hearing that I have been stilled at last, they stand at the door,
Watching the full-starred heavens that winter sees,
Will this thought rise on those who will meet my face no more,
"He was one who had an eye for such mysteries"?

And will any say when my bell of quittance is heard in the gloom,
And a crossing breeze cuts a pause in its outrollings,
Till they rise again, as they were a new bell's boom,
"He hears it not now, but used to notice such things?"

THE DISSEMBLERS

"It was not you I came to please,
Only myself," flipped she;
"I like this spot of phantasies,
And thought you far from me."
But O, he was the secret spell
That led her to the lea!

"It was not she who shaped my ways,
Or works, or thoughts," he said.
"I scarcely marked her living days,
Or missed her much when dead."
But O, his joyance knew its knell
When daisies hid her head!

FIRST OR LAST

(SONG)

If grief come early
Joy comes late,
If joy come early
Grief will wait;
Aye, my dear and tender!

Wise ones joy them early
While the cheeks are red,
Banish grief till surly
Time has dulled their dread.

And joy being ours
Ere youth has flown,
The later hours
May find us gone;
Aye, my dear and tender!

THE SECOND NIGHT

(BALLAD)

I missed one night, but the next I went;
It was gusty above, and clear;
She was there, with the look of one ill-content,
And said: "Do not come near!"

—"I am sorry last night to have failed you here,
And now I have travelled all day;
And it's long rowing back to the West-Hoe Pier,
So brief must be my stay."

—"O man of mystery, why not say
Out plain to me all you mean?
Why you missed last night, and must now away
Is—another has come between!"

—"O woman so mocking in mood and mien,
So be it!" I replied:
"And if I am due at a differing scene
Before the dark has died,

"'Tis that, unresting, to wander wide
Has ever been my plight,
And at least I have met you at Cremyll side
If not last eve, to-night."

—"You get small rest—that read I quite;
And so do I, maybe;
Though there's a rest hid safe from sight
Elsewhere awaiting me!"

A mad star crossed the sky to the sea,
Wasting in sparks as it streamed,
And when I looked back at her wistfully
She had changed, much changed, it seemed.

The sparks of the star in her pupils gleamed,
She was vague as a vapour now,
And ere of its meaning I had dreamed
She'd vanished—I knew not how.

I stood on, long; each cliff-top bough,
Like a cynic nodding there,
Moved up and down, though no man's brow
But mine met the wayward air.

Still stood I, wholly unaware
Of what had come to pass,
Or had brought the secret of my new Fair
To my old Love, alas!

I went down then by crag and grass
To the boat wherein I had come.
Said the man with the oars: "This news of the lass
Of Edgcumbe, is sharp for some!

"Yes: found this daybreak, stiff and numb
On the shore here, whither she'd sped
To meet her lover last night in the glum,
And he came not, 'tis said.

"And she leapt down, heart-hit. Pity she's dead:
So much for the faithful-bent!" . .
I looked, and again a star overhead
Shot through the firmament.

THE SEVEN TIMES

The dark was thick. A boy he seemed at that time
Who trotted by me with uncertain air;
"I'll tell my tale," he murmured, "for I fancy
A friend goes there? . . ."

Then thus he told. "I reached—'twas for the first time—
A dwelling. Life was clogged in me with care;
I thought not I should meet an eyesome maiden,
But found one there.

"I entered on the precincts for the second time—
'Twas an adventure fit and fresh and fair—
I slackened in my footsteps at the porchway,
And found her there.

"I rose and travelled thither for the third time,
The hope-hues growing gayer and yet gayer
As I hastened round the boscage of the outskirts,
And found her there.

"I journeyed to the place again the fourth time
(The best and rarest visit of the rare,
As it seemed to me, engrossed about these goings),
And found her there.

"When I bent me to my pilgrimage the fifth time
(Soft-thinking as I journeyed I would dare
A certain word at token of good auspice),
I found her there.

"That landscape did I traverse for the sixth time,
And dreamed on what we purposed to prepare;
I reached a tryst before my journey's end came,
And found her there.

"I went again—long after—aye, the seventh time;
The look of things was sinister and bare
As I caught no customed signal, heard no voice call,
Nor found her there.

"And now I gad the globe—day, night, and any time,
To light upon her hiding unaware,
And, maybe, I shall nigh me to some nymph-niche,
And find her there!"

"But how," said I, "has your so little lifetime
Given roomage for such loving, loss, despair?
A boy so young!" Forthwith I turned my lantern
Upon him there.

His head was white. His small form, fine aforetime,
Was shrunken with old age and battering wear,
An eighty-years-long plodder saw I pacing
Beside me there.

SNOW IN THE SUBURBS

Every branch big with it,
Bent every twig with it;
Every fork like a white web-foot;
Every street and pavement mute:

Some flakes have lost their way, and grope
back upward, when
Meeting those meandering down they turn
and descend again.
The palings are glued together like a wall,
And there is no waft of wind with the
fleecy fall.

A sparrow enters the tree,
Whereon immediately
A snow-lump thrice his own slight size
Descends on him and showers his head
and eyes,
And overturns him,
And near inurns him,
And lights on a nether twig, when its
brush
Starts off a volley of other lodging lumps
with a rush.

The steps are a blanched slope,
Up which, with feeble hope,
A black cat comes, wide-eyed and thin;
And we take him in.

WILLIAM ERNEST HENLEY

[August 23, 1849–July 12, 1903]

William Ernest Henley, poet, critic, dramatist, and editor, was born at Gloucester and attended the Crypt Grammar School there. His literary promise won for him the friendship of the headmaster, Thomas Edward Brown, himself a poet of real talent. Brown's influence, Henley wrote, was to him "like a call from the world outside, the great, quick, living world." Before Henley was twelve years old he contracted tuberculosis of the bone which eventually resulted in amputation of one foot. In 1874, refusing to follow the advice of his doctors that he have the other foot amputated, he went to Edinburgh Infirmary to be under the care of Dr. Lister, the famous pioneer in antiseptic surgery. For twenty months or more he was in bed there, writing poignantly of his thoughts and experiences in hospital, receiving calls from friends and from talented persons who read his hospital poems, and fighting to save his remaining foot, a fight which he finally won. One of his talented visitors was Robert Louis Stevenson, Stevenson's visit marking the beginning of a very close friendship and of a fruitful literary partnership. In 1877 Henley became the editor of *London*, a position which he gave up in 1882 in order to accept the editorship of the *Magazine of Art*. In 1889 he took over the editorship of the *National Observer*, the paper to which Kipling contributed his *Barrack-Room Ballads*. In 1888 his own *Book of Verses* appeared, part of its contents being the poems written some years before in hospital. His volume of criticism, *Views and Reviews*, was published in 1890. *London Voluntaries*, another volume of poems, which had appeared as *The Song of the Sword* in 1892, came from the press in 1893. In 1892, also, three plays, the product of the Henley-Stevenson literary partnership, appeared.

Henley's courage carried him through fifty-four years of life, a number of which were years of such suffering as would have broken a less indomitable spirit. But Henley was not to be broken. Out of the night that covered him came his defiant call, "My head is bloody, but unbowed." Not till the death of his little daughter Margaret (the "Reddy" of Barrie's *Sentimental Tommy*) did he show any sign that "the bludgeonings of chance" were beating him down. He continued working to the last notwithstanding, and was engaged in writing the preface of the Tudor Bible when he died. A limited edition of his works appeared in six volumes in 1908.

From IN HOSPITAL

II WAITING

A SQUARE, squat room (a cellar on promotion),
Drab to the soul, drab to the very daylight;
Plasters astray in unnatural-looking tinware;
Scissors and lint and apothecary's jars.

Here, on a bench a skeleton would writhe from,
Angry and sore, I wait to be admitted;
Wait till my heart is lead upon my stomach,
While at their ease two dressers do their chores.

One has a probe—it feels to me a crowbar.
A small boy sniffs and shudders after blue-
stone.
A poor old tramp explains his poor old ulcers.
Life is (I think) a blunder and a shame.

XXVIII DISCHARGED

CARRY me out
Into the wind and the sunshine,
Into the beautiful world.

O, the wonder, the spell of the streets!
The stature and strength of the horses,
The rustle and echo of footfalls,
The flat roar and rattle of wheels!
A swift tram floats huge on us . . .
It's a dream?
The smell of the mud in my nostrils
Blows brave—like a breath of the sea!

As of old,
Ambulant, undulant drapery,
Vaguely and strangely provocative,
Flutters and beckons. O, yonder—
Is it?—the gleam of a stocking!
Sudden, a spire
Wedged in the mist! O, the houses,
The long lines of lofty, grey houses,
Cross-hatched with shadow and light!
These are the streets. . . .
Each is an avenue leading
Whither I will!

Free . . .!
Dizzy, hysterical, faint,
I sit, and the carriage rolls on with me
Into the wonderful world.

The Old Infirmary, Edinburgh, 1773–75

BALLADE OF DEAD ACTORS

WHERE are the passions they essayed,
And where the tears they made to flow?
Where the wild humours they portrayed
For laughing worlds to see and know?
Othello's wrath and Juliet's woe?
Sir Peter's whims and Timon's gall?
And Millamant and Romeo?
Into the night go one and all.

Where are the braveries, fresh or frayed?
The plumes, the armours—friend and foe?
The cloth of gold, the rare brocade,
The mantles glittering to and fro?
The pomp, the pride, the royal show?
The cries of war and festival?
The youth, the grace, the charm, the glow?
Into the night go one and all.

The curtain falls, the play is played:
The Beggar packs beside the Beau;
The Monarch troops, and troops the Maid;
The Thunder huddles with the Snow.
Where are the revellers high and low?
The clashing swords? The lover's call?
The dancers gleaming row on row?
Into the night go one and all.

Envoy

Prince, in one common overthrow
The Hero tumbles with the Thrall:
As dust that drives, as straws that blow,
Into the night go one and all.

1888

INVICTUS

OUT of the night that covers me,
Black as the Pit from pole to pole,
I thank whatever gods may be
For my unconquerable soul.

In the fell clutch of circumstance
I have not winced nor cried aloud.
Under the bludgeonings of chance
My head is bloody, but unbowed.

Beyond this place of wrath and tears
Looms but the Horror of the shade,
And yet the menace of the years
Finds, and shall find, me unafraid.

It matters not how strait the gate,
  How charged with punishments the scroll,
I am the master of my fate:
  I am the captain of my soul.

1875

WHILE THE WEST IS PALING

WHILE the west is paling
  Starshine is begun.
While the dusk is failing
  Glimmers up the sun.

So, till darkness cover
  Life's retreating gleam,
Lover follows lover,
  Dream succeeds to dream.

Stoop to my endeavour,
  O my love, and be
Only and for ever
  Sun and stars to me.

1876

O, FALMOUTH IS A FINE TOWN

O, FALMOUTH is a fine town with ships in the bay,
And I wish from my heart it's there I was to-day;
I wish from my heart I was far away from here,
Sitting in my parlour and talking to my dear.
  For it's home, dearie, home—it's home I want to be.
  Our topsails are hoisted, and we'll away to sea.
  O, the oak and the ash and the bonnie birken tree
  They're all growing green in the old countrie.

In Baltimore a-walking a lady I did meet
With her babe on her arm, as she came down the street;
And I thought how I sailed, and the cradle standing ready
For the pretty little babe that has never seen its daddie.
  And it's home, dearie, home . . .

O, if it be a lass, she shall wear a golden ring;
And if it be a lad, he shall fight for his king:
With his dirk and his hat and his little jacket blue
He shall walk the quarter-deck as his daddie used to do.
  And it's home, dearie, home . . .

O, there's a wind a-blowing, a-blowing from the west,
And that of all the winds is the one I like the best,
For it blows at our backs, and it shakes our pennon free,
And it soon will blow us home to the old countrie.
  For it's home, dearie, home—it's home I want to be.
  Our topsails are hoisted, and we'll away to sea.
  O, the oak and the ash and the bonnie birken tree
  They're all growing green in the old countrie.

1878

NOTE—The burthen and the third stanza are old.

A LATE LARK TWITTERS

A LATE lark twitters from the quiet skies;
And from the west,
Where the sun, his day's work ended,
Lingers as in content,
There falls on the old, grey city
An influence luminous and serene,
A shining peace.

The smoke ascends
In a rosy-and-golden haze. The spires
Shine, and are changed. In the valley
Shadows rise. The lark sings on. The sun,
Closing his benediction,
Sinks, and the darkening air
Thrills with a sense of the triumphing night—
Night with her train of stars
And her great gift of sleep.

So be my passing!
My task accomplished and the long day done,
My wages taken, and in my heart
Some late lark singing,

Let me be gathered to the quiet west,
The sundown splendid and serene,
Death.

1888

OR EVER THE KNIGHTLY YEARS

Or ever the knightly years were gone
With the old world to the grave,
I was a King in Babylon
And you were a Christian Slave.

I saw, I took, I cast you by,
I bent and broke your pride.
You loved me well, or I heard them lie,
But your longing was denied.
Surely I knew that by and by
You cursed your gods and died.

And a myriad suns have set and shone
Since then upon the grave
Decreed by the King of Babylon
To her that had been his Slave.

The pride I trampled is now my scathe,
For it tramples me again.
The old resentment lasts like death,
For you love, yet you refrain.
I break my heart on your hard unfaith,
And I break my heart in vain.

Yet not for an hour do I wish undone
The deed beyond the grave,
When I was a King in Babylon
And you were a Virgin Slave.

1888

ON THE WAY TO KEW

On the way to Kew,
By the river old and gray,
Where in the Long Ago,
We laughed and loitered so,
I met a ghost to-day,
A ghost that told of you—
A ghost of low replies
And sweet, inscrutable eyes
Coming up from Richmond
As you used to do.

By the river old and gray,
The enchanted Long Ago
Murmured and smiled anew.
On the way to Kew,
March had the laugh of May,
The bare boughs looked aglow,
And old immortal words
Sang in my breast like birds,
Coming up from Richmond
As I used with you.

With the life of Long Ago
Lived my thought of you.
By the river old and gray
Flowing his appointed way
As I watched I knew
What is so good to know—
Not in vain, not in vain,
Shall I look for you again
Coming up from Richmond
On the way to Kew.

1888

WHERE FORLORN SUNSETS

Where forlorn sunsets flare and fade
On desolate sea and lonely sand,
Out of the silence and the shade
What is the voice of strange command
Calling you still, as friend calls friend
With love that cannot brook delay
To rise and follow the ways that wend
Over the hills and far away?

Hark in the city, street on street
A roaring reach of death and life,
Of vortices that clash and fleet
And ruin in appointed strife,
Hark to it calling, calling clear,
Calling until you cannot stay
From dearer things than your own most dear
Over the hills and far away?

Out of the sound of the ebb-and-flow,
Out of the sight of lamp and star,
It calls you where the good winds blow,
And the unchanging meadows are:
From faded hopes and hopes agleam,
It calls you, calls you night and day
Beyond the dark into the dream
Over the hills and far away.

1892

GULLS IN AN AËRY MORRICE

Gulls in an aëry morrice
Gleam and vanish and gleam . . .
The full sea, sleepily basking,
Dreams under skies of dream.

Gulls in an aëry morrice
Circle and swoop and close . . .
Fuller and ever fuller
The rose of the morning blows.

Gulls, in an aëry morrice
Frolicking, float and fade . . .
O, the way of a bird in the sunshine,
The way of a man with a maid!

SPACE AND DREAD AND THE DARK

Space and dread and the dark—
Over a livid stretch of sky
Cloud-monsters crawling, like a funeral train
Of huge, primeval presences
Stooping beneath the weight
Of some enormous, rudimentary grief;
While in the haunting loneliness
The far sea waits and wanders with a sound
As of the trailing skirts of Destiny,
Passing unseen
To some immitigable end
With her grey henchman, Death.

What larve, what spectre is this
Thrilling the wilderness to life
As with the bodily shape of Fear?
What but a desperate sense,
A strong foreboding of those dim
Interminable continents, forlorn
And many-silenced, in a dusk
Inviolable utterly, and dead
As the poor dead it huddles and swarms and styes
In hugger-mugger through eternity?

Life—life—let there be life!
Better a thousand times the roaring hours
When wave and wind,
Like the Arch-Murderer in flight
From the Avenger at his heel,
Storm through the desolate fastnesses
And wild waste places of the world!

Life—give me life until the end,
That at the very top of being,
The battle-spirit shouting in my blood,
Out of the reddest hell of the fight
I may be snatched and flung
Into the everlasting lull,
The immortal, incommunicable dream.

1892

MADAM LIFE'S A PIECE IN BLOOM

Madam Life's a piece in bloom
Death goes dogging everywhere:
She's the tenant of the room,
He's the ruffian on the stair.

You shall see her as a friend,
You shall bilk him once and twice;
But he'll trap you in the end,
And he'll stick you for her price.

With his kneebones at your chest,
And his knuckles in your throat,
You would reason—plead—protest!
Clutching at her petticoat;

But she's heard it all before,
Well she knows you've had your fun,
Gingerly she gains the door,
And your little job is done.

1877

GERARD MANLEY HOPKINS

[June 11, 1844–June 8, 1889]

Gerard Manley Hopkins, lover of music all his life, was born at Stratford, Essex, and had for his first teacher an aunt who coached him in music and drawing. At the age of ten he entered Sir Robert Cholmondeley's Grammar School at Highgate, where, fortunately for the young

Gerard, R. W. Dixon, poet, artist, historian, just out of Oxford, was a master. Hopkins won a number of school prizes at Highgate, and in 1863, as a result of his winning an exhibition for Balliol College, went to Oxford. At Oxford he came under the influence of Jowett, who "was seeing every Balliol undergraduate every week," and of Walter Pater, whose liberal philosophy and "many-hued language" made the same significant impression on Hopkins that it made on so many of the sensitive young undergraduates. Although he was "placed in the English Church by the good Providence of God," Hopkins, while still more than half a year from his degree, wrote to Dr. Newman and told him that he was anxious to become a Catholic, a desire in which he was opposed by some of his Oxford friends and which, when his father heard of it, led him to write to his son's Oxford tutors in "very deep sorrow." Nevertheless Hopkins was received into the Society of Jesus in 1868, first burning his early verse and resolving "to write no more [poetry]." After a few months with Newman at Birmingham, followed by service as a missionary in Liverpool, he obtained a church in Oxford, and in 1884 was appointed to a fellowship in the Catholic University at Dublin, where he spent the remaining five years of his life. When he died, his poems, in manuscript, went to Dr. Robert Bridges, who had remained perhaps the closest of the young friends he made at Oxford. Not till 1918 did Dr. Bridges publish the slim volume which contains Hopkins's "really wonderful achievements in rhythm."

HEAVEN–HAVEN

A NUN TAKES THE VEIL

I HAVE desired to go
Where springs not fail,
To fields where flies no sharp and sided hail
And a few lilies blow.

And I have asked to be
Where no storms come,
Where the green swell is in the havens dumb,
And out of the swing of the sea.

1918

THE HABIT OF PERFECTION

ELECTED Silence, sing to me
And beat upon my whorlèd ear,
Pipe me to pastures still and be
The music that I care to hear.

Shape nothing, lips; be lovely-dumb:
It is the shut, the curfew sent
From there where all surrenders come
Which only makes you eloquent.

Be shellèd, eyes, with double dark
And find the uncreated light:
This ruck and reel which you remark
Coils, keeps, and teases simple sight.

Palate, the hutch of tasty lust,
Desire not to be rinsed with wine:
The can must be so sweet, the crust
So fresh that come in fasts divine!

Nostrils, your careless breath that spend
Upon the stir and keep of pride,
What relish shall the censers send
Along the sanctuary side!

O feel-of-primrose hands, O feet
That want the yield of plushy sward,
But you shall walk the golden street
And you unhouse and house the Lord.

And, Poverty, be thou the bride
And now the marriage feast begun,
And lily-coloured clothes provide
Your spouse not laboured-at nor spun.

1918

GOD'S GRANDEUR

THE world is charged with the grandeur of God.
It will flame out, like shining from shook foil;
It gathers to a greatness, like the ooze of oil
Crushed. Why do men then now not reck his rod?
Generations have trod, have trod, have trod;

And all is seared with trade; bleared, smeared with toil;
And wears man's smudge and shares man's smell: the soil
Is bare now, nor can foot feel, being shod.

And for all this, nature is never spent;
There lives the dearest freshness deep down things;
And though the last lights off the black West went
Oh, morning, at the brown brink eastward, springs—
Because the Holy Ghost over the bent
World broods with warm breast and with ah! bright wings.

1918

SPRING

NOTHING is so beautiful as spring—
When weeds, in wheels, shoot long and lovely and lush;
Thrush's eggs look little low heavens, and thrush
Through the echoing timber does so rinse and wring
The ear, it strikes like lightnings to hear him sing;
The glassy peartree leaves and blooms, they brush
The descending blue; that blue is all in a rush
With richness; the racing lambs too have fair their fling.

What is all this juice and all this joy?
A strain of the earth's sweet being in the beginning
In Eden garden.—Have, get, before it cloy,
Before it cloud, Christ, lord, and sour with sinning,
Innocent mind and Mayday in girl and boy,
Most, O maid's child, thy choice and worthy the winning.

1918

THE WINDHOVER

TO CHRIST OUR LORD

I CAUGHT this morning morning's minion, kingdom of daylight's dauphin, dapple-dawn-drawn Falcon, in his riding
Of the rolling level underneath him steady air, and striding
High there, how he rung upon the rein of a wimpling wing
In his ecstasy! then off, off forth on swing,
As a skate's heel sweeps smooth on a bow-bend: the hurl and gliding
Rebuffed the big wind. My heart in hiding
Stirred for a bird,—the achieve of, the mastery of the thing!

Brute beauty and valour and act, oh, air, pride, plume, here
Buckle! AND the fire that breaks from thee then, a billion
Times told lovelier, more dangerous, O my chevalier!

No wonder of it: shéer plód makes plough down sillion
Shine, and blue-bleak embers, ah my dear,
Fall, gall themselves, and gash gold-vermilion.

1918

PIED BEAUTY

GLORY be to God for dappled things—
For skies of couple-colour as a brinded cow;
For rose-moles all in stipple upon trout that swim;
Fresh-firecoal chestnut-falls; finches' wings;
Landscape plotted and pieced—fold, fallow, and plough;
And áll trádes, their gear and tackle and trim.

All things counter, original, spare, strange;
Whatever is fickle, freckled (who knows how?)
With swift, slow; sweet, sour; adazzle, dim;
He fathers-forth whose beauty is past change:
Praise him.

1918

SPELT FROM SIBYL'S LEAVES

EARNEST, earthless, equal, attuneable, ' vaulty, voluminous, . . stupendous
Evening strains to be tíme's vást, ' womb-of-all, home-of-all, hearse-of-all night.
Her fond yellow hornlight wound to the west, ' her wild hollow hoarlight hung to the height

Waste; her earliest stars, earl-stars, | stárs principal, overbend us,
Fíre-féaturing heaven. For earth | her being has unbound, her dapple is at an end, astray or aswarm, all throughther, in throngs; | self ín self steepèd and páshed—qúite
Disremembering, dísmémbering | áll now. Heart, you round me right
With: Óur évening is over us; óur night | whélms, whélms, ánd will end us.
Only the beak-leaved boughs dragonish | damask the tool-smooth bleak light; black,
Ever so black on it. Óur tale, O óur oracle! | Lét life, wáned, ah lét life wind
Off hér once skéined stained véined varíety | upon, áll on twó spools; párt, pen, páck
Now her áll in twó flocks, twó folds—black, white; | right, wrong; reckon but, reck but, mind
But thése two; wáre of a wórld where bút these | twó tell, each off the óther; of a rack
Where, selfwrung, selfstrung, sheathe- and shelterless, | thóughts agaínst thoughts ín groans grínd.

1918

THE LEADEN ECHO AND THE GOLDEN ECHO

(MAIDENS' SONG FROM ST. WINEFRED'S WELL)

The Leaden Echo

How to kéep—is there ány any, is there none such, nowhere known some, bow or brooch or braid or brace, láce, latch or catch or key to keep
Back beauty, keep it, beauty, beauty, beauty, . . . from vanishing away?
Ó is there no frowning of these wrinkles, rankèd wrinkles deep,
Dówn? no waving off of these most mournful messengers, still messengers, sad and stealing messengers of grey?
No there's none, there's none, O no there's none,
Nor can you long be, what you now are, called fair,
Do what you may do, what, do what you may,
And wisdom is early to despair:
Be beginning; since, no, nothing can be done
To keep at bay
Age and age's evils, hoar hair,
Ruck and wrinkle, drooping, dying, death's worst, winding sheets, tombs and worms and tumbling to decay;
So be beginning, be beginning to despair.
O there's none; no no no there's none:
Be beginning to despair, to despair,
Despair, despair, despair, despair.

The Golden Echo

Spare!
There ís one, yes I have one (Hush there!);
Only not within seeing of the sun,
Not within the singeing of the strong sun,
Tall sun's tingeing, or treacherous the tainting of the earth's air,
Somewhere elsewhere there is ah well where! one,
Ońe. Yes I can tell such a key, I do know such a place,
Where whatever's prized and passes of us, everything that's fresh and fast flying of us, seems to us sweet of us and swiftly away with, done away with, undone,
Undone, done with, soon done with, and yet dearly and dangerously sweet
Of us, the wimpled-water-dimpled, not-by-morning-matchèd face,
The flower of beauty, fleece of beauty, too too apt to, ah! to fleet,
Never fleets móre, fastened with the tenderest truth
To its own best being and its loveliness of youth: it is an everlastingness of, O it is an all youth!
Come then, your ways and airs and looks, locks, maiden gear, gallantry and gaiety and grace,
Winning ways, airs innocent, maiden manners, sweet looks, loose locks, long locks, lovelocks, gaygear, going gallant, girlgrace—
Resign them, sign them, seal them, send them, motion them with breath,
And with sighs soaring, soaring síghs deliver
Them; beauty-in-the-ghost, deliver it, early now, long before death
Give beauty back, beauty, beauty, beauty, back to God, beauty's self and beauty's giver.

See; not a hair is, not an eyelash, not the least lash lost; every hair
Is, hair of the head, numbered.
Nay, what we had lighthanded left in surly the mere mould
Will have waked and have waxed and have walked with the wind what while we slept,
This side, that side hurling a heavyheaded hundredfold
What while we, while we slumbered.
O then, weary then why should we tread? O why are we so haggard at the heart, so care-coiled, care-killed, so fagged, so fashed, so cogged, so cumbered,
When the thing we freely fórfeit is kept with fonder a care,
Fonder a care kept than we could have kept it, kept
Far with fonder a care (and we, we should have lost it) finer, fonder
A care kept.—Where kept? Do but tell us where kept, where.—
Yonder.—What high as that! We follow, now we follow.—Yonder, yes yonder, yonder,
Yonder.

1918

NO WORST, THERE IS NONE

No worst, there is none. Pitched past pitch of grief,
More pangs will, schooled at forepangs, wilder wring.
Comforter, where, where is your comforting?
Mary, mother of us, where is your relief?
My cries heave, herds-long; huddle in a main, a chief
Woe, world-sorrow; on an age-old anvil wince and sing—
Then lull, then leave off. Fury had shrieked "No ling-
ering! Let me be fell: force I must be brief."

O the mind, mind has mountains; cliffs of fall
Frightful, sheer, no-man-fathomed. Hold them cheap
May who ne'er hung there. Nor does long our small
Durance deal with that steep or deep. Here! creep,
Wretch, under a comfort serves in a whirlwind: all
Life death does end and each day dies with sleep.

1918

I WAKE AND FEEL THE FELL OF DARK

I wake and feel the fell of dark, not day.
What hours, O what black hoürs we have spent
This night! what sights you, heart, saw; ways you went!
And more must, in yet longer light's delay.
With witness I speak this. But where I say
Hours I mean years, mean life. And my lament
Is cries countless, cries like dead letters sent
To dearest him that lives alas! away.

I am gall, I am heartburn. God's most deep decree
Bitter would have me taste: my taste was me;
Bones built in me, flesh filled, blood brimmed the curse.
Selfyeast of spirit a dull dough sours. I see
The lost are like this, and their scourge to be
As I am mine, their sweating selves; but worse.

1918

THOU ART INDEED JUST

Justus quidem tu es, Domine, si disputem tecum: verumtamen justa loquar ad te: Quare via impiorum prosperatur? &c.

Thou art indeed just, Lord, if I contend
With thee; but, sir, so what I plead is just.
Why do sinners' ways prosper? and why must
Disappointment all I endeavour end?

Wert thou my enemy, O thou my friend,
How wouldst thou worse, I wonder, than thou dost
Defeat, thwart me? Oh, the sots and thralls of lust
Do in spare hours more thrive than I that spend,
Sir, life upon thy cause. See, banks and brakes
Now, leavèd how thick! lacèd they are again
With fretty chervil, look, and fresh wind shakes

Them; birds build—but not I build; no, but strain,
Time's eunuch, and not breed one work that wakes.
Mine, O thou lord of life, send my roots rain.

1918

THE BUGLER'S FIRST COMMUNION

A BUGLER boy from barrack (it is over the hill
There)—boy bugler, born, he tells me, of Irish
Mother to an English sire (he
Shares their best gifts surely, fall how things will),

This very very day came down to us after a boon he on
My late being there begged of me, overflowing
Boon in my bestowing,
Came, I say, this day to it—to a First Communion.

Here he knelt then in regimental red.
Forth Christ from cupboard fetched, how fain I of feet
To his youngster take his treat!
Low-latched in leaf-light housel his too huge godhead.

There! and your sweetest sendings, ah divine,
By it, heavens, befall him! as a heart Christ's darling, dauntless;
Tongue true, vaunt- and tauntless;
Breathing bloom of a chastity in mansex fine.

Frowning and forefending angel-warder
Squander the hell-rook ranks sally to molest him;
March, kind comrade, abreast him;
Dress his days to a dexterous and starlight order.

How it dóes my heart good, visiting at that bleak hill,
When limber liquid youth, that to all I teach
Yields tender as a pushed peach,
Hies headstrong to its wellbeing of a self-wise self-will!

Then though I should tread tufts of consolation
Dáys áfter, só I in a sort deserve to
And do serve God to serve to
Just such slips of soldiery Christ's royal ration.

Nothing élse is like it, no, not all so strains
Us: fresh youth fretted in a bloomfall all portending
That sweet's sweeter ending;
Realm both Christ is heir to and thére réigns.

O now well work that sealing sacred ointment!
O for now charms, arms, what bans off bad
And locks love ever in a lad!
Let mé though see no more of him, and not disappointment

Those sweet hopes quell whose least me quickenings lift,
In scarlet or somewhere of some day seeing
That brow and bead of being,
An our day's God's own Galahad. Though this child's drift

Seems by a divíne doom chánnelled, nor do I cry
Disaster there; but may he not rankle and roam
In backwheels though bound home?—
That left to the Lord of the Eucharist, I here lie by;

Recorded only, I have put my lips on pleas
Would brandle adamantine heaven with ride and jar, did
Prayer go disregarded:
Forward-like, but however, and like favourable heaven heard these.

1918

ALFRED EDWARD HOUSMAN

[March 26, 1859–May 1, 1936]

ALFRED EDWARD HOUSMAN, native of Shropshire, the westernmost county of mid-England, prepared for the university at Bromsgrove School in Worcestershire and then entered St. John's College, Oxford. He was graduated with a thorough classical education and became in 1882 a Higher Division Clerk in the British Patent Office. During the ten years that he held this clerkship he gave his hours that were not taken up by routine duties to diligent study of the classics, and in 1892 was made Professor of Latin in University College, London. This position he held until 1911, when he became Professor of Latin at Cambridge University and a Fellow of Trinity College (Cambridge), posts which he held up to the time of his death. Only two small volumes of poetry came from Housman's pen, the first, *A Shropshire Lad* (1896), containing sixty-three short poems; and, twenty-six years later, the second, containing forty-one poems and called, with some significance, *Last Poems*. In the brief foreword to *Last Poems* Mr. Housman said that he was not likely to write much more, that he could no longer expect to be revisited by the continuous excitement under which he wrote the greater part of his earlier book. Lightfoot lads and rose-lipt maidens who die young, lads who lie under the land they "used to plough," the grim burden swaying in clanking gallows chains, "soldiers marching all to die," the thinker's agonized clutching at his heart—these are Housman's favorite subjects. Few poets of any age have equaled him in depicting, with blend of bitterness and wistfulness, man's sense of the inconstancy of time, his forebodings of change, the finality with which his youthful sports and loves and friendships are swept away.

From A SHROPSHIRE LAD

II

LOVELIEST of trees, the cherry now
Is hung with bloom along the bough,
And stands about the woodland ride
Wearing white for Eastertide.

Now, of my threescore years and ten,
Twenty will not come again,
And take from seventy springs a score,
It only leaves me fifty more.

And since to look at things in bloom
Fifty springs are little room,
About the woodlands I will go
To see the cherry hung with snow.

VI

WHEN the lad for longing sighs,
  Mute and dull of cheer and pale,
If at death's own door he lies,
  Maiden, you can heal his ail.

Lovers' ills are all to buy:
  The wan look, the hollow tone,
The hung head, the sunken eye—
  You can have them for your own.

Buy them, buy them; eve and morn
  Lovers' ills are all to sell.
Then you can lie down forlorn;
  But the lover will be well.

VII

WHEN smoke stood up from Ludlow,
  And mist blew off from Teme,
And blithe afield to ploughing
  Against the morning beam
  I strode beside my team,

The blackbird in the coppice
  Looked out to see me stride,
And hearkened as I whistled

The trampling team beside,
And fluted and replied:

"Lie down, lie down, young yeoman;
What use to rise and rise?
Rise man a thousand mornings
Yet down at last he lies,
And then the man is wise."

I heard the tune he sang me,
And spied his yellow bill;
I picked a stone and aimed it
And threw it with a will.
Then the bird was still.

Then my soul within me
Took up the blackbird's strain,
And still beside the horses
Along the dewy lane
It sang the song again:

"Lie down, lie down, young yeoman;
The sun moves always west;
The road one treads to labor
Will lead one home to rest,
And that will be the best."

IX

On moonlit heath and lonesome bank
The sheep beside me graze,
And yon the gallows used to clank
Fast by the four cross ways.

A careless shepherd once would keep
The flocks by moonlight there,
And high amongst the glimmering sheep
The dead man stood on air.

They hang us now in Shrewsbury jail;
The whistles blow forlorn,
And trains all night groan on the rail
To men that die at morn.

There sleeps in Shrewsbury jail tonight,
Or wakes, as may betide,
A better lad, if things went right,
Than most that sleep outside.

And naked to the hangman's noose
The morning clocks will ring
A neck God made for other use
Than strangling in a string.

And sharp the link of life will snap,
And dead on air will stand
Heels that held up as straight a chap
As treads upon the land.

So here I'll watch the night and wait
To see the morning shine,
When he will hear the stroke of eight
And not the stroke of nine;

And wish my friend as sound a sleep
As lads' I did not know,
That shepherded the moonlit sheep
A hundred years ago.

XIII

When I was one-and-twenty
I heard a wise man say,
"Give crowns and pounds and guineas,
But not your heart, away;
Give pearls away and rubies,
But keep your fancy free."
But I was one-and-twenty—
No use to talk to me.

When I was one-and-twenty
I heard him say again,
"The heart out of the bosom
Was never given in vain;
'Tis paid with sighs a plenty
And sold for endless rue."
And I am two-and-twenty,
And oh, 'tis true, 'tis true.

XVII

Twice a week the winter thorough
Here stood I to keep the goal;
Football then was fighting sorrow
For the young man's soul.

Now in Maytime to the wicket
Out I march with bat and pad;
See the son of grief at cricket
Trying to be glad.

Try I will—no harm in trying;
Wonder 'tis how little mirth
Keeps the bones of man from lying
On the bed of earth.

XIX. TO AN ATHLETE DYING YOUNG

The time you won your town the race
We chaired you through the market-place;

Man and boy stood cheering by,
And home we brought you shoulder-high.

Today, the road all runners come,
Shoulder-high we bring you home,
And set you at your threshold down,
Townsman of a stiller town.

Smart lad, to slip betimes away
From fields where glory does not stay
And early though the laurel grows
It withers quicker than the rose.

Eyes the shady night has shut
Cannot see the record cut,
And silence sounds no worse than cheers
After earth has stopped the ears.

Now you will not swell the rout
Of lads that wore their honors out,
Runners whom renown outran
And the name died before the man.

So set, before its echoes fade,
The fleet foot on the sill of shade,
And hold to the low lintel up
The still-defended challenge-cup.

And round that early-laureled head
Will flock to gaze the strengthless dead,
And find unwithered on its curls
The garland briefer than a girl's.

XXIII

THE lads in their hundreds to Ludlow come in for the fair;
 There's men from the barn and the forge and the mill and the fold,
The lads for the girls and the lads for the liquor are there,
 And there with the rest are the lads that will never be old.

There's chaps from the town and the field and the till and the cart,
 And many to count are the stalwart, and many the brave,
And many the handsome of face and the handsome of heart,
 And few that will carry their looks or their truth to the grave.

I wish one could know them, I wish there were tokens to tell
 The fortunate fellows that now you can never discern;
And then one could talk with them friendly and wish them farewell
 And watch them depart on the way that they will not return.

But now you may stare as you like and there's nothing to scan;
 And brushing your elbow unguessed-at and not to be told
They carry back bright to the coiner the mintage of man,
 The lads that will die in their glory and never be old.

XXVII

"Is my team ploughing,
 That I was used to drive
And hear the harness jingle
 When I was man alive?"

Aye, the horses trample,
 The harness jingles now;
No change though you lie under
 The land you used to plough.

"Is football playing
 Along the river shore,
With lads to chase the leather,
 Now I stand up no more?"

Aye, the ball is flying,
 The lads play heart and soul;
The goal stands up, the keeper
 Stands up to keep the goal.

"Is my girl happy,
 That I thought hard to leave,
And has she tired of weeping
 As she lies down at eve?"

Aye, she lies down lightly,
 She lies not down to weep;
Your girl is well contented.
 Be still, my lad, and sleep.

"Is my friend hearty,
 Now I am thin and pine,
And has he found to sleep in
 A better bed than mine?"

Yes, lad, I lie easy,
I lie as lads would choose;
I cheer a dead man's sweetheart—
Never ask me whose.

XXVIII. THE WELSH MARCHES

High the vanes of Shrewsbury gleam
Islanded in Severn stream;
The bridges from the steepled crest
Cross the water east and west.

The flag of morn in conqueror's state
Enters at the English gate;
The vanquished eve, as night prevails,
Bleeds upon the road to Wales.

Ages since the vanquished bled
Round my mother's marriage-bed;
There the ravens feasted far
About the open house of war.

When Severn down to Buildwas ran,
Colored with the death of man,
Couched upon her brother's grave
The Saxon got me on the slave.

The sound of fight is silent long
That began the ancient wrong;
Long the voice of tears is still
That wept of old the endless ill.

In my heart it has not died,
The war that sleeps on Severn side;
They cease not fighting, east and west,
On the marches of my breast.

Here the truceless armies yet
Trample, rolled in blood and sweat,
They kill and kill and never die;
And I think that each is I.

None will part us, none undo
The knot that makes one flesh of two,
Sick with hatred, sick with pain,
Strangling—When shall we be slain?

When shall I be dead and rid
Of the wrong my father did?
How long, how long, till spade and hearse
Put to sleep my mother's curse?

XLIII. THE IMMORTAL PART

When I meet the morning beam,
Or lay me down at night to dream,
I hear my bones within me say,
"Another night, another day.

"When shall this slough of sense be cast,
This dust of thoughts be laid at last,
The man of flesh and soul be slain
And the man of bone remain?

"This tongue that talks, these lungs that shout,
These thews that hustle us about,
This brain that fills the skull with schemes,
And its humming hive of dreams—

"These today are proud in power
And lord it in their little hour;
The immortal bones obey control
Of dying flesh and dying soul.

"'Tis long till eve and morn are gone;
Slow the endless night comes on,
And late to fullness grows the birth
That shall last as long as earth.

"Wanderers eastward, wanderers west,
Know you why you cannot rest?
'Tis that every mother's son
Travails with a skeleton.

"Lie down in the bed of dust
Bear the fruit that bear you must;
Bring the eternal seed to light,
And morn is all the same as night.

"Rest you so from trouble sore,
Fear the heat o' the sun no more,
Nor the snowing winter wild,
Now you labor not with child.

"Empty vessel, garment cast,
We that wore you long shall last
—Another night, another day."
So my bones within me say.

Therefore they shall do my will
Today while I am master still,
And flesh and soul, now both are strong,
Shall hale the sullen slaves along,

Before this fire of sense decay,
This smoke of thought blow clean away,
And leave with ancient night alone
The steadfast and enduring bone.

LIV

WITH rue my heart is laden
For golden friends I had,
For many a rose-lipt maiden
And many a lightfoot lad.

By brooks too broad for leaping
The lightfoot boys are laid;
The rose-lipt girls are sleeping
In fields where roses fade.

LX

Now hollow fires burn out to black,
And lights are guttering low;
Square your shoulders, lift your pack,
And leave your friends and go.

Oh, never fear, man, naught's to dread,
Look not left nor right;
In all the endless road you tread
There's nothing but the night.

LXI. HUGHLEY STEEPLE

THE vane on Hughley steeple
Veers bright, a far-known sign,
And there lie Hughley people,
And there lie friends of mine.
Tall in their midst the tower
Divides the shade and sun,
And the clock strikes the hour
And tells the time to none.

To south the headstones cluster,
The sunny mounds lie thick;
The dead are more in muster
At Hughley than the quick.
North, for a soon-told number,
Chill graves the sexton delves,
And steeple-shadowed slumber
The slayers of themselves.

To north, to south, lie parted,
With Hughley tower above,
The kind, the single-hearted,
The lads I used to love.
And, south or north, 'tis only
A choice of friends one knows,
And I shall ne'er be lonely
Asleep with these or those.

LXII

"TERENCE, this is stupid stuff:
You eat your victuals fast enough;
There can't be much amiss, 'tis clear,
To see the rate you drink your beer.
But, oh, good Lord, the verse you make,
It gives a chap the bellyache.
The cow, the old cow, she is dead;
It sleeps well, the horned head.
We poor lads, 'tis our turn now
To hear such tunes as killed the cow.
Pretty friendship 'tis to rime
Your friends to death before their time
Moping melancholy mad.
Come, pipe a tune to dance to, lad."

Why, if 'tis dancing you would be,
There's brisker pipes than poetry.
Say, for what were hop-yards meant,
Or why was Burton built on Trent?
Oh, many a peer of England brews
Livelier liquor than the Muse,
And malt does more than Milton can
To justify God's ways to man.
Ale, man, ale's the stuff to drink
For fellows whom it hurts to think;
Look into the pewter pot
To see the world as the world's not.
And faith, 'tis pleasant till 'tis past,
The mischief is that 'twill not last.
Oh, I have been to Ludlow fair
And left my necktie God knows where,
And carried half way home, or near,
Pints and quarts of Ludlow beer.
Then the world seemed none so bad,
And I myself a sterling lad;
And down in lovely muck I've lain,
Happy till I woke again.
Then I saw the morning sky—
Heigho, the tale was all a lie;
The world, it was the old world yet,
I was I, my things were wet,
And nothing now remained to do
But begin the game anew.

Therefore, since the world has still
Much good, but much less good than ill,
And while the sun and moon endure
Luck's a chance, but trouble's sure,
I'd face it as a wise man would,
And train for ill and not for good.

'Tis true, the stuff I bring for sale
Is not so brisk a brew as ale;
Out of a stem that scored the hand
I wrung it in a weary land.
But take it—if the smack is sour,
The better for the embittered hour;
It should do good to heart and head
When your soul is in my soul's stead;
And I will friend you, if I may,
In the dark and cloudy day.

There was a king reigned in the East;
There, when kings will sit to feast,
They get their fill before they think
With poisoned meat and poisoned drink.
He gathered all that springs to birth
From the many-venomed earth;
First a little, thence to more,
He sampled all her killing store;
And easy, smiling, seasoned sound,
Sate the king when healths went round.
They put arsenic in his meat
And stared aghast to watch him eat;
They poured strychnine in his cup
And shook to see him drink it up.
They shook, they stared as white's their shirt;
Them it was their poison hurt.
—I tell the tale that I heard told.
Mithridates, he died old.

1896

LIONEL PIGOT JOHNSON

[March 15, 1867–October 4, 1902]

LIONEL PIGOT JOHNSON, a native of Broadstairs, Kent, went to school at Durdham Down, Clifton, and at Winchester School, where he won prizes and medals for excellence in English literature and in writing essays and verse. In 1885 he won a scholarship at New College, Oxford, which he entered in October 1886. At Oxford he fell under the spell of Walter Pater and at the same time, strangely enough, imitated the prose style of his famous namesake, Samuel Johnson. He left Oxford in 1890 deeply in debt for expensive books and prints he had bought while a student, and for a year or more worked hard in London at writing reviews in order to quiet his creditors. Although Johnson had been born into a family whose church was the Anglican Church, even before he went to Oxford he had begun to question the principles of that Church. His doubts grew, and much of his reading after he left Oxford was Roman Catholic theology and many of his friends were Catholic priests. In 1891 he became a Catholic and thought for a time of taking orders. "Asceticism, reverence for Catholic tradition, sympathy with Catholic mysticism, and a love of the niceties, rather than the splendors, of ritual became prominent in the subject matter of his poems," the first collection of which appeared in 1895. In 1897 his second volume, *Ireland, with other Poems*, was published. His work in this volume has led some critics to speak of him as the only impressive figure in the Irish literary revival who was not an Irishman. A fall on Fleet Street in September 1902 fractured his skull and brought about his death.

ORACLES—I

LET not any withering Fate,
With her all too sombre thread,
Flying from the Ivory Gate,
Make thy soul discomforted:
From the nobler Gate of Horn,
Take the blessing of the morn.
Eyes bent full upon the goal,
Whatso be the prize of it:
Tireless feet, and crystal soul,
With good heart, the salt of wit:
These shall set thee in the clear
Spirits' home and singing sphere.

Hush thy melancholy breath,
Wailing after fair days gone:

Make thee friends with kindly Death,
That his long dominion,
With a not too bitter thrall,
Hold thee at the end of all.

Sorrow, angel of the night,
Sorrow haughtily disdains
Invocation by our light
Agonies, and passing pains:
Sorrow is but unto pure
Cloven hearts their balm and cure.

1886

ORACLES—II

And yet, what of the sorrowing years,
Their clouds and difficult event?
Here is a kindlier way than tears,
A fairer way than discontent:
The passionate remembrances,
That wake at bidding of the air:
Fancies, and dreams, and fragrances,
That charmed us, when they were.

So breathed the hay, so the rose bloomed,
Ah! what a thousand years ago!
So long imprisoned and entombed,
Out of our hearts the old joys flow:
Peace! present sorrows: lie you still!
You shall not grow to memories:
The ancient hours live yet, to kill
The sorry hour, that is.

1887

ESCAPE

She bared her spirit to her sorrow:
On the circling hills the morrow
Trembled, but it broke not forth:
Winds blew from the snowy North.

My soul! my sorrow! What wind bloweth,
Knows the wayless way, it goeth?
But before all else, we know
Death's way is the way to go.

She knew no more than that: she only
Knew, that she was left and lonely.
Left? But she had loved! And lone?
She had loved! But love had gone.

So out into the wintry weather
Soul and sorrow fled together:
On the moor day found her dead:
Snow on hands, and heart, and head.

1888

TO OCEAN HAZARD: GIPSY

Burning fire, or blowing wind;
Starry night, or glowing sun:
All these thou dost bring to mind,
All these match thee, one by one:
Ocean is thy name, most fair!
Strangest name, for thee to bear.

Daughter of the sun, and child
Of the wind upon the waste;
Daughter of the field and wild:
Thee, what oceans have embraced?
What great waves have cradled thee,
That thy name is of the sea?

In thy beauty, the red earth,
Full of gold and jewel stone,
Flames and burns: thy happy birth
Made and marked thee for her own.
Winds held triumph in the trees:
Thou wast lying on earth's knees.

For thine ancient people keep
Still their march from land to land:
Ever upon earth they sleep,
Woods and fields on either hand.
Not upon the barren sea
Have thy people dandled thee.

Closer they, than other men,
To the heart of earth have come:
First the wilderness, and then
Field and forest, gave them home:
All their days, their hearts, they must
Give to earth: and then their dust.

Was it, that they heard the sea
In the surging pinewood's voice:
As they pondered names, for thee
Fair enough; so made their choice,
Hailed thee Ocean, hailed thee queen
Over glades of tossing green?

1888

BY THE STATUE OF KING CHARLES AT CHARING CROSS

Sombre and rich, the skies;
Great glooms, and starry plains.
Gently the night wind sighs;
Else a vast silence reigns.

The splendid silence clings
Around me: and around
The saddest of all kings
Crowned, and again discrowned.

Comely and calm, he rides
Hard by his own Whitehall:
Only the night wind glides:
No crowds, nor rebels, brawl.

Gone, too, his Court: and yet,
The stars his courtiers are:
Stars in their stations set;
And every wandering star.

Alone he rides, alone,
The fair and fatal king:
Dark night is all his own,
That strange and solemn thing.

Which are more full of fate:
The stars; or those sad eyes?
Which are more still and great:
Those brows; or the dark skies?

Although his whole heart yearn
In passionate tragedy:
Never was face so stern
With sweet austerity.

Vanquished in life, his death
By beauty made amends:
The passing of his breath
Won his defeated ends.

Brief life, and hapless? Nay:
Through death, life grew sublime.
Speak after sentence? Yea:
And to the end of time.

Armoured he rides, his head
Bare to the stars of doom:
He triumphs now, the dead,
Beholding London's gloom.

Our wearier spirit faints,
Vexed in the world's employ:
His soul was of the saints;
And art to him was joy.

King, tried in fires of woe!
Men hunger for thy grace:
And through the night I go,
Loving thy mournful face.

Yet, when the city sleeps;
When all the cries are still:
The stars and heavenly deeps
Work out a perfect will.

1889

A DREAM OF YOUTH

With faces bright, as ruddy corn,
Touched by the sunlight of the morn;
With rippling hair; and gleaming eyes,
Wherein a sea of passion lies;
Hair waving back, and eyes that gleam
With deep delight of dream on dream;
With full lips, curving into song;
With shapely limbs, upright and strong:
The youths on holy service throng.

Vested in white, upon their brows
Are wreaths fresh twined from dewy boughs:
And flowers they strow along the way,
Still dewy from the birth of day.
So, to each reverend altar come,
They stand in adoration: some
Swing up gold censers; till the air
Is blue and sweet, with smoke of rare
Spices, that fetched from Egypt were.

In voices of calm, choral tone,
Praise they each God, with praise his own:
As children of the Gods, is seen
Their glad solemnity of mien:
So fair a spirit of the skies
Is in their going: and their eyes
Look out upon the peopled earth,
As theirs were some diviner birth:
And clear and courtly is their mirth.

Lights of the labouring world, they seem:
Or, to the tired, like some fresh stream.
Their dignity of perfect youth
Compels devotion, as doth truth:

So right seems all, they do, they are.
Old age looks wistful, from afar,
To watch their beauty, as they go,
Radiant and free, in ordered row;
And fairer, in the watching, grow.

Fair though it be, to watch unclose
The nestling glories of a rose,
Depth on rich depth, soft fold on fold:
Though fairer be it, to behold
Stately and sceptral lilies break
To beauty, and to sweetness wake:
Yet fairer still, to see and sing,
One fair thing is, one matchless thing:
Youth, in its perfect blossoming.

The magic of a golden grace
Brings fire and sweetness on each face:
Till, from their passage, every heart
Takes fire, and sweetness in the smart:
Till virtue lives, for all who own
Their majesty, in them alone:
Till careless hearts, and idle, take
Delight in living, for their sake;
Worship their footsteps, and awake.

Beside the tremulous, blue sea,
Clear at sunset, they love to be:
And they are rarely sad, but then.
For sorrow touches them, as men,
Looking upon the calm of things,
That pass, and wake rememberings
Of holy and of ancient awe;
The charm of immemorial Law:
What we see now, the great dead saw!

Upon a morn of storm, a swan,
Breasting the cold stream, cold and wan,
Throws back his neck in snowy length
Between his snowy wings of strength:
Against him the swift river flows,
The proudlier he against it goes,
King of the waters! For his pride
Bears him upon a mightier tide:
May death not be by youth defied?

But the red sun is gone: and gleams
Of delicate moonlight waken dreams,
Dreams, and the mysteries of peace:
Shall this fair darkness ever cease?
Here is no drear, no fearful Power,
But life grows fuller with each hour,
Full of the silence, that is best:
Earth lies, with soothed and quiet breast,
Beneath the guardian stars, at rest.

At night, behold them! Where lights burn
By moonlit olives, see them turn
Full faces toward the sailing moon,
Nigh lovelier than beneath high noon!
Throw back their comely moulded throats,
Whence music on the night wind floats!
And through the fragrant hush of night
Their lustrous eyes make darkness bright:
Their laugh loads darkness with delight.

Almost the murmuring sea is still:
Almost the world obeys their will.
Such youth moves pity in stern Fates,
And sure death wellnigh dominates:
Their passion kindles such fair flame,
As from divine Achilles came:
A vehement ardour thrills their breasts,
And beauty's benediction rests
On earth, and on earth's goodliest guests.

The music of their sighing parts
A silence: and their beating hearts
Beat to a measure of despair:
Ah! how the fire of youth is fair,
Yet may not be for ever young!
But night hath yielded; there hath sprung
Morning upon the throne of night:
Day comes, with solemnizing light:
Consuming sorrows take to flight.

Magnificent in early bloom,
Like Gods, they triumph over gloom:
All things desirable are theirs,
Of beauty and of wonder, heirs:
Their cities, vassals are, which give
Them thanks and praise, because they live
Strong, they are victors of dismay;
Fair, they serve beauty every day;
Young, the sun loves to light their way.

Where now is death? Where that gray land?
Those fearless eyes, those white brows grand,
That take full sunlight and sweet air
With rapture true and debonair,
These have not known the touch of death!
The world hath winds: these forms have breath.
But, should death come, should dear life set,
Calm would each go: *Farewell! forget*
Me dead: live you serenely yet.

See them! The springing of the palm
Is nought, beside their gracious calm:
The rippling of cool waters dies
To nought, before their clear replies:
The smile, that heralds their bright thought
Brings down the splendid sun to nought.
See them! They walk the earth in state:
In right of perfect youth, held great:
On whom the powers of nature wait.

No sceptre theirs, but they are kings:
Their forms and words are royal things.
Their simple friendship is a court,
Whither the wise and great resort.
No homage of the world, they claim:
But in all places lives their fame.
Sun, moon, and stars; the earth, the sea;
Yea! all things, that of beauty be,
Honour their true divinity.

1889

BAGLEY WOOD

The night is full of stars, full of magnificence:
Nightingales hold the wood, and fragrance loads the dark.
Behold, what fires august, what lights eternal! Hark,
What passionate music poured in passionate love's defence!
Breathe but the wafting wind's nocturnal frankincense!
Only to feel this night's great heart, only to mark
The splendours and the glooms, brings back the patriarch,
Who on Chaldæan wastes found God through reverence.

Could we but live at will upon this perfect height,
Could we but always keep the passion of this peace,
Could we but face unshamed the look of this pure light,
Could we but win earth's heart, and give desire release:
Then were we all divine, and then were ours by right
These stars, these nightingales, these scents: then shame would cease.

1890

UPON A DRAWING

Not in the crystal air of a Greek glen,
Not in the houses of imperial Rome,
Lived he, who wore this beauty among men:
No classic city was his ancient home.
What happy country claims his fair youth then,
Her pride? and what his fortunate lineage?
Here is no common man of every day,
This man, whose full and gleaming eyes assuage
Never their longing, be that what it may:
Of dreamland only he is citizen,
Beyond the flying of the last sea's foam.

Set him beneath the Athenian olive trees,
To speak with Marathonians: or to task
The wise serenity of Socrates;
Asking, what other men dare never ask.
Love of his country and his gods? Not these
The master thoughts, that comfort his strange heart,
When life grows difficult, and the lights dim:
In him is no simplicity, but art
Is all in all, for life and death, to him:
And whoso looks upon that fair face, sees
No nature there: only a magic mask.

Or set this man beside the Roman lords,
To vote upon the fate of Catiline;
Or in a battle of stout Roman swords,
Where strength and virtue were one thing divine:
Or bind him to the cross with Punic cords.
Think you, this unknown and mysterious man
Had played the Roman, with that wistful smile,
Those looks not moulded on a Roman plan,
But full of witcheries and secret guile?
Think you, those lips had framed true Roman words,
Whose very curves have something Sibylline?

Thou wouldst but laugh, were one to question thee:
Laugh with malign, bright eyes, and curious joy.
Thou'rt fallen in love with thine own mystery!
And yet thou art no Sibyl, but a boy.
What wondrous land within the unvoyaged sea
Haunts then thy thoughts, thy memories, thy dreams?

Nay! be my friend; and share with me thy
 past:
If haply I may catch enchaunting gleams,
Catch marvellous music, while our friendship
 last:
Tell me thy visions: though their true home be
Some land that was a legend in old Troy.

1890

TO MORFYDD

A VOICE on the winds,
A voice by the waters,
 Wanders and cries:
Oh! what are the winds?
And what are the waters?
 Mine are your eyes!

Western the winds are,
And western the waters,
 Where the light lies:
Oh! what are the winds?
And what are the waters?
 Mine are your eyes!

Cold, cold, grow the winds,
And wild grow the waters,
 Where the sun dies:
Oh! what are the winds?
And what are the waters?
 Mine are your eyes!

And down the night winds,
And down the night waters,
 The music flies:
Oh! what are the winds?
And what are the waters?
Cold be the winds,
And wild be the waters,
 So mine be your eyes!

1891

THE PRECEPT OF SILENCE

I KNOW you: solitary griefs,
Desolate passions, aching hours!
I know you: tremulous beliefs,
Agonized hopes, and ashen flowers!

The winds are sometimes sad to me;
The starry spaces, full of fear:
Mine is the sorrow on the sea,
And mine the sigh of places drear.

Some players upon plaintive strings
Publish their wistfulness abroad:
I have not spoken of these things,
Save to one man, and unto God.

1893

"TO WEEP IRISH"

LONG Irish melancholy of lament!
Voice of the sorrow, that is on the sea:
Voice of that ancient mourning music sent
From Rama childless: the world wails in thee.

The sadness of all beauty at the heart,
The appealing of all souls unto the skies,
The longing locked in each man's breast apart,
Weep in the melody of thine old cries.

Mother of tears! sweet Mother of sad sons!
All mourners of the world weep Irish, weep
Ever with thee: while burdened time still runs,
Sorrows reach God through thee, and ask for
 sleep.

And though thine own unsleeping sorrow yet
Live to the end of burdened time, in pain:
Still sing the song of sorrow! and forget
The sorrow, in the solace, of the strain.

1893

THE DARK ANGEL

DARK Angel, with thine aching lust
To rid the world of penitence:
Malicious Angel, who still dost
My soul such subtile violence!

Because of thee, no thought, no thing,
Abides for me undesecrate:
Dark Angel, ever on the wing,
Who never reachest me too late!

When music sounds, then changest thou
Its silvery to a sultry fire:
Nor will thine envious heart allow
Delight untortured by desire.

Through thee, the gracious Muses turn
To Furies, O mine Enemy!
And all the things of beauty burn
With flames of evil ecstasy.

Because of thee, the land of dreams
Becomes a gathering place of fears:
Until tormented slumber seems
One vehemence of useless tears.

When sunlight glows upon the flowers,
Or ripples down the dancing sea:
Thou, with thy troop of passionate powers,
Beleaguerest, bewilderest, me.

Within the breath of autumn woods,
Within the winter silences:
Thy venomous spirit stirs and broods,
O Master of impieties!

The ardour of red flame is thine,
And thine the steely soul of ice:
Thou poisonest the fair design
Of nature, with unfair device.

Apples of ashes, golden bright;
Waters of bitterness, how sweet!
O banquet of a foul delight,
Prepared by thee, dark Paraclete!

Thou art the whisper in the gloom,
The hinting tone, the haunting laugh:
Thou art the adorner of my tomb,
The minstrel of mine epitaph.

I fight thee, in the Holy Name!
Yet, what thou dost, is what God saith:
Tempter! should I escape thy flame,
Thou wilt have helped my soul from Death:

The second Death, that never dies,
That cannot die, when time is dead:
Live Death, wherein the lost soul cries,
Eternally uncomforted.

Dark Angel, with thine aching lust!
Of two defeats, of two despairs:
Less dread, a change to drifting dust,
Than thine eternity of cares.

Do what thou wilt, thou shalt not so,
Dark Angel! triumph over me:
Lonely, unto the Lone I go;
Divine, to the Divinity.

1893

A FRIEND

His are the whitenesses of soul,
That Virgil had: he walks the earth
A classic saint, in self-control,
And comeliness, and quiet mirth.

His presence wins me to repose:
When he is with me, I forget
All heaviness: and when he goes,
The comfort of the sun is set.

But in the lonely hours I learn
How I can serve and thank him best:
God! trouble him: that he may turn
Through sorrow to the only rest.

1894

DESIDERIA

The angels of the sunlight clothe
In England the corn's golden ears,
Round me: yet would that I to-day
Saw sunlight on the Hill of Howth,
And sunlight on the Golden Spears,
And sunlight upon Dublin Bay.

In hunger of the heart I loathe
These happy fields: I turn with tears
Of love and longing, far away:
To where the heathered Hill of Howth
Stands guardian, with the Golden Spears,
Above the blue of Dublin Bay.

1894

SYLVAN MORFYDD

White Morfydd through the woods
Went on a moonlit night:
Never so pure a sight
As that, as white
White Morfydd in the woods.

White Morfydd through the woods
Moved, as a spirit might:
The cool leaves with delight
Stirred round the white
White Morfydd in the woods.

White Morfydd through the woods
Went lonely and went bright:
She was those woodlands' light,
My lost, most white
White Morfydd in the woods.

1901

RUDYARD KIPLING

[December 30, 1865–January 17, 1936]

Rudyard Kipling, who was born in Bombay, India, was named Rudyard after an English lake where his artist father, John Lockwood Kipling, and his mother, Alice McDonald, first met. At the time of his son's birth John Lockwood Kipling was professor of Architectural Sculpture in the British School of Art at Bombay. Young Kipling spent the first six years of his life in India, a sensitive period for a precocious child, during which he was deeply impressed by the strange country in which he was born and developed a strong love for it. In 1871 he was sent to England and for six years lived with a severe, exacting family from which he was taken in 1877 by his father, who then sent him to the United Services College at Westward Ho, Devonshire. This was nothing more than a makeshift public school, the scene of Kipling's story *Stalky & Co.* In 1880, when he had finished at the school, he chose to return to India and become a journalist rather than enter Cambridge or Oxford. When he was seventeen he became a reporter on an Indian newspaper, writing, in addition to the items demanded by his position, stories and verses which began to appear in his own and in other Indian papers. The seven years he spent as reporter, sub-editor, and editor in India gave him a wide and intimate knowledge of Indian and Anglo-Indian life, and when he left India in 1890 to see what his chances were with English and American publishers, his mind was filled with strange and stirring scenes and with characters unknown to the pages of English books. Unsuccessful in his efforts to interest New York publishers in the stories and verses he had with him, he went on to London where, to his surprise, *Departmental Ditties*, *Plain Tales from the Hills*, and other volumes that he had published in India, were not widely known. An English publishing house brought out these books soon after Kipling's arrival in London, however; and since they met with tremendous success, he at once stepped into high place in literature.

In 1892 Kipling married Caroline Balestier, the sister of Wolcott Balestier, a young American whom he had met in London and with whom he had collaborated in the writing of a novel, *The Naulahka.* He and his bride went on a long wedding trip which took them almost around the world and ended at Brattleboro, Vermont, where for several years they lived in the unique house that Kipling built. Here he wrote the first *Jungle Book* for his little daughter, who died young, and here, too, he wrote most of the poems of *The Seven Seas*, and the volume of short stories, *Many Inventions.* In 1896 he returned to England, soon after going on a journey to South Africa. In the autumn of 1899 he came back to America and for weeks lay in New York desperately ill with pneumonia. Recovered at last, he went back to the manor-house of Bateman's Burwash in Sussex where he lived quietly afterwards except for the trying years of the Great War, which took from him his only son.

In 1907 Kipling was awarded the Nobel Prize in Literature, the inscription accompanying the Award reading: "In consideration of the power of observation, originality of imagination, and also the manly strength in the art of perception and delineation that characterize the writings of this world-renowned author."

Kipling's poetry, once it became known, took by storm the English public of the 'nineties and the early twentieth century. There were the ironists, of course, who said that he was no poet at all, who insisted that the true note of poetry is not to be heard in the booming of the British drum or in the "tinka-tinka-tink" of banjos in Anglo-Indian barracks. Doubtless there was much truth in what they said of these first poems. But in some of the later poems the rightly attuned ear catches a note whose timbre is unmistakable, the note of the lyre. In the choicest of his more recent work the Kipling of the Empire and the Seven Seas laid aside the drum and banjo and touched the strings of a purer instrument.

[The selections from Kipling are reprinted here in the order in which they appear in *Rudyard Kipling's Verse, Inclusive Edition* (1927), by special arrangement with Mr. Kipling, with his literary agents, A. P. Watt and Son, London, and with his American publishers, Doubleday, Doran and Company, Garden City.]

THE SONG OF THE BANJO

You couldn't pack a Broadwood half a mile—
You mustn't leave a fiddle in the damp—
You couldn't raft an organ up the Nile,
And play it in an Equatorial swamp.
I travel with the cooking-pots and pails—
I'm sandwiched 'tween the coffee and the pork—
And when the dusty column checks and tails,
You should hear me spur the rearguard to a walk!

With my "*Pilly-willy-winky-winky-popp!*"
[Oh, it's any tune that comes into my head!]
So I keep 'em moving forward till they drop;
So I play 'em up to water and to bed.

In the silence of the camp before the fight,
When it's good to make your will and say your prayer,
You can hear my *strumpty-tumpty* overnight,
Explaining ten to one was always fair.
I'm the Prophet of the Utterly Absurd,
Of the Patently Impossible and Vain—
And when the Thing that Couldn't has occurred,
Give me time to change my leg and go again.

With my "*Tumpa-tumpa-tumpa-tumpa-tump!*"
In the desert where the dung-fed camp-smoke curled.
There was never voice before us till I led our lonely chorus,
I—the war-drum of the White Man round the world!

By the bitter road the Younger Son must tread,
Ere he win to hearth and saddle of his own,—
'Mid the riot of the shearers at the shed,
In the silence of the herder's hut alone—
In the twilight, on a bucket upside down,
Hear me babble what the weakest won't confess—
I am Memory and Torment—I am Town!
I am all that ever went with evening dress!

With my "*Tunka-tunka-tunka-tunka-tunk!*"
[So the lights—the London Lights—grow near and plain!]
So I rowel 'em afresh towards the Devil and the Flesh,
Till I bring my broken rankers home again.

In desire of many marvels over sea,
Where the new-raised tropic city sweats and roars,
I have sailed with Young Ulysses from the quay
Till the anchor rumbled down on stranger shores.
He is blooded to the open and the sky,
He is taken in a snare that shall not fail,
He shall hear me singing strongly, till he die,
Like the shouting of a backstay in a gale.

With my "*Hya! Heeya! Heeya! Hullah! Haul!*"
[Oh the green that thunders aft along the deck!]
Are you sick o' towns and men? You must sign and sail again,
For it's "Johnny Bowlegs, pack your kit and trek!"

Through the gorge that gives the stars at noon-day clear—
Up the pass that packs the scud beneath our wheel—
Round the bluff that sinks her thousand fathom sheer—
Down the valley with our guttering brakes asqueal:
Where the trestle groans and quivers in the snow,
Where the many-shedded levels loop and twine.
Hear me lead my reckless children from below
Till we sing the Song of Roland to the pine!

With my "*Tinka-tinka-tinka-tinka-tink!*"
[Oh the axe has cleared the mountain, croup and crest!]
And we ride the iron stallions down to drink,
Through the cañons to the waters of the West!

And the tunes that mean so much to you alone—
Common tunes that make you choke and blow your nose—
Vulgar tunes that bring the laugh that brings the groan—
I can rip your very heartstrings out with those;
With the feasting, and the folly, and the fun—
And the lying, and the lusting, and the drink,
And the merry play that drops you, when you're done,
To the thoughts that burn like irons if you think.

With my "*Plunka-lunka-lunka-lunka-lunk!*"
Here's a trifle on account of pleasure past,
Ere the wit that made you win gives you eyes to see your sin
And—the heavier repentance at the last!

Let the organ moan her sorrow to the roof—
I have told the naked stars the Grief of Man!
Let the trumpet snare the foeman to the proof—
I have known Defeat, and mocked it as we ran!
My bray ye may not alter nor mistake
When I stand to jeer the fatted Soul of Things,
But the Song of Lost Endeavour that I make,
Is it hidden in the twanging of the strings?

With my "*Ta-ra-rara-rara-ra-ra-rrrp!*"
[Is it naught to you that hear and pass me by?]
But the word—the word is mine, when the order moves the line
And the lean, locked ranks go roaring down to die!

The grandam of my grandam was the Lyre—
[O the blue below the little fisher-huts!]
That the Stealer stooping beachward filled with fire,
Till she bore my iron head and ringing guts!
By the wisdom of the centuries I speak—
To the tune of yestermorn I set the truth—
I, the joy of life unquestioned—I, the Greek—
I, the everlasting Wonder-song of Youth!

With my "*Tinka-tinka-tinka-tinka-tink!*"
[What d'ye lack, my noble masters! What d'ye lack?]
So I draw the world together link by link
Yea, from Delos up to Limerick and back!

1894

THE LAST CHANTEY

"And there was no more sea."

Thus said the Lord in the Vault above the Cherubim,
Calling to the Angels and the Souls in their degree:
"Lo! Earth has passed away
On the smoke of Judgment Day.
That Our word may be established shall We gather up the sea?"

Loud sang the souls of the jolly, jolly mariners:
"Plague upon the hurricane that made us furl and flee!
But the war is done between us,
In the deep the Lord hath seen us—
Our bones we'll leave the barracout', and God may sink the sea!"

Then said the soul of Judas that betrayèd Him:
"Lord, hast Thou forgotten Thy covenant with me?
How once a year I go
To cool me on the floe?
And Ye take my day of mercy if Ye take away the sea."

Then said the soul of the Angel of the Off-shore Wind:
(He that bits the thunder when the bull-mouthed breakers flee):
"I have watch and ward to keep
O'er Thy wonders on the deep,
And Ye take mine honour from me if Ye take away the sea!"

Loud sang the souls of the jolly, jolly mariners:
"Nay, but we were angry, and a hasty folk are we.
If we worked the ship together
Till she foundered in foul weather,
Are we babes that we should clamour for a vengeance on the sea?"

Then said the souls of the slaves that men threw overboard:
"Kennelled in the picaroon a weary band were we;
But Thy arm was strong to save,
And it touched us on the wave,
And we drowsed the long tides idle till Thy Trumpets tore the sea."

Then cried the soul of the stout Apostle Paul to God:
"Once we frapped a ship, and she laboured woundily.
There were fourteen score of these,
And they blessed Thee on their knees,
When they learned Thy Grace and Glory under Malta by the sea!"

Loud sang the souls of the jolly, jolly mariners,
Plucking at their harps, and they plucked unhandily:
"Our thumbs are rough and tarred,
And the tune is something hard—
May we lift a Deepsea Chantey such as seamen use at sea?"

Then said the souls of the gentlemen-adventurers—
Fettered wrist to bar all for red iniquity:
"Ho, we revel in our chains
O'er the sorrow that was Spain's!
Heave or sink it, leave or drink it, we were masters of the sea!"

Up spake the soul of a grey Gothavn 'speckshioner—
(He that led the flenching in the fleets of fair Dundee):
"Oh, the ice-blink white and near,
And the bowhead breaching clear!
Will Ye whelm them all for wantonness that wallow in the sea?"

Loud sang the souls of the jolly, jolly mariners,
Crying: "Under Heaven, here is neither lead nor lee!
Must we sing for evermore
On the windless, glassy floor?
Take back your golden fiddles and we'll beat to open sea!"

Then stooped the Lord, and He called the good sea up to Him,
And 'stablishèd its borders unto all eternity,
That such as have no pleasure
For to praise the Lord by measure,
They may enter into galleons and serve Him on the sea.

Sun, Wind, and Cloud shall fail not from the face of it,
Stinging, ringing spindrift, nor the fulmar flying free;
And the ships shall go abroad
To the Glory of the Lord
Who heard the silly sailor-folk and gave them back their sea!

1892

THE LONG TRAIL

There's a whisper down the field where the year has shot her yield,
And the ricks stand grey to the sun,
Singing: "Over then, come over, for the bee has quit the clover,
And your English summer's done."

You have heard the beat of the off-shore wind,
And the thresh of the deep-sea rain;
You have heard the song—how long? how long?
Pull out on the trail again!

Ha' done with the Tents of Shem, dear lass,
We've seen the seasons through,
And it's time to turn on the old trail, our own trail, the out trail,
Pull out, pull out, on the Long Trail—the trail that is always new!

It's North you may run to the rime-ringed sun
Or South to the blind Horn's hate;
Or East all the way into Mississippi Bay,
Or West to the Golden Gate—
Where the blindest bluffs hold good, dear lass,
And the wildest tales are true,
And the men bulk big on the old trail, our own trail, the out trail,
And life runs large on the Long Trail—the trail that is always new.

The days are sick and cold, and the skies are grey and old,
And the twice-breathed airs blow damp;
And I'd sell my tired soul for the bucking beam-sea roll
Of a black Bilbao tramp,
With her load-line over her hatch, dear lass,
And a drunken Dago crew,
And her nose held down on the old trail, our own trail, the out trail
From Cadiz south on the Long Trail—the trail that is always new.

There be triple ways to take, of the eagle or the snake,
Or the way of a man with a maid;
But the sweetest way to me is a ship's upon the sea
In the heel of the North-East Trade.
Can you hear the crash on her bows, dear lass,
And the drum of the racing screw,
As she ships it green on the old trail, our own trail, the out trail,
As she lifts and 'scends on the Long Trail—the trail that is always new?

See the shaking funnels roar, with the Peter at the fore,
And the fenders grind and heave,
And the derricks clack and grate, as the tackle hooks the crate,
And the fall-rope whines through the sheave;
It's "Gang-plank up and in," dear lass,
It's "Hawsers warp her through!"
And it's "All clear aft" on the old trail, our own trail, the out trail,
We're backing down on the Long Trail—the trail that is always new.

O the mutter overside, when the port-fog holds us tied,
And the sirens hoot their dread,
When foot by foot we creep o'er the hueless viewless deep
To the sob of the questing lead!
It's down by the Lower Hope, dear lass,
With the Gunfleet Sands in view,
Till the Mouse swings green on the old trail, our own trail, the out trail,
And the Gull Light lifts on the Long Trail—the trail that is always new.

O the blazing tropic night, when the wake's a welt of light
That holds the hot sky tame,
And the steady fore-foot snores through the planet-powdered floors
Where the scared whale flukes in flame!
Her plates are flaked by the sun, dear lass,
And her ropes are taut with the dew,
For we're booming down on the old trail, our own trail, the out trail,
We're sagging south on the Long Trail—the trail that is always new.

Then home, get her home, where the drunken rollers comb,
And the shouting seas drive by,
And the engines stamp and ring, and the wet bows reel and swing,
And the Southern Cross rides high!

Yes, the old lost stars wheel back, dear lass,
That blaze in the velvet blue.
They're all old friends on the old trail, our own trail, the out trail,
They're God's own guide on the Long Trail—the trail that is always new.

Fly forward, O my heart, from the Foreland to the Start—
We're steaming all too slow,
And it's twenty thousand mile to our little lazy isle
Where the trumpet-orchids blow!
You have heard the call of the off-shore wind
And the voice of the deep-sea rain;
You have heard the song. How long—how long?
Pull out on the trail again!

The Lord knows what we may find, dear lass,
And The Deuce knows what we may do—
But we're back once more on the old trail, our own trail, the out trail,
We're down, hull-down, on the Long Trail—the trail that is always new!

1892

SUSSEX

God gave all men all earth to love,
But since our hearts are small,
Ordained for each one spot should prove
Belovèd over all;
That, as He watched Creation's birth,
So we, in godlike mood,
May of our love create our earth
And see that it is good.

So one shall Baltic pines content,
As one some Surrey's glade,
Or one the palm-grove's droned lament
Before Levuka's Trade.
Each to his choice, and I rejoice
The lot has fallen to me
In a fair ground—in a fair ground—
Yea, Sussex by the sea!

No tender-hearted garden crowns,
No bosomed woods adorn
Our blunt, bow-headed, whale-backed Downs,
But gnarled and writhen thorn—
Bare slopes where chasing shadows skim,
And, through the gaps revealed,
Belt upon belt, the wooded, dim,
Blue goodness of the Weald.

Clean of officious fence or hedge,
Half-wild and wholly tame,
The wise turf cloaks the white cliff edge
As when the Romans came.
What sign of those that fought and died
At shift of sword and sword?
The barrow and the camp abide,
The sunlight and the sward.

Here leaps ashore the full Sou'west
All heavy-winged with brine,
Here lies above the folded crest
The Channel's leaden line;
And here the sea-fogs lap and cling,
And here, each warning each,
The sheep-bells and the ship-bells ring
Along the hidden beach.

We have no waters to delight
Our broad and brookless vales—
Only the dewpond on the height
Unfed, that never fails—
Whereby no tattered herbage tells
Which way the season flies—
Only our close-bit thyme that smells
Like dawn in Paradise.

Here through the strong and shadeless days
The tinkling silence thrills;
Or little, lost, Down churches praise
The Lord who made the hills:
But here the Old Gods guard their round,
And, in her secret heart,
The heathen kingdom Wilfrid found
Dreams, as she dwells, apart.

Though all the rest were all my share,
With equal soul I'd see
Her nine-and-thirty sisters fair,
Yet none more fair than she.
Choose ye your need from Thames to Tweed,
And I will choose instead
Such lands as lie 'twixt Rake and Rye,
Black Down and Beachy Head.

I will go out against the sun
Where the rolled scarp retires,
And the Long Man of Wilmington
Looks naked toward the shires;

And east till doubling Rother crawls
  To find the fickle tide,
By dry and sea-forgotten walls,
  Our ports of stranded pride.

I will go north about the shaws
  And the deep ghylls that breed
Huge oaks and old, the which we hold
  No more than Sussex weed;
Or south where windy Piddinghoe's
  Begilded dolphin veers
And red beside wide-bankèd Ouse
  Lie down our Sussex steers.

So to the land our hearts we give
  Till the sure magic strike,
And Memory, Use, and Love make live
  Us and our fields alike—
That deeper than our speech and thought,
  Beyond our reason's sway,
Clay of the pit whence we were wrought
  Yearns to its fellow-clay.

God gives all men all earth to love,
  But since man's heart is small,
Ordains for each one spot shall prove
  Belovèd over all.
Each to his choice, and I rejoice
  The lot has fallen to me
In a fair ground—in a fair ground—
  Yea, Sussex by the sea!

1902

WHEN EARTH'S LAST PICTURE IS PAINTED

When Earth's last picture is painted and the tubes are twisted and dried,
When the oldest colours have faded, and the youngest critic has died,
We shall rest, and, faith, we shall need it—lie down for an æon or two,
Till the Master of All Good Workmen shall put us to work anew.

And those that were good shall be happy: they shall sit in a golden chair;
They shall splash at a ten-league canvas with brushes of comets' hair.
They shall find real saints to draw from—Magdalene, Peter, and Paul;
They shall work for an age at a sitting and never be tired at all!

And only The Master shall praise us, and only The Master shall blame;
And no one shall work for money, and no one shall work for fame,
But each for the joy of the working, and each, in his separate star,
Shall draw the Thing as he sees It for the God of Things as They are!

1892

RECESSIONAL

God of our fathers, known of old,
  Lord of our far-flung battle-line,
Beneath whose awful Hand we hold
  Dominion over palm and pine—
Lord God of Hosts, be with us yet,
Lest we forget—lest we forget!

The tumult and the shouting dies;
  The Captains and the Kings depart:
Still stands Thine ancient sacrifice,
  An humble and a contrite heart.
Lord God of Hosts, be with us yet,
Lest we forget—lest we forget!

Far-called, our navies melt away;
  On dune and headland sinks the fire:
Lo, all our pomp of yesterday
  Is one with Nineveh and Tyre!
Judge of the Nations, spare us yet,
Lest we forget—lest we forget!

If, drunk with sight of power, we loose
  Wild tongues that have not Thee in awe,
Such boastings as the Gentiles use,
  Or lesser breeds without the Law—
Lord God of Hosts, be with us yet,
Lest we forget—lest we forget!

For heathen heart that puts her trust
  In reeking tube and iron shard,
All valiant dust that builds on dust,
  And guarding, calls not Thee to guard,
For frantic boast and foolish word—
Thy mercy on Thy people, Lord!

1897

TOMLINSON

Now Tomlinson gave up the ghost at his house in Berkeley Square,
And a Spirit came to his bedside and gripped him by the hair—

A Spirit gripped him by the hair and carried him far away,
Till he heard as the roar of a rain-fed ford the roar of the Milky Way:
Till he heard the roar of the Milky Way die down and drone and cease,
And they came to the Gate within the Wall where Peter holds the keys.
"Stand up, stand up now, Tomlinson, and answer loud and high
The good that ye did for the sake of men or ever ye came to die—
The good that ye did for the sake of men on little earth so lone!"
And the naked soul of Tomlinson grew white as a rain-washed bone.
"O I have a friend on earth," he said, "that was my priest and guide,
And well would he answer all for me if he were at my side."
—"For that ye strove in neighbour-love it shall be written fair,
But now ye wait at Heaven's Gate and not in Berkeley Square:
Though we called your friend from his bed this night, he could not speak for you,
For the race is run by one and one and never by two and two."
Then Tomlinson looked up and down, and little gain was there,
For the naked stars grinned overhead, and he saw that his soul was bare.
The Wind that blows between the Worlds, it cut him like a knife,
And Tomlinson took up the tale and spoke of his good in life.
"O this I have read in a book," he said, "and that was told to me,
And this I have thought that another man thought of a Prince in Muscovy."
The good souls flocked like homing doves and bade him clear the path,
And Peter twirled the jangling Keys in weariness and wrath.
"Ye have read, ye have heard, ye have thought," he said, "and the tale is yet to run:
By the worth of the body that once ye had, give answer—what ha' ye done?"
Then Tomlinson looked back and forth, and little good it bore,
For the darkness stayed at his shoulder-blade and Heaven's Gate before:—
"O this I have felt, and this I have guessed, and this I have heard men say,
And this they wrote that another man wrote of a carl in Norroway."
"Ye have read, ye have felt, ye have guessed, good lack! Ye have hampered Heaven's Gate;
There's little room between the stars in idleness to prate!
O none may reach by hired speech of neighbour, priest, and kin
Through borrowed deed to God's good need that lies so fair within;
Get hence, get hence to the Lord of Wrong, for the doom has yet to run,
And . . . the faith that ye share with Berkeley Square uphold you, Tomlinson!"

* * *

The Spirit gripped him by the hair, and sun by sun they fell
Till they came to the belt of Naughty Stars that rim the mouth of Hell.
The first are red with pride and wrath, the next are white with pain,
But the third are black with clinkered sins that cannot burn again:
They may hold their path, they may leave their path, with never a soul to mark,
They may burn or freeze, but they must not cease in the Scorn of the Outer Dark.
The Wind that blows between the Worlds, it nipped him to the bone,
And he yearned to the flare of Hell-gate there as the light of his own hearth-stone.
The Devil he sat behind the bars, where the desperate legions drew,
But he caught the hasting Tomlinson and would not let him through.
"Wot ye the price of good pit-coal that I must pay?" said he,
"That ye rank yoursel' so fit for Hell and ask no leave of me?
I am all o'er-sib to Adam's breed that ye should give me scorn,
For I strove with God for your First Father the day that he was born.
Sit down, sit down upon the slag, and answer loud and high

The harm that ye did to the Sons of Men or ever you came to die."
And Tomlinson looked up and up, and saw against the night
The belly of a tortured star blood-red in Hell-Mouth light;
And Tomlinson looked down and down, and saw beneath his feet
The frontlet of a tortured star milk-white in Hell-Mouth heat.
"O I had a love on earth," said he, "that kissed me to my fall;
And if ye would call my love to me I know she would answer all."
—"All that ye did in love forbid it shall be written fair,
But now ye wait at Hell-Mouth Gate and not in Berkeley Square:
Though we whistled your love from her bed to-night, I trow she would not run,
For the sin ye do by two and two ye must pay for one by one!"
The Wind that blows between the Worlds, it cut him like a knife,
And Tomlinson took up the tale and spoke of his sins in life:—
"Once I ha' laughed at the power of Love and twice at the grip of the Grave,
And thrice I ha' patted my God on the head that men might call me brave."
The Devil he blew on a brandered soul and set it aside to cool:—
"Do ye think I would waste my good pit-coal on the hide of a brain-sick fool?
I see no worth in the hobnailed mirth or the jolthead jest ye did
That I should waken my gentlemen that are sleeping three on a grid."
Then Tomlinson looked back and forth, and there was little grace.
For Hell-Gate filled the houseless soul with the Fear of Naked Space.
"Nay, this I ha' heard," quo' Tomlinson, "and this was noised abroad,
And this I ha' got from a Belgian book on the word of a dead French lord."
—"Ye ha' heard, ye ha' read, ye ha' got, good lack! and the tale begins afresh—
Have ye sinned one sin for the pride o' the eye or the sinful lust of the flesh?"
Then Tomlinson he gripped the bars and yammered, "Let me in—
For I mind that I borrowed my neighbour's wife to sin the deadly sin."
The Devil he grinned behind the bars, and banked the fires high:
"Did ye read of that sin in a book?" said he; and Tomlinson said, "Ay!"
The Devil he blew upon his nails, and the little devils ran,
And he said: "Go husk this whimpering thief that comes in the guise of a man:
Winnow him out 'twixt star and star, and sieve his proper worth:
There's sore decline in Adam's line if this be spawn of earth."
Empusa's crew, so naked-new they may not face the fire,
But weep that they bin too small to sin to the height of their desire,
Over the coal they chased the Soul, and racked it all abroad,
As children rifle a caddis-case or the raven's foolish hoard.
And back they came with the tattered Thing, as children after play,
And they said: "The soul that he got from God he has bartered clean away.
We have threshed a stook of print and book, and winnowed a chattering wind,
And many a soul wherefrom he stole, but his we cannot find.
We have handled him, we have dandled him, we have seared him to the bone,
And Sire, if tooth and nail show truth he has no soul of his own."
The Devil he bowed his head on his breast and rumbled deep and low:—
"I'm all o'er-sib to Adam's breed that I should bid him go.
Yet close we lie, and deep we lie, and if I gave him place,
My gentlemen that are so proud would flout me to my face;
They'd call my house a common stews and me a careless host,
And—I would not anger my gentlemen for the sake of a shiftless ghost."
The Devil he looked at the mangled Soul that prayed to feel the flame,

And he thought of Holy Charity, but he thought of his own good name:—
"Now ye could haste my coal to waste, and sit ye down to fry.
Did ye think of that theft for yourself?" said he; and Tomlinson said, "Ay!"
The Devil he blew an outward breath, for his heart was free from care:—
"Ye have scarce the soul of a louse," he said, "but the roots of sin are there.
And for that sin should ye come in were I the lord alone.
But sinful pride has rule inside—ay, mightier than my own.
Honour and Wit, fore-damned they sit, to each his Priest and Whore;
Nay, scarce I dare myself go there, and you they'd torture sore. 110
Ye are neither spirit nor spirk," he said; "ye are neither book nor brute—
Go, get ye back to the flesh again for the sake of Man's repute.
I'm all o'er-sib to Adam's breed that I should mock your pain,
But look that ye win to worthier sin ere ye come back again.
Get hence, the hearse is at your door—the grim black stallions wait—
They bear your clay to place to-day. Speed, lest ye come too late!
Go back to Earth with a lip unsealed—go back with an open eye,
And carry my word to the Sons of Men or ever ye come to die:
That the sin they do by two and two they must pay for one by one,
And . . . the God that you took from a printed book be with you, Tomlinson!" 120

1891

THE FEMALE OF THE SPECIES

When the Himalayan peasant meets the he-bear in his pride,
He shouts to scare the monster, who will often turn aside.
But the she-bear thus accosted rends the peasant tooth and nail.
For the female of the species is more deadly than the male.

When Nag the basking cobra hears the careless foot of man,
He will sometimes wriggle sideways and avoid it if he can.
But his mate makes no such motion where she camps beside the trail.
For the female of the species is more deadly than the male.

When the early Jesuit fathers preached to Hurons and Choctaws,
They prayed to be delivered from the vengeance of the squaws.
'Twas the women, not the warriors, turned those stark enthusiasts pale.
For the female of the species is more deadly than the male.

Man's timid heart is bursting with the things he must not say,
For the Woman that God gave him isn't his to give away;
But when hunter meets with husband, each confirms the other's tale—
The female of the species is more deadly than the male.

Man, a bear in most relations—worm and savage otherwise,—
Man propounds negotiations, Man accepts the compromise.
Very rarely will he squarely push the logic of a fact
To its ultimate conclusion in unmitigated act.

Fear, or foolishness, impels him, ere he lay the wicked low,
To concede some form of trial even to his fiercest foe.
Mirth obscene diverts his anger—Doubt and Pity oft perplex
Him in dealing with an issue—to the scandal of The Sex!

But the Woman that God gave him, every fibre of her frame
Proves her launched for one sole issue, armed and engined for the same;
And to serve that single issue, lest the generations fail,
The female of the species must be deadlier than the male.

She who faces Death by torture for each life beneath her breast
May not deal in doubt or pity—must not swerve for fact or jest.
These be purely male diversions—not in these her honour dwells.
She the Other Law we live by, is that Law and nothing else.

She can bring no more to living than the powers that make her great
As the Mother of the Infant and the Mistress of the Mate.
And when Babe and Man are lacking and she strides unclaimed to claim
Her right as femme (and baron), her equipment is the same.

She is wedded to convictions—in default of grosser ties:
Her contentions are her children, Heaven help him who denies!—
He will meet no suave discussion, but the instant, white-hot, wild,
Wakened female of the species warring as for spouse and child.

Unprovoked and awful charges—even so the she-bear fights,
Speech that drips, corrodes, and poisons—even so the cobra bites,
Scientific vivisection of one nerve till it is raw
And the victim writhes in anguish—like the Jesuit with the squaw!

So it comes that Man, the coward, when he gathers to confer
With his fellow-braves in council, dare not leave a place for her
Where, at war with Life and Conscience, he uplifts his erring hands
To some God of Abstract Justice—which no woman understands.

And Man knows it! Knows, moreover, that the Woman that God gave him
Must command but may not govern—shall enthral but not enslave him.
And *She* knows, because She warns him, and Her instincts never fail,
That the Female of Her Species is more deadly than the Male.

1911

"FUZZY-WUZZY"

(*Soudan Expeditionary Force*)

We've fought with many men acrost the seas,
An' some of 'em was brave an' some was not:
The Paythan an' the Zulu an' Burmese;
But the Fuzzy was the finest o' the lot.
We never got a ha'porth's change of 'im:
'E squatted in the scrub an' 'ocked our 'orses,
'E cut our sentries up at Sua*kim*,
An' 'e played the cat an' banjo with our forces.
So 'ere's *to* you, Fuzzy-Wuzzy, at your 'ome in the Soudan;
You're a pore benighted 'eathen but a first-class fightin' man;
We gives you your certificate, an' if you want it signed
We'll come an' 'ave a romp with you whenever you're inclined.

We took our chanst among the Kyber 'ills,
The Boers knocked us silly at a mile,
The Burman give us Irriwaddy chills,
An' a Zulu *impi* dished us up in style:
But all we ever got from such as they
Was pop to what the Fuzzy made us swaller;
We 'eld our bloomin' own, the papers say,
But man for man the Fuzzy knocked us oller.
Then 'ere's *to* you, Fuzzy-Wuzzy, an' the missis and the kid;
Our orders was to break you, an' of course we went an' did.
We sloshed you with Martinis, an' it wasn't 'ardly fair;
But for all the odds agin' you, Fuzzy-Wuz, you broke the square.

'E 'asn't got no papers of 'is own,
'E 'asn't got no medals nor rewards,
So *we* must certify the skill 'e's shown,
In usin' of 'is long two-'anded swords:
When 'e's 'oppin' in an' out among the bush
With 'is coffin-'eaded shield an' shovel-spear,
An 'appy day with Fuzzy on the rush
Will last an 'ealthy Tommy for a year.

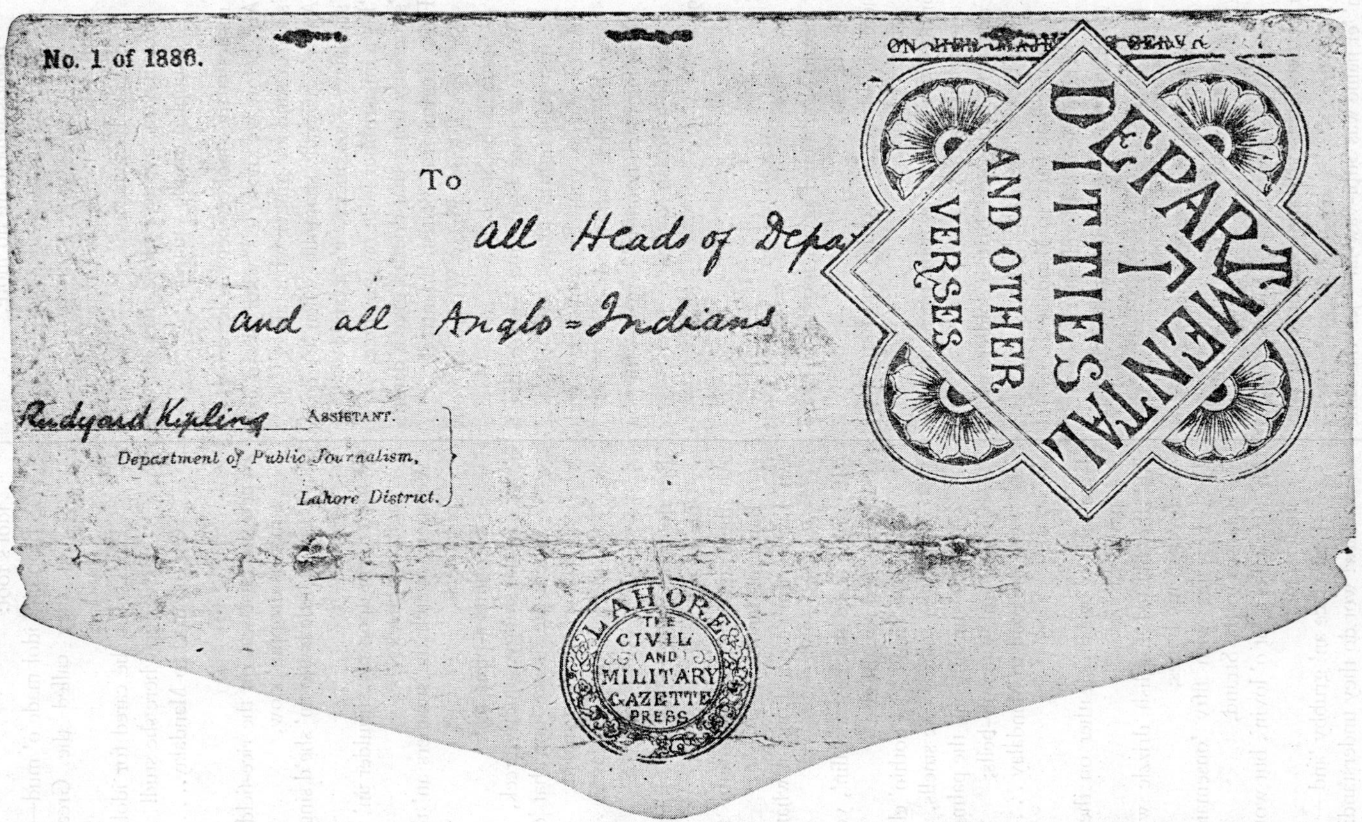

Cover of the Rare No. 1 of Kipling's *Departmental Ditties*. (See Appendix I.)

So 'ere's *to* you, Fuzzy-Wuzzy, an' your friends which are no more,
If we 'adn't lost some messmates we would 'elp you to deplore.
But give an' take's the gospel, an' we'll call the bargain fair,
For if you 'ave lost more than us, you crumpled up the square!

'E rushes at the smoke when we let drive,
An', before we know, 'e's 'ackin' at our 'ead;
'E's all 'ot sand an' ginger when alive,
An' 'e's generally shammin' when 'e's dead.
'E's a daisy, 'e's a ducky, 'e's a lamb!
'E's a injia-rubber idiot on the spree,
'E's the on'y thing that doesn't give a damn
For a Regiment o' British Infantree!
So 'ere's *to* you, Fuzzy-Wuzzy, at your 'ome in the Soudan;
You're a pore benighted 'eathen but a first-class fightin' man;
An' 'ere's *to* you, Fuzzy-Wuzzy, with your 'ayrick 'ead of 'air—
You big black boundin' beggar—for you broke a British square!

1890

MANDALAY

By the old Moulmein Pagoda, lookin' eastward to the sea,
There's a Burma girl a-settin', and I know she thinks o' me;
For the wind is in the palm-trees, and the temple-bells they say:
"Come you back, you British soldier; come you back to Mandalay!"
Come you back to Mandalay,
Where the old Flotilla lay:
Can't you 'ear their paddles chunkin' from Rangoon to Mandalay?
On the road to Mandalay,
Where the flyin'-fishes play,
An' the dawn comes up like thunder outer China 'crost the Bay!

'Er petticoat was yaller an' 'er little cap was green,
An' 'er name was Supi-yaw-lat—jes' the same as Theebaw's Queen,
An' I seed her first a-smokin' of a whackin' white cheroot,
An' a-wastin' Christian kisses on an 'eathen idol's foot:
Bloomin' idol made o' mud—
Wot they called the Great Gawd Budd—
Plucky lot she cared for idols when I kissed 'er where she stud!
On the road to Mandalay . . .

When the mist was on the rice-fields an' the sun was droppin' slow,
She'd git 'er little banjo an' she'd sing "*Kulla-lo-lo!*"
With 'er arm upon my shoulder an' 'er cheek agin my cheek
We useter watch the steamers an' the *hathis* pilin' teak.
Elephints a-pilin' teak
In the sludgy, squdgy creek,
Where the silence 'ung that 'eavy you was 'arf afraid to speak!
On the road to Mandalay . . .

But that's all shove be'ind me—long ago an' fur away,
An' there ain't no 'busses runnin' from the Bank to Mandalay;
An' I'm learnin' 'ere in London what the ten-year soldier tells:
"If you've 'eard the East a-callin', you won't never 'eed naught else."
No! you won't 'eed nothin' else
But them spicy garlic smells,
An' the sunshine an' the palm-trees an' the tinkly temple-bells;
On the road to Mandalay . . .

I am sick o' wastin' leather on these gritty pavin'-stones,
An' the blasted English drizzle wakes the fever in my bones;
Tho' I walks with fifty 'ousemaids outer Chelsea to the Strand,
An' they talks a lot o' lovin', but wot do they understand?
Beefy face an' grubby 'and—
Law! wot do they understand?
I've a neater, sweeter maiden in a cleaner, greener land!
On the road to Mandalay . . .

Ship me somewheres east of Suez, where the best is like the worst,
Where there aren't no Ten Commandments an' a man can raise a thirst;
For the temple-bells are callin', an' it's there that I would be—
By the old Moulmein Pagoda, looking lazy at the sea;
    On the road to Mandalay,
    Where the old Flotilla lay,
    With our sick beneath the awnings when we went to Mandalay!
    O the road to Mandalay,
    Where the flyin'-fishes play,
    An' the dawn comes up like thunder outer China 'crost the Bay!

1890

JOBSON'S AMEN

"BLESSÈD be the English and all their ways and works.
Cursèd be the Infidels, Hereticks, and Turks!"
"Amen," quo' Jobson, "but where I used to lie
Was neither Candle, Bell nor Book to curse my brethren by.

"But a palm-tree in full bearing, bowing down, bowing down,
To a surf that drove unsparing at the brown, walled town—
Conches in a temple, oil-lamps in a dome—
And a low moon out of Africa said: 'This way home!' "

"Blessèd be the English and all that they profess.
Cursèd be the Savages that prance in nakedness!"
"Amen," quo' Jobson, "but where I used to lie
Was neither shirt nor pantaloons to catch my brethren by:

"But a well-wheel slowly creaking, going round, going round,
By a water-channel leaking over drowned, warm ground—
Parrots very busy in the trellised pepper-vine—
And a high sun over Asia shouting: 'Rise and shine!' "

"Blessèd be the English and everything they own.
Cursèd be the Infidels that bow to wood and stone!"
"Amen," quo' Jobson, "but where I used to lie
Was neither pew nor Gospelleer to save my brethren by:

"But a desert stretched and stricken, left and right, left and right,
Where the piled mirages thicken under white-hot light—
A skull beneath a sand-hill and a viper coiled inside—
And a red wind out of Libya roaring: 'Run and hide!' "

"Blessèd be the English and all they make or do.
Cursèd be the Hereticks who doubt that this is true!"
"Amen," quo' Jobson, "but where I mean to die
Is neither rule nor calliper to judge the matter by:

"But Himalaya heavenward-heading, sheer and vast, sheer and vast,
In a million summits bedding on the last world's past—
A certain sacred mountain where the scented cedars climb,
And—the feet of my Belovèd hurrying back through Time!"

1917

COLD IRON

"GOLD is for the mistress—silver for the maid—
Copper for the craftsman cunning at his trade."
"Good!" said the Baron, sitting in his hall,
"But Iron—Cold Iron—is master of them all."

So he made rebellion 'gainst the King his liege,
Camped before his citadel and summoned it to siege.
"Nay!" said the cannoneer on the castle wall,
"But Iron—Cold Iron—shall be master of you all!"

Woe for the Baron and his knights so strong,
When the cruel cannon-balls laid 'em all along
He was taken prisoner, he was cast in thrall,
And Iron—Cold Iron—was master of it all!

Yet his King spake kindly (ah, how kind a Lord!)
"What if I release thee now and give thee back thy sword?"
"Nay!" said the Baron, "mock not at my fall,
For Iron—Cold Iron—is master of men all."

"Tears are for the craven, prayers are for the clown—
Halters for the silly neck that cannot keep a crown."
"As my loss is grievous, so my hope is small,
For Iron—Cold Iron—must be master of men all!"

Yet his King made answer (few such Kings there be!)
"Here is Bread and here is Wine—sit and sup with me.
Eat and drink in Mary's Name, the whiles I do recall
How Iron—Cold Iron—can be master of men all!"

He took the Wine and blessed it. He blessed and brake the Bread,
With His own Hands He served Them, and presently He said:
"See! These Hands they pierced with nails, outside My city wall,
Show Iron—Cold Iron—to be master of men all.

"Wounds are for the desperate, blows are for the strong.
Balm and oil for weary hearts all cut and bruised with wrong.
I forgive thy treason—I redeem thy fall—
For Iron—Cold Iron—must be master of men all!"

"Crowns are for the valiant—sceptres for the bold!
Thrones and powers for mighty men who dare to take and hold!"
"Nay!" said the Baron, kneeling in his hall,
"But Iron—Cold Iron—is master of men all!
Iron out of Calvary is master of men all!"

1909

EDDI'S SERVICE

(A. D. 687)

Eddi, priest of St. Wilfrid
In his chapel at Manhood End,
Ordered a midnight service
For such as cared to attend.

But the Saxons were keeping Christmas,
And the night was stormy as well.
Nobody came to service,
Though Eddi rang the bell.

"'Wicked weather for walking,"
Said Eddi of Manhood End.
"But I must go on with the service
For such as care to attend."

The altar-lamps were lighted,—
An old marsh-donkey came,
Bold as a guest invited,
And stared at the guttering flame.

The storm beat on at the windows,
The water splashed on the floor,
And a wet, yoke-weary bullock
Pushed in through the open door.

"How do I know what is greatest,
How do I know what is least?
That is My Father's business,"
Said Eddi, Wilfrid's priest.

"But—three are gathered together—
Listen to me and attend.
I bring good news, my brethren!"
Said Eddi of Manhood End.

And he told the Ox of a Manger
And a Stall in Bethlehem,
And he spoke to the Ass of a Rider,
That rode to Jerusalem.

They steamed and dripped in the chancel,
They listened and never stirred,
While, just as though they were Bishops,
Eddi preached them The Word,

Till the gale blew off on the marshes
And the windows showed the day,
And the Ox and the Ass together
Wheeled and clattered away.

And when the Saxons mocked him,
Said Eddi of Manhood End,
"I dare not shut His chapel
On such as care to attend."

1910

SHIV AND THE GRASSHOPPER

SHIV, who poured the harvest and made the winds to blow,
Sitting at the doorways of a day of long ago,
Gave to each his portion, food and toil and fate,
From the King upon the *guddee*[1] to the Beggar at the gate.
All things made he—Shiva the Preserver.
Mahadeo! Mahadeo! He made all,—
Thorn for the camel, fodder for the kine,
And Mother's heart for sleepy head, O little Son of mine!

Wheat he gave to rich folk, millet to the poor,
Broken scraps for holy men that beg from door to door;
Cattle to the tiger, carrion to the kite,
And rags and bones to wicked wolves without the wall at night.
Naught he found too lofty, none he saw too low—
Parbati beside him watched them come and go;
Thought to cheat her husband, turning Shiv to jest—
Stole the little grasshopper and hid it in her breast.
So she tricked him, Shiva the Preserver.
Mahadeo! Mahadeo, turn and see!
Tall are the camels, heavy are the kine,
But this was Least of Little Things, O little Son of mine!

When the dole was ended, laughingly she said,
"Master, of a million mouths is not one unfed?"
Laughing, Shiv made answer, "All have had their part,
Even he, the little one, hidden 'neath thy heart."
From her breast she plucked it, Parbati the thief,

Throne.

Saw the Least of Little Things gnawed a new-grown leaf!
Saw and feared and wondered, making prayer to Shiv,
Who hath surely given meat to all that live!
All things made he—Shiva the Preserver.
Mahadeo! Mahadeo! He made all,—
Thorn for the camel, fodder for the kine,
And Mother's heart for sleepy head, O little Son of mine!

1894

THE FAIRIES' SIEGE

I HAVE been given my charge to keep—
Well have I kept the same!
Playing with strife for the most of my life,
But this is a different game.
I'll not fight against swords unseen,
Or spears that I cannot view—
Hand him the keys of the place on your knees—
'Tis the Dreamer whose dreams come true!

Ask him his terms and accept them at once.
Quick, ere we anger him, go!
Never before have I flinched from the guns,
But this is a different show.
I'll not fight with the Herald of God
(I know what his Master can do!)
Open the gate, he must enter in state,
'Tis the Dreamer whose dreams come true!

I'd not give way for an Emperor,
I'd hold my road for a King—
To the Triple Crown I would not bow down—
But this is a different thing.
I'll not fight with the Powers of Air,
Sentry, pass him through!
Drawbridge let fall, 'tis the Lord of us all,
The Dreamer whose dreams come true!

THE CAPTIVE

NOT with an outcry to Allah nor any complaining
He answered his name at the muster and stood to the chaining.
When the twin anklets were nipped on the leg-bars that held them,

He brotherly greeted the armourers stooping to weld them.
Ere the sad dust of the marshalled feet of the chain-gang swallowed him,
Observing him nobly at ease, I alighted and followed him.
Thus we had speech by the way, but not touching his sorrow—
Rather his red Yesterday and his regal To-morrow,
Wherein he statelily moved to the clink of his chains unregarded,
Nowise abashed but contented to drink of the potion awarded.
Saluting aloofly his Fate, he made haste with his story,
And the words of his mouth were as slaves spreading carpets of glory
Embroidered with names of the Djinns—a miraculous weaving—
But the cool and perspicuous eye overbore unbelieving.
So I submitted myself to the limits of rapture—
Bound by this man we had bound, amid captives his capture—
Till he returned me to earth and the visions departed.
But on him be the Peace and the Blessing; for he was great-hearted!

ROAD-SONG OF THE *BANDAR-LOG*

HERE we go in a flung festoon,
Half-way up to the jealous moon!
Don't you envy our pranceful bands?
Don't you wish you had extra hands?
Wouldn't you like if your tails were—*so*—
Curved in the shape of a Cupid's bow?
Now you're angry, but—never mind,
Brother, thy tail hangs down behind!

Here we sit in a branchy row,
Thinking of beautiful things we know;
Dreaming of deeds that we mean to do,
All complete, in a minute or two—
Something noble and grand and good,
Won by merely wishing we could.
Now we're going to—never mind,
Brother, thy tail hangs down behind!

All the talk we ever have heard
Uttered by bat or beast or bird—
Hide or fin or scale or feather—
Jabber it quickly and all together!
Excellent! Wonderful! Once again!
Now we are talking just like men.
Let's pretend we are . . . Never mind!
Brother, thy tail hangs down behind!
This is the way of the Monkey-kind!

Then join our leaping lines that scumfish through the pines,
That rocket by where, light and high, the wild-grape swings.
By the rubbish in our wake, and the noble noise we make,
Be sure—be sure, we're going to do some splendid things!

1894

IF

IF you can keep your head when all about you
Are losing theirs and blaming it on you,
If you can trust yourself when all men doubt you,
But make allowance for their doubting too;
If you can wait and not be tired by waiting,
Or being lied about, don't deal in lies,
Or being hated don't give way to hating,
And yet don't look too good, nor talk too wise:

If you can dream—and not make dreams your master;
If you can think—and not make thoughts your aim;
If you can meet with Triumph and Disaster
And treat those two impostors just the same;
If you can bear to hear the truth you've spoken
Twisted by knaves to make a trap for fools,
Or watch the things you gave your life to, broken,
And stoop and build 'em up with worn-out tools:

If you can make one heap of all your winnings
And risk it on one turn of pitch-and-toss,
And lose, and start again at your beginnings
And never breathe a word about your loss;

If you can force your heart and nerve and sinew
To serve your turn long after they are gone,
And so hold on when there is nothing in you
Except the Will which says to them: "Hold on!"

If you can talk with crowds and keep your virtue,
Or walk with Kings—nor lose the common touch,
If neither foes nor loving friends can hurt you,
If all men count with you, but none too much;
If you can fill the unforgiving minute
With sixty seconds' worth of distance run,
Yours is the Earth and everything that's in it,
And—which is more—you'll be a Man, my son!

1910

THE BEE-BOY'S SONG

Bees! Bees! Hark to your bees!
"Hide from your neighbors as much as you please,
But all that has happened, to us *you must tell,*
Or else we will give you no honey to sell!"

A maiden in her glory,
Upon her wedding-day,
Must tell her Bees the story,
Or else they'll fly away.
Fly away—die away—
Dwindle down and leave you!
But if you don't deceive your Bees,
Your Bees will not deceive you.

Marriage, birth or buryin',
News across the seas,
All you're sad or merry in,
You must tell the Bees.
Tell 'em coming in an' out,
Where the Fanners fan,
'Cause the Bees are just about
As curious as a man!

Don't you wait where trees are,
When the lightnings play,
Nor don't you hate where Bees are,
Or else they'll pine away.
Pine away—dwine away—
Anything to leave you!
But if you never grieve your Bees,
Your Bees'll never grieve you.

1906

THE ONLY SON

She dropped the bar, she shot the bolt, she fed the fire anew,
For she heard a whimper under the sill and a great grey paw came through.
The fresh flame comforted the hut and shone on the roof-beam,
And the Only Son lay down again and dreamed that he dreamed a dream.
The last ash fell from the withered log with the click of a falling spark,
And the Only Son woke up again, and called across the dark:—
"Now was I born of womankind and laid in a mother's breast?
For I have dreamed of a shaggy hide whereon I went to rest.
And was I born of womankind and laid on a father's arm?
For I have dreamed of clashing teeth that guarded me from harm.
And was I born an Only Son and did I play alone?
For I have dreamed of comrades twain that bit me to the bone.
And did I break the barley-cake and steep it in the tyre?
For I have dreamed of a youngling kid new-riven from the byre:
For I have dreamed of a midnight sky and a midnight call to blood
And red-mouthed shadows racing by, that thrust me from my food.
'Tis an hour yet and an hour yet to the rising of the moon,
But I can see the black roof-tree as plain as it were noon.
'Tis a league and a league to the Lena Falls where the trooping blackbuck go;
But I can hear the little fawn that bleats behind the doe.

'Tis a league and a league to the Lena Falls where the crop and the upland meet,
But I can smell the wet dawn-wind that wakes the sprouting wheat.

Unbar the door. I may not bide, but I must out and see
If those are wolves that wait outside or my own kin to me!"

* * *

She loosed the bar, she slid the bolt, she opened the door anon,
And a grey bitch-wolf came out of the dark and fawned on the Only Son!

THE GLORY OF THE GARDEN

Our England is a garden that is full of stately views,
Of borders, beds and shrubberies and lawns and avenues,
With statues on the terraces and peacocks strutting by;
But the Glory of the Garden lies in more than meets the eye.

For where the old thick laurels grow, along the thin red wall,
You find the tool- and potting-sheds which are the heart of all;
The cold-frames and the hot-houses, the dung-pits and the tanks,
The rollers, carts and drain-pipes, with the barrows and the planks.

And there you'll see the gardeners, the men and 'prentice boys
Told off to do as they are bid and do it without noise;
For, except when seeds are planted and we shout to scare the birds,
The Glory of the Garden it abideth not in words.

And some can pot begonias and some can bud a rose,
And some are hardly fit to trust with anything that grows;
But they can roll and trim the lawns and sift the sand and loam,
For the Glory of the Garden occupieth all who come.

Our England is a garden, and such gardens are not made
By singing:—"Oh, how beautiful!" and sitting in the shade,
While better men than we go out and start their working lives
At grubbing weeds from gravel-paths with broken dinner-knives.

There's not a pair of legs so thin, there's not a head so thick,
There's not a hand so weak and white, nor yet a heart so sick,
But it can find some job that's crying to be done,
For the Glory of the Garden glorifieth every one.

Then seek your job with thankfulness and work till further orders,
If it's only netting strawberries or killing slugs on borders;
And when your back stops aching and your hands begin to harden,
You will find yourself a partner in the Glory of the Garden.

Oh, Adam was a gardener, and God who made him sees
That half a proper gardener's work is done upon his knees,
So when your work is finished, you can wash your hands and pray
For the Glory of the Garden, that it may not pass away!
And the Glory of the Garden it shall never pass away!

RAHERE

Rahere, King Henry's Jester, feared by all the Norman Lords
For his eye that pierced their bosoms, for his tongue that shamed their swords;
Feed and flattered by the Churchmen—well they knew how deep he stood
In dark Henry's crooked counsels—fell upon an evil mood.

Suddenly, his days before him and behind him seemed to stand
Stripped and barren, fixed and fruitless, as those leagues of naked sand
When St. Michael's ebb slinks outward to the bleak horizon-bound,
And the trampling wide-mouthed waters are withdrawn from sight and sound.

Then a Horror of Great Darkness sunk his spirit and, anon,
(Who had seen him wince and whiten as he turned to walk alone)
Followed Gilbert the Physician, and muttered in his ear,
"Thou hast it, O my brother?" "Yea, I have it," said Rahere.

"So it comes," said Gilbert smoothly, "man's most immanent distress.
'Tis a humour of the Spirit which abhorreth all excess;
And, whatever breed the surfeit—Wealth, or Wit, or Power, or Fame
(And thou hast each) the Spirit laboureth to expel the same.

"Hence the dulled eye's deep self-loathing—hence the loaded leaden brow;
Hence the burden of Wanhope that aches thy soul and body now.
Ay, the merriest fool must face it, and the wisest Doctor learn;
For it comes—it comes," said Gilbert, "as it passes—to return."

But Rahere was in his torment, and he wandered, dumb and far,
Till he came to reeking Smithfield where the crowded gallows are.
(Followed Gilbert the Physician) and beneath the wry-necked dead,
Sat a leper and his woman, very merry, breaking bread.

He was cloaked from chin to ankle—faceless, fingerless, obscene—
Mere corruption swaddled man-wise, but the woman whole and clean;
And she waited on him crooning, and Rahere beheld the twain,
Each delighting in the other, and he checked and groaned again.

"So it comes,—it comes," said Gilbert, "as it came when Life began.
'Tis a motion of the Spirit that revealeth God to man.
In the shape of Love exceeding, which regards not taint or fall,
Since in perfect Love, saith Scripture, can be no excess at all.

"Hence the eye that sees no blemish—hence the hour that holds no shame.
Hence the Soul assured the Essence and the Substance are the same.
Nay, the meanest need not miss it, though the mightier pass it by;
For it comes—it comes," said Gilbert, "and, thou seest, it does not die!"

1926

GIPSY VANS

Unless you come of the gipsy stock
That steals by night and day,
Lock your heart with a double lock
And throw the key away.
Bury it under the blackest stone
Beneath your father's hearth,
And keep your eyes on your lawful own
And your feet to the proper path.
Then you can stand at your door and mock
When the gipsy-vans come through . . .
For it isn't right that the Gorgio stock
Should live as the Romany do.

Unless you come of the gipsy blood
That takes and never spares,
Bide content with your given good
And follow your own affairs.
Plough and harrow and roll your land,
And sow what ought to be sowed;
But never let loose your heart from your hand,
Nor flitter it down the road!
Then you can thrive on your boughten food
As the gipsy-vans come through . . .
For it isn't nature the Gorgio blood
Should love as the Romany do.

Unless you carry the gipsy eyes
That see but seldom weep,
Keep your head from the naked skies
Or the stars'll trouble your sleep.
Watch your moon through your window-pane
And take what weather she brews;
But don't run out in the midnight rain
Nor home in the morning dews.
Then you can huddle and shut your eyes
As the gipsy-vans come through . . .
For it isn't fitting the Gorgio ryes
Should walk as the Romany do.

Unless you come of the gipsy race
  That counts all time the same,
Be you careful of Time and Place
  And judgment and Good Name:
Lose your life for to live your life
  The way that you ought to do;
And when you are finished, your God and your wife
  And the Gipsies'll laugh at you!
Then you can rot in your burying-place
  As the gipsy-vans come through . . .
For it isn't reason the Gorgio race
  Should die as the Romany do.

1926

GEORGE MEREDITH

[February 12, 1828–May 18, 1909]

George Meredith was born in Portsmouth, the grandson of Melchizedek Meredith, a prosperous tailor and naval outfitter who closely resembled "the Great Mel" in *Evan Harrington.* He had private teaching at Portsmouth and at Southsea, and when he was fourteen went to the Moravian school at Neuwied, Germany. In 1844 he went into a lawyer's office in London, but law soon losing its attraction for him, he gave almost his entire attention to literature. In 1849 he married one of his literary friends, Thomas Love Peacock's widowed daughter, who was nine years older than he. The marriage proved to be a "union of an ever-diverse pair," and in 1858 his wife deserted him and their young son. In 1862, the year after Mrs. Meredith's death, Meredith published *Modern Love*, a poem of fifty sonnet-like stanzas arising out of his unhappy marriage. Meanwhile he had published in 1851 a volume of poems that won the praise of Tennyson and other artists but was not successful with the English public. In 1859, too, his first important novel, *The Ordeal of Richard Feverel*, although it was well received by the critics and by his fellow writers, had fallen upon a cold and unresponsive public. Driven to do something that would bring him some money, Meredith took up journalism of different kinds, reviewing, acting as foreign correspondent to the *Morning Post*, reading for a publisher, serving for a while as editor of the *Fortnightly*. As a publisher's reader he rejected *East Lynne*, Butler's *The Way of All Flesh*, and a manuscript of Bernard Shaw's, but he gave encouragement to Hardy and Gissing. As a foreign correspondent he was sent to the Italian front in 1866. Journalism was not attractive to him—he called it "Egyptian bondage"—and he soon gave it up.

In 1864, after a year or two of sharing a house in London with Swinburne and Rossetti, he had married Marie Vulliamy, with whom, in 1867, he settled for eighteen years of happiness at Flint Cottage, facing Box Hill, in Surrey. He published several novels in the years immediately preceding his second marriage and, once settled at Flint Cottage, he wrote with amazing energy. It was not till 1879, however, when he published *The Egoist*, that he achieved fame; and even then he had to wait till 1885 to obtain general popularity with *Diana of the Crossways.*

All his life Meredith, who desired above everything else to be known as a poet, continued to write poetry. Among his volumes of poems, in addition to those already named, are *Poems and Lyrics of the Joy of Earth* (1883), *Ballads and Poems of Tragic Life* (1887), *A Reading of Earth* (1888), *Odes in Contribution to the Song of French History* (1898), *A Reading of Life* (1901), and *Last Poems* (1909).

Like Swinburne he worships not God, but the Earth, "our stern, genial mother." His poetry, possessing an extraordinary concentration and compression, is even more difficult than his prose, but in many of his pages he achieves notable beauty of phrase and form.

JUGGLING JERRY

I

PITCH here the tent, while the old horse grazes:
By the old hedge-side we'll halt a stage.
It's nigh my last above the daisies:
My next leaf'll be man's blank page.
Yes, my old girl! and it's no use crying:
Juggler, constable, king, must bow.
One that outjuggles all's been spying
Long to have me, and he has me now.

II

We've travelled times to this old common:
Often we've hung our pots in the gorse.
We've had a stirring life, old woman
You, and I, and the old grey horse.
Races, and fairs, and royal occasions,
Found us coming to their call:
Now they'll miss us at our stations:
There's a Juggler outjuggles all!

III

Up goes the lark, as if all were jolly!
Over the duck-pond the willow shakes.
Easy to think that grieving's folly,
When the hand's firm as driven stakes!
Ay, when we're strong, and braced, and manful,
Life's a sweet fiddle: but we're a batch
Born to become the Great Juggler's han'ful:
Balls he shies up, and is safe to catch.

IV

Here's where the lads of the village cricket:
I was a lad not wide from here:
Couldn't I whip off the bail from the wicket?
Like an old world those days appear!
Donkey, sheep, geese, and thatched ale-house
—I know them!
They are old friends of my halts, and seem,
Somehow, as if kind thanks I owe them:
Juggling don't hinder the heart's esteem.

V

Juggling's no sin, for we must have victual:
Nature allows us to bait for the fool.
Holding one's own makes us juggle no little;
But, to increase it, hard juggling's the rule.
You that are sneering at my profession,
Haven't you juggled a vast amount?
There's the Prime Minister, in one Session,
Juggles more games than my sins'll count.

VI

I've murdered insects with mock thunder:
Conscience, for that, in men don't quail.
I've made bread from the bump of wonder:
That's my business, and there's my tale.
Fashion and rank all praised the professor:
Ay! and I've had my smile from the Queen:
Bravo, Jerry! she meant: God bless her!
Ain't this a sermon on that scene?

VII

I've studied men from my topsy-turvy
Close, and, I reckon, rather true.
Some are fine fellows: some, right scurvy:
Most, a dash between the two.
But it's a woman, old girl, that makes me
Think more kindly of the race:
And it's a woman, old girl, that shakes me
When the Great Juggler I must face.

VIII

We two were married, due and legal:
Honest we've lived since we've been one.
Lord! I could then jump like an eagle:
You danced bright as a bit o' the sun.
Birds in a May-bush we were! right merry!
All night we kiss'd, we juggled all day.
Joy was the heart of Juggling Jerry!
Now from his old girl he's juggled away.

IX

It's past parsons to console us:
No, nor no doctor fetch for me:
I can die without my bolus;
Two of a trade, lass, never agree!
Parson and Doctor!—don't they love rarely
Fighting the devil in other men's fields!
Stand up yourself and match him fairly:
Then see how the rascal yields!

X

I, lass, have lived no gipsy, flaunting
Finery while his poor helpmate grubs:
Coin I've stored, and you won't be wanting:
You shan't beg from the troughs and tubs.
Nobly you've stuck to me, though in his
kitchen
Many a Marquis would hail you Cook!
Palaces you could have ruled and grown rich
in,
But your old Jerry you never forsook.

XI

Hand up the chirper! ripe ale winks in it;
Let's have comfort and be at peace.
Once a stout draught made me light as a linnet.
Cheer up! the Lord must have his lease.
May be—for none see in that black hollow—
It's just a place where we're held in pawn,
And, when the Great Juggler makes as to swallow,
It's just the sword-trick—I ain't quite gone!

XII

Yonder came smells of the gorse, so nutty,
Gold-like and warm: it's the prime of May.
Better than mortar, brick and putty,
Is God's house on a blowing day.
Lean me more up the mound; now I feel it:
All the old heath-smells! Ain't it strange?
There's the world laughing, as if to conceal it,
But He's by us, juggling the change.

XIII

I mind it well, by the sea-beach lying,
Once—it's long gone—when two gulls we beheld,
Which, as the moon got up, were flying
Down a big wave that sparked and swelled.
Crack, went a gun: one fell: the second
Wheeled round him twice, and was off for new luck:
There in the dark her white wing beckon'd:—
Drop me a kiss—I'm the bird dead-struck!

1859

MODERN LOVE

I

By this he knew she wept with waking eyes:
That, at his hand's light quiver by her head,
The strange low sobs that shook their common bed
Were called into her with a sharp surprise,
And strangled mute, like little gaping snakes,
Dreadfully venomous to him. She lay
Stone-still, and the long darkness flowed away
With muffled pulses. Then, as midnight makes
Her giant heart of Memory and Tears
Drink the pale drug of silence, and so beat
Sleep's heavy measure, they from head to feet
Were moveless, looking through their dead black years,
By vain regret scrawled over the blank wall.
Like sculptured effigies they might be seen
Upon their marriage-tomb, the sword between;
Each wishing for the sword that severs all.

II

It ended, and the morrow brought the task.
Her eyes were guilty gates, that let him in
By shutting all too zealous for their sin:
Each sucked a secret, and each wore a mask.
But, oh, the bitter taste her beauty had!
He sickened as at breath of poison-flowers:
A languid humour stole among the hours,
And if their smiles encountered, he went mad,
And raged deep inward, till the light was brown
Before his vision, and the world, forgot,
Looked wicked as some old dull murder-spot.
A star with lurid beams, she seemed to crown
The pit of infamy: and then again
He fainted on his vengefulness, and strove
To ape the magnanimity of love,
And smote himself, a shuddering heap of pain.

XIV

What soul would bargain for a cure that brings
Contempt the nobler agony to kill?
Rather let me bear on the bitter ill,
And strike this rusty bosom with new stings!
It seems there is another veering fit,
Since on a gold-haired lady's eyeballs pure
I looked with little prospect of a cure,
The while her mouth's red bow loosed shafts of wit.
Just heaven! can it be true that jealousy
Has decked the woman thus? and does her head
Swim somewhat for possessions forfeited?
Madam, you teach me many things that be.
I open an old book, and there I find
That "Women still may love whom they deceive."
Such love I prize not, madam: by your leave,
The game you play at is not to my mind.

XX

I am not of those miserable males
Who sniff at vice and, daring not to snap,
Do therefore hope for heaven. I take the hap
Of all my deeds. The wind that fills my sails

Wm Shirley Brooks
from the author.

MODERN LOVE

AND

POEMS OF THE ENGLISH ROADSIDE,

WITH

Poems and Ballads.

BY

GEORGE MEREDITH,

AUTHOR OF 'THE SHAVING OF SHAGPAT,' 'THE ORDEAL OF RICHARD FEVEREL,' ETC.

LONDON:
CHAPMAN & HALL, 193, PICCADILLY.
1862.

Presentation Copy of *Modern Love.* (See Appendix I.)

Propels; but I am helmsman. Am I wrecked,
I know the devil has sufficient weight
To bear: I lay it not on him, or fate.
Besides, he's damned. That man I do suspect
A coward, who would burden the poor deuce
With what ensues from his own slipperiness.
I have just found a wanton-scented tress
In an old desk, dusty for lack of use.
Of days and nights it is demonstrative,
That, like some aged star, gleam luridly.
If for those times I must ask charity,
Have I not any charity to give?

XXII

What may the woman labour to confess?
There is about her mouth a nervous twitch.
'Tis something to be told, or hidden:—which?
I get a glimpse of hell in this mild guess.
She has desires of touch, as if to feel
That all the household things are things she knew.
She stops before the glass. What sight in view?
A face that seems the latest to reveal!
For she turns from it hastily, and tossed
Irresolute steals shadow-like to where
I stand; and wavering pale before me there,
Her tears fall still as oak-leaves after frost.
She will not speak. I will not ask. We are
League-sundered by the silent gulf between.
You burly lovers on the village green,
Yours is a lower, and a happier star!

XXVI

Love ere he bleeds, an eagle in high skies,
Has earth beneath his wings: from reddened eve
He views the rosy dawn. In vain they weave
The fatal web below while far he flies.
But when the arrow strikes him, there's a change.
He moves but in the track of his spent pain,
Whose red drops are the links of a harsh chain,
Binding him to the ground, with narrow range.
A subtle serpent then has Love become.
I had the eagle in my bosom erst:
Henceforward with the serpent I am cursed.
I can interpret where the mouth is dumb.
Speak, and I see the side-lie of a truth.
Perchance my heart may pardon you this deed:
But be no coward:—you that made Love bleed,
You must bear all the venom of his tooth!

XXXIV

Madam would speak with me. So, now it comes:
The Deluge or else Fire! She's well; she thanks
My husbandship. Our chain on silence clanks.
Time leers between, above his twiddling thumbs.
Am I quite well? Most excellent in health!
The journals, too, I diligently peruse.
Vesuvius is expected to give news:
Niagara is no noisier. By stealth
Our eyes dart scrutinizing snakes. She's glad
I'm happy, says her quivering under-lip.
"And are not you?" "How can I be?" "Take ship!
For happiness is somewhere to be had."
"Nowhere for me!" Her voice is barely heard.
I am not melted, and make no pretence.
With commonplace I freeze her, tongue and sense.
Niagara or Vesuvius is deferred.

XLVI

At last we parley: we so strangely dumb
In such a close communion! It befell
About the sounding of the Matin-bell,
And lo! her place was vacant, and the hum
Of loneliness was round me. Then I rose,
And my disordered brain did guide my foot
To that old wood where our first love-salute
Was interchanged: the source of many throes!
There did I see her, not alone. I moved
Toward her, and made proffer of my arm.
She took it simply, with no rude alarm;
And that disturbing shadow passed reproved.
I felt the pained speech coming, and declared
My firm belief in her, ere she could speak.
A ghastly morning came into her cheek,
While with a widening soul on me she stared.

1862

DIRGE IN WOODS

A WIND sways the pines,
And below
Not a breath of wild air;
Still as the mosses that glow
On the flooring and over the lines
Of the roots here and there.
The pine-tree drops its dead;
They are quiet, as under the sea.

Overhead, overhead
Rushes life in a race,
As the clouds the clouds chase;
And we go,
And we drop like the fruits of the tree,
Even we,
Even so.

1870

LOVE IN THE VALLEY

UNDER yonder beech-tree single on the green-sward,
Couched with her arms behind her golden head,
Knees and tresses folded to slip and ripple idly,
Lies my young love sleeping in the shade.
Had I the heart to slide an arm beneath her,
Press her parting lips as her waist I gather slow,
Waking in amazement she could not but embrace me:
Then would she hold me and never let me go?

* * *

Shy as the squirrel and wayward as the swallow,
Swift as the swallow along the river's light
Circleting the surface to meet his mirrored winglets,
Fleeter she seems in her stay than in her flight.
Shy as the squirrel that leaps among the pine-tops,
Wayward as the swallow overhead at set of sun,
She whom I love is hard to catch and conquer,
Hard, but O the glory of the winning were she won!

* * *

When her mother tends her before the laughing mirror,
Tying up her laces, looping up her hair,
Often she thinks, were this wild thing wedded,
More love should I have, and much less care.
When her mother tends her before the lighted mirror,
Loosening her laces, combing down her curls,
Often she thinks, were this wild thing wedded,
I should miss but one for many boys and girls.

* * *

Heartless she is as the shadow in the meadows
Flying to the hills on a blue and breezy noon.
No, she is athirst and drinking up her wonder:
Earth to her is young as the slip of the new moon.
Deals she an unkindness, 'tis but her rapid measure,
Even as in a dance; and her smile can heal no less:
Like the swinging May-cloud that pelts the flowers with hailstones
Off a sunny border, she was made to bruise and bless.

* * *

Lovely are the curves of the white owl sweeping
Wavy in the dusk lit by one large star.
Lone on the fir-branch, his rattle-note unvaried,
Brooding o'er the gloom, spins the brown eve-jar.
Darker grows the valley, more and more forgetting:
So were it with me if forgetting could be willed.
Tell the grassy hollow that holds the bubbling well-spring,
Tell it to forget the source that keeps it filled.

Stepping down the hill with her fair companions,
Arm in arm, all against the raying West,
Boldly she sings, to the merry tune she marches,
Brave in her shape, and sweeter unpossessed.
Sweeter, for she is what my heart first awaking
Whispered the world was; morning light is she.
Love that so desires would fain keep her changeless;
Fain would fling the net, and fain have her free.

* * *

Happy happy time, when the white star hovers
Low over dim fields fresh with bloomy dew,
Near the face of dawn, that draws athwart the darkness,
Threading it with colour, like yewberries the yew.

Thicker crowd the shades as the grave East deepens
Glowing, and with crimson a long cloud swells.
Maiden still the morn is; and strange she is, and secret;
Strange her eyes; her cheeks are cold as cold sea-shells.

* * *

Sunrays, leaning on our southern hills and lighting
Wild cloud-mountains that drag the hills along,
Oft ends the day of your shifting brilliant laughter
Chill as a dull face frowning on a song.
Ay, but shows the South-West a ripple-feathered bosom
Blown to silver while the clouds are shaken and ascend
Scaling the mid-heavens as they stream, there comes a sunset
Rich, deep like love in beauty without end.

* * *

When at dawn she sighs, and like an infant to the window
Turns grave eyes craving light, released from dreams,
Beautiful she looks, like a white water-lily
Bursting out of bud in havens of the streams.
When from bed she rises clothed from neck to ankle
In her long nightgown sweet as boughs of May,
Beautiful she looks, like a tall garden lily
Pure from the night, and splendid for the day.

* * *

Mother of the dews, dark eye-lashed twilight,
Low-lidded twilight, o'er the valley's brim,
Rounding on thy breast sings the dew-delighted skylark,
Clear as though the dewdrops had their voice in him.
Hidden where the rose-flush drinks the rayless planet,
Fountain-full he pours the spraying fountain-showers.
Let me hear her laughter, I would have her ever
Cool as dew in twilight, the lark above the flowers.

* * *

All the girls are out with their baskets for the primrose;
Up lanes, woods through, they troop in joyful bands.
My sweet leads: she knows not why, but now she loiters,
Eyes the bent anemones, and hangs her hands.
Such a look will tell that the violets are peeping,
Coming the rose: and unaware a cry
Springs in her bosom for odours and for colour,
Covert and the nightingale; she knows not why.

* * *

Kerchiefed head and chin she darts between her tulips,
Streaming like a willow grey in arrowy rain:
Some bend beaten cheek to gravel, and their angel
She will be; she lifts them, and on she speeds again.
Black the driving raincloud breasts the iron gateway:
She is forth to cheer a neighbour lacking mirth.
So when sky and grass met rolling dumb for thunder
Saw I once a white dove, sole light of earth.

* * *

Prim little scholars are the flowers of her garden,
Trained to stand in rows, and asking if they please.
I might love them well but for loving more the wild ones:
O my wild ones! they tell me more than these.
You, my wild one, you tell of honied field-rose,
Violet, blushing eglantine in life; and even as they,
They by the wayside are earnest of your goodness,
You are of life's, on the banks that line the way.

* * *

Peering at her chamber the white crowns the red rose,
Jasmine winds the porch with stars two and three.
Parted is the window; she sleeps; the starry jasmine
Breathes a falling breath that carries thoughts of me.
Sweeter unpossessed, have I said of her my sweetest?
Not while she sleeps: while she sleeps the jasmine breathes,
Luring her to love; she sleeps; the starry jasmine
Bears me to her pillow under white rose-wreaths.

Yellow with birdfoot-trefoil are the grass-glades;
Yellow with cinquefoil of the dew-grey leaf;
Yellow with stonecrop; the moss-mounds are yellow;
Blue-necked the wheat sways, yellowing to the sheaf.
Green-yellow bursts from the copse the laughing yaffle:
Sharp as a sickle is the edge of shade and shine:
Earth in her heart laughs looking at the heavens,
Thinking of the harvest: I look and think of mine.

* * *

This I may know: her dressing and undressing
Such a change of light shows as when the skies in sport
Shift from cloud to moonlight; or edging over thunder
Slips a ray of sun; or sweeping into port
White sails furl; or on the ocean borders
White sails lean along the waves leaping green.
Visions of her shower before me, but from eyesight
Guarded she would be like the sun were she seen.

* * *

Front door and back of the mossed old farmhouse
Open with the morn, and in a breezy link
Freshly sparkles garden to stripe-shadowed orchard,
Green across a rill where on sand the minnows wink.
Busy in the grass the early sun of summer
Swarms, and the blackbird's mellow fluting notes
Call my darling up with round and roguish challenge:
Quaintest, richest carol of all the singing throats!

* * *

Cool was the woodside; cool as her white dairy
Keeping sweet the cream-pan; and there the boys from school,
Cricketing below, rushed brown and red with sunshine;
O the dark translucence of the deep-eyed cool!
Spying from the farm, herself she fetched a pitcher
Full of milk, and tilted for each in turn the beak.
Then a little fellow, mouth up and on tiptoe,
Said, "I will kiss you": she laughed and leaned her cheek.

* * *

Doves of the fir-wood walling high our red roof
Through the long noon coo, crooning through the coo.
Loose droop the leaves, and down the sleepy roadway
Sometimes pipes a chaffinch; loose droops the blue.
Cows flap a slow tail knee-deep in the river,
Breathless, given up to sun and gnat and fly.
Nowhere is she seen; and if I see her nowhere,
Lightning may come, straight rains and tiger sky.

* * *

O the golden sheaf, the rustling treasure-armful!
O the nutbrown tresses nodding interlaced!
O the treasure-tresses one another over
Nodding! O the girdle slack about the waist!
Slain are the poppies that shot their random scarlet
Quick amid the wheatears: wound about the waist,

Gathered, see these brides of Earth one blush of ripeness!
O the nutbrown tresses nodding interlaced!

* * *

Large and smoky red the sun's cold disk drops,
Clipped by naked hills, on violet shaded snow:
Eastward large and still lights up a bower of moonrise,
Whence at her leisure steps the moon aglow.
Nightlong on black print-branches our beech-tree
Gazes in this whiteness: nightlong could I.
Here may life on death or death on life be painted.
Let me clasp her soul to know she cannot die!

* * *

Gossips count her faults; they scour a narrow chamber
Where there is no window, read not heaven or her.
"When she was a tiny," one aged woman quavers,
Plucks at my heart and leads me by the ear.
Faults she had once as she learnt to run and tumbled:
Faults of feature some see, beauty not complete.
Yet, good gossips, beauty that makes holy
Earth and air, may have faults from head to feet.

* * *

Hither she comes; she comes to me; she lingers,
Deepens her brown eyebrows, while in new surprise
High rise the lashes in wonder of a stranger;
Yet am I the light and living of her eyes.
Something friends have told her fills her heart to brimming,
Nets her in her blushes, and wounds her, and tames.—
Sure of her haven, O like a dove alighting,
Arms up, she dropped: our souls were in our names.

* * *

Soon will she lie like a white-frost sunrise.
Yellow oats and brown wheat, barley pale as rye,
Long since your sheaves have yielded to the thresher,
Felt the girdle loosened, seen the tresses fly.
Soon will she lie like a blood-red sunset.
Swift with the to-morrow, green-winged Spring!
Sing from the South-West, bring her back the truants,
Nightingale and swallow, song and dipping wing.

* * *

Soft new beech-leaves, up to beamy April
Spreading bough on bough a primrose mountain, you,
Lucid in the moon, raise lilies to the skyfields,
Youngest green transfused in silver shining through:
Fairer than the lily, than the wild white cherry:
Fair as in image my seraph love appears
Borne to me by dreams when dawn is at my eyelids:
Fair as in the flesh she swims to me on tears.

* * *

Could I find a place to be alone with heaven,
I would speak my heart out: heaven is my need.
Every woodland tree is flushing like the dogwood,
Flashing like the whitebeam, swaying like the reed.
Flushing like the dogwood crimson in October;
Streaming like the flag-reed South-West blown;
Flashing as in gusts the sudden-lighted whitebeam:
All seem to know what is for heaven alone.

1878

LUCIFER IN STARLIGHT

On a starred night Prince Lucifer uprose.
Tired of his dark dominion swung the fiend
Above the rolling ball in cloud part screened,
Where sinners hugged their spectre of repose.
Poor prey to his hot fit of pride were those.
And now upon his western wing he leaned,
Now his huge bulk o'er Afric's sands careened,
Now the black planet shadowed Arctic snows.
Soaring through wider zones that pricked his scars

Mary Meredith
from George

POEMS:

BY

GEORGE MEREDITH.

EOS! blest Goddess of the Morning, hear
The blind Orion praying on thy hill,
And in thine odorous breath his spirit steep,
That he, the soft gold of thy gleaming hand
Passing across his heavy lids, sealed down
With weight of many nights, and night-like days
May feel as keenly as a new-born child,
And, through it, learn as purely to behold
The face of nature. * * * *
His blind eyes wept.

R. H. Horne's "ORION."

LONDON:
JOHN W. PARKER AND SON,
WEST STRAND.

A Presentation Copy of *Poems* [1851]. (See Appendix I.)

With memory of the old revolt from Awe,
He reached the middle height, and at the stars,
Which are the brain of heaven, he looked, and sank.
Around the ancient track marched, rank on rank,
The army of unalterable law.

1883

THE STATE OF AGE

Rub thou thy battered lamp: nor claim nor beg
Honours from aught about thee. Light the young.
Thy frame is as a dusty mantle hung,
O grey one! pendant on a loosened peg.
Thou art for this our life an ancient egg,
Or a tough bird: thou hast a rudderless tongue,
Turning dead trifles, like the cock of dung,
Which runs, Time's contrast to thy halting leg.
Nature, it is most sure, not thee admires.
But hast thou in thy season set her fires
To burn from Self to Spirit through the lash,
Honoured the sons of Earth shall hold thee high:
Yea, to spread light when thy proud letter I
Drops prone and void as any thoughtless dash.

NATURE AND LIFE

I

Leave the uproar: at a leap
Thou shalt strike a woodland path,
Enter silence, not of sleep,
Under shadows, not of wrath;
Breath which is the spirit's bath
In the old Beginnings find,
And endow them with a mind,
Seed for seedling, swathe for swathe.
That gives Nature to us, this
Give we her, and so we kiss.

II

Fruitful is it so: but hear
How within the shell thou art,
Music sounds; nor other near
Can to such a tremor start.
Of the waves our life is part;
They our running harvests bear:
Back to them for manful air,
Laden with the woodland's heart!
That gives Battle to us, this
Give we it, and good the kiss.

MEDITATION UNDER STARS

What links are ours with orbs that are
So resolutely far:
The solitary asks, and they
Give radiance as from a shield:
Still at the death of day,
The seen, the unrevealed.
Implacable they shine
To us who would of Life obtain
An answer for the life we strain
To nourish with one sign.
Nor can imagination throw
The penetrative shaft: we pass
The breath of thought, who would divine
If haply they may grow
As Earth; have our desire to know;
If life comes there to grain from grass,
And flowers like ours of toil and pain;
Has passion to beat bar,
Win space from cleaving brain;
The mystic link attain,
Whereby star holds on star.

Those visible immortals beam
Allurement to the dream:
Ireful at human hungers brook
No question in the look.
For ever virgin to our sense,
Remote they wane to gaze intense:
Prolong it, and in ruthlessness they smite
The beating heart behind the ball of sight:
Till we conceive their heavens hoar,
Those lights they raise but sparkles frore,
And Earth, our blood-warm Earth, a shuddering prey
To that frigidity of brainless ray.

Yet space is given for breath of thought
Beyond our bounds when musing: more
When to that musing love is brought,
And love is asked of love's wherefore.
'Tis Earth's, her gift; else have we nought:
Her gift, her secret, here our tie.
And not with her and yonder sky?
Bethink you: were it Earth alone

Breeds love, would not her region be
The sole delight and throne
Of generous Deity?

To deeper than this ball of sight
Appeal the lustrous people of the night.
Fronting yon shoreless, sown with fiery sails,
It is our ravenous that quails,
Flesh by its craven thirsts and fears distraught.
The spirit leaps alight,
Doubts not in them is he,
The binder of his sheaves, the sane, the right:
Of magnitude to magnitude is wrought,
To feel it large of the great life they hold:
In them to come, or vaster intervolved,
The issues known in us, our unsolved solved:
That there with toil Life climbs the self-same Tree,
Whose roots enrichment have from ripeness dropped.

So may we read and little find them cold:
Let it but be the lord of Mind to guide
Our eyes; no branch of Reason's growing lopped;
Nor dreaming on a dream; but fortified
By day to penetrate black midnight; see,
Hear, feel, outside the senses; even that we,
The specks of dust upon a mound of mould,
We who reflect those rays, though low our place,
To them are lastingly allied.

So may we read, and little find them cold:
Not frosty lamps illumining dead space,
Not distant aliens, not senseless Powers.
The fire is in them whereof we are born;
The music of their motion may be ours.
Spirit shall deem them beckoning Earth and voiced
Sisterly to her, in her beams rejoiced.
Of love, the grand impulsion, we behold
The love that lends her grace
Among the starry fold.
Then at new flood of customary morn,
Look at her through her showers,
Her mists, her streaming gold,
A wonder edges the familiar face:
She wears no more that robe of printed hours;
Half strange seems Earth, and sweeter than her flowers.

1888

SONG IN THE SONGLESS

THEY have no song, the sedges dry,
And still they sing.
It is within my breast they sing,
As I pass by.
Within my breast they touch a string,
They wake a sigh.
There is but sound of sedges dry;
In me they sing.

1900

YOUTH IN AGE

ONCE I was part of the music I heard
On the boughs or sweet between earth and sky,
For joy of the beating of wings on high
My heart shot into the breast of the bird.

I hear it now and I see it fly,
And a life in wrinkles again is stirred,
My heart shoots into the breast of the bird,
As it will for sheer love till the last long sigh.

WILLIAM MORRIS

[March 24, 1834–October 3, 1896]

BORN the son of a prosperous bill-broker, William Morris inherited a considerable fortune. All his life he had, therefore, a liberty of action denied less fortunate men. He used it greatly and generously. As a child he had a passion for Gothic art and architecture. It is said that at the age of eight he saw the Church of Minster in Thanet and was able to describe it in detail fifty years later. In Morris's first year at Oxford (he entered Exeter College, Oxford, in 1853) Ruskin published *The Stones of Venice*, and Morris was profoundly influenced by the chapter on the Nature of Gothic. Ruskin pointed out that in the Gothic each workman had a chance of expressing himself, whereas in later architecture he merely did what he was told. At Oxford Morris gave up his idea of studying for the church and in 1856 was articled to George Edmund Street, an architect whose headquarters were then in Oxford. During this year (1856) Morris, Burne-Jones, and some of their friends published *The Oxford and Cambridge Magazine*, which won them the friendship of Rossetti and brought them under the conquering sway of that powerful personality. Morris ultimately quarrelled with Rossetti—but that was nearly twenty years later. In 1857 Morris moved to London, returning to Oxford in the later months of the year with Rossetti to fresco the Oxford Union. In this year also he wrote most of the poems which were published in *The Defence of Guenevere* (1858).

In 1859 Morris married Jane Burden and built for her the delightful "Red House." When he came to furnish it he found that household furnishings commercially produced were incredibly ugly, and so Morris, with his friends, set about designing the wall papers and furniture themselves. Out of this venture grew Morris, Marshall, Faulkner and Co., founded in 1861 with a capital of £7,—£1 contributed by each of the seven partners, of whom Rossetti was one. Although the partnership was later dissolved, the work of the firm went on until Morris's death in a valiant war against encroaching ugliness. Church decoration was one of the originally conceived objects, but the work of the firm in the handicrafts was more important. It produced furniture, metal and glass wares of all sorts, hand-wrought jewelry, wall papers, printed cottons, woven carpets, tapestries, and similar products of the minor arts, and Morris was the guiding spirit. The principle was that of honest craftsmanship, with the worker himself a sharer in the artistry, and the designer either the actual worker himself or kept close to the worker and his materials. This was in opposition to the commercial principle in which the designer worked on paper far from his materials, and the worker produced as a mechanical slave. For workers, the firm, as it developed, drew boys from a Boys' Home, not looking for genius, and produced talented craftsmen out of available average human material. Morris himself became the master craftsman among master craftsmen.

Poetry had been put aside for some years. In 1866 Morris began the composition of the narratives for *The Earthly Paradise. The Life and Death of Jason* grew too large for the original plan and was published separately in 1867, *The Earthly Paradise* following in three volumes, 1868–70. A new interest also was growing up in his varied and active life. In 1870 he was associated in a translation of the *Volsunga Saga* and in 1871 he visited Iceland. His interest was always in a new and direct civilization as opposed to one complicated and commercialized. This turn to the North led him to design and write his epic, *Sigurd the Volsung and the Fall of the Niblungs* (1876), which he thought his greatest work, although posterity has ventured to differ in opinion.

Morris's interest in the work of the honest artist's hands was continuous, although other activities diverted him. He wrote and illuminated manuscript, in an age of cheap printing. It was from the preparation of a beautiful manuscript of the *Æneid* that he was led into a translation. He became annoyed at the dyes his firm was obliged to use and was led into a study (1875–76) of old books and herbals to rediscover the secret of vegetable dyes. And from about 1877 until 1890 he was active politically. His first connections with active organizations were with the Eastern Question Association (1876), designed to prevent a conservative government from encouraging Turkish atrocities in Bulgaria, and with the Society for the Protection of Ancient Buildings (1877), designed to prevent atrocities upon his beloved Gothic buildings closer home.

But for the worker with beautiful things he desired a beautiful life and he saw, finally, this life to be inseparably connected with economic and political conditions. At first Morris pinned his faith on the liberal political elements. In 1883 he became associated with the Social-Democratic Federation—a group of London workingmen's clubs and, when this broke up in 1884, the Socialist League followed. Morris abandoned it in 1890 when it turned Anarchist and when he felt, "Between you and me the League don't get on—except like a cow's tail—downwards."

He had written much for the *Commonweal*, the magazine of the League, and in his later years had done many prose stories. *A Dream of John Ball* (1888) is perhaps the most striking of his later productions. In his later years his chief interest was the Kelmscott Press (named after the beautiful country house he had bought in 1871). Morris designed three fonts of type for this press, carefully studying first the earlier printers whose types he thought were close to the grace and honesty of the great calligraphers who preceded printing. The Kelmscott *Chaucer*, for long ranked as the most beautiful of printed books, was printed from a type he designed.

RIDING TOGETHER

For many, many days together
The wind blew steady from the East;
For many days hot grew the weather,
About the time of our Lady's Feast.

For many days we rode together,
Yet met we neither friend nor foe;
Hotter and clearer grew the weather,
Steadily did the East wind blow.

We saw the trees in the hot, bright weather,
Clear-cut, with shadows very black
As freely we rode on together
With helms unlaced and bridles slack.

And often as we rode together,
We, looking down the green-bank'd stream,
Saw flowers in the sunny weather,
And saw the bubble-making bream.

And in the night lay down together,
And hung above our heads the rood,
Or watch'd night-long in the dewy weather,
The while the moon did watch the wood.

Our spears stood bright and thick together,
Straight out the banners stream'd behind,
As we gallop'd on in the sunny weather,
With faces turn'd towards the wind.

Down sank our threescore spears together,
As thick we saw the pagans ride;
His eager face in the clear fresh weather,
Shone out that last time by my side.

Up the sweep of the bridge we dash'd together,
It rock'd to the crash of the meeting spears,
Down rain'd the buds of the dear spring weather,
The elm-tree flowers fell like tears.

There, as we roll'd and writhed together,
I threw my arms above my head,
For close by my side, in the lovely weather,
I saw him reel and fall back dead.

I and the slayer met together,
He waited the death-stroke there in his place,
With thoughts of death, in the lovely weather,
Gapingly mazed at my madden'd face.

Madly I fought as we fought together;
In vain: the little Christian band
The pagans drown'd, as in stormy weather,
The river drowns low-lying land.

They bound my blood-stain'd hands together,
They bound his corpse to nod by my side:
Then on we rode, in the bright March weather,
With clash of cymbals did we ride.

We ride no more, no more together;
My prison-bars are thick and strong,
I take no heed of any weather,
The sweet Saints grant I live not long.

1856

THE CHAPEL IN LYONESS

SIR OZANA LE CURE HARDY. SIR GALAHAD. SIR BORS DE GANYS

Sir Ozana. All day long and every day,
From Christmas-Eve to Whit-Sunday,
Within that Chapel-aisle I lay,
And no man came a-near.

Naked to the waist was I,
And deep within my breast did lie,
Though no man any blood could spy,
The truncheon of a spear.

No meat did ever pass my lips
Those days. Alas! the sunlight slips
From off the gilded parclose, dips,
And night comes on apace.

My arms lay back behind my head;
Over my raised-up knees was spread
A samite cloth of white and red;
A rose lay on my face.

Many a time I tried to shout;
But as in dream of battle-rout,
My frozen speech would not well out;
I could not even weep.

With inward sigh I see the sun
Fade off the pillars one by one,
My heart faints when the day is done,
Because I cannot sleep.

Sometimes strange thoughts pass through my head;
Not like a tomb is this my bed,
Yet oft I think that I am dead;
That round my tomb is writ,

"Ozana of the hardy heart,
Knight of the Table Round,
Pray for his soul, lords, of your part;
A true knight he was found."

Ah! me, I cannot fathom it. [*He sleeps.*

Sir Galahad. All day long and every day,
Till his madness pass'd away,
I watch'd Ozana as he lay
Within the gilded screen.

All my singing moved him not;
As I sung my heart grew hot,
With the thought of Launcelot
Far away, I ween.

So I went a little space
From out the chapel, bathed my face
In the stream that runs apace
By the churchyard wall.

There I pluck'd a faint wild rose,
Hard by where the linden grows,
Sighing over silver rows
Of the lilies tall.

I laid the flower across his mouth;
The sparkling drops seem'd good for drouth;
He smiled, turn'd round towards the south,
Held up a golden tress.

The light smote on it from the west;
He drew the covering from his breast,
Against his heart that hair he pressed;
Death him soon will bless.

Sir Bors. I enter'd by the western door;
I saw a knight's helm lying there;
I raised my eyes from off the floor,
And caught the gleaming of his hair.

I stept full softly up to him;
I laid my chin upon his head;
I felt him smile; my eyes did swim,
I was so glad he was not dead.

I heard Ozana murmur low,
"There comes no sleep nor any love."
But Galahad stoop'd and kiss'd his brow:
He shiver'd; I saw his pale lips move.

Sir Ozana. There comes no sleep nor any love;
Ah me! I shiver with delight.
I am so weak I cannot move;
God move me to thee, dear, to-night!
Christ help! I have but little wit:
My life went wrong; I see it writ,

"Ozana of the hardy heart,
Knight of the Table Round,
Pray for his soul, lords, on your part;
A good knight he was found."

Now I begin to fathom it. [*He dies.*

Sir Bors. Galahad sits dreamily:
What strange things may his eyes see,
Great blue eyes fix'd full on me?
On his soul, Lord, have mercy.

Sir Galahad. Ozana, shall I pray for thee?
  Her cheek is laid to thine;
No long time hence, also I see
  Thy wasted fingers twine
Within the tresses of her hair
  That shineth gloriously,
Thinly outspread in the clear air
  Against the jasper sea.

1856

SUMMER DAWN

PRAY but one prayer for me 'twixt thy closed lips,
  Think but one thought of me up in the stars.
The summer night waneth, the morning light slips,
  Faint and grey 'twixt the leaves of the aspen, betwixt the cloud-bars,
That are patiently waiting there for the dawn:
  Patient and colourless, though Heaven's gold
Waits to float through them along with the sun.
Far out in the meadows, above the young corn,
  The heavy elms wait, and restless and cold
The uneasy wind rises; the roses are dun;
Through the long twilight they pray for the dawn,
Round the lone house in the midst of the corn.
  Speak but one word to me over the corn,
  Over the tender, bow'd locks of the corn.

1856

THE DEFENCE OF GUENEVERE

BUT, knowing now that they would have her speak,
She threw her wet hair backward from her brow,
Her hand close to her mouth touching her cheek,

As though she had had there a shameful blow,
And feeling it shameful to feel ought but shame
All through her heart, yet felt her cheek burned so,

She must a little touch it; like one lame
She walked away from Gauwaine, with her head
Still lifted up; and on her cheek of flame

The tears dried quick; she stopped at last and said:
"O knights and lords, it seems but little skill
To talk of well-known things past now and dead.

"God wot I ought to say, I have done ill,
And pray you all forgiveness heartily!
Because you must be right, such great lords; still

"Listen, suppose your time were come to die,
And you were quite alone and very weak;
Yea, laid a dying while very mightily

"The wind was ruffling up the narrow streak
Of river through your broad lands running well:
Suppose a hush should come, then some one speak:

" 'One of these cloths is heaven, and one is hell,
Now choose one cloth for ever; which they be,
I will not tell you, you must somehow tell

" 'Of your own strength and mightiness; here, see!'
Yea, yea, my lord, and you to ope your eyes,
At foot of your familiar bed to see

"A great God's angel standing, with such dyes,
Not known on earth, on his great wings, and hands,
Held out two ways, light from the inner skies

"Showing him well, and making his commands
Seem to be God's commands, moreover, too,
Holding within his hands the cloths on wands;

"And one of these strange choosing cloths was blue,
Wavy and long, and one cut short and red;
No man could tell the better of the two.

"After a shivering half-hour you said,
'God help! heaven's colour, the blue;' and he said, 'Hell.'
Perhaps you then would roll upon your bed,

"And cry to all good men that loved you well,
'Ah Christ! if only I had known, known, known;'
Launcelot went away, then I could tell,

"Like wisest man how all things would be, moan,
And roll and hurt myself, and long to die,
And yet fear much to die for what was sown.

"Nevertheless you, O Sir Gauwaine, lie;
Whatever may have happened through these years,
God knows I speak truth, saying that you lie."

Her voice was low at first, being full of tears,
But as it cleared, it grew full loud and shrill,
Growing a windy shriek in all men's ears,

A ringing in their startled brains, until
She said that Gauwaine lied, then her voice sunk,
And her great eyes began again to fill,

Though still she stood right up, and never shrunk,
But spoke on bravely, glorious lady fair!
Whatever tears her full lips may have drunk,

She stood, and seemed to think, and wrung her hair,
Spoke out at last with no more trace of shame,
With passionate twisting of her body there:

"It chanced upon a day that Launcelot came
To dwell at Arthur's court: at Christmas-time
This happened; when the heralds sung his name,

" 'Son of King Ban of Benwick,' seemed to chime
Along with all the bells that rang that day,
O'er the white roofs, with little change of rhyme.

"Christmas and whitened Winter passed away,
And over me the April sunshine came,
Made very awful with black hail-clouds, yea,

"And in the Summer I grew white with flame,
And bowed my head down—Autumn, and the sick
Sure knowledge things would never be the same,

"However often Spring might be most thick
Of blossoms and buds, smote on me, and I grew
Careless of most things, let the clock tick, tick,

"To my unhappy pulse, that beat right through
My eager body; while I laughed out loud,
And let my lips curl up at false or true,

"Seemed cold and shallow without any cloud.
Behold, my judges, then the cloths were brought:
While I was dizzied thus, old thoughts would crowd,

"Belonging to the time ere I was bought
By Arthur's great name and his little love;
Must I give up for ever then, I thought,

"That which I deemed would ever round me move
Glorifying all things; for a little word,
Scarce ever meant at all, must I now prove

"Stone-cold for ever? Pray you, does the Lord
Will that all folks should be quite happy and good?
I love God now a little, if this cord

"Were broken, once for all what striving could
Make me love anything in earth or heaven?
So day by day it grew, as if one should

"Slip slowly down some path worn smooth and even,
Down to a cool sea on a summer day;
Yet still in slipping there was some small leaven

"Of stretched hands catching small stones by the way,
Until one surely reached the sea at last,
And felt strange new joy as the worn head lay

"Back, with the hair like sea-weed; yea, all past
Sweat of the forehead, dryness of the lips,
Washed utterly out by the dear waves o'ercast,

"In the lone sea, far off from any ships!
Do I not know now of a day in Spring?
No minute of that wild day ever slips

"From out my memory; I hear thrushes sing,
And wheresoever I may be, straightway
Thoughts of it all come up with most fresh sting:

"I was half mad with beauty on that day,
And went without my ladies all alone,
In a quiet garden walled round every way;

"I was right joyful of that wall of stone,
That shut the flowers and trees up with the sky,
And trebled all the beauty: to the bone,

"Yea, right through to my heart, grown very shy
With weary thoughts, it pierced, and made me glad;
Exceedingly glad, and I knew verily,

"A little thing just then had made me mad;
I dared not think, as I was wont to do,
Sometimes, upon my beauty; if I had

"Held out my long hand up against the blue,
And, looking on the tenderly darken'd fingers,
Thought that by rights one ought to see quite through,

"There, see you, where the soft still light yet lingers,
Round by the edges; what should I have done,
If this had joined with yellow spotted singers,

"And startling green drawn upward by the sun?
But shouting, loosed out, see now! all my hair,
And trancedly stood watching the west wind run

"With faintest half-heard breathing sound—why there
I lose my head e'en now in doing this;
But shortly listen—In that garden fair

"Came Launcelot walking; this is true, the kiss
Wherewith we kissed in meeting that spring day,
I scarce dare talk of the remember'd bliss,

"When both our mouths went wandering in one way,
And aching sorely, met among the leaves;
Our hands being left behind strained far away.

"Never within a yard of my bright sleeves
Had Launcelot come before—and now, so nigh!
After that day why is it Guenevere grieves?

"Nevertheless you, O Sir Gauwaine, lie,
Whatever happened on through all those years,
God knows I speak truth, saying that you lie.

"Being such a lady could I weep these tears
If this were true? A great queen such as I
Having sinn'd this way, straight her conscience sears;

"And afterwards she liveth hatefully,
Slaying and poisoning, certes never weeps,—
Gauwaine be friends now, speak me lovingly.

"Do I not see how God's dear pity creeps
All through your frame, and trembles in your mouth?
Remember in what grave your mother sleeps,

"Buried in some place far down in the south,
Men are forgetting as I speak to you;
By her head sever'd in that awful drouth

"Of pity that drew Agravaine's fell blow,
I pray your pity! let me not scream out
For ever after, when the shrill winds blow

"Through half your castle-locks! let me not shout
For ever after in the winter night
When you ride out alone! in battle-rout

"Let not my rusting tears make your sword light!
Ah! God of mercy, how he turns away!
So, ever must I dress me to the fight,

"So—let God's justice work! Gauwaine, I say,
See me hew down your proofs: yea, all men know
Even as you said how Mellyagraunce one day,

"One bitter day in *la Fausse Garde*, for so
All good knights held it after, saw—
Yea, sirs, by cursed unknightly outrage; though

"You, Gauwaine, held his word without a flaw,
This Mellyagraunce saw blood upon my bed—
Whose blood then pray you? is there any law

"To make a queen say why some spots of red
Lie on her coverlet? or will you say,
'Your hands are white, lady, as when you wed,

" 'Where did you bleed?' and must I stammer out, 'Nay,
I blush indeed, fair lord, only to rend
My sleeve up to my shoulder, where there lay

" 'A knife-point last night:' so must I defend
The honour of the Lady Guenevere?
Not so, fair lords, even if the world should end

"This very day, and you were judges here
Instead of God. Did you see Mellyagraunce
When Launcelot stood by him? what white fear

"Curdled his blood, and how his teeth did dance,
His side sink in? as my knight cried and said,
'Slayer of unarm'd men, here is a chance!

" 'Setter of traps, I pray you guard your head,
By God, I am so glad to fight with you,
Stripper of ladies, that my hand feels lead

" 'For driving weight; hurrah now! draw and do,
For all my wounds are moving in my breast,
And I am getting mad with waiting so.'

"He struck his hands together o'er the beast,
Who fell down flat, and grovell'd at his feet,
And groan'd at being slain so young—'at least.'

"My knight said, 'Rise you, sir, who are so fleet
At catching ladies, half-arm'd will I fight,
My left side all uncovered!' then I weet,

"Up sprang Sir Mellyagraunce with great delight
Upon his knave's face; not until just then
Did I quite hate him, as I saw my knight

"Along the lists look to my stake and pen
With such a joyous smile, it made me sigh
From agony beneath my waist-chain, when

"The fight began, and to me they drew nigh;
Ever Sir Launcelot kept him on the right,
And traversed warily, and ever high

"And fast leapt caitiff's sword, until my knight
Sudden threw up his sword to his left hand,
Caught it, and swung it; that was all the fight,

"Except a spout of blood on the hot land;
For it was hottest summer; and I know
I wonder'd how the fire, while I should stand,

"And burn, against the heat, would quiver so,
Yards above my head; thus these matters went:
Which things were only warnings of the woe

"That fell on me. Yet Mellyagraunce was shent,
For Mellyagraunce had fought against the Lord;
Therefore, my lords, take heed lest you be blent

"With all this wickedness; say no rash word
Against me, being so beautiful; my eyes,
Wept all away the grey, may bring some sword

"To drown you in your blood; see my breast rise,
Like waves of purple sea, as here I stand;
And how my arms are moved in wonderful wise,

"Yea, also at my full heart's strong command,
See through my long throat how the words go up
In ripples to my mouth; how in my hand

"The shadow lies like wine within a cup
Of marvellously colour'd gold; yea, now
This little wind is rising, look you up,

"And wonder how the light is falling so
Within my moving tresses: will you dare,
When you have looked a little on my brow,

"To say this thing is vile? or will you care
For any plausible lies of cunning woof,
When you can see my face with no lie there

"For ever? am I not a gracious proof—
'But in your chamber Launcelot was found'—
Is there a good knight then would stand aloof,

"When a queen says with gentle queenly sound:
'O true as steel, come now and talk with me,
I love to see your step upon the ground

" 'Unwavering, also well I love to see
That gracious smile light up your face, and hear
Your wonderful words, that all mean verily

" 'The thing they seem to mean: good friend, so dear
To me in everything, come here to-night,
Or else the hours will pass most dull and drear;

" 'If you come not, I fear this time I might
Get thinking over much of times gone by,
When I was young, and green hope was in sight:

" 'For no man cares now to know why I sigh;
And no man comes to sing me pleasant songs,
Nor any brings me the sweet flowers that lie

" 'So thick in the gardens; therefore one so longs
To see you, Launcelot; that we may be
Like children once again, free from all wrongs

" 'Just for one night.' Did he not come to me?
What thing could keep true Launcelot away
If I said, 'Come'? there was one less than three

"In my quiet room that night, and we were gay;
Till sudden I rose up, weak, pale, and sick,
Because a bawling broke our dream up, yea,

"I looked at Launcelot's face and could not speak,
For he looked helpless too, for a little while;
Then I remember how I tried to shriek,

"And could not, but fell down; from tile to tile
The stones they threw up rattled o'er my head
And made me dizzier; till within a while

"My maids were all about me, and my head
On Launcelot's breast was being soothed away
From its white chattering, until Launcelot said—

"By God! I will not tell you more to-day,
Judge any way you will—what matters it?
You know quite well the story of that fray,

"How Launcelot still'd their bawling, the mad fit
That caught up Gauwaine—all, all, verily,
But just that which would save me; these things flit.

"Nevertheless you, O Sir Gauwaine, lie;
Whatever may have happen'd these long years,
God knows I speak truth, saying that you lie!

"All I have said is truth, by Christ's dear tears."

She would not speak another word, but stood
Turn'd sideways; listening, like a man who hears

His brother's trumpet sounding through the wood
Of his foes' lances. She lean'd eagerly,
And gave a slight spring sometimes, as she could

At last hear something really; joyfully
Her cheek grew crimson, as the headlong speed
Of the roan charger drew all men to see,
The knight who came was Launcelot at good need.

1858

CONCERNING GEFFRAY TESTE NOIRE

AND if you meet the Canon of Chimay,
As going to Ortaise you well may do,
Greet him from John of Castel Neuf, and say
All that I tell you, for all this is true.

This Geffray Teste Noire was a Gascon thief,
Who, under shadow of the English name,
Pilled all such towns and countries as were lief
To King Charles and St. Denis; thought it blame

If anything escaped him; so my lord,
  The Duke of Berry, sent Sir John Bonne Lance,
And other knights, good players with the sword,
  To check this thief, and give the land a chance.

Therefore we set out bastides round the tower
  That Geffray held, the strong thief! like a king,
High perch'd upon the rock of Ventadour,
  Hopelessly strong, by Christ! it was mid spring,

When first I joined the little army there
  With ten good spears; Auvergne is hot; each day
We sweated armed before the barrier,
  Good feats of arms were done there often—eh?

Your brother was slain there? I mind me now
  A right good man-at-arms, God pardon him!
I think 't was Geffray smote him on the brow
  With some spiked axe, and while he totter'd, dim

About the eyes, the spear of Alleyne Roux
  Slipped through his camaille and his throat; well, well!
Alleyne is paid now; your name Alleyne too?
  Mary! how strange—but this tale I would tell—

For spite of all our bastides, damned Blackhead
  Would ride abroad whene'er he chose to ride,
We could not stop him; many a burgher bled
  Dear gold all round his girdle; far and wide

The villaynes dwelt in utter misery
  'Twixt us and thief Sir Geffray; hauled this way
By Sir Bonne Lance at one time; he gone by,
  Down comes this Teste Noire on another day.

And therefore they dig up the stone, grind corn,
  Hew wood, draw water, yea, they lived, in short,
As I said just now, utterly forlorn,
  Till this our knave and blackhead was outfought.

So Bonne Lance fretted, thinking of some trap
  Day after day, till on a time he said:
"John of Newcastle, if we have good hap,
  We catch our thief in two days." "How?" I said.

"Why, Sir, to-day he rideth out again,
  Hoping to take well certain sumpter mules
From Carcassonne, going with little train,
  Because, forsooth, he thinketh us mere fools;

"But if we set an ambush in some wood,
  He is but dead; so, Sir, take thirty spears
To Verville forest, if it seem you good."
  Then felt I like the horse in Job, who hears

The dancing trumpet sound, and we went forth;
  And my red lion on the spear-head flapped,
As faster than the cool wind we rode North,
  Towards the wood of Verville; thus it happed.

We rode a soft space on that day while spies
  Got news about Sir Geffray; the red wine
Under the road-side bush was clear; the flies,
  The dragon-flies I mind me most, did shine

In brighter arms than ever I put on;
  So—"Geffray," said our spies, "would pass that way
Next day at sundown;" then he must be won;
  And so we enter'd Verville wood next day,

In the afternoon; through it the highway runs,
  'Twixt copses of green hazel, very thick,
And underneath, with glimmering of suns,
  The primroses are happy; the dews lick

The soft green moss. "Put cloths about your arms,
  Lest they should glitter; surely they will go
In a long thin line, watchful for alarms
  With all their carriages of booty; so,—

"Lay down my pennon in the grass—Lord God!
  What have we lying here? will they be cold,
I wonder, being so bare, above the sod,
  Instead of under? This was a knight too, fold

"Lying on fold of ancient rusted mail;
No plate at all, gold rowels to the spurs,
And see the quiet gleam of turquoise pale
Along the ceinture; but the long time blurs

"Even the tinder of his coat to nought,
Except these scraps of leather; see how white
The skull is, loose within the coif! He fought
A good fight, maybe, ere he was slain quite.

"No armour on the legs too; strange in faith—
A little skeleton for a knight though—ah!
This one is bigger, truly without scathe
His enemies escaped not—ribs driven out far—

"That must have reach'd the heart, I doubt—how now,
What say you, Aldovrand—a woman? why?"
"Under the coif a gold wreath on the brow,
Yea, see the hair not gone to powder, lie,

"Golden, no doubt, once—yea, and very small—
This for a knight; but for a dame, my lord,
These loose-hung bones seem shapely still, and tall,—
Didst ever see a woman's bones, my lord?"

Often, God help me! I remember when
I was a simple boy, fifteen years old,
The Jacquerie froze up the blood of men
With their fell deeds, not fit now to be told:

God help again! we enter'd Beauvais town,
Slaying them fast, whereto I help'd, mere boy
As I was then; we gentles cut them down,
These burners and defilers, with great joy.

Reason for that, too, in the great church there
These fiends had lit a fire, that soon went out,
The church at Beauvais being so great and fair—
My father, who was by me, gave a shout

Between a beast's howl and a woman's scream,
Then, panting, chuckled to me: "John, look! look!
Count the dames' skeletons!" From some bad dream
Like a man just awaked, my father shook;

And I, being faint with smelling the burnt bones,
And very hot with fighting down the street,
And sick of such a life, fell down, with groans
My head went weakly nodding to my feet.—

—An arrow had gone through her tender throat,
And her right wrist was broken; then I saw
The reason why she had on that war-coat,
Their story came out clear without a flaw;

For when he knew that they were being waylaid,
He threw it over her, yea, hood and all;
Whereby he was much hack'd, while they were stay'd
By those their murderers; many an one did fall

Beneath his arm, no doubt, so that he clear'd
Their circle, bore his death-wound out of it;
But as they rode, some archer least afear'd
Drew a strong bow, and thereby she was hit.

Still as he rode he knew not she was dead,
Thought her but fainted from her broken wrist,
He bound with his great leathern belt—she bled?
Who knows! he bled too, neither was there miss'd

The beating of her heart, his heart beat well
For both of them, till here, within this wood,
He died scarce sorry; easy this to tell;
After these years the flowers forget their blood.—

How could it be? never before that day,
However much a soldier I might be,
Could I look on a skeleton and say
I care not for it, shudder not—now see,

Over those bones I sat and pored for hours,
And thought, and dream'd, and still I scarce could see

The small white bones that lay upon the flowers,
But evermore I saw the lady; she

With her dear gentle walking leading in,
By a chain of silver twined about her wrists,
Her loving knight, mounted and arm'd to win
Great honour for her, fighting in the lists.

O most pale face, that brings such joy and sorrow
Into men's hearts—yea, too, so piercing sharp
That joy is, that it marcheth nigh to sorrow
For ever—like an overwinded harp.

Your face must hurt me always: pray you now,
Doth it not hurt you too? seemeth some pain
To hold you always, pain to hold your brow
So smooth, unwrinkled ever; yea, again,

Your long eyes where the lids seem like to drop,
Would you not, lady, were they shut fast, feel
Far merrier? there so high they will not stop,
They are most sly to glide forth and to steal

Into my heart; *I kiss their soft lids there,*
And in green gardens scarce can stop my lips
From wandering on your face, but that your hair
Falls down and tangles me, back my face slips.

Or say your mouth—I saw you drink red wine
Once at a feast; how slowly it sank in,
As though you fear'd that some wild fate might twine
Within that cup, and slay you for a sin.

And when you talk your lips do arch and move
In such wise that a language new I know
Besides their sound; they quiver, too, with love
When you are standing silent; know this, too,

I saw you kissing once; like a curved sword
That bites with all its edge, did your lips lie,
Curled gently, slowly, long time could afford
For caught-up breathings; like a dying sigh

They gather'd up their lines and went away,
And still kept twitching with a sort of smile,
As likely to be weeping presently,—
Your hands too—how I watch'd them all the while!

"Cry out St. Peter now," quoth Aldovrand;
I cried "St. Peter," broke out from the wood
With all my spears; we met them hand to hand,
And shortly slew them; natheless, by the rood,

We caught not Blackhead then, or any day;
Months after that he died at last in bed,
From a wound pick'd up at a barrier-fray;
That same year's end a steel bolt in the head,

And much bad living kill'd Teste Noire at last;
John Froissart knoweth he is dead by now,
No doubt, but knoweth not this tale just past;
Perchance then you can tell him what I show.

In my new castle, down beside the Eure,
There is a little chapel of squared stone,
Painted inside and out; in green nook pure
There did I lay them, every wearied bone;

And over it they lay, with stone-white hands
Clasped fast together, hair made bright with gold;
This Jacques Picard, known through many lands,
Wrought cunningly; he's dead now—I am old.

1858

THE GILLIFLOWER OF GOLD

A GOLDEN gilliflower to-day
I wore upon my helm alway,
And won the prize of this tourney.
Hah! hah! la belle jaune giroflée.

However well Sir Giles might sit,
His sun was weak to wither it,
Lord Miles's blood was dew on it:
Hah! hah! la belle jaune giroflée.

Although my spear in splinters flew,
From John's steel-coat, my eye was true;
I wheel'd about, and cried for you,
Hah! hah! la belle jaune giroflée.

Yea, do not doubt my heart was good,
Though my sword flew like rotten wood,
To shout, although I scarcely stood,
Hah! hah! la belle jaune giroflée.

My hand was steady too, to take
My axe from round my neck, and break
John's steel-coat up for my love's sake.
Hah! hah! la belle jaune giroflée.

When I stood in my tent again,
Arming afresh, I felt a pain
Take hold of me, I was so fain—
Hah! hah! la belle jaune giroflée.

To hear: "*Honneur aux fils des preux!*"
Right in my ears again, and shew
The gilliflower blossom'd new.
Hah! hah! la belle jaune giroflée.

The Sieur Guillaume against me came,
His tabard bore three points of flame
From a red heart: with little blame,—
Hah! hah! la belle jaune giroflée.

Our tough spears crackled up like straw;
He was the first to turn and draw
His sword, that had nor speck nor flaw,—
Hah! hah! la belle jaune giroflée.

But I felt weaker than a maid,
And my brain, dizzied and afraid,
Within my helm a fierce tune play'd,—
Hah! hah! la belle jaune giroflée.

Until I thought of your dear head,
Bow'd to the gilliflower bed,
The yellow flowers stain'd with red;—
Hah! hah! la belle jaune giroflée.

Crash! how the swords met, "*giroflée!*"
The fierce tune in my helm would play,
"*La belle! la belle! jaune giroflée!*"
Hah! hah! la belle jaune giroflée.

Once more the great swords met again,
"*La belle! la belle!*" but who fell then?
Le Sieur Guillaume, who struck down ten;—
Hah! hah! la belle jaune giroflée.

And as with mazed and unarm'd face,
Toward my own crown and the Queen's place,
They led me at a gentle pace
Hah! hah! la belle jaune giroflée.

I almost saw your quiet head
Bow'd o'er the gilliflower bed,
The yellow flowers stain'd with red.—
Hah! hah! la belle jaune giroflée.

1858

SHAMEFUL DEATH

THERE were four of us about that bed;
The mass-priest knelt at the side,
I and his mother stood at the head,
Over his feet lay the bride;
We were quite sure that he was dead,
Though his eyes were open wide.

He did not die in the night,
He did not die in the day,
But in the morning twilight
His spirit pass'd away,
When neither sun nor moon was bright,
And the trees were merely grey.

He was not slain with the sword,
Knight's axe, or the knightly spear,
Yet spoke he never a word
After he came in here;
I cut away the cord
From the neck of my brother dear.

He did not strike one blow,
For the recreants came behind,
In a place where the hornbeams grow,
A path right hard to find,
For the hornbeam boughs swing so,
That the twilight makes it blind.

They lighted a great torch then,
When his arms were pinion'd fast,
Sir John the knight of the Fen,
Sir Guy of the Dolorous Blast,
With knights threescore and ten,
Hung brave Lord Hugh at last.

I am threescore and ten,
And my hair is all turn'd grey,
But I met Sir John of the Fen
Long ago on a summer day,
And am glad to think of the moment when
I took his life away.

I am threescore and ten,
And my strength is mostly pass'd,
But long ago I and my men,
When the sky was overcast,

And the smoke roll'd over the reeds of the fen,
Slew Guy of the Dolorous Blast.

And now, knights all of you,
I pray you pray for Sir Hugh,
A good knight and a true,
And for Alice, his wife, pray too.

1858

THE EVE OF CRÉCY

Gold on her head, and gold on her feet,
And gold where the hems of her kirtle meet,
And a golden girdle round my sweet;—
Ah! qu'elle est belle La Marguerite.

Margaret's maids are fair to see,
Freshly dress'd and pleasantly;
Margaret's hair falls down to her knee;—
Ah! qu'elle est belle La Marguerite.

If I were rich I would kiss her feet,
I would kiss the place where the gold hems meet,
And the golden girdle round my sweet:—
Ah! qu'elle est belle La Marguerite.

Ah me! I have never touch'd her hand,
When the arrière-ban goes through the land,
Six basnets under my pennon stand;—
Ah! qu'elle est belle La Marguerite.

And many an one grins under his hood:
"Sir Lambert de Bois, with all his men good,
Has neither food nor firewood;"—
Ah! qu'elle est belle La Marguerite.

If I were rich I would kiss her feet,
And the golden girdle of my sweet,
And thereabouts where the gold hems meet;
Ah! qu'elle est belle La Marguerite.

Yet even now it is good to think,
While my few poor varlets grumble and drink
In my desolate hall, where the fires sink,—
Ah! qu'elle est belle La Marguerite.

Of Margaret sitting glorious there,
In glory of gold and glory of hair,
And glory of glorious face most fair;—
Ah! qu'elle est belle La Marguerite.

Likewise to-night I made good cheer,
Because this battle draweth near:
For what have I to lose or fear?—
Ah! qu'elle est belle La Marguerite.

For, look you, my horse is good to prance
A right fair measure in this war-dance,
Before the eyes of Philip of France;—
Ah! qu'elle est belle La Marguerite.

And sometime it may hap, perdie,
While my new towers stand up three and three,
And my hall gets painted fair to see,
Ah! qu'elle est belle La Marguerite—

That folks may say: "Times change, by the rood,
For Lambert, banneret of the wood,
Has heaps of food and firewood;—
Ah! qu'elle est belle La Marguerite;—

"And wonderful eyes, too, under the hood
Of a damsel of right noble blood:"
St. Ives, for Lambert of the Wood!—
Ah! qu'elle est belle La Marguerite.

1858

THE JUDGMENT OF GOD

"Swerve to the left, son Roger," he said,
"When you catch his eyes through the helmet-slit,
Swerve to the left, then out at his head,
And the Lord God give you joy of it!"

The blue owls on my father's hood
Were a little dimm'd as I turn'd away;
This giving up of blood for blood
Will finish here somehow to-day.

So when I walk'd out from the tent,
Their howling almost blinded me;
Yet for all that I was not bent
By any shame. Hard by, the sea

Made a noise like the aspens where
We did that wrong, but now the place
Is very pleasant, and the air
Blows cool on any passer's face.

And all the wrong is gather'd now
Into the circle of these lists—
Yea, howl out, butchers! tell me how
His hands were cut off at the wrists;

And how Lord Roger bore his face
  A league above his spear-point, high
Above the owls, to that strong place
  Among the waters—yea, yea, cry:

"What a brave champion we have got!
  Sir Oliver, the flower of all
The Hainault knights." The day being hot,
  He sat beneath a broad white pall,

White linen over all his steel;
  What a good knight he look'd! his sword
Laid thwart his knees; he liked to feel
  Its steadfast edge clear as his word.

And he look'd solemn: how his love
  Smiled whitely on him, sick with fear!
How all the ladies up above
  Twisted their pretty hands; so near

The fighting was—Ellayne! Ellayne!
  They cannot love like you can, who
Would burn your hands off, if that pain
  Could win a kiss—am I not true

To you for ever? therefore I
  Do not fear death or anything;
If I should limp home wounded, why,
  While I lay sick you would but sing,

And soothe me into quiet sleep.
  If they spat on the recreant knight,
Threw stones at him, and cursed him deep,
  Why then—what then; your hand would light

So gently on his drawn-up face,
  And you would kiss him, and in soft
Cool scented clothes would lap him, pace
  The quiet room and weep oft,—oft

Would turn and smile, and brush his cheek
  With your sweet chin and mouth; and in
The order'd garden you would seek
  The biggest roses—any sin.

And these say: "No more now my knight,
  Or God's knight any longer"—you,
Being than they so much more white,
  So much more pure and good and true,

Will cling to me for ever—there,
  Is not that wrong turn'd right at last
Through all these years, and I wash'd clean?
  Say, yea, Ellayne; the time is past,

Since on that Christmas-day last year
  Up to your feet the fire crept,
And the smoke through the brown leaves sere
  Blinded your dear eyes that you wept;

Was it not I that caught you then,
  And kiss'd you, on the saddle-bow?
Did not the blue owl mark the men
  Whose spears stood like the corn a-row?

This Oliver is a right good knight,
  And must needs beat me, as I fear,
Unless I catch him in the fight,
  My father's crafty way—John, here!

Bring up the men from the south gate,
  To help me if I fall or win,
For even if I beat, their hate
  Will grow to more than this mere grin.

1858

THE SAILING OF THE SWORD

Across the empty garden-beds,
  When the Sword went out to sea,
I scarcely saw my sisters' heads
  Bowed each beside a tree.
I could not see the castle-leads,
  When the Sword went out to sea.

Alicia wore a scarlet gown,
  When the Sword went out to sea,
But Ursula's was russet brown:
  For the mist we could not see
The scarlet roofs of the good town,
  When the Sword went out to sea.

Green holly in Alicia's hand,
  When the Sword went out to sea;
With sere oak-leaves did Ursula stand;
  Oh! yet alas for me!
I did but bear a peel'd white wand,
  When the Sword went out to sea.

O, russet brown and scarlet bright,
  When the Sword went out to sea,
My sisters wore; I wore but white:
  Red, brown, and white, are three;
Three damozels; each had a knight,
  When the Sword went out to sea.

Sir Robert shouted loud, and said,
  When the Sword went out to sea,

"Alicia, while I see thy head,
  What shall I bring for thee?"
"O, my sweet Lord, a ruby red:"
  The Sword went out to sea.

Sir Miles said, while the sails hung down,
  When the Sword went out to sea,
"O, Ursula! while I see the town,
  What shall I bring for thee?"
"Dear knight, bring back a falcon brown:"
  The Sword went out to sea.

But my Roland, no word he said
  When the Sword went out to sea,
But only turn'd away his head;
  A quick shriek came from me:
"Come back, dear lord, to your white maid!"
  The Sword went out to sea.

The hot sun bit the garden-beds
  When the Sword came back from sea;
Beneath an apple-tree our heads
  Stretched out toward the sea;
Gray gleamed the thirsty castle-leads,
  When the Sword came back from sea.

Lord Robert brought a ruby red,
  When the Sword came back from sea,
He kissed Alicia on the head:
  "I am come back to thee;
'T is time, sweet love, that we were wed,
  Now the Sword is back from sea!"

Sir Miles he bore a falcon brown,
  When the Sword came back from sea;
His arms went round tall Ursula's gown:
  "What joy, O love, but thee?
Let us be wed in the good town,
  Now the Sword is back from sea!"

My heart grew sick, no more afraid,
  When the Sword came back from sea;
Upon the deck a tall white maid
  Sat on Lord Roland's knee;
His chin was press'd upon her head,
  When the Sword came back from sea!

1858

OLD LOVE

"You must be very old, Sir Giles,"
  I said; he said: "Yea, very old:"
Whereat the mournfullest of smiles
  Creased his dry skin with many a fold.

"They hammer'd out my basnet point
  Into a round salade," he said,
"The basnet being quite out of joint,
  Natheless the salade rasps my head."

He gazed at the great fire a while:
  "And you are getting old, Sir John;"
(He said this with that cunning smile
  That was most sad;) "we both wear on,

"Knights come to court and look at me,
  With eyebrows up, except my lord,
And my dear lady, none I see
  That know the ways of my old sword."

(My lady! at that word no pang
  Stopp'd all my blood.) "But tell me, John,
Is it quite true that pagans hang
  So thick about the east, that on

"The eastern sea no Venice flag
  Can fly unpaid for?" "True," I said,
"And in such way the miscreants drag
  Christ's cross upon the ground, I dread

"That Constantine must fall this year."
  Within my heart; "These things are small;
This is not small, that things outwear
  I thought were made for ever, yea, all,

"All things go soon or late;" I said—
  I saw the duke in court next day;
Just as before, his grand great head
  Above his gold robes dreaming lay,

Only his face was paler; there
  I saw his duchess sit by him;
And she—she was changed more; her hair
  Before my eyes that used to swim,

And make me dizzy with great bliss
  Once, when I used to watch her sit—
Her hair is bright still, yet it is
  As though some dust were thrown on it.

Her eyes are shallower, as though
  Some grey glass were behind; her brow
And cheeks the straining bones show through
  Are not so good for kissing now.

Her lips are drier now she is
  A great duke's wife these many years,
They will not shudder with a kiss
  As once they did, being moist with tears.

Also her hands have lost that way
Of clinging that they used to have;
They look'd quite easy, as they lay
Upon the silken cushions brave

With broidery of the apples green
My Lord Duke bears upon his shield.
Her face, alas! that I have seen
Look fresher than an April field,

This is all gone now; gone also
Her tender walking; when she walks
She is most queenly I well know,
And she is fair still:—as the stalks

Of faded summer-lilies are,
So is she grown now unto me
This spring-time, when the flowers star
The meadows, birds sing wonderfully.

I warrant once she used to cling
About his neck, and kiss'd him so,
And then his coming step would ring
Joy-bells for her,—some time ago.

Ah! sometimes like an idle dream
That hinders true life overmuch,
Sometimes like a lost heaven, these seem.—
This love is not so hard to smutch.

1858

THE WIND

Ah! no, no, it is nothing, surely nothing at all,
Only the wild-going wind round by the garden-wall,
For the dawn just now is breaking, the wind beginning to fall.
Wind, wind! thou art sad, art thou kind?
Wind, wind, unhappy! thou art blind,
Yet still thou wanderest the lily-seed to find.

So I will sit, and think and think of the days gone by,
Never moving my chair for fear the dogs should cry,
Making no noise at all while the flambeau burns awry.
For my chair is heavy and carved, and with sweeping green behind
It is hung, and the dragons thereon grin out in the gusts of the wind;
On its folds an orange lies, with a deep gash cut in the rind.
Wind, wind! thou art sad, art thou kind?
Wind, wind, unhappy! thou art blind,
Yet still thou wanderest the lily-seed to find.

If I move my chair it will scream, and the orange will roll out far,
And the faint yellow juice ooze out like blood from a wizard's jar;
And the dogs will howl for those who went last month to the war.
Wind, wind! thou art sad, art thou kind?
Wind, wind, unhappy! thou art blind,
Yet still thou wanderest the lily-seed to find.

So I will sit and think of love that is over and past,
O! so long ago—yes, I will be quiet at last;
Whether I like it or not, a grim half-slumber is cast
Over my worn old brains, that touches the roots of my heart,
And above my half-shut eyes the blue roof 'gins to part,
And show the blue spring sky, till I am ready to start
From out of the green-hung chair; but something keeps me still,
And I fall in a dream that I walked with her on the side of a hill,
Dotted—for was it not spring?—with tufts of the daffodil.
Wind, wind! thou art sad, art thou kind?
Wind, wind, unhappy! thou art blind,
Yet still thou wanderest the lily-seed to find.

And Margaret, as she walked, held a painted book in her hand;
Her finger kept the place; I caught her; we both did stand
Face to face, on the top of the highest hill in the land.
Wind, wind! thou art sad, art thou kind?
Wind, wind, unhappy! thou art blind,
Yet still thou wanderest the lily-seed to find.

I held to her long bare arms, but she shuddered away from me,

While the flush went out of her face as her head fell back on a tree,
And a spasm caught her mouth, fearful for me to see;

And still I held to her arms till her shoulder touched my mail;
Weeping, she tottered forward, so glad that I should prevail,
And her hair went over my robe, like a gold flag over a sail.
Wind, wind! thou art sad, art thou kind?
Wind, wind, unhappy! thou art blind,
Yet still thou wanderest the lily-seed to find.

I kissed her hard by the ear, and she kissed me on the brow,
And then lay down on the grass, where the mark on the moss is now,
And spread her arms out wide while I went down below.
Wind, wind! thou art sad, art thou kind?
Wind, wind, unhappy! thou art blind,
Yet still thou wanderest the lily-seed to find.

And then I walked for a space to and fro on the side of the hill,
Till I gathered and held in my arms great sheaves of the daffodil,
And when I came again my Margaret lay there still.

I piled them high and high above her heaving breast—
How they were caught and held in her loose ungirded vest!
But one beneath her arm died, happy so to be prest!
Wind, wind! thou art sad, art thou kind?
Wind, wind, unhappy! thou art blind,
Yet still thou wanderest the lily-seed to find.

Again I turned my back and went away for an hour;
She said no word when I came again, so, flower by flower,
I counted the daffodils over, and cast them languidly lower.
Wind, wind! thou art sad, art thou kind?
Wind, wind, unhappy! thou art blind,
Yet still thou wanderest the lily-seed to find.

My dry hands shook and shook as the green gown showed again,
Cleared from the yellow flowers, and I grew hollow with pain,
And on to us both there fell from the sun-shower drops of rain.
Wind, wind! thou art sad, art thou kind?
Wind, wind, unhappy! thou art blind,
Yet still thou wanderest the lily-seed to find.

Alas! alas! there was blood on the very quiet breast,
Blood lay in the many folds of the loose ungirded vest,
Blood lay upon her arm where the flower had been prest.

I shrieked and leapt from my chair, and the orange rolled out far,
The faint yellow juice oozed out like blood from a wizard's jar;
And then in marched the ghosts of those that had gone to the war.

I knew them by the arms that I was used to paint
Upon their long thin shields; but the colors were all grown faint,
And faint upon their banner was Olaf, king and saint.
Wind, wind! thou art sad, art thou kind?
Wind, wind, unhappy! thou art blind,
Yet still thou wanderest the lily-seed to find.

1858

THE BLUE CLOSET

The Damozels

Lady Alice, Lady Louise,
Between the wash of the tumbling seas
We are ready to sing, if so ye please;
So lay your long hands on the keys;
Sing, "*Laudate pueri.*"

And ever the great bell overhead
Boom'd in the wind a knell for the dead,
Though no one toll'd it, a knell for the dead.

Lady Louise

Sister, let the measure swell
Not too loud; for you sing not well
If you drown the faint boom of the bell;
He is weary, so am I.

And ever the chevron overhead
Flapp'd on the banner of the dead;
(Was he asleep, or was he dead?)

LADY ALICE

Alice the Queen, and Louise the Queen,
Two damozels wearing purple and green,
Four lone ladies dwelling here
From day to day and year to year;
And there is none to let us go;
To break the locks of the doors below,
Or shovel away the heaped-up snow;
And when we die no man will know
That we are dead; but they give us leave,
Once every year on Christmas-eve,
To sing in the Closet Blue one song;
And we should be so long, so long,
If we dared, in singing; for dream on dream,
They float on in a happy stream;
Float from the gold strings, float from the keys,
Float from the open'd lips of Louise;
But, alas! the sea-salt oozes through
The chinks of the tiles of the Closet Blue;

And ever the great bell overhead
Booms in the wind a knell for the dead,
The wind plays on it a knell for the dead.

[*They sing all together*]

How long ago was it, how long ago,
He came to this tower with hands full of snow?

"Kneel down, O love Louise, kneel down," he said,
And sprinkled the dusty snow over my head.

He watch'd the snow melting, it ran through my hair,
Ran over my shoulders, white shoulders and bare.

"I cannot weep for thee, poor love Louise,
For my tears are all hidden deep under the seas;

"In a gold and blue casket she keeps all my tears,
But my eyes are no longer blue, as in old years;

"Yea, they grow grey with time, grow small and dry,
I am so feeble now, would I might die."

And in truth the great bell overhead
Left off his pealing for the dead,
Perchance, because the wind was dead.

Will he come back again, or is he dead?
O! is he sleeping, my scarf round his head?

Or did they strangle him as he lay there,
With the long scarlet scarf I used to wear?

Only I pray thee, Lord, let him come here!
Both his soul and his body to me are most dear.

Dear Lord, that loves me, I wait to receive
Either body or spirit this wild Christmas-eve.

Through the floor shot up a lily red,
With a patch of earth from the land of the dead,
For he was strong in the land of the dead.

What matter that his cheeks were pale,
His kind kiss'd lips all grey?
"O, love Louise, have you waited long?"
"O, my lord Arthur, yea."

What if his hair that brush'd her cheek
Was stiff with frozen rime?
His eyes were grown quite blue again,
As in the happy time.

"O, love Louise, this is the key
Of the happy golden land!
O, sisters, cross the bridge with me,
My eyes are full of sand.
What matter that I cannot see,
If ye take me by the hand?"

And ever the great bell overhead,
And the tumbling seas mourn'd for the dead;
For their song ceased, and they were dead.

1858

THE TUNE OF SEVEN TOWERS

No one goes there now;
For what is left to fetch away
From the desolate battlements all arow,
And the lead roof heavy and gray?
"Therefore," said fair Yoland of the flowers,
"This is the tune of Seven Towers."

No one walks there now,
  Except in the white moonlight
The white ghosts walk in a row;
  If one could see it, an awful sight—
"*Listen!" said fair Yoland of the flowers,*
"*This is the tune of Seven Towers.*"

But none can see them now,
  Though they sit by the side of the moat,
Feet half in the water, there in a row,
  Long hair in the wind afloat.
"*Therefore," said fair Yoland of the flowers,*
"*This is the tune of Seven Towers.*"

If any will go to it now,
  He must go to it all alone,
Its gates will not open to any row
  Of glittering spears—will *you* go alone?
"*Listen!" said fair Yoland of the flowers,*
"*This is the tune of Seven Towers.*"

By my love go there now,
  To fetch me my coif away,
My coif and my kirtle, with pearls arow,
  Oliver, go today!
"*Therefore," said fair Yoland of the flowers,*
"*This is the tune of Seven Towers.*"

I am unhappy now,
  I cannot tell you why;
If you go, the priests and I in a row
  Will pray that you may not die.
"*Listen!" said fair Yoland of the flowers,*
"*This is the tune of Seven Towers.*"

If you will go for me now,
  I will kiss your mouth at last;
        [*She sayeth inwardly.*]
(*The graves stand gray in a row*),
  Oliver, hold me fast!
"*Therefore," said fair Yoland of the flowers,*
"*This is the tune of Seven Towers.*"

1858

THE HAYSTACK IN THE FLOODS

HAD she come all the way for this,
To part at last without a kiss?
Yea, had she borne the dirt and rain
That her own eyes might see him slain
Beside the haystack in the floods?
Along the dripping leafless woods,
The stirrup touching either shoe,
She rode astride as troopers do;
With kirtle kilted to her knee,
To which the mud splash'd wretchedly;
And the wet dripp'd from every tree
Upon her head and heavy hair,
And on her eyelids broad and fair;
The tears and rain ran down her face.

By fits and starts they rode apace,
And very often was his place
Far off from her; he had to ride
Ahead, to see what might betide
When the roads cross'd; and sometimes, when
There rose a murmuring from his men,
Had to turn back with promises;
Ah me! she had but little ease;
And often for pure doubt and dread
She sobb'd, made giddy in the head
By the swift riding; while, for cold,
Her slender fingers scarce could hold
The wet reins; yea, and scarcely, too,
She felt the foot within her shoe
Against the stirrup: all for this,
To part at last without a kiss
Beside the haystack in the floods.

For when they near'd that old soak'd hay,
They saw across the only way
That Judas, Godmar, and the three
Red running lions dismally
Grinn'd from his pennon, under which
In one straight line along the ditch,
They counted thirty heads.

                                    So then,
While Robert turn'd round to his men,
She saw at once the wretched end,
And, stooping down, tried hard to rend
Her coif the wrong way from her head,
And hid her eyes; while Robert said:
"Nay, love, 'tis scarcely two to one;
At Poictiers where we made them run
So fast—why, sweet my love, good cheer,
The Gascon frontier is so near,
Nought after this."

                                    But, "O," she said,
"My God! my God! I have to tread
The long way back without you; then
The court at Paris; those six men;

The Haystack in the Floods. (1)

Had she come all the way for this
To part at last without a kiss?
Yea, had she born the dirt and rain
That her own eyes might see him slain
Beside the haystack in the floods?

Along the dripping leafless woods
The stirrup touching either shoe
She rode astride as troopers do;
With kirtle kilted to her knee
To which the mud splashed wretchedly,
And the wet dripped from every tree
Upon her head and heavy hair
And on her eyelids broad and fair
The tears and rain ran down her face

By fits and starts they rode apace,
And very often was his place
Far off from her; he had to ride
Ahead, to see what might betide
When the roads crossed; and sometimes, when
There rose a murmuring from his men
Had to turn back with promises;
Ah me! she had but little ease
and often for pure doubt & dread
She sobbed, made giddy in the head
By the swift riding, while for cold.

A Page of Morris's Manuscript. (See Appendix I.)

The gratings of the Chatelet;
The swift Seine on some rainy day
Like this, and people standing by,
And laughing, while my weak hands try
To recollect how strong men swim.
All this, or else a life with him,
For which I should be damned at last;
Would God that this next hour were past!"

He answer'd not, but cried his cry,
"St. George for Marny!" cheerily;
And laid his hand upon her rein.
Alas! no man of all his train
Gave back that cheery cry again;
And, while for rage his thumb beat fast
Upon his sword-hilt, some one cast
About his neck a kerchief long,
And bound him.

Then they went along
To Godmar; who said: "Now, Jehane,
Your lover's life is on the wane
So fast, that, if this very hour
You yield not as my paramour,
He will not see the rain leave off—
Nay, keep your tongue from gibe and scoff,
Sir Robert, or I slay you now."

She laid her hand upon her brow,
Then gazed upon the palm, as though
She thought her forehead bled, and "No,"
She said, and turn'd her head away,
As there were nothing else to say,
And everything were settled: red
Grew Godmar's face from chin to head:
"Jehane, on yonder hill there stands
My castle, guarding well my lands:
What hinders me from taking you,
And doing that I list to do
To your fair wilful body, while
Your knight lies dead?"

A wicked smile
Wrinkled her face, her lips grew thin,
A long way out she thrust her chin:
"You know that I should strangle you
While you were sleeping; or bite through
Your throat, by God's help—ah!" she said,
"Lord Jesus, pity your poor maid!
For in such wise they hem me in,
I cannot choose but sin and sin,
Whatever happens: yet I think
They could not make me eat or drink,
And so should I just reach my rest."
"Nay, if you do not my behest,
O Jehane! though I love you well,"
Said Godmar, "would I fail to tell
All that I know?" "Foul lies," she said.
"Eh! lies, my Jehane? by God's head,
At Paris folks would deem them true!
Do you know, Jehane, they cry for you,
'Jehane the brown! Jehane the brown!
Give us Jehane to burn or drown!'—
Eh—gag me, Robert!—sweet my friend,
This were indeed a piteous end
For those long fingers, and long feet,
And long neck, and smooth shoulders sweet;
An end that few men would forget
That saw it—So, an hour yet:
Consider, Jehane, which to take
Of life or death!"

So, scarce awake,
Dismounting, did she leave that place,
And totter some yards: with her face
Turn'd upward to the sky she lay,
Her head on a wet heap of hay,
And fell asleep: and while she slept,
And did not dream, the minutes crept
Round to the twelve again; but she,
Being waked at last, sigh'd quietly,
And strangely childlike came, and said:
"I will not." Straightway Godmar's head,
As though it hung on strong wires turn'd
Most sharply round, and his face burn'd.

For Robert—both his eyes were dry,
He could not weep, but gloomily
He seem'd to watch the rain; yea, too,
His lips were firm; he tried once more
To touch her lips; she reach'd out, sore
And vain desire so tortured them,
The poor grey lips, and now the hem
Of his sleeve brush'd them.

With a start
Up Godmar rose, thrust them apart;
From Robert's throat he loosed the bands
Of silk and mail; with empty hands
Held out, she stood and gazed, and saw
The long bright blade without a flaw
Glide out from Godmar's sheath, his hand
In Robert's hair; she saw him bend

Back Robert's head; she saw him send
The thin steel down; the blow told well,
Right backward the knight Robert fell,
And moan'd as dogs do, being half dead,
Unwitting, as I deem: so then
Godmar turn'd grinning to his men,
Who ran, some five or six, and beat
His head to pieces at their feet.

Then Godmar turn'd again and said:
"So Jehane, the first fitte is read!
Take note, my lady, that your way
Lies backward to the Chatelet!"
She shook her head and gazed awhile
At her cold hands with a rueful smile,
As though this thing had made her mad.

This was the parting that they had
Beside the haystack in the floods.

1858

TWO RED ROSES ACROSS THE MOON

There was a lady lived in a hall,
Large of her eyes and slim and tall;
And ever she sung from noon to noon,
Two red roses across the moon.

There was a knight came riding by
In early spring, when the roads were dry;
And he heard that lady sing at the noon,
Two red roses across the moon.

Yet none the more he stopp'd at all,
But he rode a-gallop past the hall;
And left that lady singing at noon,
Two red roses across the moon.

Because, forsooth, the battle was set,
And the scarlet and blue had got to be met,
He rode on the spur till the next warm noon:
Two red roses across the moon.

But the battle was scatter'd from hill to hill,
From the windmill to the watermill;
And he said to himself, as it near'd the noon,
Two red roses across the moon.

You scarce could see for the scarlet and blue,
A golden helm or a golden shoe:
So he cried, as the fight grew thick at the noon,
Two red roses across the moon!

Verily then the gold bore through
The huddled spears of the scarlet and blue;
And they cried, as they cut them down at the noon,
Two red roses across the moon!

I trow he stopp'd when he rode again
By the hall, though draggled sore with the rain;
And his lips were pinch'd to kiss at the noon
Two red roses across the moon.

Under the may she stoop'd to the crown,
All was gold, there was nothing of brown,
And the horns blew up in the hall at noon,
Two red roses across the moon.

1858

PRAISE OF MY LADY

My lady seems of ivory,
Forehead, straight nose, and cheeks that be
Hollow'd a little mournfully.
Beata mea Domina!

Her forehead, overshadow'd much
By bows of hair, has a wave such
As God was good to make for me.
Beata mea Domina!

Not greatly long my lady's hair,
Nor yet with yellow colour fair,
But thick and crispèd wonderfully:
Beata mea Domina!

Heavy to make the pale face sad,
And dark, but dead as though it had
Been forged by God most wonderfully
—Beata mea Domina!—

Of some strange metal, thread by thread,
To stand out from my lady's head,
Not moving much to tangle me.
Beata mea Domina!

Beneath her brows the lids fall slow,
The lashes a clear shadow throw
Where I would wish my lips to be.
Beata mea Domina!

Her great eyes, standing far apart,
Draw up some memory from her heart,
And gaze out very mournfully;
—Beata mea Domina!—

So beautiful and kind they are,
But most times looking out afar,
Waiting for something, not for me.
Beata mea Domina!

I wonder if the lashes long
Are those that do her bright eyes wrong,
For always half tears seem to be
—Beata mea Domina!—

Lurking below the underlid,
Darkening the place where they lie hid—
If they should rise and flow for me!
Beata mea Domina!

Her full lips being made to kiss,
Curl'd up and pensive each one is;
This makes me faint to stand and see.
Beata mea Domina!

Her lips are not contented now,
Because the hours pass so slow
Towards a sweet time: (pray for me),
—Beata mea Domina!—

Nay, hold thy peace! for who can tell;
But this at least I know full well,
Her lips are parted longingly,
—Beata mea Domina!—

So passionate and swift to move,
To pluck at any flying love,
That I grow faint to stand and see.
Beata mea Domina!

Yea! there beneath them is her chin,
So fine and round, it were a sin
To feel no weaker when I see
—Beata mea Domina!—

God's dealings; for with so much care
And troublous, faint lines wrought in there,
He finishes her face for me.
Beata mea Domina!

Of her long neck what shall I say?
What things about her body's sway,
Like a knight's pennon or slim tree
—Beata mea Domina!—

Set gently waving in the wind;
Or her long hands that I may find
On some day sweet to move o'er me?
Beata mea Domina!

God pity me though, if I miss'd
The telling, how along her wrist
The veins creep, dying languidly
—Beata mea Domina!—

Inside her tender palm and thin.
Now give me pardon, dear, wherein
My voice is weak and vexes thee.
Beata mea Domina!

All men that see her any time,
I charge you straightly in this rhyme,
What, and wherever you may be,
—Beata mea Domina!—

To kneel before her; as for me,
I choke and grow quite faint to see
My lady moving graciously.
Beata mea Domina!

1858

From THE LIFE AND DEATH OF JASON

I I Know a Little Garden-Close

I KNOW a little garden-close,
Set thick with lily and red rose,
Where I would wander if I might
From dewy morn to dewy night,
And have one with me wandering.

And though within it no birds sing,
And though no pillared house is there,
And though the apple-boughs are bare
Of fruit and blossom, would to God
Her feet upon the green grass trod,
And I beheld them as before.

There comes a murmur from the shore,
And in the close two fair streams are,
Drawn from the purple hills afar,
Drawn down unto the restless sea:
Dark hills whose heath-bloom feeds no bee,
Dark shore no ship has ever seen,
Tormented by the billows green
Whose murmur comes unceasingly
Unto the place for which I cry.

For which I cry both day and night,
For which I let slip all delight,
Whereby I grow both deaf and blind,
Careless to win, unskilled to find,
And quick to lose what all men seek.

Yet tottering as I am and weak,
Still have I left a little breath
To seek within the jaws of death
An entrance to that happy place,
To seek the unforgotten face,
Once seen, once kissed, once reft from me
Anigh the murmuring of the sea.

II O Death, That Maketh Life So Sweet

O death, that maketh life so sweet,
O fear, with mirth before thy feet,
What have ye yet in store for us,
The conquerors, the glorious?

Men say: "For fear that thou shouldst die
To-morrow, let to-day pass by
Flower-crowned and singing;" yet have we
Passed our to-day upon the sea,
Or in a poisonous unknown land,
With fear and death on either hand,
And listless when the day was done
Have scarcely hoped to see the sun
Dawn on the morrow of the earth,
Nor in our hearts have thought of mirth.
And while the world lasts, scarce again
Shall any sons of men bear pain
Like we have borne, yet be alive.

So surely not in vain we strive
Like other men for our reward;
Sweet peace and deep, the chequered sward
Beneath the ancient mulberry-trees,
The smooth-paved gilded palaces,
Where the shy thin-clad damsels sweet
Make music with their gold-ringed feet.
The fountain court amidst of it,
Where the short-haired slave maidens sit,
While on the veined pavement lie
The honied things and spicery
Their arms have borne from out the town.

The dancers on the thymy down
In summer twilight, when the earth
Is still of all things but their mirth,
And echoes borne upon the wind
Of others in like way entwined.

The merchant-town's fair market-place,
Where over many a changing face
The pigeons of the temple flit,
And still the outland merchants sit
Like kings above their merchandise,
Lying to foolish men and wise.

Ah! if they heard that we were come
Into the bay, and bringing home
That which all men have talked about,
Some men with rage, and some with doubt,
Some with desire, and some with praise;
Then would the people throng the ways,
Nor heed the outland merchandise,
Nor any talk, from fools or wise,
But tales of our accomplished quest.

What soul within the house shall rest
When we come home? The wily king
Shall leave his throne to see the thing;
No man shall keep the landward gate,
The hurried traveller shall wait
Until our bulwarks graze the quay,
Unslain the milk-white bull shall be
Beside the quivering altar-flame;
Scarce shall the maiden clasp for shame
Over her breast the raiment thin
The morn that Argo cometh in.

Then cometh happy life again
That payeth well our toil and pain
In that sweet hour, when all our woe
But as a pensive tale we know,
Nor yet remember deadly fear;
For surely now if death be near,
Unthought-of is it, and unseen
When sweet is, that hath bitter been.

1867

From THE EARTHLY PARADISE

I An Apology

Of Heaven or Hell I have no power to sing,
I cannot ease the burden of your fears,
Or make quick-coming death a little thing,
Or bring again the pleasure of past years,
Nor for my words shall ye forget your tears,
Or hope again, for aught that I can say,
The idle singer of an empty day.

But rather, when aweary of your mirth,
From full hearts still unsatisfied ye sigh,
And, feeling kindly unto all the earth,
Grudge every minute as it passes by,
Made the more mindful that the sweet days die—
Remember me a little then, I pray,
The idle singer of an empty day.

The heavy trouble, the bewildering care
That weighs us down who live and earn our bread,
These idle verses have no power to bear;
So let me sing of names remembered,
Because they, living not, can ne'er be dead,
Or long time take their memory quite away
From us poor singers of an empty day.

Dreamer of dreams, born out of my due time,
Why should I strive to set the crooked straight?
Let it suffice me that my murmuring rhyme
Beats with light wing against the ivory gate,
Telling a tale not too importunate
To those who in the sleepy region stay,
Lulled by the singer of an empty day.

Folk say, a wizard to a northern king
At Christmas-tide such wondrous things did show,
That through one window men beheld the spring,
And through another saw the summer glow,
And through a third the fruited vines a-row,
While still, unheard, but in its wonted way,
Piped the drear wind of that December day.

So with this Earthly Paradise it is,
If ye will read aright, and pardon me,
Who strive to build a shadowy isle of bliss
Midmost the beating of the steely sea,
Where tossed about all hearts of men must be;
Whose ravening monsters mighty men shall slay,
Not the poor singer of an empty day.

II March

Slayer of the winter, art thou here again?
O welcome, thou that bring'st the summer nigh!
The bitter wind makes not thy victory vain,
Nor will we mock thee for thy faint blue sky.
Welcome, O March! whose kindly days and dry
Make April ready for the throstle's song,
Thou first redresser of the winter's wrong!

Yea, welcome, March! and though I die ere June,
Yet for the hope of life I give thee praise,
Striving to swell the burden of the tune
That even now I hear thy brown birds raise,
Unmindful of the past or coming days;
Who sing: "O joy! a new year is begun:
What happiness to look upon the sun!"

Ah, what begetteth all this storm of bliss
But Death himself, who crying solemnly,
E'en from the heart of sweet Forgetfulness,
Bids us, "Rejoice, lest pleasureless ye die.
Within a little time must ye go by.
Stretch forth your open hands, and while ye live
Take all the gifts that Death and Life may give."

III June

O June, O June, that we desired so,
Wilt thou not make us happy on this day?
Across the river thy soft breezes blow
Sweet with the scent of beanfields far away,
Above our heads rustle the aspens grey,
Calm is the sky with harmless clouds beset,
No thought of storm the morning vexes yet.

See, we have left our hopes and fears behind
To give our very hearts up unto thee;
What better place than this then could we find
By this sweet stream that knows not of the sea,
That guesses not the city's misery,
This little stream whose hamlets scarce have names,
This far-off, lonely mother of the Thames?

Here then, O June, thy kindness will we take;
And if indeed but pensive men we seem,
What should we do? thou wouldst not have us wake
From out the arms of this rare happy dream
And wish to leave the murmur of the stream,
The rustling boughs, the twitter of the birds,
And all thy thousand peaceful happy words.

IV The Lady of the Land

Argument: A certain man, having landed on an island in the Greek Sea, found there a beautiful damsel, whom he fain would have delivered from a strange and dreadful doom, but failing herein, he died soon afterwards.

It happened once, some men of Italy
Midst the Greek Islands went a sea-roving,
And much good fortune had they on the sea:

Of many a man they had the ransoming,
And many a chain they gat, and goodly thing;
And midst their voyage to an isle they came,
Whereof my story keepeth not the name.

Now though but little was there left to gain,
Because the richer folk had gone away,
Yet since, by this, of water they were fain,
They came to anchor in a land-locked bay,
Whence in a while some went ashore to play,
Going but lightly armed in twos or threes,
For midst that folk they feared no enemies.

And of these fellows that thus went ashore,
One was there who left all his friends behind;
Who going inland ever more and more,
And being left quite alone, at last did find
A lonely valley sheltered from the wind,
Wherein, amidst an ancient cypress wood,
A long-deserted ruined castle stood.

The wood, once ordered in fair grove and
glade,
With gardens overlooked by terraces,
And marble-pavéd pools for pleasure made,
Was tangled now, and choked with fallen
trees;
And he who went there, with but little ease
Must stumble by the stream's side, once made
meet
For tender women's dainty wandering feet.

The raven's croak, the low wind choked
and drear,
The baffled stream, the gray wolf's doleful
cry,
Were all the sounds that mariner could hear,
As through the wood he wandered painfully;
But as unto the house he drew anigh,
The pillars of a ruined shrine he saw,
The once fair temple of a fallen law.

No image was there left behind to tell
Before whose face the knees of men had
bowed;
An altar of black stone, of old wrought well,
Alone beneath a ruined roof now showed
The goal whereto the folk were wont to
crowd,
Seeking for things forgotten long ago,
Praying for heads long ages laid a-low.

Close to the temple was the castle-gate,
Doorless and crumbling; there our fellow
turned,
Trembling indeed at what might chance to
wait
The prey entrapped, yet with a heart that
burned
To know the most of what might there be
learned,
And hoping somewhat too, amid his fear,
To light on such things as all men hold dear.

Noble the house was, nor seemed built for
war,
But rather like the work of other days,
When men, in better peace than now they are,
Had leisure on the world around to gaze,
And noted well the past times' changing
ways;
And fair with sculptured stories it was
wrought,
By lapse of time unto dim ruin brought.

Now as he looked about on all these
things,
And strove to read the moldering histories,
Above the door an image with wise wings,
Whose unclad limbs a serpent seemed to
seize,
He dimly saw, although the western breeze,
And years of biting frost and washing rain,
Had made the carver's labor wellnigh vain.

But this, though perished sore, and worn
away,
He noted well, because it seemed to be,
After the fashion of another day,
Some great man's badge of war, or armory,
And round it a carved wreath he seemed to
see;
But taking note of these things, at the last
The mariner beneath the gateway passed.

And there a lovely cloistered court he
found,
A fountain in the midst, o'erthrown and dry,
And in the cloister briers twining round
The slender shafts; the wondrous imagery
Outworn by more than many years gone by,
Because the country people, in their fear
Of wizardry, had wrought destruction here;

And piteously these fair things had been maimed—
There stood great Jove, lacking his head of might;
Here was the archer, swift Apollo, lamed;
The shapely limbs of Venus hid from sight
By weeds and shards; Diana's ankles light
Bound with the cable of some coasting ship;
And rusty nails through Helen's maddening lip.

Therefrom unto the chambers did he pass,
And found them fair still, midst of their decay,
Though in them now no sign of man there was,
And everything but stone had passed away
That made them lovely in that vanished day;
Nay, the mere walls themselves would soon be gone
And naught be left but heaps of moldering stone.

But he, when all the place he had gone o'er,
And with much trouble clomb the broken stair,
And from the topmost turret seen the shore
And his good ship drawn up at anchor there,
Came down again, and found a crypt most fair,
Built wonderfully beneath the greatest hall;
And there he saw a door within the wall,

Well-hinged, close-shut; nor was there in that place
Another on its hinges—therefore he
Stood there and pondered for a little space,
And thought, "Perchance some marvel I shall see,
For surely here some dweller there must be,
Because this door seems whole, and new, and sound,
While naught but ruin I can see around."

So with that word, moved by a strong desire,
He tried the hasp, that yielded to his hand,
And in a strange place, lit as by a fire
Unseen but near, he presently did stand;
And by an odorous breeze his face was fanned,
As though in some Arabian plain he stood,
Anigh the border of a spice-tree wood.

He moved not for a while, but looking round,
He wondered much to see the place so fair,
Because, unlike the castle above ground,
No pillager or wrecker had been there;
It seemed that time had passed on otherwhere,
Nor laid a finger on this hidden place,
Rich with the wealth of some forgotten race.

With hangings, fresh as when they left the loom,
The walls were hung a space above the head;
Slim ivory chairs were set about the room;
And in one corner was a dainty bed,
That seemed for some fair queen appareléd;
And marble was the worst stone of the floor,
That with rich Indian webs was covered o'er.

The wanderer trembled when he saw all this,
Because he deemed by magic it was wrought;
Yet in his heart a longing for some bliss,
Whereof the hard and changing world knows naught,
Arose and urged him on, and dimmed the thought
That there perchance some devil lurked to slay
The heedless wanderer from the light of day.

Over against him was another door
Set in the wall; so, casting fear aside,
With hurried steps he crossed the varied floor,
And there again the silver latch he tried,
And with no pain the door he opened wide,
And entering the new chamber cautiously
The glory of great heaps of gold could see.

Upon the floor uncounted medals lay,
Like things of little value; here and there
Stood golden caldrons, that might well outweigh
The biggest midst an emperor's copper-ware,
And golden cups were set on tables fair,
Themselves of gold; and in all hollow things
Were stored great gems, worthy the crowns of kings.

The walls and roof with gold were overlaid,
And precious raiment from the wall hung down;
The fall of kings that treasure might have stayed,

Or gained some longing conqueror great renown,
Or built again some god-destroyed old town;
What wonder, if this plunderer of the sea
Stood gazing at it long and dizzily?

But at the last his troubled eyes and dazed
He lifted from the glory of that gold,
And then the image, that, wellnigh erased,
Over the castle-gate he did behold,
Above a door well wrought in colored gold
Again he saw—a naked girl with wings
Enfolded in a serpent's scaly rings.

And even as his eyes were fixed on it
A woman's voice came from the other side,
And through his heart strange hopes began to flit
That in some wondrous land he might abide
Not dying, master of a deathless bride;
So o'er the gold he scarcely now could see
He went, and passed this last door eagerly.

Then in a room he stood wherein there was
A marble bath, whose brimming water yet
Was scarcely still; a vessel of green glass
Half full of odorous ointment was there set
Upon the topmost step that still was wet,
And jeweled shoes and women's dainty gear
Lay cast upon the varied pavement near.

In one quick glance these things his eyes did see,
But speedily they turned round to behold
Another sight, for throned on ivory
There sat a girl, whose dripping tresses rolled
On to the floor in waves of gleaming gold,
Cast back from such a form as, erewhile shown
To one poor shepherd, lighted up Troy town.

Naked she was; the kisses of her feet
Upon the floor a dying path had made
From the full bath unto her ivory seat;
In her right hand, upon her bosom laid,
She held a golden comb; a mirror weighed
Her left hand down; aback her fair head lay,
Dreaming, awake, of some long vanished day.

Her eyes were shut, but she seemed not to sleep;
Her lips were murmuring things unheard and low,
Or sometimes twitched as though she needs must weep
Though from her eyes the tears refused to flow;
And oft with heavenly red her cheek did glow,
As if remembrance of some half-sweet shame
Across the web of many memories came.

There stood the man, scarce daring to draw breath
For fear the lovely sight should fade away;
Forgetting heaven, forgetting life and death,
Trembling for fear lest something he should say
Unwitting, lest some sob should yet betray
His presence there, for to his eager eyes
Already did the tears begin to rise.

But as he gazed, she moved, and with a sigh
Bent forward, dropping down her golden head;
"Alas, alas! another day gone by,
Another day and no soul come," she said;
"Another year, and still I am not dead!"
And with that word once more her head she raised,
And on the trembling man with great eyes gazed.

Then he imploring hands to her did reach,
And toward her very slowly 'gan to move
And with wet eyes her pity did beseech,
And seeing her about to speak, he strove
From trembling lips to utter words of love;
And with a look she stayed his doubtful feet,
And made sweet music as their eyes did meet.

For now she spoke in gentle voice and clear,
Using the Greek tongue that he knew full well:
"What man art thou, that thus hast wandered here,
And found this lonely chamber where I dwell?
Beware, beware! for I have many a spell;
If greed of power and gold have led thee on,
Not lightly shall this untold wealth be won.

"But if thou com'st here, knowing of my tale,
In hope to bear away my body fair,
Stout must thine heart be, nor shall that avail
If thou a wicked heart in thee dost bear;
So once again I bid thee to beware,
Because no base man things like this may see,
And live thereafter long and happily."

"Lady," he said, "in Florence is my home,
And in my city noble is my name;
Neither on peddling voyage am I come,
But, like my fathers, bent to gather fame;
And though thy face has set my heart a-flame,
Yet of thy story nothing do I know,
But here have wandered heedlessly enow.

"But since the sight of thee mine eyes did bless,
What can I be but thine? what wouldst thou have?
From those thy words, I deem from some distress
By deeds of mine thy dear life I might save;
Oh, then, delay not! if one ever gave
His life to any, mine I give to thee;
Come, tell me what the price of love must be?—

"Swift death, to be with thee a day and night
And with the earliest dawning to be slain?
Or better, a long year of great delight,
And many years of misery and pain?
Or worse, and this poor hour for all my gain?
A sorry merchant am I on this day;
E'en as thou willest, so must I obey."

She said, "What brave words! Naught divine am I,
But an unhappy and unheard-of maid,
Compelled by evil fate and destiny
To live, who long ago should have been laid
Under the earth within the cypress shade.
Hearken awhile, and quickly shalt thou know
What deed I pray thee to accomplish now.

"God grant indeed thy words are not for naught!
Then shalt thou save me, since for many a day
To such a dreadful life I have been brought.
Nor will I spare with all my heart to pay
What man soever takes my grief away;
Ah! I will love thee, if thou lovest me
But well enough my savior now to be.

"My father lived a many years agone,
Lord of this land, master of all cunning,
Who ruddy gold could draw from out gray stone,
And gather wealth from many an uncouth thing;
He made the wilderness rejoice and sing,
And such a leech he was that none could say
Without his word what soul should pass away.

"Unto Diana such a gift he gave,
Goddess above, below, and on the earth,
That I should be her virgin and her slave
From the first hour of my most wretched birth;
Therefore my life had known but little mirth
When I had come unto my twentieth year
And the last time of hallowing drew anear.

"So in her temple had I lived and died
And all would long ago have passed away,
But ere that time came, did strange things betide,
Whereby I am alive unto this day;
Alas, the bitter words that I must say!
Ah! can I bring my wretched tongue to tell
How I was brought unto this fearful hell?

"A queen I was; what gods I knew I loved,
And nothing evil was there in my thought,
And yet by love my wretched heart was moved
Until to utter ruin I was brought!
Alas! thou sayest our gods were vain and naught;
Wait, wait, till thou hast heard this tale of mine—
Then shalt thou think them devilish or divine.

"Hearken! in spite of father and of vow,
I loved a man; but for that sin I think
Men had forgiven me—yea, yea, even thou;
But from the gods the full cup must I drink,
And into misery unheard of sink,
Tormented, when their own names are forgot,
And men must doubt e'er if they lived or not.

"Glorious my lover was unto my sight,
Most beautiful—of love we grew so fain
That we at last agreed that on a night
We should be happy, but that he were slain
Or shut in hold; and neither joy nor pain
Should else forbid that hoped-for time to be;
So came the night that made a wretch of me.

"Ah! well do I remember all that night,
When through the window shone the orb of June,
And by the bed flickered the taper's light,
Whereby I trembled, gazing at the moon;
Ah me! the meeting that we had, when soon
Into his strong, well-trusted arms I fell,
And many a sorrow we began to tell.

"Ah me! what parting on that night we had!
I think the story of my great despair
A little while might merry folk make sad;
For, as he swept away my yellow hair
To make my shoulder and my bosom bare,
I raised mine eyes, and shuddering could behold
A shadow cast upon the bed of gold;

"Then suddenly was quenched my hot desire,
And he untwined his arms; the moon, so pale
A while ago, seemed changed to blood and fire,
And yet my limbs beneath me did not fail,
And neither had I strength to cry or wail,
But stood there helpless, bare, and shivering,
With staring eyes still fixed upon the thing.

"Because the shade that on the bed of gold
The changed and dreadful moon was throwing down
Was of Diana, whom I did behold,
With knotted hair, and shining girt-up gown,
And on the high white brow, a deadly frown
Bent upon us, who stood scarce drawing breath,
Striving to meet the horrible sure death.

"No word at all the dreadful goddess said,
But soon across my feet my lover lay,
And well indeed I knew that he was dead;
And would that I had died on that same day!
For in a while the image turned away,
And without words my doom I understood,
And felt a horror change my human blood.

"And there I fell, and on the floor I lay
By the dead man, till daylight came on me,
And not a word thenceforward could I say
For three years; till of grief and misery,
The lingering pest, the cruel enemy,
My father and his folk were dead and gone,
And in this castle I was left alone.

"And then the doom foreseen upon me fell,
For Queen Diana did my body change
Into a fork-tongued dragon flesh and fell,
And through the island nightly do I range,
Or in the green sea mate with monsters strange,
When in the middle of the moonlit night
The sleepy mariner I do affright.

"But all day long upon this gold I lie,
Within this place, where never mason's hand
Smote trowel on the marble noisily;
Drowsy I lie, no folk at my command,
Who once was called the Lady of the Land;
Who might have bought a kingdom with a kiss,
Yea, half the world with such a sight as this."

And therewithal, with rosy fingers light,
Backward her heavy-hanging hair she threw,
To give her naked beauty more to sight;
But when, forgetting all the things he knew,
Maddened with love unto the prize he drew,
She cried, "Nay, wait! for wherefore wilt thou die;
Why should we not be happy, thou and I?

"Wilt thou not save me? Once in every year
This rightful form of mine that thou dost see
By favor of the goddess have I here
From sunrise unto sunset given me,
That some brave man may end my misery.
And thou—art thou not brave? can thy heart fail,
Whose eyes e'en now are weeping at my tale?

"Then listen! when this day is overpast,
A fearful monster shall I be again,
And thou mayst be my savior at the last—
Unless, once more, thy words are naught and vain.
If thou of love and sovereignty art fain,
Come thou next morn, and when thou seest here
A hideous dragon, have thereof no fear.

"But take the loathsome head up in thine hands,
And kiss it, and be master presently
Of twice the wealth that is in all the lands,
From Cathay to the head of Italy;
And master also, if it pleaseth thee,
Of all thou praisest as so fresh and bright,
Of what thou callest crown of all delight.

"Ah! with what joy then shall I see again
The sunlight on the green grass and the trees,
And hear the clatter of the summer rain,
And see the joyous folk beyond the seas;
Ah, me! to hold my child upon my knees,
After the weeping of unkindly tears,
And all the wrongs of these four hundred years.

"Go now, go quick! leave this gray heap of stone;
And from thy glad heart think upon thy way,
How I shall love thee—yea, love thee alone,
That bringest me from dark death unto day;
For this shall be thy wages and thy pay;
Unheard-of wealth, unheard-of love is near,
If thou hast heart a little dread to bear."

Therewith she turned to go; but he cried out,
"Ah! wilt thou leave me then without one kiss,
To slay the very seeds of fear and doubt,
That glad tomorrow may bring certain bliss?
Hast thou forgotten how love lives by this,
The memory of some hopeful close embrace,
Low whispered words within some lonely place?"

But she, when his bright glittering eyes she saw,
And burning cheeks, cried out, "Alas, alas!
Must I be quite undone, and wilt thou draw
A worse fate on me than the first one was?
Oh, haste thee from this fatal place to pass!
Yet, ere thou goest, take this, lest thou shouldst deem
Thou hast been fooled by some strange mid-day dream."

So saying, blushing like a new-kissed maid,
From off her neck a little gem she drew,
That, 'twixt those snowy rose-tinged hillocks laid,
The secrets of her glorious beauty knew;
And ere he well perceived what she would do,
She touched his hand, the gem within it lay,
And, turning, from his sight she fled away.

Then at the doorway where her rosy heel
Had glanced and vanished, he awhile did stare,
And still upon his hand he seemed to feel
The varying kisses of her fingers fair;
Then turned he toward the dreary crypt and bare,
And dizzily throughout the castle passed,
Till by the ruined fane he stood at last.

Then weighing still the gem within his hand,
He stumbled backward through the cypress wood,
Thinking the while of some strange lovely land,
Where all his life should be most fair and good
Till on the valley's wall of hills he stood,
And slowly thence passed down unto the bay
Red with the death of that bewildering day.

The next day came, and he, who all the night
Had ceaselessly been turning in his bed,
Arose and clad himself in armor bright,
And many a danger he rememberéd—
Storming of towns, lone sieges full of dread,
That with renown his heart had borne him through—
And this thing seemed a little thing to do.

So on he went, and on the way he thought
Of all the glorious things of yesterday,
Naught of the price whereat they must be bought,
But ever to himself did softly say,
"No roaming now, my wars are passed away;
No long dull days devoid of happiness,
When such a love my yearning heart shall bless."

Thus to the castle did he come at last,
But when unto the gateway he drew near,
And underneath its ruined archway passed
Into the court, a strange noise did he hear,
And through his heart there shot a pang of fear;
Trembling, he gat his sword into his hand,
And midmost of the cloisters took his stand.

But for a while that unknown noise increased,
A rattling, that with strident roars did blend,
And whining moans; but suddenly it ceased—
A fearful thing stood at the cloister's end,
And eyed him for a while, then 'gan to wend

Adown the cloisters, and began again
That rattling, and the moan like fiends in pain.

And as it came on toward him, with its teeth
The body of a slain goat did it tear,
The blood whereof in its hot jaws did seethe,
And on its tongue he saw the smoking hair;
Then his heart sank, and standing trembling there,
Throughout his mind wild thoughts and fearful ran,
"Some fiend she was," he said, "the bane of man."

Yet he abode her still, although his blood
Curdled within him. The thing dropped the goat,
And creeping on, came close to where he stood,
And raised its head to him, and wrinkled throat;
Then he cried out and wildly at her smote,
Shutting his eyes, and turned and from the place
Ran swiftly, with a white and ghastly face.

But little things rough stones and tree-trunks seemed,
And if he fell, he rose and ran on still.
No more he felt his hurts than if he dreamed;
He made no stay for valley or steep hill;
Heedless, he dashed through many a foaming rill,
Until he came unto the ship at last,
And with no word into the deep hold passed.

Meanwhile the dragon, seeing him clean gone,
Followed him not, but crying horribly,
Caught up within her jaws a block of stone
And ground it into powder, then turned she,
With cries that folk could hear far out at sea,
And reached the treasure set apart of old,
To brood above the hidden heaps of gold.

Yet was she seen again on many a day
By some half-waking mariner, or heard,
Playing amid the ripples of the bay,
Or on the hills making all things afeard,
Or in the wood, that did that castle gird,
But never any man again durst go
To seek her woman's form, and end her woe.

As for the man, who knows what things he bore?
What mournful faces peopled the sad night,
What wailings vexed him with reproaches sore,
What images of that nigh-gained delight!
What dreamed caresses from soft hands and white,
Turning to horrors ere they reached the best!
What struggles vain, what shame, what huge unrest!

No man he knew; three days he lay and raved,
And cried for death, until a lethargy
Fell on him, and his fellows thought him saved;
But on the third night he awoke to die;
And at Byzantium doth his body lie
Between two blossoming pomegranate trees,
Within the churchyard of the Genoese.

V October

O love, turn from the unchanging sea and gaze
Down these grey slopes upon the year grown old,
A-dying mid the autumn-scented haze,
That hangeth o'er the hollow in the wold,
Where the wind-bitten ancient elms enfold
Grey church, long barn, orchard, and red-roofed stead,
Wrought in dead days for men a long while dead.

Come down, O love; may not our hands still meet,
Since still we live to-day, forgetting June,
Forgetting May, deeming October sweet—
O hearken, hearken! through the afternoon,
The grey tower sings a strange old tinkling tune!
Sweet, sweet, and sad, the toiling year's last breath,
Too satiate of life to strive with death.

And we too—will it not be soft and kind,
That rest from life, from patience and from pain;
That rest from bliss we know not when we find;
That rest from Love which ne'er the end can gain?—
Hark, how the tune swells that erewhile did wane!
Look up, love!—ah, cling close and never move!
How can I have enough of life and love?

VI Song

From *Cupid and Psyche*

O PENSIVE, tender maid, downcast and shy,
Who turnest pale e'en at the name of love,
And with flushed face must pass the elm-tree by,
Ashamed to hear the passionate grey dove
Moan to his mate, thee too the god shall move,
Thee too the maidens shall ungird one day,
And with thy girdle put thy shame away.

What then, and shall white winter ne'er be done
Because the glittering frosty morn is fair?
Because against the early-setting sun
Bright show the gilded boughs, though waste and bare?
Because the robin singeth free from care?
Ah! these are memories of a better day
When on earth's face the lips of summer lay.

Come then, beloved one, for such as thee
Love loveth, and their hearts he knoweth well,
Who hoard their moments of felicity,
As misers hoard the medals that they tell,
Lest on the earth but paupers they should dwell:
"We hide our love to bless another day;
The world is hard, youth passes quick," they say.

Ah, little ones, but if ye could forget
Amidst your outpoured love that you must die,
Then ye, my servants, were death's conquerors yet,
And love to you should be eternity,
How quick soever might the days go by:
Yes, ye are made immortal on the day
Ye cease the dusty grains of time to weigh.

Thou hearkenest, love? O, make no semblance then
That thou art loved, but as thy custom is
Turn thy grey eyes away from eyes of men.
With hands down-dropped, that tremble with thy bliss,
With hidden eyes, take thy first lover's kiss;
Call this eternity which is to-day,
Nor dream that this our love can pass away.

VII Song

From *Ogier the Dane*

HÆC

In the white-flowered hawthorn brake,
Love, be merry for my sake;
Twine the blossoms in my hair,
Kiss me where I am most fair—
Kiss me, love! for who knoweth
What thing cometh after death?

ILLE

Nay, the garlanded gold hair
Hides thee where thou art most fair;
Hides the rose-tinged hills of snow—
Ah, sweet love, I have thee now!
Kiss me, love! for who knoweth
What thing cometh after death?

HÆC

Shall we weep for a dead day,
Or set Sorrow in our way?
Hidden by my golden hair,
Wilt thou weep that sweet days wear?
Kiss me, love! for who knoweth
What thing cometh after death?

ILLE

Weep, O Love, the days that flit,
Now, while I can feel thy breath;
Then may I remember it
Sad and old, and near my death.
Kiss me, love! for who knoweth
What thing cometh after death!

VIII Song

From *The Story of Acontius and Cydippe*

Fair is the night and fair the day,
Now April is forgot of May,
Now into June May falls away;
Fair day, fair night, O give me back
The tide that all fair things did lack
Except my love, except my sweet!

Blow back, O wind! thou art not kind,
Though thou art sweet; thou hast no mind
Her hair about my sweet to wind;
O flowery sward, though thou art bright,
I praise thee not for thy delight,
Thou hast not kissed her silver feet.

Thou know'st her not, O rustling tree,
What dost thou then to shadow me,
Whose shade her breast did never see?
O flowers, in vain ye bow adown!
Ye have not felt her odorous gown
Brush past your heads my lips to meet.

Flow on, great river—thou mayst deem
That far away, a summer stream,
Thou sawest her limbs amidst thee gleam
And kissed her foot, and kissed her knee,
Yet get thee swift unto the sea!
With nought of true thou wilt me greet.

And thou that men call by my name,
O helpless one, hast thou no shame
That thou must even look the same,
As while agone, as while agone,
When thou and she were left alone,
And hands, and lips, and tears did meet?

Grow weak and pine, lie down to die,
O body in thy misery,
Because short time and sweet goes by;
O foolish heart, how weak thou art!
Break, break, because thou needs must part
From thine own love, from thine own sweet!

1870

IX Song

From *The Hill of Venus*

Before our lady came on earth
Little there was of joy or mirth;
About the borders of the sea
The sea-folk wandered heavily;
About the wintry river side
The weary fishers would abide.

Alone within the weaving-room
The girls would sit before the loom,
And sing no song, and play no play;
Alone from dawn to hot mid-day,
From mid-day unto evening,
The men afield would work, nor sing,
'Mid weary thoughts of man and God,
Before thy feet the wet ways trod.

Unkissed the merchant bore his care,
Unkissed the knights went out to war,
Unkissed the mariner came home,
Unkissed the minstrel men did roam.

Or in the stream the maids would stare,
Nor know why they were made so fair;
Their yellow locks, their bosoms white,
Their limbs well wrought for all delight,
Seemed foolish things that waited death,
As hopeless as the flowers beneath
The weariness of unkissed feet:
No life was bitter then, or sweet.

Therefore, O Venus, well may we
Praise the green ridges of the sea
O'er which, upon a happy day,
Thou cam'st to take our shame away.
Well may we praise the curdling foam
Amidst the which thy feet did bloom,
Flowers of the gods; the yellow sand
They kissed atwixt the sea and land;
The bee-beset ripe-seeded grass,
Through which thy fine limbs first did pass;
The purple-dusted butterfly,
First blown against thy quivering thigh;
The first red rose that touched thy side,
And over-blown and fainting died;
The flickering of the orange shade,
Where first in sleep thy limbs were laid;
The happy day's sweet life and death,
Whose air first caught thy balmy breath—
Yea, all these things well praised may be,
But with what words shall we praise thee—
O Venus, O thou love alive,
Born to give peace to souls that strive?

1868–1870

SONGS *from* LOVE IS ENOUGH

I

Love is enough: have no thought for to-morrow
If ye lie down this even in rest from your pain,
Ye who have paid for your bliss with great sorrow;
For as it was once so it shall be again.
Ye shall cry out for death as ye stretch forth in vain

Feeble hands to the hands that would help but they may not,
Cry out to deaf ears that would hear if they could;
Till again shall the change come, and words your lips say not
Your hearts make all plain in the best wise they would
And the world ye thought waning is glorious and good:

And no morning now mocks you and no nightfall is weary,
The plains are not empty of song and of deed:
The sea strayeth not, nor the mountains are dreary;
The wind is not helpless for any man's need,
Nor falleth the rain but for thistle and weed.

O surely this morning all sorrow is hidden,
All battle is hushed for this even at least;
And no one this noontide may hunger, un-bidden
To the flowers and the singing and the joy of your feast
Where silent ye sit midst the world's tale increased.

Lo, the lovers unloved that draw nigh for your blessing!
For your tale makes the dreaming whereby yet they live
The dreams of the day with their hopes of re-dressing,
The dreams of the night with the kisses they give,
The dreams of the dawn wherein death and hope strive.

Ah what shall we say then, but that earth threatened often
Shall live on for ever that such things may be,
That the dry seed shall quicken, the hard earth shall soften,
And the spring-bearing birds flutter north o'er the sea,
That earth's garden may bloom round my love's feet and me?

II

Love is enough: it grew up without heeding
In the days when ye knew not its name nor its measure,
And its leaflets untrodden by the light feet of pleasure
Had no boast of the blossom, no sign of the seeding,
As the morning and evening passed over its treasure.

And what do ye say then?—that Spring long departed
Has brought forth no child to the softness and showers;
—That we slept and we dreamed through the Summer of flowers;
We dreamed of the Winter, and waking dead-hearted
Found Winter upon us and waste of dull hours.

Nay, Spring was o'er happy and knew not the reason,
And Summer dreamed sadly, for she thought all was ended
In her fulness of wealth that might not be amended;
But this is the harvest and the garnering season,
And the leaf and the blossom in the ripe fruit are blended.

It sprang without sowing, it grew without heeding,
Ye knew not its name and ye knew not its measure,
Ye noted it not 'mid your hope and your pleasure;
There was pain in its blossom, despair in its seeding,
But daylong your bosom now nurseth its treasure.

III

LOVE is enough: draw near and behold me,
Ye who pass by the way to your rest and your laughter,
And are full of the hope of the dawn coming after;
For the strong of the world have bought me and sold me
And my house is all wasted from threshold to rafter.
—Pass by me, and hearken, and think of me not!

Cry out and come near; for my ears may not hearken,
And my eyes are grown dim as the eyes of the dying.
Is this the gray rack o'er the sun's face a-flying?
Or is it your faces his brightness that darken?
Comes a wind from the sea, or is it your sighing?
—Pass by me and hearken, and pity me not!

Ye know not how void is your hope and your living:
Depart with your helping lest yet ye undo me!
Ye know not that at nightfall she draweth near to me,
There is soft speech between us and words of forgiving
Till in dead of the midnight her kisses thrill through me.
—Pass by me and hearken, and waken me not!

Wherewith will ye buy it, ye rich who behold me?
Draw out from your coffers your rest and your laughter,
And the fair gilded hope of the dawn coming after!
Nay this I sell not,—though ye bought me and sold me,—
For your house stored with such things from threshold to rafter.
—Pass by me, I hearken, and think of you not!

IV

LOVE is enough: through the trouble and tangle
From yesterday's dawning to yesterday's night
I sought through the vales where the prisoned winds wrangle,
Till, wearied and bleeding, at end of the light
I met him, and we wrestled, and great was my might.

O great was my joy, though no rest was around me,
Though 'mid wastes of the world were we twain all alone,
For methought that I conquered and he knelt and he crowned me,
And the driving rain ceased, and the wind ceased to moan,
And through clefts of the clouds her planet outshone.

O through clefts of the clouds 'gan the world to awaken,
And the bitter wind piped, and down drifted the rain,
And I was alone—and yet not forsaken,
For the grass was untrodden except by my pain:
With a Shadow of the Night had I wrestled in vain.

And the Shadow of the Night and not Love was departed;
I was sore, I was weary, yet Love lived to seek;
So I scaled the dark mountains, and wandered sad-hearted
Over wearier wastes, where e'en sunlight was bleak,
With no rest of the night for my soul waxen weak.

With no rest of the night; for I waked 'mid a story
Of a land wherein Love is the light and the lord,
Where my tale shall be heard, and my wounds gain a glory,
And my tears be a treasure to add to the hoard
Of pleasure laid up for his people's reward.

Ah, pleasure laid up! haste thou onward and listen,
For the wind of the waste has no music like this,
And not thus do the rocks of the wilderness glisten:
With the host of his faithful through sorrow and bliss
My Lord goeth forth now, and knows me for his.

V

Love is enough: cherish life that abideth,
Lest ye die ere ye know him, and curse and misname him;
For who knows in what ruin of all hope he hideth,
On what wings of the terror of darkness he rideth?
And what is the joy of man's life that ye blame him
For his bliss grown a sword, and his rest grown a fire?

Ye who tremble for death, or the death of desire,
Pass about the cold winter-tide garden and ponder
On the rose in his glory amidst of June's fire,
On the languor of noontide that gathered the thunder,
On the morn and its freshness, the eve and its wonder:
Ye may wake it no more—shall Spring come to awaken?

Live on, for Love liveth, and earth shall be shaken
By the wind of his wings on the triumphing morning,
When the dead, and their deeds that die not, shall awaken,
And the world's tale shall sound in your trumpet of warning,
And the sun smite the banner called Scorn of the Scorning,
And dead pain ye shall trample, dead fruitless desire,
As ye wend to pluck out the new world from the fire.

VI

Love is enough: while ye deemed him a-sleeping,
There were signs of his coming and sounds of his feet;
His touch it was that would bring you to weeping,
When the summer was deepest and music most sweet:
In his footsteps ye followed the day to its dying,
Ye went forth by his gown-skirts the morning to meet;
In his place on the beaten-down orchard-grass lying,
Of the sweet ways ye pondered yet left for life's trying.

Ah, what was all dreaming of pleasure anear you,
To the time when his eyes on your wistful eyes turned,
And ye saw his lips move, and his head bend to hear you,
As new-born and glad to his kindness ye yearned?
Ah, what was all dreaming of anguish and sorrow,
To the time when the world in his torment was burned,
And no god your heart from its prison might borrow,
And no rest was left, no to-day, no to-morrow?

All wonder of pleasure, all doubt of desire,
All blindness, are ended, and no more ye feel
If your feet tread his flowers or the flames of his fire,
If your breast meet his balms or the edge of his steel.
Change is come, and past over, no more strife, no more learning:
Now your lips and your forehead are sealed with his seal,
Look backward and smile at the thorns and the burning.
—Sweet rest, O my soul, and no fear of returning!

VII

Love is enough: ho ye who seek saving,
Go no further; come hither; there have been who have found it,
And these know the House of Fulfilment of Craving;
These know the Cup with the roses around it;
These know the World's Wound and the balm that hath bound it:
Cry out, the World heedeth not, "Love, lead us home!"

He leadeth, He hearkeneth, He cometh to you-ward;
Set your faces as steel to the fears that assemble
Round his goad for the faint, and his scourge for the froward:
Lo his lips, how with tales of last kisses they tremble!
Lo his eyes of all sorrow that may not dissemble!
Cry out, for he heedeth, "O Love, lead us home!"

O hearken the words of his voice of compassion:
"Come cling round about me, ye faithful who sicken
Of the weary unrest and the world's passing fashion!
As the rain in mid-morning your troubles shall thicken,
But surely within you some Godhead doth quicken,
As ye cry to me heeding, and leading you home.

"Come—pain ye shall have, and be blind to the ending!
Come—fear ye shall have, 'mid the sky's overcasting!
Come—change ye shall have, for far are ye wending!
Come—no crown ye shall have for your thirst and your fasting,
But the kissed lips of Love and fair life everlasting!
Cry out, for one heedeth, who leadeth you home!"

Is he gone? was he with us?—ho ye who seek saving,
Go no further; come hither; for have we not found it?
Here is the House of Fulfilment of Craving;
Here is the Cup with the roses around it;
The World's Wound well healed, and the balm that hath bound it:
Cry out! for he heedeth, fair Love that led home.

1873

OF THE PASSING AWAY OF BRYNHILD

From *The Story of Sigurd the Volsung*

Once more on the morrow-morning fair shineth the glorious sun,
And the Niblung children labour on a deed that shall be done.
For out in the people's meadows they raise a bale on high,
The oak and the ash together, and thereon shall the Mighty lie;
Nor gold nor steel shall be lacking, nor savour of sweet spice,
Nor cloths in the Southlands woven, nor webs of untold price:
The work grows, toil is as nothing; long blasts of the mighty horn
From the topmost tower out-wailing o'er the woeful world are borne.

But Brynhild lay in her chamber, and her women went and came,
And they feared and trembled before her, and none spake Sigurd's name;
But whiles they deemed her weeping, and whiles they deemed indeed
That she spake, if they might but hearken, but no words their ears might heed;
Till at last she spake out clearly:

"I know not what ye would;
For ye come and go in my chamber, and ye seem of wavering mood
To thrust me on, or to stay me; to help my heart in woe,
Or to bid my days of sorrow midst nameless folly go."

None answered the word of Brynhild, none knew of her intent;
But she spake: "Bid hither Gunnar, lest the sun sink o'er the bent,
And leave the words unspoken I yet have will to speak."

Then her maidens go from before her, and that lord of war they seek,
And he stands by the bed of Brynhild and strives to entreat and beseech,
But her eyes gaze awfully on him, and his lips may learn no speech.
And she saith:
"I slept in the morning, or I dreamed in the waking-hour,
And my dream was of thee, O Gunnar, and the bed in thy kingly bower,
And the house that I blessed in my sorrow, and cursed in my sorrow and shame,
The gates of an ancient people, the towers of a mighty name:
King, cold was the hall I have dwelt in, and no brand burned on the hearth;
Dead-cold was thy bed, O Gunnar, and thy land was parched with dearth:
But I saw a great King riding, and a master of the harp,
And he rode amidst the foemen, and the swords were bitter-sharp,
But his hand in the hand-gyves smote not, and his feet in the fetters were fast,
While many a word of mocking at his speechless face was cast.
Then I heard a voice in the world: 'O woe for the broken troth,
And the heavy Need of the Niblungs, and the Sorrow of Odin the Goth!
Then I saw the halls of the strangers, and the hills, and the dark-blue sea,
Nor knew of their names and their nations, for earth was afar from me,
But brother rose up against brother, and blood swam over the board,
And women smote and spared not, and the fire was master and lord.
Then, then was the moonless mid-mirk, and I woke to the day and the deed,
The deed that earth shall name not, the day of its bitterest need.
Many words have I said in my life-days, and little more shall I say:
Ye have heard the dream of a woman, deal with it as ye may:
For meseems the world-ways sunder, and the dusk and the dark is mine,
Till I come to the hall of Freyia, where the deeds of the Mighty shall shine.' "

So hearkened Gunnar the Niblung, that her words he understood,
And he knew she was set on the death-stroke, and he deemed it nothing good:
But he said: "I have hearkened, and heeded thy death and mine in thy words:
I have done the deed and abide it, and my face shall laugh on the swords;
But thee, woman, I bid thee abide here till thy grief of soul abate;
Meseems nought lowly nor shameful shall be the Niblung fate;
And here shalt thou rule and be mighty, and be Queen of the measureless Gold,
And abase the Kings and upraise them; and anew shall thy fame be told,
And as fair shall thy glory blossom as the fresh fields under the spring."

Then he casteth his arms about her, and hot is the heart of the King
For the glory of Queen Brynhild and the hope of her days of gain,
And he clean forgetteth Sigurd and the foster-brother slain:
But she shrank aback from before him, and cried: "Woe worth the while
For the thoughts ye drive back on me, and the memory of your guile!

The Kings of Earth were gathered, the wise of men were met;
On the death of a woman's pleasure their glorious hearts were set,
And I was alone amidst them—Ah, hold thy peace hereof!
Lest the thought of the bitterest hours this little hour should move."

He rose abashed from before her, and yet he lingered there;
Then she said: "O King of the Niblungs, what noise do I hearken and hear?
Why ring the axes and hammers, while feet of men go past,
And shields from the wall are shaken, and swords on the pavement cast,
And the door of the treasure is opened, and the horn cries loud and long,
And the feet of the Niblung children to the people's meadows throng?"

His face was troubled before her, and again she spake and said:
"Meseemeth this is the hour when men array the dead;
Wilt thou tell me tidings, Gunnar, that the children of thy folk
Pile up the bale for Guttorm, and the hand that smote the stroke?"

He said: "It is not so, Brynhild; for that Giuki's son was burned
When the moon of the middle heaven last night toward dawning turned."

They looked on each other and spake not; but Gunnar gat him gone,
And came to his brother Hogni, the wise-heart Giuki's son,
And spake: "Thou art wise, O Hogni; go in to Brynhild the Queen,
And stay her swift departing; or the last of her days hath she seen."

"It is nought, thy word," said Hogni; "wilt thou bring dead men aback,
Or the souls of Kings departed midst the battle and the wrack?
Yet this shall be easier to thee than the turning Brynhild's heart;
She came to dwell among us, but in us she had no part;
Let her go her ways from the Niblungs with her hand in Sigurd's hand.
Will the grass grow up henceforward where her feet have trodden the land?"

"O evil day," said Gunnar, "when my Queen must perish and die!"

"Such oft betide," saith Hogni, "as the lives of men flit by;
But the evil day is a day, and on each day groweth a deed,
And a thing that never dieth; and the fateful tale shall speed.
Lo now, let us harden our hearts and set our brows as the brass,
Lest men say it, 'They loathed the evil and they brought the evil to pass.'"

So they spake, and their hearts were heavy, and they longed for the morrow morn,
And the morrow of to-morrow, and the new day yet to be born.

But Brynhild cried to her maidens: "Now open ark and chest,
And draw forth queenly raiment of the loveliest and the best,
Red rings that the Dwarf-lords fashioned, fair cloths that the Queens have sewed
To array the bride for the mighty, and the traveller for the road."

They wept as they wrought her bidding and did on her goodliest gear;
But she laughed mid the dainty linen, and the gold-rings fashioned fair:
She arose from the bed of the Niblungs, and her face no more was wan;
As a star in the dawn-tide heavens, mid the dusky house she shone:
And they that stood about her, their hearts were raised aloft
Amid their fear and wonder: then she spake them kind and soft:

"Now give me the sword, O maidens, wherewith I sheared the wind
When the Kings of Earth were gathered to know the Chooser's mind."

All sheathed the maidens brought it, and feared the hidden blade,
But the naked blue-white edges across her knees she laid,
And spake: "The heaped-up riches, the gear my fathers left,
All dear-bought woven wonders, all rings from battle reft,
All goods of men desired, now strew them on the floor,
And so share among you, maidens, the gifts of Brynhild's store."

They brought them mid their weeping, but none put forth a hand
To take that wealth desired, the spoils of many a land:
There they stand and weep before her, and some are moved to speech,
And they cast their arms about her and strive with her, and beseech
That she look on her loved-ones' sorrow and the glory of the day.
It was nought; she scarce might see them, and she put their hands away
And she said: "Peace, ye that love me! and take the gifts and the gold
In remembrance of my fathers and the faithful deeds of old."

Then she spake: "Where now is Gunnar, that I may speak with him?
For new things are mine eyes beholding and the Niblung house grows dim,
And new sounds gather about me that may hinder me to speak
When the breath is near to flitting, and the voice is waxen weak."

Then upright by the bed of the Niblungs for a moment doth she stand,
And the blade flasheth bright in the chamber, but no more they hinder her hand
Than if a God were smiting to rend the world in two:
Then dulled are the glittering edges, and the bitter point cleaves through
The breast of the all-wise Brynhild, and her feet from the pavement fail,
And the sigh of her heart is hearkened mid the hush of the maidens' wail.
Chill, deep is the fear upon them, but they bring her aback to the bed,
And her hand is yet on the hilts, and sidelong droopeth her head.

Then there cometh a cry from withoutward, and Gunnar's hurrying feet
Are swift on the kingly threshold, and Brynhild's blood they meet.
Low down o'er the bed he hangeth and hearkeneth for her word,
And her heavy lids are opened to look on the Niblung lord,
And she saith:
"I pray thee a prayer, the last word in the world I speak,
That ye bear me forth to Sigurd, and the hand my hand would seek;
The bale for the dead is builded, it is wrought full wide on the plain,
It is raised for Earth's best Helper, and thereon is room for twain:
Ye have hung the shields about it, and the Southland hangings spread,
There lay me adown by Sigurd and my head beside his head:
But ere ye leave us sleeping, draw his Wrath from out the sheath,
And lay that Light of the Branstock, and the blade that frighted death
Betwixt my side and Sigurd's, as it lay that while agone,
When once in one bed together we twain were laid alone:
How then when the flames flare upward may I be left behind?
How then may the road he wendeth be hard for my feet to find?
How then in the gates of Valhall may the door of the gleaming ring
Clash to on the heel of Sigurd, as I follow on my King?"

Then she raised herself on her elbow, but again her eyelids sank,
And the wound by the sword-edge whispered, as her heart from the iron shrank,
And she moaned: "O lives of man-folk, for unrest all overlong
By the Father were ye fashioned; and what hope amendeth wrong?
Now at last, O my belovèd, all is gone; none else is near,
Through the ages of all ages, never sundered, shall we wear."

Scarce more than a sigh was the word, as back on the bed she fell,
Nor was there need in the chamber of the passing of Brynhild to tell;
And no more their lamentation might the maidens hold aback,
But the sound of their bitter mourning was as if red-handed wrack
Ran wild in the Burg of the Niblungs, and the fire were master of all.

Then the voice of Gunnar the war-king cried out o'er the weeping hall:
"Wail on, O women forsaken, for the mightiest woman born!
Now the hearth is cold and joyless, and the waste bed lieth forlorn.
Wail on, but amid your weeping lay hand to the glorious dead,
That not alone for an hour may lie Queen Brynhild's head:
For here have been heavy tidings, and the Mightiest under shield
Is laid on the bale high-builded in the Niblungs' hallowed field.
Fare forth! for he abideth, and we do Allfather wrong,
If the shining Valhall's pavement await their feet o'erlong."

Then they took the body of Brynhild in the raiment that she wore,
And out through the gate of the Niblungs the holy corpse they bore,
And thence forth to the mead of the people, and the high-built shielded bale:
Then afresh in the open meadows breaks forth the women's wail
When they see the bed of Sigurd and the glittering of his gear;
And fresh is the wail of the people as Brynhild draweth anear,
And the tidings go before her that for twain the bale is built,
That for twain is the oak-wood shielded and the pleasant odours spilt.

There is peace on the bale of Sigurd, and the Gods look down from on high,
And they see the lids of the Volsung close shut against the sky.
As he lies with his shield beside him in the Hauberk all of gold,
That has not its like in the heavens, nor has earth of its fellow told;
And forth from the Helm of Aweing are the sunbeams flashing wide,
And the sheathèd Wrath of Sigurd lies still by his mighty side.
Then cometh an elder of days, a man of the ancient times,
Who is long past sorrow and joy, and the steep of the bale he climbs;
And he kneeleth down by Sigurd, and bareth the Wrath to the sun
That the beams are gathered about it, and from hilt to blood-point run,
And wide o'er the plain of the Niblungs doth the Light of the Branstock glare,
Till the wondering mountain-shepherds on that star of noontide stare,
And fear for many an evil; but the ancient man stands still
With the war-flame on his shoulder, nor thinks of good or of ill,
Till the feet of Brynhild's bearers on the topmost bale are laid,
And her bed is dight by Sigurd's; then he sinks the pale white blade
And lays it 'twixt the sleepers, and leaves them there alone—
He, the last that shall ever behold them,—and his days are well-nigh done.

Then is silence over the plain; in the noon shine the torches pale
As the best of the Niblung Earl-folk bear fire to the builded bale:

Then a wind in the west ariseth, and the white flames leap on high,
And with one voice crieth the people a great and mighty cry,
And men cast up hands to the heavens, and pray without a word,
As they that have seen God's visage, and the voice of the Father have heard.

They are gone—the lovely, the mighty, the hope of the ancient Earth:
It shall labour and bear the burden as before that day of their birth:
It shall groan in its blind abiding for the day that Sigurd hath sped,
And the hour that Brynhild hath hastened, and the dawn that waketh the dead:
It shall yearn, and be oft-times holpen, and forget their deeds no more,
Till the new sun beams on Baldur, and the happy sealess shore.

1876

THE DAY IS COMING

Come hither, lads, and hearken, for a tale there is to tell,
Of the wonderful days a-coming, when all shall be better than well.

And the tale shall be told of a country, a land in the midst of the sea,
And folk shall call it England in the days that are going to be.

There more than one in a thousand in the days that are yet to come,
Shall have some hope of the morrow, some joy of the ancient home.

For then, laugh not, but listen to this strange tale of mine,
All folk that are in England shall be better lodged than swine.

Then a man shall work and bethink him, and rejoice in the deeds of his hand,
Nor yet come home in the even too faint and weary to stand.

Men in that time a-coming shall work and have no fear
For to-morrow's lack of earning and the hunger-wolf anear.

I tell you this for a wonder, that no man then shall be glad
Of his fellow's fall and mishap to snatch at the work he had.

For that which the worker winneth shall then be his indeed,
Nor shall half be reaped for nothing by him that sowed no seed.

O strange new wonderful justice! But for whom shall we gather the gain?
For ourselves and for each of our fellows, and no hand shall labour in vain.

Then all Mine and all Thine shall be Ours, and no more shall any man crave
For riches that serve for nothing but to fetter a friend for a slave.

And what wealth then shall be left us when none shall gather gold
To buy his friend in the market, and pinch and pine the sold?

Nay, what save the lovely city, and the little house on the hill,
And the waste and the woodland beauty, and the happy fields we till;

And the homes of ancient stories, the tombs of the mighty dead;
And the wise men seeking out marvels, and the poet's teeming head;

And the painter's hand of wonder; and the marvellous fiddle-bow,
And the banded choirs of music: all those that do and know.

For all these shall be ours and all men's, nor shall any lack a share
Of the toil and the gain of living in the days when the world grows fair.

Ah! such are the days that shall be! But what are the deeds of to-day
In the days of the years we dwell in, that wear our lives away?

Why, then, and for what are we waiting? There are three words to speak;
WE WILL IT, and what is the foeman but the dream-strong wakened and weak?

O why and for what are we waiting? while our brothers droop and die,
And on every wind of the heavens a wasted life goes by.

How long shall they reproach us where crowd on crowd they dwell,
Poor ghosts of the wicked city, the gold-crushed hungry hell?

Through squalid life they laboured, in sordid grief they died,
Those sons of a mighty mother, those props of England's pride.

They are gone; there is none can undo it, nor save our souls from the curse;
But many a million cometh, and shall they be better or worse?

It is we must answer and hasten, and open wide the door
For the rich man's hurrying terror, and the slow-foot hope of the poor.

Yea, the voiceless wrath of the wretched, and their unlearned discontent,
We must give it voice and wisdom till the waiting-tide be spent.

Come, then, since all things call us, the living and the dead,
And o'er the weltering tangle a glimmering light is shed.

Come, then, let us cast off fooling, and put by ease and rest,
For the Cause alone is worthy till the good days bring the best.

Come, join in the only battle wherein no man can fail,
Where whoso fadeth and dieth, yet his deed shall still prevail.

Ah! come, cast off all fooling, for this, at least, we know:
That the Dawn and the Day is coming, and forth the Banners go.

1884

THE VOICE OF TOIL

I HEARD men saying, Leave hope and praying,
All days shall be as all have been;
To-day and to-morrow bring fear and sorrow,
The never-ending toil between.

When Earth was younger mid toil and hunger,
In hope we strove, and our hands were strong;
Then great men led us, with words they fed us,
And bade us right the earthly wrong.

Go read in story their deeds and glory,
Their names amidst the nameless dead;
Turn then from lying to us slow-dying
In that good world to which they led;

Where fast and faster our iron master,
The thing we made, for ever drives,
Bids us grind treasure and fashion pleasure
For other hopes and other lives.

Where home is a hovel and dull we grovel,
Forgetting that the world is fair;
Where no babe we cherish, lest its very soul perish;
Where mirth is crime, and love a snare.

Who now shall lead us, what god shall heed us
As we lie in the hell our hands have won?
For us are no rulers but fools and befoolers,
The great are fallen, the wise men gone.

I heard men saying, Leave tears and praying,
The sharp knife heedeth not the sheep;
Are we not stronger than the rich and the wronger,
When day breaks over dreams and sleep?

Come, shoulder to shoulder ere the world grows older!
Help lies in nought but thee and me;
Hope is before us, the long years that bore us
Bore leaders more than men may be.

Let dead hearts tarry and trade and marry,
And trembling nurse their dreams of mirth,
While we the living our lives are giving
To bring the bright new world to birth.

Come, shoulder to shoulder ere earth grows older!
The Cause spreads over land and sea;
Now the world shaketh, and fear awaketh,
And joy at last for thee and me.

1884

TO THE MUSE OF THE NORTH

O MUSE that swayest the sad Northern Song,
Thy right hand full of smiting and of wrong,
Thy left hand holding pity, and thy breast
Heaving with hope of that so certain rest;
Thou, with the gray eyes kind and unafraid,
The soft lips trembling not, though they have said
The doom of the World and those that dwell therein,
The lips that smile not though thy children win
The fated Love that draws the fated Death—
O, borne adown the fresh stream of thy breath,
Let some word reach my ears and touch my heart,
That, if it may be, I may have a part
In that great sorrow of thy children dead
That vexed the brow, and bowed adown the head,
Whitened the hair, made life a wondrous dream,
And death the murmur of a restful stream,
But left no stain upon those souls of thine
Whose greatness through the tangled world doth shine.
O Mother, and Love and Sister all in one,
Come thou; for sure I am enough alone
That thou thine arms about my heart shouldst throw,
And wrap me in the grief of long ago.

1891

A DEATH SONG

WHAT cometh here from west to east awending?
And who are these, the marchers stern and slow?
We bear the message that the rich are sending
Aback to those who bade them wake and know.
Not one, not one, nor thousands must they slay,
But one and all if they would dusk the day.

We asked them for a life of toilsome earning,
They bade us bide their leisure for our bread;
We crave to speak to tell our woeful learning:
We come back speechless, bearing back our dead.
Not one, not one, nor thousands must they slay,
But one and all if they would dusk the day.

They will not learn; they have no ears to hearken.
They turn their faces from the eyes of fate;
Their gay-lit halls shut out the skies that darken.
But, lo! this dead man knocking at the gate.
Not one, not one, nor thousands must they slay,
But one and all if they would dusk the day.

Here lies the sign that we shall break our prison;
Amidst the storm he won a prisoner's rest;
But in the cloudy dawn the sun arisen

The Burghers' Battle.

Thick rise the spear-shafts o'er the land
That erst the harvest bore;
The sword is heavy in the hand,
And we return no more.

The light wind waves the Ruddy Fox,
Our banner of the war,
And ripples ~~through~~ in the Running Ox,
And we return no more.

Across our stubble acres now
The teams go four and four;
But out-worn elders guide the plough,
And we return no more.

And now the women heavy-eyed
Turn through the open door
From gazing down the highway wide,
Where we return no more.

The shadows of the ~~[illegible]~~ fruited close
Dapple the feast-hall floor;
There lie our dogs and dream and doze,
And we return no more.

Down from the minster tower today
Fall the soft chimes of yore
Amidst the chattering jackdaws' play:
And we return no more.

But underneath the streets are still;
Noon—and the market's o'er!

A Manuscript Page of *The Burghers' Battle*. (See Appendix I.)

Brings us our day of work to win the best.
Not one, not one, nor thousands must they slay,
But one and all if they would dusk the day.

1891

AGNES AND THE HILL-MAN

TRANSLATED FROM THE DANISH

Agnes went through the meadows a-weeping,
Fowl are a-singing.
There stood the hill-man heed thereof keeping.
Agnes, fair Agnes!
"Come to the hill, fair Agnes, with me,
The reddest of gold will I give unto thee!"

Twice went Agnes the hill round about,
Then wended within, left the fair world without.

In the hillside bode Agnes, three years thrice told o'er,
For the green earth sithence fell she longing full sore.

There she sat, and lullaby sang in her singing,
And she heard how the bells of England were ringing.

Agnes before her true-love did stand:
"May I wend to the church of the English Land?"

"To England's Church well mayst thou be gone,
So that no hand thou lay the red gold upon.

"So that when thou art come the churchyard anear
Thou cast not abroad thy golden hair.

"So that when thou standest the church within
To thy mother on bench thou never win.

"So that when thou hearest the high God's name,
No knee unto earth thou bow to the same."

Hand she laid on all gold that was there,
And cast abroad her golden hair.

And when the church she stood within
To her mother on bench straight did she win.

And when she heard the high God's name,
Knee unto earth she bowed to the same.

When all the mass was sung to its end
Home with her mother dear did she wend.

"Come, Agnes, into the hillside to me,
For thy seven small sons greet sorely for thee!"

"Let them greet, let them greet, as they will have to do;
For never again will I hearken thereto!"

Weird laid he on her, sore sickness he wrought,
Fowl are a-singing.
That self-same hour to death was she brought.
Agnes, fair Agnes.

1891

ICELAND FIRST SEEN

Lo, from our loitering ship a new land at last to be seen;
Toothed rocks down the side of the firth on the east guard a weary wide lea,
And black slope the hill-sides above, striped adown with their desolate green:
And a peak rises up on the west from the meeting of cloud and of sea,
Foursquare from base unto point like the building of Gods that have been,
The last of that waste of the mountains all cloud-wreathed and snow-flecked and gray,
And bright with the dawn that began just now at the ending of day.

Ah! what came we forth for to see that our hearts are so hot with desire?
Is it enough for our rest the sight of this desolate strand,
And the mountain-waste voiceless as death but for winds that may sleep not nor tire?

Why do we long to wend forth through the length and breadth of a land,
Dreadful with grinding of ice, and record of scarce hidden fire,
But that there 'mid the gray grassy dales sore scarred by the ruining streams
Lives the tale of the Northland of old and the undying glory of dreams?

O land, as some cave by the sea where the treasures of old have been laid,
The sword it may be of a king whose name was the turning of fight;
Or the staff of some wise of the world that many things made and unmade,
Or the ring of a woman maybe whose woe is grown wealth and delight.
No wheat and no wine grows above it, no orchard for blossom and shade;
The few ships that sail by its blackness but deem it the mouth of a grave;
Yet sure when the world shall awaken, this too shall be mighty to save.

Or rather, O land, if a marvel it seemeth that men ever sought
Thy wastes for a field and a garden fulfilled of all wonder and doubt,
And feasted amidst of the winter when the fight of the year had been fought,
Whose plunder all gathered together was little to babble about:
Cry aloud from thy wastes, O thou land, "Not for this nor for that was I wrought
Amid waning of realms and of riches and death of things worshipped and sure;
I abide here the spouse of a God, and I made and I make and endure."

O Queen of the grief without knowledge, of the courage that may not avail,
Of the longing that may not attain, of the love that shall never forget,
More joy than the gladness of laughter thy voice hath amidst of its wail:
More hope than of pleasure fulfilled amidst of thy blindness is set;
More glorious than gaining of all, thine unfaltering hand that shall fail:
For what is the mark on thy brow but the brand that thy Brynhild doth bear?
Lone once, and loved and undone by a love that no ages outwear.

Ah! when thy Balder comes back, and bears from the heart of the Sun,
Peace and the healing of pain, and the wisdom that waiteth no more;
And the lilies are laid on thy brow 'mid the crown of the deeds thou hast done;
And the roses spring up by thy feet that the rocks of the wilderness wore—
Ah! when thy Balder comes back and we gather the gains he hath won,
Shall we not linger a little to talk of thy sweetness of old,
Yea, turn back awhile to thy travail whence the gods stood aloof to behold?

1891

ARTHUR WILLIAM EDGAR O'SHAUGHNESSY

[March 14, 1844–January 30, 1881]

At seventeen Arthur William Edgar O'Shaughnessy became a transcriber in the library of the British Museum. After two years of this he was made an assistant in the department of natural history, and for the rest of his life, instead of giving his attention to old French literature, as he would have liked to do, he had to study the various ways of preserving fishes. In 1870 he surprised his associates, who did not suspect his poetic gift, by publishing a volume of melodious verse, *Epic of Women and Other Poems*. This volume was praised by Swinburne, and it won for O'Shaughnessy the attention and friendship of Rossetti. *Lays of France* followed in 1872 and *Music and Moonlight* in 1874. The death of his wife in 1879—he had married in 1873—dealt him a weakening blow, and two years later, at the age of thirty-seven, he contracted a cold and died. In the same year (1881) his last volume, *Songs of a Worker*, was published posthumously. O'Shaughnessy's themes are unimportant, but his pure lyrical talent gave to poetry some unforgettable melodies.

THE FOUNTAIN OF TEARS

If you go over desert and mountain,
Far into the country of sorrow,
To-day and to-night and to-morrow,
And maybe for months and for years;
You shall come, with a heart that is bursting
For trouble and toiling and thirsting,
You shall certainly come to the fountain
At length,—to the Fountain of Tears.

Very peaceful the place is, and solely
For piteous lamenting and sighing,
And those who come living or dying
Alike from their hopes and their fears;
Full of cypress-like shadows the place is,
And statues that cover their faces:
But out of the gloom springs the holy
And beautiful Fountain of Tears.

And it flows and it flows with a motion
So gentle and lovely and listless,
And murmurs a tune so resistless
To him who hath suffered and hears—
You shall surely—without a word spoken,
Kneel down there and know your heart broken,
And yield to the long curb'd emotion
That day by the Fountain of Tears.

For it grows and it grows, as though leaping
Up higher the more one is thinking;
And ever its tunes go on sinking
More poignantly into the ears:
Yea, so blessèd and good seems that fountain,
Reached after dry desert and mountain,
You shall fall down at length in your weeping
And bathe your sad face in the tears.

Then, alas! while you lie there a season,
And sob between living and dying,
And give up the land you were trying
To find mid your hopes and your fears;
—O the world shall come up and pass o'er you;
Strong men shall not stay to care for you,
Nor wonder indeed for what reason
Your ways should seem harder than theirs.

But perhaps, while you lie, never lifting
Your cheek from the wet leaves it presses,
Nor caring to raise your wet tresses
And look how the cold world appears,—
O perhaps the mere silences round you—
All things in that place grief hath found you,
Yea, e'en to the clouds o'er you drifting,
May soothe you somewhat through your tears.

You may feel, when a falling leaf brushes
Your face, as though some one had kissed you;
Or think at least some one who missed you
Hath sent you a thought,—if that cheers;
Or a bird's little song, faint and broken,
May pass for a tender word spoken:
—Enough, while around you there rushes
That life-drowning torrent of tears.

And the tears shall flow faster and faster,
Brim over, and baffle resistance,
And roll down bleared roads to each distance
Of past desolation and years;
Till they cover the place of each sorrow,
And leave you no past and no morrow:
For what man is able to master
And stem the great Fountain of Tears?

But the floods of the tears meet and gather;
The sound of them all grows like thunder:
—O into what bosom, I wonder,
Is poured the whole sorrow of years?
For Eternity only seems keeping
Account of the great human weeping:
May God then, the Maker and Father—
May He find a place for the tears!

1870

From CHAITIVEL

Hath any loved you well, down there,
Summer or winter through?
Down there, have you found any fair
Laid in the grave with you?

Is death's long kiss a richer kiss
  Than mine was wont to be—
Or have you gone to some far bliss
  And quite forgotten me?

What soft enamouring of sleep
  Hath you in some soft way?
What charmed death holdeth you with deep
  Strange lure by night and day?
—A little space below the grass,
  Out of the sun and shade;
But worlds away from me, alas,
  Down there where you are laid?

My bright hair's waved and wasted gold,
  What is it now to thee—
Whether the rose-red life I hold
  Or white death holdeth me?
Down there you love the grave's own green,
  And evermore you rave
Of some sweet seraph you have seen
  Or dreamt of in the grave.

There you shall lie as you have lain,
  Though in the world above,
Another live your life again,
  Loving again your love:
Is it not sweet beneath the palm?
  Is not the warm day rife
With some long mystic golden calm
  Better than love and life?

The broad quaint odorous leaves like hands
  Weaving the fair day through,
Weave sleep no burnished bird withstands
  While death weaves sleep for you;
And many a strange rich breathing sound
  Ravishes morn and noon:
And in that place you must have found
  Death a delicious swoon.

Hold me no longer for a word
  I used to say or sing:
Ah, long ago you must have heard
  So many a sweeter thing:
For rich earth must have reached your heart
  And turned the faith to flowers;
And warm wind stolen, part by part,
  Your soul through faithless hours.

And many a soft seed must have won
  Soil of some yielding thought,
To bring a bloom up to the sun
  That else had ne'er been brought;
And, doubtless, many a passionate hue
  Hath made that place more fair,
Making some passionate part of you
  Faithless to me down there.

1872

ODE

We are the music makers,
  And we are the dreamers of dreams,
Wandering by lone sea-breakers,
  And sitting by desolate streams;—
World-losers and world-forsakers,
  On whom the pale moon gleams;
Yet we are the movers and shakers
  Of the world for ever, it seems.

With wonderful deathless ditties
We build up the world's great cities,
  And out of a fabulous story
  We fashion an empire's glory:
One man with a dream, at pleasure,
  Shall go forth and conquer a crown;
And three with a new song's measure
  Can trample a kingdom down.

We, in the ages lying
  In the buried past of the earth,
Built Nineveh with our sighing,
  And Babel itself in our mirth;
And o'erthrew them with prophesying
  To the old of the new world's worth;
For each age is a dream that is dying,
  Or one that is coming to birth.

1874

SONG

I made another garden, yea,
  For my new love;
I left the dead rose where it lay,
  And set the new above.
Why did the summer not begin?
  Why did my heart not haste?
My old love came and walked therein,
  And laid the garden waste.

She entered with her weary smile,
  Just as of old;
She looked around a little while,
  And shivered at the cold.

Her passing touch was death to all,
  Her passing look a blight:
She made the white rose-petals fall,
  And turned the red rose white.

Her pale robe, clinging to the grass,
  Seemed like a snake
That bit the grass and ground, alas!
  And a sad trail did make.
She went up slowly to the gate;
  And there, just as of yore,
She turned back at the last to wait,
  And say farewell once more.

1874

SONG

HAS summer come without the rose,
  Or left the bird behind?
Is the blue changed above thee,
  O world! or am I blind?
Will you change every flower that grows,
Or only change this spot,
Where she who said, I love thee,
  Now says, I love thee not?

The skies seemed true above thee,
  The rose true on the tree;
The bird seemed true the summer through,
  But all proved false to me.

1874

A LOVE SYMPHONY

ALONG the garden ways just now
  I heard the flowers speak;
The white rose told me of your brow,
  The red rose of your cheek;
The lily of your bended head,
  The bindweed of your hair:
Each looked its loveliest and said
  You were more fair.

I went into the wood anon,
  And heard the wild birds sing
How sweet you were; they warbled on,
  Piped, trilled the self-same thing.
Thrush, blackbird, linnet, without pause,
  The burden did repeat,
And still began again because
  You were more sweet.

And then I went down to the sea,
  And heard it murmuring too,
Part of an ancient mystery,
  All made of me and you.
How many a thousand years ago
  I loved, and you were sweet—
Longer I could not stay, and so
  I fled back to your feet.

1881

COVENTRY KERSEY DIGHTON PATMORE

[July 23, 1823–November 26, 1896]

COVENTRY KERSEY DIGHTON PATMORE, the son of an indifferent writer who liked to pose as a sportsman and man of the world, was born at Woodford Green, in Epping Forest. At sixteen he was sent to a branch of the Collège de France, at St. Germaine, where while he was improving his French, he acquired a prejudice against everything French (except the language) that remained with him all his life. In 1844 he published *Poems*, some of which he said he wrote when he was sixteen or seventeen and some, in order to fill out the volume, "while the printer's boy was waiting." On the whole the little book was pretty well received, but there was some unfavorable criticism, *Blackwood*, as was to be expected, directing at it a typical *Blackwood* attack. Thackeray predicted that the author would some day be a genius, and Monckton Milnes, the first open champion of Keats as a poet of the first rank, believed in young Patmore and got him a much needed appointment as a supernumerary assistant in the Department of Printed Books in the British Museum. In 1847 Patmore married Emily Andrews. There followed fifteen years of happy married life, the Patmores opening their home to Tennyson, Browning, Ruskin, Carlyle, and other literary men. The influence of Mrs. Patmore upon her husband's work was very great; his dedication to her of *The Angel in the House* with the words, "To the memory of her by whom and for whom I became a Poet," was not far from the truth.

Soon after Mrs. Patmore's death in 1862 Patmore went to Rome, where he was to meet his friend Aubrey de Vere, a fervent Roman Catholic eager to win the poet to the Church. Here he met Miss Marianne Byles, a recent convert of Cardinal Manning's, of whom he wrote, "I had never before beheld so beautiful a personality, and this beauty seemed to be the pure effulgence of Catholic sanctity." Perhaps she, as much as anything the Church had to offer, led him to embrace the Catholic faith. When he asked her to marry him, however, he found that she had made a solemn "religious promise never to marry." From this promise she was relieved by dispensation, and in midsummer of 1864 the marriage took place. Marianne Byles Patmore was a woman of fortune, and Patmore, no longer compelled to work for a living, gave up his post in the British Museum and bought an estate in the Ashdown Forest, the improvement of which resulted in a beautiful country place which he called Heron's Ghyll. During his years here (1866–1874) he wrote the nine odes which were later published as *The Unknown Eros*. In 1874 he made a profitable sale of Heron's Ghyll and the next year settled in the manor-house of the old town of Hastings. The second Mrs. Patmore died in 1880, but Patmore, who married a third time the next year, continued living in Hastings till 1891. Much of his best work he wrote during the Hastings period. Upon leaving Hastings he went to live at the Lodge, Lymington, in Hampshire. Soon after he settled in the Lodge his health failed, and he died five years later. His body was laid in the Roman Catholic portion of the cemetery at Lymington.

WIND AND WAVE

The wedded light and heat,
Winnowing the witless space,
Without a let,
What are they till they beat
Against the sleepy sod, and there beget
Perchance the violet!
Is the One found,
Amongst a wilderness of as happy grace,
To make Heaven's bound;
So that in Her
All which it hath of sensitively good
Is sought and understood
After the narrow mode the mighty Heavens prefer?
She, as a little breeze
Following still Night,
Ripples the spirit's cold, deep seas
Into delight;
But, in a while,
The immeasurable smile
Is broke by fresher airs to flashes blent
With darkling discontent;
And all the subtle zephyr hurries gay,
And all the heaving ocean heaves one way,
T'ward the void sky-line and an unguess'd weal;
Until the vanward billows feel
The agitating shallows, and divine the goal,
And to foam roll,
And spread and stray
And traverse wildly, like delighted hands,
The fair and fleckless sands;
And so the whole
Unfathomable and immense
Triumphing tide comes at the last to reach
And burst in wind-kiss'd splendours on the deaf'ning beach,
Where forms of children in first innocence
Laugh and fling pebbles on the rainbow'd crest
Of its untired unrest.

1877

WINTER

I, SINGULARLY moved
To love the lovely that are not beloved,
Of all the Seasons, most
Love Winter, and to trace
The sense of the Trophonian pallor on her face.
It is not death, but plenitude of peace;

And the dim cloud that does the world enfold
Hath less the characters of dark and cold
Than warmth and light asleep,
And correspondent breathing seems to keep
With the infant harvest, breathing soft below
Its eider coverlet of snow.
Nor is in field or garden anything
But, duly look'd into, contains serene
The substance of things hoped for, in the Spring,
And evidence of Summer not yet seen.
On every chance-mild day
That visits the moist shaw,
The honeysuckle, 'sdaining to be crost
In urgence of sweet life by sleet or frost,
'Voids the time's law
With still increase
Of leaflet new, and little, wandering spray;
Often, in sheltering brakes,
As one from rest disturb'd in the first hour,
Primrose or violet bewilder'd wakes,
And deems 'tis time to flower;
Though not a whisper of her voice he hear,
The buried bulb does know
The signals of the year,
And hails far Summer with his lifted spear.
The gorse-field dark, by sudden, gold caprice,
Turns, here and there, into a Jason's fleece;
Lilies, that soon in Autumn slipp'd their gowns of green,
And vanish'd into earth,
And came again, ere Autumn died, to birth,
Stand full-array'd, amidst the wavering shower,
And perfect for the Summer, less the flower;
In nook of pale or crevice of crude bark,
Thou canst not miss,
If close thou spy, to mark
The ghostly chrysalis,
That, if thou touch it, stirs in its dream dark;
And the flush'd Robin, in the evenings hoar,
Does of Love's Day, as if he saw it, sing;
But sweeter yet than dream or song of Summer or Spring
Are Winter's sometime smiles, that seem to well
From infancy ineffable;
Her wandering, languorous gaze,
So unfamiliar, so without amaze,
On the elemental, chill adversity,
The uncomprehended rudeness; and her sigh
And solemn, gathering tear,
And look of exile from some great repose, the sphere
Of ether, moved by ether only, or
By something still more tranquil.

1877

THE AZALEA

There, where the sun shines first
Against our room,
She train'd the gold Azalea, whose perfume
She, Spring-like, from her breathing grace dispersed.
Last night the delicate crests of saffron bloom,
For this their dainty likeness watch'd and nurst,
Were just at point to burst.
At dawn I dream'd, O God, that she was dead,
And groan'd aloud upon my wretched bed,
And waked, ah, God, and did not waken her,
But lay, with eyes still closed,
Perfectly bless'd in the delicious sphere
By which I knew so well that she was near,
My heart to speechless thankfulness composed.
Till 'gan to stir
A dizzy somewhat in my troubled head—
It *was* the azalea's breath, and she *was* dead!
The warm night had the lingering buds disclosed,
And I had fall'n asleep with to my breast
A chance-found letter press'd
In which she said,
"So, till to-morrow eve, my Own, adieu!
Parting's well-paid with soon again to meet,
Soon in your arms to feel so small and sweet,
Sweet to myself that am so sweet to you!"

1877

DEPARTURE

It was not like your great and gracious ways!
Do you, that have nought other to lament,
Never, my Love, repent
Of how, that July afternoon,
You went,
With sudden, unintelligible phrase,

And frighten'd eye,
Upon your journey of so many days,
Without a single kiss, or a good-bye?
I knew, indeed, that you were parting soon;
And so we sate, within the low sun's rays,
You whispering to me, for your voice was weak,
Your harrowing praise.
Well, it was well,
To hear you such things speak,
And I could tell
What made your eyes a growing gloom of love,
As a warm South-wind sombres a March grove.
And it was like your great and gracious ways
To turn your talk on daily things, my Dear,
Lifting the luminous, pathetic lash
To let the laughter flash,
Whilst I drew near,
Because you spoke so low that I could scarcely hear.
But all at once to leave me at the last,
More at the wonder than the loss aghast,
With huddled, unintelligible phrase,
And frighten'd eye,
And go your journey of all days
With not one kiss, or a good-bye,
And the only loveless look the look with which you pass'd:
'Twas all unlike your great and gracious ways.

1877

THE TOYS

My little Son, who look'd from thoughtful eyes
And moved and spoke in quiet grown-up wise,
Having my law the seventh time disobey'd,
I struck him, and dismiss'd
With hard words and unkiss'd,
His Mother, who was patient, being dead.
Then, fearing lest his grief should hinder sleep,
I visited his bed,
But found him slumbering deep,
With darken'd eyelids, and their lashes yet
From his late sobbing wet.
And I, with moan,
Kissing away his tears, left others of my own;
For, on a table drawn beside his head,
He had put, within his reach,
A box of counters and a red-vein'd stone,
A piece of glass abraded by the beach
And six or seven shells,
A bottle with bluebells
And two French copper coins, ranged there with careful art,
To comfort his sad heart.
So when that night I pray'd
To God, I wept, and said:
Ah, when at last we lie with tranced breath,
Not vexing Thee in death,
And Thou rememberest of what toys
We made our joys,
How weakly understood,
Thy great commanded good,
Then, fatherly not less
Than I whom Thou hast moulded from the clay,
Thou'lt leave Thy wrath, and say,
"I will be sorry for their childishness."

1877

MAGNA EST VERITAS

Here, in this little Bay,
Full of tumultuous life and great repose,
Where, twice a day,
The purposeless, glad ocean comes and goes,
Under high cliffs, and far from the huge town,
I sit me down.
For want of me the world's course will not fail:
When all its work is done, the lie shall rot;
The truth is great, and shall prevail,
When none cares whether it prevail or not.

1877

"IF I WERE DEAD"

"If I were dead, you'd sometimes say, Poor Child!"
The dear lips quiver'd as they spake,
And the tears brake
From eyes which, not to grieve me, brightly smiled.
Poor Child, poor Child!
I seem to hear your laugh, your talk, your song.
It is not true that Love will do no wrong.

Poor Child!
And did you think, when you so cried and smiled,
How I, in lonely nights, should lie awake,
And of those words your full avengers make?
Poor Child, poor Child!
And now, unless it be
That sweet amends thrice told are come to thee,
O God, have Thou *no* mercy upon me!
Poor Child!

1877

REGINA CŒLI

Say, did his sisters wonder what could Joseph see
In a mild, silent little Maid like thee?
And was it awful, in that narrow house,
With God for Babe and Spouse?
Nay, like thy simple, female sort, each one
Apt to find Him in Husband and in Son,
Nothing to thee came strange in this.
Thy wonder was but wondrous bliss:
Wondrous, for, though
True Virgin lives not but does know,
(Howbeit none ever yet confess'd,)
That God lies really in her breast,
Of thine He made His special nest!
And so
All mothers worship little feet,
And kiss the very ground they've trod;
But, ah, thy little Baby sweet
Who was indeed thy God!

1878

CHRISTINA GEORGINA ROSSETTI

[December 5, 1830–December 29, 1894]

Christina Georgina Rossetti, the youngest of the four children of Gabriele Rossetti, a talented Italian exile, and his wife, Frances M. L. Polidori, was born in London and baptized in the Church of England, of which her mother was a devout member. The Rossetti family lived plainly but comfortably on a small sum—perhaps less than £300 a year—, mingling little with the English families around them, although Mrs. Rossetti was wholly English on her mother's side, but receiving a "constant and copious" stream of Italian "exiles, patriots, politicians, literary men, musicians, good-natured Neapolitans, keen Tuscans, emphatic Romans," who claimed old acquaintanceship with Gabriele Rossetti or who were confessed celebrity-hunters. Up to the time when Christina was ten years old her mother's parents lived in the country and the little girl delighted in visiting at their Buckinghamshire home, where she came to love the fields and gardens, the ponds, and even the noisy frogs. Before she was twelve years old Christina exhibited her first written verses, *To My Mother*, which were privately printed by her grandfather Polidori, a childish tribute pointing to the filial love that was hers throughout life.

In 1848 James Collinson, a painter, who had given up his membership in the Church of England and become a Catholic, fell in love with Miss Rossetti and proposed marriage to her. She liked him, but unable to bring herself to the point of marrying a Catholic, refused him. Thinking that he desired the lady more than the Church, Collinson returned to the English Church and was promptly accepted by Christina. His conscience troubled him, however, and he returned to the Catholic faith, only to have Christina break their engagement. The experience dealt a blow to her peace of mind from which she did not recover, her brother said, for many years.

Several years later Charles Bagot Cayley, a scholar of high type, proposed to her. Him she declined also, probably because she attributed the indefiniteness of his religious belief to indifference to religion itself, an indifference that she could not wittingly bring close to herself by marriage bonds. William Rossetti, her brother and biographer, said that she loved Cayley deeply and permanently as long as he lived and that after his death she cherished his memory to the last day of her own life.

Miss Rossetti's most beautiful love poem is *Monna Innominata*, a sonnet sequence to which she gave a brief prefatory note indicating that the poem was merely a literary exercise. But it is unmistakably autobiographical, growing out of her experiences with the minor Pre-Raphaelite, Collinson, and the scholar, Charles Cayley.

Miss Rossetti was a tender, sincere, affectionate person, who regulated her whole life by religion. In an age of scepticism she showed unquestioning faith in the Church and she was intolerant of an *Evidences of Christianity*. Her ultimate reply to any argument that challenged her reasons for belief was the simple but final "My faith is faith." Yet, as is proved by her attitude toward certain creative works which those of her religious zeal but without her artist's judgment would have considered forbidden, she could see a glory existing side by side with what she believed blasphemous or, at the least, shockingly wicked. She greatly admired her brother Dante's brilliant young friend Swinburne, and when his *Atalanta in Calydon* appeared she read it with fearful pleasure, after the first reading pasting a slip of paper over the dread line in which God is called the supreme evil so that her pure heart should not suffer an affront when she read the poem again.

Her first work after the volume privately printed by her grandfather was a set of beautiful lyrics published in *The Germ*, one of them the notable *Dream*. *Goblin Market and Other Poems* appeared in 1862, and *The Prince's Progress* in 1866. *Goblin Market*, which brought her much attention, made the way for "the new poetry" of her brother and the other Pre-Raphaelite poets more easy than it would have been otherwise. A dozen or more other volumes appeared before her death, most of them deeply religious in tone, and after her death a volume of *New Poems* was published. It is not too much to say, perhaps, that Miss Rossetti is the greatest English poetess.

DEDICATORY SONNET

SONNETS are full of love, and this my tome
Has many sonnets: so here now shall be
One sonnet more, a love sonnet, from me
To her whose heart is my heart's quiet home,
To my first Love, my Mother, on whose knee
I learnt love-lore that is not troublesome;
Whose service is my special dignity,
And she my lodestar while I go and come.
And so because you love me, and because
I love you, Mother, I have woven a wreath
Of rhymes wherewith to crown your honoured name;
In you not fourscore years can dim the flame
Of love, whose blessed glow transcends the laws
Of time and change and mortal life and death.

April, 1880

SONG

WHEN I am dead, my dearest,
Sing no sad songs for me;
Plant thou no roses at my head,
Nor shady cypress-tree:
Be the green grass above me
With showers and dewdrops wet;
And if thou wilt, remember,
And if thou wilt, forget.

I shall not see the shadows,
I shall not feel the rain;
I shall not hear the nightingale
Sing on, as if in pain:
And dreaming through the twilight
That doth not rise nor set,
Haply I may remember,
And haply may forget.

12 December, 1848

DREAM-LAND

WHERE sunless rivers weep
Their waves into the deep,
She sleeps a charmèd sleep:
Awake her not.
Led by a single star,
She came from very far
To seek where shadows are
Her pleasant lot.

She left the rosy morn,
She left the fields of corn,
For twilight cold and lorn
And water springs.
Through sleep, as through a veil,
She sees the sky look pale,
And hears the nightingale
That sadly sings.

Rest, rest, a perfect rest
Shed over brow and breast;
Her face is toward the west,
The purple land.
She cannot see the grain
Ripening on hill and plain;
She cannot feel the rain
Upon her hand.

Rest, rest, for evermore
Upon a mossy shore;
Rest, rest at the heart's core
Till time shall cease:
Sleep that no pain shall wake,
Night that no morn shall break,
Till joy shall overtake
Her perfect peace.

April, 1849

AFTER DEATH

THE curtains were half drawn, the floor was swept
And strewn with rushes, rosemary and may
Lay thick upon the bed on which I lay,
Where through the lattice ivy-shadows crept.
He leaned above me, thinking that I slept
And could not hear him; but I heard him say:
"Poor child, poor child": and as he turned away
Came a deep silence, and I knew he wept.
He did not touch the shroud, or raise the fold
That hid my face, or take my hand in his,
Or ruffle the smooth pillows for my head:
He did not love me living; but once dead
He pitied me; and very sweet it is
To know he still is warm though I am cold.

28 April, 1849

REST

O EARTH, lie heavily upon her eyes;
Seal her sweet eyes weary of watching, Earth;
Lie close around her; leave no room for mirth
With its harsh laughter, nor for sound of sighs.
She hath no questions, she hath no replies,
Hushed in and curtained with a blessed dearth
Of all that irked her from the hour of birth;
With stillness that is almost Paradise.
Darkness more clear than noonday holdeth her,
Silence more musical than any song;
Even her very heart has ceased to stir:
Until the morning of Eternity
Her rest shall not begin nor end, but be;
And when she wakes she will not think it long.

15 May, 1849

LIFE HIDDEN

ROSES and lilies grow above the place
Where she sleeps the long sleep that doth not dream.
If we could look upon her hidden face,
Nor shadow would be there, nor garish gleam
Of light; her life is lapsing like a stream
That makes no noise but floweth on apace
Seawards, while many a shade and shady beam
Vary the ripples in their gliding chase.
She doth not see, but knows; she doth not feel,
And yet is sensible; she hears no sound,
Yet counts the flight of time and doth not err.
Peace far and near, peace to ourselves and her:
Her body is at peace in holy ground,
Her spirit is at peace where Angels kneel.

23 July, 1849

REMEMBER

REMEMBER me when I am gone away,
Gone far away into the silent land;
When you can no more hold me by the hand,
Nor I half turn to go yet turning stay.
Remember me when no more, day by day,
You tell me of our future that you plann'd:
Only remember me; you understand
It will be late to counsel then or pray.
Yet if you should forget me for a while
And afterwards remember, do not grieve:
For if the darkness and corruption leave
A vestige of the thoughts that once I had,
Better by far you should forget and smile
Than that you should remember and be sad.

25 July, 1849

A PORTRAIT

I

SHE gave up beauty in her tender youth,
Gave all her hope and joy and pleasant ways;
She covered up her eyes lest they should gaze
On vanity, and chose the bitter truth.
Harsh towards herself, towards others full of ruth,
Servant of servants, little known to praise,
Long prayers and fasts trenched on her nights and days:
She schooled herself to sights and sounds uncouth,
That with the poor and stricken she might make
A home, until the least of all sufficed
Her wants; her own self learned she to forsake,
Counting all earthly gain but hurt and loss.
So with calm will she chose and bore the cross,
And hated all for love of Jesus Christ.

21 November, 1850

II

They knelt in silent anguish by her bed,
And could not weep; but calmly there she lay.
All pain had left her; and the sun's last ray
Shone through upon her, warming into red
The shady curtains. In her heart she said:
"Heaven opens; I leave these and go away:
The Bridegroom calls,—shall the Bride seek to stay?"
Then low upon her breast she bowed her head.
O lily-flower, O gem of priceless worth,
O dove with patient voice and patient eyes,
O fruitful vine amid a land of dearth,
O maid replete with loving purities,
Thou bowedst down thy head with friends on earth
To raise it with the saints in Paradise.

24 February, 1847

THE THREE ENEMIES

THE FLESH

"SWEET, thou art pale."
"More pale to see,
Christ hung upon the cruel tree
And bore His Father's wrath for me."

"Sweet, thou art sad."
"Beneath a rod
More heavy, Christ for my sake trod
The winepress of the wrath of God."

"Sweet, thou art weary."
"Not so Christ:
Whose mighty love of me sufficed
For Strength, Salvation, Eucharist."

"Sweet, thou art footsore."
"If I bleed,
His feet have bled: yea, in my need
His Heart once bled for mine indeed."

THE WORLD

"Sweet, thou art young."
"So He was young
Who for my sake in silence hung
Upon the Cross with Passion wrung."

"Look, thou art fair."
"He was more fair
Than men, Who deigned for me to wear
A visage marred beyond compare."

"And thou hast riches."
"Daily bread:
All else is His; Who living, dead,
For me lacked where to lay His Head."

"And life is sweet."
"It was not so
To Him, Whose Cup did overflow
With mine unutterable woe."

THE DEVIL

"Thou drinkest deep."
"When Christ would sup
He drained the dregs from out my cup:
So how should I be lifted up?"

"Thou shalt win Glory."
"In the skies,
Lord Jesus, cover up mine eyes
Lest they should look on vanities."

"Thou shalt have Knowledge."
"Helpless dust,
In Thee, O Lord, I put my trust:
Answer Thou for me, Wise and Just."

"And Might."
"Get thee behind me. Lord,
Who has redeemed and not abhorred
My soul, O keep it by Thy Word."

15 June, 1851

THREE SEASONS

"A cup for hope!" she said,
In springtime ere the bloom was old;
The crimson wine was poor and cold
By her mouth's richer red.

"A cup for love!" how low,
How soft the words; and all the while
Her blush was rippling with a smile
Like summer after snow.

"A cup for memory!"
Cold cup that one must drain alone:
While autumn winds are up and moan
Across the barren sea.

Hope, memory, love:
Hope for fair morn, and love for day,
And memory for the evening gray
And solitary dove.

18 June, 1853

THE BOURNE

Underneath the growing grass,
Underneath the living flowers,
Deeper than the sound of showers:
There we shall not count the hours
By the shadows as they pass.

Youth and health will be but vain,
Beauty reckoned of no worth:
There a very little girth
Can hold round what once the earth
Seemed too narrow to contain.

17 February, 1854

ECHO

Come to me in the silence of the night;
Come in the speaking silence of a dream;
Come with soft rounded cheeks and eyes as bright
As sunlight on a stream;
Come back in tears,
O memory, hope, love of finished years.

O dream how sweet, too sweet, too bitter sweet,
Whose wakening should have been in Paradise,
Where souls brimful of love abide and meet;
Where thristing longing eyes
Watch the slow door
That opening, letting in, lets out no more.

Yet come to me in dreams, that I may live
My very life again though cold in death:
Come back to me in dreams, that I may give
Pulse for pulse, breath for breath:
Speak low, lean low,
As long ago, my love, how long ago!

18 December, 1854

MAY

I cannot tell you how it was;
But this I know: it came to pass—
Upon a bright and breezy day
When May was young; ah, pleasant May!
As yet the poppies were not born
Between the blades of tender corn;
The last eggs had not hatched as yet,
Nor any bird foregone its mate.

my Bible Class". I write as
our Grandfather printed, "con
amore"! pray pardon me if
I run into the irrelevant.
As to myself, I present at
present one only date,
Christina Georgina Rossetti
born December 5 – 1830;
when the date of my death
completes my career it will
be seen whether any more data
are worth recording. Allow me
meanwhile to <u>lend</u> you the
book of mine you refer to: this
is all of the sort, except that

Page of a Letter from Christina Rossetti to H. Buxton Forman. (See Appendix I.)

I cannot tell you what it was;
But this I know: it did but pass.
It passed away with sunny May,
With all sweet things it passed away,
And left me old, and cold, and gray.

20 November, 1855

TO THE END

There are lilies for her sisters—
(Who so cold as they?)—
And heartsease for one I must not name
When I am far away.
I shall pluck the lady lilies
And fancy all the rest:
I shall pluck the bright-eyed heartsease
For her sake I love the best:
As I wander on with weary feet
Toward the twilight shadowy west.

O bird that flyest eastward
Unto that sunny land,
Oh, wilt thou light on lilies white
Beside her whiter hand?
Soft summer wind that breathest
Of perfumes and sweet spice,
Ah tell her what I dare not tell
Of watchful waiting eyes,
Of love that yet may meet again
In distant Paradise.

I go from earth to heaven
A dim uncertain road,
A houseless pilgrim through the world
Unto a sure abode:
While evermore an Angel
Goes with me day and night,
A ministering spirit
From the land of light,
My holy fellow-servant sent
To guide my steps aright.

I wonder if the Angels
Love with such love as ours,
If for each other's sake they pluck
And keep eternal flowers.
Alone I am and weary,
Alone yet not alone:
Her soul talks with me by the way
From tedious stone to stone,
A blessed Angel treads with me
The awful paths unknown.

When will the long road end in rest,
The sick bird perch and brood?
When will my Guardian fold his wings
At rest in the finished good?
Lulling, lulling me off to sleep:
While Death's strong hand doth roll
My sins behind his back,
And my life up like a scroll,
Till through sleep I hear kind Angels
Rejoicing at the goal.

If her spirit went before me
Up from night to day,
It would pass me like the lightning
That kindles on its way.
I should feel it like the lightning
Flashing fresh from heaven:
I should long for heaven sevenfold more,
Yea and sevenfold seven:
Should pray as I have not prayed before,
And strive as I have not striven.

She will learn new love in heaven,
Who is so full of love;
She will learn new depths of tenderness
Who is tender like a dove.
Her heart will no more sorrow,
Her eyes will weep no more:
Yet it may be she will yearn
And look back from far before:
Lingering on the golden threshold
And leaning from the door.

18 December, 1855

IN AN ARTIST'S STUDIO

One face looks out from all his canvases,
One selfsame figure sits or walks or leans:
We found her hidden just behind those screens,
That mirror gave back all her loveliness.
A queen in opal or in ruby dress,
A nameless girl in freshest summer-greens,
A saint, an angel—every canvas means
The same one meaning, neither more or less.
He feeds upon her face by day and night,
And she with true kind eyes looks back on him,
Fair as the moon and joyful as the light:
Not wan with waiting, not with sorrow dim;
Not as she is, but was when hope shone bright;
Not as she is, but as she fills his dream.

24 December, 1856

A BETTER RESURRECTION

I HAVE no wit, no words, no tears;
My heart within me like a stone
Is numbed too much for hopes or fears.
Look right, look left, I dwell alone;
I lift mine eyes, but dimmed with grief
No everlasting hills I see;
My life is in the falling leaf:
O Jesus, quicken me!

My life is like a faded leaf,
My harvest dwindled to a husk;
Truly my life is void and brief
And tedious in the barren dusk;
My life is like a frozen thing,
No bud nor greenness can I see:
Yet rise it shall,—the sap of Spring;
O Jesus, rise in me!

My life is like a broken bowl,
A broken bowl that cannot hold
One drop of water for my soul
Or cordial in the searching cold;
Cast in the fire the perished thing;
Melt and remould it, till it be
A royal cup for Him my King:
O Jesus, drink of me!

30 June, 1857

A BIRTHDAY

My heart is like a singing bird
Whose nest is in a watered shoot;
My heart is like an apple-tree
Whose boughs are bent with thickset fruit;
My heart is like a rainbow shell
That paddles in a halcyon sea;
My heart is gladder than all these
Because my love is come to me.

Raise me a dais of silk and down;
Hang it with vair and purple dyes;
Carve it in doves and pomegranates,
And peacocks with a hundred eyes;
Work it in gold and silver grapes,
In leaves and silver fleurs-de-lys;
Because the birthday of my life
Is come, my love is come to me.

18 November, 1857

ADVENT

This Advent moon shines cold and clear,
These Advent nights are long;
Our lamps have burned year after year,
And still their flame is strong.
"Watchman, what of the night?" we cry,
Heart-sick with hope deferred:
"No speaking signs are in the sky,"
Is still the watchman's word.

The Porter watches at the gate,
The servants watch within;
The watch is long betimes and late,
The prize is slow to win.
"Watchman, what of the night?" But still
His answer sounds the same:
"No daybreak tops the utmost hill,
Nor pale our lamps of flame."

One to another hear them speak,
The patient virgins wise:
"Surely He is not far to seek,"—
"All night we watch and rise."
"The days are evil looking back,
The coming days are dim;
Yet count we not His promise slack,
But watch and wait for Him."

One with another, soul with soul,
They kindle fire from fire:
"Friends watch us who have touched the goal."
"They urge us, come up higher."
"With them shall rest our waysore feet,
With them is built our home,
With Christ."—"They sweet, but He most sweet,
Sweeter than honeycomb."

There no more parting, no more pain,
The distant ones brought near,
The lost so long are found again,
Long lost but longer dear:
Eye hath not seen, ear hath not heard,
Nor heart conceived that rest,
With them our good things long deferred,
With Jesus Christ our Best.

We weep because the night is long,
We laugh, for day shall rise,
We sing a slow contented song
And knock at Paradise.

Weeping we hold Him fast Who wept
  For us,—we hold Him fast;
And will not let Him go except
  He bless us first or last.

Weeping we hold Him fast to-night;
  We will not let Him go
Till daybreak smite our wearied sight,
  And summer smite the snow:
Then figs shall bud, and dove with dove
  Shall coo the livelong day;
Then He shall say, "Arise, My love,
  My fair one, come away."

2 May, 1858

UP-HILL

Does the road wind up-hill all the way?
  Yes, to the very end.
Will the day's journey take the whole long day?
  From morn to night, my friend.

But is there for the night a resting-place?
  A roof for when the slow dark hours begin.
May not the darkness hide it from my face?
  You cannot miss that inn.

Shall I meet other wayfarers at night?
  Those who have gone before.
Then must I knock, or call when just in sight?
  They will not keep you standing at that door.

Shall I find comfort, travel-sore and weak?
  Of labor you shall find the sum.
Will there be beds for me and all who seek?
  Yea, beds for all who come.

29 June, 1858

AT HOME

When I was dead, my spirit turned
  To seek the much-frequented house:
I passed the door, and saw my friends
  Feasting beneath green orange-boughs;
From hand to hand they pushed the wine,
  They sucked the pulp of plum and peach;
They sang, they jested, and they laughed,
  For each was loved of each.

I listened to their honest chat:
  Said one: "To-morrow we shall be
Plod plod along the featureless sands,
  And coasting miles and miles of sea."
Said one: "Before the turn of tide
  We will achieve the eyrie-seat."
Said one: "To-morrow shall be like
  To-day, but much more sweet."

"To-morrow," said they, strong with hope,
  And dwelt upon the pleasant way:
"To-morrow," cried they, one and all,
  While no one spoke of yesterday.
Their life stood full at blessed noon;
  I, only I, had passed away:
"To-morrow and to-day," they cried;
  I was of yesterday.

I shivered comfortless, but cast
  No chill across the table-cloth;
I, all-forgotten, shivered, sad
  To stay, and yet to part how loth:
I passed from the familiar room,
  I who from love had passed away,
Like the remembrance of a guest
  That tarrieth but a day.

29 June, 1858

GOBLIN MARKET

Morning and evening
Maids heard the goblins cry:
"Come buy our orchard fruits,
Come buy, come buy:
Apples and quinces,
Lemons and oranges,
Plump unpecked cherries,
Melons and raspberries,
Bloom-down-cheeked peaches,
Swart-headed mulberries,
Wild free-born cranberries,
Crab-apples, dewberries,
Pine-apples, blackberries,
Apricots, strawberries;—
All ripe together
In summer weather,—
Morns that pass by,
Fair eves that fly;
Come buy, come buy:
Our grapes fresh from the vine,
Pomegranates full and fine,

Dates and sharp bullaces,
Rare pears and greengages,
Damsons and bilberries,
Taste them and try:
Currants and gooseberries,
Bright-fire-like barberries,
Figs to fill your mouth,
Citrons from the South,
Sweet to tongue and sound to eye;
Come buy, come buy."

Evening by evening
Among the brookside rushes,
Laura bowed her head to hear,
Lizzie veiled her blushes:
Crouching close together
In the cooling weather,
With clasping arms and cautioning lips,
With tingling cheeks and finger-tips.
"Lie close," Laura said,
Pricking up her golden head:
"We must not look at goblin men,
We must not buy their fruits:
Who knows upon what soil they fed
Their hungry thirsty roots?"
"Come buy," call the goblins
Hobbling down the glen.
"O," cried Lizzie, "Laura, Laura,
You should not peep at goblin men."
Lizzie covered up her eyes,
Covered close lest they should look;
Laura reared her glossy head,
And whispered like the restless brook:
"Look, Lizzie, look, Lizzie,
Down the glen tramp little men.
One hauls a basket,
One bears a plate,
One lugs a golden dish
Of many pounds' weight.
How fair the vine must grow
Whose grapes are so luscious;
How warm the wind must blow
Through those fruit bushes."
"No," said Lizzie: "No, no, no;
Their offers should not charm us,
Their evil gifts would harm us."
She thrust a dimpled finger
In each ear, shut eyes and ran:
Curious Laura chose to linger
Wondering at each merchant man.
One had a cat's face,
One whisked a tail,
One tramped at a rat's pace,
One crawled like a snail,
One like a wombat prowled obtuse and furry,
One like a ratel tumbled hurry skurry.
She heard a voice like voice of doves
Cooing all together:
They sounded kind and full of loves
In the pleasant weather.

Laura stretched her gleaming neck
Like a rush-imbedded swan,
Like a lily from the beck,
Like a moonlit poplar branch,
Like a vessel at the launch
When its last restraint is gone.

Backwards up the mossy glen
Turned and trooped the goblin men,
With their shrill repeated cry,
"Come buy, come buy."
When they reached where Laura was
They stood stock still upon the moss,
Leering at each other,
Brother with queer brother;
Signalling each other,
Brother with sly brother.
One set his basket down,
One reared his plate;
One began to weave a crown
Of tendrils, leaves, and rough nuts brown
(Men sell not such in any town);
One heaved the golden weight
Of dish and fruit to offer her:
"Come buy, come buy," was still their cry.
Laura stared but did not stir,
Longed but had no money:
The whisk-tailed merchant bade her taste
In tones as smooth as honey,
The cat-faced purr'd,
The rat-paced spoke a word
Of welcome, and the snail-paced even was heard;
One parrot-voiced and jolly
Cried "Pretty Goblin" still for "Pretty Polly";—
One whistled like a bird.

But sweet-tooth Laura spoke in haste:
"Good folk, I have no coin;
To take were to purloin:
I have no copper in my purse,

I have no silver either,
And all my gold is on the furze
That shakes in windy weather
Above the rusty heather."
"You have much gold upon your head,"
They answered altogether:
"Buy from us with a golden curl."
She clipped a precious golden lock,
She dropped a tear more rare than pearl,
Then sucked their fruit globes fair or red:
Sweeter than honey from the rock,
Stronger than man-rejoicing wine,
Clearer than water flowed that juice;
She never tasted such before,
How should it cloy with length of use?
She sucked and sucked and sucked the more
Fruits which that unknown orchard bore;
She sucked until her lips were sore;
Then flung the emptied rinds away,
But gathered up one kernel stone,
And knew not was it night or day
As she turned home alone.

Lizzie met her at the gate
Full of wise upbraidings:
"Dear, you should not stay so late,
Twilight is not good for maidens;
Should not loiter in the glen
In the haunts of goblin men.
Do you not remember Jeanie,
How she met them in the moonlight,
Took their gifts both choice and many,
Ate their fruits and wore their flowers
Plucked from bowers
Where summer ripens at all hours?
But ever in the noonlight
She pined and pined away;
Sought them by night and day,
Found them no more, but dwindled and grew
 gray;
Then fell with the first snow,
While to this day no grass will grow
Where she lies low:
I planted daisies there a year ago
That never blow.
You should not loiter so."
"Nay, hush," said Laura:
"Nay, hush, my sister:
I ate and ate my fill,
Yet my mouth waters still;
To-morrow night I will
Buy more,"—and kissed her.
"Have done with sorrow;
I 'll bring you plums to-morrow
Fresh on their mother twigs,
Cherries worth getting;
You cannot think what figs
My teeth have met in,
What melons icy-cold
Piled on a dish of gold
Too huge for me to hold,
What peaches with a velvet nap,
Pellucid grapes without one seed:
Odorous indeed must be the mead
Whereon they grow, and pure the wave they
 drink,
With lilies at the brink,
And sugar-sweet their sap."

Golden head by golden head,
Like two pigeons in one nest
Folded in each other's wings,
They lay down in their curtained bed:
Like two blossoms on one stem,
Like two flakes of new-fall'n snow,
Like two wands of ivory
Tipped with gold for awful kings.
Moon and stars gazed in at them,
Wind sang to them lullaby,
Lumbering owls forbore to fly,
Not a bat flapped to and fro
Round their rest:
Cheek to cheek and breast to breast
Locked together in one nest.

Early in the morning
When the first cock crowed his warning,
Neat like bees, as sweet and busy,
Laura rose with Lizzie:
Fetched in honey, milked the cows,
Aired and set to rights the house,
Kneaded cakes of whitest wheat,
Cakes for dainty mouths to eat,
Next churned butter, whipped up cream,
Fed their poultry, sat and sewed;
Talked as modest maidens should:
Lizzie with an open heart,
Laura in an absent dream,
One content, one sick in part;
One warbling for the mere bright day's de-
 light,
One longing for the night.

At length slow evening came:
They went with pitchers to the reedy brook;
Lizzie most placid in her look,
Laura most like a leaping flame.
They drew the gurgling water from its deep;
Lizzie plucked purple and rich golden flags,
Then turning homeward said: "The sunset flushes
Those furthest loftiest crags;
Come, Laura, not another maiden lags,
No wilful squirrel wags,
The beasts and birds are fast asleep."
But Laura loitered still among the rushes
And said the bank was steep.

And said the hour was early still,
The dew not fall'n, the wind not chill:
Listening ever, but not catching
The customary cry,
"Come buy, come buy,"
With its iterated jingle
Of sugar-baited words:
Not for all her watching
Once discerning even one goblin
Racing, whisking, tumbling, hobbling;
Let alone the herds
That used to tramp along the glen,
In groups or single,
Of brisk fruit-merchant men.

Till Lizzie urged: "O Laura, come;
I hear the fruit-call, but I dare not look:
You should not loiter longer at this brook:
Come with me home.
The stars rise, the moon bends her arc,
Each glow-worm winks her spark,
Let us get home before the night grows dark;
For clouds may gather
Though this is summer weather,
Put out the lights and drench us through;
Then if we lost our way what should we do?"

Laura turned cold as stone
To find her sister heard that cry alone,
That goblin cry,
"Come buy our fruits, come buy."
Must she then buy no more such dainty fruit?
Must she no more such succous pasture find,
Gone deaf and blind?
Her tree of life drooped from the root:
She said not one word in her heart's sore ache;
But peering thro' the dimness, naught discerning,
Trudged home, her pitcher dripping all the way;
So crept to bed, and lay
Silent till Lizzie slept;
Then sat up in a passionate yearning,
And gnashed her teeth for balked desire, and wept
As if her heart would break.

Day after day, night after night,
Laura kept watch in vain,
In sullen silence of exceeding pain.
She never caught again the goblin cry:
"Come buy, come buy";—
She never spied the goblin men
Hawking their fruits along the glen:
But when the noon waxed bright
Her hair grew thin and gray;
She dwindled, as the fair full moon doth turn
To swift decay, and burn
Her fire away.

One day remembering her kernel-stone
She set it by a wall that faced the south;
Dewed it with tears, hoped for a root,
Watched for a waxing shoot,
But there came none;
It never saw the sun,
It never felt the trickling moisture run:
While with sunk eyes and faded mouth
She dreamed of melons, as a traveller sees
False waves in desert drouth
With shade of leaf-crowned trees,
And burns the thirstier in the sandful breeze.

She no more swept the house,
Tended the fowls or cows,
Fetched honey, kneaded cakes of wheat,
Brought water from the brook:
But sat down listless in the chimney-nook
And would not eat.

Tender Lizzie could not bear
To watch her sister's cankerous care,
Yet not to share.
She night and morning
Caught the goblins' cry:
"Come buy our orchard fruits,
Come buy, come buy."

Beside the brook, along the glen,
She heard the tramp of goblin men,
The voice and stir
Poor Laura could not hear;
Longed to buy fruit to comfort her,
But feared to pay too dear.
She thought of Jeanie in her grave,
Who should have been a bride;
But who for joys brides hope to have
Fell sick and died
In her gay prime,
In earliest winter-time,
With the first glazing rime,
With the first snow-fall of crisp winter-time.

Till Laura, dwindling,
Seemed knocking at Death's door:
Then Lizzie weighed no more
Better and worse,
But put a silver penny in her purse,
Kissed Laura, crossed the heath with clumps of
furze
At twilight, halted by the brook;
And for the first time in her life
Began to listen and look.

Laughed every goblin
When they spied her peeping:
Came towards her hobbling,
Flying, running, leaping,
Puffing and blowing,
Chuckling, clapping, crowing,
Clucking and gobbling,
Mopping and mowing,
Full of airs and graces,
Pulling wry faces,
Demure grimaces,
Cat-like and rat-like,
Ratel and wombat-like,
Snail-paced in a hurry,
Parrot-voiced and whistler,
Helter-skelter, hurry skurry,
Chattering like magpies,
Fluttering like pigeons,
Gliding like fishes,—
Hugged her and kissed her;
Squeezed and caressed her;
Stretched up their dishes,
Panniers and plates:
"Look at our apples
Russet and dun,
Bob at our cherries,
Bite at our peaches,
Citrons and dates,
Grapes for the asking,
Pears red with basking
Out in the sun,
Plums on their twigs;
Pluck them and suck them,
Pomegranates, figs."

"Good folk," said Lizzie,
Mindful of Jeanie,
"Give me much and many";—
Held out her apron,
Tossed them her penny.
"Nay, take a seat with us,
Honor and eat with us,"
They answered grinning:
"Our feast is but beginning.
Night yet is early,
Warm and dew-pearly,
Wakeful and starry:
Such fruits as these
No man can carry;
Half their bloom would fly,
Half their dew would dry,
Half their flavor would pass by.
Sit down and feast with us,
Be welcome guest with us,
Cheer you and rest with us."
"Thank you," said Lizzie; "but one waits
At home alone for me:
So, without further parleying,
If you will not sell me any
Of your fruits though much and many,
Give me back my silver penny
I tossed you for a fee."
They began to scratch their pates,
No longer wagging, purring,
But visibly demurring,
Grunting and snarling.
One called her proud,
Cross-grained, uncivil;
Their tones waxed loud,
Their looks were evil.
Lashing their tails
They trod and hustled her,
Elbowed and jostled her,
Clawed with their nails,
Barking, mewing, hissing, mocking,
Tore her gown and soiled her stocking,

Twitched her hair out by the roots,
Stamped upon her tender feet,
Held her hands and squeezed their fruits
Against her mouth to make her eat.

White and golden Lizzie stood,
Like a lily in a flood,—
Like a rock of blue-veined stone
Lashed by tides obstreperously,—
Like a beacon left alone
In a hoary roaring sea,
Sending up a golden fire,—
Like a fruit-crowned orange-tree
White with blossoms honey-sweet
Sore beset by wasp and bee,—
Like a royal virgin town
Topped with gilded dome and spire
Close beleaguered by a fleet
Mad to tug her standard down.

One may lead a horse to water,
Twenty cannot make him drink.
Though the goblins cuffed and caught her,
Coaxed and fought her,
Bullied and besought her,
Scratched her, pinched her black as ink,
Kicked and knocked her,
Mauled and mocked her,
Lizzie uttered not a word;
Would not open lip from lip
Lest they should cram a mouthful in;
But laughed in heart to feel the drip
Of juice that syrupped all her face
And lodged in dimples of her chin,
And streaked her neck which quaked like curd.
At last the evil people,
Worn out by her resistance,
Flung back her penny, kicked their fruit
Along whichever road they took,
Not leaving root or stone or shoot.
Some writhed into the ground,
Some dived into the brook
With ring and ripple,
Some scudded on the gale without a sound,
Some vanished in the distance.

In a smart, ache, tingle,
Lizzie went her way;
Knew not was it night or day;
Sprang up the bank, tore through the furze,
Threaded copse and dingle,
And heard her penny jingle
Bouncing in her purse,—
Its bounce was music to her ear.
She ran and ran
As if she feared some goblin man
Dogged her with gibe or curse
Or something worse:
But not one goblin skurried after,
Nor was she pricked by fear;
The kind heart made her windy-paced
That urged her home quite out of breath with haste
And inward laughter.

She cried "Laura," up the garden,
"Did you miss me?
Come and kiss me.
Never mind my bruises,
Hug me, kiss me, suck my juices
Squeezed from goblin fruits for you,
Goblin pulp and goblin dew.
Eat me, drink me, love me;
Laura, make much of me:
For your sake I have braved the glen
And had to do with goblin merchant men."

Laura started from her chair,
Flung her arms up in the air,
Clutched her hair:
"Lizzie, Lizzie, have you tasted
For my sake the fruit forbidden?
Must your light like mine be hidden,
Your young life like mine be wasted,
Undone in mine undoing
And ruined in my ruin,
Thirsty, cankered, goblin-ridden?"
She clung about her sister,
Kissed and kissed and kissed her:
Tears once again
Refreshed her shrunken eyes,
Dropping like rain
After long sultry drouth;
Shaking with aguish fear, and pain,
She kissed and kissed her with a hungry mouth.

Her lips began to scorch,
That juice was wormwood to her tongue,
She loathed the feast:
Writhing as one possessed she leaped and sung,
Rent all her robe, and wrung

Her hands in lamentable haste,
And beat her breast.
Her locks streamed like the torch
Borne by a racer at full speed,
Or like the mane of horses in their flight,
Or like an eagle when she stems the light
Straight toward the sun,
Or like a caged thing freed,
Or like a flying flag when armies run.

Swift fire spread through her veins, knocked at her heart,
Met the fire smouldering there
And overbore its lesser flame;
She gorged on bitterness without a name:
Ah! fool, to choose such part
Of soul-consuming care!
Sense failed in the mortal strife:
Like the watch-tower of a town
Which an earthquake shatters down,
Like a lightning-stricken mast,
Like a wind-uprooted tree
Spun about,
Like a foam-topped waterspout
Cast down headlong in the sea,
She fell at last;
Pleasure past and anguish past,
Is it death or is it life?

Life out of death.
That night long Lizzie watched by her,
Counted her pulse's flagging stir,
Felt for her breath,
Held water to her lips, and cooled her face
With tears and fanning leaves:
But when the first birds chirped about their eaves,
And early reapers plodded to the place
Of golden sheaves,
And dew-wet grass
Bowed in the morning winds so brisk to pass,
And new buds with new day
Opened of cup-like lilies on the stream,
Laura awoke as from a dream,
Laughed in the innocent old way,
Hugged Lizzie but not twice or thrice;
Her gleaming locks showed not one thread of gray,
Her breath was sweet as May,
And light danced in her eyes.

Days, weeks, months, years
Afterwards, when both were wives
With children of their own;
Their mother-hearts beset with fears,
Their lives bound up in tender lives;
Laura would call the little ones
And tell them of her early prime,
Those pleasant days long gone
Of not-returning time:
Would talk about the haunted glen,
The wicked, quaint fruit-merchant men,
Their fruits like honey to the throat,
But poison in the blood;
(Men sell not such in any town;)
Would tell them how her sister stood
In deadly peril to do her good,
And win the fiery antidote:
Then joining hands to little hands
Would bid them cling together,
"For there is no friend like a sister,
In calm or stormy weather,
To cheer one on the tedious way,
To fetch one if one goes astray,
To lift one if one totters down,
To strengthen whilst one stands."

27 April, 1859

LIFE AND DEATH

LIFE is not sweet. One day it will be sweet
To shut our eyes and die:
Nor feel the wild-flowers blow, nor birds dart by
With flitting butterfly,
Nor grass grow long above our heads and feet,
Nor hear the happy lark that soars sky high,
Nor sigh that spring is fleet and summer fleet,
Nor mark the waxing wheat,
Nor know who sits in our accustomed seat.

Life is not good. One day it will be good
To die, then live again;
To sleep meanwhile: so not to feel the wane
Of shrunk leaves dropping in the wood,
Nor hear the foamy lashing of the main,
Nor mark the blackened bean-fields, nor where stood
Rich ranks of golden grain,
Only dead refuse stubble clothe the plain:
Asleep from risk, asleep from pain.

24 April, 1863

SOMEWHERE OR OTHER

Somewhere or other there must surely be
The face not seen, the voice not heard,
The heart that not yet—never yet—ah me!
Made answer to my word.

Somewhere or other, may be near or far;
Past land and sea, clean out of sight;
Beyond the wandering moon, beyond the star
That tracks her night by night.

Somewhere or other, may be far or near;
With just a wall, a hedge, between;
With just the last leaves of the dying year
Fallen on a turf grown green.

Towards November, 1863

WEARY IN WELL-DOING

I would have gone; God bade me stay:
I would have worked; God bade me rest.
He broke my will from day to day,
He read my yearnings unexpressed,
And said them nay.

Now I would stay; God bids me go:
Now I would rest; God bids me work.
He breaks my heart tossed to and fro,
My soul is wrung with doubts that lurk
And vex it so.

I go, Lord, where Thou sendest me;
Day after day I plod and moil:
But, Christ my God, when will it be
That I may let alone my toil
And rest with Thee?

22 October, 1864

AMOR MUNDI

"O where are you going with your love-locks flowing,
On the west wind blowing along this valley track?"
"The downhill path is easy, come with me an it please ye,
We shall escape the uphill by never turning back."

So they two went together in glowing August weather,
The honey-breathing heather lay to their left and right;
And dear she was to doat on, her swift feet seemed to float on
The air like soft twin pigeons too sportive to alight.

"Oh, what is that in heaven where grey cloud-flakes are seven,
Where blackest clouds hang riven just at the rainy skirt?"
"Oh, that 's a meteor sent us, a message dumb, portentous,
An undeciphered solemn signal of help or hurt."

"Oh, what is that glides quickly where velvet flowers grow thickly,
Their scent comes rich and sickly?"—"A scaled and hooded worm."
"Oh, what 's that in the hollow, so pale I quake to follow?"
"Oh, that 's a thin dead body which waits the eternal term."

"Turn again, O my sweetest,—turn again, false and fleetest:
This beaten way thou beatest, I fear, is hell's own track."
"Nay, too steep for hill mounting; nay, too late for cost counting:
This downhill path is easy, but there's no turning back."

21 February, 1865

ITALIA, IO TI SALUTO

To come back from the sweet South, to the North
Where I was born, bred, look to die;
Come back to do my day's work in its day,
Play out my play—
Amen, amen, say I.

To see no more the country half my own,
Nor hear the half familiar speech,
Amen, I saw; I turn to that bleak North
Whence I came forth—
The South lies out of reach.

But when our swallows fly back to the South,
To the sweet South, to the sweet South,
The tears may come again into my eyes
On the old wise,
And the sweet name to my mouth.

Towards July, 1865

A DAUGHTER OF EVE

A FOOL I was to sleep at noon,
And wake when night is chilly
Beneath the comfortless cold moon;
A fool to pluck my rose too soon,
A fool to snap my lily.

My garden-plot I have not kept;
Faded and all-forsaken,
I weep as I have never wept:
Oh it was summer when I slept,
It's winter now I waken.

Talk what you please of future spring
And sun-warmed sweet to-morrow:—
Stripped bare of hope and every thing,
No more to laugh, no more to sing,
I sit alone with sorrow.

30 September, 1865

"TO-DAY FOR ME"

SHE sitteth still who used to dance,
She weepeth sore and more and more:—
Let us sit with thee weeping sore,
O fair France!

She trembleth as the days advance
Who used to be so light of heart:—
We in thy trembling bear a part,
Sister France!

Her eyes shine tearful as they glance:
"Who shall give back my slaughtered sons?
"Bind up," she saith, "my wounded ones."—
Alas, France!

She struggles in a deathly trance,
As in a dream her pulses stir,
She hears the nations calling her,
"France, France, France!"

Thou people of the lifted lance,
Forbear her tears, forbear her blood:
Roll back, roll back, thy whelming flood,
Back from France.

Eye not her loveliness askance,
Forge not for her a galling chain;
Leave her at peace to bloom again,
Vine-clad France.

A time there is for change and chance,
A time for passing of the cup:
And One abides can yet bind up
Broken France.

A time there is for change and chance:
Who next shall drink the trembling cup,
Wring out its dregs and suck them up
After France?

Towards January, 1871

BIRD RAPTURES

THE sunrise wakes the lark to sing,
The moonrise wakes the nightingale.
Come darkness, moonrise, every thing
That is so silent, sweet, and pale:
Come, so ye wake the nightingale.

Make haste to mount, thou wistful moon,
Make haste to wake the nightingale:
Let silence set the world in tune
To hearken to that wordless tale
Which warbles from the nightingale.

O herald skylark, stay thy flight
One moment, for a nightingale
Floods us with sorrow and delight.
To-morrow thou shalt hoist the sail;
Leave us to-night the nightingale.

Before 1876

TREAD SOFTLY

TREAD softly! all the earth is holy ground.
It may be, could we look with seeing eyes,
This spot we stand on is a Paradise
Where dead have come to life and lost been found,
Where Faith has triumphed, Martyrdom been crowned,
Where fools have foiled the wisdom of the wise;
From this same spot the dust of saints may rise,
And the King's prisoners come to light unbound.
O earth, earth, earth, hear thou thy Maker's Word;

He & She.

"Should one of us remember,
And one of us forget,
I wish I knew what each will do:—
But who can tell as yet?"

"Should one of us remember,
And one of us forget,
I promise you what I will do:—
And I'm content to wait for you,
And not be sure as yet."

Copy of *He and She* in the Author's Handwriting. (See Appendix I.)

"Thy dead thou shalt give up, nor hide thy slain."
Some who went weeping forth shall come again
Rejoicing from the east or from the west,
As doves fly to their windows, love's own bird
Contented and desirous to the nest.

Before 1882

HE AND SHE

"Should one of us remember,
And one of us forget,
I wish I knew what each will do,
But who can tell as yet?"

"Should one of us remember,
And one of us forget,
I promise you what I will do—
And I'm content to wait for you,
And not be sure as yet."

Before 1882

DE PROFUNDIS

Oh why is heaven built so far,
Oh why is earth set so remote?
I cannot reach the nearest star
That hangs afloat.

I would not care to reach the moon,
One round monotonous of change;
Yet even she repeats her tune
Beyond my range.

I never watch the scattered fire
Of stars, or sun's far-trailing train,
But all my heart is one desire,
And all in vain:

For I am bound with fleshly bands,
Joy, beauty, lie beyond my scope;
I strain my heart, I stretch my hands,
And catch at hope.

Before 1882

O MY HEART'S HEART

"Amor che a nullo amato amar perdona." [1]
DANTE

"Amor m'addusse in si gioiosa spene." [2]
PETRARCA

O my heart's heart, and you who are to me
More than myself myself, God be with you,
Keep you in strong obedience leal and true
To Him whose noble service setteth free;
Give you all good or see we can forsee,
Make your joys many and your sorrows few,
Bless you in what you bear and what you do,
Yea, perfect you as He would have you be.
So much for you; but what for me, dear friend?
To love you without stint and all I can,
To-day, to-morrow, world without an end;
To love you much and yet to love you more,
As Jordan at his flood sweeps either shore;
Since woman is the helpmeet made for man.

Before 1882

SLEEPING AT LAST

Sleeping at last, the trouble and tumult over,
Sleeping at last, the struggle and horror past,
Cold and white, out of sight of friend and of lover,
Sleeping at last.

No more a tired heart downcast or overcast,
No more pangs that wring or shifting fears that hover,
Sleeping at last in a dreamless sleep locked fast.

Fast asleep. Singing birds in their leafy cover
Cannot wake her, nor shake her the gusty blast.
Under the purple thyme and the purple clover
Sleeping at last.

Circa 1893

[1] "Love, who exempts no loved one from loving." [2] "Love led me into such joyous hope."

Down into the green hollow of the ingathering wave,
So would I slip, and sink, and drown, in her grassy grave.

For is not my desire there, hidden away under the cloudy night
Of her long hair that was my valley of whispers and delight—

And in her two white hands, like still swans on a frozen lake,
Hath she not my heart that I have hidden there for dear love's sake?

Alas, there is no sighing song, no breath in the silence there:
Not even the white moth that loves death flits through her hair

As the bird of Brigid, made of foam and the pale moonwhite wine
Of dreams, flits under the sombre windless plumes of the pine.

I hear a voice crying, crying, crying: is it the wind
I hear, crying its old weary cry time out of mind?

The grey wind weeps, the grey wind weeps, the grey wind weeps:
Dust on her breast, dust on her eyes, the grey wind weeps!

1900

A SONG OF DREAMS

ONE came to me in the night
And said *Arise!*
I rose, phantom-white;
Far was my flight
To a star shaken with light
In the heart of the skies.

Through seven spheres I fled,
Opal and rose and white,
Emerald, violet, red,
Through azure as I led,
And the coronal on my head
With seven moons was bright.

What wonder that the day
Swings slowly through slow hours!
My heart leaps when the grey
Husht feet of Night are astray,
And I hear her wild bells play
On her starry towers.

1907

ROBERT LOUIS STEVENSON

[November 13, 1850–December 3, 1894]

Thin-legged, thin-chested, slight unspeakably,
Neat-footed and weak-fingered; in his face—
Lean, large-boned, curved of beak, and touched with race,
Bold-lipped, rich-tinted, mutable as the sea,
The brown eyes radiant with vivacity—
There shines a brilliant and romantic grace,
A spirit intense and rare, with trace on trace
Of passion and impudence and energy.
Valiant in velvet, light in ragged luck,
Most vain, most generous, sternly critical,
Buffoon and poct, lover and sensualist;
A deal of Ariel, just a streak of Puck,
Much Antony, of Hamlet most of all,
And something of the Shorter-Catechist.

So wrote Henley, when he lay in Edinburgh Infirmary, of his bedside visitor, Robert Louis Stevenson. Stevenson, "thin-chested, slight unspeakably," was frail from babyhood and, once he reached young manhood, was forced to begin a long series of pilgrimages in search of a climate that might help him to break the hold tuberculosis was getting upon him. He was born in

Edinburgh, Scotland, and when he was eight years old he almost died of a gastric fever which left him greatly weakened for months. The nine years beginning with 1858 he spent in school in his home city, his family hoping that he would become a civil engineer; indeed, he progressed far enough in engineering to win a silver medal for a paper he wrote suggesting improvements in lighthouse apparatus. His earliest work was an anonymous pamphlet, *The Pentland Rising* (1866).

Enjoying the outdoor life associated with engineering but finding it too much for his delicate health, Stevenson took up law, and was called to the bar in 1875. In this year he made his first visit to the forest of Fontainebleau, where in 1876 he met the American, Mrs. Osbourne, who was later to become his wife. He made no attempt to practice law, but spent the years 1875–1879 in wandering through France, Germany, and Scotland, and recording his experiences in *An Inland Voyage* (1878) and *Travels with a Donkey* (1879).

Mrs. Osbourne returned to America in 1878, and in the autumn of the next year Stevenson heard of her illness. He went at once to California, but his resources were so limited that the trip's hardships seriously affected his health. He married Mrs. Osbourne in 1880, and they moved to a desolate mining camp, where *The Silverado Squatters* was begun.

From then until his death in 1894, Stevenson's life was interrupted every few months by his pilgrimages for health. There were two periods spent at Davos in Switzerland (divided by some time in Scotland) where he wrote *Familiar Studies of Men and Books* (1882), the *New Arabian Nights* (1882), and *Treasure Island* (1883); over a year at Marseilles, and three years at Bournemouth, England, whence, in 1885, appeared, after long indecision, the simple and lovely *A Child's Garden of Verses*. In 1886 *Dr. Jekyll and Mr. Hyde* captured the public's taste, and in the next year appeared *Underwoods*, his second book of poems.

From England, he went to America again, spending a winter at Saranac Lake in the Adirondacks, where he wrote *The Master of Ballantrae*. Thence he went to New Jersey and to California, and shipped westward over the Pacific to the Marquesas, Tahiti, Honolulu, the leper colony at Molokai, the Gilbert Islands, and Australia, finally ending at Samoa in 1890. The last four years of his life were spent at Vailima, where he interested himself in the political affairs of the natives and their king, Mataafa, and was much reverenced by them. In 1893 he went for a change of scene to the Sandwich Islands, but fell ill and returned to Samoa.

On December 3, 1894, he had been dictating *Weir of Hermiston*, seemingly in his normal health. While chatting gaily with Mrs. Stevenson on the veranda of the Vailima house, he was stricken with apoplexy and died a few hours later. The next day sixty sorrowing natives carried their Tusitala to the precipitous peak of Vaea, where he had hoped he might be buried with the blue Pacific beneath him. Shortly after was raised a tablet inscribed with lines from his *Requiem:*

Here he lies where he longed to be;
Home is the sailor, home from sea,
And the hunter home from the hill.

LOOKING FORWARD[1]

WHEN I am grown to man's estate
I shall be very proud and great,
And tell the other girls and boys
Not to meddle with my toys.

A GOOD PLAY

WE built a ship upon the stairs
All made of the back-bedroom chairs,
And filled it full of sofa pillows
To go a-sailing on the billows.

[1] The first eleven titles in this group of Stevenson's poems are from *A Child's Garden of Verses*, first published in 1885.

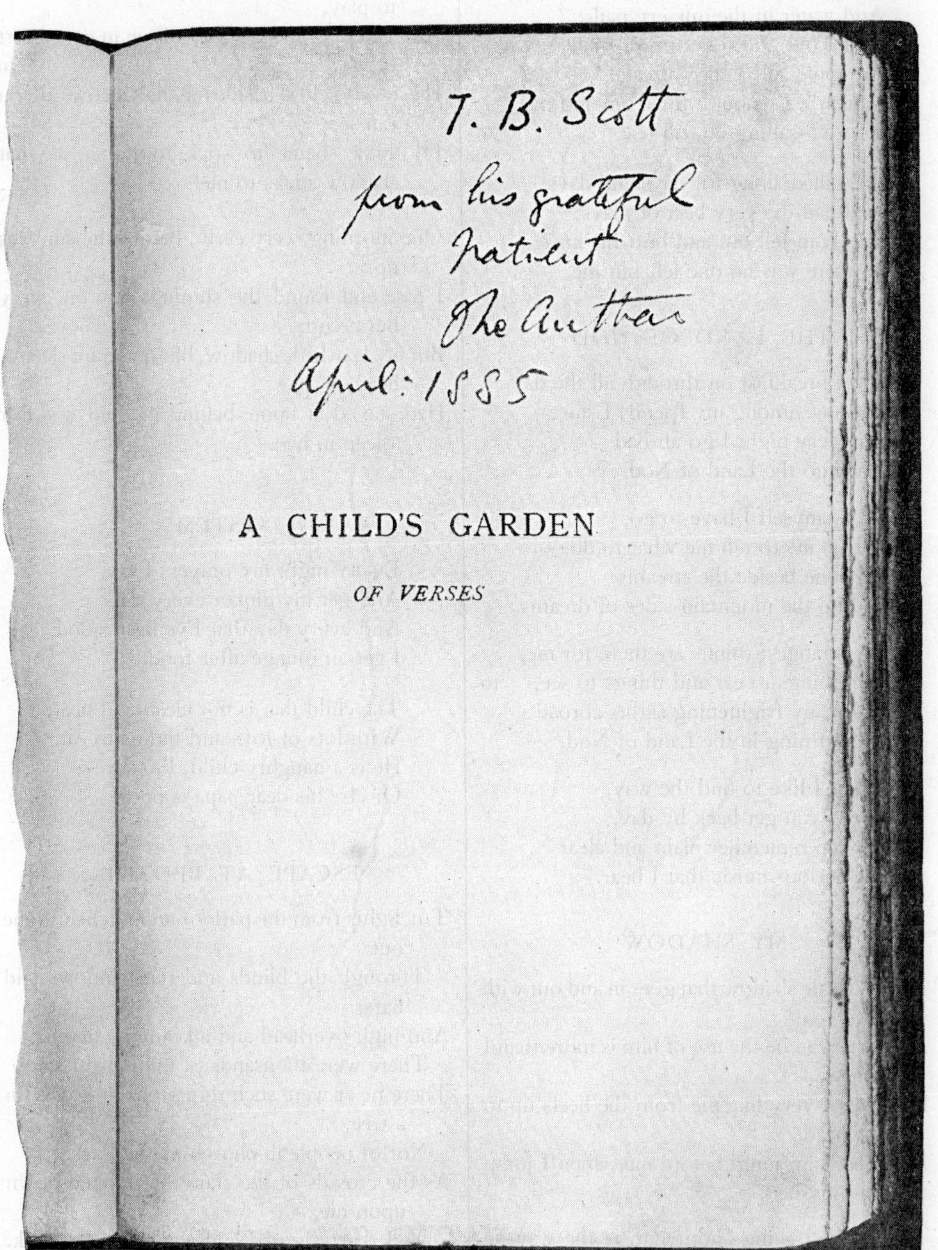

Presentation Copy to Dr. Thomas Bodley Scott. (See Appendix I.)

We took a saw and several nails,
And water in the nursery pails;
And Tom said, "Let us also take
An apple and a slice of cake;"—
Which was enough for Tom and me
To go a-sailing on, till tea.

We sailed along for days and days,
And had the very best of plays;
But Tom fell out and hurt his knee,
So there was no one left but me.

THE LAND OF NOD

From breakfast on through all the day
At home among my friends I stay,
But every night I go abroad
Afar into the Land of Nod.

All by myself I have to go,
With none to tell me what to do—
All alone beside the streams
And up the mountain-sides of dreams.

The strangest things are there for me,
Both things to eat and things to see,
And many frightening sights abroad
Till morning in the Land of Nod.

Try as I like to find the way,
I never can get back by day,
Nor can remember plain and clear
The curious music that I hear.

MY SHADOW

I have a little shadow that goes in and out with me,
And what can be the use of him is more than I can see.
He is very, very like me from the heels up to the head;
And I see him jump before me, when I jump into my bed.

The funniest thing about him is the way he likes to grow—
Not at all like proper children, which is always very slow;
For he sometimes shoots up taller like an india-rubber ball,
And he sometimes gets so little that there's none of him at all.

He hasn't got a notion of how children ought to play,
And can only make a fool of me in every sort of way.
He stays so close beside me, he's a coward you can see;
I'd think shame to stick to nursie as that shadow sticks to me!

One morning, very early, before the sun was up,
I rose and found the shining dew on every buttercup;
But my lazy little shadow, like an arrant sleepy-head,
Had stayed at home behind me and was fast asleep in bed.

SYSTEM

Every night my prayers I say,
And get my dinner every day;
And every day that I've been good,
I get an orange after food.

The child that is not clean and neat,
With lots of toys and things to eat,
He is a naughty child, I'm sure—
Or else his dear papa is poor.

ESCAPE AT BEDTIME

The lights from the parlour and kitchen shone out
Through the blinds and the windows and bars;
And high overhead and all moving about,
There were thousands of millions of stars.
There ne'er were such thousands of leaves on a tree,
Nor of people in church or the Park,
As the crowds of the stars that looked down upon me,
And that glittered and winked in the dark.

The Dog, and the Plough, and the Hunter, and all,
And the star of the sailor, and Mars,
These shone in the sky, and the pail by the wall
Would be half full of water and stars.

They saw me at last, and they chased me with cries,
And they soon had me packed into bed;
But the glory kept shining and bright in my eyes,
And the stars going round in my head.

MARCHING SONG

Bring the comb and play upon it!
Marching, here we come!
Willie cocks his highland bonnet,
Johnnie beats the drum.

Mary Jane commands the party,
Peter leads the rear;
Feet in time, alert and hearty,
Each a Grenadier!

All in the most martial manner
Marching double-quick;
While the napkin like a banner
Waves upon the stick!

Here's enough of fame and pillage,
Great commander Jane!
Now that we've been round the village,
Let's go home again.

THE COW

The friendly cow all red and white,
I love with all my heart:
She gives me cream with all her might,
To eat with apple-tart.

She wanders lowing here and there,
And yet she cannot stray,
All in the pleasant open air,
The pleasant light of day;

And blown by all the winds that pass
And wet with all the showers,
She walks among the meadow grass
And eats the meadow flowers.

HAPPY THOUGHT

The world is so full of a number of things,
I'm sure we should all be as happy as kings.

GOOD AND BAD CHILDREN

Children, you are very little,
And your bones are very brittle;
If you would grow great and stately,
You must try to walk sedately.

You must still be bright and quiet,
And content with simple diet;
And remain, through all bewild'ring,
Innocent and honest children.

Happy hearts and happy faces,
Happy play in grassy places—
That was how, in ancient ages,
Children grew to kings and sages.

But the unkind and the unruly,
And the sort who eat unduly,
They must never hope for glory—
Theirs is quite a different story!

Cruel children, crying babies,
All grow up as geese and gabies,
Hated, as their age increases,
By their nephews and their nieces.

THE SWING

How do you like to go up in a swing,
Up in the air so blue?
Oh, I do think it the pleasantest thing
Ever a child can do!

Up in the air and over the wall,
Till I can see so wide,
Rivers and trees and cattle and all
Over the countryside—

Till I look down on the garden green,
Down on the roof so brown—
Up in the air I go flying again,
Up in the air and down!

IT IS THE SEASON[1]

It is the season now to go
About the country high and low,
Among the lilacs hand in hand,
And two by two in fairy land.

[1] This and the following poems from Stevenson are all from *Underwoods*, first published in 1887 and expanded in later editions.

The brooding boy, the sighing maid,
Wholly fain and half afraid,
Now meet along the hazel'd brook
To pass and linger, pause and look.

A year ago, and blithely paired,
Their rough-and-tumble play they shared;
They kissed and quarrelled, laughed and cried,
A year ago at Eastertide.

With bursting heart, with fiery face,
She strove against him in the race;
He unabashed her garter saw,
That now would touch her skirts with awe.

Now by the stile ablaze she stops,
And his demurer eyes he drops;
Now they exchange averted sighs
Or stand and marry silent eyes.

And he to her a hero is
And sweeter she than primroses;
Their common silence dearer far
Than nightingale or mavis are.

Now when they sever wedded hands,
Joy trembles in their bosom-strands,
And lovely laughter leaps and falls
Upon their lips in madrigals.

IN THE STATES

WITH half a heart I wander here
As from an age gone by,
A brother—yet though young in years,
An elder brother, I.

You speak another tongue than mine,
Though both were English born.
I towards the night of time decline,
You mount into the morn.

Youth shall grow great and strong and free,
But age must still decay:
To-morrow for the States—for me,
England and Yesterday.

SAN FRANCISCO

A CAMP

THE bed was made, the room was fit,
By punctual eve the stars were lit;
The air was still, the water ran,
No need was there for maid or man,
When we put up, my ass and I,
At God's green caravanserai.

[1] From *Travels with a Donkey*

SKERRYVORE

FOR love of lovely words, and for the sake
Of those, my kinsmen and my countrymen,
Who early and late in the windy ocean toiled
To plant a star for seamen, where was then
The surfy haunt of seals and cormorants:
I, on the lintel of this cot, inscribe
The name of a strong tower.

SKERRYVORE: THE PARALLEL

HERE all is sunny, and when the truant gull
Skims the green level of the lawn, his wing
Dispetals roses; here the house is framed
Of kneaded brick and the plumed mountain pine,
Such clay as artists fashion and such wood
As the tree-climbing urchin breaks. But there
Eternal granite hewn from the living isle
And dowelled with brute iron, rears a tower
That from its wet foundation to its crown
Of glittering glass, stands, in the sweep of winds,
Immovable, immortal, eminent.

MY HOUSE

MY house, I say. But hark to the sunny doves
That make my roof the arena of their loves,
That gyre about the gable all day long
And fill the chimneys with their murmurous song:
Our house, they say; and *mine*, the cat declares
And spreads his golden fleece upon the chairs;
And *mine* the dog, and rises stiff with wrath
If any alien foot profane the path.
So, too, the buck that trimmed my terraces,
Our whilom gardener, called the garden his;
Who now, deposed, surveys my plain abode
And his late kingdom, only from the road.

THE VAGABOND

(*To an air of Schubert*)

GIVE to me the life I love,
Let the lave go by me,

Picklerez-vous toujours? (Remember [illegible])
I wish you would come down. When would you?

Yours
Le Picklem

He pickled low, he pickled loud
He ~~[illegible]~~ not for the smiling crowd,
Over a scene confused and curly
He pickled late, he pickled early.
He pickled slow; he pickled fast –
~~[illegible]~~ at least he hoped he might at last;
He pickled wrong; he pickled right –
~~[illegible]~~ at least he hoped at last he might.
He pickled up, he pickled down
And was the brightness of his town.

2 Richruffels will cost to you; one is for Lemon whose ~~name~~ address I forgot. [illegible]

Last Page of a Letter from Stevenson. (See Appendix I.)

Give the jolly heaven above
And the byway nigh me.
Bed in the bush with stars to see,
Bread I dip in the river—
There's the life for a man like me,
There's the life for ever.

Let the blow fall soon or late,
Let what will be o'er me;
Give the face of earth around
And the road before me.
Wealth I seek not, hope nor love,
Nor a friend to know me;
All I seek the heaven above
And the road below me.

Or let autumn fall on me
Where afield I linger,
Silencing the bird on tree,
Biting the blue finger:
White as meal the frosty field—
Warm the fireside haven—
Not to autumn will I yield,
Not to winter even!

Let the blow fall soon or late,
Let what will be o'er me;
Give the face of earth around
And the road before me.
Wealth I ask not, hope nor love,
Nor a friend to know me.
All I ask the heaven above
And the road below me.

THE UNFORGOTTEN—II

SHE rested by the Broken Brook,
She drank of Weary Well,
She moved beyond my lingering look,
Ah, whither none can tell!

She came, she went. In other lands,
Perchance in fairer skies,
Her hands shall cling with other hands,
Her eyes to other eyes.

She vanished. In the sounding town,
Will she remember too?
Will she recall the eyes of brown
As I recall the blue?

DITTY

(*To an air from Bach*)

THE cock shall crow
In the morning grey,
The bugles blow
At the break of day:
The cock shall sing and the merry bugles ring,
And all the little brown birds sing upon the spray.

The thorn shall blow
In the month of May,
And my love shall go
In her holiday array:
But I shall lie in the kirkyard nigh
While all the little brown birds sing upon the spray.

TO DOCTOR HAKE

(*On receiving a copy of verses*)

IN the belovèd hour that ushers day,
In the pure dew, under the breaking grey,
One bird, ere yet the woodland quires awake,
With brief reveille summons all the brake:
Chirp, chirp, it goes; nor waits an answer long;
And that small signal fills the grove with song.

Thus on my pipe I breathed a strain or two;
It scarce was music, but 'twas all I knew.
It was not music, for I lacked the art,
Yet what but frozen music filled my heart?
Chirp, chirp, I went, nor hoped a nobler strain;
But Heaven decreed I should not pipe in vain,
For, lo! not far from there, in secret dale,
All silent, sat an ancient nightingale.
My sparrow notes he heard; thereat awoke;
And with a tide of song his silence broke.

I HAVE TROD

I HAVE trod the upward and the downward slope;
I have endured and done in days before;
I have longed for all, and bid farewell to hope;
And I have lived and loved, and closed the door.

Under the wide and starry sky
Dig the grave and let me lie.
Glad did I live and gladly die,
And I laid me down with a will.

Here may the winds about me blow;
Here the clouds may come and go;
Here shall be rest for evermo,
And the heart for aye shall be still.

This be the verse you grave for me:
Here he lies where he longed to be;
Home is the sailor, home from sea,
And the hunter home from the hill.

The Unpublished Version of Stevenson's *Requiem.* (See Appendix I.)

TO THE MUSE

RESIGN the rhapsody, the dream,
 To men of larger reach;
Be ours the quest of a plain theme,
 The piety of speech.

As monkish scribes from morning break
 Toiled till the close of light,
Nor thought a day too long to make
 One line or letter bright:

We also with an ardent mind,
 Time, wealth and fame forgot,
Our glory in our patience find
 And skim, and skim the pot:

Till last, when round the house we hear
 The evensong of birds,
One corner of blue heaven appear
 In our clear well of words.

Leave, leave it then, muse of my heart!
 Sans finish and sans frame,
Leave unadorned by needless art
 The picture as it came.

APEMAMA

AN END OF TRAVEL

LET now your soul in this substantial world
Some anchor strike. Be here the body moored:
This spectacle immutably from now
The picture in your eye; and when time strikes,
And the green scene goes on the instant blind,
The ultimate helpers, where your horse to-day
Conveyed you dreaming, bear your body dead.

VAILIMA

EVENSONG

THE embers of the day are red
Beyond the murky hill.
The kitchen smokes: the bed
In the darkling house is spread:
The great sky darkens overhead,
And the great woods are shrill.
So far have I been led,
Lord, by Thy will:
So far I have followed, Lord, and wondered still.

The breeze from the embalmèd land
Blows sudden toward the shore,
And claps my cottage door.
I hear the signal, Lord—I understand.
The night at Thy command
Comes. I will eat and sleep and will not question more.

VAILIMA

ARTHUR SYMONS

[February 28, 1865–]

ARTHUR SYMONS was born in Wales of Cornish parentage. He had no settled home in boyhood, which perhaps contributed later to his cosmopolitanism. His schooling was obtained in various private schools but his real and wide learning in the arts was of the sort which was self-taught and long-learned rather than the product of schools. He is reported to have produced at the age of nine a poem entitled "The Lord Is Good,"—a title in striking contrast to some of his later work. However this may be, in 1886, when twenty-one, he published his *An Introduction to the Study of Browning*, followed soon by his first volume of poems, *Days and Nights* (1889), and in the late 'eighties and early 'nineties he was a contributor to the *Athenæum* and the *Saturday Review* and he was associated with Dowson, Lionel Johnson, and Yeats in the Rhymers' Club. London was his headquarters, but Symons was extending his mental and physical travel. Rome, Venice, Seville, and Paris he visited in these and later years. The Paris which fascinated him was the Paris of the Cabarets painted by Toulouse-Lautrec. Here also he developed his interest in the ballet which colored so many of his poems, and it is interesting to note that in

Who's Who of 1933 Symons still lists as his favorite recreations, "Hearing and playing music, seeing dancing." The strongest poetic influences which came to bear upon him at this time were those of Baudelaire and Verlaine, and they were powerful ones.

The eighteen-nineties loom large in Symons's life. Following his *Days and Nights* he published (aside from criticism) *Silhouettes* (1892), *London Nights*, published in 1894 and dedicated to Verlaine, and *Amoris Victima* (1897). In 1895 he edited the brilliant *Savoy Magazine* which carried, as not the least of its attractions, the brilliant but disturbing illustrations of Aubrey Beardsley. It is the Symons of this period who is best known—the uncompromising editor of a magazine whose contributors delighted in upsetting the middle classes in the name of pure art; and himself the author of poems written under decadent continental influences in which, perhaps over often, he wrote of ladies loved lightly and not too well, but always with an appreciation of the situation. The Symons of this picture is somewhat an exaggeration of the excited 'nineties. In 1906 in dedicating his *Studies in Seven Arts* to his wife, whom he married in 1901, he wrote: "In my endeavour to master what I have called the universal science of beauty, I owe more to you than to technical books or to technical people; because in you there is some hardly conscious instinct which turns toward beauty unerringly, like the magnet, at the attraction of every vital current." As a poet Symons is sometimes the appreciator of a frail and passing mood or evanescent scene; he is always quick and sensitive, and a brilliant stylist in the sense that he can express the mood or scene. And his poetry is but a part of his cultivation of "the universal science of beauty." He is an æsthete but one of range and intelligence, and his criticism is a part of his "universal science of beauty." Although considered a figure of the nineties he has published poetry fairly continuously up to *Jezebel Mort and Other Poems* (1931) and his criticism, to give only part of the purely literary, runs from his Browning study of 1886 through studies of the Symbolist Movement, the Romantic Movement, of Blake, and of Baudelaire, to one of Thomas Hardy. He has translated, among others, from Gabriele D'Annunzio, Zola, and Baudelaire, and has either edited or introduced at least thirty other volumes ranging in character from Henri Murger's *Vie de Bohème* to an edition of *Cymbeline*. His *Studies in the Seven Arts* (1906), which includes among its twenty-eight papers essays on Rodin, Eleanora Duse, Beethoven, and Wagner, indicates that he has not limited himself to literature alone in his pursuit of "the universal science."

OF CHARITY

A BEGGAR died last night; his soul
Went up to God, and said:
"I come uncalled, forgive it, Lord;
I died for want of bread."

Then answered him the Lord of heaven:
"Son, how can this thing be?
Are not my saints on earth? and they
Had surely succoured thee."

"Thy saints, O Lord," the beggar said,
"Live holy lives of prayer;
How should they know of such as we?
We perish unaware.

"They strive to save our wicked souls
And fit them for the sky;
Meanwhile, not having bread to eat,
(Forgive!) our bodies die."

Then the Lord God spake out of heaven
In wrath and angry pain:
"O men, for whom my Son hath died,
My Son hath lived in vain!"

1889

RAIN ON THE DOWN

NIGHT, and the down by the sea,
And the veil of rain on the down;
And she came through the mist and the rain to
me
From the safe warm lights of the town.

The rain shone in her hair,
And her face gleamed in the rain;
And only the night and the rain were there
As she came to me out of the rain.

1892

BEFORE THE SQUALL

THE wind is rising on the sea,
The windy white foam-dancers leap;
And the sea moans uneasily,
And turns to sleep, and cannot sleep.

Ridge after rocky ridge uplifts
Wild hands, and hammers at the land,
Scatters in liquid dust, and drifts
To death among the dusty sand.

On the horizon's nearing line,
Where the sky rests, a visible wall,
Grey in the offing, I divine
The sails that fly before the squall.

1892

AN ANGEL OF PERUGINO

HAVE I not seen your face before
Where Perugino's angels stand
In those calm circles, and adore
With singing throat and lifted hand,

And pale hair folded crescent-wise,
About the placid forehead curled,
And the pale piety of eyes
Steadfast with peace upon the world?

I pause and watch you as you lean
Out of the doorway of your house,
With eyes grown happier to have seen
The Umbrian halo on your brows.

1892

EMMY

EMMY'S exquisite youth and her virginal air,
Eyes and teeth in the flash of a musical smile,
Come to me out of the past, and I see her there
As I saw her once for a while.

Emmy's laughter rings in my ears, as bright,
Fresh and sweet as the voice of a mountain brook,
And still I hear her telling us tales that night,
Out of Boccaccio's book.

There, in the midst of the villainous dancing-hall,
Leaning across the table, over the beer,
While the music maddened the whirling skirts of the ball,
As the midnight hour drew near,

There with the women, haggard, painted and old,
One fresh bud in a garland withered and stale,
She, with her innocent voice and her clear eyes, told
Tale after shameless tale.

And ever the witching smile, to her face beguiled,
Paused and broadened, and broke in a ripple of fun,
And the soul of a child looked out of the eyes of a child,
Or ever the tale was done.

O my child, who wronged you first, and began
First the dance of death that you dance so well?
Soul for soul: and I think the soul of a man
Shall answer for yours in hell.

1892

GIPSY LOVE

THE gipsy tents are on the down,
The gipsy girls are here;
And it's O to be off and away from the town
With a gipsy for my dear!

We'd make our bed in the bracken
With the lark for a chambermaid;
The lark would sing us awake in the morning,
Singing above our head.

We'd drink the sunlight all day long
With never a house to bind us;
And we'd only flout in a merry song
The world we left behind us.

We would be free as birds are free
The livelong day, the livelong day;
And we would lie in the sunny bracken
With none to say us nay.

The gipsy tents are on the down,
The gipsy girls are here;
And it's O to be off and away from the town
With a gipsy for my dear!

1892

IN FOUNTAIN COURT

THE fountain murmuring of sleep,
A drowsy tune;
The flickering green of leaves that keep
The light of June;
Peace, through a slumbering afternoon,
The peace of June.

A waiting ghost, in the blue sky,
The white curved moon;
June, hushed and breathless, waits, and I
Wait too, with June;
Come, through the lingering afternoon,
Soon, love, come soon.

1892

AT BURGOS

MIRACULOUS silver-work in stone
Against the blue miraculous skies,
The belfry towers and turrets rise
Out of the arches that enthrone
That airy wonder of the skies.

Softly against the burning sun
The great cathedral spreads its wings;
High up, the lyric belfry sings.
Behold Ascension Day begun
Under the shadow of those wings!

1892

AT DAWN

SHE only knew the birth and death
Of days, when each that died
Was still at morn a hope, at night
A hope unsatisfied.

The dark trees shivered to behold
Another day begin;
She, being hopeless, did not weep
As the grey dawn came in.

1892

KISSES

SWEET, can I sing you the song of your kisses?
How soft is this one, how subtle this is,
How fluttering swift as a bird's kiss that is,
As a bird that taps at a leafy lattice;
How this one clings and how that uncloses
From bud to flower in the way of roses;
And this through laughter and that through
weeping
Swims to the brim where Love lies sleeping;
And this in a pout I snatch, and capture
That in the ecstasy of rapture,
When the odorous red-rose petals part
That my lips may find their way to the heart
Of the rose of the world, your lips, my rose.
But no song knows
The way of my heart to the heart of my rose.

1895

HALLUCINATION: I

ONE petal of a blood-red tulip pressed
Between the pages of a Baudelaire:
No more; and I was suddenly aware
Of the white fragrant apple of a breast
On which my lips were pastured; and I knew
That dreaming I remembered an old dream.
Sweeter than any fruit that fruit did seem,
Which, as my hungry teeth devoured it, grew
Ever again, and tantalised my taste.
So, vainly hungering, I seemed to see
Eve and the serpent and the apple-tree,
And Adam in the garden, and God laying
waste
Innocent Eden, because man's desire,
Godlike before, now for a woman's sake
Descended through the woman to the snake.
Then as my mouth grew parched, stung as
with fire
By that white fragrant apple, once so fair,
That seemed to shrink and spire into a flame,
I cried, and wakened, crying on your name:
One blood-red petal stained the Baudelaire.

1895

VENETA MARINA

THE masts rise white to the stars,
White on the night of the sky,
Out of the water's night,
And the stars lean down to them white.
Ah! how the stars seem nigh;
How far away are the stars!

And I too under the stars,
Alone with the night again,
And the water's monotone;

I and the night alone,
And the world and the ways of men
Farther from me than the stars.

1895

WHITE MAGIC

Against the world I closed my heart,
And, half in pride and half in fear,
I said to Love and Lust: Depart,
None enters here.

A gipsy witch has glided in,
She takes her seat beside my fire;
Her eyes are innocent of sin,
Mine of desire.

She holds me with an unknown spell,
She folds me in her heart's embrace;
If this be love, I cannot tell:
I watch her face.

Her sombre eyes are happier
Than any joy that found a voice;
Since I am happiness to her,
I too rejoice.

And I have closed the door again,
Against the world I close my heart;
I hold her with my spell; in vain
Would she depart.

I hold her with a surer spell,
Beyond her magic, and above:
If hers be love, I cannot tell,
But mine is love.

1895

A PRAYER TO SAINT ANTHONY OF PADUA

Saint Anthony of Padua, whom I bear
In effigy about me, hear my prayer:
Kind saint who findest what is lost, I pray,
Bring back her heart: I lost it yesterday.

1895

THE OBSCURE NIGHT OF THE SOUL

From San Juan de la Cruz

Upon an obscure night,
Fevered with love in love's anxiety,
(O hapless-happy plight!)
I went, none seeing me,
Forth from my house where all things quiet be.

By night, secure from sight,
And by the secret stair, disguisedly,
(O hapless-happy plight!)
By night, and privily,
Forth from my house where all things quiet be.

Blest night of wandering,
In secret, where by none might I be spied,
Nor I see anything;
Without a light or guide,
Save that which in my heart burnt in my side.

That light did lead me on,
More surely than the shining of noontide,
Where well I knew that one
Did for my coming bide;
Where he abode might none but he abide.

O night that didst lead thus,
O night more lovely than the dawn of light,
O night that broughtest us,
Lover to lover's sight,
Lover with loved in marriage of delight!

Upon my flowery breast,
Wholly for him, and save himself for none,
There did I give sweet rest
To my beloved one;
The fanning of the cedars breathed thereon.

When the first moving air
Blew from the tower, and waved his locks aside,
His hand, with gentle care,
Did wound me in the side,
And in my body all my senses died.

All things I then forgot,
My cheek on him who for my coming came:
All ceased, and I was not,
Leaving my cares and shame
Among the lilies, and forgetting them.

WITHIN A DAINTY GARDEN-CLOSE

From An Old French Song-Book

Within a dainty garden-close
My love hath built a happy bower;
There clove doth grow and gillyflower,
Also the lily and the rose.

This garden is so good and fair,
With every pretty flower bedight,
A man might take his pleasure there
The whole day long and all the night.

Ah me for the dear garden's guest,
The nightingale and his sweet lay,
At evening and at break of day:
When he is tired, he taketh rest.

I saw her pluck, by two and three,
Violets in a meadow green,
The fairest I did ever see,
The sweetest that were ever seen.

I gaze upon her as she goes,
O white she is, and white as cream,
And soft as any little lamb,
And rosy as a little rose.

SEA-WIND

From Stéphane Mallarmé

The flesh is sad, alas! and all the books are read.
Flight, only flight! I feel that birds are wild to tread
The floor of unknown foam, and to attain the skies!
Nought, neither ancient gardens mirrored in the eyes,
Shall hold this heart that bathes in waters its delight,
O nights! nor yet my waking lamp, whose lonely light
Shadows the vacant paper, whiteness profits best,
Nor the young wife who rocks her baby on her breast.
I will depart! O steamer, swaying rope and spar,
Lift anchor for exotic lands that lie afar!
A weariness, outworn by cruel hopes, still clings
To the last farewell handkerchief's last beckonings!
And are not these, the masts inviting storms, not these
That an awakening wind bends over wrecking seas,
Lost, not a sail, a sail, a flowering isle, ere long?
But, O my heart, hear thou, hear thou the sailors' song!

LOVE AND SLEEP

I have laid sorrow to sleep;
Love sleeps.
She who oft made me weep
Now weeps.

I loved, and have forgot,
And yet
Love tells me she will not
Forget.

She it was bid me go;
Love goes
By what strange ways, ah! no
One knows.

Because I cease to weep,
She weeps.
Here by the sea in sleep,
Love sleeps.

1897

THE RETURN

A little hand is knocking at my heart,
And I have closed the door.
"I pray thee, for the love of God, depart:
Thou shalt come in no more."

"Open, for I am weary of the way.
The night is very black.
I have been wandering many a night and day.
Open. I have come back."

The little hand is knocking patiently;
I listen, dumb with pain.
"Wilt thou not open any more to me?
I have come back again."

"I will not open any more. Depart.
I, that once lived, am dead."
The hand that had been knocking at my heart
Was still. "And I?" she said.

There is no sound, save, in the winter air,
The sound of wind and rain.
All that I loved in all the world stands there,
And will not knock again.

1897

THE UNLOVED

These are the women whom no man has loved.
Year after year, day after day has moved
These hearts with many longings, and with tears,
And with content; they have received the years
With empty hands, expecting no good thing;
Life has passed by their doors, not entering.
In solitude, and without vain desire,
They have warmed themselves beside a lonely fire;
And, without scorn, beheld as in a glass
The blown and painted leaves of Beauty pass.
Their souls have been made fragrant with the spice
Of costly virtues lit for sacrifice;
They have accepted Life, the unpaid debt,
And looked for no vain day of reckoning.

Yet
They too in certain windless summer hours
Have felt the stir of dreams, and dreamed the powers
And the exemptions and the miracles
And the cruelty of Beauty. Citadels
Of many-walled and deeply-moated hearts
Have suddenly surrendered to the arts
Of so compelling magic; entering,
They have esteemed it but a little thing
To have won so great a conquest; and with haste
They have cast down, and utterly laid waste,
Tower upon tower, and sapped their roots with flame;
And passed on that eternity of shame
Which is the way of Beauty on the earth.
And they have shaken laughter from its mirth,
To be a sound of trumpets and of horns
Crying the battle-cry of those red morns
Against a sky of triumph.

On some nights
Of delicate Springtide, when the hesitant lights
Begin to fade, and glimmer, and grow warm,
And all the softening air is quick with storm,
And the ardours of the young year, entering in,
Flush the grey earth with buds; when trees begin
To feel a trouble mounting from their roots,
And all their green life blossoming into shoots,
They too, in some obscure, unblossoming strife,
Have felt the stirring of the sap of life.
And they have wept, with bowed heads; in the street
They hear the twittering of little feet,
The rocking of the cradles in their hearts.

This is a mood, and, as a mood, departs
With the dried tears; and they resume the tale
Of the dropt stitches; these must never fail
For a dream's sake; nor, for a memory,
The telling of a patient rosary.

1899

BY THE POOL AT THE THIRD ROSSES

I heard the sighing of the reeds
In the grey pool in the green land,
The sea-wind in the long reeds sighing
Between the green hill and the sand.

I heard the sighing of the reeds
Day after day, night after night;
I heard the whirring wild ducks flying,
I saw the sea-gulls' wheeling flight.

I heard the sighing of the reeds
Night after night, day after day,
And I forgot old age, and dying,
And youth that loves, and love's decay.

I heard the sighing of the reeds
At noontide and at evening,
And some old dream I had forgotten
I seemed to be remembering.

I hear the sighing of the reeds:
Is it in vain, is it in vain
That some old peace I had forgotten
Is crying to come back again?

1899

FRANCIS THOMPSON

[December 18, 1859–November 13, 1907]

Francis Thompson, son of a doctor, Charles Thompson, who was a convert to Catholicism, received an early education at Ushaw College, near Durham, which accorded with the principles of his father's embraced belief. He hoped to enter the priesthood, but was dissuaded. In 1876, following his father's wishes, he went to Owen's College, Manchester, to study medicine. But it seemed that Francis was not so much interested in the health of bodies as that of souls, for he failed his examinations three times. In November, 1885, he set out for London to make his own way and for five years there suffered intense poverty, securing only light employment with a London bootmaker. Constant illness pressed the employment of opium upon him. He was fortunate, however, in finding in Wilfrid Meynell, the editor of *Merrie England*, a friendly critic for his first poems. Wilfrid and his wife, Alice, took the young poet under their wings, and persuaded him to toil through a long convalescence in a hospital. His first volume (*Poems*, 1893) was praised sympathetically by Coventry Patmore in the *Fortnightly Review*. From 1893 to 1897 he lived in a Franciscan monastery in Pantasaph, North Wales, where he continued to produce verses which confirmed the idea of his genius held by Patmore and Meynell. Illness, however, limited the output of his poems; *Sister Songs* appeared in 1895 (it was dedicated to Mrs. Meynell's children) and *New Poems* in 1897. Later he lived in a Capuchin monastery in Tanlasapt. His prose contributions to the *Academy* and the *Athenæum*, as well as his treatise *Health and Holiness* (1905), reveal great power, but he will be remembered chiefly as a poet. Besides two saints' lives, one on Loyola (1909) and the other on John Baptist de la Salle (1911), he wrote a bold and brilliant essay on Shelley, full of imaginative impressionism and striking felicities. He died in London of tuberculosis, and was buried at Kensal Green.

Francis Thompson's talent is one of extreme complexity. Through his mysticism and symbolism he works with the Romantics of the earlier part of his century, and confesses his love for the Elizabethans, but it is really to the subtle "metaphysical" poets of the seventeenth century that he bends his knee lowest. His style is one of elaborate ornamentation, suggesting a debt to the Pre-Raphaelites and Patmore; it is now and again a trifle affected and there is much of the eccentric in his poetically compounded neologisms. Almost supremely beautiful is the majesty and suffering written down in *The Hound of Heaven*, and the power of its inspiration carries one to impressive heights.

DAISY

Where the thistle lifts a purple crown
  Six foot out of the turf,
And the harebell shakes on the windy hill—
  O breath of the distant surf!—

The hills look over on the South,
  And southward dreams the sea;
And with the sea-breeze hand in hand
  Came innocence and she.

Where 'mid the gorse the raspberry
  Red for the gatherer springs,
Two children did we stray and talk
  Wise, idle, childish things.

She listened with big-lipped surprise,
  Breast-deep mid flower and spine:
Her skin was like a grape whose veins
  Run snow instead of wine.

Creccas Cottage,
~~MONASTERY,~~
PANTASAPH,
HOLYWELL.

Monday.

Dear Mr. Patmore,

Many thanks for your kind pains with the poem. I shall defer writing more particularly about it to-day, for there are one or two points I want to discuss at some length. I send you now a little thing which I think I should flinch from A. M. seeing. She would be indignant at the "mighty cruelties." I think you will not. Like Cromwell, I take it, you would disdain that your painter

First Page of a Letter to Coventry Patmore. (See Appendix I.)

should omit a wart.

I have received the book you forwarded — a worthless Yankee "epic" on Columbus, inscribed by the author to "Francis Thompson Esq., care of Coventry Patmore Esq., with kind regards to both!" By some enclosed "Notices" I see that he has sent his book to Newman and Aubrey de Vere. In our case the economical fellow has apparently tried to kill two poets with one stone — a very heavy one.

Yours always,

Francis Thompson.

Second Page of a Letter to Coventry Patmore. (See Appendix I.)

She knew not those sweet words she spake,
  Nor knew her own sweet way;
But there's never a bird, so sweet a song
  Thronged in whose throat that day.

Oh, there were flowers in Storrington
  On the turf and on the spray;
But the sweetest flower on Sussex hills
  Was the Daisy-flower that day!

Her beauty smoothed earth's furrowed face.
  She gave me tokens three:—
A look, a word of her winsome mouth,
  And a wild raspberry.

A berry red, a guileless look,
  A still word,—strings of sand!
And yet they made my wild, wild heart
  Fly down to her little hand.

For standing artless as the air,
  And candid as the skies,
She took the berries with her hand,
  And the love with her sweet eyes.

The fairest things have fleetest end,
  Their scent survives their close:
But the rose's scent is bitterness
  To him that loved the rose.

She looked a little wistfully,
  Then went her sunshine way:—
The sea's eye had a mist on it,
  And the leaves fell from the day.

She went her unremembering way,
  She went and left in me
The pang of all the partings gone,
  And partings yet to be.

She left me marvelling why my soul
  Was sad that she was glad;
At all the sadness in the sweet,
  The sweetness in the sad.

Still, still I seemed to see her, still
  Look up with soft replies,
And take the berries with her hand,
  And the love with her lovely eyes.

Nothing begins, and nothing ends,
  That is not paid with moan;
For we are born in other's pain,
  And perish in our own.

1893

THE POPPY

To Monica

SUMMER set lip to earth's bosom bare,
And left the flushed print in a poppy there:
Like a yawn of fire from the grass it came,
And the fanning wind puffed it to flapping flame.

With burnt mouth, red like a lion's, it drank
The blood of the sun as he slaughtered sank,
And dipped its cup in the purpurate shine
When the Eastern conduits ran with wine.

Till it grew lethargied with fierce bliss,
And hot as a swinked gipsy is,
And drowsed in sleepy savageries,
With mouth wide a-pout for a sultry kiss.

A child and man paced side by side,
Treading the skirts of eventide;
But between the clasp of his hand and hers
Lay, felt not, twenty withered years.

She turned, with the rout of her dusk South hair,
And saw the sleeping gipsy there:
And snatched and snapped it in swift child's whim,
With—"Keep it, long as you live!"—to him.

And his smile, as nymphs from their laving meres,
Trembled up from a bath of tears;
And joy, like a mew sea-rocked apart,
Tossed on the waves of his troubled heart.

For *he* saw what she did not see,
That—as kindled by its own fervency—
The verge shrivelled inward smoulderingly:
And suddenly 'twixt his hand and hers
He knew the twenty withered years—
No flower, but twenty shrivelled years.

"Was never such thing until this hour,"
Low to his heart he said; "the flower
Of sleep brings wakening to me,
And of oblivion, memory."

"Was never this thing to me," he said,
"Though with bruisèd poppies my feet are red!"
And again to his own heart very low:
"Oh child! I love, for I love and know;

"But you, who love nor know at all
The diverse chambers in Love's guest-hall,
Where some rise early, few sit long:
In how differing accents hear the throng
His great Pentecostal tongue;

"Who know not love from amity,
Nor my reported self from me;
A fair fit gift is this, meseems,
You give—this withering flower of dreams.

"O frankly fickle, and fickly true,
Do you know what the days will do to you?
To your love and you what the days will do,
O frankly fickle, and fickly true?

"You have loved me, Fair, three lives—or days;
'Twill pass with the passing of my face.
But where *I* go, your face goes too,
To watch lest I play false to you.

"I am but, my sweet, your foster-lover,
Knowing well when certain years are over
You vanish from me to another;
Yet I know, and love, like the foster-mother.

"So, frankly fickle, and fickly true!
For my brief life-while I take from you
This token, fair and fit, meseems,
For me—this withering flower of dreams."

The sleep-flower sways in the wheat its head,
Heavy with dreams, as that with bread:
The goodly grain and the sun-flushed sleeper
The reaper reaps, and Time the reaper.

I hang 'mid men my needless head,
And my fruit is dreams, as theirs is bread:
The goodly men and the sun-hazed sleeper
Time shall reap, but after the reaper
The world shall glean of me, me the sleeper.

Love, love! your flower of withered dream
In leavèd rhyme lies safe, I deem,
Sheltered and shut in a nook of rhyme,
From the reaper man, and his reaper Time.

Love! *I* fall into the claws of Time:
But lasts within a leavèd rhyme
All that the world of me esteems—
My withered dreams, my withered dreams.

1893

THE HOUND OF HEAVEN

I FLED Him, down the nights and down the days;
I fled Him, down the arches of the years;
I fled Him, down the labyrinthine ways
Of my own mind; and in the mist of tears
I hid from Him, and under running laughter.
Up vistaed hopes I sped;
And shot, precipitated,
Adown Titanic glooms of chasmèd fears,
From those strong Feet that followed, followed after.
But with unhurrying chase,
And unperturbèd pace,
Deliberate speed, majestic instancy,
They beat—and a Voice beat
More instant than the Feet—
"All things betray thee, who betrayest Me."

I pleaded, outlaw-wise,
By many a hearted casement, curtained red,
Trellised with intertwining charities;
(For, though I knew His love Who followèd,
Yet was I sore adread
Lest, having Him, I must have naught beside.)
But, if one little casement parted wide,
The gust of His approach would clash it to:
Fear wist not to evade, as Love wist to pursue.
Across the margent of the world I fled,
And troubled the gold gateways of the stars,
Smiting for shelter on their clangèd bars;
Fretted to dulcet jars
And silvern chatter the pale ports o' the moon.
I said to Dawn: Be sudden—to Eve: Be soon;
With thy young skiey blossoms heap me over
From this tremendous Lover—
Float thy vague veil about me, lest He see!
I tempted all His servitors, but to find
My own betrayal in their constancy,
In faith to Him their fickleness to me,
Their traitorous trueness, and their loyal deceit.
To all swift things for swiftness did I sue;
Clung to the whistling mane of every wind.
But whether they swept, smoothly fleet,

The long savannahs of the blue;
Or whether, Thunder-driven,
They clanged his chariot 'thwart a heaven,
Plashy with flying lightnings round the spurn o' their feet:—
Fear wist not to evade as Love wist to pursue.
Still with unhurrying chase,
And unperturbèd pace,
Deliberate speed, majestic instancy,
Came on the following Feet,
And a Voice above their beat—
"Naught shelters thee, who wilt not shelter Me."

I sought no more that after which I strayed
In face of man or maid;
But still within the little children's eyes
Seems something, something that replies,
They at least are for me, surely for me!
I turned me to them very wistfully;
But just as their young eyes grew sudden fair
With dawning answers there,
Their angel plucked them from me by the hair.
"Come then, ye other children, Nature's—share
With me" (said I) "your delicate fellowship;
Let me greet you lip to lip,
Let me twine with you caresses,
Wantoning
With our Lady-Mother's vagrant tresses,
Banqueting
With her in her wind-walled palace,
Underneath her azured daïs,
Quaffing, as your taintless way is,
From a chalice
Lucent-weeping out of the dayspring."
So it was done:
I in their delicate fellowship was one—
Drew the bolt of Nature's secrecies.
I knew all the swift importings
On the wilful face of skies;
I knew how the clouds arise
Spumèd of the wild sea-snortings;
All that's born or dies
Rose and drooped with; made them shapers
Of mine own moods, or wailful or divine;
With them joyed and was bereaven.
I was heavy with the even,
When she lit her glimmering tapers
Round the day's dead sanctities.
I laughed in the morning's eyes.
I triumphed and I saddened with all weather,
Heaven and I wept together,
And its sweet tears were salt with mortal mine;
Against the red throb of its sunset-heart
I laid my own to beat,
And share commingling heat;
But not by that, by that, was eased my human smart.
In vain my tears were wet on Heaven's grey cheek.
For ah! we know not what each other says,
These things and I; in sound *I* speak—
Their sound is but their stir, they speak by silences.
Nature, poor stepdame, cannot slake my drouth;
Let her, if she would owe me,
Drop yon blue bosom-veil of sky, and show me
The breasts o' her tenderness:
Never did any milk of hers once bless
My thirsting mouth.
Nigh and nigh draws the chase.
With unperturbèd pace,
Deliberate speed, majestic instancy;
And past those noisèd Feet
A voice comes yet more fleet—
"Lo! naught contents thee, who content'st not Me."

Naked I wait Thy love's uplifted stroke!
My harness piece by piece Thou hast hewn from me,
And smitten me to my knee;
I am defenceless utterly.
I slept, methinks, and woke,
And, slowly gazing, find me stripped in sleep.
In the rash lustihead of my young powers,
I shook the pillaring hours
And pulled my life upon me; grimed with smears,
I stand amid the dust o' the mounded years—
My mangled youth lies dead beneath the heap.
My days have crackled and gone up in smoke,

Have puffed and burst as sun-starts on a stream.
Yea, faileth now even dream
The dreamer, and the lute the lutanist;
Even the linked fantasies, in whose blossomy twist
I swung the earth a trinket at my wrist,
Are yielding; cords of all too weak account
For earth with heavy griefs so overplussed.
Ah! is Thy love indeed
A weed, albeit an amaranthine weed,
Suffering no flowers except its own to mount?
Ah! must—
Designer infinite!—
Ah! must Thou char the wood ere Thou canst limn with it?
My freshness spent its wavering shower i' the dust;
And now my heart is as a broken fount,
Wherein tear-drippings stagnate, spilt down ever
From the dank thoughts that shiver
Upon the sighful branches of my mind.
Such is; what is to be?
The pulp so bitter, how shall taste the rind?
I dimly guess what Time in mists confounds;
Yet ever and anon a trumpet sounds
From the hid battlements of Eternity;
Those shaken mists a space unsettle, then
Round the half-glimpsèd turrets slowly wash again.
But not ere him who summoneth
I first have seen, enwound
With glooming robes purpureal, cypress-crowned;
His name I know, and what his trumpet saith.
Whether man's heart or life it be which yields
Thee harvest, must Thy harvest-fields
Be dunged with rotten death?

Now of that long pursuit
Comes on at hand the bruit;
That Voice is round me like a bursting sea:
"And is thy earth so marred,
Shattered in shard on shard?
Lo, all things fly thee, for thou fliest Me!
Strange, piteous, futile thing!
Wherefore should any set thee love apart?
Seeing none but I makes much of naught" (He said),
"And human love needs human meriting:
How hast thou merited—
Of all man's clotted clay the dingiest clot?
Alack, thou knowest not
How little worthy of any love thou art!
Whom wilt thou find to love ignoble thee,
Save Me, save only Me?
All which I took from thee I did but take,
Not for thy harms,
But just that thou might'st seek it in My arms.
All which thy child's mistake
Fancies as lost, I have stored for thee at home:
Rise, clasp My hand, and come!"

Halts by me that footfall:
Is my gloom, after all,
Shade of His hand, outstretched caressingly?
"Ah, fondest, blindest, weakest,
I am He Whom thou seekest!
Thou dravest love from thee, who dravest Me."

1893

From A CORYMBUS FOR AUTUMN

(Lines 79–150)

Or higher, holier, saintlier when, as now,
All Nature sacerdotal seems, and thou.
The calm hour strikes on yon golden gong,
In tones of floating and mellow light
A spreading summons to even-song:
See how there
The cowlèd Night
Kneels on the Eastern sanctuary-stair.
What is this feel of incense everywhere?
Clings it round folds of the blanch-amiced clouds,
Upwafted by the solemn thurifer,
The mighty Spirit unknown,
That swingeth the slow earth before the embannered Throne?
Or is't the Season under all these shrouds
Of light, and sense, and silence, makes her known
A presence everywhere,
An inarticulate prayer,
A hand on the soothed tresses of the air?
But there is one hour scant
Of this Titanian, primal liturgy;

As there is but one hour for me and thee,
Autumn, for thee and thine hierophant,
Of this grave-ending chant.
Round the earth still and stark
Heaven's death-lights kindle, yellow spark by spark,
Beneath the dreadful catafalque of the dark.

And I had ended there:
But a great wind blew all the stars to flare,
And cried, "I sweep the path before the moon!
Tarry ye now the coming of the moon,
For she is coming soon";
Then died before the coming of the moon.
And she came forth upon the trepidant air,
In vesture unimagined-fair,
Woven as woof of flag-lilies;
And curdled as of flag-lilies
The vapour at the feet of her,
And a haze about her tinged in fainter wise;
As if she had trodden the stars in press,
Till the gold wine spurted over her dress,
Till the gold wine gushed out round her feet;
Spouted over her stainèd wear,
And bubbled in golden froth at her feet,
And hung like a whirlpool's mist round her.

Still, mighty Season, do I see't,
Thy sway is still majestical!
Thou hold'st of God, by title sure,
Thine indefeasible investiture,
And that right round thy locks are native to;
The heavens upon thy brow imperial,
This huge terrene thy ball,
And o'er thy shoulders thrown wide air's depending pall.
What if thine earth be blear and bleak of hue?
Still, still the skies are sweet!
Still, Season, still thou hast thy triumphs there!
How have I, unaware,
Forgetful of my strain inaugural,
Cleft the great rondure of thy reign complete,
Yielding thee half, who hast indeed the all?
I will not think thy sovereignty begun
But with the shepherd Sun
That washes in the sea the stars' gold fleeces;
Or that with Day it ceases,
Who sets his burning lips to the salt brine,
And purples it to wine;
While I behold how ermined Artemis
Ordainèd weed must wear,
And toil thy business;
Who witness am of her,
Her too in autumn turned a vintager;
And, laden with its lampèd clusters bright,
The fiery-fruited vineyard of this night.

1893

A FALLEN YEW

It seemed corrival of the world's great prime,
Made to un-edge the scythe of Time,
And last with stateliest rhyme.

No tender Dryad ever did indue
That rigid chiton of rough yew,
To fret her white flesh through:

But some god like to those grim Asgard lords,
Who walk the fables of the hordes
From Scandinavian fjords,

Upheaved its stubborn girth, and raised unriven,
Against the whirl-blast and the levin,
Defiant arms to Heaven.

When doom puffed out the stars, we might have said,
It would decline its heavy head,
And see the world to bed.

For this firm yew did from the vassal leas,
And rain and air, its tributaries,
Its revenues increase,

And levy impost on the golden sun,
Take the blind years as they might run,
And no fate seek or shun.

But now our yew is strook, is fallen—yea,
Hacked like dull wood of every day
To this and that, men say.

Never!—To Hades' shadowy shipyards gone,
Dim barge of Dis, down Acheron
It drops, or Lethe wan.

Stirred by its fall—poor destined bark of Dis!—
Along my soul a bruit there is
Of echoing images,

Reverberations of mortality:
Spelt backward from its death, to me
Its life reads saddenedly.

Its breast was hollowed as the tooth of eld;
And boys, there creeping unbeheld,
A laughing moment dwelled.

Yet they, within its very heart so crept,
Reached not the heart that courage kept
With winds and years beswept.

And in its boughs did close and kindly nest
The birds, as they within its breast,
By all its leaves caressed.

But bird nor child might touch by any art
Each other's or the tree's hid heart,
A whole God's breadth apart;

The breadth of God, the breadth of death and life!
Even so, even so, in undreamed strife
With pulseless Law, the wife,—

The sweetest wife on sweetest marriage-day,—
Their souls at grapple in mid-way,
Sweet to her sweet may say:

"I take you to my inmost heart, my true!"
Ah, fool! but there is one heart you
Shall never take him to!

The hold that falls not when the town it got,
The heart's heart, whose immurèd plot
Hath keys yourself keep not!

Its ports you cannot burst—you are withstood—
For him that to your listening blood
Sends precepts as he would.

Its gates are deaf to Love, high summoner;
Yea, love's great warrant runs not there:
You are your prisoner.

Yourself are with yourself the sole consortress
In that unleaguerable fortress;
It knows you not for portress.

Its keys are at the cincture hung of God;
Its gates are trepidant to His nod;
By Him its floors are trod.

And if His feet shall rock those floors in wrath,
Or blest aspersion sleek His path,
Is only choice it hath.

Yea, in that ultimate heart's occult abode
To lie as in an oubliette of God,
Or in a bower untrod,

Built by a secret Lover for His Spouse;—
Sole choice is this your life allows,
Sad tree, whose perishing boughs
So few birds house!

1893

SISTER SONGS

From Part the Second

I (Lines 381–447)

Thou canst foreshape thy word;
The poet is not lord
Of the next syllable may come
With the returning pendulum;
And what he plans to-day in song,
To-morrow sings it in another tongue.
Where the last leaf fell from his bough,
He knows not if a leaf shall grow;
Where he sows he doth not reap,
He reapeth where he did not sow;
He sleeps, and dreams forsake his sleep
To meet him on his waking way.
Vision will mate him not by law and vow:
Disguised in life's most hodden-grey,
By the most beaten road of everyday
She waits him, unsuspected and unknown.
The hardest pang whereon
He lays his mutinous head may be a Jacob's stone.
In the most iron crag his foot can tread
A Dream may strew her bed,
And suddenly his limbs entwine,
And draw him down through rock as sea-nymphs might through brine.

But, unlike those feigned temptress-ladies who
In guerdon of a night the lover slew,
When the embrace has failed, the rapture fled,
Not he, not he, the wild sweet witch is dead!
And though he cherisheth
The babe most strangely born from out her death,
Some tender trick of her it hath, maybe,—.
It is not she!

Yet, even as the air is rumorous of fray
Before the first shafts of the sun's onslaught
From gloom's black harness splinter,
And Summer move on Winter
With the trumpet of the March, and the pennon of the May;
As gesture outstrips thought;
So haply, toyer with ethereal strings,
Are thy blind repetitions of high things
The murmurous gnats whose aimless hoverings
Reveal song's summer in the air;
The outstretched hand, which cannot thought declare,
Yet is thought's harbinger.
These strains the way for thine own strains prepare;
We feel the music moist upon this breeze,
And hope the congregating poesies.
Sundered yet by thee from us
Wait, with wild eyes luminous,
All thy winged things that are to be;
They flit against thee, Gate of Ivory!
They clamour on the portress Destiny,—
"Set her wide, so we may issue through,
Our vans are quick for that they have to do!"
Suffer still your young desire;
Your plumes but bicker at the tips with fire;
Tarry their kindling—they will beat the higher.
And thou, bright girl, not long shalt thou repeat
Idly the music from thy mother caught;
Not vainly has she wrought,
Not vainly from the cloudward-jetting turret
Of her aërial mind for thy weak feet
Let down the silken ladder of her thought.
She bare thee with a double pain,
Of the body and the spirit;
Thou thy fleshly weeds hast ta'en,
Thy diviner weeds inherit!
The precious streams which through thy young lips roll
Shall leave their lovely delta in thy soul.

II (Lines 602–662)

Ah, help, my Dæmon, that hast served me well!
Not at this last, oh, do not me disgrace!
I faint, I sicken, darkens all my sight,
As, poised upon this unprevisioned height,
I lift into its place
The utmost aery traceried pinnacle.
So; it is builded, the high tenement,
—God grant!—to mine intent:
Most like a palace of the Occident,
Up-thrusting, toppling maze on maze,
Its mounded blaze,
And washèd by the sunset's rosy waves,
Whose sea drinks rarer hue from those rare walls it laves.
Yet wail, my spirits, wail!
So few therein to enter shall prevail.
Scarce fewer could win way, if their desire
A dragon baulked, with involuted spire,
And writhen snout spattered with yeasty fire.
For at the elfin portal hangs a horn
Which none can wind aright
Save the appointed knight
Whose lids the fay-wings brushed when he was born.
All others stray forlorn,
Or glimpsing, through the blazoned windows scrolled.
Receding labyrinths lessening tortuously
In half obscurity;
With mystic images, inhuman, cold,
That flameless torches hold.
But who can wind that horn of might.
(The horn of dead Heliades) aright,—
Straight
Open for him shall roll the conscious gate;
And light leap up from all the torches there,
And life leap up in every torchbearer,
And the stone faces kindle in the glow,
And into the blank eyes the irids grow,
And through the dawning irids ambushed meanings show.
Illumined this wise on,

He threads securely the far intricacies,
With brede from Heaven's wrought vesture overstrewn;
Swift Tellus' purfled tunic, girt upon
With the blown chlamys of her fluttering seas;
And the freaked kirtle of the pearlèd moon:
Until he gain the structure's core, where stands—
A toil of magic hands—
The unbodied spirit of the sorcerer,
Most strangely rare,
As is a vision remembered in the noon;
Unbodied, yet to mortal seeing clear,
Like sighs exhaled in eager atmosphere.
From human haps and mutabilities
It rests exempt, beneath the edifice
To which itself gave rise;
Sustaining centre to the bubble of stone
Which, breathed from it, exists by it alone.
Yea, ere Saturnian earth her child consumes,
And I lie down with outworn ossuaries,
Ere death's grim tongue anticipates the tomb's
Siste viator, in this storied urn
My living heart is laid to throb and burn,
Till end be ended, and till ceasing cease.

III (Lines 736–792)

—BUT lo! at length the day is lingered out,
At length my Ariel lays his viol by;
We sing no more to thee, child, he and I;
The day is lingered out:
In slow wreaths folden
Around yon censer, spherèd, golden,
Vague Vesper's fumes aspire;
And, glimmering to eclipse,
The long laburnum drips
Its honey of wild flame, its jocund spilth of fire.

Now pass your ways, fair bird, and pass your ways,
If you will;
I have you through the days!
And flit or hold you still,
And perch you where you list
On what wrist,—
You are mine through the times!
I have caught you fast for ever in a tangle of sweet rhymes.
And in your young maiden morn
You may scorn,
But you must be
Bound and sociate to me;
With this thread from out the tomb my dead hand shall tether thee!

* * *

Go, Sister-songs, to that sweet Sister-pair
For whom I have your frail limbs fashionèd,
And framèd feateously;—
For whom I have your frail limbs fashionèd
With how great shamefastness and how great dread,
Knowing you frail, but not if you be fair,
Though framèd feateously;
Go unto them from me.
Go from my shadow to their sunshine sight,
Made for all sights' delight;
Go like twin swans that oar the surgy storms
To bate with pennoned snows in candent air:
Nigh with abasèd head,
Yourselves linked sisterly, that Sister-pair,
And go in presence there;
Saying—"Your young eyes cannot see our forms,
Nor read the yearning of our looks aright;
But Time shall trail the veilings form our hair,
And cleanse your seeing with his euphrasy
(Yea, even your bright seeing make more bright,
Which is all sights' delight),
And ye shall know us for what things we be.

"Whilom, within a poet's calyxed heart,
A dewey love we trembled all apart;
Whence it took rise
Beneath your radiant eyes,
Which misted it to music. We must long,
A floating haze of silver subtile song,
Await love-laden
Above each maiden
The appointed hour that o'er the hearts of you—
As vapours into dew
Unweave, whence they were wove,—
Shall turn our loosening musics back to love."

1895

From ODE TO THE SETTING SUN

I Prelude

The wailful sweetness of the violin
Floats down the hushèd waters of the wind,
The heart-strings of the throbbing harp begin
To long in aching music. Spirit-pined,

In wafts that poignant sweetness drifts, until
The wounded soul ooze sadness. The red sun,
A bubble of fire, drops slowly toward the hill,
While one bird prattles that the day is done.

O setting Sun, that as in reverent days
Sinkest in music to thy smoothèd sleep,
Discrowned of homage, though yet crowned with rays,
Hymned not at harvest more, though reapers reap:

For thee this music wakes not. O deceived,
If thou hear in these thoughtless harmonies
A pious phantom of adorings reaved,
And echo of fair ancient flatteries!

Yet, in this field where the Cross planted reigns,
I know not what strange passion bows my head
To thee, whose great command upon my veins
Proves thee a god for me not dead, not dead!

For worship it is too incredulous,
For doubt—oh, too believing-passionate!
What wild divinity makes my heart thus
A fount of most baptismal tears?—Thy straight

Long beam lies steady on the Cross. Ah me!
What secret would thy radiant finger show?
Of thy bright mastership is this the key?
Is *this* thy secret, then? And is it woe?

Fling from thine ear the burning curls, and hark
A song thou hast not heard in Northern day;
For Rome too daring, and for Greece too dark,
Sweet with wild things that pass, that pass away!

II And Now, O Shaken from Thine Antique Throne

(Lines 155–238)

And now, O shaken from thine antique throne,
And sunken from thy cœrule empery,
Now that the red glare of thy fall is blown
In smoke and flame about the windy sky,
Where are the wailing voices that should meet
From hill, stream, grove, and all of mortal shape
Who tread thy gifts, in vineyards as stray feet
Pulp the globed weight of juiced Iberia's grape?
Where is the threne o' the sea?
And why not dirges thee
The wind, that sings to himself as he makes stride
Lonely and terrible on the Andèan height?
Where is the Naiad 'mid her sworded sedge?
The Nymph wan-glimmering by her wan fount's verge?
The Dyrad at timid gaze by the wood-side?
The Oread jutting light
On one up-strainèd sole from the rock-ledge?
The Nereid tip-toe on the scud o' the surge,
With whistling tresses dank athwart her face,
And all her figure poised in lithe Circean grace?
Why withers their lament?
Their tresses tear-besprent,
Have they sighed hence with trailing garment-hem?
O sweet, O sad, O fair,
I catch your flying hair,
Draw your eyes down to me, and dream on them!

A space, and they fleet from me. Must ye fade—
O old, essential candours, ye who made
The earth a living and a radiant thing—
And leave her corpse in our strained, cheated arms?
Lo ever thus, when Song with chorded charms

Draws from dull death his lost Eurydice,
Lo ever thus, even at consummating,
Even in the swooning minute that claims her his,
Even as he trembles to the impassioned kiss
Of reincarnate Beauty, his control
Clasps the cold body, and forgoes the soul!
Whatso looks lovelily
Is but the rainbow on life's weeping rain.
Why have we longings of immortal pain,
And all we long for mortal? Woe is me,
And all our chants but chaplet some decay,
As mine this vanishing—nay, vanished Day.
The low sky-line dusks to a leaden hue,
No rift disturbs the heavy shade and chill,
Save one, where the charred firmament lets through
The scorching dazzle of Heaven; 'gainst which the hill,
Out-flattened sombrely,
Stands black as life against eternity.
Against eternity?
A rifting light in me
Burns through the leaden broodings of the mind:
O blessèd Sun, thy state
Uprisen or derogate
Dafts me no more with doubt; I seek and find.

If with exultant tread
Thou foot the Eastern sea,
Or like a golden bee
Sting the West to angry red,
Thou dost image, thou dost follow
That King-Maker of Creation,
Who, ere Hellas hailed Apollo,
Gave thee, angel-god, thy station;
Thou art of Him a type memorial.
Like Him thou hang'st in dreadful pomp of blood
Upon thy Western rood;
And His stained brow did vail like thine to night,
Yet lift once more Its light,
And, risen, again departed from our ball,
But when It set on earth arose in Heaven.
Thus hath He unto death His beauty given:
And so of all which form inheriteth
The fall doth pass the rise in worth;
For birth hath in itself the germ of death,
But death hath in itself the germ of birth.
It is the falling acorn buds the tree,
The falling rain that bears the greenery,
The fern-plants moulder when the ferns arise.
For there is nothing lives but something dies,
And there is nothing dies but something lives.
Till skies be fugitives,
Till Time, the hidden root of change, updries,
Are Birth and Death inseparable on earth;
For they are twain yet one, and Death is Birth.

1879

"WHERETO ART THOU COME?"

"Friend, whereto art thou come?" Thus Verity;
Of each that to the world's sad Olivet
Comes with no multitude, but alone by night,
Lit with the one torch of his lifted soul,
Seeking her that he may lay hands on her;
Thus: and waits answer from the mouth of deed.
Truth is a maid, whom men woo diversely;
This, as a spouse; that, as a light-o'-love,
To know, and having known, to make his brag.
But woe to him that takes the immortal kiss,
And not estates her in his housing life,
Mother of all his seed! So he betrays,
Not Truth, the unbetrayable, but himself:
And with his kiss's rated traitor-craft
The Haceldama of a plot of days
He buys, to consummate his Judasry
Therein with Judas' guerdon of despair.

1897

A DEAD ASTRONOMER

STEPHEN PERRY, S.J.

Starry amorist, starward gone,
Thou art—what thou didst gaze upon!
Passed through thy golden garden's bars,
Thou seest the Gardener of the Stars.

She, about whose moonèd brows
Seven stars make seven glows,
Seven lights for seven woes;

She, like thine own Galaxy,
All lustres in one purity:—
What said'st thou, Astronomer,
When thou did'st discover *her?*
When thy hand its tube let fall,
Thou found'st the fairest Star of all!

1897

ENVOY

Go, songs, for ended is our brief, sweet play;
Go, children of swift joy and tardy sorrow:
And some are sung, and that was yesterday,
And some unsung, and that may be to-morrow.

Go forth; and if it be o'er stony way,
Old joy can lend what newer grief must borrow:
And it was sweet, and that was yesterday,
And sweet is sweet, though purchasèd with sorrow.

Go, songs, and come not back from your far way:
And if men ask you why ye smile and sorrow,
Tell them ye grieve, for your hearts know To-day,
Tell them ye smile, for your eyes know To-morrow.

1897

"BY REASON OF THY LAW"

HERE I make oath—
Although the heart that knows its bitterness
Hear loath,
And credit less—
That he who kens to meet Pain's kisses fierce
Which hiss against his tears,
Dread, loss, nor love frustrate,
Nor all iniquity of the froward years
Shall his inurèd wing make idly bate,
Nor of the appointed quarry his staunch sight
To lose observance quite;
Seal from half-sad and all-elate
Sagacious eyes
Ultimate Paradise;
Nor shake his certitude of haughty fate.
Pacing the burning shares of many dooms,
I with stern tread do the clear-witting stars
To judgment cite,
If I have borne aright
The proving of their pure-willed ordeal.
From food of all delight
The heavenly Falconer my heart debars,
And tames with fearful glooms
The haggard to His call;
Yet sometimes comes a hand, sometimes a voice withal,
And she sits meek now, and expects the light.
In this Avernian sky,
This sultry and incumbent canopy
Of dull and doomed regret;
Where on the unseen verges yet, O yet,
At intervals,
Trembles, and falls,
Faint lightning of remembered transient sweet—
Ah, far too sweet
But to be sweet a little, a little sweet, and fleet;
Leaving this pallid trace,
This loitering and most fitful light, a space,
Still some sad space,
For Grief to see her own poor face:—
Here where I keep my stand
With all o'er-anguished feet,
And no live comfort near on any hand;
Lo, I proclaim the unavoided term,
When this morass of tears, then drained and firm,
Shall be a land—
Unshaken I affirm—
Where seven-quired psalterings meet;
And all the gods move with calm hand in hand,
And eyes that know not trouble and the worm.

1897

THE DREAD OF HEIGHT

If ye were blind, ye should have no sin: but now ye say: We see: therefore your sin remaineth.

John 9:41.

NOT the Circean wine
Most perilous is for pain:
Grapes of the heavens' star-loaden vine,
Whereto the lofty-placed
Thoughts of fair souls attain,
Tempt with a more retributive delight,
And do disrelish all life's sober taste.

'Tis to have drunk too well
The drink that is divine,
Maketh the kind earth waste,
And breath intolerable.

Ah me!
How shall my mouth content it with mortality?
Lo, secret music, sweetest music,
From distances of distance drifting its lone flight,
Down the arcane where Night would perish in night,
Like a god's loosened locks slips undulously:
Music that is too grievous of the height
For safe and low delight,
Too infinite
For bounded hearts which yet would girth the sea!

So let it be,
Though sweet be great, and though my heart be small:
So let it be,
O music, music, though you wake in me
No joy, no joy at all;
Although you only wake
Uttermost sadness, measure of delight,
Which else I could not credit to the height,
Did I not know,
That ill is statured to its opposite;
Did I not know,
And even of sadness so,
Of utter sadness, make
Of extreme sad a rod to mete
The incredible excess of unsensed sweet,
And mystic wall of strange felicity.
So let it be,
Though sweet be great, and though my heart be small,
And bitter meat
The food of gods for men to eat;
Yea, John ate daintier, and did tread
Less ways of heat,
Than whom to their wind-carpeted
High banquet-hall,
And golden love-feasts, the fair stars entreat.

But ah! withal,
Some hold, some stay,
O difficult Joy, I pray,
Some arms of thine,
Not only, only arms of mine!
Lest like a weary girl I fall
From clasping love so high,
And lacking thus thine arms, then may
Most hapless I
Turn utterly to love of basest rate;
For low they fall whose fall is from the sky.
Yea, who me shall secure
But I, of height grown desperate,
Surcease my wing, and my lost fate
Be dashed from pure
To broken writhings in the shameful slime:
Lower than man, for I dreamed higher,
Thrust down, by how much I aspire,
And damned with drink of immortality?
For such things be,
Yea, and the lowest reach of reeky Hell
Is but made possible
By foreta'en breath of Heaven's austerest clime.
These tidings from the vast to bring
Needeth not doctor nor divine,
Too well, too well
My flesh doth know the heart-perturbing thing;
That dread theology alone
Is mine,
Most native and my own;
And ever with victorious toil
When I have made
Of the deific peaks dim escalade,
My soul with anguish and recoil
Doth like a city in an earthquake rock,
As at my feet the abyss is cloven then,
With deeper menace than for other men,
Of my potential cousinship with mire;
That all my conquered skies do grow a hollow mock,
My fearful powers retire,
No longer strong,
Reversing the shook banners of their song.

Ah, for a heart less native to high Heaven,
A hooded eye, for jesses and restraint,
Or for a wild accipitrine to pursue!—
The veil of tutelar flesh to simple livers given,
Or those brave-fledging fervours of the Saint,
Whose heavenly falcon-craft doth never taint,
Nor they in sickest time their ample virtue mew.

1897

From THE NIGHT OF FOREBEING

I (Lines 64–105)

A HIGHER and a solemn voice
I heard through your gay-hearted noise;
A solemn meaning and a stiller voice
Sounds to me from far days when I too shall rejoice,
Nor more be with your jollity at strife.
O prophecy
Of things that are, and are not, and shall be!
The great-vanned Angel March
Hath trumpeted
His clangorous "Sleep no more" to all the dead—
Beat his strong vans o'er earth, and air, and sea.
And they have heard;
Hark to the *Jubilate* of the bird
For them that found the dying way to life!
And they have heard,
And quicken to the great precursive word;
Green spray showers lightly down the cascade of the larch;
The graves are riven,
And the Sun comes with power amid the clouds of heaven!
Before his way
Went forth the trumpet of the March;
Before his way, before his way
Dances the pennon of the May!
O Earth, unchilded, widowed Earth, so long
Lifting in patient pine and ivy-tree
Mournful belief and steadfast prophecy,
Behold how all things are made true!
Behold your bridegroom cometh in to you,
Exceeding glad and strong.
Raise up your eyes, O raise your eyes abroad!
No more shall you sit sole and vidual,
Searching, in servile pall,
Upon the hieratic night the star-sealed sense of all:
Rejoice, O barren, and look forth abroad!
Your children gathered back to your embrace
See with a mother's face;
Look up, O mortals, and the portent heed!
In very deed,
Washed with new fire to their irradiant birth,
Reintegrated are the heavens and earth;
From sky to sod,
The world's unfolded blossom smells of God.

II (Lines 198–225)

Shade within shade! for deeper in the glass
Now other imaged meanings pass;
And as the man, the poet there is read.
Winter with me, alack!
Winter on every hand I find:
Soul, brain, and pulses dead,
The mind no further by the warm sense fed,
The soul weak-stirring in the arid mind,
More tearless-weak to flash itself abroad
Than the earth's life beneath the frost-scorched sod.
My lips have drought, and crack,
By laving music long unvisited.
Beneath the austere and macerating rime
Draws back constricted in its icy urns
The genial flame of Earth, and there
With torment and with tension does prepare
The lush disclosures of the vernal time.
All joys draw inward to their icy urns,
Tormented by constraining rime,
And there
With undelight and throe prepare
The bounteous efflux of the vernal time.
Nor less beneath compulsive Law
Rebukèd draw
The numbèd musics back upon my heart;
Whose yet-triumphant course I know
And prevalent pulses forth shall start,
Like cataracts that with thunderous hoof charge the disbanding snow.

III (Lines 320–368)

Not without fortitude I wait
The dark majestical ensuit
Of destiny, nor peevish rate
Calm-knowledged Fate.
I, that no part have in the time's bragged way,
And its loud bruit;
I, in this house so rifted, marred,
So ill to live in, hard to leave;
I, so star-weary, over-warred,
That have no joy in this your day—
Rather foul fume englutting, that of day
Confounds all ray—
But only stand aside and grieve;
I yet have sight beyond the smoke,
And kiss the gods' feet, though they wreak
Upon me stroke and again stroke;
And this my seeing is not weak.

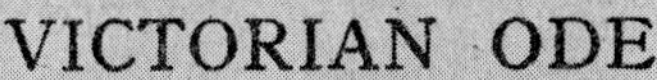

VICTORIAN ODE

BY

FRANCIS THOMPSON.

To Katharine Tynan Hinkson,
Ten years ago my sympathizer,
When I had few sympathizers.
Francis Thompson.
Xmas, 1897.

Presentation Copy to Mrs. Hinkson. (See Appendix I.)

The Woman I behold, whose vision seek
All eyes and know not; t'ward whom climb
The steps o' the world, and beats all wing of rhyme,
And knows not; 'twixt the sun and moon
Her inexpressible front enstarred
Tempers the wrangling spheres to tune;
Their divergent harmonies
Concluded in the concord of her eyes,
And vestal dances of her glad regard.
I see, which fretteth with surmise
Much heads grown unsagacious-grey,
The slow aim of wise-hearted Time,
Which folded cycles within cycles cloak:
We pass, we pass, we pass; this does not pass away,
But holds the furrowing earth still harnessed to its yoke.
The stars still write their golden purposes
On heaven's high palimpsest, and no man sees,
Nor any therein Daniel; I do hear
From the revolving year
A voice which cries:
"All dies;
Lo, how all dies! O seer,
And all things too arise:
All dies, and all is born;
But each resurgent morn, behold, more near the Perfect Morn."

Firm is the man, and set beyond the cast
Of Fortune's game, and the iniquitous hour,
Whose falcon soul sits fast,
And not intends her high sagacious tour
Or ere the quarry sighted; who looks past
To slow much sweet from little instant sour,
And in the first does always see the last.

1897

THE HEART—II

O NOTHING, in this corporal earth of man,
That to the imminent heaven of his high soul
Responds with colour and with shadow, can
Lack correlated greatness. If the scroll
Where thoughts lie fast in spell of hieroglyph
Be mighty through its mighty habitants;
If God be in His Name; grave potence if
The sounds unbind of hieratic chants;
All's vast that vastness means. Nay, I affirm
Nature is whole in her least things exprest,
Nor know we with what scope God builds the worm.
Our towns are copied fragments from our breast;
And all man's Babylons strive but to impart
The grandeurs of his Babylonian heart.

1897

TO A SNOWFLAKE

WHAT heart could have thought you?—
Past our devisal
(O filigree petal!)
Fashioned so purely,
Fragilely, surely,
From what Paradisal
Imagineless metal,
Too costly for cost?
Who hammered you, wrought you
From argentine vapour?—
"God was my shaper.
Passing surmisal,
He hammered, He wrought me,
From curled silver vapour,
To lust of His mind:—
Thou could'st not have thought me!
So purely, so palely,
Tinily, surely,
Mightily, frailly,
Insculped and embossed,
With His hammer of wind,
And His graver of frost."

1897

IN HER PATHS

AND she has trod before me in these ways!
I think that she has left here heavenlier days;
And I do guess her passage, as the skies
Of holy Paradise
Turn deeply holier,
And, looking up with sudden new delight,
One knows a seraph-wing has passed in flight.
The air is purer for her breathing, sure!
And all the fields do wear
The beauty fallen from her;
The winds do brush me with her robe's allure.
'Tis she has taught the heavens to look sweet,
And they do but repeat

The heaven, heaven, heaven of her face!
The clouds have studied going from her grace!
The pools whose marges have forgot the tread
Of Naiad, disenchanted, fled,
  A second time must mourn,
  Bereaven and forlorn.

Ah, foolish pools and meads! You did not see
Essence of old, essential pure as she.
For this was even that Lady, and none other,
The man in me calls "Love," the child calls "Mother."

1913

AN ARAB LOVE-SONG

The hunchèd camels of the night[1]
Trouble the bright
And silver waters of the moon.
The Maiden of the Morn will soon
Through Heaven stray and sing,
Star gathering.
Now while the dark about our loves is strewn,
Light of my dark, blood of my heart, O come!
And night will catch her breath up, and be dumb.

Leave thy father, leave thy mother
And thy brother;
Leave the black tents of thy tribe apart!
Am I not thy father and thy brother,
And thy mother?
And thou—what needest with thy tribe's black tents
Who hast the red pavilion of my heart?

1913

[1] Cloud-shapes observed by travellers in the East.

LOVE AND THE CHILD

"Why do you so clasp me,
  And draw me to your knee?
Forsooth, you do but chafe me,
  I pray you let me be:
I will be loved but now and then
  When it liketh me!"

So I heard a young child,
  A thwart child, a young child
Rebellious against love's arms,
  Make its peevish cry.

To the tender God I turn:—
  "Pardon, Love most High!
For I think those arms were even Thine,
  And that child was even I."

1913

TO W. M.

O tree of many branches! One thou hast
Thou barest not, but grafted'st on thee. Now,
Should all men's thunders break on thee, and leave
Thee reft of bough and blossom, that one branch
Shall cling to thee, my Father, Brother, Friend,
Shall cling to thee, until the end of end.

1913

LINES FOR A DRAWING OF OUR LADY OF THE NIGHT

This, could I paint my inward sight,
This were Our Lady of the Night:

She bears on her front's lucency
The starlight of her purity:

For as the white rays of that star
The union of all colours are,

She sums all virtues that may be
In her sweet light of purity.

The mantle which she holds on high
Is the great mantle of the sky.

Think, O sick toiler, when the night
Comes on thee, sad and infinite,

Think, sometimes, 'tis our own Lady
Spreads her blue mantle over thee,

And folds the earth, a wearied thing,
Beneath its gentle shadowing;

Then rest a little; and in sleep
Forget to weep, forget to weep!

1913

THE KINGDOM OF GOD

"In no Strange Land"

O WORLD invisible, we view thee,
O world intangible, we touch thee,
O world unknowable, we know thee,
Inapprehensible, we clutch thee!

Does the fish soar to find the ocean,
The eagle plunge to find the air—
That we ask of the stars in motion
If they have rumour of thee there?

Not where the wheeling systems darken,
And our benumbed conceiving soars!—
The drifts of pinions, would we hearken,
Beats at our own clay-shuttered doors.

The angels keep their ancient places;
Turn but a stone, and start a wing!
'Tis ye, 'tis your estrangèd faces,
That miss the many-splendoured thing.

But (when so sad thou canst not sadder)
Cry;—and upon thy so sore loss
Shall shine the traffic of Jacob's ladder
Pitched betwixt Heaven and Charing Cross.

Yea, in the night, my Soul, my daughter,
Cry,—clinging Heaven by the hems;
And lo, Christ walking on the water,
Not of Gennesareth, but Thames!

1913

THE SINGER SAITH OF HIS SONG

THE touches of man's modern speech
Perplex her unacquainted tongue;
There seems through all her songs a sound
Of falling tears. She is not young.

Within her eyes' profound arcane
Resides the glory of her dreams;
Behind her secret cloud of hair.
She sees the Is beyond the Seems.

Her heart sole-towered in her steep spirit,
Somewhat sweet is she, somewhat wan;
And she sings the songs of Sion
By the streams of Babylon.

1913

JAMES THOMSON

[November 23, 1834–June 3, 1882]

JAMES THOMSON, the son of a sailor who was disabled by paralysis when young James was six years old, and of a deeply religious mother who died when he was eight, was born at Port Glasgow, Scotland. After his mother's death he was placed in an orphanage, where he lived eight years, playing the part of a normal schoolboy in the sports and games of his fellows and showing superior ability in his studies. His unusual mental capacity led his guardians to decide that he should be an army schoolmaster, and in 1850 he entered the Royal Military College, Chelsea. Having finished his course at the college, Thomson became a teacher in the regimental school at Ballincolig, near Cork. In this position he lived in the home of the garrison-master, where he met Matilda Weller, a young girl who, if she had lived, might have saved him from becoming an inhabitant of the "City of Dreadful Night." She died about two years after their meeting, however, and ever after Sorrow pursued him, "whispering that death is better than life, that life is but a disease." After ten years as army schoolmaster Thomson was discharged from the army in the fall of 1862 for a trivial offense. For some years after, he did hack work in London and held numerous positions, none of them for an impressive period of time. He was in America for eight months in 1872 as the secretary of an English organization, "The Champion Gold and Silver Mines Company." He was in Spain for two months in 1873 as special correspondent for the New York *World*. This position failing, he returned to London to devote himself to literature exclusively, and in 1874 his *City of Dreadful Night*, the poem that brought him his first recognition, appeared in four installments in the *National Reformer*. The years 1874 to 1881 Thomson spoke of as his "seven songless years," a period during which he lived in cheap lodgings supporting himself by selling hack verse, writing some good criticism, suffering from insomnia and melancholy, and yielding to periodic debauches of drinking.

In 1880 his first volume of poetry, *The City of Dreadful Night, and Other Poems*, appeared and won high praise from Meredith. Encouraged by the modest success of this book, Thomson published another volume of poems the same year and, the following year, a volume of prose. Neither book was successful and the poet relapsed into his old despair. By the spring of 1882 his friends knew that tragedy was not far. His melancholia grew and he suffered from what may almost be called alcoholic madness. Still he wrote—several beautiful poems, one terrible one, *Insomnia*, in which he describes the horror of his sleepless nights. Before the year was half out he was laid to rest in Highgate Cemetery. There was no religious service, but at the grave one of his friends paid "feeling tribute to the virtues of the man and the genius of the poet."

ONCE IN A SAINTLY PASSION

ONCE in a saintly passion
  I cried with desperate grief,
"O Lord, my heart is black with guile,
  Of sinners I am chief."
Then stooped my guardian angel
  And whispered from behind,
"Vanity, my little man,
  You're nothing of the kind."

From SUNDAY UP THE RIVER

I I LOOKED OUT INTO THE MORNING

I LOOKED out into the morning,
  I looked out into the west:
The soft blue eye of the quiet sky
  Still drooped in dreamy rest;

The trees were still like clouds there,
  The clouds like mountains dim;
The broad mist lay, a silver bay
  Whose tide was at the brim.

I looked out into the morning,
  I looked out into the east:
The flood of light upon the night
  Had silently increased;

The sky was pale with fervor,
  The distant trees were gray,
The hill-lines drawn like waves of dawn
  Dissolving in the day.

I looked out into the morning,
  Looked east, looked west, with glee;
O richest day of happy May,
  My love will spend with me!

II "OH, WHAT ARE YOU WAITING FOR"

"OH, what are you waiting for here, young man?
What are you looking for over the bridge?"
A little straw hat with the streaming blue ribbons
  Is soon to come dancing over the bridge.

Her heart beats the measure that keeps her feet dancing,
  Dancing along like a wave o' the sea;
Her heart pours the sunshine with which her eyes glancing
  Light up strange faces in looking for me.

The strange faces brighten in meeting her glances;
  The strangers all bless her, pure, lovely, and free.
She fancies she walks, but her walk skips and dances,
  Her heart makes such music in coming to me.

Oh, thousands and thousands of happy young maidens
  Are tripping this morning their sweethearts to see;

But none whose heart beats to a sweeter love-cadence
  Than hers who will brighten the sunshine for me.

"Oh, what are you waiting for here, young man?
  What are you looking for over the bridge?"
A little straw hat with the streaming blue ribbons;
  —And here it comes dancing over the bridge!

XV GIVE A MAN A HORSE HE CAN RIDE

GIVE a man a horse he can ride,
  Give a man a boat he can sail;
And his rank and wealth, his strength and health,
  On sea nor shore shall fail.

Give a man a pipe he can smoke,
  Give a man a book he can read;
And his home is bright with a calm delight,
  Though the room be poor indeed.

Give a man a girl he can love,
  As I, O my Love, love thee;
And his heart is great with the pulse of Fate,
  At home, on land, on sea.

XVII LET MY VOICE RING OUT

LET my voice ring out and over the earth,
  Through all the grief and strife,
With a golden joy in a silver mirth:
    Thank God for Life!

Let my voice swell out through the great abyss
  To the azure dome above,
With a chord of faith in the harp of bliss:
    Thank God for Love!

Let my voice thrill out beneath and above,
  The whole world through:
O my Love and Life, O my Life and Love,
    Thank God for you!

XVIII THE WINE OF LOVE IS MUSIC

THE wine of Love is music,
  And the feast of Love is song;
And when Love sits down to the banquet,
    Love sits long;

Sits long and ariseth drunken,
  But not with the feast and the wine;
He reeleth with his own heart,
  That great rich Vine.

1869

E. B. B.

THE white-rose garland at her feet,
  The crown of laurel at her head,
Her noble life on earth complete,
  Lay her in the last low bed
For the slumber calm and deep:
  "He giveth His beloved sleep."

Soldiers find their fittest grave
  In the field whereon they died;
So her spirit pure and brave
  Leaves the clay it glorified
To the land for which she fought
With such grand impassioned thought.

Keats and Shelley sleep at Rome,
  She in well-loved Tuscan earth;
Finding all their death's long home
  Far from their old home of birth.
Italy, you hold in trust
Very sacred English dust.

Therefore this one prayer I breathe,—
  That you yet may worthy prove
Of the heirlooms they bequeath
  Who have loved you with such love:
Fairest land while land of slaves
Yields their free souls no fit graves.

WILLIAM BLAKE

HE came to the desert of London town
  Gray miles long;
He wandered up and he wandered down,
  Singing a quiet song.

He came to the desert of London town,
  Mirk miles broad;
He wandered up and he wandered down,
  Ever alone with God.

There were thousands and thousands of human kind
  In this desert of brick and stone;
But some were deaf and some were blind,
  And he was there alone.

At length the good hour came; he died
As he had lived, alone.
He was not missed from the desert wide;
Perhaps he was found at the Throne.

1866

THE CITY OF DREADFUL NIGHT

PROEM

Lo, thus, as prostrate, "In the dust I write
My heart's deep languor and my soul's sad tears."
Yet why evoke the spectres of black night
To blot the sunshine of exultant years?
Why disinter dead faith from mouldering hidden?
Why break the seals of mute despair unbidden,
And wail life's discords into careless ears?

Because a cold rage seizes one at whiles
To show the bitter old and wrinkled truth
Stripped naked of all vesture that beguiles,
False dreams, false hopes, false masks and modes of youth; 11
Because it gives some sense of power and passion
In helpless impotence to try to fashion
Our woe in living words howe'er uncouth.

Surely I write not for the hopeful young,
Or those who deem their happiness of worth,
Or such as pasture and grow fat among
The shows of life and feel nor doubt nor dearth,
Or pious spirits with a God above them
To sanctify and glorify and love them,
Or sages who foresee a heaven on earth.

For none of these I write, and none of these
Could read the writing if they deigned to try:
So may they flourish, in their due degrees,
On our sweet earth and in their unplaced sky.
If any cares for the weak words here written,
It must be some one desolate, Fate-smitten,
Whose faith and hope are dead, and who would die.

Yes, here and there some weary wanderer
In that same city of tremendous night,
Will understand the speech, and feel a stir
Of fellowship in all-disastrous fight;
"I suffer mute and lonely, yet another
Uplifts his voice to let me know a brother
Travels the same wild paths though out of sight."

O sad Fraternity, do I unfold
Your dolorous mysteries shrouded from of yore?
Nay, be assured; no secret can be told
To any who divined it not before:
None uninitiate by many a presage
Will comprehend the language of the message,
Although proclaimed aloud for evermore.

I

The City is of Night; perchance of Death,
But certainly of Night; for never there
Can come the lucid morning's fragrant breath
After the dewy dawning's cold grey air;
The moon and stars may shine with scorn or pity;
The sun has never visited that city,
For it dissolveth in the daylight fair.

Dissolveth like a dream of night away;
Though present in distempered gloom of thought
And deadly weariness of heart all day.
But when a dream night after night is brought
Throughout a week, and such weeks few or many
Recur each year for several years, can any
Discern that dream from real life in aught?

For life is but a dream whose shapes return,
Some frequently, some seldom, some by night
And some by day, some night and day: we learn,
The while all change and many vanish quite,
In their recurrence with recurrent changes
A certain seeming order; where this ranges
We count things real; such is memory's might.

A river girds the city west and south,
The main north channel of a broad lagoon,
Regurging with the salt tides from the mouth;
Waste marshes shine and glister to the moon

For leagues, then moorland black, then stony ridges;
Great piers and causeways, many noble bridges,
Connect the town and islet suburbs strewn.

Upon an easy slope it lies at large,
And scarcely overlaps the long curved crest
Which swells out two leagues, from the river marge.
A trackless wilderness rolls north and west,
Savannahs, savage woods, enormous mountains,
Bleak uplands, black ravines with torrent fountains;
And eastward rolls the shipless sea's unrest.

The city is not ruinous, although
Great ruins of an unremembered past,
With others of a few short years ago
More sad, are found within its precincts vast.
The street-lamps always burn; but scarce a casement
In house or palace front from roof to basement
Doth glow or gleam athwart the mirk air cast.

The street-lamps burn amidst the baleful glooms,
Amidst the soundless solitudes immense
Of rangèd mansions dark and still as tombs.
The silence which benumbs or strains the sense
Fulfils with awe the soul's despair unweeping:
Myriads of habitants are ever sleeping,
Or dead, or fled from nameless pestilence!

Yet as in some necropolis you find
Perchance one mourner to a thousand dead,
So there; worn faces that look deaf and blind
Like tragic masks of stone. With weary tread,
Each wrapt in his own doom, they wander, wander,
Or sit foredone and desolately ponder
Through sleepless hours with heavy drooping head.

Mature men chiefly, few in age or youth,
A woman rarely, now and then a child:
A child! If here the heart turns sick with ruth
To see a little one from birth defiled,
Or lame or blind, as preordained to languish
Through youthless life, think how it bleeds with anguish
To meet one erring in that homeless wild.

They often murmur to themselves, they speak
To one another seldom, for their woe
Broods maddening inwardly and scorns to wreak
Itself abroad; and if at whiles it grow
To frenzy which must rave, none heeds the clamor.
Unless there waits some victim of like glamour,
To rave in turn, who lends attentive show.

The City is of Night, but not of Sleep;
There sweet sleep is not for the weary brain;
The pitiless hours like years and ages creep,
A night seems termless hell. This dreadful strain
Of thought and consciousness which never ceases,
Or which some moments' stupor but increases,
This, worse than woe, makes wretches there insane.

They leave all hope behind who enter there:
One certitude while sane they cannot leave,
One anodyne for torture and despair;
The certitude of Death, which no reprieve
Can put off long; and which divinely tender,
But waits the outstretched hand to promptly render
That draught whose slumber nothing can bereave.

II

Because he seemed to walk with an intent
I followed him; who, shadowlike and frail,
Unswervingly though slowly onward went,
Regardless, wrapt in thought as in a veil:
Thus step for step with lonely sounding feet
We travelled many a long dim silent street.

At length he paused: a black mass in the gloom,
A tower that merged into the heavy sky;
Around, the huddled stones of grave and tomb:
Some old God's-acre now corruption's sty:

He murmured to himself with dull despair,
Here Faith died, poisoned by this charnel air.

Then turning to the right went on once more,
And travelled weary roads without suspense;
And reached at last a low wall's open door,
Whose villa gleamed beyond the foliage dense:
He gazed, and muttered with a hard despair,
Here Love died, stabbed by its own worshipped pair.

Then turning to the right resumed his march,
And travelled streets and lanes with wondrous strength,
Until on stooping through a narrow arch
We stood before a squalid house at length:
He gazed, and whispered with a cold despair,
Here Hope died, starved out in its utmost lair.

When he had spoken thus, before he stirred,
I spoke, perplexed by something in the signs
Of desolation I had seen and heard
In this drear pilgrimage to ruined shrines:
When Faith and Love and Hope are dead indeed,
Can Life still live? By what doth it proceed?

As whom his one intense thought overpowers,
He answered coldly, Take a watch, erase
The signs and figures of the circling hours,
Detach the hands, remove the dial-face;
The works proceed until run down; although
Bereft of purpose, void of use, still go.

Then turning to the right paced on again,
And traversed squares and travelled streets whose glooms
Seemed more and more familiar to my ken;
And reached that sullen temple of the tombs;
And paused to murmur with the old despair,
Here Faith died, poisoned by this charnel air.

I ceased to follow, for the knot of doubt
Was severed sharply with a cruel knife:
He circled thus for ever tracing out
The series of the fraction left of Life;
Perpetual recurrence in the scope
Of but three terms, dead Faith, dead Love, dead Hope.

III

Although lamps burn along the silent streets;
Even when moonlight silvers empty squares
The dark holds countless lanes and close retreats;
But when the night its sphereless mantle wears
The open spaces yawn with gloom abysmal,
The sombre mansions loom immense and dismal,
The lanes are black as subterranean lairs.

And soon the eye a strange new vision learns:
The night remains for it as dark and dense,
Yet clearly in this darkness it discerns
As in the daylight with its natural sense;
Perceives a shade in shadow not obscurely,
Pursues a stir of black in blackness surely,
Sees spectres also in the gloom intense.

The ear, too, with the silence vast and deep
Becomes familiar though unreconciled;
Hears breathings as of hidden life asleep,
And muffled throbs as of pent passions wild,
Far murmurs, speech of pity or derision;
But all more dubious than the things of vision,
So that it knows not when it is beguiled.

No time abates the first despair and awe,
But wonder ceases soon; the weirdest thing
Is felt least strange beneath the lawless law
Where Death-in-Life is the eternal king;
Crushed impotent beneath this reign of terror,
Dazed with such mysteries of woe and error,
The soul is too outworn for wondering.

IV

He stood alone within the spacious square
Declaiming from the central grassy mound,
With head uncovered and with streaming hair,
As if large multitudes were gathered round:
A stalwart shape, the gestures full of might,
The glances burning with unnatural light:—

As I came through the desert thus it was,
As I came through the desert: All was black,
In heaven no single star, on earth no track;
A brooding hush without a stir or note,
The air so thick it clotted in my throat;
And thus for hours; then some enormous things
Swooped past with savage cries and clanking wings:
But I strode on austere;
No hope could have no fear.

As I came through the desert thus it was,
As I came through the desert: Eyes of fire
Glared at me throbbing with a starved desire;
The hoarse and heavy and carnivorous breath
Was hot upon me from deep jaws of death;
Sharp claws, swift talons, fleshless fingers cold
Plucked at me from the bushes, tried to hold:
But I strode on austere;
No hope could have no fear.

As I came through the desert thus it was,
As I came through the desert: Lo you, there,
That hillock burning with a brazen glare;
Those myriad dusky flames with points a-glow
Which writhed and hissed and darted to and fro;
A Sabbath of the Serpents, heaped pell-mell
For Devil's roll-call and some *fête* of Hell:
Yet I strode on austere;
No hope could have no fear.

As I came through the desert thus it was,
As I came through the desert: Meteors ran
And crossed their javelins on the black sky-span;
The zenith opened to a gulf of flame,
The dreadful thunderbolts jarred earth's fixed frame:
The ground all heaved in waves of fire that surged
And weltered round me sole there unsubmerged:
Yet I strode on austere;
No hope could have no fear.

As I came through the desert thus it was,
As I came through the desert: Air once more,
And I was close upon a wild sea-shore;
Enormous cliffs arose on either hand,
The deep tide thundered up a league-broad strand;
White foambelts seethed there, wan spray swept and flew;
The sky broke, moon and stars and clouds and blue:
And I strode on austere;
No hope could have no fear.

As I came through the desert thus it was,
As I came through the desert: On the left
The sun arose and crowned a broad crag-cleft;
There stopped and burned out black, except a rim,
A bleeding eyeless socket, red and dim;
Whereon the moon fell suddenly south-west,
And stood above the right-hand cliffs at rest:
Still I strode on austere;
No hope could have no fear.

As I came through the desert thus it was,
As I came through the desert: From the right
A shape came slowly with a ruddy light;
A woman with a red lamp in her hand,
Bareheaded and barefooted on that strand;
O desolation moving with such grace!
O anguish with such beauty in thy face!
I fell as on my bier,
Hope travailed with such fear.

As I came through the desert thus it was,
As I came through the desert: I was twain,
Two selves distinct that cannot join again;
One stood apart and knew but could not stir,
And watched the other stark in swoon and her;
And she came on, and never turned aside,
Between such sun and moon and roaring tide:
And as she came more near
My soul grew mad with fear.

As I came through the desert thus it was,
As I came through the desert: Hell is mild
And piteous matched with that accursèd wild;

A large black sign was on her breast that bowed,
A broad black band ran down her snow-white shroud;
That lamp she held was her own burning heart,
Whose blood-drops trickled step by step apart;
The mystery was clear;
Mad rage had swallowed fear.

As I came through the desert thus it was,
As I came through the desert: By the sea
She knelt and bent above that senseless me;
Those lamp-drops fell upon my white brow there,
She tried to cleanse them with her tears and hair;
She murmured words of pity, love, and woe,
She heeded not the level rushing flow:
And mad with rage and fear,
I stood stonebound so near.

As I came through the desert thus it was,
As I came through the desert: When the tide
Swept up to her there kneeling by my side,
She clasped that corpse-like me, and they were borne
Away, and this vile me was left forlorn;
I know the whole sea cannot quench that heart,
Or cleanse that brow, or wash those two apart:
They love; their doom is drear,
Yet they nor hope nor fear;
But I, what do I here?

V

How he arrives there none can clearly know;
Athwart the mountains and immense wild tracts,
Or flung a waif upon that vast sea-flow,
Or down the river's boiling cataracts:
To reach it is as dying fever-stricken;
To leave it, slow faint birth intense pangs quicken;
And memory swoons in both the tragic acts.

But being there one feels a citizen;
Escape seems hopeless to the heart forlorn:
Can Death-in-Life be brought to life again?
And yet release does come; there comes a morn
When he awakes from slumbering so sweetly
That all the world is changed for him completely,
And he is verily as if new-born.

He scarcely can believe the blissful change,
He weeps perchance who wept not while accurst;
Never again will he approach the range
Infected by that evil spell now burst:
Poor wretch! who once hath paced that dolent city
Shall pace it often, doomed beyond all pity,
With horror ever deepening from the first.

Though he possess sweet babes and loving wife,
A home of peace by loyal friendships cheered,
And love them more than death or happy life,
They shall avail not; he must dree his weird;
Renounce all blessings for that imprecation,
Steal forth and haunt that builded desolation,
Of woe and terrors and thick darkness reared.

VI

I sat forlornly by the river-side,
And watched the bridge-lamps glow like golden stars
Above the blackness of the swelling tide,
Down which they struck rough gold in ruddier bars;
And heard the heave and splashing of the flow
Against the wall a dozen feet below.

Large elm-trees stood along that river-walk;
And under one, a few steps from my seat,
I heard strange voices join in stranger talk,
Although I had not heard approaching feet;
These bodiless voices in my waking dream
Flowed dark words blending with the sombre stream:—

And you have after all come back; come back.
I was about to follow on your track.
And you have failed: our spark of hope is black.

That I have failed is proved by my return:
The spark is quenched, nor ever more will burn.
But listen; and the story you shall learn.

I reached the portal common spirits fear,
And read the words above it, dark yet clear,
"Leave hope behind, all ye who enter here":

And would have passed in, gratified to gain
That positive eternity of pain,
Instead of this insufferable inane.

A demon warder clutched me, Not so fast;
First leave your hopes behind!—But years have passed
Since I left all behind me, to the last:

You cannot count for hope, with all your wit,
This bleak despair that drives me to the Pit:
How could I seek to enter void of it?

He snarled, What thing is this which apes a soul,
And would find entrance to our gulf of dole
Without the payment of the settled toll?

Outside the gate he showed an open chest:
Here pay their entrance fees the souls unblest;
Cast in some hope, you enter with the rest.

This is Pandora's box; whose lid shall shut,
And Hell-gate too, when hopes have filled it; but
They are so thin that it will never glut.

I stood a few steps backwards, desolate;
And watched the spirits pass me to their fate,
And fling off hope, and enter at the gate.

When one casts off a load he springs upright,
Squares back his shoulders, breathes with all his might,
And briskly paces forward strong and light:

But these, as if they took some burden, bowed;
The whole frame sank; however strong and proud
Before, they crept in quite infirm and cowed.

And as they passed me, earnestly from each
A morsel of his hope I did beseech,
To pay my entrance; but all mocked my speech.

Not one would cede a tittle of his store
Though knowing that in instants three or four
He must resign the whole for evermore.

So I returned. Our destiny is fell;
For in this Limbo we must ever dwell,
Shut out alike from Heaven and Earth and Hell.

The other sighed back, Yea; but if we grope
With care through all this Limbo's dreary scope,
We yet may pick up some minute lost hope;

And, sharing it between us, entrance win,
In spite of fiends so jealous for gross sin:
Let us without delay our search begin.

VII

Some say that phantoms haunt those shadowy streets,
 And mingle freely there with sparse mankind;
And tell of ancient woes and black defeats,
 And murmur mysteries in the grave enshrined:
But others think them visions of illusion,
Or even men gone far in self-confusion;
 No man there being wholly sane in mind.

And yet a man who raves, however mad,
 Who bares his heart and tells of his own fall,
Reserves some inmost secret good or bad:
 The phantoms have no reticence at all:
The nudity of flesh will blush though tameless,
The extreme nudity of bone grins shameless,
 The unsexed skeleton mocks shroud and pall.

I have seen phantoms there that were as men
 And men that were as phantoms flit and roam;
Marked shapes that were not living to my ken,
 Caught breathings acrid as with Dead Sea foam:

The City rests for man so weird and awful,
That his intrusion there might seem unlawful,
And phantoms there may have their proper home.

VIII

While I still lingered on that river-walk,
And watched the tide as black as our black doom,
I heard another couple join in talk,
And saw them to the left hand in the gloom
Seated against an elm bole on the ground,
Their eyes intent upon the stream profound.

"I never knew another man on earth
But had some joy and solace in his life,
Some chance of triumph in the dreadful strife:
My doom has been unmitigated dearth."

"We gaze upon the river, and we note
The various vessels large and small that float,
Ignoring every wrecked and sunken boat."

"And yet I asked no splendid dower, no spoil
Of sway or fame or rank or even wealth;
But homely love with common food and health,
And nightly sleep to balance daily toil."

"This all-too humble soul would arrogate
Unto itself some signalising hate
From the supreme indifference of Fate!"

"Who is most wretched in this dolorous place?
I think myself; yet I would rather be
My miserable self than He, than He
Who formed such creatures to His own disgrace.

"The vilest thing must be less vile than Thou
From whom it had its being, God and Lord!
Creator of all woe and sin! abhorred,
Malignant and implacable! I vow

"That not for all Thy power furled and unfurled,
For all the temples to Thy glory built,
Would I assume the ignominious guilt
Of having made such men in such a world."

"As if a Being, God or Fiend, could reign,
At once so wicked, foolish, and insane,
As to produce men when He might refrain!

"The world rolls round for ever like a mill;
It grinds out death and life and good and ill;
It has no purpose, heart or mind or will.

"While air of Space and Time's full river flow
The mill must blindly whirl unresting so:
It may be wearing out, but who can know?

"Man might know one thing were his sight less dim;
That it whirls not to suit his petty whim,
That it is quite indifferent to him.

"Nay, does it treat him harshly as he saith?
It grinds him some slow years of bitter breath,
Then grinds him back into eternal death."

IX

It is full strange to him who hears and feels,
When wandering there in some deserted street,
The booming and the jar of ponderous wheels,
The trampling clash of heavy ironshod feet:
Who in this Venice of the Black Sea rideth?
Who in this city of the stars abideth
To buy or sell as those in daylight sweet?

The rolling thunder seems to fill the sky
As it comes on; the horses snort and strain,
The harness jingles, as it passes by;
The hugeness of an overburthened wain:
A man sits nodding on the shaft or trudges
Three parts asleep beside his fellow-drudges:
And so it rolls into the night again.

What merchandise? whence, whither, and for whom?
Perchance it is a Fate-appointed hearse,
Bearing away to some mysterious tomb
Or Limbo of the scornful universe
The joy, the peace, the life-hope, the abortions
Of all things good which should have been our portions,
But have been strangled by that City's curse.

X

The mansion stood apart in its own ground;
In front thereof a fragrant garden-lawn,
High trees about it, and the whole walled round:
The massy iron gates were both withdrawn;
And every window of its front shed light,
Portentous in that City of the Night.

But though thus lighted it was deadly still
As all the countless bulks of solid gloom:
Perchance a congregation to fulfil
Solemnities of silence in this doom,
Mysterious rites of dolor and despair
Permitting not a breath of chant or prayer?

Broad steps ascended to a terrace broad
Whereon lay still light from the open door;
The hall was noble, and its aspect awed,
Hung round with heavy black from dome to floor;
And ample stairways rose to left and right
Whose balustrades were also draped with night.

I paced from room to room, from hall to hall,
Nor any life throughout the maze discerned;
But each was hung with its funereal pall,
And held a shrine, around which tapers burned,
With picture or with statue or with bust,
All copied from the same fair form of dust:

A woman very young and very fair:
Beloved by bounteous life and joy and youth,
And loving these sweet lovers, so that care
And age and death seemed not for her in sooth:
Alike as stars, all beautiful and bright,
These shapes lit up that mausoléan night.

At length I heard a murmur as of lips,
And reached an open oratory hung
With heaviest blackness of the whole eclipse;
Beneath the dome a fuming censer swung;
And one lay there upon a low white bed,
With tapers burning at the foot and head:

The Lady of the images: supine,
Deathstill, lifesweet, with folded palms she lay:
And kneeling there as at a sacred shrine
A young man wan and worn who seemed to pray:
A crucifix of dim and ghostly white
Surmounted the large altar left in night:—

The chambers of the mansion of my heart,
In every one whereof thine image dwells,
Are black with grief eternal for thy sake.

The inmost oratory of my soul,
Wherein thou ever dwellest quick or dead,
Is black with grief eternal for thy sake.

I kneel beside thee and I clasp the cross
With eyes for ever fixed upon that face
So beautiful and dreadful in its calm.

I kneel here patient as thou liest there;
As patient as a statue carved in stone,
Of adoration and eternal grief.

While thou dost not awake I cannot move;
And something tells me thou wilt never wake,
And I alive feel turning into stone.

Most beautiful were Death to end my grief,
Most hateful to destroy the sight of thee,
Dear vision better than all death or life.

But I renounce all choice of life or death,
For either shall be ever at thy side,
And thus in bliss or woe be ever well.—

He murmured thus and thus in monotone,
Intent upon that uncorrupted face,
Entranced except his moving lips alone:
I glided with hushed footsteps from the place.
This was the festival that filled with light
That palace in the City of the Night.

XI

What men are they who haunt these fatal glooms,
And fill their living mouths with dust of death,
And make their habitations in the tombs,
And breathe eternal sighs with mortal breath,
And pierce life's pleasant veil of various error
To reach that void of darkness and old terror
Wherein expire the lamps of hope and faith?

They have much wisdom yet they are not wise,
They have much goodness yet they do not well,
(The fools we know have their own Paradise,
The wicked also have their proper Hell);
They have much strength but still their doom is stronger,
Much patience but their time endureth longer,
Much valor but life mocks it with some spell.

They are most rational and yet insane:
An outward madness not to be controlled;
A perfect reason in the central brain,
Which has no power, but sitteth wan and cold,
And sees the madness, and foresees as plainly
The ruin in its path, and trieth vainly
To cheat itself refusing to behold.

And some are great in rank and wealth and power,
And some renowned for genius and for worth;
And some are poor and mean, who brood and cower
And shrink from notice, and accept all dearth
Of body, heart and soul, and leave to others
All boons of life: yet these and those are brothers,
The saddest and the weariest men on earth.

XII

Our isolated units could be brought
To act together for some common end?
For one by one, each silent with his thought,
I marked a long loose line approach and wend
Athwart the great cathedral's cloistered square,
And slowly vanish from the moonlit air.

Then I would follow in among the last:
And in the porch a shrouded figure stood,
Who challenged each one pausing ere he passed,
With deep eyes burning through a blank white hood,
Whence come you in the world of life and light
To this our City of Tremendous Night?—

From pleading in a senate of rich lords
For some scant justice to our countless hordes
Who toil half-starved with scarce a human right:
I wake from daydreams to this real night.

From wandering through many a solemn scene
Of opium visions, with a heart serene
And intellect miraculously bright:
I wake from daydreams to this real night.

From making hundreds laugh and roar with glee
By my transcendent feats of mimicry,
And humor wanton as an elfish sprite:
I wake from daydreams to this real night.

From prayer and fasting in a lonely cell,
Which brought an ecstasy ineffable
Of love and adoration and delight:
I wake from daydreams to this real night.

From ruling on a splendid kingly throne
A nation which beneath my rule has grown
Year after year in wealth and arts and might:
I wake from daydreams to this real night.

From preaching to an audience fired with faith
The Lamb who died to save our souls from death,
Whose blood hath washed our scarlet sins wool-white:
I wake from daydreams to this real night.

From drinking fiery poison in a den
Crowded with tawdry girls and squalid men,
Who hoarsely laugh and curse and brawl and fight:
I wake from daydreams to this real night.

From picturing with all beauty and all grace
First Eden and the parents of our race,
A luminous rapture unto all men's sight:
I wake from daydreams to this real night.

From writing a great work with patient plan
To justify the ways of God to man,
And show how ill must fade and perish quite:
I wake from daydreams to this real night.

From desperate fighting with a little band
Against the powerful tyrants of our land,
To free our brethren in their own despite:
I wake from daydreams to this real night.

Thus, challenged by that warder sad and stern,
Each one responded with his countersign,
Then entered the cathedral; and in turn
I entered also, having given mine;
But lingered near until I heard no more,
And marked the closing of the massive door.

XIII

Of all things human which are strange and wild
This is perchance the wildest and most strange,
And showeth man most utterly beguiled,
To those who haunt that sunless City's range;
That he bemoans himself for aye, repeating
How time is deadly swift, how life is fleeting,
How naught is constant on the earth but change.

The hours are heavy on him and the days;
The burden of the months he scarce can bear;
And often in his secret soul he prays
To sleep through barren periods unaware,
Arousing at some longed-for date of pleasure;
Which having passed and yielded him small treasure,
He would outsleep another term of care.

Yet in his marvellous fancy he must make
Quick wings for Time, and see it fly from us;
This Time which crawleth like a monstrous snake,
Wounded and slow and very venomous;
Which creeps blindwormlike round the earth and ocean,
Distilling poison at each painful motion,
And seems condemned to circle ever thus.

And since he cannot spend and use aright
The little time here given him in trust,
But wasteth it in weary undelight
Of foolish toil and trouble, strife and lust,
He naturally claimeth to inherit
The everlasting Future, that his merit
May have full scope; as surely is most just.

O length of the intolerable hours,
O nights that are as æons of slow pain,
O Time, too ample for our vital powers,
O Life, whose woeful vanities remain
Immutable for all of all our legions
Through all the centuries and in all the regions,
Not of your speed and variance *we* complain.

We do not ask a longer term of strife,
Weakness and weariness and nameless woes:
We do not claim renewed and endless life
When this which is our torment here shall close,
An everlasting conscious inanition!
We yearn for speedy death in full fruition,
Dateless oblivion and divine repose.

XIV

Large glooms were gathered in the mighty fane,
With tinted moongleams slanting here and there;
And all was hush: no swelling organ-strain,
No chant, no voice or murmuring of prayer;
No priests came forth, no tinkling censers fumed,
And the high altar space was unillumed.

Around the pillars and against the walls
Leaned men and shadows; others seemed to brood
Bent or recumbent in secluded stalls.
Perchance they were not a great multitude
Save in that city of so lonely streets
Where one may count up every face he meets.

All patiently awaited the event
Without a stir or sound, as if no less
Self-occupied, doomstricken, while attent.
And then we heard a voice of solemn stress
From the dark pulpit, and our gaze there met
Two eyes which burned as never eyes burned yet:

Two steadfast and intolerable eyes
Burning beneath a broad and rugged brow;
The head behind it of enormous size,
And as black fir-groves in a large wind bow,
Our rooted congregation, gloom-arrayed,
By that great sad voice deep and full were swayed:—

O melancholy Brothers, dark, dark, dark!
O battling in black floods without an ark!
O spectral wanderers of unholy Night!

My soul hath bled for you these sunless years,
With bitter blood-drops running down like tears:
Oh, dark, dark, dark, withdrawn from joy and light!

My heart is sick with anguish for your bale!
Your woe hath been my anguish; yea, I quail
And perish in your perishing unblest,
And I have searched the heights and depths, the scope
Of all our universe, with desperate hope
To find some solace for your wild unrest.

And now at last authentic word I bring,
Witnessed by every dead and living thing;
Good tidings of great joy for you, for all:
There is no God; no Fiend with names divine
Made us and tortures us; if we must pine,
It is to satiate no Being's gall.

It was the dark delusion of a dream,
That living Person conscious and supreme,
Whom we must curse for cursing us with life;
Whom we must curse because the life He gave
Could not be buried in the quiet grave,
Could not be killed by poison or by knife.

This little life is all we must endure,
The grave's most holy peace is ever sure,
We fall asleep and never wake again;
Nothing is of us but the mouldering flesh,
Whose elements dissolve and merge afresh
In earth, air, water, plants, and other men.

We finish thus; and all our wretched race
Shall finish with its cycle, and give place
To other beings, with their own time-doom;
Infinite æons ere our kind began;
Infinite æons after the last man
Has joined the mammoth in earth's tomb and womb.

We bow down to the universal laws,
Which never had for man a special clause
Of cruelty or kindness, love or hate;
If toads and vultures are obscene to sight,
If tigers burn with beauty and with might,
Is it by favor or by wrath of fate?

All substance lives and struggles evermore
Through countless shapes continually at war,
By countless interactions interknit:
If one is born a certain day on earth,
All times and forces tended to that birth,
Not all the world could change or hinder it.

I find no hint throughout the Universe
Of good or ill, of blessing or of curse;
I find alone Necessity Supreme;
With infinite Mystery, abysmal, dark,
Unlighted ever by the faintest spark,
For us the flitting shadows of a dream.

O Brothers of sad lives! they are so brief;
A few short years must bring us all relief:
Can we not bear these years of laboring breath?
But if you would not this poor life fulfil,
Lo, you are free to end it when you will,
Without the fear of waking after death.—

The organ-like vibrations of his voice
Thrilled through the vaulted aisles and died away;
The yearning of the tones which bade rejoice
Was sad and tender as a requiem lay:
Our shadowy congregation rested still
As brooding on that "End it when you will."

XV

Wherever men are gathered, all the air
Is charged with human feeling, human thought;
Each shout and cry and laugh, each curse and prayer,
Are into its vibrations surely wrought;
Unspoken passion, wordless meditation,
Are breathed into it with our respiration;
It is with our life fraught and over-fraught.

So that no man there breathes earth's simple breath,
As if alone on mountains or wide seas;
But nourishes warm life or hastens death
With joys and sorrows, health and foul disease,
Wisdom and folly, good and evil labors,
Incessant of his multitudinous neighbors;
He in his turn affecting all of these.

That City's atmosphere is dark and dense,
Although not many exiles wander there,
With many a potent evil influence,
Each adding poison to the poisoned air;
Infections of unutterable sadness,
Infections of incalculable madness,
Infections of incurable despair.

XVI

Our shadowy congregation rested still,
As musing on that message we had heard
And brooding on that "End it when you will";
Perchance awaiting yet some other word;
When keen as lightning through a muffled sky
Sprang forth a shrill and lamentable cry:—

The man speaks sooth, alas! the man speaks sooth:
We have no personal life beyond the grave;
There is no God; Fate knows nor wrath nor ruth:
Can I find here the comfort which I crave?

In all eternity I had one chance,
One few years' term of gracious human life:
The splendors of the intellect's advance,
The sweetness of the home with babes and wife;

The social pleasures with their genial wit;
The fascination of the worlds of art,
The glories of the worlds of nature, lit
By large imagination's glowing heart;

The rapture of mere being, full of health;
The careless childhood and the ardent youth,
The strenuous manhood winning various wealth,
The reverend age serene with life's long truth:

All the sublime prerogatives of Man;
The storied memories of the times of old,
The patient tracking of the world's great plan
Through sequences and changes myriad-fold.

This chance was never offered me before;
For me the infinite Past is blank and dumb:
This chance recurreth never, nevermore;
Blank, blank for me the infinite To-come.

And this sole chance was frustrate from my birth,
A mockery, a delusion; and my breath
Of noble human life upon this earth
So racks me that I sigh for senseless death.

My wine of life is poison mixed with gall,
My noonday passes in a nightmare dream,
I worse than lose the years which are my all:
What can console me for the loss supreme?

Speak not of comfort where no comfort is,
Speak not at all: can words make foul things fair?
Our life's a cheat, our death a black abyss:
Hush and be mute envisaging despair.—

This vehement voice came from the northern aisle,
Rapid and shrill to its abrupt harsh close;
And none gave answer for a certain while,
For words must shrink from these most wordless woes;
At last the pulpit speaker simply said,
With humid eyes and thoughtful drooping head:—

My Brother, my poor Brothers, it is thus;
This life itself holds nothing good for us,
But it ends soon and nevermore can be;
And we knew nothing of it ere our birth,
And shall know nothing when consigned to earth:
I ponder these thoughts and they comfort me.

XVII

How the moon triumphs through the endless nights!
How the stars throb and glitter as they wheel
Their thick processions of supernal lights
Around the blue vault obdurate as steel!
And men regard with passionate awe and yearning
The mighty marching and the golden burning,
And think the heavens respond to what they feel.

Boats gliding like dark shadows of a dream,
Are glorified from vision as they pass
The quivering moonbridge on the deep black stream;
Cold windows kindle their dead glooms of glass

To restless crystals; cornice, dome, and column
Emerge from chaos in the splendor solemn;
  Like faëry lakes gleam lawns of dewy grass.

With such a living light these dead eyes shine,
  These eyes of sightless heaven, that as we gaze
We read a pity, tremulous, divine,
  Or cold majestic scorn in their pure rays:
Fond man! they are not haughty, are not tender;
There is no heart or mind in all their splendor,
  They thread mere puppets all their marvellous maze.

If we could near them with the flight unflown,
  We should but find them worlds as sad as this,
Or suns all self-consuming like our own
  Enringed by planet worlds as much amiss:
They wax and wane through fusion and confusion;
The spheres eternal are a grand illusion,
  The empyréan is a void abyss.

XVIII

I wandered in a suburb of the north,
  And reached a spot whence three close lanes led down,
Beneath thick trees and hedgerows winding forth
  Like deep brook channels, deep and dark and lown:
The air above was wan with misty light,
The dull grey south showed one vague blur of white.

I took the left-hand lane and slowly trod
  Its earthen footpath, brushing as I went
The humid leafage; and my feet were shod
  With heavy languor, and my frame downbent,
With infinite sleepless weariness outworn,
So many nights I thus had paced forlorn.

After a hundred steps I grew aware
  Of something crawling in the lane below;
It seemed a wounded creature prostrate there
  That sobbed with pangs in making progress slow,
The hind limbs stretched to push, the fore limbs then
To drag; for it would die in its own den.

But coming level with it I discerned
  That it had been a man; for at my tread
It stopped in its sore travail and half-turned,
  Leaning upon its right, and raised its head,
And with the left hand twitched back as in ire
Long grey unreverend locks befouled with mire.

A haggard filthy face with bloodshot eyes,
  An infamy for manhood to behold.
He gasped all trembling, What, you want my prize?
  You leave, to rob me, wine and lust and gold
And all that men go mad upon, since you
Have traced my sacred secret of the clue?

You think that I am weak and must submit;
  Yet I but scratch you with this poisoned blade,
And you are dead as if I clove with it
  That false fierce greedy heart. Betrayed! betrayed!
I fling this phial if you seek to pass,
And you are forthwith shrivelled up like grass.

And then with sudden change, Take thought! take thought!
  Have pity on me! it is mine alone.
If you could find, it would avail you naught;
  Seek elsewhere on the pathway of your own:
  For who of mortal or immortal race
The lifetrack of another can retrace?

Did you but know my agony and toil!
  Two lanes diverge up yonder from this lane;
My thin blood marks the long length of their soil;
  Such clue I left, who sought my clue in vain:
My hands and knees are worn both flesh and bone;
I cannot move but with continual moan.

But I am in the very way at last
  To find the long-lost broken golden thread
Which reunites my present with my past,
  If you but go your own way. And I said,
I will retire as soon as you have told
Whereunto leadeth this lost thread of gold.

And so you know it not! he hissed with scorn;
  I feared you, imbecile! It leads me back
From this accursèd night without a morn,
  And through the deserts which have else no track,
And through vast wastes of horror-haunted time,
  To Eden innocence in Eden's clime:

And I become a nursling soft and pure,
  An infant cradled on its mother's knee,
Without a past, love-cherished and secure;
  Which if it saw this loathsome present Me,
Would plunge its face into the pillowing breast,
And scream abhorrence hard to lull to rest.

He turned to grope; and I retiring brushed
  Thin shreds of gossamer from off my face,
And mused, His life would grow, the germ uncrushed;
He should to antenatal night retrace,
And hide his elements in that large womb
Beyond the reach of man-evolving Doom.

And even thus, what weary way were planned,
  To seek oblivion through the far-off gate
Of birth, when that of death is close at hand!
  For this is law, if law there be in Fate:
What never has been, yet may have its when;
The thing which has been, never is again.

XIX

The mighty river flowing dark and deep,
  With ebb and flood from the remote seatides
Vague-sounding through the City's sleepless sleep,
  Is named the River of the Suicides;
For night by night some lorn wretch over-weary,
And shuddering from the future yet more dreary,
  Within its cold secure oblivion hides.

One plunges from a bridge's parapet,
  As by some blind and sudden frenzy hurled;
Another wades in slow with purpose set
  Until the waters are above him furled;
Another in a boat with dream-like motion
Glides drifting down into the desert ocean,
  To starve or sink from out the desert world.

They perish from their suffering surely thus,
  For none beholding them attempts to save,
The while each thinks how soon, solicitous,
  He may seek refuge in the self-same wave;
Some hour when tired of ever-vain endurance
Impatience will forerun the sweet assurance
  Of perfect peace eventual in the grave.

When this poor tragic-farce has palled us long,
  Why actors and spectators do we stay?—
To fill our so-short *rôles* out right or wrong;
  To see what shifts are yet in the dull play
For our illusion; to refrain from grieving
Dear foolish friends by our untimely leaving:
  But those asleep at home, how blest are they!

Yet it is but for one night after all:
  What matters one brief night of dreary pain?
When after it the weary eyelids fall
  Upon the weary eyes and wasted brain;
And all sad scenes and thoughts and feelings vanish
In that sweet sleep no power can ever banish,
  That one best sleep which never wakes again.

XX

I sat me weary on a pillar's base,
  And leaned against the shaft; for broad moonlight
O'erflowed the peacefulness of cloistered space,
  A shore of shadow slanting from the right:
The great cathedral's western front stood there,
A wave-worn rock in that calm sea of air.

Before it, opposite my place of rest,
  Two figures faced each other, large, austere:
A couchant sphinx in shadow to the breast,
  An angel standing in the moonlight clear;
So mighty by magnificence of form,
They were not dwarfed beneath that mass enorm.

Upon the cross-hilt of a naked sword
  The angel's hands, as prompt to smite, were held;
His vigilant intense regard was poured
  Upon the creature placidly unquelled,
Whose front was set at level gaze which took
No heed of aught, a solemn trance-like look.

And as I pondered these opposèd shapes
My eyelids sank in stupor, that dull swoon
Which drugs and with a leaden mantle drapes
The outworn to worse weariness. But soon
A sharp and clashing noise the stillness broke,
And from the evil lethargy I woke.

The angel's wings had fallen, stone on stone,
And lay there shattered; hence the sudden sound:
A warrior leaning on his sword alone
Now watched the sphinx with that regard profound;
The sphinx unchanged looked forthright, as aware
Of nothing in the vast abyss of air.

Again I sank in that repose unsweet,
Again a clashing noise my slumber rent;
The warrior's sword lay broken at his feet:
An unarmed man with raised hands impotent
Now stood before the sphinx, which ever kept
Such mien as if with open eyes it slept.

My eyelids sank in spite of wonder grown;
A louder crash upstartled me in dread:
The man had fallen forward, stone on stone,
And lay there shattered, with his trunkless head
Between the monster's large quiescent paws,
Beneath its grand front changeless as life's laws.

The moon had circled westward full and bright,
And made the temple-front a mystic dream,
And bathed the whole enclosure with its light,
The sworded angel's wrecks, the sphinx supreme:
I pondered long that cold majestic face
Whose vision seemed of infinite void space.

XXI

Anear the centre of that northern crest
Stands out a level upland bleak and bare,
From which the city east and south and west
Sinks gently in long waves; and thronèd there
An Image sits, stupendous, superhuman,
The bronze colossus of a wingèd Woman,
Upon a graded granite base foursquare.

Low-seated she leans forward massively,
With cheek on clenched left hand, the forearm's might
Erect, its elbow on her rounded knee;
Across a clasped book in her lap the right
Upholds a pair of compasses; she gazes
With full set eyes, but wandering in thick mazes
Of sombre thought beholds no outward sight.

Words cannot picture her; but all men know
That solemn sketch the pure sad artist wrought
Three centuries and threescore years ago,
With phantasies of his peculiar thought:
The instruments of carpentry and science
Scattered about her feet, in strange alliance
With the keen wolf-hound sleeping undistraught;

Scales, hour-glass, bell, and magic-square above;
The grave and solid infant perched beside,
With open winglets that might bear a dove,
Intent upon its tablets, heavy-eyed;
Her folded wings as of a mighty eagle,
But all too impotent to lift the regal
Robustness of her earth-born strength and pride;

And with those wings, and that light wreath which seems
To mock her grand head and the knotted frown
Of forehead charged with baleful thoughts and dreams,
The household bunch of keys, the housewife's gown
Voluminous, indented, and yet rigid
As if a shell of burnished metal frigid;
The feet thick shod to tread all weakness down;

The comet hanging o'er the waste dark seas,
The massy rainbow curved in front of it,
Beyond the village with the masts and trees;
The snaky imp, dog-headed, from the Pit,
Bearing upon its batlike leathern pinions
Her name unfolded in the sun's dominions,
The "Melencolia" that transcends all wit.

Thus has the artist copied her, and thus
  Surrounded to expound her form sublime,
Her fate heroic and calamitous;
  Fronting the dreadful mysteries of Time,
Unvanquished in defeat and desolation,
Undaunted in the hopeless conflagration
  Of the day setting on her baffled prime.

Baffled and beaten back she works on still,
  Weary and sick of soul she works the more,
Sustained by her indomitable will;
  The hands shall fashion and the brain shall pore
And all her sorrow shall be turned to labor,
Till death the friend-foe piercing with his sabre
  That mighty heart of hearts ends bitter war.

But as if blacker night could dawn on night,
  With tenfold gloom on moonless night unstarred,
A sense more tragic than defeat and blight,
  More desperate than strife with hope debarred,
More fatal than the adamantine Never
Encompassing her passionate endeavor
  Dawns glooming in her tenebrous regard:

The sense that every struggle brings defeat
  Because Fate holds no prize to crown success;
That all the oracles are dumb or cheat
  Because they have no secret to express;
That none can pierce the vast black veil uncertain
Because there is no light beyond the curtain;
  That all is vanity and nothingness.

Titanic from her high throne in the north,
  That City's sombre Patroness and Queen,
In bronze sublimity she gazes forth
  Over her Capital of teen and threne,
Over the river with its isles and bridges,
The marsh and moorland, to the stern rockridges,
  Confronting them with a coëval mien.

The moving moon and stars from east to west
  Circle before her in the sea of air;
Shadows and gleams glide round her solemn rest.
  Her subjects often gaze up to her there:
The strong to drink new strength of iron endurance,
The weak new terrors; all, renewed assurance
  And confirmation of the old despair.

1874

OSCAR WILDE

[October 15, 1856–November 30, 1900]

Oscar Wilde was born in Dublin the son of Sir William Robert Wilde, an Irish surgeon and antiquary. He attended college at the University of Dublin and at Oxford. His scholastic record at Oxford, which he left in 1878, was good; he won the Newdigate prize for poetry there; he led a movement founded on the principle of "art for art's sake;" he indulged himself in so many eccentricities and affectations that he attracted wide attention and became the idol of a host of youthful admirers. In 1881 he published *Poems*, his first volume of verse. After a tour in America in 1882, in which he preached the gospel of beauty to unheeding ears, he returned to London for a quiet life of several years, but in 1888 entered upon a most active literary career, writing poetry, plays, and various kinds of prose fiction. His plays *Lady Windermere's Fan* (1892), *Salomé* (1893), and *The Importance of Being Earnest* (1895) are brilliant with epigram and telling phrase. Wilde was often attacked for his daring opinions, and frequent charges were brought against his moral character. In 1895 he sued the Marquis of Queensberry for libel. Counter suit was brought against him, with the result that he was proved guilty of sexual abnormalities and sentenced to Reading jail for two years. His last literary works were an apologetic account of his life, written in jail, and his powerful *Ballad of Reading Gaol* (1898). After his release from prison he lived a wretched, aimless life for a few years on the Continent and finally died of cerebral meningitis in Paris. Wilde the poet has lost something because of Wilde the man, but his poetry will continue to be read by those who turn to poetry for its sensuous qualities. Not every reader, however, can overlook the "curious taint, the faint malodorous corruption" that is present in much of his most striking work.

LES SILHOUETTES

From IMPRESSIONS

THE sea is flecked with bars of grey,
The dull dead wind is out of tune,
And like a withered leaf the moon
Is blown across the stormy bay.

Etched clear upon the pallid sand
Lies the black boat: a sailor boy
Clambers aboard in careless joy
With laughing face and gleaming hand.

And overhead the curlews cry,
Where through the dusky upland grass
The young brown-throated reapers pass,
Like silhouettes against the sky.

1877

HELAS!

To drift with every passion till my soul
Is a stringed lute on which all winds can play,
Is it for this that I have given away
Mine ancient wisdom, and austere control?
Methinks my life is a twice-written scroll
Scrawled over on some boyish holiday
With idle songs for pipe and virelay,
Which do but mar the secret of the whole.
Surely there was a time I might have trod
The sunlit heights, and from life's dissonance
Struck one clear chord to reach the ears of God:
Is that time dead? lo! with a little rod
I did but touch the honey of romance—
And must I lose a soul's inheritance?

1881

REQUIESCAT

TREAD lightly, she is near,
Under the snow,
Speak gently, she can hear
The daisies grow.

All her bright golden hair
Tarnished with rust,
She that was young and fair
Fallen to dust.

Lily-like, white as snow,
She hardly knew
She was a woman, so
Sweetly she grew.

Coffin-board, heavy stone,
Lie on her breast,
I vex my heart alone,
She is at rest.

Peace, Peace, she cannot hear
Lyre or sonnet,
All my life's buried here,
Heap earth upon it.

1881

From ROME UNVISITED

AND yet what joy it were for me
To turn my feet unto the south,
And journeying towards the Tiber mouth
To kneel again at Fiesole!

And wandering through the tangled pines
That break the gold of Arno's stream,
To see the purple mist and gleam
Of morning on the Apennines.

By many a vineyard-hidden home,
Orchard and olive-garden grey,
Till from the drear Campagna's way
The seven hills bear up the dome!

1881

From THE BURDEN OF ITYS

THE harmless rabbit gambols with its young
Across the trampled towing-path, where late
A troop of laughing boys in jostling throng
Cheered with their noisy cries the racing eight;

The gossamer, with ravelled silver threads,
Works at its little loom, and from the dusky red-eaved sheds
Of the lone Farm a flickering light shines out
  Where the swinked shepherd drives his bleating flock
Back to their wattled sheep-cotes, a faint shout
  Comes from some Oxford boat at Sandford lock,
And starts the moor-hen from the sedgy rill,
And the dim lengthening shadows flit like swallows up the hill.

The heron passes homeward to the mere,
  The blue mist creeps among the shivering trees,
Gold world by world the silent stars appear,
  And like a blossom blown before the breeze
A white moon drifts across the shimmering sky,
Mute arbitress of all thy sad, thy rapturous threnody.

She does not heed thee, wherefore should she heed,
  She knows Endymion is not far away,
'Tis I, 'tis I, whose soul is as the reed
  Which has no message of its own to play,
So pipes another's bidding, it is I,
Drifting with every wind on the wide sea of misery.

Ah! the brown bird has ceased: one exquisite trill
  About the sombre woodland seems to cling
Dying in music, else the air is still,
  So still that one might hear the bat's small wing.
Wander and wheel above the pines, or tell
Each tiny dew-drop dripping from the blue-bell's brimming cell.

And far away across the lengthening wold,
  Across the willowy flats and thickets brown,
Magdalen's tall tower tipped with tremulous gold
  Marks the long High Street of the little town,
And warns me to return; I must not wait,
Hark! 'tis the curfew booming from the bell at Christ Church gate.

1881

ENDYMION

(FOR MUSIC)

THE apple trees are hung with gold,
  And birds are loud in Arcady,
The sheep lie bleating in the fold,
The wild goat runs across the wold,
But yesterday his love he told,
  I know he will come back to me.
O rising moon! O lady moon!
  Be you my lover's sentinel,
  You cannot choose but know him well,
For he is shod with purple shoon,
You cannot choose but know my love,
  For he a shepherd's crook doth bear,
And he is soft as any dove,
  And brown and curly is his hair.

The turtle now has ceased to call
  Upon her crimson-footed groom,
The grey wolf prowls about the stall,
The lily's singing seneschal
Sleeps in the lily-bell, and all
  The violet hills are lost in gloom.
O risen moon! O holy moon!
  Stand on the top of Helice,
  And if my own true love you see,
Ah! if you see the purple shoon,
The hazel crook, the lad's brown hair,
  The goat-skin wrapped about his arm,
Tell him that I am waiting where
  The rushlight glimmers in the Farm.

The falling dew is cold and chill,
  And no bird sings in Arcady,
The little fauns have left the hill,
Even the tired daffodil
Has closed its gilded doors, and still
  My lover comes not back to me.
False moon! False moon! O waning moon!
  Where is my own true lover gone,
  Where are the lips vermilion,
The shepherd's crook, the purple shoon?
Why spread that silver pavilion,
  Why wear that veil of drifting mist?
Ah! thou hast young Endymion,
  Thou hast the lips that should be kissed!

Three milkwhite doves are lying dead,
There is blood upon her hand
Three white lilies are flecked with red,
There is blood on the river sand.

Two that ride from the North and East,
And two from the South and West,
For the black ravens a goodly feast,
For the Kings daughter rest.

One man that loves her true,
(Crimson and red is the stain of gore)
He hath duggen a grave by the darksome yew,
One grave will do for four,

No moon in the still heaven,
In the black water none,
The sins on her soul are seven
The sin upon his is one

Oscar O'F. Wills Wilde.

S.M. Magdalen College
Oxford

Manuscript Page of an Early Version of *The Dole of the King's Daughter*.
(See Appendix I.)

THEOCRITUS

A VILLANNELLE

O SINGER of Persephone!
In the dim meadows desolate
Dost thou remember Sicily?

Still through the ivy flits the bee
Where Amaryllis lies in state;
O Singer of Persephone!

Simætha calls on Hecate
And hears the wild dogs at the gate:
Dost thou remember Sicily?

Still by the light and laughing sea
Poor Polypheme bemoans his fate;
O Singer of Persephone!

And still in boyish rivalry
Young Daphnis challenges his mate;
Dost thou remember Sicily?

Slim Lacon keeps a goat for thee,
For thee the jocund shepherds wait;
O Singer of Persephone!
Dost thou remember Sicily?

THE SPHINX

IN a dim corner of my room for longer than my fancy thinks
A beautiful and silent Sphinx has watched me through the shifting gloom.

Inviolate and immobile she does not rise, she does not stir
For silver moons are naught to her and naught to her the suns that reel.

Red follows grey across the air, the waves of moonlight ebb and flow
But with the Dawn she does not go and in the night-time she is there.

Dawn follows Dawn and Nights grow old and all the while this curious cat
Lies crouching on the Chinese mat with eyes of satin rimmed with gold.

Upon the mat she lies and leers and on the tawny throat of her
Flutters the soft and silky fur or ripples to her pointed ears.

Come forth, my lovely seneschal! so somnolent, so statuesque!
Come forth you exquisite grotesque! half woman and half animal!

Come forth my lovely languorous Sphinx! and put your head upon my knee!
And let me stroke your throat and see your body spotted like the Lynx!

And let me touch those curving claws of yellow ivory and grasp
The tail that like a monstrous Asp coils round your heavy velvet paws!

* * *

A thousand weary centuries are thine while I have hardly seen
Some twenty summers cast their green for Autumn's gaudy liveries.

But you can read the Hieroglyphs on the great sandstone obelisks,
And you have talked with Basilisks, and you have looked on Hippogriffs.

O tell me, were you standing by when Isis to Osiris knelt?
And did you watch the Egyptian melt her union for Antony

And drink the jewel-drunken wine and bend her head in mimic awe
To see the huge proconsul draw the salted tunny from the brine?

And did you mark the Cyprian kiss white Adon on his catafalque?
And did you follow Amenalk, the God of Heliopolis?

And did you talk with Thoth, and did you hear the moon-horned Io weep?
And know the painted kings who sleep beneath the wedge-shaped Pyramid?

* * *

Lift up your large black satin eyes which are like cushions where one sinks!
Fawn at my feet, fantastic Sphinx! and sing me all your memories!

Sing to me of the Jewish maid who wandered with the Holy Child,
And how you led them through the wild, and how they slept beneath your shade.

Sing to me of that odorous green eve when couching by the marge
You heard from Adrian's gilded barge the laughter of Antinous

And lapped the stream and fed your drouth and watched with hot and hungry stare
The ivory body of that rare young slave with his pomegranate mouth!

Sing to me of the Labyrinth in which the twy-formed bull was stalled!
Sing to me of the night you crawled across the temple's granite plinth

When through the purple corridors the screaming scarlet Ibis flew
In terror, and a horrid dew dripped from the moaning Mandragores,

And the great torpid crocodile within the tank shed slimy tears,
And tare the jewels from his ears and staggered back into the Nile,

And the priests cursed you with shrill psalms as in your claws you seized their snake
And crept away with it to slake your passion by the shuddering palms.

* * *

Who were your lovers? who were they who wrestled for you in the dust?
Which was the vessel of your lust? What Leman had you, every day?

Did giant Lizards come and crouch before you on the reedy banks?
Did Gryphons with great metal flanks leap on you in your trampled couch?

Did monstrous hippotami come sidling toward you in the mist?
Did gilt-scaled dragons writhe and twist with passion as you passed them by?

And from the brick-built Lycian tomb what horrible Chimera came
With fearful heads and fearful flame to breed new wonders from your womb?

Or had you shameful secret quests and did you hurry to your home
Some Nereid coiled in amber foam with curious rock crystal breasts?

Or did you treading through the froth call to the brown Sidonian
For tidings of Leviathan, Leviathan or Behemoth?

Or did you when the sun was set climb up the cactus-covered slope
To meet your swarthy Ethiop whose body was of polished jet?

Or did you while the earthen skiffs dropped down the grey Nilotic flats
At twilight and the flickering bats flew round the temple's triple glyphs

Steal to the border of the bar and swim across the silent lake
And slink into the vault and make the Pyramid your lúpanar

Till from each black sarcophagus rose up the painted swathèd dead?
Or did you lure unto your bed the ivory-horned Tragelaphos?

Or did you love the god of flies who plagued the Hebrews and was splashed
With wine unto the waist? or Pasht, who had green beryls for her eyes?

Or that young god, the Tyrian, who was more amorous than the dove
Of Ashtaroth? or did you love the god of the Assyrian

Whose wings, like strange transparent talc, rose high above his hawk-faced head,
Painted with silver and with red and ribbed with rods of Oreichalch?

Or did huge Apis from his car leap down and lay before your feet
Big blossoms of the honey-sweet and honey-coloured nenuphar?

* * *

How subtle-secret is your smile! Did you love none then? Nay, I know
Great Ammon was your bedfellow! He lay with you beside the Nile!

The river-horses in the slime trumpeted when they saw him come
Odorous with Syrian galbanum and smeared with spikenard and with thyme.

He came along the river bank like some tall galley argent-sailed,
He strode across the waters, mailed in beauty, and the waters sank.

He strode across the desert sand: he reached the valley where you lay:
He waited till the dawn of day: then touched your black breasts with his hand.

You kissed his mouth with mouths of flame: you made the hornèd god your own:
You stood behind him on his throne: you called him by his secret name.

You whispered monstrous oracles into the caverns of his ears:
With blood of goats and blood of steers you taught him monstrous miracles.

White Ammon was your bedfellow! Your chamber was the steaming Nile!
And with your curved archaic smile you watched his passion come and go.

* * *

With Syrian oils his brows were bright: and widespread as a tent at noon
His marble limbs made pale the moon and lent the day a larger light.

His long hair was nine cubits' span and coloured like that yellow gem
Which hidden in their garment's hem the merchants bring from Kurdistan.

His face was as the must that lies upon a vat of new-made wine:
The seas could not insapphirine the perfect azure of his eyes.

His thick soft throat was white as milk and threaded with the veins of blue:
And curious pearls like frozen dew were broidered on his flowing silk.

* * *

On pearl and porphyry pedestalled he was too bright to look upon:
For on his ivory breast there shone the wondrous ocean-emerald,

That mystic moonlight jewel which some diver of the Colchian caves
Had found beneath the blackening waves and carried to the Colchian witch.

Before his gilded galiot ran naked vine-wreathed corybants,
And lines of swaying elephants knelt down to draw his chariot,

And lines of swarthy Nubians bare up his litter as he rode
Down the great granite-paven road between the nodding peacock-fans.

The merchants brought him steatite from Sidon in their painted ships:
The meanest cup that touched his lips was fashioned from a chrysolite.

The merchants brought him cedar chests of rich apparel bound with cords:
His train was borne by Memphian lords: young kings were glad to be his guests.

Ten hundred shaven priests did bow to Ammon's altar day and night,
Ten hundred lamps did wave their light through Ammon's carven house—and now

Foul snake and speckled adder with their young ones crawl from stone to stone
For ruined is the house and prone the great rose-marble monolith!

Wild ass or trotting jackal comes and couches in the mouldering gates:
Wild satyrs call unto their mates across the fallen fluted drums.

And on the summit of the pile the blue-faced ape of Horus sits
And gibbers while the fig-tree splits the pillars of the peristyle.

* * *

The God is scattered here and there: deep hidden in the windy sand
I saw his giant granite hand still clenched in impotent despair.

And many a wandering caravan of stately negroes silken-shawled,
Crossing the desert halts appalled before the neck that none can span.

And many a bearded Bedouin draws back his yellow-striped burnous
To gaze upon the Titan thews of him who was thy paladin.

Go, seek his fragments on the moor and wash them in the evening dew,
And from their pieces make anew thy mutilated paramour!

Go, seek them where they lie alone and from their broken pieces make
Thy bruisèd bedfellow! And wake mad passions in the senseless stone!

Charm his dull ear with Syrian hymns! he loved your body! oh, be kind,
Pour spikenard on his hair, and wind soft rolls of linen round his limbs!

Wind round his head the figured coins! stain with red fruits those pallid lips!
Weave purple for his shrunken hips! and purple for his barren loins!

* * *

Away to Egypt! Have no fear. Only one God has ever died.
Only one God has let His side be wounded by a soldier's spear.
But these, thy lovers, are not dead. Still by the hundred-cubit gate
Dog-faced Anubis sits in state with lotus-lilies for thy head.

Still from his chair of porphyry gaunt Memnon strains his lidless eyes
Across the empty land, and cries each yellow morning unto thee.

And Nilus with his broken horn lies in his black and oozy bed
And till thy coming will not spread his waters on the withering corn.

Your lovers are not dead, I know. They will rise up and hear your voice
And clash their cymbals and rejoice and run to kiss your mouth! And so,

Set wings upon your argosies! Set horses to your ebon car!
Back to your Nile! Or if you are grown sick of dead divinities

Follow some roving lion's spoor across the copper-coloured plain,
Reach out and hale him by the mane and bid him be your paramour!

Couch by his side upon the grass and set your white teeth in his throat
And when you hear his dying note lash your long flanks of polished brass

And take a tiger for your mate, whose amber sides are flecked with black,
And ride upon his gilded back in triumph through the Theban gate,

And toy with him in amorous jests, and when he turns, and snarls, and gnaws,
O smite him with your jasper claws! and bruise him with your agate breasts!

Why are you tarrying? Get hence! I weary of your sullen ways,
I weary of your steadfast gaze, your somnolent magnificence.

Your horrible and heavy breath makes the light flicker in the lamp,
And on my brow I feel the damp and dreadful dews of night and death.

Your eyes are like fantastic moons that shiver in some stagnant lake,
Your tongue is like a scarlet snake that dances to fantastic tunes,

Your pulse makes poisonous melodies, and your black throat is like the hole
Left by some torch or burning coal on Saracenic tapestries.

Away! The sulphur-coloured stars are hurrying through the Western gate!
Away! Or it may be too late to climb their silent silver cars!

See, the dawn shivers round the grey gilt-dialled towers, and the rain
Streams down each diamonded pane and blurs with tears the wannish day.

What snake-tressed fury fresh from Hell, with uncouth gestures and unclean,
Stole from the poppy-drowsy queen and led you to a student's cell?

What songless tongueless ghost of sin crept through the curtains of the night,
And saw my taper burning bright, and knocked, and bade you enter in.

Are there not others more accursed, whiter with leprosies than I?
Are Abana and Pharphar dry that you come here to slake your thirst?

Get hence, you loathsome mystery! Hideous animal, get hence!
You wake in me each bestial sense, you make me what I would not be.

You make my creed a barren sham, you wake foul dreams of sensual life,
And Atys with his blood-stained knife were better than the thing I am.

False Sphinx! False Sphinx! By reedy Styx old Charon, leaning on his oar,
Waits for my coin. Go thou before, and leave me to my crucifix,

Whose pallid burden, sick with pain, watches the world with wearied eyes,
And weeps for every soul that dies, and weeps for every soul in vain.

1894

THE TRUE KNOWLEDGE

. . . ἀναγκαίως δ' ἔχει
βίον θερίζειν ὥστε χάρπιμον στάχυν,
καὶ τὸν μὲν εἶναι τὸν δὲ μή.

Thou knowest all; I seek in vain
What lands to till or sow with seed—
The land is black with briar and weed,
Nor cares for falling tears or rain.

Thou knowest all; I sit and wait
With blinded eyes and hands that fail,
Till the last lifting of the veil
And the first opening of the gate.

Thou knowest all; I cannot see.
I trust I shall not live in vain,
I know that we shall meet again
In some divine eternity.

THE BALLAD OF READING GAOL

I

He did not wear his scarlet coat,
For blood and wine are red,
And blood and wine were on his hands
When they found him with the dead,
The poor dead woman whom he loved,
And murdered in her bed.

He walked amongst the Trial Men
In a suit of shabby grey;
A cricket cap was on his head,
And his step seemed light and gay;
But I never saw a man who looked
So wistfully at the day.

I never saw a man who looked
With such a wistful eye
Upon that little tent of blue
Which prisoners call the sky,
And at every drifting cloud that went
With sails of silver by.

I walked, with other souls in pain,
Within another ring,
And was wondering if the man had done
A great or little thing,
When a voice behind me whispered low,
"*That fellow's got to swing.*"

Dear Christ! the very prison walls
Suddenly seemed to reel,
And the sky above my head became
Like a casque of scorching steel;
And, though I was a soul in pain,
My pain I could not feel.

I only knew what hunted thought
Quickened his step, and why
He looked upon the garish day
With such a wistful eye;
The man had killed the thing he loved,
And so he had to die.

* * *

Yet each man kills the thing he loves,
By each let this be heard,
Some do it with a bitter look,
Some with a flattering word,
The coward does it with a kiss,
The brave man with a sword!

Some kill their love when they are young,
And some when they are old;
Some strangle with the hands of Lust,
Some with the hands of Gold:
The kindest use a knife, because
The dead so soon grow cold.

Some love too little, some too long,
Some sell, and others buy;
Some do the deed with many tears,
And some without a sigh:

The Ballad of Reading Gaol

By

C. 3. 3.

Ernest Dowson
from his
friend and admirer
the author

Leonard Smithers
Royal Arcade London W
Mdcccxcviii

Feb. 98.

Presentation Copy of *The Ballad of Reading Gaol.* (See Appendix I.)

For each man kills the thing he loves,
  Yet each man does not die.

He does not die a death of shame
  On a day of dark disgrace,
Nor have a noose about his neck,
  Nor a cloth upon his face,
Nor drop feet foremost through the floor
  Into an empty space.

* * *

He does not sit with silent men
  Who watch him night and day;
Who watch him when he tries to weep,
  And when he tries to pray;
Who watch him lest himself should rob
  The prison of its prey.

He does not wake at dawn to see
  Dread figures throng his room,
The shivering Chaplain robed in white,
  The Sheriff stern with gloom,
And the Governor all in shiny black,
  With the yellow face of Doom.

He does not rise in piteous haste
  To put on convict-clothes,
While some coarse-mouthed Doctor gloats, and notes
  Each new and nerve-twitched pose,
Fingering a watch whose little ticks
  Are like horrible hammer-blows.

He does not know that sickening thirst
  That sands one's throat, before
The hangman with his gardener's gloves
  Slips through the padded door,
And binds one with three leathern thongs,
  That the throat may thirst no more.

He does not bend his head to hear
  The Burial Office read,
Nor, while the terror of his soul
  Tells him he is not dead,
Cross his own coffin, as he moves
  Into the hideous shed.

He does not stare upon the air
  Through a little roof of glass:
He does not pray with lips of clay
  For his agony to pass;
Nor feel upon his shuddering cheek
  The kiss of Caiaphas.

II

Six weeks our guardsman walked the yard,
  In the suit of shabby grey:
His cricket cap was on his head,
  And his step seemed light and gay,
But I never saw a man who looked
  So wistfully at the day.

I never saw a man who looked
  With such a wistful eye
Upon that little tent of blue
  Which prisoners call the sky,
And at every wandering cloud that trailed
  Its ravelled fleeces by.

He did not wring his hands, as do
  Those witless men who dare
To try to rear the changeling Hope
  In the cave of black Despair:
He only looked upon the sun,
  And drank the morning air.

He did not wring his hands nor weep,
  Nor did he peek or pine,
But he drank the air as though it held
  Some healthful anodyne;
With open mouth he drank the sun
  As though it had been wine!

And I and all the souls in pain,
  Who tramped the other ring,
Forgot if we ourselves had done
  A great or little thing,
And watched with gaze of dull amaze
  The man who had to swing.

And strange it was to see him pass
  With a step so light and gay,
And strange it was to see him look
  So wistfully at the day,
And strange it was to think that he
  Had such a debt to pay.

* * *

For oak and elm have pleasant leaves
  That in the spring-time shoot:
But grim to see is the gallows-tree,
  With its adder-bitten root,
And, green or dry, a man must die
  Before it bears its fruit!

The loftiest place is that seat of grace
  For which all worldlings try:
But who would stand in hempen band
  Upon a scaffold high,

And through a murderer's collar take
His last look at the sky?

It is sweet to dance to violins
When Love and Life are fair:
To dance to flutes, to dance to lutes
Is delicate and rare:
But it is not sweet with nimble feet
To dance upon the air!

So with curious eyes and sick surmise
We watched him day by day,
And wondered if each one of us
Would end the self-same way,
For none can tell to what red Hell
His sightless soul may stray.

At last the dead man walked no more
Amongst the Trial Men,
And I knew that he was standing up
In the black dock's dreadful pen,
And that never would I see his face
In God's sweet world again.

Like two doomed ships that pass in storm
We had crossed each other's way:
But we made no sign, we said no word,
We had no word to say;
For we did not meet in the holy night,
But in the shameful day.

A prison wall was round us both,
Two outcast men we were:
The world had thrust us from its heart,
And God from out His care:
And the iron gin that waits for Sin
Had caught us in its snare.

III

In Debtor's Yard the stones are hard,
And the dripping wall is high,
So it was there he took the air
Beneath the leaden sky,
And by each side a Warder walked,
For fear the man might die.

Or else he sat with those who watched
His anguish night and day;
Who watched him when he rose to weep,
And when he crouched to pray;
Who watched him lest himself should rob
Their scaffold of its prey.

The Governor was strong upon
The Regulations Act:
The Doctor said that Death was but
A scientific fact:
And twice a day the Chaplain called,
And left a little tract.

And twice a day he smoked his pipe,
And drank his quart of beer:
His soul was resolute, and held
No hiding-place for fear;
He often said that he was glad
The hangman's hands were near.

But why he said so strange a thing
No warder dared to ask:
For he to whom a watcher's doom
Is given as his task,
Must set a lock upon his lips,
And make his face a mask.

Or else he might be moved, and try
To comfort or console:
And what should Human Pity do
Pent up in Murderers' Hole?
What word of grace in such a place
Could help a brother's soul?

* * *

With slouch and swing around the ring
We trod the Fools' Parade!
We did not care: we knew we were
The Devil's Own Brigade:
And shaven head and feet of lead
Make a merry masquerade.

We tore the tarry rope to shreds
With blunt and bleeding nails;
We rubbed the doors, and scrubbed the floors,
And cleaned the shining rails:
And, rank by rank, we soaped the plank,
And clattered with the pails.

We sewed the sacks, we broke the stones,
We turned the dusty drill:
We banged the tins, and bawled the hymns,
And sweated on the mill:
But in the heart of every man
Terror was lying still.

So still it lay that every day
Crawled like a weed-clogged wave:
And we forgot the bitter lot
That waits for fool and knave,

Till once, as we trampled in from work,
  We passed an open grave.

With yawning mouth the yellow hole
  Gaped for a living thing;
The very mud cried out for blood
  To the thirsty asphalt ring:
And we knew that ere one dawn grew fair
  Some prisoner had to swing.

Right in we went, with soul intent
  On Death and Dread and Doom:
The hangman, with his little bag,
  Went shuffling through the gloom:
And each man trembled as he crept
  Into his numbered tomb.

* * *

That night the empty corridors
  Were full of forms of Fear,
And up and down the iron town
  Stole feet we could not hear,
And through the bars that hide the stars
  White faces seemed to peer.

He lay as one who lies and dreams
  In a pleasant meadow-land,
The watchers watched him as he slept,
  And could not understand
How one could sleep so sweet a sleep
  With a hangman close at hand.

But there is no sleep when men must weep
  Who never yet have wept:
So we—the fool, the fraud, the knave—
  That endless vigil kept,
And through each brain on hands of pain
  Another's terror crept.

Alas! it is a fearful thing
  To feel another's guilt!
For, right within, the sword of Sin
  Pierced to its poisoned hilt,
And as molten lead were the tears we shed
  For the blood we had not spilt.

The Warders with their shoes of felt
  Crept by each padlocked door,
And peeped and saw, with eyes of awe,
  Grey figures on the floor,
And wondered why men knelt to pray
  Who never prayed before.

All through the night we knelt and prayed,
  Mad mourners of a corse!
The troubled plumes of midnight were
  The plumes upon a hearse:
And bitter wine upon a sponge
  Was the savour of Remorse.

* * *

The grey cock crew, the red cock crew,
  But never came the day:
And crooked shapes of Terror crouched,
  In the corners where we lay:
And each evil sprite that walks by night
  Before us seemed to play.

They glided past, they glided fast,
  Like travellers through a mist:
They mocked the moon in a rigadoon
  Of delicate turn and twist,
And with formal pace and loathsome grace
  The phantoms kept their tryst.

With mop and mow, we saw them go,
  Slim shadows hand in hand:
About, about, in ghostly rout
  They trod a saraband:
And the damned grotesques made arabesques,
  Like the wind upon the sand!

With the pirouettes of marionettes,
  They tripped on pointed tread:
But with flutes of Fear they filled the ear,
  As their grisly masque they led,
And loud they sang, and long they sang,
  For they sang to wake the dead.

"*Oho!*" they cried, "*The world is wide,*
  But fettered limbs go lame!
And once, or twice, to throw the dice
  Is a gentlemanly game,
But he does not win who plays with Sin
  In the secret House of Shame."

No things of air these antics were,
  That frolicked with such glee:
To men whose lives were held in gyves,
  And whose feet might not go free,
Ah! wounds of Christ! they were living things,
  Most terrible to see.

Around, around, they waltzed and wound;
  Some wheeled in smirking pairs;
With the mincing step of a demirep
  Some sidled up the stairs:

And with subtle sneer, and fawning leer,
  Each helped us at our prayers.

The morning wind began to moan,
  But still the night went on:
Through its giant loom the web of gloom
  Crept till each thread was spun:
And, as we prayed, we grew afraid
  Of the Justice of the Sun.

The moaning wind went wandering round
  The weeping prison-wall:
Till like a wheel of turning steel
  We felt the minutes crawl:
O moaning wind! what had we done
  To have such a seneschal?

At last I saw the shadowed bars,
  Like a lattice wrought in lead,
Move right across the whitewashed wall
  That faced my three-plank bed,
And I knew that somewhere in the world
  God's dreadful dawn was red.

At six o'clock we cleaned our cells,
  At seven all was still,
But the sough and swing of a mighty wing
  The prison seemed to fill,
For the Lord of Death with icy breath
  Had entered in to kill.

He did not pass in purple pomp,
  Nor ride a moon-white steed.
Three yards of cord and a sliding board
  Are all the gallows' need:
So with rope of shame the Herald came
  To do the secret deed.

We were as men who through a fen
  Of filthy darkness grope:
We did not dare to breathe a prayer,
  Or to give our anguish scope:
Something was dead in each of us,
  And what was dead was Hope.

For Man's grim Justice goes its way,
  And will not swerve aside:
It slays the weak, it slays the strong,
  It has a deadly stride:
With iron heel it slays the strong,
  The monstrous parricide!

We waited for the stroke of eight:
  Each tongue was thick with thirst:
For the stroke of eight is the stroke of Fate
  That makes a man accursed,
And Fate will use a running noose
  For the best man and the worst.

We had no other thing to do,
  Save to wait for the sign to come:
So, like things of stone in a valley lone,
  Quiet we sat and dumb:
But each man's heart beat thick and quick,
  Like a madman on a drum!

With sudden shock the prison-clock
  Smote on the shivering air,
And from all the gaol rose up a wail
  Of impotent despair,
Like the sound that frightened marshes hear
  From some leper in his lair.

And as one sees most fearful things
  In the crystal of a dream,
We saw the greasy hempen rope
  Hooked to the blackened beam,
And heard the prayer the hangman's snare
  Strangled into a scream.

And all the woe that moved him so
  That he gave that bitter cry,
And the wild regrets, and the bloody sweats,
  None knew so well as I:
For he who lives more lives than one
  More deaths than one must die.

IV

There is no chapel on the day
  On which they hang a man:
The Chaplain's heart is far too sick,
  Or his face is far too wan,
Or there is that written in his eyes
  Which none should look upon.

So they kept us close till nigh on noon,
  And then they rang the bell,
And the Warders with their jingling keys
  Opened each listening cell,
And down the iron stair we tramped,
  Each from his separate Hell.

Out into God's sweet air we went,
  But not in wonted way,
For this man's face was white with fear,
  And that man's face was grey,

And I never saw sad men who looked
So wistfully at the day.

I never saw sad men who looked
With such a wistful eye
Upon that little tent of blue
We prisoners called the sky,
And at every careless cloud that passed
In happy freedom by.

But there were those amongst us all
Who walked with downcast head,
And knew that, had each got his due,
They should have died instead:
He had but killed a thing that lived,
Whilst they had killed the dead.

For he who sins a second time
Wakes a dead soul to pain,
And draws it from its spotted shroud,
And makes it bleed again,
And makes it bleed great gouts of blood,
And makes it bleed in vain!

* * *

Like ape or clown, in monstrous garb
With crooked arrows starred,
Silently we went round and round,
The slippery asphalt yard;
Silently we went round and round
And no man spoke a word.

Silently we went round and round,
And through each hollow mind
The Memory of dreadful things
Rushed like a dreadful wind,
And Horror stalked before each man,
And Terror crept behind.

The Warders strutted up and down,
And kept their herd of brutes,
Their uniforms were spick and span,
And they wore their Sunday suits,
But we knew the work they had been at,
By the quicklime on their boots.

For where a grave had opened wide,
There was no grave at all:
Only a stretch of mud and sand
By the hideous prison-wall,
And a little heap of burning lime,
That the man should have his pall.

For he has a pall, this wretched man,
Such as few men can claim:
Deep down below a prison-yard,
Naked for greater shame,
He lies, with fetters on each foot,
Wrapt in a sheet of flame!

And all the while the burning lime
Eats flesh and bone away,
It eats the brittle bone by night,
And the soft flesh by day,
It eats the flesh and bone by turns,
But it eats the heart alway.

* * *

For three long years they will not sow
Or root or seedling there:
For three long years the unblessed spot
Will sterile be and bare,
And look upon the wondering sky
With unreproachful stare.

They think a murderer's heart would taint
Each simple seed they sow.
It is not true! God's kindly earth
Is kindlier than men know,
And the red rose would but blow more red,
The white rose whiter blow.

Out of his mouth a red, red rose!
Out of his heart a white!
For who can say by what strange way,
Christ brings His will to light,
Since the barren staff the pilgrim bore
Bloomed in the great Pope's sight?

But neither milk-white rose nor red
May bloom in prison air;
The shard, the pebble, and the flint,
Are what they give us there:
For flowers have been known to heal
A common man's despair.

So never will wine-red rose or white,
Petal by petal, fall
On that stretch of mud and sand that lies
By the hideous prison-wall,
To tell the men who tramp the yard
That God's Son died for all.

* * *

Yet though the hideous prison-wall
Still hems him round and round,

And a spirit may not walk by night
  That is with fetters bound,
And a spirit may but weep that lies
  In such unholy ground,

He is at peace—this wretched man—
  At peace, or will be soon:
There is no thing to make him mad,
  Nor does Terror walk at noon,
For the lampless Earth in which he lies
  Has neither Sun nor Moon.

They hanged him as a beast is hanged:
  They did not even toll
A requiem that might have brought
  Rest to his startled soul,
But hurriedly they took him out,
  And hid him in a hole.

They stripped him of his canvas clothes,
  And gave him to the flies:
They mocked the swollen purple throat,
  And the stark and staring eyes:
And with laughter loud they heaped the shroud
  In which their convict lies.

The Chaplain would not kneel to pray
  By his dishonoured grave:
Nor mark it with that blessed Cross
  That Christ for sinners gave,
Because the man was one of those
  Whom Christ came down to save.

Yet all is well; he has but passed
  To life's appointed bourne:
And alien tears will fill for him
  Pity's long-broken urn,
For his mourners will be outcast men,
  And outcasts always mourn.

V

I know not whether Laws be right,
  Or whether Laws be wrong;
All that we know who lie in gaol
  Is that the wall is strong;
And that each day is like a year,
  A year whose days are long.

But this I know; that every Law
  That men have made for Man,
Since first Man took his brother's life,
  And the sad world began,
But straws the wheat and saves the chaff
  With a most evil fan.

This too I know—and wise it were
  If each could know the same—
That every prison that men build
  Is built with bricks of shame,
And bound with bars lest Christ should see
  How men their brothers maim.

With bars they blur the gracious moon,
  And blind the goodly sun:
And they do well to hide their Hell,
  For in it things are done
That Son of God nor Son of Man
  Ever should look upon!

* * *

The vilest deeds like poison weeds,
  Bloom well in prison-air;
It is only what is good in Man
  That wastes and withers there:
Pale Anguish keeps the heavy gate,
  And the Warder is Despair.

For they starve the little frightened child
  Till it weeps both night and day:
And they scourge the weak, and flog the fool,
  And gibe the old and grey,
And some grow mad, and all grow bad,
  And none a word may say.

Each narrow cell in which we dwell
  Is a foul and dark latrine,
And the fetid breath of living Death
  Chokes up each grated screen,
And all, but Lust, is turned to dust
  In Humanity's machine,

The brackish water that we drink
  Creeps with a loathsome slime,
And the bitter bread they weigh in scales
  Is full of chalk and lime,
And Sleep will not lie down, but walks
  Wild-eyed, and cries to Time.

* * *

But though lean Hunger and green Thirst
  Like asp with adder fight,
We have little care of prison fare,
  For what chills and kills outright
Is that every stone one lifts by day
  Becomes one's heart by night.

With midnight always in one's heart,
  And twilight in one's cell,
We turn the crank, or tear the rope,
  Each in his separate Hell,
And the silence is more awful far
  Than the sound of a brazen bell.

And never a human voice comes near
  To speak a gentle word:
And the eye that watches through the door
  Is pitiless and hard:
And by all forgot, we rot and rot,
  With soul and body marred.

And thus we rust Life's iron chain
  Degraded and alone:
And some men curse, and some men weep,
  And some men make no moan:
But God's eternal Laws are kind
  And break the heart of stone.

* * *

And every human heart that breaks,
  In prison-cell or yard,
Is as that broken box that gave
  Its treasure to the Lord,
And filled the unclean leper's house
  With the scent of costliest nard.

Ah! happy they whose hearts can break
  And peace of pardon win!
How else may man make straight his plan
  And cleanse his soul from Sin?
How else but through a broken heart
  May Lord Christ enter in?

And he of the swollen purple throat,
  And the stark and staring eyes,
Waits for the holy hands that took
  The Thief to Paradise;
And a broken and a contrite heart
  The Lord will not despise.

The man in red who reads the Law
  Gave him three weeks of life,
Three little weeks in which to heal
  His soul of his soul's strife,
And cleanse from every blot of blood
  The hand that held the knife.

And with tears of blood he cleansed the hand,
  The hand that held the steel:
For only blood can wipe out blood,
  And only tears can heal:
And the crimson stain that was of Cain
  Became Christ's snow-white seal.

VI

In Reading gaol by Reading town
  There is a pit of shame,
And in it lies a wretched man
  Eaten by teeth of flame,
In a burning winding-sheet he lies,
  And his grave has got no name.

And there, till Christ call forth the dead,
  In silence let him lie:
No need to waste the foolish tear,
  Or heave the windy sigh:
The man had killed the thing he loved,
  And so he had to die.

And all men kill the thing they love,
  By all let this be heard,
Some do it with a bitter look,
  Some with a flattering word,
The coward does it with a kiss,
  The brave man with a sword!

1898

WILLIAM BUTLER YEATS

[June 13, 1865–January 28, 1939]

William Butler Yeats, son of the artist, John Yeats, was born at Sandymount, Dublin. His mother was the daughter of a merchant and shipowner in Sligo, a town in the wildest part of Ireland, where William Butler spent much of his early boyhood. About the time he was ten years old his family moved to London and he began attending the Godolphin School, Hammersmith. At fifteen he went to live with his mother's family at Sligo and attended school in Dublin. These were impressionable days for the boy, and at the old town by the sea he drank in the strange tales told by sailors and fishing people of ghosts and fairies and of

"the dark folk who lived in souls
Of passionate men."

In *The Celtic Twilight* (1893), a book of Irish stories and fancies, he drew upon his memories of the old Sligo days.

Because his father wished him to become an artist, Yeats studied at the Metropolitan School of Art, Dublin, for a time. He liked a library better than a studio, however, and he spent more time in "reading translations—or making them—from Gaelic tales and poems" and in sitting "by the turf fires in old Connaught, listening to the folk tales of the peasantry," than in the study of art. About this time, too, he and George William Russell, together with a number of able and restless youths in the University of Dublin, became interested in theosophy and Buddhism, interests quite to be expected in one of Yeats's temperament.

In 1884 his first poem, *The Island of Statues*, was published in the *Dublin University Review*, and in 1886 *Mosada*, his first book, appeared. The next year he went to London to live, where he did journalistic writing, compiled several volumes of fairy stories and folk stories, assisted in the editing of Blake's works, wrote reviews and articles for magazines, and became associated with the Rhymers' Club, the group of "decadents" of which Dowson, Symons, and Lionel Johnson were members. Influenced by the work of Sir Samuel Ferguson, forerunner of the Celtic revival in literature, he published in 1889 *The Wanderings of Oisin*, the volume which assured him high place in poetry. *Poems*, (1895), *The Secret Rose* (1897), *The Wind Among the Reeds* (1899), *The Green Helmet* (1912), *The Wild Swans at Coole* (1919), and *The Tower* (1928), are the chief volumes of poetry that followed *Oisin*.

But Yeats's writing was not done in poetry alone. He published a number of books of prose, among them the early *Celtic Twilight*, *Discoveries* (1907), *The Cutting of an Agate* (1912), and the memorable *Autobiographies* (1927), containing *Reveries over Childhood and Youth* and *The Trembling of the Veil.* In the 'nineties his interest turned to the drama, and in 1899 he became prominent as one of the founders of the Irish National Theatre. Some of the plays he wrote for the Theatre were *Cathleen ni Houlihan*, *On Baile's Strand*, *The Hour-Glass*, *Deirdre*, and *The Shadowy Waters.*

In 1922 Yeats was made a senator of the Irish Free State, and he also served the state as inspector of schools and censor of the cinema. In 1923 he received the Nobel Prize in literature, the inscription accompanying the award reading: "For his consistently emotional poetry which in the strictest artistic form expresses a people's spirit."

DOWN BY THE SALLEY GARDENS

Down by the salley gardens my love and I did meet;
She passed the salley gardens with little snow-white feet.
She bid me take love easy, as the leaves grow on the tree,
But I, being young and foolish, with her would not agree.

In a field by the river my love and I did stand,
And on my leaning shoulder she laid her snow-white hand.
She bid me take life easy, as the grass grows on the weirs;
But I was young and foolish, and now am full of tears.

1889

THE ROSE OF THE WORLD

Who dreamed that beauty passes like a dream?
For these red lips, with all their mournful pride,
Mournful that no new wonder may betide,
Troy passed away in one high funeral gleam,
And Usna's children died.

We and the labouring world are passing by:
Amid men's souls, that waver and give place
Like the pale waters in their wintry race,
Under the passing stars, foam of the sky,
Lives on this lonely face.

Bow down, archangels, in your dim abode:
Before you were, or any hearts to beat,
Weary and kind one lingered by His seat;
He made the world to be a grassy road
Before her wandering feet.

1893

THE LAKE ISLE OF INNISFREE

I will arise and go now, and go to Innisfree,
And a small cabin build there, of clay and wattles made:
Nine bean-rows will I have there, a hive for the honey-bee,
And live alone in the bee-loud glade.

And I shall have some peace there, for peace comes dropping slow,
Dropping from the veils of the morning to where the cricket sings;
There midnight's all a glimmer, and noon a purple glow,
And evening full of linnet's wings.

I will arise and go now, for always night and day
I hear lake water lapping with low sounds by the shore;
While I stand on the roadway, or on the pavements grey,
I hear it in the deep heart's core.

1893

THE SONG OF WANDERING AENGUS

I went out to the hazel wood,
Because a fire was in my head,
And cut and peeled a hazel wand
And hooked a berry to a thread;
And when white moths were on the wing,
And moth-like stars were flickering out,
I dropped the berry in a stream
And caught a little silver trout.

When I had laid it on the floor
I went to blow the fire aflame,
But something rustled on the floor,
And some one called me by my name:
It had become a glimmering girl
With apple blossom in her hair
Who called me by my name and ran
And faded through the brightening air.

Though I am old with wandering
Through hollow lands and hilly lands,
I will find out where she has gone,
And kiss her lips and take her hands;
And walk among long dappled grass,
And pluck till time and times are done
The silver apples of the moon,
The golden apples of the sun.

1899

THE OLD MEN ADMIRING THEMSELVES IN THE WATER

I heard the old, old men say,
"Everything alters,
And one by one we drop away."
They had hands like claws, and their knees
Were twisted like the old thorn-trees
By the waters.
I heard the old, old men say,
"All that's beautiful drifts away
Like the waters."

1904

THE RAGGED WOOD

O hurry where by water among the trees
The delicate-stepping stag and his lady sigh,
When they have but looked upon their images—
Would none had ever loved but you and I!

13

Mary Bruin

Your looks are all the candle-light I need

Shawn Bruin

Once a fly dancing in a beam of the sun,
Or the light wind blowing out of the dawn
Could fill your heart with dreams none other knew
But now the indissoluble sacrament
Has mixed your heart that was most proud & cold
With my warm heart for ever; the sun & moon
Must fade & heaven be rolled up like a scroll;
But your white spirit still walks by my spirit.

(A voice singing in the wood)

Maurteen Bruin ~~(goes to door)~~

There's some one singing. Why it's but a child
It sang, 'the lonely of heart is withered away'
A strange song for a child, but she sings sweetly
Listen listen. (goes to door)

Mary Bruin

O cling close to me
Because I have said wicked things tonight

The Voice

The wind blows out of the gates of the ~~Day~~ day,
The wind blows over the lonely of heart
And the lonely of heart is withered away
While the faeries dance in a place apart
Shaking their milk white feet in a ring
Tossing their milk white arms in the air;
For they hear the wind laugh & murmur & sing
Of a land where even the old are fair
And even the wise are merry of tongue;
But I heard a reed of Coolaney say
'When the wind has laughed & murmured & sung,
The lonely of heart is withered away'

Page from the Manuscript of Yeats's *The Land of Heart's Desire.*
(See Appendix I.)

Or have you heard that sliding silver-shoed
Pale silver-proud queen-woman of the sky,
When the sun looked out of his golden hood?—
O that none ever loved but you and I!

O hurry to the ragged wood, for there
I will drive all those lovers out and cry—
O my share of the world, O yellow hair!
No one has ever loved but you and I.

1904

THE WILD SWANS AT COOLE

THE trees are in their autumn beauty,
The woodland paths are dry,
Under the October twilight the water
Mirrors a still sky;
Upon the brimming water among the stones
Are nine-and-fifty swans.

The nineteenth autumn has come upon me
Since I first made my count;
I saw, before I had well finished,
All suddenly mount
And scatter wheeling in great broken rings
Upon their clamorous wings.

I have looked upon those brilliant creatures,
And now my heart is sore.
All's changed since I, hearing at twilight,
The first time on this shore,
The bell-beat of their wings above my head,
Trod with a lighter tread.

Unwearied still, lover by lover,
They paddle in the cold
Companionable streams or climb the air;
Their hearts have not grown old;
Passion or conquest, wander where they will,
Attend upon them still.

But now they drift on the still water
Mysterious, beautiful;
Among what rushes will they build,
By what lake's edge or pool
Delight men's eyes when I awake some day
To find they have flown away?

1919

A PRAYER FOR MY DAUGHTER

ONCE more the storm is howling, and half hid
Under this cradle-hood and coverlid
My child sleeps on. There is no obstacle
But Gregory's wood and one bare hill
Whereby the haystack- and roof-levelling wind,
Bred on the Atlantic, can be stayed;
And for an hour I have walked and prayed
Because of the great gloom that is in my mind.

I have walked and prayed for this young child an hour
And heard the sea-wind scream upon the tower,
And under the arches of the bridge, and scream
In the elms above the flooded stream;
Imagining in excited reverie
That the future years had come,
Dancing to a frenzied drum,
Out of the murderous innocence of the sea.

May she be granted beauty and yet not
Beauty to make a stranger's eye distraught,
Or hers before a looking-glass, for such,
Being made beautiful overmuch,
Consider beauty a sufficient end,
Lose natural kindness and maybe
The heart-revealing intimacy
That chooses right, and never find a friend.

Helen being chosen found life flat and dull
And later had much trouble from a fool,
While that great Queen, that rose out of the spray,
Being fatherless could have her way
Yet chose a bandy-leggèd smith for man.
It's certain that fine women eat
A crazy salad with their meat
Whereby the Horn of Plenty is undone.

In courtesy I'd have her chiefly learned;
Hearts are not had as a gift but hearts are earned
By those that are not entirely beautiful;
Yet many, that have played the fool
For beauty's very self, has charm made wise,
And many a poor man that has roved,
Loved and thought himself beloved,
From a glad kindness cannot take his eyes.

May she become a flourishing hidden tree
That all her thoughts may like the linnet be,
And have no business but dispensing round
Their magnanimities of sound,
Nor but in merriment begin a chase,
Nor but in merriment a quarrel.
O may she live like some green laurel
Rooted in one dear perpetual place.

My mind, because the minds that I have loved,
The sort of beauty that I have approved,
Prosper but little, has dried up of late,
Yet knows that to be choked with hate
May well be of all evil chances chief.
If there's no hatred in a mind,
Assault and battery of the wind
Can never tear the linnet from the leaf.

An intellectual hatred is the worst,
So let her think opinions are accursed.
Have I not seen the loveliest woman born
Out of the mouth of Plenty's horn,
Because of her opinionated mind
Barter that horn and every good
By quiet natures understood
For an old bellows full of angry wind?

Considering that, all hatred driven hence,
The soul recovers radical innocence
And learns at last that it is self-delighting,
Self-appeasing, self-affrighting,
And that its own sweet will is Heaven's will;
She can, though every face should scowl
And every windy quarter howl
Or every bellows burst, be happy still.

And may her bridegroom bring her to a house
Where all's accustomed, ceremonious;
For arrogance and hatred are the wares
Peddled in the thoroughfares.
How but in custom and in ceremony
Are innocence and beauty born?
Ceremony's a name for the rich horn,
And custom for the spreading laurel tree.

1921

THE APPENDIX

I. THE ILLUSTRATIONS

II. BIBLIOGRAPHIES AND NOTES

III. INDEX OF AUTHORS, TITLES, AND FIRST LINES OF POETRY

APPENDIX I

THE ILLUSTRATIONS

The facsimiles used in illustrating this volume are reproduced from originals in the collection of Mr. William T. H. Howe, with the exception of Matthew Arnold's *Longing*, which is used by permission of the Yale University Press.

PAGE 49.—A Copy of *Tears, Idle Tears*, Made for Frederick Locker (-Lampson).

The copy is dated "20th Feby, 1873," and is practically identical with the text as printed on p. 48 f. It appeared in the first version of *The Princess*, published in 1847. Tennyson told James Knowles, editor of the *Nineteenth Century*, that the song was inspired by a visit to Tintern Abbey "when the woods were all yellowing with autumn seen through the ruined windows. It is what I have always felt even from a boy, and what as a boy I called, the 'passion of the past.'" Cf. *The Ancient Sage* (p. 193), particularly lines 216 ff., and *Far—Far—Away* (p. 206).

Frederick Locker, anthologist and writer of brilliant *vers de société*, was one of Tennyson's dearest friends. In 1870 the Tennysons made proximity to Mr. Locker and his wife a primary consideration in selecting a house in London. Tennyson and Locker frequently took morning walks in the park, and went together on several trips to the Continent. Locker later added to his name "Lampson," the family name of his second wife.

PAGE 95.—Rossetti's Drawing of Tennyson Reading *Maud*.

On September 27, 1855, Tennyson read *Maud* aloud to a group of friends—Robert and Mrs. Browning, Mrs. Browning's sister Arabella (Barrett), and Dante Gabriel and William Michael Rossetti. Sitting unobserved in a corner, Dante Gabriel Rossetti made a rapid but good portrait of Tennyson, which he later gave to Browning. It is this drawing to which Rossetti refers in a letter to Allingham (p. 664). According to W. M. Rossetti, Tennyson did not know of the picture, at the time or afterward.

When *Maud* had been read through (with Tennyson interrupting himself frequently to comment upon individual passages), Browning read *Fra Lippo Lippi*, and the party broke up at two-thirty A.M. The inscription is the first line of the poem.

PAGE 113.—A Presentation Copy of *Maud*.

After Tennyson finished reading *Maud* on the occasion just noted, he inscribed the book to Mrs. Browning, and dated it

Monday, September 27. [1855]
13 Dorset St Manchester Sq.

The words "Robert &" before Mrs. Browning's name are in her handwriting and were evidently added later.

PAGE 217.—Letter to Mrs. Browning Announcing the Birth of Hallam Tennyson.

Chapel House
Twickenham

August 11th [1852]

My dear Mrs Browning

I wrote to you once before this morning. I now write again to tell you what I am sure your womans & poets heart will rejoice in that my wife was delivered of a fine boy at 9½ a.m. this day & that both she & the child are doing well. I never saw any face so radiant with all high & sweet expression as hers when I saw her some time after

ever yours truly
A. Tennyson

Hallam was the Tennysons' first child. Mrs. Browning sympathized with Tennyson's happiness; on September 2 she wrote to a friend: "Mr. Tennyson has a little son and wrote me such three [*sic*] happy notes on the occasion that I really never liked him so well before. I do like men who are not ashamed to be happy beside a cradle. . . ."

PAGE 289.—A Page of Browning's Manuscript.

Dramatic Romances.
Incident of the French Camp.

I

You know, we French stormed Ratisbon:
A mile or so away
On a little mound, Napoleon
Stood on our storming-day;
With neck out-thrust, you fancy how
Legs wide, arms locked behind,
As if to balance the prone brow
Oppressive with its mind.

This is the first page of the manuscript of *Dramatic Romances*. The poem was first published in Number III of *Bells and Pomegranates*, which was called *Dramatic Lyrics*. There it was linked, under the group title of *Camp and Cloister*, with the *Soliloquy of the Spanish Cloister*. (See the Chronological List, p. 227.) Later, when Browning collected his writings, he re-classified this poem as a "Dramatic Romance."

PAGE 339.—A Page of Browning's Revised Proof-Copy.

This proof of *Red Cotton Night-Cap Country* is extremely interesting because of the changing of all the proper names occurring in the poem. The incidents narrated had actually happened in France only a short time before, and Browning's publisher feared the possibility of a libel action if the characters were not thoroughly disguised. Browning consulted Lord Coleridge, the Attorney-General; and it was directly on his advice that Browning altered the names in the proof.

PAGE 376.—A Presentation Copy from Browning to His Son.

"Pen" was the family nickname for Robert Wiedemann Barrett Browning (born 1849). In a letter from Paris in 1851, Mrs. Browning wrote: "He has taken to calling himself 'Peninni,' which sounds something like a fairy's name, though he means it for 'Wiedeman.'" Hawthorne, visiting the Brownings in 1858, was given a different interpretation ". . . Pennini . . . is a diminutive of Apennino, which was bestowed upon him at his first advent into the world because he was so very small, there being a statue in Florence of colossal size called Apennino."

PAGE 531.—A Copy of *Longing* in Arnold's Handwriting.

This poem was first published in *Empedocles on Etna and Other Poems* (1852). In Arnold's final arrangement of his poems, it is the last of five poems included under the heading, *Faded Leaves*.

PAGE 636.—Manuscript of Rossetti's Sonnet Inscription for Shelley's Couch.

Percy Bysshe Shelley.

(Inscription for the couch, still preserved, on which he passed the last night of his life)

'Twixt those twin worlds,—the world of Sleep, which gave
No dream to warn,—the tidal world of Death,
Which the earth's sea, as the earth, replenisheth,—
Shelley, Song's orient sun, to breast the wave,
Rose from this couch that morn. Ah! did he brave
Only the sea?—or did man's deed of hell
Engulph his bark 'mid mists impenetrable? . . .
No eye discerned, nor any power might save.

When that mist cleared, O Shelley! what dread veil
Was rent for thee, to whom far-darkling Truth
Reigned sovereign guide through thy brief ageless youth?

Was the Truth *thy* Truth, Shelley?—Hush! All-Hail,
Past doubt, thou gav'st it; and in Truth's bright sphere
Art first of praisers, being most praisèd here.

Written in 1870, this sonnet was published in *Ballads and Sonnets* (1881), as the fifth of a group called *Five English Poets*. The other four, in order, are Chatterton, Blake, Coleridge, and Keats.

PAGE 655.—Presentation Copy from Rossetti to Dr. Heimann.

Dr. Adolf Heimann was the professor of German at University College. About 1842, according to W. M. Rossetti, Dr. Heimann one day presented himself at the Rossetti home, offering to teach German to the children in exchange for lessons in Italian. He was amiable as well as learned, and quickly became an intimate friend of the whole Rossetti family. The friendship was long-lasting, as the date (1864) on this presentation copy reveals.

PAGE 709.—Stanzas 7 and 36 of *Dolores* in Swinburne's Handwriting.

Note that these stanzas were at first numbered 9 and 10. Swinburne mentions the business of expanding the poem in a letter (in 1865) to Charles Augustus Howell, whom he addresses as "Infame libertin": "I have added yet four more jets of boiling and gushing infamy to the perennial and poisonous fountain of *Dolores*." Then, in a postscript to the same letter: "Since writing the above I have added ten verses to *Dolores*—très-infâmes et très-bien tournés."

PAGE 737.—A Page of Early Swinburne Manuscript.

Queen Yseult

Canto
§ 1 Of the birth of Sir Tristram, & how he voyaged into Ireland

In the noble days were shown
Deeds of good knights many one,
Many worthy wars were done.

It was time of scath & scorn
When at breaking of the morn
Tristram the good knight was born.

He was fair & well to see
As his mother's child might be.
Many happy wars had he,

Slew Moronde the knight alone,
Wherefrom all the ill begun
That on Blancheflour was done.

This, Swinburne's earliest narrative poem, is a juvenile attempt to treat the Tristram theme, later done so effectively in *Tristram of Lyonesse*. The story of Tristram and Iseult captured Swinburne's fancy while he was at Eton (1849–1853), and he began to write it while at Oxford (1856–1860). In its form, manner, and diction there is a strong flavor of Morris and the pre-Raphaelites. The poem was intended to consist of ten cantos, but only six were ever written. The first canto appeared in a periodical called *Undergraduate Papers* in December 1857; the remaining cantos were not published until 1918, and then in an edition of only thirty copies.

PAGE 777.—Manuscript Copy of the Opening Sonnet from *A Sequence of Sonnets on the Death of Robert Browning*.

This is the first sonnet of the sequence; the seventh and last is printed on page 776. The manuscript reads:

A Sequence of Sonnets
On the Death of Robert Browning

I.

The clearest eyes in all the world they read
With sense more keen & spirit of sight more true
Than burns & thrills in sunrise, when the dew
Flames, & absorbs the glory round it shed,

As they the light of ages quick & dead,
  Closed now, forsake us: yet the shaft that slew
  Can slay not one of all the works we knew,
Nor death discrown that many-laurelled head.

The works of words whose life seems lightning wrought,
And moulded of unconquerable thought,
  And quickened with imperishable flame,
Stand fast & shine & smile, assured that nought
  May fade of all their myriad-moulded fame,
  Nor England's memory clasp not Browning's name.

The words altered in the ninth line were "divine & deathless"; the earlier wording of the fourteenth line is undecipherable.

Browning died in Italy on December 12, 1889. This first sonnet is dated December 13; the second, third, and fourth sonnets are dated December 14, and the fifth, sixth, and seventh, December 15.

PAGE 811.—Copy of a Poem in Robert Bridges' Handwriting.

PAX HOMINIBUS BONÆ VOLUNTATIS

  A frosty Xmas eve | when the stars were shining
Fared I forth alone | where westward falls the hill
And from many a village | in the water'd valley
Distant music reached me | peals of bells aringing:
The constellated sounds | ran sprinkling on earth's floor
As the dark vault above | with stars was spangled o'er.

  Then sped my thought to keep | that first Xmas of all
When the shepherds watching | by their fields ere the dawn
Heard music in the fields | and marvelling c^d not tell
Whether it were angels | or the bright stars singing.

  Now blessed be the towers | that crown England so fair
That stand up strong in prayer | unto God for our souls:
Blessed be their founders |, said I, an' our country folk
Who are ringing for Christ | in the belfries tonight
With arms lifted to clutch | the rattling ropes that race
Into the dark above | and the mad romping din.

  But to me heard afar | it was heav'nly † music
Angels song comforting | as the comfort of Christ
When he spake tenderly | to his sorrowful flock;
The old words came to' me | by the riches of time
Mellow'd and transfigured | as I stood on the hill
Hark'ning in the aspect | of th' eternal silence.

R. B. 1913

† I find I have written "heavenly" in all my copies for my original "starry," & I can't copy afresh, so I leave it.

Written in 1913, this was sent by Bridges to the King. His Majesty sent it to *The Times* for publication. It was collected in *October and Other Poems* (1920) under the title *Noël: Christmas Eve, 1913*, the Latin phrase remaining as a subtitle. Note the carefully marked cæsuras. The word "heavenly" was correctly printed "starry" when the poem was collected.

PAGE 820.—Title-page of *Poems* by the Brontë Sisters.

Emily Brontë's poems were published in this volume over the pseudonym of "Ellis Bell"; Charlotte was "Currer" and Anne was "Acton"—each of the sisters preserving her own initials.

This venture in verse was not very successful. It was of this edition (now very rare) that Charlotte Brontë wrote to Thomas De Quincey on June 16, 1847:

Sir:

My relatives, Ellis and Acton Bell and myself, heedless of the repeated warnings of various respectable publishers, have committed the rash act of printing a volume of poems.

The consequences predicted have, of course, overtaken us; our book is found to be a drug; no man needs it or heeds it; in the space of a year our publisher has disposed but of two copies, and by what painful efforts he succeeded in getting rid of those two, himself only knows.

Before transferring the edition to the trunk-makers, we have decided on distributing as presents a few copies of what we cannot sell—we beg to offer you one in acknowledgment of the pleasure and profit we have often and long derived from your works—

I am sir

Yours very respectfully

Currer Bell.

PAGE 823.—A Page of Emily Brontë's Manuscript.

And voiceless, soul[l]ess, messenger
Thy presence waked a thrilling tone
That comforts me while thou art here
And will sustain when thou art gone.

Emily Jane Brontë. December—1837

Song by Julius Angora

Awake! awake! how loud the stormy morning
Calls up to life the nations resting round;
Arise, Arise, is it the voice of mourning
That breaks our slumber with so wild a sound?

The voice of mourning? Listen to its pealing[:]
That shout of triumph drowns the sigh of woe[;]
Each tortured heart forgets its wonted feeling,
Each faded cheek resumes its longlost glow.

Our souls are full of gladness, God has given
Our arms to victory, our foes to death;
The crimson ensign waves its sheet in heaven,

The stanza at the head of the page is the seventh and last of a poem called *To a Wreath of Snow*, dated December, 1837. In one manuscript it is signed by "A. G. Alaisda." The *Song by Julius Angora* belongs to the same time. Though these poems were written in 1837, when Emily Brontë was nineteen, they were not printed until 1902. The five concluding lines of the *Song by Julius Angora* (not on the page reproduced) follow:

The sea-green standard lies in dust beneath.

Patriots! no stain is on your country's glory;
Soldiers! preserve that glory bright and free;
Let Almedore in peace and battle gory
Be still a nobler name for victory!

PAGE 837.—A Presentation Copy to Talfourd.

Inscribed "To T. N. Serjt. Talfourd with the author's compliments. August, 1844."

Sir Thomas Noon Talfourd was a serjeant at law (later a judge) and wrote on both legal and literary matters. His most famous work was *Ion, A Tragedy in Five Acts*, issued privately in 1835, and first produced, with great success, on May 26, 1836. He was well known in the literary world; Dickens, not long after the success of *Ion*, dedicated the *Pickwick Papers* to him.

PAGE 857.—A Piece of Mrs. Browning's Manuscript.

Seventh stanza omitted by an oversight, from the 'Tale of Villafranca'—

(Insert it between the sixth and seventh as printed in the Atheneum.)

'A great deed in this world of ours?
Unheard of the pretence is.

It threatens plainly the great Powers,
Is fatal in all senses.
A just deed in the world? call out
The rifles! be not slack about
The national defences.'

Elizabeth Barrett Browning
Florence. 1859.

A Tale of Villafranca was printed in the *Athenæum* September 24, 1859, two months after the Peace of Villafranca (July 11, 1859) by which, for political or prudential reasons, Napoleon III withdrew his support from the Italian patriots and their fight for unity and independence. Mrs. Browning had been heart and soul for the Italian cause, and was so deeply affected by this disappointing setback that she had an attack of severe illness, from which her health never fully recovered.

PAGE 883.—A Presentation Copy from Davidson to Gissing.

The volume is inscribed to "George Gissing from John Davidson. 25 Dec. '95." Gissing, in his diary for December 25, 1895, records a series of odd dreams of the preceding night, and then notes: "Letter from Davidson, saying he sends me his new volume, and asking me to lunch next Saturday."

PAGE 905.—A Stanza of the *Rubáiyát* (last but one) in Persian Script, with FitzGerald's Signature.

This is the close of a letter to George Borrow, dated May 24, 1857. The passages immediately preceding the quotation read:

Your book [*The Romany Rye*] was put into my hands a week ago just as I was leaving London; so I e'en carried it down here, and have been reading it under the best Circumstances:—at such a Season—in the Fields as they now are—and in company with a Friend I love best in the world—who scarce ever reads a Book, but knows better than I do what they are made of from a hint.

Well, lying in a Paddock of his, I have been travelling along with you to Horncastle, etc.,—in a very delightful way for the most part; something as I have travelled, and love to travel, with Fielding, Cervantes, and Robinson Crusoe—and a smack of all these there seems to me, with something beside, in your book. But, as will happen in Travel, there were some spots I didn't like so well—and didn't like *at all:* and sometimes wished to myself that I, a poor 'Man of Taste,' had been at your Elbow (who are a Man of much more than Taste) to direct you, or get you by some means to pass lightlier over some places. But you wouldn't have heeded me, and won't heed me, and *must* go your own way, I think—And in the parts I least like, I am yet thankful for honest, daring, and original Thought and Speech such as one hardly gets in these mealy-mouthed days. It was very kind of you to send me your book. . . .

Now I shall finish this large sheet with a Tetrastich of one Omar Khayyam who was an Epicurean Infidel some 500 years ago:

[Yon rising Moon that looks for us again—
How oft hereafter will she wax and wane;
How oft hereafter rising look for us
Through this same Garden—and for one in vain!]

and am yr's very truly
Edward FitzGerald

This letter was written in the year when FitzGerald was first reading Omar, two years before the first publication of the *Rubáiyát*. Borrow was an accomplished linguist and translator, so that a quotation addressed to him in Persian was no mere pleasantry, as it might seem at first glance.

PAGE 915.—Two Stanzas in Hardy's Handwriting.

These stanzas are the first two of the six-stanza poem, *Shelley's Skylark* (p. 914), which was first published in *Poems of the Past and Present* (1902).

PAGE 921.—A Page of Hardy's Manuscript.

These are the first five stanzas of *At a House in Hampstead*, dated July 1920, and published in *Late Lyrics* (1922):

At a House in Hampstead

(Sometime the Dwelling of John Keats.)

O Poet, come you haunting here
Where streets have crept up all around
And never a nightingale pours one
Full throated sound?

Drawn from your drowse by the far Gaunt Gate,
Thought you to find all just the same
Here shining, as in hours of old,
If you but came?

What will you do in your surprise
At seeing that changes wrought in Rome
Are wrought yet more on the misty hill
One time your home?

Will you wake windwafts on these stairs?
Swing the doors open noisily?
Show as a troubled ghost beside
Your ancient tree?

Or will you, softening, the while
You further & yet further look;
Learn that a laggard few would fain
Preserve your nook? . . .

In Hardy's final version, "crept" in line 2 became "stolen"; "far Gaunt Gate" in line 5 became "Seven famed Hills"; "hill" in line 11 became "slope"; and the much-changed words in line 15 finally became "umbraged."

Page 957.—Cover of the Rare No. 1 of Kipling's *Departmental Ditties.*

This cover is an imitation of an official public document envelope. The crossed-out frank in the corner reads "On Her Majesty's Service Only," and the imprint on the flap is in imitation of a rupee. The volume contains twenty-six poems—eleven "Departmental Ditties" and fifteen "other poems."

Kipling in 1892 referred to this as his first book, although it had been preceded by a volume called *School Boy Lyrics* which his parents had had printed in a small edition at Lahore in 1881, while he was still in school at Westward Ho.

Page 969.—Presentation Copy of *Modern Love.*

Inscribed to "Mrs Shirley Brooks from the author." Mrs. Brooks was the wife of Charles William Shirley Brooks, novelist, playwright, journalist, and editor of *Punch*—a close personal friend of Meredith.

Page 975.—A Presentation Copy of *Poems.*

The inscription is to "Mary Meredith [his wife] from George." Appearing in 1851, this was Meredith's first published volume.

The quotation on the title-page, from Richard Hengist Horne's *Orion*, is interesting. Horne was highly thought of in his time both as a poet and as a critic. Meredith gave Horne a copy of *Poems* inscribed with a glowing tribute to Horne's "generous appreciation and trusty criticism."

Page 997.—A Page of Morris's Manuscript.

These are the first twenty-five lines of *The Haystack in the Floods* (see p. 996). This poem was published in Morris's first volume of poetry, *The Defence of Guenevere and Other Poems* (1858). At the age of twenty-four, intensely interested in the Middle Ages, he was already capable of producing such masterpieces of understanding as this.

Page 1023.—A Manuscript Page of *The Burghers' Battle.*

These are the first twenty-six lines of the poem:

The Burghers' Battle

Thick rise the spear-shafts o'er the land
That erst the harvest bore,
The sword is heavy in the hand,
And we return no more.

The light wind waves the Ruddy Fox,
Our banner of the war,
And ripples in the Running Ox,
And we return no more.

Across our stubble acres now
The teams go four and four,
But out-worn elders guide the plough,
And we return no more.

And now the women heavy-eyed
Turn through the open door
From gazing down the highway wide,
Where we return no more.

The shadows of the fruited close
Dapple the feast-hall floor;
There lie our dogs and dream and doze,
And we return no more.

Down from the minster tower today
Fall the soft chimes of yore
Amidst the chattering jackdaws play:
And we return no more.

But underneath the streets are still;
Noon—and the market's o'er!

Written a short time before, this poem was published in *Poems by the Way* at the Kelmscott Press in 1891. Buxton Forman referred to it as "that truly great ballad."

PAGE 1037.—Page of a Letter from Christina Rossetti to H. Buxton Forman.

This page here reproduced reads:

my Bible Class—." I write, as our Grandfather printed, "con amore"! pray pardon me if I run into the irrelevant.

As to myself I have at present one only date, Christina Georgina Rossetti born December 5. 1830. When the date of my death completes my career it will be seen whether any more data are worth recording. Allow me meanwhile to LEND you the book of mine you refer to: this is all of the sort, except that

This letter is dated from 30 Torrington Square (Bloomsbury), October 26, 1885. It is eleven pages long, and is mostly about the life and works of her sister, Maria Francesca Rossetti, in answer to a request from Forman for information for a book he was writing on the Rossetti family.

Henry (or Harry) Buxton Forman was a Post Office official who, being interested in literature, wrote about literary people. He began his literary career by writing a group of magazine articles (later collected under the title of *Our Living Poets*) in 1869. Through these articles he met Dante Gabriel Rossetti, and became a family friend. His work on Shelley and Keats is his principal claim to remembrance.

PAGE 1049.—Copy of *He and She* in the Author's Handwriting.

The manuscript version is identical, except for minor variations in punctuation, with the poem as printed on p. 1050.

PAGE 1055.—Presentation Copy to Dr. Thomas Bodley Scott.

Dr. T. B. Scott was a Bournemouth physician who attended Stevenson in his illness there, not only as a physician but as a personal friend. Dr. Scott died only a few years ago, while Mayor of Bournemouth. Stevenson commemorated his services in the general medical dedication to *Underwoods*:

"But one name I have kept on purpose to the last, because it is a household word with me, and because if I had not received favours from so many hands and in so many quarters of the world, it should have stood upon this page alone: that of my friend Thomas Bodley Scott of Bournemouth. Will he accept this, although shared among so many, for a dedication to himself? and when next my ill-fortune (which has thus its pleasant side) brings him hurrying to me when he would fain sit down to meat or lie down to rest, will he care to remember that he takes this trouble for one who is not fool enough to be ungrateful?"

PAGE 1059.—Last Page of a Letter from Stevenson.

picklerez-vous toujours? (Romance of Boilgod)

I wish you would come down. When could you?

Yours

Le Pickleur

He pickled low, he pickled loud
He recked not of the smiling crowd,
Over a scale [?] confused and curly
He pickled late, he pickled early.
He pickled slow; he pickled fast—
At least he hoped he might at last;
He pickled wrong; he pickled right—
At least he hoped at last he might.
He pickled up, he pickled down
And was the bugbear of his town.

2 Kidnappeds will come to you; one is for Leman [?] whose [the canceled word is *name*] address I forget. Head gone.

This is the last page of a four-page letter dated from Bournemouth, 1886, and addressed to his cousin, R. A. M. Stevenson ("My dear Bob").

During the spring and summer of 1886 Stevenson spent a great deal of his spare time trying to learn a little about the theory and practice of music. He put in a great deal of time "pickling" (to use his own word) at the piano. He went so far as to try his hand at composition, and sent one of his efforts to R. A. M. Stevenson, who knew something of music, for criticism. This dabbling with music may have provided, in some part, the background for the amusing piano incidents in *The Wrong Box* (1888).

PAGE 1061.—The Unpublished Version of Stevenson's *Requiem.*

Under the wide and starry sky
Dig the grave and let me lie.
Glad did I live and gladly die,
And I laid me down with a will.

Here may the winds about me blow;
Here the clouds may come and go;
Here shall be rest for evermo,
And the heart for aye shall be still.

This be the verse you grave for me:
Here he lies where he longed to be;
Home is the sailor, home from sea,
And the hunter home from the hill.

The first and third stanzas of this manuscript version are the poem as published (first in *Underwoods*, 1887). The second stanza was omitted from the published version, and the last three lines were printed in italics.

PAGES 1070 and 1071.—Two Pages of a Letter to Coventry Patmore.

Creccas Cottage,
Pantasaph,
Holywell.
Monday.

Dear Mr. Patmore,

Many thanks for your kind pains with the poem. I shall defer writing more particularly about it to-day, for there are one or two points I want to discuss at some length. I send you now a little thing which I think I should flinch from A.M. seeing. She would be indignant at the "mighty cruelties." I think you will not. Like Cromwell, I take it, you would disdain that your painter should omit a wart.

I have received the book you forwarded—a worthless Yankee "epic" on Columbus, inscribed by the author to "Francis Thompson Esq., care of Coventry Patmore Esq., with kind regards to both." By some enclosed "Notices" I see that he has sent his book to Newman and Aubrey de Vere. In our case the economical fellow has apparently tried to kill two poets with one stone—a very heavy one.

Yours always,
Francis Thompson.

Coventry Patmore had met Francis Thompson through the Meynells, and both men profited for years by mutual sympathy. Patmore made occasional "retreats" at Pontypool, Pantasaph, and Stonyhurst. From Pantasaph in 1894 he wrote to his wife: "I spend part of my day with Francis Thompson, who is a delightful companion, full of the best talk. . . ."

The "A.M." mentioned in the first paragraph is Alice Meynell. The authorship and identity of the irritating "Yankee 'epic'" are not known.

Page 1085.—Presentation Copy to Mrs. Hinkson.

The volume is inscribed "To Katharine Tynan Hinkson, / Ten years ago my sympathizer, / When I had few sympathizers. / Francis Thompson. / Xmas, 1897."

Katharine Tynan, an Irish poet (who was married to H. A. Hinkson in 1893), had been, as the inscription indicates, one of the small group of sympathetic writers who, with Wilfrid and Alice Meynell, had given Thompson's poetry its earliest praise.

Thompson memorialized his friendship in a poem written to her (*The Sere of the Leaf*) on the occasion of her visit to London in 1889.

Page 1109.—Manuscript Page of an Early Version of *The Dole of the King's Daughter*.

The poem in full consists of eight stanzas, of which these are the last four, and was first published in the *Dublin University Magazine* for June 1876 (Vol. LXXXVII, No. 522), under the title of *The Dole of the King's Daughter*. (*For a painting.*) When it was reprinted in Wilde's *Poems*, in 1881, the subtitle was changed from "For a painting" to "Breton." The variations between the first version of these stanzas (printed in the first column) and the final one (in the second column) show somewhat of the maturing of Wilde's artistry.

Manuscript Version	Final Version
Three milk white doves are lying dead,	What do they there so stark and dead?
There is blood upon her hand,	(There is blood upon her hand)
Three white lilies are flecked with red,	Why are the lilies flecked with red?
There is blood on the river sand.	There is no blood on the river sand.
Two that ride from the North and East,	There are two that ride from the south and east,
And two from the South and West,	And two from the north and west,
For the black ravens a goodly feast,	For the black raven a goodly feast,
For the Kings daughter rest.	For the King's daughter rest.
One man that loves her true,	There is one man who loves her true,
(Crimson and red is the stain of gore.)	(Red, O red, is the stain of gore!)
He hath duggen a grave by the darksome yew,	He hath duggen a grave by the darksome yew,
One grave will do for four.	(One grave will do for four.)
No moon in the still heaven,	No moon in the still heaven,
In the black water none,	In the black water none,
The sins on *her* soul are seven	The sins on her soul are seven,
The sin upon his is one.	The sin upon his is one.
Oscar O'F. Wills Wilde.	
S.M. Magdalen College	
Oxford.	

Page 1115.—Presentation Copy of *The Ballad of Reading Gaol*.

Inscribed to "Ernest Dowson from his friend and admirer the author. Feb. *. *8*8." This title-page is that of the first edition, published early in 1898. Wilde had been convicted of a crime against public morality in 1895 and imprisoned for two years at hard labor in Reading Gaol. This powerful poem was inspired by his prison experiences. "C. 3. 3." was Wilde's prison number, and indicated that his cell was Number 3 on the third landing in Gallery C.

PAGE 1125.—Page from the Manuscript of Yeats's *The Land of Heart's Desire.*

These are lines 222–247 of the play, and read:

Mary Bruin 13

Your looks are all the candles that I need

Shawn Bruin

Once a fly dancing in a beam of the sun,
Or the light wind blowing out of the dawn
Could fill your heart with dreams none other knew
But now the indissoluble sacrament
Has mixed your heart that was most proud & cold
With my warm heart for ever; the sun & moon
Must fade & heaven be rolled up like a scroll;
But your white spirit still walks by my spirit.
(A voice sings in the wood)

Maurteen Bruin ~~(going to door)~~

There's some one singing. Why, it's but a child
It sang, 'The lonely of heart is withered away'
A strange song for a child, but she sings sweetly
Listen listen. (goes to door)

Mary Bruin

O cling close to me
Because I have said wicked things to-night

The voice

The wind blows out of the gates of the day,
The wind blows over the lonely of heart
And the lonely of heart is withered away
While the faeries dance in a place apart
Shaking their milk white feet in a ring
Tossing their milk white arms in the air;
For they hear the wind laugh & murmur & sing
Of a land where even the old are fair
And even the wise are merry of tongue;
But I heard a reed of Coolaney say
'When the wind has laughed & murmured & sung
The lonely of heart is withered away'

APPENDIX II

BIBLIOGRAPHIES AND NOTES

The editors of *Victorian and Later English Poets* are greatly indebted to Tom B. Haber, Ph.D., of the English department, Ohio State University, for the preparation of all the bibliographies included in the following pages. While these bibliographies are frankly selective, an attempt has been made to indicate all the more important books and articles dealing with each poet—editions of works as well as biographical and critical discussions. The descriptive comments accompanying the entries give the student some clear notion of the nature and value of each.

Biographical accounts of the poets precede each group of selections throughout the text. Additional biographical facts are given in the following notes only when needed to help in the understanding of some particular poem.

Guides in heavy-faced type are inserted to indicate the pages on which poems begin, and elsewhere to enable the user easily to locate passages in the prose material to which notes refer.

ALFRED, LORD TENNYSON

BIBLIOGRAPHY

I. WORKS

Complete Works, ed. by Hallam Tennyson. Eversley Edition. 6 vols. (Macmillan: New York, 1908.) The authoritative edition, containing a Memoir by the editor and the (often disturbingly accurate) annotations of the poet himself. The same editor has a one-volume edition (Macmillan, New York, 1913).

Complete Works, ed. by Elisabeth L. Cary. 8 vols. (Putnam: New York, 1909.) The comprehensive Centenary Edition, equipped with a general preface by the editor and separate critical introductions; illustrated by F. S. Coburn and Gustave Doré.

Poetic and Dramatic Works. 7 vols. (Houghton: Boston, 1929.) A fine limited edition, valuable for its illustrations of the Tennyson country by C. S. Olcott.

Poetic and Dramatic Works, ed. by W. J. Rolfe. Cambridge Edition. (Houghton: Boston, 1898.) A very satisfactory one-volume collection, provided with an introductory Memoir.

Poems, ed. by Henry van Dyke. (Scribner: New York, 1920.) A well-chosen selection, equipped with a worth-while editorial introduction.

Alfred, Lord Tennyson, An Anthology, chosen by F. L. Lucas. (Cambridge University Press: 1932.) The contents include most of the standard selections, plus some excerpts and early poems; the introduction presents the standard criticism, effectively couched.

Selected Poems, ed. by Marjorie H. Nicolson. (Houghton: Boston, 1924.) An ably-compiled anthology, edited especially for college use.

The Best of Tennyson, ed. by W. J. Graham. (Nelson: New York, 1930.) One of the low-priced Nelson English Series: the poems are well chosen, representing all phases of the poet's work.

Poems, ed. by J. F. A. Pyre. (Scribner: New York, 1925.) A useful student-edition, provided with a helpful introduction by the editor.

Poems. 2 vols. (Dutton: New York, 1928.) A good inexpensive edition, with an introduction by Ernest Rhys. Vol. I contains the poems 1830–1856; Vol. II, the poems 1857–1869.

Tennyson and Browning, ed. by Guy Boas. (Nelson: New York, 1925.) A "tiger-lily and rose" anthology of the two poets, represented under the titles Patriotism, Art, Love, Faith, etc.

Early Poems, ed. by J. C. Collins. (Methuen: London, 1900.) An edition for the special student; contains the many variorum readings of the *juvenilia*, together with critical introductions, commentaries, and notes.

Unpublished Early Poems, ed. by Charles Tennyson. (Macmillan: New York, 1932.) An edition prepared from original manuscripts by the poet's grandson.

Idylls of the King, ed. by Elizabeth Nitchie. (Macmillan: New York, 1928.) The best edition for student reading: the introduction gives a full account of the Arthurian tradition.

In Memoriam, ed. by H. C. Beeching. (Methuen: London, 1923.) The best edition for use in college classes, provided with notes and useful commentary.

The Devil and the Lady, ed. by Charles Tennyson. (Macmillan: New York, 1930.) A limited edition of the three-act play written when the poet was fourteen years old and hitherto unpublished.

II. BIOGRAPHY AND CRITICISM

Alden, R. M. *Alfred Tennyson, How to Know Him.* (Bobbs: Indianapolis, 1917.) Gives an analysis of all the important lyrics, with "some account of the general character and structure of the great works."

Baker, A. E. *A Concordance to the Poetical and Dramatic Works of Alfred, Lord Tennyson.* (Macmillan: New York, 1914.) A useful compilation, providing verbal indices to the poetry as contained in the large Macmillan edition, the *Poems* in the Life by Hallam Tennyson, and the Sands edition of the suppressed poems.

Baker, A. E. *A Tennyson Dictionary.* (Dutton: New York, 1916.) The purpose of this work is "to identify and describe the . . . characters, place-names, etc. . . . created or utilized by the poet."

Benson, A. C. *Alfred Tennyson.* (Methuen: London, 1904.) A well-rounded biography, assembling the critical canon, but contributing little of novelty.

Bowden, Mrs. Marjorie. *Tennyson in France.* (Manchester University Press: 1930.) Chiefly important for the light cast on the influence of Tennyson on the French symbolist school; points out that the era of his real significance dates from the 'sixties.

Bradley, A. C. *A Commentary on Tennyson's "In Memoriam."* (Macmillan: London, 1929.) Detailed commentary, section by section, with tracing of parallel passages and annotation, based on extensive research and study of the text of the poem; the introduction discusses its significance in the poet's life and some of the leading ideas in the elegy.

Ellison, Mrs. Edith N. *A Child's Recollections of Tennyson.* (Dutton: New York, 1906.) Fascinating reminiscences of the favored childhood of the author, who associated with the Tennyson family while living on the Isle of Wight.

Fausset, H. I' A. *Tennyson, A Modern Portrait.* (Cape: London, 1929.) Admitting that Tennyson's incarnation of the recent Victorian period makes final judgment on his genius impossible, this study essays to discover in his life and works "those artistic and moral values which Plato named eternal."

Gatty, Alfred. *A Key to Lord Tennyson's "In Memoriam."* (Bell: London, 1911.) The earliest detailed handbook to the elegy, furnishing an analysis for each poem; the preface contains interesting personal sketches of the poet and elucidates the background of the elegy. Many of the notes were furnished by Tennyson himself.

Genung, J. F. *Tennyson's "In Memoriam": Its Purpose and Its Structure.* (Houghton: Boston, 1884.) An analytical study of the chronology and outline of the poem, considered as containing three cycles, preceded by an introduction; provides commentary on separate groups of poems.

Gingerich, S. F. *Wordsworth, Tennyson, and Browning.* (Wahr: Ann Arbor, 1911.) Names Tennyson the "mystical successor" of Wordsworth, with less insistence upon duty, but with greater mobility of will.

Gwynn, S. L. *Tennyson; A Critical Study.* (Blackie: London, 1899.) Quotes freely from contemporary critical opinions and summarizes the poet's social, political, and religious views; chiefly concerned with Tennyson the artist and the analysis of his style and metre; makes many comparisons with English poets and others: Vergil and De Musset among these.

Japikse, Cornelia G. *The Dramas of Alfred, Lord Tennyson.* (Macmillan: New York, 1926.) The authoritative work on the subject: finds that, as literature, the dramas contain "some of the poet's noblest work"; as pieces for the stage, none but *Harold* are entirely satisfactory.

Johnson, R. B. *Tennyson and His Poetry.* (Harrap: London, 1924.) An admirable introduction: devoted to the idea of presenting the poet's art by a careful survey of the places and conditions under which it was produced; quotes liberally.

Lang, Andrew. *Alfred Tennyson.* (Dodd: New York, 1901.) A study by a professed Victorian enthusiast, answering many adverse criticisms; the chapter on *In Memoriam* represents typical Victorian judgment.

Lounsbury, T. R. *The Life and Times of Tennyson,* ed. by W. L. Cross. (Yale University Press: 1915.) A brilliantly written posthumous work: carries only to 1850, but one of the best references for the youth and early manhood of the poet.

Luce, Morton. *A Handbook to the Works of Alfred, Lord Tennyson.* (Bell: London, 1908.) The standard work on this subject, frequently reprinted; concludes with a convenient chronological table of the poet's publications.

Lyall, Sir Alfred. *Tennyson.* English Men of Letters series. (Macmillan: New York, 1902.) A satisfactory short biography, comprising the bulk of the accepted critical opinion.

Napier, G. G. *Homes and Haunts of Alfred Tennyson.* (Macmillan: London, 1892.) A valuable accessory to the study of Tennyson's poetry, showing how it often grew out of local associations and was definitely colored by them.

Nicolson, H. G. *Tennyson: Aspects of His Life, Character, and Poetry.* (Houghton: Boston, 1925.) An admirably written Life, spiced with much anecdotal chat; the last third of the book contains valuable critical comment on the major poems.

Pyre, J. F. A. *The Formation of Tennyson's Style.* (University of Wisconsin Press: 1921.) Applies statistical methods to the analysis of the poet's conscious art, chiefly in reference to the preparation of the 1842 volume; the chapter "Mastering Blank Verse" is illuminating.

Scaife, C. H. O. *The Poetry of Alfred Tennyson.* (Cobden: London, 1930.) An attempt to reintroduce the poet to moderns; recalls his interest in scientific advancement; holds that he fathered many of the ideals of present-day verse.

Smith, Jean Pauline. *The Aesthetic Nature of Tennyson.* (White: New York, 1920.) Shows that, of the three elements of poetry — simplicity, sensuousness, passion — the second was a much stronger element in Tennyson's work than is generally recognized; the wealth of sense-impressions to which he was keenly alive is illustrated here, with interesting comparisons to Keats and Browning.

Smyser, W. E. *Tennyson.* (Eaton: New York, 1906.) "Written in accordance with a single purpose—to present as simply and directly as possible those poems of Tennyson in which he has given expression to the fundamental principles of his faith."

Tennyson, Hallam. *Alfred, Lord Tennyson: A Memoir.* 2 vols. (Macmillan: New York, 1898.) The authoritative Life: "in its clear construction and outright simplicity a remarkable literary achievement"; includes a considerable portion of the Tennyson correspondence.

Tennyson, Hallam. *Tennyson and His Friends.* (Macmillan: New York, 1911.) A re-sifting of the material used in the foregoing work, with a tendency toward a more easy, reminiscential tone.

Turnbull, A. *Life and Writings of Alfred, Lord Tennyson.* (Scribner: New York, 1915.) A recommended brief biography; concludes with a chronology of the poet's chief works.

Van Dyke, Henry. *Studies in Tennyson.* (Scribner: New York, 1920.) A companion volume to *Select Poems of Tennyson*, containing essays on various phases of the poet's development, of which perhaps the best is "Milton and Tennyson," showing comparisons and contrasts.

Waugh, Arthur. *Alfred, Lord Tennyson.* (Webster: New York, 1894.) An outstanding work: has held its place as the best of the brief biographies.

Wolfe, Humbert. *Tennyson.* (Faber: London, 1930.) A discussion, principally of *Maud*, rhapsodic and not over-informative; illustrative of a certain modern trend in criticism.

III. ARTICLES FROM BOOKS

Abercrombie, Lascelles. "Tennyson," in *Revaluations*, ed. by A. C. Ward. (Oxford University Press: 1931.) Interprets *Maud*, "Lucretius," *In Memoriam*, and the *Idylls* as the poet's greatest achievements; points out his many successful efforts to attain the heroic manner.

Dawson, W. J. "Lord Tennyson," and six other essays in *Makers of English Poetry*. (Revell: New York, 1906.) The titles are "Treatment of Nature," "Love and Woman," "Society and Politics," "*The Idylls of the King*," "A Religious Poet," and "*In Memoriam*." Bring together the accepted critical attitudes, but with little original judgment.

Drinkwater, John. "Tennyson's Diction," "Tennyson's Influence," "*The Idylls of the King*," in *Victorian Poetry*. (Doran: New York, 1924.) The first essay remarks the poet's exactness in his description of natural details, which is substantially free from literary borrowings; claims originality also for his verbal luxuriance. The second essay points out traces of the poet's work in Arnold, Rossetti, Morris, and Swinburne. The last essay is a reply to Tennyson's detractors.

Elton, Oliver. "Tennyson," in *Modern Studies*. (Arnold: London, 1907.) Holds that the character of the poet excels his expressed ideas; finds his greatest achievement in his landscape-imagery and his description of mixed feeling.

Gosse, E. W. "Tennyson, and After," in *Questions at Issue*. (Heinemann: London, 1893.) A reflex of feeling following the poet's burial in Westminster Abbey, expressing a conservative's regret that poetry should be made to bear the debasing test of public interest.

Grierson, H. J. C. "The Tennysons," in *The Cambridge History of English Literature*, XIII. (Putnam: New York, 1917.) Provides an excellent brief account of Alfred's verse-experiments; comments judiciously on the *Idylls*, praising the poet's ear and sense of color.

Grierson, H. J. C. "Tennyson, Browning, and Some Others," in *Lyrical Poetry of the Nineteenth Century*. (Harcourt: New York, 1929.) Comments on Tennyson's enlarging of the lyric's power of expressing subtle feeling, though showing no novelty of passion or theme.

Henley, W. E. "Tennyson," in *Views and Reviews*. (Macmillan: London, 1921.) Briefly suggests interesting contrasts between the St. Agnes poems of Keats and Tennyson; remarks the latter's development and his mastery of his materials.

Lucas, F. L. "Tennyson," in *Eight Victorian Poets*. (Cambridge University Press: 1930.) Provides a biographical sketch of anecdotal piquancy; lauds the poet as the unparalleled interpreter of the sea.

Mackail, J. W. "Tennyson," in *Studies of English Poets*. (Longmans: New York, 1926.) Acclaims the poet as the representative of his age and as a master of the lyric and the elegy; traces the poet's advance through his many editions, remarking his long-lived lyric gift.

Meynell, Alice. "Some Thoughts of a Reader of Tennyson," in *Hearts of Controversy*. (Scribner: New York, 1918.) Remarks the adverse reaction, explaining some of its legitimate objections; pleads for a new appreciation of Tennyson's "wildness."

More, P. E. "Tennyson," in *Shelburne Essays*, Seventh Series. (Putnam: New York, 1910.) Identifies the poet as the most complete representative of his nation; recounts some anecdotes illustrating his love of recluseness; bewails the "prettiness" of his lyrical verse and the compromise of the *Idylls*.

Noyes, Alfred. "Tennyson and Some Recent Critics," in *Some Aspects of Modern Poetry*. (Stokes: New York, 1924.) Shows that the poet himself was one of the most outspoken arraigners of the Victorianism which is now suffering its reaction; goes on to point out subtle harmonies in his verse and echoes of "the great style."

Saintsbury, George. "Tennyson," in *Corrected Impressions*. (Dodd: New York, 1895.) Describes a Tennysonian's reminiscences of his first reading; finds the greatest charm of the poet to lie in his "slow and dreamy music."

Shanks, Edward. "The Return of Tennyson," in *Second Essays on Literature*. (Collins: London, 1927.) Sees the reasons for Tennyson's resurgence in the many new biographies and historical studies of him and his age; praises the "clean economy" of his verse-narratives.

Stephen, Leslie. "The Life of Tennyson," in *Studies of a Biographer*, II. (Putnam: New York, 1907.) A broad review of the *Memoir* by Hallam Tennyson, quoting many other critical opinions, and concluding that the poet's power lay chiefly in his "perfect utterance of emotions."

Stevenson, Lionel. "Alfred Tennyson," in *Darwin Among the Poets*. (University of Chicago Press: 1932.) Recalls that the poet anticipated the central theories of Darwin; points out his efforts to reconcile them and religion by reaffirming immortality and denouncing materialism.

Swinburne, A. C. "Tennyson and Musset," in *Miscellanies*. (Scribner: New York, 1911.) Beginning with praise of "Rizpah," sets Tennyson definitely above the French poet, glancing obliquely however at "the Morte d'Albert, or Idylls of the Prince Consort."

Walker, Hugh. "Tennyson" and "Tennyson and Browning," in *The Greater Victorian Poets*. (Swan: London, 1895.) The first essay comments on the early poems and the revisions; points out faults of characterization in the *Idylls*, with praise for the lyrical passages; the second essay remarks the tougher grain of the poetry of Tennyson's closing years.

IV. ARTICLES FROM PERIODICALS

Boas, F. S. "*The Idylls of the King* in 1921," *Nineteenth Century*, XC, 819–30 (Nov., 1921). Shows that Tennyson's heavy devaluation arises from an unfortunate struggle between the medieval and modern motifs in the *Idylls*.

Cressman, E. D. "Classical Poems of Tennyson," *Classical Journal*, XXIV, 98–111 (Nov., 1928). A survey of the poems upon classical subjects in the light of the information afforded by the *Memoir* by Hallam Tennyson.

Howe, M. A. DeWolfe. "The Tennysons at Farringford," *Cornhill Magazine*, LXIII, 447–57 (Oct., 1927). Gives an interesting series of personal events, drawn from the unpublished papers of Mrs. James T. Fields, who left a journal-record of her visits with the poet.

Howe, M. L. "Dante Gabriel Rossetti's Comments on *Maud*," *Modern Language Notes*, XLIX, 290–3 (May, 1934). Based on Rossetti's letters to William Allingham: the comments are not unqualifiedly flattering.

Macy, John. "Tennyson, the Perfect Laureate," *Bookman*, LXIX, 375–86 (June, 1929). A plea for a modern revival of Tennyson, pointing out his technical skill and his admirable treatment of subjects.

Magnus, Laurie. "Tennyson a Hundred Years After," *Cornhill*, LXVI, 660–70 (June, 1929). A survey of the poet's attitude toward France and his composition of the Arthurian stories.

Rawnsley, W. F. "Personal Recollections of Tennyson," *Nineteenth Century*, XCVII, 1–9; 190–6 (Jan., Feb., 1925). Interesting *personalia*, beginning with the poet's Shiplake residence from 1850, and continuing to his last years at Farringford.

Smyser, W. E. "Romanticism in Tennyson and his Pre-Raphaelite Illustrators," *North American Review*, CXCII, 504–15 (Oct., 1910). Shows how Pre-Raphaelite concepts were introduced into illustrated editions by Millais, Hunt, and Rossetti.

Tennyson, Charles. "Tennyson's Unpublished Poems," *Nineteenth Century*, CIX, 367–80; 495–508, 625–36, 756–64 (March to June, 1931). A sifting of material not used in Hallam Tennyson's *Memoir;* prints the texts of many juvenile and other unpublished pieces, many of which supply variants to the published versions.

Thomson, J. C. "Suppressed Poems of Tennyson," *Harper's Magazine*, CVIII, 70–74 (Dec., 1903). A review of various uncollected poems which Tennyson contributed to magazines, with passing comment on those which were not reprinted from the 1830, 1833, and 1842 volumes.

Traill, D. H. "Aspects of Tennyson," *Nineteenth Century*, XXXII, 952–66 (Dec., 1892). From an obituary viewpoint assays the enduring parts of Tennyson's work; finds his strength in his depiction of elemental human feeling.

Warren, Herbert. "The Real Tennyson," *Nineteenth Century*, XCIV, 507–19 (Oct., 1923). Recalls a conversation with the poet; reviews the vicissitudes of his reputation; rebukes some asperities of modern critics.

Weatherhead, L. D. "Tennyson's Afterworld," *London Quarterly Review*, CXLIV, 157–74 (Oct., 1925). An inquiry, based on *In Memoriam*, of the poet's belief in immortality: it is eclectic and poetical, not philosophical.

NOTES

Page 5. CLARIBEL

The poems *Lilian* and *Claribel* which appeared in Tennyson's first volume (that of 1830), are interesting melody studies, although the sensitive ear will not find pleasing what Mr. Harold Nicolson calls the "lispings of *Claribel*." The loneliness and quiet loveliness of the churchyard in this poem are beautifully suggested by the fitness of the descriptive details which the young poet selected. "It is not quite certain," said George Brimley in 1855, "what the precise feeling of the melody is,—whether it expresses a grief that, finding no consolation in its memories or hopes, is deepened by the sweet sights and sounds of the quiet churchyard; or a grief that finds in these a soothing influence." Tennyson said that the "ladies" of his early poems were evolved from his own consciousness. The name Claribel was probably suggested by Spenser (*The Faerie Queene*, Book II, Canto IV), for whose work Tennyson, especially in his youth, had great admiration.

15. *lintwhite*. The European linnet.
19. *runnel crispeth*. The little stream ripples.

SONG

There is a definite sentimental touch in this poem, but one feels clearly the earnestness and sincerity of the poet in his attempt to express the wistfulness with which the human heart lingers over beauty that it loves and that it knows is soon to pass away.

Page 6. MARIANA

This ballad, with its Lincolnshire scenery, was suggested to Tennyson by Shakespeare's picture, in *Measure for Measure* (Act III, sc. 1, l.

277), of Mariana sitting dejected in the moated grange awaiting her lover, Angelo, who has deserted her. It is correct to say that the "lispings of *Claribel*" and other defects that marred Tennyson's early work disappeared as he developed as a music-maker; but there are few if any of his later ballads that equal in impressiveness *Mariana* with the fine monotony of its "aweary—dreary" refrain, its carefully measured lines, and its sense of some dread thing about to happen.

See *Mariana in the South* (text p. 14), and the note to that poem, below.

8. *moated grange.* A large country house with a moat or water-filled ditch surrounding it. No particular house was in the poet's mind.

18. *trance.* To charm, or hold unnaturally still.

40. *marish-mosses.* Marsh mosses.

RECOLLECTIONS OF THE ARABIAN NIGHTS

Mr. Nicolson points out that Tennyson was not impressed by "the different, the adventurous," and says that he gave them but little attention. In some of his earliest poems, however, notably *Recollections of the Arabian Nights,* the young poet felt the thrill that comes from dreaming of far-off lands and horizons, the dwelling-place of wonders unmatched in the familiar homeland. The poem, a young man's dream of beauty, suggests comparison with Keats for its sensuousness. In his review of Tennyson's 1830 volume in *Blackwood's Edinburgh Magazine* Christopher North branded most of the poems in its pages as "miserable" or "dismal drivel," but he praised this poem and *Mariana.*

Tennyson tells us that when the poem was written he had read only a translation from the French of the *Arabian Nights.*

11. *Haroun Alraschid.* Caliph of Bagdad from 786 to 809, and chief character in the *Arabian Nights.* The name means *Aaron the Just.* Under the rule of Haroun, who was a patron of learning, music, and art, Bagdad, a Mesopotamian city on the Tigris river, flourished and became famous.

23. *platans.* Plane trees.

47. *rivage.* A bank or shore (of a river).

64. *tiars.* Crowns.

70. *bulbul.* A Persian songbird frequently mentioned in poetry.

101. *pleasance.* A source of pleasure; a delight.

105. *tamarisks.* The tamarisk is a tree or shrub with white or pinkish flowers, native to the eastern Mediterranean region and tropical Asia.

106. *rosaries.* Rose gardens.

125. *twisted silvers.* Silver candlesticks in spiral ("twisted") shape.

127. *mooned domes.* The crescent moon is the emblem of Islam, the religion of the Moslems.

134. *the Persian girl.* "Noureddin, the fair Persian," in the *Arabian Nights.*

Page 8. THE KRAKEN

The Kraken was a fabulous Scandinavian sea serpent, described by Erik Pontoppidan (1698–1764), a Norwegian bishop, in his *Naturaï History of Norway* (1755).

In his attack on Tennyson's volume of 1830, Christopher North wrote, in wicked gaiety, of this poem: "Mercy on us! Alfred becomes a—Kraken! Leviathan, 'wallowing unwieldy, enormous in his gait,' he despises as we would a minnow; his huge ambition will not suffer him to be 'very like a whale'; he must be a—Kraken. And such a Kraken, too, as would have astonished Pontoppidan." Then, quoting the poem, North mocked the sensitive young poet with this appeal: "The gentle reader who understands that sonnet will perhaps have the goodness to interpret for us the following oracular sentence, which from childhood has been to us a great mystery: 'An old horse came in to be shaved; curse you, where's the suds? The estate was entailed to male heirs; and poor Mrs. Molly lost all her apple-dumplings.'" (See the letter to Christopher North, text p. 212, and the note to that letter, below. See also Rossetti's sonnet, *Mac Cracken*, text p. 656.)

THE POET

This poem is important as expressing the beliefs of the youthful Tennyson as to the mission of the poet. The doctrine of the poet's having a "mission" was instilled in Tennyson's mind in his Cambridge days by the "Apostles" (see introductory sketch of Tennyson, text p. 1), and he never grew out of the belief that it was his mission as a poet to teach and to lead and direct.

3. *the hate of hate.* Hallam Tennyson said, "My father denounced hate and scorn as if they were the 'sins against the Holy Ghost.'"

13. *Indian reeds.* Arrows. The idea of the blowpipe through which the arrows were blown is also suggested.

15. *Calpe unto Caucasus.* Calpe (Gibraltar), one of the Pillars of Hercules, was the western limit of the ancient world. Caucasus was the eastern limit.

19. *arrow-seeds of the field flower.* The seeds of the dandelion.

Page 9. TO J. M. K.

John (Jack) Mitchell Kemble (1807–1857), to whom this sonnet is addressed, was a Cambridge student, a member of the "Apostles" (see note to *The Poet*, above). He was believed by the "Apostles" to have a philosophical and religious turn of mind and came to be known at their Saturday night meetings for his pronouncement that the world was one great thought, "and he was thinking it." He did not, however, "shoot arrows of lightnings from a throne mounted in Heaven." Instead of becoming a preacher he became a learned scholar in Anglo-Saxon.

THE MILLER'S DAUGHTER

Of this poem Tennyson said, "If I thought at all of any mill, it was that of Trumpington, near Cambridge." See extract, "I am told," etc., text p. 211.

When Wordsworth's death, in 1850, left the Laureateship vacant, a number of poets were mentioned for the honor. Tennyson stood fourth on the list submitted to the Queen, the names of Leigh Hunt, Henry Taylor, and Sheridan Knowles preceding his. Some writers say that the influence of the Prince Consort, who was greatly moved by *In Memoriam*, led the Queen to select Tennyson. Another report, that of Mr. George Napier, says that the Queen was so touched by the simple strains of *The Miller's Daughter* that in face of all opposition she conferred "the much-coveted wreath on its author."

This "simple story of true sweet-hearting and married love" is of course on the black list of those who find fault with Tennyson for his sentimentality and his praise of what may be called the homely, pleasing family virtues, the tender delicacies of the household. Mr. I. A. Richards says that it figures as one of the favorites of the anthologies through its "bad eminence."

80. *dimpled beck*. A beck is a small brook. When its bed is stony the surface of the brook becomes dimpled or rippled.

Page 12. BUONAPARTE

The battles referred to in this sonnet, in which the young Englishman sings robustiously of his country's prowess, occurred in the Napoleonic Wars.

3. *island queen*. England.
4. *Ind to Ind*. East India to West India.
5. *wooden walls*. Battleships.
8. *Coptic sands*. A reference to the Battle of the Nile (1798), in which Admiral Nelson defeated the French fleet and caused the failure of Napoleon's expedition to Egypt. Coptic, as used here, means Egyptian.
9. *Elsinore*. In 1801 the Danish fleet in the harbor of Copenhagen was defeated by the English. Elsinore is a Danish seaport.
12. *Trafalgar*. In 1805 the English fleet under Nelson defeated the combined French and Spanish fleets off Cape Trafalgar, Spain.
13. *late he learned humility*. A reference to the Battle of Waterloo (1815), which ended Napoleon's career.
14. *Gideon school'd*. See Judges 8 : 16.

THE LADY OF SHALOTT

While he was still a very young man Tennyson became deeply interested in "the haunted region of Celtic romance." Although he tells us that he first lighted upon Malory's *Morte d'Arthur*, that "most pleasant jumble and summary of the legends about Arthur," when he was little more than a boy, he did not take *The Lady of Shalott* from Malory but from an Italian romance, *Donna di Scalotta* ("Lady of Scalott"). The word "Scalott," the poet said, he changed to "Shalott" because the latter had a softer sound. In Malory's version of the story, which Tennyson used in his Idyll, *Lancelot and Elaine*, the home of the heroine was Astolat. Shalott and Astolat, he explained, were "the same words."

The two dates at the end of the poem indicate that it was published first in the 1832 volume and again, practically rewritten, in 1842. In so far as the British public was concerned the 1832 book was a disastrous failure. At the end of the ten years of silence to which Tennyson was sentenced by the reception of the volume of 1832 (see introductory note to Tennyson), came *Poems*, containing many of the poems of the earlier volume "improved and modified in some cases . . . almost beyond recognition."

The sheer beauty of the poem as a piece of music and the interest it awakens as a story are not the only noteworthy things about it; it has, in addition to these, an allegorical or symbolical significance the clue to which, the poet said, is in the closing lines of Part II: "the new-born love for something, for some one in the wide world from which she has been so long excluded, takes her out of the region of shadows into that of realities."

5. *Camelot*. A city in Cornwall, the legendary seat of King Arthur's court.
84. *Galaxy*. The Milky Way.

Page 14. MARIANA IN THE SOUTH

When Tennyson and Arthur Hallam journeyed to the Pyrenees in the summer of 1830 with funds for the Spanish patriots, they came upon a range of country in southern France which exactly corresponded to the poet's preconceived idea of barrenness. This barren scenery forms the background of *Mariana in the South*, and its portraiture, wrote Hallam, "is most faithful." The poem is a variation on the theme of *Mariana* (text p. 6). Mr. Nicolson, who counts it somewhat against Tennyson that the scenery in his dramatic poems can be so easily identified, points out that the "sense of drought" in this poem comes from its having been "written in a diligence near Perpignan."

9. *"Ave Mary."* The salutation of Gabriel and of Elizabeth to the Virgin Mary, combined, as

now used in the Roman Catholic Church, with a prayer to her as Mother of God.

85. *a dry cicala.* The cicada, often called locust. Its prolonged shrill note, shriller (apparently) and heard more frequently in hot, dry weather, seems to intensify the oppression of drought and heat.

90. *Hesper.* The evening star.

Page 15. ŒNONE

Tennyson's interest in classical stories led him to write a number of so-called "classical" poems—*Œnone, The Lotos-Eaters* (text p. 22), *Ulysses* (p. 37), *Tithonus* (p. 116), *Lucretius* (p. 134), and others.

Of this poem, which was worked over for the 1842 *Poems* until it was almost unrecognizable as the *Œnone* of 1832 (see p. 213a, l. 51), Professor Archibald MacMechan writes: "Tennyson calls it 'Œnone'; but its true title is 'The Judgment of Paris,' a favorite subject of poets and painters. The merely sensual is eliminated by the device of letting the goddesses be seen through a woman's eyes; but the picture loses little of its Titianesque color thereby. It carries on the modern treatment of classic legend, which Keats began. It is not the revival of a Greek myth; which were impossible; the Greek myth is used as a mould, or form into which is poured the poet's new gold. Not only Athene's speech, but Here's conception of power is modern: the bribe of Aphrodite is of all time." (MacMechan, in *Select Poems of Tennyson*, p. 238.)

See note to Rossetti's *Troy Town*, below, and see also Swinburne's remark concerning *Œnone* in his letter to Lord Houghton, text p. 791.

Œnone, a nymph of Mt. Ida, was the wife of Paris, son of King Priam of Troy. As a result of his decision in the beauty contest of the three goddesses, Paris was awarded Helen, "the most beautiful of women," for whom he deserted Œnone.

1. *a vale in Ida.* Mt. Ida, in the Troad, northwestern Asia Minor. Ancient Troy was the capital of the Troad. Tennyson, who never saw the Troad, drew largely upon the scenery in the Valley of Cauteretz in the Pyrenees for this poem. See *In the Valley of Cauteretz*, text p. 117.

2. *Ionian hills.* Hills of Greece.

3–9. *The swimming vapour . . . to the sea.* Hallam Tennyson wrote that the memories of the Pyrenean country were a "continued source of inspiration" to the poet.

10. *Gargarus.* The highest point of Mt. Ida.

37. *daughter of a River-God.* The river-god, her father, was Cebrenus, of the Cebren, a little river of the Troad.

39–40. *walls . . . music.* According to the legend, the walls of Troy were built to the music of Apollo's lyre.

51. *Simois.* A small stream flowing into the Scamander, a river whose source is on Mt. Ida.

65. *fruit . . . Hesperian gold.* The Hesperides, daughters of Atlas or Hesperus, king of the Western Land, guarded the golden apples in the Gardens of the West.

72. *Oread.* A mountain nymph.

74. *married brows.* Eyebrows that meet.

79. *Peleus.* King of Thessaly, who invited all the gods except Eris, goddess of discord, to witness his marriage with Thetis, a sea nymph. Incensed, Eris tossed among the guests the apple of discord inscribed with the words "To the fairest." Thus rose the feud (l. 80) leading to the Judgment of Paris, his desertion of Œnone, and the Trojan War.

81. *Iris.* Goddess of the rainbow, the swift-footed messenger of Zeus and Herè.

83–4. *Herè . . . Pallas and Aphroditè.* These were the three goddesses who claimed the prize for beauty. Herè (Juno) was queen of heaven, Pallas (Minerva) goddess of wisdom, and Aphroditè (Venus) goddess of love.

102. *peacock.* The peacock was sacred to Herè.

126. *A shepherd . . . yet king-born.* Before the birth of Paris, Hecuba, his mother, dreamed that she gave birth to a burning brand. The dream was interpreted as meaning that her child would bring destruction upon Troy. When Paris was born, Priam, his father, gave him to a slave to expose on Mt. Ida. There a bear nursed him for five days, after which he was found by a shepherd who brought him up as his own son.

151. *Sequel of guerdon.* A reward to follow or to be given for choosing her—almost bribing.

170. *Idalian.* Idalium, a town in Cyprus, was sacred to Aphroditè.

171. *Paphian.* There was a famous temple of Aphroditè in Paphos, an ancient city in Cyprus.

195. *wanton pard.* Sportive leopard.

204. *They came.* Probably the Trojan shipbuilders for ship timber.

220. *The Abominable.* Eris.

242. *I will not die alone.* Œnone, who had the gift of prophecy, had exacted a promise from Paris that he would come to her for healing if he were wounded in the war which she foresaw. Remembering this agreement, he had himself taken to her when he was struck by an arrow. She refused to help him, however, and sent him back to Troy to die. Later she repented and followed him, but finding him dead, she killed herself.

259. *Cassandra.* The daughter of Priam and Hecuba. Apollo gave her the gift of prophecy, but when she spurned him he punished her by bringing it to pass that no man believed her prophecy. She tried again and again to warn her countrymen against the Greeks, and when Troy fell Agamemnon took her as a slave to Mycenae, where she was slain by Clytemnestra.

Page 18. THE PALACE OF ART

If *The Poet* (text p. 8) is an expression of Tennyson's creed in the 1830 volume, *The Palace of Art* may be considered such an expression for the volume of 1832. In these verses, which he said were the embodiment of his "belief that the Godlike life is with man and for man," the poet depicts the failure of a cultured intellectual to find in art all the satisfying and abiding values that are necessary to the highest human development. The belief in the self-sufficiency of art—"art for art's sake"—is a heresy. Tennyson tells us that Richard Trench (one of the "Apostles") had said to him when they were students at Trinity, "Tennyson, we cannot live in art."

See introductory note to *The Vision of Sin*, below, and Rossetti's letter (No. IV), text p. 659.

15–16. *Saturn whirls . . . luminous ring.* Saturn is encircled by a broad belt of luminous matter upon which it casts its shadow. The planet is of course rotating, but the shadow is motionless ("stedfast").

30. *lent broad verge.* Offered a far view.

49. *traced.* Carved or ornamented.

61–92. In these lines the scenes on the tapestries (arras) and the decorations of the rooms are taken from living Nature. "Every landscape fair" is done in these decorations.

79–80. *prodigal in oil . . . wind.* Olive trees grew on the uplands. Tennyson said, "The underside of the olive leaf is white."

93–128. These lines describe legendary figures and scenes as they are represented in the decoration of the Palace.

99. *St. Cecily.* St. Cecilia, the patron saint of musicians and of sacred music; according to legend, the inventor of the organ.

102. *Houris.* Nymphs of the Mohammedan paradise.

103. *Islamite.* A Moslem, an orthodox Mohammedan.

105. *Uther's . . . son.* King Arthur. He was wounded by the invading Saxons on the battlefield of Camlan. The wound referred to here is that given him by his rebellious nephew, Modred, one of the knights of the Round Table.

107. *Avalon.* An earthly paradise in the western seas, where Arthur got his sword and where he was taken to recover from his wounds.

111. *Ausonian king.* Numa Pompilius, a legendary king of Rome, sought the advice of the wood-nymph Egeria. Italy is poetically called Ausonia.

113. *engrail'd.* Indented at the edge with small concave curves.

115. *Indian Cama.* The Hindu god of love, son of Brahma.

117. *Europa.* A princess of Phœnicia, who, while she was gathering flowers, was abducted and carried off to Crete by Zeus, in the form of a white bull.

121. *Ganymede.* A very beautiful Trojan boy who was carried off to Olympus by the eagle of Zeus to be cupbearer to the gods.

131. With this line begins an enumeration of the great whose portraits honor the Palace.

137. *the Ionian father.* Homer.

146. *cycles of the human tale.* For several lines following l. 146, historical scenes depicted in the Palace in some art form are described.

149 ff. These lines describe the condition and the state of mind of the French people at the time of the Revolution. The "beast of burden" has been spoken of as symbolizing slavery, the "tiger," rebellion, the "athlete," democracy, and the "sick man," anarchy.

163–4. *Plato . . . Verulam . . . know.* Plato, the Greek philosopher, and Bacon (Lord Verulam) may be fitly characterized as "the first of those who know."

171. *Memnon.* The statue of Memnon, near Thebes in Egypt, was said to give forth music like that of a harpstring when the first rays of the morning sun fell upon it.

186. *Anadems.* Garlands.

203–4. *devil . . . deep.* Suggested by the incident related in Luke 8 : 33, in which the devils Jesus casts out of a man enter a herd of swine and drive them into the lake.

219. *Herod.* The angel of the Lord smote Herod because "he gave not God the glory." See Acts 12 : 21–3.

227. "*Mene.*" At the time of Belshazzar's feast a hand wrote the phrase "Mene, mene, tekel, upharsin" on the wall of the palace. The prophet Daniel interpreted the writing to mean, "God hath numbered thy kingdom, and finished it." See Daniel 5 : 25–6.

242. *fretted.* Wrinkled, worm-eaten.

253. *A star.* The soul.

255. *Circumstance.* An "old phrase for the surrounding sphere of the heavens" (Palgrave).

Page 22. THE LOTOS-EATERS

The Lotophagi or Lotos-Eaters were a people inhabiting a coast visited by Ulysses in his wanderings. Their "flowery food," the fruit of the lotos (also lotus) tree, made those who ate it indolent, given to daydreaming, and "forgetful of the homeward way." Ulysses escaped by leading his men who had eaten of the lotos back to the ships and binding them fast. (*Odyssey*, Bk. IX, 83 ff.) The beautiful land of the Lotos-Eaters, "In which it seemed always afternoon," is not that of "the peaceable folk of Libya" whom Ulysses visited, but only an idealized Torquay. The underlying idea of the poem, like that of *The Palace of Art*, is the moral wrong of trying to escape human duties and responsibilities.

11. *Slow-dropping veils of thinnest lawn.* See letter to S. E. Dawson, text p. 222a, ll. 19 ff.

23. *galingale.* A grasslike plant.

44. *island home.* Ithaca, an island off the west coast of Greece.

46–173. These lines, composing the choric song, are sung by the mariners, who have eaten of the lotos.

133. *amaranth.* An imaginary flower, supposed never to fade.

moly. A fabulous herb said by Homer to have been used by Ulysses to counteract the spells of Circe.

142. *acanthus-wreath.* The acanthus leaf was used in the making of garlands and in decorations.

169–70. *Elysian . . . asphodel.* The asphodel is a plant of the lily kind. It is a flower much mentioned by poets, English poets usually identifying it with the daffodil. Homer makes it grow in the Elysian Fields.

Page 24. A DREAM OF FAIR WOMEN

2. *The Legend of Good Women.* A poem by Chaucer in which he tells the stories of famous women who, even at great price to themselves, were constant in love.

5. *Dan.* A title of respect, from the Latin *dominus,* "master."

7. *spacious . . . Elizabeth.* The Elizabethan period was one of great and varied literary activity.

27. *tortoise.* In ancient warfare, troops attacking a walled city often interlocked their shields over their heads, the formation resembling the back of a tortoise (Latin *testudo*).

85. *a lady.* Helen, the beautiful Greek woman carried off to Troy by Paris. The act led to the Trojan War.

95. *Many drew swords and died.* I.e., in the Trojan War.

100. *one.* Iphigenia. The fleet which Agamemnon had assembled at Aulis for the expedition against Troy could not sail because Artemis, goddess of the chase, wrathful at his slaying a stag that was sacred to her, had "laid the winds" and would not bid them rise. Calchas, a soothsayer, prophesied that the fleet could not sail unless Agamemnon sacrificed his daughter, Iphigenia, to appease the goddess. According to Tennyson, Agamemnon actually performed the sacrifice of Iphigenia, but the most frequent version of the legend is that Artemis took pity upon her, rescued her, and accepted the sacrifice of a hind in her place.

126–7. *One sitting . . . A queen.* Cleopatra (69–30 B.C.), who became queen of Egypt in 51 B.C. Tennyson said that in describing the queen he was thinking of Shakespeare's Cleopatra; he knew perfectly well, he added, that Cleopatra of Egypt was a Greek.

139. *cold-blooded Cæsar.* Octavius Cæsar, who did not fall under her spell as did Julius Cæsar and Mark Antony.

145. *Libyan.* African.

146. *Canopus.* A star in the constellation Argo. Next to Sirius it is the brightest fixed star.

150. *Hercules . . Antony.* Antony claimed descent from Hercules and imitated him in dress.

155. *with a worm.* A false report that Cleopatra was dead drove Antony to suicide as Octavius approached Alexandria. Then, failing to win Octavius and fearing that he would take her captive to Rome, Cleopatra killed herself by allowing a snake (worm) to strike her.

178. *some one coming.* Jephthah's daughter. When Jephthah (Judges 11 : 30 ff.) went out against the Ammonites he vowed that if victory were given to him he would sacrifice whatever came forth first from his house to meet him on his return. His daughter came first, and he "did with her according to his vow."

179. *crested bird.* Logically the cock; but since the cock is a commonplace fowl, most editors call the "crested bird" the lark.

197. *Gileadite.* Jephthah, as a native of Gilead.

199. *Mizpeh's.* Jephthah's house was in Mizpeh.

203–4. *a thousand times . . . die.* She would gladly die a thousand times rather than have her father break his vow.

214. *my maiden blame.* Hebrew women were considered to be covered with shame if they died without a son. Jephthah's daughter withdrew to the mountains for a period before her death in order to mourn her virginity.

237. *it is written.* In Judges 11 : 33.

239. *Arnon.* A river emptying into the Dead Sea.

243. *Thridding.* Threading.

Boskage. Thickets.

251. *Rosamond.* Rosamond Clifford, the mistress of Henry II, said to have been poisoned by Henry's jealous queen, Eleanor (l. 255), in 1177.

258–9. *Egyptian . . . Fulvia's waist.* Cleopatra substitutes the name of Fulvia, Antony's first wife, of whom she was fiercely jealous, for Eleanor of Aquitaine, Henry's queen.

263. *captain of my dreams.* Venus, the morning star. Venus, goddess of love and beauty, may well serve as the inspirer of this dream of fair women.

266. *her.* Margaret Roper (1505–1544), daughter of Sir Thomas More, who was beheaded in 1535 for high treason. It is said that she purchased his head a month after it had been exposed on London Bridge, preserved it in spices, and caused it to be buried with her.

267. *Joan of Arc.* The national heroine of

France, who led the French army to victory over the English in 1428. Finally the English took her prisoner and burned her at the stake as a witch in 1431.

269–71. *her.* Eleanor, wife of Edward I, accompanied him to the Holy Land in 1269. When he was stabbed with a poisoned dagger, she sucked the poison from his wound.

Page 28. ST. AGNES' EVE

St. Agnes was a Christian virgin of the third century who, when she was twelve years old, was martyred in Rome through the persecution of Diocletian. She is venerated as the pattern of innocence and the patron of young girls. It was popularly believed that by performing certain ceremonies on the eve of her feast (January 21) a maiden would have a vision of the man she was destined to marry. In this poem a pure sister of the church, who longs for a vision of the Heavenly Bridegroom, is the speaker.

See Keats's *The Eve of St. Agnes*, in *English Romantic Poets*, p. 586.

16. *argent round.* The silver moon.

Page 29. YOU ASK ME, WHY, THO' ILL AT EASE

Tennyson denied the report that he listened to a speech by Spedding, one of the Apostles, at the Cambridge Union, and was so impressed by it that he went home and wrote this poem and the two immediately following it in the text the same evening. The three poems show the poet's interest in political and social questions of his day. In them he voices the conservatism and conventionalism that were a part of him all his life. The good advice spoken in *Love Thou Thy Land* is precisely what one must expect from a writer who believes the function or business of the poet to be what Tennyson said it was in *The Poet* (text p. 8). All three of the poems, too, augur Laureate gifts.

11. *slowly broadens down.* See extract beginning, "The English public think" (text p. 208).

OF OLD SAT FREEDOM ON THE HEIGHTS

See introductory note to *You Ask Me, Why, Tho' Ill at Ease*, above.

14. *isle-altar.* England.

15. *Who . . . forks.* Britannia, who symbolizes Great Britain, is represented as carrying the trident of Neptune, god of the sea, to indicate her control of the seas.

Page 30. LOVE THOU THY LAND, WITH LOVE FAR-BROUGHT

See introductory note to *You Ask Me, Why, Tho' Ill at Ease*, above.

12. *lime.* Deceive, ensnare.

37–40. *For . . . form.* A reference to the old belief that the nature of a body was determined by the proportion of heat, cold, moistness, and dryness found in it.

64. *contrivances of Power.* A reference to battleships and, possibly, airships, as in *Locksley Hall* (text p. 38, ll. 119–124).

Page 31. THE EPIC

Mr. Harold Nicolson says that some idea of the details and general atmosphere of Tennyson's Trinity College days may be got by attention to Everard Hall, the poet in this prologue and in the epilogue to the *Morte d'Arthur*. He finds also a number of "other undergraduate touches" in this poem, in the prelude to *The Princess*, and in *The Gardener's Daughter*.

3. *the sacred bush.* The mistletoe.

10. *cutting eights.* Engaging in fancy skating; cutting designs on the ice with skates.

15. *church-commissioners.* In 1835–1836 the Ecclesiastical Commission was established, one of its duties being to administer the revenues of the Church of England.

16. *Geology and schism.* A reference to the "conflict between religion and science."

38. *twelve books of mine.* The *Morte d'Arthur* was written and published before Tennyson had written the twelve *Idylls of the King*. In playful pretense he speaks of the "twelve books" and says that the eleventh, *Morte d'Arthur*, was "pick'd" from the hearth on which the others were burned. Some forty years after, the *Idylls* were completed in twelve books.

50–1. *oes and aes . . Deep-chested music.* Tennyson, whose voice was very deep, read "with a broad north country vowel."

MORTE D'ARTHUR

See introductory note to *The Lady of Shalott*, above.

This poem, which formed the nucleus of the twelve sections of the *Idylls of the King*, Tennyson revised and finally incorporated in the *Idylls* with the title *The Passing of Arthur* (see letter XVI, to the Duke of Argyll, text p. 219). It was written before the poet had conceived of the possibility of a cycle of stories with a "deeper meaning"; its interest therefore is purely a story interest.

4. *Lyonnesse.* In Arthurian legend a country that lay between Cornwall and the Scilly Islands and included Land's End. It was the land of mystery whence Arthur came, and is said to have sunk beneath the sea.

21. *Camelot.* See note to l. 5 of *The Lady of Shalott*, above.

23. *Merlin.* The magician or wizard, the wise man of King Arthur's court.

31. *samite*. A heavy silk fabric.
80. *lief*. Beloved, precious.
139. *streamer . . . morn*. The aurora borealis or northern lights.
140. *isles of winter*. Icebergs.
186. *Dry*. Harsh.
232. *light*. The star of Bethlehem.
240. *The old . . . new*. In 1842, when the *Morte d'Arthur* appeared, the Oxford movement and the movement for amelioration of the social and industrial conditions of the working classes were at their height. The Corn Law agitation was active and Parliamentary reform and Catholic Emancipation had actually been accomplished. In England, certainly, the "old order" was yielding place.
259. *Avilion*. Avalon. See note to l. 107 of *The Palace of Art*, above.

Page 35. DORA

This poem, one of the English idylls, i.e., descriptive and narrative pieces dealing with simple rural or village life, was in part suggested to Tennyson by Mary Russell Mitford's pastoral, "Dora Creswell," in her volume, *Our Village*. Tennyson said of it that since it had to be told in the simplest poetical language, the writing of it gave him much trouble. The style and the manner of the poem remind one more of Wordsworth than of Tennyson. It reminded Carlyle of the Book of Ruth, and Wordsworth liked it so well that he told Tennyson he had been trying all his life to write a pastoral like it. Most lovers of Wordsworth, however, would insist that *Dora* falls far short of both the elder poet's *Michael* and his *Margaret*.

Page 37. ULYSSES

Tennyson said that this poem, which was written soon after Arthur Hallam's death, gave perhaps more simply than anything in *In Memoriam* his feelings about the need of going forward and braving the struggle of life. The chief source of the poem is Dante, who in the *Inferno*, XXVI, 90–120, makes Ulysses tell the poets that when he departed from Circe neither affection for his son, piety for his father, nor love for his wife Penelope chilled his ardor to gain experience of the world and to know human vice and worth. He set forth on the deep open sea, he said, with his small, faithful company in one little ship, and after long wandering, when he and his companions were old and slow, reached the bounds of the world set by Hercules. There he addressed his faithful band: "O brothers, who through a hundred thousand perils have reached the West, to this so little vigil of your senses that remains be ye unwilling to deny the experience, following the sun, of the world that hath no people. . . . Ye were not made to live as brutes, but for pursuit of virtue and of knowledge." There is a passage in the *Odyssey* telling that Ulysses arrived safe at his home in Ithaca after the fall of Troy, and another in which it is foretold that after his return to Ithaca he will set forth on a mysterious voyage. The scene of Tennyson's poem is Ithaca. The poem is noteworthy for its beauty of phrase, its fine dramatic quality, and the high courage which it voices.

For Swinburne's comment on *Ulysses* see his letter to Lord Houghton, text p. 792b, ll. 18 ff.
3. *an aged wife*. Penelope.
10. *rainy Hyades*. A V-shaped cluster of stars in the constellation Taurus, believed by the ancients to indicate the coming of rainy weather when they rose with the sun.
63. *the Happy Isles*. The Islands of the Blessed, in the Western Ocean, came to be identified with the Elysian Fields as the dwelling place of just men after death.
64. *Achilles*. The son of Peleus. He became to the Greeks the type of youthful strength, beauty, valor, and chivalry. He was the foremost hero of the Trojan War. The death which sent him to the Happy Isles resulted from an arrow wound inflicted upon him by Paris.
69. *strong in will*. The doctrine of the unconquerable will was a favorite with Tennyson.

Page 38. LOCKSLEY HALL

Despite the fact that this poem was roundly ridiculed by the critics when it first appeared and that it is still a favorite piece at which the modern Tennyson-baiters jibe, it is a faithful study of one kind of youthful behavior under disappointment in love. Suicide, dissipation, despair, bravado, and Byronic fuming—any one of these acts or states may be expected of the young man whose sweetheart forces upon him the realization that love is not "love for evermore." To think caustically of the poem because the greatly upset youth of twenty does not speak a deep and finished philosophy is to confess unfamiliarity with the adolescent mind. *Locksley Hall*, Tennyson said, "represents young life, its good side, its deficiencies, and its yearnings." The situation in the poem is not circumscribed in place or time—the speaker may represent young America of today as well as he represented young England of Tennyson's day. See extract, "I am told," etc., text p. 211.
1. *Comrades*. The course of a hunting expedition having led the youth to his old home, Locksley Hall, he stops to muse while his companions continue the chase.
8. *Orion*. The most conspicuous constellation in the sky.
9. *the Pleiads*. A loose cluster of stars in the constellation Taurus.

19. *iris . . . dove.* The rainbow colors on the dove's neck grow brighter at mating time.
75. *the poet sings.* Dante, in the *Inferno*, V, 121–3, wrote: "There is no greater sorrow than to remember happy times when one is in misery."
79. *he.* Amy's husband.
104. *laid with sound.* A reference to the belief, once common, that heavy cannonading brought on calm.
121–4. Most readers see in these lines a prophecy of modern aviation and battle in the air.
135. *a hungry people.* The reference is to the "dangerous growth of democracy, felt in the discontent which preceded the Revolution of 1848." (Van Dyke, *Poems by Tennyson*, p. 406.)
138. *the process of the suns.* The flight of time.
150. *motions.* Impulses, feelings.
155. *Mahratta-battle.* The youthful speaker was born in India, the son of a British soldier who was slain in battle against the Mahrattas, a people of India.
180. *Joshua's moon in Ajalon.* In Joshua 10 : 12–13 Joshua commanded the moon to stand still in the valley of Ajalon "until the people had avenged themselves upon their enemies."
182. *grooves.* When Tennyson went from Liverpool to Manchester by the first train (1830), he thought the wheels ran in grooves. It was a dark night, and there was such a great crowd at the station that he could not see the wheels. He made l. 182 on that trip.
184. *cycle of Cathay.* A very long period of time spent in China. But Cathay (China) stands for the Orient as contrasted with the Western world (Europe).
186. *weigh the Sun.* In 1838–1842 Francis Baily interested minds like Tennyson's with a series of experiments for determining the mean density of the earth and the weight of the sun.

Page 43. GODIVA

Godiva, according to a legend which may have some truth in it, was the wife of one Leofric, who, about 1040, was Earl of Mercia and Lord of Coventry. When she asked him to remit a burdensome tax which he had imposed on the people he jestingly told her that he would do so if she rode naked through the town. She took him at his word and made the ride. The only person in the town mean enough to look at her was a tailor who was called, from his act, Peeping Tom. He was miraculously stricken blind.
3. *three tall spires.* The spires of the three churches, St. Michael's, Trinity, and Christ.
28. *Esau's hand.* Esau, the son of Isaac, was remarkable for the hair which covered his hands and body. See Genesis 25 : 25, and 27 : 16–23.

Page 44. SIR GALAHAD

In Malory's *Morte d'Arthur* Galahad is by enchantment the son of Lancelot and Elaine, daughter of King Pelles (not the maid of Astolat). He is predestined by his purity to achieve the quest of the Holy Grail. The Grail, according to some medieval legends, was the platter from which Christ ate at the Last Supper and in which Joseph of Arimathea later received the Saviour's blood at the Cross; according to others it was identified with the wine cup used by Christ at the Last Supper. The Grail was brought to Glastonbury, Britain, by Joseph when he was driven from Palestine, and there it was preserved for generations. If approached by any but a pure and holy person, it would be borne away and vanish. Its keepers having become impure, it disappeared and thereafter was an object of search to numerous knights. The quest was to be undertaken only by one who was perfectly chaste in thought, word, and act. Of King Arthur's knights only Percivale, Galahad, and Bors achieved the quest. The Galahad of this poem is the counterpart of the pure sister of the Church in *St. Agnes' Eve*, text p. 28.
25. *stormy crescent.* The moon on a night of storm.
43. *stoles.* Here the meaning is "long cloaks."
61. *maiden knight.* A scrupulously pure knight. In the *Morte d'Arthur*, Book XVII, Chap. XXII, Joseph of Arimathea says to Sir Galahad, "Thou hast been a clean maiden, as I have been and am."
69–72. Tennyson had himself experienced what he called "a kind of waking trance" from boyhood. For a remark of his that seems to have some bearing on this experience see text p. 209b, ll. 12–23. In *The Holy Grail* (text p. 163, ll. 907–15), he makes Arthur undergo the experience.

Page 45. MOVE EASTWARD, HAPPY EARTH

6. *Thy silver sister-world.* This has been called Venus, as the morning star, but the glow seen over the earth's "dark shoulder," followed by the rising of the "sister-world," more nearly fits the moon.

THE VISION OF SIN

"[*The Vision of Sin*] is reminiscent of *The Palace of Art*, painting the same surrender to sensuous luxury, but with a more curt and savage hatred. It is a poem full of wormy circumstance, a ghastly caricature of an hysterical hell, in which a creature more fiend than man indulges his 'maudlin gall' by mocking at every fair and cleanly thing in the world, and drinking himself into madness. Sin is far more subtle and far less melodramatic than such poetical panic would have us believe, yet the poem contains two lines of remarkable insight:

> 'We are men of ruin'd blood:
> Therefore comes it we are wise.'"
> (Hugh I'Anson Fausset, in *Tennyson, A Modern Portrait*, p. 104.)

The poem, which deals with the sins of youth and the inevitable disillusionment, bitterness, and cynicism which follow, shows us first the youth entering upon a wild orgy in a palace, and then, much later, the same youth, now a man "of ruined blood," jeering before the hideous attendants of a vile inn, the Dragon, at friendship, virtue, love, and all other things of good repute.

See Rossetti's letter (No. IV), text p. 659.

3. *horse with wings*. Pegasus, according to legend the mount of poets. The youth had superior talent and high hopes, but he did not have the will to restrain his low desires.

41. *Furies*. The goddesses of vengeance. *Graces*. Goddesses of charm and beauty.

96. *rouse*. A carousal, a drinking frolic.

141–2. *hue Of that cap*. A reference to the blood-red Liberty-cap of the French Revolutionists.

179. *Vivat Rex*. Long live the King.

189. *Buss*. Kiss.

224. *God made Himself an awful rose of dawn.* Asked the meaning of this line, Tennyson said: "The power of explaining such concentrated expressions of the imagination is very different from that of writing them."

Page 48. BREAK, BREAK, BREAK

Of this poem, inspired by the death of Arthur Hallam, and "made in a Lincolnshire lane at 5 o'clock in the morning between blossoming hedges," Mr. Alfred Noyes writes, in *Some Aspects of Modern Poetry*, p. 173: "This brief poem is a simple but very perfect example of the way in which rhythm and meter bring the thought of the poet into harmony with the pulsations of the universe; the swinging tides, the moving ships, and the beating heart of man all seeming to discover their common measure as he translates them into music, and entering thereby into some wider communion with the Eternal."

SONGS FROM THE PRINCESS

The theme of *The Princess*, which Mr. Henry van Dyke called "one of the minor poems of a major poet," is the equality of the sexes and the proper sphere of woman, a theme whose grave nature "is often a disturbing element in the easy enjoyment of a poem which is essentially a fantasy." The princess, Ida, who had been betrothed in childhood to a prince, becomes a champion of woman's rights and establishes a college in which to educate women in isolation from men. The prince and two companions disguise themselves as women students and are admitted to the college. Two tutors discover the identity of the three young men but keep their discovery secret. Later Princess Ida herself detects the deceit, and although the prince has rescued her from drowning, she remains unshaken in her determination to emancipate woman through isolation from man and drives the three young men out of her domain to the peril of their lives. At this critical time the father of the prince comes to attack the college with his army. Champions of the princess appear, and the settlement of the matter is staked on a combat between fifty warriors led by the prince and fifty led by Princess Ida's mighty brother, Arac. The prince's forces are defeated, and he and his two comrades are wounded. Womanly pity now asserts itself; the college is turned into a hospital, the girl students nurse the wounded men, and Princess Ida, yielding to the love she has always felt, gives her heart to the prince.

Like *The Palace of Art*, this poem voices the need of normal human feelings in every situation in which normal men and women find themselves. No arbitrary plan to suppress such feelings can possibly succeed.

A paragraph which is omitted from the letter to S. E. Dawson as it appears in the text, p. 221, bears directly upon the songs and explains the importance of the child, Lady Psyche's daughter, for the poem:

"I may tell you that the songs were not an afterthought. Before the first edition came out I deliberated with myself whether I should put songs in between the separate divisions of the poem; again, I thought, the poem will explain itself; but the public did not see that the child, as you say, was the heroine of the piece, and at last I conquered my laziness and inserted them. You would be still more certain that the child was the true heroine if, instead of the first song as it now stands,

> As thro' the land at eve we went,

I had printed the first song which I wrote, 'The losing of the child.' The child is sitting on the bank of a river, and playing with flowers; a flood comes down; a dam has been broken through; the child is borne down by the flood; the whole village distracted; after a time the flood has subsided; the child is thrown safe and sound again upon the bank, and all the women are in raptures. I quite forget the words of the ballad, but I think I may have it somewhere."

It is really the child that softens the heart of the princess and makes her feel that she is a woman with a woman's tender love for children.

Four of the songs—*Tears, Idle Tears, O Swallow, Swallow, Now Sleeps the Crimson Petal*, and *Come Down, O Maid*—appeared in the 1847 edition of *The Princess;* the others were added as interludes between the parts of the poem in 1850.

I AS THRO' THE LAND

In 1576 Richard Edwards published a lyric the theme of which was, "the falling out of faithful friends renewing is of love," a theme very similar to that of *As Thro' the Land.*

II SWEET AND LOW

This familiar and beautiful lullaby, though sung by the women of the college, expresses their tender feeling toward children.

III THE SPLENDOUR FALLS

Tennyson said that when he was at the Lakes of Killarney, Ireland, in 1848, he heard "eight distinct echoes" of a bugle blown beneath the "Eagle's nest." It is said that some of the fame of these lakes as a place of romantic scenery is to be attributed to this beautiful lyric.

IV TEARS, IDLE TEARS

This, for many understanding readers the most impressive of the *Songs*, is sung by "a maid, Of those beside her" in Ida's tent. Tennyson once said to his son: "The passion of the past, the abiding in the transient, was expressed in *Tears, Idle Tears*, which was written in the yellowing autumntide at Tintern Abbey, full for me of its by-gone memories. Few know that it is a blank verse lyric." (*Memoir*, I, 253.)

Page 50. V SWALLOW, SWALLOW

At the completion of *Tears, Idle Tears* the princess asks the prince (who is disguised as a woman) to sing a song of promise, not one that "moans about the retrospect." The prince sings the *Swallow* song, in which a lover in the north, seeing a swallow flying southward in the autumn, bids it take a message to his sweetheart in the south.

VI THY VOICE IS HEARD

Lilia, that one of Ida's maids who would be like her, sings this song, the theme of which is the nerving of the warrior for combat by the memory of his wife and babes.

VII HOME THEY BROUGHT

This song, which is sung after the battle in which the prince and his comrades are wounded, expresses the motive of *The Princess*—the power of love for children—from a point of view different from those of the preceding songs. The child rescues its widowed mother from despair.

VIII OUR ENEMIES HAVE FALL'N

Princess Ida, holding Psyche's babe in her arms, sings this song of triumph over the defeat of the Prince's forces. It is not a song of relentless triumph, however, for at its close Ida offers the wounded men "the tender ministries Of female hands and hospitality."

Page 51. IX ASK ME NO MORE

The princess has scorned love, but, like the elemental forces of nature, it is irresistible, and in the end she needs must yield to it.

X NOW SLEEPS THE CRIMSON PETAL

Watching at night by the side of the wounded prince, Princess Ida reads this song aloud.

7. *Danaë to the stars.* Danaë, the beautiful daughter of a king of Argos, was imprisoned by her father in a brazen tower, but Zeus visited her in the form of a golden shower.

XI COME DOWN, O MAID

This "small sweet Idyl" is also read by the princess as she watches by the side of the wounded prince. She feels love calling her from the lofty heights to his home in the "smiling valleys" where true happiness awaits her. Tennyson considered this idyl as "amongst his most successful work."

12. *foxlike in the vine.* Cf. Song of Solomon 2:15—"Take us the foxes, the little foxes, that spoil the vines."

13. *the silver horns.* Snow-capped mountain peaks. This song, written in Switzerland, describes the Alpine heights and gorges and the "sweet, rich valleys."

15. *firths of ice.* Glaciers.

29–31. These lines have called forth much praise for their beauty.

IN MEMORIAM A. H. H.

A. H. H., in whose memory this poem was written, was Arthur Henry Hallam, son of the historian, Henry Hallam, and intimate friend of Tennyson from the Cambridge days of the two young men to the time of Hallam's death, September 15, 1833. Arthur Hallam and Tennyson were "Apostles" at Cambridge (see text p. 1), they traveled together in France and Spain and in other parts of the Continent, and they had the greatest admiration and respect for each other's powers of mind and purity of heart. Hallam, who had become engaged to Tennyson's sister Emily, died very suddenly—of apoplexy, the medical record said—"in Vienna's fatal walls," while on a continental tour with his father. His body was taken to England and buried at Clevedon, Somersetshire, on the Bristol Channel, January 3, 1834.

The lyrics which compose the poem were not written consecutively, but at intervals, the period of composition stretching out to seventeen years at least. Tennyson said that the "way of [the poem's] being written was so queer that if there were a blank space I would put in a poem." Despite the irregularity of composition there is a satisfying coherence in the lyrics composing the elegy, and "a clear advance toward a definite goal of thought and feeling" is discoverable by the careful reader. *In Memoriam* "is a poem, *not* an actual biography," said Tennyson, ". . . a kind of *Divina Commedia*, ending with happiness. . . . The different moods of sorrow as in a drama are dramatically given, and my conviction that fear, doubts, and suffering will find answer to relief only through Faith in a God of Love. 'I' is not always the author speaking of himself, but the voice of the human race speaking through him." (*Memoir*, I, 305.)

Tennyson said that the poem fell into "nine natural groups," marking the stages of his grief, the progress and development of his thought. His nine groups were as follows: (1) I–VIII; (2) IX–XIX; (3) XX–XXVII; (4) XXVIII–XLIX; (5) L–LVIII; (6) LIX–LXXI; (7) LXXII–XCVIII; (8) XCIX–CIII; (9) CIV–CXXXI.

Mr. John F. Genung and Professor A. C. Bradley agree in arranging the cantos of the poem as follows: (1) I–XXVII; (2) XXVIII–LXXVII; (3) LXXVIII–CIII; (4) CIV–CXXXI. These scholars, in harmony with a remark of Tennyson's that the divisions of the poem were made by the Christmastide sections, mark their divisions with these sections (XXVIII, LXXVIII, CIV). The first of these divisions, which Bradley names "To the First Christmas," refers to the first Christmas after Hallam's death, the second to the Christmas of the next year. The third refers, not to the Christmas of the next again, as might be expected, but to that of 1837 (see note to CIV below). Professor Bradley suggests also a twofold division of the poem, basing this division on the fact that with section LXXVIII grief, which up to that point has been the predominant feeling of the poet, begins to give way to joy. Most analysts, however, consider section LXXXV the one in which the transition from grief to joy begins. (For Professor Bradley's subdivisions see his *A Commentary on Tennyson's "In Memoriam,"* pp. 30–35. Genung's subdivisions are given in his *Tennyson's "In Memoriam,"* p. 90. Other arrangements of the poem are recorded in Eugene Parsons's *In Memoriam*, p. 138.)

There have been many conflicting opinions concerning *In Memoriam*. Some objectors to the poem have called it professedly but not truly philosophical. Others criticise "the wearisome plaintiveness—the almost whining tone—of the earlier portions." In a "Journal" entry for January, 1851, Emerson wrote: "*In Memoriam* is the commonplaces of condolence among good Unitarians in the first week of mourning. The consummate skill of the versification is the sole merit." Mr. Henry van Dyke said that none of the poems that have blossomed in the valley of the shadow of death "is more rich in significance, more perfect in beauty of form and spirit, or more luminous with the triumph of light and love over darkness and mortality, than *In Memoriam*, the greatest of English elegies" (*The Poetry of Tennyson*, p. 131). A truer characterization than any of these, perhaps, is that of Louis Cazamian, who says on p. 1202 of *A History of English Literature:* "*In Memoriam* reflects in every line the moral and religious conflict of the century in the aspect it assumed about 1850, and the poem will always bear the ineffaceable stamp of this date. Yet the thoughts therein expressed are deep enough to make the conflict not so much one of a particular epoch, as of all time; they voice universal emotions."

[PROLOGUE]

Obiit MDCCCXXXIII. "He died in 1833."

In the prologue (ll. 1–44), which was the last part of the poem to be composed, Tennyson voices his conviction that only through faith can man understand the eternal purpose of God and know the certainty of immortality.

5. *orbs of light and shade*. The earth and the other planets, half in sunlight, half in shadow.

27–8. *mind and soul . . . as before*. "Before the growth of knowledge disturbed their union," i.e., when there was still an age of faith.

32. *thy light*. The light of knowledge.

42. *wasted youth*. Youth made waste by sorrow.

Page 52. I

45. *him*. Goethe, whom Tennyson gave a place "foremost among the moderns as a lyrical poet," because of his being "consummate in so many different styles." (*Memoir*, II, 392.)

II

67. *the clock*. The church-tower clock.

72. *thousand years*. The yew lives to be very old. Wordsworth wrote of an old Keswick guide who believed that a gigantic yew fallen along a road over which he conducted tourists was "in existence before the flood."

III

87. *my own*. Sorrow's, not the poet's.

Page 53. V

117. *weeds.* Garments.

VII

165. *Dark house.* No. 67 Wimpole Street, London, a house belonging to Henry Hallam, the residence of his son Arthur while he was studying law.

Page 54. IX

201. *Fair ship.* The vessel that carried Hallam's body from the Continent to England. The vessel sailed from Trieste, which, although an Austrian port, had the "air of an Italian city."
210. *Phosphor.* The morning star.
220. Cf. section LXXIX.

X

235–6. *kneeling hamlet . . grapes of God.* The communion altar or table is often placed in the chancel of an English church, and near the altar or under it the members of the church were sometimes buried.
240. *tangle.* Seaweed.

XI

245. *wold.* Upland plain.
246. *furze.* A spiny evergreen shrub.
247. *gossamers.* Strands of cobweb.
251. *lessening towers.* The church towers, a striking feature of Lincolnshire landscapes, are pictured as diminishing in the distance as the country stretches away to the seacoast.

Page 55. XIII

293. *many years.* A vocative; or in apposition with "Time."

XV

This section should be compared with section XI.

330. *thy motions.* Those of the ship.

Page 56. XVI

342. *calm despair and wild unrest.* Note that these expressions are repeated, the first from XI, 256, the second from XV, 335. The poet is bewildered by the swift alternation of calm despair and wild unrest.

XVIII

Professor A. C. Bradley says that this poem on the burial is in keeping with Tennyson's statement that *In Memoriam* was not strictly biographical. This burial poem *precedes* the first Christmas section, but the burial did not really occur until after Christmas, 1833 (January 3, 1834). Moreover, Hallam was buried, not in Clevedon churchyard, but in Clevedon church; and Tennyson did not see Clevedon till years later.

389. *bear the head.* Hallam's pallbearers were workers on the estate of Clevedon Court, which had been his mother's early home.
394–5. Cf. II Kings 4 : 34.

XIX

This lyric is said to have been written in Tintern Abbey, which is on the Wye, a river flowing into the Severn a short distance above Clevedon. Vienna, the place of Hallam's death, is on the Danube.
407. *hushes half the babbling Wye.* The tide comes up into the Wye for about half its course, arrests its flow to the sea, and silences it through very fullness (l. 409).

Page 57. XX

A further contrast between "the lesser griefs" that lack no voice and the anguish which is dumb for very depth.

XXI

In this lyric the poet resents certain charges that he thinks may be made against him—(1) sentimentalism and hence insincerity (ll. 443–4), (2) vanity (ll. 445–8), (3) selfish isolation in days when stirring things are abroad (ll. 449–56).
437–40. It should be remembered that Hallam was not buried in the open churchyard, but in the church itself. These lines, therefore, represent another departure from the biographical (see note to XVIII, above). Professor Bradley remarks that "the conventions of the classical pastoral elegy, in which the singer is supposed to be a shepherd," occur only here and there in *In Memoriam*, and "perhaps generally with a jarring effect." Probably few readers would say that a "jarring effect" results from the use of these conventions in these particular lines.
451–2. These lines have been thought to refer to the Chartist movement of 1837–1848, a movement for amelioration of the social and industrial condition of the working classes.
454–5. Probably a reference to the discovery of Neptune. Professor Bradley thinks that Tennyson may not have referred to any one discovery, but he considers the phrase, "to feel from world to world" "beautifully appropriate to the process by which the existence of Neptune was guessed at."

XXIII

496. *Pan.* The god of flocks and pastures, of forests and their wild life, of "universal nature."

506. *Argive*. Grecian.
508. *Arcady*. Arcadia (poetical *Arcady*) was a mountainous and picturesque region of Greece, celebrated for its rustic innocence and untroubled quiet.

Page 58. XXIV

511–2. A reference to sunspots.

XXVI

552. *proper scorn*. Self-scorn.

XXVII

565–8. With these lines the poem is seen to have completed a definite stage of progress. Professor Bradley suggests that the phrases "I hold it true," and "loved and lost" may be intended to indicate this accomplishment by reminding the reader of ll. 45 and 59 in section I.

XXVIII

573. *four hamlets round*. These hamlets near the old Tennyson home at Somersby are thought to be Tetford, Hagg, Langton, and Ormsby.
577–80. Each church seems to have four bells, the peals of which are finely interpreted by the four phrases of ll. 579–80.
581. *This year*. 1833, as is proved by XXX, l. 620.

Page 59. XXX

612. *one mute Shadow*. The dead friend, Hallam, not Death.
626–36. *"They do not die" . . . Hope was born*. See the two extracts, text p. 210, the one beginning "The life after death," the other, "If the immediate life after death."

XXXI

637. *Lazarus*. The brother of Mary and Martha, who was raised from the dead by Christ. See John 11 : 32–44. For Browning's treatment of the story see *An Epistle*, text p. 326. For a treatment of the story in a totally different spirit from that of Tennyson or Browning see L. N. Andreyev's *Lazarus*, in *Best Russian Short Stories*.
648. *Olivet*. A hill near Jerusalem.
651. *He*. Lazarus.
652. *that Evangelist*. St. John, whose Gospel contains the story.

Page 60. XXXII

663. *bathes the Saviour's feet*. When Christ was at the home of Lazarus, Mary took ointment of spikenard and anointed his feet and wiped them with her hair.

XXXIII

The Mary-spirit of simple faith, which is marked by purity, blessedness, and active goodness, must be respected by the man whose religion is an intellectual one and who holds himself answerable to no authority but his conscience.

XXXIV

689. *round . . . orb*. The earth and the sun.

XXXV

711. *Æonian hills*. Hills everlasting.
722. *Satyr-shape*. Satyrs were sylvan demigods, often represented with the ears and the tail of a horse.

XXXVI

When questions about Christ came to Tennyson in writing, he would tell his son "to answer for him that he had given his belief in *In Memoriam*," especially in this section.
725–8. *truths in manhood . . . current coin*. Though the great spiritual truths are inseparable from the idea of human nature ("manhood"), they are nevertheless only dimly known to man through his intuition alone, and to Christ, whose life made them so clear that all may understand them, man must "yield all blessing."
733. *the Word*. "The Word as used by St. John, the Revelation of the Eternal Thought of the Universe"—cf. John 1 : 14. (*Memoir*, I, 312.)
739. *wild eyes*. Of island savages.

Page 61. XXXVII

741. *Urania*. The Muse of astronomy, here conceived of as the goddess of heavenly or lofty poetry.
746. *Parnassus*. A mountain in Greece, sacred to Apollo and the Muses.
747. *laurel*. This tree or shrub, the foliage of which was used to crown poets, grew freely on Mt. Parnassus.
749. *Melpomene*. The Muse of tragedy usually, but here of elegy.

XXXIX

This section, written in April, 1868, appeared first in 1870, this late date of composition making understandable the action of the poet in l. 778, an action which would be puzzling on the part of one who had addressed the yew only a few months before in the words of section II.
779. *fruitful cloud and living smoke*. The cloud of smoke is pollen (hence "fruitful," "living").

XL

805. *unto thee.* Hallam.

Page 62. XLI

835–6. These lines probably refer to the horror of the lower world, described by Dante and, to some degree, by Virgil. *Forgotten* (l. 836) is puzzling. Bradley suggests "forgotten by Heaven."

XLII

852. *the mind.* The poet's mind.

XLIII

Mr. F. W. Robertson sums up the idea of this section in these words: "If death be unconscious trance, love, as after sleep, will begin again."

858. The soul, like a flower, closes at night.

871. *spiritual prime.* The reawakening of spirits on resurrection dawn.

XLIV

For a long discussion of this section see Bradley's *A Commentary on Tennyson's "In Memoriam,"* pp. 125–36.

876. *shut the doorways of his head.* This phrase has been interpreted as referring (1) to the closing of the sutures of the skull in the growing child, or (2) to the closing of the organs of sense by death.

882. *Lethean.* Lethe was the river of forgetfulness.

Page 63. XLVI

916. *those five years.* The five years of friendship between Hallam and Tennyson.

XLVII

In this section Tennyson rejects the idea that in the next world personality will disappear and each soul will remerge "in the general Soul."

XLVIII

The idea of this section is that the poet's "short swallow-flights of song" are expressions of his feelings, not philosophical discussions of his doubts and questions.

XLIX

955. *a shiver'd lance.* A broken ray of light.

961. *thy look.* "Thy" refers to the traveller of XXI, l. 441.

L

In this section the poet breathes a prayer for the spirit of the lost Hallam to be near him when faith in God fails him and men's actions convict them of pettiness and evil.

976. *a Fury slinging flame.* The Furies are represented as carrying torches.

Page 64. LI

The wisdom that comes through death would lead the dead to make divine allowance for all human failure. Hence the poet wants the spirit of Hallam near his side.

LII

1011. *the sinless years.* The record of the highest ideal, i.e., the life of Christ.

LIII

Of lines 1021–4 Tennyson said: "There's a passionate heart of nature in a rake sometimes—the nature that yields emotionally may come straighter than a prig's."

LIV

However marred by pain, sin, doubts, and bad heredity, every life, the poet trusts, will reach a goal of good—not one will be wasted or destroyed. Lines 1041–4 voice this belief for the lower animals, a thing which leads Bradley to say that he knows of no other expression by Tennyson of the thought that animals may live again.

Page 65. LV

When his faith is shaken by the ruthlessness of nature toward the individual, the poet clings blindly to the larger hope and calls to the shadowy embodiment of his longing, the Lord of all.

1059–60. These lines indicate Tennyson's familiarity with the phenomena of natural selection, of which Darwin was to write in *The Origin of Species* (1859).

LVI

1074–5. *cliff . . . gone.* Geological studies have disclosed the fossils of numerous forms of life that have become extinct.

1098. *thy voice.* Hallam's.

LVII

For an interesting discussion in which he rejects the claims that have been made for this section as the turning point in the poem, see Bradley's *A Commentary on Tennyson's "In Memoriam,"* pp. 28–9.

1105. *your cheeks are pale.* Those of the poet's fellow-mourners for Hallam.

1115. *"Ave."* Hail, greetings. Literally, "Be well." Used by the Romans as a farewell address to the dead.

LVIII

1125. *high Muse.* Probably Urania. See note to XXXVII, l. 741.

LIX

This section, which was added in the fourth edition of the poem (1851), should be contrasted with III and compared with LXVI.

Page 66. LX

The sections LX to LXV are concerned with the question, "Does my dead friend remember me?" the poet's desire that Hallam should think of him holding strong throughout the group.

1145. *nobler.* Very noble. (Not a comparative in the usual English sense.)

LXI

1162. *change.* Exchange.

1168. *blanch'd with darkness.* Weak, frail, like plants grown without sunlight.

1169. *doubtful shore.* The earth.

1172. *soul of Shakespeare.* The poet can point to no greater intellect than Shakespeare's, to no soul capable of greater love for a friend than his. R. H. Shepherd says "the allusion indicates a deep and probably recent study of the sonnets of Shakespeare."

LXII

1173. *Tho'.* Equivalent to "yet."

1177. *declined.* Looked down, stooped.

LXIV

Tennyson is said to have composed this lyric while he was walking down the Strand.

1206. *golden keys.* Symbols of high public office.

Page 67. LXV

Bradley remarks that this is perhaps the first happy lyric in *In Memoriam.* In it the sorrowing poet ceases to worry about remembrance and rejoices in the thoughts that Love is too precious to be lost, and that the old friendship is dear to both the living and the dead.

LXVI

1237. *You.* Some person—probably a friend—who has seen the poet's gloom and who now wonders at the change in him, is addressed.

LXVII

1255. *broad water of the west.* The Severn. It is about nine miles wide where it empties into Bristol Channel.

1268. *Thy tablet.* Hallam's tablet is in the centre of the western wall of the aisle almost opposite the organ, underneath which is the vault where the body lies.

LXVIII

"In dreams, by an illusion, the sadness of the mourner is transferred to the lost, and he is conceived of as sad too." (Robertson.)

LXIX

1288. *chatter'd.* The chatterers, said one writer, were those whose lives had not been deepened by sorrow.

1298. *angel of the night.* An angel of "the night of sorrow, the divine Thing in the gloom," said Tennyson.

Page 68. LXX

1317. *beyond the will.* As the strivings to "see the features right" cease and the poet yields to sleep, his soul is soothed by a sudden flashing forth of the face he loved so well.

LXXI

1324. *thro' summer France.* A reference to the travels in France made by Hallam and Tennyson in the summer of 1830. The re-creation of their experiences at that time is singularly vivid.

LXXII

The thought of the poet goes in bitterness to the first anniversary of Hallam's death, September 15. His mood, says Beeching, is one of "wild grief, entirely desperate."

1339. *blow the poplar white.* By turning up the under side of the leaves.

Page 69. LXXIV

1387. *the wise below.* The wise among the dead rather than the wise now on earth. Each interpretation, however, has a number of champions.

LXXV

1401. *these fading days.* Days that quickly fall away.

LXXVI

1418. *secular abyss.* Of time, or of ages.

1420. *mouldering of a yew.* The comparison is suggested by the fact that the yew lives to a great age. See note to section II, l. 72.

1421. *matin songs.* The poems of the great early poets.

1425. *these.* Yew and oak.

LXXVII

In this section, which ends the second cycle of the poem, the singer insists that he will sing his love because to utter love is sweet. He is under no illusion that his songs will bring him fame.

1429–32. *What hope . . . of time.* Things near us are seen in false proportion. And so modern rhyme, as it recedes in time, will thin out and appear greatly contracted; i.e., it will decrease more and more in import.

LXXVIII

1445. *Christmas.* Christmas of 1834, the second after Hallam's death. Note the contrast between this Christmas and that of the preceding year, a contrast in weather and a contrast in the mood and feelings of the household and of the poet himself. Cf. sections XXX and CV.

1449. *yule-clog.* The log burnt on Christmas eve.

1455. *mimic picture. Tableaux vivants,* or charades.

Page 70. LXXIX

1465. "*More than my brothers are to me.*" See IX, l. 220.

1466. *thee.* Charles, Tennyson's older brother.

1468. *in fee.* In complete possession.

1482. *he.* Hallam.

LXXX

"If Hallam had lived and I had died," the poet fancies in this section, "he would have turned his sorrow into gain."

1492. *stay'd.* Supported, sustained.

1497. *His credit.* The behavior with which I credit him in case of my fancied death (ll. 1489–96).

LXXXI

Bradley, who insists that "could I have said" is a question, says that the first stanza of this section is unintelligible unless an interrogation mark is placed after "ear."

1511. *grain.* His love for Hallam.

LXXXII

1519. *these.* The "changes" of l. 1514.

Page 71. LXXXIII

1529. *the northern shore.* England.

1530. *new-year.* Spring.

1533. *the clouded noons.* The noons (days) are cloudy in England before springtime.

LXXXIV

Another section whose subject is what might have been.

1559. *cypress of her orange flower.* Hallam's death changed the orange blossoms (symbol of marriage) of Emily Tennyson to cypress (symbol of mourning).

1563–4. *I see . . . fire.* One commentator remarks upon the unfortunate fact that these, which he considers the finest lines in this lyric, recall Lamb's *Dream Children.*

LXXXV

This poem was addressed to Edmund Law Lushington (the "true in word" of l. 1597), an "Apostle," professor of Greek at the University of Glasgow, and Tennyson's brother-in-law by his marriage to the poet's sister Cecilia in 1842. Some commentators consider the poem the turning point in the elegy, the point, that is, where grief begins to yield to joy. Bradley, in an interesting discussion of this question, rejects both LVII and LXXXV and selects LXXVIII, the second Christmas poem, as the turning point. (For Bradley's discussion see his *A Commentary on Tennyson's "In Memoriam,"* pp. 27–9.) The poet is concerned with replying to three questions in the section: (1) what kind of life he is leading, (2) whether sorrow has dimmed or sustained his trust in things above, and (3) whether love for Hallam has made him incapable of other loves.

1613. *Intelligences.* Angels.

1620. *cycled times.* Successive periods of human progress.

1626. *O heart.* Hallam's, when he was living.

1659. *all-assuming.* All-devouring.

1677. *nature.* Human nature.

Page 73. LXXXVI

Tennyson is said to have quoted this poem frequently as giving "pre-eminently his sense of the joyous peace in Nature."

1716–7. *breathing bare . . . space.* Clearing the clouds from the sky.

1719. *shadowing . . . horned flood.* Darkening the winding river.

LXXXVII

1729. *reverend walls.* Trinity College, Cambridge.

1743. *walk of limes.* Trinity Avenue.

1749 ff. *we held debate,* etc. A reference to the "Apostles" group and their discussions.

1767–8. *over . . . Angelo.* According to the *Memoir* (I, 38), Tennyson wrote these lines "from what Arthur Hallam said after reading of the prominent ridge of bone over the eyes of Michael Angelo: 'Alfred, look over my eyes; surely I have the bar of Michael Angelo.'"

LXXXVIII

1769. *Wild bird.* The nightingale.

1770. *quicks.* The quickset or hawthorn hedges.

1773. *fierce extremes.* The extremes are grief and melancholy on one side and joy and delight on the other.

Page 74. LXXXIX

1782. *this flat lawn.* The lawn at Somersby, Tennyson's home. Hallam's visits at Somersby are lived over by the poet in happy retrospect in this section.

1792. *purlieus of the law.* The Inner Temple, London, where Hallam studied law.

1804. *Tuscan poets.* Dante and Petrarch.

1816. *Socratic dream.* As found in Plato, who was a great favorite of Hallam's.

1827–8. *crimson-circled . . . grave.* Venus, setting, sinks into the sea. According to the nebular hypothesis, the sun is the nuclear remains of a great nebulous cloud from which the planets were hurled into space. In a sense, therefore, the sun may be spoken of as the father of the planets.

XC

1836. *This bitter seed.* The ideas expressed in ll. 1837–52.

XCI

1860. *sea-blue bird.* The kingfisher.

1862. *in time.* In the life on earth.

Page 75. XCII

Belief in the idea, advanced by some analysts, that in these lines Tennyson rejects spiritualism as a means of bringing back the dead, is not essential to an understanding of them. He merely means that any vision, any realization of Hallam's presence to the *senses,* would be unconvincing—a "canker of the brain," an hallucination.

XCIII

1897. *thy sightless range.* Where Hallam ranges invisible.

1903. *the frame.* The body.

XCV

On a summer night, left alone in the garden at Somersby once frequented by Hallam, Tennyson reads over his friend's letters, and suddenly the soul of Hallam is flashed on the soul of the poet.

1930. *the filmy shapes.* Night-moths.

1956. *The living soul.* Tennyson once remarked: "I've often had a strange feeling of being wound and wrapped in the Great Soul."

1963. *my trance.* Tennyson is writing of his own experience here. He once said to a friend: "Sometimes as I sit here alone in this great room I get carried away out of sense and body, and rapt into mere existence, till the accidental touch or movement of one of my own fingers is like a great shock and blow and brings the body back with a terrible start."

Page 76. XCVI

Mr. Beeching calls this a poem of Faith and Doubt, suggested by the eighth quatrain of XCV.

1986. *Sweet-hearted, you.* Some woman of simple faith.

1989. *one.* Hallam. In a sonnet Hallam spoke of doubt making "an unkind December of [his] spring," a remark which seems to have some bearing on ll. 1991–4.

2006–8. See Exodus, chapters 19 and 32.

XCVII

2009. *My love.* The poet's love, which he personifies and treats as finding an echo of itself everywhere.

2014. *thee.* Hallam.

2023. *earnest.* Proof, pledge, assurance.

Page 77. XCVIII

2045. *You.* Tennyson's brother Charles, who in 1836 planned to go to Vienna on his wedding trip.

2047. *I was there with him.* In July, 1832.

2051. *wisp.* The will-o'-the-wisp.

2053–4. The poet never went to Vienna.

2061. *Gnarr.* Snarl, or growl.

2065. *mother town.* Metropolis.

XCIX

2077. *Risest thou thus, dim dawn, again.* The second anniversary of Hallam's death, September 15 (see section LXXII).

C

This section and the three immediately following it allude to the removal of the Tennyson family from Somersby to High Beech, Epping Forest, in 1837. In taking leave of the old home the poet feels Hallam's presence everywhere.

Page 78. CI

In this poem he lingers on the things loved in his childhood at the old home.

2127. *the lesser wain.* Ursa Minor, usually called the Little Dipper, in the northern heavens.

2129. *gird.* Encircle.

2130. *hern and crake.* Heron and corncrake.

2138. *glebe.* Cultivated land.

CII

2147. *Two spirits.* "The first," Tennyson said, "is the love of the native place; the second, the same love enhanced by the memory of the friend."

CIII

This is a dream or allegory of the voyage of life which brings the poet content.

2170. *maidens.* Tennyson said these were "the muses, arts—all that makes life beautiful here, which we hope will pass with us beyond the grave." In so far as the allegory applies to the life of the poet and not to human life in general, the maidens symbolize his own aspirations and activities within the spheres over which they preside as Muses.

2172. *river.* The river is life, flowing from "the high—the divine" ("hidden summits," l. 2171).

2181. *must go.* In death.

2189–90. "The great progress of the age, as well as the opening of another world" (Tennyson).

2191–6. Symbolic of the growth—intellectually, artistically, spiritually—of the poet.

2195. *Anakim.* Giants, sons of Anak; see Numbers 13 : 33.

2216. *they enter'd in.* See note to l. 2170 above.

Page 79. CIV

This is the *third Christmas poem* after Hallam's death, but it does not commemorate the *third Christmas*, that of 1835. For that year and for 1836 there were no Christmas poems. The Christmas of 1837 is the subject of this section.

2223. *A single church.* Waltham Abbey, some two or three miles from Beech Hill House, in Epping Forest, which became the new home of the Tennysons in 1837.

CV

2235. *stranger's land.* A reference to the new home.

2244. *dying use.* The changing custom. In the new home the family does not celebrate Christmas as it did at Somersby.

2250. *bowl of wassail.* Ale or wine flavored with spices, sugar, toast, etc.

Mantle warm, Redden brightly, blush.

2257. *rising worlds.* Rising stars.

2260. *closing cycle rich in good.* The final period, sometimes called the Golden Age, when life will be perfect.

CVI

2288. *the thousand years of peace.* The thousand years mentioned in Revelation, chapter 20, during which holiness is to be triumphant.

2292. *the Christ that is to be.* The poet said that one of his meanings of this was [the time] "when Christianity without bigotry will triumph" and "when the controversies of creeds should have vanished." (*Memoir*, I, 326.)

Page 80. CVII

2293. *day . . . born.* February 1, 1838, the twenty-seventh anniversary of Hallam's birth.

2304. *iron horns.* Ice-covered branches.

2305. *drifts.* Some analysts say the poet meant "snow," others "clouds," and still others "winds."

CVIII

In this section the poet voices the futility of "barren faith" and "vacant yearning" and expresses his conviction that through sorrow he may become wise.

CIX

In the six poems beginning with this section, the poet, searching for the "fruit" of sorrow-wisdom, finds it in studying and in exalting as an ideal the noble character of Hallam.

2344. *April.* Youthful.

2356. Note the connection of CIX with CVIII, from l. 2331 to this line.

Page 81. CX

The subject is the influence of the noble character of Hallam.

2358. *of rathe and riper years.* Both the younger and the elder.

2363. *serpent.* Deceiver, liar.

CXI

2377. *churl.* Rude, uncultivated.

2379. *golden ball.* The decoration of the crown and the scepter of a king.

2394. *villain.* Common, vulgar, ignoble.

2395. *Drew in.* Narrowed.

CXII

2401. Note linking of this section with CVIII, l. 2331, through this line.

2402. *with temperate eyes.* Undazzled, with little enthusiasm.

2403. *glorious insufficiencies.* The phrase is not applied to Hallam. The poet is not saying that he is compelled to a choice between "glorious insufficiencies" and "narrower perfectness" (l. 2404). He holds both of them of slight import, for both fall far short of Hallam.

2408. *the lesser lords of doom.* "Those," said Tennyson, "that have free will but less intellect."

CXIII

2417. This line indicates the connection of the section with CVIII through l. 2331.

2424. Cf. extract beginning "He [Hallam] would have been," text p. 207.

Page 82. CXIV

Robertson comments: "Knowledge [is] less high than charity. In [Hallam] both were blended."

2440. *Her pillars*. An allusion to "the pillars of Hercules, the farthest boundary of the ancient mariners" (Beeching).

2446. *cannot . . . death*. Unequal to the fight because she cannot prove a life after death.

2448. *Pallas*. Pallas (Minerva), goddess of wisdom, sprang from the head of Zeus.

2453. *higher hand*. The hand of wisdom.

2458. This line connects the poem with CVIII, l. 2331, through the idea of wisdom.

CXV

2466. *burgeons . . . quick*. Bud the interlacing hedges of hawthorn, etc.

2467. *squares*. Fields.

2472. *sightless song*. Cf. Shelley's lines *To a Skylark*.

CXVI

2487. *meets the year*. The year is thought of as beginning in spring.

2488. *crescent prime*. Growing, advancing spring.

CXVII

2509–12. References to the hourglass, the sundial, the clock, and the heavenly bodies as recorders of time occur in these lines.

CXVIII

2514. *The giant*. The Titan Cronus, god of harvests, came erroneously to be called the god of time because of confusion of his name with Chronos ("Time").

2516. *As dying Nature's earth and lime*. As perishable, like the body, which is composed in part of earth and lime.

2520–3. These lines allude to the ideas of Laplace in his nebular hypothesis (early nineteenth century).

2528. For a discussion of the obscurities of the passage beginning with this line see Bradley's *A Commentary on Tennyson's "In Memoriam,"* pp. 214–5.

Page 83. CXIX

Contrast this section, in which the poet writes of a second visit to the house in Wimpole Street, with section VII, in which he recounts his first visit there after Hallam's death.

2544. *smell the meadow*. Possibly from loads of hay. For other possible explanations, see Bradley, p. 216.

CXX

2553. *I have not wasted breath*. In opposing the idea that death is the end of all.

2556. *Like Paul*. See I Corinthians 15 : 32.

2561–4. A protest against materialism—but not against evolution—couched in ironical language. For a discussion of Tennyson's purpose in italicizing "born" (l. 2564), see Bradley, p. 217.

CXXI

2565. *Sad Hesper*. The evening star, which, since it shines after sunset, looks down upon man as he ceases from labor and gives himself to sleep.

2573. *Bright Phosphor*. The morning star, which rises before the sun, and hence looks down upon a world waking to labor.

2581–2. *Hesper-Phosphor . . . is one*. As the evening star, Venus was called Hesper[us] by the ancients; as the morning star, Phosphor[us]. For a period of about 290 days Venus is the evening star; then for about the same period it becomes the morning star.

CXXII

The analysts do not agree on the questions as to (1) what occasion is referred to by "then" (l. 2585), and (2) whether or not the poet had in mind a still earlier time when he wrote "again" (l. 2588) and "once more" (l. 2589). Genung and Benham say that Tennyson referred to XCV, particularly to the trance there described. Bradley, though agreeing that CXXII is reminiscent of the trance in XCV, says that the last nine lines of CXXII point back very clearly to LXXXVI. But he also has another interpretation which seems even "likelier" to him. For his discussion see his *A Commentary*, pp. 219–26.

2602. *a bow*. Rainbow colors.

2603. *wizard lightnings*. Probably the idea was suggested by the aurora borealis.

Page 84. CXXIII

This beautiful poem could not have been written by one whose sense of wonder was not deeply stirred by the study of geology. Cf. ll. 259–65 of *Ode on the Death of the Duke of Wellington*, text p. 87.

CXXIV

2617–9. *That which . . . All*. Something there is—the infinite unknown—whose presence we feel both in moments of faith and in those of doubt, and our understanding cannot tell us whether its proper designation is He, They, One, or All.

CXXV

In whatever mood the poet sang, whatever bitterness was in his song, Love was in his singing—Love that will abide with him even till he go out into the deep to seek his friend.

CXXVII

2675–6. *fool-fury . . . dead.* The reference may be to the revolution of July, 1830, which forced Charles X to go into exile. Genung thinks that Tennyson had in mind the French revolutionary movement of 1848.
2683. *brute.* Ponderous.
2684. *Æon.* The period that the universe has existed.

Page 85. CXXVIII

2690. *he.* Love, of l. 2689.
2695. *throned races.* The dominant peoples; races now in power.
2711–2. *all . . . an end.* All, even the eddies (l. 2693) and degradations or retrogressions (l. 2695), work together toward some great end and purpose.

CXXX

Van Dyke, pointing out that in this poem Tennyson feels the spirit of Hallam to be in all nature, says that his idea is not like the pantheism of Shelley in *Adonais*, stanzas XLII and XLIII. Hallam, though dead, is still the object of the poet's ever deepening affection.

CXXXI

See extract beginning, "Yes, it is true," text p. 209, for a remark which Tennyson made in January, 1869, bearing on this section.
2741. *living will.* Free will in man, his "higher and enduring part" (Tennyson).
2743. *spiritual rock.* See I Corinthians 10 : 4.

[EPILOGUE]

2747. *conquer'd years.* See section I, l. 57.
The conclusion, or epilogue (ll. 2753–2896), has for its subject the marriage of Tennyson's youngest sister, Cecilia, to Professor Edmund Lushington, October 10, 1842. Thus *In Memoriam,* which "begins with a funeral," ends, as Tennyson said, "with a marriage—begins with death and ends in promise of a new life."
2758. *he.* Hallam.
2760. *that dark day.* The day of Hallam's death.
2802. *feet . . . dead.* Her feet on the vaults of the dead who are buried beneath the floor of the church.
2838. *stiller guest.* Hallam.

Page 87. THE EAGLE

Mr. Alfred Noyes, commenting on the "extraordinarily vivid and terse picture of *The Eagle,*" says, "Nobody who has ever stood upon a mountain at any great height, over a lively sea, with a brisk wind blowing, can fail to recognize the vivid truth of that line,

> The wrinkled sea beneath him crawls.

Not only in the simplicity and precision of the phrasing is it masterly; but its music also is alive. The long vowel-sound of the word upon which the rhyme falls gives the very sound of the brawling waves in the caverns below. The line moves and shines and sounds like the sea; and yet there is not a trace of effort. It is as lucid and simple as all greatness always is. Not a rhyme is forced. Nothing is affected. Everything is concentrated on expressing as perfectly as possible the picture that the poet had in his mind." (Noyes, in *Some Aspects of Poetry,* p. 163.)

ODE ON THE DEATH OF THE DUKE OF WELLINGTON

Arthur Wellesley, Duke of Wellington, was the idol of the British nation at the time of his death, September 14, 1852. He had a distinguished career first as a military man and then as a statesman, the high point in his military career being his defeat of Napoleon at the Battle of Waterloo, 1815. This poem was published November 18, 1852, the day of Wellington's burial under the dome of Saint Paul's Cathedral, in "London's central roar." Professor Alden, in his *Tennyson,* p. 70, speaks of the poem as "a notable example of 'free rhythm.' The opening strophe," he says, "suggests the irregular movement of the crowds in the streets, on the day when the duke is to be buried. In the second our attention is turned toward St. Paul's Cathedral, and in the third the procession begins to move. Later we approach the cathedral, and hear the sound of tolling bell mingle with that of the music within. The movement of the remaining strophes is one of thought rather than action, but at the close we find ourselves inside the cathedral, hearing the dead march, the 'Dust to dust' of the burial service, and the final prayer."
See extract beginning "Writing to order," text p. 210.
37. *iron nerve.* Wellington's tenacity and coolness led to his being nicknamed the "Iron Duke."
42. *World-victor's victor.* Wellington was the victor in his contest with Napoleon, the "World-victor."
49. *cross of gold.* St. Paul's is surmounted by a golden cross.
56. A reference to the fact that the names of

Wellington's conquests were inscribed on the funeral car in letters of gold.

64–6. *many a clime . . . victory.* Wellington won victories for the English in Holland, India, Denmark, Portugal, Spain, France, Belgium.

80–2. Lord Nelson, one of England's greatest admirals, speaks these lines. He was killed at the Battle of Trafalgar in 1805 and is buried in St. Paul's.

99–100. *Assaye . . . few.* A town in Hindostan, where in 1803 Wellington (then General Wellesley) won his first great victory, "his fiery few"—not 5000—defeating a force of over 40,000.

105. *labour'd rampart-lines.* Those which in 1809–1810 Wellington constructed for the purpose of fortifying Lisbon and a large area around it. In 1813 he forced the French across the Pyrenees into France.

123. *loud sabbath.* Waterloo was fought on Sunday.

129. *Heaven . . . ray.* It is said that just as the British and Germans charged the French and overthrew them the light of the setting sun broke through the clouds that had obscured it all day and glittered on the bayonets of the victors.

137. *Baltic and the Nile.* Battles in which Nelson defeated Napoleon's forces. See note to ll. 8 and 9 of *Buonaparte*, above.

172. *guard . . . coasts.* Wellington was very active in 1844–1845 in insisting upon the repair of England's coast defences and the increase of her naval and military equipment.

188. *Truth-teller . . . Alfred.* Alfred the Great was so called.

194. *Followed . . . lands.* Austria alone of all the European powers did not have a military representative at the funeral.

196. *all her stars.* Wellington in addition to his successive titles of baron, viscount, earl, marquis, and duke, was a knight of twenty-six orders and a marshal of eight nations.

256–7. These lines form another instance of the poet's frequent expression of his belief in human immortality.

Page 91. THE CHARGE OF THE LIGHT BRIGADE

The indecisive battle of Balaklava, in which the English cavalry made the heroic charge here described, was fought October 25, 1854, between the Russian army and the allied English, French, and Turkish troops. Tennyson wrote the poem after reading in *The Times* a description of the cavalry charge in which was used the phrase, "some one had blundered." The poem made Tennyson "known to a completely new audience, with whom otherwise he could scarcely have gained contact, not only to the soldiers . . . but also to all the commonplace elements in the nation, indifferent to poetry in general, but ready to embrace a poet who gave expression to a transient mood engendered by war fever." (Hugh I'Anson Fausset, in *Tennyson*, pp. 185–6.) With this poem Tennyson became "a revered and representative Laureate." See letter to John Forster, text pp. 215–16.

12. *Some one had blunder'd.* This was probably one Lord Lucan, who did not understand the exact meaning of an order from his superior, and himself ordered Lord Cardigan, leader of the Light Cavalry, to charge.

18–20. *Cannon . . . of them.* The Russian forces were stationed at the end of a long valley both sides of which were held by their infantry and cavalry. The charging "Light Brigade" was therefore exposed to cannon fire from both the sides and the front.

38. *Not the six hundred.* Only 198 of the 670 men composing the "Light Brigade" returned. (It is perhaps unnecessary to remark that the exact number of casualties has been and probably always will be a disputed point.)

THE DAISY

This poem is the record of a journey to Italy made by the poet and Mrs. Tennyson in the summer of 1851.

5. *Turbìa.* A village in the western Riviera. Its name comes from a ruin, the remains of which are a mute testimonial of the "Roman strength" which erected it to commemorate the subjugation of the Ligurian tribes.

13. *campanili.* Bell towers.

23. *Cogoletto.* A town about fifteen miles from Genoa which claims to be the birthplace of Columbus.

37. *that hall.* Probably the Palazzo Ducale at Genoa.

43. *Cascinè.* The park of Florence.

44. *Boboli's ducal bowers.* Gardens behind the Pitti Palace.

46. *duomo.* The cathedral of Florence.

51–2. *Reggio . . . Parma . . . Lodi . . . Piacenza.* Italian cities.

55–6. The description fits many of the Lombard churches.

57 ff. Next to St. Peter's and the cathedral of Seville, the cathedral at Milan is the largest in Europe. From its roof one has a glorious view of the Alps, that of Monte Rosa being especially impressive.

75–6. *Virgilian . . . Maxume.* The phrase "Lari Maxume" (Larius the greatest [of those mighty lakes]) from Virgil's *Georgics*, kept ringing in his ears.

78. *Lariano.* The name of the boat came from Larius, the Latin name of Lake Como.

79. *that fair port.* Varenna, on the eastern shore of the lake.

80. *Theodolind.* Daughter of Garibald, duke of Bavaria, who according to tradition ended

her days (she died in 628) in the castle above Varenna.

84. *agavè.* The century plant.

86. *Splügen.* One of the passes over the Alps, a short distance from the northern end of Como.

93. *So dear a life.* The late Hallam Tennyson, born August 11, 1852.

95. *this dark city.* Edinburgh, the city on the "clouded Forth," where Tennyson was visiting.

Page 93. THE SONG OF THE BROOK

The brook in this, one of Tennyson's best-known nature lyrics, is an imaginary one, not the Somersby brook which the poet loved so well. The poem is part of an idyll—*The Brook*—in which one Lawrence Aylmer, returned to his English home after an absence of twenty years, loiters by the brook he loved in his youth and repeats the poem—*The Song* composed years before by his brother, long since dead in Italy.

9. *Philip's farm.* Philip Willows is a farmer who has a prominent place in the idyll.

47. *shingly.* Gravelly; strewn with stones or coarse gravel.

Page 94. MAUD; A MONODRAMA

PART I

Tennyson called this poem, which he liked to read aloud, "a little *Hamlet*, the history of a morbid poetic soul, under the blighting influence of a recklessly speculative age. He is the heir of madness," he continued, "an egotist with the makings of a cynic, raised to sanity by a pure and holy love which elevates his whole nature, passing from the height of triumph to the lowest depth of misery, driven into madness by the loss of her whom he has loved, and, when he has at length passed through the fiery furnace, and has recovered his reason, giving himself up to work for the good of mankind through the unselfishness born of his great passion. . . . The peculiarity of this poem is that different phases of passion in one person take the place of different characters." (*Memoir*, I, 396.)

The poem, which Mr. Lascelles Abercrombie says is Tennyson's supreme achievement, is composed of 28 monologues in most of which the introspective hero tells his life story, beginning with an account of the strange death of his father, of the ruin of his family, and of the influence upon him of the villainies in the world due to the domination of commerce; passing to the awakening and progress of his love for Maud, a fatal passion which ended in the slaying of her brother, the hero's flight abroad, and the horrors of madness and the madhouse; and concluding with the slow reawakening of the hero to his responsibilities in a world of men who are flying to arms under the colors of Britain. Several of the monologues are love lyrics, among them the poignant "O let the solid ground"; "Come into the garden, Maud"; and the moving "O that 'twere possible," which, if it is not a pure love lyric, may be called a lyric of passionate grief; in Swinburne's words, "the poem of deepest charm and fullest delight of pathos and melody . . . written by Tennyson."

It has been suggested by Nicolson and others that the morbidly sensitive young man whose soliloquies tell the story of *Maud* is Tennyson himself. Alden in his *Tennyson* finds in the hero of *Maud* a striking resemblance to the young man of *Locksley Hall.* He points out, however, that Tennyson does not present the temperament and behavior of the youth in *Maud* as those of a typical youth, but rather "as exceptional, even pathological."

The appearance of *Maud* aroused the critics, some of whom shuddered at its "positively hideous cacophony" and its outrageous silliness. Many found it "morbid" and "degenerate," and one indignant scribe wrote the following note to the author:

"Sir,

"I used to worship you, but now I hate you. I loathe and detest you. You beast! So you've taken to imitating Longfellow! Yours in Aversion, —"

See letters X and XI (text p. 216) and XIII (p. 218).

41. *centre-bits.* Tools used for boring holes. "Sleep must lie down armed" against thieves, who frequently use these tools.

45. *Mammonite . . . fee.* In his *Past and Present* Carlyle relates the story of three children whose parents poisoned them in order to get from a burial society £3 8s. per child, this amount being legally due to the parents of a child upon its death.

46. *Timour . . . bones.* A reference to Tamurlane or Timur the Lame, a Mongol conqueror, who in the 14th century extended his rule over parts of Turkestan, Siberia, Persia, and India by terror and desolation.

144. *Isis.* An Egyptian goddess of motherhood and fertility.

147. *Poland . . fail.* Probably a reference to Nicholas of Russia's severe treatment of Poland in 1831, which resulted in the absorption of Poland by Russia; and to the failure of the Hungarians in their revolt against Austria in 1849.

233. *Assyrian Bull.* The bull, frequently figured in Assyrian sculpture, is represented with hair curled.

243. *hustings.* The platform from which candidates for Parliament were formerly nominated.

251. *cap and bells*. The headdress sometimes worn by court fools and professional jesters.
295. *Viziers*. High executive officers in certain Mohammedan countries.
366–73. *came one . . . put down war*. Tennyson was accused of attacking John Bright, the earnest Quaker reformer and statesman who opposed England's participation in the Crimean War, the war which restored the hero of *Maud* to sanity. Tennyson's answer to the charge was that he did not even know, at the time he wrote the poem, that Bright was a Quaker. The hero is not attacking Bright or the Quakers in this passage, but those who want peace at any price.
435. *left the daisies rosy*. When she stepped across the meadow her feet bent down the daisies so that their rose-colored under sides could be seen.
441. *King Charley*. A spaniel.
464. *Gorgonised*. The face of Medusa, one of the three Gorgons of Greek mythology, was so terrible that "whoso looked upon it was instantly turned into stone."
509. *seventh Heaven*. The last and highest of the abodes of bliss of the Mohammedan and of the cabalist systems; hence the abiding place of supreme rapture.
544. *Oread*. A mountain nymph.
551. *Arab arch*. The swiftness and grace of the Arab is said to be due to the high instep.
615–16. *Sighing for Lebanon . . . cedar*. The poet greatly admired a cedar of Lebanon in the grounds of Farringford, his Isle of Wight home. Much of the scenery of *Maud* is taken from that of Farringford.
625. *the thornless garden*. The Garden of Eden.
634. *A sad astrology*. Astrology is the pseudo-science which treats of the influence of the stars upon human affairs. Now that he is accepted, the stars are "fair," going in and out "at merry play" among the branches of the cedar under which he reclines and ceasing to be "tyrants in [their] iron skies."
653–9. *why should Love . . . "himself more dear*." Love is intensified by the thought of death and separation.
666. *false death*. Sleep.
717–26. *she said . . . have sworn*. See section VII, Part I (text p. 100).

Section XXII. Mr. Humbert Wolfe calls this section "one of the greatest love-poems in the English language." He writes of Tennyson's poetic flights in the poem under the symbol of the soaring lark that in the ninth stanza makes "one last ascent before the wings come to rest in their high haven." Then, quoting the tenth and the eleventh stanzas, he says: "And so passing beyond a cloud, dyed with the sun, the bird is home with the ultimate song of which it was the feathered image. All the harshnesses, all the twists, all the turns, all the expectations in Part I of the poem have conspired to create that moment. It is the summary, the meaning, and the justification of them all." He concludes, "*Maud*, might, indeed, perhaps should, have ended there. It is hard after that passing into the sunset to come back to the first stanza of Part II, and verse as angry-formless as the passion that led to the slaying of Maud's brother in the duel." (*Tennyson*, p. 44.)

Page 108. PART II

This division of the poem deals with the hero's feeling and behavior after the fatal duel. He has fled to Brittany, but he cannot escape his horror. He feels himself going mad, and after he hears of Maud's death madness does indeed seize upon him, and in the madhouse he conceives of himself as long dead, but buried in so shallow a grave that he cannot escape the ghastly babble of the dead men who ever go about him. There is no peace even in the grave.
26. *Christless code*. The code or unwritten law which approved the system of dueling.
32. *ghastly Wraith*. The phantom of Maud.
49. *shell*. Tennyson said that this shell, "undestroyed amid the storm, perhaps symbolizes to him [the hero] his own first and highest nature preserved amid the storms of passion." But this is not the chief significance of the scene. Mr. Alfred Noyes quotes a remark of Jowett's—"No poem since Shakespeare seems to show equal power of the same kind, or equal knowledge of human nature"—and then selects this passage of "the shell" as an "example of Tennyson's Shakespearean power of depicting human nature and the tremendous forces that attack the soul." He finds nothing with which to compare the musing of the blood-guilty exile over the fragile shell except the musing of Hamlet over what seem to be trivialities. Many critics have passed the section by without comment and some have ridiculed it; but certainly those who understand the strange vagaries of the human mind as derangement approaches it or as it is bent by overpowering emotion will feel that here, if never again, Tennyson depicted with something of Shakespearean penetration the behavior of man under the stress of "the tremendous forces that attack his soul."
96. *Lamech*. In Genesis 4 : 23 Lamech "said unto his wives . . . 'Hear my voice . . . hearken unto my speech: for I have slain a man to my wounding, and a young man to my hurt.'"
Section IV. It is said that the poem *Maud* grew out of a remark to Tennyson by Sir John Simeon to the effect that he should elaborate into a story the first four lines of this section, a version of which appeared in 1837 in an annual, *The Tribute*.

280. *the prophecy given of old.* Probably a reference to "there is nothing covered, that shall not be revealed . . . upon the housetops," of Luke 12 : 2–3.
290. *him.* Maud's brother.
291. *wolf.* Maud's father.
296. *the rat.* The Jacobites said that the brown Norwegian rat, which drove out the English rat, came to England in 1714 with the House of Hanover. Hence they called it "the Hanover rat."
317. *the keeper.* Maud's brother.
318. *a dead man.* The speaker himself.
326. *the second corpse.* Maud's brother. The first is his own father, killed, he believes, by Maud's father.

Page 114. PART III

Some readers of Tennyson's time did not like this section because, they said, it showed that the poet loved war and wished to excite his country to war. Hallam Tennyson defends his father from the charge by pointing to the *Epilogue to the Heavy Brigade* which contains the lines,

> . . . who loves War for War's own sake
> Is fool, or crazed, or worse;

and by saying that the poet looked eagerly forward to the time when the "Parliament of man, the Federation of the world," should be a reality.
6. *the Charioteer.* This is a constellation, as are also Gemini (l. 7), Orion (l. 8), and the Lion (l. 14).
36. *dreary phantom.* The "ghastly Wraith" of Part II, section I, l. 32.
45. *a giant liar.* Nicholas I of Russia.

Page 115. TURN, FORTUNE, TURN THY WHEEL

IN LOVE, IF LOVE BE LOVE

These two songs—the first sung by Enid, the second, by Vivien—are from the *Idylls of the King.* Van Dyke describes the second as "a sweet and tender rhyme, containing one of Tennyson's most quotable phrases."

Page 116. TITHONUS

Tithonus was the son of Laomedon, king of Troy. His youthful beauty won for him the love of Aurora, who secured immortality for him but forgot to ask for eternal youth. In time therefore he grew old and helpless and shrivelled and finally slept in a cradle like a child. As life became more and more a burden to him, he prayed to Aurora to remove him from the world, and she changed him to a grasshopper.
39. *the wild team.* Aurora's golden chariot was drawn by white horses.
63. *Ilion.* Troy. Apollo was believed to have built the walls of Troy to the music of his lyre.
73–6. *Thou seëst . . . silver wheels.* Nicolson speaks of "the infinite beauty" of these concluding lines.

Page 117. *From* AYLMER'S FIELD

Aylmer's Field is a poem which tells the story of Sir Aylmer Aylmer, "that almighty man," and his lady, whose cruel opposition to the love of their daughter and a young man, the brother of their rector, led to the daughter's early death from fever and to the young man's stabbing himself to death. To Lady Aylmer's request that the rector "speak before the people of her child," the "harrow'd brother" consented and spoke so openly and so bitterly from the text, "My house is left unto me desolate," that the lady swooned under his voice and died within the month, and her lord became an imbecile whose tongue could shape but one word—"desolate."
Lines 635–43 immediately precede the rector's devastating words. Lines 644–74 are the first thirty-one lines, or about one-quarter, of his speech.
638. *Eight . . . left.* "Noah, and Shem, and Ham, and Japheth, the sons of Noah, and Noah's wife, and the three wives of his sons." (Genesis 7 : 13.)
644. *"Gash . . . Baäl."* A reference to the words used by Elijah in rebuking the prophets of the heathen god (I Kings 18 : 19–40).

IN THE VALLEY OF CAUTERETZ

In August, 1861, Tennyson revisited the beautiful valley of Cauteretz in the Pyrenees mountains. He had tramped through the valley with Arthur Hallam in the summer of 1830, when the two young men made their expedition for the purpose of helping the Spanish revolutionists under Torréjos. Tennyson said that he wrote the poem "after hearing the voice of the torrent seemingly sound deeper as the night grew."
4. *two and thirty years ago.* This should be "one and thirty." The inaccuracy annoyed the poet greatly.

MILTON

Tennyson had great admiration for Milton and said that the splendor of his greatest passages could not be matched in English. He included him too in a list of writers of the stateliest English prose.
Alcaic meter was invented by Alcaeus, a lyric poet of Mytilene, about 600 B.C., and was used freely by Horace and other early poets. In this poem Tennyson imitated the Greek alcaics, which had a freer and lighter movement than the Horatian. The scansion of the first four

lines of the *Milton* alcaics may be indicated thus:

5. *Gabriel, Abdiel.* In *Paradise Lost* Gabriel is "chief of the angelic guards," and Abdiel the angel who alone opposes Satan's efforts to stir his subordinate angels to revolt.

Page 118. THE FLOWER

Tennyson told J. B. Selkirk in a letter that the "I" in this poem did not mean "A. T." (Alfred Tennyson) and that "the flower" was not his own verses. In a note on the poem he described it as "a universal apologue."

A DEDICATION

This poem was addressed to Lady Tennyson.

THE VOYAGE

Another of the thousand and one instances in which a voyage on boundless oceans is used to symbolize the search for an ideal.

Page 119. ENOCH ARDEN

It is said that this poem was suggested to Tennyson by the sculptor and poet Thomas Woolner, one of the original Pre-Raphaelite brethren. In 1859 Mrs. Tennyson asked Woolner to "give A. something to do," and in 1860 she wrote him and said that a worthy subject for A. would be beyond all price to her—a subject "which would fix him, whether he would or no." Woolner responded with "The Fisherman's Story," which under Tennyson's hands became *Enoch Arden*. The poem achieved great popularity with the English public, but the intellectuals and the "ferocious young" did not like it, and there was a third class of critics that charged it with being immoral and with glorifying concubinage. These last charges worried the Queen, who was a great admirer of the poem, and there is a story that she drove to Farringford and laid her doubts before the Laureate himself. Tennyson's reply, the essence of which was that many enviable acts of heroism occur among the poor and lowly, and that he is a happy being who can understand such acts and not condemn the actors, calmed the Queen. As she left the presence of the poet she called down God's blessing on Enoch Arden and said softly, "He did right, after all."

1–9. *Long . . . the down.* As an example of what he means by saying that Tennyson is at his best in direct and simple narrative Mr. Nicolson calls attention to these lines descriptive of the sea-village. He might well have included, as exemplifying the same thing, the fine lines (568–95) descriptive of the tropic island on which the luckless Enoch was marooned.

910–11. *the little port Had seldom seen a costlier funeral.* Mr. Nicolson says that *Enoch Arden* appeals to him as a well-constructed and a moving poem, *with the exclusion of the last line.* On the other hand Lascelles Abercrombie, who says that some of the charges of Victorianism made against Tennyson are unfair, finds in the epithet *costlier* "the masterstroke of the poem." "It sums up the whole social psychology of 'the little port,'" he writes; "a costly funeral is just the mark of respect such a community would pay to an Enoch Arden. It is not a trait of Victorian manners; it is mere human nature. And assuredly it was no Victorian sentimentalizing that made Tennyson thus set it down without comment, without even irony; it was the genuine sympathy with human nature that comes from clearly understanding it." (Lascelles Abercrombie, in *Revaluations*, p. 63.)

Page 130. NORTHERN FARMER (OLD STYLE)

This poem grew out of the dying words of a Lincolnshire farm bailiff—"God A'mighty little knows what He's about, a-taking me. An' Squire will be so mad an' all." Tennyson said that he conjectured the man from this one speech. The dialect and feeling of the "Northern Farmer" poems are so true that a Lincolnshire farmer's daughter exclaimed on hearing them read: "That's Lincoln labourers' talk, and I thought Mr. Tennyson was a gentleman." (*Memoir*, II, 10.)

1. *'asta beän.* Hast thou been.
   liggin'. Lying.
3. *moänt 'a.* Mayn't have.
5. *a says.* He says.
7. *point.* Pint.
10. *'issén.* Himself.
11. *an 's toithe.* And his tithe.
14. *a cast oop.* He brought up against me.
    barne. Child, baby.
16. *raäte.* The poor tax.
23. *'Siver.* However.
27. *summun said.* Someone said. (David, in Psalm 116:11—"I said in my haste, 'All men are liars.'")
28. *stubb'd.* Prepared for cultivation by grubbing out the stubs.
30. *boggle.* Ghost.
32. *raäved an' rembled.* Tore up and threw away.
33. *Keäper's it wur.* The gamekeeper's ghost it was.
36. *at 'soize.* At the assizes (trial, hearing).
37. *Dubbut.* Do but.

40. *Yows.* Ewes.
41. *Nobbut.* Only.
42. *ta-year.* This year.
thruff. Through
43. *'ud nobbut.* Would only.
46. *saws.* Sows, plants.
48. *Michaelmas.* A church festival falling on September 29.
49. *'aäpoth.* A halfpenny's worth.
52. *cauve.* Calve.
hoälms. Low flat land bordering a stream.
53. *quoloty.* Quality, the gentry.
54. *thessén.* Themselves.
sewer-loy. Surely.
58. *howd.* Hold.
61. *kittle.* Boiler. The thresher run by the steam engine was introduced in Lincolnshire in 1848.
62. *Huzzin' an' maäzin'.* Worrying and astonishing.
66. *'toättler.* Teetotaler.
a's hallus i' the owd taäle. He's always telling the same story.
67. *Floy.* Fly.

Page 132. NORTHERN FARMER (NEW STYLE)

The speaker in this poem is a prosperous independent farmer who owns his land. This type of farmer succeeded the bailiff (old style) or the farmer who managed the land of another. Tennyson heard that the favorite remark of a well-to-do neighbor of his was: "When I canters my 'erse along the ramper (highway) I 'ears 'proputty, proputty, proputty'" (*Memoir*, II, 9); and from this the poem came.

1. *'erse's.* Horse's.
2. *Proputty.* Property.
14. *scoors o' gells.* Scores of girls.
24. *as 'ant nowt.* That has nothing.
25. *weänt 'a nowt.* Won't have anything.
28. *ligs.* Lies. *shere.* Shire, county.
41. *esh.* Ash.
52. *tued an' moil'd.* Tugged and drudged.
53. *beck.* Stream, brook.
54. *Feyther run oop.* Father's land ran up (or reached).
55. *brig.* Bridge.

Page 134. WAGES

Sir Oliver Lodge said that Tennyson "by his strong majestic attitude saved the faith of thousands who else would have been overwhelmed." In support of this statement he named a number of poems in which the poet rendered a special service to humanity when it was passing through a most trying period of revolution in thought. *In Memoriam* stands first in Lodge's list, but a number of shorter poems are there too, among them *Vastness, The Voice and the Peak, By an Evolutionist, Flower in the Crannied Wall, The Higher Pantheism,* and this poem in which Tennyson expresses his sure belief that the power to go on is the only satisfying reward for moral excellence in man.

6. *The wages of sin is death.* Quoted from Romans 6 : 23.

LUCRETIUS

Titus Lucretius Carus (96–55 B.C.) was a Roman poet, philosopher, and scientist. In his remarkable poem, *De Rerum Natura* ("Of the Nature of Things"), he holds to the materialistic theory that the facts of the universe, man included, are sufficiently explained by the existence and nature of matter. He does not believe in life after death and argues, therefore, that man should not fear to die. Religion he rejects as the ignoble creature of fear and superstition. His wife Lucilia, mistaking his indifference to her as a result of his philosophical broodings for growing coldness, gave him a love potion. The effect was madness, and tortured by the unbearable backward "wrenching of his will," he killed himself. The *Lucretius* of Tennyson is closely Lucretian in thought.

11. *Hexameter. De Rerum Natura* is written in hexameters.
13. *Teacher . . . divine.* Epicurus (342–270 B.C.), founder of the philosophy of Epicureanism, which teaches that pleasure is the only good and the end of all morality. The best expression of his philosophy is in Lucretius's *De Rerum Natura.*
44–6. *the dog . . . woodland.* The dog hunts in dreams.
47. *Sylla.* Sulla (138–78 B.C.), a Roman general and statesman, who put to death thousands of his enemies throughout Italy and finally became so powerful that he had himself declared dictator for an unlimited time.
50. *Cadmean teeth.* A reference to the story of Cadmus, the founder of Thebes. He slew a dragon, the teeth of which, when he had sown them, produced a band of armed warriors who fought one another until only five were left.
52. *Hetairai.* Mistresses, courtezans.
54. *mulberry-faced Dictator's.* In his *Plutarch's Lives* Clough says that scurrilous Athenian jesters called Sylla a "mulberry sprinkled over with meal."
61. *Helen.* Helen of Troy.
65. *Ilion.* Troy.
68–9. *I would . . . thee.* Because he did not approve of any sacrifice or offering to Venus. In *De Rerum Natura* Lucretius holds that "the course of the world can be explained without resorting to divine intervention, his object being to free mankind from terror of the gods." It is not piety, he said, "to sprinkle the altars with the streaming blood of beasts."
70. *prœmion.* Proem, introduction, invocation. The invocation to *De Rerum Natura* is addressed to Venus.

82. *Mavors.* An archaic name for Mars, god of war.

85–8. *her . . . abroad.* Venus as the briber or temptress of Paris. See *Œnone,* text p. 15.

89–90. *her . . . tears.* Venus as the lover of Adonis, the beautiful young hunter who was killed by a wild boar.

91. *beardless apple-arbiter.* Paris.

93. *the great Sicilian.* Empedocles (500?—430? B.C.) a Greek philosopher, of Agrigentum, Sicily. See note to Arnold's *Last Song of Callicles,* below.

94. *Calliope.* The Muse of epic poetry.

95. *Kypris.* Cypris, an epithet of Aphrodite, Venus.

96–8. *popular name . . . Nature.* In his invocation to *De Rerum Natura* Lucretius addresses Venus as goddess of the productive power of nature, the bringer forth "of the eternal generations."

114. *If all be atoms.* Lucretius believed in the atomic theory of Democritus the Greek. According to the theory, "the beginning and the end of every existing object and phenomenon find their causes in the association and the dissipation of material particles called atoms."

118. *I . . . his.* I follow or copy Epicurus.

119. *Memmius. De Rerum Natura* was dedicated to Caius Memmius Gemellus.

125. *Delius.* This and Hyperion (l. 126) are names that were applied to Apollo.

147–9. *Plato . . . Gods.* In *Phaedo,* VI, Plato says: "Men are as it were in ward, and a man ought not to free himself from it, or to run away."

182. *Picus and Faunus.* Old Italian gods of agriculture. Lucretius laughs at the unknown "he" who first fashioned the story that created these garden gods; but he finds more to laugh at in himself, who might easily people the garden, wood, or mountain with nymphs, fauns, oreads, and satyrs if he should see the arbutus tottering and all the treetops quivering with the wind.

193. *him I proved impossible.* In *De Rerum Natura,* II, 700; V, 837 ff., 878 ff.

194. *Twy-natured.* Two- or double-natured.

218. *sweet, Epicurean life.* The epicureanism taught by Lucretius was not that of unbridled bodily pleasure. He meant by the life of pleasure one of prudence, honor, and justice, and he held that the taking away of his desires made for man's happiness.

219–22. *monster . . being.* The effect of the love potion.

235. *her.* Lucretia, the virtuous wife of Lucius Tarquinius Collatinus, who was raped by Sextus, son of King Tarquin the Proud and cousin of her husband. She told the story to her husband and to Lucretius her father, made them swear vengeance on Sextus, and then plunged a dagger into her heart. Her bleeding body was carried to Rome. The incensed Romans dethroned Tarquin, drove his family into exile, and took oath that Rome should never again have a king.

259–62. *golden work . . . hell.* See *De Rerum Natura,* IV, 8, 9 ff.; III, 978–1023.

260. *Ixionian wheel.* Ixion, a king of the Lapithae, was bound to an endlessly revolving wheel in the underworld for aspiring to the love of Hera.

261. *Fury's ringlet-snake.* The three Furies were represented as having snakes for hair.

Page 138. THE HIGHER PANTHEISM

Simply defined, pantheism is the doctrine that the universe conceived of as a whole is God. Higher pantheism is more far-reaching. It does not limit God by the finite universe, but holds that He transcends it. In the words (approximately) of Van Dyke, it adds to the pantheistic concept that "God is [immanent] in the Visible All" the higher concept that "the Visible All is not the whole of God." See note to *Wages,* above, the extract beginning, "Yes, it is true" (text p. 209), and Swinburne's parody, *The Higher Pantheism in a Nutshell* (text p. 765).

FLOWER IN THE CRANNIED WALL

In a note Tennyson said the flower was plucked out of a wall at "Waggoners Wells," near Haslemere. Woolner's heroic statue of the poet in Lincoln cathedral yard represents him holding a flower in his hand. See note to *Wages,* above.

ENGLAND AND AMERICA IN 1782

When this poem was published in the *New York Ledger* of January 6, 1872, it was accompanied by a note from Tennyson in which he said the speaker was "a liberal Englishman at the time of our recognition of American Independence." Robert Bonner, the proprietor of the *Ledger,* is said to have paid Tennyson £1000 for this poem.

19. *Hampden.* John Hampden (1594–1643), a member of Parliament famous for his leadership in the struggle against the imposition of ship-money, a tax to provide ships for the king's service. Hampden was virtually fighting against taxation without representation, a principle which fired the colonies to rebellion against England.

IN THE GARDEN AT SWAINSTON

Swainston, in the Isle of Wight, was the home of Sir John Simeon, one of Tennyson's three most intimate friends. The other two, with Sir John making the three dead men of this poem, were Arthur Hallam and Henry Lushington, to whom Tennyson dedicated *The Princess. Maud* was partly written in the Swainston garden.

15–16. *thou . . . three.* Simeon died in 1870, Lushington in 1855, and Hallam in 1833.

Page 139. *From* IDYLLS OF THE KING

The *Idylls of the King* consist of twelve poems which tell the story of King Arthur, beginning with his mysterious birth, following the long line of events that resulted in the failure of his high design in the Round Table, and ending with his strange passing into the mystery—the great deep—from which he came. The story of King Arthur had a lifelong interest for Tennyson, his first poem on the subject appearing in 1832 (*The Lady of Shalott*) and his last in 1885. The *Idylls* is therefore the work of almost a lifetime, and Tennyson believed it to be one of "the two predominating achievements of both his life and his art." (The other was *In Memoriam.*) When Tennyson composed the earliest numbers of the *Idylls*, he did not think of them as parts of one great poem, but by 1855 or thereabout the idea of uniting the several Arthur poems that he had published came into his mind. In 1885 he rounded out the story with *Balin and Balan*, and in 1888 arranged the set of twelve in the following order:

Dedication (to Prince Albert)

1.	*The Coming of Arthur*	1869
2.	*Gareth and Lynette*	1872
3.	*The Marriage of Geraint*	1859
4.	*Geraint and Enid*	1859
5.	*Balin and Balan*	1885
6.	*Merlin and Vivien*	1859
7.	*Lancelot and Elaine*	1859
8.	*The Holy Grail*	1869
9.	*Pelleas and Ettarre*	1869
10.	*The Last Tournament*	1871
11.	*Guinevere*	1859
12.	*The Passing of Arthur*	1842

To the Queen (Victoria)

Sources of the *Idylls*

The chief source of the *Idylls* was Malory's *Morte d'Arthur* (1485), a book which Tennyson came to know when he was still a boy. Nennius's *Historia Britonum* (c. 800), Geoffrey of Monmouth's *Historia Regum Britanniae* (1139), and Ellis's *Specimens of Early English Metrical Romances* (1805) also influenced the *Idylls*. The story of *Geraint and Enid* the poet took from the *Mabinogion*, a collection of Welsh tales which he may have read in the original and which he certainly read in a translation by Lady Charlotte Guest.

Summary of the *Idylls* not in the text

In *Gareth and Lynette* the court of Arthur is pictured in its early days of innocence and promise. Gareth, Arthur's nephew, serving in the court as a kitchen knave, is permitted by the king (who alone knows who he is) to go to the aid of class-conscious Lynette, whose sister is imperilled in her castle by four knights. Lynette, who wanted Lancelot for her champion, is indignant to think that she should be given a kitchen knave. She bitterly reviles him as they ride along, but after he has overthrown the hostile knights, she admires him for his even temper and his noble achievements and offers him her love.

The Marriage of Geraint tells the love story of the handsome knight, Geraint, for "Enid the Good," daughter of Yniol, a knight who had been robbed of his earldom by his powerful nephew. Intent in his pursuit of a knight, one of whose party had insulted the Queen, Geraint finds shelter at nightfall in the ruinous castle of Yniol and there falls in love with Enid. He learns of Yniol's bad treatment at the hands of his nephew and discovers that the knight whose punishment he seeks is this same nephew. Next day he meets the nephew in a tournament, defeats him, and under threat of death compels him to go to Arthur's court and crave pardon for the insult done the Queen and to restore his earldom to Yniol. He then takes Enid to the court, presents her to the Queen, who "clothed her for her bridals like the sun," and, as he had promised her father, "makes her truly his true wife." After a period of great happiness at the court with his bride, Geraint hears the rumor that "rose about the queen" and is seized with horror lest Enid should suffer taint because of her affection for Guinevere. With Arthur's permission he withdraws from the court and goes with Enid to his own princedom, where he "sinks into uxorious idleness." A remark of Enid's—"O me, I fear that I am no true wife"—spoken "piteously" at the thought that she might be the cause of his idleness, he misunderstands and believes to be a confession of the same guilt as Guinevere's.

In *Geraint and Enid* appears the first effect upon the court of the guilt of Lancelot and the Queen. Geraint, madly suspicious of Enid because of her "piteously" spoken words (related in *The Marriage of Geraint*), posts away into a bandit-haunted wilderness, compelling her to ride a long way ahead of him and forbidding her to speak to him. He meets with many adventures, the most formidable being an encounter with Earl Limours, a wicked knight and former suitor of Enid's, and with Earl Doorm, a conscienceless freebooter whose power no man had been able to stand against. Throughout all these encounters the devotion of Enid to the suspicious Geraint never falters, and through her constancy she wins back his wavering love.

Balin and Balan. Balin, a fiery but upright

knight of Arthur's court, comes to suspect that Lancelot and the Queen, to whom he was deeply devoted, are in love. From much brooding on this thought he is seized by a madness and leaves the court. His suspicions finally confirmed by the perfidious Vivien, he tears the Queen's token from his shield in a rage, stamps it "into defacement," and hurls it "among the forest weeds." His brother Balan, who had been sent by Arthur upon the quest of a demon, arrives on the scene at the moment of Balin's raging, and thinking him the demon for which he has been seeking, falls upon him and slays him, but not until he himself has received a mortal wound at the hand of the violent Balin. (In this *Idyll* the seed of evil sowed by Lancelot and the Queen is shown "ripening into a crop of disaster.")

In *Merlin and Vivien* the wily Vivien, "whose sin was Guinevere's in a lower and wickeder form," and who hated Arthur because her father had been killed in battle against him, makes her way to his court in order to sow discontent and suspicion, and even tries to tempt Arthur himself. Failing in her evil design, she withdraws from court and sets herself to learn the secret of the magic power of Merlin, who typifies wisdom and who, up to the time of her attempts to ensnare him, had used his power "in the service of the Ideal as embodied in Arthur." Finally he yields to her cajolements and, held prisoner in a hollow oak by her use of his own charms, he can no longer aid in thwarting Sense in its war against Soul.

Pelleas and Ettarre tells the story of the trusting and loyal knight Pelleas and the wanton Ettarre. Ettarre, who has scorned the love of Pelleas, pretends to love him when she thinks that he may win a prize for her at the tournament. After he has been victorious in the contests and has chosen her the Queen of Beauty, she once more disdains his love and sends three evil knights to slay him. He defeats them and while he hesitates in confusion as to what course to take, Gawain, the "light-of-love," comes riding by, hears Pelleas's story, and promises to aid him. But Gawain too proves treacherous, and Pelleas, more bewildered than ever, speeds to the court to tell his story. On the way he learns from Percivale of the guilt of Lancelot and the Queen, and believing that their sin is the cause of his own disaster, fights with Lancelot and is overthrown. The poem ends with a scene between Lancelot and the Queen in which each looks hard upon the other as they realize "the dolorous day to be." (See note to *A Worm within a Rose*, below.)

The Last Tournament. In the "Tournament of the Dead Innocence," the last tournament held at Arthur's court, Arthur realizes that the glory of the Round Table has departed. "The laws that ruled the tournament were broken," and where once were honesty and loyalty, obedience and high honor in men and women, are now broken oaths and disloyalty, disobedience, debased manhood and womanhood. The champion in the tournament—fit irony—is Tristram, disloyal husband of Isolt of Brittany and paramour of Isolt, the wife of King Mark of Cornwall. He takes the prize he has won—a ruby necklace—to his paramour, and as he clasps it round her neck and bows "to kiss the jewell'd throat," Mark, the jealous husband, steals up behind him—"Mark's way"—and cleaves "him through the brain." Arthur, returning to the Hall in the "autumn-dripping gloom," learns that Guinevere has fled and hears his court fool sobbing, "I shall never make thee smile again."

The Passing of Arthur. With this *Idyll*, describing Arthur's last great battle in the dying year, the poem closes. Sir Bedivere, the last of Arthur's knights, relates the final scenes in the life of the King—the warning spoken by the ghost of Gawain; the driving of Modred and his traitor band to the very "sunset bound of Lyonesse"; the man-to-man meeting of Arthur and Modred in which Arthur slew the traitor and himself received a mortal wound; the "lightnings in the splendour of the moon" made by the brand Excalibur as Bedivere hurled it out above the mere; the marvellous arm that rose from the water and drew the brand under; and the funeral barge, with the three weeping Queens, which received the dying Arthur and which Bedivere gazed upon as it moved away until it

Look'd one black dot against the verge of dawn.

Critical judgment has been by no means undivided as to the merits of the *Idylls* as a whole or indeed of each idyll as a poem in itself. Nicolson, while admitting that he would omit the *Idylls* if he were making an anthology of Tennyson's poetry which has an appeal to the literary taste of today, nevertheless speaks of *The Passing of Arthur* as a "magnificent poem magnificently treated"; of *Lancelot and Elaine*, with all its blemishes, as a story handled "with admirable delicacy"; and of *The Last Tournament* as a "remarkable achievement in the creation of atmosphere." Carlyle saw in the *Idylls* "the inward perfection of vacancy." Meredith wrote of *The Holy Grail:* "The lines are satin lengths, the figures Sèvres china . . . To think! . . . that the foremost poet of the country goes on fluting of creatures that have not a breath of vital humanity in them, and doles us out his regular five-feet with the old trick of the vowel endings." Abercrombie says: "The *Idylls of the King* are full of splendid and lovely things; the imagination lives delighted in a series of exquisite moments; but these do not form a whole; not . . . a whole of any importance beyond the mere sequence of the moments, certainly not the whole which Tennyson intended . . . a symbolic interpretation, in terms of these moments, of human nature and human destiny." (*Revaluations*, p. 67.) Drinkwater calls the actual poetic achievement of the *Idylls* very great. Matthew Arnold wrote after reading them, "The fault I find with Tennyson in his *Idylls of the King* is that the peculiar charm and aroma of the Middle Ages he does not give in them. . . . Tennyson, with all his temperament and artistic skill, is deficient in intellectual power." Swinburne called them the "Morte d'Albert, or Idylls of the Prince Consort." Between the ardent Tennysonians who see nothing but high excellence in the poem and the scoffers who find nothing in it to praise are the critics whose fine understanding, "experience of literature and its function," and sure instinct for beauty lead them inevitably to just pronouncement upon it. Of this number are Nicolson and Abercrombie, quoted above; and here too is Cazamian with his comment: "Some of his characters [in the *Idylls*] are living, and it must be admitted that the touch of the writer, the artist or the musician in language, has never been more exquisite. But at the same time one cannot forget the essential artificiality of this imaginative epic, at once mystic and moralizing."

Page 139. THE COMING OF ARTHUR

1. *Cameliard*. A mystic kingdom, which, like all the places in the *Idylls*, is not to be definitely located.
5. *many a petty king*. Before the coming of Arthur Britain included many small kingdoms. Arthur united them.
13. *Aurelius*. Brother of King Uther.
14. *Uther*. Arthur's father.
17. *Table Round*. The table about which Arthur's knights sat. The table was made round so that it might have neither head nor foot. Hence no knight sat above or below his fellows, and Arthur himself sat among his knights as an equal, not as a superior.
20. *Cameliard was waste*. Before Arthur came. For some lines from this point the "back story" is given.
36. *Urien*. Husband of Arthur's sister and king of North Wales.
43. *not Uther's son*. There are many references in this Idyll to the doubt concerning Arthur's birth.
63. *A doubt*. As to Arthur's parentage.
72. *son of Gorloïs*. The first husband of Arthur's mother, Ygerne. After the death of Gorloïs Ygerne married Uther, but it was rumored that Gorloïs, not Uther, was the father of Arthur (ll. 184–210).
73. *son of Anton*. The "old knight and ancient friend of Uther" to whom Merlin entrusted the child Arthur (ll. 211–36).
94. *he*. Tennyson.
96–9. *world . . . star*. More than mortal power is Arthur's here. Tennyson's, like many other myths of Arthur, attributed magic powers to the king.
103. *long-lanced battle*. Horsemen in battle array.
106. *the Powers*. Divinities that watched over Arthur.
119. *brands*. Swords.
124–5. *loved . . . most*. Lancelot.
141. *holp*. Helped.
160. *holpen*. Helped.
166. *cuckoo chased*. Cuckoos lay their eggs in the nests of other birds. The owners of the nest rightfully attempt to chase the invaders away.
208. *night of the new year*. Arthur's passing was on the last night of the year.
213. *holden*. Held.
237. *King*. Leodogran.
244. *Bellicent*. Daughter of Gorloïs and Ygerne and so half-sister of Arthur.
256. *Uther's peerage*. Apparently the followers of Uther shouted their approval of Arthur at his coronation.
271. *thro' the cross*. A stained window containing the image of Christ on the cross admits the sunlight in colored rays.
275. *three fair queens*. These have been interpreted as Faith, Hope, and Charity. Tennyson said: "They mean that and they do not. They are three of the noblest of women."
282. *Lady of the Lake*. In the old romances Lancelot is instructed in the Christian faith by the Lady of the Lake. Apparently she symbolizes Religion.
284. *samite*. A silk fabric.
288. *minster gloom*. The gloom of the church in which Arthur's coronation took place.
294. *Excalibur*. In the Middle Ages it was the custom to name a warrior's sword.
298. *elfin Urim*. Urim, a Hebrew word of doubtful origin, seems to mean "flames" here, describing the brightness of the little (elfin) jewels.
322. *Modred . . . doors*. Modred, a deceitful sneak from his first appearance in the *Idylls*, is the chief traitor in *The Passing of Arthur*.
325. "*What know I?*" Bellicent cannot clear up the mystery. Arthur's birth, symbolizing the coming of the Soul from the great unknown, must remain mysterious.
362. *Shrunk . . . changeling*. It was an old belief that fairies sometimes stole human babies and left their own wizened offspring in exchange.
379. *ninth one*. The ninth wave, according to old belief, was higher and more powerful than the preceding eight.

380. *full of voices.* Supernatural voices.
382–91. This description of Arthur's coming, which is Tennyson's own, is in keeping with the idea of the coming of the Soul out of the great deep (l. 410).
401. *riddling triplets.* The bards and magicians of old time often spoke in riddles.
431. *hind.* Peasant, farmer.
476. *Lords from Rome.* Arthur had yet to break the power of Rome over Britain.

Page 145. LANCELOT AND ELAINE

Elaine "is Tennyson's loveliest fantasy of womanhood, characterless, but pure, faithful in love, and infinitely pathetic. She is above sex and outside the burden of life and worldly interpretation. She speaks as

'a little helpless innocent bird
That has but one plain passage of few notes,
Will sing the simple passage o'er and o'er
For all an April morning.'

The moral conflict of one whose 'honour rooted in dishonour stood' is conducted beyond the range of her personality, as a catechism cannot consort with music. The intrigues of Guinevere and Lancelot in this episode satisfy all Tennyson's desire to inform his readers how a lawless passion can corrupt love and mar the features. On the maiden he expends his faultless artistry as on no other character in the 'Idylls.' The guilty Queen is the rose harbouring the invisible worm, but Elaine floats down the stream of murmuring verse a lily without stain. She is the essence of pure art and April innocence." (H. I'A. Fausset, *Tennyson, A Modern Portrait*, pp. 209–10.)
2. *Astolat.* Said to be Guildford, in Surrey.
22. *Caerlyle.* Carlisle in Cumberland.
23. *Caerleon.* In Monmouthshire. It was the traditional capital of Arthur.
Camelot. See note to *The Lady of Shalott*, above.
35. *Lyonesse.* See note to *Morte d'Arthur*, l. 4, above.
53. *shingly scaur.* A steep height covered with pebbles.
75. *the place.* London.
94. *lets.* Hinders, keeps, prevents.
110. *allow'd.* Recognized as right or appropriate.
118. *devoir.* Duty.
196. *wot.* Knows.
269. *glanced.* Turned their talk to.
279. *Badon hill.* The final battle in which Arthur drove out the Saxon invaders was fought here. It is thought to be Bradbury Hill, Dorsetshire. All the battles mentioned in ll. 287–300 are mystical, and the places named therefore cannot be located.
293. *Lady's Head.* Image of the Virgin Mary.
297. *wild white Horse.* The Saxon emblem.
338. *rathe.* Early.
422. *Pendragon.* Literally, head, leader. A title of Uther, Arthur's father, now given by the amazed youth to Arthur himself.
535. *Gawain.* Brother of Gareth and nephew of Arthur. A prominent knight, but a trouble-maker and scandalmonger.
660. *Ramp.* Leaping.
766. *wit.* Know.
795. *strange-statued gate.* The mystical carved gateway of Camelot is described in detail in *Gareth and Lynette*, ll. 209–26.
798. *His own far blood.* His distant relatives.
880. *ghostly grace.* The vision of the Queen.
883. *rough sickness.* The sickness from his physical wound.
1015–16. *Phantom . . . a death.* The banshee of Celtic folklore, whose wailing or mournful singing was thought to be a warning of the near approach of death.
1092. *ghostly man.* Priest.
1134. *that stream.* The Thames. According to l. 76 Arthur was holding court at London.
1140. *the black decks.* Cf. *The Lady of Shalott.*
1170. *oriel.* A deeply-recessed window.
1178. *tawnier.* The neck of the cygnet is yellowish, that of the grown swan pure white.
1183. *rumours.* Gawain's tales about Lancelot and Elaine.
1198. *of the Lake.* So called because in the old stories he was reared in the castle of the Lady of the Lake.
1217. *her pearls.* See l. 601.
1256–7. *Sir Percivale . . . Sir Galahad.* It is fitting that the two purest knights should bear the body of the lily maid, Elaine.
1319. *that shrine.* The burial place of kings.
1417–18. See Malory, XXI, 9, 10.

Page 163. THE HOLY GRAIL

See note to *Sir Galahad*, above.
15. *puff'd . . smoke.* The pollen of the yew, blown by the wind. Cf. *In Memoriam*, ll. 788–9.
43. *What is it?* See note to *Sir Galahad*, above.
48. *Aromat.* Arimathea, a town in Palestine.
50. *Moriah.* Mt. Moriah, near Jerusalem. In Matthew 27 : 50–3, is told the story of the wandering of the dead after the crucifixion.
52. *winter thorn.* This thorn is said to have sprung from the staff used by Joseph in his wanderings from the Holy Land to Britain.
61. *Arviragus.* Said to have been a king of Britain from 44 to 72 A.D.
135. *Galahad.* In Malory's *Morte d'Arthur* he is (by enchantment) the son of Lancelot and Elaine (not the Elaine of Astolat, but daughter of King Pelles), "cousin nigh unto Joseph of Arimathie." He is destined by reason of his immaculate purity to succeed in his quest for the Holy Grail.
172. *The Siege perilous.* Siege = seat. The seat

of danger at the Round Table, reserved for the knight destined to achieve the quest of the Holy Grail and fatal to all others. This seat or chair has been variously interpreted—as symbolizing Knowledge, as representing the seat occupied by Christ Himself at the Last Supper, as standing for "the temptation of sense." Tennyson characterized it as "spiritual imagination."

175–6. *Merlin . . . lost.* The exact meaning is not clear. Merlin both in the medieval romances and in Tennyson's *Merlin and Vivien* falls a victim to the treacherous arts of Vivien.

218. *under Camelot.* Camelot was on a hill.

225. *had you known.* Would you had known.

232. *four great zones.* These represent the stages through which the knights must pass before they can achieve the quest. In a more general sense they may represent the stages of human progress.

250. *twelve great battles.* See *Lancelot and Elaine*, ll. 285 ff. (text p. 149).

251–3. *Nay . . . Excalibur.* See *Morte d'Arthur*, ll. 27 ff. (text p. 32).

263. *golden dragon.* The symbol of sovereignty among the Britons, a symbol connected especially with Uther, Arthur's father. It is, of course, the symbol of Arthur.

264. *the hold.* That mentioned in l. 207.

273. *Darken'd.* Because he saw in the vow of his knights the doom of the Round Table. They had not the spiritual insight to succeed in the quest.

287. Cf. Matthew 11 : 7.

300. *Taliessin.* Most famous of the early Welsh poets—about 500 A.D. In this speech Arthur means to say that because Taliessin sings and because Lancelot is so strong in conflict those who have no poetry in them think they must sing and those who are indifferent knights think they are Lancelots. So because Galahad, who is really fit for the quest, has seen the Grail, all the others, who are not fit at all, needs must vow that they will ride until they find and see it. They will fail because, though they are valiant knights, they are not Galahads or Percivales in spiritual character.

346–7. *necks . . . dragons.* The galleries were on supports carved in figures of dragons.

350. *wyvern . . . swan.* Heraldic devices. A wyvern is a two-legged dragon. A griffin is half lion, half eagle.

358. *Gate of the Three Queens.* See *Gareth and Lynette*, ll. 209–26.

361–439. In his quest Sir Percivale finds that all things he had believed to be precious are but vanity: pleasure of sense (ll. 380–9), pleasure of home and family (ll. 391–400), splendor of wealth (ll. 402–19), high place among men (ll. 421–36).

449. *she.* Humility.

452–3. *star . . . east.* She is compared to the star of Bethlehem which led the Wise Men of the East to the manger in which lay the infant Christ.

462. *sacring.* Consecrating.

526. *spiritual city.* Cf. Revelation 21 : 10 ff., for the new Jerusalem.

539. *gate of Arthur's wars.* The wars were "done in weird devices" on the gate. See *Gareth and Lynette*, ll. 209–26.

541. *ancient books.* See l. 59.

545. *breviary.* Prayer book.

558. *market-cross.* In the Middle Ages a cross was erected in the market place of most European towns.

612. *yule is cold.* The Christmas log is burned out; i.e., Christmas is past.

639. *maddening what he rode.* Goading his horse to a frenzy.

643. *a lion in the way.* His guilty love for the Queen.

646. *his former madness.* Guinevere's anger at Lancelot because she believed he was in love with Elaine, daughter of King Pelles, resulted in his madness. See Malory's *Morte d'Arthur*, XI, 9, and XII, 4.

661. *Paynim . . . circles.* Paynim = pagan. Bors was said to have met "some remnants of the old fire-worshippers." The circles (of stone) were their temples or places of worship.

667. *he.* The sun.

681. *seven . . . Round.* The Great Bear, which, the knights said, in revolving around the pole-star made a circle in the heavens like the Round Table.

714–17. *ruin . . . hall.* The city began to go to ruin after the knights, obedient to their vow (ll. 195–202), left it and set out on the quest of the Holy Grail. Arthur speaks as if the gale of l. 726 were the immediate cause of the havoc, but the ruin, which symbolizes the coming failure of the Round Table, was inevitable and needed no immediate cause. The figures overthrown are carved ornaments. The unicorn was a fabulous one-horned beast resembling the horse, the basilisk was a dragon-like monster, the cockatrice was half fowl and half reptile, and the talbot a large-nosed hunting dog.

720. *tithe.* A tenth part.

729. See l. 240.

759. *him of Cana.* A reference to the marriage feast at Cana. When the wine failed Jesus turned water into wine. The ruler of the feast, drinking, but not knowing that the wine was made of water, said to the bridegroom, "Thou hast kept the good wine until now." (John 2 : 1–10.)

810. *Carbonek.* This castle, in the "Terre Foraine," was built, so legend said, to be the abode of the Holy Grail.

840. *seventimes-heated.* See Daniel 3 : 19.

862. *deafer . . . cat.* Darwin said (*Origin of Species*): "In monstrosities, the correlations

between quite distinct parts are very curious . . . Some instances of correlation [given in St. Hilaire] are quite whimsical: thus cats which are entirely white and have blue eyes are generally deaf."

Page 175. GUINEVERE

2. *Almesbury.* The abbey or "holy house" to which Guinevere retired (modern Amesbury) is about eight miles from Salisbury and a mile and a half from Stonehenge. The old abbey church is still standing.
4. *novice.* One who has entered a religious house and is still on probation.
10. *Modred.* See note to l. 554, below.
16. *Hengist.* A traditional leader of the Jutes, who landed at Ebbsfleet about 449. He and his brother, Horsa, founded the kingdom of Kent.
28. *Enid . . . Vivien.* Enid was the devoted wife of Geraint, one of Arthur's knights. Vivien was the daughter of a man slain in battle against Arthur. In *Merlin and Vivien* is told the story of her treachery to Merlin. So wily and unprincipled was she that in the early days of the Round Table her presence at court would not have been tolerated.
64. *the Powers.* Conscience.
127. *weald.* An open country.
147. *housel . . . shrift.* Sacrament . . . confession.
154. *waging . . . Lancelot.* Because he believed Guinevere had fled with Lancelot.
166. "*Late, late, so late!*" The song of the novice is probably founded upon the parable of the virgins, Matthew 25:1–13.
194. *traitor.* In Arthur's absence Modred had usurped the throne.
286. *Gorloïs.* Duke of Cornwall and husband of Igraine or Ygerne. Uther Pendragon assumed his likeness and won her for his wife. Of their union Arthur was born. See note to *The Coming of Arthur*, l. 72.
289. *Bude and Bos.* Districts in Cornwall.
292. *dark Tintagil.* A castle on the north coast of Cornwall. Its ruins are still to be seen.
294. *by miracle.* In Malory Arthur proves his kingly mettle by drawing a sword from a stone into which it had been fastened by magic power.
345. *doom of fire.* Eternal punishment by fire.
378. See *The Coming of Arthur*, ll. 446 ff.
395. *Pendragonship.* See note to *Lancelot and Elaine*, l. 422.
419–20. *child . . . honour'd.* She was the daughter of Leodogran.
424. *the craft of kindred.* A reference to the treachery of Modred, Arthur's nephew.
485. *Tristram and Isolt.* In *The Last Tournament* Tristram won a carcanet of rubies. Instead of giving it to his wife, Isolt of Brittany, he gave it to his paramour, Isolt, the wife of Mark, "the Cornish king." Mark surprised him as he was clasping the rubies round the queen's neck and "clove him through the brain."
500. *Usk.* The city in which Arthur was crowned and held his court was Caerleon-upon-Usk.
534–5. *fierce . . . death.* Under the old English law a queen who was unfaithful to her husband was guilty of treason, the punishment for which was burning at the stake.
550–3. Mr. Abercrombie says that anything that is disliked in Tennyson is called "Victorian," and quotes these lines (to the colon) as evidence of understanding in Tennyson that goes beyond the understanding of his critics. "How often has this passage been held up as the very type of Victorian self-righteousness!" he writes. "Why, it is the one real touch of downright human nature in Arthur's character; for the moment it makes a man of him, instead of a tediously allegorical piece of symbolism. The divorce courts are full of people who feel as Arthur did. . . . The feeling seldom emerges in intelligible form; but Tennyson, in the very midst of his solemn allegory, seizes on it and makes it, for once, unforgettably articulate. And just when his art penetrates to the heart of average human nature, the critics call him Victorian!" (Lascelles Abercrombie, in *Revaluations*, p. 64.)
554. *I . . . thee.* Tennyson quoted from an old chronicler—"God has not made since Adam was, the man more perfect than Arthur." Yet in the early stories of Arthur, as told by these same chroniclers, Arthur was once guilty of unlawful love, a passion for his half-sister, Bellicent, and from their union sprang the traitorous Modred. In the *Idylls* Tennyson makes Arthur the perfect character. In everything he is the "blameless king."

Page 183. A WORM WITHIN A ROSE

"This tender rhyme" vexed the heart of Pelleas at the end of his third night of vain waiting for the return of Gawain, the "light-of-love," from his self-appointed mission of winning for Pelleas the love of the heartless Ettarre. The song is prophetic of the evil which is about to be disclosed to the luckless Pelleas.

Page 184. THE VOICE AND THE PEAK

See note to *Wages*, above.
The theme of the poem is that everything in the material universe must pass away—nothing is abiding but the spiritual.
Stanza IX may be taken as an explanation of higher pantheism. (See *The Higher Pantheism*, text p. 138).

HAPLESS DOOM OF WOMAN

This song, from Act V, scene 2 of *Queen Mary*, is sung by the Queen when she learns that both her people and her husband hate her.

THE REVENGE

The occurrence which this poem commemorates is as follows: In 1591 an English fleet of six ships, sent to the Azores to capture Spanish treasure ships coming from the West Indies, was compelled to retreat before a Spanish fleet of fifty-three vessels. Sir Thomas Howard, commander of the English fleet, escaped with five of the ships, but Sir Richard Grenville, in command of the *Revenge*, would not leave until he had taken his sick on board. Attempting to cut his way through the whole of the enemy squadron, he was attacked by fifteen of the largest Spanish ships, and surrendered only after all of his men but twenty were killed and he himself was mortally wounded. Tennyson's version of the story was taken mainly from an account of the battle written by Sir Walter Raleigh, a cousin of Grenville.

1. *Flores*. That one of the Azores farthest west.
2. *a pinnace*. The Earl of Cumberland sent a pinnace to warn Howard of the approach of the Spanish fleet.
7. *ships of the line*. Of the line of battle.
12. *Inquisition*. The tribunal or court established by the Roman Catholic Church for the purpose of discovering and punishing heretics was extremely severe in Spain in the 16th century.
17. *Bideford*. The birthplace of Sir Richard Grenville.
30. *Seville*. A Spanish province.
31. *Don*. A Spanish title.
108. *He was devil*. Froude writes that the Spaniards told stories of Grenville's draining three or four glasses of wine and then crushing the glasses with his teeth and swallowing them.
117. *sea . . . Spain*. The storm was so severe that most of the Spanish vessels were destroyed.

Page 187. *From* THE LOVER'S TALE

Tennyson's statement of the argument of the poem was as follows: "Julian, whose cousin and foster-sister, Camilla, had been wedded to his friend and rival, Lionel, endeavors to narrate the story of his own love for her, and the strange sequel. He speaks of having been haunted by visions and the sound of bells, tolling for a funeral, and at last ringing for a marriage; but he breaks away, overcome, as he approaches the Event, and a witness to it completes the tale."

The lines given in the text are spoken by the cousin and lover of Camilla just after she, never suspecting the character of his love for her, has told him of her love for another.

DE PROFUNDIS (OUT OF THE DEEP)

There are two greetings to the newborn child in this poem, begun, it is said, on the day of the birth of the poet's son, Hallam (see text p. 217). In the first the child is addressed as merely a human being, its birth a result of purely physical causes easily explained by even an elementary knowledge of biological science. The deep whence came the child is "the vast ocean of matter," which has contained potentially for a million aeons all that is to come from it. In the second the child is addressed as having come from a still greater deep, the world of spirit, the *true* world behind the veil,

"Whereon the Spirit of God moves as he will";

and the child is no longer a human creature but himself a spirit. In the first the poet is stricken with wonder at the miracle of physical appearance, of sheer animal coming-to-be; in the second, the greater miracle of human personality, the wonder that "thou art thou," overwhelms him, and he breaks forth into "The Human Cry," a prayer "of self-prostration before the Infinite."

For an illuminating explanation of *De Profundis* as Tennyson himself saw it, see note by Mr. Wilfrid Ward in *The Works of Tennyson*, edited by Hallam, Lord Tennyson, pp. 970 ff.

Page 188. RIZPAH

This dramatic monologue, of which Swinburne said that "the poet never lived . . . whose glory would not be heightened by . . . [its] attribution . . . to his hand," had its origin in a story Tennyson read in a penny magazine, the story of an old eighteenth-century woman of Brighton whose son had been hanged for highway robbery. The body of the boy was left hanging on the gallows until the clothes and flesh were gone, and as the bones dropped to the ground, the mother made nightly visits to the spot—the stormier the weather the more frequent her visits—, gathered them up, and storing them away until she had taken the last one, buried them "in the dead silence of the night . . . in the hallowed enclosure of old Shoreham Churchyard." In the poem the grief-maddened mother is dying and is telling the story to an evangelist or sister of mercy who has come to pray with her.

The title was suggested by II Samuel 21 : 8 ff.

38. *ships . . . by*. The gallows stood near the sea.
51. *Flesh of my flesh*. Cf. Genesis 2 : 23.
58. *holy ground*. The graveyard was a consecrated spot in which her boy, having been executed, could not be buried.
62. *Full . . . mercy*. Cf. Psalm 86 : 15.
65. *black cap*. English judges about to pass sentence of death put on a black cap.
66. *first . . . first*. Cf. Matthew 19 : 30.
73. *Election*. The doctrine of predestination to mercy and salvation.

Reprobation. The doctrine of predestination to eternal damnation. The dying woman is familiar with the beliefs of the church that she thinks may bear on the fate of her son.

Page 190. "FRATER AVE ATQUE VALE" (BROTHER, HAIL AND FAREWELL)

In 1880 Tennyson and his son Hallam visited Sirmione, the peninsula on the Lago di Garda where once had been the villa of Catullus, a Roman poet of the first century B.C. At that time this poem was written.

Mr. Abercrombie, writing in *Revaluations* (p. 65), said that Tennyson could set all sorts of rich and subtle experiences to a tune of words irresistibly self-commending; "as when he came to Sirmio and remembered Catullus with the death of his own brother in his mind." Abercrombie cites *In the Garden at Swainston* (text p. 138) and *To Virgil* (stanza III particularly) as two more poems of which his remark on the poet's command of word music is true. He concludes with the comment that "Such inevitable music needs no critical reasoning in its favour; this is enough to give language that 'elevation' above its usual nature of which the critic said that the office was not persuasion but transport: it acts directly on the aesthetic sensibility." (*Revaluations*, p. 66.)

1. *Desenzano.* A town on Lake Garda in northern Italy.

2. "*O venusta Sirmio!*" "O beautiful Sirmio," a quotation from Catullus.

5. "*Ave atque Vale.*" Quoted from a poem of Catullus in which he takes everlasting leave of his brother.

6. *Tenderest . . . poets.* See extract beginning, "Catullus says," text p. 209.

8. *Lydian.* The Etruscans, who lived near Lake Garda, were believed to be of Lydian origin.

TO VIRGIL

See note to "*Frater Ave atque Vale*," above.

Tennyson, who has often been called "England's Virgil," was a great admirer of the Roman poet.

The Mantuans, mentioned in the note following the title, are the natives of Mantua, the Etruscan town in which Virgil was born.

1–4. The references in these lines are to characters and events celebrated in Virgil's *Aeneid*—the fall of Troy, the death of Dido of Carthage, etc.

6. *Works and Days.* A poem by Hesiod, a Greek poet of the 8th century B.C.

9–12. A reference to the character of Virgil's *Georgics*.

13. *Tityrus.* A fortunate freedman and shepherd in Virgil's first *Eclogue*.

15–16. An incident of *Eclogue 6*.

17. *Pollio.* C. Asinius Pollio, a patron of Virgil, "chanted" in *Eclogue* 4.

21–2. Suggested by *Aeneid*, Book VI.

23–4. See *Aeneid*, Book I, 462.

27–8. Echoed from *Aeneid*, Book VI.

37. *Mantovano.* A complimentary reference to Virgil's birthplace.

Page 191. FREEDOM

In elucidation of this poem, which voices the poet's belief that governmental and social changes and reforms, to be wholesome, must be a gradual growth, this sentence from Bacon's essay *Of Innovations* has been cited: "It were good . . . that men in their innovations would follow the example of time itself; which indeed innovateth greatly, but quietly, and by degrees scarce to be perceived."

3. *Parthenon.* A temple of Athena, on the Acropolis at Athens.

4. *Capitol.* The temple of Jupiter at Rome.

Page 192. VASTNESS

See note to *Wages*, above.

Tennyson made the following comment on this poem: "What matters anything in this world without full faith in the Immortality of the Soul and of Love?"

9. *Innocence . . . milk.* Cf. Exodus 23 : 19, and 34 : 26.

12. *all-heal.* A number of plants, among them woundwort, yarrow, and mistletoe, are so called because of supposed medicinal qualities.

28. *He . . . Cross.* Cf. Galatians 5 : 24.

36. This line has been the subject of some debate, some readers believing that a new voice speaks it, others that it is spoken by the old voice in a revulsion of feeling, and still others that Tennyson himself, experiencing a sudden instinctive recognition that Hallam is not gone forever, is the speaker.

Page 193. THE ANCIENT SAGE

Tennyson said that the ideas expressed in this poem are what he would have believed if he had lived "a thousand summers ere the time of Christ," but that his present belief included Christianity. The voice of the Sage in the poem is that of Tennyson himself. The youth whose verses call forth the remarks of the Sage is a poet who, Mr. Van Dyke says, "shares the creed of Omar Khayyam." The poem, which Tennyson thought one of the best of his later work, he wrote after reading the life and the maxims of the Chinese philosopher, Lao-tze.

31. *the Nameless.* Tennyson said that the misuses of the word "God" made him prefer another name.

146–9. *poet . . . name.* Swift, who was insane

from 1740 to the time of his death in 1745, has been mentioned as an example.

216–28. Van Dyke points to this passage as one which shows the intensely personal character of the poem. The "Passion of the Past" was a very strong passion with the poet, for whom speculation upon the distant in time or space had a real fascination. His poetry frequently voices his love for the mystic in distance and for the sound of far-off bells, his wonder at what lies beyond receding horizons, and his memories of the half-forgotten things of childhood. The "shadowy Platonic doctrine of a prenatal state" discoverable in this passage he uses not as an argument for immortality but, like Wordsworth, as "an element in our instincts of immortality." These lines should be compared with *Tears, Idle Tears* (text p. 48), *Far—Far—Away* (text p. 206), and with Wordsworth's *Ode: Intimations of Immortality*.

229–39. See *In Memoriam*, XCV, ll. 1953–68, for another reference to the state of trance or ecstasy described here.

Page 196. LOCKSLEY HALL SIXTY YEARS AFTER

In this poem, published forty-four years after *Locksley Hall*, the youth of that poem, now a garrulous old man of eighty, has returned to the ancestral Hall with his grandson to attend the funeral of the man who so many decades ago won from him the "shallow-hearted" Amy for wife. In the years that elapsed between the writing of *Locksley Hall* and the publication of *Locksley Hall Sixty Years After* Tennyson, who may be said to have begun life with a "suspicion of democracy," came to distrust and loathe it, even though he may not have believed that he did. The speaker in this poem, therefore, speaks with the voice of the changed Tennyson. He no longer rails at a rival whose success in love, he believed in the first poem, was due to his money. Instead he fears the strength of the mob, and he is maddened by "the uneducated, ignorant cry of 'Forward.'" There is bitterness in the heart of the aged poet as he sees "the closing century threatened with an inner decay."

29. *he . . . pride.* He had been a Crusader.

82. *Timur.* See note to *Maud*, l. 46, above.

83–4. *Edward's . . . flames.* In the reign of Edward VI (1547–1553) Protestantism became the state religion of England. When Mary I succeeded him in 1553 she repealed the religious statutes made in his reign, and in her effort to restore the Roman Catholic religion put to death more than 300 persons. Among those who were burned at the stake were Bishops Ridley and Latimer and Archbishop Cranmer.

88. *Rome . . . Cæsar . . . Peter.* A reference to the persecution of the Christians by the pagan Roman emperors and of non-Catholics by the Roman Catholic Church.

90. *Celtic Demos.* The word "Demos" means commons or common people. Linguistically the ancient Gauls (of France) were Celtic. The poet is thinking of the excesses of the French Revolution.

95–6. A reference, Tennyson said, to modern Irish cruelties.

100. *Saint . . . Assisi.* An Italian friar (1182–1226), founder of the order of Franciscans. The special note in his teaching was joyousness and love of nature.

103. *Chaos . . . Chaos.* Tennyson is contrasting two schools of thought, that which conceives of the universe as an orderly and harmonious system and that which conceives of it as subject to no law.

115. *Russia . . . barrier.* Control of the "Indian barrier," Afghanistan, was the persistent dream of Russia in the 19th century. In 1837 England announced "the principle that the integrity of Afghanistan is necessary to the safety of India."

116. *voices . . . field.* Voices of the laboring classes, of the masses.

123. *hustings-liar.* The candidates for Parliament spoke from a platform called the hustings.

131. *Voices.* The masses.

139–50. Tennyson disliked the realistic novel of the 'eighties. It was an evil, shameless thing, un-English in essence; and Zola, the French naturalistic novelist, was largely to blame for its vogue.

157. *Jacobinism . . . Jacquerie.* Irrational opposition to orderly government. The Jacquerie, a revolt of French peasants against the nobles in 1358, gave its name to any revolt of peasants and then to the peasant class.

185. *Hesper.* The evening star.
the poet. Homer.

201. *king of sacred song.* David, in the Psalms.

224. *warrens.* Tenements or districts for the poor as crowded as rabbit warrens.

278. *Angel . . . tomb.* See Matthew 28:1–7.

Page 204. MERLIN AND THE GLEAM

In this, Tennyson's poetical biography, "the Gleam," so the poet said, "signifies . . . the higher poetic imagination." The usual interpretation of the poem is as follows: the second stanza is a reference to the youthful work of the poet; in the third he writes of the "ten years of silence" to which he was condemned by the severe criticism of his early volumes and by his sorrow at the death of Hallam; the fourth and fifth refer to the romantic and idyllic poetry characteristic of the volume of 1842; the sixth centers upon the epic tales of the Round Table; the seventh, in which the personality of King Arthur and that of Arthur Hallam are fused in the poet's mind, has to do with the creation of *In Memoriam;* the eighth sings of the brightening of the Gleam and of its hovering before the poet "all but in Heaven" as in old age he came "to the land's last limit." Mr. Nicolson, who writes that although the poem was intended to be an historical document it is not historical, does not accept this simple chronological interpretation. For his discussion of the "mystifying discrepancy" which stands in the way of his belief, see his *Tennyson*, pp. 122–3.

14. *learn'd*. Taught. (An obsolete use of the word.)

Page 205. BY AN EVOLUTIONIST

See note to *Wages*, above.

Hallam Tennyson said that his father believed in evolution from the time of his Cambridge days, and that he "brought it into poetry." Cf. Browning's *Rabbi Ben Ezra*, text p. 353.

Page 206. FAR—FAR—AWAY

Van Dyke wrote of this poem: "The emotion so delicately expressed is the attraction of the distant—in landscape, in sound, in the antenatal past." See note to lines 216–18 of *The Ancient Sage*, above, and compare the poem with *Tears, Idle Tears*, text p. 48.

3. *Far—far—away?* These words, Tennyson said, had always a strange charm for him.

THE THROSTLE

This poem, of which it is not incorrect to write, "Words by Tennyson, music by the missel-thrush," was composed in the poet's eightieth year. It "is a miracle of freshness wrought by the immortal spring in Tennyson's heart, in very spite of pain and age." (Van Dyke, *Poems by Tennyson*, p. 317.)

JUNE BRACKEN AND HEATHER

In 1892 Tennyson's last volume, *The Death of Œnone*, was published. The dedicatory poem in this volume, *June Bracken and Heather*, an "incomparable tribute of love untouched by age," was addressed to Mrs. Tennyson. Mr. Nicolson says that the detractors of Tennyson would do well to read more often such a piece as *June Bracken and Heather*.

CROSSING THE BAR

Tennyson wrote this poem, which his son called the crown of his life's work, in his eighty-first year. At the time of composition he was crossing the Solent on his way home to Farringford, after the serious illness of 1888–1889 at Aldworth. A few days before his death he said to his son, "Mind you put *Crossing the Bar* at the end of all editions of my poems." The poem should be compared with Browning's *Prospice*, text p. 361.

Page 207.

EXTRACTS FROM CONVERSATIONS, ETC.

207a, l. 24. *Descartes*. René Descartes (1596–1650), a French mathematician, physicist, and philosopher, the founder of the school of philosophy known as Cartesian.

207a, l. 27. *Lycidas*. An elegiac poem by Milton commemorating the death of Edward King, who had been a fellow student of Milton's at Cambridge.

207b, l. 5. *Theseus*. A Greek hero. He rid Attica of Procrustes and other evildoers, slew the Minotaur, conquered the Amazons, took part in the Caledonian boar hunt, etc. In the British Museum there is a statue of Theseus taken from the east pediment of the Parthenon.

207b, ll. 8–9. *Sir Edward Lytton Bulwer*. English novelist and dramatist (1803–1873), best known, perhaps, for his *The Last Days of Pompeii*. He opposed the granting of a pension to Tennyson, whom he called "School-Miss Alfred."

207b, l. 30. *Odium literarium*. The jealousies of men of letters!

207b, ll. 44–5. *Major prœteritis majorque futuris Regibus*. Greater than kings of bygone ages and greater than kings yet to be.

Page 208.

208a, l. 17. *Robertson*. The "well known and much beloved Frederick Robertson," preacher at Trinity Chapel, Brighton. He wrote a review of *The Princess* that pleased Tennyson, and he believed that *In Memoriam* contained "the best things that have been said on the future state."

208a, ll. 44–50. *Self-reverence . . . scorn of consequence*. These lines are from *Œnone*. (See text p. 17, ll. 142–8.)

Page 209.

209b, l. 43. *Catullus*. See note to *Frater Ave atque Vale*, above.

Page 210.

210a, l. 15. *Heber's*. Reginald Heber (1783–1826), bishop of Calcutta; poet and hymn writer.

210a, l. 29. *Mr. Rawnsley*. Drummond Rawnsley, rector of Halton. Both he and his father, who had been rector before him, were very intimate friends of the Tennyson family.

210a, l. 47. *Froude*. James Anthony Froude (1818–1894), English historian and man of letters.

210b, l. 6. *Lightfoot*. Joseph B. Lightfoot (1828–1889), divine and scholar. Chaplain to Queen Victoria and bishop of Durham.

210b, l. 36. *French Alexandrines*. The French Alexandrine is a line of twelve syllables.

210b, l. 41. *Béranger's Chansons.* Pierre Jean de Béranger (1780–1857), a French lyric poet. The French *chanson* is typically a lyric of smooth rhythm intended for singing.

210b, ll. 42–3. "*O par pitié, lui dit ma belle, Vieillard, épargnez nos amours.*" "O, I beseech you, old man," said my fine lady to me, "spare our love."

210b, l. 44. *Sully Prudhomme.* A French poet (1839–1907), recipient of the Nobel prize for literature, 1901.

210b, l. 46. *Alfred de Musset.* French poet, dramatist, and story writer (1810–1857).

Page 211.

211b, l. 28. *Bruno.* Giordano Bruno (1548–1600), an Italian philosopher.

211b, l. 40. *Spinoza.* Baruch (or Benedict) Spinoza (1632–1677), a Dutch Jewish philosopher.

Page 212. LETTERS

212a, ll. 23–4. *Memoria Technica of Mr. Gray.* Dr. Richard Gray, rector of Hinton, Devonshire, published a work on "artificial memory" in 1730. "So great was the demand for it," wrote another "Memoria Technica" man almost a hundred years later, "that six editions were soon exhausted."

212a, l. 42. *Christopher North.* The pseudonym of John Wilson, reviewer for *Blackwood's Edinburgh Magazine.* His sharp attacks on Tennyson's 1830 volume and on some of his later work greatly disturbed and depressed the poet.

212a, l. 46. "*the star of little Britain.*" In one of his reviews North said that it was the "unlucky lot of Alfred Tennyson . . . to be elevated to the throne of Little Britain."

212a, l. 51. *Maga.* A colloquial name applied to *Blackwood's Magazine.*

212b, l. 2. *Criticism and Taste.* This "Satyre" was the work of John Lake (l. 8), a Scotch tailor who had "perpetrated several poems and plays now absolutely forgotten," and who had not been successful in finding a market for his literary wares. He felt no special bitterness toward Christopher North, but when North's criticisms of Tennyson appeared in *Blackwood's*, Lake, although he confessed that he had never read a poem of Tennyson's, defended the poet against his critic by writing *Criticism and Taste.* The doggerel lines with which the "Satyre" ended included the words of encouragement given to Tennyson by North:

And yet, "of us if he will take advice,"
"Us," in whose hands all power and talent lies,
"The day may come", "with our assistance," he
"May grow expanding to a stately tree;"
But if he pride or disobedience "shews,
Assuredly he to oblivion goes."

Lake sent his defense to Tennyson and probably suggested that he should encourage its circulation. This the poet refused to do, and apparently fearing that the appearance of Lake's defense would lead to further attacks upon himself by *Blackwood's*, he made haste to write this apologetic letter to Christopher North. North probably never replied to the letter.

212b, ll. 13–14. *silly . . . North.* The "silly squib" Tennyson inserted in the volume of 1832. It was as follows:—

To Christopher North

You did late review my lays,
Crusty Christopher;
You did mingle blame and praise,
Rusty Christopher.
When I learnt from whom it came,
I forgave you all the blame,
Musty Christopher;
I could *not* forgive the praise,
Fusty Christopher.

Page 213.

213a, l. 4. *Conrade and Borachio.* Characters in Shakespeare's *Much Ado About Nothing.*

213a, l. 19. *James Spedding* (1808–1881) was one of the "Apostles" at Cambridge. In 1841 he began studying Bacon and for more than thirty years devoted himself with unflagging industry to research on Bacon and his age and to editing Bacon's works. Tennyson, who in his Cambridge days pronounced Spedding the wisest man he knew, always reckoned him among his most trusted friends and counsellors.

213a, l. 27. *Fitzgerald.* See introductory note to FitzGerald, text p. 903.

"*par nobile fratrum.*" A fine pair of friends! (FitzGerald counted Spedding his "earliest and dearest friend.")

213a, l. 35. *Charles.* The poet's brother. When he inherited the property of Sam Turner, his great-uncle, he assumed the name of Turner.

213a, l. 42. *John Heath.* At an "Apostle" dinner in 1833 which Tennyson did not attend, Heath was "full to the brim" of enquiries after the "Poet of the Apostles." Tennyson visited Heath at his home near Dorking in the summer of 1834.

Mill. John Stuart Mill (1806–1873), philosopher, logician, and profound student of literature, history, political economy, and mathematics. Mill's review, which, in spite of Tennyson's protest, appeared in the *London Review* in July, 1835, has been characterized as the only criticism of Tennyson of the period which still remains worth reading after the lapse of a century. For an excellent discussion of this review, see Lounsbury's *The Life and Times of Tennyson*, pp. 346–52.

213b, l. 10. *Emily Sellwood.* Miss Sellwood became Mrs. Tennyson in 1850.

Page 214.

214a, l. 13. *Kenilworth.* The ruins of this historic castle, which goes back to Henry I's reign and which was destroyed by Cromwell's forces, are in Kenilworth, a Warwickshire town four miles north of Warwick. It serves as the background for Scott's *Kenilworth.*

214a, l. 15. *Warwick.* The historic castle of the Warwick family, famous in English history, is located at Warwick, a town some seven miles from Stratford-on-Avon and a few miles south of Kenilworth.

214a, l. 29. *Guy's tower.* One of the principal towers of Warwick castle. It stands—128 feet high—on the right of the approach to the castle, and by some peculiarity of the contour of the land seems higher than Caesar's tower, the flanking tower on the left, whose height is 147 feet.

214a, l. 32. *Admiral van Tromp.* Martin Harpertzoon Tromp (1597–1653), a Dutch naval officer who was victor in more than thirty sea fights. A victory over the Spanish fleet in 1639 resulted in his being made admiral of Holland.

214a, l. 33. *Rembrandt.* Rembrandt van Rijn (1606–1669) was a Dutch painter.

Machiavelli. Niccolo Machiavelli (1469–1527), a Florentine statesman and political writer.

214a, l. 34. *Titian.* Titian (1477–1576) was a Venetian painter.

214a, l. 39. *foolish fellow painted it white.* In 1793 Edmond Malone (1741–1812), an Irish critic and author who had written much about Shakespeare, caused the vicar of Stratford, James Davenport, to have the bust of Shakespeare painted white. In 1861 the white paint was removed, and the original colors—auburn for the hair and beard, hazel for the eyes, scarlet for the doublet, and white for the collars and cuffs—were restored. Much satirical criticism was directed at Malone for his stupidity.

214a, l. 40. *Johnny Combe.* A wealthy bachelor with whom Shakespeare had had many business dealings. He died in 1614. A clause in his will read, "To Mr. William Shakespeare five pounds." His tomb is near Shakespeare's in the chancel of Stratford Church.

214b, l. 31. *Edmund Lushington.* See note to *In Memoriam,* LXXXV, above.

214b, l. 36. *Bolton Abbey.* The ruins of this abbey, in which Mary Queen of Scots was imprisoned for a while, are in Yorkshire. The note referred to in l. 38 is a quotation from Whitaker's *The History and Antiquities of the Deanery of Craven* appended to Wordsworth's *The White Doe of Rylstone,* a poem relating the legend of the doe that frequented Bolton Abbey churchyard. One sentence of the quotation reads, "Whatever the most fastidious taste could require to constitute a perfect landscape, is not only found here, but in its proper place." A traditional story of the founding of Bolton Abbey is the subject of Wordsworth's poem, *The Force of Prayer.*

Page 215.

215a, l. 16. *Aubrey de Vere.* An Irish poet (1814–1902). Besides writing poetry De Vere wrote a number of prose works, critical and miscellaneous.

215a, l. 46. "*Take . . . unreproved.*" Line 21 of Wordsworth's *Address to Kilchurn Castle, upon Loch Awe.*

215b, l. 28. *Gerald Massey.* A minor Victorian poet (1828–1907) whose first volume of verse appeared in 1847. As the editor of a paper for working men he wrote a number of significant articles on social and political reform. The "captivating volume" to which Tennyson refers was probably Massey's *The Ballad of Babe Christabel and Other Lyrical Poems,* 1854.

215b, l. 47. *John Forster.* Forster was editor of the *Examiner* from 1847 to 1855. He wrote a number of favorable reviews of Tennyson's work.

Page 216.

216a, l. 4. *Chapman.* Probably Sir Frederick Edward Chapman (1815–1893), general. He directed operations during the latter part of the siege at Sebastopol.

216a, l. 35. *Moxon.* Edward Moxon (1801–1858) became a publisher in London in 1830. He published for Southey, Wordsworth, Landor, Tennyson, and Browning.

216b, l. 1. *The Rev. G. G. Bradley.* Bradley was a neighbor of Tennyson's at Farringford. When Bradley was head master of Marlborough school, Tennyson entered his son Hallam in that school, and in reply to a question by the Queen said, "I am not sending my son to Marlborough—I am sending him to Bradley." After a most successful experience as head master at Marlborough Bradley became head of an Oxford college, and eventually Dean of Westminster.

216b, ll. 17–18. *Apollodorus . . . X.* The meaning is puzzling. X is probably Christopher North. It is possible that when Tennyson characterized the gifted X as a "pompholygous, broad-blown Apollodorus" he was thinking of the Greek Apollodorus, author of the *Library,* written, probably, in the first or second century A.D. J. G. Frazer calls the *Library* the "dull compilation of a commonplace man, who relates without one touch of imagination or one spark of enthusiasm the long series of fables and legends which inspired the immortal productions of Greek poetry and the splendid creations of Greek art."

216b, l. 23. *George Brimley* (1819–1857), essayist and critic, contributed to the *Cambridge Essays* of 1855 a study of Tennyson's poems which, in so far as the long poems, *The Princess, In Memoriam*, and *Maud*, were concerned, attempted merely "to place the reader in the true point of view, and examine certain prejudices against them which have obtained currency among us."

Page 218.

218a, l. 30. *Dr. Mann*. Robert James Mann (1817–1886). He studied medicine at University College, London, acting as dresser for the celebrated Liston at the hospital connected with that college. He lived in Natal from 1857 to 1866. He published a number of books on meteorological, astronomical, governmental, and medical subjects. He gained the favor of Tennyson by his paper *Tennyson's Maud Vindicated; an Explanatory Essay*.

218b, l. 16. *W. M. Thackeray*, the novelist, became editor of the *Cornhill Magazine* upon its founding in 1860. His urgent request that Tennyson "send them something" (see letter XV, text p. 219) was the occasion of this letter.

Page 219.

219a, l. 6. *The Duke of Argyll*. George John Douglas Campbell, eighth duke of Argyll (1823–1900). Tennyson was introduced to him in 1851 and from that time to the poet's death Argyll was one of his most valued friends. In 1859 Argyll, who had predicted that the *Idylls of the King* would be understood and admired by many who were incapable of understanding and appreciating many of Tennyson's poems, tested his prediction on Macaulay by giving him *Guinevere*. Macaulay, he reported, was delighted with the poem and could not find a single fault in it. In choosing Macaulay for his test the Duke was careful to make clear that he did not place the great essayist among those "incapable of understanding and appreciating" Tennyson.

219a, l. 15. *Guizot*. François Pierre Guillaume Guizot (1787–1874), French historian and statesman. He was ambassador of France in London, 1840, and after the fall of the French monarchy in 1848 he was again in London for about a year.

219a, l. 26. *Crabbe*. George Crabbe (1754–1832), poet, characterized by Horace Smith as "Pope in worsted stockings," and by Byron as "nature's sternest painter, yet the best."

219a, l. 30. *Sangreal*. The Duke and the Duchess of Argyll had urged Tennyson to attempt the topic of the Holy Grail.

219b, ll. 30–1. *about . . . Fisherman*. Working on *Enoch Arden*.

219b, ll. 50–51. *Cockneys . . . Freshwater*. At Farringford, which is near the village of Freshwater, Tennyson was much annoyed by celebrity hunters.

Page 220.

220a, l. 1. *Lord Lorne*. Marquis of Lorne, title of the eldest son of the Duke of Argyll.

220a, l. 10. *Corniche*. The name given to the picturesque road leading from Nice, France, to Genoa, Italy. See notes to *The Daisy*, above.

220a, l. 29. *Lionel . . . Dr. Hunt*. Tennyson's younger son Lionel was born in 1854. Dr. Hunt was probably his schoolmaster.

220a, l. 36. *Francis T. Palgrave* (1824–1897), poet and critic, and for ten years professor of poetry at Oxford. In the years 1850–1855, when he was vice-principal of Kneller Hall, Twickenham, he became a close friend of Tennyson. He is best known, perhaps, for his *Golden Treasury of Songs and Lyrics*, first published in 1861.

220b, l. 5. *Max Müller*. Friedrich (1823–1900), son of the German poet Wilhelm Müller, was naturalized a British subject under the name of Frederick Max-Müller. From 1854 to 1868 he was professor of modern European languages at Oxford University, and for more than twenty years one of the curators of the Bodleian Library.

220b, l. 16. *Jowett*. Benjamin Jowett (1817–1893), master of Balliol College, Oxford, and regius professor of Greek at Oxford. His essays and translations gave him high place among the writers of his time.

220b, l. 30. *Lord Houghton*. Richard Monckton Milnes, first Lord Houghton (1809–1885), was one of the "Apostles" at Cambridge. His chief title to remembrance rests on the part he played in moulding public opinion on literary matters and on the assistance he gave to young writers. He secured a pension for Tennyson and was one of the earliest champions of Swinburne. Tennyson's letter was written on the occasion of Lady Houghton's death, March 6, 1874.

Page 221.

221a, l. 6. *S. E. Dawson*. Tennyson said that he wrote this letter in criticism of an edition of *The Princess* brought out by "Dawson, of Canada." Dawson (1833–1916), who was a bookseller and publisher, was king's printer of Canada for eighteen years and president of the Royal Society of Canada in 1907.

221a, l. 18. *two whole lines*. The reference is to ll. 31 and 32 of *The Voice and the Peak*, text p. 184.

221b, l. 33. *in the Prometheus*. Lines 156 ff. of Act II, scene 1, of Shelley's *Prometheus*—"A wind arose among the pines," etc.

ROBERT BROWNING

BIBLIOGRAPHY

I. WORKS

Complete Works, ed. by F. G. Kenyon. 10 vols. Century Edition. (Smith: London, 1912.) Generally accepted as the best text; also valuable for introductory notes to the poems.

Complete Poetical Works, ed. by Augustine Birrell. (Macmillan: New York, 1915.) The most complete edition, providing an authoritative text. An appendix includes Kenyon's 1915 edition of *New Poems*.

Complete Works, ed. by Charlotte Porter and Helen A. Clarke. 12 vols. Camberwell Edition. (Crowell: New York, 1912.) The standard edition for its time, and sound in its criticism; the text is based upon the edition of 1888–1889, revised by the poet. Vol. I contains an essay, "Browning's Place in Literature," by W. L. Phelps.

Complete Poetical and Dramatic Works, ed. by G. W. Cooke. 6 vols. (Houghton: Boston, 1899.) A useful edition, frequently preferred for its critical apparatus.

Complete Poetic and Dramatic Works, ed. by H. E. Scudder. Cambridge Edition. (Houghton: Boston, 1895.) A good edition for use in schools, equipped with a biographical sketch; a thin-paper edition is available, dating 1905.

The Reader's Browning, ed. by Walter Graham. (American Book Company: New York, 1934.) One of the best of the recent partial editions; the editor supplies an introduction, notes, and a selected bibliography.

Tennyson and Browning, ed. by Guy Boas. (Nelson: New York, 1925.) A "tiger-lily-and-rose" anthology of the two poets, whose selections are grouped under the headings Patriotism, Art, Love, Faith, etc.

Select Poems, ed. by A. J. George. (Little: Boston, 1905.) An excellent selection, providing full and valuable literary and biographical commentary.

Robert Browning: Humanist, ed. by Arthur Compton-Rickett. (Jenkins: London, 1924.) Arranges selections under the headings The Poet of Nature, The Poet of Men and Women, Songs and Fantasies, The Poet's Outlook on Life; the introduction follows this outline also.

Poems and Plays. 2 vols. (Dutton: New York, 1930.) A desirable inexpensive collection, provided with an introduction by Arthur Waugh: Vol. I includes the poetry, 1833–1844; Vol. II, 1844–1864.

Shorter Poems, ed. by W. C. DeVane. (Crofts: New York, 1934.) A convenient collection of the lyrics and dramatic monologues; concludes with a selected bibliography.

New Poems by Robert Browning and Elizabeth Barrett Browning, ed. by Sir F. G. Kenyon. (Macmillan: New York, 1915.) Provides a small body of not generally known and new (about 25) poems, chiefly *juvenilia*. The most valuable part of the book is the information which the editor supplies concerning Miss Barrett's criticism of her future husband's poems.

Sordello, ed. by A. J. Whyte. (Dent: London, 1913.) The best edition of the poem, providing an introduction to each book, together with full notes.

The Ring and the Book. (Dutton: New York, 1932.) A good cheap edition, furnished with a brief introduction by C. W. Hodell; an appendix provides a few pages of notes.

The Ring and the Book, ed. by M. J. Moses and Helen A. Clarke. (Crowell: New York, 1927.) The best, though not the latest, edition of Browning's masterpiece; Moses furnishes a critical introduction,—notes by Clarke.

The Letters of Robert Browning and Elizabeth Barrett Barrett, 1845–1846, ed. by Robert W. B. Browning. 2 vols. (Harper: New York, 1926.) The entire correspondence as transmitted from the father to his son, the editor.

Letters to Miss Isa Blagden, ed. by A. J. Armstrong. (Baylor University Press: Waco, Texas, 1923.) Without shedding much light on the poet's literary work, these letters are valuable biographically for the years 1861–72.

Letters, collected by T. J. Wise and ed. by T. L. Hood. (Yale University Press: 1933.) Revealing little of the poet in Browning, these letters (1838–1887) with their annotations show him "as a man among men in the Victorian age."

Intimate Glimpses from Browning's Letter File. (Baylor University Press: Waco, Texas, 1934.) An interesting assembly of Browning correspondence, chosen from letters in the Baylor University collection of Browningiana.

Twenty-Two Unpublished Letters of Elizabeth Browning and Robert Browning. (United Feature Syndicate: New York, 1936.) The letters date from Oct. 2, 1846 to June 24, 1855, and are addressed to Mrs. Browning's sisters, Henrietta and Arabella. They throw much light on the early married life of the two poets and their new relations with the Barrett family. Prefaced by a statement from Major Altham, grandson of Captain Surtees Cook, who married Henrietta Barrett.

II. BIOGRAPHY AND CRITICISM

Berdoe, Edward. *The Browning Cyclopedia*. (Macmillan: New York, 1916.) An exhaustive survey of the sources of the poems; brings forward explanatory literary and historical material.

Brockington, A. A. *Browning and the Twentieth Century*. (Oxford University Press: 1932.) Furnished with abundant quotation, this study attempts to demonstrate (not always successfully) Browning's influence in the present century.

Brooke, S. A. *The Poetry of Robert Browning*. (Crowell: New York, 1902.) Rationalizes the philosophy underlying the whole of Browning's verse, following the headings Nature, Human Life, Art, Love, etc.; provides searching criticism of separate poems.

Broughton, L. N., and Stelter, B. F. *A Concordance to the Poems of Robert Browning*. 2 vols. (Stechert: New York, 1924.) An invaluable aid to the study of the poet, giving the reader access to his complete poetic vocabulary.

Browning, Fannie Barrett. *Some Memories of Robert Browning*. (Jones: Boston, 1928.) Provides interesting reminiscence by the poet's daughter-in-law, supplements what was previously known about the poet's last days and his funeral.

Burdett, Osbert, *The Brownings*. (Houghton: Boston, 1929.) Sheds no new light upon the work of the poets, but of interest for the analysis of the extensive correspondence and the revelation of a contact in which "poetry was not the only grace."

Burt, Emma. *The Seen and Unseen in Browning*. (Blackwell: Oxford, 1923.) Six essays revealing the mystical aspects of the poet in six of his major pieces; the best are upon "Abt Vogler" and "A Grammarian's Funeral."

Campbell, Lily B. *The Grotesque in the Poetry of Robert Browning*. (University of Texas Press: 1907.) A satisfactory review of this significant phase in the poet's work; concludes with a brief bibliography.

Cassidy, J. *A Study of Browning's "The Ring and the Book."* (Houghton: Boston, 1924.) Retaining the sectional divisions of the poem, this prose paraphrase relates the story as told by the poet's original characters.

Chesterton, G. K. *Robert Browning*. English Men of Letters series. (Macmillan: New York, 1925.) An outstanding short biography, abounding in journalistic flamboyancy, but recommended as a stimulating diversion.

Clarke, Helen A. *Browning and His Century*. (Doubleday: New York, 1912.) A centenary study of the relation of the poet to contemporary thought; contains a number of illustrations from photographs.

Clarke, Helen A. *Browning's England*. (Baker: New York, 1908.) An indispensable book for the study of the poet's native background; following a general discussion, the author analyzes a number of single poems, pointing out their inspiration and local color.

Clarke, Helen A. *Browning's Italy*. (Baker: New York, 1907.) Filled with abundant quotation, including many excerpts from *Sordello* and *The Ring and the Book*, this study shows the results of Browning's Italian residence upon a large body of his poetry.

Cook, A. K. *A Commentary upon Browning's "The Ring and the Book."* (Oxford University Press: 1920.) An exhaustive study of the materials of the poem, providing annotation of the poet's language and his numerous, often far-fetched allusions.

Cooke, G. W. *A Guide-Book to the Poetic and Dramatic Works of Robert Browning*. (Houghton: Boston, 1891.) Aims to provide fuller reference than the Orr *Handbook*, but errs on the side of bulkiness.

Corson, Hiram. *An Introduction to the Study of Robert Browning's Poetry*. (Heath: Boston, 1903.) A recommended book for the beginner who desires not a substitute but a motive for his reading.

DeVane, W. C. *Browning's Parleyings: The Autobiography of a Mind*. (Yale University Press: 1927.) A discussion of the effect exercised by the interlocutors of the poems upon Browning; most interesting is the revelation of the poet's own views on human conduct and the world of art.

DeVane, W. C. *A Browning Handbook*. (Crofts: New York, 1935.) Provides helpful annotations on the poems and classifies the pertinent facts established by much study of the poet; the preface furnishes a biographical sketch.

Douglas, James. *Robert Browning*. (Hodder: London, 1903.) An ably written essay on the poet, with the actual biographical material relegated to a tabulated appendix. Illustrations from the Browning Number (Nov., 1902) of the London *Bookman*.

Dowden, Edward. *The Life of Robert Browning*. (Dutton: New York, 1917.) A recommended biography, relating the material of Browning's poetry to the events of his life; provides excellent comment on separate poems.

Duckworth, F. R. G. *Browning: Background and Conflict*. (Dutton: New York, 1932.) A study of the poet's reputation in the 1850's, the 1890's, and the 1920's; the best chapter is the last, "The White Light." W. L. Phelps contributes an introduction.

Fotheringham, James. *Studies in the Mind and Art of Robert Browning*. (Marshall: London, 1900.) Presents a definitely academic series of comments on separate poems and the poet's work as a whole; however, Browning himself cordially praised its acute interpretation.

Gingerich, S. F. *Wordsworth, Tennyson, and Browning*. (Wahr: Ann Arbor, 1911.) Acclaims Browning as the "greatest psychologist of human souls"—great because of his optimism in the face of the facts of experience.

Gosse, E. W. *Robert Browning—Personalia*. (Houghton: Boston, 1890.) One of the earliest sources for intimate details of the poet's life; contains reminiscences and evaluations of the man and the poet.

Griffin, W. H. *The Life of Robert Browning*, completed and ed. by H. C. Minchin. (Macmillan: New York, 1910). One of the standard sources for the biographical data; offers little original criticism, but provides much information on the origin and reception of many of the major poems.

Griggs, E. H. *The Poetry and Philosophy of Browning*. (Huebsch: New York, 1905.) Purporting to be a handbook to the poetry of Browning, this booklet contains a syllabus of six inspiring lectures on the poet's principal themes and attitudes.

Harrington, V. C. *Browning Studies*. (Badger: Boston, 1915.) A series of entertaining essays, rearranged from classroom lectures.

Hatcher, H. H. *The Versification of Robert Browning*. (Ohio State University Press: 1928.) A catalogued analysis of the poet's metrical features; comments on his rapid composition and his reluctance to revise.

Herford, C. H. *Robert Browning*. (Dodd: New York, 1905.) Presents a reliable biographical account, especially valuable for its study of the poet's "joy in soul."

Hodell, C. W., ed. *The Old Yellow Book*. (Dutton: New York, 1927.) The most accessible edition of this important source book, translated by the editor.

Jones, Sir Henry. *Browning as a Philosophical and Religious Teacher*. (Maclehose: Glasgow, 1912.) The authoritative work on this subject; useful for the advanced student who can sympathize with its exegetical method.

Jones, R. M. *Mysticism in Robert Browning*. (Macmillan: New York, 1924.) Admitting that the poet does not exhibit trance-like or ecstatic mystical qualities, this brief study discovers the basis of a real mysticism in certain personal experiences which establish a certitude of God's existence.

Kenyon, F. G., ed. *Robert Browning and Alfred Domett.* The correspondence 1840–1846; also provides generous running commentary and thus brings together a full discussion of the friendship between the poet and the original of "Waring"—mentioned also in "Time's Revenges" and "The Guardian Angel."

Kingsland, W. G. *Robert Browning, Chief Poet of the Age.* (Jarvis: London, 1887.) One of the most readable of the rhapsodic earlier criticisms, "addressed primarily to beginners in the study of Browning's poems."

Loth, David. *The Brownings: A Victorian Idyll.* (Tudor: New York, 1935.) Offering little new in matters of fact, this book presents the interesting history of the London courtship and the residence of the two poets in Italy; concludes with a humorous fling at the Browning Societies.

Lounsbury, T. R. *The Early Literary Career of Robert Browning.* (Scribner: New York, 1911.) Consists of lectures on the following subjects: "*Pauline* and *Paracelsus*," "*Strafford* and *Sordello*," "*Bells and Pomegranates*"; describes the reviewers' attitudes up to 1846.

Marzials, F. T. *Browning.* (Bell: London, 1905.) A compact, readable Life, recommended as an introduction; concludes with a seven-page bibliography.

Mayne, Ethel C. *Browning's Heroines.* (Chatto: London, 1913.) An earnest, sophisticated study of the poet's delineation of feminine characters.

Orr, Mrs. Alexandra L. *Life and Letters of Robert Browning.* (Houghton: Boston, 1908.) An interesting but too facile interpretation; includes many remarks by the poet on his own work. The edition has been revised by F. G. Kenyon.

Orr, Mrs. Alexandra L. *A Handbook to the Works of Robert Browning.* (Bell: London, 1902.) "Originally intended to be a primer," this valuable work, authorized by the poet himself, has expanded through many editions; it provides easy analyses for practically all of the poems.

Phelps, W. L. *Robert Browning.* (Bobbs: Indianapolis, 1932.) Draws together the gist of the author's many writings on this subject, adding some new material; valuable for its interpretations of single poems.

Pottle, F. A. *Shelley and Browning: A Myth and Some Facts.* (Pembroke Press: Chicago, 1923.) A full discussion of Browning's first interest in Shelley, whose influence is seen as a liberating factor, turning definitely to the idea of poetry being self-revelation; contains a foreword by W. L. Phelps.

Powell, J. W. *Confessions of a Browning Lover.* (Abingdon Press: New York, 1918.) A charmingly written record of adventures in the poet's world of men and ideas; concludes with an analysis of "Prospice."

Rain, Thomas. *Browning for Beginners.* (Sonnenschein: London, 1904.) A series of diverting essays on the poet, mingling humor and good taste.

Rhys, Ernest. *Browning and His Poetry.* (Harrap: London, 1918.) A combined Life and anthology; useful for the beginner by providing an inviting approach to the poetry.

Russell, Mrs. Frances T. *One Word More on Browning.* (Stanford University Press: 1927.) Free from academic posturing, the criticism is fresh and stimulating, even though enthusiasm and wit sometimes take the place of judgment; contains bibliographies for the poetry of Mr. and Mrs. Browning.

Sharp, William. *The Life of Robert Browning.* (Scott: London, 1890.) A well-written brief biography, although hastily composed upon the occasion of the poet's death.

Sim, Mrs. Frances M. *Robert Browning, the Poet and the Man, 1833–1846.* (Appleton: New York, 1923.) A popular account of the life of the poet up to the date of his marriage; contains no literary criticism of any importance.

Sim, Mrs. Frances M. *Robert Browning, Poet and Philosopher, 1850–1889.* (Unwin: London, 1923.) A continuation of the former work, showing the deepening of the poet's thought and expression; provides analyses of many of the major poems.

Sim, Mrs. Frances M. *Robert Browning and Elizabeth Barrett.* (Golden Vista Press: London, 1930.) A brief account of the courtship and marriage; suggests that Miss Barrett is memorialized in *Fifine* and parts of *The Ring and the Book.*

Symons, Arthur. *An Introduction to the Study of Browning.* (Dutton: New York, 1923.) Particularly concerned with the poetry, furnishing a critical analysis of the many poems under review; the original form of this study was highly commended by Browning himself.

Treves, Sir Frederick. *The Country of "The Ring and the Book."* (Cassell: New York, 1929.) Reconstructs in an interesting way the story of the poem, providing local color and the background of human associations.

Waugh, Arthur. *Robert Browning.* (Small: Boston, 1900.) The best of the briefer Lives, judicious and well written; concludes with a two-page bibliography.

Whiting, Lilian. *The Brownings: Their Life and Art.* (Little: Boston, 1917.) Based on documents in the possession of the poets' descendants, this book provides new light on the last phase of Browning's life.

III. ARTICLES FROM BOOKS

Birrell, Augustine. "On the Alleged Obscurity of Mr. Browning's Poetry," in *Obiter Dicta.* (Stock: London, 1896.) Remarks that most of the obscurity is dissipated upon reading the much-maligned poems; ardently commends the poet's strength and versatility.

Dawson, W. J. "Robert Browning" and five other essays, in *Makers of English Poetry.* (Revell: New York, 1906.) Titles: "Philosophy of Life," "Spirit of Religion," "Attitude to Christianity," "Significance in Literature," "Concluding Survey": —these essays assemble the older critical opinion, providing little of novelty.

Drinkwater, John. "Some Letters from Matthew Arnold to Robert Browning," in *A Book for Bookmen.* (Doran: New York, 1927.) A collection of fourteen letters (with annotations by Mr. Drinkwater), showing the cordial relations existing between the two poets.

Drinkwater, John. "Browning's Diction," in *Victorian Poetry*. (Doran: New York, 1924.) Makes comparisons with Tennyson and Byron; remarks also the "Browningesque" strain, which is colored with the grotesque.

Gosse, Edmund. "Browning in France," in *More Books on the Table*. (Scribner: New York, 1923.) Records the service rendered to the poet by Joseph Milsand, who in 1851 contributed to Paris reviews favorable criticisms of Browning's poetry.

Grierson, H. J. C. "Tennyson, Browning, and Some Others," in *Lyrical Poetry of the Nineteenth Century*. (Harcourt: New York, 1929.) Compares Tennyson's virtuosity with Browning's wider range; discusses Browning's variety and his love for the climactic moment.

Hearn, Lafcadio. "Studies in Browning," in *Pre-Raphaelite and Other Poets*. (Dodd: New York, 1922.) Furnishes an easy introduction to the philosophy of the poet; analyzes many of the poems, seeing Browning as the greatest poet of human character since Shakespeare.

Inge, W. R. "The Mysticism of Robert Browning," in *Studies of English Mystics*. (Murray: London, 1906.) Founds the poet's mysticism on his belief in a spiritual world and his teleological convictions; shows how he brings this attitude into his analyses of human nature.

Jones, Sir Henry. "Robert Browning and Elizabeth Barrett Browning," in *The Cambridge History of English Literature*, XIII. (Putnam: New York, 1917.) Provides an excellent summary of the composition and reception of Browning's early work, his dramas, and the later longer poems.

Lucas, F. L., "Browning," in *Eight Victorian Poets*. (Cambridge University Press: 1930.) Makes frequent contrasts between Browning and Tennyson; remarks the contradictions and prosiness of Browning's verse, redeemed by a "few human figures that still speak to us and a few lyrics that still sing."

More, P. E. "Why is Browning Popular?" in *Shelburne Essays*, Third Series. (Putnam: New York, 1905.) Answers the question by pointing to the poet's skill in describing mixed feelings, with which readers feel a natural sympathy.

Morley, John. "On *The Ring and the Book*," in *Studies in Literature*. (Macmillan: New York, 1891.) Traces amid the details of the poem the elements which constitute its unity; sees its humanity as its great achievement.

Nevinson, H. W. "The Poet of the Grotesque," in *Books and Personalities*. (Lane: London, 1905.) Criticizes Chesterton's Life of Browning, finding it admirable as a character sketch, but too indiscriminate in its praise of the poet's works, which, except for the two volumes of his own selection, are destined to oblivion.

Parrott, T. M. "The Vitality of Browning," in *Studies of a Booklover*. (Pott: New York, 1904.) Praises the poet's optimism and intellectual curiosity, briefly reviewing his life, and commenting upon the impetus he gave to the modern realistic movement.

Pater, Walter. "Browning," in *Essays from "The Guardian."* (Macmillan: London, 1901.) A favorable review of Symons's *Introduction to the Study of Browning;* concludes with a eulogy of the poet's skill in interpreting human motives.

Saintsbury, George. "Browning," in *Corrected Impressions*. (Dodd: New York, 1895.) Explodes the obscurity complaint; praises many of the dramatic lyrics, but shies off from *The Ring and the Book;* comments on the poet's "generous and indomitable spirit."

Santayana, George. "The Poetry of Barbarism," in *Interpretations of Poetry and Religion*. (Scribner: New York, 1900.) A corrective for the popular idolizing of Browning.

Scott, Dixon. "The Homeliness of Browning," in *Men of Letters*. (Hodder: London, 1923.) Praises the poet as "the laureate of life in undress," expressing a desire to free him from the monopoly of the Browning Clubs.

Shanks, Edward. "Robert Browning," in *Second Essays on Literature*. (Collins: London, 1927.) Points out the lack of autobiographical material in the poet's work; severely criticizes his obscurities; finds his best work in the *Men and Women* series.

Stevenson, Lionel. "Robert Browning," in *Darwin Among the Poets*. (University of Chicago Press: 1932.) Comments on the young poet's lack of interest in science, but refers to significant passages in *Paracelsus* and *Pauline;* remarks his later self-possession in his belief in the anthropocentric universe, controlled by God.

Walker, Hugh. "Browning, 1833–46," and "Browning, 1850–69," in *The Greater Victorian Poets*. (Swan: London, 1895.) The first essay, after analyzing the early poems, notes the gain of proportion over grotesqueness in the poet's middle period. The second essay remarks the dominance of types in the later poems.

Woodberry, G. E. "On Browning's Death," in *Makers of Literature*. (Macmillan: London, 1900.) A review of the poet's literary theory and his tolerant attitude toward his type-figures, best illustrated in his dramatic monologues; lauds his vigorous draftsmanship, which makes him one of "the heirs of the masculine intellect."

IV. ARTICLES FROM PERIODICALS

Crawford, A. W. "Browning's 'Cleon,'" *Journal of English and Germanic Philology*, XXVI, 485–90 (Winter, 1927). Attempts to show that the poem was written as a complement to Arnold's *Empedocles on Ætna*.

Cressman, E. D. "Classical Poems of Robert Browning," *Classical Journal*, XXIII, 198–207 (Dec., 1927). Analyzes some twenty complete poems dealing with classical subjects.

Cunliffe, J. W. "Elizabeth Barrett's Influence on Browning's Poetry," *Publications of the Modern Language Association*, XXIII, 169–83 (June, 1908). Finds Browning's inspiration prominent in his wife's later work, her influence seen as more subtle and indirect; believes that Mrs. Browning's death is the cause of the obscurity of the lyrical tone under the heavier casuistry of Browning's later verse.

DeVane, W. C. "The Landscape of 'Childe Roland,'" *Publications of the Modern Language Association*, XL, 426–32 (June, 1925). Finds the genesis of the scarred landscape in Gerard de Lairesse's *Art of Painting*, which the poet read as a child.

Elliott, G. R. "Shakespeare's Significance for Browning," *Anglia*, XXXII, 90–162 (Jan., 1909). A very valuable article: points out definite relationship by reference to "facts in the poet's life, letters, and work"; sees Shakespeare as the principal reason for Browning's desire to write a great tragedy.

Fonblanque, Ethel de. "The Influence of Italy on the Poetry of the Brownings," *Fortnightly Review*, XCII, 327–44 (Aug., 1909). Reviews the poets' itinerary and places of residence, providing the background of many of their poems.

Gloder, H. "Browning's 'Childe Roland,'" *Publications of the Modern Language Association*, XXXIX, 963–78 (Dec., 1924). Shows how the poet's subconscious mind wrought the landscape and motif of the poem out of nursery-tale heroics and medieval legend.

Lubbock, Percy. "Browning's Work," *Quarterly Review*, CCXVII, 437–57 (Oct., 1912). A review of the ten-volume Kenyon edition, remarking the changes of popular opinion upon Browning; sees the poet's final biography in his work.

Phelps, W. L. "Robert Browning on Spiritualism," *Yale Review*, XXIII, 125–38 (Autumn, 1933). Shows the poet carrying his skepticism into a number of seances, quoting also letters in which Browning describes his experiences.

Raymond, W. O. "Browning and Higher Criticism," *Publications of the Modern Language Association*, XLIV, 590–621 (June, 1929). Shows the poet's reaction to the religious thought of his day: the orthodoxy of most of his poems, his dislike of Higher Criticism, and his stand on the basis of human experience.

Ritchie, Anne T. "Robert and Elizabeth Barrett Browning," *Harper's Magazine*, LXXXIV, 832–55 (May, 1892). An interesting and valuable review of the life of the Brownings, filled with many reminiscential notes.

Stephen, Leslie. "Browning's Casuistry," *Living Age*, CCXXXVI, 257–71 (Jan. 31, 1903). A review of Brooke's study of the poet; comments on Browning's teaching that the errors of an individual may be stages in his evolution.

NOTES

In the text of the Browning material in this anthology, there are explanatory notes and introductions to many of the poems, printed in the form of footnotes. The notes which follow do not reprint commentary already available in the footnotes referred to, but are designed to amplify and supplement these footnotes. It will often be found, therefore, that the omission here of an expected note on a Browning poem is explained by the fact that the point in question has already been explained in some detail in a footnote in the text.

Page 230. PIPPA PASSES

Introduction

230a, l. 14. *Asolo in the Trevisan.* Asolo is a small town about thirty miles from Venice in the province of Treviso. Silk growing and spinning were the chief industry of the district.

Page 231.

231a, l. 29. *St. Agnes' nipple.* Pippa probably has in mind some painting in the church of St. Agnes, a virgin martyr of the fourth century, whose beauty was so great it excited the admiration of all the young noblemen of Rome but who resolved to live as the spouse of Christ. See note on Tennyson's *St. Agnes' Eve*, above.

231a, l. 30. *Turk bird.* The common turkey.

231b, l. 1. *weevil and chafer.* Destructive insects of the beetle family.

231b, ll. 22–3. *Sebald . . . Luca.* The young lover and the despised old husband.

231b, l. 34. *Possagno church.* The church at Possagno, four miles from Asolo, was designed by the sculptor Canova and therefore was a fitting place for the wedding of Jules.

Page 232.

232a, l. 28. *our turret.* Presumably a turret in the ruined city walls of Asolo.

232a, l. 31. *each to each.* Luigi and his mother, not the lizards of l. 30.

Page 233. *I.—Morning*

233a, ll. 25–7. *St. Mark's . . . belfry . . . Vicenza . . . Padua.* From Asolo on a clear day the Cathedral of St. Mark and the Campanile (belfry) at Venice would be visible, also the cities of Vicenza and Padua.

233b, l. 17. *wittol.* A man who knows of his wife's infidelity and submits to it.

233b, l. 25. *Capuchin.* A monk of the Capuchin branch of the Franciscan order.

Page 234.

234a, l. 12. *coil.* Fuss.

Page 237. *[Interlude:] Talk by the Way*

The interludes, pitched in a lower key than the four sections of the play, were designed to give contrast and relief. The wit in them is so allusive that it may be questioned if they serve their dramatic purpose adequately or even indeed if they are so very witty after all.

237a, l. 29. *Giovacchino.* A young poet whose good character is indicated by the fact that he has dropped out of the group, declining to have any part in the cruel joke which is the basis of the episode following. He has taken flight from some passion of his own, either dishonorable or impossible, and the other students ridicule him for treating love as a disease instead of enjoying it, regardless of honor. They suggest (ll. 41–5) that he write an epic with Æsculapius, the god of medicine, for hero, and other divinities assisting in the cure of the lovesick.

237b, l. 40. *Canova.* Antonio Canova (1757–1832), the sculptor, was born at Possagno near Asolo, and many of his pieces were in the vicinity.

Page 238.

238a, l. 40. *Pietà.* A virgin with the dead Christ upon which Canova was working at the time of his death.

238b, l. 13. *Malamocco.* A town on an island of the same name which forms part of the boundary of the harbor of Venice.

238b, l. 14. *Alciphron.* A Greek epistolary writer of the second century A.D.

238b, l. 19. *lire.* Plural of *lira*, the basic coin in Italian currency.

238b, l. 22. *Tydeus at the Academy.* Jules had done a statue of Tydeus, an Homeric hero, which he had shown in the Academy of Fine Arts at Venice.

Page 239.

239a, l. 1. *Hannibal Scratchy.* A burlesque on the name of the painter Annibale Caracci.

239a, l. 19. *the little girl.* Pippa.

II.—Noon

Swinburne in a letter accused Browning of stealing a plot from Diderot and spoiling it, and the reference is to this episode in *Pippa Passes.* (See note on postscript to Swinburne letter XVI, text p. 800.)

239b, l. 14. *Psyche's robe.* One of the statues in Jules's studio was of Psyche.

239b, ll. 30–1. *Minion, a Coluthus . . . Bessarion.* Minion = favorite. Coluthus was a sixth-century Greek epic poet, most of whose works were lost but whose poem on *The Rape of Helen* was discovered by Cardinal Bessarion, a noted Greek scholar, in the fifteenth century.

239b, ll. 37–8. *He said,* etc. The quotation is from the *Odyssey*, XXII, 10. Antinous was one of the suitors of Penelope. Ulysses upon his return shot them down with his great bow. Antinous was the first to fall, pierced in the neck by the "bitter shaft."

239b, l. 41. *Almaign Kaiser.* German Emperor.

Page 240.

240a, l. 3. *Hippolyta.* Queen of the Amazons.

240a, l. 8. *bay-filletted and thunder-free.* According to ancient belief the laurel (or bay) was a protection against lightning and a man who wore a wreath of it would be safe.

240a, l. 10. *those who slew Hipparchus.* Harmodius and Aristogeiton killed the tyrant in 514 B.C. The daggers which they used were concealed in myrtle branches which the assassins carried at the Panathenaic festival.

240a, l. 24. *Violet and parsley crowns.* The leaves of a species of parsley, our celery, were used by the ancients in garlands because of their strong fragrance.

240b, l. 6. *But marble!—'neath my tools.* Rolfe roughly paraphrases the succeeding passage as follows: "The capabilities of marble are numberless; it may have the clearness of air, the brilliance of diamond; it is at one moment metal, and at another, flesh; it is even flame-like when the passion of the workman wakes an answering passion."

Page 242.

242a, ll. 27–8. *You I shall not meet: If I dreamed,* etc. He will never meet the Phene of whom he dreamed because she never existed; saying this much is enough to waken him from the dream.

242b, l. 16. *all this.* Queenship with all that it entails.

242b, l. 21. *jesses.* The straps fitted around the leg of a hawk, to which the line held by the falconer is attached.

Page 243.

243a, ll. 5–6. *Like my own Psyche . . . visionary butterfly.* The statue of Psyche by Jules, in the folds of the gown of which he had concealed Phene's supposed letters (see p. 239b, l. 14) showed Psyche with a butterfly alighting on her lips—the butterfly being the symbol of the soul. Phene with her new soul resembles this figure.

[*Interlude:*] *Talk by the Way*

243b, l. 9. *Bishop's Intendant's money.* How it was to be earned is disclosed in Act IV. See p. 251b, ll. 5–31.

243b, l. 15. *grig.* Cricket, supposedly a very lively insect.

243b, l. 19. *Koenigsberg, Prussia Improper.* One portion of the kingdom of Prussia was long called "Prussia Proper," to distinguish it from the other provinces of the kingdom. Koenigsberg is just outside of "Prussia Proper."

243b, l. 29. *posy.* Poesy, verse motto.

243b, ll. 31–5. *How Moses,* etc. For anyone who wishes to pursue Bluphocks's rhymes to the source, the biblical references are Exodus 8:20–21 and 10:4; Jonah 1:1–2; Numbers 22:23–31.

243b, l. 33. *harshish.* Harsh.

Page 244.

244a, l. 5. *Lupine-seed.* A kind of pulse, no very suitable food for a man of Bluphocks's temperament.

244a, l. 10. *zwanzigers.* An Austrian coin worth about fifteen cents.

244a, l. 20. *Metternich.* The Austrian prime minister from 1809 to 1848. See note to l. 19 of *The Italian in England,* below.

244a, l. 29. *Panurge consults Hertrippa.* Panurge is the handsome and witty young man in Rabelais's *Gargantua and Pantagruel* who resolves on marriage and consults various people concerning the step. Hertrippa the philosopher-magician gave him most alarming predictions.

244a, l. 30. *King Agrippa.* Acts 26 : 27.

244a, ll. 33–4. *your head and a ripe musk-melon,* etc. The point is that the melon would be worth half a zwanziger and the head therefore worth nothing.

244b, ll. 4–6. *if Signor Luigi leaves home to-night . . . well and good.* The police, aware of Luigi as a possible conspirator, have been misinformed somehow of the extent of his plans. Therefore the ironic situation arises that, if he leaves for Vienna intending to assassinate the Emperor, he will be allowed to pass freely, but if he stays innocently at home as his mother tries to persuade him to do, he will be arrested on the suspicion of lurking about to meet conspirators. This mistake of the police must be understood to clarify what otherwise seem inconsistencies in the third act.

III.—Evening

244b, l. 41. *old Franz.* Francis I, Emperor of Austria.

Page 245.

245a, l. 4. *Your Pellicos.* Silvio Pellico (1788–1854), an Italian patriot and writer, was a member of the Carbonari. He spent eleven years in prison and wrote a pathetic account of this experience. He was released in 1830.

245a, l. 15. *they visit night by night.* The patriotic leaders haunt his dreams. His mother hints, on the basis of this, that his mind is unbalanced.

245b, ll. 1–2. *I go This evening.* See the note above on 244b, ll. 4–6, concerning the police misunderstanding of his purpose.

Page 246.

246a, ll. 33–4. *Andrea . . . Pier . . . Gualtier.* Conspirators who have preceded Luigi.

246b, l. 14. *How first the Austrians got these provinces.* In 1813 the Austrian armies overran much of northern Italy and secured further concessions at the Congress of Vienna. Their occupation of northern Italy was legalized by the Treaty of Vienna in 1815.

246b, l. 26. *"I am the bright and morning-star."* See Revelation 22 : 16.

246b, l. 27. *"I give the morning-star."* "And he that overcometh, and keepeth my works unto the end, to him will I give power over the nations. . . . And I will give him the morning star." (Revelation 2 : 26, 28.)

Page 247.

247a, l. 10. *The Titian at Treviso.* In the cathedral at Treviso there is an altarpiece, an Annunciation, by Titian.

247a, l. 14. *A king lived long ago.* Originally published in 1835, this song was much revised for use in the drama.

Page 248. [*Interlude:*] *Talk by the Way*

248a, ll. 8–9. *fig-peckers, Lampreys and red Breganze-wine.* A bird that feeds on figs, an eel-like fish considered a delicacy, and a north Italian wine.

Page 249. *IV.—Night*

249b, l. 1. *Messina.* A large seaport in Sicily.

249b, l. 2. *Assumption Day.* The ascent of the Virgin is celebrated August 15th.

249b, l. 12. *Ascoli, Fermo, and Fossombruno.* Towns in central Italy.

Page 250.

250a, ll. 39–42. *Forli . . . Cesena.* Towns of east central Italy on the route from Bologna to Rimini.

Page 251.

251b, l. 17. *English knave.* Bluphocks. See p. 243a, ll. 7–15.

Page 252. [*Epilogue*]

252a, l. 15. *dray.* Nest.

252a, l. 18. *hedge-shrew and lob-worm.* A field mouse and a species of worm similar to an earthworm, but larger.

252a, l. 21. *thanks for your counsel, my Zanze.* No thanks, is what Pippa means. Zanze is the Third Girl of the Interlude between Acts III and IV. See p. 249a, ll. 31–4.

252b, l. 40. *Brenta.* A river in northern Italy.

Page 253.

253a, l. 13. *Full complines.* A compline is the religious exercise which completes the service of the day. In the Catholic service the compline is the last division of the breviary.

253a, l. 15. *twats.* In answer to an inquiry from Furnival, Browning explained that he found the word in a volume of royalist rhymes and that "the word struck me as a distinctive part of a nun's attire that might fitly pair off with the cowl appropriated to a monk."

CAVALIER TUNES

The so-called "Long Parliament" elected in 1640 was dominated by the Puritans and was hostile to Charles I. John Pym and John Hampden were two of the chief parliamentary leaders and (Sir Arthur) Hazelrig, (Nathaniel) Fiennes, and young Harry (Sir Henry Vane the younger) aided Pym and Hampden. Matters reached a crisis and in August, 1642, the king went to Nottingham where he was joined by his nephew, Prince Rupert of Bavaria, who became his great cavalry leader. And at Nottingham the king at once raised the royal standard—an act equivalent to declaring that a state of war existed, and one that was a summons to loyal subjects to rally to his assistance.

It is against this background of civil war that Browning's three poems are set. The Cavaliers were the supporters of the king. The Roundheads were the parliamentary party, so called because they cropped their hair short while the Cavaliers continued the courtly Renaissance tradition of wearing curls.

Browning's series of three poems represents phases of the civil struggle which followed the raising of the royal standard. *Marching Along* shows the spirit of the Cavaliers rallying to the standard at Nottingham. *Give a Rouse* belongs to a period after there has been heavy fighting but before the final outcome of the struggle is certain. It is a song by a lion-hearted old Cavalier who has had his son shot down beside him in battle by "Noll's" (Cromwell's) troopers (see stanza III) but who is still "ripe for fight" for his king. *Boot and Saddle* reflects the final period when the war was going against the Cavaliers. The Cavalier is mounting his troop to go to the relief of his own Castle Brancepeth besieged by Roundheads and defended by his wife. The query "Who?" in l. 13 is an abbreviation for "Who is defending the castle?" And the answer is, "My wife, of course!" Browning brings out admirably the gallantry and recklessness of the Cavalier type.

Page 254. THE LOST LEADER

Asked if this poem referred to Wordsworth and his defection from the cause of liberalism, Browning wrote Dr. Grosart on Feb. 24, 1875: "I have been asked the question you now address me with, and as duly answered it, I can't remember how many times; there is no sort of objection to one more assurance or rather confession, on my part, that I *did* in my hasty youth presume to use the great and venerated personality of Wordsworth as a sort of painter's model; one from which this or the other particular feature may be selected and turned to account; had I intended more, above all, such a boldness as portraying the entire man, I should not have talked about 'handfuls of silver and bits of ribbon.' These never influenced the change of politics in the great poet, whose defection, nevertheless, accompanied as it was by a regular face-about of his special party, was to my juvenile apprehension, and even mature consideration, an event to deplore. But just as in the tapestry on my wall I can recognize figures which have *struck out* a fancy, on occasion, that though truly enough thus derived, yet would be preposterous as a copy, so, though I dare not deny the original of my little poem, I altogether refuse to have it considered as the 'very effigies' of such a moral and intellectual superiority."

Mrs. Orr (*Life and Letters of Robert Browning*, pp. 191–2) quotes a letter written in September of the same year in which Browning repeats the point that although Wordsworth was his model, the portrait is not complete. "I undoubtedly had Wordsworth in my mind—but simply as 'a model'; you know, an artist takes one or two striking traits in the features of his 'model' and uses them to start his fancy on a flight which may end far enough from the good man or woman who happens to be 'sitting' for nose and eye. . . . But once call my fancy-portrait *Wordsworth*—and how much more ought one to say—how much more would not I have attempted to say!"

Page 255. "HOW THEY BROUGHT THE GOOD NEWS FROM GHENT TO AIX"

"There is no sort of historical foundation," wrote Browning, "about 'Good News from Ghent.' I wrote it under the bulwark of a vessel off the African coast, after I had been at sea long enough to appreciate even the fancy of a gallop on the back of a certain good horse 'York,' then in my stable at home. It was written in pencil on the fly-leaf of Bartoli's *Simboli*, I remember." On another occasion Browning declared that he wrote from "a merely general impression of the characteristic warfare and besieging which abound in the Annals of Flanders."

The ride would be slightly less than one hundred miles by road. W. J. Rolfe calculates the distances as follows: Ghent to Lokeren 12 miles; Lokeren to Boom 16 miles; Boom to Düffeld (Duffel) 12 miles. Mecheln (Malines) is south of the route but close enough so that the cathedral chimes could be heard. Düffeld to Aershot 15 miles; Aershot to Hasselt 24 miles and approximately 80 from Ghent. It is here that Dirck's horse goes down. Looz and Tongres are off the direct route and Dalhem is unidentified—probably a village very near Aix.

Page 256. GARDEN FANCIES

The linking of two such dissimilar poems as *The Flower's Name* and *Sibrandus Schafnaburgensis* under a common title may seem odd until one considers the question—just what sort of company is desirable in a garden? A girl—yes. A book—yes. But certainly not a book such as Sibrandus wrote! Better a copy of Rabelais and a good bottle of wine.

Sibrandus Schafnaburgensis with its worms, owls, beetles, and toadstools reveals an approach to nature very different from that of the roses-and-lilies school of poets. This poem is of course jocular in tone. Browning was always interested in odd and "ugly" living things and was perfectly willing to admit them to his serious poems. See for example the lichens and midges in *By the Fire-Side* (text pp. 280–1, ll. 48 and 70), the landscapes in *The Flight of the Duchess* (p. 305–6, ll. 20–30), *Childe Roland to the Dark Tower Came* (p. 323, ll. 55–78), and the pet spider mentioned in Browning's letters (text p. 476a, ll. 30–40). Chesterton has a striking passage on this quality in Browning: "There is one very curious idea into which we have been hypnotised by the more eloquent poets, and that is that nature in the sense of what is ordinarily called the country is a thing entirely stately and beautiful as those terms are commonly understood. The whole world of the fantastic, all things top-heavy, lop-sided, and nonsensical are conceived as the work of man, gargoyles, German jugs, Chinese pots, political caricatures, burlesque epics, the pictures of Mr. Aubrey Beardsley and the puns of Robert Browning. But in truth a part, and a very large part, of the sanity and power of nature lies in the fact that out of her comes all this instinct of caricature. Nature may present itself to the poet too often as consisting of stars and lilies; but these are not poets who live in the country; they are men who go to the country for inspiration and could no more live in the country than they could go to bed in Westminster Abbey. Men who live in the heart of nature, farmers and peasants, know that nature means cows and pigs and creatures more humorous than can be found in a whole sketchbook of Callot. And the element of the grotesque in art, like the element of the grotesque in nature, means, in the main, energy, the energy which takes its own forms and goes its own way. Browning's verse, in so far as it is grotesque, is not complex and artificial; it is natural and in the legitimate tradition of nature. The verse sprawls like the trees, dances like the dust; it is ragged like the thundercloud, it is top-heavy like the toadstool. Energy which disregards the standard of classical art is in nature as it is in Browning. The same sense of the uproarious force in things which makes Browning dwell on the oddity of a fungus or a jellyfish makes him dwell on the oddity of a philosophical idea. Here, for example, we have a random instance from 'The Englishman in Italy' of the way which Browning, when he was most Browning, regarded physical nature.

'And pitch down his basket before us,
  All trembling alive
With pink and grey jellies, your sea-fruit;
  You touch the strange lumps,
And mouths gape there, eyes open, all manner
  Of horns and of humps,
Which only the fisher looks grave at.'

Nature might mean flowers to Wordsworth and grass to Walt Whitman, but to Browning it really meant such things as these, the monstrosities and living mysteries of the sea. And just as these strange things meant to Browning energy in the physical world, so strange thoughts and strange images meant to him energy in the mental world." (G. K. Chesterton, *Robert Browning*, p. 149–50.)

19. *pont-levis*. Drawbridge.

61. *John Knox*. A stern and earnest Calvinistic preacher of the sixteenth century.

Page 258.

SOLILOQUY OF THE SPANISH CLOISTER

A study of the innocent, flower-loving Friar Lawrence seen through the eyes of a venomous monk who hates him and who in his attitude toward Lawrence reveals his own vicious nature.

10. *Salve tibi*. Hail to thee.

49. *text in Galatians*. In Galatians 3: 10 it is stated, "Cursed is every one that continueth not in all things which are written in the book of the law to do them"—which would cover everything in the Book of Deuteronomy. Galatians 5: 19–21 give seventeen works of the flesh. But Browning's precise "twenty-nine distinct damnations" have puzzled the mathematically minded. The solution of the mystery may be that Browning had no specific text in mind—nor do the needs of his poem require one—and that "Galatians" rhymed conveniently with "damnations." Had he had Galatians 5: 19–21 in mind his meter would have allowed him to say "seventeen" just as easily as "twenty-nine."

70. *Hy, Zy, Hine*. It is generally assumed that these syllables represent the sound of vesper bells striking in on the soliloquy. DeVane suggests it may be the beginning of an imprecation against Laurence.

Page 259. THE LABORATORY

The subtitle, "Ancien Régime" (Old Order), indicates that this poem was set in France, possibly in the later sixteenth century under the Regency of Catherine de' Medici. Poisoning as a fine art and an instrument of policy was developed in Renaissance Italy. Catherine while Queen and Regent of France was accused (quite falsely) of introducing the device into France.

19–20. *an earring . . . a filigree basket.* According to report, various ingenious devices were employed to bring the victim into contact with the poison. A deadly powder might be dusted on the handle of a fan. It would be only courteous in offering the fan to the victim to present the handle while the poisoner held the unpoisoned fan end. The Borgias were reputed to have a ring with a lion's head for signet. The lion's tongue, with the pressure of a handclasp, darted out and injected the poison.

Page 260. CRISTINA

"In *Cristina*, four of Browning's fundamental articles of faith are expressed: the doctrine of the elective affinities; the doctrine of success through failure; the doctrine that time is measured not by the clock and the calendar, but by the intensity of spiritual experiences; the doctrine that life on earth is a trial and a test, the result of which will be seen in the higher and happier development when the soul is freed from the limitations of time and space." (William Lyon Phelps, *Robert Browning: How to Know Him*, p. 116.)

Page 261. MEETING AT NIGHT
PARTING AT MORNING

These two poems are spoken by the same man, the second indicating the necessity of a life of activity as well as of love, to a man.

In l. 3 of *Parting*, "him" refers to the sun.

Page 263. LOVE AMONG THE RUINS

The construction of this poem is one of balance and antithesis. The first four stanzas split—in each there are three lines devoted to the present peaceful scene, three lines to the splendor of the past. The fifth is a transitional stanza—between peace and splendor stands a living girl. In the last two stanzas the balance is between dead splendor and living love.

Page 264. UP AT A VILLA—DOWN IN THE CITY

This lively picture of Italian life may be compared with that given in *The Englishman in Italy* (text p. 297).

39. *diligence.* Stage coach.

43. *At the post-office*, etc. In Latin countries much of the news of the day, official and unofficial, can be found on bulletin boards or on placards in the city. In l. 43, for example, the "scene-picture" is a poster announcing a new play, and in l. 44 there is the announcement of the execution of three revolutionaries ("liberal thieves"—who opposed the Austrian rule).

52. See note below on Rossetti's *Mary's Girlhood* for the Seven Sorrows of our Lady symbolized by the seven swords.

Page 266. A TOCCATA OF GALUPPI'S

The speaker is playing the faded old eighteenth-century music and it sets him to dreaming of the people who heard this plaintive tune when it was fresh. The seventh stanza tells the warning it carried to a pair of Venetian lovers and the eighth their response to it—a turning back to kisses. Beginning in the twelfth stanza (ll. 35–45) we have what the tune says now to a modern Englishman.

6. *wed the sea with rings.* In an annual ceremony the Doge, the chief magistrate of Venice, flung a ring into the Adriatic—symbolizing the wedding of the city with that sea and its domination of the Adriatic.

Page 271. "DE GUSTIBUS——"

The title is taken from the Latin proverb, *De gustibus non est disputandum*—There is no disputing about tastes.

4. *cornfield . . . with poppies.* A wheat-field; and in Europe in spring poppies grow like weeds in the wheat so that when a passing breeze bends the young grain, great streaks of scarlet show through the green.

40. *Queen Mary's saying.* In 1588, the last year of Queen Mary's reign, the French recaptured Calais—the last possession of the English crown in France. Queen Mary grieved so much that she said that if her heart could be laid bare the word "Calais" would be found cut upon it.

Page 272. HOME-THOUGHTS, FROM ABROAD

DeVane considers as improbable the tradition that Browning wrote this poem on his first voyage to Italy (1838) and thinks it "more likely" that he wrote it in the spring of 1845 after his return from his second Italian voyage.

HOME-THOUGHTS, FROM THE SEA

This poem, according to Mrs. Orr, was written on shipboard on Browning's first voyage to Italy, but DeVane thinks it belongs to his second voyage—that of 1844. His ship passed near the scene of English naval victories. Saint Vincent and Trafalgar are capes in the southwest of Spain. Off Saint Vincent Nelson defeated the Spanish fleet and at Trafalgar he gained his greatest victory, defeating the combined French and Spanish fleets. It was in Cadiz Bay that these fleets were drawn up for the battle.

Page 273. SAUL

From the biblical narrative (I Samuel 16 : 14–23) Browning took simply the fact that David did play before Saul and freed him of an evil spirit, expanding this bare fact into what has been recognized as one of his most important poems on religious themes. The first nine stanzas were completed before he met Elizabeth Barrett. He was in doubt as to whether to print them in *Dramatic Romances and Lyrics* (1845). Elizabeth was emphatic that the fragment should be printed and the poem later completed. On August 27, 1845, she wrote Robert: "He [Saul] was tormented by an evil spirit—but how, we are not told . . . and the consolation is not obliged to be definite . . . is it? A singer was sent for as a singer—and all that you are called upon to be true to, are the general characteristics of David the chosen, standing between his sheep and his dawning hereafter, between innocence and holiness, and with what you speak of as the 'gracious gold locks' besides the chrism of the prophet, on his own head—and surely you have been happy in the tone and spirit of these lyrics. . . . The whole conception of the poem, I like . . . and the execution is exquisite up to this point—and the sight of Saul in the tent, just struck out of the dark by that sunbeam, 'a thing to see,' . . . not to say that afterwards when he is visibly 'caught in his fangs' like the king serpent, . . . the sight is grander still. How could you doubt about this poem. . . ."

The last ten stanzas were written in Italy and the poem first appeared in its complete form in *Men and Women* (1855).

Saul's recovery goes through various stages and in the course of it David becomes transformed from the singer to the prophet; this progress is marked by the nature of David's songs.

36–60. David plays on his harp. Note that his songs include a reaping song, a wine song, a funeral chant, a marriage song and a religious chorus—i.e., the songs of men at work and play, in sorrow, in joy, and exaltation—a full panorama of life; and Saul's interest is aroused.

68–96. The actual words of David's song to the aroused Saul in praise of the richness and greatness of life. Saul responds and yet asks more.

147–90. David attempts to add the "more." He sings not of the richness of this world but of the soul and the glory of Saul's service to his people. Although David is chanting to the accompaniment of his harp the passage is less lyrical than ll. 68–96.

238–312. David's prophetic speech. David first thinks that his love for this man might exceed God's love and then, overcome, realizes that God's love must be greater than any man's love. He sees Saul's present suffering as a preparation for the next world (conclusion of XVII) and prophesies the coming of Christ (conclusion of XVIII).

Page 280. MY STAR

9. *dartles*. Browning coined the word, using the verb "to dart" as a base.

BY THE FIRE-SIDE

The incidents of the poem are purely imaginary. It expresses Browning's conception of a happy married life with a happy past and a serene future. As such it could not fail to be colored by his affection for Elizabeth Barrett and ll. 113–14 are descriptive of her. The scenery is that of a little mountain gorge near the baths of Lucca where the Brownings spent the summers of 1849 and 1853.

The poem is developed in three planes of time. The man, now middle-aged, is sitting by the fire. He projects his imagination forward to dream of what old age will be like, and then memories crowd in of the time of his courtship in Italy. First he thinks of a walk which had been a particular favorite with them, and then of the very day when amidst these scenes he had declared his love for her. Between the two Italian scenes there is a passage in the present (ll. 101–25) in which he looks across the room at his wife reading. From this point on, to the conclusion of the poem, he is speaking to her directly but "mutely"—i.e., he is telling the story in his mind, sure that her perfect sympathy will divine what he is thinking of. See note on *Two in the Campagna*, below.

70. *midge*. See comment on Browning's approach to nature in note on *Garden Fancies*, above.

132. *The great Word*. "Behold I make all things new. And he said unto me, write: for these words are true and faithful" (Revelation 21 : 5). "True and faithful" must have been words ringing in Browning's mind as he wrote.

Page 284. TWO IN THE CAMPAGNA

DeVane notes that "the same failure of love is expressed in Matthew Arnold's line in *Isolation* [l. 4 of *To Marguerite—Continued*],

'We mortal millions live *alone*.'

The perfect contrast to *Two in the Campagna* is provided in *By the Fire-Side* where love achieves perfect understanding."

Page 285. MISCONCEPTIONS

11. *dalmatic*. A robe worn by kings on state occasions. Also worn by bishops at the celebration of Mass.

A SERENADE AT THE VILLA

The speaker had ventured out on a sultry, thunderous night to serenade his beloved. He wonders what she thought at hearing his song. Was his presence in the dark and storm heartening to her as an omen that there was one ready to guard her through life (ll. 28–34), or was his presence but an added exasperation on an unpleasant night?

25. *passed away*. Gone away.

Page 286. ANOTHER WAY OF LOVE

The speaker is a woman. The implication is that her love for the man is as perfect as the June season and his boredom with the season implies boredom with her love. In stanza III, identifying herself with June, she gives her answer—she may blossom for another lover, "indulgent to redness and sweetness," or she may scorn love.

6. *discover*. Make known.

RESPECTABILITY

Professor Corson summarizes the situation: "These two unconventional Bohemian lovers strolling together at night, at their own sweet will, see down the court along which they are strolling three lampions flare, which indicate some big place or other where the respectables do congregate; and the woman says to the companion, with a humorous sarcasm, 'Put forward your best foot!' that is, we must be very correct passing along here in this brilliant light." (*Introduction to Browning*, p. 110.)

21. *Institute*. The Institute of France, of which the French Academy is a subdivision, was founded in 1795 to promote science, literature, and art. In this poem it may be considered as a symbol of entrenched orthodoxy.

22. *Guizot receives Montalembert*. A newly elected member of the Institute was formally received by his colleagues. Guizot went through the conventional ceremonial although he and Montalembert were political enemies.

Page 287. LOVE IN A LIFE

LIFE IN A LOVE

These two poems are complementary. In both love eludes him, but the titles are significant. In the first he tries to capture love in this life to complete it. In the second he comes finally to the understanding that he can make a life out of the quest.

Page 288. MEMORABILIA

Browning as a boy, probably in his thirteenth year, picked up a copy of *Queen Mab* and soon after, his mother bought him all of Shelley's published works. Browning's enthusiasm for Shelley lasted all through his youth and the middle years of his manhood. Browning wrote little prose for publication, but one of his most important pieces was an essay on Shelley, published in 1852 as the foreword of an edition of letters which were later proved to be mostly forgeries. This poem was written in the winter of 1853–1854 at Rome.

9. *I crossed a moor*, etc. The unappreciative individual who had casually mentioned Shelley was as flat and as uninteresting as a moor. But there was the eagle-feather of the name! DeVane quotes Kingsland's account of the encounter which inspired the poem. Browning "was in the shop . . . of a bookseller when a stranger to himself entered, and commenced a conversation with the bookseller on Shelley—stating, *inter alia*, that he had seen and spoken to him. While thus conversing, the stranger suddenly turned round, and burst into a laugh on observing how Browning was staring at him with blanched face: 'and,' said the poet, 'I have not yet forgotten how strangely the sight of one who had spoken with Shelley affected me.'"

THE PATRIOT

The subtitle is ironic and a commentary on the fickleness of the mob at all times and places. The patriot speaks as he is being driven to the scaffold just one year after roses were scattered in his path. There is no specific historical basis for the poem.

Page 290. MY LAST DUCHESS

This is one of the most masterly of Browning's dramatic monologues with its full revelation through small details of action of the character of the duke, his former duchess, and of the tragedy which has occurred. The speaker is an imaginary Duke of Ferrara who is negotiating with a neighboring count for the hand of his daughter, and he explains to an envoy of the count just why the previous Duchess of Ferrara had been unsatisfactory.

3. *Fra Pandolf*. An imaginary artist, as is Claus of Innsbruck (l. 56).

6. *by design*. "To have some occasion for telling the story, and illustrating part of it." (Browning's explanation in 1889 in reply to a questionnaire from The Day's End Club of Exeter, reported in *Cornhill Magazine*, March, 1917.) It may be inferred also that in telling the story the Duke is issuing a subtle warning that he expects different conduct from his next wife.

25. *Sir, 'twas all one! My favour at her breast*, etc. "An excuse—mainly to himself—for taking revenge on one who had unwittingly wounded his absurdly pretentious vanity, by failing to recognize his superiority in even the most trifling matters." (Browning's explanation in *Cornhill Magazine*, March, 1917.)

45. *I gave commands*. Professor Hiram Corson inquired concerning this line and Browning replied, "Yes, I meant that the commands were that she be put to death," adding after a

pause, "or he might have had her shut up in a convent."

Page 291. THE BOY AND THE ANGEL

44. *my little human praise.* The little tradesman's apprentice praised with a full heart, and with God that honest voice equalled in value the greatest. Even the Angel Gabriel was unable to replace the apprentice. Cf. *Pippa Passes*, text p. 232b, ll. 6–17.

Page 292. INSTANS TYRANNUS

The title, which means "the threatening tyrant," was suggested by Horace, the third ode in Book III. Horace's lines translate, "The just man, firm of purpose, is not to be turned aside by the heat of the mob nor the brow of the threatening tyrant." Browning makes his victim weak to show that even the most abject creature, when in the right, can call upon spiritual forces mightier than the worldly.

44. *gravamen.* The heart of a grievance or complaint.

Page 293. THE GLOVE

Poullain de St. Croix in his *Essais historiques sur Paris* is the source of this story which has also been used by Schiller and Leigh Hunt. "One day whilst Francis I amused himself with looking at a combat between his lions, a lady, having let her glove drop, said to De Lorge, 'If you would have me believe you love me as much as you swear you do, go and bring back my glove.' De Lorge went down, picked up the glove from amidst the ferocious beasts, returned, and threw it in the lady's face; and in spite of all her advances and cajoleries would never look at her again." In the original, the lady's character scarcely commands respect. Browning, characteristically, takes a novel approach and uses the story as the test of a man's love rather than the revelation of a woman's shallowness, and his conception of the woman is different from that of his predecessors. The incident is related through the lips of Pierre Ronsard, a famous French poet of the court of Francis I, who as a member of that gay and witty court might be expected to understand the subtleties and finesses of love.

12. *Naso.* Ovid (Publius Ovidius Naso), a Latin poet.

14. *Ixions.* Ixion loved Juno. She sent to him a cloud in her shape which he embraced. The "cloudlets" of l. 11 are explained by this legend.

163. *our brute been Nemean.* One of the labors of Hercules was to kill the especially ferocious Nemean lion.

191. *theorbo.* Browning represents the poet as having told his story while strumming on his theorbo, an instrument like a lute.

Page 295. TIME'S REVENGES

46. *the Florentine.* Dante. It is the irony of time's revenge that this poet in a garret, who is indifferent to the friend who loves him, would rather be trampled by the selfish woman who does not love him than surpass one of the great poets of the world.

THE ITALIAN IN ENGLAND

Mazzini, the Italian revolutionary leader, spent seven years of his exile in England. He told Browning that he had read this poem to a group of refugees to show how an Englishman could sympathize with them—a fact of which Browning was proud. Like Byron and Shelley before them, both Elizabeth and Robert Browning were sympathetic with the Italian patriots who were trying to throw off Austrian domination. The speaker of this poem, now a refugee in England, is recalling the manner of his escape after some unsuccessful plot. There is no specific historical basis for the incident, but the time is sometime between 1823 and 1848.

8. *Charles.* Charles Albert, Prince of Carignano, a member of the younger branch of the House of Savoy. He was educated simply in a public school, which would have made possible his boyhood contact with the speaker. Charles Albert encouraged an uprising in 1823 but soon after left his friends in the lurch.

19. *Metternich.* Metternich, an Austrian, was the astutest statesman of post-Napoleonic Europe. He was the leader of the reactionary forces, and was bitterly hated by all liberals.

75. *duomo.* The cathedral.

Page 297. THE ENGLISHMAN IN ITALY

Mrs. Sutherland Orr describes this poem as "a vivid picture of Italian peasant-life on the plain of Sorrento: the occasion being an outbreak of the well-known hot wind—the 'scirocco'—which in this case has brought with it a storm of rain. A little frightened peasant girl has taken refuge by the side of the Englishman, who is apparently lodging in her mother's cottage. And he is diverting her attention by describing his impressions of the last twenty-four hours." There is no narrative. The picture is based upon direct observation and catches the liveliness of Italian life. Compare this picture with that given in *Up at a Villa—Down in the City* (text p. 264).

47. *frails.* Baskets.

55–61. *pitch down his basket*, etc. See comment on Browning's approach to nature in note on *Garden Fancies*, above.

75. *all bare-legged is dancing.* In the making of wine the peasants put the grapes in vats and crushed them by treading on them barefooted.

251. *Feast of the Rosary's Virgin.* Annually thanks are given to Our Lady of the Rosary in

commemoration of the naval victory of the Catholic powers over the Turks at Lepanto. At Sorrento, where this poem is set, the image of the Virgin is carried through the streets with ceremonies which Browning describes in the lines which follow.

265. *Bellini nor Auber.* Composers. The fiddlers, fifers, drummers, and trumpeters weren't afraid of the music and went at it with vigor. What happened to the music, Browning does not say.

289–92. *debate . . . Corn-laws. . . . If 'twere proper, Scirocco should vanish.* The Corn Laws, which had been a cause of agitation in England for years, put a tariff on grain and, being a tax on food, bore heavily on the common people. Peel, in October, 1845, asked his cabinet to agree to repeal, and in 1846 the laws actually were repealed. Browning's lines mean that there is just as much sense in *debating* a question of that sort as in debating whether we should be happier without the Scirocco. The answer is obvious.

Page 300. IN A GONDOLA

Browning wrote "The first stanza was written to illustrate Maclise's picture (The Serenade) for which he was anxious to get some line or two. I had not seen it, but from Forster's description gave it to him in his room, impromptu. When I did see it I thought the serenade too jolly, somewhat, for the notion I got from Forster, and I took the subject in my own way." His own way was to write a lyrical tragedy of love under the shadow of death. The Three whom the lovers try to evade are Gian and Paul (see ll. 106–7) and an unnamed individual most feared of all—either her husband or her father.

113. *Lido's . . . graves.* There was a Jewish cemetery near the Lido.

141. *lory.* A species of parrot.

151–4. *snake . . . Roman girls.* At various periods in history, including ancient Rome and postwar Paris, snakes have been kept as pets by the ultra-sophisticate.

Page 305. THE FLIGHT OF THE DUCHESS

On July 25, 1845, Browning wrote Elizabeth, "So much for this 'Duchess'—which I shall ever rejoice in—wherever was a bud, even, in that strip of May-bloom, a live musical bee hangs now" (after her approval of the poem). Browning in his youth had overheard a woman singing "Following the Queen of the Gipsies, O!" (probably a version of *The Raggle-Taggle Gypsies*) and the phrase haunted him. Some years later he began *The Flight of the Duchess* on this theme but was interrupted. Several years later, and some months after the actual publication of the first part of the poem in *Hood's Magazine,* a guest in the same house in which he was staying made the chance remark that "the deer had already to break the ice in the pond." The sentence caught Browning's fancy (see ll. 217–18); he wrote it up and went on to complete *The Flight of the Duchess* as it now stands. There had been considerable alteration in Browning's conception. He wrote Elizabeth, "But, as I conceived the poem, it consisted entirely of the Gipsy's description of the life the Lady was to lead with her future Gipsy lover—a *real* life, not an unreal one like that with the Duke. And as I meant to write it, all their wild adventures would have come out and the insignificance of the former vegetation have been deducible only." As written, we have a picture of the unreal life and must surmise much concerning the real gipsy life that is to be.

2. *I was the man.* The one whom the Duke designated to take the Gipsy to the Duchess—that is how he knows the story. See l. 440.

20–30. *greater, wilder country.* See comment on Browning's approach to nature in note on *Garden Fancies,* above.

66. *comfort when he died.* I.e., after the Kaiser made a courtier of him, he was glad to die.

78–80. *merlin . . . falcon-lanner.* Types of hawks used in falconry.

130. *urochs or buffle.* Wild bulls or buffalo.

249. *Venerers, Prickers, and Verderers.* Medieval terms for huntsmen, light horsemen, and guardians of the forest law (game wardens).

263. *wind a mort.* Blow to announce the kill.

273. *sealed.* In hunting with falcons, the hawk was hooded when on the wrist. The hood was removed when the bird was launched.

322. "A canon in music is a piece wherein the subject is repeated, in various keys; and, being strictly obeyed in the repetition, becomes the 'canon'—the imperative *law*—to what follows. Fifty of such parts would be indeed a notable peal; to manage three is enough of an achievement for a good musician." (Browning's explanation.)

480. *tomans.* Persian coins.

864–5. *morion . . . hauberk.* Pieces of medieval armor.

910. *Orson the wood-knight.* Orson as a baby was carried off and suckled by a bear. He grew up to be the terror of the forests but was redeemed by his brother. He appears in the *Romance of Valentine and Orson.*

Page 316. A GRAMMARIAN'S FUNERAL

The speaker is a disciple of the dead scholar. He tells of the grammarian's passion for knowledge, interspersing, in parentheses, directions to his companions who are bearing the body to the mountain top. Browning in other poems has illustrated the love of art and the love of luxury of the Renaissance. Here he is illustrating the passionate intellectual curiosity which was another pronounced characteristic of the period. In this poem he has performed the remarkable feat of making a hero out of a pedant and Browning's attitude here might be compared to that he exhibited in *Sibrandus Schafnaburgensis* (text p. 257).

34. *Lyric Apollo.* I.e., the grammarian had not turned to his studies because he was fit for nothing else, but, handsome as a god, he had deliberately turned away from the opportunities open to such a man.

129–31. *Hoti . . . Oun . . . De. Hoti* and *Oun* are Greek participles meaning "that" and "then." Concerning *De,* meaning "towards," Browning wrote to *The News,* Nov. 21, 1874: "That this is not to be confounded with the accentuated 'De, meaning *but,*' was 'the doctrine' which the Grammarian bequeathed to those capable of receiving it."

Page 318. THE STATUE AND THE BUST

Lines 226–50, pointing the moral of the story, express one of Browning's fundamental ideas.

22. *encolure.* Mane.

36. *Because of a crime.* Cosimo de' Medici and his grandson Lorenzo exercised almost absolute power in Florence, destroying the freedom of the early republic. The Florentines were less disturbed about the "crime" than was Browning, for they called Cosimo "Pater Patriae" (roughly, "Father of his Country") and Lorenzo was known as "The Magnificent."

95. *Petraja.* A suburb of Florence where the duke had a villa.

169. Luca, Andrea, and Giovanni della Robbia were masters in handling the glazed bisque ware which became an important manufacture in Florence and was afterwards called by their family name. The last of this great trio, however, had died twenty years before the duke was born.

Page 322. PORPHYRIA'S LOVER

This poem was first grouped with another—*Johannes Agricola in Meditation,* which is not included in the anthology—under the general title *Madhouse Cells.* One may wonder if by cancelling the general title Browning implied that he had decided the lover to be not so very mad after all!

"CHILDE ROLAND TO THE DARK TOWER CAME"

From Edgar's song to which Browning refers in his subtitle he borrowed only a line and developed the idea it suggested in his own way—

Child Rowland to the dark tower came,
His word was still,—Fie, foh, and fum,
I smell the blood of a British man.
(*King Lear,* III, iv, 171–3.)

Perhaps no other poem of Browning's has been so much be-allegorized as *Childe Roland.* J. T. Nettleship, in his *Robert Browning: Essays and Thoughts,* pp. 89–114, gives one of the most elaborate interpretations and Arlo Bates in the *Critic* (April 26, 1886) gives one less elaborate. Either of these may be consulted. A sentence from Bates on the conclusion is of interest: "The nominal issue of the conflict is no matter, because the real issue is here; with the universe against him, with the realization of all this, dauntless he gives his challenge." Mrs. Sutherland Orr, who stood somewhat in the position of official interpreter, cautioned against seeking for any "intended lesson" in the poem, as did Browning himself. However, J. W. Chadwick (in the *Christian Register,* Jan. 19, 1888) reported an interview with Browning: "I further asked him if he had ever said that he only wrote *Childe Roland* for its realistic imagery, without any moral purpose—a notion to which Mrs. Sutherland Orr has given currency; and he protested that he never had. When I asked him if constancy to an ideal—'He that endureth to the end shall be saved'—was not a sufficient understanding of the central purpose of the poem, he said, 'Yes, just about that.'" Browning might quite easily have assured Chadwick that constancy in the quest was a central idea in the poem—which it is—without intending that symbolic values should be found in every detail of the poem.

See comment on Browning's approach to nature in the note on *Garden Fancies.* Chesterton in connection with this poem points out that other poets had escaped from conventional gardens and written of wild landscapes of the Byronic type, but Browning has gone farther and written of "mean" landscapes. "The sense of scrubbiness in nature, as of a man unshaved, had never been conveyed with this enthusiasm and primeval gusto before."

48. *estray.* Technically, a strayed animal; in this case, Childe Roland.

68. *bents.* Coarse grasses.

80. *colloped.* Probably means that the muscles of the neck stood out in ropelike ridges.

114. *bespate.* Spattered.

130. *pad.* Trample.

141–2. *harrow fit to reel Men's bodies out like silk.* I.e., it suggested some instrument of torture to stretch and twist men's bodies.

143. *Tophet.* Hell.

160. *Apollyon's.* The devil's. The name Apollyon is used in Revelation 9: 11.

Page 326. "TRANSCENDENTALISM: A POEM IN TWELVE BOOKS"

One poet (who is doing the speaking) criticizes another who is writing a poem in twelve books after the transcendental method—i.e., he is trying to leave out of his poetry all the concrete pictures which appeal to the senses and, transcending the brave show of this world, is trying to attain to pure idea. It won't do! says the other poet, and, in proof, contrasts two sages, Boehme and John of Halberstadt, one of whom had plenty of ideas about flowers and one of whom could call flowers into being. This last is the proper method for a poet.

AN EPISTLE

Karshish in his travels has written back to his teacher, Abib, a series of letters, of which this poem is supposed to be the twenty-second, recording various bits of medical information he has picked up in his journey. He records the case history of the man Lazarus—the remarkable cure and the mental effects following his illness. Karshish is well-trained in the medicine of his day and his approach is essentially scientific, but at the same time, like the good physician that he is, Karshish recognizes that there is something in the case which he has not fully diagnosed. His thinking as a result is a blend of analytical skepticism and wonder, and the originality of Browning's poem lies in the curious blend. This treatment may be compared with Tennyson's rather colorless handling of the Lazarus theme in *In Memoriam* (text pp. 59–60, sections XXXI–II). The biblical account is in John 11 : 1–44.

11. *wily vapour*. Christian thought all through the Middle Ages conceived of the soul at the moment of death as returning to God in the shape of a small babe on the exhalation of the last breath. Karshish theoretically would not have been familiar with this conception, but Browning must have seen it often portrayed in Italian paintings with which he was familiar.

43. *tertians*. Intermittent fevers or persons suffering from them.

55. *gum-tragacanth*. A medicinal gum.

60. *Zoar*. A city in Palestine.

103. *fume*. Crazy idea.

167. *our lord*. The aged scholar with whom both Abib and Karshish studied.

177. *Greek fire*. A chemical mixture which burns under water. Lazarus on occasion (see preceding lines) looks at the wise men of this world much as the great sage of line 67 looked at Abib and Karshish when they recklessly recited potent charms—as children playing with dangerous fire.

252. *which happened when the earthquake fell*. At the time of the crucifixion, as told in the Bible, there was an earthquake. See Matthew 27 : 50–51.

281. *borage*. A medicinal herb.

Page 331. FRA LIPPO LIPPI

The speaker is the painter-monk who has just been snapped up by the watch (the police) while he is trying to slip quietly home. The seizure gives him a great fright. After he has named his patron, the great Cosimo de' Medici, and the watch has released him, he feels better, and feels impelled to explain to the captain of the watch just why he happens to be wandering about at that hour. The explanation involves a life story and an important theory of art.

The paragraph in Vasari's *Lives of the Painters* which suggested to Browning the situation tells how Cosimo, knowing Lippo's habits, tried to keep him inside by the simple device of locking his door, and Lippo escaped by the equally simple device of going out the window in the manner described in the poem. Cosimo learned of the escapade and, resolving not to risk a valuable painter's neck again, left his door unlocked, keeping him in afterwards only by persuasion.

23. *pilchards*. A cheap fish.

53. *Flower o' the broom*. A species of Italian folksong is the stornello, which the peasants improvise while at work. The first line of five syllables usually ends in the name of a flower which sets the rhyme. Stornelli are three lines long but Lippo improvises in couplets.

67. *Saint Laurence*. The church of San Lorenzo near what was then the Medici Palace (now known as the Riccardi).

117. *gentleman processional and fine*. Fine gentlemen carrying candles in a religious procession.

121. *the Eight*. The Eight Priors were the chief magistrates of Florence.

130. *antiphonary's marge*. The margin of the antiphonary, the Roman Catholic service book compiled by Gregory the Great and containing all that is sung in the choir.

148. *cribs*. Cheats or small thefts.

149–50. *altar-foot . . . safe*. A church was sacred ground and a wrongdoer who took sanctuary there was safe from private vengeance; neither could he be seized by legal authorities.

189. *Here's Giotto*. The first great master of the Florentine school. Giotto died in 1337 and Lippo was born in 1412(?), so the Prior was trying to cancel out about a century of development. Even so, the Prior underestimated Giotto's realistic power, for legend has it that, as a boyish prank, Giotto painted a fly on the nose of a madonna his teacher Cimabue was painting and did it so vividly that Cimabue, coming back to work on his canvas, was deceived and tried to "shoo" the creature off.

196. *Herodias*. For the story of Herod, Herodias, and Salome, see Matthew 14 : 1–12.

228. *the rings in front*. Fixed in the stonework in the facades of Italian Renaissance palaces were a series of rings and brackets. A torch or a banner could be fixed in the bracket and the horse of a visiting cavalier tied to the ring.

276. Browning in a letter to Dowden in 1866 denied that he was in error in making Masaccio the pupil of Lippo and attempted to justify his position (see the *Letters of Robert Browning* edited by Thurman L. Hood, p. 104). Nevertheless Browning was wrong.

307. *cullion's hanging face*. The cullion is the rascal who had a "gullet's-gripe" on Lippo (l. 20) and whom Lippo thought looked like Judas (l. 25). Lippo has recovered his good humor but he hasn't forgotten that first grip on his throat and he thinks the man obviously has the face of one born to be hanged.

323. *Saint Laurence*. Was martyred by being roasted on a gridiron. See l. 328.

346. *Something in Sant' Ambrogio's!* According to Vasari, Lippo's altarpiece at Sant' Ambrogio's—"Coronation of the Virgin"—was done fairly early in his career, before he came under the patronage of Cosimo. The necessities of Browning's poem made it necessary for Lippo, when he told the watch to go and see something of his, to refer them to an important painting near at hand—hence Browning's reference to Sant' Ambrogio's. Lippo's enthusiasm for "a sweet angelic slip of a thing" (l. 370) whom he planned to put in the picture-to-be, suggests that Browning perhaps also had in the back of his mind another altarpiece (a "Nativity") described by Vasari and done later for the nuns of Santa Margherita at Prato. After it was completed, Lippo eloped with the novice who had posed for the Madonna.

361. *Out of the corner*. Renaissance artists often painted their own portraits as one of the minor figures in a large canvas, just as Lippo plans to put himself down in one corner of the painting.

374–5. *Saint John . . . his camel hair*. "And John was clothed with camel's hair, and with a girdle of skin about his loins; and he did eat locusts and wild honey." See Mark 1:6.

381. *hot cockles*. An old-fashioned game in which one player with his eyes covered is struck from behind and then tries to guess which of the other players hit him.

Page 337. ANDREA DEL SARTO

15. *Fiesole*. A beautiful suburb on a hillside overlooking Florence.

65. *Legate's talk*. The Legate was the delegate of the Pope.

93–7. *Morello's outline*, etc. A mountain peak north of Florence. The mountain and Andrea, the craftsman, are alike in being "unmoved by men's blame." But both are fixed in their present stature—a cardinal fault in Browning's opinion. Andrea's rivals make the effort for more. See l. 87, and especially l. 97: "A man's reach should exceed his grasp."

99. *Placid and perfect*, etc. Cf. *Old Pictures in Florence*, ll. 81–144 (text pp. 268–9).

106. *Vasari*. Giorgio Vasari (1512–1574), a painter himself, was an art historian also. It was from his *Lives of the Painters* that Browning drew material for this poem and for *Fra Lippo Lippi*.

162. *this face beyond*. Lucrezia's face waiting for him at home in Florence.

178. *The Roman's*. Raphael's.

212. *melancholy little house*. Andrea spent much of the money given him by Francis I in building for Lucrezia a small villa which she wished.

241. *scudi*. A scudo was at that time worth about a dollar.

Page 341. THE BISHOP ORDERS HIS TOMB AT ST. PRAXED'S CHURCH

Browning's poems of the Renaissance illustrate many aspects of that many-sided period. In this poem he shows its fundamental amorality, and its love of luxury, as shown in the late Renaissance when the spirit of the period might be described as "over-ripe" and approaching degeneracy. Be it noted, however, that the Bishop, with all his luxuriousness, has a passion for good Latin which makes him akin to Browning's grammarian (text p. 316). The Bishop is speaking from his deathbed to his illegitimate sons whom he politely calls nephews. It may be an intentional irony on Browning's part to have the luxury-loving Bishop, who hopes to cling to his precious stones even after death, buried in the church of St. Praxedes—a virgin who distributed her wealth to the poor. Her character adds to the irony of l. 75 in which the Bishop offers to pray to her to grant his sons desirable mistresses. Browning shortened the name, possibly for purposes of rhythm, possibly to make easier the Bishop's later confusion of sexes.

Ruskin says of the poem: "Robert Browning is unerring in every sentence he writes of the Middle Ages; always vital, right, and profound; so that in the matter of art, with which we have been specially concerned, there is hardly a principle connected with the medieval temper, that he has not struck upon in those seemingly careless and too rugged rhymes of his. . . . I know no other piece of modern English prose or poetry in which there is so much told, as in these lines, of the Renaissance spirit—its worldliness, inconsistency, pride, hypocrisy, ignorance of itself, love of art, of luxury, and of good Latin. It is nearly all that I said of the central Renaissance in thirty pages of the *Stones of Venice*, put into as many lines, Browning's being also the antecedent work. The worst of it is that this kind of concentrated writing needs so much *solution* before the reader can fairly get the good of it, that people's patience fails them, and they give the thing up as insoluble; though, truly, it ought to be to the current of common thought like Saladin's talisman, dipped in clear water, not soluble altogether, but making the element medicinal." (*Modern Painters*, Vol. IV, ch. 20, secs. 32, 34.)

1. *vanity, saith the preacher.* Ecclesiastes 1 : 2.

21. *pulpit o' the epistle side.* Right-hand side facing the altar. From this side the epistle is read by the priest acting as celebrant.

31. *onion-stone.* An inferior kind of marble called by the Italians *cipollino* because it splits into coats like an onion (*cipolla*).

35. *So much was saved if aught were missed.* When the church burned down nearly everything was saved and no one was surprised that a few things were missing after the catastrophe. One of the "missing" items was the lump of *lapis lazuli* which the Bishop himself had stolen.

41. *olive-frail.* A "frail" is a basket—in this case for olives.

46. *Frascati.* In the Alban hills near Rome. An especially delicate wine is produced in the district.

49. *in the Jesu Church.* There was a group representing the Trinity at the altar of St. Ignatius in the church of Il Gesu.

51. *Swift . . . years.* Freely quoted from Job 7 : 6.

66. *travertine.* A species of limestone. Rather a lovely building stone, but cheap in comparison to marble.

87. *clasped a crook.* A bishop's crozier, or staff, was a symbolic representation of a shepherd's crook, the bishop being the shepherd of his flock.

88. *straight as stone can point.* On many Renaissance and medieval tombs were carved recumbent figures of the occupant. The Bishop, lying on his deathbed, takes the position of such a rigid stone figure.

95. *St. Praxed at his sermon on the mount.* The dying Bishop here attributes the Saviour's sermon on the mount to the virgin St. Praxedes (cf. ll. 59–60). "The blunder . . .," wrote Browning, "is the result of the dying man's haziness; he would not reveal himself as he does but for that."

108. *a vizor and a Term.* A mask and a bust on a square pillar. The decoration would be rather easily carved and undistinguished.

Page 343. CLEON

Cleon, a Greek poet of the first century A.D., writes to Protus, a tyrant, answering certain philosophical questions Protus has raised. Both belong to the exhausted end of a great civilization which had once been young and vigorous and this fact colors both question and answer. Cleon is unaware of decay and not ashamed of his period nor of his own work, but his very defense of it suffers from a lack of *élan vital*. The religious element also enters—he has been unable to establish any certainties beyond the physical *now*, and, by an irony of intellectual pride, he is led to reject the possibility of immortality or the comfort of religious faith. See introductory note to Arnold's *Last Song of Callicles*, below.

The three questions raised by Protus are—(1) In spite of the present subtle civilization, has there been any real progress since the men of the heroic age? Cleon answers, "Yes," but the very reasons he gives admit defeat. His era cannot do better in any field, but it can combine (ll. 43–157). (2) Is not progress really failure?—Man's understanding of all the joy he could take out of the physical world increases intensely but his physical ability actually to take it increases not at all. Cleon sorrowfully agrees (ll. 158–272). (3) Is not the artist, who lives on in his works, an exception to the common fate of mankind? Cleon denies this—showing how to live and actual living being different entirely. He is growing old, as is Protus (ll. 273–334).

The motto, "As certain also of your own poets have said" is from Acts 17 : 28, and the verse concludes, "For we are also his offspring." The implication is, considering the full passage in Acts 17 : 23–28, that Cleon, although intellectual pride leads him to reject the one opportunity of escape through faith from the limitations of his intellectualism (see ll. 337–53), is yet also of His offspring, and seeks gropingly for truth and God. See especially Acts 17 : 23.

1. *sprinkled isles.* Greek civilization spread from Greece proper over the Aegean Islands and the coasts of Asia Minor.

47. *epos*, etc. Epic engraved on plates of gold.

51. *sun-god on the phare.* A statue of Apollo mounted on a lighthouse.

132. *drupe.* Browning is comparing the cultivated and the wild fruit.

Page 347. ONE WORD MORE

9. *but one.* Only one person might see the sonnets—possibly a girl named Margherita whom Raphael is said to have loved in Rome.

21. *wonder at Madonnas.* Browning then mentions specifically Raphael's Sistine Madonna now at Dresden, the Madonna of Foligno at Rome, the Madonna del Granduca at Florence and La Belle Jardinière in the Louvre in Paris.

32. *Dante . . . paint an angel.* Dante, as he tells in the *Vita Nuova* (XXXV), on the first anniversary of the death of Beatrice prepared to paint, out of memory, her portrait as an angel. Certain people of importance broke in on him. Browning (l. 45) conceives them to have been the same sort of people Dante damned in his *Inferno*.

57. *Bice.* Short for Beatrice, Dante's beloved, referred to in ll. 32 and 54.

73–4. *Wherefore? . . . He who smites the rock,*

etc. Wherefore (l. 71) "be the man and leave the artist?" Because the artist is like Moses smiting the rock for water (Exodus 17 : 1–7) for a thankless people. But "Did he love one face" (l. 100), then no sacrifice would be too great for him to make to supply the life-giving water.

95. *Egypt's flesh-pots.* See Exodus 16 : 3.

101–2. *Jethro's Daughter . . Æthiopian bond-slave.* Jethro's daughter was Moses's wife Zipporah (Exodus 2 : 21). Moses also married an Ethiopian slave (Numbers 12 : 1).

125. *missal-marge.* The margin of her prayer book.

145. *Here in London.* This dedicatory poem was written in London where the two poets had gone from Italy for a short stay in 1855.

146. *thrice-transfigured.* Together Browning and Elizabeth had seen the new moon over Fiesole (l. 148), a suburb of Florence, had seen the full moon back of the church of San Miniato (l. 150) which overlooks Florence from a hillside opposite Fiesole, and now (l. 153) they see the waning moon over London.

160. *mythos.* A reference to the legend of Diana's love for Endymion, the theme of Keats's *Endymion.*

163. *Zoroaster.* Founder of the Persian religion. He studied the stars.

164. *Galileo.* Constructor of the first telescope. His discoveries about the heavenly bodies, supporting the Copernican theory, particularly his statement that the earth revolved on an axis instead of being fixed, were branded as heresy by the church.

165. *dumb to Keats.* See note on l. 160, above.

Page 350. *From* JAMES LEE'S WIFE

IV ALONG THE BEACH

In the cycle of nine poems which make up *James Lee's Wife,* each presents a scene in the growing estrangement of the husband from the faithful wife. Here she speaks and her analytical approach reveals a certain hopelessness, a recognition that there can be no real reconciliation.

VII AMONG THE ROCKS

The earth is old and warm and wise, and the wife understands the distillation of its wisdom expressed in ll. 9–12.

Page 351. ABT VOGLER

DeVane notes that Browning's own music teacher was a pupil of Vogler and that thus the poet himself was schooled in Vogler's system of music. Vogler was a great extemporiser, and Weber, one of his pupils, says, "Never did Vogler in his extemporization drink more deeply at the source of all beauty than when, before his three dear boys, as he liked to call us [Weber, Meyerbeer, and Gänsbacker], he drew from the organ angelic voices and words of thunder." See note on text p. 353. The very fact that Vogler was a great improviser would make him acutely conscious of the evanescence of sound. Recorded music could be reproduced; not so extemporization.

23. *Rome's dome.* The dome of St. Peter's at Rome. It is illuminated for certain religious festivals.

Page 353. RABBI BEN EZRA

1. *Grow old along with me.* Matthew Arnold, who lacked Browning's buoyant optimism, disagreed so sharply with Browning's conception of old age that he composed an answer (*Growing Old,* text p. 569).

24. *Irks care the crop-full bird?* Is the bird with a full crop worried by care?

81. *adventure brave and new.* The new life.

151. *Potter's wheel.* Most commentators refer to Isaiah 64 : 8 as the source of the image of the potter's wheel. Fitzgerald in the *Rubáiyát* (text p. 910, ll. 325–60) employs the same figure and points out in a note that the image is widespread in Oriental literature.

Page 356. CALIBAN UPON SETEBOS

In *The Tempest,* Caliban is the "savage and deformed" servant of Prospero and his daughter Miranda, contrasting with their other servant, the "airy spirit," Ariel. Browning conceives Caliban as a rudimentary and savage intellect pondering upon the nature of deity and creating God in his own image—Setebos being, according to Elizabethan voyagers, the god of the Patagonians. The capriciousness of Setebos is his most apparent characteristic to Caliban and Caliban's own feeling toward his god is consequently one of fear. He creeps into a secret cave to do his meditating, lest Setebos spy him, and to make assurance doubly sure, he talks in the third person—the responsibility for this dangerous talk thus resting on a mysterious "he," not on Caliban. In the poem the third person pronoun capitalized ("Him") refers to Setebos; uncapitalized, it refers to Caliban. And in an excess of caution Caliban frequently omits his own pronoun. (Example: "'Thinketh, He dwelleth i' the cold o' the moon," l. 25.) Toward the end of the poem (ll. 202 et seq.) Caliban forgets his caution and allows himself to use the personal pronoun. Thinking the matter over afterward, and after the conclusion of the poem, he doubtless regretted it and considered that this gave the raven (of l. 286) the really disastrous evidence against him.

Page 360. CONFESSIONS

The dying speaker is talking to the priest who has come to confess him, but there is little regret in his confession.

23. *two eyes except.* Except the two eyes of the girl who was waiting for him.
28. *Oes.* Plural of "o."

Page 361. PROSPICE

The title means, "Look forward." This poem, with its rugged vigor of expression, should be compared to Tennyson's *Crossing the Bar* (text p. 206). Both poets express a confidence in immortality. Cf. also *Epilogue* (text p. 382).

Page 363. APPARENT FAILURE

In the summer of 1856 at the time of the baptism of Louis Napoleon (referred to in ll. 1–3), only child of Napoleon III, Browning was in Paris and rather a gruesome whim caused him to visit the morgue. Seven years later when a newspaper story informed him the building was to be destroyed he recalled the episode and wrote this poem.

Page 366. NED BRATTS

1. *'Twas Bedford Special Assize.* The Court of Assizes was sitting in Bedford.
52. *Publican.* Saloonkeeper.
71. *Public.* Public house, saloon.
79. *noggin.* Cup of liquor.
82. *midden.* Manure-heap.
91. *clipping.* Stealing.
97. *houghed.* Hamstrung.
114. *Gammer.* Old wife.
117. *Bagman.* A species of travelling salesman.
fuddling-cap. The cap he wore to a drinking party; "fuddle" meaning to confuse with liquor.
119. *Gaffer.* Old man.
157. *Dives in the wain,* etc. *Dives* means "a rich man," but has come to be used as a proper name. The story of Dives is told in Luke 16:19–25. Ned in his excitement is thoroughly mixed-up at this point. A "wain" is a farm wagon and "Charles's Wain" is a constellation. Moreover, Charles II was King of England. Ned gets his rich man, his kings, and his constellations mixed.
175. *marle.* An earthy deposit containing lime, much used as a fertilizer.
215. *Destruction.* The City of Destruction in *Pilgrim's Progress*. From this point in Browning's poem to l. 247 there are frequent references to characters, places, and episodes in Bunyan's book. Bratts makes a personal application of the fable to his own case.

Page 374. ADAM, LILITH, AND EVE

Under the pressure of fear two women speak the truth to one man—and then retract it. Lilith, according to legend, was the witch who was Adam's wife before the creation of Eve. Adam forms his own conclusions and says little.

Page 375. SONGS FROM FERISHTAH'S FANCIES

Ferishtah, going upon his daily way through Ispahan, encounters certain people and situations and draws conclusions from them. There are twelve of the *Fancies* and to each is appended a lyric which expresses the central idea from a somewhat different point of view. The lyrics included in the anthology should be judged purely for their value as lyrics, independent of context, but for the curious, a summary of their place in the volume is given.

I. ROUND US THE WILD CREATURES

Attached to *The Eagle*, number one of the *Fancies*, in which Ferishtah sees an eagle feeding some young ravens, the mother bird being dead. From this Ferishtah derives the idea that he himself should "work, eat, then feed who lack." The lovers in the lyric do not isolate themselves in their happiness any more than had the eagle in his freedom.

II. MAN I AM AND MAN WOULD BE

Attached to number four, *The Family*, in which three sons and a husband react differently to the decision of a doctor that the mother's leg must be amputated. The moral in brief is that in the face of such a catastrophe we cannot be sure what is right or what is God's intent, but we must retain our humanity of heart, not approach it with a cocksureness of brain which discards humanity.

III. FIRE IS IN THE FLINT

Attached to number five, *The Sun*, in which Ferishtah discusses the Incarnation with a man who is outraged at the statement that God once demeaned himself to the point of assuming human shape on earth. Ferishtah uses the sun as a symbol.

IV. ASK NOT ONE LEAST WORD OF PRAISE

Attached to number eleven, *A Pillar at Sebzevar*, in which Ferishtah decides that knowledge is never complete in that we are always altering theories or adding information, whereas love is a complete thing in spite of the fact that we do not know its real source and only know its effects on us.

Page 377. SUMMUM BONUM

The Latin title means, "the highest good."

Page 380. REPHAN

The theme of this poem is an old one in literature—that of the man from Mars or the moon come to this earth—but Browning characteristically gives it an unexpected twist and, incidentally, re-expresses in his last volume one of his fundamental ideas. The man from the star Rephan does not ridicule the imperfections of life on the earth—he sees in them the opportunity for growth as opposed to the dead perfection of Rephan. (Compare *Old Pictures in Florence*, ll. 81–136, text pp. 268–9.) Browning took the title (which is the Coptic proper name for Saturn and was sometimes spelled Remphan) from Acts 7 : 43.

Page 380. *From* THE RING AND THE BOOK

The text (pp. 382–90) carries an introduction narrating in some detail the Franceschini murder case of 1698 which Browning chose to present through the lips of contemporary witnesses who differed in their ideas of the guilt involved. The introduction emphasizes these differences. The text prints the statements of the three principals—the woman who was killed, the man who tried to save her, and the man who killed her. The first footnote on each of text pp. 390, 417, and 440 will serve to place the extracts in relation to the events as told in the introduction. A word might be added to the footnote of p. 440 to the effect that Guido, self-possessed on the witness stand, went to pieces in the death cell and showed the truth. In the text there are sufficient footnotes to clarify such other important points as need explanation. The murder was committed on January 2, 1698, and the murderers were executed on February 22, following.

Page 471. FOREWORD TO A SOUL'S TRAGEDY

471b, ll. 1–4. The *Camera della Segnatura*, where the pomegranate appeared before the explaining historian, was a room in the Vatican, frescoed by Raphael. The portrait of Dante by Giotto is presumably that in the Bargello at Florence, although the pomegranate is not clear. Neither is it clear in the other possible portrait—in the Louvre in Paris.

471b, ll. 5–9. *the Bellari and Vasari . . . simbolo delle buone opere*, etc. Historians of painting such as Bellari and Vasari would come after to explain that the pomegranate was a "symbol of good work—the pomegranate was therefore used [embroidered] on the vestments of the priest among the Hebrews."

Page 472. SELECTIONS FROM THE LETTERS OF ROBERT BROWNING AND ELIZABETH BARRETT

472b, l. 14. *your verses*. Miss Barrett's *Poems* of 1844. In *Lady Geraldine's Courtship* Miss Barrett had written:

"Or from Browning some 'Pomegranate'
which, if cut deep down the middle,
Shows a heart within blood-tinctured, of
veined humanity."

Browning consequently had an excuse to address her. The admiration of the two poets for one another's work preceded the correspondence.

472b, l. 50. *Kenyon*. John Kenyon, Elizabeth Barrett's second cousin. He early tried to arrange a meeting between the two and it was at Kenyon's urging that Browning first gathered courage to write to Elizabeth. Always a staunch supporter of the two poets, Kenyon at his death in 1856 left Elizabeth six thousand guineas and Robert four thousand that they might be free of money worries.

Page 474.

474a, l. 23. *Alla cara memoria*, etc. "To the beloved memory of Torquato Tasso, Doctor Bernadini offers the following song, *O thou. . . .*"

474a, l. 42–5. *Mr. Fellows . . . Lycians*. Between 1839 and 1844 Sir Charles Fellows made four trips to Asia Minor which aroused great interest in England. The subject was fresh in Browning's mind, as only the year before (1844) Fellows had made his fourth trip and shipped home twenty-seven cases of marbles which were set up in the British Museum in the Lycian Saloon.

474b, l. 41–2. *cognate creature . . . by stick and string*. That similar creature, a puppet, worked by strings from a stick; a puppet also would come down "flop" when the end of the play was reached and the curtain drawn.

Page 475.

475b, l. 4. *εἴδωλον*. *Likeness*.

475b, ll. 48–50. *A great dramatic power . . . formal drama*. Browning's published work in 1843–1844 (Numbers IV–VI of the *Bells and Pomegranates;* see chronological list, text p. 227) had consisted entirely of dramas.

Page 476.

476a, ll. 31–2. *petted . . . garden spider*. See comment on Browning's approach to nature in note on *Garden Fancies*. Browning refers also to this spider in a letter to R. H. Horne, Dec., 1842: "A picturesque bit of ghastliness: in this little writing-room of mine are two sculls, each on its bracket by the window; few brooms trouble walls and ceiling, you may be sure—so here has a huge field-spider woven his platform —web from the under-jaw of one of these sculls to the window-sill—and (the two sole remaining teeth keeping the jaws just enough apart) the spider's self is on the watch with each great arm wide out in a tooth-socket—thus." And Browning drew a sketch.

476b, l. 33. *Kirke White* (1785–1806). White, the son of a butcher, secured a scholarship to Cambridge, where he literally worked himself to death. Southey published his literary remains. The lines Browning quotes are from *Fragment* (reprinted in Stephens, Beck, and Snow, *English Romantic Poets*, p. 791).

Page 477.

477a, l. 33. *Paracelsus.* A reference to Browning's poem of that name. Mrs. Browning has in mind the indomitable aspiration and vigor of the hero, not the disasters which befell him.

Page 478.

478a, ll. 19–21. *Prometheus . . . Milton's ground.* Miss Barrett had previously translated Aeschylus's *Prometheus Bound* (1833). Browning in his letter of March 12 had suggested to her a drama on the Promethean theme and outlined it to her. Her comment on treading Milton's "ground" is a reference to her *A Drama of Exile* (1844).

478a, l. 46. [*Letter*] *VII.* This letter was written immediately after Browning's first call on Miss Barrett in Wimpole Street

478b, l. 23. [*Letter*] *VIII.* On Friday, May 23, Miss Barrett wrote Browning referring emphatically to some expressions in a previous letter of his as "fancies,—which you will not say over again, nor unsay, but *forget at once,* and *for ever, having said at all*" and threatening to break off all communication if he repeated them, and on the following Sunday she returned the offending letter, which Browning burned—the only letter in the series to be destroyed. Number VIII in the text is the letter which closes the incident in the correspondence.

It has been asserted that Browning's destroyed letter contained a proposal of marriage. The correspondence (*The Letters of Robert Browning and Elizabeth Barrett Barrett,* I, 74–83) gives no confirmation of this, but seems to indicate that Browning wrote rather wildly of her immense superiority to him and of his gratefulness for the association.

478b, l. 44. *Luria.* The hero of Browning's play of the same name.

Page 479.

479b, ll. 5–6. *I lost what I loved best in the world.* Miss Barrett's favorite brother was drowned off Torquay. He accompanied her to Torquay where she was sent for her health and was allowed, at Elizabeth's prayers, to remain with her, although her father wished him to return to London. Had her father's wishes been obeyed the brother would not have been drowned and Elizabeth morbidly considered herself responsible for his death.

Page 480.

480b, l. 12. [*Letter*] *X.* Miss Barrett had some means of her own, inherited from her mother's family, so she was financially independent of her father and bound only by what she thought were the obligations of her duty and affection. The trip to Italy (she planned to go to Pisa) would have been a wise move for her health and was a cherished dream of her spirit. Her father arbitrarily and without explanation forbade it in 1845. The following year when a similar situation arose, Elizabeth eloped with Browning.

Page 482.

482a, ll. 30–3. *certain noble extravagances . . . made me happy.* A reference to the previous letter. See especially text p. 481b, ll. 40 et seq.

Page 483.

483b, ll. 3–4. *jamais je n'ai pas été,* etc. "I have never been loved as I love."

483b, l. 19. *de profundis amavi.* "From the depths I loved."

483b, l. 33. [*Letter*] *XIV.* Browning's reply to this letter on the duality of his appearance to her—the letter-writer and the Tuesday-caller—is given in the text, Letter XVII. See especially p. 486a, ll. 17–23.

Page 484.

484a, l. 17. [*Letter*] *XV.* From preceding letters in the correspondence it is apparent that Browning on one of his visits had suggested going to her father and asking to be accepted formally as a suitor. The suggestion threw Elizabeth into a panic. She recalled how abruptly a suitor of her sister Henrietta had been dismissed and Henrietta, for the crime of seeming to "feel a little," had been made to suffer and do penance until she was driven into hysterics and Elizabeth herself—although quite healthy at the time—in the strain of the situation had fainted while going to Henrietta's assistance. It was Elizabeth's fear that if ever her father learned of their love, Browning would be forbidden the house and his letters would be intercepted—making all communication impossible.

484b, l. 19. *If it had not been for you.* See note on p. 479b, ll. 5–6 (Letter IX).

484b, l. 44. *Pisa-business.* See note on p. 480b, l. 12 (Letter X).

Page 486.

486b, ll. 13–15. "*Tragedy*" . . . *Luria.* The eighth and last pamphlet of the *Bells and Pomegranates* published in 1846 contained *A Soul's Tragedy* and *Luria.*

486b, l. 29. *Selah.* The whole letter is clearly one of emotional and intellectual shorthand, the full meaning dependent upon a recent conversation perfectly clear to Robert and Elizabeth and unknown to anyone else. Conjecture might assert that Elizabeth (at that date a far more famous and fluent poet than Robert) had shrewdly and honestly told the truth—that he was greater than she, and that association between his genius and her talent meant her eclipse. To that idea Robert indignantly refuses to say "Amen" ("so be it"). Lines 29–30 apparently quote Elizabeth who used the Hebraic word "Selah" rather carelessly (its exact meaning being unknown).

Page 487.

487b, l. 19. *Arabel and Flush.* Elizabeth's sister Arabella and her pet spaniel Flush, perhaps the best beloved pet in literary history.

Page 488.

488a, l. 7. *Severn.* Joseph Severn, the painter, who accompanied Keats to Italy and attended him in his last illness in Rome.

488b, l. 12. [*Letter*] *XXII.* The journals of Benjamin Robert Haydon the painter, to which this letter refers, were contained in twenty-six folio volumes. Haydon had enjoyed the friendship of many of the leading men of his time, but a career which contained many brilliant successes ended in frustration, defeat, and poverty. Many men had held a high opinion of Haydon's talent, but no one had ever thought quite so highly of it as did Haydon himself. His last exhibition was a failure and he had the mortification of seeing Tom Thumb, the dwarf, who was on exhibition in the same building, drawing crowds. In his bitterness, Haydon committed suicide. See also Letters XXIII and XXV.

Page 489.

489a, l. 33. *the poor writer.* Haydon. See note on 488b, l. 12.

Page 490.

490a, l. 6. *Ah Flush, Flush.* Flush, who knew a rival for Elizabeth Barrett's affection when he saw one, had bitten Robert Browning. He repeated the offense a few days later. See Letter XXVII.

490a, l. 49. *Laocoon.* The priest Laocoön's two sons were in the toils of crushing serpents and, coming to their aid, Laocoön was also entangled and crushed.

Page 491.

491b, ll. 33–4. *the hatefulness of this state of things.* Browning was in the awkward situation of being the secretly accepted suitor with whom Elizabeth was planning an elopement, whereas outwardly he was only a casual afternoon caller. Some unexplained episode had just occurred which embarrassed and angered him. See later in this letter (p. 493a, ll. 13–32) and the beginning of Letter XXIX.

Page 492.

492a, l. 13. *end of September at very latest.* The sudden decision of Elizabeth's father to move his household from London to a place in the country forced action and Elizabeth and Robert were married on September 12, 1846.

Page 493.

493a, l. 16. *Mr. Hunter.* See note on 491b, ll. 33–4. Apparently Mr. Hunter had been talking in terms Browning did not like about some case Browning fancied to be similar to that of his own and Elizabeth's. Browning would like to get him outside and thrash him.

493b, l. 10. *a position unworthy of you.* See notes on p. 491b, ll. 33–4 and p. 493a, l. 16.

MATTHEW ARNOLD

BIBLIOGRAPHY

I. WORKS

Complete Works. 15 vols. (Macmillan: London, 1903–4.) The most comprehensive edition; the final volume contains a useful bibliography. Vols. I and II contain the poetry; the Letters (last three volumes) are edited by G. W. E. Russell.

Poems, 1849–1867, ed. by A. T. Quiller-Couch. (Oxford University Press: 1926.) Includes the body of the six volumes of Arnold's poetry; the editor provides an introduction; notes supplied by G. St. Quintin.

Select Poems, ed. by E. E. Hale, Jr. (Heath: Boston, 1908.) A good book of selections, fully equipped with introduction and notes.

Poems. (Dutton: New York, 1927.) Contains an introduction by R. A. Scott-James, together with Arnold's prefaces of 1853 and 1854. Divisions: Early Poems, Lyric, Narrative, Elegiac, and Dramatic Poems.

Selections, ed. by R. E. C. Houghton. (Methuen: London, 1929.) A sifted harvest of the best of Arnold's poetry, chosen on the principle that "reading is the simplest and the most innocent manner of living in the best company."

Essays and Poems, ed. by F. W. Roe. (Harcourt: New York, 1928.) One of the best selections of its kind, provided with an introduction by the editor.

Prose and Poetry, ed. by A. L. Bouton. (Scribner: New York, 1927.) A recommended collection, including a good range of the essays and the most frequently anthologized poems.

Letters, 1848–1888, ed. by G. W. E. Russell. 2 vols. (Macmillan: New York, 1895.) Chosen from the correspondence remaining with the poet's family, who, respecting his desire that he should not be made the subject of a biography, permitted the publication of a limited number of his letters.

Unpublished Letters, ed. by Arnold Whitridge. (Yale University Press: 1923.) From correspondence of the poet to his sister, covering the period 1849–60, containing many references to his poems. Included also are portions of Arnold's correspondence with Sainte-Beuve and Cardinal Newman.

Letters to Arthur Hugh Clough, ed. by H. F. Lowry. (Oxford University Press: 1932.) An illuminating revelation of Arnold's inner life is found in these letters (56 in number), dating 1845–1862. The chief theme is the art of poetry; contains also the one letter from Clough which escaped destruction. The introductory essay is noteworthy.

II. BIOGRAPHY AND CRITICISM

Bickley, F. L. *Matthew Arnold and His Poetry*. (Dodge: New York, 1911.) One of the best of the briefer Lives, forming an easy introduction to the study of the poet.

Chambers, Edmund. *Matthew Arnold*. (Milford: London, 1932.) A Warton lecture, this appreciation offers interesting suggestions on the poems to Marguerite; praises Arnold's fastidiousness, particularly in "Thyrsis"; remarks the pervasive elegiac element in his poetry.

Dawson, W. H. *Matthew Arnold and His Relation to the Thought of Our Time*. (Putnam: New York, 1904.) A rather "heavy" treatment of Arnold's theories and influence, under the headings Culture, Religion, Politics; concludes with a bibliography of Arnold's works.

Houghton, R. E. C. *The Influence of the Classics on the Poetry of Matthew Arnold*. (Blackwell: Oxford, 1923.) Illuminates some of the best passages in Arnold by placing them beside their classical sources; shows that Arnold gained from the classics not only a profound influence on his style and choice of theme, but a poise and a restraint evident in his treatment of modern problems.

Kingsmill, Hugh. *Matthew Arnold*. (Dial Press: New York, 1928.) A recommended biography, giving the outward facts of the poet's life, together with an analysis of his inner sensuous development, which the biographer thinks was curbed by Arnold's father.

Paul, H. W. *Matthew Arnold*. English Men of Letters series. (Macmillan: London, 1925.) An excellent summary, giving the gist of practically all the important biographical data; makes abundant quotation and reference to Arnold's prose and poetry.

Russell, G. W. E. *Matthew Arnold*. (Scribner: New York, 1904.) Providing a minimum of comment on Arnold's writing, this study is "a survey of the effect which he produced on the thought and action of his age."

Saintsbury, George. *Matthew Arnold*. (Dodd: New York, 1909.) An authoritative critical study, written to "help the reader who wants criticism"; places Arnold's poetry in a class with that of Gray, combining the poet and the critic; compares him also with Dryden and Coleridge.

Sells, Iris E. *Matthew Arnold and France*. (Cambridge University Press: 1935.) A none-too-well supported study of French influence upon Arnold; Sand and Sénancour appear most prominently, but little new relevant material is presented here. An appendix includes "Lines Written on the Seashore at Eaglehurst," composed at the age of thirteen and not previously published.

Sherman, S. P. *Matthew Arnold, How to Know Him*. (Bobbs: Indianapolis, 1917.) An excellent study, showing the survival of the poet's classical ideals in the age of rising democracy; endeavors to probe the secret of his melancholy.

III. ARTICLES FROM BOOKS

Birrell, Augustine. "Matthew Arnold," in *Res Judicatae*. (Scribner: New York, 1892.) A rather unsympathetic review of the poet's relation to his time; praises his verse for its "grave and manly sincerity."

Brooke, S. A. "Matthew Arnold," in *Four Poets*. (Duckworth: London, 1913.) Discusses the effects of the poet's modified stoical creed; reviews the material of his published works and their reception.

Dawson, W. J. "Matthew Arnold," in *Makers of English Poetry*. (Revell: New York, 1906.) Provides the accepted critical judgments on Arnold's poetry; shows how in many ways he was the most representative man of his age.

Drinkwater, John. "Tennyson's Influence: The Diction of Arnold," in *Victorian Poetry*. (Doran: New York, 1924.) Notes Arnold's facility in "linked sweetness," which he strengthens with a prose temper.

Drinkwater, John. "Some Letters from Matthew Arnold to Robert Browning," in *A Book for Bookmen*. (Doran: New York, 1927.) Presents fourteen letters (annotated by Mr. Drinkwater) which reveal the cordial relations existing between the two poets.

Galton, A. H. "Mr. Matthew Arnold," in *Urbana Scripta*. (Stock: London, 1885.) Goes little beyond the salient material of the Russell edition of the Letters, except to add "a few pleasant notes, chiefly about dachshunds."

Garrod, H. W. "The Poetry of Matthew Arnold" and "Matthew Arnold as Critic," in *Poetry and the Criticism of Life*. (Harvard University Press: 1931.) The first essay reviews the "Marguerite" episode and its later significance; points out the median importance of "Sohrab and Rustum": the second essay indicates the enduring elements of Arnold's prose.

Gosse, E. W. "Matthew Arnold," in *More Books on the Table*. (Scribner: New York, 1923.) An account of the reception of Arnold's various volumes of poetry; points to the paradox of his complexity and his profound originality.

Grierson, H. J. C. "Lord Byron: Arnold and Swinburne," in *The Background of English Literature* (Chatto: London, 1925.) Reviews Arnold's challenge, which Swinburne fiercely took up; attempts a fair arbitration of the issues involved.

Grierson, H. J. C. "Arnold and the Pre-Raphaelite Group," in *The Lyrical Poetry of the Nineteenth Century*. (Harcourt: New York, 1929.) Traces Arnold's indebtedness to the Romantic poets; shows the influence of the Greeks in his swing from virtuosity to a simpler style.

Harper, G. M. "Matthew Arnold and the Zeitgeist," in *Spirit of Delight*. (Holt: New York, 1928.) Attempts to summarize the influence of Arnold on his own generation, by his religious teaching, his work for educational reform, and his social and political criticism.

Henley, W. E. "Arnold," in ***Views and Reviews***.

(Macmillan: London, 1921.) Praises the poet's restraint and judgment in choice of themes, deprecating "Merope," and naming "Balder Dead" his best poem.

Johnson, L. P. "Matthew Arnold," in *Post Liminium*, ed. by Thomas Whittemore. (Mathews: London, 1911.) Discusses the profound influence from Arnold's father; points out the persistent humanism of the poet's work.

Jones, W. L. "Matthew Arnold, Arthur Hugh Clough, James Thomson," in *The Cambridge History of English Literature*, XIII. (Putnam: New York, 1917.) Points out the influence of Greek letters, Goethe, and Wordsworth in Arnold's poetry; comments on the irony of his pessimism in the face of these sources of strength.

Lucas, F. L. "Arnold," in *Eight Victorian Poets*. (Cambridge University Press: 1930.) Reminds us of the poet's "Biblical element"; gently rails at his melancholy, but praises it as sublimated in "Thyrsis."

Parrott, T. M. "The Poetry of Matthew Arnold," in *Studies of a Booklover*. (Pott: New York, 1904.) Points out the prevailing classicism of the poet, briefly reviews his publications and their major pieces, and remarks his vigorous humanism.

Quiller-Couch, A. T. "Matthew Arnold," in *Studies in Literature*, First Series. (Putnam: New York, 1918.) Hastily reviews the biographical facts; denies to the poet the highest inspiration but admits his steadying influence in the poetry of 1850 and later.

Raleigh, Walter. "Matthew Arnold," in *Some Authors*. (Oxford University Press: 1923.) Forms the preface to an edition of *Essays in Criticism* (1912), remarking that "in a sense, the critic in Matthew Arnold killed the poet, and killed him young."

Saintsbury, George. "Matthew Arnold," in *Corrected Impressions*. (Dodd: New York, 1895.) Provides many contemporary reflections on the poet's career; remarks his lack of dramatic power; concludes that as a poet his influence is "not wholly benign."

Stephen, Leslie. "Matthew Arnold," in *Studies of a Biographer*, II. (Putnam: New York, 1907.) Sets Arnold at his best on an equality with Tennyson; mildly deprecates his melancholy and his love for catchwords.

Swinburne, A. C. "Matthew Arnold's New Poems," in *Essays and Studies*. (Chatto: London, 1888.) Looking back upon the earlier volumes, reviews the publication of 1867; laments metrical faults, praises "Thyrsis," and points out the poet's lack of sympathy with French culture.

Walker, Hugh. "Matthew Arnold," in *The Greater Victorian Poets*. (Sonnenschein: London, 1895.) Analyzes the poet's criticism of life as expressed in a number of his pieces, which reveal "an incarnation of the classical spirit."

White, Greenough. "Arnold's Character as Revealed in His Poems," in *Matthew Arnold and the Spirit of the Age*. (Putnam: New York, 1898.) Shows the depth of Arnold's pessimism, relieved by his tenderness of heart and his patience, which deepened into stoicism.

Williams, S. T. "Three Aspects of Arnold's Poetry," and "Theory and Practice in the Poetry of Arnold," in *Studies in Victorian Literature*. (Dutton: New York, 1923.) The first essay discusses the poet's skill in creating moods, the submergence of narrative in his philosophy, and his Hellenism. The second essay reviews Arnold's many critical definitions and shows how his own poetry squares with them.

Woodberry, G. E. "Matthew Arnold," in *Makers of Literature*. (Macmillan: New York, 1900.) Shows the poet to be a Wordsworthian with a difference; laments the infrequency of the "burst of native song"; comments appreciatively on the Letters.

IV. ARTICLES FROM PERIODICALS

Benson, A. C. "Leaves of the Tree: Matthew Arnold," *North American Review*, CXCIV, 136–52 (July, 1911). A recollection of early first-hand impressions, giving some biographical information, together with some analyses of the poet's temperament as revealed in his life and his writings.

Chesterton, G. K. "Matthew Arnold," *Bookman*, XVI, 116–20 (Oct., 1902). A brief, penetrating review of the artistic and critical principles which Arnold supported as "the most serious man alive."

Elliott, G. R. "The Arnoldian Lyric Melancholy," *Publications of the Modern Language Association*, XXXVIII, 929–33 (Dec., 1923). Defines the spirit as the ideal of a settled calm, not the reflex of ecstasy, as with many of the Romantics; "The Buried Life" is analyzed as the key to Arnold's nature.

Foerster, Norman. "Matthew Arnold and American Letters Today," *Sewanee Review*, XXX, 298–306 (July, 1922). Beginning with one of Arnold's critical passages on the Romantic period, shows how American writers are falling into dangers against which Arnold spoke—"dealing with unrealities, and their forms are deformities."

Gummere, R. M. "Matthew Arnold," *Quarterly Review*, CCXLI, 142–55 (Jan., 1924). Shows the influence of Arnold's father upon him; names Arnold the proponent for "real culture as opposed to vocationalism."

Knickerbocker, W. S. "Matthew Arnold's Theory of Poetry," *Sewanee Review*, XXXIII, 440–50 (Oct., 1925). Shows Arnold's firm stand on the moral obligations of poetry, insisting that in his disillusion "there is no despair."

Knickerbocker, W. S. "Semaphore: Arnold and Clough," *Sewanee Review*, XLI, 152–74 (Jan., 1933). Making frequent reference to Lowry's publication of Arnold's Letters to Clough, reviews the stimulating effects of the contact between the two poets, even though their intra-individual differences were never bridged.

Lawrence, E. P. "Matthew Arnold in America," *Philological Quarterly*, X, 62–79 (Jan., 1931). An interesting report of Arnold's 1883 visit, based on newspaper comment and Arnold's letters and essays.

Montague, C. E. "Matthew Arnold," *London Mercury*, XIX, 278–84 (Jan., 1929). Impressions of one sight of Arnold and early reading of the poet and critic; invites a new perusal of Arnold's poetry.

Nicolson, Marjorie. "The Real Scholar Gipsy," *Yale Review*, XVIII, 347–63 (Dec., 1929). Traces the story of the hero of Arnold's poem, Van Helmont—a legend which Arnold knew very imperfectly and pieced together with liberal improvisation.

Orrick, J. B. "Matthew Arnold and America," *London Mercury*, XX, 389–97 (Aug., 1929). A review of Arnold's lectures on the first of his American visits, impressions received and given, and his reports to his English audience.

Romer, V. L. "Matthew Arnold and Some French Poets," *Nineteenth Century*, XCIX, 869–80 (June, 1926). Provides a valuable discussion of Arnold's debt to Sénancour, Lamartine, Guérin, and Vigny.

Sadler, M. E. "Matthew Arnold," *Nineteenth Century*, XCIII, 199–207; 366–77 (Feb., Mar., 1923). A centenary tribute: makes comparisons with Gray, and remarks Arnold's English staunchness and his service to education.

Stoddard, R. H. "Matthew Arnold as a Poet," *North American Review*, CXLVI, 657–62 (June, 1888). Reviews the materials of the poet's early publications; sees his poetry as the outgrowth of the spiritual unrest of his age.

Tinker, C. B. "Arnold's Poetic Plans," *Yale Review*, XXII, 782–93 (June, 1933). Cites Arnold's notation (1849) of his plans for work in that year; shows how the reason for his comparative failure to meet his own requirements lay in his self-obsession.

Warren, T. H. "The Life and Literary Work of Arnold," *Quarterly Review*, CCII, 221–49 (Jan., 1905). A review of several studies of Arnold, this essay points out the many paradoxical strains in Arnold's character and shows his impress upon the thought of his own day.

White, H. C. "Matthew Arnold and Goethe," *Publications of the Modern Language Association*, XXXVI, 436–53 (Sept., 1921). Chiefly a study of the effect of Goethe's critical theory upon Arnold, who "owed the general direction of his ideas to Goethe."

Wilkinson, W. C. "Matthew Arnold As Poet," *North American Review*, CLXXXVIII, 666–81 (Nov., 1908). A destructive review of "Sohrab and Rustum," pointing out syntactic lapses and narrative faults.

NOTES

Page 505. QUIET WORK

As an illustration of his belief that there is little or nothing mystical for Arnold in the "sweet influence of the Pleiades"; that "the planetary and stellar motions appear to him matchless patterns of quiet eternal activity," Mr. Stuart Sherman cites this poem, *Self-Dependence* (text p. 522), and *A Summer Night* (text p. 523).

MYCERINUS

"After Chephren, Mycerinus, son of Cheops, reigned over Egypt. He abhorred his father's courses, and judged his subjects more justly than any of their kings had done. To him there came an oracle from the city of Buto, to the effect that he was to live but six years longer, and to die in the seventh year from that time." (Herodotus.)

Arnold "took the story of Mycerinus and treated it with a brief nobility of imaginative and sympathetic thought which was rare in so young a poet. The King's father had been unjust, cruel, a wicked king. He had lived long and happily. The son had believed in justice, kindness, good government, and practised them; yet the gods condemned him to die in six years. He had governed himself, sacrificed himself, and this was his reward for giving up the joy of life. 'Then have I cleansed my heart in vain.' There is then no justice, no morality in the gods. Or they are themselves slaves of a necessity beyond them, or careless, in their leisured pleasure, of mankind. I scorn them; and, men of Egypt, if you wish to please them, do wrong, indulge in injustice, be like my father, then they will give you length of days. For me, I will give my six years to revel, to youthful joys, and so farewell.

"Nor does Arnold, in that passing mood, altogether blame him. At least, the king knew his aim and followed it. It is curious to read the lines in which Arnold expresses this. He would not have approved the life, but he approved—since the king had deliberately chosen that life—the firmness and clearness of his choice, the settled purpose of his soul—

he, within,
Took measure of his soul, and knew its strength,
And by that silent knowledge, day by day,
Was calm'd, ennobled, comforted, sustain'd."

(Stopford Brooke, in *Four Poets*, p. 75.)

See note to *The Sick King of Bokhara*, below.

Page 508. TO A FRIEND

Mr. Stanley T. Williams, in his *Studies in Victorian Literature*, speaks of the "very different forms" in which Arnold expresses "his absorption in Greek literature," and gives as illustrations the *Notebooks*, the lectures *On Translating Homer*, and this poem.

2. *the old man*. Homer, the great Greek epic poet, who, according to tradition, was blind.

3. *Wide Prospect . . . Fen*. The Wide Prospect is Europe, the Asian Fen, Asia. "The name Europe (Εὐρώπη, *the wide prospect*) probably describes the European coast to the Greeks on the coast of Asia Minor opposite. The name Asia, again, comes, it has been thought, from the muddy fens of the rivers of Asia Minor."—Arnold. Arnold's etymologies, it may be remarked, will not impress the philologist in the same way that they impress the lover of poetry.

4. *Tmolus Hill, and Smyrna Bay*. Tmolus is a

mountain in Lydia, Asia Minor. Smyrna Bay or Gulf cuts into Asia Minor on the west. Smyrna, on the gulf, was one of the seven cities that claimed to be the birthplace of Homer.

6. *Halting slave.* Epictetus (first century A.D.), a Stoic philosopher who taught at Rome and later at Nicopolis, in Epirus, Greece. He was a freedman and is said to have been lame and poor. He was banished from Rome by the Emperor Domitian, "Vespasian's brutal son."

7. *Arrian.* Flavius Arrian (100?–170?), a Greek historian who was a pupil of Epictetus.

8–14. *But be his . . . its child.* The reference is to Sophocles (496?–406 B.C.), one of the three great Attic tragedians. He was born at Colonus, a village not far from Athens. His plays are remarkable for their calmness and serenity, qualities which Arnold revered and to which much of his poetry owes its charm.

THE SICK KING IN BOKHARA

"The conception of a moral law is a favorite idea in Arnold's poetry. Not only is it a theme which seems to link these two poems [*Mycerinus* and *The Sick King in Bokhara*], but it finds expression in *Sohrab and Rustum*, *Balder Dead*, and in many shorter poems. Moreover, to the idea itself and its interpretation Arnold sacrifices a great deal. For what interests a lover of narrative poetry as he reads *Mycerinus* and *The Sick King in Bokhara* is the lack of emphasis upon dramatic situations. Both these poems have marked possibilities as dramatic poems. But, as in *Empedocles on Etna*, Arnold cares for the idea. The oracle in *Mycerinus*, the slave's sin in *The Sick King in Bokhara* are merely grist for Arnold's purpose,—the development of thought." (Williams, *Studies in Victorian Literature*, pp. 119–20.)

Pursuing still further the idea set forth in the above quotation, Mr. Williams points out that Mycerinus learned to submit to the law, and that to the king in Bokhara came the revelation that the slave whom he had killed had a higher conception of the law than he himself possessed.

Bokhara was a former state in Russian central Asia; Bokhara is also the name of the capital. The state is now a part of the Soviet Socialist Republic of Uzbek.

1. *just Vizier.* The Vizier was a minister or councilor of state.

12. *Ferdousi's.* Ferdousi or Firdusi (940–1020), sometimes called the Persian Homer, was the epic poet of Persia. His great poem, *Shah-namah* ("Book of Kings"), "a real Eastern epic that glows with colors unknown in our Western verses," contains the story of Sohrab and Rustum.

17. *the Registàn.* The market place.

24. *Allah.* The Supreme Being of the Mohammedans.

31. *Moollah.* A Moollah, or Mullah, is a learned teacher or expounder of the law and dogmas of Islam.

62–3. *the stream Of Samarcand.* Samarcand, a city east of Bokhara, took its water supply from the Zerafshan River.

109. *the Ulemas.* The scholars who were the authorities in Moslem religion and law.

166. *Mervè.* A city south of Bokhara.

167. *The Shiah dogs.* The Shiites or Shiahs are of that branch of the Moslems who do not acknowledge the body of traditions respecting Mohammed as any part of the law.

168. *Orgunjè.* A city on the Amu (Oxus) River, in central Asia.

173. *kaffirs.* A name applied loosely to all unbelievers by the Mohammedans.

229. *nard.* Ointment.

Page 511. WRITTEN IN EMERSON'S ESSAYS

In 1853 Arnold, writing to Clough, spoke of Emerson as being "very thin and ineffectual, and self-defensive only"; but thirty years later, in his lecture on Emerson, he praised him as "a friend and aider of all who would live in the spirit," although he did not admit him into high place as a poet, a prose writer, or a philosopher. In this same lecture, too, he included the voice of Emerson among the great voices, one that forty years before, when he was an undergraduate at Oxford, brought to his ear from beyond the Atlantic "a strain as new, and moving, and unforgettable" as the strain of Newman, Carlyle, or Goethe.

See letters (Nos. XXII and XXIII), text pp. 603–4.

SHAKESPEARE

See lines 62–6 of *Heine's Grave*, text p. 578.

1–3. *Others . . . knowledge.* The secret of Shakespeare's supreme greatness baffles the "searching of mortality." The greatness of other poets is understandable; not so that of Shakespeare.

IN HARMONY WITH NATURE

In this sonnet, which is addressed to a preacher who had urged his hearers to be "in harmony with nature," Arnold contradicts the idea which he voices in the last six lines of *The Youth of Nature* (text p. 528). Mr. Stuart Sherman quotes the poem as evidence that Arnold thought of Nature as "enigmatic, a dark-browed sphinx, a cruel or rather indifferent spectator mocking the vain fever of man's small activities."

TO A REPUBLICAN FRIEND, 1848

The "republican friend" was Arthur Hugh Clough (see text p. 860), who in a letter to a friend said of the French Revolution of 1848, "If it were not for all these blessed revolutions, I should sink into hopeless lethargy." The Revolution prompted him and Arnold to a rapid exchange of letters, in one of which Arnold said, "Certainly the present spectacle in France is a fine one." Ten days later, however, in a letter to his sister he wrote, "I do not say that these people in France have much dreamed of the deepest wants of man, or are likely to enlighten the world much on the subject." Nevertheless he and Clough agreed, he told her, on the question of the Revolution "like two lambs in a world of wolves."

Page 512. CONTINUED

3. *France proclaims*. The reference is to the establishment of the republic in 1848.

A QUESTION

Fausta, to whom the "question" is addressed, was Arnold's sister Jane, who became Mrs. W. E. Forster in 1850.

From THE STRAYED REVELLER

These words are spoken to Ulysses by a youthful reveller, the beloved of Bacchus, who entered the palace of Circe while she and Ulysses were away hunting and drank of her magic bowl that sent

> The bright procession
> Of eddying forms

sweeping through his soul. He has just told Ulysses that the gods, who can see all things on earth, are happy, and that the wise bards can behold all things and sing them, but only at great labor and pain to themselves, the gods exacting for a song the price that the singer become what he sings. Even as he talks the goddess and Ulysses begin to fade, to swim, to waver before him, and he calls again for the magic cup which has power to give him the "bright procession" without pain.

261. *Silenus*. The oldest of the satyrs, son of Hermes or of Pan. He fostered the infant Bacchus and became his companion when he grew up.

265. *Fauns*. Italian deities of fields and herds represented as having human shape, with pointed ears, small horns, goats' feet, and sometimes a goat's tail.

270. *Ulysses*. See introductory note to Tennyson's *Ulysses*, above. In his wanderings Ulysses reached the island of Ææa, the home of Circe. She gave a magic potion to the men whom he sent inland to explore and changed them into swine. Ulysses, who drank of the magic cup without harm to himself and forced Circe to restore his men to their natural form, dwelt in Circe's palace for a year.

275. *Mænad*. A nymph attendant upon Dionysus (Bacchus).

281. *Iacchus*. Bacchus, god of wine.

Page 513. THE FORSAKEN MERMAN

Of this poem, which Swinburne said had "all the fanciful pitiful beauty of dreams and legends born in grey windy lands on shores and hillsides whose life is quiet and wild," Mr. A. Clutton-Brock writes: "*The Forsaken Merman*, the freest of all his poems, is still full of the early world, forsaken and seeming to reproach us for forsaking it. It is the same myth taking another form, the same longing for an impossible simplicity and youth of all things, here found in the depths of the sea. . . It is a myth of two worlds, neighbouring yet separate, with rumours and whispers of each one reaching the other; the bells and the song of Margaret are heard by the Merman, and Margaret remembers her little mer-children and hears the Merman singing—

> There dwells a loved one,
> But cruel is she!
> She left lonely for ever
> The kings of the sea.

There is much of Arnold's poetry, measured, outwardly calm, full of good advice, in which he tries to be another Goethe, to forget this sense of two worlds, as if he were Margaret herself spinning in the upper world of the little grey church on the shore; and one side of him was indeed the official, the critic, the smiling man of the world; but he too hears snatches of the Merman's song, and when he hears it he is a divine poet." (*Essays on Literature and Life*, pp. 132–3.)

13. *Margaret*. Sir Edmund Chambers sees in this name a hint of the "daughter of France" who appeared as Marguerite in the love lyrics which Arnold gathered together in 1857 under the title of *Switzerland*. See the poems from *Parting* (text p. 520), *Isolation. To Marguerite* (p. 520), and *To Marguerite—Continued* (p. 521).

69. *sea-stocks*. Sea gillyflowers.

82. *shut . . . door*. The door is closed against the Merman in accordance with the popular belief that supernatural beings or those of another world are denied Heaven and the blessings of Christianity.

Page 514. IN UTRUMQUE PARATUS

The title, which means "prepared for either," points clearly to the theme of the poem. If nature and man are of divine origin, let man prepare himself for the full understanding of life and "the all-pure fount" by "lonely pureness." If, on the other hand, man seems to be the "sole to awake" in a world not shaped by the divine and in his pride sees a great difference between himself and his brother-world at his feet, let him beware of boasting, lest at the last it be forced upon him that, like his lowly brother-world, he too but seems.

Page 515. A MODERN SAPPHO

Sappho, called the "Tenth Muse" by Plato, was a Greek lyric poet who, in the seventh century B.C., lived on the island of Lesbos in the Ægean Sea. When Phaon, a handsome youth with whom she fell in love, looked coldly upon her, she is said to have thrown herself into the sea. Through her lyrics, which are exquisite songs of love and nature—often unrequited love—sounds a recurring note of sadness quite in keeping with their passionate mood. In Arnold's poem a modern Sappho sings of the same theme which inspired the Lesbian Sappho so long ago.

See notes to Swinburne's *Sapphics*, below.

Page 516. RESIGNATION

Swinburne called this poem "an unspotted and unbroken model of high calm thought couched in pure and faultless words." He found in it "a serene spell, a sad supremacy of still music that softens and raises into wisdom the passionless and gentle pain of patience; the charm of earth and sorrowful magic of things everlasting; the spell that is upon the patient hills and immutable rocks, at work and asleep, in the 'life of plants and stones and rain'; the life to which we too may subdue our souls and be wise." (Swinburne, *Works*, XV, 86.)

Sir Edmund Chambers believes that the elegiac temper which pervades Arnold's poetry is its peculiar characteristic. He points out that Arnold's elegy ("as is common with elegy") often has an idyllic setting and names *The Scholar-Gipsy* and *Thyrsis* as two obvious examples. He selects as illustrations also lines 170–88 of this poem and the first fifteen lines of *Bacchanalia* (text p. 570), and concludes with this comment: "For such writing I will venture to borrow the phrase of a poetess who herself wrote no poetry, 'It calls home the heart to quietness.'"

For Fausta, to whom the poem is addressed, see note to *A Question*, above.

3. *Mecca*. An Arabian city, the birthplace of Mohammed and holy city of the Moslems.

4. *warriors*. Crusaders seeking to recover the Holy Land from the Moslems.

7. *Lydian*. Lydia was an ancient country of western Asia Minor.

9. *Goth . . . Hun*. The Goths were an ancient Teutonic race which in the early centuries of the Christian Era overran the Roman Empire. The Huns were a barbarous Asiatic people who near the middle of the fifth century gained control of much of central and eastern Europe, even forcing Rome to pay tribute.

13. *Euxine*. The Black Sea.

41. *wayside inn*. The inn at Wythburn, Cumberland. The tramp to the sea, which is the subject of ll. 40–85, was probably made in 1839, when Arnold was seventeen years old. He was then living at Grasmere, where Dr. Arnold had established his home in order that his family might escape from the ugliness of the country around Rugby.

44. *leader*. Dr. Thomas Arnold, the poet's father.

77. *noisy town*. Keswick.

208. *Orpheus*. See note to ll. 38–9 of *Memorial Verses*, below.

265–70. Mr. Hugh Kingsmill points out that in these lines Arnold uses Nature as an image of his own resigned attitude towards life. In *Self-Dependence* (text p. 522) he makes of her an exemplar of right conduct, and in *Morality* (p. 522) he sees her as a force free from the "limitations that fetter human beings."

Page 518. MEMORIAL VERSES

Arnold wrote this poem at the request of Edward Quillinan, Wordsworth's son-in-law. The fact that he wrote to Clough soon after the poem was completed and said, "I have . . . dirged W. W. *in the grand style* and need thy rapture therewith," is not to be interpreted as evidence that he held either Wordsworth or the poem in light esteem. In many of his letters to Clough Arnold spoke playfully—even irreverently—of persons and things of dignity and fineness, a circumstance not at all unusual in the correspondence of young men as intimate as were he and Clough. In *Crabb Robinson's Correspondence with the Wordsworth Circle* (II, 769) is a note from Quillinan in which he calls the poem "a triple Epicede on your Friends Wordsworth and Goethe, and on Byron who, I think . . . is not tall enough for the other two." The note closes with the remark that "Arnold has a good deal of poetry in him; and it will come out in spite of all the heathen gods and goddesses that hold him in enchantment."

It is not a rare thing to hear Wordsworth spoken of as the teacher of Arnold. Arnold called himself a Wordsworthian and doubtless his poetry owes something to Wordsworth, but it is perhaps too much to say that Wordsworth was his teacher. Mr. Stuart Sherman, writing of this poem, said that the voice Arnold "lends to the 'solemn hills' has a far grimmer message than that delivered by the sage of Cockermouth," and Sir Edmund Chambers warns the enthusiast against pushing the parallel between Wordsworth and Arnold too far. "What Arnold felt most clearly in Wordsworth's reaction to nature and life," Chambers says, "was joy." But Arnold, seeing "the whole of life unroll before him, just as Wordsworth might have done," felt that it was a life

"Whose secret is not joy, but peace."

Mr. Chambers sees no parallel either between Wordsworth's conviction "of a universal harmony in things," a conviction "based on mystic intuition rather than logical reasoning," and Arnold's incoherent "vision of the scheme of things entire." The "philosophic optimism" so confidently set forth by Wordsworth in *Tintern Abbey* had no place in the mind of the poet of *Resignation*. Cf. *The Youth of Nature* (text p. 528), and see letters XI (text p. 598) and XX (text p. 603).

1–2. *Goethe . . . cease.* The tomb of Goethe, who died in 1832, is in Weimar, Germany. Byron died in 1824 while engaged in helping the Greeks in their revolt against Turkey.

5. *Wordsworth's tomb.* Wordsworth died in 1850.

6–14. *When . . . strife.* Although Arnold wrote to Clough in 1848 of the spoiling of the whole locality of the Lake of Geneva by "the omnipresence there of that furiously flaring bethiefed rushlight, the vulgar Byron," in 1863, in his *Essays in Criticism*, he pronounced Byron, with all his weaknesses, "the greatest natural force, the greatest elementary power . . . in our literature since Shakespeare."

15–33. *When Goethe's . . . happiness.* The impression made upon Arnold by Goethe was second only to that made by Wordsworth. In 1864 he wrote in a letter to Lady de Rothschild: "They are the two moderns (very different) I most care for."

38–9. *Orpheus . . . Hades.* When Eurydice, wife of the Thracian poet and musician, Orpheus, died, he descended into Hades and so pleased Pluto by his music that the god allowed him to lead her back to earth on condition that he should not look behind him till he reached the upper world. Over-anxious, he broke the condition, and Eurydice vanished.

72. *Rotha.* Grasmere, where Wordsworth is buried, is near this little stream.

Page 519. LAST SONG OF CALLICLES

This song is sung by the young harp-player, Callicles, just after Empedocles, a learned and eloquent Sicilian philosopher in banishment, has thrown himself into the crater of Mt. Etna. Empedocles was driven to his desperate deed by a "fierce, man-hating mood," and Callicles, whose harp-playing Empedocles loved and who felt himself drawn, he knew not how, to the philosopher, had followed him at a distance up the mountainside, hoping "to relax his settled gloom" by the sweet strains of the harp. The hope of Callicles was vain, however; he had begun and completed his song before he was aware that Empedocles, "in wrath and gloom," had plunged into the crater.

Arnold did not include *Empedocles* in the edition of his poems of 1853, and only included it in the 1867 volume because of Browning's insistence. Writing of the omission of the poem from the 1853 volume, Mr. A. Clutton-Brock suggests that *Empedocles on Etna* is the story of "a divided personality, the inner truth about Arnold himself, which, as soon as he told it, he wished to suppress because it was indeed a conflict in himself to which he could see no solution." The final song of Callicles, in sharp contrast to the "wrath and gloom" voiced by Empedocles, is "the other, irreconcilable part of Arnold himself," the Arnold who at the same time that he saw bitterness and disillusionment on every side yet longed for "a golden age of sunlight, of the Mediterranean, of the morning of the world." Cf. introductory note to *The Austerity of Poetry*, below.

Browning, who believed that Empedocles seemed precisely in the condition of despair to which Greek paganism would lead a profound mind, is said to have had Arnold's poem in mind when he wrote his own *Cleon* (text p. 343).

7. *Helicon.* A mountain in Bœotia, in Greece, supposed by the Greeks to be the residence of Apollo and the Muses.

11. *Thisbe.* A town in Bœotia.

30. *the Nine.* The nine Muses. See note to l. 27 of Swinburne's *Sapphics*, below.

Page 520. *From* PARTING
ISOLATION. TO MARGUERITE
TO MARGUERITE—CONTINUED

These three pieces belong in the group of nine poems known as the "Marguerite poems," or the "Switzerland series," the first eight of which appeared in the years from 1849 to 1857 and the last, *The Terrace at Berne*, in 1867. Despite the fact that members of Arnold's family insisted that the poet declared Marguerite to be imaginary, there is much reason to believe that she was real, a French girl, probably a governess or companion, with "sweet blue eyes" and "soft ash-colour'd hair," living in Thun, a town in German Switzerland. *Parting* seems to have for its subject the first year of the lovers' acquaintance, which was probably 1846 or 1847. The other poems in the group deal with the second year, by which time Marguerite's love had well-nigh faded. Professor T. M. Parrott pronounces *To Marguerite—Continued* the "loveliest of Arnold's poems of love." It is worth noting, he says, that the "poem deals, not with the rapture of possession, nor with the unutterable sadness of remembered kisses after death, but with the sense of that predestined solitude of the soul which even love is unable to overcome." (*Studies of a Booklover*, p. 21.)

The reference in ll. 20–4 of *Isolation* is to the story of Selene, goddess of the moon, and Endymion, the handsome young hunter or shepherd of Mt. Latmos in Caria. Seeing him asleep one night, the goddess fell in love with the youth, and forsaking her "starry height" stole down and kissed him.

For Browning's treatment of the idea expressed in l. 4 of *To Marguerite—Continued* see *Two in the Campagna* (text p. 284).

Page 521. DESPONDENCY

Mr. S. P. Sherman, in his *Matthew Arnold* (p. 55), speaks of three phases of disillusionment experienced by Arnold in his young manhood. He was disillusioned concerning: (1) love and human relationships, (2) his own powers and his career, and (3) God and the universe. Sherman quotes this poem, ll. 16–30 of *Growing Old* (text p. 569), and *The Progress of Poesy* (text p. 569), in support of his belief that Arnold was early disillusioned about his poetic powers, a disillusionment which doubtless had some bearing on his early abandonment of the career of poetry.

SELF-DECEPTION

This is another of the many compositions in which the poet, brooding upon the longing of the "tremulous, eager being," voices his disillusionment about the gifts of man and asks the painful question, whether for him there is some satisfying end. Man at best seems but to be "in some unknown Power's employ." See the note to *Despondency*, above.

Page 522. SELF-DEPENDENCE

Being like the stars, living as they live, offers a refuge from the weariness and disillusionment that are human. H. W. Paul, in his *Matthew Arnold*, admits that the lines of this poem are pretty, but says that the consolation they offer "never dried a single tear." See note to *Quiet Work*, above, and to ll. 265–70 of *Resignation*, above.

MORALITY

Earnest, agonizing struggle toward good is the distinctive characteristic of man. He is "harried" by a morality of which nature knows nothing and which is the mark of his kinship with God. In 1852 Clough advised his sweetheart, who was unhappy because he was going to America, to read this poem for consolation. See note to ll. 265–70 of *Resignation*, above.

Page 523. A SUMMER NIGHT

Professor Parrott speaks of this composition as "perhaps the very highest poetic expression of the mingled despair and fortitude, the disgust with the world and the relief to be found in the contemplation of nature, which go to make up the essential undertone of most of Arnold's verse." (*Studies of a Booklover*, p. 20.) See note to *Quiet Work*, above.

37–50. These lines describe the life symbolized by the slave, as lines 51–73 describe that symbolized by the madman.

Page 524. THE BURIED LIFE

The subject of this poem, in which Arnold tells us that even love is "too weak to unlock the heart" and let it speak in fullness, is man's longing to know his actual, hidden self.

Page 525. STANZAS IN MEMORY OF THE AUTHOR OF "OBERMANN"

The author of *Obermann*, a psychological romance describing the sentimental speculations and aspirations of a melancholy egoist, was the French novelist, Étienne Pivert de Sénancour (1770–1846). The scene in which *Obermann* is laid was probably connected in Arnold's mind with his journey to Thun, Switzerland, in 1846 or 1847, which resulted in his love affair with the French girl, Marguerite. (See note to *Isolation. To Marguerite*, and *To Marguerite—Continued*, above.) This, Mr. Hugh Kingsmill says, would account for "the mournful sincerity of this poem." Arnold has been unfavorably criticized for comparing the work of Sénancour with that of Wordsworth and Goethe.

See *Obermann Once More* (text p. 574), and introductory note to that poem, below.

5. *abandon'd baths.* At Leuk, a village in the canton of Valais.

50. *one.* Wordsworth.

51. *one.* Goethe, whose tomb is in Weimar, Germany. Cf. *Memorial Verses* (text p. 518) for both Wordsworth and Goethe.

89. *son of Thetis.* Achilles, the Greek hero of the Trojan war. When Lycaon, son of King Priam, was defeated by Achilles, he begged for mercy. Achilles, remembering the slaying of his great friend, Patroclus, replied: "Do thou too die; Patroclus, who was better far than thou, is dead, and behold what kind of man I am; I too must die" (*Iliad*, XXI, 34 ff.).

114. *Jaman.* An Alpine peak.

121. *Lake Leman.* Lake Geneva.

164. *Vevey and Meillerie.* Towns on Lake Geneva.

179. *Capital of Pleasure.* Paris.

Page 527. LINES WRITTEN IN KENSINGTON GARDENS

In quiet Kensington Gardens—western London—, hearing only vaguely "men's impious uproar" in the streets hard by, the poet lies musing over the peace of glade and forest, of bird song, "blowing daisies," and "fragrant grass," and prays the calm soul of all things that he may feel, even "amid the city's jar," the presence of the abiding peace, the "perfecting silence," which is revealed in every aspect of Nature.

24. *Pan.* An Arcadian god of shepherds, herdsmen, and hunters.

37–40. *Calm . . . mar.* Mr. H. W. Paul says that the spirit of Pantheism voiced in these lines has never been more beautifully expressed except by Wordsworth. (For Pantheism see note to Tennyson's *The Higher Pantheism*, above.)

Page 528. THE YOUTH OF NATURE

This tribute to Wordsworth, written soon after that poet's death in 1850, reflects Arnold's love for the beauty of the Lake Country and establishes in the mind of the careful reader the belief that as a poet of natural beauty Arnold is the "direct inheritor of Wordsworth." The poem contrasts the eternal life of Nature, her freshness and changelessness through the ages, with the brief and fleeting life of man. Cf. *Memorial Verses* (text p. 518), and see introductory note to that poem and to *In Harmony with Nature*, above. See also letter XX (text p. 603).

2. *the lake.* Grasmere, in the Lake District.

8. *Rydal and Fairfield.* Rydal Mount, about two miles from Grasmere, was the home of Wordsworth from 1813 to 1850. Fairfield is a mountain near Rydal Mount.

15. *Pillar.* A high rock in the mountains near Wordsworth's home, celebrated in his poem, *The Brothers.*

16. *Ennerdale Lake.* In Cumberland, seven miles northeast of the market town, Egremont.

18. *The Evening Star.* The cottage of Michael in Wordsworth's *Michael.* The cottage, which stood above Grasmere, took its name from the fact that its evening light could be seen so far.

19. *Grasmere.* The village (near the north end of Grasmere Lake) where Wordsworth lived from 1799 to 1850. His four homes in or near Grasmere village were Dove Cottage, Allan Bank, the rectory, and Rydal Mount.

21. *Michael.* See note to l. 18, above.

23. *Quantock coombs.* The Quantock Hills are in Somerset. Coombs are narrow valleys.

24. *Ruth.* In her "wandering, over dale and hill," Ruth, in Wordsworth's *Ruth,* tramped the Quantock Hills.

28. *Age . . . condemned.* In his youth Wordsworth sympathized with the French revolutionists. Soon, however, he saw their excesses as the product of "human ignorance and guilt," and his praise turned to condemnation. In the last book of *The Prelude* he arraigns his age as one "too weak to tread the ways of truth."

33. *brethren . . . peers.* Probably Coleridge and Southey, poets who were closely associated with Wordsworth.

34. *Theban seer.* The blind prophet, Tiresias, fleeing with his Theban countrymen, who had been defeated in battle, drank from a fountain on Mt. Tilphusa, in Bœotia, and died because of the coldness of its water.

37. *Copais.* A lake near Thebes.

38. *Helicon.* See note to l. 7 of *Last Song of Callicles*, above.

40. *Parnassus.* A mountain in Bœotia sacred to Apollo.

77. *Mighty Mother.* Cybele, "Mother of the Gods," who was worshipped on Mt. Ida, in Mysia, Asia Minor.

Page 529. THE FUTURE

Arnold once said that he had a perfect passion for clear water. Mr. H. F. Lowry, in his *Letters of Matthew Arnold to Arthur Hugh Clough* (p. 34), finds this passion symbolical of "Arnold's lucid mind and character, his love of simplicity and his purity of thought and diction," and speaks of the fascination of studying the figures of river and stream as they appear in Arnold's poems. Mr. Lowry points out the elaborate imaging of life as a river in this poem, a river upon whose "widening course"

. . . the stars come out, and the night-wind
Brings up the stream
Murmurs and scents of the infinite sea.

36. *Rebekah.* In Genesis 24 is told the story of how the servant of Abraham, who had been sent to find a wife for Isaac, came at evening to a well "without the city of Nahor," found Rebekah drawing water there, tried her by a rigorous test, and pronounced her fit to be the wife of Isaac.

45. *Moses.* According to Exodus 3, the angel of the Lord appeared to Moses in a flame of fire out of the midst of a bush as he was keeping the flock of Jethro at "the backside of the desert" near Mt. Horeb.

Page 530. LONGING

This poem, one of the group of five poems called "Faded Leaves," has the same biographical interest that is to be found in the Switzerland group. The Marguerite of "Switzerland" is almost surely the lady longed for in "Faded Leaves." See note to extract from *Parting, Isolation. To Marguerite,* and *To*

Marguerite—Continued, above. Critics have pointed out that in *Longing* one feels the pang at the poet's heart and hears his cry "uttered in pure lyrical abandon."

Page 532. TRISTRAM AND ISEULT

Tristram, a famous hero of Celtic legend, lying wounded in Brittany, has sent a message to Iseult the Beautiful begging her to come to him, and is waiting for her reply.

In a letter to Clough (August 25, 1853) Arnold said that J. A. Froude had suggested that he should use an extract from Dunlop's *History of Fiction* as a preface to *Tristram and Iseult*, this being a better way to tell the story, Froude believed, than it would be for Arnold to tell it in his own words. Arnold liked the suggestion, and used the following extract from Dunlop as a preface.

"In the court of his uncle King Marc, the king of Cornwall, who at this time resided at the castle of Tyntagel, Tristram became expert in all knightly exercises.—The king of Ireland, at Tristram's solicitations, promised to bestow his daughter Iseult in marriage on King Marc. The mother of Iseult gave to her daughter's confidante a philtre, or love-potion, to be administered on the night of her nuptials. Of this beverage Tristram and Iseult, on their voyage to Cornwall, unfortunately partook. Its influence, during the remainder of their lives, regulated the affections and destiny of the lovers.

"After the arrival of Tristram and Iseult in Cornwall, and the nuptials of the latter with King Marc, a great part of the romance is occupied with their contrivances to procure secret interviews.—Tristram, being forced to leave Cornwall on account of the displeasure of his uncle, repaired to Brittany, where lived Iseult with the White Hands.—He married her—more out of gratitude than love.—Afterwards he proceeded to the dominions of Arthur, which became the theatre of unnumbered exploits.

"Tristram, subsequent to these events, returned to Brittany, and to his long-neglected wife. There, being wounded and sick, he was soon reduced to the lowest ebb. In this situation, he dispatched a confidant to the queen of Cornwall, to try if he could induce her to follow him to Brittany, etc." (Dunlop's *History of Fiction*.)

On March 4, 1886, Arnold wrote from Munich to Mrs. Arnold: ". . . went to the opera to see *Tristram and Iseult*. . . . I have managed the story better than Wagner. The second act is interminable and without any action. The hero and the heroine sit on a sofa and sing to one another about light and darkness, and their connexion with love. . . . At the end of the second act . . . I was quite worn out and came away. The third act is better, I imagine. But even in that less is made of the story than might be made." (*Letters of Matthew Arnold*, Vol. II, p. 374.) See introductory note to Swinburne's *Tristram and Iseult*, below.

TRISTRAM

9. *What Knight is this*. Note that the story is told partly by dialogue and partly by simple narrative.

23. *Lyoness*. Lyonesse, the home of Tristram, was a country fabled to have been formerly contiguous to Cornwall. See note to l. 4 of Tennyson's *Morte d'Arthur*, above.

161. *pleasaunce-walks*. Walks in the pleasure ground, or formal garden, near a mansion.

164. *fay*. Faith.

194. *chatelaine*. The lady of a château or castle.

203. *Launcelot's . . . Gard*. Joyous Gard, said to have been near Berwick, in the north of England, was the residence of Lancelot, the most famous knight of King Arthur's Round Table. See *Lancelot and Elaine* (text p. 145).

236. *chivalry of Rome*. According to early story Tristram, as one of King Arthur's knights, fought against the Romans, the Gauls, and the Scandinavians.

258. *leaguer*. Siege.

269. *wife*. Iseult of Brittany, known as Iseult of the White Hands.

Page 536. ISEULT OF IRELAND

85. *name . . . sorrow*. The name Tristram is perhaps connected with the Latin *tristis*, meaning *sad, sorrowful*.

169. *mullion'd windows*. Windows with slender bars or piers dividing the panes.

Page 538. ISEULT OF BRITTANY

Mr. Stuart P. Sherman called this canto "incomparably the finest third of the poem." He gave it high praise for "the fresh idyllic charm of its landscape, its touching humanity, its tone of tranquil melancholy, and its metrical regularity." Some critics have disapproved of the prominence given to the life of Iseult and her children in Brittany in this canto on the ground that the abrupt shifting of interest from the lovers to Tristram's wife and children mars the unity of the poem.

22. *fell-fare's*. The fell-fare, or fieldfare, is a thrush.

26. *stagshorn*. This may be the ground pine a kind of fern, or a kind of moss.

30. *missel-thrush*. A large European thrush which feeds on the berries of the mistletoe.

92. *prie-dieu*. A praying-desk, devotion-chair.

97. *seneschal*. A steward or major-domo.

143–4. *Cæsar . . . knight*. According to the historian Suetonius, Julius Cæsar wept when he heard of the conquests of the youthful Alexander the Great.

147. *Prince Alexander.* Alexander the Great, son of Philip of Macedon and King of Macedon 336–323 B.C. He died of fever in Babylon.

149. *Soudan.* Soldan or Sultan.

156. *Broce-liande.* In Arthurian legend, a magic forest in Brittany, where Merlin was enchanted by Vivien. See note to Tennyson's *Merlin and Vivien* (*Idylls of the King*), above.

197. *dingles.* Dells, small valleys.

216. *wimple.* A head-covering—linen, silk, etc.—formerly worn by women.

Page 541. SOHRAB AND RUSTUM

The story told in this poem is taken from the *Shah-namah* ("Book of Kings"), the great Persian epic written in the tenth century A.D. by Firdusi. Rustum, who had "the power of a lion," was a famous Persian hero. The combat between him and his son Sohrab took place in the reign of the weak king Kai Kaous, but Arnold places it in the reign of the great Kai Khosroo, possibly Cyrus the Great (sixth century B.C.). Giving the story a date, however, does not mean that it has a definite historical basis; it is to be taken as a myth or legend rather than as an historical tale.

In a note accompanying the poem, which he said he wrote with more pleasure than anything he had yet done, Arnold quoted the following from Sir John Malcolm's *History of Persia:* "The young Sohrab was the fruit of one of Rustum's early amours [with Tahmineh, a Tartar princess]. He had left his mother, and sought fame under the banners of Afrasiab, whose armies he commanded; and soon obtained a renown beyond that of all contemporary heroes but his father. He had carried death and dismay into the ranks of the Persians, and had terrified the boldest warriors of that country, before Rustum encountered him, which at last that hero resolved to do, under a feigned name. They met three times. The first time, they parted by mutual consent, though Sohrab had the advantage. The second, the youth obtained a victory, but granted life to his unknown father. The third was fatal to Sohrab, who, when writhing in the pangs of death, warned his conqueror to shun the vengeance that is inspired by parental woes, and bade him dread the rage of the mighty Rustum, who must soon learn that he had slain his son Sohrab. These words, we are told, were as death to the aged hero; and when he recovered from a trance, he called in despair for proofs of what Sohrab had said. The afflicted and dying youth tore open his mail, and showed his father a seal which his mother had placed on his arm when she discovered to him the secret of his birth, and bade him seek his father. The sight of his own signet rendered Rustum quite frantic: he cursed himself, attempted to put an end to his existence, and was only prevented by the efforts of his expiring son. After Sohrab's death, he burnt his tents and all his goods, and carried the corpse to Seistan, where it was interred. The army of Turan was, agreeably to the last request of Sohrab, permitted to cross the Oxus unmolested. . . . To reconcile us to the improbability of this tale we are informed that Rustum could have had no idea his son was in existence. The mother of Sohrab had written to him her child was a daughter, fearing to lose her darling infant if she revealed the truth; and Rustum, as before stated, fought under a feigned name, an usage not uncommon in the chivalrous combats of those days."

Sir Edmund Chambers pronounces *Sohrab and Rustum* a noble poem, the fruit of Arnold's constant preoccupation with Homer, whose works, the poet said, for one or two years were seldom out of his hands. "But it is no mere transcript from Homer," Mr. Chambers writes. "It is Homeric in its large utterance, its forthrightness, its constant use of expanded similes; un-Homeric and modern in its concentration on a theme of family relationship such as Homer only lightly touches, in the more conscious elaboration of its decorative passages, and above all in the enveloping presence of the river Oxus, which is a recurrent note throughout, and culminates in the magnificent *finale*, . . . where the father and the son are left alone on the darkling plain, and the Oxus, regardless and serene, moves onward to the Aral sea." (*Matthew Arnold, Warton Lecture on English Poetry, British Academy*, 1932, p. 12.) See introductory note to *The Sick King in Bokhara*, above.

2. *Oxus.* A large river of central Asia, flowing from the Caucasus mountains to the Aral Sea.

3. *Tartar.* The Tartars were nomadic tribes of central and northern Asia. Those figuring in the poem lived between Turan, or Turkestan, and the Caspian Sea. Their Persian foes came from South Persia (Iran).

11. *Peran-Wisa.* The Tartar leader.

15. *Pamere.* A plateau in the Caucasus mountains, 13,000 feet above the sea.

25. *thick-piled.* Having thick, heavy nap.

38. *Afrasiab.* The Tartar king.

40. *Samarcand.* A city in Turkestan famous for its caravan commerce; the "silken Samarcand" of Keats.

42. *Ader-baijan.* A province in Persia, the home of Sohrab's mother, Tahmineh.

82. *Seistan.* A region east of the Persian gulf, bordering Afghanistan and Persia.

85. *Persian King.* Kai Khosroo. (See l. 223 and introductory note to the poem.)

101. *Kara-Kul.* A division of country in south-central Asia.

107. *Haman.* In the *Shah-namah* Haman is the chief leader.

111–16. *As when . . . sea-board.* An example of the expanded simile, which Mr. Chambers (see introductory note) points out as a Homeric quality in the poem. In the *Iliad* (III, 1–8), Homer uses the same figure—marching cranes—to describe the Trojan army.

113. *Casbin.* A city in northern Persia.

114. *Elburz.* A mountain range on the northern border of Persia.

Aralian. Of the Aral, the sea into which the Oxus flows.

115. *frore.* Frozen; old past participle of *freeze.*

119. *Bokhara.* See introductory note to *The Sick King in Bokhara,* above.

120. *Khiva.* A district south of the Aral Sea.

ferment . . . mares. The drink made from mare's milk is called kumiss.

121. *Toorkmuns.* A Turkish race living in central Asia.

122. *Tukas.* A people from northwest Persia.

Salore. A people living east of the Caspian Sea.

123. *Attruck.* A river in northern Persia.

128. *Ferghana.* A district in Turkestan, east of Samarcand.

129. *Jaxartes.* A river of Turan (now Turkestan) emptying into the Aral Sea. Its present name is Sir or Syr.

131. *Kipchak.* A district east of the Aral Sea.

132. *Kalmucks.* Nomadic Mongols in western Siberia.

Kuzzaks. Cossack tribes inhabiting parts of Russia.

133. *Kirghizzes.* Wandering tribes from northern Turan (Turkestan).

138. *Ilyats of Khorassan.* Tribes. Khorassan was a province in northeastern Persia.

160. *Cabool.* Kábul, the chief city of Afghanistan.

161. *Indian Caucasus.* A mountain range, the Hindu-Koosh, between Turan and Afghanistan.

167. *stop their breath.* Stop talking.

200. *falcon.* For centuries falconry was a popular sport in Persia.

217. *Iran's.* Iran is the Persian name for Persia.

223. *Kai Khosroo.* See introductory note, above.

230. *helpless girl.* See introductory note above, and ll. 607–9.

232. *snow-haired Zal.* Zal, Rustum's father, was said to have been born with snow-white hair. Disgraced by this, he was left as an infant in the Elburz mountains to die, but a griffin rescued and cared for him.

257. *plain arms.* The device which Rustum regularly wore on his shield was the griffin, the marvelous creature that had saved his father. In this man to man combat, in order to conceal his identity, he would wear no device.

277. *Dight.* Arrayed, decorated.

286. *Bahrein.* Islands famous for pearl fisheries in the Persian Gulf.

288. *tale.* Number, count.

412. *Hyphasis or Hydaspes.* Rivers in northern India, now known as the Sutley and the Jhelum.

452. *autumn-star.* Sirius, the Dog Star. The rising of this star at the same time that the sun rose was thought by the ancients to be a baleful occurrence, one which accounted for the sultriness of the late summer and for the maladies, especially fevers, prevalent at that time.

592. *Koords.* A people of northwestern Persia.

596. *bruited up.* Noised abroad. The French for *noise* is "bruit."

626. *His wandering guest.* Rustum, "wandering" in search of Ruksh, his lost horse, had gone "in that long-distant summer-time," to the kingdom of Samengan, in Ader-baijan, the king of which was the father of Tahmineh, Sohrab's mother.

679. *griffin.* See note to l. 232.

701. *threw . . . hair.* In certain countries the grief-stricken or sorrowful express their feelings by throwing dust or ashes on their heads. Cf. Job 2:12: "They rent every one his mantle and sprinkled dust upon their heads."

725. *writ . . . be.* The belief that the manner and moment of one's death are foreordained in Heaven is a vital part of many religions of the East.

751. *Helmund* and *Zirrah* (l. 752) are in Seistan.

763–4. *Moorghab . . . Tejend, Kohik.* Rivers in Afghanistan.

765. *Sir.* See note to l. 129.

831–4. *When thou . . . his grave.* A puzzling passage. The meaning is probably the simple one that Rustum will not have peace until he has returned from a journey which he is to make "far into the north" with Kai Khosroo, the Persian king. The king's journey to the north he was to make in order to prepare for death.

861. *Jemshid.* A legendary Persian king, the founder of Persepolis, the Persian name of which means "the throne of Jemshid." According to the *Shah-namah* he ruled for seven hundred years.

878. *Chorasmian waste.* The desert of Chorasmia, south of the Aral Sea.

880. *Orgunjè.* A small town on the Oxus, near the Aral Sea.

Page 553. PHILOMELA

There are several versions of the Philomela-Procne story, which is the subject of this poem. The version which Arnold uses is as follows: Tereus, king of Daulis in Phocis, Greece, married Procne, daughter of King Pandion of

Attica and sister of Philomela. After a few years the affections of Tereus turned toward Philomela, and in order to be free to marry her he cut out Procne's tongue, concealed her in the country, and gave out the story that she was dead. Procne, however, found a way of informing her sister of her mistreatment by weaving the story into a tapestry. Horrified, Philomela went to the aid of her sister, and the two women killed Itylus, Procne's son by Tereus, served his flesh to Tereus, and fled. Discovering the crime, Tereus pursued the fleeing sisters so hotly that they had to call upon the gods for deliverance. The gods answered their prayer by turning Philomela into a swallow and Procne into a nightingale. According to Ovid and a number of other Latin writers it was Philomela who was changed into a nightingale and Procne into a swallow. Arnold, like most modern poets, adopts the version in which Philomela is identified with the nightingale.

See Swinburne's *Itylus*, text p. 700.

18. *Thracian.* Tereus is frequently referred to as King of Thrace.

27. *Cephissian.* The Cephissus was a river in Phocis.

28. *Eugenia.* Probably an imaginary person.

Page 554. REQUIESCAT

Of this poem, the title of which means "May she rest," Professor Parrott writes: "If a reader cannot see its flawless perfection; if he cannot feel its tender beauty and solemn pathos, culminating, as it does, in one inevitable and unforgettable line, he is indeed to be pitied, but not to be argued with." (*Studies of a Booklover*, p. 24.)

2. *yew.* The leaves and branches of the yew, a common graveyard tree, are associated with death and mourning.

13. *cabin'd.* Confined, restrained, shut up as in a cabin. The word is in sharp contrast with "vasty hall" (l. 16).

THE SCHOLAR-GIPSY

Arnold quoted "the oft-read tale" from "Glanvil's book" as a note bearing upon the story of the poem: "There was very lately a lad in the University of Oxford, who was by his poverty forced to leave his studies there; and at last to join himself to a company of vagabond gipsies. Among these extravagant people, by the insinuating subtilty of his carriage, he quickly got so much of their love and esteem as that they discovered to him their mystery. After he had been a pretty while exercised in the trade, there chanced to ride by a couple of scholars, who had formerly been of his acquaintance. They quickly spied out their old friend among the gipsies; and he gave them an account of the necessity which drove him to that kind of life, and told them that the people he went with were not such impostors as they were taken for, but that they had a traditional kind of learning among them, and could do wonders by the power of imagination, their fancy binding that of others: that himself had learned much of their art, and when he had compassed the whole secret, he intended, he said, to leave their company, and give the world an account of what he had learned." (Joseph Glanvil, *Vanity of Dogmatizing*, 1661.)

For an intimate description of the country of this poem and of *Thyrsis*, and for some of the stories familiar to many generations of Oxford students, see Henry W. Taunt's *Matthew Arnold's "Scholar-Gipsy" and "Thyrsis."* Miss Marjorie Nicolson, writing in the *Yale Review* for December, 1929, says that when Glanvil, who had been a student at Oxford, wrote the words which prompted Arnold to write *The Scholar-Gipsy*, "he knew the scholar-gipsy only as the subject of a tale told at Oxford and at Cambridge—and doubtless at many a continental university—localized usually in the place where it was told." Ten years later the real scholar-gipsy in the person of Baron Francis Mercury van Helmont crossed the path of Glanvil and told him the tale of the scholar-gipsy and many another tale in "broken language—Dutch, and French, and German, with a smattering of Latin, and, as time went on, more and more English." Van Helmont, who was the son of Jean Baptiste van Helmont, "last of the alchemists, first of the great chemists," was a most romantic figure, and had long been famous for his wanderings over the continent of Europe among all manner of men when, in 1670, he turned his face toward England. He remained in England, a fascinating adventurer, alchemist, and philosopher, the intimate of Henry More, leader of the Cambridge Platonists, until 1684, at which time he returned to the continent. He died in 1698 in his middle eighties. He was never a gipsy plain and simple, and never an Oxford student; but he was a gipsy in the sense in which one who has wandered widely over the earth is a gipsy, and he was a scholar in the sense in which those who have had much experience of men and books are scholars. The glamour the youthful mind throws round such as he is sufficient to account for the wide circulation of tales like that recorded by Glanvil.

"Matthew Arnold did not know the true story of his scholar-gipsy," Miss Nicolson concludes. "The ghost which haunts the long Oxfordshire twilight is his, not Helmont's. Yet there is much in *The Scholar-Gipsy* which was true of this original 'of pregnant parts and quick inventive brain,' who 'roam'd the world with that wild brotherhood.' He, too, was a 'glad perennial youth . . . exempt from age.'" The words of Arnold's poem are as fitting to the real as to the imagined scholar-gipsy.

November 30, 1853, Arnold said in a letter to Clough: "I am glad you like the Gipsy Scholar—but what does it *do* for you? Homer *animates*—Shakespeare *animates*—in its poor way I think Sohrab and Rustum *animates*—the Gipsy Scholar at best awakens a pleasing melancholy. But this is not what we want.

> The complaining millions of men
> Darken in labour and pain—

what they want is something to *animate* and *ennoble* them—not merely to add zest to their melancholy or grace to their dreams.—I believe a feeling of this kind is the basis of my nature—and of my poetics." (H. F. Lowry, *The Letters of Matthew Arnold to Arthur Hugh Clough*, p. 146.)

Mr. S. P. Sherman says that in this poem Arnold "betrays his poetical sympathy with an impulse which in his own conduct he severely checked, the impulse to drift and wander irresponsibly."

See introductory note to *Thyrsis*, below.

See Tennyson's letter X (text p. 216), and Arnold's letter IV (text p. 595).

2. *wattled cotes*. Sheds or sheepfolds made of wattles—that is, bundles of interwoven twigs.

10. *the quest*. The search for the scholar-gipsy, who, rumor said, "long was seen to stray" about the countryside.

13. *cruse*. Jug or vessel containing water or other drink.

25. *convolvulus*. Bindweed or morning-glory.

30. *Oxford's Towers*. Cf. *Thyrsis*, l. 19.

31. *Glanvil's book*. See introductory note to the poem, above.

42. *erst*. Formerly.

57. *Hurst*. Cumner Hurst, a hill about three miles southwest of Oxford.

58. *Berkshire*. The Thames, at Oxford, flows between Oxfordshire and Berkshire.

59. *ingle-bench*. Chimney-corner bench.

74. *Bab-lock-hithe*. A ferry about two miles west of Cumner village.

76. *the punt's rope chops round*. Sir Edmund Chambers quotes this line as an example of "Arnold's desire for literal fidelity of visual rendering." The poet did not write, "the slow punt swings round," a more elegant line than the other but lacking in accuracy, since "the punt [ferry-boat] at Bab-lock-hithe is so fixed as to make a moving bridge which cannot swing round."

79. *Wychwood bowers*. Wychwood Forest is twelve miles or more northwest of Oxford.

83. *dance . . . May*. Fyfield is a village about seven miles southwest of Oxford. The Fyfield maidens gathered near the elm, probably the great elm of Tubney, a mile from Fyfield, for their maypole festivities.

91. *Godstow Bridge*. Over the Thames about two miles above Oxford.

95. *lasher*. A pool below a weir, or dam.

111. *Bagley Wood*. On the Berkshire side of the Thames, about three miles below Oxford.

115. *Thessaly*. This classic name was given by Oxford students to the tract of land lying between the northern outskirts of Bagley Wood and the south bank of the Thames.

120. *the spark from heaven*. See ll. 48–50.

125. *Hinksey*. North and South Hinksey—"the two Hinkseys" of *Thyrsis*—lie between Oxford and Cumner, to the south of the main road.

129. *Christ-church hall*. The dining hall of Christ Church College. This college, near the north bank of the Thames, is clearly seen from the Cumner hills.

147. *teen*. Sorrow.

149. *the just-pausing Genius*. Various interpretations of this phrase have been made. One commentator suggests that Genius means the spirit of death, and that his "just-pausing" is in keeping with the brief moment of man's life. Another, that the Genius or guardian spirit of man, which presides over his fortunes and ultimately conducts him out of the world, pauses a moment before departing from him. Still another, that *just-pausing* means justly-pausing, the attendant Genius decreeing that it is "but fair that man should be allowed to show his own ineffectiveness before being taken hence."

182–3. *one . . . suffer'd*. Who the "one" of this passage is is uncertain. Coleridge has been mentioned, as have Carlyle and Tennyson. The fact that in the first edition of the poem *one* was spelled with a capital "O" and that in subsequent editions this was changed to a small "o" has been held to indicate that no particular person was meant. A writer in English *Notes and Queries* said that Arnold meant Tennyson and that he was thinking of ll. 5–8 of Section V of *In Memoriam*. Mr. E. A. G. Lamborn questions the naming of Tennyson here on the ground that Arnold speaks so disparagingly of Tennyson's intellectual powers that he would hardly have thought of him as "our wisest" (l. 191).

190. *anodynes*. Drugs to alleviate pain.

208–9. *Averse . . . turn*. Æneas, the "false friend" of Queen Dido of Carthage, deserted her. Virgil in his *Æneid*, VI, 469–72, thus describes their meeting in Hades:

> "But on the ground
> She fixed averted eyes. For all he spoke
> Moved her no more than if her frowning brow
> Were changeless flint or carved in Parian stone.
> Then, after pause, away in wrath she fled."
> (Trans. by Theodore C. Williams.)

232. *Tyrian trader.* The Phœnicians, an ancient people living in Phœnicia, on the coast of Syria, were great traders. Their two chief cities were Tyre and Sidon, from the former of which comes Arnold's "Tyrian."
234. *Lifting . . . creepers.* The boat thrust aside the vegetation overhanging from the shore.
236. *Ægean.* The Ægean Sea is between Greece and Asia Minor.
238. *Chian wine.* The isle of Chios, in the Ægean, was famous for its wine.
239. *tunnies.* A kind of fish, weighing sometimes as much as a thousand pounds.
244. *Midland waters.* A literal translation of "Mediterranean Sea."
245. *the Syrtes.* The ancient name of two gulfs, Sidra and Cabes, on the northern coast of Africa, opposite Sicily.
247. *western straits.* Straits of Gibraltar.
249. *Iberians.* Ancient inhabitants of the Spanish peninsula.

Page 558. HAWORTH CHURCHYARD

Haworth, in Yorkshire, nine miles northwest of the city of Bradford, was the gloomy moorland village to which Patrick Brontë moved his family when his daughter Charlotte was four years old. With the exception of a few years, Charlotte Brontë spent her entire life in this village, and when she died, March 31, 1855, she was buried in Haworth church

"... on the crest of the hill,
Lonely and bleak."

Of Harriet Martineau, the other of the "two gifted women" (l. 8), who was a neighbor of Arnold's at Fox How, he wrote to his mother in May, 1855:

My dearest Mother,

As to the poem in *Fraser*, I hope K. sent you a letter I wrote to her on that subject, in which I told her that I knew absolutely nothing of Harriet Martineau's works or debated matters—had not even seen them, that I know of, nor do I ever mention her creed with the slightest applause, but only her boldness in avowing it. The want of independence of mind, the shutting their eyes and professing to believe what they do not, the running blindly together in herds, for fear of some obscure danger and horror if they go alone, is so eminently a vice of the English, I think, of the last hundred years—has led them, and is leading them into such scrapes and bewilderment, that I cannot but praise a person whose one effort seems to have been to deal perfectly honestly and sincerely with herself, although for the speculations into which this effort has led her I have not the slightest sympathy. I shall never be found to identify myself with her and her people, but neither shall I join, nor have I the least community of feeling with, her attackers. And I think a perfectly impartial person may say all in her praise that I have said [i.e., in *Haworth Churchyard*].

M. A.

1. *Loughrigg.* An "ascent," or fell, over 1000 feet high, south of Rydal Water, Westmorland.
2. *Rotha.* A river flowing by the Grasmere churchyard (the place of Wordsworth's burial) and emptying into Rydal Water.
4. *Four years since.* In 1850 Charlotte Brontë visited the English Lakes and met Mrs. Gaskell, Miss Martineau, Arnold, and other interesting men and women. In 1851 she was the guest of Miss Martineau at Ambleside, Westmorland. On the occasion of the first visit the "two gifted women" called on Arnold at Fox How one evening. After they had gone Arnold wrote the following note, dated December 21, to Miss Wightman (who the next year became Mrs. Arnold): "At seven came Miss Martineau and Miss Brontë (Jane Eyre); talked to Miss Martineau (who blasphemes frightfully) about the prospects of the Church of England, and, wretched man that I am, promised to go and see her cow-keeping miracles [some experiments on a farm of two acres] to-morrow—I, who hardly know a cow from a sheep. I talked to Miss Brontë (past thirty and plain, with expressive gray eyes, though) of her curates, of French novels, and her education in a school at Brussels, and sent the lions roaring to their dens at half-past nine, and came to talk to you."
4–6. *house . . . son-in-law.* The house of Edward Quillinan, "a man sweet, generous, and humane." See note to *Memorial Verses*, above.
11–12. *feign'd . . . life.* Charlotte Brontë's *Jane Eyre*, which has been described as a story of "overwhelming passion," was published in 1847.
15. *fiction.* Miss Martineau's first successful writing was a nine-volume series of stories in illustration of political economy. They are now characterized as an "unreadable mixture of fiction, founded on rapid cramming, with raw masses of the dismal science."
17. *History . . . mind.* Miss Martineau's numerous writings included treatises on these subjects.
18–19. *wrote . . . book.* In an autograph album.
30–3. *elder . . . Summons.* Miss Martineau, who was fourteen years older than Charlotte Brontë, began suffering from a disease of the heart in 1855. Believing death near, she set to work on her autobiography. She did not die, however, until 1876, twenty-one years after she first expected the "last summons."
55. *Keighley.* Manufacturing town in the West Riding of Yorkshire about five miles northeast of Haworth.

59. *Poach.* Plow through mud.
80–1. *preceded . . . band.* Maria and Elizabeth Brontë, elder sisters of Charlotte, died in 1825, Maria at the age of twelve, Elizabeth at eleven.
90–2. *She . . . graceful.* Anne, the youngest of the sisters, who died in 1849. Arnold is mistaken in placing her grave at Haworth. She died at Scarborough, where late in her illness she had gone with a last hope, and there "she lies alone." As further evidence of the gentleness and sweetness which Arnold commends in her, the words of one of her biographers concerning her last resting-place may be quoted: "To that choice she would have submitted—gently."
92–100. *she . . . soul.* This passage refers to Emily Brontë, the author of *Wuthering Heights* and that one of the sisters possessing the true poetic gift. By the "too bold dying song" (l. 99) Arnold probably refers to Emily's last poem, *No Coward Soul Is Mine* (text p. 824), in which she gives bold utterance to her creed.
101–11. These lines refer to Patrick Branwell Brontë, the brother of the gifted sisters. See the introductory sketch to Emily Brontë (text p. 818).

Page 559. STANZAS FROM THE GRANDE CHARTREUSE

Professor Parrott, writing of this "lament for a dead faith," says that it is "the highest expression in the elegiac mood of the theme that Arnold treated with supreme lyric power in *Dover Beach.*" The poem not only reveals "the poet's own divided mind" but also stands as a typical utterance of the Mid-Victorian philosopher whose thinking has been influenced by the rationalistic science of his time. Arnold was not alone in his belief that the Christian faith was but "a dead time's exploded dream." La Grande Chartreuse, in the mountains near Grenoble, France, was the chief house or monastery of the Carthusians, an austere religious order founded by St. Bruno in 1086. The present building, which dates from 1678, was the chief house of the order from that date until 1903, at which time the monks were compelled to leave France under the provisions of the Associations Law, a law passed by the French Parliament, July 1, 1901, restricting religious orders, dissolving monastic associations, and secularizing education. Arnold had made a visit to the Grande Chartreuse in 1852.
4. *Saint Laurent.* A village five or six miles from the monastery.
10. *Dead Guier's stream.* The Guiers Mort River is near the monastery.
14. *scars.* Steep, rocky heights.
18. *Courrerie.* A mountain village near the monastery.
42. *Host.* Bread consecrated in the Eucharist, or Mass.
77. *anchorites.* Religious hermits.
83. *Runic stone.* A stone bearing runes, i.e., letters or signs used by the Teutonic, or Germanic, peoples from about the third century A.D.
85. *two worlds.* One is the old age of simple faith destroyed for Arnold with the advance of religious disillusionment upon his spirit; the other, a new age in which he hoped he would find a satisfying and abiding faith to take the place of that which he had lost. Sherman quotes ll. 67–96 in support of his belief that however much Arnold loved John Henry Newman, leader of the Oxford Movement, the movement itself left him cold.
99. *sciolists.* Superficial pretenders to knowledge.
115. *Achilles . . . tent.* At the siege of Troy, Achilles, who had proved himself one of the mightiest of the Greek warriors, quarrelled with Agamemnon over the possession of the captive maid, Briseis. As a result of the quarrel he withdrew to his tent and refused to take further part in the siege. The Greeks fared so badly without him that Briseis was returned to him. He still refused to fight, but when Patroclus, his dearly beloved friend, was slain, he leaped into his chariot and sped forth to deal death and destruction to the Trojans. It may be that Arnold saw in this inactivity of Achilles something that reminded him of the two years of study and meditation (1843–1845) that Newman engaged in before he entered the Roman Catholic Church.
133–8. *Byron . . . own.* Byron's exile from England was the result of several circumstances, most prominent being his separation from Lady Byron after a stormy year of married life, his publishing of some pro-Gallican stanzas, *On the Star of the Legion of Honour*, and some charges concerning his conduct with his half-sister, the Hon. Augusta Byron, wife of her first cousin, Col. George Leigh. It was "the excommunicating voice of society" that drove the poet from London. Macaulay wrote of his going: "The howl of contumely followed him across the sea, over the Alps; it gradually waxed fainter; it died away. . . . His poetry became more popular than it had ever been; and his complaints were read with tears by thousands and tens of thousands who had never seen his face." He died at Missolonghi, on the shores of Ætolia, Greece.
139–42. *Shelley . . . bay.* About a year after his marriage to Mary Godwin in 1816 Shelley went to Italy, where he was drowned in 1822 in the Gulf of Spezzia. Some of his most beautiful poems were written during this Italian period, poems marked both by the "rapturous

and ecstatic note" and by the melancholy which led Arnold to speak of their "lovely wail."

146. *Obermann*. See note to *Stanzas in Memory of the Author of "Obermann,"* above.

149. *Fontainebleau*. A city south of Paris.

154. *weeds*. Garments of mourning.

Page 562. SAINT BRANDAN

Brandan (also Brendan and Brandon, *c.* 484–578) was an Irish saint, the hero of a legendary voyage in search of the earthly paradise, the "Promised Land of the Saints," supposed to be an island in the North Atlantic. The story of his voyage ranks among the most celebrated of the medieval sagas of western Europe. The poem is Arnold's version of one of the impressive incidents of the voyage.

7. *Hebrides*. Islands northwest of Scotland.

8. *monastery-lights*. For several centuries, beginning with the fifth, many monasteries were founded in England, Scotland, and the neighboring islands by Irish monks.

18–20. *hair . . . Judas*. Judas Iscariot, the betrayer of Christ, is traditionally represented as having red hair.

40. *Joppa*. A seaport of Palestine; the modern Jaffa.

43. *sirocco*. A hot south wind.

THYRSIS

In his essay, *Matthew Arnold's New Poems*, Swinburne wrote: "There are in the English language three elegiac poems so great that they eclipse and efface all the elegiac poetry we know; all of Italian, all of Greek. It is only because the latest born is yet new to us that it can seem strange or rash to say so. The 'Thyrsis' of Mr. Arnold makes a third with 'Lycidas' and 'Adonais.' It is not so easy as those may think who think by rote and praise by prescription to strike the balance between them. The first, however, remains first, and must remain; its five opening lines are to me the most musical in all known realms of verse; there is nothing like them; and it is more various, more simple, more large and sublime than the others; lovelier and fuller it cannot be.

The leader is fairest,
But all are divine.

The least pathetic of the three is 'Adonais,' which indeed is hardly pathetic at all; it is passionate, subtle, splendid; but 'Thyrsis,' like 'Lycidas,' has a quiet and tender undertone which gives it something of sacred. Shelley brings fire from heaven, but these bring also 'the meed of some melodious tear.' There is a grace ineffable, a sweet sound and sweet savour of things past, in the old beautiful use of the language of shepherds, of flocks and pipes: the spirit is none the less sad and sincere because the body of the poem has put on this dear familiar raiment of romance; because the crude and naked sorrow is veiled and chastened with soft shadows and sounds of a 'land that is very far off'; because the verse remembers and retains a perfume and an echo of Grecian flutes and flowers,

Renews the golden world, and holds through all
The holy laws of homely pastoral,
Where flowers and founts, and nymphs and semi-gods,
And all the Graces find their old abodes."

(*Complete Works*, Vol. XV, pp. 91–2.)

April 7, 1866, Arnold wrote in a letter to his mother: "Tell him [his brother Edward] that the diction of the poem [*Thyrsis*] was modelled on that of Theocritus, whom I have been much reading during the two years this poem has been forming itself, and that I meant the diction to be so artless as to be almost heedless. . . . The images are all from actual observation. . . . The cuckoo on the wet June morning I heard in the garden at Woodford, and all those three stanzas you like are reminiscences of Woodford. Edward has, I think, fixed on the two stanzas I myself like best in 'O easy access' and 'And long the way appears.' I also like 'Where is the girl' and the stanza before it, but that is because they bring certain places and moments before me. . . . It is probably too *quiet* a poem for the general taste, but I think it will stand wear."

The poem both "commemorates the author's friend, Arthur Hugh Clough," and in the words (approximately) of Professor H. F. Lowry, consecrates the love of both Arnold and Clough for the countryside round Oxford. Mr. Stopford Brooke said that *The Scholar-Gipsy* and *Thyrsis* are the two best poems Arnold wrote. He pointed out that both are engaged with Clough, and hence illustrate and supplement one another. All that is said in the poem "is brought into unity by the pervasiveness of the one emotion of memorial and loving friendship." Like Professor Lowry, Mr. Brooke felt the presence of another emotion in the two poems—the love of Oxford and of the countryside round about as the home of the poet's youthful heart.

See Arnold's letters X (text p. 598), and XII (p. 599).

2. *two Hinkseys*. See note to l. 125 of *The Scholar-Gipsy*, above.

3. *haunted mansion*. A reference to a witch legend associated with a ruined house in North Hinksey, and well-known to the villagers.

4. *Sibylla's name*. When Arnold was a student at Oxford, he and his fellow walkers often passed a "pub" in South Hinksey, kept by a certain Sibylla Kerr whose name was on the sign in

front. Years later, at the time celebrated in this poem, the name had disappeared, the keeper probably having died in the meantime.

10. *Thyrsis.* Clough. The name is a conventional one in pastoral poetry.

11. *Childsworth Farm.* About three miles from Oxford.

12. *elm-tree.* Sir Edmund Chambers says that Mr. A. D. Godley, tracing the course Arnold must have taken on the footpath from Childsworth Farm to Cumner Hurst, concluded that the elm must have been on the top of the Hurst (hillock). Chambers himself believes that it was a noble tree a "little farther along on the same walk," standing "bare on its lonely ridge," in the great field between Chawley Farm and Cumner village. Both these trees fell in a great gale in December, 1929.

14. *Ilsley Downs.* In West Berkshire.

15. *youthful Thames.* The Thames is about fifty yards wide at Oxford.

19. *sweet city.* Oxford.

29. *Gipsy-Scholar.* See *The Scholar-Gipsy* (text p. 554), and the notes to that poem, above.

35. *shepherd-pipes . . . assay'd.* I.e., composed poetry.

36–7. *many . . . lost.* Arnold had not published any poetry for some time.

40. *Thyrsis . . . away.* Clough resigned his fellowship in Oriel College, Oxford, in 1848, because "he could not honestly remain in a university where he had to subscribe to the Thirty-nine Articles of the Church of England."

45. *silly.* Simple.

48–9. *piping . . . rage.* Much of Clough's poetry reflects his doubts and spiritual unrest.

80. *Corydon.* Arnold. Like Thyrsis (see note to l. 10), the name is a conventional one in pastoral poetry.

82–4. *Sicilian . . . fate.* When one of the pastoral poets of Sicily was lost to his mates, one of his survivors would write a lament for him; as the passing of Bion, a Greek poet of the second century B.C., was commemorated by the *Lament for Bion*, written by his friend, Moschus.

85. *unpermitted . . . flow.* Only the dead were permitted to pass over the River Styx.

86. *Pluto's brow.* Pluto, god of the underworld, took Proserpine from the vale of Enna (l. 95), in Sicily, where she was gathering flowers, to be his wife in his underworld kingdom. See Swinburne's *The Garden of Proserpine* (text p. 715), and the notes to that poem, below.

90. *Orpheus.* See note to l. 38 of *Memorial Verses*, above.

92. *Dorian.* Sicilian.

99. *Cumner.* Hills near Oxford.

106. *Fyfield tree.* See note to *The Scholar-Gipsy*, l. 83, above.

107. *fritillaries.* Flowers resembling the lily.

109. *Ensham . . . Sandford.* Villages near Oxford.

123. *Wytham flats.* The low plain between the Thames and Wytham village northwest of Oxford.

135. *sprent.* Sprinkled.

137. *pausefully.* To make it pause.

155. *Berkshire.* The county south of Oxford.

160. *the Tree.* See note to ll. 12–14, above.

167. *Arno-vale.* Clough, who died in Italy, was buried in Florence by the River Arno.

175. *boon.* Benign, bounteous.

177. *great Mother.* See note to l. 77 of *The Youth of Nature*, above.

183–5. *Phrygian . . . Daphnis.* Lityerses, a Phrygian king, engaged Daphnis, a Sicilian shepherd and the founder of pastoral poetry, in a reaping contest. Hercules helped Daphnis win and so saved his life, since Lityerses put to death all those whom he defeated in his reaping contests. The Lityerses-song was sung by Greek reapers.

187. *blinded eyes.* According to one story Daphnis was blinded by a nymph to whom he proved unfaithful. Hermes, his father, took him to heaven and created a fountain on the spot whence he had taken him.

217. *Hurst.* See note to *The Scholar-Gipsy*, l. 57, above.

Page 566. EAST LONDON

In his *Matthew Arnold* (p. 87) S. P. Sherman quotes this sonnet and the sonnet entitled *The Better Part* (text p. 567), and says of them that though they are not better poetry than many of the passages in *The Scholar-Gipsy*, "they are much closer to the center of Arnold's thought and feeling at maturity."

2. *Bethnal Green.* A district of poverty and squalor in London.

4. *Spitalfields.* A section of London long known for its silk weaving.

WEST LONDON

1. *Belgrave Square.* A fashionable West End residential section in London.

Page 567. THE BETTER PART

See introductory note to *East London*, above. The last five lines of the poem have been quoted as illustrative of the manly tone and temper characteristic of Arnold's poetry. Arnold, who pronounced the poetic Muse to be

> a hidden ground
> Of thought and of austerity within,

may be called a poet of doubt but certainly not a poet of despair.

WORLDLY PLACE

3. *Marcus Aurelius.* Roman emperor (161–180 A.D.), famous for his reflective and philo-

sophical writings. Arnold esteemed especially the old Roman's *Meditations,* the following extract from which bears upon this poem: "Wheresoever thou mayest live, there it is in thy power to live well and happy. But thou mayest live at the Court; there then also mayest thou live well and happy." (V, 15.) The first series of Arnold's *Essays in Criticism* concludes with an eloquent appreciation of the Roman philosopher.

AUSTERITY OF POETRY

In this poem, it may be said, Arnold gives us an insight into his dual nature. His Muse has her moments of appearing "radiant, adorn'd outside," but she is more often profoundly thoughtful and sober, not to say severe. In a letter he wrote in his young manhood he confessed that he laughed too much and expressed a fear that his friends might suspect that he was laughing when he meant to be serious. Perhaps the essay *Hebraism and Hellenism,* which he published in 1868, would not have suggested itself to one whose soul had not experienced both of these disciplines.

1. *son of Italy.* Giacopone di Todi, a poet of the thirteenth century, whose bride was killed in the fall of a platform at a public feast.

Page 568. DOVER BEACH

Professor Woodberry quotes ll. 29–34 of this poem in support of his belief that Arnold in his treatment of man's life is "either very austere or very pessimistic. If the feeling is moral," Woodberry writes, "the predominant impression is of austerity; if it is intellectual, the predominant impression is of sadness; he was not insensible to the charm of life, but he feels it in his senses only to deny it in his mind." The passage quoted is "the contradiction of sense and thought, the voice of a regret grounded in the intellect (for if it were vital and grounded in the emotions, it would become despair); the creed of illusion and futility in life, which is the characteristic note of Arnold, and the reason of his acceptance by many minds." (G. E. Woodberry, *Makers of Literature,* pp. 21–2).

15. *Sophocles.* See note to ll. 8–14 of *To a Friend,* above.

29–37. *Ah, love . . . by night.* Cf. *The Buried Life,* ll. 79–98 (text p. 524).

PALLADIUM

The Palladium was an image of the goddess Pallas Athena at Troy. It was said to have fallen from heaven at the time of the founding of the city. As long as it remained in Troy the city could not be taken, and hence the Greeks tried in every way to get possession of it. Finally Odysseus and Diomede entered the temple of Pallas by an underground passage and bore the image off to the Greek camp, an exploit which soon made possible the capture of the city.

1. *Simois.* The Simois and Xanthus (l. 14) were small rivers near Troy.

3. *Hector.* Son of King Priam of Troy and a great warrior.

Ilium. Troy. So called after Ilus, the founder of the city.

15. *Ajax.* A famous Greek hero at the siege of Troy who was chosen to fight against Hector.

16. *Helen.* Wife of Menelaus, king of Sparta. Paris, brother of Hector, took her to Troy, an act which precipitated the Trojan War.

Page 569. GROWING OLD

See note to *Despondency,* above, and cf. Browning's *Rabbi Ben Ezra* (text p. 353).

THE PROGRESS OF POESY

See note to *Despondency,* above.

2. *strikes the rock.* In Exodus 17:6 Moses, in obedience to the Lord's command, smote the rock in Horeb with his rod so that the water might gush forth for the thirsting Israelites.

Page 570. A WISH

Sir Edmund Chambers speaks of the sincerity and simplicity of this poem in which the poet wishes that at his deathbed there may be no doctor and no "brother-doctor of the soul." Mr. Chambers sees both irony and pathos in the fact that Arnold, the apostle of quiet, who asks in this poem to be spared "the whispering, crowded room" and the "ceremonious air" attendant upon death, died while running to catch a tram.

In November, 1873, Arnold said in a letter to his sister: "I have a curious letter from the State of Maine in America, from a young man who wished to tell me that a friend of his, lately dead, had been especially fond of my poem *A Wish,* and often had it read to him in his last illness. They were both—the writer and his friend—of a class too poor to buy books, and had met with the poem in a newspaper." (*Letters,* Vol. I, p. 126.)

PIS-ALLER

In this poem, the title of which means "The Last Resource," Arnold dismisses in contempt the narrow religionist who does not arrive at his ideas of man's relation to God through an intelligent consideration of the question, but finds a sure and easy answer to it in the meaningless jargon of his creed.

BACCHANALIA

This poem compares the wild dance of Mænads, breaking in upon the shepherd's love of the quiet in Nature, with the new age, "thundering and bursting in torrents" upon the poet, and scattering the peace and beauty of the past. The title means a festival of Bacchus, the god of wine.

1–15. See introductory note to *Resignation*, above.

1–19. In the first version of the poem these lines described a reaping scene. In the revision of the poem for the collection of 1869 they were turned into the present mowing scene, the reason being, Mr. Chambers suggests, that Arnold's fastidiousness would not allow him to make the dog-rose blossom in a reaping scene, since its blooms are gone before harvest-time.

5. *wain*. Wagon.

28. *Mænads*. Bacchantes, women who engaged in celebrating the orgiastic festival of Bacchus.

30. *Iacchus*. Bacchus.

107. *Pitt*. William Pitt (1708–1778), a famous English statesman.

108. *Phidias*. A famous Greek sculptor (500?–432? B.C.).

109. *Raphael*. A great Italian painter (1483–1520).

Page 572. RUGBY CHAPEL

In a letter to his mother, dated August 8, 1867, Arnold expressed his belief that she would take pleasure in this poem, and confessed that he had often wanted to say it to her but had foreborne because he did not like his own saying of his "things." He was moved to write the poem by an article in the *Edinburgh Review* by Fitzjames Stephen depicting Dr. Thomas Arnold as "a narrow bustling fanatic." He felt, he said, that in writing it he had done "something to fix the true legend" about his father; "and this," he concluded, "is much." Stephen's article that offended Arnold was a review of Thomas Hughes's *Tom Brown's Schooldays*, the story of an ordinary schoolboy at Rugby under Dr. Arnold's headmastership. In his review Stephen accused the headmaster of want of humor. This lack of humor so affected the Rugby boy, he wrote, that "he never ties his shoes without asserting a principle; [and] when he puts on his hat he 'founds himself' on an eternal truth."

On August 13, 1859, Stephen published in the *Saturday Review* an article entitled "Mr. Matthew Arnold on the Italian Question," the article being an answer to a pamphlet Arnold had written some weeks before. On the same day Arnold said in a letter to his sister, Mrs. Forster, "There is a very clever and long answer to the pamphlet in to-day's *Saturday Review*, by Fitzjames Stephen, the man who ill-treated papa in reviewing 'Tom Brown.' He is exceedingly civil this time and no one can complain of his tone."

13. *my father*. Dr. Thomas Arnold became headmaster of Rugby in 1828. He died suddenly in 1842 and was buried in the chapel of the school.

162–5. *Servants . . . mind*. An echo of Galatians 4:7, "Wherefore thou art no more a servant, but a son"; and of John 15:15, "For the servant knoweth not what his lord doeth."

190. *Ye*. The servants of God referred to in l. 162.

Page 574. OBERMANN ONCE MORE

Contrasting this poem with *Stanzas in Memory of the Author of "Obermann"* (text p. 525), Mr. Stopford Brooke sees in the Arnold of the later poem a different person from him who wrote the earlier *Obermann*. The "Obermann" of the first poem, Mr. Brooke writes, was a restless stranger (like Matthew Arnold) in the world in which he found himself, and he fled to a chalet in the Swiss mountains to seek the peace and quiet that were missing from his world. He was not successful in escaping pain and melancholy, but nevertheless he found a peace he had never known before by renouncing the world that had wounded his soul. Arnold applauds Obermann for his boldness in making this renunciation and consigns half of his own soul to him and nature, knowing that the other half must remain in the unhappy world in which it has been placed by fate. He prays that it may live there, like Obermann, "unsoiled by wrong," and bear the pain of "miserable days."

Fifteen years later Arnold, sickened by "interminable hours" in the "haunts of strife," slips his chain and goes once more in thought to the mountain chalet of Obermann.

> . . . still and sudden, Obermann
> On the grass

stands near him, reviews for him the history of the world from the beginning of the Christian Era, and beseeches him not to despair but to

> tell
> Hope to a world new-made,

and employ "what still of strength is left" in "lifting mankind again." The vision ended, the poet, raising his eyes to "the upcrowding hills," sees the morning break, fit symbol of the new dawn lighting a world that has been too long in darkness.

The Arnold of the earlier *Obermann*, Mr. Brooke believes, could see no vision of a new dawn.

Motto: *Savez-vous . . . d'un monde?* "Do you know anything that heals sorrow for a lost world?"

1. *Glion*. A mountain village above the Castle of Chillon, which is on the east shore of Lake Geneva, Switzerland.

3. *prank*. Adorn, deck.

14. *Avant.* A village near Glion.
20. *the pass.* The Col de Jaman.
23. *Allière.* A district near Lake Geneva.
24. *Walls . . . came.* Montbovon, a town Byron visited. (See his Journal, in his *Works,* Vol. III, p. 258.)
25–6. *river . . . birth-name.* The River Saane becomes the Sarine below Montbovon.
31. *Jaman.* A peak that rises above the pass.
43. *An eremite.* A hermit.
100. *Appian Way.* The great paved highway from ancient Rome to Brundisium. Begun by Appius Claudius Cæcus, about 312 B.C., it is the oldest and most famous of the Roman roads, and its pavement, 14 to 18 feet wide, is still in use in places.
174. *Syrian town.* Jerusalem.
179. *not yet to.* Not yet closed.
201. *the storm.* The French Revolution.
225. *mask of union.* The union was an appearance, a mask only, not real.
232. *See . . . new.* From Revelation 21:5 "And he that sat upon the throne said, 'Behold, I make all things new.'"
268. *Sèvres.* A suburb of Paris, on the River Seine.
336. *rocks of Naye.* The Rochers de Naye at the east end of Lake Geneva.
337. *Sonchaud.* This and Malatrait (l. 339) are mountainous districts east of Lake Geneva.
340. *Valais.* A Swiss canton above Lake Geneva.
341. *Velan.* A high Alpine peak.

Page 578. HEINE'S GRAVE

Heinrich Heine (1797–1856) German poet and journalist, born of Jewish parents, lived in Paris from 1831 to the end of his life. Only twice after he went to Paris did he return to his native land and then only for brief visits. In 1845 a spinal disease attacked him and from the spring of 1848 condemned him to eight years of terrible suffering on a "mattress grave" (see ll. 13–22 of the poem). His body lies in the cemetery of Montmartre, Paris. He was most famous as a lyrical poet, pre-eminent in wit and raillery. His deathbed remark is characteristic: "Dieu me pardonnera: c'est son métier" (God will pardon me: it is his *métier* [calling, specialty, line]). In his *Essays in Criticism,* First Series, Arnold has an essay on Heine.

37–54. Possibly a reference to the biting ironical powers often displayed by Heine in his criticisms. "Bitter spirits" were his kindred.
57. *laurell'd rock.* Virgil's tomb is near Naples; Dante's (l. 62), at Ravenna, Italy; Shakespeare's (l. 65), at Stratford on the River Avon.
70–2. *sharp . . . England.* As a result of a visit to England in 1828 Heine criticized the sordidly commercial spirit of English life and the brutal egoism of the ordinary Englishman. He missed in England too the finer literary and artistic tastes of the continent and was repelled by the austerity of English religious sentiment and observance.
88. *Titan.* The Titans were a massive, dim-featured race, with an earthly rather than celestial grandeur. They were the embodiment of mighty force, dull to beauty, intelligence, light. In war with the Olympian gods they were overthrown.
94. *Atlanteän.* From Atlas, the giant of Greek story who supported the world on his shoulders.
135–6. *blond . . . Kaiser.* Probably a reference to Frederick I of Germany (1122–1190), surnamed Barbarossa, or Red Beard. During most of his reign he was engaged in struggle with the powerful Italian cities which formed the Lombard League. One of these—Milan—he captured in 1158. He became Holy Roman Emperor in 1155.
153. *Hartz.* Mountains in central Germany.
168. *Brocken-tower.* In the Hartz mountains.
183. *Ilse.* A river in the Hartz mountains.
188. *iron cross.* A cross erected by Count Anton von Stolberg-Wernigerode on the peak Ilstenstein as a memorial to his friends killed in the wars of 1813–1815.
218–32. Mr. Stuart Sherman said that Arnold is most bracing when he stands by a grave. "His most inspiriting lines," he wrote, "are his commemorative poems." The prayer voiced in these lines and the poems *Rugby Chapel* and *Memorial Verses* for Wordsworth are some of the illustrations which Mr. Sherman offered (*Matthew Arnold,* p. 88).

Page 581. THE STUDY OF POETRY

This essay, in which Arnold proposes his famous touchstone theory of criticism, was written as the general introduction to T. H. Ward's anthology, *The English Poets,* published in 1880.

581a, ll. 1–17. "*The future . . . poetry.*" These lines are quoted from the closing paragraph of Arnold's contribution to a work called *The Hundred Greatest Men* (1879).
581a, ll. 43–45. "*the impassioned . . . science.*" In Wordsworth's preface to the second edition of *Lyrical Ballads* (1800).
581b, l. 16. *Sainte-Beuve.* Charles Augustin Sainte-Beuve (1804–1869), a French critic whose "extraordinary delicacy of tact and judgment in literature" greatly impressed Arnold. In some respects he may be considered the master of Arnold in the art of criticism.
581b, l. 44. *poetry . . . life.* This famous phrase, now instantly associated with Arnold, was first used in 1864 in his essay on Joubert.

Page 582.

582b, l. 21. *Pellisson.* Paul Pellisson (1624–1693), a French author. He was the historiographer to the king and the friend of Madeleine De Scudéry, voluminous writer of French romances.

582b, ll. 23–24. *politesse . . . rampante.* "Barren and cringing civility."

582b, l. 28. *M. Charles d'Héricault.* One of the editors of an edition of Clément Marot's poems (1868–1872). Marot (1497–1544) was a French Protestant whose sonnets and pastorals and translations of the Psalms had considerable influence on the English poets of his time. Marot is mentioned in Browning's *The Glove*, text p. 293.

Page 583.

583b, l. 34. *Imitation. De Imitatione Christi*, the famous book of the Augustinian monk, Thomas à Kempis (1380–1471).

583b, ll. 35–37. *Cum . . . principium.* "Although you may have read and known many things, it is always necessary to get back to one principle."

583b, l. 49. *Cædmon.* The earliest important religious poet in Old English literature. He died about 680 A.D.

Page 584.

584a, l. 2. *M. Vitet.* Ludovic Vitet (1802–1873), French dramatist and politician.

584a, l. 4. *Chanson de Roland.* During the Middle Ages *Chansons des Gestes*, long historical verse romances, mostly connected with Charlemagne, were popular in France. They were the work of trouvères and troubadours, and were rendered by *jongleurs* in open places, cloisters, and castles. The legend of Roland, one of Charlemagne's most famous paladins, who met his death at Roncevaux, has been handed down in the greatest of the *Chansons*, the *Chanson de Roland*. Turoldus (l. 12) has not been identified, but is probably the name of the reciting minstrel.

Page 585.

585a, ll. 8–9. *Henry the Fourth.* Part 2, III, i, 18–20.

585a, l. 13. *Hamlet.* Act V, ii, 361–362.

585a, l. 20. *Miltonic passage.* In *Paradise Lost*, I, 599–602.

585a, ll. 26–27. *"And . . . overcome." Ibid.*, I, 108–109.

585a, ll. 31–32. *"which . . . world." Ibid.*, IV, 271.

585b, l. 30. *Aristotle's . . . observation.* In section 9 of *Poetics*.

Page 586.

586a, l. 34. *langue d'oc.* The Romance dialects of the southerly provinces of France;—so-called owing to the use of *oc* in expressing affirmation, in contrast with the *langue d'oïl*, of the basin of the Loire and North.

586b, l. 12. *Brunetto Latini.* Although Latini (*c.* 1230–*c.* 1294) was probably not Dante's tutor, Dante acknowledged his debt to him.

586b, ll. 14–15. *"la . . . gens."* "The language is more beautiful and more widely known."

586b, l. 17. *Christian of Troyes.* A French poet of the last half of the twelfth century. Arnold's quotation comprises lines 30–39 of the *Cligés*.

586b, l. 48. *that stanza.* The seven-line and the eight-line stanzas in heroic verse, much used by Chaucer, were imitated from Old French poetry.

Page 587.

587a, l. 2. *Wolfram of Eschenbach.* A medieval German poet, best remembered for his epic, *Parzival*.

587a, l. 30. *right comment.* In Dryden's *Preface to the Fables*, 1700.

587a, l. 48. *Gower.* John Gower (*c.* 1330–1408), an English poet, author of *Confessio Amantis*.

587b, l. 20. *"O . . . virginitee!"* slightly misquoted by Arnold from *The Prioress's Tale*. The line is "O martir souded to virginitee!"

Page 588.

588b, l. 9. *poor Villon.* François Villon, a gifted poetic rogue, was born in or near Paris in 1431.

Page 589.

589a, ll. 15–18. *Dryden . . . "that . . . fathers."* In *An Essay of Dramatic Poesy*, 1688.

589a, ll. 18–19. *Cowley . . . poetry.* So Dryden said in his *Preface to the Fables*.

589a, ll. 19–25. *"there . . . perfect."* In *Preface to the Fables*.

589a, l. 37. *Wordsworth and Coleridge.* Wordsworth's views were expressed in his *Essay, Supplementary to the Preface* (1815); Coleridge's, in *Biographia Literaria* (1817).

589b, l. 12. *Gades.* Phœnician colony, founded about 1100 B.C. on the present site of Cadiz, Spain.

589b, l. 13. *Aurora.* The dawn of day, or the East.

Ganges. The principal river of India, regarded as sacred by the Hindus.

589b, ll. 19–23. *"And . . . poem."* In *An Apology for Smectymnus*.

589b, ll. 26–31. *"What . . . write."* From Dryden's *Postscript to the Reader* in the translation of Virgil's *Æneid* (1697).

Page 590.

590a, ll. 25–26. *"A milk-white Hind . . . ranged."* The opening lines of *The Hind and the Panther*.

590a, ll. 31–32. *"To . . . own." Imitations of Horace*, Book II, Satire 2, ll. 143–4.

590b, ll. 43–48. *"Mark . . . Wrong"* from *On the Death of Robert Dundas, Esq.*

590b, l. 51. *Clarinda's love-poet, Sylvander.*

Clarinda was the name assumed by Mrs. Maclehose, a young grass widow whom Burns met in 1784. A silly boy-and-girl love immediately sprang up between the two, and though they were both in Edinburgh, they wrote to each other every day and sometimes twice a day for a period of three months. In the correspondence Burns used the name Sylvander.

Page 591.

591a, ll. 2–8. "*These . . . stupid.*" In a letter to Mr. Thomson, October 19, 1794.

591a, ll. 44–51. "*Leeze . . . day.*" A stanza from *The Holy Fair.*

591b, ll. 26–33. "*The sacred . . . feeling.*" From *Epistle: To a Young Friend.*

591b, ll. 35–42. "*Who . . . resisted.*" From *Address to the Unco' Guid, or the Rigidly Righteous.*

591b, ll. 45–48. "*To make . . . human life.*" From *Epistle to Dr. Blacklock.*

Page 592.

592b, ll. 6–9. "*Thou . . . will!*" From *Winter: A Dirge.*

Page 593.

593a, l. 24. "*Pinnacled . . . inane.*" The last line of Act III, sc. IV, of Shelley's *Prometheus Unbound.*

593a, ll. 28–31. "*On . . . fire.*" *Ibid.*, II, v, 1–4.

ARNOLD'S LETTERS

593b, l. 40. *Mrs. Forster.* The poet's eldest sister, Jane, the wife of W. E. Forster. August 13, 1859, Arnold said to her in a letter, "You and Clough are . . . the two people I in my heart care most to please by what I write." "K" was a pet name for Mrs. Forster, dating from the nursery. See note to *A Question*, above.

Page 594.

594a, l. 43. *Rentool.* Robert Stephen Rintoul (1787–1858), a journalist of Scotch birth. He gained such a name for boldness and independence as editor of the *Dundee Advertiser* that some of his friends induced him to try his fortune as an editor in London, and in 1826 he joined the staff of the *Atlas.* In 1828, after a quarrel with the *Atlas* proprietors, he established the *Spectator*, a weekly that from the beginning was a "model of exact journalism, alike in matter and form." This paper still survives.

594b, l. 1. *L'd Landsdowne.* Henry Petty-Fitzmaurice (1780–1863), third marquis of Landsdowne, began his second term as president of the Council in 1846. In this office he was charged with the administration of public instruction, and in 1847 he procured for his secretary, Matthew Arnold, an inspectorship of schools.

594b, l. 2. *Foster.* The reference must be to John Forster (not Foster), who was editor of the *Examiner* from 1847 to 1855.

594b, l. 3. *Froude.* See note to p. 210a, l. 47 and introductory note to *Tristram and Iseult*, above.

Chapman. Probably John Chapman (1822–1894), physician, author, and publisher. In 1851 he became editor and proprietor of the *Westminster Review.*

594b, l. 7. *Grey's or William's!* Probably the 3rd Earl Grey (1802–1894). William was W. E. Forster.

594b, l. 14. *Eckerman.* Johann Eckermann, German author (1792–1854), was the faithful attendant of Goethe from 1803 to the year of Goethe's death. His record of Goethe's conversations has been translated into English.

594b, l. 30. *Dingle.* Dingle Bank, in Liverpool, the home of Arnold's sister, Mrs. J. W. Cropper.

594b, l. 36. *Edward.* Arnold's younger brother.

Page 595.

595a, l. 5. *just finished a poem.* The poem referred to was *Balder Dead.* In a later letter, Arnold wrote: "I felt sure William would be interested in *Balder Dead* from what I know of his Scandinavian interests."

595a, l. 11. *Sainte-Beuve.* See note to *The Study of Poetry*, p. 581b, l. 16, above.

595a, l. 17. *Revue des deux mondes.* In 1854 Arthur Dudley had an article in the *Revue* (VII, 1136) entitled "La Poesie Anglaise depuis Shelley; Mathew Arnold et Alexandre Smith," in which he designated Arnold and Smith as "Shelleyites" and spoke of Arnold as the most distinguished disciple of Shelley.

595a, l. 22. *Westminster quarrel.* In 1851 Harriet Martineau, in collaboration writh one Atkinson, published *Letters on the Laws of Man's Social Nature and Development.* The antitheological views expressed in the writing—Atkinson was an avowed atheist—gave much offense to Englishmen, especially to Miss Martineau's brother James. He reviewed her work very severely and expressed disappointment in her atheistic tendencies. The conflict was partly recorded in *The Westminster Review*, and hence, probably, the name "Westminster quarrel."

595a, l. 23. *Miss Martineau.* See notes to *Haworth Churchyard*, above.

595a, l. 24. *Pelops.* Son of Tantalus. Upon all of the six sons of Pelops great woes fell because of the dying curse of Myrtilus, a charioteer whom Pelops threw into the sea.

595a, l. 33. *Louisa Twining.* A versatile lady (1820–1912), interested in genealogy, social work, and art.

595a, l. 38. *Walrond.* Theodore Walrond, a college friend of Arnold's. Arnold, his brother, Clough, and Walrond formed "a little interior company" at Balliol for sports and pleasures. Each Sunday morning they breakfasted together in Clough's rooms and discussed politics, literature, and problems of state.

595b, l. 41–42. *deprimirter Stimmung.* A low-spirited mood; in the dumps.

Page 596.

596a, l. 6. *Merope.* "A Tragedy," published in 1858. Arnold said that he meant his readers "to see in it a specimen of the world created by the Greek imagination." Soon after it was published he wrote to his sister saying that the poem "was not going to take" as he wished.

596a, l. 12. *Time's . . . acting.* Rachel (1821–1857), born in Mumpf, Switzerland, of poor Jewish parents, was a French actress. Her real name was Elizabeth (or Eliza) Felix. A French director discovered her when, in childhood, she and her sister were singing on the streets of Paris, and made her a famous tragic heroine. In his *Irish Essays* Arnold wrote: "I remember how in my youth after the first sight of the divine Rachel at the Edinburgh Theatre in the part of Hermione, I followed her to Paris and for two months never missed one of her representations."

596a, l. 15. *Adrienne Lecouvreur.* A famous French tragic actress (1692–1730).

596a, l. 16. *Night and Morning.* A novel (1845) by Edward Bulwer Lytton.

596a, l. 22. *Corsican brothers.* A play translated by Boucicault from the French, and produced in 1848.

596a, l. 27. *Kotzebue.* August von Kotzebue (1761–1819), a German dramatist, author of a large number of sentimental plays.

596a, l. 51. *Grote.* George Grote (1794–1871), M. P. for the City of London from 1832 to 1841, retired from parliament in order to devote himself to historical work. His "excellent remarks on the liberties Sophocles took" are in his famous *History of Greece,* a work in eight volumes, to the composition of which he gave almost thirty years.

596b, l. 11. *Michelet.* Jules Michelet, a French historian (1798–1874).

596b, l 23. *Polyphontes.* King of Messinia, a character in *Merope.* He murdered his brother, Cresphontes, and forced the widow, Merope, to marry him.

596a, l. 40. *Louis Napoleon.* Napoleon III, Emperor of the French (1852–1870).

Page 597.

597a, l. 10. *Etruria.* An ancient country of Italy, now Tuscany and part of Umbria.

597a, l. 11. *L'uomo del secolo.* "The man of the century."

597a, l. 15. *Lord Cowley.* Henry Richard Wellesley, first Earl Cowley (1804–1884). Ambassador to Switzerland, to the Germanic confederation (1851), and at Paris. Prominent in various negotiations of state.

597a, l. 28. *coup d'œil.* "Glance."

597a, l. 38. *Lord Derby.* Edward Henry Stanley, fifteenth Earl of Derby (1826–1893). He was at Rugby under Dr. Arnold, and at Cambridge he was one of "The Apostles." He attained considerable prominence as a statesman.

597a, l. 42. *William's appearance at Leeds.* In 1859 Forster was invited by the Liberals of Leeds "to come forward" with Sir Edward Baines. Forster, though afterwards regarded as a liberal of the conservative type, was chosen as the parliamentary candidate of the advanced party. Baines defeated him by a scant 63 votes.

597a, l. 46. *Willy's sake.* William Delafield Arnold, the poet's younger brother, died in April, 1859, about a month and a half before this letter was written.

597a, l. 50. *Queen Pomare.* Queen Pomare IV, a well-known native ruler of Tahiti (Society Islands). Her reign ran from 1827 to 1877. She figures in Melville's *Omoo.*

597a, l. 51. *Vaucluse.* A department in Southern France.

597b, l. 6. *Meurice's.* A well known hotel on the Rue de Rivoli.

597b, l. 8. *Miss Arnold.* Arnold's youngest sister, Frances.

597b, l. 22. *my Report.* Arnold's report on elementary education on the Continent was reprinted in 1861 under the title, *The Popular Education of France with Notices of That of Holland and Switzerland.*

Page 598.

598a, l. 22. *ex cathedra.* With authority.

598a, l. 27. *Claude.* Claude Lorrain (real name Claude Gelée), French painter in Italy (1600–1682).

598a, l. 28. *Murillo.* Bartolomé Esteban-Murillo, Spanish religious and genre painter (1618–1687).

598a, ll. 47–48. *thousand . . . both.* February 11, 1861, Forster, who was the candidate of a large majority of liberal electors, was elected to Parliament to represent Bradford. Since he had no opposition in this election, Arnold knew that his success was assured; hence his "thousand congratulations" a few days before the election was held.

598b, l. 6. *Dicky.* Arnold's son.

598b, l. 12. *Clough.* See text pp. 501 and 860.

598b, l. 37. *Lingen.* William Ralph Lingen (1819–1905) had been a fellow at Balliol when Arnold was there. In 1849 he was made Education Secretary.

598b, l. 45. *J. Dykes Campbell* (1838–1895) studied Tennyson closely for some years and made a collection of early editions of his work. Leslie Stephen described him as the "type of Scotsman which appreciates Burns's poetry more than the theology of John Knox." He is best known, perhaps, as the biographer and editor of Coleridge.

Page 599.

599a, l. 23. *J. C. Shairp* (1819–1885) was a close friend of Arnold and Clough at Balliol. He became in turn a master at Rugby, principal of St. Andrews, and professor of poetry at Oxford.

599a, l. 40. *Sellar.* William Young Sellar (1825–1890), professor of Latin in Edinburgh University. He and Arnold were close friends at Balliol.

599a, ll. 41–42. *Multi . . . adhibenda.* "Different people have different opinions; hence one should not be too trusting."

599a, l. 42. See note to l. 34 (p. 583b) of *The Study of Poetry*, above.

599b, l. 18. *Valeat quantum.* "May it succeed as well as may be."

599b, l. 27. *Mr. Boyle.* George David Boyle (1828–1901), dean of Salisbury. He developed a precocious interest in the Oxford movement and numbered Newman among his close friends.

599b, l. 36. *Milman.* Henry Hart Milman (1791–1868), dean of St. Paul's. His *History of the Jews* (1830) created consternation among the orthodox. Newman reviewed it unfavorably in the *British Critic* as late as January, 1841, and in his *Apologia* he records the unfavorable impression it made on him.

Page 600.

600a, l. 17. *Butler.* Bishop Joseph Butler (1692–1752). In 1736 he published his *Analogy of Religion*, a defense of the Christian religion against the Deists by showing that their natural religion is open to the same objections as revelation.

600a, l. 27. *Lamennais.* Hugues Félicité Robert de Lamennais (1782–1854), French religious and political writer.

600a, l. 35. *Gregories.* The Roman Catholic Church has had among its Popes sixteen Gregories and thirteen Innocents (l. 36).

600b, ll. 7–8. *Cornhill Magazine.* A monthly periodical founded in 1860, with Thackeray as first editor.

600b, l. 17. *Great Prophecy.* In 1872 Arnold published *A Bible-Reading for Schools.* The book reached a fourth edition in 1875 and was reprinted in that year for general use with the title, *The Great Prophecy of Israel's Restoration.*

Page 601.

601a, l. 41. *Princess Alice.* Second daughter and third child of Queen Victoria. Princess Alice married Prince Louis of Hesse, referred to in this same letter.

601a, l. 43. *Pitti.* One of the two principal art galleries of Florence, Italy.

601b, l. 19. *Lady de Rothschild.* The wife of Sir Anthony de Rothschild, at whose "grand place," Aston Clinton, Arnold was frequently a guest. She was an enthusiastic admirer of Arnold, and he characterized her to his mother as his "unapproached favourite."

602a, l. 3. *Dean Stanley.* Arthur Penrhyn Stanley (1815–1881), Dean of Westminster. He was at Rugby under Dr. Thomas Arnold, and in 1844 published the *Life of Dr. Arnold.*

Page 602.

602a, l. 27. *Butler. Bishop Butler and the Zeit-Geist*, two lectures delivered by Arnold before the Edinburgh Philosophical Institution, January 4 and 7, 1876.

602a, l. 42. *Sarazin's.* Sarazin was a French army-surgeon in Algeria, who translated Arnold's *Literature and Dogma.*

602b, l. 10. *Bishop of Derry.* William Alexander (1824–1911), who was made bishop of Derry in 1867. In the same year he was a candidate for the professorship of poetry at Oxford, but was defeated by Sir Francis Doyle. A lecture on Arnold's poetry which Alexander gave at Dublin in 1863 was full of suggestiveness and of nice critical distinction. In 1877 Arnold, thinking that the Bishop might be a candidate for the post again, wrote to a friend: "To the Bishop of Derry I am in some degree pledged, having promised to vote for him at the last election. . . . You may have seen that I was asked to stand, but I have definitely refused. A theological election for a literary post is an odious thing, and that is what we should have had. Besides, I really think it better that the same man should not be professor more than once."

602b, l. 14. *Morley.* John Morley, who was for fifteen years editor of the *Fortnightly Review* and for two years editor of the *Pall Mall Gazette.* He was also editor of the English Men of Letters Series. In 1876, the year of this letter, Morley was deep in a series of French studies and hence in close touch with French writers and affairs. Among his publications arising out of these studies were *Voltaire* (1872), *Rousseau* (1873), and *Diderot and the Encyclopædists* (1878).

602b, l. 15. *G. Sand.* George Sand was the pseudonym of Armandine Lucile Aurore Dupin, Baronne Dudevant (1804–1876), French novelist.

Renan. Ernest Renan (1823–1892), a Breton by birth, and a learned French writer, philologist, and historian.

602b, ll. 16–17. *Je lui . . . voyageant.* "I gave her the impression of a youthful journeying Milton."

602b, l. 33. *praises . . . poem. Light* for August 31, 1878, praised and quoted *Switzerland.* See introductory note to *Parting; Isolation,* etc., above.

602b, l. 46. *Robert Buchanan.* Poet, novelist, dramatist (1841–1921).

Page 603.

603a, l. 2. *Horsley.* A village in Surrey. It is not far from Pains Hill Cottage, where Arnold lived from 1873 to 1888.

603a, l. 14. *Eton speech.* An address on the value of the classics, delivered before the Eton Literary Society, April 5, 1879.

603a, l. 40. *send . . . Scherer.* Edmond Scherer (1815–1889), French critic, theologian, and politician. One of Arnold's "admirable habits as a critic was, on points of doubt relating to English literature, to resort to foreign opinion."

603b, l. 2. *Chilterns.* The Chiltern Hills in Buckinghamshire. They are noted for their beautiful beech-woods.

603b, l. 13. *Duchess of Norfolk.* Cardinal Newman was staying at the time with the Duke and the Duchess of Norfolk in St. James's Square.

603b, l. 51. *Yates Thompsons.* Henry Yates Thompson purchased the *Pall Mall Gazette* in 1881 and made it into a liberal organ supporting Gladstone, with John Morley as editor. Mrs. Thompson was a daughter of the publisher, George Smith.

Page 604

604b, l. 6. *Fanny Lucy.* Mrs. Arnold, whose maiden name was Frances Lucy Wightman.

604b, l. 48. *Mr. Carnegie.* Andrew Carnegie (1837–1919), Scottish-American steel manufacturer and philanthropist.

Page 605.

605a, l. 18. *Cleveland.* Grover Cleveland, who was elected twenty-second President of the United States in 1884.

605a, l. 27. *Henry A. Jones* (1851–1929), member of a Welsh dissenting family, was a dramatist. *Saints and Sinners* (1884) was one of his most successful plays.

605b, l. 31. *Nelly.* Arnold's younger daughter.

DANTE GABRIEL ROSSETTI

BIBLIOGRAPHY

I. WORKS

Complete Works, ed. by W. M. Rossetti. Siddal Edition. 7 vols. (Ellis: London, 1900–1.) The most desirable complete edition, though latterly hard to obtain; each volume contains a prefatory note by the editor.

Collected Works, ed. by W. M. Rossetti. 2 vols. (Ellis: London, 1890.) An authoritative edition, equipped with a preface and full notes.

Complete Poetical Works, ed. by W. M. Rossetti. 2 vols. (Little: Boston, 1905.) An excellent edition for student-use, reproducing many of the poet's paintings; furnished with a brief preface by the editor.

Dante Gabriel Rossetti: An Anthology, ed. by F. L. Lucas. (Cambridge University Press: 1933.) An excellent representation, though unwisely offering but fragments of some of the sonnets; the preface contrasts the sensualist and idealist in Rossetti.

Poems and Translations, 1850–1870. (Oxford University Press: 1914.) A collection recommended for general reading; contains the bulk of the Dante material, the first form of *The House of Life*, together with "Hand and Soul."

The House of Life, ed. by P. F. Baum. (Harvard University Press: 1928.) A scholarly edition of the sequence, which probably contains the secret of the poet's inner life, to which the editor by suggestive notes and a fine introduction has attempted to provide a clue.

Dante and His Circle, ed. by W. M. Rossetti. (Ellis: London, 1900.) The most desirable edition of Rossetti's anthology, furnished with a critical essay by the editor.

Family Letters, ed. by W. M. Rossetti. 2 vols. (Roberts: Boston, 1895.) Indispensable for an understanding of the inner life of the man; the editor includes a valuable Memoir, which with a dedication and preface forms Vol. I.

Letters of D. G. Rossetti to His Publisher, F. S. Ellis, ed. by Oswald Doughty. (Scholartis Press: London, 1928.) Interesting for the light cast upon the story of the disinterred poems and for the revelation of the poet's timidity to adverse criticism; the editor's introduction also represents this material in a bold light.

Letters to William Allingham, 1854–1870, ed. by G. B. Hill. (Stokes: New York, 1898.) The record of a long friendship, providing a mine of information concerning Rossetti's most productive period; contains many references to Elizabeth Siddal.

II. BIOGRAPHY AND CRITICISM

Benson, A. C. *Rossetti.* English Men of Letters series. (Macmillan: New York, 1904.) A recommended Life, interestingly written, condensing the essential biographical data.

Boas, Mrs. F. S. *Rossetti and His Poetry.* (Harrap: London, 1914.) A brief introduction to the man and his poetry, approaching his art through the facts of his life; contains many selections from his poems.

Cary, Elisabeth L. *The Rossettis.* (Putnam: New York, 1907.) An excellent introductory study; the conclusions on Dante Gabriel owe much to the author's acquaintance with an extensive correspondence in possession of Mr. Samuel Bancroft of Wilmington, Delaware.

Dunn, H. T. *Recollections of Dante Gabriel Rossetti and His Circle*, ed. by Gale Pedrick. (Mathews: London, 1904.) Covers the last twenty years of the poet's life; the writer, as William Rossetti says, knew the poet more intimately than did anyone else. The volume concludes with notes by the editor.

Hueffer, F. M. *Rossetti: A Critical Essay on His Art.* (Dutton: New York, 1902.) Chiefly concerned with Rossetti the painter; recommended for its list of fifty-three reproductions of cartoons, portraits, and caricatures.

Hunt, Violet. *The Wife of Rossetti: Her Life and Death.* (Dutton: New York, 1932.) Written from first-hand information, this frank and passionate exposition sets forth the "sad and strange" story of the main figure, showing the pathos of the clash of her personality with that of her husband.

Knight, Joseph. *The Life of Dante Gabriel Rossetti.* (Scott: London, 1887.) A good brief biography, perhaps the best of the earlier Lives, and still useful. Bibliography by J. P. Anderson.

Larg, David. *Trial by Virgins.* (Davies: London, 1933.) An interesting study of the "possible mental reactions" of Rossetti, Elizabeth Siddal, and their friends; much prominence is given to the fact of Rossetti's foreign antecedents.

Marillier, H. C. *Dante Gabriel Rossetti.* 2 vols. (Macmillan: New York, 1904.) Primarily a study of the artist's inner development; critically sound and engagingly written.

Mégroz, R. L. *Dante Gabriel Rossetti: Painter Poet of Heaven in Earth.* (Faber: London, 1928.) Part I is devoted to biographical facts and the initiation into Rossetti's personality; Part II offers a number of suggestive criticisms. The major poems are supplied with illuminating commentary.

Rossetti, Helen M. Madox. *The Life and Work of Dante Gabriel Rossetti.* (Virtue: London, 1902.) A monograph in tribute to Rossetti's pictorial art and his association with the Pre-Raphaelite movement; offers some good reproductions of his paintings, with textual comment.

Stephens, F. G. *Dante Gabriel Rossetti, Painter and Poet.* (Seeley: London, 1894.) Primarily a book for the student of Rossetti's painting; contains a good collection of reproductions.

Waller, R. D. *The Rossetti Family, 1824–1854.* (Manchester University Press: 1932.) Centering attention on Gabriele Rossetti, this study also contains many references to his talented children; it concludes with the death of the father, when Dante Gabriel was twenty-five.

Waugh, Evelyn. *Rossetti: His Life and Works.* (Dodd: New York, 1928.) Although an unsympathetic study, provides an interesting comparison between the man's poetry and painting, the latter considered as his greatest work; the biographical facts are presented in the modern tone of "novelized" memoir-writing.

Winwar, Frances. *Poor Splendid Wings.* (Little: Boston, 1933.) A biographical narrative, revealing many of the personalities of the Pre-Raphaelite brotherhood, but turning the spotlight upon Rossetti, who is studied as the artist and the man of passion.

Wood, Esther. *Dante Rossetti and the Pre-Raphaelite Movement.* (Low: London, 1894.) One of the still-useful earlier studies, aiming to describe the movement "more as an ethical than an aesthetic revolution"; only the final chapter deals with Rossetti's poetry, which is held to be secondary in his mind to his painting.

III. ARTICLES FROM BOOKS

Brooke, S. A. "Dante Gabriel Rossetti," in *Four Poets.* (Duckworth: London, 1913.) Makes comparisons with Keats, whose love of the medieval led him away from the present; praises the studied symbolism of *The House of Life;* comments on Rossetti's Italian warmth in his love poetry and on his mysticism.

Dawson, W. J. "Dante Gabriel Rossetti," in *Makers of English Poetry.* (Revell: New York, 1906.) Interesting for its presentation of the Victorian distaste for Rossetti's description of love; comments on his wide following and influence.

Hearn, Lafcadio. "Studies in Rossetti," in *Pre-Raphaelite and Other Poets.* (Dodd: New York, 1922.) Provides an easy approach to the work of the poet, analyzing many selections.

Lucas, F. L. "Dante Gabriel Rossetti," in *Eight Victorian Poets.* (Cambridge University Press: 1930.) Remarks the poet's connection with Pre-Raphaelitism; finds in him "the passions as well as the dreaminess of the South."

Pater, Walter, "Dante Gabriel Rossetti," in *Appreciations.* (Macmillan: London, 1920.) Comments warmly on "The Blessed Damozel" as an example of Pre-Raphaelite art; defines Rossetti as the poet of a small but select audience.

Swinburne, A. C. "The Poems of Dante Gabriel Rossetti," in *Essays and Studies.* (Chatto: London, 1888.) Has enthusiastic praise for *The House of Life* and other single poems, particularly the ballads and "The Burden of Nineveh."

Symons, Arthur. "Dante Gabriel Rossetti," in *Figures of Several Centuries.* (Constable: London, 1916.) Briefly comments upon the personal and novel force which the poet contributed to English verse.

Thompson, A. H. "The Rossettis, William Morris, and Swinburne," in *The Cambridge History of English Literature,* XIII. (Putnam: New York, 1917.) Describes Rossetti's connections with the Pre-Raphaelites, praises his dramatic and pictorial faculties and his skill as a translator.

Welby, T. E. "Rossetti," in *The Victorian Romantics, 1850–1870.* (Howe: London, 1929.) Rossetti is seen in many places in this study as the artist adventuring among Pre-Raphaelitism, developing his art in his contributions to fledgling periodicals, and carrying "pencil and brush into his verse."

Williams, S. T. "Two Poems by Rossetti," in *Studies in Victorian Literature.* (Dutton: New York, 1923.) Comments on the broad popularity of "The Blessed Damozel" and "Jenny"—another early poem which expresses the poet's concept of earthly beauty.

Woodberry, G. E. "A Literary Portrait of Rossetti," in *Studies of a Litterateur.* (Harcourt: New York, 1921.) A brief survey of Rossetti as a romantic and mystic, pointing out the not entirely happy joining in him of the painter and poet.

IV. ARTICLES FROM PERIODICALS

Burgum, E. B. "Rossetti and the Ivory Tower," *Sewanee Review,* XXXVII, 431–46 (Oct., 1929).

Sees Rossetti's Pre-Raphaelitism as his chief stumbling-block in his failure to compromise earthly and spiritual beauty; appeals for a new evaluation of his poetry on its intellectual side.

Howe, M. L. "Dante Gabriel Rossetti's Comments on *Maud*," *Modern Language Notes*, XLIX, 290–93 (May, 1934). Based on Rossetti's letters to William Allingham:—the comments are not entirely laudatory.

Knickerbocker, K. L. "Rossetti's 'The Blessed Damozel,'" *Studies in Philology*, XXIX, 485–504 (July, 1932). Scouts the precocity theory of the poem by showing how its alterations matured it into a work of genius, in which middle-life biographical features appear; finds influences from Dante, Shelley, and Keats.

Mather, F. J., Jr. "The Rossettis," *London Bookman*, XLIX, 139–47 (Apr., 1919). A study of the antecedents of the family, dwelling particularly on the relations of the members to each other; comments on a number of Dante Gabriel's sonnets and ballads.

Milner, George. "On Some Marginalia Made by D. G. Rossetti in a Copy of Keats' Poems," *Englische Studien*, LXI, 211–19 (May, 1927). Based on Rossetti's copy of the 1868 Moxon edition; indicates Rossetti's preferences among Keats's poems.

Morse, B. J. "Dante Gabriel Rossetti and Dante Alighieri," *Englische Studien*, LXVIII, 227–48 (Sept., 1933). Discusses Rossetti's interest in Dante from childhood, his translations and interpretations, and the superficial influence of the *Vita Nuova* on Rossetti's poetry.

Shanks, E. B. "Dante Gabriel Rossetti," *London Mercury*, XVIII, 67–78 (May, 1928). Sees Rossetti's poetry as merely the memorializing of his moods, written only for himself and a few friends.

Shine, Hill. "The Influence of Keats upon Rossetti," *Englische Studien*, LXI, 183–210 (May, 1926). Bases the study upon Rossetti's *marginalia* in his copy of Keats's poetry; traces influences in themes, situations, descriptions, and poetic figures.

Smith, Garnet. "Dante Gabriel Rossetti," *Contemporary Review*, CXXXIII, 624–31 (May, 1928). A eulogistic survey of the poet's work, showing in it the interaction of painting and poetry.

Symons, Arthur. "A Note on Rossetti," *North American Review*, CCIV, 128–34 (July, 1916). Points out Rossetti's sensitiveness to human crises, compares his poetic scope to Blake's.

Tisdel, F. M. "Rossetti's *House of Life*," *Modern Philology*, XV, 257–76 (Sept., 1917). An attempt to date the sonnets after 1869 and a re-examination of some usually supposed to be earlier, leaving only six unplaced; traces a strong autobiographical element throughout the sequence.

Turner, A. M. "Rossetti's Reading and His Critical Opinions," *Publications of the Modern Language Association*, XLII, 465–91 (June, 1927). An essay "to reconstruct the literary interests of Rossetti and define his tendencies as a critic"; concludes that his field of reading was specialized and that he was a Romantic, intuitive critic.

Waller, R. D. "'The Blessed Damozel,'" *Modern Language Review*, XXVI, 129–41 (April, 1931). Reviews the antecedents of the poem, finding most influential Dante, Petrarch, and Shelley.

Wallerstein, Ruth. "Bancroft MSS of Rossetti's Sonnets," *Modern Language Notes*, XLIV, 279–84 (May, 1929). A study of the variants in the collection of Mrs. Samuel Bancroft of Wilmington, Delaware, furnishing the text of two hitherto unpublished sonnets.

Wallerstein, Ruth. "Personal Experience in Rossetti's *House of Life*," *Publications of the Modern Language Association*, XLII, 492–504 (June, 1927). Examines the dates and grouping of the sonnets; attempts to identify autobiographical references.

Waugh, Evelyn. "D. G. Rossetti: A Centenary Criticism," *Fortnightly Review*, CXXIII, 595–604 (May, 1928). Bases a survey of Rossetti's development as an artist and a man upon his five paintings: The Annunciation, Launcelot and Guinever, Beata Beatrix, Monna Vanna, Proserpine.

Winwar, Frances. "Dante Gabriel's or William Michael's," *Publications of the Modern Language Association*, XLVIII, 312–5 (March, 1933). An attempt to establish the authorship of some Rossetti sonnets published by the Duke University Press.

NOTES

Page 611. THE BLESSED DAMOZEL

"Among pieces where the mystical feeling is by necessity of subject most simple and most on the surface, 'The Blessed Damozel' should be noticed, a poem in which wild longing, and the shame of life, and despair of separation, and the worship of love, are wrought into a palpable dream, in which the heaven that exists as if for the sake of the beloved is as real as the earthly things about the lover, while these are scarcely less strange or less pervaded with a sense of his passion, than the things his imagination has made. The poem is as profoundly sweet and touching and natural as any in the book, that is to say, as any in the whole range of modern poetry. At first sight the leap from this poem to the 'Jenny' may seem very great, but there is in fact no break in the unity of the mind that imagined both these poems; rather one is the necessary complement to the other." (William Morris, "Poems by Dante Gabriel Rossetti," *Academy*, May 14, 1870.)

See notes on *Jenny*, below.

Rossetti in some *Sentences and Notes* of 1866 made some remarks concerning Coleridge which might be considered in their application to himself:

"Moderation is the highest law of poetry. Experimental as Coleridge sometimes becomes, his *best* work is tuned but never twanged; and this is his great distinction from almost all others who venture as far. . . . I was one of those whose little is their own." (Rossetti, *Collected Works* [1886], I, 511–12.)

The Blessed Damozel was first written in 1847 when Rossetti was eighteen and was published in *The Germ* in 1850. As the Introduction to Rossetti says (text p. 608), the germinal idea derived from Poe's *The Raven* by a curious inverse process. "I saw at once," said Rossetti, "that Poe had done the utmost it was possible to do with the grief of the lover on earth, and I determined to reverse the conditions and give utterance to the yearning of the loved one in heaven." The poem was revised and appeared in 1856 in Morris's *The Oxford and Cambridge Magazine* and was further revised for the *Poems* of 1870 and 1881. It is therefore in its final form the result of years of polishing and is not representative of Rossetti's state of artistic development at the age of eighteen. Two critical comments have frequently been made on this poem. The first is to call attention to portions of it as representative of the accurate visualization of the painter carried over into poetry. For example in the first stanza there is a girl with lilies in her hand and stars in her hair, but stars and lilies cannot be painted in the general. Rossetti makes it a definite three lilies and seven stars and places the girl in a definite pose. The second frequent comment is on the sense of nearness and farness in the poem, the curious mixture of intimacy and immensity.

10. *meetly*. appropriately.

54. *The stars sang in their spheres*. For poetic effect Rossetti has apparently confused two conceptions. According to Ptolemaic (pre-Copernican) astronomy the stars and planets were set in spheres which made music as they rotated. In Job 38:7 there is the phrase "When the morning stars sang together."

105. *five handmaidens*. The Virgin is attended by five female saints whose names were chosen by Rossetti for the music he could make of them rather than for any particular significance to the poem of the story of the saint.

Page 612. MY SISTER'S SLEEP

The exactitude of detail in this poem has led some to believe that it was based upon some event in the poet's life. It was, however, purely imaginary.

Page 613. THE PORTRAIT

"In printed notices of my brother's poems I have often seen the supposition advanced that this poem was written after the death of his wife, in relation to some portrait he had painted of her during her lifetime. The supposition is very natural—yet not correct. The poem was in fact an extremely early one, and purely imaginary,—perhaps, in the first draft of it, as early as 1847; it was afterwards considerably revised." (W. M. Rossetti's note.) In the revision Rossetti may, however, very well have written in his feeling for his wife, although without any specific portrait in mind.

Page 614. AVE

Rossetti in 1869, as a preliminary before settling on the poems to be included in the 1870 volume, had his poems privately printed. To *Ave* he put a note: "This hymn was written as a prolog to a series of designs. Art still identifies herself with all faiths for her own purposes: and the emotional influence here employed demands above all an inner standing point."

56. *garments in the stream*. Rossetti (1855) did a water color showing the Virgin steeping clothes in a stream as Gabriel approached.

63. *Long years when It was Finished*. The years after the Crucifixion and before Mary's Assumption into Heaven.

65. *darkness in the house of John*. Rossetti did (1858) a water color on this subject.

Page 616. ON REFUSAL OF AID BETWEEN NATIONS

Rossetti at the time of writing was moved by the national struggles of Italy and Hungary against Austrian domination, and was exasperated by the indifference with which other nations looked on.

THE CARD-DEALER

When this poem first appeared in the *Athenæum* (Oct. 23, 1852) Rossetti subtitled it *From a Picture* and added a note, "The picture is one painted by the late Theodore von Holst; and represents a beautiful woman, richly dressed, who is sitting at a lamp-lit table, dealing out cards, with a peculiar fixedness of expression." The original title was "The Card-dealer, or Vingt-et-un." Vingt-et-un is a gambling game of high stakes and swift play. Rossetti seized on the opportunity to expand the significance of his figure and make her play at Life and Death.

THE STAFF AND SCRIP

Rossetti took this story from the *Gesta Romanorum* where it was entitled "Of Ingratitude," but he changed the sense of it drastically. In the original the pilgrim fought after receiving the lady's promise that if he died she would preserve his staff and scrip in her private chamber. She promised and he died. Some years later, being in high prosperity, she was able to choose a husband from three neighboring kings (representing the Devil, the World, and the Flesh) and as she went out from her chamber she ordered the staff and scrip removed (symbolizing a putting away of the memorials of our Saviour's love) because they were rather shabby. Rossetti omits most of the moral element, and exacts no promise from the lady. Her unfaithfulness to a promise which exists in the original and not in Rossetti's ballad will be rectified in heaven.

54. *grame.* Grief.

84. *He writ.* Her name, as also upon his shield (l. 88) he painted her portrait.

182. *they.* The staff and scrip.

188–90. *soul . . . in the scrip . . . dust of palm.* In other words, with more than ten years passed, the pilgrim was forgotten and no longer an essential part of her life.

196–7. *they shake To gusts in chapel.* The staff and scrip, which are now preserved in a chapel instead of in her chamber.

211. *Not tithed.* Not fractioned or reduced in heaven by the inevitable decay of mortality.

Page 619. SISTER HELEN

The foundation of this story is the old superstition that if one could secure something which had had contact with an enemy—it might be a bit of cloth which had been worn or, better still, a fingernail paring or a lock of hair—and if one, with proper incantations, embedded the object in a waxen image, one could torture the enemy by torturing the image. The usual method was to stick pins in the wax, but Helen chose to melt it slowly before a fire.

The theme as developed by Rossetti has a chilly and restrained horror. Helen proceeds with a deadly, emotionless persistency about her task. The desperate men who ride up to intercede for Keith of Ewern (his brothers and the great baron, his father) never gain admittance to the locked chamber where the waxen image melts. A terrified small brother, only half-comprehending, reports their words to Helen. The image crumbles, a death-knell tolls, and Helen cries out, for her witchcraft means damnation of her own soul.

Rossetti's prestige has prevented much consideration of his use of the refrain. In *Sister Helen* with its variations, Rossetti used the refrain more effectively than anywhere else. The question, however, can be fairly raised whether or not it is an irritating interruption and an easy technical trick. The question is fairer in the case of *Troy Town* (on which see notes). Evelyn Waugh makes one of the most intelligent pro-Rossetti comments on this question:

"It is part of the underlying sensuality of Rossetti's poetry that it really needs to be read aloud. The actual form in which words are presented has a great influence in determining their psychological effect. With Rossetti the shape of his poems upon paper means nothing, but the vocal sound of them means everything. The peculiar resonance so much remarked upon in his own voice has to be evoked before many of his rhythms and rhymes, particularly the feminine rhymes which he employed so extensively, can be appreciated. Read these for yourself purely intellectually, without pronouncing the words, and the effect is lost; read them aloud and loudly, allowing the voice to fall into softness at the end of the lines, and if it does not make you feel shy, Rossetti's intention is in some way realised.

"A particularly notable example of this is *Troy Town*, with its refrain in each verse:

(O Troy Town!)
(Oh, Troy's down!)
(Tall Troy's on fire!)

"And *Sister Helen*, where the refrain undergoes slight modulation at each repetition:

(O Mother, Mary Mother,
Three days to-day between Hell and Heaven!)

(O Mother, Mary Mother,
What sight to-night, between Hell and Heaven?)

(O Mother, Mary Mother,
Shall God not hear between Hell and Heaven?), etc.

"Read aloud, these refrains achieve exactly the effect for which they were designed, exercising a hypnotic influence on the hearer, drawing him into the poem, making it hauntingly memorable, and giving it a certain liturgical solemnity. But printed upon a page, the effect is exactly the opposite. One sees the italics coming, and finds them an interruption which one overcomes by skipping. There is something slightly ludicrous in reading these repetitions silently to oneself; a sort of shyness throws up an immediate barrier to the poet which is the more serious as the reader is the more sensitive." (Evelyn Waugh, *Rosselti*, pp. 156–7.)

Page 622. THE BURDEN OF NINEVEH

Nineveh, Persepolis, and Babylon, great capitals of fallen empires, have become symbols of the oblivion which threatens greatness. Rossetti is dilating on this theme as he observes a statue from Nineveh which has been dug up by cheap Arab labor and hauled by truck to a London museum where it will be exhibited to schoolboys. Rossetti extends the theme to London, wondering whether it in turn might not be excavated by Australian archæologists and he also extends the theme beyond fallen cities to fallen gods. (See note on l. 109.)

14. *mitred Minotaur.* The minotaur in Greek mythology was half bull and half man. Mitred, as Rossetti uses the word, roughly means "crowned"; apparently the statue carried some sort of headgear which suggested to Rossetti the mitre of a Roman Catholic bishop.

53. *Sheltered his Jonah with a gourd.* This refers to Jonah 3:4–6, 10, and 4:1, 5–6:

"And Jonah began to enter into the city a day's journey, and he cried, and said, Yet forty days, and Nineveh shall be overthrown.

"So the people of Nineveh believed God, and proclaimed a fast, and put on sackcloth, from the greatest of them even to the least of them.
"For word came unto the king of Nineveh, and he arose from his throne, and he laid his robe from him, and covered him with sackcloth, and sat in ashes. . . .
"And God saw their works, that they turned from their evil way; and God repented of the evil, that he had said that he would do unto them; and he did it not.
"But it displeased Jonah exceedingly, and he was very angry.
"So Jonah went out of the city, and sat on the east side of the city, and there made him a booth, and sat under it in the shadow, till he might see what would become of the city.
"And the Lord God prepared a gourd, and made it to come up over Jonah, that it might be a shadow over his head, to deliver him from his grief. So Jonah was exceeding glad of the gourd."

76. *school-foundations*. Schoolboys. In England if one is a scholarship winner at an endowed school one is said to be "on the foundation."

88. *unblest abode*. The British Museum.

109. *Isis or Ibis*. Isis, the goddess of fecundity, was the wife of Osiris and the chief female divinity of ancient Egypt. Statues and drawings represented her as having the head of a cow. The ibis was a bird sacred to the Egyptians.

113. *teraphim*. Household images of the ancient Hebrews.

122. *cities of the lake of salt*. The cities of Sodom and Gomorrah, which were great cities before Nineveh was built and which were destroyed (Genesis 19 : 24–5). Rossetti is carrying out his theme of destroyed greatness. The "lake of salt" (and the "brackish lake" of l. 128) is the Dead Sea.

126. *Jonah bore abroad*, etc. See note on l. 53.

162. *kerb and rut*. The American spelling would be "curb(stone)" for "kerb" and the meaning is "commonplace crowds of the street."

164. *ranks in gypsum quaintly cut*. Gypsum in its compact state appears as alabaster and, in a less dignified form, goes to make up "plaster of Paris." Rossetti, by the use of the word "gypsum," was apparently trying to emphasize the unhumanness and image quality to him of the crowds which passed before him at the moment. He may possibly have had in the back of his mind (note the verb "strut," l. 163) the curiously frozen postures of the ancient Egyptian figures in the illustrations for what is commonly called "The Book of the Dead."

Page 624. TROY TOWN

Rossetti makes an unusual approach to the story of Helen of Troy (who was Queen of Sparta before she eloped) and Paris, in that he makes Helen the indirect seducer. Behind the story of Paris and Helen was the story of a feast of the gods into which was flung the golden "Apple of Discord" marked "For the Fairest." With Juno, Minerva, and Venus present there was indeed discord. Paris had been called in to decide and decided in favor of Venus. (See ll. 57–9.) Tennyson treats the Judgment of Paris in *Œnone* and has Venus promise him the fairest wife in all the world. Rossetti has Helen, already in love, approach Venus to bring about Paris's passion. And so Cupid (the son of Venus) takes another golden arrow (the "dart" of l. 85) and shoots it into the heart of Paris.

Whether the refrain, in spite of Waugh's brilliant defense (see notes on *Sister Helen*), has any significance may be doubted. Max Nordau, in his *Degeneration*, says of the refrains of a similar poem (*Eden Bower*): "As a matter of course, between these absolutely senseless phrases and the strophe which each interrupts, there is not the remotest connection. They are strung together without any reference to their meaning, but only because they rhyme." Nordau considers this sort of procedure a mild form of mania which he calls "echolalia."

Page 626. THE BALLAD OF DEAD LADIES

The theme of fallen greatness or vanished beauty was common in the Middle Ages, but Villon's exquisite handling of it in the *Ballade des Dames du Temps Jadis* has associated the theme with his name in the minds of most readers. Villon included the poem in his *Le Grand Testament* after stanza XLI and followed it with the *Ballade des Seigneurs du Temps Jadis*—"Of the Lords of Other Days."

The ladies mentioned by Villon and Rossetti are: Flora, a celebrated Roman courtesan mentioned in Juvenal; in Villon's text there is a mysterious Archipiades, whom Rossetti translates as Hipparchia, a Greek courtesan; Thais, an Athenian courtesan, was with Alexander the Great at the burning of the palace of the Persian kings at Persepolis.

Héloïse and Abelard were heroine and hero of one of the famous love tragedies of the middle ages. The queen of l. 13 was Marguerite, Queen of Burgundy, who, according to legend, enticed students into her palace (the Tour de Nesle in Paris) and, when her whim was gratified, had them flung in the Seine. Buridan was a professor in the University of Paris who, according to report, in his younger days had fallen into the queen's clutches but was saved when he fell into a barge laden with straw which his pupils had placed under the tower to catch him. There is no historical basis for the story.

Blanche may be Blanche of Castile, mother of St. Louis (Louis IX of France). Bertha Broadfoot ("Berte au grant pié") was the tall wife of Pepin the Short and the mother of Charlemagne. Beatrice and Alice cannot be identified with any assurance. Ermengarde was Arembour, heiress to the county of Maine, who married Foulque V, Count of Anjou (d. 1126), allying the two powerful estates. Joan is of course Joan of Arc.

It may be noticed that the character of the ladies changes as the poem advances but the refrain remains the same.

SONGS

Very rarely did Rossetti choose purely to sing. When he did write the pure lyric he did it with a grace and clarity which makes comment unnecessary.

For those who are interested in such information—the woodspurge is a member of the spurge family (which has over 250 genera) and it emits a milky fluid. The honeysuckle is a fragrant plant about which humming birds are frequently to be found on a spring evening.

Page 628. SONNETS FOR PICTURES

I MARY'S GIRLHOOD

The picture upon which the first sonnet is based, the "Ecce Ancilla Domini," is simple in its composition—an awed girl, rather shrinking, crouches on her bed and faces the archangel Gabriel who presents to her a lily. Entering the window is a dove which represents the Holy Ghost.

The picture upon which the second sonnet is based was first in point of time and is complicated both in composition and symbolism. W. M. Rossetti thus describes the picture: "Perhaps Rossetti had never been forestalled in representing an ideal scene of the home-life of the Virgin Mary with her parents; certainly not in the particular invention which this picture embodies. The Virgin, aged about seventeen, is shown working at an embroidery under the eye of her mother St. Anna. The embroidery represents a lily, the emblem of purity, which she copies from a plant watered by a child-angel. The father St. Joachim is behind, trailing up a vine. The Holy Ghost, in the form of a dove, is also present. The head of the Virgin was painted from Christina Rossetti, that of St. Anna from our mother: both very faithful likenesses. The vase containing the lily is mounted upon six large volumes lettered with the names of virtues, Charity being the uppermost. There are numerous other details, each with a symbolic or spiritual meaning; and I will venture to say that every one of the meanings is well conceived and rightly indicated." (W. M. Rossetti, *Dante Gabriel Rossetti, His Family Letters*, I, 142–3.)

The seven-thorned briar and seven-leaved palm symbolize the Seven Sorrows and the Seven Joys of Our Lady. The Seven Sorrows were (1) the prophecy of Simeon, (2) the flight into Egypt, (3) her grief at the loss of the child Jesus before finding him again in the temple, (4) the sight of Christ bearing the cross on the road to Calvary, (5) the Crucifixion, (6) the piercing of Christ's side by the spear, (7) the entombment. The Seven Joys were (1) the Annunciation, (2) the visitation and the birth of John the Baptist, (3) the nativity of Christ, (4) the adoration of the Magi, (5) the presentation of Jesus in the temple, (6) the finding of the lost Jesus (cf. the third Sorrow recounted in Luke 2 : 41–51), (7) the Assumption.

Page 629. II FOR "A VENETIAN PASTORAL"

In the original Giorgione, through a tunnel of distance and across a warm green hillside one can see on this hot day a pastoral group (of four, two cavaliers and two women) of which this woman is the center.

III FOR "THE WINE OF CIRCE"

Circe was the enchantress who appears in the Odyssey and who had the power of transforming men, with a draught of her wine, into beasts (see ll. 9–10)—the particular type of beast, whether tiger or hog, being dependent on the character of the man.

Helios (l. 5) was a sun god (the son of Hyperion) and Hecatè was a goddess with power over the moon, earth, and the underworld. In late myths she is the goddess of witchcraft.

IV FIAMMETTA

Fiammetta was the mistress of Boccaccio, and Rossetti thus translated one of Boccaccio's sonnets to that lady:

Of His Last Sight of Fiammetta

Round her red garland and her golden hair
  I saw a fire about Fiammetta's head;
  Thence to a little cloud I watched it fade,
Than silver or than gold more brightly fair;
And like a pearl that a gold ring doth bear,
  Even so an angel sat therein, who sped
  Alone and glorious throughout heaven, array'd
In sapphires and in gold that lit the air.
Then I rejoiced as hoping happy things,
Who rather should have then discerned how God
  Had haste to make my lady all His own,
Even as it came to pass. And with these stings
  Of sorrow, and with life's most weary load
    I dwell, who fain would be where she is gone.

Rossetti's painting (of 1878) was an illustration of the opening two lines of this sonnet, for he shows Fiammetta aureoled ("a fire about Fiammetta's head") and surrounded by flowers (the "red garland"). Rossetti's poem is a poem to his illustration of the poem by Boccaccio—which makes the relationship somewhat involved.

V "FOUND"

The first line of this sonnet should be balanced against the last and be considered as hinting the true conclusion. A country girl has gone up to London and fallen into evil ways. Her country lover who had searched for her fruitlessly goes up to London carrying in a cart a calf which he intended to sell. He encounters the girl and Rossetti's picture portrays the moment when she is "found."

The grief of the unfortunate calf which had to pose for the picture is described in one of Rossetti's letters (text p. 658b, ll. 30–50).

Page 630. JENNY

References to this poem occur in Rossetti's letters in the text, pp. 667a, l. 33, and 672b, ll. 20 et seq., the second being the more important.

Morris analyzed this poem in some detail in his review of Rossetti's *Poems* in the *Academy* and linked it, strangely enough, to *The Blessed Damozel*. See introductory material to that poem.

"The subject is difficult for a modern poet to deal with, but necessary for a man to think of; it is thought of here with the utmost depths of feeling, pity, and insight, with no mawkishness on the one hand, no coarseness on the other: and carried out with perfect simplicity and beauty. It is so strong, unforced, and full of nature, that I think it the poem of the whole book that would be most missed if it were away. With all this, its very simplicity and directness make it hard to say much about it: but it may be noticed, as leading to the consideration of one side of Mr. Rossetti's powers, how perfectly the *dramatic* quality of the soliloquiser is kept: his pity, his protest against the hardness of nature and chance never make him didactic, or more or less than a man of the world, any more than his 'Shame of his own shame' makes him brutal, though in the inevitable flux and reflux of feeling and habit and pleasure he is always seeming on the verge of touching one or other of these extremes. How admirably, too, the conclusion is managed with that dramatic breaking of day, and the effect that it gives to the chilling of enthusiasm and remorse, which it half produces and is half typical of; coming after the grand passage about lust that brings to a climax the musings over so much beauty and so many good things apparently thrown away causelessly." (William Morris, "Poems by Dante Gabriel Rossetti," *Academy*, May 14, 1870.)

Motto: *Vengeance of Jenny's case,* etc. Mistress Quickly is the servant of Dr. Caius in Shakespeare's *Merry Wives of Windsor*. For the original form of this speech (which makes possible Rossetti's use of it) see *Merry Wives of Windsor*, Act IV, scene 1.

Page 634. THE HOUSE OF LIFE

The title of Rossetti's sequence was derived from astrology, but Rossetti used the term "House" rather vaguely. In astrology the heavens (both above and below the horizon) are divided into twelve parts, each named—the House of Life being one of them. Rossetti, however, presents no complete philosophy of life although he does treat of certain of its passionate crises.

A portion of the sequence appeared in 1870, although some of the sonnets had been composed much earlier—perhaps as much as twenty years before—and the completed *House of Life* appeared in 1881. To term it a sequence is perhaps misleading, as one poem does not lead to another with any logical progression, nor is there any story told. There is, however, a coherence of tone which unifies the sequence. In the background of the whole lies the tragic love story of Rossetti and Elizabeth Siddal (see text pp. 608–9). That this affair colored Rossetti's thinking ever after, there can be no doubt; but there are indications, clear enough, that in some of the sonnets Rossetti was thinking of other women. Therefore the sequence should not be considered as a poem to "A Woman."

The sultry and intense atmosphere of the series has often been commented upon—in fact, Buchanan in his famous attack, *The Fleshly School of Poetry*, drew his most telling quotations from *The House of Life*. That Rossetti's flowers were hothouse flowers, exotic and gorgeous, rather than simple violets by a windy wayside, no one has ever denied. And to admit as much is not to deny their beauty. Rossetti's admirers have always pointed out that paralleling his physical sumptuousness in *The House of Life* there is another quality, a sense of the spiritual which lies beyond the physical. Mr. P. F. Baum (in his edition of *The House of Life*) analyzes at some length the relationship of the physical to the spiritual in Rossetti.

"A difficulty faces us, however, in certain of Rossetti's so-called 'fleshly' passages, and it is, of course, toward these that I have been aiming. In seeking to give expression to the real which lies behind the actual, the poet must frankly undertake to 'communicate the incommunicable,' and this he does by the use of symbols. Symbolism, or the representation of one thing by another, is not only the basis of language, but the special method of poetic language. But symbolism works upon many different levels, varying according to the relation or remoteness of the thing expressed to the thing suggested. Here lies the concealed danger—*latet anguis*—which has brought error and misconception down upon Rossetti's head. In sonnet XXI, 'Love-Sweetness,' the octave describes the more or less carnal delights of love. These Rossetti accepts as natural or normal and has no desire to make us suppose they are symbolic (in the simple sense of the term).

Her mouth's culled sweetness by thy kisses shed
On cheeks and neck and eyelids, and so led
Back to her mouth which answers there for all,

he says. This is a frankly sensuous description of a frankly sensuous affair. There is no other symbolism here than the most elementary symbolism of language. But the sestet of the sonnet puts the matter in a different light: What is sweeter than this, he says, except that without which it would not be sweet at all, namely, the spiritual love which is known only through the physical. The same idea appears in sonnet XXVIII, 'Soul-Light,' where 'after the fulness of all (fleshly) rapture' there gleams in her eyes 'a yet more hungering thrill'—that of the soul.

"Here we have, of course, simple mysticism in one of its aspects: the communication of the unknowable through the knowable. But here also is the danger which I have mentioned, and a danger which in Rossetti is likely to be a stumbling-block if not a fault—that the symbol itself may stand in the light of the thing symbolized. It is well known that in some of the early forms of Maryolatry the excessive worship of the Virgin's eyes and lips and breasts became an end in itself, and the symbol usurped the spiritual power. Rossetti is not free from liability to this charge. He may deny the intention—and does, rightly and sincerely, no doubt. But the fact remains, though one must call it an artistic rather than a moral fault. I repeat: it is not always thus perhaps in Rossetti's 'fleshly' passages; but where a blemish is to be acknowledged, this distinction meets the requirements of explanation.

"Rossetti carried symbolism beyond such a simple stage as this, however. Not only is human love, in its ordinary process, a counterpart and image of the divine, but all that intercourse with the eternal idealisms which is desired and denied to mortal man, all that striving to rise from the phenomena of living to Life itself, all that eager passionate struggling through mysteries up to the great Mystery—in a word, all that worship which innate religion craves, is but 'in some way a transformation of the sexual passion'—at once a sexual and mystical passion. Woman—her eyes, her lips, her breasts—the visible human loveliness and charm, is an occult presentation of the divine parts and attributes. She is beauty, she is love, she is the supreme god. Through her the embodied soul reaches and arrives to pure Idea. Through her, through a mortal, we other mortals ascend to the immortal summits. This is 'no deliberate worship of Baal and Ashtoreth'; it is 'a love which appertains to the category of reasoned affections no more; its place is with the visions of saints, the intuitions of philosophers, in Plato's ideal world.'

"To grant all this—a natural and unconscious Platonism—to Rossetti is very high praise indeed, but it is not unjustified for parts of 'The House of Life.' It is no more than adequate for sonnet LXXVII, 'Soul's Beauty'—as Myers (from whom I have just quoted) makes sufficiently plain; and this Rossetti is manifestly visible in the first sonnet of the sequence and (somewhat flatteringly) in the last; and in lesser degree here and there through the series, as, for example, in 'The Dark Glass' (XXXIV). But of course Rossetti is not wholly with the great mystics; he cannot dwell constantly in their white light. The *selva selvaggia ed aspra e forte* presses too closely upon him, and too often he sees only

As at the end of some deep avenue
A tender glamour of day.

It is much, however, that he had seen the vision, though he held to it but fitfully; and, if one were to indulge in a pleading which is as futile as it is unnecessary, one might maintain that his failings on the side of 'fleshliness' are simply the tokens of his great desire for the great truth, the shadows which are humanly inseparable from the light." (Paull Franklin Baum, *The House of Life*, pp. 23–6.)

II. Bridal Birth. The transitions of thought in this sonnet are difficult to follow. The child of the octave is Love—Love in its infancy. At the start of the sestet it is Love mature, the love god born and serving the lovers. At the conclusion Love is the creator, the father of their souls at the time of death when all else goes and only love remains, and the halo of the love god's hair is their only light.

Page 635.

V. Heart's Hope. "Love in the individual, according to the rather obscure utterance of the sestet, or six concluding lines, stands a portion of the eternal love of the ages past and to come, a thing in which mortal worship of the best is signified and sublimated. The reading of the octave is simple. In the attempt to analyze love, and to separate what is earthly from what is heavenly, there is in Rossetti's idea profanity. Soul and body the woman beloved and responsible becomes a part of the man. The twain are one, and the love which binds them is the one Divine effluence not to be distinguished from Divinity." (Joseph Knight, *Life of Dante Gabriel Rossetti*, pp. 163–4.)

4. *which Israel crossed.* Exodus 14 : 15–29.

XI. The Love-Letter. The poet is addressing the letter which has been "warmed by her hand," etc.

Page 637.

XVIII. Genius in Beauty. "Beauty like hers is a king of genius—a mysterious quality like the sublimity of Homer or Dante or Michelangelo. . . . The octave celebrates the richness of her beauty, the sestet its imperishability." (Baum, *op. cit.*)

XXI. Love-Sweetness. See introductory material quoted from Baum, and sonnet XXVIII.

Page 638.

XXVII. Heart's Compass.

6–7. *Whose eyes the sun-gate,* etc. These lines are obscure. Apparently the flash of her eyes suggests (are "oracular") the furthest fires of the soul, i.e., in the living eye we see the soul and it unbars the "sun-gate" to give us this glimpse.

XXVIII. Soul-Light. See note on sonnet XXI.

XXXIV. The Dark Glass. See introductory material from Baum (*op. cit.*) on this sonnet as representative of Rossetti's mysticism.

XXXVI. Life-in-Love. The fourteenth line refers to the glorious hair of Elizabeth Siddal, of which Rossetti preserved a tress, but the opening suggests that another woman has given him new life among his mournful memories.

XXXVIII. The Morrow's Message.

2. *Yesterday's son.* Today is the son of the *happy* yesterday. Could all that happiness have come in the end to this present abjection and grief?

9. *malisons.* Maledictions, curses.

Page 639.

XLI. Through Death to Love. The octave is difficult because, advancing a series of vague and terrifying images, Rossetti holds his thought in suspension until ll. 7–8. These are images of Death—Death which overshadows every life. The sestet declares there is another power, and then (ll. 12–14) turns from the general statement to the particular case. Tell me, my heart, whose Lord is Love, the poet asks, what door at which an angel ever knocked hath guest as fire-fledged as thine?

13–14. *angel-greeted . . . wing-winnowed.* According to simple medieval faith it was not incredible that angels should walk the earth in disguise and at nightfall ask for shelter in human habitations, nor that, having been treated in a christian spirit, they should help in the winnowing of the grain by the beating of their invisible wings.

XLVII. Broken Music. Hesitantly he has at last come back to poetic expression and personal release. The poetry is like the sound of the sea-shell—something from the past. But the voice of the lost one strikes across it. (The antecedent of "her" in l. 13 is "soul" in l. 9.)

XLIX–LII. Willowwood, 1–4. William Michael Rossetti considered that the general theme of these sonnets was the pangs of severance—possibly by death, but he was more inclined to believe caused by circumstances on earth. The significance of the title lies in the fact that the weeping willow is a symbol of faithfulness in grief.

L. 3. *souls disused,* etc. Souls with a faded, lingering memory of a former life, not yet reborn to another active life.

Page 640.

LI. 3. *soul-struck widowhood.* Widowhood implies, of course, division from the loved one, so deep and profound in this case that it has struck to the soul.

13. *her.* The soul.

LII. 10–11. *She . . . her.* The loved one.

Page 641.

LXIX. Autumn Idleness.

12. *the lost hours,* etc. In the hours which he loses idling he relives the lost hours of the past.

Page 642.

LXXVII. Soul's Beauty. This sonnet, as the footnote in the text (p. 642) indicates, was written for one of Rossetti's pictures. The sibyl with a palm branch in her hand is seated on a throne beneath a stone canopy—phrases in the poem are dictated by this original. A sibyl was a priestess of the gods, usually of Apollo, and it was this figure that Rossetti chose to include in *The House of Life* under the title he gave it.

LXXVIII. Body's Beauty. See note on sonnet LXXVII. This poem is less definitely descriptive of the picture on which it is based than is the preceding sonnet but it is perhaps more subtly interpretive. In the picture, against a background of roses, Lilith is combing her luxurious hair. Scent and hair and their sensual power are a predominant motif in the poem.

1. *Lilith.* The witch who is supposed to have delighted Adam before the creation of Eve.

6. *subtly of herself contemplative.* In the picture, Lilith is watching with a certain drowsy assurance in a hand mirror the effect of her hair as she combs it.

LXXXIII. Barren Spring.

3–4. *And now before . . . Stoops as it swoops.* The girl is both merry and blushful as she tries to control her skirts in the wind. And the spring is like her.

XCVII. A Superscription. A shell from the dead sea (Sea of Death?) has been washed up at his feet and grimly "No-more" holds it to his ear that he may hear the dim murmur from it, just as "No-more" holds up a mirror which holds the now intolerable shadow of what had once had the substance and form of Life and Love. But "No-more" is very still and quiet. Only, if ever the guilty man looks away from the mirror or tries to escape the shell, looking towards Peace in another love, then "No-more" will make him turn again to face his memories, the "ambush" at his heart.

A superscription means a writing-over. The title may mean that if there is any new effort at love, memory will write over it a cancellation.

Page 643.

CI. The One Hope.

8. *amulet.* The charm which will solve all this desperation of passion and death and separation about which Rossetti has written one hundred sonnets.

10. *scriptured petals.* The amulet (l. 8) is a flower on the petals of which may be written ("scriptured") the answer to the riddle.

13. *the one Hope's one name.* It is impossible to say whether this refers to the name of the one lady truly loved whom he shall rejoin in Paradise, or "Love" conceived in terms of Paradise rather than the Earth, with a power to tranquilize all the fever which has gone before.

THE CLOUD CONFINES

"Rossetti wrote this poem (in 1871) in a highly serious mood of mind: he intended it to be a definite expression of his conceptions, indefinite as they were, upon problems which no amount of knowledge and experience can make other than mysterious and unfathomable. In writing to me he said that the lyric was 'not meant to be a trifle'; and he consulted me as to whether it might be better to leave the last four lines as they stand, or to substitute other lines 'on the theory hardly of annihilation but of absorption.' He also wrote to Mr. W. Bell Scott in the same connexion, saying: 'I cannot suppose that any particle of life is "extinguished," though its permanent individuality may be more than questionable. Absorption is not annihilation; and it is even a real retributive future for the special atom of life to be re-embodied (if so it were) in a world which its own former identity had helped to fashion for pain or pleasure.' Franz Hueffer, who edited the Tauchnitz Edition of Rossetti's 'Ballads and Sonnets,' thought 'The Cloud Confines' 'his highest effort in the field of contemplative, not to say philosophic verse.'" (W. M. Rossetti's note in the *The Works of Dante Gabriel Rossetti* [London, 1911], p. 669.)

Page 644. THE KING'S TRAGEDY

". . . That the character of James I of Scotland, the poet-king whose youth was spent as a prisoner in England, and whose turbulent reign was one long effort to repress the disorders of a kingdom in which violence and crime had reigned unchecked, should appeal to Rossetti, was natural. While taking, however, an historical basis for the story, and adhering so far to the truth as to introduce into his poem some stanzas from James's poem of 'The King's Quhair,' Rossetti did not hesitate, for the purpose of effect, to depart from strict historical accuracy, especially in regard to the circumstances under which the king, by retiring to the Charterhouse he had erected at Perth, facilitated the operations of his murderers. He naturally retained the supernatural element, which no one who knows his affinities for such subjects will be surprised to find is the most effective portion of the poem, and is, moreover, treated in the very spirit of the old ballads. Less consonant with this ballad spirit is the assigning the task of narration to Kate Barlass, or Catherine Douglas, the heroine of the murder, whose arm thrust through the socket from which the bolt had been withdrawn, is the means of temporarily arresting the assassins.

"The historical incidents, the interruption of the siege of Roxbro' hold by the news of the disaffection of the nobles, the rapid return of the king, the arrest of Sir Robert Graeme, and the temporary repression of rebellion, are told with spirit. With the start of the regal cavalcade for Perth and the meeting with the crone, whose mysterious predictions fail to turn the king from his purpose, the poem rises into sublimity, and the execution from this point forward is such as Rossetti alone could have afforded. Little in imaginative literature is more noteworthy for weird power and appropriateness than the message of the witch woman. . . .

"Supernatural intervention such as this is frequent in ancient poetry and fiction, and is ordinarily futile. Rossetti's employment of it is always prosperous. If ever supernatural interference is justifiable, it is in a case such as this, where through those misty highlands, in which the traditions of wraith and spectre linger longest, a gallant king is riding to his doom at the hands of traitors. In striking contrast with the unpretentious nature of the sibyl is the effect of her presence upon inanimate nature. At the charms of the Lapland witches, 'the labouring moon eclipses.' Nature, in awe, accords to the spectral presence of the old woman the attention the king refuses, and furnishes the poet with opportunity for those descriptions of the wrath or affright of the earth and heavens, in which he was most at home. The woman, of course, appears once more when the curtain is rising on the tragedy, and equally, of course, her warning voice is once more heard and unheeded. . . . In the hands of small men supernatural machinery of this description is a dangerous device; in those of a master of the craft its influence is irresistible. The effect of this episode, for such, in a way, it is, in binding together the parts of a story the action of which is diffuse, and in giving the whole tragic dignity and solemnity, cannot be over-estimated. Without it the story would be no more than a fairly spirited narrative; with it it impresses us as do the sombre scenes in a great tragedy." (Joseph Knight, *Life of Dante Gabriel Rossetti*, pp. 155–8.)

James's elder brother, the heir to the throne, was murdered and his father for safety's sake sent the young James, then twelve, to France. Henry IV of England, however, captured him on the journey (1406) and refused to accept ransom. Henry V on his accession transferred the prisoner to Windsor Castle, where he was kindly treated. It was at Windsor that James wrote his poem *The King's Quhair*, some stanzas of which (indicated by italics) Rossetti adapted for his ballad. A treaty was finally made between Scotland and England by which Scotland agreed to pay a ransom and James agreed to marry a noble English lady—Jane Beaufort, daughter of the Earl of Somerset. The two were married in England and entered Scotland in 1424, being crowned at Scone according to the Scottish tradition on May 21, 1424. Rossetti refers to these events in the earlier part of his ballad.

176. *'Twixt the Duchray and the Dhu.* Castle Duchray stands beside a stream of the same name in the extreme south of the country of Perth. Dhu is a lake in Aberdeenshire in the north of Scotland.

414. *Voidee-cup.* A voidee is a collation consisting of wine, cakes, etc., taken before retiring to rest or before the departure of guests.

442. *arrased wall.* Hung with arras, tapestry.

462. *dule to dree.* Two obsolete dialectal words, meaning "grief to bear."

545. *at the palm he play'd.* The French *jeu de paume*, a primitive form of tennis.

Page 654. ROSSETTI'S LETTERS

654a, l. 4. *William Allingham* (1824–1889). Allingham's family had been settled in Ireland since the days of Elizabeth and there he was born and grew up. He worked in the customs in Ireland but made almost annual trips to London where he made the acquaintance of Leigh Hunt, Carlyle, Tennyson, and Rossetti (among others), by whom he was highly regarded. His first volume of poems (1850) was immediately withdrawn; his second, *Day and Night Songs* (1854) figures frequently in this correspondence. It was successful enough to have a second edition the next year, with additional material and illustrations by Hughes, Millais, and Rossetti.

654a, l. 8. *Cayley.* Charles Bagot Cayley, at one time in love with Christina Rossetti. See text pp. 1032–3.

654a, l. 20. *Poems.* The work referred to was Rossetti's translations from the Italian.

Page 656.

656a, l. 8. *The Kraken.* See text p. 8.

656b, l. 3. *there.* In New South Wales. Three years before Woolner had entered a competition to do a statue for Wordsworth's tomb (referred to in ll. 16–18) and in his disappointment at the rejection of his design he had gone out to Australia. The immediate project under discussion in the letter was a statue to William Charles Westworth of New South Wales for which Woolner hoped to get the commission.

656b, l. 30. *Hunt has written.* Hunt was in Egypt.

"Thomas Seddon wrote from Egypt (no date given):—'Old Hunt came to join me yesterday, for I have spent the principal part of the last two months in a tomb, just at the back of the Sphinx, away from all the petty evening bustle of an hotel. We began in a tent, but a week's experience showed that the tomb possessed in comfort what it lost in picturesqueness. It is a spacious apartment, 25 feet by 14 feet, and about 6 feet high. My end is matted, and I recline, dine, and sleep on a sumptuous divan consisting of a pair of iron trestles with two soft boards laid across them. Poor Hunt is half-bothered out of his life here in painting figures; but, between ourselves, he is rather *exigeant* in expecting Arabs and Turks in this climate to sit still (standing) for six or eight hours. Don't tell any one this, not even Rossetti.'" (George Birkbeck Hill, *Letters of Dante Gabriel Rossetti to William Allingham*, p. 41.)

Page 657.

657a, ll. 4–5. *Satire and Satirists.* Written by James Hannay (1827–1873). After his withdrawal from the navy, Hannay devoted much of his energy to letters. The volume in question was made up of a series of lectures which Hannay had given the year before at the Literary Institution in Portman Square.

657a, l. 17. *Day and Night Songs.* By Allingham. Rossetti and Millais each did one illustration for the volume and Arthur Hughes did eight. Rossetti's was for *The Maids of Elfen-Mere*.

657a, l. 22. *Miss S.* Elizabeth Siddal.

657b, l. 26. *Smith.* George Smith of the publishing firm of Smith and Elder.

657b, l. 50. *The Chief of Zanquebar.* Was apparently mentioned in Hunt's letter but the meaning of the allusion has been lost.

Page 658.

658a, l. 5. *Firmilian.* By W. E. Aytoun. "*Firmilian* was written [by Aytoun] in ridicule of the extravagant themes and style of Bailey, Dobell, and A. Smith. It was, however, so full of imagination in fine rhythmical swing, that its object was mistaken, and what was meant for caricature was accepted as serious poetry." (*Dictionary of National Biography.*)

658a, l. 13. *Wuthering Heights.* Emily Brontë's famous novel, published in 1847.

658a, l. 16. *Sidonia.* William Meinhold's *Sidonia the Sorceress*, for which Rossetti had a "positive passion."

658a, l. 19. *Mrs. Brownrigg.* A celebrated murderess who was deservedly hanged in 1767.

658b, l. 21. *Working Men's College.* Birkbeck Hill (pp. 87–8) quotes, from Ruskin's *Preterita*, Ruskin's own comment on the school:

"... I knew of its masters only the Principal, F. D. Maurice, and my own friend Rossetti. It is to be remembered of Rossetti with loving honour, that he was the only one of our modern painters who taught disciples for love of them. He was really not an Englishman, but a great Italian tormented in the Inferno of London; doing the best he could, and teaching the best he could; but the 'could' shortened by the strength of his animal passions, without any trained control, or guiding faith. . . .

"So the college went on—collecting, carpentering, sketching, Bible criticising, etc., virtually with no head; but only a clasp to the strap of its waist, and as many heads as it had students. The leaven of its affectionate temper has gone far; but how far also the leaven of its pride, and defiance of everything above it, nobody quite knows. . . . And finally, in this case, and many more, I have very clearly ascertained that the only proper school for workmen is of the work their fathers bred them to, under masters able to do better than any of their men, and with common principles of honesty and the fear of God to guide the firm." (*Letters to Allingham*, pp. 87, 88.)

658b, l. 31. *calf and cart.* The picture Rossetti was painting, which included a calf and a cart, was called "Found." See sonnet on the picture, text p. 629, and note on the sonnet, above.

Page 659.

659a, l. 14. *my ballad.* May refer to *The Staff and Scrip.*

659a, l. 43. *a certain lady.* Elizabeth Siddal.

659b, l. 26. *Working Men's College.* See note on 658b, l. 21. Madox Brown was also a teacher at the college, which was founded in 1854.

Page 660.

660a, l. 17. *unlucky job.* The illustration referred to in the footnote in the text.

660a, l. 22. *Miss Siddal's designs.* None were included in the illustrated Tennyson after all.

660b, l. 5. *The returned MSS.* Of Rossetti's *Early Italian Poets.*

660b, l. 39. *design beyond designation.* The same "unlucky" illustration cut by Dalziel.

Page 661.

661a, l. 5. *hanging committee.* Of the R. A. (Royal Academy).

"Seddon wrote on May 3, 1855:—'The Academy opens on Monday. The hangers were of the old school, and they have kicked out everything tainted with Praeraphaelitism. My *Pyramids*, and a head in chalk of Hunt's; and all our friends are stuck out of sight or rejected. Millais's picture was put where it could not be seen. . . . He carried his point by threatening to take away his picture and resign at once, unless they re-hung him, which they did. He told them his mind very freely, and said they were jealous of all rising men, and turned out or hung their pictures where they could not be seen.'" (Quoted by Birkbeck Hill, *op. cit.*, p. 128.)

661a, l. 24. *Cimabue.* By Frederic Leighton, later Lord Leighton and President of the R. A. The full title of the picture was *Cimabue's Madonna Carried in Procession Through the Streets of Florence.*

661b, l. 31. *The Music Master.* This poem was included in Allingham's *Day and Night Songs*, second edition.

Page 662.

662a, l. 32. *that thing of Dalziel's.* The unfortunate illustration referred to in 660a, l. 17.

Page 663.

663a, l. 11–12. *certain ones . . . now dated Nice.* Letters from Elizabeth Siddal who, thanks to Ruskin's generosity, had been able to go to Nice on the French Riviera for her health.

663a, ll. 19–33. *Old Blake . . . drawings*, etc. The drawings referred to in Rossetti's letter may be found in Lawrence Binyon's *Engraved Designs of William Blake* (1926) where also occurs the following note: "In a rather pompous and patronizing preface Hayley tells how 'to amuse the Artist in his patient labour,' he 'chanced to compose, in hours of exercise and leisure, a few Ballads upon anecdotes relating to animals.' Blake was induced to engrave some drawings he had made for the ballads. It was proposed to publish monthly numbers at half a crown, each containing a ballad and three engravings; the whole to be completed in fifteen numbers. But few copies were sold, and only four numbers, in blue paper wrappers, appeared. The fourth number is rare. Though so unsuccessful, the project was resumed in 1805, when a small book of ballads was issued with small engravings by Blake." (Pp. 56–7.)

663b, l. 15. *id.* One penny.

663b, l. 47. *Old Pictures.* See text p. 267 and footnote.

Page 664.

664a, l. 4. *Squarcialupe*, etc. Appear in Browning's *Sordello.*

664a, l. 13. *Dutch boors.* The Flemish school of painting.

664a, l. 17. *Sermon to the Jews.* Browning's *Holy Cross Day.*

664a, l. 19. *Milsand.* In 1863 Browning rededicated *Sordello* to Milsand. See text p. 471. Milsand's article on Browning appeared in the *Revue des Deux Mondes*, August 15, 1851.

664a, l. 22. *Pauline.* Browning's first published volume. The book was a rare one because the poet soon withdrew it from circulation.

664a, l. 44. *I made a sketch.* The sketch is reproduced in the text, p. 95. See also note on it, text p. 1131.

664b, l. 35. *Porphyrio and Madeline.* Based upon Keats's *The Eve of St. Agnes*, although Rossetti misspells the hero's name.

Page 665.

665a, ll. 4–5. *Delacroix . . . Ingres.* Delacroix, a superb colorist, was the leader of the French romantic school of painting; Ingres, an older man by nearly twenty years, adhered to the classical tradition, saying proudly, "I am a conservative of sound doctrines, not an innovator." Delacroix was the more popular in his own day, but it was Ingres who influenced such dissimilar later painters as Gaugin, Puvis de Chavannes and Degas.

665a, l. 13. *The Mystake.* What Rossetti called P. J. Bailey's *The Mystic.*

665a, l. 21. *Oxford and Cambridge Magazine.* This magazine (published 1856) led to a friendship between Rossetti and Morris and Burne-Jones. See text p. 609. Of this magazine says Birkbeck Hill (pp. 175–8):

". . . The mention of this magazine brings back to my memory a little front parlour in a small lodging-house in Pembroke Street, Oxford, in which, in the Michaelmas term of 1855, I heard a knot of eager young men talk of the forthcoming first number. They were all my seniors in standing, some of them by two or three years. I was only in my second term. . . .

"I was introduced to this little fraternity by the future editor of the magazine, William Fulford, a poet of no mean power. It was, in fact, 'a nest of singing birds,' who, night after night, were found together in the close neighbourhood of Dr. Johnson's old college, often in the college itself. It was a new world into which I was brought. I knew nothing of art and nothing of Tennyson, Browning, and Ruskin. The subjects which I had always heard discussed were never discussed here, while matters on which I had never heard any one speak formed here the staple of the talk. I recall how, one evening, the nineteenth century was denounced for its utter want of poetry. This was more than I could bear, for the nineteenth century was almost an object of adoration in my father's house. I ventured to assert that it could boast, at all events, of one piece of poetry—the steam-engine. The roar of laughter which burst forth nearly overwhelmed me. The author of *The Earthly Paradise* almost overturned his chair as he flung himself backwards, overpowered with mirth. I was too much abashed to explain that I was recalling the sight I had once had of an engine rushing through the darkness along a high embankment, drawing after it a cloud of flame and fiery steam."

665a, l. 28. *Jones.* Better known as Burne-Jones.

665a, l. 34. *the Germ.* The magazine published by the P.R.B. in 1850. See text p. 608.

665a, l. 51. *Aurora Leigh.* By Mrs. Browning.

665b, l. 37. *capital tales.* Morris contributed prose romances such as *Golden Wings, The Hollow Land,* and *Gertha's Lovers* to the *Oxford and Cambridge Magazine.*

665b, l. 40. *The Chapel in Lyoness.* See text p. 980.

665b, l. 42. *Golden Wings.* A prose tale which appeared in the *Oxford and Cambridge Magazine*, December, 1856. The hoax was probably perpetrated by one of Morris's fellow editors instead of by the printer as Rossetti suggests. The simple insertion of the adjective "old" into a romantic story sent an elderly knight and lady through incidents unbecoming to their years of discretion with a ludicrous result.

Page 666.

666a, l. 8. *The Blue Closet.* See text p. 994.

666b, l. 17. *Spiritualism.* Browning hated to have his wife dabbling with the subject and Rossetti, although four or five years later he was inclined to believe, was at this time very skeptical. Hill (p. 204) gives an incident of these séances:

"Madox Brown wrote on April 9, 1868: 'Blank gave a spirit *soirée*, at which Rossetti attended, and flowers grew under Blank's hands out of the dining-table and eau de Cologne was squirted over the guests in the dark; but Gabriel, growing irreverent, and addressing the S.'s by the too familiar appellation of "Bogies," they squirted plain (it must be hoped *clean*) water over those present and withdrew. So the report runs—I was not there.'"

Page 667.

667a, l. 44. *The Bride's Chamber*. Published finally only in 1881 with the title *The Bride's Prelude*.

667b, l. 30. *Colney Hatch*. A lunatic asylum.

Page 668.

668a, l. 15. *Ours*, etc. The child was born dead.

668a, l. 50. *Topsy's house*. Morris's "Red House." See text p. 978.

668b, l. 1. *We are organising*, etc. Morris, Marshall, Faulkner and Co. See text p. 978.

668b, l. 40. [Ford] *Madox Brown* (1821–1893). Because of limited finances Brown's parents were living abroad at the time of his birth and much of his time in his youth and early manhood was spent on the continent. His father encouraged his artistic bent and gave him training at Bruges, Ghent and Antwerp. Brown was extremely precocious and had exhibited with some success at Ghent as early as 1837 and exhibited at the English Academy in 1841. It was to Brown that Rossetti turned for instruction when he sickened of the formal schools. (See text p. 607.) Brown was on affectionate terms with the Pre-Raphaelite Brotherhood but was never officially one of the group because he did not believe in coteries. Moreover his own style was already formulated while the rest were developing theirs and he disapproved of the minute realism of some of the early P.R.B. pictures. Later his own style was somewhat colored by that of his friends.

668b, l. 47. *Janey*. Jane Burden Morris.

Page 669.

669a, l. 15. *Tupper*. Martin Tupper, the author of *Proverbial Philosophy*. Rossetti in his sentiment on "Man, fattening" is Tupperizing in burlesque fashion.

669a, l. 48. *"funny."* The name given to a frail type of boat which capsizes very easily.

669b, l. 16. *the wretch Gambart*. Ernest Gambart, an art dealer, had commissioned a painting, paid for it in advance, and expected to get it.

669b, l. 26. *Charles Eliot Norton* (1827–1908). A famous American scholar, professor of the history of art at Harvard from 1875 to 1898. In his trips abroad he made the friendship of many distinguished men. Besides being the literary executor of such distinguished Americans as J. R. Lowell and Emerson, he acted in the same capacity for Carlyle and Ruskin—an evidence of the esteem in which he was held.

670b, l. 8. *Fields of Boston*. James T. Fields (1817–1881) of Ticknor and Fields, perhaps the most distinguished publishing house in America at the time. Among other properties this firm controlled the *Atlantic Monthly*.

670b, l. 24. *Gudrun*. In the cycle of poems which make up *The Earthly Paradise*, this is the second of the stories told in November.

670b, l. 46. *Stillman*. William James Stillman (1828–1901), an artist and journalist, and for many years an American consular official abroad. Among his friends he numbered Ruskin and the Brownings as well as Rossetti.

Page 671.

671a, l. 9. *F. S. Ellis*. Rossetti's publisher. This and the other letters to Ellis reprinted in the text are interesting as showing Rossetti's attention to details in connection with his forthcoming (1870) volume, particularly his arrangements to assure it—in advance, so far as that was possible—of a favorable press reception. Page 671a, ll. 31 et seq., although expressed in no very decorous imagery, show that Rossetti was expecting the attack from Buchanan which ultimately came in the article *The Fleshly School of Poetry*.

ALGERNON CHARLES SWINBURNE

BIBLIOGRAPHY

I. WORKS

Complete Works, ed. by Edmund Gosse and T. J. Wise. Bonchurch Edition. 20 vols. (Wells: New York, 1925–7.) The definitive edition, limited, containing all of Swinburne that can be published; the poetry is found in Vols. I–VI, dramas VII–X; Vol. XIX contains the revised Life by Gosse; Vol. XX has a complete bibliography, a revision of Wise's 1919–20 work.

Collected Poetical Works, 2 vols. (Heinemann: London, 1924.) A cheap compendious edition, recommended for introductory reading.

Poems, ed. by Ernest Rhys. (Boni: New York, 1925.) A good edition for classroom use; contains a brief preface by the editor.

Posthumous Poems, ed. by Edmund Gosse and T. J. Wise. (Lane: New York, 1918.) A collection of interest chiefly from the historical viewpoint; prefaced by a short critical sketch.

Selected Poems, ed. by W. M. Payne. (Heath: Boston, 1905.) An edition providing helpful notes and an introduction which is of much historical interest as an early American apology for the poet.

Selections, ed. by H. M. Burton. (Cambridge University Press: 1927.) Includes many of the less familiar pieces, the purpose of the edition being to demonstrate the poet's variable and erratic method; the introduction provides a beginner's approach.

Selected Poems, ed. by Humbert Wolfe. (Lane: London, 1928.) The interesting introduction sees the poet as a Victorian in spirit, not iconoclastic or sensual; illustrations by Harry Clarke.

"Hyperion" and Other Poems, ed. by Georges Lafourcade. (Faber: London, 1927.) The introductory essay on Swinburne and Keats explains the later poet's interest in Keats's fragment, which demonstrated the "Greek touch"—the faculty Swinburne attempted to cultivate in his unfinished juvenile poem.

"Atalanta in Calydon": A Facsimile of the First Edition. (Oxford University Press: 1930.) The preface by Georges Lafourcade undertakes the study of the composition and the history of the MS, and comments authoritatively on the poem itself, finding its interest largely historical.

Dramas, ed. by Arthur Beatty. (Crowell: New York, 1909.) An inexpensive collection, recommended for student use.

Letters, ed. by Thomas Hake and Arthur Compton-Rickett. (Murray: London, 1918.) Not included in the Bonchurch Edition; contains also some personal recollections of the poet. The letters to Watts-Dunton comprise the middle third of the volume.

Letters, ed. by Edmund Gosse and T. J. Wise. 2 vols. (Dodd: New York, 1919.) The best separate edition of the Letters.

II. BIOGRAPHY AND CRITICISM

Chew, S. C. *Swinburne*. (Little: Boston, 1929.) An enthusiastic re-appraisal of the man and the poet, providing a clear biographical narrative, with many critical comments on his work; ranks him first of the later Victorians.

Drinkwater, John. *Swinburne: An Estimate*. (Dent: London, 1924.) The most valuable chapters are "Lyric Technique" and "Lyric Thought," which praise the poet's skill in metric and combat the idea that he is lacking in thought.

Gosse, E. W. *The Life of Algernon Charles Swinburne*. (Macmillan: New York, 1917.) The standard Life "without rival in critical tact"; devotes little time to the last phase of the poet's life; sets highest the second series of *Poems and Ballads*.

Henderson, W. B. D. *Swinburne and Landor*. (Macmillan: London, 1918.) A study of much insight and subtlety: shows that Landor's influence was deeper than a merely literary one, determining the tone of Swinburne's thought and contributing to his inner development.

Hyder, C. K. *Swinburne's Literary Career and Fame*. (Duke University Press: 1933.) Concerned chiefly with the poet and the world of criticism, its effect upon him and his reaction to it; limits the study to England and America.

Kernahan, Coulson. *Swinburne As I Knew Him*. (Lane: London, 1919.) An interesting narrative of the last phase of the poet's life, recording many of his conversations; prefaced by four letters not included in the Bonchurch Edition.

Lafourcade, Georges. *Swinburne: A Literary Biography*. (Bell: London, 1932.) Brilliantly written and ably supported, this study presents Swinburne as the forerunner and example of modernism in literature, as it traces the man through the varied phases of his career.

Leith, Mrs. Disney. *Algernon Charles Swinburne*. (Putnam: New York, 1917.) An excellent résumé of the biographical facts by the poet's cousin, offering much first-hand material; touches mainly upon the period of his youth. Prints a number of letters not included in the Bonchurch Edition.

Nicolson, Harold. *Swinburne*. English Men of Letters series. (Macmillan: New York, 1926.) An interesting brief biography, tinged with mild satire, showing the effect upon Swinburne's poetry of his almost exclusively bookish contacts during his creative period.

Rutland, W. R. *Swinburne: A Nineteenth-Century Hellene*. (Blackwell: Oxford, 1931.) Offers fine analyses of *Atalanta* and *Erechtheus;* sees Swinburne as the genius of Attic drama, reincarnate in English letters.

Thomas, Edward. *Algernon Charles Swinburne: A Critical Study*. (Kennerley: New York, 1912.) Gives only conventional criticism, comments on the poet's mastery of rhythm, devotes much space to the aesthetic shortcomings of *Atalanta*.

Watts-Dunton, Mrs. Clara. *The Home Life of Swinburne*. (Philpot: London, 1922.) An intimate record of the last period of the poet's life,—kindly and amusing.

Welby, T. E. *A Study of Swinburne*. (Doran: New York, 1926.) A thoroughly reliable study, with much attention given to separate discussion of the major poems: freedom is seen as the poet's one prevailing passion. The fine concluding chapter is nearly the whole gospel on Swinburne.

Woodberry, G. E. *Swinburne*. (Macmillan: New York, 1912.) The first American book devoted to Swinburne: an eloquent appreciation of the poet's work, studying it as a development from passion to meditativeness.

Wratislaw, Theodore. *Algernon Charles Swinburne*. (Greening: London, 1900.) The first effort at a full-length biography, necessarily incomplete; desultory and undiscriminating on the critical side.

III. ARTICLES FROM BOOKS

Beerbohm, Max. "No. 2, The Pines: Reminiscences of Swinburne," in *And Even Now*. (Dutton: New York, 1921.) A chatty and capable review of various *personalia;* laughs off the critics' attack on Swinburne's hatred of the Boers.

Bennett, Arnold. "Swinburne," in *Books and Persons*. (Doran: New York, 1917.) Frankly accepts the sensuality of Swinburne's poetry and scoffs at his apologists who would dress him in saintly robes.

Brandes, Georg. "Algernon Charles Swinburne," in *Creative Spirits of the Nineteenth Century*. Trans. by R. B. Anderson. (Crowell: New York, 1923.) Considers Swinburne the greatest lyricist of the English-speaking world; finds his vigor and daring equal to Wagner's.

Carman, Bliss. "Mr. Swinburne's Poetry," in *The Poetry of Life*. (Page: Boston, 1905.) Maintains that the fascination of Swinburne does not endure because of his failure to appeal to our reason.

Clutton-Brock, Arthur. "Algernon Charles Swinburne," in *Essays on Books*. (Methuen: London, 1921.) Originally a review of Gosse's Life: calls the poet a "wonderful visitor," the more admirable because the more perverse.

Eliot, T. S. "Swinburne As Poet," in *The Sacred Wood*. (Methuen: London, 1920.) Names the poet's diffusiveness as "one of his glories," speaking of his language as vital in itself, independent of the world of objects.

Elton, Oliver. "Mr. Swinburne's Poems," in *Modern Studies*. (Arnold: London, 1907.) Singles out for praise *Songs Before Sunrise*, *Poems and Ballads* (second series), *Tristram*, and *The Tale of Balen*.

Gosse, E. W. "Swinburne," in *Portraits and Sketches*. (Heinemann: London, 1924.) Full of vivid reminiscence: describes many of the poet's personal traits, comments on his visits in France, remarks his passages with Browning.

Grierson, H. J. C. "Lord Byron: Arnold and Swinburne," in *The Background of English Literature*. (Chatto: London, 1925.) Recalls Swinburne's attack on Arnold's categorical statements in his preface to a selection of Byron's poetry; attempts to judge the whole issue dispassionately.

Hearn, Lafcadio. "Studies in Swinburne," in *Pre-Raphaelite and Other Poets*. (Dodd: New York, 1922.) Provides an easy approach to the poet, analyzing many of his lyrics; demonstrates his technical brilliance.

Kellett, E. E. "Swinburne," in *Reconsiderations*. (Cambridge University Press: 1928.) Insists that the poet is more than a master of sound; finds reasons for his unpopularity in his indifference to religion and patriotism.

Lucas, F. L. "Swinburne," in *Authors Dead and Living*. (Macmillan: New York, 1926.) The view of an uncompromising classicist: says of the poet "he is like the sea, but the sea within a cave, limited yet sublime in his energy."

Lucas, F. L. "Swinburne," in *Eight Victorian Poets*. (Cambridge University Press: 1930.) Remarks the poet's persistent spirit of revolt and of youth; ranks him with Byron as the apostle "of eloquence and of Liberty."

Lyall, A. C. "Characteristics of Mr. Swinburne's Poetry," in *Studies in Literature and History*. (Murray: London, 1915.) Grants the poet chief rank among the lyricists of the later nineteenth century.

Mackail, J. W. "Swinburne," in *Studies of English Poets*. (Longmans: New York, 1926.) Finds the best poetry in the 'sixties and 'seventies; comments upon the poet's interest in Greece and contemporary Italy; names him "the last of the great Victorian poets."

Marks, Jeanette. "Stigmata," in *Genius and Disaster*. (Adelphi Press: New York, 1925.) Shows a curious perversion of criticism: explains the poet in terms of microbes.

More, P. E. "Swinburne," in *Shelburne Essays*, Third Series. (Putnam: New York, 1905.) An unsympathetic review of the decadent element in the poet's work; at some length laments his wordiness and unrestraint.

Noyes, Alfred. "Swinburne's Tragedies," in *Some Aspects of Modern Poetry*. (Stokes: New York, 1924.) Enthusiastically calls our attention to the "welded line" and the dramatic power of *Chastelard* and *Bothwell;* remarks *Marino Faliero* as the best of the later plays.

Quiller-Couch, A. T. "Mr. Swinburne's Later Manner," in *Adventures in Criticism*. (Cassell: London, 1896.) Acclaiming the poet as "a god-like voice chanting in the void," shows how his development has discouraged would-be imitators.

Quiller-Couch, A. T. "Swinburne," in *Studies in Literature*, First Series. (Putnam: New York, 1918.) Recalls the sensation created by *Poems and Ballads;* comments on Gosse's Life, reviewing a number of biographical details.

Saintsbury, George. "Mr. Swinburne," in *Corrected Impressions*. (Dodd: New York, 1895.) Comments on the reception of *Poems and Ballads;* praises the speed of the poet's lines and his great metrical versatility.

Symons, Arthur. "Algernon Charles Swinburne," in *Figures of Several Centuries*. (Dutton: New York, 1916.) Reviews the poet's estimates of his own work; analyzes a number of poems in the 1904 volume, holding that the poet will be popular only among those who love poetry for its own sake.

Thomas, Edward. "Swinburne," in *A Literary Pilgrim in England*. (Dodd: New York, 1917.) Offers some interesting biographical data and valuable literary comment.

Thompson, A. H. "The Rossettis, William Morris, and Swinburne," in *The Cambridge History of English Literature*, XIII. (Putnam: New York, 1917.) Recalls the effect of *Poems and Ballads;* selects as best *Tristram of Lyonesse;* remarks a decline in Swinburne's later volumes.

Welby, T. E. "Swinburne," in *The Victorian Romantics, 1850–1870*. (Howe: London, 1929.) Many scattered references point out Swinburne's contribution to the movement, but his work is seen as chiefly valuable for its own sake.

Woodberry, G. E. "Swinburne," in *Literary Essays*. (Harcourt: New York, 1920.) Lauds the poet's passion for liberty; remarks his continental enthusiasms, particularly for Hugo; sets highest his lyrical quality, his rendering of the experience of passion, and his concept of faith and nature.

IV. ARTICLES FROM PERIODICALS

Bailey, John. "Swinburne," *Quarterly Review*, CCXXVIII, 228–48 (July, 1917). Rebukes the assertion in Gosse's Life that Swinburne had no real interest in Italian politics; warmly praises his language and melody.

Barlow, George. "The Spiritual Side of Mr. Swinburne's Genius," *Contemporary Review*, LXXXVIII, 231–50 (Aug., 1905). A curious example of many favorable reviews of the period; Swinburne is regarded as "one of the world's very great spiritual poets"; "soul-passion" is read into *Tristram*.

Gosse, E. W. "Swinburne's Unpublished Writings," *Fortnightly Review*, CII, 255–67 (Aug., 1914). Describes a part of the valuable Wise collection: *Ode to Mazzini*, *In the Twilight*,

Border Ballads, The Triameron, The Chronicle of Queen Fredegond, etc.

Hyder, C. K. "Swinburne's *Laus Veneris,*" *Publications of the Modern Language Association,* XLV, 1202–13 (Dec., 1930). Traces the source of the poem to a German ballad which appeared in *Once A Week,* August 17, 1861, containing the medieval legend.

Hyder, C. K. "Swinburne and the Popular Ballad," *Publications of the Modern Language Association,* XLIX, 295–309 (March, 1934). Follows the ballad through Swinburne's poetry from 1866 forward; analyzes themes and characteristics, noting the poet's infusion of a philosophic note.

Jones, G. A. "Notes on Swinburne's *Song of Italy,*" *Modern Language Notes,* XXXII, 200–7 (April, 1917). Establishes the fact that Swinburne's interest in Italian affairs went deeper than a mere revolutionary enthusiasm; provides historical notes on many lines of the poem.

LeGallienne, Richard. "Swinburne's Poetry," *North American Review,* CLXXXIII, 792–5 (Oct., 1906). Defends Swinburne against being caricatured as the poet of lust; names *Tristram* the greatest love-poem in the language.

Morley, John. "Mr. Swinburne's New Poems," *Living Age,* CCCXXIX, 587–92 (June, 1926). Reprints the anonymous article which (August 4, 1866) severely reviewed Swinburne's *Poems and Ballads,* causing Moxon, the publisher, to withdraw the book from sale.

Peck, H. T. "Swinburne and the Swinburnians," *Bookman,* XXIX, 374–84 (June, 1909). Discusses the poet as a rebel against convention; points out his influence upon his contemporaries, granting that he will be appreciated by only a few.

Watts-Dunton, Mrs. Clara. "My Recollections of Swinburne," *Nineteenth Century,* XC, 219–29; 438–47 (Aug., Sept., 1921). A fascinating account of Swinburne the man as the writer knew him; later incorporated into her book, *The Home Life of Swinburne.*

Waugh, Arthur. "The Swinburne Letters and Our Debt to the Victorian Era," *Nineteenth Century,* LXXXIV, 1021–34 (Dec., 1918). One of the best reviews of the Hake and Compton-Rickett collection of the poet's Letters.

NOTES

Page 679. A SONG IN TIME OF ORDER, 1852

In 1852, the year Napoleon III mounted the throne of France, the forces of tyranny and repression restored "order" in Europe by suppressing revolutionary republicanism. Republicans were in despair, and in this poem Swinburne sings the defiant song of three of them who are leaving an oppressed Europe behind and seeking on the sea the liberty they love.

38. *a Pope.* A reference to Pius IX, who was driven from Rome by Garibaldi. He was restored by French troops in 1849.

39. *Buonaparte.* Louis Buonaparte, i.e., Napoleon III.

50. *From Cayenne to the Austrian whips.* Cayenne is the capital of French Guiana, to which country political prisoners were banished. *Austrian whips* is an allusion to the Austrian oppression of Italy.

FAUSTINE

In *Notes on Poems and Reviews* Swinburne writes as follows of the origin and meaning of this poem:

". . . 'Faustine' is the reverie of a man gazing on the bitter and vicious loveliness of a face as common and as cheap as the morality of reviewers, and dreaming of past lives in which this fair face may have held a nobler or fitter station; the imperial profile may have been Faustina's, the thirsty lips a Mænad's, when first she learnt to drink blood or wine, to waste the loves and ruin the lives of men; through Greece and again through Rome she may have passed with the same face which now comes before us dishonoured and discrowned. Whatever of merit or demerit there may be in the verses, the idea that gives them such life as they have is simple enough; the transmigration of a single soul, doomed as though by accident from the first to all evil and no good, through many ages and forms, but clad always in the same type of fleshly beauty. The chance which suggested to me this poem was one which may happen any day to any man—the sudden sight of a living face which recalled the well-known likeness of another dead for centuries: in this instance, the noble and faultless type of the elder Faustina, as seen in coin and bust. Out of that casual glimpse and sudden recollection these verses sprang and grew."

Ruskin said of this poem, "[It makes me] all hot, like pies with the Devil's fingers in them." And again, "It's glorious!"

The salutation to Faustine, the empress—"Ave Faustina . . . salutant"—was suggested to the poet by the traditional words spoken by the Roman gladiators as they were about to engage in mortal combat: "Hail Caesar, Emperor! those about to die, salute thee."

49–50. *cast seven devils out Of Magdalene.* See Luke 8 : 2: " . . . Mary called Magdalene, out of whom went seven devils."

57. *I know what queen at first you were.* This is a reference to the "elder Faustina" mentioned in Swinburne's note above. She was the notorious wife of Antoninus Pius, Roman emperor (138–161 A.D.). When Swinburne speaks of her "as seen in coin and bust," he probably has in mind a bust of her that is in the Vatican. Her daughter, Faustina the younger, was the wife of Marcus Aurelius, Roman emperor (161–180)

and philosopher. She was even more notorious than her mother.

90. *teen.* Grief, sorrow.

99. *Bacchanal.* A devotee of Bacchus.

100. *The first Faustine.* Cf. Swinburne's comment on the idea of transmigration of souls in the introductory note above.

117. *Sapphic song.* A reference to Sappho, the celebrated lyric poetess of Mitylene. See note to *Sapphics*, below.

130. *epicene.* Common to both sexes.

146. *Lampsacene.* Priapus, god of the creative power of man, beast, and plant. He was worshipped with wanton and lascivious ceremonials at Lampsacus, a city in Asia Minor.

Page 681. *From* ATALANTA IN CALYDON

Swinburne said that his purpose in *Atalanta in Calydon* was "to do something original in English which might in some degree reproduce for English readers the likeness of a Greek tragedy, with possibly something more of its true poetic life and charm than could have been expected from the authors of *Caractacus* [W. Mason] and *Merope* [Matthew Arnold]." See letters IV (text p. 793), XV (p. 799), and XXIX (p. 806). The argument with which he introduced the tragedy was as follows:

"Althæa, daughter of Thestius and Eurythemis, queen of Calydon, being with child of Meleager her first-born son, dreamed that she brought forth a brand burning; and upon his birth came the three Fates and prophesied of him three things, namely these; that he should have great strength of his hands, and good fortune in this life, and that he should live no longer when the brand then in the fire were consumed: wherefore his mother plucked it forth and kept it by her. And the child being a man grown sailed with Jason after the fleece of gold, and won himself great praise of all men living; and when the tribes of the north and west made war upon Ætolia, he fought against their army and scattered it. But Artemis, having at the first stirred up these tribes to war against Œneus king of Calydon, because he had offered sacrifice to all the gods saving her alone, but her he had forgotten to honour, was yet more wroth because of the destruction of this army, and sent upon the land of Calydon a wild boar which slew many and wasted all their increase, but him could none slay, and many went against him and perished. Then were all the chief men of Greece gathered together, and among them Atalanta daughter of Iasius the Arcadian, a virgin; for whose sake Artemis let slay the boar, seeing she favoured the maiden greatly; and Meleager having despatched it gave the spoil thereof to Atalanta, as one beyond measure enamoured of her; but the brethren of Althæa his mother, Toxeus and Plexippus, with such others as misliked that she only should bear off the praise whereas many had borne the labour, laid wait for her to take away her spoil; but Meleager fought against them and slew them; whom when Althæa their sister beheld and knew to be slain of her son, she waxed for wrath and sorrow like as one mad, and taking the brand whereby the measure of her son's life was meted to him, she cast it upon a fire; and with the wasting thereof his life likewise wasted away, that being brought back to his father's house he died in a brief space; and his mother also endured not long after for very sorrow; and this was his end, and the end of that hunting."

The tragedy opens with a prologue spoken by the Chief Huntsman in the presence of the Greek heroes and huntsmen who have gathered for the chase and who are awaiting the rising sun. Beginning with an invocation to Aurora, "Maiden, and mistress of the months and stars," the voice of the Huntsman rises, with the growing light, into a prayer to Apollo and a plea to Artemis that they may aid in the slaying of the Calydonian boar.

WHEN THE HOUNDS OF SPRING

Commenting upon the presentation of this chorus invocation to Artemis, Mr. Harold Nicolson says: "With the concluding lines of the Prologue, the Chorus of fifteen Ætolian virgins advance slowly for . . . [the first song of the chorus as a whole], bearing wreaths of flowers for the altar of Artemis, and as the Chief Huntsman closes his monologue, they slide gently into the famous processional anapaests, pacing [in] rhythmic movement . . . while the dawn breaks slowly over Calydon." (*Swinburne*, p. 77.)

2. *mother of months.* Artemis, goddess of the moon. In the fourth act of *Prometheus Unbound* Shelley speaks of the moon as "the mother of the months."

6. *Itylus.* See note to Arnold's *Philomela*, above, and to *Itylus*, below.

28. *The light that loses, the night that wins.* In winter the days grow shorter and the nights longer.

38. *oat.* The shepherd's pipe of oaten straw.

39. *satyr.* A sylvan deity or demigod, often represented with the tail and ears of a horse or goat and given to merriment and lasciviousness.

41. *Pan . . . Bacchus.* Pan is a god of flocks and pastures, of forests and their wild life. Bacchus is the god of wine. See note to *A Nympholept*, below.

44. *Mænad . . . Bassarid.* A mænad was a female worshipper of Bacchus, in worshipping whom she engaged in wild orgies. A Bassarid was a Thracian mænad or worshipper of Bacchus.

47–8. *And screen . . . maiden hid. Screen* refers to the *maiden hid,* and *leave in sight* to *the god pursuing.*

Page 682. BEFORE THE BEGINNING OF YEARS

The theme of this chorus, which follows Althæa's plaint against the cruel Artemis, who in her final act of revenge caused Meleager to fall in love with Atalanta, is "the making of man." Its philosophy is the philosophy of despair. Man is the victim, the sport, of the gods.

3–4. *Time, with a gift . . . glass that ran.* Ascribing tears to Time and a glass to Grief is an unusual inversion of attributes. It is a rather startling example of antithesis and paradox, perhaps, as one critic suggests, Swinburne's expression of "his sense of the identity that may underlie formal distinction."

WE HAVE SEEN THEE, O LOVE

The ten lines of this poem introduce a chorus on the coming of Love in the form of Venus.

1–2. *We have seen thee . . . the wings of a dove.* Cf. Song of Solomon, 4 : 1—"Behold, thou art fair, my love; behold, thou art fair; thou hast doves' eyes within thy locks."

10. *Fate is the name of her; and his name is Death.* "The curse of Venus." The coming of Love brings tragedy and Death—which is illustrated in the play itself.

Page 683. NOT AS WITH SUNDERING OF THE EARTH

This chorus on the suddenness of fate is sung after Althæa, having learned that her son has slain her two brothers in a quarrel over the division of the spoils, "like as one mad," goes to burn the brand "whereby the measure of her son's life was meted to him."

THE DEATH OF MELEAGER

Mr. Harold Nicolson calls this "final Kommos [a lament sung in parts alternating between the chief actor and actors and the chorus] the most memorable and exquisitely symphonic achievement of all Swinburne's poetry." (*Swinburne*, p. 85.)

20. *Arcadia.* A mountainous and picturesque region in the heart of Greece.

Calydon. A city of Ætolia, Greece, with the district surrounding it.

95. *From the Acroceraunian snow to the ford of the fleece of gold.* The Acroceraunian mountains are in Epirus, northwestern Greece. The ford of the fleece of gold is the Hellespont, so called because Helle fell off the ram of the golden fleece into the strait and was drowned.

99. *Chersonese.* A region north of the Hellespont, now known as Gallipoli.

100. *Bosphorus.* A strait connecting the Black or Pontic Sea with the Sea of Marmora.

115. *narrowing Symplegades.* A reference to the two rocks at the entrance of the Black Sea, which dashed together at intervals but became fixed when the ship Argo passed between them.

Propontis. The Sea of Marmora.

125. *Helle.* The Hellespont. See note to line 95.

Page 686. A BALLAD OF LIFE

This ballad and *A Ballad of Death* (p. 687) are good examples of the early work of Swinburne as it was influenced by Pre-Raphaelitism. Love of sensuous beauty, an attitude of ecstasy, ornateness of style, chaste intensity, elaborate personification, vague symbolism—all these show the Pre-Raphaelite influence.

William Michael Rossetti said of these poems: "[They] are Italian canzoni of the exactest type, such as Dante, Cavalcanti, Petrarca, and the other medieval, with many modern, poets of Italy have written; more especially taking the tinge which works of this class have assumed in Mr. Dante G. Rossetti's volume of translations, *The Early Italian Poets.*"

76. *Borgia.* Lucrezia Borgia (1480–1519), Duchess of Ferrara. She was a daughter of Pope Alexander VI and sister of Cesare Borgia. A woman of great beauty and a patroness of learning and the arts, she was nevertheless notorious for her wickedness and crimes. Cf. letter to Paulina, Lady Trevelyan, text p. 791a, ll. 22–5.

Page 687. A BALLAD OF DEATH

See introductory note to *A Ballad of Life,* above.

10. *gorget.* An ornamental band for the neck.

11–12. *O Love's lute . . . therein.* Cf. the Church of England prayer book version of Psalm 137 : 2.

19. *kisses . . . wine.* Cf. Song of Solomon, 1 : 2: "Let him kiss me with the kisses of his mouth; for thy love is better than wine."

41. *sendaline.* A silken fabric used for garments in the Middle Ages. Written also *sendal* and *cendal.*

Page 688. LAUS VENERIS

In the *Notes on Poems and Reviews* Swinburne wrote as follows of this poem, the title of which means "Praise of Venus":

"To me it seemed that the tragedy began with the knight's return to Venus—began at the point where hitherto it had seemed to leave off. The immortal agony of a man lost after all repentance—cast down from fearful hope into fearless despair—believing in Christ and bound to Venus—desirous of penitential pain, and damned to joyless pleasure—this, in my eyes, was the kernel and nucleus of a myth comparable only to that of the foolish virgins and bearing the same burden. The tragic touch of the story is this: that the knight who has renounced Christ believes in him; the lover who has embraced Venus disbelieves in her. Vainly and in despair he would make the best of that which is the worst—vainly remonstrate with God, and argue on the side he would fain desert. Once accept or admit the least admixture of pagan worship, or of modern thought, and the whole story collapses into froth and smoke. It was not till my poem was completed that I received from the hands of its author the admirable pamphlet of Charles Baudelaire on Wagner's 'Tannhäuser.' If anyone desires to see, expressed in better words than I can command, the conception of the mediaeval Venus which it was my aim to put into verse, let him turn to the magnificent passage in which M. Baudelaire describes the fallen goddess, grown diabolic among ages that would not accept her as divine. In another point, as I then found, I concur with the great musician and his great panegyrist. I have made Venus the one love of her knight's whole life, as Mary Stuart of Chastelard's; I have sent him, poet and soldier, fresh to her fierce embrace. Thus only both legend and symbol appear to me noble and significant. Light loves and harmless errors must not touch the elect of heaven or of hell. The queen of evil, the lady of lust, will endure no rival but God; and when the vicar of God rejects him, to her only can he return to abide the day of his judgment in weariness and sorrow and fear."

The stanza of the poem was adapted from the stanza pattern of the *Rubáiyát* (text p. 903), a poem of which Swinburne wrote that he was one of its "earliest English admirers." See the letter (XXVII) to Clement K. Shorter, text p. 805. The reader should note that the third lines of the first and second stanzas rhyme, as do those of the third and fourth, the fifth and sixth, and so on.

25. *Horsel*. According to medieval story the Court of Venus was held in the caverns of the Horselberg, the Mountain of Venus, in central Germany. In medieval legend she enticed persons into these caverns, and by music, revelry, and sensuous pleasure kept them from returning. The theme of Wagner's opera *Tannhäuser* centers about the entrance of the German knight, Tannhäuser, into the enchanted cavern of the Venusberg (symbolic of sensual passion).

133. *Adonis*. A beautiful youth, beloved by Venus. He was killed by a wild boar, and so great was the grief of Venus that the gods required him to spend only half (one-third, some versions of the story say) of the year in Hades.

172. *Nathless*. Nevertheless.

173–96. *Sin, is it sin . . . on her the fire of hell.* These lines may be quoted as evidence of the reasonableness of an article in the *Examiner* of September 22, 1866, which declared, Mr. Samuel Chew says, that Swinburne "in his treatment of lascivious subjects subordinated the 'animalism' of the theme to an emphasis upon the nemesis which pursues those who submit themselves to lust." Commenting upon this article, Mr. Chew points out that the poet sometimes shocked and scandalized deliberately, but insists that in *Laus Veneris*, *Dolores*, and in other poems "there is discoverable, implicit if not explicit, Dante's lesson [*Inferno*, V, 37–9]:

'Intesi ch' a così fatto tormento
ènno dannati i peccator carnali,
che la ragion sommettono al talento.'"

("I understood that to this torment sad
The carnal sinners are condemned, in whom
Reason by lust is swayed."—Carey.)

186. *The ladies that were queens*. Such ladies as Helen of Troy and Cleopatra.

191–2. *Trodden as grapes . . . by the fiery feet.* Cf. Isaiah 63 : 2–3.

197. *lote-leaf*. Lotus leaf. See Tennyson's *The Lotos-Eaters* (text p. 22).

198. *The queen*. Cleopatra.

200. *Semiramis*. A mythical Assyrian queen, noted for her beauty, wisdom, and voluptuousness, and reputed to have been the builder of Babylon.

210. *blinkard*. Weak-eyed, stupid.

252. *teen*. Grief.

267. The word *slot* refers to the track or trail of an animal, which may be followed by scent or by print.

271–2. *springe . . . gin's grip*. A springe and a gin are traps or devices for catching game.

278. *vair*. The skin of a species of squirrel, once used as fur for the dresses of kings, nobles, and prelates.

283. *Magdalen*. See Luke 7 : 37–8.

352. *sweet-souled father*. Urban IV, who was Pope from 1261 to 1264.

355–6. *The spot . . . bleached with it.* Cf. Jeremiah 13 : 23: "Can the Ethiopian change his skin, or the leopard his spots?"

390. *she came out of the naked sea*. According to tradition Venus, whose Greek name is Aphrodite, meaning *foam-born*, rose from the sea.

424. *thunder of the trumpets*. The sounding of the trumpet on the Day of Judgment.

Explicit Laus Veneris. "Here ends the Praise of Venus."

Page 694. THE TRIUMPH OF TIME

This, "the most enduring of all Swinburne's single lyrics," arose out of the refusal of Miss Jane Faulkner, the "graceful and vivacious" niece and adopted daughter of Sir John Simon, to marry him. This young woman, Sir Edmund Gosse writes, gave the poet roses and "played and sang to him." He believed that she was in love with him—he called her his "sweet one love"—and made her a sudden and ardent offer of marriage. Shaken by the violence of the poet's declaration, Miss Faulkner laughed in his face. Grieved and angered, the rejected lover wrote this poem of his soul that for a time must walk "in a bleak blown space," but that in the end will go "back to the great sweet mother, Mother and lover of men, the sea." Swinburne said that this poem, *Dolores* (p. 707), and *The Garden of Proserpine* (p. 715) were biographical "beyond the rest." See note to *The Garden of Proserpine*, below.

65. *Mother of loves*. The sea.

83. *the great third wave*. The third wave, in the popular mind, was thought to be higher and more powerful than the two preceding it.

101–4. In the original draft of the poem these lines were:

But now you are cloven in twain, rent,
Flesh of his flesh, but heart of my heart,
And deep in me is the bitter root
And sweet for him is the lifelong flower.

Very little is known of Miss Faulkner. "Imagination," one writer says, "is left with nothing but her pet name—Boo—to play with." It is not even known whether or not the lady married, but certainly the implication of these lines is that she rejected Swinburne for another lover.

156. *the fates are three*. In Greek mythology Clotho spins the thread of life, Lachesis determines its length, Atropos cuts it off.

253. *swords . . . seven*. See l. 52 of Browning's *Up at a Villa—Down in the City*, text p. 265, and note to Rossetti's *Mary's Girlhood*, sonnet 2, above.

321. *singer . . . old*. A reference to the story of the love of Jaufre (Geoffrey) Rudel, a Provençal poet of the 12th century and a prince of Blaya, for the Countess of Tripoli. The poet, who had heard of the beauty of the Countess, set out for Tripoli to see her. He arrived mortally ill and died in the arms of the Countess.

Page 699. A LEAVE-TAKING

This is another of the poems inspired by the unhappy outcome of the author's love for Miss Jane Faulkner, his "sweet one love." See note to *The Triumph of Time*, above.

Page 700. ITYLUS

The version of the Procne-Philomela story used by Swinburne in this poem differs in one respect from that used by Arnold in *Philomela*. In Swinburne's version it is Philomela whose tongue is cut out, Tereus having done this in order to keep her from informing Procne that he had ravished her. It is Philomela therefore who weaves the tapestry in *Itylus*. In each version Tereus greatly wrongs one of the sisters, sister goes to the aid of sister, Itylus is slain and served to his father as food, and the fleeing sisters are changed into birds.

Swinburne tells us that he composed this lyric in a garden in Fiesole, "while the air was full of the songs of nightingales."

48. *The feast of Daulis*. The feast at which Tereus ate of the flesh of his son Itylus (see note to Arnold's *Philomela*, above). Daulis, a town of Phocis, near Delphi (but not near the Thracian sea), was the capital of the monarchy of Tereus.

52. *The woven web*. A reference to the weaving of her story into a piece of cloth by Philomela.

Page 701. HYMN TO PROSERPINE

"The Heraclitean doctrine that all things are in flux and that nothing remains . . . is at the foundation of such philosophy as is discoverable in [Swinburne's] 'Poems and Ballads'; and it is best set forth in the dramatic monologue of the 'Hymn to Proserpine,' sung by an Epicurean after the proclamation of Christianity at Rome. Proserpina is the goddess of Change; she has overcome Olympus; in the end she will conquer Christianity." (Samuel C. Chew, *Swinburne*, pp. 94–5.)

The Edict of Milan, a proclamation by the Emperor Constantine in 313 recognizing Christianity, marked the passing of paganism and the triumph of the new faith. In the reign of Julian (331–363) paganism regained something of what it had lost, but (according to tradition) the dying words of Julian, who had renounced Christianity were these which Swinburne uses as the motto of the poem: "Vicisti, Galilæe"—"Thou hast conquered, Galilean."

The spirit of new paganism voiced by the epicurean singer of the hymn is in harmony with Swinburne's own thought and philosophy. He called this poem and the *Hymn of Man* (p. 742) "the deathsong of spiritual decadence and the birthsong of spiritual renascence." See letter to Paulina, Lady Trevelyan (text p. 794).

2. *Goddess and maiden and queen*. Proserpine was the wife of Pluto and queen of the lower world. She is called *maiden* because Pluto stole her from her mother—Ceres—when she was a young girl and took her to his dominions.

5. *feet of the dove*. The dove was sacred to Venus.

9. *the bays*. The poet's crown of laurel leaves.

24. *The laurel, the palms*. These were sacred to the gods.

36. *things Lethean*. Things that cause forgetfulness, as the waters of the river Lethe were said to do.

43–4. *O lips . . . gibbeted Gods*. One evidence

of the ascetic spirit of the early Christians was their veneration of martyred saints. Racks and rods are suggestive both of the persecution of early Christians and of their self-inflicted torture.

46. *the end.* The ages to come. The singer describes his vision of the coming ages by comparing life to a boundless ocean, where "the wave of the world" rolls "under the whitening wind of the future" (l. 54).

73. *Cytherean.* Venus (Aphrodite); see ll. 85–7.

75. *Of the maiden thy mother.* The Virgin Mary.

80. *mother of Rome.* Aphrodite.

91. *I turn to her.* I.e., to Proserpine.

97. *poppies.* The poppy, sacred to Proserpine, queen of the lower world, is the flower of sleep, of oblivion.

108. *A little soul.* The line from Epictetus from which this is adapted is, "Thou art a little soul bearing up a corpse."

Page 703. ILICET

The Latin title means "Have done," "All is over." It implies that death is the end of all consciousness—no more joy or sorrow, no more pleasure or pain, no more tears or laughter. There is no hope that the dust that has gone down into the grave shall ever live again; death is "An end, an end, an end of all" (l. 42).

6. *the poppied sleep.* See note on l. 97 of *Hymn to Proserpine*, above.

Page 705. A MATCH

This beautiful lyric was suggested to Swinburne by an Old French love song, *Les Transformations*. He had both a scholar's and a poet's interest in the work of the older French writers, and several of his pieces owe their inspiration to this interest.

A Match has been more often parodied than any other of Swinburne's poems except *Dolores* (p. 707). The parodist who uses his art upon such a charming melody as *A Match* may be justly accused of lacking in finer feeling, but not even the most jealous lover of the poem can fail to catch the spirit of fun—and truth—in such lines as Tom Hood the Younger's—

If you were but a jingle,
And I were but a rhyme,
We'd keep this up for ever,
Nor think it very clever
A grain of sense to mingle
At times with simple chime;
If you were but a jingle,
And I were but a rhyme.

And again those of Mortimer Collins:

If wit were always radiant,
And wine were always iced,
And bores were kicked out straightway
Through a convenient gateway;
Then down the years' long gradient
'Twere sad to be enticed,
If wit were always radiant,
And wine were always iced.

A BALLAD OF BURDENS

The transience of beauty, the inconstancy of love, the vanity of all sensuous pleasures—even of the *innocent* delights of man—these are the theme of this ballad. In the very midst of the joy awakened by beauty, by love, by all delights, forebodings of the last hour "shod with fire from hell," are inescapable.

Page 707. IN MEMORY OF WALTER SAVAGE LANDOR

Swinburne was both a strong hater and an extravagant hero-worshipper. Stinging words for those who had offended him are frequent in his letters, and he has several times confessed his hero-worship, once in these words: "I feel my betters in my blood; they send a heat and sting all through one at first sight. And the delight of feeling small and giving in when one does get sight of them is beyond words." For Landor he felt extreme adoration.

See the following letters: to Lord Houghton, text p. 791; to Paulina, Lady Trevelyan, p. 793; to E. C. Stedman, p. 795; to Edmund Gosse, pp. 797 and 800.

1. *the flower-town.* Florence, Italy, where Landor died at the age of eighty-nine in 1864.

4. *Freedom and spring.* Both Landor and Swinburne were very deeply interested in Italy's struggle for freedom from Austria. Florence became the capital of united Italy in 1865.

21. *I came.* In the spring of 1864 Swinburne visited Landor at Florence, and by his bowing and uncontrolled hand-kissing so embarrassed and overwhelmed the old poet that he was asked to leave at once. Swinburne wrote an apology, which brought him a second invitation. The second invitation resulted in a pleasant and satisfactory interview between the two poets.

DOLORES

"I have striven here to express that transient state of spirit through which a man may be supposed to pass, foiled in love and weary of loving, but not yet in sight of rest; seeking refuge in those 'violent delights' which 'have violent ends,' in fierce and frank sensualities which at least profess to be no more than they are. This poem, like *Faustine*, is so distinctly symbolic and fanciful that it cannot justly be amenable to judgment as a study in the school of realism. The spirit, bowed and discolored by suffering and by passion (which are indeed the same thing and the same word), plays for awhile with its pleasures and its pains, mixes and distorts them with a sense half-humorous and half-mournful, exults in bitter and doubtful emotions:

Moods of fantastic sadness, nothing worth.

It sports with sorrow, and jests against itself; cries out for freedom and confesses the chain; decorates with the name of goddess, crowns anew as the mystical Cotytto, some woman, real or ideal, in whom the pride of life with its companion lusts is incarnate. In her lover's half-shut eyes, her fierce unchaste beauty is transfigured, her cruel sensual eyes have a meaning and a message; there are memories and secrets in the kisses of her lips. She is the darker Venus, fed with burnt-offering and blood-sacrifice; the veiled image of that pleasure which men impelled by satiety and perverted by power have sought through ways as strange as Nero's before and since his time; the daughter of lust and death, and holding of both her parents; Our Lady of Pain, antagonist alike of trivial sins and virtues: no Virgin, and unblessed of men; no mother of the Gods or God; no Cybele, served by sexless priests or monks, adored of Origen or Atys; no likeness of her in Dindymus or Loreto." (Swinburne in *Notes on Poems and Reviews*, in Vol. 16 of the *Complete Works*, pp. 360–1.)

Swinburne's contention that Dolores, which he referred to as a "perennial and poisonous fountain," is "merely the first of a sedate trilogy," is unconvincing. He is more reasonable when he says that poems like *Dolores* were written as "a protest against the idyllic and tender optimism of Tennyson." "On such grounds," Mr. Harold Nicolson says, "it is possible to base a defense, which gives them not merely an intellectual reason for existence, but an actual coherence and meaning." (*Swinburne*, p. 106.) See note to illustration of p. 709 in text p. 1133. See also note to *The Garden of Proserpine*, below.

Notre-Dame des Sept Douleurs. Our Lady of the Seven Sorrows.

9. *Seven sorrows . . . Virgin*. See note to Rossetti's sonnet, *Mary's Girlhood*, above. The good people, Swinburne's contemporaries, were shocked by the poet's shameless contrasting of Mary the Madonna with Dolores the anti-Madonna. In *Laus Veneris* and in the *Hymn to Proserpine* he contrasts Mary with Venus.

19. *O tower not of ivory*. Cf. Song of Solomon 7:4.

51. *Libitina . . . Priapus*. Libitina (the Tuscan) was an ancient Italian goddess of death or burial. At her temple in Rome all essentials for burial were kept and a coin was deposited for every person who died. This conception of her led to her identification with Proserpina, goddess of death, but also goddess of gardens, fertility, vegetation. As "Venus Libitina," Libitina was associated with wanton pleasure. Priapus, a Greek deity, son of Dionysus and Aphrodite, was the god of husbandry and fertility. He was worshipped with voluptuous rites.

175–6. *cypress . . . death*. In making cypress the emblem of love and myrtle that of death Swinburne reverses the tradition. See note to ll. 3–4 of *Before the Beginning of Years*, above.

223. *Thalassian*. Venus. The word, which means "born of the sea," suggests the story of Venus's rising from ocean foam.

228. *The children of change*. The early Christians.

229. *the blood of thy foemen*. A reference to the persecution of the Christians by the Roman emperors, who were, of course, pagans, believers in Venus.

230. *A sand*. The arena of the Coliseum, where great spectacles were made out of the persecutions of the Christians.

231. *As one smote them*. The Emperor Nero.

244. *limbs too delicious for death*. Probably a reference to the imperial torturings of women and children for their Christian faith.

245. *thy gardens . . . live torches*. Tacitus writes that under Nero Christians "were set fire to, and when day declined were burned to serve for nocturnal lights."

249–56. *with flame all around . . . a thunder of lyres*. An allusion to the traditional story that Nero played upon the harp and sang while Rome was burning.

265–80. It is such passages as these two stanzas that led Mr. Harold Nicolson to speak of the "sadistic jingle of *Dolores*" and to quote Landor's words—"From the mysteries of religion the veil is seldom to be drawn, from the mysteries of love never. For this offense the gods take away from us our freshness of heart and our susceptibilities of pure delight." Mr. Nicolson points out that the poems which deal with "the supreme crises of physical sensation" "become inevitably but fugitive things not good to treasure." This he believes to be "true of all poetry which deals exclusively with sensuality"; and he charges "the seventeen studies of highly specialized sexual stimulation . . . among [Swinburne's] Poems and Ballads" (one of which is *Dolores*) with possessing "the additional defect of being based on an experience which is not only transitory but also eccentric." (Nicolson's *Swinburne*, p. 105).

281. *All shrines that were Vestal are flameless*. Six "Vestal Virgins" kept the fire of Vesta, Roman goddess of the hearth and home, always burning.

299. *Alciphron once or Arisbe*. Alciphron was a Greek rhetorician of the second century A.D. He was the author of letters supposed to have been written by celebrated courtesans. Arisbe, in Greek legend, was the wife of Priam of Troy.

Just what significance for the poem Swinburne found in the names is not clear.

303. *the garden god.* Priapus, wooden images of whom were placed in Roman gardens. He was armed with a club and a sickle and was thought to be watching for thieves.

307. *the pearl of his oyster.* An allusion to the cult of Priapus at Lampsacus in Asia Minor.

311. *thy father.* Priapus; see note to l. 51, above.

326. *Ipsithilla.* In *Carmina 32* Catullus sings of a lover, Hypsithilla.

330. *the Phrygian.* Cybele. Swinburne described Cybele as "served by sexless priests or monks." She was to be contrasted, therefore, with Venus, "Our Lady of Pain" for the greater restraint of her devotees.

333. *Ida.* Mt. Ida in Asia Minor, a seat of the worship of Cybele.

340. *Catullus.* A Roman poet (87–54 B.C.), famous for his graceful and exquisite love lyrics. See Tennyson's *Frater Ave atque Vale*, text p. 190.

345. *Dindymus.* A mountain in Phrygia, sacred to Cybele. From her shrine on the mountain she passed through the surrounding lands in a chariot drawn by lions.

371. *rod to a serpent.* An allusion to the story in Exodus 7 : 8–10, in which the Lord promises to change Aaron's rod into a serpent, so that Pharaoh shall see a miracle.

380. *Sin's child . . . Death.* In *Paradise Lost*, Death is the son of Sin and Satan.

405–6. *Lampsacus . . . Aphaca.* Cities in Asia Minor where worship of Venus and Priapus was prominent.

409. *Cotytto.* A Thracian goddess whose worship was similar to that of Cybele. Wild and licentious orgies marked her festival.

410. *Astarte or Ashtaroth.* The Phoenician goddess of fecundity and sexual love. Astarte is the Greek form of the name; Ashtaroth or Ashtoreth was the form used by the Canaanites.

Page 713. MADONNA MIA

Swinburne has done no more beautiful work than this exquisite little Pre-Raphaelite picture of "My Lady." Like *A Ballad of Life* and *A Ballad of Death*, it is a good illustration of the Pre-Raphaelitism of the early Swinburne.

18. *vair.* See note to l. 278 of *Laus Veneris*, above.

Page 714. LOVE AT SEA

See letter X, to E. C. Stedman, text p. 796.

Page 715. THE GARDEN OF PROSERPINE

"The literary source of [this poem] is very probably not classical. But the psychological source is not hard to find. The explanation given in *Notes on Poems and Reviews*, which makes it merely a pendant to *Dolores*, . . . has no value . . . and is most unjust and inadequate. . . The feeling which is expressed in *The Garden of Proserpine* is deeper and of far greater artistic significance than would be the mere physical reaction and impotence resulting from physical excess. It is the reaction of the soul to the weary, grievous fever of living; the aspiration of the spirit that has in its youth found that all is pain and vanity towards an hereafter that will at least no more be life. And there is probably no more consummate piece of conscious art, and virtuosity that makes one hold one's breath, in English than this song of that garden in the everlasting twilight": [here Mr. Rutland quotes ll. 65–72.] (William R. Rutland, in *Swinburne*, pp. 273–4.)

This is one of the three poems which, the poet said, "beyond the rest were biographical." The other two are *The Triumph of Time*, which arose, as is pointed out in the note to that poem, out of the one real love he found in life—Jane Faulkner,—a love which may have been "the tragic destruction of all his faith in women"; and *Dolores*, which expresses "the passion with which he had sought relief, in the madness of the fleshly Venus, from his ruined dreams of the heavenly." *The Garden of Proserpine* expressed, he wrote, "that brief total pause of passion and of thought, when the spirit, without fear or hope of good things or evil, hungers and thirsts only after the perfect sleep."

4. *dreams of dreams.* Life and its realities become so far away and futile to the dweller in the garden of Proserpine that they are remembered as dreams, not as experiences that ever were.

27. *buds of poppies.* The poppy, the flower of oblivion, was sacred to Proserpine. She was often represented as wearing a garland of poppies.

59. *Forgets the earth her mother.* Proserpine was the daughter of Demeter, goddess of grains and fruits, of sowing and reaping—in short, she was the daughter of the mother-earth. While gathering flowers in the Sicilian fields she was seized by Pluto and carried off to his underground realm, Hades, the kingdom of darkness and death. Demeter wandered long over the earth hunting her, and finally prevailed upon the gods to allow Proserpine to spend half of each year—some versions of the story say a third—in the upper world. The myth of Demeter and Proserpine (Persephone) arose out of the ever-recurring birth and death of nature with the changing of the seasons.

Page 716. SAPPHICS

In this poem Swinburne uses a poetic form which is an imitation of the stanza used by Sappho, the "Lesbian nightingale," a celebrated Greek lyric poetess of the seventh and sixth centuries B.C. Many exquisitely beautiful fragments of her poems remain, but only two exist in their entire form. Swinburne wrote of her: "Judging even from the mutilated fragments fallen within our reach from the broken altar of her sacrifice of song, I for one have always agreed with all Grecian tradition in thinking Sappho to be beyond all question and comparison the very greatest poet that ever lived."

9. *Aphrodite.* The goddess of love.

13. *the doves.* The dove was sacred to Aphrodite, who was often represented as drawn by doves.

16. *Mitylene.* A city on the island of Lesbos, in the Ægean Sea. Lesbos is one of

"... the isles of Greece,
Where burning Sappho loved and sung."

27. *nine Muses about Apollo.* The Muses, who in Greek story presided over song, the different kinds of poetry, and the arts and sciences, were the daughters of Zeus and Mnemosyne. They were Calliope (epic poetry), Clio (history), Erato (amatory poetry), Euterpe (lyric poetry), Melpomene (tragedy), Polymnia or Polyhymnia (sacred poetry), Terpsichore (dancing and choral song), Thalia (comedy), and Urania (astronomy). As god of music and poetry Apollo was associated with the Muses.

29. *the tenth.* Plato called Sappho "the tenth Muse."

49–55. *Saw the Lesbians . . . Full of Music.* Possibly a reference to the story that Sappho was the head of a school of girls who devoted themselves to the writing of poetry.

76. *Purged not in Lethe.* Unable to secure oblivion by drinking from Lethe, the stream of forgetfulness in Hades.

Page 717. DEDICATION

This, the dedication to the first series of *Poems and Ballads* (July, 1866), was addressed to Sir Edward Burne-Jones (1833–1898), the greatest of the Pre-Raphaelite painters in England. Romantic atmosphere and poetic feeling make his pictures highly appealing to lovers of Pre-Raphaelite art. He was a pupil of Rossetti's and a friend of Swinburne's.

7. *bay-leaf.* Laurel, used in honorary garlands or crowns.

17. *seven years' traces.* The time of the composition of *Poems and Ballads* is fixed in the years from 1859 to 1865 by this expression.

23. *myrtles.* Wreaths of myrtle were used to crown poets.

27–8. *Faustine . . . Juliette.* Names of women appearing in the 1866 volume of *Poems and Ballads.*

45. *dreaming in class-time.* A reference to the time when, as a schoolboy at Eton, the poet "poured forth torrents of verse." Swinburne entered Eton when he was twelve and remained there a little over four years. Edmund Gosse, Swinburne's biographer, holds that the pieces in *Poems and Ballads* cannot go back to the Eton days, since the poet said that at eighteen he "burned every scrap of MS. he had in the world." Even if this is true, the poet may have easily remembered some of the burnt poems and recreated them for the 1866 volume.

81. *the world of your hands.* The artistic creations—the paintings—of Burne-Jones.

Page 718. BEFORE DAWN

This *aubade*, or lyric piece suggestive of morning, is one of the occasional poems of Swinburne that show his interest in French lyrists. (See note to *A Match,* above.) The theme is "the fair but fleeting passion of love," the development of which is marked by the poet's characteristic emphasis on sensual suggestion.

Page 719. THE LEPER

Mr. T. S. Eliot, in *The Sacred Wood,* names this poem, *Laus Veneris,* and *The Triumph of Time* as three poems which any volume of selections from Swinburne "should certainly contain"; and Mr. Harold Nicolson pronounces it "almost as macabre as Tennyson's *Happy,* which it may possibly have suggested." Mr. Chew finds in it a taste for the macabre arising out of the poet's early admiration for Rossetti's work and his interest in Beddoes's *Death's Jest-Book.* The critics and readers of its time quite generally condemned the poem as revolting and listed it as the worst of the "foul stuff" of its author. In *The Spectator* of September 15, 1866, Mr. Robert Buchanan published his amusing *The Session of the Poets,* an account of a meeting which was stampeded when young Mr. Swinburne arose and made a characteristic speech. Buchanan tells us that the session was peaceful until, at the supper hour,

Up jumped, with his neck stretching out like a gander,
Master Swinburne, and squeal'd, glaring out thro' his hair,
"All virtue is bosh! Hallelujah for Landor!
I disbelieve wholly in everything!—There!"

This sensational pronouncement disconcerted the poets. Arnold rushed away, and Tennyson caught the fainting Miss Ingelow in his arms. The situation was desperate

Till Tennyson, flaming and red as a gipsy,
Struck his fist on the table and utter'd a shout:
"To the door with the boy! Call a cab! He is tipsy!"
And they carried the naughty young gentleman out.

Page 721. AVE ATQUE VALE

When Swinburne read in the newspapers of April 19, 1866, the news of Baudelaire's death (which turned out to be a false report) he wrote to a friend, saying that he hoped to write a little notice of the French poet's death and that he wanted to lay hold of any facts he could. The notice he withheld, of course, when he got the news that though Baudelaire had been and still was very ill, he was not dead. More than a year later another report of the sick poet's death reached Swinburne, and again he wrote to his friend, George Powell: "I am writing a sort of lyric dirge for my poor Baudelaire which I think is good as far as it has gone. But London and business or (worse) society are awful clogs on poetry." But a second time Baudelaire was not dead and Swinburne laid aside his elegy in disgust. Some three months later Baudelaire really died, and Swinburne once more took up his elegy, revised it, and, after waiting a little while to make sure that the dead poet was indeed dead, published it in the *Fortnightly Review*.

Swinburne considered Baudelaire "one of the most exquisite, most delicate, and most perfect poets of the century—perfect in sound, in color, in taste of meter, and in tone of emotion."

For Swinburne's references to the poem see letters X and XXIX, text pp. 796 and 806.

"We are struck . . . by the insistence laid on the farewell theme and the irrevocability of Baudelaire's fate. Written in the first period of Mazzinian fervour, *Ave atque Vale* displays on the part of Swinburne a consciousness that one stage of his career is now closing and that he must turn to new inspirations." (Georges Lafourcade, in *Swinburne, a Literary Biography*, p. 194.)

". . . This grave and stately threnody has a soberness, a dignity, which distinguish it among the fervid writings of its author. Nowhere else has Swinburne come nearer to the majesty and depth of emotion of the purest Greek literature, nor clothed his thought in severer language." (William R. Rutland, in *Swinburne, a Nineteenth Century Hellene*, p. 311.)

Title: *Ave atque Vale*. "Hail and Farewell."

Motto: *Nous devrions . . . bien ingrats*. These verses from Baudelaire's *Les Fleurs du Mal* (The Flowers of Evil) may be translated as follows: "Yet we should bear to him some flowers; the dead, the pitiful dead, have great sorrows, and when October, pruner of ancient trees, blows its melancholy winds about their mounds, then indeed they must deem the living very ingrate."

1. *rose . . . laurel*. The rose is a symbol of love; rue, herb of grace, is for pity; laurel is for the making of garlands with which to honor the poet.

2. *the veil of thee*. The body of Baudelaire.

5. *Dryads*. Wood nymphs.

8. *Half-faded fiery blossoms*. Baudelaire's *Les Fleurs du Mal* are, as the name suggests, poems of a bitter and passionate nature.

11. *tropic feet*. In 1841–1842 Baudelaire visited India.

14–18. *Thine ears knew . . . supreme head of song*. There is a legend that the Lesbian poetess, Sappho, "the supreme head of song," threw herself into the sea from the rocks of Leucas, an island in the Ionian group, because Phaon, a beautiful youth with whom she was in love, looked coldly upon her.

50. *dead yew-leaves*. The "graveyard yew" is a symbol of mourning.

59. *pale Titan-woman*. A reference to Baudelaire's poem, *La Géante* (The Giantess).

83. *Proserpine's veiled head*. See note to *The Garden of Proserpine*, above.

120–1. *Orestes-like . . . severed hair*. In the opening scene of Æschylus' *Choëphore* where Orestes and Electra, his sister, are at the tomb of their father, Agamemnon, who was murdered by his wife, Clytemnestra, and her paramour, Ægisthus, Orestes offers as a sacrifice to the dead a lock of his hair, a symbol of mourning.

123. *head of Him, the King*. Agamemnon, the conqueror of Troy.

131. *most high Muses*. See note to l. 27 of *Sapphics*, above.

134. *lord of light*. Apollo, god of the sun and of poetry and song.

138–9. *Thy lips . . . with bitter bread*. A reference to the "sad and strange things . . . the languid lurid beauty . . . the dangerous hothouse scents" that mark Baudelaire's *Les Fleurs du Mal*.

146. *laurel with thy cypress crown*. The laurel, sacred to poetry, is mingled with the cypress, symbol of death.

155. *the ways Lethean*. The paths of oblivion.

157. *obscure Venus of the hollow hill*. See note to l. 25 of *Laus Veneris*, above.

158. *Cytherean*. Aphrodite (Venus) was said to have risen from the foam of the sea near the island of Cythera.

160. *Erycine*. Venus was called Erycine from Mt. Eryx, in Sicily, where a temple for her worship in the finer aspects of her divinity was erected.

166. *staff shall break in blossom*. After Tannhäuser had spent a year with Venus in her Venusberg cavern, he repented of his sin and asked the Pope for absolution. The Pope replied that he would grant no forgiveness unless his staff broke into bloom as a sign of God's pity for the erring knight. The knight returned to Venus, and soon after he was gone the Pope's staff broke into blossom.

192. *sadder than the Niobean womb*. The four-

teen children of Niobe were slain by Apollo and Diana because of her proud boast that she had more children than their mother, Latona.

Page 724. SUPER FLUMINA BABYLONIS

In 1831 the exiled Giuseppe Mazzini stirred thousands of Italians from their lethargic indifference toward the tyranny of Austria by his famous manifesto addressed to "Young Italy." "Italy's resurrection" as a result of this rousing of her sons, the theme of the poem, Swinburne chants "in words of lofty eloquence and ethical intensity." (Chew's *Swinburne*, p. 107.) See the letter to William Sharp, text p. 806.

When Swinburne died Meredith said of him in a letter to the *Times* (April 15, 1909): "Had Italy been native to him he would have borne the renown of a poet fired on the instant to deliver himself orally. And had he been Italian, the glow of a people's adoration would have clad him during life."

The title, which means "By the rivers of Babylon," is taken from Psalms 137 : 1, the fine elegy commemorating the constancy of the Jews in captivity in Babylon. Mr. William R. Rutland, who says that in its supreme moments Swinburne's art combines the Hellenic and the Hebraic in its thought, mentions this poem and *Mater Dolorosa* as pieces in which the poet reaches out "to the sacred scriptures and the sacred places of the Jew and the Christian." (*Swinburne*, p. 224.)

45. *the horn of Eridanus*. The delta of the Po River, the ancient Greek name of which was Eridanus.

65. *Gethsemane*. The garden near Jerusalem which was the scene of the agony of Jesus before the crucifixion.

67. *Aceldama*. The scene of the suicide of Judas (Acts 1 : 18), identified with the "potter's field" of Matthew 27 : 7–8, and called the "field of blood" because purchased with the thirty pieces of silver which Judas received for betraying Christ.

73. *an angel's similitude*. The angel of l. 121.

125. *Golgotha*. The place of Christ's crucifixion.

Page 726. HERTHA

This poem Swinburne considered his greatest single piece because he found in it "the most of lyric force and music combined with the most of condensed and clarified thought." Lafourcade sees in the poem evidences of ideas gained by the poet from much reading—from "Cleanthes' *Hymn to God*, Blake, Emily Brontë, Tennyson's *Higher Pantheism*, Whitman, Schopenhauer, and Darwin." Hertha was the ancient Teutonic goddess of the earth (the "Mater Terra" of Tacitus), of fertility, and of growth. In the poem Swinburne speaks in her name, and his conception of the goddess is that she is "an active, living, and growing force . . . 'the vital principle of matter,'" the world-soul.

"It seems to me that Swinburne's triumph [in *Hertha*] lies . . in having made of the scientific law of evolution a spiritual necessity; the natural compulsion to grow, live, and change, apart from any idea of perfection or progress of the species, has never been rendered in a finer or more powerful way than in this stanza" [ll. 136–40]. (Georges Lafourcade, *Swinburne, a Literary Biography*, p. 177.)

15. *before God was, I am*. God's words to Moses, "I AM THAT I AM" (Exodus 3 : 14), and Jesus' "Before Abraham was, I am" (John 8 : 58), probably suggested these words of Hertha. The phrase "I am," coming from Hertha, the world-soul or vital principle, has a much vaster application than when spoken by any mere (in comparison with Hertha) god.

20–40. *I am stricken . . . the dust which is God*. The thought of these lines suggests the "doctrine of identity" advanced by Emerson in his poem *Brahma*.

41–62. The situation of man in these lines, in which the world-soul challenges his knowledge and wisdom with a series of questions, is similar to that of Job when the voice of the Lord sounded out of the whirlwind and overwhelmed him with questions to which he could answer only, "I will lay mine hand upon my mouth." (See Job 38, 39, and 40 : 1–4.)

64. *Nor tripod nor throne*. Nor priest nor king. The tripod was an altar, supported by three legs, on which the priestess of Apollo at Delphi sat to deliver the oracles.

67. *Born, and not made*. These lines set forth the idea of the principle of growth, the spiritual necessity of evolution, and deny any special act of creation.

88. *the lights*. Religious creeds and dogmas.

99. *The life-tree*. The great ash tree, in Norse myth symbolizing the universe. Thus Hertha speaks of herself as the spirit of the universe.

156–60. *I bid . . . of me fair*. Swinburne said that Hertha "prefers liberty to bondage, Mazzini to Buonaparte," and is a "good republican"; for in "liberty only can man's soul reach its full stature and growth."

181. *his twilight*. In Norse myth the "twilight of the gods" is the period when the world is destroyed in the conflict between the gods and the giants and the powers of Hel. There is to be, however, a regenerated world, for a few of the minor gods escape the conflict.

Page 729. THE PILGRIMS

In this dialogue between men who are in love with "the fair, soft present" and the Pilgrims, those who devote themselves to the service of enthralled humanity and abandon all things to follow their Lady of Liberty, Swinburne "achieves as austere a moral utterance as any of the century." (Chew, *Swinburne*, p. 108.)

1. *lady of love.* From the replies of the Pilgrims we find their lady of love to be Liberty, inspirer of "the inward soul" of the human race.

56. *Than sister or wife,* etc. Cf. Luke 14:26—"If any man come to me, and hate not his father, and mother, and wife, and children, and brethren, and sisters, yea, and his own life also, he cannot be my disciple."

87. *bring death lives . . . to sow.* In I Corinthians 15:36–8, St. Paul writes: ". . . that which thou sowest is not quickened, except it die: and that which thou sowest, thou sowest not that body that shall be, but bare grain . . . but God giveth it a body as it hath pleased him, and to every seed his own body."

Page 730. TO WALT WHITMAN IN AMERICA

When Swinburne wrote this poem he was an extreme admirer of the "strong-winged soul with prophetic lips," Walt Whitman, the prophet of Democracy in America. In 1862 he had become intimately acquainted with three great poetry books—FitzGerald's *Rubáiyát*, Baudelaire's *Fleurs du Mal*, and Whitman's *Leaves of Grass*, all of which markedly influenced his work, *Leaves of Grass* leaving its impress especially on the poems in adoration of "the earth-god Freedom" in the volume *Songs before Sunrise.* Whitman's great poem to Lincoln, *When Lilacs Last in the Dooryard Bloom'd*, Swinburne pronounced "the most sonorous anthem ever chanted in the church of the world." After some years of hero-worship of the American poet, Swinburne, probably because of the influence of Watts-Dunton, repudiated him and in his *Whitmania* (1887) wrote this: "Mr. Whitman's Eve is a drunken apple-woman, indecently sprawling in the slush and garbage of the gutter amid the rotten refuse of her overturned fruit-stall; but Mr. Whitman's Venus is a Hottentot wench under the influence of cantharides and adulterated rum." (*Complete Works*, Vol. 15, p. 316.) John Burroughs said that Whitman was not disturbed by this attack. "He looks upon Swinburne," Burroughs wrote, "as a sort of abnormal creature, full of wind and gas, but not worth attending to. . . . Walt has no stomach for his poetry. He is a mere puff of mephitic gas." (Quoted from Hyder's *Swinburne's Literary Career*, Duke University Press, p. 220. Hyder credits it to Clara Barrus's *Life and Letters of John Burroughs*, I, 288–9.) See letter to Edmund Gosse, text p. 804.

73. *the stake-net.* A fishing net.

115 ff. *Not as one man,* etc. Christ died once that man might be free, but in every age the earth-god Freedom must go to the cross.

125. *the stripe.* The mark made by a whip or scourge.

Page 732. COR CORDIUM

On Shelley's tomb at Rome are inscribed the words "Cor Cordium" ("Heart of Hearts"). Of *Songs before Sunrise*, in which *Cor Cordium* was published, Swinburne said: "My other books are books; *Songs before Sunrise* is myself." The volume reflects the poet's passionate love of freedom, his devotion to Italy, his hatred of priestcraft and kingcraft, his trust in world revolution, and his admiration of men who, like Shelley, spoke in fearless voice the ideals that were dearest to their hearts.

For another passage in which Swinburne speaks high praise of Shelley see ll. 151 ff. of *In the Bay* (text p. 755), and see also the notes to that poem, below. See the letter to Sir Sidney Lee, text p. 804.

MATER TRIUMPHALIS

In this poem the "triumphant mother" of Man is Liberty. She subdues death and breaks the bands of hell; who hears her not, "A nameless sign of death shall his name be"; having sinned sometimes, she is sinless; her sons, though she slay them, will gladly die.

". . . Liberty is the most real thing in Swinburne's experience. . . . His delight in the sea, in the wind, in light, in the life of the seabird giving its wings to the storm, acquires deeper significance, since these are among the symbols of liberty. All his loves and hates gain intensity in ministering to a liberty apprehended successively as *mater dolorosa*, *mater triumphalis*, the mother, the beloved, the bride of man's soul, the infinitely bountiful, the implacable goddess demanding bitter sacrifices of man. . . . Incomparably holy, she is no aloof divinity awaiting a peculiar tribute. . . . Towards her . . . he can be by turns filial and passionate, her son, her servant, her lover, her prophet." (T. Earle Welby, in *A Study of Swinburne*, pp. 124–5.)

Sir Edmund Gosse, though he speaks high praise of the poems in *Songs before Sunrise*, the volume that contains this poem, is puzzled nevertheless by the "apparent causelessness of the emotion, and the vain violence as of a whirlwind in a vacuum." Mr. Harold Nicolson is annoyed by the "almost revivalist attitude" of the poet, the "shrill rhetoric in which he claims the functions of a prophet" in such lines as

I am the trumpet at thy lips, thy clarion
  Full of thy cry, sonorous with thy breath;
The grave of souls born worms and creeds grown carrion
  Thy blast of judgment fills with fires of death.

147. *Æschylean.* Having the characteristics of Æschylus, the "father of Greek tragedy."

148. *Sappho.* See note to *Sapphics*, above.

Page 735. THE SONG OF THE STANDARD

This is another of the *Songs before Sunrise* that, like *Super Flumina Babylonis* (text p. 724), may be classified as an elegiac for Italy.

2. *republican.* Italy, which had gained its freedom at this time, was a limited monarchy under Victor Emmanuel, but Swinburne still yearned deeply for an Italian republic.

5–6. *Red . . . white . . . Green.* The colors of the Italian flag.

24. *Twice hast thou spoken a message.* The first time was when imperial Rome was the ruler of the ancient world (ll. 25–7). In speaking of a second occasion Swinburne has in mind the great part played by Rome and Italy in the Renaissance (ll. 28–30).

Page 736. THE OBLATION

In this poem Liberty, devotion to which is Swinburne's ruling passion in *Songs before Sunrise,* is the mistress of the poet, and he the lover at her feet, whose life depends on his love for her.

TRISTRAM AND ISEULT

Tristram is the hero of a medieval romance originally not connected with the Arthurian cycle of romances, but early incorporated into it with Tristram represented as a knight of the Round Table. The chief medieval version, in French, dates from about 1170. There is also a voluminous prose form of the story. Tristram is sent to Ireland by King Mark of Cornwall, his uncle, to fetch the king's bride, Iseult (or Isolde) the Beautiful, and on the return voyage he and Iseult partake of a potion which renders them permanently in love. According to the version adopted by Tennyson in his *Idylls of the King,* Tristram is cloven through the head by King Mark, who surprises him with Iseult. According to that followed by Matthew Arnold in *Tristram and Iseult,* he flees to Brittany, where he marries another Iseult, called Iseult of the White Hand. Being wounded, he sends for Iseult the Beautiful to come and cure him. She comes, but too late to save him, and she too goes down to death. In Swinburne's *Tristram of Lyonesse* is told the story of Tristram's first visit to the court of the king of Ireland, his subsequent mission to fetch Iseult to be Mark's bride, his love for Queen Iseult, his separation from her, and his marriage with Iseult of Brittany. Later, when he lies near to death, he sends for Queen Iseult. The messenger is to hoist a white sail if Iseult is returning with him. He does so, but Iseult, Tristram's "virgin wife," tells him that the sail is black, and he dies before Iseult the queen reaches his side. In Wagner's opera, *Tristan und Isolde,* there is only one Isolde, the wife of Mark. The lovers are discovered by the king, and Tristan lets himself be wounded by the king's squire, and then, in his castle, awaits the ship of Isolde. She comes, and he, desiring to meet her as when first he saw her, with bleeding wounds, tears off the bandage and dies in her arms. Isolde falls dead on his body.

More recent "Tristrams" have been done by John Masefield (in the dramatic form) and by Edwin Arlington Robinson. The Dedicatory Epistle which Swinburne published with the Prelude (1871), is as follows:

"My aim was simply to present that story, not diluted and debased as it had been in our own time by other hands, but undefaced by improvement and undeformed by transformation, as it was known to the age of Dante wherever the chronicles of romance found hearing from Ercildoune to Florence; and not in the epic or romantic form of sustained or continuous narrative, but mainly through a succession of dramatic scenes or pictures with descriptive settings or backgrounds."

See note to *Queen Yseult,* text p. 1133.

1. *Love, that is first and last,* etc. The poem begins with a magnificent apostrophe to Love as the animating spirit of the Universe.

26. *terrene things.* Things of the earth.

42. *these twain.* Tristram and Iseult.

83. *lamping.* Shining, brilliant.

86–156. *sweet shining signs . . . of space and timeless time.* There is nothing more Swinburnian in Swinburne than "this jewelled enumeration of the zodiac of famous lovers," with its luxuriant fluency of words, its music and glowing color, and its splendor of images and comparisons.

90. *Queen Helen.* See note on l. 85 of *A Dream of Fair Women,* above.

Queen Guenevere. The beautiful queen of King Arthur. The story of her love for Lancelot du Lac is told in the *Idylls of the King,* text pp. 139 ff.

91. *sphery signs.* The signs of the zodiac. The poet finds a heroine of love for each sign.

100. *star of Hero.* Hero was a priestess of Aphrodite, beloved of Leander, who swam the Hellespont every night, guided by a torch on her tower, in order to be with her. Finally when he was drowned, Hero in her grief threw herself into the sea.

101. *The star that Marlowe sang.* The story of Hero and Leander is the subject of a poem by Marlowe.

104. *Alcyone.* Halcyone, the daughter of Æolus, god of the winds. In grief over the drowning of her husband, Ceyx, she threw herself into the sea. The gods, in pity, changed both her and Ceyx into kingfishers.

105. *the wind-foot year.* The swift-going year.

110. *My birth-month star.* April was Swinburne's "birth-month."

111. *Iseult.* See introductory note to this poem.

114. *Rosamond.* See note on *A Dream of Fair Women*, l. 251, above.

116–18. *Flares like . . . flying sail with fire.* An allusion to the story of Dido, the queen of Carthage at the time that Æneas landed on her shore (Virgil's *Æneid*, IV). She fell in love with him, and when he sailed away after a year's stay with her, she built a funeral pyre and slew herself upon it with his sword. It was her blazing pyre that lighted up his flying sail.

121. *Juliet.* The heroine of Shakespeare's *Romeo and Juliet*, the scene of which is laid in Verona (hence *Veronese* of l. 124).

129. *Cleopatra.* See note on *A Dream of Fair Women*, l. 127, above.

132. *Sweet tears for Phaethon.* When Phaethon drove the chariot of the sun so close to the earth that the earth caught fire, Zeus struck him with a thunderbolt and hurled him into the river Eridanus (Po). His grief-stricken sisters, the Heliades, wept so bitterly that they were turned into poplar trees, and their tears, which continued to flow, fell into the stream as amber.

136. *Francesca's.* The punishment of Francesca da Rimini and Paolo for their great but guilty love is told in Dante's *Inferno*.

138. *Thisbe.* According to Ovid, Thisbe was a maid of ancient Babylon beloved of Pyramus. They chose a tomb as a trysting place because their parents objected to their love. Thisbe, approaching the tomb, saw a lion which had just killed an ox. Fleeing, she lost her veil, which the lion mauled and smeared with blood. Pyramus came upon the bloodstained veil, and believing Thisbe dead, killed himself. Later, when Thisbe found his dead body, she killed herself. Chaucer refers to the story in his *Legend of Good Women* and Shakespeare burlesques it in *A Midsummer Night's Dream.*

142. *Angelica's.* In Boiardo's *Orlando Innamorato* and in Ariosto's *Orlando Furioso*, Angelica, the beautiful daughter of Galafron, king of Cathay, drives her lover Orlando, chief of the paladins and "a perfect knight, invincible and invulnerable," mad because of her fickleness toward him.

155. *antiphones.* Musical responses; alternate singing or chanting by groups of a choir.

185. *And hers.* "Hers" refers to Beatrice, the Florentine lady immortalized by Dante.

191–2. *For these too . . . Saw Dante.* In the fifth canto of Dante's *Inferno* Dante sees Swinburne's "twain," Tristram and Iseult, suffering the same punishment that multitudes of other guilty lovers are suffering—the fate of being tossed about in the dark air unceasingly by blasts of hell.

239. *So many and many.* Swinburne has in mind the large number of artists—poets, musicians, writers in prose—who have told the story of Tristram and Iseult. See the introductory note to the poem, above.

Page 741. MATER DOLOROSA

This poem, like *Mater Triumphalis* (text p. 732), is another from the volume *Songs before Sunrise* whose theme is one aspect of Liberty as the mother of man—the sorrowful mother here, in "stained raiment," all but slain by "the kings of the earth," fallen by the wayside and awaiting the hour when her dead face shall "shine as the face of the sun." See note to *Mater Triumphalis*, above.

Citoyen, lui dit, etc. "'Citizen,' Enjolras said to him, 'my mother is the Republic.'"

41–2. *their children . . . the light of her eyes.* The hatred of kings and priests is a frequently sounded note in the *Songs before Sunrise.* It is too simple an explanation of social evils to find their sources always in kings and priests; but some of the ills of Italy which Swinburne had in mind doubtless go back to such sources. The phrase "the light of her eyes" refers, of course, to the light in the eyes of Liberty.

Page 742. HYMN OF MAN

Of this poem—another of the *Songs before Sunrise*—Swinburne wrote: "I have in my head a sort of Hymn for this Congress—as it were a 'Te Hominem Laudamus' ['We praise thee, O Man'] to sing the human triumph over 'things' [l. 65]—the opposing forces of life and nature—and over the God of his own creation, till he attains truth, self-sufficience, and freedom." By "this Congress" he meant an anti-Catholic Council called by the Italian radical, Ricciardi, to meet in Naples in December, 1869, the same time that the Œcumenical Council was to be in session at Rome.

The Œcumenical Council of 1869–1870—a Council of the entire church which is conducted under the presidency of the Pope or his legates, and the decrees of which receive papal confirmation—held under the presidency of Pius IX, decreed papal infallibility and adopted a syllabus condemning the liberal doctrines of the age. This action added to Swinburne's burning hatred of the Pope, whom he now conceived of as an enemy of freedom, just as he believed Napoleon III and, for that matter, all emperors and kings to be its enemies.

For Ricciardi's anti-Catholic Council Swinburne and W. M. Rossetti prepared a declaration of sympathy in which Swinburne's most significant paragraph was the following:

"The Liberty we believe in is one and indivisible: without free thought there can be no free life. That democracy of the spirit without which the body, personal or social, can enjoy but a false freedom, must, by the very law of its being, confront a man-made theocracy to destroy it. Ideal or actual, the Church or priests, and the Republic, are natural and internecine enemies. Freedom, which comes by the law of the life of man—flame of his spirit, root and heart and blood and muscle of his manhood—can take no truce with the creeds or miscreeds which inflict, not (as some kings of our past) upon the flesh, but upon the souls of men, the hideous and twofold penalty of blindness and eviration. She expects no non-natural message from above or from without; but only that which comes from within—faith, born of man, in man, which passes in contagious revelation from spirit again to spirit without authority and without sign. Truth, Right, Freedom are self-sufficing, and claim service from the soul that suffices to itself." (Quoted in Lafourcade's *Swinburne*, p. 173.)

To Swinburne's indignation, Ricciardi's anti-Council was dispersed by the authorities soon after it met, the thin excuse for their action being a quarrel between the Italian and French members of the anti-Council which ended, they said, in the acclaiming of the French Republic. Unable to get his declaration published by authority of the anti-Council and failing also to find an English printer to bring it out, Swinburne finished his "Hymn for this Congress," which he had begun some time before, and called it the *Hymn of Man*. The poem, therefore, is not "a tide of vague and purposeless rhetoric." It was written for a definite occasion, its author having a very clear purpose in mind.

85. *sing with the spheres.* An allusion to the ancient belief that the stars sang in their courses. See note to l. 54 of *The Blessed Damozel*, above.

99. *thou that bringest a sword.* In Matthew 10:34 Christ says, "Think not that I am come to send peace on earth; I came not to send peace, but a sword."

104. *For bread, and thou gavest a stone.* A satirical application of the words of Christ in the Sermon on the Mount (Matthew 7:9)—"Or what man is there of you, whom if his son ask bread, will he give him a stone?"

124. *tripod.* See note on l. 64 of *Hertha*, above.
tree. The cross.

135. *body . . . meat.* From Christ's Sermon on the Mount, Matthew 6:25—"Is not the life more than meat, and the body than raiment?"

155. *consonant.* Harmonious.

167 ff. *Cry aloud; for your God,* etc. In these lines Swinburne is making satirical use of words that approximate those spoken by the prophet Elijah when he rebuked and destroyed the prophets of Baal (I Kings 18:19–40). Elijah defied Baal and showed him to be a weak and powerless deity in whom "there was no voice" for his people when they called upon his name. Even as Elijah mocked the followers of Baal and shouted "Cry aloud!" so Swinburne in the poem mocks the followers of the Christian God with Elijah's "Cry aloud" and with his own "O fools, he was God, and is dead."

184. *ears . . . dumb.* An approximation of the language of the Psalmist in Psalm 115:4–6, again with the satirical inversion. The Psalmist is speaking of idols, the images of the heathen gods, as having eyes that see not and ears that hear not; Swinburne attributes such blindness and deafness to the Psalmist's deity, the God of Israel himself.

200. *Glory to Man in the highest!* An inversion of the "Glory to God in the highest" of Luke 2:14. The climactic thought expressed in the last two lines of the poem must have been in Swinburne's mind for some time before the poem was completed, although, as he quoted them in a letter written early in 1870, the lines had not been given the form in which they appear in the text. As he quoted them they read:

> "And the love-song of earth as thou diest
> sounds over the graves of her kings
> Glory to Man in the highest! for man is the
> master of things."

In the letter in which he so quoted the conclusion he said, "It [the poem] might end somehow thus with a cry of triumph over the decadence of a receding Deity." In its first form the poem was finished not later than February 5, 1870, and it received its present form in the August following.

Page 746. A VISION OF SPRING IN WINTER

This poem, *A Forsaken Garden* (text p. 748), *The Year of the Rose*, and *A Ballad of Dreamland* (text p. 749), all of the *Poems and Ballads* of 1878, make up a group of "magical lyrics" of which Mr. Edmund Gosse said, the "witchery of exquisite sound, the tone of the Æolian harp, . . . is found here in its most harmonious ecstasy." There is finely missing from them the "torrent of palpitating and trumpeting music" of the earlier odes and choruses. Somewhat wistfully Mr. Gosse concludes his study with the remark that the "delicate, tremulous melody" of these poems was scarcely ever heard again in Swinburne's poetry.

Mr. T. Earle Welby is impressed by the "subdual and spiritualization [in these poems] of the hitherto clamorous music." He finds in the Swinburne of these lyrics "moods of dejection, of wistfulness, of pensive acquiescence."

1–36. It is said that these lines were composed by Swinburne as he slept, after the manner in which Coleridge is said to have fashioned the fragment *Kubla Khan*.

5. *mother-month.* Writing to John Morley concerning the publication of this poem in the *Fortnightly Review* for April, 1875, Swinburne said: "I think . . . April should be the time

of the year for its birth—especially as it begins and ends with a reference to the 'birthmonth.'" Swinburne was born in April.

26. *plenilune.* The time of full moon.

61–72. *I would not bid thee,* etc. One detects here the tendency to retrospection, the wistful yearning for the light and love "that has been," even while the poet denies such yearning. Certainly he sends his "love back to the lovely time."

Page 748. A FORSAKEN GARDEN

See introductory note to *A Vision of Spring in Winter,* above.

The scene of *A Forsaken Garden* is East Dene, Bonchurch, Isle of Wight. Swinburne spent much of his childhood and youth on the moors of Northumberland around his grandfather's home, which was near the town of Capheaton, and at East Dene in the southern part of the Isle of Wight. The haunting, melancholy beauty of the lines is perfectly fitted to the pensive theme, the slow but inevitable encroachment of the sea upon the English coast, with the resulting desolation of garden and flowers, of loves and lovers. Cf. the last twelve lines of Swinburne's *Tristram of Lyonesse.*

Page 749. A BALLAD OF DREAMLAND

See introductory note to *A Vision of Spring in Winter,* above.

This poem is an excellent example of the English adaptation from the French form known as the *ballade.* A ballade usually has three stanzas of seven, eight, or ten lines, followed by a quatrain termed the *envoi.* The last line of each of the four divisions is identical and is known as the refrain. If the refrain is designated by C, the rhyme scheme of the eight-line ballade may be indicated by the formula:

3 ababbcbC plus bcbC.

Except in the refrain no rhyme word should be repeated.

A BALLAD OF FRANÇOIS VILLON

François Villon (b. 1431) was a French poet, a poor scholar of the university of Paris, a vagabond, who lived a short, riotous life and narrowly escaped hanging for theft. He was famed for his ballades and other songs arising out of his own experiences. Swinburne translated his *La Belle Heaulmière.*

For an explanation of the ballade form see note to *A Ballad of Dreamland,* above.

1. *golden morn.* The Renaissance.

2. *the dusk of dolorous years.* The dusk, darkness, of the Middle Ages.

6. *song new-born.* Villon struck a new note in poetry. His verse, characterized by raciness, wit, irony, and fine polish, had much influence upon later poets.

14. *plume-plucked gaol-birds.* Villon was the "brains" and the leader of a band of thieves and vagabonds in Paris. He himself was several times arrested, and members of his band were constantly in trouble with the law.

32. *A harlot was thy nurse, a God thy sire.* A reference to the base, debauched life led by Villon. The god, his sire, was Apollo.

33. *assoiled.* Atoned for.

Page 750. THE LAST ORACLE

Julian, who became emperor of Rome in 361 A.D., made an effort to restore paganism in all its magnificence. At the same time he surprised his subjects by issuing an edict of toleration and so, as emperor, did not persecute the Christians. His disbelief in Christianity and espousal of paganism arose out of his study of philosophy at Athens, where he was allowed to go by permission of Constantius II, who had massacred the royal family at Rome. Julian, who according to Gibbon was a special devotee of the Sun God (Apollo), was surnamed "the Apostate" because of his attempt to save Hellenism and rescue the world from "the wail of Galileans" with their "hymns of wrath and wrong." His effort failed, however, and dying, he is said to have spoken sadly the words, "Thou hast conquered, Galilean."

In his early work Swinburne presents the law of change as alone lasting amid the flux of all things. Later, as his thought developed, stability amid change is the possession of the human spirit. In this poem he has discovered "steadfastness in one aspect of human achievement: in Art and Song. His affirmation of the immortality of Apollo is the sign of his confidence in the eternity of Art." (Samuel C. Chew, in *Swinburne,* p. 144.)

See note to *Hymn to Proserpine,* above.

11. *thy true last lover.* The emperor Julian. See introductory note.

18. *the Graces took hands with the Hours.* In Greek mythology the Graces were beautiful maidens, sister goddesses, represented as intimate with the Muses, and oftenest as attendants of Eros, Aphrodite, and Dionysus. They were commonly mentioned as three—Aglaia (brilliance), Euphrosyne (joy), and Thalia (bloom)—and were regarded as the inspirers of the qualities that give charm to nature, wisdom, love, social intercourse, etc. The Hours (Horae) were goddesses of the seasons, and hence of orderliness both in nature and society. Dike (justice), Eirene (peace), and Eunomia (wise legislation) are the three mentioned by Hesiod, the Greek epic poet.

23. *Paian.* An expression used in addressing Apollo as the god of healing and, later, as the god of battle.

54. *all Gods that waned and grew.* This idea is in keeping with Swinburne's belief in the flux of all things. Even gods rise and fall in the continuing succession of changes. Nothing is permanent but change itself.

Page 752. TRIADS

In this group of three (Triads) closely related three-stanza poems Swinburne voices the timeless question over which the philosophic and poetical mind loves yearningly to brood—the question, namely, of the essential nature of reality. In the first triad he puts the question in several concrete forms; in the second he tells us that none knows the answer with ear or with eye; and in the third he promises that in the light of one hour, the hour when life looks into "death's strange eyes," the secret shall "be secret no more."

9. *kye.* Cows. The word is Scottish.

10. *lime.* The linden tree. Its flowers are rich in honey.

Page 753. IN THE BAY

This poem has been called "the first fruit in verse of Swinburne's devotion to the Elizabethan dramatists." In it he ascribes great glory to the spirit of Marlowe, pays tribute to Webster, Ford, Beaumont and Fletcher, "the twin-souled brethren of the single wreath," and to Shakespeare, the mighty master of them all. The beauty of sunset across the bay arouses in the poet thoughts of a land beyond the sunset, a place of deathless souls we fain would win, and he pleads with these mighty ones to send earthward one sound of their lyres, of their fire, one spark.

Cf. *Christopher Marlowe, William Shakespeare,* and *John Webster* (text p. 767).

See letter to William Sharp, text p. 806.

10. *freak.* Streak.

31. *Hades.* The abode of the dead, usually conceived of as a dark and gloomy subterranean realm.

Elysium. The dwelling place of the happy souls after death.

32. *Lethe.* A river of Hades whose water when drunk caused forgetfulness of the past.

34. *Stygian web.* The Styx, the principal river of the lower world, had to be crossed by those who were going to the regions of the dead. It was said to flow seven times around the lower world; hence *web.*

37. *these twain.* The poets' words and their souls.

46. *First lights to lighten.* Marlowe (1564–1593) was the first English writer to write great tragedies and the first to use blank verse in the modern sense of the term.

50. *Titan . . . Titaness.* The comparison to the Titans is suggested by the greatness of Marlowe as a writer of tragedies. Jonson spoke of Marlowe's "mighty line."

59. *Sirius.* A star of the constellation Canis Major, the brightest star in the heavens.

90–6. *Like spray these waves . . . fit harbourage for thy soul.* The Spanish (or "Invincible") Armada, sent by Philip II of Spain against England in 1588, was in great part destroyed by the English fleet and by storms. The sea was a glorious symbol of liberty to Swinburne, and he here writes with enthusiasm of its power and violence.

97. *in her green south fields, a poor man's child.* Marlowe, a native of Canterbury, in southern England, was the son of a shoemaker. See letter to Sir Sidney Lee, text p. 804.

100–2. *wild world . . . godlike boy.* In 1593 Marlowe, who was under accusation of atheism, was stabbed to death in a tavern quarrel.

129. *he that rose our mightiest.* Shakespeare.

142–4. *The twin-souled brethren . . . all men's heart's delight.* Francis Beaumont and John Fletcher. They are always named together because they were so closely associated in the writing of plays. Their plays were fully as popular as Shakespeare's in their time, as these lines indicate.

145. *that fixed fervour.* The reference is to John Ford (1586–1639?). He wrote mostly tragedy.

148. *the incestuous prisoner's bride-house bars.* An allusion to the story told in one of Ford's tragedies, *'Tis Pity She's a Whore.*

149–50. *And thine . . . before the sun.* Marlowe, whose soul is next to Shakespeare, "the sun."

152. *Phosphor.* The morning star. It is fitting that the star of dawn should be the star of the youthful Marlowe and Shelley.

157–8. *You twain . . . Down the steep darkness.* Marlowe and Shelley died "in the same swift year of manhood," each at twenty-nine.

159. *Apollonian tears.* Tears wept by Apollo, god of poetry, for "these youthful twain."

190–1. *fang-drawn worm . . . wound you living.* A reference to the violent attacks made upon the character and deeds of Marlowe and Shelley in their lifetimes. Just before Marlowe was killed a warrant for his arrest as an atheist had been issued. Shelley, too, was violently attacked for his atheism (he wrote a pamphlet on *The Necessity of Atheism*), for his hatred of oppression of all kinds, and for his ideas looking toward world liberation. Swinburne would see greatness in these two men because they were fearless opponents of two ideas to which he himself was hostile—priestcraft and kingcraft.

Page 757. AT PARTING

In this lyric, one of the *Poems and Ballads* of 1878, Swinburne expresses the wistful yearning of man over the transience of love, whether it be pure and spiritual or guilty and sensual.

RELICS

This poem, when first printed—in the *Fortnightly Review* for 1873—bore the title *North and South.* It was inspired by tender memories of San Gimignan (l. 55), the "little laurelled town of towers," in Tuscany, surrounded by ancient walls, and with thirteen of its original fifty towers still standing. In 1864, when Swinburne made his second tour to Italy, his imagination was fired by the fact that San Gimignan[o] contained the "hall which saw Dante speaking" when he was seeking help for Florence.

2. *White laurustine.* A shrub which, though native to the Mediterranean countries, is widely cultivated in Europe for its evergreen leaves and fragrant white or pink flowers. The flower, "a white star made of memory," awakens in the poet thoughts of the "keen-faced promontory" where he had first seen it growing; and then, his mind set going, he conjures up a message that the "soft Italian bloom" must bring him of the sweet day and the night in its far-off southern clime.

57–8. *breached walls . . . Called of Saint Fina.* The chapel "called of Saint Fina," a local saint of San Gimignano who died at the age of fifteen, was built in the fifteenth century.

Page 758. THALASSIUS

Thalassius, which means "from the sea," is Swinburne's spiritual autobiography, his *Apologia pro Vita Sua.* In it he presents symbolically the deep truths which he fervently believes underlie his life. He expresses his consciousness of the divine gift of song and of his kinship with the sun and stars, the waters and the winds. He is the child of Sun and Sea (Apollo and Cymothoe). Apollo, the sun-god, woos Cymothoe, symbol of the sea (ll. 16–36), and of his wooing is born "a sun-child whiter than the sunlit snows." "He that found the sea-flower" was Landor, and it is through his "high songs" that the boy learns to love love, to hate tyranny, to worship Liberty, and to believe in hope. So clothed, the youth tries "the spring-flowered ways." Love, "God-featured" and "lovelier than all men," meets him and for a while is mute and "flowerlike sweet"; but suddenly he cries, "Thou fool, my name is death," and disappears. The earth becomes bitter now and the heaven, and even the sea and the sun fail the youth, and to escape from that which is searing his heart he rides for many a night the vine-leafed, rose-hung ways directed only by the "light of his dread lady's hot sweet hungering eyes." Disillusionment and satiety come in the wake of reveling and lust and with them the desire for cleanliness; and the youth bethinks him of his mother and goes "back to the grey sea-banks" and is restored. In the end Apollo appears and in "the old great voice" bestows upon the poet heart and mouth the sound of song, and on his purged soul "the sense of all the sea."

See note to *In Memory of Walter Savage Landor*, above.

In a letter which Swinburne wrote to E. C. Stedman in reply to a request for some facts about his life he said:

"As for the sea, its salt *must* have been in my blood before I was born. I can remember no earlier enjoyment than being held up naked in my father's arms and brandished between his hands, then shot like a stone from a sling through the air, shouting and laughing with delight, head foremost into the coming wave—which could only have been the pleasure of a very little fellow. I remember being afraid of other things, but never of the sea. But this is enough of infancy; only it shows the *truth* of my endless passionate returns to the sea in all my verse."

2. *April sea.* Swinburne's birth-month was April.

15. *Oread's hair.* Oreads were nymphs of mountains and hills.

18. *Cymothoe.* One of the nereids, or sea nymphs.

53. *hyaline.* A poetic term applied to the sea to indicate smoothness and clearness.

59. *laurel-laden hair.* A reference to the poet's garland of honor which is Landor's due.

61. *bayleaf bloom.* Honorary garlands were made of bay, or laurel.

88–9. *And gladly . . . lie dead.* Landor wrote an inscription in Latin for the Spanish patriots who died defending their land against the Napoleonic invasion in 1811–1812. These lines constitute a free translation of that inscription.

205. *like a sea-mew.* Mr. Chew, in *Swinburne*, p. 3, says: "The image of the sea bird here and in various other poems implies an awareness not only of his physical frailty—'so birdlike slight and light'—but of his isolation from ordinary ways of life—'a fosterling and fugitive on earth.'"

222. *ineluctable.* Inescapable.

339–56. *red hand of Rome . . . the lithe-limbed mime.* This description of the revels at Rome under Nero should be compared with those passages in *Dolores* dealing with the same subject.

344. *must.* Fresh or unfermented juice of grapes or other fruit; here meaning blood in the arena.

370. *furred Bassarides.* Devotees of Bacchus, god of wine, in whose celebration they indulged in wild orgies. Their garments were probably made of skins of the fox.

373. *his flesh took fire of theirs.* Probably a symbolic reference to the state the poet was in when he wrote the first series of *Poems and*

Ballads. Among the poems in the text that were in this volume are *The Leper* (p. 719), *The Triumph of Time* (p. 694), *Hymn to Proserpine* (p. 701), *The Garden of Proserpine* (p. 715), *Laus Veneris* (p. 688), *Dolores* (p. 707), and *Fausline* (p. 679). The last three, which Mr. Nicolson classifies as "Poems of Passion," may be considered typical products of that period of the poet's life which he had in mind when he wrote "his flesh took fire of theirs."

409. *panther-throned beside Erigone*. Erigone, the daughter of Icarius, committed suicide when her father was murdered by shepherds who thought that wine he had given them was poison. Her presence in these revels is fitting because of her association, through her father, with Dionysus, the god of wine, to whom the panther was sacred.

455–60. *wild mares in Thessaly*, etc. Boreas, the north wind, taking the form of a stallion, became the sire, by the mares of Ericthonius, of twelve horses as swift as the wind over land and sea. Cf. *Iliad*, XX, 223.

459. *levin's*. Flash's.

483–500. "*Child of my sunlight . . . sense of all the sea.*" Apollo, god of the sun and poetry, as father of Swinburne is addressing these words to him.

Page 765. THE HIGHER PANTHEISM IN A NUTSHELL

This poem, a parody on Tennyson's *The Higher Pantheism* (text p. 138), is one of the several examples of Swinburne's ridiculing the beliefs of the Laureate. He was entirely out of sympathy with most of Tennyson's beliefs concerning the human and the divine, especially with his position toward immortality, and with Browning's fervently expressed optimism. In an unpublished poem in the collection of Mr. Thomas Wise, who has made a valuable bibliography of Swinburne's writings, the poet said of such beliefs:

This satisfies our Browning,
And this delights our Tennyson:
And soothed Britannia simpers in serene applause.

(Quoted by C. K. Hyder in *Swinburne's Literary Career and Fame*, p. 19.)

Page 766. NEPHELIDIA

In this poem, the title of which means *Cloudlets*, Swinburne parodies the extreme redundancy and alliteration that sometimes marked his own work. In another parody, *Poeta Loquitur*, he writes in playful mockery of some of his ideas:

If a person conceive an opinion
That my verses are stuff that will wash,
Or my muse has one plume on her pinion,
That person's opinion is bosh.
My philosophy, politics, free-thought!
Are worth not three skips of a flea,
And the emptiest thoughts that can be thought
Are mine on the sea.

ON THE DEATHS OF THOMAS CARLYLE AND GEORGE ELIOT

This sonnet may be taken as evidence that in the presence of death even a Swinburne, whose hatred of Carlyle has been characterized as "unreasoning, persistent, and . . . venomous," can hide his venom and pay, if not the highest, at least fitting, tribute to the genius whom he had so bitterly attacked in life. The death of George Eliot, whom in general he liked but of whom he wrote some unkind or uncomplimentary things in *A Note on Charlotte Brontë*, moved the poet more than that of Carlyle. He was especially impressed, as the last two lines of the sonnet show, by George Eliot's tender, loving treatment of children in her stories.

Page 767. *From* SONNETS ON ENGLISH DRAMATIC POETS

See letter to E. C. Stedman, text p. 802.

I CHRISTOPHER MARLOWE

Swinburne was enthusiastic in his admiration for the Elizabethan dramatists, and of Marlowe (1564–1593) "he was all his life an ecstatic disciple."

See *In the Bay*, text p. 753, and the note to that poem, above; see also the letter to Sir Sidney Lee, text p. 804.

2. *Son first-born of the morning*. See note to *In the Bay*, l. 46, above.

9–10. "*If all the pens . . . their masters' thoughts.*" These lines are from Marlowe's *Tamburlaine*, Part 1, Act 5, scene 1.

II WILLIAM SHAKESPEARE

Cf. Matthew Arnold's *Shakespeare*, text p. 511, and Swinburne's *In the Bay*, text p. 753.

III BEN JONSON

In this sonnet Swinburne praises Jonson (1572–1637) for the wide range of his poetic powers. In the lyric, in comedy, in tragedy, in the masque, in elegy, and in satire he excelled—his genius was "bounteous, multiform."

V PHILIP MASSINGER

Swinburne called Massinger (1583–1640) "the most temperate, studious, and conscientious of the successors of Shakespeare." The "still warm concord" of Massinger's "tune" was first heard (probably) in his play *The Duke of Milan*, written about 1618. England was at comparative peace at this time, but clouds were gathering and Mars was reddening (l. 6) for the civil war of 1642–1646 between the Royalists and Parliamentarians.

7. *like a sound of silver speech of stars.* Swinburne is impressed by what critics have called the "solemn eloquence of Massinger's sustained and even flow of language."

10–11. *High melancholy lights . . . brows of revel.* His solemn eloquence was "tinged with a melancholy which suggests a sermon," writes Robert Boyle in the *Dictionary of National Biography;* and again, "he seldom sinks into the trivial."

VII JOHN WEBSTER

Eighteenth century critics wrote of "the more than earthly wildness" of Webster's dramas, and Charles Lamb, to whose justness of view Swinburne bore powerful testimony, recognized the surpassing genius of Webster (1580?–1625?) as a writer of tragedy. One realizes the fitness of Swinburne's description in this sonnet of Webster's "more than earthly wildness" when one learns that Webster approached nearer to Shakespeare in tragic power than any other of his contemporaries.

Page 768. VIII THOMAS DECKER

Swinburne characterized Decker (1570?–1641) as "a man of gentle, modest, shiftless, and careless nature, irritable and placable, eager and unsteady, full of excitable kindliness and deficient in strenuous principle."

6–7. *What charm of joy-bells . . . note they blow.* Swinburne praised Decker's lyric note, his pathos, his tenderness and fancy.

11. *o'er a dense and doleful city.* Decker wrote especially of London and for the cockneys. He was "almost alone in his sympathy for the world of the craftsmen and the ragtag and bobtail of the streets." (Legouis and Cazamian, *A History of English Literature*, p. 482.)

A CHILD'S LAUGHTER

In *Tristram of Lyonesse*, of 1882, and in many of his books of poems following that date Swinburne published much verse describing babies and young children and expressing his love for them. Tenderness toward children was a genuine feeling in Swinburne. In 1864 he wrote of Andrea del Sarto's "round-limbed babies in red chalk outline, with full blown laughter in their mouths and eyes; such flowers of flesh and live fruits of man, as only a great love and liking for new-born children could have helped him to render"; and in his sonnet on the death of George Eliot (text p. 766) he speaks of

> "the loveliest lamp for earthly feet
> The light of little children, and their love."

The subject of a number of the poems to children was Watts-Dunton's little nephew, Herbert Mason, for whom, when the lad came to Putney to live, Swinburne conceived a great affection. See concluding paragraph of the letter to Paul Hamilton Hayne, text p. 803.

OF SUCH IS THE KINGDOM OF HEAVEN

The title is from Matthew 19 : 14—"Jesus said, 'Suffer little children, and forbid them not, to come unto me: for of such is the kingdom of heaven.'"

3–4. *the crowning star . . . world's head.* The North Star, Polaris, the brightest of the seven stars in the constellation *Ursa Minor.*

Page 769. A BABY'S DEATH

The last two tercets of this poem seem to indicate that Swinburne wrote it in memory of some particular baby. The editors have been unable to identify the child.

72. *Sovereign of arts, and angel.* Michelangelo (Michael Angelo) (1475–1564), one of the greatest figures in the world of art. He was supreme as a sculptor and painter, and he was also a poet, an architect, and a military engineer. In Revelation 12 : 7–9 the archangel Michael is mentioned as warring against Satan and his forces in the upper regions. He is a mighty figure in Milton's *Paradise Lost.*

Page 770. THE ROUNDEL

The roundel is an English modification of the rondeau, its refrain coming after the first and last of three tercets and fitting into the rhyme scheme, which may be diagramed thus: *abaB* (refrain), *bab*, *abaB*. The rondeau is a French poetic form, running on two rhymes and consisting usually of thirteen lines and an unrhymed refrain taken from the beginning of the first line. The rhymes and refrain are generally arranged: *aabba*, *aab*, refrain, *aabba*, refrain.

A Century of Roundels (rondeaux), from which this and other poems in the same form in the text are taken, Swinburne wrote, we are told, for self-discipline and for the purpose of placing some restraint upon a pen that was too facile in the production of flowing numbers. Writing all these poems in the fixed form of the roundel slowed his pen but little, however, for he began and completed the whole volume in a very few months.

IN GUERNSEY

Victor Hugo, with a number of Frenchmen who had fled from France to escape the vengeance of Napoleon III, was expelled by the English government in 1855 from the island of Jersey, in the English Channel. Hugo finally settled on the island of Guernsey, also in the Channel, and remained there till 1870. In May, 1876, Swinburne went on a trip to the island and wrote of it to a friend that he had never seen anything so charming. Only one thing was missing to make his holiday there perfect—the presence of the hero whom he worshipped, Victor Hugo. For a number of years up to 1890 Watts (see introductory sketch to Swinburne, text p. 677) took Swinburne to the seashore once or twice a year to allow the poet to satisfy his great passion for swimming. In September, 1882, he went again to Guernsey, and it was on this visit that, while giving his body and soul to the sea (l. 16), he had the Dantean vision which he records in stanzas (roundels) IV, V, and VI.

46. *whin.* A spiny, evergreen herb common in Europe. It is often used for fuel.

52. *Farinata's eyes.* Farinata degli Uberti, a once famous Florentine whom Dante finds in the sixth circle of Hell. Farinata, lying in his (open) fiery tomb, holds discourse with Dante (*Inferno*, X).

53. *Geryon stands.* In Dante's *Inferno* (XVII–XVIII) Geryon, the symbol of Fraud, is guardian of the Eighth Circle of Hell, the place where traitors are punished. He has the face of a just man, hairy arms, and a forked tail.

80. *This eyrie was the homeless eagle's nest.* A reference to Guernsey as the refuge of Hugo, "the homeless eagle." Hugo delighted Swinburne by asking the poet to visit him at Hauteville House, his residence in Guernsey, a year or two before he left the island.

Page 772. LINES ON THE MONUMENT OF GIUSEPPE MAZZINI

Mazzini, the Italian patriot and revolutionary agitator, who was another of Swinburne's heroes, died in 1872. In 1888 Swinburne wrote to his mother concerning Mazzini: "I am very glad you saw the statue tho' not the tomb of my beloved friend and leader—I may call him so as he was good enough to reckon me among his friends and disciples. I wish you had seen him living. His face was indeed 'as it had been the face of an angel.'"

The monument to Mazzini is in Genoa, where he was born.

See note to *Super Flumina Babylonis*, above.

11. *Alighieri.* Dante. See note to *In Guernsey*, above.

12. *Angelo.* Michelangelo. See note to *A Baby's Death*, above.

25–8. *But this man . . . she did rise.* Swinburne considered Mazzini the liberator of his mother Italy.

Page 773. *From* A MIDSUMMER HOLIDAY

A Midsummer Holiday consists of nine poems composing "the chronicle of an excursion through the country." Although in his nature poems Swinburne often turns a striking phrase and occasionally advances an arresting idea, he is not a great poet of nature. He did not have the power or the patience to hold himself to the close and sustained observation of natural phenomena which is necessary to one who would report them intimately and with sympathetic understanding. Only two or three of the nine pieces in *A Midsummer Holiday* are marked by qualities that are essentially poetical. The three appearing in the present text are (approximately) ballades. See note to *A Ballad of Dreamland*, above.

I ON A COUNTRY ROAD

1. *low pleached lanes.* Lanes shaded by a canopy of interlaced boughs.

II IN THE WATER

This poem is a rapturous expression of Swinburne's love of the sea and his passion for swimming in its waters. Cf. *The Lake of Gaube*, text p. 785.

28. *her cliffs that I clomb.* In late December, 1854, Swinburne determined to climb Culver Cliff, the eastern headland of the Isle of Wight, as a means of testing his nerve in face of death. According to tradition the precipice was impregnable from the seaside, and Swinburne, who was successful in scaling a height which no human being had ever dared before him, received fearful acclaim for his hazardous feat.

Page 774. III ON THE VERGE

This poem is a strikingly beautiful expression of the commonplace. Standing on the verge of the sea and looking out over its restless bosom, the poet is troubled by the question that hundreds of poets and philosophers and vast multitudes of the mute and inglorious have asked themselves in a like situation—whether "death have life or life have death for goal." Swinburne, like all the other questioners, finds no answer. "Silence answering only strikes response reverberate on the soul." Dignity, poise, reverence for nature, resignation to fate, fearlessness—all are in these lines.

1. *Here begins . . . world's end.* The North Sea, which is an arm of the North Atlantic and so may be said to stretch without boundary to "the world's end" around the Pole. These waters, the poet fancies, are free, without "a worldwide shore's control," such as other English seas have.

Page 775. IN TIME OF MOURNING

This poem Swinburne wrote in memory of Victor Hugo, whose death occurred May 22, 1885. Cf. *In Guernsey*, text p. 770.

THE WINDS

The singer of this lament is a Scotch maiden whose lover has been lost at sea.

1. *fa'.* Fall.

3. *gin*. If.
wan. Dark.
4. *I wot weel wad I rest*. "I know well I would rest."
12. *gang*. Go.
13. *a'*. All.
16. *ae*. One.

Page 776. ON THE DEATH OF ROBERT BROWNING

Swinburne wrote seven sonnets on the death of Browning. Browning's death occurred December 12, 1889, and Swinburne's sonnet group on the occasion is dated December 13–15, 1889. This sonnet is the one that concludes the group.

6. "*Look forth*." This is a translation of the word *Prospice*, which is the title of a celebrated lyric by Browning on the subject of death. See text p. 361.

A NYMPHOLEPT

This poem reflects, Swinburne said, "the effect of inland or woodland solitude—the splendid oppression of nature at noon which found utterance of old in words of such singular and everlasting significance as panic and nympholepsy." Mr. T. Earle Welby thinks the poem Swinburne's finest lyric in the last twenty years of his life, and "one of the profoundest nature poems in the language."

The poet, in the deep mid-wood at noon, is filled with "dread of a strange thing near," dread that is so deep, so dim, so sacred that it "is wellnigh sweet," and which he attributes to the unseen presence of the god who is all—Pan. While he is stricken by the fearful thought that his eyes may see Pan and he be seized, like the men of old, with the frenzy (nympholepsy) of panic, he becomes aware of "a form, a face, a wonder to sense and sight." It is the sweet spirit of nature, and seeing her he feels the beauty of the earth; fear changes to desire, desire to delight and love. The sense of impending evil passes away, but as the first intensity of his delight and love tempers, the uncertain question arises in his mind—if haply the heart of the "unknown sweet spirit" be kind and her gifts good. There is no direct answer, but "Pan's dim frown wanes," and the sense "of imminent ill to be" which the poet felt in the woodland solitude passes strangely away. Heaven is as earth, earth as heaven; and all, even the poet, is but a dream of the "sweet spirit." See letter to William Sharp, text p. 806.

14. *the one God, Pan*. Since the word Pan was understood (erroneously) by the Orphics to mean *All*, Pan, the god of woods and fields, came in time to be considered the summation of the varied and numerous attributes of the several pagan deities. Hence he was elevated to the point at which he became a symbol of the universe and a personification of nature.

48. *bent-grass . . . couch-grass*. Bent grass is stiff and wiry; couch grass is a creeping grass which spreads rapidly.

54. *tongueless as she*, etc. Philomela. See notes to Arnold's *Philomela* and Swinburne's *Itylus*, above.

126. *the God who art all*. Another reference to Pan based upon the interpretation of his name, which was probably *ho Paōn*, the feeder, as *to Pan*, the All.

136. *Typho labours*. Typho, called also Typhoeus and Typhon, was a fearful monster of gigantic size who made war against Zeus. Zeus overcame him and according to one version of the story imprisoned him under Mt. Etna. His struggles to escape caused volcanic eruptions ("Etna shudders with passion and pain volcanic") and earthquakes.

138–40. *felt and feared thee . . heights were Pan's*. A reference to the sudden terror which, according to the myth, Pan inspired in human beings, especially those, like herdsmen, or shepherds, in remote and lonely places, and which, from his name, was called *panic*.

197. *What light, what shadow*, etc. At this point the poet becomes aware of the presence of the sweet spirit of nature, a spirit whose loveliness banishes the sinister which is inseparable from nature as she is symbolized by Pan.

Page 783. A CHANNEL PASSAGE

On the night of August 23, 1855, Swinburne was on a boat going from Ostend (not Calais) to England, the last stage of a trip he had been making with his uncle in Germany and other countries in western Europe. A storm of such violence broke over the Channel that the poet's uncle, Colonel Ashburnham, who had seen long service in India, swore that it could be matched only in the tropics. For young Swinburne the three hours of storm were a period "of supreme and supernal joy." He delighted in the lightning flashes, the winds, and the wild freedom of the waters. The thrilling experience lived in his memory all his life, and at various times, widely separated in point of years, was the subject of his pen.

Lafourcade recommends reading the following descriptions of this storm as an interesting study in style: (1) The account in *The Times* for August 25, 1855 (for the dullness of the journalese); (2) the opening paragraph in Swinburne's *Essays and Studies* (for "fine rhythmical prose"); and finally (3) this poem (for "ponderous anapests").

15. *fraught*. Cargo, load.

18. *heart of Ind*. Suggested, perhaps, by the vows of Colonel Ashburnham, Swinburne's uncle and companion on the boat, that he had seen no storms like this out of India.

Page 784. NORTHUMBERLAND

Swinburne spent much of his childhood and early youth on the wild moors that surrounded the home of his grandfather, Sir John Swinburne, in Northumberland, the northernmost county of England. Here he could climb, ride, or swim to his heart's content, and here too he could brood over his most glorious symbol of freedom, "the white wandering waste of sea far north."

28. *Their hearts . . . Flodden side.* In 1513 the English under the Earl of Surrey defeated the Scots under James IV at Flodden Field, a hill in Northumberland near the Scottish border.

29. *hers who rode the waves.* Grace Darling (1815–1842) a native of Bamborough, Northumberland. Her father was the keeper of the Longstone (Farne Islands) lighthouse. On September 7, 1838, the *Forfarshire,* with sixty-three persons aboard, struck on the Farne Islands. Darling saw the wreck from the lighthouse, and by a combination of daring, strength, and skill he and his daughter succeeded in reaching it and rescuing five of the survivors. A second trip, made by Darling and two of the rescued men, brought to safety the four remaining survivors. The Darlings were given a gold medal for their heroism.

33. *Joyous Gard.* The residence of Lancelot of the Lake, reputed to have been at or near Berwick, Northumberland.

46. *Our Collingwood.* British naval commander (1750–1810), a native of Newcastle-on-Tyne, Northumberland.

though Nelson. See note to *Ode on the Death of the Duke of Wellington,* above.

Page 785. THE LAKE OF GAUBE

In the spring of 1862 Swinburne went to the Pyrenees, where he swam "through the still stronger chill of the darkness from shore to shore" of the mysterious Lake of Gaube—this to the overawing of the natives, who believed in the fearful tradition that he who swam in Gaube was doomed to certain death.

In his *Studies in Prose and Poetry* (1894) Swinburne wrote the following concerning Lake Gaube and his visit there:

"The fiery exuberance of flowers among which the salamanders glide like creeping flames, radiant and vivid, up to the skirt of the tragic little pine-wood at whose heart the fathomless lake lies silent, with a dark dull gleam on it as if of half-tarnished steel; the deliciously keen and exquisite shock of a first plunge under its tempting and threatening surface, more icy cold in spring than the sea in winter; the ineffable and breathless purity of the clasping water in which it seems to savour of intrusive and profane daring that a swimmer should take his pleasure . . . the sport of catching and taming a salamander till it became the pleasantest as well as the quaintest of dumb four-footed friends; the beauty of its purple-black coat of scaled armour inlaid with patches of dead-leaf gold, its shining eyes and its flashing tongue—these things, of which a humbler hand could write at greater length than this, would require such a hand as Hugo's to do them any sort of justice."

1–8. These lines form a most impressive passage dealing with the majestic sovereignty of the sun, an orb, a god, may one say, to whom in Swinburne's poetry much tribute is paid.

10–25. These lines give the poet's impressions of the salamanders which he describes in the quotation from *Studies in Prose and Poetry,* above.

25–8. *even as fear . . . dark as death.* A reference to the tradition that anyone who dared to bathe in the Lake of Gaube must surely die.

33–54. This passage describes the dive, the plunge of "the downward swimmer," the "love of his body and soul for the darkling delight of the soundless lake."

Page 787. IN A ROSARY

The thought in the last stanza of this poem descriptive of the beauty of roses is similar to that of Wordsworth in the concluding stanza of *I Wandered Lonely as a Cloud* (*English Romantic Poets,* p. 66). Wordsworth's daffodils

> flash upon that inward eye
> Which is the bliss of solitude

long after they have perished; just as Swinburne's roses

> live and shine on memory, free
> . . . from fear of death or change.

Page 788. BURNS: AN ODE

In this tribute to Burns, Swinburne uses the measure employed by Burns in *A Bard's Epitaph* and in so many other poems that it is not inaccurate to speak of it as his favorite poetic melody. Swinburne admired Burns especially for his manly sense of liberty and for his boldness in voicing his dislike of people and principles of a kind that Swinburne himself found highly offensive.

7–42. There is much of irreverence in Burns's poetry. He lashes both the church and the clergy, and he is influenced by none of the orthodox creeds in arriving at his own beliefs. Like Emerson, he pokes fun at the Devil. He jests at the "doctrine" of eternal damnation, and the Puritan conscience is a thing which he can never take seriously. Calvin (l. 25) is John Calvin (1509–1564), the French theologian and reformer, originator of the dogma of Scottish Presbyterianism. He made much of punishment by hell-fire for those predestined to damnation.

67. *The daisy . . . cleft.* A reference to Burns's poem *To a Mountain Daisy*, in which he sadly regrets having turned down the flower with his plough.

73–90. *But Chaucer's daisy . . . Burns may claim.* These lines point out that in certain fields of poetry Burns was surpassed by Chaucer, Dunbar, and Villon. William Dunbar (1465?–1530?) was a Scottish poet, author of *The Dance of the Sevin Deidly Synnis*, of which poem Swinburne was thinking when he wrote ll. 77–8. For Villon, see *A Ballad of Francis Villon*, text p. 749, and the introductory note to that poem, above.

112. *bent.* A field, pasture, or heath.
byre. A cow house.

Page 789. SWINBURNE'S LETTERS

789a, l. 11. *Aurora Leigh.* A narrative poem by Elizabeth Barrett Browning.

789a, l. 16. *Rosamond.* An early play of Swinburne's, not yet published when this letter was written.

789a, l. 17. *Peter Harpdon.* William Morris's poem, *Sir Peter Harpdon's End.* It appeared in *The Defence of Guenevere and Other Poems* (1858).

789b, l. 9. *The Golden House.* Swinburne changed the title of *Rudel in Paradise* (l. 10) to *The Golden House.* The poem seems to be lost.

789b, l. 16. *Nichol.* See introductory sketch to Swinburne, text, foot of p. 675.

Page 790.

790a, l. 8. *Eglamor.* A troubadour in Browning's *Sordello*, over whom Sordello, the chief figure in the poem, triumphs as a poet. The historical Sordello was a thirteenth-century troubadour mentioned repeatedly by Dante in his *Purgatorio.*

790b, l. 18. *Dobell.* Sydney Dobell (1824–1874), a member of the "Spasmodic School" of poets ridiculed by W. E. Aytoun. He is a mere name now, but in his heyday he influenced Tennyson (in *Maud* especially) and Mrs. Browning.

790b, l. 19. *Tupper.* Martin Farquhar Tupper (1810–1889). His *Proverbial Philosophy*, commonplace maxims and reflections couched in rhythmical form, achieved extraordinary popularity. See note to p. 669a, l. 15, above.

Paulina, Lady Trevelyan, was the first wife of Sir Walter Calverley Trevelyan, a naturalist and a liberal patron of the fine arts. She exercised a wholesome influence on Swinburne. Her death occurred in 1866.

Page 791.

791a, l. 18. *out of Boccaccio. The Two Dreams*, originally entitled *The White Hind.*

791a, l. 25. *her hair as is kep.* See note to l. 76 of *A Ballad of Life*, above.

791a, l. 42. *the British Murray.* A reference to the British guide-books, the publication of which was suggested to John Murray (1778–1843) by the fact that his publishing house brought out Mrs. Starke's *Guide for Travellers on the Continent* in 1820. Several of the guide-books in the Murray series were written by the third John Murray (1808–1892), son of the John Murray mentioned above. The founder of the publishing house was also a John Murray (1745–1793).

791b, l. 4. *Ratbert and Ruy Blas.* Ratbert is a character in Hugo's *L'Italie*, which is a section of his *La Légende des Siècles*. *Ruy Blas* is a drama by Hugo.

791b, l. 21. *Giorgione.* A Venetian painter (1478?–1511).

791b, l. 22. *Gabriel.* Dante Gabriel Rossetti.

791b, l. 23. *Stephen.* The first Christian martyr. He was accused of blasphemy and stoned to death (Acts 6 and 7).

791b, l. 24. *Carpaccio.* An Italian painter (*c.* 1450–*c.* 1522).

791b, l. 26. *Velasquez.* A Spanish painter (1599–1660).

791b, l. 27. *Uccello.* An Italian painter (1396–1475).

791b, l. 33. *Sir Walter.* Lady Trevelyan's husband.

791b, l. 41. *Garibaldi.* An Italian patriot (1807–1882).

Lord Houghton. Richard Monckton Milnes (1809–1885), afterward Lord Houghton, was a man of taste and culture whom Swinburne met in 1861 and with whom he was soon on most friendly terms. Lord Houghton "was immensely useful" to the poet, though in some ways his influence was not for the best.

Page 792.

792a, l. 42. *mieux conservé.* Better preserved.

792a, l. 46. *Titian.* A Venetian painter (1477–1576).

792b, l. 2. *chez moi.* At my house.

792b, l. 48. *rimailleur inédit.* A writer of bad verse.

Page 793.

793a, l. 42. *Lewes's.* G. H. Lewes (1817–1878), a versatile writer, author of a *Life of Goethe.*

793a, l. 50. *Mr. Carlyle's volumes. The History of Frederick the Great*, published in six volumes from 1858 to 1865.

793b, ll. 13–14. *letter at the end of vol. 4.* This letter of "May 5th (16th)," 1744, written in London by George Lyttelton, "now an official in Prince Fred's household," to his father, contains the news that the King of Prussia (Frederick) is confined because of madness arising out of excessive drinking. The writer wonders at the effect upon the fate of Europe this occurrence may have at this critical time, and quotes Lord Chesterfield as saying that Frederick "is only thought to be *mad* in Germany, because he has *more wit than* other Germans."

793b, l. 17. "*A God-intoxicated man.*" By the "God-intoxicated man" Swinburne meant Cromwell, a sympathetic interpretation of whom Carlyle published in 1845 under the title of *The Letters and Speeches of Oliver Cromwell.* The phrase probably arose out of the characterization of Spinoza (1632–1677) as a "Gott-trunkener Mensch" by Hardenberg (Novalis) (1772–1801). The poet, although he quite regularly voices his hostility toward kings, nevertheless places Frederick's "clear, cold purity of pluck" far above the "splendid pietism" of Cromwell.

793b, l. 31. *Leonidas.* King of Sparta (491–480 B.C.), the hero of the defense of the pass of Thermopylæ.

Joshua. The leader of the Israelites in their invasion and settlement of Canaan.

793b, l. 32. *Marathon.* The battle of Marathon in 490 B.C. resulted in the defeat of the Persians by the Greeks under Miltiades.

Gilgal. The name, which means "circle of sacred stones," is given to several places in western Palestine.

793b, l. 37. *Boädicea.* A queen of the Iceni in the east of Britain, who led a revolt against the Romans, but was defeated and took her own life.

Page 794.

794b, l. 3. *Moxon's series.* Edward Moxon (1801–1858), a publisher and verse-writer, his first publication being Lamb's *Album Verses.* He published for Southey, Wordsworth, Landor, Tennyson, Browning, Swinburne, and others.

Lord Lytton. Edward Bulwer Lytton (1803–1873), with whom Swinburne lived for some time, was a versatile writer, known best for his novel, *The Last Days of Pompeii.* It was his advice that led Swinburne to change from the publishing house of Moxon to that of Hotten.

794b, l. 30. *The book.* Refers to *Poems and Ballads.*

Page 795.

Thomas Purnell (1834–1889) was a London journalist. He founded a club known as the "Decemviri," of which Swinburne, Whistler, and Joseph Knight were members. It was Purnell who introduced Swinburne to Mazzini.

795b, l. 6. *Close, Buchanan.* John Close (1816–1891) published tracts of verse. As printer at Kirby Stephen he attracted patrons by his rhyming. All his life he wrote "metrical balderdash." Robert W. Buchanan (1841–1901) attacked the Pre-Raphaelites in a pseudonymous article (1871) entitled *The Fleshly School of Poetry.* Swinburne retorted with *Under the Microscope.* Buchanan was a voluminous writer of verse, but of little poetry.

E. C. Stedman (1833–1908) was an American poet and critic.

Page 796.

John H. Ingram (1849–1916) was a literary critic and popular writer. His most talked of work was *The True Chatterton,* though his articles on Poe were also well-known.

Page 797.

797a, l. 37. *Mr. Frederick Locker.* Locker (1821–1895), who took the name of Locker-Lampson in 1885, is known especially for his light verse, the first volume of which appeared in 1857.

797a, l. 41. *Mr. Whistler.* James M'Neill Whistler (1834–1903), a distinguished American painter and etcher, who removed to England in 1863, and whom Swinburne met in Paris that year. Swinburne's poem, *Before the Mirror,* was inspired by Whistler's "The Little White Girl."

Joseph Knight (1829–1907), who was a journalist, a lover of poetry, and a great student of dramatic literature, came to know Swinburne in the late 'sixties, became his close friend, and proved serviceable to him in a number of ways.

797b, ll. 25–6. *Sir C. Dilke.* Charles Wentworth Dilke (1843–1911) was a liberal statesman and the author of *Greater Britain* (1868), the record of a tour through many parts of the British Empire. He was proprietor of the *Athenæum* and of *Notes and Queries.*

Sir Edmund Gosse (1849–1928) became assistant librarian in the British Museum in 1867, translator to the Board of Trade in 1875, and librarian to the House of Lords in 1904, a post which he held for ten years. He published essays on Norwegian, Swedish, Danish, and Dutch poets, wrote an excellent life of Ibsen, *Life and Letters of John Donne,* lives of Gray, Jeremy Taylor, Sir Thomas Browne, and numerous other books. He was a very close friend of Swinburne and his life of the poet is invaluable.

Page 798.

798a, l. 11. *Scott.* William Bell Scott (1811–1890), a poet and artist, a friend of Swinburne and Rossetti. He was the author of five volumes of verse, the best of which is of a mystical and metaphysical nature.

798a, l. 12. *Watts.* Walter Theodore Watts-Dunton (1832–1914), the literary critic—once a solicitor—who befriended Swinburne and in whose care the poet lived from 1879 to the time of his death.

798a, l. 37. *the Veronese.* Catullus had a country home at Sirmio on Lake Garda. Cf. Tennyson's "*Frater Ave atque Vale,*" text p. 190, and note on that poem.

Page 799.

799a, l. 7. *Wain[e]wright.* Thomas Griffiths Wainewright (1794–1852), a painter and magazine writer, who poisoned his sister-in-law, his uncle, his mother-in-law, and a friend. Dickens's *Hunted Down* and Bulwer-Lytton's *Lucretia* were suggested by his crimes. His personality, as artist and poisoner, has interested several latter-day writers, notably Oscar Wilde in *Pen, Pencil and Poison,* and A. G. Allen in T. Seccombe's *Twelve Bad Men.*

799b, l. 26. *Trelawny.* Edward John Trelawny (1792–1881), Shelley's friend, who was present at Leghorn when Shelley was drowned. He wrote *Adventures of a Younger Son* and *Records of Shelley, Byron, and the Author.*

John Morley (1838–1923), statesman and writer. He was editor of the *Fortnightly Review* from 1867 to 1882, and opened the pages of this publication to Swinburne at a time when the poet was chafing over his inability to find an editor who would print his critical prose.

Page 800.

800a, l. 8. *Trollope.* Anthony Trollope (1815–1882), post-office clerk, novelist, author of books of travel. *The Warden, Barchester Towers,* and *The Last Chronicle of Barset* are perhaps his best-known novels.

800a, l. 9. *Braddon.* Mary Elizabeth Braddon (Mrs. Maxwell) (1837–1915), who became famous with her novel *Lady Audley's Secret* (1862).

800a, l. 25. *Leconte de Lisle* (1818–1894), the foremost poet of his generation, both in thought and in expression, was the leader of the "Parnassiens," a school of young French poets who affected "Olympian calm," and so shunned "Romantic storm, stress, and subjectivism."

800a, l. 41. *plagiarism from Diderot.* Swinburne believed that Browning took the episode of Jules and Phene, in the second part of *Pippa Passes* (see text p. 239), from Diderot. In a letter to John Morley, dated February 13, 1876, he wrote: "If Browning did not consciously steal and unconscionably spoil in the stealing, the episode of Jules the sculptor's marriage in *Pippa Passes* from the 'Histoire de Mme. de la Pommeraye et du Marquis des Arcis,' in *Jacques le Fataliste,* then all incredible coincidences must henceforth be held credible. The minute I saw the gist of Diderot's story I recognized the admirable original of a decidedly unadmirable copy. As the work of a slighted woman's revenge, the conception seems to me most terribly and almost grandly natural; as the device of a male crew of jealous rival artists, absurdly false, and repulsive by reason of its absurdity."

800b, l. 22. *Fouquier-Tinville petit-fils.* Antoine-Quentin Fouquier-Tinville (1746–1795) died on the guillotine after having sent innumerable victims to the guillotine in his capacity as public accuser for the French Revolutionary Tribunal. Swinburne calls the editor of *The Times* "grandson" (*petit-fils*) of Fouquier-Tinville because criticisms of *The Times* have "guillotined" so many British writers.

800b, l. 36. *grivoises.* Licentious, ribald.

Page 801.

801a, l. 7. *merum sal cum mero melle.* Pure wit (salt) with pure sweetness (honey).

801a, l. 27. *facile principem.* Easily the first man.

801b, l. 19. *Cowley.* Abraham Cowley (1618–1667), a poet and prose writer, author of an epical romance of "Pyramus and Thisbe" when he was ten years old. *The Mistress, Pindarique Odes,* and *Verses on Several Occasions* are other poetical works of his. Among his prose titles are *A Discourse by Way of Vision concerning Oliver Cromwell* and *Essays.*

801b, l. 34. *Etheredge.* Sir George Etheredge (1634?–1691?), a writer of comedies, author of *The Comical Revenge, or Love in a Tub,* important as the first example of English prose comedy. Other comedies of his are *The Man of Mode* and *She Would If She Could.*

801b, l. 35. *Aphra Behn.* Mrs. Aphra Behn (1640–1689) wrote fifteen plays between 1671 and 1689, the most popular of which was *The Rover.* She also wrote poems and novels. Her novel, *Oroonoko, or the History of the Royal Slave,* is said to be the first English philosophical novel containing dissertations on abstract subjects, such as the religion of humanity.

Page 802.

802a, l. 16. *venerable and revered father.* Sir Henry Taylor (1800–1886), the author of *Philip von Artevelde* and other plays in verse, and a number of poems.

802a, l. 37. *pièce de résistance.* The main thing.

802b, l. 46. *Wolfe's tribute.* James Wolfe (1727–1759), commander of the British troops at Quebec (1759), is said to have recited Gray's *Elegy Written in a Country Churchyard* to his officers as they were floating quietly down the river to make a surprise attack on the French. When he finished the poem he paused and then said solemnly: "Gentlemen, I would rather have written that poem than take Quebec tomorrow."

Page 803.

John Churton Collins (1848–1908), a professor of English at the University of Birmingham, was the author of *Studies in Shakespeare; Studies in Poetry and Criticism; Voltaire, Montesquieu, and Rousseau in England;* and numerous other scholarly writings. Collins and Swinburne were at one time close friends, but in a critical article which Collins wrote he attacked Swinburne's criticism and brought on a controversy that destroyed the friendship.

Paul Hamilton Hayne (1830–1886) was an American poet, a native of Charleston, South Carolina.

803b, l. 1. *Mr. Burroughs'.* John Burroughs (1837–1921), an American naturalist and author.

803b, l. 15. *Mr. Horne.* Richard Henry Horne (1803–1884), author of the epic *Orion, The Death of Marlowe, Ballad Romances,* and others. See note for p. 975 (text p. 1137).

803b, l. 20. *"In the wide waste there still is a tree."* This is l. 46 of Byron's *Stanzas to Augusta.*

803b, l. 34. *Manfred.* A dramatic poem by Byron.

803b, l. 38. *"Hall of Arimanes."* In *Manfred,* Manfred, guilty of some inexpiable crime, visits the Hall of Arimanes (the principle of evil), refuses submission to the spirits of evil, bids them call up the dead, and has a vision of Astarte, the woman whom he has loved.

Page 804.

Sir Sidney Lee (1859–1926), an English man of letters, editor of the *Dictionary of National Biography,* and author of many books on literary men and subjects.

See *In the Bay,* text p. 753, and *Christopher Marlowe,* text p. 767.

804a, l. 43. *Canterbury.* Marlowe's birthplace.

804b, l. 17. *Giordano Bruno.* An Italian philosopher (1548?–1599?) who saw God as the unity reconciling spirit and matter.

Sir Edmund Burne-Jones (1833–1898) was the greatest of the painters who came under the influence of the Pre-Raphaelite movement in England.

804b, l. 30. *Palamon and Arcite.* Palamon and Arcite are rivals for the love of Emilia in Chaucer's *Knight's Tale.*

Page 805.

805a, l. 13. *Joyous Gard.* See note to l. 33 of *Northumberland,* above.

Clement K. Shorter (1857–1926) was an English journalist and critic.

805b, l. 13. *Mr. Whitley Stokes.* Stokes (1830–1909) was an Irish Celtic scholar, jurist, and Indian official.

805b, l. 46. *Mr. Nicholls.* The Rev. A. B. Nicholls, who became the husband of Charlotte Brontë, June 29, 1854.

Page 806.

806a, ll. 12–13. *Martha Brown.* A servant of the Brontës in their home, The Parsonage, at Haworth.

806a, l. 25. *Vittoria Colonna.* A famous Italian poetess (1490–1547) and friend of Michelangelo.

William Sharp. See text p. 1051.

806b, l. 38. *Sark.* One of the Channel Islands, a bailiwick of Guernsey. It is the Garden of Cymodoce in Swinburne's poem of that name. Mr. Gosse tells us that Swinburne was "quite infatuated . . . with this rocky islet" and after his visit there in 1876 said that he would like to be the king of Sark.

WILFRID SCAWEN BLUNT

BIBLIOGRAPHY

I. WORKS

Poetical Works. 2 vols. (Macmillan: London, 1928.) The most comprehensive collection of Blunt's poetry.

Poems. (Knopf: New York, 1923.) A selection made by Floyd Dell, with the approval of the author, from the 1923 London edition.

Poetry of Wilfrid Blunt. (Heinemann: London, 1898.) A selection arranged by W. E. Henley and George Wyndham, containing the bulk of the preferred poems of Blunt.

My Diaries. (Secker: London, 1932.) The most recent edition of Blunt's personal narrative, containing a foreword by Lady Gregory.

II. BIOGRAPHY AND CRITICISM

Chew, S. C. "Wilfrid Scawen Blunt; An Intimate View," *North American Review,* CCXVII, 664–75 (May, 1923). Describes a visit to the poet's Sussex home; bases his claim to fame on the love lyrics, in which he proves himself to be an upholder of the Byronic tradition.

Fenlon, J. F. "Wilfrid Scawen Blunt," *Catholic World,* CXVI, 357–69 (Dec., 1922). A brief biographical review, showing Blunt's religious antecedents and the decay of his faith.

Graham, R. B. C. "Wilfrid Scawen Blunt," *English Review,* XXXV, 486–92 (Dec., 1922). Describes the poet's home as it has remained since his death; names his love sonnets his best work.

O'Connor, T. P. "Wilfrid Scawen Blunt," *Living Age,* CCCXV, 157–63 (Oct. 21, 1922). A reminiscence of a visit at Blunt's Sussex residence, recalling his wide variety of interests.

Tynan, Katharine. "Wilfrid Scawen Blunt," *Catholic World,* XLVII, 370–8 (June, 1888). Analyzes *The Bedouins of the Euphrates, Son-*

nets and Songs, and *Love Sonnets of Proteus;* shows the poet's strong interest in contemporary politics.

Watson, William. "Poetry by Men of the World," *Living Age*, CLXXXIV, 85–90 (Jan. 11, 1890). Shows the poet's efforts toward liberalizing verse forms and his preference for assonance over rhyme.

White, N. I. "Wilfrid Blunt's Diaries," *South Atlantic Quarterly*, XXI, 360–4 (Oct., 1922). Points out the conscious unity of the *Diaries* and their wide range of interests.

NOTES

"... Above all things the verse of Blunt is sincere. The Byronic tradition, a scanty stream in later English verse, flows at its clearest in his poetry. If there is introspection, there is nothing in it anticipative of the eighteen-nineties. There is not mere morbid, self-deceitful brooding, but pitiless, clear-sighted self-analysis. [His love poetry] reveals 'the loved one as fully as it expresses the lover'; it is 'a love-poetry that searches even while it sings.' Here is a man honest with himself and with the Beloved and with the world, bringing loyalty even to the service of those relationships wherein disloyalty most often plays a part." (Samuel C. Chew, in the *New Republic*, XXIII, 250.)

"When the Victorian era was at its height and every poet was decking himself out in abstract garments—when the fashion of romantic unreality was as strong as ours is today of realism—Blunt had the honesty of insight into his own feelings to write differently from the rest, in a way that interested him, to write about real people of this world in actual situations and about places he had actually seen. Today that alone would not distinguish him, but coming when it did, eccentrically in the midst of Victorian vagueness, it denoted an extraordinary strength of mind. That strength, that original and honest look at things, gave him a wisdom and passion of utterance that are acceptable even now, and make him far more readable than most of his contemporaries. It is impossible to approach him with condescension. He knows too much; he sees too far into the same difficult and basic strugglings in life which we have made grave and monstrous today." (Maurice Lesemann, in *Poetry*, September, 1923.)

Page 808. THE MORTE D'ARTHUR

2. *Table Round*. For this and all the other proper names appearing in the poem see Tennyson's *Morte D'Arthur* (p. 31), *Sir Galahad* (p. 44), and *The Idylls of the King* (pp. 139–183). See also the notes to these poems.

ROBERT BRIDGES

BIBLIOGRAPHY

I. WORKS

Poetical Works, 6 vols. (Oxford University Press: 1929–30.) A reprint of the edition of 1898–1905; the appendix of each volume furnishes brief notes.

Shorter Poems. (Oxford University Press: 1931.) A convenient re-issue of Vol. II of the above-named edition, also including selections from *Later Poems* (1912), *October* (1920), and *New Verse* (1926).

The Testament of Beauty. (Oxford University Press: 1930.) The second issue of Bridges' final work in poetry; this edition incorporates the author's last revisions.

Poetical Works. (Oxford University Press: 1912.) Complete for its date, except for the eight plays.

New Verse, Written in 1921. (Oxford University Press: 1925.) Contains besides the 1921 pieces a number of earlier lyrics.

II. BIOGRAPHY AND CRITICISM

Kelshall, T. *Robert Bridges*. (Scott: London, 1924.) A general discussion, intended to serve as an introduction to the man and his work; praises his variety and his scholarship.

McKay, G. L. *A Bibliography of Robert Bridges*. (Oxford University Press: 1933.) Based on the Daniel check list of 1895 and the Modern Authors publication, 1921; adds the privately printed pieces, the Yattendon Hymns; attempts to identify the *editio princeps* for each item.

Smith, Nowell C. *Notes on "The Testament of Beauty."* (Oxford University Press: 1931.) A scholarly résumé of the philosophy of the poem and its technical features; adds explanations of unfamiliar allusions.

Warren, T. H. *Robert Bridges*. (Oxford University Press: 1913.) A brief enthusiastic review of the poet's work and influence, including many readings from his poetry.

Young, F. E. B. *Robert Bridges: A Critical Study*. (Secker: London, 1914.) Disregarding biographical details, pretends only to express the writer's enthusiasm for the "peculiar excellencies which have made the work of Robert Bridges so great a personal joy"; chapter VII offers an analysis of his prosody.

III. ARTICLES FROM BOOKS

Dowden, Edward. "The Poetry of Robert Bridges," in *New Studies in Literature*. (Paul: London, 1895.) Praises the poet's keen appreciation of objects in nature; pleads for a wider knowledge of his sonnets; analyzes several of his dramas.

Freeman, John. "Robert Bridges," in *The Moderns*. (Scott: London, 1915.) Compares the poet's metrical technique with Tennyson's; comments on Bridges' "joyousness of life" and his patriotic fervor.

Hearn, Lafcadio. "Robert Bridges," in *Pre-Raphaelite and Other Poets*. (Dodd: New York, 1922.)

Admits, but refuses to lament, that the number of the poet's readers is not large; analyzes "Eros," "On a Dead Child," and "Nightingales."

Hind, C. L. "Robert Bridges," in *More Authors and I.* (Dodd: New York, 1922.) Recalls the appointment to the laureateship, which the poet wears gracefully, despite some lack of popularity.

Squire, J. C. "The Attack on Mr. Bridges," in *Books in General,* Third Series. (Hodder: London, 1921.) A defense of the traditions of the laureateship, protesting against the complaint that the incumbent laureate must versify to earn his salary.

Symons, Arthur. "Robert Bridges," in *Studies in Prose and Verse.* (Dutton: New York, 1904.) Finds the poet's charm in his simple lyrics, his appeal to "direct though delicate emotions"—which are marked with temperance and content.

Ward, A. C. "Robert Bridges: 'The Testament of Beauty,' " in *The Nineteen-Twenties.* (Methuen: London, 1933.) Briefly remarks the poem as a revival in English of "the grand manner"; sees Bridges as a guiding voice in an age of disillusionment.

IV. ARTICLES FROM MAGAZINES

Boas, Cicely. "The Metre of 'The Testament of Beauty,' " *London Mercury,* XXII, 147–53 (June, 1930). Justifies the poem's irregularities of metre and rhythm on the score of the poet's search for a suitable medium.

Colum, Padraic. "Robert Bridges and Thomas Hardy," *New Republic,* XII, 47–9 (Aug. 11, 1917). Wonders that Bridges has had to wait so long for popularity; contrasts his epicureanism with Hardy's stoicism.

Davison, Edward. "In Praise of the Poet Laureate," *Fortnightly Review,* CXXX, 66–79 (July, 1928). Rebukes the neglect which the poet has suffered in England; traces his happier moods through some of his descriptive lyrics; sees a real philosophic depth in his easy conventionality.

Magnus, Laurie. " 'The Testament of Beauty,' " *Cornhill Magazine,* LXVIII, 527–38 (May, 1930). Provides a stimulating analysis of the poem, finding in it influences from Darwin.

Twitchett, E. G. "The Poetry of Robert Bridges," *London Mercury,* XXI, 136–45 (Dec., 1929). Traces the poet's progress through his many volumes; praises *The Growth of Love* as a successful sonnet sequence; remarks of "The Testament of Beauty" that "there has been nothing like it since Lucretius."

Waugh, Arthur. "Robert Bridges," *Fortnightly Review,* CXXXIII, 832–43 (June, 1930). A sympathetic assay of the poet's technical excellence and his unusual learning; analyzes "The Testament of Beauty."

NOTES

"It appears to me that the first quality to be recognized in the poetry of Mr. Bridges is its austerity. Alone among our modern poets, he does not attempt to deafen us with sound or blind us with dazzling color. The determination of writers, in all languages, at this end of a century, to excite their readers upon every occasion and to be forever producing electrical effects upon the senses, is a feature which will probably attract the notice of future historians of literature. In Mr. Kipling—so far as he can be considered a poet—this habit reaches its extremity. In his ballads the note is invariably forced: the rain "threshes," the rollers are "drunken," the islands are "painted vermilion." With Mr. Bridges the opposite is always the case. He pushes reticence to the point of dryness, and in his anxiety not to do wrong to the sacred dignity of beauty, he neglects those sensuous aspects of it which all the world has learnt to demand from the poet. Hence there are passages and even whole pages in his work which the absence of any species of ornament makes exceedingly difficult for a modern attention to follow." (Edmund Gosse, in the *Independent,* January, 1900, p. 107.)

"The secret of the charm of Mr. Bridges's lyrics may seem difficult to explain; there is an elusive simplicity about them; but we come to love them, as we love some English garden that we know, or some corner of English country; they do not force their beauties on our notice, they have a kind of shyness; but they yield an intimate delight, which, once found, is lasting. A perfect sincerity is matched by an exquisite truth and precision. And behind a certain austerity of manner we come to feel a deep reality of feeling. No English poet has given in his verse so true a taste of English country, its grays and greens, its silvery horizons, its rich quiet, its lanes and flowers, above all its trees and singing birds; none has noted so unerringly the features of its seasons." (Laurence Binyon, in the *Living Age,* October, 1918, p. 156.)

Page 812. THERE IS A HILL BESIDE THE SILVER THAMES

22. *myosote.* Forget-me-not.
23. *flower-de-lys.* Lily or iris.
30. *nenuphars.* Water-lilies.
62. *gibbous.* The moon is gibbous when its bright part is greater than semicircle and less than circle.

Page 813. LONDON SNOW

Mr. Charles Williams says that no other poet of Bridges' time equalled him in his power to persuade the reader of the real existence of such abstractions as Virtue, Honour, Truth, and Beauty. This singular prerogative of Bridges' verse, Williams believes, arose out of his surpassing presentation of "concrete instances of these abstractions." In the famous *London Snow,* Beauty is a living and significant thing.

Page 814. THE PHILOSOPHER TO HIS MISTRESS

THOU DIDST DELIGHT MY EYES

THE FULL MOON FROM HER CLOUDLESS SKIES

AWAKE, MY HEART

These four lyrics are examples of Bridges' exquisite love poems. Mr. Williams, who considers *Awake, My Heart* one of the finest love poems of the last century, is especially impressed by its "strength without violence."

Page 815. I LOVE ALL BEAUTEOUS THINGS

MY EYES FOR BEAUTY PINE

Edward Dowden wrote of Bridges nearly fifty years ago: "All he has to tell is that he loves beauty, and loves love; and all he has done is to praise God in the best of ways by making some beautiful things." The passing of years has made of Dowden's statement only a half-truth. It is true in that "the essence of all the poet's philosophy is his pursuit of the spirit of Beauty, and his discovery that Beauty's home is always in the house of Love." The idea pointed out by Dowden is doubtless the mainspring for all the poet's thought, but "it is far from being the sum of his message and achievement."

I NEVER SHALL LOVE THE SNOW AGAIN

This touching poem commemorates the death of Maurice Waterhouse, the brother of Mrs. Bridges.

"Bridges is given to elegiac strains," said Milton Bronner, in the *Bookman*. "The best of his art is the lyric that muses, that ponders, that sighs, 'Alas!' that weeps gently, that breaks into an elegy."

Page 816. NIGHTINGALES

The subtle cadences and the haunting music of this lyric express the high creative gift of the poet, his exact knowledge of metrics, and even his nice philological scholarship.

PATER FILIO

The title means, "The Father to the Son." For an elaborate comment on the poem see Lafcadio Hearn's *Pre-Raphaelite and Other Poems*, pp. 417–9. *Pater Filio* is not strictly a poem of childhood, but it is closely akin to such poetry. Hearn says that Bridges has treated no topic "more exquisitely and touchingly than certain phases of childhood, the poetry of childhood, the purity of childhood, the pathos of childhood. I do not think that any one except Patmore, and Patmore only in one poem, *The Toys* (text p. 1031), has ever approached him."

EMILY BRONTË

BIBLIOGRAPHY

I. WORKS

Poems of Charlotte Brontë and Patrick Branwell Brontë (Vol. I); *Poems of Emily Jane Brontë and Anne Brontë* (Vol. II), ed. by T. J. Wise and J. A. Symington. (Blackwell: Oxford, 1934.) The definitive edition of the entire body of the Brontë poetry, distinctive for 28 pages of facsimiles of Emily's poems.

Complete Poems, ed. by C. K. Shorter. (Doran: New York, 1924.) The best one-volume collection: includes all previously printed pieces, together with the material of the privately published editions; bibliography and complete notes by C. W. Hatfield.

Complete Poems, ed. by C. K. Shorter. (Hodder: London, 1910.) The first well-edited collection, prefaced by an essay by W. R. Nicoll.

Emily Jane Brontë: Poems. (Selwyn: London, 1923.) Interesting for its inclusion of Charlotte Brontë's notes on her sister's poetry.

Brontë Poems: Selections from the Poetry of Charlotte, Emily, Anne, and Branwell Brontë, ed. by A. C. Benson. (Putnam: New York, 1915.) Valuable for its introduction, in which the editor explains why the selections from Emily's poetry take up one-half of the space: without her genius, the poetry of the other three would have been forgotten.

Two Poems: "Love's Rebuke," and "Remembrance," ed. by Fannie E. Ratchford. (Martin: Austin, Texas, 1934.) Provides the text of the two poems, with a discussion of the shadowy Gondal epic.

II. BIOGRAPHY AND CRITICISM

Shorter, C. K. *The Brontës: Life and Letters.* 2 vols. (Scribner: New York, 1908.) The most complete biography, incorporating the *Charlotte Brontë and Her Sisters* (1905) and including over 700 letters.

Simpson, Charles. *Emily Brontë.* (Scribner: New York, 1930.) Containing the substance of most of the older sources, gives some new material respecting Emily's desk, papers, etc. The illustrations, some reproduced from paintings by the author, are especially inviting.

Sugden, K. A. R. *A Short History of the Brontës.* (Oxford University Press: 1929.) A summary of the information obtainable about this remarkable literary household; the tone of the book is clear and judicious.

Willis, Irene C. *The Brontës.* (Duckworth: London, 1933.) A compressed story of the lives of the several Brontë personalities in their Haworth parsonage.

Wilson, Romer. *All Alone: The Life and Private History of Emily Jane Brontë.* (Chatto: London, 1928.) An interesting attempt to construct, out of the biographical data, the psychic foundations of the inner development of the writer which emerged in her poetry and prose.

III. ARTICLES FROM BOOKS

Drinkwater, John. "The Brontës as Poets," in *Prose Papers*. (Mathews: London, 1917.) A review of the Benson edition: remarks the infrequency of Emily's poetic inspiration; dates her best work after 1843.

Gosse, Edmund. "The Challenge of the Brontës," in *Some Diversions of a Man of Letters*. (Scribner: New York, 1919.) Though devoted chiefly to Charlotte, deals with a number of local facts and traditions associated with the Brontë family.

Jack, A. A. "The Brontës," in *The Cambridge History of English Literature*, XIII. (Putnam: New York, 1917.) Maintains for Emily Brontë's poems that "they are on the edge of greatness"; finds in them fuller self-expression than in her novel.

Meynell, Alice. "Charlotte and Emily Brontë," in *Hearts of Controversy*. (Scribner: New York, 1918.) The latter part of the essay deals with Emily, whose imagery is described as simple, in contrast with her sister's love for complex figures; the influence of environment is shown.

Powys, J. C. "Emily Brontë," in *Suspended Judgments*. (Shaw: New York, 1916.) Chiefly a study of Emily Brontë's great novel, but affording a good brief sketch of her Yorkshire *milieu* and an impressionistic analysis of her philosophy.

Swinburne, A. C. "Emily Brontë," in *Miscellanies*. (Scribner: New York, 1911.) Concerned mainly with the writer's prose, but undertakes a general survey of her inner nature and her methods of composition.

Symons, Arthur. "Emily Brontë," in *Figures of Several Centuries*. (Constable: London, 1916.) Points out the personal intensity of the poet's few lyrics.

IV. ARTICLES FROM PERIODICALS

Bradner, Leicester. "The Growth of *Wuthering Heights*," *Publications of the Modern Language Association*, XLVIII, 129–46 (March, 1933). A review of the Gondal poetry (especially the "A. G. A. Poems" and the "Julius Group"), showing how the author was here trying her hand at characterization in unconscious preparation for her novel.

Chadwick, Esther A. "Emily Brontë," *Nineteenth Century*, LXXXVI, 677–87 (Oct., 1919). Comments on Emily's strategic position in the Brontë household; attempts to show the sources of her inspiration.

Chadwick, Esther A. "Haworth Parsonage: The Home of the Brontës," *Nineteenth Century*, CIII, 133–44 (Jan., 1928). An interesting room-by-room tour of the parsonage, describing the library, relics, etc.

Cook, Davidson. "Emily Brontë's Poems," *Nineteenth Century*, C, 248–62 (Aug., 1926). Describes the manuscripts of the poems; reviews Charlotte's often unlucky hand in their editing and publication; concludes with a discussion of the poems first printed in America.

Dodds, Madeleine. "Gondaliand," *Modern Language Review*, XVIII, 9–21 (Jan., 1923), XXI, 373–9 (Oct., 1926). Traces the idea of the dream-kingdom through the Brontë Journals; shows how much of the feeling of the poetry was carried into *Wuthering Heights*. The second article discusses the parts which the various members of the Brontë family contributed to the legend.

NOTES

"It is upon her capacity for experience, her intensity of life, her acceptance of its tragedies, that her lyrical power is founded. The moorland air, with all that it has of sweet and wild, becomes a part of her poetry because it has already become a part of herself. Death, the memory of death, and what seems almost a preference for its associations, characterize her work for the same reason. And all is clothed in reconciling music, because the beauty of the world, answering the rectitude of her soul, compels her to music as the only satisfying statement of the truth of things. Montaigne wrote many essays, and Socrates lived and died, to illuminate a principle which to Emily Brontë was breath and being. She called it liberty, and Englishmen need ask no better name. But liberty is the consequence; the essence is the perception that all growth is from within, that all accepted experience sustains, and that its flower is harmony. The reader of Emily Brontë's lyrics encounters gloom; for the graveyard was next door to Haworth Parsonage, and her mother and sisters lay there. He encounters so much gloom that he may well wonder why the prevailing impression he receives is an impression of warmth and light. Snow falls, the winds moan, the moors are drenched with rain—those lonely moors haunted by violence and vain regret; but in the midst of all is a spirit of heroic mould, a spirit to which all that is adverse in nature appears delightful because it calls forth power, and all that is bleak and desolate appears holy because it prompts to communion; a spirit which, early schooled in misfortune, the wearing siege of perverse destiny leaves ever impregnable, a triumphant personality built upon calamity and disaster, upon suffering and solitude." (*Living Age*, July 24, 1915; reprinted from *The London Times*.)

Page 818. THE PHILOSOPHER

Miss May Sinclair writes of this poem: "... this woman, destitute ... of all metaphysical knowledge or training, reared in the narrowest and least metaphysical of creeds, did yet contrive to express in one poem of four irregular verses all the hunger and thirst after the 'Absolute' that ever moved a human soul, all the bewilderment and agony inflicted by the unintelligible spectacle of existence, the intolerable triumph of evil over good, and did conceive an image and a vision of the transcendent reality that holds, as in crystal, all the philosophies that were ever worthy of the name." (*The Three Brontës*, p. 176.)

Page 819. REMEMBRANCE

It is not known whose death is the subject of this poem, but it seems improbable—Miss Sinclair's indignant denial of a sweetheart of Emily Brontë notwithstanding—that any one who has not experienced a stirring personal emotion could write so "inspired and vehement a song of passionate human love."

Page 824. NO COWARD SOUL IS MINE

For Arnold's reference to this poem, which Miss Sinclair characterizes as "an astonishing poem to have come from a girl in a country parsonage in the 'forties," see ll. 92–100 of his *Haworth Churchyard*, text p. 558. See also the note to ll. 92–100 of that poem.

THOMAS EDWARD BROWN

BIBLIOGRAPHY

I. WORKS

Collected Poems, ed. by H. F. Brown, H. G. Dakyns, and W. E. Henley. (Macmillan: New York, 1900.) A comprehensive collection, comprising the bulk of the four earlier volumes and magazine verse, together with 27 poems not previously published.

Poems, ed. by H. F. B(rown) and H. G. D(akyns). (Macmillan: London, 1908.) A reprint of the foregoing edition, provided with an introduction and notes.

Letters. 2 vols. (Dutton: New York, 1900.) The introductory memoir by S. T. Irwin offers an excellent biographical sketch, concluding with reminiscences of two school associates.

II. BIOGRAPHY AND CRITICISM

Thomas Edward Brown: A Memorial Volume, 1830–1930. (Cambridge University Press: 1930.) A fine collection of essays, reminiscential in part, including appreciations by Canon Wilson, A. T. Quiller-Couch, Henry Newbolt, Professor Boas, and others. Offers a valuable bibliography.

Simpson, S. G. *Thomas Edward Brown, the Manx Poet*. (Scott: London, 1907.) The only effort at a lengthy appraisal of the poet: based on unpublished correspondence in possession of his family and other *personalia* from friends.

III. ARTICLES FROM BOOKS AND PERIODICALS

Abercrombie, Lascelles. "T. E. Brown," *Nineteenth Century*, CVII, 716–28 (May, 1930). Provides a fine discussion of Brown's poetry, praising his "subtly elaborate language."

Boas, F. S. "T. E. Brown," in *The Eighteen-Eighties*, ed. by Walter de la Mare. (Cambridge University Press: 1930.) Finds in the poet's *Fo'c's'le Yarns* a refreshing contrast to the pedagogic career of the author.

Drinkwater, John. "Browning's Influence: T. E. Brown," in *Victorian Poetry*. (Doran: New York, 1924.) Remarks in Brown's poetry something of his elder's love of dramatic contrast and clipped rhetoric.

Hughes-Games, S. H. W. "The Rev. Thomas Edward Brown: Poet," *Fortnightly Review*, LXXIV, 765–77 (Nov., 1900). Points out Brown's service in embalming the Manx dialect in his poetry; reviews the facts of his biography, which find frequent reflection in his poems.

Quiller-Couch, A. T. "T. E. B.," *Monthly Review*, I, 152–64 (Oct., 1900). Reviews Brown's unexciting biography; praises his classical learning and his skill as a letter-writer.

Spender, Constance. "The Poetry of Thomas Edward Brown," *Contemporary Review*, CXXVII, 359–66 (Mar., 1925). Finds Brown's Manx dialect one bar to his popularity; calls his "philosophical yarn" *The Doctor* the poet's masterpiece.

Strachan, L. R. M. "The Poet of Manxland," *Englische Studien*, XXXIV, 350–62 (Dec., 1904). Shows Brown's intimacy with scenes of his homeland, in which most of his poetry is laid; makes comparisons with Wordsworth and Browning.

Tarver, J. C. "T. E. Brown: Manxman, Scholar, Poet," *Nineteenth Century*, LXXXVIII, 1020–5 (Dec., 1920). Provides some pen-sketches and personal recollections of the poet; finds a clearer revelation of the man in his letters than in his poetry.

Tuell, Annie K. "T. E. B.," *Bookman*, LXXI, 290–8 (June, 1930). Comments on the local spirit in Brown's letters and the *Fo'c's'le Yarns;* points out some of the best of his mystical lyrics.

NOTES

"In the poetry not Anglo-Manx but Brown's own lyrical, speculative, descriptive, religious, there is perhaps a finer value and a more than minor originality, not only in the free-ranging verse in days before freedom of verse got itself talked about much. Resemblances to better known poets are evident enough, as is natural where reading and sympathy went wide. Among the English poets Wordsworth was his declared choice, though he suggests more often the anguished or the buoyant Clough in the animal verve of some nature verses and in the gallant pitting of his spirit against the universal secret." (Annie Kimball Tuell, in the *Bookman*, June, 1930, p. 296.)

"[Brown's language in the best of his lyrics] is no longer dialect, but . . . literary English pregnant with the ever varying intonation of *speech*. This is the result of the meter. It is not . . . 'free verse'; for the rhythm is persistently and definitely a formal rhythm. But instead of modulations being fitted into a scheme, the scheme is made to depend on the modulations. The secret of it is, in fact, that the natural cadences of speech are allowed to determine the length of the line. This sounds simple; but in execution it is apt to prove exceedingly difficult. Its supreme practitioner is Coventry Patmore in his odes; but T. E. Brown comes very near him. . . .

"This power of making subtly elaborate language move with the apparent freedom of natural speech is the most striking thing in the technique of Brown's lyrical verse; and whenever he uses this power he exerts on any sensitive ear an extraordinary fascination, however slight the topic. . . . But his lyrical topics are as a rule far from slight." (Lascelles Abercrombie, in the *Nineteenth Century*, CVII, 727.)

Page 825. PEGGY'S WEDDING

Brown had an "indefatigable interest, whether humorous or tragic, in the thing called character. . . . It is just this blessed gift of seeing people as they are, and not as they ought to be, which makes Brown the man of men, and so the poet among poets that he is. Take *Peggy's Wedding*, for instance, and you will see at once that it is imitated from Swift; but you will also see, if you have any taste of letters in you, that it is infinitely better art than Swift's, in that it gives you, with a touch of force perhaps, but with not so much as the hint of a departure from the big lines of human nature, two characters whom you have never met before, but whom you will know to your dying day." (W. E. Henley, in *Essays*, p. 392.)

Page 829. ST. BEE'S HEAD

This bold promontory stands at the westernmost point of Cumberland, England. The St. Bee's light rises 300 feet above the sea.

Page 830. AN OXFORD IDYLL

10. "*horty.*" Haughty.
14. *aitches*. H's.
15. *point-device*. Perfectly correct.
16. "*Burton.*" An English ale.

Page 831. IN MEMORIAM

1. *Braddan*. Brown's father was vicar of Kirk Braddan, near Douglas, Isle of Man, and Brown always writes lovingly of the Braddan country.

CAROL

8. *Withouten dreed.* Without dread; i.e., without doubt.
10. *hight.* Called.
12. *rouncy.* A riding horse.
17. *Cathay.* China.
24. *dromedar.* A camel of unusual speed.
26. *Samarkand.* A city in Turkestan.

CLIMBING

3. *joyaunce*. Delight.
24. *bilberry*. A European species of blueberry.
27. *Natheless*. Nevertheless.

Page 832. O GOD TO THEE I YIELD

Brown wrote this poem in memory of his son Braddan, who died at the age of seven.

SAD! SAD!

In reading this "poem of pain and inquiry" one is reminded of the anguished Clough.

Page 833. MY GARDEN

1. *wot*. Knows.

ELIZABETH BARRETT BROWNING

BIBLIOGRAPHY

I. WORKS

Complete Works, ed. by Charlotte Porter and Helen A. Clarke. 6 vols. (Crowell: New York, 1900.) The definitive autograph edition, equipped with an introduction and full notes.

Complete Poetical Works, ed. by Harriet W. Preston. Cambridge Edition. (Houghton: Boston, 1900.) A recommended edition for the student; prefaced with a biographical sketch by the editor.

Poetical Works, ed. by F. G. Kenyon. (Macmillan: New York, 1897.) The first complete edition of the poetry, containing a preface by the editor.

Poetical Works, with Two Prose Essays. (Oxford University Press: 1932.) A good edition for use in schools; gives the standard text of the poetry and the two essays: "Some Account of the Greek Christian Poets" and "The Book of the Poets."

New Poems of Robert Browning and Elizabeth Barrett Browning, ed. by Sir F. G. Kenyon. (Macmillan: New York, 1915.) Provides a small body of new (about 25) and not generally known poems—chiefly *juvenilia;* the most valuable part of the book is the information which the editor supplies concerning Miss Barrett's criticism of her future husband's poems.

Sonnets from the Portuguese, ed. by Charlotte Porter and Helen A. Clarke. (Crowell: New York, 1933.) A valuable edition for special study, fully equipped with introduction and notes.

The Letters of Robert Browning and Elizabeth Barrett Barrett, 1845–1846, ed. by Robert W. B. Browning. 2 vols. (Harper: New York, 1926.) The entire correspondence as transmitted from Robert Browning to his son, the editor.

Letters, ed. by F. G. Kenyon. (Macmillan: New York, 1899.) A good edition of fascinating material, which is not included in the preceding; the editor supplies biographical information of the correspondents.

Elizabeth Barrett Browning: Letters to Her Sister,

ed. by Leonard Huxley. (Murray: London, 1930.) Gives the text of the extensive correspondence with Mrs. Henrietta Cook, 1846–59.

Twenty-Two Unpublished Letters of Elizabeth Browning and Robert Browning. (United Feature Syndicate: New York, 1935.) The letters date from Oct. 2, 1846 to June 24, 1855; they are addressed to Mrs. Browning's sisters, Henrietta and Arabella. They throw much light on the early married life of the Brownings and their new relations with the Barrett family. Prefaced by a statement from Major Altham, grandson of Captain Surtees Cook, who married Henrietta Barrett.

II. BIOGRAPHY AND CRITICISM

Boas, Mrs. Louise S. *Elizabeth Barrett Browning.* (Longmans: New York, 1930.) Setting aside the task of literary criticism, this simple biography is concerned chiefly with the story of Mrs. Browning's courtship and married life.

Burdett, Osbert. *The Brownings.* (Houghton: Boston, 1929.) Offers little critical comment, but analyzes the extensive correspondence; demonstrates the enduring basis of the wedded life of the Brownings, in which "poetry was not the only grace."

Clarke, Isabel C. *Elizabeth Barrett Browning: A Portrait.* (Hutchinson: London, 1929.) An interesting history of the courtship, following with lucid memorable scenes of the Italian days; provides a human background for certain of Mrs. Browning's poems.

Creston, Dormer. *Andromeda in Wimpole Street.* (Dutton: New York, 1930.) A "novelized" biography of the poet, based largely on correspondence, carrying up to the Italian period.

Gould, Elizabeth P. *The Brownings and America.* (Poet-Lore: Boston, 1904.) An ably written account of the reception of the two poets' work in America.

Lenanton, Mrs. Carola M. *Miss Barrett's Elopement.* (Hodder: London, 1929.) Another of the numerous "fictionized" biographies of the poet; the story begins with her twenty-sixth year.

Loth, David. *The Brownings, a Victorian Idyll.* (Tudor: New York, 1934.) Presents an appealing account of the home life of the poets, discussing their poetry as the fulfillment of human contacts.

Lubbock, Percy. *Elizabeth Barrett Browning in Her Letters.* (Smith: London, 1906.) A condensed study, based on the correspondence, with annotations providing a narrative sequence.

Royds, Kathleen E. *Elizabeth Barrett Browning and Her Poetry.* (Harrap: London, 1918.) One of the best of the briefer lives; includes considerable quotation from Mrs. Browning's poetry.

Shackford, Martha H. *E. B. Browning: R. H. Horne—Two Studies.* (Wellesley Press: 1935.) A refreshing reminder of Mrs. Browning's warm humanity and humor, which enabled her to analyze better than many contemporaries the smugness of "the pewter age."

Sim, Mrs. Frances M. *Robert Browning and Elizabeth Barrett.* (Golden Vista Press: London, 1930.) A brief account of the courtship and marriage; suggests that Miss Barrett is memorialized in *Fifine* and parts of *The Ring and the Book.*

Whiting, Lilian. *A Study of Elizabeth Barrett Browning.* (Little: Boston, 1902.) An uncritical but interesting biography, written chiefly from the enthusiasms arising from visits to places connected with the events of the poet's life.

Whiting, Lilian. *The Brownings; Their Life and Art.* (Little: Boston, 1917.) Based on documents of the family, this book treats chiefly of the last phase of Browning's life.

Willis, Irene C. *Elizabeth Barrett Browning.* (Viking: New York, 1928.) Determined to show the poet apart from her husband's life, this study reveals many of the inconsequential facts of her life, giving little critical material.

Woolf, Virginia. *Flush: A Biography.* (Harcourt: New York, 1933.) With a clever and amusing playing-up of Flush as the chief character, this biography provides a valuable dog's-eye view of the Barrett family and their associates.

III. ARTICLES FROM BOOKS AND PERIODICALS

Cunliffe, J. W. "Elizabeth Barrett's Influence on Browning's Poetry," *Publications of the Modern Language Association*, XXIII, 169–83 (June, 1908). Finds Browning's inspiration prominent in his wife's later work, her influence seen as more subtle and indirect; believes that Mrs. Browning's death is the cause of the obscurity of the lyrical tone under the heavier casuistry of Browning's later verse.

Fonblanque, Ethel de. "The Influence of Italy on the Poetry of the Brownings," *Fortnightly Review*, XCII, 327–44 (Aug., 1909). Reviews the itinerary and residences of the poets, providing the background of many of their poems.

Gosse, E. W. "*Sonnets from the Portuguese,*" in *Critical Kit-Kats.* (Scribner: New York, 1914.) Relates the circumstances of the writing and publication of the sonnets; traces influences, analyzes the style and content of the cycle, finding its sincerity its outstanding merit.

Hickey, Emily. "Elizabeth Barrett Browning: Woman and Poet," *Nineteenth Century*, LXXIV, 164–84 (July, 1913). A useful biographical survey, concluding with critical comment on some of the poems; shows the continuation of the work of the poet by Francis Thompson.

Huxley, Leonard. "Mrs. Browning and Her Father's Forgiveness," *Cornhill Magazine*, LXXIV, 331–5 (Mar., 1933). Prints a new letter from the poet to her sister (dated May 15, 1857), showing Mrs. Browning's "deep appreciation of the smallest concession on his part."

Jones, Sir Henry. "Robert Browning and Elizabeth Barrett Browning," in *The Cambridge History of English Literature*, XIII. (Putnam: New York, 1917.) Comments on Miss Barrett's early work, the effect of her romance on her poetry, and her later passionate interest in contemporary history.

Ritchie, Anne T. "Robert and Elizabeth Browning," *Harper's Magazine*, LXXXIV, 832–55 (May, 1892). An interesting and worth-while review of the life of the two poets, filled with many reminiscential notes.

Woolf, Virginia. "*Aurora Leigh,*" in *The Second Common Reader.* (Harcourt: New York, 1932.) Points out the baneful results of Miss Barrett's long invalidism on her poetry, especially on *Aurora Leigh.*

NOTES

"No English contemporary poet by profession has left us work so full of living fire. Fire is the element in which her genius lives and breathes; it has less hold on earth than Tennyson's or Browning's or Miss Ingelow's, and less aërial impulse, less fantastic or spiritual aspiration, than Miss Rossetti's. But all these noble poets seem to play with life and passion like actors or like students if compared with her. The devout and undevout imaginations which caught hold on her passionate fancy and her sensitive conscience flew up at once into utterance, and became as Marlowe's—'all air and fire'; which by no means always 'made her verses clear' as those of that prince of poets. Nor was the fine madness of her inspiration always such as 'rightly should possess a poet's brain.' But in moral ardor and ethical energy it is unlike any other woman's; and the peculiar passion which it gave to her very finest work, the rush and glow and ardor of aspiring and palpitating life, cannot properly be compared with the dominant or distinctive quality of any other poet. . . ." (Algernon Charles Swinburne, in *Aurora Leigh*, in *Complete Works*, XVI, 3.)

"'In melodiousness and splendour of poetic gift Mrs. Browning stands . . . first among women,' says a critic [P. Bayne, in *Great Englishwomen*]. She may not, as he goes on to say, have the knowledge of life, the insight into character of some, but a poet's far more essential qualities are here, usefulness, fervor, a noble aspiration, and, above all, tender, far-reaching nature, loving and beloved, and touching the hearts of her readers with some virtue from its depths." (Lady Ritchie, in *Dictionary of National Biography*.)

Page 836. COWPER'S GRAVE

The grave of William Cowper (1731–1800) is in Cowper Chapel, Dereham Church, Norfolk, England. About 1754 Cowper, who was of a nervous temperament, began to suffer from attacks of melancholy. These progressed in seriousness, and a few years after their first appearance Cowper, unnerved at the thought of taking an examination for a clerkship in the House of Lords, actually became insane. Upon his recovery he went to the village of Olney, where he turned seriously to literary work, and in 1779 appeared as a writer with the publication of the *Olney Hymns*. In 1794 he suffered another attack of insanity which put an end to his creative work.

19. *madness-cloud . . . him.* In his morbid mental condition Cowper believed that God had forsaken him. See ll. 44–52.

21–24. *And . . . slumber.* In a number of his poems Cowper portrayed nature faithfully and sympathetically.

25. *hares.* Cowper tamed hares in order to find something to employ his mind, and found that caring for them relieved his melancholy. See his poem, *Epitaph on a Hare.*

33–38. Cf. Cowper's poem, *On the Receipt of My Mother's Picture.*

51. *Immanuel.* The name, which means "God with us," is applied to the Christ.

52. "*My . . . forsaken.*" On the cross Christ cried, "My God, my God, why hast thou forsaken me?" (Matthew 27 : 46.)

Page 839. THE CRY OF THE CHILDREN

William Henry Hudson, writing of this poem and of Hood's *The Song of the Shirt*, said that "in each case a voice was found for despair hitherto inarticulate, in each case those who could not speak for themselves found one to speak for them with all the eloquence of sympathy; and the world was forced to give heed." The poem was suggested by the report of a commission appointed to investigate the subject of child labor. Commenting on the rhythm of the poem, Mrs. Browning said that the first stanza came into her head in a hurricane and she was obliged to make the other stanzas like it.

The motto, from the *Medea* of Euripides, means, "Alas, my children, why do you look upon me?"

Page 844. SONNETS FROM THE PORTUGUESE

Elizabeth Barrett wrote this sonnet sequence during the exciting days of her love-making with Robert Browning. She did not give it to the poet until several months after they had taken up their residence in Italy. Edmund Gosse tells the following story (in *Critical Kit-Kats*) of Mrs. Browning's breaking the news to Browning: "One day early in 1847, their breakfast being over, Mrs. Browning went upstairs, while her husband stood at the window watching the street till the table should be cleared. He was presently aware of some one behind him, although the servant was gone. It was Mrs. Browning, who held him by the shoulder to prevent his turning to look at her, and at the same time pushed a packet of papers into the pocket of his coat. She told him to read that and to tear it up if he did not like it; and then she fled again to her own room." Browning, who was completely carried away by the beauty of the sonnets, said afterward: "I dared not reserve to myself the finest sonnets written in any language since Shakespeare's." Mrs. Browning pleaded that the poems were too intimate a confession to be given to the public, and they were first privately printed. Browning finally had his way, however, and in 1850 they were published with the title, chosen by Browning to hide their exact nature, of *Sonnets from the Portuguese.*

In the words (approximately) of Houston Peterson in his *Book of Sonnet Sequences:* In this sequence into which she poured her pent-up emotions, ranging from a surprised despair to an ecstatic idolatry, "Mrs. Browning not only surpassed all those that had preceded her, except Shakespeare, but all that were to follow, with the possible exception of Rossetti. In this sequence she had not only written her own masterpiece, but perhaps the masterpiece among long poems by women."

Sonnet I

1. *Theocritus.* A celebrated Greek poet of the third century B.C. Thirty idylls or pastoral poems bear his name. See note on Oscar Wilde's *Theocritus*, below.

Sonnet II

5. *amerce.* To deprive, punish.
7. *death-weights.* Small weights laid on the eyelids of a corpse to keep them closed.

Page 845. *Sonnet III*

7. *gages.* Pledges.
12. *cypress-tree.* Symbolical of death.
13. *chrism.* Consecrated oil used for anointing the head.

Sonnet V

2. *Electra.* Daughter of Agamemnon, who was murdered by his wife, Clytemnestra, and her paramour, Ægisthus. As a part of his plan to avenge the murder, Orestes, the brother of Electra, caused a report that he was dead to be spread abroad, and carrying what he pretended were his own ashes in a funeral urn, gave them to Electra, whom he mistook for a domestic. So violent was her grief that Orestes knew her for his sister, and together they slew both Clytemnestra and Ægisthus.
11. *laurels.* Poets were honored with crowns of laurel.

Page 846. *Sonnet IX*

12. *Venice-glass.* It was once believed that poison would crack or break Venetian glassware, which is very delicate and fragile.

Sonnet XI

6. *Aornus.* A mountain in India.

Page 847. *Sonnet XIX*

1. *Rialto.* A famous marble bridge over the Grand Canal, Venice.
5. *Pindar.* The greatest lyric poet of ancient Greece (about 522–443 B.C.).
7. *nine . . . Muse-brows.* For the nine Muses see note to l. 27 of Swinburne's *Sapphics*, above.
8. *bay-crown.* Laurel crown for a poet.

Page 849. *Sonnet XXVII*

10. *asphodel.* A flower of which the daffodil or narcissus may be representative.

Sonnet XXX

4. *acolyte.* One who lights and carries the altar candles, prepares the wine and water for the Mass, etc.

Page 850. *Sonnet XXXIII*

1. *pet-name.* Browning's pet-name for Mrs. Browning was "Ba."

Page 851. *Sonnet XXXIX*

10. *God's infliction.* Her illness.

Sonnet XL

5. *Mussulmans.* Mohammedans.
Giaours. The name, meaning infidel, is applied by Turks to Christians and to others who are not Mohammedan.
7. *Polypheme.* The one-eyed Cyclops who imprisoned Odysseus and his companions in a cavern and ate six of them. Odysseus made him drunk, pierced his eye with a stake, and escaped.

Page 852. *From* AURORA LEIGH

"Mrs. Browning's longest narrative poem, *Aurora Leigh,* is conceived and wrought out in close harmony with [her] ideals of what should be the sphere and the aims of poetry. The story concerns the life of a young girl [Aurora Leigh] half-Italian and half-English, who grows up in an old-fashioned country house in England in the midst of books and of nature, who chooses letters for a profession, and who goes to London and captures the world with her poetry. Her love for her cousin [Romney Leigh], a keenly intellectual social reformer, an apostle of statistics and political economy—furnishes the conventional *motif* of passion for the narrative. But though thus ostensibly portraying the life of a visionary girl and though continually revealing the world through her eyes, the poem is really an interpretation and criticism of the entire age in which it was written. The characters are drawn from the whole range of English society; the incident is widely varied and typical and yet not extravagant or out of the bounds of daily experience; the analysis of motive and of the play of the social forces which in large measure determine the action is searching and suggestive; and the poem is continually—too continually for the taste of some uncourageous readers—unfolding the ways of God to man as they reveal themselves through the fortunes and the fates of the actors in the story. There is withal much glowing rhetoric—often brilliantly imaginative, albeit sometimes florid and hysterical—concerning the economic and social and artistic questions that were most canvassed in the later 'fifties. And everywhere the reader is kept within sound of the busy rumor of daily life; he breathes the actual air of the smoky London streets; he explores squalid tenements; he watches the pageantry of church weddings; he flashes on railway journeys across the continent; he is never for long allowed to lose sight of the expressive visage of the great world of fact." (Lewis E. Gates, in the *Critic*, Feb., 1900.)

Page 852. *Extract I*

2. *Marian Erle.* The outcast daughter of a tramp. She is rescued by Romney Leigh, who proposes marriage to her. The plan for the wedding fails.
23. *Malvern Hill.* Between Worcester and Hereford counties, England.
126. *Name . . . thunder-shelf.* Call down curses from Heaven. Swear.

Page 854. *Extract II*

13. *Potiphar's.* The wife of Potiphar, an Egyptian official to whom Joseph was sold as a slave, attempted to seduce Joseph. See Genesis 39.

Extract III

21. *Their age, not Charlemagne's.* Charlemagne (742–814) became king of the Franks (768) and emperor of the West (800). In this passage Mrs. Browning expresses her emphatic opinion that poets should deal with their own age rather than with the past.
25. *Roland . . . Roncesvalles.* Roland was a celebrated hero of French romances of chivalry. He was the nephew of Charlemagne and was defeated and killed at Roncesvalles, Spain, in 778, when Charlemagne was fighting the Saracens.
31. *Fleet Street.* A celebrated street in London, the center of the district for newspapers and printing offices.
58. *Jacob's . . . rams.* The reference is to the story of Jacob's peeling "white strakes" on "rods of fresh poplar, almond, and plane" and using them on the flocks of Laban in such a way that the feebler in the flocks became "Laban's and the stronger Jacob's." (Genesis 30 : 28–41.)
107. *King . . . asses.* For the story referred to, see I Samuel 9 : 5 et seq.

Page 856. A MUSICAL INSTRUMENT

Pan, the Greek god of pasture and forest, flocks and herds, invented the shepherd's pipe, or flute.

MOTHER AND POET

Turin. A city in the north of Italy, was the capital of the kingdom of Italy from 1861 to 1865.
Gaeta. A port on the Mediterranean in the province of Caserta, Italy.
37. *Ancona.* A city in Italy on the Adriatic.
50. *Viva l'Italia!* Long live Italy!
66. *five wounds.* Christ's feet and hands were pierced by nails and his side was wounded with a spear.
77. *wicked queen.* Maria Sophia, wife of Francis II, King of the Two Sicilies. He was driven from his kingdom when the fortress of Gaeta fell, February, 1861.
79. *Cavalli.* Giovanni Cavalli (1808–1879) invented a type of cannon.
84. *King Victor.* Victor Emanuel II (1820–1878) was proclaimed King of Italy in 1861.

ARTHUR HUGH CLOUGH

BIBLIOGRAPHY

I. WORKS

Poems and Prose Remains, ed. by Blanche S. Clough. (Macmillan: London, 1869.) The first collected edition, provided with a selection from the letters of Clough and a memoir by the editor, the poet's wife.

Poems, ed. by H. S. Milford. (Oxford University Press: 1910.) A good book of selections, recommended for general reading.

"The Bothie" and Other Poems, ed. by Ernest Rhys. (Scott: London, 1896.) Gives the gist of Clough's best poetry, together with a brief editorial preface.

II. BIOGRAPHY AND CRITICISM

Osborne, J. I. *Arthur Hugh Clough.* (Constable: London, 1920.) A well-written biography, with a fine sympathy for Clough's personal problems; sees his limited field as the result of his self-imposed restrictions of conscience.

Waddington, Samuel. *Arthur Hugh Clough.* (Bell: London, 1883.) An appreciative study, drawing largely upon notices and reviews, with extracts from various writers who were personally acquainted with Clough; discusses his association with the Tractarian Movement; points out the autobiographical significance of *The Bothie* and *Amours de Voyage.*

III. ARTICLES FROM BOOKS AND PERIODICALS

Bagehot, Walter. "Mr. Clough's Poems," in *Literary Studies*, II. (Dutton: New York, 1911.) Comments on Clough's realism and his skill in English hexameters; gives an analysis of *Amours de Voyage.*

Brooke, S. A. "Arthur Hugh Clough," in *Four Victorian Poets.* (Duckworth: London, 1913.)

Remarks the intense personal tone of the poet's work, which however qualifies him to stand "in the porch, not in the temple of the Muses."

Gosse, E. W. "Clough," in *Books on the Table.* (Heinemann: London, 1921.) Finds a "faint perennial interest" in a few of the lyrics; agrees that Osborne is right in pronouncing that traces of Wordsworth's influence are slight in Clough's mature work—suggests echoes of Longfellow.

Jones, W. L. "Matthew Arnold, Hugh Clough, James Thomson," in *The Cambridge History of English Literature*, XIII. (Putnam: New York, 1917.) Discusses the introspective qualities of Clough's poetry; laments his unfortunate choice of metre.

Knickerbocker, W. S. "Semaphore: Arnold and Clough," *Sewanee Review*, XLI, 152–74 (Jan., 1933). Based on Lowry's publication of Arnold's Letters to Clough; reviews the long duration of the fruitful friendship of the two poets.

Lucas, F. L. "Clough," in *Eight Victorian Poets.* (Cambridge University Press: 1930.) Comments on the poet's spiritual unrest; remarks the decline of his later work, naming him a poet of promise, cut short by a lack of vitality.

Patmore, Coventry. "Arthur Hugh Clough," in *Principle in Art.* (Bell: London, 1889.) Explains how Clough exercised much greater influence on his contemporaries than the bulk of his poetry would seem to warrant; shows that, although much of his work was marred by doubt and introspection, he attained fine expression in *The Bothie.*

Turner, A. M. "A Study of Clough's 'Mari Magno,'" *Publications of the Modern Language Association*, XLIV, 569–89 (June, 1929). A review of the sources of Clough's six narratives in his last volume of verse; Chaucer and Crabbe are named as significant influences.

Welby, T. E. "Clough," in *Back Numbers.* (Smith: New York, 1930.) Comments briefly on Clough's failure to realize his early promise, which was, however, partly redeemed in *The Bothie.*

White, Greenough. "The Character of A. H. Clough as Revealed in His Poems," in *Matthew Arnold and the Spirit of the Age.* (Putnam: New York, 1898.) Naming Clough "a modern Hamlet," this essay points out the unsatisfied indecision in his life and his poetry.

NOTES

"Clough cannot be ranked, on the basis of pure poetic achievement, in the same class with Arnold. . . . He has left, to be sure, in the *Bothie of Tober-na-Vuolich*, a richly fragrant idyll of country life, which is almost unique in its union of humor and transfiguring passion in the treatment of everyday English incident. A few of his lyrics, too, where fate seems to have guided him into melody, are memorable for their simple beauty of phrase as well as for their spiritual ardor. But in the main—let it be said with all possible respect to his eulogist in *Thyrsis*—Clough was but a bungling workman in verse. He must nearly always be read with allowances. And yet his poetry is historically of high interest because of its sensitive reflection of the spirit of his age." (Lewis E. Gates, in the *Critic*, February, 1900.)

". . . In Clough a great natural satirist and storyteller was smothered not by his own doubts but by the doubts thrust upon him by his friends. Born in a happier time, a less superficially introspective time, he would, I believe, have found a place beside Dryden and Byron as one of the greatest of the English in the satiric mode. All the circumstances of his life and time combined to defeat this—Dr. Arnold, the false expectations of his friends, the hatred of his age for clear Attic laughter, and above all its immense appetite for morbid self-analysis. He was in truth Dipsychus, but the Tempter against whom he was struggling, and to whom in the end he submitted, was not the spirit of Evil, but the spirit of Prussian jack-booted Good. Again and again his valiant spirit made desperately gay sorties outside the walls of the besieged city. But in vain. For there were traitors within the gate, who lifted their eyebrows at his gallant adventures into the open. Till in the end he reconciled himself to the starvation diet of the invested city of his soul, and lived the life of the professional martyr assigned to him by the temper of the times. But for all that he had flung down his glove more than once, and Time, as Lowell prophesied, is picking it up for him." (Humbert Wolfe, in *The Eighteen-Sixties*, edited by John Drinkwater, p. 50.)

Page 863. THE MUSIC OF THE WORLD AND OF THE SOUL

Arnold, who referred to this poem as "the one about 2 musics," said that as a metrical curiosity it did not seem to him happy.

Page 865. IN A LECTURE-ROOM

Writing to Clough in 1847, Arnold said that in reading Clough's poetry he was repeatedly reminded of Milton. The third line of this poem he characterized as "Miltonically thought and expressed."

τὸ καλὸν

The title, which means "the beautiful," refers here to moral excellence.

17. *Summum Pulchrum.* The highest beauty.

QUA CURSUM VENTUS

The title means, "Whither the winds [direct] their course"; or more freely, "As the wind flows so the course of the vessel." Virgil's *Aeneid* (III, 269) contains the Latin phrase. The poem is said to have grown out of Clough's reaction against William George Ward, his tutor in mathematics at Balliol. Ward, who turned from Tractarianism to Catholicism, became intensely interested in Clough largely because of the young scholar's intellectuality and his sincere seeking for truth. He questioned the youth "on every possible subject," with the result that Clough finally pronounced "the vortex of Philosophism and Discussion (whereof Ward is the centre), the most exhausting exercise in the world." Many years later Ward, who confessed that he had been prematurely forcing Clough's mind, said: "I cannot to this day think of all this without a bitter pang of self-reproach." (Wilfrid Ward, in *William George Ward and the Oxford Movement*, p. 110.)

"WEN GOTT BETRÜGT, IST WOHL BETROGEN"

The title is an old German proverb meaning, "Whom God deludes is well deluded."
7. *Apollo and the Nine.* See note to l. 27 of Swinburne's *Sapphics*, above.
8. "*the vision . . . divine.*" From Wordsworth's *Excursion*, I, 79.

Page 866. "BLANK MISGIVINGS OF A CREATURE MOVING ABOUT IN WORLDS NOT REALIZED"

This is one of the first of many poems in which one may read the "story of Clough's believing heart and doubting head."

Page 867. THE NEW SINAI

Sinai is the mountain on which Moses received the Law (the Ten Commandments) from God. (See Exodus 19, 20, and 34.)
36. *Olympus*. A mountain in Greece believed in ancient times to be the home of the gods.
37. *Avernian woods*. On the shore of Lago d'Averno, a lake occupying an extinct crater in Campania, Italy, eight miles west of Naples.
56. *Mécanique Céleste*. A celestial mechanism.
82. *Golden Calf*. An image made by Aaron and worshipped by the Israelites (Exodus 32:1–4). Arnold several times spoke of this poem, which he greatly admired, as "the Calf Poem."
105. *Man*. Moses. There was a thick cloud on Sinai when Moses received the Law.
112. *brother-Priest*. Aaron.

Page 868. THE QUESTIONING SPIRIT

Arnold admired this poem for its "trueness to its purpose," its depth of feeling.

Page 869. BETHESDA

This poem is a sequel to *The Questioning Spirit*. The pool of Bethesda, near Jerusalem, was believed to have curative powers. (See John 5:1–9.)
28. Lethe. The river of forgetfulness in Hades.
35. *take . . . go*. The command of Jesus to the sick man at Bethesda (John 5:5–9).

SEHNSUCHT

The title means "longing."

Page 870. PESCHIERA

Peschiera was a fortress in the province of Verona, Italy, on an island in the Mincio. It was taken by the Piedmontese from the Austrians, in 1848, but it again fell into the hands of the Austrians in 1849.
5. *tricolour*. The Italian flag—red, white, and green.
9. *Croat*. A native of Croatia, formerly a crownland within the Dual Monarchy of Austria-Hungary.
14. *Brescia*. Capital of the province of Brescia, in Lombardy, Italy. It revolted from Austria in 1848, and in 1849 was the only Lombard town to rally to Charles Albert, king of Sardinia (Piedmont); but it was taken in a few days by the Austrians.

Page 871. ALTERAM PARTEM

The title means, "*On the other side.*"
18. *Peschiera*. See note on *Peschiera*, above.

IN THE DEPTHS

2. *nobler Muse*. Melpomene, the muse of tragedy. See note to line 27 of Swinburne's *Sapphics*, above.

From DIPSYCHUS

"*Dipsychus* is a delicately sure, analytic record [in about 2000 lines], half-lyrical and half-dramatic, of the typical moods of sad recollection, distrust, hesitation, and final acquiescence, with which many men of Clough's day who had listened long to the music of romantic poetry turned back . . . from vague dreaming and laid hold of the tasks of conventional life. "The scene of the poem is laid in Venice, and at the start the hero, Dipsychus, the Double-Minded, a young Englishman of exceptional fineness of temperament, comes before us very much in the guise of one of the Romantic wanderers of the preceding poetic age. He soliloquizes over the fantastic splendor of the scenes around him, bewails in good set terms the vileness of human society, and turns with true Romantic queasiness to nature for consolation. . . . The reader feels from the very start that he is looking out upon actual throngs of moving men and women, is caught in the veritable swirl of the world's business. [At the conclusion of the poem Dipsychus, who] has been considering and reconsidering his relation to the world, . . . finally elects for the world of action and resigns himself to practical life . . . [at the same time remaining] in his heart true to his idealistic dreaming." (Lewis E. Gates, in the *Critic*, February, 1900.)

"All some very cultured people know of [Clough] . . . is that 'his piping took a troubled sound.' It is no conceit to realize that, if Arnold's poem [*Thyrsis*] has fixed one aspect of his friend and given him an extra fame, it has helped to obscure and prevent the knowledge of that other Clough, high-spirited, deeply imaginative, and full of gusto. It has let critics rest content to see in *Dipsychus* a conventional lament for faith departed, rather than a humorous and penetrating psychological study." (Howard Foster Lowry, in *The Letters of Matthew Arnold to Arthur Hugh Clough*, p. 21.)

See note on *The Latest Decalogue*, below.

1. "*There is no God.*" The Spirit speaks this poem to Dipsychus, who all night had dreamed that a bell kept tolling in his ears, "There is no God."

Page 872. SAY NOT THE STRUGGLE NOUGHT AVAILETH

Stanley T. Williams points to this poem as an example of his belief that a dauntless hope in the face of fact inspired some of Clough's best writing.

IN STRATIS VIARUM

The title means, "In narrow streets."

1–2. *Blessed . . . believed.* See John 20:29.

Page 873. QUI LABORAT, ORAT

The title means, "He who labors, prays."

ὕμνος ἄυμνος

The title means, "The unsung hymn."

Page 874. COME HOME, COME HOME!

This and the six poems immediately following it, which were composed either during Clough's voyage across the Atlantic in 1852, or during his year of residence in America as a teacher and lecturer, were published under the general title of *Songs in Absence.* Many of the "songs in absence" are addressed to Miss Blanche Smith, who later became Mrs. Clough.

Page 875. YE FLAGS OF PICCADILLY

1. *flags of Piccadilly.* Flagstones of Piccadilly, a famous London street of fine houses, clubs, and shops.

COME BACK, COME BACK

22. *Gordian knot.* A knot tied by Gordius, mythical founder of the kingdom of Phrygia. An oracle having declared that he who could untie it should be master of Asia, Alexander the Great, who could not loosen it, cut it with his sword.

Page 876. WHERE LIES THE LAND

1. This line is taken almost verbatim from Wordsworth's sonnet beginning "Where lies the land to which yon ship must go?"

THROUGH A GLASS DARKLY

The title was suggested by I Corinthians 13:12—"For now we see through a glass darkly."

3. *John tells us.* In I John 3:2.

Page 877. ITE DOMUM SATURÆ VENIT HESPERUS

In this poem a peasant girl muses over her absent lover while she is driving home her three cows, Rose, Provence, and La Palie. The title means, "Go home content; the evening star is come." In Virgil's tenth *Eclogue* a goatherd says to his herd, "Go home full-fed; Hesperus comes."

"WITH WHOM IS NO VARIABLENESS, NEITHER SHADOW OF TURNING"

The title is from James 1:17—"Father of lights, with whom is no variableness, neither shadow of turning."

Page 878. THE LATEST DECALOGUE

The Decalogue is the Ten Commandments. On page 44 of John Drinkwater's *The Eighteen-Sixties*, Humbert Wolfe is quoted as follows: "The spirit of *Dipsychus*—as I have called it, the mid-Victorian *Faust*—is admirably conveyed in *The Latest Decalogue*—a poem probably written not much later, in which is one of the most convincing pieces of short satire in the language." See note on *Dipsychus*, above.

"PERCHÈ PENSA? PENSANDO S'INVECCHIA"

The title means "Why think? By thinking you grow old."

EASTER DAY—I

S. T. Williams writes that the mind, in considering Clough, "turns instinctively to the ironical *Latest Decalogue* or the despairing poems on *Easter Day.* The latter," he concludes, "are, indeed heart-broken poems."

12. *where . . first.* In the tomb of Joseph of Arimathæa. See Matthew 27:57–60.

24–26. *women . . . Him.* See Matthew 28; Mark 16:5; Luke 24:4; John 20:22.

28. *Peter . . . Ten.* After the Resurrection "Jesus shewed himself again to the disciples at the sea of Tiberias." See John 21; see also Luke 24:34–43, and John 20:19–25.

29. *Saul.* Jesus appeared to Saul on the road

to Damascus, blinded him with a great light, and cried out, "Why persecutest thou me?" See Acts 9:3–4.

30. *late Creed*. The Nicene Creed, formulated by the First Council of Nicæa, A.D. 325, affirmed the resurrection of Christ, as did also the Apostles' Creed, the date of which is uncertain.

33–34. *The Ten saw*. In Luke 24 it is related that Jesus suddenly stood in the midst of the disciples, quieted them when they were terrified at his appearance, and asked them for food.

35. *Emmaüs*. A village near Jerusalem.

Capernaum's Lake. The sea of Galilee. The city of Capernaum was on its shores.

39. "*some*" . . . "*doubt*." See Matthew 28:17.

98–99. *Set . . . corrupt*. See Matthew 6:20.

110. *catch not men*. Jesus, walking by the sea of Galilee, saw Simon and Andrew casting a net into the sea, and said to them, "Come ye after me, and I will make you to become fishers of men." See Mark 1:16–17.

Page 880.

In *Easter Day II* the poet continues his ironical study of the risen Christ. His thoughts no longer arise out of his "secret self," but are prompted by a voice which, though it admits that "He lies and moulders low," still insists that "In . . . the true creed . . . Christ is yet risen."

JOHN DAVIDSON

BIBLIOGRAPHY

I. WORKS

Poems. (Boni: New York, 1924.) A recommended inexpensive edition, containing a preface by R. M. Wenley and a brief bibliography.

Selected Poems. (Lane: London, 1905.) An excellent representation, including the best of the volumes issued separately 1891–1902.

John Davidson: Poetry. (Benn: London, 1925.) One of the Augustan Books of Modern Poetry, edited by Edward Thompson; contains a selected bibliography.

II. BIOGRAPHY AND CRITICISM

Archer, William. "John Davidson," in *Poets of the Younger Generation*. (Lane: New York, 1902.) Points out the poet's lack of dramatic fitness; finds beauty and power in his blank verse and ballads.

Bronner, Milton. "John Davidson, Poet of Anarchy," *Forum*, XLIV, 305–20 (Sept., 1910). Indicates a strong autobiographical note in Davidson's verse; sees the *Ballads and Songs* as his most characteristic work; regrets the egomania which overcame the last phase of his life.

Fineman, Hayim. *John Davidson: A Study of the Relation of His Ideas to His Poetry*. (University of Pennsylvania Press: 1916.) Relates the poet's reactions against Victorian tradition; points out the influence of Nietzsche; analyzes some ballads and semi-dramatic poems.

Hind, C. L. "John Davidson," in *More Authors and I*. (Dodd: New York, 1922.) Provides a racy biography; sets high value on *Fleet Street Eclogues*.

Johnson, L. P. "John Davidson," in *Reviews and Critical Papers*. (Mathews: London, 1921.) An enthusiastic review of *Ballads and Songs*, pointing out the poet's originality in diction and sentiment.

Le Gallienne, Richard. "Mr. John Davidson's Poetry," *Nineteenth Century*, XXXV, 952–5 (June, 1894). Selects *Fleet Street Eclogues* as the poet's maturest work, unsurpassed in "their whimsical association of incongruities."

Quiller-Couch, A. T. "Mr. John Davidson," in *Adventures in Criticism*. (Putnam: New York, 1925.) Praises the vigor and poetic sureness of the five early dramas; finds in the ballads greater excellence of language than of theme.

Traill, H. D. "Two Modern Poets," *Fortnightly Review*, LXIII, 401–7 (Mar., 1895). A somewhat unkindly exposition of metrical peculiarities in Davidson's verse; finds his "strongest work" in *Ballads and Poems*.

Young, Filson. "The New Poetry," *Fortnightly Review*, XCI, 138–52 (Jan., 1909). Points out the poet's Scotch predilection for religious themes; opines that the very scope and fervor of his message have failed to gain for him a definite following.

NOTES

". . . We must take him [Davidson] as he is, the faults of his manner with the merits, and remarkable merits they are, of his matter; and these again with the occasional crudities of thought and violences of imagery by which here and there they are still marred. . . .

"It is, indeed, when Mr. Davidson seems most anxious to be 'up-to-date' that he is least admirable; and conversely [in] his poems of pure fancy, or of pure psychology, two subjects essentially dateless, he is at his best. Then it is that we meet, as in the *Ballad of a Nun*, with a descriptive stanza so full of wonderful word-magic as [ll. 21–24], or one which strikes so profound a note as this [ll. 25–28] and this [ll. 37–40].

"No better proof of the authenticity of the poet's inspiration could, perhaps, be cited than the *Ballad of a Nun*. The poem trembles throughout on the verge of extravagance; it is saved only, but saved everywhere, by the intensity and sincerity with which it has so obviously been felt." (H. D. Traill, in *Fortnightly Review*, LXIII, pp. 403 and 405.)

Page 881. A BALLAD OF A NUN

Davidson once wrote: "Liberty of utterance, spontaneity, is the mark of the highest poetry. To be spontaneous is the whole art of poetry and especially distinguishes it from the artifice of poetry." In this remark he touched upon his chief defect as a poet—lack of genius for fine finish; and in it, too, he unwittingly revealed why the ballad was his favorite poetic form—the ballad, with its "impetuous, spontaneous movement, its ability to tell a story by leaps and bounds, rather than by carefully and closely constructed narrative." Mr. Milton Bronner called this poem in many ways Davidson's most successful ballad, "most resplendent in its verse magic, at the same time shocking to people of piety, and leading superficial critics to class him for all time with the English decadent school of poets. Here, for the first time, Davidson showed his tendency to use the holy things of the new Testament as so many myths to be applied to poetic uses."

The story of "the nun who goes out to see the world" and who, when she returns to the convent wan with spent passion, finds that in her absence she was impersonated by the Virgin Mother, is well known in medieval literature.

Page 884. THE VENGEANCE OF THE DUCHESS

1. *Austerlitz.* Napoleon I defeated the Austrians and Russians at Austerlitz, a town in Austria, on December 2, 1805.
2. *Illyria.* A region on the eastern shores of the Adriatic. It formed part of the Franco-Napoleonic empire, but reverted to Austria in 1815.
9–10. *churl . . . kingdom-breaker.* Napoleon I.
16. *Idria.* A mining town in Italy. Its mines of quicksilver are the second richest in the world.
24. *cinnabar.* Mercuric sulphide, an ore of mercury.

Page 886. A BALLAD OF HEAVEN

7. *flags.* Paving stones.
25, 32, 36. *adagio, andante, scherzo.* Musical terms indicating slow, moderately slow, and quick, respectively.
64. *unscored work.* Music not written.
104. *music . . . spheres.* A reference to the ancient belief that the stars made music in their courses.

Page 887. A BALLAD OF HELL

24. *missal.* Book of the mass.
61. *poppet.* A term of endearment.

Page 888. SUMMER

3. *Leda's twins.* Castor and Pollux, twin brothers, sons of Zeus and Leda, were made a constellation known as *Gemini* or the Twins.

Page 889. A RUNNABLE STAG

Padraic Colum said, "Davidson's best ballad is not the *Ballad of a Nun;* is not *The Vengeance of the Duchess;* it is the free and fantastic ballad of *A Runnable Stag.*"

A stag is "runnable" when it has reached a certain age or maturity, this period being indicated by the presence of at least two tines at the top of the antler.

1. *broom.* A shrub with small leaves and showy yellow flowers.
3. *harboured.* Traced to its place of refuge.
coomb. A narrow ravine-like valley.
4. *feathered . . . up-wind.* Put the hounds on the trail, which led against the wind.
6. *stag of warrant.* Of value; of the age or size to be hunted.
7. *kingly crop.* A noble pair of antlers.
8. *brow . . . tray.* The main stem of the antler of the red deer is called the beam. The first tine or point branching from the beam is the brow antler, the next is the bay, the third the tray or royal antler.
11. *harbourer.* The man who tracked the deer to its refuge.
12. *brocket.* A male red deer two years old. Its antlers are not branched.
17. *beamed and tined.* Fully antlered.
19. *tufted.* Beat—trying to start the stag.
29. *copse was drawn.* The thicket was searched.
30. "*Tally ho!*" The huntsman's halloo at sight of the stag.
85. *Severn Sea.* Bristol Channel, into which the Severn River empties.

Page 890. THE CHILTERNS

The Chiltern Hills, a chalk range noted for its beautiful beech-woods, are in Buckinghamshire, England.

AUSTIN DOBSON

BIBLIOGRAPHY

I. WORKS

Complete Poetical Works, ed. by Alban Dobson. (Oxford University Press: 1923.) Undoubtedly the most complete edition—by the son of the poet; contains all of the Paul (1920) collection, together with 54 "War Rondeaus" and other miscellaneous pieces. A few pages of notes and a bibliographical index conclude the volume.

Collected Poems. (Paul: London, 1920.) The most complete collection made by the poet himself, secondary only to the Oxford Edition; a few notes are supplied in the appendix.

Selected Poems. (Oxford University Press: 1924.) The most convenient book of selections, substantially the same as the 1905 London Edition; contains an explanatory foreword by Alban Dobson.

An Anthology of Prose and Verse by Austin Dobson, ed. by Alban Dobson. (Dutton: New York,

1922.) A recommended collection, prefaced by an essay by Edmund Gosse; concludes with a three-page bibliography.

II. BIOGRAPHY AND CRITICISM

Dobson, Alban. *Austin Dobson: Some Notes.* (Oxford University Press: 1928.) *Miscellania*, which avowedly are materials for a future biography; contains also essays by Edmund Gosse and George Saintsbury.

Dobson, Alban. "Austin Dobson Causerie," *Cornhill Magazine*, LVIII, 149–62 (Feb., 1925). A series of informal remarks on the poet's relations with his publishers and other literary men, adding notes concerning the various editions of Dobson's poetry.

Dobson, Alban. "Austin Dobson: Some Letters from His Friends," *Cornhill Magazine*, LXIII, 129–46, 366–81, 496–510 (Aug., Sept., Oct., 1927). A selection of letters dating from 1867 to 1893: throw much light on Dobson's relations with English and French writers of his day.

Ellis, S. M. "Austin Dobson," in *Mainly Victorian.* (Hutchinson: London, 1925.) Contributes the briefest of biographical sketches; comments on a few of the poet's finest lyrics.

Gosse, E. W. "Austin Dobson," in *Silhouettes.* (Scribner: New York, 1925.) Maintains that Dobson's popularity accounts for his undervaluation by the critics, who do not yet appreciate his real genius; finds most enjoyment in judicious selections from his verse.

Gosse, E. W. "Austin Dobson," *Quarterly Review*, CCXXXVII, 53–67 (Jan., 1922). Remarks the "noiseless regularity" of the poet's life; reviews his many publications, pointing out his return in the latter part of his career to many of his earlier themes.

Lipscombe, H. C. "Horace and the Poetry of Austin Dobson," *American Journal of Philology*, L, 1–20 (Jan., 1929). Shows by abundant quotation Dobson's interest in Horace's human types and technical brilliance.

Noyes, Alfred. "The Poems of Austin Dobson," in *Some Aspects of Modern Poetry.* (Stokes: New York, 1924.) Bases the poet's claim to fame on his "rare felicities"; compares his ballads to Longfellow's; points out some technical failures in Dobson's verse.

Stedman, E. C. "Austin Dobson," in *Genius and Other Essays.* (Moffat: New York, 1911.) Finds Dobson at his best in his descriptions of a faded age, but insists upon his realism; praises his "refreshing variety."

Symons, Arthur. "Austin Dobson," in *Studies in Prose and Verse.* (Dutton: New York, 1904.) Remarks the poet's apparent lightness of sentiment as an evasion from the stress of deeper emotions; finds his best work in the themes of bygone days.

Welby, T. E. "Austin Dobson," in *Back Numbers.* (Constable: London, 1929.) Questions whether there was not a sort of pathos in Dobson's deliberate reticence upon the more serious aspects of life; remarks that his too-keen sense of man's position between two eternities might have caused him to shun taking issue with the heroic problems of life.

Weygandt, Cornelius. "Austin Dobson, Augustan," in *Tuesdays at Ten.* (University of Pennsylvania Press: 1928.) Sees the poet as a sentimentalist at core, but gifted with a restraint that saves him from bathos; praises his skill in capturing the social graces of a vanished age.

NOTES

"Mr. Dobson's poetry, except for a few serious poems, is all a diversion. His object is not to glorify reality, but to relieve us from it for a little while. He always has the air of one who has schooled himself to be content with small pleasures, and who would like his readers to share his enjoyment of them. Yet he is a true poet, for his sense of beauty is quickened by little things, as the sense of beauty of the great poets is quickened by great things. Little relics from the past, old gardens with their scents and flowers, are significant to his imagination, as flaming sunsets and deep passions are significant to the imaginations of the great poets. They mean to him more than he can state in set terms; and it is this overplus of meaning that expresses itself in the beauty of his verse, and that makes him a poet, and his versifying something more than an amusing game. His trifles are connected with life and not mere ornaments like the china images to which he compares them, and he can, on the rare occasions when he chooses to do so, write serious poetry." (*Living Age*, CCXLVI, 887. Quoted from *The London Times*.)

"Little concerned with the vain racket of the life about us, Austin Dobson moved in a delicate world of his own, a microcosm where everything was fragrant and harmonious, and where the past and the present were mingled in the clearness of a rose-colored air. The charm of his wit and the lucidity of his fancy were controlled by the scruples of a fastidious artist; and, when much that is violent has sunken into oblivion forever, his writings may still float towards posterity on the stream of their purity and perfection." (Edmund Gosse, in the *Quarterly Review*, CCXXXVII, 67.)

Page 891. A SONG OF THE FOUR SEASONS

7. *speedwell.* Any of several species of veronica, with small blue or white flowers.

20. *wain.* A wagon.

28. *ingle.* Chimney corner; hearth.

Page 892. THE PARADOX OF TIME

Pierre de Ronsard (1524–1585) was a French lyric poet, celebrated for his light verse. The quotation may be translated,

"Time goes, time goes, my lady!
Alas! it is not time, but we."

TO A GREEK GIRL

1. *thyme*. A shrub with aromatic leaves.
15. *Pan*. The arcadian god of shepherds, herdsmen, hunters, of woods and fields, and, finally, the personification of all nature.
26. *Thamis*. The Thames River.
27. *fill . . . reams*. Fill much paper with verse.
29. *Alcestis*. The wife of Admetus, who had been granted immortality provided some one could be found to die in his stead. She offered herself, died, and was buried; but Heracles, who was hospitably entertained by Admetus on the day of Alcestis's burial, went to her tomb, defeated Death, and rescued her.

ARS VICTRIX

This poem, the title of which means "art victorious," was adapted from Gautier's poem *L'Art*, in his *Emaux et camées*. Gautier (1811–1872) was a French poet and novelist of the Romantic movement.
6. *loosely-sandalled verse*. Comedy.
8. *buskin*. Tragedy.
15. *Paros*. An island in the Ægean Sea famous for its fine marble.
17. *Satyr*. A Greek woodland deity.
18. *Syracuse*. An ancient Greek city in Sicily famous for bronze work.
26. *Erycine*. Venus, whose chariot was drawn by doves.
27. *Sirens*. Mythical women who lived on rocky isles and lured seafarers with enchanting music.
32. *Tiberius*. Emperor of Rome (14–37 A.D.).

Page 893. THE LADIES OF ST. JAMES'S

St. James's is a fashionable district in London. The motto from Virgil means "I love Phyllida (Phyllis) more than all others."
11. *Ombre*. A card game popular in the 18th century.
47. *Shrove-tide*. The days, usually three, immediately before Lent.

Page 894. TWO SERMONS

2. "*Stranger's Pew*." A church pew reserved for strangers.
7. *St. Cecily*. Cecilia, the patron saint of sacred music.

A GARDEN SONG

W. E. H. was William Ernest Henley.
12. *Alcinoüs*. The prosperous king of Phæacia, who hospitably entertained Ulysses. He was celebrated for his gardens.
24. *Pierides*. A collective name of the Muses, so called from Pieria, the seat of their worship. See note to l. 27 of Swinburne's *Sapphics*, above.

Page 895. HOUSEHOLD ART

1. "*Mine . . . cot*." From Rogers's *A Wish*.
2. *Greenaway*. Kate Greenaway (1846–1901), English artist, wrote and illustrated books for children.
14. *au delà*. To the great beyond.

FOR A COPY OF HERRICK

Robert Herrick (1591–1674) was an English poet who sang, he said,

". . . of maypoles, hock-carts, wassails, wakes,
Of bridegrooms, brides, and of their bridal cakes."

4. *Barley-break*. An ancient rural game.

ROSE-LEAVES

The motto for this group of triolets means, "Without weighing, without waiting."

Circe

For Circe, sorceress and coquette, see note to l. 270 of Arnold's *The Strayed Reveller*, above.

A Greek Gift

A Greek gift is one given with a treacherous purpose.
29. *Plats . . . Rôts*. Chapter heading on main dishes, secondary dishes, and roasts in a cookbook by Jules Gouffé, a celebrated French chef. The book was translated into English in 1868 by Alphonse Gouffé, the Queen's head pastrycook.

"Urceus Exit"

The title was suggested by a passage in Horace's *The Art of Poetry*, ll. 21–22, which Ben Jonson translated as follows:

. . . "A great jar to be shaped,
Was meant at first; why forcing still about
Thy labouring wheel, comes scarce a pitcher out?"

Dobson, like Horace, has in mind the poem that promises to be great but turns out slight.

"WITH PIPE AND FLUTE"

This poem, a rondeau in form (see note to Swinburne's *The Roundel*, p. 1271, above), is inscribed to Edmund Gosse.
1. *Pan*. He invented the flute.
7. *Arcady*. Any region of simple pleasure, rustic innocence, untroubled quiet; from Arcadia, Greece.
11. *Beersheba . . . Dan*. From limit to limit. Dan was once the northern limit of Palestine, and Beersheba the southern.
12. *Apollo*. The god of poetry and music.
13. *night-jar*. A bird with a harsh, unpleasant cry.

Page 896. FOR A COPY OF THEOCRITUS

See note to l. 1 of Mrs. Browning's *Sonnets from the Portuguese*, above.

THE BALLAD OF IMITATION

The quotation introducing this ballade (the term is not to be confused with *ballad*) means, freely, "Even the planting of cabbages is imitation." See note to Swinburne's *A Ballad of Dreamland*, p. 1267, above.

2. *Chopin or Spohr*. 19th century composers. Chopin was French-Polish, and Spohr was German.

4. *Arnes and Purcells*. Arne and Purcell were English composers of music in the eighteenth and seventeenth centuries respectively.

6. "*Wandering Jew.*" In medieval story a Jew who treated Christ contemptuously, on His way to the crucifixion, was condemned by Him to wander over the earth until the Second Advent.

7. *Beethoven*. Famous Prussian composer (1770–1827).

14. *Gainsborough*. An eighteenth-century English portrait and landscape painter.

23. *Pegasus*. In Greek myth a winged horse, the mount of poets.

Page 897. THE BALLAD OF THE BORE

The motto from Horace means, "Some time a chatterbox shall talk him out."

12. *Juggernaut*. In Hindu mythology the idol of the god Vishnu. The idol was dragged in an enormous car.

AN EPITAPH

The motto from Hugo means, "One can read no name there."

Page 898. ON THE FUTURE OF POETRY

17. *Pindus Hill*. A mountain range in Greece, here symbolizing the "ancient way" of poetry.

40. *Hector's wife*. Andromache, whose grief at the slaying of Hector in the siege of Troy is one of the most pathetic subjects in Greek story.

ERNEST DOWSON

BIBLIOGRAPHY

I. WORKS

Complete Poems. (Medusa Head Press: New York, 1928.) A fine limited edition, illustrated by Elinore Blaisdell.

Poems. (Dodd: New York, 1924.) A fairly comprehensive collection: the preface by Arthur Symons, written upon the occasion of the poet's death, is a eulogistic but well-balanced survey of Dowson's retired life and his unique art.

Poems. (Lane: New York, 1915.) A desirable edition, prefaced by the Symons memoir; contains four illustrations by Aubrey Beardsley.

Poems and Prose. (Modern Library: New York, 1932.) A convenient inexpensive collection, containing the memoir by Symons.

II. BIOGRAPHY AND CRITICISM

Brégy, Katherine. "Ernest Dowson: An Interpretation," *Catholic World*, C, 193–205 (Nov., 1914). A study of the poet's aestheticism; points out the origin of decadent and pessimistic strains; draws comparisons with Lionel Johnson.

Flower, Newman. "Ernest Dowson," *London Bookman*, LXIV, 148–50 (Sept., 1926). A pen-picture of Dowson as the defeated poet of "Cynara" with a brief note upon the story of the background of the poem.

Plarr, V. G. *Ernest Dowson, 1888–1897*. (Gomme: New York, 1914.) Without being a biography, contains a part of the materials for one: unpublished letters, reminiscences, *marginalia*, etc.; includes also a bibliography by H. G. Harrison.

Symons, Arthur. "Ernest Dowson," in *Studies in Prose and Verse*. (Dutton: New York, 1904.) Begins with an interesting biographical sketch founded largely upon reminiscences of the poet; comments upon his sensuousness, his Latin love of restraint, and tendency to the *macabre*.

Thomas, W. R. "Ernest Dowson at Oxford," *Nineteenth Century*, CIII, 560–6 (Apr., 1928). Intended to enlarge a phase in Symons's memoir; gives many recollections covering Dowson's five terms at Queen's College.

NOTES

"Poetry as a philosophy did not exist for him; it existed solely as the loveliest of the arts. He loved the elegance of Horace, all that was most complex in the simplicity of Poe, most bird-like in the human melodies of Verlaine. He had the pure lyric gift, unweighted or unballasted by any other quality of mind or emotion; and a song, for him, was music first, and then whatever you please afterwards, so long as it suggested, never told, some delicate sentiment, a sigh or a caress; finding words, at times, as perfect as . . . [those] of a poem headed, 'O Mors! quam amara est memoria, tuo homini pacem habenti in substantiis suis.'" (Arthur Symons, in *Fortnightly Review*, LXVII, 955.)

"Dowson is the poet symbolic of the eighteen-nineties—His work is the logical conclusion of the æstheticism of Rossetti and Swinburne and of the influence of the doctrine of *l'art pour l'art* of the later French romanticists. He has removed from his poetry everything except his own narrow circle of sensations, and these, with the sickening sense of sin that lies behind them, he has tortured himself to express with exquisite perfection. Even his sense of sin, except in a few places, seems an artistic rather than a moral value, some self-mutilation necessary to make complete the presentation of his sensations. It was as if Dowson were fulfilling in his poetry the precepts of Walter Pater and recording moments of sensation to the utter exclusion of all moral and philosophical comment. Wilde, the bulk of whose verse belongs to the eighties, never achieved this with equal force, and despite his wide personal influence on the period, he seldom approached Dowson's quality as a poet. Many of Dowson's companions in that decade shared his purposes temporarily and then turned to achieve other things; so Mr. Arthur Symons, who developed in the twentieth century as a prose writer and a critic, and Mr. W. B. Yeats, who left the London of the nineties to found a new Irish national poetry. Even Lionel Johnson was governed by other loyalties, in which his classicism and his Irish attachments had a part. But Dowson in his brief life gathered into his own distress, and his own darkly beautiful lyrics, all that this final movement in English romanticism had to express. (B. Ifor Evans, in *English Poetry in the Later Nineteenth Century*, p. 315.)

Page 899. VITAE SUMMA BREVIS SPEM NOS VETAT INCOHARE LONGAM

The title from Horace (*Odes*, Bk. I, Ode 4, l. 15) means, "The brief span of life forbids us to entertain a long hope."

This poem is a perfect expression of the motives frequent in Latin lyrical poetry—"the brevity of life and the fading of things that once were beautiful." No one else has equalled it in English, and hardly has it been surpassed by the Latin singers themselves.

AMOR PROFANUS

The title means "profane love."

22. *Lalage.* Another instance of the Horatian influence upon Dowson. Lalage is a lady in one of Horace's *Odes* (Bk. II, Ode 5).

Page 900. NON SUM QUALIS ERAM BONAE SUB REGNO CYNARÆ

The title, taken from Horace's *Odes* (Bk. IV, Ode 1, ll. 3–4), means, "I am not what I once was under the spell of the sweet Cynara." The situation in the poem is not that of Horace's ode, but rather that of the *Cynthia* of Propertius, another Latin poet whose work impressed Dowson.

O MORS! QUAM AMARA EST MEMORIA TUA HOMINI PACEM HABENTI IN SUBSTANTIIS SUIS

See first introductory note to Dowson, quoted from Symons, above.

The title from Horace's *Odes* means, "O Death, how bitter is thy memory to a man who has peace in the possession of his worldly goods."

Of this poem Arthur Symons said: "There, surely, the music of silence speaks, if it has ever spoken. The words seem to tremble back into the silence which their whisper has interrupted, but not before they have created for us a mood, such a mood as the Venetian Pastoral attributed to Giorgione renders in painting."

Page 901. IN TEMPORE SENECTUTIS

The title means "in old age."

EXTREME UNCTION

In the Catholic Church the sacrament administered to one in danger of death is called "extreme unction."

16. *Viaticum.* The Communion when given to one dying.

Page 902. IMPENITENTIA ULTIMA

The title, interpreted freely, means "impenitent to the end."

17. Dowson once said that his ideal of a line of verse was the line of Poe:

"The viol, the violet, and the vine,"

and that the letter "v" was the most beautiful of the letters, and could not be brought into verse too often.

EDWARD FITZGERALD

BIBLIOGRAPHY

I. WORKS

Variorum and Definitive Edition of Poetical and Prose Writings, ed. by George Bentham. 7 vols. (Doubleday: New York, 1902–3.) The preferred edition for the special student; includes a complete bibliography and notes, together with an introduction by E. W. Gosse; the first three volumes contain the various editions of the *Rubáiyát*.

FitzGerald's Rubáiyát of Omar Khayyám, ed. by Edward Heron-Allen. (Quaritch: London, 1899.) Collated from the translator's manuscripts of the original quatrains, of which facsimiles and literal translations are provided. It is shown that FitzGerald sometimes produced one quatrain from more than one Persian original, and again used a half-ruba'i for a full-length stanza.

Rubáiyát of Omar Khayyám, Translated by Edward FitzGerald. (Crowell: New York, 1921.) Recommended for its clear presentation of the variants in the five original printings.

Letters and Literary Remains, ed. by W. A. Wright. 7 vols. (Macmillan: London, 1902–3.) Incorporating various collections, 1889–1901, contains the major portion of the correspondence—about 700 letters; prefaced by an outline-biography.

Letters to Fanny Kemble, ed. by W. A. Wright. (Macmillan: New York, 1895.) A complete collection of the correspondence, 1871–1883, a part of which had appeared in the *Temple Bar Magazine* and in the 1889, 3-volume edition.

Edward FitzGerald and Bernard Barton, ed. by F. R. Barton. (Putnam: New York, 1924.) Gives the text of about 60 letters addressed to FitzGerald's Quaker friend, 1839–1848; other letters and notes by the editor weave a biographical story carrying to 1856.

Letters to Bernard Quaritch, 1853–1883, ed. by C. Q. Wrentmore. (Quaritch: London, 1926.) Contains about 100 letters to FitzGerald's publisher of the first edition of his Persian translation.

A FitzGerald Friendship, ed. by N. C. Hannay. (Rudge: New York, 1932.) Includes 60 new letters, addressed to William Bodham Donne; footnotes supplied in collaboration with Catharine B. Johnson provide abundant explanatory material.

Some New Letters, ed. by F. R. Barton. (Williams: London, 1923.) Contains a foreword by Viscount Grey of Falloden.

II. BIOGRAPHY AND CRITICISM

Benson, A. C. *Edward FitzGerald*. English Men of Letters series. (Macmillan: New York, 1925.) A good concise biography, providing only the accepted facts, but containing original matter of a critical nature.

Blyth, James. *Edward FitzGerald, "Posh," "Herring Merchants."* (Longmans: London, 1908.) Includes 30 letters to Joseph Fletcher, the poet's longshore companion and partner; the letters are woven into an interesting biography.

Glyde, John. *The Life of Edward FitzGerald*. (Stone: Chicago, 1900.) The first extended Life of the poet, written from information gleaned from many first-hand sources; quotes many letters and some variant passages from the poet's work. Introduction by Edward Clodd.

Tutin, J. R. *A Concordance of FitzGerald's Translation of the Rubáiyát of Omar Khayyám*. (Macmillan: New York, 1900.) A full index to the use of each word contained in the final version of the translation, and the variations in the earlier editions.

Weir, T. H. *Omar Khayyám, the Poet*. (Dutton: New York, 1927). A revelation of the Persian poet through the oldest authentic manuscript sources; a collation of extensive magazine material contributed by the author over a number of years.

Wright, Thomas. *The Life of Edward FitzGerald*. 2 vols. (Scribner: New York, 1904.) A thoroughgoing work, founded chiefly on hitherto unpublished material, together with first-hand information derived from FitzGerald's many friends: first published the circumstances of the writing of *Euphranor*.

III. ARTICLES FROM BOOKS

Gosse, E. W. "Edward FitzGerald," in *Critical Kit-Kats*. (Scribner: New York, 1914.) Comments on the poet's small but diverse circle of friends, his slow rise to public notice, and his revision of his translations and adaptations.

Hearn, Lafcadio. "Edward FitzGerald and the *Rubáiyát*," in *Interpretations of Literature*, I. (Dodd: New York, 1915.) A brief informal review of the background and sentiment of the poems.

More, P. E. "Kipling and FitzGerald," in *Shelburne Essays*, Second Series. (Putnam: New York, 1905.) Hails the Persian translation as an onset against stolid Anglo-Saxon tradition, besides being memorable for its verbal beauty.

Platt, A. "Edward FitzGerald," in *Nine Essays*. (Cambridge University Press: 1927.) One of the best essays on the subject of FitzGerald's translation of the Persian poems and his Letters; scholarly, and engagingly written.

Stoddard, R. H. "Edward FitzGerald," in *Under the Evening Lamp*. (Scribner: New York, 1892.) Names the poet an "unambitious man of letters" but unforgettable for his work in translation; praises his letters and remarks his wide literary acquaintance.

Thompson, A. H. "Edward FitzGerald," in *The Cambridge History of English Literature*, XIII. (Putnam: New York, 1917.) Discusses the poet's various translations, particularly the *Rubáiyát*.

Welby, T. E. "FitzGerald," in *Back Numbers*. (Smith: New York, 1930.) Briefly reviews the story of the first publication of the quatrains; comments on the rise of the Omar cult; points out in FitzGerald's style the influence of Dryden.

Woodberry, G. E. "Edward FitzGerald," in *Literary Memoirs of the Nineteenth Century*. (Harcourt: New York, 1921.) Dwells kindly on the poet's exaggerated patriotism; points out his changing attitudes toward Tennyson; shows the vital strain of classicism in his work.

IV. ARTICLES FROM PERIODICALS

Blake, W. B. "Poetry, Time, and Edward FitzGerald," *Dial*, XLVI, 177–80 (Mar. 16, 1909). Shows FitzGerald's sensuous love of the past; praises his Letters and regrets his inability to seek out the sterner aspects of life.

Gribble, Francis. "Edward FitzGerald," *Fortnightly Review*, XCI, 647–57 (Apr., 1909). Throws out a miscellaneous variety of parallels with many English and continental writers; points out amusing eccentricities in FitzGerald's character.

Harris, May. "A Victorian Pagan," *Sewanee Review*, XXXIV, 309–17 (July, 1926). Traces the best work of the poet to his indolence and egotistical seclusion; these also account for his small output.

Hutchinson, H. G. "Edward FitzGerald," *Quarterly Review*, CCLVI, 279–301 (Apr., 1931). Reviews the standard biographical data; analyzes some revisions in the editions of the *Rubáiyát*.

Murray, J. A. "Omar Khayyám," *Fortnightly Review*, LXVI, 848–55 (Dec., 1896). A description of Nishápúr and its surroundings; gives the few facts known of Omar's life and a brief review of his philosophy.

Torrey, Bradford. "Edward FitzGerald," *Atlantic Monthly*, LXXXVI, 617–29 (Nov., 1900).

Gently deplores FitzGerald's lack of ambition; finds the best revelation of the man in his Letters, which indicate his astonishingly wide range of reading.

NOTES

Page 903. THE RUBÁIYÁT OF OMAR KHAYYÁM

E. B. Cowell, professor of Sanskrit at Cambridge, made a copy of the Ouseley MSS. of Omar for FitzGerald in 1856 and in May of the next year, FitzGerald was writing pleasantly to Cowell, "When in Bedfordshire I put away almost all Books except Omar Khayyám, which I could not help looking over in a Paddock covered with Buttercups and brushed by a delicious Breeze, while a dainty racing Filly of W. Browne's came startling up to wonder and snuff about me." The poem is melancholy, but there are roses and wine in it, and FitzGerald read it among buttercups.

A biographer has well explained the alliance of profound despondency, which is the tone of the poem, with delight in the transient beauties which are the very cause of the despondency. Says Benson: "As to the *motif* of the poem, FitzGerald himself sums up in a sad and tender epigram, as far as so evasive a thing can be summarised, the underlying thought. In 1877, sending the book to his friend Laurence, he wrote: 'I know you will thank me (for the book), and I think you will feel a sort of *triste Plaisir* in it, as others besides myself have felt. *It is a desperate sort of thing, unfortunately at the bottom of all thinking men's minds; but made Music of.*'

"To translate that exquisite sentence into more scientific and harsher terminology, the poem is probably the most beautiful and stately presentation of Agnosticism ever made, with its resultant Epicureanism. Omar does not go to the wine-jar only that he may forget, but that he may also remember. He feeds on honey-dew and drinks the milk of paradise that he may banish for a little the terror of the unknown, the bewildered mystery of life, the pain, the shame, the fear, and the dark shadow that nearer or further lies across the road; thus much to forget; and then he is perchance, enabled to remember the sweet days, the spring and the budding rose; to remember that though the beginning and the end are dark, yet that the God of Pain and Death is also the maker of the fair world, the gracious charm of voice and hand and eye . . . of all the sights and sounds that fill the heart full and leave it yearning, unsatisfied with the pain that is itself a joy." (A. C. Benson, *Edward FitzGerald*, English Men of Letters Series, pp. 114–15.)

FitzGerald's translation appeared in 1859 with 75 quatrains. It attracted no attention and was finally dumped on the penny bookstalls of Quaritch's in London. There it was discovered by the Rossetti circle, who were delighted with it. (See Swinburne Letter XXVII, text p. 805, for an account of the episode.) The second edition of 1868 was much revised and expanded to 110 quatrains. The other two editions to appear in FitzGerald's lifetime (1872 and 1879) were reduced to 101 quatrains and further revised.

FitzGerald handled his material with some freedom, condensing, combining, translating oriental imagery into terms comprehensible to the West, but retaining the spirit. He wrote to Cowell, "I suppose very few People have ever taken such Pains in Translation as I have; though certainly not to be literal. But at all Cost, a Thing must *live:* with a transfusion of one's own worse Life if one can't retain the Original's better. Better a live Sparrow than a stuffed Eagle. . . ." And the translation is nearer to a live Persian nightingale than the live sparrow FitzGerald would have been content to make it.

Heron-Allen states that 49 quatrains are "beautiful paraphrases" of a single quatrain original; 44 are "composite," being drawn from two or more originals; 8 are drawn from other poets or combinations of other poets with Omar.

To illustrate the way FitzGerald used his materials there is given below Heron-Allen's literal translation of the materials FitzGerald used in some of his most-quoted stanzas:

XI and XII

If a loaf of wheaten bread be forthcoming,
A gourd of wine, and a thigh-bone of mutton,
And then, if thou and I be sitting in the wilderness,—
That were a joy not within the power of any Sultan.

I desire a flask of ruby wine and a book of verses
Just enough to keep me alive, and half a loaf is needful,
And then, that thou and I should sit in the wilderness,
Is better than the kingdom of a Sultan.

XIII

They say that the Garden of Eden is pleasant with houris:
I say that the juice of the grape is pleasant.
Hold fast this cash and keep thy hand from that credit,
For the noise of drums, brother, is pleasant from afar.

XIV

The rose said: I brought a gold-scattering hand,
Laughing, laughing, have I blown into the world,
I snatched the noose-string from off the head of my purse and I am gone!
I flung into the world all the ready money that I had.

LXVI–LXVII

Already on the Day of Creation, beyond the heavens, my soul
Searched for the Tablet and Pen, and for heaven and hell;
At last the Teacher said to me with His enlightened judgment,
"Tablet and Pen, and heaven and hell, are within thyself."

The heavenly vault is a girdle (cast) from my weary body.
Jihun is a water-course worn by my filtered tears,
Hell is a spark from my useless worries,
Paradise is a moment of time when I am tranquil.

LXXI

From the beginning was written what shall be;
Unhaltingly the Pen (writes) and is heedless of good and bad;
On the First Day He appointed everything that must be—
Our grief and our efforts are vain.

The following line by line notes are based on FitzGerald's notes, with abridgments and additions.

5. *False morning.* "A transient light on the horizon about an hour before the . . . True Dawn; a well-known Phenomenon in the East."

13. *the New Year.* The Persian New Year began with the Vernal Equinox. "'The sudden approach and rapid advance of the Spring,' says Mr. Binning, 'are very striking. Before the Snow is well off the Ground, the Trees burst into Blossom, and the Flowers start forth from the Soil.'"

15–16. *White hand of Moses . . . Jesus from the Ground suspires.* "'The White Hand of Moses.' Exodus iv. 6; where Moses draws forth his Hand—not, according to the Persians, '*leprous as Snow,*'—but *white,* as our May-blossom in Spring perhaps. According to them also the Healing Power of Jesus resided in His Breath."

17. *Iram.* A garden "now sunk somewhere in the Sands of Arabia."

18. *Jamshyd's Sev'n-ring'd Cup.* It symbolized the seven heavens, seven planets, seven seas, etc., "and was a divining cup."

21–22. *David's lips are lockt; but in . . . Pehleví.* The sweet voice of David is mentioned frequently in Persian poetry. Pehleví, FitzGerald believed (erroneously, according to Heron-Allen) to be "the old Heroic Sanskrit of Persia," a language which did not change with the vulgar speech of the people.

29. *Naishápúr.* Omar's native place, where he died.

36. *Jamshyd . . Kaikobád.* "The *roi soleil* of early Persian history, and the Kaianian dynasty—Kai Kobad, Kai Kawus, Kai Khosru, etc." (Heron-Allen.)

39–40. *Zál and Rustum . . Hátim.* Rustum was the Hercules of Persia and Zál his father. Hátim was celebrated for his generosity. Cf. Arnold's *Sohrab and Rustum,* text p. 541.

52. *distant Drum.* "Beaten outside a palace."

56. *its Treasure.* "That is, the Rose's Golden Centre."

65. *Caravanserai.* An inn at which caravans stopped overnight.

71. *Bahrám, that great Hunter.* "Bahrám Gúr—*Bahram of the Wild Ass*—a Sassanian Sovereign—had also his Seven Castles (like the King of Bohemia!) each of a different Colour: each with a Royal Mistress within; each of whom tells him a Story, as told in one of the most famous Poems of Persia, written by Amír Khusraw: all these Sevens also figuring (according to Eastern Mysticism) the Seven Heavens; and perhaps the Book itself that Eighth, into which the Mystical Seven transcend, and within which they revolve. The Ruins of Three of those Towers are yet shown by the Peasantry; as also the Swamp in which Bahrám sunk, like the Master of Ravenswood, while pursuing his *Gúr.*" (Gúr = Wild Ass.)

75. *Hyacinth.* The flower was named after a youth accidentally killed by Apollo, and is said to have sprung up from the earth where his blood fell.

84. *Sev'n thousand Years.* "A thousand years to each planet," FitzGerald somewhat cryptically explains. Heron-Allen translates the original literally as follows:

When, to-morrow, we depart from the face of the earth
We shall be equal with those who went seven thousand years ago.

96. *Sans.* Without.

99. *Muezzín.* A Mohammedan public crier who calls the people to prayer.

119. *forbidden Wine.* Mohammedanism forbids the use of wine.

122. *Saturn.* "The Lord of the Seventh Heaven."

127. *talk . . . of Me and Thee.* "Of some dividual Existence or Personality distinct from the Whole."

148. *"Gently, Brother."* "One of the Persian Poets—Attár, I think—has a pretty story

about this. A thirsty Traveller dips his hand into a Spring of Water to drink from. By and by comes another who draws up and drinks from an earthen Bowl, and then departs, leaving his Bowl behind him. The first Traveller takes it up for another draught; but is surprised to find that the same Water which had tasted sweet from his own hand tastes bitter from the earthen Bowl. But a Voice—from Heaven, I think—tells him the clay from which the Bowl is made was once *Man;* and, into whatever shape renewed, can never lose the bitter flavour of Mortality."

153–4. *drop . . . for Earth to drink of.* "The custom of throwing a little Wine on the ground before drinking still continues in Persia, and perhaps generally in the East. Mons. Nicolas considers it 'un signe de libéralité, et en même temps un avertissement que le buveur doit vider sa coupe jusqu'à la dernière goutte.' Is it not more likely an ancient Superstition; a Libation to propitiate Earth, or make her an Accomplice in the illicit Revel? Or, perhaps, to divert the Jealous Eye by some sacrifice of superfluity, as with the Ancients of the West? With Omar we see something more is signified; the precious Liquor is not lost, but sinks into the ground to refresh the dust of some poor Wine-worshipper foregone.

"Thus Háfiz, copying Omar in so many ways: 'When thou drinkest Wine pour a draught on ground. Wherefore fear the Sin which brings to another Gain?'"

164. *Minister of Wine.* The maiden who pours the wine.

169. *Angel of the darker Drink.* Azrael, the Angel of Death.

179–80. *dark Ferrásh Strikes.* Heron-Allen translates this literally:

Khayyam! thy body surely resembles a tent;
The soul is a Sultan and the halting-place is
  the perishable world,
The ferrash of fate, preparing for the next
  halting-place,
Will overthrow this tent when the Sultan has
  arisen.

In other words the ferrash of fate, preparing for the next halting-place, destroys this tent (body) when the Sultan (soul) arises.

183. *Eternal Sákí.* Saki is a wine-bearer or wine-pourer.

198. *Alif.* First letter of the Arabic alphabet.

203. *from Máh to Máhi.* "From fish to moon."

223–4. *I Was never deep in anything but—Wine.* Omar is jesting at his own studies. He was a very learned man and "deep" in many things.

225. *Computations,* etc. Omar was one of the astronomers employed to reform the calendar.

234. *The Two and Sovonty jarring Socts.* The seventy-two religions which were supposed to divide the world.

237. *The mighty Mahmúd.* The quatrain is allusive. A sultan Mahmúd conquered the dark people of India. So in this quatrain another sultan is to conquer the dark fears of the soul.

235. *I must abjure.* A reference to the Mohammedan prohibition of the use of wine.

270. *Magic Shadow-shapes.* "Fánúsi khiyál, a Magic-lantern still used in India; the cylindrical Interior being painted with various Figures, and so lightly poised and ventilated as to revolve round the lighted Candle within."

277. *The Ball.* Refers to the game of Polo.

298–9. *Foal Of Heav'n Parwín and Mushtarí.* Parwín and Mushtarí are the Pleiades and Jupiter; the Foal, judging from the literal text, was the Sun. The meaning of the quatrain is that when the constellations were created Omar's destiny was pre-ordained. See l. 300 and ll. 290–1.

317. *Gin.* Trap.

325. *As under cover,* etc. "Here begins the section devoted especially to the talking pots in the workshop of the potter—it ends at quatrain No. 90. In the first edition this section was entitled Kuza-nama—the 'Potbook' or 'Book of Pots.' It may be observed that the quatrains in this section are not so closely rendered from recognisable originals as the other quatrains composing FitzGerald's poem. This may be accounted for by the fact that the comparison between the human form—the Personal Ego—and a pot made of earth by the Supreme Potter (if one may be allowed the phrase) is constantly recurrent in all ruba'iyat attributed to Omar Khayyám. The section is therefore to a great extent a poetical reflection upon this phase of the philosophy of the ruba'iyat." (Heron-Allen.)

326. *Ramazán.* The month of fasting in which no food is eaten from dawn to sunset. See note on l. 358.

346. *Súfi.* A member of a Persian sect of mystics.

358. *The little Moon.* "At the close of the Fasting Month, Ramazan (which makes the Musulman unhealthy and unamiable) the first Glimpse of the New Moon (who rules their division of the Year) is looked for with the utmost Anxiety, and hailed with acclamation. Then it is that the Porter's Knot may be heard—toward the *Cellar.*"

THOMAS HARDY

BIBLIOGRAPHY

I. WORKS

Collected Poems. (Macmillan: New York, 1928.) An aggregation of the seven volumes of lyrics published during the life of the poet, 1898–1925.

Winter Words in Various Moods and Metres. (Macmillan: New York, 1928.) The single posthumous volume of poetry.

Selected Poems. (Macmillan: London, 1917.) A recommended book of selections, containing the best of Hardy's lyrics, narrative and reflective poems, war poems, and lyrics from *The Dynasts.*

The Dynasts. (Macmillan: New York, 1931.) A convenient edition of the epic, complete in one volume.

The Dynasts, selections, ed. by J. F. Fowler. (Macmillan: New York, 1928.) Choice scenes from the dramatic epic, intended to serve as an introduction to the beginning reader; the editor's notes provide the consecutiveness necessary to gain a comprehensive view of the whole poem.

The Famous Tragedy of the Queen of Cornwall. (Macmillan: New York, 1923.) A limited, numbered edition of the play, which is not included in the *Collected Poems;* it purports to be a "new version of an old story, arranged as a play for mummers."

II. BIOGRAPHY AND CRITICISM

Abercrombie, Lascelles. *Thomas Hardy: A Critical Study.* (Viking: New York, 1927.) The last two chapters discuss the poetry, as depending not upon the emotional property of individual words, but upon word-patterns; *The Dynasts* is seen as "the characteristic poem of our age" and akin to *Faust, Prometheus Bound,* and *Paradise Lost.*

Brennecke, Ernest, Jr. *Thomas Hardy's Universe: A Study of a Poet's Mind.* (Unwin: London, 1924.) An inquiry into the sources of Hardy's pessimism, showing the predominant influence of Schopenhauer and of Greek tragedy.

Brennecke, Ernest, Jr. *The Life of Thomas Hardy.* (Greenberg: New York, 1925.) Weak on the biographical side, this work is really a commentary on Hardy's poetry and prose and an analysis of his art.

Chew, S. C. *Thomas Hardy, Poet and Novelist.* (Knopf: New York, 1928.) A reliable, though brief, introduction to Hardy's works, sketching in his environment and outlining his intellectual scope; bibliography, pages 185–96.

Child, H. H. *Thomas Hardy.* (Holt: New York, 1925.) Chapter III deals in a general way with Hardy's poetry, showing its development from the four volumes of the early lyrics to *The Dynasts,* which is interpreted as giving most clearly the author's "view of life which the novels had adumbrated."

Elliott, A. E. *Fatalism in the Works of Thomas Hardy.* (University of Pennsylvania Press: 1935.) Traces through the prose and poetry the five fatalistic motifs: Chance, Nature, Time, Woman, Convention. Concludes that Hardy evolved no consistent philosophy but wavered between determinism and the doctrine of chance.

Firor, Ruth A. *Folkways in Thomas Hardy.* (University of Pennsylvania Press: 1931.) Establishes conclusively the importance of folklore in Hardy, by tracing the origins of ancient and medieval legend found in his prose and poetry; provides a ten-page bibliography.

Hardy, Florence E. *The Early Life of Thomas Hardy, 1840–1891.* (Macmillan: New York, 1928.) A compilation by Mrs. Hardy of her husband's literary *miscellania,* with her own notations, providing a fairly consecutive story; a prominent opinion is that Hardy was by choice a poet, but turned to the novel to make a living.

Hardy, Florence E. *The Later Years of Thomas Hardy, 1892–1928.* (Macmillan: New York, 1930.) This, together with the foregoing item, is indispensable to students of Hardy; most valuable are the author's own comments on his work in prose and verse, expressed in his letters, memoranda, and diary.

Hickson, E. C. *The Versification of Thomas Hardy.* (University of Pennsylvania Press: 1931.) A systematic catalogue of the poet's subject-material, rhythmical features, stanzaic forms, figures, vocabulary, and other technicalities.

Holland, Clive. *Thomas Hardy, O. M.* (Jenkins: London, 1933.) A first-hand study of the personality of Hardy and many of the scenes of his poetry and prose; attractively illustrated by Douglas Snowden.

McDowall, A. S. *Thomas Hardy: A Critical Study.* (Faber: London, 1931.) A comprehensive essay to analyze Hardy's artistic method; the latter portion of the book devotes a section to the discussion of the symbolism of *The Dynasts.*

Symons, Arthur. *A Study of Thomas Hardy.* (Sawyer: London, 1927.) Primarily concerned with Hardy's prose, but in the conclusion points out in his poetry the same satiric, poignant themes that prevail in his novels.

III. ARTICLES FROM BOOKS

Ellis, S. M. "Thomas Hardy: His Lyrics," in *Mainly Victorian.* (Hutchinson: London, 1925.) A review of the poet's 1922 volume; defines his pessimism as a view of the world as *sad* rather than bad.

Freeman, John. "Thomas Hardy," in *Moderns.* (Scott: London, 1916.) After a discussion of the novels, comments on several of the lyrics; briefly surveys *The Dynasts,* and sums up the novelist and poet as "an Elizabethan reborn."

Gosse, E. W. "The Lyrical Poetry of Thomas Hardy," in *Some Diversions of a Man of Letters.* (Scribner: New York, 1919.) Briefly scans the volumes of verse since 1898; remarks the poet's indifference to melody, his pessimism, distrust of nature, and Wessex spokesmanship.

Johnson, L. P. "Mr. Hardy's Later Prose and Verse," in *Post Liminium,* ed. by Thomas Whittemore. (Mathews: London, 1911.) Finds in many lyrics the sombre tones of Hardy's settled pessimism.

Lucas, F. L. "Hardy," in *Eight Victorian Poets.* (Cambridge University Press: 1930.) Remarks the writer's distrust of nature even in his most perfect intimacy; discovers in his pessimism the dominance of pity; points out his advantage in surviving the Victorian era.

Murry, J. M. "The Poetry of Thomas Hardy," in *Aspects of Literature.* (Collins: London, 1920.) Tries to take a view of the poetry distinctly uninfluenced by the prose; finds that Hardy's artistic power and unity proceed from his "plenary vision of life."

Quiller-Couch, A. T. "The Poetry of Thomas Hardy," in *Studies in Literature*, First Series. (Putnam: New York, 1918.) Defends the idea that, though the poet's pessimism may not appeal to youth, it is an inspiring challenge; admires Hardy's love of the English countryside.

Stevenson, Lionel. "Thomas Hardy," in *Darwin among the Poets*. (University of Chicago Press: 1932.) Notes the poet's acceptance of Darwinism, with no effort to reconcile it with religion; traces his philosophic growth, showing that his pessimism springs from his denial of purpose in the cosmic forces of creation.

Strong, Sir Archibald. "The Poetry of Thomas Hardy," in *Four Studies*. (Preece: Adelaide, 1932.) Well describes and praises Hardy's poetry, without offering essentially new criticism.

Sturgeon, Mary C. "Thomas Hardy," in *Studies of Contemporary Poets*. (Harrap: London, 1920.) Traces the poet's intellectual development, and discusses his scientific attitude, particularly in *The Dynasts*.

Symons, Arthur. "A Note on the Genius of Thomas Hardy," in *Figures of Several Centuries*. (Constable: London, 1916.) Remarks the "tremulous, half-inarticulate" tones of the poet; comments on the poetry of the novels.

IV. ARTICLES FROM PERIODICALS

Colum, Padraic. "Robert Bridges and Thomas Hardy," *New Republic*, XII, 47–9 (Aug. 11, 1917). Rather disparagingly contrasts Hardy the stoic with Bridges the epicurean.

Columbine, W. B. "The Poems of Thomas Hardy," *Westminster Review*, CLII, 180–4 (Aug., 1899). Reviews Hardy's *Wessex Poems*, dividing them into narrative and philosophical types; cautiously remarks that the book "does not detract from his reputation."

Dickinson, T. H. "Thomas Hardy's *The Dynasts*," *North American Review*, CXCV, 526–42 (Apr., 1912). Points out the unenthusiastic reception of the epic drama, finding a reason in its new technique; outlines the action of the poem, calling it a work "of first magnitude."

Elliott, G. R. "Spectral Etching in the Poetry of Thomas Hardy," *Publications of the Modern Language Association*, XLIII, 1185–95 (Dec., 1928). Sees the poet's disillusion as the cause of his "drab, ironic spiritualism," which is the natural companion of his sincerity and simplicity.

Ellis, S. M. "Some Personal Recollections of Thomas Hardy," *Fortnightly Review*, CXXIX, 393–406 (Mar., 1928). A survey of a fourteen-year-old friendship, providing interesting background material for many of the poems and novels; points out the cheer and geniality of Hardy's conversation.

Fairley, B. "Notes on the Form of *The Dynasts*," *Publications of the Modern Language Association*, XXXIV, 401–15 (Sept., 1919). Reads the poem as a unique experiment, in which "explicitness takes its widest reach"; names Goethe as Hardy's most evident model.

Fletcher, J. G. "Thomas Hardy's Poetry: An American View," *Poetry*, XVI, 43–9 (Apr. 1920). Points out in Hardy's poetry sharp contrasts to the Romantic and Victorian ideals; names him "the most homogeneous of all English poets."

Grey, Rowland. "Woman in the Poetry of Thomas Hardy," *Fortnightly Review*, CXXV, 34–46 (Jan., 1926). Scouts the idea that Hardy has no variety of types; shows how his sombre tone overlays his romantic stories; suggests influences from Browning.

Hall, J. A. "The 'Thing' of Mr. Hardy's Poetry," *Adelphi*, III, 364–7 (Oct., 1925). Begins with Hardy's concept of deity as expressed in his *The Dynasts;* shows the real height of the poet's courage in his persistence to sing in the presence of the "sense-bound" Thing—Hardy's God.

Harper, G. M. "Hardy, Hudson, Housman," *Scribner's Magazine*, LXXVIII, 151–7 (Aug., 1925). Comments on Hardy's double purpose in raising anew religious questions and in dealing creatively with human problems; reflects on the "faith reduced to a minimum," revealed in *The Dynasts*.

Hone, J. M. "The Poetry of Mr. Hardy," *London Mercury*, V, 396–405 (Feb., 1922). A naïve review of Hardy's favorite themes and methods; names him "a sentimental poet at his best."

King, R. W. "The Lyrical Poems of Thomas Hardy," *London Mercury*, XV, 157–70 (Dec., 1926). Finds an introduction to the poems not through Browning or Wordsworth but through William Barnes, an obscure Wessex poet; maintains that Hardy's intense subjectivity dominates all his lyric verse.

Nairne, A. "The Poetry of Thomas Hardy," *Living Age*, CCCII, 175–8 (July 19, 1919). Points out the poet's unswerving love of humanity, whence arises the pathos of his poetry; suggests influences from the World War.

Noyes, Alfred. "The Poetry of Hardy," *North American Review*, CXCIV, 96–105 (July, 1911). Defends Hardy's poetry against the charge of prosaism; shows his keen appreciation of beauty and analyzes the action of *The Dynasts*.

Parker, W. M. "My Visit to Thomas Hardy," *Cornhill Magazine*, LXVI, 149–57 (Feb., 1929). A glowing report of a personal interview, wherein Hardy discusses the value of reading poetry in cultivating a prose style and issues sundry criticisms on younger novelists.

Smith, R. M. "Philosophy in Thomas Hardy's Poetry," *North American Review*, CCXX, 330–40 (Dec., 1924). Admitting that Hardy's sombre themes deter many readers, shows a part of the foundation of the poet's thought to lie in his interesting religion; points out this philosophy in *The Dynasts*.

Valakis, A. P. "The *Moira* of Æschylus and the Immanent Will of Thomas Hardy," *Classical Journal*, XXI, 431–42 (March, 1926). Reviewing fatalistic teaching in various motifs in *The Dynasts* and the novels, points out differences and similarities in the Æschylean doctrine of Fate.

Whitmore, C. E. "Mr. Hardy's *Dynasts* as Tragic Drama," *Modern Language Notes*, XXXIX, 455–60 (Dec., 1924). Discusses the action of the drama on the levels of the supernatural figures, historical figures, minor participants, and the level of stage directions; points out kinship with medieval sacred drama and oratorio.

NOTES

"... Many of [Hardy's] poems are stark transcripts of human experience in moments when passion, or jealousy, or the irony of circumstance reflects unrelieved the grimness of life. So frequent are these poems that there arises from Hardy's poetry a permanent image of human frustration: a man and a woman are thrown together by the irony of circumstance and from their union arises a moment of passion which they call love, only to discover that its aftermath is a dreary record of semblance and deceit. The mood varies but the theme is the same [in poem after poem].

"...The true position of Hardy in these lyrics of human inadequacy can only be estimated historically. They are in part a protest against the idealization of love in the poetry surrounding him, from Browning's conception that love is the centre of successful human activity, to Rossetti's apotheosis of the earthly Eros. Read with these poems as a background, Hardy's short lyrics, economical in phrase and pungent in the expression of their dark realism, recall the poetry of the century to moods in life which it had forgotten." (B. Ifor Evans, in *English Poetry in the Later Nineteenth Century*, pp. 183–4.)

[Hardy] "records with microscopic exactitude, preserving a flawless artistic integrity. . . . In his short poems he fuses all that he has learned from the past and endured in the present, in a supreme imaginative vision with masterly and original craft in words and subtle ironic sense. He realizes that the true satisfaction of life lies in imaginative conflict. Whatever their ultimate purpose, men are alive only while they struggle. When they grow aware of the futility of their effort, and yet strive to fashion something from it, they become noble and tragic. Such is Hardy; but his despair is mitigated by tenderness and pity for his fellows . . . With a wistful understanding he surveys the human scene." (Siegfried Sassoon, in *Great Names*, as quoted in Louis Untermeyer's *Modern British Poetry*, p. 131.)

"From beginning to end the poetry of Thomas Hardy is the very voice of pessimism, but it is the pessimism of Shakespeare's tragedies, a pessimism so profound that it goes down to the depths where construction begins. The motto of it might be, 'Life's a poor player!' With the Book of Ecclesiastes it would cry, 'All is vanity!' and with Job it would sometimes be tempted to curse the Omnipotent Dramatist and die; but what it really does is to find the connections, likes, harmonies, ironic harmonies, perhaps, but still harmonies, between one detail of the world and another. For that is the whole business of art. It finds meanings, bitter meanings apparently and primarily, but still meanings, in the meaningless. It finds in the chaotic a little order, rhythm, and music; and this, so far as it goes, is—as the very name of poetry implies—not destructive, but constructive. . . .

". . . The poetry of Thomas Hardy is meat for the strong; but so is the book of Ecclesiastes, and the 'pessimism' of both is so profound that it postulates without affirming a passionate gospel. For there is one reality that they leave us—the grim reality of infinite passion, infinite pain; and infinite compassion, too." (Alfred Noyes, in *The North American Review*, CXCIV, 101–2, and 104.)

Page 912. NEUTRAL TONES

R. W. King, writing in the *London Mercury* (Dec., 1926), comments on the remarkable uniformity of quality in Hardy's poems of the earliest and of the most recent date. "Already in the group of a dozen love lyrics belonging to 1865–7," Mr. King writes, "there is no mistaking the note of the real Hardy. The best of these, *Neutral Tones*, has a theme—the 'bitter-sweet jest' of love—which he was to make all his own. This [poem] has a touch of the crudity of youth; but it has, too, most of the qualities we find in the later lyrics. There is the simple, almost colloquially plain-spoken diction, the flicks of alliteration which give emphasis rather than adornment, the indifference to bright colouring in description—tending therefore, in Hardy's own phrase, to an effect of 'even monochrome and curving line.' And in sum there is a kind of acrid clarity in both thought and style. One detects precisely the same flavor in a much later lyric like *The Darkling Thrush*, written in 1900."

Page 913. GOD-FORGOTTEN

This poem may be pointed to as exemplifying Hardy's "peculiar attitude of blaming God for human troubles." Generally, however, he imagines for "deity a sort of lackadaisical existence which has none of the potency of Fate, and which deserves far more pity than blame—he pities God's incapacity for pity."

Page 914. SHELLEY'S SKYLARK

Of Shelley's *To a Skylark*, written at Leghorn in 1820, Mrs. Shelley said that it was prompted by his "listening to the carolling of the bird, aloft in the azure sky of Italy!" Lascelles Abercrombie classifies this poem as one of those fairly numerous pieces which "may roughly be called epigrams; things hovering between prose and poetry. They usually versify some curiosity of thought, some reflection from the unexpected aspect of things, some ironical comment on life and death." This poem, "pondering the fate of that 'little ball of feather and bone,' 'that tiny pinch of priceless dust,'" slight things though they are, is "certainly pleasing and, somehow memorable."

THE DARKLING THRUSH

See note to *Neutral Tones*, above.

In the *North American Review* for July, 1911, Alfred Noyes called this elegy for the closing century a "lyric of rugged strength, that peculiar strength which comes from understatement and the sense of something in reserve; a lyric of such pathos and beauty as can be compared with the best that has ever been done in our great lyrical language."

1. *coppice*. A wood or thicket.

10. *Century's corpse*. The nineteenth century just ending.

Page 916. THE MAN HE KILLED

This poem "oddly touches (though from above) the Kipling of *Barrack-Room Ballads*."

4. *nipperkin*. About a half-pint of liquor.

Page 917. THE SACRILEGE

Hardly any of the places mentioned in this ballad are to be found in modern geographies of England or in travelers' guides to that island. Hardy frequently disguised the scene of a narrative by inventing a name for it. *Moor* (l. 2) is an extensive area of wild or waste land; *tor* (l. 10) is a hill; *deane* (l. 114) is a vale or valley. *Mendip* (l. 90) is a range of hills in Somerset; the Severn (l. 98) is a river flowing into Bristol Channel.

Page 919. A POET

14. *Two . . . him*. Hardy was twice married. The first Mrs. Hardy, who died in 1912, was the woman "with bright hair flapping free" in his wistful poem, *Beeny Cliff;* the second Mrs. Hardy, whom he married in 1914, dedicated "To the Dear Memory" her two excellent books, *The Early Life of Thomas Hardy* and *The Later Years of Thomas Hardy*.

TO SHAKESPEARE

"A comparison of this poem with the other tributes gathered together in the tercentary volume of homage to Shakespeare brings out strikingly the originality of Hardy's genius. He approaches even so well-worn a theme from an angle that demonstrates his idiosyncrasy. The motive is once more [as so often in Hardy] the contrast between the apparent and the real significance of human endeavor. What did Shakespeare's fellow-citizens know of his greatness?" (Samuel C. Chew, in *Thomas Hardy*, p. 155.)

Cf. Arnold's *Shakespeare,* text p. 511, and see the note to that poem

15. *Avon*. Stratford, the Warwick town in which Shakespeare was born, is on the Avon River.

Page 920. THE BLINDED BIRD

Mr. A. Nairne points to this poem as evidence of the truth of his statement that Hardy loved men and the innocent creatures which, "like men, suffer the mystery of life, and cheerfully play in it their unasked for, inevitable part." The poem was prompted by Hardy's dislike of a practice once very common—the blinding of songbirds to make them sing.

THE OXEN

According to a widespread folk belief, oxen kneel at the hour of Christ's birth as they did before the manger in Bethlehem.

13. *barton*. A farmyard.
coomb. A valley.

Page 922. THE SECOND NIGHT

19. *Cremyll*. A town in Cornwall.
44. *Edgcumbe*. A mountain in Cornwall.
47. *glum*. Gloom.

WILLIAM ERNEST HENLEY

BIBLIOGRAPHY

I. WORKS

Works. 5 vols. (Macmillan: London, 1921.) The poems are found in Vol. I; *Lyra Heroica* comprises Vol. V, of which the notes provide an insight into Henley's critical points of view.

Works. 7 vols. (Nutt: London, 1908.) The first collected edition: Vols. I and II contain the poetry; Vol. VII, the plays.

Poems. (Scribner: New York, 1928.) The most recent American edition; complete, and the most desirable single-volume collection.

Plays. (Macmillan: London, 1921.) Contains the four plays (written in collaboration with Stevenson): *Deacon Brodie*, *Beau Austin*, *Admiral Guinea*, and the blood-and-thunder *Macaire*.

II. BIOGRAPHY AND CRITICISM

Cornford, L. C. *William Ernest Henley*. (Houghton: Boston, 1913.) A good introductory study of the writer and his age; chapter V discusses his poetry, which represents his "quest of the spirit immanent in every manifestation of life."

Williamson, Kennedy. *W. E. Henley*. (Shaylor: London, 1930.) A most readable biography, written from abundant first-hand information, showing Henley's friendships and battles with many literary figures of his day.

III. ARTICLES FROM BOOKS AND PERIODICALS

Blackburn, Vernon. "William Ernest Henley," *Fortnightly Review*, LXXX, 232–8 (Aug., 1903). Recalls Henley's great journalistic activities and his authority as a critic; names him "the most modest artist of his generation."

Drinkwater, John. "William Ernest Henley," in *The Muse in Council.* (Houghton: Boston, 1925.) Fairly points out the poet's defects, giving compensatory quotation from his better pieces; reviews his work as a critic.

Hind, C. L. "W. E. Henley," in *Authors and I.* (Lane: London, 1921.) Describes a meeting between Henley and Francis Thompson; points out the persistence of Henley's poetic vigor amid the pressure of his editorial and critical activity.

Low, Sidney. "W. E. Henley, Some Memories and Impressions," *Cornhill Magazine,* XV, 411–22 (Sept., 1903). Recalls Henley's courage in his physical distresses and his work with the *National Observer;* eulogizes his lyric charm.

Neff, Marietta. "The Place of Henley," *North American Review,* CCXI, 555–63 (Apr., 1920). Discounts the idea of Henley's imitation of other poets; values him for his "independence and sanity."

Nichols, W. B. "The Influence of Henley," *Living Age,* CCCX, 88–92 (July 9, 1921). Sees some permanent worth in Henley's criticism, but places highest his reputation as a poet of lyrical quality.

Noyes, Alfred. "The Poetry of W. E. Henley," in *Some Aspects of Modern Poetry.* (Stokes: New York, 1924.) Brings into relief some biographical details; praises the poet's portrait-sonnets.

Schappes, M. U. "William Ernest Henley's Principles of Criticism," *Publications of the Modern Language Association,* XLVI, 1289–1301 (Dec., 1931). A survey of Henley's editorial tenets, which were that criticism means interpretation, is subjective but systematic, and should view art as self-complete.

Shanks, Edward. "W. E. Henley," in *First Essays on Literature.* (Collins: London, 1923.) Remarks the waning of Henley's vogue; feels that, though his poetry is frequently marked by vigor and freshness, "almost all of it is vitiated by an insincere violence of expression."

Shields, Roden. "A Blurred Memory of Childhood," *Cornhill Magazine,* XIX, 223–8 (Aug., 1905). A recollection of hospital days in the Edinburgh Infirmary by one who occupied a cot near Henley's.

Stephen, Herbert. "Henley as a Contemporary and an Editor," *London Mercury,* XIII, 387–400 (Feb., 1926). Relates personal passages with Henley the editor, who is described as a staunch friend and a gallant fighter.

Symons, Arthur. "Some Makers of Modern Verse," *Forum,* LXVI, 476–88 (Dec., 1921). Reviews some editorial dealings with Henley; draws many comparisons between the poet and his contemporaries.

Symons, Arthur. "Modernity in Verse," in *Studies in Two Literatures.* (Secker: London, 1924.) Takes account of Henley's revolutionary tendencies in poetry, pointing out his models in Meredith, Patmore, Whitman, and others; reviews *In Hospital* and *London Voluntaries.*

Yeats, W. B. "Four Years, 1887–1891," *London Mercury,* IV, 129–40 (June, 1921). Sections IV and V recall conversations with Henley, who is described as a master among many younger poets.

NOTES

"Henley was the painter of miniatures, the maker of cameos. There are some rough, and even brutal, passages in his poems; but his art, taken as a whole, was delicate, precise, and finished. When he set to work, the violence that one noticed in his talk, the over-emphasis of his intellectual temper, died away; in his best passages he has the subtle restraint, the economy of material, and the careful manipulation of the artist-workman. He will live through his lyric passages and his vignettes, in prose and verse. No man of our time has expressed a mood of the emotions with more absolute appropriateness and verbal harmony, and that is lyric poetry in its essence." (Sidney Law, in the *Cornhill Magazine,* XV, 420.)

"Henley's verse, whenever it has been good, has always been a whisper, or a pathetic cry, or a lilt which seems to come from a long way off, like the sound of dance music in a village fair, heard across the fields. His brave lamentings over himself, and the pains of his body, in the 'Hospital' poems; his impressions of streets and parks and water and the city seasons in the 'London Voluntaries'; all the fleeting snatches of song which he has scattered up and down his pages, have a personal quality and strike a personal note. They are often speech rather than song; but, after all, there is room for speech in poetry when it is the utterance of an interesting personality, and really says something. Some of them are quite evanescent song, giving us the delight of music, with the least possible accompaniment of words. But in much of his verse, and notably in his patriotic pamphlet 'For England's Sake,' Henley shouts at the top of his voice, and his voice is not suited for shouting." (Arthur Symons, in *The Forum,* LXVI, 487.)

Page 925. WAITING

In Hospital, the remarkable book from which the poems *Waiting* and *Discharged* were taken, was written in the Old Infirmary, Edinburgh, while Henley was a patient there. Louis Untermeyer characterizes the hospital verses as "vivid precursors of free verse . . ., sharp with the sights, sensations, even the actual smells, of the sick-room."

10. *bluestone.* Copper sulphate, or blue vitriol. It was once used as an emetic.

BALLADE OF DEAD ACTORS

This poem was dedicated to Henley's brother Ted, whose promising career on the stage was cut short by death when he was only thirty-seven.

For an explanation of the ballade form, see note to Swinburne's *A Ballad of Dreamland,* above.

6. *Sir Peter.* Sir Peter Teazle, in Sheridan's *School for Scandal.*

Timon. In Shakespeare's *Timon of Athens.*

7. *Millamant.* The heroine of Congreve's *The Way of the World.*

20. *Thunder . . . Snow.* Stage machines for making thunder and snow.

INVICTUS

The title of this poem, which has been called "a portrait of the artist, painted by himself," means "unconquered."

This defiance of the "Everlasting No" (the voice of Evil in the world) is similar to Carlyle's eloquent defiance in the chapter on "The Everlasting No" in *Sartor Resartus.*

"The poem is great," writes Kennedy Williamson, in *W. E. Henley* (p. 35), "because the truculence of the writer's utterance was matched by the truculence of his experience."

"This famous battle cry is altogether un-Victorian. Neither the orthodox Christian nor the scientist can feel that he is the master of his fate. But it is the man who will not rationalize about either point of view who can feel this and who substitutes for thought his own moods and emotions." (C. E. Andrews and M. O. Percival, in *Poetry of the Nineties,* p. 13.)

Page 926. O, FALMOUTH IS A FINE TOWN

Falmouth, the small seaport that is the home of the sailor who sings this song, is in Cornwall.

7. *birken.* Birch.

A LATE LARK TWITTERS

This is an "In Memoriam" poem for Margaret Boyle, Mrs. Henley's sister.

5. *city.* London.

15–16. *night . . . sleep.* This phrase—"all monosyllables—is the kind of phrase that echoes in the secret places of the soul and comes back to the memory in the elemental hours of a man's life. It is one of the great phrases that seem so perfectly fitting as almost to be integral and organic with the things that they describe." (Kennedy Williamson, in *W. E. Henley,* p. 184.)

Page 927. OR EVER THE KNIGHTLY YEARS

This poem, Henley's favorite among his own verses, was dedicated to the distinguished dramatic critic, William Archer. With the public the poem generally takes second place, first place being given to *Invictus.*

ON THE WAY TO KEW

Kew, famous for its botanical garden, and Richmond are suburbs of London a little way up the Thames.

GERARD MANLEY HOPKINS

BIBLIOGRAPHY

I. WORKS

Poems, ed. by Robert Bridges. (Oxford University Press: 1931.) The second edition of Hopkins's poetry, containing comprehensive notes and an appendix of poems additional to the first edition; prefaced by a critical essay by Charles Williams.

Letters to Robert Bridges, Vol. I; *Correspondence with Richard Watson Dixon,* Vol. II, ed. by C. C. Abbott. (Oxford University Press: 1935.) Provides proof of Hopkins's influence upon Bridges' metrical experiments; the two-sided Dixon correspondence discusses the relationship of poetry and religion.

II. BIOGRAPHY AND CRITICISM

Lahey, G. F. *The Life of Father Gerard Manley Hopkins.* (Oxford University Press: 1930.) The most recent and probably the standard biography; the chapters describing the poet's relations with Newman and Patmore bring him out of the hermit life in which he so largely dwelt.

Lappin, H. A. "Gerard Hopkins and His Poetry," *Catholic World,* CIX, 501–12 (July, 1919). Rather severely condemns Bridges's editorial supervision; quotes many passages of Hopkins's poetry for analysis.

Murry, J. M. "Gerard Manley Hopkins," in *Aspects of Literature.* (Collins: London, 1920.) Finds the poet's chief melodic models in Shelley and Keats; names "The Golden Echo" his best lyric.

Phare, Elsie E. *The Poetry of Gerard Manley Hopkins.* (Cambridge University Press: 1933.) The first detailed critical study of Hopkins's work; compares him with Wordsworth, dilating upon the Victorian poet's "love of wildness."

Richards, I. A. "Gerard Hopkins," *Dial,* LXXXI, 195–203 (Sept., 1926). Points out that most of the reader's difficulty with Hopkins's verse arises rather from the poet's oddities of manner than obscurity of thought; quotes and analyzes several selections to illustrate Hopkins's themes and technique.

Zabel, M. D. "Gerard Manley Hopkins," *Poetry,* XXXVII, 152–61 (Dec., 1930). Shows Hopkins's freedom from models and tradition, quoting passages illustrating his metrical experiments.

NOTES

". . . Even in polyphonic prose, which made a definite attempt to be contrapuntal, there has been no modern poetry attaining to the amazing effect of lines in Hopkins. His mind discarded ordinary word sequences and grammatical arrangements, creating for itself an original order which has its own habits of ingenious displacement and irregularity, making sometimes grace and sometimes grandeur. He can halt a sentence, a verse, retard it with a broken preposition, then set it spinning with a participle to gather momentum until it collects its own climax. Verbal indulgences, so easily faults of diffuseness, are here less faults than a curious, purposive colliding and jamming, an overlapping and telescoping of images and words in an effort toward sustained music and sense. Extravagance of a kind is the inevitable result, but extravagance so integrated, so disciplined to intention, that the accomplishment never sinks to mere lavishness. The will is never relaxed." (Hildegarde Flanner, in the *New Republic*, LXV, 331.)

Page 929. HEAVEN-HAVEN

This poem was originally composed of seven quatrains. Father Lahey speaks of its delicacy, which "suggests, and almost surpasses Tennyson, even at his best." It is said that Hopkins wrote the poem as a result of the deep impression made upon him by a long conversation with Canon (afterwards Abbot) Raynal, of the Benedictine monastery, near Hereford, England, in 1865.

THE HABIT OF PERFECTION

27–28. *lily-coloured . . . spun.* Suggested by the "Consider-the-lilies-of-the-field" passage, Matthew 6:28–29.

GOD'S GRANDEUR

This sonnet is one of the few poems in which Hopkins voiced his preoccupation with the theme of God's presence in Nature. However "seared with trade" the world, yet God broods over it "with warm breast and bright wings." Other poems showing the same interest are *Hurrahing in Harvest*, *The Starlight Night*, and the ecstatic *Spring*, in which the joy and charm of Nature in spring are made to go far back to the days of man's innocence and companionship with God in the primitive Eden.

3–4. *ooze . . . Crushed.* The oil made of crushed olives.

Page 930. SPRING

See preceding note on *God's Grandeur.*

THE WINDHOVER

The windhover is the kestrel, a falcon.

[Hopkins] "uses words always as tools, an attitude towards them which the purist and grammarian can never understand. He was clear, too, that his poetry was for the ear, not for the eye, a point that should be noted before we proceed to *The Windhover*, which, unless we begin by listening to it, may *only* bewilder us. To quote from a letter: 'Indeed, when, on somebody's returning me the *Eurydice*, I opened and read some lines as one commonly reads, whether prose or verse, with the eyes, so to say, only, it struck me aghast with a kind of raw nakedness and unmitigated violence I was unprepared for: but take breath and read it with the ears, as I always wish to be read, and my verse becomes all right.' I have to confess that *The Windhover* only became all right for me, in the sense of perfectly clear and explicit, intellectually satisfying as well as emotionally moving, after many readings and several days of reflection.

"The dedication at first sight is puzzling. Hopkins said of this poem that it was the best thing he ever wrote, which is to me in part the explanation. It sounds like an echo of the offering made . . . when his early poems were burnt. For a while I thought that the apostrophe, 'O my chevalier!' . . . had reference to Christ. I take it now to refer only to the poet, though the moral ideal, embodied of course for Hopkins in Christ, is before the mind.

"Some further suggestions . . . may save the reader trouble. . . . *Kingdom of daylight's dauphin*—I see (unnecessarily) the falcon as a miniature sun, flashing so high up. *Rung upon the rein*—a term from the *manège*, ringing a horse—causing it to circle round one on a long rein. *My heart in hiding*—as with other good poets I have come to expect that when Hopkins leaves something which looks at first glance as though it were a concession to rhyme or a mere pleasing jingle of words, some really important point is involved. Why in hiding? Hiding from what? Does this link up with 'a billion times told lovelier, more dangerous, O my chevalier'? What is the greater danger and what the less? I should say the poet's heart is in hiding from Life, has chosen a safer way, and that the greater danger is the greater exposure to temptation and error than a more adventurous, less sheltered course (sheltered by Faith?) brings with it. Another, equally plausible reading would be this: Renouncing the Glamour of the outer life of adventure, the poet transfers its qualities of audacity to the inner life. (*Here* is the bosom, the inner consciousness.) The greater danger is that to which the moral hero is exposed. Both readings may be combined, but pages of prose would be required for a paraphrase of the result. The last three lines carry the thought of the achievement possible through renunciation further, and explain, with the image of the ash-covered fire, why the dangers of the inner life are greater. So much for the sense, but the close has a strange, weary, almost exhausted rhythm, and the word 'gall' has an extraordinary force, bringing out painfully the shock with which the sight of the soaring bird has jarred the poet into an unappeased discontent." (I. A. Richards, in *The Dial*, LXXXI, 197–99.)

For other analyses of the poem, which, like much impressive poetry, has been variously interpreted, see E. E. Phare's *The Poetry of Gerard Manley Hopkins*, pp. 130 ff.

Herbert Read characterizes *The Windhover* as completely objective in its senseful catalogue and sees in the dedication "To Christ our Lord," an effort by Hopkins to sublimate his poetic powers. This, he says, does not remove the naked sensualism of the poem. It is at once a tribute to the glory of God and to the senses.

11. *sillion.* A ridge made in plowing.

PIED BEAUTY

Herbert Read quotes Hopkins's criticism of Keats in which he implies that "the poet, by nature a dreamer and a sensualist, only raises himself to greatness by concerning himself with 'great causes, as liberty and religion.'" In a poem like *Pied Beauty,* Read writes, we see openly enacted the process by which Hopkins so sublimated his poetic powers: "After a catalogue of dappled things, things which owe their beauty to contrast, inconsistency, and change, Hopkins concludes by a neat inversion—an invocation to God who, fathering forth such things, is Himself changeless." (Quoted from Read's essay, *The Poetry of Gerard Manley Hopkins.*)

3. *stipple.* Dotted or spotted with color.

10. *past change.* In James 1:17 God is characterized as one "with whom is no variableness, neither shadow of turning."

SPELT FROM SIBYL'S LEAVES

The Sibyl was a prophetess whose prophecies, written on leaves, were blown into terrible disorder by the winds.

"If we compare those poems . . . which were conceived definitely within the circle of Hopkins's theology with those which transcend it, we shall find difficulty in resisting the conclusion that the poet in him was often oppressed and stifled by the priest. In this case the conflict which seems to lie behind and prompt all Hopkins's better poems is temporarily resolved through a stoic acceptance of sacrifice. An asceticism which fails to reach ecstasy and accepts the failure. All Hopkins's poems are in this sense poems of defeat. This will perhaps become clearer if we turn to *Spelt from Sibyl's Leaves* . . .

" . . . The heart speaks after 'Heart you round me right' to the end, applying in the moral sphere the parable of the passing away of all the delights, accidents, nuances, the 'dapple' of existence, to give place to the awful dichotomy of right and wrong. It is characteristic of this poet that there is no repose for him in the night of traditional morality. As the terrible last line shows, the renunciation of all the myriad temptations of life brought no gain. It was all loss. The present order of 'black, white; right, wrong' was an afterthought and an intentional rearrangement; the original order was more orthodox. *Let life, waned*—the imperative mood carries through to the end; let life part, pen, pack, let life be aware of. *All throughther* = each through the other." (I. A. Richards, in *The Dial*, LXXXI, 199–200.)

Page 931. THE LEADEN ECHO AND THE GOLDEN ECHO

Of this poem, which Hopkins considered his most musical piece, he wrote to Robert Bridges in 1880: "You shall also see the *Leaden Echo* when finished. The reason, I suppose, why you feel it carry the reader along with it is that it is dramatic and meant to be popular. It is a song for St. Winefred's maidens to sing."

[The poem] "is as *baroque,* as extravagant a piece of workmanship as ever issued from the seventeenth century. The first verse falls heavily, both in sound and in meaning, representing as it does the Echo of Lead: the second trips along with a rather precious grace, swaying under its load of fluttering femininities . . . the way in which Hopkins has exploited the musical resources of the language, contriving . . . never to sacrifice sense to sound [is praiseworthy]. At the same time . . . [the poem] is not one . . . by which Hopkins may be said to stand or fall. It is more of a pretty piece than any other of his poems: in spite of all its charm it is somehow trivial. . . .

"The didactic intention in [the poem] is very slight. The idea that whosoever loveth his youth shall lose it and whosoever resigns it willingly shall find it is a tenuous theme almost overburdened with the variations which the poet plays on it." (E. E. Phare, in *Gerard Manley Hopkins*, pp. 122–3.)

38–41. In October, 1882 Hopkins wrote to Bridges concerning these lines: "'Nay, what we lighthanded' etc. means 'Nay, more: the seed that we so carelessly and freely flung into the dull furrow, and then forgot it, will have come to ear meantime' etc."

Page 932. NO WORST, THERE IS NONE

This is one of the four sonnets which, so Hopkins wrote to Bridges (Sept. 1, 1885), "came like inspirations unbidden and against my will."

I WAKE AND FEEL THE FELL OF DARK

Another of the sonnets that "came unbidden." E. E. Phare (Mrs. Austin Duncan-Jones) suggests a comparison of this, "the most majestic, the bleakest of all Hopkins's sonnets," with one of Herbert's "Affliction" poems "in which his reproaches suddenly give way to a protestation of the staunchest affection." Herbert, she feels, is held by the heart; Hopkins clings to faith "only by the reason and the will."

1. *fell*. Skin, fleece, covering.

THOU ART INDEED JUST

Herbert Read places this sonnet and the two immediately preceding it in the text in a group expressive of doubt rather than of belief. Read quotes this "last terrible" sonnet, which dates from the very year of the poet's death, as evidence of the truth of his (Read's) belief that "the sonnets themselves are complete in their gloom, awful in their anguish."

The first three lines of the poem translate the Latin motto, which is the first verse of Jeremiah 12 as it appears in *Biblia Sacra Latina* (the Vulgate).

11. *fretty chervil*. An aromatic herb whose pinnately divided leaves may suggest fretwork.

Page 933. THE BUGLER'S FIRST COMMUNION

E. E. Phare remarks that this poem is "spoilt by the presence of one image after another which does nothing more than startle, which will not melt away into the consistency of the poem as a whole." (*The Poetry of Gerard Manley Hopkins*, p. 16). She admits that the poem contains many felicitous lines and phrases, but she finds it "discordant and somehow false."

12. *housel*. The Eucharist or sacrament of the Lord's Supper.

18. *squander*. Disperse.

46. *brandle*. Shake.

ALFRED EDWARD HOUSMAN

BIBLIOGRAPHY

I. WORKS

A Shropshire Lad. (Holt: New York, 1928.) The authorized American edition of Housman's first volume of verse.

A Shropshire Lad. (Illustrated Editions Company: New York, 1932.) A pleasing edition, illustrated with designs by Elinore Blaisdell.

Last Poems. (Holt: New York, 1928.) The standard American edition of Housman's second volume of poetry.

II. ARTICLES FROM BOOKS AND PERIODICALS

Archer, William. "A. E. Housman," in *Poets of the Younger Generation*. (Lane: New York, 1902.) Analyzes the "three main topics" of the *Shropshire Lad:* pessimism, patriotism, wistful cynicism.

Brannin, James. "Alfred Housman," *Sewanee Review*, XXXIII, 191–8 (Apr., 1925). Besides noting the classic flavor of the poet's two volumes, points out also traces of Heine and Burns.

Drinkwater, John. "A. E. Housman's *Last Poems*," in *The Muse in Council*. (Houghton: Boston, 1925.) Briefly remarks the continued tone of pessimism and the artistic perfection of the new lyrics.

Ellis, S. M. "A. E. Housman," in *Mainly Victorian*. (Hutchinson: London, 1925.) A review of the second volume, commenting pointedly on outstanding lines and stanzas.

Garrod, H. W. "Mr. A. E. Housman," in *The Profession of Poetry*. (Oxford University Press: 1929.) Holds that Housman's scholarship is "an anodyne for the wounds which poetry has wrought in him"; points out resemblances to Swift; rather severely criticizes the false pastoralism in *A Shropshire Lad*.

Gosse, E. W. "*A Shropshire Lad*," in *More Books on the Table*. (Scribner, New York, 1923.) Discusses both volumes of verse; points out resemblances to Heine.

Harper, G. M. "Hardy, Hudson, Housman," *Scribner's Magazine*, LXXVIII, 151–7 (Aug., 1925). Compares Housman's lyric note with Burns's; laying aside the "pessimistic" label, commends the poet's courage and honesty.

Hind, C. L. "The Housmans," in *Authors and I*. (Lane: London, 1921.) Briefly reviews *A Shropshire Lad*, pointing out its cold, caustic irony and its tenderness and lyric beauty.

MacDonald, J. F. "The Poetry of A. E. Housman," *Queen's Quarterly*, XXXI, 114–37 (Oct., 1923). Believing Housman's place to be secure with Gray, points out his many felicities in diction and his metrical skill, particularly as shown in the *Last Poems;* holds that his peculiar appeal is based on his frank stoicism (by many miscalled pessimism), which emphasizes the virtues of courage and an intense joy in the beauties of nature and human relations.

Priestley, J. B. "Mr. A. E. Housman," in *Figures in Modern Literature*. (Lane: London, 1924.) Provides trenchant commentary on selected lines and stanzas from Housman's poetry.

Sapir, Edward. "A. E. Housman's *Last Poems*," *Dial*, LXXV, 188–91 (Aug., 1923). Finds in the second volume "less drama, less interested amusement in the process, a more explicit concern with the journey's end"; insists that the poet is not creating a new vogue, but is definitely apart from the temper of his age.

Tinker, C. B. "Housman's Poetry," *Yale Review*, XXV, 84–95 (Autumn, 1935). An enthusiastic review of the poet's outstanding themes and moods, praising his aloofness, the high level of his art, and his power of evoking emotion.

NOTES

". . . For poetic beauty in the strictest sense of the term, beauty that in this case depends almost wholly on sound and on those suggestions, now vague and again vivid, which are produced by sound, we must go back to Keats to find an equal quantity of verse by any one poet which excels them . . . [Housman's] poems have entered my heart through the porches of my ears. Among this great artist's cunning devices we find unexpected and strangely suggestive checks in tunes that are flowing smoothly; deep words brought from afar, and set like blazing planets in a Milky Way of simple English; hidden harmonies, through rhyme and alliteration and cadence, which please like the rippling of unnoticed rills." (G. M. Harper, in *Scribner's Magazine*, LXXVIII, 157.)

"Purely as writing . . . *A Shropshire Lad* is incomparable. Owing nothing to any poet of his own generation and showing no influence other than Heine's, Housman's verse is condensed to the uttermost, stripped of every superfluous ornament, pared and precise. Not the least of his triumph is the mingling of pungent humor and poignance in lines of haunting melody. Possibly the outstanding virtue is the seemingly artless but extraordinarily skillful simplicity of tone. This is song sharpened, acid-flavored, yet always song." (Louis Untermeyer, in *Modern British Poetry*, p. 254.)

Page 934. *From* A SHROPSHIRE LAD

II

Mr. A. C. Ward, remarking on the simplicity of Housman's work and the sureness with which he creates beauty by rigid exclusion of ornament, says that this poem contains only one epithet of beauty, and no adjectives of color. "The exquisite picture is built up by means of four principal words—three nouns and one adjective: *bloom*, *white* ('wearing white for Easter-tide'), *snow*, and *loveliest*.

VII

1. *Ludlow.* A town in Shropshire situated above the confluence of the Teme and the Corve.

Page 935. *IX*

"Hanging in chains was called keeping sheep by moonlight."—Housman's note.

9. *Shrewsbury.* The county town of Shropshire.

XIII

Cf. Yeats's *Down by the Salley Gardens*, text p. 1123.

XIX To an Athlete Dying Young

11. *laurel.* Symbolic of victory.

Page 937. *XXVIII The Welsh Marches*

The borderland, or Welsh Marches, between England and Wales, was for many centuries the scene of fierce fighting between the native Celts and the Saxons and Normans.

1. *Shrewsbury.* Shrewsbury is on the Severn River.

13. *Buildwas.* A town on the Severn about twelve miles below Shrewsbury.

Page 938. *LIV*

"In a beautiful lyric ["With rue my heart is laden"] the quintessence of regret is revealed with a master's touch. Some of Housman's lyrics have all the grace of the little songs of the Shakespearean era." (Holbrook Jackson, in the *Living Age*, CCCII, 730.)

LXI Hughley Steeple

Hughley is a small town near Shrewsbury.

LXII

18. *Burton . . . Trent.* Burton-upon-Trent, in Derbyshire, is "famous," says Baedeker, for its sixteen breweries, one of which was founded in 1777 by the Messrs. Bass.

22. *justify . . . man.* In *Paradise Lost* (I, 26) Milton states in these words his purpose in writing that epic.

29–58. Holbrook Jackson, writing in the *Living Age* (September 20, 1919), doubts that Housman's confession that he has often been to Ludlow Fair and left his necktie God knows where, is to be taken literally; but he sees in ll. 43–58 an explanation of Housman's attitude to his own muse that is to be accepted by the reader letter for letter.

59. *a king.* Mithridates, a famous king of Pontus, in Asia Minor on the shore of the Black Sea, is said to have become inured to poisons by starting with small doses and gradually increasing the size of the dose until he could withstand the effect of any amount.

LIONEL PIGOT JOHNSON

BIBLIOGRAPHY

I. WORKS

Poetical Works. (Mathews: London, 1915.) A recommended complete edition, containing a preface by Ezra Pound.

Poems, ed. by Louise I. Guiney. (Mathews: London, 1912.) A comprehensive selection, supplied with a brief introduction by the editor.

Lionel Pigot Johnson: Poems. (Benn: London, 1932.) One of the convenient Augustan Books of Poetry; concludes with a short bibliography.

Some Winchester Letters. (Macmillan: New York, 1919.) Contains a biographical note and a brief introduction to the letters.

II. ARTICLES FROM BOOKS AND PERIODICALS

Boyd, Ernest. "Lionel Johnson," in *Ireland's Literary Renaissance.* (Knopf: New York, 1922.)

The first section of chapter IX defines Johnson's share in the poetry revival and compares him with Yeats.

Colby, Elbridge. "The Poetry and Prose of Lionel Johnson," *Catholic World*, XCVI, 721–32; XCVII, 52–63 (Mar., Apr., 1913). Points out the poet's two chief inspirations: the Catholic faith and Ireland, which fused in his best poetry.

Guiney, Louise I. "Of Lionel Johnson," *Atlantic Monthly*, XC, 856–62 (Dec., 1902). A eulogy of Johnson's devotion to his high ideals as an artist; commends his lack of prejudice and his spiritual courage.

Hind, C. L. "Lionel Johnson," in *More Authors and I*. (Dodd: New York, 1922.) Recalls the poet's love of solitude, and other *personalia;* names him a "devoted disciple" of Pater.

More, P. E. "Two Poets of the Irish Movement," in *Shelburne Essays*, First Series. (Putnam: New York, 1904.) Names Johnson a "poet of failure" but of a firmer fibre than Yeats; selects *Ireland* as his most characteristic poem.

O'Brien, E. J. "Lionel Johnson," *Poet-Lore*, XXVI, 405–8 (May, 1915). Comments on the poet's love of seclusion and of the past; praises his ability to objectify his enthusiasms.

Scott, Dixon. "Lionel Johnson's Prose," in *Men of Letters*. (Hodder: London, 1923.) A review of *Post Liminium*, praising the purity and quiet vigor of Johnson's prose.

Waugh, Arthur. "Lionel Johnson," in *Tradition and Change*. (Dutton: New York, 1919.) Recalls college days with the poet; follows his literary ventures in London; identifies him as a poet "standing somewhat aloof from the spirit of his generation."

Weygandt, Cornelius. "Lionel Johnson: English Irishman," in *Tuesdays at Ten*. (University of Pennsylvania Press: 1928.) Reminds us of the poet's precocity; comments on his devotion to Ireland and his attraction to England; places him in the same category with Marvell, Collins, and Arnold.

Yeats, W. B. "Lionel Johnson," in *Collected Works*, VIII. (Shakespere Head: Stratford, 1908.) Remarks the poet's unworldliness, seen most clearly in his "ecstasy of combat," which represents his attitude toward divinity.

NOTES

" . . . The proud melancholy charm of his finest stanzas rests upon the severest adherence to the laws and by-laws of rhythm; in no page of his was there ever a rhetorical trick or an underbred rhyme. Excess and show were foreign to him. The real shortcoming of his verse lies in its Latin strictness and asceticism, somewhat repellent to any readers but those of his own temper. Its emotional glow is a shade too moral, and it is only after a league of stately pacing that fancy is let go with a looser rein. . . . Lionel Johnson, even as a beginner, was of so jealous an integrity that his youthful numbers are in their detail almost scandalously free from *parentalia.* Is it not, surely, by some supernatural little joke that his most famous line,—

'Lonely unto the Lone I go,'

had been anticipated by Plotinus? . . . To one who looks well into the structure of his poems, they are like the roof of Milan Cathedral, 'gone to seed with pinnacles,' full of voweled surprises, and exquisitely devotional elaborations, given in the zest of service, and meant to be hidden from mundane eyes. Yet they have the grace to appear much simpler than they are. The groundwork, at least, is always simple: his usual metre is iambic or trochaic, and the English alexandrine he made his own." (Louise Imogen Guiney, in *The Atlantic Monthly*, XC, 858.)

[The] "dominant note [of Johnson's poetry] is meditation, not passion. It is not poetry that stirs the pulses; its ardors are intellectual. It is a little remote; it is often severe; it leaves one, at first reading, somewhat cold. But as one reads, the quiet felicity of the imagery, the meditative charm of the thought, the grave beauty of the phrasing gradually take possession of the reader's mind and rule it. Such verse is not an incantation; it weaves no spell, unless its power, continually exerted and continually renewed, upon the reader's reluctance, be a spell of the most magical sort. One feels its beauty, as Pater says of Wordsworth, only at the price of certain adjustments and renunciations; but the beauty is there, and one's admiration of it is the more durable for not being easily yielded. Little of it is devoted to the passion of love, in spite of the poet's youth, and that little, almost without exception, is dedicated to a love that is spiritualized by distance or by death. There is, indeed, almost no 'human interest' in these poems, not even that which centres in the poet himself, for he effaces himself as completely as it is possible to do in verse so entirely subjective. It is upon the emotion, the imagery, that our attention is fixed, not upon the poet who feels and sees." (Charles H. A. Wager, in the *Dial*, LX, 372.)

Page 939. ORACLES—I

1–2. *Fate . . . thread.* One of the Fates spun the thread of life, another determined its length, the third cut it.

3. *Ivory Gate.* In classic story the gate of the abode of Sleep through which dreams come forth.

5. *Gate of Horn.* That gate of the abode of Sleep through which *true* dreams come forth.

Page 941. BY THE STATUE OF KING CHARLES AT CHARING CROSS

An equestrian statue of Charles I, who was beheaded by the Parliamentary party in 1649, was erected at Charing Cross, near Trafalgar Square, London, in 1674.

10. *Whitehall*. The ancient royal palace near Charing Cross. It was burned in 1698, and the banquet-hall, now a royal chapel, alone remains.

31–32. The bravery and dignity of Charles in the face of death did much to shake the power of the Parliamentary party and speed the Restoration.

35. *Speak after sentence?* Charles asked permission to speak after sentence of death was passed upon him, but it was refused because he had not recognized the right of the court to try him.

44. *art . . . joy*. Charles had a very fine collection of paintings.

A DREAM OF YOUTH

96. *Achilles*. The type to the Greeks of youthful strength, beauty, and chivalry, who withdrew in wrath from the Trojan War because his captive, Briseis, was taken from him by Agamemnon.

Page 943. BAGLEY WOOD

Bagley Wood is on the Berkshire side of the Thames, about three miles below Oxford.

8. *Chaldean*. Chaldea was an ancient region in Asia on the Euphrates River and the Persian Gulf. The Chaldeans were much impressed by the beauty and majesty of the stars.

UPON A DRAWING

13. *Marathonians*. Natives of Marathon, a plain and a town in Greece.

14. *Socrates*. An Athenian philosopher (B.C. 469–399).

24. *Catiline*. A Roman conspirator (B.C. 108?–62).

27. *Punic*. Carthaginian. From the Roman point of view treacherous, faithless.

33. *Sibylline*. Mysterious, like the oracles embodied in the *Sibylline Books*.

Page 944. TO MORFYDD

Johnson told W. B. Yeats that he made this love song out of three lines in Welsh which he heard a woman singing at her door while he was on a walking tour in Wales. Yeats questions the truth of the poet's statement, wondering whether Johnson really knew Welsh, and intimating that he but wished to hide that he shared in the emotion:

"O, what are the winds?
And what are the waters?
Mine are your eyes!"

There was a Welsh maiden Morfudd (Morfydd) prominent in the loves and the poems of Dafydd Ab Gwilym, a Welsh bard of the 13th century.

"TO WEEP IRISH"

Charles H. A. Wager finds missing from Johnson's poems on Irish subjects "the note of intensity for which we listen in poetry dedicated to the hopes and sorrows of an unhappy people." Johnson does not wring the heart for Ireland or quicken the pulses in the way in which Swinburne, for example, did for Italy when he sang the woes of that unhappy land.

THE DARK ANGEL

13–14. *Muses . . . Furies*. For the Muses see note to l. 27 of Swinburne's *Sapphics*, p. 1260, above. In Greek myth the Furies were the avenging deities, who executed the curses pronounced upon criminals, tortured the guilty with the stings of conscience, or inflicted famines and pestilences.

36. *Paraclete*. The Holy Ghost or Spirit. As St. John uses the term he means man's guardian spirit; Johnson addresses his dark angel by the term.

55. *Lonely . . . go*. See first introductory note on Johnson.

Page 945. DESIDERIA

The title means "longings."

4. *Hill of Howth*. At the mouth of the river Liffey, which empties into Dublin Bay, on the east coast of Ireland.

RUDYARD KIPLING

BIBLIOGRAPHY

I. WORKS

Rudyard Kipling's Verse: Inclusive Edition, 1885–1932. (Doubleday: Garden City, 1934.) The recommended edition, containing over sixty pieces not found in the collection of 1927.

Poems, 1886–1929. 3 vols. (Doubleday: Garden City, 1930.) A worth-while collection, presenting the poems in chronological order; concludes with a useful glossary.

Poems. (Crowell: New York, 1928.) A recommended collection, furnished with a biographical introduction by N. H. Dole.

A Kipling Anthology. (Methuen: London, 1922.) One of the many convenient books of selections from the poems.

Letters of Travel. (Doubleday: Garden City, 1920.) A collection of correspondence covering the time 1892–1913.

II. BIOGRAPHY AND CRITICISM

Braybrooke, Patrick. *Kipling and His Soldiers*. (Daniel: London, 1926.) A pleasant analysis, though offering little novelty; finds Kipling's chief claim to fame in his humanitarianism.

Charles, C. *Rudyard Kipling: His Life and Works.* (Hewetson: London, 1911.) One of the few extant full-length attempts in Kipling's biography, necessarily incomplete, but assembling and aptly presenting the available data.

Durand, R. A. *A Handbook to the Poetry of Rudyard Kipling.* (Hodder: London, 1917.) A meticulous annotation of poems appearing in *Departmental Ditties, Barrack-Room Ballads, The Seven Seas, The Five Nations, Songs from Books, A School History of England,* and chapter-headings for the prose narratives.

Hopkins, R. T. *The Kipling Country.* (Appleton: New York, 1925.) Filled with interesting illustrations, this volume reveals Kipling's English backgrounds, which are pertinently discussed in relation to his poetry in chapters XV and XVI.

Mansfield, M. F., ed. *A Kipling Notebook.* (Mansfield: New York, 1899.) Also issued under the title *Kiplingiana,* this volume provides a miscellany of biographical and literary notes on the author's prose and verse.

Munson, Arley. *Kipling's India.* (Doubleday: New York, 1915.) One of the finest books of its kind: superbly illustrated from photographs, with captions quoted from Kipling's poetry and prose; the "tour" begins at Bombay and ends at Mandalay.

Young, W. A. *A Dictionary of the Characters and Scenes in the Stories and Poems of Rudyard Kipling.* (Routledge: London, 1921.) The introduction provides brief reviews of the books published up to 1911; the dictionary proper contains about 4,000 entries.

III. ARTICLES FROM BOOKS

Archer, William. "Rudyard Kipling," in *Poets of the Younger Generation.* (Lane: New York, 1902.) Has enthusiastic praise for the *Barrack-Room Ballads;* acclaims Kipling as one of the great English patriotic poets.

Chevrillon, André. "Rudyard Kipling," in *Three Studies in English Literature.* Trans. by Florence Simmonds. (Heinemann: London, 1922.) A vivid and picturesque presentation of the poet and novelist as the best modern example of the tradition of Defoe and Carlyle—the militant Puritan.

Dobrée, Bonamy. "Rudyard Kipling," in *The Lamp and the Lute.* (Oxford University Press: 1929.) Finds Kipling at his best in his realistic acceptance of the world as it is, in his admiration of the Empire; insists that judgment on his final place in literature must wait until the passing of that popularity which some of his least worthy qualities have inspired.

Kernahan, Coulson. "Rudyard Kipling," in *Six Famous Living Poets.* (Butterworth: London, 1922.) By abundant quotation shows the vigorous patriotic note in the poet's work; analyzes many outstanding poems and groups supporting a single prominent theme.

Maurois, André. "Rudyard Kipling," in *Prophets and Poets.* Trans. by Hamish Miles. (Harper: New York, 1935.) Sees the poet as the exponent of a modern heroic society, in which British imperialism is the outstanding element.

More, P. E. "Kipling and FitzGerald," in *Shelburne Essays,* Second Series. (Putnam: New York, 1905.) A review of *The Seven Seas:* founds Kipling's popularity on his strong imperialistic strain, which at its best is nobly prophetic and inspiring.

Phelps, W. L. "Rudyard Kipling," in *The Advance of English Poetry in the Twentieth Century.* (Dodd: New York, 1918.) Identifies Kipling as "the spokesman for the Anglo-Saxon breed"; points out his great following, lay and clerical.

Scott, Dixon. "The Meekness of Mr. Rudyard Kipling," in *Men of Letters.* (Hodder: London, 1923.) Deprecates the author's admission that the quality of his work has declined; calls attention to his integrity of language and his skill in character-portrayal.

Shanks, Edward. "Mr. Rudyard Kipling," in *Second Essays on Literature.* (Collins: London, 1927.) Finds Kipling's best work in his short stories, with only occasional success in his poetry, most of which is effective rhetoric.

Squire, J. C. "Mr. Kipling's Later Verse," in *Books in General,* Third Series. (Hodder: London, 1921.) A rather caustic review of *The Years Between:* Kipling's lapses in his political and martial poetry are pointed out in all their bad rhetoric.

IV. ARTICLES FROM PERIODICALS

Dowden, Edward. "The Poetry of Kipling," *Critic,* XXXVIII, 219–24 (Mar., 1901). Admires Kipling's cosmopolitan spirit, which expresses itself romantically through the facts of real experience; analyzes the poet's idea of God.

Ferguson, J. D. "The Poetry of Rudyard Kipling," *Forum,* L, 396–411 (Sept., 1913). Complains of the lack of sound criticism of Kipling's poetry; discusses the ideas of many of the better-known poems.

Gilmer, H. W. "The Classical Element in the Poems of Rudyard Kipling," *Classical Weekly,* XIV, 178–81 (Apr. 25, 1921). Finds the most obvious evidences in the poet's mythological allusions, many of which are pointed out in various places in his poetry; concludes that Kipling's classical knowledge was derived from secondary sources.

Lord, L. E. "Two Imperial Poets: Horace and Kipling," *Classical Journal,* XVI, 261–70 (Feb., 1921). Finds a major identity in the fact that both poets are great "imperial laureates"; points out some similarities in metric and peculiarities in diction.

Maurice, A. B. "Kipling's Verse People," *Bookman,* IX, 57–61 (Mar., 1899). Locates the "most tangible" people in the *Barrack-Room Ballads,* where the poet's range is widest and he is at home in the East.

Overton, Grant. "Kipling's Career," *Bookman,* LXI, 65–73 (Mar., 1925). Can find no great novelty in Kipling's work, which impresses by its youthful exuberance; insists that the real man eludes the student of the poetry.

Schuyler, Montgomery. "Rudyard Kipling as a Poet," *Forum,* XXII, 406–13 (Dec., 1896). Admitting the variety of the poet's metrical patterns, criticizes the importunity of his rhymes and cadences; traces a thread of melancholy in the poems, which contrasts with their prevailing confidence and briskness.

NOTES

"Kipling is interested in the external life of men, their appearance, their actions, their speech. He cares little for their thoughts and nothing for their theories. . . . [He] finds inspiration not in the ruling classes or the thinking classes but in the people who are in the thick of life, the workers, fighters, explorers, or tramps. He dislikes conventional people, conventional actions, and conventional language—and above all, hypocrisy. The world of people who do not conform, the Victorians ignored or sentimentalized, or else excused by placing them back in those wicked old unenlightened times when people did such things, for time whitewashes the blackness of evil. But Kipling wrote of the British soldier, sailor, and tramp as he knew them, without apology for their swearing or their sinning. . . .

"To Kipling the poetry of life is action. He loves people who do difficult things, who show courage in struggling with obstacles. He admires the engineer, the border-thief, Tommy Atkins, and the explorer for their stout-hearted fighting qualities, and for their sincerity and manliness. And he admires these qualities anywhere in the world, under brown skins or white, in enemies and lawbreakers as well as in friends." (C. E. Andrews and M. O. Percival, in *Poetry of the Nineties*, pp. 11–12.)

See the first introductory note to Robert Bridges, above.

Page 947. THE SONG OF THE BANJO

1. *Broadwood.* A piano.
7. *tails.* Straggles.
35. *rowel 'em.* Spur them.
39. *Ulysses.* See Tennyson's *Ulysses*, text p. 37, and the note to that poem.
41. *blooded.* Having the blood or temperament that makes him a wanderer.
44. *backstay.* A rope or wire supporting the mast of a ship.
48. *"Johnny . . . trek!"* Suggested by the Cape-Dutch song of Johnny with the limping leg.
54. *many-shedded levels.* Places covered with sheds to keep snow and rocks from falling on roads or railroad tracks.
56. *Song of Roland.* See Arnold's *The Study of Poetry*, text p. 584, and the note to that reference on p. 1231.
87. *the Stealer.* Hermes, who among his varied functions was the god of thieves, invented the lyre by stretching strings across a tortoise shell.
96. *Delos . . . Limerick.* Delos, in the Ægean Sea, was the birthplace of Apollo, the god of music; Limerick, in Ireland, is associated with the nonsense verse-form known as the limerick. The banjo boasts of its accomplishments in music of every kind and place.

Page 948. THE LAST CHANTEY

"And . . . sea." Part of the description of the end of the world as related in Revelation 21:1. A chantey is a song with a boisterous chorus sung by sailors as they heave the capstan or windlass or hoist heavy weights.
10. *barracout'.* The barracuda, a carnivorous West Indian fish.
11–14. *Judas . . . floe.* A reference to the legend that Judas Iscariot was permitted to leave Hell each Christmas day and "stanch with ice his burning breast" for one hour. See Arnold's *Saint Brandan*, text p. 562.
27. *Kennelled . . . picaroon.* Confined like dogs in a slave ship.
32. *frapped a ship.* Strengthened a ship by passing cables around it. St. Paul's story is told in Acts 27:37–44, and 28:1–2.
woundily. Excessively.
35. *Malta.* Paul's ship was wrecked near the island of Malta, in the Mediterranean.
46. *Gothavn 'speckshioner.* The 'speckshioner, or inspector, who is the chief harpooner on a whaling vessel, directs the flenching, or slicing of blubber from the whale. He was probably from Godhaven or Godthaav, fishing ports in north Greenland and south Greenland respectively, although it is possible that Kipling intended a pun in "Gothavn," in which case the word is to be taken as equivalent to "damned" or even a more profane expression.
47. *Dundee.* A town in Scotland near the North Sea.
49. *bowhead.* The right whale of the Arctic.
breaching. Breaking or leaping from the water.
52. *neither lead nor lee.* Neither open channel (in an icefield) nor sheltered anchorage.
62. *spindrift.* Blown spray.
fulmar. An Arctic sea bird.

Page 949. THE LONG TRAIL

9. *Tents of Shem.* Shem, Noah's eldest son, was the traditional ancestor of the Semitic peoples. "God shall enlarge Japheth (Noah's youngest son, traditional ancestor of the European races), and he shall dwell in the tents of Shem." (Genesis 9:27.) Kipling has in mind houses with their comforts and conveniences.
13. *rime-ringed.* Frost-ringed.
14. *Horn's hate.* The waters about Cape Horn, southern point of South America, are rough and treacherous.
16. *Golden Gate.* The strait forming the entrance to San Francisco bay.
23. *beam-sea roll.* The roll of the sea in a line with the beam, or at right angles with the keel.

24. *Bilboa.* A port in Spain on the Bay of Biscay.

tramp. A vessel not making regular trips between the same ports, but picking up cargo wherever it can.

29–30. *eagle . . . maid.* See Proverbs 30:18–19—"There be three things which are too wonderful for me, yea, four which I know not: the way of an eagle in the air; the way of a serpent upon a rock; the way of a ship in the midst of the sea; and the way of a man with a maid."

32. *Trade.* Trade wind.

37. *Peter.* The hoisting of the blue Peter, a flag, is a signal of immediate starting.

40. *fall-rope.* Any rope used for hoisting, as in a derrick.

42. *Hawsers.* Large ropes or lines for towing or securing vessels.

warp. To move a vessel by hauling on a line.

48. *lead.* A mass of lead used in sounding for depth.

49–52. *Lower Hope . . . Gunfleet Sands . . . Gull Light.* Points on the way from the London Docks, down the Thames, into the English Channel.

51. *Mouse.* A lightship, showing the way.

64. *Southern Cross.* A constellation in the southern hemisphere.

69. *Foreland.* A cape at the northern point of the Devon coast.

Start. A cape at the southern extremity of the Devon coast.

Page 951. SUSSEX

Sussex was the home shire of Kipling from 1900 to the time of his death in 1936. Drinkwater includes this poem among a number of poems from recent writers as illustrations from literature of a "particular loyalty that is characteristic" of the poets of our own age, if not peculiar to them—the frequency with which they map out for us their chosen landscapes. Never before, he says, has the use of place-names "been given so freely the creative value that it often beautifully has in the literature of today." (*Patriotism in Literature*, p. 143.)

12. *Levuka's Trade.* The trade wind in Levuka, one of the Fiji Islands.

19. *Downs.* The treeless chalk uplands along the south and southeast coast of England.

24. *Weald.* Open country. As a Sussex provincialism the name "Weald" is given to the large woodland tract extending from the Downs, with which it runs parallel, to the Surrey hills.

31. *barrow.* An ancient burial mound.

43. *dewpond.* An artificial pond on the downs, filled and kept up by the condensation of dews, mist, etc.

55. *Wilfrid.* St. Wilfrid (634–709), Archbishop of York. He converted the Saxons in Sussex to Christianity.

59. *nine-and-thirty sisters.* There are forty shires or counties in England.

61. *Tweed.* A river in Scotland flowing into the North Sea.

63. *Rake.* A town in the western part of Sussex.

Rye. A town in the eastern part of Sussex.

64. *Black Down.* In Surrey.

Beachy Head. The southern point of Sussex. In naming the four places of ll. 63–64 Kipling is roughly bounding his loved Sussex.

67. *Long . . . Wilmington.* A figure in Sussex, 230 feet high, cut out of the chalk and supposed to be of Celtic or Saxon origin. One theory makes it a representation of the ancient hero, Beowulf.

69. *Rother.* A Sussex river.

73. *shaws.* Thickets.

74. *ghylls.* Wooded ravines.

77. *Piddinghoe's.* A church in Sussex. The dolphin weather vane is in reality a representation of an Ouse salmon.

79. *Ouse.* A Sussex river.

Page 952. WHEN EARTH'S LAST PICTURE IS PAINTED

The title *L'Envoi* is often given to this poem since it appeared under that title as the concluding poem in the volume *The Seven Seas.* There has been some comment on the poem as an "example of skillful use of allusion merely as a technical display."

RECESSIONAL

In the Anglican church service as the clergy and choir are retiring in procession, the choir sings a hymn known as the recessional. In 1897 England celebrated with the Diamond Jubilee the sixtieth anniversary of Victoria's accession to the throne. Kipling, feeling that there was too strong a disposition among Englishmen to boast of the great power and extent of the Empire, wrote the *Recessional* as a warning against the evils of unlicensed imperialism.

4. *palm and pine.* A reference to the far separated boundaries of the Empire.

9–10. *sacrifice . . heart.* Cf. Psalms 51:17—"The sacrifices of God are a broken spirit; a broken and a contrite heart, O God, thou wilt not despise."

16. *Nineveh.* The once famous capital of ancient Assyria. It is now so completely blotted out that it can be studied only by excavation.

Tyre. Once a famous maritime city in Phoenicia; now an unimportant port known as Sur.

21–22. *Gentiles . . Law.* See Romans 2:14—"For when the Gentiles, which have not the law, do by nature the things contained in the

law, these, having not the law, are a law unto themselves."
26. *reeking . . . shard.* Gun and shell.

TOMLINSON

1. *Berkeley Square.* One of the most aristocratic of London squares.
22. *Muscovy.* Russia. It has been conjectured that "Prince" in this line refers to Tolstoy.
30. *Carl in Norroway.* The Norwegian playwright, Ibsen, has been mentioned as the possible "Carl in Norroway." The works and ideas of Tolstoy and Ibsen would of course be much read and discussed by the type of person who lived in Berkeley Square.
35. *doom.* Judgment.
47. *Wot.* Know.
49. *o'er-sib.* Too closely related.
85. *Empusa.* A terrifying being associated with Hecate. She tortured souls in Hell.
88. *caddis-case.* The larvæ of the caddis fly live in and drag around cases or tubes of silk covered with shells, gravel, bits of wood, etc.
91. *stook.* Pile, stack.
99. *stews.* A low resort, dive.
111. *spirk.* Sprout, shoot. Possibly indicating "vegetable kingdom."

Page 956. "FUZZY-WUZZY"

Somewhat timidly A. C. Ward suggests that Kipling's parade of "malformed and crippled words," the speech of his soldiers and sailors, with its "dropped consonants and distorted vowels, its sprinkling of foreign words . . . , and its technical jargon" may be an offense against literary good manners. Kipling, Ward writes, "was a cultured Anglo-Indian, and although he travelled widely and studied the British soldier at close quarters, 'cockney' was virtually a foreign tongue to him. In his use of this dialect, therefore, he was performing a literary trick, not employing a natural medium of expression. . . . A born Cockney knows that a 'foreigner' is speaking, and suspects that the fellow is trying, condescendingly, to talk down to his level." (*Twentieth Century Literature*, pp. 106–7.)
The Soudan is a region along the southern border of the Sahara Desert and the upper Nile. The natives, called "Fuzzy-Wuzzies" by the British soldiers because of their woolly hair, rebelled against English and Egyptian rule in 1881 and remained unconquered till 1898.
Soudan . . . Force. An English army, led by General Graham, was sent to Khartum in 1884 to relieve General Gordon, who was besieged by the Soudanese.
3. *Paythan.* An Afghan.
Zulu. A Bantu tribesman of Natal.
Burmese. Natives of Burma.
7. *Suakim.* The headquarters, on the Red Sea, of the army fighting the Soudanese.
13. *Kyber 'ills.* Mountains on the Afghanistan border.
14. *Boers . . . mile.* The Dutch in South Africa. They were famous for accuracy in long-range rifle shooting.
15. *Irriwaddy.* A river in Burma.
16. *Zulu impi.* Zulu regiment. In 1879 the Zulus defeated an English force of 4000 men.
23. *Martinis.* Rifles, named for their Swiss inventor.
24. *broke the square.* Pierced the hollow square, at the battle of Tamai, 1884. The hollow square was a regular formation of the British army in open warfare.

Page 958. MANDALAY

England acquired Burma by conquest in 1885–1886, since which time she has kept an army of occupation there. Mandalay is a city in Burma on the Irrawaddy river. Rangoon (l. 7) is a city near the mouth of the Irrawaddy, about 370 miles below Mandalay.
1. *Moulmein Pagoda.* A Buddhist temple at Moulmein, a city in lower Burma.
6. *old Flotilla.* The boats of the Irrawaddy Flotilla Company, plying between Rangoon and Mandalay.
12. *Supi-yaw-lat.* Supaiyah Lat, wife of Thebaw, king of Burma from 1876 to 1885.
16. *Budd.* Buddha.
22. *hathis.* Elephants trained to pile up teak logs.
37. *Chelsea.* A pleasant residential suburb of London.
Strand. One of the busiest and most important streets in London.

Page 959. JOBSON'S AMEN

24. *Libya.* In Northern Africa, west of Egypt.
28. *calliper.* A measuring instrument.

Page 960. EDDI'S SERVICE

Eddi, who was skilled in the Roman method of chanting, was selected by Wilfrid to act as choirmaster in his churches. He wrote the life of Wilfrid, a work of the highest interest and value, probably used by the Venerable Bede. The incident related in the poem had its origin in the long series of disheartening experiences undergone by Wilfrid and his associates before they converted the Saxons.
1. *St. Wilfrid.* See note to l. 55 of *Sussex*, above. The South Saxons were the last of the Germanic groups to be brought to Christianity.
25. *three . . . together.* "For where two or three are gathered together in my name there am I in the midst of them." (Matthew 18:20.)
31–32. *Rider . . . Jerusalem.* Christ rode into Jerusalem on an ass. See Matthew 21 and Zechariah 19:9.

Page 961. SHIV AND THE GRASSHOPPER

1. *Shiv.* Siva, one of the supreme deities of Hinduism.
6. *Mahadeo.* Mahadeva, one of the thousand and more titles given to Shiv.
14. *Parbati.* Parvati, consort of Shiv (Siva).

THE FAIRIES' SIEGE

19. *Triple Crown.* The Pope's crown.

THE CAPTIVE

1. *Allah.* The Supreme Being of the Mohammedans.
2. *anklets . . . legbars.* Fetters were fastened on the legs.
8. *red.* Memorable, happy.
12–13. *words . . . weaving.* He spoke with wondrous eloquence and fascination. In Mohammedan tradition the Djinns are supernatural beings.

Page 962. ROAD-SONG OF THE *BANDAR-LOG*

Bandar = monkey; *log* = people. In Kipling's jungle stories, the monkey race, portrayed as chatterers or poseurs.
26. *scumfish.* The meaning is uncertain.

IF—

Patrick Braybrooke condemns this poem, which, he says, "is open to grave objections on the ground of not being a logical conclusion to a number of suppositions: 'If' cannot with any truth be classed as real poetry; it is more than anything else 'moral' verse, written almost in journalistic vein." He believes that the "vast popularity" of the poem is due to its appearing "as a piece of idealism. . . . The public loves idealism," he writes, "especially when it knows that it is so impossible of attainment that the falling short cannot weigh too heavily on the conscience." (In *Kipling and His Soldiers*, p. 149.)
32. *you'll be a Man.* Braybrooke, quoted above, insists that the individual who measures up to Kipling's requirements would be neither what the usual criticism makes him—a god, nor what the poet calls him—a Man, but a prig.

Page 963. THE BEE-BOY'S SONG

The Bee-Boy is a character in *Puck of Pook's Hill.*
Cf. Whittier's poem, *Telling the Bees.* Both poems are founded on the superstition of informing the bees of all births, deaths, and marriages in the family.
18. *Fanners.* When the temperature of a bee hive gets too low, the bees fan vigorously with their wings to produce heat. Fanning also serves as the earliest exercise of the young bees and aids in hastening the evaporation of water from the newly gathered honey.

THE ONLY SON

13. *tyre.* A kind of sweet wine.
14. *byre.* A cow house.
19. *Lena Falls.* The river Lena is in Siberia.

Page 964. THE GLORY OF THE GARDEN

"To Rudyard Kipling gardening is a solemn rite, and Sussex is all his garden. 'One does not like gardening,' we can hear him exclaim. 'One worships gardens. Gardening is a religion.' The note recurs again and again in his work." (R. Thurston Hopkins, in *The Kipling Country*, p. 230.)
26. *netting.* Covering, as with straw.

RAHERE

7. *St. Michael's.* St. Michael's Mount, a rocky islet in Mount's Bay off the Cornwall coast.
22. *Smithfield.* From an early period to the reign of Henry IV, Smithfield in London was the usual place of execution. Under the Tudors many persons were burned here for their religious convictions. William Wallace, Wat Tyler, Anne Askew, and others of famous or notorious name perished at Smithfield.

Page 965. GIPSY VANS

11. *Gorgio.* A corruption of gajo, a nongipsy.
12. *Romany.* A gipsy.
35. *ryes.* Gentlemen.

GEORGE MEREDITH

BIBLIOGRAPHY

I. WORKS

Poetical Works, ed. by G. M. Trevelyan. (Scribner: New York, 1928.) A comprehensive edition, containing a good editorial preface and brief notes.

Last Poems. (Scribner: New York, 1909.) The only separate edition of Meredith's final volume of verse.

Selected Poems. (Scribner: New York, 1897.) The best book of selections—one of the few obtainable.

Modern Love, ed. by Richard Le Gallienne. (Kennerley: New York, 1909.) A recommended edition of the sonnet-sequence, prefaced by a critical essay by the editor.

Letters, ed. by W. M. Meredith. 2 vols. (Scribner: New York, 1912.) A selection by Meredith's son; provided with many biographical notes: necessarily the basis of all later biographies.

"Unpublished Letters of Meredith," ed. by R. E. G. George, *Nineteenth Century*, CIII, 149–62 (Feb., 1928). Prints seven letters written late in life to a young lady whose name is not given.

II. BIOGRAPHY AND CRITICISM

Able, A. H., 3d. *George Meredith and Thomas Love Peacock.* (University of Pennsylvania Press: 1933.) A textual proof of the generally admitted influences; prominently concerned with Meredith's prose, although scattered poetic borrowings are also pointed out.

Butcher, Alice M. *Memories of George Meredith.* (Constable: London, 1919.) Written with no intention of being even a partial biography, these recollections of a forty-year acquaintance with Meredith "contain a contemporaneous record of his sayings."

Chislett, W., Jr., *George Meredith: A Study and an Appraisal.* (Badger: Boston, 1925.) Fragmentary and inconclusive; the section "The Content of Meredith's Poetry" provides sketchy analyses of some of the separate poems.

Crees, J. H. E. *George Meredith: A Study of his Works and Personality.* (Blackwell: Oxford, 1918.) A well-tempered, enthusiastic report of an avowed Meredithian: most valuable are the chapters "Meredith's Poetry and Philosophy," and "Meredith the Artist."

Curle, R. H. P. *Aspects of George Meredith.* (Dutton: New York, 1908.) A somewhat superficial study of a number of phases of Meredith's work in prose and poetry; chapter IV, "Lyrical View of Nature," is illustrated with many quotations from his verse.

Ellis, S. M. *George Meredith: His Life and Friends in Relation to His Work.* (Richards: London, 1920.) Contains the substance of many years of research in *personalia;* especially valuable for backgrounds of the novels, identifying many of the characters drawn from real life.

Gretton, Mrs. Mary S. *The Writings and Life of George Meredith.* (Oxford University Press: 1926.) Tracing a biographical thread, this study is concerned chiefly with Meredith's artistic development; chapter IV provides a good analysis of *Modern Love.*

Hammerton, J. A. *George Meredith, His Life and Art in Anecdote and Criticism.* (Grant: Edinburgh, 1911.) A satisfactory fulfillment of the two aims of this study: to bring the artist out from the mass of contemporary criticism and to provide an account of the man's career and friendships; chapter XI discusses the poetry.

Le Gallienne, Richard. *George Meredith, Some Characteristics.* (Lane: London, 1900.) Provides little biographical data, but abounds in convincing critical summaries, chiefly eulogistic in tone. Includes a bibliography by John Lane.

Photiadès, Constantin. *George Meredith.* Trans. by Arthur Price. (Scribner: New York, 1913.) An informal chapter describing a visit with Meredith is followed by a brief biographical sketch; the last two chapters contain some penetrating comments on his poetry.

Priestley, J. B. *George Meredith.* English Men of Letters series. (Macmillan: New York, 1926.) Chiefly valuable for its discussion of Meredith's prose; sets out to show that his works were the outgrowth of his self-condemnation.

Sencourt, R. E. *The Life of George Meredith.* (Scribner: New York, 1929.) An ably written Life, done with "an almost uninterrupted reference to sources," with no attempt at final judgments; much space is given to the analysis of the poetry.

Trevelyan, G. M. *The Poetry and Philosophy of George Meredith.* (Scribner: New York, 1920.) An excellent handbook to the poems: useful as an approach in beginning acquaintance with Meredith.

III. ARTICLES FROM BOOKS

Burdett, Osbert. "George Meredith," in *Critical Essays.* (Faber: London, 1925.) Founds the poet's claim to originality on his "identification of Nature with Intelligence"—humanity and natural forces being twin inspirers of his lyricism.

Dowden, Edward. "Mr. Meredith in His Poems," in *New Studies in Literature.* (Paul: London, 1902.) Comments on the poet's didacticism and his love of earth, counting *Modern Love* his most significant work.

Elton, Oliver. "Mr. George Meredith," in *Modern Studies.* (Arnold: London, 1907.) Remarks Meredith's perseverance in the face of neglect; analyzes the characters of the novels; discusses his worship of the pagan divinity of earth; contrasts his prose and verse.

Hearn, Lafcadio. "The Poetry of George Meredith," in *Pre-Raphaelite and Other Poets.* (Dodd: New York, 1922.) Comments upon "King Harald's Trance," "Archduchess Anne," "The Nuptials of Attila," and other poems; concludes that Meredith is "the poet of men of culture."

Henley, W. E. "Meredith," in *Views and Reviews.* (Macmillan: London, 1921.) After a cursory review concludes with an irritated thrust at the poet's impenetrability but singles out "The Nuptials of Attila" for praise.

Hind, C. L. "George Meredith," in *Authors and I.* (Lane: London, 1921.) Describes a visit with Meredith at Box Hill; values his poetry for its spirit of youth and courage.

Quiller-Couch, A. T. "The Poetry of George Meredith," in *Studies in Literature,* First Series. (Putnam: New York, 1918.) Reviews some of the easier narrative poems, points out a road of understanding into the poet's more difficult pieces; names *Love in the Valley* one of the greatest love-songs in the language.

Stevenson, Lionel. "George Meredith," in *Darwin among the Poets.* (University of Chicago Press: 1932.) Shows how the poet's uncompromising acceptance of Darwinism led him to a scientific materialism, which included the idea of immortality "through service to the race."

Strong, A. T. "An Essay on Nature in Wordsworth and Meredith," in *Three Studies in Shelley.* (Oxford University Press: 1921.) Shows an agreement in the poets' belief in the benevolence of Nature, with Meredith's belief in the theory of evolution contrasting with Wordsworth's idea of personal immortality.

Symons, Arthur. "George Meredith as a Poet," in *Figures of Several Centuries.* (Dutton: New York, 1916.) Names *Modern Love* the poet's masterpiece; laments his stubborn, ill-forged verse as a whole.

Welby, T. E. "George Meredith," in *Back Numbers*. (Smith: New York, 1930.) Naming Meredith as one of the great malcontents in English poetry, briefly points out his "admirable cruelty" in various untraditional lyrics.

Young, W. T. "George Meredith, Samuel Butler, George Gissing," in *The Cambridge History of English Literature*, XIII. (Putnam: New York, 1917.) Discusses Meredith's novelty in verse-technique; sees his perfection in the "Lucifer" sonnet.

IV. ARTICLES FROM PERIODICALS

Armstrong, Martin. "The Poetry of George Meredith," *North American Review*, CCXIII, 354–61 (Mar., 1921). Names Meredith a poet of "the explicitly philosophic type," whose ideas are drawn from a study of Nature and pointed with the comic spirit.

Bailey, E. J. "A Note on Mr. Meredith's *Modern Love*," *Forum*, XL, 245–54 (Sept., 1908). Attempts to clarify the meaning of the sequence by outlining a plot through it; compares the sequence with Shakespeare's Sonnets, rather than other Victorian sequences.

Bailey, John. "Poetry of Meredith," *Fortnightly Review*, XCII, 32–46 (July, 1909). Admitting obscurity and unpleasantness, insists on our recognition of Meredith's optimism and vigor; points out kinships and contrasts with Shelley; analyzes the *Odes* to France.

Clodd, Edward "George Meredith, Some Recollections," *Fortnightly Review*, XCII, 19–31 (July, 1909). Refers to many conversations of Meredith and Peacock; notes how frequently Meredith's friends appear in his novels.

Collins, J. P. "Conversations with Meredith," *North American Review*, CXCVI, 830–43 (Dec., 1912). A recollection of two visits, quoting conversations at length.

Edgar, Pelham. "Poetry of George Meredith," *Living Age*, CCLV, 744–51 (Dec. 21, 1907). Interprets Meredith as a philosopher-poet, with a new stoic insight into Nature.

Granville-Barker, H. "Three Victorians and the Theatre," *Fortnightly Review*, CXXXI, 655–72 (May, 1929). Meredith is the leading figure in this sketch, which discusses his *Idea of Comedy* and *The Sentimentalists*, where there is seen a genuine dramatic promise, thwarted by the author's lack of sympathy with the middle classes.

Hardy, Thomas. "George Meredith: A Reminiscence," *Nineteenth Century*, CIII, 145–8 (Feb., 1928). A centenary tribute, recalling Hardy's first meeting with Meredith and later passages between them.

Koszul, A. H. "An Unpublished Sonnet by George Meredith," *Nineteenth Century*, CIX, 1–3 (Jan., 1931). The sonnet is addressed to P. A. Labouchère, a native of Nantes, whose relationship with Meredith is obscure; the theme of the sonnet is Meredith's admiration for French satirists.

Le Gallienne, Richard. "George Meredith's Poetry," *Forum*, XLIII, 441–7 (Apr., 1910). Admitting that Meredith's audience will be a small one, points to his wide range of subjects and his joy in natural objects.

Slaughter, Gertrude. "A Poet's Wisdom," *North American Review*, CCVII, 82–90 (Jan., 1918). An airy colloquy between an American and an Englishman who find in Meredith a timely interpreter of some of the issues involved in the troublous present.

Young, Joan. "Meredith," *London Mercury*, XVII, 563–74 (Mar., 1928). A centenary appreciation, giving a thumbnail biography; praises the poet's *Odes* to France, calling attention to his desire to be remembered as a poet.

NOTES

Page 967. JUGGLING JERRY

". . . But one result of my hard education since the publication of my boy's book in '51 (those poems were written before I was twenty) has been that I rarely write save from the suggestion of something actually observed. I mean, that I rarely write verse. Thus my Jugglers, Beggars, etc., I have met on the road, and have idealized but slightly. I desire to strike the poetic spark out of absolute human clay. And in doing so I have the fancy that I do solid work—better than a carol in mid air . . ." (George Meredith, *Letters*, I, 45.)

25. *cricket*. play cricket.

27. *whip off the bail from the wicket*. A term from the English game of cricket, roughly equivalent in baseball terminology to: "Couldn't I make a snappy put-out?" In cricket the batter sometimes scores over a hundred runs before being put out, and hence ability to put him out promptly has its value.

49. *from my topsy-turvy*. Jerry, as a travelling entertainer, would be a tumbler as well as a juggler.

67. *bolus*. A large pill.

81. *chirper*. A "pick-me-up."

Page 968. MODERN LOVE

Modern Love is a sequence of fifty poems, each of sixteen lines, dealing with the tortured thoughts and feelings of a modern couple. Husband and wife have been drifting apart and with a pang he sees her attracted by another man. In turn he pays a surface attention to another woman. None of this is openly admitted, and husband and wife preserve toward one another and the world at large an attitude of highly civilized good manners and forbearance. Underneath this surface of good manners there is the ebb and flow of the old emotions—attraction and repulsion, jealousy, anger, and affection—but the old emotions filtered through two fine and highly sophisticated temperaments.

For the origin of the poem, see the first paragraph of the biographical sketch of Meredith, text p. 966.

1. "He" and "she" are the husband and wife; they are lying side by side at midnight.

14. *sculptured effigies.* On top of many tombs in European churches there is a carved recumbent figure of the occupant.

XIV. This poem is contorted in expression. The "nobler agony" of l. 2 is his present suffering, but he would not bargain for any cure which substituted contempt for his wife for his present suffering. The point of the remark is explained in l. 14—his wife is jealous of the other woman and he says that if she should try to win him back while continuing to play with the other man, he would scorn her. "Madam" is the wife, as is "the woman" of l. 10.

XX. In the previous poem he has been torn by conflicting emotions and asks himself "Could I hurt her? heaven and hell! But I could hurt her cruelly!"

XXII. In the previous poem the wife has fainted under stress of emotion when a friend, deeply in love, tells of his new happiness and asks their blessing as happily wedded lovers.

XXVI. The wife makes advances toward an explanation and he stops her with conventional talk. In a previous section (XXIV) he himself had been tempted to make the advance, but pride had checked him.

XLVI. He interrupts an interview between her and the other man. In l. 14 he assures her of his confidence that she has not been unfaithful in deed.

Page 974. LUCIFER IN STARLIGHT

9. *scars.* Received in the war with heaven. The conception of the scarred Lucifer derives from Milton:

"Darkened so, yet shone
Above them all the Archangel: but his face
Deep scars of thunder had entrenched, and care
Sat on his faded cheek. . . ."
(*Paradise Lost*, I, 599–602.)

Page 976. NATURE AND LIFE

". . . His feeling for nature is not—at least in its root, however it may be with the flower—the Wordsworthian sense

'Of something far more deeply interfused,
Whose dwelling is the light of setting suns.'

He prefers the word earth to the more abstract word nature, and hugs reality. . . .

"But a true lover of Earth must be a hardy lover, caring for more than her soothing touch and soft caress, able to read her heart even though she should frown or seem cold and indifferent. Mr. Meredith is bent above all to understand her meanings that are severe, yet kind in their severity; those ways of hers which train us for the battle-field rather than the bower. . . .

"But does Earth indeed care at all for her offspring, Man? Are not the laws of nature regardless of humanity, and ruthless in their blind persistence? Mr. Meredith has no desire to cheat himself with words; above all else he seeks reality. Is there, then, in truth this opposition between man and nature? Is there this breach of continuity in the universe, or rather is not man the crowning part of nature—nature evolving itself, or being evolved, into mind and soul? And are not the laws of human nature her laws? Man's loving-kindness, his mercifulness, his passion for righteousness, are they not the flower and fruit of her long obscure endeavour? Is not in truth their root in her? And what if the seeming cruelty of Earth to her child, Man, be no more than a wholesome severity, needed in order that he may advance through brain to soul, and from bestial up to spiritual? . . ." (Edward Dowden, *New Studies in Literature*, pp. 38–45.)

"Does not all science (the mammoth balloon, to wit) tell us that when we forsake earth, we reach up to a frosty, inimical Inane? For my part I love and cling to earth, as the one piece of God's handiwork which we possess. I admit that we can refashion; but of earth must be the material.—Yours faithful, George Meredith." (George Meredith, *Letters*, I, 157.)

6–7. *In the old Beginnings . . . mind.* To the elemental ("Beginnings") qualities of Nature man brings "mind" which makes possible the interpretation of nature. Therefore man gives seed for seed towards the growth of the future.

12–14. *within the shell thou art*, etc. Man is like a shell with his own music inside him. Nothing near (in nature) can respond ("to such a tremor start") so sharply to outside stimulation.

15. *Of the waves.* The ocean and struggle of life.

17. *Back to them.* We belong in the "manful" struggle of the waves, but should take back to them "the woodland's heart."

MEDITATION UNDER STARS

See introductory material to *Nature and Life*, above.

4. *as from a shield.* The light shines back from a shield but we cannot see through it or get an answer.

37. *love is asked of love's wherefore.* The succeeding lines state that love is the gift of Earth but that it also comes from the universe of which our earth is a part. If it belonged to Earth alone, Earth would be the throne of the Deity.

48–52. *It is our ravenous that quails . . . binder of his sheaves.* "When flesh quails before the starry sky, the spirit is filled with joy at the sight, doubting not that 'in them' (the stars) is Deity or Reason, the harvester." (Trevelyan's note.)

WILLIAM MORRIS

BIBLIOGRAPHY

I. WORKS

Collected Works, ed. by May Morris. 24 vols. Kelmscott Edition. (Longmans: London, 1910–15.) The most desirable, complete edition, with introductions by the editor (the poet's daughter), which provide valuable biographical and critical information. The poems and translations are contained in the first thirteen volumes.

Poems, ed. by P. R. Colwell. (Crowell: New York, 1904.) An edition especially suitable for use in schools; provided with valuable notes and a four-page bibliography.

Poems, selected and ed. by H. Newbolt. (Nelson: London, 1923.) A good inexpensive one-volume text.

The Early Romances of William Morris in Prose and Verse. (Dent: London, 1913.) A recommended edition, with a brief critical preface by Alfred Noyes.

Stories in Prose, Stories in Verse, Shorter Poems, Lectures, and Essays, ed. by G. D. H. Cole. (Nonesuch Press: London, 1934.) An admirable recent collection containing *News from Nowhere* and *A Dream of John Ball*, together with representative selections from the shorter and longer poems.

The Life and Death of Jason, ed. by E. Maxwell. (Milford: London, 1914.) The most desirable edition for student use; fully equipped with introduction and notes.

Selections from the Prose Works, ed. by A. H. R. Ball. (Cambridge University Press: 1931.) The best book of prose selections; the admirable introduction provides sound criticism and discusses the author's relations with Ruskin and Carlyle.

II. BIOGRAPHY AND CRITICISM

Bloomfield, Paul. *William Morris.* (Barker: London, 1934.) A most readable study, dwelling on the craftsmanship of the artist in many fields and his enduring interest in socialism.

Cary, Elisabeth L. *William Morris, Poet, Craftsman, Socialist.* (Putnam: New York, 1902.) Founded on Mackail's Life, lacking biographical detail, and "showing only the man and his work as they appeared to the outer public"; contains a worth-while chapter on the poetry.

Clutton-Brock, Arthur. *William Morris, His Work and Influence.* (Holt: New York, 1914.) Relying extensively upon Mackail's Life and Miss Morris's introductions, this brief study attempts to interpret the work of Morris to later time.

Compton-Rickett, Arthur. *William Morris, a Study in Personality.* (Dutton: New York, 1913.) An effort "to reconstruct the man just as he spoke and worked," with no attempt at final judgments; introduction by R. B. C. Graham. Part II deals with the poetry.

Crow, G. H. *William Morris, Designer.* (Studio Publications: London, 1935.) A well-presented story of Morris's career, based on Mackail's Life; offers many striking illustrations in color.

Drinkwater, John. *William Morris, a Critical Study.* (Kennerley: New York, 1912.) A scholarly, sympathetic review of the man and his numerous artistic pursuits; chapters II, IV, and V deal with the poetry.

Evans, B. I. *William Morris and His Poetry.* (Harrap: London, 1925.) Intended primarily as an introduction; presents the facts of Morris's life in such a manner as to serve as commentary on his poetry, which is generously quoted throughout.

Glasier, J. B. *William Morris and the Early Days of the Socialist Movement.* (Longmans: London, 1921.) Points out Morris's neo-humanism as the essential fire of his genius; although containing little critical material, gives a vivid picture of the poet's artistic nature.

Mackail, J. W. *The Life of William Morris.* (Longmans: New York, 1922.) The authoritative biography, intimate and impartial; provides the facts of Morris's life, as well as sound estimates of his work.

Noyes, Alfred. *William Morris*, English Men of Letters series. (Macmillan: New York, 1908.) A satisfactory biography, where more detailed works are not needed; valuable for its critical appreciations.

Vallance, Aymer. *William Morris, His Art, His Writings, and His Public Life.* (Bell: London, 1909.) "Makes no claim to be a biography," but provides an invaluable record of Morris's varied activities; illustrated at the poet's suggestion with his own designs.

Weekley, Montague. *William Morris.* (Duckworth: London, 1934.) An excellent brief Life, emphasizing throughout Morris's hearty masculinity and his unaffected attitude toward his art; concludes with a brief bibliography.

III. ARTICLES FROM BOOKS

Brooke, S. A. "William Morris," in *Four Victorian Poets.* (Duckworth: London, 1913.) Notes the poet's love for the earth and his absorption into an ideal world; analyzes several of the verse-narratives.

Cole, G. D. H. "William Morris," in *Revaluations*, ed. by A. C. Ward. (Oxford University Press: 1931.) Shows the decline of Morris's poetic vitality, competing with his many other interests; insists that the man is not to be judged by his poetry alone, but from a view of all his work, including his propaganda.

Dawson, W. J. "William Morris," in *The Makers of English Poetry.* (Revell: New York, 1906.) Points out the poet's sense of color, his delight in nature, and his aversion to flowery phrases; comments on his derivation from Chaucer.

Drinkwater, John. "William Morris and the State," in *Prose Papers.* (Mathews: London,

1917.) Recalls Morris's belief in art as the great rectifier of human ills; concludes with an interesting comment on Morris's dislike of Milton.

Hearn, Lafcadio. "William Morris," in *Pre-Raphaelite and Other Poets*. (Dodd: New York, 1922.) Valuable as an introduction to Morris's life and art; analyzes many poems, praising especially *The Story of Sigurd*.

Lang, Andrew. "Mr. Morris's Poems," in *Adventures among Books*. (Longmans: London, 1905.) Shows Morris's predilection for the fourteenth century; points out his wide range from his earlier to later verse, expressing dissatisfaction at his translations from the classics.

Lucas, F. L. "William Morris," in *Eight Victorian Poets*. (Cambridge University Press: 1930.) Remarks the man's vigorous life; names *The Earthly Paradise* his best-known work, but grants that he is "not on the highway of literature."

Mackail, J. W. "William Morris," in *Studies of English Poets*. (Longmans: New York, 1926.) A popular review of the artist's many-sided interests, poetry being the sublime vision comprehending all; in his socialism the practical man is said to emerge.

More, P. E. "William Morris," in *Shelburne Essays*, Seventh Series. (Putnam: New York, 1910.) Describes the writer's restlessness; analyzes *The Earthly Paradise* and *Sigurd*.

Saintsbury, George. "Mr. William Morris," in *Corrected Impressions*. (Dodd: New York, 1895.) Provides reminiscences on the effect of the *Guenevere* volume, *The Life and Death of Jason*, and *The Earthly Paradise*.

Scott, Dixon. "The First Morris," in *Men of Letters*. (Hodder: London, 1923.) An enthusiastic review of the *Guenevere* volume, where the magic of the poet is present, as it was not in any of his later volumes; analyzes the influence of Rossetti.

Swinburne, A. C. "Morris's *Life and Death of Jason*," in *Essays and Studies*. (Chatto: London, 1888.) Remarks the poet's advance from earlier verse, praising the narrative vigor and descriptive clarity of the poem.

Symons, Arthur. "William Morris," in *Studies in Two Literatures*. (Secker: London, 1924.) Illustrates the vital connection between the socialist and the poet in Morris; shows him to be of the line of Chaucer and Spenser.

Thompson, A. H. "The Rossettis, William Morris, and Swinburne," in *The Cambridge History of English Literature*, XIII. (Putnam: New York, 1917.) Remarks the influence of Rossetti upon Morris, whose verse-narratives and epics are analyzed as most representative of his work.

Welby, T. E. "William Morris," in *The Victorian Romantics, 1850–1870*. (Howe: London, 1929.) A number of scattered references point to the importance of Morris's early work, his contribution to Pre-Raphaelitism by his interest in many arts and crafts, and his essential independence in his varied activities.

Yeats, W. B. "The Happiest of the Poets," in *Collected Works*, VI. (Shakespere Head: Stratford, 1908.) Recalls Morris's fortune in finding an ideal world of escape from reality; commends his sincerity and fidelity to his abstract scheme of life.

IV. ARTICLES FROM PERIODICALS

Clutton-Brock, Arthur. "The Later Poems of William Morris," *Living Age*, CCLI, 241–5 (Oct. 27, 1906). Reveals the hand of Morris at his best in *Sigurd* and *Poems by the Way*.

Cockerell, T. D. A. "William Morris and the World Today," *Dial*, LIX, 544–8 (Dec. 9, 1915). Recalls Morris's activities in the Socialist movement, in which his mind worked constructively and upward; indicates some of his social ideals in his prose and verse.

Crane, Walter. "William Morris," *Scribner's Magazine*, XXII, 88–99 (July, 1897). Valuable for its reproductions of Morris's designs for books, tapestries, wallpapers, etc.

Hewlett, H. G. "The Poems of Mr. Morris," *Contemporary Review*, XXV, 100–24 (Dec., 1874). An enthusiastic review of Morris's publications, 1858–1873; sees him poised on a skepticism which may settle to a secure conviction.

Lubbock, Percy. "The Poetry of William Morris, *Quarterly Review*, CCXV, 482–504 (Oct., 1911). Maintains that Morris's work proceeded from a fully developed imagination, in which tentative experiment played little part; provides an excellent review of the poet's entire output.

Moorhouse, E. H. "Aspects of William Morris," *Fortnightly Review*, XCVIII, 464–76 (Sept., 1912). Praises Morris's achievements as belonging to a heroic age; indicates his love of medievalism as expressed in many of his lyrics and the breadth that expanded throughout all his work.

Myers, F. W. H. "Modern Poets and the Meaning of Life," *Nineteenth Century*, XXXIII, 93–111 (Jan., 1893). Closely identifies the emotions of Morris's poetry with his mental life; shows how he maintained his personal integrity in the face of a cosmic hopelessness.

Parry, J. J. "A Note on the Prosody of William Morris," *Modern Language Notes*, XLIV, 306–9 (May, 1929). Calls attention to the poet's unorthodox rhyme and metric, which are traced to his imitation of certain prosodic features in Welsh poetry.

Sharp, William. "William Morris, the Man and His Work," *Atlantic Monthly*, LXXVIII, 768–81 (Dec., 1896). An enthusiastic survey of the poet and craftsman; provides a good biographical outline and an insight into Morris's inner life.

NOTES

Page 980. THE CHAPEL IN LYONESS

This poem, like certain others by Morris, has a vagueness of outline. The central situation is perfectly clear—the wounded Ozana of the Hardy Heart, who has been watched over by Galahad and is visited by Sir Bors—is dying with a tress of woman's hair in his fingers. He has forgotten her recent visit to him and moans, "There comes no sleep nor any love." Upon this situation Morris elaborates to create an atmosphere and a sense of mystery—

which remains unexplained. Rossetti in his letters (text p. 665b, l. 41) refers to this poem as "glorious."

Ozana was one of the knights who was wounded defending Guenevere from Meliagrance (see note on p. 983, ll. 167–8), but the present poem seems to have no connection with that episode.

Lyoness was the homeland of Sir Tristram—a shadowy country of romance with no very definite geographic location.

Page 981. SUMMER DAWN

This poem had originally appeared in *The Oxford and Cambridge Magazine,* the first line reading "Pray but one prayer for us," etc.; as the poem appeared in *The Defence of Guenevere* volume, "me" was substituted for "us."

THE DEFENCE OF GUENEVERE

"*Guenevere* and the rest are still read with admiration by people who find *Jason* dull and *Sigurd* doggerel. Crammed into that first little collection, bursting from those mediaeval scenes of lust and blood and sacrifice, are all the evidences of poetical genius. . . . The tormented soul of Guenevere cries out with a devastating shrillness: there the queen writhes, now humbly coaxing, now proudly drawing herself up to invoke the fire from heaven; and gleaming across the page one sees the grinning teeth of caitiff knights, and the chill of dungeons is conjured up, and strikes like a frightful miasma on the cheek. Those mediaeval figures, so unbridled in their good and evil passions, are very explicit. With their reasonings and arguments they are prepared to ride trampling down the neat stanzas lest their grim meanings be left in doubt. The Middle Ages were dear to Morris, and he had (what is not very apparent in *Guenevere*) some illusions about them, but obviously far fewer than the twentieth-century man-in-the-street, who easily persuades himself that the whole period was no more than a series of variations on *The Haystack in the Floods*—a theme of rapine and murder." (Paul Bloomfield, *William Morris,* pp. 87–8.)

The Defence of Guenevere is at points difficult to follow because it presupposes a knowledge of the story of Lancelot, Guenevere, and King Arthur as told by Malory. The poem is the last speech to her accusers of a desperate woman who expects to be condemned to be burned at the stake and who is hoping against hope for the arrival of her lover to save her from this fate. It has the incoherence and intensity of that situation, and it refers to the story (but does not tell the story) which had brought her to that pass.

Agravaine and Mordred had laid a trap. The king had been persuaded to take a hunting trip for the day and then to send back word that he would not return that night. The queen sent for Lancelot, and Mordred and Agravaine with twelve other knights, fully armed, trapped Lancelot, unarmed, in the queen's chamber.

Malory (Book XX, chapter IV) describes the fight which followed:

"And therewith Sir Launcelot wrapped his mantle about his arm well and surely; and by then they had gotten a great form out of the hall, and therewithal they rashed at the door. Fair lords, said Sir Launcelot, leave your noise and your rashing, and I shall set open this door, and then may ye do with me what it liketh you. Come off then, said they all, and do it, for it availeth thee not to strive against us all; and therefore let us into this chamber, and we shall save thy life until thou come to King Arthur. Then Launcelot unbarred the door, and with his left hand he held it open a little, so that but one man might come in at once; and so anon there came striding a good knight, a much man and large, and his name was Colgrevance of Gore, and he with a sword strake at Sir Launcelot mightily; and he put aside the stroke, and gave him such a buffet upon the helmet, that he fell groveling dead within the chamber door, and then Sir Launcelot with great might drew that dead knight within the chamber door; and then Sir Launcelot with the help of the queen and her ladies was lightly armed in Sir Colgrevance's armour.

"And ever stood Sir Agravaine and Sir Mordred crying: Traitor knight, come out of the queen's chamber. Leave your noise, said Sir Launcelot unto Sir Agravaine, for wit you well, Sir Agravaine, ye shall not prison me this night; and therefore an ye do by my counsel, go ye all from this chamber door, and make not such crying and such manner of slander as ye do; for I promise you by my knighthood, an ye will depart and make no more noise, I shall as to-morn appear afore you all before the king, and then let it be seen which of you all, and either else ye all, that will accuse me of treason; and there I shall answer you as a knight should, that hither I came to the queen for no manner of mal-engin, and that will I prove and make it good upon you with mine hands. Fie on thee, traitor, said Sir Agravaine and Sir Mordred, we will have thee, maugre thy head, and slay thee if we list; for we let thee wit, we have the choice of King Arthur, to save thee or to slay thee. Ah sirs, said Sir Launcelot, is there none other grace with you? then keep yourselves.

"So then Sir Launcelot set all open the chamber door, and mightily and knightly he strode in amongst them; and anon at the first buffet he slew Sir Agravaine. And twelve of his fellows, within a little while after, he laid them cold to the earth, for there was none of the twelve that might stand Sir Launcelot one buffet. Also Sir Launcelot wounded Sir Mordred, and he fled with all his might. And then Sir Launcelot returned again unto the queen, and said: Madam, now wit you well all our true love is brought to an end, for now will King Arthur ever be my foe; and therefore, madam, an it like you that I may have you with me, I shall save you from all manner adventures dangerous. That is not best, said the queen; meseemeth now ye have done so much harm, it will be best ye hold you still with this. And if ye see as to-morn they will put me unto the death, then may ye rescue me as ye think best. I will well, said Sir Launcelot, for have ye no doubt while I am living I shall rescue you. And then he kissed her, and either gave other a ring; and so there he left the queen, and went until his lodging."

Lancelot took immediate counsel with his friends and they vowed to support him, even against the king. And Sir Bors said, "Insomuch as ye were taken with her, whether ye did right or wrong, it is now your part to hold with the queen, that she be not slain and put to a mischievous death."

Meanwhile, Mordred, the sole survivor of the attacking party, had reported the whole affair of the entrapment and battle to the king, who commanded that the Queen should be burned.

8. *Gauwaine.* Morris, in making Gawaine the Queen's chief accuser, departs from Malory's account. According to Malory, Gawaine was the staunchest defender of the Queen and Lancelot. He tried to prevent the ambuscade, he tried later to persuade Arthur that the two might have been together perfectly innocently, and finally when the King ordered him to be the one to bring the Queen to the fire he flatly refused to have anything to do with the proceedings. The king then ordered Gawaine's younger brothers Gaheris and Gareth to do so. Both protested but, being younger men, were obliged to bow to the king's will. Both, however, refused to wear armor in token of their refusal to defend the burning. In the confusion which followed the charge of Lancelot and his knights to Guenevere's rescue both Gareth and Gaheris were killed by Lancelot himself. Thereafter Gawaine vowed revenge.

22. *One of these cloths.* The significance of the choice offered Guenevere lies in the color and length of the cloths (see ll. 34–5), blue being the color of faithfulness and red that of passion. She was offered the choice (l. 80) after her meeting with Lancelot, and the implication of her speech is that she chose the blue—"heaven's colour"—and it proved to be that of hell.

Tradition concedes that the love of Guenevere and Lancelot was more than platonic. Within the limits of this specific poem, however, there is nothing which concedes Guenevere's guilt. In the Malory account Gawaine supplies an explanation of how Lancelot could have been in the queen's chamber quite innocently. Lancelot's own friends, however, forbear to ask whether he was there "for right or wrong."

46. *Nevertheless you, O Sir Gauwaine, lie.* See notes above on l. 8 and l. 22.

62. *at Christmas-time.* It was the second springtime after this Christmas that Lancelot first kissed her. See ll. 132–40.

153. *Remember in what grave your mother sleeps.* Gaheris, a brother of Gawaine, had discovered his mother in bed with Sir Lamorak and with a single blow had struck off her head. In l. 157 Morris incorrectly assigns the deed to Agravaine, another brother.

167–8. *See me hew down your proofs . . . Mellyagraunce,* etc. "Your accusation will be disproved just as was that previous false accusation which Meliagrance made." Guenevere is referring to a previous occasion when Lancelot had saved her from the stake, an occasion when what had started out as a May-party ended up in an ordeal by battle. The queen with ten of her knights, without armor but carrying swords, went a-maying on a pleasant morning. Meliagrance, who had long loved the queen, saw his opportunity and attacked the party with a large force of fully armed men. The queen's knights defended her valiantly but when more than half of them had fallen and all were wounded Guenevere interceded. She promised to go to Meliagrance's castle if she could bring the knights and tend their wounds. And so the party moved to his castle. Meanwhile a child had escaped from the May-party and carried the news of these happenings to Sir Lancelot. Lancelot arrived at the castle in time to prevent any further wrong being done. Meliagrance had been so terrified at Lancelot's coming that he had begged forgiveness of the queen and, although it was Lancelot's impulse to kill him offhand, he was spared at the queen's intercession. That night the wounded men were put in the queen's room that she might attend them and what followed Malory (Book XIX, chapters v and vi) relates:

". . . Sir Launcelot made a promise with the queen that the same night Sir Launcelot should come to a window outward toward the garden; and that window was y-barred with iron, and there Sir Launcelot promised to meet her when all folks were asleep. . . ."

". . . Then when season was, they went unto their chambers, but in no wise the queen would not suffer the wounded knights to be from her, but that they were laid within draughts by her chamber, upon beds and pillows, that she herself might see to them, that they wanted nothing."

". . . Then Sir Launcelot took his sword in his hand, and privily went to a place whereas he had espied a ladder to-forehand, and that he took under his arm, and bare it through the garden, and set it up to the window, and there anon the queen was ready to meet him. And then they made either to other their complaints of many divers things, and then Sir Launcelot wished that he might have come in to her. Wit ye well, said the queen, I would as fain as ye, that ye might come in to me. Would ye, madam, said Sir Launcelot, with your heart that I were with you? Yea, truly, said the queen. Now shall I prove my might, said Sir Launcelot, for your love; and then he set his hands upon the bars of iron, and he pulled at them with such a might that he brast them clean out of the stone walls, and therewithal one of the bars of iron cut the brawn of his hand throughout to the bone; and then he leapt into the chamber to the queen. Make ye no noise, said the queen, for my wounded knights lie here fast by me. And when he saw his time that he might tarry no longer he took his leave and departed at the window, and put it together as well as he might again, and so departed unto his own chamber; and there he told Sir Lavaine how he was hurt. Then Sir Lavaine dressed his hand and staunched it, and put upon it a glove, that it should not be espied; and so the queen lay long in her bed until it was nine of the clock.

"Then Sir Meliagrance went to the queen's chamber, and found her ladies there ready clothed. . . . What aileth you, madam, said Sir Meliagrance, that ye sleep thus long? And right therewithal he opened the curtain for to behold her; and then was he ware of the blood of Sir Launcelot's hurt hand. When Sir Meliagrance espied that blood, then he deemed in himself that she was false to the king, and that it was the blood of some of the wounded knights. Ah, madam, said Sir Meliagrance, now I have found you a false traitress unto my lord Arthur; for now I prove well it was not for nought that ye laid these wounded knights within the bounds of your chamber; therefore I will call you of treason. . . ."

Lancelot, asserting that none of the ten knights had been in the Queen's bed (as, indeed, none had), undertook to defend the Queen's honor in trial by battle. He very nearly failed to appear at the appointed time and place (in which case Guenevere would have been burnt) because Meliagrance at a moment when Lancelot was unwary had sprung a trap in the floor and pitched him into a dungeon. Lancelot escaped and arrived just in time. The episode and the fight between the two knights is referred to in ll. 167–220.

169. *la Fausse Garde.* The false stronghold or castle. The castle to which Lancelot carried off Guenevere just after the close of this poem was called Joyous Garde.

188–9. *Slayer of unarm'd men . . . Setter of traps.* See note on ll. 167–8.

200. *half-arm'd will I fight.* According to Malory, when Meliagrance refused to stand up and be killed, Lancelot enticed him to his feet by offering to fight half-armed.

207. *waist-chain.* Guenevere was chained to the stake at the time of the trial by battle.

Page 985. CONCERNING GEFFRAY TESTE NOIRE

John of Castel Neuf in his old age is telling of an incident of his young manhood. The recollection really embraces three episodes which are interlaced—(1) the ambush of Geffray, (2) the story of the skeletons as John had reconstructed it in his imagination, and (3) an incident in his youth when he was fighting the Jacquerie in the streets of Beauvais.

Geoffrey of the Black Head was a Breton who took the strong castle of Ventador in Gascony by treachery and then harried the neighboring provinces. He had a reputation for cruelty. He was besieged in 1388 by Sir William Lignac, Sir John Bonne Lance (Good Lance) and "dyvers other knightes and squiers" but Ventador was so strong that they failed to take it. Geoffrey, however, was wounded and as he took evil care of himself he died from the effects, after having appointed his nephew Alleyne Roux as his successor. There are references to Geoffrey in the *Chronicle* of Froissart. (Berner's trans. in the Tudor Translations, Vol. III, p. 60; Vol. V, 251; 254–7.)

1. *Canon of Chimay.* Froissart, the chronicler.

8. *King Charles and St. Denis.* Charles V of France. St. Denis was the patron saint of the French. Geoffrey allied himself with the English because of the greater possibilities of plunder.

52. *the horse in Job.* See Job 39:21–2.—"He paweth in the valley, and rejoiceth in his strength: he goeth on to meet the armed men. He mocketh at fear, and is not affrighted; neither turneth he back from the sword."

96. *Didst ever see a woman's bones, my lord?* Lines 97–116 answer this question in recalling an episode when John was fifteen and was fighting the Jacquerie in the streets of Beauvais. The revolt of the Jacquerie (so-called because Jacques was a common name) was a revolt of the peasants provoked by their suffering in the Hundred Years' War and fought with extreme ferocity on both sides. It broke out in the Île de France itself and around Beauvais in the spring of 1358.

117. *her tender throat.* That of the female skeleton. The poem now returns to John's reconstruction of what had happened.

181. *Cry out St. Peter.* Events of the ambush

break in on his reverie concerning the lives of the skeleton.

Page 988. THE GILLIFLOWER OF GOLD

The poem recalls the deeds of glory performed in honor of his lady by a knight in a tournament.

4. *la belle jaune giroflée.* The beautiful yellow gilliflower.
6. *it.* The flower, which the knight was wearing as his lady's token.
25. *Honneur aux fils des preux!* Honor to the sons of valiant knights.
30. *tabard.* A loose cloak worn by knights over their armor and usually emblazoned with the knight's coat of arms.

Page 990. THE EVE OF CRÉCY

Alfred Noyes considered this poem lyrically the finest piece of music in the volume in which it appeared (*The Defence of Guenevere*) and declared the refrain to be "for once perfectly 'right.'"

The poem is spoken by the French knight, Sir Lambert de Bois. In his poverty he broods on what he may win in battle the next day: glory, wealth—and Marguerite! The irony and pathos of the situation lie in the fact that in the battle of Crécy (1346) the French were overwhelmingly defeated by the English, and the victory of footmen and archers over mounted knights dealt feudalism a blow from which it never recovered. Sir Lambert is dreaming on the night before the end of his world.

4. *Ah! qu'elle est belle*, etc. "Ah, but she is beautiful, is Margaret!"
14. *arrière-ban.* The proclamation calling men to arms; also the troops thus called.
15. *six basnets*, etc. Six helmeted men.

THE JUDGMENT OF GOD

Morris again uses the technique he so often employs of taking a principal character, fully informed of events which have preceded, and making him speak at a crisis in the story. The reader must deduce the events which precipitated the crisis. Sir Roger, a recreant and outcast knight, hated by all but his beloved Ellayne, is speaking just before he goes out to trial by battle which shall finally end a long blood feud (see ll. 7–8 and 73–80). Roger is in a somber mood but he regrets none of his crimes, because, after all, he has won Ellayne, and the crimes were long ago (l. 56 and ll. 61–3).

The significance of the title lies in the fact that the knight was about to face trial by battle. The belief was that in trials by the various "ordeals"—of fire, of water, of battle, etc.—God dictated the outcome.

Professor Maynadier, although he is writing specifically of Morris's Arthurian poems, makes a comment which is applicable to all of Morris's mediæval work: ". . . These . . . have a singing fascination, and they are full of vivid, highly colored mediæval pictures; they transport you, whether their intangibility irritates or pleases you, into a remote, poetical Middle Age, which for the time being, unreal as it is, you accept as real. You may never be quite satisfied with these poems, because of their too little substance and their too much length and color and imagery; but their spontaneity must rouse your wonder. They seem to have come from Morris's pen as naturally as if this man of the nineteenth century, who deplored the sky-polluting smoke of its factories and the roar and clatter of its steam engines, had lived in the earlier ages of which he wrote. . . ." (Howard Maynadier, *The Arthur of the English Poets*, pp. 362–3.)

See also the introductory note to *The Blue Closet*, below.

Page 991. THE SAILING OF THE SWORD

See quotation from Mackail in notes on *The Blue Closet*, below, although this poem has more of a ballad quality.

37. *no word he said.* This is the one of the three who brings back a wife upon his knee. See ll. 63–4.

Page 992. OLD LOVE

John in this poem can be assumed to be middle-aged; Sir Giles is very old.

17. *at that word no pang.* After all these years his old love has no longer power to move him.
25. *Constantine.* Constantinople.

Page 993. THE WIND

The insignia on the banners referred to in ll. 83–4 make it clear that the speaker is a Norwegian, the reference to Olaf, king and saint, being to Olaf II of Norway who was canonized after his death. But the geographic location has no bearing on the meaning of the poem, which is not clear. The knight is recalling the scene of the death of his beloved. She had resisted him but had surrendered, glad that he should prevail (l. 44), and had kissed him. The why or how of her mortal wound remains unexplained.

Page 994. THE BLUE CLOSET

"Between the charm of the Malory poems and that of the Froissart poems the choice is one of personal feeling. But the part of the volume which one gathers to represent its spirit and form most intimately to many lovers of poetry, is neither of these. It consists of the poems of a wholly unbased and fantastic romance, in which any traceable poetical influence is that of Poe rather than of Browning. Their very names—such names as 'The Blue Closet,' or 'The Sailing of the Sword,' or 'Two Red Roses across the Moon'—are taken straight out of dreamland. . . . Never perhaps has poetry come nearer to what some theorists have laid down as its goal, the emotional effect of music, than in some of these remarkable pieces—'The Wind,' 'Spellbound,' 'Near Avalon.' Even now, to those to whom they have been long familiar, their faint beauty comes back, ever and again, like a fugitive and haunting scent, or the vague trouble of a dream remembered in a dream." (J. W. Mackail, *The Life of William Morris*, I, 133–4.) Some sketches and water-colors of Rossetti's of this period carry the same titles as poems by Morris, notably *The Blue Closet* and *The Tune of Seven Towers*. Morris's poems were apparently an effort to capture the atmosphere of Rossetti's work in another artistic medium, which would account for their mysteriousness and vagueness of outline. Rossetti (see text p. 666a, l. 8) considered the poem "stunning."

5. *Laudate pueri*. Let the children praise, the opening words of a version of the *Te Deum*.

Page 995. THE TUNE OF SEVEN TOWERS

See note on *The Blue Closet*.

Page 996. THE HAYSTACK IN THE FLOODS

This poem is one of the most remarkable examples of Morris's power to visualize an anguished scene (cf. *The Defence of Guenevere*) and create a sense of intense actuality in his mediæval narratives. The story occurs in the fourteenth century during the Hundred Years' War and shortly after the battle of Poictiers (1356). Robert of Marny, an English knight, is riding with his mistress Jehane through the south of France toward Gascony. Once across the frontier of the province of Gascony they were safe, as Gascony was at that time held by the English. But they are ambushed before they can reach it, and the poem starts at the moment of the ambush.

42. *coif*. A small tight-fitting hat. She tries to pull it down over her eyes to shut out the scene.

51. *those six men*. Her judges.

52. *the Chatelet*. A prison in Paris.

56. *To recollect how strong men swim*. That is, she would be thrown into the Seine and be subjected to the trial by water to test her innocence, a procedure which had unfortunate results for the victim whatever the outcome. If she sank and drowned God had taken her and she was innocent. If the water "refused" her (i.e., if she did not drown), she was guilty and would be burned.

Page 999. TWO RED ROSES ACROSS THE MOON

This poem, like *The Blue Closet* and *The Tune of Seven Towers*, is a study in color, but its story can be discerned. The knight's color was gold, and the colors of the enemies he had to fight were scarlet and blue. In spite of his apparent indifference to the lady's song of the roses, the knight remembers it in battle and uses it as a war-cry. There is the appropriate happy ending.

33. *Under the may*. The May-tree (hawthorn): a small tree blossoming very profusely and fragrantly in the spring.

PRAISE OF MY LADY

4. *Beata mea Domina!* My blessed lady.

Page 1000. *From* THE LIFE AND DEATH OF JASON

Morris had originally intended for inclusion in *The Earthly Paradise* a narrative on the quest of the Golden Fleece by Jason and the Argonauts. When he actually came to write it, the poem outgrew his original conception and became too long for any possible inclusion in the collection. It was published in 1867, and its great success encouraged Morris to complete *The Earthly Paradise*.

I Know a Little Garden-Close

The ship of the adventurers had put in at Mysia for water and Hylas wandered away from the party. A group of sea-nymphs fell in love with him and delegated one of their number to charm him. This poem is the song she sings to put him to sleep. The other nymphs then appear and carry him down into the depth of the stream. The episode occurs at the close of the fourth book.

Page 1001. *O Death, that Maketh Life So Sweet*

This song is sung by Orpheus in the twelfth book to encourage his companions.

38. *outland*. Foreign.

42–3. *bringing home That which all men have talked about*. The Golden Fleece, the object of their quest.

60. *Argo*. The name of their ship, from which the group were called the Argonauts.

From THE EARTHLY PARADISE

Morris conceived the idea of a collection of narrative poems bound together much as were Chaucer's *Canterbury Tales* by a prologue and interludes which should provide a setting and excuse for the narratives, and *The Earthly Paradise*, published in instalments from 1868 to 1870, was the final result. The pattern of the poem was ingenious. He indulged the fancy that somewhere might have existed, surviving into the fourteenth century, an isolated community carrying on the old Greek tradition, and representative of the golden age. The scheme also provides that in a time of pestilence and ruin in Europe, "Certain gentlemen and mariners of Norway," to quote Morris's *Argument*, "having considered all that they had heard of the Earthly Paradise, set sail to find it, and after many troubles and the lapse of many years came old men to a Western land." There great honor was done to them and they were entertained at semi-monthly feasts for a year, alternately one of the hosts and one of the guests telling a story. The ingenuity of the scheme is two-fold. First it put at his disposal all the stories of both the Greek and the northern epic cycles. The leader of the expedition, moreover, had spent his youth at Byzantium, which gave a contact with the stories of the East, and in the party there were also a Breton and a Swabian. The second great virtue of the scheme lay in the fact that the old stories were now being told by men of the fourteenth century, with all the possibility this offered of adjusting them to Morris's own passion for the mediæval.

J. W. Mackail states this point clearly. ". . . It is, for instance, one of the commonest criticisms made of the Greek stories in 'The Earthly Paradise,' that the atmosphere and treatment are not Greek but mediæval; that the feelings, incidents, and decoration are neither those of classical poetry, nor yet of the stories of ancient Greece as interpreted and modernized by the taste of the present day. This is precisely true, and precisely what Morris meant. Ancient Greek poetry he admired for its own qualities, and appreciated more than is generally known—a criticism which he once made on Pindar showed insight much greater than that of the average classical scholar—but its way was not his way; and still less his way was the sort of modernization, beautiful and touching as that is, which other poets of this age have applied to the Greek legends—the method of Tennyson in 'Œnone' or 'Tiresias,' the method of Matthew Arnold in 'Empedocles,' the method of Mr. Swinburne in 'Atalanta in Calydon.' To Morris the mediæval method—using the term to cover the whole period of four or five centuries from the age of the *chansons de geste* and the Icelandic epic to the close of the Middle Ages in Chaucer—was beyond all question or comparison the best; was so much the best that it was practically the only one. To adopt this method, however naturally it came to him, without warning, and, as it were, in the air, would put a needless strain on the intelligence of his public. It was prepared for, nay more, it was rendered both natural and appropriate, by this device of laying the scene of the stories themselves at the end of the fourteenth century, and telling them as they would have been told then: as they were in fact told then in Western Europe, but with the greater sweetness of tone and purity of line, the less mystic or fantastic turn, which might be expected from a purely Greek tradition; and with something also of that stately Greek melancholy which seems inherent in the Hellenic blood, and clings, the shadow of its brightness, to the whole of ancient Greek poetry from Homer to Theocritus." (J. W. Mackail, *The Life of William Morris*, I, 180–1.)

Page 1002. *March*

In the volume there is a lyric for each month, all done in the seven-line stanza of the old "rhyme royal" so much used by Chaucer.

The Lady of the Land

This is the second story for June. Morris took his fable from Mandeville's *Voiage and Travaile* but the theme of the enchanted maiden waiting to be rescued by a knight is common enough—witness such varied stories as *The Sleeping Beauty* or the old ballad of *Kemp Owynne.* Morris, it will be noted (by a comparison with the extract from Mandeville which follows), follows the events of his source rather closely but has elaborated descriptive detail and, more important, supplied a motive for the curse and the release—a violation of virginity (not of love) has caused the doom to fall, a true love kiss will repeal it. The visitor turns a silver handle on the door and comes into a room filled with gold—but if he kisses her for power or gold the kiss will be of no avail and he is warned to beware. (See ll. 222–3.)

Mandeville's account reads as follows:

"Some Men seyn, that in the Ile of Lango is yit the Doughtre of Ypocras, in forme and lykeness of a gret Dragoun, that is a hundred Fadme of lengthe, as Men seyn: For I have not seen hire. And thei of the Isles callen hire, Lady of the Lond. And sche lyethe in an olde castelle, in a Cave, and schewethe twyes or thryes in the Yeer. And sche dothe none harm to no Man, but yif Men done hire harm. And sche was thus chaunged and transformed, from a fair Damysele, in-to lykenesse of a Dragoun, be a Goddesse, that was clept Deane. And Men seyn, that sche schalle so endure in that forme of a Dragoun, unto the tyme that a Knyghte come; that is so hardy, that dar come to hire and kiss hire on the Mouthe: And then schalle sche turne ayen to hire owne Kynde, and ben a Woman ayen: But aftre that sche schalle not liven longe. And it is not long siththen, that a Knyghte of the Rodes, that was hardy and doughty in Armes, seyde that he wolde kyssen hire. And whan he was upon his Coursere, and wente to the Castelle, and entred into the Cave, the Dragoun lifte up hire Hed ayenst him. And whan the Knyghte saw hire in that Forme so hidous and so horrible, he fleyghe awey. And the Dragoun bare the Knyghte upon a Roche, mawgre his Hede; and from that Roche, sche caste him in-to the See: and so was lost bothe Hors and Man. And also a yonge Man, that wiste not of the Dragoun, wente out of a Schipp, and wente thorghe the Ile, til that he come to the Castelle, and cam in to the Cave; and wente so longe, til that he fond a Chambre, and there he saughe a Damysele, that kembed hire Hede, and lokede in a Myrour; and sche hadde meche Tresoure abouten hire: and he trowed, that sche hadde ben a comoun Woman, that dwelled there to receyve Men to Folye. And he abode, tille the Damysele saughe the Schadewe of him in the Myrour. And sche turned hire toward him, and asked hym, what he wolde. And he seyde, he wolde ben hire Lemman or Paramour. And sche asked him, yif that he were a Knyghte. And he seyde, nay. And than sche seyde, that he myghte not ben hire Lemman: But sche bad him gon ayen unto his Felowes, and make him Knyghte, and come ayen upon the Morwe, and sche scholde come out of the Cave before him; and thanne come an kysse hire on the mowthe, and have no Drede; "for I schalle do the no maner harm, alle be it that thou see me in Lykenesse of a Dragoun. For thoughe thou see me hidouse and horrible to loken onne, I do the to wytenc, that it is made be Enchauntement. For withouten doute, I am non other than thou seest now, a Woman; and therefore drede the noughte. And yif thou kysse me, thou schalt have all this Tresoure, and be my Lord, and Lord also of all that Ile." And he departed fro hire and wente to his Felowes to Shippe, and leet make him Knyghte, and cam ayen upon the Morwe, for to Kysse this Damysele. And when he saughe hire comen out of the Cave, in forme of a Dragoun, so hidouse and so horrible, he hadde so grete drede, that he fleyghe ayen to the Schippe; and sche folewed him. And whan sche saughe, that he turned not ayen, sche began to crye, as a thing that hadde meche Sorwe; and thanne sche turned ayen, in-to hire Cave; and anon the Knyghte dyede. And siththen hidrewards, myghte no Knyghte se hire, but that he dyede anon. But when a Knyghte comethe, that is so hardy to kisse hire, he schalle not dye; but he schall turne the Damysele in-to hire righte Forme and kyndely Schapp, and he schal be Lord of alle the Contreyes and Iles aboveseyd." (*The Voiage and Travaile of Sir John Maundeville*, ch. IV.)

79–84. *There stood great Jove.* There is apparently a symbolic value to the mutilation of these images. Jove, the highest of the gods and presumably the wisest, has no head; the swift Apollo is lamed; Diana, goddess of the moon which moves across unfettered skies, is chained; Helen of Troy, whose kisses "launched a thousand ships and burned the topless towers of Ilium," has rusty nails through her lip.

181–2. *Cast back from such a form as . . . lighted up Troy town.* The beauty of Helen of Troy has become symbolic of the supreme in feminine beauty. Paris, a shepherd prince, carried her off from her husband to Troy. The Greeks thereupon besieged Troy and after a ten-year siege, captured and burned the city. (See notes on *Œnone.*)

251. *A sorry merchant.* Morris explicitly makes clear that he is a merchant; see l. 234. The point here is that he is a bad bargainer and will except any terms—even destruction—for a single hour with her. The Mandeville account is indefinite as to his business.

324–5. *The moon . . . seemed changed to blood.* The chaste goddess Diana, to whom the girl had been dedicated by her father, was goddess of the moon.

353. *flesh and fell.* Fell means skin. The phrase is graphic when fully realized. The woman has been changed into a dragon—in skin and in the meat within the skin.

Page 1010. *Song* from *Ogier the Dane*

Haec and *Ille* are She and He. The song was overheard by Ogier. It was sung by two young voices, but in its conclusion (ll. 21–2) carried to him a foreboding note.

Song from *The Story of Acontius and Cydippe*

A group of mariners have come ashore at Delos, an island of the Cyclades, and are in a lovely spring garden. Beautiful as is the spot, they long for more and a young man sings this song.

The narrative is the first story of October in the cycle.

Page 1011. *Song* from *The Hill of Venus*

"The story tells of a certain man who by strange adventure fell into the power of Venus, and who, repenting of his life with her, was fain to return to the world and amend all, but might not; for his repentance was rejected of men, by whomsoever it was accepted."

The knight is seeking his beloved when he hears this song in the distance sung by "young men and girls thin-clad and garlanded, too full of love a word of speech to say, Except in Song."

The Hill of Venus was the second story of February and was the last narrative in the volume.

Page 1012. SONGS *from* LOVE IS ENOUGH

Love is Enough; or the Freeing of Pharamond: a Morality was begun in 1871 after Morris's return from Iceland and finished the following year, its elaborate composition causing Morris a good deal of difficulty. It was published in 1873.

" . . . In 1873 he published *Love is Enough*. . . . The story is a Celtic legend, which he took from *The Mabinogion*, telling of the hero king Pharamond, wise ruler and brave soldier, who becomes a listless dreamer, distraught by visions of an ideal love. He leaves his kingdom, and sets forth with one faithful companion, Oliver, wandering over land and sea until he finds in a lowly maid the fulfilment of his dreams. Pharamond returns, after surviving many perils, to find his throne usurped and the loyalty of his subjects dead, yet he is content to lose kingship and all worldly comforts for love. The morality is performed before an emperor and empress at their marriage festivities, while the rustic lovers, Giles and Joan, watch the emperor and empress as well as the play itself; their role resembles that of a Greek chorus. In this elaborate framework, Morris set beautiful lyrics, and proved again his skill in handling a variety of metres. . . . " (Montague Weekley, *William Morris*, pp. 81–2.)

Page 1015. OF THE PASSING AWAY OF BRYNHILD

The story of Sigurd (or Siegfried) is widespread among the northern peoples. Wagner based his series of operas upon the German version, Morris turned to the Icelandic versions, of which there are several. The elder *Edda* told the story in verse form and the so-called *Völsungasaga* (of which, although the story is centuries older, the earliest manuscript dates from the beginning of the thirteenth century) retold the story in prose. It was this latter version Morris used. See also note on *Iceland First Seen*.

Volsung and Niblung are "House" or "family" names. Sigurd is the last of the Volsungs. Gunnar is a Niblung, the son of Giuki. Behind the passage given in the text there is a long, complicated, and bloody story, full of fighting and intense passion, and the passage suffers from not being in its context and therefore lacking the cumulative value of the full story.

Odin for disobedience had placed Brynhild, the Valkyrie (the Valkyrie were handmaidens of Odin who watched over battlefields and chose those who were to be slain), in a trance and condemned her to fall in love with a mortal. It was Sigurd, the hero, who awakened her, and the two had plighted troth. But Sigurd fell into the hands of the Niblungs and a too-scheming mother gave him a potion which caused him to forget Brynhild and marry into the Niblungs, becoming Gunnar's brother-in-law. Gunnar in turn loved Brynhild but he could not ride through the ring of flames which surrounded her and it was Sigurd, himself forgetful of the past and assuming Gunnar's shape, who did so. The two slept (Sigurd in Gunnar's form) with his sword between them and Brynhild married the real Gunnar. The deceit came out and it was Brynhild herself who urged the Niblungs to bring about Sigurd's death—Sigurd himself now bitterly awakened from the effects of the potion. Involved in the story amongst other things are a dragon, a ring, and a treasure of gold. But the passage given in the text relates to the human values of the story. Twice Brynhild slept with Sigurd, a sword between—once when he was in Gunnar's form, and once on their funeral pyre.

3. *bale*. Funeral pyre.

44. *Freyia*. The goddess of love and beauty who also presides over the regions of the dead.

72. *Guttorm*. The Niblung who accomplished Sigurd's death.

141. *draw his Wrath from out the sheath*. Warriors named their swords and "Wrath" was the name of Sigurd's sword.

Page 1020. THE DAY IS COMING

Morris's sympathy with the working man was very real. When the Social Democratic Federation disappointed him (see introductory note, text pp. 978–9) he was one of the leading spirits in the formation of the Socialist League in late 1884. The first issue of the official organ of the League, *The Commonweal*, appeared in February, 1885, and it carried a manifesto which has been thus summarized:

" . . . The first issue opened with an introductory column, written and signed by William Morris, in which he observed: 'It is our duty to attack unsparingly the miserable system which would make all civilization end in a society of rich and poor, of slaves and slave-owners'; and again: 'We assume as a matter of course that a government of privileged persons, hereditary and commercial, cannot act usefully towards the community; their position forbids it; their arrangements for the distribution of the plunder of the workers, their struggles for the national share of the exploitation of barbarous peoples are nothing to us, except so far as they may give us an opportunity of instilling Socialism into men's minds.' The manifesto, which occupied, as it were, with the Socialist League the corresponding position to the programme of the Federation, made no direct reference to that body, but by the very way in which its paragraphs were worded its policy was lifted at once on to a higher and broader platform than that of the Social Democratic Federation. The object of the League was stated to be to destroy all 'distinctions of classes and nationalities.' And whereas 'the workers, although they produce all the wealth of Society, have no control over its production or distribution,' the League proposed to alter all this 'from the foundation: the land, the capital, the machinery, factories, workshops, stores, means of transit, mines, banking, all means of production and distribution of wealth, must be declared and treated as the common property of all.' And further, 'as to mere politics, Absolutism, Constitutionalism, Republicanism, have all been tried in our day and under our present social system, and all alike have failed in dealing with the real evils of life. Nor . . . will certain incomplete schemes of social reform . . solve the question. Co-operation so-called—that is, competitive co-operation for profit' will not do; neither will nationalization of the land alone. . . No better solution would be that of State Socialism. . . . No number of merely administrative changes, until the workers are in possession of all political power, would make any real approach to Socialism. The Socialist League therefore aims at the realization of complete Revolutionary Socialism, and well knows that this can never happen in any one country without the help of the workers of all civilization. 'For us,' proceeds the manifesto, 'neither geographical boundaries, political history, race, nor creed makes rivals or enemies; for us there are no nations, but only varied masses of workers and friends, whose mutual sympathies are checked or perverted by groups of masters and fleecers whose interest it is to stir up rivalries and hatreds between the dwellers in different lands. . . . '" (Aymer Vallance, *William Morris*, pp. 331–2.)

Before the year 1885 was out Morris found himself in a police court, under not very glorious circumstances. A comrade from his branch of the League had been arrested. "When he, with the other seven, was brought up before the magistrate, Morris was present in court. The magistrate, Mr. Saunders, having delivered himself of some general remarks, sentenced one prisoner to two months' hard labour, and fined the rest.

"At this there was an uproar: cries of 'Shame!' hoots and hisses. Then, according to Morris, 'the police simply hustled me and others out with shoves and pushes; when I got to the door I turned round and expostulated with the policeman for his shoving, and the beggar immediately collared me and swore I had hit him and had broken his helmet. . . . ' Result: Morris himself now stood before Mr. Saunders, and the following dialogue took place.

"Mr. Saunders: 'What are you?'

"Morris: 'I am an artist and a literary man, pretty well known, I think, throughout Europe.'

"Mr. Saunders: 'I suppose you did not intend to do this?'

"Morris: 'I never struck him at all.'

"Mr. Saunders: 'Well, I will let you go.'

"Morris: 'But I have not done anything.'

"Mr. Saunders: 'Well, you can stay if you like.'

"Morris: 'I don't want to stay.'

"He was discharged. Afterwards he was sorry for having added to his description of himself as an artist and literary man what he did add. 'It's the only time I've had to bounce about myself, and I'll never do it again.'" (Paul Bloomfield, *William Morris*, p. 230.)

The Socialist movement had more serious and more violent days. There was Sunday, November 13, 1887, when the police forbade them to speak in Trafalgar Square and when, defending the British right of free speech, they vowed they would speak. Squadrons of the mounted Life Guards and battalions of the Foot Guards were called out to support the police. Ultimately they did *not* speak although Cunningham Grahame, very bloody, did somehow break through the police cordon into the Square. On that day a young man named Bernard Shaw marched with William Morris. And some days later Morris stood in a drizzling rain by the grave of a young workman who had died of wounds incurred that day and said, "Our friend who lies here has had a hard life, and met with a hard death; and if society had been differently constituted, his life might have been a delightful, a beautiful, and a happy one. It is our business to begin to organize for the purpose of seeing that such things shall not happen; and to try and make this earth a beautiful and happy place."

Page 1021. THE VOICE OF TOIL

See notes on *The Day Is Coming*, above.

Page 1022. A DEATH SONG

See introductory note to *The Day Is Coming*, above. The "one" referred to in this poem as slain was the young workman (Alfred Linnell) injured in the disturbances of November 13, 1887.

Page 1024. AGNES AND THE HILL-MAN

The hill-man would be a gnome.

35. *Weird*. A charm, although the word more commonly means "fate."

ICELAND FIRST SEEN

Morris visited Iceland in 1871 and in 1873 but his enthusiasm for the Icelandic literature was of long standing. In 1860 he began to learn the language with Eirikr Magnusson so that he could read the sagas in the original, and in 1870, with Magnusson, he did a prose translation of the *Völsungasaga*.

21. *be mighty to save.* That is, the great Icelandic tradition would be a regenerative force in the world.

34. *Brynhild.* See note on *Of the Passing Away of Brynhild*.

36. *Balder.* The Norse sun god—god of peace, goodness, brightness, and wisdom.

ARTHUR O'SHAUGHNESSY

BIBLIOGRAPHY

I. WORKS

Poems, ed. by W. A. Percy. (Yale University Press: 1923.) A selection intended to take the place of the original four volumes (1870–1881); the brief introduction comments on the poet's lyric ecstasy and his originality.

II. BIOGRAPHY AND CRITICISM

"Arthur O'Shaughnessy's Poems," *Contemporary Review*, CXXVI, 125–8 (July, 1924). Reviews the Percy edition: prints some of the best-known stanzas from the poetry, showing the poet's "exquisite tenderness of touch."

Clarke, G. H. "Arthur O'Shaughnessy's Poetry," *Sewanee Review*, XXXI, 486–9 (Oct., 1923). A review of the Percy collection: points out a favorite motif of the poet—the dead speaking to the living.

Gosse, E. W. "Arthur O'Shaughnessy," in *Silhouettes*. (Scribner: New York, 1925.) Describes the poet's work as "flute-music, not strong in quality, nor wide in range, but of a piercing tenderness"; shows the persistence of a strain of introspective melancholy in the poet's best work.

Moulton, Mrs. Louise C. *Arthur O'Shaughnessy, His Life and His Work, with Selections from His Poems*. (Stone: Chicago, 1894.) An interesting account of the poet as a member of the circle of Rossetti and Ford Madox Brown; explains how his beauty and melancholy derive from the facts of his short, difficult career.

NOTES

[O'Shaughnessy] "was a member of the Rossetti circle, but he certainly gave more than he received. The perfect music of his verse is a vehicle for deep thought on mystic themes, and though he is plainly a Victorian, he is nearer to Browning in thought than to those such as Swinburne and Rossetti, whose liquid music has kinship with his. Some critics have spoken in faint praise of O'Shaughnessy, but in fact his poetry is wearing better than that of most of the Victorians, certainly better than the technical achievements of Swinburne. Swinburne, of course, was the greater artist and moved on a larger stage, but somehow today Swinburne's superb technique seems artificial beside O'Shaughnessy's 'exquisite tenderness of touch.'" (*The Contemporary Review*, CXXVI, 128.)

"His quality is, above all, individual. Here is a poet who had no range, no profundity or originality of thought, no interest, so far as his art reveals, in everyday life, or simple joys and sorrows, or heroic deeds, no ability to construct or invent a tale because facts in themselves meant nothing to him. Yet here is a poet, authentically of the sacred band, blessed with the divine gusto. This he is because of the gift of music and the gift of ecstasy. The latter not infrequently failed him, leaving his verse with only a swooning sweetness, flat and flavorless. But when the ecstasy was upon him he had, as Palgrave put it, 'the exquisite tenderness of touch, the melody and delicacy of his favorite composer, Chopin.' He is a singer or nothing." (William Alexander Percy, in *Poems of Arthur O'Shaughnessy*, pp. 2–3.)

Page 1026. *From* CHAITIVEL

Chaitivel (the wretched one) becomes the accepted lover of Sarrazine long after Pharamond, her first lover, to whom she had vowed her body forever, had been slain in battle. Filled with her new love for Chaitivel and moved by something like pity for Pharamond, she sings this song—

"Singing it idly to the birds
And finding as she went along
Mere wanton music in the words."

Pharamond, though he lay in a grave "beyond so many a sea," bound in meshes of her soft, gold hair, heard, and realizing that she was about to give her body to another, "rose up . . . pale and terrible in blood-stained mail," slew Sarrazine, and dragged her body "inward to his hell forever." Her soul he could not slay and he, the fiend, and Chaitivel, the man, go on fighting each other for its possession

" till some final gloom
Shall end all things and God entomb
Eternity!"

"If I were passing the Siren Isles, one of the songs I know I should hear drifting across the waves would be that which Sarrazine sang to her dead lover in 'Chaitivel':

'Hath any loved you well,' etc.

A hackneyed stanza form, no single unusual or colorful word, indeed an almost complete series of monosyllables, no tangible thought, yet magic—and magic continued for seven stanzas!" (William Alexander Percy, in *Poems of Arthur O'Shaughnessy*, pp. 3–4.)

Page 1027. ODE

1. *We.* The poets.

19–20. *Nineveh . . . Babel.* Nineveh, the splendid capital of the ancient Assyrian Empire, and Babel, the great tower erected in the land of Shinar (Genesis 11), could not have been had not men been dreamers of dreams.

SONG

"Some of his lyrics, such as . . . 'I made another garden,' 'Has summer come without the rose?' may be pronounced flawless. Their tender plaintiveness, imaginative grace, and delightful melody give them an enduring charm. Some of them have a delicate and ominous beauty drawn from sadness, like the first hectic of autumn, which seems to enhance the loveliness of the year while presaging its decay. (*The Athenæum*, Feb. 5, 1881, p. 196.)

COVENTRY PATMORE

BIBLIOGRAPHY

I. WORKS

Selected Poems, ed. by Derek Patmore. (Chatto: London, 1931.) A recommended edition, prepared by the poet's great-grandson; the introduction gives a short biographical sketch and judicious critical hints.

Poems. (Bell: London, 1906.) A convenient one-volume edition, prefaced with a sympathetic memoir by Basil Champneys.

Poetry of Pathos and Delight, ed. by Alice Meynell. (Putnam: New York, 1896.) A brief but inclusive list of selections from the best of Patmore's work in verse.

The Angel in the House; Victories of Love, ed. by Alice Meynell. (Routledge: London, 1905.) The best edition of the final arrangement of Patmore's four love poems; the editor furnishes a brief introduction.

II. BIOGRAPHY AND CRITICISM

Burdett, Osbert. *The Idea of Coventry Patmore.* (Oxford University Press: 1921.) A clear exposition of the poet's concept of married love, making abundant reference to his poetry and prose.

Champneys, Basil. *Memoirs and Correspondence of Coventry Patmore.* 2 vols. (Bell: London, 1900.) The authoritative biography, written from an intimate acquaintance with the poet and his family; of much importance in recommending Patmore to a somewhat estranged public. Includes a second prefatory note by the wife of the poet.

Gosse, E. W. *Coventry Patmore.* (Scribner: New York, 1905.) A penetrating study of the writer and his aims and accomplishments; affords many glimpses of Tennyson and the Pre-Raphaelite circle.

Page, Frederick. *Patmore: A Study in Poetry.* (Oxford University Press: 1933.) A book for special students of Patmore: the author's object is to evaluate *The Angel in the House* and to analyze the metrics of *The Unknown Eros.*

Patmore, Derek. *Portrait of My Family.* (Harper: New York, 1935.) A frank and entertaining study; the biographer attains a remarkable objectivity in his depiction of the inner life of the poet and his family circle.

III. ARTICLES FROM BOOKS AND PERIODICALS

Drinkwater, John. "Browning's Influence: Coventry Patmore," in *Victorian Poetry.* (Doran: New York, 1924.) Remarks the younger poet as the outstanding disciple of Browning; points also to seventeenth-century influences.

Fleming, W. K. "Coventry Patmore," *Life and Letters*, IV, 27–40 (Jan., 1930). Deals largely with the man's religious life, which found frequent expression in his verse; comments on the decay of his reputation as a poet.

Freeman, John. "Coventry Patmore," in *The Moderns.* (Scott: London, 1916.) Analyzes some of the odes of *The Unknown Eros;* values the poet as an interpreter of the world of the spirit.

Freeman, John. "Coventry Patmore," in *English Portraits and Essays.* (Hodder: London, 1924.) Provides judicious comments upon *The Angel in the House* and *The Unknown Eros;* finds Patmore's excellence in his genius for concentration.

Gosse, E. W. "The Laureate of Wedded Love," in *More Books on the Table.* (Scribner: New York, 1923.) A review of Burdett's study; shows how Patmore's ideas were hampered by his unfortunate choice of scene.

Hind, C. L. "Coventry Patmore," in *More Authors and I.* (Dodd: New York, 1922.) Recalls personal contacts with the poet; briefly reviews his publications.

Johnson, L. P. "Coventry Patmore's Genius," in *Post Liminium*, ed. by Thomas Whittemore. (Mathews: London, 1911.) A review of Champneys' *Memoirs;* dwells upon Patmore's unsocial temperament and his high devotion to his art.

Quiller-Couch, A. T. "Coventry Patmore," in *Studies in Literature*, Third Series. (Cambridge University Press: 1933.) Reviews the biographical facts, comments amusingly upon Patmore's theory of love, and finds his last work his best.

Symons, Arthur. "Coventry Patmore," in *Studies in Two Literatures.* (Secker: London, 1924.) Shows the advance of *The Unknown Eros* over *The Angel in the House;* reviews the *Religio Poetæ.*

Symons, Arthur. "Coventry Patmore," in *Figures of Several Centuries.* (Constable: London, 1916.) Prints and reviews a number of Patmore's letters; comments on the Life by Gosse.

NOTES

"The austere figure of Coventry Patmore stands strangely apart from the other poets of the Victorian age. He owed next to nothing to his predecessors, and he has scarcely at all affected the poetry of later days. He stalked in his narrow field, casting hardly more than an indifferent glance at the work of his contemporaries. His poetry has an individuality so deep and so curious that its appeal must always be as dumb to most people as it is intense to a few. He raised a new flower, unique in its bold shape and color, but he contrived to spread round it a desert which effectually deters the casual adventurer. And yet this grim recluse, who appears to stamp so summarily upon any conciliatory overture from the world at large, stands almost alone in literature for the interpretation and the defense of one of the most normal and least recondite elements of human life" [married love, "the only expression of perfect felicity attainable by man"]. (Percy Lubbock, in the *Quarterly Review*, CCVIII, 356.)

Page 1029. WINTER

5. *Trophonian.* Trophonius, probably originally an earth-god, is said to have built the first temple of Apollo at Delphi. All who consulted the oracle of Trophonius returned melancholy and dejected in appearance.

15–6. *substance . . . seen.* "Now faith is the substance of things hoped for, the evidence of things not seen." (Hebrews 11:1.)

18. *shaw.* A thicket, grove.

33. *Jason's fleece.* The Golden Fleece, which was placed in a sacred grove and guarded by a sleepless dragon, was won by Jason with the help of Medea.

Page 1030. THE AZALEA

This poem and the four immediately following it are from *The Unknown Eros*.

Louis Garvin writes in the *Fortnightly Review* (LXI, 216) of "the little group of pathetic poems" by Patmore "that utter so intolerable a sharp note of human pathos." "These," Mr. Garvin says, "may possibly be held the greatest of all . . . Patmore's poems. They are certainly the most perfect. It might conceivably be argued that there is in the poems called mystical a didactic note distasteful to spirits not prepared for the word. It might be said that the mystical odes are not overheard, and that even in *St. Valentine's Day* a sensitive ear may detect the accent of address. It is very different with the little poems in which are articulated griefs that all who live can feel. *Departure, The Azalea, Farewell, The Toys, If I Were Dead*—these utter the most penetrating cry in lyric poetry. All other sorrow seems diffuse, nerveless, trivial beside this sorrow. Compared with their strange quality, that surgery of literal expression, other styles, all styles, the very idea of style, seem artificial. They are intolerable in their simplicity and calm and great reality of utterance—fulfilled with the sense of tears in mortal things. And in these poems the sensation of *overhearing* what is said becomes extraordinarily acute, and the voice of this pain goes shuddering to the quick of pathos. . . .

"*Departure* and *The Azalea* are so brief and in every word so perfect that they cannot be quoted from. The note of mortal pathos is sharpest, perhaps, in *Departure*. In *The Azalea* there is an unearthly subtlety as well as a cruel reality of anguish. It is so small a poem to convey so powerful a vicissitude of emotion; and it ends upon a strange note: 'sadder than sorrow, sweeter than delight.' Recent literature [this was written in 1897] has shown a remarkable movement of sympathy with children, but *If I Were Dead* and *The Toys* are probably worth all else that has been written. These ruthful little pieces go to the root of the matter.

'It is not true that love will do no wrong,
Poor child, poor child.'

The Toys, however, closes with an apologue for all the children of men, which makes the whole poem indescribably characteristic in its play of nameless pathos, sad humor, insight into human nature, the Dantesque faith so untainted by pietism."

DEPARTURE

This poem, a tribute to Patmore's first wife, Emily, is an example of the supreme quality that occasionally came into his work. Percy Lubbock wrote of it: " . . . Tragedy is at first bewilderment, hardly more than a sense of disquiet. It is this moment which is seized with such wonderful insight in the poem 'Departure,' a picture of grief which does not yet perceive that it is grief."

Page 1031. THE TOYS

See note to *The Azalea*, above, and to Bridges' *Pater Filio*, above.

6. *Mother . . . dead.* Mrs. Patmore died in 1862, leaving to Patmore the care of the six children of the family. "The constant strain of responsibility for these young motherless creatures," wrote Edmund Gosse, "was very trying to his nerves."

MAGNA EST VERITAS

9. *The truth is great.* This is a translation of the Latin title.

"IF I WERE DEAD"

See note to *The Azalea*, above.

Page 1032. REGINA COELI

The title means, "Queen of Heaven."

CHRISTINA ROSSETTI

BIBLIOGRAPHY

I. WORKS

Poetical Works, ed. by W. M. Rossetti. (Macmillan: London, 1924.) The authoritative edition, combining the seven previously published volumes, beside 12 hitherto unpublished pieces; contains a memoir, together with full annotations, etc.

Poems, ed. by Alice Meynell. (Blackie: London, 1923.) A recommended edition, valuable for the excellent introduction, supplied by the editor.

Selected Poems, ed. by C. B. Burke. (Macmillan: New York, 1913.) The best book of selections, well equipped with notes and an introduction.

Goblin Market. (Lippincott: Philadelphia, 1933.) One of the most interesting of many special editions of the poem—illustrated by Arthur Rackham.

Family Letters, ed. by W. M. Rossetti. (Scribner: New York, 1908.) Provides a world of personal information, clarified by the editorship of the poet's brother.

II. BIOGRAPHY AND CRITICISM

Bell, Mackenzie. *Christina Rossetti, a Biographical and Critical Study*. (Roberts: Boston, 1898.) The standard Life, by an intimate friend of the Rossetti family: still the accepted source book for the facts of the poet's life. Bibliography by J. P. Anderson.

Birkhead, Edith. *Christina Rossetti and Her Poetry*. (Harrap: London, 1930.) Combines a review of the poet's life with criticism of her work, of which much is quoted; sees her refusal of Cayley as arising from a fear of violating a romantic ideal.

Cary, Elisabeth L. *The Rossettis*. (Putnam: New York, 1907.) The last two chapters are devoted to somewhat unsympathetic criticism of Christina; finds much of her best work in her sonnets.

Sandars, Mary F. *The Life of Christina Rossetti*. (Hutchinson: London, 1930.) The most recent full biography, finely illustrated; replete with personal details, it is also valuable for its insight into the creative mind of the poet and for its interpretations of her poetry.

Shove, Fredegond. *Christina Rossetti: A Study*. (Cambridge University Press: 1931.) Though this study "in no way pretends to be a Life" of the poet, it points out the foundation of her poetic impulse: love for living things; provides also an adequate discussion of her prose.

Stuart, Dorothy M. *Christina Rossetti*. (Oxford University Press: 1931.) An able short biography, defining without demeaning the poet's subtle magic; sees her as ostensibly aloof from contemporary movements, but influenced by many past and present writers.

Thomas, Eleanor W. *Christina Georgina Rossetti*. (Columbia University Press: 1931.) The biographical section emphasizes the religious element in the life of the poet; the criticism discusses her love for allegory and her otherworldliness.

Waller, R. D. *The Rossetti Family, 1824–1854*. (Manchester University Press: 1932.) This study is concerned with Gabriele Rossetti and his talented children; concludes with the death of the father, when Christina was 23; she seems to occupy the center of the writer's interest in the children.

III. ARTICLES FROM BOOKS

Bald, Marjorie A. "Christina Rossetti," in *Women Writers of the Nineteenth Century*. (Cambridge University Press: 1923.) Finds the basis for the poet's poignant intensity in the two facts of her experience: death and renunciation; discusses her symbolism and the irregularity of her habits of composition.

Gosse, E. W. "Christina Rossetti," in *Critical Kit-Kats*. (Scribner: New York, 1914.) Calls attention to the contributions to *The Germ;* suggests the influence of the poet on the metric of Swinburne. Remarks the English color of the poet's work, which unites the ideals of physical beauty and religion.

More, P. E. "Christina Rossetti," in *Shelburne Essays*, Third Series. (Putnam: New York, 1905.) A lukewarm review of the 1904 collection; comments on its spirit of passivity and otherworldliness.

Woolf, Virginia. "I Am Christina Rossetti," in *The Second Common Reader*. (Harcourt: New York, 1932.) An exalted review of Miss Sandars' Life, pointing out its success in reviewing the life of the author of *Goblin Market*.

IV. ARTICLES FROM PERIODICALS

Evans, B. I. "The Sources of Christina Rossetti's *Goblin Market*," *Modern Language Review*, XXVIII, 156–65 (Apr., 1933). Finds a possible source in Keightley's *The Fairy Mythology* (which Christina read as a child) and Allingham's *The Fairies*, together with recollections from *The Arabian Nights* and Shakespeare.

Greene, Kathleen C. "Christina Georgina Rossetti," *Cornhill Magazine*, LXIX, 662–70 (Dec., 1930). A sedate and satisfactory review of the poet's life and work; points out Dante's predominant influence.

Hueffer, F. M. "The Character of Christina Rossetti," *Fortnightly Review*, XCV, 422–9 (Mar., 1911). Discusses the poet as an introspective modern, who felt little literary connection with the past.

Kent, Muriel. "Christina Rossetti: A Reconsideration," *Contemporary Review*, CXXXVIII, 759–67 (Dec., 1930). Compares the poet with Swinburne; comments on her wide range of interests and her information on out-of-the-way subjects; foresees a rise in her future reputation.

Lowther, George. "Christina Rossetti," *Contem-*

porary Review, CIV, 681–9 (Nov., 1913). Reviews a number of the poet's lyrics, naming her "the saint among the poets."

Mather, F. J., Jr. "The Rossettis," *Bookman*, XLIX, 139–47 (Apr., 1919). Describes the family as Holman Hunt knew them in 1848; reviews details in the lives and works of Christina and her brothers.

Sharp, William. "Some Reminiscences of Christina Rossetti," *Atlantic Monthly*, LXXV, 736–49 (June, 1895). Recalls many *personalia*, quoting letters and conversations of the poet; comments on her recent illness and death.

Watts-Dunton, Theodore. "Reminiscences of Christina Rossetti," *Nineteenth Century*, XXXVII, 355–66 (Feb., 1895). Relates the story of many visits at the Rossetti home, providing a wealth of interesting anecdotal information.

Waugh, Arthur. "Christina Rossetti," *Nineteenth Century*, CVIII, 787–98 (Dec., 1930). Reviews the biographical data; points out the reconciliation of the poet's delight in the world of sense with her religious spirit; bases her fame on her sincerity and clearness of vision.

NOTES

"Her customary music is sad, often poignantly sad. Her lyrics have that *desiderium*, that obstinate longing for something lost out of life, which Shelley's have, although her Christian faith gives her regret a more resigned and sedate character than his possesses. In the extremely rare gift of song-writing Miss Rossetti has been singularly successful. Of the poets of our time she stands next to Lord Tennyson in this branch of the art, in the spontaneous and complete quality of her *Lieder*, and in her propriety for the purpose of being sung. . . . Her music is very delicate, and it is no small praise to her that she it is who, of living verse-writers, has left the strongest mark on the metrical nature of that miraculous artificer of verse, Mr. Swinburne. In his 'Poems and Ballads,' as other critics have long ago pointed out, as was shown when that volume first appeared, several of Miss Rossetti's discoveries were transferred to his more scientific and elaborate system of harmonies, and adapted to more brilliant effects. . . . From the first a large section of Miss Rossetti's work has been occupied with sacred and devotional themes. Through this most rare and difficult department of the art, which so few essay without breaking on the Scylla of doctrine on the one hand, or being whirled in the Charybdis of commonplace dullness on the other, she has steered with extraordinary success. Her sacred poems are truly sacred, and yet not unpoetical. As a religious poet of our time she has no rival but Cardinal Newman, and it could only be schismatic prejudice or absence of critical faculty which should deny her a place, as a poet, higher than that of our exquisite master of prose. To find her exact parallel it is at once her strength and her snare that we must go back to the middle of the seventeenth century. She is the sister of George Herbert; she is of the family of Crashaw, of Vaughan, of Wither." (Edmund Gosse, *Christina Rossetti*, *Century Magazine*, XLVI, 216–7.)

Page 1033. SONG (WHEN I AM DEAD, MY DEAREST)

W. M. Rossetti, Christina's editor, says this poem probably has been oftener quoted and set to music than any other lyric by her.

Page 1035. A PORTRAIT

The second of these two sonnets was written for the death of Lady Isabella Howard, the first was originally entitled *Saint Elizabeth of Hungary*. In combining the two under the present title the poet apparently intended to dedicate both to Lady Isabella.

Page 1038. IN AN ARTIST'S STUDIO

The reference is to Dante Gabriel Rossetti and Elizabeth Siddal.

Page 1039. A BIRTHDAY

A parody of this poem so much amused Christina that she pasted it into her copy of her *Poems* (1875). The parody reads:

An Unexpected Pleasure

(After Christina G. Rossetti)

My heart is like one asked to dine
  Whose evening dress is up the spout;
My heart is like a man would be
  Whose raging tooth is half pulled out.
My heart is like a howling swell
  Who boggles on his upper C;
My heart is madder than all these—
  My wife's mamma has come to tea.

Raise me a bump upon my crown,
  Bang it till green in purple dies;
Feed me on bombs and fulminates,
  And turncocks of a medium size.
Work me a suit in crimson apes
  And sky-blue beetles on the spree;
Because the mother of my wife
  Has come—and means to stay with me.

ADVENT

Advent is a period of the church year including the four Sundays before Christmas.

Part of this poem was set to music and sung for Christina's funeral service.

Page 1040. GOBLIN MARKET

Mackenzie Bell in his biography of Christina Rossetti (pp. 206–7) quotes from an essay by J. A. Noble which says that *Goblin Market* may be "read and enjoyed merely as a charming fairy-fantasy, and as such it is delightful and satisfying; but behind the simple story of the two children and the goblin fruit-sellers is a little spiritual drama of love's vicarious redemption, in which the child redeemer goes into the wilderness to be tempted of the devil, that by her painful conquest she may succour and save the sister who has been vanquished and all but slain. The luscious juices of the goblin fruit, sweet and deadly when sucked by selfish greed, become bitter and medicinal when spilt in unselfish conflict."

Bell doubts that Christina had any such didactic intention, but the interpretation is there for those who want it.

The poem was originally called *A Peep at the Goblins—To M. F. R.*, M. F. R. being Maria Francesca Rossetti, Christina's sister. The poem then had some obscure connection in the author's mind with her sister. W. M. Rossetti, a brother, wrote to Bell concerning this poem, "I don't remember that there were at that time any personal circumstances of a marked kind: but I certainly think (with you) that the lines at the close, 'There is nothing like a sister,' etc. (l. 562), indicate *something:* apparently C(hristina) considered herself to be chargeable with some sort of spiritual backsliding against which Maria's influence had been exercised beneficially. I have more than once heard C(hristina) aver that the poem has not any profound or ulterior meaning—it is just a fairy story: yet one can discern that it implies at any rate this much—That to succumb to a temptation makes one a victim to that same continuous temptation; that the remedy does not always lie with oneself; and that a stronger and more righteous will may prove of avail to restore one's lost estate."

Page 1047. AMOR MUNDI

"... I take it that both her personages are female: one of them a woman, the other the World in feminine shape. The first speaker is the woman, who inquires of the World who is figured with 'love-locks,' and as 'dear to doat on,' and who is afterwards pronounced 'false and fleetest.' The reader can take or reject this opinion as he likes, for I do not remember ever hearing the point settled by Christina. In her arrangement of her poems when collected, she put *Up-hill* next after *Amor Mundi;* a significant juxtaposition, done no doubt with intention. . . ." (W. M. Rossetti's note.)

ITALIA IO TI SALUTO

The title means, "Italy, I salute you."

Page 1048. "TO-DAY FOR ME"

The defeats of France in the Franco-Prussian war of 1870 occasioned this poem.

TREAD SOFTLY

This is the tenth sonnet of a sequence, *Later Life: A Double Sonnet of Sonnets*, there being twenty-eight poems in the sequence, which explains the expression "double sonnet" in the sub-title—twice the fourteen lines of the form. The theme of the sequence is religious, with frequent reference to Christian love.

Page 1050. O MY HEART'S HEART

This is the fifth sonnet of the sequence of fourteen called *Monna Innominata* ("The Unnamed Lady"). Christina added a prose foreword saying that before Dante sang his Beatrice and Petrarch his Laura there must have been many unnamed ladies sung by less conspicuous poets. "Had such a lady spoken for herself, the portrait left us might have appeared more tender, if less dignified, than any drawn even by a devoted friend." In the *Monna Innominata* series the lady speaks for herself. Christina's brother considered the prose foreword a "blind" to draw off attention from the intensely personal quality of the sonnets.

SLEEPING AT LAST

Her brother believes this to be the very last poem Christina ever wrote—a fitting conclusion.

WILLIAM SHARP

BIBLIOGRAPHY

I. WORKS

Writings of Fiona Macleod. 7 vols. (Duffield: New York, 1909–10.) The first collection, prepared by the author's wife according to instructions given before his death; Vol. VII contains the poems and dramas.

Selected Writings, ed. by Mrs. William Sharp. 4 vols. (Duffield: New York, 1912.) The authoritative edition of the choice poetry and prose.

Songs and Poems, Old and New. (Stock: London, 1909.) The recommended comprehensive edition, containing the substance of five volumes published 1879–1905, together with much magazine verse.

Flower o' the Vine. (Webster: New York, 1892.) Prefaced by a critical sketch by the poet's friend, T. A. Janvier; in addition to the *Romantic Ballads* and *Sospiri di Roma*, contains also the *Poems of Phantasy*.

II. BIOGRAPHY AND CRITICISM

Gilman, Lawrence. "The Art of Fiona Macleod," *North American Review*, CLXXXIII, 674–6 (Oct., 1906). Shows the variety and depth of the Fiona literature, in which the Celtic spirit is expressed in a new and intense beauty.

Goddard, Ethel. "'The Winged Destiny' and Fiona Macleod," *Fortnightly Review*, LXXXII, 1037–44 (Dec., 1904). An enthusiastic review of the new Fiona volume, which with others of its kind should win for the author the title "the Celtic William Morris."

Janvier, Catharine. "Fiona Macleod and Her Creator, William Sharp," *North American Review*, CLXXXIV, 718–32 (Apr., 1907). Prints some correspondence between the writer and William Sharp, together with records of other *personalia*, showing the care which Sharp took in preserving the secret of his dual personality.

King, Georgiana G. "Fiona Macleod," *Modern Language Notes*, XXXIII, 352–6 (June, 1918). An attempt to define the tenuous Celtic folklore behind the writings of the shadowy Fiona Macleod.

Le Gallienne, Richard. "The Mystery of Fiona Macleod," *Forum*, XLV, 170–9 (Feb., 1911). Recalls the flurry caused by the writer's penetration of the secret of the dual authors; finds the "mystery" in the persistent mediocrity of the work done under the name of William Sharp.

Rhys, Ernest. "William Sharp and Fiona Macleod," *Century Magazine*, LXXIV, 111–17 (May, 1907). A reminiscence, written upon the occasion of Sharp's death, of a long acquaintance with him; names Fiona Macleod the "greatest of his illusions."

Sharp, Elizabeth A. *William Sharp* (*Fiona Macleod.*) 2 vols. (Heinemann: London, 1910.) The authoritative biography, compiled by the writer's wife; makes much of the mystery of his dual personality, quotes from his diary and from numerous letters.

NOTES

"The 'Fiona' literature . . . ranges easily through the domain of pure fantasy, of fable and allegory, of speculation, of æsthetic discussion, of symbolized fiction, and of verse. The voice has spoken many tongues, but always the accent of the mystic has persisted, has persisted and increased in poignancy and aloofness; so that in her later work it is frankly, and without the palliation of pictorial or symbolical setting, the speech and vision of the dreaming mind that is offered us. One will miss the essential note of this writing if one fails to see in it, as its prime possession, the confessions and aspirations of a spirit swayed, beyond any other impulse, by a passionate consciousness and a special revelation of all beauty. Beyond any other writer whom one may allege for the comparison, this writer has chosen to saturate her work in beauty. The sense of it is, for her, a perpetual touchstone—a touchstone for the apperception of sheer natural presences, of dream and vision and intimation, of that miraculous and supra sensuous world in which the spirit of the essential mystic has its intensest life." (Lawrence Gilman, in the *North American Review*, CLXXXIII, 674.)

"'Fiona Macleod' was the greatest of his own creations in fiction. She had never any existence whatever except in his brain, and yet she was a living, real personality with all the charm of the most delicate and sympathetic womanhood. . . . He felt his Celtic poetry intensely; he took enormous pains about it. . . . He had an idea—perhaps a fanciful one—that he had enemies in the press, and that to give his Celtic muse the best chance she should be wholly dissociated from his name. In this way 'Fiona' came into the world. . . . She soon ceased to be a mere pseudonym. He gradually perfected his own conception until she became a thing of perfect womanhood, and . . . the greatest of his characters." (Richard Whiteing, in the London *Sphere:* quoted in *Current Literature*, XL, 151.)

Page 1051. THE MOON-CHILD

In his dedication to W. B. Yeats of *Foam of the Past*, from which this poem is taken, Sharp said: "Perhaps, if you have not seen, or heard, my little Moon-Child, you remember her from long ago, and her loneliness when she sang

'I have no playmate but the tide.'

For all poetry is in a sense memory: all art, indeed, is a mnemonic gathering of the innumerable and lost into the found and unique."

Page 1052. THE VISION

B. Ifor Evans, who is displeased by the presence of what he calls "a small cohort of romantically colored adjectives and nouns" in many of the poems both of William Sharp and of Fiona Macleod, says that Sharp "had a poetic quality which appeared most clearly when his verbal fluency could be restrained." This quality, he believes, is found even more consistently in the earlier poems than in those of the Fiona period. He characterizes *The Vision* as one of the "short-line lyrics of the Fiona period" which shows high poetic quality. (The student should note that all the poems included in the text belong to the Fiona period.)

DEIRDRÊ IS DEAD

Deirdrê, sometimes called the Irish Helen, was the daughter of Fedlimid, harper to King Conchobar of Ulster. So beautiful was she that it had been prophesied that her beauty would bring banishment and death to heroes. Conchobar, intending her for his wife, had her brought up in solitude. By accident she met and fell in love with Naoise, the son of Usnach, who with his two brothers, Ardan and Ainnle, carried her away to Scotland. Conchobar lured them back and treacherously beheaded them, and Deirdrê took her own life.

The House of Usna, from which the motto of the poem is taken, is a play of Sharp's written in 1900.

21. *Brigid.* Brigit, the Vesta, or Minerva, of the heathen Irish, goddess of fire and fertility and of poetic inspiration.

ROBERT LOUIS STEVENSON

BIBLIOGRAPHY

I. WORKS

Complete Poems. (Scribner: New York, 1905.) The recommended edition of the poetry, containing prefaces by Stevenson's wife; includes also music for several of the lyrics.

Complete Poetical Works. (Heinemann: London, 1924.) Vol. XX of the complete Skerryvore Edition; contains notes by Lloyd Osbourne and Mrs. Stevenson.

Poems, ed. by Ernest Rhys. (Dutton: New York, 1925.) A good inexpensive collection, including *A Child's Garden of Verses, Underwoods, Songs of Travel,* and *Ballads.*

Poems, ed. by W. P. Trent. (Crowell: New York, 1900.) Preserves the arrangement of the four singly published volumes; the introduction is a restrained tribute to Stevenson's skill in verse.

Poems. (Chatto: London, 1922.) A convenient one-volume selection, including *Underwoods, Ballads,* and *Songs of Travel,* together with some prefatory notes by Stevenson.

Poems, Hitherto Unpublished. (Bibliophile Society: Boston, 1921.) A privately printed, limited edition, furnished with notes by G. S. Hellman and W. P. Trent; noteworthy for its facsimile reproductions.

Letters, ed. by Sidney Colvin. 5 vols. (Heinemann: London, 1924.) The editor corrects some scribal errors and provides full notes and an introduction.

Vailima Letters. (Nelson: London, 1928.) A desirable separate reprint of this correspondence, all of which was contained in the item listed above.

II. BIOGRAPHY AND CRITICISM

Baildon, H. B. *Robert Louis Stevenson.* (Chatto: London, 1901.) Making no pretense to be a full Life, this study is an outgrowth of a long personal acquaintance; much of the material had appeared in *Englische Studien.*

Balfour, Graham. *The Life of Robert Louis Stevenson.* (Scribner: New York, 1915.) The authoritative Life, by Stevenson's cousin; written from the conviction that "all biography would be autobiography if it could" and therefore replete with references made by Stevenson to his life and work.

Chesterton, G. K. *Robert Louis Stevenson.* (Dodd: New York, 1927.) An analysis of the development of the writer's personality and the changes of his views on art and life; the facts in Stevenson's life are skillfully marshalled to support the design of the book.

Dark, Sidney. *Robert Louis Stevenson.* (Hodder: London, 1931.) Shows the background of Stevenson's life and work to lie in his Scotch Presbyterian training, which is taken partly to account for his Victorian popularity.

Japp, A. H. *Robert Louis Stevenson.* (Laurie: London, 1905.) On the whole, a sound, enthusiastic summary of the writer's work and the spirit behind it; the first book to print many Stevenson letters and other significant contemporary documents.

Lockett, W. G. *Robert Louis Stevenson at Davos.* (Hurst: London, 1934.) The author, for many years British consul at Davos, describes Stevenson's two-year recuperation period at the Swiss resort, commenting on his literary associations there, particularly with J. A. Symonds and Horatio Brown.

Masson, Rosaline O. *The Life of Robert Louis Stevenson.* (Chambers: Edinburgh, 1924.) A biography Boswellian in its exactness, containing many letters hitherto unpublished; shows Stevenson in the role of an overcomer of obstacles; offers little literary criticism.

Masson, Rosaline O., ed. *I Can Remember Robert Louis Stevenson.* (Chambers: Edinburgh, 1925.) A collection of about 100 personal reminiscences of friends and school comrades; especially interesting are those of Gosse, Colvin, Barrie, and Archer.

Osbourne, Lloyd. *An Intimate Portrait of R. L. S.* (Scribner: New York, 1924.) A record of personal association, told by Stevenson's stepson, describing their travels, residences abroad, their collaboration, etc.

Steuart, J. A. *Robert Louis Stevenson: A Critical Biography.* (Low: London, 1926.) A fresh reappraisal of the writer and an attempt to analyze the temperament and ideals of the man, who is represented as erratic, capricious, and vagrant, in spite of the studied excellence of his work.

Swinnerton, Frank. *R. L. Stevenson, A Critical Study.* (Doran: New York, 1923.) A somewhat stringent study of Stevenson's work, particularly his poetry; denies him a place among great English writers.

III. ARTICLES FROM BOOKS

Freeman, John. "Robert Louis Stevenson," in *English Portraits and Essays.* (Hodder: London, 1924.) Concerned chiefly with the prose-writer: discusses his theories of art and his use of the materials of life; the final section remarks the infrequency of beauty in his verse.

Garrod, H. W. "The Poetry of R. L. Stevenson," in *The Profession of Poetry.* (Oxford University Press: 1929.) Discounts heavily the encyclopedic Boston Bibliophile publication of Stevenson's poetry; selects as best the *Songs of Travel;* pleads for a fifty-poem anthology.

Gosse, E. W. "Mr. Robert Louis Stevenson as a Poet," in *Questions at Issue.* (Heinemann: London, 1893.) Praises the *Child's Garden* and *Underwoods;* ventures that they will live as long as Stevenson's best novels.

Gosse, E. W. "Robert Louis Stevenson," in *Critical Kit-Kats.* (Scribner: New York, 1914.) A series of chatty reminiscences; the writings reviewed are only those which Gosse heard planned or discussed by the author and his friends.

Johnson, L. P. "R. L. Stevenson," in *Post Liminium*, ed. by Thomas Whittemore. (Mathews: London, 1911.) A discussion of Stevenson as the "wandering Scot," reminding us of the notable effect of foreign travel upon his prose and poetry.

Lang, Andrew. "Recollections of Robert Louis Stevenson," in *Adventures among Books*. (Longmans: London, 1905.) A series of picturesque views of Stevenson as man and writer, presented with enthusiasm and respect for his ability to attract varied types of readers.

Noyes, Alfred. "Stevenson," in *Some Aspects of Modern Poetry*. (Stokes: New York, 1924.) Discusses the enduring reputation of the poet; shows the relationship between his theories of art and his productions.

IV. ARTICLES FROM PERIODICALS

Benson, E. F. "The Myth of Robert Louis Stevenson," *London Mercury*, XII, 268–83, 372–84 (July, Aug., 1925). Delicately exposes the egotistical weakness of the man; remarks his oversedulousness as a writer and his lack of clearness in his critical pronouncements.

Burriss, E. E. "Classical Culture of Robert Louis Stevenson," *Classical Journal*, XX, 271–9 (Feb., 1925). Admitting Stevenson's lack of academic interest, points out the influence of many classical writers, notably Vergil, Martial, Horace, Cicero, Tacitus, and others.

Clarke, W. E. "Robert Louis Stevenson in Samoa," *Yale Review*, X, 275–96 (Jan., 1921). A recollection of a visit to Samoa, describing Stevenson's hospitality, his habits of work, and his interest in native government.

Colvin, Sidney. "Some Personal Recollections of Stevenson," *Scribner's Magazine*, LXVII, 338–54 (Mar., 1920). A rare and useful human document, beginning with Stevenson at 23 and carrying to his departure from Great Britain in 1887.

Jessop, Alexander. "The Poetry of Stevenson," *Poet Lore*, XVIII, 396–401 (Sept., 1907). Shows the strong impressionistic note in Stevenson's poetry, with the appeal immediate and direct — "the intimate poetry of personal relations."

Masson, Flora. "Scottish Homes and Haunts of Robert Louis Stevenson," *Living Age*, CCLXX, 72–80 (July 8, 1911). A description of Stevenson's associations with the houses in which he lived in and near Edinburgh: the town-house in Heriot Row, the Manse in Colinton Dell, and the cottage in the Pentland Hills.

Millard, Bailey. "Some Rare Glimpses of Stevenson," *Bookman*, XXVIII, 442–9 (Jan., 1909). Recommended for four unusual photographs, illustrating (as does the main part of the article) Stevenson's Samoa days.

NOTES

"... Nearly all [of Stevenson's poetry is] good reading and more interesting than a good deal of poetry with a higher reputation. Some of his blank verse pieces are a little dull ... and only a Scotchman can read the Scotch poems with perfect ease; but the rest, when once you have begun them, lead you on to the end just like his stories and his essays....

"... Verse-making was not Stevenson's peculiar craft; and therefore he could but seldom put all the weight of his thought and all the strength of his emotion into it; but he was not content either to prose in his verses, or to leave them rough, like some prose writers such as Emerson." (From the *London Times:* quoted in the *Living Age*, CCLIII, 245.)

Of *A Child's Garden of Verses*, from which the first eleven poems in the text were taken, E. C. Stedman wrote: "Now, as a minor but genuine example of poetic art, not alone for art's sake, but for dear nature's sake—in the light of whose maternal smile all art must thrive and blossom if at all,—take *A Child's Garden of Verses*. ... This is a real addition to the lore for children, and to that for man, to whom the child is father. The flowers of this little garden spring from the surplusage of a genius that creates nothing void of charm and originality. Thanks, then, for the fresh, pure touch, for the revelation of childhood with its vision of the lands of Nod and Counterpane, and of those next-door Foreign Lands spied from cherry-tree top, and beyond the trellised wall." (*Victorian Poets*, p. 468.)

Louis Untermeyer, who speaks of the *Garden* as a poetry-book "which is equally at home in the nursery and the library," believes that it is second only to *Mother Goose* "in its simplicity and universal appeal." (*Modern British Poetry*, p. 189.)

Page 1056. ESCAPE AT BEDTIME

9. *Dog ... Hunter*. Constellations.
10. *star of the sailor*. The North Star.

Page 1057. GOOD AND BAD CHILDREN

18. *gabies*. Dunces, simpletons.

Page 1058. IN THE STATES

In the autumn of 1879 Stevenson made his first voyage to America—a hurried one prompted by the illness of Mrs. Osbourne, whom he married in 1880. On this visit he spent most of his time at San Francisco and Monterey.

A CAMP

5. *ass*. This was Modestine, the mouse-colored "diminutive she-ass," of "kindly eye and determined under-jaw," the donkey of the famous *Travels*.
6. *caravanserai*. An inn. The word carries the idea of a resting place for caravans.

SKERRYVORE

In 1884–87 Stevenson lived at "Skerryvore," 61 Alum Chine Road, Bournemouth, a fashionable watering-place in Hampshire, England. He named the house Skerryvore after the famous lighthouse built by his uncle, Alan Stevenson, on the dangerous rock Skerryvore, fourteen miles southwest of the island of Tiree of the Inner Hebrides.

4. *star.* Lighthouse.

SKERRYVORE: THE PARALLEL

8. *dowelled.* Fastened with dowels, or pins, that fit into holes.

tower. A lighthouse. Skerryvore tower is the finest example for mass combined with elegance of outline of any extant rock tower. On its lone rock fourteen miles from any land, its great body of 4300 tons of granite has stood unshaken since 1844.

MY HOUSE

3. *gyre.* Fly in curved flight.

THE VAGABOND

Schubert (1797–1828) was an Austrian composer.

2. *lave.* The rest.

Page 1060. THE UNFORGOTTEN—II

It is a common remark that Stevenson's poetry "lacks some of the enticing aspects of his prose writings." Now and then, however, critics find in his work a poem with qualities which no prose expression could surpass or, indeed, equal. Such a poem is *The Unforgotten*, whose impressive first stanza unites a lyric spontaneity and grave simplicity to match Wordworth's

She dwelt among the untrodden ways,
Beside the springs of Dove,
A maid whom there were none to praise
And very few to love.

DITTY

Bach. Johann Sebastian Bach (1685–1750), famous German composer and musician.

TO DOCTOR HAKE

Thomas Gordon Hake (1809–95) was a physician and poet. Stevenson sent the poem to Hake from New York in September, 1887, inclosed in a letter to W. E. Henley.

Page 1062. TO THE MUSE

Apemama, the place named at the end of the poem, is one of the Gilbert Islands—in the Pacific on the equator—which Stevenson visited when he was a traveler in the South Seas, 1888–90.

18. *sans.* Without.

AN END OF TRAVEL

Vailima, which means "Five Rivers," was Stevenson's 400-acre estate on Upolu Island, Samoa. Here he spent the last four years of his life.

ARTHUR SYMONS

BIBLIOGRAPHY

I. EDITIONS

Collected Works. 9 vols. (Secker: London, 1924.) The first comprehensive collection, containing the poetry in vols. I, II, and III; preserves the prefaces of the original separate volumes.

Poems. 2 vols. (Heinemann: London, 1902.) A reprint (with minor changes) of selections from *Days and Nights*, *Silhouettes*, *London Nights*, *Amoris Victima*, and *Images of Good and Evil;* the selections from the last two volumes are reproduced with practically no alterations.

Tragedies. (Lane: New York, 1916.) Contains the text of *The Harvesters*, *The Death of Agrippina*, and *Cleopatra in Judaea.*

II. BIOGRAPHY AND CRITICISM

Murdock, W. G. B. *The Work of Arthur Symons.* (Gray: Edinburgh, 1907.) An earnest attempt to enlarge the circle of Symons's readers in England; as a poet he is praised as a faultless technician of great fecundity and delicacy of expression, and as a sincere humanitarian.

Welby, T. E. *Arthur Symons, A Critical Study.* (Philpot: London, 1925.) A thorough critical study of Symons's prose and poetry, showing the influence of French æsthetic theory upon his work.

III. ARTICLES FROM BOOKS AND PERIODICALS

Archer, William. "Arthur Symons," in *Poets of the Younger Generation.* (Lane: New York, 1902.) Points out in the poet's work the influence of Browning and Verlaine; inclines to lament his introspective self-criticism; sets highest the *Amoris Victima.*

Gribble, Francis. "The Pose of Mr. Arthur Symons," *Fortnightly Review*, XC, 127–36 (July, 1908). An unfriendly review of Symons's relation with the public; the wide range of his critical viewpoints seems to indicate a dissipation rather than a useful exercise of his abilities.

More, P. E. "Arthur Symons," in *Shelburne Essays*, First Series. (Putman: New York, 1909.) Notes the change in the poet from his early illusions to realism, ending in pessimism, which represents the "first full and sincere expression of decadence in English."

Urban, W. M. "Arthur Symons and Impressionism," *Atlantic Monthly*, CXIV, 384–93 (Sept., 1914). A thoughtful review of Symons's aesthetic principles; concludes that his most characteristic poetry is an expression of his "spiritual avarice."

Waugh, Arthur. "The Tragedies of Mr. Arthur Symons," in *Tradition and Change.* (Dutton: New York, 1919.) A laudatory review of *Cleopatra in Judaea, The Death of Agrippina,* and *The Harvesters,* the last being read as the masterpiece among the entire work of the poet and dramatist.

NOTES

Arthur Symons is that peculiar type—an æsthete not afraid of but rather seeking reality, within, however, certain circumscribed intellectual limits. He does not intend to let "realism" impose upon him and disturb his comfort, æsthetic or physical. So far as it can supply him with a selected "sensation," he is responsive to the real world, is an acute recorder of physical fact from whom those who write realistic prose might well take lessons. Nevertheless his approach is primarily æsthetic. As one critic says, "his *metier* [is] the abstraction of beauty from life. He is always conscious of himself as an instrument of sensation" (W. M. Urban, *Atlantic Monthly,* CXIV, 384). But beyond the recording of fact or "sensation," Symons enjoys the mood induced by the fact, and still beyond the mood is Symons the æsthete to enjoy the total effect—rather aloof from the real world in which the effect started. The contradiction between realist and æsthete is reconciled in that gradual distillation. Symons inherits the Walter Pater doctrine that sensation is important in and for itself, but he inherits it at a time when continental "realism" is pressing upon the English literati and is therefore obliged, being aloof of mind, to approach his sensations warily, like a cat dainty of paw but with bristles aquiver.

Page 1063. RAIN ON THE DOWN

A down is a tract of open upland. An Englishman speaking of "the Downs" is usually referring to the chalk uplands along the south coast of England.

Page 1064. AN ANGEL OF PERUGINO

Pietro Perugino (1446–1524), Italian painter, was the teacher of Raphael. His canvases are marked by a tranquillity of temper—the figures, broad of brow and serene of eye and bathed in a soft clear light, gaze out at one sweetly and simply.

12. *Umbrian halo.* The Umbrian school of painting was named from the province of Umbria whence its leaders came.

EMMY

8. *Boccaccio's book. The Decameron* (which Giovanni Boccaccio completed about 1353) has the reputation of being a storehouse of lively tales.

Page 1065. AT BURGOS

Burgos Cathedral (located in the city of that name, the capital of old Castile) is one of the great Spanish gothic cathedrals. It was built of white limestone ("silver-work in stone").

9. *Ascension Day.* Fortieth day after Easter and one of the great Christian festival days, the celebration of Christ's Ascension to heaven.

HALLUCINATION: I

2. *pages of a Baudelaire.* Charles Baudelaire published in 1857 his *Les Fleurs du Mal* (*The Flowers of Evil*), a volume of magnificently wrought poetry which was, however,—because of the nature of its subjects and approach—more acclaimed by the artistically minded than by the bourgeoisie.

VENETA MARINA

The title means, "The Harbor of Venice."

Page 1066. WHITE MAGIC

In popular usage the word "magic" is identified with "black magic"—the employment of super-physical powers to cause evil and unhappiness. The reverse of this—the causing of good and happiness—would be "white magic."

A PRAYER TO SAINT ANTHONY OF PADUA

St. Anthony of Padua (1195–1231), called in his own day "Malleus Hereticorum" ("The Hammer of the Heretics") because of his fierce onslaughts on false doctrine, is especially to be invoked "for the recovery of things lost." There is a delicate irony in Symons's appeal to this severe Franciscan saint for assistance in recovering the heart of his lost mistress. Heretics are "lost," and upon whom would it be more appropriate to call than St. Anthony, "The Hammer of the Heretics"?

THE OBSCURE NIGHT OF THE SOUL

The poem is a translation from San Juan de La Cruz (1542–1591), a Spanish priest of great piety, who founded the order of the barefoot Carmelites in Spain. He also wrote mystical poetry. The love expressed in the poem, although phrased in terms of romantic love, is the love of the seeker struggling through the dark of the world and finally reaching Christ.

Page 1067. SEA-WIND

The poem is a translation of Stéphane Mallarmé's *Brise Marine.* Mallarmé (1842–1898) was one of the leaders of the French *Sym-*

boliste school of poetry whose theories Symons helped to introduce in the nineties to a poetic group in England which was receptive toward a purely æsthetic attitude (as opposed to the worshippers of action, such as Kipling). Yeats in his *Autobiography* reports that Symons "fresh from Paris" attended the Rhymer's Club, and talked of Impressionism.

Page 1068. BY THE POOL AT THE THIRD ROSSES

Symons printed this as the second of a group of five poems under the general heading, "In Ireland."

FRANCIS THOMPSON

BIBLIOGRAPHY

I. WORKS

Works, ed. by Wilfrid Meynell. 3 vols. (Scribner: New York, 1913.) The definitive edition; Volumes I and II contain the poetry.

Collected Poetry. (Hodder: London, 1924.) A recommended edition, arranging the poems in the order of their publication.

Complete Poetical Works. (Boni: New York, 1919.) A convenient reprint from the 1913 Meynell edition, containing a preface by Wilfrid Meynell.

Poems, ed. by T. L. Connolly. (Century: New York, 1932.) An edition for the special student; well supplied with biographical and textual notes, concluding with a useful bibliography.

Selected Poems, ed. by Wilfrid Meynell. (Scribner: New York, 1930.) An attractive one-volume selection, with a biographical note by the editor.

The Hound of Heaven, ed. by M. A. Kelly. (Reilly: Philadelphia, 1916.) Contains a biographical sketch and notes by the editor and an introduction by Katherine Brégy.

II. BIOGRAPHY AND CRITICISM

La Gorce, Agnes de. *Francis Thompson*. Trans. by H. F. Kynaston-Snell. (Oates: London, 1933.) Written from a theological point of view; shows that religion was the center of Thompson's life as an artist.

Le Buffe, F. P. *"The Hound of Heaven": An Interpretation*. (Macmillan: New York, 1921.) An essay by a Jesuit father to bring out the depth of the religious significance of the ode; offers 62 pages of notes, analyzing the poem phrase by phrase.

Mégroz, R. L. *Francis Thompson, the Poet of Earth in Heaven*. (Faber: London, 1927.) Provides a brief biographical review and launches into a rather bewildering array of antecedent and contemporary writers, with whom Thompson is compared or by whom he was allegedly influenced.

Meynell, Everard. *The Life of Francis Thompson*. (Scribner: New York, 1926.) Provides an insight into the personality of the poet and the convictions born out of his inner struggle; contains also an adequate notice of his literary work, his style, his Latinisms, etc.

Thomson, John. *Francis Thompson: Poet and Mystic*. (Simpkin: London, 1922.) This (the third) edition reviews the troublous life of the poet: enthusiastically praises his art, finding it the expression of a "seventeenth-century poet born in the nineteenth."

Wright, T. H. *Francis Thompson and His Poetry*. (Harrap: London, 1927.) A sympathetic review of the poet's work, illuminated by numerous quotations.

III. ARTICLES FROM BOOKS

Archer, William. "Francis Thompson," in *Poets of the Younger Generation*. (Lane: New York, 1902.) Furnished with many quotations, illustrating the poet's fertility of imagination, his love for Latinisms, and his distaste for fixed verse-forms.

Freeman, John. "Francis Thompson," in *The Moderns*. (Scott: London, 1915.) Presents an analysis of *The Hound of Heaven*; finds the ultimate value of Thompson's verse in its "expression of eternal truth."

More, P. E. "Francis Thompson," in *Shelburne Essays*, Seventh Series. (Putnam: New York, 1910.) Hesitatingly admits the poet's genius, finding in *The Hound of Heaven* the most perfect accord of his powers.

Symons, Arthur. "Francis Thompson," in *Dramatis Personae*. (Bobbs: Indianapolis, 1923.) Places *The Hound of Heaven* first among the poet's work; equally appraises *A Corymbus for Autumn*. Notes the stationary quality of Thompson's poetry, weighted with its verbal luxuriance.

Weygandt, Cornelius. "Francis Thompson, Poet and Pariah," in *Tuesdays at Ten*. (University of Pennsylvania Press: 1928.) Sets the poet at the head of his contemporaries; points to his originality and love of luxuriant detail; believes that he will live through separate great lines.

IV. ARTICLES FROM PERIODICALS

Brégy, Katherine. "The Poetry of Francis Thompson," *Catholic World*, LXXXI, 605–14 (Aug., 1905). Discusses Thompson's verse under the headings Love Poems and Devotional Pieces; points to his dramatic sense in showing his difference from Crashaw.

Hamilton, G. R. "Wit and Beauty," *London Mercury*, XIV, 606–20 (Oct., 1926). Thompson is here contrasted with Donne, who could not make peace between his medieval and modern concepts; the Victorian poet found the Heavenly Vision in the midst of the materialism of his day and was able to record it adequately.

Johnson, Leslie. "Modern Mysticism," *Quarterly Review*, CCXX, 227–32 (Jan., 1914). Points out in *The Hound of Heaven* and elsewhere the record of the poet's religious experience, which he cherishes even though it is far short of perfection.

Lewis, C. M. "The Poetry of Thompson," *Yale Review*, IV, 99–114 (Oct., 1914). Describes the rescue of the poet by the Meynells; passes severe judgment upon his eccentricities in verse.

Twitchett, E. G. "Francis Thompson," *London Mercury*, XXVII, 58–64 (Nov., 1932). Has nothing but condemnation for the poet's extravagances, but admits his true fire in his best work.

Tynan, Katharine. "Thompson's Place in Poetry," *Fortnightly Review*, XCIII, 349–60 (Feb., 1910). Puts Thompson in the company of Crashaw and Shelley; points out his "humility and humanity."

NOTES

"Magnificently faulty at times, magnificently perfect at others. The ardours of poetry taking you triumphantly by storm: a surging sea of verse, rising and falling and irresistibly advancing. Drunk with his inspiration, sometimes helplessly so: more often he is fired and quickened and remains master of himself. He has done more to harm the English language than the worst American newspapers: *corruptio optimi pessima* ["the worst corruption is the corruption of the best"]. He has the opulent, prodigal manner of the seventeenth century; a profusion of imagery, sometimes excessive and false: and another profusion and opulence, that of Shelley in his lyrical choruses. Beneath the outward manner a passionate reality of thought: profound, pathetic, full of faith without fear. Words that if you pricked them would bleed . . . Incapable of prettiness and pettiness: for good or bad always vehement and burning, and—to use a despised word—sublime. *Sublime* rather than *noble*. Too fevered to be austere: a note of ardent suffering, not of endurance." (Quoted from Lionel Johnson by Katharine Tynan, in the *Fortnightly Review*, XCIII, 355.) Mrs. Tynan calls this sound criticism, but she believes that Johnson was thinking too much of the excesses of Thompson's poetry; as when, in *A Corymbus for Autumn*, he made

"The sopped sun, toper as ever drank hard
Totty with thine October tankard," etc.

Page 1069. DAISY

In an essay, *Finis Coronat Opus*, Thompson wrote: "I met a child today; a child with great candour of eyes . . . she knew not that hell was in my soul, she knew only that softness was in my gaze. She had been gathering wild flowers, and offered them to me . . . I was inexpressibly pleased and touched."

Who Daisy was is not known. Thompson knew her as a village child with eight brothers and sisters, "the last four, all flowers—Rose, Daisy, Lily, and Violet."

9. *gorse*. A prickly shrub, furze.

21. *Storrington*. A village in Sussex where Thompson was living when he met the village child.

Page 1072. THE POPPY

Monica, to whom the poem was dedicated, was the daughter of Thompson's benefactors, Wilfrid and Alice Meynell. She was fifteen years old when she gave the poppy to Thompson, the incident occurring when he and the Meynell children were on one of their frequent picnics in the fields about Friston, in Suffolk. After Thompson's death the poppy was found in a copy of his own poems that he kept near him.

10. *swinked*. Toiling, drudging.

THE HOUND OF HEAVEN

Thompson began this poem when he was struggling against the drug habit during his life at the Priory in Storrington, the haven which the Meynells found for him when they rescued him from the London streets. All the heartburnings of his outcast days find a voice in the poem.

"He is at home among the stars, his soul keeping the loftiest company, however ill his body fared on earth. The flight of *The Hound of Heaven* is through the stars, and through the stars the feet of the Pursuer. I know nothing in literature which has the sense of flight and pursuit like this. The sound of the flying feet beats through the magnificent passages, till it dies off in the exquisite cessation and silence of the close when the pursued is taken to the breast of the Pursuer. This poem more than any other must be Francis Thompson's warrant for immortality." (Katharine Tynan, in the *Fortnightly Review*, XCIII, 357.)

Burne-Jones said of the poem: "Since Gabriel's 'Blessed Damozel' no mystical words have so touched me."

24. *wist*. Knew.

25. *margent*. Border.

26–29. *troubled . . . moon*. The soul in its flight disturbed the very stars and agitated into sound even the gates of the moon. The passage contrasts the harassed flight of the soul with the calm and "unperturbed pace" of God's pursuit.

41. *savannahs*. Great level stretches.

72. *Lucent-weeping*. Overflowing with light.

118–119. *shook . . . me*. Suggested by the story of Samson, who "killed many more at his death than he had killed before in his life" when he shook the pillars of the temple of Dagon and brought it down on the Philistines and on his own head. See Judges 16: 29–30.

123. *sun-starts*. Bubbles.

126. *linked fantasies*. Poetic imaginings, fancies.

131. *amaranthine*. Immortal like the amaranth, an imaginary never-fading flower. It was fabled that no other plant could grow near it.

135. *limn*. To draw, as with charcoal.

150. *purpureal*. Of purple, a royal color.

cypress crowned. Cypress symbolizes sorrow and death.

156. *bruit*. Noise.

159. *shard*. Fragment.

Page 1075. *From* A CORYMBUS FOR AUTUMN

"Such a poem as *A Corymbus for Autumn* shows his genius at its faultiest, although it is never more unmistakably genius. It is like a dance of Bacchantes." (Katharine Tynan, in the *Fortnightly Review*, XCIII, 355.)

The Latin "corymbus" means a cluster of flowers. Thompson uses it in the poem to mean a cluster of grapes or berries, such as the bacchanals used in crowning their wine god, Bacchus.

80. *sacerdotal.* Priestly.

84–104. Mrs. Tynan quotes these lines as an example of a noble passage occurring among passages of startling excess. These lines, she says, after "the dabbled spilt wine and blood and fire of the opening passages," come coolly, "like moonlight and starlight and the dark!"

88. *blanch-amiced.* Blanch = white; amiced = shaped like an amice, the oblong piece of white linen worn by priests at the Mass.

89. *thurifer.* One who carries a censer or thurible.

98. *Titanian, primal liturgy.* The magnificent primitive liturgy of an autumnal sunset. The poet speaks of the phenomena of the sunset and of the coming of night in the language of his church. These phenomena are so many ceremonies performed by Nature for the earth, which, in a scant hour after the sun has gone, will lie "still and stark," with "Heaven's death-lights," the stars, burning about it like candles by the dead.

100. *hierophant.* An expositor of sacred mysteries.

104. *catafalque.* A draped or canopied funeral stage. Here, more fittingly, the canopy of darkness.

111. *trepidant.* Trembling.

117. *trodden . . . press.* An allusion to the custom of treading upon grapes to crush out the juice.

144. *Artemis.* The moon.

148. *a vintager.* See ll. 117–122.

Page 1076. A FALLEN YEW

The falling of an old yew tree on the playground at St. Cuthbert's College, in Ushaw, where Thompson was in school from 1870 to 1877, is said to have inspired this poem.

1. *corrival.* A companion.

4. *Dryad.* A wood nymph, inhabiting a tree.
indue. Put on.

5. *chiton.* An ancient Greek tunic.

7. *Asgard.* In Norse myth the abode of the gods.

11. *levin.* Lightning.

16. *leas.* Meadows.

23–4. *Hacked . . . that.* The Ushaw students made crosses, paper-knives, etc. of their old playground yew.

25. *Hades.* The lower world.

26. *Dis.* Pluto, god of the lower world.
Acheron. The river of darkness in Hades.

27. *Lethe.* The river of forgetfulness in Hades.

43–79. In these lines "Thompson gives us a supreme development of that great truth of life . . . [that] there is a necessary and inviolable reticence in human nature itself and it is folly for man to attempt to explore or violate its realms." (The Rev. Terrence L. Connolly, in *Poems of Francis Thompson*, p. 404.)

74. *oubliette.* A dungeon whose only entrance is through the top.

76. *Lover.* God.
His Spouse. Man's soul.

Page 1077. SISTER SONGS

The sisters—Madeline, who is addressed in the poem as Sylvia, and Monica—were the children of Mr. and Mrs. Wilfrid Meynell. Thompson gave them the poem as a Christmas gift in 1891.

In Part I the poet, who in the Proem invites the children of Spring to sing with him the praise of Sylvia, sees Spring's first children, the leaves and buds and flowers, trooping to his call, and realizes that her unseen children, the flower elves, the Hours and Dryades, have come to join in festal dance at the feet of Spring and Sylvia. Part II is dedicated to the "elder nursling of the nest," Monica, whose association with the poet, beginning at the time of his rescue by her father and mother, gave to his despairing soul a living proof of the reality of Beauty—"not the visible, tangible beauty of nature, not the visible worshipful beauty of Woman's queenly form, but an invisible, intangible, inapprehensible Beauty." (Albert A. Cock, in the *Dublin Review*, October, 1911.)

382–435. A musical and eloquent essay on the nature of poetry and poetic inspiration.

398. *Jacob's stone.* Jacob "took . . . stones . . . for his pillows, and lay down to sleep. And he dreamed." (Genesis 28: 11–12.)

403. *temptress-ladies.* The sirens.

429. *Gate of Ivory.* See note to l. 3 of Johnson's *Oracles–I*, above.

437. *music . . . mother.* Mrs. Meynell was a poet.

602. *Daemon.* The spirit of poetry or poetic inspiration.

608. *high tenement.* His poem.

610–14. *palace . . . laves.* A great Gothic structure.

617–19. *Scarce . . . fire.* Still using the imagery of the Gothic palace, Thompson writes of the bewildering strangeness of the poem he has created.

631. *Heliades.* The three daughters of the Sun (Helios), who wept for their brother Phaëthon

until they were changed into poplar trees and their tears became amber.

637. *irids*. The poet's plural for iris—irises, or irides.

642. *Tellus*. Goddess of the earth, especially of cultivated fields.

purfled. Ornamented.

643. *chlamys*. A short mantle, or cloak.

657. *Saturnian*. A reference to Saturn as the god of seed-time and harvest.

658. *ossuaries*. Burial urns.

660. *Siste viator*. "Stop, traveler!" Often inscribed on tombstones.

storied urn. The poem.

737. *Ariel . . . viol by*. Ceases from poetry. Suggested by the famous passage in Shakespeare's *Tempest* (Act V, scene 1, ll. 50–57), sometimes called the dramatist's "farewell to his art."

742. *Vesper's fumes*. Evening clouds resembling incense.

744. *laburnum*. A shrub bearing bright yellow flowers.

761. *feateously*. Elegantly.

770. *candent*. Glowing.

774–80. The poet realized that the poem was beyond the understanding of the children for whom it was created. Complete appreciation must wait for the future when they should no longer be children.

777. *euphrasy*. A plant thought to be of use in the treatment of blindness.

Page 1080. *From* ODE TO THE SETTING SUN

1–4. The description of music in the opening lines of the poem, which was written in the Storrington days just after the poet's escape from the drug habit, was inspired by the playing of three wandering musicians in the streets of the village.

9. *reverent days*. In the days of sun-worship.

15. *reaved*. Taken away.

17. *field . . . Cross*. The Field of the Cross, in which the *Ode* was begun, is in the grounds of the Premonstratensian Priory, at Storrington. A large cross, erected on a mound in this field to face the west, stood out clearly before the poet against the sunset glow as he looked toward the Sussex hills.

155–80. A lament for the passing of the ancient deities who in the days of pagan Greece would have wailed their lord, the Sun, sunken from his "cœrule empery."

162. *Iberia*. Spain and Portugal.

163. *threne*. Threnody, a song of lamentation.

167. *Naiad*. Nymph, or divinity of fountain or stream.

169. *Dryad*. Nymph of forest or tree.

170. *Oread*. Mountain nymph.

172. *Nereid*. Sea nymph.

174. *Circean*. Of Circe, daughter of Helios (Sun) and an ocean nymph. See note to l. 270 of Arnold's *The Strayed Reveller*, above.

181. *they*. The nymphs.

182. *candours*. Radiance, brightness, innocent beliefs. As the sun fades our outstretched arms embrace the corpse of earth just as Orpheus clasped only the cold body of his spouse, Eurydice, when his music so charmed the gods of Hades that they allowed her to return to the upper world with him. The poet makes his own version of the story of Orpheus and Eurydice.

201. *the hill*. The mound on which stood the cross in the Priory grounds (see note to l. 17, above). The light gleaming through a rift in the clouds (l. 205) enlightens not only the poet's eye but also his mind. Doubt passes (l. 209), the secret of the sun (l. 28) becomes clear. It images God, the "King-Maker of Creation" (l. 215), who set it in its station in the heavens. In its rising and setting, too, it is emblematic of Christ in his birth and death. Setting, it hangs upon a rood (cross) "in dreadful pomp of blood," but, rising, it comes forth in a glorious resurrection.

216. *Hellas*. Greece.

Page 1081. "WHERETO ART THOU COME?"

When Judas gave Jesus the telltale kiss of betrayal at Gethsemane, Jesus said to him, "Friend, whereto art thou come?" (See Matthew 26: 47–50.)

1. *Thus Verity*. Thus (saith) Truth.

2. *Olivet*. The Garden of Gethsemane is on Olivet, a low range of hills near Jerusalem.

8. *light-o'-love*. One inconstant in love.

12. *seed*. Thoughts and actions.

14. *rated*. Offered, settled, bargained for.

15. *Haceldama*. In "the proper tongue of the dwellers in Jerusalem," the name of the potter's field which was purchased with the thirty pieces of silver, the blood money given to Judas for betraying Christ. The word means "the field of blood." (See Matthew 27: 7–8 and Acts 1: 19, and note to l. 67 of Swinburne's *Super Flumina Babylonis*, p. 1262 above.)

17. *guerdon of despair*. A halter. Judas hanged himself.

A DEAD ASTRONOMER

Father Perry died in December, 1889, on a ship off the coast of French Guiana, where he had been making observations on a solar eclipse. This poem, first published in April, 1890, in Wilfrid Meynell's magazine, *Merry England*, gained much attention at once. Thompson said that he meant it "merely for a pretty, gracefully turned fancy; what the Elizabethans would have called an excellent conceit."

5. *She*. Our Lady, the Virgin Mary. For her seven woes see the note to Rossetti's *Mary's Girlhood*, above.

12. *tube*. Telescope.

13. *fairest Star*. Our Lady.

Page 1082. ENVOY

This poem appeared as the postscript (envoy) for the volume entitled *New Poems* (1897).

"BY REASON OF THY LAW"

1–15. In these lines the poet asserts his sure knowledge that nothing—dread, frustrate love, even the sum of all iniquity—can turn him who knows the inner meaning of bitterness and suffering from his faith in the reality of an ultimate Paradise and his belief in final reward. Rightly understood, "the fierceness of pain is a kiss, not a curse." It is the law of man's being that his faith and trust in the final good shall increase as the bitterness of his life increases.

9. *bate.* In falconry, to beat the wings with impatience.

22. *heavenly Falconer.* God, who "tames with fearful gloom" the haggard, or hawk, of l. 24.

27. *Avernian.* Dark, lowering, suffocating. Lake Avernus, in Italy, which occupies the crater of an extinct volcano, is said to have been so overhung with suffocating gases in ancient days that birds attempting to fly over it fell dead.

47. *seven-quired psalterings.* Songs sung by the complete angelic quire. The best-known arrangement of the celestial hierarchy is one of nine orders instead of seven.

49. *worm.* Probably death.

THE DREAD OF HEIGHT

"*The Dread of Height* is a cry from the depths into which the poet has fallen after having made 'Of the deific peaks dim escalade.'" In much of Thompson's poetry the "dark night of the soul" follows hard upon the moment of beatific vision. "These alternations of rapture and despair were in part the result of his poverty-stricken, opium-harassed life. Worn out with the passion of successive height and depth, the poet envies those who walk steadily on their chosen elevation:

'Ah, for a heart less native to high Heaven,
A hooded eye, for jesses and restraint,
Or for a will accipitrine to pursue!'"

(C. E. Andrews and M. O. Percival, in *Poetry of the Nineties*, pp. 26 and 27.)

1. *Circean wine.* A magic potion like that which Circe, the beautiful magician, used in changing into swine the men sent by Ulysses to explore her island. See note to l. 270 of *Ode to the Setting Sun*, above.

16. *arcane.* Secret place.

42. *John.* Saint John the Baptist, who ate locusts and wild honey. (Mark 1: 6; Matthew 3: 4.)

90. *Jesses.* Straps fastened round the leg of a hawk for attaching the leash.

91. *accipitrine.* The accipiter is a bird of prey —falcon, hawk.

92. *tutelar.* Protecting.

94. *heavenly . . . taint.* Never tainted or corrupted by the pursuit of heavenly quarry.

95. *sickest time.* Time of greatest despair, desolation, bitterness.

mew. When the falcon mews, or molts, his flight is impaired.

Page 1084. *From* THE NIGHT OF FOREBEING

The title was suggested to Thompson by this passage from Sir Thomas Browne's *Urn Burial* (chap. 5, paragraph 17): "Pious spirits, who pass their days in raptures of futurity, made little more of this world than the world that was before it, while they lay obscure in the chaos of preordination and night of our forebeings. And if any have been so happy as truly to understand Christian annihilation, ecstasis, exolution, liquefaction, transformation, the kiss of the spouse, gustation of God and ingression into the divine shadow, they have already had a handsome anticipation of heaven; the glory of the world is surely over, and the earth in ashes unto them."

65. *your . . . noise.* Leaves, grass, winds, flowers, birds, even the "slug-abed snail"— all the poet's "elemental co-mates"—are addressed as "you" and "your" in the opening lines of the poem, bade to continue their joyous tendance on the steps of Spring, and not to seem sad that the strange heart of the poet "should be so little glad."

71–2. *great-vanned . . . trumpeted.* Great-winged March has blown his trumpet of the winds to wake the sleeping earth. The sub-title of the poem is *An Ode after Easter.*

76. *Jubilate* [*Deo omnis terra*]. "Sing joyfully [to God, all the earth]."

79. *quicken . . . precursive.* Receive life at the precursory, or premonitory, word.

88–9. *Lifting . . . prophecy.* The pine and ivy tree, remaining green throughout the period of the winter-death, are prophetic of the awakening (the resurrection) of all the things of earth in the spring.

94. *vidual.* Like a widow; widowed.

96. *hieratic.* Consecrated to sacred uses.

100. *mortals . . . heed.* See, O men, in the awakening of the earth in the spring a divine sign that man shall live again.

198–225. The poet describes the failure of poetic inspiration, a frequent theme of his verse. (See *Sister Songs*, ll. 602–62, text p. 1078.) In lines 200–212 he writes of the period (winter) of poetic unproductiveness, when inspiration fails (lies dead); but "heeding the portent" of the miraculous revival of earth in the springtime, he sees "other imaged meanings" in it and knows (ll. 213–25) that the icebound floods of poetry shall be unloosed in their own spring and burst forth again like cataracts. In the use of the word "rime" (l. 210) he has in mind the two meanings—frost and identity of sound between words.

320–68. The poet recognizes his unfitness for the present life on earth and reaffirms his absolute belief in the voice that he hears in the revolving year calling out a promise of "the Perfect Morn."

321. *ensuit.* Suite.

322. *rate.* Berate.

326. *this house.* His body, ill, weakened by poverty, marred by the use of opium.

329. *your day.* The phrase may mean "the present," or it may indicate a return to the idea with which the poem opens. (See note to l. 65 above.)

337. *Woman.* The Virgin Mary, Our Lady. Father Connolly, in *The Poems of Francis Thompson*, p. 467, suggests three interpretations of the word, each involving an attribute of Mary. He prefers the interpretation of Mary as a type of God's love for Man.

353. *palimpsest.* Manuscript, the original writing on which has been erased to make room for more. Men in different ages have ascribed meaning to the writing of the stars which later ages have rejected. The significance of the word seems to rest upon the idea that it carries of scratching out or erasing the original writing, but it is possible that Thompson used it merely as a poetical word and with no thought of its special significance.

354. *Daniel.* Daniel interpreted the mysterious handwriting on the wall which foretold the fall of Babylon. (See Daniel 5.)

Page 1086. THE HEART—II

13. *Babylon.* Symbolic of grandeur and material wealth.

TO A SNOW-FLAKE

Of these lines, which he calls "a poetry upon the borderland between word-conjuring and the imaginative realization of things," Max Eastman writes: "Consider them, not because they lack all other poetry, but because they lack all other greatness in poetry, than the greatness of a creation in the flavors of words. A sensuous if delicate cloud is hung before us, hiding the snow-flake, or even the God, we may have thought of, but hiding it in order to ravish us away with a mystery of names. As a builder of these magic clouds, dwelling upon them forever, and even to the ruin of his melody and rhythm, Francis Thompson has hardly been excelled." (*Enjoyment of Poetry*, p. 159.)

10. *argentine.* Silvery.

Page 1087. AN ARAB LOVE-SONG

Chesterton said of these lines: "A mediaeval illuminator would have jumped out of his sandals to illustrate that." (*Eyes of Youth*, p. xvi.)

LOVE AND THE CHILD

Thompson once said that all human love was to him a symbol of divine love.

TO W. M.

W. M. = Wilfrid Meynell.

1. *tree . . . branches.* The Meynells had seven children.

Page 1088. THE KINGDOM OF GOD

This poem, which "expresses the essence of Thompson's religion," was first published with the title, "In No Strange Land" (see Psalms 137: 4), and with the sub-title, "The Kingdom of God Is Within You" (see Luke 17: 21). Professor W. L. Phelps, who considers it "one of the greatest poems of the twentieth century," finds in its defective rhymes and its roughness of rhythm a reminder of "some of Donne's shaggy and splendid verse." Miss Wilkinson sees in it the same spiritual authenticity that is in *The Hound of Heaven*.

"His language, though its complete significance eludes us, gives us . . . unforgettable glimpses of his meaning. Such phrases as 'Beats at our own clay-shuttered doors' and 'the many-splendoured thing'; such visions as those of

'The traffic of Jacob's ladder
Pitched betwixt Heaven and Charing Cross'

and

'Christ walking on the water,
Not of Gennesareth, but Thames,'

even apart from their context, are felt to be of the kind that makes 'the mind a mansion for all lovely things, the memory as a dwelling-place for all sweet sounds and harmonies.'" (E. A. G. Lamborn, in *Poetic Values*, p. 206.)

19. *Jacob's ladder.* "And he dreamed, and behold a ladder set upon the earth, and the top of it reached to heaven: and behold the angels of God ascending and descending on it." (Genesis 28: 12.)

20. *Charing Cross.* The hub of London. It is the site of one of the several crosses erected in 1290 by Edward I to mark the spots where the coffin of Queen Eleanor rested on its funeral journey to Westminster. See note to Johnson's *By the Statue of King Charles at Charing Cross*, above.

24. *Gennesareth.* The Sea of Galilee. (See Matthew 14: 25.)

JAMES THOMSON

BIBLIOGRAPHY

I. WORKS

Complete Poetical Works, ed. by Bertram Dobell. 2 vols. (Reeves: London, 1895.) The standard edition of Thomson's poetry, superseding the three original issues; the editor adds a judicious but warmly appreciative memoir, which is one of the few authoritative sources of the poet's life.

Poems, ed. by G. H. Gerould. (Holt: New York, 1927.) Recommended as an introduction to the poet; abandoning the chronological order, the editor has arranged the best pieces in a climaxing series concluding with *The City of Dreadful Night* and *The Doom of a City*.

"The City of Dreadful Night" and Other Poems, ed. by Bertram Dobell. (Dobell: London, 1922.) A good representative selection, with a valuable biographical notice by the editor.

II. BIOGRAPHY AND CRITICISM

Dobell, Bertram. *The Laureate of Pessimism*. (Dobell: London, 1910.) A brief appreciative review of the life and character of the poet, whose work is studied as the outgrowth of the facts of his experience.

Meeker, J. E. *The Life and Poetry of James Thomson*. (Yale University Press: 1917.) An illuminating "essay to sketch the poet's life, using his poems and his prose chronologically as a key to his inner development."

Salt, H. S. *The Life of James Thomson*. (Watts: London, 1914.) The authoritative Life, the basis of most of the later studies of the poet; out of print and almost unobtainable.

III. ARTICLES FROM BOOKS AND PERIODICALS

Hoffman, Harold. "An Angel in the City of Dreadful Night," *Sewanee Review*, XXXII, 317–35 (July, 1924). Following a brief biographical sketch, attempts an interpretation of the poem; compares Thomson's poetic psychology with Shelley's, who is the "angel" in the poem.

Jones, W. L. "Matthew Arnold, Arthur Hugh Clough, James Thomson," in *The Cambridge History of English Literature*, XIII. (Putnam: New York, 1917.) Sympathetically reviews Thomson's chequered career; praises *The City of Dreadful Night*.

Marks, Jeannette. "Disaster and Poetry: A Study of James Thomson," *North American Review*, CCXII, 93–109 (July, 1920). A study of the effect of intemperance on the poet's life and work, which his weakness inclined him to pattern after greater models.

More, P. E. "James Thomson," in *Shelburne Essays*, Fifth Series. (Putnam: New York, 1908.) Outlines a concise biographical sketch; shows Thomson's pessimism to be the natural maturity of the scientific interpretation of life.

Simcox, G. A. "A New Poet," *Fortnightly Review*, XXXIV, 31–41 (July, 1880). A commendatory review of Thomson's new 1880 volume; attempts a superficial interpretation of *The City of Dreadful Night*.

Symons, Arthur. "James Thomson," in *Studies in Two Literatures*. (Secker: London, 1924.) Points out the poet's sense of incompleteness, even in his best work; names as his chief influences Shelley, Browning, and Heine.

Welby, T. E. "James Thomson," in *Back Numbers*. (Smith: New York, 1930.) Laments the fact that Thomson became the victim of his one great poem; comments briefly on his stylistic defects.

Zabel, M. D. "James Thomson's Poems," *Poetry*, XXXII, 229–33 (July, 1928). Points to the imagery of *The City* as the poet's "one design of real mastery"; names him the hero of his own City.

NOTES

"James Thomson was of no group, was in truth among the most solitary of our [Victorian Romantics] . . . He has, intermittently, a great style of his own, surpassing Dante Gabriel Rossetti himself in the filling of lines with sonorous Latinate polysyllabic phrases; he can set the walls of his chapel of disbelief rocking with the reverberation of his tremendous double rhymes; he can accumulate the symbols of disaster with extraordinary resource so that when it seems impossible to add anything which shall not diminish the total effect there shall indeed be some dreadful gain,

As if blacker night could dawn on night
With tenfold gloom on moonless night unstarred.

"But his only security is in monotony. The moment he escapes from *The City of Dreadful Night* to walk otherwise than in a circle, or under changeful skies, his style becomes uncertain, a mixture of Shelley, Heine, Browning, and refined vulgarism." (T. Earle Welby, in *The Victorian Romantics*, p. 70.)

Page 1089. *From* SUNDAY UP THE RIVER

Sunday up the River, a group of twenty idylls, or songs, was published in October, 1869, in *Fraser's Magazine*, which was at that time edited by the historian, James Anthony Froude. Froude was so impressed by the poem that he invited its author to breakfast with him, an invitation which Thomson eagerly accepted. Breaking into the pages of *Fraser's* this one time, however, and winning the momentary attention of Froude did not bring the poet the cultured audience he probably hoped for. Neither the public nor the critics noticed the poem, and Thomson made no more attempts to publish his work in *Fraser's*. Thomson called this group of poems "An Idyll of Cockaigne"

—the land of cockneys. The word "Cockaigne" also suggests a country of idleness and luxury.

Page 1090. E. B. B.

11. *land . . . fought.* In several poems—*e.g.* *Casa Guidi Windows*—Mrs. Browning wrote with enthusiasm for the cause of Italian liberty.

Page 1091. THE CITY OF DREADFUL NIGHT

"'The City of Dreadful Night' may be characterized as a somber, darkly wrought composition toned to a minor key from which it never varies. It is a mystical allegory, the outgrowth of broodings on hopelessness and spiritual desolation. The legend of Dürer's *Melancholia* is marvelously transcribed, and the isometric interlude, 'As I came through the Desert thus it was,' is only surpassed by Browning's 'Childe Roland.' The cup of pessimism, with all its conjuring bitterness, is drunk to the dregs in this enshrouded, and again lurid, but always remarkable poem." (E. C. Stedman, in *Victorian Poets*, p. 456.)

The City of Dreadful Night is Thomson's "deepest confession of despair, his acknowledgment of those realities around whose laws so much confusion had been thrown. It is a rejection of all Will and Mind from the universe, the victory of that negation which hovers like a threat over the [Victorian] period. In the stanzas whose appeal to us is now damaged by their verbosity and heavy pomp, we see what an Inferno a sensitive weakling made of his environment. The imagery of the dreadful city is Thomson's one design of real mastery: the dark stronghold of denials, mysteries, and dispirited fancies, shot through, at times, by a saving light, but in the end brooding eternally on the banks of its River of Death. In the massive pictorial effect, built as it is out of dreams and longings, a strong insight defines itself. The distorted prospects and vistas over which Melancholia presides give a panorama of nightmare and delusion, it is true, but the poem mounts unforgettably toward the somber majesty of grief. In the city the poet sees men destined,

The strong to drink new strength of iron endurance,
The weak new terrors; all, renewed assurance
And confirmation of the old despair.

But he is that city's lonely hero, realizing his isolation and knowing that his fellows never admit the idea of brotherhood or the leadership of new wisdom." (Morton Dauwen Zabel, in *Poetry*, XXII, 232–3.)

92. *necropolis.* A city of the dead.

120. *leave . . . there.* Dante saw these words written over the gate to hell (*Inferno*, Canto III, l. 9).

136. *God's-acre.* Graveyard.

232. *Sabbath of the Serpents.* A midnight orgy of demons, evil spirits, etc. held annually under the leadership of Satan.

327. *dolent.* Sorrowful.

333. *dree his weird.* Endure, bear his fate.

373. *Pandora's box.* A box given to Pandora by Zeus, inclosing all human ills. When she opened it all the ills escaped and spread over the earth.

391. *fell.* Cruel.

392. *Limbo.* The abode of souls barred from heaven through no fault of their own.

472. *Venice . . . Sea.* The City of Dreadful Night.

620. *blood . . . wool-white.* See Isaiah 1: 18.

631. *justify . . . man.* Milton thus announced his purpose in writing *Paradise Lost* in line 26 of Book I of that epic.

882. *lown.* Calm, quiet.

1055. *sad artist.* Albrecht Dürer (1471–1528), painter, engraver, sculptor, and architect, the greatest artist of the German Renaissance. One of his famous engravings is the *Melancholia.*

1113. *teen.* Sorrow.
threne. Lamentation.

OSCAR WILDE

BIBLIOGRAPHY

I. WORKS

The Writings of Oscar Wilde. (Wise: New York, 1931.) The most comprehensive of recent one-volume collections, containing representations from the poems, short stories, plays, novels, letters, and other prose pieces.

Works of Oscar Wilde. (Collins: London, 1933.) An inclusive, low-priced edition, desirable for its fifteen illustrations by Donia Nachshen.

Poems. (Brentano: New York, 1910.) A recommended edition, containing a biographical introduction by Temple Scott.

Selected Poems. (Methuen: London, 1925.) One of the best of many books of selections from Wilde's poetry.

Poems and Fairy-Tales. (Cerf: New York, 1932.) A convenient (Modern Library) edition of selected verse and prose fantasias.

Letters after Reading. 2 vols. (Reynolds: New York, 1921.) A limited edition of Wilde's correspondence with Robert Ross.

Sixteen Letters, ed. by John Rothenstein. (Coward: New York, 1930.) The letters are from Wilde to William Rothenstein, dating from 1891–1900; notes are supplied to the correspondence by the editor.

Some Letters to Alfred Douglas, ed. by A. C. Dennison, Jr. and Harrison Post. (Nash: San Francisco, 1924.) The time covered by the correspondence is 1892–1897; also contains an essay by A. S. W. Rosenbach.

II. BIOGRAPHY AND CRITICISM

Braybrooke, Patrick. *Oscar Wilde, A Study.* (Braithwaite: London, 1930.) One of many "enthusiastic" studies of Wilde's engaging personality, dwelling on his conversational wit and his literary achievements.

Harris, Frank. *Oscar Wilde: His Life and Confessions.* (Covici: New York, 1930.) Provides the fullest discussion of many of the controversial topics of Wilde's life; includes Shaw's *My Memories of Oscar Wilde* and the hitherto unpublished "confession" of Lord Alfred Douglas.

Ransome, Arthur. *Oscar Wilde, A Critical Study.* (Secker: London, 1912.) An interesting, seriously written study; selects *Intentions* as Wilde's most representative book.

Renier, G. J. *Oscar Wilde.* (Appleton: New York, 1933.) A brief commonsense story of Wilde's life, tracing the steps by which he rose to success and describing the causes and stages of his moral collapse.

Sherard, R. H. *The Life of Oscar Wilde.* (Dodd: New York, 1928.) A good portrait of the man and the artist, but unfortunately weakened by an effort to prove that Wilde was "martyred" for lapses which Sherard believes demand pity rather than condemnation.

Sherard, R. H. *Oscar Wilde Twice Defended.* (Argus Press: Chicago, 1935.) A re-statement of the defensive pronouncements of the foregoing work, briefly refuting the hostile charges of Harris and Gide.

Symons, Arthur. *A Study of Oscar Wilde.* (Sawyer: London, 1930.) A brief digest of many previous contributions; sees the man as a personality rather than as an artist; comments on his works, making comparisons with other contemporary productions.

III. ARTICLES FROM BOOKS

Birnbaum, Martin. "Oscar Wilde," in *Fragments and Memories.* (Mathews: London, 1920.) An interesting brief account of Wilde's friendship with Clyde Fitch, including delicious fragments of their correspondence (most of which was destroyed), quotations from Wilde's Paris notebook, accounts of his American lectures, and a few of his last letters from Paris.

Lynd, Robert. "Oscar Wilde," in *The Art of Letters.* (Fisher: London, 1920.) A short review of Ransome's study, maintaining that language, in its excess, was a vice with Wilde.

Powys, J. C. "Oscar Wilde," in *Suspended Judgments.* (Shaw: New York, 1916.) Admits Wilde's fascination but complains of his lack of "that large, cool spaciousness," which the greater masters produce; supports many of his attacks on the society of his day.

Shanks, Edward. "Oscar Wilde," in *Second Essays on Literature.* (Collins: London, 1927.) Selects "The Sphinx" and "The Ballad of Reading Gaol" as Wilde's most persuasive and original work; concludes that the man was greater than his output.

Sherman, S. P. "Oscar Wilde," in *Critical Woodcuts.* (Scribner: New York, 1926.) A chatty review of Wilde as a public figure who failed deplorably in his lifelong task of divorcing art from morality.

IV. ARTICLES FROM PERIODICALS

Bendz, Ernst. "The Real Oscar Wilde," *Englische Studien*, L, 309–19 (Dec., 1916). A discussion of the facts and the theories of Wilde's life involved in Sherard's biography; insists that the character of Wilde must remain an enigma.

Cooper-Prichard, A. H. "Reminiscences of Oscar Wilde," *Cornhill Magazine*, LXVIII, 144–54 (Feb., 1930). Reviews an acquaintance of many years, showing the spontaneity of Wilde's conversational wit.

Esdaile, A. "The New Hellenism," *Fortnightly Review*, XCIV, 706–22 (Oct., 1910). Sketches the facts in Wilde's biography; emphasizes his discipleship to Pater; shows the simplification of his art as expressed in his final writings.

Glaenzer, R. B. "The Story of 'The Ballad of Reading Gaol,'" *Bookman*, XXXIII, 376–81 (June, 1911). Shows how much of the philosophy of the poem is implicit in Wilde's early work; gives the facts of the composition of the poem.

Shanks, Edward. "Oscar Wilde," *London Mercury*, X, 278–87 (July, 1924). Points out Wilde's large following on the continent; scathes the extravagances of his earlier poetry; denies the existence of any real decadent strain in him.

Yeats, W. B. "Four Years, 1887–1891," *London Mercury*, IV, 129–40 (June, 1921). Sections VI, VIII, IX describe Yeats's first meeting with Wilde and recall Wilde's conversational charm, providing some amusing notes on his family.

NOTES

"The poetry of Wilde is a poetry that seeks escape from the world in an Endymion-like pursuit of sensuous beauty. It is overrich with ornamental diction and outdoes Keats in love of colors and odors." (C. E. Andrews and M. O. Percival, in *Poetry of the Nineties*, p. 18.)

Page 1107. LES SILHOUETTES

This poem is one of a number in which Wilde used the stanza of *In Memoriam.* Cf. *Rome Unvisited*, *The Sphinx*, and *The True Knowledge.*

HÉLAS!

The title means, "Alas!"

Richard Le Gallienne said of this poem: "Here thus early is the genuine cry *de profundis*, the spiritual cry which is to be heard like an undertone of anguish in almost all Wilde's writings—

'And must I lose a soul's inheritance?'"

The strange and pathetic prophecy voiced in this sonnet of self-analysis is deeply impressive.

7. *virelay.* A poem or song with two rhymes to a stanza, variously arranged.

REQUIESCAT

In this little prayer for the repose of his sister, Isola, who died in childhood, the poet wrote with a simplicity and tenderness that are puzzling to those who think of him as affected and unfeeling. Cf. Arnold's *Requiescat,* text p. 554, and see the note to that poem.

From THE BURDEN OF ITYS

For two versions of the story of Itys, or Itylus, see Arnold's *Philomela,* text p. 553, and Swinburne's *Itylus,* text p. 700. See also the notes to these poems, pp. 1221 and 1256 above, respectively. There are other versions of the story—one in which Itys, the son of Zethus and Ædon was slain by mistake by Ædon, she believing that she was killing the oldest son of Niobe, of whose large family of children she was envious. In the poem, which consists of about 350 lines, Wilde asks the English nightingale to sing of Grecian themes, a request which enables him to make a poetic catalogue of classic myths. The selection given comprises the last six stanzas of the poem.

5. *gossamer.* A small spider.

9. *wattled sheep-cotes.* A shelter for sheep, made of twigs or withes.

10. *Sandford lock.* The first of the thirty-three locks in the Thames on the way from Oxford to London is at the village of Sandford, about three miles below Oxford.

18. *threnody.* Song of lamentation—here sung by the nightingale for the slain Itys.

20. *Endymion.* The beautiful young hunter or shepherd with whom Selene, goddess of the moon, fell in love.

33. *Magdalen's tall tower.* Magdalen is often considered the most beautiful college in Oxford. The belfry tower, completed in 1504, "is one of the glories of the city."

34. *High . . . town.* Hawthorne called High Street in Oxford "the noblest old street in England."

36. *curfew . . . Christ Church.* "Great Tom," the 7-ton bell at Christ Church, an Oxford college begun by Cardinal Wolsey, gives out 101 strokes at 9:05 each evening. With the last stroke the various college gates are closed.

Page 1108. ENDYMION

2. *Arcady.* Arcadia, a region of simple pleasure, innocence, and untroubled quiet.

10. *shoon.* Shoes.

15. *turtle.* The turtledove.

18. *singing seneschal.* Steward; here, the bee.

22. *Helice.* Possibly a poetic adaptation of Helicon, a mountain of Boeotia sacred to the Muses. Helice, a huntress beloved of Zeus, was changed by the jealous Hera into a constellation, the Great Bear.

Page 1110. THEOCRITUS

Theocritus was a Greek pastoral poet who lived in the third century B.C. His *Idylls,* depicting the everyday life of the people of Sicily, are the first examples of pastoral poetry in Greek literature. Cf. sonnet I of Elizabeth Barrett Browning's *Sonnets from the Portuguese,* text p. 844.

A villanelle is a form of poem of 19 lines on two rhymes (especially French).

1. *Persephone.* See note to l. 59 of Swinburne's *The Garden of Proserpine,* p. 1259, above.

5. *Amaryllis.* A shepherdess in Theocritus's *Idylls.*

7. *Simætha.* A woman who in Theocritus's *Idyll II* is represented as endeavoring to regain the lost affections of a lover by means of magic art, practiced at midnight under the full moon.

Hecate. A mysterious goddess often confused with Selene, Artemis, and Persephone. She haunted graveyards and crossroads, and her coming was announced by the howling of dogs.

11. *Polypheme.* The Cyclops who imprisoned Odysseus and his companions in a cave and whom Odysseus blinded in order that he and his men might escape.

14. *Daphnis.* A Sicilian shepherd who invented pastoral story and song. A possible explanation of Daphnis's challenge may be found in the note to ll. 183–5 of Arnold's *Thyrsis,* p. 1227, above.

16. *Lacon.* A shepherd. In *Idyll V* he and Comatas, a goatherd, meet, spar at one another in bantering dialogue, and engage in a singing contest.

THE SPHINX

"Wilde's reputation as a poet rests entirely on two pieces [*The Sphinx* and *The Ballad of Reading Gaol*], both of which are derivative in style and yet both of which have a life of their own. *The Sphinx* gives its author's age as under twenty, which, to speak with frankness, I cannot bring myself to believe. It is much too remarkable an exercise in literary decoration for this to be possible, when one compares it with the other works of the same kind.

"It *is* remarkable, and it *is* an exercise. But for Baudelaire and Swinburne it could never have been written. Cato and the fascination of sin, the names of precious stones and other 'stunning' words, as Rossetti called them, a sinister disillusionment with life and hints at strange vices—it is hard to say what in this is the contribution of the poet. Perhaps the form: for the stanza of *In Memoriam* undergoes a definite and interesting change when it is written as a couplet, with the rhymes concealed and not dwelt on. It takes on a different movement, very characteristic and rather impressive. This is, I fancy, Wilde's one invention in literary technique.

"But so much will not explain the definite impression made on us that the poem is a valid work of art, and not to be dismissed as derivative or insincere, though both these faults could be shown in it. But what is to be made of such a passage as this [ll. 53–72]? When the undergraduate (or so, at least, it used to be) reads this for the first time, his heart leaps up, for he beholds what an immense amount of entertainment can be got of mere words. And one's instinct still is to say of *The Sphinx:* This is great fun! For it is entirely something, and it is equally certainly nothing on a higher level than that. The extravagance of the decoration is at once self-conscious and naïve. The ideas are mere counters, and the poem expresses no feeling, unless it be a delight in verbal and metrical virtuosity. But as such it exists and has an enduring spark of life in it." (Edward Shanks, in the *London Mercury*, Vol. X, 281–2.)

T. Earle Welby says that Swinburne's *Cleopatra*, a poem which he designates as "that minor masterpiece of decadent poetry," and which Swinburne never reprinted after George Meredith "persuaded him that it was no more than a farrago of the commonplaces of his poetical style," was without doubt the model for *The Sphinx*.

19. *Hieroglyphs*. Characters in the picture writing of the ancient Egyptians.

20. *Basilisks*. Fabulous reptiles, blasting by their breath or look.

Hippogriffs. Fabulous winged beasts, half horse and half griffin.

21. *Isis*. An Egyptian goddess of motherhood and fertility.

Osiris. The Egyptian god of the underworld and judge of the dead.

22. *the Egyptian*. Cleopatra.

24. *tunny*. A large oceanic fish used as food.

25. *the Cyprian*. Aphrodite.

Adon. Adonis.

26. *Heliopolis*. A city of ancient Egypt on the lower Nile near Memphis.

27. *Thoth*. In Egyptian religion the scribe of the gods, the measurer of time, and inventor of numbers.

Io. The daughter of a river god, Io was changed into a heifer by Hera. She wandered into Egypt and there was restored to her original shape.

34. *Antinous*. A youth of remarkable beauty, who was a favorite of the Emperor Hadrian (Adrian). He was drowned in the Nile in A.D. 122.

37. *Labyrinth*. A place of intricate passage built by Daedalus for Minos, king of Crete. In it was confined the Minotaur, a monster, half man and half bull.

39. *Ibis*. A large bird common in the Nile basin and venerated by the ancient Egyptians.

40. *Mandragores*. The mandrake is common in northern Africa. It is the subject of many superstitions.

46. *Leman*. A paramour.

48. *Gryphons*. Monsters, half lion and half eagle.

51. *Lycian tomb*. Lycia was an ancient land in Asia Minor.

Chimera. A horrible flame-vomiting she-monster.

54. *Nereid*. A sea nymph.

55. *Sidonian*. Of Sidon, an ancient seaport of Phoenicia.

60. *Glyphs*. Carved figures, incised or in relief.

62. *lupanar*. A brothel.

64. *Tragelaphos*. A fictitious animal combining the forms of goat and stag.

65. *flies . . . Hebrews*. If Wilde was thinking of the plague of flies that is described in the eighth chapter of *Exodus*, either he is confused in his details or he has purposely changed them. In the *Exodus* story it was the Egyptians, not the Hebrews, who were plagued by a "grievous swarm of flies."

66. *Pasht*. A cat-headed goddess of the ancient Egyptians.

67. *Tyrian*. Probably Tammuz, who was identified with the West Semitic Adonis. Just as Adonis was associated with Aphrodite, so Tammuz was associated with Istar, the Babylonian goddess of love. Ezekiel 8: 4 speaks of the "women weeping for Tammuz."

68. *Ashtaroth*. The Ashtoreth of the Old Testament, the eastern equivalent of the Greek Aphrodite, goddess of love. The dove was beloved of her.

god of the Assyrian. Assur or Ashur.

70. *Oreichalch*. Wilde seems to have made this word by using approximations of two Greek combining forms—*oreo*, suggesting *mountain*, and *chalco*, meaning *copper*, *brass*. The wings were ribbed, he means, with bronze or brass.

71. *Apis*. A sacred bull worshipped by the ancient Egyptians.

72. *nenuphar*. Water lily.

74. *Ammon*. A supreme god of the Egyptians in the Theban religion.

76. *galbanum*. A gum resin of aromatic odor.

spikenard. A fragrant ointment of the ancients.

thyme. A shrub with pungent aromatic leaves.

90. *Kurdistan*. An extensive region of Western Asia, divided among Turkey, Iraq, and Persia.

97. *Colchian*. Of Colchis, an ancient district of

Asia Minor at the eastern extremity of the Black Sea. The witch was Medea, the famous sorceress, daughter of the Colchian king, Æetes.
99. *galiot.* A small, swift galley once much used on the Mediterranean.
corybants. The attendants of Cybele at the wild orgiastic rites celebrating her worship.
103. *steatite.* A variety of talc, grayish green or brown in color.
104. *chrysolite.* Any of several yellow or greenish gems.
106. *Memphian.* Memphis was an ancient Egyptian city.
110. *monolith.* A block of stone shaped into a pillar, statue, etc.
113. *Horus.* The Egyptian god of light.
119. *Bedouin.* A nomadic Arab of the desert.
burnous. A cloaklike garment and hood worn by Arabs and Moors.
120. *paladin.* Knight errant. Originally any of the Twelve Peers of Charlemagne's court.
132. *Anubis.* An ancient Egyptian deity, the ruler of the dead.
133–4. *Memnon . . . morning.* An allusion to the "vocal Memnon," a colossal statue near Thebes which was said to give forth musical notes when struck by the rays of the rising sun. Memnon was the name the Greeks gave to Amenhotep III, whom the statue represented.
162. *student's cell.* Wilde is said to have written *The Sphinx* in his Oxford days. (See introductory note to the poem, second sentence.)
166. *Abana and Pharphar.* Rivers of Damascus (2 Kings 5: 12), the "lucid streams" of Milton (*Paradise Lost*, Book I, l. 469).
167–74. Le Gallienne hears the *De Profundis* sounding tragically in these lines.
170. *Atys.* A beautiful Phrygian youth. Cybele fell in love with him, and, because he wished to marry another, drove him mad. He fled to a forest, emasculated himself, and died.
171. *Styx.* The principal river of Hades.
Charon. The ferryman of Hades who rowed the dead across the Acheron, the underworld river of woe.

Page 1114. THE TRUE KNOWLEDGE

The fragment from Euripides introducing this poem may be translated—"It is necessary to cut down life as one does the fruitful ear of corn, for one to live, another to die."
B. Ifor Evans says that the imitation of the *In Memoriam* measure in Wilde's early pieces does not seem accidental, since Wilde, like Tennyson, explored "his spiritual experience in these early quatrain poems."

THE BALLAD OF READING GAOL

On May 27, 1895, Wilde was convicted on a "statutory charge" (see sketch of Wilde, text p. 1106) and sentenced to two years' imprisonment with hard labor in Reading Gaol, Berkshire. While a prisoner he wrote the striking apologetic account of his life, *De Profundis*, the only work of composition he accomplished during his imprisonment. There is reason to believe that the immediate inspiration of *The Ballad of Reading Gaol*, which was written at Berneval, France, after his release, was Housman's *On Moonlit Heath*, a poem which Wilde probably saw in August, 1897. The crime whose consequences are so fearfully portrayed in *Reading Gaol* was the murder of his wife by a former trooper of the Royal Horse Guards, one Charles T. Woolridge. Woolridge was hanged July 7, 1896. The poem has been pointed to again and again as "a terrible exposure of the barbarities of the English prison system," but it is better, perhaps, to think of it as an expression of the absolute horror felt by the sensitive poet at the thought, the abstract idea, of imprisonment and legal murder. A short time before his sentence ended he wrote (in *De Profundis*): "I tremble with pleasure when I think that on the very day of my leaving prison both the laburnum and the lilac will be blooming in the gardens."
7. *Trial Men.* Prisoners upon whom sentence has been passed by a preliminary court and who may have a chance to appeal.
96. *Caiaphas.* A high priest of the Jews who presided at the trial of Jesus. Judas bargained with him for the thirty pieces of silver to be paid for the kiss of betrayal. See Matthew 26.
118. *anodyne.* A drug that eases pain.
173. *gin.* Trap.
175. *Debtor's Yard.* A portion of the exercise ground in the prison formerly set apart for prisoners for debt.
188. *Regulations Act.* An act providing for the supervision of prisoners by the government and compelling humane treatment of them.
217. *We . . . shreds.* To make oakum for calking vessels.
291. *rigadoon.* A lively dance.
298. *saraband.* A slow Spanish dance.
301. *pirouettes of marionettes.* Spinning on the points of the toes like dancing puppets.
434. *arrows.* The marks used to indicate prison garb.
456. *pall.* Coffin cloth or cover.
485–6. *staff . . . sight.* See note to l. 166 of Swinburne's *Ave atque Vale*, p. 1261, above.
589–90. *midnight . . . cell.* In *De Profundis* Wilde wrote: "The very sun and moon seem taken from us. Outside the day may be blue and gold, but the light that creeps down through the thickly muffled glass of the small iron-barred window beneath which one sits is grey and niggard. It is always twilight in one's cell, as it is always twilight in one's heart."
609–12. *box . . . nard.* While Christ "sat at meat" at the home of Simon the leper, a

woman with a box of precious spikenard came into his presence, broke open the box, and poured the spikenard on his head. See Mark 14: 3–9.

621–2. *holy . . . Paradise.* See Luke 23: 39–43.

623–4. *broken . . . despise.* "A broken and a contrite heart, O God, thou wilt not despise" (Psalms 51: 17).

625. *man in red.* The judge who sentenced the prisoner to death.

WILLIAM BUTLER YEATS

BIBLIOGRAPHY

I. WORKS

Collected Works. 8 vols. (Chapman: London, 1908.) The most comprehensive collection: Vol. I includes the lyrical and narrative poems; Vols. II–IV, the plays; Vol. VIII, a bibliography by Allan Wade.

Collected Poems. (Macmillan: New York, 1933.) The most complete edition of the poetry alone, containing many significant revisions.

Collected Plays. (Macmillan: New York, 1935.) The most convenient full edition, containing 21 selections; a companion-volume to the item above.

Selected Poems. (Macmillan: London, 1929.) Bears the interest of showing the poet's preferences from his own work and his notes on the occasions and sources of many of the selections.

The Winding Stair and Other Poems. (Macmillan: London, 1933.) A late separate volume of verse, containing the notes of austerity and reminiscential tenderness that have marked Yeats's recent poetry.

The King of the Great Clock-Tower, Commentaries, and Poems. (Cuala Press: Dublin, 1934.) One of the most significant of the recent books by Yeats produced by Elizabeth Corbet Yeats, the sister of the poet.

A Full Moon in March. (Macmillan: London, 1935.) Includes two revisions (one prose, one verse) of the prose *King of the Great Clock-Tower;* many of the other poems express a resurgence of the writer's interest in contemporary affairs.

II. BIOGRAPHY AND CRITICISM

Hone, J. M. *William Butler Yeats.* (Dodd: New York, 1916.) A record of Yeats's attachment to various patriotic movements, showing his later interest in the social and literary life of his country.

Krans, H. S. *W. B. Yeats and the Irish Literary Revival.* (McClure: New York, 1904.) Intended as an introduction to Yeats, showing his contribution to his times; chapters II and III discuss his poetry.

Pollock, J. H. *William Butler Yeats.* (Duckworth: London, 1935.) A well-balanced survey of Yeats's long poetical career, demonstrating his power in evoking and vivifying local Irish tradition.

Reid, Forrest. *W. B. Yeats: A Critical Study.* (Secker: London, 1915.) Reviews the whole of Yeats's work to date, making many comparisons between earlier and later pieces. Concludes that the poet has frequently been underrated, but never overrated.

Wrenn, C. L. *W. B. Yeats: A Literary Study.* (Murby: London, 1920.) Without discounting Yeats's immense service to Irish drama, briefly contends that he is in no true sense a dramatist, but essentially a lyric poet; discusses the sources of his symbolism and his great debt to Blake.

III. ARTICLES FROM BOOKS

Archer, William. "William Butler Yeats," in *Poets of the Younger Generation.* (Lane: New York, 1902.) Comments on the poet's blending of the artistic and the primitive; analyzes his *Wanderings of Oisin* and some of the plays.

Boyd, E. A. "William Butler Yeats," in *Ireland's Literary Renaissance.* (Knopf: New York, 1922.) Chapters VI, VII, and VIII deal with Yeats's poems, plays, and prose. He is named predominantly the poet, but weakest in his mysticism; his interest in the drama is seen as the reason for his diminishing lyrical power.

Ellis, S. M. "W. B. Yeats," in *Mainly Victorian.* (Hutchinson: London, 1924.) Offers a thumbnail biographical sketch, outlining the poet's wide circle of acquaintances and his interest in the National Movement in Ireland.

Figgis, D. "Mr. W. B. Yeats's Poetry," in *Studies and Appreciations.* (Dent: London, 1912.) Studies the preoccupation of Yeats's poetry with a "strange underworld," which is neither that of Celtic mythology, nor yet of mysticism, though drawing from both; points out the poet's effort to catch the spirit and music of "the shadowy people of the earth."

Hind, C. L. "W. B. Yeats," in *Authors and I.* (Lane: London, 1921.) Briefly comments on Yeats as "a good poet, a good prose-writer, and good to look upon"; describes a reading in the poet's rooms in London.

More, P. E. "Two Poets of the Irish Movement," in *Shelburne Essays,* First Series. (Putnam: New York, 1909.) Sees Yeats as the poet of a "long tradition of defeat" which has turned him away from reality to a "Celtic twilight of defeated dreams"; points out beauties in phraseology.

Murry, J. M. "Mr. Yeats's Swan-Song," in *Aspects of Literature.* (Collins: London, 1920.) Points out with some regret the tenuousness of thought in the *Wild Swans at Coole* volume; feels that the poet was overmastered by his vision and failed in the adequate expression of it.

Shanks, Edward. "The Later Poetry of Mr. W. B. Yeats," in *First Essays on Literature.* (Collins: London, 1923.) Comments that Yeats has found a field distinctly his own, which he can describe in a diction "curiously bare and economical."

Sturgeon, Mary C. "William Butler Yeats," in *Studies of Contemporary Poets.* (Harrap: London, 1920.) Sees the poet as his country's artistic incarnation; remarks his foundation upon native legend and his appeal to the Celtic spirit.

Symons, Arthur. "Mr. W. B. Yeats," in *Studies in Prose and Verse*. (Dutton: New York, 1904.) Names Yeats the "only one among the younger English poets who has the whole poetical temperament"; praises his dramas for the perfect suiting of language to the narrative.

Weygandt, Cornelius. "With Yeats in the Woods of Coole," in *Tuesdays at Ten*. (University of Pennsylvania Press: 1928.) Describes a visit with the poet, wherein were pointed out backgrounds for a number of his lyrics.

IV. ARTICLES FROM PERIODICALS

Jackson, Schuyler. "William Butler Yeats," *London Mercury*, XI, 396–410 (Feb., 1925). Sees Yeats's development as a successful outcome of his experimenting with his own personality.

Jones, Llewellyn. "Later Poetry of W. B. Yeats," *North American Review*, CCXIX, 499–506 (Apr., 1924). Commends the *Wild Swans at Coole* volume as best illustrating Yeats's sincerity and simplicity; shows that the poet grows in originality as he grows in experience.

Macleod, Fiona. "The Later Work of Mr. W. B. Yeats," *North American Review*, CLXXV, 473–85 (Oct., 1902). Finds in the *Wind Among the Reeds* a new significant note; candidly points out the dramatic incapabilities of the play-poems, which seem to require a new classification.

Stace, W. T. "The Faery Poetry of Mr. W. B. Yeats," *Living Age*, CCLXXVI, 483–90 (Feb., 22, 1913). Discusses the role of Oisin in Yeats's poetry; shows that his ideas of fairies constitute his real philosophy of life, which is best when nearest to nature.

NOTES

"... What poet has sown more pure beauty along the secret paths of life? What poet has more consistently wrestled with his angel? Mr. Yeats has used poetry as a method of life. To him it has been both goad and pilgrimage. If he has offered us no conclusion, do we not know that life itself offers us no conclusion but death, which is still a hazard? Better a fiddler than a teller of inconsequential truths! This poet has caught his tunes from the wandering air and wind: how should it be that he should not wander, that he should not be wind-driven? Yet with his wavering bow he has drawn sweet music even out of the impersonal deeps. To that music he has set many songs, with burdens ever the same—'Seek on earth that which you have found in heaven.' And that wise, sweet singing we shall never forget." (Schuyler Jackson, in the *London Mercury*, XI, 410.)

"In *The Green Helmet and Other Poems*, *Responsibilities*, and *The Wild Swans at Coole*, there is a marked change of method; the magic of the Celtic world is replaced by the reality of this. The newer lyrics show not only a greater realism than do the earlier poems, but also increasing freedom of rhythm which, in the last-named volume, at least, approaches that of modern free verse. Moreover, an obscurity, present in the poet's previous lyrics, is intensified. Nevertheless, whatever liberties the author takes, the reader cannot fail to realize that here is the deliberate experimentation of a master. Never has Mr. Yeats painted a picture with more movement and color than the title poem of *The Wild Swans at Coole*." (Norreys Jephson O'Connor, in *Changing Ireland*, p. 79.)

Page 1123. DOWN BY THE SALLEY GARDENS

Cf. Housman's *When I Was One and Twenty*, text p. 935.

1. *salley*. Willow. The word is a dialect form for sallow.

Page 1124. THE ROSE OF THE WORLD

The rose is "a type of the perfect abstract principle of Beauty, of which all beautiful forms and emotions are but partial manifestations." (J. H. Pollock, in *William Butler Yeats*, p. 90.)

"... The quality symbolized as The Rose differs from the Intellectual Beauty of Shelley and Spenser in that I have imagined it as suffering with man and not as something pursued and seen from afar." (Yeats's note, 1925.)

4. *Troy . . . gleam*. The Trojan War, in which Troy was burned, was really brought about by the beauty of a woman—Helen of Troy.
5. *Usna's children*. See note to Sharp's *Deirdrê Is Dead*, above.

THE LAKE ISLE OF INNISFREE

When Yeats was a boy of fifteen or sixteen he remarked to his uncle that one does not know a countryside till one knows it at night, and informed him that he was going to walk round Lough Gill, a lake in the county of Sligo, and sleep in a wood. His uncle approved of the plan, not knowing that the lad had devised it in order that he might see the little island of Innisfree, which was opposite Slish Wood, where he meant to sleep. His interest in the island had been awakened by his father's reading to him from Thoreau's *Walden*, and he had planned to live there some day in a cottage, seeking wisdom, as Thoreau had sought it, in isolation. The revival in the poet's memory of this long-gone incident by the sound of water tinkling in a London shop window is said to have been the immediate inspiration of the poem.

Drinkwater, in discussing "Patriotism of Place," doubts the correctness of those critics who contend that "the name of a place in verse in itself can have no significance," that it is "but a tinkling prettiness unless it happens to have in it something of personal reminiscence for the reader. I have never been to Ireland and I do not know where Innisfree is. But I know that the name as Mr. Yeats here uses it has a specific emotional value that is distinct from its easy syllabic grace. It not only specifies a place, it adds firmness of expression to a patriotic mood.

'The rhyme of the poet
Modulates the king's affairs,'

says Emerson. And the name of a place on a poet's tongue may influence the national destiny." (John Drinkwater, in *Patriotism in Literature*, pp. 145–6.)

2. *Wattles*. Rods laid on a roof to support the thatch.

THE SONG OF WANDERING AENGUS

"Angus—the god of youth, beauty, and poetry. He reigned in Tir-nam-Oge, the country of the young." (Yeats's note.)

Page 1126. THE WILD SWANS AT COOLE

Coole Park, in County Galway, western Ireland, was the home of Lady Gregory.

25–30. J. H. Pollock says that he can see no fitting parallel for these lines "other than Keats's *Ode on a Grecian Urn;* both exhibit the passionate desire to fix for eternity the essentially fugitive beauty of a moment."

A PRAYER FOR MY DAUGHTER

7–9. *walked . . . child.* ". . . In most cases children, being objective projections of our personality, provide a partial solution of that complex in which every introverted character finds itself at moments in its relation with the world. But in Dr. Yeats's case his two children appear to serve but as fresh material for subjective self-torment." (J. H. Pollock, in *William Butler Yeats*, pp. 62–3.)

25. *Helen*. Of Troy.

27. *great Queen*. Aphrodite.

29. *bandy-legged smith*. Hephæstus—the Roman Vulcan—the smith of the gods, was the husband of Aphrodite.

APPENDIX III

INDEX OF AUTHORS, TITLES, AND FIRST LINES OF POETRY

Authors' names are set in black face type, titles are set in italics, and first lines of poetry are set in roman type. When a part or all of the first line of a poem is used as the title, the entry is by first line only.